THE CRITICAL TRADITION

Classic Texts and Contemporary Trends

THE CRITICAL TRADITION

Classic Texts and Contemporary Trends

Shorter Third Edition

Edited by

David H. Richter

*Queens College
of the City University of New York*

bedford/st.martin's
Macmillan Learning

Boston | New York

For Bedford/St. Martin's

Vice President, Editorial, Macmillan Higher Education Humanities: Edwin Hill
Editorial Director, English and Music: Karen S. Henry
Executive Editor: Vivian Garcia
Senior Executive Editor: Steve Scipione
Production Editor: Lidia MacDonald-Carr
Production Manager, Humanities: Joe Ford
Marketing Manager: Sandra McGuire
Project Management: MPS Limited
Permissions Manager: Kalina Ingham
Senior Art Director: Anna Palchik
Cover Design: William Boardman
Composition: MPS Limited
Printing and Binding: RR Donnelley and Sons

Manufactured in the United States of America.

1   0   9   8   7   6
f   e   d   c   b   a

For information, write: Bedford/St. Martin's, 75 Arlington Street, Boston, MA 02116   (617–399–4000)

ISBN: 978–1–319–01118–5

Acknowledgments
Text acknowledgments and copyrights appear at the back of the book on pages 1155–58, which constitute an extension of the copyright page. Art acknowledgments and copyrights appear on the same page as the art selections they cover. It is a violation of the law to reproduce these selections by any means whatsoever without the written permission of the copyright holder.

Preface to the Shorter Third Edition

> The "canon of theory" introduces into the institutional context of literary pedagogy (the graduate seminar) a syllabus whose symptomatic function is to signify precisely methodological "rigor," rather than the taste or discrimination which for so long determined the ideological protocols of literary criticism. . . . Those authors or texts designated as "theoretical" are now increasingly capable of being introduced to students in traditional routinized forms, even by means of anthologies.
> — JOHN GUILLORY, *Cultural Capital* (1993)

In the late 1960s, when I started teaching, literary criticism was primarily an arcane subspecialty of historical research, in which scholars quarreled about Philip Sidney's distinction between "poesy" and "poetry" or the relative influence of Horace and Longinus on Samuel Johnson. My own interest in literary theory as an ongoing as well as a historic concern, stimulated by University of Chicago professors Wayne Booth, Sheldon Sacks, Norman Maclean, and Richard McKeon, then seemed a harmless oddity to most of my colleagues at Queens College. One of them, since guilty of a metacritical book himself, warned me authoritatively over lunch that I was wasting my time with theory because there was no future in it.

THE FIRST WAVE

By then, of course, the revolution had already begun that would end by making critical theory the roiling pivot point of the profession of letters, the one topic the fans of Philip Roth and the devotees of Lady Mary Wroth might have in common. The turbulence and clash of ideas had begun decades before on the Continent, but those of us in the provinces, who read French and German haltingly and Russian not at all, didn't experience the explosion of theory until the mid 1970s, as structuralism and semiotics, deconstruction, Lacanian psychology, Althusserian Marxism, Russian formalism, phenomenology, and reception theory rode successive waves into our awareness. A profession that a few years before had been hacking out dozens of progressively less plausible ways of misreading *The Turn of the Screw* was now lit up with a rush of ideas, a dozen disparate systems with enormous philosophical reach and scope. Many of those systems were capable also of informing and channeling the social imperatives of women and minorities seeking a theoretical manifestation of their need for greater freedom and power. To academics like me the sense of liberation was palpable, echoing Wordsworth's sentiments about a revolution two hundred years past: "Great it was in that dawn to be alive / But to be young was very heaven." The first edition of *The Critical Tradition* was conceived in the rush of that era, as a tool to help my own students and those like them all over the Americas, many of them innocent of philosophy of any sort, take tentative steps toward joining the magnificent conversation going on about them. Its aim was not merely to provide an anthology of contemporary theory, with examples of all the latest trends, but a book that could locate and present the sources of the new theory within Western intellectual history going back to Plato.

The revolution was, after all, reshaping our sense of intellectual history, forcing us to broaden our horizons. Anglo-American feminist theory, like that of Elaine Showalter and Sandra Gilbert, needed to be understood against the backdrop of Germaine de Staël, Virginia Woolf, Simone de Beauvoir, and other forebears who served either as sources of inspiration or as antagonists. Understanding Derrida required one to understand not only the theories of structuralism and semiotics against which he had reacted: he presumes in the reader the knowledge of Plato, Kant, Hegel, Nietzsche, and Heidegger, some of whom were comparative strangers to traditional literary criticism courses. On the other side, with the waning of the hegemony of New Critical explication, the differences between the various New Critics, like Allen Tate, John Crowe Ransom, and Cleanth Brooks, no longer seemed as profound as they once did, and the New Criticism itself receded to a trend within the larger formalist movement in the earlier part of the twentieth century that also comprehended such disparate theorists as Victor Shklovsky and R. S. Crane. An entire tradition of rhetorical theory going back to classical times, whose centrality depended on that of the New Criticism, was displaced. But original thinkers like Kenneth Burke, who had once been seen within the context of New Criticism, now assumed unique places in the pantheon.

THE SECOND WAVE: PRACTICES AND PIDGINS

Intellectual revolutions too have their Thermidors, and not long after *The Critical Tradition* appeared in 1989, it became clear that the era of Grand Theory was coming to an end. No longer did each year bring a rediscovered thinker with the significance of Bakhtin, a new theory with the impact of deconstruction. Theory had moved into a period of consolidation, when it was being used not for its own sake, but to make possible a new sort of encounter with a text or a group of related texts. Critical practices that had emerged since the beginning of the revolution, engaged in "gender studies," "New Historicism," and, broadest of all, "cultural studies," began to dominate the graduate and undergraduate study of literature.

People began to engage in loose talk about the arrival of a post-theoretical age, and Terry Eagleton published a book titled *After Theory* (2003). But of course theory had not disappeared. The new critical discourses were so thoroughly imbued with contemporary theory that they were incomprehensible in isolation from their theoretical origins. Really coming to terms with the methodology behind the New Historicism involved reading all sorts of abstract texts: practitioners like Stephen Greenblatt and Jerome McGann as well as theorists like Clifford Geertz and Hayden White and Michel Foucault. And to do things properly one would have to read the theorists who had most influenced them: not only Clifford Geertz on the semiotics of culture but also Max Weber and Emile Durkheim and Claude Lévi-Strauss; not only Hayden White on the tropics of history but also Jacques Derrida and Ludwig Wittgenstein; not only Michel Foucault on the genealogies of power/knowledge but also Martin Heidegger and the later Nietzsche. The bases for gender studies and cultural studies would be even wider and more diverse.

The process of consolidating and simplifying the elaborate and difficult Grand Theories into workable critical practices involved creating a pidgin, in much the same way people manage to communicate across language barriers by forming a *lingua franca* for trade and barter during interludes between hostilities. This critical pidgin was encouraged by the way universities avoided the creation of "schools" of like-minded thinkers such as those you find on the Continent, and instead filled slots so as to create the greatest possible diversity. English departments that had acquired a Lacanian or a reception theorist to be fashionable didn't feel the need of a breeding pair. This tendency to isolate individuals using a particular theoretical vocabulary from one another had the consequence that, while they could use their chosen critical language in all its purity in their own classroom and at conferences, they had to use some other sort of discourse to talk with their colleagues. The result was a carnival of jostling jargons, in which purity of rhetoric took second place to the pragmatics of discourse. A gender theorist like Judith Butler could derive her notions about sex and society from Foucault, but her rhetorical ploys might be taken from Derrida and J. L. Austin, and never mind that these thinkers might otherwise be strange bedfellows. An important innovator in postcolonial theory, such as Gayatri Spivak, was unlikely to talk purely like a feminist or a Marxist or a deconstructionist, but rather like a combination of all three.

If all this has given literary studies a sense of common purpose that we have lacked since the hegemony of the New Criticism, there are also potentially disturbing consequences. One problem is that pidgins are defective languages that suppress the more complex features of the different critical languages that compose them. Critical pidgins adopt terms without necessarily adopting the full philosophy out of which the terms emerge. When we try to say something for ourselves without understanding how each of those sets of ideas works, the result is often gobbledygook composed of different and irreconcilable terminologies. One reads "theory-damaged" discourse that sounds plausible but really makes no sense, like the following sentences taken from a recent book: "Bakhtin's reading of the process of self-realization is the opposite of Lacan's. If for Lacan there is an inevitable dismemberment of a total self, for Bakhtin there is a continual movement toward a self that is never total but always capable of further realization." It would take a long time to explain everything that is wrong with this formulation, though one might begin with the fact that in Lacan there is no "total self" to be dismembered except as an Imaginary construct. But the main problem lies not in such details, but in the unexamined assumption that Bakhtin's use of the word *self* and Lacan's have enough in common to allow them to be juxtaposed in this way.

The only way to avoid this kind of muddle is to understand Bakhtin and Lacan in their own terms. Otherwise, we are at the mercy of hybrid practices with internal contradictions, formed from some elements that aspire to be "scientific" and empirical (such as structural linguistics) along with others that are deeply hostile to science and positivism (such as Foucault's genealogies of discursive practices); some elements that are humanistic and pluralistic (such as the work of Habermas), and others (such as Derrida's) that are profoundly distrustful of the relics of the Enlightenment. So while a synthesis of critical practices may have been desperately needed to correct the excesses of the era of Grand Theory, an understanding of theory is more desperately needed than ever to avoid the incoherence of an eclectic critical practice.

THE THIRD WAVE

In recent years these syncretic trends have continued to proliferate, as the study of literature has become just one area in a widening arena of textual criticism. Critical tools for studying literature have been applied to other artistic cultural productions like film and television, radio plays and comic books, painting and photography—and vice versa. Analytic approaches to narrative originally used to study novels and short stories have found application to medical case histories and the narratives judges create in writing legal decisions. Historical movements in architecture and home furnishing—such as the eighteenth-century vogue in England and France for chinoiserie—are today thought of not as capricious episodes of fashion, but as part of a larger cultural plenum shared with all the other fine and useful arts and determined by changes in trading relationships and other economic and social trends. Cultural studies has in fact turned back upon itself in ecocriticism, which attempts to understand how culture comes to define its opposite, nature, and to explore the changing relationship between civilization and the wild. Science studies, legal studies, business studies: new fields like these attempt to interrogate the paradigms of knowledge taught to and accepted by professionals in these areas. Most eclectic of all, perhaps, is the field of global studies, which uses every resource of the social sciences and humanities to analyze how the forces of power, money, and culture have shaped a planet that began to become one world since the voyages of discovery some five hundred years ago. The result of all this has been that, although institutional structures within academe have remained more or less stable—most professors still teach and most students still earn degrees within departments—my own research projects and those of most of my doctoral students, colleagues, and friends have become ever more interdisciplinary.

The other clear change of the last decade has been the demise of the traditional literary canon as a basis for the curriculum in humanities courses. The persistent attacks on the traditional canon as a gentleman's club for dead white European males provoked culture wars beginning in the 1980s, but those wars are over now. Research on the history of literary evaluation revealed that, despite the long-term agreement on the significance of Homer and the Bible, the canon of the vernacular literatures had always been in flux. Most teachers understood that there was no way to teach any permanent list as "the best that has been known and thought in the world," that the best we could do would be to teach different ways of reading whatever texts retained cultural importance today. The emphasis on the contemporary and the postmodern did not mean eliminating all the old favorites—indeed, Shakespeare and Jane Austen have as many followers as they have ever had—but the culture of the university had approved so many new major writers, and so many new areas of study, that no one could rationally feel guilty any more about what got left out of the selection taken by undergraduate and graduate students. Our students, living in a postmodern culture that insistently recycles the cultural icons of the past, thus needed to read Defoe's *Robinson Crusoe* not only for its historical importance but in order to understand Coetzee's *Foe* and Tournier's *Vendredi*, or Dickens' *Great Expectations* in order to understand the versions by Kathy Acker and Peter Carey.

With contemporary cultural value taking clear precedence over other versions of merit, the curriculum began to give greater attention to ethnic literatures, particularly by writers of African American, Asian, and Latino/Hispanic descent, and abroad to the contemporary literature of Africa, South Asia, and the Caribbean, where so much of the most innovative poetry and fiction of the last decades has been written. With this shift, postcolonial theory has become a major growth area. Originating in the politics of identity within nation-states carved out of European empires, postcolonial theory has since been applied to American literature (based on the view that the United States was formed by absorbing territories inhabited by other cultures in a process of internal colonization). The theory behind contemporary and historical ethnic studies has tended to borrow from postcolonial theory and its sources. But of course these studies are not limited to the contemporary: they can even be read back onto biblical texts, where the Israelites appear first as the conquering hegemons of Canaan, later as a conquered people at risk of cultural absorption by the Eastern empires of Babylon and Persia.

If most of the forces in the third wave of theory have been centrifugal—exploding the canon of literature and viewing literature against the countless other arenas of life—at least one, cognitive psychology, seems to be seeking a new center within, in the activities of the human mind. Philology could reveal the poem and its patterns, and rhetoric could give us some inkling of how audiences reacted, but until recently the key aesthetic moment was a mystery, a "black box" whose workings were hidden to us. Experimental psychology, however, has begun to shine some light on mind and brain, how literary tropes (like metaphor) are involved in all cognition, how the aesthetic moment happens, and how literary texts engage and occasionally test the limits of cognitive functioning.

AND NOW: A COMPACT CRITICAL TRADITION

This understanding of our current moment in the evolution of literary and cultural studies underlies this latest—*compact*—incarnation of *The Critical Tradition*. But some purely practical considerations came into play as well. The complete third edition contained 182 selections and weighed in at two kilos, close to five pounds, physically straining backs and backpacks alike, with much more material than even the most extensive full-year course would require. Both faculty and students expressed the need for a shorter, lighter anthology that could still present the full range of critical thought from Plato and Aristotle to the latest contemporary theory. The current edition is a slimmed-down version of the bulky third edition, which nevertheless retains the texts that instructors most esteemed and most enjoyed teaching (insofar as we were able to obtain permission from copyright holders to reprint those texts).

This volume, as in the full edition, is organized in two parts. Part One, Classic Texts, presents a history of criticism through thirty-eight selections by twenty-eight major critics from Plato to Susan Sontag. Part Two contains fifty-five readings grouped into nine chapters on contemporary critical trends. Postcolonial theory has been broken out from its previous position as one of several areas within cultural studies to a separate chapter. But since it shares with contemporary African American, Latino, and Asian studies the issues of cultural identity, nationality, liminality, and contact zones, I have incorporated postcolonial and ethnic studies into a single coherent chapter.

Even in this condensed format, *The Critical Tradition* contains such varied ideas in such complex relationships that I have retained (and, as much as possible, brought up to date) the extensive apparatus—what Alexander Pope disdained as "dull duty"—that makes the works collected here easier to assimilate. The book begins with an introduction that explores the ways in which theorists have tried to chart the terrain of criticism. The first half of this introduction describes the ineluctable fourfold classifications of critical theories from M. H. Abrams's *The Mirror and the Lamp*, evaluates the powers and limitations of the Abrams map, its general biases and unspoken assumptions, and then discusses other quite different ways of mapping critical tasks and methods. I also include a section that focuses on the relation of theory to the sort of textual criticism and analysis students will find in their research into academic journals, with some practical advice on how to "unpack" the elaborate skein of theoretical assumptions that underlie and imbue literary discourse in what we ironically call our "post-theoretical" age.

In Part One, each reading is prefaced with an extensive headnote that places the text within the context of the author's life and works, explores the key issues of each reading and its relationship with other readings, and occasionally analyzes troublesome twists in the argumentation. For the readings by contemporary academic theorists and critics composing Part Two, the biographical headnotes before each selection are necessarily briefer, but each of the chapters is prefaced by a substantial introduction. These introductions, addressed to the serious reader, cover the origins, the general approach, and the variations in theory and practice of each of the nine movements. Individual readings are analyzed primarily to mark out their place within larger critical trends. The introductions try to navigate between the Scylla of commentary that expresses only the prejudices of the editor and the Charybdis of neutralist mumbling that expresses nothing. The intent was to provide an even-handed overview of each critical movement or issue, showing both its power and its limitations. Finally, following the headnotes to Part One and the introductions to

Part Two, selected bibliographies direct the interested reader to further works by and about the authors and their critical approaches. The texts in both parts are annotated to save the reader's time in tracking down allusions, to highlight the cross-references between one text and another, and to fill in the argument where the text has been abridged.

Although Part Two sorts its selections into nine "schools," it need hardly be said that even centrally placed "members" of a "school" swear no allegiance to its doctrines; despite the "fallacies" and "heresies" of the New Critics, there were no recorded excommunications. We need to bear in mind that some theorists bridge categories, as is becoming more and more usual these days. Pierre Bourdieu, one of the theoretical lights of cultural studies, is a Marxist sociologist, while Julia Kristeva, here represented as a feminist, has made major contributions to psychoanalysis and semiotics. Michel Foucault, influential everywhere these days, appears in two chapters of the book as a poststructuralist and as a gender theorist. Therefore, an additional table of contents that places theorists in alternative categories appears after Part Two. The book concludes with an index to proper names and major critical terms, which, together with the cross-references in the annotations, should help the reader understand the shifting skeins of influence upon which the critical tradition is built. "Let us now be told no more," as Samuel Johnson said with both weariness and pride, "of 'the dull duty of an editor.'"

ACKNOWLEDGMENTS

Although the title page might suggest a solo performance, no book the size and complexity of *The Critical Tradition* can be created alone. At every stage, from the initial impulse to produce the book to the final corrections in this revised edition, I have depended on the assistance and collaboration of colleagues within academia and publishing. At Bedford/St. Martin's, first and foremost were Chuck Christensen and Joan Feinberg, who believed in the project and made it happen. Steve Scipione developed the first edition and worked out the myriad details that made it the teaching text it became, and Kathy Retan masterminded the adventurous revision that reshaped the book for the needs of the twenty-first century. Elizabeth Schaaf guided the production crew that turned messy masses of manuscript into aesthetically pleasing objects. For the third edition, Steve Scipione again helped me imagine how the book might be improved as a pedagogical tool, and Emily Berleth and Linda DeMasi shouldered the task of guiding an even larger and more daunting manuscript through the production process. Jennifer Blanksteen not only cleared permissions (a task that can drive anyone crazy) but developed the book with unfailing intelligence and energy, wit, and good humor. Carrie Shanafelt, once my brilliant and charming research assistant, now professor of English at Fairleigh Dickinson, contributed dozens of cogent and erudite headnotes. For this shorter version of the third edition, I am again grateful to Steve Scipione and Kathy Retan for their development efforts and indebted to acquisition editor Vivian Garcia and literature publisher Karen Henry for giving the project the green light. I thank Virginia Creeden for clearing permissions,

Lidia MacDonald-Carr and Anoop Chaturvedi for their hard work in the book's production, and Joy Fisher Williams for her marketing efforts.

I am also thankful to the literary critics, theorists, and teachers of literary theory who, during the development of one or another of the editions, have provided helpful suggestions and pointed comments on the choice of contents and editorial materials. They include Beate Allert of Purdue University; Emily Anderson of Knox College; Robert F. Barsky of Vanderbilt University; Raymond L. Baubles Jr. of Western Connecticut State University; Michael Beard of the University of North Dakota; Greg Bentley of Mississippi State University; Jill Benton of Pitzer College; Kathryn N. Benzel of the University of Nebraska, Kearney; Mark Boren of University of North Carolina at Wilmington; Glen Brewster of Westfield State College; Theron Britt of the University of Memphis; Suzanne L. Bunkers of Mankato State University; William E. Cain of Wellesley College; Michael Calabrese of California State University, Los Angeles; Wes Chapman of Illinois Wesleyan University; Joseph J. Colavito of the University of Arizona; Glen Colburn of Morehead State University; Michael Colson of Allan Hancock College; Frederick Crews of the University of California, Berkeley; Ashley J. Cross of Manhattan College; Robert Denham of Roanoke College; Victoria deZwaan of Trent University; Brian Diemert of Brescia University College; Martha Diede of Western Carolina University; Joseph Dupras of the University of Alaska, Fairbanks; Bernard Duyfhuizen of the University of Wisconsin, Eau Claire; Neil Easterbrook of Texas Christian University; Marilyn Edelstein of Santa Clara University; Lee Erickson of Marshall University; Anne Fairbanks of Hastings College; Susan Felch of Calvin College; Thomas Ferraro of Duke University; Daniel Fineman of Occidental College; Jane Fisher of Canisius College; Peter Fitz of the University of Baltimore; Elizabeth Flynn of Michigan Technological University; Joseph Francavilla of Columbus State University; Dean Franco of Wake Forest University; Stephen Goldsmith of the University of California, Berkeley; Stephen Greenblatt of Harvard University; Marshall Gregory of Butler University; Robin Grey of the University of Illinois, Chicago; Susan Gubar of Indiana University Bloomington; Nira Gupta-Casale of Kean University; David Halliburton of Stanford University; Michael Hancher of the University of Minnesota; James Hans of Wake Forest University; Barbara Leah Harmon of Wellesley College; Lee Harrod of The College of New Jersey; Cary Henson of the University of Wisconsin, Oshkosh; Frank Hoffman of Susquehanna University; Norman N. Holland of the University of Florida; John R. Holmes of the Franciscan University of Steubenville; Harriet Hustis of The College of New Jersey; Earl Ingersoll of the State University of New York, Brockport; Michael C. Jordan of the University of St. Thomas; Linda Karell of Montana State University, Bozeman; Meegan Kennedy of Harvard University; William Kenney of Manhattan College; Mark Koch of St. Mary's College; Catherine Gunther Kodat of Hamilton College; Augustus M. Kolich of St. Xavier University; Janet Sanders Land of Gardner-Webb University; Page R. Laws of Norfolk State University; L. B. Lebim of Lock Haven University; Pericles Lewis of Yale University; Mary Libertin of Shippensburg University of Pennsylvania; Lawrence Lipking of Northwestern University; Jun Liu of California State University, Los Angeles; Zhang Longxi of the University of California,

Riverside; Carol Schaechterle Loranger of Wright State University; Paul Lukacs of Loyola College in Maryland; Kathleen Lundeen of Western Washington University; Mark Lussier of Arizona State University; Steven Mailloux of the University of California, Irvine; Bruce Martin of Drake University; Felix Martínez-Bonati of Columbia University; Bill McCarron of East Texas State University; Janet McNew of Illinois Wesleyan University; Robert McRuer of George Washington University; Michael Meyer of the University of Connecticut, Storrs; Nancy K. Miller of the Graduate Center, City University of New York; Christian Moraru of the University of North Carolina, Greensboro; Eileen Morgan of the State University of New York, Oneonta; Bradford Mudge of the University of Colorado, Denver; Patrick Murphy of University of Central Florida; Michael Murrin of the University of Chicago; James W. Newcomb of Memphis State University; Eric W. Nye of the University of Wyoming; Charles O'Neill of St. Thomas Aquinas College; Edward O'Shea of the State University of New York, Oswego; Windy C. Petrie of Colorado Christian University; Jan Plug of the University of Western Ontario; Mary Poovey of New York University; Ronald Primeau of Central Michigan University; Ben Railton of Fitchburg State University; Catherine Rainwater of St. Edward's University; Luz Elena Ramirez of California State University, San Bernardino; Herman Rapaport of Wayne State University; James A. W. Rembert of The Citadel; Michael Karl Ritchie of Arkansas Tech University; Lance Rivers of Lake Superior State University; Thomas M. Rivers of the University of Southern Indiana; John G. Roberts of the University of Rochester; Doug Robinson of the University of Mississippi; Lisa Schnell of the University of Vermont, Burlington; Michael Sexson of Montana State University; William Sheidley of the University of Southern Colorado; Faiza Shereen of the University of Dayton; Elaine Showalter of Princeton University; Anne B. Simpson of California State Polytechnic University, Pomona; Barbara Herrnstein Smith of Duke University; Mark Trevor Smith of Southwest Missouri State University; Jack Solomon of California State University, Northridge; James Sosnoski of Miami University; Patricia Meyer Spacks of the University of Virginia; Henry Staten of the University of Washington; Gary Lee Stonum of Case Western Reserve University; David Suchoff of Colby College; Susan Suleiman of Harvard University; James Sullivan of California State University at Los Angeles; Leon Surette of the University of Western Ontario; John Sykes of Wingate College; Brook Thomas of the University of California, Irvine; Calvin Thomas of Georgia State University; Jane Tompkins of Duke University; Steven Venturino of Loyola University; David Wagenknecht of Boston University; Jim Warren of Washington and Lee University; Michelle Warren of the University of Miami; Jack W. Weaver of Winthrop University; Keith Welsh of Webster University; David Willbern of the State University of New York, Buffalo; Dolora Chapelle Wojciehowski of the University of Texas, Austin; Steven J. Zani of Lamar University; and Clarisse Zimra of Southern Illinois University, Carbondale. Many of these reviewers have changed institutions, retired, or passed on since the first edition of *The Critical Tradition* was published, but at a certain point in time all left their mark on the book.

While all these scholars and teachers have influenced the book's form and content, I would like to single out for particular mention James Phelan of Ohio State

University, who read the entire manuscript of the first edition, whose perceptive commentary helped me to clarify and rethink my entrenched opinions, and whose unfailing tact and generosity of spirit made his suggestions easy to take.

In addition to these participants in formal reviewing procedures, the table of contents and sections of the manuscript were read by friends whose formal or casual suggestions I have shamelessly incorporated. These include Don Bialostosky of Pennsylvania State University; Brian Corman of the University of Toronto (who told me all about Aphra); Bob Folkenflik of the University of California, Irvine; Susan K. Harris and William J. Harris of the University of Kansas; Donald McQuade of the University of California, Berkeley; Laura Wadenpfuhl of New Jersey City University (who never spared me); and my colleagues at Queens College and/or the Graduate Center of the City University of New York: Barbara Bowen (who talked about gender and cultural studies with me), Nancy Comley (who has read everything), Tom Hayes (who helped me with Lacan and Žižek), Carrie Hintz, David Kazanjian (who taught me how to teach Spivak), Bill Kelly, Steve Kruger (who put me straight about queer theory), Rich McCoy, Charles Molesworth, Tony O'Brien, Blanford Parker, Michael Sargent (who explained the *querelle*), Barbara Shollar, Chris Suggs, Joe Wittreich, and Susan Zimmerman. My research for the third edition was carried out at the British Library, the Mina Rees Library at the CUNY Graduate Center, the New York Public Library, the Rosenthal Library of Queens College, and—hey—over the Internet. The index was produced and compiled on my own little Dell computer, and you don't want to know.

In closing, I recall the ghostly voices of those who taught me literary theory at the University of Chicago, including Wayne Booth, Norman Maclean, and Elder Olson, along with R. S. Crane, Richard McKeon, and Shelly Sacks, who taught me the uses of theory. From the thousands of students in the undergraduate and graduate literary criticism courses I have taught at Queens College and the CUNY Graduate Center over the last forty-five years, I have learned what was clear and what opaque about the theoretical texts we studied together. I have tried to put some of that knowledge to work in this book, and I plan to continue learning from them.

And finally, I dedicate this edition of *The Critical Tradition* to Golde, my wife, my partner, my love.

Contents

Part Two

CONTEMPORARY TRENDS IN LITERARY CRITICISM   409

THE CRITICAL TRADITION

Classic Texts and Contemporary Trends

INTRODUCTION

Everybody . . . would be willing to admit, as a general proposition, that the critical faculty is lower than the inventive. But is it true that criticism is really, in itself, a baneful and injurious employment?
— MATTHEW ARNOLD, *The Function of Criticism at the Present Time* (1864)

What if criticism is a science as well as an art?
— NORTHROP FRYE, *The Function of Criticism at the Present Time* (1949)

Criticism is not literature, and the pleasure of criticism is not the pleasure of literature. . . . But experience suggests that the two pleasures go together, and the pleasure of criticism makes literature and its pleasure the more readily accessible.
— LIONEL TRILLING, Preface to *Literary Criticism: An Introductory Reader* (1970)

The . . . general and well publicized curricular crisis of the "humanities" suggests that the ambivalence of theory with respect to the literary syllabus is itself related to long-term developments in the educational institution. For the "canon of theory" introduces into the institutional context of literary pedagogy . . . a syllabus whose symptomatic function is to signify precisely methodological "rigor," rather than the taste or discrimination which for so long determined the ideological protocols of literary criticism.
— JOHN GUILLORY, *Cultural Capital* (1993)

In the Socratic dialogues of the early fourth century B.C.E., Plato raised skeptical questions about the value of art and literature that have provoked responses from artists and philosophers from Aristotle's day to our own. In striving to rescue poetry from the exile to which Socrates had condemned it, the defenders of literature have had to recast the questions Plato answered with such assurance. We are still asking the same questions today: What is the nature of the work of art? What are its sources in the artist, in the literary scene, in the society for which it is produced? What are its properties, uses, powers, and value? How is the nature of literature circumscribed by the properties of language itself, by the gender of the writer or the reader, by the intrinsic limitations of the human mind? What are literature's effects on individuals and on communities? Questions like these remain at the heart of the critical tradition. They have inspired an ongoing conversation that is continually modified by new voices from different cultural matrices, which join in with other critical languages, other norms, other views of the world. The proliferation in the past four decades of new critical theories and practices is a sign that the inquiring and speculative spirit of that critical tradition is thriving as never before. But the very abundance of voices and vocabularies can be intimidating to the newcomer seeking to enter the conversation.

The discussion that follows is intended as a guide to the two key problems of theoretical discourse: synthesis and analysis. The first is aimed at understanding the relationships of the great variety of critical theories to each other, drawing maps of the critical terrain, elucidating the various ways our ideas about the nature of litera-ture and the tasks of criticism have been organized. Learning this terrain is the surest way to take one's own bearings and find one's own voice. The second is aimed at understanding how to take critical discourse apart, how to unpack the theoretical assumptions that lie underneath the surface — which, as we shall see, is something one can do best when already provided with a map.

MAPPING CRITICAL THEORIES

M. H. Abrams and the Traditional Classification

In his influential treatise on romantic views of art, *The Mirror and the Lamp* (1953), the literary historian M. H. Abrams distinguished among four different types of literary theories, and the map he drew of these distinctions is still valuable as a place to start thinking about the history of criticism.

Historically, the first type, the mimetic theories of classical antiquity, focused on the relationship between the outside world and the work of art. These theories posited that poetry could best be understood as an imitation, a representation, a copy of the physical world.

The second type, the rhetorical, emphasized the relationship between the work of art and its audience — either how the literary work should be formed to please and instruct its audience, or what that audience should be like in order to appreciate literature correctly. These theories held that to attain its proper effect, the poem must be shaped by both the poet's innate talent and the rules of art. Such theories, most popular during the later classical period, the Middle Ages, and the Renaissance, began to decline toward the end of the eighteenth century.

The third type, which Abrams called expressive, stressed the relationship between the work of art and the artist, particularly the special faculties of mind and soul that the artist brings to the act of creation. These theories proliferated during the late eighteenth and most of the nineteenth centuries.[1]

[1] Although it is possible to specify when mimetic, rhetorical, and expressive theories flourished, it must be understood that all three continue to be influential. Even when theory is not progressing along certain lines, the old questions are asked of new texts. Thus the movie reviewer who wonders whether *Braveheart* accurately depicts battle conditions in medieval Scotland is as much a mimetic critic as Aristotle.

The fourth type, which developed around the beginning of the twentieth century, played down the connections of the work of art with the exterior world, the audience, and the artist. These formal theories stressed the purely aesthetic relationship between the parts of a work of literature, analyzing its "themes" or "motifs" as if a literary text were a form of classical music or an abstract painting, and strove for a quasi-scientific objectivity. Such theories probably prevail today, since thousands of teachers and scholars who might deny allegiance to any theory actually adhere to formalist principles. In their explicit claims to possessing the highest truth about literature, however, formal theories now face a great deal of competition.

One version of the Abrams map might look like Figure 1. The world of criticism is not as clear or as neat as this diagram suggests. Abrams himself points out that a label such as "mimetic" or "expressive" indicates only the primary orientation of a theory: "Any reasonable theory takes account of all four elements." A mimetic theorist (such as Aristotle) might have much to say about how works of art affect an audience or about the artist, but his views often derive directly from his mimetic principles. When Aristotle suggests in *Poetics*, Chapter 4, for example, that poets of noble character took up the art of tragedy and those of baser character created comedy, his rationale is that nobler poets are better able to understand and then to imitate in poetic language the noble characters of tragedy. In this sense, Aristotle's mimetic orientation comes through even when he takes up the problem of poetic creativity.

Abrams's notion of critical orientation helps us distinguish the disparate rationales behind the same piece of conventional wisdom. A mimetic critic, for instance, might enjoin an aspiring poet to observe human nature well, the more accurately to imitate human actions in his poetry. A rhetorical critic might advise the poet in the very same words, but in order to prompt the poet to discover what pleases the various classes and age groups that comprise his audience. As the notes to Part One of

Figure 1

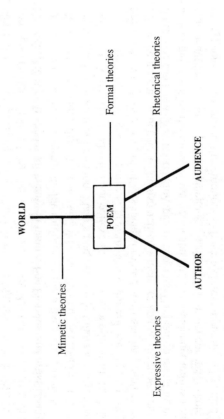

this collection show, the various dicta of Plato and Aristotle, shorn of their mimetic logic, reappear in the works of rhetorical, expressive, and objective critics to bolster markedly different arguments.

Each of these four orientations covers a great deal of ground, and the fact that two critics are both mimetic in orientation does not guarantee that they agree. Quite the contrary: Whereas critics with different principles merely tend to miss each other's points, those who share a theoretical orientation are likely to clash in an interesting and violent way. A brief consideration of Plato (p. 25), Aristotle (p. 46), and Plotinus, three of the more influential mimetic critics, can reveal how some of these disagreements take shape.

Differences within Theoretical Orientations

Plato's view of art derives from a complicated metaphysics and a relatively simple notion of imitation. Imitation, for Plato, is the creation of an *eidolon*. The artist makes an "image" — a degraded copy — of the external world, which is analogous to the image formed in a mirror (it lasts longer than a mirror image, but not being eternal, the difference is not significant). Plato's worldview is idealist, which means that he takes the material world, the world of the senses, to be a copy of an eternal world of Ideas. Works of art, in their turn, are copies of material things, and hence copies of copies. For Plato, art is therefore an activity inferior to artisanship (the making of useful objects), first, because art copies rather than creates a material object, and second, because an artist needs only to know the appearances of things, not their real nature. Plato also worried that imitation might weaken the individual spirit by arousing passion and corrupt the body politic through its distance from the truth.

Six centuries later, the Neoplatonic philosopher Plotinus developed a mimetic theory of art that generally conformed with that of Plato but drew vastly different conclusions about the value of art. In the idealism of Plotinus, although imitation is still basically copying, the artist imitates not the material world but the Ideas themselves. A sculptor carving a statue of Zeus makes not a marble copy of a flesh-and-blood man but a representation of what Power and Majesty might be like if those concepts could become visible. The Idea of Beauty resides within the artist, shaping his conceptions as it shapes all beauty in nature. For Plotinus, the artist is superior to the artisan because Beauty, the Idea informing the artist's craft, is higher than Utility, which informs that of the artisan. Whereas Plotinus accepted Plato's metaphysics and his notion of imitation, Plato's pupil Aristotle fundamentally disagreed with both. A materialist who did not believe in an eternal world of Ideas, Aristotle saw everything as subject to process, growth, and change. Poets, by imitating the process by which one state of affairs metamorphoses into another, capture in language the general principles of human action, which are among the most important things one can know. Nor is imitation merely copying: The poet, in imitating human action, purifies it of the dross of the accidental and the incidental, unifies it into a plot, beautifies it with expressive language, and molds it into a concrete whole with the capacity to command the emotions. Those feelings, aroused and guided by a complex imitation, can cleanse rather than weaken the individual, and can serve the state rather than harm it, by draining off passions and frustrations that might lead to political instability.

Just as mimetic thinkers could agree that art was primarily a matter of imitation but differ about what the world was like, what aspect of that world the artists imitated, and what sort of process imitation actually was, so rhetorical theorists also had their differences about the ends and means of artistic production. The main question for them was how to construct a work of art so that it would affect an audience properly. Horace (p. 73), one of the earliest and most influential of the rhetorical theorists, thought that poems should "either delight, or instruct, or if possible accomplish both ends at once," but later critics subtly redrew his specifications. For moralists like Dante (p. 100) or Samuel Johnson (p. 158), the more significant purpose was instruction, delight being merely a means to that didactic end. Sir Philip Sidney (p. 112) and John Dryden gave delight a more equal role. Although many theorists took "delight" and "instruction" as general and indivisible qualities to be sought in poetry, others elaborately classified the arts according to the varieties of pleasure and benefit that should reside in each.

And for which audience should the poet write? Horace's audience is apparently limited to the upper classes — the *senatores* and *equites* of the early Roman Empire; what the middle-class sellers of beans care about is not the concern of the aristocratic writer. Sidney assumes a universal contemporary audience, but there too the universe may be implicitly restricted to gentlemen — indeed, perhaps even English gentlemen, whom Sidney thinks provincial relative to those in Italy, even though they may be models of cultivation relative to those of Ireland and Scotland. Dryden's debaters in *An Essay of Dramatic Poesy* (1665) posit national audiences with specific national characteristics, not a strange move for a piece written during the Restoration, when King Charles and his court had arrived from a long exile in France. And in Samuel Johnson's analysis, Shakespeare's greatness inheres in his ability to affect people of other countries and much later eras. In the eighteenth century, when the question of taste had become an important one in literary theory, Horace's problem, the adaptation of work to audience, had, in effect, been inverted. For critics like David Hume, the most important issue was not how poems should be shaped to please audiences but why some members of the audience were better adapted to appreciate the arts than others. (This is an issue that is not likely to come up until the audience for art has become split between different classes that have been educated in different ways.)

In similar fashion, expressive theorists concurred that art manifested the artist's sensibility even as they disputed the source of that sensibility. Many nineteenth-century Romantics agreed that the key faculty was the imagination — although they differed sharply on how that faculty worked. Later expressive theorists found the source of poetry in the artist's unconscious mind. For one group of psychological critics, the followers of Sigmund Freud (p. 309), a poem, like a dream, was the imagined fulfillment of an individual artist's unconscious wish; for another group, the followers of Carl Gustav Jung (p. 326), all art evinced archetypal imagery common to the entire human race. For critics like Northrop Frye, the artist expresses the "dream of mankind," which is contained not in the collective unconscious but in a literary tradition that speaks through us all. For sociohistorical critics, followers of Karl Marx (p. 247) or Hippolyte Taine, artists inadvertently expressed the ideologies of their times, conveying their understanding of the world in ways determined by their position within the class struggle and their moment in history.

In the twentieth century, formalists have differed about both what sort of form should be sought and where it could be found. The New Critics discovered form in a dialectical thrust and counterthrust of themes; neo-Aristotelians in a complex link-age of plot, language, technique, and purpose; and structuralists and semioticians in repeated patterns of language. Just as in the eighteenth century, there is a split between those critics investigating the various principles of form within literature and those exploring the reader's capacity to discover form or to supply it when it is not to be found. These variations and developments within major critical orienta-tions seem to embody the behavior of biological organisms that proliferate to fill up a new ecological niche. Once a mode like expressive criticism had become estab-lished, it was almost inevitable that every aspect of the poet's psyche, conscious and unconscious, would be held up to scrutiny as a source of the creative spirit. A more difficult question is why changes in critical orientation occur — why mimetic criti-cism gave way to rhetorical or rhetorical to expressive.

Such epochs seem to be analogous to scientific revolutions, described by Thomas Kuhn in *The Structure of Scientific Revolutions* (1962). Over one or two generations, the previous "paradigm," a vast structure of assumptions, principles, and methods, gives way and is replaced by another for a variety of reasons — new facts that need explaining, new theories that cannot be reconciled with the present paradigm, a scientific community that has lost intellectual cohesion over its basic principles. The causes of such "revolutions" in critical tradition, where Kuhn's model is less exact, might include the creation of new literary works and styles; shifts in the canon (the informal list of the literary works that are held to be significant); developments in the other arts, in philosophy, and in other humanistic disciplines; and changes in politics and society.

Changes in Theoretical Paradigms

The first critical revolution was when Plato and his doctrine of imitation displaced the Sophists, who saw literature as essentially a function of language. Because few writ-ings of the Sophists have survived, too little is known about that revolution to hazard any explanation of Plato's triumph. The second major shift, from mimetic to rhetorical criticism, might have developed partly from a misreading of Aristotle's *Poetics*, a document of enormous authority, if one more respected than understood. (As late as the age of Dryden and Johnson, critics quoted — or misquoted — Aristotle while ignoring his central ideas, methods, and principles.) Though the *Poetics* views art as the imitation of human action, the product is not a simple copy. It differs from the natural process it represents in its form, its material (language instead of action), its technique, and its purpose. These four "causes," as Aristotle termed them, all con-tribute equally in defining the special character of a particular work of art. But one of them — purpose — is, so to speak, more equal than the rest, since it largely dictates the others. Purpose, for Aristotle, refers to the potential capacity of a work to move human beings in a certain way, not its actual effect on an audience.

One can easily imagine, however, how internal purpose could be altered to external effect, and how the four-cause structure of Aristotelian imitation might be simplified to the means/end argument we find in Horace. There were surely external reasons as well for mimetic theories to give way to rhetorical ones. The development in late republican Rome of a publishing industry (using hand-copying), serving a far-flung and disparate literary audience, may have fostered a critical scene different from that of post-Periclean Athens, where the poet's audience was the tight-knit coterie within the polis.

The revolution from rhetorical to expressive criticism may also have been partly the result of social change. The reading public grew enormously in the eighteenth century as formerly illiterate classes became avid consumers of literature. The new cadres of less-educated readers made taste an issue in criticism as it had never been before. As theorists investigating taste examined the inner experience of readers, they found that the faculties behind good taste, the capacities that made ideal readers — delicate imagination, good sense, wide experience — were the same as those that made the best poets. Creation and appreciation were more closely allied than one might have supposed, for the audience passively reenacted what the poets had actively created. Poetic creativity was therefore a refined but not a mysterious process: It could be investigated and understood.

The twentieth-century shift from expressive to formal criticism was not a total revolution: Biographical, psychological, sociological, and myth criticism continued to develop alongside the several varieties of formalism. But in a sense, formalism grew out of the exhaustion of expressive criticism. Literature, once thought to grow organically from the artistic imagination, which, as Samuel Taylor Coleridge (p. 222) said, was "coexistent with the conscious will," was increasingly seen as deriving from forces beyond the artist's control (milieu, class, unconscious drives, the collective unconscious). The poet appeared to be less an agent and more a catalyst in the act of creation,[2] while poetry, like music, painting, and sculpture, became increasingly abstract. And in the demotic twentieth century, audience reaction has seemed an even less plausible guide to art than in the eighteenth. The eighteenth-century split between refined and popular art, which had been partially repaired during the Victorian era, re-emerged in the 1890s to become an ongoing fixture of twentieth-century culture.

As a result, criticism was left with almost nowhere to go. With the principle of imitation stymied by the vogue of abstraction, the fashion of the impersonal artist nullifying the romantic appeal to expression, and the fragmented and unreliable audience undermining rhetorical criticism, the only avenue left was an appeal to pure form. These developments seem to have been felt all over Europe and America after World War I, and they culminated in a variety of formalist movements: Russian formalism,

---

[2]The cult of impersonality in poetry and of the poet as the catalyst will be found in the criticism of T. S. Eliot (p. 318), one of the founders of the New Criticism.

structuralism, the New Criticism, neo-Aristotelianism. Another factor, exterior to art and criticism, was the development of the modern university, within which departments of literature, structured like those of the natural and social sciences, may have sought for a comparably "objective" and "scientific" mode of literary study, which the varieties of formalism could supply.[3]

During the most recent revolution, which began in the years since Abrams drew up his map, many literary theorists have viewed literature as the free play of signifiers. In this view, words — the signifiers — no longer have an innocent connection to their meanings — the signified; and the relation of language and meaning is not transparent. Instead of testifying to the truth and beauty of the world, instead of expressing the personality (or impersonality) of the author, instead of delighting and instructing its audience, instead of presenting an abstract aesthetic form, language now expresses the circularity of meaning, contemplates the paradoxes of its own making. The text is no longer the poem isolated in the center of the diagram. Rather textuality — the condition of inscription within language — is implicated in all our knowledge of the world, of reading, of expression. History is no longer the inferior of poetry, as Aristotle thought, nor its master, as Karl Marx suggested. History cannot even be opposed to poetry, for both of them are equally texts; they may be seen as discursive practices, modes of power/knowledge that need to be analyzed using the rules of New Historicism and cultural studies. Thus we have returned full circle to the position of the Sophists, for whom everything was ruled by the art of rhetoric. A key question for the future of theory is whether the key topics of textuality, language, and discursive practice will remain at the center of critical study or whether some new revolution may not lurk over the horizon.

Other Maps of the Critical Terrain

Abrams's map of the spectrum of critical theory is useful as far as it goes. But maps have a way of reducing the number of dimensions, inevitably distorting even as they clarify the actual landscape. The points of Abrams's compass should not be taken as natural, self-evident, or unquestionable. Like any other theoretical construct, Abrams's map includes areas of blindness as well as insight, and its limitations derive from its unstated assumptions. By differentiating between "rhetorical" and "objective" theories, for example, Abrams seems to presume that the text can have a meaning apart from what it means to its readers. In practice, however, many formalist critics have relied heavily for their analysis on what an "ideal" or "potential" reader would make of the text. Nor can Abrams's map comfortably accommodate forms of criticism (Marxist and otherwise) that view the text, author, and reader as determined, collectively or separately, by the processes of history. (Abrams may think that an author expresses his or her age, but while this will do for some forms of historical criticism, it will not adequately characterize neo-Marxist criticism, New Historicism, or cultural studies.)

[3] Cf. Richard Ohmann, *English in America* (New York: Oxford University Press, 1976), and Gerald Graff, *Professing Literature: An Institutional History* (Chicago: University of Chicago Press, 1987).

Another limitation of the Abrams map — or at least of how many readers have employed it — is the specious linearity it imposes upon the history of criticism. It seems to imply that mimetic thought was confined to classical antiquity and that everyone shifted from rhetorical to expressive criticism around the end of the eighteenth century. Not only did rhetorical criticism continue to be practiced throughout the nineteenth and twentieth centuries, but (as Robert Marsh has shown) one essential pattern of romantic criticism flourished during what is typically considered the neoclassical period. The prestige of the Abrams map should not mask the importance of other theorists and critics (such as James "Hermes" Harris or Walter Scott) whose work implicitly challenges Abrams's notion of historical succession.

One way of transcending the limitations of the Abrams map is by formulating other maps whose limitations are different. The Abrams map groups literary theories in terms of the critical principle on which each rests. Both R. S. Crane (p. 457) and Norman Friedman have, at different times, constructed a different sort of map to clarify the interrelationships of critical tasks and the variety of approaches to a given literary work. The form of these maps is not a group of adjacent territories, but a series of concentric circles, with the work itself in the middle. A single composite map combining the essential features of both might look something like Figure 2 on page 10.

This map is one way of visualizing the relationship of various modes of literary interpretation to one another. Its bias is its suggestion that a poem is determined most intimately by the requirements of form, both its own organic shape and the institutional shapes that culture bequeaths to art. (For example, the terseness of a sonnet — its fourteen-line structure — is a formal issue.) As long as form accounts adequately for an aspect of a given work, no explanation need be sought elsewhere.

But when form is exhausted, one must turn directly to the poet, both to the poet's conscious life (biographical interpretation) and to the poet's unconscious fantasies and defenses (psychological interpretation). The circle is broader here, too, because what biographical and psychological interpretation reveals will cover the whole of the artist's work. Still broader modes of interpretation, sociological and historical, will link that work with others written by authors of the same class in the same era — or explain the differences among works written from different class perspectives and at different times. Broadest of all (and hence least explanatory of any given work) are interpretations based on human universals. One such universal is the collective unconscious of Carl Gustav Jung, whose archetypes are said to run through all imaginative literature and art. Another is the ethical wisdom that can give works of literature long-term significance across cultural boundaries.[4]

Neither of these maps of the critical tasks assigns an explicit spot to the most traditional job of the critic: judging the quality of a literary work. In effect, academic critics indicate their preferences by what they choose to spend their time interpreting (although this implicit procedure is currently being questioned in a wide-ranging debate

[4]For further discussion of this "concentric" map of critical theory, see R. S. Crane, "Questions and Answers in the Teaching of Literary Texts," in *The Idea of the Humanities,* vol 2. (Chicago: University of Chicago Press, 1966); and Norman Friedman, "Pluralism Exemplified: *Great Expectations* and *The Great Gatsby,*" in *Form and Meaning in Fiction* (Athens: University of Georgia Press, 1975).

over the literary canon). And both maps, it will be noted, place the work in the center, thus implying that the text is the still and stable point around which the complex world of critical thought revolves — which seems reasonable enough, since it went unquestioned for over two thousand years. But this dogma is precisely what a good deal of audience-centered criticism is challenging today, and maps like those of Abrams and Crane/Friedman will be seen as seriously distortive by those who feel that the text is not a stable entity or that it is determined by the reader. At the same time, any map that placed the reader in the center would be thought severely distorted by critics of many other persuasions. But how is a map to avoid a center?

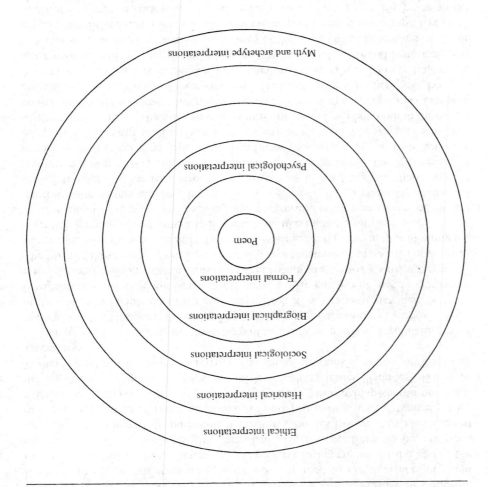

Figure 2

Semantic Maps: Ideas about Method

One map of sufficient generality and neutrality might be derived from the semantics of Richard McKeon. It would group critics according to their methods, or modes of thought, rather than their central topic. Whereas the Abrams map groups Plato with Aristotle and Plotinus because of the centrality in all three of the principles of mimesis, the McKeon map would emphasize Plato's dialectical method — his habit of analogizing the structure of an upper realm (the world of Ideas) to a lower realm (the world of Matter). Aristotle does not work that way, though Plotinus does. Later critics with different principles, like the expressive critic Samuel Taylor Coleridge and the formal critic Cleanth Brooks (p. 449), adopted the same dialectical method.

Dialectic is one of four abstract methods of proceeding, which include the operational, the problematic, and the logistic, that McKeon calls modes of thought. Walter Davis, in *The Act of Interpretation*, has defined them succinctly: Dialectic is a method of assimilation to a model whereby comprehensive truths are approximated or embodied. Operational thought is a method of discrimination and postulation whereby arbitrary formulations are interpreted in order to distinguish the different legitimate perspectives on a topic. The problematic is a method of inquiry that separates questions into the distinct disciplines in which particular problems are determined and solved. Logistic thought is a method of composition in which irreducible least parts are put together by means of invariable laws.[5]

Dialectical thinkers, such as Plato and Georg Wilhelm Friedrich Hegel, see the world as a bound and interconnected whole, with a lower realm (defined by terms like *becoming* or *consciousness*) and an upper realm (that of *being* or *self-consciousness*). Such a pattern runs through all of reality, and each aspect of life — religion, politics, ethics, aesthetics — can be analyzed in the same way using analogous terms.

But where dialectical thought is intrinsically interdisciplinary, problematic thought is discipline-bound. Problematic thinkers, such as Aristotle and John Dewey, see the world as containing a number of irreconcilable things and therefore find no single method that will answer all questions, no single set of terms that can be used to grapple with all problems. The initial task of problematic thinking is to separate disciplines according to their scope, determining their bounds and establishing a method of inquiry according to the nature of the discipline itself.

[5]Walter A. Davis, *The Act of Interpretation: A Critique of Literary Reason* (Chicago: University of Chicago Press, 1978), pp. 93–94. McKeon's grid is too complex to do justice to here, since it contains three other dimensions as well: A dialectical thinker might have comprehensive, simple, reflexive, or actional principles. There are also quadripartite distinctions for a thinker's organization and interpretation. The result is sixteen categories that generate 256 possible positions. McKeon's own mode of thought is, of course, operationalist — his grid is a way of talking about the relation among modes of discourse. Richard McKeon's clearest exposition of his semantics occurs in an essay called "Philosophic Semantics and Philosophic Discovery," widely circulated among his students but unpublished at his death. It was published posthumously in Richard P. McKeon, *Freedom and History and Other Essays,* ed. Zahava K. McKeon (Chicago: University of Chicago Press, 1990). See also his article "Philosophy and Method" in *Journal of Philosophy* 48 (1951): 653–81; and "Imitation and Poetry," in his book *Thought, Action and Passion* (Chicago: University of Chicago Press, 1954). See also the exposition of McKeon in Walter A. Davis, "Critical Theory and Philosophic Method," in *The Act of Interpretation,* pp. 88–119.

Like dialectical thinkers, operational thinkers take a holistic view of the universe, but for them, the whole is determined not by the nature of things, but by the way people view them and talk about them. There is no higher realm of being or truth: The way people see things is all there is. The role of operational thought, in Cicero or in Kenneth Burke (p. 385), is to clarify discourse, to reduce the ambiguities that arise from using common language to describe disparate perspectives.

Like problematic thinkers, logistic thinkers avoid the holistic; but unlike them, they have a single method, which is associated with but not limited to modern science: breaking down phenomena into their least parts and then discovering the laws by which those parts are interrelated. This method is clearest in sciences like chemistry and physics, which are concerned with particles and forces, but a logistic approach has also been made to politics (by Niccolò Machiavelli), ethics (by René Descartes and Thomas Hobbes), and social structure (by Claude Lévi-Strauss, p. 503).

Applied to literature, dialectical thought often takes poetry to be a mode of thinking, while problematic thought often takes it to be a mode of making. Operational thought considers literature as one of many forms of discourse; logistic thought considers litera-ture as data in its scientific analysis of the parts of a text, confident that parts make up a whole. Another map might be created, in other words, gathering dialectical thinkers (like Plato, Plotinus, Coleridge, and Hegel) into one group, problematic thinkers (like Aristotle) into another, logistic thinkers (like Freud or Lévi-Strauss) into a third, and operational thinkers (like Alexander Pope, p. 146, and Kenneth Burke) into a fourth. This map would be more historically complicated than Abrams's since competing modes of thought would operate within a given age, but it would suggest some impor-tant linkages across the centuries that should not be ignored.[6]

It is useful to be able to refer to three maps rather than one, but in the long run, all maps are inadequate and none is wholly innocent. That is, any map, no matter how apparently objective and pluralistic, is certain to contain certain implicit assumptions con-genial to some theorists and anathema to others. Abrams's map is that of a historical critic seeking a set of distinctions that will allow him to write a history of critical thought, particularly one that will help him make sense of the transition between the eighteenth century and the romantic age. Crane, the formalist, draws a map that puts formalism in the center, the implicit starting point for any further study of the text. McKeon's map, though contemporary with Abrams's, looks like something a structuralist might devise, with spatial vectors that replace linear causality. Maps are like Ludwig Wittgenstein's ladder in the *Tractatus Logico-Philosophicus* (1922): We can climb only with their assistance, but once we have ascended, we throw them to the ground. Once we outgrow the maps we are given, we learn to do without them — or do as our three mapmakers did: Make our own.

[6]Applied to the critical revolution of the past three decades, the McKeon map might suggest that operational thought, hitherto one element among many, moved into the vanguard, as once dialectical Marxists began (after Louis Althusser, p. 740) to consider history as a text rather than a force, as once logistical psychoanalysts began (after Jacques Lacan, p. 645) to think of the unconscious as a mode of discourse rather than a hidden space. Similarly, the Derridean revolution consists in the displacement of grammar (in Ferdinand de Saussure's logistical approach, p. 492) by rhetoric.

Traditional literature courses typically impose a method and an order on the disparate texts of one period or one author. In contrast, a course in critical theory will often call into question the very myths of order the traditions of culture have handed down. The study of critical theory tends to raise the ultimate questions about literature and its relation to life without establishing an ultimate order, because the clash of one principle, one method, one logic with another cannot be evaded. To the extent that these oppositions are genuinely understood, we are unlikely to end by resolving their differences into a tidy and harmonious chorus. We can, however, set the voices at play, engage them in contrapuntal dialogue with each other, and enter that dialogue ourselves. And in discoursing with some of the most probing minds that have trained their gaze upon literature, we become participants in an ancient and exalted conversation.

UNPACKING CRITICAL THEORIES

Having first ascended to an overview of theory as a whole, we now need to descend to where theory meets practical criticism, where theory informs talk about literary texts, for there are some very practical reasons why those who want to study literature need to understand literary theory. Any research we do into a poem, a play, or a novel is certain to bring us into contact with contemporary critical essays, essays that, whether or not they explicitly support a particular literary theory, use theoretical vocabulary as a kind of shorthand to indicate the writer's critical assumptions.

At one time academic articles were expected to be written in a transparent language that could be easily understood by the educated layman, but today we need to be able to "unpack" the author's language to discover the theory or, more often, theories underlying the literary discourse. Even book reviews in popular magazines by non-academic writers can have us reaching for the dictionary of literary terms and make us grateful for whatever grounding in theory we have. For instance, in his *New Yorker* review of Colm Tóibín's novel about Henry James, John Updike raises issues about the recent vogue of the historical novel and the postmodern uses of the recorded past in ways that presume that the reader is familiar with theories of postmodernism such as those of Jean Baudrillard and Fredric Jameson:

> Fiction about actual historical persons, so intrinsically conflicted and impure, feels like part of postmodernism's rampant eclecticism. True, examples exist before the twentieth century, in, say, Tolstoy's depiction of Napoleon and the Russian general Kutuzov in "War and Peace," and in the portraits of the poet Petronius, the emperor Nero, and the saint Peter in Sienkiewicz's "Quo Vadis?" But until truth became thoroughly relative, and image seized priority over fact, and the historical past became an attic full of potentially entertaining trinkets, the famous dead were allowed to rest in the record they left in their documents and documented deeds, in their letters and the accounts of their contemporaries.[7]

Articles in learned journals are even more explicitly steeped in theoretical discourses, and it may be even more difficult to unpack the structure of assumptions, because

---

[7]John Updike, "Silent Master," *The New Yorker* (June 28, 2004): 98.

today's critics are less likely to raise questions that are purely formalist or purely Marxist or purely psychoanalytic. More than likely we will discover that we need to unpack a complicated eclectic mixture of literary theories, such as we find in the following example, taken from a remarkable essay by Jay Ladin.[8] Here are the first four paragraphs, in which Ladin makes his intentions and his methods clear — to those who know how to read him:

"So Anthracite, to live": Emily Dickinson and American Literary History[9]

It was R. P. Blackmur who described the phrase "So Anthracite, to live" as "beyond bearing awkward to read" (42).[10] Even now, when we have had seven more decades to grow accustomed to Dickinson's peculiar diction, "So Anthracite, to live" is a shockingly awkward phrase, one of many in Dickinson's unruly oeuvre. Twentieth-century American poetry experiments with norm-defying diction, but how did a woman in the early 1860s come to write phrases such as "So Anthracite, to live"? To put it differently, how should American literary history account for Emily Dickinson?

For the most part, as Margaret Dickie points out, it hasn't. "[E]ven when she is acknowledged as a great writer, Dickinson has never found a central place in American literary history . . . Dickinson remains an anomaly . . . fit into a largely masculine history . . . as an eccentric woman isolated from the main concerns of the day" (186, 187).[11] Dickinson is fortunate to have achieved even anomaly status. Though the nineteenth century was a boom era for American women poets — as Paula Bennett notes, "by the last decades of the century, women poets were beginning to out-publish men even in the most exclusive and prestigious venues" — none but Dickinson have entered the canons of American literary history (216). Dickie argues that the marginalization of Dickinson and eclipse of other nineteenth-century women authors are symptoms of the same androcentric astigmatism and that alloting Dickinson a central role in American literary history will bring other women's achievements into proper focus: "[A] literary history that would include women writers should start with Dickinson and redo the conventional story by fitting literary history around the poet, considering both how she defines the period and how literary history might be redone if she were placed at its center" (187). But fitting American literary history around Dickinson is easier said than done, because both Dickinson's claim to a place in that history and her relegation to its margins derive in large part from the innovative approach to poetic language apparent in phrases such as "So Anthracite, to live" — an approach unparalleled among female (or, for that matter, male) nineteenth-century American poets.

For the most part, scholars have swerved around the question of how Dickinson's use of language relates to that of her contemporaries.[12] Studies that focus on Dickinson's

[8] *Emily Dickinson Journal* 13, no. 1 (2004): 19–50. [Slightly revised by the author.]

[9] From Emily Dickinson's poem "More Life - went out - when He went," Fr415. [Ladin] [The number Fr415 refers to the numbering of Emily Dickinson's poems as established in the Ralph W. Franklin edition (Cambridge: Harvard University Press, 1999).]

[10] R. P. Blackmur, *Language as Gesture* (New York: Harcourt Brace, 1962).

[11] Margaret Dickie, "Emily Dickinson in History and Literary History," in *Challenging Boundaries: Gender and Periodization*, eds. Joyce W. Warren and Margaret Dickie (Athens: University of Georgia Press, 2000).

[12] Dickie's efforts to recenter American literary history focus on establishing Dickinson as a writer engaged with the major political event of her era — the Civil War. Like most content-oriented studies of Dickinson, Dickie says little about how Dickinson uses language. [Ladin]

language tend either to treat her innovations as unique idiosyncrasies or to present her as a sort of wrinkle in time, a modernist poet born fifty or a hundred years early.[13] Both these approaches avoid relating Dickinson's poetics to those of her contemporaries; both isolate Dickinson from her milieu. Historicizing studies that locate Dickinson in cultural context generally ignore the peculiarity of Dickinson's poetic language.[14] Even studies that focus on aspects of Dickinson's poetics, such as Christine Ross' recent "Uncommon Measures," which places Dickinson's prosody in the context of practices promoted in nineteenth-century textbooks, tend to overlook her deviant diction.[15] But to move Dickinson to the center of American literary history — and, by extension, to fashion "a literary history that would include women writers" as central rather than peripheral figures — we must understand how Dickinson's "anomalous" treatment of language relates to the more normative language of her contemporaries. That is, we must read Dickinson's work as an example of, rather than an exception to, nineteenth-century women's poetry, before we can take up Dickie's challenge to "consider both how [Dickinson] defines the period and how literary history" — i.e., the history which leads to and through Dickinson into the feverish poetic innovation of the twentieth century — "might be redone if she were placed at its center."

To bring the common ground between Dickinson's treatment of language and that of her peers into focus, this essay, like many other recent studies of Dickinson, adapts concepts introduced by Mikhail Bakhtin for the study of novels to poetic analysis.[16] Specifically, I argue that Dickinson transfigures common nineteenth-century linguistic materials, themes and rhetorical modes into previously unheard-of diction such as "So Anthracite, to live" by tipping the balance of what Bakhtin calls "centripetal and centrifugal forces" from the centripetally-weighted modes characteristic of most nineteenth-century poetry to centrifugally-weighted modes that became a mainstay of twentieth-century American modernist poetry. Building on recent work by Paula Bennett, I argue that Dickinson's precociously modernist treatment of language represents not an isolated literary mutation, but a conscious engagement with — and reaction against — the flourishing mid-nineteenth-century American women's poetry scene. By examining Dickinson's early letters and poems, I show that Dickinson's precociously modernist configuration of centripetal and centrifugal forces evolved from a technique that Bakhtin calls "novelization" which was common in nineteenth-century prose, and had already been adapted to poetic uses by other nineteenth-century women poets by the 1850s, when Dickinson began to write seriously. Finally, I consider how American literary history looks when Dickinson is placed at its center, focusing on Dickinson's crucial but complex relation to the tradition of American

[13]For example, Cristanne Miller's landmark study *Emily Dickinson: A Poet's Grammar* catalogues and analyzes the interpretive implications of Dickinson's idiosyncratic diction and punctuation with little attempt to relate Dickinson's techniques to those of other nineteenth-century poets. David Porter's *Dickinson: The Modern Idiom*, the most extended presentation of Dickinson in relation to twentieth-century modernist poetry, argues that Dickinson should be read as the "first practitioner" of "an extreme . . . American modernism" (1). [Ladin]

[14]See for example Domhnall Mitchell's fine *Emily Dickinson: Monarch of Perception*, which notes Dickinson's polysemy but does not address the difference between her poetic language and that of her contemporaries. [Ladin]

[15]For example, Ross' discussion of "My Reward for Being - was this" (Fr375) does not note the oddity of language such as "When Thrones - accost my Hands - / With 'Me - Miss - Me' - / I'll unroll - Thee -." [Ladin]

[16]Bakhtin-influenced scholars of poetry have long noted that Bakhtin's insistence that poetry is monoglossic does not hold true for many texts. Indeed, Gerald Bruns has suggested that American poetry is inherently heteroglossic. [Ladin]

women's poetry, and the deep continuities between nineteenth-century American verse and the twentieth-century poetic practices that Dickinson's work prefigures.

The problem, as Ladin announces in his title, is the relationship of Emily Dickinson to American literary history. But Ladin begins with the observation, not of a literary historian, but of a New Critic, R. P. Blackmur, about the difficulty "beyond bearing" of Dickinson's poetic diction in the last line of her poem "More Life — went out — when He went." This leads Ladin to the key paradox: Dickinson's use of language is "shock-ing" and "experimental," akin to the poetics of the modernist poets of the 1920s, such as T. S. Eliot, Ezra Pound, and Marianne Moore (who were the heroes of the New Critics). But to view Dickinson purely as a "precocious modernist" writing in the 1860s would be to isolate her from the literary history of her own period. Previous writers have found contemporary themes in Dickinson, such as the devastation of the Civil War, but have not accounted for her poetics. Ladin wants simultaneously to do justice to the originality of Dickinson's poetic techniques and to view her as a woman of her time.

Two other recent theoretical movements stand in the background of Ladin's problem and have assisted Ladin with his quest: feminism and New Historicism (see respectively Chapters 7 and 6). Feminist scholarship like that of Paula Bennett has made us aware that women were publishing poetry in great volume in the important periodicals of the nineteenth century, and has unearthed once-forgotten female poets who were Emily Dickinson's peers in her own period. And the New Historicism has made clear that "history is textual" and that the writers of a given period are often responding not only to their peers in the literary world but also to genres at the margins of the literary (sermons, eulogies, legal tracts, advertisements). In the course of his essay, Ladin will quote a conventional eulogy on Abraham Lincoln by Phineas Gurley as one example of what Dickinson's obituary poem, "More Life," was explicitly reacting against. And he will quote a poem by Sarah Louise Forten published in William Lloyd Garrison's *Liberator* as proof that Dickinson's radical poetics were not hers alone.

But the theorist who provides Ladin with the important tools for his mission is Mikhail Bakhtin (see the selection from "Discourse in the Novel," pp. 352–61). Bakhtin discusses how novelists of the nineteenth century, such as Charles Dickens, created their satirical narrative voices by importing and juxtaposing for comic effect catch phrases used by various trades and professions, by the classes and the masses. This discussion is Ladin's key to what Dickinson is doing. In effect, Ladin argues, Dickinson shifts this technique from prose to poetry, where the catch phrases belong to a disembodied voice rather than literary characters, and are juxtaposed within the confines of brief lyrics that react against the conventional sentiments of contempo-rary poetic discourse.

So in the article as a whole Ladin accounts for Dickinson as a writer of her time, in reacting against the conventional poetry of her day and in using the techniques of the nineteenth-century comic novel, but also as a great original in adapting those techniques to poetry. And he accounts for why Dickinson, despite her grounding in the nineteenth century, also appears to us as a precocious modernist: because the "centrifugal" qualities of Dickinson's poetry are similar to that of modernists like

Eliot and Moore, even though those modernists came to their poetics through a different route.

Unpacking Ladin's essay is relatively easy because he is a lucid writer who is at great pains to indicate his sources and his critical affiliations. He also has a single key critical figure (Mikhail Bakhtin) at the center of his approach to Dickinson. But not all critical discourse is so lucid, or based on a single theoretical approach.

At the other end of the range, both of difficulty of the language and complexity of the argument, is the following passage, taken from the first pages of Gayatri Chakravorty Spivak's Introduction to Ranajit Guha's *Subaltern Studies*:[17]

> The work of the Subaltern Studies group offers a theory of change. The insertion of India into colonialism is generally defined as a change from semi-feudalism into capitalist subjection. Such a definition theorizes the change within the great narrative of the modes of production and, by uneasy implication, within the narrative of the transition from feudalism to capitalism. Concurrently, this change is seen as the inauguration of politicization for the colonized. The colonial subject is seen as emerging from those parts of the indigenous elite which come to be loosely described as "bourgeois nationalist." The Subaltern Studies group seems to me to be revising this general definition and its theorization by proposing at least two things: first, that the moment(s) of change be pluralized and plotted as confrontations rather than transition (they would thus be seen in relation to histories of domination and exploitation rather than within the great modes-of-production narrative) and, secondly, that such changes are signaled or marked by a functional change in sign-systems. The most important functional change is from the religious to the militant. There are, however, many other functional changes in sign-systems indicated in these collections: from crime to insurgency, from bondsman to worker, and so on.
>
> The most significant outcome of this revision or shift in perspective is that the agency of change is located in the insurgent or the "subaltern." A functional change in a sign-system is a violent event. Even when it is perceived as "gradual," or "failed," or yet "reversing itself," the change itself can only be operated by the force of a crisis. Yet, if the space for a change (necessarily also an addition) had not been there in the prior function of the sign-system, the crisis could not have made the change happen. The change in signification-function supplements the previous function. The Subaltern Studies collective scrupulously annotates this double movement.
>
> They generally perceive their task as making a theory of consciousness or culture rather than specifically a theory of change. It is because of this, I think, that the force of crisis, *although never far from their argument*, is not systematically emphasized in their work, and sometimes disarmingly alluded to as "impingement," "combination," "getting caught up in a general wave," "circumstances for unification," "reasons for change," "ambiguity," "unease," "transit[ion]," "bringing into focus"; even as it is also described as "switch," "catching fire" and, pervasively, as "turning upside down" — all critical concept-metaphors that would indicate force. Indeed, a general sobriety of tone will not allow them to emphasize sufficiently that they are themselves bringing hegemonic historiography to crisis. This leads them to describe the clandestine operation of supplementarity as the inexorable speculative logic of the dialectic. In this they seem to me to do themselves a disservice, for, as self-professed dialecticians, they open themselves to older debates between

[17]New York: Oxford University Press, 1988.

spontaneity and consciousness or structure and history. Their actual practice, which I will argue, is closer to deconstruction, would put these oppositions into question. A theory of change as the site of the displacement of function between sign-systems — which is what they oblige me to read in them — is a theory of reading in the strongest possible general sense. The site of displacement of the function of signs is the name of reading as active transaction between past and future. This transactional reading as (the possibility of) ac-tion, even at its most dynamic, is perhaps what Antonio Gramsci meant by 'elaboration,' *e-laborare*, working out. If seen in this way, the work of the Subaltern Studies group re-peatedly makes it possible for us to grasp that the concept-metaphor of the 'social text' is not the reduction of real life to the page of a book. My theoretical intervention is a modest attempt to remind us of this. (3–5)

The key to unpacking this difficult passage involves locating where Spivak stands in relation to the Subaltern Studies group she is introducing. Since she is writing an introduction to a collection of their essays, one might expect to find her in general agreement with them. But it is quite clear from the tone of the opening lines that her attitude seems to be one of critique rather than of univocal praise. Spivak would agree that, relative to the currently available histories of social change in India, Subaltern Studies offers a massive improvement, but all the same, Spivak is not entirely happy with the way the group has characterized the social history it chronicles and with its own efforts at historiography.

Even this may be difficult to pick up because the history books touching India and imperialism that most of us are likely to have actually read are not on the horizon of Spivak's essay. Standard "world studies" history textbooks discuss the colonization of India in the eighteenth century and its emancipation in the mid-twentieth century in terms that emphasize India as a land exploited but also modernized and given a set of enlightened civil institutions by Great Britain, and this story of colonization and emancipation is told in terms of the major personalities involved: John Clive and Warren Hastings, Gandhi and Nehru, and Mountbatten. This story, whatever its value, is not on Spivak's map at all.

The historiography against which Spivak views the Subaltern Studies group as an improvement is traditional Marxist historiography, which would inevitably represent the colonization of India in terms of what Spivak calls "the great narrative of modes of production," as a possession acquired and exploited by the burgeoning industrial capitalists of England, first because of the need for access to exotic imports (such as tea and spices), but later, as the nineteenth century progressed, as a captive market for the export of English industrial goods. Spivak talks of the "uneasy implication" of this narrative. What she is uneasy about is the fact that the protagonist of colonial history in Marx's grand narrative of modes of production is not the native Indian, but the English bureaucrat and industrialist (who by pushing capitalism to its limits will bring about the proletarian revolution). The natives of India, within this narrative, are not agents or, as Spivak puts it, "subjects." They are mere objects, victims of exploita-tion, for most of the history of the Raj. Similarly, the story of the emancipation of India in the mid-twentieth century is the story of "bourgeois nationalists" seeking self-rule in order to exploit Indian workers themselves instead of having them exploited by industrialists living abroad, and the active agents will predictably be the elite classes of postcolonial India. Again there is no room for the masses.

Spivak goes on to claim that the Subaltern Studies group proposes to write a different history based on the ideas of the Marxist thinker Antonio Gramsci (1891–1937). It was Gramsci who coined the term "subaltern" in the sense of the subject who is dominated by the physical power of the state and not merely by its ideological apparatus. (For further information, see the introduction to Marxist Criticism, p. 693.) This revised history would allow a greater active role to the masses, would view them as "workers" with a collective or class consciousness rather than as "bondsmen" or slaves with at best an individual hatred for their owners or exploiters. Similarly, Gramsci would view their rebellions against the systems set up by the British as "insurgency" (collective opposition) instead of "crime" (individuals breaking laws). This in turn would allow the Subaltern Studies group to write what has been called "history from the bottom up": the emancipation of India would be viewed as the result of the efforts of the masses rather than as the victory of elite bourgeois leaders like Nehru.

Spivak is definitely in favor of "history from the bottom up," but she feels that the Subaltern Studies group is selling itself short by not comprehending that "a functional change in a sign system is a violent event." Even more revolutionary than the insurgency of the masses against the British Raj, for Spivak, is the crisis in historiography that the Subaltern Studies group is forcing upon Marxist thought. At bottom, her critique of Subaltern Studies is that it has not paid sufficient attention to the revolutionary implications of its own activities. Despite occasionally falling back into vague terms like *gradual* or *transition*, the Subaltern Studies group has actually caused a change in the sign-systems of history.

Here Spivak is speaking as a deconstructionist rather than as a Marxist: A change in discourse is in this context a revolution more powerful than the storming of the Bastille. When she refers to the Subaltern Studies group's "theory of change . . . between sign-systems" as "a theory of reading," Spivak is appealing to Paul de Man's *Allegories of Reading*; when she refers to it as employing the "operation of supplementarity," Spivak is appealing to Jacques Derrida's *Of Grammatology*. In both cases she sees the rhetorical moves of deconstruction as evading "older debates" within Marxism (such as the debate about the value of class consciousness versus that of spontaneity), which she sees as leading nowhere. Spivak sees Gramsci's language as deconstructing the discourse of Karl Marx, and the changes in the language of history of the Subaltern Studies group as revolutionizing the narratives about subaltern insurgency.

This is only the start of a far more complex essay; later on, Spivak will critique the Subaltern Studies group in terms of the dilemmas about representing consciousness. When the educated historian writes about the activities of the illiterate masses (who necessarily cannot write their own history), it is the historian's thought process that necessarily takes over and thereby effaces the consciousness of those whose chronicler he is. And finally Spivak analyzes the even more intense dilemma of the representation of the Indian woman and the way femininity operates within patriarchal Indian society. Spivak points out how "woman" (as the Othered subordinate to "man") becomes a metaphor for India as a whole, in the scheme of colonial social relations, and how that metaphor effaces, even more completely, the consciousness of actual Indian women.

At this point, if the unpacking has been a success, one can go back to the Spivak passage and understand its drift. But how does one do that for oneself? We can go back over the steps in the process, which can be generalized as follows:

1. *Identify the sources the writer is using.* In the case of Ladin, the key source, apart from Emily Dickinson herself, is Mikhail Bakhtin's "Discourse and the Novel," quoted in the fourth paragraph and discussed at length later in the essay. The New Critical reading of Blackmur is there primarily to demonstrate how challenging Dickinson's discourse could be even to critics who valorized modern poetry, and the various studies of Dickinson cited are primarily "touchstones." Ladin discusses to show that he is aware of previous work on American literary history and on Dickinson's poetics and that he is not repeating already published studies.

In the case of Spivak, the key sources are Gramsci and Marx, Derrida and de Man. And one of the things that makes Spivak so difficult to penetrate is that, of the four, only Gramsci is mentioned in Spivak's text. We are expected to understand that her general topic is Marxist historiography through Spivak's use of phrases that explicitly echo Marx's texts, like "capitalist subjection" and "great narrative of the modes of production." Similarly, although Spivak mentions "deconstruction," the name Derrida is not mentioned; we are expected to pick this up because terms like "supplement" and "supplementarity" connect up with Derrida's arguments about discourse in *Of Grammatology* (see the introduction to structuralism and deconstruction, p. 470).

How does the reader pick up covert references of that sort? One might as well be honest about the fact that writing like Spivak's can be obscure even to highly trained scholars. The reader of *The Critical Tradition*, however, will find by consulting the index that "supplement" leads one to Derrida, and that Gramsci is discussed at length in terms of his influence on Althusser and Eagleton. Even in Ladin's essay, it would not be obvious to everyone who R. P. Blackmur is or what set of ideas about poetry he stands for (Blackmur, too, can be found in the index to *The Critical Tradition* and is identified as a New Critic on p. 416).

2. *Determine the writer's stance toward sources.* Ladin finds he needs to critique two varieties of Dickinson criticism: formal criticism that detaches Dickinson from history, as though one could be a modernist poet half a century before modernist poetry began to be written; and *historical* criticism that places Dickinson in her own time in terms of the subject matter touched on in her poetry, but does not bother to account for Dickinson's formal innovations, as though these were an unimportant part of her reputation. Ladin's critique is not mean-spirited or even snarky, but it makes clear that the question he is working on is one that should interest any serious reader of Dickinson. Ladin is not critical of either Dickinson or Bakhtin. His primary difficulty is in getting them together, since Bakhtin's discussion of "centrifugal" and "centripetal" writing in "Discourse and the Novel" is, as the title suggests, primarily aimed at explaining how prose fiction (including narrative poetry, such as Pushkin's *Eugene Onegin*) works as a speech act. Since Bakhtin does not discuss lyric poetry as such, and at one point suggests that the lyric is not dialogical, Ladin has to work

hard, in a key section of his article not reproduced here, to show that Bakhtin's ideas apply fruitfully to Dickinson.

Spivak's tone is quite different: She is making a "theoretical intervention" to "remind" the Subaltern Studies group of what is genuinely revolutionary about their historiography. Rather than considering them as misguided or wrong-headed, she thinks that they are going about things the right way but are theoretically woolly: They need to understand better than they do exactly how right they are. For Spivak, furthermore, the deconstructionists de Man and Derrida are also revolutionaries operating in the realm of discourse (Spivak's view, though, is not the only possible one: In the 1990s leftist writers attacked deconstruction as a politically suspect evasion of ideology). Despite her own commitment to Marxism, Spivak holds Marx's "grand narrative" at arm's length: For postcolonial theory, Marx needs to be revised or, as she would put it, "deconstructed" by Gramsci in order to allow agency and a subject position to the "subaltern" under the Raj.

3. *Identify the writer's theoretical commitments.* At this point we are pretty well placed to understand where both Ladin and Spivak are coming from in the cited passages.

Ladin seems committed to a literary history that will do justice to both the content and form of the poetic text. Like some New Historicists, he understands the poet to be in dialogue with other cultural discourses in society, literary and otherwise, and understands that this dialogue may be a reaction against conventional utterances as well as a reproduction of those utterances. Taking poetry as a speech-act, Ladin finds the ideas of Mikhail Bakhtin useful in analyzing the ways in which a writer has travestied or re-accented the speech-acts of others, but has discarded Bakhtin's notion that this play of language has no place in lyric poetry.

Spivak, for her part, is a postcolonial theorist whose understanding of social change owes a great deal to the neo-Marxist Gramsci, who saw change occurring through social conflict at diverse zones of contact and who stressed the agency of the subaltern fighting an insurgency against state power. Like the deconstructionists, she views textuality as a pervasive condition, and she sees the possibility for revolution in new forms of discourse, new ways of "reading" society as text. She is also concerned with the issue of who is allowed to speak for whom: how the subject position of oppressed classes can be effaced even by those from the literate elites who defend those classes and how the subject position of women can be effaced by the men who presume to tell their story.

This three-step process is just one possible way of blazing a trail into criticism that depends crucially on rhetorical moves licensed by literary and cultural theory. But it should be clear from the analysis of Ladin and Spivak that any process of unpacking is going to depend at least in part on having maps of the critical terrain. To analyze we need to synthesize, but of course to read the texts that we will later synthesize we need to have analyzed them. It sounds like a vicious circle, where in order to understand anything we need first to have understood everything.

There is a name for this vicious circle — "the hermeneutic circle" — but it's actually a virtuous circle or perhaps a spiral. We enter it every time we interpret any text, including the words you are reading right now, words that have countless meanings, individually and in combination — ask any dictionary. But as we grope for the overall intention, however crudely, we remove ambiguities, which in turn allows us to refine our sense of the whole, which eliminates more ambiguities, and so on.

And that power is what is working for us here, as our unpacking not only reveals the sense of criticism but helps us revise our maps of the terrain. Our prior sense of what Bakhtin is all about allows us to understand Jay Ladin, but reading Jay Ladin has also expanded and corrected our sense of what Bakhtin is all about. Unpacking criticism thus gives us a sense of the possible reach of theory that we couldn't have gotten from reading theory alone.

CLASSIC TEXTS IN LITERARY CRITICISM

Plato

ca. 427–347 B.C.E.

"All of Western philosophy is but a footnote to Plato," Alfred North Whitehead once said, and it is true in the sense that most of the historically significant issues with which philosophy has been concerned — the nature of being, the question of how we know things, the purposes of right action, the structure of an ordered society, the meaning of love and beauty — were issues that he raised. Later philosophers, including Plato's great pupil Aristotle, have disagreed not only with his results but also with his ways of setting up the questions, and their argument with Plato makes up much of the history of thought. Nor have later thinkers always merely disagreed with and revised Plato: Century after century has witnessed a renaissance of his system of thought, most notably in the Neoplatonists of the second century C.E., the Cambridge Platonists of the latter seventeenth century, and the idealists of the romantic movement. Later thinkers, including Plotinus, Sir Philip Sidney (p. 112), and Percy Bysshe Shelley (p. 227), directly take up Plato's challenge, but his shadow falls, as Whitehead said, over all of Western thought.

For contemporary readers the most difficult concept in Plato's thought is his *idealism* — the doctrine of a permanent realm of eternal Forms that shape our mutable material world. In a philosophy class students might be asked to contrast the "Idea of the Desk" — the concept of a thing to write on that also holds one's papers — with the physical object in the classroom. The former is timeless and pure, while the latter is time-bound: It came into being, exists for a time, will soon vanish. Nor is the material desk a *perfect* desk: Its very materiality precludes it. Presumably, the Idea of the Desk must have preceded the material desk and caused it, in effect, to be created. A carpenter who is not merely copying an existing desk must be working from some inner awareness of this Idea.

This approach is a time-honored way of introducing Plato's ideas, but it tends to lead our thought downward, to wondering, for example, whether there is a Platonic Idea of a pencil shaving or of manure. Actually, despite their vulgarity, these are perfectly sound Platonic questions. The usual solution is to assume that formless things — mud, sawdust, and so on — have no Forms because they are in fact formless matter. The real problem is that the explanation removes Plato's ideas from common human thought. Few of us are acquainted, other than in theory, with the ideas of things like desks. Nor is it apparent at first glance that the Idea of a Desk is a higher or better thing than a material desk; it is certainly much harder to do one's work on.

It may be more helpful to think of a geometry class, where one operates with perfect circles, right angles, and parallel lines, and where one learns to prove theorems — or eternal truths — about them. It is understood that the diagrams drawn to illustrate the theorems, however neatly done, are imperfect representations of the lines and angles of the theorem. Here, on a mathematical level, one is working with the Ideal and the Material, and it is the Ideal — the proof, not the diagram — which counts. This may be why the door to Plato's school, the Academy, had a warning on it: "Let no one ignorant of geometry enter here."

The mathematics prerequisite, so to speak, had a good reason: Those who had already wrestled with the Idea of the Right Triangle in proving the Pythagorean theorem were prepared to understand the higher ideas of Truth, Goodness, and Beauty that Plato believed shape all human knowledge, right action, artistic endeavor, and love.

Plato developed his idealism in reaction against the notions of the Sophists. They have a poor reputation today — the word *sophistry* testifies to that — but the original Sophists were not a set of quibblers but a diverse group of teachers of what we would now call rhetoric and composition, the language arts. Some of the major Sophists, like Gorgias and Lysias, are known today because Plato used them as debating opponents for his spokesman, Socrates. The Sophists claimed that their science of language could lead to the knowledge of truth and virtue. Against this, Plato thought it danger-ous to suppose that the highest realities — Truth, Goodness, and Beauty — had the flickering impermanence of human words, and his world of ideas may derive from his fear that, like language, even matter could be shaped to cheat and deceive.

REPUBLIC, BOOK X

Book X is the most influential discussion of art in the Platonic canon. Its central thesis — that poets have no place in Plato's perfect state save as writers of hymns to the gods and songs in praise of great leaders — has stung devotees of the arts for the last two thousand years.

Book X is at the end of the *Republic,* the longest of the dialogues, which opens with the issue of whether Might makes Right. This harsh question leads Socrates and his two friends to consider the question What is Justice? Socrates' hypothesis is that Justice is knowing one's place and performing its duties — but how can one know and act properly in the imperfect Athenian polis? This question leads Socrates to fashion a model state, a republic governed by a natural elite of guardians, in which it would be possible, as it is not in Athens, to understand one's place and its duties. But how should the guardians be educated to rule? They must learn a great many other things, but at the center of their training is philosophy. And it is in answering *this* question — Of what does philosophy consist? — that Socrates presents his hierar-chical portrait of the physical and mental universe: the myth of the divided line. In simplified form, the diagram Socrates draws looks like this:

MODES OF BEING	MODES OF MENTAL ACTIVITY
Ideas	Knowing
Mathematical Forms	Understanding
Material Things	Opinion
Images	Conjecture

The first horizontal line separates the eternal world of true Being from the world of Becoming, the material things that are begotten, born, and die. The vertical line separates modes of existence from the modes of thought appropriate to them. For Plato the word *know* applies only to Ideas, but about material animals, plants, and human artifacts we can at best hold correct opinions, and with respect to mere images we can only hazard guesses.

In this context, the discussion of art in Book X is logically sound. First of all, Plato identifies art as imitation, positing that what artists do (as they have claimed in the centuries before and after Plato) is hold the mirror up to nature: They copy the appearances of men, animals, and objects in the physical world. But if this is the case, then the artistic object is merely an image, slightly but not more meaningfully permanent than a reflection in a pool of water. And the intelligence that went into its creation need involve nothing more than conjecture. (Notice that Socrates is not being redundant when he twice proves the inferiority of art: The first time he proves the inferiority of the *mode of being* of art; the second, its inferiority as a *mode of mental activity*.) As a result, art cannot be justified as an activity worthy in its own right. The poets may stay as servants of the state if they teach piety and virtue, but the pleasures of art are condemned as inherently corrupting to citizens and guardians alike.

ION

Much of the *Ion* is reasonably consistent with the *Republic,* and a good deal more entertaining if we allow ourselves to enjoy the spectacle of Socrates exposing the vanity and pretensions of the none-too-bright performer for whom the dialogue is named. (The moment when Ion declares that he is the greatest general in Athens as well as its greatest rhapsode is made richer if one remembers that at the purported time of the discourse, Athens was fighting for its survival in the Peloponnesian War.) Here, as in the *Republic,* Socrates exposes the inferiority of art as a way of knowing.

Where *Ion* differs from the *Republic* is in the suggestion contained in the image of the magnet as a metaphor of divine inspiration. Just as a magnet attracts iron and passes that attraction along, so the muse inspires the artist, who inspires the interpreter, who inspires the audience. The chain runs from the god to Homer to Ion to the applauding citizens. If this view of art is true, then it is divine, not inferior stuff.

Reconciling this notion of art with the contrary position in *Republic,* Book X, has been attempted in a number of different ways. One way is to suppose that Plato changed his mind, but that would mean trying to discover which, the *Ion* or the *Republic,* is the later dialogue (we have only conjectural datings) and deciding whether his first or second thoughts were the more trustworthy.

Another possibility is to suppose that the *Ion* is an essentially ironic (as well as humorous) dialogue, and that Socrates does not seriously respect inspiration. The Greek word translated as "inspiration" is *enthousiasmós,* and its literal meaning is closer to "demonic possession" than to the English derivative "enthusiasm." It is hard to believe that the rationalistic Plato could commend such a state. But on the other side, Socrates *does* praise such an experience elsewhere, in the *Phaedrus,* the principal dialogue on love and beauty, where poetry finds its place along with prophecy and love as forms of divine madness, the gods' most precious gifts to humanity. There Socrates claims that the state of *enthousiasmos* allows a dim but gripping memory of the Ideas, the eternal Forms of Truth, Goodness, and Beauty, which the soul experienced directly prior to its incarnation. This doctrine is narrated as a myth, but it is surely not ironic in context.

Perhaps most plausibly, the discrepancies between *Ion* and *Republic* may be ascribed to their different contexts. In *Republic* Socrates is imagining a perfect state, one that must be designed to run without benefit of chance, luck, or divine intervention. Its rulers must therefore act rightly out of permanently dependable knowledge, not occasional inspiration. In the *Ion* Socrates is discoursing about the actual world, where poets may be generally foolish and ignorant, but can sometimes be heard to speak holy truths in tongues given them by the gods.

Plato did not set down his philosophy in the usual form of a set of treatises, but rather in dialogues. Indeed, in the Seventh Letter, Plato claims that he never wrote down his philosophy at all because it could not be written down. What he seems to have meant is that the published dialogues represent philosophy as an *activity* rather than as a set of received doctrines. But Plato may also have meant the dialogues to *stimulate* philosophy: The dialogues cause us to philosophize as we read and reason and argue with the positions taken by Socrates and his interlocutors.

But if the liveliness and depth of the dialogues remain unequaled, their form creates problems of interpretation and consistency. At times we wonder whether Socrates is being serious or ironic, whether he is always speaking directly for Plato. And a position held in one dialogue may be renounced in another. Both these issues emerge in the *Republic*, Book X, and in the *Ion*.

Selected Bibliography

Cavarnos, Constantine. *Plato's Theory of Fine Art*. Athens: Astir, 1973.

Else, Gerald F. *Plato and Aristotle on Poetry*. Chapel Hill: University of North Carolina Press, 1986.

Fortenbaugh, William W., and Lewis Ayres, eds. *The Passionate Intellect: The Transformation of the Classical Traditions*. New Brunswick: Rutgers University Press, 1995.

Friedländer, Paul. *Plato*. New York: Pantheon, 1958–69.

Gadamer, Hans-Georg. "Plato und die Dichter." In *Platos Dialektische Ethik und andere Studien*. Hamburg: F. Meiner, 1968.

Gebauer, Gunter. *Mimesis: Culture — Art — Society*. Berkeley: University of California Press, 1995.

Greene, William Chase. "Plato's View of Poetry." *Harvard Studies in Classical Philology* 29 (1918): 1–75.

Grube, G. M. A. *Plato's Thought*. London: Methuen, 1935.

Gulley, Norman. *Plato's Theory of Knowledge*. London: Methuen, 1962.

Havelock, Eric. *Preface to Plato*. Cambridge: Harvard University Press, 1963.

Lodge, Rupert C. *Plato's Theory of Art*. New York: Humanities Press, 1953.

Marback, Richard. *Plato's Dream of Sophistry*. Columbia: University of South Carolina Press, 1999.

Murdoch, Iris. *The Fire and the Sun: Why Plato Banished the Artists.* Oxford: Clarendon Press, 1972.

Murray, James S. "Disputation, Deception and Dialectic: Plato on the True Rhetoric (Phaedrus 261–266)." *Philosophy and Rhetoric* 21, no. 4 (1988): 279–87.

Nightingale, Andrea Wilson. *Genres in Dialogue: Plato and the Construct of Philosophy.* Cambridge: Cambridge University Press, 1996.

Oates, Whitney J. *Plato's View of Art.* New York: Scribner, 1972.

Partee, Morriss Henry. *Plato's Poetics: The Authority of Beauty.* Salt Lake City: University of Utah Press, 1981.

Shorey, Paul. *What Plato Said.* Chicago: University of Chicago Press, 1933.

Sinaiko, Herman J. *Love, Knowledge and Discourse in Plato.* Chicago: University of Chicago Press, 1965.

Switzer, Robert. "The Topology of Madness: Philosophical Seduction in Plato's *Phaedrus*." *Alif: Journal of Comparative Poetics* 14 (1994): 6–36.

Taylor, A. E. *Plato.* 1929; Ann Arbor: University of Michigan Press, 1960.

Republic, Book X

Of the many excellences which I perceive in the order of our State, there is none which upon reflection pleases me better than the rule about poetry.

To what do you refer?

To our refusal to admit the imitative kind of poetry, for it certainly ought not to be received; as I see far more clearly now that the parts of the soul have been distinguished.

What do you mean?

Speaking in confidence, for you will not denounce me to the tragedians and the rest of the imitative tribe, all poetical imitations are ruinous to the understanding of the hearers, unless as an antidote they possess the knowledge of the true nature of the originals.

Explain the purport of your remark.

Well, I will tell you, although I have always from my earliest youth had an awe and love of Homer which even now makes the words falter on my lips, for he seems to be the great captain and teacher of the whole of that noble tragic company;

Translated by Benjamin Jowett. The speakers are Socrates and Glaucon.

but a man is not to be reverenced more than the truth, and therefore I will speak out.

Very good, he said.

Listen to me then, or rather, answer me.

Put your question.

Can you give me a general definition of imitation? for I really do not myself understand what it professes to be.

A likely thing, then, that I should know.

There would be nothing strange in that, for the duller eye may often see a thing sooner than the keener.

Very true, he said; but in your presence, even if I had any faint notion, I could not muster courage to utter it. Will you inquire yourself?

Well then, shall we begin the inquiry at this point, following our usual method: Whenever a number of individuals have a common name, we assume that there is one corresponding idea or form: — do you understand me?

I do.

Let us take, for our present purpose, any instance of such a group; there are beds and tables in the world — many of each, are there not?

Yes.

But there are only two ideas or forms of such furniture — one the idea of a bed, the other of a table.

True.

And the maker of either of them makes a bed or he makes a table for our use, in accordance with the idea — that is our way of speaking in this and similar instances — but no artificer makes the idea itself: how could he?

Impossible.

And there is another artificer — I should like to know what you would say of him.

Who is he?

One who is the maker of all the works of all other workmen.

What an extraordinary man!

Wait a little, and there will be more reason for your saying so. For this is the craftsman who is able to make not only furniture of every kind, but all that grows out of the earth, and all living creatures, himself included; and besides these he can make earth and sky and the gods, and all the things which are in heaven or in the realm of Hades under the earth.

He must be a wizard and no mistake.

Oh! you are incredulous, are you? Do you mean that there is no such maker or creator, or that in one sense there might be a maker of all these things but in another not? Do you see that there is a way in which you could make them all yourself?

And what way is this? he asked.

An easy way enough; or rather, there are many ways in which the feat might be quickly and easily accomplished, none quicker than that of turning a mirror round and round — you would soon enough make the sun and the heavens, and the earth and yourself, and other animals and plants, and furniture and all the other things of which we were just now speaking, in the mirror.

Yes, he said; but they would be appearances only.

Very good, I said, you are coming to the point now. And the painter too is, as I conceive, just such another — a creator of appearances, is he not?

Of course.

But then I suppose you will say that what he creates is untrue. And yet there is a sense in which the painter also creates a bed? Is there not?

Yes, he said, but here again, an appearance only.

And what of the maker of the bed? Were you not saying that he too makes, not the idea which according to our view is the real object denoted by the word bed, but only a particular bed?

Yes, I did.

Then if he does not make a real object he cannot make what is, but only some semblance of existence; and if any one were to say that the work of the maker of the bed, or of any other workman, has real existence, he could hardly be supposed to be speaking the truth.

Not, at least, he replied, in the view of those who make a business of these discussions.

No wonder, then, that his work too is an indistinct expression of truth.

No wonder.

Suppose now that by the light of the examples just offered we inquire who this imitator is?

If you please.

Well then, here we find three beds: one existing in nature, which is made by God, as I think that we may say — for no one else can be the maker?

No one, I think.

There is another which is the work of the carpenter?

Yes.

And the work of the painter is a third?

Yes.

Beds, then, are of three kinds, and there are three artists who superintend them: God, the maker of the bed, and the painter?

Yes, there are three of them.

God, whether from choice or from necessity, made one bed in nature and one only; two or more such beds neither ever have been nor ever will be made by God.

Why is that?

Because even if He had made but two, a third would still appear behind them of which they again both possessed the form, and that would be the real bed and not the two others.

Very true, he said.

God knew this, I suppose, and He desired to be the real maker of a real bed, not a kind of bed, and therefore He created a bed which is essentially and by nature one only.

So it seems.

Shall we, then, speak of Him as the natural author or maker of the bed?

Yes, he replied; inasmuch as by the natural process of creation, He is the author of this and of all other things.

And what shall we say of the carpenter — is not he also the maker of a bed?

Yes.

But would you call the painter an artificer and maker?

Certainly not.

Yet if he is not the maker, what is he in relation to the bed?

I think, he said, that we may fairly designate him as the imitator of that which the others make.

Good, I said; then you call him whose product is third in the descent from nature, an imitator?

Certainly, he said.

And so if the tragic poet is an imitator, he too is thrice removed from the king and from the truth; and so are all other imitators.

That appears to be so.

Then about the imitator we are agreed. And what about the painter? — Do you think he tries to imitate in each case that which originally exists in nature, or only the creation of artificers?

The latter.

As they are or as they appear? you have still to determine this.

What do you mean?

I mean to ask whether a bed really becomes different when it is seen from different points of view, obliquely or directly or from any other point of view? Or does it simply appear different, without being really so? And the same of all things.

Yes, he said, the difference is only apparent.

Now let me ask you another question: Which is the art of painting designed to be — an imitation of things as they are, or as they appear — of appearance or of reality?

Of appearance, he said.

Then the imitator is a long way off the truth, and can reproduce all things because he lightly touches on a small part of them, and that part an image. For example: A painter will paint a cobbler, carpenter, or any other artisan, though he knows nothing of their arts; and, if he is a good painter, he may deceive children or simple persons when he shows them his picture of a carpenter from a distance, and they will fancy that they are looking at a real carpenter.

Certainly.

And surely, my friend, this is how we should regard all such claims: Whenever any one informs us that he has found a man who knows all the arts, and all things else that anybody knows, and every single thing with a higher degree of accuracy than any other man — whoever tells us this, I think that we can only retort that he is a simple creature who seems to have been deceived by some wizard or imitator whom he met, and whom he thought all-knowing, because he himself was unable to analyze the nature of knowledge and ignorance and imitation.

Most true.

And next, I said, we have to consider tragedy and its leader, Homer; for we hear some persons saying that these poets know all the arts; and all things human; where virtue and vice are concerned, and indeed all divine things too; because the good poet cannot compose well unless he knows his subject, and he who has not this knowledge can never be a poet. We ought to consider whether here also there may not be a similar illusion. Perhaps they may have come across imitators and been deceived by them; they may not have remembered when they saw their works that these were thrice removed from the truth, and could easily be made without any knowledge of the truth, because they are appearances only and not realities? Or, after all, they may be in the right, and good poets do really know the things about which they seem to the many to speak so well?

The question, he said, should by all means be considered.

Now do you suppose that if a person were able to make the original as well as the image, he would seriously devote himself to the image-making branch? Would he allow imitation to be the ruling principle of his life, as if he had nothing higher in him?

I should say not.

But the real artist, who had real knowledge of those things which he chose also to imitate, would be interested in realities and not in imitations; and would desire to leave as memorials of himself works many and fair; and, instead of being the author of encomiums, he would prefer to be the theme of them.

Yes, he said, that would be to him a source of much greater honor and profit.

Now let us refrain, I said, from calling Homer or any other poet to account regarding those arts to which his poems incidentally refer: We will not ask them, in case any poet has been a doctor and not a mere imitator of medical parlance, to show what patients have been restored to health by a poet, ancient or modern, as they were by Asclepius; or what disciples in medicine a poet has left behind him, like the Asclepiads. Nor shall we press the same question upon them about the education of man, which are the chiefest and noblest subjects of his poems, and we may fairly ask him about them. "Friend Homer," then we say to him, "if you are only in the second remove from truth in what you say of virtue, and not in the third — not an image maker, that is, by our definition, an imitator — and if you are able to discern what pursuits make men better or worse in private or public life, tell us what State was ever better governed by your help? The good order of Lacedaemon is due to Lycurgus, and many other cities great and small have been similarly benefited by others; but who says that you have been a good legislator to them and have done them any good? Italy and Sicily boast of Charondas, and there is Solon who is renowned among us; but what city has anything to say about you?" Is there any city which he might name?

I think not, said Glaucon; not even the Homerids themselves pretend that he was a legislator.

Well, but is there any war on record which was carried on successfully owing to his leadership or counsel?

There is not.

Or is there anything comparable to those clever improvements in the arts, or in other operations, which are said to have been due to men of practical genius such as Thales the Milesian or Anacharsis the Scythian?

There is absolutely nothing of the kind.

But, if Homer never did any public service, was he privately a guide or teacher of any? Had he in his lifetime friends who loved to associate with him, and who handed down to posterity a Homeric way of life, such as was established by Pythagoras who was especially beloved for this reason and whose followers are to this day conspicuous among others by what they term the Pythagorean way of life?

Nothing of the kind is recorded of him. For surely, Socrates, Creophylus, the companion of Homer, that child of flesh, whose name always makes us laugh, might be more justly ridiculed for his want of breeding, if what is said is true, that Homer was greatly neglected by him in his own day when he was alive?

Yes, I replied, that is the tradition. But can you imagine, Glaucon, that if Homer had really been able to educate and improve mankind — if he had been capable of knowledge and not been a mere imitator — can you imagine, I say, that he would not have attracted many followers, and been honored and loved by them? Protagoras of Abdera, and Prodicus of Ceos, and a host of others, have only to whisper to their contemporaries: "You will never be able to manage either your own house or your own State until you appoint us to be your ministers of education" — and this ingenious device of theirs has such an effect in making men love them that their companions all but carry them about on their shoulders. And is it conceivable that the contemporaries of Homer, or again of Hesiod, would have allowed either of them to go about as rhapsodists, if they had really been able to help mankind forward in virtue? Would they not have been as unwilling to part with them as with gold, and have compelled them to stay at home with them? Or, if the master would not stay, then the disciples would have followed him about everywhere, until they had got education enough?

Yes, Socrates, that, I think, is quite true.

Then must we not infer that all these poetical individuals, beginning with Homer, are only imitators, who copy images of virtue and the other themes of their poetry, but have no contact with the truth? The poet is like a painter who, as we have already observed, will make a likeness of a cobbler though he understands nothing of cobbling; and his picture is good enough for those who know no more than he does, and judge only by colors and figures.

Quite so.

In like manner the poet with his words and phrases[1] may be said to lay on the colors of the several arts, himself understanding their nature only enough to imitate them; and other people, who are as ignorant as he is, and judge only from his words, imagine that if he speaks of cobbling, or of military tactics, or of anything else, in meter and harmony and rhythm, he speaks very well — such is the sweet influence which melody and rhythm by nature have. For I am sure that you know what a poor appearance the works of poets make when stripped of the colors which art puts upon them, and recited in simple prose. You have seen some examples?

Yes, he said.

They are like faces which were never really beautiful, but only blooming, seen when the bloom of youth has passed away from them?

Exactly.

Come now, and observe this point: The imitator or maker of the image knows nothing, we have said, of true existence; he knows appearances only. Am I not right?

Yes.

Then let us have a clear understanding, and not be satisfied with half an explanation.

Proceed.

Of the painter we say that he will paint reins, and he will paint a bit?

Yes.

And the worker in leather and brass will make them?

Certainly.

But does the painter know the right form of the bit and reins? Nay, hardly even the workers in brass and leather who make them; only the horseman who knows how to use them — he knows their right form.

Most true.

And may we not say the same of all things?

What?

That there are three arts which are concerned with all things: one which uses, another which makes, a third which imitates them?

Yes.

And the excellence and beauty and rightness of every structure, animate or inanimate, and of every action of man, is relative solely to the use for which nature or the artist has intended them.

True.

Then beyond doubt it is the user who has the greatest experience of them, and he must report to the maker the good or bad qualities which develop themselves in use; for example, the flute player will tell the flute maker which of his flutes is satisfactory to the performer; he will tell him how he ought to make them, and the other will attend to his instructions?

Of course.

So the one pronounces with knowledge about the goodness and badness of flutes, while the other, confiding in him, will make them accordingly?

True.

The instrument is the same, but about the excellence or badness of it the maker will possess a correct belief, since he associates with one who knows, and is compelled to hear what he has to say; whereas the user will have knowledge?

True.

But will the imitator have either? Will he know from use whether or not that which he paints is correct or beautiful? or will he have right opinion from being compelled to associate with another who knows and gives him instructions about what he should paint?

Neither.

Then an imitator will no more have true opinion than he will have knowledge about the goodness or badness of his models?

I suppose not.

The imitative poet will be in a brilliant state of intelligence about the theme of his poetry?

Nay, very much the reverse.

And still he will go on imitating without knowing what makes a thing good or bad, and may be expected therefore to imitate only that which appears to be good to the ignorant multitude?

Just so.

Thus far then we are pretty well agreed that the imitator has no knowledge worth mentioning of what he imitates. Imitation is only a kind of play

[1] Or, "with his nouns and verbs." [Tr.]

or sport, and the tragic poets, whether they write in iambic or in heroic verse,² are imitators in the highest degree?

Very true.

And now tell me, I conjure you — this imitation is concerned with an object which is thrice removed from the truth?

Certainly.

And what kind of faculty in man is that to which imitation makes its special appeal?

What do you mean?

I will explain: The same body does not appear equal to our sight when seen near and when seen at a distance?

True.

And the same objects appear straight when looked at out of the water, and crooked when in the water; and the concave becomes convex, owing to the illusion about colors to which the sight is liable. Thus every sort of confusion is revealed within us; and this is that weakness of the human mind on which the art of painting in light and shadow, the art of conjuring, and many other ingenious devices impose, having an effect upon us like magic.

True.

And the arts of measuring and numbering and weighing come to the rescue of the human understanding — there is the beauty of them — with the result that the apparent greater or less, or more or heavier, no longer have the mastery over us, but give way before the power of calculation and measuring and weighing?

Most true.

And this, surely, must be the work of the calculating and rational principle in the soul?

To be sure.

And often when this principle measures and certifies that some things are equal, or that some are greater or less than others, it is, at the same time, contradicted by the appearance which the objects present?

True.

But did we not say that such a contradiction is impossible — the same faculty cannot have

contrary opinions at the same time about the same thing?

We did; and rightly.

Then that part of the soul which has an opinion contrary to measure can hardly be the same with that which has an opinion in accordance with measure?

True.

And the part of the soul which trusts to measure and calculation is likely to be the better one?

Certainly.

And therefore that which is opposed to this is probably an inferior principle in our nature?

No doubt.

This was the conclusion at which I was seeking to arrive when I said that painting or drawing, and imitation in general, are engaged upon productions which are far removed from truth, and are also the companions and friends and associates of a principle within us which is equally removed from reason, and that they have no true or healthy aim.

Exactly.

The imitative art is an inferior who from intercourse with an inferior has inferior offspring.

Very true.

And is this confined to the sight only, or does it extend to the hearing also, relating in fact to what we term poetry?

Probably the same would be true of poetry.

Do not rely, I said, on a probability derived from the analogy of painting; but let us once more go directly to that faculty of the mind with which imitative poetry has converse, and see whether it is good or bad.

By all means.

We may state the question thus: Imitation imitates the actions of men, whether voluntary or involuntary, on which, as they imagine, a good or bad result has ensued, and they rejoice or sorrow accordingly. Is there anything more?

No, there is nothing else.

But in all this variety of circumstances is the man at unity with himself — or rather, as in the instance of sight there was confusion and opposition in his opinions about the same things, so here also is there not strife and inconsistency in his life? Though I need hardly raise the question again, for I remember that all this has been already

²Dramatists wrote in iambic verse and epic poets in dactylic hexameters — "heroic" verse.

admitted; and the soul has been acknowledged by us to be full of these and ten thousand similar oppositions occurring at the same moment?

And we were right, he said.

Yes, I said, thus far we were right; but there was an omission which must now be supplied.

What was the omission?

Were we not saying that a good man, who has the misfortune to lose his son or anything else which is most dear to him, will bear the loss with more equanimity than another?

Yes, indeed.

But will he have no sorrow, or shall we say that although he cannot help sorrowing, he will moderate his sorrow?

The latter, he said, is the truer statement.

Tell me: will he be more likely to struggle and hold out against his sorrow when he is seen by his equals, or when he is alone in a deserted place?

The fact of being seen will make a great difference, he said.

When he is by himself he will not mind saying many things which he would be ashamed of anyone hearing, and also doing many things which he would not care to be seen doing?

True.

And doubtless it is the law and reason in him which bids him resist; while it is the affliction itself which is urging him to indulge his sorrow?

True.

But when a man is drawn in two opposite directions, to and from the same object, this, as we affirm, necessarily implies two distinct principles in him?

Certainly.

One of them is ready to follow the guidance of the law?

How do you mean?

The law would say that to be patient under calamity is best, and that we should not give way to impatience, as the good and evil in such things are not clear, and nothing is gained by impatience; also, because no human thing is of serious importance, and grief stands in the way of that which at the moment is most required.

What is most required? he asked.

That we should take counsel about what has happened, and when the dice have been thrown, according to their fall, order our affairs in the way which reason deems best; not, like children who have had a fall, keeping hold of the part struck and wasting time in setting up a howl, but always accustoming the soul forthwith to apply a remedy, raising up that which is sickly and fallen, banishing the cry of sorrow by the healing art.

Yes, he said, that is the true way of meeting the attacks of fortune.

Well then, I said, the higher principle is ready to follow this suggestion of reason?

Clearly.

But the other principle, which inclines us to recollection of our troubles and to lamentation, and can never have enough of them, we may call irrational, useless, and cowardly?

Indeed, we may.

Now does not the principle which is thus inclined to complaint, furnish a great variety of materials for imitation? Whereas the wise and calm temperament, being always nearly equable, is not easy to imitate or to appreciate when imitated, especially at a public festival when a promiscuous crowd is assembled in a theater. For the feeling represented is one to which they are strangers.

Certainly.

Then the imitative poet who aims at being popular is not by nature made, nor is his art intended, to please or to affect the rational principle in the soul; but he will appeal rather to the lachrymose and fitful temper, which is easily imitated?

Clearly.

And now we may fairly take him and place him by the side of the painter, for he is like him in two ways: first, inasmuch as his creations have an inferior degree of truth — in this, I say, he is like him; and he is also like him in being the associate of an inferior part of the soul; and this is enough to show that we shall be right in refusing to admit him into a State which is to be well ordered, because he awakens and nourishes this part of the soul, and by strengthening it impairs the reason. As in a city when the evil are permitted to wield power and the finer men are put out of the way, so in the soul of each man, as we shall maintain, the imitative poet implants an evil constitution, for he indulges the irrational nature which has no discernment of greater and less, but thinks the same thing at one time great and at another small — he is an imitator of images and is very far removed from the truth.

Exactly.

But we have not yet brought forward the heaviest count in our accusation: The power which poetry has of harming even the good (and there are very few who are not harmed) is surely an awful thing?

Yes, certainly, if the effect is what you say.

Hear and judge: The best of us, as I conceive, when we listen to a passage of Homer or one of the tragedians, in which he represents some hero who is drawing out his sorrows in a long oration, or singing and smiting his breast — the best of us, you know, delight in giving way to sympathy, and are in raptures at the excellence of the poet who stirs our feelings most.

Yes, of course I know.

But when any sorrow of our own happens to us, then you may observe that we pride ourselves on the opposite quality — we would fain be quiet and patient; this is considered the manly part, and the other which delighted us in the recitation is now deemed to be the part of a woman.

Very true, he said.

Now can we be right in praising and admiring another who is doing that which any one of us would abominate and be ashamed of in his own person?

No, he said, that is certainly not reasonable.

Nay, I said, quite reasonable from one point of view.

What point of view?

If you consider, I said, that when in misfortune we feel a natural hunger and desire to relieve our sorrow by weeping and lamentation, and that this very feeling which is starved and suppressed in our own calamities is satisfied and delighted by the poets; the better nature in each of us, not having been sufficiently trained by reason or habit, allows the sympathetic element to break loose because the sorrow is another's; and the spectator fancies that there can be no disgrace to himself in praising and pitying anyone who, while professing to be a brave man, gives way to untimely lamentation; he thinks that the pleasure is a gain, and is far from wishing to lose it by rejection of the whole poem. Few persons ever reflect, as I should imagine, that the contagion must pass from others to themselves. For the pity which has been nourished and strengthened in the misfortunes of others is with difficulty repressed in our own.

How very true!

And does not the same hold also of the ridiculous? There are jests which you would be ashamed to make yourself, and yet on the comic stage, or indeed in private, when you hear them, you are greatly amused by them, and are not at all disgusted at their unseemliness; the case of pity is repeated: there is a principle in human nature which is disposed to raise a laugh, and this, which you once restrained by reason because you were afraid of being thought a buffoon, is now let out again; and having stimulated the risible faculty at the theater, you are betrayed unconsciously to yourself into playing the comic poet at home.

Quite true, he said.

And the same may be said of lust and anger and all the other affections, of desire and pain and pleasure, which are held to be inseparable from every action — in all of them poetry has a like effect; it feeds and waters the passions instead of drying them up; she lets them rule, although they ought to be controlled if mankind are ever to increase in happiness and virtue.

I cannot deny it.

Therefore, Glaucon, I said, whenever you meet with any of the eulogists of Homer declaring that he has been the educator of Hellas, and that he is profitable for education and for the ordering of human things, and that you should take him up again and again and get to know him and regulate your whole life according to him, we may love and honor those who say these things — they are excellent people, as far as their lights extend; and we are ready to acknowledge that Homer is the greatest of poets and first of tragedy writers; but we must remain firm in our conviction that hymns to the gods and praises of famous men are the only poetry which ought to be admitted into our State. For if you go beyond this and allow the honeyed Muse to enter, either in epic or lyric verse, not law and the reason of mankind, which by common consent have ever been deemed best, but pleasure and pain will be the rulers in our State.

That is most true, he said.

And now since we have reverted to the subject of poetry, let this our defense serve to show the reasonableness of our former judgment in sending away out of our State an art having the tendencies which we have described; for reason constrained us. But that she may not impute to us any harshness or want of politeness, let us tell her that there is an ancient quarrel between philosophy and poetry; of which there are many proofs, such as the saying of "the yelping hound howling at her lord," or of one "mighty in the vain talk of fools," and "the mob of sages circumventing Zeus," and the "subtle thinkers who are beggars after all,"[3] and there are innumerable other signs of ancient enmity between them. Notwithstanding this, let us assure the poetry which aims at pleasure, and the art of imitation, that if she will only prove her title to exist in a well-ordered State we shall be delighted to receive her — we are very conscious of her charms; but it would not be right on that account to betray the truth. I dare say, Glaucon, that you are as much charmed by her as I am, especially when she appears in Homer?

Yes, indeed, I am greatly charmed.

Shall I propose, then, that she be allowed to return from exile, but upon this condition only — that she make a defense of herself in some lyrical or other meter?

Certainly.

And we may further grant to those of her defenders who are lovers of poetry and yet not poets the permission to speak in prose on her behalf: let them show not only that she is pleasant but also useful to States and to human life, and we will listen in a kindly spirit; for we shall surely be the gainers if this can be proved, that there is a use in poetry as well as a delight?

Certainly, he said, we shall be the gainers.

If her defense fails, then, my dear friend, like other persons who are enamored of something, but put a restraint upon themselves when they think their desires are opposed to their interests, so too must we after the manner of lovers give her up, though not without a struggle. We too are inspired by that love of such poetry which the education of noble States has implanted in us, and therefore we shall be glad if she appears at her best and truest; but so long as she is unable to make good her defense, this argument of ours shall be a charm to us, which we will repeat to ourselves while we listen to her strains; that we may not fall away into the childish love of her which captivates the many. At all events we are well aware that poetry, such as we have described, is not to be regarded seriously as attaining to the truth; and he who listens to her, fearing for the safety of the city which is within him, should be on his guard against her seductions and make our words his law.

Yes, he said, I quite agree with you.

Yes, I said, my dear Glaucon, for great is the issue at stake, greater than appears, whether a man is to be good or bad. And what will any one be profited if under the influence of honor or money or power, aye, or under the excitement of poetry, he neglect justice and virtue?

Yes, he said; I have been convinced by the argument, as I believe that anyone else would have been.

[3]Socrates is alluding to various proverbs, otherwise unknown, denigrating both poets and philosophers.

Ion

SOCRATES: Welcome, Ion! And whence come you now to pay us a visit? From your home in Ephesus?

ION: No, Socrates, I come from Epidaurus and the festival of Asclepius.[1]

SOCRATES: What! Do the citizens of Epidaurus, in honoring the god, have a contest between rhapsodes[2] too?

ION: Indeed they do. They have every sort of musical competition.

SOCRATES: So? And did you compete? And how did you succeed?

Translated by Lane Cooper.
[1]Greek god of medicine; his festival, like that of other minor divinities connected with Apollo, was the occasion for artistic performances and competitions.

[2]Professional actors who delivered recitations of poetry, especially of Homer and the other epic poets.

ION: We carried off first prize, Socrates.

SOCRATES: Well done! See to it, now, that we win the Panathenaea also.

ION: It shall be so, God willing.

SOCRATES: I must say, Ion, I am often envious of you rhapsodists in your profession. Your art requires of you always to go in fine array, and look as beautiful as you can, and meanwhile you must be conversant with many excellent poets, and especially with Homer, the best and most divine of all. You have to understand his thought, and not merely learn his lines. It is an enviable lot! In fact, one never could be a rhapsode if one did not comprehend the utterances of the poet, for the rhapsode must become an interpreter of the poet's thought to those who listen, and to do this well is quite impossible unless one knows just what the poet is saying. All that, of course, will excite one's envy.

ION: What you say is true, Socrates; to me, at all events, this aspect of the art has given the most concern. And I judge that I, of all men, have the finest things to say on Homer, that neither Metrodorus of Lampsacus, nor Stesimbrotus of Thasos, nor Glaucon, nor anyone else who ever lived, had so many reflections, or such fine ones, to present on Homer as have I.

SOCRATES: That is pleasant news, Ion, for obviously you will not begrudge me a display of your talent.

ION: Not at all. And, Socrates, it really is worthwhile to hear how well I have embellished Homer. In my opinion I deserve to be crowned with a wreath of gold by the Homeridae.³

SOCRATES: Another time I shall find leisure to hear your recitation. At the moment do but answer me so far. Are you skilled in Homer only, or in Hesiod and Archilochus as well?

ION: No, only in regard to Homer; to me that seems enough.

SOCRATES: Is there any point on which both Homer and Hesiod say the same thing?

ION: Indeed, I think so; there are many cases of it.

SOCRATES: In those cases, then, would you interpret what Homer says better than what Hesiod says?

ION: In the cases where they say the same, Socrates, I should do equally well with both.

SOCRATES: But what about the cases where they do not say the same? For example, take the art of divination. Homer and Hesiod both speak of it.

ION: Quite so.

SOCRATES: Well then, where they say the same on the art of divination, and where they differ on it, would you interpret better what these two poets say, or would one of the diviners, one of the good ones, do so?

ION: One of the diviners.

SOCRATES: But suppose you were a diviner. If you were competent to explain the passages where they agree, would you not be competent to explain as well the passages where they differ?

ION: Manifestly, yes.

SOCRATES: How is it, then, that you are skilled in Homer, but not in Hesiod or the other poets? Does Homer treat of matters different from those that all the other poets treat of? Wasn't his subject mainly war, and hasn't he discussed the mutual relations of men good and bad, or the general run as well as special craftsmen, the relations of the gods to one another and to men, as they forgather, the phenomena of the heavens and occurrences in the underworld, and the birth of gods and heroes? Are not these the subjects Homer dealt with in his poetry?

ION: What you say is true, Socrates.

SOCRATES: And what about the other poets? Haven't they dealt with these same themes?

ION: Yes, but, Socrates, not in the same way.

SOCRATES: How so? In a worse way than he?

ION: Far worse.

SOCRATES: He in a better way?

ION: Better indeed, I warrant you.

SOCRATES: Well now, Ion darling, tell me. When several persons are discussing number, and one of them talks better than the rest, there will be someone who distinguishes the good speaker?

ION: I agree.

SOCRATES: It will be the same one who distinguishes those who are speaking badly, or will it be another?

ION: No doubt the same.

SOCRATES: And this will be the one who knows the art of numbers?

³A group of poets who claimed descent from Homer, or more generally in this case, the admirers of Homer.

ION: Yes.

SOCRATES: Tell me. When several are discussing diet, and what foods are wholesome, and one of them speaks better than the rest, will a given person see the excellence of the best speaker, and another the inferiority of the worst, or will the same man distinguish both?

ION: Obviously, I think, the same.

SOCRATES: Who is he? What is he called?

ION: The doctor.

SOCRATES: We may therefore generalize, and say: When several persons are discussing a given subject, the man who can distinguish the one who is talking well on it, and the one who is talking badly, will always be the same. Or, if he does not recognize the one who is talking badly, then, clearly, neither will he recognize the one who is talking well, granted that the subject is the same.

ION: That is so.

SOCRATES: Then the same man will be skilled with respect to both?

ION: Yes.

SOCRATES: Now you assert that Homer and the other poets, among them Hesiod and Archilochus, all treat of the same subjects, yet not all in the same fashion, but the one speaks well, and the rest of them speak worse.

ION: And what I say is true.

SOCRATES: Then you, if you can recognize the poet who speaks well, could also recognize the poets who speak worse, and see that they speak worse.

ION: So it seems.

SOCRATES: Well then, my best of friends, when we say that Ion has equal skill in Homer and all other poets, we shall not be mistaken. It must be so, since you yourself admit that the same man will be competent to judge of all who speak of the same matters, and that the poets virtually all deal with the same subjects.

ION: Then what can be the reason, Socrates, for my behavior? When anyone discusses any other poet, I pay no attention, and can offer no remark of any value. I frankly doze. But whenever anyone mentions Homer, immediately I am awake, attentive, and full of things to say.

SOCRATES: The riddle is not hard to solve, my friend. No, it is plain to everyone that not from art and knowledge comes your power to speak concerning Homer. If it were art that gave you power, then you could speak about all the other poets as well. There is an art of poetry as a whole? Am I not right?

ION: Yes.

SOCRATES: And is not the case the same with any other art you please, when you take it as a whole? The same method of inquiry holds for all the arts? Do you want some explanation, Ion, of what I mean by that?

ION: Yes, Socrates, upon my word I do. It gives me joy to listen to you wise men.

SOCRATES: I only wish you were right in saying that, Ion. But "wise men"! That means you, the rhapsodists and actors, and the men whose poems you chant, while I have nothing else to tell besides the truth, after the fashion of the ordinary man. For example, take the question I just now asked you. Observe what a trivial and commonplace remark it was that I uttered, something anyone might know, when I said that the inquiry is the same whenever one takes an art in its entirety. Let us reason the matter out. There is an art of painting taken as a whole?

ION: Yes.

SOCRATES: And there are and have been many painters, good and bad?

ION: Yes indeed.

SOCRATES: Now, take Polygnotus, son of Aglaophon. Have you ever seen a man with the skill to point out what is good and what is not in the works of Polygnotus, but without the power to do so in the works of other painters? A man who, when anybody shows the works of other painters, dozes off, is at a loss, has nothing to suggest, but when he has to express a judgment on one particular painter, say Polygnotus or anyone else you choose, wakes up, and is attentive, and is full of things to say?

ION: No, on my oath, I never saw the like.

SOCRATES: Or, again, take sculpture. Have you ever seen a man with the skill to judge the finer works of Daedalus, son of Metion, or of Epeus, son of Panopeus, or of Theodorus of Samos, or the works of any other single sculptor, but, confronted by the works of other sculptors, is at a loss, and dozes off, without a thing to say?

ION: No, on my oath, I never saw one.

SOCRATES: Yet further, as I think, the same is true of playing on the flute, and on the harp, and

ION: On that I cannot contradict you, Socrates. But of this thing I am conscious, that I excel all men in speaking about Homer, and on him have much to say, and that everybody else avers I do it well, but on the other poets I do not. Well then, see what that means.

SOCRATES: I do see, Ion, and in fact will proceed to show you what to my mind it betokens. As I just now said, this gift you have of speaking well on Homer is not an art; it is a power divine, impelling you like the power in the stone Euripides called the magnet, which most call "stone of Heraclea." This stone does not simply attract the iron rings, just by themselves; it also imparts to the rings a force enabling them to do the same thing as the stone itself, that is, to attract another ring, so that sometimes a chain is formed, quite a long one, of iron rings, suspended from one another. For all of them, however, their power depends upon that loadstone. Just so the Muse. She first makes men inspired, and then through these inspired ones others share in the enthusiasm, and a chain is formed, for the epic poets, all the good ones, have their excellence, not from art, but are inspired, possessed, and thus they utter all these admirable poems. So is it also with the good lyric poets: as the worshiping Corybantes[4] are not in their senses when they dance, so the lyric poets are not in their senses when they make these lovely lyric poems. No, when once they launch into harmony and rhythm, they are seized with the Bacchic transport, and are possessed — as the bacchants, when possessed, draw milk and honey from the rivers, but not when in their senses. So the spirit of the lyric poet works, according to their own report. For the poets tell us, don't they, that the melodies they bring us are gathered from rills that run with honey, out of glens and gardens of the Muses, and they bring them as the bees do of honey, flying like the bees? And what they

say is true, for a poet is a light and winged thing, and holy, and never able to compose until he has become inspired, and is beside himself, and reason is no longer in him. So long as he has this in his possession, no man is able to make poetry or to chant in prophecy. Therefore, since their making is not by art, when they utter many things and fine about the deeds of men, just as you do about Homer, but is by lot divine — therefore each is able to do well only that to which the Muse has impelled him — one to make dithyrambs, another panegyric odes, another choral songs, another epic poems, another iambs. In all the rest, each one of them is poor, for not by art do they utter these, but by power divine, since if it were by art that they knew how to treat one subject finely, they would know how to deal with all the others too. Herein lies the reason why the deity has bereft them of their senses, and uses them as ministers, along with soothsayers and godly seers; it is in order that we listeners may know that it is not they who utter these precious revelations while their mind is not within them, but that it is the god himself who speaks, and through them becomes articulate to us. The most convincing evidence of this statement is offered by Tynnichus of Chalcis, who never composed a single poem worth recalling, save the song of praise which everyone repeats, wellnigh the finest of all lyrical poems, and absolutely what he called it, an "Invention of the Muses." By this example above all, it seems to me, the god would show us, lest we doubt, that these lovely poems are not of man or human workmanship, but are divine and from the gods, and that the poets are nothing but interpreters of the gods, each one possessed by the divinity to whom he is in bondage. And to prove this, the deity on purpose sang the loveliest of all lyrics through the most miserable poet, isn't it so, Ion? Don't you think that I am right?[5]

ION: You are indeed, I vow! Socrates, your words in some way touch my very soul, and it does seem to me that by dispensation from above good poets convey to us these utterances of the gods.

SOCRATES: Well, and you rhapsodists, again, interpret the utterances of the poets?

[4]Female worshippers of Dionysus whose rites drove them to frenzy; cf. Euripides, *The Bacchae.*

[5]In the preceding speech, the language spoken by Socrates takes on the rhythms of the dithyramb — the traditional hymn to Dionysus — as though he himself were in an inspired state.

ION: There also you are right.

SOCRATES: Accordingly, you are interpreters of interpreters?

ION: Undeniably.

SOCRATES: Wait now, Ion; tell me this. And answer frankly what I ask you. Suppose you are reciting epic poetry well, and thrill the spectators most deeply. You are chanting, say, the story of Odysseus as he leaped up to the dais, unmasked himself to the suitors, and poured the arrows out before his feet, or of Achilles rushing upon Hector, or one of the pitiful passages, about Andromache, or Hecuba, or Priam. When you chant these, are you in your senses? Or are you carried out of yourself, and does not your soul in an ecstasy conceive herself to be engaged in the actions you relate, whether they are in Ithaca, or Troy, or wherever the story puts them?

ION: How vivid, Socrates, you make your proof for me! I will tell you frankly that whenever I recite a tale of pity, my eyes are filled with tears, and when it is one of horror or dismay, my hair stands up on end with fear, and my heart goes leaping.

SOCRATES: Well now, Ion, what are we to say of a man like that? There he is, at a sacrifice or festival, got up in holiday attire, adorned with golden chaplets, and he weeps, though he has lost nothing of his finery. Or he recoils with fear, standing in the presence of more than twenty thousand friendly people, though nobody is stripping him or doing him damage. Shall we say that the man is in his senses?

ION: Never, Socrates, upon my word. That is strictly true.

SOCRATES: Now then, are you aware that you produce the same effects in most of the spectators too?

ION: Yes, indeed, I know it very well. As I look down at them from the stage above, I see them, every time, weeping, casting terrible glances, stricken with amazement at the deeds recounted. In fact, I have to give them very close attention, for if I set them weeping, I myself shall laugh when I get my money, but if they laugh, it is I who have to weep at losing it.

SOCRATES: Well, do you see that the spectator is the last of the rings I spoke of, which receive their force from one another by virtue of the loadstone? You, the rhapsodist and actor, are the middle ring, and the first one is the poet himself. But it is the deity who, through all the series, draws the spirit of men wherever he desires, transmitting the attractive force from one into another. And so, as from the loadstone, a mighty chain hangs down, of choric dancers, masters of the chorus, undermasters, obliquely fastened to the rings which are suspended from the Muse. One poet is suspended from one Muse, another from another; we call it being "possessed," but the fact is much the same, since he is *held*. And from these primary rings, the poets, others are in turn suspended, some attached to this one, some to that, and are filled with inspiration, some by Orpheus, others by Musaeus. But the majority are possessed and held by Homer, and, Ion, you are one of these, and are possessed by Homer. And whenever anyone chants the work of any other poet, you fall asleep, and haven't a thing to say, but when anybody gives tongue to a strain of this one, you are awake at once, your spirit dances, and you have much to say, for not by art or science do you say of Homer what you say, but by dispensation from above and by divine possession. So the worshiping Corybantes have a lively feeling for that strain alone which is of the deity by whom they are possessed, and for that melody are well supplied with attitudes and utterances, and heed no others. And so it is with you, Ion. When anyone mentions Homer, you are ready, but about the other poets you are at a loss. You ask me why you are ready about Homer and not about the rest. Because it is not by art but by lot divine that you are eloquent in praise of Homer.

ION: Well put, I grant you, Socrates. And yet I should be much surprised if by your argument you succeeded in convincing me that I am possessed or mad when I praise Homer. Nor do I think that you yourself would find me so if you heard me speaking upon Homer.

SOCRATES: And indeed I wish to hear you, but not until you have answered me as follows. On what point in Homer do you speak well? Not on all points, I take it.

ION: I assure you, Socrates, I do it on every point, without exception.

SOCRATES: Yet not, I fancy, on those matters of which you happen to be ignorant, but Homer tells of?

ION: And the matters Homer tells of, and I do not know, what are they?

SOCRATES: Why, does not Homer in many passages speak of arts, and have much to say about them? About driving a chariot, for instance; if I can recollect the lines, I'll repeat them to you.

ION: No, let me do it, for I know them.

SOCRATES: Then recite for me what Nestor says to Antilochus, his son, where he warns him to be careful at the turning post, in the lay of the horse race in honor of Patroclus.

ION:
Thyself lean slightly in the burnished car
To the left of them, then call upon the off horse
With goad and voice; with hand give him free rein.
And at the post let the near horse come so close
That the nave of the well-wrought wheel shall seem
To graze the stone. Which yet beware to strike!6

SOCRATES: That will do. Now, Ion, in these lines, which will be more capable of judging whether Homer speaks aright or not, a doctor or a charioteer?

ION: The charioteer, do doubt.

SOCRATES: Because that is his art, or for some other reason?

ION: No, because it is his art.

SOCRATES: Each separate art, then, has had assigned to it by the deity the power of knowing a particular occupation? I take it that what we know by the pilot's art we do not know by the art of medicine as well.

ION: No indeed.

SOCRATES: And what we know by medical art we do not know by the builder's art as well.

ION: No indeed.

SOCRATES: Well, and so it is with all the arts? What we know by one of them, we do not know by another? But before you answer that, just tell me this. Do you allow a distinction between arts? One differs from another?

ION: Yes.

SOCRATES: Now with me the mark of differentiation is that one art means the knowledge of one kind of thing, another art the knowledge of another, and so I give them their respective names. Do you do that?

6*Iliad* 23:335. [Tr.]

ION: Yes.

SOCRATES: If they meant simply knowledge of the same things, why should we distinguish one art from another? Why call them different, when both would give us the same knowledge? For example, take these fingers, I know that there are five of them, and you know the same as I about them. Suppose I asked you if we knew this same matter, you and I, by the same art, that of arithmetic, or by different arts. I fancy you would hold that we knew it by the same?

ION: Yes.

SOCRATES: Then tell me now what just a little while ago I was on the point of asking you. Does that seem true to you of all the arts — that, necessarily, the same art makes us know the same, another art not the same, but, if it really is another art, it must make us know something else?

ION: That is my opinion, Socrates.

SOCRATES: Well then, if one does not possess a given art, one will not be capable of rightly knowing what belongs to it in word or action?

ION: That is true.

SOCRATES: Then, in the lines which you recited, which will have the better knowledge whether Homer speaks aright or not, you or a charioteer?

ION: The charioteer.

SOCRATES: Doubtless because you are a rhapsode, and not a charioteer?

ION: Yes.

SOCRATES: The rhapsode's art is different from the charioteer's?

ION: Yes.

SOCRATES: If it is another art, then, it is a knowledge also about other matters.

ION: Yes.

SOCRATES: Now what about the passage in which Homer tells how Hecamede, Nestor's concubine, gave the wounded Machaon the broth to drink? The passage runs something like this:

She grated goat's-milk cheese in Pramnian wine,
With brazen grater, adding onion as a relish to the brew.7

7*Iliad* 11:639-40. [Tr.]

On the question whether Homer here speaks properly or not, is it for the art of the physician, or the rhapsode's art, to discriminate aright?

ION: The art of the physician.

SOCRATES: What of this? The passage in which Homer says:

> She plunged to the bottom like a leaden sinker
> Which, mounted on the horntip from a field ox,
> Speeds its way bringing mischief to voracious fish.[8]

What shall we say? Is it rather for the art of fishing, or the rhapsode's art, to decide on what the verses mean, and whether they are good or not?

ION: Obviously, Socrates, it is for the art of fishing.

SOCRATES: Reflect now. Suppose that you were questioning, and asked me, "Now, Socrates, you find it is for these several arts to judge in Homer, severally, what appertains to each of them. Come then, pick me out the passages concerning the diviner, and the diviner's art, the kind of things that appertain to him, regarding which he must be able to discern whether the poetry is good or bad?" Observe how easily and truly I can answer you. The poet does, in fact, treat of this matter in the *Odyssey* too — for example, when a scion of Melampus, the diviner Theoclymenus, says to the wooers:

> Ah, wretched men, what bane is this ye suffer? Shrouded in night
> Are your heads and your faces and your limbs below,
> And kindled is the voice of wailing, and cheeks are wet with tears.
> And the porch is full of ghosts; the hall is full of them,
> Hastening hellward beneath the gloom, and the sun
> Has perished out of heaven, and an evil mist infolds the world.[9]

And he treats of it in many places in the *Iliad* — for instance, in the lay of the battle at the wall. There he says:

> For, as they were eager to pass over, a bird approached them,
> An eagle of lofty flight, skirting the host on the left,

And in its talons bearing a monstrous blood-red serpent,
> Still alive and struggling; nor had it yet forgot the joy of battle.
> Writhing back, it smote the bird that held it, upon the breast
> Beside the neck, and the bird did cast it from him,
> In the agony of pain, to the earth,
> And dropped it in the middle of the throng.
> And, with a cry, himself went flying on the gusty wind.[10]

These passages, I contend, and others like them, appertain to the diviner to examine and to judge.

ION: And, Socrates, you are right.

SOCRATES: And you are right too, Ion, when you say so. Come now, you do for me what I have done for you. From both the *Odyssey* and *Iliad* I picked out for you the passages belonging to the doctor, the diviner, and the fisherman; now you likewise, since you are better versed than I in Homer, pick out for me the sort of passages, Ion, that concern the rhapsode and the rhapsode's art, the passages it befits the rhapsode, above all other men, to examine and to judge.

ION: *All* passages, Socrates, is what I say.

SOCRATES: Surely, Ion, you don't mean *all!* Are you really so forgetful? Indeed, it would ill become a man who is a rhapsode to forget.

ION: Why? What am I forgetting?

SOCRATES: Don't you remember how you stated that the art of the rhapsode was different from the charioteer's?

ION: I remember.

SOCRATES: Well, and you admitted also that, being different, it had another field of knowledge?

ION: Yes.

SOCRATES: Well then, by your own account the art of rhapsody will not know everything, nor the rhapsode either.

ION: The exceptions, Socrates, are doubtless only such matters as that.

SOCRATES: In "such matters" you must include approximately all the other arts. Well, as the rhapsode does not know the subject matter of them all, what sort of matters *will* he know?

---

[8]*Iliad* 24:80–82. [Tr.]
[9]*Odyssey* 20:351–56. [Tr.]

[10]*Iliad* 12:200–08. [Tr.]

ION: The kind of thing, I judge, that a man would say, and a woman would say, and a slave and a free man, a subject and a ruler — the suitable thing for each.

SOCRATES: You mean, the rhapsode will know better what the ruler of a ship in a storm at sea should say than the pilot?

ION: No, in that case the pilot will know better.

SOCRATES: But suppose it is the ruler of a sick man. Will the rhapsode know better what the ruler should say than the doctor?

ION: No, not in that case, either.

SOCRATES: But you say, 'the kind of speech that suits a slave.'

ION: Yes.

SOCRATES: You mean, for instance, if the slave is a cowherd, it is not he who will know what one should say to quiet angry cattle, but the rhapsode?

ION: Surely not.

SOCRATES: Well, 'the kind of speech that suits a woman' — one who spins — about the working up of wool?

ION: No.

SOCRATES: Well, the rhapsodist will know ''the kind of speech that suits a man'' — a general exhorting his soldiers?

ION: Yes! that is the sort of thing the rhapsodist will know.

SOCRATES: What! Is the rhapsode's art the general's?

ION: At all events I ought to know the kind of speech a general should make.

SOCRATES: Indeed, you doubtless have the talents of a general, Ion! And suppose you happened to have skill in horsemanship, along with skill in playing on the lyre, you would know when horses were well or badly ridden, but if I asked you, ''By which art, do you know that horses are well managed — is it because you are a horseman, or because you play the lyre?'' What answer would you give me?

ION: I should say, ''It is by my skill as horseman.''

SOCRATES: Then, too, if you were picking out good players on the lyre, you would admit that you discerned them by your art in playing the lyre, and not by your art as horseman?

ION: Yes.

SOCRATES: But when you know of military matters, do you know them because you are competent as a general, or as a rhapsode?

ION: I cannot see a bit of difference.

SOCRATES: What, no difference, you say? You mean to call the art of the rhapsode and the art of the general a single art, or two?

ION: To me, there is a single art.

SOCRATES: And so, whoever is an able rhapsode is going to be an able general as well?

ION: Unquestionably, Socrates.

SOCRATES: And then, whoever happens to be an able general is an able rhapsode too.

ION: No, I do not think that holds.

SOCRATES: But you think the other does? That whoever is an able rhapsode is an able general too?

ION: Absolutely!

SOCRATES: Well, and you are the ablest rhapsodist in Greece?

ION: Yes, Socrates, by far.

SOCRATES: And the ablest general, Ion? The ablest one in Greece?

ION: You may be sure of it, for, Socrates, I learned this also out of Homer.

SOCRATES: Then, Ion, how in heaven's name is this? You are at once the ablest general and ablest rhapsodist among the Greeks, and yet you go about Greece performing as a rhapsode, but not as general. What think you? The Greeks are in great need of a rhapsode adorned with a wreath of gold, and do not need a general at all?[11]

ION: It is because my native city, Socrates, is under your dominion, and your military rule, and has no need whatever of a general. As for yours and Lacedaemon, neither would choose me for general; you think yourselves sufficient to yourselves.

SOCRATES: Excellent Ion, you know who Apollodorus is, of Cyzicus, don't you?

ION: What might he be?

SOCRATES: The man whom the Athenians at various times have chosen for their general, although he is an alien. The same is true of Phanosthenes.

[11]The dialogue occurs during the Peloponnesian War, which Athens eventually lost to Sparta.

of Andros, and Heraclides of Clazomenae, also aliens, who nevertheless, when they had shown their competence, were raised to the generalship by the city, and put in other high positions. And Ion of Ephesus, will she not elect him general, and accord him honors, if his worth becomes apparent? Why, you inhabitants of Ephesus are originally Athenians, are you not, and Ephesus is a city inferior to none? But the fact is, Ion, that if you are right, if it really is by art and knowledge that you are able to praise Homer, then you do me wrong. You assure me that you have much fine knowledge about Homer, and you keep offering to display it, but you are deceiving me. Far from giving the display, you will not even tell me what subject it is on which you are so able, though all this while I have been entreating you to tell. No, you are just like Proteus; you twist and turn, this way and that, assuming every shape, until finally you elude my grasp and reveal yourself as a general. And all in order not to show how skilled you are in the lore concerning Homer! So if you are an artist, and, as I said just now, if you only promised me a display on Homer in order to deceive me, then you are at fault. But if you are not an artist, if by lot divine you are possessed by Homer, and so, knowing nothing, speak many things and fine about the poet, just as I said you did, then you do no wrong. Choose, therefore, how you will be called by us, whether we shall take you for a man unjust, or for a man divine.

ION: The difference, Socrates, is great. It is far lovelier to be deemed divine.

SOCRATES: This lovelier title, Ion, shall be yours, to be in our minds divine, and not an artist, in praising Homer.

Aristotle

384–322 B.C.E.

Unlike his teacher Plato, who was a native-born Athenian aristocrat, Aristotle was a *metic* — a foreigner with a green card, as it were — the son of a doctor from Thrace. Aristotle's origins may help explain why Plato's idealism had so little ultimate appeal for him. As a skilled biologist from Macedonia, an impoverished military state, Aristotle may have been loath to dismiss physical reality as an illusion. Certainly for Aristotle the universal *processes* of nature, the eternal laws of change, were not mere signs of the mutable, inferior character of the world of Becoming compared with the unalterable world of Ideas. They possessed immense significance.

Aristotle spent many years in Plato's Academy, learning its philosophy and its methods of argumentation, but his own school, the Lyceum, rejected Plato's idealism in favor of a materialism that investigated every aspect of the physical world. If Plato is the father of Western philosophy, Aristotle is the father of most of the sciences. Although Aristotle was often wildly wrong about details (Galileo's disproof of his speculations on gravity is the most famous instance), his systematizing of thought made science as we know it possible.

Aristotle's immense philosophical output may be divided into treatises on three types of science: the *theoretical* sciences, like logic or physics, which aimed at improving thought itself — one's general ideas on a particular subject; the *practical* sciences, like ethics and politics, whose goal lay in the realm of human action; and the *productive* sciences, like rhetoric and poetics, whose purpose was in making something. Here already, one can see a major difference from Plato, whose *Republic* combined speculation on metaphysics, ethics, politics, music, poetry, and much else. For Plato, thought was *holistic:* All was ultimately One and could be known through one dialectical method. For Aristotle, the world was not One but Many, and investigating it meant adapting one's methods and principles to the subject under consideration. This is the *problematic* method, and it is rare in the history of philosophy, where most thinkers have preferred universal dialectic to institutionalized improvisation. At the same time, Aristotle's mode of organization has clearly prevailed over Plato's in the structure of the modern university, where specialized departments of physics, psychology, literature, and music pursue their disparate disciplines by different methodologies.

Textual scholars believe the *Poetics* to be what is technically termed an *esoteric* treatise — it was circulated privately, within the Lyceum — rather than an *exoteric* one meant for general publication. It can be compared to a teacher's lecture notes, brief and pointed, but meant to be filled out with further examples and arguments during presentation. Where the text seems dogmatic or disconnected or downright obscure, we should be tolerant — this was not the form in which Aristotle's students received it. There are other sources of obscurity, of course—the usual gaps that appear in transmitting and translating a verbal text more than two thousand years old. In Chapter 6, for example, Aristotle tells us that he will speak of comedy later, but never returns to the subject. It has been presumed for centuries that the treatise on comedy was a second book of the *Poetics* that had been lost forever. In 1839 a manuscript was discovered containing what some scholars believe to be a brief summary of the lost *Poetics II,* but whether this material is genuinely Aristotelian is still controversial.

ORGANIZATION AND METHOD

As a treatise on productive science, the *Poetics* takes as its topic the making of a work of art, specifically a dramatic or epic tragedy. Although the *Poetics* was later misread as a how-to manual, Aristotle was only presenting the general *principles* of dramatic construction as they applied to the poetry and theater of his age; he was not dispensing tips for the practicing tragedian. Later critics attacked the drama of their day for not conforming to Aristotle's rules, often without understanding the reasons behind his general statements or the highly empirical basis of the *Poetics.* It would be as much a mistake to fault Aristotle for not being able to anticipate every development in the drama over the last two millennia.

Productive science relies on Aristotle's method of four-cause analysis in which an artifact is defined by its shape (the formal cause), its composition (the material cause), its manner of construction (the efficient cause), and its end or purpose (the final cause).[1] Thus, in the poetics of hammers, that tool might be defined by its shape (a long handle to give leverage, a flat striking surface), its materials (hard metal for the head, light but strong wood or plastic for the handle), its manner of construction (the relation and attachments of the parts), and its purpose (pounding nails). In defining a dramatic or epic tragedy, the same method of definition is used. Here the material is language, rhythm, and harmony; the form is the imitation of a serious action; the manner is dramatic or narrative (as the case may be); and the end is the *katharsis* of pity and fear (about which more will be said later). The first four chapters of the *Poetics* discuss the causes of tragedy (among the other arts) and prepare the reader for the famous definition of tragedy in Chapter 6.

(Note that Aristotle never formally defines more general categories like *poetry* or *drama.* For him these are not legitimate genres. They are not definable because they do not have all their causes in common. Those things called poetry are similar in formal and material causes; those called drama in formal, material, and efficient causes; but because they do not have similar final causes, they remain congeries of many things rather than one definite species. Aristotle is a genre critic, in other words, not by choice but because of the demands of his systematic method.)

Having defined tragedy, Aristotle analyzes its qualitative parts (plot, character, thought, diction, song, and spectacle) and then examines each part successively, beginning with the most important — plot. Nearly half of the *Poetics* is devoted to the analysis of plot, and here again the same four-cause organization is used. Aristotle considers plot *form* (its general character, length, relation to history,

[1]The method of analysis is itself discussed in the *Posterior Analytics,* one of Aristotle's major treatises on logic.

the course of the action, and so on), plot *materials* (devices like recognition and reversal or the tragic deed), and plot *handling*. All these technical issues are explained ultimately in terms of the *purpose* of plot, the *katharsis*. In Chapter 13, he argues deductively that *hamartia* — the tragic protagonist's character flaw — derives directly from the nature of the tragic emotions of pity and fear. Later he moves from plot to the formal and material aspects of character, thought, and so on. Throughout, his method is rigorous, though what remains of the *Poetics* is not complete and there are occasional interruptions or interpolations (like Chapter 12).

ARISTOTELIAN IMITATION

Although Aristotle, like Plato, considers poetry a form of mimetic art, he surprisingly does not think that art itself is necessarily or essentially imitative. (Thus without having experienced abstract art or even discussing it, he does not preclude its possibility.)[2] Another surprise is the title of the treatise, since the word *poiētikēs* in Greek means "things that are made or crafted." The point is that for Aristotle, poetic art is not, as Plato thought, merely copying; It is a creative act.

One reason poetics cannot be simple copying is that art involves the translation of reality into another medium. Just as the portrait sculptor translates the human countenance into clay or stone, the poet translates action into language. Nor can the poet merely translate his materials raw. Even if he does not invent his plots, but takes them, as many Greek tragedians did, from the historical or mythological record, he selectively reshapes the action to make it more universal and thus more powerfully tragic. Divesting the historical action of the accidental and the incidental,[3] he pares away unnecessary prologue until he has a probable sequence of actions leading inexorably to the protagonist's doom. If this is done well, the bare summary of a tragic plot should have something of the tragic effect. After he has constructed the plot, he must compose it verbally using extraordinary, "embellished" language and compose it visually for the stage. The whole process is a complex one — of making, not of mere imitation — that requires keeping the ultimate end in constant view.

For Plato, that artists were not always faithful to the truth counted against them; for Aristotle, artists must disregard incidental facts to search for deeper *universal* truths. For Plato, Pygmalion's statue, which came to life, would be the transcendent triumph of art; for Aristotle, a statue that was merely true to life would not be art at all.

KATHARSIS

One of the most controversial passages in the *Poetics* is contained in the passage on the final cause of tragedy: The play, "through incidents arousing pity and fear

[2]In the sentence where Aristotle tells us that poetry is a form of imitation, he uses not the usual verb *eimi* ("be"), but rather *tugkhanō*, "happen to be."

[3]"Poetry . . . is more philosophical and more significant than history, for poetry is more concerned with the universal, and history more with the individual." This is a crucial passage in the *Poetics* (see p. 56). The issue for Aristotle seems to be that we can learn more from the universal principles that poets must abstract in creating their plots than from the messy, contingent realities the historian is forced to deal with. This is the paradox behind the saying "Truth is stranger than fiction." Precisely — the poets who create fictions must jettison the strange accidents that shape the events of this world.

effects their *katharsis*."[4] But what does *katharsis* mean and what is "katharted"? Three possible translations of *katharsis* are "clarification," "purification," and "purgation"; and what is clarified, purified, or purged must be either the "incidents" or the emotions of "pity and fear."

According to the classical scholar Leon Golden, *katharsis* means "clarification," and it is the tragic *incidents* that are clarified: The process of poetic imitation, by stripping all accident and contingency from the tragic fall of the noble protagonist, reveals as clearly as possible how such things can happen. Tragedy here has an educative function. The "purification" theory, which has a long history beginning with the Renaissance theorists Lodovico Castelvetro and Francesco Robortello, suggests that tragedy has the function of tempering (or hardening) the emotions by revealing to the audience the proper objects of pity and fear.

The oldest theory holds that *katharsis* means "purgation," the violent driving-out of the emotions of pity and fear. This theory is supported by the only other instance in which Aristotle uses *katharsis* in the context of the arts, in a passage from the *Politics:*

> Music should be studied . . . for the sake of . . . many benefits . . . [one of which is] purgation (the word purgation we use at present without any explanation, but when hereafter we speak of poetry we will treat the subject with more precision). For feelings such as pity and fear, or, again, enthusiasm, exist very strongly in some souls, and have more or less influence over all. Some persons fall into a religious frenzy, whom we see . . . when they have used the sacred melodies, restored as though they had found healing and purgation. Those who are influenced by pity or fear, and every emotional nature, must have a like experience, and others in so far as each is susceptible to such emotions, and all are in a manner purged and their souls lightened and delighted. (*Politics* 1341[b] 35 to 1342[a] 15)

Aristotle thought that the *Poetics* would clarify the *Politics* rather than the other way around, but the context of this passage is clear enough: Unpleasant feelings may be relieved through music or poetry. When the experience is over, the soul is "lightened and delighted." After seeing a performance of *Oedipus the King* or *King Lear*, spectators are no longer gripped by pity and fear; rather they are exhausted, cleansed, emptied of emotion. The primary meaning of the word *katharsis*, preserved in the English cognate "cathartic," is the action of a powerful laxative. A doctor's son, Aristotle perhaps could not resist using a familiar medical metaphor for the experience.

Selected Bibliography

Belfiore, Elizabeth. *Tragic Pleasures: Aristotle on Plot and Emotion.* Princeton: Princeton University Press, 1992.

Butcher, S. H. *Aristotle's Theory of Poetry and Fine Art.* New York: Macmillan, 1902.

Cooper, Lane. *The Poetics of Aristotle: Its Meaning and Influence.* 1923; New York: Cooper Square, 1963.

Cronk, Nicholas. "Aristotle, Horace and Longinus: The Conception of Reader Response." In *The Cambridge History of Literary Criticism, III: The Renaissance*, ed. Glyn P. Norton, 199–204. Cambridge: Cambridge University Press, 1999.

[4]Editor's literal translation.

Else, Gerald F. *Aristotle's Poetics: The Argument.* Cambridge: Harvard University Press, 1957.

——. *Plato and Aristotle on Poetry.* Chapel Hill: University of North Carolina Press, 1986.

Fergusson, Francis. "On the Poetics." *Tulane Drama Review* 4 (1960): 23–32.

House, Humphrey. *The Poetics of Aristotle in England.* London: R. Hart-Davis, 1956.

Janko, Richard. *Aristotle on Comedy.* Berkeley: University of California Press, 1984.

Lucas, F. L. *Tragedy: Serious Drama in Relation to Aristotle's Poetics.* New York: Macmillan, 1958.

Modrak, Deborah K. W. *Aristotle: The Power of Perception.* Chicago: University of Chicago Press, 1987.

——. *Aristotle's Theory of Language and Meaning.* Cambridge: Cambridge University Press, 2001.

Olson, Elder. *Aristotle's Poetics and English Literature.* Chicago: University of Chicago Press, 1965.

——. "The Poetic Method of Aristotle: Its Powers and Limitations." In *On Value Judgments in the Arts and Other Essays.* Chicago: University of Chicago Press, 1976.

Rorty, Amelie Oksenberg, ed. *Essays on Aristotle's Poetics.* Princeton: Princeton University Press, 1992.

Watson, Walter. *The Lost Second Book of Aristotle's Poetics.* Chicago: University of Chicago Press, 2012.

Poetics

Translated by Leon Golden.

1

Let us discuss the art of poetry, itself, and its species, describing the character of each of them, and how it is necessary to construct plots if the poetic composition is to be successful and, furthermore, the number and kind of parts to be found in the poetic work, and as many other matters as are relevant. Let us follow the order of nature, beginning with first principles.

Now epic poetry, tragedy, comedy, dithyrambic poetry, and most forms of flute and lyre playing all happen to be, in general, imitations, but they differ from each other in three ways: either because the imitation is carried on by different means or because it is concerned with different kinds of objects or because it is presented, not in the same, but in a different manner.

For just as some artists imitate many different objects by using color and form to represent them (some through art, others only through habit), other artists imitate through sound, as indeed, in the arts mentioned above; for all these accomplish imitation through rhythm and speech and harmony, making use of these elements separately or in combination. Flute playing and lyre playing, for example, use harmony and rhythm alone; and this would also be true of any other arts (for example, the art of playing the shepherd's pipe) that are similar in character to these. Dancers imitate by using rhythm without harmony, since they imitate characters, emotions, and actions by rhythms that are arranged into dance-figures.

The art that imitates by words alone, in prose and in verse, and in the latter case, either combines various meters or makes use of only one, has been nameless up to the present time. For we cannot assign a common name to the mimes of Sophron and Xenarchus and the Socratic dialogues; nor would we have a name for such an imitation if someone should accomplish it through trimeters or elegiacs or some other such meter, except that the public at large by joining the term "poet" to a meter gives writers such names as "elegiac poets" and "epic poets." Here the public classifies all those who write in meter as poets and completely misses the point that the capacity to produce an imitation is the essential characteristic of the poet. The public is even accustomed to apply the name "poet" to those who publish a medical or scientific treatise in verse, although Homer has nothing at all in common with Empedocles except the meter. It is just to call Homer a poet, but we must consider Empedocles a physicist rather than a poet.

And in the same way, if anyone should create an imitation by combining all the meters as Chairemon did when he wrote *The Centaur,* a rhapsody composed by the use of all the meters, he must also be designated a poet. Concerning these matters let us accept the distinctions we have just made.

There are some arts that use all the means that have been discussed, namely, rhythm and song and meter, as in the writing of dithyrambs and nomic poetry[1] and in tragedy and comedy. A difference is apparent here in that some arts use all the various elements at the same time, whereas others use them separately. These, then, are what I call the differences in the artistic means through which the imitation is accomplished.

2

Artists imitate men involved in action and these must either be noble or base since human character regularly conforms to these distinctions, all of us being different in character because of some quality of goodness or evil. From this it follows that the objects imitated are either better than or worse than or like the norm. We find confirmation of this observation in the practice of our painters. For Polygnotus represents men as better, Pauson as worse, and Dionysius as like the norm.[2] It is clear that each of the above-mentioned forms of imitation will manifest differences of this type and will be different through its choosing, in this way, a different kind of object to imitate.

Even in dancing, flute-playing, and lyre-playing it is possible for these differences to exist, and they are seen also in prose, and in verse that does not make use of musical accompaniment, as is shown by the fact that Cleophon represents men like the norm, Homer as better, and both Hegemon the Thasian (who was the first writer of parodies) and Nicochares, the author of the *Deiliad,* as worse.[3] The same situation is found in dithyrambic and nomic poetry,[4] as we see in the way Timotheus and Philoxenus handled the Cyclops theme.[5] It is through the same distinction in objects that we differentiate comedy from tragedy, for the former takes as its goal the representation of men as worse, the latter as better, than the norm.

3

There is, finally, a third factor by which we distinguish imitations, and that is the manner in which the artist represents the various types of object. For, using the same means and imitating the same kinds of object, it is possible for the poet on different occasions to narrate the story (either speaking in the person of one of his characters as Homer does or in his own person without changing roles)[6] or to have the imitators performing and acting out the entire story.

---

[1]The dithyramb was originally a choral ode sung in honor of Dionysus, whereas nomic poetry was originally concerned with texts taken from the epic and was presented with a flute or lyre accompaniment. [Tr.]

[2]Polygnotus was one of the great painters of the fifth century B.C. Neither Pauson nor Dionysius are identified with certainty. [Tr.]

[3]Not much is known about the poets other than Homer mentioned here. Cleophon was a dramatic or epic writer; a small fragment of a parody of Hegemon of Thasos is preserved in Athenaeus; we have no further certain information about Nicochares. [Tr.]

[4]There is a lacuna in the text at this point where the name of another writer of nomic poetry was probably mentioned. [Tr.]

[5]Timotheus was a dithyrambic poet who lived in Miletus from 450 to 360 B.C.; Philoxenus was a dithyrambic poet who lived in Cythera from 436 to 380 B.C. [Tr.]

[6]The translation given of this phrase is based on the traditional text, which has been accepted by Butcher, Hardy, and Kassel. On philosophical and linguistic grounds, Bywater prefers to emend the text of the passage so that it reads as follows: "Given both the same means and the same kind of object for imitation, one may either (1) speak at one moment in narrative and at another in an assumed character, as Homer does; or (2) one may remain the same throughout, without any such change; or (3) the imitators may represent the whole story dramatically, as though they were actually doing the things described." [Tr.]

As we said at the beginning, imitations are to be distinguished under these three headings: means, object, and manner. Thus, in one way, Sophocles is the same kind of imitative artist as Homer, since they both imitate noble men; but in another sense, he resembles Aristophanes, since they both imitate characters as acting and dramatizing the incidents of the story. It is from this, some tell us, that these latter kinds of imitations are called "dramas," because they present characters who "dramatize" the incidents of the plot.

By the way, it is also for this reason that the Dorians claim to be the originators of both tragedy and comedy. The Megarians — both those in Megara itself, who assert that comedy arose when democracy was established among them, and those Megarians in Sicily, who point out that their poet Epicharmus far antedates Chionides and Magnes[7] — claim to have originated comedy; in addition, some of the Dorians in the Peloponnesus claim to be the originators of tragedy. As proof of their contentions, they cite the technical terms they use for these art forms; for they say that they call the towns around their city *komai*, but that the Athenians call their towns *demoi*. By this they argue that the root of the name "comedian" is not derived from *komazein* [the word for "reveling"] but from *komai* [their word for the towns], that the comic artists visited in their wanderings after they had been driven in disgrace from the city. In support of their claim to be the originators of "drama," they point out that the word for "doing" is *dran* in their dialect, whereas Athenians use the word *prattein* for this concept.

Concerning the number and kind of distinctions that characterize "imitations," let us accept what has been said above.

4

Speaking generally, the origin of the art of poetry is to be found in two natural causes. For the process of imitation is natural to mankind from childhood on: Man is differentiated from other animals because he is the most imitative of them, and he learns his first lessons through imitation; and we observe that all men find pleasure in imitations. The proof of this point is what actually happens in life. For there are some things that distress us when we see them in reality, but the most accurate representations of these same things we view with pleasure — as, for example, the forms of the most despised animals and of corpses. The cause of this is that the act of learning is not only most pleasant to philosophers but, in a similar way, to other men as well, only they have an abbreviated share in this pleasure. Thus men find pleasure in viewing representations because it turns out that they learn and infer what each thing is — for example, that this particular object is that kind of object; since if one has not happened to see the object previously, he will not find any pleasure in the imitation qua imitation but rather in the workmanship or coloring or something similar.

Since imitation is given to us by nature, as are harmony and rhythm (for it is apparent that meters are parts of the rhythms), men, having been naturally endowed with these gifts from the beginning and then developing them gradually, for the most part, finally created the art of poetry from their early improvisations.

Poetry then diverged in the directions of the natural dispositions of the poets. Writers of greater dignity imitated the noble actions of noble heroes; the less dignified sort of writers imitated the actions of inferior men, at first writing invectives as the former writers wrote hymns and encomia. We know of no "invective" by poets before Homer, although it is probable that there were many who wrote such poems; but it is possible to attribute them to authors who came after Homer — for example, the *Margites* of Homer himself, and other such poems. In these poems, the fitting meter came to light, the one that now bears the name "iambic" [i.e., invective] because it was originally used by men to satirize each other. Thus, of our earliest writers, some were heroic and some iambic poets. And just as Homer was especially the poet of noble actions (for he not only handled these well but he also made his

[7]Not much is known, beyond what Aristotle tells us in the *Poetics*, about these three comic writers who lived in the early part of the fifth century B.C. [Tr.]

imitations dramatic), so also he first traced out the form of comedy by dramatically presenting not invective but the ridiculous. For his *Margites* has the same relation to comedy as the *Iliad* and *Odyssey* have to tragedy. But when tragedy and comedy began to appear, poets were attracted to each type of poetry according to their individual natures, one group becoming writers of comedies in place of iambics, and the other, writers of tragedies instead of epics because these genres were of greater importance and more admired than the others.

Now then, the consideration of whether or not tragedy is by now sufficiently developed in its formal elements, judged both in regard to its essential nature and in regard to its public performances, belongs to another discussion. What is relevant is that it arose, at first, as an improvisation (both tragedy and comedy are similar in this respect) on the part of those who led the dithyrambs, just as comedy arose from those who led the phallic songs that even now are still customary in many of our cities. Tragedy, undergoing many changes (since our poets were developing aspects of it as they emerged), gradually progressed until it attained the fulfillment of its own nature. Aeschylus was the first to increase the number of actors from one to two; he also reduced the role of the chorus and made the dialogue the major element in the play. Sophocles increased the number of actors to three and introduced scene painting. Then tragedy acquired its magnitude. Thus by developing away from a satyr-play of short plots and absurd diction, tragedy achieved, late in its history, a dignified level. Then the iambic meter took the place of the tetrameter. For the poets first used the trochaic tetrameter because their poetry was satyric and very closely associated with dance; but when dialogue was introduced, nature itself discovered the appropriate meter. For the iambic is the most conversational of the meters — as we see from the fact that we speak many iambs when talking to each other, but few [dactylic] hexameters, and only when departing from conversational tone. Moreover, the number of episodes was increased. As to the other elements by which, we are told, tragedy was embellished, we must consider them as having been mentioned by us. For it would probably be an enormous task to go through each of these elements one by one.

5

As we have said, comedy is an imitation of baser men. These are characterized not by every kind of vice but specifically by "the ridiculous," which is a subdivision of the category of "deformity." What we mean by "the ridiculous" is some error or ugliness that is painless and has no harmful effects. The example that comes immediately to mind is the comic mask, which is ugly and distorted but causes no pain.

Now then, the successive changes in the history of tragedy and the men who brought them about have been recorded; but the analogous information about the history of comedy is lacking because the genre was not treated, at the beginning, as a serious art form. It was only recently that the archons began to grant choruses to the comic poets; until then, the performers were all volunteers. And it was only after comedy had attained some recognizable form that we began to have a record of those designated as "comic poets." Who introduced masks or prologues, who established the number of actors, and many other matters of this type, are unknown. The creation of plots came first from Sicily, where it is attributed to Epicharmus and Phormis; and it was first Crates among the Athenian poets who departed from iambic [or invective] poetry and began to write speeches and plots of a more universal nature.

Now epic poetry follows the same pattern as tragedy insofar as it is the imitation of noble subjects presented in an elevated meter. But epic differs from tragedy in that it uses a single meter, and its manner of presentation is narrative. And further, there is a difference in length. For tragedy attempts, as far as possible, to remain within one circuit of the sun or, at least, not depart from this by much. Epic poetry, however, has no limit in regard to time, and differs from tragedy in this respect; although at first the poets proceeded in tragedy in the same way as they did in epic. Some of the parts of a poem are common to both tragedy and epic, and some belong to tragedy alone. Therefore, whoever can judge what is good and bad in tragedy can also do this in regard to epic. For whatever parts epic poetry has, these are also found in tragedy; but, as we have said, not all of the parts of tragedy are found in epic poetry.

6

We shall speak about the form of imitation that is associated with hexameter verse and about comedy later.[8] Let us now discuss tragedy, bring-ing together the definition of its essence that has emerged from what we have already said. Tragedy is, then, an imitation of a noble and complete action, having the proper magnitude;[9] it employs language that has been artistically enhanced by each of the kinds of linguistic adorn-ment, applied separately in the various parts of the play; it is presented in dramatic, not narrative form, and achieves, through the representation of pitiable and fearful incidents, the catharsis of such pitiable and fearful incidents. I mean by "language that has been artistically enhanced," that which is accompanied by rhythm and har-mony and song; and by the phrase "each of the kinds of linguistic adornment applied separately in the various parts of the play," I mean that some parts are accomplished by meter alone and others, in turn, through song.

And since [in drama] agents accomplish the imitation by acting the story out, it follows, first of all, that the arrangement of the spectacle should be, of necessity, some part of the tragedy as would be melody and diction; also; for these are the means through which the agents accom-plish the imitation. I mean by diction the act, itself, of making metrical compositions, and by

melody, what is completely obvious. Since the imitation is of an action and is accomplished by certain agents, the sort of men these agents are is necessarily dependent upon their "character" and "thought." It is, indeed, on the basis of these two considerations that we designate the quality of actions, because the two natural causes of human action are thought and character. It is also in regard to these that the lives of all turn out well or poorly. For this reason we say that tragic plot is an imitation of action.

Now I mean by the plot the arrangement of the incidents, and by character that element in accordance with which we say that agents are of a certain type; and by thought I mean that which is found in whatever things men say when they prove a point or, it may be, express a general truth. It is necessary, therefore, that tragedy as a whole have six parts in accordance with which, as a genre, it achieves its particular quality. These parts are plot, character, diction, thought, spectacle, and melody. Two of these parts come from the means by which the imita-tion is carried out: one from the manner of its presentation, and three from the objects of the imitation. Beyond these parts there is nothing left to mention. Not a few poets, so to speak, employ these parts; for indeed, every drama has [theoretically] spectacle, character, plot, diction, song, and thought.

The most important of these parts is the arrangement of the incidents; for tragedy is not an imitation of men, per se, but of human action and life and happiness and misery. Both happi-ness and misery consist in a kind of action; and the end of life is some action, not some quality.[10] Now according to their characters men have cer-tain qualities; but according to their actions they are happy or the opposite. Poets do not, therefore, create action in order to imitate character; but character is included on account of the action. Thus the end of tragedy is the presentation of the individual incidents and of the plot; and the end is, of course, the most significant thing of all. Furthermore, without action tragedy would be

[8] Aristotle discusses the epic in Chs. 23 and 24, but the section of the Poetics dealing with comedy seems to have been written but lost. Various Aristotelian scholars (including Richard Janko and Walter Watson) have attempted to recon-struct what a poetics of comedy would be like.

[9] There is no word in the Greek text for "proper," but I have followed the practice of several other translators who add a modifier to the term "magnitude" where it is logically warranted. The term "representation" has also been added to the final clause of this sentence because of Aristotle's insis-tence that the pleasure of tragedy is achieved through imita-tion (Ch. 14, ll. 18–19). See L. Golden, "Catharsis," TAPA 93 (1962): 58. [Tr.]

[10] The text is corrupt here. The translation follows an emendation suggested by Vahlen and accepted by Bywater and Hardy. [Tr.]

impossible, but without character it would still be possible. This point is illustrated both by the fact that the tragedies of many of our modern poets are characterless, and by the fact that many poets, in general, experience this difficulty. Also, to take an example from our painters, Zeuxis illustrates the point when compared to Polygnotus; for Polygnotus is good at incorporating character into his painting, but the work of Zeuxis shows no real characterization at all. Furthermore, if someone arranges a series of speeches that show character and are well-constructed in diction and thought, he will not, by this alone, achieve the end of tragedy; but far more will this be accomplished by the tragedy that employs these elements rather inadequately but, nevertheless, has a satisfactory plot and arrangement of incidents. In addition to the arguments already given, the most important factors by means of which tragedy exerts an influence on the soul are parts of the plot, the reversal, and the recognition. We have further proof of our view of the importance of plot in the fact that those who attempt to write tragedies are able to perfect diction and character before the construction of the incidents, as we see, for example, in nearly all of our early poets.

The first principle, then, and to speak figuratively, the soul of tragedy, is the plot; and second in importance is character. A closely corresponding situation exists in painting. For if someone should paint by applying the most beautiful colors, but without reference to an overall plan, he would not please us as much as if he had outlined the figure in black and white. Tragedy, then, is an imitation of an action; and it is, on account of this, an imitation of men acting.

Thought is the third part of tragedy and is the ability to say whatever is pertinent and fitting to the occasion, which, in reference to the composition of speeches, is the essential function of the arts of politics and rhetoric. As proof of this we point out that our earlier poets made their characters speak like statesmen, and our contemporary poets make them speak like rhetoricians. Now character is that part of tragedy which shows an individual's purpose by indicating, in circumstances where it is not clear, what sort of things he chooses or rejects. Therefore those speeches do not manifest character in which there is absolutely nothing that the speaker chooses or rejects. Thought we find in those speeches in which men show that something is or is not, or utter some universal proposition.

The fourth literary part is diction, and I mean by diction, as has already been said, the expression of thoughts through language which, indeed, is the same whether in verse or prose.

Of the remaining parts, melody is the greatest of the linguistic adornments; and spectacle, to be sure, attracts our attention but is the least essential part of the art of poetry. For the power of tragedy is felt even without a dramatic performance and actors. Furthermore, for the realization of spectacle, the art of the costume designer is more effective than that of the poet.

7

Now that we have defined these terms, let us discuss what kind of process the arrangement of incidents must be, since this is the first and most important element of tragedy. We have posited that tragedy is the imitation of a complete and whole action having a proper magnitude. For it is possible for something to be a whole and yet not have any considerable magnitude. To be a whole is to have a beginning and a middle and an end. By a "beginning" I mean that which is itself not, by necessity, after anything else but after which something naturally is or develops. By an "end" I mean exactly the opposite: that which is naturally after something else, either necessarily or customarily, but after which there is nothing else. By a "middle" I mean that which is itself after something else and which has something else after it. It is necessary, therefore, that well-constructed plots not begin by chance, anywhere, nor end anywhere, but that they conform to the distinctions that have been made above.

Furthermore, for beauty to exist, both in regard to a living being and in regard to any object that is composed of separate parts, not only must there be a proper arrangement of the component elements, but the object must also be of a magnitude that is not fortuitous. For beauty is determined by magnitude and order; therefore, neither would a very small animal be beautiful (for one's view of the animal is not clear, taking place, as it does, in an almost unperceived length of time), nor is a very large animal beautiful (for then one's view does not occur all at once, but, rather, the unity and wholeness of the animal are lost to the viewer's sight as would happen, for example, if we should come across an animal a thousand miles in length). So that just as it is necessary in regard to bodies and animals for there to be a proper magnitude — and this is the length that can easily be perceived at a glance — thus, also, there must be a proper length in regard to plots, and this is one that can be easily taken in by the memory. The limit of length in regard to the dramatic contests and in terms of the physical viewing of the performance is not a matter related to the art of poetry. For if it were necessary for a hundred tragedies to be played, they would be presented by timing them with water clocks as we are told happened on some occasions in the past. The limit, however, that is set in regard to magnitude by the very nature of the subject itself is that whatever is longer (provided it remains quite clear) is always more beautiful. To give a general rule, we say that whatever length is required for a change to occur from bad fortune to good or from good fortune to bad through a series of incidents that are in accordance with probability or necessity, is a sufficient limit of magnitude.

8

A plot is a unity not, as some think, merely if it is concerned with one individual, for in some of the many and infinitely varied things that happen to any one person, there is no unity. Thus, we must assert, there are many actions in the life of a single person from which no overall unity of action emerges. For this reason all those poets seem to have erred who have written a *Heracleid* and a *Theseid* and other poems of this type; for they think that since Heracles was one person it is appropriate for his story to be one story. But Homer, just as he was superior in other respects, also seems to have seen this point well, whether through his technical skill or his native talent, since in making the *Odyssey* he did not include all the things that ever happened to Odysseus. (For example, it happened that Odysseus was wounded on Parnassus and that

he feigned madness at the time of the call to arms; but between these two events there is no necessary or probable relation.) Homer, rather, organized the *Odyssey* around one action of the type we have been speaking about and did the same with the *Iliad*. Necessarily, then, just as in other forms of imitation, one imitation is of one thing, so also, a plot, since it is an imitation of an action, must be an imitation of an action that is one and whole. Moreover, it is necessary that the parts of the action be put together in such a way that if any one part is transposed or removed, the whole will be disordered and disunified. For that whose presence or absence has no evident effect is not part of the whole.

9

It is apparent from what we have said that it is not the function of the poet to narrate events that have actually happened, but rather, events such as might occur and have the capability of occurring in accordance with the laws of probability or necessity. For the historian and the poet do not differ by their writing in prose or verse (the works of Herodotus might be put into verse but they would, nonetheless, remain a form of history both in their metrical and prose versions). The difference, rather, lies in the fact that the historian narrates events that have actually happened, whereas the poet writes about things as they might possibly occur. Poetry, therefore, is more philosophical and more significant than history, for poetry is more concerned with the universal, and history more with the individual. By the universal I mean what sort of man turns out to say or do what sort of thing according to probability or necessity — this being the goal poetry aims at, although it gives individual names to the characters whose actions are imitated. By the individual I mean a statement telling, for example, "what Alcibiades did or experienced."

Now then, this point has already been made clear in regard to comedy; for the comic poets, once they have constructed the plot through probable incidents, assign any names that happen to occur to them, and they do not follow the procedure of the iambic poets who write about specific individuals. In regard to tragedy, however, our poets cling to the names of the heroes of the past on the principle that whatever is clearly capable of happening is readily believable. We cannot be sure that whatever has not yet happened is possible; but it is apparent that whatever has happened is also capable of happening for, if it were not, it could not have occurred. Nevertheless in some tragedies one or two of the names are well known and the rest have been invented for the occasion; in others not even one is well known, for example, Agathon's *Antheus*,[11] since in this play both the incidents and the names have been invented, and nonetheless they please us. Thus we must not seek to cling exclusively to the stories that have been handed down and about which our tragedies are usually written. It would be absurd, indeed, to do this since the well-known plots are known only to a few, but nevertheless please everyone. It is clear then from these considerations that it is necessary for the poet to be more the poet of his plots than of his meters, insofar as he is a poet because he is an imitator and imitates human actions. If the poet happens to write about things that have actually occurred, he is no less the poet for that. For nothing prevents some of the things that have actually occurred from belonging to the class of the probable or possible, and it is in regard to this aspect that he is the poet of them.

Of the simple plots and actions the episodic are the worst; and I mean by episodic a plot in which the episodes follow each other without regard for the laws of probability or necessity. Such plots are constructed by the inferior poets because of their own inadequacies, and by the good poets because of the actors. For since they are writing plays that are to be entered in contests (and so stretch the plot beyond its capacity) they are frequently forced to distort the sequence of action.

Since the imitation is not only a complete action but is also of fearful and pitiable incidents, we must note that these are intensified when they occur unexpectedly, yet because of one another. For there is more of the marvelous in them if they occur this way than if they occurred spontaneously and by chance. Even in regard to coincidences, those seem to be most astonishing that appear to have some design associated with them. We have an example of this in the story of the statue of Mitys in Argos killing the man who caused Mitys' death by falling upon him as he was a spectator at a festival.[12] The occurrence of such an event, we feel, is not without meaning and thus we must consider plots that incorporate incidents of this type to be superior ones.

10

Plots are divided into the simple and the complex, for the actions of which the plots are imitations are naturally of this character. An action that is, as has been defined, continuous and unified I call simple when its change of fortune arises without reversal and recognition, and complex when its change of fortune arises through recognition or reversal or both. Now these aspects of the plot must develop directly from the construction of the plot itself, so that they occur from prior events either out of necessity or according to the laws of probability. For it makes quite a difference whether they occur *because* of those events or merely *after* them.

11

Reversal is the change of fortune in the action of the play to the opposite state of affairs, just as has been said; and this change, we argue, should be in accordance with probability and necessity. Thus, in the *Oedipus* the messenger comes to cheer Oedipus and to remove his fears in regard to his mother; but by showing him who he actually is he accomplishes the very opposite effect. And in *Lynceus*, Lynceus is being led away to die and Danaus is following to kill him; but it turns out, because of the action that has taken place, that Danaus dies and Lynceus is saved. Recognition, as the same indicates, is a change from ignorance to knowledge, bringing about either a state of

---

[11]Agathon was a late fifth-century B.C. tragic poet whose work has not survived except in fragments. He appears, prominently, in Plato's *Symposium*. [Tr.]

[12]I have followed Butcher's, Hardy's, and Bywater's interpretation of this passage. Others, however, understand the phrase to mean "when he was looking at the statue." [Tr.]

friendship or one of hostility on the part of those who have been marked out for good fortune or bad. The most effective recognition is one that occurs together with reversal, for example, as in the *Oedipus*. There are also other kinds of recognition for, indeed, what we have said happens, in a way, in regard to inanimate things, even things of a very casual kind; and it is possible, further, to "recognize" whether someone has or has not done something. But the type of recognition that is especially a part of the plot and the action is the one that has been mentioned. For such a recognition and reversal will evoke pity or fear, and we have defined tragedy as an imitation of actions of this type; and furthermore, happiness and misery will appear in circumstances of this type.

Since this kind of recognition is of persons, some recognitions that belong to this class will merely involve the identification of one person by another when the identity of the second person is clear; on other occasions it will be necessary for there to be a recognition on the part of both parties: for example, Iphigenia is recognized by Orestes from her sending of the letter; but it is necessary that there be another recognition of him on her part.

Now then, these are two parts of the plot, reversal and recognition, and there is also a third part, suffering. Of these, reversal and recognition have been discussed; the incident of suffering results from destructive or painful action such as death on the stage, scenes of very great pain, the infliction of wounds, and the like.

12

The parts of tragedy that we must view as formal elements we have discussed previously; looking at the quantitative aspect of tragedy and the parts into which it is divided in this regard, the following are the distinctions to be made: prologue, episode, exode, and the choral part, which is divided into parode and stasimon. These are commonly found in all plays, but only in a few are found songs from the stage and *kommoi*. The prologue is the complete section of a tragedy before the parode of the chorus; an episode is the complete section of a tragedy between complete choric songs; the exode is the complete section of a tragedy after which there is no song of the chorus. Of the choral part, the parode is the entire first speech of the chorus, the stasimon is a song of the chorus without anapaests and trochees, and a *kommos* is a lament sung in common by the chorus and the actors. The parts of tragedy that we must view as formal elements we have discussed previously; the above distinctions have been made concerning the quantitative aspects of tragedy, and the parts into which it is divided in this regard.

13

What goals poets must aim at, which difficulties they must be wary of when constructing their plots, and how the proper function of tragedy is accomplished are matters we should discuss after the remarks that have just been made.

Since the plots of the best tragedies must be complex, not simple, and the plot of a tragedy must be an imitation of pitiable and fearful incidents (for this is the specific nature of the imitation under discussion), it is clear, first of all, that unqualifiedly good human beings must not appear to fall from good fortune to bad; for that is neither pitiable nor fearful: it is, rather, repellent. Nor must an extremely evil man appear to move from bad fortune to good fortune for that is the most untragic situation of all because it has none of the necessary requirements of tragedy; it both violates our human sympathy and contains nothing of the pitiable or fearful in it. Furthermore, a villainous man should not appear to fall from good fortune to bad. For, although such a plot would be in accordance with our human sympathy, it would not contain the necessary elements of pity and fear; for pity is aroused by someone who undeservedly falls into misfortune, and fear is evoked by our recognizing that it is someone like ourselves who encounters this misfortune (pity, as I say, arising for the former reason, fear for the latter). Therefore the emotional effect of the situation just mentioned will be neither pitiable nor fearful. What is left, after our considerations, is someone in between these extremes. This would be a person who is neither perfect in virtue and justice, nor one who falls into misfortune through vice and depravity; but rather, one who succumbs through some miscalculation. He must also be a person who enjoys great reputation and good fortune, such as Oedipus, Thyestes, and other illustrious men from similar families. It is necessary, furthermore, for the well-constructed plot to have a single rather than a double construction, as some urge, and to illustrate a change of fortune not from bad fortune to good but, rather, the very opposite, from good fortune to bad, and for this to take place not because of depravity but through some great miscalculation on the part of the type of person we have described (or a better rather than a worse one).

A sign of our point is found in what actually happens in the theater. For initially, our poets accepted any chance plots; but now the best tragedies are constructed about a few families, for example, about Alcmaeon, Oedipus, Orestes, Meleager, Thyestes, Telephon, and any others who were destined to experience, or to commit, terrifying acts. For as we have indicated, artistically considered, the best tragedy arises from this kind of plot. Therefore, those critics make the very mistake that we have been discussing who blame Euripides because he handles the material in his tragedies in this way, and because many of his plots end in misfortune. For this is, indeed, the correct procedure, as we have said. The very great proof of this is that on the stage and in the dramatic contests such plays appear to be the most tragic, if they are properly worked out; and Euripides, even if in other matters he does not manage things well, nevertheless appears to be the most tragic of the poets. The second ranking plot, one that is called first by some, has a double structure of events, as in the *Odyssey,* ending in opposite ways for the better and worse characters. It seems to be first on account of the inadequacy of the audience. For our poets trail along writing to please the tastes of the audience. But this double structure of events involves a pleasure that is not an appropriate pleasure of tragedy but rather of comedy. For in comedy, whoever are the greatest enemies in the story — for example, Orestes and Aegisthus — becoming friends at the end, go off together, and no one is killed by anyone.

14

Pity and fear can arise from the spectacle and also from the very structure of the plot, which is the superior way and shows the better poet. The poet should construct the plot so that even if the action is not performed before spectators, one who merely hears the incidents that have occurred both shudders and feels pity from the way they turn out. That is what anyone who hears the plot of the *Oedipus* would experience. The achievement of this effect through the spectacle does not have much to do with poetic art and really belongs to the business of producing the play. Those who use the spectacle to create not the fearful but only the monstrous have no share in the creation of tragedy; for we should not seek every pleasure from tragedy but only the one proper to it.

Since the poet should provide pleasure from pity and fear through imitation, it is apparent that this function must be worked into the incidents. Let us try to understand what type of occurrences appear to be terrifying and pitiable. It is, indeed, necessary that any such action occur either between those who are friends or enemies to each other, or between those who have no relationship, whatsoever, to each other. If an enemy takes such an action against an enemy, there is nothing pitiable in the performance of the act or in the intention to perform it, except the suffering itself. Nor would there be anything pitiable if neither party had any relationship with the other. But whenever the tragic incidents occur in situations involving strong ties of affection — for example, if a brother kills or intends to kill a brother or a son a father or a mother a son or a son a mother or commits some equally terrible act — there will be something pitiable. These situations, then, are the ones to be sought. Now, it is not possible for a poet to alter completely the traditional stories. I mean, for example, the given fact that Clytemnestra dies at the hands of Orestes, and Eriphyle at the hands of Alcmaeon; but it is necessary for the poet to be inventive and skillful in adapting the stories that have been handed down. Let us define more clearly what we mean by the skillful adaptation of a story. It is possible for the action to occur, as our early poets handled it, with the characters knowing and understanding what they are doing, as indeed Euripides makes Medea kill her children. It is also possible to have the deed done with those who accomplish the terrible deed in ignorance of the identity of their victim, only later recognizing the relationship — as in Sophocles' *Oedipus*. The incident, here, is outside the plot, but we find an example of such an incident in the play itself, in the action of Astydamas's *Alcmaeon* or of Telegonus in the *Wounded Odysseus*,[13] and there is further a third type in addition to these that involves someone who intends to commit some fatal act through ignorance of his relationship to another person but recognizes this relationship before doing it. Beyond these possibilities, there is no other way to have an action take place. For it is necessary either to do the deed or not and either knowingly or in ignorance.

Of these possibilities, the case in which one knowingly is about to do the deed and does not is the worst; for it is repellent and not tragic because it lacks the element of suffering. Therefore, no one handles a situation this way, except rarely; for example, in the *Antigone*, Haemon is made to act in this way toward Creon. To do the deed knowingly is the next best way. Better than this is the case where one does the deed in ignorance and after he has done it recognizes his relationship — for the repellent aspect is not present, and the recognition is startling. But the most effective is the final type, for example, in the *Cresphontes*, where Merope is going to kill her son and does not, but, on the contrary, recognizes him, and in the *Iphigenia*, where a sister is involved in a similar situation with a brother, and in the *Helle*, where a son who is about to surrender his mother recognizes her.[14]

It is for this reason that, as we have said previously, tragedies are concerned with a few families. For proceeding not by art, but by trial and error, poets learned how to produce the appropriate effect in their plots. They are compelled, therefore, to return time and again to that number of families in which these terrifying events have occurred. We have now spoken sufficiently about the construction of the incidents and of what type the plot must be.

15

In regard to character, there are four points to be aimed at. First and foremost, character should be good. If a speech or action has some choice connected with it, it will manifest character, as has been said, and the character will be good if the choice is good. Goodness is possible for each class of individuals. For, both a woman and a slave have their particular virtues even though the former of these is inferior to a man, and the latter is completely ignoble.[15] Second, character must be appropriate. For it is possible for a person to be manly in terms of character, but it is not appropriate for a woman to exhibit either this quality or the intellectual cleverness that is associated with men. The third point about character is that it should be like reality, for this is different from making character virtuous and making it appropriate, as we have defined these terms. The fourth aspect of character is consistency. For even if it is an inconsistent character who is the subject of the imitation (I refer to the model that suggested the kind of character being imitated), it is nevertheless necessary for him to be consistently inconsistent. We have an example of unnecessarily debased character in the figure of Menelaus in the *Orestes*, of unsuitable and inappropriate character in the lament of Odysseus in the *Scylla* and the speech of Melanippe, and of inconsistency of character in *Iphigenia at Aulis* where the heroine's role as a suppliant does not fit in with her character as it develops later in the play.

In character, as in the construction of the incidents, we must always seek for either the necessary or the probable, so that a given type of person says or does certain kinds of things, and

[13]Astydamas was a fourth-century B.C. poet; the *Wounded Odysseus* may have been a play by Sophocles. [Tr.]

[14]The *Cresphontes* and the *Iphigenia*, the former no longer extant, are plays by Euripides. We have no further information concerning the *Helle*. [Tr.]

[15]Aristotle's word for "good" here, *chrestén*, means "valuable" rather than "noble." Aristotle is distinguishing between the intrinsic value of personages (he considered women and slaves to be inferior beings) and the instrumental value of their ethical choices to the drama in which they figure. Aristotle's point is that character must serve the ends of the drama, and that *motiveless* choice, which has no effect on the action — like Menelaus's cowardice in Euripides' *Orestes* — is to be avoided.

one event follows another according to necessity or probability. Thus, it is apparent that the resolutions of the plots should also occur through the plot itself and not by means of the deus ex machina, as in the *Medea,* and also in regard to the events surrounding the department of the fleet in the *Iliad.* The deus ex machina must be reserved for the events that lie outside the plot, either those that happened before it that are not capable of being known by men, or those that occur after that need to be announced and spoken of beforehand. For we grant to the gods the power of seeing all things. There should, then, be nothing improbable in the action; but if this is impossible, it should be outside the plot as, for example, in Sophocles' *Oedipus.*

Because tragedy is an imitation of the nobler sort of men it is necessary for poets to imitate good portrait painters. For even though they reproduce the specific characteristics of their subjects and represent them faithfully, they also paint them better than they are. Thus, also, the poet imitating men who are prone to anger or who are indifferent or who are disposed in other such ways in regard to character makes them good as well, even though they have such characteristics, just as Agathon[16] and Homer portray Achilles.

It is necessary to pay close attention to these matters and, in addition, to those that pertain to the effects upon an audience that follow necessarily from the nature of the art of poetry. For, indeed, it is possible frequently to make mistakes in regard to these. We have spoken sufficiently about these matters in our published works.

16

What we mean by "recognition" we have indicated previously. Of the kinds of recognition that occur, there is one, first of all, that is least artistic, which poets mainly use through the poverty of their inspiration. This is the form of recognition that is achieved through external signs; some of these are birthmarks, for example, "the

---

[16]I have followed Butcher, Hardy, and Bywater in reading the name of the tragic poet here. Other scholars accept a manuscript reading of the word meaning "good." [Tr.]

spearhead which the Earth-born are accustomed to bear," or the "stars" such as Carcinus wrote about in his *Thyestes.* Then there are characteristics that we acquire after birth. Of these some are found on the body, for example, scars; and others are external to the body, such as necklaces, and as another example, the ark through which the recognition is accomplished in the *Tyro.* It is also possible to employ these recognitions in better and worse ways; for example, Odysseus was recognized through his scar in one way by the nurse and in another way by the swineherds. Now those recognitions are less artistic that depend on signs as proof, as well as all that are similar to these; but those that derive from the reversal of action, as in the Bath Scene of the *Odyssey,* are better.

In second place come those recognitions that have been contrived for the occasion by the poet and are therefore inartistic. For example, the way Orestes in the *Iphigenia* makes known that he is Orestes; for Iphigenia made herself known through the letter, but he himself says what the poet wishes him to say but not what the plot requires. Therefore this type of recognition is rather close to the error that has already been mentioned; for it would have been just as possible for him to carry tokens with him. Another example of this type of recognition is the use of the "voice of the shuttle" in the *Tereus* of Sophocles.

The third type arises from our being stimulated by something that we see to remember an event that has an emotional significance for us. This type of recognition occurs in the *Cyprioe* of Dicaeogenes where the sight of the painting brings forth tears, and also in the story of Alcinous where Odysseus hears the lyre player and, reminded of his past fortunes, weeps; in both instances, it was by their emotional reactions that the characters were recognized.

The fourth type of recognition occurs through reasoning, for example, in the *Choëphoroe* it is achieved by the deduction: Someone like me has come; there is no one resembling me except Orestes; he, therefore, has come. Another recognition of this type was suggested by Polyidus the Sophist in regard to Iphigenia; for it was reasonable for Orestes to infer that, since his sister was

Again, in the *Tydeus* of Theodectes, the deduction is made that he who had come to find a son was, himself, to perish. Another example is in the *Phinidae* where the women, when they had seen the place, inferred their destiny; that since they had been exposed there, they were fated to die there.

There is also a type of composite recognition from false reasoning on the part of another character.[17] for example, in the story of Odysseus, the False Messenger; for he said that he would know the bow that he had not seen, but it is false reasoning to suppose through this that he would recognize it again (as if he had seen it before).[18]

The best recognition is the one that arises from the incidents themselves, striking us, as they do, with astonishment through the very probability of their occurrence as, for example, in the action of the *Oedipus* of Sophocles and in the *Iphigenia*, where it is reasonable for the heroine to wish to dispatch a letter. Such recognitions alone are accomplished without contrived signs and necklaces. The second-best type of recognition is the one that is achieved by reasoning.

17

In constructing plots and working them out with diction, the poet must keep the action as much as possible before his eyes. For by visualizing the events as distinctly as he can, just as if he were present at their actual occurrence, he will discover what is fitting for his purpose, and there will be the least chance of incongruities escaping his notice. A sign of this is found in the criticism that is made of Carcinus. For Amphiaraus is coming back from the temple, a point that would have escaped the audience's notice if it had not actually seen it; and on the stage the play failed

[17] I have followed Bywater in accepting an emendation meaning "another" in place of the manuscript reading "audience" followed by Kassel and Hardy. [Tr.]

[18] In this passage, Bywater notes that, "both text and interpretation here are in the highest degree doubtful." I have followed his interpretation of this difficult passage. Except for the *Choëphoroe*, we do not have any information about the plays mentioned in the previous paragraph. [Tr.]

because the audience was annoyed at this incongruity.[19]

As much as is possible the poet should also work out the action with gestures. For, given poets of the same natural abilities, those are most persuasive who are involved in the emotions they imitate: for example, one who is distressed conveys distress, and one who is enraged conveys anger most truly. Therefore, the art of poetry is more a matter for the well-endowed poet than for the frenzied one. For poets marked by the former characteristic can easily change character, whereas those of the latter type are possessed.

In regard to arguments, both those that already are in existence and those he himself invents, the poet should first put them down in universal form and then extend them by adding episodes. I mean that the poet should take a general view of the action of the play, like, for example, the following. A young girl had been sacrificed and had disappeared in a way that was obscure to the sacrificers. She settled in another country in which it was the custom to sacrifice strangers to the goddess, and she came to hold the priesthood for this sacrifice. Later, it turned out that the brother of the priestess came to this country (the fact that the god commanded him to come is outside the argument; the purpose of his coming is outside of the plot). When he came he was seized, and on the point of being sacrificed he made himself known, either as Euripides handled the situation or as Polyidus arranged it, by his saying, in a very reasonable way, that not only had it been necessary for his sister to be sacrificed but also for him; and from this came his deliverance. After this, when the names have already been assigned, it is necessary to complete the episodes. The episodes must be appropriate, as, for example, the madness of Orestes through which he was captured and his deliverance through purification.

In drama, the episodes are short, but epic achieves its length by means of them. For the argument of the *Odyssey* is not long: A certain man is away from home for many years, closely

[19]Carcinus was a fifth-century B.C. tragic poet; nothing further is known of the play mentioned here. [Tr.]

watched by Poseidon but otherwise completely alone. His family at home continually faces a situation where his possessions are being squandered by the suitors who plot against his son. Storm-driven, he arrives home and, having made certain people acquainted with him, he attacks the suitors and, while destroying his enemies, is himself saved. This is the essence of the story; everything else is episode.

18

In every tragedy, we find both the complication and the resolution of the action. Frequently some matters outside the action together with some within it comprise the complication, and the rest of the play consists of the resolution. By complication I mean that part of the play from the beginning up to the first point at which the change occurs to good or to bad fortune. By resolution I mean the part of the play from the beginning of the change in fortune to the end of the play. For example, in the *Lynceus* of Theodectes, the complication comprises everything done before the action of the play begins and the seizing of the child, and, in turn, of the parents; the resolution comprises all that happens from the accusation of murder to the end of the play.[20]

There are four kinds of tragedy (for that number of parts has been mentioned): the complex, which consists wholly in reversal and recognition; the tragedies of suffering, for example, the *Ajaxes* and *Ixions* that have been written; the tragedies of character, for example, the *Phthiotian Women* and the *Peleus*.[21] And a fourth type [the tragedy of spectacle], for example, is *The Daughters of Phorcis* and *Prometheus*[22] and

those plays that take place in Hades. Now it is necessary to attempt, as much as possible, to include all elements in the play, but if that is not possible, then as many as possible and certainly the most important ones. This is especially so now, indeed, when the public unjustly criticizes our poets. For although there have been poets who were outstanding in regard to each kind of tragedy, the public now demands that one man be superior to the particular virtue of each of his predecessors.

It is correct to speak of a tragedy as different from or similar to another one on the basis of its plot more than anything else: that is, in regard to an action having the same complication and resolution. Many poets are skillful in constructing their complications, but their resolutions are poor. It is, however, necessary for both elements to be mastered.

The poet, as has frequently been said, must remember not to make a tragedy out of an epic body of incidents (by which I mean a multiple plot), [as would be the case], for example, if someone should construct a plot out of the entire *Iliad*. For, there, because of the length, the parts take on the appropriate magnitude, but the same plot used in the drama turns out quite contrary to one's expectations. A sign of this is that so many as have written about the entire destruction of Troy (and not of sections of it, as Euripides) or about the entire story of Niobe (and not just a part, as Aeschylus) either completely fail on stage or do badly, since even Agathon failed for this reason alone. But in their reversals and in their simple plots, these poets aim with marvelous accuracy at the effects that they wish for: that is, whatever is tragic and touches our human sympathy. This occurs whenever a clever but evil person is deceived, as Sisyphus, or a brave but unjust man is defeated. Such an event is probable, as Agathon says, because it is probable for many things to occur contrary to probability.

It is necessary to consider the chorus as one of the actors and as an integral part of the drama; its involvement in the action should not be in Euripides' manner but in Sophocles'. In the hands of our later poets, the songs included in the play are no more a part of that particular plot than

[20]The text is in dispute here. Bywater, following a suggestion of Susemihl, translates the passage 1456ᵃ, 7–10, at this point in the text. Butcher, Hardy, and Kassel retain the traditional reading that I have followed in my translation. [Tr.]

[21]*The Phthiotian Women* and *Peleus,* neither now extant, were probably written by Sophocles. The *Lynceus,* mentioned above and at 1. 9 in Ch. 11, is also no longer extant. [Tr.]

[22]*The Daughters of Phorcis* and *Prometheus* are both by Aeschylus; Bywater identifies them as lost satyr-plays and does not connect the latter play with the famous *Prometheus Bound.* [Tr.]

they are of any other tragedy. They have been sung, therefore, as inserted pieces from the time Agathon first introduced this practice. And yet what difference does it make whether one sings an inserted song or adopts a speech or a whole episode from one play into another?

19

We have already spoken about other matters; it remains for us to discuss diction and thought. Concerning thought, let it be taken as given what we have written in the *Rhetoric*, for this is more appropriately a subject of that discipline. All those matters pertain to thought that must be presented through speech; and they may be subdivided into proof and refutation and the production of emotional effect, for example, pity or fear or anger or other similar emotions. Indications of the importance or insignificance of anything also fall under this heading. It is clear that we must employ thought also in actions in the same ways [as in speech] whenever we aim at the representation of the pitiable, the terrible, the significant, or the probable, with the exception of this one difference — that the effects arise in the case of the incidents without verbal explanation, whereas in the speech they are produced by the speaker and arise because of the speech. For what would be the function of the speaker if something should appear in the way that is required without being dependent on the speech?

Concerning diction one kind of study involves the forms of diction that are investigated by the art of elocution and are the concern of the individual who considers this his guiding art, for example, what a command is and what a prayer is, and threat and question and answer and any other such matters. For in regard to the knowledge or ignorance of these matters, no censure worth taking seriously can be made against the art of poetry. Why should any one accept as an error Protagoras's censure of Homer on the grounds that when he said, "Sing, O goddess, of the wrath . . ." he gave a command, although he really wished to utter a prayer. For Protagoras says to order someone to do something or not is a command. Let us, therefore,

disregard such a consideration as being a principle of some other art, not the art of poetry.

20

The following parts comprise the entire scope of diction: letter, syllable, connective, noun, verb, inflection, and sentence. A letter is an indivisible sound; not every such sound is a letter, however, but only one from which a compound sound can be constructed. For I would call none of the individual sounds uttered by wild animals letters. The subdivisions of this category of "letters" are vowel, semivowel, and mute. A vowel is a sound that is audible without the contact of any of the physical structures of the mouth.[23] a semivowel is a sound that is audible with the contact of some of the physical structures of the mouth, for example, the S and R sounds; and a mute is a letter produced by the contact of the physical structures of the mouth, but inaudible in itself, although it becomes audible when it is accompanied by letters that are sounded, for example, the G and D sounds. These letters differ in the positions taken by the mouth to produce them, in the places in the mouth where they are produced, in aspiration and smoothness, in being long or short and, furthermore, in having an acute, grave, or middle [circumflex] pitch accent. The detailed investigation concerning these matters belongs to the study of metrics.

A syllable is a nonsignificant sound constructed from a mute and a vowel. For, indeed, GR without an A is a syllable and also with it, for example, GRA. However, it is the business of the art of metrics also to investigate distinctions in this area.[24]

A connective is a nonsignificant sound that neither hinders nor promotes the creation of one significant sound from many sounds and that

[23] I have followed Butcher and Hardy in seeing this passage as a reference to the physical means of producing speech. Bywater disputes this interpretation and argues that the ambiguous term *prosbole* does not refer to the impact of the physical structures of the mouth but to the addition of one letter to another. [Tr.]

[24] The passage that begins here is corrupt and contains many difficulties of interpretation. [Tr.]

is not appropriate to place at the beginning of a speech that stands independently, for example, *men, dē, toi, de.* Or it is a nonsignificant sound that is naturally able to make one significant sound from a number of sounds, for example, *amphi, peri,* and others like them. There is also a kind of connective that is a nonsignificant sound that shows the beginning, end, or division of a sentence and that may naturally be placed at either end or in the middle of a sentence.

A noun is a compound significant sound, not indicating time, no part of which is significant by itself. For in compound nouns we do not consider each part of the compound as being significant in itself; for example, in the name "Theodore" the root *dor* [gift] has no significance.

A verb is a compound significant sound indicating time, no part of which is significant by itself in the same way as has been indicated in regard to nouns. For "man" or "white" do not tell us anything about "when"; but "he goes" or "he has gone" indicate the present and the past.

Inflection is a characteristic of a noun or verb signifying the genitive or dative relation, or other similar ones, or indicating the singular or plural, that is, man or men, or is concerned with matters that fall under the art of elocution, for example, questions and commands; for the phrases, "Did he go?" or "Go!" involve inflections of the verb in regard to these categories.

A speech is a compound, significant sound some of whose parts are significant by themselves. For not every speech is composed of verbs and nouns but it is possible to have a speech without verbs (for example, the definition of man). However, part of the speech will always have some significance, for example, "Cleon" in the phrase "Cleon walks." A speech is a unity in two ways. Either it signifies one thing or it is a unity through the joining together of many speeches. For example, the *Iliad* is a unity by the process of joining together many speeches, and the definition of man by signifying one thing.

21

Nouns are either simple, by which I mean constructed solely from nonsignificant elements, for example *gē* [earth], or compound. This latter category is divided into nouns that are constructed from both significant and nonsignificant elements (except that neither element is significant within the compound word itself) and nouns that are composed solely out of significant elements. Nouns may also be made up of three, four, or more parts, for example, many of the words in the Massilian vocabulary, such as Hermocaicoxanthus. . . .[25]

Every word is either standard, or is a strange word, or is a metaphor, or is ornamental, or is a coined word, or is lengthened, or contracted, or is altered in some way. I mean by standard, words that everyone uses, and by a strange word, one that foreigners use. Thus, it is apparent, the same word can be both strange and ordinary but not, of course, to the same persons. The word *sigunon* [spear] is ordinary for the Cyprians and strange to us.

Metaphor is the transference of a name from the object to which it has a natural application; this transference can take place from genus to species or species to genus or from species to species or by analogy. I mean by "from genus to species," for example, "This ship of mine stands there." For to lie at anchor is a species of standing. An example of the transference from species to genus, "Odysseus has truly accomplished a myriad of noble deeds." For a myriad is the equivalent of "many," for which the poet now substitutes this term. An example of the transference from species to species is "having drawn off life with a sword" and also "having cut with unyielding bronze." For here to draw off is to cut and to cut is called to draw off, for both are subdivisions of "taking away."

I mean by "transference by analogy" the situation that occurs whenever a second element is related to a first as a fourth is to a third. For the poet will then use the fourth in place of the second or the second in place of the fourth, and sometimes poets add the reference to which the transferred term applies. I mean, for example, that a cup is related to Dionysus as a shield is to Ares. The poet will, therefore, speak of the cup as the

[25]There is a lacuna in the text here. Some editors accept Diel's conjecture, "praying to father Zeus," as the completion of this line. [Tr.]

shield of Dionysus and the cup of Ares. The same situation occurs in regard to the relation of old age to life and evening to day. A poet will say that evening is the old age of day, or however Empedocles expressed it, and that old age is the evening of life or the sunset of life. In some situations, there is no regular name in use to cover the analogous relation, but nevertheless the related elements will be spoken of by analogy; for example, to scatter seed is to sow, but the scattering of the sun's rays has no name. But the act of sowing in regard to grain bears an analogous relation to the sun's dispersing of its rays, and so we have the phrase ''sowing the god-created fire.'' It is also possible to use metaphor in a different way by applying the transferred epithet and then denying some aspect that is proper to it — for example, if one should call the shield not the cup of Ares but the wineless cup.[26] A coined word is one that is not in use among foreigners but is the invention of the poet. There seem to be some words of this type, for example, horns [*kerata*] called ''sprouters'' [*ernuges*], and a priest [*iereus*] called ''supplicator'' [*arētēr*].

A word may be lengthened or contracted. It is lengthened if it makes use of a longer vowel than is usual for it, or a syllable is inserted in it; and it is contracted if any element is removed from it. An example of lengthening is *poleōs* to *poleōs* and *Pēleidou* to *Pēleiadeō*; an example of contraction is *krī* and *dō* and *ops* in ''*mia ginetai amphoterōn ops.*''

A word is altered whenever a poet utilizes part of the regular name for the object he is describing and invents part anew, for example, in the phrase ''*dexiteron kata mazon*''[27] the use of *dexiteron* in place of *deksion*.

Nouns are subdivided into masculine, feminine, and neuter. Those are masculine that end in nu, rho, and sigma and in the two letters psi and ksi that are constructed in combination with sigma. Those nouns are feminine that end in the vowels that are always long, the eta and omega, and that end (in regard to the vowels subject to lengthening) in the lengthened alpha. Thus it turns out that there are an equal number of terminations for masculine and feminine nouns since psi and ksi are subdivisions of sigma. No noun ends in a mute nor in a short vowel. Only three end in iota, *meli*, *kommi*, *peperi*, and five end in upsilon. Neuter nouns end in these vowels and in nu and sigma.

22

Diction achieves its characteristic virtue in being clear but not mean. The clearest style results from the use of standard words; but it is also mean, as can be seen in the poetry of Cleophon and Sthenelus. A really distinguished style varies ordinary diction through the employment of unusual words. By unusual I mean strange words and metaphor and lengthened words and everything that goes beyond ordinary diction. But if someone should write exclusively in such forms the result would either be a riddle or a barbarism. A riddle will result if someone writes exclusively in metaphor; and a barbarism will result if there is an exclusive use of strange words. For it is in the nature of a riddle for one to speak of a situation that actually exists in an impossible way. Now it is not possible to do this by the combination of strange words; but it can be done by metaphor, for example, ''I saw a man who welded bronze on another man by fire,'' and other metaphors like this. A statement constructed exclusively from strange words is a barbarism.

It is therefore necessary to use a combination of all these forms. The employment of strange words and metaphor and ornamental words and the other forms of speech that have been mentioned will prevent the diction from being ordinary and mean; and the use of normal speech will keep the diction clear. The lengthening and contraction of words and alterations in them contribute in no small measure to the diction's clarity and its elevation above ordinary diction. For because such words are different they will prevent the diction from being ordinary through their contrast with the ordinary expression; and

[26]Editors have noted that a definition of the term ''ornamental word'' belongs in the text at this point, although it is missing from the manuscripts. [Tr.]

[27]The phrase quoted comes from the *Iliad* 5:393 and means ''at her right breast.'' Two words meaning ''right'' are quoted to illustrate Aristotle's point here. [Tr.]

because they have a share in the customary word, they will keep the diction clear.

Thus, the criticism is not well-taken on the part of those who censure this way of using language and who mock the poet, as the elder Euclid did, on the grounds that it is easy to write poetry if you are allowed to lengthen forms as much as you want; Euclid composed a satiric verse in the very words he used, *Epicharēn eidon Marathōnade badizonta* and *ouk an g'eramenos ton ekeinou elleboron*.[28]

Now then, the employment of the technique of lengthening in excess is ridiculous, and moderation is a quality that is commonly needed in all aspects of diction. For, indeed, if one employs metaphors and strange words and other forms in an inappropriate way and with intended absurdity, he can also accomplish the same effect. When the ordinary words are inserted in the verse, it can be seen how great a difference the appropriate use of lengthening makes in epic poetry. If someone should also change the strange words and metaphors and other forms to ordinary words, he would see the truth of what we have said. For example, Aeschylus and Euripides wrote the same iambic line, but Euripides changed one word and instead of using a standard one employed a strange one; his line thus has an elegance to it, whereas the other is mean. For Aeschylus wrote in his *Philoctetes*:

phagediana hē mou sarkas esthiei podos
[this cancerous sore eats the flesh of my leg].

Euripides in place of "eats" substitutes *thoinatai* [feasts upon]. A similar situation would occur in the line

nun de m'eōn oligos te kai outidanos kai aeikēs[29]

if someone should substitute the ordinary words

nun de m'eōn mikros te kai asthenikos kai aeidēs

or if we changed the line

diphron aeikelion katatheis oligēn te trapezan[30]

to

diphron moxtheřon katatheis mikran te trapezan

or for *ēiones booosin*, we substituted *ēiones krazousin*.[31] Furthermore, Ariphrades mocked the tragedians because no one would use their style in conversation; for example, the word order *dōmatōn apo* in place of *apo dōmatōn*, and the word *sethen*, and the phrase *egō de nin*, and the word order *Achilleōs peri* in place of *peri Achilleōs*, and many other similar expressions. For he missed the point that the virtue of all these expressions is that they create an unusual element in the diction by their not being in ordinary speech.

It is a matter of great importance to use each of the forms mentioned in a fitting way, as well as compound words and strange ones, but by far the most important matter is to have skill in the use of metaphor. This skill alone it is not possible to obtain from another, and it is, in itself, a sign of genius. For the ability to construct good metaphors implies the ability to see essential similarities.

In regard to words, compounds are especially suitable for dithyrambs, strange words for heroic verse, and metaphors for iambic verse; in heroic verse all the forms mentioned are serviceable; but in iambic verse, because as much as possible it imitates conversation, only those words are appropriate that might be used in prose.

Of this nature are standard words, metaphors, and ornamental words.

Now, then, concerning tragedy and the imitation that is carried out in action, let what has been said suffice.

---

[28]This passage offers a number of difficulties in text and interpretation. The essential point is that the prosaic lines quoted can be technically turned into verse if enough licenses are allowed. The first phrase may be translated "I saw Epichares going to Marathon." The text of the second phrase is corrupt and does not have a clear meaning as it stands. [Tr.]

[29]A passage quoted from *Odyssey* 9:515, meaning "someone small, worthless, and unseemly." [Tr.]

[30]A passage quoted from *Odyssey* 20:259, meaning "having set down [for him] an unseemly chair and a small table." [Tr.]

[31]A passage quoted from *Iliad* 17:265, meaning "the shores cry out." [Tr.]

Concerning that form of verse imitation that is narrative, it is necessary to construct the plot as in tragedy in a dramatic fashion, and concerning a single action that is whole and complete (having a beginning, middle, and end) so that, like a single integrated organism, it achieves the pleasure natural to it.

The composition of incidents should not be similar to that found in our histories, in which it is necessary to show not one action but one period of time and as many things as happened in this time, whether they concern one man or many, and whether or not each of these things is related to the others. For just as there occurred in the same period of time a sea battle at Salamis and a battle with the Carthaginians in Sicily, but these did not at all lead to a common goal, thus also in the sequence of time, occasionally one event happens after another without there being a common goal to join them.

However, almost all the poets commit this error. Also in this, then, Homer would appear to be of exceptional skill in relation to other poets, as we have already said, since he did not attempt to write about the complete war, although it had a beginning and end; for that would have been a very large subject and could not have been taken in easily in a single view; or even if its magnitude were moderate, the story still would be tangled because of the diversity of incidents. But note how although treating only one part of the war, he also introduces many of the other episodes in the war, for example, the catalogue of ships and others, by which he gives variety to his poem. Others write about one man and about one period and one action with diverse parts, for example, the poet who wrote the *Cypria* and the *Little Iliad*. Therefore from the *Iliad* and *Odyssey* one or two tragedies apiece are constructed; but from the *Cypria* many tragedies are constructed and from the *Little Iliad* eight, for example, *The Award of the Arms*, *Philoctetes*, *Neoptolemus*, *Eurypylus*, *The Beggar*, *The Laconian Woman*, *The Sack of Troy*, *The Return Voyage*, and a *Simon*, and a *Women of Troy*.[32]

[32]Butcher and Kassel bracket the names of the last two plays as being later additions to the original text of the *Poetics*. [Tr.]

Moreover, it is necessary for epic poetry to exhibit the same characteristic forms as tragedy; for it is either simple or complex, displays character or suffering, and is composed of the same parts, with the exception of song and spectacle. In epic, there is also a necessity for reversals, recognitions, and the depiction of suffering. Here too, thought and diction must be handled with skill. Homer used all these elements first and in a proper way. For each of his poems is well constructed; the *Iliad* is simple and exhibits suffering, whereas the *Odyssey* is complex (for there is recognition throughout) and shows character. In addition to these matters, Homer outstrips all others in diction and thought.

Epic differs from tragedy in regard to the length of the plot, and the meter. The sufficient limit of length has been mentioned, for we have noted that it must be possible to take in the plot's beginning and end in one view. This would occur if the plots were shorter than those of the old epics but would extend to the length of the number of tragedies that are designated for one performance. For the purpose of extending its length, epic poetry has a very great capacity that is specifically its own, since it is not possible in tragedy to imitate many simultaneous lines of action but only that performed by the actors on the stage. But because of the narrative quality of epic it is possible to depict many simultaneous lines of action that, if appropriate, become the means of increasing the poem's scope. This has an advantage in regard to the elegance of the poem and in regard to varying the interest of the audience and for constructing a diverse sequence of episodes. For the rapid overloading of tragedies with the same kind of incident is what makes tragedies fail.

The heroic meter has been found appropriate to epic through practical experience. If someone should write a narrative imitation in another meter, or in a combination of meters, we would feel it to be inappropriate. For the heroic is the stateliest and most dignified meter, and therefore it is especially receptive to strange words and metaphors, for narrative poetry in this regard is exceptional among the forms of imitation; the iambic and the trochaic tetrameter are expressive of motion, the latter being a dance meter and the former displaying the quality of action. Furthermore, it makes a very strange impression if someone combines these meters as Chairemon did. Therefore, no one has written a long poem in a meter other than the heroic; but, as we said, nature herself teaches us to choose the appropriate meter.

Homer deserves praise for many qualities and, especially, because alone of the poets he is not ignorant of the requirements of his craft. For it is necessary for the poet himself to speak in his own person in the poem as little as possible, because he is not fulfilling his function as an imitator when he appears in this way. Now the other poets are themselves active performers throughout the poem, and they perform their imitative function infrequently and in regard to only a few objects. Homer, on the other hand, when he has made a brief prelude immediately brings in a man or woman or some other character; and all his figures are expressive of character, and none lacks it.

Now then, it is necessary in tragedy to create the marvelous, but the epic admits, even more, of the irrational, on which the marvelous especially depends, because the audience does not see the person acting. The whole business of the pursuit of Hector would appear ridiculous on the stage with some men standing about and not pursuing and Achilles nodding at them to keep them back; but in the narrative description of epic, this absurdity escapes notice.

The marvelous is pleasant, and the proof of this is that everyone embellishes the stories he tells as if he were adding something pleasant to his narration. Homer has especially taught others how it is necessary to lie, and this is through the employment of false reasoning. For whenever one event occurs or comes into existence and is naturally accompanied by a second event, men think that whenever this second event is present the first one must also have occurred or have come into existence. This, however, is a fallacy. Therefore, if the first event mentioned is false but there is another event that must occur or come into existence when the first event occurs, we feel compelled to join the two events in our thought. For our mind, through knowing that the second event is true, falsely reasons that the first event must have occurred or have come into existence also. There is an example of this type of fallacy in the Bath Scene in the *Odyssey*.

The use of impossible probabilities is preferable to that of unpersuasive possibilities. We must not construct plots from irrational elements, and we should especially attempt not to have anything irrational at all in them; but if this is not possible, the irrational should be outside the plot (as in Oedipus's ignorance of how Laius died); it should not be in the drama itself, as occurs in the *Electra* concerning those who bring news of the Pythian games, or in the *Mysians,* concerning the man who has come from Tegea to Mysia without speaking. To say that without the use of such incidents the plot would have been ruined is ridiculous. For it is necessary, right from the beginning, not to construct such plots.

If the poet takes such a plot and if it appears to admit of a more probable treatment, the situation is also absurd,[33] since it is clear that even the improbable elements in the *Odyssey* concerning the casting ashore of Odysseus would not be bearable if a poor poet had written them. Here the poet conceals the absurdity by making it pleasing through his other skillful techniques. It is necessary to intensify the diction only in those parts of the poem that lack action and are unexpressive of character and thought. For too brilliant a diction conceals character and thought.

25

Concerning the number and character of the problems that lead to censure in poetry and the ways in which this censure must be met, the following considerations would be apparent to those who study the question. Since the poet is an imitator, like a painter or any maker of likenesses, he must carry out his imitations on all occasions in one of three possible ways. Thus, he must imitate

---

[33]Butcher and Hardy, following a different punctuation of the text, interpret this passage to mean that it is possible to admit some element of the irrational to the plot; others feel that the Greek text does not make adequate sense as it stands. I have followed Bywater's punctuation and interpretation of this passage. [Tr.]

the things that were in the past, or are now, or that people say and think to be or those things that ought to be. The poet presents his imitation in standard diction, as well as in strange words and metaphors and in many variations of diction, for we grant this license to poets. In addition to this, there is not the same standard of correctness for politics and poetry, nor for any other art and poetry. In regard to poetry itself, two categories of error are possible, one essential, and one accidental. For if the poet chose to imitate but imitated incorrectly through lack of ability,[34] the error is an essential one; but if he erred by choosing an incorrect representation of the object (for example, representing a horse putting forward both right hooves) or made a technical error, for example, in regard to medicine or any other art, or introduced impossibilities of any sort, the mistake is an accidental, not an essential, one.

As a result, we must meet the criticisms of the problems encountered in poetry by taking these points into consideration. First, in regard to the problems that are related to the essential nature of art: if impossibilities have been represented, an error has been made; but it may be permissible to do this if the representation supports the goal of the imitation (for the goal of an imitation has been discussed) and if it makes the section in which it occurs, or another part of the poem, more striking. An example of such a situation is the pursuit of Hector in the *Iliad*. If, indeed, the goal of the imitation admits of attainment as well, or better, when sought in accordance with technical requirements, then it is incorrect to introduce the impossible. For, if it is at all feasible, no error should be committed at all. Further, we must ascertain whether an error originates from an essential or an accidental aspect of the art. For it is a less important matter if the artist does not know that a hind does not have horns than if he is unskillful in imitating one. In addition, the criticism that a work of art is not a truthful representation can be met by the argument that it represents the situation as it should be. For example, Sophocles said that he himself created characters

such as should exist, whereas Euripides created ones such as actually do exist. If neither of the above is the case, the criticism must be met by reference to men's opinions, for example, in the myths that are told about the gods. For, perhaps, they do not describe a situation that is better than actuality, nor a true one, but they are perhaps the real one. Perhaps, at any rate, with men's opinions. Perhaps the situation described by the artist is not better than actuality but was one that actually existed in the past, for example, the description of the arms that goes, "The spears were standing upright on their butt spikes"; for once this was customary, as it is now among the Illyrians. Now to judge the nobility or ignobility of any statement made or act performed by anyone, we must not only make an investigation into the thing itself that has been said or done, considering whether it is noble or ignoble, but we must also consider the one who does the act or says the words in regard to whom, when, by what means, and for what purpose he speaks or acts — for example, whether the object is to achieve a greater good or to avoid a greater evil.

We must meet some kinds of criticism by considering the diction, for example, by reference to the use of a strange word, as in the phrase, *oureas men prōton*.[35] The word *oureas* here could cause some difficulty because perhaps the poet does not mean mules but guards. Dolon's statement, "I who was badly formed,"[36] has a similar difficulty involved in it: for he does not mean that he was misshapen in body but that he was ugly, because the Cretans use *eueidēs* [of fair form] to denote "handsome." A difficulty might arise in the phrase "mix the drink purer,"[37] which does not mean stronger, as if for drunkards, but faster. Difficulties arise in thoughts that are expressed in metaphors, for example, "All the gods and men slept the entire night through," which is said at the same time as "When truly he turned his gaze upon the Trojan plain, and hears the sound of flutes and pipes." "All" is used here metaphorically in place of "many," since "all" is some

34There is a lacuna in the text here that I have filled by translating Bywater's suggested reading, *hēmarte de di'*. [Tr.]

35Quoted from *Iliad* 1:50. The phrase means "first of all, the mules." [Tr.]

36Quoted from *Iliad* 10:316. [Tr.]

37Quoted from *Iliad* 11:202. [Tr.]

division of "many." The phrase "alone, she has no share"[38] shows a similar use of metaphor, since the best-known one is "alone." A problem may arise from the use of accent; Hippias the Thasian solved such a problem in the phrase, *didomen de oi* and similarly, in the phrase, *to men hoi katapythetai ombrō*.[39] Some difficulties are solved through punctuation, for example, in Empedocles' statement that "Suddenly things became mortal that had previously learned to be immortal and things unmixed before mixed."[40] Some problems are solved by reference to ambiguities, for example, "more than two-thirds of night has departed" because "more" is ambiguous here.[41] Some difficulties are met by reference to customary usages in our language. Thus, we call "wine" the mixture of water and wine; and it is with the same justification that the poet writes of "a greave of newly wrought tin"; and iron workers are called *chalkeas,* literally, copper smiths; and it is for this reason that Ganymede is called the wine pourer of Zeus, although the gods do not drink wine. This would also be justified through metaphor.

Whenever a word seems to signify something contradictory, we must consider how many different meanings it might have in the passage quoted; for example, in the phrase "the bronze spear was held there," we must consider how many different senses of "to be held" are possible, whether by taking it in this way or that one might best understand it. The procedure is opposite to the one that Glaucon mentions in which people make an unreasonable prior assumption and, having themselves made their decree, they draw their conclusions, and then criticize the poet as if he had said whatever they think he has said if it is opposed to their thoughts. We have had this experience in regard to discussion of the character Icarius.[42] People assume that he was a Spartan; but then it appears ridiculous that Telemachus did not meet him in Sparta when he visited there. Perhaps the situation is as the Cephallenians would have it, for they say that Odysseus married amongst them and that there was an Icadius involved, but no Icarius. Thus, it is probable that the difficulty has arisen through a mistake.

Speaking generally, the impossible must be justified in regard to the requirements of poetry, or in regard to what is better than actuality, or what, in the opinion of men, is held to be true. In regard to the art of poetry, we must prefer a persuasive impossibility to an unpersuasive possibility. Perhaps it is impossible[43] for the kind of men Zeuxis painted to exist; but they illustrate what is better than the actual. For whatever is a model must express superior qualities. The irrational must be justified in regard to what men say and also on the grounds that it is, sometimes, not at all irrational. For it is reasonable that some things occur contrary to reason.

We must consider contradictions in the same way as the refutation of arguments is carried on: that is, with reference to whether the same object is involved, and in the same relationship, and in the same sense, so that the poet, indeed, has contradicted himself in regard to what he himself says or what a sensible person might assume. There is justifiable censure for the presence of irrationality and depravity where, there being no necessity for them, the poet makes no use of them, as Euripides' handling of Aegeus in the *Medea* (in regard to the irrational) or in the same poet's treatment of the character of Menelaus in the *Orestes* (in regard to depravity). Criticisms of poetry, then, derive from five sources: either that the action is impossible or that it is irrational or that it is morally harmful or that it is contradictory or that it contains technical errors. The

---

[38] Quoted from *Iliad* 18:489. [Tr.]

[39] The problem here is that words that are spelled the same way, when given different accents, change their meaning. In the first phrase quoted, *didomen* can be either a present indicative or an infinitive used as an imperative, depending on the way in which it is accented; in the second phrase, *ou* can be either a relative pronoun or a negative adverb, depending on the way in which it is accented. [Tr.]

[40] The problem treated here is the effect that punctuation has on the meaning of a sentence. Thus, by means of different punctuations the word "before" in Empedocles' statement could be referred either to the phrase that precedes it, "things unmixed," or to the word that follows it, "mixed." [Tr.]

[41] The word "more" has a form in Greek that can also be translated as "full." [Tr.]

[42] In Homer, Icarius is Penelope's father. [Tr.]

[43] Translating *kai ei adunaton,* suggested by Vahlen to fill a lacuna in the text at this point. [Tr.]

26

The problem of whether epic or tragedy is the better type of imitation might be raised. For if whatever is less common is better, that art would be superior that is directed at the more discriminating audience; and it is very clear that the art that imitates every detail is common. For on the grounds that the audience does not see the point unless they themselves add something, the actors make quite a commotion; for example, the poorer sort of flute players roll about the stage if they must imitate a discus throw and drag their leader about if they are playing the *Scylla.* Now tragedy is considered to be of the same character that our older actors attribute to their successors; for, indeed, Mynescus called Callippides an ape on the grounds of overacting, and such an opinion was also held about Pindarus. As these two types of actor are related to each other, so the whole art of tragedy is thought to be related to epic by some people, who then conclude that epic is oriented toward a reasonable audience that does not at all require gestures, but that tragedy is disposed toward a less sophisticated audience. If, then, tragedy is directed toward a more common audience, it would be clear that it is the inferior art form.

Now then, first, this accusation is made against the art of acting, not poetry, since it is possible to overdo gestures both in epic recitations as Sosistratus did, and in song competitions as Mnasitheus the Opuntian did. Then, too, not every movement is to be rejected, if dancing indeed is not to be condemned, but only the movements of the ignoble, a point that was criticized in Callippides and now in others, since, it was charged, they were not representing freeborn women. Further, tragedy even without action achieves its function just as epic does; for its character is apparent simply through reading. If, then, tragedy is better in other respects, this

defect is not essential to it. We argue, next, that it *is* better since it contains all of the elements that epic has (for it is even possible to use epic meter in tragedy) and, further, it has no small share in music and in spectacle, through which pleasure is very distinctly evoked. Tragedy also provides a vivid experience in reading as well as in actual performance. Further, in tragedy the goal of the imitation is achieved in a shorter length of time (for a more compact action is more pleasant than one that is much diluted). I mean, for example, the situation that would occur if someone should put Sophocles' *Oedipus* into an epic as long as the *Iliad.* Further, the imitation of an epic story is less unified than that of tragedy (a proof of this is that a number of tragedies can be derived from any one epic). So that if epic poets write a story with a single plot, that plot is either presented briefly and appears to lack full development, or, if it follows the accustomed length of epic, it has a watered-down quality (I mean, for example, if the epic should be composed of very many actions in the same way as the *Iliad* and *Odyssey* have many such elements that also have magnitude in themselves). And yet these poems are constructed in the best possible way and are, as much as possible, the imitations of a single action.

If, then, tragedy is superior in all these areas and, further, in accomplishing its artistic effect (for it is necessary that these genres create not any chance pleasure, but the one that has been discussed as proper to them), it is apparent that tragedy, since it is better at attaining its end, is superior to epic.

Now then, we have expressed our view of tragedy and epic, both in general, and in their various species, and of the number and differences in their parts, as well as of the causes of their effectiveness or ineffectiveness, and the criticisms that can be directed against them, and the ways in which these criticisms must be answered. . . .⁴⁴

answers to these criticisms must be sought from the solutions, twelve in number, that we have discussed.

⁴⁴One of our manuscripts, Riccardianus 46, continues the text briefly at this point. The continuation seems to read, "Now as to iambic poetry and comedy. . . ." [Tr.]

Horace
65–8 B.C.E.

Quintus Horatius Flaccus was the son of a freed slave but received an excellent education in the private academies of Rome. Following the assassination of Julius Caesar, Horace fought in the ill-fated army of Marcus Brutus but was allowed to return to Rome at the amnesty. He served for a time as a clerk in government offices, but his talent as a poet and satirist came to the attention of Virgil, who introduced him to the renowned Roman patron Maecenas. Maecenas provided Horace with encouragement and money, and ultimately, the farm in the Sabine hills to which he retired.

The *Ars Poetica (The Art of Poetry),* also known as the *Epistle to the Pisos,* was composed as a letter of advice in verse to the two sons of Lucius Calpurnius Piso, both of whom had poetic ambitions. Because it is a verse letter, it lacks the careful composition and exhaustive organization of a treatise on the art of poetry; Horace's aim was to blend witty reminders and sage maxims in an entertaining way.

Like Pope's *Essay on Criticism* (p. 147), the *Ars Poetica* contains dozens of lines and phrases that passed into the Latin language (and to an extent into English) as proverbs or catch phrases. We still speak of "purple patches" in prose, a phrase Horace coined. *Bonus dormitat Homerus* is the familiar "even Homer sometimes nods." *Parturiunt montes, nascetur ridiculus mus* (the mountains labor, giving birth to a ridiculous mouse) has become an adage for any pretentious activity. (The meaning of some of Horace's maxims has become garbled over the years: *Ut pictura poesis* [a poem is like a picture] was Horace's way of saying that some poems repay close scrutiny while others appeal through their broad outlines; it has been misinterpreted to suggest that Horace saw spatial form in poetry.)

To a reader expecting system, the organization of the *Ars Poetica* can be baffling. It is traditionally divided into three parts: lines 1–41 of the Latin original are on *poesis* or subject matter; lines 42–294 on *poema* or technique; and lines 295–476 on *poeta* or the poet. But in fact, Horace's wildfire ideas always outrace any system or organization that can be devised, and the reader should be prepared for rapid and unexpected transitions from one topic to another.

In the Middle Ages and the Renaissance, the *Ars Poetica* was often regarded as a commentary on Aristotle's *Poetics.* Though undoubtedly Horace had read Aristotle and occasionally echoes some of his remarks, the two thinkers have little in common. Where Aristotle suggests that tragedy uses iambic meter because it is closest to natural human speech, Horace offers two other rationales: literary tradition and the fact that iambics are better able to drown out a noisy and inattentive audience. Aristotle's explanation derives from his principle of *mimesis;* Horace's from his understanding of the expectations and the physical boisterousness of the *audience.*

Although Horace pays lip service to *mimesis* from time to time, what is really important to him is audience response. The poet should stick to traditional subjects, he tells us, but treat them in a new way. Poetic language should be novel, but not too novel — and the only way of judging the mean here is by closely observing the audience and the literary marketplace. Regardless of his innate genius, the poet must learn his art, especially the conventions that guide his audience in their expectations. Some of these, like the use of iambics in drama, may be more than mere conventions: They may reflect enduring aspects of human nature. Others, like Horace's dictum that a tragedy should have neither more nor less than five acts, were pure formalities. From Horace's point of view, such a distinction makes no difference, and indeed, he does not differentiate between rules and conventions. All alike need to be observed if the poet is to succeed in gaining a hearing from a fastidious and often captiously critical audience.

At the center of the Ars Poetica is Horace's statement of the ultimate aim of poetry: *aut prodesse aut delectare*, to teach or to delight — or both if possible, because the poet's audience, made up of diverse types, will require both: the *equites*, the knightly class, insist upon amusement, while the *senatores* want profitable lessons. The poet must understand their demands — and even those of the middle classes, the "roast-beans-and-chestnuts crowd" who applaud what is simple and exciting.

Like Aristotle, Horace assumes that different genres have their proper subject matter, technical devices, and effects; for example, that tragedy will concern dire events, be written in the highest style, and cause the audience to weep. But while for Aristotle, genres come into existence as if by the laws of nature and are scientifically comprehensible as emergent outgrowths of natural human impulses, for Horace genres do not have to make sense: They are just *there*. They exist, by accident as far as he is concerned, as predefined parts of the literary scene into which the poet comes, and the poet learns their rules as any prudent traveler in a strange country would learn the laws.

Unlike Plato and Aristotle, Horace is very much the worldly philosopher, and it is possible to misunderstand and cheapen the values by which he operates. Though Horace tells us that the successful author's book "will bring in money for Sosius and Son" — the Roman family that ran an operation copying manuscripts much in demand — he is not a prostitute producing verses to order. It is not vulgar commercial success Horace worships. For Horace, the author's reward is not money but fame. His ambition is to be read and praised, his terror to be ignored or laughed at. For Horace the poet was not a private man, but a public servant, like a successful statesman or ruler; both wore their laurels with pride, and their rewards came from the same public source.

Selected Bibliography

Brink, C. O. *Horace on Poetry.* Cambridge: Cambridge University Press, 1963.

D'Alton, J. F. *Horace and His Age.* London: Longmans Green, 1917.

Dettmer, Helena. *Horace: A Study in Structure.* Hildesheim and New York: Olms-Weidmann, 1983.

Freudenberg, Kirk. *The Walking Muse: Horace on the Theory of Satire.* Princeton: Princeton University Press, 1993.

Frischer, Bernard. *Shifting Paradigms: New Approaches to Horace's Ars Poetica.* Atlanta: Scholars Press, 1991.

Goad, Caroline. *Horace in the English Literature of the Eighteenth Century.* New Haven: Yale University Press, 1918.

Hack, R. K. "The Doctrine of Literary Forms." *Harvard Studies in Classical Philology* 27 (1916): 1–65.

Hardison, O. B., and Leon Golden, eds. *Horace for Students of Literature: The* Ars Poetica *and Its Tradition.* Gainesville: University Press of Florida, 1995.

Herrick, Marvin T. *The Fusion of Horatian and Aristotelian Literary Criticism.* Urbana: University of Illinois Press, 1946.

Perrot, Jacques. *Horace.* New York: New York University Press, 1964.

Showerman, Grant. *Horace and His Influence.* London: Longmans Green, 1922.

Stack, Frank. *Pope and Horace: Studies in Imitation.* Cambridge and New York: Cambridge University Press, 1985.

West, David. *Reading Horace.* Edinburgh: Edinburgh University Press, 1967.

Wood, Allen G. *Literary Satire and Theory: A Study of Horace, Boileau, and Pope.* New York: Garland, 1985.

The Art of Poetry

Humano capiti cervicem pictor equinam

Suppose you'd been asked to come for a private view
Of a painting wherein the artist had chosen to join
To a human head the neck of a horse, and gone on
To collect some odds and ends of arms and legs
And plaster the surface with feathers of differing
    colors,
So that what began as a lovely woman at the top
Tapered off into a slimy, discolored fish —
Could you keep from laughing, my friends?
    Believe me, dear Pisos,
Paintings like these look a lot like the book of a writer
Whose weird conceptions are just like a sick man's
    dreams,
So that neither the head nor the foot can be made
    to apply
To a single uniform shape. "But painters and poets
Have always been equally free to try anything."
We writers know that, and insist that such license
    be ours,
And in turn extend it to others — but not to the
    extent
Of mating the mild with the wild, so that snakes
    are paired
With birds, and tigers with lambs.
                                To works that begin
On a stately note and promise more grandeur to come
A couple of colorful patches are artfully stitched

To shimmer and shine, some sequins like these, for
    instance,
When the altar or grove of Diana, or perhaps it's a
    rainbow,
Or the Rhine is being described: "The sinuous stream
Rustles daintily, tastefully, on midst the sylvan
    scene."
But you put it in just the wrong place! You draw cy-
    press trees
Particularly well? But you're paid to hit off the
    likeness
Of the desperate sailor swimming away from his
    shipwreck!
This thing began as a wine jar: how come it comes
Off the wheel at last as a milk jug? Make what you
    want,
So long as it's one and the same, complete and entire.

O father, and sons who deserve a father like yours,
We poets are too often tricked into trying to achieve
A particular kind of perfection: I studiously try
To be brief, and become obscure; I try to be smooth,
And my vigor and force disappear; another assures us
Of something big which turns out to be merely
    pompous.
Another one crawls on the ground because he's too
    safe,
Too much afraid of the storm. The poet who strives
To vary his single subject in wonderful ways
Paints dolphins in woods and foaming boars on the
    waves.

Translated by Smith Palmer Bovie.

Avoiding mistakes, if awkwardly done, leads to error.
Nearby the gladiators' school there's a craftsman
who molds
In bronze with special skill the lifelike shapes
Of fingernails and straying strands of hair,
But the whole result of his work is much less happy,
He can't represent the figure complete and entire.
If I were to try to cast a good piece of writing,
I'd no more prefer to be like this fellow than live
With my nose at an angle, no matter how much
admired
I was for my coal-black hair and coal-black eyes.
Take up a subject equal to your strength, O writers,
And mull over well what loads your shoulders will
bear,
And what they will not. The man who chooses a
subject
He can really manage won't be at a loss for the words
Or the logical order they go in. As for order itself,
Its power and charm consist, if I'm not mistaken,
In saying just then what ought to be said at that point,
Putting some things off, leaving others out, for the
present:
The author of the promised work must choose and
discard.
In weaving your words, make use of care and good
taste:
You've done it right, if a clever connection of phrases
Makes a good old word look new. If you have to
display
Some recondite matter in brand-new terms, you
can forge
Words never heard in the pre-tunic days of Cethegus;
License is given, on condition that you use it with
care.
New-fashioned words, just coined, will soon gain
currency,
If derived from a Grecian source, *and* in small
amounts.
Will the Roman refuse the license to Vergil and
Varius
And grant it to Plautus and Caecilius?[1] And why
should I

Be refused the right to put in my bit, if I can,
When the language of Ennius and Cato enriched
the speech
Of our native land and produced some new terms
for things?
It has always been granted, and always will be, to
produce
Words stamped with the date of the present. As
trees change their leaves
When each year comes to its end, and the first fall
first,
So the oldest words die first and the newborn thrive
In the manner of youth, and enjoy life. All that we are
And have is in debt to death, as are all our
projects:[2]
The Portus Julius where Neptune is at home on the
land
And protects our ships from his storms — a
princely achievement;
The Pontine marshes, inhabitable only for boats
And plagues in the past, but now a food-bearing land
That feels the weight of the plow and feeds nearby
towns;
The straightening-out of the Tiber that used to wreak
havoc
On fields of grain but has now learned to mend its
ways —
All these projects, whatever men make, will perish,
And the fame and dignity of speech are equally
mortal.
Much that has once dropped out will be born again,
And much of our language now held in high repute
Will fall to the ground if UTILITY so decrees,
With which rests the final decision, the ultimate
standard,
The legal existence, of speech.
                              Homer has showed us
The meter to use to describe sad wars and great deeds
Of kings and princes. The uneven couplet that joined
One verse to another was first adapted to grief,
But elegy easily turned into epigrammatic
Couplets expressive of thanks for prayers
answered.
          Who wrote these first little couplets? The critics
are STILL

[1]Horace's point is that Plautus and Caecilius, a century earlier, had made new Latin words out of good Greek ones, but his contemporaries Vergil and Varius were being criticized for the same artistic license.

[2]The creation of a sheltered harbor at Ostia, the draining of the Pontine marshes, and the straightening of the Tiber were three of Augustus's great civic achievements.

Disputing the subject; the case is still on the books.
Fury equipped Archilochus[3] with his iambics:
The foot slipped into the comic sock as neatly
As into the tragic boot, so dramatists used it
To make their dialogue heard, even over the noise
The audience was making — the rhythm of
  purposeful action.
The muse entrusted to lyric verse the accounts
Of gods and the children of gods, of a winning boxer,
Of a prize-winning race horse, the laments of young
  lads in love,
The intoxicating freedom of wine. If I can't observe
These distinctions of form and tone, do I really
  deserve
To be hailed as a poet? Why, from a false sense of
  shame,
Do I prefer being ignorant to learning? A good comic
  sequence
Just won't submit to treatment in the meters of
  tragedy.
Likewise, Thyestes' feast[4] resents being told
In strains more nearly like those that comedy needs
In the vein of everyday life. Let each of the styles
Be assigned to the places most proper for it to
  maintain.
Of course, now and then even comedy raises her
  voice:
Angry old Chremes swells up like a supersorehead;
And the Tragedy of Telephus, the Plight of Peleus,
  stoop
To the muse of prose for words of grief when, poor
Or exiled, either hero discards the bombast
That jars on our ears and his wordsafootandahalflong,
To let his lament wing its way to the hearer's heart.

It isn't enough for poems to be things of beauty:
Let them STUN the hearer and lead his heart where
  they will.
A man's face is wreathed in smiles when he sees
  someone smile;
It twists when he sees someone cry; if you expect *me*
To burst into tears, you have to feel sorrow yourself.
Then your woes will fasten on me, O Telephus,
  Peleus;

If you speak incongruous lines, I'll snooze or I'll
  giggle.
Touching words most become the sorrowful
  countenance,
Blistering threats the enraged, playful remarks
The cheerful, suitably dignified speech the severe.
For nature first forms us, deep in our hearts, to
  respond
To the changing guise of our fortunes; she makes
  us take heart
Or drives us wild or bends us down to the ground
And let us writhe over inconsolable grief;
Then she brings these emotions out by using the
  tongue
To interpret them. If a speaker's words don't accord
With his fortunes, the Roman knights and those
  wretched wights
Who bought only standing room will both rock the
  house
With uproarious laughter. It will make a great deal
  of difference
Who's speaking: a god or a hero, a wise old man,
Or a fervent fellow in the flower of youth, or a
  matron,
A *powerful* matron, a busy old nurse, or a merchant,
A wandering merchant, or a man who farms the
  green field,
Or the Colchian or Assyrian type, or a man bred at
  Thebes,
A man bred at Argos.
           You should either stick to tradition
Or invent a consistent plot. If you bring back
  Achilles,
Have him say how laws don't apply to him, have
  prowess
Prevail over status, make him ruthless, impatient
  and fierce,
And ANGRY! Let Medea be wild, inconquerably so,
Ino tearful, Io "lost"; let Ixion
Go back on his word; let Orestes be sadly depressed.
If it's something as yet untried you put on the stage
And you dare construct a new character, you must
  keep
To the end the same sort of person you started out
  with,
And make your portrayal consistent.
                It's hard to write
Of familiar concerns in a new and original way.
You're better off telling the story of Troy in five acts

---

[3]Greek satiric poet of the sixth century B.C.E.
[4]As an act of revenge, Atreus served a feast to his brother
Thyestes, consisting of Thyestes' own children.

Than being the first to foist something new and
untried
On the world. In the public domain you'll have
private rights
If you keep from loitering around the most com-
mon places
And from dawdling on the easiest path, and take
pains to refrain
From translating faithfully word for word, and
don't leap
Right down the close-scooped well of the source
you draw on,
Precluded by shame or the laws of your task from
lifting
Your foot up over the edge. And don't begin
As the Cyclic poet once did:" 'And now I shall sing
Of the fortune of Priam and famous war of that king.'"
What could issue from the mouth that made such
an opening?
Mountains will labor, a funny little mouse will be
born.
To take on less is a much more sensible labor:
"Tell me, O Muse, of the man who, after Troy fell,
Came to know well all manner of cities and men."[5]
This writer plans to send up not smoke from the
flames
But light from the smoke, to deliver some marvel-
ous events:
Antiphates, giants, Scylla, Charybdis, the Cyclops.
Diomedes' return is not traced back to begin
With Meleager's death. The Trojan War doesn't start
With the egg of the twins.[6] He is eager to get to the
point
And hurries the reader along to the middle of
things,
As if they were already known, and simply leaves
out
Whatever he thinks he can't bring off shining and
clear,
And devises so well, intermingling the true and the
false,
That the middle part fits with the first, the last with
the middle.

[5] The opening lines of Homer's *Odyssey*.
[6] Meleager, Diomedes' uncle, died before he was born.
Helen of Troy was born from one of Leda's eggs; her twin
brothers Castor and Polydeukes were born from the other.

Now hear what I and the rest of your listeners expect
If you want them to sit there and wait till the curtain
comes down
And the cantor intones *"vos plaudite"*[7] . . . now is
the time."
Make careful note of the way each age group
behaves,
And apply the right tone to their changeable natures
and years.
The child who by now knows how to reel off his
words,
And plant his feet squarely beneath him, likes most
of all
To play with his friends; he flies into rage like a flash
And forgets it equally fast, and changes every hour.
The beardless youth, finally free of his guardian,
Rejoices in horse and hounds and the sun-drenched
grass
Of the Campus Martius: he is putty in your hands
to mold
To evil courses, resentful of warning advisers;
Slow to provide for his needs but recklessly fast
To spend his money, enthusiastic, intense,
But quick to transfer his affections. As his interests
change,
The man is seen in the manly style of his life:
He looks for wealth and for friends, is a slave to
success.
Is wary of making a move he will soon be concerned
To undo. A great many troubles harass the old man,
Either because he keeps on trying for gain
And yet won't touch what he has, worried and afraid
To use it, or perhaps because in all that he does
He's slow and phlegmatic, and keeps postponing
his pleasures.
Conscious of the rainy days he should be prepared
for.
"Difficult," always complaining, ready to praise
The good old days when he was a boy and reprove
And disapprove of the young. As the years come
along,
They bring along much that is fine; as they disappear,
They take many fine things away. In portraying our
roles,
We will dwell on the matters best suited and best
attached

[7] "Applaud."

To the age in question, and not let the old men's parts
Be assigned to a youth or the manly parts to a boy.

The events are either enacted on stage or described
As having occurred. But things entrusted to the ear
Impress our minds less vividly than what is exposed
To our trustworthy eyes so that a viewer informs
    himself
Of precisely what happened. Still, you are not to
    show
On stage what ought to take place backstage: remove
From our eyes the substance of things an eloquent
    messenger
Will soon be ready to state in person. Medea
Must not butcher her boys in front of the people;
Unspeakable Atreus should not cook up human flesh
Before our eyes, nor should Procne change into a
    bird,
Or Cadmus into a snake. Whatsoever such stuff
You *show* me, I won't believe it, I'll simply detest it.

The play that expects to be asked for another
    performance
Once it's been given, should be just five acts long,
No more, no less. A god must not intervene
Unless the action tangles itself in such knots
That only a divine deliverer can work the denoue-
    ment;
A fourth actor should not try to come forward to
    speak.[8]

The chorus should be handled as one of the actors
    and play
An important part, singing between episodes
What advances the plot and fits in well with the
    action.
Let it favor the good and offer them friendly
    advice,
Control the wrathful and develop a fondness for
    soothing
With quiet words the fearful in heart. Let it praise
    plain living,
The blessings of justice, the laws, and the doors left
    open
By Peace. Let the chorus respect the secrets it's told.

[8]Latin and Greek plays had more than three characters, but by convention, no more than three speaking actors in addition to the chorus were allowed on stage at the same time. See Aristotle's *Poetics*, Ch. 4.

Let it pray to the gods, devoutly imploring that
    fortune
Return to the unhappy low and depart from the proud.

The present-day brass-bound flute produces a tone
That rivals the trumpet's, unlike the primitive pipe,
With its thin, clear tone and one or two stops, war-
    bling woodnotes
To give the chorus the pitch, and provide an
    accompaniment —
A sound that could nevertheless carry in the
    uncrowded halls
When virtuous, decent, well-behaved folk came
    together.
But after a victorious people began to acquire
More land, and surround their cities with larger walls,
And drink to the Genius in broad daylight without
    shame,
More license entered the rhythms and modes of the
    music.
How could these rough country types be expected
    to judge,
Just off from work, mixed in with the city crowd,
The uncouth sitting next to the wealthy? And so
    the flute player
Added movement and gesture to the primitive style
And fluttered his robe as he strutted around the stage.
New notes increased the restricted range of the lyre,
And unrestrained wit produced a new form of
    eloquence,
So that even the thought, which had been such a
    fine detective
Of useful clues and prophet of future events,
Now resembled the unclear, ambiguous dictates of
    Delphi.

The writer who vied for the paltry prize of a goat
With tragic song, soon bared shaggy satyrs to view
On the stage, coarsely probing for laughs without
    losing dignity —
Some pleasant device and novel attraction like this
Being all that could make the spectator stay on and
    watch
After having fulfilled the ritual rites of the occasion,
And drunk a good bit, and been freed from the nor-
    mal restraints.
But those laughing, bantering satyrs will have to be
    told
To transform the mood from the grave to the gay
    with some care

And not let a god or a hero, previously seen
Coming out from his palace clad in royal crimson
and gold,
Move into a dingy shack and a low way of talking
Or, avoiding the depths, climb too fantastically high.
For tragedy, not condescending to mouth low lines,
Joins the satyrs but briefly, and not without some
hesitation,
Like a matron commanded to dance on a festive
occasion.
I assure you, good Pisos, if I write a satyr play,
I will not use only commonplace nouns and verbs
Or "plain words," nor try to depart from the tragic
tone
To the point where it makes no difference whether
Davus is speaking
With maudlin Pythias (who's just swiped some
dough from old Simo)
Or Silenus, tutor and guide to his heavenly ward.[9]
I shall set my sights on familiar things: anyone
Will think he can do as well but will soon find he can't
When he tries it and sweats and strains to bring it off.
The order and inner coherence and careful connection
Are what make your writing take hold: your major
success
Consists in mastering the language that is common
to all.
I incline to believe that when fauns trot in from the
woods,
They ought not to act as if they were reared in the
gutter
And virtually lived in the Forum, with citified ways
And prettified lays like those of young-bloods-
about-town,
Or resort to indecent remarks and crack dirty jokes.
The better-class patrons may take offense (the
freeborn,
The knights, the wealthy) and refuse to award the
crown,
As it were, unwilling to see in a favorable light
What the roast-beans-and-chestnuts[10] crowd find so
entertaining.
A short syllable followed by a long is of course an
iambus.

It moves along fast, so a verse consisting of six
Full-fledged iambic stresses has come to be known
As iambic trimeter. But recently, to come to our ears
More slowly and solemnly, father iambus adopted
A firm-footed son, the spondee. Affable and kind
Though he was, the iambus did not admit the young
man
On equal terms into this partnership, but reserved
The second and fourth foot all for himself. This
iambus
Appears but rarely in the "fine old" trimeters of
Accius,
And the spondaic stress in the lines which Ennius
heavily
Launched on the stage is a sign of hasty production
Or a fault to be chalked up to careless ignorance of
style.
Not every critic can spot the lines that don't quite
scan right,
And Roman poets have been granted too much
indulgence.
Shall I therefore run wild and write without any
restrictions
Or consider that everyone is bound to see my
mistakes
And cautiously keep well within the bounds of
indulgence?
I may have avoided the fault without rating praise.
Thumb through your Greek examples by day and
by night!
Your ancestors praised both the wit and rhythms of
Plautus?
For admiring both of these things they were *too*
tolerant,
Not to say dense, if you and I can distinguish
A crudeness in phrasing from lapidary strength of
wit,
And catch the legitimate beat with our fingers and
ears.
Thespis is said to have discovered the unknown style
Of the tragic muse, and to have carted his plays
about,
With actors singing the lines and performing the
parts,
Their faces smeared with a paste concocted from
wine lees —
So they trudged around in road shows, reveling in
tragedy.

[9] Davus outwits Simo in Terence's *Andria;* Pythias is a character from his *Eunuchus;* Silenus was the tutor of the god Bacchus.

[10] Snacks sold outside Roman theaters.

Aeschylus thought up the masks and distinctive
  costumes;
He built the first stage on a platform of several
  small boards
And taught his actors a lofty manner of speech
And a stately, high-booted stride. These tragic arts
Were succeeded by Old Comedy, whose many
  good points
Should be noted. From freedom that form declined
  into license
And fell upon violent ways that required regulation.
The law was obeyed and the chorus then lapsed
  into silence,
Deprived of its right to insult and abuse its victims.

Our Roman poets have left no style untried
And have not been the least deserving when they
  have dared
To desert the traces of Greece and dwell on affairs
Originating here among us, on our native designs,
Whether tragic or comic. Latium would be as
  triumphant
In language as in character and military might
If a single one of her poets could endure the effort
And time-consuming, slow discipline of the file.
Oh, descendants of Numa, turn your backs on the
  poem
Which many a day and many a diligent erasure
Have not corrected, which a sensitive, newly-pared
  nail
Has not run over and checked, at the least, ten times.

Because Democritus held that *genius was all*
And the miserable practice of art far inferior to it,
And denied that sensible poets rated a place
On Helicon's heights,[11] most poets neglect their
  appearance —
They won't cut their nails or their beards, they
  won't take a bath,
They wander off somewhere alone. For surely the
  name
And the fame of the poet will attach itself to that
  dome
Which has never entrusted itself to the shears of
  Licinus,[12]
Which trips for treatment to three times as many
  psychiatrists

[11]Helicon was the mountain sacred to the Muses.
[12]A well-known Roman barber.

As even Switzerland harbors have failed to set
  straight.[13]
What a fool am I to purge myself of my bile
Seasonably, every spring! If I'd only refrained,
I'd be unsurpassed as a poet. But perhaps it's not
  worth it
To lose your head and then write verses instead,
So I'll play the whetstone's part, giving edge to the
  steel,
Without being able to cut. And though I write
  nothing,
I'll point out the writer's mission and function and
  show
Him where his best material lies and what
Nurtures and shapes the poet, what best accords
With his role, what worst, where the right path
  goes, and the wrong.

The principal source of all good writing is wisdom.
The Socratic pages will offer you ample material,
And with the matter in hand, the words will be
  quick to follow.
A man who has learned what is owing to country
  and friends,
The love that is due a parent, a brother, a guest,
What the role of a judge or senator chiefly requires,
What part is played by the general sent off to war,
Will surely know how to write the appropriate lines
For each of his players. I will bid the intelligent
  student
Of the imitative art to look to the model of life
And see how men act, to bring his speeches alive.
At times a play of no particular merit,
Artistically lacking in strength and smoothness of
  finish
But with vivid examples of character drawn true
  to life,
Will please the audience and hold their attention
  better
Than tuneful trifles and verses empty of thought.

[13]*Psychiatrists . . . Switzerland*: The translator here
indulges in an anachronism to avoid a complicated explanation. The geographical reference in Horace's Latin is not to
Switzerland but to Antycra, a town famous for producing
black hellebore, a poisonous plant that, in legend, was used
by the physician Melampus to cure the madness of three
daughters of the King of Argos. Horace's general point is that
poets, supposed to be men of genius, affect to be both uncouth
and mad.

To the Greeks the muse gave genius, the Greeks
she endowed
With eloquent speech and greed for nothing but
praise.
Our Roman lads learn arithmetic and divide
The unit into its hundreds. "The Son of
Albinus —
You here today? All right, your turn to recite!
Subtract a twelfth from five-twelfths, and what
have you left?"
Come on, Albinus Minus — don't think so hard!'
"One-third, Sir." "Fine! You'll keep track of your
money, you will.
Now take that original sum and add on a twelfth.
How much?" "One-half." When once the corrosive
concern
For petty cash has tainted our minds, can we hope
to write poems
To be oiled with cedar and kept in smooth cypress
cases?
Poets would either delight or enlighten the reader,
Or say what is both amusing and really worth
using.
But when you instruct, be brief, so the mind can
clearly
Perceive and firmly retain. When the mind is full,
Everything else that you say just trickles away.
Fictions that border on truth will generate pleasure,
So your play is not to expect automatic assent
To whatever comes into its head, nor to draw forth
a child
Still alive from Lamia's stomach after she's dined.
Our elders will chase off the stage what is merely
delightful;
Our young bloods will pass up the works that
merely make sense.
He wins every vote who combines the sweet and
the useful,
Charming the reader and warning him equally well.
This book will bring in money for Sosius and Son,
Booksellers, travel across the sea, and extend
Its author's fame a long distance into the future.
There still may be some oversights, and we may be
willing
To overlook them, for the string won't always play
back
What the hand had in mind; quite often you ask for
a flat

And get back a sharp. You brandish your bow at
the target,
But the arrow won't always fly home. If happy
effects
Figure more, I won't take offense at the few bad
spots
Which either carelessness let slip onto the page
Or human nature took too little pains to avert.
And what's the truth here? If a slave who copies
out books
Keeps making the same mistake no matter how often
He's warned, he can't be excused; if a harpist
keeps striking
The same wrong note, he'll be laughed at. I would
reserve
The role of Choerilus for poets who strike some-
thing *good*[14]
Two or three times in the course of a largely
flawed work.
Which makes me laugh as a matter of sheer
amazement.
Good Homer sometimes nods, which gives me a
jerk —
But sleep may well worm its way into any long work!
A poem is much like a painting: one will please more
If you see it close up, another if seen from a distance;
One prefers being viewed in the shade, while the
other
Prefers being seen in broad daylight and doesn't
shrink back
From the piercing glance of the critic. One pleased
once;
The other will always please, though it's called for
ten times.
Let me say to the older of you two boys, and remind
You to take it to heart, no matter how wise you
may be
And well directed to the right by your father's
voice:
The doctrine of the mean does not correctly apply
To all things, but rather to a few quite definite
matters.
The average lawyer, consultant or trial attorney,

[14]Choerilus was an epic poet of the fourth century B.C.E. who was offered a piece of gold by Alexander the Great for every *good* verse celebrating his victories. He died poor.

May lack Messalla's delivery, may not know as much
As Aulus Cascellius, and still be of no little worth.
But men and gods and booksellers WON'T PUT UP
WITH SECOND-RATE POETS. If the orchestra playing
    at dinner
Is all out of tune, if the ointment offered each guest
Is lumpy, if sour Sardinian honey is served
With the poppy seeds, the party is spoiled all the
    more;
It could have gone on perfectly, simply without them.
So a poem, designed and destined to afford the soul
Genuine pleasure, if it falls somewhat short of the
    top,
Sinks right down to the bottom. If a man can't play,
He avoids the weapons drill going on in the Campus.
And if he can't handle the ball or discus or hoop,
He stands off, lest he provoke the justified laughter
Of spectators crowded around and forming the circle.
But someone who doesn't know how dares fashion
    verses.
Why not? He's free, freeborn, in fact, and his income
Is rated at a knightly sum, has a fine reputation.

But you, my dear fellow, will refrain from speak-
    ing or acting
Without Minerva's consent? That shows good
    judgment
And a sound attitude. If you ever do write some-
    thing, though,
Be sure to expose it to such ears as Tarpa the
    Censor's,
And your father's, and mine. Then put the parch-
    ment away
For a good nine years! What you haven't yet
    published
You can always destroy, but once a word is let go,
It can't be called back.
                    When primitive men roamed the forests,
Orpheus, the sacred interpreter of heavenly will,
Turned them away from killing and living like beasts
And hence is said to have tamed wild lions and tigers.
Amphion is said, as founder of the city of Thebes,
To have moved the stones and led them wherever
    he wished
By the sound of his lyre and the winning appeal of
    his voice.
This was the wisdom of former times: to distinguish
Public from private concerns and sacred from
    common,

To forbid impromptu liaisons and make rules for
    marriage,
To build towns and carve out the laws on pillars of
    wood.
The poets who taught by expressing these things
    were acclaimed:
They and their works were considered divine. After
    them,
Tyrtaeus and Homer won wide renown by sharpening
Masculine minds to a warlike pitch with their poems.
Oracles were uttered in song, and a way of life
Pointed out, along gnomic lines. The favor of kings
Was courted in verse, and festival joy was found
As the suitable end to periods of long, hard
    work —
Lest you make excuses for Apollo, the god of song,
Or the muse so skilled with the lyre.
                            The question is raised
Whether nature or art makes a poem deserving of
    praise.
I fail to see what good either learning can be
Which is not veined with natural wealth or primi-
    tive genius.
Each needs the other's help and friendly alliance.
The racer who wants to win has learned, as a boy,
To strain and train, shiver and sweat, stay away
From women and wine. The flute player who gets
    to play
At the Pythian games has long since studied and
    shuddered
In the presence of his teacher. Today, it's enough
    just to say:
"I PEN these marvelous POEMS — I'm a Creative
    Person.
The last one's a dirty shirt. I won't get left back,
Admitting I just don't know what I've never yet
    learned."

Like the auctioneer who collects a crowd for a sale,
The poet with property or money put out in loans
Is ordering flatterers to make a profit from him.
But when he can serve a nice little dinner for
    friends,
Or put up the bail for a poor man who's not a good
    risk,
Or rescue one held in the gloomy grip of the law,
I'll marvel if the lucky man can always distinguish
    the false friend from the true.
                            And if you have given,

Or intend to give, a present to someone, don't take
him
To hear, still glowing with joy, some verses you've
written.
He'll shout out "Fine! Oh, *excellent! How* superb!"
Go pale at the sombre parts, even squeeze out a drop
Of dew from his friendly eyes, and pound on the
ground
With his foot to keep time, and dance a bit for
sheer joy.
Just as hired mourners often behave much better at
funerals
Than those sincerely bereaved, so the man who
pretends
Makes more perpetual emotion than your honest
admirer.
Kings are said to ply with drink after drink
And put through the ordeal by wine the man they
would test
As worthy of the royal friendship. And if you
would write,
Don't ever forget: there's a motive concealed in
the fox.
If you read something out to Quintilius,[15] he'd usu-
ally say,
"You could straighten out *this,* or *that.*" And if,
after trying
Two or three times with no luck, you'd said you
could *not*
Improve on the passage, he'd tell you to strike it
right out
And hand back to the anvil those verses that came
out so bent,
To be hammered into shape once again. Then, if
you preferred
Standing by your mistake to changing it, he'd waste
not a word
Or an ounce of energy more, and not interfere
With your loving, alone and unrivaled, yourself
and your work.
The fair-minded, thoughtful man will reproach the
verses
That come out spineless and flat, find fault with the
clumsy

And rhythmically harsh; with a straight black
stroke of the pen
He will line out disorganized parts; your elegant
effects
He will simply cut out; he will force you to let in
more light
On the dark passages, point out ambiguous phrasing,
And note what ought to be changed, a real Richard
Bentley,[16]
Who won't stop to say, "But why should I harass
a friend
With these minor repairs?" These minor repairs
will create
A major disaster, once that friend is exposed
To a hostile reception and unfriendly jeers in public.

The mad poet only makes sensible people avoid him
And fear to touch him, as if he were plagued by the
itch
Or the royal disease of jaundice (yellow as gold
And worth a king's ransom to cure) or St. Vitus'
dance
Or lunatic frenzy. Kids chase after and taunt him.
With his head held high, he strolls off belching his
lines,
Like a fowler whose eyes are steadily trained on
the merles —
And then if he falls down a well or into a pit —
He may yell long and loud for help: "To the res-
cue! This way,
Fellow citizens!" None will care to come pull him
out.
And if someone *should have* the urge to lend him
a hand
And let down a rope, I will say, "But how do you
know
He hasn't intentionally thrown himself in and
doesn't
Want to be saved?" and then I will tell of the death
Of the Sicilian poet. Because Empedocles wished
To be thought an immortal god, he leaped into Etna,
This cool customer, to his fiery fate. We are left
To conclude that poetic justice or poetic license
Includes suicide. To save some person from death

15A Roman critic of the second century B.C.E.; Horace is using the name to denote some man of taste.

16Another anachronism by the translator. Bentley (1662–1742) was a British critic who corrected Pope's translation of Homer. Horace's Latin refers to Aristarchus of Samothrace (220–143 B.C.E.), who wrote scholarly commentary on Homer.

Against his will is just as wrong as to kill him.
This isn't the first time it's happened, and if he's
  pulled out,
He will not necessarily be made over into a man
And put aside his desire for a memorable end.

It's not quite clear what drove him to write, in the
  first place —
Did he sprinkle his well-wrought urine on ancestral
  ashes?
Or blasphemously joggle the ground at some sacred
  spot?

At any rate, he's got it bad; and, bold as a bear,
If he's strong enough to have smashed in the fret-
  work of bars
That kept him confined to his cage, he's on a
  rampage,
Stampeding unlearned and learned alike, in his rage
To recite. Once he's caught you, he'll hang on with
  all his might;
The leech just clings to your skin and never gives in
Until bloated with blood; *he'll* never run out of breath
But will read you and read you and read you and
  read you to death.

Longinus

First Century C.E.

One of the most controversial aspects of "On the Sublime" has been its author-ship. The oldest manuscript, from the tenth century, calls the author "Dionysius Longinus." The name is too apt to be true. Each of its two halves belongs to a great Greco-Roman philosopher, Dionysius of Halicarnassus (who wrote under Augustus Caesar) and Cassius Longinus (who died nearly three centuries later, in 273 C.E.). But neither of these men is a plausible candidate to have written "On the Sublime." The literary opinions of Longinus are inconsistent with those of Dionysius, while Cassius Longinus, who wrote during the most brutally chaotic period of the Empire, is unlikely to have penned Chapter 44, which discusses the causes of literary decline in an era of universal peace.

The style and historical allusions suggest a date during the quiet reigns of Nerva and Trajan, toward the end of the first century. The quotation in Chapter 9 from the Old Testament book of Genesis would be an extraordinary allusion for a pagan author to make, and it has been suggested that Longinus may have been either a Hellenized Jew (perhaps of the circle of Philo Judaeus[1]) or a Greek with Jewish connections.

Unlike Plato, who concerned himself with common features of artistic works in general, Longinus is interested in a special quality, sublimity or elevation, which is possessed by some works but not others. Unlike Aristotle, whose poetics dealt with the particular characteristics of different literary forms, Longinus's sublimity is a quality that transcends generic boundaries. It can be found in drama or epic or lyric — or even in rhetoric or history or theology. Longinus's approach might be called "qualitative criticism," and it constitutes the third enduring method of literary theory, with descendants from Burke to Bakhtin. "On the Sublime" is related in one sense to the rhetorical criticism of Horace and others — its principal topics seem to be author, work, and audience — but where Horace differentiated between a high, a middle, and a low style, Longinus is concerned only with the first. And Longinus is far more methodical in exploring his more limited subject than Horace.

The argument of "On the Sublime" can be easily outlined. In Chapters 1 and 2 Longinus defines the Sublime as that quality within a discourse that produces "not persuasion but transport" (*ekstasis*) within the audience. He then questions whether there is such an art — whether it is purely a matter of inspiration or whether there are basic principles at work. Much of the actual argument itself has been lost, but from the rest of the essay, which presents five components of the art, it is clear on which side Longinus comes down. In Chapters 3 through 7, Longinus discusses the traps that lie on all sides of the target, those faults in literature that result from try-ing for the sublime and missing the mark. There are faults of commission, such as

[1]Philo may be the "philosopher" in Ch. 44 whom Longinus attempts to confute.

trying too hard (bombast, pedantry, hysteria), and there are faults of omission, such as frigidity of tone.

In Chapter 8, Longinus outlines the remainder of his essay, which successively treats the five sources (beyond language itself) of the Sublime. First are high thoughts (Chapters 9–15) and second, strong passions (not included but promised in a separate treatise), both of which are innate within the artist. Next are rhetorical figures (Chapters 16–29), then noble diction (Chapters 30–38 and 43), and finally, elevated composition (Chapters 39–42), all of which are the product of art and must be learned.

Just as important as Longinus's systematic method is the clarity and vigor with which he pursues it. He always has an apt quotation ready to exemplify a literary fault or grace, and for a judicial critic, there is nothing mean-spirited about his tone or temper.

Longinus's treatise "On the Sublime" was not influential in its own time. Its importance dates only from the Renaissance; it was published by Francesco Robortello in 1554 and translated by Nicolas Boileau in 1674. Soon thereafter it became common property, and poet-critics like John Dryden drew upon its central issues. During the eighteenth century, the Sublime was considered to be of great significance in opposition to the beautiful (a dichotomy treated by Edmund Burke, Immanuel Kant, and many others), and Longinus's brilliance as a critic was much appreciated. In his *Essay on Criticism,* Alexander Pope conveys the typical Augustan sentiments about the author of "On the Sublime":

> Thee, bold Longinus! all the Nine inspire,
> And bless their critic with a poet's fire:
> An ardent judge, who, zealous in his trust,
> With warmth gives sentence, yet is always just;
> Whose own example strengthens all his laws;
> And is himself that great Sublime he draws.

But Longinus was more admired than imitated in the eighteenth century — except on one occasion by Pope, who wrote a travesty of "On the Sublime" in "The Art of Sinking in Poetry," explaining (with delicious examples from contemporary works) the sources of the quality of Bathos. In the nineteenth century, his overt influence and reputation declined somewhat, perhaps owing to his antidemocratic political beliefs, but his method of qualitative criticism was paradoxically revived in thinkers like Matthew Arnold, Walter Pater, and most recently Mikhail Bakhtin.

Selected Bibliography

Apfel, Henrietta Veit. *Literary Quotation and Allusion in Demetrius' Peri hermeneias and Longinus' Peri hypsos.* New York: Columbia University Library, 1935.

Ashfield, Andrew, and Peter De Bolla. *The Sublime: A Reader.* Cambridge: Cambridge University Press, 1993.

Brody, Jules. *Boileau and Longinus.* Geneva: Droz, 1953.

Davidson, Hugh M. "The Literary Arts of Longinus and Boileau." In *Studies in Seventeenth-Century French Literature,* ed. Jean Demonest. Ithaca: Cornell University Press, 1962.

Fuhrmann, Manfred. *Die Dichtungstheorie der Antike.* Darmstadt: Wissenschaftliche Buchgesellschaft, 1993.

Guerlac, Suzanne, and Frances Ferguson. "Longinus and the Subject of the Sublime." *New Literary History*, 16:2 (Winter 1985): 275–97.

Henn, T. R. *Longinus and English Criticism.* Cambridge: Cambridge University Press, 1934.

Marin, Demetrio St. *Bibliography of the Essay on the Sublime.* N.p. 1967.

Olson, Elder. "The Argument of Longinus's *On the Sublime.*" In *On Value Judgments in the Arts and Other Essays.* Chicago: University of Chicago Press, 1976.

Rosenberg, Alfred. *Longinus in England.* Berlin: Meyer und Müller, 1937.

Russell, D. A., ed. *"Longinus" on the Sublime.* Oxford: Clarendon Press, 1964.

From *On the Sublime*

Translated by W. Rhys Roberts.

I

You will remember, my dear Postumius Terentianus, that when we examined together the treatise of Caecilius on the Sublime, we found that it fell below the dignity of the whole subject, while it failed signally to grasp the essential points, and conveyed to its readers but little of that practical help which it should be a writer's principal aim to give. In every systematic treatise two things are required. The first is a statement of the subject; the other, which although second in order ranks higher in importance, is an indication of the methods by which we may attain our end. Now Caecilius seeks to show the nature of the sublime by countless instances as though our ignorance demanded it, but the consideration of the means whereby we may succeed in raising our own capacities to a certain pitch of elevation he has, strangely enough, omitted as unnecessary. 2. However, it may be that the man ought not so much to be blamed for his shortcomings as praised for his happy thought and his enthusiasm. But since you have urged me, in my turn, to write a brief essay on the sublime for your special gratification, let us consider whether the views I have formed contain anything which will be of use to public men. You will yourself, my friend, in accordance with your nature and with what is fitting, join me in appraising each detail with the utmost regard for truth; for he answered well who, when asked in what qualities

we resemble the gods, declared that we do so in benevolence and truth. 3. As I am writing to you, my good friend, who are well versed in literary studies, I feel almost absolved from the necessity of premising at any length that sublimity is a certain distinction and excellence in expression, and that it is from no other source than this that the greatest poets and writers have derived their eminence and gained an immortality of renown. 4. The effect of elevated language upon an audience is not persuasion but transport. At every time and in every way imposing speech, with the spell it throws over us, prevails over that which aims at persuasion and gratification. Our persuasions we can usually control, but the influences of the sublime bring power and irresistible might to bear, and reign supreme over every hearer. Similarly, we see skill in invention, and due order and arrangement of matter, emerging as the hard-won result not of one thing nor of two, but of the whole texture of the composition, whereas Sublimity flashing forth at the right moment scatters everything before it like a thunderbolt, and at once displays the power of the orator in all its plenitude. But enough; for these reflections, and others like them, you can, I know well, my dear Terentianus, yourself suggest from your own experience.

2

First of all, we must raise the question whether there is such a thing as an art of the sublime or lofty. Some hold that those are entirely in error who would bring such matters under the precepts of art. A lofty tone, says one, is innate, and does not come by teaching; nature is the only art that can compass it. Works of nature are, they think, made worse and altogether feebler when wizened by the rules of art. 2. But I maintain that this will be found to be otherwise if it be observed that, while nature as a rule is free and independent in matters of passion and elevation, yet is she wont not to act at random and utterly without system. Further, nature is the original and vital underlying principle in all cases, but system can define limits and fitting seasons, and can also contribute the safest rules for use and practice. Moreover, the expression of the sublime is more exposed to danger when it goes its own way without the guidance of knowledge — when it is suffered to be unstable and unballasted — when it is left at the mercy of mere momentum and ignorant audacity. It is true that it often needs the spur, but it is also true that it often needs the curb. 3. Demosthenes expresses the view, with regard to human life in general, that good fortune is the greatest of blessings, while good counsel, which occupies the second place, is hardly inferior in importance, since its absence contributes inevitably to the ruin of the former. This we may apply to diction, nature occupying the position of good fortune, art that of good counsel. Most important of all, we must remember that the very fact that there are some elements of expression which are in the hands of nature alone, can be learnt from no other source than art. If, I say, the critic of those who desire to learn were to turn these matters over in his mind, he would no longer, it seems to me, regard the discussion of the subject as superfluous or useless. . . .

3

> Quell they the oven's far-flung splendour-glow!
> Ha, let me but one hearth-abider mark —
> One flame-wreath torrent-like I'll whirl on high;
> I'll burn the roof, to cinders shrivel it —
> Nay, now my chant is not of noble strain.[1]

[1]Aeschylus, *Oreithyia*.

Such things are not tragic but pseudo-tragic — "flame-wreaths," and "belching to the sky," and Boreas represented as a "flute-player," and all the rest of it. They are turbid in expression and confused in imagery rather than the product of intensity, and each one of them, if examined in the light of day, sinks little by little from the terrible into the contemptible. But since even in tragedy, which is in its very nature stately and prone to bombast, tasteless tumidity is unpardonable, still less, I presume, will it harmonize with the narration of fact. 2. And this is the ground on which the phrases of Gorgias of Leontini are ridiculed when he describes Xerxes as the "Zeus of the Persians" and vultures as "living tombs." So is it with some of the expressions of Callisthenes which are not sublime but high-flown, and still more with those of Cleitarchus, for the man is frivolous and blows, as Sophocles has it,

> On pigmy hautboys: mouthpiece have they none.

Other examples will be found in Amphicrates and Hegesias and Matris, for often when these writers seem to themselves to be inspired they are in no true frenzy but are simply trifling. 3. Altogether, tumidity seems particularly hard to avoid. The explanation is that all who aim at elevation are so anxious to escape the reproach of being weak and dry that they are carried, as by some strange law of nature, into the opposite extreme. They put their trust in the maxim that "failure in a great attempt is at least a noble error." 4. But evil are the swellings, both in the body and in diction, which are inflated and unreal, and threaten us with the reverse of our aim; for nothing, say they, is drier than a man who has the dropsy. While tumidity desires to transcend the limits of the sublime, the defect which is termed puerility is the direct antithesis of elevation, for it is utterly low and mean and in real truth the most ignoble vice of style. What, then, is this puerility? Clearly, a pedant's thoughts, which begin in learned trifling and end in frigidity. Men slip into this kind of error because, while they aim at the uncommon and elaborate and most of all at the attractive, they drift unawares into the tawdry and affected. 5. A third, and closely allied, kind of defect in matters of passion is that which Theodorus used to call *parenthyrsus*. By this is meant unseasonable and empty passion, where no passion is required, or immoderate, where moderation is needed. For men are often carried away, as if by intoxication, into displays of emotion which are not caused by the nature of the subject, but are purely personal and wearisome. In consequence they seem to hearers who are in no wise affected to act in an ungainly way. And no wonder: for they are beside themselves, while their hearers are not. But the question of the passions we reserve for separate treatment.

4

Of the second fault of which we have spoken — frigidity — Timaeus supplies many examples. Timaeus was a writer of considerable general ability, who occasionally showed that he was not incapable of elevation of style. He was learned and ingenious, but very prone to criticize the faults of others while blind to his own. Through his passion for continually starting novel notions, he often fell into the merest childishness. 2. I will set down one or two examples only of his manner, since the greater number have been already appropriated by Caecilius. In the course of a eulogy on Alexander the Great, he describes him as "the man who gained possession of the whole of Asia in fewer years than it took Isocrates to write his *Panegyric* urging war against the Persians." Strange indeed is the comparison of the man of Macedon with the rhetorician. How plain it is, Timaeus, that the Lacedaemonians, thus judged, were far inferior to Isocrates in prowess, for they spent thirty years in the conquest of Messene, whereas he composed his *Panegyric* in ten. 3. Consider again the way in which he speaks of the Athenians who were captured in Sicily. "They were punished because they had acted impiously towards Hermes and mutilated his images, and the infliction of punishment was chiefly due to Hermocrates the son of Hermon, who was descended, in the paternal line, from the outraged god." I am surprised, beloved Terentianus, that he does not write with regard to the despot Dionysius that "Dion and Heracleides deprived him of his sovereignty because he had acted impiously towards Zeus and Heracles." 4. But why speak of Timaeus when even those

heroes of literature, Xenophon and Plato, though trained in the school of Socrates, nevertheless sometimes forget themselves for the sake of such paltry pleasantries? Xenophon writes in the *Polity of the Lacedaemonians:*[2] "You would find it harder to hear their voice than that of busts of marble, harder to deflect their gaze than that of statues of bronze; you would deem them more modest than the very maidens in their eyes."[2] It was worthy of an Amphicrates and not of a Xenophon to call the pupils of our eyes "modest maidens." Good heavens, how strange it is that the pupils of the whole company should be believed to be modest notwithstanding the common saying that the shamelessness of individuals is indicated by nothing so much as the eyes! "Thou sot, that hast the eyes of a dog,"[3] as Homer has it. 5. Timaeus, however, has not left even this piece of frigidity to Xenophon, but clutches it as though it were hid treasure. At all events, after saying of Agathocles that he abducted his cousin, who had been given in marriage to another man, from the midst of the nuptial rites, he asks, "Who could have done this had he not had wantons, in place of maidens, in his eyes?" 6. Yes, and Plato (usually so divine) when he means simply *tablets* says, "They shall write and preserve *cypress memorials*[4] in the temples." And again, "As touching walls, Megillus, I should hold with Sparta that they be suffered to lie asleep in the earth and not summoned to arise."[5] The expression of Herodotus to the effect that beautiful women are "eye-smarts" is not much better.[6] This, however, may be condoned in some degree since those who use this particular phrase in his narrative are barbarians and in their cups, but not even in the mouths of such characters is it well that an author should suffer, in the judgment of posterity, from an unseemly exhibition of triviality.

2 Xenophon, *On the Government of the Lacedaimonians* 3:5. [Tr.]

3 Homer, *Iliad* 1:225. [Tr.]

4 Plato, *Laws* 5:741c. [Tr.]

5 Plato, *Laws* 6:778d [Tr.]

6 Herodotus, *History* 5:18. [Tr.]

5

All these ugly and parasitical growths arise in literature from a single cause, that pursuit of novelty in the expression of ideas which may be regarded as the fashionable craze of the day. Our defects usually spring, for the most part, from the same sources as our good points. Hence, while beauties of expression and touches of sublimity, and charming elegances withal, are favorable to effective composition, yet these very things are the elements and foundation, not only of success, but also of the contrary. Something of the kind is true also of variations and hyperboles and the use of the plural number, and we shall show subsequently the dangers to which these seem severally to be exposed. It is necessary now to seek and to suggest means by which we may avoid the defects which attend the steps of the sublime.

6

The best means would be, my friend, to gain, first of all, clear knowledge and appreciation of the true sublime. The enterprise is, however, an arduous one. For the judgment of style is the last and crowning fruit of long experience. Nonetheless, if I must speak in the way of precept, it is not impossible perhaps to acquire discrimination in these matters by attention to some such hints as those which follow.

7

You must know, my dear friend, that it is with the sublime as in the common life of man. In life nothing can be considered great which it is held great to despise. For instance, riches, honors, distinctions, sovereignties, and all other things which possess in abundance the external trappings of the stage, will not seem, to a man of sense, to be supreme blessings, since the very contempt of them is reckoned good in no small degree, and in any case those who could have them, but are high-souled enough to disdain them, are more admired than those who have them. So also in the case of sublimity in poems and prose writings, we must consider whether some supposed examples have not simply the appearance of elevation with many

idle accretions, so that when analyzed they are found to be mere vanity — objects which a noble nature will rather despise than admire. 2. For, as if instinctively, our soul is uplifted by the true sublime; it takes a proud flight, and is filled with joy and vaunting, as though it had itself produced what it has heard. 3. When therefore, a thing is heard repeatedly by a man of intelligence, who is well versed in literature, and its effect is not to dispose the soul to high thoughts, and it does not leave in the mind more food for reflection than the words seem to convey, but falls, if examined carefully through and through, into disesteem, it cannot rank as true sublimity because it does not survive a first hearing. For that is really great which bears a repeated examination, and which it is difficult or rather impossible to withstand, and the memory of which is strong and hard to efface. 4. In general, consider those examples of sublimity to be fine and genuine which please all and always. For when men of different pursuits, lives, ambitions, ages, languages, hold identical views on one and the same subject, then that verdict which results, so to speak, from a concert of discordant elements makes our faith in the object of admiration strong and unassailable.

8

There are, it may be said, five principal sources of elevated language. Beneath these five varieties there lies, as though it were a common foundation, the gift of discourse, which is indispensable. First and most important is the power of forming great conceptions, as we have elsewhere explained in our remarks on Xenophon. Secondly, there is vehement and inspired passion. These two components of the sublime are for the most part innate. Those which remain are partly the product of art. The due formation of figures deals with two sorts of figures, first those of thought and secondly those of expression. Next there is noble diction, which in turn comprises choice of words, and use of metaphors, and elaboration of language. The fifth cause of elevation — one which is the fitting conclusion of all that have preceded it — is dignified and elevated composition. Come now, let us consider what is involved in each of these varieties, with this one remark by way of preface, that Caecilius has omitted some of the five divisions, for example, that of passion. 2. Surely he is quite mistaken if he does so on the ground that if it seems to him that they are by nature one and these two, sublimity and passion, are a unity, and inseparable. For some passions are found which are far removed from sublimity and are of a low order, such as pity, grief and fear; and on the other hand there are many examples of the sublime which are independent of passion, such as the daring words of Homer with regard to the Aloadae, to take one out of numberless instances.

> Yea, Ossa in fury they strove to upheave on Olympus on high,
> With forest-clad Pelion above, that thence they might step to the sky.[7]

And so of the words which follow with still greater force:

> Ay, and the deed had they done.

3. Among the orators, too, eulogies and ceremonial and occasional addresses contain on every side examples of dignity and elevation, but are for the most part void of passion. This is the reason why passionate speakers are the worst eulogists, and why, on the other hand, those who are apt in encomium are the least passionate. 4. If, on the other hand, Caecilius thought that passion never contributes at all to sublimity, and if it was for this reason that he did not deem it worthy of mention, he is altogether deluded. I would affirm with confidence that there is no tone so lofty as that of genuine passion, in its right place, when it bursts out in a wild gust of mad enthusiasm and as it were fills the speaker's words with frenzy.

9

Now the first of the conditions mentioned, namely elevation of mind, holds the foremost rank among them all. We must, therefore, in this case also, although we have to do rather with an endowment than with an acquirement, nurture our souls (as far as that is possible) to thoughts sublime, and make them always pregnant; so to say, with noble inspiration. 2. In what way, you may ask, is this to be done? Elsewhere I have written as follows: "Sublimity is the echo of a great soul." Hence also a bare idea, by itself and without a spoken word, sometimes excites admiration just because of the greatness of soul implied. Thus the silence of Ajax in the Underworld is great and more sublime than words.[8] 3. First, then, it is absolutely necessary to indicate the source of this elevation, namely, that the truly eloquent must be free from low and ignoble thoughts. For it is not possible that men with mean and servile ideas and aims prevailing throughout their lives should produce anything that is admirable and worthy of immortality. Great accents we expect to fall from the lips of those whose thoughts are deep and grave. 4. Thus it is that stately speech comes naturally to the proudest spirits. [You will remember the answer of] Alexander to Parmenio when he said "For my part I had been well content."[9]

. . . the distance from earth to heaven; and this might well be considered the measure of Homer no less than of Strife. 5. How unlike to this the expression which is used of Sorrow by Hesiod, if indeed the *Shield* is to be attributed to Hesiod,

> Rheum from her nostrils was trickling.[10]

The image he has suggested is not terrible but rather loathsome. Contrast the way in which Homer magnifies the higher powers:

> And far as a man with his eyes through the sea-line haze may discern,
> On a cliff as he sitteth and gazeth away o'er the wine-dark deep,
> So far at a bound do the loud-neighing steeds of the Deathless leap.[11]

He makes the vastness of the world the measure of their leap. The sublimity is so overpowering as naturally to prompt the exclamation that if the divine steeds were to leap thus twice in succession they would pass beyond the confines of the

---

[7] Homer, *Odyssey* 11:315–16. [Tr.]

[8] Homer, *Odyssey* 11:543. [Tr.]

[9] From Arrian's *Anabasis of Alexander.* A lacuna in the manuscript follows.

[10] Hesiod, *The Shield of Heracles,* 267. [Tr.]

[11] Homer, *Iliad* 5:770–72. [Tr.]

world. 6. How transcendent also are the images in the Battle of the Gods:

> Far round wide heaven and Olympus echoed his clarion of thunder;
> And Hades, king of the realm of shadows, quaked thereunder.
> And he sprang from his throne, and he cried aloud in the dread of his heart
> Lest o'er him earth-shaker Poseidon should cleave the ground apart,
> And revealed to Immortals and mortals should stand those awful abodes,
> Those mansions ghastly and grim, abhorred of the very Gods.[12]

You see, my friend, how the earth is torn from its foundations, Tartarus itself is laid bare, the whole world is upturned and parted asunder, and all things together — heaven and hell, things mortal and things immortal — share in the conflict and the perils of that battle!

7. But although these things are awe-inspiring, yet from another point of view, if they be not taken allegorically, they are altogether impious, and violate our sense of what is fitting. Homer seems to me, in his legends of wounds suffered by the gods, and of their feuds, reprisals, tears, bonds, and all their manifold passions, to have made, as far as lay within his power, gods of the men concerned in the Siege of Troy, and men of the gods. But whereas we mortals have death as the destined haven of our ills if our lot is miserable, he portrays the gods as immortal not only in nature but also in misfortune. 8. Much superior to the passages respecting the Battle of the Gods are those which represent the divine nature as it really is — pure and great and undefiled; for example, what is said of Poseidon in a passage fully treated by many before ourselves:

> Her far-stretching ridges, her forest-trees, quaked in dismay,
> And her peaks, and the Trojans' town, and the ships of Achaia's array,
> Beneath his immortal feet, as onward Poseidon strode.

> Then over the surges he drave: leapt sporting before the God
> Sea-beasts that uprose all around from the depths, for their king they knew,
> And for rapture the sea was disparted, and onward the car-steeds flew.[13]

9. Similarly, the legislator of the Jews, no ordinary man, having formed and expressed a worthy conception of the might of the Godhead, writes at the very beginning of his Laws, "God said," — what? "Let there be light, and there was light; let there be land, and there was land."[14] 10. Perhaps I shall not seem tedious, my friend, if I bring forward one passage more from Homer — this time with regard to the concerns of *men* — in order to show that he is wont himself to enter into the sublime actions of his heroes. In his poem the battle of the Greeks is suddenly veiled by mist and baffling night. Then Ajax, at his wits' end, cries:

> Zeus, Father, yet save thou Achaia's sons from beneath the gloom,
> And make clear day, and vouchsafe unto us with our eyes to see!
> So it be but in light, destroy us![15]

That is the true attitude of an Ajax. He does not pray for life, for such a petition would have ill beseemed a hero. But since in the hopeless darkness he can turn his valor to no noble end, he chafes at his slackness in the fray and craves the boon of immediate light, resolved to find a death worthy of his bravery, even though Zeus should fight in the ranks against him. 11. In truth, Homer in these cases shares the full inspiration of the combat, and it is neither more nor less than true of the poet himself that

> Mad rageth he as Arês the shaker of spears, or as mad flames leap
> Wild-wasting from hill unto hill in the folds of a forest deep,
> And the foam-froth fringeth his lips.[16]

---

[12]Homer, *Iliad* 20:61–65. [Tr.]

[13]Homer, *Iliad* 13:18–19, 27–29. The second line belongs at the beginning of the last quotation; it is *Iliad* 20:60.
[14]Genesis 1:3, slightly misquoted.
[15]Homer, *Iliad* 17:645–47. [Tr.]
[16]Homer, *Iliad* 15:605–7. [Tr.]

He shows, however, in the *Odyssey* (and this further observation deserves attention on many grounds) that, when a great genius is declining, the special token of old age is the love of marvellous tales. 12. It is clear from many indications that the *Odyssey* was his second subject. A special proof is the fact that he introduces in that poem remnants of the adventures before Ilium as episodes, so to say, of the Trojan War. And indeed, he there renders a tribute of mourning and lamentation to his heroes as though he were carrying out a long-cherished purpose. In fact, the *Odyssey* is simply an epilogue to the Iliad:

> There lieth Ajax the warrior wight, Achilles is there,
> There is Patroclus, whose words had weight as a God he were:
> There lieth mine own dear son.[17]

13. It is for the same reason, I suppose, that he has made the whole structure of the Iliad, which was written at the height of his inspiration, full of action and conflict, while the *Odyssey* for the most part consists of narrative, as is characteristic of old age. Accordingly, in the *Odyssey* Homer may be likened to a sinking sun, whose grandeur remains without its intensity. He does not in the *Odyssey* maintain so high a pitch as in those poems of Ilium. His sublimities are not evenly sustained and free from the liability to sink; there is not the same profusion of accumulated passions, nor the supple and oratorical style, packed with images drawn from real life. You seem to see henceforth the ebb and flow of greatness, and a fancy roving in the fabulous and incredible, as though the ocean were withdrawing into itself and were being laid bare within its own confines. 14. In saying this I have not forgotten the tempests in the Odyssey and the story of the Cyclops and the like. If I speak of old age, it is neverthe-less the old age of Homer. The fabulous element, however, prevails throughout this poem over the real. The object of this digression has been, as I said, to show how easily great natures in their decline are sometimes diverted into absurdity, as in the incident of the wine-skin, and of the

men who were fed like swine by Circe (*whin-ing porkers*, as Zoilus called them), and of Zeus like a nestling nurtured by the doves, and of the hero who was without food for ten days upon the wreck, and of the incredible tale of the slaying of the suitors.[18] For what else can we term these things than veritable dreams of Zeus? 15. These observations with regard to the *Odyssey* should be made for another reason — in order that you may know that the genius of great poets and prose-writers, as their passion declines, finds its final expression in the delineation of character. For such are the details which Homer gives, with an eye to characterization, of life in the home of Odysseus; they form as it were a comedy of manners.

10

Let us next consider whether we can point to anything further that contributes to sublimity of style. Now, there inhere in all things by nature certain constituents which are part and parcel of their substance. It must needs be, therefore, that we shall find one source of the sublime in the systematic selection of the most important ele-ments, and the power of forming, by their mutual combination, what may be called one body. The former process attracts the hearer by the choice of the ideas, the latter by the aggregation of those chosen. For instance, Sappho everywhere chooses the emotions that attend delirious passion from its accompaniments in actual life. Wherein does she demonstrate her supreme excellence? In the skill with which she selects and binds together the most striking and vehement circumstances of passion:

> 2. Peer of Gods he seemeth to me, the blissful
> Man who sits and gazes at thee before him,
> Close beside thee sits, and in silence hears thee
> Silverly speaking,
> Laughing love's low laughter. Oh this, this only

---

[17] Homer, *Odyssey* 3:109–11. [Tr.]

[18] Five incidents from the *Odyssey*. The Cyclops at 9:192; Aiolos's wineskin at 10:17; the metamorphosis at 10:237; Zeus's doves at 12:62; Odysseus's fast at 12:447; the slaying of the suitors at 22:79–380.

Stirs the troubled heart in my breast to tremble!
For should I but see thee a little moment,
   Straight is my voice hushed;

Yea, my tongue is broken, and through and
   through me
'Neath the flesh impalpable fire runs tingling;
Nothing see mine eyes, and a noise of roaring
   Waves in my ear sounds;

Sweat runs down in rivers, a tremor seizes
All my limbs, and paler than grass in autumn,
Caught by pains of menacing death, I falter,
   Lost in the love-trance.

3. Are you not amazed how at one instant she summons, as though they were all alien from herself and dispersed, soul, body, ears, tongue, eyes, color? Uniting contradictions, she is, at one and the same time, hot and cold, in her senses and out of her mind, for she is either terrified or at the point of death. The effect desired is that not one passion only should be seen in her, but a concourse of the passions. All such things occur in the case of lovers, but it is, as I said, the selection of the most striking of them and their combination into a single whole that has produced the singular excellence of the passage. In the same way Homer, when describing tempests, picks out the most appalling circumstances. 4. The author of the *Arimaspeia* thinks to inspire awe in the following way:

A marvel exceeding great is this withal to my
   soul —
Men dwell on the water afar from the land, where
   deep seas roll.
Wretches are they, for they reap but a harvest of
   travail and pain,
Their eyes on the stars ever dwell, while their
   hearts abide in the main.
Often, I ween, to the Gods are their hands upraised
   on high,
And with hearts in misery heavenward-lifted in
   prayer do they cry.

It is clear, I imagine, to everybody that there is more elegance than terror in these words. 5. But what says Homer? Let one instance be quoted from among many:

And he burst on them like as a wave swift-rushing
   beneath black clouds,
Heaved huge by the winds, bursts down on a ship,
   and the wild foam shrouds

From the stem to the stern her hull, and the storm-
   blast's terrible breath
Roars in the sail, and the heart of the shipmen
   shuddereth
In fear, for that scantly upborne are they now from
   the clutches of death.[19]

6. Aratus has attempted to convert this same expression to his own use:

And a slender plank averteth their death.

Only, he has made it trivial and neat instead of terrible. Furthermore, he has put bounds to the danger by saying *A plank keeps off death.* After all, it *does* keep it off. Homer, however, does not for one moment set a limit to the terror of the scene, but draws a vivid picture of men continually in peril of their lives, and often within an ace of perishing with each successive wave. Moreover, he has in the words ὑπὲκ θανάτοιο, forced into union, by a kind of unnatural compulsion, prepositions not usually compounded.[20] He has thus tortured his line into the similitude of the impending calamity, and by the constriction of the verse has excellently figured the disaster, and almost stamped upon the expression the very form and pressure of the danger, ὑπὲκ θανάτοιο φέρονται. 7. This is true also of Archilochus in his account of the shipwreck, and of Demosthenes in the passage which begins "It was evening," where he describes the bringing of the news.[21] The salient points they selected, one might say, according to merit and massed them together, inserting in the midst nothing frivolous, mean, or trivial. For these faults mar the effect of the whole, just as though they introduced chinks or fissures into stately and co-ordered edifices, whose walls are compacted by their reciprocal adjustment.

II

An allied excellence to those already set forth is that which is termed *amplification*. This figure is employed when the narrative or the course

---

[19]Homer, *Iliad* 15:624–28. [Tr.]
[20]The point is that Homer has created an unusual compound word — *hypek*, out of *hyper* ("up") and *ek* ("out of"): "up out of death."
[21]Demosthenes, *On the Crown*, 169. [Tr.]

of a forensic argument admits, from section to section, of many starting points and many pauses, and elevated expressions follow, one after the other, in an unbroken succession and in an ascending order. 2. And this may be effected either by way of the rhetorical treatment of commonplaces, or by way of intensification (whether events or arguments are to be strongly presented), or by the orderly arrangement of facts or of passions; indeed, there are innumerable kinds of amplification. Only, the orator must in every case remember that none of these methods by itself, apart from sublimity, forms a complete whole, unless indeed where pity is to be excited or an opponent to be disparaged. In all other cases of amplification, if you take away the sublime, you will remove as it were the soul from the body. For the vigor of the amplification at once loses its intensity and its substance when not resting on a firm basis of the sublime. 3. Clearness, however, demands that we should define concisely how our present precepts differ from the point under consideration a moment ago, namely the marking-out of the most striking conceptions and the unification of them; and wherein, generally, the sublime differs from amplification.

12

Now the definition given by the writers on rhetoric does not satisfy me. Amplification is, say they, discourse which invests the subject with grandeur. This definition, however, would surely apply in equal measure to sublimity and passion and figurative language, since they too invest the discourse with a certain degree of grandeur. The point of distinction between them seems to me to be that sublimity consists in elevation, while amplification embraces a multitude of details. Consequently, sublimity is often comprised in a single thought, while amplification is universally associated with a certain magnitude and abundance. 2. Amplification (to sum the matter up in a general way) is an aggregation of all the constituent parts and topics of a subject, lending strength to the argument by dwelling upon it, and differing herein from proof that, while the latter demonstrates the matter under investigation. . . .

With his vast riches Plato swells, like some sea, into a greatness which expands on every side. 3. Wherefore it is, I suppose, that the orator in his utterance shows, as one who appeals more to the passions, all the glow of a fiery spirit. Plato, on the other hand, firm-planted in his pride and magnificent stateliness, cannot indeed be accused of coldness, but he has not the same vehemence. 4. And it is in these same respects, my dear friend Terentianus, that it seems to me (supposing always that we Greeks are allowed to have an opinion upon the point) that Cicero differs from Demosthenes in elevated passages. For the latter is characterized by sublimity which is for the most part rugged, Cicero by profusion. Our orator,[22] owing to the fact that in his vehemence — aye, and in his speed, power and intensity — he can as it were consume by fire and carry away all before him, may be compared to a thunderbolt or flash of lightning. Cicero, on the other hand, it seems to me, after the manner of a widespread conflagration, rolls on with all-devouring flames, having within him an ample and abiding store of fire, distributed now at this point now at that, and fed by an unceasing succession. 5. This, however, you will be better able to decide; but the great opportunity of Demosthenes' high-pitched elevation comes where intense utterance and vehement passion are in question, and in passages in which the audience is to be utterly enthralled. The profusion of Cicero is in place where the hearer must be flooded with words, for it is appropriate to the treatment of commonplaces, and to perorations for the most part and digressions, and to all descriptive and declamatory passages, and to writings on history and natural science, and to many other departments of literature.

13

To return from my digression. Although Plato thus flows on with noiseless stream, he is nonetheless elevated. You know this because you have read the Republic and are familiar with his

22 Demosthenes. He is "our" orator because Longinus is a Greek writing to a Roman.

manner. "Those," says he, "who are destitute of wisdom and goodness and are ever present at carousals and the like are carried on the downward path, it seems, and wander thus throughout their life. They never look upwards to the truth, nor do they lift their heads, nor enjoy any pure and lasting pleasure, but like cattle they have their eyes ever cast downwards and bent upon the ground and upon their feeding-places, and they graze and grow fat and breed, and through their insatiate desire of these delights they kick and butt with horns and hoofs of iron and kill one another in their greed."[23]

2. This writer shows us, if only we were willing to pay him heed, that another way (beyond anything we have mentioned) leads to the sublime. And what, and what manner of way, may that be? It is the imitation and emulation of previous great poets and writers. And let this, my dear friend, be an aim to which we steadfastly apply ourselves. For many men are carried away by the spirit of others as if inspired, just as it is related of the Pythian priestess when she approaches the tripod, where there is a rift in the ground which (they say) exhales divine vapor. By heavenly power thus communicated she is impregnated and straightway delivers oracles in virtue of the afflatus. Similarly from the great natures of the men of old there are borne in upon the souls of those who emulate them (as from sacred caves) what we may describe as *effluences,* so that even those who seem little likely to be possessed are thereby inspired and succumb to the spell of the others' greatness. 3. Was Herodotus alone a devoted imitator of Homer? No, Stesichorus even before his time, and Archilochus, and above all Plato, who from the great Homeric source drew to himself innumerable tributary streams. And perhaps we should have found it necessary to prove this, point by point, had not Ammonius and his followers selected and recorded the particulars. 4. This proceeding is not plagiarism; it is like taking an impression from beautiful forms or figures or other works of art. And it seems to me that there would not have been so fine a bloom of perfection on Plato's philosophical doctrines, and that he would not in many cases have found

his way to poetical subject matter and modes of expression, unless he had with all his heart and mind struggled with Homer for the primacy, entering the lists like a young champion matched against the man whom all admire, and showing perhaps too much love of contention and breaking a lance with him as it were, but deriving some profit from the contest nonetheless. For, as Hesiod says, "This strife is good for mortals."[24] And in truth that struggle for the crown of glory is noble and best deserves the victory in which even to be worsted by one's predecessors brings no discredit.

14

Accordingly it is well that we ourselves also, when elaborating anything which requires lofty expression and elevated conception, should shape some idea in our minds as to how perchance Homer would have said this very thing, or how it would have been raised to the sublime by Plato or Demosthenes or by the historian Thucydides. For those personages, presenting themselves to us and inflaming our ardor and as it were illumining our path, will carry our minds in a mysterious way to the high standards of sublimity which are imaged within us. 2. Still more effectual will it be to suggest this question to our thoughts, "What sort of hearing would Homer, had he been present, or Demosthenes have given to this or that when said by me, or how would they have been affected by the other?" For the ordeal is indeed a severe one, if we presuppose such a tribunal and theater for our own utterances, and imagine that we are undergoing a scrutiny of our writings before these great heroes, acting as judges and witnesses. 3. A greater incentive still will be supplied if you add the question, "In what spirit will each succeeding age listen to me who have written thus?" But if one shrinks from the very thought of uttering aught that may transcend the term of his own life and time, the conceptions of his mind must necessarily be incomplete, blind, and as it were untimely born, since they are by no means brought to the perfection needed to ensure a futurity of fame.

[23]Plato, *Republic* 9:586a. [Tr.]

[24]Hesiod, *Works and Days,* 24. [Tr.]

It remains however (as I will not hesitate to add) in recognition of your love of knowledge) to clear up, my dear Terentianus, a question which a certain philosopher has recently mooted. "I wonder," he says, "as no doubt do many others, how it happens that in our time there are men who have the gift of persuasion to the utmost extent, and are well fitted for public life, and are keen and ready, and particularly rich in all the charms of language, yet there no longer arise really lofty and transcendent natures unless quite exceptionally. So great and worldwide a dearth of high utterance attends our age." 2. "Can it be," he continued, "that we are to accept the trite explanation that democracy is the kind nursing-mother of genius, and that literary power may be said to share its rise and fall with democracy and democracy alone? For freedom, it is said, has power to feed the imaginations of the lofty-minded and to inspire hope, and where it prevails there spreads abroad the eagerness of mutual rivalry and the emulous pursuit of the foremost place. 3. Moreover, owing to the prizes which are open to all under popular government, the mental excellences of the orator are continually exercised and sharpened, and as it were rubbed bright, and shine forth (as it is natural they should) with all the freedom which inspires the doings of the state. Today," he went on, "we seem in our boyhood to learn the lessons of a righteous servitude, being all but enswathed in its customs and observances, when our thoughts are yet young and tender, and never tasting the fairest and most productive source of eloquence (by which," he added, "I mean freedom), so that we emerge in no other guise than that of sublime flatterers." 4. This is the reason, he maintained, why no slave ever becomes an orator, although all other faculties may belong to menials. In the slave there immediately burst out signs of fettered liberty of speech, of the dungeon as it were, of a man habituated to buffetings. 5. "For the day of slavery," as Homer has it, "takes away half our manhood."25 "Just as," he proceeded, "the cages (if what I hear is true) in which are kept the Pygmies, commonly called

25Homer, *Odyssey* 17:322. [Tr.]

nani, not only hinder the growth of the creatures confined within them, but actually attenuate them through the bonds which beset their bodies, so one has aptly termed all servitude (though it be most righteous) the cage of the soul and a public prisonhouse." 6. I answered him thus: "It is easy, my good sir, and characteristic of human nature, to find fault with the age in which one lives. But consider whether it may not be true that it is not the world's peace that ruins great natures, but far rather this war illimitable which holds our desires in its grasp, aye, and further still those passions which occupy as with troops our present age and utterly harry and plunder it. For the love of money (a disease from which we all now suffer sorely) and the love of pleasure make us their thralls, or rather, as one may say, drown us body and soul in the depths, the love of riches being a malady which makes men petty, and the love of pleasure one which makes them most ignoble. 7. On reflection I cannot discover how it is possible for us, if we value boundless wealth so highly, or (to speak more truly) deify it, to avoid allowing the entrance into our souls of the evils which are inseparable from it. For vast and unchecked wealth is accompanied, in close conjunction and step for step as they say, by extravagance, and as soon as the former opens the gates of cities and houses, the latter immediately enters and abides. And when time has passed the pair build nests in the lives of men, as the wise say, and quickly give themselves to the rearing of offspring, and breed ostentation, and vanity, and luxury, no spurious progeny of theirs, but only too legitimate. If these children of wealth are permitted to come to maturity, straightway they beget in the soul inexorable masters — insolence, and lawlessness, and shamelessness. 8. This must necessarily happen, and men will no longer lift up their eyes or have any further regard for fame, but the ruin of such lives will gradually reach its complete consummation and sublimities of soul fade and wither away and become contemptible, when men are lost in admiration of their own mortal parts and omit to exalt that which is immortal. 9. For a man who has once accepted a bribe for a judicial decision cannot be an unbiased and upright judge of what is just and honorable (since to the man who is venal his own interests must seem honorable and just), and the same is true where the entire life of each of us is ordered by bribes, and huntings after the death of others, and the laying of ambushes for legacies, while gain from any and every source we purchase — each one of us — at the price of life itself, being the slaves of pleasure. In an age which is ravaged by plagues so sore, is it possible for us to imagine that there is still left an unbiased and incorruptible judge of works that are great and likely to reach posterity, or is it not rather the case that all are influenced in their decisions by the passion for gain? 10. Nay, it is perhaps better for men like ourselves to be ruled than to be free, since our appetites, if let loose without restraint upon our neighbors like beasts from a cage, would set the world on fire with deeds of evil. 11. Summing up, I maintained that among the banes of the natures which our age produces must be reckoned that half-heartedness in which the life of all of us with few exceptions is passed, for we do not labor or exert ourselves except for the sake of praise and pleasure, never for those solid benefits which are a worthy object of our own efforts and the respect of others. 12. But "'tis best to leave these riddles unresolved,"[26] and to proceed to what next presents itself, namely the subject of the Passions, about which I previously undertook to write in a separate treatise. These form, as it seems to me, a material part of discourse generally and of the Sublime itself.

[26]Euripides, *Electra,* 379. [Tr.]

Dante Alighieri
1265–1321

Dante Alighieri was born in Florence, the son of Alighiero Alighieri of the lesser nobility. His mother died when Dante was quite young, and his father, whom Dante mentions seldom and then only formally, remarried and produced a large second family. Dante was well educated, probably by the Franciscans; his rhetoric tutor was Brunetto Latini. Around 1285, Dante married Gemma Donati, by whom he had two sons and two daughters. Gemma's influence on his life pales, however, beside the radiance of another Florentine noblewoman, Bice Portinari, whom Dante dubbed "Beatrice," the bringer of blessing. Dante's contacts with Beatrice (who married Simone dei Bardi) were undoubtedly few and platonic in the years before her death in 1290, but she became his lifelong Muse and his guide through Paradise in the *Commedia*.

Although Dante experimented with verse in his twenties (under the influence of the poet Guido Cavalcanti), his life was devoted to public affairs: He fought in 1289 in the battle of Campaldino, spoke in the Florentine assembly, and became one of the six priors of Florence. While Dante was away from Florence on a diplomatic mission in 1300, factional warfare broke out: a rival party came to power and convicted Dante in absentia of graft and corruption in office. Under sentence of death if he returned, Dante spent the rest of his life abroad, where he learned "how salt is the bread of exile and how steep the stairs of another." Except for the *Vita Nuova*, which was written in Florence in 1292, most of Dante's works are the product of his exile, including the *Convivio* ("The Banquet," 1304–08), the *De Monarchia* (1308), and his masterpiece, the *Commedia* (1306–14) — "Divina" was added by its readers. Dante's literary life was spent wandering between Verona (where his patrons included Can Grande della Scala) and other intellectual centers such as Bologna and Paris. He finally settled in Ravenna, where he died in 1321.

Dante's letter to Can Grande is the most familiar exposition of medieval semiotic theory: the ideas are not original with Dante, but have a long and distinguished history. In the sixth century, St. Augustine had claimed in *Of the Value of Belief* that the Old Testament was to be interpreted as "history, etiology, analogy, and allegory." During the Middle Ages, the Hebrew bible was interpreted not only as the literal history of the Israelites, but as prefiguring events in the life of Christ. And in the thirteenth century, St. Thomas Aquinas's *Summa Theologica* had codified this mode of interpreting scripture:

That first signification whereby words signify things belongs to the first sense, the historical. . . . That signification whereby things signified by words have themselves also a signification is called the spiritual sense. . . . Now this spiritual sense has a threefold division. . . . So far as the things of the Old Law signify the things of the New Law, there is the allegorical sense. . . . So far as the things done in Christ . . . are signs of what we ought to do, there is the moral sense. . . . But so far as they signify what relates to eternal glory, there is the anagogical sense.

Dante's principal innovation, if indeed it is an innovation, is in applying these principles of symbolic meaning to something other than sacred scripture — to his

Commedia, a poetical work written in the "vulgar" language of common speech. Some medievalists (the followers of D. W. Robertson) have suggested that this multivalent mode of reading was part of the freight of medieval literacy, and that even apparently secular texts (like Chaucer's *Canterbury Tales,* or Boccaccio's *Decameron*) were automatically read in this manner. Whether this was actually the case is controversial, but certainly with the coming of the Renaissance, this mode of reading began to fade away, and the notion that all literature was potentially ambiguous — indeed, that the mark of literature was ambiguity and multiplicity of interpretation — would not return until Northrop Frye and William Empson in the middle of the twentieth century.

Selected Bibliography

Alighieri, Dante. *The Divine Comedy.* Translated and with a commentary by Charles S. Singleton. Princeton: Princeton University Press, 1970–75.

Dunbar, Helen Flanders. *Symbolism in Medieval Thought.* New Haven: Yale University Press, 1929.

Ginsberg, Warren. *Dante's Aesthetics of Being.* Ann Arbor: University of Michigan Press, 1999.

Hollander, Robert. *Allegory in Dante's Commedia.* Princeton: Princeton University Press, 1969.

Kirkpatrick, Robin. *Dante's Paradiso and the Limitations of Modern Criticism: A Study of Style and Poetic Theory.* Cambridge: Cambridge University Press, 1978.

Pietrobono, Luigi. "L'epistola a Can Grande." *Giornale dantesco* 4 (1939): 3–51.

Saley, John V. *Dante and the English Romantics.* New York: Columbia University Library, 1960.

Singleton, Charles S. *Dante Studies.* 2 vols. Cambridge: Harvard University Press, 1954–58.

Tock, J. F. *L'etterno piacer: Aesthetic Ideas in Dante.* Oxford: Clarendon Press, 1984.

Toynbee, Paget Jackson. *Dante in English Literature from Chaucer to Cary.* 2 vols. London: Methuen, 1909.

From *Letter to Can Grande della Scala*

5. As the Philosopher says in the second book of the *Metaphysics,* "As a thing is with respect to being, so it is with respect to truth";[1] and the reason for this is that the truth concerning a thing, which consists in the truth as its subject, is the perfect image of the thing as it is. And so, of all things which have being, some are such that they have absolute being in themselves, others such that their being is dependent upon a relationship with something else: they exist at the same time with something which is their correlative, as is the case with father and son, master and servant, double and half, the whole and the parts, and many other such things. Because such things depend for their being upon another thing, it follows that their truth would depend upon the truth of the other; not knowing the "half," its "double" could not be understood, and so with the other cases.

Translated by Robert S. Haller.

[1]Aristotle, *Metaphysics* 2.1 [Tr.]

6. Therefore, if one should wish to present an introduction to a part of a work, it is necessary to present some conception of the whole work of which it is a part. For this reason I, who wish to present something in the form of an introduction to the above-mentioned part of the whole *Comedy*,² have decided to preface it with some discussion of the whole work, in order to make the approach to the part easier and more complete. There are six questions, then, which should be asked at the beginning about any doctrinal work: what is its subject, its form, its agent, its end, the title of the book, and its branch of philosophy. In three cases the answers to these questions will be different for the part of the work I propose to give you than for the whole, that is, in the cases of its subject, form, and title, while in the other three, as will be clear upon inspection, they will be the same. Thus these first three should be specifically asked in a discussion of the whole work, after which the way will be clear for an introduction to the part. Let us, then, ask the last three questions about the whole but also about the part itself.

7. For the clarification of what I am going to say, then, it should be understood that there is not just a single sense in this work; it might rather be called *polysemous*, that is, having several senses. For the first sense is that which is contained in the letter, while there is another which is contained in what is signified by the letter. The first is called literal, while the second is called allegorical, or moral or anagogical. And in order to make this manner of treatment clear, it can be applied to the following verses: '"When Israel went out of Egypt, the house of Jacob from a barbarous people, Judea was made his sanctuary, Israel his dominion."³ Now if we look at the letter alone, what is signified to us is the departure of the sons of Israel from Egypt during the time of Moses; if at the allegory, what is signified to us is our redemption through Christ; if at the moral sense, what is signified to us is the conversion of the soul from the sorrow and misery of sin to the state of grace; if at the anagogical, what is signified to us is the departure of the sanctified soul from bondage to the corruption of this world into the freedom of eternal glory. And although these mystical senses are called by various names, they may all be called allegorical, since they are all different from the literal or historical. For allegory is derived from the Greek *alleon*, which means in Latin *alienus* ("belonging to another") or *diversus* ("different").

8. This being established, it is clear that the subject about which these two senses play must also be twofold. And thus it should first be noted what the subject of the work is when taken according to the letter, and then what its subject is when understood allegorically. The subject of the whole work, then, taken literally, is the state of souls after death, understood in a simple sense; for the whole movement of the work turns upon this and about this. If on the other hand the work is taken allegorically, the subject is man, in the exercise of his free will, earning or becoming liable to the rewards or punishments of justice.

9. And the form is twofold: the form of the treatise and the form of the treatment. The form of the treatise is threefold, according to its three kinds of division. The first division is that which divides the whole work into three canticles. The second is that which divides each canticle into cantos. The third, that which divides the cantos into rhymed units. The form or manner of treatment is poetic, fictive, descriptive, digressive, and transumptive, and it as well consists in definition, division, proof, refutation, and the giving of examples.

10. The title of the work is, '"Here begins the Comedy of Dante Alighieri, a Florentine by birth but not in character." To understand the title, it must be known that comedy is derived from *comos*, "a village," and *oda*, "a song," so that a comedy is, so to speak, "a rustic song." Comedy, then, is a certain genre of poetic narrative differing from all others. For it differs from tragedy in its matter, in that tragedy is tranquil and conducive to wonder at the beginning, but foul and conducive to horror at the end, or catastrophe, for which reason it is derived from *tragos*, meaning "goat," and *oda*, making it, as it were, a "goat song," that is, foul as a goat is foul.

²His *Divine Comedy*.

³Psalm 113:1–2 (114:1–2 in the King James version). [Tr.]

This is evident in Seneca's tragedies. Comedy, on the other hand, introduces a situation of adversity, but ends its matter in prosperity, as is evident in Terence's comedies. And for this reason some writers have the custom of saying in their salutations, by way of greeting, "a tragic beginning and a comic ending to you." And, as well, they differ in their manner of speaking. Tragedy uses an elevated and sublime style, while comedy uses an unstudied and low style, which is what Horace implies in the *Art of Poetry* where he allows comic writers occasionally to speak like the tragic, and also the reverse of this:

> Yet sometimes even comedy elevates its voice, and angry Chremes rages in swelling tones; and in tragedy Telephus and Peleus often lament in prosaic speeches. . . .[4]

So from this it should be clear why the present work is called the *Comedy*. For, if we consider the matter, it is, at the beginning, that is, in Hell, foul and conducive to horror, but at the end, in Paradise, prosperous, conducive to pleasure, and welcome. And if we consider the manner of speaking, it is unstudied and low, since its speech is the vernacular, in which even women communicate. There are, besides these, other genres of poetic narrative, such as pastoral verse, elegy, satire, and the hymn of thanksgiving, as could also be gathered from Horace in his *Art of Poetry*. But there is no purpose to discussing these at this time.

11. Now it can be explained in what manner the part I have offered you may be assigned a subject. For if the subject of the whole work, on the literal level, is the state of souls after death, in an absolute, not in a restricted sense, then the subject of this part is the same state, but restricted to the state of blessed souls after death. And if the subject of the whole work, considered allegorically, is man, through exercise of free will, earning or becoming liable to the rewards or punishments of justice, then it is evident that the subject in this part is restricted to man's becoming eligible, to the extent he has earned them, for the rewards of justice.

12. And in the same manner the form of this part follows from the form ascribed to the whole. For if the form of the whole treatise is threefold, then the form in this part is twofold, that is, the division into cantos and into rhymed units. This part could not have the first division as its form, since this part itself is [a product] of the first division.

13. The title of the book also follows; for while the title of the whole book is, as was said earlier, "Here begins the Comedy, etc.," the title of this part is, "Here begins the third canticle of Dante's *Comedy*, etc., which is called *Paradise*."

14. Having settled these three questions, where the answer was different for the part than for the whole, it remains to deal with the other three, where the answers will not be different for either the part or the whole. The agent, then, in the whole and in the part, is he who has been mentioned above; and he is clearly so throughout.

15. The end of the whole and of the part could be multiple, that is, both immediate and ultimate. But, without going into details, it can be briefly stated that the end of the whole as of the part is to remove those living in this life from the state of misery and to lead them to the state of happiness.

16. The branch of philosophy which determines the procedure of the work as a whole and in this part is moral philosophy, or ethics, inasmuch as the whole and this part have been conceived for the sake of practical results, not for the sake of speculation. So even if some parts or passages are treated in the manner of speculative philosophy, this is not for the sake of the theory, but for a practical purpose, following that principle which the Philosopher advances in the second book of the *Metaphysics*, that "practical men sometimes speculate about things in their particular and temporal relations."[5]

[4] Horace, *Art of Poetry*, 93–96. [Tr.] See Horace, p. 77.

[5] Aristotle, *Metaphysics* 2.1.

Christine de Pisan

1365–ca. 1431

Christine de Pisan, one of the most remarkable literary women of the Middle Ages, was born in Venice, daughter of civil councillor Tommaso di Benvenuto da Pizzano, a citizen of both scientific and medical accomplishments. Shortly after Christine's birth, Tommaso became Court Astrologer to Charles V of France, a position he held until Charles's death in 1380. During the quarrelsome regency at the time of the minority of Charles VI, Tommaso's salary and perquisites were cut, the family's fortunes declined, and, after a long illness, he died around 1385. Meanwhile, however, Christine had received a literary education at court that would have been unusual for a nobleman of the time, much less a woman.[1] This was owing to her father's encouragement, but over her mother's protests; as Christine put it in *The Book of the City of Ladies* (1405), "Your father, who was a great scientist and philosopher, did not believe that women were worth less by knowing science; rather . . . he took great pleasure from seeing your inclination to learning. The feminine opinion of your mother, however, who worked to keep you busy with spinning and silly girlishness . . . was the major obstacle" (II.37.4).[2] In 1380, Christine was married — apparently happily — to a rising young courtier from Picardy, Estienne de Castel, notary to the King, by whom she had three children, including at least one son and one daughter who survived into adulthood. Estienne, traveling with the court to Beauvais, died during an epidemic in 1390, leaving Christine to deal with the responsibility of her mother and three children while Estienne's inheritance was tied up in legal disputes. She had to go to work, and the work she chose was literature. For more than two decades starting around 1393, Christine was what today would be called a professional writer, working in most of the dominant prose and poetical genres of her day: lyric and narrative poetry, penitential psalms and proverbs, biography and history, literary criticism; as well she produced a courtesy manual and even an essay on military strategy compiled from classical authors. She tended to give her personal slant to conventional forms: Her poem on the mutability of fortune, for example, in addition to giving well-known cases of historical figures raised and then thrown down by Fortune's Wheel, presents her own life as a case in point.

Christine was an exceptionally successful writer. Her patrons included King Charles VI of France, for whom she wrote a biography of his father, Louis the dauphin; Charles King of Navarre; Jean duc de Berry; and Charles the Bold and Jean Sans Peur, dukes of Burgundy; and she was invited to the courts of London and Milan. Her works were translated into English, Italian, and other vernacular languages, and she carefully supervised, as few vernacular writers had done, the

[1]Christine wrote exclusively in the French vernacular, but must have known how to read Latin in order to participate in the fifteenth-century debate known as the *Querelle de la Rose*, from which the following selection is taken.

[2]Christine de Pisan. *The Book of the City of Ladies*. Translated and with an introduction by Earl Jeffrey Richards (New York: Persea, 1982), II.37.4.

illumination of her manuscripts. Christine seems to have fallen silent around the time of the Burgundian massacres at Paris in 1418, and she is thought to have secluded herself in her daughter's convent, St. Louis de Poissy. But she emerged once more to write *La Ditié de Jehanne d'Arc* (1429), the only celebratory poem on Joan of Arc written in Joan's lifetime. After this there is only silence, and it is supposed that Christine died at Poissy around 1431.

The *Querelle de la Rose,* a literary debate that took place in the opening years of the fifteenth century, pitted Christine and her powerful ally Jean Gerson, the chancellor of the University of Paris, against the humanist royal secretaries Gontier and Pierre Col and Jean de Montreuil, provost of Lille, in a moralistic attack on the literary quality and effect of the *Roman de la Rose,* one of the masterworks of the Middle Ages. Enormously influential on Chaucer and his contemporaries, the *Roman de la Rose* (or *Romance of the Rose*), is an allegorical love poem begun around 1225 by Guillaume de Lorris and completed and augmented around 1275 by Jean de Meun, which describes the ultimately successful quest of a lover for the mystical and fleshly Rose. As usual, time has been on the side of the *Rose*'s defenders, rather than the moralists, and it may not be easy to understand what so disturbed Christine and Gerson. Christine seems to view her society as spiritually adrift and to attribute this lack of standards in part to the popularity of attractive but immoral literature. As E. J. Richards puts it, "The French court was left to its own devices during the frequent spells of insanity which plagued Charles VI. Charles' queen, Isabella of Bavaria, led a licentious and frivolous existence. Not surprisingly, Christine and Gerson connected the immorality of their day with the popularity of the *Rose*."[3]

For Christine, the *Rose* was also threatening because it reinforced the dominant misogyny of the Middle Ages, representing women as unchaste objects of desire. Men get away with such misrepresentation, Christine says, because they own the pen and thus "can tell endless tales and keep the best parts for themselves" with impunity; "my answer is that women did not write these books. . . . They know they stand wrongfully accused. If women had written these books, I know full well the matter would have been handled differently." Christine finds the *Rose* shameful, not merely for its sexual frankness, but for the manners and morals it attributes to women.

In her later, more explicitly feminist treatise, *The Book of the City of Ladies,* written as an antidote to Ovid's *Remedia amoris* and to Boccaccio's stories in *De mulieribus claris,* Christine sets forth representations of admirable women from the present as well as legendary times, middle-class dames as well as noblewomen and queens. The treatise is not merely a defense of women against the standard masculine accusations, but a reinscription of femininity suggesting that standard male virtues — including learning, bravery, leadership, and magnanimity — are not limited to men at all, that women have been capable of them in the past and would be so more frequently were their opportunities less limited by restrictive social roles. By the end of her life, Christine found her vision of the ideal woman embodied in Joan of Arc, whom she represented as a chaste but heroic girl whose courage and fortitude could lead France to secular and spiritual salvation.

[3]From E. J. Richards's introduction to *The Book of the City of Ladies* (New York: Persea, 1982), pp. 31–32.

Selected Bibliography

Altmann, Barbara K., Deborah L. McGrady, and Charity Cannon Willard. *Christine de Pizan: A Casebook.* New York: Routledge, 2003.

Baird, Joseph L. and John R. Kane, eds. *La Querelle de la Rose: Letters and Documents.* Chapel Hill: North Carolina Studies in Romance Languages and Literatures, 1978.

Brown-Grant, Rosalind. *Christine de Pizan and the Moral Defense of Women: Reading Beyond Genre.* Cambridge Studies in Medieval Literature 40. Cambridge: Cambridge University Press, 1999.

Christine de Pisan. *Oeuvres Poétiques,* ed. Maurice Roy, 3 vols. 1886; New York: Johnson Reprint Corporation, 1965.

———. *The Book of the City of Ladies.* Translated and with an introduction by Earl Jeffrey Richards. New York: Persea, 1982.

Kelly, F. Douglas. "Reflections on the Role of Christine de Pisan as a Feminist Writer." *Sub-Stance* 2 (1972): 63–71.

McLeod, Enid. *The Order of the Rose: The Life and Ideas of Christine de Pizan.* Totowa, NJ: Rowman and Littlefield, 1976.

Quilligan, Maureen. *The Allegory of Female Authority: Christine de Pizan's Cité de Dames.* Ithaca: Cornell University Press, 1991.

Willard, Charity Cannon. *Christine de Pizan: Her Life and Works.* New York: Persea, 1984.

Yenal, Edith. *Christine de Pisan: A Bibliography.* Metuchen, NJ: Scarecrow Press, 1989.

From *La Querelle de la Rose*

To the very competent and wise person, Master John,[1] Secretary of the King our Lord and Provost of Lisle.

Reverence, honor, and due respect to you, Lord Provost of Lisle, esteemed Master, sage in morals, lover of knowledge, steeped in learning, and expert in rhetoric; from me, Christine de Pisan, a woman weak in understanding and inadequate in learning — for which things may your sagacity not hold in scorn the smallness of my reasons; rather may it take into account my feminine weakness. It has pleased you out of your goodness (for which I say thanks) to send me a small treatise expressed in fine language and true-seeming reasons. Your treatise was written, as I gather from your own words, to oppose critics of certain parts of the *Roman de la Rose,* to give firm support to the work, and to approve it and its authors, and in particular Meun.[2] Having read and considered your letter and having understood it, within the limits of my ability, I disagreed with your remarks and shared the opinion of the learned man to whom your letter was addressed. Therefore, although your letter was not addressed to me and did not require a reply, nevertheless I wish to say, to divulge, and to maintain openly that (saving your good grace) you are in grave error to give such lavish and unjustified praise to Meun's book — one which could better be called plain idleness[3] than useful work, in my judgment. You severely criticize his opponents and say, "that a great thing is therein

[1]Christine writes "Jehan Johannes," which was a frequent designation for Jean de Monteuil. [Trs.]

[2]Monteuil's original treatise, the first document in the debate known as *La Querelle de la Rose,* has been lost.

[3]Christine's word here is *oisiveté.* Is this not a half-amused allusion to Lady *Oiseuse,* keeper of the wicket gate of the garden in the *Roman de la Rose?* Not only is the garden kept by Lady Idleness, but also the entire romance, which, for all the effort and industry that went into it, is mere trifling "idleness." [Trs.]

Translated by Joseph L. Baird and John R. Kane.

to be understood," "that what a third party says gives a better testimony," "has constructed and erected through great study and at great length." Yet may my daring to repudiate and find fault with an author so worthy and so subtle not seem presumption in me. Rather, take heed of the firm conviction which has moved me to oppose some opinions contained in your letter. In truth, a mere assertion not justified by law can be re-argued without prejudice. I am not, I confess, learned nor schooled in the subtle language, which would make my arguments dazzling, a language which you indeed can display with a fine array of carefully polished words. Nevertheless, I will not hesitate to express my opinion bluntly in the vernacular, although I may not be able to express myself elegantly.

But why did I say before that Meun's work could best be called idleness? Certainly, it seems to me that any trivial thing, even though it is treated, composed, and accomplished with great labor and difficulty, can be called idle, or worse than idle, insofar as evil follows from it. Yet because of the great and widespread fame of the said romance, I had long desired to read it, and once I had gained the knowledge to understand subtle matters somewhat, I did read and consider it at length, to the best of my ability. It is true that the subject matter did not please me in certain parts and so I skipped over it as quickly as a cock over hot embers; therefore, I have not read it in every detail. Nevertheless, some things have remained in my memory which my judgment strongly condemned, and still cannot approve, despite the contrary praise of other people. It is quite true that my small understanding finds great prettiness there; in some parts, he expresses himself very well indeed, using beautiful terms and graceful leonine rhyme. He could not have treated his subject more subtly or more skillfully. But I agree with the opinion (which you clearly oppose, it seems to me) that he speaks too dishonorably in some parts of the *Roman de la Rose,* even when he speaks through the character he calls Reason, who names the secret members plainly by name. You, in fact, support Meun and say that such frankness is perfectly reasonable, maintaining that in the things God has made there is no ugliness, and consequently no need to eschew

their names. To this I say and confess that truly God created all things pure and clean coming from himself and that in the State of Innocence it would not have been wrong to name them; but by the pollution of sin man became impure, and his original sin has remained with us, as Holy Scripture testifies. I can make this clear by a comparison: God made Lucifer beautiful above all the angels and gave him a very solemn and beautiful name, but then Lucifer was reduced by his sin to horrible ugliness; whereupon, the name, albeit very beautiful in itself, now, because of the impression of the person, creates horror in those who hear it.

Further, you point out that Jesus Christ calls the women sinners *meretrix,*[4] etc. But I can explain to you why he called them by that name, because the name *meretrix* is not particularly dishonorable to utter considering the vileness of the thing named, and, in fact, it could have been more basely said even in Latin. Thus should modesty be respected when speaking publicly of things about which Nature herself is ashamed. Saving your reverence and the author's, I say that you commit great wrong against the noble virtue of modesty, which by its nature bridles indecency and dishonorable conduct in words and deeds. Holy Scripture makes clear in many places that this is a great wrong, outside the range of decent conduct and good morals. Moreover, I affirm that the indecent name should not be avoided by substituting the word "relics" for it. I suggest to you that the name does not make the thing dishonorable, but the thing, the name. Therefore, in my humble opinion, one should speak about such matters soberly and only when necessary, as in certain particular cases, such as sickness or other genuine need. Just as our first parents hid their private parts instinctively, so ought we to do in deed and in word.

Further, I cannot be silent about a subject that so displeases me: that the function of Reason, whom he even calls the daughter of God, should be to propound such a dictum as the one I found in the chapter where Reason says to the Lover,

[4]See Matthew XXI.31–32; Luke XV.30. [Trs.] *Meretrix* is Latin for prostitute.

''In the amorous war, it is better to deceive than to be deceived.'' And truly, Master Jean de Meun, I dare say that Reason denied her heavenly father in that teaching, for He taught an utterly different doctrine. If you hold one of these two to be better than the other, it would follow that both are good, and this cannot be. I hold a contrary opinion: it is far less evil, clearly, to be deceived than to deceive.

Further, let us consider the subject matter or choice of words, which many people find reprehensible. Dear Lord! What horrible stuff! What an affront to honor! What reprehensible teachings recorded in the chapter about the Old Woman! In God's name, what can one find there but sophistical exhortations filled with ugliness and things horrible to recall? Ha, you who have beautiful daughters! If you really want to introduce them to the honorable life, give them, give them, I say, this book so that they may learn from the *Roman de la Rose* ways to distinguish Good from Evil — what am I saying! — rather Evil from Good! To what purpose or to what profit is it that the hearers of this book have their ears assailed by so much sinfulness?

Then, in the chapter about jealousy, my God, what great good can be observed there! What need to record the dishonorable things and the shameful words, which are common enough in the mouths of the unfortunate people impassioned by this sickness! What good example or preparation for life could this be? And the wickedness which is there recorded of women! Many people attempt to excuse him by saying that it is the Jealous Man who speaks and that in truth Meun does no more than God himself did when He spoke through the mouth of Jeremiah! But whatever lying additions he may have made, he certainly could not have rendered worse or abased the condition of women more! Ha! When I remember the deceits, the hypocrisies, and the conduct dissembled within marriage and outside it, which one can find in this book — certainly, I consider these to be beautiful and edifying tales for one to hear!

Further, what great marvels does the character that he calls Genius the priest say! Surely, the works of Nature would have completely fallen into disuse long since, if he had not so greatly

recommended them! But, my God, who could show or convince me what profit there is in the great argument full of vituperation that he calls a sermon (as if to deride holy preaching), which, he says, Genius delivers? It contains too many dishonorable things, names, sophistical words, fanning the flames of those secrets of Nature which ought to be left tacit and not named. Moreover, the ''sermon'' is superfluous, for a work which is of the very order of Nature cannot, obviously, fail. If it were not so, then it would be good for the maintenance of human generation to invent and say exciting and inflaming words and terms in order to stimulate man to continue that work.

Yet the author does more, if I remember well; for the life of me I can't understand to what purpose. For in the said sermon he adduces, as a comparison, paradise and its joys. He says truly enough that the virtuous will go to that place, but he concludes that everyone, men and women alike, should know how to perform and exercise the functions of Nature; nor in this does he make any exception of law, as if he wished to say, and indeed says plainly, that they will all be saved. And by this it appears that he wishes to maintain that the sin of lechery is nothing, rather a virtue, which is error and against the law of God. Ha! what seed and what doctrine! What great good can come of it! I believe that many have left the world because of it and entered religion, or become hermits because of that holy message, or come out of the evil life and been saved by such exhortation! Certainly (I dare say it, no matter whom it offends), this never came from anywhere but a heart corrupted and abandoned to dissolution and vice, which can be the cause of great sin and unbecoming conduct.

And again, for God's sake, let us look a little further to see what profit there can possibly be in his excessive, impetuous, and most untruthful criticism and denigration of women as exceedingly wicked creatures! He declares that their conduct is filled with all manner of perversity, with which condemnations, even with all the give and take among his characters, he cannot fully gorge himself. For if you wish to tell me that the Jealous Man does this as a man overcome by passion, I fail to see how he fulfills the teaching of Genius, for

Genius so fully recommends and exhorts men to bed them and to perform the act which he praises so highly. And this Genius, more than any of the characters, makes great attacks on women, saying, in fact, "Flee, flee, flee from the deadly serpent."[5] Then he declares that men should pursue them unremittingly. Here is a glaring contradiction, evilly intended: to order men to flee what he wishes them to pursue, and to pursue what he wishes them to flee. But since women are so perverse, he ought not to command men to approach them at all. For he who fears a problem ought to eschew it. And it is for this reason that he so strongly forbids a man to tell his secret to a woman, who is so eager to know it (as he records), although I simply do not know where the devil he found so much nonsense and so many useless words, which are there laid out by a long process. But I pray all those who truly hold this teaching authentic and put so much faith in it, that they kindly tell me how many men they have seen accused, killed, hanged, and publicly rebuked by the accusations of their women? I think you will find them few and far between. Nevertheless, it would be good and praiseworthy counsel for a man to keep his affairs to himself for the greatest security, for he who does so is rich above all men. Indeed, not long ago I heard tell of a man who was accused and hanged on account of having revealed himself to a friend whom he trusted. But I think that few have come before a judge with accusations or complaints of such horrible evil, such disloyalties, and such wickedness which he says women know how to commit so maliciously and underhandedly. It is indeed secret when nobody sees it. As I have said previously on this subject in my work called "L'Epistre au Dieu d'Amours," where are those countries and kingdoms which have been ruined by the great evils of women? If it be not presumptuous, let us speak of the great crimes that one can attribute to even the worst and most deceitful of women. What do they do? In what ways do they deceive you? If they ask you for money from your purse, which they cannot get from you by a ruse or cannot take themselves, do not give it to them if you do not wish to. And if you say that they have made a fool of you, don't let them. Do they go into your house

to woo, pursue, or rape you? It would be good to know how they deceive you. And, besides, he speaks superficially and wrongly about married women who deceive their husbands in this way, for he could know nothing of the married state by experience, and therefore he spoke of it only in generalities. I do not understand what good purpose this can serve or what good can come of it, save to impede the good and peace that is in marriage, and to render the husbands who hear so much babbling and extravagance (if they believe such things) suspicious and less affectionate toward their wives. God, what exhortation! How profitable it is! But truly since he blamed all women in general, I am constrained to believe that he never had acquaintance of, or regular contact with, any honorable or virtuous woman. But by having resort to many dissolute women of evil life (as lechers commonly do), he thought, or feigned to know, that all women were of that kind; for he had known no others. And if he had blamed only the dishonorable ones and counseled men to flee them, it would have been a good and just teaching. But no, without exception he accuses them all. But if, beyond all the bounds of reason, the author took it upon himself to accuse or judge them without justification, the ones accused ought not to be blamed for it. Rather, he should be blamed who carried his argument to the point where it was simply not true, since the contrary is so obvious. For if he and all his henchmen had sworn it in this matter (let no one take offense), there have been, there are, and there will be more virtuous women, more honorable, better bred, and even more learned, and from whom more great good has come forth into the world than ever did from his person. Similarly, there have been women well schooled in worldly conduct and virtuous morals, and many who have effected a reconciliation with their husbands and have borne their concerns and their secrets and their passions calmly and discreetly, despite the fact that their husbands were crude and brutish toward them. One finds proof enough of this in the Bible and in other ancient histories, women such as Sarah, Rebecca, Esther, Judith, and many others. And even in our own time we have seen in France many virtuous women, great ladies and others of our ladies of France: the holy devout Queen Jeanne; Queen Blanche; the Duchess of Orleans,

---

[5]Cf. Vergil, *Bucolica*, III.92–93. [Trs.]

daughter of the King of France; the Duchess of Anjou, who is now called Queen of Sicily; and many others — all of whom had such great beauty, chastity, honor, and wisdom. And also women of lesser rank, like Madame de la Ferté, wife of Monsieur Pierre de Craon, who did much that was praiseworthy; besides many others, whom I pass over for lack of time.

And do not believe or let anyone else think, dear Sir, that I have written this defense, out of feminine bias, merely because I am a woman. For, assuredly, my motive is simply to uphold the pure truth, since I know by experience that the truth is completely contrary to those things I am denying. And it is precisely because I am a woman that I can speak better in this matter than one who has not had the experience, since he speaks only by conjecture and by chance. But above all these things, pray let us consider what the aim of the aforementioned treatise is: for as the proverb says, "By the intent a case is concluded." Thus may be seen and noted what can be profitable in that excessively horrible and shameful conclusion.[6] I call it shameful and so very dishonorable that I dare say that nobody who loves virtue and honor will hear it without being totally confounded by shame and abomination at hearing described, expressed, and distorted in dishonorable fictions what modesty and reason should restrain well-bred folk from even thinking about. Yet, further, I dare say that even the goliards[7] would have been horrified to read or hear it in public, in decent places, and before people whom they would have considered virtuous. But who could praise a work which can be neither read nor quoted at the table of queens, of princesses, and of worthy women, who would surely, on hearing it, be constrained to cover their blushing faces? And if you wish to excuse him by saying that by means of a pretty novelty it pleases him to put the purpose of love through such figures, I answer you that in this work he tells us nothing new. Does one not know how men normally behave with women? If he had told us something about bears or lions or birds or other strange creatures, this would have been matter for laughing on account of the fable, but there is no novelty in this that he tells us. And certainly it could have been done more pleasantly, far more agreeably and by means of more courteous terms, a method which would have been more pleasing to handsome and decent lovers and to every other virtuous person.

Thus, without being more prolix, although a great deal more could be said, and said better, I do not know how, according to my small capacity and weak judgment, to consider this book useful in any way. But it seems so very manifest to me that a great labor was expended on it which produced nothing of value, although my judgment concedes that Master Jean de Meun was a very great, learned, and eloquent clerk. But he would have been able to produce so much better a work, more profitable, and of higher sentiment, if he had applied himself to it, and that he did not do so is great loss. I suppose, however, that perhaps the great carnality with which he was filled caused him to abandon himself to desire rather than to the good of his soul, for by one's actions generally the inclinations are known. Notwithstanding, I do not condemn the *Roman de la Rose* entirely, for it does indeed contain some good things, and its style is poetically pleasing, but therein lies the greater peril, for the more authentic the good the more faith one puts in the evil. And in this way many learned men have sometimes sown great errors by intermingling good and evil and by covering the errors over with truth and virtue. Thus if his priest Genius can say, "Flee, flee, the evil serpent hidden in the grass"; I can say, "Flee the malice concealed in the shadow of goodness and virtue."

Therefore, I say this in conclusion to you, dear Sir, and to all your allies who praise this work so highly and make so much of it that you dare and presume to minimize almost all other works by comparison — I say that it does not merit such praise (saving your good grace) and that you do great wrong to the more deserving works. For a work without usefulness, contributing nothing to the general or personal good (even though we concede it to be delightful, the fruit of great work and labor), in no way deserves praise. And

---

[6]Christine refers here, of course, to the thinly veiled description of the sexual act which concludes the *Roman de la Rose.* [Trs.]

[7]The goliards were satiric poets of the thirteenth and fourteenth centuries.

as in former times the triumphant Romans would not attribute praise or honor to anything if it was not to the utility of the Republic, let us look to their example to see whether we can crown this Romance. But having considered the afore-mentioned things and numerous others we have touched on, I consider it more fitting to bury it in fire than to crown it with laurel, although you call it a mirror of good living and, for men of all classes, an example of good social conduct and of the wise, moral life. But to the contrary (sav-ing your grace) I call it an exhortation to vice, a comfort to dissolute life, a doctrine full of decep-tion, the way to damnation, a public defamer, the cause of suspicion and misbelieving, the shame of many people, and possibly the occasion of heresy. But I know well that you will excuse it by replying to me that therein he enjoins man to do the good but to eschew the evil. But my reasoning is better, for I can show that there is no point in reminding human nature, which is natu-rally inclined to evil, that it limps on one foot, in the hope that it will then walk straighter. Do you wish to speak of all the good which can be found in this book? Certainly, far more virtuous things, eloquently expressed, closer to the truth, and more profitable to the decorous and moral life can be found in many other books — books written by certain philosophers and by teach-ers of our faith, like Aristotle, Seneca, St. Paul, St. Augustine, and others, as you well know. For these testify and teach how to pursue virtue and flee vice more clearly and plainly than Master Jean de Meun has ever been able to do. But such teachings are not usually heard or remembered by fleshly men. They are like the thirsty invalid who, when the doctor permits him to drink, does so gladly and excessively, for the lust for drink-ing leads him to believe that now it will do him no harm.[8] If by God's grace you were restored to the light and purity of a clear conscience, freed from the stain and pollution of sin or any sinful intent, and purged by the prick of contri-tion which reveals the secrets of conscience and condemns self-will — and may God grant it to you and to all others — then you would be more receptive to truth and thus would make a different judgment of the *Rose;* perhaps you would wish that you had never seen it. So much suffices. And may it not be imputed to me as folly, arro-gance, or presumption, that I, a woman, should dare to reproach and call into question so subtle an author, and to diminish the stature of his work, when he alone, a man, has dared to under-take to defame and blame without exception an entire sex.

[8]The passage is somewhat difficult to translate, because the comparison contains only its first term and is not com-pletely worked out. Cf. Ovid, *Amores,* III.iv.18. [Trs.]

Sir Philip Sidney

1554–1586

As a skilled courtier, scholar, soldier, and poet, Philip Sidney was the pattern of the English Renaissance gentleman. After attending Shrewsbury School and Christ Church College at Oxford, and making a grand tour of the continent, he established himself at Elizabeth's court, where he joined the faction led by one of the Queen's favorites, his uncle Robert Dudley, Earl of Leicester. Sidney ended his short life as military governor in Flanders during the Dutch wars. His heroic death at the battle of Zutphen was the stuff of legend: Sidney is said to have courteously declined water and medical attention in favor of a lowlier fellow soldier, a deed that made him a model of the chivalric ideal. But notwithstanding his nobility of birth and spirit, Sidney's unique talents and personality would have procured him success and fame. His *Arcadia* (1593), a romance alternating prose with poetry, established a tradition for the English pastoral; it was a best-seller for over two centuries and was crucial to the development of the English novel. And his *Apology for Poetry*, written in 1583 and published in 1595, was the first significant piece of literary criticism in the English language. (The essay is also known as *The Defence of Poetry*, the title of a slightly earlier version.)

The occasion of *An Apology for Poetry* was to refute *The Schoole of Abuse* (1579), a moralistic attack on poetry written by Puritan minister Stephen Gosson and dedicated (without leave) to Sidney himself. In constructing his *apologia* — Greek for a legal defense — Sidney addressed himself less to Gosson than to Plato, whose *Republic* provides most of the ammunition the Puritan divine expended against poetry. Sidney's *Apology* is structured according to the principles of medieval rhetoric like a good legal brief, with an introduction that draws the reader into the case while offering reassurance of the ethical rightness of the speaker, a central argumentative section, a set of answers to objections, and a glowing peroration. The contemporary reader must have patience, however, with the slow Senecan amble of Sidney's sentences. They were formed before muscularity became the mainstay of English prose. The reader who gets lost will be glad of another characteristic of Renaissance prose: Sidney signals all his transitions with a rapid and elegant summary of the preceding section.

Sidney opens the systematic section of the *Apology* with a definition of poetry, which he calls "an art of imitation, for so Aristotle termeth it in his word *mimesis*, that is to say, a representing, counterfeiting, or figuring forth. . . ." The definition suggests an affinity with Aristotle that is more apparent than real, for Sidney concludes with the Horatian phrase ". . . with this end, to teach and delight." Like many Renaissance theorists, Sidney appeals to mimesis not because it is a crucial principle, but in order to set limits to his subject. He wants to differentiate that class of poetry he will discuss, fictions based on human action, from hymns and psalms on the one hand and philosophy or history or natural science written in verse on the other. The distinction is needed: The two latter types of poetry were not under attack as were fictions. But the end, "to teach and delight," is the pivotal phrase.

Sidney's world, like Plato's, is structured hierarchically and holistically. Like Plato also, he sees the sciences and arts all directed to a single end, "the mistress-knowledge, by the Greeks called *architectonike*, which stands . . . in the knowledge of a man's self, in the ethic and politic consideration, with the end of well doing and not of well knowing only." Horsemanship — the art Sidney begins his *Apology* by mentioning — is no end in itself but serves the art of the soldier, just as the soldier's art serves the statesman's; the ultimate goal is right action.

The arts are judged by their distance from that architectonic goal: the closer, the higher. Thus divinity, Sidney concedes, must be the highest of the sciences, and with this no merely earthly art, including poetry, can compete. It is only against the other major sublunary disciplines — law, history, and philosophy — that Sidney pits the poets. Which of these arts will best serve to make men better? Once the question is so phrased, poetry excels. For law at best keeps us from evil: Its function is not to make us good. Ethical philosophy will help us with the moral distinctions, but philosophy, although it teaches us what virtue is, will not *move* us to virtuous action. History occasionally teaches sound moral lessons — yet just as often its examples are immoral: how the evil triumphed or the virtuous were slain. Only poetry always provides poetic justice to move us to virtuous action, and by the pleasure it gives, move us to go on reading it. Poetry does not merely teach and delight; for Sidney it delights *in order to* teach.

Sidney's aesthetic principle, then, is Horatian, while his metaphysics owes much to Plato. Because of this, whenever he quotes and glosses Aristotle, he subtly alters and distorts his meaning. On page 123, for instance, Sidney argues for the poets and against the claims of history by quoting *Poetics,* Chapter 9, that "poetry is *philosophoteron* and *spoudaioteron,* that is to say, it is more philosophical and more studiously serious than history. . . . because poesy dealeth with *katholou,* that is to say, with the universal consideration, and the history with *kathekaston,* the particular. . . ." The quotation is accurate as far as it goes, but within the same paragraph, Sidney loses track of the distinction between the universal and the particular, substituting one more consistent with his basic Platonism between the *ideal* and the *real.* ("But if the question be . . . whether it be better to have it set down as it should be, or as it was, then certainly is more doctrinable [instructive] the feigned Cyrus in Xenophon than the true Cyrus in Justin. . . .")

The central argument in Sidney is based on poetry's "works and parts" — Elizabethan English for its *effects* and *genres.* After he has shown the superiority of poetry to law, history, and philosophy, he reviews the major genres of poetry to show that they are all instructive, or at least not injurious.

That done, Sidney runs through Gosson's four major objections to poetry in *The Schoole of Abuse.* The first, that there are more fruitful arts than poetry, his main argument has already disposed of. The second is an objection to fiction in general: that poets by the very nature of their trade must be liars. Here Sidney claims benefit of poetic license: that "the poet nothing affirmeth"; fictions are not asserted or received as verifiable truth and therefore can never deceive, as the statements of the historian or the scientist might.

The third objection, that "poetry abuseth man's wit," Sidney turns on its head. He admits that immoral poetry and fictions exist, but these constitute an abuse of the art, not a reflection of its deepest nature. In fact, the possible damage poetry may do, if its ends are perverted, is a reflection of poetry's importance — just as the improper use of the art of medicine will lead to illness and death. The fourth, that the poets were banished from Plato's republic, Sidney refutes with arguments ad hominem — that Plato, as a philosopher, was naturally in competition with the poets. While Sidney also expresses shock at Plato's frank discussions of homoerotic love (in the *Phaedrus* and the *Symposium*), in truth he wants Plato on his side, not on Gosson's, and his most serious argument here is that Plato banished poetry not because it was evil in its nature but only to avoid its possible abuses — such as the teaching of falsehoods about the nature of God. He thus assimilates the last objection to the previous one.

For many, the most interesting section of the *Apology for Poetry* is Sidney's digression on the arts in contemporary England, which he considered to be in a bad way. Applying the strict standards of Renaissance poetics to home-grown English verse and drama, Sidney finds most of his fellow poets admirable for their natural genius but lamentably ignorant about the rules and regulations that Horatian aesthetics had evolved for literary art. Several of Sidney's accusations about the English theater — its neglect of the three unities of time, place, and action; mixing of comic scenes into tragedy, polluting genres that ought to be kept pure; indecorous portrayal of violence on the stage — will be debated nearly a century later in John Dryden's *An Essay of Dramatic Poesy* and laid to rest after another century in Samuel Johnson's "Preface to *Shakespeare*." What Sidney thought to be immutable laws of art came to be seen, more and more, as mere conventions, useful in their day but no longer valid.

Sidney and his strictures on the artist's need for study and practice may seem pedantic unless we remember what was always before the well-traveled Sidney's eyes: how recently England had emerged from provincial barbarism into the sunlight of Elizabethan courtliness, and how much the English still needed to learn from the older cultures of Europe and the classical world. If these are the broad outlines of the *Apology*, this critical work repays close study as well. An undergraduate in one of my recent classes, Janet Strunk, noted that the word "poesy" itself switches gender in the course of the essay, and with the aid of a computer file of the essay we were able to confirm that, seven times referred to as "he" in the earlier sections of the essay, "poesy" becomes a "she" for Sidney three times toward its end.[1] Is this abstract gender bending one more aspect of the Elizabethan fascination with cross-dressing, with which Sidney himself plays in the *Arcadia?* Or is it simply the argumentative context that dictates gender here? At the outset of the essay, poetry is portrayed as engaged in a contest to prove its excellence and virtue against rival sciences like philosophy and history, and, like a participant in one of the formal Elizabethan tournaments, must be gendered masculine. By the end of the essay,

[1]For example, "But I list not to defend poesy with the help of her underling historiography" (p. 134): "Sweet Poesy, that hath anciently had kings . . . not only to favor poets, but to be poets; and of our nearer times can present for her patrons a Robert, king of Sicily . . ." (p. 134): "[drama] like an unmannerly daughter showing a bad education, causeth her mother poesy's honesty to be called in question" (p. 137). In the early part of the *Apology*, we often get sentences like this: "Nay truly, though I yield that poesy may not only be abused, but that, being abused, by the reason of his sweet charming force, it can do more hurt than any other army of words" (p. 131).

though, poesy has become not the contender but what is contended for, the prize for which England's writers strive against those of other nations, the feminine reward of masculine valor. Such hidden metaphors remind us, if we needed such reminding, that the *Apology* was written by the Elizabethan age's foremost lyric poet, who could not help bringing his talents and wit into everything he did.

Selected Bibliography

Curtright, Travis. "Sidney's Defense of Poetry: Ethos and the Ideas." *Ben Jonson Journal* 10 (2003): 101–15.

Devereux, James A. "The Meaning of Delight in Sidney's Defense of Poesy." *Studies in the Literary Imagination* 15 (1982): 85–97.

Jacobson, Daniel. "Sir Philip Sidney's Dilemma: On the Ethical Function of Narrative Art." *Journal of Aesthetics and Art Criticism* 54, no. 4 (1996): 327–36.

Levao, Ronald. *Renaissance Minds and Their Fictions: Cusanus, Sidney, Shakespeare.* Berkeley: University of California Press, 1985.

Mason, H. A. "An Introduction to Literary Criticism by Way of Sidney's Apologie for Poetrie." *Cambridge Quarterly* 12, no. 2–3 (1984): 79–173.

McCoy, Richard C. *Sir Philip Sidney: Rebellion in Arcadia.* New Brunswick: Rutgers University Press, 1979.

Myrick, Kenneth Orne. *Sir Philip Sidney as a Literary Craftsman.* Cambridge: Harvard University Press, 1935.

Robinson, Forrest Glen. *The Shape of Things Known: Sidney's Apology in Its Philosophical Tradition.* Cambridge: Harvard University Press, 1972.

Spingarn, J. E. *A History of Literary Criticism in the Renaissance.* New York: Columbia University Press, 1912.

Stump, Donald V. "Sidney's Concept of Tragedy in the Apology and the Arcadia." *Studies in Philology* 79 (1982): 78–99.

Ulreich, John C., Jr. "Poets Only Deliver: Sidney's Conception of Mimesis." *Studies in the Literary Imagination* 15 (1982): 67–84.

Weiner, Andrew D. *Sir Philip Sidney and the Poetics of Protestantism.* Minneapolis: University of Minnesota Press, 1978.

An Apology for Poetry

When the right virtuous Edward Wotton and I were at the Emperor's Court together, we gave ourselves to learn horsemanship of John Pietro Pugliano, one that with great commendation had the place of an esquire in his stable. And he, according to the fertileness of the Italian wit, did not only afford us the demonstration of his practice, but sought to enrich our minds with the contemplations there which he thought most precious. But with none I remember mine ears were at any time more loaden, than when (either angered with slow payment, or moved with our learnerlike admiration) he exercised his speech in the praise of his faculty. He said soldiers were the noblest estate of mankind, and horsemen the noblest of soldiers. He said they were the masters of war and ornaments of peace; speedy goers and strong abiders; triumphers both in camps and courts. Nay, to so unbelieved a point he proceeded, as that no earthly thing bred such wonder to a prince as to be a good horseman. Skill of government was but a *pedanteria*[1] in comparison. Then would he add certain praises, by telling what a peerless beast a horse was, the only serviceable courtier without flattery, the beast of most beauty, faithfulness, courage, and such more, that, if I had not been a piece of a logician before I came to him, I think he would have persuaded me to have wished myself a horse. But thus much at least with his no few words he drove into me, that self-love is better than any gilding to make that seem gorgeous wherein ourselves are parties. Wherein, if Pugliano's strong affection and weak arguments will not satisfy you, I will give you a nearer example of myself, who (I know not by what mischance) in these my not old years and idlest times having slipped into the title of a poet, am provoked to say something unto you in the defense of that my unelected vocation, which if I handle with more good will than good reasons, bear with me, since the scholar is to be pardoned that followeth the steps of his master. And yet I must say that, as I have just cause to make a pitiful defense of poor Poetry, which from almost the highest estimation of learning is fallen to be the laughingstock of children, so have I need to bring some more available proofs, since the former is by no man barred of his deserved credit, the silly latter hath had even the names of philosophers used to the defacing of it, with great danger of civil war among the Muses.

And first, truly, to all them that professing learning inveigh against poetry may justly be objected, that they go very near to ungratefulness, to seek to deface that which, in the noblest nations and languages that are known, hath been the first light-giver to ignorance, and first nurse, whose milk by little and little enabled them to feed afterwards of tougher knowledges. And will they now play the hedgehog that, being received into the den, drove out his host, or rather the vipers, that with their birth kill their parents? Let learned Greece in any of her manifold sciences be able to show me one book before Musaeus, Homer, and Hesiod, all three nothing else but poets. Nay, let any history be brought that can say any writers there before them, if they were

not men of the same skill, as Orpheus, Linus, and some other are named, who, having been the first of that country that made pens deliverers of their knowledge to their posterity, may justly challenge to be called their fathers in learning, for not only in time they had this priority (although in itself antiquity be venerable) but went before them, as causes to draw with their charming sweetness the wild untamed wits to an admiration of knowledge. So, as Amphion was said to move stones with his poetry to build Thebes, and Orpheus to be listened to by beasts — indeed stony and beastly people.[2] So among the Romans were Livius Andronicus, and Ennius. So in the Italian language the first that made it aspire to be a treasure-house of science were the poets Dante, Boccaccio, and Petrarch. So in our English were Gower and Chaucer. After whom, encouraged and delighted with their excellent foregoing, others have followed, to beautify our mother tongue, as well in the same kind as in other arts. This did so notably show itself that the philosophers of Greece durst not a long time appear to the world but under the masks of poets. So Thales, Empedocles, and Parmenides sang their natural philosophy in verses; so did Pythagoras and Phocylides their moral counsels; so did Tyrtaeus in war matters, and Solon in matters of policy; or rather, they, being poets, did exercise their delightful vein in those points of highest knowledge, which before lay hid to the world. For that wise Solon was directly a poet it is manifest, having written in verse the notable fable of the Atlantic Island, which was continued by Plato.

And truly, even Plato, whosoever well considereth shall find that in the body of his work, though the inside and strength were philosophy, the skin as it were and beauty depended most of poetry: for all standeth upon dialogues, wherein he feigneth many honest burgesses of Athens to speak of such matters, that, if they had been set on the rack, they would never have confessed them, besides his poetical describing the circumstances of their meetings, as the well ordering of a banquet, the delicacy of a walk, with interlacing

[1]Pedantry: useless book-learning.

[2]Sidney's notion of poetry's power derives from Horace's *Art of Poetry*. See p. 83.

mere tales, as Gyges' ring, and others, which who knoweth not to be flowers of poetry did never walk into Apollo's garden.[3]

And even historiographers (although their lips sound of things done, and verity be written in their foreheads) have been glad to borrow both fashion and perchance weight of poets. So Herodotus entitled his history by the name of the nine Muses;[4] and both he and all the rest that followed him either stole or usurped of poetry their passionate describing of passions, the many particularities of battles, which no man could affirm, or, if that be denied me, long orations put in the mouths of great kings and captains, which it is certain they never pronounced. So that, truly, neither philosopher nor historiographer could at the first have entered into the gates of popular judgments, if they had not taken a great passport of poetry, which in all nations at this day, where learning flourisheth not, is plain to be seen, in all which they have some feeling of poetry. In Turkey, besides their lawgiving divines, they have no other writers but poets. In our neighbor country Ireland, where truly learning goeth very bare, yet are their poets held in a devout reverence. Even among the most barbarous and simple Indians where no writing is, yet have they their poets, who make and sing songs, which they call *areytos,* both of their ancestors' deeds and praises of their gods — a sufficient probability that, if ever learning come among them, it must be by having their hard dull wits softened and sharpened with the sweet delights of poetry. For until they find a pleasure in the exercises of the mind, great promises of much knowledge will little persuade them that know not the fruits of knowledge. In Wales, the true remnant of the ancient Britons, as there are good authorities to show the long time they had poets, which they called bards, so through all the conquests of Romans, Saxons, Danes, and Normans, some of whom did seek to ruin all memory of learning from among them, yet do their poets, even to this day, last; so as it is not more notable in soon beginning than in long continuing. But since the authors of most of our sciences were the Romans, and before them the Greeks, let us a little stand upon their authorities, but even so far as to see what names they have given unto this now scorned skill.

Among the Romans a poet was called *vates,* which is as much as a diviner, foreseer, or prophet, as by his conjoined words *vaticinium* and *vaticinari* is manifest: so heavenly a title did that excellent people bestow upon this heart-ravishing knowledge. And so far were they carried into the admiration thereof, that they thought in the chanceable hitting upon any such verses great foretokens of their following fortunes were placed. Whereupon grew the word of *sortes Virgilianae*[5] when, by sudden opening Virgil's book, they lighted upon any verse of his making: whereof the histories of the emperors' lives are full, as of Albinus, the governor of our island, who in his childhood met with this verse, *"Arma amens capio nec sat rationis in armis"*;[6] and in his age performed it: which, although it were a very vain and godless superstition, as also it was to think that spirits were commanded by such verses — whereupon this word charms, derived of *carmina,*[7] cometh — so yet serveth it to show the great reverence those wits were held in. And altogether not without ground, since both the Oracles of Delphos and Sibylla's prophecies were wholly delivered in verses. For that same exquisite observing of number and measure in words, and that high flying liberty of conceit proper to the poet, did seem to have some divine force in it.

And may not I presume a little further, to show the reasonableness of this word *vates,* and say that the holy David's Psalms are a divine poem? If I do, I shall not do it without the testimony of great learned men, both ancient and modern. But even the name Psalms will speak for me, which, being interpreted, is nothing but "songs"; then that it is fully written in meter, as all learned Hebricians agree, although the rules be not yet

---

[3]The myth of Gyges' ring appears in *Republic,* Book II, and other myths appear in other dialogues; Plato also occasionally writes prose that modulates into dithyrambic verse, as in the *Ion* and the *Phaedrus.*

[4]Each of the nine books of Herodotus's *History* is titled with the name of one of the Muses.

[5]The Virgilian lots: a method of fortune-telling using a random passage from the *Aeneid.*

[6]"Insane, I seize my weapons; there's no sense in weapons. . . ." *Aeneid* 2:314.

[7]Songs.

fully found: lastly and principally, his handling his prophecy, which is merely poetical. For what else is the awaking his musical instruments, the often and free changing of persons, his notable *prosopopoeias*,[8] when he maketh you, as it were, see God coming in his majesty, his telling of the beasts' joyfulness, and hills' leaping, but a heavenly poesy, wherein almost he showeth himself a passionate lover of that unspeakable and everlasting beauty to be seen by the eyes of the mind, only cleared by faith? But truly now having named him, I fear me I seem to profane that holy name, applying it to poetry, which is among us thrown down to so ridiculous an estimation. But they that with quiet judgments will look a little deeper into it, shall find the end and working of it such, as, being rightly applied, deserveth not to be scourged out of the church of God.

But now, let us see how the Greeks named it, and how they deemed of it. The Greeks called him a "poet," which name hath, as the most excellent, gone through other languages. It cometh of this word *poiein*, which is "to make": wherein, I know not whether by luck or wisdom, we Englishmen have met with the Greeks in calling him a *maker:* which name, how high and incomparable a title it is, I had rather were known by marking the scope of other sciences than by my partial allegation.

There is no art delivered to mankind that hath not the works of nature for his principal object, without which they could not consist, and on which they so depend, as they become actors and players, as it were, of what nature will have set forth. So doth the astronomer look upon the stars, and, by that he seeth, setteth down what order nature hath taken therein. So do the geometrician and arithmetician in their diverse sorts of quantities. So doth the musician in times tell you which by nature agree, which not. The natural philosopher thereon hath his name, and the moral philosopher standeth upon the natural virtues, vices, and passions of man; and "follow nature" (saith he) "therein, and thou shalt not err." The lawyer saith what men have determined; the historian what men have done. The grammarian speaketh only of the rules of speech; and the rhetorician

8Personifications.

and logician, considering what in nature will soonest prove and persuade, thereon give artificial rules, which still are compassed within the circle of a question according to the proposed matter. The physician weigheth the nature of a man's body, and the nature of things helpful or hurtful unto it. And the metaphysic, though it be in the second and abstract notions, and therefore be counted supernatural, yet doth he indeed build upon the depth of nature. Only the poet, disdaining to be tied to any such subjection, lifted up with the vigor of his own invention, doth grow in effect another nature, in making things either better than nature bringeth forth, or, quite anew, forms such as never were in nature, as the Heroes, Demigods, Cyclopes, Chimeras, Furies, and such like: so as he goeth hand in hand with nature, not enclosed within the narrow warrant of her gifts, but freely ranging only within the zodiac of his own wit.

Nature never set forth the earth in so rich tapestry as divers poets have done — neither with pleasant rivers, fruitful trees, sweet-smelling flowers, nor whatsoever else may make the too much loved earth more lovely. Her world is brazen, the poets only deliver a golden. But let those things alone, and go to man — for whom as the other things are, so it seemeth in him her uttermost cunning is employed — and know whether she have brought forth so true a lover as Theagenes, so constant a friend as Pylades, so valiant a man as Orlando, so right a prince as Xenophon's Cyrus, so excellent a man every way as Virgil's Aeneas. Neither let this be jestingly conceived, because the works of the one be essential, the other in imitation or fiction; for any understanding knoweth the skill of the artificer standeth in that idea or foreconceit of the work, and not in the work itself. And that the poet hath that idea is manifest, by delivering them forth in such excellency as he hath imagined them. Which delivering forth also is not wholly imaginative, as we are wont to say by them that build castles in the air: but so far substantially it worketh, not only to make a Cyrus, which had been but a particular excellency, as nature might have done, but to bestow a Cyrus upon the world, to make many Cyruses, if they will learn aright why and how that maker made him.

Neither let it be deemed too saucy a comparison to balance the highest point of man's wit with the efficacy of nature; but rather give right honor to the heavenly Maker of that maker, who, having made man to his own likeness, set him beyond and over all the works of that second nature: which in nothing he showeth so much as in poetry, when with the force of a divine breath he bringeth things forth far surpassing her doings, with no small argument to the incredulous of that first accursed fall of Adam, since our erected wit maketh us know what perfection is, and yet our infected will keepeth us from reaching unto it. But these arguments will by few be understood, and by fewer granted. Thus much (I hope) will be given me, that the Greeks with some probability of reason gave him the name above all names of learning. Now let us go to a more ordinary opening of him, that the truth may be more palpable: and so I hope, though we get not so unmatched a praise as the etymology of his names will grant, yet his very description, which no man will deny, shall not justly be barred from a principal commendation.

Poesy therefore is an art of imitation, for so Aristotle termeth it in his word *mimesis*,[9] that is to say, a representing, counterfeiting, or figuring forth — to speak metaphorically, a speaking picture; with this end, to teach and delight.[10] Of this have been three several kinds. The chief, both in antiquity and excellency, were they that did imitate the inconceivable excellencies of God. Such were David in his Psalms; Solomon in his Song of Songs, in his Ecclesiastes, and Proverbs; Moses and Deborah in their Hymns; and the writer of Job, which, beside other, the learned Emanuel Tremellius and Franciscus Junius do entitle the poetical part of the Scripture. Against these none will speak that hath the Holy Ghost in due holy reverence.

In this kind, though in a full wrong divinity, were Orpheus, Amphion, Homer in his *Hymns,* and many other, both Greeks and Romans, and this poesy must be used by whosoever will follow St. James's counsel in singing psalms when they are merry, and I know is used with the fruit of comfort by some, when, in sorrowful pangs of their death-bringing sins, they find the consolation of the never-leaving goodness.

The second kind is of them that deal with matters, philosophical: either moral, as Tyrtaeus, Phocylides, and Cato; or natural, as Lucretius and Virgil's *Georgics;* or astronomical, as Manilius and Pontanus; or historical, as Lucan; which who mislike, the fault is in their judgments quite out of taste, and not in the sweet food of sweetly uttered knowledge. But because this second sort is wrapped within the fold of the proposed subject, and takes not the course of his own invention, whether they properly be poets or no let grammarians dispute; and go to the third, indeed right poets, of whom chiefly this question ariseth, betwixt whom and these second is such a kind of difference as betwixt the meaner sort of painters, who counterfeit only such faces as are set before them, and the more excellent, who, having no law but wit, bestow that in colors upon you which is fittest for the eye to see, as the constant though lamenting look of Lucretia, when she punished in herself another's fault.

Wherein he painteth not Lucretia whom he never saw, but painteth the outward beauty of such a virtue. For these third be they which most properly do imitate to teach and delight, and to imitate borrow nothing of what is, hath been, or shall be; but range, only reined with learned discretion, into the divine consideration of what may be, and should be. These be they that, as the first and most noble sort may justly be termed *vates,* so these are waited on in the excellentest languages and best understandings, with the foredescribed name of poets; for these indeed do merely make to imitate, and imitate both to delight and teach, and delight to move men to take that goodness in hand, which without delight they would fly as from a stranger, and teach, to make them know that goodness whereunto they are moved: which being the noblest scope to which ever any learning was directed, yet want there not idle tongues to bark at them. These be subdivided into sundry more special denominations. The most notable be the heroic, lyric, tragic, comic, satiric, iambic, elegiac, pastoral, and certain others, some of these being termed according to the matter they deal with, some by the sorts of verses they liked

[9]Aristotle, *Poetics,* Ch. I; see p. 50.
[10]Horace, *Art of Poetry;* see p. 82.

best to write in; for indeed the greatest part of poets have apparelled their poetical inventions in that numbrous kind of writing which is called verse — indeed but apparelled, verse being but an ornament and no cause to poetry, since there have been many most excellent poets that never versified, and now swarm many versifiers that need never answer to the name of poets. For Xenophon, who did imitate so excellently as to give us effigiem iusti imperii,[11] "the portraiture of a just empire," under name of Cyrus (as Cicero saith of him), made therein an absolute heroical poem.[12] So did Heliodorus in his sugared invention of that picture of love in Theagenes and Chariclea; and yet both these writ in prose: which I speak to show that it is not rhyming and versing that maketh a poet — no more than a long gown maketh an advocate, who though he pleaded in armor should be an advocate and no soldier. But it is that feigning notable images of virtues, vices, or what else, with that delightful teaching, which must be the right describing note to know a poet by, although indeed the senate of poets hath chosen verse as their fittest raiment, meaning, as in matter they passed all in all, so in manner to go beyond them — not speaking (table talk fashion or like men in a dream) words as they chanceably fall from the mouth, but peising[13] each syllable of each word by just proportion according to the dignity of the subject.

Now therefore it shall not be amiss first to weigh this latter sort of poetry by his works, and then by his parts,[14] and, if in neither of these anatomies he be condemnable, I hope we shall obtain a more favorable sentence. This purifying of wit, this enriching of memory, enabling of judgment, and enlarging of conceit, which commonly we call learning, under what name soever it come forth, or to what immediate end soever it be directed, the final end is to lead and draw us to as high a perfection as our degenerate souls, made worse by their clayey lodgings, can be capable of. This, according to the inclination

of the man, bred many formed impressions. For some that thought this felicity principally to be gotten by knowledge and no knowledge to be so high and heavenly as acquaintance with the stars, gave themselves to astronomy; others, persuading themselves to be demigods if they knew the causes of things, became natural and supernatural philosophers; some an admirable delight drew to music; and some the certainty of demonstration to the mathematics. But all, one and other, having this scope — to know, and by knowledge to lift up the mind from the dungeon of the body to the enjoying his own divine essence. But when by the balance of experience it was found that the astronomer looking to the stars might fall into a ditch, that the inquiring philosopher might be blind in himself, and the mathematician might draw forth a straight line with a crooked heart, then, lo, did proof, the overruler of opinions, make manifest that all these are but serving sciences, which, as they have each a private end in themselves, so yet are they all directed to the highest end of the mistress-knowledge, by the Greeks called architectonike,[15] which stands (as I think) in the knowledge of a man's self, in the ethic and politic consideration, with the end of well doing and not of well knowing only — even as the saddler's next end is to make a good saddle, but his farther end to serve a nobler faculty, which is horsemanship; so the horseman's to soldiery, and the soldier not only to have the skill, but to perform the practice of a soldier. So that the ending end of all earthly learning being virtuous action, those skills, that most serve to bring forth that, have a most just title to be princes over all the rest. Wherein we can show the poet's nobleness, by setting him before his other competitors, among whom as principal challengers step forth the moral philosophers, whom me thinketh, I see coming towards me with a sullen gravity, as though they could not abide vice by daylight, rudely clothed for to witness outwardly their contempt of outward things, with books in their hands against glory, whereto they set their names, sophistically speaking against subtlety,

11Sidney is praising Xenophon's Cyropaedia, or Education of Cyrus.

12Cf. Aristotle, Poetics, Ch. 9; see p. 56.

13Weighing, evaluating.

14"Works" and "parts" are, in modern English, effects and genres.

15In Aristotle, the controlling principle of something. For Sidney, the ultimate end of knowledge is the Greek ideal of sophrosyne: self-knowledge and self-mastery.

and angry with any man in whom they see the foul fault of anger. These men casting largesse as they go of definitions, divisions, and distinctions, with a scornful interrogative do soberly ask whether it be possible to find any path so ready to lead a man to virtue as that which teacheth what virtue is — and teacheth it not only by delivering forth his very being, his causes, and effects, but also by making known his enemy, vice (which must be destroyed), and his cumbersome servant, passion (which must be mastered), by showing the generalities that containeth it, and the specialties that are derived from it; lastly, by plain setting down, how it extendeth itself out of the limits of a man's own little world to the government of families, and maintaining of public societies.

The historian scarcely giveth leisure to the moralist to say so much, but that he, laden with old mouse-eaten records, authorizing himself (for the most part) upon other histories, whose greatest authorities are built upon the notable foundation of hearsay; having much ado to accord differing writers and to pick truth out of partiality; better acquainted with a thousand years ago than with the present age, and yet better knowing how this world goeth than how his own wit runneth; curious for antiquities and inquisitive of novelties; a wonder to young folks and a tyrant in table talk, denieth, in a great chafe, that any man for teaching of virtue, and virtuous actions, is comparable to him. "I am '*lux vitae, temporum magistra, vita memoriae, nuntia vetustatis,*'" &c.[16]

The philosopher (saith he)

> teacheth a disputative virtue, but I do an active. His virtue is excellent in the dangerless Academy of Plato, but mine showeth forth her honorable face in the battles of Marathon, Pharsalia, Poitiers, and Agincourt. He teacheth virtue by certain abstract considerations, but I only bid you follow the footing of them that have gone before you. Old-aged experience goeth beyond the fine-witted philosopher, but I give the experience of many ages. Lastly, if he make the song book, I put the learner's hand to the lute; and if he be the guide, I am the light.

Then would he allege you innumerable examples, conferring story by story, how much the wisest senators and princes have been directed by the credit of history, as Brutus, Alphonsus of Aragon, and who not, if need be? At length the long line of their disputation maketh a point in this, that the one giveth the precept, and the other the example.

Now, whom shall we find (since the question standeth for the highest form in the school of learning) to be moderator? Truly, as me seemeth, the poet; and if not a moderator, even the man that ought to carry the title from them both, and much more from all other serving sciences. Therefore compare we the poet with the historian, and with the moral philosopher; and, if he go beyond them both, no other human skill can match him. For as for the Divine, with all reverence it is ever to be excepted, not only for having his scope as far beyond any of these as eternity exceedeth a moment, but even for passing each of these in themselves.

And for the lawyer, though Jus be the daughter of justice, and justice the chief of virtues, yet because he seeketh to make men good rather *formidine poenae* than *virtutis amore*,[17] or, to say righter, doth not endeavor to make men good, but that their evil hurt not others, having no care, so he be a good citizen, how bad a man he be: therefore, as our wickedness maketh him necessary, and necessity maketh him honorable, so is he not in the deepest truth to stand in rank with these who all endeavor to take naughtiness away, and plant goodness even in the secretest cabinet of our souls. And these four are all that any way deal in that consideration of men's manners, which being the supreme knowledge, they that best breed it deserve the best commendation.

The philosopher therefore and the historian are they which would win the goal, the one by precept, the other by example. But both, not having both, do both halt. For the philosopher, setting down with thorny argument the bare rule, is so hard of utterance, and so misty to be conceived, that one that hath no other guide but his shall wade

---

[16]"The light of life, the master of the times, the life of memory, the messenger of antiquity." Cicero, *On Oratory* 2.9:36.

[17]Rather through fear of punishment than through love of virtue.

in him till he be old before he shall find sufficient cause to be honest. For his knowledge standeth so upon the abstract and general, that happy is that man who may understand him, and more happy that can apply what he doth understand.

On the other side, the historian, wanting the precept, is so tied, not to what should be but to what is, to the particular truth of things and not to the general reason of things, that his example draweth no necessary consequence, and therefore a less fruitful doctrine.

Now doth the peerless poet perform both: for whatsoever the philosopher saith should be done, he giveth a perfect picture of it in someone by whom he presupposeth it was done; so as he coupleth the general notion with the particular example. A perfect picture I say, for he yieldeth to the powers of the mind an image of that whereof the philosopher bestoweth but a wordish description: which doth neither strike, pierce, nor possess the sight of the soul so much as that other doth.

For as in outward things, to a man that had never seen an elephant or a rhinoceros, who should tell him most exquisitely all their shapes, color, bigness, and particular marks, or of a gorgeous palace the archi- tecture, with declaring the full beauties might well make the hearer able to repeat, as it were by rote, all he had heard, yet should never satisfy his inward conceits with being witness to itself of a true lively knowledge; but the same man, as soon as he might see those beasts well painted, or the house well in model, should straightways grow, without need of any description, to a judicial comprehending of them: so no doubt the philosopher with his learned definition — be it of virtue, vices, matters of public policy or private government — replenisheth the memory with many infallible grounds of wisdom, which, notwithstanding, lie dark before the imagina- tive and judging power, if they be not illuminated or figured forth by the speaking picture of poesy.

Tully[18] taketh much pains, and many times not without poetical helps, to make us know the force of our country hath in us. Let us but hear old Anchises speaking in the midst of Troy's flames, or see Ulysses in the fullness of all Calypso's delights bewail his absence from barren and

beggarly Ithaca. Anger, the Stoics say, was a short madness: let but Sophocles bring you Ajax on a stage, killing and whipping sheep and oxen, thinking them the army of Greeks, with their chieftains Agamemnon and Menelaus, and tell me if you have not a more familiar insight into anger than finding in the schoolmen his genus and dif- ference. See whether wisdom and temperance in Ulysses and Diomedes, valor in Achilles, friend- ship in Nisus and Euryalus, even to an ignorant man carry not an apparent shining, and, contrarily, the remorse of conscience in Oedipus, the soon repenting pride of Agamemnon, the self-devouring cruelty in his father Atreus, the violence of ambition in the two Theban brothers, the sour- sweetness of revenge in Medea, and, to fall lower, the Terentian Gnatho and our Chaucer's Pandar so expressed that we now use their names to signify their trades; and finally, all virtues, vices, and pas- sions so in their own natural seats laid to the view, that we seem not to hear of them, but clearly to see through them. But even in the most excellent deter- mination of goodness, what philosopher's counsel can so readily direct a prince, as the feigned Cyrus in Xenophon; or a virtuous man in all fortunes, as Aeneas in Virgil; or a whole commonwealth, as the way of Sir Thomas More's *Utopia*? I say the way, because where Sir Thomas More erred, it was the fault of the man and not of the poet, for that way of patterning a commonwealth was most absolute, though he perchance hath not so abso- lutely performed it. For the question is, whether the feigned image of poesy or the regular instruc- tion of philosophy hath the more force in teaching: wherein if the philosophers have more rightly showed themselves philosophers than the poets have attained to the high top of their profession, as in truth, "*mediocribus esse poetis, / Non dii, non homines, non concessere columnae*",[19] it is, I say again, not the fault of the art, but that by few men that art can be accomplished.

Certainly, even our Saviour Christ could as well have given the moral commonplaces of uncharitableness and humbleness as the divine narration of Dives and Lazarus; or of disobedi- ence and mercy, as that heavenly discourse of

18 Cicero.

19 "But men and gods and booksellers won't put up / With second-rate poets." Horace, *Art of Poetry*; see p. 83.

the lost child and the gracious father; but that his through-searching wisdom knew the estate of Dives burning in hell, and of Lazarus being in Abraham's bosom, would more constantly (as it were) inhabit both the memory and judgment. Truly, for myself, meseems I see before my eyes the lost child's disdainful prodigality, turned to envy a swine's dinner: which by the learned divines are thought not historical acts, but instructing parables. For conclusion, I say the philosopher teacheth, but he teacheth obscurely, so as the learned only can understand him; that is to say, he teacheth them that are already taught. But the poet is the food for the tenderest stomachs, the poet is indeed the right popular philosopher, whereof Aesop's tales give good proof: whose pretty allegories, stealing under the formal tales of beasts, make many, more beastly than beasts, begin to hear the sound of virtue from these dumb speakers.

But now may it be alleged that, if this imagining of matters be so fit for the imagination, then must the historian needs surpass, who bringeth you images of true matters, such as indeed were done, and not such as fantastically or falsely may be suggested to have been done. Truly, Aristotle himself, in his discourse of poesy, plainly determineth this question, saying that poetry is *philosophoteron* and *spoudaioteron*, that is to say, it is more philosophical and more studiously serious than history. His reason is, because poesy dealeth with *katholou*, that is to say, with the universal consideration, and the history with *kathekaston*, the particular: "now," saith he, "the universal weighs what is fit to be said or done, either in likelihood or necessity (which the poesy considereth in his imposed names), and the particular only marks whether Alcibiades did, or suffered, this or that."[20] Thus far Aristotle: which reason of his (as all his) is most full of reason. For indeed, if the question were whether it were better to have a particular act truly or falsely set down, there is no doubt which is to be chosen, no more than whether you had rather have Vespasian's picture right as he was, or at the painter's pleasure nothing resembling. But if the question be for your own use and learning, whether it be better to

have it set down as it should be, or as it was, then certainly is more doctrinable the feigned Cyrus in Xenophon than the true Cyrus in Justin, and the feigned Aeneas in Virgil than the right Aeneas in Dares Phrygius.[21]

As to a lady that desired to fashion her countenance to the best grace, a painter should more benefit her to portrait a most sweet face, writing Canidia upon it, than to paint Canidia as she was, who, Horace sweareth, was foul and ill favored.

If the poet do his part aright, he will show you in Tantalus, Atreus, and such like, nothing that is not to be shunned; in Cyrus, Aeneas, Ulysses, each thing to be followed; where the historian, bound to tell things as things were, cannot be liberal (without he will be poetical) of a perfect pattern, but, as in Alexander or Scipio himself, show doings, some to be liked, some to be misliked. And then how will you discern what to follow but by your own discretion, which you had without reading Quintus Curtius? And whereas a man may say, though in universal consideration of doctrine the poet prevaileth, yet that the history, in his saying such a thing was done, doth warrant a man more in that he shall follow.

The answer is manifest: that if he stand upon that *was* — as if he should argue, because it rained yesterday, therefore it should rain today — then indeed it hath some advantage to a gross conceit; but if he know an example only informs a conjectured likelihood, and so go by reason, the poet doth so far exceed him, as he is to frame his example to that which is most reasonable, be it in warlike, politic, or private matters; where the historian in his bare *was* hath many times that which we call fortune to overrule the best wisdom. Many times he must tell events whereof he can yield no cause: or, if he do, it must be poetical. For that a feigned example hath as much force to teach as a true example (for as for to move, it is clear, since the feigned may be tuned to the highest key of passion), let us take one example wherein a poet and a historian do concur.

[20]Aristotle, *Poetics,* Ch. 9; see p. 56.

[21]A slippage of terms characteristic of Sidney has just occurred. Aristotle's distinction between the universal and the particular has just become a distinction between the ideal and the real, which will support Sidney's defense of the moral function of poetry.

Herodotus and Justin do both testify that Zopyrus, King Darius's faithful servant, seeing his master long resisted by the rebellious Babylonians, feigned himself in extreme disgrace of his king: for verifying of which, he caused his own nose and ears to be cut off, and so flying to the Babylonians, was received, and for his known valor so far credited, that he did find means to deliver them over to Darius. Much like matter doth Livy record of Tarquinius and his son. Xenophon excellently feigneth such another stratagem performed by Abradates in Cyrus's behalf. Now would I fain know, if occasion be presented unto you to serve your prince by such an honest dissimulation, why you do not as well learn it of Xenophon's fiction as of the other's verity — and truly so much the better, as you shall save your nose by the bargain: for Abradates did not counterfeit so far. So then the best of the historian is subject to the poet; for whatsoever action, or faction, whatsoever counsel, policy, or war stratagem the historian is bound to recite, that may the poet (if he list) with his imitation make his own, beautifying it both for further teaching, and more delighting, as it pleaseth him, having all, from Dante's heaven to his hell, under the authority of his pen. Which if I be asked what poets have done so, as I might well name some, yet say I, and say again, I speak of the art, and not of the artificer.

Now, to that which commonly is attributed to the praise of histories, in respect of the notable learning is gotten by marking the success, as though therein a man should see virtue exalted and vice punished — truly that commendation is peculiar to poetry, and far off from history. For indeed poetry ever setteth virtue so out in her best colors, making Fortune her well-waiting handmaid, that one must needs be enamored of her. Well may you see Ulysses in a storm, and in other hard plights; but they are but exercises of patience and magnanimity, to make them shine the more in the near-following prosperity. And of the contrary part, if evil men come to the stage, they ever go out (as the tragedy writer answered to one that misliked the show of such persons) so manacled as they little animate folks to follow them. But the historian, being captived to the truth of a foolish world, is many times a

terror from well doing, and an encouragement to unbridled wickedness.

For see we not valiant Miltiades rot in his fetters: the just Phocion and the accomplished Socrates put to death like traitors: the cruel Severus live prosperously; the excellent Severus miserably murdered; Sylla and Marius dying in their beds; Pompey and Cicero slain then, when they would have thought exile a happiness?

See we not virtuous Cato driven to kill himself, and rebel Caesar so advanced that his name yet, after 1,600 years, lasteth in the highest honor? And mark but even Caesar's own words of the forenamed Sylla (who in that only did honestly, to put down his dishonest tyranny). *Literas nescivit*,[22] as if want of learning caused him to do well. He meant it not by poetry, which, not content with earthly plagues, deviseth new punishments in hell for tyrants, nor yet by philosophy, which teacheth *Occidendos esse*;[23] but no doubt by skill in history, for that indeed can afford your Cypselus, Periander, Phalaris, Dionysius, and I know not how many more of the same kennel, that speed well enough to their abominable injustice or usurpation. I conclude, therefore, that he excelleth history, not only in furnishing the mind with knowledge, but in setting it forward to that which deserveth to be called and accounted good: which setting forward, and moving to well doing, indeed setteth the laurel crown upon the poet as victorious, not only of the historian, but over the philosopher, howsoever in teaching it may be questionable.

For suppose it be granted (that which I suppose with great reason may be denied) that the philosopher, in respect of his methodical proceeding, doth teach more perfectly than the poet, yet do I think that no man is so much *philophiloso-phos*[24] as to compare the philosopher, in moving, with the poet.

And that moving is of a higher degree than teaching, it may by this appear, that it is well-nigh the cause and the effect of teaching. For who will be taught, if he be not moved with desire to be taught, and what so much good doth that teaching

22 He did not know literature.

23 They must be put to death.

24 A lover of philosophy.

bring forth (I speak still of moral doctrine) as that it moveth one to do that which it doth teach? For, as Aristotle saith, it is not *gnosis* but *praxis*[25] must be the fruit. And how *praxis* cannot be, without being moved to practice, it is no hard matter to consider.

The philosopher showeth you the way, he informeth you of the particularities, as well of the tediousness of the way, as of the pleasant lodging you shall have when your journey is ended, as of the many by-turnings that may divert you from your way. But this is to no man but to him that will read him, and read him with attentive studious painfulness; which constant desire whosoever hath in him, hath already passed half the hardness of the way, and therefore is beholding to the philosopher but for the other half. Nay truly, learned men have learnedly thought that where once reason hath so much over-mastered passion as that the mind hath a free desire to do well, the inward light each mind hath in itself is as good as a philosopher's book; seeing in nature we know it is well to do well, and what is well and what is evil, although not in the words of art which philosophers bestow upon us. For out of natural conceit the philosophers drew it; but to be moved to do that which we know, or to be moved with desire to know, *Hoc opus, hic labor est.*[26]

Now therein of all sciences (I speak still of human, and according to the humane conceits) is our poet the monarch. For he doth not only show the way, but giveth so sweet a prospect into the way, as will entice any man to enter into it. Nay, he doth, as if your journey should lie through a fair vineyard, at the first give you a cluster of grapes, that, full of that taste, you may long to pass further. He beginneth not with obscure definitions, which must blur the margent[27] with interpretations, and load the memory with doubtfulness; but he cometh to you with words set in delightful proportion, either accompanied with, or prepared for, the well-enchanting skill of music; and with a tale forsooth he cometh unto you, with a tale which holdeth children from play, and old men from the chimney corner. And, pretending no more, doth intend the winning of the mind with wickedness to virtue: even as the child is often brought to take most wholesome things by hiding them in such other as have a pleasant taste: which, if one should begin to tell them the nature of aloes or rhubarb they should receive, would sooner take their physic at their ears than at their mouth. So is it in men (most of which are childish in the best things, till they be cradled in their graves): glad they will be to hear the tales of Hercules, Achilles, Cyrus, and Aeneas; and, hearing them, must needs hear the right description of wisdom, valor, and justice; which, if they had been barely, that is to say philosophically, set out, they would swear they be brought to school again.

That imitation whereof poetry is, hath the most conveniency to nature of all other, insomuch that, as Aristotle saith, those things which in themselves are horrible, as cruel battles, unnatural monsters, are made in poetical imitation delightful. Truly, I have known men, that even with reading *Amadis de Gaule* (which God knoweth wanteth much of a perfect poesy) have found their hearts moved to the exercise of courtesy, liberality, and especially courage.

Who readeth Aeneas carrying old Anchises on his back, that wisheth not it were his fortune to perform so excellent an act? Whom do not the words of Turnus move, the tale of Turnus having planted his image in the imagination? — *"Fugientem haec terra videbit? / Usque adeone mori miserum est?"*[28] Where the philosophers, as they scorn to delight, so must they be content little to move, saving wrangling whether virtue be the chief or the only good, whether the contemplative or the active life do excel: which Plato and Boethius well knew, and therefore made Mistress Philosophy very often borrow the masking raiment of Poesy. For even those hard-hearted evil men who think virtue a school name, and know no other good but *indulgere genio,*[29] and therefore despise the austere admonitions

---

[25]Not abstract knowledge but action.

[26]"That is the labor, that is the task." Virgil, *Aeneid* 6:129.

[27]The margins of the page, where the notes to a text were then placed.

[28]"And shall the land see me fleeing? And after all, is death so sad a thing?" *Aeneid* 12:645–46.

[29]To indulge one's nature.

of the philosopher, and feel not the inward reason they stand upon, yet will be content to be delighted — which is all the good fellow poet seemeth to promise — and so steal to see the form of goodness, which seen they cannot but love ere themselves be aware, as if they took a medicine of cherries. Infinite proofs of the strange effects of his poetical invention might be alleged; only two shall serve, which are so often remembered as I think all men know them.

The one of Menenius Agrippa, who, when the whole people of Rome had resolutely divided themselves from the Senate, with apparent show of utter ruin, though he were (for that time) an excellent orator, came not among them upon trust of figurative speeches or cunning insinuations, and much less with farfetched maxims of philosophy, which (especially if they were Platonic) they must have learned geometry before they could well have conceived; but forsooth he behaves himself like a homely and familiar poet. He telleth them a tale, that there was a time when all the parts of the body made a mutinous conspiracy against the belly, which they thought devoured the fruits of each other's labor; they concluded they would let so unprofitable a spender starve. In the end, to be short (for the tale is notorious, and as notorious that it was a tale), with punishing the belly they plagued themselves. This applied by him wrought such effect in the people, as I never read that ever words brought forth but then so sudden and so good an alteration; for upon reasonable conditions a perfect reconcilement ensued. The other is of Nathan the Prophet, who, when the holy David had so far forsaken God as to confirm adultery with murder, when he was to do the tenderest office of a friend, in laying his own shame before his eyes, sent by God to call again so chosen a servant, how doth he it but by telling of a man whose beloved lamb was ungratefully taken from his bosom? — the application most divinely true, but the discourse itself feigned. Which made David (I speak of the second and instrumental cause) as in a glass to see his own filthiness, as that heavenly Psalm of Mercy well testifieth.

By these, therefore, examples and reasons, I think it may be manifest that the poet, with that same hand of delight, doth draw the mind more effectually than any other art doth: and so a conclusion not unfitly ensueth, that, as virtue is the most excellent resting place for all worldly learning to make his end of, so poetry, being the most familiar to teach it, and most princely to move towards it, in the most excellent work is the most excellent workman. But I am content not only to decipher him by his works (although works in commendation or dispraise must ever hold an high authority), but more narrowly will examine his parts: so that, as in a man, though all together may carry a presence full of majesty and beauty, perchance in some one defectious piece we may find a blemish. Now in his parts, kinds, or species (as you list to term them), it is to be noted that some poesies have coupled together two or three kinds, as tragical and comical, whereupon is risen the tragicomical. Some, in the like manner, have mingled prose and verse, as Sannazzaro and Boethius. Some have mingled matters heroical and pastoral. But that cometh all to one in this question, for, if severed they be good, the conjunction cannot be hurtful. Therefore, perchance forgetting some, and leaving some as needless to be remembered, it shall not be amiss in a word to cite the special kinds, to see what faults may be found in the right use of them.

Is it then the pastoral poem which is misliked? For perchance where the hedge is lowest they will soonest leap over. Is the poor pipe disdained, which sometime out of Meliboeus's mouth can show the misery of people under hard lords or ravening soldiers, and again, by Tityrus, what blessedness is derived to them that lie lowest from the goodness of them that sit highest; sometimes, under the pretty tales of wolves and sheep, can include the whole considerations of wrong doing and patience; sometimes show that contention for trifles can get but a trifling victory; where perchance a man may see that even Alexander and Darius, when they strave who should be cock of this world's dunghill, the benefit they got was that the afterlivers may say, *"Haec memini et victum frustra contendere Thyrsin: / Ex illo Corydon Corydon est tempore nobis."*[30]

30. "I remember those things, and that conquered Thyrsis strove in vain: Since then Corydon is for us Corydon." Virgil, *Eclogues 7:69–70.*

Or is it the lamenting elegiac, which in a kind heart would move rather pity than blame, who bewails with the great philosopher Heraclitus the weakness of mankind and the wretchedness of the world; who surely is to be praised, either for compassionate accompanying just causes of lamentation, or for rightly pointing out how weak be the passions of woefulness? Is it the bitter but wholesome iambic, which rubs the galled mind, in making shame the trumpet of villainy with bold and open crying out against naughtiness? Or the satiric, who *"omne vafer vitium ridenti tangit amico",*[31] who sportingly never leaveth until he make a man laugh at folly, and, at length ashamed, to laugh at himself, which he cannot avoid, without avoiding the folly; who, while *"circum praecordia ludit,"*[32] giveth us to feel how many headaches a passionate life bringeth us to; how, when all is done, *"est Ulubris animus si nos non deficit aequus?"*[33]

No, perchance it is the comic, whom naughty play-makers and stage-keepers have justly made odious. To the argument of abuse I will answer after. Only thus much now is to be said, that the comedy is an imitation of the common errors of our life, which he representeth in the most ridiculous and scornful sort that may be, so as it is impossible that any beholder can be content to be such a one.

Now, as in geometry the oblique must be known as well as the right, and in arithmetic the odd as well as the even, so in the actions of our life who seeth not the filthiness of evil wanteth a great foil to perceive the beauty of virtue. This doth the comedy handle so in our private and domestical matters, as with hearing it we get as it were an experience, what is to be looked for of a niggardly Demea, of a crafty Davus, of a flattering Gnatho, of a vainglorious Thraso; and not only to know what effects are to be expected, but to know who be such, by the signifying badge given them by the comedian. And little reason

hath any man to say that men learn evil by seeing it so set out; since, as I said before, there is no man living but, by the force truth hath in nature, no sooner seeth these men play their parts, but wisheth them in *pistrinum;*[34] although perchance the sack of his own faults lie so behind his back that he seeth not himself dance the same measure; whereto yet nothing can more open his eyes than to find his own actions contemptibly set forth. So that the right use of comedy will (I think) by nobody be blamed, and much less of the high and excellent tragedy, that openeth the greatest wounds, and showeth forth the ulcers that are covered with tissue; that maketh kings fear to be tyrants, and tyrants manifest their tyrannical humors; that, with stirring the affects of admiration and commiseration, teacheth the uncertainty of this world, and upon how weak foundations gilden roofs are builded; that maketh us know, *"Qui sceptra saevus duro imperio regit, / Timet timentes, metus in auctorem redit."*[35]

But how much it can move, Plutarch yieldeth a notable testimony of the abominable tyrant Alexander Pheraeus, from whose eyes a tragedy, well made and represented, drew abundance of tears, who, without all pity, had murdered infinite numbers, and some of his own blood, so as he, that was not ashamed to make matters for tragedies, yet could not resist the sweet violence of a tragedy.

And if it wrought no further good in him, it was that he, in despite of himself, withdrew himself from hearkening to that which might mollify his hardened heart. But it is not the tragedy they do mislike; for it were too absurd to cast out so excellent a representation of whatsoever is most worthy to be learned. Is it the lyric that most displeaseth, who with his tuned lyre, and well-accorded voice, giveth praise, the reward of virtue, to virtuous acts, who gives moral precepts, and natural problems, who sometimes raiseth up his voice to the height of the heavens, in singing the lauds of the immortal God? Certainly, I must confess my own barbarousness, I never heard the

---

[31]"The rogue touches every vice while making his friend laugh." Persius, *Satires* 1:116–17.

[32]"He plays about the heartstrings." From the passage above.

[33]"Happiness is to be found, even in Ulubrae [a dead city], so long as we don't lose our sense of proportion." Horace, *Epistles* I.11:30.

[34]A treadmill for slaves.

[35]"The savage ruler who wields the sceptre with a hard hand / Fears the timid, and thus fear returns to its author." Seneca, *Oedipus,* 705–06.

most accomplished kind of poetry.[36] For as the image of each action stirreth and instructeth the mind, so the lofty image of such worthies most inflameth the mind with desire to be worthy, and informs with counsel how to be worthy. Only let Aeneas be worn in the tablet of your memory, how he governeth himself in the ruin of his country, in the preserving his old father, and carrying away his religious ceremonies, in obeying the god's commandment to leave Dido, though not only all passionate kindness, but even the human consideration of virtuous gratefulness, would have craved other of him; how in peace, how in storms, how in sports, how in war; how besieged, how besieging, how to strangers, how to allies, how to enemies, how to his own; lastly, how in his inward self, and how in his outward government, and I think, in a mind not prejudiced with a prejudicating humor, he will be found in excellency fruitful, yea, even as Horace saith, "*melius Chrysippo et Crantore.*"[37]

But truly I imagine it falleth out with these poet-whippers, as with some good women, who often are sick, but in faith they cannot tell where. So the name of poetry is odious to them, but neither his cause nor effects, neither the sum that contains him nor the particularities descending from him, give any fast handle to their carping dispraise.

Since then poetry is of all human learning the most ancient and of most fatherly antiquity, as from whence other learnings have taken their beginnings; since it is so universal that no learned nation doth despise it, nor no barbarous nation is without it; since both Roman and Greek gave divine names unto it, the one of *prophesying*, the other of *making*, and that indeed that name of *making* is fit for him, considering that whereas other arts retain themselves within their subject, and receive, as it were, their being from it, the poet only bringeth his own stuff, and doth not

36 It was characteristic of Renaissance criticism to favor epic over tragedy — unlike Aristotle, who in *Poetics*, Ch. 26, had favored the concise tragedy over the full-blown epic.

37 "Better than Chrysippus and Crantor." Horace, *Epistles* 1.2:4. Horace claims that Homer teaches virtue better than the above-mentioned two philosophers.

old song of Percy and Douglas that I found not my heart moved more than with a trumpet; and yet is it sung but by some blind crowder, with no rougher voice than rude style; which, being so evil appareled in the dust and cobwebs of that uncivil age, what would it work, trimmed in the gorgeous eloquence of Pindar? In Hungary I have seen it the manner at all feasts, and other such meetings, to have songs of their ancestors' valor; which that right soldierlike nation think the chiefest kindlers of brave courage. The incomparable Lacedaemonians did not only carry that kind of music ever with them to the field, but even at home, as such songs were made, so were they all content to be the singers of them, when the lusty men were to tell what they did, the old men what they had done, and the young men what they would do. And where a man may say that Pindar many times praiseth highly victories of small moment, matters rather of sport than virtue; as it may be answered, it was the fault of the poet, and not of the poetry, so indeed the chief fault was in the time and custom of the Greeks, who set those toys at so high a price that Philip of Macedon reckoned a horse race won at Olympus among his three fearful felicities. But as the inimitable Pindar often did, so is that kind most capable and most fit to awake the thoughts from the sleep of idleness, to embrace honorable enterprises.

There rests the heroical, whose very name (I think) should daunt all backbiters; for by what conceit can a tongue be directed to speak evil of that which draweth with it no less champions than Achilles, Cyrus, Aeneas, Turnus, Tydeus, and Rinaldo? Who doth not only teach and move to a truth, but teacheth and moveth to the most high and excellent truth; who maketh magnanimity and justice shine throughout all misty fearfulness and foggy desires; who, if the saying of Plato and Tully be true, that who could see virtue would be wonderfully ravished with the love of her beauty — this man sets her out to make her more lovely in her holiday apparel, to the eye of any that will deign not to disdain until they understand. But if anything be already said in the defense of sweet Poetry, all concurreth to the maintaining the heroical, which is not only a kind, but the best and

learn a conceit out of a matter, but maketh matter for a conceit; since neither his description nor his end containeth any evil, the thing described cannot be evil; since his effects be so good as to teach goodness and to delight the learners; since therein (namely in moral doctrine, the chief of all knowledges) he doth not only far pass the historian, but, for instructing, is well-nigh comparable to the philosopher, and, for moving, leaves him behind him; since the Holy Scripture (wherein there is no uncleanness) hath whole parts in it poetical, and that even our Saviour Christ vouchsafed to use the flowers of it; since all his kinds are not only in their united forms but in their severed dissections fully commendable; I think (and think I think rightly) the laurel crown appointed for triumphing captains doth worthily (of all other learnings) honor the poet's triumph. But because we have ears as well as tongues, and that the lightest reasons that may be will seem to weigh greatly, if nothing be put in the counter-balance, let us hear, and, as well as we can, ponder, what objections may be made against this art, which may be worthy either of yielding or answering.

First, truly I note not only in these *mysomousoi,* "poet-haters," but in all that kind of people who seek a praise by dispraising others, that they do prodigally spend a great many wandering words in quips and scoffs, carping and taunting at each thing, which, by stirring the spleen, may stay the brain from a thorough beholding the worthiness of the subject.

Those kind of objections, as they are full of very idle easiness, since there is nothing of so sacred a majesty but that an itching tongue may rub itself upon it, so deserve they no other answer, but, instead of laughing at the jest, to laugh at the jester. We know a playing wit can praise the discretion of an ass, the comfortableness of being in debt, and the jolly commodity of being sick of the plague. So of the contrary side, if we will turn Ovid's verse, *"Ut lateat virtus proximitate mali,"* that "good lie hid in nearness of the evil," Agrippa will be as merry in showing the vanity of science as Erasmus was in commending of folly. Neither shall any man or matter escape some touch of these smiling railers. But for Erasmus and Agrippa, they had another foundation than the superficial part would promise.

Marry, these other pleasant faultfinders, who will correct the verb before they understand the noun, and confute others' knowledge before they confirm their own, I would have them only remember that scoffing cometh not of wisdom; so as the best title in true English they get with their merriments is to be called good fools, for so have our grave forefathers ever termed that humorous kind of jesters. But that which giveth greatest scope to their scorning humors is rhyming and versing. It is already said (and, as I think truly said) it is not rhyming and versing that maketh poesy. One may be a poet without versing, and a versifier without poetry. But yet presuppose it were inseparable (as indeed it seemeth Scaliger judgeth) truly it were an inseparable commendation.[38] For if *oratio* next to *ratio,* "speech" next to "reason," be the greatest gift bestowed upon mortality, that cannot be praiseless which doth most polish that blessing of speech; which considers each word, not only (as a man may say) by his forcible quality, but by his best measured quantity, carrying even in themselves a harmony (without, perchance, number, measure, order, proportion be in our time grown odious). But lay aside the just praise it hath, by being the only fit speech for music (music, I say, the most divine striker of the senses), thus much is undoubtedly true, that if reading be foolish without remembering, memory being the only treasurer of knowledge, those words which are fittest for memory are likewise most convenient for knowledge.

Now, that verse far exceedeth prose in the knitting up of the memory, the reason is manifest — the words (besides their delight, which hath a great affinity to memory) being so set as one word cannot be lost but the whole work fails; which accuseth itself, calleth the remembrance back to itself, and so most strongly confirmeth it. Besides, one word so, as it were, begetting another, as, be it in rhyme or measured verse, by the former a man shall have a near guess to the follower: lastly, even they that have taught the art of memory have showed nothing so apt for it as a certain room divided into many

[38]In his *Poetics,* Julius Caesar Scaliger claimed that what the poet made was verses; Aristotle identified the poet's primary product as the imitation of a human action.

places well and thoroughly known. Now, that hath the verse in effect perfectly, every word having his natural seat, which seat must needs make the words remembered. But what needeth more in a thing so known to all men? Who is it that ever was a scholar that doth not carry away some verses of Virgil, Horace, or Cato, which in his youth he learned, and even to his old age serve him for hourly lessons? But the fitness it hath for memory is notably proved by all deliv-ery of arts: wherein for the most part, from gram-mar to logic, mathematic, physic, and the rest, the rules chiefly necessary to be borne away are compiled in verses. So that, verse being in itself sweet and orderly, and being best for memory, the only handle of knowledge, it must be in jest that any man can speak against it. Now then go we to the most important imputations laid to the poor poets. For aught I can yet learn, they are these. First, that there being many other more fruitful knowledges, a man might better spend his time in them than in this. Secondly, that it is the mother of lies. Thirdly, that it is the nurse of abuse, infecting us with many pestilent desires, with a siren's sweetness drawing the mind to the serpent's tale of sinful fancy — and herein, especially, comedies give the largest field to ear (as Chaucer saith) — how both in other nations and in ours, before poets did soften us, we were full of courage, given to martial exercises, the pillars of manlike liberty, and not lulled asleep in shady idleness with poets' pastimes. And lastly, and chiefly, they cry out with an open mouth, as if they outshot Robin Hood, that Plato banished them out of his commonwealth.[39] Truly, this is much, if there be much truth in it. First, to the first, that a man might better spend his time is a reason indeed: but it doth (as they say) but *petere principium*:[40] for if it be, as I affirm, that no learning is so good as that which teacheth and moveth to virtue, and that none can both teach and move thereto so much as poetry, then is the conclusion manifest that ink and paper cannot be to a more profitable purpose employed. And certainly, though a man should grant their first assumption, it should follow (methinks) very

unwillingly, that good is not good because better is better. But I still and utterly deny that there is sprung out of earth a more fruitful knowledge. To the second therefore, that they should be the principal liars, I answer paradoxically, but truly, I think truly, that of all writers under the sun the poet is the least liar, and, though he would, as a poet can scarcely be a liar. The astronomer, with his cousin the geometrician, can hardly escape, when they take upon them to measure the height of the stars.

How often, think you, do the physicians lie, when they aver things good for sicknesses, which afterwards send Charon a great number of souls drowned in a potion before they come to his ferry? And no less of the rest, which take upon them to affirm. Now, for the poet, he nothing affirms, and therefore never lieth. For, as I take it, to lie is to affirm that to be true which is false; so as the other artists, and especially the historian, affirming many things, can, in the cloudy knowl-edge of mankind, hardly escape from many lies. But the poet (as I said before) never affirmeth. The poet never maketh any circles about your imagination, to conjure you to believe for true what he writes. He citeth not authorities of other histories, but even for his entry calleth the sweet Muses to inspire into him a good invention; in truth, no laboring to tell you what is, or is not, but what should or should not be. And therefore, though he recount things not true, yet because he telleth them not for true, he lieth not — without we will say that Nathan lied in his speech, before alleged, to David; which as a wicked man durst scarce say, so think I none so simple would say that Aesop lied in the tales of his beasts: for who thinks that Aesop writ it for actually true were well worthy to have his name chronicled among the beasts he writeth of.

What child is there that, coming to a play, and seeing *Thebes* written in great letters upon an old door, doth believe that it is Thebes? If then a man can arrive, at that child's age, to know that the poets' persons and doings are but pictures what should be, and not stories what have been, they will never give the lie to things not affirmatively but allegorically and figuratively written. And therefore, as in history, looking for truth, they go away full fraught with falsehood, so in poesy,

[39]Plato, *Republic*, see pp. 35-37.

[40]To beg the question — assume what one needs to prove.

looking for fiction, they shall use the narration but as an imaginative ground plot of a profitable invention.

But hereto is replied, that the poets give names to men they write of, which argueth a conceit of an actual truth, and so, not being true, proves a falsehood. And doth the lawyer lie then, when under the names of John a Stile and John a Noakes he puts his case? But that is easily answered. Their naming of men is but to make their picture the more lively, and not to build any history; painting men, they cannot leave men nameless. We see we cannot play at chess but that we must give names to our chessmen; and yet, methinks, he were a very partial champion of truth that would say we lied for giving a piece of wood the reverend title of a bishop. The poet nameth Cyrus or Aeneas no other way than to show what men of their fames, fortunes, and estates should do.

Their third is, how much it abuseth men's wit, training it to wanton sinfulness and lustful love: for indeed that is the principal, if not the only, abuse I can hear alleged. They say the comedies rather teach than reprehend amorous conceits. They say the lyric is larded with passionate sonnets, the elegiac weeps the want of his mistress, and that even to the heroical Cupid hath ambitiously climbed. Alas, Love, I would thou couldst as well defend thyself as thou canst offend others. I would those on whom thou dost attend could either put thee away, or yield good reason why they keep thee. But grant love of beauty to be a beastly fault (although it be very hard, since only man, and no beast, hath that gift to discern beauty); grant that lovely name of Love to deserve all hateful reproaches (although even some of my masters the philosophers spent a good deal of their lamp-oil in setting forth the excellency of it); grant, I say, whatsoever they will have granted; that not only love, but lust, but vanity, but (if they list) scurrility, possesseth many leaves of the poets' books: yet think I, when this is granted, they will find their sentence may with good manners put the last words foremost, and not say that poetry abuseth man's wit, but that man's wit abuseth poetry.

For I will not deny but that man's wit may make poesy, which should be *eikastike*, which some learned have defined, "figuring forth good things," to be *phantastike,* which doth, contrariwise, infect the fancy with unworthy objects, as the painter, that should give to the eye either some excellent perspective, or some fine picture, fit for building or fortification, or containing in it some notable example, as Abraham sacrificing his son Isaac, Judith killing Holofernes, David fighting with Goliath, may leave those, and please an ill-pleased eye with wanton shows of better hidden matters. But what, shall the abuse of a thing make the right use odious? Nay truly, though I yield that poesy may not only be abused, but that being abused, by the reason of his sweet charming force, it can do more hurt than any other army of words, yet shall it be so far from concluding that the abuse should give reproach to the abused, that contrariwise it is a good reason, that whatsoever, being abused, doth most harm, being rightly used (and upon the right use each thing conceiveth his title), doth most good.

Do we not see the skill of physic (the best rampire[41] to our often-assaulted bodies), being abused, teach poison, the most violent destroyer? Doth not knowledge of law, whose end is to even and right all things, being abused, grow the crooked fosterer of horrible injuries? Doth not (to go to the highest) God's word abused breed heresy, and his name abused become blasphemy? Truly, a needle cannot do much hurt, and as truly (with leave of ladies be it spoken) it cannot do much good. With a sword thou mayest kill thy father, and with a sword thou mayest defend thy prince and country. So that, as in their calling poets the fathers of lies they say nothing, so in this their argument of abuse they prove the commendation.

They allege herewith, that before poets began to be in price our nation hath set their heart's delight upon action, and not upon imagination, rather doing things worthy to be written, than writing things fit to be done. What that beforetime was, I think scarcely Sphinx can tell, since no memory is so ancient that hath the precedence of poetry. And certain it is that, in our plainest homeliness, yet never was the Albion nation without poetry. Marry, this argument, though it be leveled against poetry, yet is it indeed a

[41]Rampart, defense.

chainshot against all learning, or bookishness, as they commonly term it. Of such mind were certain Goths, of whom it is written that, having in the spoil of a famous city taken a fair library, one hangman, belike, fit to execute the fruits of their wits, who had murdered a great number of bodies, would have set fire to it. "No," said another very gravely, "take heed what you do, for while they are busy about these toys, we shall with more leisure conquer their countries."

This indeed is the ordinary doctrine of ignorance, and many words sometimes I have heard spent in it: but because this reason is generally against all learning, as well as poetry, or rather, all learning but poetry; because it were too large a digression to handle, or at least too superfluous (since it is manifest that all government of action is to be gotten by knowledge, and knowledge best by gathering many knowledges, which is reading), I only, with Horace, to him that is of that opinion, "*jubeo stultum esse libenter*";[42] for as for poetry itself, it is the freest from this objection. For poetry is the companion of the camps. I dare undertake, Orlando Furioso, or honest King Arthur, will never displease a soldier: but the quiddity of *ens* and *prima materia*[43] will hardly agree with a corselet. And therefore, as I said in the beginning, even Turks and Tartars are delighted with poets. Homer, a Greek, flourished before Greece flourished. And if to a slight conjecture a conjecture may be opposed, truly it may seem, that, as by him their learned men took almost their first light of knowledge, so their active men received their first motions of courage. Only Alexander's example may serve, who by Plutarch is accounted of such virtue, that fortune was not his guide but his footstool; whose acts speak for him, though Plutarch did not — indeed the Phoenix of warlike princes. This Alexander left his schoolmaster, living Aristotle, behind him, but took dead Homer with him. He put the philosopher Callisthenes to death for his seeming philosophical, indeed mutinous, stubbornness, but the chief thing he ever was

heard to wish for was that Homer had been alive. He well found he received more bravery of mind by the pattern of Achilles than by hearing the definition of fortitude: and therefore, if Cato misliked Fulvius for carrying Ennius with him to the field, it may be answered that, if Cato misliked it, the noble Fulvius liked it, or else he had not done it: for it was not the excellent Cato Uticensis (whose authority I would much more have reverenced), but it was the former, in truth a bitter punisher of faults, but else a man that had never well sacrificed to the Graces. He misliked and cried out upon all Greek learning, and yet, being eighty years old, began to learn it, belike fearing that Pluto understood not Latin. Indeed, the Roman laws allowed no person to be carried to the wars but that he that was in the soldier's roll, and therefore, though Cato misliked his unmustered persons, he misliked not his work. And if he had, Scipio Nasica, judged by common consent the best Roman, loved him. Both the other Scipio brothers, who had by their virtues no less surnames than of Asia and Afric, so loved him that they caused his body to be buried in their sepulcher. So as Cato's authority being but against his person, and that answered with so far greater than himself, is herein of no validity. But now indeed my burden is great; now Plato's name is laid upon me, whom I must confess, of all philosophers I have ever esteemed most worthy of reverence, and with great reason, since of all philosophers he is the most poetical. Yet if he will defile the fountain out of which his flowing streams have proceeded, let us boldly examine with what reasons he did it. First truly, a man might maliciously object that Plato, being a philosopher, was a natural enemy of poets. For indeed, after the philosophers had picked out of the sweet mysteries of poetry the right discerning true points of knowledge, they forthwith, putting it in method, and making a school art of that which the poets did only teach by a divine delightfulness, beginning to spurn at their guides, like ungrateful 'prentices, were not content to set up shops for themselves, but sought by all means to discredit their masters; which by the force of delight being barred them, the less they could overthrow them, the more they hated them. For indeed, they found for Homer seven cities strove who should have

42"I ask him to be a fool as much as he likes." Horace, *Satires* 1:63.

43The whatness of being and primal matter. Sidney uses scholastic terms here.

him for their citizen; where many cities banished philosophers as not fit members to live among them. For only repeating certain of Euripides' verses, many Athenians had their lives saved of the Syracusians, when the Athenians themselves thought many philosophers unworthy to live.

Certain poets, as Simonides and Pindarus, had so prevailed with Hiero the First, that of a tyrant they made him a just king; where Plato could do so little with Dionysius, that he himself of a philosopher was made a slave. But who should do thus, I confess, should require the objections made against poets with like cavillation against philosophers; as likewise one should do that should bid one read *Phaedrus* or *Symposium* in Plato, or the discourse of love in Plutarch, and see whether any poet do authorize abominable filthiness, as they do. Again, a man might ask out of what commonwealth Plato did banish them. In sooth, thence where he himself alloweth community of women. So as belike this banishment grew not for effeminate wantonness, since little should poetical sonnets be hurtful when a man might have what woman he listed. But I honor philosophical instructions, and bless the wits which bred them: so as they be not abused, which is likewise stretched to poetry.

St. Paul himself, who yet, for the credit of poets, allegeth twice two poets, and one of them by the name of a prophet, setteth a watchword upon philosophy — indeed upon the abuse. So doth Plato upon the abuse, not upon poetry. Plato found fault that the poets of his time filled the world with wrong opinions of the gods, making light tales of that unspotted essence, and therefore would not have the youth depraved with such opinions. Herein may much be said; let this suffice: the poets did not induce such opinions, but did imitate those opinions already induced. For all the Greek stories can well testify that the very religion of that time stood upon many and many-fashioned gods, not taught so by the poets, but followed according to their nature of imitation. Who list may read in Plutarch the discourses of Isis and Osiris, of the cause why oracles ceased, of the divine providence, and see whether the theology of that nation stood not upon such dreams which the poets indeed superstitiously observed, and truly (since they had not the light of Christ) did much

better in it than the philosophers, who, shaking off superstition, brought in atheism. Plato therefore (whose authority I had much rather justly construe than unjustly resist) meant not in general of poets, in those words of which Julius Scaliger saith, *"Qua authoritate barbari quidam atque hispidi abuti velint ad poetas e republica exigendos"*;[44] but only meant to drive out those wrong opinions of the Deity (whereof now, without further law, Christianity hath taken away all the hurtful belief), perchance (as he thought) nourished by the then esteemed poets. And a man need go no further than to Plato himself to know his meaning: who, in his dialogue called *Ion,* giveth high and rightly divine commendation to poetry. So as Plato, banishing the abuse, not the thing, not banishing it, but giving due honor unto it, shall be our patron and not our adversary. For indeed I had much rather (since truly I may do it) show their mistaking of Plato (under whose lion's skin they would make an asslike braying against poesy) than go about to overthrow his authority; whom, the wiser a man is, the more just cause he shall find to have in admiration; especially since he attributeth unto poesy more than myself do, namely, to be a very inspiring of a divine force, far above man's wit, as in the afore-named dialogue is apparent.

Of the other side, who would show the honors have been by the best sort of judgments granted them, a whole sea of examples would present themselves: Alexanders, Caesars, Scipios, all favorers of poets; Laelius, called the Roman Socrates, himself a poet, so as part of *Heautontimorumenos*[45] in Terence was supposed to be made by him, and even the Greek Socrates, whom Apollo confirmed to be the only wise man, is said to have spent part of his old time in putting Aesop's fables into verses. And therefore, full evil should it become his scholar Plato to put such words in his master's mouth against poets. But what need more? Aristotle writes the *Art of Poesy:* and why, if it should not be written? Plutarch teacheth the use to be gathered of them, and how, if they should not be read? And who reads Plutarch's either history or philosophy,

[44]"Barbarous and rude men would abuse this authority to drive poets out of the republic." Scaliger, *Poetics* I:2.
[45]*The Self-Tormentor.*

shall find he trimmeth both their garments with guards of poesy. But I list not to defend poesy with the help of her underling historiography. Let it suffice that it is a fit soil for praise to dwell upon; and what dispraise may set upon it, is either easily overcome, or transformed into just commendation. So that, since the excellencies of it may be so easily and so justly confirmed, and the low-creeping objections so soon trodden down; it not being an art of lies, but of true doctrine; not of effeminateness, but of notable stirring of courage; not of abusing man's wit, but of strengthening man's wit; not banished, but honored by Plato: let us rather plant more laurels for to engarland our poets' heads (which honor of being laureate, as besides them only triumphant captains wear, is a sufficient authority to show the price they ought to be had in) than suffer the ill-favoring breath of such wrongspeakers once to blow upon the clear springs of poesy.

But since I have so long a career in this matter, methinks, before I give my pen a full stop, it shall be but a little more lost time to inquire why England (the mother of excellent minds) should be grown so hard a stepmother to poets, who certainly in wit ought to pass all other, since all only proceedeth from their wit, being indeed makers of themselves, not takers of others. How can I but exclaim, "*Musa, mihi causas memora, quo numine laeso!*"[46] Sweet Poesy, that hath anciently had kings, emperors, senators, great captains, such as, besides a thousand others, David, Adrian, Sophocles, Germanicus, not only to favor poets, but to be poets; and of our nearer times can present for her patrons a Robert, king of Sicily, the great King Francis of France, King James of Scotland; such cardinals as Bembus and Bibbiena; such famous preachers and teachers as Beza and Melanchthon; so learned philosophers as Fracastorius and Scaliger; so great orators as Pontanus and Muretus; so piercing wits as George Buchanan; so grave counselors as, besides many, but before all, that Hospital of France, than whom (I think) that realm never brought forth a more accomplished judgment, more firmly builded upon virtue — I say, these, with numbers of others, not

only to read others' poesies, but to poetize for others' reading — that poesy, thus embraced in all other places, should only find in our time a hard welcome in England, I think the very earth lamenteth it, and therefore decketh our soil with fewer laurels than it was accustomed. For heretofore poets have in England also flourished, and, which is to be noted, even in those times when the trumpet of Mars did sound loudest. And now that an overfaint quietness should seem to strew the house for poets, they are almost in as good reputation as the mountebanks at Venice. Truly even that, as of the one side it giveth great praise to poesy, which like Venus (but to better purpose) hath rather be troubled in the net with Mars than enjoy the homely quiet of Vulcan; so serves it for a piece of a reason why they are less grateful to idle England, which now can scarce endure the pain of a pen. Upon this necessarily followeth, that base men with servile wits undertake it, who think it enough if they can be rewarded of the printer. And so as Epaminondas is said, with the honor of his virtue, to have made an office, by his exercising it, which before was contemptible, to become highly respected, so these, no more but setting their names to it, by their own disgracefulness disgrace the most graceful poesy. For now, as if all the Muses were got with child, to bring forth bastard poets, without any commission they do post over the banks of Helicon, till they make the readers more weary than post-horses, while, in the meantime, they, "*quis meliore luto finxit praecordia Titan,*"[47] are better content to suppress the outflowing of their wit, than, by publishing them, to be accounted knights of the same order. But I, that, before ever I durst aspire unto the dignity, am admitted into the company of the paper-blurrers, do find the very true cause of our wanting estimation is want of desert, taking upon us to be poets in despite of Pallas. Now, wherein we want desert were a thankworthy labor to express: but if I knew, I should have mended myself. But I, as I never desired the title, so have I neglected the means to come by it. Only, overmastered by some thoughts, I yielded an inky tribute unto them. Marry, they that delight in poesy itself should

---

[46] "Tell me the reason, Muse: what was the injury to her divinity?" Virgil, *Aeneid* I:8.

[47] "Whom the Titan has formed out of finer clay," Juvenal, *Satires* 14:35.

seek to know what they do, and how they do, and, especially, look themselves in an unflattering glass of reason, if they be inclinable unto it. For poesy must not be drawn by the ears; it must be gently led, or rather it must lead; which was partly the cause that made the ancient-learned affirm it was a divine gift, and no human skill; since all other knowledges lie ready for any that hath strength of wit; a poet no industry can make, if his own genius be not carried unto it; and therefore is it an old proverb, *Orator fit, poeta nascitur.*[48] Yet confess I always that as the fertilest ground must be manured, so must the highest-flying wit have a Daedalus to guide him. that Daedalus, they say, both in this and in other, hath three wings to bear itself up into the air of due commendation: that is, art, imitation, and exercise. But these, neither artificial rules nor imitative patterns, we much cumber ourselves withal. Exercise indeed we do, but that very forebackwardly: for where we should exercise to know, we exercise as having known: and so is our brain delivered of much matter which never was begotten by knowledge. For, there being two principal parts — matter to be expressed by words and words to express the matter — in neither we use art or imitation rightly. Our matter is *quodlibet*[49] indeed, though wrongly performing Ovid's verse, *"Quicquid conabar dicere, versus erat":*[50] never marshaling it into an assured rank, that almost the readers cannot tell where to find themselves.

Chaucer, undoubtedly, did excellently in his *Troilus and Cressida;* of whom, truly, I know not whether to marvel more, either that he in that misty time could see so clearly, or that we in this clear age walk so stumblingly after him. Yet had he great wants, fit to be forgiven in so reverent antiquity. I account the *Mirror of Magistrates* meetly furnished of beautiful parts, and in the Earl of Surrey's lyrics many things tasting of a noble birth, and worthy of a noble mind. The *Shepherd's Calendar* hath much poetry in his eclogues, indeed worthy the reading, if I be not deceived. That same framing of his style to an old rustic language I dare not allow, since

neither Theocritus in Greek, Virgil in Latin, nor Sannazzaro in Italian did affect it. Besides these, do I not remember to have seen but few (to speak boldly) printed, that have poetical sinews in them: for proof whereof, let but most of the verses be put in prose, and then ask the meaning; and it will be found that one verse did but beget another, without ordering at the first what should be at the last; which becomes a confused mass of words, with a tingling sound of rhyme, barely accompanied with reason.

Our tragedies and comedies (not without cause cried out against), observing rules neither of honest civility nor of skillful poetry, excepting *Gorboduc* (again, I say, of those that I have seen), which notwithstanding, as it is full of stately speeches and well-sounding phrases, climbing to the height of Seneca's style, and as full of notable morality, which it doth most delightfully teach, and so obtain the very end of poesy, yet in truth it is very defectious in the circumstances, which grieveth me, because it might not remain as an exact model of all tragedies. For it is faulty both in place and time, the two necessary companions of all corporal actions.[51] For where the stage should always represent but one place, and the uttermost time presupposed in it should be, both by Aristotle's precept and common reason, but one day, there is both many days, and many places, inartificially[52] imagined. But if it be so in *Gorboduc,* how much more in all the rest, where you shall have Asia of the one side, and Afric of the other, and so many other underkingdoms, that the player, when he cometh in, must ever begin with telling where he is, or else the tale will not be conceived? Now ye shall have three ladies walk to gather flowers and then we must believe the stage to be a garden. By and by we hear news of shipwreck in the same place, and then we are to blame if we accept it not for a rock.

Upon the back of that comes out a hideous monster, with fire and smoke, and then the miserable beholders are bound to take it for a cave. While in the meantime two armies fly in, represented with four swords and bucklers, and

[48]The orator is made; the poet is born.

[49]An impromptu performance.

[50]"Whatever I tried to say was verse." Ovid, *Tristia* IV. 10:26.

[51]*Gorboduc* fails to satisfy the unities of place and time, which Sidney ascribes to Aristotle.

[52]Unartistically.

then what hard heart will not receive it for a pitched field? Now, of time they are much more liberal: for ordinary it is that two young princes fall in love. After many traverses, she is got with child, delivered of a fair boy; he is lost, groweth a man, falls in love, and is ready to get another child; and all this in two hours' space: which, how absurd it is in sense, even sense may imagine, and art hath taught, and all ancient examples justified, and, at this day, the ordinary players in Italy will not err in. Yet will some bring in an example of *Eunuchus*[53] in Terence, that containeth matter of two days, yet far short of twenty years. True it is, and so was it to be played in two days, and so fitted to the time it set forth. And though Plautus hath in one place done amiss, let us hit with him, and not miss with him. But they will say, How then shall we set forth a story, which containeth both many places and many times? And do they not know that a tragedy is tied to the laws of poesy, and not of history; not bound to follow the story, but having liberty, either to feign a quite new matter, or to frame the history to the most tragical conveniency? Again, many things may be told which cannot be showed, if they know the difference betwixt reporting and representing. As, for example, I may speak (though I am here) of Peru, and in speech digress from that to the description of Calicut; but in action I cannot represent it without Pacolet's horse. And so was the manner the ancients took, by some nuncius[54] to recount things done in former time or other place. Lastly, if they will represent an history, they must not (as Horace saith) begin *ab ovo*,[55] but they must come to the principal point of that one action which they will represent. By example this will be best expressed. I have a story of young Polydorus, delivered for safety's sake, of great riches, by his father Priam to Polymnestor, king of Thrace, in the Trojan war time. He, after some years, hearing the overthrow of Priam, for to make the treasure his own, murdereth the child. The body of the child is taken up by Hecuba. She, the same day, findeth a slight

[53] Actually the *Self-Tormentor*, not the Eunuch.

[54] Messenger.

[55] "From the egg"; Horace praises Homer for not beginning his tale of the Trojan war with the egg from which Helen was hatched. See the *Art of Poetry*, p. 78.

to be revenged most cruelly of the tyrant. Where now would one of our tragedy writers begin, but with the delivery of the child? Then should he sail over into Thrace, and so spend I know not how many years, and travel numbers of places. But where doth Euripides? Even with the finding of the body, leaving the rest to be told by the spirit of Polydorus. This need no further to be enlarged; the dullest wit may conceive it. But besides these gross absurdities, how all their plays be neither right tragedies, nor right comedies, mingling kings and clowns, not because the matter so carrieth it, but thrust in clowns by head and shoulders, to play a part in majestical matters, with neither decency nor discretion, so as neither the admiration and commiseration, nor the right sportfulness, is by their mongrel tragicomedy obtained. I know Apuleius did somewhat so, but that is a thing recounted with space of time, not represented in one moment: and I know the ancients have one or two examples of tragicomedies, as Plautus hath *Amphitrio*. But, if we mark them well, we shall find that they never, or very daintily, match hornpipes and funerals. So falleth it out that, having indeed no right comedy, in that comical part of our tragedy we have nothing but scurrility, unworthy of any chaste ears, or some extreme show of doltishness, indeed fit to lift up a loud laughter, and nothing else: where the whole tract of a comedy should be full of delight, as the tragedy should be still maintained in a well-raised admiration. But our comedians think there is no delight without laughter; which is very wrong, for though laughter may come with delight, yet cometh it not of delight, as though delight should be the cause of laughter; but well may one thing breed both together. Nay, rather in themselves they have, as it were, a kind of contrariety: for delight we scarcely do but in things that have a conveniency to ourselves or to the general nature: laughter almost ever cometh of things most disproportioned to ourselves and nature. Delight hath a joy in it, either permanent or present. Laughter hath only a scornful tickling. For example, we are ravished with delight to see a fair woman, and yet are far from being moved to laughter. We laugh at deformed creatures, wherein certainly we cannot delight. We delight in good chances, we laugh at mischances;

we delight to hear the happiness of our friends, or country, at which he were worthy to be laughed at that would laugh. We shall, contrarily, laugh sometimes to find a matter quite mistaken and go down the hill against the bias, in the mouth of some such men, as for the respect of them one shall be heartily sorry, yet he cannot choose but laugh; and so is rather pained than delighted with laughter. Yet deny I not but that they may go well together. For as in Alexander's picture well set out we delight without laughter, and in twenty mad antics we laugh without delight, so in Hercules, painted with his great beard and furious countenance, in woman's attire, spinning at Omphale's commandment, it breedeth both delight and laughter. For the representing of so strange a power in love procureth delight: and the scornfulness of the action stirreth laughter. But I speak to this purpose, that all the end of the comical part be not upon such scornful matters as stirreth laughter only, but, mixed with it, that delightful teaching which is the end of poesy. And the great fault even in that point of laughter, and forbidden plainly by Aristotle, is that they stir laughter in sinful things, which are rather execrable than ridiculous; or in miserable, which are rather to be pitied than scorned.[56] For what is it to make folks gape at a wretched beggar, or a beggarly clown; or, against the law of hospitality, to jest at strangers, because they speak not English so well as we do? What do we learn, since it is certain *"Nil habet infelix paupertas durius in se, / Quam quod ridiculos homines facit"*?[57] But rather a busy loving courtier, a heartless threatening Thraso, a self-wise–seeming schoolmaster, an awry-transformed traveler — these if we saw walk in stage names, which we play naturally, therein were delightful laughter, and teaching delightfulness: as in the other, the tragedies of Buchanan do justly bring forth a divine admiration. But I have lavished out too many words of this play matter. I do it because, as they are excelling parts of poesy, so is there none so much used in England, and none can be more pitifully abused; which, like an

unmannerly daughter showing a bad education, causeth her mother poesy's honesty to be called in question. Other sorts of poetry almost have we none, but that lyrical kind of songs and sonnets: which, Lord, if he gave us so good minds, how well it might be employed, and with how heavenly fruit, both private and public, in singing the praises of the immortal beauty, the immortal goodness of that God who giveth us hands to write and wits to conceive; of which we might well want words, but never matter; of which we could turn our eyes to nothing, but we should ever have new budding occasions. But truly many of such writings as come under the banner of unresistible love, if I were a mistress, would never persuade me they were in love; so coldly they apply fiery speeches, as men that had rather read lovers' writings, and so caught up certain swelling phrases (which hang together like a man which once told me the wind was at northwest, and by south, because he would be sure to name winds enough), than that in truth they feel those passions, which easily (as I think) may be betrayed by that same forcibleness or *energia* (as the Greeks call it) of the writer. But let this be a sufficient though short note, that we miss the right use of the material point of poesy.

Now, for the outside of it, which is words, or (as I may term it) diction, it is even well worse. So is that honey-flowing matron eloquence appareled, or rather disguised, in a courtesanlike painted affectation: one time with so farfetched words, they may seem monsters, but must seem strangers, to any poor Englishman; another time, with coursing of a letter, as if they were bound to follow the method of a dictionary; another time, with figures and flowers, extremely winter-starved. But I would this fault were only peculiar to versifiers, and had not as large possession among prose-printers, and (which is to be marveled) among many scholars, and (which is to be pitied) among some preachers. Truly I could wish, if at least I might be so bold to wish in a thing beyond the reach of my capacity, the diligent imitators of Tully and Demosthenes (most worthy to be imitated) did not so much keep Nizolian paper books of their figures and phrases, as by attentive translation (as it were) devour them whole, and make them wholly theirs. For now they cast sugar and spice upon every dish

---

[56]Sidney may be thinking of Ch. 5 of the *Poetics*, but this is not Aristotle's point there.

[57]"The worst thing about poverty is that it makes people ridiculous." Juvenal, *Satires* 2:152–53.

that is served to the table, like those Indians, not content to wear earrings at the fit and natural place of the ears, but they will thrust jewels through their nose and lips, because they will be sure to fine.

Tully, when he was to drive out Catiline, as it were with a thunderbolt of eloquence, often used that figure of repetition, "*Vivit. Vivit? Imo in Senatum venit,*" &c.[58] Indeed, inflamed with a well-grounded rage, he would have his words (as it were) double out of his mouth, and so do that artificially which we see men do in choler naturally. And we, having noted the grace of those words, hale them in sometime to a familiar epistle, when it were too much choler to be choleric. Now for similitudes in certain printed discourses, I think all herberists, all stories of beasts, fowls, and fishes are rifled up, that they come in multitudes to wait upon any of our conceits; which certainly is as absurd a surfeit to the ears as is possible: for the force of a similitude not being to prove anything to a contrary disputer, but only to explain to a willing hearer; when that is done, the rest is a most tedious prattling, rather overswaying the memory from the purpose whereto they were applied, than any whit informing the judgment, already either satisfied, or by similitudes not to be satisfied. For my part, I do not doubt, when Antonius and Crassus, the great forefathers of Cicero in eloquence, the one (as Cicero testifieth) pretended not to know art, the other not to set by it, because with a plain sensibleness they might win credit of popular ears; which credit is the nearest step to persuasion; which persuasion is the chief mark of oratory — I do not doubt (I say) that but they used these knacks very sparingly; which, who doth generally use, any man may see doth dance to his own music; and so to be noted by the audience more careful to speak curiously than truly.

Undoubtedly (at least to my opinion undoubtedly) I have found in divers small-learned courtiers a more sound style than in some professors of learning: of which I can guess no other cause, but that the courtier, following that which by practice he findeth fittest to nature, therein (though he know it not) doth according to art,

though not by art: where the other, using art to show art, and not to hide art (as in these cases he should do), flieth from nature, and indeed abuseth art.

But what? Methinks I deserve to be pounded for straying from poetry to oratory: but both have such an affinity in this wordish consideration, that I think this digression will make my meaning receive the fuller understanding — which is not to take upon me to teach poets how they should do, but only, finding myself sick among the rest, to show some one or two spots of the common infection grown among the most part of writers: that, acknowledging ourselves somewhat awry, we may bend to the right use both of matter and manner: whereto our language giveth us great occasion, being indeed capable of any excellent exercising of it. I know some will say it is a mingled language. And why not so much the better, taking the best of both the other? Another will say it wanteth grammar. Nay truly, it hath that praise, that it wanteth grammar: for grammar it might have, but it needs it not; being so easy of itself, and so void of those cumbersome differences of cases, genders, moods, and tenses, which I think was a piece of the Tower of Babylon's curse, that a man should be put to school to learn his mother tongue. But for the uttering sweetly and properly the conceits of the mind, which is the end of speech, that hath it equally with any other tongue in the world; and is particularly happy in compositions of two or three words together, near the Greek, far beyond the Latin: which is one of the greatest beauties can be in a language.

Now, of versifying there are two sorts, the one ancient, the other modern: the ancient marked the quantity of each syllable, and according to that framed his verse; the modern observing only number (with some regard of the accent), the chief life of it standeth in that like sounding of the words, which we call rhyme. Whether of these be the most excellent, would bear many speeches. The ancient (no doubt) more fit for music, both words and tune observing quantity, and more fit lively to express divers passions, by the low and lofty sound of the well-weighed syllable. The latter likewise, with his rhyme, striketh a certain music to the ear: and, in fine, since it doth delight, though by another way, it obtains the same purpose: there being in either sweetness, and wanting in neither majesty. Truly the English, before any other vulgar language I know, is fit for both sorts: for, for the ancient, the Italian is so full of vowels that it must ever be cumbered with elisions; the Dutch so, of the other side, with consonants, that they cannot yield the sweet sliding fit for a verse; the French, in his whole language, hath not one word that hath his accent in the last syllable saving two, called *antepenultima;* and little more hath the Spanish: and, therefore, very gracelessly may they use dactyls. The English is subject to none of these defects.

Now, for the rhyme, though we do not observe quantity, yet we observe the accent very precisely: which other languages either cannot do, or will not do so absolutely. That *caesura,* or breathing place in the midst of the verse, neither Italian nor Spanish have, the French, and we, never almost fail of. Lastly, even the very rhyme itself the Italian cannot put in the last syllable, by the French named the "masculine rhyme," but still in the next to the last, which the French call the "female," or the next before that, which the Italians term *sdrucciola.* The example of the former is *buono:suono,* of the *sdrucciola, femina:semina.* The French, of the other side, hath both the male, as *bon:son,* and the female, as *plaise:taise,* but the *sdrucciola* he hath not: where the English hath all three, as *due:true, father:rather, motion:potion,* with much more which might be said, but that I find already the triflingness of this discourse is much too much enlarged. So that since the ever-praise-worthy poesy is full of virtue-breeding delightfulness, and void of no gift that ought to be in the noble name of learning; since the blames laid against it are either false or feeble; since the cause why it is not esteemed in England is the fault of poet-apes, not poets; since, lastly, our tongue is most fit to honor poesy, and to be honored by poesy; I conjure you all that have had the evil luck to read this ink-wasting toy of mine, even in the name of the nine Muses, no more to scorn the sacred mysteries of poesy, no more to laugh at the name of *poets,* as though they were next inheritors to fools, no more to jest at the reverent title of a *rhymer;* but to believe, with Aristotle, that they were the ancient treasurers of the Grecians'

divinity; to believe, with Bembus,[59] that they were first bringers-in of all civility; to believe, with Scaliger, that no philosopher's precepts can sooner make you an honest man than the reading of Virgil; to believe, with Clauserus, the translator of Cornutus, that it pleased the heavenly Deity, by Hesiod and Homer, under the veil of fables, to give us all knowledge, logic, rhetoric, philosophy, natural and moral, and *Quid non?;*[60] to believe, with me, that there are many mysteries contained in poetry, which of purpose were written darkly, lest by profane wits it should be abused; to believe, with Landino, that they are so beloved of the gods that whatsoever they write proceeds of a divine fury; lastly, to believe themselves, when they tell you they will make you immortal by their verses.

Thus doing, your name shall flourish in the printers' shops; thus doing, you shall be of kin to many a poetical preface; thus doing, you shall be most fair, most rich, most wise, most all; you shall dwell upon superlatives. Thus doing, though you be *"libertino patre natus,"* you shall suddenly grow *"Herculea proles," "si quid mea carmina possunt."*[61] Thus doing, your soul shall be placed with Dante's Beatrix, or Virgil's Anchises. But if (fie of such a but) you be born so near the dull-making cataract of Nilus that you cannot hear the planetlike music of poetry, if you have so earth-creeping a mind that it cannot lift itself up to look to the sky of poetry, or rather, by a certain rustical disdain, will become such a mome as to be a momus of poetry; then, though I will not wish unto you the ass's ears of Midas, nor to be driven by a poet's verses (as Bubonax was) to hang himself, nor to be rhymed to death, as is said to be done in Ireland; yet thus much curse I must send you, in the behalf of all poets, that while you live, you live in love, and never get favor for lacking skill of a sonnet, and, when you die, your memory die from the earth for want of an epitaph.

[59]Pietro Bembo (1470–1547), Italian scholar and critic.
[60]What not?
[61]"Thus doing, though you be 'the son of a freed slave,' you shall suddenly grow 'Herculean offspring,' 'if my poems can do anything.'" The quotations are from Horace, Ovid, and Virgil.

Aphra Behn

1640?–1689

Aphra Behn is considered the first Englishwoman to have lived by her pen, but her birthplace and maiden name and many of the facts of her life are still either cloaked in darkness or subjects of controversy. One theory has it that she was born Aphra Johnson, daughter of the barber Bartholomew Johnson of the cathedral town of Canterbury, and that she came by her education through the aristocratic Colepeper family when her mother became wet nurse to one of its children. Another is that she was the "Ayfara" born the same year to John and Amy Amis (of unknown occupation) in Wye. And it is generally agreed that at some time she traveled at some time between 1658 and 1663 to Surinam (now the independent country of Suriname) on the north equatorial coast of South America, which until its loss to the Dutch in 1665 had been a British colony. She stayed in Surinam at the plantation of the governor-general, Lord Willoughby, and there collected the factual background for her most famous narrative, *Oronoko, or The Royal Slave* (published 1688), including the names and personal habits of the ruling gentry. She apparently brought back to England a cloak of feathers of native manufacture, which was used as a costume in a Dryden play. Yet there is no evidence that her father, like that of the narrator of *Oronoko*, had been appointed lieutenant-governor of the colony.

On her return to England (she said she was eighteen but may have been somewhat older), she married a merchant of Dutch extraction named Behn, and she was known by that name from then on. Behn himself does not appear in her later writings, and some have surmised that he may have died or separated from Aphra before 1666. She had, along with her verbal ability and skill at intrigue, a connection to the government through the theatrical producer Thomas Killigrew. As a result of his recommendation, Aphra Behn had a personal interview with Charles II and was sent by Charles's foreign minister, Lord Arlington, to spy for England in Antwerp. Behn brought back and transmitted intelligence gathered by others about Admiral de Wit's plans to assault English vessels in their harbors at the outset of the Second Dutch War (1665–67). Her information might have been valuable had it been credited. It was disregarded, however, and Behn found herself seriously in debt because she wrongly believed that the Crown would pay the expenses she incurred in its service. In the late 1660s, Behn was jailed in debtor's prison, but she was soon bailed out and began her literary career as a playwright around 1670.

Her plays, mainly comedies of intrigue like those of George Etherege and William Wycherley, were performed primarily by Killigrew's "King's Company" during the next two decades. Behn kept herself very busy, as was required in an age when the playwright's "royalties" were the receipts from the third night's performance and irregular "author's rights" thereafter — a risky business when many plays did not run even three nights. At least thirteen of her plays were produced between 1670 and 1687. Her works for the theater include *The Forced Marriage* (1670); *The Dutch Lover* (1673); *Abdelazer; or, The Moor's Revenge* (1676); *The Rover; or, The Banished Cavalier, Part I* (1677); *Sir Patient Fancy* (1678); *The Feign'd*

Courtesans; or, A Night's Intrigue (1679); *The Roundheads; or, The Good Old Cause* (1681); *The Rover, Part II* (1681); *The City Heiress; or, Sir Timothy Treat-all* (1682); *The Lucky Chance; or, An Alderman's Bargain* (ca. 1686); and *The Widow Ranter,* the first British play set in America (published posthumously in 1690).

Though some of Behn's plays have been successfully revived, as in recent London productions of *The Rover* and *The Lucky Chance,* today Behn is better known as an innovator in prose fiction who created the "factual fictions" that Daniel Defoe was later to bring to greater perfection. The narrative of *Oroonoko, or The Royal Slave* is filled with the sort of gritty, concrete details that suggest the narrator was an eyewitness to real happenings. Its ideology is equally surprising for its day: *Oroonoko* is intensely anti-imperialistic, attacking the base venality and cruelty of the European colonists and settlers. Indeed, the novel was instrumental in establishing the convention of the "noble savage," which dominated Western culture in the era of Rousseau. On the other hand, *Oroonoko* was not in any sense (as it has frequently been called) an antislavery novel. The novel takes the institution of slavery for granted; its African hero himself captures and sells others into slavery, and resents only that he, a prince, has been tricked into bondage. Behn's other stories and novels include *Love Letters Between a Noble-Man and His Sister* (1684), a reconstruction of the scandal surrounding a Whig lord who had eloped with his sister-in-law; and *The Fair Jilt* (1688), based upon an incident Behn observed in The Hague in the 1660s. Behn also published her *Poems on Several Occasions* in 1684. Behn's health began to fail in the early 1680s and she died in 1689, the year of the Glorious Revolution; she is buried in Westminster Abbey.

In the Preface to her quarto edition of *The Dutch Lover* (1673), Behn takes on the "phlegmatick, white, ill-favour'd, wretched Fop" who complained on opening night "that they were to expect a woful Play, God damn him, for it was a woman's." Like her near-contemporary, Mary Astell, Behn presumes that women are "as capable of knowledge, of whatever sort" as men, if granted the same access to education. But given the male audience for her plays, she does not argue this directly, stressing instead that education is hardly a playwright's first requirement. The "immortal Shakespeare" had no more learning himself "than often falls to women's share," and even the more educated Ben Jonson "was no such Rabbi neither." Those who most overestimate the poet's need for learning are often, she suggests, those who have absorbed the least education themselves. Given that native genius and invention are more important than learning and the rules of art, there is little bar to women excelling in the arts: ". . . except our most unimitable Laureat [John Dryden] . . . I know of none that write . . . but that a woman may well hope to reach their greatest heights," says Behn. If in those words she was immodestly thinking of herself, as one may suspect, most of today's readers would agree that Behn achieved those heights.

Selected Bibliography

Chibka, Robert L. "'Oh! Do Not Fear a Woman's Invention': Truth, Falsehood and Fiction in Aphra Behn's *Oroonoko.*" *Texas Studies in Literature and Language* 30 (1988): 510–37.
Duffy, Maureen. *The Passionate Shepherdess: Aphra Behn,* 1640–1689. London: Cape, 1977.

Goreau, Angeline. *Reconstructing Aphra: A Social Biography of Aphra Behn.* New York: Dial Press, 1980.

Hutner, Heidi, ed. *Rereading Aphra Behn: History, Theory and Criticism.* Charlottesville: University Press of Virginia, 1993.

O'Donnell, Mary Ann. "Tory Wit and Unconventional Woman: Aphra Behn." In *Women Writers of the Seventeenth Century,* eds. Katharina M. Wilson and Frank J. Warnke. Athens: University of Ohio Press, 1989. 349–72.

Todd, Janet, ed. *Aphra Behn Studies.* New York and London: Cambridge University Press, 1996.

An Epistle to the Reader
from *The Dutch Lover*

Good, Sweet, Honey, Sugar-Candied READER.

Which I think is more than anyone has called you yet, I must have a word or two with you before you do advance into the Treatise: but 'tis not to beg your pardon for diverting you from your affairs, by such an idle Pamphlet as this is, for I presume you have not much to do and therefore are to be obliged to me for keeping you from worse employment, and if you have a better you may get you gone about your business: but if you will misspend your Time, pray lay the fault upon yourself; for I have dealt pretty fairly in the matter, told you in the Title Page what you are to expect within. Indeed, had I hung a sign of the Immortality of the Soul, of the Mystery of Godliness, or of Ecclesiastical Policie, and then had treated you with Indiscerpibility and Essential Spissitude (words, which though I am no competent Judge of, for want of Languages, yet I fancy strongly ought to mean just nothing) with a company of Apocryphal midnight Tales cull'd out of the choicest Insignificant Authors; if I had only proved in Folio that Appolonius was a naughty knave, or had presented you with two or three of the worst principles transcrib'd out of the peremptory and ill-natur'd (though pretty inge-nious) Doctor of Malmsbury[1] undigested and ill-manag'd by a silly, saucy, ignorant, impertinent, ill educated Chaplain I were then indeed suffi-ciently in fault; but having inscrib'd Comedy on the beginning of my Book, you may guess pretty near what penny-worths you are like to have, and ware your money and your time accordingly. I would not yet be understood to lessen the dignity of Playes, for surely they deserve a place among the middle if not the better sort of Books: for I have heard the most of that which bears the name of Learning, and which has abused such quanti-ties of Ink and Paper, and continually employs so many ignorant, unhappy souls for ten, twelve, twenty years in the University (who yet poor wretches think they are doing something all the while) as Logick etc. and several other things (that shall be nameless lest I misspell them) are much more absolutely nothing than the errantest Play that e'er was writ. Take notice, Reader, I do not assert this purely upon my own knowledge, but I think I have known it very fully prov'd, both sides being fairly heard, and even some ingenious opposers of it most abominably baff'd in the Argument: Some of which I have got so perfectly by rote, that if this were a proper place for it, I am apt to think myself could almost make it clear; and as I would not undervalue Poetry, so neither am I altogether of their Judgement who believe no wisdom in the world beyond it. I have often heard indeed (and read) how much the World was anciently oblig'd to it for most of that which they call'd Science, which my want of letters makes me less assured of than others happily may be: but I have heard some wise men say that no considerable part of useful knowledge

---

[1]Behn is referring to the political philosopher Thomas Hobbes as Doctor of Malmsbury.

was this way communicated, and on the other way, that it hath serv'd to propogate so many idle superstitions, as all the benefits it hath or can be guilty of, can never make sufficient amends for; which unaided by the unlucky charms of Poetry, could never have possest a thinking Creature such as man. However true this is, I am myself well able to affirm that none of all our English Poets, and least the Dramatique (so I think you call them) can be justly charg'd with too great reformation of men's minds or manners, and for that I may appeal to general experiment, if those who are the most assiduous Disciples of the Stage, do not make the fondest and the lewdest Crew about this Town; for if you should unhappily converse them through the year, you will not find one Dram of sense amongst a Club of them, unless you will allow for such a little Link-Boy's[2] Ribaldry thick larded with unseasonable oaths & impudent defiance of God, and all things serious; and that at such a senseless damn'd unthinking rate, as, if 'twere well distributed, would spoil near half the Apothecaries trade, and save the sober people of the Town the charge of Vomits; And it was smartly said (how prudently I cannot tell) by a late learned Doctor, who, though himself no great asserter of a Deity, (as you'll believe by that which follows) yet was observed to be continually persuading of this sort of men (if I for once may call them so) of the necessity and truth of our Religion; and being ask'd how he came to bestir himself so much this way, made answer that it was because their ignorance and indiscreet debauch made them a scandal to the profession of Atheism. And for their wisdom and design I never knew it reach beyond the invention of some notable expedient, for the speedier ridding them of their Estate, (a devilish clog to Wit and Parts), than other grouling Mortals know, or battering half-a-dozen fair new Windows in a Morning after their debauch, whilst the dull unjantee[3]

[2]A boy hired to carry a "link" (a torch made of tow dipped in pitch) to light his employer through the otherwise unlit streets. As observers of the nocturnal habits of the dissipated men and women of Charles II's London, link-boys could be expected to have seen everything and to have a street-wise sense of humor about it all.

[3]Variant of "unjaunty," characterizing the stay-at-home sleepers, as opposed to the hellraisers battering their windows at dawn.

Rascal they belong to is fast asleep. But I'll proceed no farther in their character, because that miracle of Wit (in spite of Academick frippery) the mighty Echard[4] hath already done it to my satisfaction; and whoever undertakes a Supplement to anything he hath discourst, had better for their reputation be doing nothing.

Besides this Theam is worn too thread-bare by the whiffling would-be Wits of the Town, and of both the stone-blind-eyes of the Kingdom. And therefore to return to that which I before was speaking of, I will have leave to say that in my judgement the increasing number of our latter Plays have not done much more towards the amending of men's Morals, or their Wit, than hath the frequent Preaching, which this last age hath been pester'd with, (indeed without all Controversie they have done less harm) nor can I once imagine what temptation anyone can have to expect it from them; for sure I am no Play was ever writ with that design. If you consider Tragedy, you'll find their best of Characters unlikely patterns for a wise man to pursue: For he that is the Knight of the Play, no sublunary feats must serve his Dulcinea; for if he can't bestrid the Moon, he'll ne'er make good his business to the end, and if he chance to be offended, he must without considering right or wrong confound all things he meets, and put you half-a-score likely tall fellows into each pocket; and truly if he come not something near this Pitch I think the Tragedy's not worth a farthing; for Playes were certainly intended for the exercising of men's passions not their understandings, and he is infinitely far from wise that will bestow one moment's meditation on such things: And as for Comedie, the finest folks you meet with there are still unfitter for your imitation, for though within a leaf or two of the Prologue, you are told that they are people of Wit, good Humour, good Manners, and all that: yet if the Authors did not kindly add their proper names, you'd never know them by their Characters; for whatsoe'er's the matter, it hath happen'd so spightfully in several Playes, which have been prettie well

[4]Probably John Eachard (1636–1697), author of a contemporary satire, *The Grounds and Occasions of the Contempt of the Clergy* (1670).

received of late, that even those persons that
were meant to be the ingenious Censors of the
Play, have either prov'd the most debauch'd, or
most unwittie people in the Company; nor is this
error very lamentable, since as I take it Comedie
was never meant, either for a converting or a
conforming Ordinance: In short, I think a Play
the best divertisement that wise men have: but I
do also think them nothing so who do discourse
as formallie about the rules of it, as if 'twere
the grand affair of humane life. This being my
opinion of Plays, I studied only to make this as
entertaining as I could, which whether I have
been successful in, my gentle Reader, you may
for your shilling judge. To tell you my thoughts
of it, were to little purpose, for were they very
ill, you may be sure I would not have expos'd
it; nor did I so till I had first consulted most of
those who have a reputation for judgement of
this kind; who were at least so civil (if not kind)
to it as did encourage me to venture it upon
the Stage, and in the Press: Nor did I take their
single word for it, but us'd their reasons as a
confirmation of my own.

Indeed that day 'twas Acted first, there comes
me into the Pit, a long, lither, phlegmatick,
white, ill-favour'd, wretched Fop, an Officer in
Masquerade newly transported with a Scarf &
Feather out of France, a sorry Animal that has
nought else to shield it from the uttermost contempt of all mankind, but that respect which we
afford to Rats and Toads, which though we do not
well allow to live, yet when considered as a part
of God's Creation, we make honourable mention
of them. A thing, Reader — but no more of such
a Smell: This thing, I tell ye, opening that thing,
serves it for a mouth, out issued such a noise as
this to those that sate about it, that they were to
expect a woful Play, God damn him, for it was
a woman's. Now how this came about I am not
sure, but I suppose he brought it piping hot from
some who had with him the reputation of a vil-
lanous Wit: for Creatures of his size of sense
talk without all imagination, such scraps as they
pick up from other folks. I would not for a world
be taken arguing with such a propertie as this:
but if I thought there were a man of any tolerable parts, who could upon mature deliberation

distinguish well his right hand from his left, and
justly state the difference between the number of
sixteen and two, yet had this prejudice upon him;
I would take a little pains to make him know how
much he errs. For waving the examination why
women having equal education with men, were
not as capable of knowledge, of whatsoever sort
as well as they; I'll only say as I have touch'd
before, that Plays have no great room for that
which is men's great advantage over women, that
is Learning: We all well know that the immortal
Shakespeare's Plays (who was not guilty of much
more of this than often falls to women's share)
have better pleas'd the World than Johnson's[5]
works, though by the way 'tis said that Benjamin
was no such Rabbi neither, for I am inform'd that
his Learning was but Grammar high; (sufficient
indeed to rob poor Salust of his best orations) and
it hath been observ'd that they are apt to admire
him most confoundedly, who have just such a
scantling of it as he had; and I have seen a man
the most severe of Johnson's Sect, sit with his Hat
remov'd less than a hair's breadth from one sullen
posture for almost three hours at The Alchymist;
who at that excellent Play of Harry the Fourth
(which yet I hope is far enough from Farce) hath
very hardly kept his Doublet whole; but affectation hath always had a greater share both in the
action and discourse of men than truth and judgement have; and for our Modern ones, except our
most unimitable Laureat, I dare to say I know of
none that write at such a formidable rate, but that
a woman may well hope to reach their greatest
heights. Then for their musty rules of Unity, and
God knows what besides, if they meant anything,
they are enough intelligible and as practicble by
a woman; but really methinks they that disturb
their heads with any other rule of Plays besides
the making them pleasant, and avoiding of scurrility, might much better be employed in studying
how to improve men's too imperfect knowledge

[5]The Roman writer Sallust, like Shakespeare's contemporary, Ben Jonson, was known for using language remote
from that of common life. Behn asserts that Jonson's comedy The Alchemist provokes only a "sullen posture," while
Shakespeare's history play Henry IV, with comic scenes
involving Falstaff, causes even an admirer of Jonson almost
to split his doublet with laughter.

of that ancient English Game which hight long Laurence:[6] And if Comedy should be the picture of ridiculous mankind I wonder anyone should think it such a sturdy task, whilst we are furnish'd with such precious Originals as him I lately told you of; if at least that Character do not dwindle into Farce, and so become too mean an entertainment for those persons who are us'd to think. Reader, I have a complaint or two to make to you and I have done; Know then that this Play was hugely injur'd in the Acting, for 'twas done so imperfectly as never any was before, which did more harm to this than it could have done to any of another sort; the Plot being busie (though I think not intricate) and so requiring a continual attention, which being interrupted by the intolerable negligence of some that acted in it, must needs much spoil the beauty on't. My Dutch Lover spoke but little of what I intended for him, but supplied it with a great deal of idle stuff, which I was wholly unacquainted with until I had heard it first from him; so that Jack-pudding ever us'd to do: which though I knew before, I gave him yet the Part, because I knew him so acceptable to most o'th' lighter Periwigs about the Town, and he indeed did vex me so, I could almost be angry: Yet, but Reader, you remember, I suppose, a fusty piece of Latine[7] that has past from hand to hand this thousand years they say (and how much longer I can't tell) in favour of the dead. I intended him a habit much more notably ridiculous, which if ever it be important was so here, for many of the Scenes in the three last Acts depended upon the mistakes of the Colonel for Haunce, which the ill-favour'd likeness of their Habits is suppos'd to cause. Lastly my Epilogue was promis'd me by a Person who had surely made it good, if any, but he failing of his word, deput'd one, who has made it as you see, and to make out your penyworth you have it here. The Prologue is by misfortune lost. Now, Reader, I have eas'd my mind of all I had to say, and so sans farther complyment, Adieu.

[6]Janet Todd's new edition of Aphra Behn's works defines a "Long Lawrence" as an instrument marked with signs about three inches long like a short ruler or totem with eight sides. Each side had a different set of markings of strokes, zigzags, and crosses. The ancient English game with the same name was played (particularly at Christmas), by rolling the Long Lawrence; each player would win or lose pins or tokens according to which side came up. The name itself may have come from the marks on the instrument, which resembled the bars of a gridiron, on which St. Lawrence was martyred. Todd cites Alice Bertha Gomme, *The Traditional Games of England, Scotland, and Ireland* (1894).

[7]The "fusty bit of Latine . . . in favour of the dead" is probably the proverb "De mortuis nil nisi bonum": Of the dead speak nothing but good. The application is to Edward Angel, the actor who played the male lead in *The Dutch Lover* and whose ad-libbing of lines and vulgar stage business caused the scandal Behn is discussing: Angel had died in the interval between the production and publication of the play.

Alexander Pope

1688–1744

Born into a Roman Catholic family in the year the last Catholic monarch of England, James II, was forced to abdicate his throne, Alexander Pope was legally barred from a university education and from many careers. From his wet nurse he caught a severe case of spinal tuberculosis, which left him dwarfed, twisted, and delicate of constitution. Nevertheless, with the private education provided by his father, a well-to-do merchant of London just retired to Windsor Forest, Pope crafted himself into the prodigy and soon into the poet of eighteenth-century England, its laureate in all but name. His translations of the *Iliad* and the *Odyssey* (1720 and 1725) not only made him a fortune in royalties, they set the poetic standard for the age; his *Essay on Man* (1733) became its optimistic and rationalistic creed. What has best survived, however, are his satires, delicate fantasies like *The Rape of the Lock* (1714), or vitriolic diatribes like *An Epistle to Dr. Arbuthnot* (1735) and the *Dunciad* (1728–43).

The *Essay on Criticism*, published in 1711 and written possibly as early as 1707, belongs to Pope's earliest years, when he "lisp'd in numbers, and the numbers came." It would be astonishing for any nineteen-year-old, however learned, to make an original contribution to literary theory, and in fact, the *Essay on Criticism* is original only in that it is addressed to critics rather than to poets. But since Pope considered it the critic's first duty to endeavor to comprehend fully and disinterestedly the poem's form, matter, and end, the *Essay* easily and often shifts its focus from qualities of criticism to qualities of poetry. Pope's central ideas are the standard poetic notions of the Augustan Age, drawn from a variety of classical and Renaissance sources — from Horace and Quintilian to Boileau and Dryden — but these well-worn truths he imbues with a clarity and brilliance of expression.

The central and recurring image of the *Essay on Criticism* is that of the eternal war between critics, who judge according to a rigid system of regulations, and poets, hemmed in by such rules and longing to soar. By and large, although Pope presents the poets' perspective, he sides with the critics. While he insists that "Some beauties yet no precepts can declare / For there's a happiness as well as care," and admits that poets can through genius "snatch a grace beyond the reach of art," he also warns them that remorseless criticism will justly clip their wings should they depart from the precedent of the rules and practices of the ancients. The critics come in for a lashing in Part II, where they are attacked for partial readings, partial both in the sense that their praise and blame depend on the congruence of their party politics with that of the poet, and in the sense that they take only a single aspect of a poem into account without understanding its end or how it relates to the chosen means.

Pope's demonstrations of prosody and imagery here have become classic citations. Pope's tendency to use his central terms in a variety of related but distinct ways can be confusing. "Nature" is sometimes used to signify the objective world of creation and other times to mean human nature or the instinctual basis of our humanity. "Art" can be opposed to "Nature" in any of the following senses: It can be the world of human invention, as opposed to that of divine creation; it can be technique and craft, as opposed to creative instinct; it can be the rules behind a skill, as opposed to the skill itself; it can be (as in its usual modern meaning) the class of objects created by human intelligence and creativity. "Wit" is even more ambiguous than "Art" and "Nature" and can partake of either realm: It may mean "sense" or "intelligence" or "verbal facility" or "genius" or "creative power," or it may signify a person with any of these qualities — or just an educated person in general. These shifts, which are not announced, can create an immense and bewildering compression of meaning. When Pope claims that nature is "at once the source, and end, and test of Art," he may be using both Nature and Art in three different senses. Context is a guide here, and fortunately, the context is enhanced by Pope's tendency to repeat each of his ideas at least once before moving on to the next.

What may be more problematic for the reader is Pope's tendency to draw a distinction only to collapse it later on. Like Sidney, Pope suggests that the poet requires natural genius, a knowledge of the rules of art, and an education based on the classics to provide models for imitation. But art and nature, creation and imitation, turn out to be false dichotomies. The rules of art remain "Nature still, but Nature methodiz'd"; Virgil discovers that imitating Nature and imitating Homer are "the same." Pope in 1711 is content to leave such contradictions unresolved as poetic paradoxes; in later hands, like those of David Hume and Immanuel Kant, these issues will recur as evidence of inward mental structures common to humanity.

Selected Bibliography

Empson, William. "'Wit' in the *Essay on Criticism.*" *Hudson Review* 2 (1950): 559–77.
Fenner, Arthur, Jr. "The Unity of Pope's *Essay on Criticism.*" *Philological Quarterly* 39 (1960): 435–56.
Griffin, Dustin. *Alexander Pope: The Poet in the Poems.* Princeton: Princeton University Press, 1978.
Hooker, E. N. "Pope on Wit: The Essay on Criticism." *Hudson Review* 2 (1950): 84–100.
Stack, Frank. *Pope and Horace: Studies in Imitation.* Cambridge and New York: Cambridge University Press, 1985.
Warren, Austin. *Pope as Critic and Humanist.* Princeton: Princeton University Press, 1929.
Wood, Allen G. *Literary Satire and Theory: A Study of Horace, Boileau, and Pope.* New York: Garland, 1985.

An Essay on Criticism

— *Si quid novisti rectius istis,*
   Candidus imperti; si non, his utere mecum.[1]

[1]"If you know better maxims, impart them to me; if not, use these with me." Horace, *Epistles* 6:1.

PART I

'Tis hard to say, if greater want of skill
Appear in writing or in judging ill;
But of the two less dangerous is the offense
To tire our patience than mislead our sense.

Some few in that, but numbers err in this.
Ten censure wrong for one who writes amiss;
A fool might once himself alone expose,
Now one in verse makes many more in prose.
'Tis with our judgments as our watches, none
Go just alike, yet each believes his own.
In poets as true genius is but rare,
True taste as seldom is the critic's share;
Both must alike from Heaven derive their light,
These born to judge, as well as those to write.
Let such teach others who themselves excel,
And censure freely who have written well.
Authors are partial to their wit,[2] 'tis true.
But are not critics to their judgment too?
Yet if we look more closely, we shall find
Most have the seeds of judgment in their mind:
Nature affords at least a glimmering light;
The lines, though touched but faintly, are drawn
right.
But as the slightest sketch, if justly traced,
Is by ill coloring but the more disgraced,
So by false learning is good sense defaced:
Some are bewildered in the maze of schools,[3]
And some made coxcombs Nature meant but
fools.
In search of wit these lose their common sense,
And then turn critics in their own defense:
Each burns alike, who can, or cannot write,
Or with a rival's or an eunuch's spite.
All fools have still an itching to deride,
And fain would be upon the laughing side.
If Maevius[4] scribble in Apollo's spite,
There are who judge still worse than he can
write.
Some have at first for wits, then poets passed,
Turned critics next, and proved plain fools at
last.
Some neither can for wits nor critics pass,
As heavy mules are neither horse nor ass.
Those half-learn'd witlings, numerous in our
isle,
As half-formed insects on the banks of Nile:[5]
Unfinished things, one knows not what to call,

Their generation's so equivocal:
To tell them would a hundred tongues require:
Or one vain wit's, that might a hundred tire.
But you who seek to give and merit fame,
And justly bear a critic's noble name.
Be sure yourself and your own reach to know,
How far your genius, taste, and learning go;
Launch not beyond your depth, but be discreet,
And mark that point where sense and dullness
meet.
Nature to all things fixed the limits fit,
And wisely curbed proud man's pretending wit.
As on the land while here the ocean gains,
In other parts it leaves wide sandy plains;
Thus in the soul while memory prevails,
The solid power of understanding fails;
Where beams of warm imagination play,
The memory's soft figures melt away.
One Science[7] only will one genius fit,
So vast is art, so narrow human wit.[8]
Not only bounded to peculiar arts,
But oft in those confined to single parts.
Like kings we lose the conquests gained before,
By vain ambition still to make them more:
Each might his several province well command,
Would all but stoop to what they understand.
First follow Nature, and your judgment frame
By her just standard, which is still the same:
Unerring Nature, still divinely bright,
One clear, unchanged, and universal light,
Life, force, and beauty must to all impart,
At once the source, and end, and test of art.
Art from that fund each just supply provides,
Works without show, and without pomp pre-
sides.
In some fair body thus the informing soul
With spirits feeds, with vigor fills the whole,
Each motion guides, and every nerve sustains;
Itself unseen, but in the effects remains.
Some, to whom Heaven in wit has been profuse.
Want as much more to turn it to its use;
For wit[9] and judgment often are at strife,
Though meant each other's aid, like man and
wife.

[2] Artistic genius.
[3] Scholastic learning.
[4] A legendarily bad poet, known only through contemptuous references by both Virgil and Horace.
[5] Insects were supposed to be spontaneously generated by river mud and other similar matter.
[6] Count,
[7] Branch of knowledge.
[8] Here, mental power.
[9] Here, imagination.

'Tis more to guide than spur the Muse's steed,[10]
Restrain his fury than provoke his speed;
The wingéd courser, like a generous horse,
Shows most true mettle when you check his
    course.
    Those rules of old discovered, not devised,
Are Nature still, but Nature methodized;
Nature, like liberty, is but restrained
By the same laws which first herself ordained.
    Hear how learn'd Greece her useful rules
    indites,
When to repress and when indulge our flights:
High on Parnassus'[11] top her sons she showed,
And pointed out those arduous paths they trod;
Held from afar, aloft, the immortal prize,
And urged the rest by equal steps to rise.
Just precepts thus from great examples given,
She drew from them what they derived from
    Heaven.
The generous critic fanned the poet's fire,
And taught the world with reason to admire.
Then criticism the Muse's handmaid proved,
To dress her charms, and make her more
    beloved:
But following wits from that intention strayed,
Who could not win the mistress, wooed the
    maid;
Against the poets their own arms they turned,
Sure to hate most the men from whom they
    learned.
So modern 'pothecaries, taught the art
By doctors' bills to play the doctor's part,
Bold in the practice of mistaken rules,
Prescribe, apply, and call their masters fools.[12]
Some on the leaves of ancient authors prey,
Nor time nor moths e'er spoiled so much as they.
Some dryly plain, without invention's aid,
Write dull receipts[13] how poems may be made.
These leave the sense their learning to display,
And those explain the meaning quite away.
    You then whose judgment the right course
    would steer,
Know well each ancient's proper character;

His fable, subject, scope in every page;
Religion, country, genius of his age:
Without all these at once before your eyes,
Cavil you may, but never criticize.
Be Homer's works your study and delight,
Read them by day, and meditate by night;
Thence form your judgment, thence your max-
    ims bring,
And trace the Muses upward to their spring.
Still with itself compared, his text peruse;
And let your comment be the Mantuan Muse.[14]
    When first young Maro in his boundless mind
A work to outlast immortal Rome designed,
Perhaps he seemed above the critic's law,
And but from Nature's fountains scorned to
    draw;
But when to examine every part he came,
Nature and Homer were, he found, the same.
Convinced, amazed, he checks the bold design, ⎤
And rules as strict his labored work confine ⎬
As if the Stagirite[15] o'erlooked each line. ⎦
Learn hence for ancient rules a just esteem;
To copy Nature is to copy them.
    Some beauties yet no precepts can declare,
For there's a happiness as well as care.[16]
Music resembles poetry, in each   ⎤
Are nameless graces which no methods teach, ⎬
And which a master hand alone can reach.   ⎦
If, where the rules not far enough extend
(Since rules were made but to promote their end)
Some lucky license answers to the full
The intent proposed, that license is a rule.
Thus Pegasus, a nearer way to take,
May boldly deviate from the common track.
From vulgar bounds with brave disorder part,
And snatch a grace beyond the reach of art,
Which without passing through the judgment,
    gains
The heart, and all its end at once attains.
In prospects thus, some objects please our eyes, ⎤
Which out of Nature's common order rise,   ⎬
The shapeless rock, or hanging precipice.   ⎦
Great wits sometimes may gloriously offend,
And rise to faults true critics dare not mend;

---

[10]Pegasus, the winged horse associated with the Muses.
[11]Hill where the Muses gathered.
[12]Pope refers to a contemporary dispute between doctors
and druggists, who were invading each other's territories.
[13]Recipes.

[14]Virgil, born in Mantua: his last name, mentioned in the
next line, was Maro.
[15]Aristotle, born in Stagira.
[16]Beauty that transcends the taking of pains.

But though the ancients thus their rules invade,
(As kings dispense with laws themselves have
made)
Moderns, beware! or if you must offend
Against the precept, ne'er transgress its end;
Let it be seldom, and compelled by need;
And have at least their precedent to plead.
The critic else proceeds without remorse,
Seizes your fame, and puts his laws in force.
I know there are, to whose presumptuous
thoughts
Those freer beauties, even in them, seem faults.
Some figures monstrous and misshaped appear,
Considered singly, or beheld too near,
Which, but proportioned to their light or place,
Due distance reconciles to form and grace.[17]
A prudent chief not always must display
His powers in equal ranks and fair array,
But with the occasion and the place comply,
Conceal his force, nay seem sometimes to fly.
Those oft are stratagems which errors seem,
Nor is it Homer nods, but we that dream.[18]
Still green with bays each ancient altar stands
Above the reach of sacrilegious hands,
Secure from flames, from envy's fiercer rage,
Destructive war, and all-involving age.
See, from each clime the learn'd their incense
bring!
Here in all tongues consenting paeans ring!
In praise so just let every voice be joined,
And fill the general chorus of mankind.
Hail, bards triumphant! born in happier days,
Immortal heirs of universal praise!
Whose honors with increase of ages grow,
As streams roll down, enlarging as they flow;
Nations unborn your mighty names shall sound,
And worlds applaud that must not yet be found!
Oh, may some spark of your celestial fire,
The last, the meanest of your sons inspire,
(That on weak wings, from far, pursues your
flights,

[17]Pope alludes to the "ut pictura poesis" passage in Horace's Art of Poetry, which stresses that some poems, like some paintings, need to be looked at from afar, not scrutinized in detail.
[18]Where Horace claims in the Art of Poetry to be "indignant even when it is the great Homer who falls asleep on the job." Pope suggests that the critic rather than the poet may be at fault.

Glows while he reads, but trembles as he writes)
To teach vain wits a science little known,
To admire superior sense, and doubt their own!

PART II

Of all the causes which conspire to blind
Man's erring judgment, and misguide the mind,
What the weak head with strongest bias rules,
Is pride, the never-failing vice of fools.
Whatever Nature has in worth denied,
She gives in large recruits of needful pride;
For as in bodies, thus in souls, we find
What wants in blood and spirits swelled with
wind:
Pride, where wit fails, steps in to our defense,
And fills up all the mighty void of sense.
If once right reason drives that cloud away,
Truth breaks upon us with resistless day.
Trust not yourself; but your defects to know,
Make use of every friend — and every foe.
A little learning is a dangerous thing;[19]
Drink deep, or taste not the Pierian spring.
There shallow draughts intoxicate the brain,
And drinking largely sobers us again.
Fired at first sight with what the Muse imparts,
In fearless youth we tempt the heights of arts,
While from the bounded level of our mind
Short views we take, nor see the lengths behind;
But more advanced, behold with strange surprise
New distant scenes of endless science rise!
So pleased at first the towering Alps we try,
Mount o'er the vales, and seem to tread the sky,
The eternal snows appear already past,
And the first clouds and mountains seem the last;
But those attained, we tremble to survey
The growing labors of the lengthened way,
The increasing prospect tires our wandering
eyes,
Hills peep o'er hills, and Alps on Alps arise!
A perfect judge will read each work of wit
With the same spirit that its author writ:
Survey the whole, nor seek slight faults to find
Where Nature moves, and rapture warms the
mind;
Nor lose, for that malignant dull delight,
The generous pleasure to be charmed with wit.

[19]Pieria, near Mt. Olympus, was sacred to the Muses.

But in such lays as neither ebb nor flow,
Correctly cold, and regularly low,
That, shunning faults, one quiet tenor keep,
We cannot blame indeed — but we may sleep.
In wit, as nature, what affects our hearts
Is not the exactness of peculiar parts;
'Tis not a lip, or eye, we beauty call,
But the joint force and full result of all.
Thus when we view some well-proportioned
    dome[20]
(The world's just wonder, and even thine, O
    Rome!),
No single parts unequally surprise,
All comes united to the admiring eyes:
No monstrous height, or breadth, or length
    appear;
The whole at once is bold and regular.
    Whoever thinks a faultless piece to see,
Thinks what ne'er was, nor is, nor e'er shall be.
In every work regard the writer's end,
Since none can compass more than they intend;
And if the means be just, the conduct true,
Applause, in spite of trivial faults, is due.
As men of breeding, sometimes men of wit,
To avoid great errors must the less commit,
Neglect the rules each verbal critic lays,
For not to know some trifles is a praise.
Most critics, fond of some subservient art,
Still make the whole depend upon a part:
They talk of principles, but notions prize,
And all to one loved folly sacrifice.
    Once on a time La Mancha's knight,[21] they say,
A certain bard encountering on the way,
Discoursed in terms as just, with looks as sage,
As e'er could Dennis,[22] of the Grecian stage;
Concluding all were desperate sots and fools
Who durst depart from Aristotle's rules.
Our author, happy in a judge so nice,
Produced his play, and begged the knight's
    advice;
Made him observe the subject and the plot,

The manners, passions, unities; what not?
All which exact to rule were brought about,
Were but a combat in the lists left out.
"What! leave the combat out?" exclaims the
    knight.
"Yes, or we must renounce the Stagirite."
"Not so, by Heaven!" he answers in a rage,
"Knights, squires, and steeds must enter on the
    stage."
"So vast a throng the stage can ne'er contain."
"Then build a new, or act it in a plain."
    Thus critics of less judgment than caprice,
Curious,[23] not knowing, not exact, but nice,
Form short ideas, and offend in arts
(As most in manners), by a love to parts.
    Some to conceit[24] alone their taste confine,
And glittering thoughts struck out at every line;
Pleased with a work where nothing's just or fit,
One glaring chaos and wild heap of wit.
Poets, like painters, thus unskilled to trace
The naked nature and the living grace,
With gold and jewels cover every part,
And hide with ornaments their want of art.
    True wit is Nature to advantage dressed,
What oft was thought, but ne'er so well
    expressed;
Something whose truth convinced at sight we
    find,
That gives us back the image of our mind.
As shades more sweetly recommend the light,
So modest plainness sets off sprightly wit;
For works may have more wit than does them
    good,
As bodies perish through excess of blood.
    Others for language all their care express,
And value books, as women men, for dress.
Their praise is still — the style is excellent;
The sense they humbly take upon content.[25]
Words are like leaves; and where they most
    abound,
Much fruit of sense beneath is rarely found.
False eloquence, like the prismatic glass,
Its gaudy colors spreads on every place;
The face of Nature we no more survey,

[20]Of St. Peter's Basilica.
[21]Don Quixote. The episode is not in Cervantes but in a sequel written under the name of Alonzo Fernandez de Avellaneda and translated into English around 1705.
[22]John Dennis (1657–1734), a playwright and critic who had argued for the application of classical rules to the English stage.

[23]Pedantically careful; "nice" in the same line means "overrefined."
[24]Figures of speech.
[25]On faith.

All glares alike, without distinction gay.
But true expression, like the unchanging sun,
Clears and improves whate'er it shines upon;
It gilds all objects, but it alters none.
Expression is the dress of thought, and still
Appears more decent as more suitable.
A vile conceit in pompous words expressed
Is like a clown in regal purple dressed:
For different styles with different subjects sort,
As several garbs with country, town, and court.
Some by old words to fame have made pretense,
Ancients in phrase, mere moderns in their sense.
Such labored nothings, in so strange a style,
Amaze the unlearn'd, and make the learned
  smile;
Unlucky as Fungoso[26] in the play,
These sparks with awkward vanity display
What the fine gentleman wore yesterday;
And but so mimic ancient wits at best,
As apes our grandsires in their doublets dressed.
In words as fashions the same rule will hold,
Alike fantastic if too new or old:
Be not the first by whom the new are tried,
Nor yet the last to lay the old aside.
But most by numbers[27] judge a poet's song,
And smooth or rough with them is right or
  wrong.
In the bright Muse though thousand charms con-
  spire,
Her voice is all these tuneful fools admire,
Who haunt Parnassus but to please their ear,
Not mend their minds; as some to church repair,
Not for the doctrine, but the music there.
These equal syllables alone require,
Though oft the ear the open vowels tire,
While expletives their feeble aid do join,
And ten low words oft creep in one dull line:
While they ring round the same unvaried chimes,
With sure returns of still expected rhymes;
Where'er you find "the cooling western breeze,"
In the next line, it "whispers through the trees";
If crystal streams "with pleasing murmurs
  creep,"
The reader's threatened (not in vain) with
  "sleep";

Then, at the last and only couplet fraught
With some unmeaning thing they call a thought,
A needless Alexandrine[28] ends the song
That, like a wounded snake, drags its slow length
  along.
Leave such to tune their own dull rhymes, and
  know
What's roundly smooth or languishingly slow;
And praise the easy vigor of a line
Where Denham's strength and Waller's sweet-
  ness join.
True ease in writing comes from art, not chance,
As those move easiest who have learned to
  dance.
'Tis not enough no harshness gives offense,
The sound must seem an echo to the sense.
Soft is the strain when Zephyr gently blows,
And the smooth stream in smoother numbers flows;
But when loud surges lash the sounding shore,
The hoarse, rough verse should like the torrent
  roar.
When Ajax strives some rock's vast weight to
  throw,
The line too labors, and the words move slow;
Not so when swift Camilla[29] scours the plain,
Flies o'er the unbending corn, and skims along
  the main.
Hear how Timotheus'[30] varied lays surprise,
And bid alternate passions fall and rise!
While at each change the son of Libyan Jove
Now burns with glory, and then melts with love;
Now his fierce eyes with sparkling fury glow,
Now sighs steal out, and tears begin to flow:
Persians and Greeks like turns of nature found
And the world's victor stood subdued by sound!
The power of music all our hearts allow.
And what Timotheus was is Dryden now.
Avoid extremes; and shun the fault of such
Who still are pleased too little or too much.

[26]A character in Ben Jonson's *Every Man out of His Humour* (1599).
[27]Prosody.

[28]Line of iambic hexameter, usually broken in the middle.
[29]Camilla was an Amazonian warrior allied to Turnus in Virgil's *Aeneid*.
[30]Pope retells the story of Dryden's *Alexander's Feast*: how Alexander the Great's bard, Timotheus, was able to subdue the conqueror of the world through his art. The "son of Libyan Jove" is Alexander, who claimed descent from Ammon after conquering Egypt.

At every trifle scorn to take offense:
That always shows great pride, or little sense.
Those heads, as stomachs, are not sure the best,
Which nauseate all, and nothing can digest.
Yet let not each gay turn thy rapture move;
For fools admire, but men of sense approve:
As things seem large which we through mists
  descry,
Dullness is ever apt to magnify.

    Some foreign writers, some our own despise;
The ancients only, or the moderns prize.
Thus wit, like faith, by each man is applied
To one small sect, and all are damned beside.
Meanly they seek the blessing to confine,
And force that sun but on a part to shine,
Which not alone the southern wit sublimes,
But ripens spirits in cold northern climes;
Which from the first has shone on ages past,
Enlights the present, and shall warm the last;
Though each may feel increases and decays,
And see now clearer and now darker days.
Regard not then if wit be old or new,
But blame the false and value still the true.

    Some ne'er advance a judgment of their own,
But catch the spreading notion of the town;
They reason and conclude by precedent,
And own stale nonsense which they ne'er invent.
Some judge of authors' names, not works, and
  then
Nor praise nor blame the writings, but the men.
Of all this servile herd the worst is he
That in proud dullness joins with quality,
A constant critic at the great man's board,
To fetch and carry nonsense for my lord.
What woeful stuff this madrigal would be
In some starved hackney sonneteer or me!
But let a lord once own the happy lines,
How the wit brightens! how the style refines!
Before his sacred name flies every fault,
And each exalted stanza teems with thought!

    The vulgar thus through imitation err;
As oft the learn'd by being singular;
So much they scorn the crowd, that if the throng
By chance go right, they purposely go wrong.
So schismatics the plain believers quit,
And are but damned for having too much wit.
Some praise at morning what they blame at
  night,
But always think the last opinion right.

A Muse by these is like a mistress used,
This hour she's idolized, the next abused;
While their weak heads like towns unfortified,
'Twixt sense and nonsense daily change their
  side.
Ask them the cause; they're wiser still, they say;
And still tomorrow's wiser than today.
We think our fathers fools, so wise we grow;
Our wiser sons, no doubt, will think us so.
Once school divines[31] this zealous isle o'er-
  spread;
Who knew most sentences was deepest read.
Faith, Gospel, all seemed made to be disputed,
And none had sense enough to be confuted.
Scotists and Thomists now in peace remain
Amidst their kindred cobwebs in Duck Lane.[32]
If faith itself has different dresses worn,
What wonder modes in wit should take their
  turn?
Oft, leaving what is natural and fit,
The current folly proves the ready wit;
And authors think their reputation safe,
Which lives as long as fools are pleased to laugh.

    Some valuing those of their own side or mind,
Still make themselves the measure of mankind:
Fondly[33] we think we honor merit then,
When we but praise ourselves in other men.
Parties in wit attend on those of state,
And public faction doubles private hate.
Pride, Malice, Folly against Dryden rose,
In various shapes of parsons, critics, beaux;
But sense survived, when merry jests were past;
For rising merit will buoy up at last.
Might he return and bless once more our eyes,
New Blackmores and new Milbourns must
  arise.[34]
Nay, should great Homer lift his awful head,
Zoilus[35] again would start up from the dead.
Envy will merit, as its shade, pursue,
But like a shadow, proves the substance true;
For envied wit, like Sol eclipsed, makes known
The opposing body's grossness, not its own.

[31]Scholastic theologians.
[32]Street of used bookstores.
[33]Foolishly.
[34]Richard Blackmore had attacked Dryden's dramas, Luke
Milbourn his translation of the *Aeneid.*
[35]Zoilus was a severe critic of Homer of the fourth century B.C.E.

When first that sun too powerful beams displays,
It draws up vapors which obscure its rays;
But even those clouds at last adorn its way,
Reflect new glories, and augment the day.
Be thou the first true merit to befriend;
His praise is lost who stays till all commend.
Short is the date, alas! of modern rhymes,
And 'tis but just to let them live betimes.
No longer now that golden age appears,
When patriarch wits survived a thousand years:
Now length of fame (our second life) is lost,
And bare threescore is all even that can boast;
Our sons their fathers' failing language see,
And such as Chaucer is shall Dryden be.[36]
So when the faithful pencil has designed
Some bright idea of the master's mind,
Where a new world leaps out at his command,
And ready Nature waits upon his hand;
When the ripe colors soften and unite,
And sweetly melt into just shade and light;
When mellowing years their full perfection give,
And each bold figure just begins to live,
The treacherous colors the fair art betray,
And all the bright creation fades away!
Unhappy wit, like most mistaken things,
Atones not for that envy which it brings.
In youth alone its empty praise we boast,
But soon the short-lived vanity is lost:
Like some fair flower the early spring supplies,
That gaily blooms, but even in blooming dies.
What is this wit, which must our cares employ?
The owner's wife, that other men enjoy;
Then most our trouble still when most admired,
And still the more we give, the more required;
Whose fame with pains we guard, but lose with
ease,
Sure some to vex, but never all to please;
'Tis what the vicious fear, the virtuous shun,
By fools 'tis hated, and by knaves undone!
If wit so much from ignorance undergo,
Ah, let not learning too commence its foe!
Of old those met rewards who could excel,
And such were praised who but endeavored well;
Though triumphs were to generals only due,
Crowns were reserved to grace the soldiers too.

Now they who reach Parnassus' lofty crown
Employ their pains to spurn some others down;
And while self-love each jealous writer rules,
Contending wits become the sport of fools:
But still the worst with most regret commend,
For each ill author is as bad a friend.
To what base ends, and by what abject ways,
Are mortals urged through sacred[37] lust of
praise!
Ah, ne'er so dire a thirst of glory boast,
Nor in the critic let the man be lost!
Good nature and good sense must ever join;
To err is human, to forgive divine.
But if in noble minds some dregs remain
Nor yet purged off, of spleen and sour disdain,
Discharge that rage on more provoking crimes,
Nor fear a dearth in these flagitious[38] times.
No pardon vile obscenity should find,
Though wit and art conspire to move your mind;
But dullness with obscenity must prove
As shameful sure as impotence in love.
In the fat age of pleasure, wealth, and ease
Sprung the rank weed, and thrived with large
increase:
When love was all an easy monarch's[39] care,
Seldom at council, never in a war;
Jilts[40] ruled the state, and statesmen farces writ;
Nay, wits had pensions, and young lords had wit:
The fair sat panting at a courtier's play,
And not a mask[41] went unimproved away;
The modest fan was lifted up no more,
And virgins smiled at what they blushed before.
The following license of a foreign reign[42]
Did all the dregs of bold Socinus drain;
Then unbelieving priests reformed the nation,
And taught more pleasant methods of salvation;
Where Heaven's free subjects might their rights
dispute,
Lest God himself should seem too absolute:

[36] The Middle English in which Chaucer wrote had become
unintelligible by Pope's time.

[37] Accursed.
[38] Wicked.
[39] Charles II (reigned 1660–85).
[40] Charles's mistresses.
[41] Women wearing a vizard mask, whose concealment
allowed one to behave immorally without scandal.
[42] The reign of William III (1689–1701), who came from
Holland. Socinus, in the next line, was the name of two
Renaissance Italian theologians whose doctrines denied the
divinity of Christ and the efficacy of the Atonement.

Pulpits their sacred satire learned to spare,
And Vice admired to find a flatterer there!
Encouraged thus, wit's Titans braved the skies,
And the press groaned with licensed blas-
   phemies.
These monsters, critics! with your darts engage,
Here point your thunder, and exhaust your rage!
Yet shun their fault, who, scandalously nice,
Will needs mistake an author into vice;
All seems infected that the infected spy,
As all looks yellow to the jaundiced eye.

PART III

   Learn then what morals Critics ought to show,
For 'tis but half a judge's task to know.
'Tis not enough Taste, Judgment, Learning join;
In all you speak let Truth and Candour shine;
That not alone what to your Sense is due
All may allow, but seek your friendship too.
   Be silent always when you doubt your Sense,
And speak, tho' sure, with seeming diffidence.
Some positive persisting fops we know,
Who if once wrong will needs be always so;
But you with pleasure own your errors past,
And make each day a critique on the last.
   'Tis not enough your counsel still be true;
Blunt truths more mischief than nice falsehoods
   do.
Men must be taught as if you taught them not,
And things unknown proposed as things forgot.
Without good breeding truth is disapprov'd;
That only makes superior Sense belov'd.
   Be niggards of advice on no pretence,
For the worst avarice is that of Sense.
With mean complacence ne'er betray your trust,
Nor be so civil as to prove unjust.
Fear not the anger of the wise to raise;
Those best can bear reproof who merit praise.
   'Twere well might critics still this freedom take,
But Appius[43] reddens at each word you speak,
And stares tremendous, with a threat'ning eye,
Like some fierce tyrant in old tapestry.
Fear most to tax an honourable fool,
Whose right it is, uncensured to be dull:

Such without Wit, are poets when they please,
As without Learning they can take degrees.[44]
Leave dangerous truths to unsuccessful satires,
And flattery to fulsome dedicators;
Whom, when they praise, the world believes no
   more
Than when they promise to give scribbling o'er.
'Tis best sometimes your censure to restrain,
And charitably let the dull be vain;
Your silence there is better than your spite,
For who can rail so long as they can write?
Still humming on their drowsy course they keep,
And lash'd so long, like tops, are lash'd asleep.
False steps but help them to renew the race,
As, after stumbling, jades will mend their pace.
What crowds of these, impenitently bold,
In sounds and jingling syllables grown old,
Still run on poets, in a raging vein,
Ev'n to the dregs and squeezings of the brain,
Strain out the last dull dropping of their sense,
And rhyme with all the rage of impotence!
   Such shameless bards we have; and yet 'tis true
There are as mad abandon'd critics too.
The bookful blockhead ignorantly read,
With loads of learned lumber in his head,
With his own tongue still edifies his ears,
And always list'ning to himself appears.
All books he reads, and all he reads assails,
From Dryden's Fables down to Durfey's Tales.[45]
With him most authors steal their works, or buy;
Garth did not write his own Dispensary.[46]
Name a new play, and he's the poet's friend;
Nay, show'd his faults — but when would poets
   mend?
No place so sacred from such fops is barr'd,
Nor is Paul's church more safe than Paul's
   churchyard:[47]
Nay, fly to altars, there they'll talk you dead;
For fools rush in where angels fear to tread.
Distrustful sense with modest caution speaks,

[43]See n. 22. Dennis wrote an unsuccessful play, *Appius and Virginia* (1709).

[44]Sons of peers were allowed to take degrees at Oxford and Cambridge without meeting the usual requirements.
[45]Thomas Durfey (1653–1723), author of popular songs, tales, plays, and other entertainments.
[46]Samuel Garth (1661–1719), physician-poet who wrote a didactic poem called "The Dispensary."
[47]Where booksellers plied their trade.

It still looks home, and short excursions makes;
But rattling nonsense in full volleys breaks,
And never shock'd, and never turn'd aside,
Bursts out, resistless, with a thund'ring tide.
But where's the man who counsel can bestow,
Still pleas'd to teach, and yet not proud to know?
Unbiass'd or by favour or by spite;
Not dully prepossess'd nor blindly right;
Tho' learn'd, well bred, and tho' well bred sin-
        cere;
Modestly bold, and humanly severe:
Who to a friend his faults can freely show,
And gladly praise the merit of a foe;
Bless'd with a taste exact, yet unconfin'd,
A knowledge both of books and humankind;
Gen'rous converse; a soul exempt from pride;
And love to praise, with reason on his side?
Such once were critics; such the happy few,
Athens and Rome in better ages knew.
The mighty Stagyrite first left the shore,
Spread all his sails, and durst the deeps explore;
He steer'd securely, and discover'd far,
Led by the light of the Mæonian star.[48]
Poets, a race long unconfin'd and free,
Still fond and proud of savage liberty,
Receiv'd his laws, and stood convinc'd 'twas fit
Who conquer'd Nature should preside o'er Wit.
Horace still charms with graceful negligence,
And without method talks us into sense;
Will, like a friend, familiarly convey
The truest notions in the easiest way.
He who, supreme in judgment as in wit,
Might boldly censure as he boldly writ,
Yet judg'd with coolness, though he sung with
        fire;
His precepts teach but what his works inspire.
Our critics take a contrary extreme,
They judge with fury, but they write with
        phlegm;
Nor suffers Horace more in wrong translations
By Wits, than Critics in as wrong quotations.
See Dionysius[49] Homer's thoughts refine,
And call new beauties forth from ev'ry line!

48 Homer, whose birthplace, according to tradition, was Mæonia.
49 Dionysius of Halicarnassus (first century B.C.E.), literary critic and historian.

Fancy and art in gay Petronius[50] please,
The Scholar's learning with the courtier's ease.
In grave Quintilian's[51] copious work we find
The justest rules and clearest method join'd.
Thus useful arms in magazines we place,
All ranged in order, and disposed with grace,
But less to please the eye then arm the hand,
Still fit for use, and ready at command.
Thee, bold Longinus![52] all the Nine inspire,
And bless their critic with a poet's fire:
An ardent judge, who, zealous in his trust,
With warmth gives sentence, yet is always just;
Whose own example strengthens all his laws,
And is himself that great sublime he draws.
Thus long succeeding critics justly reign'd,
License repress'd, and useful laws ordain'd:
Learning and Rome alike in empire grew,
And arts still follow'd where her eagles flew;
From the same foes at last both felt their doom,
And the same age saw learning fall and Rome.
With tyranny then superstition join'd,
As that the body, this enslaved the mind;
Much was believ'd, but little understood,
And to be dull was construed to be good;
A second deluge learning thus o'errun,
And the monks finish'd what the Goths begun.
At length Erasmus, that great injur'd name,
(The glory of the priesthood and the shame!)
Stemm'd the wild torrent of a barb'rous age,
And drove those holy Vandals off the stage.
But see! each Muse in Leo's[53] golden days
Starts from her trance, and trims her wither'd
        bays.
Rome's ancient genius, o'er its ruins spread,
Shakes off the dust, and rears his rev'rend head.
Then sculpture and her sister arts revive;
Stones leap'd to form, and rocks began to live;
With sweeter notes each rising temple rung;
A Raphael painted and a Vida[54] sung:
Immortal Vida! on whose honour'd brow

50 Petronius Arbiter (?–65 C.E.), author of the Satyricon.
51 Quintilian (35–95), rhetorician and author of Institutio Oratoria.
52 The nine Muses.
53 Leo X, originally Giovanni de' Medici (1475–1521), whose pontificate was "golden" from the artistic commissions given out.
54 Marco Girolamo Vida (1480–1566), Italian critic, poet, and author of De arte poetica.

The poet's bays and critic's ivy grow:
Cremona now shall ever boast thy name,
As next in place to Mantua,[55] next in fame!
     But soon by impious arms from Latium
     chased,
Their ancient bounds the banish'd Muses pass'd;
Thence arts o'er all the northern world advance,
But critic learning flourish'd most in France;
The rules a nation born to serve obeys,
And Boileau[56] still in right of Horace sways.
But we, brave Britons, foreign laws despised,
And kept unconquer'd and uncivilized;
Fierce for the liberties of wit, and bold,
We still defied the Romans, as of old.
Yet some there were, among the sounder few
Of those who less presumed and better knew,
Who durst assert the juster ancient cause,
And here restor'd Wit's fundamental laws.
Such was the Muse whose rules and practice tell
"Nature's chief masterpiece is writing well."[57]
Such was Roscommon,[58] not more learn'd than
     good,

With manners gen'rous as his noble blood;
To him the wit of Greece and Rome was known,
And every author's merit but his own.
Such late was Walsh[59] — the Muse's judge and
     friend,
Who justly knew to blame or to commend;
To failings mild but zealous for desert,
The clearest head, and the sincerest heart.
This humble praise, lamented Shade! receive;
This praise at least a grateful Muse may give:
The Muse whose early voice you taught to sing,
Prescribed her heights, and pruned her tender
     wing,
(Her guide now lost), no more attempts to rise,
But in low numbers short excursions tries;
Content if hence th' unlearn'd their wants may
     view,
The learn'd reflect on what before they knew;
Careless of censure, nor too fond of fame;
Still pleas'd to praise, yet not afraid to blame;
Averse alike to flatter or offend;
Not free from faults, nor yet too vain to mend.

[55]Birthplace of Virgil.
[56]Nicolas Boileau-Despréaux (1636–1711), French poet
and critic, whose *Art poétique* is one of the sources of Pope's
ideas.
[57]From Buckingham's "Essay on Poetry."
[58]Wentworth Dillon, Earl of Roscommon (1633–1685),
poet, critic, and translator of Horace.

[59]William Walsh (1663–1708), Pope's friend, who had
advised the young poet that he could make his mark by striving for correctness.

Samuel Johnson

1709–1784

Samuel Johnson, the "Great Cham of Literature," is the magisterial personality that dominates the late eighteenth century in England with his insistent moralism, his unflappable common sense, and his tragic vision of life. The only son of a provincial book dealer, whose formal education came to an end after an impecunious year at Oxford, Johnson made himself into the most broadly learned man of his age.

He arrived in London in 1737, just around the time the system of patrician patronage (which had supported John Dryden so well) was giving way to the one familiar today, in which authors bargain with publishers for their material support. In his thirties, Johnson joined the army of hack writers who eked out their living by producing for the Grub Street booksellers the journalism, travel books, occasional essays, translations, and histories for which the new middle-class reading public hankered. From 1747 to 1755, in sickness and sorrow, Johnson labored virtually alone on his massive *Dictionary of the English Language;* its appearance made Johnson's reputation, became the standard dictionary for over half a century, and helped to standardize the chaotic English tongue. He wrote major works in every important literary genre of his age: They include satirical poems like "London" (1739) and "The Vanity of Human Wishes" (1749); the fable *Rasselas* (1759); the tragedy *Irene* (1749); weekly essays for *The Rambler* (1750–52), *The Adventurer* (1753–54), and *The Idler* (1758–60); an authoritative edition of Shakespeare (1763); and a massive series of biographical and critical essays, *Lives of the Poets,* on all the significant English writers of the seventeenth and eighteenth centuries (1779–81).

Johnson's criticism, like that of Sidney and Dryden and most of his own contemporaries, derives its principles from Horace: He conceives of the literary work as a piece of rhetoric to be judged by the impact it makes upon the audience. But those trying to place Johnson within the broad spectrum of rhetorical criticism should note that he takes the didactic purpose of literature far more seriously than either Horace or Dryden, and that his insistence on the universal character of poetry differentiates him from such Platonizing critics as Sidney.

"The end of writing is to instruct; the end of poetry is to instruct by pleasing," he declared in his Preface to *Shakespeare,* and this *locus classicus* dominates the rest of his theory. Didacticism is surely the keynote in his essay on the novel in *The Rambler,* No. 4 (1750). While Johnson admits that literature should imitate life and that the novel is therefore an improvement over the romance, he sees no reason why writers should not be selective about what aspects of life they choose to imitate. The plots of novels should end with poetic justice, and in presenting characters, novelists should strive to exhibit "the most perfect idea of virtue" in their heroes, not to present characters at once fascinating and deeply flawed. The date of the essay suggests that Johnson may have been reacting specifically to Fielding's *Tom Jones* (1749) and its scapegrace hero, but the viewpoint he presents is not topical, and it was one with which his entire age was in sympathy.

If the aim of poetry is "to instruct by pleasing," then we might inquire how that is brought about. The answer, also found in the Preface to *Shakespeare*, runs briefly thus: "Nothing can please many, and please long, but just representations of general nature." Poetry must be deeply true to life, not because art is a matter of imitation, but because the truth of accurate representation holds us longer than any artful fancy could: "The pleasures of sudden wonder are soon exhausted, and the mind can only repose on the stability of truth."

Precisely what Johnson means by "general nature" is glossed in *Rasselas*, Chapter 10, where Imlac tells the Prince that "the business of the poet . . . is to examine, not the individual, but the species; to remark general properties and large appearances: he does not number the streaks of the tulip. . . . He . . . must neglect the minuter discriminations, which one may have remarked, and another have neglected, for those characteristics which are alike obvious to vigilance and carelessness." Johnson's insistence on the universality of poetry is very similar to Aristotle's, but his point is Horatian: If the literary work is to please a universal audience, it must deal broadly with the world we all know, not with special issues of interest to a few.

From Johnson's universalizing perspective, the old topics of rhetorical criticism — the three unities, generic integrity, decorum of the stage — finally recede to the status of mere conventions, and conventions that were not those of Shakespeare's era. With all due reverence to the venerable antiquity of these doctrines, Johnson refutes their assumptions so thoroughly that it becomes difficult to see how they influenced so many for so long. At every point, Johnson insists that "there is always an appeal open from criticism to nature," and the old dogmas wither in the brutal spotlight of Johnson's common sense. The unities of time and place, he says, derive from "the supposed necessity of making the drama credible"; but in fact, no one in the audience believes for an instant that the things happening on stage are actually occurring. The audience's enjoyment indeed depends upon their sense that they are watching fiction. Critics have claimed that by mixing comic with tragic scenes, the passions are interrupted and the drama is deprived of emotional force. This reasoning, Johnson insinuates, is "so specious [attractive] that it is received as true even by those who in daily experience feel it to be false." To critics who object to the apparent indecorum of Shakespeare's presenting King Claudius of Denmark as a drunkard, Johnson scoffs that "these are the petty cavils of petty minds."

Those who are accustomed to believe that Shakespeare could do no wrong may be surprised by Johnson's strictly judicial appraisal of the bard's faults and virtues. Johnson's didactic streak, in fact, is offended by Shakespeare's amorality, and Shakespeare's greatness is rescued only by his surpassing universality and trueness to life. In his stray judgments on Shakespeare, however, Johnson can be very shrewd — as when he states that Shakespeare's "tragedy seems to be skill, his comedy to be instinct."

The pleasures of reading Johnson's criticism are not merely intellectual. In his hands criticism becomes literature, delighting as well as instructing, and the source of the pleasure is Johnson's unique personality. We value his wisdom as much as his learning, and his tragic vision as much as his ebullient combativeness. He speaks of readers "willing to be thought wicked, if they may be allowed to be wits," and of writers who ''are willing to hope from posterity what the present age refuses, and flatter themselves that the regard which is yet denied by envy, will be at last bestowed by time.'' He refers to the way ''the common satiety of life sends us all in quest'' of fantastic but worthless novelties; and reminds us that love ''is only one of many passions, and . . . has no great influence upon the sum of life.'' It is then that we sense the presence of the very human sage who felt so deeply 'The Vanity of Human Wishes.''

Selected Bibliography

Bate, Walter Jackson. *The Achievement of Samuel Johnson*. Chicago: University of Chicago Press, 1978.

Battersby, James L. *Rational Praise and Natural Lamentation: Johnson, Lycidas and Principles of Criticism*. Rutherford, NJ: Fairleigh Dickinson University Press, 1980.

Damrosch, Leopold. *The Uses of Johnson's Criticism*. Charlottesville: University Press of Virginia, 1976.

Fussell, Paul. *Samuel Johnson and the Life of Writing*. New York: Norton, 1986.

Hagstrum, Jean H. *Samuel Johnson's Literary Criticism*. 1952; Chicago: University of Chicago Press, 1967.

Jenkins, Ralph Eugene. *Some Sources of Samuel Johnson's Literary Criticism*. Austin: University of Texas Press, 1969.

Keast, W. R. "Theoretical Foundations of Johnson's Criticism." In *Critics and Criticism: Ancient and Modern*, ed. R. S. Crane. Chicago: University of Chicago Press, 1952.

Mahoney, John L. "The True Story: Poetic Law and License in Johnson's Criticism." In *Ideas, Aesthetics, and Inquiries in the Early Modern Era*, vol. 6, ed. Kevin L. Cope, 185–98. New York: AMS Press, 2001.

Smallwood, Philip. *Johnson's Critical Presence: Image, History, Judgment*. Aldershot, England: Ashgate, 2003.

Stock, R. D. *Samuel Johnson and Neoclassical Dramatic Theory: The Literary Content of the "Preface to Shakespeare."* Lincoln: University of Nebraska Press, 1973.

The Rambler, No. 4

Simul et jucunda et idonea dicere vitæ.

— HORACE, *Ars Poetica,* 334

And join both profit and delight in one

— CREECH

The works of fiction, with which the present generation seems more particularly delighted, are such as exhibit life in its true state, diversified only by accidents that daily happen in the world, and influenced by passions and qualities which are really to be found in conversing with mankind.

This kind of writing may be termed not properly the comedy of romance, and is to be conducted nearly by the rules of comic poetry. Its province is to bring about natural events by easy means, and to keep up curiosity without the help of wonder: it is therefore precluded from the machines and expedients of the heroic romance, and can neither employ giants to snatch away a lady from the nuptial rites, nor knights to bring her back from captivity; it can neither bewilder its personages in deserts, nor lodge them in imaginary castles.

I remember a remark made by Scaliger[1] upon Pontanus, that all his writings are filled with the same images; and that if you take from him his lilies and his roses, his satyrs and his dryads, he

[1]Julius Caesar Scaliger, *Poetics* 5:4.

will have nothing left that can be called poetry. In like manner almost all the fictions of the last age will vanish, if you deprive them of a hermit and a wood, a battle and a shipwreck.

Why this wild strain of imagination found reception so long in polite and learned ages, it is not easy to conceive; but we cannot wonder that while readers could be procured, the authors were willing to continue it; for when a man had by practice gained some fluency of language, he had no further care than to retire to his closet, let loose his invention, and heat his mind with incredibilities; a book was thus produced without fear of criticism, without the toil of study, without knowledge of nature, or acquaintance with life.

The task of our present writers is very different; it requires, together with that learning which is to be gained from books, that experience which can never be attained by solitary diligence, but must arise from general converse and accurate observation of the living world. Their performances have, as Horace expresses it, *plus oneris quantum veniæ minus*, little indulgence, and therefore more difficulty.[2] They are engaged in portraits of which every one knows the original, and can detect any deviation from exactness of resemblance. Other writings are safe, except from the malice of learning, but these are in danger from every common reader; as the slipper ill executed was censured by a shoemaker who happened to stop in his way at the Venus of Apelles.[3]

But the fear of not being approved as just copiers of human manners, is not the most important concern that an author of this sort ought to have before him. These books are written chiefly to the young, the ignorant, and the idle, to whom they serve as lectures of conduct, and introductions into life. They are the entertainment of minds unfurnished with ideas, and therefore easily susceptible of impressions; not fixed by principles, and therefore easily following the current of fancy; not informed by experience, and consequently open to every false suggestion and partial account.

That the highest degree of reverence should be paid to youth, and that nothing indecent should be suffered to approach their eyes or ears, are precepts extorted by sense and virtue from an ancient writer, by no means eminent for chastity of thought. The same kind, though not the same degree, of caution, is required in every thing which is laid before them, to secure them from unjust prejudices, perverse opinions, and incongruous combinations of images.

In the romances formerly written, every transaction and sentiment was so remote from all that passes among men, that the reader was in very little danger of making any applications to himself; the virtues and crimes were equally beyond his sphere of activity; and he amused himself with heroes and with traitors, deliverers and persecutors, as with beings of another species, whose actions were regulated upon motives of their own, and who had neither faults nor excellencies in common with himself.

But when an adventurer is levelled with the rest of the world, and acts in such scenes of the universal drama, as may be the lot of any other man; young spectators fix their eyes upon him with closer attention, and hope, by observing his behaviour and success, to regulate their own practices, when they shall be engaged in the like part.

For this reason these familiar histories may perhaps be made of greater use than the solemnities of professed morality, and convey the knowledge of vice and virtue with more efficacy than axioms and definitions. But if the power of example is so great as to take possession of the memory by a kind of violence, and produce effects almost without the intervention of the will, care ought to be taken, that, when the choice is unrestrained, the best examples only should be exhibited; and that which is likely to operate so strongly, should not be mischievous or uncertain in its effects.

The chief advantage which these fictions have over real life is, that their authors are at liberty, though not to invent, yet to select objects, and to cull from the mass of mankind, those individuals upon which the attention ought most to be employed; as a diamond, though it cannot be made, may be polished by art, and placed in such a situation, as to display that lustre which before was buried among common stones.

[2]Horace, *Epistles* II.1:70.
[3]Pliny, *Natural History* 35:84–85.

It is justly considered as the greatest excellency of art, to imitate nature; but it is necessary to distinguish those parts of nature, which are most proper for imitation: greater care is still required in representing life, which is so often discoloured by passion, or deformed by wickedness. If the world be promiscuously described, I cannot see of what use it can be to read the account; or why it may not be as safe to turn the eye immediately upon mankind as upon a mirror which shows all that presents itself without discrimination.

It is therefore not a sufficient vindication of a character, that it is drawn as it appears; for many characters ought never to be drawn; nor of a narrative, that the train of events is agreeable to observation and experience; for that observation which is called knowledge of the world, will be found much more frequently to make men cunning than good. The purpose of these writings is surely not only to show mankind, but to provide that they may be seen hereafter with less hazard; to teach the means of avoiding the snares which are laid by Treachery for Innocence, without infusing any wish for that superiority with which the betrayer flatters his vanity; to give the power of counteracting fraud, without the temptation to practise it; to initiate youth by mock encounters in the art of necessary defence, and to increase prudence without impairing virtue.

Many writers, for the sake of following nature, so mingle good and bad qualities in their principal personages, that they are both equally conspicuous; and as we accompany them through their adventures with delight, and are led by degrees to interest ourselves in their favour, we lose the abhorrence of their faults, because they do not hinder our pleasure, or, perhaps, regard them with some kindness, for being united with so much merit.

There have been indeed splendidly wicked, whose endowments threw a brightness on their crimes, and whom scarce any villainy made perfectly detestable, because they never could be wholly divested of their excellencies; but such have been in all ages the great corrupters of the world, and their resemblance ought no more to be preserved, than the art of murdering without pain.

Some have advanced, without due attention to the consequences of this notion, that certain virtues have their correspondent faults, and therefore that to exhibit either apart is to deviate from probability. Thus men are observed by Swift to be "grateful in the same degree as they are resentful." This principle, with others of the same kind, supposes man to act from a brute impulse, and pursue a certain degree of inclination, without any choice of the object; for, otherwise, though it should be allowed that gratitude and resentment arise from the same constitution of the passions, it follows not that they will be equally indulged when reason is consulted; yet, unless that consequence be admitted, this sagacious maxim becomes an empty sound, without any relation to practice or to life.

Nor is it evident, that even the first motions to these effects are always in the same proportion. For pride, which produces quickness of resentment, will obstruct gratitude, by unwillingness to admit that inferiority which obligation implies; and it is very unlikely that he who cannot think he receives a favour, will acknowledge or repay it.

It is of the utmost importance to mankind, that positions of this tendency should be laid open and confuted; for while men consider good and evil as springing from the same root, they will spare the one for the sake of the other, and in judging, if not of others at least of themselves, will be apt to estimate their virtues by their vices. To this fatal error all those will contribute, who confound the colours of right and wrong, and instead of helping to settle their boundaries, mix them with so much art, that no common mind is able to disunite them.

In narratives where historical veracity has no place, I cannot discover why there should not be exhibited the most perfect idea of virtue: of virtue not angelical, nor above probability, for what we cannot credit, we shall never imitate, but the highest and purest that humanity can reach, which, exercised in such trials as the various revolutions of things shall bring upon it, may, by conquering some calamities, and enduring others, teach us what we may hope, and what we can perform. Vice, for vice is necessary to be shown, should always disgust; nor should the graces of gaiety, or the dignity of courage, be so united with it, as to reconcile it to the mind. Wherever it appears, it should raise hatred by the malignity of its practices, and contempt by the meanness of its stratagems: for while it is supported by either parts or spirit, it will be seldom heartily abhorred. The Roman tyrant was content to be hated, if he was but feared; and there are thousands of the readers of romances willing to be thought wicked, if they may be allowed to be wits. It is therefore to be steadily inculcated, that virtue is the highest proof of understanding, and the only solid basis of greatness; and that vice is the natural consequence of narrow thoughts; that it begins in mistake, and ends in ignominy.

Rasselas, Chapter 10

IMLAC'S HISTORY CONTINUED

"Wherever I went, I found that Poetry was considered as the highest learning, and regarded with a veneration somewhat approaching to that which man would pay to the Angelick Nature. And it yet fills me with wonder, that, in almost all countries, the most ancient poets are considered as the best: whether it be that every other kind of knowledge is an acquisition gradually attained, and poetry is a gift conferred at once; or that the first poetry of every nation surprised them as a novelty, and retained the credit by consent which it received by accident at first: or whether the province of poetry is to describe Nature and Passion, which are always the same, and the first writers took possession of the most striking objects for description, and the most probable occurrences for fiction, and left nothing to those that followed them, but transcription of the same events, and new combinations of the same images. Whatever be the reason, it is commonly observed that the early writers are in possession of nature, and their followers of art: that the first excel in strength and invention, and the latter in elegance and refinement.

"I was desirous to add my name to this illustrious fraternity. I read all the poets of Persia and Arabia, and was able to repeat by memory the volumes that are suspended in the mosque of Mecca. But I soon found that no man was ever great by imitation. My desire of excellence impelled me to transfer my attention to nature and to life. Nature was to be my subject, and men to be my auditors: I could never describe what I had not seen: I could not hope to move those with delight or terrour, whose interests and opinions I did not understand.

"Being now resolved to be a poet, I saw every thing with a new purpose; my sphere of attention was suddenly magnified: no kind of knowledge was to be overlooked. I ranged mountains and deserts for images and resemblances, and pictured upon my mind every tree of the forest and flower of the valley. I observed with equal care the crags of the rock and the pinnacles of the palace. Sometimes I wandered along the mazes of the rivulet, and sometimes watched the changes of the summer clouds. To a poet nothing can be useless. Whatever is beautiful, and whatever is dreadful, must be familiar to his imagination: he must be conversant with all that is awfully vast or elegantly little. The plants of the garden, the animals of the wood, the minerals of the earth, and meteors of the sky, must all concur to store his mind with inexhaustible variety: for every idea is useful for the inforcement or decoration of moral or religious truth; and he, who knows most, will have most power of diversifying his scenes, and of gratifying his reader with remote allusions and unexpected instruction.

"All the appearances of nature I was therefore careful to study, and every country which I have surveyed has contributed something to my poetical powers."

"In so wide a survey, said the prince, you must surely have left much unobserved. I have lived, till now, within the circuit of these mountains, and yet cannot walk abroad without the sight of something which I had never beheld before, or never heeded."

"The business of a poet, said Imlac, is to examine, not the individual, but the species; to remark general properties and large appearances: he does not number the streaks of the tulip, or describe the different shades in the verdure of the forest. He is to exhibit in his portraits of nature such prominent and striking features, as recal the original to every mind; and must neglect the minuter discriminations, which one may have remarked, and another have neglected, for those characteristicks which are alike obvious to vigilance and carelessness.

"But the knowledge of nature is only half the task of a poet; he must be acquainted likewise with all the modes of life. His character requires that he estimate the happiness and misery of every condition; observe the power of all the passions in all their combinations, and trace the changes of the human mind as they are modified by various institutions and accidental influences of climate or custom, from the spriteliness of infancy to the despondence of decrepitude. He must divest himself of the prejudices of his age or country; he must consider right and wrong in their abstracted and invariable state; he must disregard present laws and opinions, and rise to general and transcendental truths, which will always be the same: he must therefore content himself with the slow progress of his name; contemn the applause of his own time, and commit his claims to the justice of posterity. He must write as the interpreter of nature, and the legislator of mankind, and consider himself as presiding over the thoughts and manners of successive generations; as a being superiour to time and place. His labour is not yet at an end: he must know many languages and many sciences; and, that his stile may be worthy of his thoughts, must, by incessant practice, familiarize to himself every delicacy of speech and grace of harmony."

Immanuel Kant

1724–1804

It is an irony of the history of philosophy that the most revolutionary thinker of the eighteenth century, an unwitting founder of the romantic movement, should have lived a life whose restriction and regularity were the stuff of legend. Immanuel Kant, son of a saddlemaker, was born and educated in the Prussian seaport of Königsberg, became professor of philosophy at the university, and died without traveling more than forty miles from his birthplace. His self-discipline was so stringent and his routine so invariable that Königsbergers reputedly set their watches by him: He was awakened daily at five A.M., read for two hours, lectured to his students for two hours, wrote for two hours, and then went to a restaurant for his midday meal, where, at the height of his fame, crowds of strangers would gather to see and hear him.

Kant began his career as a scientist rather than a metaphysician (his collected works include treatises on earthquakes and lunar volcanoes), and he may have turned to philosophy to determine for himself the boundaries between the physical questions that may result in positive knowledge and the moral and aesthetic questions that can only produce further speculation.

In his *Critique of Pure Reason* (1781), Kant shifted the entire basis of our understanding of perception by showing how the mind, previously considered a passive receptor of objective sense data, instead actively *creates* the sensual world of which we are conscious. But because each mind has essentially the same equipment and performs the same operations, and because these creative operations occur prior to consciousness, we are able — in fact, we are forced — to experience the world of the senses as though it were objectively present. This theory of the mind has had immense influence on critical theory. (See the headnote for Samuel Taylor Coleridge on p. 218 for a fuller discussion of Kant's theory of perception.) In his *Critique of Judgment* (1790), Kant takes a similar tack. Just as the sensual world is the product of our subjective mental processes rather than of objective features, so our judgments of beauty are also subjective. The beauty of a work of art or a natural landscape exists nowhere but in the eye of the beholder. Yet because of their special qualities, aesthetic judgments seem to have an objective character and to reflect universal rather than individual concerns.

Kant has an unenviable reputation as one of the most perversely difficult of philosophers. His language tends to be abstract, it is true, but he proceeds slowly and delights in giving examples. The major problem readers often have with the *Critique of Judgment* involves their misunderstanding of the exact nature of the questions Kant is trying to answer. He is not trying, as Plato might have done, to define the essence of Beauty, since for him, such essences have no meaning. Nor is he concerned, as Aristotle was, to note what features good works of art have in common. His interest is in the mind, not in the object: He is more of a psychologist than a metaphysician. His overriding question might be paraphrased as follows: When a person looks at a flower or listens to a symphony and experiences it as beautiful, what propositions does that moment of aesthetic judgment strictly entail? When someone looks at Velasquez's *Las Meninas* and exclaims in aesthetic delight, what mental experience is implicit in that exclamation? Kant analyzes that mental experience in a vigorous and systematic way, by running it through his list of categories (Quality, Quantity, Relation, Modality).

The first issue is Quality: What sort of mental process underlies the judgment that a work of art or of nature is beautiful? Here Kant distinguishes beauty from two other types of judgments, those of utility and ethical goodness. Something is useful when it is good for an individual (though it may not benefit anybody else); ethically good things — virtuous actions — are universally beneficial, since it is to each person's collective advantage that everyone act justly. But to judge something as beautiful is to approve of it *freely*, without considering individual or collective interests. (Obviously some works of art — like a Frank Lloyd Wright house — can be functional as well as beautiful, but the judgment of beauty, strictly speaking, has nothing to do with function.) Personal satisfaction in a thing of beauty, therefore, is entirely *disinterested*.

The second issue is Quantity. Some judgments we make — that something is *pleasant*, for example — are *singular*: We apply them purely as individuals. Someone might enjoy raspberries but without any sense that others should agree; if a friend says he detests raspberries, a rational reaction is "All the more for me!" Other judgments are *universal*: We apply them as individuals but with a sense that our judgment holds for all humankind. Ethical judgments are universal in this sense. If we are morally outraged at, for example, the Iranian persecution of the Bahá'í faith, our judgment is combined with a sense that everyone ought to agree with us. According to Kant, the judgment of taste is *universal*, like moral judgments, not *singular*, like the judgment that something is pleasant; for to judge a thing as beautiful is also to *impute* that judgment implicitly to everyone else. Kant is not saying that aesthetic judgments are *in practice* universal, that everyone in fact agrees about what is and is not beautiful; he knew that human tastes differ enormously. His point is only that the *disinterested* quality of our sense of beauty makes us feel that, since there is nothing peculiar about us or our situation, everyone similarly placed ought to make the same judgment.

The third issue in the judgment of taste has to do with the "relations of purposes" inherent in it, which is the closest Kant comes to talking about the nature of beauty. His contemporaries had proposed that beauty was a matter of simple charm (Winckelmann) or the contemplation of perfection (Wolff). Kant disagreed: For him the central experience in a beautiful object is the form of "purposiveness without purpose" (*Zweckmässigkeit ohne Zweck*). That is, works of art and natural beauty evince relationships of parts to whole or means to end that are *like* artifacts that have purposes. The intricacy of the interaction of themes in a Bach fugue or the pattern of petals in a chrysanthemum is like the patterned intricacy of a precisely tooled machine; but the machine is made to serve another end — an exterior purpose — while the formal purposiveness in the fugue or the flower is an end in itself. However, Kant is never talking about what is objectively *in* the object we find beautiful. He is talking about the psychological experience of judgment and this sense of purposiveness-without-purpose as something that takes hold within us.

Kant's thesis under his final category, Modality, seems to follow from all that has gone before: Taste is an *exemplary* judgment. By this Kant means that our aesthetic feelings do not seem to be merely random; rather, they feel as though they were the *necessary* consequence of a rule, but one we cannot state. Our sense of beauty seems to be formed prior to conceptual knowledge, and its basis seems to be common sense. As a result, there can be (indeed, must be) disagreements about taste. But, as the proverb states, there cannot be *disputations* about taste, since there are no general, *a priori* principles to which we can rationally appeal.

In the second book, Kant takes up another common topic of late eighteenth-century aesthetics: the differences between the beautiful and the sublime. Consistently, Kant's interest is in psychological processes rather than in realities; he is less concerned to explain what things we consider sublime than to help us understand the motions of the mind when we experience it. Motion is important here, for the sublime is psychologically *dynamic,* while the beautiful is a matter of restful contemplation.

The movement of the mind that constitutes the sublime resembles one or the other of two mental acts: cognition or desire. But herein lies the paradox. We judge something to be sublime precisely when cognition fails — when in looking up into the starry sky, for instance, we experience a height, or depth, or magnitude that defies reason or is beyond our power to comprehend. On the other hand, it may be that the principles of rational desire are overthrown. When we contemplate something horrible and dangerous, like rocky cliffs or a storm at sea, and yet manage to stifle the imaginative desire to flee, we also experience the sublime. This means that the sublime depends on human reason, with its attendant limitations. An angelic or divine mind could experience the beautiful, as Kant defines it, but an omnipotent and omniscient God could not find his own handiwork sublime.

In Section 49, near the end of the *Critique of Judgment,* Kant shifts his interest from the (chiefly) eighteenth-century issue of *taste* to the quintessentially romantic issue of *genius,* from the psychological qualities involved in the reception of beauty to those involved in its creation.[1] His discussion is not developed at great length or in detail, but one can see in it many of the ideas that later German critics, such as Schiller, were to take up and that students of German philosophy, such as Coleridge, were to import into the English tradition.

Here we begin with Kant's presentation of the imagination as the primary mental faculty in genius, and one that is primarily *creative and intuitive* rather than *rational and cognitive.* The imagination indulges in the free play of spirit, breaking the laws that bind rational thought (though it follows laws of its own) and "creating another nature . . . out of the material that actual nature gives it." Genius consists of the ability

[1]Kant here also shifts his attention away from the beauty of nature to that of art. Where Hume's essay on taste had taken the response of the spectator to *art* (especially poetry) as the typical moment of aesthetic judgment, Kant instead presented taste as the response to nature ("flowers," he says, "are typical free beauties"). Perhaps this is because in nature the forms of animals, plants, and landscapes seem clearly ends in themselves and our response to them almost unconditioned by social motives.

to seize and make concrete this free play of spirit and then to embody it in a material that will make it universally communicable. In this final process, the imagination must work unfettered yet somehow under the control of the understanding. This enables the creator to get *outside* the creative process in order to assess the product of the imagination as it would appear to the spirit of another. Artists must therefore be at once creators and consumers: They must approach their creations from the outside, via their faculty of taste, to shape and mold them into proper form.

But on the other side, the consumer of art must also be, potentially, at least, a producer, because the product of the artist's free play is what Kant calls an *aesthetical idea*. Unlike a *rational idea*, an aesthetical idea calls up the faculty of cognition only to defeat it by employing more thought in the representation than we can clearly grasp. To comprehend aesthetical ideas embodied in a poem or painting requires the free play of the listener's or viewer's imagination as well.

In a sense, however, Kant had appealed to this free play of the spirit even in the earlier sections of the *Critique of Judgment* — particularly when he defined beauty as a product of the subjective sense of purposiveness (rational structure) cut loose from purpose itself. How could it be anything but a free play of the mind, untrammeled by the usually utilitarian (or ethical) notions of purpose, that could succeed in thus divorcing form from goal.

Selected Bibliography

Allison, Henry E. *Kant's Theory of Taste: A Reading of the Critique of Aesthetic Judgment.* Cambridge: Cambridge University Press, 2001.

Cassirer, H. W. *Commentary on Kant's Critique of Judgment.* London: Methuen, 1938.

Cohen, Ted, and Paul Guyer, eds. *Essays in Kant's Aesthetics.* Chicago: University of Chicago Press, 1982.

Coleman, Francis X. J. *The Harmony of Reason: A Study in Kant's Aesthetics.* Pittsburgh: University of Pittsburgh Press, 1974.

Crawford, Donald W. *Kant's Aesthetic Theory.* Madison: University of Wisconsin Press, 1974.

Gasché, Rodolphe, Mieke Bal, and Hent de Vries. *The Idea of Form: Rethinking Kant's Aesthetics.* Stanford: Stanford University Press, 2003.

Guyer, Paul. *Kant and the Claims of Taste.* Cambridge: Harvard University Press, 1979.

Jaspers, Karl. *Kant.* Munich: R. Piper, 1975.

McCloskey, Mary A. *Kant's Aesthetic.* Basingstoke, Hampshire: Macmillan, 1987.

Richardson, Robert Allan. *Aesthetics and Freedom: A Critique of Kant's Analysis of Beauty.* New Haven: Yale University Press, 1969.

Rogerson, Kenneth F. *Kant's Aesthetics: The Roles of Form and Expression.* Lanham, MD: University Press of America, 1986.

Schaper, Eva. *Studies in Kant's Aesthetics.* Edinburgh: University of Edinburgh Press, 1979.

Zimmerman, R. L. "Kant: The Aesthetic Judgment." *Journal of Aesthetics and Art Criticism* 21 (1963): 333–44.

From *Critique of Judgment*

First Book.
Analytic of the Beautiful

FIRST MOMENT. OF THE JUDGMENT OF TASTE,[1] ACCORDING TO QUALITY

1. The Judgment of Taste Is Aesthetical

In order to distinguish whether anything is beautiful or not, we refer the representation, not by the understanding to the object for cognition, but by the imagination (perhaps in conjunction with the understanding) to the subject and its feeling of pleasure or pain. The judgment of taste is therefore not a judgment of cognition, and is consequently not logical but aesthetical, by which we understand that whose determining ground can be *no other than subjective*. Every reference of representations, even that of sensations, may be objective (and then it signifies the real element of an empirical representation), save only the reference to the feeling of pleasure and pain, by which nothing in the object is signified, but through which there is a feeling in the subject as it is affected by the representation.

To apprehend a regular, purposive building by means of one's cognitive faculty (whether in a clear or a confused way of representation) is something quite different from being conscious of this representation as connected with the sensation of satisfaction. Here the representation is altogether referred to the subject and to its feeling of life, under the name of the feeling of pleasure or pain. This establishes a quite separate faculty of distinction and of judgment, adding nothing to cognition, but only comparing the given representation in the subject with the whole faculty of representations, of which the mind is conscious in the feeling of its state. Given representations in a judgment can be empirical (consequently, aesthetical); but the judgment which is formed by means of them is logical, provided they are referred in the judgment to the object. Conversely, if the given representations are rational, but are referred in a judgment simply to the subject (to its feeling), the judgment is so far always aesthetical.

2. The Satisfaction Which Determines the Judgment of Taste Is Disinterested

The satisfaction which we combine with the representation of the existence of an object is called "interest." Such satisfaction always has reference to the faculty of desire, either as its determining ground or as necessarily connected with its determining ground. Now when the question is if a thing is beautiful, we do not want to know whether anything depends or can depend on the existence of the thing, either for myself or for anyone else, but how we judge it by mere observation (intuition or reflection). If anyone asks me if I find that palace beautiful which I see before me, I may answer: I do not like things of that kind which are made merely to be stared at. Or I can answer like that Iroquois Sachem, who was pleased in Paris by nothing more than by the cook shops. Or again, after the manner of Rousseau, I may rebuke the vanity of the great who waste the sweat of the people on such superfluous things. In fine, I could easily convince myself that if I found myself on an uninhabited island without the hope of ever again coming among men, and could conjure up just such a splendid building by my mere wish, I should not even give myself the trouble if I had a sufficiently comfortable hut. This may all be admitted and approved, but we are not now talking of this. We wish only to know if this mere representation of the object is accompanied in me with satisfaction, however indifferent I may be as regards the existence of the object of this representation. We easily see that, in saying it is

Translated by J. H. Bernard.

[1]The definition of "taste" which is laid down here is that it is the faculty of judging of the beautiful. But the analysis of judgments of taste must show what is required in order to call an object beautiful. The moments to which this judgment has regard in its reflection I have sought in accordance with the guidance of the logical functions of judgment (for in a judgment of taste a reference to the understanding is always involved). I have considered the moment of quality first because the aesthetical judgment upon the beautiful first pays attention to it. [Kant]

beautiful and in showing that I have taste, I am concerned, not with that in which I depend on the existence of the object, but with that which I make out of this representation in myself. Everyone must admit that a judgment about beauty, in which the least interest mingles, is very partial and is not a pure judgment of taste. We must not be in the least prejudiced in favor of the existence of the things, but be quite indifferent in this respect, in order to play the judge in things of taste.

We cannot, however, better elucidate this proposition, which is of capital importance, than by contrasting the pure disinterested² satisfaction in judgments of taste with that which is bound up with an interest, especially if we can at the same time be certain that there are no other kinds of interest than those which are to be now specified.

3. The Satisfaction in the Pleasant Is Bound Up with Interest

That which pleases the senses in sensation is "*pleasant.*" Here the opportunity presents itself of censuring a very common confusion of the double sense which the word "sensation" can have, and of calling attention to it. All satisfaction (it is said or thought) is itself sensation (of a pleasure). Consequently everything that pleases is pleasant because it pleases (and according to its different degrees or its relations to other pleasant sensations it is *agreeable, lovely, delightful, enjoyable*, etc.). But if this be admitted, then impressions of sense which determine inclination, fundamental propositions of reason which determine the will, mere reflective forms of intuition which determine the judgment, are quite the same as regards the effect upon the feeling of pleasure. For this would be pleasantness in the sensation of one's state; and since in the end all the operations of our faculties must issue in the practical and unite in it as their goal,

we could suppose no other way of estimating things and their worth than that which consists in the gratification that they promise. It is of no consequence at all how this is attained, and since then the choice of means alone could make a difference, men could indeed blame one another for stupidity and indiscretion, but never for baseness and wickedness. For thus they all, each according to his own way of seeing things, seek one goal, that is, gratification.

If a determination of the feeling of pleasure or pain is called sensation, this expression signifies something quite different from what I mean when I call the representation of a thing (by sense, as a receptivity belonging to the cognitive faculty) sensation. For in the latter case the representation is referred to the object, in the former simply to the subject, and is available for no cognition whatever, not even for that by which the subject *cognizes itself*.

In the above elucidation we understand by the word "sensation" an objective representation of sense; and, in order to avoid misinterpretation, we shall call that which must always remain merely subjective and can constitute absolutely no representation of an object by the ordinary term "feeling." The green color of the meadows belongs to *objective* sensation, as a perception of an object of sense; the pleasantness of this belongs to *subjective* sensation by which no object is represented, i.e., to feeling, by which the object is considered as an object of satisfaction (which does not furnish a cognition of it).

Now that a judgment about an object by which I describe it as pleasant expresses an interest in it, is plain from the fact that by sensation it excites a desire for objects of that kind; consequently the satisfaction presupposes, not the mere judgment about it, but the relation of its existence to my state, so far as this is affected by such an object. Hence we do not merely say of the pleasant, *it pleases*, but, *it gratifies*. I give to it no mere assent, but inclination is aroused by it; and in the case of what is pleasant in the most lively fashion there is no judgment at all upon the character of the object, for those persons who always lay themselves out for enjoyment (for that is the word describing intense gratification) would fain dispense with all judgment.

²A judgment upon an object of satisfaction may be quite *disinterested*, but yet very *interesting*, i.e., not based upon an interest, but bringing an interest with it; of this kind are all pure moral judgments. Judgments of taste, however, do not in themselves establish any interest. Only in society is it *interesting* to have taste: the reason of this will be shown in the sequel. [Kant]

4. The Satisfaction in the Good Is Bound Up with Interest

Whatever by means of reason pleases through the mere concept is *good*. That which pleases only as a means we call *good for something* (the useful), but that which pleases for itself is *good in itself.* In both there is always involved the concept of a purpose, and consequently the relation of reason to the (at least possible) volition, and thus a satisfaction in the *presence* of an object or an action, i.e., some kind of interest.

In order to find anything good, I must always know what sort of a thing the object ought to be, i.e., I must have a concept of it. But there is no need of this to find a thing beautiful. Flowers, free delineations, outlines intertwined with one another without design and called conventional foliage, have no meaning, depend on no definite concept, and yet they please. The satisfaction in the beautiful must depend on the reflection upon an object, leading to any concept (however indefinite), and it is thus distinguished from the pleasant, which rests entirely upon sensation.

It is true, the pleasant seems in many cases to be the same as the good. Thus people are accustomed to say that all gratification (especially if it lasts) is good in itself, which is very much the same as to say that lasting pleasure and the good are the same. But we can soon see that this is merely a confusion of words, for the concepts which properly belong to these expressions can in no way be interchanged. The pleasant, which, as such, represents the object simply in relation to sense, must first be brought by the concept of a purpose under principles of reason, in order to call it good, as an object of the will. But that there is involved a quite different relation to satisfaction in calling that which gratifies at the same time *good* may be seen from the fact that, in the case of the good, the question always is whether it is mediately or immediately good (useful or good in itself); but on the contrary in the case of the pleasant, there can be no question about this at all, for the word always signifies something which pleases immediately. (The same is applicable to what I call beautiful.)

Even in common speech men distinguish the pleasant from the good. Of a dish which stimulates the taste by spices and other condiments we say unhesitatingly that it is pleasant, though it is at the same time admitted not to be good; for though it immediately *delights* the senses, yet mediately, i.e., considered by reason which looks to the after results, it displeases. Even in the judging of health we may notice this distinction. It is immediately pleasant to everyone possessing it (at least negatively, i.e., as the absence of all bodily pains). But in order to say that it is good, it must be considered by reason with reference to purposes, viz., that it is a state which makes us fit for all our business. Finally, in respect of happiness, everyone believes himself entitled to describe the greatest sum of the pleasantness of life (as regards both their number and their duration) as a true, even as the highest, good. However, reason is opposed to this. Pleasantness is enjoyment. And if we were concerned with this alone, it would be foolish to be scrupulous as regards the means which procure it for us, or to care whether it is obtained passively by the bounty of nature or by our own activity and work. But reason can never be persuaded that the existence of a man who merely lives for *enjoyment* (however busy he may be in this point of view) has a worth in itself, even if he at the same time is conducive as a means to the best enjoyment of others and shares in all their gratifications by sympathy. Only what he does, without reference to enjoyment, in full freedom and independently of what nature can procure for him passively, gives an absolute worth to his presence in the world as the existence of a person; and happiness, with the whole abundance of its pleasures, is far from being an unconditioned good.[3]

However, notwithstanding all this difference between the pleasant and the good, they both agree in this that they are always bound up with an interest in their object; so are not only the pleasant (§ 3), and the mediate good (the useful) which is pleasing as a means toward pleasantness

[3]An obligation to enjoyment is a manifest absurdity. Thus the obligation to all actions which have merely enjoyment for their aim can only be a pretended one, however spiritually it may be conceived (or decked out), even if it is a mystical, or so-called heavenly, enjoyment. [Kant]

5. Comparison of the Three Specifically Different Kinds of Satisfaction

The pleasant and the good have both a reference to the faculty of desire, and they bring with them, the former a satisfaction pathologically conditioned (by impulses, *stimuli*), the latter a pure practical satisfaction which is determined not merely by the representation of the object but also by the represented connection of the subject with the existence of the object. It is not merely the object that pleases, but also its existence. On the other hand, the judgment of taste is merely *contemplative;* i.e., it is a judgment which, indifferent as regards the existence of an object, compares its character with the feeling of pleasure and pain. But this contemplation itself is not directed to concepts; for the judgment of taste is not a cognitive judgment (either theoretical or practical), and thus is not *based* on concepts, nor has it concepts as its *purpose.*

The pleasant, the beautiful, and the good designate then three different relations of representations to the feeling of pleasure and pain, in reference to which we distinguish from one another objects or methods of representing them. And the expressions corresponding to each, by which we mark our complacency in them, are not the same. That which *gratifies* a man is called *pleasant;* that which merely *pleases* him is *beautiful;* that which is *esteemed* or *approved* by him, i.e., that to which he accords an objective worth, is *good.* Pleasantness concerns irrational animals also, but beauty only concerns men, i.e., animal, but still rational, beings — not merely *qua* rational (e.g., spirits), but *qua* animal also — and the good concerns every rational being in general. This is a proposition which can only be completely established and explained in the sequel. We may say that, of all these three kinds of satisfaction, that of taste in the beautiful

is alone a disinterested and *free* satisfaction; for no interest, either of sense or of reason, here forces our assent. Hence we may say of satisfaction that it is related in the three aforesaid cases to *inclination,* to *favor,* or to *respect. Now favor* is the only free satisfaction. An object of inclination and one that is proposed to our desire by a law of reason leave us no freedom in forming for ourselves anywhere an object of pleasure. All interest presupposes or generates a want, and, as the determining ground of assent, it leaves the judgment about the object no longer free.

As regards the interest of inclination in the case of the pleasant, everyone says that hunger is the best sauce, and everything that is eatable is relished by people with a healthy appetite; and thus a satisfaction of this sort shows no choice directed by taste. It is only when the want is appeased that we can distinguish which of many men has or has not taste. In the same way there may be manners (conduct) without virtue, politeness without good will, decorum without modesty, etc. For where the moral law speaks there is no longer, objectively, a free choice as regards what is to be done; and to display taste in its fulfillment (or in judging of another's fulfillment of it) is something quite different from manifesting the moral attitude of thought. For this involves a command and generates a want, while moral taste only plays with the objects of satisfaction, without attaching itself to one of them.

Explanation of the Beautiful Resulting from the First Moment

Taste is the faculty of judging of an object or a method of representing it by an *entirely disinterested* satisfaction or dissatisfaction. The object of such satisfaction is called *beautiful.*[4]

[4]Ueberweg points out (*History of Philosophy,* II, 528, English translation) that Mendelssohn had already called attention to the disinterestedness of our satisfaction in the beautiful. "It appears," says Mendelssohn, "to be a particular mark of the beautiful, that it is contemplated with quiet satisfaction, that it pleases, even though it be not in our possession, and even though we be never so far removed from the desire to put it to our use." But, of course, as Ueberweg remarks, Kant's conception of disinterestedness extends far beyond the idea of merely not desiring to possess the object. [Tr.]

SECOND MOMENT. OF THE JUDGMENT OF TASTE, ACCORDING TO QUANTITY

6. The Beautiful Is That Which Apart from Concepts Is Represented as the Object of a Universal Satisfaction

This explanation of the beautiful can be derived from the preceding explanation of it as the object of an entirely disinterested satisfaction. For the fact of which everyone is conscious, that the satisfaction is for him quite disinterested, implies in his judgment a ground of satisfaction for all men. For since it does not rest on any inclination of the subject (nor upon any other premeditated interest), but since the person who judges feels himself quite *free* as regards the satisfaction which he attaches to the object, he cannot find the ground of this satisfaction in any private conditions connected with his own subject, and hence it must be regarded as grounded on what he can presuppose in every other person. Consequently he must believe that he has reason for attributing a similar satisfaction to everyone. He will therefore speak of the beautiful as if beauty were a characteristic of the object and the judgment logical (constituting a cognition of the object by means of concepts of it), although it is only aesthetical and involves merely a reference of the representation of the object to the subject. For it has this similarity to a logical judgment that we can presuppose its validity for all men. But this universality cannot arise from concepts; for from concepts there is no transition to the feeling of pleasure or pain (except in pure practical laws, which bring an interest with them such as is not bound up with the pure judgment of taste). Consequently the judgment of taste, accompanied with the consciousness of separation from all interest, must claim validity for every man, without this universality depending on objects. That is, there must be bound up with it a title to subjective universality.

7. Comparison of the Beautiful with the Pleasant and the Good by Means of the Above Characteristic

As regards the pleasant, everyone is content that his judgment, which he bases upon private feeling and by which he says of an object that it pleases him, should be limited merely to his own person. Thus he is quite contented that if he says, "Canary wine is pleasant," another man may correct his expression and remind him that he ought to say, "It is pleasant *to me*." And this is the case not only as regards the taste of the tongue, the palate, and the throat, but for whatever is pleasant to anyone's eyes and ears. To one, violet color is soft and lovely; to another, it is washed out and dead. One man likes the tone of wind instruments, another that of strings. To strive here with the design of reproving as incorrect another man's judgment which is different from our own, as if the judgments were logically opposed, would be folly. As regards the pleasant, therefore, the fundamental proposition is valid: *Everyone has his own taste* (the taste of sense).

The case is quite different with the beautiful. It would (on the contrary) be laughable if a man who imagined anything to his own taste thought to justify himself by saying: "The object (the house we see, the coat that person wears, the concert we hear, the poem submitted to our judgment) is beautiful *for me*." For he must not call it *beautiful* if it merely pleases him. Many things may have for him charm and pleasantness — no one troubles himself at that — but if he gives out anything as beautiful, he supposes in others the same satisfaction; he judges not merely for himself, but for everyone, and speaks of beauty as if it were a property of things. Hence he says "the *thing* is beautiful"; and he does not count on the agreement of others with this his judgment of satisfaction, because he has found this agreement several times before, but he *demands* it of them. He blames them if they judge otherwise and he denies them taste, which he nevertheless requires from them. Here, then, we cannot say that each man has his own particular taste. For this would be as much as to say that there is no taste whatever, i.e., no aesthetical judgment which can make a rightful claim upon everyone's assent.

At the same time we find as regards the pleasant that there is an agreement among men in their judgments upon it in regard to which we deny taste to some and attribute it to others, by this not meaning one of our organic senses, but a faculty of judging in respect of the pleasant generally. Thus we say of a man who knows how to entertain his guests with pleasures (of enjoyment for all the senses), so that they are all pleased, "he has taste." But here the universality is only taken comparatively; and there emerge rules which are only *general* (like all empirical ones), and not *universal*, which latter the judgment of taste upon the beautiful undertakes or lays claim to. It is a judgment in reference to sociability, so far as this rests on empirical rules. In respect of the good it is true that judgments make rightful claim to validity for everyone; but the good is represented *only by means of a concept* as the object of a universal satisfaction, which is the case neither with the pleasant nor with the beautiful.

8. The Universality of the Satisfaction Is Represented in a Judgment of Taste Only as Subjective

This particular determination of the universality of an aesthetical judgment, which is to be met with in a judgment of taste, is noteworthy, not indeed for the logician, but for the transcendental philosopher. It requires no small trouble to discover its origin, but we thus detect a property of our cognitive faculty which without this analysis would remain unknown.

First, we must be fully convinced of the fact that in a judgment of taste (about the beautiful) the satisfaction in the object is imputed to *every-one*, without being based on a concept (for then it would be the good). Further, this claim to universal validity so essentially belongs to a judgment by which we describe anything as *beautiful* that, if this were not thought in it, it would never come into our thoughts to use the expression at all, but everything which pleases without a concept would be counted as pleasant. In respect of the latter, everyone has his own opinion; and no one assumes in another agreement with his judgment of taste, which is always the case in a judgment of taste about beauty. I may call the first the taste of sense, the second the taste of reflection, so far as the first lays down mere private judgments and the second judgments supposed to be generally valid (public), but in both cases aesthetical (not practical) judgments about an object merely in respect of the relation of its representation to the feeling of pleasure and pain. Now here is

something strange. As regards the taste of sense, not only does experience show that its judgment (of pleasure or pain connected with anything) is not valid universally, but everyone is content not to impute agreement with it to others (although actually there is often found a very extended con-currence in these judgments). On the other hand, the taste of reflection has its claim to the universal validity of its judgments (about the beautiful) rejected often enough, as experience teaches, although (as it may find it possible actually does) to represent judgments which can demand this universal agreement. In fact it imputes this to everyone for each of its judgments of taste, without the persons that judge disputing as to the possibility of such a claim, although in particular cases they cannot agree as to the correct applica-tion of this faculty.

Here we must, in the first place, remark that a universality which does not rest on concepts of objects (not even on empirical ones) is not logi-cal but aesthetical; i.e., it involves no objective quantity of the judgment, but only that which is subjective. For this I use the expression *general validity*, which signifies the validity of the ref-erence of a representation, not to the cognitive faculty, but to the feeling of pleasure and pain for every subject. (We can avail ourselves also of the same expression for the logical quantity of the judgment, if only we prefix "objective" to "uni-versal validity," to distinguish it from that which is merely subjective and aesthetical.)

A judgment with *objective universal valid-ity* is also always valid subjectively; i.e., if the judgment holds for everything contained under a given concept, it holds also for everyone who represents an object by means of this concept. But from a *subjective universal validity*, i.e., aestheti-cal and resting on no concept, we cannot infer that which is logical because that kind of judg-ment does not extend to the object. But, therefore, the aesthetical universality which is ascribed to a judgment must be of a particular kind, because it does not unite the predicate of beauty with the concept of the object, considered in its whole logical sphere, and yet extends it to the whole sphere of judging persons.

In respect of logical quantity, all judgments of taste are *singular* judgments. For because I must refer the object immediately to my feeling of pleasure and pain, and that not by means of concepts, they cannot have the quantity of objective generally valid judgments. Nevertheless, if the singular representation of the object of the judgment of taste, in accordance with the conditions determining the latter, were transformed by comparison into a concept, a logically universal judgment could result therefrom. E.g., I describe by a judgment of taste the rose that I see as beautiful. But the judgment which results from the comparison of several singular judgments, "Roses in general are beautiful," is no longer described simply as aesthetical, but as a logical judgment based on an aesthetical one. Again the judgment, "The rose is pleasant" (to use) is, although aesthetical and singular, not a judgment of taste but of sense. It is distinguished from the former by the fact that the judgment of taste carries with it an *aesthetic quantity* of universality, i.e., of validity for everyone, which cannot be found in a judgment about the pleasant. It is only judgments about the good which, although they also determine satisfaction in an object, have logical and not merely aesthetical universality, for they are valid of the object as cognitive of it, and thus are valid for everyone.

If we judge objects merely according to concepts, then all representation of beauty is lost. Thus there can be no rule according to which anyone is to be forced to recognize anything as beautiful. We cannot press [upon others] by the aid of any reasons or fundamental propositions our judgment that a coat, a house, or a flower is beautiful. People wish to submit the object to their own eyes, as if the satisfaction in it depended on sensation; and yet, if we then call the object beautiful, we believe that we speak with a universal voice, and we claim the assent of everyone, although on the contrary all private sensation can only decide for the observer himself and his satisfaction.

We may see now that in the judgment of taste nothing is postulated but such a *universal voice,* in respect of the satisfaction without the intervention of concepts, and thus the *possibility* of an aesthetical judgment that can, at the same time, be regarded as valid for everyone. The judgment of taste itself does not *postulate* the agreement of everyone (for that can only be done by a logically universal judgment because it can adduce reasons); it only *imputes* this agreement to everyone, as a case of the rule in respect of which it expects, not confirmation by concepts, but assent from others. The universal voice is, therefore, only an idea (we do not yet inquire upon what it rests). It may be uncertain whether or not the man who believes that he is laying down a judgment of taste is, as a matter of fact, judging in conformity with that idea; but that he refers his judgment thereto, and consequently that it is intended to be a judgment of taste, he announces by the expression "beauty." He can be quite certain of this for himself by the mere consciousness of the separating off everything belonging to the pleasant and the good from the satisfaction which is left; and this is all for which he promises himself the agreement of everyone — a claim which would be justifiable under these conditions, provided only he did not often make mistakes, and thus lay down an erroneous judgment of taste. . . .

Explanation of the Beautiful Resulting from the Second Moment

The *beautiful* is that which pleases universally without requiring a concept.

THIRD MOMENT. OF JUDGMENTS OF TASTE, ACCORDING TO THE RELATION OF THE PURPOSES WHICH ARE BROUGHT INTO CONSIDERATION IN THEM

10. Of Purposiveness in General

If we wish to explain what a purpose is according to its transcendental determinations (without presupposing anything empirical like the feeling of pleasure), we say that the purpose is the object of a concept, insofar as the concept is regarded as the cause of the object (the real ground of its possibility); and the causality of a *concept* in respect of its *object* is its purposiveness (*forma finalis*). Where then not merely the cognition of an object but the object itself (its form and existence) is thought as an effect only possible by means of the concept of this latter, there we think a purpose. The representation of the effect is here the determining ground of its cause and precedes it. The consciousness of the causality of a representation, for *maintaining* the subject in the same state, may here generally denote what we call pleasure; while on the other hand pain is that representation which contains the ground of the determination of the state of representations into their opposite of restraining or removing them.[5]

The faculty of desire, so far as it is determinable to act only through concepts, i.e., in conformity with the representation of a purpose, would be the will. But an object, or a state of mind, would even an action is called purposive, although its possibility does not necessarily presuppose the representation of a purpose, merely because its possibility can be explained and conceived by us only so far as we assume for its ground a causality according to purposes, i.e., in accordance with a will which has regulated it according to the representation of a certain rule. There can be, then, purposiveness without purpose, so far as we do not place the causes of this form in a will, but yet can only make the explanation of its possibility intelligible to ourselves by deriving it from a will. Again, we are not always forced to regard what we observe (in respect of its possibility) from the point of view of reason. Thus we can at least observe a purposiveness according to form, without basing it on a purpose (as the material of the *nexus finalis*), and remark it in objects, although only by reflection.

11. The Judgment of Taste Has Nothing at Its Basis but the Form of the Purposiveness of an Object (or of Its Mode of Representation)

Every purpose, if it be regarded as a ground of satisfaction, always carries with it an interest — as the determining ground of the judgment — about the object of pleasure. Therefore no subjective purpose can lie at the basis of the judgment of taste. But also the judgment of taste can be determined by no representation of an objective purpose, i.e., of the possibility of the object itself in accordance with principles of purposive combination, and consequently by no concept of the good, because it is an aesthetical and not a cognitive judgment. It therefore has to do with no *concept* of the character and internal or external possibility of the object by means of this or that cause, but merely with the relation of the representative powers to one another, so far as they are determined by a representation.

Now this relation in the determination of an object as beautiful is bound up with the feeling of pleasure, which is declared by the judgment of taste to be valid for everyone; hence a pleasantness accompanying the representation can as little contain the determining ground of the judgment as the representation of the perfection of the object and the concept of the good can. Therefore it can be nothing else than the subjective purposiveness in the representation of an object without any purpose (either objective or subjective), and thus it is the mere form of purposiveness in the representation by which an object is *given* to us, so far as we are conscious of it, which constitutes the satisfaction that we without a concept judge to be universally communicable; and, consequently, this is the determining ground of the judgment of taste.

12. The Judgment of Taste Rests on A Priori Grounds

To establish *a priori* the connection of the feeling of a pleasure or pain as an effect, with any representation whatever (sensation or concept) as its cause, is absolutely impossible; for that would be a particular causal relation which (with objects of experience) can always only be cognized *a posteriori* and through the medium of experience itself. We actually have, indeed, in the *Critique of Practical Reason*, derived from universal moral concepts *a priori* the feeling of respect (as a special and peculiar modification of feeling which will not strictly correspond either to the pleasure or the pain that we get from empirical objects). But there we could go beyond the bounds of experience and call in a causality which rested

[5] Mr. Herbert Spencer expresses much more concisely what Kant has in his mind here. "Pleasure . . ." is a feeling which we seek to bring into consciousness and retain there; pain is . . . a feeling which we seek to get out of consciousness and to keep out." *Principles of Psychology*, 125. [Tr.]

on a supersensible attribute of the subject, viz., freedom. And even there, properly speaking, it was not this *feeling* which we derived from the idea of the moral as cause, but merely the determination of the will. But the state of mind which accompanies any determination of the will is in itself a feeling of pleasure and identical with it, and therefore does not follow from it as its effect. This last must only be assumed if the concept of the moral as a good precedes the determination of the will by the law, for in that case the pleasure that is bound up with the concept could not be derived from it as from a mere cognition.

Now the case is similar with the pleasure in aesthetical judgments, only that here it is merely contemplative and does not bring about an interest in the object, while on the other hand in the moral judgment it is practical.[6] The consciousness of the mere formal purposiveness in the play of the subject's cognitive powers, in a representation through which an object is given, is the pleasure itself, because it contains a determining ground of the activity of the subject in respect of the excitement of its cognitive powers, and therefore an inner causality (which is purposive) in respect of cognition in general, without however being limited to any definite cognition, and consequently contains a mere form of the subjective purposiveness of a representation in an aesthetical judgment. This pleasure is in no way practical, neither like that arising from the pathological ground of pleasantness, nor that from the intellectual ground of the presented good. But yet it involves causality, viz., of *maintaining* without further design the state of the representation itself and the occupation of the cognitive powers. We *linger* over the contemplation of the beautiful because this contemplation strengthens and reproduces itself,

which is analogous to (though not of the same kind as) that lingering which takes place when a physical charm in the representation of the object repeatedly arouses the attention, the mind being passive. . . .

16. The Judgment of Taste, by Which an Object Is Declared to Be Beautiful Under the Condition of a Definite Concept, Is Not Pure

There are two kinds of beauty: free beauty (*pulchritudo vaga*), or merely dependent beauty (*pulchritudo adhaerens*). The first presupposes no concept of what the object ought to be; the second does presuppose such a concept and the perfection of the object in accordance therewith. The first is called the (self-subsistent) beauty of this or that thing; the second, as dependent upon a concept (conditioned beauty), is ascribed to objects which come under the concept of a particular purpose.

Flowers are free natural beauties. Hardly anyone but a botanist knows what sort of a thing a flower ought to be; and even he, though recognizing in the flower the reproductive organ of the plant, pays no regard to this natural purpose if he is passing judgment on the flower by taste. There is, then, at the basis of this judgment no perfection of any kind, no internal purposiveness, to which the collection of the manifold is referred. Many birds (such as the parrot, the hummingbird, the bird of paradise) and many seashells are beauties in themselves, which do not belong to any object determined in respect of its purpose by concepts, but please freely and in themselves. So also delineations *à la grecque,* foliage for borders or wall papers, mean nothing in themselves; they represent nothing — no object under a definite concept — and are free beauties. We can refer to the same class what are called in music phantasies (i.e., pieces without any theme), and in fact all music without words.

In the judging of a free beauty (according to the mere form), the judgment of taste is pure. There is presupposed no concept of any purpose which the manifold of the given object is to serve, and which therefore is to be represented in it. By such a concept the freedom of the imagination

---

[6]Cf. *Metaphysic of Morals,* Introduction I. "The pleasure which is necessarily bound up with the desire (of the object whose representation affects feeling) may be called *practical* pleasure, whether it be cause or effect of the desire. On the contrary, the pleasure which is not necessarily bound up with the desire of the object, and which, therefore, is at bottom not a pleasure in the existence of the object of the representation, but clings to the representation only, may be called mere contemplative pleasure or *passive satisfaction.* The feeling of the latter kind of pleasure we call *taste.*" [Tr.]

which disports itself in the contemplation of the figure would be only limited.

But human beauty (i.e., of a man, a woman, or a child), the beauty of a horse, or a building (be it church, palace, arsenal, or summer house), presupposes a concept of the purpose which determines what the thing is to be, and consequently a concept of its perfection; it is therefore adherent beauty. Now as the combination of the pleasant (in sensation) with beauty, which properly is only concerned with form, is a hindrance to the purity of the judgment of taste, so also is its purity injured by the combination with beauty of the good (viz., that manifold which is good for the thing itself in accordance with its purpose).

We could add much to a building which would immediately please the eye if only it were not to be a church. We could adorn a figure with all kinds of spirals and light but regular lines, as the New Zealanders do with their tattooing, if only it were not the figure of a human being. And again this could have much finer features and a more pleasing and gentle cast of countenance provided it were not intended to represent a man, much less a warrior.

Now the satisfaction in the manifold of a thing in reference to the internal purpose which determines its possibility is a satisfaction grounded on a concept; but the satisfaction in beauty is such as presupposes no concept, but is immediately bound up with the representation through which the object is given (not through which it is thought). If now the judgment of taste in respect of the beauty of a thing is made dependent on the purpose in its manifold, like a judgment of reason, and thus limited, it is no longer a free and pure judgment of taste.

It is true that taste by this combination of aesthetical with intellectual satisfaction, insmuch as it becomes fixed; and though it is not universal, yet in respect to certain purposively determined objects it becomes possible to prescribe rules for it. These, however, are not rules of taste, but merely rules for the unification of taste with reason, i.e., of the beautiful with the good, by which the former becomes available as an instrument of design in respect of the latter. Thus the tone of mind which is self-maintaining and of subjective universal validity

is subordinated to the way of thinking which can be maintained only by painful resolve, but is of objective universal validity. Properly speaking, however, perfection gains nothing by beauty, or beauty by perfection; but when we compare the representation by which an object is given to us with the object (as regards what it ought to be) by means of a concept, we cannot avoid considering along with it the sensation in the subject. And thus when both states of mind are in harmony our whole faculty of representative power gains.

A judgment of taste, then, in respect of an object with a definite internal purpose, can only be pure if either the person judging has no concept of this purpose or else abstracts from it in his judgment. Such a person, although forming an accurate judgment of taste in judging of the object as free beauty, would yet by another who considers the beauty in it only as a dependent attribute (who looks to the purpose of the object) be blamed and accused of false taste, although both are right in their own way — the one in reference to what he has before his eyes, the other in reference to what he has in his thought. By means of this distinction we can settle many disputes about beauty between judges of taste, by showing that the one is speaking of free, the other of dependent, beauty — that the first is making a pure, the second an applied, judgment of taste. . . .

Explanation of the Beautiful Derived from This Third Moment

Beauty is the form of the *purposiveness* of an object, so far as this is perceived in it without any *representation of a purpose.*[7]

[7]It might be objected to this explanation that there are things in which we see a purposive form without cognizing any purpose in them, like the stone implements often gotten from old sepulchral tumuli with a hole in them, as if for a handle. These, although they plainly indicate by their shape a purposiveness of which we do not know the purpose, are nevertheless not described as beautiful. But if we regard a thing as a work of art, that is enough to make us admit that its shape has reference to some design and definite purpose. And hence there is no immediate satisfaction in the contemplation of it. On the other hand a flower, e.g., a tulip, is regarded as beautiful, because in perceiving it we find a certain purposiveness which, in our judgment, is referred to no purpose at all. [Kant]

FOURTH MOMENT. OF THE JUDGMENT OF TASTE, ACCORDING TO THE MODALITY OF THE SATISFACTION IN THE OBJECT

18. What the Modality in a Judgment of Taste Is

I can say of every representation that it is at least *possible* that (as a cognition) it should be bound up with a pleasure. Of a representation that I call *pleasant* I say that it *actually* excites pleasure in me. But the *beautiful* we think as having a *necessary* reference to satisfaction. Now this necessity is of a peculiar kind. It is not a theoretical objective necessity, in which case it would be cognized *a priori* that everyone *will feel* this satisfaction in the object called beautiful by me. It is not a practical necessity, in which case, by concepts of a pure rational will serving as a rule for freely acting beings, the satisfaction is the necessary result of an objective law and only indicates that we absolutely (without any further design) ought to act in a certain way. But the necessity which is thought in an aesthetical judgment can only be called exemplary, i.e., a necessity of the assent of *all* to a judgment which is regarded as the example of a universal rule that we cannot state. Since an aesthetical judgment is not an objective cognitive judgment, this necessity cannot be derived from definite concepts and is therefore not apodictic. Still less can it be inferred from the universality of experience (of a complete agreement of judgments as to the beauty of a certain object). For not only would experience hardly furnish sufficiently numerous vouchers for this, but also, on empirical judgments, we can base no concept of the necessity of these judgments.

19. The Subjective Necessity, Which We Ascribe to the Judgment of Taste, Is Conditioned

The judgment of taste requires the agreement of everyone, and he who describes anything as beautiful claims that everyone *ought* to give his approval to the object in question and also describe it as beautiful. The *ought* in the aesthetical judgment is therefore pronounced in accordance with all the data which are required for judging, and yet is only conditioned. We ask for the agreement of everyone else, because we have for it a ground that is common to all; and we could count on this agreement, provided we were always sure that the case was correctly subsumed under that ground as rule of assent.

20. The Condition of Necessity Which a Judgment of Taste Asserts Is the Idea of a Common Sense

If judgments of taste (like cognitive judgments) had a definite objective principle, then the person who lays them down in accordance with this latter would claim an unconditioned necessity for his judgment. If they were devoid of all principle, like those of the mere taste of sense, we would not allow them in thought any necessity whatever. Hence they must have a subjective principle which determines what pleases or displeases only by feeling and not by concepts, but yet with universal validity. But such a principle could only be regarded as a *common sense,* which is essentially different from common understanding which people sometimes call common sense (*sensus communis*); for the latter does not judge by feeling but always by concepts, although ordinarily only as by obscurely represented principles.

Hence it is only under the presupposition that there is a common sense (by which we do not understand an external sense, but the effect resulting from the free play of our cognitive powers) — it is only under this presupposition, I say, that the judgment of taste can be laid down. . . .

Explanation of the Beautiful Resulting from the Fourth Moment

The *beautiful* is that which without any concept is cognized as the object of a *necessary* satisfaction.

GENERAL REMARK ON THE FIRST SECTION OF THE ANALYTIC

If we seek the result of the preceding analysis, we find that everything runs up into this concept of taste — that it is a faculty for judging an object in reference to the imagination's *free conformity to law*. Now, if in the judgment of taste the imagination must be considered in its freedom, it is in the first place not regarded as reproductive, as it is subject to the laws of association, but as productive and spontaneous (as the author of arbitrary forms of possible intuition). And although in the apprehension of a given object of sense it is tied to a definite form of this object and so far has no free play (such as that of poetry), yet it may readily be conceived that the object can furnish it with such a form containing a collection of the manifold as the imagination itself, if it were left free, would project in accordance with the conformity to law of the understanding in general. But that the *imaginative power should be free and yet of itself conformed to law*, i.e. bringing autonomy with it, is a contradiction. The understanding alone gives the law. If, however, the imagination is compelled to proceed according to a definite law, its product in respect of form is determined by concepts as to what it ought to be. But then, as is above shown, the satisfaction is not that in the beautiful, but in the good (in perfection, at any rate in mere formal perfection), and the judgment is not a judgment of taste. Hence it is a conformity to law without a law; and a subjective agreement of the imagination and understanding — without such an objective agreement as there is when the representation is referred to a definite concept of an object — can subsist along with the free conformity to law of the understanding (which is also called purposiveness without purpose) and with the peculiar feature of a judgment of taste.

Now geometrically regular figures, such as a circle, a square, a cube, etc., are commonly adduced by critics of taste as the simplest and most indisputable examples of beauty, and yet they are called regular because we can only represent them by regarding them as mere presentations of a definite concept which prescribes the rule of the figure (according to which alone it is possible). One of these two must be wrong, either that judgment of the critic which ascribes beauty to the said figures, or ours which regards purposiveness apart from a concept as requisite for beauty.

Hardly anyone will say that a man must have taste in order that he should find more satisfaction in a circle than in a scrawled outline, in an equilateral and equiangular quadrilateral than in one which is oblique, irregular, and as it were deformed; for this belongs to the ordinary understanding and is not taste at all. Where, e.g., our design is to judge of the size of an area or to make intelligible the relation of the parts of it, when divided, to one another and to the whole, then regular figures and those of the simplest kind are needed, and the satisfaction does not rest immediately on the aspect of the figure, but on its availability for all kinds of possible designs. A room whose walls form oblique angles, or a parterre of this kind, even every violation of symmetry in the figure of animals (e.g., being one-eyed), of buildings, or of flower beds, displeases because it contradicts the purpose of the thing, not only practically in respect of a definite use of it, but also when we pass judgment on it as regards any possible design. This is not the case in the judgment of taste, which when pure combines satisfaction or dissatisfaction — without reference to its use or to a purpose — with the mere *consideration* of the object.

The regularity which leads to the concept of an object is indeed the indispensable condition (*conditio sine qua non*) for grasping the object in a single representation and determining the manifold in its form. This determination is a purpose in respect of cognition, and in reference to this it is always bound up with satisfaction (which accompanies the execution of every, even problematical, design). There is here, however, merely the approval of the solution satisfying a problem, and not a free and indefinite purposive entertainment of the mental powers with what we call beautiful, where the understanding is at the service of imagination, and not *vice versa*.

In a thing that is only possible by means of design — a building, or even an animal — the regularity consisting in symmetry must express the unity of the intuition that accompanies the concept of purpose, and this regularity belongs to cognition. But where only a free play of the representative powers (under the condition, however, that the understanding is to suffer no shock thereby) is to be kept up, in pleasure gardens, room decorations, all kinds of tasteful furniture, etc., regularity that shows constraint is avoided as much as possible. Thus in the English taste in gardens or in bizarre taste in furniture, the freedom of the imagination is pushed almost near to the grotesque, and in this separation from every constraint of rule we have the case where taste can display its greatest perfection in the enterprises of the imagination.

All stiff regularity (such as approximates to mathematical regularity) has something in it repugnant to taste; for our entertainment in the contemplation of it lasts for no length of time, but it rather, insofar as it has not expressly in view cognition or a definite practical purpose, produces weariness. On the other hand, that with which imagination can play in an unstudied and purposive manner is always new to us, and one does not get tired of looking at it. Marsden, in his description of Sumatra, makes the remark that the free beauties of nature surround the spectator everywhere and thus lose their attraction for him.[8] On the other hand, a pepper garden, where the stakes on which this plant twines itself form parallel rows, had much attractiveness for him if he met with it in the middle of a forest. And he hence infers that wild beauty, apparently irregular, only pleases as a variation from the regular beauty of which one has seen enough. But he need only have made the experiment of spending one day in a pepper garden to have been convinced that, if the understanding has put itself in accordance with the order that it always needs by means of regularity, the object will not entertain for long — nay, rather it will impose a burdensome constraint upon the imagination. On the other hand, nature, which there is prodigal in its variety even to luxuriance, that is subjected to no constraint of artificial rules, can supply constant food for taste. Even the song of birds, which we can bring under no musical rule, seems to have more freedom, and therefore more for taste, than a song of a human being which is produced in accordance with all the rules of music; for we very much sooner weary of the latter if it is repeated often and at length. Here, however, we probably confuse our participation in the mirth of a little creature that we love with the beauty of its song,

[8]W. Marsden, *The History of Sumatra* (London, 1783), p. 113. [Tr.]

for if this were exactly imitated by man (as sometimes the notes of the nightingale are), it would seem to our ear quite devoid of taste.

Again, beautiful objects are to be distinguished from beautiful views of objects (which often on account of their distance cannot be more clearly cognized). In the latter case taste appears, not so much in what the imagination *apprehends* in this field, as in the impulse it thus gets to *fiction,* i.e., in the peculiar fancies with which the mind entertains itself, while it is continually being aroused by the variety which strikes the eye. An illustration is afforded, e.g., by the sight of the changing shapes of a fire on the hearth or of a rippling brook; neither of these has beauty, but they bring with them a charm for the imagination because they entertain it in free play.

Second Book.
Analytic of the Sublime

23. Transition from the Faculty Which Judges of the Beautiful to That Which Judges of the Sublime

The beautiful and the sublime agree in this that both please in themselves. Further, neither presupposes a judgment of sense nor a judgment logically determined, but a judgment of reflection. Consequently the satisfaction belonging to them does not depend on a sensation, as in the case of the pleasant, nor on a definite concept, as in the case of the good; but it is nevertheless referred to concepts, although indeterminate ones. And so the satisfaction is connected with the mere presentation of the object or with the faculty of presentation, so that in the case of a given intuition this faculty or the imagination is considered as in agreement with the *faculty of concepts* of understanding or reason, regarded as promoting these latter. Hence both kinds of judgments are *singular,* and yet announce themselves as universally valid for every subject; although they lay claim merely to the feeling of pleasure, and not to any cognition of the object.

But there are also remarkable differences between the two. The beautiful in nature is connected with the form of the object, which consists in having definite boundaries. The sublime, on the other hand, is to be found in a formless object, so far as in it or by occasion of it *boundlessness* is represented, and yet its totality is also present to thought. Thus the beautiful seems to be regarded as the presentation of an indefinite concept of understanding, the sublime as that of a like concept of reason. Therefore the satisfaction in the one case is bound up with the representation of *quality*, in the other with that of *quantity*. And the latter satisfaction is quite different in kind from the former, for the beautiful directly brings with it a feeling of the furtherance of life, and thus is compatible with charms and with the play of the imagination. But the feeling of the sublime is a pleasure that arises only indirectly; viz., it is produced by the feeling of a momentary checking of the vital powers and a consequent stronger outflow of them, so that it seems to be regarded as emotion — not play, but earnest in the exercise of the imagination. Hence it is incompatible with physical charm; and as the mind is not merely attracted by the object but is ever being alternately repelled, the satisfaction in the sublime does not so much involve a positive pleasure as admiration or respect, which rather deserves to be called negative pleasure.

But the inner and most important distinction between the sublime and beautiful is, certainly, as follows. (Hence, as we are entitled to do, we only bring under consideration in the first instance the sublime in natural objects, for the sublime of art is always limited by the conditions of agreement with nature.) Natural beauty (which is independent) brings with it a purposiveness in its form by which the object seems to be, as it were, preadapted to our judgement, and thus constitutes in itself an object of satisfaction. On the other hand, that which excites in us, without any reasoning about it, but in the mere apprehension of it, the feeling of the sublime may appear, as regards its form, to violate purpose in respect of the judgement, to be unsuited to our presentative faculty, and as it were to do violence to the imagination; and yet it is judged to be only the more sublime.

Now we may see from this that, in general, we express ourselves incorrectly if we call any *object of nature* sublime, although we can quite correctly call many objects of nature beautiful. For how can that be marked by an expression of approval which is apprehended in itself as being a violation of purpose? All that we can say is that the object is fit for the presentation of a sublimity which can be found in the mind, for no sensible form can contain the sublime properly so-called. This concerns only ideas of the reason which, although no adequate presentation is possible for them, by this inadequateness that admits of sensible presentation are aroused and summoned into the mind. Thus the wide ocean, disturbed by the storm, cannot be called sublime. Its aspect is horrible; and the mind must be already filled with manifold ideas if it is to be determined by such an intuition to a feeling itself sublime, as it is incited to abandon sensibility and to busy itself with ideas that involve higher purposiveness.

Independent natural beauty discovers to us a technique of nature which represents it as a system in accordance with laws, the principle of which we do not find in the whole of our faculty of understanding. That principle is the principle of purposiveness, in respect of the use of our judgement in regard to phenomena, which requires that these must not be judged as merely belonging to nature in its purposeless mechanism, but also as belonging to something analogous to art. It therefore actually extends, not indeed our cognition of natural objects, but our concept of nature, which is now regarded not as mere mechanism but as art. This leads to profound investigations as to the possibility of such a form. But in what we are accustomed to call sublime there is nothing at all that leads to particular objective principles and forms of nature corresponding to them; so far from it is that, for the most part, nature excites the ideas of the sublime in its chaos or in its wildest and most irregular disorder and desolation, provided size and might are perceived. Hence, we see that the concept of the sublime is not nearly so important or rich in consequences as the concept of the beautiful; and that, in general, it displays nothing purposive in nature itself, but only in that possible use of our intuitions of it by which there is produced in us a feeling of a purposiveness quite independent of nature. We must seek a ground external to ourselves for the beautiful of nature, but seek it for the sublime merely in ourselves and in our attitude of thought, which introduces sublimity into the representation of nature.

This is a very needful preliminary remark, which quite separates the ideas of the sublime from that of a purposiveness of *nature* and makes the theory of the sublime a mere appendix to the aesthetical judging of that purposiveness, because by means of it no particular form is represented in nature, but there is only developed a purposive use which the imagination makes of its representation.

24. Of the Divisions of an Investigation into the Feeling of the Sublime

As regards the division of the moments of the aesthetical judging of objects in reference to the feeling of the sublime, the Analytic can proceed according to the same principle as was adopted in the analysis of judgments of taste. For as an act of the aesthetical reflective judgment, the satisfaction in the sublime must be represented just as in the case of the beautiful — according to *quantity* as universally valid, according to *quality* as devoid of *interest,* according to *relation* as subjective purposiveness, and according to *modality* as necessary. And so the method here will not diverge from that of the preceding section, unless indeed we count it a difference that in the case where the aesthetical judgment is concerned with the form of the object we began with the investigation of its quality, but here, in view of the formlessness which may belong to what we call sublime, we will begin with quantity, as the first moment of the aesthetical judgment as to the sublime. The reason for this may be seen from the preceding paragraph.

But the analysis of the sublime involves a division not needed in the case of the beautiful, viz., a division into the *mathematically* and the *dynamically sublime.*

For the feeling of the sublime brings with it as its characteristic feature a *movement* of the mind bound up with the judging of the object, while in the case of the beautiful taste presupposes and maintains the mind in *restful* contemplation. Now this movement ought to be judged as subjectively purposive (because the sublime pleases us), and thus it is referred through the imagination either to the *faculty of cognition* or *of desire.* In either reference the purposiveness of the given representation ought to be judged only in respect of this *faculty* (without purpose or interest), but

in the first case, it is ascribed to the object as a *mathematical* determination of the imagination, in the second as *dynamical.* And hence we have this twofold way of representing the sublime.

A. OF THE MATHEMATICALLY SUBLIME

25. Explanation of the Term Sublime

We call that *sublime* which is *absolutely great.* But to be great and to be a great something are quite different concepts (*magnitudo* and *quantitas*). In like manner to say simply (*simpliciter*) that anything is *great* is quite different from saying that it is *absolutely great* (*absolute, non comparative magnum*). The latter is *what is great beyond all comparison.* What now is meant by the expression that anything is great or small or of medium size? It is not a pure concept of understanding that is thus signified; still less is it an intuition of sense; and just as little is it a concept of reason, because it brings with it no principle of cognition. It must therefore be a concept of judgment or derived from one, and a subjective purposiveness of the representation in reference to the judgment must lie at its basis. That anything is a magnitude (*quantum*) may be cognized from the thing itself, without many comparisons of it with other things, viz., if there is a multiplicity of the homogeneous constituting one thing. But to cognize *how great* it is always requires some other magnitude as a measure. But because the judging of magnitude depends, not merely on multiplicity (number), but also on the magnitude of the unit (the measure), and since, to judge of the magnitude of this latter again requires another as measure with which it may be compared, we see that the determination of the magnitude of phenomena can supply no absolute concept whatever of magnitude, but only a comparative one.

If now I say simply that anything is great, it appears that I have no comparison in view, at least none with an objective measure, because it is thus not determined at all how great the object is. But although the standard of comparison is merely subjective, yet the judgment nonetheless claims universal assent; "this man is beautiful" and "he is tall" are judgments, not limited merely

judging of things as great or small extends to everything, even to all their characteristics; thus we describe beauty as great or small. The reason of this is to be sought in the fact that whatever we present in intuition according to the precept of the judgment (and thus represent aesthetically) is always a phenomenon, and thus a quantum.

But if we call anything, not only great, but absolutely great in every point of view (great beyond all comparison), i.e., sublime, we soon see that it is not permissible to seek for an adequate standard of this outside itself, but merely in itself. It is a magnitude which is like itself alone. It follows hence that the sublime is not to be sought in the things of nature, but only in our ideas; but in which of them it lies must be reserved for the "Deduction."

The foregoing explanation can be thus expressed: *The sublime is that in comparison with which everything else is small.* Here we easily see that nothing can be given in nature, however great it is judged by us to be, which could not, if considered in another relation, be reduced to the infinitely small; and conversely there is nothing so small which does not admit of extension by our imagination to the greatness of a world if compared with still smaller standards. Telescopes have furnished us with abundant material for making the first remark, microscopes for the second. Nothing, therefore, which can be an object of the senses is, considered on this basis, to be called sublime. But because there is in our imagination a striving toward infinite progress and in our reason a claim for absolute totality, regarded as a real idea, therefore this very inadequateness for that idea in our faculty for estimating the magnitude of things of sense excites in us the feeling of a supersensible faculty. And it is not the object of sense, but the use which the judgment naturally makes of certain objects on behalf of this latter feeling that is absolutely great, and in comparison every other use is small. Consequently it is the state of mind produced by a certain representation with which the reflective judgment is occupied, and not the object, that is to be called sublime.

We can therefore append to the preceding formulas explaining the sublime this other: *The sublime is that, the mere ability to think which*

to the judging subject, but, like theoretical judgments, demanding the assent of everyone.

In a judgment by which anything is designated simply as great, it is not merely meant that the object has a magnitude, but that this magnitude is superior to that of many other objects of the same kind, without, however, any exact determination of this superiority. Thus there is always at the basis of our judgment a standard which we assume as the same for everyone; this, however, is not available for any logical (mathematically definite) judging of magnitude, but only for aesthetical judging of the same, because it is a merely subjective standard lying at the basis of the reflective judgment upon magnitude. It may be empirical, as, e.g., the average size of the men known to us, of animals of a certain kind, trees, houses, mountains, etc. Or it may be a standard given *a priori*, through which the defects of the judging subject, is limited by the subjective conditions of presentation *in concreto*, as, e.g., in the practical sphere, the greatness of a certain virtue or of the public liberty and justice in a country, or, in the theoretical sphere, the greatness of the accuracy or the inaccuracy of an observation or measurement that has been made, etc.

Here it is remarkable that, although we have no interest whatever in an object — i.e., its existence is indifferent to us — yet its mere size, even if it is considered as formless, may bring a satisfaction with it that is universally communicable and that consequently involves the consciousness of a subjective purposiveness in the use of our cognitive faculty. This is not indeed a satisfaction in the object (because it may be formless), as in the case of the beautiful, in which the reflective judgment finds itself purposively determined in reference to cognition in general, but a satisfaction in the extension of the imagination by itself. If (under the above limitation) we say simply of an object "it is great," this is no mathematically definite judgment, but a mere judgment of reflection upon the representation of it, which is subjectively purposive for a certain use of our cognitive powers in the estimation of magnitude; and we always then bind up with the representation a kind of respect, as also a kind of contempt, for what we simply call "small." Further, the

shows a faculty of the mind surpassing every standard of sense. . . .

27. Of the Quality of the Satisfaction in Our Judgments upon the Sublime

The feeling of our incapacity to attain to an idea *which is a law for us* is *respect*. Now the idea of the comprehension of every phenomenon that can be given us in the intuition of a whole is an idea prescribed to us by a law of reason, which recognizes no other measure, definite, valid of everyone, and invariable, than the absolute whole. But our imagination, even in its greatest efforts, in respect of that comprehension which we expect from it of a given object in a whole of intuition (and thus with reference to the presentation of the idea of reason) exhibits its own limits and inadequacy, although at the same time it shows that its destination is to make itself adequate to this idea regarded as a law. Therefore the feeling of the sublime in nature is respect for our own destination, which, by a certain subreption, we attribute to an object of nature (conversion of respect for the idea of humanity in our own subject into respect for the object). This makes intuitively evident the superiority of the rational determination of our cognitive faculties to the greatest faculty of our sensibility.

The feeling of the sublime is therefore a feeling of pain arising from the want of accordance between the aesthetical estimation of magnitude formed by the imagination and the estimation of the same formed by reason. There is at the same time a pleasure thus excited, arising from the correspondence with rational ideas of this very judgment of the inadequacy of our greatest faculty of sense, in so far as it is a law for us to strive after these ideas. In fact it is for us a law (of reason) and belongs to our destination to estimate as small, in comparison with ideas of reason, everything which nature, regarded as an object of sense, contains that is great for us; and that which arouses in us the feeling of this supersensible destination agrees with that law. Now the greatest effort of the imagination in the presentation of the unit for the estimation of magnitude indicates a reference to something *absolutely great,* and consequently a reference to the law of reason, which bids us take this alone as our highest measure of magnitude. Therefore the inner perception of the inadequacy of all sensible standards for rational estimation of magnitude indicates a correspondence with rational laws; it involves a pain, which arouses in us the feeling of our supersensible destination, according to which it is purposive and therefore pleasurable to find every standard of sensibility inadequate to the ideas of understanding.

The mind feels itself *moved* in the representation of the sublime in nature, while in aesthetical judgments about the beautiful it is in *restful* contemplation. This movement may (especially in its beginning) be compared to a vibration, i.e., to a quickly alternating attraction toward, and repulsion from, the same object. The transcendent (toward which the imagination is impelled in its apprehension of intuition) is for the imagination like an abyss in which it fears to lose itself; but for the rational idea of the supersensible it is not transcendent, but in conformity with law to bring about such an effort of the imagination, and consequently here there is the same amount of attraction as there was of repulsion for the mere sensibility. But the judgment itself always remains in this case only aesthetical, because, without having any determinate concept of the object at its basis, it merely represents the subjective play of the mental powers (imagination and reason) as harmonious through their very contrast. For just as imagination and *understanding,* in judging of the beautiful, generate a subjective purposiveness of the mental powers by means of their harmony, so in this case imagination and *reason* do so by means of their conflict. That is, they bring about a feeling that we possess pure self-subsistent reason, or a faculty for the estimation of magnitude, whose superiority can be made intuitively evident only by the inadequacy of that faculty imagination which is itself unbounded in the presentation of magnitudes (of sensible objects).

The measurement of a space (regarded as apprehension) is at the same time a description of it, and thus an objective movement in the act of imagination and a progress. On the other hand, the comprehension of the manifold in the unity — not of thought but of intuition — and consequently the comprehension of the successively apprehended elements in one glance is a regress which annihilates the condition of time in this progress of the imagination and makes *coexistence* intuitable. It is therefore (since the time series is a condition of the internal sense and of an intuition) and subjective movement of the imagination, by which it does violence to the internal sense; this must be the more noticeable, the greater the quantum in which the imagination comprehends in one intuition. The effort, therefore, to receive in one single intuition a measure for magnitude that requires a considerable time to apprehend is a kind of representation which, subjectively considered, is contrary to purpose; but objectively, as requisite for the estimation of magnitude, it is purposive. Thus that very violence which is done to the subject through the imagination is judged as purposive *in reference to the whole determination* of the mind.

The *quality* of the feeling of the sublime is that it is a feeling of pain in reference to the faculty by which we judge aesthetically of an object, which pain, however, is represented at the same time as purposive. This is possible through the fact that the very incapacity in question discovers the consciousness of an unlimited faculty of the same subject, and that the mind can only judge of the latter aesthetically by means of the former.

In the logical estimation of magnitude, the impossibility of ever arriving at absolute totality, by means of the progress of the measurement of things of the sensible world in time and space, was cognized as objective, i.e., as an impossibility of *thinking* the infinite as entirely given, and not as merely subjective or that there was only an incapacity to *grasp* it. For there we have not to do with the degree of comprehension in an intuition regarded as a measure, but everything depends on a concept of number. But in aesthetical estimation of magnitude, the concept of number must disappear or be changed, and the comprehension of the imagination in reference to the unit of measure (thus avoiding the concepts of a law of the successive production of concepts of magnitude) is alone purposive for it. If now a magnitude almost reaches the limit of our faculty of comprehension in an intuition, and yet the imagination is invited by means of numerical magnitudes (in respect of which we are conscious that our faculty is unbounded) to aesthetical comprehension in a

greater unit, then we mentally feel ourselves confined aesthetically within bounds. But nevertheless the pain in regard to the necessary extension of the imagination for accordance with that which is unbounded in our faculty of reason, viz., the idea of the absolute whole, and consequently the very unpurposiveness of the faculty of imagination for rational ideas and the arousing of them, are represented as purposive. Thus it is that the aesthetical judgment itself is subjectively purposive for the reason as the source of ideas, i.e., as the source of an intellectual comprehension for which all aesthetical comprehension is small, and there accompanies the reception of an object as sublime a pleasure, which is only possible through the medium of a pain.

B. OF THE DYNAMICALLY SUBLIME IN NATURE

28. Of Nature Regarded as Might

Might is that which is superior to great hindrances. It is called *dominion* if it is superior to the resistance of that which itself possesses might. Nature, considered in an aesthetical judgment as might that has no dominion over us, is *dynamically sublime*.

If nature is to be judged by us as dynamically sublime, it must be represented as exciting fear (although it is not true conversely that every object which excites fear is regarded in our aesthetical judgment as sublime). For in aesthetical judgments (without the aid of concepts) superiority to hindrances can only be judged according to the greatness of the resistance. Now that which we are driven to resist is an evil and, if we do not find our faculties a match for it, is an object of fear. Hence nature can be regarded by the aesthetical judgment as might, and consequently as dynamically sublime, only so far as it is considered an object of fear.

But we can regard an object as *fearful* without being afraid *of it*, viz., if we judge of it in such a way that we merely *think* a case in which we would wish to resist it and yet in which all resistance would be altogether vain. Thus the virtuous man fears God without being afraid of Him, because to wish to resist Him and His commandments he thinks is a case that *he* need not apprehend. But in every such case that he thinks as not impossible, he cognizes Him as fearful.

He who fears can form no judgment about the sublime in nature, just as he who is seduced by inclination and appetite can form no judgment about the beautiful. The former flies from the sight of an object which inspires him with awe, and it is impossible to find satisfaction in a terror that is seriously felt. Hence the pleasurableness arising from the cessation of an uneasiness is *a state of joy*. But this, on account of the deliverance from danger which is involved, is a state of joy when conjoined with the resolve that we shall no more be exposed to the danger; we cannot willingly look back upon our sensations of danger, much less seek the occasion for them again.

Bold, overhanging, and as it were threatening rocks; clouds piled up in the sky, moving with lightning flashes and thunder peals; volcanoes in all their violence of destruction; hurricanes with their track of devastation; the boundless ocean in a state of tumult; the lofty waterfall of a mighty river, and such like — these exhibit our faculty of resistance as insignificantly small in comparison with their might. But the sight of them is the more attractive, the more fearful it is, provided only that we are in security; and we willingly call these objects sublime, because they raise the energies of the soul above their accustomed height and discover in us a faculty of resistance of a quite different kind, which gives us courage to measure ourselves against the apparent almightiness of nature.

Now, in the immensity of nature and in the insufficiency of our faculties to take in a standard proportionate to the aesthetical estimation of the magnitude of its *realm,* we find our own limitation, although at the same time in our rational faculty we find a different, nonsensuous standard, which has that infinity itself under it as a unity, in comparison with which everything in nature is small, and thus in our mind we find a superiority to nature even in its immensity. And so also the irresistibility of its might, while making us recognize our own physical impotence, considered as beings of nature, discloses to us a faculty of judging independently of and a superiority over nature, on which is based a kind of self-preservation entirely different from that which can be attacked and brought into danger by external nature. Thus humanity in our person remains unhumiliated, though the individual might have to submit to this dominion. In this way nature is not judged to be sublime in our aesthetical judgments insofar as it excites fear, but because it calls up that power in us (which is not nature) of regarding as small the things about which we are solicitous (goods, health, and life), and of regarding its might (to which we are no doubt subjected in respect of these things) as nevertheless without any dominion over us and our personality to which we must bow where our highest fundamental propositions, and their assertion or abandonment, are concerned. Therefore nature is here called sublime merely because it elevates the imagination to a presentation of those cases in which the mind can make felt the proper sublimity of its destination, in comparison with nature itself.

This estimation of ourselves loses nothing through the fact that we might regard ourselves as safe in order to feel this inspiriting satisfaction and that hence, as there is no seriousness in the danger, there might be also (as might seem to be the case) just as little seriousness in the sublimity of our spiritual faculty. For the satisfaction here concerns only the *destination* of our faculty which discloses itself in such a case, so far as the tendency to this destination lies in our nature, while its development and exercise remain incumbent and obligatory. And in this there is truth and reality, however conscious the man may be of his present actual powerfulness, when he turns his reflection to it.

No doubt this principle seems to be too farfetched and too subtly reasoned, and consequently seems to go beyond the scope of an aesthetical judgment; but observation of men proves the opposite and shows that it may lie at the root of the most ordinary judgments, although we are not always conscious of it. For what is that which is, even to the savage, an object of the greatest admiration? It is a man who shrinks from nothing, who fears nothing, and therefore does not yield to danger, but rather goes to face it vigorously with the most complete deliberation. Even in the most highly civilized state this peculiar veneration for the soldier remains, though only under the condition that he exhibit all the virtues of peace, gentleness, compassion, and even a becoming care for his own person; because even by these it is recognized that his mind is unsubdued by danger. Hence whatever disputes there may be about the superiority of the respect which is to be accorded them, in the comparison of a statesman and a general, the aesthetical judgment decides for the latter. War itself, if it is carried on with order and with a sacred respect for the rights of citizens, has something sublime in it, and makes the disposition of the people who carry it on thus only the more sublime, the more numerous are the dangers to which they are exposed and in respect of which they behave with courage. On the other hand, a long peace generally brings about a predominant commercial spirit and, along with it, low selfishness, cowardice, and effeminacy, and debases the disposition of the people.

It appears to conflict with this solution of the concept of sublime, so far as sublimity is ascribed to might, that we are accustomed to represent God as presenting Himself in His wrath and yet in His sublimity, in the tempest, the storm, the earthquake, etc.; and that it would be foolish and criminal to imagine a superiority of our minds over these works of His and, as it seems, even over the designs of such might. Hence it would appear that no feeling of the sublimity of our own nature, but rather subjection, abasement, and a feeling of complete powerlessness, is a fitting state of mind in the presence of such an object; and this is generally bound up with the idea of it during natural phenomena of this kind. In religion in general, prostration, adoration with bent head, with contrite, anxious demeanor and voice, seems to be the only fitting behavior in presence of the Godhead, and hence most peoples have adopted and still observe it. But this state of mind is far from being necessarily bound up with the idea of the *sublimity* of a religion and its object. The man who is actually afraid, because he finds reasons for fear in himself, while conscious by his culpable disposition of offending against a might whose will is irresistible and at the same time just, is not in the frame of mind for admiring the divine greatness. For this a mood of calm contemplation and a quiet free judgment are needed. Only if he is conscious of an upright disposition pleasing to God do those operations of might serve to awaken in him the idea of the sublimity of this Being, for then he recognizes in himself a sublimity of disposition conformable to His will; and thus he is raised above the fear of such operations of nature, which he no longer regards as outbursts of His wrath. Even humility, in the shape of a stern judgment upon his own faults — which otherwise, with a consciousness of good intentions, could be easily palliated from the frailty of human nature — is a sublime state of mind, consisting in a voluntary subjection of himself to the pain of remorse, in order that the causes of this may be gradually removed. In this way religion is essentially distinguished from superstition. The latter establishes in the mind, not reverence for the sublime, but fear and apprehension of the all-powerful Being to whose will the terrified man sees himself subject, without according Him any high esteem. From this nothing can arise but a seeking of favor and flattery, instead of a religion which consists in a good life.[9]

Sublimity, therefore, does not reside in any-thing of nature, but only in our mind, in so far as we can become conscious that we are superior to nature within, and therefore also to nature without us (so far as it influences us). Everything that excites this feeling in us, e.g., the *might of* nature which calls forth our forces, is called then (although improperly) sublime. Only by suppos-ing this idea in ourselves and in reference to it are we capable of attaining to the idea of the sublim-ity of that Being which produces respect in us, not merely by the might that it displays in nature, but rather by the faculty which resides in us of judging it fearlessly and of regarding our destination as sublime in respect of it. . . .

[9]In the *Philosophical Theory of Religion*, Pt. I (Abbott's trans., p. 360), Kant, as here, divides "all religions into two classes — *favor-seeking* religion (mere worship) and *moral* religion, that is, the religion *of a good life*'; and he concludes that "amongst all the public religions that have ever existed the Christian alone is moral.'." [Tr.]

49. Of the Faculties of the Mind That Constitute Genius

We say of certain products of which we expect that they should at least in part appear as beautiful art, they are without *spirit*,[10] although we find nothing to blame in them on the score of taste. A poem may be very neat and elegant, but without spirit. A history may be exact and well arranged, but without spirit. A festal discourse may be solid and at the same time elaborate, but without spirit. Conversation is often not devoid of entertainment, but it is without spirit; even of a woman we say that she is pretty, an agreeable talker, and courteous, but without spirit. What then do we mean by spirit?

Spirit, in an aesthetical sense, is the name given to the animating principle of the mind. But that by means of which this principle animates the soul, the material which it applies to that purpose, is what puts the mental powers purposively into swing, i.e., into such a play as maintains itself and strengthens the mental powers in their exercise.

Now I maintain that this principle is no other than the faculty of presenting *aesthetical ideas.* And by an aesthetical idea I understand that representation of the imagination which occasions much thought, without however any definite thought, i.e., any *concept,* being capable of being adequate to it; it consequently cannot be completely compassed and made intelligible by language. We easily see that it is the counterpart (pendant) of a *rational idea,* which conversely is a concept to which no *intuition* (or representation of the imagination) can be adequate.

The imagination (as a productive faculty of cognition) is very powerful in creating another nature, as it were, out of the material that actual nature gives it. We entertain ourselves with it when experience becomes too commonplace, and by it we remold experience, always indeed in accordance with analogical laws, but yet also in accordance with principles which occupy a higher place in reason (laws, too, which are just as natural to us as those by which understanding

comprehends empirical nature). Thus we feel our freedom from the law of association (which attaches to the empirical employment of imagination), so that the material supplied to us by nature in accordance with this law can be worked up into something different which surpasses nature.

Such representations of the imagination we may call *ideas,* partly because they at least strive after something which lies beyond the bounds of experience and so seek to approximate to a presentation of concepts of reason (intellectual ideas), thus giving to the latter the appearance of objective reality, but especially because no concept can be fully adequate to them as internal intuitions. The poet ventures to realize to sense,[11] rational ideas of invisible beings, the kingdom of the blessed, hell, eternity, creation, etc.; or even if he deals with things of which there are examples in experience — e.g., death, envy and all vices, also love, fame, and the like — he tries, by means of imagination, which emulates the play of reason in its quests after a maximum, to go beyond the limits of experience and to present them to sense with a completeness of which there is no example in nature. This is properly speaking the art of the poet, in which the faculty of aesthetical ideas can manifest itself in its entire strength. But this faculty, considered in itself, is properly only a talent (of the imagination).

If now we place under a concept a representation of the imagination belonging to its presentation, but which occasions in itself more thought than can ever be comprehended in a definite concept and which consequently aesthetically enlarges the concept itself in an unbounded fashion, the imagination is here creative, and it brings the faculty of intellectual ideas (the reason) into movement; i.e., by a representation more thought (which indeed belongs to the concept of the object) is occasioned than can in it be grasped or made clear.

Those forms which do not constitute the presentation of a given concept itself but only, as approximate representations of the imagination, express the consequences bound up with it and its relationship to other concepts, are called (aesthetical) *attributes* of an object whose concept

---

[10]In English we would rather say "without soul," but I prefer to translate "*Geist*" consistently by "spirit," to avoid the confusion of it with "*Seele.*" [Tr.]

[11]Ventures to make real for the senses.

as a rational idea cannot be adequately presented. Thus Jupiter's eagle with the lightning in its claws is an attribute of the mighty king of heaven, as the peacock is of his magnificent queen. They do not, like *logical attributes*, represent what lies in our concepts of the sublimity and majesty of creation, but something different, which gives occasion to the imagination to spread itself over a number of kindred representations that arouse more thought than can be expressed in a concept determined by words. They furnish an *aesthetical idea*, which for that rational idea takes the place of logical presentation; and thus, as their proper office, they enliven the mind by opening out to it the prospect into an illimitable field of kindred representations. But beautiful art does this not only in the case of painting or sculpture (in which the term "attribute" is commonly employed); poetry and rhetoric also get the spirit that animates their works simply from the aesthetical attributes of the object, which accompany the logical and stimulate the imagination, so that it thinks more by their aid, although in an undeveloped way, than could be comprehended in a concept and therefore in a definite form of words. For the sake of brevity, I must limit myself to a few examples only.

When the great king in one of his poems expresses himself as follows:

Oui, finissons sans trouble et mourons sans regrets,
En laissant l'univers comblé de nos bienfaits.
Ainsi l'astre du jour au bout de sa carrière,
Répand sur l'horizon une douce lumière;
Et les derniers rayons qu'il darde dans les airs,
Sont les derniers soupirs qu'il donne à l'univers;[12]

he quickens his rational idea of a cosmopolitan disposition at the end of life by an attribute which the imagination (in remembering all the pleasures

of a beautiful summer day that are recalled at its close by a serene evening) associates with that representation, and which excites a number of sensations and secondary representations for which no expression is found. On the other hand, an intellectual concept may serve conversely as an attribute for a representation of sense, and so can quicken this latter by means of the idea of the supersensible, but only by the aesthetical element, that subjectively attaches to the concept of the latter, being here employed. Thus, for example, a certain poet says, in his description of a beautiful morning:

The sun arose
As calm from virtue springs.

The consciousness of virtue, if we substitute it in our thoughts for a virtuous man, diffuses in the mind a multitude of sublime and restful feelings, and a boundless prospect of a joyful future, to which no expression that is measured by a definite concept completely attains.[13]

In a word, the aesthetical idea is a representation of the imagination associated with a given concept, which is bound up with such a multiplicity of partial representations in its free employment that for it no expression marking a definite concept can be found; and such a representation, therefore, adds to a concept much ineffable thought, the feeling of which quickens the cognitive faculties, and with language, which is the mere letter, binds up spirit also.

The mental powers, therefore, whose union (in a certain relation) constitutes genius are imagination and understanding. In the employment of the imagination for cognition, it submits to the constraint of the understanding and is subject to the

---

12."Yes, let us end without sadness and let us die without regrets, in leaving the world filled with our good deeds. So the day-star, at the end of its course, sheds a gentle light on the horizon; and the last rays that it darts into the air are the last sighs which it gives to the world." [Ed.] Barni quotes these lines as occurring in one of Frederick the Great's French poems: "Épître au maréchal Keith, sur les vaines terreurs de la mort et les frayeurs d'une autre vie" [Letter to Marshal Keith on the Pointless Terror of Death and Fears of Another Life]; but I have not been able to verify his reference. Kant here translates them into German. [Tr.]

13.Perhaps nothing more sublime was ever said and no sublimer thought ever expressed than the famous inscription on the Temple of Isis (Mother Nature): 'I am all that is and that was and that shall be, and no mortal hath lifted my veil.' Segner availed himself of this idea in a *suggestive* vignette prefixed to his *Natural Philosophy*, in order to inspire beforehand the pupil whom he was about to lead into that temple with a holy awe, which should dispose his mind to serious attention. [Kant] J. A. de Segner (1704-1777) was Professor of Natural Philosophy at Göttingen and the author of several scientific works of repute. [Tr.]

limitation of being conformable to the concept of the latter. On the contrary, in an aesthetical point of view it is free to furnish unsought, over and above that agreement with a concept, abundance of undeveloped material for the understanding, to which the understanding paid no regard in its concept but which it applies, though not objectively for cognition, yet subjectively to quicken the cognitive powers and therefore also indirectly to cognitions. Thus genius properly consists in the happy relation between these faculties, which no science can teach and no industry can learn, by which ideas are found for a given concept; and, on the other hand, we thus find for these ideas the expression by means of which the subjective state of mind brought about by them, as an accompaniment of the concept, can be communicated to others. The latter talent is, properly speaking, what is called spirit; for to express the ineffable element in the state of mind implied by a certain representation and to make it universally communicable — whether the expression be in speech or painting or statuary — this requires a faculty of seizing the quickly passing play of imagination and of unifying it in a concept (which is even on that account original and discloses a new rule that could not have been inferred from any preceding principles of examples) that can be communicated without any constraint of rules.

If, after this analysis, we look back to the explanation given above of what is called *genius,* we find: first, that it is a talent for art, not for science, in which clearly known rules must go beforehand and determine the procedure. Secondly, as an artistic talent it presupposes a definite concept of the product as the purpose, and therefore understanding; but it also presupposes a representation (although an indeterminate one) of the material, i.e., of the intuition, for the presentment of this concept, and, therefore a relation between the imagination and the understanding. Thirdly, it shows itself, not so much in the accomplishment of the proposed purpose in a presentment of a definite concept, as in the enunciation or expression of aesthetical ideas which contain abundant material for that very design; and consequently it represents the imagination as free from all guidance of rules and yet as purposive in reference to the presentment of

the given concept. Finally, in the fourth place, the unsought, undesigned subjective purposiveness in the free accordance of the imagination with the legality of the understanding presupposes such a proportion and disposition of these faculties as no following of rules, whether of science or of mechanical imitation, can bring about, but which only the nature of the subject can produce.

In accordance with these suppositions, genius is the examplary originality of the natural gifts of a subject in the *free* employment of his cognitive faculties. In this way the product of a genius (as regards what is to be ascribed to genius and not to possible learning or schooling) is an example, not to be imitated (for then that which in it is genius and constitutes the spirit of the work would be lost), but to be followed by another genius, whom it awakens to a feeling of his own originality and whom it stirs so to exercise his art in freedom from the constraint of rules, that thereby a new rule is gained for art; and thus his talent shows itself to be exemplary. But because a genius is a favorite of nature and must be regarded by us as a rare phenomenon, his example produces for other good heads a school, i.e., a methodical system of teaching according to rules, so far as these can be derived from the peculiarities of the products of his spirit. For such persons beautiful art is so far imitation, to which nature through the medium of a genius supplied the rule.

But this imitation becomes a mere *aping* if the scholar *copies* everything down to the deformities, which the genius must have let pass only because he could not well remove them without weakening his idea. This mental characteristic is meritorious only in the case of a genius. A certain *audacity* in expression — and in general many a departure from common rules — becomes him well, but it is in no way worthy of imitation; it always remains a fault in itself which we must seek to remove, though the genius is, as it were, privileged to commit it, because the inimitable rush of his spirit would suffer from overanxious carefulness. *Mannerism* is another kind of aping, viz., of mere *peculiarity* (originality) in general, by which a man separates himself as far as possible from imitators, without however possessing the talent to be at the same time *exemplary*. There are indeed in general two ways (*modi*) in which such a man may put together his notions of expressing himself; the one is called a *manner* (*modus aestheticus*), the other a *method* (*modus logicus*). They differ in this, that the former has no other standard than the *feeling* of unity in the presentment, but the latter follows definite *principles;* hence the former alone avails for beautiful art. But an artistic product is said to show *mannerism* only when the exposition of the artist's idea is *founded* on its very singularity and is not made appropriate to the idea itself. The ostentatious (*précieux*), contorted, and affected manner adopted to differentiate oneself from ordinary persons (though devoid of spirit) is like the behavior of a man of whom we say that he hears himself talk, or who stands and moves about as if he were on a stage in order to be stared at; this always betrays a bungler.

Mary Wollstonecraft
1759–1797

The most important British feminist writer of the eighteenth century was born in London. Her grandfather, a prosperous silk weaver, had left her father a small fortune, with which he bought a farm in Yorkshire in 1768, setting himself up as gentry. But expensive habits, lack of experience at farming, and addiction to drink turned this venture into a failure. He sold the farm and returned to London in 1774, a pattern he then repeated with another farm in Wales. Wollstonecraft's childhood was embittered as much by the preference given her elder brother — who was formally educated for the law, whereas she and her sisters were left to scrape together learning as they could — as by her family's impoverishment and her father's drunken brutality. Her solace was two close friendships with intelligent women who assisted in her self-development: Jane Arden in Yorkshire and Fanny Blood in London.

For ten years from the age of nineteen, Wollstonecraft took on most of the jobs available to genteel women at that time: She served as companion to a rich tradesman's widow; she managed and taught in schools for young ladies at Islington and Stoke Newington; she was governess to the two daughters of Viscount Kingsborough. All the while she continued to educate herself, participating in conversations with the men of letters with whom her work brought her into contact, and reading the literature and philosophy of the Enlightenment period, particularly that of Jean-Jacques Rousseau, whose work on education both inspired and outraged her. She also became aware of the pitfalls fate digs for women: Her sister Eliza was devastated by post-partum depression and lost custody of her child; her friend Fanny Blood died of childbed fever in the weeks following a premature childbirth.

Back in London, Wollstonecraft began her career as a writer, working primarily for Joseph Johnston, publisher of the liberal *Analytical Review*, and specializing primarily in works on education. *Thoughts on the Education of Daughters* (1787) was her first monograph; over the next two years she published a proto-feminist novel called *Mary*, a highly successful children's book, *Original Stories from Real Life* (1788), a reader for women, and book-length translations from both French and German on moral education. In 1790, the direction of her work changed. The parliamentarian Edmund Burke published *Reflections on the Revolution in France*, in response to a pro-Jacobin sermon by Richard Price, a minister in Wollstonecraft's circle. Wollstonecraft responded swiftly with *A Vindication of the Rights of Men*, meeting Burke's personal attacks on Price with insinuations of her own, and arguing that the French Revolution was not to be judged by the momentary violence of the march on Versailles, but by the National Assembly's passage of the Declaration of Rights of Man and the Citizen.

Wollstonecraft quickly followed this success — which may, as William Godwin thought, have made her for a time "the most famous woman in the world" — with her most important work, *A Vindication of the Rights of Woman* (1792), from which a selection appears below. Wollstonecraft's central argument is that the traditional education of women has been in the art of pleasing men, and the accomplishments that women acquired — music and dancing, painting and penmanship — serve to make them decorative objects fit for a seraglio, but not to make them fit companions for intelligent men who want to converse on the important subjects of the day, like science and philosophy. Men have established their superiority by this arrangement, Wollstonecraft argues, but not their own felicity, since marriages would be happier if the partners were on an equal intellectual footing. And since not all women become wives, cared for by wealthy men, women should be encouraged to study other matters as well, like business, law, and politics, to become more useful citizens, in coeducational public schools supported by government funds. Wollstonecraft's controversial tract sold out two editions in a year and was widely attacked as well as defended (Horace Walpole called her "a hyena in petticoats").

In the years following the two *Vindications*, Wollstonecraft became involved in a series of intense romantic involvements: with the Swiss-German painter Henry Fuseli, whose wife objected to sharing him; with an American officer and adventurer named Gilbert Imlay, whom she met in France during the most violent phase of the French Revolution (and by whom she had a child out of wedlock, named Fanny, after her late friend); and with the philosopher and radical social critic William Godwin. Godwin had argued in his celebrated tract *Political Justice* (1793) that marriage and the family are regressive features of society, which should teach us to love each of our fellow citizens alike, and Wollstonecraft had argued that marriage under English law took away any rights women had to their property and their own persons. She was in fact hard at work on a second feminist novel, *Maria, or The Wrongs of Woman*, which delineates in scarifying detail the failure of English law and social practice to protect married women from violence, fraud, and patriarchal power. But she and Godwin had become lovers, and once Mary became pregnant, they were forced to break with principle and marry (in March 1797) because of the social and legal penalties their child would otherwise have had to bear. On August 30, 1797, Mary delivered a healthy girl, whom they named Mary; the child would one day marry the poet Shelley and achieve fame as the author of *Frankenstein*. But the placenta failed to deliver, puerperal fever set in, and Wollstonecraft died in London on September 10. After her death Godwin published an affectionate memoir of Wollstonecraft's life, and an edition of his late wife's unfinished novel, *Maria*.

Selected Bibliography

Conger, Syndy M. *Mary Wollstonecraft and the Language of Sensibility*. Rutherford, NJ: Fairleigh Dickinson UP, 1996.

Falco, Maria, ed. *Feminist Interpretations of Mary Wollstonecraft*. University Park: Penn State UP, 1996.

Kelly, Gary. *Revolutionary Feminism: The Mind and Career of Mary Wollstonecraft*. New York: St. Martin's, 1992.

Poovey, Mary. *The Proper Lady and the Woman Writer*. Chicago: U Chicago P, 1984.

Taylor, Barbara. *Mary Wollstonecraft and the Feminist Imagination*. New York: Cambridge UP, 2003.

Todd, Janet. *Mary Wollstonecraft: A Revolutionary Life.* New York: Columbia UP, 2000.
———. *Mary Wollstonecraft: An Annotated Bibliography.* New York: Garland, 1976.
Todd, Janet, and Marilyn Butler, eds. *The Works of Mary Wollstonecraft,* 7 vols. London: Pickering, 1989.
Wardle, Ralph, ed. *Collected Letters of Mary Wollstonecraft.* Ithaca: Cornell UP, 1979.

From *A Vindication of the Rights of Woman*

CHAPTER III: THE PREVAILING OPINION OF A SEXUAL CHARACTER DISCUSSED

Women, as well as despots, have now perhaps more power than they would have if the world, divided and subdivided into kingdoms and families, were governed by laws deduced from the exercise of reason; but in obtaining it, to carry on the comparison, their character is degraded, and licentiousness spread through the whole aggregate of society. The many become pedestal to the few. I, therefore, will venture to assert that till women are more rationally educated, the progress of human virtue and improvement in knowledge must receive continual checks. And if it be granted that woman was not created merely to gratify the appetite of man, or to be the upper servant who provides his meals and takes care of his linen, it must follow that the first care of those mothers or fathers who really attend to the education of females should be, if not to strengthen the body, at least not to destroy the constitution by mistaken notions of beauty and female excellence; nor should girls ever be allowed to imbibe the pernicious notion that a defect can, by any chemical process of reasoning, become an excellence. In this respect I am happy to find that the author of one of the most instructive books that our country has produced for children, coincides with me in opinion. I shall quote his pertinent remarks to give the force of his respectable authority to reason.[1, 2]

But should it be proved that woman is naturally weaker than man, whence does it follow that it is

---

[1] A respectable old man gives the following sensible account of the method he pursued when educating his daughter: "I endeavoured to give both to her mind and body a degree of vigour which is seldom found in the female sex. As soon as she was sufficiently advanced in strength to be capable of the lighter labours of husbandry and gardening I employed her as my constant companion. Selene — for that was her name — soon acquired a dexterity in all these rustic employments which I considered with equal pleasure and admiration. If women are in general feeble both in body and mind it arises less from nature than from education. We encourage a vicious indolence and inactivity which we falsely call delicacy. Instead of hardening their minds by the severer principles of reason and philosophy, we breed them to useless arts which terminate in vanity and sensuality. In most of the countries which I had visited they are taught nothing of an higher nature than a few modulations of the voice or useless postures of the body; their time is consumed in sloth or trifles and trifles become the only pursuit capable of interesting them. We seem to forget that it is upon the qualities of the female sex that our own domestic comforts and the education of our children must depend. And what are the comforts or the education which a race of beings corrupted from their infancy and unacquainted with all the duties of life are fitted to bestow? To touch a musical instrument with useless skill, to exhibit their cultural or affected graces to the eyes of indolent and debauched young men, to dissipate their husband's patrimony in riotous and unnecessary expenses: these are the only arts cultivated by women in most of the polished nations I had seen. And the consequences are uniformly such as may be expected to proceed from such polluted sources — private and public servitude. But Selene's education was regulated by different views, and conducted upon severer principles — if that can be called severity which opens the mind to a sense of moral and religious duties, and most effectually arms it against the inevitable evils of life." — Mr. Day's *Sandford and Merton,* vol. iii. [Wollstonecraft]

[2] Thomas Day (1748–1789), a British follower of Rousseau, wrote *Sandford and Merton* (1783) as a didactic novel explicating his theories about education.

natural for her to become still weaker than nature intended her to be? Arguments of this cast are an insult to common sense, and savour of passion. The divine right of husbands, like the divine right of kings, may, it is to be hoped, in this enlightened age, be contested without danger; and though conviction may not silence many boisterous disputants, yet, when any prevailing prejudice is attacked, the wise will consider, and leave the narrow-minded to rail with thoughtless vehemence at innovation. The mother who wishes to give true dignity of character to her daughter must, regardless of the sneers of ignorance, proceed on a plan diametrically opposite to that which Rousseau[3] has recommended with all the deluding charms of eloquence and philosophical sophistry, for his eloquence renders absurdities plausible, and his dogmatic conclusions puzzle, without convincing, those who have not ability to refute them. Throughout the whole animal kingdom every young creature requires almost continual exercise, and the infancy of children, conformable to this intimation, should be passed in harmless gambols that exercise the feet and hands, without requiring very minute direction from the head, or the constant attention of a nurse. In fact, the care necessary for self-preservation is the first natural exercise of the understanding, as little inventions to amuse the present moment unfold the imagination.

But these wise designs of nature are counter-acted by mistaken fondness or blind zeal. The child is not left a moment to its own direction — particularly a girl — and thus rendered dependent. Dependence is called natural. To preserve personal beauty — woman's glory — the limbs and faculties are cramped with worse than Chinese bands,[4] and the sedentary life which they are condemned to live, whilst boys frolic in the open air, weakens the muscles and relaxes the nerves. As for Rousseau's remarks, which have since been echoed by several writers, that they have naturally, that is, from their birth, independent of

education, a fondness for dolls, dressing, and talking, they are so puerile as not to merit a serious refutation. That a girl, condemned to sit for hours together listening to the idle chat of weak nurses, or to attend at her mother's toilet, will endeavour to join the conversation, is, indeed, very natural; and that she will imitate her mother or aunts, and amuse herself by adorning her lifeless doll, as they do in dressing her, poor innocent babe! is undoubtedly a most natural consequence. For men of the greatest abilities have seldom had sufficient strength to rise above the surrounding atmosphere; and if the pages of genius have always been blurred by the prejudices of the age, some allowance should be made for a sex, who, like kings, always see things through a false medium. Pursuing these reflections, the fondness for dress, conspicuous in woman, may be easily accounted for, without supposing it the result of a desire to please the sex on which they are dependent. The absurdity, in short, of supposing that a girl is naturally a coquette, and that a desire connected with the impulse of nature to propagate the species, should appear even before an improper education has, by heating the imagination, called it forth prematurely, is so unphilosophical, that such a sagacious observer as Rousseau would not have adopted it, if he had not been accustomed to make reason give way to his desire of singularity, and truth to a favourite paradox. Yet thus to give a sex to mind was not very consistent with the principles of a man who argued so warmly, and so well, for the immortality of the soul. But what a weak barrier is truth when it stands in the way of an hypothesis! Rousseau respected — almost adored virtue — and yet he allowed himself to love with sensual fondness. His imagination constantly prepared inflammable fuel for his inflammable senses; but, in order to reconcile his respect for self-denial, fortitude, and those heroic virtues, which a mind like his could not coolly admire, he labours to invert the law of nature, and broaches a doctrine pregnant with mischief, and derogatory to the character of supreme wisdom. His ridiculous stories, which tend to prove that girls are naturally attentive to their persons, without laying any stress on daily example, are below contempt. And that a little miss should have such a correct taste as to neglect the pleasing amusement of

[3]Wollstonecraft alludes to the educational theories of the French philosopher Jean-Jacques Rousseau (1712–1778) as expressed in his novel *Emile, or Education* (1762).

[4]Alluding to the practice of binding the feet of aristocratic Chinese wives, which deformed the limbs so that the woman was unable to walk.

making O's, merely because she perceived that it was an ungraceful attitude, should be selected with the anecdotes of the learned pig.[5]

I have, probably, had an opportunity of observing more girls in their infancy than J. J. Rousseau. I can recollect my own feelings, and I have looked steadily around me; yet, so far from coinciding with him in opinion respecting the first dawn of the female character, I will venture to affirm, that a girl, whose spirits have not been damped by inactivity, or innocence tainted by false shame, will always be a romp, and the doll will never excite attention unless confinement allows her no alternative. Girls and boys, in short, would play harmlessly together, if the distinction of sex was not inculcated long before nature makes any difference. I will go further, and affirm, as an indisputable fact, that most of the women, in the circle of my observation, who have acted like rational creatures, or shown any vigour of intellect, have accidentally been allowed to run wild, as some of the elegant formers of the fair sex would insinuate.

The baneful consequences which flow from inattention to health during infancy and youth extend further than is supposed — dependence of body naturally produces dependence of mind; and how can she be a good wife or mother, the greater part of whose time is employed to guard against or endure sickness? Nor can it be expected that a woman will resolutely endeavour to strengthen her constitution and abstain from enervating indulgences, if artificial notions of beauty, and false descriptions of sensibility, have been early entangled with her motives of action. Most men are sometimes obliged to bear with bodily inconveniences, and to endure, occasionally, the inclemency of the elements; but genteel women are, literally speaking, slaves to their bodies, and glory in their subjection.

I once knew a weak woman of fashion, who was more than commonly proud of her delicacy and sensibility. She thought a distinguishing taste and puny appetite the height of all human perfection, and acted accordingly. I have seen this weak sophisticated being neglect all the duties of life, yet recline with self-complacency on a sofa, and boast of her want of appetite as a proof of delicacy that extended to, or, perhaps, arose from, her exquisite sensibility; for it is difficult to render intelligible such ridiculous jargon. Yet, at the moment, I have seen her insult a worthy old gentlewoman, whom unexpected misfortunes had made dependent on her ostentatious bounty, and who, in better days, had claims on her gratitude. Is it possible that a human creature could have become such a weak and depraved being, if, like the Sybarites,[6] dissolved in luxury, everything like virtue had not been worn away, or never impressed by precept, a poor substitute, it is true, for cultivation of mind, though it serves as a fence against vice?

Such a woman is not a more irrational monster than some of the Roman emperors, who were depraved by lawless power. Yet, since kings have been more under the restraint of law, and the curb, however weak, of honour, the records of history are not filled with such unnatural instances of folly and cruelty, nor does the despotism that kills virtue and genius in the bud, hover over Europe with that destructive blast which desolates Turkey, and renders the men, as well as the soil, unfruitful.[7]

Women are everywhere in this deplorable state; for, in order to preserve their innocence, as ignorance is courteously termed, truth is hidden from them, and they are made to assume an artificial character before their faculties have acquired any strength. Taught from their infancy that beauty is woman's sceptre, the mind shapes

---

[5] "I once knew a young person who learned to write before she learned to read, and began to write with her needle before she could use a pen. At first, indeed she took it into her head to make no letter than the O: this letter she was constantly making of all sizes and always the wrong way. Unluckily one day as she was intent on this employment, she happened to see herself in the looking-glass; when, taking a dislike to the constrained attitude in which she sat while writing she threw away her pen like another Pallas and determined against making the O any more. Her brother was also equally averse to writing; it was the confinement however and not the constrained attitude that most disgusted him." — Rousseau's *Emilius*. [Wollstonecraft alludes to a pig, shown in London and Norwich in 1785, who had been trained to spell words and solve arithmetic problems by pointing at cards with its snout.]

[6] The ancient Greek natives of Sybaris were notorious voluptuaries.

[7] The Ottoman Empire, known for the prevalence of despotism and cruelty among its sultans, was in serious decline in the decades before the publication of Wollstonecraft's *Vindication*; under Sultan Abdul Hamid I (who ruled 1774–1789), several of its provinces rebelled against rule from Istanbul, and it lost territory, including the Crimea, to wars with Russia.

itself to the body, and roaming round its gilt cage, only seeks to adore its prison. Men have various employments and pursuits which engage their attention, and give a character to the opening mind; but women, confined to one, and having their thoughts constantly directed to the most insignificant part of themselves, seldom extend their views beyond the triumph of the hour. But were their understanding once emancipated from the slavery to which the pride and sensuality of man and their short-sighted desire, like that of dominion in tyrants, of present sway, has sub-jected them, we should probably read of their weaknesses with surprise. I must be allowed to pursue the argument a little further. Perhaps, if the existence of an evil being were allowed, who, in the allegorical language of Scripture, went about seeking whom he should devour,[8] he could not more effectually degrade the human character, than by giving a man absolute power.

This argument branches into various ramifica-tions. Birth, riches, and every extrinsic advantage that exalt a man above his fellows, without any mental exertion, sink him in reality below them. In proportion to his weakness, he is played upon by designing men, till the bloated monster has lost all traces of humanity. And that tribes of men, like flocks of sheep, should quietly follow such a leader, is a solecism that only a desire of present enjoyment and narrowness of understanding can solve. Educated in slavish dependence, and ener-vated by luxury and sloth, where shall we find men who will stand forth to assert the rights of man, or claim the privilege of moral beings, who should have but one road to excellence? Slavery to monarchs and ministers, which the world will be long in freeing itself from, and whose deadly grasp stops the progress of the human mind, is not yet abolished.

Let not men then in the pride of power, use the same arguments that tyrannic kings and venal ministers have used, and fallaciously assert that woman ought to be subjected because she has always been so. But, when man, governed by rea-sonable laws, enjoys his natural freedom, let him despise woman, if she do not share it with him;

and, till that glorious period arrives, in descant-ing on the folly of the sex, let him not overlook his own.

Women, it is true, obtaining power by unjust means, by practising or fostering vice, evidently lose the rank which reason would assign them, and they become either abject slaves or capri-cious tyrants. They lose all simplicity, all dignity of mind, in acquiring power, and act as men are observed to act when they have been exalted by the same means.

It is time to effect a revolution in female manners — time to restore to them their lost dignity — and make them, as a part of the human species, labour by reforming themselves to reform the world. It is time to separate unchange-able morals from local manners. If men be demi-gods, why let us serve them! And if the dignity of the female soul be as disputable as that of animals — if their reason does not afford suf-ficient light to direct their conduct whilst unerr-ing instinct is denied — they are surely of all creatures the most miserable! and, bent beneath the iron hand of destiny, must submit to be a fair defect in creation. But to justify the ways of Providence respecting them, by pointing out some irrefragable reason for thus making such a large portion of mankind accountable and not accountable, would puzzle the subtlest casuist.

The only solid foundation for morality appears to be the character of the Supreme Being; the harmony of which arises from a balance of attributes, — and, to speak with reverence, one attribute seems to imply the necessity of another. He must be just, because He is wise; He must be good, because He is omnipotent. For to exalt one attribute at the expense of another equally noble and necessary, bears the stamp of the warped reason of man — the homage of passion. Man, accustomed to bow down to power in his savage state, can seldom divest himself of this barbarous prejudice, even when civilisation determines how much superior mental is to bodily strength; and his reason is clouded by these crude opinions, even when he thinks of the Deity. His omnipotence is made to swallow up, or preside over His other attributes, and those morals are supposed to limit His power irreverently, who think that it must be regulated by His wisdom. I disclaim that specious

[8] Wollstonecraft is alluding to 1 Peter 5:8.

humility which, after investigating nature, stops at the Author. The High and Lofty one, who inhabiteth eternity, doubtless possesses many attributes of which we can form no conception; but Reason tells me that they cannot clash with those I adore — and I am compelled to listen to her voice. It seems natural for man to search for excellence, and either to trace it in the object that he worships, or blindly to invest it with perfection, as a garment. But what good effect can the latter mode of worship have on the moral conduct of a rational being? He bends to power; he adores a dark cloud, which may open a bright prospect to him, to burst in angry, lawless fury, on his devoted head — he knows not why. And, supposing that the Deity acts from the vague impulse of an undirected will, man must also follow his own, or act according to rules, deduced from principles which he disclaims as irreverent. Into this dilemma have both enthusiasts and cooler thinkers fallen, when they laboured to free men from the wholesome restraints which a just conception of the character of God imposes.

It is not impious thus to scan the attributes of the Almighty: in fact, who can avoid it that exercises his faculties? For to love God as the fountain of wisdom, goodness, and power, appears to be the only worship useful to a being who wishes to acquire either virtue or knowledge. A blind unsettled affection may, like human passions, occupy the mind and warm the heart, whilst, to do justice, love mercy, and walk humbly with our God, is forgotten. I shall pursue this subject still further, when I consider religion in a light opposite to that recommended by Dr. Gregory,[9] who treats it as a matter of sentiment or taste.

To return from this apparent digression. It were to be wished that women would cherish an affection for their husbands, founded on the same principle that devotion ought to rest upon. No other firm base is there under heaven — for let them beware of the fallacious light of sentiment; too often used as a softer phrase for sensuality. It follows then, I think, that from their infancy women should either be shut up like Eastern princes, or educated in such a manner as to be able to think

and act for themselves. Why do men halt between two opinions, and expect impossibilities? Why do they expect virtue from a slave, from a being whom the constitution of civil society has rendered weak, if not vicious? Still I know that it will require a considerable length of time to eradicate the firmly rooted prejudices which sensualists have planted; it will also require some time to convince women that they act contrary to their real interest on an enlarged scale, when they cherish or affect weakness under the name of delicacy, and to convince the world that the poisoned source of female vices and follies, if it be necessary, in compliance with custom, to use synonymous terms in a lax sense, has been the sensual homage paid to beauty: — to beauty of features; for it has been shrewdly observed by a German writer[10] that a pretty woman, as an object of desire, is generally allowed to be so by men of all descriptions; whilst a fine woman, who inspires more sublime emotions by displaying intellectual beauty, may be overlooked or observed with indifference, by those men who find their happiness in their gratification of their appetites. I foresee an obvious retort — whilst man remains such an imperfect being as he appears hitherto to have been, he will, more or less, be the slave of his appetites; and those women obtaining most power who gratify a predominant one, the sex is degraded by a physical, if not by a moral necessity.

This objection has, I grant, some force; but while such a sublime precept exists, as, "Be pure as your heavenly Father is pure";[11] it would seem that the virtues of man are not limited by the Being who alone could limit them; and that he may press forward without considering whether he steps out of his sphere by indulging such a noble ambition. To the wild billows it has been said, "Thus far shalt thou go, and no farther; and here shall thy proud waves be stayed."[12] Vainly then do they beat and foam, restrained by the power that confines the struggling planets in their orbits, matter yields to the great governing Spirit. But an immortal soul, not restrained by mechanical laws and struggling to free itself from the shackles

---

[9]Dr. John Gregory (1724–1773) was the author of the widely read conduct book, *A Father's Legacy to His Daughters* (1774).

[10]Immanuel Kant's *Observations on the Feelings of the Beautiful and the Sublime* (1764).

[11]1 John 3:3.

[12]Job 38:11.

of matter, contributes to, instead of disturbing, the order of creation, when, co-operating with the Father of spirits, it tries to govern itself by the invariable rule that, in a degree, before which our imagination faints, regulates the universe.

Besides, if women be educated for dependence, that is, to act according to the will of another fallible being, and submit, right or wrong, to power, where are we to stop? Are they to be considered as viceregents allowed to reign over a small domain, and answerable for their conduct to a higher tribunal, liable to error? It will not be difficult to prove that such delegates will act like men subjected by fear, and make their children and servants endure their tyrannical oppression. As they submit without reason, they will, having no fixed rules to square their conduct by, be kind, or cruel, just as the whim of the moment directs; and we ought not to wonder if sometimes, galled by their heavy yoke, they take a malignant pleasure in resting it on weaker shoulders.

But, supposing a woman, trained up to obedience, be married to a sensible man, who directs her judgment without making her feel the servility of her subjection, to act with as much propriety by this reflected light as can be expected when reason is taken at secondhand, yet she cannot ensure the life of her protector; he may die and leave her with a large family. A double duty devolves on her; to educate them in the character of both father and mother; to form their principles and secure their property. But, alas! she has never thought, much less acted for herself. She has only learned to please[13] men, to depend gracefully on them; yet, encumbered with children, how is she to obtain another protector — a husband to supply the place of reason? A rational man, for we are not treading on romantic ground, though he may think her a pleasing docile creature, will not choose to marry a family for love, when the world contains many more pretty creatures. What is then to become of her? She either falls an easy prey to some mean fortune-hunter, who defrauds her children of their paternal inheritance, and renders her miserable; or becomes the victim of discontent and blind indulgence. Unable to educate her sons, or impress them with respect; — for it is not a play on words to assert, that people are never respected, though filling an important station, who are not respectable. — she pines under the anguish of unavailing impotent regret. The serpent's tooth enters into her very soul, and the vices of licentious youth bring her with sorrow, if not with poverty also, to the grave.

This is not an overcharged picture; on the contrary, it is a very possible case, and something similar must have fallen under every attentive eye. I have, however, taken it for granted, that she was well disposed, though experience shows, that the blind may as easily be led into a ditch as along the beaten road. But supposing, no very improbable conjecture, that a being only taught to please must still find her happiness in pleasing; — what an example of folly, not to say vice, will she be to her innocent daughters! The mother will be lost in the coquette, and, instead of making friends of her daughters, view them with eyes askance, for they are rivals — rivals more cruel than any other, because they invite a comparison, and drive her from the throne of beauty, who has never thought of a seat on the bench of reason.

It does not require a lively pencil, or the discriminating outline of a caricature, to sketch the

13,"In the union of the sexes, both pursue one common object, but not in the same manner. From their diversity in this particular, arises the first determinate difference between the moral relations of each. The one should be active and strong, the other passive and weak; it is necessary the one should have both the power and the will and that the other should make little resistance. This principle being established it follows that woman is expressly formed to please the man: if the obligation be reciprocal also and the man ought to please in his turn it is not so immediately necessary; his great merit is in his power, and he pleases merely because he is strong. This I must confess is not one of the refined maxims of love: it is however one of the laws of nature prior to love itself. If woman be formed to please and be subjected to man, it is her place, doubtless, to render herself agreeable to him instead of challenging his passion. The violence of his desires depends on her charms; it is by means of these she should urge him to the exertion of those powers which nature hath given him. The most successful method of exciting them, is, to render such exertion necessary by resistance; as in that case self-love is added to desire and the one triumphs in the victory which the other is obliged to acquire. Hence arise the various modes of attack and defence between the sexes; the boldness of one sex and the timidity of the other; — and in a word that bashfulness and modesty with which nature hath armed the weak in order to subdue the strong." — Rousseau's *Emilius.* I shall make no other comment on this ingenious passage than just to observe that it is the philosophy of lasciviousness. [Wollstonecraft]

domestic miseries and petty vices which such a mistress of a family diffuses. Still she only acts as a woman ought to act, brought up according to Rousseau's system. She can never be reproached for being masculine, or turning out of her sphere; nay, she may observe another of his grand rules, and, cautiously preserving her reputation free from spot, be reckoned a good kind of woman. Yet in what respect can she be termed good? She abstains, it is true, without any great struggle, from committing gross crimes; but how does she fulfil her duties? Duties! in truth she has enough to think of to adorn her body and nurse a weak constitution.

With respect to religion, she never presumed to judge for herself; but conformed, as a dependent creature should, to the effects of a good education! These the virtues of man's helpmate![14]

I must relieve myself by drawing a different picture. Let fancy now present a woman with a tolerable understanding, for I do not wish to leave the line of mediocrity, whose constitution, strengthened by exercise, has allowed her body to acquire its full vigour; her mind, at the same time, gradually expanding itself to comprehend the moral duties of life, and in what human virtue and dignity consist. Formed thus by the discharge of the relative duties of her station, she marries from affection, without losing sight of prudence, and looking beyond matrimonial felicity, she secures her husband's respect before it is necessary to exert mean arts to please him and feed a dying flame, which nature doomed to expire when the object became familiar, when friendship and forbearance take place of a more ardent affection. This is the natural death of love, and domestic peace is not destroyed by struggles to prevent its extinction. I also suppose the husband to be virtuous; or she is still more in want of independent principles. Fate, however, breaks this tie. She is left a widow,

perhaps without a sufficient provision; but she is not desolate! The pang of nature is felt; but after time has softened sorrow into melancholy resignation, her heart turns to her children with redoubled fondness, and anxious to provide for them, affection gives a sacred heroic cast to her maternal duties. She thinks that not only the eye sees her virtuous efforts from whom all her comfort now must flow, and whose approbation is life; but her imagination, a little abstracted and exalted by grief, dwells on the fond hope that the eyes which her trembling hand closed, may still see how she subdues every wayward passion to fulfil the double duty of being the father as well as the mother of her children. Raised to heroism by misfortunes, she represses the first faint dawning of a natural inclination, before it ripens into love, and in the bloom of life forgets her sex — forgets the pleasure of an awakening passion, which might again have been inspired and returned. She no longer thinks of pleasing, and conscious dignity prevents her from priding herself on account of the praise which her conduct demands. Her children have her love, and her brightest hopes are beyond the grave, where her imagination often strays. I think I see her surrounded by her children, reaping the reward of her care. The intelligent eye meets hers, whilst health and innocence smile on their chubby cheeks, and as they grow up the cares of life are lessened by their grateful attention. She lives to see the virtues which she endeavoured to plant on principles, fixed into habits, to see her children attain a strength of character sufficient to enable them to endure adversity without forgetting their mother's example. The task of life thus fulfilled, she calmly waits for the sleep of death, and rising from the grave, may say — "Behold, Thou gavest me a talent, and here are five talents."[15]

I wish to sum up what I have said in a few words, for I here throw down my gauntlet, and deny the existence of sexual virtues, not excepting modesty. For man and woman, truth, if I understand the meaning of the word, must be the same; yet the fanciful female character, so prettily drawn by poets and novelists, demanding the sacrifice of truth and sincerity, virtue becomes

[14]"O how lovely, exclaims Rousseau, speaking of Sophia, is her ignorance! Happy is he who is destined to instruct her! She will never pretend to be the tutor of her husband but will be content to be his pupil. Far from attempting to subject him to her taste she will accommodate her self to his. She will be more estimable to him than if she was learned he will have a pleasure in instructing her." — Rousseau's *Emilius*. I shall content myself with simply asking how friendship can subsist when love expires between the master and his pupil. [Wollstonecraft]

[15]Wollstonecraft alludes to the parable of the talents, Matthew 25: 14–30.

a relative idea, having no other foundation than utility, and of that utility men pretend arbitrarily to judge, shaping it to their own convenience. Women, I allow, may have different duties to fulfil; but they are *human* duties, and the principles that should regulate the discharge of them, I sturdily maintain, must be the same. To become respectable, the exercise of their understanding is necessary, there is no other foundation for independence of character; I mean explicitly to say that they must only bow to authority of reason, instead of being the *modest* slaves of opinion. In the superior ranks of life how seldom do we meet with a man of superior abilities, or even common acquirements? The reason appears to me clear, the state they are born in was an unnatural one. The human character has ever been formed by the employments the individual, or class, pursues; and if the faculties are not

sharpened by necessity, they must remain obtuse. The argument may fairly be extended to women; for, seldom occupied by serious business, the pursuit of pleasure gives that insignificancy to their character which renders the society of the *great* so insipid. The same want of firmness, produced by a similar cause, forces them both to fly from themselves to noisy pleasures, and artificial passions, till vanity takes place of every social affection, and the characteristics of humanity can scarcely be discerned. Such are the blessings of civil governments, as they are at present organised, that wealth and female softness equally tend to debase mankind, and are produced by the same cause; but allowing women to be rational creatures, they should be incited to acquire virtues which they may call their own, for how can a rational being be ennobled by anything that is not obtained by its *own* exertions?

William Wordsworth

1770–1850

William Wordsworth was born in Cockermouth, Cumberlandshire, the son of an attorney who was steward to a noble lord, and raised in the Lake District in northwest England among hills and lakes and their rustic inhabitants and sojourners, whom he would celebrate in his poetry. Though orphaned at thirteen, Wordsworth managed to attend St. John's College, Cambridge. Taking his degree in 1791, Wordsworth spent a year on the Continent absorbing the sights and the spirit of the French Revolution in its most idealistic phase. On his return to England, Wordsworth wrote *Descriptive Sketches* and met an admirer of that volume, Samuel Taylor Coleridge, who was to be a major poetical and intellectual influence. Together, Wordsworth and Coleridge (mostly Wordsworth) wrote *Lyrical Ballads* (1798), the premier volume of English Romanticism. Although the critics were harsh ("This will never do," Francis Jeffrey began in his notorious attack), the public was not, and a second edition was published in 1800, to which Wordsworth contributed a preface, his single major piece of literary criticism, reprinted here.[1]

Most of Wordsworth's best poetry was written in a single decade, 1797–1807; during this period he wrote not only *Lyrical Ballads* but *Poems in Two Volumes* (1807), including the "Intimations of Immortality" Ode, and *The Prelude* (1805, published 1850). By his forties, when he published *The Excursion* (1814), he was in decline, though he continued to write long into his eighth decade. In old age he had become an institution, and Queen Victoria appointed him poet laureate in 1843.

The Preface to *Lyrical Ballads* is a transitional work between the rhetorical/mimetic literary theory of the eighteenth century and the expressive theories of the nineteenth. As an argument it is at odds with itself. Part of the confusion derives from Wordsworth's revisions: Most of the original 1800 version of the Preface adheres to a mode of thought (though not, of course, a thesis) that Samuel Johnson would readily have understood, whereas the 1802 version and subsequent editions ally the essay with later expressive theories of literature.

The occasion of the Preface was Wordsworth's desire to defend two of the revolutionary aspects of *Lyrical Ballads*: their use of a plain style and their rustic subject matter. He does so by attacking the poetic diction of the latter eighteenth century as artificial and meaningless. His memorable analysis of Thomas Gray's "Sonnet on the Death of Mr. Richard West" demonstrates how little of that brief poem actually functions in making its elegiac impression.[2]

When he discusses the subject and style of *Lyrical Ballads*, however, Wordsworth calls on the values the eighteenth century already revered. Why did he choose to write about "low and rustic life"? Because there "the essential passions of the heart

---

[1]Reprinted here is the 1802 version of the Preface to *Lyrical Ballads*, which includes the "What is a poet?" section, among other revisions.

[2]Not everyone has agreed with Wordsworth: Later readers of Gray's sonnet, including the poet Gerard Manley Hopkins, have argued that the contrast between the flowery poetic diction (lines 1–4 and 9–12) and the plain earnest speech (lines 6–8 and 13–14) was intended by Gray as part of the elegiac effect. And recent gender criticism, taking off from the passionate attachment of Gray to Richard West, have seen the patently artificial language of the sonnet as a way of testifying to a grief whose erotic intensity cannot be fully acknowledged.

find a better soil in which they can attain their maturity, are under less restraint," and because "the manners of rural life . . . are most easily comprehended; and are more durable." This recalls Johnson's dictum that the poet who wishes to become a classic should choose to imitate "general nature" rather than topical but evanescent manners. Why did Wordsworth choose to write in the plain style, and what is the role of the reader?' "I have proposed to myself to imitate, and, as far as is possible, to adopt the very language of men. . . . to keep my reader in the company of flesh and blood, persuaded that by so doing I shall interest him." At the same time, he hopes to "enlighten the understanding" of the reader and "strengthen and purify" his affections. It sounds as if Wordsworth, however revolutionary his style and subject matter, was defending his poetic practice in the most traditional terms as an attempt to "please many and please long" by providing "just representations of general nature."

Wordsworth thus far seems to be claiming that in *Lyrical Ballads* he was imitating the manners, passions, and actions of rustic Englishmen for the delight and instruction of his audience, but the sections added in 1802 suggest a very different approach to poetry: That poetry is created less by representing what is in the outside world than by attending to the voice within. These passages focus on the poet and the genesis of poetry. But once he had defined poetry as "the spontaneous overflow of powerful feelings," it becomes necessary to explain how the feelings of his preferred humble rustics, such as Goody Blake and Harry Gill, can overflow from a university-educated son of a country lawyer. Wordsworth's solution is to posit for the poet a special internal makeup. The poet is "endued with more lively sensibility, more enthusiasm and tenderness . . . a greater knowledge of human nature, and a more comprehensive soul, than are supposed to be common among mankind." Most important, the poet can express "those thoughts and feelings which," voluntarily or not, "arise in him without immediate external excitement." At times the poet can "let himself slip into an entire delusion, and even confound and identify his own feelings with" those of the people he describes. The poet is thus able to internalize something he has seen and experienced and call it up in himself as though he were participating in it.

As he discusses the process of poetic imagination and composition, Wordsworth erodes the mimetic/rhetorical framework with which he has begun by claiming that the feeling will not be precisely the same when it is imaginatively "recollected in tranquillity" as in immediate experience: It will be purified, on the one hand, but it will "fall short" of reality on the other. The validity of the feeling the poet conveys therefore is not measurable by its accuracy, as a mimetic theory would suggest; it must be measured by a subjective, internal measure: The poet's "faith that no words, which *his* fancy or imagination can suggest, will be to be compared with those which are the emanations of reality and truth."

Wordsworth's theories of poetic diction would be criticized by his friend Coleridge (in *Biographia Literaria,* Ch. 17), his theory of poetic process and imagination refined and replaced by more sophisticated versions, and his vision of the high status and purposes of poetry superseded by the celestial ascending rhetoric of Shelley. But in the Preface to *Lyrical Ballads,* Wordsworth created the first and one of the most lasting apologies for the Romantic Movement in poetry and for the expressive theory of literature that underpinned its other beliefs.

Selected Bibliography

Barstow, Marjorie Latta. *Wordsworth's Theory of Poetic Diction*. New Haven: Yale University Press, 1917.

Berman, Douglas Scott. "The 'Other' Wordsworth: Philosophy, Art, and the Pursuit of the 'Real' in the Preface to *Lyrical Ballads*." *Concentric: Literary and Cultural Studies* 27, no. 1 (2001): 111–28.

Clancey, Richard W. *Wordsworth's Classical Undersong: Education, Rhetoric and Poetic Truth*. New York: St. Martin's Press, 2000.

Hirsch, E. D. *Wordsworth and Schelling*. New Haven: Yale University Press, 1960.

Jackson, Wallace. *The Probable and the Marvelous: Blake, Wordsworth and the Eighteenth-Century Critical Tradition*. Athens: University of Georgia Press, 1978.

Jones, Henry John Franklin. *The Egotistical Sublime: A History of Wordsworth's Imagination*. London: Chatto and Windus, 1960.

Knapp, Steven. *Personification and the Sublime: Milton to Coleridge*. Cambridge: Harvard University Press, 1985.

Peacock, M. L., Jr. *Critical Opinions of William Wordsworth*. Baltimore: Johns Hopkins University Press, 1950.

Smith, Nowell C., ed. *Wordsworth's Literary Criticism*. Bristol, Eng.: Bristol Classical Press, 1980.

Thorpe, C. D. "The Imagination: Coleridge versus Wordsworth." *Philological Quarterly* 18 (1939): 1–18.

Wlecke, Albert O. *Wordsworth and the Sublime*. Berkeley: University of California Press, 1973.

Preface to *Lyrical Ballads*

The first volume of these poems has already been submitted to general perusal. It was published, as an experiment, which, I hoped, might be of some use to ascertain, how far, by fitting to metrical arrangement a selection of the real language of men in a state of vivid sensation, that sort of pleasure and that quantity of pleasure may be imparted, which a poet may rationally endeavour to impart.

I had formed no very inaccurate estimate of the probable effect of those poems: I flattered myself that they who should be pleased with them would read them with more than common pleasure: and, on the other hand, I was well aware, that by those who should dislike them they would be read with more than common dislike. The result has differed from my expectation in this only, that I have pleased a greater number, than I ventured to hope I should please.

For the sake of variety, and from a consciousness of my own weakness, I was induced to request the assistance of a friend, who furnished me with the poems of the *Ancient Mariner*, the "Foster-Mother's Tale," the *Nightingale*, and the poem entitled *Love*. I should not, however, have requested this assistance, had I not believed that the poems of my friend would in a great measure have the same tendency as my own, and that, though there would be found a difference, there would be found no discordance in the colours of our style; as our opinions on the subject of poetry do almost entirely coincide.

Several of my friends are anxious for the success of these poems from a belief, that, if the views with which they were composed were indeed realized, a class of poetry would be produced, well adapted to interest mankind permanently, and not unimportant in the multiplicity, and in the quality of its moral relations: and on this account they have advised me to prefix a systematic defence of the theory, upon which the poems were written. But I was unwilling to undertake the task, because I knew that on this occasion the reader would look coldly upon my arguments, since I might be suspected of having been principally influenced by the selfish and foolish hope of *reasoning* him into an approbation of these particular poems: and I was still more unwilling to undertake the task, because, adequately to display my opinions, and fully to enforce my arguments, would require a space wholly disproportionate to the nature of a preface. For to treat the subject with the clearness and coherence, of which I believe it susceptible, it would be necessary to give a full account of the present state of the public taste in this country, and to determine how far this taste is healthy or depraved; which, again, could not be determined, without pointing out, in what manner language and the human mind act and react on each other, and without retracing the revolutions, not of literature alone, but likewise of society itself. I have therefore altogether declined to enter regularly upon this defence; yet I am sensible, that there would be some impropriety in abruptly obtruding upon the public, without a few words of introduction, poems so materially different from those, upon which general approbation is at present bestowed.

It is supposed, that by the act of writing in verse an author makes a formal engagement that he will gratify certain known habits of association; that he not only thus apprizes the reader that certain classes of ideas and expressions will be found in his book, but that others will be carefully excluded. This exponent or symbol held forth by metrical language must in different eras of literature have excited very different expectations: for example, in the age of Catullus, Terence, and Lucretius and that of Statius or Claudian; and in our own country, in the age of Shakespeare and Beaumont and Fletcher, and that of Donne and Cowley, or Dryden, or Pope. I will not take upon me to determine the exact import of the promise which by the act of writing in verse an author, in the present day, makes to his reader; but I am certain, it will appear to many persons that I have not fulfilled the terms of an engagement thus

voluntarily contracted. They who have been accustomed to the gaudiness and inane phraseology of many modern writers, if they persist in reading this book to its conclusion, will, no doubt, frequently have to struggle with feelings of strangeness and awkwardness: they will look round for poetry, and will be induced to inquire by what species of courtesy these attempts can be permitted to assume that title. I hope therefore the reader will not censure me, if I attempt to state what I have proposed to myself to perform; and also (as far as the limits of a preface will permit), to explain some of the chief reasons which have determined me in the choice of my purpose: that at least he may be spared any unpleasant feeling of disappointment, and that I myself may be protected from the most dishonourable accusation which can be brought against an author, namely, that of an indolence which prevents him from endeavouring to ascertain what is his duty, or, when his duty is ascertained, prevents him from performing it.

The principal object, then, which I proposed to myself in these poems was to choose incidents and situations from common life and to relate or describe them, throughout, as far as was possible, in a selection of language really used by men; and, at the same time, to throw over them a certain colouring of imagination, whereby ordinary things should be presented to the mind in an unusual way; and, further, and above all, to make these incidents and situations interesting by tracing in them, truly though not ostentatiously, the primary laws of our nature: chiefly, as far as regards the manner in which we associate ideas in a state of excitement. Low and rustic life was generally chosen, because in that condition, the essential passions of the heart find a better soil in which they can attain their maturity, are less under restraint, and speak a plainer and more emphatic language; because in that condition of life our elementary feelings co-exist in a state of greater simplicity, and, consequently, may be more accurately contemplated, and more forcibly communicated; because the manners of rural life germinate from those elementary feelings; and, from the necessary character of rural occupations, are most easily comprehended; and are more durable; and lastly, because in that condition the passions of men are incorporated with the beautiful and permanent forms of nature. The language, too, of these men is adopted (purified indeed from what appear to be its real defects, from all lasting and rational causes of dislike or disgust) because such men hourly communicate with the best objects from which the best part of language is originally derived; and because, from their rank in society and the sameness and narrow circle of their intercourse, being less under the influence of social vanity they convey their feelings and notions in simple and unelaborated expressions. Accordingly, such a language, arising out of repeated experience and regular feelings, is a more permanent, and a far more philosophical language, than that which is frequently substituted for it by poets, who think that they are conferring honour upon themselves and their art, in proportion as they separate themselves from the sympathies of men, and indulge in arbitrary and capricious habits of expression, in order to furnish food for fickle tastes, and fickle appetites, of their own creation.

I cannot, however, be insensible of the present outcry against the triviality and meanness both of thought and language, which some of my contemporaries have occasionally introduced into their metrical compositions; and I acknowledge, that this defect, where it exists, is more dishonourable to the writer's own character than false refinement or arbitrary innovation, though I should contend at the same time that it is far less pernicious in the sum of its consequences. From such verses the poems in these volumes will be found distinguished at least by one mark of difference, that each of them has a worthy *purpose*. Not that I mean to say, that I always began to write with a distinct purpose formally conceived; but I believe that my habits of meditation have so formed my feelings, as that my descriptions of such objects as strongly excite those feelings, will be found to carry along with them a *purpose*. If in this opinion I am mistaken, I can have little right to the name of a poet. For all good poetry is the spontaneous overflow of powerful feelings: but though this be true, poems to which any value can be attached, were never produced on any variety of subjects but by a man, who being possessed of more than usual organic sensibility, had also thought long and deeply. For our continued influxes of feeling are modified and directed by our thoughts, which are indeed the representatives of all our past feelings; and, as by contemplating the relation of these general representatives to each other we discover what is really important to men, so, by the repetition and continuance of this act, our feelings will be connected with important subjects, till at length, if we be originally possessed of much sensibility, such habits of mind will be produced, that, by obeying blindly and mechanically the impulses of those habits, we shall describe objects, and utter sentiments, of such a nature and in such connection with each other, that the understanding of the being to whom we address ourselves, if he be in a healthful state of association, must necessarily be in some degree enlightened, and his affections ameliorated.

I have said that each of these poems has a purpose. I have also informed my reader what this purpose will be found principally to be: namely to illustrate the manner in which our feelings and ideas are associated in a state of excitement. But, speaking in language somewhat more appropriate, it is to follow the fluxes and refluxes of the mind when agitated by the great and simple affections of our nature. This object I have endeavoured in these short essays to attain by various means; by tracing the maternal passion through many of its more subtle windings, as in the poems of the *Idiot Boy* and the *Mad Mother;* by accompanying the last struggles of a human being, at the approach of death, cleaving in solitude to life and society, as in the poem of the "Forsaken Indian"; by showing, as in the stanzas entitled "We Are Seven," the perplexity and obscurity which in childhood attend our notion of death, or rather our utter inability to admit that notion; or by displaying the strength of fraternal, or to speak more philosophically, of moral attachment when early associated with the great and beautiful objects of nature, as in The Brothers; or, as in the incident of "Simon Lee," by placing my reader in the way of receiving from ordinary moral sensations another and more salutary impression than we are accustomed to receive from them. It has also been part of my general purpose to attempt to sketch characters under the influence of less impassioned feelings, as in the "Two April Mornings," "The Fountain," "The Old Man Travelling," "The Two Thieves," etc. characters of which the elements are simple, belonging rather to nature than to manners, such as exist now, and will probably always exist, and which from their constitution may be distinctly and profitably contemplated. I will not abuse the indulgence of my reader by dwelling longer upon this subject; but it is proper that I should mention one other circumstance which distinguishes these poems from the popular poetry of the day; it is this, that the feeling therein developed gives importance to the action and situation, and not the action and situation to the feeling. My meaning will be rendered perfectly intelligible by referring my reader to the poems entitled "Poor Susan" and the "Childless Father," particularly to the last stanza of the latter poem.

I will not suffer a sense of false modesty to prevent me from asserting, that I point my reader's attention to this mark of distinction, far less for the sake of these particular poems than from the general importance of the subject. The subject is indeed important! For the human mind is capable of being excited without the application of gross and violent stimulants; and he must have a very faint perception of its beauty and dignity who does not know this, and who does not further know, that one being is elevated above another, in proportion as he possesses this capability. It has therefore appeared to me, that to endeavour to produce or enlarge this capability is one of the best services in which, at any period, a writer can be engaged; but this service, excellent at all times, is especially so at the present day. For a multitude of causes, unknown to former times, are now acting with a combined force to blunt the discriminating powers of the mind, and unfitting it for all voluntary exertion to reduce it to a state of almost savage torpor. The most effective of these causes are the great national events which are daily taking place, and the increasing accumulation of men in cities, where the uniformity of their occupations produces a craving for extraordinary incident, which the rapid communication of intelligence hourly gratifies.[1] To this tendency of life and manners the literature and theatrical exhibitions of the country have conformed themselves. The invaluable works of our elder writers, I had

almost said the works of Shakespeare and Milton, are driven into neglect by frantic novels, sickly and stupid German tragedies, and deluges of idle and extravagant stories in verse.[2] — When I think upon this degrading thirst after outrageous stimulation, I am almost ashamed to have spoken of the feeble effort with which I have endeavoured to counteract it; and, reflecting upon the magnitude of the general evil, I should be oppressed with no dishonourable melancholy, had I not a deep impression of certain inherent and indestructible qualities of the human mind, and likewise of certain powers in the great and permanent objects that act upon it which are equally inherent and indestructible; and did I not further add to this impression a belief, that the time is approaching when the evil will be systematically opposed, by men of greater powers, and with far more distinguished success.

Having dwelt thus long on the subjects and aim of these poems, I shall request the reader's permission to apprize him of a few circumstances relating to their *style*, in order, among other reasons, that I may not be censured for not having performed what I never attempted. The reader will find that personifications of abstract ideas rarely occur in these volumes; and, I hope, are utterly rejected as an ordinary device to elevate the style, and raise it above prose. I have proposed to myself to imitate, and, as far as is possible, to adopt the very language of men; and assuredly such personifications do not make any natural or regular part of that language. They are, indeed, a figure of speech occasionally prompted by passion, and I have made use of them as such; but I have endeavoured utterly to reject them as a mechanical device of style, or as a family language which writers in metre seem to lay claim to by prescription. I have wished to keep my reader in the company of flesh and blood, persuaded that by so doing I shall interest him. I am, however, well aware that others who pursue a different track may interest him likewise; I do not interfere with their claim, I only wish to prefer a different claim of my own. There will also be found in these

---

[1]Wordsworth refers to the French Revolution and the war between England and France that followed.

[2]Wordsworth alludes to the vogue of the Gothic novel, which lasted from the early 1790s until about 1825.

volumes little of what is usually called poetic diction; I have taken as much pains to avoid it as others ordinarily take to produce it; this I have done for the reason already alleged, to bring my language near to the language of men, and further, because the pleasure which I have proposed to myself to impart is of a kind very different from that which is supposed by many persons to be the proper object of poetry. I do not know how without being culpably particular I can give my reader a more exact notion of the style in which I wished these poems to be written than by informing him that I have at all times endeavoured to look steadily at my subject, consequently, I hope that there is in these poems little falsehood of description, and that my ideas are expressed in language fitted to their respective importance. Something I must have gained by this practice, as it is friendly to one property of all good poetry, namely, good sense; but it has necessarily cut me off from a large portion of phrases and figures of speech which from father to son have long been regarded as the common inheritance of poets. I also have thought it expedient to restrict myself still further, having abstained from the use of many expressions, in themselves proper and beautiful, but which have been foolishly repeated by bad poets, till such feelings of disgust are connected with them as it is scarcely possible by any art of association to overpower.

If in a poem there should be found a series of lines, or even a single line, in which the language, though naturally arranged and according to the strict laws of metre, does not differ from that of prose, there is a numerous class of critics, who, when they stumble upon these prosaisms as they call them, imagine that they have made a notable discovery, and exult over the poet as over a man ignorant of his own profession. Now these men would establish a canon of criticism which the reader will conclude he must utterly reject, if he wishes to be pleased with these volumes. And it would be a most easy task to prove to him, that not only the language of a large portion of every good poem, even of the most elevated character, must necessarily, except with reference to the metre, in no respect differ from that of good prose, but likewise that some of the most interesting parts of the best poems will be found to be strictly the language of prose, when prose is well written. The truth of this assertion might be demonstrated by innumerable passages from almost all the poetical writings, even of Milton himself. I have not space for much quotation; but, to illustrate the subject in a general manner, I will here adduce a short composition of Gray, who was at the head of those who by their reasonings have attempted to widen the space of separation betwixt prose and metrical composition, and was more than any other man curiously elaborate in the structure of his own poetic diction.

In vain to me the smiling mornings shine,
And reddening Phoebus lifts his golden fire:
The birds in vain their amorous descant join,
Or cheerful fields resume their green attire:
These ears alas! for other notes repine;
A different object do these eyes require;
My lonely anguish melts no heart but mine;
And in my breast the imperfect joys expire;
Yet Morning smiles the busy race to cheer,
And new-born pleasure brings to happier men;
The fields to all their wonted tribute bear;
To warm their little loves the birds complain.
I fruitless mourn to him that cannot hear
And weep the more because I weep in vain.[3]

It will easily be perceived that the only part of this sonnet which is of any value is the lines printed in italics: it is equally obvious, that, except in the rhyme, and in the use of the single word "fruitless" for fruitlessly, which is so far a defect, the language of these lines does in no respect differ from that of prose.

By the foregoing quotation I have shown that the language of prose may yet be well adapted to poetry; and I have previously asserted that a large portion of the language of every good poem can in no respect differ from that of good prose. I will go further. I do not doubt that it may be safely affirmed, that there neither is, nor can be, any essential difference between the language of prose and metrical composition. We are fond of tracing the resemblance between poetry and painting, and, accordingly, we call them sisters: but where shall we find bonds of connection

[3]Thomas Gray, "Sonnet on the Death of Mr. Richard West."

sufficiently strict to typify the affinity betwixt metrical and prose composition? They both speak by and to the same organs; the bodies in which both of them are clothed may be said to be of the same substance, their affections are kindred and almost identical, not necessarily differing even in degree; poetry[4] sheds no tears "such as Angels weep," but natural and human tears; she can boast of no celestial ichor that distinguishes her vital juices from those of prose; the same human blood circulates through the veins of them both.

If it be affirmed that rhyme and metrical arrangement of themselves constitute a distinction which overturns what I have been saying on the strict affinity of metrical language with that of prose, and paves the way for other artificial distinctions which the mind voluntarily admits, I answer that the language of such poetry as I am recommending is, as far as is possible, a selection of the language really spoken by men; that this selection, wherever it is made with true taste and feeling, will of itself form a distinction far greater than would at first be imagined, and will entirely separate the composition from the vulgarity and meanness of ordinary life; and, if metre be superadded thereto, I believe that a dissimilitude will be produced altogether sufficient for the gratification of a rational mind. What other distinction would we have? Whence is it to come? And where is it to exist? Not, surely, where the poet speaks through the mouths of his characters: it cannot be necessary here, either for elevation of style, or of any of its supposed ornaments: for, if the poet's subject be judiciously chosen, it will naturally, and upon fit occasion, lead him to passions the language of which, if selected truly and judiciously, must necessarily be dignified and variegated, and alive with metaphors and figures. I forbear to speak of an incongruity

[4]I here use the word "poetry" (though against my own judgment) as opposed to the word prose, and synonymous with metrical composition. But much confusion has been introduced into criticism by this contradistinction of poetry and prose, instead of the more philosophical one of poetry and prose, instead of science. The only strict antithesis to prose is metre; nor is this, in truth, a *strict* antithesis, because lines and passages of metre so naturally occur in writing prose, that it would be scarcely possible to avoid them, even were it desirable. [Wordsworth.]

which would shock the intelligent reader, should the poet interweave any foreign splendour of his own with that which the passion naturally suggests: it is sufficient to say that such addition is unnecessary. And, surely, it is more probable that those passages, which with propriety abound with metaphors and figures, will have their due effect, if, upon other occasions where the passions are of a milder character, the style also be subdued and temperate.

But, as the pleasure which I hope to give by the poems I now present to the reader must depend entirely on just notions upon this subject, and, as it is in itself of the highest importance to our taste and moral feelings, I cannot content myself with these detached remarks. And if, in what I am about to say, it shall appear to some that my labour is unnecessary, and that I am like a man fighting a battle without enemies, I would remind such persons, that, whatever may be the language outwardly holden by men, a practical faith in the opinions which I am wishing to establish is almost unknown. If my conclusions are admitted, and carried as far as they must be carried if admitted at all, our judgments concerning the works of the greatest poets both ancient and modern will be far different from what they are at present, both when we praise, and when we censure: and our moral feelings influencing, and influenced by these judgments will, I believe, be corrected and purified.

Taking up the subject, then, upon general grounds, I ask what is meant by the word poet? What is a poet? To whom does he address himself? And what language is to be expected from him? He is a man speaking to men: a man, it is true, endued with more lively sensibility, more enthusiasm and tenderness, who has a greater knowledge of human nature, and a more comprehensive soul, than are supposed to be common among mankind; a man pleased with his own passions and volitions, and who rejoices more than other men in the spirit of life that is in him; delighting to contemplate similar volitions and passions as manifested in the goings-on of the universe, and habitually impelled to create them where he does not find them. To these qualities he has added a disposition to be affected more than other men by absent things as if they were present; an ability of conjuring up in himself passions, which are indeed far from being the same as those produced by real events, yet (especially in those parts of the general sympathy which are pleasing and delightful) do more nearly resemble the passions produced by real events, than any thing which, from the motions of their own minds merely, other men are accustomed to feel in themselves; whence, and from practice, he has acquired a greater readiness and power in expressing what he thinks and feels, and especially those thoughts and feelings which, by his own choice, or from the structure of his own mind, arise in him without immediate external excitement.

But, whatever portion of this faculty we may suppose even the greatest poet to possess, there cannot be a doubt but that the language which it will suggest to him, must, in liveliness and truth, fall far short of that which is uttered by men in real life, under the actual pressure of those passions, certain shadows of which the poet thus produces, or feels to be produced, in himself. However exalted a notion we would wish to cherish of the character of a poet, it is obvious, that, while he describes and imitates passions, his situation is altogether slavish and mechanical, compared with the freedom and power of real and substantial action and suffering. So that it will be the wish of the poet to bring his feelings near to those of the persons whose feelings he describes, nay, for short spaces of time perhaps, to let himself slip into an entire delusion, and even confound and identify his own feelings with theirs; modifying only the language which is thus suggested to him, by a consideration that he describes for a particular purpose, that of giving pleasure. Here, then, he will apply the principle on which I have so much insisted, namely, that of selection; on this he will depend for removing what would otherwise be painful or disgusting in the passion; he will feel that there is no necessity to trick out or to elevate nature: and, the more industriously he applies this principle, the deeper will be his faith that no words, which *his* fancy or imagination can suggest, will be to be compared with those which are the emanations of reality and truth.

But it may be said by those who do not object to the general spirit of these remarks, that, as it is impossible for the poet to produce upon all occasions language as exquisitely fitted for the passion as that which the real passion itself suggests, it is proper that he should consider himself as in the situation of a translator, who deems himself justified when he substitutes excellences of another kind for those which are unattainable by him; and endeavours occasionally to surpass his original, in order to make some amends for the general inferiority to which he feels that he must submit. But this would be to encourage idleness and unmanly despair. Further, it is the language of men who speak of what they do not understand; who talk of poetry as of a matter of amusement and idle pleasure; who will converse with us as gravely about a *taste* for poetry, as they express it, as if it were a thing as indifferent as a taste for rope-dancing, or frontiniac or sherry. Aristotle, I have been told, hath said, that poetry is the most philosophic of all writing:[5] it is so: its object is truth, not individual and local, but general, and operative; not standing upon external testimony, but carried alive into the heart by passion; truth which is its own testimony, which gives strength and divinity to the tribunal to which it appeals, and receives them from the same tribunal. Poetry is the image of man and nature. The obstacles which stand in the way of the fidelity of the biographer and historian, and of their consequent utility, are incalculably greater than those which are to be encountered by the poet who has an adequate notion of the dignity of his art. The poet writes under one restriction only, namely, that of the necessity of giving immediate pleasure to a human being possessed of that information which may be expected from him, not as a lawyer, a physician, a mariner, an astronomer or a natural philosopher, but as a man. Except this one restriction, there is no object standing between the poet and the image of things; between this, and the biographer and historian there are a thousand.

Nor let this necessity of producing immediate pleasure be considered as a degradation of the poet's art. It is far otherwise. It is an acknowledgment of the beauty of the universe, an

---

[5]Aristotle, *Poetics*, Ch. 9. One notes that Wordsworth misquotes Aristotle by hearsay.

acknowledgment the more sincere because it is not formal, but indirect; it is a task light and easy to him who looks at the world in the spirit of love: further, it is a homage paid to the native and naked dignity of man, to the grand elementary principle of pleasure, by which he knows, and feels, and lives, and moves. We have no sympathy but what is propagated by pleasure: I would not be misunderstood; but wherever we sympathize with pain it will be found that the sympathy is produced and carried on by subtle combinations with pleasure. We have no knowledge, that is, no general principle drawn from the contemplation of particular facts, but what has been built up by pleasure, and exists in us by pleasure alone. The man of science, the chemist and mathematician, whatever difficulties and disgusts they may have had to struggle with, know and feel this. However painful may be the objects with which the anatomist's knowledge is connected, he feels that his knowledge is pleasure; and where he has no pleasure he has no knowledge. What then does the poet? He considers man and the objects that surround him as acting and reacting upon each other, so as to produce an infinite complexity of pain and pleasure; he considers man in his own nature and in his ordinary life as contemplating this with a certain quantity of immediate knowledge, with certain convictions, intuitions, and deductions which by habit become of the nature of intuitions; he considers him as looking upon this complex scene of ideas and sensations, and finding every where objects that immediately excite in him sympathies which, from the necessities of his nature, are accompanied by an overbalance of enjoyment. To this knowledge which all men carry about with them, and to these sympathies in which without any other discipline than that of our daily life we are fitted to take delight, the poet principally directs his attention. He considers man and nature as essentially adapted to each other, and the mind of man as naturally the mirror of the fairest and most interesting qualities of nature. And thus the poet, prompted by this feeling of pleasure which accompanies him through the whole course of his studies, converses with general nature with affections akin to those, which, through labour and length of time, the man of science has raised up in himself, by conversing

with those particular parts of nature which are the objects of his studies. The knowledge both of the poet and the man of science is pleasure; but the knowledge of the one cleaves to us as a necessary part of our existence, our natural and unalienable inheritance; the other is a personal and individual acquisition, slow to come to us, and by no habitual and direct sympathy connecting us with our fellow-beings. The man of science seeks truth as a remote and unknown benefactor; he cherishes and loves it in his solitude: the poet, singing a song in which all human beings join with him, rejoices in the presence of truth as our visible friend and hourly companion. Poetry is the breath and finer spirit of all knowledge; it is the impassioned expression which is in the countenance of all science. Emphatically may it be said of the poet, as Shakespeare hath said of man, "that he looks before and after." He is the rock of defence of human nature; an upholder and preserver, carrying every where with him relationship and love. In spite of difference of soil and climate, of language and manners, of laws and customs, in spite of things silently gone out of mind and things violently destroyed, the poet binds together by passion and knowledge the vast empire of human society, as it is spread over the whole earth, and over all time. The objects of the poet's thoughts are every where; though the eyes and senses of man are, it is true, his favourite guides, yet he will follow wheresoever he can find an atmosphere of sensation in which to move his wings. Poetry is the first and last of all knowledge — it is as immortal as the heart of man. If the labours of men of science should ever create any material revolution, direct or indirect, in our condition, and in the impressions which we habitually receive, the poet will sleep then no more than at present, but he will be ready to follow the steps of the man of science, not only in those general indirect effects, but he will be at his side, carrying sensation into the midst of the objects of the science itself. The remotest discoveries of the chemist, the botanist, or mineralogist, will be as proper objects of the poet's art as any upon which it can be employed, if the time should ever come when these things shall be familiar to us, and the relations under which they are contemplated by the followers of these respective sciences shall be manifestly and palpably material to us as enjoying and suffering beings. If the time should ever come when what is now called science, thus familiarized to men, shall be ready to put on, as it were, a form of flesh and blood, the poet will lend his divine spirit to aid the transfiguration, and will welcome the being thus produced, as a dear and genuine inmate of the household of man. — It is not, then, to be supposed that any one, who holds that sublime notion of poetry which I have attempted to convey, will break in upon the sanctity and truth of his pictures by transitory and accidental ornaments, and endeavour to excite admiration of himself by arts, the necessity of which must manifestly depend upon the assumed meanness of his subject.

What I have thus far said applies to poetry in general; but especially to those parts of composition where the poet speaks through the mouths of his characters; and upon this point it appears to have such weight that I will conclude, there are few persons, of good sense, who would not allow that the dramatic parts of composition are defective, in proportion as they deviate from the real language of nature, and are coloured by a diction of the poet's own, either peculiar to him as an individual poet, or belonging simply to poets in general, to a body of men who, from the circumstance of their compositions being in metre, it is expected will employ a particular language.

It is not, then, in the dramatic parts of composition that we look for this distinction of language; but still it may be proper and necessary where the poet speaks to us in his own person and character. To this I answer by referring my reader to the description which I have before given of a poet. Among the qualities which I have enumerated as principally conducing to form a poet, is implied nothing differing in kind from other men, but only in degree. The sum of what I have there said is, that the poet is chiefly distinguished from other men by a greater promptness to think and feel without immediate external excitement, and a greater power in expressing such thoughts and feelings as are produced in him in that manner. But these passions and thoughts and feelings are the general passions and thoughts and feelings of men. And with what are they connected? Undoubtedly with our moral sentiments and animal sensations, and

with the causes which excite these; with the operations of the elements and the appearances of the visible universe; with storm and sunshine, with the revolutions of the seasons, with cold and heat, with loss of friends and kindred, with injuries and resentments, gratitude and hope, with fear and sorrow. These, and the like, are the sensations and objects which the poet describes, as they are the sensations of other men, and the objects which interest them. The poet thinks and feels in the spirit of the passions of men. How, then, can his language differ in any material degree from that of all other men who feel vividly and see clearly? It might be *proved* that it is impossible. But supposing that this were not the case, the poet might then be allowed to use a peculiar language, when expressing his feelings for his own gratification, or that of men like himself. But poets do not write for poets alone, but for men. Unless therefore we are advocates for that admiration which depends upon ignorance, and that pleasure which arises from hearing what we do not understand, the poet must descend from this supposed height, and, in order to excite rational sympathy, he must express himself as other men express themselves. To this it may be added, that while he is only selecting from the real language of men, or, which amounts to the same thing, composing accurately in the spirit of such selection, he is treading upon safe ground, and we know what we are to expect from him. Our feelings are the same with respect to metre; for, as it may be proper to remind the reader, the distinction of metre is regular and uniform, and not like that which is produced by what is usually called poetic diction, arbitrary, and subject to infinite caprices upon which no calculation whatever can be made. In the one case, the reader is utterly at the mercy of the poet respecting what imagery or diction he may choose to connect with the passion, whereas, in the other, the metre obeys certain laws, to which the poet and reader both willingly submit because they are certain, and because no interference is made by them with the passion but such as the concurring testimony of ages has shown to heighten and improve the pleasure which co-exists with it.

It will now be proper to answer an obvious question, namely, why, professing these opinions, have I written in verse? To this, in addition to such answer as is included in what I have already said, I reply in the first place, because, however I may have restricted myself, there is still left open to me what confessedly constitutes the most valuable object of all writing whether in prose or verse, the great and universal passions of men, the most general and interesting of their occupations, and the entire world of nature, from which I am at liberty to supply myself with endless combinations of forms and imagery. Now, supposing for a moment that whatever is interesting in these objects may be as vividly described in prose, why am I to be condemned, if to such description I have endeavoured to superadd the charm which, by the consent of all nations, is acknowledged to exist in metrical language? To this, by such as are unconvinced by what I have already said, it may be answered, that a very small part of the pleasure given by poetry depends upon the metre, and that it is injudicious to write in metre, unless it be accompanied with the other artificial distinctions of style with which metre is usually accompanied, and that by such deviation more will be lost from the shock which will be thereby given to the reader's associations, than will be counterbalanced by any pleasure which he can derive from the general power of numbers. In answer to those who still contend for the necessity of accompanying metre with certain appropriate colours of style in order to the accomplishment of its appropriate end, and who also, in my opinion, greatly underrate the power of metre in itself, it might perhaps, as far as relates to these poems, have been almost sufficient to observe, that poems are extant, written upon more humble subjects, and in a more naked and simple style than I have aimed at, which poems have continued to give pleasure from generation to generation. Now, if nakedness and simplicity be a defect, the fact here mentioned affords a strong presumption that poems somewhat less naked and simple are capable of affording pleasure at the present day; and, what I wished chiefly to attempt, at present, was to justify myself for having written under the impression of this belief. But I might point out various causes why, when the style is manly, and the subject of some importance, words metrically arranged will long continue to impart such a pleasure to mankind as he who is sensible of the extent of that pleasure will be desirous to impart. The end of poetry is to produce excitement in co-existence with an overbalance of pleasure. Now, by the supposition, excitement is an unusual and irregular state of the mind; ideas and feelings do not in that state succeed each other in accustomed order. But, if the words by which this excitement is produced are in themselves powerful, or the images and feelings have an undue proportion of pain connected with them, there is some danger that the excitement may be carried beyond its proper bounds. Now the co-presence of something regular, something to which the mind has been accustomed in various moods and in a less excited state, cannot but have great efficacy in tempering and restraining the passion by an inter-texture of ordinary feeling, and of feeling not strictly and necessarily connected with the passion. This is unquestionably true, and hence, though the opinion will at first appear paradoxical, from the tendency of metre to divest language in a certain degree of its reality, and thus to throw a sort of half consciousness of unsubstantial existence over the whole composition, there can be little doubt but that more pathetic situations and sentiments, that is, those which have a greater proportion of pain connected with them, may be endured in metrical composition, especially in rhyme, than in prose. The metre of the old ballads is very artless; yet they contain many passages which would illustrate this opinion, and, I hope, if the following poems be attentively perused, similar instances will be found in them. This opinion may be further illustrated by appealing to the reader's own experience of the reluctance with which he comes to the reperusal of the distressful parts of *Clarissa Harlowe*, or the *Gamester*.[6] While Shakespeare's writings, in the most pathetic scenes, never act upon us as pathetic beyond the bounds of pleasure — an effect which, in a much greater degree than might at first be imagined, is to be ascribed to small, but continual and regular impulses of pleasurable surprise from the metrical arrangement. — On the other hand (what it must be allowed will much more frequently happen) if the poet's words

[6] Samuel Richardson's *Clarissa* (1747–48) and Edward Moore's *The Gamester* (1753).

should be incommensurate with the passion, and inadequate to raise the reader to a height of desirable excitement, then, (unless the poet's choice of his metre has been grossly injudicious) in the feelings of pleasure which the reader has been accustomed to connect with metre in general, and in the feeling, whether cheerful or melancholy, which he has been accustomed to connect with that particular movement of metre, there will be found something which will greatly contribute to impart passion to the words, and to effect the complex end which the poet proposes to himself.

If I had undertaken a systematic defence of the theory upon which these poems are written, it would have been my duty to develop the various causes upon which the pleasure received from metrical language depends. Among the chief of these causes is to be reckoned a principle which must be well known to those who have made any of the arts the object of accurate reflection; I mean the pleasure which the mind derives from the perception of similitude in dissimilitude. This principle is the great spring of the activity of our minds, and their chief feeder. From this principle the direction of the sexual appetite, and all the passions connected with it take their origin: it is the life of our ordinary conversation; and upon the accuracy with which similitude in dissimilitude, and dissimilitude in similitude are perceived, depend our taste and our moral feelings. It would not have been a useless employment to have applied this principle to the consideration of metre, and to have shown that metre is hence enabled to afford much pleasure, and to have pointed out in what manner that pleasure is produced. But my limits will not permit me to enter upon this subject, and I must content myself with a general summary.

I have said that poetry is the spontaneous overflow of powerful feelings: it takes its origin from emotion recollected in tranquillity: the emotion is contemplated till by a species of reaction the tranquillity gradually disappears, and an emotion, kindred to that which was before the subject of contemplation, is gradually produced, and does itself actually exist in the mind. In this mood successful composition generally begins, and in a mood similar to this it is carried on; but the emotion, of whatever kind and in whatever degree, from various causes is qualified by various pleasures, so that in describing any passions whatsoever, which are voluntarily described, the mind will upon the whole be in a state of enjoyment. Now, if nature be thus cautious in preserving in a state of enjoyment a being thus employed, the poet ought to profit by the lesson thus held forth to him, and ought especially to take care, that whatever passions he communicates to his reader, those passions, if his reader's mind be sound and vigorous, should always be accompanied with an overbalance of pleasure. Now the music of harmonious metrical language, the sense of difficulty overcome, and the blind association of pleasure which has been previously received from works of rhyme or metre of the same or similar construction, an indistinct perception perpetually renewed of language closely resembling that of real life, and yet, in the circumstance of metre, differing from it so widely, all these imperceptibly make up a complex feeling of delight, which is of the most important use in tempering the painful feeling which will always be found intermingled with powerful descriptions of the deeper passions. This effect is always produced in pathetic and impassioned poetry; while, in lighter compositions, the ease and gracefulness with which the poet manages his numbers are themselves confessedly a principal source of the gratification of the reader. I might perhaps include all which it is *necessary* to say upon this subject by affirming, what few persons will deny, that, of two descriptions, either of passions, manners, or characters, each of them equally well executed, the one in prose and the other in verse, the verse will be read a hundred times where the prose is read once. We see that Pope by the power of verse alone, has contrived to render the plainest common sense interesting, and even frequently to invest it with the appearance of passion. In consequence of these convictions I related in metre the tale of *Goody Blake and Harry Gill*, which is one of the rudest of this collection. I wished to draw attention to the truth that the power of the human imagination is sufficient to produce such changes even in our physical nature as might almost appear miraculous. The truth is an important one; the fact (for it is a *fact*) is a valuable illustration of it. And I have the satisfaction of knowing that it has been communicated to many

Having thus explained a few of the reasons why I have written in verse, and why I have chosen subjects from common life, and endeavoured to bring my language near to the real language of men, if I have been too minute in pleading my own cause, I have at the same time been treating a subject of general interest; and it is for this reason that I request the reader's permission to add a few words with reference solely to these particular poems, and to some defects which will probably be found in them. I am sensible that my associations must have sometimes been particular instead of general, and that, consequently, giving to things a false importance, sometimes from diseased impulses I may have written upon unworthy subjects; but I am less apprehensive on this account, than that my language may frequently have suffered from those arbitrary connexions of feelings and ideas with particular words and phrases, from which no man can altogether protect himself. Hence I have no doubt, that, in some instances, feelings even of the ludicrous may be given to my readers by expressions which appeared to me tender and pathetic. Such faulty expressions, were I convinced they were faulty at present, and that they must necessarily continue to be so, I would willingly take all reasonable pains to correct. But it is dangerous to make these alterations on the simple authority of a few individuals, or even of certain classes of men; for where the understanding of an author is not convinced, or his feelings altered, this cannot be done without great injury to himself: for his own feelings are his stay and support; and, if he sets them aside in one instance, he may be induced to repeat this act till his mind loses all confidence in itself, and becomes utterly debilitated. To this it may be added, that the reader ought never to forget that he is himself exposed to the same errors as the poet, and perhaps in a much greater degree: for there can be no presumption in saying, that it is not probable he will be so well acquainted with the various stages of meaning through which words have passed, or with the fickleness or stability of the relations of particular ideas to each other; and above all, since he is so much less interested in the subject, he may decide lightly and carelessly.

Long as I have detained my reader, I hope he will permit me to caution him against a mode of false criticism which has been applied to poetry in which the language closely resembles that of life and nature. Such verses have been triumphed over in parodies of which Dr. Johnson's stanza is a fair specimen.

I put my hat upon my head,
And walked into the Strand,
And there I met another man
Whose hat was in his hand.

Immediately under these lines I will place one of the most justly admired stanzas of the "Babes in the Wood."

These pretty Babes with hand in hand
Went wandering up and down;
But never more they saw the Man
Approaching from the Town.

In both these stanzas the words, and the order of the words, in no respect differ from the most unimpassioned conversation. There are words in both, for example, "the Strand," and "the Town," connected with none but the most familiar ideas; yet the one stanza we admit as admirable, and the other as a fair example of the superlatively contemptible. Whence arises this difference? Not from the metre, not from the language, not from the order of the words; but the *matter* expressed in Dr. Johnson's stanza is contemptible. The proper method of treating trivial and simple verses to which Dr. Johnson's stanza would be a fair parallelism is not to say, this is a bad kind of poetry, or this is not poetry; but this wants sense; it is neither interesting in itself, nor can *lead* to any thing interesting; the images neither originate in that sane state of feeling which arises out of thought, nor can excite thought or feeling in the reader. This is the only sensible manner of dealing with such verses: Why trouble yourself about the species till you have previously decided upon the genus? Why take pains to prove that an ape is not a Newton when it is self-evident that he is not a man?

I have one request to make of my reader, which is, that in judging these poems he would decide by his own feelings genuinely, and not by reflection upon what will probably be the judgment of others. How common is it to hear a person say, "I myself do not object to this style of composition or this or that expression, but to such and such classes of people it will appear mean or ludicrous." This mode of criticism, so destructive of all sound unadulterated judgment, is almost universal: I have therefore to request, that the reader would abide independently by his own feelings, and that if he finds himself affected he would not suffer such conjectures to interfere with his pleasure.

If an author by any single composition has impressed us with respect for his talents, it is useful to consider this as affording a presumption, that, on other occasions where we have been displeased, he nevertheless may not have written ill or absurdly; and, further, to give him so much credit for this one composition as may induce us to review what has displeased us with more care than we should otherwise have bestowed upon it. This is not only an act of justice, but in our decisions upon poetry especially, may conduce in a high degree to the improvement of our own taste: for an *accurate* taste in poetry and in all the other arts, as Sir Joshua Reynolds has observed,[7] is an *acquired* talent, which can only be produced by thought and a long continued intercourse with the best models of composition. This is mentioned, not with so ridiculous a purpose as to prevent the most inexperienced reader from judging for himself (I have already said that I wish him to judge for himself), but merely to temper the rashness of decision, and to suggest, that, if poetry be a subject on which much time has not been bestowed, the judgment may be erroneous; and that in many cases it necessarily will be so.

I know that nothing would have so effectually contributed to further the end which I have in view as to have shown of what kind the pleasure is, and how that pleasure is produced, which is confessedly produced by metrical composition

essentially different from that which I have here endeavoured to recommend: for the reader will say that he has been pleased by such composition; and what can I do more for him? The power of any art is limited; and he will suspect, that, if I propose to furnish him with new friends, it is only upon condition of his abandoning his old friends. Besides, as I have said, the reader is himself conscious of the pleasure which he has received from such composition, composition to which he has peculiarly attached the endearing name of poetry; and all men feel an habitual gratitude, and something of an honourable bigotry for the objects which have long continued to please them: we not only wish to be pleased, but to be pleased in that particular way in which we have been accustomed to be pleased. There is a host of arguments on these feelings; and I should be the less able to combat them successfully, as I am willing to allow, that, in order entirely to enjoy the poetry which I am recommending, it would be necessary to give up much of what is ordinarily enjoyed. But, would my limits have permitted me to point out how this pleasure is produced, I might have removed many obstacles, and assisted my reader in perceiving that the powers of language are not so limited as he may suppose; and that it is possible that poetry may give other enjoyments, of a purer, more lasting, and more exquisite nature. This part of my subject I have not altogether neglected; but it has been less my present aim to prove, that the interest excited by some other kinds of poetry is less vivid, and less worthy of the nobler powers of the mind, than to offer reasons for presuming, that, if the object which I have proposed to myself were adequately attained, a species of poetry would be produced, which is genuine poetry; in its nature well adapted to interest mankind permanently, and likewise important in the multiplicity and quality of its moral relations.

From what has been said, and from a perusal of the poems, the reader will be able clearly to perceive the object which I have proposed to myself: he will determine how far I have attained this object; and, what is a much more important question, whether it be worth attaining; and upon the decision of these two questions will rest my claim to the approbation of the public.

[7]Wordsworth refers to Joshua Reynolds's *Discourses* on art, probably a passage in Discourse 12 (*Works*, 2:95. London: Cadell and Davies, 1797.)

Samuel Taylor Coleridge

1772–1834

Coleridge's father, a parson in rural Devonshire, died when his son was nine years old. Thereafter Coleridge was educated at Christ's Hospital school as a charity student and then at Jesus College, Cambridge, which he left in 1794 without a degree. He became involved with Robert Southey's protosocialist pantisocracy scheme and in 1795 married Southey's sister-in-law, Sara Fricker, with whom he was deeply unhappy. That same year he was introduced to William Wordsworth, and the two "lake poets" collaborated on the seminal Romantic work of *Lyrical Ballads* (1798), in which Coleridge published "The Rime of the Ancient Mariner." Although he had experimented with opium as early as 1797, Coleridge did not become fully addicted until 1803 and remained so until 1816, when Dr. James Gillman attempted, with some success, to wean him gradually from the drug. Coleridge published *Christabel and Other Poems*, including the title poem "Christabel" and "Kubla Khan," in 1816, and his critical testament, *Biographia Literaria*, in 1817. The latter, together with some of Coleridge's Shakespeare lectures, comprises some of the richest critical theory the English Romantic Movement produced.

Coleridge based his ideas about the nature of imagination and art on his reading in the late 1790s of Kant and Kant's student Schelling. To understand fully what Coleridge intends in the *Biographia Literaria* requires a short detour into the history of the philosophy of mind.

KANT AND THE MIND

Immanuel Kant's most difficult and important work is probably the *Critique of Pure Reason*, in which his central concern is the way the mind operates. Since we are necessarily unaware of many of the operations of the mind, Kant is forced to focus on the most fleeting of our sensations; in fact he must generate a large-scale set of abstract notions in order to account for the mental output of which we are aware. The debate about mind that Kant joined in the eighteenth century was in some ways much like the debate in post–World War II psychology between the behaviorists and the mentalists.

Nearly a century before Kant, John Locke, in the *Essay Concerning Human Understanding* (1690), had attempted to establish the ultimate behaviorist position. Locke posited that the mind is a *tabula rasa*, a blank slate upon which experience writes. All ideas are derived from two sources: sense experience and the ability of the mind to contemplate itself. Locke tried to show that one could explain the most complex notions of the mind as aggregations of simple ideas. All the mind has to be able to do, by and large, is to place current sensations in memory and recall them on demand, to form simple ideas by associating and comparing current with past sense data, and to be able to associate and compare the simple ideas that result to build up more complex ones. In Locke's notion, the mind is like a computer with data inputs (the senses), an information storage/retrieval system, and some very simple programs, endlessly iterated, to process and compare the data.

Locke's picture of the mind as a simple machine influenced the thought of the entire eighteenth century (the novelist Laurence Sterne based *Tristram Shandy* on the workings and misworkings of Lockean associationism). But over the course of the century, Locke's system came to seem less and less adequate to account for the world as we know it. One problem was that Locke's philosophy assumed a sharp distinction between the inner world of mind and the outer world of matter. But since, as the philosopher George Berkeley argued, we know the world of matter only through mind, skeptics might doubt the very existence of the material world.

Another problem (raised by David Hume) concerned causality, surely the most important of the simple ideas by which we make sense of the phenomenal world. When we say that event A caused event B, we minimally mean that A is included in the ground of being of B. But when we see (on a billiard table, for example) the red ball hit the white ball (A) and the white ball move into the pocket (B), it is not clear that we know this much. What we know is that two events show spatial contiguity (the balls touched) and temporal succession (B followed A). But spatial contiguity and temporal succession do not add up to causality. If a baseball player were to scratch his nose and then hit a home run, would the scratching be thought the *cause* of the homer? Hume suggested that we attribute causality only where we have seen consistency of behavior. Only if there were a pattern in which nose-scratching led to home runs would we say that the former caused the latter; only on the basis of long experience with billiard balls do we say that the motion of the red ball causes that of the white. But this adds only subjective mental habit to the objective spatiotemporal contact we had before, and we seem just as far as ever from what we mean by cause.

Berkeley questioned the existence of the physical world that provides Locke's sense data and experience, and Hume raised doubts about whether the behavioristic mind Locke had assumed could effectually process its data in the way we know it does. The problem, it was becoming clear, was that the human mind had to be more complicated in its workings than Locke had thought. In fact, in order to account for what the mind can do, Kant was forced to attribute a great many more features of our sense of reality to the subjective mind.

For Kant, the external world consists of *noumena,* things whose existence we have to assume but about which we can form no clear idea. As the noumena impinge upon our senses, the mind actively (not passively as Locke claimed) processes the data into "representations." First the datum is marked with our identity — as *ours.* Then it is labeled for space and time — which for Kant were features of mind rather than of matter. Then it is run through the Kantian categories of the understanding and marked for quality, quantity, substance, relation, and so on. The noumena enter the mind; what emerges is phenomena, the world as it appears to us. For Kant, then, the phenomenal world is not *given;* it is *created* by us at every conscious moment through the processing system he calls the productive imagination. Since all minds contain the same mechanisms, we all perceive phenomena consistently and in roughly the same ways: The features of the outside world appear objectively real to us, although they are largely produced by the subjective workings of the mind.

COLERIDGE ON THE IMAGINATION

The above is a more elaborate explanation of what Coleridge is trying to say in a single enigmatic sentence of Chapter 13 of the *Biographia Literaria.* "The primary imagination I hold to be the living Power and prime Agent of all human Perception, and as a repetition in the finite mind of the eternal act of creation in the infinite I AM." What Kant had called the productive imagination, Coleridge renamed the primary: that mental faculty by which we create the world of our perceptions at each moment of consciousness. Just as God created the *noumena,* man creates the *phenomena.*

If the primary imagination is responsible for perception, the *secondary* imagina-tion is responsible for art. It is, Coleridge says, "an echo" of the primary, and like an echo it is similar to but weaker than what it echoes. Like the primary imagination, it is a creative faculty, but even when the imagination operates, it may not wholly displace the phenomenal world. Unlike the primary imagination, the power of the secondary imagination varies from individual to individual. Where the primary imagination creates the perceptual world without our desiring it, the secondary is "co-existing with," and at least partially responsive to, "the conscious will." It oper-ates by dissolving, diffusing, dissipating the perceptual world and creating another world in its place — or at least minimally reshaping the perceptual world into a more idealized and unified picture. The more complete the process of dissolution and recreation, the more fantastic the art form produced; the less complete, the more realistic. Coleridge has thus accounted for the differences between his poetry and that of his friend Wordsworth.

At the end of Chapter 13, Coleridge differentiates between fancy and imagina-tion. Imagination — the secondary imagination described above — is a fully cre-ative activity that, in effect, produces a new perceptual world. Fancy, on the other hand, is an inferior activity, since it operates entirely within the usual perceptual world; it is an activity describable in purely Lockean terms as the willful conjunc-tion of ideas that are normally distinct (like placing an elephant's head on the body of a camel).

COLERIDGE ON POEMS AND POETRY

In Chapter 14 Coleridge differentiates between *poem* and *poetry* — which are almost but not quite related as product to process. The procedure by which Coleridge defines "poem" is laborious but not entirely lucid. The confusion largely stems from an internal conflict. On the one hand Coleridge wants to evaluate as he defines, to define the *legitimate* as opposed to the *mere* poem; on the other hand, he also knows well that the word *poem* is generally used to apply to any composition in verse — good, bad, or indifferent. In trying to have it both ways, Coleridge muddies his argument. First, he grudgingly concedes that mere rhyming mnemonics "may be given the name of poem." But the real process of definition is more involved.

In Coleridge's definition there are two criteria: "object" or purpose and "superficial form." A poem has as its immediate purpose "pleasure not truth" and is thus differ-entiated from history or science. And it is written in verse: rhyme or meter or both conjointly. In effect, Coleridge specifies the following outline for major genres of poetry and prose:

	IMMEDIATE OBJECT	
	PLEASURE	TRUTH
SUPERFICIAL FORM:		
RHYME AND/OR METER	Poem	Mnemonic
PROSE	Novel	History or science

This outline seems mechanical enough — but then Coleridge asks a revealing question: If we turned a work of prose fiction into verse, would that make it a poem? The obvious answer would be "yes," but Coleridge says it would not: "Nothing can permanently please, which does not contain in itself the reason why it is so, and not otherwise." In a genuine poem, the linguistic and ideological content justifies the "perpetual and distinct attention to each part" that meter excites in us. A novel versified might look like a poem, but it would be dreadful in effect, since its texture would not be tightly woven enough to bear up under the sort of attention we would give it *as verse.* In legitimate poems, on the other hand, form and content, structure and texture, are interconnected: They are designed to stand the intense scrutiny that meter provokes.

The broad principle to which Coleridge appeals is that of *organic form,* in his famous discussion of Shakespeare where he contrasts the merely mechanical form that it is possible to impose upon materials with the organic form that grows out of the nature of the materials themselves. The "superficial" form in a genuine poem is, in fact, not superficial at all: It is an integral part of the poem's design.

Having defined "poem," Coleridge turns to "poetry," which to him is not a collective term for poems but an independent category. Poetry, he says, may be written in prose rather than in verse; and it may occur in works whose immediate object is truth rather than pleasure. More positively, his definition of poetry has "been in part anticipated in [some of the remarks] on the Fancy and Imagination": Less coyly, poetry is the verbal product of the "poetic genius" — the secondary imagination as defined in Chapter 13.

Long poems, Coleridge asserts, cannot be all poetry; conversely, much that is poetry is not in the form of a poem. In fact, so disparate are the two definitions that one might wonder why there needs to be *any* poetry whatever in the poem. The definitions only appear to be disconnected, however. What links them is Coleridge's concept of "organic form." If organic form is implicit in his definition of "poem," it is even more obvious that the distinction between organic and mechanical form is essentially that between imagination and fancy. Organicism is an essential characteristic of the workings of the secondary imagination in recreating an idealized, unified, and coherent fictive universe.

From Biographia Literaria

From Chapter 13

The IMAGINATION then, I consider either as primary, or secondary. The primary IMAGINATION I hold to be the living Power and prime Agent of all human Perception, and as a repetition in the finite mind of the eternal act of creation in the infinite I AM. The secondary Imagination I consider as an echo of the former, co-existing with the conscious will, yet still as identical with the primary in the *kind* of its agency, and differing only in *degree*, and in the *mode* of its operation. It dissolves, diffuses, dissipates, in order to recreate; or where this process is rendered impossible, yet still at all events it struggles to idealize and to unify. It is essentially vital, even as all objects (*as* objects) are essentially fixed and dead.

FANCY, on the contrary, has no other counters to play with, but fixities and definites. The Fancy is indeed no other than a mode of Memory emancipated from the order of time and space; while it is blended with, and modified by that empirical phenomenon of the will, which we express by the word CHOICE. But equally with the ordinary memory the Fancy must receive all its materials ready made from the law of association.

Chapter 14

Occasion of the Lyrical Ballads, and the objects originally proposed — Preface to the second edition — The ensuing controversy, its causes and acrimony —

Selected Bibliography

Barth, J. Robert. *The Symbolic Imagination: Coleridge and the Romantic Tradition.* Princeton: Princeton University Press, 1977.

Christensen, Jerome. *Coleridge's Blessed Machine of Language.* Ithaca: Cornell University Press, 1981.

Corrigan, Timothy. *Coleridge, Language and Criticism.* Athens: University of Georgia Press, 1982.

Fogle, R. H. *The Idea of Coleridge's Criticism.* Berkeley: University of California Press, 1962.

Hamilton, Paul. *Coleridge's Poetics.* Oxford: Blackwell, 1983.

Harding, Anthony John. *Coleridge and the Inspired Word.* Kingston, Ont.: McGill-Queen's University Press, 1985.

Kooy, Michael John. *Coleridge, Schiller, and Aesthetic Education.* Basingstoke, Eng.: Palgrave, 2002.

Marks, Emerson. *Coleridge on the Language of Verse.* Princeton: Princeton University Press, 1981.

McKenzie, Gordon. *Organic Unity in Coleridge.* Berkeley: University of California Press, 1939.

Read, Herbert Edward. *Coleridge as a Critic.* London: Faber and Faber, 1949.

Richards, Ivor Armstrong. *Coleridge on Imagination.* 3rd ed. London: Routledge and Kegan Paul, 1962.

Sharma, L. S. *Coleridge: His Contribution to English Criticism.* New Delhi: Arnold-Heinemann, 1981.

Thorpe, C. D. "Coleridge as Aesthetician and Critic." *Journal of the History of Ideas* 1 (1944): 387–414.

Philosophic definitions of a poem and poetry with scholia.

During the first year that Mr. Wordsworth and I were neighbours,[1] our conversations turned frequently on the two cardinal points of poetry, the power of exciting the sympathy of the reader by a faithful adherence to the truth of nature, and the power of giving the interest of novelty by the modifying colors of imagination. The sudden charm, which accidents of light and shade, which moon-light or sun-set diffused over a known and familiar landscape, appeared to represent the practicability of combining both. These are the poetry of nature. The thought suggested itself (to which of us I do not recollect) that a series of poems might be composed of two sorts. In the one, the incidents and agents were to be, in part at least, supernatural; and the excellence aimed at was to consist in the interesting of the affections by the dramatic truth of such emotions, as would naturally accompany such situations, supposing them real. And real in *this* sense they have been to every human being who, from whatever source of delusion, has at any time believed himself under supernatural agency. For the second class, subjects were to be chosen from ordinary life; the characters and incidents were to be such, as will be found in every village and its vicinity, where there is a meditative and feeling mind to seek after them, or to notice them, when they present themselves.

In this idea originated the plan of the "Lyrical Ballads"; in which it was agreed, that my endeavours should be directed to persons and characters supernatural, or at least romantic; yet so as to transfer from our inward nature a human interest and a semblance of truth sufficient to procure for these shadows of imagination that willing suspension of disbelief for the moment, which constitutes poetic faith. Mr. Wordsworth, on the other hand, was to propose to himself as his object, to give the charm of novelty to things of every day, and to excite a feeling analogous to the supernatural, by awakening the mind's attention from the lethargy of custom, and directing it to the loveliness and the wonders of the world before us; an inexhaustible treasure, but for which, in consequence of the film of familiarity and selfish solicitude we have eyes, yet see not, ears that hear not, and hearts that neither feel nor understand.

With this view I wrote "The Ancient Mariner," and was preparing among other poems, "The Dark Ladie," and the "Christabel," in which I should have more nearly realized my ideal, than I had done in my first attempt. But Mr. Wordsworth's industry had proved so much more successful, and the number of his poems so much greater, that my compositions, instead of forming a balance, appeared rather an interpolation of heterogeneous matter. Mr. Wordsworth added two or three poems written in his own character, in the impassioned, lofty, and sustained diction, which is characteristic of his genius. In this form the "Lyrical Ballads" were published; and were presented by him, as an *experiment,* whether subjects, which from their nature rejected the usual ornaments and extra-colloquial style of poems in general, might not be so managed in the language of ordinary life as to produce the pleasureable interest, which it is the peculiar business of poetry to impart. To the second edition he added a preface of considerable length; in which, notwithstanding some passages of apparently a contrary import, he was understood to contend for the extension of this style to poetry of all kinds, and to reject as vicious and indefensible all phrases and forms of style that were not included in what he (unfortunately, I think, adopting an equivocal expression) called the language of *real* life. From this preface, prefixed to poems in which it was impossible to deny the presence of original genius, however mistaken its direction might be deemed, arose the whole long-continued controversy. For from the conjunction of perceived power with supposed heresy I explain the inveteracy and in

[1] In 1797.

some instances, I grieve to say, the acrimonious passions, with which the controversy has been conducted by the assailants.

Had Mr. Wordsworth's poems been the silly, the childish things, which they were for a long time described as being; had they been really distinguished from the compositions of other poets merely by meanness of language and inanity of thought; had they indeed contained nothing more than what is found in the parodies and pretended imitations of them; they must have sunk at once, a dead weight, into the slough of oblivion, and have dragged the preface along with them. But year after year increased the number of Mr. Wordsworth's admirers. They were found too not in the lower classes of the reading public, but chiefly among young men of strong sensibility and meditative minds; and their admiration (inflamed perhaps in some degree by opposition) was distinguished by its intensity, I might almost say, by its *religious* fervor. These facts, and the intellectual energy of the author, which was more or less consciously felt, where it was outwardly and even boisterously denied, meeting with sentiments of aversion to his opinions, and of alarm at their consequences, produced an eddy of criticism, which would of itself have borne up the poems by the violence, with which it whirled them round and round. With many parts of this preface, in the sense attributed to them, and which the words undoubtedly seem to authorize; I never concurred; but on the contrary objected to them as erroneous in principle, and as contradictory (in appearance at least) both to other parts of the same preface, and to the author's own practice in the greater number of the poems themselves. Mr. Wordsworth in his recent collection has, I find, degraded this prefatory disquisition to the end of his second volume, to be read or not at the reader's choice. But he has not, as far as I can discover, announced any change in his poetic creed. At all events, considering it as the source of a controversy, in which I have been honored more than I

deserve by the frequent conjunction of my name with his, I think it expedient to declare once for all, in what points I coincide with his opinions, and in what points I altogether differ. But in order to render myself intelligible I must previously, in as few words as possible, explain my ideas, first, of a POEM; and secondly, of POETRY itself, in kind, and in *essence*.

The office of philosophical *disquisition* consists in just *distinction*; while it is the privilege of the philosopher to preserve himself constantly aware, that distinction is not division. In order to obtain adequate notions of any truth, we must intellectually separate its distinguishable parts; and this is the technical *process* of philosophy. But having so done, we must then restore them in our conceptions to the unity, in which they actually co-exist; and this is the *result* of philosophy. A poem contains the same elements as a prose composition; the difference therefore must consist in a different combination of them, in consequence of a different object being proposed. According to the difference of the object will be the difference of the combination. It is possible, that the object may be merely to facilitate the recollection of any given facts or observations by artificial arrangement; and the composition will be a poem, merely because it is distinguished from prose by metre, or by rhyme, or by both conjointly. In this, the lowest sense, a man might attribute the name of a poem to the well-known enumeration of the days in the several months;

Thirty days hath September,
April, June, and November, &c.

and others of the same class and purpose. And as a particular pleasure is found in anticipating the recurrence of sounds and quantities, all compositions that have this charm superadded, whatever be their contents, *may* be entitled poems.

So much for the superficial *form*. A difference of object and contents supplies an additional ground of distinction. The immediate purpose may be the communication of truths; either of truth absolute and demonstrable, as in works of science; or of facts experienced and recorded, as in history. Pleasure, and that of the highest and most permanent kind, may *result* from the *attainment* of the end; but it is not itself the immediate end. In other works the communication of pleasure may be the immediate purpose; and though truth, either moral or intellectual, ought to be the *ultimate* end, yet this will distinguish the character of the author, not the class to which the work belongs. Blest indeed is that state of society, in which the immediate purpose would be baffled by the perversion of the proper ultimate end; in which no charm of diction or imagery could exempt the Bathyllus even of an Anacreon, or the Alexis of Virgil, from disgust and aversion![2]

But the communication of pleasure may be the immediate object of a work not metrically composed; and that object may have been in a high degree attained, as in novels and romances. Would then the mere superaddition of metre, with or without rhyme, entitle *these* to the name of poems? The answer is, that nothing can permanently please, which does not contain in itself the reason why it is so, and not otherwise. If metre be superadded, all other parts must be made consonant with it. They must be such, as to justify the perpetual and distinct attention to each part, which an exact correspondent recurrence of accent and sound are calculated to excite. The final definition then, so deduced, may be thus worded. A poem is that species of composition, which is opposed to works of science, by proposing for its *immediate* object pleasure, not truth; and from all other species (having *this* object in common with it) it is discriminated by proposing to itself such delight from the *whole,* as is compatible with a distinct gratification from each component *part.*

Controversy is not seldom excited in consequence of the disputants attaching each a different meaning to the same word; and in few instances has this been more striking, than in disputes concerning the present subject. If a man chooses to call every composition a poem, which is rhyme, or measure,

or both, I must leave his opinion uncontroverted. The distinction is at least competent to characterize the writer's intention. If it were subjoined, that the whole is likewise entertaining or affecting, as a tale, or as a series of interesting reflections, I of course admit this as another fit ingredient of a poem, and an additional merit. But if the definition sought for be that of a *legitimate* poem, I answer, it must be one, the parts of which mutually support and explain each other; all in their proportion harmonizing with, and supporting the purpose and known influences of metrical arrangement. The philosophic critics of all ages coincide with the ultimate judgement of all countries, in equally denying the praises of a just poem, on the one hand, to a series of striking lines or distiches, each of which, absorbing the whole attention of the reader to itself, disjoins it from its context, and makes it a separate whole, instead of an harmonizing part; and on the other hand, to an unsustained composition, from which the reader collects rapidly the general result, unattracted by the component parts. The reader should be carried forward, not merely or chiefly by the mechanical impulse of curiosity, or by a restless desire to arrive at the final solution; but by the pleasureable activity of mind excited by the attractions of the journey itself. Like the motion of a serpent, which the Egyptians made the emblem of intellectual power; or like the path of sound through the air; at every step he pauses and half recedes, and from the retrogressive movement collects the force which again carries him onward. "Præcipitandus est *liber* spiritus," says Petronius Arbiter most happily.[3] The epithet, *liber,* here balances the preceding verb; and it is not easy to conceive more meaning condensed in fewer words.

But if this should be admitted as a satisfactory character of a poem, we have still to seek for a definition of poetry. The writings of PLATO, and Bishop TAYLOR, and the "Theoria Sacra" of BURNET, furnish undeniable proofs that poetry

---

[2]Anacreon's Ode 29 to Bathyllus, and Virgil's *Eclogue* 2.

[3]"The free spirit must be hurried onward." Petronius, *Satyricon,* 118.

of the highest kind may exist without metre, and even without the contra-distinguishing objects of a poem. The first chapter of Isaiah (indeed a very large portion of the whole book) is poetry in the most emphatic sense; yet it would be not less irrational than strange to assert, that pleasure, and not truth, was the immediate object of the prophet. In short, whatever *specific* import we attach to the word, poetry, there will be found involved in it, as a necessary consequence, that a poem of any length neither can be, nor ought to be, all poetry. Yet if an harmonious whole is to be produced, the remaining parts must be preserved in *keeping* with the poetry; and this can be no otherwise effected than by such a studied selection and artificial arrangement, as will partake of *one*, though not a *peculiar* property of poetry. And this again can be no other than the property of exciting a more continuous and equal attention than the language of prose aims at, whether colloquial or written.

My own conclusions on the nature of poetry, in the strictest use of the word, have been in part anticipated in the preceding disquisition on the fancy and imagination. What is poetry? is so nearly the same question with, what is a poet? that the answer to the one is involved in the solution of the other. For it is a distinction resulting from the poetic genius itself, which sustains and modifies the images, thoughts, and emotions of the poet's own mind.

The poet, described in *ideal* perfection, brings the whole soul of man into activity, with the subordination of its faculties to each other, according to their relative worth and dignity. He diffuses a tone and spirit of unity, that blends, and (as it were) *fuses*, each into each, by that synthetic and magical power, to which we have exclusively appropriated the name of imagination. This power, first put in action by the will and understanding, and retained under their irremissive, though gentle and unnoticed, controul (*laxis effertur habenis*)[4] reveals itself in the balance or reconciliation of opposite or discordant qualities: of sameness, with difference; of the general, with the concrete; the idea, with the image; the individual, with the representative; the sense of novelty and freshness, with old and familiar objects; a more than usual state of emotion, with more than usual order; judgement ever awake and steady self-possession, with enthusiasm and feeling profound or vehement; and while it blends and harmonizes the natural and the artificial, still subordinates art to nature; the manner to the matter; and our admiration of the poet to our sympathy with the poetry. "Doubtless," as Sir John Davies observes of the soul (and his words may with slight alteration be applied, and even more appropriately, to the poetic IMAGINATION)

Doubtless this could not be, but that she turns
Bodies to spirit by sublimation strange,
As fire converts to fire the things it burns,
As we our food into our nature change.

From their gross matter she abstracts their forms,
And draws a kind of quintessence from things;
Which to her proper nature she transforms
To bear them light on her celestial wings.

Thus does she, when from individual states
She doth abstract the universal kinds;
Which then re-clothed in divers names and fates
Steal access through our senses to our minds.[5]

Finally, GOOD SENSE is the BODY of poetic genius, FANCY its DRAPERY, MOTION its LIFE, and IMAGINATION the SOUL that is everywhere, and in each; and forms all into one graceful and intelligent whole.

[4] "Carried on with slackened reins." Petrarch, *Epistola Barbato Sulmonensi*, 39.
[5] Sir John Davies, *Nosce Teipsum: Of the Soule of Man and the Immortality Thereof*, 4:11–13.

Percy Bysshe Shelley

1792–1822

The most radical English poet since Milton, Percy Bysshe Shelley wrote in proud rebellion against his conservative and aristocratic roots: His grandfather was a land-owning baronet, his father a member of Parliament. Shelley was educated at Eton and Oxford, from which he was sent down at the age of eighteen for publishing a tract advocating atheism. In London, he came under the influence of the philosopher William Godwin, whose *Political Justice* questioned the foundations of the English state. Though already married to Harriet Westbrook, Shelley fell in love with Godwin's daughter Mary, and in 1814 eloped with her to France; they were able to marry only after Harriet's suicide, in 1816. In financial straits and anathematized by the British public for his political opinions as well as his sexual immorality, Shelley moved to Italy the next year. There he wrote his most impressive works: *Prometheus Unbound* (1819), *The Masque of Anarchy* (1819), *Epipsychidion* (1821), and *Adonais* (1821). He had just embarked on his most ambitious poem, *The Triumph of Life,* when he drowned in July of 1822 in a boating accident in the Gulf of Spezia.

Like Sir Philip Sidney's *An Apology for Poetry,* Shelley's *A Defence of Poetry* (written in 1821, though not published until 1840) is a reply to Plato's attacks on mimetic art in *Republic,* Book X (p. 29). It should not be surprising that in the period after Kant and his successors, Shelley's riposte would depend on the notion of mental faculties and their powers. He thus begins the *Defence* with the parallel dialectical oppositions of *tò logizeín* and *tò poieîn,* reason and imagination, analysis and synthesis. His purpose is to refute Plato's attack on the mimetic artist as inferior to the artisan in knowledge and understanding by insisting that the poetic faculty is equal and complementary to logical reason.

The reader who scans *A Defence of Poetry* in search of a systematic approach to Romantic critical theory, however, will be disappointed. Although the essay begins austerely enough with what appears to be a set of logical distinctions, philosophical rigor is soon abandoned. Indeed, some readers may find Shelley's prose disjointed and contradictory, apparently unplanned in organization, at times almost incoherent. But if we set aside system and rigor and attend instead to Shelley's ideals and imagery, the essay yields an inspiring vision, rather like that at the conclusion of *Adonais,* of how the Romantic poets saw themselves and the place of poetry in human society. Perhaps the first and third sections of *A Defence of Poetry* (pp. 229–33 and 243–46) should be read as we read a lyric, through key metaphors.

The first of these metaphors likens the mind to an Aeolian lyre, struck to melody by the wind of its "external and internal impressions." Shelley develops this metaphor further: The mind produces not just melody but harmony as well, and the spontaneous song of the child is an expression of delight in this harmony, an effect the child prolongs by recalling its cause. It is here, deep in human nature, that Shelley locates the impulse to produce art, for poetry is nothing but the adult analogy to this process.

Toward the end of the *Defence,* in discussing the haphazard nature of poetic inspiration Shelley likens the mind of the poet to "a fading coal which some invisible influence, like an inconstant wind, awakens to transitory brightness." Again, the external world is like a wind, forcible but insubstantial, while the mind is like a physical object that can make light or heat or melody. Perhaps nothing suggests Shelley's deep affinity to Plato more than this; it is as if the mind and its ideas are real, while the external physical world is not.

Shelley is most Platonic in opposition to his master. Where Plato ejected the poets from his Republic, Shelley makes them its masters, calling them "the unacknowledged legislators of the World." He begins with the idea that "every original language near to its source is in itself the chaos of a cyclic [i.e. epic] poem." We might think of poetry as a special use of language that arranges a harmony between sound and meaning, but all language does that. Whoever creates any new word or names any unnamed feature of the sensual world is, in effect, a poet. Language is everywhere a network of living, dying, and dead metaphors, statements of the likenesses between one aspect of experience and another. We talk of "the iron curtain," we play the game of "cat's cradle": Both are poetic metaphors. And language embalms metaphors in its etymologies: At one time the verb *transgress* literally signified "straying from the herd." In shaping language, the poets — these innova-tors of language, who are not necessarily identical with the canonized poets from Homer to Shelley himself — have in effect shaped human thought, and thus molded society and human relations.

But it is not enough for Shelley to find a poetic act somewhere behind any use of language. He claims that poetry, in any age removed from the primitive *source* of language, recaptures for humanity, by metaphor and harmony, the immediacy of life and experience, an immediacy that is lost by the use of logical, analytical thought and language. For Shelley, the world is veiled from human participation by dead thought and language, and it is the poets alone who are able to penetrate and "lift the veil from the hidden beauty of the world."

In the course of this argument, the words *poetry* and *poet* shift their ground away from pure aesthetics. A poet is anyone who can synthesize a vision of the world and express that apprehended synthesis in language. Thus the great philosophers, Plato among them, are revealed to be nothing other than poets. And conversely, since poets' visions are necessarily of the eternal truths of the human spirit, Shakespeare, Dante, and Milton must be seen as "philosophers of the very loftiest power."

The development of these general ideas is interrupted by a long middle section (pp. 233–43), which was inspired less by Plato than by *The Four Ages of Poetry* (1820), a pamphlet by Shelley's friend, the satirist Thomas Love Peacock. Perhaps influenced by the Italian philosopher Giambattista Vico, Peacock posited a cyclical theory of the history of Western civilization: Both history and poetry had by then gone through two cycles with four phases in each.

Each cycle begins with an "age of iron," like the archaic period or the Middle Ages, when the poet is essentially a bard paid to flatter in verse the exploits of mili-tary chieftains. There follows an "age of gold," a tough but harmonious civilization, like Periclean Athens or Elizabethan England, which produces the finest poetry, the

Homers and the Shakespeares. From then on, however, the increasing encroachment of scientific knowledge limits the scope of poetry. There arrives an "age of silver," a polished and classicizing civilization that gives rise to the Virgils and the Miltons and Popes. Finally comes the decadence of the "age of brass," in which poetry is mere nostalgic archaism, like the later Roman Empire — or the English Romantic period. At last, the destruction of civilization itself — the fall of the Roman Empire in the first cycle — puts an end to the decay and allows a new age of iron to begin. The bulk of *A Defence of Poetry* is a reply to Peacock's attack on Romantics and Romanticism, which takes the form of a progressive (rather than a cyclical) theory of history and of the poetry that grew up alongside (and in Shelley's view helped to form) political institutions.

Selected Bibliography

Bloom, Harold. *Shelley's Mythmaking.* New Haven: Yale University Press, 1959.

Damm, Robert F. *A Tale of Human Power: Art and Life in Shelley's Poetic Theory.* Oxford, OH: Miami University Press, 1970.

Gallagher, Catherine. "Formalism and Time." *Modern Language Quarterly* 61, no.1 (2000): 229–51.

Grabo, C. H. *The Magic Plant: The Growth of Shelley's Thought.* Chapel Hill: University of North Carolina Press, 1936.

Milnes, Tim. "Centre and Circumference: Shelley's Defence of Philosophy." *European Romantic Review* 15, no.1 (2004): 3–22.

Notopoulos, J. A. *The Platonism of Shelley.* Durham: Duke University Press, 1949.

Schulze, Earl J. *Shelley's Theory of Poetry: A Reappraisal.* The Hague: Mouton, 1966.

Shawcross, John, ed. *Shelley's Literary and Philosophical Criticism.* London: H. Frowde, 1909.

Solve, Melvin T. *Shelley: His Theory of Poetry.* Chicago: University of Chicago Press, 1927.

A Defence of Poetry

Or Remarks Suggested by an Essay Entitled "The Four Ages of Poetry"

According to one mode of regarding those two classes of mental action, which are called reason and imagination, the former may be considered as mind contemplating the relations borne by one thought to another, however produced; and the latter, as mind acting upon those thoughts so as to colour them with its own light, and composing from them, as from elements, other thoughts, each containing within itself the principle of its own integrity. The one is the τὸ ποιεῖν,[1] or the principle of synthesis, and has for its objects those forms which are common to universal nature and existence itself; the other is the τὸ λογίζειν,[2] or principle of analysis, and its action regards the relations of things, simply as relations; considering thoughts, not in their integral unity, but as the algebraical representations which conduct to certain general results. Reason is the enumeration of quantities

[1]Making.
[2]Reasoning.

already known: imagination is the perception of the value of those quantities, both separately and as a whole. Reason respects the differences, and imagination the similitudes of things. Reason is to Imagination as the instrument to the agent, as the body to the spirit, as the shadow to the substance.

Poetry, in a general sense, may be defined to be "the expression of the imagination": and poetry is connate with the origin of man. Man is an instrument over which a series of external and internal impressions are driven, like the alternations of an ever-changing wind over an Æolian lyre, which move it by their motion to ever-changing melody. But there is a principle within the human being, and perhaps within all sentient beings, which acts otherwise than in the lyre, and produces not melody alone, but harmony, by an internal adjustment of the sounds or motions thus excited to the impressions which excite them. It is as if the lyre could accommodate its chords to the motions of that which strikes them, in a determined proportion of sound; even as the musician can accommodate his voice to the sound of the lyre. A child at play by itself will express its delight by its voice and motions; and every inflexion of tone and every gesture will bear exact relation to a corresponding antitype in the pleasurable impressions which awakened it: it will be the reflected image of that impression; and as the lyre trembles and sounds after the wind has died away, so the child seeks, by prolonging in its voice and motions the duration of the effect, to prolong also a consciousness of the cause. In relation to the objects which delight a child, these expressions are what poetry is to higher objects. The savage (for the savage is to ages what the child is to years) expresses the emotions produced in him by surrounding objects in a similar manner; and language and gesture, together with plastic or pictorial imitation, become the image of the combined effect of those objects, and of his apprehension of them. Man in society, with all his passions and his pleasures, next becomes the object of the passions and pleasures of man; an additional class of emotions produces an augmented treasure of expressions; and language, gesture, and the imitative arts, become at once the representation and the medium, the pencil and the picture, the chisel and the statue, the chord and the harmony. The social sympathies, or those laws from which as from its elements society results,

begin to develope themselves from the moment that two human beings coexist; the future is contained within the present as the plant within the seed; and equality, diversity, unity, contrast, mutual dependence, become the principles alone capable of affording the motives according to which the will of a social being is determined to action, inasmuch as he is social; and constitute pleasure in sensation, virtue in sentiment, beauty in art, truth in reasoning, and love in the intercourse of kind. Hence men, even in the infancy of society, observe a certain order in their words and actions, distinct from that of the objects and the impressions represented by them, all expression being subject to the laws of that from which it proceeds. But let us dismiss those more general considerations which might involve an enquiry into the principles of society itself, and restrict our view to the manner in which the imagination is expressed upon its forms.

In the youth of the world, men dance and sing and imitate natural objects, observing in these actions, as in all others, a certain rhythm or order. And, although all men observe a similar, they observe not the same order, in the motions of the dance, in the melody of the song, in the combinations of language, in the series of their imitations of natural objects. For there is a certain order or rhythm belonging to each of these classes of mimetic representation, from which the hearer and the spectator receive an intenser and purer pleasure than from any other: the sense of an approximation to this order has been called taste, by modern writers. Every man in the infancy of art, observes an order which approximates more or less closely to that from which this highest delight results: but the diversity is not sufficiently marked, as that its gradations should be sensible, except in those instances where the predominance of this faculty of approximation to the beautiful (for so we may be permitted to name the relation between this highest pleasure and its cause) is very great. Those in whom it exists in excess are poets, in the most universal sense of the word; and the pleasure resulting from the manner in which they express the influence of society or nature upon their own minds, communicates itself to others, and gathers a sort of reduplication from that community. Their language is vitally metaphorical; that is, it marks the before unapprehended relations of things, and perpetuates their apprehension, until the words which represent them, become through time signs for portions or classes of thoughts instead of pictures of integral thoughts; and then if no new poets should arise to create afresh the associations which have been thus disorganized, language will be dead to all the nobler purposes of human intercourse. These similitudes or relations are finely said by Lord Bacon to be "the same footsteps of nature impressed upon the various subjects of the world"[3] — and he considers the faculty which perceives them as the storehouse of axioms common to all knowledge. In the infancy of society every author is necessarily a poet, because language itself is poetry; and to be a poet is to apprehend the true and the beautiful, in a word the good which exists in the relation, subsisting, first between existence and perception, and secondly between perception and expression. Every original language near to its source is in itself the chaos of a cyclic poem: the copiousness of lexicography and the distinctions of grammar are the works of a later age, and are merely the catalogue and the form of the creations of Poetry.

But Poets, or those who imagine and express this indestructible order, are not only the authors of language and of music, of the dance and architecture and statuary and painting: they are the institutors of laws, and the founders of civil society and the inventors of the arts of life and the teachers, who draw into a certain propinquity with the beautiful and the true that partial apprehension of the agencies of the invisible world which is called religion. Hence all original religions are allegorical, or susceptible of allegory, and like Janus have a double face of false and true. Poets, according to the circumstances of the age and nation in which they appeared, were called in the earlier epochs of the world legislators or prophets: a poet essentially comprises and unites both these characters.[4] For he not only beholds intensely the present as it is, and discovers those laws according to which present things ought to be ordered, but he beholds the future in the present, and his thoughts are the germs of the flower and the fruit of latest time. Not that I

assert poets to be prophets in the gross sense of the word, or that they can foretell the form as surely as they foreknow the spirit of events: such is the pretence of superstition which would make poetry an attribute of prophecy, rather than prophecy an attribute of poetry. A Poet participates in the eternal, the infinite, and the one; as far as relates to his conceptions, time and place and number are not. The grammatical forms which express the moods of time, and the difference of persons and the distinction of place are convertible with respect to the highest poetry without injuring it as poetry, and the choruses of Æschylus, and the book of Job, and Dante's Paradise would afford, more than any other writings, examples of this fact, if the limits of this essay did not forbid citation. The creations of sculpture, painting, and music, are illustrations still more decisive.

Language, colour, form, and religious and civil habits of action are all the instruments and materials of poetry; they may be called poetry by that figure of speech which considers the effect as a synonime of the cause. But poetry in a more restricted sense expresses those arrangements of language, and especially metrical language, which are created by that imperial faculty, whose throne is curtained within the invisible nature of man. And this springs from the nature itself of language, which is a more direct representation of the actions and passions of our internal being, and is susceptible of more various and delicate combinations, than colour, form, or motion, and is more plastic and obedient to the controul of that faculty of which it is the creation. For language is arbitrarily produced by the Imagination and has relation to thoughts alone; but all other materials, instruments and conditions of art, have relations among each other, which limit and interpose between conception and expression. The former is as a mirror which reflects, the latter as a cloud which enfeebles, the light of which both are mediums of communication. Hence the fame of sculptors, painters and musicians, although the intrinsic powers of the great masters of these arts, may yield in no degree to that of those who have employed language as the hieroglyphic of their thoughts, has never equalled that of poets in the restricted sense of the term; as two performers of equal skill will produce unequal effects from

[3]Francis Bacon, *The Advancement of Learning.* 3:1.
[4]Cf. Philip Sidney, *An Apology for Poetry;* see p. 115.

We have thus circumscribed the meaning of the word Poetry within the limits of that art which is the most familiar and the most perfect expression of the faculty itself. It is necessary however to make the circle still narrower, and to determine the distinction between measured and unmeasured language; for the popular division into prose and verse is inadmissible in accurate philosophy.

Sounds as well as thoughts have relation both between each other and towards that which they represent, and a perception of the order of those relations has always been found connected with a perception of the order of the relations of thoughts. Hence the language of poets has ever affected a certain uniform and harmonious recurrence of sound, without which it were not poetry, and which is scarcely less indispensable to the communication of its influence, than the words themselves, without reference to that peculiar order. Hence the vanity of translation; it were as wise to cast a violet into a crucible that you might discover the formal principle of its colour and odour, as seek to transfuse from one language into another the creations of a poet. The plant must spring again from its seed or it will bear no flower — and this is the burthen of the curse of Babel.

An observation of the regular mode of the recurrence of this harmony in the language of poetical minds, together with its relation to music, produced metre, or a certain system of traditional forms of harmony of language. Yet it is by no means essential that a poet should accommodate his language to this traditional form, so that the harmony which is its spirit, be observed. The practise is indeed convenient and popular, and to be preferred, especially in such composition as includes much form and action: but every great poet must inevitably innovate upon the example of his predecessors in the exact structure of his peculiar versification. The distinction between poets

and prose writers is a vulgar error. The distinction between philosophers and poets has been anticipated. Plato was essentially a poet — the truth and splendour of his imagery and the melody of his language is the most intense that it is possible to conceive. He rejected the measure of the epic, dramatic, and lyrical forms, because he sought to kindle a harmony in thoughts divested of shape and action, and he forbore to invent any regular plan of rhythm which would include, under determinate forms, the varied pauses of his style. Cicero sought to imitate the cadence of his periods but with little success. Lord Bacon was a poet.[5] His language has a sweet and majestic rhythm, which satisfies the sense, no less than the almost superhuman wisdom of his philosophy satisfies the intellect; it is a strain which distends, and then bursts the circumference of the hearer's mind, and pours itself forth together with it into the universal element with which it has perpetual sympathy. All the authors of revolutions in opinion are not only necessarily poets as they are inventors, nor even as their words unveil the permanent analogy of things by images which participate in the life of truth; but as their periods are harmonious and rhythmical and contain in themselves the elements of verse; being the echo of the eternal music. Nor are those supreme poets, who have employed traditional forms of rhythm on account of the form and action of their subjects, less capable of perceiving and teaching the truth of things, than those who have omitted that form. Shakespeare, Dante and Milton (to confine ourselves to modern writers) are philosophers of the very loftiest power.

A poem is the very image of life expressed in its eternal truth. There is this difference between a story and a poem, that a story is a catalogue of detached facts, which have no other bond of connexion than time, place, circumstance, cause and effect; the other is the creation of actions according to the unchangeable forms of human nature, as existing in the mind of the creator, which is itself the image of all other minds. The one is partial, and applies only to a definite period of time, and a certain combination of events which can never again recur; the other is universal, and contains within

⁵See the *Filum Labyrinthi* and the *Essay on Death* particularly. [Shelley]

itself the germ of a relation to whatever motives or actions have place in the possible varieties of human nature. Time, which destroys the beauty and the use of the story of particular facts, stript of the poetry which should invest them, augments that of Poetry, and for ever developes new and wonderful applications of the eternal truth which it contains. Hence epitomes have been called the moths of just history; they eat out the poetry of it. The story of particular facts is as a mirror which obscures and distorts that which should be beautiful: Poetry is a mirror which makes beautiful that which is distorted.

The parts of a composition may be poetical, without the composition as a whole being a poem. A single sentence may be considered as a whole though it be found in a series of unassimilated portions; a single word even may be a spark of inextinguishable thought. And thus all the great historians, Herodotus, Plutarch, Livy, were poets; and although the plan of these writers, especially that of Livy, restrained them from developing this faculty in its highest degree, they make copious and ample amends for their subjection, by filling all the interstices of their subjects with living images.

Having determined what is poetry, and who are poets, let us proceed to estimate its effects upon society.

Poetry is ever accompanied with pleasure: all spirits on which it falls, open themselves to receive the wisdom which is mingled with its delight. In the infancy of the world, neither poets themselves nor their auditors are fully aware of the excellence of poetry: for it acts in a divine and unapprehended manner, beyond and above consciousness; and it is reserved for future generations to contemplate and measure the mighty cause and effect in all the strength and splendour of their union. Even in modern times, no living poet ever arrived at the fulness of his fame; the jury which sits in judgement upon a poet, belonging as he does to all time, must be composed of his peers: it must be impanelled by Time from the selectest of the wise of many generations. A Poet is a nightingale, who sits in darkness and sings to cheer its own solitude with sweet sounds; his auditors are as men entranced by the melody of an unseen musician, who feel that they are moved and softened, yet know not whence or why. The poems of Homer and his contemporaries were the delight of infant Greece; they were the elements of that social system which is the column upon which all succeeding civilization has reposed. Homer embodied the ideal perfection of his age in human character; nor can we doubt that those who read his verses were awakened to an ambition of becoming like to Achilles, Hector and Ulysses: the truth and beauty of friendship, patriotism and persevering devotion to an object, were unveiled to the depths in these immortal creations: the sentiments of the auditors must have been refined and enlarged by a sympathy with such great and lovely impersonations, until from admiring they imitated, and from imitation they identified themselves with the objects of their admiration. Nor let it be objected, that these characters are remote from moral perfection, and that they can by no means be considered as edifying patterns for general imitation. Every epoch under names more or less specious has deified its peculiar errors; Revenge is the naked Idol of the worship of a semi-barbarous age; and Self-deceit is the veiled Image of unknown evil before which luxury and satiety lie prostrate. But a poet considers the vices of his contemporaries as the temporary dress in which his creations must be arrayed, and which cover without concealing the eternal proportions of their beauty. An epic or dramatic personage is understood to wear them around his soul, as he may the antient armour or the modern uniform around his body; whilst it is easy to conceive a dress more graceful than either. The beauty of the internal nature cannot be so far concealed by its accidental vesture, but that the spirit of its form shall communicate itself to the very disguise, and indicate the shape it hides from the manner in which it is worn. A majestic form and graceful motions will express themselves through the most barbarous and tasteless costume. Few poets of the highest class have chosen to exhibit the beauty of their conceptions in its naked truth and splendour; and it is doubtful whether the alloy of costume, habit, etc., be not necessary to temper this planetary music for mortal ears.

The whole objection however of the immorality of poetry rests upon a misconception of the manner in which poetry acts to produce the moral improvement of man. Ethical science arranges the elements which poetry has created, and propounds schemes and proposes examples of civil and domestic life: nor is it for want of admirable doctrines that men hate, and despise, and censure, and deceive, and subjugate one another. But Poetry acts in another and diviner manner. It awakens and enlarges the mind itself by rendering it the receptacle of a thousand unapprehended combinations of thought. Poetry lifts the veil from the hidden beauty of the world, and makes familiar objects be as if they were not familiar; it reproduces all that it represents, and the impersonations clothed in its Elysian light stand thenceforward in the minds of those who have once contemplated them, as memorials of that gentle and exalted content which extends itself over all thoughts and actions with which it coexists. The great secret of morals is Love; or a going out of our own nature, and an identification of ourselves with the beautiful which exists in thought, action, or person, not our own. A man, to be greatly good, must imagine intensely and comprehensively; he must put himself in the place of another and of many others; the pains and pleasures of his species must become his own. The great instrument of moral good is the imagination; and poetry administers to the effect by acting upon the cause. Poetry enlarges the circumference of the imagination by replenishing it with thoughts of ever new delight, which have the power of attracting and assimilating of their own nature all other thoughts, and which form new intervals and interstices whose void for ever craves fresh food. Poetry strengthens that faculty which is the organ of the moral nature of man, in the same manner as exercise strengthens a limb. A Poet therefore would do ill to embody his own conceptions of right and wrong, which are usually those of his place and time, in his poetical creations, which participate in neither. By this assumption of the inferior office of interpreting the effect, in which perhaps after all he might acquit himself but imperfectly, he would resign the glory in a participation in the cause. There was little danger that Homer, or any of the eternal poets, should have so far misunderstood themselves as to have abdicated this throne of their widest dominion. Those in whom the poetical faculty, though great, is less intense, as Euripides,

Lucan, Tasso, Spenser, have frequently affected a moral aim, and the effect of their poetry is diminished in exact proportion to the degree in which they compel us to advert to this purpose.

Homer and the cyclic poets were followed at a certain interval by the dramatic and lyrical Poets of Athens, who flourished contemporaneously with all that is most perfect in the kindred expressions of the poetical faculty; architecture, painting, music, the dance, sculpture, philosophy, and we may add the forms of civil life. For although the scheme of Athenian society was deformed by many imperfections which the poetry existing in Chivalry and Christianity have erased from the habits and institutions of modern Europe; yet never at any other period has so much energy, beauty, and virtue, been developed; never was blind strength and stubborn form so disciplined and rendered subject to the will of man, or that will less repugnant to the dictates of the beautiful and the true, as during the century which preceded the death of Socrates. Of no other epoch in the history of our species have we records and fragments stamped so visibly with the image of the divinity in man. But it is Poetry alone, in form, in action, or in language, which has rendered this epoch memorable above all others, and the storehouse of examples to everlasting time. For written poetry existed at that epoch simultaneously with the other arts, and it is an idle enquiry to demand which gave and which received the light, which all as from a common focus have scattered over the darkest periods of succeeding time. We know no more of cause and effect than a constant conjunction of events: Poetry is ever found to coexist with whatever other arts contribute to the happiness and perfection of man. I appeal to what has already been established to distinguish between the cause and the effect.

It was at the period here adverted to, that the Drama had its birth; and however a succeeding writer may have equalled or surpassed those few great specimens of the Athenian drama which have been preserved to us, it is indisputable that the art itself never was understood or practised according to the true philosophy of it, as at Athens. For the Athenians employed language, action, music, painting, the dance, and religious institutions, to produce a common effect in the representation of the highest idealisms of passion and of power; each division in the art was made perfect in its kind by artists of the most consummate skill, and was disciplined into a beautiful proportion and unity one towards another. On the modern stage a few only of the elements capable of expressing the image of the poet's conception are employed at once. We have tragedy without music and dancing; and music and dancing without the highest impersonations of which they are the fit accompaniment, and both without religion and solemnity. Religious institution has indeed been usually banished from the stage. Our system of divesting the actor's face of a mask, on which the many expressions appropriated to his dramatic character might be moulded into one permanent and unchanging expression, is favourable only to a partial and inharmonious effect; it is fit for nothing but a monologue, where all the attention may be directed to some great master of ideal mimicry. The modern practice of blending comedy with tragedy, though liable to great abuse in point of practise, is undoubtedly an extension of the dramatic circle; but the comedy should be as in *King Lear,* universal, ideal, and sublime. It is perhaps the intervention of this principle which determines the balance in favour of *King Lear* against the *Œdipus Tyrannus* or the *Agamemnon,* or, if you will, the trilogies with which they are connected;[6] unless the intense power of the choral poetry, especially that of the latter, should be considered as restoring the equilibrium. *King Lear,* if it can sustain this comparison, may be judged to be the most perfect specimen of the dramatic art existing in the world; in spite of the narrow conditions to which the poet was subjected by the ignorance of the philosophy of the Drama which has prevailed in modern Europe. Calderón in his religious *Autos*[7] has attempted to fulfil some of the high conditions of dramatic representation

neglected by Shakespeare; such as the establishing a relation between the drama and religion, and the accommodating them to music and dancing; but he omits the observation of conditions still more important, and more is lost than gained by a substitution of the rigidly-defined and ever-repeated idealisms of a distorted superstition for the living impersonations of the truth of human passion.

But we digress. — The Author of the Four Ages of Poetry[8] has prudently omitted to dispute on the effect of the Drama upon life and manners. For, if I know the knight by the device of his shield, I have only to inscribe Philoctetes or Agamemnon or Othello[9] upon mine to put to flight the giant sophisms which have enchanted him, as the mirror of intolerable light, though on the arm of one of the weakest of the Paladins, could blind and scatter whole armies of necromancers and pagans. The connexion of scenic exhibitions with the improvement or corruption of the manners of men, has been universally recognized: in other words, the presence or absence of poetry in its most perfect and universal form has been found to be connected with good and evil in conduct and habit. The corruption which has been imputed to the drama as an effect, begins, when the poetry employed in its constitution ends: I appeal to the history of manners whether the periods of the growth of the one and the decline of the other have not corresponded with an exactness equal to any other example of moral cause and effect.

The drama at Athens, or wheresoever else it may have approached to its perfection, coexisted with the moral and intellectual greatness of the age. The tragedies of the Athenian poets are as mirrors in which the spectator beholds himself, under a thin disguise of circumstance, stript of all but that ideal perfection and energy which every one feels to be the internal type of all that he loves, admires, and would become. The imagination is enlarged by a sympathy with pains and passions so mighty, that they distend in their

---

[6]The *Agamemnon* by Aeschylus is the first play of the *Oresteia* trilogy. Sophocles' *Oedipus Tyrannos* is not part of an extant trilogy, though he wrote plays connected with the Oedipus story twenty years earlier *(Antigone)* and twenty years later *(Oedipus at Colonus).*

[7]The *autos* of the Spanish dramatist Calderón (1600–1681) were short religious allegorical dramas.

[8]Shelley's friend, Thomas Love Peacock (1785–1866).

[9]Tragic protagonists of Sophocles, Aeschylus, and Shakespeare, respectively.

conception the capacity of that by which they are conceived; the good affections are strengthened by pity, indignation, terror and sorrow; and an exalted calm is prolonged from the satiety of this high exercise of them into the tumult of familiar life; even crime is disarmed of half its horror and all its contagion by being represented as the fatal consequence of the unfathomable agencies of nature: error is thus divested of its wilfulness; men can no longer cherish it as the creation of their choice. In a drama of the highest order there is little food for censure or hatred; it teaches rather self-knowledge and self-respect. Neither the eye nor the mind can see itself, unless reflected upon that which it resembles. The drama, so long as it continues to express poetry, is as a prismatic and many-sided mirror, which collects the brightest rays of human nature and divides and reproduces them from the simplicity of these elementary forms, and touches them with majesty and beauty, and multiplies all that it reflects, and endows it with the power of propagating its like wherever it may fall.

But in periods of the decay of social life, the drama sympathizes with that decay. Tragedy becomes a cold imitation of the form of the great masterpieces of antiquity, divested of all harmonious accompaniment of the kindred arts; and often the very form misunderstood: or a weak attempt to teach certain doctrines, which the writer considers as moral truths; and which are usually no more than specious flatteries of some gross vice or weakness with which the author in common with his auditors are infected. Hence what has been called the classical and domestic drama. Addison's *Cato* is a specimen of the one; and would it were not superfluous to cite examples of the other? To such purposes Poetry cannot be made subservient. Poetry is a sword of lightning, ever unsheathed, which consumes the scabbard that would contain it. And thus we observe that all dramatic writings of this nature are unimaginative in a singular degree; they affect sentiment and passion; which, divested of imagination, are other names for caprice and appetite. The period in our own history of the grossest degradation of the drama is the reign of Charles II when all forms in which poetry had been accustomed to be expressed became hymns to the triumph of kingly power over liberty and virtue. Milton stood

alone illuminating an age unworthy of him. At such periods the calculating principle pervades all the forms of dramatic exhibition, and poetry ceases to be expressed upon them. Comedy loses its ideal universality: wit succeeds to humour; we laugh from self-complacency and triumph instead of pleasure; malignity, sarcasm and contempt, succeed to sympathetic merriment; we hardly laugh, but we smile. Obscenity, which is ever blasphemy against the divine beauty in life, becomes, from the very veil which it assumes, more active if less disgusting: it is a monster for which the corruption of society for ever brings forth new food, which it devour's in secret.

The drama being that form under which a greater number of modes of expression of poetry are susceptible of being combined than any other, the connexion of poetry and social good is more observable in the drama than in whatever other form: and it is indisputable that the highest perfection of human society has ever corresponded with the highest dramatic excellence; and that the corruption or the extinction of the drama in a nation where it has once flourished, is a mark of a corruption of manners, and an extinction of the energies which sustain the soul of social life. But, as Machiavelli says of political institutions, that life may be preserved and renewed, if men should arise capable of bringing back the drama to its principles. And this is true with respect to poetry in its most extended sense: all language, institution and form, require not only to be produced but to be sustained: the office and character of a poet participates in the divine nature as regards providence, no less than as regards creation.

Civil war, the spoils of Asia, and the fatal predominance first of the Macedonian, and then of the Roman arms were so many symbols of the extinction or suspension of the creative faculty in Greece. The bucolic writers, who found patronage under the lettered tyrants of Sicily and Egypt, were the latest representatives of its most glorious reign. Their poetry is intensely melodious; like the odour of the tuberose, it overcomes and sickens the spirit with excess of sweetness; whilst the poetry of the preceding age was as a meadow-gale of June mingles the fragrance of all the flowers of the field, and adds a quickening and harmonizing spirit of its own which endows the sense with a power of sustaining its extreme delight. The bucolic and erotic delicacy in written poetry is correlative with that softness in statuary, music, and the kindred arts, and even in manners and institutions which distinguished the epoch to which we now refer. Nor is it the poetical faculty itself, or any misapplication of it, to which this want of harmony is to be imputed. An equal sensibility to the influence of the senses and the affections is to be found in the writings of Homer and Sophocles: the former especially has clothed sensual and pathetic images with irresistible attractions. Their superiority over these succeeding writers consists in the presence of those thoughts which belong to the inner faculties of our nature, not in the absence of those which are connected with the external; their incomparable perfection consists in an harmony of the union of all. It is not what the erotic writers have, but what they have not, in which their imperfection consists. It is not inasmuch as they were Poets, but inasmuch as they were not Poets, that they can be considered with any plausibility as connected with the corruption of their age. Had that corruption availed so as to extinguish in them the sensibility to pleasure, passion and natural scenery, which is imputed to them as an imperfection, the last triumph of evil would have been achieved. For the end of social corruption is to destroy all sensibility to pleasure; and therefore it is corruption. It begins at the imagination and the intellect as at the core, and distributes itself thence as a paralyzing venom, through the affections into the very appetites, until all become a torpid mass in which sense hardly survives. At the approach of such a period, Poetry ever addresses itself to those faculties which are the last to be destroyed, and its voice is heard, like the footsteps of Astræa, departing from the world.[10] Poetry ever communicates all the pleasure which men are capable of receiving: it is ever still the light of life; the source of whatever of beautiful, or generous, or true can have place in an evil time. It will readily be confessed that those among the luxurious citizens of Syracuse and Alexandria who were delighted with the poems of Theocritus, were less cold, cruel and sensual than

---

[10]Astraea was the goddess of justice who fled Earth for Heaven once the reign of Zeus began.

the remnant of their tribe. But corruption must have utterly destroyed the fabric of human society before Poetry can ever cease. The sacred links of that chain have never been entirely disjoined, which descending through the minds of many men is attached to those great minds, whence as from a magnet the invisible effluence is sent forth, which at once connects, animates and sustains the life of all. It is the faculty which contains within itself the seeds at once of its own and of social renovation. And let us not circumscribe the effects of the bucolic and erotic poetry within the limits of the sensibility of those to whom it was addressed. They may have perceived the beauty of those immortal compositions, simply as fragments and isolated portions: those who are more finely organized, or born in a happier age, may recognize them as episodes to that great poem, which all poets, like the co-operating thoughts of one great mind, have built up since the beginning of the world.

The same revolutions within a narrower sphere had place in antient Rome; but the actions and forms of its social life never seem to have been perfectly saturated with the poetical element. The Romans appear to have considered the Greeks as the selectest treasuries of the selectest forms of manners and of nature, and to have abstained from creating in measured language, sculpture, music or architecture, anything which might bear a particular relation to their own condition, whilst it should bear a general one to the universal constitution of the world. But we judge from partial evidence; and we judge perhaps partially. Ennius, Varro, Pacuvius, and Accius, all great poets, have been lost. Lucretius is in the highest, and Virgil in a very high sense, a creator. The chosen delicacy of the expressions of the latter is as a mist of light which conceals from us the intense and exceeding truth of his conceptions of nature. Livy is instinct with poetry. Yet Horace, Catullus, Ovid, and generally the other great writers of the Virgilian age, saw man and nature in the mirror of Greece. The institutions also and the religion of Rome were less poetical than those of Greece, as the shadow is less vivid than the substance. Hence poetry in Rome, seemed to follow rather than accompany the perfection of political and domestic society. The true Poetry of Rome lived in its institutions;

for whatever of beautiful, true and majestic they contained could have sprung only from the faculty which creates the order in which they consist. The life of Camillus, the death of Regulus; the expectation of the Senators, in their godlike state, of the victorious Gauls; the refusal of the Republic to make peace with Hannibal after the battle of Cannae, were not the consequences of a refined calculation of the probable personal advantage to result from such a rhythm and order in the shews of life, to those who were at once the poets and the actors of these immortal dramas. The imagination beholding the beauty of this order, created it out of itself according to its own idea: the consequence was empire, and the reward ever-living fame. These things are not the less poetry, *quia carent vate sacro.*[11] They are the episodes of the cyclic poem written by Time upon the memories of men. The Past, like an inspired rhapsodist, fills the theatre of everlasting generations with their harmony.

At length the antient system of religion and manners had fulfilled the circle of its revolution. And the world would have fallen into utter anarchy and darkness, but that there were found poets among the authors of the Christian and Chivalric systems of manners and religion, who created forms of opinion and action never before conceived; which, copied into the imaginations of men, became as generals to the bewildered armies of their thoughts. It is foreign to the present purpose to touch upon the evil produced by these systems: except that we protest, on the ground of the principles already established, that no portion of it can be imputed to the poetry they contain.

It is probable that the astonishing poetry of Moses, Job, David, Solomon and Isaiah had produced a great effect upon the mind of Jesus and his disciples. The scattered fragments preserved to us by the biographers of this extraordinary person, are all instinct with the most vivid poetry. But his doctrines seem to have been quickly distorted. At a certain period after the prevalence of a system of opinions founded upon those promulgated by him, the three forms into which Plato had distributed the faculties of mind underwent a sort of apotheosis, and became the object of the worship of the civilized world. Here it is to be confessed that

"Light seems to thicken," and
The crow makes wing to the rooky wood,
Good things of day begin to droop and drowze,
And night's black agents to their preys do rouze.[12]

But mark how beautiful an order has sprung from the dust and blood of this fierce chaos! how the World, as from a resurrection, balancing itself on the golden wings of knowledge and of hope, has reassumed its yet unwearied flight into the Heaven of time. Listen to the music, unheard by outward ears, which is as a ceaseless and invisible wind, nourishing its everlasting course with strength and swiftness.

The poetry in the doctrines of Jesus Christ, and the mythology and institutions of the Celtic[13] conquerors of the Roman empire, outlived the darkness and the convulsions connected with their growth and victory, and blended themselves into a new fabric of manners and opinion. It is an error to impute the ignorance of the dark ages to the Christian doctrines or the predominance of the Celtic nations. Whatever of evil their agencies may have contained sprung from the extinction of the poetical principle, connected with the progress of despotism and superstition. Men, from causes too intricate to be here discussed, had become insensible and selfish: their own will had become feeble, and yet they were its slaves, and thence the slaves of the will of others: lust, fear, avarice, cruelty and fraud, characterised a race amongst whom no one was to be found capable of *creating* in form, language, or institution. The moral anomalies of such a state of society are not justly to be charged upon any class of events immediately connected with them, and those events are most entitled to our approbation which could dissolve it most expeditiously. It is unfortunate for those who cannot distinguish words from thoughts, that many of these anomalies have been incorporated into our popular religion.

11"Because they lack a sacred prophet/poet." Horace, *Odes* IV.9:28.

12Shakespeare, *Macbeth*, III.ii.50–53.

13Shelley uses "Celtic" to refer to Germanic tribes (like those Caesar fought), not the aboriginal inhabitants of the British Isles.

It was not until the eleventh century that the effects of the poetry of the Christian and Chivalric systems began to manifest themselves. The principle of equality had been discovered and applied by Plato in his Republic, as the theoretical rule of the mode in which the materials of pleasure and of power produced by the common skill and labour of human beings ought to be distributed among them. The limitations of this rule were asserted by him to be determined only by the sensibility of each, or the utility to result to all. Plato, following the doctrines of Timæus and Pythagoras, taught also a moral and intellectual system of doctrine comprehending at once the past, the present, and the future condition of man. Jesus Christ divulged the sacred and eternal truths contained in these views to mankind, and Christianity, in its abstract purity, became the exoteric expression of the esoteric doctrines of the poetry and wisdom of antiquity. The incorporation of the Celtic nations with the exhausted population of the South, impressed upon it the figure of the poetry existing in their mythology and institutions. The result was a sum of the action and reaction of all the causes included in it; for it may be assumed as a maxim that no nation or religion can supersede any other without incorporating into itself a portion of that which it supersedes. The abolition of personal and domestic slavery, and the emancipation of women from a great part of the degrading restraints of antiquity were among the consequences of these events.

The abolition of personal slavery is the basis of the highest political hope that it can enter into the mind of man to conceive. The freedom of women produced the poetry of sexual love. Love became a religion, the idols of whose worship were ever present. It was as if the statues of Apollo and the Muses had been endowed with life and motion and had walked forth among their worshippers; so that earth became peopled by the inhabitants of a diviner world. The familiar appearance and proceedings of life became wonderful and heavenly; and a paradise was created as out of the wrecks of Eden. And as this creation itself is poetry, so its creators were poets; and language was the instrument of their art: "Galeotto

fù il libro, e chi lo scrisse."[14] The Provençal Trouveurs, or inventors, preceded Petrarch, whose verses are as spells, which unseal the inmost enchanted fountains of the delight which is in the grief of Love. It is impossible to feel them without becoming a portion of that beauty which we contemplate: it were superfluous to explain how the gentleness and the elevation of mind connected with these sacred emotions can render men more amiable, more generous, and wise, and lift them out of the dull vapours of the little world of self. Dante understood the secret things of love even more than Petrarch. His *Vita Nuova* is an inexhaustible fountain of purity of sentiment and language: it is the idealized history of that period, and those intervals of his life which were dedicated to love. His apotheosis of Beatrice in Paradise and the gradations of his own love and her loveliness, by which as by steps he feigns himself to have ascended to the throne of the Supreme Cause, is the most glorious imagination of modern poetry. The acutest critics have justly reversed the judgement of the vulgar, and the order of the great acts of the "Divine Drama," in the measure of the admiration which they accord to the Hell, Purgatory and Paradise. The latter is a perpetual hymn of everlasting love. Love, which found a worthy poet in Plato alone of all the antients, has been celebrated by a chorus of the greatest writers of the renovated world; and the music has penetrated the caverns of society, and its echoes still drown the dissonance of arms and superstition. At successive intervals, Ariosto, Tasso, Shakespeare, Spenser, Calderón, Rousseau, and the great writers of our own age, have celebrated the dominion of love, planting as it were trophies in the human mind of that sublimest victory over sensuality and force. The

[14]"That book was a Galeotto [legend of Sir Galahad], and so was he that wrote it." Dante, *Inferno* 5:137. The quotation is spoken by Francesca di Rimini, an adulterous wife Dante meets in Hell, who recounts how her affair with Paolo Malatesta began over a book of chivalric romance. Galahad introduced his uncle Lancelot to Queen Guinevere and so began their adulterous liaison; hence "Galeotto" in Italian can mean a go-between.

true relation borne to each other by the sexes into which human kind is distributed has become less misunderstood; and if the error which confounded diversity with inequality of the powers of the two sexes has become partially recognized in the opinions and institutions of modern Europe, we owe this great benefit to the worship of which Chivalry was the law, and poets the prophets.

The poetry of Dante may be considered as the bridge thrown over the stream of time, which unites the modern and antient world. The distorted notions of invisible things which Dante and his rival Milton have idealized, are merely the mask and the mantle in which these great poets walk through eternity enveloped and disguised. It is a difficult question to determine how far they were conscious of the distinction which must have subsisted in their minds between their own creeds and that of the people. Dante at least appears to wish to mark the full extent of it by placing Riphæus, whom Virgil calls *justissimus unus*, in Paradise[15] and observing a most heretical caprice in his distribution of rewards and punishments. And Milton's poem contains within itself a philosophical refutation of that system of which, by a strange and natural antithesis, it has been a chief popular support. Nothing can exceed the energy and magnificence of the character of Satan as expressed in *Paradise Lost*. It is a mistake to suppose that he could ever have been intended for the popular personification of evil. Implacable hate, patient cunning, and a sleepless refinement of device to inflict the extremest anguish on an enemy, these things are evil; and although venial in a slave are not to be forgiven in a tyrant; although redeemed by much that ennobles his defeat in one subdued, are marked by all that dishonours his conquest in the victor. Milton's Devil as a moral being is as far superior to his God as one who perseveres in some purpose which he has conceived to be excellent in spite of adversity and torture, is to one who in the cold security of undoubted triumph inflicts the most horrible revenge upon his enemy, not from

15"The one who is most just." Virgil, *Aeneid* 2.426. Dante finds him, to his surprise (since he was a pagan), in Paradise (*Paradiso* 20:67–69).

any mistaken notion of inducing him to repent of a perseverance in enmity, but with the alleged design of exasperating him to deserve new torments. Milton has so far violated the popular creed (if this shall be judged to be a violation) as to have alleged no superiority of moral virtue to his God over his Devil. And this bold neglect of a direct moral purpose is the most decisive proof of the supremacy of Milton's genius. He mingled as it were the elements of human nature, as colours upon a single pallet, and arranged them into the composition of his great picture according to the laws of epic truth; that is, according to the laws of that principle by which a series of actions of the external universe and of intelligent and ethical beings is calculated to excite the sympathy of succeeding generations of mankind. The *Divina Commedia* and *Paradise Lost* have conferred upon modern mythology a systematic form; and when change and time shall have added one more superstition to the mass of those which have arisen and decayed upon the earth, commentators will be learnedly employed in elucidating the religion of ancestral Europe, only not utterly forgotten because it will have been stamped with the eternity of genius.

Homer was the first, and Dante the second epic poet: that is, the second poet the series of whose creations bore a defined and intelligible relation to the knowledge, and sentiment, and religion, and political conditions of the age in which he lived, and of the ages which followed it, developing itself in correspondence with their development. For Lucretius had limed the wings of his swift spirit in the dregs of the sensible world; and Virgil, with a modesty which ill became his genius, had affected the fame of an imitator even whilst he created anew all that he copied; and none among the flock of mock-birds, though their notes were sweet, Apollonius Rhodius, Quintus Calaber Smyrnaeus, Nonnus, Lucan, Statius, or Claudian, have sought even to fulfil a single condition of epic truth. Milton was the third Epic Poet. For if the title of epic in its highest sense be refused to the *Aeneid*, still less can it be conceded to the *Orlando Furioso*, the *Gerusalemme Liberata*, the *Lusiad*, or the *Fairy Queen*.

Dante and Milton were both deeply penetrated with the antient religion of the civilized world; and its spirit exists in their poetry probably in the same proportion as its forms survived in the unreformed worship of modern Europe. The one preceded and the other followed the Reformation at almost equal intervals. Dante was the first religious reformer, and Luther surpassed him rather in the rudeness and acrimony, than in the boldness of his censures of papal usurpation. Dante was the first awakener of entranced Europe; he created a language in itself music and persuasion out of a chaos of inharmonious barbarisms. He was the congregator of those great spirits who presided over the resurrection of learning; the Lucifer[16] of that starry flock which in the thirteenth century shone forth from republican Italy, as from a heaven, into the darkness of the benighted world. His very words are instinct with spirit; each is as a spark, a burning atom of inextinguishable thought; and many yet lie covered in the ashes of their birth, and pregnant with a lightning which has yet found no conductor. All high poetry is infinite; it is as the first acorn, which contained all oaks potentially. Veil after veil may be undrawn, and the inmost naked beauty of the meaning never exposed. A great Poem is a fountain for ever overflowing with the waters of wisdom and delight; and after one person and one age has exhausted all its divine effluence which their peculiar relations enable them to share, another and yet another succeeds, and new relations are ever developed, the source of an unforeseen and an unconceived delight.

The age immediately succeeding to that of Dante, Petrarch, and Boccaccio, was characterized by a revival of painting, sculpture, music, and architecture. Chaucer caught the sacred inspiration, and the superstructure of English literature is based upon the materials of Italian invention.

But let us not be betrayed from a defence into a critical history of Poetry and its influence on Society. Be it enough to have pointed out the effects of poets, in the large and true sense of the word, upon their own and all succeeding times and to revert to the partial instances cited as illustrations of an opinion the reverse of that attempted to be established in the Four Ages of Poetry.

But poets have been challenged to resign the civic crown to reasoners and mechanists on another plea. It is admitted that the exercise of the imagination is most delightful, but it is alleged that of reason is more useful. Let us examine as the grounds of this distinction, what is here meant by Utility. Pleasure or good in a general sense, is that which the consciousness of a sensitive and intelligent being seeks, and in which when found it acquiesces. There are two kinds of pleasure, one durable, universal, and permanent; the other transitory and particular. Utility may either express the means of producing the former or the latter. In the former sense, whatever strengthens and purifies the affections, enlarges the imagination, and adds spirit to sense, is useful. But the meaning in which the Author of the Four Ages of Poetry seems to have employed the word utility is the narrower one of banishing the importunity of the wants of our animal nature, the surrounding men with security of life, the dispersing the grosser delusions of superstition, and the conciliating such a degree of mutual forbearance among men as may consist with the motives of personal advantage.

Undoubtedly the promoters of utility in this limited sense, have their appointed office in society. They follow the footsteps of poets, and copy the sketches of their creations into the book of common life. They make space, and give time. Their exertions are of the highest value so long as they confine their administration of the concerns of the inferior powers of our nature within the limits due to the superior ones. But whilst the sceptic destroys gross superstitions, let him spare to deface, as some of the French writers have defaced, the eternal truths charactered upon the imaginations of men. Whilst the mechanist abridges, and the political œconomist combines, labour, let them beware that their speculations, for want of correspondence with those first principles which belong to the imagination, do not tend, as they have in modern England, to exasperate at once the extremes of luxury and want. They have exemplified the saying, "To him that hath, more shall be given; and from him that hath not, the little that he hath shall be taken away."[17] The rich have become richer, and the poor have become poorer; and the vessel of the state is driven

---

[16]Shelley intends here the literal sense of "bearer of light."

[17]Matthew 25:29.

between the Scylla and Charybdis of anarchy and despotism. Such are the effects which must ever flow from an unmitigated exercise of the calculating faculty.

It is difficult to define pleasure in its highest sense; the definition involving a number of apparent paradoxes. For, from an inexplicable defect of harmony in the constitution of human nature, the pain of the inferior is frequently connected with the pleasures of the superior portions of our being. Sorrow, terror, anguish, despair itself are often the chosen expressions of an approximation to the highest good. Our sympathy in tragic fiction depends on this principle; tragedy delights by affording a shadow of the pleasure which exists in pain. This is the source also of the melancholy which is inseparable from the sweetest melody. The pleasure that is in sorrow is sweeter than the pleasure of pleasure itself. And hence the saying, "It is better to go to the house of mourning, than to the house of mirth."[18] Not that this highest species of pleasure is necessarily linked with pain. The delight of love and friendship, the extacy of the admiration of nature, the joy of the perception and still more of the creation of poetry is often wholly unalloyed. The production and assurance of pleasure in this highest sense is true utility. Those who produce and preserve this pleasure are Poets or poetical philosophers.

The exertions of Locke, Hume, Gibbon, Voltaire, Rousseau,[19] and their disciples, in favour of oppressed and deluded humanity, are entitled to the gratitude of mankind. Yet it is easy to calculate the degree of moral and intellectual improvement which the world would have exhibited, had they never lived. A little more nonsense would have been talked for a century or two; and perhaps a few more men, women, and children, burnt as heretics. We might not at this moment have been congratulating each other on the abolition of the Inquisition in Spain. But it exceeds all imagination to conceive what would have been the moral condition of the world if neither Dante, Petrarch, Boccaccio, Chaucer,

Shakespeare, Calderón, Lord Bacon, nor Milton, had ever existed: if Raphael and Michael Angelo had never been born: if the Hebrew poetry had never been translated: if a revival of the study of Greek literature had never taken place: if no monuments of antient sculpture had been handed down to us: and if the poetry of the religion of the antient world had been extinguished together with its belief. The human mind could never, except by the intervention of these excitements, have been awakened to the invention of the grosser sciences, and that application of analytical reasoning to the aberrations of society, which it is now attempted to exalt over the direct expression of the inventive and creative faculty itself.

We have more moral, political and historical wisdom, than we know how to reduce into practise; we have more scientific and œconomical knowledge than can be accommodated to the just distribution of the produce which it multiplies. The poetry in these systems of thought, is concealed by the accumulation of facts and calculating processes. There is no want of knowledge respecting what is wisest and best in morals, government, and political œconomy, or at least, what is wiser and better than what men now practise and endure. But we let "I dare not wait upon I would," like the poor cat i' the adage."[20] We want the creative faculty to imagine that which we know; we want the generous impulse to act that which we imagine; we want the poetry of life: our calculations have outrun conception; we have eaten more than we can digest. The cultivation of those sciences which have enlarged the limits of the empire of man over the external world, has, for want of the poetical faculty, proportionally circumscribed those of the internal world; and man, having enslaved the elements, remains himself a slave. To what but a cultivation of the mechanical arts in a degree disproportioned to the presence of the creative faculty, which is the basis of all knowledge, is to be attributed the abuse of all invention for abridging and combining labour, to the exasperation of the inequality of mankind? From what other cause has it arisen that the discoveries which should have lightened have

---

[18]Ecclesiastes 7:2.

[19]I follow the classification adopted by the author of the Four Ages of Poetry. But Rousseau was essentially a poet. The others, even Voltaire, were mere reasoners. [Shelley]

[20]Shakespeare, *Macbeth*, I.vii:44–45.

added a weight to the curse imposed on Adam? Poetry, and the principle of Self, of which money is the visible incarnation, are the God and the Mammon of the world.

The functions of the poetical faculty are twofold; by one it creates new materials of knowledge, and power and pleasure; by the other it engenders in the mind a desire to reproduce and arrange them according to a certain rhythm and order which may be called the beautiful and the good. The cultivation of poetry is never more to be desired than at periods when, from an excess of the selfish and calculating principle, the accumulation of the materials of external life exceed the quantity of the power of assimilating them to the internal laws of human nature. The body has then become too unwieldy for that which animates it.

Poetry is indeed something divine. It is at once the centre and circumference of knowledge; it is that which comprehends all science, and that to which all science must be referred. It is at the same time the root and blossom of all other systems of thought: it is that from which all spring, and that which adorns all; and that which, if blighted, denies the fruit and the seed, and withholds from the barren world the nourishment and the succession of the scions of the tree of life. It is the perfect and consummate surface and bloom of things; it is as the odour and the colour of the rose to the texture of the elements which compose it, as the form and the splendour of unfaded beauty to the secrets of anatomy and corruption. What were Virtue, Love, Patriotism, Friendship &c. — what were the scenery of this beautiful Universe which we inhabit — what were our consolations on this side of the grave — and what were our aspirations beyond it — if Poetry did not ascend to bring light and fire from those eternal regions where the owl-winged faculty of calculation dare not ever soar? Poetry is not like reasoning, a power to be exerted according to the determination of the will. A man cannot say, "I will compose poetry." The greatest poet even cannot say it: for the mind in creation is as a fading coal which some invisible influence, like an inconstant wind, awakens to transitory brightness: this power arises from within, like the colour of a flower which fades and changes as it is developed, and the conscious portions of our natures are unprophetic either of its approach or its departure.

Could this influence be durable in its original purity and force, it is impossible to predict the greatness of the results: but when composition begins, inspiration is already on the decline, and the most glorious poetry that has ever been communicated to the world is probably a feeble shadow of the original conception of the poet. I appeal to the greatest Poets of the present day, whether it be not an error to assert that the finest passages of poetry are produced by labour and study. The toil and the delay recommended by critics can be justly interpreted to mean no more than a careful observation of the inspired moments, and an artificial connexion of the spaces between their suggestions by the intertexture of conventional expressions; a necessity only imposed by a limitedness of the poetical faculty itself. For Milton conceived the *Paradise Lost* as a whole before he executed it in portions. We have his own authority also for the Muse having "dictated" to him the "unpremeditated song,"[21] and let this be an answer to those who would allege the fifty-six various readings of the first line of the *Orlando Furioso*. Compositions so produced are to poetry what mosaic is to painting. This instinct and intuition of the poetical faculty is still more observable in the plastic and pictorial arts: a great statue or picture grows under the power of the artist as a child in the mother's womb, and the very mind which directs the hands in formation is incapable of accounting to itself for the origin, the gradations, or the media of the process.

Poetry is the record of the best and happiest moments of the happiest and best minds. We are aware of evanescent visitations of thought and feeling sometimes associated with place or person, sometimes regarding our own mind alone, and always arising unforeseen and departing unbidden, but elevating and delightful beyond all expression: so that even in the desire and the regret they leave, there cannot but be pleasure, participating as it does in the nature of its object. It is as it were the interpenetration of a diviner nature through our own; but its footsteps are like those of a wind over a sea, which the coming calm erases, and whose traces remain only as on the wrinkled sand which paves it. These and corresponding conditions of being are

[21]Milton, *Paradise Lost*, 9:21–24.

experienced principally by those of the most delicate sensibility and the most enlarged imagination; and the state of mind produced by them is at war with every base desire. The enthusiasm of virtue, love, patriotism, and friendship is essentially linked with these emotions; and whilst they last, self appears as what it is, an atom to a Universe. Poets are not only subject to these experiences as spirits of the most refined organization, but they can colour all that they combine with the evanescent hues of this ethereal world; a word, a trait in the representation of a scene or a passion, will touch the enchanted chord, and reanimate, in those who have ever experienced these emotions, the sleeping, the cold, the buried image of the past. Poetry thus makes immortal all that is best and most beautiful in the world; it arrests the vanishing apparitions which haunt the interlunations of life, and veiling them or in language or in form sends them forth among mankind, bearing sweet news of kindred joy to those with whom their sisters abide — abide, because there is no portal of expression from the caverns of the spirit which they inhabit into the universe of things. Poetry redeems from decay the visitations of the divinity in man.

Poetry turns all things to loveliness; it exalts the beauty of that which is most beautiful, and it adds beauty to that which is most deformed: it marries exultation and horror, grief and pleasure, eternity and change; it subdues to union under its light yoke all irreconcilable things. It transmutes all that it touches, and every form moving within the radiance of its presence is changed by wondrous sympathy to an incarnation of the spirit which it breathes: its secret alchemy turns to potable gold the poisonous waters which flow from death through life; it strips the veil of familiarity from the world, and lays bare the naked and sleeping beauty which is the spirit of its forms.

All things exist as they are perceived: at least in relation to the percipient. "The mind is its own place, and of itself can make a heaven of hell, a hell of heaven."[22] But poetry defeats the curse which binds us to the accident of surrounding impressions. And whether it spreads its own figured curtain or withdraws life's dark veil from before the scene of things, it equally

creates for us a being within our being. It makes us the inhabitants of a world to which the familiar world is a chaos. It reproduces the common universe of which we are portions and percipients, and it purges from our inward sight the film of familiarity which obscures from us the wonder of our being. It compels us to feel that which we perceive, and to imagine that which we know. It creates anew the universe after it has been annihilated in our minds by the recurrence of impressions blunted by reiteration. It justifies that bold and true word of Tasso — *Non merita nome di creatore, se non Iddio ed il Poeta.*[23]

A Poet, as he is the author to others of the highest wisdom, pleasure, virtue and glory, so he ought personally to be the happiest, the best, the wisest, and the most illustrious of men. As to his glory, let Time be challenged to declare whether the fame of any other institutor of human life be comparable to that of a poet. That he is the wisest, the happiest, and the best, inasmuch as he is a poet, is equally incontrovertible: the greatest poets have been men of the most spotless virtue, of the most consummate prudence, and, if we could look into the interior of their lives, the most fortunate of men: and the exceptions, as they regard those who possessed the poetic faculty in a high yet inferior degree, will be found on consideration to confirm rather than destroy the rule. Let us for a moment stoop to the arbitration of popular breath, and usurping and uniting in our own persons the incompatible characters of accuser, witness, judge and executioner, let us decide without trial, testimony, or form, that certain motives of those who are "there sitting where we dare not soar,"[24] are reprehensible. Let us assume that Homer was a drunkard, that Virgil was a flatterer, that Horace was a coward, that Tasso was a madman, that Lord Bacon was a peculator, that Raphael was a libertine, that Spenser was a poet laureate.[25] It is inconsistent with this division

---

[22] Milton, *Paradise Lost*, 1:254–55.

[23] "Nobody merits the title of Creator save God and the Poet." The line is quoted thus in Serassi's *Life of Torquato Tasso.*

[24] Milton, *Paradise Lost*, 4:829.

[25] Poet laureate may seem an odd member of this sequence, unless we remember that the current laureate was Robert Southey, a personal and political enemy of Shelley's.

of our subject to cite living poets, but Posterity has done ample justice to the great names now referred to. Their errors have been weighed and found to have been dust in the balance: if their sins "were as scarlet, they are now white as snow"; they have been washed in the blood of the mediator and the redeemer Time. Observe in what a ludicrous chaos the imputations of real or fictitious crime have been confused in the contemporary calumnies against poetry and poets; consider how little is, as it appears — or appears, as it is; look to your own motives, and judge not, lest ye be judged.

Poetry, as has been said, in this respect differs from logic, that it is not subject to the controul of the active powers of the mind, and that its birth and recurrence has no necessary connexion with consciousness or will. It is presumptuous to determine that these are the necessary conditions of all mental causation, when mental effects are experienced insusceptible of being referred to them. The frequent recurrence of the poetical power, it is obvious to suppose, may produce in the mind an habit or order and harmony correlative with its own nature and with its effects upon other minds. But in the intervals of inspiration, and they may be frequent without being durable, a poet becomes a man, and is abandoned to the sudden reflux of the influences under which others habitually live. But as he is more delicately organized than other men, and sensible to pain and pleasure, both his own and that of others, in a degree unknown to them, he will avoid the one and pursue the other with an ardour proportioned to this difference. And he renders himself obnoxious to calumny, when he neglects to observe the circumstances under which these objects of universal pursuit and flight have disguised themselves in one another's garments.

But there is nothing necessarily evil in this error, and thus cruelty, envy, revenge, avarice, and the passions purely evil, have never formed any portion of the popular imputations on the lives of poets.

I have thought it most favourable to the cause of truth to set down these remarks according to the order in which they were suggested to my mind by a consideration of the subject itself, instead of following that of the treatise that excited me to make them public. Thus although devoid of the formality of a polemical reply; if the view they contain be just, they will be found to involve a refutation of the Four Ages of Poetry, so far at least as regards the first division of the subject. I can readily conjecture what should have moved the gall of the learned and intelligent author of that paper; I confess myself like him unwilling to be stunned by the Theseids of the hoarse Codri of the day. Bavius and Mævius undoubtedly are, as they ever were, insufferable persons.[26] But it belongs to a philosophical critic to distinguish rather than confound.

The first part of these remarks has related to Poetry in its elements and principles; and it has been shewn, as well as the narrow limits assigned them would permit, that what is called poetry, in a restricted sense, has a common source with all other forms of order and of beauty according to which the materials of human life are susceptible of being arranged, and which is poetry in an universal sense.

The second part will have for its object an application of these principles to the present state of the cultivation of Poetry, and a defence of the attempt to idealize the modern forms of manners and opinion, and compel them into a subordination to the imaginative and creative faculty.[27] For the literature of England, an energetic developement of which has ever preceded or accompanied a great and free developement of the national will, has arisen as it were from a new birth. In spite of the low-thoughted envy which would undervalue contemporary merit, our own will be a memorable age in intellectual achievements, and we live among such philosophers and poets as surpass beyond comparison any who have appeared since the last national struggle for civil and religious liberty. The most unfailing herald, companion, and follower of the awakening of a great people to work a beneficial change in opinion or institution, is Poetry. At such periods

---

[26]Codrus, Bavius, and Maevius are traditional examples of bad poets cited by Juvenal, Horace, and Virgil.
[27]The "second part" was never written.

there is an accumulation of the power of communicating and receiving intense and impassioned conceptions respecting man and nature. The persons in whom this power resides, may often, as far as regards many portions of their nature, have little apparent correspondence with that spirit of good of which they are the ministers. But even whilst they deny and abjure, they are yet compelled to serve, the Power which is seated upon the throne of their own soul. It is impossible to read the compositions of the most celebrated writers of the present day without being startled with the electric life which burns within their words.

They measure the circumference and sound the depths of human nature with a comprehensive and all-penetrating spirit, and they are themselves perhaps the most sincerely astonished at its manifestations, for it is less their spirit than the spirit of the age. Poets are the hierophants of an unapprehended inspiration, the mirrors of the gigantic shadows which futurity casts upon the present, the words which express what they understand not, the trumpets which sing to battle, and feel not what they inspire: the influence which is moved not, but moves. Poets are the unacknowledged legislators of the World.

Karl Marx

1818–1883

Karl Marx, the chief philosopher and theorist of modern socialism, was born into a comfortable middle-class home in Trier, Germany. The son of a lawyer who converted from Judaism to Lutheranism, Marx studied law at Bonn and Berlin before turning to philosophy and taking his Ph.D. at Jena in 1841. He became editor of the *Rheinische Zeitung* in 1842, but his calls for radical reform led to its suppression in 1843. That same year he emigrated to Paris, where he began his lifelong partnership with Friedrich Engels, committed himself to socialism, and commenced his study of the works of the classical economists. Within a year he was expelled from France for his radical views, and he settled for the next three years in Brussels.

Marx's evolving theories, although recorded in 1846, were not published until 1932, as *The German Ideology*. In 1847 he joined the Communist League and with Engels wrote *The Communist Manifesto,* which was published in 1848 just before revolution swept the continent. Exiled from most European centers, in 1849 Marx settled permanently in London to a life of poverty, chronic illness, and arduous, unflagging devotion to the cause of world communism. *A Contribution to the Critique of Political Economy* was published in 1859, and the next twelve years saw the founding of the First International Working Men's Council (1864) and the publication of both the first volume of his monumental *Capital* (1867) and *The Civil War in France* (1871), an analysis of the brutally suppressed Paris Commune of 1871. Marx's last years, clouded by ill health and by the deaths of his eldest daughter and wife, were less precarious financially owing to the pension that Engels settled on him in 1869.

Marx is usually classified as a "dialectical materialist." Like his teacher Hegel, Marx believed that historical transformations occur through a *dialectic* of thesis, antithesis, and synthesis, whereby each historical force calls into being its Other so that the two opposites negate each other and ultimately give rise to a third force, which transcends this opposition. But while Hegel was an idealist who believed in spiritual forces that bend and transform the material world, Marx was a materialist who contended that "it is not the consciousness of men that determines their being, but, on the contrary, their social being that determines their consciousness."

Marx argues in *The German Ideology* that the ultimate moving force of human history is economics, or perhaps one should use the older and broader term "political economy," since in Marxist thought the engine of change is a fusion of political and social as well as economic issues. Each society lives by certain "forces of production" — the methods and techniques by which it produces food, clothing, shelter, and the other necessities of life — and by the "social relations of production" these methods create. In an economy based on sheep raising, for example, the shepherds work alone and relate primarily to the flock owner, while an economy based on manufacturing demands a division of labor, which in turn requires elaborate patterns of cooperation among workers and a hierarchy of managers. These modes of production and their accompanying social relations are the foundation *(Grundlage)* of a culture.

Marx posited that major historical changes occur not as a result of spiritual contradictions, as Hegel had thought, but because of economic ones. (It is in this sense
that, as the cliché puts it, Marx stood Hegel on his head.) Feudalism, for example,
was a relatively stable system as long as it was based on local agriculture; but as
trade began to generate wealth, feudal rulers became rich and powerful by taxing
it and secured their power by giving their towns and traders maximum freedom of
action. By so doing, they created two rival centers of power, the feudal countryside and the bourgeois city. In the city, the merchants and manufacturers formed
cooperative social relationships with one another and recognized their mutual
class interests, which were not always in harmony with those of the agricultural
feudatories. It was inevitable that eventually the bourgeoisie of the tightly organized city would gain ascendancy over the feudal lords, who were unaccustomed
to cooperation. Conflict between feudal lords and the middle classes broke out
most violently in bourgeois revolutions, like the English Civil War in the 1640s
and the French Revolution of the 1790s. Marx devoted most of his efforts to demonstrating that capitalism was developing the same sorts of internal contradictions
as feudalism and to predicting the course of the proletarian revolution that would
displace it.

One of these key internal contradictions that flourish within capitalism, as Marx
explained in the 1844 *Manuscripts*, involves the alienation of the worker. Workers
depend on labor to provide the means to continue living, but the more dependent
they become on this external factor, the less their lives belong to them. The products of their labor, too, belong to the capitalist, not to the workers. And Marx goes
on to show that this alienation has a spiritual dimension as well: Laboring for
themselves, workers affirm themselves, but in working for the capitalist, workers
deny themselves. Work becomes a punishment they willingly inflict on themselves, a form of slavery from which they are free only while they are performing
their animal functions of eating, sleeping, and reproducing themselves. They feel
human only when they are behaving like animals, and like mere animals when they
are working for their livelihood.

If the material foundation of a culture is economic, the spiritual superstructure
(*Überbau*) finds expression in the culture's *ideology*. Marx used the term *ideology*
to denote the culture's collective consciousness of its own being — comprising all
its elaborate codes of law, politics, religion, art, and philosophy. By and large, the
ideology of a society will be consistent with and supportive of its dominant material
basis. One would expect, for example, that a society whose economy is based on
herds of livestock (like that of the Old Testament Hebrews) would erect a paternalistic monarchy and believe in a fatherly God of their own profession ("The Lord
is my shepherd; I shall not want"). This does not mean that art always expresses
only the sentiments of the dominant class. All the implicit contradictions and conflicts within the economic base are likely to find some sort of expression within
the ideological superstructure. For example, the aspiration of the capitalist middle
classes to equality with the great lords emerges in literature as early as Chaucer's

Canterbury Tales, in the Merchant's sentiment that tradesmen too may possess "gentilesse." But the term *ideology* in Marx's usage often has the connotation of "false consciousness," a set of illusions fostered by the dominant class in order to ensure social stability — and its own continued dominance. Marx was notoriously hostile to religious visions of equality in heaven that defused the proletarian desire for greater equality here on earth. Literature too might be "the opium of the people" to the extent that vicarious participation in the struggles of upper–middle-class life would undermine the natural solidarity of the working classes. Indeed, merely representing the world as it is as a coherent social structure has the conservative force of making the present into an icon: It implies that, since things are thus, they cannot be otherwise.

Art and literature are therefore dependent ideological features of the dominant socioeconomic system, changing as the base changes but usually reflecting the values of the hegemonic class. In part, this is true for obvious economic reasons: Making art is one way of earning a living and those who create art must flatter, or at least not affront, their patrons, those in a position to pay for it. Note, for example, the aristocratic bias of Shakespeare's plays in a day when theaters were licensed by the Crown and theatrical companies were sponsored by courtiers, or the fact that genre painting depicting bourgeois interiors with stunning detail arose in seventeenth-century Dutch society, which was dominated by merchants.

But beyond conscious pandering, there is Marx's broader assumption that individuals can only think the thoughts that are thinkable in their society. If Shakespeare regarded Jack Cade (in 2 *Henry VI*) or the plebeian rebels of *Coriolanus* as bringers of chaos, chances are no one else in Shakespeare's still-feudal society could imagine how a democratic commonwealth might function. Similarly, Dickens was able to understand and represent the immense human misery produced by the Industrial Revolution and the gospel of wealth, but he was unable to envision any solution for that misery, other than a change of heart from acquisitiveness to benevolence on the part of wealthy capitalists.

On the other hand, in artistic matters at least, individuals can continue to think thoughts that their society no longer considers thinkable. Why the art of the distant past, based on social and political relationships that have long been superseded, should still have such an intense effect upon later audiences, is a question that long troubled Marx and his followers. The immense appeal of Greek art to the German middle class (including Marx) is one of the more perplexing issues Marx treats in the selection from *Contribution to a Critique of Political Economy.* It is a problem he solves as a collective case of emotional nostalgia: Just as our sentimental attachment to our own personal childhood depends on the fact that we will never have to live it over again, so Greek art reflects the idyllic childhood of the human race. For Marx, the lucidity and force of Greek literature and sculpture are captivating precisely because the hard life, the meager diet, the tyrants, and the slaves that produced it are things we no longer have to endure.

The Alienation of Labor[1]
from Economic and Philosophic
Manuscripts of 1844

In political economy[2] and its terminology, we have shown that the laborer sinks to the level of a commodity and indeed becomes the most miserable commodity possible, that the misery of the laborer stands in an inverse relationship to the power and size of his production, that the natural result of competition is the accumulation of capital in a few hands, which is the most frightening type of monopoly, that finally the

difference between the ground-renter[3] and the capitalist[4] as well as the difference between the farmer-renter and the factory laborer disappears and the entire society must fall into two classes: those with property and those propertyless souls who labor.

Political economy begins with the fact of private property. It does not explain this fact to us. It describes the material process of private property — by which it actually passes from hand

Translated by Richard Hooker.

[1]A note on terminology: Marx uses two terms to describe this phenomenon: *Entfremdung* (estrangement) and *Entäuss-erung* (alienation): these words are by and large interchangeable (the real title of this essay is "The Estrangement of Labor"). Estrangement means "dividing, separating," or "making foreign." Estrangement of labor means "separating" labor from the laborer, separating the product of labor from the laborer, etc. Alienation of labor can be understood in largely the same terms: "making labor something foreign to the laborer," "making the product of labor something alien to the laborer."

[2]"Political economy," (in German: *Nationalökonomie*, "the economy of nations") is what we would call "macroeconomics," that is economics of large systems. The principal authors of political economy for Marx are Adam Smith, David Ricardo, David Hume, and Thomas Malthus.

[3]A "ground-renter" for Marx is a person in a largely pre-industrial society who owns land and rents it out to people who produce goods from that land. Historically, in pre-industrial societies, land tends to accumulate in only a very few hands, and the bulk of people within these societies are renters. A ground-renter is the prototype for the "capitalist" in an industrial society.

[4]The capitalist in European economics is understood as a person who accumulates the material of production, factories, raw materials, etc., and who pays laborers wages in order to produce various goods. The capitalist is essentially rational: he or she calculates the acquisition and disposal of materials and wage-labor in order to produce extra wealth, profit, which accumulates to the capitalist as a reward for accurate calculation.

Selected Bibliography

Ahearn, Edward. *Marx and Modern Fiction.* New Haven: Yale University Press, 1989.

Berlin, Isaiah. *Karl Marx: His Life and Environment*, 4th ed. New York: Oxford University Press, 1996.

Demetz, Peter. *Marx, Engels, and the Poets: Origins of Marxist Literary Criticism.* Chicago: University of Chicago Press, 1967.

Dowling, William P. *Jameson, Althusser, Marx: An Introduction to The Political Unconscious.* Ithaca: Cornell University Press, 1984.

Foucault, Michel. *Remarks on Marx.* London: Autonomedia, 1991.

Kedourie, Elie. *Lectures on Hegel and Marx.* London: Blackwell, 1991.

Lifshitz, Mikhail. *The Philosophy of Art of Karl Marx*, 1933; London: Plato Press, 1973.

Marx, Karl, and Friedrich Engels. *Marx and Engels on Literature and Art.* St. Louis: Telos Press, 1973.

Mazlish, Bruce. *The Meaning of Karl Marx.* New York: Oxford University Press, 1984.

Wilson, H. T. *Marx's Critical-Dialectical Procedure.* New York: Routledge, 1990.

to hand — in general, abstract formulas, which it then raises to the status of *laws*. It does not *understand* these laws, that is, it does not show how the existence of private property comes about. Political economy gives no explanation concerning the foundation of the division between labor and capital and between capital and land. When, for instance, it describes the relationship between wage-labor and the profit of capital, its fundamental point of departure is the interest of the capitalist, that is, it accepts as given what it should be explaining. In the same way, competition is used to explain everything. It is explained using external circumstances. How far these external, seemingly magical circumstances originate in a necessary process, political economy teaches us nothing. We have seen, that exchange itself appears to be some magical occurrence. The only wheels which political economy sets in motion are *greed* and *the war between the greedy: competition.* . . .

We have now to explain the real connections between private property, greed, the division of labor, capital, and land, the connection between exchange and competition, between value and the devaluation of humans, between monopoly and competition, etc., and between this entire estrangement and the money system. . . .

We must start our investigation from a *real* fact of political economy.

The laborer becomes poorer the more wealth he produces, indeed, the more powerful and wide-ranging his production becomes. The laborer becomes a cheaper commodity the more commodities he creates. With the *increase in value* of the world of things arises in direct proportion the *decrease of value* of human beings. Labor does not only produce commodities, it produces itself and the laborer as a *commodity*, and in relation to the level at which it produces commodities.[5]

This fact defines more than this: the object, which labor produces, its product, confronts the laborer as a strange thing, as a *power independent*

of the producer. The product of labor is labor, which fixes itself in the object, it becomes a thing, it is the *objectification*[6] of labor. The "making real," or realization,[7] of labor is its objectification. The realization of labor appears in political economy as the "making unreal," or loss of reality[8] of, the laborer, objectification as the *loss of and slavery to the object*, appropriation as *estrangement*, as *alienation*.

The realization of labor manifests itself so much as a loss of reality, that the worker becomes unreal to the point that he starves to death. The objectification of labor manifests itself so much as a loss of objects, that the laborer is robbed of the most necessary objects, not only to maintain his own life, but even objects to labor with. Indeed, labor itself becomes an object, which only with the greatest effort and with random interruptions can be acquired. Appropriation of objects manifests itself so much as estrangement, that, the more objects the laborer produces, the fewer he can own and so he plunges deeper under the mastery of his product: capital.

In this definition — that the laborer is related to the *product of his labor* as a *strange, foreign* object, — lies all these consequences. For from this hypothesis the following becomes clear: the more the laborer labors, as well as the more powerful the alien, object world which he builds over himself becomes, the poorer he himself becomes, that is, his inner world, as he owns less. The same thing occurs in religion. The more people place in God, the less they retain in themselves. The laborer places his life in the object; but now it [his life] belongs less to him than to the object. Therefore, the more this happens, the more deprived of objects the laborer becomes. What

---

[5]What Marx is arguing is that wage-labor becomes something that can be bought and sold just like any other object. The more important products become, the less important humans as laborers become.

[6]*Vergegenständlichung*, often translated as "reification": "the making into a thing," that is, labor turned into an object. Labor becomes an object rather than a thing people do; as a result, the laborer becomes an object rather than a human being.

[7]*Verwirklichung*, meaning literally "the making real"; this is what the word "realization" means, that is, "making real."

[8]*Entwirklichung*, "making unreal"; this is the opposite of *Verwirklichung*, "the making real." In other words, labor "made real" in its product "makes unreal" the laborer; that is, the laborer is no longer a person who is laboring, but rather the products he or she produces. The products are more "valuable" than the people who produce them.

the product of his labor is, he is not. Therefore, the greater this product, the less he becomes. The alienation of the laborer in his product has this significance: since his labor is an object, not only does this labor become a separate existence, but it is also separate from him, independent, alien to his existence and a self-sufficient power which exists above him, that the life, which he has bestowed on the object, confronts him as something hostile and strange.

XXIII. Let us now treat more closely objectification, the production of the laborer and its estrangement, the loss of objects, its products.

The laborer can create nothing without nature, without the sensual, material world. It is the stuff on which labor realizes itself, on which it acts, and from which and with which it produces.

Just as nature provides the *means of life* for labor, in the sense that labor cannot live without objects, which it uses, but also it provides the *means of life* in a narrower sense, namely the means to sustain the physical existence of the *laborer*.

Therefore, the more the laborer through his labor appropriates the external world, sensuous nature, the more he deprives himself of the *means of life* in this double meaning: first, more and more the sensuous external world stops being an object proper to his labor, that is, to be a *means of life* to his labor; second: more and more the sensuous external world stops being a *means of life* in the second sense: means to sustain the physical existence of the laborer.

In this double sense the worker becomes a slave to his objects; first: he receives an *object of labor*, that is, *labor*; and second: he receives a *means of subsistence*. In the first instance, he can exist as a laborer; in the second instance, he can exist as a *physical subject*. The result of this slavery is that he can maintain himself as a *physical subject* only if he is a *laborer*, and that he can maintain himself as a *laborer* only if he is a *physical subject*. . . .

Political economy hides completely the estrangement of labor in its real existence in that it does not treat the direct, unmediated relationship between the laborer (labor) and production. Labor produces wonderful works for

the rich, but it produces poverty for the worker. It produces palaces, but hovels for the laborer. It produces beauty, but deformity for the laborer. It replaces labor with machines, but at the same time it throws the laborer into the most barbarous labor and at the same time makes the laborer into a machine. It produces intelligence and culture, but it produces senselessness and cretinism for the laborer.

The direct, unmediated relationship between labor and its product is the relationship between laborers and the objects of their production. The relationship between the wealthy man and the objects of production and to production itself is only a *consequence* of these primary relationships. And it, in fact, proves these primary relationships. We will treat these in later pages. Therefore, when we ask what the essential relationship of labor is, we are asking about the relationship of *labor* to production.

Up until this point, we have been treating the estrangement, the alienation of the laborer in only one sense, that is, his relationship to the products of his labor. But this estrangement displays itself not only in the products, but also in the *act of production*, in the *producing activity* itself. How can it happen that the laborer becomes estranged from the product of his activity if in the act of production he does not become estranged from himself? The product is only the sum of the activity, that is, production. If the product of labor is alienation, then production itself must be active alienation, the alienation of activity, the activity of alienation. In the estrangement of the objects of labor is summed up the estrangement, the alienation of the laboring activity itself. What then makes up the alienation of labor?

First, that labor is *alien* to the laborer, that is, that it does not make up his existence, that he does not affirm himself in his labor, but rather denies himself; he does not feel happy, but rather unhappy; he does not grow physically or mentally, but rather tortures his body and ruins his mind. The laborer feels himself first to be other than his labor and his labor to be other than himself. He is at home when he is not laboring, and when he is laboring he is not at home. His labor is not voluntary, but constrained, *forced labor*. Therefore, it does not meet a need, but rather it is a means to meet some need alien to it. Its estranged character becomes obvious when one sees that as soon as there is no physical or other coercion, labor is avoided like the plague. This alienated labor, this labor, in which human beings alienate themselves from themselves, is a labor of self-denial and self-torture. Finally, the alienation of labor manifests itself to the laborer in that this labor does not belong to him, but to someone else; it does not belong to him; while he is doing it he does not belong to himself, but to another. . . . the activity of the laborer is not his own activity. It belongs to someone else, it is the loss of his self.

The result, therefore, is that the human being (the laborer) does not feel himself to be free except in his animal functions: eating, drinking, and reproducing, at his best in his dwelling or in his clothing, etc., and in his human functions he is no more than an animal. The animal becomes human and the human becomes animal.

Eating, drinking, and reproducing, etc., are real human functions. However, in the abstraction which draws them out of the circle of other human activities and makes them the sole activity to be sought after, they are animal.

We have treated the act of the estrangement of practical, human activity, labor, as having two senses: 1.) The relationship of the laborer to the *product of labor* as a strange object having power over the laborer. This relationship is moreover a relationship to the sensuous, external world, in which the objects of nature confront the laborer as a dominating, strange, and hostile world. 2.) The relationship of labor as an *act of production* within labor itself. This relationship is a relationship of the laborer to his activity as if it were estranged, as if it didn't belong to him, activity as sorrow, strength as weakness, producing as emasculation, the laborer's *own* physical and mental energy, his individual life — what is life without activity? — is an activity which turns against him, does not depend on him, does not belong to him. This is *self-alienation*, where before we had the estrangement of the *thing*.

XXIV. We have now to demonstrate how a third aspect of *estranged labor* derives from these two.

Human beings . . . believe themselves to represent the real, living species, in that they believe themselves to be *universal*; they believe themselves to represent, therefore, a free being.

The life of the species, which applies to both humans and animals, consists in the physical, in which humans, just as animals, derive their life from inorganic nature, and the more universal man is in comparison to animals, the more universal is the sphere of inorganic nature, on which he lives. . . . Physically, human beings live only on the products of nature, whether they might appear in the form of food, heating, clothing, dwellings, etc. The universality of humanity manifests itself practically even in this universality, in which the whole of nature becomes the *inorganic* body of human beings, both inasmuch as it is 1.) a direct means for life, and 2.) the material, the object and the instrument of humanity's life-activity. Nature is the inorganic body of humanity insofar as it is not a human body. Humanity lives on nature, which means that nature is humanity's *body* with which it must remain in objective dialogue with or else perish. That the physical and mental life of human beings depends on nature has another sense: nature depends on itself since human beings are part of nature.

Estranged labor estranges human beings from 1.) nature and 2.) from themselves in their own active function, their life-activity, and from this, it estranges human beings from their *species*; estranged labor makes the *species-being* only the means for the individual life. First, it estranges the species life from the individual life, and second, it makes the individual life in its abstraction the purpose of the species life, even in its abstracted and estranged form.

First, labor appears to human beings, labor which is the *life-activity*, the *productive life* itself, only as a *means* to meet some need, the need of maintaining physical existence. The productive life is also the species life. It is life engendering life. In the art of life-activity lies the entire character of the species, its species-character, and the species-character of humanity consists of free, conscious activity. Life itself manifests itself as a *means of life*.

The animal is its own life-activity. It does not distinguish itself from it. It is *it*. Humanity makes its life-activity itself an object of will and consciousness. It has conscious life-activity. . . . Conscious life-activity distinguishes human beings from animals. . . . human life is an object that belongs to humanity, this is its species-being. For this reason its activity is free activity. Estranged labor reverses this relationship, so that human beings, because they have conscious being, make their life-activity, their existence, a means for existence. . . .

Estranged labor works thus:

3.) *the species-being of humanity*, in that nature and its mental species-property, confronts humanity as a strange existence, as a *means* to its *individual existence*. It estranges humanity from its own body, as it does the external, natural world, as it does his mental existence, his *human existence*.

4.) A direct consequence of the estrangement of the humans from the product of their labor, from their life-activity, from their species-being, is the *estrangement of humans from humans*. When a human confronts himself as a stranger, so he confronts another human as a stranger. The relationship of humans to their labor, to the product of their labor, and to themselves, is also the relationship of humans to each other, and to the labor of others and to the objects of others.

Moreover, this fact, that the individual is estranged from his species-being means that the individual is estranged from other individuals, since each of them is estranged from their own species-being.

The self-estrangement of individuals, in fact, every relationship in which individuals stand in relationship to themselves, is first realized in the relationship that individuals have with other individuals. Therefore, within the relationship of estranged labor, each individual treats others with the same standard and relative position that he finds himself in.

XXV. We began with a fact of political economy, the estrangement of the laborer and his production. We have produced the idea of this fact: *estranged, alienated* labor. We have analyzed this idea, therefore, we have analyzed a fact of political economy.

We must now see how this idea of estranged, alienated labor expresses and produces itself in actuality.

If the product of labor is foreign to me, if it confronts me as a foreign power, to whom, then, does it belong?

When my own activity does not belong to me, when it is a coerced activity, to whom then does it belong?

It belongs to a being *other* than myself.

Who is this being? . . .

This foreign being, to whom labor and the product of labor belong, in whose service labor and in whose benefit the product of labor is brought into existence, can only be another *human being*.

When the product of labor does not belong to the laborer, when a strange, foreign power confronts and dominates him, this can only be possible if it belongs to *a human being other than the laborer*. When his activity is agony to the laborer, it can only be a *delight* and joy to another. Not gods, not nature, but only human beings themselves can be this strange, foreign power over other human beings.

One should consider that in the proposition stated above man's relationship to himself is first and foremost an *objective, actual* relationship only through his relationship to other men. Therefore, if the product of his labor, of his labor turned into an object, is in relation to him a *foreign, hostile*, powerful, independent object, then his relation to it is such that it is an object mastered by a man foreign, hostile, powerful, and independent of him. If his own activity is for him an unfree activity, then he sees his activity as being done in the service, under the lordship, under the coercion and under the yoke of another man.

Every self-estrangement of people from themselves and from nature manifests itself in the relationship they establish between themselves, nature, and other humans differentiated from themselves. . . . In the *practical*, real world, self-estrangement can only manifest itself in the practical, real relationships between other people. The medium, through which estrangement arises, is itself *practical*. Through estranged labor, humans not only produce their relationship to the object and to the act of production as a power foreign and hostile to them, they produce also the relationship in which their production and their product stands in relationship to other humans as well as the relationship between themselves and other men. Just as the laborer gives birth to his own production as his reality, as his strife, just as he gives birth to his own product as a loss, as a product not to be owned by him, so he gives birth to the mastery of that man, who has produced nothing, over production and over the product. Just as he estranges himself from his own activity, so he confers ownership to a stranger over this activity which does not really belong to him.

We have until now treated only this relationship from the side of the laborer, and we shall later treat this relationship from the side of the non-laborer.

Therefore, through *estranged, alienated labor* the laborer gives birth to his relationship to his labor as something alien and external to him. This relationship of the laborer to his labor gives birth to the relationship of that labor to the capitalist, or whatever one wishes to name the "labor-master." *Private property* is also the product, the result, the natural consequence of *alienated labor*, of the alienated relationship of the laborer to nature and to himself.

Therefore, private property arises from the analysis of the idea of *alienated labor*, that is, of *alienated humanity*, of estranged labor, of estranged life, of *estranged* humanity.

In political economy we have derived this idea of *alienated labor* (of *alienated life*) as a result of the *circulation of private property*. But it is manifest in the analysis of this idea that even though private property appears as the ground, as the foundation of alienated labor, it is rather the consequence of it . . .

This explanation can shed light on several conflicts unsolved until now:

1.) Political economy begins with the notion that labor is the soul of production, yet it gives nothing to labor and everything to private property. . . . We now see, however, that this blatant contradiction is a contradiction of *estranged labor* with itself and that political economy only has drawn out the laws of estranged labor.

We can also see that wages and private property are identical: wages, which is the product, the object of labor, for which labor sells itself, are the necessary consequence of the estrangement of labor, just as in wage labor work itself is not an end in itself, but rather appears as a servant of the wage. . . .

XXVI. A coerced *rise in wages*, therefore . . . is nothing more than a better *salary for slaves* and would not recover for the laborer or for labor its human meaning and dignity.

Indeed, the *equality of salaries* . . . would only change the relationship of each laborer to his labor into the relationship of all humans to their labor. Society would then become an abstract capitalist.

Wages are an unmediated, direct result of estranged labor, and estranged labor is the unmediated, direct source of private property. If the one falls, the other must fall.

2.) From the relationship of estranged labor to private property follows the conclusion that the liberation of society from private property, etc., from servitude, expresses its *political* form in the *emancipation of the laborer*, and not only the emancipation of the laborer, for in the emancipation of the laborer is contained the emancipation of all humanity, and it contains this because the entirety of human servitude is involved in the relationship of the laborer to production and all relationships of servitude are only modifications and consequences of this primary relationship.

Consciousness Derived from Material Conditions from *The German Ideology*

Translated by R. Pascal.

The premises from which we begin are not arbitrary ones, but real premises from which abstraction can only be made in the imagination. They are the real individuals, their activity, and the material conditions under which they live, both those which they find already existing and those produced by their activity. These premises can thus be verified in a purely empirical way.

The first premise of all human history is, of course, the existence of living human individuals. Thus the first fact to be established is the physical organization of these individuals and their consequent relation to the rest of nature. Of course, we cannot here go either into the actual physical nature of man, or into the natural conditions in which man finds himself — geological, oro-hydrographical, climatic, and so on. The writing of history must always set out from these natural bases and their modification in the course of history through the action of man.

Men can be distinguished from animals by consciousness, by religion, or anything else you like. They themselves begin to distinguish themselves from animals as soon as they begin to *produce* their means of subsistence, a step which is conditioned by their physical organization. By producing their means of subsistence men are indirectly producing their actual material life.

The way in which men produce their means of subsistence depends first of all on the nature of the actual means they find in existence and have to reproduce. This mode of production must not be considered simply as being the reproduction of the physical existence of the individuals. Rather it is a definite form of activity of these individuals, a definite form of expressing their life, a definite *mode of life* on their part. As individuals express their life, so they are. What they are, therefore, coincides with their production, both with *what* they produce and with *how* they produce. The nature of individuals thus depends on the material conditions determining their production.

This production only makes its appearance with the increase of population. In its turn this presupposes the intercourse of individuals with one another. The form of this intercourse is again determined by production.

The relations of different nations among themselves depend upon the extent to which each has developed its productive forces, the division of labor, and internal intercourse.[1] This statement is generally recognized. But not only the relation of one nation to others, but also the whole internal structure of the nation itself depends on the stage of development reached by its production and its internal and external intercourse. How far the productive forces of a nation are developed is shown most manifestly by the degree to which the division of labor has been carried. Each new productive force, insofar as it is not merely a quantitative extension of productive forces already known, (for instance, the bringing into cultivation of fresh land), brings about a further development of the division of labor.

The division of labor inside a nation leads at first to the separation of industrial and commercial from agricultural labor, and hence to the separation of town and country and a clash of interests between them. Its further development leads to the separation of commercial from industrial labor. At the same time through the division of labor there develop further, inside these various branches, various divisions among individuals cooperating in definite kinds of labor. The relative position of these individual groups is determined by the methods employed in

[1]Markets within the economy of the nation.

agriculture, industry, and commerce (patriarchalism, slavery, estates, classes). These same conditions are to be seen (given a more developed intercourse) in the relations of different nations to one another.

The various stages of development in the division of labor are just so many different forms of ownership; i.e., the existing stage in the division of labor determines also the relations of individuals to one another with reference to the material, instrument, and product of labor.

The first form of ownership is tribal ownership. It corresponds to the undeveloped stage of production, at which a people lives by hunting and fishing, by the rearing of beasts or, in the highest stage, agriculture. In the latter case it presupposes a great mass of uncultivated stretches of land. The division of labor is at this stage still very elementary and is confined to a further extension of the natural division of labor imposed by the family. The social structure is therefore limited to an extension of the family; patriarchal family chieftains; below them the members of the tribe; finally slaves. The slavery latent in the family only develops gradually with the increase of population, the growth of wants, and with the extension of external relations, of war or of trade.

The second form is the ancient communal and State ownership which proceeds especially from the union of several tribes into a city by agreement or by conquest, and which is still accompanied by slavery. Beside communal ownership we already find movable, and later also immovable, private property developing, but as an abnormal form subordinate to communal ownership. It is only as a community that the citizens hold power over their laboring slaves, and on this account alone, therefore, they are bound to the form of communal ownership. It is the communal private property which compels the active citizens to remain in this natural form of association over against their slaves. For this reason the whole structure of society based on this communal ownership, and with it the power of the people, decays in the same measure as immovable private property evolves. The division of labor is already more developed. We already find the antagonism of town and country; later the antagonism between those states which represent town interests and those which represent country, and inside the towns themselves the antagonism between industry and maritime commerce. The class relation between citizens and slaves is now completely developed.

The whole interpretation of history appears to be contradicted by the fact of conquest. Up till now violence, war, pillage, rape, and slaughter, etc. have been accepted as the driving force of history. Here we must limit ourselves to the chief points and take therefore only a striking example — the destruction of an old civilization by a barbarous people and the resulting formation of an entirely new organization of society. (Rome and the barbarians; Feudalism and Gaul; the Byzantine Empire and the Turks.) With the conquering barbarian people war itself is still, as hinted above, a regular form of intercourse, which is the more eagerly exploited as the population increases, involving the necessity of new means of production to supersede the traditional and, for it, the only possible, crude mode of production. In Italy it was, however, otherwise. The concentration of landed property (caused not only by buying-up and indebtedness but also by inheritance, since loose living being rife and marriage rare, the old families died out and their possessions fell into the hands of a few) and its conversion into grazing-land (caused not only by economic forces still operative today but by the importation of plundered and tribute-corn and the resultant lack of demand for Italian corn) brought about the almost total disappearance of the free population. The very slaves died out again and again, and had constantly to be replaced by new ones. Slavery remained the basis of the whole productive system. The plebeians, mid-way between freemen and slaves, never succeeded in becoming more than a proletarian rabble. Rome indeed never became more than a city; its connection with the provinces was almost exclusively political and could therefore easily be broken again by political events.

With the development of private property, we find here for the first time the same conditions which we shall find again, only on a more extensive scale, with modern private property. On the one hand the concentration of private property, which began very early in Rome (as the Licinian agrarian law² proves), and proceeded very rapidly from the time of the civil wars and especially under the Emperors; on the other hand, coupled with this, the transformation of the plebeian small peasantry into a proletariat, which, however, owing to its intermediate position between propertied citizens and slaves, never achieved an independent development.

The third form of ownership is feudal or estate-property. If antiquity started out from the town and its little territory, the Middle Ages started out from the country. This different starting-point was determined by the sparseness of the population at that time, which was scattered over a large area and which received no large increase from the conquerors. In contrast to Greece and Rome, feudal development therefore extends over a much wider field, prepared by the Roman conquests and the spread of agriculture at first associated with it. The last centuries of the declining Roman Empire and its conquest by the barbarians destroyed a number of productive forces; agriculture had declined, industry had decayed for want of a market, trade had died out or been violently suspended, the rural and urban population had decreased. From these conditions and the mode of organizations of the conquest determined by them, feudal property developed under the influence of the Germanic military constitution. Like tribal and communal ownership, it is based on a community; but the directly producing class standing over against it is not, as in the case of the ancient community, the slaves, but the enserfed small peasantry. As soon as feudalism is fully developed, there also arises antagonism to the towns. The hierarchical system of land ownership, and the armed bodies of retainers associated with it, gave the nobility power over the serfs. This feudal organization was, just as much as the ancient communal ownership, an association against a subjected producing class; but the form of association and the relation to the direct producers were different because of the different conditions of production.

This feudal organization of land-ownership had its counterpart in the towns in the shape of corporative property, the feudal organization of trades. Here property consisted chiefly in the labor of each individual person. The necessity for association against the organized robber-nobility, the need for communal covered markets in an age when the industrialist was at the same time a merchant, the growing competition of the escaped serfs swarming into the rising towns, the feudal structure of the whole country: these combined to bring about the guilds. Further, the gradually accumulated capital of individual craftsmen and their stable numbers, as against the growing population, evolved the relation of journeyman and apprentice, which brought into being in the towns a hierarchy similar to that in the country.

Thus the chief form of property during the feudal epoch consisted on the one hand of landed property with serf-labor chained to it, and on the other of individual labor with small capital commanding the labor of journeymen. The organization of both was determined by the restricted conditions of production — the small-scale and primitive cultivation of the land, and the craft type of industry. There was little division of labor in the heyday of feudalism. Each land bore in itself the conflict of town and country and the division into estates was certainly strongly marked: but apart from the differentiation of princes, nobility, clergy, and peasants in the country, and masters, journeymen, apprentices, and soon also the rabble of casual laborers in the towns, no division of importance took place. In agriculture it was rendered difficult by the strip-system, beside which the cottage industry of the peasants themselves emerged as another factor. In industry there was no division of labor at all in the individual trades themselves, and very little between them. The separation of industry and commerce was found already in existence in older towns; in the newer it only developed later, when the towns entered into mutual relations.

The grouping of larger territories into feudal kingdoms was a necessity for the landed nobility as for the towns. The organization of the ruling class, the nobility, had, therefore, everywhere a monarch at its head.

²A law dating to the early days of the Republic that prevented the dispersal of estates by providing that the eldest son inherited the landed property.

The fact is, therefore, that definite individuals who are productively active in a definite way enter into these definite social and political relations. Empirical observation must in each separate instance bring out empirically, and without any mystification and speculation, the connection of the social and political structure with production. The social structure and the State are continually evolving out of the life-process of definite individuals, but of individuals, not as they may appear in their own or other people's imagination, but as they really are; i.e., as they are effective, produce materially, and are active under definite material limits, presuppositions, and conditions independent of their will.

The production of ideas, of conceptions, of consciousness, is at first directly interwoven with the material activity and the material intercourse of men, the language of real life. Conceiving, thinking, the mental intercourse of men, appear at this stage as the direct efflux of their material behavior. The same applies to mental production as expressed in the language of the politics, laws, morality, religion, metaphysics of a people. Men are the producers of their conceptions, ideas, etc.—real, active men, as they are conditioned by a definite development of their productive forces and of the intercourse corresponding to these, up to its furthest forms. Consciousness can never be anything else than conscious existence, and the existence of men is their actual life-process. If in all ideology men and their circumstances appear upside down as in a *camera obscura*,[3] this phenomenon arises just as much from their historical life-process as the inversion of objects on the retina does from their physical life-process.

[3]Marx refers to the fact that the lens of a camera inverts the image while projecting it onto the plate or film.

In direct contrast to German philosophy which descends from heaven to earth, here we ascend from earth to heaven. That is to say, we do not set out from what men say, imagine, conceive, nor from men as narrated, thought of, imagined, conceived, in order to arrive at men in the flesh. We set out from real, active men, and on the basis of their real life-process we demonstrate the development of the ideological reflexes and echoes of this life-process. The phantoms formed in the human brain are also, necessarily, sublimates of their material life-process, which is empirically verifiable and bound to material premises. Morality, religion, metaphysics, all the rest of ideology and their corresponding forms of consciousness, thus no longer retain the semblance of independence. They have no history, no development; but men, developing their material production and their material intercourse, alter, along with this their real existence, their thinking and the products of their thinking. Life is not determined by consciousness, but consciousness by life. In the first method of approach the starting point is consciousness taken as the living individual; in the second it is the real living individuals themselves, as they are in actual life, and consciousness is considered solely as *their* consciousness.

This method of approach is not devoid of premises. It starts out from the real premises and does not abandon them for a moment. Its premises are men, not in any fantastic isolation or abstract definition, but in their actual, empirically perceptible process of development under definite conditions. As soon as this active life-process is described, history ceases to be a collection of dead facts as it is with the empiricists (themselves still abstract), or an imagined activity of imagined subjects, as with the idealists.

On Greek Art in Its Time
from A Contribution to the Critique of Political Economy

THE MODE OF PRODUCTION OF MATERIAL LIFE DETERMINES THE SOCIAL, POLITICAL, AND INTELLECTUAL PROCESSES OF LIFE

In the social production which men carry on they enter into definite relations that are indispensable and independent of their will; these relations of production correspond to a definite stage of development of their material forces of production. The sum total of these relations of production constitutes the economic structure of society — the real foundation, on which rises a legal and political superstructure and to which correspond definite forms of social consciousness. The mode of production in material life determines the social, political, and intellectual life processes in general. It is not the consciousness of men that determines their being, but, on the contrary, their social being that determines their consciousness. At a certain stage of their development, the material forces of production in society come in conflict with the existing relations of production or — what is but a legal expression for the same thing — with the property relations within which they have been at work before. From forms of development of the forces of production these relations turn into their fetters. Then begins an epoch of social revolution. With the change of the economic foundation the entire immense superstructure is more or less rapidly transformed. In considering such transformations a distinction should always be made between the material transformation of the economic conditions of production which can be determined with the precision of natural science, and the legal, political, religious, aesthetic, or philosophic — in short, ideological — forms in which men become conscious of this conflict and

Translated by Nahum Isaac Stone.

fight it out. Just as our opinion of an individual is not based on what he thinks of himself, so can we not judge of such a period of transformation by its own consciousness, on the contrary this consciousness must be explained rather from the contradictions of material life, from the existing conflict between the social forces of production and the relations of production. No social order ever disappears before all the productive forces for which there is room in it have been developed; and new higher relations of production never appear before the material conditions of their existence have matured in the womb of the old society itself. Therefore, mankind always sets itself only such tasks as it can solve; since, looking at the matter more closely, we will always find that the task itself arises only when the material conditions necessary for its solution already exist or are at least in the process of formation. In broad outlines we can designate the Asiatic, the ancient, the feudal, and the modern bourgeois modes of production as so many epochs in the progress of the economic formation of society. The bourgeois relations of production are the last antagonistic form of the social process of production — antagonistic not in the sense of individual antagonism, but of one arising from the social conditions of life of the individuals; at the same time the productive forces developing in the womb of bourgeois society create the material conditions for the solution of that antagonism. This social formation constitutes, therefore, the closing chapter of the prehistoric stage of human society.

On Greek Art in Its Time

It is well known that certain periods of highest development of art stand in no direct connection with the general development of society, nor with the material basis and the skeleton structure of its organization. Witness the example of the Greeks as compared with the modern nations or even Shakespeare. As regards certain forms of art, as e.g., the epos, it is admitted that they can never be produced in the world-epoch making form as soon as art as such comes into existence; in other words, that in the domain of art certain important forms of it are possible only at a low stage of its development. If that be true of the mutual relations of different forms of art within the domain of art itself, it is far less surprising that the same is true of the relation of art as a whole to the general development of society. The difficulty lies only in the general formulation of these contradictions. No sooner are they specified than they are explained. Let us take for instance the relation of Greek art and of that of Shakespeare's time to our own. It is a well-known fact that Greek mythology was not only the arsenal of Greek art, but also the very ground from which it had sprung. Is the view of nature and of social relations which shaped Greek imagination and Greek [art] possible in the age of automatic machinery, and railways, and locomotives, and electric telegraphs? Where does Vulcan come in as against Roberts & Co.; Jupiter, as against the lightning rod; and Hermes, as against the Credit Mobilier?[1] All mythology masters and dominates and shapes the forces of nature in and through the imagination; hence it disappears as soon as man gains mastery over the forces of nature. What becomes of the Goddess Fame side by side with Printing House Square?[2] Greek art presupposes the existence of Greek mythology; i.e., that nature and even the form of society are wrought up in popular fancy in an unconsciously artistic fashion. That is its material. Not, however, any mythology taken at random, nor any accidental unconsciously artistic elaboration of nature (including under the latter all objects, hence [also] society). Egyptian mythology could never be the soil or womb which would give birth to Greek art. But in any event [there had to be] *a* mythology. In no event [could Greek art originate] in a society which excludes any mythological explanation of nature, any mythological attitude towards it and which requires from the artists an imagination free from mythology.

Looking at it from another side: is Achilles possible side by side with powder and lead? Or is the *Iliad* at all compatible with the printing press and steam press? Does not singing and reciting and the muses necessarily go out of existence with the appearance of the printer's bar, and do not, therefore, disappear the prerequisites of epic poetry?

But the difficulty is not in grasping the idea that Greek art and epos are bound up with certain forms of social development. It rather lies in understanding why they still constitute with us a source of aesthetic enjoyment and in certain respects prevail as the standard and model beyond attainment.

A man can not become a child again unless he becomes childish. But does he not enjoy the artless ways of the child and must he not strive to reproduce its truth on a higher plane? Is not the character of every epoch revived perfectly true to nature in child nature? Why should the social childhood of mankind, where it had obtained its most beautiful development, not exert an eternal charm as an age that will never return? There are ill-bred children and precocious children. Many of the ancient nations belong to the latter class. The Greeks were normal children. The charm their art has for us does not conflict with the primitive character of the social order from which it had sprung. It is rather the product of the latter, and is rather due to the fact that the unripe social conditions under which the art arose and under which alone it could appear can never return.

[1]Marx wittily compares ancient and modern institutions; Vulcan was the god of manufactures, while Roberts & Co. was a munitions maker; Jupiter controlled the lightning as now the lightning rod does; Hermes was the god of thieves, while the Credit Mobilier was a large financial institution.

[2]Where the London *Times* was printed.

Matthew Arnold

1822–1888

Matthew Arnold was born in Laleham, Middlesex, but in 1828 moved to Rugby, where his father, Dr. Thomas Arnold, the sage and humane spirit of *Tom Brown's School Days*, had been appointed headmaster. Arnold went to Winchester, then to Rugby, to Balliol College of Oxford, and then to a fellowship at Oriel. In 1851 Arnold left academia, became an inspector of schools (a position he held for thirty-five years), and married Frances Lucy Wightman. His chief volumes of poetry were *Empedocles on Etna* (1852); *Poems* (1853); *Poems, Second Series* (1855); *Merope, a Tragedy* (1858); and *New Poems* (1867). His chief critical publications were *Essays in Criticism*, First Series (1865); *Culture and Anarchy* (1869); *Literature and Dogma* (1873); and *Essays in Criticism, Second Series* (1888). Arnold was elected professor of poetry at Oxford in 1857 and held the position for ten years. He died unexpectedly in 1888.

Some passages in Arnold's criticism have struck commentators as Aristotelian, notably a section from his preface to *Poems* (1853), which insists that human action, rather than the consciousness of the poet, is the true subject of poetry:

What are the eternal objects of poetry, among all nations and at all times? They are actions; human actions; possessing an inherent interest in themselves, and which are to be communicated in an interesting manner by the art of the poet. Vainly will the latter imagine that he has everything in his power; that he can make an intrinsically inferior action . . . delightful . . . by his treatment of it. . . . I fearlessly assert that *Hermann and Dorothea, Childe Harold, Jocelyn, The Excursion*, leave the reader cold in comparison with the effect produced on him by the latter books of the *Iliad*, by the *Oresteia*, or by the episode of Dido. . . .

If to know and to cite Aristotle is to be Aristotelian, then Arnold was one of the most loyal Aristotelians the nineteenth century produced. Indeed, in the essay included here, Arnold alludes to *Poetics*, Chapter 9, that poetry is a higher thing than history, because poetry is *philosophoteron kai spoudaioteron*, the more philosophical and more nobly serious human activity.

But in fact, Arnold's conception of literature is far from the gist and method of the *Poetics*. For Aristotle the poem's only duty is to be good in the way of its kind, and he resolutely differentiated between the genres of poetry and between poetry and all other forms of creativity. Aristotle's sense of the discreteness of activities and the primacy of form over content — both intellectual and spiritual — would be totally foreign to Arnold's way of thinking. For Arnold, form as an issue in itself never comes up.

Even the word *criticism* in "The Function of Criticism at the Present Time" (1864) is far broader than *literary* criticism: It denominates literature itself as a "criticism of life." Literature and literary criticism alike engage in a comprehensive critique of the entire culture. And while Arnold seems at times to be discussing literature as such, art is never for art's sake: Literature is of interest to him primarily as an index to and a banner of the society that produced it. In this sense Arnold is as holistic a critic as Plato in *Republic,* Book X. In another sense, however, Arnold entirely inverts Plato, for he views art as one possible salvation for an inhumane society rather than as a potential source of pollution in a utopia. Instead of being, as in Plato, a distorting mirror of reality, art for Arnold is one way of increasing the accuracy of one's spiritual vision — and a corrective for the illusions of political propaganda.

In one passage of "The Function of Criticism," for example, Arnold quotes some of the dithyrambically optimistic oratory of contemporary parliamentarians Charles Adderley and John Arthur Roebuck, who viewed Victorian society as not merely perfectible but as nearly perfected. Arnold responds not with a quotation from the classics but rather with a sordid newspaper paragraph about a "shocking child murder" committed at Nottingham by a workhouse girl named Wragg. Arnold asks us to imagine "the workhouse, the dismal Mapperly hills . . . the gloom, the smoke, the cold, the strangled illegitimate child. . . . And the final touch, — short, bleak, and inhuman: *Wragg is in custody.*" The passage is astonishing in a work of literary criticism. In a way, though, it is the center of the essay. This quotation represents the lowest level at which literature — the imaginative recreation of human existence — can be "criticism of life": minimally, by ironically exploding the pretenses of current ideology. But criticism of life has other phases. At its best literature can reawaken in us a sense of what it would mean to be fully human — a reawakening that Arnold sensed was needed more than ever in his mechanical age.

Because of what literature is capable of at its best, Arnold is concerned that we recognize what is best and not mistake cheaper merchandise for the genuine article. This form of elitism inspired "The Study of Poetry" (1880) and its doctrine of "touchstones" — lines of poetry that supposedly characterize the highest flights of the human spirit. When we hear a line of poetry, Arnold recommends that we compare it immediately to those lines in literature that are most sublime: "*In la sua voluntade è nostra pace*" from Dante's *Paradiso,* or "Absent thee from felicity awhile" from *Hamlet.*

As a method of literary criticism, "touchstonery" had been exploded a century before, in Johnson's *Preface to Shakespeare*: "He that tries to recommend [Shakespeare] by select quotations, will succeed like the pedant in Hierocles, who, when he offered his house to sale, carried a brick in his pocket as a specimen." One problem with touchstonery is obvious: It valorizes the single, sublime line to the neglect of every other aspect of literature: plot, characterization, consistency of tone, originality of thought. Less obviously, perhaps, it devalues genres other than epic and tragedy. Within Arnold's essay itself it is clear that the comic genius of Chaucer must be placed below the soberer Milton, even below François Villon. The brilliant eighteenth-century wits who devoted themselves to satire and comedy fall, by Arnold's standard, below the salt.

While it would be hard to defend Arnold's touchstones as a mode of literary analysis, it is important to understand their historical significance as well as the general importance of the sublime in Arnold's thought. Arnold's age was also that of Charles Darwin and Herbert Spencer and David Friedrich Strauss. With science beginning to undermine the tenets of revealed religion, with philosophy becoming either too abstruse or too pragmatic to provide consolation and solace, Arnold felt that poetry could provide the new Word for which humanity was listening. "More and more," Arnold prophesies, "mankind will discover that we have to turn to poetry to interpret life for us, to console us, to sustain us. Without poetry, our science will appear incomplete; most of what now passes with us for religion and philosophy will be replaced by poetry." Culture would be grounded in literature, and Arnold was determined that if the culture was not to decline or vanish, that foundation would have to be revelatory of humanity's highest spiritual aspirations.

Arnold expected that the trends he saw would continue or accelerate, but as is usual with human affairs, this did not precisely happen. Revealed religion revived in the decade of Arnold's death, and the pendulum has swung back and forth several times since then. In many regions of America, Darwinian evolution is on the defensive, at least in the public schools, and one might as easily fear the possibility that religion might subvert science in the popular mind. But what has come to pass in the last few decades — a culture grounded not in poetry but in television and dedicated not to the sublime but to the lowest common denominator — might well have been Arnold's worst nightmare.

Selected Bibliography

Boutellier, Victor N. *Imaginative Reason: The Continuity of Arnold's Critical Effort.* Bern: Franke, 1977.

Buckley, Vincent. *Poetry and Morality: Studies in the Criticism of Matthew Arnold, T. S. Eliot, and F. R. Leavis.* London: Chatto and Windus, 1959.

Carroll, Joseph. *The Cultural Theory of Matthew Arnold.* Berkeley: University of California Press, 1982.

Donoghue, Denis. "Three Ways of Reading." *Southern Review* 34, no.2 (1998): 383–401.

Eells, John Shepard. *The Touchstones of Matthew Arnold.* New York: Bookman Associates, 1955.

Garrod, Heathcote William. *Poetry and the Criticism of Life.* New York: Russell and Russell, 1963.

Knickerbocker, William S. "Matthew Arnold's Theory of Poetry." *Sewanee Review* 33 (1925): 440–50.

Perkins, David. "Arnold and the Function of Literature." *ELH* 18 (1951): 287–309.

Stange, G. Robert. *Matthew Arnold: The Poet as Humanist.* Princeton: Princeton University Press, 1967.

Stone, Donald D. *Communications with the Future: Matthew Arnold in Dialogue.* Ann Arbor: University of Michigan Press, 1997.

Trilling, Lionel. *Matthew Arnold.* New York: Norton, 1939.

Wills, Anthony Aldwin. *Matthew Arnold's Literary and Religious Thought.* Stanford: Stanford University Press, 1968.

The Function of Criticism at the Present Time

Many objections have been made to a proposition which, in some remarks of mine on translating Homer, I ventured to put forth; a proposition about criticism, and its importance at the present day. I said: "Of the literature of France and Germany, as of the intellect of Europe in general, the main effort, for now many years, has been a critical effort; the endeavour, in all branches of knowledge, theology, philosophy, history, art, science, to see the object as in itself it really is." I added, that owing to the operation in English literature of certain causes, "almost the last thing for which one would come to English literature is just that very thing which now Europe most desires, — criticism"; and that the power and value of English literature was thereby impaired. More than one rejoinder declared that the importance I here assigned to criticism was excessive, and asserted the inherent superiority of the creative effort of the human spirit over its critical effort. And the other day, having been led by an excellent notice of Wordsworth[1] published in the *North British Review,* to turn again to his biography, I found, in the words of this great man, whom I, for one, must always listen to with the profoundest respect, a sentence passed on the critic's business, which seems to justify every possible disparagement of it. Wordsworth says in one of his letters:

The writers in these publications [the Reviews], while they prosecute their inglorious employment,

can not be supposed to be in a state of mind very favourable for being affected by the finer influences of a thing so pure as genuine poetry.[2]

And a trustworthy reporter of his conversation quotes a more elaborate judgment to the same effect:

Wordsworth holds the critical power very low, infinitely lower than the inventive; and he said today that if the quantity of time consumed in writing critiques on the works of others were given to original composition, of whatever kind it might be, it would be much better employed; it would make a man find out sooner his own level, and it would do infinitely less mischief. A false or malicious criticism may do much injury to the minds of others, a stupid invention, either in prose or verse, is quite harmless.[3]

It is almost too much to expect of poor human nature, that a man capable of producing some effect in one line of literature, should, for the greater good of society, voluntarily doom himself to impotence and obscurity in another. Still less is this to be expected from men addicted to the composition of the "false or malicious criticism," of which Wordsworth speaks. However, everybody would admit that a false or malicious criticism had better never have been written. Everybody, too, would be willing to admit, as a general proposition, that the critical faculty is lower than the inventive. But is it true that criticism is really, in itself, a baneful and injurious employment; is it true that all time given to writing critiques on the works of others would be much better employed if it were given to original composition, of whatever kind this may be? Is it true that Johnson had better have gone on producing more *Irenes* instead of writing his *Lives of the Poets;* nay, is it certain that Wordsworth himself was better employed in making his Ecclesiastical Sonnets than when he made his celebrated Preface,

---

[1] I cannot help thinking that a practice, common in England during the last century, and still followed in France, of printing a notice of this kind,—a notice by a competent critic,—to serve as an introduction to an eminent author's works, might be revived among us with advantage. To introduce all succeeding editions of Wordsworth, Mr. Sharp's notice (it is permitted, I hope, to mention his name) might, it seems to me, excellently serve; it is written from the point of view of an admirer, nay, of a disciple, and that is right; but then the disciple must be also, as in this case he is, a critic, a man of letters, not, as too often happens, some relation or friend with no qualification for his task except affection for his author. [Arnold.] J. C. Sharp's "Wordsworth: The Man and Poet" appeared in *North British Review* 61 (1864): 1–54.

[2] Letter of January 12, 1816, to Bernard Barton in *The Letters of William and Dorothy Wordsworth* (ed. Ernest de Selincourt, revised by Mary Moorman and Alan G. Hill), 3: 269.
[3] William Knight, *Life of William Wordsworth* (1889) 3: 438.

so full of criticism, and criticism of the works of others? Wordsworth was himself a great critic, and it is to be sincerely regretted that he has not left us more criticism; Goethe was one of the greatest of critics, and we may sincerely congratulate ourselves that he has left us so much criticism. Without wasting time over the exaggeration which Wordsworth's judgment on criticism clearly contains, or over an attempt to trace the causes, — not difficult I think to be traced, — which may have led Wordsworth to this exaggeration, a critic may with advantage seize an occasion for trying his own conscience, and for asking himself of what real service, at any given moment, the practice of criticism either is, or may be made, to his own mind and spirit, and to the minds and spirits of others.

The critical power is of lower rank than the creative. True; but in assenting to this proposition, one or two things are to be kept in mind. It is undeniable that the exercise of a creative power, that a free creative activity, is the highest function of man; it is proved to be so by man's finding in it his true happiness. But it is undeniable, also, that men may have the sense of exercising this free creative activity in other ways than in producing great works of literature or art; if it were not so, all but a very few men would be shut out from the true happiness of all men. They may have it in well-doing, they may have it in learning, they may have it even in criticizing. This is one thing to be kept in mind. Another is, that the exercise of the creative power in the production of great works of literature or art, however high this exercise of it may rank, is not at all epochs and under all conditions possible; and that therefore labour may be vainly spent in attempting it, which might with more fruit be used in preparing for it, in rendering it possible. This creative power works with elements, with materials; what if it has not those materials, those elements, ready for its use? In that case it must surely wait till they are ready. Now in literature, — I will limit myself to literature, for it is about literature that the question arises, — the elements with which the creative power works are ideas; the best ideas, on every matter which literature touches, current at the time. At any rate we may lay it down as certain that in modern literature no manifestation of the creative power not working

with these can be very important or fruitful. And I say *current* at the time, not merely accessible at the time; for creative literary genius does not principally show itself in discovering new ideas: that is rather the business of the philosopher: the grand work of literary genius is a work of synthesis and exposition, not of analysis and discovery; its gift lies in the faculty of being happily inspired by a certain intellectual and spiritual atmosphere, by a certain order of ideas, when it finds itself in them; of dealing divinely with these ideas, presenting them in the most effective and attractive combinations, — making beautiful works with them, in short. But it must have the atmosphere, it must find itself amidst the order of ideas, in order to work freely; and these it is not so easy to command. This is why great creative epochs in literature are so rare; this is why there is so much that is unsatisfactory in the production of many men of real genius; because for the creation of a masterwork of literature two powers must concur, the power of the man and the power of the moment, and the man is not enough without the moment; the creative power has, for its happy exercise, appointed elements, and those elements are not in its own control.

Nay, they are more within the control of the critical power. It is the business of the critical power, as I said in the words already quoted, "in all branches of knowledge, theology, philosophy, history, art, science, to see the object as in itself it really is." Thus it tends, at last, to make an intellectual situation of which the creative power can profitably avail itself. It tends to establish an order of ideas, if not absolutely true, yet true by comparison with that which it displaces; to make the best ideas prevail. Presently these new ideas reach society; the touch of truth is the touch of life, and there is a stir and growth everywhere; out of this stir and growth come the creative epochs of literature.

Or, to narrow our range, and quit these considerations of the general march of genius and of society, considerations which are apt to become too abstract and impalpable, — everyone can see that a poet, for instance, ought to know life and the world before dealing with them in poetry; and life and the world being, in modern times, very complex things, the creation of a modern poet, to be worth much, implies a great critical effort behind it; else it must be a comparatively poor, barren, and short-lived affair. This is why Byron's poetry had so little endurance in it, and Goethe's so much; both Byron and Goethe had a great productive power, but Goethe's was nourished by a great critical effort providing the true materials for it, and Byron's was not; Goethe knew life and the world, the poet's necessary subjects, much more comprehensively and thoroughly than Byron. He knew a great deal more of them, and he knew them much more as they really are.

It has long seemed to me that the burst of creative activity in our literature, through the first quarter of this century, had about it, in fact, something premature; and that from this cause its productions are doomed, most of them, in spite of the sanguine hopes which accompanied and do still accompany them, to prove hardly more lasting than the productions of far less splendid epochs. And this prematureness comes from its having proceeded without having its proper data, without sufficient materials to work with. In other words, the English poetry of the first quarter of this century, with plenty of energy, plenty of creative force, did not know enough. This makes Byron so empty of matter, Shelley so incoherent, Wordsworth even, profound as he is, yet so wanting in completeness and variety. Wordsworth cared little for books, and disparaged Goethe. I admire Wordsworth, as he is, so much that I cannot wish him different; and it is vain, no doubt, to imagine such a man different from what he is, to suppose that he could have been different. But surely the one thing wanting to make Wordsworth an even greater poet than he is, — his thought richer, and his influence of wider application, — was that he should have read more books, among them, no doubt, those of that Goethe whom he disparaged without reading him.

But to speak of books and reading may easily lead to a misunderstanding here. It was not really books and reading that lacked to our poetry at this epoch; Shelley had plenty of reading, Coleridge had immense reading. Pindar and Sophocles — as we all say so glibly, and often with so little discernment of the real import of what we are saying — had not many books; Shakespeare was no deep reader. True; but in the Greece of Pindar and Sophocles, in the England of Shakespeare, the poet lived in a current of ideas in the highest degree animating and nourishing to the creative power; society was, in the fullest measure, permeated by fresh thought, intelligent and alive; and this state of things is the true basis for the creative power's exercise, — in this it finds its data, its materials, truly ready for its hand; all the books and reading in the world are only valuable as they are helps to this. Even when this does not actually exist, books and reading may enable a man to construct a kind of semblance of it in his own mind, a world of knowledge and intelligence in which he may live and work: this is by no means an equivalent, to the artist, for the nationally diffused life and thought of the epochs of Sophocles or Shakespeare, but, besides that it may be a means of preparation for such epochs, it does really constitute, if many share in it, a quickening and sustaining atmosphere of great value. Such an atmosphere the many-sided learning and the long and widely combined critical effort of Germany formed for Goethe, when he lived and worked. There was no national glow of life and thought there as in the Athens of Pericles, or the England of Elizabeth. That was the poet's weakness. But there was a sort of equivalent for it in the complete culture and unfettered thinking of a large body of Germans. That was his strength. In the England of the first quarter of this century, there was neither a national glow of life and thought, such as we had in the age of Elizabeth, nor yet a culture and a force of learning and criticism, such as were to be found in Germany. Therefore the creative power of poetry wanted, for success in the highest sense, materials and a basis; a thorough interpretation of the world was necessarily denied to it.

At first sight it seems strange that out of the immense stir of the French Revolution and its age should not have come a crop of works of genius equal to that which came out of the stir of the great productive time of Greece, or out of that of the Renascence, with its powerful episode the Reformation. But the truth is that the stir of the French Revolution took a character which essentially distinguished it from such movements as these. These were, in the main, disinterestedly intellectual and spiritual movements; movements in which the human spirit looked for its satisfaction in itself and in the increased play of its own activity: the French Revolution took a political, practical character. The movement which went on in France under the old régime, from 1700 to 1789, was far more really akin than that of the Revolution itself to the movement of the Ren-ascence; the France of Voltaire and Rousseau told far more powerfully upon the mind of Europe than the France of the Revolution. Goethe reproached this last expressly with having "thrown quiet cul-ture back."[4] Nay, and the true key to how much in our Byron, even in our Wordsworth, is this!—that they had their source in a great movement of feeling, not in a great movement of mind. The French Revolution, however,—that object of so much blind love and so much blind hatred,—found undoubtedly its motive-power in the intel-ligence of men and not in their practical sense;—this is what distinguishes it from the English Revolution of Charles the First's time; this is what makes it a more spiritual event than our Revolution, an event of much more powerful and worldwide interest, though practically less suc-cessful:—it appeals to an order of ideas which are universal, certain, permanent. 1789 asked of a thing, Is it rational? 1642 asked of a thing, Is it legal? Or, when it went furthest, Is it according to conscience? This is the English fashion; a fash-ion to be treated, within its own sphere, with the highest respect; for its success, within its own sphere, has been prodigious. But what is law in one place, is not law in another; what is law here today, is not law even here tomorrow; and as for conscience, what is binding on one man's conscience is not binding on another's; the old woman who threw her stool at the head of the surpliced minister in St. Giles's Church at Edinburgh[5] obeyed an impulse to which millions of the human race may be permitted to remain strangers. But the prescriptions of reason are absolute, unchanging, of universal validity; *to count by tens is the easiest way of counting,* — that is a proposition of which every one, from here to the Antipodes, feels the force; at least, I should say so, if we did not live in a country where it is not impossible that any morning we find a letter in *The Times* declaring that a decimal

coinage is an absurdity.[6] That a whole nation should have been penetrated with an enthusiasm for pure reason, and with an ardent zeal for mak-ing its prescriptions triumph, is a very remark-able thing, when we consider how little of mind, or anything so worthy and quickening as mind, comes into the motives which alone, in general, impel great masses of men. In spite of the extrav-agant direction given to this enthusiasm, in spite of the crimes and follies in which it lost itself, the French Revolution derives from the force, truth, and universality of the ideas which it took for its law, and from the passion with which it could inspire a multitude for these ideas, a unique and still living power; it is — it will probably long remain — the greatest, the most animating event in history. And, as no sincere passion for the things of the mind, even though it turns out in many respects an unfortunate passion, is ever quite thrown away and quite barren of good, France has reaped from hers one fruit — the natural and legitimate fruit, though not precisely the grand fruit she expected: she is the country in Europe where *the people* is most alive.

But the mania for giving an immediate politi-cal and practical application to all these fine ideas of the reason was fatal. Here an Englishman is in his element: on this theme we can all go on for hours. And all we are in the habit of saying on it has undoubtedly a great deal of truth. Ideas cannot be too much prized in and for themselves, can-not be too much lived with; but to transport them abruptly into the world of politics and practice, violently to revolutionize this world to their bid-ding, — that is quite another thing. There is the world of ideas and there is the world of practice; the French are often for suppressing the one and the English the other; but neither is to be sup-pressed. A member of the House of Commons said to me the other day: "That a thing is an anomaly, I consider to be no objection to it what-ever." I venture to think he was wrong; that a thing *is* an anomaly is an objection to it, but absolutely and in the sphere of ideas: it is not necessarily, under such and such circumstances, or at such and such a moment, an objection to it in the sphere of

[4]In Goethe's 'The Four Seasons': Spring."

[5]Jenny Geddes did this on July 23, 1637.

[6]A decimal coinage bill was introduced and withdrawn in 1863.

politics and practice. Joubert has said beautifully: "C'est la force et la droit qui règlent toutes choses dans le monde; la force en attendant le droit." (Force and right are the governors of this world; force till right is ready.)[7] *Force till right is ready;* and till right is ready, force, the existing order of things, is justified, is the legitimate ruler. But right is something moral, and implies inward recognition, free assent of the will; we are not ready for right, — *right,* so far as we are concerned, *is not ready,* — until we have attained this sense of seeing it and willing it. The way in which for us it may change and transform force, the existing order of things, and become, in its turn, the legitimate ruler of the world, should depend on the way in which, when our time comes, we see it and will it. Therefore for other people enamoured of their own newly discerned right, to attempt to impose it upon us as ours, and violently to substitute their right for our force, is an act of tyranny, and to be resisted. It sets at nought the second great half of our maxim, *force till right is ready.* This was the grand error of the French Revolution; and its movement of ideas, by quitting the intellectual sphere and rushing furiously into the political sphere, ran, indeed, a prodigious and memorable course, but produced no such intellectual fruit as the movement of ideas of the Renascence, and created, in opposition to itself, what I may call an *epoch of concentration.* The great force of that epoch of concentration was England; and the great voice of that epoch of concentration was Burke. It is the fashion to treat Burke's writings on the French Revolution as superannuated and conquered by the event; as the eloquent but unphilosophical tirades of bigotry and prejudice. I will not deny that they are often disfigured by the violence and passion of the moment, and that in some directions Burke's view was bounded, and his observation therefore at fault; but on the whole, and for those who can make the needful corrections, what distinguishes these writings is their profound, permanent, fruitful, philosophical truth; they contain the true philosophy of an epoch of concentration, dissipate the heavy atmosphere which its own nature is apt to engender round it, and make its resistance rational instead of mechanical.

But Burke is so great because, almost alone in England, he brings thought to bear upon politics, he saturates politics with thought; it is his accident that his ideas were at the service of an epoch of concentration, not of an epoch of expansion; it is his characteristic that he so lived by ideas, and had such a source of them welling up within him, that he could float even an epoch of concentration and English Tory politics with them. It does not hurt him that Dr. Price and the Liberals were enraged with him; it does not even hurt him that George the Third and the Tories were enchanted with him. His greatness is that he lived in a world which neither English Liberalism nor English Toryism is apt to enter; — the world of ideas, not the world of catchwords and party habits. So far is it from being really true of him that he "to party gave up what was meant for mankind,"[8] that at the very end of his fierce struggle with the French Revolution, after all his invectives against its false pretensions, hollowness, and madness, with his sincere conviction of its mischievousness, he can close a memorandum on the best means of combating it, some of the last pages he ever wrote, — the *Thoughts on French Affairs,* in December 1791, — with these striking words:

> The evil is stated, in my opinion, as it exists. The remedy must be where power, wisdom, and information, I hope, are more united with good intentions than they can be with me. I have done with this subject, I believe, for ever. It has given me many anxious moments for the last two years. *If a great change is to be made in human affairs, the minds of men will be fitted to it; the general opinions and feelings will draw that way. Every fear, every hope will forward it; and then they who persist in opposing this mighty current in human affairs, will appear rather to resist the decrees of Providence itself, than the mere designs of men. They will not be resolute and firm, but perverse and obstinate.*

That return of Burke upon himself has always seemed to me one of the finest things in English literature, or indeed in any literature. That is what I call living by ideas; when one side of a question has long had your earnest support, when all your feelings are engaged, when you hear all round

----

[7]Jean Joubert, *Pensées* (1877), 2:178.

[8]From Oliver Goldsmith's poem "Retaliation" (1774).

you no language but one, when your party talks this language like a steam-engine and can imagine no other. — still to be able to think, still to be irresistibly carried, if so it be, by the current of thought to the opposite side of the question, and, like Balaam, to be unable to speak anything *but what the Lord has put in your mouth.*[9] I know nothing more striking, and I must add that I know nothing more un-English.

For the Englishman in general is like my friend the Member of Parliament, and believes, point-blank, that for a thing to be an anomaly is absolutely no objection to it whatever. He is like the Lord Auckland of Burke's day, who, in a memorandum on the French Revolution, talks of "certain miscreants, assuming the name of philosophers, who have presumed themselves capable of establishing a new system of society." The Englishman has been called a political animal, and he values what is political and practical so much that ideas easily become objects of dislike in his eyes, and thinkers "miscreants," because ideas and thinkers have rashly meddled with politics and practice. This would be all very well if the dislike and neglect confined themselves to ideas transported out of their own sphere, and meddling rashly with practice; but they are inevitably extended to ideas as such, and to the whole life of intelligence; practice is everything, a free play of the mind is nothing. The notion of the free play of the mind upon all subjects being a pleasure in itself, being an object of desire, being an essential provider of elements without which a nation's spirit, whatever compensations it may have for them, must, in the long run, die of inanition, hardly enters into an Englishman's thoughts. It is noticeable that the word *curiosity*, which in other languages is used in a good sense, to mean, as a high and fine quality of man's nature, just this disinterested love of a free play of the mind on all subjects, for its own sake, — it is noticeable, I say, that this word has in our language no sense of the kind, no sense but a rather bad and disparaging one. But criticism, real criticism, is essentially the exercise of this very quality; it obeys an instinct prompting it to know the best that is known and thought in the world, irrespectively of practice, politics, and everything of the kind; and to value knowledge and thought as they approach this best, without the intrusion of any other considerations whatever. This is an instinct for which there is, I think, little original sympathy in the practical English nature, and what there was of it has undergone a long benumbing period of blight and suppression in the epoch of concentration which followed the French Revolution.

But epochs of concentration cannot well endure for ever; epochs of expansion, in the due course of things, follow them. Such an epoch of expansion seems to be opening in this country. In the first place all danger of a hostile forcible pressure of foreign ideas upon our practice has long disappeared; like the traveller in the fable, therefore, we begin to wear our cloak a little more loosely. Then, with a long peace, the ideas of Europe steal gradually and amicably in, and mingle, though in infinitesimally small quantities at a time, with our own notions. Then, too, in spite of all that is said about the absorbing and brutalizing influence of our passionate material progress, it seems to me indisputable that this progress is likely, though not certain, to lead in the end to an apparition of intellectual life; and that man, after he has made himself perfectly comfortable and has now to determine what to do with himself next, may begin to remember that he has a mind and that the mind may be made the source of great pleasure. I grant it is mainly the privilege of faith, at present, to discern this end to our railways, our business, and our fortune-making; but we shall see if, here as elsewhere, faith is not in the end the true prophet. Our ease, our travelling, and our unbounded liberty to hold just as hard and securely as we please to the practice to which our notions have given birth, all tend to beget an inclination to deal a little more freely with these notions themselves, to canvass them a little, to penetrate a little into their real nature. Flutterings of curiosity, in the foreign sense of the word, appear amongst us, and it is in these that criticism must look to find its account. Criticism first; a time of true creative activity, perhaps, — which, as I have said, must inevitably be preceded amongst us by a time of criticism, — hereafter, when criticism has done its work.

[9] Numbers 22:38.

It is of the last importance that English criticism should clearly discern what rule for its course, in order to avail itself of the field now opening to it, and to produce fruit for the future, it ought to take. The rule may be summed up in one word, — *disinterestedness.* And how is criticism to show disinterestedness? By keeping aloof from practice; by resolutely following the law of its own nature, which is to be a free play of the mind on all subjects which it touches; by steadily refusing to lend itself to any of those ulterior, political, practical considerations about ideas which plenty of people will be sure to attach to them, which perhaps ought often to be attached to them, which in this country at any rate are certain to be attached to them quite sufficiently, but which criticism has really nothing to do with. Its business is, as I have said, simply to know the best that is known and thought in the world, and by in its turn making this known, to create a current of true and fresh ideas. Its business is to do this with inflexible honesty, with due ability; but its business is to do no more, and to leave alone all questions of practical consequences and applications, questions which will never fail to have due prominence given to them. Else criticism, besides being really false to its own nature, merely continues in the old rut which it has hitherto followed in this country, and will certainly miss the chance now given to it. For what is at present the bane of criticism in this country? It is that practical considerations cling to it and stifle it; it subserves interests not its own; our organs of criticism are organs of men and parties having practical ends to serve, and with them those practical ends are the first thing and the play of mind the second; so much play of mind as is compatible with the prosecution of those practical ends is all that is wanted. An organ like the *Revue des Deux Mondes,* having for its main function to understand and utter the best that is known and thought in the world, existing, it may be said, as just an organ for a free play of the mind, we have not; but we have the *Edinburgh Review,* existing as an organ of the old Whigs, and for as much play of the mind as may suit its being that; we have the *Quarterly Review,* existing as an organ of the Tories, and for as much play of mind as may suit its being that; we have the *British Quarterly Review,* existing as an organ of the political Dissenters, and for as much play of mind as may suit its being that; we have *The Times,* existing as an organ of the common, satisfied, well-to-do Englishman, and for as much play of mind as may suit its being that. And so on through all the various fractions, political and religious, of our society; every fraction has, as such, its organ of criticism, but the notions of combining all fractions in the common pleasure of a free disinterested play of mind meets with no favour. Directly this play of mind wants to have more scope, and to forget the pressure of practical considerations a little, it is checked, it is made to feel the chain; we saw this the other day in the extinction, so much to be regretted, of the *Home and Foreign Review;* perhaps in no organ of criticism in this country was there so much knowledge, so much play of mind; but these could not save it: the *Dublin Review* subordinates play of mind to the practical business of English and Irish Catholicism, and lives. It must needs be that men should act in sects and parties, that each of these sects and parties should have its organ, and should make this organ subserve the interests of its action; but it would be well, too, that there should be a criticism, not the minister of these interests, not their enemy, but absolutely and entirely independent of them. No other criticism will ever attain any real authority or make any real way towards its end, — the creating a current of true and fresh ideas.

It is because criticism has so little kept in the pure intellectual sphere, has so little detached itself from practice, has been so directly polemical and controversial, that it has so ill accomplished, in this country, its best spiritual work; which is to keep man from a self-satisfaction which is retarding and vulgarizing, to lead him towards perfection, by making his mind dwell upon what is excellent in itself, and the absolute beauty and fitness of things. A polemical practical criticism makes men blind even to the ideal imperfection of their practice, makes them willingly assert its ideal perfection, in order the better to secure it against attack; and clearly this is narrowing and baneful for them. If they were reassured on the practical side, speculative considerations of ideal perfection they might be brought to entertain, and their spiritual horizon would thus gradually widen. Mr. Adderley says to the Warwickshire farmers:

Talk of the improvement of breed! Why, the race we ourselves represent, the men and women, the old Anglo-Saxon race, are the best breed in the whole world. . . . The absence of a too enervating climate, too unclouded skies, and a too luxurious nature, has produced so vigorous a race of people, and has rendered us so superior to all the world.

Mr. Roebuck says to the Sheffield cutlers:

I look around me and ask what is the state of England? Is not property safe? Is not every man able to say what he likes? Can you not walk from one end of England to the other in perfect security? I ask you whether, the world over or in past history, there is anything like it? Nothing, I pray that our unrivalled happiness may last.[10]

Now obviously there is a peril for poor human nature in words and thoughts of each exuberant self-satisfaction, until we find ourselves safe in the streets of the Celestial City.

Das wenige verschwindet leicht dem Blicke
Der vorwärts sieht, wie viel noch übrig bleibt —[11]

says Goethe; the little that is done seems nothing when we look forward and see how much we have yet to do. Clearly this is a better line of reflection for weak humanity, so long as it remains on this earthly field of labour and trial.

But neither Mr. Adderley nor Mr. Roebuck is by nature inaccessible to considerations of this sort. They only lose sight of them owing to the controversial life we all lead, and the practical form which all speculation takes with us. They have in view opponents whose aim is not ideal, but practical; and in their zeal to uphold their own practice against these innovators, they go so far as even to attribute to this practice an ideal perfection. Somebody has been wanting to introduce a six-pound franchise, or to abolish church-rates, or to collect agricultural statistics by force, or to diminish local self-government. How natural, in reply to such proposals, very likely improper or ill-timed,

to go a little beyond the mark and to say stoutly: "Such a race of people as we stand, so superior to all the world! The old Anglo-Saxon race, the best breed in the whole world! I pray that our unrivalled happiness may last! I ask you whether, the world over or in past history, there is anything like it?" And so long as criticism answers this dithyramb by insisting that the old Anglo-Saxon race would be still more superior to all others if it had no church-rates, or that our unrivalled happiness would last yet longer with a six-pound franchise, so long will the strain, "The best breed in the whole world!" swell louder and louder, everything ideal and refining will be lost out of sight, and both the assailed and their critics will remain in a sphere, to say the truth, perfectly unvital, a sphere in which spiritual progression is impossible. But let criticism leave church-rates and the franchise alone, and in the most candid spirit, without a single lurking thought of practical innovation, confront with our dithyramb this paragraph on which I stumbled in a newspaper immediately after reading Mr. Roebuck:

A shocking child murder has just been committed at Nottingham. A girl named Wragg left the work-house there on Saturday morning with her young illegitimate child. The child was soon afterwards found dead on Mapperly Hills, having been strangled. Wragg is in custody.[12]

Nothing but that; but, in juxtaposition with the absolute eulogies of Mr. Adderley and Mr. Roebuck, how eloquent, how suggestive are those few lines! "Our old Anglo-Saxon breed, the best in the whole world!" — how much that is harsh and ill-favoured there is in this best! Wragg! If we are to talk of ideal perfection, of "the best in the whole world," has anyone reflected what a touch of grossness in our race, what an original shortcoming in the more delicate spiritual percep-tions, is shown by the natural growth amongst us of such hideous names, — Higginbottom, Stiggins, Bugg! In Ionia and Attica they were luckier in this respect than "the best race in the world"; by the Ilissus there was no Wragg, poor thing! And

---

[10]These speeches were reported in the London *Times* on September 17, 1863, and August 19, 1864, respectively.

[11]Goethe, *Iphigenia on Tauris*, I.ii.91–92.

[12]The crime was committed on September 10, 1864. Elizabeth Wragg was sentenced to twenty years in prison in March of the following year.

"our unrivalled happiness"; — what an element of grimness, bareness, and hideousness mixes with it and blurs it; the workhouse, the dismal Mapperly Hills, — how dismal those who have seen them will remember; — the gloom, the smoke, the cold, the strangled illegitimate child! "I ask you whether, the world over or in past history, there is anything like it?" Perhaps not, one is inclined to answer; but at any rate, in that case, the world is very much to be pitied. And the final touch, — short, bleak, and inhuman: *Wragg is in custody.* The sex lost in the confusion of our unrivalled happiness; or (shall I say?) the superfluous Christian name lopped off by the straightforward vigour of our old Anglo-Saxon breed! There is profit for the spirit in such contrasts as this; criticism serves the cause of perfection by establishing them. By eluding sterile conflict, by refusing to remain in the sphere where alone narrow and relative conceptions have any worth and validity, criticism may diminish its momentary importance, but only in this way has it a chance of gaining admittance for those wider and more perfect conceptions to which all its duty is really owed. Mr. Roebuck will have a poor opinion of an adversary who replies to his defiant songs of triumph only by murmuring under his breath, *Wragg is in custody;* but in no other way will these songs of triumph be induced gradually to moderate themselves, to get rid of what in them is excessive and offensive, and to fall into a softer and truer key.

It will be said that it is a very subtle and indirect action which I am thus prescribing for criticism, and that, by embracing in this manner the Indian virtue of detachment and abandoning the sphere of practical life, it condemns itself to a slow and obscure work. Slow and obscure it may be, but it is the only proper work of criticism. The mass of mankind will never have any ardent zeal for seeing things as they are; very inadequate ideas will always satisfy them. On these inadequate ideas reposes, and must repose, the general practice of the world. That is as much as saying that whoever sets himself to see things as they are will find himself one of a very small circle; but it is only by this small circle resolutely doing its own work that adequate ideas will ever get current at all. The rush and roar of practical life will always have a dizzying and attracting effect upon the most collected spectator, and tend to draw him into its vortex; most of all will this be the case where that life is so powerful as it is in England. But it is only by remaining collected, and refusing to lend himself to the point of view of the practical man, that the critic can do the practical man any service; and it is only by the greatest sincerity in pursuing his own course, and by at last convincing even the practical man of his sincerity, that he can escape misunderstandings which perpetually threaten him.

For the practical man is not apt for fine distinctions, and yet in these distinctions truth and the highest culture greatly find their account. But it is not easy to lead a practical man — unless you reassure him as to your practical intentions, you have no chance of leading him — to see that a thing which he has always been used to look at from one side only, which he greatly values, and which, looked at from that side, quite deserves, perhaps, all the prizing and admiring which he bestows upon it, — that this thing, looked at from another side, may appear much less beneficent and beautiful, and yet retain all its claims to our practical allegiance. Where shall we find language innocent enough, how shall we make the spotless purity of our intentions evident enough, to enable us to say to the political Englishman that the British Constitution itself, which, seen from the practical side, looks such a magnificent organ of progress and virtue, seen from the speculative side, — which its compromises, its love of facts, its horror of theory, its studied avoidance of clear thoughts, — that, seen from this side, our august Constitution sometimes looks, — forgive me, shade of Lord Somers! — a colossal machine for the manufacture of Philistines? How is Cobbett to say this and not be misunderstood, blackened as he is with the smoke of a lifelong conflict in the field of political practice? how is Mr. Carlyle to say it and not be misunderstood, after his furious raid into this field with his *Latter-day Pamphlets*? how is Mr. Ruskin, after his pugnacious political economy? I say, the critic must keep out of the region of immediate practice in the political, social, humanitarian sphere, if he wants to make a beginning for that more free speculative treatment of things, which may perhaps one day make its benefits felt even in this sphere, but in a natural and thence irresistible manner.

Do what he will, however, the critic will still remain exposed to frequent misunderstandings, and nowhere so much as in this country. For here people are particularly indisposed even to comprehend that without this free disinterested treatment of things, truth and the highest culture are out of the question. So immersed are they in practical life, so accustomed to take all their notions from this life and its processes, that they are apt to think that truth and culture themselves can be reached by the processes of this life, and that it is an impertinent singularity to think of reaching them in any other. "We are all *terrae filii*,"[13] cries their eloquent advocate; "all Philistines together. Away with the notion of proceeding by any other course than the course dear to the Philistines: let us have a social movement, let us organize and combine a party to pursue truth and new thought, let us call it *the liberal party*, and let us all stick to each other, and back each other up. Let us have no nonsense about independent criticism, and intellectual delicacy, and the few and the many. Don't let us trouble ourselves about foreign thought; we shall invent the whole thing for ourselves as we go along; if one of us speaks well, applaud him; if one of us speaks ill, applaud him too; we are all in the same movement, we are all liberals, we are all in pursuit of truth." In this way the pursuit of truth becomes really a social, practical, pleasurable affair, almost requiring a chairman, a secretary, and advertisements; with the excitement of an occasional scandal, with a little resistance to give the happy sense of difficulty overcome; but, in general, plenty of bustle and very little thought. To act is so easy, as Goethe says; to think is so hard! It is true that the critic has many temptations to go with the stream, to make one of the party movement, one of these *terrae filii*; it seems ungracious to refuse to be a *terrae filius*, when so many excellent people are; but the critic's duty is to refuse, or, if resistance is in vain, at least to cry with Obermann: *Périssons en résistant.*[14]

How serious a matter it is to try and resist, I had ample opportunity of experiencing when I ventured some time ago to criticize the celebrated first volume

---

13 Children of earth.

14 "Let us perish while resisting." Étienne de Sénancour, *Obermann* (1804).

---

of Bishop Colenso.[15] The echoes of the storm which was then raised I still, from time to time, hear grumbling round me. That storm arose out of a misunderstanding almost inevitable. It is a result of no little culture to attain to a clear perception that science and religion are two wholly different things; the multitude will for ever confuse them; but happily that is of no great real importance, for while the multitude imagines itself to live by its false science, it does really live by its true religion. Dr. Colenso, however, in his first volume did all he could to strengthen the confusion,[16] and to make it dangerous. He did this with the best intentions, I freely admit, and with the most candid ignorance that this was the natural effect of what he was doing; but, says Joubert, "Ignorance, which in matters of morals extenuates the crime, is itself, in intellectual matters, a crime of the first order."[17] I criticized Bishop Colenso's speculative confusion. Immediately there was a cry raised: "What is this? here is a liberal attacking a liberal. Do not you belong to the movement? are not you a friend of truth? Is not Bishop Colenso in pursuit of truth? then speak with proper respect of his book. Dr. Stanley is another friend of truth, and you speak with proper respect of his book; why make these invidious differences? both books are excellent, admirable, liberal; Bishop Colenso's perhaps the most so, because it is the boldest, and will have the best practical consequences for the liberal cause. Do you want to encourage to the attack of a brother

---

15 So sincere is my dislike to all personal attack and controversy, that I abstain from reprinting, at this distance of time from the occasion which called them forth, the essays in which I criticized Dr. Colenso's book; I feel bound, however, after all that has passed, to make here a final declaration of my sincere impenitence for having published them. Nay, I cannot forbear repeating yet once more, for his benefit and that of his readers, this sentence from my original remarks upon him: *There is truth of science and truth of religion; truth of science does not become truth of religion till it is made religious.* And I will add: *Let us have all the science there is from the men of science; from the men of religion let us have religion.* [Arnold] The essays in which Arnold criticized John William Colenso's *The Pentateuch and the Book of Joshua Critically Examined* (1863) were "The Bishop and the Philosopher" and "Dr. Stanley's Lectures on the Jewish Church," published in 1863.

16 It has been said I make it "a crime against literary criticism and the higher culture to attempt to inform the ignorant." Need I point out that the ignorant are not informed by being confirmed in a confusion? [Arnold]

17 Joubert, *Pensées,* 2:311.

liberal his, and your, and our implacable enemies, the *Church and State Review* or the *Record,* — the High Church rhinoceros and the Evangelical hyaena? Be silent, therefore; or rather speak, speak as loud as ever you can, and go into ecstasies over the eighty and odd pigeons."

But criticism cannot follow this coarse and indiscriminate method. It is unfortunately possible for a man in pursuit of truth to write a book which reposes upon a false conception. Even the practical consequences of a book are to genuine criticism no recommendation of it, if the book is, in the highest sense, blundering. I see that a lady who herself, too, is in pursuit of truth, and who writes with great ability, but a little too much, perhaps, under the influence of the practical spirit of the English liberal movement, classes Bishop Colenso's book and M. Renan's[18] together, in her survey of the religious state of Europe, as facts of the same order, works, both of them, of "great importance"; "great ability, power, and skill"; Bishop Colenso's, perhaps, the most powerful; at least, Miss Cobbe[19] gives special expression to her gratitude that to Bishop Colenso "has been given the strength to grasp, and the courage to teach, truths of such deep import." In the same way, more than one popular writer has compared him to Luther. Now it is just this kind of false estimate which the critical spirit is, it seems to me, bound to resist. It is really the strongest possible proof of the low ebb at which, in England, the critical spirit is, that while the critical hit in the religious literature of Germany is Dr. Strauss's book,[20] in that of France M. Renan's book, the book of Bishop Colenso is the critical hit in the religious literature of England. Bishop Colenso's book reposes on a total misconception of the essential elements of the religious problem, as that problem is now presented for solution. To criticism, therefore, which seeks to have the best that is known and thought on this problem, it is, however well meant, of no importance whatever. Mr. Renan's book attempts a new synthesis of the elements furnished to us by the Four Gospels. It attempts, in my opinion, a

synthesis, perhaps premature, perhaps impossible, certainly not successful. Up to the present time, at any rate, we must acquiesce in Fleury's sentence on such recastings of the Gospel story: *Quiconque s'imagine la pouvoir mieux écrire, ne l'entend pas.*[21] M. Renan had himself passed by anticipation a like sentence on his own work, when he said: "If a new presentation of the character of Jesus were offered to me, I would not have it; its very clearness would be, in my opinion, the best proof of its insufficiency." His friends may with perfect justice rejoin that at the sight of the Holy Land, and of the actual scene of the Gospel story, all the current of M. Renan's thoughts may have naturally changed, and a new casting of that story irresistibly suggested itself to him; and that this is just a case for applying Cicero's maxim: Change of mind is not inconsistency — *nemo doctus unquam mutationem consilii inconstantiam dixit esse.*[22] Nevertheless, for criticism, M. Renan's first thought must still be the truer one, as long as his new casting so fails more fully to commend itself, more fully (to use Coleridge's happy phrase about the Bible) to *find* us. Still M. Renan's attempt is, for criticism, of the most real interest and importance, since, with all its difficulty, a fresh synthesis of the New Testament *data,* — not a making war on them, in Voltaire's fashion, not a leaving them out of mind, in the world's fashion, but the putting a new construction upon them, the taking them from under the old, adoptive, traditional, unspiritual point of view and placing them under a new one, — is the very essence of the religious problem, as now presented; and only by efforts in this direction can it receive a solution.

Again, in the same spirit in which she judges Bishop Colenso, Miss Cobbe, like so many earnest liberals of our practical race, both here and in America, herself sets vigorously about a positive reconstruction of religion, about making a religion of the future out of hand, or at least setting about making it; we must not rest, she and they are always thinking and saying, in negative criticism, we must be creative and constructive; hence we

---

[18]Ernest Renan, *La Vie de Jesus* (1863).

[19]Frances Power Cobbe in *Broken Lights: An Inquiry into the Present Condition and Future Prospects of Religious Faith* (1864).

[20]David Friedrich Strauss's *Leben Jesus* (1835).

[21]"Whoever imagines himself able to write it better, does not understand it." Claude Fleury, *Ecclesiastical History* (1722).

[22]Cicero, *To Atticus* 16.17:3.

have such works as her recent *Religious Duty*, and works still more considerable, perhaps, by others, which will be in everyone's mind. These works often have much ability; they often spring out of sincere convictions, and a sincere wish to do good; and they sometimes, perhaps, do good. Their fault is (if I may be permitted to say so) one which they have in common with the British College of Health, in the New Road. Everyone knows the British College of Health; it is that building with the lion and the statue of the Goddess Hygeia before it; at least I am sure about the lion, though I am not absolutely certain about the goddess Hygeia. This building does credit, perhaps, to the resources of Dr. Morrison and his disciples; but it falls a good deal short of one's idea of which a British College of Health ought to be. In England, where we hate public interference and love individual enterprise, we have a whole crop of places like the British College of Health; the grand name without the grand thing. Unluckily, creditable to individual enterprise as they are, they tend to impair our taste by making us forget what more grandiose, noble, or beautiful character properly belongs to a public institution. The same may be said of the religions of the future of Miss Cobbe and others. Creditable, like the British College of Health, to the resources of their authors, they yet tend to make us forget what more grandiose, noble, or beautiful character properly belongs to religious construc- tions. The historic religions, with all their faults, have had this: it certainly belongs to the religious sentiment, when it truly flowers, to have this; and we impoverish our spirit if we allow a religion of the future without it. What then is the duty of criticism here? To take the practical point of view, to applaud the liberal movement and all its works, — its New Road religions of the future into the bargain, — for their general utility's sake? By no means; but to be perpetually dissatisfied with these works, while they perpetually fall short of a high and perfect ideal.

For criticism, these are elementary laws; but they never can be popular, and in this country they have been very little followed, and one meets with immense obstacles in following them. That is a reason for asserting them again and again. Criticism must maintain its independence of the practical spirit and its aim. Even with

well-meant efforts of the practical spirit it must express dissatisfaction, if in the sphere of the ideal they seem impoverishing and limiting. It must not hurry on to the goal because of its practical importance. It must be patient, and know how to wait; and flexible, and know how to attach itself to things and how to withdraw from them. It must be apt to study and praise elements that for the fulness of spiritual perfection are wanted, even though they belong to a power which in the prac- tical sphere may be maleficent. It must be apt to discern the spiritual shortcomings or illusions of powers that in the practical sphere may be benefi- cent. And this without any notion of favouring or injuring, in the practical sphere, one power or the other; without any notion of playing off, in this sphere, one power against the other. When one looks, for instance, at the English Divorce Court, — an institution which perhaps has its practical conveniences, but which in the ideal sphere is so hideous; an institution which neither makes divorce impossible nor makes it decent, which allows a man to get rid of his wife, or a wife of her husband, but makes them drag one another first, for the public edification, through a mire of unutterable infamy, — when one looks at this charming institution, I say, with its crowded benches, its newspaper-reports, and its money- compensations, this institution in which the gross unregenerate British Philistine has indeed stamped an image of himself, — one may be per- mitted to find the marriage-theory of Catholicism refreshing and elevating. Or when Protestantism, in virtue of its supposed rational and intellectual origin, gives the law to criticism too magisteri- ally, criticism may and must remind it that its pretensions, in this respect, are illusive and do it harm; that the Reformation was a moral rather than an intellectual event; that Luther's theory of grace no more exactly reflects the mind of the spirit than Bossuet's philosophy of history[23] reflects it; and that there is no more antecedent probability of the Bishop of Durham's stock of ideas being agreeable to perfect reason than of Pope Pius the Ninth's. But criticism will not on that account forget the achievements of Protestantism in the practical

[23] Jacques-Bénigne Bossuet, *Discourse on Universal History* (1681).

and moral sphere; nor that, even in the intellectual sphere, Protestantism, though in a blind and stumbling manner, carried forward the Renascence, while Catholicism threw itself violently across its path.

I lately heard a man of thought and energy[24] contrasting the want of ardour and movement which he now found amongst young men in this country with what he remembered in his own youth, twenty years ago. "What reformers we were then!" he exclaimed; "what a zeal we had! how we canvassed every institution in Church and State, and were prepared to remodel them all on first principles!" He was inclined to regret, as a spiritual flagging, the lull which he saw. I am disposed rather to regard it as a pause in which the turn to a new mode of spiritual progress is being accomplished; everything was long seen, by the young and ardent amongst us, in inseparable connection with politics and practical life; we have pretty well exhausted the benefits of seeing things in this connection, we have got all that can be got by so seeing them. Let us try a more disinterested mode of seeing them; let us betake ourselves more to the serener life of the mind and spirit. This life, too, may have its excesses and dangers; but they are not for us at present. Let us think of quietly enlarging our stock of true and fresh ideas, and not, as soon as we get an idea or half an idea, be running out with it into the street, and trying to make it rule there. Our ideas will, in the end, shape the world all the better for maturing a little. Perhaps in fifty years' time it will in the English House of Commons be an objection to an institution that it is an anomaly, and my friend the Member of Parliament will shudder in his grave. But let us in the meanwhile rather endeavour that in twenty years' time it may, in English literature, be an objection to a proposition that it is absurd. That will be a change so vast, that the imagination almost fails to grasp it. *Ab integro saeclorum nascitur ordo.*[25]

If I have insisted so much on the course which criticism must take where politics and religion are concerned, it is because, where these burning matters are in question, it is most likely to

go astray. I have wished, above all, to insist on the attitude which criticism should adopt towards everything; on its right tone and temper of mind. Then comes the question as to the subject-matter which criticism should most seek. Here, in general, its course is determined for it by the idea which is the law of its being; the idea of a disinterested endeavour to learn and propagate the best that is known and thought in the world, and thus to establish a current of fresh and true ideas. By the very nature of things, as England is not all the world, much of the best that is known and thought in the world cannot be of English growth, must be foreign; by the nature of things, again, it is just this that we are least likely to know, while English thought is streaming in upon us from all sides, and takes excellent care that we shall not be ignorant of its existence; the English critic, therefore, must dwell much on foreign thought, and with particular heed on any part of it, which, while significant and fruitful in itself, is for any reason specially likely to escape him. Again, judging is often spoken of as the critic's one business, and so in some sense it is; but the judgment which almost insensibly forms itself in a fair and clear mind, along with fresh knowledge, is the valuable one; and thus knowledge, and ever fresh knowledge, must be the critic's great concern for himself; and it is by communicating fresh knowledge, and letting his own judgment pass along with it, — but insensibly, and in the second place not the first, as a sort of companion and clue, not as an abstract lawgiver, — that he will generally do most good to his readers. Sometimes, no doubt, for the sake of establishing an author's place in literature, and his relation to a central standard (and if this is not done, how are we to get at our *best in the world?*) criticism may have to deal with a subject-matter so familiar that fresh knowledge is out of the question, and then it must be all judgment; an enunciation and detailed application of principles. Here the great safeguard is never to let oneself become abstract, always to retain an intimate and lively consciousness of the truth of what one is saying, and, the moment this fails us, to be sure that something is wrong. Still, under all circumstances, this mere judgment and application of principles is, in itself, not the most satisfactory work to the critic; like mathematics,

[24]Charles Thomas Baring, Bishop of Durham (1861–79).
[25]"Order is born from the renewal of the ages." Virgil, *Eclogues* 4:5

it is tautological, and cannot well give us, like fresh learning, the sense of creative activity.

But stop, someone will say; all this talk is of no practical use to us whatever; this criticism of yours is not what we have in our minds when we speak of criticism; when we speak of critics and criticism, we mean critics and criticism of the current English literature of the day; when you offer to tell criticism its function, it is to this criticism that we expect you to address yourself. I am sorry for it, for I am afraid I must disappoint these expectations. I am bound by my own definition of criticism: *a disinterested endeavour to learn and propagate the best that is known and thought in the world.* How much of current English literature comes into this "best that is known and thought in the world"? Not very much, I fear; certainly less, at this moment, than of the current literature of France or Germany. Well, then, am I to alter my definition of criticism, in order to meet the requirements of a number of practising English critics, who, after all, are free in their choice of a business? That would be making criticism lend itself just to one of those alien practical consider-ations, which, I have said, are so fatal to it. One may say, indeed, to those who have to deal with the mass — so much better disregarded — of current English literature, that they may at all events endeavour, in dealing with this, to try it, so far as they can, by the standard of the best that is known and thought in the world; one may say, that to get anywhere near this standard, every critic should try and possess one great literature, at least, besides his own; and the more unlike his own, the better. But, after all, the criticism I am really concerned with, — the criticism which alone can much help us for the future, the criticism which, throughout Europe, is at the present day meant, when so much stress is laid on the importance of criticism and the critical spirit, — is a criticism which regards Europe as being, for intellectual and spiritual purposes, one great confederation, bound to a joint action and working to a common result; and whose mem-bers have, for their proper outfit, a knowledge of Greek, Roman, and Eastern antiquity, and of one

another. Special, local, and temporary advantages being put out of account, that modern nation will in the intellectual and spiritual sphere make most progress, which most thoroughly carries out this programme. And what is that but saying that we too, all of us, as individuals, the more thoroughly we carry it out, shall make the more progress?

There is so much inviting us! — what are we to take? what will nourish us in growth towards perfection? That is the question which, with the immense field of life and of literature lying before him, the critic has to answer; for himself first, and afterwards for others. In this idea of the critic's business the essays brought together in the fol-lowing pages have had their origin; in this idea, widely different as are their subjects, they have, perhaps, their unity.

I conclude with what I said in the beginning: to have the sense of creative activity is the great happiness and the great proof of being alive, and it is not denied to criticism to have it; but then criticism must be sincere, simple, flexible, ardent, ever widening its knowledge. Then it may have, in no contemptible measure, joyful sense of creative activity; a sense which a man of insight and con-science will prefer to what he might derive from a poor, starved, fragmentary, inadequate creation. And at some epochs no other creation is possible.

Still, in full measure, the sense of creative activity belongs only to genuine creation; in lit-erature we must never forget that. But what true man of letters ever can forget it? It is no such common matter for a gifted nature to come into possession of a current of true and living ideas, and to produce amidst the inspiration of them, that we are likely to underrate it. The epochs of Aeschylus and Shakespeare make us feel their pre-eminence. In an epoch like those is, no doubt, the true life of a literature; there is the promised land, towards which criticism can only beckon. That promised land it will not be ours to enter, and we shall die in the wilderness: but to have desired to enter it, to have saluted it from afar, is already, perhaps, the best distinction among contemporaries; it will certainly be the best title to esteem with posterity.

Friedrich Nietzsche
1844–1900

Friedrich Wilhelm Nietzsche was born in 1844, the son of a Saxon pastor. He was educated at the universities of Bonn and Leipzig, took his degrees in philology, and was appointed professor at the University of Basel in 1869. The selection included here is from Nietzsche's first book, *The Birth of Tragedy from the Spirit of Music* (1872). *The Birth of Tragedy* is unusual among Nietzsche's works in having a sustained and coherent argument: In his later works, he intentionally became more and more aphoristic, conveying his thought in brief flashes and ironic hints. Because he died relatively young of complications from tertiary syphilis and because of nervous breakdowns in the decade before his death, some of his critics have suggested that he was incapable of sustained argument almost from the outset of his career. This is unfair to Nietzsche, who, like Plato, was in rebellion against the stultifying philosophical treatise. His aim was to stimulate thought in others, and for this he was willing to risk being misunderstood. As a result, he has been misunderstood as few philosophers ever have been. Nietzsche was neither nationalistic nor racist nor anti-Semitic, for example, so it is hideously ironic that less than a generation after his death, his ideas, perverted almost beyond recognition, were adopted as the pet philosophy of the Nazi regime.

If there is any central theme in Nietzsche's philosophy, it is his opposition to the complacent Victorian faith in progress through a rationalistic reordering of society. He saw as basic to human nature darker motives (like the will to power) than his utilitarian contemporaries were willing to acknowledge, but he also saw the possibility of self-sacrifice and transcendence. These themes appear most strongly in his ecstatic tract *Thus Spake Zarathustra* (1883–92), along with *The Joyful Wisdom* (1882) and *Beyond Good and Evil* (1886). Like Dostoevsky, Nietzsche was a reactionary whose insights into the obscene hunger of the human soul strikingly prefigured the discoveries of Freud.

APOLLO AND DIONYSUS

Nietzsche's essay begins with two opposed symbolic images: Apollo and Dionysus, dream and intoxication, plastic arts and music. The obvious question is why they should divide the aesthetic world between them. This dichotomy is best understood if we see Nietzsche as a follower — with many qualifications — of Arthur Schopenhauer. Schopenhauer's monumental treatise *The World as Will and Idea* (1819) had posited that human life reverberates between the extremes of boredom and longing — most often the latter, given the competition among the many hungry wills inhabiting the universe. To be alive, Nietzsche agreed, was to be in a state of want: The image of Tantalus, forever groping at the desired food and drink beyond his grasp, was for Nietzsche an image of humankind. Existence was, in a word, tragic.

Nietzsche saw art as civilization's most effective means of coping with this tragedy of existence. Art works by taming dream and intoxication, two primitive methods of coping with the hungry will. In dream the hunger is satiated; in intoxication the self is obliterated. In dream (as Freud and many others had noted) we retreat into a fantasy world in which our desires are all fulfilled, as they cannot be in reality. In intoxication we do not lose our desires so much as we lose *ourselves*: When drunk, our sense of self — our awareness of an inside and an outside, of a consciousness differentiated from the Other — fades away as the ego is annihilated.

THE BIRTH, AND DEATH, AND REBIRTH, OF TRAGEDY

Most of Nietzsche's treatise is a historical essay on the development of Greek trag-edy out of the religious ritual of Dionysus. It is startling to think that he developed this notion by an intuitive leap from a few hints in the classics, long before classical research established the religious origins and the ritual nature of the drama.

In the beginning was music, a chorus of dancing satyrs rhythmically, musically expressing their devotion to the god of intoxication, each Greek citizen losing his individuality within the satyr chorus. The choric dance then begins to include song, takes on language and, with it, the plastic images of Apollonian dream. For Nietzsche the essence of tragedy is now already present, before anything like a play exists, in the "Dionysiac chorus which again and again discharges itself in Apollonian images." Later still the god himself is impersonated by the choral leader, who becomes in effect the first actor. From here to the enactment of story and the addition of the second and third actors — to the drama of Aeschylus and Sophocles — it is only a short step: mere complications.

For Nietzsche, tragedy reaches its height with Aeschylus and Sophocles. Its essence in the fusion of Apollonian and Dionysiac impulses begins to be destroyed almost immediately thereafter. Nietzsche's villains are the individualism of Eurip-ides and the rationalism of Socrates, which were consistent with the lyrics of Apollo but not with the music of Dionysus. Individualism and rationalism infected Greek civilization and the Roman and Western European civilizations that followed. Tragedy now began to explore the causes of the errors of highly placed individu-als rather than expressing the essence of all human life. Even music itself began in the nineteenth century to become plastic and descriptive — Apollonian rather than Dionysian in character. This perversion of the tragic hit bottom, for Nietzsche, in the Italian opera.

The antidote for all this Nietzsche found in the music-dramas of Richard Wagner, who by 1871 had already written *Tristan und Isolde* and *Die Meistersinger* and had just produced *Das Rheingold* and *Die Walküre*, the first two segments of his massive cycle based on the *Nibelungenlied*. In Wagner's use of myth and universal types, and above all in his return of the leading role to the communal spirit of music rather than the individuation of the Apollonian image, Nietzsche saw the possibility for a rebirth of the healing qualities of art that had been lost when Greek tragedy declined. This enthusiasm with Wagner was to be short-lived. By the second edition of *The Birth of Tragedy*, Nietzsche had broken with Wagner, disgusted by his nationalism and the sickly spiritualism of his last opera, *Parsifal*.

Selected Bibliography

Danto, Arthur. *Nietzsche as a Philosopher.* New York: Macmillan, 1965.

Donadio, Stephen. *Nietzsche, Henry James, and the Artistic Will.* New York: Oxford University Press, 1976.

Gilman, Sander L. *Nietzschean Parody: An Introduction to Reading Nietzsche.* Bonn: Bouvier Verlag, 1976.

Jaspers, Karl. *Nietzsche: An Introduction to the Understanding of His Philosophical Activity.* Tucson: University of Arizona Press, 1965.

Kaufmann, Walter. *Nietzsche: Philosopher, Psychologist, Antichrist,* 3rd ed. Princeton: Princeton University Press, 1968.

Kemal, Salim, Ivan Gaskell, and Daniel W. Conway. *Nietzsche, Philosophy, and the Arts.* Cambridge, Eng.: Cambridge University Press, 1998.

Klein, Wayne. *Nietzsche and the Promise of Philosophy.* Albany: State University of New York Press, 1997.

Ludovici, Anthony. *Nietzsche and Art.* Boston: J. W. Luce, 1912.

Megill, Allan. *Prophets of Extremity: Nietzsche, Heidegger, Foucault, Derrida.* Berkeley: University of California Press, 1985.

Nehamas, Alexander. *Nietzsche: Life as Literature.* Cambridge: Harvard University Press, 1985.

Silk, M. S. *Nietzsche on Tragedy.* Cambridge and New York: Cambridge University Press, 1981.

From *The Birth of Tragedy from the Spirit of Music*

I

Much will have been gained for esthetics once we have succeeded in apprehending directly — rather than merely *ascertaining* — that art owes its continuous evolution to the Apollonian-Dionysiac duality, even as the propagation of the species depends on the duality of the sexes, their constant conflicts and periodic acts of reconciliation. I have borrowed my adjectives from the Greeks, who developed their mystical doctrines of art through plausible *embodiments,* not through purely conceptual means. It is by those two art-sponsoring deities, Apollo and Dionysos, that we are made to recognize the tremendous split, as regards both origins and objectives, between the plastic, Apollonian arts and the non-visual art of music inspired by Dionysos. The two creative tendencies developed alongside one another, usually in fierce opposition, each by its taunts forcing the other to more energetic production, both perpetuating in a discordant concord that agon[1] which the term *art* but feebly denominates: until at last, by the thaumaturgy of an Hellenic act of will, the pair accepted the yoke of marriage and, in this condition, begot Attic tragedy, which exhibits the salient features of both parents.

To reach a closer understanding of both these tendencies, let us begin by viewing them as the separate art realms of *dream* and *intoxication,* two physiological phenomena standing toward one another in much the same relationship as the Apollonian and Dionysiac. It was in a dream, according to Lucretius, that the marvelous gods and goddesses first presented themselves to the minds of men. That great sculptor, Phidias, beheld in a dream the entrancing bodies of

Translated by Francis Golffing.

[1] Tragic struggle.

more-than-human beings, and likewise, if anyone had asked the Greek poets about the mystery of poetic creation, they too would have referred him to dreams and instructed him as much as Hans Sachs instructs us in *Die Meistersinger:*

> My friend, it is the poet's work
> Dreams to interpret and to mark.
> Believe me that man's true conceit
> In a dream becomes complete:
> All poetry we ever read
> Is but true dreams interpreted.[2]

The fair illusion of the dream sphere, in the production of which every man proves himself an accomplished artist, is a precondition not only of all plastic art, but even, as we shall see presently, of a wide range of poetry. Here we enjoy an immediate apprehension of form, all shapes speak to us directly, nothing seems indifferent or redundant. Despite the high intensity with which these dream realities exist for us, we still have a residual sensation that they are illusions; at least such has been my experience — and the frequency, not to say normality, of the experience is borne out in many passages of the poets. Men of philosophical disposition are known for their constant premonition that our everyday reality, too, is an illusion, hiding another, totally different kind of reality. It was Schopenhauer who considered the ability to view at certain times all men and things as mere phantoms or dream images to be the true mark of philosophic talent. The person who is responsive to the stimuli of art behaves toward the reality of dream much the way the philosopher behaves toward the reality of existence: he observes exactly and enjoys his observations, for it is by these images that he interprets life, by these processes that he rehearses it. Nor is it by pleasant images only that such plausible connections are made: the whole divine comedy of life, including its somber aspects, its sudden balkings, impish accidents, anxious expectations, moves past him, not quite like a shadow play — for it is he himself, after all, who lives and suffers through these scenes — yet never without giving a fleeting sense of illusion; and I imagine

that many persons have reassured themselves amidst the perils of dream by calling out, "It is a dream! I want it to go on."[1] I have even heard of people spinning out the causality of one and the same dream over three or more successive nights. All these facts clearly bear witness that our inner-most being, the common substratum of humanity, experiences dreams with deep delight and a sense of real necessity. This deep and happy sense of the necessity of dream experiences was expressed by the Greeks in the image of Apollo. Apollo is at once the god of all plastic powers and the soothsaying god. He who is etymologically the "lucent" one, the god of light, reigns also over the fair illusion of our inner world of fantasy. The perfection of these conditions in contrast to our imperfectly understood waking reality, as well as our profound awareness of nature's healing powers during the interval of sleep and dream, furnishes a symbolic analogue to the soothsaying faculty and quite generally to the arts, which make life possible and worth living. But the image of Apollo must incorporate that thin line which the dream image may not cross, under penalty of becoming pathological, of imposing itself on us as crass reality; a discreet limitation, a freedom from all extravagant urges, the sapient tranquility of the plastic god. His eye must be sunlike, in keeping with his origin. Even at those moments when he is angry and ill-tempered there lies upon him the consecration of fair illusion. In an eccentric way one might say of Apollo what Schopenhauer says, in the first part of *The World as Will and Idea,* of man caught in the veil of Maya:[3] "Even as on an immense, raging sea, assailed by huge wave crests, a man sits in a little rowboat trusting his frail craft, so, amidst the furious torments of this world, the individual sits tranquilly, supported by the *principium indi-viduationis*[4] and relying on it." One might say that the unshakable confidence in that principle has received its most magnificent expression in Apollo, and that Apollo himself may be regarded as the marvelous divine image of the *principium*

---

[2] Richard Wagner, *The Mastersingers of Nuremberg,* III.1.99–104.

[3] Illusion.

[4] "The principle of individuation": that which different-iates the Self from the Other, the ego from the outside world.

individuationis, whose looks and gestures radiate the full delight, wisdom, and beauty of "illusion."

In the same context Schopenhauer has described for us the tremendous awe which seizes man when he suddenly begins to doubt the cognitive modes of experience, in other words, when in a given instance the law of causation seems to suspend itself. If we add to this awe the glorious transport which arises in man, even from the very depths of nature, at the shattering of the *principium individuationis,* then we are in a position to apprehend the essence of Dionysiac rapture, whose closest analogy is furnished by physical intoxication. Dionysiac stirrings arise either through the influence of those narcotic potions of which all primitive races speak in their hymns, or through the powerful approach of spring, which penetrates with joy the whole frame of nature. So stirred, the individual forgets himself completely. It is the same Dionysiac power which in medieval Germany drove ever increasing crowds of people singing and dancing from place to place; we recognize in these St. John's and St. Vitus' dancers the bacchic choruses of the Greeks, who had their precursors in Asia Minor and as far back as Babylon and the orgiastic Sacaea.[5] There are people who, either from lack of experience or out of sheer stupidity, turn away from such phenomena, and, strong in the sense of their own sanity, label them either mockingly or pityingly "endemic diseases." These benighted souls have no idea how cadaverous and ghostly their "sanity" appears as the intense throng of Dionysiac revelers sweeps past them.

Not only does the bond between man and man come to be forged once more by the magic of the Dionysiac rite, but nature itself, long alienated or subjugated, rises again to celebrate the reconciliation with her prodigal son, man. The earth offers its gifts voluntarily, and the savage beasts of mountain and desert approach in peace. The chariot of Dionysos is bedecked with flowers and garlands; panthers and tigers stride beneath his yoke. If one were to convert Beethoven's "Paean to Joy"[6] into a painting, and refuse to curb the imagination when

that multitude prostrates itself reverently in the dust, one might form some apprehension of Dionysiac ritual. Now the slave emerges as a freeman; all the rigid, hostile walls which either necessity or despotism has erected between men are shattered. Now that the gospel of universal harmony is sounded, each individual becomes not only reconciled to his fellow but actually at one with him — as though the veil of Maya had been torn apart and there remained only shreds floating before the vision of mystical Oneness. Man now expresses himself through song and dance as the member of a higher community; he has forgotten how to walk, how to speak, and is on the brink of taking wing as he dances. Each of his gestures betokens enchantment; through him sounds a supernatural power, the same power which makes the animals speak and the earth render up milk and honey. He feels himself to be godlike and strides with the same elation and ecstasy as the gods he has seen in his dreams. No longer the *artist,* he has himself become a *work of art:* the productive power of the whole universe is now manifest in his transport, to the glorious satisfaction of the primordial One. The finest clay, the most precious marble — man — is here kneaded and hewn, and the chisel blows of the Dionysiac world artist are accompanied by the cry of the Eleusinian mystagogues: "Do you fall on your knees, multitudes, do you divine your creator?"[7]

III

In order to comprehend this we must take down the elaborate edifice of Apollonian culture stone by stone until we discover its foundations. At first the eye is struck by the marvelous shapes of the Olympian gods who stand upon its pediments, and whose exploits, in shining bas-relief, adorn its friezes. The fact that among them we find Apollo as one god among many, making no claim to a privileged position, should not mislead us. The same drive that found its most complete representation in Apollo generated the whole

---

[5]The Babylonian "day of the false king" — a kind of Saturnalia.

[6]The setting of Schiller's "Ode to Joy" takes up most of the final movement of the Ninth Symphony.

[7]The Eleusinian Mysteries were a cult devoted to the goddess Persephone which celebrated the coming of winter and the return of spring; the quotation is from Schiller's "Ode to Joy."

Olympian world, and in this sense we may consider Apollo the father of that world. But what was the radical need out of which that illustrious society of Olympian beings sprang?

Whoever approaches the Olympians with a different religion in his heart, seeking moral elevation, sanctity, spirituality, loving-kindness, will presently be forced to turn away from them in ill-humored disappointment. Nothing in these deities reminds us of asceticism, high intellect, or duty: we are confronted by luxuriant, triumphant *existence*, which deifies the good and the bad indifferently. And the beholder may find himself dismayed in the presence of such overflowing life and ask himself what potion these heady people must have drunk in order to behold, in whatever direction they looked, Helen laughing back at them, the beguiling image of their own existence. But we shall call out to this beholder, who had already turned his back: Don't go! Listen first to what the Greeks themselves have to say of this life, which spreads itself before you with such puzzling serenity. An old legend has it that King Midas hunted a long time in the woods for the wise Silenus, companion of Dionysos, without being able to catch him. When he had finally caught him the king asked him what he considered man's greatest good. The daemon remained sullen and uncommunicative until finally, forced by the king, he broke into a shrill laugh and spoke: "Ephemeral wretch, begotten by accident and toil, why do you force me to tell you what it would be your greatest boon not to hear? What would be best for you is quite beyond your reach: not to have been born, not to *be*, to be nothing. But the second best is to die soon."

What is the relation of the Olympian gods to this popular wisdom? It is that of the entranced vision of the martyr to his torment.

Now the Olympian magic mountain[8] opens itself before us, showing us its very roots. The Greeks were keenly aware of the terrors and horrors of existence; in order to be able to live at all they had to place before them the shining fantasy of the Olympians. Their tremendous distrust

of the titanic forces of nature: *Moira*,[9] mercilessly enthroned beyond the knowable world; the vulture which fed upon the great philanthropist Prometheus; the terrible lot drawn by wise Oedipus; the curse on the house of Atreus which brought Orestes to the murder of his mother: in short, that whole Panic[10] philosophy, with its mythic examples, by which the gloomy Etruscans perished, the Greeks conquered — or at least hid from view — again and again by means of this artificial Olympus. In order to live at all the Greeks had to construct these deities. The Apollonian need for beauty had to develop the Olympian hierarchy of joy by slow degrees from the original titanic hierarchy of terror, as roses are seen to break from a thorny thicket. How else could life have been borne by a race so hypersensitive, so emotionally intense, so equipped for suffering? The same drive which called art into being as a completion and consummation of existence, and as a guarantee of further existence, gave rise also to the Olympian realm which acted as a transfiguring mirror to the Hellenic will. The gods justified human life by living it themselves — the only satisfactory theodicy[11] ever invented. To exist in the clear sunlight of such deities was now felt to be the highest good, and the only real grief suffered by Homeric man was inspired by the thought of leaving that sunlight, especially when the departure seemed imminent. Now it became possible to stand the wisdom of Silenus on its head and proclaim that it was the worst evil for man to die soon, and second worst for him to die at all. Such laments as arise now arise over short-lived Achilles, over the generations ephemeral as leaves, the decline of the heroic age. It is not unbecoming to even the greatest hero to yearn for an afterlife, though it be as a day laborer. So impetuously, during the Apollonian phase, does man's will desire to remain on earth, so identified does he become with existence, that even his lament turns to a song of praise.

It should have become apparent by now that the harmony with nature which we late-comers regard with such nostalgia, and for which Schiller

[8]The Zauberberg was the mountain where Venus lived, to which the troubadour Tannhäuser was attracted in the medieval legend. Nietzsche uses it as a symbol for a fantasy world.

[9]Destiny.
[10]Relating to Pan, the god of Nature.
[11]Explanation of divine justice.

has coined the cant term *naïve,* is by no means a simple and inevitable condition to be found at the gateway to every culture, a kind of paradise. Such a belief could have been endorsed only by a period for which Rousseau's Emile was an artist and Homer just such an artist nurtured in the bosom of nature. Whenever we encounter "naïveté" in art, we are face to face with the ripest fruit of Apollonian culture — which must always triumph first over titans, kill monsters, and overcome the somber contemplation of actuality, the intense susceptibility to suffering, by means of illusions strenuously and zestfully entertained. But how rare are the instances of true naïveté, of that complete identification with the beauty of appearance! It is this achievement which makes Homer so magnificent — Homer, who, as a single individual, stood to Apollonian popular culture in the same relation as the individual dream artist to the oneiric capacity of a race and of nature generally. The naïveté of Homer must be viewed as a complete victory of Apollonian illusion. Nature often uses illusions of this sort in order to accomplish its secret purposes. The true goal is covered over by a phantasm. We stretch out our hands to the latter, while nature, aided by our deception, attains the former. In the case of the Greeks it was the will wishing to behold itself in the work of art, in the transcendence of genius; but in order so to behold itself its creatures had first to view themselves as glorious, to transpose themselves to a higher sphere, without having that sphere of pure contemplation either challenge them or upbraid them with insufficiency. It was in that sphere of beauty that the Greeks saw the Olympians as their mirror images; it was by means of that esthetic mirror that the Greek will opposed suffering and the somber wisdom of suffering which always accompanies artistic talent. As a monument to its victory stands Homer, the naïve artist.

IV

We can learn something about the naïve artist through the analogy of dream. We can imagine the dreamer as he calls out to himself, still caught in the illusion of his dream and without disturbing it, "This is a dream, and I want to go on dreaming," and we can infer, on the one hand, that he takes deep delight in the contemplation of his dream, and, on the other, that he must have forgotten the day, with its horrible importunity, so to enjoy his dream. Apollo, the interpreter of dreams, will furnish the clue to what is happening here. Although of the two halves of life — the waking and the dreaming — the former is generally considered not only the more important but the only one which is truly lived, I would, at the risk of sounding paradoxical, propose the opposite view. The more I have come to realize in nature those omnipotent formative tendencies and, with them, an intense longing for illusion, the more I feel inclined to the hypothesis that the original Oneness, the ground of Being, ever-suffering and contradictory, time and again has need of rapt vision and delightful illusion to redeem itself. Since we ourselves are the very stuff of such illusions, we must view ourselves as the truly nonexistent, that is to say, as a perpetual unfolding in time, space, and causality — what we label "empiric reality." But if, for the moment, we abstract from our own reality, viewing our empiric existence, as well as the existence of the world at large, as the *idea* of the original Oneness, produced anew each instant, then our dreams will appear to us as illusions of illusions, hence as a still higher form of satisfaction of the original desire for illusion. It is for this reason that the very core of nature takes such a deep delight in the naïve artist and the naïve work of art, which likewise is merely the illusion of an illusion. Raphael, himself one of those immortal "naïve" artists, in a symbolic canvas has illustrated that reduction of illusion to further illusion which is the original act of the naïve artist and at the same time of all Apollonian culture. In the lower half of his *Transfiguration,* through the figures of the possessed boy, the despairing bearers, the helpless, terrified disciples, we see a reflection of original pain, the sole ground of being: "illusion" here is a reflection of eternal contradiction, begetter of all things. From this illusion there rises, like the fragrance of ambrosia, a new illusory world, invisible to those enmeshed in the first: a radiant vision of pure delight, a rapt seeing through wide-open eyes. Here we have, in a great symbol of art, both the fair world of Apollo and its substratum, the terrible wisdom of Silenus, and we can comprehend intuitively how they mutually require one another. But Apollo appears to us once again as the apotheosis of the *principium individuationis*, in whom the eternal goal of the original Oneness, namely its redemption through illusion, accomplishes itself. With august gesture the god shows us how there is need for a whole world of torment in order for the individual to produce the redemptive vision and to sit quietly in his rocking rowboat in mid-sea, absorbed in contemplation.

If this apotheosis of individuation is to be read in normative terms, we may infer that there is one norm only: the individual — or, more precisely, the observance of the limits of the individual: *sophrosyne*. As a moral deity Apollo demands self-control from his people and, in order to observe such self-control, a knowledge of self. And so we find that the esthetic necessity of beauty is accompanied by the imperatives, "Know thyself," and "Nothing too much." Conversely, excess and *hubris* come to be regarded as the hostile spirits of the non-Apollonian sphere, hence as properties of the pre-Apollonian era — the age of Titans — and the extra-Apollonian world, that is to say the world of the barbarians. It was because of his Titanic love of man that Prometheus had to be devoured by vultures; it was because of his extravagant wisdom which succeeded in solving the riddle of the Sphinx that Oedipus had to be cast into a whirlpool of crime: in this fashion does the Delphic god interpret the Greek past.

The effects of the Dionysiac spirit struck the Apollonian Greeks as titanic and barbaric; yet they could not disguise from themselves the fact that they were essentially akin to those deposed Titans and heroes. They felt more than that: their whole existence, with its temperate beauty, rested upon a base of suffering and *knowledge* which had been hidden from them until the reinstatement of Dionysos uncovered it once more. And lo and behold! Apollo found it impossible to live without Dionysos. The elements of titanism and barbarism turned out to be quite as fundamental as the Apollonian element. And now let us imagine how the ecstatic sounds of the Dionysiac rites penetrated ever more enticingly into that artificially restrained and discreet world of illusion, how this clamor expressed the whole outrageous gamut of

nature — delight, grief, knowledge — even to the most piercing cry; and then let us imagine how the Apollonian artist with his thin, monotonous harp music must have sounded beside the demoniac chant of the multitude! The muses presiding over the illusory arts paled before an art which enthusiastically told the truth, and the wisdom of Silenus cried "Woe!" against the serene Olympians. The individual, with his limits and moderations, forgot himself in the Dionysiac vortex and became oblivious to the laws of Apollo. Indiscreet extravagance revealed itself as truth, and contradiction, a delight born of pain, spoke out of the bosom of nature. Wherever the Dionysiac voice was heard, the Apollonian norm seemed suspended or destroyed. Yet it is equally true that, in those places where the first assault was withstood, the prestige and majesty of the Delphic god appeared more rigid and threatening than before. The only way I am able to view Doric art and the Doric state[12] is as a perpetual military encampment of the Apollonian forces. An art so defiantly austere, so ringed about with fortifications — an education so military and exacting — a polity so ruthlessly cruel — could endure only in a continual state of resistance against the titanic and barbaric menace of Dionysos.

Up to this point I have developed at some length a theme which was sounded at the beginning of this essay: how the Dionysiac and Apollonian elements, in a continuous chain of creations, and enhancing the other, dominated the Hellenic mind; how from the Iron Age, with its battles of Titans and its austere popular philosophy, there developed under the aegis of Apollo and the Homeric world of beauty; how this "naïve" splendor was then absorbed once more by the Dionysiac torrent, and how, face to face with this new power, the Apollonian code rigidified into the majesty of Doric art and contemplation. If the earlier phase of Greek history may justly be broken down into four major artistic epochs dramatizing the battle between the two hostile principles, then we must inquire further (lest Doric art appear to us as the acme and final goal of all these striving tendencies)

12 Sparta.

what was the true end toward which that evolution moved. And our eyes will come to rest on the sublime and much lauded achievement of the dramatic dithyramb and Attic tragedy, as the common goal of both urges; whose mysterious marriage, after long discord, ennobled itself with such a child, at once Antigone and Cassandra.[13]

V

We are now approaching the central concern of our inquiry, which has as its aim an understanding of the Dionysiac-Apollonian spirit, or at least an intuitive comprehension of the mystery which made this conjunction possible. Our first question must be: where in the Greek world is the new seed first to be found which was later to develop into tragedy and the dramatic dithyramb? Greek antiquity gives us a pictorial clue when it represents in statues, on cameos, etc., Homer and Archilochus side by side as ancestors and torch-bearers of Greek poetry, in the certainty that only these two are to be regarded as truly original minds, from whom a stream of fire flowed onto the entire later Greek world. Homer, the hoary dreamer, caught in utter abstraction, prototype of the Apollonian naïve artist, stares in amazement at the passionate head of Archilochus, soldierly servant of the Muses, knocked about by fortune. All that more recent esthetics has been able to add by way of interpretation is that here the "objective" artist is confronted by the first "subjective" artist. We find this interpretation of little use, since to us the subjective artist is simply the bad artist, and since we demand above all, in every genre and range of art, a triumph over subjectivity, deliverance from the self, the silencing of every personal will and desire; since, in fact, we cannot imagine the smallest genuine art work lacking objectivity and disinterested contemplation. For this reason our esthetic must first solve the following problem: how is the lyrical poet at all possible as artist — he who, according to the experience of all times, always says "I" and recites to us the entire chromatic scale of his passions and appetites? It is this Archilochus who most disturbs

us, placed there beside Homer, with the stridor of his hate and mockery, the drunken outbursts of his desire. Isn't he — the first artist to be called subjective — for that reason the veritable nonartist? How, then, are we to explain the reverence in which he was held as a poet, the honor done him by the Delphic oracle, that seat of "objective" art, in a number of very curious sayings?

Schiller has thrown some light on his own manner of composition by a psychological observation which seems inexplicable to himself without, however, giving him pause. Schiller confessed that, prior to composing, he experienced not a logically connected series of images but rather a *musical mood*. "With me emotion is at the beginning without clear and definite ideas; those ideas do not arise until later on. A certain musical disposition of mind comes first, and after follows the poetical idea." If we enlarge on this, taking into account the most important phenomenon of ancient poetry, by which I mean that union — nay identity — everywhere considered natural, between musician and poet (alongside which our modern poetry appears as the statue of a god without a head), then we may, on the basis of the esthetics adumbrated earlier, explain the lyrical poet in the following manner. He is, first and foremost, a Dionysiac artist, become wholly identified with the original Oneness, its pain and contradiction, and producing a replica of that Oneness as music, if music may legitimately be seen as a repetition of the world; however, this music becomes visible to him again, as in a dream similitude, through the Apollonian dream influence. That reflection, without image or idea, or original pain in music, with its redemption through illusion, now produces a second reflection as a single simile or example. The artist had abrogated his subjectivity earlier, during the Dionysiac phase: the image which now reveals to him his oneness with the heart of the world is a dream scene showing forth vividly, together with original pain, the original delight of illusion. The "I" thus sounds out of the depth of being; what recent writers on esthetics speak of as "subjectivity" is a mere figment. When Archilochus, the first lyric poet of the Greeks, hurls both his frantic love and his contempt at the daughters of Lycambes, it is not his own

---

[13]The dutiful Antigone may represent the Apollonian principle, the possessed Cassandra the Dionysiac.

passion that we see dancing before us as in an orgiastic frenzy; we see Dionysos and the maenads, we see the drunken reveler Archilochus, sunk down in sleep — as Euripides describes him for us in the *Bacchae*, asleep on a high mountain meadow, in the midday sun — and now Apollo approaches him and touches him with his laurel. The sleeper's enchantment through Dionysiac music now begins to emit sparks of imagery, poems which, at their point of highest evolution, will bear the name of tragedies and dramatic dithyrambs.

The sculptor, as well as his brother, the epic poet, is committed to the pure contemplation of images. The Dionysiac musician, himself imageless, is nothing but original pain and reverberation of the image. Out of this mystical process of un-selving, the poet's spirit feels a whole world of images and similitudes arise, which are quite different in hue, causality, and pace from the images of the sculptor or narrative poet. While the latter lives in those images and only in them, with joyful complacence, and never tires of scanning them down to the most minute features, while even the image of angry Achilles is no more for him than an *image* whose irate countenance he enjoys with a dreamer's delight in appearance — so that this mirror of appearance protects him from complete fusion with his characters — the lyrical poet, on the other hand, himself becomes his images, his images are objectified versions of himself. Being the active center of that world he may boldly speak in the first person, only his "I" is not that of the actual waking man, but the "I" dwelling, truly and eternally, in the ground of being. It is through the reflections of that "I" that the lyric poet beholds the ground of being. Let us imagine, next, how he views himself too among these reflections — as nongenius, that is, as his own subject matter, the whole teeming crowd of his passions and intentions directed toward a definite goal; and when it now appears as though the poet and the nonpoet joined to him were one, and as though the former were using the pronoun "I," we are able to see through this appearance, which has deceived those who have attached the label "subjective" to the lyrical poet. The man Archilochus, with his passionate loves and hates, is really only a vision of genius, a genius who

is no longer merely Archilochus but the genius of the universe, expressing its pain through the similitude of Archilochus the man. Archilochus, on the other hand, the subjectively willing and desiring human being, can never be a poet. Nor is it at all necessary for the poet to see only the phenomenon of the man Archilochus before him as a reflection of Eternal Being: the world of tragedy shows us to what extent the vision of the poet can remove itself from the urgent, immediate phenomenon.

Schopenhauer, who was fully aware of the difficulties the lyrical poet creates for the speculative esthetician, thought that he had found a solution, which, however, I cannot endorse. It is true that he alone possessed the means, in his profound philosophy of music, for solving this problem; and I think I have honored his achievement in these pages, I hope in his own spirit. Yet in the first part of *The World as Will and Idea* he characterizes the essence of song as follows:

The consciousness of the singer is filled with the subject of will, which is to say with his own willing. That willing may either be a released, satisfied willing (joy), or, as happens more commonly, an inhibited willing (sadness). In either case there is affect here: passion, violent commotion. At the same time, however, the singer is moved by the contemplation of nature surrounding him to experience himself as the subject of pure, unwilling ideation, and the unshakable tranquility of that ideation becomes contrasted with the urgency of his willing, its limits, and its lacks. It is the experience of this contrast, or tug of war, which he expresses in his song. While we find ourselves in the lyrical condition, pure ideation approaches us, as it were, to deliver us from the urgencies of willing; we obey, yet obey for moments only. Again and again our willing, our memory of personal objectives, distracts us from tranquil contemplation, while, conversely, the next scene of beauty we behold will yield us up once more to pure ideation. For this reason we find in song and in the lyrical mood a curious mixture of willing (our personal interest in *purposes*) and pure contemplation (whose subject matter is furnished by our surroundings); relations are sought and imagined between these two sets of experiences. Subjective mood — the affection of the will — communicates its color to the purely viewed surroundings, and vice versa. All authentic song reflects a state of mind mixed and divided in this manner.

Who can fail to perceive in this description that lyric poetry is presented as an art never completely realized, indeed a hybrid whose essence is made to consist in an uneasy mixture of will and contemplation, i.e., the esthetic and the nonesthetic conditions? We, on our part, maintain that the distinction between subjective and objective, which even Schopenhauer still uses as a sort of measuring stick to distinguish the arts, has no value whatever in esthetics; the reason being that the subject — the striving individual bent on furthering his egoistic purposes — can be thought of only as an enemy to art, never as its source. But to the extent that the subject is an artist he is already delivered from individual will and has become a medium through which the True Subject celebrates his redemption in illusion. For better or worse, one thing should be quite obvious to all of us: the entire comedy of art is not played for our own sakes — for our betterment or education, say — nor can we consider ourselves the true originators of that art realm; while on the other hand we have every right to view ourselves as esthetic projections of the veritable creator and derive such dignity as we possess from our status as art works. Only as an esthetic product can the world be justified to all eternity — although our consciousness of our own significance does scarcely exceed the consciousness a painted soldier might have of the battle in which he takes part. Thus our whole knowledge of art is at bottom illusory, seeing that as mere *knowers* we can never be fused with that essential spirit, at the same time creator and spectator, who has prepared the comedy of art for his own edification. Only as the genius in the act of creation merges with the primal architect of the cosmos can he truly know something of the eternal essence of art. For in that condition he resembles the uncanny fairy tale image which is able to see itself by turning its eyes. He is at once subject and object, poet, actor, and audience.

XIV

Let us now imagine Socrates' great Cyclops' eye — that eye which never glowed with the artist's divine frenzy — turned upon tragedy.

Bearing in mind that he was unable to look with any pleasure into the Dionysiac abysses, what could Socrates see in that tragic art which to Plato seemed noble and meritorious? Something quite abstruse and irrational, full of causes without effects and effects seemingly without causes, the whole texture so checkered that it must be repugnant to a sober disposition, while it might act as dangerous tinder to a sensitive and impressionable mind. We are told that the only genre of poetry Socrates really appreciated was the Aesopian fable. This he did with the same smiling complaisance with which honest Gellert sings the praise of poetry in his fable of the bee and the hen:

> I exemplify the use of poetry:
> To convey to those who are a bit backward
> The truth in a simile.[14]

The fact is that for Socrates tragic art failed even to "convey the truth," although it did address itself to those who were "a bit backward," which is to say to nonphilosophers: a double reason for leaving it alone.[15] Like Plato, he reckoned it among the beguiling arts which represent the agreeable, not the useful, and in consequence exhorted his followers to abstain from such unphilosophical stimulants. His success was such that the young tragic poet Plato burned all his writings in order to qualify as a student of Socrates. And while strong native genius might now and again manage to withstand the Socratic injunction, the power of the latter was still great enough to force poetry into entirely new channels.

A good example of this is Plato himself. Although he did not lag behind the naïve cynicism of his master in the condemnation of tragedy and of art in general, nevertheless his creative gifts forced him to develop an art form deeply akin to the existing form which he had repudiated. The main objection raised by Plato to the older art (that it was the imitation of an imitation and hence belonged to an even lower order

[14]Christian Fürchtegott Gellert (1715–1769), poet and novelist of the German Enlightenment; the quotation is from *Poems and Fables* (1746–48).
[15]Nietzsche alludes to Socrates' final assessment of poetry in Plato's *Republic,* Book X; see p. 29.

of empiric reality) must not, at all costs, apply to the new genre; and so we see Plato intent on moving beyond reality and on rendering the idea which underlies it. By a detour Plato the thinker reached the very spot where Plato the poet had all along been at home, and from which Sophocles, and with him the whole poetic tradition of the past, protested such a change. Tragedy had assimilated to itself all the older poetic genres. In a somewhat eccentric sense the same thing can be claimed for the Platonic dialogue, which was a mixture of all the available styles and forms and hovered between narrative, lyric, drama, between prose and poetry, once again breaking through the old law of stylistic unity. The Cynic philosophers went even farther in that direction, seeking, by their utterly promiscuous style and constant alternation between verse and prose, to project their image of the "raving Socrates" in literature, as they sought to enact it in life. The Platonic dialogue was the lifeboat in which the shipwrecked older poetry saved itself, together with its numerous offspring. Crowded together in a narrow space, and timidly obeying their helmsman Socrates, they moved forward into a new era which never tired of looking at this fantastic spectacle. Plato has furnished for all posterity the pattern of a new art form, the novel, viewed as the Aesopian fable raised to its highest power; a form in which poetry played the same subordinate role with regard to dialectic philosophy as that same philosophy was to play for many centuries with regard to theology. This, then, was the new status of poetry, and it was Plato who, under the pressure of daemonic Socrates, had brought it about. It is at this point that philosophical ideas begin to entwine themselves about art, forcing the latter to cling closely to the trunk of dialectic. The Apollonian tendency now appears disguised as logical schematism, just as we found in the case of Euripides a corresponding translation of the Dionysiac affect into a naturalistic one. Socrates, the dialectical hero of the Platonic drama, shows a close affinity to the Euripidean hero, who is compelled to justify his actions by proof and counterproof, and for that reason is often in danger of forfeiting our tragic compassion. For who among us can close his eyes to the optimistic element in the nature of dialectics, which sees a

triumph in every syllogism and can breathe only in an atmosphere of cool, conscious clarity? Once that optimistic element had entered tragedy, it overgrew its Dionysiac regions and brought about their annihilation and, finally, the leap into genteel domestic drama. Consider the consequences of the Socratic maxims: "Virtue is knowledge; all sins arise from ignorance; only the virtuous are happy" — these three basic formulations of optimism spell the death of tragedy. The virtuous hero must henceforth be a dialectician; virtue and knowledge, belief and ethics, be necessarily and demonstrably connected; Aeschylus' transcendental concept of justice be reduced to the brash and shallow principle of poetic justice with its regular *deus ex machina*.

What is the view taken of the chorus in this new Socratic-optimistic stage world, and of the entire musical and Dionysiac foundation of tragedy? They are seen as accidental features, as reminders of the origin of tragedy, which can well be dispensed with — while we have in fact come to understand that the chorus is the cause of tragedy and the tragic spirit. Already in Sophocles we find some embarrassment with regard to the chorus, which suggests that the Dionysiac floor of tragedy is beginning to give way. Sophocles no longer dares to give the chorus the major role in the tragedy but treats it as almost on the same footing as the actors, as though it had been raised from the *orchestra* onto the *scene*. By so doing he necessarily destroyed its meaning, despite Aristotle's endorsement of this conception of the chorus. This shift in attitude, which Sophocles displayed not only in practice but also in theory, was the first step toward the total disintegration of the chorus: a process whose rapid phases we can follow in Euripides, Agathon, and the New Comedy. Optimistic dialectics took up the whip of its syllogisms and drove music out of tragedy. It entirely destroyed the meaning of tragedy — which can be interpreted only as a concrete manifestation of Dionysiac conditions, music made visible, an ecstatic dream world.

Since we have discovered an anti-Dionysiac tendency antedating Socrates, its most brilliant exponent, we must now ask, "Toward what does a figure like Socrates point?" Faced with the evidence of the Platonic dialogues, we are certainly not entitled to see in Socrates merely an agent of disintegration. While it is clear that the immediate result of the Socratic strategy was the destruction of Dionysiac drama, we are forced, nevertheless, by the profundity of the Socratic experience to ask ourselves whether, in fact, art and Socratism are diametrically opposed to one another, whether there is really anything inherently impossible in the idea of a Socratic artist?

It appears that this despotic logician had from time to time a sense of void, loss, unfulfilled duty with regard to art. In prison he told his friends how, on several occasions, a voice had spoken to him in a dream, saying "Practice music, Socrates!"[16] Almost to the end he remained confident that his philosophy represented the highest art of the muses, and would not fully believe that a divinity meant to remind him of "common, popular music." Yet in order to unburden his conscience he finally agreed, in prison, to undertake that music which hitherto he had held in low esteem. In this frame of mind he composed a poem on Apollo and rendered several Aesopian fables in verse. What prompted him to these exercises was something very similar to that warning voice of his daimonion: an Apollonian perception that, like a barbarian king, he had failed to comprehend the nature of a divine effigy, and was in danger of offending his own god through ignorance. These words heard by Socrates in his dream are the only indication that he ever experienced any uneasiness about the limits of his logical universe. He may have asked himself: "Have I been too ready to view what was unintelligible to me as being devoid of meaning? Perhaps there is a realm of wisdom, after all, from which the logician is excluded? Perhaps art must be seen as the necessary complement of rational discourse?"

XIX

The best way to characterize the core of Socratic culture is to call it the culture of the opera. It is in this area that Socratism has given an open account of its intentions — a rather surprising one when we compare the evolution of the opera with the abiding Apollonian and Dionysiac truths. First I want to remind the reader of the genesis of the *stilo rappresentativo*[17] and of recitative. How did it happen that this operatic music, so wholly external and incapable of reverence, was enthusiastically greeted by an epoch which, not so very long ago, had produced the inexpressibly noble and sacred music of Palestrina? Can anyone hold the luxury and frivolity of the Florentine court and the vanity of its dramatic singers responsible for the speed and intensity with which the vogue of opera spread? I can explain the passion for a semimusical declamation, at the same period and among the same people who had witnessed the grand architecture of Palestrina's harmonies (in the making of which the whole Christian Middle Ages had conspired), only by reference to an extra-artistic tendency. To the listener who desires to hear the words above the music corresponds the singer who speaks more than he sings, emphasizing the verbal pathos in a kind of half-song. By this emphasis he aids the understanding of the words and gets rid of the remaining half of music. There is a danger that now and again the music will preponderate, spoiling the pathos and clarity of his declamation, while conversely he is always under the temptation to discharge the music of his voice in a virtuoso manner. The pseudopoetic librettist furnishes him ample opportunity for this display in lyrical interjections, repetitions of words and phrases, etc., where the singer may give himself up to the purely musical element without consideration for the text. This constant alternation, so characteristic of the *stilo rappresentativo,* between emotionally charged, only partly sung declamation and wholly musical interjections, this rapid shift of focus between concept and imagination, on the one hand, and the musical response of the listener, on the other, is so completely unnatural, equally opposed to the Dionysiac and the Apollonian spirit, that one

---

[16]In Plato's *Phaedo.*

[17]A term characterizing the opera created in the late sixteenth century by the Florentine musical society known as the *Camerata,* in which dramatic recitative alternates with florid arias expressing emotion. Operas in the current repertory written in the *stilo rappresentativo* include Monteverdi's *L'Incoronazione di Poppaea* and Purcell's *Dido and Aeneas.*

must conclude the origin of recitative to have lain outside any artistic instinct. Viewed in these terms, the recitative may be characterized as a mixture of epic and lyric declamation. And yet, since the components are so wholly disparate, the resulting combination is neither harmonious nor constant, but rather a superficial and mosaic-like conglutination, not without precedent in the realm of nature and experience. However, the inventors of recitative took a very different view of it. They, and their age with them, thought they had discovered the secret of ancient music, that secret which alone could account for the amazing feats of an Orpheus or an Amphion or, indeed, for Greek tragedy. They thought that by that novel style they had managed to resuscitate ancient Greek music in all its power; and, given the popular conception of the Homeric world, it was possible to embrace the illusion that one had at last returned to the paradisaical beginnings of mankind, in which music must have had that supreme purity, power, and innocence of which the pastoral poets wrote so movingly. Here we have touched the nerve center of opera, that genuinely modern genre. In it, art satisfies a strong need, but one that can hardly be called esthetic: a hankering for the idyll, a belief in the primordial existence of pure, artistically sensitive man. Recitative stood for the rediscovered language of that archetypal man, opera for the rediscovered country of that idyllic and heroically pure species, who in all their actions followed a natural artistic bent — who, no matter what they had to say, sang at least part of it, and who when their emotions were ever so little aroused burst into full song. It is irrelevant to our inquiry that the humanists of the time used the new image of the paradisaical artist to combat the old ecclesiastical notion of man as totally corrupt and damned: that opera thus represented the opposition dogma of man as essentially good, and furnished an antidote to that pessimism which, given the terrible instability of the epoch, naturally enlisted its strongest and most thoughtful minds. What matters here is our recognition that the peculiar attraction and thus the success of this new art form must be attributed to its satisfaction of a wholly unesthetic need: it was optimistic; it

glorified man in himself; it conceived of man as originally good and full of talent. This principle of opera has by degrees become a menacing and rather appalling claim, against which we who are faced with present-day socialist movements cannot stop our ears. The "noble savage" demands his rights: what a paradisaical prospect!

There is still a further point in support of my contention that opera is built on the same principles as our Alexandrian culture. Opera is the product of the man of theory, the critical layman, not the artist. This constitutes one of the most disturbing facts in the entire history of art. Since the demand, coming from essentially unmusical people, was for a clear understanding of the words, a renascence of music could come about only through the discovery of a type of music in which the words lorded it over the counterpoint as a master over his servant. For were not the words nobler than the accompanying harmonic system, as the soul is nobler than the body? It was with precisely that unmusical clumsiness that the combinations of music, image, and word were treated in the beginning of opera, and in this spirit the first experiments in the new genre were carried out, even in the noble lay circles of Florence, by the poets and singers patronized by those circles. Inartistic man produces his own brand of art, precisely by virtue of his artistic impotence. Having not the faintest conception of the Dionysiac profundity of music, he transforms musical enjoyment into a rationalistic rhetoric of passion in the *stilo rappresentativo*, into a voluptuous indulgence of vocal virtuoso feats; lacking imagination, he must employ engineers and stage designers; being incapable of understanding the true nature of the artist, he invents an "artistic primitive" to suit his taste, i.e., a man who, when his passions are aroused, breaks into song and recites verses. He projects himself into a time when passion sufficed to produce songs and poems — as though mere emotion had ever been able to create art. There lies at the root of opera a fallacious conception of the artistic process, the idyllic belief that every sensitive man is at bottom an artist. In keeping with this belief, opera is the expression of dilettantism in art, dictating its rules with the cheerful optimism of the theorist.

If we were to combine the two tendencies conspiring at the creation of opera into one, we might speak of an idyllic tendency of opera. Here it would be well to refer back to Schiller's account. Nature and ideal, according to Schiller, are objects of grief when the former is felt to be lost, the latter to be beyond reach. But both may become objects of joy when they are represented as actual. Then the first will produce the elegy, in its strict sense, and the second the idyll, in its widest sense. I would like to point out at once the common feature of these two conceptions in the origin of opera: here the ideal is never viewed as unattained nor nature as lost. Rather, a primitive period in the history of man is imagined, in which he lay at the heart of nature and in this state of nature attained immediately the ideal of humanity through Edenic nobility and artistry. From this supposedly perfect primitive we are all said to derive; indeed, we are still his faithful replicas. All we need do in order to recognize ourselves in that primitive is to jettison some of our later achievements, such as our superfluous learning and excess culture. The educated man of the Renaissance used the operatic imitation of Greek tragedy to lead him back to that concord of nature and ideal, to an idyllic reality. He used ancient tragedy the way Dante used Virgil, to lead him to the gates of Paradise,[18] but from there on he went ahead on his own, moving from an imitation of the highest Greek art form to a "restitution of all things," to a re-creation of man's original art world. What confidence and bonhomie these bold enterprises betokened, arising as they did in the very heart of theoretical culture! The only explanation lies in the comforting belief of the day that "essential man" is the perennially virtuous operatic hero, the endlessly piping or singing shepherd, who, if he should ever by chance lose himself for a spell, would inevitably recover himself intact; in the optimism that rises like a perfumed, seductive cloud from the depths of Socratic contemplation.

[18]In the *Divina Commedia* the pagan Virgil guided Dante through Hell and Purgatory, but handed him over to Beatrice at the gates of Paradise.

Opera, then, does not wear the countenance of eternal grief but rather that of joy in an eternal reunion. It expresses the complacent delight in an idyllic reality, or such, at least, as can be viewed as real at any moment. Perhaps people will one day come to *realize* that this supposititious reality is at bottom no more than a fantastic and foolish trifling, which should make anyone who pits against it the immense seriousness of genuine nature and of the true origins of man exclaim in disgust: "Away with that phantom!" And yet it would be self-delusion to think that, trivial as it is, opera can be driven off with a shout, like an apparition. Whoever wants to destroy opera must gird himself for battle with that Alexandrian cheerfulness that has furnished opera its favorite conceptions and whose natural artistic expression it is. As for art proper, what possible benefit can it derive from a form whose origins lie altogether outside the esthetic realm, a form which from a semimoral sphere has trespassed on the domain of art and can only at rare moments deceive us as to its hybrid origin? What sap nourishes this operatic growth if not that of true art? Are we not right in supposing that its idyllic seductions and Alexandrian blandishments may sophisticate the highest, the truly serious task of art (to deliver the eye from the horror of night, to redeem us by virtue of the healing balm of illusion, from the spastic motions of the will) into an empty and frivolous amusement? What becomes of the enduring Apollonian and Dionysiac truths in such a mixture of styles as we find in the *stilo rappresentativo;* where music acts the part of the servant, the text that of the master; where music is likened to the body, the text to the soul; where the ultimate goal is at best a periphrastic tone painting, similar to that found in the new Attic dithyramb; where music has abrogated its true dignity as the Dionysiac mirror of the universe and seems content to be the slave of appearance, to imitate the play of phenomenal forms, and to stimulate an artificial delight by dallying with lines and proportions? To a careful observer this pernicious influence of opera on music recapitulates the general development of modern music. The optimism that presided at the birth of opera and of the society represented by opera has succeeded with frightening rapidity in divesting music of its grand Dionysiac meanings and stamping it with the trivial character in a *divertissement*.[19] If we have been justified in suggesting a connection between the disappearance of the Dionysiac spirit and the spectacular, yet hitherto unexplained, degeneration of the Greek species, with what high hopes must we greet the auspicious signs of the opposite development in our own era, namely the gradual reawakening of the Dionysiac spirit! The divine power of Heracles cannot languish for ever in the service of Omphale.[20] Out of the Dionysiac recesses of the German soul has sprung a power which has nothing in common with the presuppositions of Socratic culture and which that culture can neither explain nor justify. Quite the contrary, the culture sees it as something to be dreaded and abhorred, something infinitely potent and hostile. I refer to German music, in its mighty course from Bach to Beethoven, and from Beethoven to Wagner. How can the petty intellectualism of our day deal with this monster that has risen out of the infinite deeps? There is no formula to be found, in either the reservoir of operatic filigree and arabesque or the abacus of the fugue and contrapuntal dialectics, that will subdue this monster, make it stand and deliver. What a spectacle to see our estheticians beating the air with the butterfly nets of their pedantic slogans, in vain pursuit of that marvelously volatile musical genius, their movements sadly belying their standards of "eternal" beauty and grandeur! Look at these patrons of music for a moment at close range, as they repeat indefatigably: "Beauty! Beauty!" and judge for yourselves whether they really look like the beautiful darlings of nature, or whether it would not be more correct to say that they have assumed a disguise for their own coarseness, as esthetic pretext for their barren and jejune sensibilities — take the case of Otto Jahn.[21] But liars and prevaricators ought to watch

their step in the area of German music. For amidst our degenerate culture music is the only pure and purifying flame, towards which all things move in a Heracleitean double motion.[22] All that is now called culture, education, civilization will one day have to appear before the incorruptible judge, Dionysos.

Let us now recall how the new German philosophy was nourished from the same sources, how Kant and Schopenhauer succeeded in destroying the complacent acquiescence of intellectual Socratism, how by their labors an infinitely more profound[23] and serious consideration of questions of ethics and art was made possible — a conceptualized form, in fact, of Dionysiac wisdom. To what does this miraculous union between German philosophy and music point if not to a new mode of existence, whose precise nature we can divine only with the aid of Greek analogies? For us, who stand on the watershed between two different modes of existence, the Greek example is still of inestimable value, since it embodies the violent transition to a classical, rationalistic form of suasion; only, we are living through the great phases of Hellenism in reverse order and seem at this very moment to be moving backward from the Alexandrian age into an age of tragedy. And we can't help feeling that the dawn of a new tragic age is for the German spirit only a return to itself, a blessed recovery of its true identity. For an unconscionably long time powerful forces from the outside have compelled the German spirit, which had vegetated in barbaric formlessness, to subserve their forms. But at long last the German spirit may stand before the other nations, free of the leading strings of Romance culture — provided that it continues to be able to learn from the nation from whom to learn at all is a high and rare thing, the Greeks. And was there ever a time when we needed these supreme teachers more urgently than now, as we witness the rebirth of tragedy and are in danger of not knowing either whence it comes or whither it goes?

[19]Diversion.

[20]In the legend, in atonement for killing Iphitus, Heracles was forced to wear women's clothes and learn to spin at the direction of Queen Omphale.

[21]Otto Jahn (1813–1869), a classicist and archeologist, was a contemporary of Neitzsche.

[22]Heracleitus, who believed that all matter was in flux, thought nevertheless that changes in one direction for one aspect of the universe were balanced by changes in the opposite direction for another.

[23]Nietzsche is suggesting that Kant and Schopenhauer made aesthetics a matter of pure intuition, replacing the rationalist aesthetics common since Horace.

Henry James
1843–1916

Born in America, partly formed by the French, and late in life naturalized a British subject, Henry James was a relentless experimentalist with technique and subject matter who brought a new sophistication to the art of fiction. His father, Henry James, Sr., an independently wealthy gentleman, was a philosopher and religious mystic who valued eccentricity in himself and in his offspring. Henry and his equally well-known elder brother, William, were educated at schools in England, France, Switzerland, and Germany as well as in their birthplace, New York City; their father believed that his sons could become themselves only by avoiding attachments to any master, school, place, or nation, and he also loathed the pragmatism and professionalism of the American educational system. The paradoxical result was that both Henry and William became ardent professionals — William a psychologist and philosopher, Henry a novelist and critic.

James began publishing stories in his twenties but did not find his true voice until he left America for good in 1875 to live in Paris and then settle in London. The fiction of his first period is often some variation on the "international theme" — the moral and spiritual gap between America and Europe. *The American* (1877), *Daisy Miller* (1878), and *Portrait of a Lady* (1881) made his reputation; today these works (especially the last) seem to mark a transition between the social chronicle of the nineteenth century and the twentieth-century novel of psychological realism. The novels of his middle years, like *The Princess Casamassima* (1886) and *The Tragic Muse* (1890), were less successful, and James's attempt to conquer the London stage with *Guy Domville* (1895) ended in disaster. James withdrew from London to the retirement of Lamb House in Rye, where he produced the three ambiguous and highly nuanced masterworks of his late period: *The Wings of the Dove* (1902), *The Ambassadors* (1903), and *The Golden Bowl* (1904). In the next decade, James turned from fiction to memoir, but the outbreak of World War I disturbed the quiet of his last years. As an expression of solidarity with the British cause during America's long neutrality, James applied for citizenship (granted in 1915) and worked at war relief, the exertions of which broke his own health. He died on February 26, 1916.

"The Art of Fiction" (1884) seems to promise a manual of techniques, but this is precisely what James is least willing to provide. The title in fact is not James's own but was taken from a lecture by Walter Besant, which proposed that "laws of fiction may be laid down and taught with as much precision and exactness as the laws of harmony, perspective, and proportion." While generously granting everything he can to Besant's claims, James — who had been trained as a painter — essentially disagrees that regulations and conventions in fiction comparable to those in painting and music could exist. "If there are exact sciences, there are also exact arts, and the grammar of painting is so much more definite that it makes the difference." And James might have said, *Vive la différence,* for most of the distinctions that had become current in the short history of the criticism of fiction struck him as mechani-cal and empty.

Even before the English novel existed as such, William Congreve in his preface to *Incognita* (1692) had contrasted the romance and the novel. Later critics differentiated novels of incident from novels of character. For James, these notions might make talking about the novel easier but would only make excellence in writing more difficult. "What is character," he asks, "but the determination of incident? What is incident but the illustration of character?" For James, the novel is intended to convey the felt impression of life — a seamless web of action and motive that could not be reduced to simple formulas. The only Besantine dictum James wholeheartedly endorses is the recommendation that the prospective novelist keep a notebook to record impressions.

Although James rejects all of Besant's particular recommendations, he agrees that fiction is indeed an art. Today, after Joyce and Woolf and James himself, this contention would seem to need no proof. But the Victorian novel had been created mainly by entertainers who made few claims for themselves and their trade, and the British public was used to retreating into three-volume narratives that guaranteed adventure and escape, a love story with a happy ending, and poetic justice for all. In "The Art of Fiction," James positions himself against this stultifying formula. He is also concerned to champion his own style of writing fiction, which was more subtle and inward than was common. More generally, however, he wants the novelist to have the freedom to experiment not just with subject matter and point of view but with moral issues that disturb and disquiet.

Since James sets himself squarely against the philistines, we might expect him, in the 1880s, to embrace either the naturalism of Emile Zola or the pure "art for art's sake" aestheticism of Walter Pater. In fact he enters neither camp. James holds to fairly traditional notions of realism; beauty of form is not to be pursued merely for its own sake but in the process of conveying a complex and authentic experience that rests on the contingencies of life. "Do not listen," he warns, "to those who would . . . persuade you that this heavenly messenger wings her way outside of life altogether, breathing a superfine air, and turning away her head from the truth of things." But at the same time, James does not, like Zola, expect the artist to present social conditions in a scientifically accurate way; he claimed, in fact, that Zola's deterministic philosophy "vitiated" his portraiture.

Ultimately, James's impatience with rules and formulas for fiction derives from a post-Romantic, expressive theory of art. "The deepest quality of a work of art will always be the quality of the mind of the producer. In proportion as that intelligence is fine will the novel . . . partake of the substance of beauty and truth." James's most heartfelt recommendation to the aspiring artist is not to watch his handling of point of view, but to remain open to experience, to "be one of the people on whom nothing is lost." A fine intelligence will, he is confident, find or invent the techniques needed to realize the imagined vision, while a mechanical mind, using all the arts, will never produce something worthy of lasting fame.

Selected Bibliography

Beach, Joseph Warren. *The Method of Henry James.* Philadelphia: A. Saifer, 1954.

Cameron, J. M. "History, Realism, and the Work of Henry James." *English Studies in Canada* 10 (1984): 299–316.

Da Sousa Correa, Delia. "'The Art of Fiction': Henry James as Critic." In *The Nineteenth-Century Novel: Identities,* ed. Dennis Walder, 137–56. London: Routledge, 2001.

Daugherty, Sarah B. *The Literary Criticism of Henry James.* Athens: Ohio University Press, 1981.

During, Simon. "Henry James and Me." *MLN* 118, no. 5 (2003): 1279–93.

Edel, Leon. *The Prefaces of Henry James.* Paris: Jouvé, 1931.

Hughes, Herbert Leland. *Theory and Practice in Henry James.* Ann Arbor: Edwards Bros., 1926.

Jackson, Wendell P. "Theory of the Creative Process in the 'Prefaces' of Henry James." In *Amid Visions and Revisions: Poetry and Criticism on Literature and the Arts,* ed. Burney J. Hillis, Baltimore: Morgan State University Press, 1985, pp. 59–64.

James, Henry. *The Art of the Novel: Critical Prefaces.* Introduction by R. P. Blackmur. New York: Scribner, 1934.

Roberts, Morris. *Henry James's Criticism.* Cambridge: Harvard University Press, 1929.

Veeder, William. "Image as Argument: Henry James and the Style of Criticism." *Henry James Review* 6 (1985): 172–81.

The Art of Fiction

I should not have affixed so comprehensive a title to these few remarks, necessarily wanting in any completeness upon a subject the full consideration of which would carry us far, did I not seem to discover a pretext for my temerity in the interesting pamphlet lately published under this name by Mr. Walter Besant.[1] Mr. Besant's lecture at the Royal Institution — the original form of his pamphlet — appears to indicate that many persons are interested in the art of fiction, and are not indifferent to such remarks, as those who practice it may attempt to make about it. I am therefore anxious not to lose the benefit of this favorable association, and to edge in a few words under cover of the attention which Mr. Besant is sure to have excited. There is something very encouraging in his having put into form certain of his ideas on the mystery of story-telling.

It is a proof of life and curiosity — curiosity on the part of the brotherhood of novelists as well as on the part of their readers. Only a short time ago it might have been supposed that the English novel was not what the French call *discutable.* It had no air of having a theory, a conviction, a consciousness of itself behind it — of being the expression of an artistic faith, the result of choice and comparison. I do not say it was necessarily the worse for that; it would take much more courage than I possess to intimate that the form of the novel as Dickens and Thackeray (for instance) saw it had any taint of incompleteness. It was, however, *naïf* (if I may help myself out with another French word); and evidently if it be destined to suffer in any way for having lost its *naïveté* it has now an idea of making sure of the corresponding advantages. During the period I have alluded to there was a comfortable, good-humored feeling abroad that a novel is a novel, as a pudding is a pudding and that our only business with it could be to swallow it. But within a year or two, for some reason or other, there have been signs of returning animation — the era of discussion would appear to have been to

[1]Victorian man of letters (1836–1901). Besant's lecture on the art of fiction was delivered on April 25, 1884.

a certain extent opened. Art lives upon discus-sion, upon experiment, upon curiosity, upon variety of attempt, upon the exchange of views and the comparison of standpoints; and there is a presumption that those times when no one has anything particular to say about it, and has no reason to give for practice or preference, though they may be times of honor, are not times of development — are times, possibly even, a little of dulness. The successful application of any art is a delightful spectacle, but the theory too is interesting; and though there is a great deal of the latter without the former I suspect there has never been a genuine success that has not had a latent core of conviction. Discussion, suggestion, formulation, these things are fertilizing when they are frank and sincere. Mr. Besant has set an excellent example in saying what he thinks, for his part, about the way in which fiction should be written, as well as about the way in which it should be published; for his view of the "art," carried on into an appendix, covers that too. Other laborers in the same field will doubtless take up the argument, they will give it the light of their experience, and the effect will surely be to make our interest in the novel a little more what it had for some time threatened to fail to be — a seri-ous, active, inquiring interest, under protection of which this delightful study may, in moments of confidence, venture to say a little more what it thinks of itself.

It must take itself seriously for the public to take it so. The old superstition about fiction being "wicked"[2] has doubtless died out in England; but the spirit of it lingers in a certain oblique regard directed toward any story which does not more or less admit that it is only a joke. Even the most jocular novel feels in some degree the weight of the proscription that was formerly directed against literary levity: the jocularity does not always succeed in passing for orthodoxy. It is still expected, though perhaps people are ashamed to say it, that a production which is after all only a "make-believe" (for what else is a "story"?) shall be in some degree apologetic — shall renounce the pretension of attempting really to represent

life. This, of course, any sensible, wide-awake story declines to do, for it quickly perceives that the tolerance granted to it on such a condition is only an attempt to stifle it disguised in the form of generosity. The old evangelical hostility to the novel, which was as explicit as it was narrow, and which regarded it as little less favorable to our immortal part than a stage play, was in reality far less insulting. The only reason for the existence of a novel is that it does attempt to represent life. When it relinquishes this attempt, the same attempt that we see on the canvas of the painter, it will have arrived at a very strange pass. It is not expected of the picture that it will make itself humble in order to be forgiven; and the analogy between the art of the painter and the art of novel-ist is, so far as I am able to see, complete. Their inspiration is the same, their process (allowing for the different quality of the vehicle) is the same, their success is the same. They may learn from each other, they may explain and sustain each other. Their cause is the same, and the honor of one is the honor of another. The Mahometans think a picture an unholy thing, but it is a long time since any Christian did, and it is therefore the more odd that in the Christian mind the traces (dissimulated though they may be) of a suspicion of the sister art should linger to this day. The only effectual way to lay it to rest is to emphasize the analogy to which I just alluded — to insist on the fact that as the picture is reality, so the novel is history. That is the only general description (which does it justice) that we may give of the novel. But history also is allowed to represent life; it is not, any more than painting, expected to apologize. The subject-matter of fiction is stored up likewise in documents and records, and if it will not give itself away, as they say in California, it must speak with assurance, with the tone of the historian. Certain accomplished novelists have a habit of giving themselves away which must often bring tears to the eyes of people who take their fiction seriously. I was lately struck, in reading over many pages of Anthony Trollope, with his want of discretion in this particular. In a digression, a parenthesis or an aside, he concedes to the reader that he and this trusting friend are only "making believe." He admits that the events he narrates have not really happened, and that he can give his narrative any turn the reader may like best.[3] Such a betrayal of a sacred office seems to me, I confess, a terrible crime; it is what I mean by the attitude of apology, and it shocks me every whit as much in Trollope as it would have shocked me in Gibbon or Macaulay. It implies that the novelist is less occupied in looking for the truth (the truth, of course I mean, that he assumes, the premises that we grant him, whatever they may be) than the historian, and in doing so it deprives him at a stroke of all his standing room. To represent and illustrate the past, the actions of men, is the task of either writer, and the only difference that I can see is, in proportion as he succeeds, to the honor of the novelist, consisting as it does in his having more difficulty in collecting his evidence, which is so far from being purely literary. It seems to me to give him a great character, the fact that he has at once so much in common with the philosopher and the painter; this double analogy is a magnificent heritage.

It is of all this evidently that Mr. Besant is full when he insists upon the fact that fiction is one of the *fine* arts, deserving in its turn of all the honors and emoluments that have hitherto been reserved for the successful profession of music, poetry, painting, architecture. It is impossible to insist too much on so important a truth, and the place that Mr. Besant demands for the work of the novelist may be represented, a trifle less abstractly, by saying that he demands not only that it shall be reputed artistic, but that it shall be reputed very artistic indeed. It is excellent that he should have struck this note, for his doing so indicates that there was need of it, that his proposition may be to many people a novelty. One rubs one's eyes at the thought; but the rest of Mr. Besant's essay confirms the revelation. I suspect in truth that it would be possible to confirm it still further, and that one would not be far wrong in saying that in addition to the people to whom it has never occurred that a novel ought to be artistic, there are a great many others who, if this principle were urged upon them, would be filled with an indefinable mistrust. They would find it difficult to explain their repugnance, but it would operate strongly to put them on their guard. "Art," in our Protestant communities, where so many things have got so strangely twisted about, is supposed in certain circles to have some vaguely injurious effect upon those who make it an important consideration, who let it weigh in the balance. It is assumed to be opposed in some mysterious manner to morality, to amusement, to instruction. When it is embodied in the work of the painter (the sculptor is another affair!) you know what it is: it stands there before you, in the honesty of pink and green and a gilt frame; you can see the worst of it at a glance, and you can be on your guard. But when it is introduced into literature it becomes more insidious — there is danger of its hurting you before you know it. Literature should be either instructive or amusing, and there is in many minds an impression that these artistic preoccupations, the search for form, contribute to neither end, interfere indeed with both. They are too frivolous to be edifying, and too serious to be diverting; and they are moreover priggish and paradoxical and superfluous. That, I think, represents the manner in which the latent thought of many people who read novels as an exercise in skipping would explain itself if it were to become articulate. They would argue, of course, that a novel ought to be "good," but they would interpret this term in a fashion of their own, which indeed would vary considerably from one critic to another. One would say that being good means representing virtuous and aspiring characters, placed in prominent positions; another would say that it depends on a "happy ending," on a distribution at the last of prizes, pensions, husbands, wives, babies, millions, appended paragraphs, and cheerful remarks. Another still would say that it means being full of incident and movement, so that we shall wish to jump ahead, to see who was the mysterious stranger, and if the stolen will was ever found, and shall not be distracted from this pleasure by any tiresome analysis or "description." But they would all agree that the "artistic" idea would spoil some of their fun. One would hold it accountable for all the description, another would see it revealed in the absence of sympathy. Its hostility to a happy ending would be evident,

---

[3]James may be thinking about such addresses to the reader as the opening of Ch. 51 in *Barchester Towers,* where the narrator worries aloud about the difficulty of writing endings.

and it might even in some cases render any ending at all impossible. The "ending" of a novel is, for many persons, like that of a good dinner, a course of dessert and ices, and the artist in fiction is regarded as a sort of meddlesome doctor who forbids agreeable aftertastes. It is therefore true that this conception of Mr. Besant's of the novel as a superior form encounters not only a negative but a positive indifference. It matters little that as a work of art it should really be as little or as much of its essence to supply happy endings, sympathetic characters, and an objective tone, as if it were a work of mechanics: the association of ideas, however incongruous, might easily be too much for it if an eloquent voice were not sometimes raised to call attention to the fact that it is at once as free and as serious a branch of literature as any other.

Certainly this might sometimes be doubted in presence of the enormous number of works of fiction that appeal to the credulity of our generation, for it might easily seem that there could be no great character in a commodity so quickly and easily produced. It must be admitted that good novels are much compromised by bad ones, and that the field at large suffers discredit from overcrowding, I think, however, that this injury is only superficial, and that the superabundance of written fiction proves nothing against the principle itself. It has been vulgarized, like all other kinds of literature, like everything else today, and it has proved more than some kinds accessible to vulgarization. But there is as much difference as there ever was between a good novel and a bad one: the bad is swept with all the daubed canvases and spoiled marble into some unvisited limbo, or infinite rubbish-yard beneath the back-windows of the world, and the good subsists and emits its light and stimulates our desire for perfection. As I shall take the liberty of making but a single criticism of Mr. Besant, whose tone is so full of the love of his art, I may as well have done with it at once. He seems to me to mistake in attempting to say so definitely beforehand what sort of an affair the good novel will be. To indicate the danger of such an error as that has been the purpose of these few pages; to suggest that certain traditions on the subject, applied *a priori*, have already had much to answer for, and that the good health of

an art which undertakes so immediately to reproduce life must demand that it be perfectly free. It lives upon exercise, and the very meaning of exercise is freedom. The only obligation to which in advance we may hold a novel, without incurring the accusation of being arbitrary, is that it be interesting. That general responsibility rests upon it, but it is the only one I can think of. The ways in which it is at liberty to accomplish this result (of interesting us) strike me as innumerable, and such as can only suffer from being marked out or fenced in by prescription. They are as various as the temperament of man, and they are successful in proportion as they reveal a particular mind, different from others. A novel is in its broadest definition a personal, a direct impression of life: that, to begin with, constitutes its value, which is greater or less according to the intensity of the impression. But there will be no intensity at all, and therefore no value, unless there is freedom to feel and say. The tracing of a line to be followed, of a tone to be taken, of a form to be filled out, is a limitation of that freedom and a suppression of the very thing that we are most curious about. The form, it seems to me, is to be appreciated after the fact: then the author's choice has been made, his standard has been indicated; then we can follow lines and directions and compare tones and resemblances. Then in a word we can enjoy one of the most charming of pleasures, we can estimate quality, we can apply the test of execution. The execution belongs to the author alone; it is what is most personal to him, and we measure him by that. The advantage, the luxury, as well as the torment and responsibility of the novelist, is that there is no limit to what he may attempt as an executant — no limit to his possible experiments, efforts, discoveries, successes. Here it is especially that he works, step by step, like his brother of the brush, of whom we may always say that he has painted his picture in a manner best known to himself. His manner is his secret, not necessarily a jealous one. He cannot disclose it as a general thing if he would; he would be at a loss to teach it to others. I say this with a due recollection of having insisted on the community of method of the artist who paints a picture and the artist who writes a novel. The painter *is* able to teach the rudiments of his practice, and it is possible, from the study of good work (granted the aptitude), both to learn how to paint and to learn how to write. Yet it remains true, without injury to the *rapprochement,* that the literary artists would be obliged to say to his pupil much more than the other, "Ah, well, you must do it as you can!" It is a question of degree, a matter of delicacy. If there are exact sciences, there are also exact arts, and the grammar of painting is so much more definite that it makes the difference.

I ought to add, however, that if Mr. Besant says at the beginning of his essay that the "laws of fiction may be laid down and taught with as much precision and exactness as the laws of harmony, perspective, and proportion," he mitigates what might appear to be an extravagance by applying his remark to "general" laws, and by expressing most of these rules in a manner with which it would certainly be unaccommodating to disagree. That the novelist must write from his experience, that his "characters must be real and such as might be met with in actual life"; that "a young lady brought up in a quiet country village should avoid descriptions of garrison life," and "a writer whose friends and personal experiences belong to the lower middle-class should carefully avoid introducing his characters into society"; that one should enter one's notes in a common-place book; that one's figures should be clear in outline; that making them clear by some trick of speech or of carriage is a bad method, and "describing them at length" is a worse one; that English Fiction should have a "conscious moral purpose"; that "it is almost impossible to estimate too highly the value of careful workmanship — that is, of style"; that "the most important point of all is the story," that "the story is everything": these are principles with most of which it is surely impossible not to sympathize. That remark about the lower middle-class writer and his knowing his place is perhaps rather chilling; but for the rest I should find it difficult to dissent from any one of these recommendations. At the same time, I should find it difficult positively to assent to them, with the exception, perhaps, of the injunction as to entering one's notes in a common-place book. They scarcely seem to me to have the quality that Mr. Besant attributes to the rules of the novelist — the "precision and

exactness" of "the laws of harmony, perspective, and proportion." They are suggestive, they are even inspiring, but they are not exact, though they are doubtless as much so as the case admits of: which is a proof of that liberty of interpretation for which I just contended. For the value of these different injunctions — so beautiful and so vague — is wholly in the meaning one attaches to them. The characters, the situation, which strike one as real will be those that touch and interest one most, but the measure of reality is very difficult to fix. The reality of Don Quixote or of Mr. Micawber is a very delicate shade; it is a reality so colored by the author's vision that, vivid as it may be, one would hesitate to propose it as a model: one would expose one's self to some very embarrassing questions on the part of a pupil. It goes without saying that you will not write a good novel unless you possess the sense of reality; but it will be difficult to give you a recipe for calling that sense into being. Humanity is immense, and reality has a myriad forms; the most one can affirm is that some of the flowers of fiction have the odor of it, and others have not; as for telling you in advance how your nosegay should be composed, that is another affair. It is equally excellent and inconclusive to say that one must write from experience; to our supposititious aspirant such a declaration might savor of mockery. What kind of experience is intended, and where does it begin and end? Experience is never limited, and it is never complete; it is an immense sensibility, a kind of huge spider-web of the finest silken threads suspended in the chamber of consciousness, and catching every air-borne particle in its tissue. It is the very atmosphere of the mind; and when the mind is imaginative — much more when it happens to be that of a man of genius — it takes to itself the faintest hints of life, it converts the very pulses of the air into revelations. The young lady living in a village has only to be a damsel upon whom nothing is lost to make it quite unfair (as it seems to me) to declare to her that she shall have nothing to say about the military. Greater miracles have been seen than that, imagination assisting, she should speak the truth about some of these gentlemen. I remember an English novelist, a woman of genius, telling me that she was much commended for the impression

all its other merits (including that conscious moral purpose of which Mr. Besant speaks) help-lessly and submissively depend. If it be not there they are all as nothing, and if these be there, they owe their effect to the success with which the author has produced the illusion of life. The cul-tivation of this success, the study of this exquisite process, form, to my taste, the beginning and the end of the art of the novelist. They are his inspiration, his despair, his reward, his torment, his delight. It is here in very truth that he com-petes with life; it is here that he competes with his brother the painter in his attempt to render the look of things, the look that conveys their mean-ing, to catch the color, the relief, the expression, the surface, the substance of the human spectacle. It is in regard to this that Mr. Besant is well inspired when he bids him take notes. He cannot possibly take too many, he cannot possibly take enough. All life solicits him, and to "render" the simplest surface, to produce the most momentary illusion, is a very complicated business. His case would be easier, and the rule would be more exact, if Mr. Besant had been able to tell him what notes to take. But this, I fear, he can never learn in any manual; it is the business of his life. He has to take a great many in order to select a few, he has to work them up as he can, and even the guides and philosophers who might have most to say to him must leave him alone when it comes to the applications of precepts, as we leave the painter in communion with his palette. That his characters "must be clear in outline," as Mr. Besant says — he feels that down to his boots; but how he shall make them so is a secret between his good angel and himself. It would be absurdly simple if he could be taught that a great deal of "description" would make them so, or that on the contrary the absence of description and the cultivation of dialogue, or the absence of dialogue and the multiplication of "incident," would rescue him from his difficulties. Nothing, for instance, is more possible than that he be of a turn of mind for which this odd, literal opposition of descrip-tion and dialogue, incident and description, has little meaning and light. People often talk of these things as if they had a kind of internecine distinct-ness, instead of melting into each other at every breath, and being intimately associated parts of

she had managed to give in one of her tales of the nature and way of life of the French Protestant youth.[4] She had been asked where she learned so much about his recondite being, she had been congratulated on her peculiar opportunities. These opportunities consisted in her having once, in Paris, as she ascended a staircase, passed an open door where, in the household of a *pasteur*,[5] some of the young Protestants were seated at table round a finished meal. The glimpse made a picture; it lasted only a moment, but that moment was experience. She had got her direct personal impression, and she turned out her type. She knew what youth was, and what Protestantism; she also had the advantage of having seen what it was to be French, so that she converted these ideas into a concrete image and produced a real-ity. Above all, however, she was blessed with the faculty which when you give it an inch takes an ell, and which for the artist is a much greater source of strength than any accident of residence or of place in the social scale. The power to guess the unseen from the seen, to trace the implication of things, to judge the whole piece by the pattern, the condition of feeling life in general so com-pletely that you are well on your way to knowing any particular corner of it — this cluster of gifts may almost be said to constitute experience, and they occur in country and in town, and in the most differing stages of education. If experience con-sists of impressions, it may be said that impres-sions *are* experience, just as (have we not seen it?) they are the very air we breathe. Therefore, if I should certainly say to a novice, "Write from experience and experience only," I should feel that this was rather a tantalizing monition if I were not careful immediately to add, "Try to be one of the people on whom nothing is lost!"

I am far from intending by this to minimize the importance of exactness — of truth of detail. One can speak best from one's own taste, and I may therefore venture to say that the air of reality (solidity of specification) seems to me to be the supreme virtue of a novel — the merit on which

[4] Probably *The Story of Elizabeth* by Anne Thackeray, Lady Ritchie.

[5] Minister.

one general effort of expression. I cannot imagine composition existing in a series of blocks, nor conceive, in any novel worth discussing at all, of a passage of description that is not in its intention narrative, a passage of dialogue that is not in its intention descriptive, a touch of truth of any sort that does not partake of the nature of incident, or an incident that derives its interest from any other source than the general and only source of the success of a work of art — that of being illustrative. A novel is a living thing, all one and continuous, like any other organism, and in proportion as it lives will it be found, I think, that in each of the parts there is something of each of the other parts. The critic who over the close texture of a finished work shall pretend to trace a geography of items will mark some frontiers as artificial, I fear, as any that have been known to history. There is an old-fashioned distinction between the novel of character and the novel of incident which must have cost many a smile to the intending fabulist who was keen about his work. It appears to me as little to the point as the equally celebrated distinction between the novel and the romance — to answer as little to any reality. There are bad novels and good novels, as there are bad pictures and good pictures; but that is the only distinction in which I see any meaning, and I can as little imagine speaking of a novel of character as I can imagine speaking of a picture of character. When one says picture one says of character, when one says novel one says of incident, and the terms may be transposed at will. What is character but the determination of incident? What is incident but the illustration of character? What is either a picture or a novel that is *not* of character? What else do we seek in it and find in it? It is an incident for a woman to stand up with her hand resting on a table and look out at you in a certain way; or if it be not an incident I think it will be hard to say what it is. At the same time it is an expression of character. If you say you don't see it (character in *that — allons donc!*[6]), this is exactly what the artist who has reasons of his own for thinking he *does* see it undertakes to show you. When a young man makes up his mind that he has not faith enough after all to enter the church as he intended, that is an incident, though you may not hurry to the end of the chapter to see whether perhaps he doesn't change once more. I do not say that these are extraordinary or startling incidents. I do not pretend to estimate the degree of interest proceeding from them, for this will depend upon the skill of the painter. It sounds almost puerile to say that some incidents are intrinsically much more important than others, and I need not take this precaution after having professed my sympathy for the major ones in remarking that the only classification of the novel that I can understand is into that which has life and that which has it not.

The novel and the romance, the novel of incident and that of character — these clumsy separations appear to me to have been made by critics and readers for their own convenience, and to help them out of some of their occasional queer predicaments, but to have little reality or interest for the producer, from whose point of view it is of course that we are attempting to consider the art of fiction. The case is the same with another shadowy category which Mr. Besant apparently is disposed to set up — that of the "modern English novel"; unless indeed it be that in this matter he has fallen into an accidental confusion of standpoints. It is not quite clear whether he intends the remarks in which he alludes to it to be didactic or historical. It is as difficult to suppose a person intending to write a modern English as to suppose him writing an ancient English novel: that is a label which begs the question. One writes the novel, one paints the picture, of one's language and of one's time, and calling it modern English will not, alas! make the difficult task any easier. No more, unfortunately, will calling this or that work of one's fellow-artist a romance — unless it be, of course, simply for the pleasantness of the thing, as for instance when Hawthorne gave this heading to his story of *Blithedale*. The French, who have brought the theory of fiction to remarkable completeness, have but one name for the novel, and have not attempted smaller things in it, that I can see, for that. I can think of no obligation to which the "romancer" would not be held equally with the novelist; the standard of execution is equally high for each. Of course it is

⁶Get out of here!

of execution that we are talking — that being the only point of a novel that is open to contention. This is perhaps too often lost sight of, only to produce interminable confusions and cross-purposes. We must grant the artist his subject, his idea, his *donnée:*[7] our criticism is applied only to what he makes of it. Naturally I do not mean that we are bound to like it or find it interesting: in case we do not our course is perfectly simple — to let it alone. We may believe that of a certain idea even the most sincere novelist can make nothing at all, and the event may perfectly justify our belief; but the failure will have been a failure to execute, and it is in the execution that the fatal weakness is recorded. If we pretend to respect the artist at all, we must allow him his freedom of choice, in the face, in particular cases, of innumerable presumptions that the choice will not fructify. Art derives a considerable part of its beneficial exercise from flying in the face of presumptions, and some of the most interesting experiments of which it is capable are hidden in the bosom of common things. Gustave Flaubert has written a story about the devotion of a servant-girl to a parrot,[8] and the production, highly finished as it is, cannot on the whole be called a success. We are perfectly free to find it flat, but I think it might have been interesting; and I, for my part, am extremely glad he should have written it; it is a contribution to our knowledge of what can be done — or what cannot. Ivan Turgeneff has written a tale about a deaf and dumb serf and a lap-dog,[9] and the thing is touching, loving, a little masterpiece. He struck the note of life where Gustave Flaubert missed it — he fell in the face of a presumption and achieved a victory.

Nothing, of course, will ever take the place of the good old fashion of "liking" a work of art or not liking it: the most improved criticism will not abolish that primitive, that ultimate test. I mention this to guard myself from the accusation of intimating that the idea, the subject, of a novel or a picture, does not matter. It matters, to my sense, in the highest degree, and if I might put up a prayer it would be that artists should select

7. What is given.
8. *A Simple Heart.*
9. *Mumu.*

none but the richest. Some, as I have already hastened to admit, are much more remunerative than others, and it would be a world happily arranged in which persons intending to treat them should be exempt from confusions and mistakes. This fortunate condition will arrive only, I fear, on the same day that critics become purged from error. Meanwhile, I repeat, we do not judge the artist with fairness unless we say to him,

"'Oh, I grant you your starting-point, because if I did not I should seem to prescribe to you, and heaven forbid I should take that responsibility. If I pretend to tell you what you must not take, you will call upon me to tell you then what you must take; in which case I shall be prettily caught. Moreover, it isn't till I have accepted your data that I can begin to measure you. I have the standard, the pitch; I have no right to tamper with your flute and then criticize your music. Of course I may not care for your idea at all; I may think it silly, or stale, or unclean; in which case I wash my hands of you altogether. I may content myself with believing that you will not have succeeded in being interesting, but I shall, of course, not attempt to demonstrate it, and you will be as indifferent to me as I am to you. I needn't remind you that there are all sorts of tastes: who can know it better? Some people, for excellent reasons, don't like to read about carpenters; others, for reasons even better, don't like to read about courtesans. Many object to Americans. Others (I believe they are mainly editors and publishers) won't look at Italians. Some readers don't like quiet subjects; others don't like bustling ones. Some enjoy a complete illusion, others the consciousness of large concessions. They choose their novels accordingly, and if they don't care about your idea they won't, *a fortiori,* care about your treatment.'

So that it comes back very quickly, as I have said, to the liking: in spite of M. Zola, who reasoned less powerfully than he represents, and who will not reconcile himself to this absoluteness of taste, thinking that there are certain things that people ought to like, and that they can be made to like. I am quite at a loss to imagine anything (at any rate in this matter of fiction) that people *ought* to like or to dislike. Selection will be sure to take care of itself, for it has a constant motive behind it. That motive is simply experience. As people feel life, so they will feel the art that is most closely related to it. This closeness of relation is what we should never forget in talking of the effort of the novel. Many people speak of it as a factitious, artificial form, a product of ingenuity, the business of which is to alter and arrange the things that surround us, to translate them into conventional, traditional moulds. This, however, is a view of the matter which carries us but a very short way, condemns the art to an eternal repetition of a few familiar *clichés,* cuts short its development, and leads us straight up to a dead wall. Catching the very note and trick, the strange irregular rhythm of life, that is the attempt whose strenuous force keeps Fiction upon her feet. In proportion as in what she offers us we see life *without* rearrangement do we feel that we are touching the truth; in proportion as we see it *with* rearrangement do we feel that we are being put off with a substitute, a compromise and convention. It is not uncommon to hear an extraordinary assurance of remark in regard to this matter of rearranging, which is often spoken of as if it were the last word of art. Mr. Besant seems to me in danger of falling into the great error with his rather unguarded talk about "selection." Art is essentially selection, but it is a selection whose main care is to be typical, to be inclusive. For many people art means rose-colored window-panes, and selection means picking a bouquet for Mrs. Grundy.[10] They will tell you glibly that artistic considerations have nothing to do with the disagreeable, with the ugly; they will rattle off shallow commonplaces about the province of art and the limits of art till you are moved to some wonder in return as to the province and the limits of ignorance. It appears to me that no one can ever have made a seriously artistic attempt without becoming conscious of an immense increase — a kind of revelation — of freedom. One perceives in that case — by the light of a heavenly ray — that the province of art is all life, all feeling, all observation, all vision. As Mr. Besant so justly intimates, it is all experience. That is a sufficient answer to those who maintain

[10]Personification of prudery.

that it must not touch the sad things of life, who stick into its divine unconscious bosom little prohibitory inscriptions on the end of sticks, such as we see in public gardens — "It is forbidden to walk on the grass; it is forbidden to touch the flowers; it is not allowed to introduce dogs or to remain after dark; it is requested to keep to the right." The young aspirant in the line of fiction whom we continue to imagine will do nothing without taste, for in that case his freedom would be of little use to him; but the first advantage of his taste will be to reveal to him the absurdity of the little sticks and tickets. If he have taste, I must add, of course he will have ingenuity, and my disrespectful reference to that quality just now was not meant to imply that it is useless in fiction. But it is only a secondary aid; the first is a capacity of receiving straight impressions.

Mr. Besant has some remarks on the question of "the story" which I shall not attempt to criticize, though they seem to me to contain a singular ambiguity, because I do not think I understand them. I cannot see what is meant by talking as if there were a part of a novel which is the story and part of it which for mystical reasons is not — unless indeed the distinction be made in a sense in which it is difficult to suppose that any one should attempt to convey anything. "The story," if it represents anything, represents the subject, the idea, the *donnée* of the novel; and there is surely no "school" — Mr. Besant speaks of a school — which urges that a novel should be all treatment and no subject. There must assuredly be something to treat; every school is intimately conscious of that. This sense of the story being the idea, the starting-point, of the novel, is the only one that I see in which it can be spoken of as something different from its organic whole; and since in proportion as the work is successful the idea permeates and penetrates it, informs and animates it, so that every word and every punctuation-point contribute directly to the expression, in that proportion do we lose our sense of the story being a blade which may be drawn more or less out of its sheath. The story and the novel, the idea and the form, are the needle and thread, and I never heard of a guild of tailors who recommended the use of the thread without the needle, or the needle without the thread. Mr. Besant is not the only critic who may be observed to have spoken as if there were certain things in life which constitute stories, and certain others which do not. I find the same odd implication in an entertaining article in the *Pall Mall Gazette*, devoted, as it happens, to Mr. Besant's lecture. "The story," says this graceful writer, as if with a tone of opposition to some other idea, I should think it was, as every painter who, as the time for "sending in" his picture looms in the distance, finds himself still in quest of a subject — as every belated artist not fixed about his theme will heartily agree. There are some subjects which speak to us and others which do not, but he would be a clever man who should undertake to give a rule — an *index expurgatorius* — by which the story and the no-story should be known apart. It is impossible (to me at least) to imagine any such rule which shall not be altogether arbitrary. The writer in the *Pall Mall* opposes the delightful (as I suppose) novel of *Margot la Balafrée* to certain tales in which "Bostonian nymphs" appear to have "rejected English dukes for psychological reasons."11 I am not acquainted with the romance just designated, and can scarcely forgive the *Pall Mall* critic for not mentioning the name of the author, but the title appears to refer to a lady who may have received a scar in some heroic adventure. I am inconsolable at not being acquainted with this episode, but am utterly at a loss to see why it is a story when the rejection (or acceptance) of a duke is not, and why a reason, psychological or other, is not a subject when a cicatrix is. They are all particles of the multitudinous life with which the novel deals, and surely no dogma which pretends to make it lawful to touch the one and unlawful to touch the other will stand for a moment on its feet. It is the special picture that must stand or fall, according as it seem to possess truth or to lack it. Mr. Besant does not, to my sense, light up the subject by intimating that a story must, under penalty of not being a story, consist of "adventures." Why of adventures more than of green spectacles? He mentions a category of impossible things, and

among them he places "fiction without adventure." Why without adventure, more than without matrimony, or celibacy, or parturition, or cholera, or hydropathy, or Jansenism? This seems to me to bring the novel back to the hapless little *rôle* of being an artificial, ingenious thing — bring it down from its large, free character of an immense and exquisite correspondence with life. And what *is* adventure, when it comes to that and by what sign is the listening pupil to recognize it? It is an adventure — an immense one — for me to write this little article; and for a Bostonian nymph to reject an English duke is an adventure only less stirring, I should say, than for an English duke to be rejected by a Bostonian nymph. I see dramas within dramas in that, and innumerable points of view. A psychological reason is, to my imagination, an object adorably pictorial; to catch the tint of its complexion — I feel as if that idea might inspire one to Titianesque efforts. There are few things more exciting to me, in short, than a psychological reason, and yet, I protest, the novel seems to me the most magnificent form of art. I have just been reading, at the same time, the delightful story of *Treasure Island*, by Mr. Robert Louis Stevenson and, in a manner less consecutive, the last tale from M. Edmond de Goncourt, which is entitled *Chérie*. One of these works treats of murder, mysteries, islands of dreadful renown, hairbreadth escapes, miraculous coincidences and buried doubloons. The other treats of a little French girl who lived in a fine house in Paris, and died of wounded sensibility because no one would marry her. I call *Treasure Island* delightful, because it appears to me to have succeeded wonderfully in what it attempts; and I venture to bestow no epithet upon *Chérie*, which strikes me as having failed deplorably in what it attempts — that is in tracing the development of the moral consciousness of a child. But one of these productions strikes me as exactly as much of a novel as the other, and as having a "story" quite as much. The moral consciousness of a child is as much a part of life as the islands of the Spanish Main, and the one sort of geography seems to me to have those "surprises" of which Mr. Besant speaks quite as much as the other. For myself (since it comes back in the last resort, as I say, to the preference of the individual), the

11Henry James's own *An International Episode* (1879). *Margot la Balafrée* (1884) is by Fortune de Boisgobey.

picture of the child's experience has the advantage that I can at successive steps (an immense luxury, near to the "sensual pleasure" of which Mr. Besant's critic in the *Pall Mall* speaks) say Yes or No, as it may be, to what the artist puts before me. I have been a child in fact, but I have been on a quest for a buried treasure only in supposition, and it is a simple accident that with M. de Goncourt I should have for the most part to say No. With George Eliot, when she painted that country with a far other intelligence, I always said Yes.

The most interesting part of Mr. Besant's lecture is unfortunately the briefest passage — his very cursory allusion to the "conscious moral purpose" of the novel. Here again it is not very clear whether he be recording a fact or laying down a principle; it is a great pity that in the latter case he should not have developed his idea. This branch of the subject is of immense importance, and Mr. Besant's few words point to considerations of the widest reach, not to be lightly disposed of. He will have treated the art of fiction but superficially who is not prepared to go every inch of the way that these considerations will carry him. It is for this reason that at the beginning of these remarks I was careful to notify the reader that my reflections on so large a theme have no pretension to be exhaustive. Like Mr. Besant, I have left the question of the morality of the novel till the last, and at the last I find I have used up my space. It is a question surrounded with difficulties, as witness the very first that meets us, in the form of a definite question, on the threshold. Vagueness, in such a discussion, is fatal, and what is the meaning of your morality and your conscious moral purpose? Will you not define your terms and explain how (a novel being a picture) a picture can be either moral or immoral? You wish to paint a moral picture or carve a moral statue: will you not tell us how you would set about it? We are discussing the Art of Fiction; questions of art are questions (in the widest sense) of execution; questions of morality are quite another affair, and will you not let us see how it is that you find it so easy to mix them up? These things are so clear to Mr. Besant that he has deduced from them a law which he sees embodied in English Fiction, and which is "a truly admirable thing and a great

cause for congratulation." It is a great cause for congratulation indeed when such thorny problems become as smooth as silk. I may add that in so far as Mr. Besant perceives that in point of fact English Fiction has addressed itself preponderantly to these delicate questions he will appear to many people to have made a vain discovery. They will have been positively struck, on the contrary, with the moral timidity of the usual English novelist; with his (or with her) aversion to face the difficulties with which on every side the treatment of reality bristles. He is apt to be extremely shy (whereas the picture that Mr. Besant draws is a picture of boldness), and the sign of his work, for the most part, is a cautious silence on certain subjects. In the English novel (by which of course I mean the American as well), more than in any other there is a traditional difference between that which people know and that which they agree to admit that they know, that which they see and that which they speak of, that which they feel to be a part of life and that which they allow to enter into literature. There is the great difference, in short, between what they talk of in conversation and what they talk of in print. The essence of moral energy is to survey the whole field, and I should directly reverse Mr. Besant's remark and say not that the English novel has a purpose, but that it has a diffidence. To what degree a purpose in a work of art is a source of corruption I shall not attempt to inquire; the one that seems to me least dangerous is the purpose of making a perfect work. As for our novel, I may say lastly on this score that as we find it in England today it strikes me as addressed in a large degree to "young people," and that this in itself constitutes a presumption that it will be rather shy. There are certain things which it is generally agreed not to discuss, not even to mention, before young people. That is very well, but the absence of discussion is not a symptom of the moral passion. The purpose of the English novel — "a truly admirable thing, and a great cause for congratulation" — strikes me therefore as rather negative.

There is one point at which the moral sense and the artistic sense lie very near together; that is in the light of the very obvious truth that the deepest quality of a work of art will always be the quality of the mind of the producer. In proportion as that intelligence is fine will the novel, the picture, the statue partake of the substance of beauty and truth. To be constituted of such elements is, to my vision, to have purpose enough. No good novel will ever proceed from a superficial mind; that seems to me an axiom which, for the artist in fiction, will cover all needful moral ground: if the youthful aspirant take it to heart it will illuminate for him many of the mysteries of "purpose." There are many other useful things that might be said to him, but I have come to the end of my article, and can only touch them as I pass. The critic in the *Pall Mall Gazette*, whom I have already quoted, draws attention to the danger, in speaking of the art of fiction, of generalizing. The danger that he has in mind is rather, I imagine, that of particularizing, for there are some comprehensive remarks which, in addition to those embodied in Mr. Besant's suggestive lecture, might without fear of misleading him be addressed to the ingenuous student. I should remind him first of the magnificence of the form that is open to him, which offers to sight so few restrictions and such innumerable opportunities. The other arts, in comparison, appear confined and hampered; the various conditions under which they are exercised are so rigid and definite. But the only condition that I can think of attaching to the composition of the novel is, as I have already said, that it be sincere. This freedom is a splendid privilege, and the first lesson of the young novelist is to learn to be worthy of it.

"Enjoy it as it deserves [I should say to him]; take possession of it, explore it to its utmost extent, publish it, rejoice in it. All life belongs to you, and do not listen either to those who would shut you up into corners of it and tell you that it is only here and there that art inhabits, or to those who would persuade you that this heavenly messenger wings her way outside of life altogether, breathing a superfine air, and turning away her head from the truth of things. There is no impression of life, no manner of seeing it and feeling it, to which the plan of the novelist may not offer a place; you have only to remember that talents so dissimilar as those of Alexandre Dumas and Jane Austen, Charles Dickens and Gustave Flaubert have worked in this field with equal glory. Do not think too much about optimism and pessimism; try and catch the color of life itself. In France today we see a prodigious effort (that of Emile Zola, to whose solid and serious work no explorer of the capacity of the novel can allude without respect), we see an extraordinary effort vitiated by a spirit of pessimism on a narrow basis. M. Zola is magnificent, but he strikes an English reader as ignorant; he has an air of working in the dark; if he had as much light as energy, his results would be of the highest value. As for the aberrations of a shallow optimism, the ground (of English fiction especially) is strewn with their brittle particles as with broken glass. If you must indulge in conclusions, let them have the taste of a wide knowledge. Remember that your first duty is to be as complete as possible — to make as perfect a work. Be generous and delicate and pursue the prize."

Sigmund Freud

1856–1939

Sigmund Freud, the patriarch of psychoanalysis, was by no means primarily a literary critic, but his ideas have had a major influence on twentieth-century literary
theory, and his influence has been as far-reaching on those who are outraged by his
ideas as it has been on his disciples. (Freud's theory of the unconscious is given more
complete exposition in the introduction to Psychoanalytic Theory in Part Two of this
book, to which the reader is referred; see p. 627.)

Freud was born in Moravia (now part of the Czech Republic) but lived most of
his assiduous life in the imperial capital of Vienna, where he received his M.D. from
the university in 1881. He studied under Charcot in Paris, and then with Josef Breuer
in Vienna, where their collaborative investigations of the treatment of hysterical
patients, though not well received by the rest of the profession, led Freud to devise
his famed analytical technique, based on free association, to reveal the contents of
the unconscious mind. Freud's epochal *The Interpretation of Dreams* (1900) and
other groundbreaking studies met with much skeptical antagonism; nevertheless, by
1910 his fame had spread throughout Europe and had reached America.

A group calling itself "The International Psycho-Analytical Association" gathered around him, but by 1913 — the year Freud published *Totem and Taboo* — two
of its most impressive members, Carl Jung and Alfred Adler, had resigned to form
their own schools in protest against Freud's insistence on the primacy of infantile
sexuality. During and after World War I, despite hardships that included agonizing jaw cancer, Freud continued to publish important work, notably *Beyond the
Pleasure Principle* (1920) and *The Ego and the Id* (1923). His last year was spent in
London, where he fled in 1938 after the Nazi invasion of Austria.

Freud's most important general discussion of art is "Creative Writers and
Daydreaming"; it was delivered as a lecture in 1907 and published in 1908. Here
Freud draws an analogy between nocturnal dreams, daytime fantasies, and the conscious constructions of literary artists, all of which he views as disguised versions
of repressed wishes. Freud does not explain his method of dream analysis fully in
this brief essay (as he had in his earlier treatise *The Interpretation of Dreams*), but
the key to his explication is that what motivates the dream is the *pleasure principle,* in which one's unconscious desires are magically fulfilled. The unconscious
wish for pleasure or power is the latent content of the dream. But the dream as it
appears to the dreamer and is reported to the analyst consists of what Freud termed
manifest content — it is a story that has, in effect, been censored by the defenses
of the ego. One could say that latent content is to manifest content, as primary process (the basic urges and drives) is to secondary process (in which those urges and
drives are shifted, filtered, sublimated, and altered into more socially acceptable
forms). The analysis of a dream involves peeling back the ego-defenses that have
distorted the wish in order to reveal the working of the primary process beneath.

In *The Interpretation of Dreams*, Freud approaches the question of how dreams signify by treating the unconscious psyche of the dreamer as a kind of poet. The raw fantasies that make up the latent content are transformed by substitutions and analogies, so as to disinfect them, so to speak, of the unacceptable content that the dreamer has to censor from awareness. What Freud calls "displacement" is a process similar to poetic metaphor, and the process can be recursively repeated to create a more complicated code, a signifying chain of metaphors of metaphors. If displacement corresponds to metaphor, condensation corresponds to poetic metonymy or synecdoche, where several different associations to the forbidden fantasy coalesce into a single complex vision. As with a poem, a dream operates on several levels: It represents the dreamer's history, but some of its elements may need to be interpreted symbolically. Visual symbols may need to be turned into words, which in turn need to be examined for puns and other verbal transformations.

Like nocturnal dreams, Freud believes, literature contains a latent and a manifest content. According to Freud, the primary process that lurks behind popular novels (for example, ranging from *The Godfather* to *The Bridges of Madison County*) obviously embodies the ambitious and erotic wishes to dominate others and to possess loved objects, wishes that formed during the Oedipal phase of childhood development. But those same drives underlie the greatest masterpieces, like *Emma* or *The Great Gatsby*. The differences between popular fiction and literature are not in the latent content but in the way the ego's defenses are marshalled. Freud suggests that "better" fiction contains the same Oedipal fantasies but that they are expressed in a form that is more carefully and elaborately defended. Because the form is less raw, the fantasy content is more acceptable to refined readers.

Although Freud was once attacked by Jung (p. 326) for implying that the artist is sick, creating out of personal neurotic needs, it is now widely accepted that nearly all of us are at least slightly neurotic and that the artist's need to create comes not from any incapacitating lunacy but merely from a greater sensitivity to the lacks and dissatisfactions that plague us all. The primary objection to Freudian criticism of this sort is its insensitivity to aesthetic quality: Although Freud was personally deeply moved by art and literature, in his version of artistic creation, form itself enters the work of art merely as a sugar coating that allows the reader to swallow the dose of fantasy more easily. Later analytic critics, like Peter Brooks, have tried to deal more constructively with this issue, although the function of artistic form remains one of the vexing questions within the psychoanalytic approach to literature (see Brooks, p. 449).

Freud also wrote several papers analyzing particular literary texts, including *The Merchant of Venice* and *King Lear*. "The Uncanny" (1919, revised 1924), an analysis of the novella *The Sandman* (1817) by Ernst Theodor Amadeus Hoffmann, is probably the most complex and interesting of these papers. Freud takes off from Ernst Jentsch's 1906 article on the psychology of the uncanny, and his focus of interest is not the poet, as it was in "Creative Writers and Daydreaming," but the reader's experience of the text. In the first section of the paper, Freud takes apart the word *unheimlich*, German for uncanny. Its opposite, *heimlich*, has two distinct meanings: what is homey or familiar (*heim* = home) and what is hidden or concealed (*geheim* = mystery). *Unheimlich* similarly has two meanings: what is unfamiliar and what has been inadvertently revealed. The contraries thus coalesce: the *heimlich* is known but also hidden and therefore unknown; the *unheimlich* is unknown but also revealed and therefore known. (These coalescing contraries also appear in English, in the overlapping meanings of the words "canny" and "uncanny.") For Freud, these contraries describe the process of repression (making the known unknown) and also the "return of the repressed" (where what we have attempted to repress comes to light).

Freud then shows how the plot of *The Sandman*, through three repeated stages, represents the narrative of the Oedipus complex. What makes the story uncanny for readers, according to Freud, is that although it starts out as realistic, seemingly true, we suddenly find ourselves in a dream world where what should be hidden (the repressed Oedipal struggle) is instead quite clearly revealed. Freud clarifies his position, expanding it and also qualifying it. If the uncanny is the return of the repressed, then it must appear in other infantile psychic material that we repress. Uncanny stories about being buried alive relate to the wish to return to the womb, an "inter-uterine existence" that Freud calls "lascivious" because it involves fusion with the mother. Stories about doubles or döppelgangers may relate to the post-Oedipal creation of the superego, a "second self" that chides us about our sinful desires: The stories are usually about doubles that enact those desires while the protagonist stands about too repressed to act. And similarly, Freud analyzes other causes of the uncanny, haunted houses, revenants who return from death, severed hands with a will of their own. But he also discusses why this repressed material does not always strike us as uncanny in fictional form, what special literary qualities uncanny stories possess that force us to enter this forbidden world of fantasy without being aware of what we are doing.

In the very brief selection "Medusa's Head," Freud interprets a single image from a Greek myth. Published posthumously in 1940, "Medusa's Head" is interesting primarily because of what it displays about Freud himself, and secondarily because of the feminist reaction to it. Freud analyzes the decapitated head as a symbol of female castration, a visual metaphor that connects with the moment "when a boy . . . catches sight of the female genitals . . . surrounded by hair . . . those of his mother." In childhood, the episode advances the Oedipal struggle but is repressed; in adult life, the repressed returns when the decapitated female head is seen, an open mouth surrounded with snakes, an image of horror that "makes the spectator stiff." This in turn reminds Freud that the male erection can be displayed to ward off and is comforting evidence that one has come through the Oedipal struggle intact. Today's reader may feel that Freud's penultimate comment — "I am not afraid of you. I defy you. I have a penis" — reveals rather more than we wanted to know about the sage of Vienna. Certainly Freud's discourse seems disconcertingly male-oriented. The myth takes the shape it does because of what boys discover; the stiffening response to horror is what men do to ward off an evil whose deep meaning is female sexuality. Women have no part in the struggle except as objects of the male gaze, or as demonic enemies who are designated victims. It seems appropriate that the French feminist Hélène Cixous has taken the image of a triumphantly laughing Medusa as the aegis of the woman who, in spite of patriarchy, finds her own voice (see Cixous, p. 988).

Selected Bibliography

Bowie, Malcolm. *Psychoanalysis and the Future of Theory*. London: Blackwell, 1994.

Brenner, Charles. *An Elementary Textbook of Psychoanalysis*. New York: Anchor Books, 1974.

Freud, Sigmund. *The Standard Edition of the Complete Psychological Works*. 24 vols. London: Hogarth Press and the Institute for Psychoanalysis, 1940–68.

Gilman, Sander L., ed. *Introducing Psychoanalytic Theory*. New York: Brunner/Mazel, 1982.

Hoffman, Frederick J. *Freudianism and the Literary Mind*. New York: Greenwood, 1977.

Jones, Ernest. *Hamlet and Oedipus*. New York: Doubleday, 1949.

Kris, Ernst. *Psychoanalytic Exploration in Art*. New York: Schocken Books, 1962.

Royle, Nicholas. *The Uncanny*. New York: Routledge, 2003.

Sadoff, Dianne F. *Sciences of the Flesh: Representing Body and Subject in Psychoanalysis*. Stanford: Stanford University Press, 1998.

Thomas, Ronald R. *Dreams of Authority: Freud and the Fictions of the Unconscious*. Ithaca, NY: Cornell University Press.

[Creative Writers and Daydreaming]

We laymen have always been intensely curious to know — like the cardinal who put a similar question to Ariosto[1] — from what sources that strange being, the creative writer, draws his material, and how he manages to make such an impression on us with it and to arouse in us emotions of which, perhaps, we had not even thought ourselves capable. Our interest is only heightened the more by the fact that, if we ask him, the writer himself gives us no explanation, or none that is satisfactory; and it is not at all weakened by our knowledge that not even the clearest insight into the determinants of his choice of material and into the nature of the art of creating imaginative form will ever help to make creative writers of us.

If we could at least discover in ourselves or in people like ourselves an activity which was in some way akin to creative writing! An examination of it would then give us a hope of obtaining the beginnings of an explanation of the creative work of writers. And, indeed, there is some prospect of this being possible. After all, creative writers themselves like to lessen the distance between their kind and the common run of humanity; they so often assure us that every man is a poet at heart and that the last poet will not perish till the last man does.

Should we not look for the first traces of imaginative activity as early as in childhood? The child's best-loved and most intense occupation is with his play or games. Might we not say that every child at play behaves like a creative writer, in that he creates a world of his own, or, rather, rearranges the things of his world in a new way which pleases him? It would be wrong to think he does not take that world seriously; on the contrary, he takes his play very seriously and he expends large amounts of emotion on it. The opposite of play is not what is serious but what is real. In spite of all the emotion with which he cathects[2] his world of play, the child distinguishes it quite well from reality; and he likes to link his imagined objects and situations to the tangible and visible things of the real world. This linking is all that differentiates the child's "play" from "fantasying."

The creative writer does the same as the child at play. He creates a world of fantasy which he takes very seriously — that is, which he

---

Translated by I. F. Grant-Duff.

[1]Ariosto dedicated the *Orlando Furioso* to Cardinal Ippolito d'Este, who said in response, "Where did you find so many stories?" [Freud]

[2]Cathexis is the investment of *libido* energy in an activity.

invests with large amounts of emotion — while separating it sharply from reality. Language has preserved this relationship between children's play and poetic creation. It gives the name of *Spiel* ["play"] to those forms of imaginative writing which require to be linked to tangible objects and which are capable of representation. It speaks of a *Lustspiel* or *Trauerspiel* ["comedy" or "tragedy"] and describes those who carry out the representation as *Schauspieler* ["players"]. The unreality of the writer's imaginative world, however, has very important consequences for the technique of his art; for many things which, if they were real, could give no enjoyment, can do so in the play of fantasy, and many excitements which, in themselves, are actually distressing, can become a source of pleasure for the hearers and spectators at the performance of a writer's work.

There is another consideration for the sake of which we will dwell a moment longer on this contrast between reality and play. When the child has grown up and has ceased to play, and after he has been laboring for decades to envisage the realities of life with proper seriousness, he may one day find himself in a mental situation which once more undoes the contrast between play and reality. As an adult he can look back on the intense seriousness with which he once carried on his games in childhood, and, by equating his ostensibly serious occupations of today with his childhood games, he can throw off the too heavy burden imposed on him by life and win the high yield of pleasure afforded by *humor.*

As people grow up, then, they cease to play, and they seem to give up the yield of pleasure which they gained from playing. But whoever understands the human mind knows that hardly anything is harder for a man than to give up a pleasure which he has once experienced. Actually, we can never give anything up; we only exchange one thing for another. What appears to be a renunciation is really the formation of a substitute or surrogate. In the same way, the growing child, when he stops playing, gives up nothing but the link with real objects; instead of *playing,* he now *fantasies.* He builds castles in the air and creates what are called *daydreams.* I believe that most people construct fantasies at times in their lives. This is a fact which has long been overlooked and whose importance has therefore not been sufficiently appreciated.

People's fantasies are less easy to observe than the play of children. The child, it is true, plays by himself or forms a closed psychical system with other children for the purposes of a game; but even though he may not play his game in front of the grown-ups, he does not, on the other hand, conceal it from them. The adult, on the contrary, is ashamed of his fantasies and hides them from other people. He cherishes his fantasies as his most intimate possessions, and as a rule he would rather confess his misdeeds than tell anyone his fantasies. It may come about that for that reason he believes he is the only person who invents such fantasies and has no idea that creations of this kind are widespread among other people. This difference in the behavior of a person who plays and a person who fantasies is accounted for by the motives of these two activities, which are nevertheless adjuncts to each other.

A child's play is determined by wishes: in point of fact by a single wish — one that helps in his upbringing — the wish to be big and grown up. He is always playing at being "grown up," and in his games he imitates what he knows about the lives of his elders. He has no reason to conceal this wish. With the adult, the case is different. On the one hand, he knows that he is expected not to go on playing or fantasying any longer, but to act in the real world; on the other hand, some of the wishes which give rise to his fantasies are of a kind which it is essential to conceal. Thus he is ashamed of his fantasies as being childish and as being unpermissible.

But, you will ask, if people make such a mystery of their fantasying, how is it that we know such a lot about it? Well, there is a class of human beings upon whom, not a god, indeed, but a stern goddess — Necessity — has allotted the task of telling what they suffer and what things give them happiness. These are the victims of nervous illness, who are obliged to tell their fantasies, among other things, to the doctor by whom they expect to be cured by mental treatment. This is our best source of knowledge, and we have since found good reason to suppose that our patients tell us nothing that we might not also hear from healthy people.

Let us make ourselves acquainted with a few of the characteristics of fantasying. We may lay it down that a happy person never fantasies, only an unsatisfied one. The motive forces of fantasies are unsatisfied wishes, and every single fantasy is the fulfillment of a wish, a correction of unsatisfying reality. These motivating wishes vary according to the sex, character, and circumstances of the person who is having the fantasy; but they fall naturally into two main groups. They are either ambitious wishes, which serve to elevate the subject's personality; or they are erotic ones. In young women the erotic wishes predominate almost exclusively, for their ambition is as a rule absorbed by erotic trends. In young men egoistic and ambitious wishes come to the fore clearly enough alongside of erotic ones. But we will not lay stress on the opposition between the two trends; we would rather empha-size the fact that they are often united. Just as, in many altarpieces, the portrait of the donor is to be seen in a corner of the picture, so, in the majority of ambitious fantasies, we can discover in some corner or other the lady for whom the creator of the fantasy performs all his heroic deeds and at whose feet all his triumphs are laid. Here, as you see, there are strong enough motives for conceal-ment: the well-brought-up young woman is only allowed a minimum of erotic desire, and the young man has to learn to suppress the excess of self-regard which he brings with him from the spoilt days of his childhood, so that he may find his place in a society which is full of other individuals mak-ing equally strong demands.

We must not suppose that the products of this imaginative activity — the various fantasies, castles in the air and daydreams — are stereotyped or unalterable. On the contrary, they fit themselves into the subject's shifting impressions of life, change with every change in his situation, and receive from every fresh active impression what might be called a "date-mark." The relation of a fantasy to time is in general very important. We may say that it hovers, as it were, between three times — the three moments of time which our ideation involves. Mental work is linked to some current impression, some provoking occasion in the present which has been able to arouse one of the subject's major wishes. From there it harks back to a memory of an earlier experience (usually an infantile one) in which this wish was fulfilled; and it now creates a situation relating to the future which represents a fulfillment of the wish. What it thus creates is a daydream or fantasy, which carries about it traces of its origin from the occasion which provoked it and from the memory. Thus past, pres-ent, and future are strung together, as it were, on the thread of the wish that runs though them.

A very ordinary example may serve to make what I have said clear. Let us take the case of a poor orphan boy to whom you have given the address of some employer where he may perhaps find a job. On his way there he may indulge in a daydream appropriate to the situation from which it arises. The content of his fantasy will perhaps be some-thing like this. He is given a job, finds favor with his new employer, makes himself indispensable in the business, is taken into his employer's family, marries the charming young daughter of the house, and then himself becomes a director of the busi-ness, first as his employer's partner and then as his successor. In this fantasy, the dreamer has regained what he possessed in his happy childhood — the protecting house, the loving parents, and the first objects of his affectionate feelings. You will see from this example the way in which the wish makes use of an occasion in the present to construct, on the pattern of the past, a picture of the future.

There is a great deal more that could be said about fantasies; but I will only allude as briefly as possible to certain points. If fantasies become overluxuriant and overpowerful, the conditions are laid for an onset of neurosis or psychosis. Fantasies, moreover, are the immediate mental precursors of the distressing symptoms com-plained of by our patients. Here a broad bypath branches off into pathology.

I cannot pass over the relation of fantasies to dreams. Our dreams at night are nothing else than fantasies like these, as we can demonstrate from the interpretation of dreams. Language, in its unrivaled wisdom, long ago decided the question of the essen-tial nature of dreams by giving the name of *day-dreams* to the airy creations of fantasy. If the mean-ing of our dreams usually remains obscure to us in spite of this pointer, it is because of the circumstance that at night there also arise in us wishes of which we are ashamed; these we must conceal from our-selves, and they have consequently been repressed.

pushed into the unconscious. Repressed wishes of this sort and their derivatives are only allowed to come to expression in a very distorted form. When scientific work had succeeded in elucidating this factor of *dream distortion*, it was no longer difficult to recognize that night dreams are wish-fulfillments in just the same way as daydreams — the fantasies which we all know so well.

So much for fantasies. And now for the creative writer. May we really attempt to compare the imaginative writer with the "dreamer in broad daylight," and his creations with daydreams? Here we must begin by making an initial distinction. We must separate writers who, like the ancient authors of epics and tragedies, take over their material ready-made, from writers who seem to originate their own material. We will keep to the latter kind, and, for the purposes of our comparison, we will choose not the writers most highly esteemed by the critics, but the less pretentious authors of novels, romances, and short stories, who nevertheless have the widest and most eager circle of readers of both sexes. One feature above all cannot fail to strike us about the creations of these story-writers: each of them has a hero who is the center of interest, for whom the writer tries to win our sympathy by every possible means and whom he seems to place under the protection of a special providence. If, at the end of one chapter of my story, I leave the hero unconscious and bleeding from severe wounds, I am sure to find him at the beginning of the next being carefully nursed and on the way to recovery; and if the first volume closes with the ship he is in going down in a storm at sea, I am certain, at the opening of the second volume, to read of his miraculous rescue — a rescue without which the story could not proceed. The feeling of security with which I follow the hero through his perilous adventures is the same as the feeling with which a hero in real life throws himself into the water to save a drowning man or exposes himself to the enemy's fire in order to storm a battery. It is the true heroic feeling, which one of our best writers has expressed in an inimitable phrase: "Nothing can happen to *me*!" It seems to me, however, that through this revealing characteristic of invulnerability we can immediately recognize His Majesty the Ego, the hero alike of every daydream and of every story.

Other typical features of these egocentric stories point to the same kinship. The fact that all the women in the novel invariably fall in love with the hero can hardly be looked on as a portrayal of reality, but it is easily understood as a necessary constituent of a daydream. The same is true of the fact that the other characters in the story are sharply divided into good and bad, in defiance of the variety of human characters that are to be observed in real life. The "good" ones are the helpers, while the "bad" ones are the enemies and rivals, of the ego which has become the hero of the story.

We are perfectly aware that very many imaginative writings are far removed from the model of the naive daydream; and yet I cannot suppress the suspicion that even the most extreme deviations from that model could be linked with it through an uninterrupted series of transitional cases. It has struck me that in many of what are known as "psychological" novels only one person — once again the hero — is described from within. The author sits inside his mind, as it were, and looks at the other characters from outside. The psychological novel in general no doubt owes its special nature to the inclination of the modern writer to split up his ego, by self-observation, into many part-egos, and, in consequence, to personify the conflicting currents of his own mental life in several heroes. Certain novels, which might be described as "eccentric," seem to stand in quite special contrast to the types of the daydream. In these, the person who is introduced as the hero plays only a very small active part; he sees the actions and sufferings of other people pass before him like a spectator. Many of Zola's later works belong to this category. But I must point out that the psychological analysis of individuals who are not creative writers, and who diverge in some respects from the so-called norm, has shown us analogous variations of the daydream, in which the ego contents itself with the role of spectator.

If our comparison of the imaginative writer with the daydreamer, and of poetical creation with the daydream, is to be of any value, it must, above all, show itself in some way or other fruitful. Let us, for instance, try to apply to these authors' works the thesis we laid down earlier concerning the relation between fantasy and the three periods of time and the wish which runs through them; and, with its help, let us try to study the connections that exist between the life of the writer and his works. No one has known, as a rule, what expectations to frame in approaching this problem; and often the connection has been thought of in much too simple terms. In the light of the insight we have gained from fantasies, we ought to expect the fol- lowing state of affairs. A strong experience in the present awakens in the creative writer a memory of an earlier experience (usually belonging to his childhood) from which there now proceeds a wish which finds its fulfilment in the creative work. The work itself exhibits elements of the recent provok- ing occasion as well as of the old memory.

Do not be alarmed at the complexity of this for- mula. I suspect that in fact it will prove to be too exiguous a pattern. Nevertheless, it may contain a first approach to the true state of affairs; and, from some experiments I have made, I am inclined to think that this way of looking at creative writings may turn out not unfruitful. You will not forget that the stress it lays on childhood memories in the writer's life — a stress which may perhaps seem puzzling — is ultimately derived from the assumption that a piece of creative writing, like a daydream, is a continuation of, and a substitute for, what was once the play of childhood.

We must not neglect, however, to go back to the kind of imaginative works which we have to recognize, not as original creations, but as the refashioning of ready-made and familiar mate- rial. Even here, the writer keeps a certain amount of independence, which can express itself in the choice of material and in changes in it which are often quite extensive. Insofar as the material is already at hand, however, it is derived from the popular treasure-house of myths, legends, and fairy tales. The study of constructions of folk psychology such as these is far from being com- plete, but it is extremely probable that myths, for instance, are distorted vestiges of the wishful fantasies of whole nations, the *secular dreams of* youthful humanity.

You will say that, although I have put the cre- ative writer first in the title of my paper, I have told you far less about him than about fantasies. I am aware of that, and I must try to excuse it by pointing to the present state of our knowledge. All I have been able to do is to throw out some

encouragements and suggestions which, starting from the study of fantasies, lead on to the problem of the writer's choice of his literary material. As for the other problem — by what means the cre- ative writer achieves the emotional effects in us that are aroused by his creations — we have as yet not touched on it at all. But I should like at least to point out to you the path that leads from our discus- sion of fantasies to the problems of poetical effects.

You will remember how I have said that the daydreamer carefully conceals his fantasies from other people because he feels he has reasons for being ashamed of them. I should now add that even if he were to communicate them to us he could give us no pleasure by his disclosures. Such fantasies, when we learn them, repel us or at least leave us cold. But when a creative writer presents his plays to us or tells us what we are inclined to take to be his personal daydreams, we experience a great pleasure, and one which probably arises from the confluence of many sources. How the writer accomplishes this is his innermost secret; the essential *ars poetica*[3] lies in the technique of overcoming the feeling of repulsion in us which is undoubtedly connected with the barriers that rise between each single ego and the others. We can guess two of the methods used by this technique. The writer softens the character of his egoistic daydreams by altering and disguising it, and he bribes us by the purely formal — that is, aesthetic — yield of pleasure which he offers us in the presentation of his fantasies. We give the name of an *incentive bonus*, or a *forepleasure*, to a yield of pleasure such as this, which is offered to us so as to make possible the release of still greater pleasure arising from deeper psychical sources. In my opinion, all the aesthetic pleasure which a creative writer affords us has the charac- ter of a forepleasure of this kind, and our actual enjoyment of an imaginative work proceeds from a liberation of tensions in our minds. It may even be that not a little of this effect is due to the writ- er's enabling us thenceforward to enjoy our own daydreams without self-reproach or shame. This brings us to the threshold of new, interesting, and complicated inquiries; but also, at least for the moment, to the end of our discussion.

[3] Art of poetry.

Medusa's Head[1]

We have not often attempted to interpret individual mythological themes, but an interpretation suggests itself easily in the case of the horrifying decapitated head of Medusa.

To decapitate = to castrate. The terror of Medusa is thus a terror of castration that is linked to the sight of something. Numerous analyses have made us familiar with the occasion for this: it occurs when a boy, who has hitherto been unwilling to believe the threat of castration, catches sight of the female genitals, probably those of an adult, surrounded by hair, and essentially those of his mother.

The hair upon Medusa's head is frequently represented in works of art in the form of snakes, and these once again are derived from the castration complex. It is a remarkable fact that, however frightening they may be in themselves, they nevertheless serve actually as a mitigation of the horror, for they replace the penis, the absence of which is the cause of the horror. This is a confirmation of the technical rule according to which a multiplication of penis symbols signifies castration.[2]

The sight of Medusa's head makes the spectator stiff with terror, turns him to stone. Observe that we have here once again the same transformation of affect! For becoming stiff means an erection. Thus in the original situation it offers consolation to the spectator: he is still in possession of a penis, and the stiffening reassures him of the fact.

This symbol of horror is worn upon her dress by the virgin goddess Athena.[3] And rightly so, for thus she becomes a woman who is unapproachable and repels all sexual desires — since she displays the terrifying genitals of the Mother. Since the Greeks were in the main strongly homosexual, it was inevitable that we should find among them a representation of woman as a being who frightens and repels because she is castrated.

If Medusa's head takes the place of a representation of the female genitals, or rather if it isolates their horrifying effects from their pleasure-giving ones, it may be recalled that displaying the genitals is familiar in other connections as an apotropaic[4] act. What arouses horror in oneself will produce the same effect upon the enemy against whom one is seeking to defend oneself. We read in Rabelais of how the Devil took to flight when the woman showed him her vulva.[5]

The erect male organ also has an apotropaic effect, but thanks to another mechanism. To display the penis (or any of its surrogates) is to say: "I am not afraid of you. I defy you. I have a penis." Here, then, is another way of intimidating the Evil Spirit.[6]

In order to seriously substantiate this interpretation it would be necessary to investigate the origin of this isolated symbol of horror in Greek mythology as well as parallels to it in other mythologies.[7]

---

[1]"Das Medusenhaupt." First published posthumously *Internationale Zeitschrift für Psychoanalyse Imago*, 25 (1940), 105; reprinted *Gesammelte Werke*, 17 (1941), 47. The manuscript is dated May 14, 1922, and appears to be a sketch for a more extensive work. The present translation, by James Strachey, is reprinted from *International Journal for Psycho-Analysis: Imago*, 22 (1941), 69 and *Collected Papers*, 5 (1950), 105. [Tr.]

[2]This is referred to in Freud's paper on "The 'Uncanny'" (1919h), middle of Section II. [Tr.]

[3]Athena was the Greek goddess of wisdom; Freud is alluding to the snaky decoration on her dress (the aegis) in the statue of Athena now in the Parthenon museum.

[4]Used to ward off evil.

[5]See François Rabelais, *Gargantua and Pantagruel*, vol. 4, chapter 47.

[6]It may be worth quoting a footnote added by Freud to a paper of Stekel's, "Zur Psychologie des Exhibitionismus," in *Zentralbl. Psychoanal.*, 1 (1911), 495: "Dr. Stekel here proposes to derive exhibitionism from unconscious narcissistic motive forces. It seems to me probable that the same explanation can be applied to the apotropaic exhibiting found among the peoples of antiquity."[Tr.]

[7]The same topic was dealt with by Ferenczi (1923) in a very short paper which was itself briefly commented upon by Freud in his "Infantile Genital Organization of the Libido" (1923e). [Tr.]

T. S. Eliot

1888–1965

Thomas Stearns Eliot, America's most influential literary expatriate since Henry James, was born in St. Louis, Missouri, where his father was a businessman and his mother a locally renowned poet. He was educated at private schools in St. Louis and in Milton, Massachusetts, before entering Harvard, where he studied with the philosophers Bertrand Russell and George Santayana (from whom he may have derived the idea of the "objective correlative"), and the literary critic Irving Babbitt, from whom he absorbed an inveterate hostility to Romanticism. Eliot graduated from Harvard College in 1909 and spent most of the next five years in England working toward a Ph.D. in philosophy. He actually wrote his dissertation on the English neo-idealist F. H. Bradley but never returned to take his final orals. In 1914 he accepted a traveling fellowship to the University of Marburg but was stranded in England by the outbreak of World War I, stayed at Merton College, Oxford, and gradually came to make England his home. In 1915 he married Vivien Haigh-Wood, a beautiful and intelligent woman whose infidelities, emotional demands, and nervous instability made home life a misery for him: he eventually left her in 1933, and they lived apart until her death fourteen years later.

Eliot's poetic career seems to have dated from a year spent in France (1910–11), where his encounter with the French symbolists, especially Jules Laforgue, helped him to find his own voice. His first volume, *Prufrock and Other Observations* (1917), was a major contribution to the Modernist movement in poetry, characterized by the combination of hard clear images, mysterious and transcendent symbols, and an almost classical restraint of subjective feeling. In *The Waste Land* (1922), Eliot produced Modernism's epic of decay: an elegy upon the desiccation and near death of the poet's own spirit with an odd Buddhistic conclusion ambiguously suggesting the hope of renewal and rebirth. The poem, written rapidly while Eliot was recovering from a nervous breakdown in a Swiss sanatorium, was tightened drastically by his friend Ezra Pound. Eliot found a more conventional source of solace and hope in his conversion to Anglo-Catholicism in 1927. Later poems included *Journey of the Magi* (1927), *Ash Wednesday* (1930), *Old Possum's Book of Practical Cats* (1939; adapted by Andrew Lloyd Webber into *Cats*, an international theatrical success in the 1980s and 1990s), and *Four Quartets* (1943). Eliot was also a successful playwright whose dry, menacing dialogue influenced postwar dramatists such as Harold Pinter. *The Cocktail Party* (1950), his most successful play, made Eliot a good deal of money from both the London and New York productions, though *Murder in the Cathedral* (1935), a verse tragedy on St. Thomas à Becket, may be the most durable and interesting of his dramas. While he was gaining his reputation as a poet and playwright, Eliot worked first as a teacher of French and Latin, then as a clerk at Lloyds Bank, until he was made an editor at the publishing firm of Faber and Faber — which also subsidized the *Criterion*, a little magazine Eliot edited, and in which he published much of his critical writing. Eliot's criticism has been attacked as dry and pedantic, but at the time it was highly influential. Theoretical pieces like "Tradition and the Individual Talent"

(1917) were manifestos of literary Modernism. But Eliot may have been more important as a tastemaker than as a theorist: His essays on Jacobean playwrights such as Philip Massinger and Thomas Middleton helped put a vanished generation of English drama back on the stage, while those on the metaphysical poets heralded a revival of interest in such then-neglected names as John Donne and George Herbert and such virtually forgotten figures as Thomas Traherne and Lancelot Andrewes.

Most of Eliot's major poetry and criticism was written before the end of World War II, though it could be argued that his most pleasant days were spent after the war, as an honored elder statesman of letters. In 1948 he was awarded both the Nobel Prize for literature and the British Order of Merit. At the age of 69 he married his secretary, Valerie Fletcher, who shared his last happy years. He died in 1965 and was buried in East Coker, the Somerset village from which his ancestors had emigrated to America.

Eliot's literary theory does not appear in total in any single book. His most celebrated passages usually occur within an appreciation of an author or a text, and to put all of them together would require reprinting quite a number of different essays. His famous definition of an "objective correlative," so important for the development of the New Criticism, appears in an essay on *Hamlet:*

> The only way of expressing emotion in the form of art is by finding an "objective correlative"; in other words a set of objects, a situation, a chain of events which shall be the formula of that *particular* emotion; such that when the external facts, which must terminate in sensory experience, are given, the emotion is immediately evoked.[1]

His theory of the dissociation of sensibility comes in the course of an essay on the metaphysical poets:

> Something . . . had happened to the mind of England between the time of Donne or Lord Herbert of Cherbury and the time of Tennyson and Browning; it is the difference between the intellectual poet and the reflective poet. Tennyson and Browning are poets, and they think; but they do not feel their thought as immediately as the odour of a rose. A thought to Donne was an experience; it modified his sensibility. When a poet's mind is perfectly equipped for its work, it is constantly amalgamating disparate experience; the ordinary man's experience is chaotic, irregular, fragmentary. The latter falls in love, or reads Spinoza, and these two experiences have nothing to do with each other, or with the noise of the typewriter or the smell of cooking; in the mind of the poet these experiences are always forming new wholes.[2]

In context, the first quotation is designed to explain what is special about *Hamlet* — it is a play that is problematic precisely because the external causes of feeling do not match the internal effects; the second is designed to explain the characteristic tone of seventeenth-century poetry to readers whose notions of the poetic have been corrupted, in Eliot's view, by the dissociation of sensibility that set in with Milton and Dryden. Both of these ideas, however, also have direct bearing on the poetics of the Modernism that Eliot practiced. The doctrine of the objective correlative

---

[1] T. S. Eliot, "Hamlet" (1919), in *Elizabethan Essays* (New York: Haskell House, 1964), p. 61.
[2] T. S. Eliot, "The Metaphysical Poets" (1921), in *Selected Prose of T. S. Eliot,* ed. Frank Kermode (New York: Harcourt, Brace and Jovanovich; Farrar, Straus and Giroux, 1975), p. 65.

would lead to the sort of imagism practiced by both Eliot and Pound in their earliest poems, while the Modernists, just as much as Donne, were interested in exploring a varied range of the sensibilities. In addition to the heart's feelings, Eliot went on, "one must look into the cerebral cortex, the nervous system, and the digestive tracts."

"Tradition and the Individual Talent" is much more openly a manifesto for Modernism. In a voice that vacillates between a leaderly "we" and a modest "I," Eliot is clearly calling for a new "programme" for the *métier* of poetry. If the essay is a relatively difficult one, it is because of the ambiguities at the heart of what Eliot means by his two central terms, "tradition," which the poet is asked to cultivate, and "personality," which the poet must sacrifice.

Many creative writers are wary of immersing themselves in the tradition of English and American poetry because they fear that their own voices are not strong enough for the encounter and are likely to be lost in the process. Eliot argues the opposite: that a poet cannot become himself, cannot understand his own place in time, his own modernness, without an understanding of the past. As a result, the historical sense is "indispensable to anyone who would continue to be a poet beyond his twenty-fifth year." — Keats's age when he died. It is easy to understand the value Eliot places on tradition and on the historical sense that allows the poet to contemplate the current significance of the past.

What seems a bit mystical, however, is Eliot's claim that there is an "ideal order" in literary tradition.

The existing monuments form an ideal order among themselves, which is modified by the introduction of the new (the really new) work of art among them. The existing order is complete before the new work arrives; for order to persist after the supervention of novelty, the *whole* existing order must be, if ever so slightly, altered; and so the relations, proportions, values of each work of art toward the whole are readjusted; and this is conformity between the old and the new.

Since Eliot never makes clear what the basis of the "ideal order" is — how this order is *ordered* — it remains unclear how the order can be perfect and complete both before and after the introduction of a new work. Nor is it clear of what this order is composed. It is not merely an anthology of celebrated texts, the current canon, but Eliot does not discuss how far removed a work can be from current fashion and yet remain within the tradition or how far down into popular culture the tradition reaches. The difficulty with the issue of personality is not fuzziness, but the apparent contradictions with other Eliot criticism. In "Tradition," Eliot seems to be suggesting that art is, or at least ought to be, essentially impersonal: that the tradition writes itself, as it were, using the poet as a catalyst for converting emotion and thought into poetry. But in an essay on Philip Massinger in 1920, Eliot suggests that personality is necessary for high art: "Marlowe's and Jonson's comedies . . . were, as great literature is, the transformation of a personality into a personal work of art. . . . Massinger is not simply a smaller personality: his personality hardly exists. He did not, out of his own personality, build a world of art, as Shakespeare and Marlowe and Jonson built."[3]

[3] T. S. Eliot, "Philip Massinger" (1920), in *Elizabethan Essays*, p. 171.

A careful reading finds a paradox here, but no real self-contradiction. Eliot (like Proust in *Contre Sainte-Beuve*) repudiates the post-Romantic notion that the self an artist expresses is the habitual self one presents in society to intimates, friends, and acquaintances. He postulates another deeper self that is responsible for the artist's unique vision of reality and that lends that vision authority and general truth. The former "personality" is what the artist escapes from into art; the latter is the source of that art. These two definitions of "personality," which incidentally correspond to the "you" and "I" in that schizoid lyric, "The Love Song of J. Alfred Prufrock," are what Eliot puns on throughout the last section of "Tradition and the Individual Talent."

Selected Bibliography

Allan, Mowbray, *T. S. Eliot's Impersonal Theory of Poetry*. Lewisburg, PA: Bucknell University Press, 1974.

Austin, Allen. *T. S. Eliot: The Literary and Social Criticism*. Bloomington: Indiana University Press, 1971.

Brombert, Victor. *The Criticism of T. S. Eliot*. New Haven: Yale University Press, 1949.

Freed, Lewis. *T. S. Eliot: Aesthetics and History*. La Salle, IL: Open Court, 1962.

Frye, Northrop. *T. S. Eliot*. New York: Grove Press, 1963.

Habib, M. A. R. *The Early T. S. Eliot and Western Philosophy*. Cambridge: Cambridge University Press, 1999.

Lee, Brian. *Theory and Personality: The Significance of T. S. Eliot's Criticism*. London: Athlone Press, 1979.

Lu, Fei-Pai. *T. S. Eliot: The Dialectical Structure of His Theory of Poetry*. Chicago: University of Chicago Press, 1966.

Lucy, Sean. *T. S. Eliot and the Idea of Tradition*. London: Cohen and West, 1960.

Matthiessen, F. O. *The Achievement of T. S. Eliot*. New York: Oxford University Press, 1947.

Menand, Louis. *Discovering Modernism: T. S. Eliot and His Context*. New York: Oxford University Press, 1987.

Spurr, David. *Conflicts in Consciousness: T. S. Eliot's Poetry and Criticism*. Urbana: University of Illinois Press, 1983.

Tradition and the Individual Talent

I

In English writing we seldom speak of tradition, though we occasionally apply its name in deploring its absence. We cannot refer to "the tradition" or to "a tradition"; at most, we employ the adjective in saying that the poetry of so-and-so is "traditional" or even "too traditional." Seldom, perhaps, does the word appear except in a phrase of censure. If otherwise, it is vaguely approbative, with the implication, as to the work approved, of some pleasing archaeological reconstruction. You can hardly make the word agreeable in English ears without this comfortable reference to the reassuring science of archaeology.

Certainly the word is not likely to appear in our appreciations of living or dead writers. Every nation, every race, has not only its own creative, but its own critical turn of mind; and is even more oblivious of the shortcomings and limitations of its critical habits than of those of its creative genius. We know, or think we know, from the enormous mass of critical writing that has appeared in the

French language the critical method or habit of the French; we only conclude (we are such uncon-scious people) that the French are "more critical" than we, and sometimes even plume ourselves a little with the fact, as if the French were the less spontaneous. Perhaps they are; but we might remind ourselves that criticism is as inevitable as breathing, and that we should be none the worse for articulating what passes in our minds when we read a book and feel an emotion about it, for criticizing our own minds in their work of criti-cism. One of the facts that might come to light in this process is our tendency to insist, when we praise a poet, upon those aspects of his work in which he least resembles anyone else. In these aspects or parts of his work we pretend to find what is individual, what is the peculiar essence of the man. We dwell with satisfaction upon the poet's difference from his predecessors, especially his immediate predecessors; we endeavor to find something that can be isolated in order to be enjoyed. Whereas if we approach a poet without this prejudice we shall often find that not only the best, but the most individual parts of his work may be those in which the dead poets, his ancestors, assert their immortality most vigorously. And I do not mean the impressionable period of adolescence, but the period of full maturity.

Yet if the only form of tradition, of hand-ing down, consisted in following the ways of the immediate generation before us in a blind or timid adherence to its successes, "tradition" should positively be discouraged. We have seen many such simple currents soon lost in the sand; and novelty is better than repetition. Tradition is a matter of much wider significance. It cannot be inherited, and if you want it you must obtain it by great labor. It involves, in the first place, the historical sense, which we may call nearly indispensable to anyone who would continue to be a poet beyond his twenty-fifth year; and the historical sense involves a perception, not only of the pastness of the past, but of its presence; the historical sense compels a man to write not merely with his own generation in his bones, but with a feeling that the whole of the literature of Europe from Homer and within it the whole of the literature of his own country has a simulta-neous existence and composes a simultaneous

order. This historical sense, which is a sense of the timeless as well as of the temporal and of the timeless and of the temporal together, is what makes a writer traditional. And it is at the same time what makes a writer most acutely conscious of his place in time, of his own contemporaneity.

No poet, no artist of any art, has his complete meaning alone. His significance, his appreciation is the appreciation of his relation to the dead poets and artists. You cannot value him alone; you must set him, for contrast and comparison, among the dead. I mean this as a principle of aesthetic, not merely historical, criticism. The necessity that he shall conform, that he shall cohere, is not one-sided; what happens when a new work of art is created is something that happens simultaneously to all the works of art which preceded it. The existing monuments form an ideal order among themselves, which is modified by the introduction of the new (the really new) work of art among them. The existing order is complete before the new work arrives; for order to persist after the supervention of novelty, the whole existing order must be, if ever so slightly, altered; and so the relations, proportions, values of each work of art toward the whole are readjusted; and this is con-formity between the old and the new. Whoever has approved this idea of order, of the form of European, of English literature will not find it preposterous that the past should be altered by the present as much as the present is directed by the past. And the poet who is aware of this will be aware of great difficulties and responsibilities.

In a peculiar sense he will be aware also that he must inevitably be judged by the standards of the past. I say judged, not amputated, by them; not judged to be as good as, or worse or better than, the dead; and certainly not judged by the canons of dead critics. It is a judgment, a comparison, in which two things are measured by each other. To conform merely would be for the new work not really to conform at all; it would not be new, and would therefore not be a work of art. And we do not quite say that the new is more valuable because it fits in; but its fitting in is a test of its value — a test which can only be slowly and cautiously applied, for we are none of us infal-lible judges of conformity. We say: It appears to conform, and is perhaps individual, or it appears individual, and may conform; but we are hardly likely to find that it is one and not the other.

To proceed to a more intelligible exposition of the relation of the poet to the past: he can neither take the past as a lump, an indiscriminate bolus, nor can he form himself wholly on one or two private admirations, nor can he form himself wholly upon one preferred period. The first course is inadmissible, the second is an important experience of youth, and the third is a pleasant and highly desirable supplement. The poet must be very conscious of the main current, which does not at all flow invariably through the most distinguished reputations. He must be quite aware of the obvious fact that art never improves, but that the material of art is never quite the same. He must be aware that the mind of Europe — the mind of his own country — a mind which he learns in time to be much more important than his own private mind — is a mind which changes, and that this change is a development which abandons nothing en route, which does not superannuate either Shakespeare, or Homer, or the rock drawing of the Magdalenian draftsmen.[1] That this development, refinement perhaps, complication certainly, is not, from the point of view of the artist, any improvement. Perhaps not even an improvement from the point of view of the psychologist or not to the extent which we imagine; perhaps only in the end based upon a complication in economics and machinery. But the difference between the present and the past is that the conscious present is an awareness of the past in a way and to an extent which the past's awareness of itself cannot show.

Someone said: "The dead writers are remote from us because we *know* so much more than they did." Precisely, and they are that which we know.

I am alive to a usual objection to what is clearly part of my program for the métier of poetry. The objection is that the doctrine requires a ridiculous amount of erudition (pedantry), a claim which can be rejected by appeal to the lives of poets in any pantheon. It will even be affirmed that much learning deadens or perverts poetic sensibility. While, however, we persist in believing that a poet ought to know as much

as will not encroach upon his necessary receptivity and necessary laziness, it is not desirable to confine knowledge to whatever can be put into a useful shape for examinations, drawing rooms, or the still more pretentious modes of publicity. Some can absorb knowledge, the more tardy must sweat for it. Shakespeare acquired more essential history from Plutarch than most men could from the whole British Museum. What is to be insisted upon is that the poet must develop or procure the consciousness of the past and that he should continue to develop this consciousness throughout his career.

What happens is a continual surrender of himself as he is at the moment to something which is more valuable. The progress of an artist is a continual self-sacrifice, a continual extinction of personality.

There remains to define this process of depersonalization and its relation to the sense of tradition. It is in this depersonalization that art may be said to approach the condition of science. I, therefore, invite you to consider, as a suggestive analogy, the action which takes place when a bit of finely filiated platinum is introduced into a chamber containing oxygen and sulfur dioxide.

II

Honest criticism and sensitive appreciation are directed not upon the poet but upon the poetry. If we attend to the confused cries of the newspaper critics and the susurrus of popular repetition that follows, we shall hear the names of poets in great numbers; if we seek not blue-book knowledge but the enjoyment of poetry, and ask for a poem, we shall seldom find it. I have tried to point out the importance of the relation of the poem to other poems by other authors, and suggested the conception of poetry as a living whole of all the poetry that has ever been written. The other aspect of this impersonal theory of poetry is the relation of the poem to its author. And I hinted, by an analogy, that the mind of the mature poet differs from that of the immature one not precisely in any valuation of "personality," not being necessarily more interesting, or having "more to say," but rather by being a more finely perfected medium in which special, or very

[1]The Cro-Magnon cave men.

varied, feelings are at liberty to enter into new combinations.

The analogy was that of the catalyst. When the two gases previously mentioned are mixed in the presence of a filament of platinum, they form sulfurous acid. This combination takes place only if the platinum is present; nevertheless the newly formed acid contains no trace of platinum, and the platinum itself is apparently unchanged; has remained inert, neutral, and unaffected. The mind of the poet is the shred of platinum. It may partly or exclusively operate upon the experience of the man himself; but, the more perfect the artist, the more completely separate in him will be the man who suffers and the mind which creates; the more perfectly will the mind digest and transmute the passions which are its material.

The experience, you will notice, the elements which enter the presence of the transforming catalyst, are of two kinds: emotions and feelings. The effect of a work of art upon the person who enjoys it is an experience different in kind from any experience not of art. It may be formed out of one emotion, or may be a combination of several; and various feelings, inhering for the writer in particular words or phrases or images, may be added to compose the final result. Or great poetry may be made without the direct use of any emotion whatever: composed out of feelings solely. Canto XV of the *Inferno* (Brunetto Latini) is a working up of the emotion evident in the situation; but the effect, though single as that of any work of art, is obtained by considerable complexity of detail. The last quatrain gives an image, a feeling attaching to an image, which "came," which did not develop simply out of what precedes, but which was probably in suspension in the poet's mind until the proper combination arrived for it to add itself to.[2] The poet's mind is in fact a receptacle for seizing and storing up numberless feelings, phrases, images, which remain there until all the particles which can unite to form a new compound are present together.

[2] "And seemed like one of those who over the flat / And open course in the fields beside Verona / Run for the green cloth; and he seemed, at that, / Not like a loser but like the winning runner." Dante, *Inferno* 15:121–24.

If you compare several representative passages of the greatest poetry you see how great is the variety of types of combination, and also how completely any semiethical criterion of "sublimity" misses the mark. For it is not the "greatness," the intensity, of the emotions, the components, but the intensity of the artistic process, the pressure, so to speak, under which the fusion takes place, that counts. The episode of Paolo and Francesca employs a definite emotion, but the intensity of the poetry is something quite different from whatever intensity in the supposed experience it may give the impression of. It is no more intense, furthermore, than Canto XXVI, the voyage of Ulysses, which has not the direct dependence upon an emotion. Great variety is possible in the process of transmutation of emotion: the murder of Agamemnon, or the agony of Othello, gives an artistic effect apparently closer to a possible original than the scenes from Dante. In the *Agamemnon*, the artistic emotion approximates to the emotion of an actual spectator; in *Othello* to the emotion of the protagonist himself. But the difference between art and the event is always absolute; the combination which is the murder of Agamemnon is probably as complex as that which is the voyage of Ulysses. In either case there has been a fusion of elements. The ode of Keats contains a number of feelings which have nothing particular to do with the nightingale, but which the nightingale, partly, perhaps, because of its attractive name, and partly because of its reputation, served to bring together.

The point of view which I am struggling to attack is perhaps related to the metaphysical theory of the substantial unity of the soul: for my meaning is, that the poet has, not a "personality" to express, but a particular medium, which is only a medium and not a personality, in which impressions and experiences combine in peculiar and unexpected ways. Impressions and experiences which are important for the man may take no place in the poetry, and those which become important in the poetry may play quite a negligible part in the man, the personality.

I will quote a passage which is unfamiliar enough to be regarded with fresh attention in the light — or darkness — of these observations:

And now methinks I could e'en chide myself
For doting on her beauty, though her death
Shall be revenged after no common action.
Does the silkworm expend her yellow labors
For thee? For thee does she undo herself?
Are lordships sold to maintain ladyships
For the poor benefit of a bewildering minute?
Why does yon fellow falsify highways,
And put his life between the judge's lips,
To refine such a thing — keeps horse and men
To beat their valors for her? . . .[3]

In this passage (as is evident if it is taken in its context) there is a combination of positive and negative emotions: an intensely strong attraction toward beauty and an equally intense fascination by the ugliness which is contrasted with it and which destroys it. This balance of contrasted emotion is in the dramatic situation to which the speech is pertinent, but that situation alone is inadequate to it. This is, so to speak, the structural emotion, provided by the drama. But the whole effect, the dominant tone, is due to the fact that a number of floating feelings, having an affinity to this emotion by no means superficially evident, have combined with it to give us a new art emotion.

It is not in his personal emotions, the emotions provoked by particular events in his life, that the poet is in any way remarkable or interesting. His particular emotions may be simple, or crude, or flat. The emotion in his poetry will be a very complex thing, but not with the complexity of the emotions of people who have very complex or unusual emotions in life. One error, in fact, of eccentricity in poetry is to seek for new human emotions to express; and in this search for novelty in the wrong place it discovers the perverse. The business of the poet is not to find new emotions, but to use the ordinary ones and, in working them up into poetry, to express feelings which are not in actual emotions at all. And emotions which he has never experienced will serve his turn as well as those familiar to him. Consequently, we must believe that "emotion recollected in tranquility"[4] is an inexact formula. For it is neither emotion, nor recollection, nor, without distortion of meaning, tranquility. It is a concentration, and a new thing resulting from the concentration, of a very great number of experiences which to the practical and active person would not seem to be experiences at all; it is a concentration which does not happen consciously or of deliberation. These experiences are not "recollected," and they finally unite in an atmosphere which is "tranquil" only in that it is a passive attending upon the event. Of course this is not quite the whole story. There is a great deal, in the writing of poetry, which must be conscious and deliberate. In fact, the bad poet is usually unconscious where he ought to be conscious, and conscious where he ought to be unconscious. Both errors tend to make him "personal." Poetry is not a turning loose of emotion, but an escape from emotion; it is not the expression of personality, but an escape from personality. But, of course, only those who have personality and emotions know what it means to want to escape from these things.

III

ὁ δὲ νοῦς ἴσως Θειότερον τὶ καὶ ἀπαβές ἔστιν.[5]

This essay proposes to halt at the frontier of metaphysics or mysticism, and confine itself to such practical conclusions as can be applied by the responsible person interested in poetry. To divert interest from the poet to the poetry is a laudable aim: for it would conduce to a juster estimation of actual poetry, good and bad. There are many people who appreciate the expression of sincere emotion in verse, and there is a smaller number of people who can appreciate technical excellence. But very few know when there is an expression of *significant* emotion, emotion which has its life in the poem and not in the history of the poet. The emotion of art is impersonal. And the poet cannot reach his impersonality without surrendering himself wholly to the work to be done. And he is not likely to know what is to be done unless he lives in what is not merely the present, but the present moment of the past; unless he is conscious, not of what is dead, but of what is already living.

[3]Cyril Tourneur, *The Revenger's Tragedy,* III.iv.
[4]Eliot is quoting Wordsworth's "Preface to *Lyrical Ballads*"; see p. 215.

[5]"The mind may be too divine and therefore unimpassioned." Heracleitus.

Carl Gustav Jung

1875–1961

Carl Gustav Jung, the founder of analytic psychology, was born in Switzerland. The son of a philologist and pastor, from a clan of many clergymen, Jung turned his back on the ministry to pursue philosophical and medical interests. He studied at Basel (1895–1900) and Zürich, where he earned his M.D. in 1902 after working under Eugen Bleuler at the Burghölzli Psychiatric Clinic.

In 1907 Jung met Freud and quickly became the intellectual "son" for whom Freud had long been looking. But in an Oedipal struggle that Freud doubtless appreciated, Jung rapidly and thoroughly shook off his master to declare an independent vision of the mind involving less the cure of symptomatic neurosis than the pursuit of a lifelong task: the achievement of individuation, including the harmonious wholeness of conscious and unconscious. The close collaboration ended in 1912, a year after Jung became president of the International Psycho-Analytical Association, and the year when he published the clearly un-Freudian *The Psychology of the Unconscious*. In 1933 Jung became professor of psychology at the Federal Polytechnical University in Zürich, and in 1943 professor of medical psychology at the University of Basel. Immensely prolific, Jung revised and reissued much of his work. His important books include *The Psychology of Dementia* (1906), *Psychological Types* (1921), and *Psychology and Alchemy* (1944). "The Principal Archetypes" is from *Aion: Researches into the Phenomenology of the Self* (1951), a late work that tidily summarizes many of Jung's key ideas.

Jung took from Freud the notion of a structured unconscious mind, but beyond this the differences between them are profound. In Jung, the unconscious of Freud's writings is termed the "personal unconscious"; it is but a "thin layer" under the conscious mind, relatively accessible by tricks of free association and parapraxis, and therefore not of supreme significance. More important is the "collective unconscious," or racial memory, through which the spirit of the whole human species manifests itself. This deeper layer of the unconscious is not accessible through the techniques of analysis; we understand its existence through our profound response to universal symbols that appear both in dreams and in our waking lives.

Jung developed the idea of a racial memory through his study of anthropology and comparative mythology, sciences that were beginning to show interesting results by the first decade of the century. Studies like James Frazer's *The Golden Bough* (1890) had revealed striking similarities between the myths and rituals of primitive peoples around the globe, peoples who seemed to be too distant to have influenced each other directly. Jung's hypothesis was that direct influence was unnecessary, that the similar mythologies were merely differing manifestations of structures deep in the human unconscious. These structures Jung termed *archetypes*; they manifest themselves not only in myth and in dreams but in the finished art of cultures like our own in the form of symbols. Jung distinguished very strictly between the archetype itself, as a purely psychic structure, and its images: the representations the archetype takes within the symbolic fantasies created by the individual, and which then reappear in various forms in art and literature. (Later thinkers strongly influenced by Jung, such as Northrop Frye and Claude Lévi-Strauss (see p. 503), use the term *archetype* for what Jung would have called the "archetypal image.")

The archetypes and their symbols take the shape of various aspects of the Self. On the surface of the Self is the *Mask,* the face we show to the outside world. Beneath this is the *Shadow,* a demonic image of evil that represents the side of the Self that we reject. Beneath this is the *Anima,* the feminine side of the male Self, and the *Animus,* the correspondingly masculine side of the female Self. (The Animus, for males, becomes an image of the Father.) For men, the Anima, the Great Mother, is characteristically split in the shadow of the Shadow into the nurturing Mother, the tempting Whore, and the destroying Crone. Women, in turn, split the Animus into a Protector, a Lover, and a Destroying Angel. Finally there is the image of the *Spirit,* symbolized by a wise old man or woman. The four principal archetypes — Shadow, Anima, Animus, and Spirit — make up what Jung called the *Syzygy:* a quaternion composing a whole, the unified self of which people are in search. That very search for unity can take the archetypal form of the Quest, in which the Self journeys to encounter the various elements that make it up, thereby forming the relationships that constitute its individuality. The quest itself often culminates in another archetype, the Night-Sea-Journey, a voyage from life through death to a new rebirth.

In Jungian analysis, the patient recapitulates his life and looks for the ways in which symbols of the above-mentioned archetypes have been embodied within its texture. Similarly, Jungian criticism is generally involved with a search for the embodiment of these symbols within particular works of art. The pleasures of Jungian criticism often come in noting the parallels between one work and another; how, for example, Cora and Alice in *The Last of the Mohicans,* Rebecca and Rowena in *Ivanhoe,* Becky Sharp and Amelia Sedley in *Vanity Fair,* and Eustacia and Thomasin in *The Return of the Native* can all be read as variations on the Dark Lady and the White Lady — split versions of the Anima. On the other hand, since the archetypes can be found in all powerful literature, Jungian criticism can become a relatively monotonous and predictable approach, harping invariably on the same chord, finding the basic motifs of the Quest, the Shadow, and the Night-Sea-Journey in every text.

Selected Bibliography

Bodkin, Maud. *Archetypal Patterns in Poetry.* London: Oxford University Press, 1934.

Jung, Carl Gustav. *Complete Works.* 17 vols. Eds. Herbert Read, Michael Fordham, and Gerhard Adler. New York: Pantheon, 1953–.

Knapp, Bettina L. *Music, Archetype and the Writer: A Jungian View.* University College: Pennsylvania State University Press, 1988.

Rowland, Susan. *C. G. Jung and Literary Theory: The Challenge from Fiction.* Basingstoke, Eng. / New York: Macmillan–St. Martin's, 1999.

Sugg, Richard, ed. *Jungian Literary Criticism.* Evanston: Northwestern University Press, 1993.

Van Meurs, Jos. *Jungian Literary Criticism, 1920–1980: An Annotated Critical Bibliography of Works in English.* Metuchen, NJ: Scarecrow Press, 1988.

Walker, Steven F., and Robert A. Segal. *Jung and the Jungians on Myth: An Introduction.* London: Routledge, 2002.

Translated by R. F. C. Hull.

THE EGO

Investigation of the psychology of the unconscious confronted me with facts which required the formulation of new concepts. One of these concepts is the *self*. The entity so denoted is not meant to take the place of the one that has always been known as the *ego*, but includes it in a supraordinate concept. We understand the ego as the complex factor to which all conscious contents are related. It forms, as it were, the center of the field of consciousness; and, insofar as this comprises the empirical personality, the ego is the subject of all personal acts of consciousness. The relation of a psychic content to the ego forms the criterion of its consciousness, for no content can be conscious unless it is represented to a subject.

With this definition we have described and delimited the *scope* of the subject. Theoretically, no limits can be set to the field of consciousness, since it is capable of indefinite extension. Empirically, however, it always finds its limit when it comes up against the *unknown*. This consists of everything we do not know, which, therefore, is not related to the ego as the center of the field of consciousness. The unknown falls into two groups of objects: those which are outside and can be experienced by the senses, and those which are inside and are experienced immediately. The first group comprises the unknown in the outer world; the second the unknown in the inner world. We call this latter territory the *unconscious*.

The ego, as a specific content of consciousness, is not a simple or elementary factor but a complex one which, as such, cannot be described exhaustively. Experience shows that it rests on two seemingly different bases: the *somatic* and the *psychic*. The somatic basis is inferred from the totality of endosomatic perceptions, which for their part are already of a psychic nature and are associated with the ego, and are therefore conscious. They are produced by endosomatic stimuli, only some of which cross the threshold of consciousness. A considerable proportion of these stimuli occur unconsciously, that is, subliminally. The fact that they are subliminal does not necessarily mean that their status is merely physiological, any more than this would be true of a psychic content. Sometimes they are capable of crossing the threshold, that is, of becoming perceptions. But there is no doubt that a large portion of these endosomatic stimuli are simply incapable of consciousness and are so elementary that there is no reason to assign them a psychic nature — unless of course one favors the philosophical view that all life-processes are psychic anyway. The chief objection to this hardly demonstrable hypothesis is that it enlarges the concept of the psyche beyond all bounds and interprets the life-process in a way not absolutely warranted by the facts. Concepts that are too broad usually prove to be unsuitable instruments because they are too vague and nebulous. I have therefore suggested that the term "psychic" be used only where there is evidence of a will capable of modifying reflex or instinctual processes. Here I must refer the reader to my paper "On the Nature of the Psyche," where I have discussed this definition of the "psychic" at somewhat greater length.

The somatic basis of the ego consists, then, of conscious and unconscious factors. The same is true of the psychic basis: on the one hand the ego rests on the *total field of consciousness*, and on the other, on the *sum total of unconscious contents*. These fall into three groups: first, temporarily subliminal contents that can be reproduced voluntarily (memory); second, unconscious contents that cannot be reproduced voluntarily; third, contents that are not capable of becoming conscious at all. Group two can be inferred from the spontaneous irruption of subliminal contents into consciousness. Group three is hypothetical; it is a logical inference from the facts underlying group two. It contains contents which have *not yet* irrupted into consciousness, or which never will.

When I said that the ego "rests" on the total field of consciousness I do not mean that it *consists* of this. Were that so, it would be indistinguishable from the field of consciousness as a whole. The ego is only the latter's point of reference, grounded on and limited by the somatic factor described above.

Although its bases are in themselves relatively unknown and unconscious, the ego is a conscious factor par excellence. It is even acquired, empirically speaking, during the individual's lifetime. It seems to arise in the first place from the collision between the somatic factor and the environment, and, once established as a subject, it goes on developing from further collisions with the outer world and the inner.

Despite the unlimited extent of its bases, the ego is never more and never less than consciousness as a whole. As a conscious factor the ego could, theoretically at least, be described completely. But this would never amount to more than a picture of the *conscious personality;* all those features which are unknown or unconscious to the subject would be missing. A total picture would have to include these. But a total description of the personality is, even in theory, absolutely impossible, because the unconscious portion of it cannot be grasped cognitively. This unconscious portion, as experience has abundantly shown, is by no means unimportant. On the contrary, the most decisive qualities in a person are often unconscious and can be perceived only by others, or have to be laboriously discovered with outside help.

Clearly, then, the *personality as a total phenomenon* does not coincide with the ego, that is, with the conscious personality, but forms an entity that has to be distinguished from the ego. Naturally the need to do this is incumbent only on a psychology that reckons with the fact of the unconscious, but for such a psychology the distinction is of paramount importance. Even for jurisprudence it should be of some importance whether certain psychic facts are conscious or not — for instance, in adjudging the question of responsibility.

I have suggested calling the total personality which, though present, cannot be fully known, the *self.* The ego is, by definition, subordinate to the self and is related to it like a part to the whole. Inside the field of consciousness it has, as we say,

free will. By this I do not mean anything philosophical, only the well-known psychological fact of "free choice," or rather the subjective feeling of freedom. But, just as our free will clashes with necessity in the outside world, so also it finds its limits outside the field of consciousness in the subjective inner world, where it comes into conflict with the facts of the self. And just as circumstances or outside events "happen" to us and limit our freedom, so the self acts upon the ego like an *objective occurrence* which free will can do very little to alter. It is, indeed, well known that the ego not only can do nothing against the self, but is sometimes actually assimilated by unconscious components of the personality that are in the process of development and is greatly altered by them.

It is, in the nature of the case, impossible to give any general description of the ego except a formal one. Any other mode of observation would have to take account of the *individuality* which attaches to the ego as one of its main characteristics. Although the numerous elements composing this complex factor are, in themselves, everywhere the same, they are infinitely varied as regards clarity, emotional coloring, and scope. The result of their combination — the ego — is therefore, so far as one can judge, individual and unique, and retains its identity up to a certain point. Its stability is relative, because farreaching changes of personality can sometimes occur. Alterations of this kind need not always be pathological; they can also be developmental and hence fall within the scope of the normal.

Since it is the point of reference for the field of consciousness, the ego is the subject of all successful attempts at adaptation so far as these are achieved by the will. The ego therefore has a significant part to play in the psychic economy. Its position there is so important that there are good grounds for the prejudice that the ego is the center of the personality, and that the field of consciousness is the psyche *per se.* If we discount certain suggestive ideas in Leibniz, Kant, Schelling, and Schopenhauer, and the philosophical excursions of Carus and von Hartmann, it is only since the end of the nineteenth century that modern psychology, with its inductive methods, has discovered the foundations of consciousness and proved empirically the existence of a psyche outside consciousness. With this discovery the position of the ego, till then absolute, became relativized; that is to say, though it retains its quality as the center of the field of consciousness, it is questionable whether it is the center of the personality. It is part of the personality but not the whole of it. As I have said, it is simply impossible to estimate how large or how small its share is; how free or how dependent it is on the qualities of this "extra-conscious" psyche. We can only say that its freedom is limited and its dependence proved in ways that are often decisive. In my experience one would do well not to underestimate its dependence on the unconscious. Naturally there is no need to say this to persons who already overestimate the latter's importance. Some criterion for the right measure is afforded by the psychic consequences of a wrong estimate, a point to which we shall return later on.

We have seen that, from the standpoint of the psychology of consciousness, the unconscious can be divided into three groups of contents. But from the standpoint of the psychology of the personality a twofold division ensues: an "extra-conscious" psyche whose contents are *personal*, and an "extra-conscious" psyche whose contents are *impersonal* and *collective*. The first group comprises contents which are integral components of the individual personality and could therefore just as well be conscious; the second group forms, as it were, an omnipresent, unchanging, and everywhere identical *quality or substrate of the psyche per se.* This is, of course, no more than a hypothesis. But we are driven to it by the peculiar nature of the empirical material, not to mention the high probability that the general similarity of psychic processes in all individuals must be based on an equally general and impersonal principle that conforms to law, just as the instinct manifesting itself in the individual is only the partial manifestation of an instinctual substrate common to all men.

THE SHADOW

Whereas the contents of the personal unconscious are acquired during the individual's lifetime, the contents of the collective unconscious are invariably archetypes that were present from the beginning. Their relation to the instincts has been discussed elsewhere.[1] The archetypes most clearly characterized from the empirical point of view are those which have the most frequent and the most disturbing influence on the ego. These are the *shadow,* the *anima,* and the *animus.*[2] The most accessible of these, and the easiest to experience, is the shadow, for its nature can in large measure be inferred from the contents of the personal unconscious. The only exceptions to this rule are those rather rare cases where the positive qualities of the personality are repressed, and the ego in consequence plays an essentially negative or unfavorable role.

The shadow is a moral problem that challenges the whole ego-personality, for no one can become conscious of the shadow without considerable moral effort. To become conscious of it involves recognizing the dark aspects of the personality as present and real. This act is the essential condition for any kind of self-knowledge, and it therefore, as a rule, meets with considerable resistance. Indeed, self-knowledge as a psychotherapeutic measure frequently requires much painstaking work extending over a long period.

Closer examination of the dark character-istics — that is, the inferiorities constituting the shadow — reveals that they have an *emotional* nature, a kind of autonomy, and accordingly an obsessive or, better, possessive quality. Emotion, incidentally, is not an activity of the individual but something that happens to him. Affects occur usually where adaptation is weakest, and at the same time they reveal the reason for its weak-ness, namely a certain degree of inferiority and the existence of a lower level of personality. On this lower level with its uncontrolled or scarcely controlled emotions one behaves more or less like a primitive, who is not only the passive victim of his affects but also singularly incapable of moral judgment.

[1] "Instinct and the Unconscious" and "On the Nature of the Psyche," pars. 397ff. [Jung]

[2] The contents of this and the following chapter are taken from a lecture delivered to the Swiss Society for Practical Psychology, in Zurich, 1948. The material was first published in the *Wiener Zeitschrift für Nervenheilkunde und deren Grenzgebiete* I (1948): 4. [Jung]

Although, with insight and good will, the shadow can to some extent be assimilated into the conscious personality, experience shows that there are certain features which offer the most obstinate resistance to moral control and prove almost impossible to influence. These resistances are usually bound up with *projections,* which are not recognized as such, and their recognition is a moral achievement beyond the ordinary. While some traits peculiar to the shadow can be recognized without too much difficulty as one's own personal qualities, in this case both insight and good will are unavailing because the cause of the emotion appears to lie, beyond all possibility of doubt, in the *other person.* No matter how obvious it may be to the neutral observer that it is a matter of projections, there is little hope that the subject will perceive this himself. He must be convinced that he throws a very long shadow before he is willing to withdraw his emotionally-toned projections from their object.

Let us suppose that a certain individual shows no inclination whatever to recognize his projections. The projection-making factor then has a free hand and can realize its object — if it has one — or bring about some other situation characteristic of its power. As we know, it is not the conscious subject but the unconscious which does the projecting. Hence one meets with projections, one does not make them. The effect of projection is to isolate the subject from his environment, since instead of a real relation to it there is now only an illusory one. Projections change the world into the replica of one's own unknown face. In the last analysis, therefore, they lead to an auto-erotic or autistic condition in which one dreams a world whose reality remains forever unattainable. The resultant *sentiment d'incomplétude*[3] and the still worse feeling of sterility are in their turn explained by projection as the malevolence of the environment, and by means of this vicious circle the isolation is intensified. The more projections are thrust in between the subject and the environment, the harder it is for the ego to see through its illusions. A forty-five-year-old patient who had suffered from a compulsion neurosis since he was twenty and had become completely cut off from the world once said to me: "But I can never admit to myself that I've wasted the best twenty-five years of my life!"

It is often tragic to see how blatantly a man bungles his own life and the lives of others yet remains totally incapable of seeing how much the whole tragedy originates in himself, and how he continually feeds it and keeps it going. Not *consciously,* of course — for consciously he is engaged in bewailing and cursing a faithless world that recedes further and further into the distance. Rather, it is an unconscious factor which spins the illusions that veil his world. And what is being spun is a cocoon, which in the end will completely envelop him.

One might assume that projections like these, which are so very difficult if not impossible to dissolve, would belong to the realm of the shadow — that is, to the negative side of the personality. This assumption becomes untenable after a certain point, because the symbols that then appear no longer refer to the same but to the opposite sex, in a man's case to a woman and vice versa. The source of projections is no longer the shadow — which is always of the same sex as the subject — but a contrasexual figure. Here we meet the animus of a woman and the anima of a man, two corresponding archetypes whose autonomy and unconsciousness explain the stubbornness of their projections. Though the shadow is a motif as well known to mythology as anima and animus, it represents first and foremost the personal unconscious, and its content can therefore be made conscious without too much difficulty. In this it differs from anima and animus, for whereas the shadow can be seen through and recognized fairly easily, the anima and animus are much further away from consciousness and in normal circumstances are seldom if ever realized. With a little self-criticism one can see through the shadow — so far as its nature is personal. But when it appears as an archetype, one encounters the same difficulties as with anima and animus. In other words, it is quite within the bounds of possibility for a man to recognize the relative evil of his nature, but it is a rare and shattering experience for him to gaze into the face of absolute evil.

---

[3]Feeling of incompleteness.

THE SYZYGY: ANIMA AND ANIMUS

What, then, is this projection-making factor? The East calls it the "Spinning Woman"[4] — Maya, who creates illusion by her dancing. Had we not long since known it from the symbolism of dreams, this hint from the Orient would put us on the right track: the enveloping, embracing, and devouring element points unmistakably to the mother,[5] that is, to the son's relation to the real mother, to her imago, and to the woman who is to become a mother for him. His Eros is passive like a child's; he hopes to be caught, sucked in, enveloped, and devoured. He seeks, as it were, the protecting, nourishing, charmed circle of the mother, the condition of the infant released from every care, in which the outside world bends over him and even forces happiness upon him. No wonder the real world vanishes from sight!

If this situation is dramatized, as the unconscious usually dramatizes it, then there appears before you on the psychological stage a man living regressively, seeking his childhood and his mother, fleeing from a cold cruel world which denies him understanding. Often a mother appears beside him who apparently shows not the slightest concern that her little son should become a man, but who, with tireless and self-immolating effort, neglects nothing that might hinder him from growing up and marrying. You behold the secret conspiracy between mother and son, and how each helps the other to betray life.

Where does the guilt lie? With the mother, or with the son? Probably with both. The unsatisfied longing of the son for life and the world ought to be taken seriously. There is in him a desire to touch reality, to embrace the earth and fructify the field of the world. But he makes no more than a series of fitful starts, for his initiative as well as his staying power are crippled by the secret memory that the world and happiness may be

had as a gift — from the mother. The fragment of world which he, like every man, must encounter again and again is never quite the right one, since it does not fall into his lap, does not meet him half way, but remains resistant, has to be conquered, and submits only to force. It makes demands on the masculinity of a man, on his ardor, above all on his courage and resolution when it comes to throwing his whole being into the scales. For this he would need a faithless Eros, one capable of forgetting his mother and undergoing the pain of relinquishing the first love of his life. The mother, foreseeing this danger, has carefully inculcated into him the virtues of faithfulness, devotion, loyalty, so as to protect him from the moral disruption which is the risk of every life adventure. He has learnt these lessons only too well, and remains true to his mother. This naturally causes her the deepest anxiety (when, to her greater glory, he turns out to be a homosexual, for example) and at the same time affords her an unconscious satisfaction that is positively mythological. For, in the relationship now reigning between them, there is consummated the immemorial and most sacred archetype of the marriage of mother and son. What, after all, has commonplace reality to offer, with its registry offices, pay envelopes, and monthly rent, that could outweigh the mystic awe of the *hieros gamos*?[6] Or the star-crowned woman whom the dragon pursues, or the pious obscurities veiling the marriage of the Lamb?

This myth, better than any other, illustrates the nature of the collective unconscious. At this level the mother is both old and young, Demeter and Persephone, and the son is spouse and sleeping suckling rolled into one. The imperfections of real life, with its laborious adaptations and manifold disappointments, naturally cannot compete with such a state of indescribable fulfilment.

In the case of the son, the projection-making factor is identical with the mother-imago, and this is consequently taken to be the real mother. The projection can only be dissolved when the son sees that in the realm of his psyche there is an imago not only of the mother but of the daughter, the sister, the beloved, the heavenly

[4]Erwin Rousselle, "Seelische Führung im lebenden Taoismus," Pl. I, pp. 150, 170. Rousselle calls the spinning woman the "animal soul." There is a saying that runs, "The spinner sets in motion." I have defined the anima as a personification of the unconscious. [Jung]

[5]Here and in what follows, the word "mother" is not meant in the literal sense but as a symbol of everything that functions as a mother. [Jung]

[6]Sacred marriage. Jung's allusions are to the book of Revelation.

goddess, and the chthonic Baubo.[7] Every mother and every beloved is forced to become the carrier and embodiment of this omnipresent and ageless image, which corresponds to the deepest reality in a man. It belongs to him, this perilous image of Woman; she stands for the loyalty which in the interests of life he must sometimes forgo; she is the much needed compensation for the risks, struggles, sacrifices that all end in disappointment; she is the solace for all the bitterness of life. And, at the same time, she is the great illusionist, the seductress, who draws him into life with her Maya — and not only in life's reasonable and useful aspects, but into its frightful paradoxes and ambivalences where good and evil, success and ruin, hope and despair, counterbalance one another. Because she is his greatest danger she demands from a man his greatest, and if he has it in him she will receive it.

This image is "My Lady Soul," as Spitteler called her. I have suggested instead the term "anima," as indicating something specific, for which the expression "soul" is too general and too vague. The empirical reality summed up under the concept of the anima forms an extremely dramatic content of the unconscious. It is possible to describe this content in rational, scientific language, but in this way one entirely fails to express its living character. Therefore, in describing the living processes of the psyche, I deliberately and consciously give preference to a dramatic, mythological way of thinking and speaking, because this is not only more expressive but also more exact than an abstract scientific terminology, which is wont to toy with the notion that its theoretic formulations may one fine day be resolved into algebraic equations.

The projection-making factor is the anima, or rather the unconscious as represented by the anima. Whenever she appears, in dreams, visions, and fantasies, she takes on personified form, thus demonstrating that the factor she embodies possesses all the outstanding characteristics of a feminine being. She is not an invention of the conscious, but a spontaneous product of the unconscious. Nor is she a substitute figure for the mother.

On the contrary, there is every likelihood that the numinous qualities which make the mother-imago so dangerously powerful derive from the collective archetype of the anima, which is incarnated anew in every male child.

Since the anima is an archetype that is found in men, it is reasonable to suppose that an equivalent archetype must be present in women; for just as the man is compensated by a feminine element, so woman is compensated by a masculine one. I do not, however, wish this argument to give the impression that these compensatory relationships were arrived at by deduction. On the contrary, long and varied experience was needed in order to grasp the nature of anima and animus empirically. Whatever we have to say about these archetypes, therefore, is either directly verifiable or at least rendered probable by the facts. At the same time, I am fully aware that we are discussing pioneer work which by its very nature can only be provisional.

Just as the mother seems to be the first carrier of the projection-making factor for the son, so is the father for the daughter. Practical experience of these relationships is made up of many individual cases presenting all kinds of variations on the same basic theme. A concise description of them can, therefore, be no more than schematic.

Woman is compensated by a masculine element and therefore her unconscious has, so to speak, a masculine imprint. This results in a considerable psychological difference between men and women, and accordingly I have called the projection-making factor in women the animus, which means mind or spirit. The animus corresponds to the paternal Logos[8] just as the anima corresponds to the maternal Eros.[9] But I do not wish or intend to give these two intuitive concepts too specific a definition. I use Eros and Logos merely as conceptual aids to describe the fact that woman's consciousness is characterized more by the connective quality of Eros than by the discrimination and cognition associated with Logos. In men, Eros, the function of relationship, is usually less developed than Logos. In women, on the other hand, Eros is an expression of their

---

[7]The earth mother, symbol of the grave to which man goes.

[8]Reason.
[9]Love, desire.

true nature, while their Logos is often only a regrettable accident. It gives rise to misunderstandings and annoying interpretations in the family circle and among friends. This is because it consists of *opinions* instead of reflections, and by opinions I mean *a priori* assumptions that lay claim to absolute truth. Such assumptions, as everyone knows, can be extremely irritating. As the animus is partial to argument, he can best be seen at work in disputes where both parties know they are right. Men can argue in a very womanish way, too, when they are anima-possessed and have thus been transformed into the animus of their own anima. With them the question becomes one of personal vanity and touchiness (as if they were females); with women it is a question of *power*, whether of truth or justice or some other "ism" — for the dressmaker and hairdresser have already taken care of their vanity. The "Father" (i.e., the sum of conventional opinions) always plays a great role in female argumentation. No matter how friendly and obliging a woman's Eros may be, no logic on earth can shake her if she is ridden by the animus. Often the man has the feeling — and he is not altogether wrong — that only seduction or a beating or rape would have the necessary power of persuasion. He is unaware that this highly dramatic situation would instantly come to a banal and unexciting end if he were to quit the field and let a second woman carry on the battle (his wife, for instance, if she herself is not the fiery war horse). This sound idea seldom or never occurs to him, because no man can converse with an animus for five minutes without becoming the victim of his own anima. Anyone who still had enough sense of humor to listen objectively to the ensuing dialogue would be staggered by the vast number of commonplaces, misapplied truisms, clichés from newspapers and novels, shop-soiled platitudes of every description interspersed with vulgar abuse and brain-splitting lack of logic. It is a dialogue which, irrespective of its participants, is repeated millions and millions of times in all the languages of the world and always remains essentially the same.

This singular fact is due to the following circumstance: when animus and anima meet, the animus draws his sword of power and the anima ejects her poison of illusion and seduction. The outcome need not always be negative, since the two are equally likely to fall in love (a special instance of love at first sight). The language of love is of astonishing uniformity, using the well-worn formulas with the utmost devotion and fidelity, so that once again the two partners find themselves in a banal collective situation. Yet they live in the illusion that they are related to one another in the most individual way.

In both its positive and its negative aspects the anima/animus relationship is always full of "animosity," i.e., it is emotional, and hence collective. Affects lower the level of the relationship and bring it closer to the common instinctual basis, which no longer has anything individual about it. Very often the relationship runs its course heedless of its human performers, who afterwards do not know what happened to them.

Whereas the cloud of "animosity" surrounding the man is composed chiefly of sentimentality and resentment, in woman it expresses itself in the form of opinionated views, interpretations, insinuations, and misconstructions, which all have the purpose (sometimes attained) of serving the relation between two human beings. The woman, like the man, becomes wrapped in a veil of illusions by her demon-familiar, and, as the daughter who alone understands her father (that is, is eternally right in everything), she is translated to the land of sheep, where she is put to graze by the shepherd of her soul, the animus.

Like the anima, the animus too has a positive aspect. Through the figure of the father he expresses not only conventional opinion but — equally — what we call "spirit," philosophical or religious ideas in particular, or rather the attitude resulting from them. Thus the animus is a psychopomp, a mediator between the conscious and the unconscious and a personification of the latter. Just as the anima becomes, through integration, the Eros of consciousness, so the animus becomes a Logos; and in the same way that the anima gives relatedness and relationship to a man's consciousness, the animus gives to a woman's consciousness a capacity for reflection, deliberation, and self-knowledge.

The effect of anima and animus on the ego is in principle the same. This effect is extremely difficult to eliminate because, in the first place, it is uncommonly strong and immediately fills the ego-personality with an unshakable feeling of rightness and righteousness. In the second place, the cause of the effect is projected and appears to lie in objects and objective situations. Both these characteristics can, I believe, be traced back to the peculiarities of the archetype. For the archetype, of course, exists *a priori*. This may possibly explain the often totally irrational yet undisputed and indisputable existence of certain moods and opinions. Perhaps these are so notoriously difficult to influence because of the powerfully suggestive effect emanating from the archetype. Consciousness is fascinated by it, held captive, as if hypnotized. Very often the ego experiences a vague feeling of moral defeat and then behaves all the more defensively, defiantly, and self-righteously, thus setting up a vicious circle which only increases its feeling of inferiority. The bottom is then knocked out of the human relationship, for, like megalomania, a feeling of inferiority makes mutual recognition impossible, and without this there is no relationship.

As I said, it is easier to gain insight into the shadow than into the anima or animus. With the shadow, we have the advantage of being prepared in some sort by our education, which has always endeavored to convince people that they are not one-hundred-per-cent pure gold. So everyone immediately understands what is meant by "shadow," "inferior personality," etc. And if he has forgotten, his memory can easily be refreshed by a Sunday sermon, his wife, or the tax collector. With the anima and animus, however, things are by no means so simple. Firstly, there is no moral education in this respect, and secondly, most people are content to be self-righteous and prefer mutual vilification (if nothing worse!) to the recognition of their projections. Indeed, it seems a very natural state of affairs for men to have irrational moods and women irrational opinions. Presumably this situation is grounded on instinct and must remain as it is to ensure that the Empedoclean game of the hate and love of the elements shall continue for all eternity. Nature is conservative and does not easily allow her courses to be altered; she defends in the most stubborn way the inviolability of the preserves where anima and animus roam. Hence it is much

more difficult to become conscious of one's anima/animus projections than to acknowledge one's shadow side. One has, of course, to overcome certain moral obstacles, such as vanity, ambition, conceit, resentment, etc., but in the case of projections all sorts of purely intellectual difficulties are added, quite apart from the contents of the projection which one simply doesn't know how to cope with. And on top of all this there arises a profound doubt as to whether one is not meddling too much with nature's business by prodding into consciousness things which it would have been better to leave asleep.

Although there are, in my experience, a fair number of people who can understand without special intellectual or moral difficulties what is meant by anima and animus, one finds very many more who have the greatest trouble in visualizing these empirical concepts as anything concrete. This shows that they fall a little outside the usual range of experience. They are unpopular precisely because they seem unfamiliar. The consequence is that they mobilize prejudice and become taboo like everything else that is unexpected.

So if we set it up as a kind of requirement that projections should be dissolved, because it is wholesomer that way and in every respect more advantageous, we are entering upon new ground. Up till now everybody has been convinced that the idea "my father," "my mother," etc., is nothing but a faithful reflection of the real parent, corresponding in every detail to the original, so that when someone says "my father" he means no more and no less than what his father is in reality. This is actually what he supposes he does mean, but a supposition of identity by no means brings that identity about. This is where the fallacy of the *enkekalymmenos* ("the veiled one") comes in.[10] If one includes in the psychological equation X's picture of his father, which he takes for the real father, the equation will not work out, because the unknown quantity he has introduced does not tally with reality. X has overlooked the fact that his

[10]The fallacy, which stems from Eubulides the Megarian, runs: "Can you recognize your father?" Yes. "Can you recognize this veiled one?" No. "This veiled one is your father. Hence you can recognize your father and not recognize him." [Jung]

idea of a person consists, in the first place, of the possibly very incomplete picture he has received of the real person and, in the second place, of the subjective modifications he has imposed upon this picture. X's idea of his father is a complex quantity for which the real father is only in part responsible, an indefinitely larger share falling to the son. So true is this that every time he criticizes or praises his father he is unconsciously hitting back at himself, thereby bringing about those psychic consequences that overtake people who habitually disparage or overpraise themselves. If, however, X carefully compares his reactions with reality, he stands a chance of noticing that he has miscalculated somewhere by not realizing long ago from his father's behavior that the picture he has of him is a false one. But as a rule X is convinced that he is right, and if anybody is wrong it must be the other fellow. Should X have a poorly developed Eros, he will be either indifferent to the inadequate relationship he has with his father or else annoyed by the inconsistency and general incomprehensibility of a father whose behavior never really corresponds to the picture X has of him. Therefore X thinks he has every right to feel hurt, misunderstood, and even betrayed.

One can imagine how desirable it would be in such cases to dissolve the projection. And there are always optimists who believe that the golden age can be ushered in simply by telling people the right way to go. But just let them try to explain to these people that they are acting like a dog chasing its own tail. To make a person see the shortcomings of his attitude considerably more than mere "telling" is needed, for more is involved than ordinary common sense can allow. What one is up against here is the kind of fateful misunderstanding which, under ordinary conditions, remains forever inaccessible to insight. It is rather like expecting the average respectable citizen to recognize himself as a criminal.

I mention all this just to illustrate the order of magnitude to which the anima/animus projections belong, and the moral and intellectual exertions that are needed to dissolve them. Not all the contents of the anima and animus are projected, however. Many of them appear spontaneously in dreams and so on, and many more can be made conscious through active imagination. In this way we find that

thoughts, feelings, and affects are alive in us which we would never have believed possible. Naturally, possibilities of this sort seem utterly fantastic to anyone who has not experienced them himself, for a normal person "knows what he thinks." Such a childish attitude on the part of the "normal person" is simply the rule, so that no one without experience in this field can be expected to understand the real nature of anima and animus. With these reflections one gets into an entirely new world of psychological experience, provided of course that one succeeds in realizing it in practice. Those who do succeed can hardly fail to be impressed by all that the ego does not know and never has known. This increase in self-knowledge is still very rare nowadays and is usually paid for in advance with a neurosis, if not with something worse.

The autonomy of the collective unconscious expresses itself in the figures of anima and animus. They personify those of its contents which, when withdrawn from projection, can be integrated into consciousness. To this extent, both figures represent *functions* which filter the contents of the collective unconscious through to the conscious mind. They appear or behave as such, however, only so long as the tendencies of the conscious and unconscious do not diverge too greatly. Should any tension arise, these functions, harmless till then, confront the conscious mind in personified form and behave rather like systems split off from the personality, or like part souls. This comparison is inadequate in so far as nothing previously belonging to the ego-personality has split off from it: on the contrary, the two figures represent a disturbing accretion. The reason for their behaving in this way is that though the contents of anima and animus can be integrated they themselves cannot, since they are archetypes. As such they are the foundation stones of the psychic structure, which in its totality exceeds the limits of consciousness and therefore can never become the object of direct cognition. Though the effects of anima and animus can be made conscious, they themselves are factors transcending consciousness and beyond the reach of perception and volition. Hence they remain autonomous despite the integration of their contents, and for this reason they should be borne constantly in mind. This is extremely important from the therapeutic standpoint, because constant observation pays the unconscious a tribute that more or less guarantees its co-operation. The unconscious as we know can never be "done with" once and for all. It is, in fact, one of the most important tasks of psychic hygiene to pay continual attention to the symptomatology of unconscious contents and processes, for the good reason that the conscious mind is always in danger of becoming one-sided, of keeping to well-worn paths and getting stuck in blind alleys. The complementary and compensating function of the unconscious ensures that these dangers, which are especially great in neurosis, can in some measure be avoided. It is only under ideal conditions, when life is still simple and unconscious enough to follow the serpentine path of instinct without hesitation or misgiving, that the compensation works with entire success. The more civilized, the more unconscious and complicated a man is, the less he is able to follow his instincts. His complicated living conditions and the influence of his environment are so strong that they drown the quiet voice of nature. Opinions, beliefs, theories, and collective tendencies appear in its stead and back up all the aberrations of the conscious mind. Deliberate attention should then be given to the unconscious so that the compensation can set to work. Hence it is especially important to picture the archetypes of the unconscious not as a rushing phantasmagoria of fugitive images but as constant, autonomous factors, which indeed they are.

Both these archetypes, as practical experience shows, possess a fatality that can on occasion produce tragic results. They are quite literally the father and mother of all the disastrous entanglements of fate and have long been recognized as such by the whole world. Together they form a divine pair,[11] one of whom, in accordance with his Logos nature, is characterized by *pneuma* and *nous*,[12] rather like Hermes with his ever-shifting hues, while the other, in accordance with her Eros nature, wears the features of Aphrodite, Helen (Selene), Persephone, and Hecate. Both of them are unconscious powers, "gods" in fact, as the ancient world quite rightly conceived them to be. To call them by this name is to give them that central position in the scale of psychological values which has always been theirs whether consciously acknowledged or not; for their power grows in proportion to the degree that they remain unconscious. Those who do not see them are in their hands, just as typhus epidemic flourishes best when its source is undiscovered. Even in Christianity the divine syzygy has not become obsolete, but occupies the highest place as Christ and his bride the Church.[13] Parallels like these prove extremely helpful in our attempts to find the right criterion for gauging the significance of these two archetypes. What we can discover about them from the conscious side is so slight as to be almost imperceptible. It is only when we throw light into the dark depths of the psyche and explore the strange and tortuous paths of human fate that it gradually becomes clear to us how immense is the influence wielded by these two factors that complement our conscious life.

Recapitulating, I should like to emphasize that the integration of the shadow, or the realization of the personal unconscious, marks the first stage in the analytic process, and that without it a recognition of anima and animus is impossible. The shadow can be realized only through a relation to a partner, and anima and animus only through a relation to a partner of the opposite sex, because only in such a relation do their projections become operative. The recognition of the anima gives rise, in a man, to a triad, one third of which is transcendent: the masculine subject, the opposing feminine subject, and the

[11]Naturally this is not meant as a psychological definition, let alone a metaphysical one. As I pointed out in "The Relations between the Ego and the Unconscious" (pars. 296ff.), the syzygy consists of three elements: the femininity pertaining to the man and the masculinity pertaining to the woman; the experience which man has of woman and vice versa; and, finally, the masculine and feminine archetypal image. The first element can be integrated into the personality by the process of conscious realization, but the last one cannot. [Jung]

[12]Spirit and mind.

[13]"For the Scripture says, God made man male and female; the male is Christ, the female is the Church." — Second Epistle of Clement to the Corinthians, xiv, 2 (*The Apostolic Fathers* [Loeb Classics], Vol. I, London, 1912, p. 151, trans. Kirsopp Lake). In pictorial representations, Mary often takes the place of the Church. [Jung]

transcendent anima. With a woman the situation is reversed. The missing fourth element that would make the triad a quaternity is, in a man, the archetype of the Wise Old Man, which I have not discussed here, and in a woman the Chthonic Mother. These four constitute a half immanent and half transcendent quaternity, an archetype which I have called the *marriage quaternio*.[14]

14."The Psychology of the Transference," pars. 425ff. [Jung]

The marriage quaternio provides a schema not only for the self but also for the structure of primitive society with its cross-cousin marriage, marriage classes, and division of settlements into quarters. The self, on the other hand, is a God-image, or at least cannot be distinguished from one. Of this the early Christian spirit was not ignorant, otherwise Clement of Alexandria could never have said that he who knows him- self knows God.

W. E. B. Du Bois
1868–1963

The first African American intellectual leader, and the most militant and controversial civil rights leader before Martin Luther King, was born in Great Barrington, Massachusetts, soon after the ratification of the constitutional amendment abolishing slavery. William Edward Burghardt Du Bois was born free, and in fact his family on both sides had been free for generations. His mother, Mary Burghardt, had a grandfather who had been freed after fighting in the American Revolutionary War; his father, Alfred Du Bois, had fought in the Civil War. His father disappeared around the time of his birth, and Du Bois was raised by his mother with some assistance from his father's family. Du Bois attended public schools in Great Barrington, where he had his first personal experience of racial prejudice at the hands of a white female classmate, a "tall newcomer" who spurned him when he attempted to exchange "gorgeous" cards with her as with the others. Characteristically, as we read of the episode in Du Bois's *The Souls of Black Folk*, we feel the fresh sting of the young man's pain, but it is quickly reshaped into his mature meditation on the "double consciousness" of the African American, "this sense of always looking at one's self through the eyes of others," which Du Bois saw as one of the key conditions under which his race lived and, striving for equality, would have to overcome.

Du Bois's own way of overcoming it was through education. An excellent student, he was sponsored by his neighbors to attend Fisk College in Nashville (now Fisk University), from which he went on to Harvard. There Du Bois studied with the pragmatist philosophers Josiah Royce, George Santayana, and William James; his 1890 commencement address on Jefferson Davis was cited in newspapers around the country. Du Bois did graduate work in history at Harvard, then at the Universität Friedrich Wilhelm in Berlin, returning to Harvard to complete his doctorate in 1896, with a dissertation on the efforts to suppress the African slave trade to the United States. Du Bois taught classics at Wilberforce College, then left to work at the University of Pennsylvania on a pioneering sociological study, *The Philadelphia Negro* (1899), which used field research to underpin its argument that racism was at the source of many of the social problems afflicting the colored communities, including crime, broken families, and unemployment. Unemployed himself after the conclusion of his study — since Penn would not offer an African American a position on the faculty — Du Bois moved to the South, to Atlanta University, where he taught from 1897 to 1910.

Around the turn of the century, as Du Bois was writing the influential essays that would appear in *The Souls of Black Folk*, the leading spokesman for African Americans was Booker T. Washington, a former slave who had organized the Tuskegee Institute, a teacher's college and school of industrial training in Alabama. Washington's message to his race, expressed in his 1895 Atlanta address, was to strive for economic equality and, in the meanwhile, to forgo voting rights and accept second-class citizenship. Du Bois's sociological research had convinced him that white racism was the visible force behind the social, economic, and political plight of African Americans, but he was at first moderate in his critique of Washington. Then, in 1899, the horrific lynching of Sam Hose near Atlanta became the "red ray" that radicalized Du Bois and made him feel that African Americans needed another kind of leadership. In 1905 Du Bois began the Niagara Movement, an organization of educated African Americans devoted to the ideal of immediate political equality, in opposition to Washington's "Tuskegee Machine." Here he propagated the idea that the "talented tenth," the educated upper crust of African American society, owed it to the rest of their race to work selflessly for their collective advantage.

After a violent race riot in Springfield, Illinois, in 1909, Du Bois merged the Niagara Movement with that of northern liberal whites in what became the National Association for the Advancement of Colored People (NAACP). From 1910 through 1934, Du Bois was its most prominent officer and the editor of its magazine, *The Crisis*, a position that gave him an independent political pulpit to shape black public opinion. He flirted with socialism but supported the internationalist Woodrow Wilson, at a time when blacks usually voted for the party of Lincoln, and urged African Americans to "close ranks" with white America during World War I, despite the inequalities visited by racist practices on black soldiers. During the 1920s, he was a furious opponent of Marcus Garvey's "Back to Africa" movement and considered himself a supporter of the Harlem Renaissance. It was in *The Crisis* that Du Bois published his 1925 speech, "Criteria of Negro Art" (published in 1926 and reprinted on the following pages). Du Bois takes it pretty much for granted that black men like Paul Laurence Dunbar and Countee Cullen have written superb poetry, recognized as such by critics white as well as black. His worry is about the effect of that on the white audience. Will the white world assume, once aware of the success of African Americans as writers, artists, and musicians, that the race problem has already been solved, that the political and economic inequalities of America have vanished? For that reason, Du Bois argues, it is the duty of the Negro writer to portray the truth about their race, a truth that will include their struggle. At that time, when modernism was in flower, Du Bois's position that "all art is propaganda," stood in opposition to mainstream aesthetics, which saw art as an end in itself. Du Bois's critics included black intellectuals, including the "godfather" of the Harlem Renaissance, Alain Locke. Today, Du Bois's argument that one of the functions of art is to raise social consciousness seems very current indeed.

By 1934, Du Bois's political position and that of the NAACP had diverged, causing conflicts that he resolved by resigning and returning to Atlanta University. For the next ten years, Du Bois worked on a revisionist history of the Reconstruction era, a study on African and African American folkways, and his autobiography, *Dusk of Dawn* (1940). Retired from teaching in 1944, Du Bois returned to the NAACP, only to be expelled once more at the age of eighty, in 1948, for favoring the Progressive candidate, Henry Wallace, over the official NAACP candidate, Harry Truman. The last fifteen years of Du Bois's life are a chronicle of opposition, as he found himself drawn toward internationalist and Stalinist "front" organizations, and demonized by right-wing politicians. In 1961, responding to an invitation from Kwame Nkrumah, he emigrated to Ghana, where he renounced his American citizenship shortly before he died on August 27, 1963. Ironically, in the years of Du Bois's self-imposed exile, the militant civil rights movement came to fruition in the American South, and it was on the day after Du Bois's death that Martin Luther King addressed the March on Washington with his speech "I Have a Dream."

Selected Bibliography

Andrews, William, ed. *Critical Essays on W. E. B. Du Bois*, Boston: G. K. Hall, 1985.

Byerman, Keith. *Seizing the Word: History, Art, and Self in the Work of W. E. B. Du Bois*. Athens: University Georgia Press, 1994.

DeMarco, Joseph P. *The Social Thought of W. E. B. Du Bois*. Lanham, MD: University Press of America, 1983.

Du Bois, W. E. B. *Complete Works*, ed. Herbert Aptheker. 32 vols. Millwood, NY: University Press of America, 1973–1986.

Hamilton, Virginia. *W. E. B. Du Bois: A Biography*. New York: Crowell, 1972.

Lewis, David Levering. *W. E. B. Du Bois: Biography of a Race*. New York: Henry Holt, 1994.

——. *W. E. B. Du Bois: The Fight for Equality and the American Century*. New York: Henry Holt, 2000.

Marable, Manning. *W. E. B. Du Bois: Black Radical Democrat*. Boston: Twayne, 1986.

Rampersad, Arnold. *The Art and Imagination of W. E. B. Du Bois*. Cambridge: Harvard University Press, 1976.

[On Double Consciousness]
from *The Souls of Black Folk*

[B]eing a problem is a strange experience, — peculiar even for one who has never been anything else, save perhaps in babyhood and in Europe. It is in the early days of rollicking boyhood that the revelation first bursts upon one, all in a day, as it were. I remember well when the shadow swept across me. I was a little thing, away up in the hills of New England, where the dark Housatonic[1] winds between Hoosac and Taghkanic to the sea. In a wee wooden schoolhouse, something put it into the boys' and girls' heads to buy gorgeous visiting-cards — ten cents a package — and exchange. The exchange was merry, till one girl, a tall newcomer, refused my card, — refused it peremptorily, with a glance. Then it dawned upon me with a certain suddenness that I was different from the others; or like, mayhap, in heart and life and longing, but shut out from their world by a vast veil. I had thereafter no desire to tear down that veil, to creep through; I held all beyond it in common contempt, and lived above it in a region of blue sky and great wandering shadows. That sky was bluest when I could beat my mates at examination-time, or beat them at a foot-race, or even beat their stringy heads. Alas, with the years all this fine contempt began to fade; for the worlds I longed for, and all their dazzling opportunities, were theirs, not mine. But they should not keep these prizes, I said; some, all, I would wrest from them. Just how I would do it I could never decide: by reading law, by healing the sick, by telling the wonderful tales that swam

[1]The Housatonic River flows through the Berkshire Hills past his hometown of Great Barrington, between the Taghkanic (Taconic) Hills and Hoosac Mountain.

in my head. — some way. With other black boys the strife was not so fiercely sunny: their youth shrunk into tasteless sycophancy, or into silent hatred of the pale world about them and mock-ing distrust of everything white; or wasted itself in a bitter cry, Why did God make me an outcast and a stranger in mine own house? The shades of the prison-house closed round about us all: walls strait and stubborn to the whitest, but relentlessly narrow, tall, and unscalable to sons of night who must plod darkly on in resignation, or beat unavailing palms against the stone, or steadily, half hopelessly, watch the streak of blue above.

After the Egyptian and Indian, the Greek and Roman, the Teuton and Mongolian, the Negro is a sort of seventh son, born with a veil,[2] and gifted with second-sight in this American world, — a world which yields him no true self-consciousness, but only lets him see himself through the revelation of the other world. It is a peculiar sensation, this double-consciousness, this sense of always looking at one's self through the eyes of others, of measur-ing one's soul by the tape of a world that looks on in amused contempt and pity. One ever feels his two-ness, — an American, a Negro; two souls, two thoughts, two unreconciled strivings; two warring ideals in one dark body, whose dogged strength alone keeps it from being torn asunder.

The history of the American Negro is the history of this strife, — this longing to attain self-conscious manhood, to merge his double self into a better and truer self. In this merging he wishes neither of the older selves to be lost. He would not Africanize America, for America has too much to teach the world and Africa. He would not bleach his Negro soul in a flood of white Americanism, for he knows that Negro blood has a message for the world. He simply wishes to make it possible for a man to be both a Negro and an American, without being cursed and spit upon by his fellows, without having the doors of Opportunity closed roughly in his face.

This, then, is the end of his striving; to be a co-worker in the kingdom of culture, to escape both death and isolation, to husband and use his best

[2] In superstition, a seventh son and a child born with caul (bluish skin from the afterbirth) over his face are supposed to have special supernatural gifts, including a dual soul, as well as extra senses that allow them to prophesy.

powers and his latent genius. These powers of body and mind have in the past been strangely wasted, dispersed, or forgotten. The shadow of a mighty Negro past flits through the tale of Ethiopia the Shadowy and of Egypt the Sphinx. Throughout his-tory, the powers of single black men flash here and there like falling stars, and die sometimes before the world has rightly gauged their brightness. Here in America, in the few days since Emancipation, the black man's turning hither and thither in hesi-tant and doubtful striving has often made his very strength to lose effectiveness, to seem like absence of power. And yet it is not weak-ness, — it is the contradiction of double aims. The double-aimed struggle of the black artisan — on the one hand to escape white contempt for a nation of mere hewers of wood and drawers of water,[3] and on the other hand to plough and nail and dig for a poverty-stricken horde — could only result in making him a poor craftsman, for he had but half a heart in either cause. By the poverty and ignorance of his people, the Negro minister or doctor was tempted toward quackery and demagogy; and by the criticism of the other world, toward ideals that made him ashamed of his lowly tasks. The would-be black savant was confronted by the paradox that the knowledge his people needed was a twice-told tale to his white neighbors, while the knowledge which would teach the white world was Greek to his own flesh and blood. The innate love of harmony and beauty that set the ruder souls of his people a-dancing and a-singing raised but confusion and doubt in the soul of the black artist; for the beauty revealed to him was the soul-beauty of a race which his larger audience despised, and he could not artic-ulate the message of another people. This waste of double aims, this seeking to satisfy two unrec-onciled ideals, has wrought sad havoc with the courage and faith and deed of ten thousand people, — has sent them often wooing false gods[4] and invok-ing false means of salvation, and at times has even seemed about to make them ashamed of themselves.

[3] Du Bois alludes to Joshua 9:23, where the Gibeonites are made into the slaves of the Israelites, to hew wood and draw water for the house of God.

[4] Du Bois alludes to Judges 2:17, about the Israelites who forsake the Lord and "went a whoring after other gods, and bowed themselves unto them."

Criteria of Negro Art

I do not doubt but there are some in this audience who are a little disturbed at the subject of this meeting, and particularly at the subject I have chosen. Such people are thinking something like this: "How is it that an organization like this, a group of radicals trying to bring new things into the world, a fighting organization which has come up out of the blood and dust of battle, struggling for the right of black men to be ordinary human beings — how is it that an organization of this kind can turn aside to talk about Art? After all, what have we who are slaves and black to do with Art?"

Or perhaps there are others who feel a certain relief and are saying, "After all it is rather satisfactory after all this talk about rights and fighting to sit and dream of something which leaves a nice taste in the mouth."

Let me tell you that neither of these groups is right. The thing we are talking about tonight is part of the great fight we are carrying on and it represents a forward and an upward look — a pushing onward. You and I have been breasting hills, we have been climbing upward; there has been progress and we can see it day by day looking back along blood-filled paths. But as you go through the valleys and over the foothills, so long as you are climbing, the direction, — north, south, east or west, — is of less importance. But when gradually the vista widens and you begin to see the world at your feet and the far horizon, then it is time to know more precisely whither you are going and what you really want.

What do you want? What is the thing we are after? As it was phrased last night it had a certain truth: We want to be Americans, full-fledged Americans, with all the rights of other American citizens. But is that all? Do we want simply to be Americans? Once in a while through all of us there flashes some clairvoyance, some clear idea, of what America really is. We who are dark can see America in a way that white Americans can not. And seeing our country thus, are we satisfied with its present goals and ideals?

In the high school where I studied we learned most of Scott's "Lady of the Lake"[1] by heart. In after life once it was my privilege to see the lake. It was Sunday. It was quiet. You could glimpse the deer wandering in unbroken forests; you could hear the soft ripple of romance on the waters. Around me fell the cadence of that poetry of my youth. I fell asleep full of the enchantment of the Scottish border. A new day broke and with it came a sudden rush of excursionists. They were mostly Americans and they were loud and strident. They poured upon the little pleasure boat, — men with their hats a little on one side and drooping cigars in the wet corners of their mouths; women who shared their conversation with the world. They all tried to get everywhere first. They pushed other people out of the way. They made all sorts of incoherent noises and gestures so that the quiet home folk and the visitors from other lands silently and half-wonderingly gave way before them. They struck a note not evil but wrong. They carried, perhaps, a sense of strength and accomplishment, but their hearts had no conception of the beauty which pervaded this holy place.

If you tonight suddenly should become full-fledged Americans; if your color faded, or the color line here in Chicago was miraculously forgotten; suppose, too, you became at the same time rich and powerful; — what is it that you would want? What would you immediately seek? Would you buy the most powerful of motor cars and outrace Cook County? Would you buy the most elaborate estate on the North Shore? Would you be a Rotarian or a Lion or a What-not of the very last degree? Would you wear the most striking clothes, give the richest dinners and buy the longest press notices?

Even as you visualize such ideals you know in your hearts that these are not the things you really want. You realize this sooner than the average white American because, pushed aside as we have been in America, there has come to

[1]Sir Walter Scott (1771–1832) wrote the poem *Lady of the Lake* in 1810. [Huggins]

us not only a certain distaste for the tawdry and flamboyant but a vision of what the world could be if it were really a beautiful world; if we had the true spirit; if we had the Seeing Eye, the Cunning Hand, the Feeling Heart; if we had had, to be sure, not perfect happiness, but plenty of good hard work, the inevitable suffering that always comes with life; sacrifice and waiting, all that — but, nevertheless, lived in a world where men know, where men create, where they realize themselves and where they enjoy life. It is that sort of a world we want to create for ourselves and for all America.

After all, who shall describe Beauty? What is it? I remember tonight four beautiful things: The Cathedral at Cologne,[2] a forest in stone, set in light and changing shadow, echoing with sunlight and solemn song; a village of the Veys[3] in West Africa, a little thing of mauve and purple, quiet, lying content and shining in the sun; a black and velvet room where on a throne rests, in old and yellowing marble, the broken curves of the Venus of Milo[4]; a single phrase of music in the Southern South — utter melody, haunting and appealing, suddenly arising out of night and eternity, beneath the moon.

Such is Beauty. Its variety is infinite, its possibility is endless. In normal life all may have it and have it yet again. The world is full of it; and yet today the mass of human beings are choked away from it, and their lives distorted and made ugly. This is not only wrong, it is silly. Who shall right this well-nigh universal failing? Who shall let this world be beautiful? Who shall restore to men the glory of sunsets and the peace of quiet sleep?

We black folk may help for we have within us as a race new stirrings; stirrings of the beginning of a new appreciation of joy, of a new desire to create, of a new will to be; as though in this morning of group life we had awakened from some sleep that at once dimly mourns the past and dreams a splendid future; and there has come the conviction that the youth that is here today, the Negro Youth, is a different kind of Youth, because in some new way it bears this mighty

[2] A Gothic cathedral in Germany. [Huggins]

[3] One of the Mandingo peoples of Senegal. [Huggins]

[4] The Venus de Milo, a Greek statue of the goddess Aphrodite carved 130–120 B.C.E., can be seen in the Louvre Museum in Paris.

prophecy on its breast, with a new realization of itself, with new determination for all mankind.

What has this Beauty to do with the world? What? What has Beauty to do with Truth and Goodness — with the facts of the world and the right actions of men? "Nothing," the artists rush to answer. They may be right. I am but an humble disciple of art and cannot presume to say. I am one who tells the truth and exposes evil and seeks with Beauty and for Beauty to set the world right. That somehow, somewhere eternal and perfect Beauty sits above Truth and Right I can conceive, but here and now and in the world in which I work they are for me unseparated and inseparable.

This is brought to us peculiarly when as artists we face our past as a people. There has come to us — and it has come especially through the man we are going to honor tonight[5] — a realization of that past, of which for long years we have been ashamed, for which we have apologized. We thought nothing could come out of that past which we wanted to remember; which we wanted to hand down to our children. Suddenly, this same past is taking on form, color and reality, and in a half shamefaced way we are beginning to be proud of it. We are remembering that the romance of the world did not die and lie forgotten in the Middle Age; that if you want romance to deal with you must have it here and now and in your own hands.

I once knew a man and woman. They had two children, a daughter who was white and a daughter who was brown; the daughter who was white married a white man; and when her wedding was preparing the daughter who was brown prepared to go and celebrate. But the mother said, "No!" and the brown daughter went into her room and turned on the gas and died. Do you want Greek tragedy swifter than that?

Or again, here is a little Southern town and you are in the public square. On one side of the square is the office of a colored lawyer and on all

[5] Carter Godwin Woodson, 12th Spingarn Medallist [Du Bois]. Professor Woodson (1875–1950), dean at Howard University and at West Virginia State College, was the author of dozens of books and articles on African American history and sociology, known as the "father of black history," and he inaugurated what is now known as Black History Month.

the other sides are men who do not like colored lawyers. A white woman goes into the black man's office and points to the white-filled square and says, "I want five hundred dollars now and if I do not get it I am going to scream."

Have you heard the story of the conquest of German East Africa? Listen to the untold tale: There were 40,000 black men and 4,000 white men who talked German. There were 20,000 black men and 12,000 white men who talked English. There were 10,000 black men and 400 white men who talked French. In Africa then where the Mountains of the Moon raised their white and snow-capped heads into the mouth of the tropic sun, where Nile and Congo rise and the Great Lakes swim, these men fought; they struggled on mountain, hill and valley, in river, lake and swamp, until in masses they sickened, crawled and died; until the 4,000 white Germans had become mostly bleached bones; until nearly all the 12,000 white Englishmen had returned to South Africa, and the 400 Frenchmen to Belgium and Heaven; all except a mere handful of the white men died; but thousands of black men from East, West and South Africa, from Nigeria and the Valley of the Nile, and from the West Indies still struggled, fought and died. For four years they fought and won and lost German East Africa; and all you hear about it is that England and Belgium conquered German Africa for the allies!

Such is the true and stirring stuff of which Romance is born and from this stuff come the stirrings of men who are beginning to remember that this kind of material is theirs, and this vital life of their own kind is beckoning them on.

The question comes next as to the interpretation of these new stirrings, of this new spirit: Of what is the colored artist capable? We have had on the part of both colored and white people singular unanimity of judgment in the past. Colored people have said: "The work must be inferior because it comes from colored people." White people have said: "It is inferior because it is done by colored people." But today there is coming to both the realization that the work of the black man is not always inferior. Interesting stories come to us. A professor in the University of Chicago read to a class that had studied literature a passage of poetry and asked them to guess the author. They guessed a goodly

company from Shelley and Robert Browning down to Tennyson and Masefield. The author was Countée Cullen.[6] Or again the English critic John Drinkwater went down to a Southern seminary, one of the sort which "finishes" young white women of the South. The students sat with their wooden faces while he tried to get some response out of them. Finally he said, "Name me some of your Southern poets." They hesitated. He said finally, "I'll start out with your best: Paul Laurence Dunbar!"[7]

With the growing recognition of Negro artists in spite of the severe handicaps, one comforting thing is occurring to both white and black. They are whispering, "Here is a way out. Here is the real solution of the color problem. The recognition accorded Cullen, Hughes, Fauset, White[8] and others shows there is no real color line. Keep quiet! Don't complain! Work! All will be well!"

I will not say that already this chorus amounts to a conspiracy. Perhaps I am naturally too suspicious. But I will say that there are today a surprising number of white people who are getting great satisfaction out of these younger Negro writers because they think it is going to stop agitation of the Negro question. They say, "What is the use of your fighting and complaining; do the great thing and the reward is there." And many colored people are all too eager to follow this advice; especially those who are weary of the external struggle along the color line, who are afraid to fight and to whom the money of philanthropists and the alluring publicity are subtle and deadly bribes. They say, "What is the use of fighting? Why not show simply what we deserve and let the reward come to us?"

And it is right here that the National Association for the Advancement of Colored People comes upon the field, comes with its great call to a new battle, a new fight and new things to

[6]African American poet (1903–1946). Percy Bysshe Shelley (1792–1822); Robert Browning (1812–1889); Alfred, Lord Tennyson (1809–1892); and John Masefield (1878–1967) were all English poets. [Huggins]

[7]African American poet (1872–1906). [Huggins] Dunbar was born in Dayton, Ohio, and never lived in the South, though both his parents had been slaves in Kentucky.

[8]Walter White (1893–1955), author and civil rights leader. Langston Hughes (1902–1967), poet, dramatist, and fiction writer. Jessie Redmon Fauset (1882–1961), editor and novelist. [Huggins]

fight before the old things are wholly won; and to say that the Beauty of Truth and Freedom which shall some day be our heritage and the heritage of all civilized men is not in our hands yet and that we ourselves must not fail to realize.

There is in New York tonight a black woman molding clay by herself in a little bare room, because there is not a single school of sculpture in New York where she is welcome. Surely there are doors she might burst through, but when God makes a sculptor He does not always make the pushing sort of person who beats his way through doors thrust in his face. This girl is working her hands off to get out of this country so that she can get some sort of training.

There was Richard Brown.[9] If he had been white he would have been alive today instead of dead of neglect. Many helped him when he asked but he was not the kind of boy that always asks. He was simply one who made colors sing.

There is a colored woman in Chicago who is a great musician. She thought she would like to study at Fontainebleau this summer where Walter Damrosch[10] and a score of leaders of Art have an American school of music. But the application blank of this school says: 'I am a white American and I apply for admission to the school.'

We can go on the stage; we can be just as funny as white Americans wish us to be; we can play all the sordid parts that America likes to assign to Negroes; but for any thing else there is still a small place for us.

And so I might go on. But let me sum up with this: Suppose the only Negro who survived some centuries hence was the Negro painted by white Americans in the novels and essays they have written. What would people in a hundred years say of black Americans? Now turn it around. Suppose you were to write a story and put in it the kind of people you know and like and imagine. You might get it published and you might not. And the "might not" is still far bigger than the "might." The white publishers catering to white folk would say, "It is not interesting" — to white folk, natu- rally not. They want Uncle Toms, Topsies,[11] good "darkies" and clowns. I have in my office a story with all the earmarks of truth. A young man says that he started out to write and had his stories accepted. Then he began to write about the things he knew best about, that is, about his own people. He submitted a story to a magazine which said, "We are sorry, but we cannot take it." I sat down and revised my story, changing the color of the characters and the locale and sent it under an assumed name with a change of address and it was accepted by the same magazine that had refused it, the editor promising to take anything else I might send in providing it was good enough."

We have, to be sure, a few recognized and suc- cessful Negro artists; but they are not all those fit to survive or even a good minority. They are but the remnants of that ability and genius among us whom the accidents of education and opportunity have raised on the tidal waves of chance. We black folk are not altogether peculiar in this. After all, in the world at large, it is only the accident, the remnant, that gets the chance to make the most of itself; but if this is true of the white world it is infinitely more true of the colored world. It is not simply the great clear tenor of Ronald Hayes[12] that opened the ears of America. We have had many voices of all kinds as fine as his and America was as deaf as she was for years to him. Then a foreign land heard Hayes and put its imprint on him and immediately America with all its imitative snobbery woke up. We approved Hayes because London, Paris and Berlin approved him and not simply because he was a great singer.

Thus it is the bounden duty of black America to begin this great work of the creation of Beauty.

[9] Richard Lonsdale Brown (1886–1915), an African American landscape artist who was raised in West Virginia, who was "discovered" by New York artist George de Forest Brush in 1911. Brown studied with Brush and was given a one-man show at the Ovington Gallery on Fifth Avenue the following year. According to John Cuthbert of West Virginia University (personal communication), Brown "subsequently studied for a year at the Robert Gould Shaw House in Boston. During this period he was a poster artist for W. E. B. Du Bois. He died of an unspecified illness while still in his twenties."

[10] German-American conductor and composer (1862–1950). [Huggins] Fontainebleau is a chateau built by French King Francois I in a forest about 40 miles southeast of Paris, and the site of artists' colonies since the sixteenth century.

[11] Uncle Tom and Topsy are characters from Harriet Beecher Stowe's Uncle Tom's Cabin (1852). [Huggins]

[12] Internationally acclaimed African American singer (1887–1976). [Huggins]

of the preservation of Beauty, of the realization of Beauty, and we must use in this work all the methods that men have used before. And what have been the tools of the artist in times gone by? First of all, he has used the Truth — not for the sake of truth, not as a scientist seeking truth, but as one upon whom Truth eternally thrusts itself as the highest handmaid of imagination, as the one great vehicle of universal understanding. Again artists have used Goodness — goodness in all its aspects of justice, honor and right — not for sake of an ethical sanction but as the one true method of gaining sympathy and human interest.

The apostle of Beauty thus becomes the apostle of Truth and Right not by choice but by inner and outer compulsion. Free he is but his freedom is ever bounded by Truth and Justice; and slavery only dogs him when he is denied the right to tell the Truth or recognize an ideal of Justice.

Thus all Art is propaganda and ever must be, despite the wailing of the purists. I stand in utter shamelessness and say that whatever art I have for writing has been used always for propaganda for gaining the right of black folk to love and enjoy. I do not care a damn for any art that is not used for propaganda. But I do care when propaganda is confined to one side while the other is stripped and silent.

In New York we have two plays: "White Cargo" and "Congo."[13] In "White Cargo" there is a fallen woman. She is black. In "Congo" the fallen woman is white. In "White Cargo" the black woman goes down further and further and in "Congo" the white woman begins with degradation but in the end is one of the angels of the Lord.

You know the current magazine story: A young white man goes down to Central America and the most beautiful colored woman there falls in love with him. She crawls across the whole isthmus to get to him. The white man says nobly, "No." He goes back to his white sweetheart in New York.

In such cases, it is not the positive propaganda of people who believe white blood divine, infallible and holy to which I object. It is the denial of a similar right of propaganda to those who believe black blood is human, lovable and inspired with new ideals for the world. White artists themselves suffer from this narrowing of their field. They cry for freedom in dealing with Negroes because they have so little freedom in dealing with whites. DuBose Heyward writes "Porgy"[14] and writes beautifully of the black Charleston underworld. But why does he do this? Because he cannot do a similar thing for the white people of Charleston, or they would drum him out of town. The only chance he had to tell the truth of pitiful human degradation was to tell it of colored people. I should not be surprised if Octavius Roy Cohen[15] had approached the *Saturday Evening Post* and asked permission to write about a different kind of colored folk than the monstrosities he has created; but if he has, the *Post* has replied, "No. You are getting paid to write about the kind of colored people you are writing about."

In other words, the white public today demands from its artists, literary and pictorial, racial prejudgment which deliberately distorts Truth and Justice, as far as colored races are concerned, and it will pay for no other.

On the other hand, the young and slowly growing black public still wants its prophets almost equally unfree. We are bound by all sorts of customs that have come down as second-hand soul clothes of white patrons. We are ashamed of sex and we lower our eyes when people will talk of it. Our religion holds us in superstition. Our worst side has been so shamelessly emphasized that we are denying we have or ever had a worst side. In all sorts of ways we are hemmed in and our new young artists have got to fight their way to freedom.

The ultimate judge has got to be you and you have got to build yourselves up into that wide judgment, that catholicity[16] of temper which is going to enable the artist to have his widest chance for freedom. We can afford the Truth.

[13] Or *Kongo* (1926) by Kilbourn Gordon and Chester DeVonde. *White Cargo: A Play of the Primitive* (1925) by Leon Gordon. [Huggins]

[14] A 1925 novel about southern African-American life by DuBose Heyward (1885–1940). [Huggins]

[15] Cohen was an American magazine fiction writer (1891–1959) whose African American series characters included Epic Peters, a Pullman porter, and Florian Slappey, a private detective from Birmingham, Alabama, operating in Harlem.

[16] Universality.

White folk today cannot. As it is now we are handing everything over to a white jury. If a colored man wants to publish a book, he has got to get a white publisher and a white newspaper to say it is great; and then you and I say so. We must come to the place where the work of art when it appears is reviewed and acclaimed by our own free and unfettered judgment. And we are going to have a real and valuable and eternal judgment only as we make ourselves free of mind, proud of body and just of soul to all men.

And then do you know what will be said? It is already saying. Just as soon as true Art emerges; just as soon as the black artist appears, someone touches the race on the shoulder and says, "He did that because he was an American, not because he was a Negro; he was born here; he was trained here; he is not a Negro — what is a Negro anyhow? He is just human; it is the kind of thing you ought to expect."

I do not doubt that the ultimate art coming from black folk is going to be just as beautiful, and beautiful largely in the same ways, as the art that comes from white folk, or yellow, or red; but the point today is that until the art of the black folk compels recognition they will not be rated as human. And when through art they compel recognition then let the world discover if it will that their art is as new as it is old and as old as new.

I had a classmate once who did three beautiful things and died. One of them was a story of a folk who found fire and then went wandering in the gloom of night seeking again the stars they had once known and lost; suddenly out of blackness they looked up and there loomed the heavens; and what was it that they said? They raised a mighty cry: "It is the stars, it is the ancient stars, it is the young and everlasting stars!"

Mikhail Bakhtin

1895–1975

Nearly lost to the world because of Soviet political turbulence in the first half of the twentieth century, the literary and aesthetic theories of the Russian polymath Mikhail Bakhtin have, in the past four decades, exerted a spellbinding and fertile power over critical imaginations in North America and Europe. Born in Orel, Russia, Bakhtin attended the universities in Odessa and St. Petersburg. In 1920 he moved to the cultural center Vitebsk and in 1924 back to St. Petersburg (then renamed Leningrad), where he worked at the Historical Institute and became part of an intellectual circle that opposed itself to the then-fashionable philosophy of the neo-Kantian Hermann Cohen.[1]

Bakhtin's magisterial *Problems of Dostoevsky's Poetics* appeared in 1929, but its impact was stifled when a Stalinist purge sent its author into internal exile, probably because of his connections with Russian Orthodox "Old-Believers." During the next six precarious years on the border of Siberia, Bakhtin wrote the seminal essay "Discourse in the Novel" (later printed as one of the four essays in *The Dialogic Imagination*) and a study of the German *Bildungsroman* that was thought lost when it disappeared from a publishing house during the German invasion; fragments of it have since been recovered and appear in *Speech Genres and Other Late Essays*. On his return from exile in 1936, Bakhtin was offered a position at the Mordovia State Teachers' College (later University) at Saransk, where he taught until his retirement in 1961. In 1940 Bakhtin submitted a dissertation on Rabelais but was unable to defend it until after the war; when he did defend it in 1946, the dissertation's very originality worked against its acceptance. Its acceptance in 1951 and eventual publication in 1965 (as *Rabelais and His World*) lifted Bakhtin's ideas from obscurity and made them available to the international scholarly community. One important vector for the spread of his fame was Julia Kristeva, who incorporated Bakhtin's ideas about intertextuality into her early structuralist work. Meanwhile Bakhtin, in declining health from osteomyelitis, which had plagued him all his life, was able to move from Saransk to Moscow in 1969. At the end of his life he gathered around him a group of students that reportedly included the daughter of then-KGB director Yuri Andropov. At the center rather than the periphery of Russia, and no longer in danger of being purged for heterodox views, he was finally able to publish many of the seminal pieces on the philosophy of language and theory of literature that he had written fifty years before. He died in Moscow in 1975.

Given his views on the social construction of languages and the literary codes based on language, Mikhail Bakhtin has been claimed as both a Marxist and a formalist. Part of the difficulty in categorizing his work stems from the still-disputed question of Bakhtin's contribution to three books published in the late 1920s by members of his philosophical circle. Bakhtin's thought clearly informs *Marxism and the Study of*

---

[1]Cohen, who worked at the University of Marburg, is almost unknown today; he is a significant figure in intellectual history, however, because his views inspired reaction by so many other literary/philosophical theorists, including Gadamer and Heidegger.

Language (1929–30) and *Freudianism: A Critical Sketch* (1927) by V. N. Vološinov, and *The Formal Method in Literary Scholarship* (1928) by P. N. Medvedev. Some scholars have argued that Bakhtin actually wrote these attacks on Freudian psychology and formalist literary theory, publishing them, under the names of his friends. But more recent evidence suggests that these Marxist texts of the Bakhtin circle owe their orthodox slant and dialectical argumentation to their titular authors. Without these texts as part of his canon, Bakhtin can be seen as a highly individualistic theorist concerned with problems similar to the ones that engrossed Shklovsky (see p. 426) and other formalists, such as Yuri Tynyanov.

At the center of Bakhtin's ideas is the principle usually translated as *heteroglos-sia* (in the original Russian: *raznorecie*, literally 'the word of another'): the notion that the meaning of language is socially determined, that utterances reflect social values and depend for their meaning on their relation to other utterances. The idea is a familiar one in the purely linguistic context of speech-act theory: An imperative sentence can be an order, a command, a request, a plea, or a prayer, depending on who is talking to whom. We could say that Bakhtin — who was working on these ideas many years before the speech-act theorists Austin and Searle — essentially directs our attention to the *pragmatics* of literary discourse. He differentiates sharply between *dialogical* discourse, which explicitly or tacitly acknowledges the language of the Other, the controlling presence of a social context; and *monological* discourse, which tries to have its say in a vacuum. What many English and American critics find worth emulating in Bakhtin's criticism is the extraordinary sensitivity with which he succeeds in locating the various nuances — the responses to internal and external pressures — that go into the creation of dialogical fictional discourse.

But Bakhtin does not merely analyze literary pragmatics neutrally; he loathes single-voiced authoritative discourse, the unquestionable word that comes from above to dictate meaning. For Bakhtin, monologism denies the existence and valid-ity of the Other, assuming an auditor to whom one speaks without needing to listen. Instead, Bakhtin valorizes dialogism and the types of discourse he calls *double-voiced* (*dvugolosoe slovo*), in which a single sentence will bring into dialogue two or more different languages. What Bakhtin calls languages can be idiolects — the individualized discourse of a particular person — or various sorts of dialects, com-munication styles, or jargons characteristic of particular social groups: trades, pro-fessions, classes, parties, generations. The shifting planes of intention that can occur whenever one language meets another in a single discourse permit an exhilaratingly chaotic freedom of expression. Bakhtin particularly loves the various forms of parody, which mediate comically between an audience and a known prior discourse.

Thus, purity and clarity of speech, with clear levels of discourse of the sort Aristotle and Horace recommended, earn no points from Bakhtin. They suggest to him a closed and stratified society without freedom of thought, devoted to "ter-ror, dogmatism, reverence, and piety." What he values instead is the Rabelaisian carnivalization of literature: the sociolinguistic fun-fair where, as in the medieval festival or carnival, rulers and ruled mix on equal terms in a parodic rout devoted to "ambivalent laughter, blasphemy, the profanation of everything sacred, full of debasing and obscenities, familiar contact with everyone and everything."

Bakhtin consequently valorizes the novel, where heteroglossia is practically unavoidable, to poetry, which is typically single-voiced.[2] And of course some novelists are more given to heteroglossia than others — at one point Bakhtin contrasts Tolstoy, whose multifarious characters nonetheless always express the author's dogmas, with Dostoevsky, who gives some of the most striking dialogue to characters whose ideas are anathema to him, like Svidrigaïlov and Ivan Karamazov. The existence of conversation and dialogue as such does not guarantee double-voiced discourse. On the other hand, the voice of an authorial narrator, which one might expect to be entirely authoritative, may represent perspectives other than those of the characters of the fiction. Analyzing the narrator's voice in *Little Dorrit* in "Discourse and the Novel," reproduced on the following pages, Bakhtin makes us aware that Dickens's narrator is not a single univocal speaker, but embodies, paradoxically at times, various linguistic strata embedded in Victorian society, the jargons of various trades and professions, the chatter of particular segments of society, and so on. Within these "heteroglot" utterances may be included direct authorial discourse, though within a complex passage it may be impossible to say whether a particular phrase belongs to the author or to an Other whose language he is re-accenting — and it may indeed be both at once.

Bakhtin's dialogism is the basis for a broader genre-criticism, which in turn is the basis for an innovative approach to literary history. But his notion of the languages competing within an individual's speech, the way one's discourse is at the same time the discourse of an Other, lies at the heart of his critical system.

The selections reprinted here are both from *Discourse in the Novel*; in addition we have reproduced a convenient chart presenting the levels of dialogue within a discourse from *Problems in Dostoevsky's Poetics*.

Selected Bibliography

Bakhtin, Mikhail. *Rabelais and His World*. Cambridge: MIT Press, 1968.
———. *The Dialogic Imagination: Four Essays*. Austin: University of Texas Press, 1981.
———. *Problems of Dostoevsky's Poetics*. Minneapolis: University of Minnesota Press, 1984.
———. *Speech Genres, and Other Essays*. Austin: University of Texas Press, 1987.
———. *Art and Answerability: Early Philosophical Essays*. Austin: University of Texas Press, 1990.
Clark, Katerina, and Michael Holquist. *Mikhail Bakhtin*. Cambridge: Belknap Press of Harvard University, 1984.
Emerson, Caryl. *Bakhtin Across the Disciplines*. Evanston, IL: Northwestern University Press, 1995.
Holquist, Michael. *Dialogism: Bakhtin and His World*. London and New York: Routledge, 1990.
———. *Dialogism*. London: Routledge, 2002.
Medvedev, P. N. *The Formal Method in Literary Scholarship*. Baltimore: Johns Hopkins University Press, 1978.
Morson, Gary. *Bakhtin: Essays and Dialogues on His Work*. Chicago: University Press, 1986.

[2]This is not purely a question of genre. As Bakthtin himself points out, there are what he calls "novelized forms" within any genre. But historically the novel has lent itself to heteroglossia far more than lyric poetry has done.

Richter, David. "Dialogism and Poetry." *Studies in the Literary Imagination* (Spring 1990): 3–27.

Todorov, Tzvetan. *Mikhail Bakhtin: The Dialogical Principle.* Minneapolis: University of Minnesota Press, 1985.

Volosinov, V. N. *Marxism and the Philosophy of Language.* Cambridge: Harvard University Press, 1986.

The Topic of the Speaking Person
from *Discourse in the Novel*

Before, then, taking up the issue of the artistic representation of another's speech conceived as the image of a language, we should say something about the importance in extra-artistic areas of life and ideology of the topic of the speaking person and his discourse. While in the many forms available for transmitting another's speech outside the novel there is no defining concern for the images of a language, such forms are used in the novel for self-enrichment — but not before they are first transformed and subjected within it to the new holistic unity of the novel itself (and, conversely, novels have a powerful influence on the extra-artistic perception and transmission of another's discourse).

The topic of a speaking person has enormous importance in everyday life. In real life we hear speech about speakers and their discourse at every step. We can go so far as to say that in real life people talk most of all about what others talk about — they transmit, recall, weigh and pass judgment on other people's words, opinions, assertions, information; people are upset by others' words, or agree with them, contest them, refer to them and so forth. Were we to eavesdrop on snatches of raw dialogue in the street, in a crowd, in lines, in a foyer and so forth, we would hear how often the words "he says," "people say," "he said ..." are repeated, and in the conversational hurly-burly of people in a crowd, everything often fuses into one big "he says ... you say ... I say ..." Reflect how

Translated by Caryl Emerson and Michael Holquist.

The importance of this motif is in no way diminished in the higher and better-organized areas of everyday communication. Every conversation is full of transmissions and interpretations of other people's words. At every step one meets a "quotation" or a "reference" to something that a particular person said, a reference to "people say," or "everyone says," to the words of the person one is talking with, or to one's own previous words, to a newspaper, an official decree, a document, a book and so forth. The majority of our information and opinions is usually not communicated in direct form as our own, but with reference to some indefinite and general source: "I heard," "It's generally held that ...," "It is thought that ..." and so forth. Take one of the most widespread occurrences in our everyday life, conversations about some official meeting: they are all constructed on the transmission, interpretation and evaluation of various kinds of verbal performance, resolutions, the rejected and accepted corrections that are made to them and so forth. Thus talk goes on about speaking people and their words everywhere — this motif returns again and again; it either accompanies the development of the other topics in everyday life, or directly governs speech as its leading theme.

Further examples of the significance of the topic of the speaking person in everyday life would be superfluous. We need only keep our ears open to the speech sounding everywhere around us to reach such a conclusion: in the everyday speech of any person living in society, no less than half (on the average) of all the words uttered by him will be someone else's words (consciously someone else's), transmitted with varying degrees of precision and impartiality (or more precisely, partiality).

It goes without saying that not all transmitted words belonging to someone else lend themselves, when fixed in writing, to enclosure in quotation marks. That degree of otherness and purity in another's word that in written speech would require quotation marks (as per the intention of the speaker himself, how he himself determines this degree of otherness) is required much less frequently in everyday speech.

Furthermore, syntactic means for formulating the transmitted speech of another are far from exhausted by the grammatical paradigms of direct and indirect discourse: the means for its incorporation, for its formulation and for indicating different degrees of shading are highly varied. This must be kept in mind if we are to make good our claim that of all words uttered in everyday life, no less than half belong to someone else.

The speaking person and his discourse are not, in everyday speech, subjects for artistic representation, but rather they are topics in the engaged transmission of practical information. For this reason everyday speech is not concerned with forms of representation, but only with means of *transmission*. These means, conceived both as a way to formulate verbally and stylistically another's speech and as a way to provide an interpretive frame, a tool for reconceptualization and re-accenting — from direct verbatim quotation in a verbal transmission to malicious and deliberately parodic distortion of another's word, slander — are highly varied.[1]

The following must be kept in mind: that the speech of another, once enclosed in a context, is — no matter how accurately transmitted — always subject to certain semantic changes. The context embracing another's word is responsible for its dialogizing background, whose influence can be very great. Given the appropriate methods for framing, one may bring about fundamental changes even in another's utterance accurately quoted. Any sly and ill-disposed polemicist knows very well which dialogizing backdrop he should bring to bear on the accurately quoted words of his opponent, in order to distort their sense. By manipulating the effects of context, it is very easy to emphasize the brute materiality of another's words, and to stimulate dialogic reactions associated with such "brute materiality"; thus it is, for instance, very easy to make even the most serious utterance comical. Another's discourse, when introduced into a speech context, enters the speech that frames it not in a mechanical bond but in a chemical union (on the semantic and emotionally expressive level); the degree of dialogized influence, one on the other, can be enormous. For this reason we cannot, when studying the various forms for transmitting another's speech, treat any of these forms in isolation from the means for its contextualized (dialogizing) framing — the one is indissolubly linked with the other. The formulation of another's speech as well as its framing (and the context can begin preparing for the introduction of another's speech far back in the text) both express the unitary act of dialogic interaction with that speech, a relation determining the entire nature of its transmission and all the changes in meaning and accent that take place in it during transmission.

The speaking person and his discourse in everyday speech, we have said, serves as a *subject* for the engaged, practical transmission of information, and not as a *means* of representation. As a matter of fact, all everyday forms for transmitting another's discourse, as well as the changes in discourse connected with those forms — from subtle nuances in meaning and emphasis to gross externalized distortions of the verbal composition — are defined by this practical engagement. But this emphasis on engaged discourse does not exclude certain aspects of representability. In order to assess and divine the real

[1]There are different ways to falsify someone else's words while taking them to their furthest extreme, to reveal their *potential* content. Rhetoric, the art of argument, and "heuristics" explore this area somewhat. [Bakhtin]

meaning of others' words in everyday life, the following are surely of decisive significance: *who* precisely is speaking, and under *what* concrete circumstances? When we attempt to understand and make assessments in everyday life, we do not separate discourse from the personality speaking it (as we can in the ideological realm), because the personality is so materially present to us. And the entire speaking situation is very important: who is present during it, with what expression or mimicry is it uttered, with what shades of intonation? During everyday verbal transmission of another's words, the entire complex of discourse as well as the personality of the speaker may be expressed and even played with (in the form of anything from an exact replication to a parodic ridiculing and exaggeration of gestures and intonations). This representation is always subordinated to the tasks of practical, engaged transmission and is wholly determined by these tasks. This of course does not involve the artistic image of a speaking person and the artistic image of his discourse, and even less the image of a language. Nevertheless, everyday episodes involving the same person, when they become linked, already entail prose devices for the double-voiced and even double-languaged representation of another's words. These conversations about speaking persons and others' words in everyday life do not go beyond the boundaries of the superficial aspects of discourse, the weight it carries in a specific situation; the deeper semantic and emotionally expressive levels of discourse do not enter the game. The topic of a speaking person takes on quite another significance in the ordinary ideological workings of our consciousness, in the process of assimilating our consciousness to the ideological world. The ideological becoming of a human being, in this view, is the process of selectively assimilating the words of others.

When verbal disciplines are taught in school, two basic modes are recognized for the appropriation and transmission — simultaneously — of another's words (a text, a rule, a model): "reciting by heart" and "retelling in one's own words." The latter mode poses on a small scale the task implicit in all prose stylistics: retelling a text in one's own words is to a certain extent a double-voiced narration of another's words, for indeed

"one's own words" must not completely dilute the quality that makes another's words unique; a retelling in one's own words should have a mixed character, able when necessary to reproduce the style and expressions of the transmitted text. It is this second mode used in schools for transmitting another's discourse, "retelling in one's own words," that includes within it an entire series of forms for the appropriation while transmitting of another's words, depending upon the character of the text being appropriated and the pedagogical environment in which it is understood and evaluated.

The tendency to assimilate others' discourse takes on an even deeper and more basic significance in an individual's ideological becoming, in the most fundamental sense. Another's discourse performs here no longer as information, directions, rules, models and so forth — but strives rather to determine the very bases of our ideological interrelations with the world, the very basis of our behavior; it performs here as *authoritative discourse*, and as *internally persuasive discourse*.

Both the authority of discourse and its internal persuasiveness may be united in a single word — one that is *simultaneously* authoritative and internally persuasive — despite the profound differences between these two categories of alien discourse. But such unity is rarely a given — it happens more frequently that an individual's becoming, an ideological process, is characterized precisely by a sharp gap between these two categories: in one, the authoritative word (religious, political, moral; the word of a father, of adults and of teachers, etc.) that does not know internal persuasiveness; in the other the internally persuasive word that is denied all privilege, backed up by no authority at all, and is frequently not even acknowledged in society (not by public opinion, nor by scholarly norms, nor even in the legal code). The struggle and dialogic interrelationship of these categories of ideological discourse are what usually determine the history of an individual ideological consciousness.

The authoritative word demands that we acknowledge it, that we make it our own; it binds us, quite independent of any power it might have to persuade us internally; we encounter it with its authority already fused to it. The authoritative word is located in a distanced zone, organically connected with a past that is felt to be hierarchically higher. It is, so to speak, the word of the fathers. Its authority was already *acknowledged* in the past. It is a *prior* discourse. It is therefore not a question of choosing it from among other possible discourses that are its equal. It is given (it sounds) in lofty spheres, not those of familiar contact. Its language is a special (as it were, hieratic) language. It can be profaned. It is akin to taboo, i.e., a name that must not be taken in vain.

We cannot embark here on a survey of the many and varied types of authoritative discourse (for example, the authority of religious dogma, or of acknowledged scientific truth or of a currently fashionable book), nor can we survey different degrees of authoritativeness. For our purposes only formal features for the transmission and representation of authoritative discourse are important, those common to all types and degrees of such discourse.

The degree to which a word may be conjoined with authority — whether the authority is recognized by us or not — is what determines its specific demarcation and individuation in discourse; it requires a *distance* vis-à-vis itself (this distance may be valorized as positive or as negative, just as our attitude toward it may be sympathetic or hostile). Authoritative discourse may organize around itself great masses of other types of discourses (which interpret it, praise it, apply it in various ways), but the authoritative discourse itself does not merge with these (by means of, say, gradual transitions); it remains sharply demarcated, compact and inert: it demands, so to speak, not only quotation marks but a demarcation even more magisterial, a special script, for instance.[2] It is considerably more difficult to incorporate semantic changes into such a discourse, even with the help of a framing context: its semantic structure is static and dead, for it is fully complete, it has but a single meaning, the letter is fully sufficient to the sense and calcifies it.

It is not a free appropriation and assimilation of the word itself that authoritative discourse

seeks to elicit from us; rather, it demands our unconditional allegiance. Therefore authoritative discourse permits no play with the context framing it, no play with its borders, no gradual and flexible transitions, no spontaneously creative stylizing variants on it. It enters our verbal consciousness as a compact and indivisible mass; one must either totally affirm it, or totally reject it. It is indissolubly fused with its authority — with political power, an institution, a person — and it stands and falls together with that authority. One cannot divide it up — agree with one part, accept but not completely another part, reject utterly a third part. Therefore the distance we ourselves observe vis-à-vis this authoritative discourse remains unchanged in all its projections: a playing with distances, with fusion and dissolution, with approach and retreat, is not here possible.

All these functions determine the uniqueness of authoritative discourse, both as a concrete means for formulating itself during transmission and as its distinctive means for being framed by contexts. The zone of the framing context must likewise be distanced — no familiar contact is possible here either. The one perceiving and understanding this discourse is a distant descendent; there can be no arguing with him.

These factors also determine the potential role of authoritative discourse in prose. Authoritative discourse can not be represented — it is only transmitted. Its inertia, its semantic finiteness and calcification, the degree to which it is hard-edged, a thing in its own right, the impermissibility of any free stylistic development in relation to it — all this renders the artistic representation of authoritative discourse impossible. Its role in the novel is insignificant. It is by its very nature incapable of being double-voiced; it cannot enter into hybrid constructions. If completely deprived of its authority it becomes simply an object, a *relic,* or *thing.* It enters the artistic context as an alien body, there is no space around it to play in, no contradictory emotions — it is not surrounded by an agitated and cacophonous dialogic life, and the context around it dies, words dry up. For this reason images of official-authoritative truth, images of virtue (of any sort: monastic, spiritual, bureaucratic, moral, etc.) have never been successful in the novel. It suffices to mention the hopeless attempts of Gogol

[2]Often the authoritative word is in fact a word spoken by another in a foreign language (cf. for example the phenomenon of foreign-language religious texts in most cultures). [Bakhtin]

and Dostoevsky in this regard.[3] For this reason the authoritative text always remains, in the novel, a dead quotation, something that falls out of the artistic context (for example, the evangelical texts in Tolstoy at the end of *Resurrection*).[4]

Authoritative discourses may embody various contents: authority as such, or the authoritative-ness of tradition, of generally acknowledged truths, of the official line and other similar author-ities. These discourses may have a variety of zones (determined by the degree to which they are distanced from the zone of contact) with a variety of relations to the presumed listener or interpreter (the apperceptive background presumed by the discourse, the degree of reciprocation between the two and so forth).

In the history of literary language, there is a struggle constantly being waged to overcome the official line with its tendency to distance itself from the zone of contact, a struggle against vari-ous kinds and degrees of authority. In this process discourse gets drawn into the contact zone, which results in semantic and emotionally expressive (intonational) changes: there is a weakening and degradation of the capacity to generate meta-phors, and discourse becomes more reified, more concrete, more filled with everyday elements and so forth. All of this has been studied by psychology, but not from the point of view of its verbal formulation in possible inner monologues of developing human beings, the monologue that lasts a whole life. What confronts us is the complex problem presented by forms capable of expressing such a (dialogized) monologue.

When someone else's ideological discourse is internally persuasive for us and acknowledged by us, entirely different possibilities open up. Such internally persuasive discourse is of decisive significance in the evolu-tion of an individual consciousness: consciousness awakens to independent ideological life pre-cisely in a world of alien discourses surrounding

it, and from which it cannot initially separate itself; the process of distinguishing between one's own and another's discourse, between one's own and another's thought, is activated rather late in development. When thought begins to work in an independent, experimenting and discriminating way, what first occurs is a separation between internally persuasive discourse and authoritar-ian enforced discourse, along with a rejection of those congeries of discourses that do not matter to us, that do not touch us.

Internally persuasive discourse — as opposed to one that is externally authoritative — is, as it is affirmed through assimilation, tightly interwoven with "one's own word."[5] In the everyday rounds of our consciousness, the internally persuasive word is half ours and half someone else's. Its creativity and productiveness consist precisely in the fact that such a word awakens new and independent words, that it organizes masses of our words from within, and that it does not remain in an isolated and static condition. It is not so much interpreted by us as it is further, that is, freely, developed, applied to new mate-rial, new conditions; it enters into interanimating relationships with new contexts. More than that, it enters into an intense interaction, a *struggle* with other internally persuasive discourses. Our ideological development is just such an intense struggle within us for hegemony among various available verbal and ideological points of view, approaches, directions and values. The semantic structure of an internally persuasive discourse is *not finite*, it is *open*; in each of the new contexts that dialogize it, this discourse is able to reveal ever newer ways to mean.

The internally persuasive word is either a contemporary word, born in a zone of contact with unresolved contemporaneity, or else it is a word that has been reclaimed for contemporane-ity; such a word relates to its descendents as well as to its contemporaries as if *both* were contem-porary; what is constitutive for it is a special conception of listeners, readers, perceivers. Every

---

[3] Bakhtin refers to Gogol's and Dostoevsky's failed attempts to represent the ideal of holiness they believed in — such as Father Zossima in the latter's *Brothers Karamazov*.

[4] When analyzing a concrete example of authoritative discourse in a novel, it is necessary to keep in mind the fact that purely authoritative discourse may, in another epoch, be internally persuasive; this is especially true where ethics are concerned. [Bakhtin]

[5] One's own discourse is gradually and slowly wrought out of others' words that have been acknowledged and assimi-lated, and the boundaries between the two are at first scarcely perceptible. [Bakhtin]

discourse presupposes a special conception of the listener, of his apperceptive background and the degree of his responsiveness; it presupposes a specific distance. All this is very important for coming to grips with the historical life of discourse. Ignoring such aspects and nuances leads to a reification of the word (and to a muffling of the dialogism native to it).

All of the above determine the methods for formulating internally persuasive discourse during its transmission, as well as methods for framing it in contexts. Such methods provide maximal interaction between another's word and its context, for the dialogizing influence they have on each other, for the free and creative development of another's word, for a gradation of transitions. They serve to govern the play of boundaries, the distance between that point where the context begins to prepare for the introduction of another's word and the point where the word is actually introduced (its "theme" may sound in the text long before the appearance of the actual word). These methods account for other peculiarities as well, which also express the essence of the internally persuasive word, such as that word's semantic openness to us, its capacity for further creative life in the context of our ideological consciousness, its unfinishedness and the inexhaustibility of our further dialogic interaction with it. We have not yet learned from it all it might tell us; we can take it into new contexts, attach it to new material, put it in a new situation in order to wrest new answers from it, new insights into its meaning, and even wrest from it new words, of its *own* (since another's discourse, if productive, gives birth to a new word from us in response).

The means for formulating and framing internally persuasive discourse may be supple and dynamic to such an extent that this discourse may literally be *omnipresent* in the context, imparting to everything its own specific tones and from time to time breaking through to become a completely materialized thing, as another's word fully set off and demarcated (as happens in character zones). Such variants on the theme of another's discourse are widespread in all areas of creative ideological activity, and even in the narrowly scientific disciplines. Of such a sort is any gifted, creative exposition defining alien world views: such an exposition is always a free stylistic variation on another's discourse; it expounds another's thought in the style of that thought even while applying it to new material, to another way of posing the problem; it conducts experiments and gets solutions in the language of another's discourse.

In other less obvious instances we notice analogous phenomena. We have in mind first of all those instances of powerful influence exercised by another's discourse on a given author. When such influences are laid bare, the half-concealed life lived by another's discourse is revealed within the new context of the given author. When such an influence is deep and productive, there is no external imitation, no simple act of reproduction, but rather a further creative development of another's (more precisely, half-other) discourse in a new context and under new conditions.

In all these instances the important thing is not only forms for transmitting another's discourse, but the fact that in such forms there can always be found the embryonic beginnings of what is required for an artistic representation of another's discourse. A few changes in orientation and the internally persuasive word easily becomes an object of representation. For certain kinds of internally persuasive discourse can be fundamentally and organically fused with the image of a speaking person: ethical (discourse fused with the image of, let us say, a preacher), philosophical (discourse fused with the image of a wise man), sociopolitical (discourse fused with an image of a Leader). While creatively stylizing upon and experimenting with another's discourse, we attempt to guess, to imagine, how a person with authority might conduct himself in the given circumstances, the light he would cast on them with his discourse. In such experimental guesswork the image of the speaking person and his discourse become the object of creative, artistic imagination.[6]

This process — experimenting by turning persuasive discourse into speaking persons — becomes especially important in those cases where a struggle against such images has already begun, where someone is striving to liberate

[6]In Plato, Socrates serves as just such an artistic image of the wise man and teacher, an image employed for the purposes of experiment. [Bakhtin]

himself from the influence of such an image and its discourse by means of objectification, or is striving to expose the limitations of both image and discourse. The importance of struggling with another's discourse, its influence in the history of an individual's coming to ideological consciousness, is enormous. One's own discourse and one's own voice, although born of another or dynamically stimulated by another, will sooner or later begin to liberate themselves from the authority of the other's discourse. This process is made more complex by the fact that a variety of alien voices enter into the struggle for influence within an individual's consciousness (just as they struggle with one another in surrounding social reality). All this creates fertile soil for experimentally objectifying another's discourse. A conversation with an internally persuasive word that one has begun to resist may continue, but it takes on another character: it is questioned, it is put in a new situation in order to expose its weak sides, to get a feel for its boundaries, to experience it physically as an object. For this reason stylizing discourse by attributing it to a person often becomes parodic, although not crudely parodic — since another's word, having been at an earlier stage internally persuasive, mounts a resistance to this process and frequently begins to sound with no parodic overtones at all. Novelistic images, profoundly double-voiced and double-languaged, are born in such a soil, seek to objectivize the struggle with all types of internally persuasive alien discourse that had at one time held sway over the author (of such a type, for instance, is Pushkin's Onegin or Lermontov's Pechorin).[7] At the heart of the Prüfungsroman[8] is the same kind of subjective struggle with internally persuasive, alien discourse, and just such a liberation from this discourse by turning it into an object. Another illustration of what we mean here is provided by the Bildungsroman,[9] but in such novels the maturation — a selecting, ideological process — is developed as a theme within the novel, whereas in

[7] The antiheroes, respectively, of Eugene Onegin and A Hero for Our Time.
[8] Novel of testing.
[9] Novel of education.

the Prüfungsroman the subjectivity of the author himself remains outside the work.

The works of Dostoevsky, in such a view, can be seen to occupy an extraordinary and unique place. The acute and intense interaction of another's word is present in his novels in two ways. In the first place in his characters' language there is a profound and unresolved conflict with another's word on the level of lived experience ("another's word about me"), on the level of ethical life (another's judgment, recognition or non-recognition by another) and finally on the level of ideology (the world views of characters understood as unresolved and unresolvable dialogue). What Dostoevsky's characters say constitutes an arena of never-ending struggle with others' words, in all realms of life and creative ideological activity. For this reason these utterances may serve as excellent models of the most varied forms for transmitting and framing another's discourse. In the second place, the works (the novels) in their entirety, taken as utterances of their author, are the same never-ending, internally unresolved dialogues among characters (seen as embodied points of view) and between the author himself and his characters; the characters' discourse is never entirely subsumed and remains free and open (as does the discourse of the author himself). In Dostoevsky's novels, the life experience of the characters and their discourse may be resolved as far as plot is concerned, but internally they remain incomplete and unresolved.[10]

The enormous significance of the motif of the speaking person is obvious in the realm of ethical and legal thought and discourse. The speaking person and his discourse is, in these areas, the major topic of thought and speech. All fundamental categories of ethical and legal inquiry and evaluation refer to speaking persons precisely as such: conscience (the "voice of conscience," the "inner word"), repentance (a free admission, a statement of wrongdoing by the person himself), truth and falsehood, being liable and not liable, the right to vote [pravo golosa] and so on. An independent,

[10] Cf. our book Problems of Dostoevsky's Art [Problemy tvorčestva Dostoevskogo], Leningrad, 1929 (in its second and third editions, Problems of Dostoevsky's Poetics [Problemy poetiki Dostoevskogo], Moscow, 1963, Moscow, 1972). This book contains stylistic analyses of characters' utterances, revealing various forms of transmission and contextual framing. [Bakhtin]

responsible and active discourse is *the* fundamental indicator of an ethical, legal and political human being. Challenges to this discourse, provocations of it, interpretations and assessments of it, the establishing of boundaries and forms for its activity (civil and political rights), the juxtaposing of various wills and discourses and so on — all these acts carry enormous weight in the realms of ethics and the law. It is enough to point out the role played in narrowly judicial spheres by formulation, analysis and interpretation of testimony, declarations, contracts, various documents and other forms of others' utterances; finally, of course, there is legal hermeneutics.

All this calls for further study. Juridical (and ethical) techniques have been developed for dealing with the discourse of another [after it has been uttered], for establishing authenticity, for determining degrees of veracity and so forth (for example, the process of notarizing and other such techniques). But problems connected with the methods used for formulating such kinds of discourse — compositional, stylistic, semantic and other — have not as yet been properly posed.

The problem of *confession* in cases being investigated for trial (what has made it necessary and what provokes it) has so far been interpreted only at the level of laws, ethics and psychology. Dostoevsky provides a rich body of material for posing this language (of discourse): the problem of a thought, a desire, a motivation that is authentic — as in the case of Ivan Karamazov, for instance — and how these problems are exposed in words; the role of the other in formulating discourse, problems surrounding an inquest and so forth.

The speaking person and his discourse, as subject of thought and speech, is of course treated in the ethical and legal realms only insofar as it contributes to the specific interests of these disciplines. All methods for transmitting, formulating and framing another's discourse are made subordinate to such special interests and orientations. However, even there elements of an artistic representation of another's word are possible, especially in the ethical realm: for example, a representation of the struggle waged by the voice of conscience with other voices that sound in a man, the internal dialogism leading to repentance and so forth. Artistic prose, the novelistic element present in ethical tracts, especially in confessions, may be quite significant — for example, in Epictetus, Marcus Aurelius, Augustine and Petrarch we can detect the embryonic beginnings of the *Prüfungs-* and *Bildungsroman.*

Our motif carries even greater weight in the realm of religious thought and discourse (mythological, mystical and magical). The primary subject of this discourse is a being who speaks: a deity, a demon, a soothsayer, a prophet. Mythological thought does not, in general, acknowledge anything not alive or not responsive. Divining the will of a deity, of a demon (good or bad), interpreting signs of wrath or beneficence, tokens, indications and finally the transmission and interpretation of words directly spoken by a deity (revelation), or by his prophets, saints, soothsayers — all in all, the transmission and interpretation of the divinely inspired (as opposed to the profane) word are acts of religious thought and discourse having the greatest importance. All religious systems, even primitive ones, possess an enormous, highly specialized methodological apparatus (hermeneutics) for transmitting and interpreting various kinds of holy word.

The situation is somewhat different in the case of scientific thought. Here, the significance of discourse as such is comparatively weak. Mathematical and natural sciences do not acknowledge discourse as a subject in its own right. In scientific activity one must, of course, deal with another's discourse — the words of predecessors, the judgments of critics, majority opinion and so forth; one must deal with various forms for transmitting and interpreting another's word — struggle with an authoritative discourse, overcoming influences, polemics, references, quotations and so forth — but all this remains a mere operational necessity and does not affect the subject matter itself of the science, into whose composition the speaker and his discourse do not, of course, enter. The entire methodological apparatus of the mathematical and natural sciences is directed toward mastery over *mute objects, brute things,* that do not reveal themselves in words, that do not *comment on themselves.* Acquiring knowledge here is not connected with receiving and interpreting words or signs from the object itself under consideration.

In the humanities — as distinct from the natural and mathematical sciences — there arises the specific task of establishing, transmitting and interpreting the words of others (for example, the problem of sources in the methodology of the historical disciplines). And of course in the philological disciplines, the speaking person and his discourse is the fundamental object of investigation.

Philology has specific aims and approaches to its subject (the speaker and his discourse) that determine the ways it transmits and represents others' words (for example, discourse as an object of study in the history of language). However, within the limits of the humanities (and even of philology in the narrow sense) there is possible a twofold approach to another's word when it is treated as something we seek to understand.

The word can be perceived purely as an object (something that is, in its essence, a thing). It is perceived as such in the majority of the linguistic disciplines. In such a word-object even meaning becomes a thing: there can be no dialogic approach to such a word of the kind immanent to any deep and actual understanding. Understanding, so conceived, is inevitably abstract: it is completely separated from the living, ideological power of the word to mean — from its truth or falsity, its significance or insignificance, beauty or ugliness. Such a reified word-thing cannot be understood by attempts to penetrate its meaning dialogically; there can be no conversing with such a word.

In philology, however, a dialogic penetration into the word is obligatory (for indeed without it no sort of understanding is possible): dialogizing it opens up fresh aspects in the word (semantic aspects, in the broadest sense), which, since they were revealed by dialogic means, become more immediate to perception. Every step forward in our knowledge of the word is preceded by a "stage of genius" — *a sharpened dialogic relationship to the word* — that in turn uncovers fresh aspects within the word.

Precisely such an approach is needed, more concrete and that does not deflect discourse from its actual power to mean in real ideological life, an approach where objectivity of understanding is linked with dialogic vigor and a deeper penetration into discourse itself. No other approach is in fact possible in the area of poetics, or the history of literature (and in the history of ideologies in general) or to a considerable extent even in the philosophy of discourse: even the driest and flattest positivism in these disciplines cannot treat the word neutrally, as if it were a thing, but is obliged to initiate talk not only about words but in words, in order to penetrate their ideological meanings — which can only be grasped dialogically, and which include evaluation and response. The forms in which a dialogic understanding is transmitted and interpreted may, if the understanding is deep and vigorous, even come to have significant parallels with the double-voiced representations of another's discourse that we find in prose art. It should be noted that the novel always includes in itself the activity of coming to know another's word, a coming to knowledge whose process is represented in the novel.

Finally, a few words about the importance of our theme in the rhetorical genres. The speaker and his discourse is, indisputably, one of the most important subjects of rhetorical speech (and all other themes are inevitably implicated in the topic of discourse). In the rhetoric of the courts, for example, rhetorical discourse accuses or defends the subject of a trial, who is, of course, a speaker, and in so doing relies on his words, interprets them, polemicizes with them, creatively erecting *potential* discourses for the accused or for the defense (just such free creation or for the defense, but never actually uttered words, sometimes whole speeches — "as he must have said" or "as he might have said" — was a device very widespread in ancient rhetoric); rhetorical discourse tries to outwit possible retorts to itself, it passes on and compiles the words of witnesses and so forth. In political rhetoric, for example, discourse can support some candidacy, represent the personality of a candidate, present and defend his point of view, his verbal statements, or in other cases protest against some decree, law, order, announcement, occasion — that is, protest against the specific verbal utterances toward which it is dialogically aimed.

Publicistic discourse also deals with the word itself and with the individual as its agent: it criticizes a speech, an article, a point of view; it polemicizes, exposes, ridicules and so forth. When it analyzes an act it uncovers its verbal motifs, the point of view in which it is grounded, it formulates such acts in words, providing them the appropriate emphases — ironic, indignant and so on. This does not mean, of course, that the rhetoric behind the word forgets that there are deeds, acts, a reality outside words. But such rhetoric has always to do with social man, whose most fundamental gestures are made meaningful ideologically through the word, or directly embodied in words.

The importance of another's speech as a subject in rhetoric is so great that the word frequently begins to cover over and substitute itself for reality; when this happens the word itself is diminished and becomes shallow. Rhetoric is often limited to purely verbal victories over the word; when this happens, rhetoric degenerates into a formalistic verbal play. But, we repeat, when discourse is torn from reality, it is fatal for the word itself as well: words grow sickly, lose semantic depth and flexibility, the capacity to expand and renew their meanings in new living contexts — they essentially die as discourse, for the signifying word lives beyond itself, that is, it lives by means of directing its purposiveness outward. The exclusive concentration on another's discourse as a subject does not, however, *in itself* inevitably indicate such a rupture between discourse and reality.

Rhetorical genres possess the most varied forms for transmitting another's speech, and for the most part these are intensely dialogized forms. Rhetoric relies heavily on the vivid reaccentuating of the words it transmits (often to the point of distorting them completely) that is accomplished by the appropriate framing context. Rhetorical genres provide rich material for studying a variety of forms for transmitting another's speech, the most varied means for formulating and framing such speech. Using rhetoric, even a representation of a speaker and his discourse of the sort one finds in prose art is possible — but the rhetorical double-voicedness of such images is usually not very deep: its roots do not extend to the dialogical essence of evolving language itself; it is not structured on authentic heteroglossia but on a mere diversity of voices; in most cases the double-voicedness of rhetoric is abstract and thus lends itself to formal, purely logical analysis of the ideas that are parceled out in voices, an analysis that then exhausts it. For this

reason it is proper to speak of a distinctive *rhetorical* double-voicedness, or, put another way, to speak of the double-voiced rhetorical transmission of another's word (although it may involve some artistic aspects), in contrast to the double-voiced *representation* of another's word in the novel with its orientation toward the *image of a language.*

Such, then, is the importance of the speaker and his discourse as a topic in all areas of everyday, as well as verbal-ideological, life. It might be said, on the basis of our argument so far, that in the makeup of almost every utterance spoken by a social person — from a brief response in a casual dialogue to major verbal-ideological works (literary, scholarly and others) — a significant number of words can be identified that are implicitly or explicitly admitted as someone else's, and that are transmitted by a variety of different means. Within the arena of almost every utterance an intense interaction and struggle between one's own and another's word is being waged, a process in which they oppose or dialogically interanimate each other. The utterance so conceived is a considerably more complex and dynamic organism than it appears when construed simply as a thing that articulates the intention of the person uttering it, which is to see the utterance as a direct, single-voiced vehicle for expression.

That one of the main subjects of human speech is discourse itself has not up to now been sufficiently taken into consideration, nor has its crucial importance been appreciated. There has been no comprehensive philosophical grasp of all the ramifications of this fact. The specific nature of discourse as a topic of speech, one that requires the transmission and reprocessing of another's word, has not been understood: one may speak of another's discourse only with the help of that alien discourse itself, although in the process, it is true, the speaker introduces into the other's words his own intentions and highlights the context of those words in his own way. To speak of discourse as one might speak of any other subject, that is, thematically, without any dialogized transmission of it, is possible only when such discourse is utterly reified, a thing; it is possible, for example, to talk about the word in such a way in grammar, where it is precisely the dead, thing-like shell of the word that interests us.

Heteroglossia in the Novel
from Discourse in the Novel

The compositional forms for appropriating and organizing heteroglossia in the novel, worked out during the long course of the genre's historical development, are extremely heterogeneous in their variety of generic types. Each such compositional form is connected with particular stylistic possibilities, and demands particular artistic treatment of the heteroglot "languages" introduced into it. We will pause here only on the most basic forms that are typical for the majority of novel types.

The so-called comic novel makes available a form for appropriating and organizing heteroglossia that is both externally very vivid and at the same time historically profound: its classic representatives in England were Fielding, Smollett, Sterne, Dickens, Thackeray and others, and in Germany Hippel and Jean Paul.

In the English comic novel we find a comic-parodic re-processing of almost all the levels of literary language, both conversational and written that were current at the time. Almost every novel we mentioned above as being a classic representative of this generic type is an encyclopedia of all strata and forms of literary language: depending on the subject being represented, the storyline parodically reproduces first the forms of parliamentary eloquence, then the eloquence of the court, or particular forms of parliamentary protocol, or court protocol, or forms used by reporters in newspaper articles, or the dry business language of the City, or the dealings of speculators, or the pedantic speech of scholars, or the high epic style, or the style of the hypocritical moral sermon or finally the way one or another concrete and socially determined personality, the subject of the story, happens to speak.

This usually parodic stylization of generic, professional and other strata of language is sometimes interrupted by the direct authorial word (usually as an expression of pathos, of Sentimental or idyllic sensibility), which directly embodies (without any refracting) semantic and axiological intentions of the author. But the primary source of language

usage in the comic novel is a highly specific treatment of "common language." This "common language" — usually the average norm of spoken and written language for a given social group — is taken by the author precisely as the *common view*, as the verbal approach to people and things normal for a given sphere of society, as the *going point of view* and the *going value*. To one degree or another, the author distances himself from this common language, he steps back and objectifies it, forcing his own intentions to refract and diffuse themselves through the medium of this common view that has become embodied in language (a view that is always superficial and frequently hypocritical).

The relationship of the author to a language conceived as the common view is not static — it is always found in a state of movement and oscillation that is more or less alive (this sometimes is a rhythmic oscillation): the author exaggerates, now strongly, now weakly, one or another aspect of the "common language," sometimes abruptly exposing its inadequacy to its object and sometimes, on the contrary, becoming one with it, maintaining an almost imperceptible distance, sometimes even directly forcing it to reverberate with his own "truth," which occurs when the author completely merges his own voice with the common view. As a consequence of such a merger, the aspects of common language, which in the given situation had been parodically exaggerated or had been treated as mere things, undergo change. The comic style demands of the author a lively to-and-fro movement in his relation to language, it demands a continual shifting of the distance between author and language, so that first some, then other aspects of language are thrown into relief. If such were not the case the style would be monotonous or would require a greater individualization of the narrator — would, in any case, require a quite different means for introducing and organizing heteroglossia.

Against this same backdrop of the "common language," of the impersonal, going opinion, one can also isolate in the comic novel those parodic stylizations of generic, professional and other languages we have mentioned, as well as compact masses of direct authorial discourse — pathos-filled, moral-didactic, sentimental-elegiac or idyllic. In the comic novel the direct authorial word is thus realized in direct, unqualified stylizations of poetic genres (idyllic, elegiac, etc.) or stylizations of rhetorical genres (the pathetic, the moral didactic). Shifts from common language to parodying of generic and other languages and shifts to the direct authorial word may be gradual, or may be on the contrary quite abrupt. Thus does the system of language work in the comic novel.

We will pause for analysis on several examples from Dickens, from his novel *Little Dorrit*.

> (1) The conference was held at four or five o'clock in the afternoon, when all the region of Harley Street, Cavendish Square, was resonant of carriage-wheels and double-knocks. It had reached this point when Mr. Merdle came home *from his daily occupation of causing the British name to be more and more respected in all parts of the civilized globe capable of appreciation of wholewide commercial enterprise and gigantic combinations of skill and capital.* For, though nobody knew with the least precision what Mr. Merdle's business was, except that it was to coin money, these were the terms in which everybody defined it on all ceremonious occasions, and which it was the last new polite reading of the parable of the camel and the needle's eye to accept without inquiry. [book 1, ch. 33]

The italicized portion represents a parodic stylization of the language of ceremonial speeches (in parliaments and at banquets). The shift into this style is prepared for by the sentence's construction, which from the very beginning is kept within bounds by a somewhat ceremonious epic tone. Further on — and already in the language of the author (and consequently in a different style) — the parodic meaning of the ceremoniousness of Merdle's labors becomes apparent: such a characterization turns out to be "another's speech," to be taken only in quotation marks ("these were the terms in which everybody defined it on all ceremonious occasions").

Thus the speech of another is introduced into the author's discourse (the story) in *concealed form*, that is, without any of the formal markers usually accompanying such speech, whether direct or indirect. But this is not just another's speech in the same "language" — it is another's utterance in a language that is itself "other" to the author as well, in the archaicized language of oratorical genres associated with hypocritical official celebrations.

> (2) In a day or two it was announced to all the town, that Edmund Sparkler, Esquire, son-in-law of the eminent Mr. Merdle of worldwide renown, was made one of the Lords of the Circumlocution Office; and proclamation was issued, to all true believers, that this admirable *appointment was to be hailed as a graceful and gracious mark of homage, rendered by the graceful and gracious Decimus, to that commercial interest which must ever in a great commercial country — and all the rest of it, with blast of trumpet.* So, bolstered by this mark of Government homage, the *wonderful* Bank and all the other *wonderful* undertakings went on and went up; and gapers came to Harley Street, Cavendish Square, only to look at the house where the golden wonder lived. [book 2, ch. 12]

Here, in the italicized portion, another's speech in another's (official-ceremonial) language is openly introduced as indirect discourse. But it is surrounded by the hidden, diffused speech of another (in the same official-ceremonial language) that clears the way for the introduction of a form more easily perceived *as* another's speech and that can reverberate more fully as such. The clearing of the way comes with the word "Esquire," characteristic of official speech, added to Sparkler's name; the final confirmation that this is another's speech comes with the epithet "wonderful." This epithet does not of course belong to the author but to that same "general opinion" that had created the commotion around Merdle's inflated enterprises.

> (3) It was a dinner to provoke an appetite, though he had not had one. The rarest dishes, sumptuously cooked and sumptuously served; the choicest fruits, the most exquisite wines; marvels of workmanship in gold and silver, china and glass; innumerable things delicious to the senses of taste, smell, and sight, were insinuated into its composition. *O, what a wonderful man this Merdle, what a great man, what a master man, how blessedly and*

enviably endowed — in one word, what a rich man! [book 2, ch. 12]

The beginning is a parodic stylization of high epic style. What follows is an enthusiastic glorification of Merdle, a chorus of his admirers in the form of the concealed speech of another (the italicized portion). The whole point here is to expose the real basis for such glorification, which is to unmask the chorus' hypocrisy: "wonderful," "great," "master," "endowed," "rich," can all be replaced by the single word "rich." This act of authorial unmasking, which is openly accomplished within the boundaries of a single simple sentence, merges with the unmasking of another's speech. The ceremonial emphasis on glorification is complicated by a second emphasis that is indignant, ironic, and this is the one that ultimately predominates in the final unmasking words of the sentence.

We have before us a typical double-accented, double-styled hybrid construction.

What we are calling a hybrid construction is an utterance that belongs, by its grammatical (syntactic) and compositional markers, to a single speaker, but that actually contains mixed within it two utterances, two speech manners, two styles, two "languages," two semantic and axiological belief systems. We repeat, there is no formal — compositional and syntactic — boundary between these utterances, styles, languages, belief systems; the division of voices and languages takes place within the limits of a single syntactic whole, often within the limits of a simple sentence. It frequently happens that even one and the same word will belong simultaneously to two languages, two belief systems that intersect in a hybrid construction — and, consequently, the word has two contradictory meanings, two accents (examples below). As we shall see, hybrid constructions are of enormous significance in novel style.[1]

(4) But Mr. Tite Barnacle was a buttoned-up man, and consequently a weighty one. [book 2, ch. 12]

The above sentence is an example of *pseudo-objective motivation*, one of the forms for concealing another's speech — in this example, the speech

of "current opinion." If judged by the formal markers above, the logic motivating the sentence seems to belong to the author, i.e., he is formally at one with it; but in actual fact, the motivation lies within the subjective belief system of his characters, or of general opinion.

Pseudo-objective motivation is generally characteristic of novel style,[2] since it is one of the manifold forms for concealing another's speech in hybrid constructions. Subordinate conjunctions and link words ("thus," "because," "for the reason that," "in spite of," and so forth), as well as words used to maintain a logical sequence ("therefore," "consequently," etc.) lose their authorial intention, take on the flavor of someone else's language, become refracted or even completely reified.

Such motivation is especially characteristic of comic style, in which someone else's speech is dominant (the speech of concrete persons, or, more often, a collective voice).[3]

(5) As a vast fire will fill the air to a great distance with its roar, so the sacred flame which the mighty Barnacles had fanned caused the air to resound more and more with the name of Merdle. It was deposited on every lip, and carried into every ear. There never was, there never had been, there never again should be, such a man as Mr. Merdle. Nobody, as aforesaid, knew what he had done; but everybody knew him to be the greatest that had appeared. [book 2, ch. 13]

Here we have an epic, "Homeric" introduction (parodic, of course) into whose frame the crowd's glorification of Merdle has been inserted (concealed speech of another in another's language). We then get direct authorial discourse; however, the author gives an objective tone to this "aside" by suggesting that "everybody knew" (the italicized portion). It is as if even the author himself did not doubt the fact.

(6) That illustrious man and great national ornament, Mr. Merdle, continued his shining course. It began to be widely understood that one who had done society the admirable service of making *so much money out of it*, could not be suffered to remain a commoner. A baronetcy was spoken

---

[1]For more detail on hybrid constructions and their significance, see ch. 4 of the present essay. [Bakhtin]

[2]Such a device is unthinkable in the epic. [Bakhtin]

[3]Cf. the grotesque pseudo-objective motivations in Gogol. [Bakhtin]

of with confidence; a peerage was frequently mentioned. [book 2, ch. 24]

We have here the same fictive solidarity with the hypocritically ceremonial general opinion of Merdle. All the epithets referring to Merdle in the first sentences derive from general opinion, that is, they are the concealed speech of another. The second sentence — "it began to be widely understood," etc. — is kept within the bounds of an emphatically objective style, representing not subjective opinion but the admission of an objective and completely indisputable fact. The epithet "who had done society the admirable service" is completely at the level of common opinion, repeating its official glorification, but the subordinate clause attached to that glorification ("of making so much money out of it") are the words of the author himself (as if put in parentheses in the quotation). The main sentence then picks up again at the level of common opinion. We have here a typical hybrid construction, where the subordinate clause is in direct authorial speech and the main clause in someone else's speech. The main and subordinate clauses are constructed in different semantic and axiological conceptual systems.

The whole of this portion of the novel's action, which centers around Merdle and the persons associated with him, is depicted in the language (or more accurately, the languages) of hypocritically ceremonial common opinion about Merdle, and at the same time there is a parodic stylization of that everyday language of banal society gossip, or of the ceremonial language of official pronouncements and banquet speeches, or the high epic style or Biblical style. This atmosphere around Merdle, the common opinion about him and his enterprises, infects the positive heroes of the novel as well, in particular the sober Pancks, and forces him to invest his entire estate — his own, and Little Dorrit's — in Merdle's hollow enterprises.

(7) Physician had engaged to break the intelligence in Harley Street. Bar could not at once return to his inveiglements of the most enlightened and remarkable jury he had ever seen in that box, with whom, he could tell his learned friend, no shallow sophistry would go down, and no unhappily abused professional tact and skill prevail (this was the way he

meant to begin with them); so he said he would go too, and would loiter to and fro near the house while his friend was inside. [book 2, ch. 25, mistakenly given as ch. 15 in Russian text, Tr.]

Here we have a clear example of hybrid construction where within the frame of authorial speech (informative speech) — the beginning of a speech prepared by the lawyer has been inserted, "The Bar could not at once return to his inveiglements . . . of the jury . . . so he said he would go too. . . ." etc. — while this speech is simultaneously a fully developed epithet attached to the subject of the author's speech, that is, "jury." The word "jury" enters into the context of informative authorial speech (in the capacity of a necessary object to the word "inveiglements") as well as into the context of the parodic-stylized speech of the lawyer. The author's word "inveiglements" itself emphasizes the parodic nature of the re-processing of the lawyer's speech, the hypocritical meaning of which consists precisely in the fact that it would be impossible to inveigle such a remarkable jury.

(8) It followed that Mrs. Merdle, as a woman of fashion and good breeding *who had been sacrificed to wiles of a vulgar barbarian* (for Mr. Merdle was found out from the crown of his head to the sole of his foot, the moment he was found out in his pocket), must be actively championed by her order for her order's sake. [book 2, ch. 33]

This is an analogous hybrid construction, in which the definition provided by the general opinion of society — "a sacrifice to the wiles of a vulgar barbarian" — merges with authorial speech, exposing the hypocrisy and greed of common opinion.

So it is throughout Dickens' whole novel. His entire text is, in fact, everywhere dotted with quotation marks that serve to separate out little islands of scattered direct speech and purely authorial speech, washed by heteroglot waves from all sides. But it would have been impossible actually to insert such marks, since, as we have seen, one and the same word often figures both as the speech of the author and as the speech of another — and at the same time.

Another's speech — whether as storytelling, as mimicking, as the display of a thing in light of a particular point of view, as a speech deployed first in compact masses, then loosely scattered, a speech that is in most cases impersonal ("common opin-ion," "professional and generic languages") — is at none of these points clearly separated from autho-rial speech: the boundaries are deliberately flex-ible and ambiguous, often passing through a single syntactic whole, often through a simple sentence, and sometimes even dividing up the main parts of a sentence. This varied play with the boundaries of speech types, languages and belief systems is one most fundamental aspects of comic style.

Comic style (of the English sort) is based, therefore, on the stratification of common lan-guage and on the possibilities available for isolat-ing from these strata, to one degree or another, one's own intentions, without ever completely merging with them. *It is precisely the diversity of speech, and not the unity of a normative shared language, that is the ground of style.* It is true that such speech diversity does not exceed the bound-aries of literary language conceived as a linguistic whole (that is, language defined by abstract lin-guistic markers), does not pass into an authentic heteroglossia and is based on an abstract notion of language as unitary (that is, it does not require knowledge of various dialects or languages). However a mere concern for language is but the abstract side of the concrete and active (i.e., dialogically engaged) understanding of the living heteroglossia that has been introduced into the novel and artistically organized within it.

In Dickens' predecessors, Fielding, Smollett and Sterne, the men who founded the English comic novel, we find the same parodic stylization of various levels and genres of literary language, but the distance between these levels and genres is greater than it is in Dickens and the exaggera-tion is stronger (especially in Sterne). The parodic and objectivized incorporation into their work of various types of literary language (especially in Sterne) penetrates the deepest levels of literary and ideological thought itself, resulting in a par-ody of the logical and expressive structure of any ideological discourse as such (scholarly, moral and rhetorical, poetic) that is almost as radical as the parody we find in Rabelais.

Literary parody understood in the narrow sense plays a fundamental role in the way language is structured in Fielding, Smollett and Sterne (the Richardsonian novel is parodied by the first two,

and almost all contemporary novel-types are paro-died by Sterne. Literary parody serves to distance the author still further from language, to complicate still further his relationship to the literary language of his time, especially in the novel's own territory. The novelistic discourse dominating a given epoch is itself turned into an object and itself becomes a means for refracting new authorial intentions.

Literary parody of dominant novel-types plays a large role in the history of the European novel. One could even say that the most important nov-elistic models and novel-types arose precisely during this parodic destruction of preceding novelistic worlds. This is true of the work of Cervantes, Mendoza, Grimmelshausen, Rabelais, Lesage and many others.

In Rabelais, whose influence on all novelistic prose (and in particular the comic novel) was very great, a parodic attitude toward almost all forms of ideological discourse — philosophical, moral, scholarly, rhetorical, poetic and in particular the pathos-charged forms of discourse (in Rabelais, pathos almost always is equivalent to lie) — was intensified to the point where it became a parody of the very act of conceptualizing anything in language. We might add that Rabelais taunts the deceptive human word by a parodic destruc-tion of syntactic structures, thereby reducing to absurdity some of the logical and expressively accented aspects of words (for example, predica-tion, explanations and so forth). Turning away from language (by means of language, of course), discrediting any direct or unmediated intentional-ity and expressive excess (any "weighty" serious-ness) that might adhere in ideological discourse, presuming that all language is conventional and false, maliciously inadequate to reality — all this achieves in Rabelais almost the maximum purity possible in prose. But the truth that might oppose such falsity receives almost no direct intentional and verbal expression in Rabelais, it does not receive its own word — it reverberates only in the parodic and unmasking accents in which the lie is present. Truth is restored by reducing the lie to an absurdity, but truth itself does not seek words; she is afraid to entangle herself in the word, to soil herself in verbal pathos.

Rabelais' "philosophy of the word" — a philosophy expressed not as much in direct utterances as in stylistic practice — has had enormous influence on all consequent novel prose and in particular of the great representative forms of the comic novel; with that in mind we bring forward the purely Rabelaisian formulation of Sterne's Yorick, which might serve as an epigraph to the history of the most important stylistic lines of development in the European novel:

> For aught I know there might be some mixture of unlucky wit at the bottom of such Fracas : — For, to speak the truth, Yorick had an invincible dislike and opposition in his nature to gravity; — not to gravity as such; — for where gravity was wanted, he would be the most grave or serious of mortal men for days and weeks together; — but he was an enemy to the affectation of it, and declared open war against it, only as it appeared a cloak for ignorance, or for folly; and then, whenever it fell his way, however sheltered and protected, he seldom gave it much quarter.
>
> Sometimes, in his wild way of talking, he would say, That gravity was an errant scoundrel; and he would add, — of the most dangerous kind too, — because a sly one; and that, he verily believed, more honest, well-meaning people were bubbled out of their goods and money by it in one twelve-month, than by pocket-picking and shop-lifting in seven. In the naked temper which a merry heart discovered, he would say, There was no danger, — but to itself: — whereas the very essence of gravity was design, and consequently deceit; — 'twas a taught trick to gain credit of the world for more sense and knowledge than a man was worth; and that, with all its pretensions, — it was no better, but often worse, than what a French wit had long ago defined it, — viz. A mysterious carriage of the body to cover the defects of the mind; — which definition of gravity, Yorick, with great imprudence, would say, deserved to be wrote in letters of gold. [Bakhtin does not locate citation; it is from *Tristram Shandy*, vol. I, ch. II, Tr.]

Close to Rabelais, but in certain respects even exceeding him in the decisive influence he had on all of novelistic prose, is Cervantes. The English comic novel is permeated through and through with the spirit of Cervantes. It is no accident that this same Yorick, on his deathbed, quotes the words of Sancho Panza.

While the attitude toward language and toward its stratification (generic, professional and otherwise) among the German comic writers, in Hippel and especially in Jean Paul, is basically of the Sternean type, it is raised — as it is in Sterne himself — to the level of a purely philosophical problem, the very possibility of literary and ideological speech as such. The philosophical and ideological element in an author's attitude toward his own language forces into the background the play between intention and the concrete, primarily generic and ideological levels of literary language (cf. the reflection of just this in the aesthetic theories of Jean Paul).[4]

Thus the stratification of literary language, its speech diversity, is an indispensable prerequisite for comic style, whose elements are projected onto different linguistic planes while at the same time the intention of the author, refracted as it passes through these planes, does not wholly give itself up to any of them. It is as if the author has no language of his own, but does possess his own style, his own organic and unitary law governing the way he plays with languages and the way his own real semantic and expressive intentions are refracted within them. Of course this play with languages (and frequently the complete absence of a direct discourse of his own) in no sense degrades the general, deep-seated intentionality, the overarching ideological conceptualization of the work as a whole.

In the comic novel, the incorporation of heteroglossia and its stylistic utilization is characterized by two distinctive features:

(1) Incorporated into the novel are a multiplicity of "language" and verbal-ideological belief systems — generic, professional, class-and-interest-group (the language of the nobleman, the farmer, the merchant, the peasant); tendentious, everyday (the languages of rumor, of society chatter, servants' language) and so forth, but these languages are, it is true, kept primarily within the limits of the literary written and conversational language; at the same time these languages are not, in most cases, consolidated

---

[4]Intellect as embodied in the forms and the methods of verbal and ideological thought (i.e., the linguistic horizon of normal human intellectual activity) becomes in Jean Paul something infinitely petty and ludicrous when seen in the light of "reason." His humor results from play with intellectual activity and its forms. [Bakhtin]

into fixed persons (heroes, storytellers) but rather are incorporated in an impersonal form "from the author," alternating (while ignoring precise formal boundaries) with direct authorial discourse. (2) The incorporated languages and socio-ideological belief systems, while of course utilized to refract the author's intentions, are unmasked and destroyed as something false, hypocritical, greedy, limited, narrowly rational-istic, inadequate to reality. In most cases these languages — already fully formed, officially rec-ognized, reigning languages that are authoritative and reactionary — are (in real life) doomed to death and displacement. Therefore what pre-dominates in the novel are various forms and degrees of *parodic stylization* of incorporated languages, a stylization that, in the most radical, most Rabelaisian[5] representatives of this novel-type (Sterne and Jean Paul), verges on a rejection of any straightforward and unmediated serious-ness (true seriousness is the destruction of all false seriousness, not only in its pathos-charged expression but in its Sentimental one as well);[6] that is, it limits itself to a principled criticism of the word as such.

[5]It is of course impossible in the strict sense to include Rabelais himself — either chronologically or in terms of his essential character — among the representatives of comic novelists. [Bakhtin]

[6]Nevertheless sentimentality and "high seriousness" is not completely eliminated (especially in Jean Paul). [Bakhtin]

From *Problems in Dostoevsky's Poetics*

Table 1

I. Direct, unmediated discourse directed exclusively toward its referential object, as an expression of the speaker's ultimate semantic authority

II. Objectified discourse (discourse of a represented person)

1. With a predominance of sociotypical determining factors	} Various degrees of objectification.
2. With a predominance of individually characteristic determining factors	

III. Discourse with an orientation toward someone else's discourse (double-voiced discourse)

1. Unidirectional double-voiced discourse 　a. Stylization; 　b. Narrator's narration; 　c. Unobjectified discourse of a char-acter who carries out (in part) the author's intentions; 　d. *Ich-Erzählung*	} When objectification is reduced, these tend toward a fusion of voices, i.e., toward discourse of the first type.
2. Vari-directional double-voiced discourse 　a. Parody with all its nuances; 　b. Parodistic narration; 　c. Parodistic *Ich-Erzählung*; 　d. Discourse of a character who is parodically represented; 　e. Any transmission of someone else's words with a shift in accent.	} When objectification is reduced and the other's idea activated, these become internally dialogized and tend to disinte-grate into two discourses (two voices) of the first type.

Table I *(Contd.,)*

3. The active type (reflected discourse of another)
   a. Hidden internal polemic;
   b. Polemically colored autobiography and confession;
   c. Any discourse with a sideward glance at someone else's word;
   d. A rejoinder of a dialogue;
   e. Hidden dialogue

} The other discourse exerts influence from without; diverse forms of inter-relationship with another's discourse are possible here, as well as various degrees of deforming influence exerted by one discourse on the other.

The table above from *Problems in Dostoevsky's Poetics* is Bakhtin's classification of monological and dialogical discourses. Type I is monological discourse directed at a listener, neither expecting nor desiring any reply. At its most rigid such discourse is anonymous (like the signs telling us that smoking is not permitted or to be quiet in the library). Type II is monological discourse but the speaker is characterized in two possible ways, as a particular person, whose views may or may not be authoritative, or as some general sort of person. (Such sociotypes speak to us from advertisements, for example: speakers dressed as doctors recommending an over-the-counter drug, speakers dressed as mechanics recommending a particular motor oil.) Type III discourse is dialogical, directed at an audience and expecting an appropriate response.

The three subtypes vary according to whether the speaker's relationship to the listener is merely implicit (subtype 1), whether the speaker's discourse explicitly parodies another discourse (subtype 2), or whether the listener's anticipated response already operates within the speaker's discourse (subtype 3). Dickens, like Dostoevsky, was a skilled practitioner of subtypes 2 and 3, as is shown in the analysis of *Little Dorrit* in "Heteroglossia in the Novel" (see p. 363). Bakhtin's own note on his table emphasizes that the classification should not be viewed as rigid or static. Actual discourses often move rapidly from one class to another and back again, and may even belong simultaneously to different classes or even types.

Virginia Woolf

1882–1941

The novelist and critic Virginia Woolf, one of the founders of literary modernism in fiction, was born in London. The daughter of the Victorian intellectual Sir Leslie Stephen, Woolf educated herself thoroughly using the resources of her father's library and friends. On her father's death in 1904, she moved to Gordon Square in the Bloomsbury neighborhood that houses the University of London and the British Museum. There she and her sister Vanessa gathered round them that coterie of artists and intellectuals who have become known as the "Bloomsbury Group." In 1912 she married the journalist and editor Leonard Woolf, and together in 1917 they founded the Hogarth Press, a small press distinguished for publishing not only her own work but that of authors such as D. H. Lawrence and T. S. Eliot, in addition to the English translations of Sigmund Freud. Woolf's early *The Voyage Out* (1915) and *Night and Day* (1919) prepared the way for her more ambitious, experimental *Jacob's Room* (1922) and the novels for which she is most admired, *Mrs. Dalloway* (1925), *To the Lighthouse* (1927), and *The Waves* (1931). Her other novels include *Orlando: A Biography* (1928), *The Years* (1937), and *Between the Acts* (1941). While Woolf was completing *Between the Acts* during the darkest days of World War II, it was expected that at any moment the German Wehrmacht would invade the Sussex coast not far from her home — an event Woolf knew would create incomprehensible havoc for England, her Jewish husband, and herself. The invasion never came off, but at that time of crisis Woolf suffered a terrifying recurrence of the depression that had plagued her since childhood, and she drowned herself in the River Ouse.

While Woolf may be best known for her novels, she was also a prolific writer of critical essays, reviews, and autobiography: The complete edition of her essays would contain over one million words. Working rapidly for the journalistic deadlines of the weekly *Times Literary Supplement*, the *Nation and Athenaeum*, and T. S. Eliot's *Criterion*, Woolf took up in her writing individual authors, schools, and aspects of contemporary culture. Although her subjects were often dictated by journalistic assignment, she used them to explore her own central aesthetic beliefs about the bankruptcy of the realist literary tradition and the importance of what we today call *modernism*. This credo can be found in the two volumes of *The Common Reader* (1925 and 1932), in *The Death of the Moth* (1942), and in *Granite and Rainbow* (1958) published after her death. The selections that follow are taken from her well-known work of feminist theory, *A Room of One's Own* (1929).

Woolf takes her place in the world of literary criticism as both a modernist and a feminist, and as a feminist she is considerably more modern than her dates of birth and death might suggest. If the major feminist issues of the 1970s and 1980s were the critique of patriarchal culture and its attitudes toward women, the analysis of female creativity and the tradition of women's writing, and the analysis of *écriture féminine* (as French feminists termed the special quality of women's writing), the roots of all three can be found in Woolf's *A Room of One's Own*.

The most famous section of *A Room of One's Own* — a personal brief for women writers expanded from two lectures Woolf gave at Newnham and Girton Colleges — is that which traces the tragically wasted career of an imaginary "Shakespeare's sister," whose creativity and talent would have found no outlet in the society of the sixteenth century. This fictional history is the premise for a historical sketch of actual women writers and the difficulties they experienced in their work, from Aphra Behn, the first female dramatist to make a living by her pen, through the noble bluestockings of the eighteenth century, to the four major novelists of the nineteenth: Jane Austen, Emily and Charlotte Brontë, and George Eliot. In her manifesto, written in 1929, ten years after women received the vote and sixty-five years after the founding of the first women's college at Oxford, Woolf remains painfully conscious of the disparities that still exist between women and men. But she is convinced that the birth of a female Shakespeare, one with an "incandescent" spirit capable of unimpeded expression, is possible within the century — if the rest of her sisters work to prepare her way.

In the course of tracing the histories of women writers, Woolf touches on a great many issues taken up by later feminists. Her ironic commentary, set in the British Museum, on the way women have traditionally been defined and analyzed as inferiors by men previews the issues later raised by Simone de Beauvoir, Kate Millett, Mary Ellmann, and other images-of-women critics. Woolf's analysis of the women novelists of the nineteenth century — of how the adoption of a masculine prose by Charlotte Brontë and George Eliot hampered their expressiveness, and of how Austen succeeded in devising a feminine prose that allowed her to say what she needed to — anticipates current research on women's language and *écriture féminine*. And in her emphatic endorsement of Coleridge's claim that a great mind is androgynous, Woolf takes a stand on the most contested feminist question — whether there are distinct masculine and feminine modes of creativity — which would be attacked by critics like Showalter who are committed to the idea of a uniquely feminine poetics, and by French feminists such as Cixous (see p. 988) and Irigaray exploring a more polymorphous sexuality.

But in her feminism, Woolf is also very much the modernist, convinced that the key role of the artist is to create a world whose validity stands independent of the testimony and personal life of the artist herself. Like Eliot's catalytic creator, Woolf's must be impersonal and detached, with the ego shaping a sensibility but not expressing a personality. This vision accounts for some of Woolf's judgments on her major predecessors, the women who made the nineteenth-century novel what it was. Austen's delicacy and disinterestedness wins the highest acclaim, as does Emily Brontë's masterly creation of a transcendent Yorkshire world of pure poetic imagination. In *Jane Eyre,* however, Woolf spots the telltale signs of Charlotte Brontë's rage:

> She left her story, to which her entire devotion was due, to attend to some personal grievance. She remembered that she had been starved of her proper due of experience — she had been made to stagnate in a parsonage mending stockings when she wanted to wander free over the world. Her imagination swerved from indignation and we feel it swerve. . . . The portrait of Rochester is drawn in the dark. We feel the influence of fear in

it; just as we constantly feel an acidity which is the result of oppression, a buried suffering smouldering beneath her passion, a rancour which contracts those books, splendid as they are, with a spasm of pain.

As Woolf well understands, the root causes of Charlotte Brontë's aesthetic imperfections were social. It would take a miracle for any woman under the oppression of patriarchal society, deprived of the financial independence and quiet leisure that men often took for granted, to produce texts that transcend the creating self. Woolf closes her treatise by arguing that it will take the transformation of society, giving women the titular "room of one's own," to make a space where Shakespeare's future sisters can evolve.

Selected Bibliography

Banfield, Ann. *The Phantom Table: Woolf, Fry, Russell and the Epistemology of Modernism.* Cambridge: Cambridge University Press, 2000.

Bell, Quentin. *Virginia Woolf: A Biography.* New York: Harcourt, Brace and Jovanovich, 1972.

Black, Naomi. *Virginia Woolf as Feminist.* Ithaca: Cornell University Press, 2004.

Hanson, Clare. *Virginia Woolf.* London: Macmillan, 1994.

King, James. *Virginia Woolf.* New York: Norton, 1995.

Majumdar, Robin. *Virginia Woolf: An Annotated Bibliography of Criticism.* New York: Garland, 1976.

Marcus, Jane. *Art and Anger: Reading Like a Woman.* Columbus: Ohio State University Press, 1988.

Marder, Herbert. *Feminism and Art: A Study of Virginia Woolf.* Chicago: University of Chicago Press, 1968.

Moi, Toril. *Sexual/Textual Politics: Feminist Literary Theory.* London: Methuen, 1985.

Newman, Herta. *Virginia Woolf and Mrs. Brown: Toward a Realism of Uncertainty.* New York: Garland, 1996.

Rosenbaum, S. P. *Women and Fiction: The Manuscript Versions of A Room of One's Own.* Oxford: Blackwell, 1992.

Rosenman, Ellen Bayuk. *A Room of One's Own: Women Writers and the Politics of Creativity.* New York: Twayne, 1995.

Woolf, Virginia. *A Room of One's Own.* New York: Harcourt Brace, 1929.

———. *Three Guineas.* New York: Harcourt Brace, 1938.

———. *The Essays of Virginia Woolf,* ed. Andrew McNeillie. London: Hogarth Press, 1986.

[Shakespeare's Sister]
from *A Room of One's Own*

Let me imagine, since facts are so hard to come by, what would have happened had Shakespeare had a wonderfully gifted sister, called Judith, let us say. Shakespeare himself went, very probably — his mother was an heiress — to the grammar school, where he may have learnt Latin — Ovid, Virgil and Horace — and the elements of grammar and logic. He was, it is well known, a wild boy who poached rabbits, perhaps shot a deer, and had, rather sooner than he should have done, to marry a woman in the neighborhood, who bore him a child rather quicker than was right. That escapade sent him to seek his fortune in London. He had, it seemed, a taste for the theatre; he began by holding horses at the stage door. Very soon he got work in the theatre, became a successful actor, and lived at the hub of the universe, meeting everybody, knowing everybody, practising his art on the boards, exercising his wits in the streets, and even getting access to the palace of the queen. Meanwhile his extraordinarily gifted sister, let us suppose, remained at home. She was as adventurous, as imaginative, as agog to see the world as he was. But she was not sent to school. She had no chance of learning grammar and logic, let alone of reading Horace and Virgil. She picked up a book now and then, one of her brother's perhaps, and read a few pages. But then her parents came in and told her to mend the stockings or mind the stew and not moon about with books and papers. They would have spoken sharply but kindly, for they were substantial people who knew the conditions of life for a woman and loved their daughter — indeed, more likely than not she was the apple of her father's eye. Perhaps she scribbled some pages up in an apple loft on the sly, but was careful to hide them or set fire to them. Soon, however, before she was out of her teens, she was to be betrothed to the son of a neighboring wool-stapler. She cried out that marriage was hateful to her, and for that she was severely beaten by her father. Then he ceased to scold her. He begged her instead not to hurt him, not to shame him in this matter of her marriage. He would give her a chain of beads or a fine petticoat, he said; and there were tears in his eyes. How could she disobey him? How could she break his heart? The force of her own gift alone drove her to it. She made up a small parcel of her belongings, let herself down by a rope one summer's night and took the road to London. She was not seventeen. The birds that sang in the hedge were not more musical than she was. She had the quickest fancy, a gift like her brother's, for the tune of words. Like him, she had a taste for the theatre. She stood at the stage door; she wanted to act, she said. Men laughed in her face. The manager — a fat, loose-lipped man — guffawed. He bellowed something about poodles dancing and women acting — no woman, he said, could possibly be an actress. He hinted — you can imagine what. She could get no training in her craft. Could she even seek her dinner in a tavern or roam the streets at midnight? Yet her genius was for fiction and lusted to feed abundantly upon the lives of men and women and the study of their ways. At last — for she was very young, oddly like Shakespeare the poet in her face, with the same grey eyes and rounded brows — at last Nick Greene the actor-manager took pity on her; she found herself with child by that gentleman and so — who shall measure the heat and violence of the poet's heart when caught and tangled in a woman's body? — killed herself one winter's night and lies buried at some cross-roads where the omnibuses now stop outside the Elephant and Castle.[1]

That, more or less, is how the story would run, I think, if a woman in Shakespeare's day had had Shakespeare's genius. But for my part, I agree with the deceased bishop, if such he was — it

[1]Public square in London on the south bank of the Thames.

is unthinkable that any woman in Shakespeare's day should have had Shakespeare's genius. For genius like Shakespeare's is not born among labouring, uneducated, servile people. It was not born in England among the Saxons and the Britons. It is not born today among the work-ing classes. How, then, could it have been born among women whose work began, according to Professor Trevelyan,[2] almost before they were out of the nursery, who were forced to it by their parents and held to it by all the power of law and custom? Yet genius of a sort must have existed among women as it must have existed among the working classes. Now and again an Emily Brontë or a Robert Burns blazes out and proves its presence. But certainly it never got itself on to paper. When, however, one reads of a witch being ducked, of a woman possessed by devils, of a wise woman selling herbs, or even of a very remarkable man who had a mother, then I think we are on the track of a lost novelist, a suppressed poet, of some mute and inglorious Jane Austen, some Emily Brontë who dashed her brains out on the moor or mopped and mowed about the highways crazed with the torture that her gift had put her to. Indeed, I would venture to guess that Anon, who wrote so many poems without signing them, was often a woman. It was a woman Edward Fitzgerald, I think, suggested who made the ballads and the folk-songs, croon-ing them to her children, beguiling her spinning with them, or the length of the winter's night.

This may be true or it may be false — who can say? — but what is true in it, so it seemed to me, reviewing the story of Shakespeare's sister as I had made it, is that any woman born with a great gift in the sixteenth century would certainly have gone crazed, shot herself, or ended her days in some lonely cottage outside the village, half witch, half wizard, feared and mocked at. For it needs little skill in psychology to be sure that a highly gifted girl who had tried to use her gift for poetry would have been so thwarted and hindered by other people, so tortured and pulled asunder

by her own contrary instincts, that she must have lost her health and sanity to a certainty. No girl could have walked to London and stood at a stage door and forced her way into the presence of actor-managers without doing herself a violence and suffering an anguish which may have been irrational — for chastity may be a fetish invented by certain societies for unknown reasons — but were none the less inevitable. Chastity had then, it has even now, a religious importance in a woman's life, and has so wrapped itself round with nerves and instincts that to cut it free and bring it to the light of day demands courage of the rarest. To have lived a free life in London in the sixteenth century would have meant for a woman who was poet and playwright a nervous stress and dilemma which might well have killed her. Had she survived, whatever she had written would have been twisted and deformed, issuing from a strained and morbid imagination. And undoubtedly, I thought, looking at the shelf where there are no plays by women, her work would have gone unsigned. That refuge she would have sought certainly. It was the relic of the sense of chastity that dictated anonymity to women even so late as the nineteenth century. Currer Bell, George Eliot, George Sand, all the victims of inner strife as their writings prove, sought inef-fectively to veil themselves by using the name of a man. Thus they did homage to the conven-tion, which if not implanted by the other sex was liberally encouraged by them (the chief glory of a woman is not to be talked of, said Pericles, himself a much-talked-of man), that publicity in women is detestable. Anonymity runs in their blood. The desire to be veiled still possesses them. They are not even now as concerned about the health of their fame as men are, and, speak-ing generally, will pass a tombstone or a signpost without feeling an irresistible desire to cut their names on it, as Alf, Bert or Chas. must do in obedience to their instinct, which murmurs if it sees a fine woman go by, or even a dog, Ce chien est à moi.[3] And, of course, it may not be a dog, I thought, remembering Parliament Square, the Sieges Allee[4] and other avenues; it may be a piece

---

[2] George Macaulay Trevelyan (1876–1962), Regius pro-fessor of modern history at Cambridge, author of England in the Age of Wycliffe (1899) and British History in the Nineteenth Century (1922).

[3] The dog is mine.

[4] Broad avenue in Berlin.

of land or a man with curly black hair. It is one of the great advantages of being a woman that one can pass even a very fine negress without wishing to make an Englishwoman of her.

That woman, then, who was born with a gift of poetry in the sixteenth century, was an unhappy woman, a woman at strife against herself. All the conditions of her life, all her own instincts, were hostile to the state of mind which is needed to set free whatever is in the brain. But what is the state of mind that is most propitious to the act of creation, I asked. Can one come by any notion of the state that furthers and makes possible that strange activity? Here I opened the volume containing the Tragedies of Shakespeare. What was Shakespeare's state of mind, for instance, when he wrote *Lear* and *Antony and Cleopatra*? It was certainly the state of mind most favourable to poetry that there has ever existed. But Shakespeare himself said nothing about it. We only know casually and by chance that he "never blotted a line." Nothing indeed was ever said by the artist himself about his state of mind until the eighteenth century perhaps. Rousseau perhaps began it. At any rate, by the nineteenth century self-consciousness had developed so far that it was the habit for men of letters to describe their minds in confessions and autobiographies. Their lives also were written, and their letters were printed after their deaths. Thus, though we do not know what Shakespeare went through when he wrote *Lear,* we do know what Carlyle went through when he wrote the *French Revolution;* what Flaubert went through when he wrote *Madame Bovary;* what Keats was going through when he tried to write poetry against the coming of death and the indifference of the world.

And one gathers from this enormous modern literature of confession and self-analysis that to write a work of genius is almost always a feat of prodigious difficulty. Everything is against the likelihood that it will come from the writer's mind whole and entire. Generally material circumstances are against it. Dogs will bark; people will interrupt; money must be made; health will break down. Further, accentuating all these difficulties and making them harder to bear is the world's notorious indifference. It does not ask people to write poems and novels and histories; it does not need them. It does not care whether Flaubert finds the right word or whether Carlyle scrupulously verifies this or that fact. Naturally, it will not pay for what it does not want. And so the writer, Keats, Flaubert, Carlyle, suffers, especially in the creative years of youth, every form of distraction and discouragement. A curse, a cry of agony, rises from those books of analysis and confession. "Mighty poets in their misery dead" — that is the burden of their song. If anything comes through in spite of all this, it is a miracle, and probably no book is born entire and uncrippled as it was conceived.

But for women, I thought, looking at the empty shelves, these difficulties were infinitely more formidable. In the first place, to have a room of her own, let alone a quiet room or a sound-proof room, was out of the question, unless her parents were exceptionally rich or very noble, even up to the beginning of the nineteenth century. Since her pin money, which depended on the good will of her father, was only enough to keep her clothed, she was debarred from such alleviations as came even to Keats or Tennyson or Carlyle, all poor men, from a walking tour, a little journey to France, from the separate lodging which, even if it were miserable enough, sheltered them from the claims and tyrannies of their families. Such material difficulties were formidable; but much worse were the immaterial. The indifference of the world which Keats and Flaubert and other men of genius have found so hard to bear was in her case not indifference but hostility. The world did not say to her as it said to them, Write if you choose; it makes no difference to me. The world said with a guffaw, Write? What's the good of your writing?

[Austen–Brontë–Eliot]
from *A Room of One's Own*

Here, then, one had reached the early nineteenth century. And here, for the first time, I found several shelves given up entirely to the works of women. But why, I could not help asking, as I ran my eyes over them, were they, with very few exceptions, all novels? The original impulse was to poetry. The "supreme head of song" was a poetess. Both in France and in England the women poets precede the women novelists. Moreover, I thought, looking at the four famous names, what had George Eliot in common with Emily Brontë? Did not Charlotte Brontë fail entirely to understand Jane Austen? Save for the possibly relevant fact that not one of them had a child, four more incongruous characters could not have met together in a room — so much so that it is tempting to invent a meeting and a dialogue between them. Yet by some strange force they were all compelled, when they wrote, to write novels. Had it something to do with being born of the middle class, I asked; and with the fact, which Miss Emily Davies[1] a little later was so strikingly to demonstrate, that the middle-class family in the early nineteenth century was possessed only of a single sitting-room between them? If a woman wrote, she would have to write in the common sitting-room. And, as Miss Nightingale was so vehemently to complain, — "women never have an half hour . . . that they can call their own" — she was always interrupted. Still it would be easier to write prose and fiction there than to write poetry or a play. Less concentration is required. Jane Austen wrote like that to the end of her days. "How she was able to effect all this," her nephew writes in his *Memoir*, "is surprising, for she had no separate study to repair to, and most of the work must have been done in the general sitting-room, subject to all kinds of casual interruptions. She was careful that her occupation should not be suspected by servants or visitors or any persons beyond her own family party."[2]

Jane Austen hid her manuscripts or covered them with a piece of blotting-paper. Then, again, all the literary training that a woman had in the early nineteenth century was training in the observation of character, in the analysis of emotion. Her sensibility had been educated for centuries by the influences of the common sitting-room. People's feelings were impressed on her; personal relations were always before her eyes. Therefore, when the middle-class woman took to writing, she naturally wrote novels, even though, as seems evident enough, two of the four famous women here named were not by nature novelists. Emily Brontë should have written poetic plays; the over-flow of George Eliot's capacious mind should have spread itself when the creative impulse was spent upon history or biography. They wrote novels, however; one may even go further, I said, taking *Pride and Prejudice* from the shelf, and say that they wrote good novels. Without boasting or giving pain to the opposite sex, one may say that *Pride and Prejudice* is a good book. At any rate, one would not have been ashamed to have been caught in the act of writing *Pride and Prejudice*. Yet Jane Austen was glad that a hinge creaked, so that she might hide her manuscript before any one came in. To Jane Austen there was something discreditable in writing *Pride and Prejudice*. And, I wondered, would *Pride and Prejudice* have been a better novel if Jane Austen had not thought it necessary to hide her manuscript from visitors? I read a page or two to see; but I could not find any signs that her circumstances had harmed her work in the slightest. That, perhaps, was the chief miracle about it. Here was a woman about the year 1800 writing without hate, without bitterness, without fear, without protest, without preaching. That was how Shakespeare wrote, I thought, looking at *Antony and Cleopatra*; and

[1]Sarah Emily Davies (1830–1921), British feminist responsible for the admission of women to University College, London (1870) and the foundation of Girton College, Cambridge (1873).

[2]*Memoir of Jane Austen*, by her nephew, James Edward Austen-Leigh. [Woolf]

when people compare Shakespeare and Jane Austen, they may mean that the minds of both had consumed all impediments; and for that reason we do not know Jane Austen and we do not know Shakespeare, and for that reason Jane Austen pervades every word that she wrote, and so does Shakespeare. If Jane Austen suffered in any way from her circumstances it was in the narrowness of life that was imposed upon her. It was impossible for a woman to go about alone. She never travelled; she never drove through London in an omnibus or had luncheon in a shop by herself. But perhaps it was the nature of Jane Austen not to want what she had not. Her gift and her circumstances matched each other completely. But I doubt whether that was true of Charlotte Brontë, I said, opening *Jane Eyre* and laying it beside *Pride and Prejudice.*

I opened it at chapter twelve and my eye was caught by the phrase, "Anybody may blame me who likes." What were they blaming Charlotte Brontë for, I wondered? And I read how Jane Eyre used to go up on the roof when Mrs. Fairfax was making jellies and looked over the fields at the distant view. And then she longed — and it was for this that they blamed her — that "then I longed for a power of vision which might overpass that limit; which might reach the busy world, towns, regions full of life I had heard of but never seen: that then I desired more of practical experience than I possessed; more of intercourse with my kind, of acquaintance with variety of character than was here within my reach. I valued what was good in Mrs. Fairfax, and what was good in Adèle; but I believed in the existence of other and more vivid kinds of goodness, and what I believed in I wished to behold.

"Who blames me? Many, no doubt, and I shall be called discontented. I could not help it: the restlessness was in my nature; it agitated me to pain sometimes. . . .

"It is vain to say human beings ought to be satisfied with tranquillity: they must have action; and they will make it if they cannot find it. Millions are condemned to a stiller doom than mine, and millions are in silent revolt against their lot. Nobody knows how many rebellions ferment in the masses of life which people earth. Women are supposed to be very calm generally:

but women feel just as men feel; they need exercise for their faculties and a field for their efforts as much as their brothers do; they suffer from too rigid a restraint, too absolute a stagnation, precisely as men would suffer; and it is narrow-minded in their more privileged fellow-creatures to say that they ought to confine themselves to making puddings and knitting stockings, to playing on the piano and embroidering bags. It is thoughtless to condemn them, or laugh at them, if they seek to do more or learn more than custom has pronounced necessary for their sex.

"When thus alone I not unfrequently heard Grace Poole's laugh. . . ."

That is an awkward break, I thought. It is upsetting to come upon Grace Poole all of a sudden. The continuity is disturbed. One might say, I continued, laying the book down beside *Pride and Prejudice,* that the woman who wrote those pages had more genius in her than Jane Austen; but if one reads them over and marks that jerk in them, that indignation, one sees that she will never get her genius expressed whole and entire. Her books will be deformed and twisted. She will write in a rage where she should write calmly. She will write foolishly where she should write wisely. She will write of herself where she should write of her characters. She is at war with her lot. How could she help but die young, cramped and thwarted?

One could not but play for a moment with the thought of what might have happened if Charlotte Brontë had possessed say three hundred a year — but the foolish woman sold the copyright of her novels outright for fifteen hundred pounds; had somehow possessed more knowledge of the busy world, and towns and regions full of life; more practical experience, and intercourse with her kind and acquaintance with a variety of character. In those words she puts her finger exactly not only upon her own defects as a novelist but upon those of her sex at that time. She knew, no one better, how enormously her genius would have profited if it had not spent itself in solitary visions over distant fields; if experience and intercourse and travel had been granted her. But they were not granted; they were withheld; and we must accept the fact that all those good novels, *Villette, Emma, Wuthering*

Heights, *Middlemarch*, were written by women without more experience of life than could enter the house of a respectable clergyman; written too in the common sitting-room of that respectable house and by women so poor that they could not afford to buy more than a few quires of paper at a time upon which to write *Wuthering Heights* or *Jane Eyre*. One of them, it is true, George Eliot, escaped after much tribulation, but only to a secluded villa in St. John's Wood. And there she settled down in the shadow of the world's disapproval. "I wish it to be understood," she wrote, "that I should never invite any one to come and see me who did not ask for the invitation"; for was she not living in sin with a married man and might not the sight of her damage the chastity of Mrs. Smith or whoever it might be that chanced to call? One must submit to the social convention, and be "cut off from what is called the world." At the same time, on the other side of Europe, there was a young man living freely with this gipsy or with that great lady; going to the wars; picking up unhindered and uncensored all that varied experience of human life which served him so splendidly later when he came to write his books. Had Tolstoy lived at the Priory in seclusion with a married lady "cut off from what is called the world," however edifying the moral lesson, he could scarcely, I thought, have written *War and Peace*.

But one could perhaps go a little deeper into the question of novel-writing and the effect of sex upon the novelist. If one shuts one's eyes and thinks of the novel as a whole, it would seem to be a creation owning a certain looking-glass likeness to life, though of course with simplifications and distortions innumerable. At any rate, it is a structure leaving a shape on the mind's eye, built now in squares, now pagoda shaped, now throwing out wings and arcades, now solidly compact and domed like the Cathedral of Saint Sofia at Constantinople. This shape, I thought, thinking back over certain famous novels, starts in one the kind of emotion that is appropriate to it. But that emotion at once blends itself with others, for the "shape" is not made by the relation of stone to stone, but by the relation of human being to human being. Thus a novel starts in us all sorts of antagonistic and opposed emotions. Life conflicts with something that is not life. Hence the difficulty of coming to any agreement about novels, and the immense sway that our private prejudices have upon us. On the one hand, we feel You — John the hero — must live, or I shall be in the depths of despair. On the other, we feel, Alas, John, you must die, because the shape of the book requires it. Life conflicts with something that is not life. Then since life it is in part, we judge it as life. James is the sort of man I most detest, one says. Or, This is a farrago of absurdity. I could never feel anything of the sort myself. The whole structure, it is obvious, thinking back on any famous novel, is one of infinite complexity, because it is thus made up of so many different judgments, of so many different kinds of emotion. The wonder is that any book so composed holds together for more than a year or two, or can possibly mean to the English reader what it means for the Russian or the Chinese. But they do hold together occasionally very remarkably. And what holds them together in these rare instances of survival (I was thinking of *War and Peace*) is something that one calls integrity, though it has nothing to do with paying one's bills or behaving honourably in an emergency. What one means by integrity, in the case of the novelist, is the conviction that he gives one that this is the truth. Yes, one feels, I should never have thought that this could be so; I have never known people behaving like that. But you have convinced me that so it is, so it happens. One holds every phrase, every scene to the light as one reads — for Nature seems, very oddly, to have provided us with an inner light by which to judge of the novelist's integrity or disintegrity. Or perhaps it is rather that Nature, in her most irrational mood, has traced in invisible ink on the walls of the mind a premonition which these great artists confirm; a sketch which only needs to be held to the fire of genius to become visible. When one so exposes it and sees it come to life one exclaims in rapture, But this is what I have always felt and known and desired! And one boils over with excitement, and, shutting the book even with a kind of reverence as if it were something very precious, a stand-by to return to as long as one lives, one puts it back on the shelf, I said, taking *War and Peace* and putting it back in its place. If, on the other hand, these poor sentences that one takes and tests rouse first a quick and eager response with their bright colouring and their dashing gestures but there they stop: something seems to check them in their development: or if they bring to light only a faint scribble in that corner and a blot over there, and nothing appears whole and entire, then one heaves a sigh of disappointment and says, Another failure. This novel has come to grief somewhere.

And for the most part, of course, novels do come to grief somewhere. The imagination falters under the enormous strain. The insight is confused; it can no longer distinguish between the true and false; it has no longer the strength to go on with the vast labour that calls at every moment for the use of so many different faculties. But how would all this be affected by the sex of the novelist, I wondered, looking at *Jane Eyre* and the others. Would the fact of her sex in any way interfere with the integrity of a woman novelist — that integrity which I take to be the backbone of the writer? Now, in the passages I have quoted from *Jane Eyre,* it is clear that anger was tampering with the integrity of Charlotte Brontë the novelist. She left her story, to which her entire devotion was due, to attend to some personal grievance. She remembered that she had been starved of her proper due of experience — she had been made to stagnate in a parsonage mending stockings when she wanted to wander free over the world. Her imagination swerved from indignation and we feel it swerve. But there were many more influences than anger tugging at her imagination and deflecting it from its path. Ignorance, for instance. The portrait of Rochester is drawn in the dark. We feel the influence of fear in it; just as we constantly feel an acidity which is the result of oppression, a buried suffering smouldering beneath her passion, a rancour which contracts those books, splendid as they are, with a spasm of pain.

And since a novel has this correspondence to real life, its values are to some extent those of real life. But it is obvious that the values of women differ very often from the values which have been made by the other sex; naturally, this is so. Yet it is the masculine values that prevail. Speaking crudely, football and sport are "important"; the worship of fashion, the buying of clothes "trivial."

And these values are inevitably transferred from life to fiction. This is an important book, the critic assumes, because it deals with war. This is an insignificant book because it deals with the feelings of women in a drawing-room. A scene in a battlefield is more important than a scene in a shop — everywhere and much more subtly the difference of value persists. The whole structure, therefore, of the early nineteenth-century novel was raised, if one was a woman, by a mind which was slightly pulled from the straight, and made to alter its clear vision in deference to external authority. One has only to skim those old forgotten novels and listen to the tone of voice in which they were written to divine that the writer was meeting criticism; she was saying this by way of aggression, or that by way of conciliation. She was admitting that she was "only a woman," or protesting that she was "as good as a man." She met that criticism as her temperament dictated, with docility and diffidence, or with anger and emphasis. It does not matter which it was; she was thinking of something other than the thing itself. Down comes her book upon our heads. There was a flaw in the centre of it. And I thought of all the women's novels that lie scattered, like small pock-marked apples in an orchard, about the secondhand book shops of London. It was the flaw in the centre that had rotted them. She had altered her values in deference to the opinion of others.

But how impossible it must have been for them not to budge either to the right or to the left. What genius, what integrity it must have required in face of all that criticism, in the midst of that purely patriarchal society, to hold fast to the thing as they saw it without shrinking. Only Jane Austen did it and Emily Brontë. It is another feather, perhaps the finest, in their caps. They wrote as women write, not as men write. Of all the thousand women who wrote novels then, they alone entirely ignored the perpetual admonitions of the eternal pedagogue — write this, think that. They alone were deaf to that persistent voice, now grumbling, now patronising, now domineering, now grieved, now shocked, now angry, now avuncular, that voice which cannot let women alone, but must be at them, like some too conscientious governess, adjuring them, like Sir Egerton

Brydges, to be refined, dragging even into the criticism of poetry criticism of sex;[3] admonishing them, if they would be good and win, as I suppose, some shiny prize, to keep within certain limits which the gentleman in question thinks suitable:'. . . female novelists should only aspire to excellence by courageously acknowledging the limitations of their sex.'[4] That puts the matter in a nutshell, and when I tell you, rather to your surprise, that this sentence was written not in August 1828 but in August 1928, you will agree, I think, that however delightful it is to us now, it represents a vast body of opinion — I am not going to stir those old pools, I take only what chance has floated to my feet — that was far more vigorous and far more vocal a century ago. It would have needed a very stalwart young woman in 1828 to disregard all those snubs and chidings and promises of prizes. One must have been something of a firebrand to say to oneself, Oh, but they can't buy literature too. Literature is open to everybody. I refuse to allow you, Beadle though you are, to turn me off the grass. Lock up your libraries if you like; but there is no gate, no lock, no bolt that you can set upon the freedom of my mind.

But whatever effect discouragement and criticism had upon their writing — and I believe that they had a very great effect — that was unimportant compared with the other difficulty which faced them (I was still considering those early nineteenth-century novelists) when they came to set their thoughts on paper — that is that they had no tradition behind them, or one so short and partial that it was of little help. For we think back through our mothers if we are women. It is useless to go to the great men writers for help, however much one may go to them for pleasure. Lamb, Browne, Thackeray, Newman, Sterne, Dickens, De Quincey — whoever it may be — never helped a woman yet, though she may have learnt a few tricks of them and adapted them to her use. The weight, the pace, the stride of a man's mind are too unlike her own for her to lift anything substantial from him successfully. The ape is too distant to be sedulous. Perhaps the first thing she would find, setting pen to paper, was that there was no common sentence ready for her use. All the great novelists like Thackeray and Dickens and Balzac have written a natural prose, swift but not slovenly, expressive but not precious, taking their own tint without ceasing to be common property. They have based it on the sentence that was current at the time. The sentence that was current at the beginning of the nineteenth century ran something like this perhaps: ''The grandeur of their works was an argument with them, not to stop short, but to proceed. They could have no higher excitement or satisfaction than in the exercise of their art and endless generations of truth and beauty. Success prompts to exertion; and habit facilitates success.'' That is a man's sentence; behind it one can see Johnson, Gibbon and the rest. It was a sentence that was unsuited for a woman's use. Charlotte Brontë, with all her splendid gift for prose, stumbled and fell with that clumsy weapon in her hands. George Eliot committed atrocities with it that beggar description. Jane Austen looked at it and laughed at it and devised a perfectly natural, shapely sentence proper for her own use and never departed from it. Thus, with less genius for writing than Charlotte Brontë, she got infinitely more said. Indeed, since freedom and fullness of expression are of the essence of the art, such a lack of tradition, such a scarcity and inadequacy of tools, must have told enormously upon the writing of women. Moreover, a book is not made of sentences laid end to end, but of sentences built, if an image helps, into arcades or domes. And this shape too has been made by men out of their own needs for their own uses. There is no reason to think that the form of the epic or of the poetic play suits a woman any more than the sentence suits her. But all the older forms of literature were hardened and set by the time she became a writer. The novel alone was young enough to be soft in her hands — another reason, perhaps, why she wrote novels. Yet who shall say that that

[3] "[She] has a metaphysical purpose, and that is a dangerous obsession, especially with a woman, for women rarely possess men's healthy love of rhetoric. It is a strange lack in the sex which is in other things more primitive and more materialistic.'" — New Criterion, June 1928. [Woolf]

[4] "'If, like the reporter, you believe that female novelists should only aspire to excellence by courageously acknowledging the limitations of their sex (Jane Austen [has] demonstrated how gracefully this gesture can be accomplished). . . .'" — Life and Letters, August 1928. [Woolf]

even now "the novel" (I give it inverted commas to mark my sense of the words' inadequacy), who shall say that even this most pliable of all forms is rightly shaped for her use? No doubt we shall find her knocking that into shape for herself when she has the free use of her limbs; and providing some new vehicle, not necessarily in verse, for the poetry in her. For it is the poetry that is still denied outlet. And I went on to ponder how a woman nowadays would write a poetic tragedy in five acts — would she use verse — would she not use prose rather?

[The Androgynous Vision]
from *A Room of One's Own*

What does one mean by "the unity of the mind," I pondered, for clearly the mind has so great a power of concentrating at any point at any moment that it seems to have no single state of being. It can separate itself from the people in the street, for example, and think of itself as apart from them, at an upper window looking down on them. Or it can think with other people spontaneously, as, for instance, in a crowd waiting to hear some piece of news read out. It can think back through its fathers or through its mothers, as I have said that a woman writing thinks back through her mothers. Again if one is a woman one is often surprised by a sudden splitting off of consciousness, say in walking down Whitehall, when from being the natural inheritor of that civilisation, she becomes, on the contrary, outside of it, alien and critical. Clearly the mind is always altering its focus, and bringing the world into different perspectives. But some of these states of mind seem, even if adopted spontaneously, to be less comfortable than others. In order to keep oneself continuing in them one is unconsciously holding something back, and gradually the repression becomes an effort. But there may be some state of mind in which one could continue without effort because nothing is required to be held back. And this perhaps, I thought, coming in from the window, is one of them. For certainly when I saw the couple get into the taxi-cab the mind felt as if, after being divided, it had come together again in natural fusion. The obvious reason would be that it is natural for the sexes to cooperate. One has a profound, if irrational, instinct in favour of the theory that the union of man and woman makes for the greatest satisfaction, the most complete happiness. But the sight of the two people getting into the taxi and the satisfaction it gave me made me also ask whether there are two sexes in the mind corresponding to the two sexes in the body, and whether they also require to be united in order to get complete satisfaction and happiness. And I went on amateurishly to sketch a plan of the soul so that in each of us two powers preside, one male, one female; and in the man's brain, the man predominates over the woman, and in the woman's brain, the woman predominates over the man. The normal and comfortable state of being is that when the two live in harmony together, spiritually co-operating. If one is a man, still the woman part of the brain must have effect; and a woman also must have intercourse with the man in her. Coleridge perhaps meant this when he said that a great mind is androgynous.[1] It is when this fusion takes place that the mind is fully fertilised and uses all its faculties. Perhaps a mind that is purely masculine cannot create, any more than a mind that is purely feminine, I thought. But it would be well to test what one meant by man-womanly, and conversely by woman-manly, by pausing and looking at a book or two.

Coleridge certainly did not mean, when he said that a great mind is androgynous, that it is a mind that has any special sympathy with women; a mind that takes up their cause or devotes itself

[1]See *Specimens of the Table Talk of S. T. Coleridge* (London, 1837) for September 1, 1832.

to their interpretation. Perhaps the androgynous mind is less apt to make these distinctions than the single-sexed mind. He meant, perhaps, that the androgynous mind is resonant and porous; that it transmits emotion without impediment; that it is naturally creative, incandescent, and undivided. In fact one goes back to Shakespeare's mind as the type of the androgynous, of the man-womanly mind, though it would be impossible to say what Shakespeare thought of women. And if it be true that it is one of the tokens of the fully developed mind that it does not think specially or separately of sex, how much harder it is to attain that condition now than ever before. Here I came to the books by living writers, and there paused and wondered if this fact were not at the root of something that had long puzzled me. No age can ever have been as stridently sex-conscious as our own; those innumerable books by men about women in the British Museum are a proof of it. The Suffrage campaign² was no doubt to blame. It must have roused in men an extraordinary desire for self-assertion; it must have made them lay an emphasis upon their own sex and its characteristics which they would not have troubled to think about had they not been challenged. And when one is challenged, even by a few women in black bonnets, one retaliates, if one has never been challenged before, rather excessively. That perhaps accounts for some of the characteristics that I remember to have found here, I thought, taking down a new novel by Mr. A, who is in the prime of life and very well thought of, apparently, by the reviewers. I opened it. Indeed, it was delightful to read a man's writing again. It was so direct, so straightforward after the writing of women. It indicated such freedom of mind, such liberty of person, such confidence in himself. One had a sense of physical well-being in the presence of this well-nourished, well-educated, free mind, which had never been thwarted or opposed, but had had full liberty from birth to stretch itself in whatever way it liked. All this was admirable. But after reading a chapter or two a shadow seemed to lie across the page. It was

a straight dark bar, a shadow shaped something like the letter "I." One began dodging this way and that to catch a glimpse of the landscape behind it. Whether that was indeed a tree or a woman walking I was not quite sure. Back one was always hailed to the letter "I." One began to be tired of "I." Not but what this "I" was a most respectable "I"; honest and logical; as hard as a nut, and polished for centuries by good teaching and good feeding. I respect and admire that "I" from the bottom of my heart. But — here I turned a page or two, looking for something or other — the worst of it is that in the shadow of the letter "I" all is shapeless as mist. Is that a tree? No, it is a woman. But . . . she has not a bone in her body, I thought, watching Phoebe, for that was her name, coming across the beach. Then Alan got up and the shadow of Alan at once obliterated Phoebe. For Alan had views and Phoebe was quenched in the flood of his views. And then Alan, I thought, has passions; and here I turned page after page very fast, feeling that the crisis was approaching, and so it was. It took place on the beach under the sun. It was done very openly. It was done very vigorously. Nothing could have been more indecent. But . . . I had said "but" too often. One cannot go on saying "but." One must finish the sentence somehow, I rebuked myself. Shall I finish it, "But — I am bored!" But why was I bored? Partly because of the dominance of the letter "I" and the aridity, which, like the giant beech tree, it casts within its shade. Nothing will grow there. And partly for some more obscure reason. There seemed to be some obstacle, some impediment of Mr. A's mind which blocked the fountain of creative energy and shored it within narrow limits. And remembering the lunch party at Oxbridge, and the cigarette ash and the Manx cat and Tennyson and Christina Rossetti all in a bunch, it seemed possible that the impediment lay there. As he no longer hums under his breath, "There has fallen a splendid tear from the passion-flower at the gate,"³ when Phoebe crosses the beach, and she no longer replies, "My

²Women in the United Kingdom asserted their right to vote in a campaign that lasted from 1866 to 1928. (Women over 30 were given the vote in 1918; the franchise was extended to women 21–29 in 1928.)

³From *Maud* (1862) by Alfred, Lord Tennyson (1809–1892), lines 165–68. This famous passage goes on: "She is coming, my dove, my dear; She is coming, my life, my fate; / The red rose cries, 'She is near, she is near;' and the white rose weeps, / The larkspur listens, 'I hear, I hear;' and the lily whispers, 'I wait.'"

heart is like a singing bird whose nest is in a water'd shoot,"[4] when Alan approaches what can he do? Being honest as the day and logical as the sun, there is only one thing he can do. And that he does, to do him justice, over and over (I said, turning the pages) and over again. And that, I added, aware of the awful nature of the confession, seems somehow dull. Shakespeare's indecency uproots a thousand other things in one's mind, and is far from being dull. But Shakespeare does it for pleasure; Mr. A, as the nurses say, does it on purpose. He does it in protest. He is protesting against the equality of the other sex by asserting his own superiority. He is therefore impeded and inhibited and self-conscious as Shakespeare might have been if he too had known Miss Clough and Miss Davies.[5] Doubtless Elizabethan literature would have been very different from what it is if the woman's movement had begun in the sixteenth century and not in the nineteenth.

What, then, it amounts to, if this theory of the two sides of the mind holds good, is that virility has now become self-conscious — men, that is to say, are now writing only with the male side of their brains. It is a mistake for a woman to read them, for she will inevitably look for something that she will not find. It is the power of suggestion that one most misses, I thought, taking Mr. B the critic in my hand and reading, very carefully and very dutifully, his remarks upon the art of poetry. Very able they were, acute and full of learning; but the trouble was, that his feelings no longer communicated; his mind seemed separated into different chambers; not a sound carried from one to the other. Thus, when one takes a sentence of Mr. B into the mind it falls plump to the ground — dead; but when one takes a sentence of Coleridge into the mind, it explodes and gives birth to all kinds of other ideas, and that is the only sort of writing of which one can say that it has the secret of perpetual life.

But whatever the reason may be, it is a fact that one must deplore. For it means — here I had come to rows of books by Mr. Galsworthy and Mr. Kipling — that some of the finest works of our greatest living writers fall upon deaf ears. Do what she will a woman cannot find in them that fountain of perpetual life which the critics assure her is there. It is not only that they celebrate male virtues, enforce male values, and describe the world of men; it is that the emotion with which these books are permeated is to a woman incomprehensible. It is coming, it is gathering, it is about to burst on one's head, one begins saying long before the end. That picture will fall on old Jolyon's head; he will die of the shock; the old clerk will speak over him two or three obituary words; and all the swans on the Thames will simultaneously burst out singing. But one will rush away before that happens and hide in the gooseberry bushes, for the emotion which is so deep, so subtle, so symbolical to a man moves a woman to wonder. So with Mr. Kipling's officers who turn their backs; and his Sowers who sow the Seed; and his Men who are alone with their Work; and the Flag — one blushes at all these capital letters as if one had been caught eavesdropping at some purely masculine orgy. The fact is that neither Mr. Galsworthy nor Mr. Kipling has a spark of the woman in him. Thus all their qualities seem to a woman, if one may generalise, crude and immature. They lack suggestive power. And when a book lacks suggestive power, however hard it hits the surface of the mind it cannot penetrate within.

And in that restless mood in which one takes books out and puts them back again without looking at them I began to envisage an age to come of pure, of self-assertive virility, such as the letters of professors (take Sir Walter Raleigh's[6] letters, for instance) seem to forebode, and the rulers of Italy[7] have already brought into being. For one can hardly fail to be impressed in Rome by the sense of unmitigated masculinity; and whatever the

[4]The opening lines of "A Birthday" in *Goblin Market and Other Poems* (published in the same years as *Maud*, 1862), by Christina Rossetti (1830–1894), ending "Because the birthday of my life / Is come, my love is come to me."

[5]Anne Jemima Clough (1820–1892) and Emily Davies (1830–1921) were prominent in both the suffrage movement and the efforts to open Cambridge University to women. Clough served as principal of Newnham College; Davies raised money for the foundation of what eventually became Girton College.

[6]Not the Elizabethan explorer, but Sir Walter Alexander Raleigh (1861–1922), professor at Oxford and the author of dozens of studies on English literature.

[7]Benito Mussolini and his Fascist Party.

value of unmitigated masculinity upon the state, one may question the effect of it upon the art of poetry. At any rate, according to the newspapers, there is a certain anxiety about fiction in Italy. There has been a meeting of academicians whose object it is "to develop the Italian novel." "Men famous by birth, or in finance, industry or the Fascist corporations" came together the other day and discussed the matter, and a telegram was sent to the Duce expressing the hope "that the Fascist era would soon give birth to a poet worthy of it." We may all join in that pious hope, but it is doubtful whether poetry can come out of an incubator. Poetry ought to have a mother as well as a father. The Fascist poem, one may fear, will be a horrid little abortion such as one sees in a glass jar in the museum of some country town. Such monsters never live long, it is said; one has never seen a prodigy of that sort cropping grass in a field. Two heads on one body do not make for length of life.

However, the blame for all this, if one is anxious to lay blame, rests no more upon one sex than upon the other. All seducers and reformers are responsible. Lady Bessborough when she lied to Lord Granville;[8] Miss Davies when she told the truth to Mr. Greg.[9] All who have brought about a state of sex-consciousness are to blame, and it is they who drive me, when I want to stretch my faculties on a book, to seek it in that happy age, before Miss Davies and Miss Clough were born, when the writer used both sides of his mind equally. One must turn back to Shakespeare then, for Shakespeare was androgynous; and so was Keats and Sterne and Cowper and Lamb and Coleridge. Shelley perhaps was sexless. Milton and Ben Jonson had a dash too much of the male in them. So had Wordsworth and Tolstoi. In our time Proust

[8]Two well-born Regency lovers, Henrietta Spencer Ponsonby, Countess Bessborough (1761–1821), and Granville Leveson Gower, Earl Granville (1773–1846). The "lie" is in her letter to Granville, which Woolf quotes earlier: "I perfectly agree with you that no woman has any business to meddle with [politics] or any other serious business whatsoever, farther than giving her opinion (if she is ask'd)."

[9]Probably Walter Wilson Greg (1875–1959), known primarily as a textual editor of English literature, who is quoted earlier in A Room of One's Own: the "essentials of a woman's being are that they are supported by, and they minister to, men."

was wholly androgynous, if not perhaps a little too much of a woman. But that failing is too rare for one to complain of it, since without some mixture of the kind the intellect seems to predominate and the other faculties of the mind harden and become barren. However, I consoled myself with the reflection that this is perhaps a passing phase; much of what I have said in obedience to my promise to give you the course of my thoughts will seem out of date; much of what flames in my eyes will seem dubious to you who have not yet come of age.

Even so, the very first sentence that I would write here, I said, crossing over to the writing-table and taking up the page headed Women and Fiction, is that it is fatal for any one who writes to think of their sex. It is fatal to be a man or woman pure and simple; one must be woman-manly or man-womanly. It is fatal for a woman to lay the least stress on any grievance; to plead even with justice any cause; in any way to speak consciously as a woman. And fatal is no figure of speech; for anything written with that conscious bias is doomed to death. It ceases to be fertilised. Brilliant and effective, powerful and masterly, as it may appear for a day or two, it must wither at nightfall; it cannot grow in the minds of others. Some collaboration has to take place in the mind between the woman and the man before the act of creation can be accomplished. Some marriage of opposites has to be consummated. The whole of the mind must lie wide open if we are to get the sense that the writer is communicating his experience with perfect fullness. There must be freedom and there must be peace. Not a wheel must grate, not a light glimmer. The curtains must be close drawn. The writer, I thought, once his experience is over, must lie back and let his mind celebrate its nuptials in darkness. He must not look or question what is being done. Rather, he must pluck the petals from a rose or watch the swans float calmly down the river. And I saw again the current which took the boat and the undergraduate and the dead leaves; and the taxi took the man and the woman, I thought, seeing them come together across the street, and the current swept them away, I thought, hearing far off the roar of London's traffic, into that tremendous stream.

Kenneth Burke

1897–1993

Kenneth Duva Burke was born on May 5, 1897, in Pittsburgh, where he was educated through high school. He attended college at Ohio State University in Columbus and Columbia University in New York but did not take a degree; this has been amply made up for by the number of universities — over a dozen — that awarded him honorary doctorates. Burke worked as a researcher for the Laura Spelman Rockefeller Foundation, as the music critic for *The Dial* and *The Nation,* and as an editor for government publications, but his chief occupation during his long life was that of itinerant scholar and critic. Burke took literally dozens of academic appointments at prestigious institutions, but most of them, except for an eighteen-year appointment at Bennington College from 1943 to 1961, itself broken by visiting appointments elsewhere, were for a year or two. In addition to writing dozens of critical and philosophical books, Burke was a poet from his eighteenth year, and his first publication (*The White Oxen,* 1924) was a collection of short stories. Burke was married twice, to two sisters, and had three daughters by the first marriage and two sons by the second.

A quirky and individualistic thinker, Burke has often and for understandable reasons been mischaracterized as a New Critic strongly influenced by Marx and Freud. Of the same generation as Brooks and Wimsatt, Burke was interested, like the New Critics, in the poem as a verbal creation, or as he put it himself, "a dance of attitudes"; and like most twentieth-century thinkers from Lionel Trilling to William Empson, he was also interested in the two most revolutionary thinkers of the later Victorian era. Nevertheless, Burke was more a philosopher of language, which he understood as *symbolic action*, than a literary critic, a social thinker or a psychologist.

Perhaps we should begin at a very general level, with Burke's famous definition of *man*. Burke conceived of *man* not as *homo sapiens* but as *homo symbolicus,* the only being capable of using (and therefore misusing) symbols. Man is therefore also the "inventor of the negative," since negation is a product only of symbol systems: Nature may not abhor a vacuum, but only language can explore the absence of something in a world that knows only presence. Man is also "separated from his natural condition by instruments of his own making," so conditioned by language and the social aspects of life that are created within and through language that even his physiology has changed from that of the arboreal apes from which he descended. Man is also "goaded by the spirit of hierarchy," a characteristically less pleasant way of saying "moved by a sense of order."

Finally, Burke likes to say that *man* is "rotten with perfection," in that our sense of order leads us to carry out our ideas to the nth degree, regardless of the consequences. One obvious instance is Hitler's idea of racial purity. Carried out to perfection, and with full negativity, using the power that rigidly enforced hierarchies give to a leader, the symbolic enactment leads to the horrors of the Holocaust. Although

Burke's theory suggests that humanity has a drive to "perfect" such ideas in such a way, a utopian strain in Burke hopes that the strife between contrary symbol-systems (like capitalism and communism) can be indefinitely confined, with all our help, to symbolic battles, rather than exploding in that final negativity, nuclear annihilation. The idea of conflict confined to a symbolic agon, a struggle of words, brings us back to Burke and literature. Saying something is another way of doing something. Essentially, Burke assumes that human beings write literature, just as they do everything else, in an effort to achieve some personal goal. Writing is itself a drama. Authors are *agents* who *act* within a certain *scene* (their environment) by means of a certain *agency* (writing) to achieve a *purpose*. These five terms — agent, act, scene, agency, and purpose — make up the Burkean *pentad;* their "ratios," or the relationships between the terms, are crucial to his criticism. Authors do not merely write as an end in itself, nor do they write for secular reasons — to make money or achieve fame. Rather, they select their particular subjects, topics, conflicts, for reasons that go beyond the secular, usually the purgation of their own sense of sinfulness, which leads to a sense of redemption within their lives. As Burke says in "Literature as Equipment for Living," there is no room for such a thing as "pure literature" of the sort the New Critics wished to analyze. Works of art are "equipment for living," "strategies for selecting enemies and allies, for socializing losses, for warding off the evil eye, for purification, propitiation, and desanctification, consolation and vengeance, admonition and exhortation, implicit commands or instructions of one sort or another."

As an example of how the poet may socialize a loss or give himself symbolic instructions, we could take Burke's analysis of Milton's "Lycidas" in *Attitudes toward History* (1937). While a New Critic like John Crowe Ransom considered "Lycidas" "a poem nearly anonymous" in its exquisite variants on the general themes of the pastoral elegy, Burke boldly commits the intentional fallacy, even takes the poem, with its evocation of the death and resurrection of a poet, as a personal prophecy. After writing "Lycidas," Burke claims,

Milton travelled in 1638 and 1639. And for the next twenty years thereafter, with the exception of an occasional sonnet, he devoted all his energies to his polemic prose. These dates, coupled with the contents of the poem, would justify us in contending that "Lycidas" was the symbolic dying of his poetic self. . . . In "Lycidas" he testifies that he is holding his dead self in abeyance, and that it will rise again. . . . So the poet remained, for all his dying; and at the Restoration, after the political interregnum of Cromwell, he would be reborn. "Paradise Lost" is the fulfillment of his contract.[1]

Similarly, "The Rime of the Ancient Mariner" represents Coleridge's symbolic way of purging the guilt arising out of his failed marriage and his drug addiction, and of achieving an equally symbolic redemption. For Burke, the slain albatross can be equated with Sarah Coleridge, since they are "in the same equational cluster" — connected by similar imagery in "Mariner" and "The Aeolian Harp."

[1]Kenneth Burke, *Attitudes toward History,* 3rd ed. (Berkeley: University of California Press, 1984), p. 57.

Similarly, the watersnakes whom the mariner blesses as a part of nature connect with his drug addiction, which is referred to in a letter as "a scourge of ever restless, ever coiling and uncoiling serpents," while Coleridge feels "driven on from behind" — as the Mariner's ship is driven. In effect, Coleridge uses the poem to symbolically "bless" his drug addiction and "curse" his marriage — the scene of the poem itself involves a detained wedding guest who misses the ceremony, and the poem ends by denigrating marriage in favor of the brotherhood of Nature and of humanity ("to walk together to the kirk, With a goodly company").

Not only may authors have their purgative/redemptive purposes, their societies also have them (and, we might add, the "affective" fallacy means as little to Burke as the "intentional" fallacy does). Burke's analysis of Shakespeare's *Coriolanus* in *Language as Symbolic Action* (1966) presents the hero of that play as the apotheosis of the aristocracy, with all the virtues and vices of the highborn — courage, pride, stoical fortitude, snobbery, family feeling — taken to the last extreme, "rotten with perfection," as Burke liked to put it. According to Burke, the action of the tragedy shapes everything toward the sacrifice of Coriolanus as a scapegoat — a symbolic destruction of the ultimate patrician enacted at a time when the strife between patrician and plebeian in English society was already becoming virulent, although it would not erupt into civil war for another three decades. The death of Coriolanus causes the reunification of Rome and symbolically allows the English Cavaliers and Roundheads, enemies-to-be, to join in unity in a purgative/redemptive experience.

Here and in the Milton example, Burke is characteristically cavalier in his use of the facts and delights in prophecy after the fact. One could pedantically object that Milton in 1637 could not have foreseen Cromwell and his secretaryship, that Coleridge was not fully addicted to laudanum at the time he wrote "The Ancient Mariner," that Shakespeare in 1609 could not have foreseen the Civil War. But the sort of conflict Burke is talking about always runs behind and above such facts: If Milton could not have predicted Cromwell, he certainly saw the conflict within himself between poetry and politics, and if Shakespeare could not have predicted the civil war that broke out twenty-five years after his death, he certainly understood the clash between classes within his own society. The same is true of Coleridge; even if one is not willing to claim (as Burke once did) that the poet was an *incipient* addict in 1796, there was surely a deep-seated and long-standing conflict in Coleridge between affections licensed by society (symbolized by the wedding in the poem) and affections that transcend and defy the social (like the Mariner's demonic bond with the watersnakes).

Burke's method of analyzing literature turns primarily on reducing the text to its scene of conflict, then viewing that conflict as symbolic of other conflicts within other scenes — within the poet's self, family, or society, including his or her relation with intellectual forebears or poetic rivals. The "scene" for which the poem is a grand metaphor can be psychological, economic, political, sociological, even theological. And as the example of Coleridge shows, Burke is willing to read other poems or letters onto the text under analysis. Everything is relevant.

If this allegorizing and psychologizing is utterly foreign to the formalist movements against which Burke defined his own poetics, he nevertheless resembles the New Critics in his concern for symbol, language, and imagery. The notion that themes essentially reside in clusters of images, that the associations of primary terms determine their psychic meaning, is close to the New Critical method. Nevertheless, the freewheeling Burke went considerably further than the New Critics were ever comfortable with in his "joycings" — puns, usually scatological, that reduce the high-flown meaning of a passage to a physiological level. Burke's analysis of Keats's "Ode on a Grecian Urn" in *A Grammar of Motives* (1945) is relatively decorous, but in the later *A Rhetoric of Motives* (1950), the "urn" is joyced to "urine," while the final sentiment, "Beauty is truth, truth beauty," is joyced to "Body is turd, turd body." Burke is not being childishly dirty-minded here. His point is that, in any poem so concerned with transcendence, the poet tends to repress the earthly and bodily functions that are being transcended; but what is repressed returns in language that, in distorted form, conveys what the poet has been avoiding talking about. In Burke conflict is unavoidable and language always takes over — that much is certain.

Selected Bibliography

Frank, Armin Paul. *Kenneth Burke.* New York: Twayne, 1969.

Heath, Robert L. "Kenneth Burke's Break with Formalism." *Quarterly Journal of Speech 70* (1984): 132–43.

———. *Realism and Relativism: A Perspective on Kenneth Burke.* Macon, GA: Mercer University Press, 1986.

Henderson, Greig, and David Cratis Williams, eds. *Unending Conversations: New Writings by and about Kenneth Burke.* Carbondale: Southern Illinois University Press, 2001.

Rueckert, William H. *The Rhetoric of Rebirth: A Study of the Literary Theory and Critical Practice of Kenneth Burke.* Ann Arbor: University Microfilms, 1957.

———. *Kenneth Burke and the Drama of Human Relations,* 2nd ed. Berkeley: University of California Press, 1982.

Southwell, Samuel B. *Kenneth Burke and Martin Heidegger, with a Note Against Deconstruction.* Gainesville: University Presses of Florida, 1987.

Wolin, Ross. *The Rhetorical Imagination of Kenneth Burke.* Columbia: University of South Carolina Press, 2001.

White, Hayden, and Margaret Brose, eds. *Representing Kenneth Burke.* Baltimore: Johns Hopkins University Press, 1982.

Literature as Equipment for Living

Here I shall put down, as briefly as possible, a statement in behalf of what might be catalogued, with a fair degree of accuracy, as a *sociological* criticism of literature. Sociological criticism in itself is certainly not new. I shall here try to suggest what partially new elements or emphasis I think should be added to this old approach. And to make the "way in" as easy as possible, I shall begin with a discussion of proverbs.

I

Examine random specimens in *The Oxford Dictionary of English Proverbs.* You will note,

I think, that there is no "pure" literature here. Everything is "medicine." Proverbs are designed for consolation or vengeance, for admonition or exhortation, for foretelling.

Or they name typical, recurrent situations. That is, people find a certain social relationship recurring so frequently that they must "have a word for it." The Eskimos have special names for many different kinds of snow (fifteen, if I remember rightly) because variations in the quality of snow greatly affect their living. Hence, they must "size up" snow much more accurately than we do. And the same is true of social phenomena. Social structures give rise to "type" situations, subtle subdivisions of the relationships involved in competitive and coöperative acts. Many proverbs seek to chart, in more or less homey and picturesque ways, these "type" situations. I submit that such naming is done, not for the sheer glory of the thing, but because of its bearing upon human welfare. A different name for snow implies a different kind of hunt. Some names for snow imply that one should not hunt at all. And similarly, the names for typical, recurrent social situations are not developed out of "disinterested curiosity," but because the names imply a command (what to expect, what to look out for).

To illustrate with a few representative examples:

Proverbs designed for consolation: "The sun does not shine on both sides of the hedge at once." "Think of ease, but work on." "Little troubles the eye, but far less the soul." "The worst luck now, the better another time." "The wind in one's face makes one wise." "He that hath lands hath quarrels." "He knows how to carry the dead cock home." "He is not poor that hath little, but he that desireth much."

For vengeance: "At length the fox is brought to the furrier." "Shod in the cradle, barefoot in the stubble." "Sue a beggar and get a louse." "The higher the ape goes, the more he shows his tail." "The moon does not heed the barking of dogs." "He measures another's corn by his own bushel." "He shuns the man who knows him well." "Fools tie knots and wise men loose them."

Proverbs that have to do with foretelling (the most obvious are those to do with the weather): "Sow peas and beans in the wane of the moon,

Who soweth them sooner, he soweth too soon." "When the wind's in the north, the skilful fisher goes not forth." "When the sloe tree is as white as a sheet, sow your barley whether it be dry or wet." "When the sun sets bright and clear, An easterly wind you need not fear. When the sun sets in a bank, A westerly wind we shall not want."

In short: "Keep your weather eye open": be realistic about sizing up today's weather, because your accuracy has bearing upon tomorrow's weather. And forecast not only the meteorological weather, but also the social weather: "When the moon's in the full, then wit's in the wane." "Straws show which way the wind blows." "When the fish is caught, the net is laid aside." "Remove an old tree, and it will wither to death." "The wolf may lose his teeth, but never his nature." "He that bites on every weed must needs light on poison." "Whether the pitcher strikes the stone, or the stone the pitcher, it is bad for the pitcher." "Eagles catch no flies." "The more laws, the more offenders."

In this foretelling category we might also include the recipes for wise living, sometimes moral, sometimes technical: "First thrive, and then wive." "Think with the wise but talk with the vulgar." "When the fox preacheth, then beware your geese." "Venture a small fish to catch a great one." "Respect a man, he will do the more."

In the class of "typical, recurrent situations" we might put such proverbs and proverbial expressions as: "Sweet appears sour when we pay." "The treason is loved but the traitor is hated." "The wine in the bottle does not quench thirst." "The sun is never the worse for shining on a dunghill." "The lion kicked by an ass." "The lion's share." "To catch one napping." "To smell a rat." "To cool one's heels."

By all means, I do not wish to suggest that this is the only way in which the proverbs could be classified. For instance, I have listed in the "foretelling" group the proverb, "When the fox preacheth, then beware your geese." But it could obviously be "taken over" for vindictive purposes. Or consider a proverb like, "Virtue flies from the heart of a mercenary man." A poor man might obviously use it either to console himself for being poor (the implication being, "Because I am poor in money I am rich in virtue") or to strike at another (the implication being, "When he got money, what else could you expect of him but deterioration?"). In fact, we could even say that such symbolic vengeance would itself be an aspect of solace. And a proverb like "The sun is never the worse for shining on a dunghill" (which I have listed under "typical recurrent situations") might as well be put in the vindictive category. The point of issue is not to find categories that "place" the proverbs once and for all. What I want is categories that suggest their active nature. Here is no "realism for its own sake." Here is realism for promise, admonition, solace, vengeance, foretelling, instruction, charting, all for the direct bearing that such acts have upon matters of welfare.

2

Step two: Why not extend such analysis of proverbs to encompass the whole field of literature? Could the most complex and sophisticated works of art legitimately be considered somewhat as "proverbs writ large"? Such leads, if held admissible, should help us to discover important facts about literary organization (thus satisfying the requirements of technical criticism). And the kind of observation from this perspective should apply beyond literature to life in general (thus helping to take literature out of its separate bin and give it a place in a general "sociological" picture).

The point of view might be phrased in this way: Proverbs are *strategies* for dealing with *situations*. In so far as situations are typical and recurrent in a given social structure, people develop names for them and strategies for handling them. Another name for strategies might be *attitudes*.

People have often commented on the fact that there are *contrary* proverbs. But I believe that the above approach to proverbs suggests a necessary modification of that comment. The apparent contradictions depend upon differences in *attitude*, involving a correspondingly different choice of *strategy*. Consider, for instance, the apparently opposite pair: "Repentance comes too late" and "Never too late to mend." The first is admonitory. It says in effect: "You'd better look out, or you'll get yourself too far into this business." The

second is consolatory, saying in effect: "Buck up, old man, you can still pull out of this."

Some critics have quarreled with me about my selection of the word "strategy" as the name for this process. I have asked them to suggest an alternative term, so far without profit. The only one I can think of is "method." But if "strategy" errs in suggesting to some people an overly conscious procedure, "method" errs in suggesting an overly "methodical" one. Anyhow, let's look at the documents:

Concise Oxford Dictionary: "Strategy: Movement of an army or armies in a campaign, art of so moving or disposing troops or ships as to impose upon the enemy the place and time and conditions for fighting preferred by oneself" (from a Greek word that refers to the leading of an army).

New English Dictionary: "Strategy: The art of projecting and directing the larger military movements and operations of a campaign."

André Cheron, *Traité Complet d'Echecs:* "On entend par stratégie les manoeuvres qui ont pour but la sortie et le bon arrangement des pieces."[1]

Looking at these definitions, I gain courage. For surely, the most highly alembicated and sophisticated work of art, arising in complex civilizations, could be considered as designed to organize and command the army of one's thoughts and images, and to so organize them that one "imposes upon the enemy the time and place and conditions for fighting preferred by oneself." One seeks to "direct the larger movements and operations" in one's campaign of living. One "maneuvers," and the maneuvering is an "art."

Are not the final results one's "strategy"? One tries, as far as possible, to develop a strategy whereby one "can't lose." One tries to change the rules of the game until they fit his own necessities. Does the artist encounter disaster? He will "make capital" of it. If one is a victim of competition, for instance, if one is elbowed out, one is willy-nilly more jockeyed against than jockeying, one can by the solace and vengeance of art convert this very

[1] *Complete Treatise on Chess:* "Strategy signifies the maneuvers whose goal is attack and correct position."

"liability" into an "asset." One tries to fight on his own terms, developing a strategy for imposing the proper "time, place, and conditions."

But one must also, to develop a full strategy, be *realistic*. One must *size things up* properly. One cannot accurately know how things *will be,* what is promising and what is menacing, unless he accurately knows how things *are*. So the wise strategist will not be content with strategies of merely a self-gratifying sort. He will "keep his weather eye open." He will not too eagerly "read into" a scene an attitude that is irrelevant to it. He won't sit on the side of an active volcano and "see" it as a dormant plain.

Often, alas, he will. The great allurement in our present popular "inspirational literature," for instance, may be largely of this sort. It is a strategy for easy consolation. It "fills a need," since there is always a need for easy consolation — and in an era of confusion like our own the need is especially keen. So people are only too willing to "meet a man halfway" who will *play down* the realistic naming of our situation and *play up* such strategies as make solace cheap. However, I should propose a reservation here. We usually take it for granted that people who consume our current output of books on "How to Buy Friends and Bamboozle Oneself and Other People"[2] are reading as *students* who will attempt applying the recipes given. Nothing of the sort. *The reading of a book on the attaining of success is in itself the symbolic attaining of that success.* It is *while they read* that these readers are "succeeding." I'll wager that, in by far the great majority of cases, such readers make no serious attempt to apply the book's recipes. The lure of the book resides in the fact that the reader, while reading it, is then living in the aura of success. What he wants is *easy* success; and he gets it in symbolic form by the mere reading itself. To attempt applying such stuff in real life would be very difficult, full of many disillusioning problems.

Sometimes a different strategy may arise. The author may remain realistic, avoiding too easy a form of solace — yet he may get as far off the

---

[2]Burke is parodying Dale Carnegie's *How to Make Friends and Influence People* in particular, but the genre of the self-help book continues to thrive today.

track in his own way. Forgetting that realism is an aspect for foretelling, he may take it as an end in itself. He is tempted to do this by two factors: (1) an *ill-digested* philosophy of science, leading him mistakenly to assume that "relentless" naturalistic "truthfulness" is a proper end in itself, and (2) a merely *competitive* desire to outstrip other writers by being "more realistic" than they. Works thus made "efficient" by tests of competition internal to the book trade are a kind of academicism not so named (the writer usually thinks of it as the *opposite* of academicism). Realism thus stepped up competitively might be distinguished from the proper sort by the name of "naturalism." As a way of "sizing things up," the naturalistic tradition tends to become as inaccurate as the "inspirational" strategy, though at the opposite extreme.

Anyhow, the main point is this: A work like *Madame Bovary* (or its homely American translation, *Babbitt*) is the strategic naming of a situation. It singles out a pattern of experience that is sufficiently representative of our social structure, that recurs sufficiently often *mutatis mutandis,* for people to "need a word for it" and to adopt an attitude towards it. Each work of art is the addition of a word to an informal dictionary (or, in the case of purely derivative artists, the addition of a subsidiary meaning to a word already given by some originating artist). As for *Madame Bovary,* the French critic Jules de Gaultier proposed to add it to our *formal* dictionary by coining the word "Bovarysme" and writing a whole book to say what he meant by it.

Mencken's book on *The American Language,* I hate to say, is splendid. I console myself with the reminder that Mencken didn't write it. Many millions of people wrote it, and Mencken was merely the amanuensis who took it down from their dictation. He found a true "vehicle" (that is, a book that could be greater than the author who wrote it). He gets the royalties, but the job was done by a collectivity. As you read that book, you see a people who were up against a new set of typical recurrent situations, situations typical of their business, their politics, their criminal organizations, their sports. Either there were no words for these in standard English, or people didn't know them, or they didn't "sound right." So a new vocabulary arose, to "give us a word for it." I see no reason for believing that Americans are unusually fertile in word-coinage. American slang was not developed out of some exceptional gift. It was developed out of the fact that new typical situations had arisen and people needed names for them. They had to "size things up." They had to console and strike, to promise and admonish. They had to describe for purposes of forecasting. And "slang" was the result. It is, by this analysis, simply *proverbs not so named*, a kind of "folk criticism."

3

With what, then, would "sociological criticism" along these lines be concerned? It would seek to codify the various strategies which artists have developed with relation to the naming of situations. In a sense, much of it would even be "timeless," for many of the "typical," recurrent situations" are not peculiar to our own civilization at all. The situations and strategies framed in Aesop's Fables, for instance, apply to human relations now just as fully as they applied in ancient Greece. They are, like philosophy, sufficiently "generalized" to extend far beyond the particular combination of events named by them in any one instance. They name an "essence." Or, we could say that they are on a "high level of abstraction." One doesn't usually think of them as "abstract," since they are usually so concrete in their stylistic expression. But they invariably aim to discern the "general behind the particular" (which would suggest that they are good Goethe). The attempt to treat literature from the standpoint of situations and strategies suggests a variant of Spengler's notion of the "contemporaneous." By "contemporaneity" he meant corresponding stages of different cultures. For instance, if modern New York is much like decadent Rome, then we are "contemporaneous" with decadent Rome, or with some corresponding decadent city among the Mayas, etc. It is in this sense that situations are "timeless," "non-historical," "contemporaneous." A given human relationship may be at one time named in terms of foxes and lions, if there are foxes and lions about; or it may now be named in terms of salesmanship, advertising, the tactics of politicians, etc. But beneath the change in particulars, we may often discern the naming of the one situation.

So sociological criticism, as here understood, would seek to assemble and codify this lore. It might occasionally lead us to outrage good taste, as we sometimes found exemplified in some great sermon or tragedy or abstruse work of philosophy the same strategy as we found exemplified in a dirty joke. At this point, we'd put the sermon and the dirty joke together, thus "grouping by situation" and showing the range of possible particularizations. In his exceptionally discerning essay, "A Critic's Job of Work," R. P. Blackmur says, "I think on the whole his (Burke's) method could be applied with equal fruitfulness to Shakespeare, Dashiell Hammett, or Marie Corelli."[3] When I got through wincing, I had to admit that Blackmur was right. This article is an attempt to say for the method what can be said. As a matter of fact, I'll go a step further and maintain: You can't properly put Marie Corelli and Shakespeare apart until you have first put them together. First genus, then differentia. The strategy in common is the genus. The *range* or *scale* or *spectrum* of particularizations is the differentia.

Anyhow, that's what I'm driving at. And that's why reviewers sometime find in my work "intuitive" leaps that are dubious as "science." They are not "leaps" at all. They are classifications, groupings, made on the basis of some strategic element common to the items grouped. They are neither more nor less "intuitive" than *any* grouping or classification of social events. Apples can be grouped with bananas as fruits, and they can be grouped with tennis balls as round. I am simply proposing, in the social sphere, a method of classification with reference to *strategies*.

The method has these things to be said in its favor: It gives definite insight into the organization of literary works; and it automatically breaks down the barriers erected about literature as a specialized pursuit. People can classify novels by reference to three kinds, eight kinds, seventeen kinds. It doesn't matter. Students patiently copy down the professor's classification and pass examinations on it, because the range of possible academic classifications is endless. Sociological classification, as herein suggested, would derive

[3]Richard P. Blackmur, "A Critic's Job of Work" (1935), published in *Language as Gesture* (1952).

its relevance from the fact that it should apply both to works of art and to social situations outside of art.

It would, I admit, violate current pieties, break down current categories, and thereby "outrage good taste." But "good taste" has become *inert*. The classifications I am proposing would be *active*. I think that what we need is active categories.

These categories will lie on the bias across the categories of modern specialization. The new alignment will outrage in particular those persons who take the division of faculties in our universities to be an exact replica of the way in which God himself divided up the universe. We have had the Philosophy of Being; and we have had the Philosophy of Becoming. In typical contemporary specialization, we have been getting the Philosophy of the Bin. Each of these mental localities has had its own peculiar way of life, its own values, even its own special idiom for seeing, thinking, and "proving." Among other things, a sociological approach should attempt to provide a reintegrative point of view, a broader empire of investigation encompassing the lot.

What would such sociological categories be like? They would consider works of art, I think, as strategies for selecting enemies and allies, for socializing losses, for warding off evil eye, for purification, propitiation, and desanctification, consolation and vengeance, admonition and exhortation, implicit commands or instructions of one sort or another. Art forms like "tragedy" or "comedy" or "satire" would be treated as *equipments for living,* that size up situations in various ways and in keeping with correspondingly various attitudes. The typical ingredients of such forms would be sought. Their relation to typical situations would be stressed. Their comparative values would be considered, with the intention of formulating a "strategy of strategies," the "overall" strategy obtained by inspection of the lot.

Simone de Beauvoir

1908–1986

Simone-Lucie-Ernestine-Marie-Bertrand de Beauvoir was born and raised in a middle-class Parisian household that discouraged her interest in matters intellectual, but she went on to obtain a prestigious *agrégation* (postgraduate) degree in philosophy at the Sorbonne in 1929 and to write the influential feminist treatise *The Second Sex* (*Le Deuxième sexe*, 1949). While she was preparing for her degree, she met Jean-Paul Sartre, who became her companion in a lifelong nonmarital union, though it was a partnership fraught with conflicts produced by, among other things, his persistent and pointed infidelities. They were also partners in the important intellectual journal *Les Temps modernes*, a monthly that she and Sartre began in 1945 and that she continued to edit and review after Sartre's death in 1980.

After taking her *agrégé*, Beauvoir taught philosophy for thirteen years in various schools, then decided to make her living by her pen, publishing novels, essays, and travel literature. Most of her novels focus on themes of freedom, responsibility, and angst — giving concrete exposition to the issues highlighted in existentialism, the philosophy espoused by Beauvoir and Sartre. In his monumental philosophical treatise *Being and Nothingness* (*L'Être et le néant*, 1943), whose title plays off that of Heidegger's 1927 treatise, *Being and Time*, Sartre distinguishes between things, which exist purely in themselves and can be essentialized (the *en-soi*), and human beings (the *pour-soi*). As human beings we have no essence to which we aspire: Ever-changing, we are always free to make ourselves what we are, negating what we currently are and do in favor of some other mode of action and existence. Indeed one should not say that we *are*, but rather that we *become*. Our existence is contingent, unfixed, dependent on our interactions with an ever-changing environment. The responsibility for conscious choice of what we shall become at every moment of existence produces in the authentic individual the feeling of *angst*, or existential dread. So terrifying is our freedom and responsibility that we are constantly tempted by what Sartre calls bad faith (*mauvaise foi*), comforting lies by which we reassure ourselves that we have been merely formed by circumstance, that our choices are predetermined by psychic or social forces beyond our control.

Beauvoir's first novel, *She Came to Stay* (*L'Invitée*, 1943), focuses on the problems of conscience produced by conflicts within a close familial group. It also reflects the emotional upheaval in the Beauvoir-Sartre *ménage* caused by the prolonged stay of Olga Kosakiewicz, a young girl that Sartre had "adopted." *The Blood of Others* (*Le Sang des autres*, 1945) raises the issue of causes and consequences: Must a French resistance fighter consider himself responsible for the reprisals carried out by the Nazis? Her later novel, *The Mandarins* (*Les Mandarins*, 1954), a probing portrait of the French literary and intellectual establishment after World War II, won the Prix Goncourt, an award presented by that very establishment.

Beginning at the age of fifty, Beauvoir turned from philosophical fiction to autobiography and memoir. *Memoirs of a Dutiful Daughter* (*Mémoires d'une jeune fille rangée,* 1958) explores her youth and rebellion; *The Prime of Life* (*La Force de l'age,* 1960) and *The Force of Circumstance* (*La Force des choses,* 1963) continue her story into her middle age. As she grew older, Beauvoir concerned herself more and more with the problems of aging and dying, which she addressed in *A Very Easy Death* (*Une Morte très douce,* 1964), which focuses on the death of her mother; she wrote about Sartre's last illness and death in *Adieux: A Farewell to Sartre* (*Cérémonies des adieux,* 1981).

Beauvoir's magnum opus, *The Second Sex,* is one of the most important texts for twentieth-century feminism, a broad and wide-ranging attempt to review and critique the social and psychological constructions that since the Bronze Age have defined "humanity" in terms of the capacities, ideologies, and desires of the male sex, and correspondingly have positioned women as protected — even at times worshipped — but inferior: "She is defined and differentiated with reference to man and not he with reference to her; she is the incidental, the inessential as opposed to the essential. He is the Subject, he is the Absolute — she is the Other."[1]

In terms of the existential philosophy that Beauvoir developed along with Jean-Paul Sartre, this "alterity" or Otherness means that a woman is implicitly defined as *en-soi* rather than *pour-soi:* a thing rather than a person, a means to some other end rather than an end in itself. If, as existentialist philosophy suggests, the freedom to define what one is through one's choices and acts is terrifyingly difficult to accept for men, Beauvoir argues that it is almost impossible for women, who internalize and help maintain a patriarchal belief that their essential nature is to exist for the sake of others.

For Beauvoir, the destiny of Woman to be the Other begins, though it does not end, with mammalian anatomy. Unlike the controlling female queens in bee and ant societies, or the choosy (and devouring) female arachnids, whose power depends on exteriorizing their reproductive maneuvers, the human female carries the fertilized ovum inside her — a growing being that is a part of her and yet not herself, a parasite whose significance to the survival of the species makes her body an object rather than a subject, something Other even to herself.[2] When at the dawn of history man began to till the soil, woman in her fecundity was like the Earth itself, and like the Earth was made to yield her harvest for his benefit.[3] The tool-making and tool-using capacity vested more significance in man's upper-body strength and less in woman's adaptivity and endurance. Once created, patriarchy required that property descend through the male line, which in turn demanded that virtuous women be passive, acquiescent, and above all chaste, to guarantee true genetic inheritance as strictly as possible in a species whose individuals can never truly know who their father is.

---

[1]Simone de Beauvoir, *The Second Sex* (New York: Random House, 1953), p. xix.

[2]Some contemporary feminists have been critical of Beauvoir's essentialization of female inferiority and of the implication of her argument that anatomy was always destiny.

[3]Beauvoir dismisses as "a myth" the theory of some anthropologists that an early Bronze-Age matriarchal society may have preceded the development of patriarchal society. The theory is based on texts like Aeschylus's *The Eumenides,* which presupposes that the patriarchal Olympian gods had recently displaced the rule of the female principles of Earth and Night.

Beauvoir, like Hegel, sees the progress of civilization as bringing the individual closer and closer to the realization of his or her freedom, but she argues that while events like the French revolution liberated the masculine spirit from outmoded feudal social structures, the liberation of woman has been far slower in coming. She believes this is partly because women, however oppressed, are not a true class in Marx's sense: Restrictions on aristocratic women were imposed differently than on bourgeois or working-class women, and women could therefore gain no sense of common interest. The delay mainly results because women are epiphenomenal to the historically developing class struggle of men: Historical changes in women's status and choices — greater or less occupational or familial or sexual freedom — seem to depend not on what they want but on what men want of them.

In part III of *The Second Sex*, Beauvoir explores the ideological component of women's alterity: the way in which women are made to think of themselves as the Other, not by social rules or restrictions but by the myths through which societies construct the female consciousness. In "Myths: Of Women in Five Authors," Beauvoir exposes several myths that present women not as they are, but as projections of male needs, defined as whatever men need to complete themselves. These myths can be vulgar, as in Henri de Montherlant's casting of woman as mere "slimy" flesh with which man satiates himself sexually, or comparatively refined, as in D. H. Lawrence's vision of passive woman subordinating herself to the enabling transcendence of the Phallus. Or the myth can invert alterity, as in Paul Claudel's vision of woman as the holy channel through which the striving male soul may find the peace of God. Even Stendhal — who liked his women to have minds and hearts as well as bodies and souls, so that Beauvoir feels it is "a relief" to be able to talk about his complex and subtle creations — has his mythic woman. Stendhal's women — such as Madame de Rênal or la Sanseverina — are more complicated and intelligent than their male counterparts, but they are never the subject of the narrative in their own right: They are there as the Other to play their part in the maturation of the male subject, Julien Sorel or Fabrizio.[4]

The result of the construction of woman as an ideal, whatever her characteristics, Beauvoir argues, is to force women to choose between being a "woman" and being themselves. In her final section, she sees light at the end of the tunnel: In the dissatisfaction of contemporary men with the lack of womanliness of present-day women, Beauvoir senses that a parting of the ways has come and that the myth of femininity is not all-powerful. Her book itself gave a gigantic tug at that unstable ideological structure. Some present-day feminists would argue that it is necessary to go beyond Beauvoir's own dogmas, her own inherited essentialisms, such as the rigid dialectic between masculinity and femininity, but surely *The Second Sex* has a clear place on the map of today's feminist theory.

[4]Beauvoir's observations concerning Stendhal's novels are similar to what James Phelan has more recently argued about *A Farewell to Arms* — that the essential sexism of Hemingway's novel resides less in how Catherine Barkley is characterized than in the fact that the novel is structured so that the central tragedy is not her death, but Frederic Henry's having to go on living without her. It is his loss, not hers, that counts.

Selected Bibliography

Beauvoir, Simone de. *The Second Sex*. Trans. Constance Borde and Sheila Malovany-Chevallier. Random House: Alfred A. Knopf. 2009.

———. *All Said and Done*. New York: Marlowe, 1994.

Francis, Claude, and Fernande Gontier. *Simone de Beauvoir: A Life — A Love Story*. New York: St. Martin's Press, 1988.

Fullbrook, Kate, and Edward Fullbrook. *Simone de Beauvoir and Jean-Paul Sartre: The Remaking of the Twentieth-Century Legend*. New York: Basic Books, 1994.

Grosholz, Emily R., ed. *The Legacy of Simone de Beauvoir*. Oxford: Clarendon, 2004.

Keefe, Terry. *Simone de Beauvoir*. New York, St. Martin's Press, 1998.

Lundgren-Gothlin, Eva. *Sex and Existence: Simone de Beauvoir's* The Second Sex. Boston: University Press of New England, 1996.

Marks, Elaine, ed. *Critical Essays on Simone de Beauvoir*. Boston: G. K. Hall, 1987.

Moi, Toril. *Simone de Beauvoir: The Making of an Intellectual Woman*. London: Blackwell, 1994.

Pilardi, Jo-Ann. *Simone de Beauvoir Writing the Self: Philosophy Becomes Autobiography*. Westport, CT: Praeger, 1999.

Simons, Margaret A., ed. *Feminist Interpretations of Simone de Beauvoir*. University Park: Pennsylvania State University Press, 1995.

The Second Sex

MYTHS: OF WOMEN IN FIVE AUTHORS

These examples show that the great collective myths are reflected in each singular writer: woman appears to us as *flesh*; male flesh is engendered by the maternal womb and re-created in the woman lover's embrace: thus, woman is akin to *nature*, she embodies it: animal, little vale of blood, rose in bloom, siren, curve of a hill, she gives humus, sap, tangible beauty, and the world's soul to man; she can hold the keys to *poetry;* she can be *mediator* between this world and the beyond; grace or Pythia, star or witch, she opens the door to the supernatural, the surreal; she is destined to *immanence;* and through her passivity she doles out peace and harmony: but should she refuse this role, she becomes praying mantis or ogress. In any case, she appears as the *privileged Other* through whom the subject accomplishes himself: one of the measures of man, his balance, his salvation, his adventure, and his happiness.

But these myths are orchestrated differently for each individual. The *Other* is singularly defined according to the singular way the *One* chooses to posit himself. All men assert themselves as freedom and transcendence: but they do not all give the same meaning to these words. For Montherlant[1] transcendence is a state: he is the transcendent, he soars in the sky of heroes; the woman crouches on the ground, under his feet; he enjoys measuring the distance separating him from her; from time to time, he raises her to him, takes and then

---

Translation by Constance Borde and Sheila Malovany-Chevallier

[1]Henri de Montherlant (1896–1972), antifeminist author of *Les Jeune filles* (1936), *Pitié pour les femmes* (1936), *Le Démon du bien* (1937), and *Lea Lepreuses* (1939).

rejects her: never does he lower himself toward her sphere of viscous darkness. Lawrence[2] situates transcendence in the phallus; the phallus is life and power only thanks to woman: immanence is thus good and necessary; the false hero who deigns not to touch the earth, far from being a demigod, fails to be a man; woman is not despicable, she is deep wealth, hot spring; but she must renounce all personal transcendence and settle for nourishing that of her male. Claudel[3] demands the same devotion: woman is also for him the one who maintains life, while man prolongs the vital momentum by his activity; but for the Catholic everything that occurs on earth is steeped in vain immanence: the only transcendent is God; in God's eyes the active man and the woman who serves him are exactly equal; each one has to surpass his earthly condition: salvation in any case is an autonomous undertaking. For Breton[4] sexual hierarchy is inverted: action and conscious thought in which the male situates his transcendence are for him a banal mystification that engenders war, stupidity, bureaucracy, and negation of the human; it is immanence, the pure opaque presence of the real, that is the truth; true transcendence would be accomplished by the return to immanence. His attitude is the exact opposite of Montherlant's: the latter likes war because women are banished from it, Breton venerates woman because she brings peace; one confuses mind and subjectivity, he rejects the given universe: the other thinks the mind is objectively present in the heart of the world; woman compromises Montherlant because she shatters his solitude; she is, for Breton, revelation because she wrests him from subjectivity. As for Stendhal,[5] we saw that woman barely takes on a mythical value

[2]D. H. Lawrence (1885–1930), author of Sons and Lovers (1913) and Women in Love (1920).

[3]Paul Claudel (1868–1955), poet and playwright, author of L'Annonce faite à Marie (1912) and Le Soulier de satin (1937), which contains the salvation of Rodrigue by Prouhèze that Beauvoir refers to later.

[4]André Breton (1896–1966), surrealist poet and novelist, author of Nadja (1928) and L'Amour fou (1937).

[5]Marie-Henri Beyle (1783–1842), psychological novelist who wrote as Stendhal; his works include Le Rouge et le noir (1830) and La Chartreuse de Parme (1839).

for him: he considers her as also being a transcendence; for this humanist, it is in their reciprocal relations that freedoms are accomplished; and it is sufficient that the Other is simply another for life to have, according to him, a little spice; he does not seek a stellar equilibrium, he does not nourish himself with the bread of disgust; he does not expect miracles; he wishes to concern himself not with the cosmos or poetry but with freedoms.

That is, he also experiences himself as a translucent freedom. The others—and this is one of the most important points—posit themselves as transcendences but feel they are prisoners of an opaque presence in their own hearts: they project onto this woman the "unbreakable core of night." In Montherlant there is an Adlerian complex[6] where heavy bad faith is born: these pretensions and fears are what he incarnates in woman; the disgust he feels for her is what he fears to feel for himself; he intends to trample in her the ever possible proof of his own insufficiency; he asks scorn to save him; woman is the ditch in which he throws all the monsters that inhabit him.[7] Lawrence's life shows us that he suffered from an analogous complex but more purely sexual: woman in his work has the value of a compensatory myth; through her is found an exalted virility of which the writer was not very sure: when he describes Kate at Don Cipriano's feet, he believes he has won a male triumph over Frieda;[8] nor does he accept that his female companion challenges him: if she contested his aims, he would probably lose confidence in them; her role is to reassure him. He asks for peace, rest, and faith from her, just as Montherlant asks for the certitude of his

[6]Inferiority complex, feelings of self-doubt for which one may compensate by projecting the inferiority on some other person or group whom one attempts to dominate; named for psychologist Alfred Adler (1870–1937).

[7]Stendhal judged in advance the cruelties with which Montherlant amuses himself: "In indifference, what should be done? Love-taste, but without the horrors. The horrors always come from a little soul that needs reassurance of its own merits." [Beauvoir]

[8]Kate and Don Cipriano are characters in Lawrence's novel, The Plumed Serpent (1926); Frieda was Lawrence's wife.

superiority: they demand what they lack. Self-confidence is not lacking in Claudel: if he is shy, it is only the secret of God. Thus, there is no trace of the battle of the sexes. Man bravely takes on the weight of woman: she is the possibility of temptation or of salvation. For Breton it seems that man is only true through the mystery that inhabits him; it pleases him that Nadja sees that star he is going toward and that is like "a heartless flower"; his dreams, intuitions, and the spontaneous unfolding of his inner language: it is in these activities that are out of the control of will and reason that he recognizes himself: woman is the tangible figure of this veiled presence infinitely more essential than her conscious personality.

As for Stendhal, he quietly coincides with himself; but he needs woman as she does him so that his dispersed existence is gathered in the unity of a figure and a destiny; it is as for-another that the human being reaches being; but another still has to lend him his consciousness: other men are too indifferent to their peers; only the woman in love opens her heart to her lover and shelters it in its entirety. Except for Claudel, who finds a perfect[9] witness in God, all the writers we have considered expect, in Malraux's words, woman to cherish in them this "incomparable monster" known to themselves alone. In collaboration or combat, men come up against each other in their generality. Montherlant, for his peers, is a writer, Lawrence a doctrinaire, Breton a leader of a school, Stendhal a diplomat or a man of wit; it is women who reveal in one a magnificent and cruel prince, in another a disturbing animal, in still another a god or a sun or a being "black and cold … like a man struck by lightning, lying at the feet of the Sphinx,"[10] and in the other a seducer, a charmer, a lover.

For each of them, the ideal woman will be she who embodies the most exactly the *Other* able to reveal him to himself. Montherlant, the solar spirit, looks for pure animality in her; Lawrence, the phallic, demands that she sum up the female sex in its generality; Claudel defines her as a soul sister; Breton cherishes Melusina rooted in nature, he puts his hopes in the child-woman; Stendhal wants his mistress intelligent, cultivated, free of spirit and morals: an equal. But the only earthly destiny reserved to the woman equal, child-woman, soul sister, woman-sex, and female animal is always man. Regardless of the ego looking for itself through her, it can only attain itself if she consents to be his crucible. In any case, what is demanded of her is self-forgetting and love. Montherlant consents to be moved by the woman who enables him to measure his virile power; Lawrence addresses an ardent hymn to the woman who renounces herself for him; Claudel exalts the vassal, servant, and devoted woman who submits herself to God by submitting herself to the male; Breton puts his hopes in woman for humanity's salvation because she is capable of the most total love for her child and her lover; and even in Stendhal the heroines are more moving than the masculine heroes because they give themselves over to their passion with a more ardent violence; they help man to accomplish his destiny as Prouhèze contributes to Rodrigo's salvation; in Stendhal's novels, women often save their lovers from ruin, prison, or death. Feminine devotion is demanded as a duty by Montherlant and Lawrence; less arrogant, Claudel, Breton, and Stendhal admire it as a generous choice; they desire it without claiming to deserve it; but— except for the astonishing *Lamiel*[11]—all their works show they expect from woman this altruism that Comte[12] admired in and imposed on her, and which, according to him, also constituted both a flagrant inferiority and an equivocal superiority.

We could find many more examples: they would always lead to the same conclusions. In defining woman, each writer defines his general

---

[9]André Malraux (1901–76), novelist and political figure: his works include *La Condition humaine* (1933) and *Les Voix du silence* (1951).

[10]Breton's *Nadja*. [Beauvoir]

[11]Stendhal's final unfinished novel, written 1838–42, published 1889.

[12]Auguste Comte (1798–1857), French philosopher and sociologist, author of *Système de politique positive* (1851–54).

ethic and the singular idea he has of himself: it is also in her that he often registers the distance between his view of the world and his egotistical dreams. The absence or insignificance of the female element in a body of work in general is itself symptomatic; it has an extreme importance when it sums up in its totality all the aspects of the Other, as it does for Lawrence; it remains important if woman is grasped simply as another but the writer is interested in her life's individual adventure, which is Stendhal's case; it loses importance in a period like ours in which each individual's particular problems are of secondary import. However, woman as other still plays a role inasmuch as even to transcend himself, each man still needs to take consciousness of himself.

Susan Sontag

1933–2004

Susan Sontag was born in New York City but raised in Tucson, Arizona, and in Los Angeles. She began her college work at the University of California, Berkeley, but transferred to the University of Chicago, where she received her B.A. in philosophy in 1951, at the age of eighteen. She did graduate work in English and philosophy at Harvard, where she received her M.A., and further graduate study at Oxford and the Sorbonne. Sontag taught at Harvard, the University of Connecticut, Rutgers, and Columbia, but supported herself mainly through her books and periodical essays.

Though she resisted being classified "primarily as an essayist" Sontag was usually regarded as a cultural barometer, whose novels, short fiction, and screenplays were generated by her critical ideas and cultural observations. And while other theorists, such as T. S. Eliot, were primarily concerned with demonstrating the continuity of the present with the past, Sontag, who began writing in the 1960s, always appeared less concerned with the traditions than with the discontinuities of contemporary life.

One of Sontag's major roles, at the outset of her career at least, was as a conduit between America and Europe of avant-garde ideas and personalities. Theorists like Walter Benjamin and Roland Barthes, now canonical, were almost unknown in the United States when they were recommended by Sontag in 1964 as writers who "reveal the sensuous surface of art without mucking about in it" in Section 8 of "Against Interpretation." In other essays in the early 1960s, she called attention on this side of the Atlantic to writers like Nathalie Sarraute, Antonin Artaud, and Alain Robbe-Grillet.

But Sontag was not a typical literary critic. She did not wish to analyze and interpret a series of standard texts so much as to discuss the conditions for their appearance, and the cultural assumptions that underlie their production and their reception. The subjects that most appealed to her were the marginal areas of art, which sketch in the boundaries of a culture and its perceptions: the "camp" sensibility, the pornographic imagination, illness as metaphor, and photography as an art form. Despite the variety of topics, Sontag's work, according to Susan Jeffords, "is of a piece. . . . No matter what form they take, Sontag asks the same questions — about the construction and resolution of identity, about manipulation and violence as a basis for social and aesthetic encounters, about the structure and function of cultural interpretation, about the inspiration of those outside accepted social boundaries — hoping that new answers will appear as a byproduct of new form. It is paradigmatic of Sontag's position as a modernist that they do not." Although she was not a reader-response critic in any of the usual senses of the term (see the introduction to Reader-Response Theory, p. 543), Sontag was most strongly engaged by the question of how readers process texts and by the cultural uses to which literature is put. This is the central concern in "Against Interpretation."

The core of the essay is the three short sentences in Section 5: "Real art has the capacity to make us nervous. By reducing the work of art to its content and then interpreting *that*, one tames the work of art. Interpretation makes art manageable, comfortable." Interpretation, for Sontag, was a vicious and cowardly form of translation, in which the work of art is stripped of its sensuous life and reduced to a bare statement, which is then processed through the categories of the various schools of criticism (Marxist, Freudian, Christian) into a message that is inevitably familiar, indeed always already known. Appreciative and analytical criticism — not the nasty judgmental kind — has thus become the most deadly enemy of art.

The reaction to "Against Interpretation" was predictably fierce, and not merely from the Freudians and Marxists whose oxen were explicitly gored. Representatives of the New Criticism, then enjoying its hegemony, objected that they had been making Sontag's point for her all along (in such essays as Cleanth Brooks's "The Heresy of Paraphrase"). In fact, Sontag's strictures would equally apply against the New Critics, who, while granting lip service to the primacy of form, had always treated poetry as a general statement (or pseudostatement) about the world, albeit an especially complex sort of statement, riffed by paradox, irony, ambiguity, and other tropes. In New Critical terminology, theme is a part of form — and thus Sontag's dichotomy of "form" and "content" might mislead one to think she favored that school of exegesis. In fact, for Sontag any *translation* of the text into other terms is a betrayal of that text, and the *thematization* of any text always reduces it to a subartistic level.

Since "Against Interpretation" was published, there have been at least a few faltering steps toward exploring the "erotics of art" Sontag mentions. In particular, much recent psychoanalytic theory (like that of Peter Brooks) have dropped the old dichotomy between latent and manifest content and attempted to discuss the form of the text as something other than a nicely wrapped container for fantasy and defense. Some New Historicist and cultural critics have moved beyond the representative quality and the political tendency of the text. Nevertheless, since translation and thematization have always been the mainstay of academic criticism, Sontag could be certain to find, in the pages of almost every scholarly journal today, specimens of the same destructive, spiritually impoverished interpretation she rejects.

Susan Sontag died as she had lived, with great fortitude, on December 28, 2004, after a long struggle with leukemia.

Selected Bibliography

Brooks, Peter. "Death of/as Metaphor." *Partisan Review* 46 (1979): 438–44.

Jeffords, Susan. "Susan Sontag." *Modern American Critics Since 1955*, ed. Gregory Jay. Detroit: Bruccoli-Clark-Layman, 1988.

Phillips, William. "Radical Styles." *Partisan Review* 36 (1969): 388–400.

Poague, Leland, and Kathy A. Parsons. *Susan Sontag: An Annotated Bibliography: 1948–1992*. New York: Garland, 2000.

Rollyson, Carl, and Lisa Paddock. *Susan Sontag: The Making of an Icon*. New York: Norton, 2000.

Roudiez, Leon S. "Susan Sontag: Against the Ideological Grain." *World Literature Today* 57 (1983): 219–23.

Rubin, Louis D., Jr. "Susan Sontag and the Camp Followers." *Sewanee Review* 82 (1974): 503–10.

Shaw, Peter. "Two Afterthoughts on Susan Sontag." *Encounter* 58/59 (1982): 38–40.

Against Interpretation

Content is a glimpse of something, an encounter like a flash. It's very tiny — very tiny, content.

— WILLEM DE KOONING, in an interview

It is only shallow people who do not judge by appearances. The mystery of the world is the visible, not the invisible.

— OSCAR WILDE, in a letter

I

The earliest *experience* of art must have been that it was incantatory, magical; art was an instrument of ritual. (Cf. the paintings in the caves at Lascaux, Altamira, Niaux, La Pasiega, etc.) The earliest *theory* of art, that of the Greek philosophers, proposed that art was mimesis, imitation of reality.

It is at this point that the peculiar question of the *value* of art arose. For the mimetic theory, by its very terms, challenges art to justify itself.

Plato, who proposed the theory, seems to have done so in order to rule that the value of art is dubious. Since he considered ordinary material things as themselves mimetic objects, imitations of transcendent forms or structures, even the best painting of a bed would be only an "imitation of an imitation." For Plato, art is neither particularly useful (the painting of a bed is no good to sleep on), nor, in the strict sense, true. And Aristotle's arguments in defense of art do not really challenge Plato's view that all art is an elaborate *trompe l'oeil,*[1] and therefore a lie. But he does dispute Plato's idea that art is useless. Lie or no, art has a certain value according to Aristotle

because it is a form of therapy. Art is useful, after all, Aristotle counters, medicinally useful in that it arouses and purges dangerous emotions.[2]

In Plato and Aristotle, the mimetic theory of art goes hand in hand with the assumption that art is always figurative. But advocates of the mimetic theory need not close their eyes to decorative and abstract art. The fallacy that art is necessarily a "realism" can be modified or scrapped without ever moving outside the problems delimited by the mimetic theory.

The fact is, all Western consciousness of and reflection upon art have remained within the confines staked out by the Greek theory of art as mimesis or representation. It is through this theory that art as such — above and beyond given works of art — becomes problematic, in need of defense. And it is the defense of art which gives birth to the odd vision by which something we have learned to call "form" is separated off from something we have learned to call "content," and to the well-intentioned move which makes content essential and form accessory.

Even in modern times, when most artists and critics have discarded the theory of art as representation of an outer reality in favor of the theory of art as subjective expression, the main feature of the mimetic theory persists. Whether we conceive of the work of art on the model of a picture (art as a picture of reality) or on the model of a statement (art as the statement of the artist), content still comes first. The content may have changed. It may now be less figurative, less lucidly realistic. But it is still assumed that

[1]Deception of the eye.

[2]Sontag conflates Aristotle's *Poetics* with the reference to *katharsis* in the *Politics,* quoted in the introduction to Aristotle; see p. 46.

a work of art *is* its content. Or, as it's usually put today, that a work of art by definition says something. ("'What X is saying is . . . . ,'" "'What X is trying to say is . . . ,'" "'What X said is . . .'" etc., etc.)

2

None of us can ever retrieve that innocence before all theory when art knew no need to justify itself, when one did not ask of a work of art what it *said* because one knew (or thought one knew) what it *did*. From now to the end of conscious-ness, we are stuck with the task of defending art. We can only quarrel with one or another means of defense. Indeed, we have an obliga-tion to overthrow any means of defending and justifying art which becomes particularly obtuse or onerous or insensitive to contemporary needs and practice.

This is the case, today, with the very idea of content itself. Whatever it may have been in the past, the idea of content is today mainly a hindrance, a nuisance, a subtle or not so subtle philistinism.

Though the actual developments in many arts may seem to be leading us away from the idea that a work of art is primarily its content, the idea still exerts an extraordinary hegemony. I want to suggest that this is because the idea is now perpetuated in the guise of a certain way of encountering works of art thoroughly ingrained among most people who take any of the arts seriously. What the overemphasis on the idea of content entails is the perennial, never consum-mated project of *interpretation*. And, conversely, it is the habit of approaching works of art in order to *interpret* them that sustains the fancy that there really is such a thing as the content of a work of art.

3

Of course, I don't mean interpretation in the broadest sense, the sense in which Nietzsche (rightly) says, "There are no facts, only interpre-tations." By interpretation, I mean here a con-scious act of the mind which illustrates a certain code, certain "rules" of interpretation.

Directed to art, interpretation means plucking a set of elements (the X, the Y, the Z, and so forth) from the whole work. The task of interpretation is virtually one of translation. The interpreter says, Look, don't you see that X is really — or, really means — A? That Y is really B? That Z is really C?

What situation could prompt this curious proj-ect for transforming a text? History gives us the materials for an answer. Interpretation first appears in the culture of late classical antiquity, when the power and credibility of myth had been broken by the "realistic" view of the world introduced by scientific enlightenment. Once the question that haunts post-mythic consciousness — that of the *seemliness* of religious symbols — had been asked, the ancient texts were, in their pristine form, no longer acceptable. Then interpretation was summoned, to reconcile the ancient texts to "modern" demands. Thus, the Stoics, to accord with their view that the gods had to be moral, allegorized away the rude features of Zeus and his boisterous clan in Homer's epics. What Homer really designated by the adultery of Zeus with Leto, they explained, was the union between power and wisdom. In the same vein, Philo of Alexandria interpreted the literal historical narra-tives of the Hebrew Bible as spiritual paradigms. The story of the exodus from Egypt, the wandering in the desert for forty years, and the entry into the promised land, said Philo, was really an allegory of the individual soul's emancipation, tribulations, and final deliverance.[3] Interpretation thus presupposes a discrepancy between the clear meaning of the text and the demands of (later) readers. It seeks to resolve that discrep-ancy. The situation is that for some reason a text has become unacceptable; yet it cannot be discarded. Interpretation is a radical strategy for conserving an old text, which is thought too precious to repudiate, by revamping it. The inter-preter, without actually erasing or rewriting the text, *is* altering it. But he can't admit to doing this. He claims to be only making it intelligible,

[3]Dante's redaction of Philo's system appears in his letter to *Can Grande della Scala*, p. 101.

by disclosing its true meaning. However far the interpreters alter the text (another notorious example is the Rabbinic and Christian "spiritual" interpretations of the clearly erotic Song of Songs), they must claim to be reading off a sense that is already there.

Interpretation in our own time, however, is even more complex. For the contemporary zeal for the project of interpretation is often prompted not by piety toward the troublesome text (which may conceal an aggression), but by an open aggressiveness, an overt contempt for appearances. The old style of interpretation was insistent, but respectful; it erected another meaning on top of the literal one. The modern style of interpretation excavates, and as it excavates, destroys; it digs "behind" the text, to find a subtext which is the true one. The most celebrated and influential modern doctrines, those of Marx and Freud, actually amount to elaborate systems of hermeneutics, aggressive and impious theories of interpretation. All observable phenomena are bracketed, in Freud's phrase, as *manifest content.* This manifest content must be probed and pushed aside to find the true meaning — the *latent content* — beneath.[4] For Marx, social events like revolutions and wars; for Freud, the events of individual lives (like neurotic symptoms and slips of the tongue) as well as texts (like a dream or a work of art) — all are treated as occasions for interpretation. According to Marx and Freud, these events only *seem* to be intelligible. Actually, they have no meaning without interpretation. To understand *is* to interpret. And to interpret is to restate the phenomenon, in effect to find an equivalent for it.

Thus, interpretation is not (as most people assume) an absolute value, a gesture of mind situated in some timeless realm of capabilities. Interpretation must itself be evaluated, within a historical view of human consciousness. In some cultural contexts, interpretation is a liberating act. It is a means of revising, of transvaluing, of escaping the dead past. In other cultural contexts, it is reactionary, impertinent, cowardly, stifling.

[4]See the introduction to Psychoanalytic Theory, p. 627.

4

Today is such a time, when the project of interpretation is largely reactionary, stifling. Like the fumes of the automobile and of heavy industry which befoul the urban atmosphere, the effusion of interpretations of art today poisons our sensibilities. In a culture whose already classical dilemma is the hypertrophy of the intellect at the expense of energy and sensual capability, interpretation is the revenge of the intellect upon art.

Even more. It is the revenge of the intellect upon the world. To interpret is to impoverish, to deplete the world — in order to set up a shadow world of "meanings." It is to turn *the* world into *this* world. ("This world"! As if there were any other.)

The world, our world, is depleted, impoverished enough. Away with all duplicates of it, until we again experience more immediately what we have.

5

In most modern instances, interpretation amounts to the philistine refusal to leave the work of art alone. Real art has the capacity to make us nervous. By reducing the work of art to its content and then interpreting *that,* one tames the work of art. Interpretation makes art manageable, comfortable.

This philistinism of interpretation is more rife in literature than in any other art. For decades now, literary critics have understood it to be their task to translate the elements of the poem or play or novel or story into something else. Sometimes a writer will be so uneasy before the naked power of his art that he will install within the work itself — albeit with a little shyness, a touch of the good taste of irony — the clear and explicit interpretation of it. Thomas Mann is an example of such an overcooperative author. In the case of more stubborn authors, the critic is only too happy to perform the job.

The work of Kafka, for example, has been subjected to a mass ravishment by no less than three armies of interpreters. Those who read Kafka as a social allegory see case studies of the frustrations and insanity of modern bureaucracy and its ultimate issuance in the totalitarian state. Those who read Kafka as a psychoanalytic allegory see desperate revelations of Kafka's fear of his father, his castration anxieties, his sense of his own impotence, his thralldom to his dreams. Those who read Kafka as a religious allegory explain that K. in *The Castle* is trying to gain access to heaven, that Joseph K. in *The Trial* is being judged by the inexorable and mysterious justice of God.... Another *oeuvre* that has attracted interpreters like leeches is that of Samuel Beckett. Beckett's delicate dramas of the withdrawn consciousness — pared down to essentials, cut off, often represented as physically immobilized — are read as a statement about modern man's alienation from meaning or from God, or as an allegory of psychopathology.

Proust, Joyce, Faulkner, Rilke, Lawrence, Gide ... one could go on citing author after author; the list is endless of those around whom thick encrustations of interpretation have taken hold. But it should be noted that interpretation is not simply the compliment that mediocrity pays to genius. It is, indeed, *the* modern way of understanding something, and is applied to works of every quality. Thus, in the notes that Elia Kazan published on his production of *A Streetcar Named Desire*, it becomes clear that, in order to direct the play, Kazan had to discover that Stanley Kowalski represented the sensual and vengeful barbarism that was engulfing our culture, while Blanche Du Bois was Western civilization, poetry, delicate apparel, dim lighting, refined feelings and all, though a little the worse for wear to be sure. Tennessee Williams's forceful psychological melodrama now became intelligible: it was *about* something, about the decline of Western civilization. Apparently, were it to go on being a play about a handsome brute named Stanley Kowalski and a faded mangy belle named Blanche Du Bois, it would not be manageable.

6

It doesn't matter whether artists intend, or don't intend, for their works to be interpreted. Perhaps Tennessee Williams thinks *Streetcar* is about what Kazan thinks it to be about. It may be that Cocteau in *The Blood of a Poet* and in *Orpheus* wanted the elaborate readings which have been given these films, in terms of Freudian symbolism and social critique. But the merit of these works certainly lies elsewhere than in their "meanings." Indeed, it is precisely to the extent that Williams's plays and Cocteau's films do suggest these portentous meanings that they are defective, false, contrived, lacking in conviction.

From interviews, it appears that Resnais and Robbe-Grillet consciously designed *Last Year at Marienbad* to accommodate a multiplicity of equally plausible interpretations. But the temptation to interpret *Marienbad* should be resisted. What matters in *Marienbad* is the pure, untranslatable, sensuous immediacy of some of its images, and its rigorous if narrow solutions to certain problems of cinematic form.

Again, Ingmar Bergman may have meant the tank rumbling down the empty night street in *The Silence* as a phallic symbol. But if he did, it was a foolish thought. ("Never trust the teller, trust the tale," said Lawrence.) Taken as a brute object, as an immediate sensory equivalent for the mysterious abrupt armored happenings going on inside the hotel, that sequence with the tank is the most striking moment in the film. Those who reach for a Freudian interpretation of the tank are only expressing their lack of response to what is there on the screen.

It is always the case that interpretation of this type indicates a dissatisfaction (conscious or unconscious) with the work, a wish to replace it by something else.

Interpretation, based on the highly dubious theory that a work of art is composed of items of content, violates art. It makes art into an article for use, for arrangement into a mental scheme of categories.

7

Interpretation does not, of course, always prevail. In fact, a great deal of today's art may be understood as motivated by a flight from interpretation. To avoid interpretation, art may become parody. Or it may become abstract. Or it may become ("merely") decorative. Or it may become non-art. The flight from interpretation seems particularly a feature of modern painting. Abstract painting is the attempt to have, in the ordinary sense, no content; since there is no content, there can be no interpretation. Pop Art works by the opposite means to the same result; using a content so blatant, so "what it is," it, too, ends by being uninterpretable.

A great deal of modern poetry as well, starting from the great experiments of French poetry (including the movement that is misleadingly called Symbolism) to put silence into poems and to reinstate the *magic* of the word, has escaped from the rough grip of interpretation. The most recent revolution in contemporary taste in poetry — the revolution that has deposed Eliot and elevated Pound — represents a turning away from content in poetry in the old sense, an impatience with what made modern poetry prey to the zeal of interpreters.

I am speaking mainly of the situation in America, of course. Interpretation runs rampant here in those arts with a feeble and negligible avant-garde: fiction and the drama. Most American novelists and playwrights are really either journalists or gentlemen sociologists and psychologists. They are writing the literary equivalent of program music. And so rudimentary, uninspired, and stagnant has been the sense of what might be done with *form* in fiction and drama that even when the content isn't simply information, news, it is still peculiarly visible, handier, more exposed. To the extent that novels and plays (in America), unlike poetry and painting and music, don't reflect any interesting concern with changes in their form, these arts remain prone to assault by interpretation.

But programmatic avant-gardism — which has meant, mostly, experiments with form at the expense of content — is not the only defense against the infestation of art by interpretations. At least, I hope not. For this would be to commit art to being perpetually on the run. (It also perpetuates the very distinction between form and content which is, ultimately, an illusion.) Ideally, it is possible to elude the interpreters in another way, by making works of art whose surface is so unified and clean, whose momentum is so rapid, whose address is so direct that the work can be . . . just what it is. Is this possible now? It does happen in films, I believe. This is why cinema is the most alive, the most exciting, the most important of all art forms right now. Perhaps the way one tells how alive a particular art form is, is by the latitude it gives for making mistakes in it, and still being good. For example, a few of the films of Bergman — though crammed with lame messages about the modern spirit, thereby inviting interpretations — still triumph over the pretentious intentions of their director. In *Winter Light* and *The Silence,* the beauty and visual sophistication of the images subvert before our eyes the callow pseudo-intellectuality of the story and some of the dialogue. (The most remarkable instance of this sort of discrepancy is the work of D. W. Griffith.) In good films, there is always a directness that entirely frees us from the itch to interpret. Many old Hollywood films, like those of Cukor, Walsh, Hawks, and countless other directors, have this liberating anti-symbolic quality, no less than the best work of the new European directors, like Truffaut's *Shoot the Piano Player* and *Jules and Jim,* Godard's *Breathless* and *Vivre Sa Vie,* Antonioni's *L'Avventura,* and Olmi's *The Fiancés.*

The fact that films have not been overrun by interpreters is in part due simply to the newness of cinema as an art. It also owes to the happy accident that films for such a long time were just movies; in other words, that they were understood to be part of mass, as opposed to high, culture, and were left alone by most people with minds. Then, too, there is always something other than content in the cinema to grab hold of, for those who want to analyze. For the cinema, unlike the novel, possesses a vocabulary of forms — the explicit, complex, and discussable technology of camera movements, cutting, and composition of the frame that goes into the making of a film.

8

What kind of criticism, of commentary on the arts, is desirable today? For I am not saying that works of art are ineffable, that they cannot be described or paraphrased. They can be. The question is how. What would criticism look like that would serve the work of art, not usurp its place?

What is needed, first, is more attention to form in art. If excessive stress on *content* provokes the arrogance of interpretation, more extended and more thorough descriptions of *form* would silence. What is needed is a vocabulary — a descriptive, rather than prescriptive, vocabulary — for *forms*.[5] The best criticism, and it is uncommon, is of this sort that dissolves considerations of content into those of form. On film, drama, and painting respectively, I can think of Erwin Panofsky's essay, "Style and Medium in the Motion Pictures," Northrop Frye's essay "A Conspectus of Dramatic Genres," Pierre Francastel's essay "The Destruction of a Plastic Space," Roland Barthes's book *On Racine* and his two essays on Robbe-Grillet are examples of formal analysis applied to the work of a single author. (The best essays in Erich Auerbach's *Mimesis*, like "The Scar of Odysseus," are also of this type.) An example of formal analysis applied simultaneously to genre and author is Walter Benjamin's essay, "The Story Teller: Reflections on the Works of Nicolai Leskov."

Equally valuable would be acts of criticism which would supply a really accurate, sharp, loving description of the appearance of a work of art. This seems even harder to do than formal analysis. Some of Manny Farber's film criticism, Dorothy Van Ghent's essay "The Dickens World: A View from Todgers'," Randall Jarrell's essay on Walt Whitman are among the rare examples of what I mean. These essays are which reveal the sensuous surface of art without mucking about in it.

6

Transparence is the highest, most liberating value in art — and in criticism — today. Transparence means experiencing the luminousness of the thing in itself, of things being what they are. This is the

[5]One of the difficulties is that our idea of form is spatial (the Greek metaphors for form are all derived from notions of space). This is why we have a more ready vocabulary of forms for the spatial than for the temporal arts. The exception among the temporal arts, of course, is the drama; perhaps this is because the drama is a narrative (i.e. temporal) form that extends itself visually and pictorially, upon a stage. . . . What we don't have yet is a poetics of the novel, any clear notion of the forms of narration. Perhaps film criticism will be the occasion of a breakthrough here, since films are primarily a visual form, yet they are also a subdivision of literature. [Sontag]

greatness of, for example, the films of Bresson and Ozu and Renoir's *The Rules of the Game*.

Once upon a time (say, for Dante), it must have been a revolutionary and creative move to design works of art so that they might be experienced on several levels. Now it is not. It reinforces the principle of redundancy that is the principal affliction of modern life.

Once upon a time (a time when high art was scarce), it must have been a revolutionary and creative move to interpret works of art. Now it is not. What we decidedly do not need now is further to assimilate Art into Thought, or (worse yet) Art into Culture.

Interpretation takes the sensory experience of the work of art for granted, and proceeds from there. This cannot be taken for granted, now. Think of the sheer multiplication of works of art available to every one of us, superadded to the conflicting tastes and odors and sights of the urban environment that bombard our senses. Ours is a culture based on excess, on overproduction; the result is a steady loss of sharpness in our sensory experience. All the conditions of modern life — its material plenitude, its sheer crowdedness — conjoin to dull our sensory faculties. And it is in the light of the condition of our senses, our capacities (rather than those of another age), that the task of the critic must be assessed.

What is important now is to recover our senses. We must learn to *see* more, to *hear* more, to *feel* more.

Our task is not to find the maximum amount of content in a work of art, much less to squeeze more content out of the work than is already there. Our task is to cut back content so that we can see the thing at all.

The aim of all commentary on art now should be to make works of art — and, by analogy, our own experience — more, rather than less, real to us. The function of criticism should be to show *how it is what it is*, even *that it is what it is*, rather than to show *what it means*.

10

In place of a hermeneutics we need an erotics of art.

Part Two

CONTEMPORARY TRENDS
IN LITERARY CRITICISM

1

FORMALISMS: RUSSIAN FORMALISM, NEW CRITICISM, NEO-ARISTOTELIANISM

Habitualization devours works, clothes, furniture, one's wife, and the fear of war.... And art exists that one may recover the sensation of life; it exists to make one feel things, to make the stone stony. The purpose of art is to impart the sensation of things as they are perceived and not as they are known. — VICTOR SHKLOVSKY

Finding its proper symbol, defined and refined by the participating metaphors, the theme becomes a part of the reality in which we live — an insight, rooted in and growing out of concrete experience, many-sided, three-dimensional. — CLEANTH BROOKS

There are many questions that Aristotle's approach will not answer: questions about the spirit of tragedy throughout the ages, questions about how to rise from despair to faith, questions about how to use art to attack your enemies. . . . But you know there is no better cure for despair than rousing yourself and joining a great artist in his particular creative acts; there is no better proof of nobility than seeing a bit of it really work in a great piece of art; there is no more satisfactory proof of the existence of the good, the true and the beautiful than experiencing their fusion in the unique, particular achievement of a story. . . . — WAYNE C. BOOTH

The three movements discussed here cover a vast amount of geographical ground (centered in Moscow, in London and Nashville, and in Chicago), and they flourished for many decades following World War I, with their influence still felt to the present day. Whether the theoretical territories inhabited by the formalists are seen as vast or confined depends on whether one looks at the positive ideas they have espoused or at their oppositions. All three versions of formalism proposed an "intrinsic" criticism that defined and addressed the specifically literary qualities in the text, and all three began in reaction to various forms of "extrinsic" criticism that viewed the text as either the product of social and historical forces or a document making an ethical statement. But no two of the three agreed on precisely what made a text "literary," what qualities of form, language, or content differentiated it from nonliterary discourse, or what the significance of literature was for humanity. There are major discrepancies among these three movements, as one might expect, but the divergences *within* each movement are almost as striking.

RUSSIAN FORMALISM

Of the three movements, Russian formalism had the briefest flowering. It originated in Moscow in 1915 with a group of linguists and stylisticians known as OPOYAZ (Society for the Study of Poetic Language), grew for about a decade in postrevolutionary Russia, and as a movement was finally eliminated for political reasons by Joseph Stalin and his henchman Andrey Zhdanov around 1930. Most of its members either formally recanted (as did Victor Shklovsky) or emigrated (like Roman Jakobson). Their publications, suppressed in the USSR, were lost to the West until Victor Erlich's pioneering study *Russian Formalism: History — Doctrine* (1955) and Tzvetan Todorov's 1965 translation of the Formalists into French. Nevertheless, the ultimate influence of the Formalists was considerable. Roman Jakobson carried their ideas west, first to the Prague Linguistic Circle (which included Jan Mukařovský), and then to Paris, where he and Claude Lévi-Strauss helped create the structuralist movement that flourished from the early 1960s.

The origins of Russian formalism and the New Criticism show some interesting parallels, largely because the two movements developed in opposition to the same two mainstream forms of contemporary criticism. On the one hand they rejected the historicism of academic criticism, which was seen as a tedious investigation of the circumstances of poetic creation pursued in the absence of any coherent notion of poetics itself. On the other, they despised the liberal "social criticism" of reformers who wished to use literature as a means of cultural progress. What the moralist Paul Elmer More was to the New Critics, nineteenth-century socialist critics like Vissarion Belinsky, Nikolay Chernyshevsky, and Nikolay Dobrolyubov were to the Russian formalists.

Serious divergences occurred, however. The New Critics were essentially allied with the imagist poets (including T. E. Hulme, T. S. Eliot, and Ezra Pound), who viewed poetry as a means of communicating, through image and symbol, what could not be said in prose. The poetics of the New Critics centered in semantics and set the critic the task of decoding the text by explicating its tropes. The systems of individual New Critics largely differed over which of the principal figures of speech or thought — such as metaphor, irony, and ambiguity — was chosen as the master trope. The Russian formalists began by refining but ultimately rejecting the work of a nineteenth-century philologist who might be seen as a prototype New Critic. Alexander Potebnya viewed imagery as the master trope distinguishing poetry from prose, which he regarded as two distinct ways of knowing the world. This theory was embraced by the symbolist poets (like Andrey Bely and Dmitry Merezhkovsky), who looked to art to produce a mystical form of knowledge. Potebnya was as much an exemplar as he was an opponent of the formalists; he had been concerned about the line dividing the literary from the nonliterary (an issue about which the social critics cared little), and he had defined literariness as a function of language, a point of view the formalists were also to embrace.

Potebnya is chiefly known today, however, through the attack on his ideas in Victor Shklovsky's manifesto of formalism, "Art as Technique," which takes issue with the narrowness of Potebnya's conception of art in elevating metaphor and symbolism, imagery, or any single trope to master status. From Shklovsky's perspective, the central difficulty with Potebnya's conception of poetry was its obsession with semantics, with the notion that the things poetry had to express were mystically different from those of prose. For Shklovsky, the chief function of art is not to lead us to a knowledge above and beyond the world, but to restore our capacity to see a world to which use and habit have blinded us. "As perception becomes habitual, it becomes automatic," says Shklovsky, "and art exists that one may recover the sensation of life . . . of things as they are perceived and not as they are known." By its use of unaccustomed language, art makes the world strange again, so that we can see it with the freshness of a child. *Ostranenie* (defamiliarization), the concept at the center of Shklovsky's poetics, is an inversion of Samuel Johnson's notion that art "approximates the remote and familiarizes the wonderful."

The concept of defamiliarization is central to the formalist project, but the term can be used in different ways at different levels of approach to the literary object. At the most basic level of discourse, the formalists analyzed sentences taken from literary texts to see how they estranged reality as a purely aesthetic end in itself. But at the higher level where discourse becomes social, the formalists saw texts' representations of reality as a technique for defamiliarizing the social ideas of the dominant culture, and thus for challenging our automatic acceptance of these ideas. They would say, for example, that an apparently naive and incoherent narrative voice (like that of Gogol's *The Nose*) functions so as to expose the cruelty and hypocrisy of the social ideas of the time.

At a still higher and more abstract level, the formalists, as Tony Bennett has put it, "were concerned with the formal mechanisms whereby literary works tended to reveal or make strange the systems of coherence imposed on reality by the codes and conventions of other, usually earlier literary forms."[1] For example, Shklovsky's essay on *Tristram Shandy* (1921) distinguishes between *fabula* (or story), that is, the temporal-causal sequence of narrated events that comprise the raw materials of the work, and *sjuzet* (or plot), the way in which these raw materials are formally manipulated, in order to argue that *Tristram Shandy,* as Bennett puts it, "is told in such a way as to limit and reveal the narrative conventions of the time. . . ."

The distinction between *fabula* and *sjuzet* owes a great deal to another nineteenth-century forebear of the formalists, the academic literary historian Alexander Veselovsky. Around 1906, Veselovsky evolved a poetics of "motifs," in which the literary work is dissected into its smallest irreducible components, and plot is seen as a complex cluster of story-motifs, ordered, altered, and rearranged by art; Veselovsky thought that shifting motifs correlated with changes in cultural attitudes. The formalists predictably disagreed with his version of historical

---

[1]Tony Bennett, *Formalism and Marxism* (London: Methuen, 1979), p. 23.

determinism but adopted Veselovsky's techniques of thematic analysis, as exemplified by Boris Tomashevsky's "Thematics" (1925) and Vladimir Propp's *The Morphology of the Folk-Tale* (1928).

In effect, the Formalists viewed literature as a mode of construction. Poetry was defined by its use of poetic language, fiction as the craft of manipulating story materials by narrative technique. What was not a matter of construction, such as the origins and the cultural meaning of a literary work, was not specifically literary and was therefore dismissed as not a true part of poetics. The difficulty with such a view, as one historian of formalism has suggested, is that "it does not permit us to evaluate" individual texts. "But the OPOYAZ members never introduced the problems of evaluation into their system."[2]

If Shklovsky established the principal issues governing the literary qualities of texts, Roman Jakobson most succinctly defined the poetic in what would today be called semiotic fashion: as a special use of language. Poetry was "an utterance oriented toward the mode of expression"; in poetry "a word is perceived as a word and not merely as a proxy for the denoted object or an outburst of emotion. . . . Words and their arrangement . . . their outward and inward form acquire weight and value of their own."[3]

At the outset, the Russian Formalists talked as though it were the emotive quality of poetry that differentiated it from common language, but a *semantic* feature of that sort was bound to seem unsatisfactory in the long run; obviously some expressions of feeling are poetic and some are not, while a great deal of what is clearly poetry is not primarily emotional expression. Besides, emotion was a sort of content, and with such a discriminant, the formalists would have been entrapped in the notion of an external form enclosing a crude content. Jakobson's idea made it possible to drop entirely the notion of a separable content and to view poetic form as that which integrates the raw material of language into a shaped structure. Jakobson's sense of form as a dynamic shaping process thus resembles the Aristotelian *eidos*; as we shall see, it has more in common with the Chicago neo-Aristotelians' notions of form than that of the New Critics.

The work of Vladimir Propp on folklore (represented here by "Fairy Tale Transformations," p. 437) exemplifies this notion of literature as a system. Previous ways of analyzing folktales had operated at the level of the plot as a whole: the classification system of Antti Aarne (begun 1907, codified by Stith Thompson in 1932)[4] was designed to allow folklorists to compare tales from different cultures, to allow us to show the similarities of a "Cinderella" story from China and one told by the Lakota. The defect of the system is that it groups tales together in terms of the whole plot, and the factors by which tales are grouped together or separated can sometimes seem arbitrary. For example, the story most of us know as "Bluebeard" focuses on a person who marries an ogre, violates a condition the ogre imposes, and is about to be killed when he or she is saved by a rescuer. Aarne-Thompson classifies the story

---

[2]Krystyna Pomorska, "Russian Formalism in Retrospect," in *Readings in Russian Poetics*, ed. Ladislav Matejka and Krystyna Pomorska (Cambridge: MIT Press, 1971), p. 275.

[3]Victor Erlich, *Russian Formalism: History — Doctrine* (The Hague: Mouton, 1963), p. 183.

[4]Antti Aarne, *Vergleichende märchenforschung* (Helsinki, 1907); Stith Thompson, *Motif-index of Folk Literature* (Bloomington, IN, 1932–36).

as Type 312 if the rescuer is male, Type 311 if female, but whether the ogre is male or female does not make any difference.

Trying to bring greater system to the understanding of folklore and fictional plots in general, Propp analyzed a group of 100 fairy tales collected by Afanase'ev, breaking each of them down into individual plot elements, then generalizing those elements. For example, in one tale Baba Jaga (a demonic female figure in Russian folklore) gives Ivan a horse. Within one "function" (Gift), the *donor* is Baba Jaga, the *recipient* is Ivan, and the *gift* is the horse. Propp found 31 functions, usually related to the verbs in his plot element, and 120 other "components," which may correspond to nouns, adjectives, or phrases indicating where an action takes place. Propp's system seems protostructuralist; in this we can see how structuralist anthropologists like Claude Lévi-Strauss used Propp in devising their classifications of myth. But Propp is not primarily interested in creating a purely theoretical system with static symmetry; his principal object is to understand how folklore develops historically. Russia was Christianized fairly late in its history, so Propp understands tales where the hero's helpers are apostles and the villain is the devil as more recent than those where the helpers are friendly animals and the villain is a forest demon. Other historical connections may be less clear because they can move in both directions. Normally we think of romances as developing out of pre-existing folk materials, but romances can be recited and retold in the form of stories that can break down into folktales (as many of us know Greek and Roman "myths" without knowing the specific poems and romances in which they originate).

If the idea of the literary was the founding feature of Russian formalism, literary history rapidly became one of its primary concerns. For the formalists, the older modes of literary history were essentially inadequate because they had never established any strong sense of what made a particular text into literature in a given age. Without any systematic notion of the literary, the only causal mechanisms available were what Boris Eikhenbaum called "the naïve theory of 'inheritance' and 'influence' and hence naïve biographism based on individual psychology."[5] The formalists believed that at any moment a national literature was not just a collection of individual works but a system of genres. This system is hierarchical: one genre is dominant at any given time. And the genres fall into dialectical relations with each other, epic against romance, comedy against tragedy, pastoral poetry against the poetic satire. As cultures change, the literary system changes, but the dominance of genres does not follow in a clear and predictable line of succession. Shklovsky put it this way: "When literary schools change, the succession passes not from father to son, but from uncle to nephew." Applying this to early modern England, epic clearly seems the dominant genre (*The Faerie Queene, Paradise Lost*). In the eighteenth century, the philosophical poem dominates (*Essay on Man*), while epic is a depressed, even despised genre. Narrative poetry resumes its primacy in the early nineteenth century, but its form is personal and autobiographical rather than epic (*The Prelude, Childe Harold's Pilgrimage*).

[5]Boris Mikhailovich Eikhenbaum, "Literature and Literary Life," in *Moi Vramennik* (Leningrad, 1929): 52.

primarily to exterior social and economic change.

The Russian formalists held that this generic change within literary systems happens primarily by reason of formal exhaustion. A dominant genre attracts lesser talents, becomes less and less creative, more and more imitative, becomes coarse as strong sensations need to be delivered to provide literary impact. Held together by conventions, the genre becomes automatized (the mark of the non-literary, as Shklovsky says), and topples from its position. A new genre takes its place at the top, and the process repeats itself with the new dominant. This motor for literary history stands in compelling contrast with the Marxists' view that literature responds primarily to exterior social and economic change.

THE NEW CRITICISM

The Russian formalists were Underground Men, whose ideas were absent from the critical dialogue of the West until the 1960s. The New Criticism, to the contrary, is one of the more conspicuous success stories of the century, and if the movement is centered somewhat less coherently than the others, that may have been one of the principal reasons for its popularity, because the New Criticism is associated less with a body of theoretical doctrine about the nature of language and poetry than with a method of critical exegesis and explication.

The name "New Criticism" seems to have been bestowed by John Crowe Ransom in a 1941 book of that title, which examines the work of I. A. Richards and William Empson, T. S. Eliot, Yvor Winters, and the philosopher Charles W. Morris. The most important New Critics include this group, Ransom himself, and his fellow Southern "fugitive" writers Allen Tate, Cleanth Brooks, and Robert Penn Warren. Other important theorists associated with the movement include René Wellek, R. P. Blackmur, Robert B. Heilman, Austin Warren, and Murray Krieger. After this point it is hard to tell where to stop, since by the 1950s the New Critical method of poetic explication had come to dominate the teaching of literature in England and America, and most working literary critics had been touched by it in one way or another. One should look to I. A. Richards and T. S. Eliot as the primary founders of this method, the former through his philosophical theories and the latter through his critical practice and tastes.

Like the Russian formalists, Richards was mainly concerned with what differentiated poetry from common language. For him the issue was principally referentiality. Richards held that in common language we make statements that refer to matters of fact, whereas in poetry we make pseudostatements that may appear to be referential but in fact are not. Statements made in poetry cannot be verified; their function is affective rather than cognitive. A poem arouses and allays feelings through the dance of conflicting attitudes stimulated by its complex language. Such an aesthetic moment shakes up the reader's established responses to real life by stimulating the reader's experience of a sense of harmony established among opposing impulses. The form of the poem consists of these stimuli and responses within an ideal reader. (Richards's notion of poetry is at bottom a more behavioristic version of Coleridge, who held that the imagination operates by reconciling opposing qualities into an ideal unity of form.) Richards was primarily a theorist: the critical practice inherent in his ideas was taken over by his student, William Empson. Empson's *Seven Types of Ambiguity* (1930) was an attempt to establish the ways in which texts create, through ambiguity, a multiplicity of meanings, which stimulate the reader to see their harmonious reconciliation. Since it would be possible using any good dictionary to find dozens of possible meanings for the words in a short poem and thousands of possible combinations of these meanings, Empson was attacked for employing a method that, when used mechanically, would produce an inchoate cloud of possible interpretations for any text. Empson was in fact sensitive to the issue of literary intentionality and the question of how the many possible constituents of meaning coalesce into a single complex and moving idea; his epilogue to *Seven Types of Ambiguity* discusses the limits to ambiguity and the relation between audience response and authorial intent.

Two decades later, the most rigorous of the American New Critics, including Ransom and Wimsatt, would reject the reader-oriented formulation of Richards and Empson: The "affective fallacy" would insist that the form of a poem is not to be identified with the psychological process undergone by its audience. (Since this process is likely to differ in various readers, it would leave the form at best indeterminate and at worst under the control of the audience.) But purged of its affective slant, this view of form as an interplay of feelings and attitudes, like the interwoven themes of music, was to prove persuasive and fertile.

T. S. Eliot was also to lend ideas to the New Criticism. In "Tradition and the Individual Talent" Eliot spoke of literature as an "ideal order," a tradition which exists not successively in history but is somehow present simultaneously as it exerts influence upon the newly created work. (See Eliot's essay, p. 321.) This viewpoint had justified the breach between the New Criticism and the historical scholarship that had dominated the academy. In "Hamlet and His Problems," Eliot also presented the "objective correlative," the idea of one-to-one correspondence between the images in a poem and the feelings for which the image is supposed to be the formula. Given this correspondence, poetry could have emotive significance, but its themes could be discussed *objectively* in a more concrete explication of the poem's emotional content. Although these were influential ideas, Eliot was perhaps even more influential in his tastes, which valorized the poets and playwrights of the English Renaissance over the Augustans, Romantics, and Victorians who had dominated the canon, and in his critical practice, which lucidly explicated the poetry of Donne and the plays of Middleton as though they were his contemporaries.

Despite the efforts of René Wellek to give the New Criticism a pedigree in Kantian aesthetics, its development from the late 1930s on was primarily as a critical practice rather than a set of theoretical doctrines. The general theory was simply that literature was a special kind of language and that practical criticism reflects and is constrained by that principle. The most influential ideological statements tended to explain what criticism should not do, rather than what it should. Pride of place should be given to a pair of papers by William K. Wimsatt and Monroe C. Beardsley defending new critical practice against a series of "fallacies": One was "The Affective Fallacy" (1949), which rejected the notion that the poem could be defined in terms of the internal experiences of actual readers (although the New Critics, without precisely admitting to it, tended to analyze poetry in terms of the response of *ideal* readers).

Even more influential was "The Intentional Fallacy" (1946), which, consistent with Eliot's assertion of the impersonality of poetry in "Tradition and the Individual Talent," attacks the notion of the work of art as the essentially private product of the internal experience of a particular individual. The poem is defined as a public text, and its meaning by what the public norms of language allow it to mean. The text's aesthetic success or failure must be judged in those terms alone. Within its original context, the intentional fallacy was a convincing refutation of Crocean idealism, which would have located the aesthetic object in the author's lyrical intuition, and of the old historicism, which referred the meaning of the text to the circumstances of its genesis and its historical context. The intent of the intentional fallacy was to liberate the reader: Thereafter, the only apparatus one needed to read Chaucer and Shakespeare was a good text and a historical dictionary. But the ultimate effect of anti-intentionalism was to foster the irresponsible interpretation of texts, a search for originality of reading without regard to the creator's probable purposes.

There were other fallacies and heresies: the *fallacy of imitative form* attempted to cut the text off from the world it supposedly represented in order to purify the New Criticism of the mimetic principle, as it had already been purified of the expressive and affective ones. The *fallacy of neoclassic species* was aimed at R. S. Crane and the Chicago critics, whose formal theories located the text within an open system of genres. The *biographical heresy* was aimed at those who would identify the speaker of the poem with its author. In general, these treatises aimed to isolate the text as a "verbal icon" (to use Wimsatt's phrase) whose form was to be found entirely within itself. As various historians of critical theory have pointed out, the creators of this version of formalism may have had ulterior reasons for purifying the text. Many of the American New Critics were from the South, a depressed region that during and after World War II had been undergoing a social and economic revolution, which had displaced traditional values and culture. As the Marxist Terry Eagleton puts it, the New Criticism "was the ideology of an uprooted, defensive intelligentsia who reinvented in literature what they could not find in reality. Poetry was the new religion, a nostalgic haven from the alienations of industrial capitalism."[6] Poetry was not only viewed as a force opposing the crassness and secularization of modern life, but as the location of the spiritual values these critics held dear. As Cleanth Brooks once confessed, "It is no accident that so many of the [New Critics] have gone on, either to avow an orthodox religious position or else to affirm the possibility and necessity for metaphysics as a science."[7] Brooks's associates at the *Kenyon Review*, including critics like John Crowe Ransom and Allen Tate, felt that "the whole effort of the literary imagination is toward a kind of incarnation of reality in language."[8] We can see this quasi-religious impulse in the theories of John Crowe Ransom, who sought in poetry something larger than aesthetic form, something that in

[6] Terry Eagleton, *Literary Criticism: An Introduction* (Minneapolis: University of Minnesota Press, 1983), p. 47.

[7] "Metaphor and the Function of Criticism," in *Spiritual Problems in Contemporary Literature*, ed. S. R. Hooper (New York: Harper Torchbooks, 1957), p. 134.

[8] Allen Tate, quoted in Michael Millgate, "An Interview with Allen Tate," *Shenandoah* 12 (1961): 31.

The World's Body (1941) he had called "ontological": a capturing of the *body* of experience. And in criticism he was seeking a way of helping the reader recapture that essence:

> The poet perpetuates in his poem an order of existence which in actual life is constantly crumbling beneath his touch. ... For each poem even, ideally, there is distinguishable a logical object or universal, but at the same time a tissue of irrelevance from which it does not really emerge. The critic has to take the poem apart, or analyze it, for the sake of uncovering these features. With all the finesse possible, it is rude and patchy business. ... But without it there could hardly be much understanding of the value of poetry, or of the natural history behind any adult poem.[9]

For Ransom, poetry is defined by the interplay between structure and texture. Like prose, poetry has a determinate meaning (or logical structure), but in the case of poetry the determinate meaning is deformed by (among other things) the pressure of versification. The necessity of finding rhymes and rhythmic form results in an admixture of what he calls "indeterminate meaning," which may be a mere dross of verbiage that testifies to the human process of creation or may include wonderful, shockingly brilliant novelties that contribute to poetic texture.

Although there was considerable agreement on the principles of art and on the technique of literary explication that was the critic's "job of work," each New Critic developed a slightly different terminology for discussing the issues. For Cleanth Brooks, the terms equivalent to Ransom's structure and texture would be the "paraphraseable content" of a poem (which he equates with its "rational or logical structure") and its "essential structure." In "The Heresy of Paraphrase" (1947) (another heresy!), Brooks insists that the poem not only cannot be equated with its paraphrasable content, but that the content should not be seen as an inner core wrapped about in an exterior form consisting of metrical language. Harking back to Richards, in *The Well Wrought Urn* (1947) Brooks instead defines the "essential structure" of the poem as being like that of

> architecture or painting: it is a pattern of resolved stresses. Or, to move closer still . . . the structure of a poem resembles that of a ballet or musical composition. It is a pattern of resolutions and balances and harmonizations developed through a temporal scheme.[10]

The thematic criticism of the New Critics tended to operate by finding within the texture of the poem oppositions and conflicts that were resolved into a harmonious balance. The principal mediator of this resolution was poetic language, specifically the capacity of language to carry multiple meanings that could disclose hidden conflicts and tensions at the outset of the poem and converge into a harmonious balance at the end. For I. A. Richards's pupil William Empson, the proper term for this polysemic capacity of language was *ambiguity,* of which he distinguished and elaborately discussed seven distinct types. The American New Critics preferred to locate

[9]John Crowe Ransom, *The World's Body* (New York: Scribner's, 1938): 348–49.
[10]Cleanth Brooks, "The Heresy of Paraphrase" in *The Well Wrought Urn: Studies in the Structure of Poetry* (New York: Harcourt, Brace and World, 1947): p. 203.

individual master tropes (or figures of speech) that would serve as the center for their discourse. For Cleanth Brooks, the master tropes were *paradox* and *irony*, the latter defined not in its strict sense — saying the opposite of what is intended — but very broadly, as occurring whenever a statement is undercut or qualified by its context. Similarly, for Allen Tate the chief issue in poetry was the "*tension* between two opposing forces." Although the criticism of Robert Penn Warren flirted with irony, his usual master trope, like that of R. P. Blackmur, was the literary *symbol*. For Robert B. Heilman, the principal issue was the *image*, and it was through the conflict of opposing clusters of images that eventual resolution was achieved. For Murray Krieger, as for the Russian formalists, the master trope was *metaphor*. These divergences were more apparent than real, for each of these literary figures of speech and of thought was in practice broadened from its usual definition to potentially include all the others as well.

What may seem strange, especially given the contrary example of the Russian formalists, is that despite the New Critical emphasis on poetic language, none of the major theorists had any interest in contemporary discoveries in linguistics and semiotics; in fact they disdained "professionalism" in the study of language. This disdain may have been held over from the amateur's stance that the New Critics cultivated, a stance opposed to the professionalism of historical scholarship, against which the movement had originally defined itself.

As we have noted, the dominance of the New Critical thematic explication was nearly absolute through the 1960s. Even today the critical practice of many American teachers of literature owes a great deal to Cleanth Brooks and William Empson. But as a theory, the New Criticism has few current defenders, and its vitality has suffered more than one might gather by counting its remaining devotees. Nevertheless, while the New Criticism has been supplanted by a variety of other interpretive modes, these modes have been forced to define themselves against a once-dominant New Critical tradition, and in this negative sense the New Criticism still lives.

Its more important surviving legacy is the cult of the interpretation and reinterpretation of texts that makes up so much of the critic's professional life. John Crowe Ransom had begun by noting that for the poem to capture the world's body, the critic must recapture it for the common reader. The New Criticism redefined the professoriate as the priesthood of twentieth-century humanism, making the verbal icon accessible to the laity. The critic's proper job of work was the decoding of a text whose surface meaning, however evident to the average reader, is seen as insufficient. The journals and little magazines accordingly filled with interpretations, but eventually the very success of the New Critical methods bred failure. By the 1960s it had spawned an insistent hunger for reinterpretation of canonical texts (or at least for the books and articles upon which professional academic success depends). And eventually the New Criticism, within its formal strictures of fallacies and heresies, could provide for this demand only by more farfetched decodings. But if New Critical theory has been jettisoned in favor of readings based on Marxist, feminist, or deconstructionist literary theories, the view of literature as a mystery to which the critic alone has the key survives. The profession has not so readily relinquished the verbal icon.

NEO-ARISTOTELIANISM

Just as the New Criticism arose out of the New South, neo-Aristotelianism grew out of the innovative Hutchins curriculum at the University of Chicago, which replaced the traditional lecture system with a program of the close study of the "Great Books of the Western Tradition." Moved by the general intellectual ferment of the time and galvanized by the philosophical semantics of Richard McKeon, the historical scholar R. S. Crane came out in 1935 against teaching literature to undergraduates through its purely historical origins and in favor of a new approach using textual explication and aesthetics.[11] As chairman of the English department, Crane was able to hire over the next decade a number of humanists who assisted him in developing a critical theory and practice that has become known as neo-Aristotelianism or Chicago criticism; this group included Elder Olson, Norman Maclean, and W. R. Keast, in addition to McKeon and Crane himself.

Though Crane had placed himself on the side of the New Critics on the issue of history versus criticism, he and his group were scornful of New Critical theories of literature, which they considered reductive, simplistic, and a serious distortion of the nature of literature and language. As a result, the 1940s and 1950s saw an acrimonious debate in the pages of scholarly journals and little magazines, intemperate on both sides, between Crane's group and such New Critics as Brooks, Wimsatt, Warren, and Heilman. A sample taste of this rancorous relationship can be found in the Dialogue section on p. 457, where Crane criticizes Cleanth Brooks. By 1960, when the dust had settled, the New Critics held the field, primarily because their critical methods, propagated in successful textbooks like *Understanding Poetry* (1938), had revolutionized undergraduate and even secondary-school training in literature across America. The textual explications of the Chicago school, in contrast, were confined primarily to scholarly books and learned journals. And the neo-Aristotelian method of analyzing literature was a more complex approach, which did not lend itself to popularization. On the other hand, the New Criticism succeeded at the cost of ideological stagnation, while neo-Aristotelianism developed a second generation of critics (including Wayne C. Booth, Sheldon Sacks, Ralph Rader, Robert Marsh, Norman Friedman, Mary Doyle Springer, and Austin Wright) and a third generation (including Don Bialostosky, Brian Corman, Walter Davis, Barbara Foley, Elizabeth Langland, James Phelan, Peter Rabinowitz, and Adena Rosmarin), all of whom are endeavoring to revise, extend, and adapt Crane's ideas to new projects.

Aristotle's concept of *mimesis,* or imitation, is not central to Chicago criticism. The crucial Aristotelian concepts are from the *Metaphysics* rather than the *Poetics;*

---

[11]R. S. Crane, "History versus Criticism in the Study of Literature" (1935), reprinted in *The Idea of the Humanities* (Chicago: University of Chicago Press, 1967), vol. 2, pp. 3–24.

they include the *eidos*, or "shaping form," and the *synolon*, or "concrete whole" of formed matter, found in nature or manufactured by art. The *synolon* is analyzed in terms of its formal, material, efficient, and final causes. Poetic works of art are *synola* in which plot, character, and thought (the formal cause) give shape to language (the material cause) using various techniques or devices of disclosure (the efficient cause) to create an object with the power to affect a reader in various ways (the final cause).

The "concrete whole" is matter shaped by form to be "inherently meaningful and beautiful."[12] The work's power comes from the inferred sense of the whole, not from the parts; in fact our sense of the whole *as a pattern* is what governs the perceived meaning of the parts. Language, however crucial to our perception of the form, does not define poetic form as it did for the New Critics: It is only a means — and not even the most important one — to an end. Not even plot, which was so crucial for Crane's notions of form, is wholly decisive. Although our sense of the whole takes shape through our experience of the parts, we revise our sense of the parts through our growing sense of the whole to which they contribute. And while the powers of some literary works may require temporary or permanent ambiguities, many merely *potential* ambiguities within a text are cleared up by this shaping process.

R. S. Crane viewed Aristotle primarily as the founder of a positivistic and "differential" method (one opposed to Plato's idealistic and synthesizing method). In tragedy the final cause, the *dynamis*, is the catharsis of pity and fear, and Aristotle judges various Attic tragedies by how well their various elements are designed, the ultimate criterion being their capacity to effect the tragic *dynamis*. Crane wanted to extend the systematic approach of the *Poetics* to other genres with different powers, which different structures of plot, character, thought, language, and technique were designed to serve.

While other genre critics (like Northrop Frye) felt the need to map literature as a field, for the Chicago critics, genres had a different purpose. They functioned as multiple models to which the critic might look in creating strong hypotheses about the specific texts under analysis, hypotheses leading to predictions that might (like scientific hypotheses) be verified or falsified by the text itself or by features of its creation or reception. The openness and pluralism of the genre system served to make it less likely that the critic would have to distort the text to make it fit a single procrustean model. The aim was a method similar to that of science, where conjectures are tested and refuted, and false leads eliminated, until the best explanation is found. Indeed, the critical aims of the Chicago school included the attainment of power through the successful search for objective truth. They were displaced scientists, unlike most of the New Critics, whose motivations, by their own accounts, were more like those of disappointed priests seeking in literature for a new Word to replace the one the world had lost.

---

[12]Ralph Rader, "Defoe, Richardson, Joyce, and the Concept of Form in Fiction," in *Autobiography, Biography and the Novel* (Los Angeles: Clark Memorial Library, 1973), p. 29.

Selected Bibliography

Bann, Stephen, and John E. Bowlt, eds. *Russian Formalism: A Collection of Articles and Texts in Translation.* New York: Barnes and Noble, 1973.

Bennett, Tony. *Formalism and Marxism.* London: Methuen, 1979.

Blackmur, R. P. *Language as Gesture.* New York: Harcourt, Brace and World, 1952.

————. *The Lion and the Honeycomb.* New York: Harcourt, Brace and World, 1955.

————. *New Criticism in the United States.* Tokyo: Kenkyusha, 1959.

Booth, Wayne C. *The Rhetoric of Fiction.* Chicago: University of Chicago Press, 1961; 2nd edition, 1983.

————. *A Rhetoric of Irony.* Chicago: University of Chicago Press, 1974.

————. *Critical Understanding: The Powers and Limits of Pluralism.* Chicago: University of Chicago Press, 1979.

————. *The Company We Keep: An Ethics of Fiction.* Berkeley and Los Angeles: University of California Press, 1988.

Brooks, Cleanth, and Robert Penn Warren. *Understanding Poetry.* New York: Henry Holt, 1938.

————. *Modern Poetry and the Tradition.* Chapel Hill: University of North Carolina Press, 1939.

————. *The Well Wrought Urn: Studies in the Structure of Poetry.* New York: Reynal and Hitchcock, 1947.

Crane, Ronald Salmon. *Critics and Criticism: Ancient and Modern.* Chicago: University of Chicago Press, 1952.

————. *The Languages of Criticism and the Structure of Poetry.* Toronto: University of Toronto Press, 1953.

————. *The Idea of the Humanities, and Other Essays.* 2 vols. Chicago: University of Chicago Press, 1967.

Davis, Walter A. *The Act of Interpretation: A Critique of Literary Reason.* Chicago: University of Chicago Press, 1978.

Eikhenbaum, Boris Mikhailovich. *O. Henry and the Theory of the Short Story.* Ann Arbor: Dept. of Slavic Languages and Literatures of the University of Michigan, 1968.

————. *Lermontov: A Study in Literary-Historical Evaluation.* Ann Arbor: Ardis, 1981.

Eliot, Thomas Stearns. *The Sacred Wood: Essays on Poetry and Criticism.* London: Methuen, 1920.

————. *For Lancelot Andrewes.* London: Faber and Gwyer, 1928.

————. *The Use of Poetry and the Use of Criticism.* London: Faber and Faber, 1933.

Empson, William. *Seven Types of Ambiguity.* London: Chatto & Windus, 1930.

Erlich, Victor. *Russian Formalism: History — Doctrine.* The Hague: Mouton, 1955.

Foley, Barbara. *Telling the Truth: The Theory and Practice of Documentary Fiction.* Ithaca: Cornell University Press, 1986.

Friedman, Norman. *Form and Meaning in Fiction.* Athens: University of Georgia Press, 1975.

Gallagher, Catherine. "The History of Literary Criticism." *Dædalus* 126 (1997): 133–53.

Gorman, David. "A Bibliography of Russian Formalism in English." *Style* 26 (1992): 554–76.

Green, Daniel. "Literature Itself: The New Criticism and Aesthetic Experience." *Philosophy and Literature* 27 (2003): 62–79.

Jakobson, Roman. *Selected Writings.* 7 vols. The Hague: Mouton, 1962.

————. *The Framework of Language.* Ann Arbor: Graduate School of the University of Michigan, 1980.

Jancovich, Mark. *The Cultural Politics of the New Criticism.* Cambridge: Cambridge University Press, 1992.

Lemon, Lee T., and Marion J. Reis, eds. *Russian Formalist Criticism: Four Essays.* Lincoln: University of Nebraska Press, 1965.

Matejka, Ladislav, and Krystyna Pomorska, eds. *Readings in Russian Poetics.* Cambridge: MIT Press, 1971.

Medici, Anthony G. "The Restless Ghost of the New Criticism." *Style* 31 (1997): 760–73.

Olson, Elder. *Tragedy and the Theory of Drama.* Chicago: University of Chicago Press, 1962.

——. *On Value Judgments in the Arts.* Chicago: University of Chicago Press, 1976.

Phelan, James. *Worlds from Words: A Theory of Language in Fiction.* Chicago: University of Chicago Press, 1981.

——. *Reading People, Reading Plots.* Chicago: University of Chicago Press, 1991.

Propp, Vladimir. *Theory and History of Folklore.* Minneapolis: University of Minnesota Press, 1984.

Rader, Ralph. "Defoe, Richardson, Joyce, and the Concept of Form in the Novel." In *Autobiography, Biography and the Novel.* Los Angeles: William Andrews Clark Memorial Library, 1973.

——. "Fact, Theory and Literary Explanation." *Critical Inquiry* 1 (1974): 245–72.

——. "The Dramatic Monologue and Related Lyric Forms." *Critical Inquiry* 3 (1976): 131–51.

——. "The Emergence of the Novel in England: Genre in History vs. History of Genre." *Narrative* 1 (1993): 69–83.

Ransom, John Crowe. *The World's Body.* New York: Scribner's, 1938.

——. *The New Criticism.* Norfolk, CT: New Directions, 1941.

——. *Poems and Essays.* New York: Vintage, 1955.

Richards, I. A. *Principles of Literary Criticism.* New York: Harcourt Brace Jovanovich, 1924.

Richter, David H. *Fable's End: Completeness and Closure in Rhetorical Fiction.* Chicago: University of Chicago Press, 1974.

——. "The Second Flight of the Phoenix: Neo-Aristotelianism Since Crane." *The Eighteenth Century: Theory and Interpretation* 23 (1982): 27–48.

Sacks, Sheldon. *Fiction and the Shape of Belief.* Berkeley: University of California Press, 1964.

——. "Golden Birds and Dying Generations." *Comparative Literature Studies* 6 (1969): 274–91.

——. "Clarissa and the Tragic Traditions." In *Studies in Eighteenth-Century Culture,* ed. Harold E. Pagliaro. Cleveland: Case Western Reserve University Press, 1972, pp. 195–221.

Schneider, Anna-Dorothea. *Literaturkritik und Bildungspolitik: R. S. Crane, die Chicago (Neo-Aristotelian) Critics und die University of Chicago.* Heidelberg: 1994.

Shaitanov, Igor. "Aleksandr Veselovskii's Historical Poetics: Genre in Historical Poetics." *New Literary History* 32 (2001): 429–43.

Shklovsky, Victor Borisovich. *Works.* Moscow: Khudozh' Lit'ra, 1973–4.

Spurlin, William J., and Michael Fischer, eds. *The New Criticism and Contemporary Literary Theory: Connections and Continuities.* New York: Garland, 1995.

Steiner, Peter. *Russian Formalism: A Meta-Poetics.* Ithaca: Cornell University Press, 1984.

Striedter, Jurij. *Literary Structure, Evolution, and Value: Russian Formalism and Czech Structuralism Reconsidered.* Cambridge: Harvard University Press, 1989.

Tate, Allen. *Reactionary Essays on Poetry and Ideas.* New York: Scribner's, 1936.

——. *Reason in Madness: Critical Essays.* New York: G. P. Putnam, 1941.

Thompson, Ewa Majewska. *Russian Formalism and Anglo-American New Criticism: A Comparative Study.* Hawthorne, NY: Mouton, 1971.

Tynyanov, Yuri. *The Problem of Verse Language.* Ann Arbor: Ardis, 1981.

Vygotsky, L. S. *Mind in Society: The Development of Higher Psychological Processes.* Cambridge: Harvard University Press, 1978.

Warren, Austin. *Rage for Order: Essays in Criticism.* Ann Arbor: University of Michigan Press, 1948.

Wellek, René, and Austin Warren. *Theory of Literature.* New York: Harcourt, Brace and World, 1949.

———. *A History of Modern Criticism 1759–1950.* 6 vols. New Haven: Yale University Press, 1955–87.

———. *Concepts of Criticism.* New Haven: Yale University Press, 1963.

Willingham, John R. "The New Criticism: Then and Now." In *Contemporary Literary Theory,* ed. Douglas Atkins and Janice Morrow. Amherst: University of Massachusetts Press, 1989, pp. 24–41.

Wimsatt, William K. *The Verbal Icon: Studies in the Meaning of Poetry.* Lexington: University Press of Kentucky, 1954.

———. *Hateful Contraries: Studies in Literature and Criticism.* Lexington: University Press of Kentucky, 1965.

———, and Cleanth Brooks. *Literary Criticism: A Short History.* New York: Alfred A. Knopf, 1957.

Wolfson, Susan J. "Reading for Form." *Modern Language Quarterly* 61 (2000) 1–11.

Victor Shklovsky
1893–1984

The versatile Russian man of letters Victor Shklovsky was born the son of a teacher in Petersburg and studied at the university there. An outspoken founding member of the Russian literary society OPOYAZ, Shklovsky wrote one of the central theoretical statements of the formalist school ("Art as Technique," 1917) and his ideas were singled out for special denunciation by Leon Trotsky. Problems with the Bolsheviks prompted his emigration in 1921, but he returned two years later. Within a few years, after the publication of The Theory of Prose (1925), he backed away from the politically risky business of theorizing and took up other pursuits, particularly film criticism, screenwriting, and historical fiction. He wrote books on Tolstoy (1928), Mayakovsky (1940), and Dostoevsky (1957), and is also remembered for his autobiographical account of the revolutionary years, A Sentimental Journal: Memoirs 1917–1922 (1923). Ultimately, Shklovsky came to be considered an honored member of the Soviet literary establishment.

Art as Technique

"Art is thinking in images." This maxim, which even high school students parrot, is nevertheless the starting point for the erudite philologist who is beginning to put together some kind of system-atic literary theory. The idea, originated in part by Potebnya, has spread. "Without imagery there is no art, and in particular no poetry," Potebnya writes.[1] And elsewhere, "Poetry, as well as prose, is first and foremost a special way of thinking and knowing."[2]

Poetry is a special way of thinking; it is, pre-cisely, a way of thinking in images, a way which permits what is generally called "economy of mental effort," a way which makes for "a sensa-tion of the relative ease of the process." Aesthetic feeling is the reaction to this economy. This is how the academician Ovsyaniko-Kulikovsky,[3] who undoubtedly read the works of Potebnya attentively, almost certainly understood and faithfully summarized the ideas of his teacher. Potebnya and his numerous disciples consider poetry a special kind of thinking — thinking by means of images; they feel that the purpose of imagery is to help channel various objects and activities into groups and to clarify the unknown by means of the known. Or, as Potebnya wrote:

The relationship of the image to what is being clari-fied is that: (a) the image is the fixed predicate of that which undergoes change — the unchanging means of attracting what is perceived as change-able. . . . (b) the image is far clearer and simpler than what it clarifies.[4]

In other words:

Since the purpose of imagery is to remind us, by approximation, of those meanings for which the image stands, and since, apart from this, imagery is unnecessary for thought, we must be more familiar with the image than with what it clarifies.[5]

Translated by Lee T. Lemon and Marion Reis.

[1] Alexander Potebnya, *Iz zapisok po teorii slovesnosti* [Notes on the Theory of Language] (Kharkov, 1905), p. 83. [Shklovsky]

[2] Ibid., p. 97. [Shklovsky]

[3] Dmitry Ovsyaniko-Kulikovsky (1835–1920), a leading Russian scholar, was an early contributor to Marxist peri-odicals and a literary conservative, antagonistic towards the deliberately meaningless poems of the Futurists. [Tr.]

[4] Potebnya, *Iz zapisok po teorii slovesnosti*, p. 314. [Shklovsky]

[5] Ibid., p. 291. [Shklovsky]

It would be instructive to try to apply this principle to Tyutchev's comparison of summer lightning to deaf and dumb demons or to Gogol's comparison of the sky to the garment of God.[6]

"Without imagery there is no art" — "Art is thinking in images." These maxims have led to far-fetched interpretations of individual works of art. Attempts have been made to evaluate even music, architecture, and lyric poetry as imagistic thought. After a quarter of a century of such attempts Ovsyaniko-Kulikovsky finally had to assign lyric poetry, architecture, and music to a special category of imageless art and to define them as lyric arts appealing directly to the emotions. And thus he admitted an enormous area of art which is not a mode of thought. A part of this area, lyric poetry (narrowly considered), is quite like the visual arts; it is also verbal. But, much more important, visual art passes quite imperceptibly into nonvisual art; yet our perceptions of both are similar.

Nevertheless, the definition "Art is thinking in images," which means (I omit the usual middle terms of the argument) that art is the making of symbols, has survived the downfall of the theory which supported it. It survives chiefly in the wake of Symbolism, especially among the theorists of the Symbolist movement.

Many still believe, then, that thinking in images — thinking, in specific scenes of "roads and landscape" and "furrows and boundaries"[7] — is the chief characteristic of poetry. Consequently, they should have expected the history of "imagistic art," as they call it, to consist of a history of changes in imagery. But we find that images change little; from century to century, from nation to nation, from poet to poet, they flow on without changing. Images belong to no one: they are "the Lord's." The more you understand an age, the more convinced you become that the images a given poet used and which you thought his own were taken almost unchanged from another poet. The works of poets are classified or grouped according to the new techniques that poets discover and share, and according to their arrangement and development of the resources of language; poets are much more concerned with arranging images than with creating them. Images are given to poets; the ability to remember them is far more important than the ability to create them.

Imagistic thought does not, in any case, include all the aspects of art nor even all the aspects of verbal art. A change in imagery is not essential to the development of poetry. We know that frequently an expression is thought to be poetic, to be created for aesthetic pleasure, although actually it was created without such intent — e.g., Annensky's opinion that the Slavic languages are especially poetic and Andrey Bely's ecstasy over the technique of placing adjectives after nouns, a technique used by eighteenth-century Russian poets. Bely joyfully accepts the technique as something artistic, or more exactly, as intended, if we consider intention as art. Actually, this reversal of the usual adjective-noun order is a peculiarity of the language (which had been influenced by Church Slavonic). Thus a work may be (1) intended as prosaic and accepted as poetic, or (2) intended as poetic and accepted as prosaic. This suggests that the artistry attributed to a given work results from the way we perceive it. By "works of art," in the narrow sense, we mean works created by special techniques designed to make the works as obviously artistic as possible.

Potebnya's conclusion, which can be formulated "poetry equals imagery," gave rise to the whole theory that "imagery equals symbolism," that the image may serve as the invariable predicate of various subjects. (This conclusion, because it expressed ideas similar to the theories of the Symbolists, intrigued some of their leading representatives — Andrey Bely, Merezhkovsky and his "eternal companions" — and, in fact, formed the basis of the theory of Symbolism.) The conclusion stems partly from the fact that Potebnya did not distinguish between the language of poetry and the language of prose.

---

[6]Fyodor Tyutchev (1803–1873), a poet, and Nicholas Gogol (1809–52), a master of prose fiction and satire, are mentioned here because their bold use of imagery cannot be accounted for by Potebnya's theory. Shklovsky is arguing that writers frequently gain their effects by comparing the commonplace to the exceptional rather than vice versa. [Tr.]

[7]This is an allusion to Vyacheslav Ivanov's *Borozdy i mezhi [Furrows and Boundaries]* (Moscow, 1916), a major statement of Symbolist theory. [Tr.]

Consequently, he ignored the fact that there are two aspects of imagery: imagery as a practical means of thinking, as a means of placing objects within categories; and imagery as poetic, as a means of reinforcing an impression. I shall clarify with an example. I want to attract the attention of a young child who is eating bread and butter and getting the butter on her fingers. I call, "Hey, butterfingers!" This is a figure of speech, a clearly prosaic trope. Now a different example. The child is playing with my glasses and drops them, I call, "Hey, butterfingers"[8] This figure of speech is a poetic trope. (In the first example, "butterfingers" is metonymic; in the second, metaphoric — but this is not what I want to stress.)

Poetic imagery is a means of creating the strongest possible impression. As a method it is, depending upon its purpose, neither more nor less effective than other poetic techniques; it is neither more nor less effective than ordinary or negative parallelism, comparison, repetition, balanced structure, hyperbole, the commonly accepted rhetorical figures, and all those meth- ods which emphasize the emotional effect of an expression (including words or even articu- lated sounds).[9] But poetic imagery only exter- nally resembles either the stock imagery of fables and ballads or thinking in images — e.g., the example in Ovsyaniko-Kulikovsky's Language and Art in which a little girl calls a ball a little watermelon. Poetic imagery is but one of the devices of poetic language. Prose imagery is a means of abstraction: a little watermelon instead of a lampshade, or a little watermelon instead of a head, is only the abstraction of one of the object's characteris- tics, that of roundness. It is no different from saying that the head and the melon are both round. This is what is meant, but it has nothing to do with poetry.

The law of the economy of creative effort is also generally accepted. [Herbert] Spencer wrote:

On seeking for some clue to the law underly- ing these current maxims, we may see shadowed forth in many of them, the importance of econo- mizing the reader's or the hearer's attention. To so present ideas that they may be apprehended with the least possible mental effort, is the desideratum towards which most of the rules above quoted point. . . . Hence, carrying out the metaphor that language is the vehicle of thought, there seems rea- son to think that in all cases the friction and inertia of the vehicle deduct from its efficiency; and that in composition, the chief, if not the sole thing to be done, is to reduce this friction and inertia to the smallest possible amount.[10]

And R[ichard] Avenarius:

If a soul possess inexhaustible strength, then, of course, it would be indifferent to how much might be spent from this inexhaustible source; only the necessarily expended time would be important. But since its forces are limited, one is led to expect that the soul hastens to carry out the apperceptive process as expediently as possible — that is, with comparatively the least expenditure of energy, and, hence, with comparatively the best result.

Petrazhitsky, with only one reference to the gen- eral law of mental effort, rejects [William] James's theory of the physical basis of emotion, a the- ory which contradicts his own. Even Alexander Veselovsky acknowledged the principle of the economy of creative effort, a theory especially appealing in the study of rhythm, and agreed with Spencer: "A satisfactory style is precisely that style which delivers the greatest amount of thought in the fewest words." And Andrey Bely, despite the fact that in his better pages he gave numerous examples of "roughened" rhythm[11] (particularly in the examples from Baratynsky) showed the difficulties inherent in poetic epithets, also thought it necessary to speak of the law of

[8]The Russian text involves a play on the word for "hat," colloquial for "clod," "duffer," etc. [Tr.]

[9]Shklovsky is here doing two things of major importance: (1) he argues that different techniques serve a sin- gle function, and that (2) no single technique is all-important. The second permits the formalists to be concerned with any and all literary devices; the first permits them to discuss the devices from a single consistent theoretical position. [Tr.]

[10]Herbert Spencer, The Philosophy of Style (Humboldt Library, vol. 34, New York, 1882), pp. 2–3. [Shklovsky] Shklovsky's quoted reference, in Russian, preserves the idea of the original but shortens it. [Tr.]

[11]The Russian zatrudyonny means "made difficult." The suggestion is that poems with "easy" or smooth rhythms slip by unnoticed; poems that are difficult or "roughened" force the reader to attend to them. [Tr.]

the economy of creative effort in his book[12] — a heroic effort to create a theory of art based on unverified facts from antiquated sources, on his vast knowledge of the techniques of poetic creativity, and on Krayevich's high school physics text.

These ideas about the economy of energy, as well as about the law and aim of creativity, are perhaps true in their application to "practical" language; they were, however, extended to poetic language. Hence they do not distinguish properly between the laws of practical language and the laws of poetic language. The fact that Japanese poetry has sounds not found in conversational Japanese was hardly the first factual indication of the differences between poetic and everyday language. Leo Jakubinsky has observed that the law of the dissimilation of liquid sounds does not apply to poetic language.[13] This suggested to him that poetic language tolerated the admission of hard-to-pronounce conglomerations of similar sounds. In his article, one of the first examples of scientific criticism, he indicates inductively, the contrast (I shall say more about this point later) between the laws of poetic language and the laws of practical language.[14]

We must, then, speak about the laws of expenditure and economy in poetic language not on the basis of an analogy with prose, but on the basis of the laws of poetic language.

If we start to examine the general laws of perception, we see that as perception becomes habitual, it becomes automatic. Thus, for example, all of our habits retreat into the area of the unconsciously automatic; if one remembers the sensations of holding a pen or of speaking in a foreign language for the first time and compares that with his feeling at performing the action for the ten thousandth time, he will agree with us. Such habituation explains the principles by which, in ordinary speech, we leave phrases unfinished and words half expressed. In this process, ideally realized in algebra, things are replaced by symbols. Complete words are not expressed in rapid speech; their initial sounds are barely perceived. Alexander Pogodin offers the example of a boy considering the sentence "The Swiss mountains are beautiful" in the form of a series of letters: T, S, m, a, b.[15]

This characteristic of thought not only suggests the method of algebra, but even prompts the choice of symbols (letters, especially initial letters). By this "algebraic" method of thought we apprehend objects only as shapes with imprecise extensions; we do not see them in their entirety but rather recognize them by their main characteristics. We see the object as though it were enveloped in a sack. We know what it is by its configuration, but we see only its silhouette. The object, perceived thus in the manner of prose perception, fades and does not leave even a first impression; ultimately even the essence of what it was is forgotten. Such perception explains why we fail to hear the prose word in its entirety (see Leo Jakubinsky's article[16]) and, hence, why (along with other slips of the tongue) we fail to pronounce it. The process of "algebrization," the over-automatization of an object, permits the greatest economy of perceptive effort. Either objects are assigned only one proper feature — a number, for example — or else they function as though by formula and do not even appear in cognition:

> I was cleaning a room and, meandering about, approached the divan and couldn't remember whether or not I had dusted it. Since these movements are habitual and unconscious, I could not remember and felt that it was impossible to remember — so that if I had dusted it and forgot — that is, had acted unconsciously, then it was the same as if I had not. If some conscious person had been watching, then the fact could be established. If, however, no one was looking, or looking on unconsciously, if the whole complex lives of many people go on unconsciously, then such lives are as if they had never been.[17]

---

[12]*Simvolizm,* probably. [Tr.]
[13]Leo Jakubinsky, "O zvukakh poeticheskovo yazyka" ["On the Sounds of Poetic Language"], *Sborniki* I (1916): 38. [Shklovsky]
[14]Leo Jakubinsky, "Skopleniye odinakovykh plavnykh v prakticheskom i poeticheskom yazykakh" ["The Accumulation of Identical Liquids in Practical and Poetic Language"], *Sborniki* II (1917): 13–21. [Shklovsky]

[15]Alexander Pogodoin, *Yazyk, kak tvorchestvo [Language as Art]* (Kharkov, 1931), p. 42. [Shklovsky] The original sentence was in French, "*Les montaignes de la Suisse sont belles,*" with the appropriate initials. [Tr.]
[16]Jakubinsky, *Sborniki* I (1916). [Shklovsky]
[17]Leo Tolstoy's *Diary,* entry dated February 29, 1897. [Shklovsky] The date is transcribed incorrectly; it should read March 1, 1897. [Tr.]

And so life is reckoned as nothing. Habitualization devours works, clothes, furniture, one's wife, and the fear of war. "If the whole complex lives of many people go on unconsciously, then such lives are as if they had never been." And art exists that one may recover the sensation of life; it exists to make one feel things, to make the stone *stony*. The purpose of art is to impart the sensation of things as they are perceived and not as they are known. The technique of art is to make objects "unfamiliar," to make forms difficult, to increase the difficulty and length of perception because the process of perception is an aesthetic end in itself and must be prolonged. *Art is a way of experiencing the artfulness of an object; the object is not important.*

The range of poetic (artistic) work extends from the sensory to the cognitive, from poetry to prose, from the concrete to the abstract: from Cervantes's Don Quixote — scholastic and poor nobleman, half consciously bearing his humiliation in the court of the duke — to the broad but empty Don Quixote of Turgenev; from Charlemagne to the name "king" [in Russian "Charles" and "king" obviously derive from the same root, *korol*]. The meaning of a work broadens to the extent that artfulness and artistry diminish; thus a fable symbolizes more than a poem, and a proverb more than a fable. Consequently, the least self-contradictory part of Potebnya's theory is his treatment of the fable, which, from his point of view, he investigated thoroughly. But since his theory did not provide for "expressive" works of art, he could not finish his book. As we know, *Notes on the Theory of Literature* was published in 1905, thirteen years after Potebnya's death. Potebnya himself completed only the section on the fable.[18]

After we see an object several times, we begin to recognize it. The object is in front of us and we know about it, but we do not see it[19] — hence we cannot say anything significant

[18] Alexander Potebnya, *Iz leksy po teorii slovesnosti* [Lectures on the Theory of Language] (Kharkov, 1914). [Shklovksy]

[19] Victor Shklovsky, *Voskresheniye slova* [The Resurrection of the Word] (Petersburg, 1914). [Shklovsky]

about it. Art removes objects from the automatism of perception in several ways. Here I want to illustrate a way used repeatedly by Leo Tolstoy, that writer who, for Merezhkovsky at least, seems to present things as if he himself saw them, saw them in their entirety, and did not alter them.

Tolstoy makes the familiar seem strange by not naming the familiar object. He describes an object as if he were seeing it for the first time, an event as if it were happening for the first time. In describing something he avoids the accepted names of its parts and instead names corresponding parts of other objects. For example, in "Shame" Tolstoy "defamiliarizes" the idea of flogging in this way: "to strip people who have broken the law, to hurl them to the floor, and to rap on their bottoms with switches," and, after a few lines, "to lash about on the naked buttocks." Then he remarks:

Just why precisely this stupid, savage means of causing pain and not any other — why not prick the shoulders or any part of the body with needles, squeeze the hands or the feet in a vise, or anything like that?

I apologize for this harsh example, but it is typical of Tolstoy's way of pricking the conscience. The familiar act of flogging is made unfamiliar both by the description and by the proposal to change its form without changing its nature. Tolstoy uses this technique of "defamiliarization" constantly. The narrator of "Kholstomer," for example, is a horse, and it is the horse's point of view (rather than a person's) that makes the content of the story seem unfamiliar. Here is how the horse regards the institution of private property:

I understood well what they said about whipping and Christianity. But then I was absolutely in the dark. What's the meaning of "his own," "his colt"? From these phrases I saw that people thought there was some sort of connection between me and the stable. At the time I simply could not understand the connection. Only much later, when they separated me from the other horses, did I begin to understand. But even then I simply could not see what it meant when they called me "man's property." The words "my horse" referred to me, a living horse, and seemed as strange to me as the words "my land," "my air," "my water."

But the words made a strong impression on me. I thought about them constantly, and only after the most diverse experiences with people did I understand, finally, what they meant. They meant this: In life people are guided by words, not by deeds. It's not so much that they love the possibility of doing or not doing something as it is the possibility of speaking with words, agreed on among themselves, about various topics. Such are the words "my" and "mine," which they apply to different things, creatures, objects, and even to land, people, and horses. They agree that only one may say "mine" about this, that, or the other thing. And the one who says "mine" about the greatest number of things is, according to the game which they've agreed to among themselves, the one they consider the most happy. I don't know the point of all this, but it's true. For a long time I tried to explain it to myself in terms of some kind of real gain, but I had to reject that explanation because it was wrong.

Many of those, for instance, who called me their own never rode on me — although others did. And so with those who fed me. Then again, the coachman, the veterinarians, and the outsiders in general treated me kindly, yet those who called me their own did not. In due time, having widened the scope of my observations, I satisfied myself that the notion "my," not only in relation to us horses, has no other basis than a narrow human instinct which is called a sense of or right to private property. A man says "this house is mine" and never lives in it; he only worries about its construction and upkeep. A merchant says "my shop," "my dry goods shop," for instance, and does not even wear clothes made from the better cloth he keeps in his own shop.

There are people who call a tract of land their own, but they never set eyes on it and never take a stroll on it. There are people who call others their own, yet never see them. And the whole relationship between them is that the so-called "owners" treat the others unjustly.

There are people who call women their own, or their "wives," but their women live with other men. And people strive not for the good in life, but for goods they can call their own.

I am now convinced that this is the essential difference between people and ourselves. And therefore, not even considering the other ways in which we are superior, but considering just this one virtue, we can bravely claim to stand higher than men on the ladder of living creatures. The actions of men, at least those with whom I have had dealings, are guided by *words* — ours, by deeds.

The horse is killed before the end of the story, but the manner of the narrative, its technique, does not change:

> Much later they put Serpukhovsky's body, which had experienced the world, which had eaten and drunk, into the ground. They could profitably send neither his hide, nor his flesh, nor his bones anywhere.
>
> But since his dead body, which had gone about in the world for twenty years, was a great burden to everyone, its burial was only a superfluous embarrassment for the people. For a long time no one had needed him; for a long time he had been a burden on all. But nevertheless, the dead who buried the dead found it necessary to dress this bloated body, which immediately began to rot, in a good uniform and good boots; to lay it in a good new coffin with new tassels at the four corners, then to place this new coffin in another of lead and ship it to Moscow; there to exhume ancient bones and at just that spot, to hide this putrefying body, swarming with maggots, in its new uniform and clean boots, and to cover it over completely with dirt.

Thus we see that at the end of the story Tolstoy continues to use the technique even though the motivation for it [the reason for its use] is gone.

In *War and Peace* Tolstoy uses the same technique in describing whole battles as if battles were something new. These descriptions are too long to quote; it would be necessary to extract a considerable part of the four-volume novel. But Tolstoy uses the same method in describing the drawing room and the theater:

> The middle of the stage consisted of flat boards; by the sides stood painted pictures representing trees, and at the back a linen cloth was stretched down to the floor boards. Maidens in red bodices and white skirts sat on the middle of the stage. One, very fat, in a white silk dress, sat apart on a narrow bench to which a green pasteboard box was glued from behind. They were all singing something. When they had finished, the maiden in white approached the prompter's box. A man in silk with tight-fitting pants on his fat legs approached her with a plume and began to sing and spread his arms in dismay. The man in the tight pants finished his song alone; then the girl sang. After that both remained silent as the music resounded; and the man, obviously waiting to begin singing his part with her again, began to run his fingers over the hand of the girl in the white

dress. They finished their song together, and everyone in the theater began to clap and shout. But the men and women on stage, who represented lovers, start to bow, smiling and raising their hands.

In the second act there were pictures representing monuments and openings in the linen cloth representing the moonlight, and they raised lamp shades on a frame. As the musicians started to play the bass horn and counter-bass, a large number of people in black mantles poured onto the stage from right and left. The people, with something like daggers in their hands, started to wave their arms. Then still more people came running out and began to drag away the maiden who had been wearing a white dress but who now wore one of sky blue. They did not drag her off immediately, but sang with her for a long time before dragging her away. Three times they struck on something metallic behind the side scenes, and everyone got down on his knees and began to chant a prayer. Several times all of this activity was interrupted by enthusiastic shouts from the spectators.

The third act is described:

. . . But suddenly a storm blew up. Chromatic scales and chords of diminished sevenths were heard in the orchestra. Everyone ran about and again they dragged one of the bystanders behind the scenes as the curtain fell.

In the fourth act, "There was some sort of devil who sang, waving his hands, until the boards were moved out from under him and he dropped down."[20]

In *Resurrection* Tolstoy describes the city and the court in the same way; he uses a similar technique in "Kreutzer Sonata" when he describes marriage — "Why, if people have an affinity of souls, must they sleep together?" But he did not defamiliarize only those things he sneered at:

Pierre stood up from his new comrades and made his way between the campfires to the other side of the road where, it seemed, the captive soldiers were held. He wanted to talk with them. The French sentry stopped him on the road and ordered him to return. Pierre did so, but not to the campfire.

[20] The Tolstoy and Gogol translations are ours. The passage occurs in Vol. II, Part 8, Chap. 9 of the edition of *War and Peace* published in Boston by the Dana Estes Co. in 1904–1912. [Tr.]

not to his comrades, but to an abandoned, unharnessed carriage. On the ground, near the wheel of the carriage, he sat cross-legged in the Turkish fashion, and lowered his head. He sat motionless for a long time, thinking. More than an hour passed. No one disturbed him. Suddenly he burst out laughing with his robust, good natured laugh — so loudly that the men near him looked around, surprised at his conspicuously strange laughter.

"Ha, ha, ha," laughed Pierre. And he began to talk to himself. "The soldier didn't allow me to pass. They caught me, barred me. Me — me — my immortal soul. Ha, ha, ha," he laughed with tears starting in his eyes.

Pierre glanced at the sky, into the depths of the departing, playing stars. "And all this is mine, all this is in me, and all this is I." thought Pierre. "And all this they caught and put in a planked enclosure." He smiled and went off to his comrades to lie down to sleep.[21]

Anyone who knows Tolstoy can find several hundred such passages in his work. His method of seeing things out of their normal context is also apparent in his last works. Tolstoy described the dogmas and rituals he attacked as if they were unfamiliar, substituting everyday meanings for the customarily religious meanings of the words common in church ritual. Many persons were painfully wounded; they considered it blasphemy to present as strange and monstrous what they accepted as sacred. Their reaction was due chiefly to the technique through which Tolstoy perceived and reported his environment. And after turning to what he had long avoided, Tolstoy found that his perceptions had unsettled his faith.

The technique of defamiliarization is not Tolstoy's alone. I cited Tolstoy because his work is generally known.

Now, having explained the nature of this technique, let us try to determine the approximate limits of its application. I personally feel that defamiliarization is found almost everywhere form is found. In other words, the difference between Potebnya's point of view and ours is this: An image is not a permanent referent for

[21] Leo Tolstoy, *War and Peace*, IV, Part 13, Chap. 14. [Tr.]

those mutable complexities of life which are revealed through it; its purpose is not to make us perceive meaning, but to create a special perception of the object — *it creates a "vision" of the object instead of serving as a means for knowing it.*

The purpose of imagery in erotic art can be studied even more accurately; an erotic object is usually presented as if it were seen for the first time. Gogol, in "Christmas Eve," provides the following example:

> Here he approached her more closely, coughed, smiled at her, touched her plump, bare arm with his fingers, and expressed himself in a way that showed both his cunning and his conceit.
>
> "And what is this you have, magnificent Solokha?" and having said this, he jumped back a little.
>
> "What? An arm, Osip Nikiforovich!" she answered.
>
> "Hmm, an arm! *He, he, he!*" said the secretary cordially, satisfied with his beginning. He wandered about the room.
>
> "And what is this you have, dearest Solokha?" he said in the same way, having approached her again and grasped her lightly by the neck, and in the very same way he jumped back.
>
> "As if you don't see, Osip Nikiforovich!" answered Solokha, "a neck, and on my neck a necklace."
>
> "Hmm! On the neck a necklace! *He, he, he!*" and the secretary again wandered about the room, rubbing his hands.
>
> "And what is this you have, incomparable Solokha?" . . . It is not known to what the secretary would stretch his longer fingers now.

And Knut Hamsun has the following in *Hunger:* "Two white prodigies appeared from beneath her blouse."

Erotic subjects may also be presented figuratively with the obvious purpose of leading us away from their "recognition." Hence sexual organs are referred to in terms of lock and key,[22] or quilting tools,[23] or bow and arrow, or rings and marlinspikes, as in the legend of Stavyor, in which a married man does not recognize his wife, who is disguised as a warrior. She proposes a riddle:

> "Remember, Stavyor, do you recall
> How we little ones walked to and fro in the street?
> You and I together sometimes played with a
>   marlinspike —
> You had a silver marlinspike,
> But I had a gilded ring?
> I found myself at it just now and then,
> But you fell in with it ever and always."
> Says Stavyor, son of Godinovich,
> "What! I didn't play with you at marlinspikes!"
> Then Vasilisa Mikulichna: "So he says.
> Do you remember, Stavyor, do you recall,
> Now must you know, you and I together learned to
>   read and write;
> Mine was an ink-well of silver,
> And yours a pen of gold?
> But I just moistened it a little now and then,
> And I just moistened it ever and always."[24]

In a different version of the legend we find a key to the riddle:

> Here the formidable envoy Vasilyushka
> Raised her skirts to the very navel,
> And then the young Stavyor, son of Godinovich,
> Recognized her gilded ring. . . .[25]

But defamiliarization is not only a technique of the erotic riddle — a technique of euphemism — it is also the basis and point of all riddles. Every riddle pretends to show its subject either by words which specify or describe it but which, during the telling, do not seem applicable (the type: "black and white and 'red' — read — all over") or by means of odd but imitative sounds ("'Twas brillig, and the slithy toves / Did gyre and gimble in the wabe").[26]

---

[22][Dmitry] Savodnikov, *Zagadki russkovo naroda* [*Riddles of the Russian People*] (St. Petersburg, 1901), Nos. 102–107. [Shklovsky]

[23]Ibid., Nos. 588–591. [Shklovsky]

[24]A. E. Gruzinsky, ed., *Pesni, sobrannye P[avel] N. Rybnikovym* [*Songs Collected by P. N. Rybnikov*] (Moscow, 1909–1910), No. 30. [Shklovsky]

[25]Ibid., No. 171.

[26]We have supplied familiar English examples in place of Shklovsky's word-play. Shklovsky is saying that we create words with no referents or with ambiguous referents in order to force attention to the objects represented by the similar-sounding words. By making the reader go through the extra step of interpreting the nonsense word, the writer prevents an automatic response. A toad is a toad, but "tove" forces one to pause and think about the beast. [Tr.]

Even erotic images not intended as riddles are defamiliarized ("boobies," "tarts," "piece," etc.). In popular imagery there is generally something equivalent to "trampling the grass," and "breaking the guelder-rose." The technique of defamiliarization is absolutely clear in the widespread image — a motif of erotic affectation — in which a bear and other wild beasts (or a devil), with a different reason[27] for nonrecognition) do not recognize a man.

The lack of recognition in the following tale is quite typical:

A peasant was plowing a field with a piebald mare. A bear approached him and asked, "Uncle, what's made this mare piebald for you?"

"I did the piebalding myself."

"But how?"

"Let me, and I'll do the same for you."

The bear agreed. The peasant tied his feet together with a rope, took the ploughshare from the two-wheeled plough, heated it on the fire, and applied it to his flanks. He made the bear piebald by scorching his fur down to the hide with the hot ploughshare. The man untied the bear, which went off and lay down under a tree.

A magpie flew at the peasant to pick at the meat on his shirt. He caught her and broke one of her legs. The magpie flew off to perch in the same tree under which the bear was lying. Then, after the magpie, a horsefly landed on the mare, sat down, and began to bite. The peasant caught the fly, took a stick, shoved it up its rear, and let it go. The fly went to the tree where the bear and the magpie were. There all three sat.

The peasant's wife came to bring his dinner to the field. The man and his wife finished their dinner in the fresh air, and he began to wrestle with her on the ground.

The bear saw this and said to the magpie and the fly, "Holy priests! The peasant wants to piebald someone again."

The magpie said, "No, he wants to break someone's legs."

The fly said, "No, he wants to shove a stick up someone's rump."[28]

The similarity of technique here and in Tolstoy's "Kholstomer," is, I think, obvious.

Quite often in literature the sexual act itself is defamiliarized: for example, the *Decameron* refers to "scraping out a barrel," "catching nightingales," "gay wool-beating work" (the last is not developed in the plot). Defamiliarization is often used in describing the sexual organs.

A whole series of plots is based on such a lack of recognition; for example, in Afanasyev's *Intimate Tales* the entire story of "The Shy Mistress" is based on the fact that an object is not called by its proper name — or, in other words, on a game of nonrecognition. So too in Onchukov's "Spotted Petticoats," tale no. 525, and also in "The Bear and the Hare" from *Intimate Tales,* in which the bear and the hare make a "wound." Such constructions as "the pestle and the mortar," or "Old Nick and the internal regions" (*Decameron*), are also examples of the technique of defamiliarization. And in my article on plot construction I write about defamiliarization in psychological parallelism. Here, then, I repeat that the perception of disharmony in a harmonious context is important in parallelism. The purpose of parallelism, like the general purpose of imagery, is to transfer the usual perception of an object into the sphere of a new perception — that is, to make a unique semantic modification.

In studying poetic speech in its phonetic and lexical structure as well as in its characteristic distribution of words and in the characteristic thought structures compounded from the words, we find everywhere the artistic trademark — that is, we find material obviously created to remove the automatism of perception; the author's purpose is to create the vision which results from that deautomatized perception. A work is created "artistically" so that its perception is impeded and the greatest possible effect is produced through the slowness of the perception. As a result of this lingering,

27 E. R. Romanov, "Besstrashny barin" *Velikorusskiye skazki* (Zapiski Imperskovo Russkovo Geografícheskovo Obshcestva, XLII, No. 52), Belorussky sbornik, "Spravyadliy solar." ["The intrepid Russian Gentleman," *Great Russian Tales* (Notes of the Imperial Russian Geographical Society, XLII, No. 52), White Russian Anthology, "The Upright Soldier" (1886–1912).] [Shklovsky]

28 D[mitry] S. Zelenin, *Velikorusskiye skazki Permskoy gubernii* [*Great Russian Tales of the Permian Province* (St. Petersburg, 1913)], No. 70. [Shklovsky]

the object is perceived not in its extension in space, but, so to speak, in its continuity. Thus "poetic language" gives satisfaction. According to Aristotle, poetic language must appear strange and wonderful; and, in fact, it is often actually foreign: the Sumerian used by the Assyrians, the Latin of Europe during the Middle Ages, the Arabisms of the Persians, the Old Bulgarian of Russian literature, or the elevated, almost literary language of folk songs. The common archaisms of poetic language, the intricacy of the sweet new style [*dolce stil nuovo*],[29] the obscure style of the language of Arnaut Daniel with the "roughened" [*harte*] forms *which make pronunciation difficult* — these are used in much the same way. Leo Jakubinsky has demonstrated the principle of phonetic "roughening" of poetic language in the particular case of the repetition of identical sounds. The language of poetry is, then, a difficult, roughened, impeded language. In a few special instances the language of poetry approximates the language of prose, but this does not violate the principle of "roughened" form.

> Her sister was called Tatyana.
> For the first time we shall
> Wilfully brighten the delicate
> Pages of a novel with such a name.[30]

wrote Pushkin. The usual poetic language of Pushkin's contemporaries was the elegant style of Derzhavin; but Pushkin's style, because it seemed trivial then, was unexpectedly difficult for them. We should remember the consternation of Pushkin's contemporaries over the vulgarity of his expressions. He used the popular language as a special device for prolonging attention, just as his contemporaries generally used Russian words in their usually French speech (see Tolstoy's examples in *War and Peace*).

Just now a still more characteristic phenomenon is under way. Russian literary language, which was originally foreign to Russia, has so permeated the language of the people that it has blended with their conversation. On the other hand, literature has now begun to show a tendency towards the use of dialects (Remizov, Klyuyev, Essenin, and others,[31] so unequal in talent and so alike in language, are intentionally provincial) and of barbarisms (which gave rise to the Severyanin group[32]). And currently Maxim Gorky is changing his diction from the old literary language to the new literary colloquialism of Leskov.[33] Ordinary speech and literary language have thereby changed places (see the work of Vyacheslav Ivanov and many others). And finally, a strong tendency, led by Khlebnikov, to create a new and properly poetic language has emerged. In the light of these developments we can define poetry as *attenuated, tortuous* speech. Poetic speech is *formed speech*. Prose is ordinary speech — economical, easy, proper; the goddess of prose [*dea prosae*] is a goddess of the accurate, facile type, of the "direct" expression of a child. I shall discuss roughened form and retardation as the general *law* of art at greater length in an article on plot construction.[34]

Nevertheless, the position of those who urge the idea of economy of artistic energy as something which exists in and even distinguishes poetic language seems, at first glance, tenable for the problem of rhythm. Spencer's description of rhythm would seem to be absolutely incontestable:

> Just as the body in receiving a series of varying concussions, must keep the muscles ready to meet the most violent of them, as not knowing when such may come: so, the mind in receiving unarranged articulations, must keep its perspectives active enough to recognize the least easily caught sounds. And as, if the concussions recur in definite order, the body may husband its forces by adjusting the resistance needful for each concussion; so, if the syllables be rhythmically arranged, the mind may

[29]Dante, *Purgatorio*, 24:56. Dante refers to the new lyric style of his contemporaries. [Tr.]

[30]Alexander Pushkin, *Eugene Onegin*, I.ii.24.

[31]Alexey Remizov (1877–1957) is best known as a novelist and satirist; Nicholas Klyuyev (1885–1937) and Sergey Essenin (1895–1925) were "peasant poets." All three were noted for their faithful reproduction of Russian dialects and colloquial language. [Tr.]

[32]A group noted for its opulent and sensuous verse style. [Tr.]

[33]Nicholas Leskov (1831–1895), novelist and short story writer, helped popularize the *skaz*, or yarn, and hence, because of the part dialect peculiarities play in the *skaz*, also altered Russian literary language. [Tr.]

[34]Shklovsky is probably referring to his *Razvyortyvaniye syuzheta* [*Plot Development*] (Petrograd, 1291). [Tr.]

economize its energies by anticipating the attention required for each syllable.[35]

This apparently conclusive observation suffers from the common fallacy, the confusion of the laws of poetic and prosaic language. In *The Philosophy of Style* Spencer failed utterly to distinguish between them. But rhythm may have two functions. The rhythm of prose, or of a work song like "Dubinushka," permits the members of the work crew to do their necessary "groaning together" and also eases the work by making it automatic. And, in fact, it is easier to march with music than without it, and to march during an animated conversation is even easier, for the walking is done unconsciously. Thus the rhythm of prose is an important automatizing element; the rhythm of poetry is not. There is "order" in art, yet not a single column of a Greek temple stands exactly in its proper order; poetic rhythm is similarly disordered rhythm. Attempts to systematize the irregularities have been made, and such attempts are part of the current problem in the theory of rhythm. It is obvious that the systematization will not work, for in reality the problem is not one of complicating the rhythm but of disordering the rhythm — a disordering which cannot be predicted. Should the disordering of rhythm become a convention, it would be ineffective as a device for the roughening of language. But I will not discuss rhythm in more detail since I intend to write a book about it.[36]

[35]Spencer, p. 169. Again the Russian text is shortened from Spencer's original. [Tr.]

[36]We have been unable to discover the book Shklovsky promised. [Tr.]

Vladimir Propp

1895–1970

Vladimir Yakovlevich Propp is the originator of folklore studies in the mode of historical and structural typology. Initially a philologist of Russian and German, Propp in 1918 took his degree at Petersburg, where he taught from the 1930s (when the institution had become known as Leningrad University) until his death. Propp's work, such as the groundbreaking Morphology of the Folktale *(1928), was suppressed because of official suspicion of formalist influence, but Western intellectuals, notably Claude Lévi-Strauss (see Ch. 2) rescued him from obscurity in the 1960s. Among Propp's other studies are those on the origins of the tale of enchantment (1947), the Russian heroic saga (1958), and the poetics of peasant folk songs (1963). The translation of "Fairy Tale Transformations" is from* Readings in Russian Poetics *(1971).*

Fairy Tale Transformations

I

The study of the fairy tale may be compared in many respects to that of organic formation in nature. Both the naturalist and the folklorist deal with species and varieties which are essentially the same. The Darwinian problem of the origin of species arises in folklore as well. The similarity of phenomena both in nature and in our field resists any direct explanation which would be both objective and convincing. It is a problem in its own right. Both fields allow two possible points of view: either the internal similarity of two externally dissimilar phenomena does not derive from a common genetic root — the theory of spontaneous generation — or else this morphological similarity does indeed result from a known genetic tie — the theory of differentiation owing to subsequent metamorphoses or transformations of varying cause and occurrence.

In order to resolve this problem, we need a clear understanding of what is meant by similarity in fairy tales. Similarity has so far been invariably defined in terms of a plot and its variants. We find such an approach acceptable only if based upon the idea of the spontaneous generation of species. Adherents to this method do not compare plots; they feel such

Translated by C. H. Severens.

comparison to be impossible or, at the very least, erroneous.[1] Without our denying the value of studying individual plots and comparing them solely from the standpoint of their similarity, another method, another basis for comparison may be proposed. Fairy tales can be compared from the standpoint of their composition or structure; their similarity then appears in a new light.[2]

We observe that the actors in the fairy tale perform essentially the same actions as the tale progresses, no matter how different from one another in shape, size, sex, and occupation, in nomenclature and other static attributes. This determines the relationship of the constant factors to the variables. The functions of the actors are constant; everything else is a variable. For example:

1. The king sends Ivan[3] after the princess; Ivan departs.
2. The king sends Ivan after some marvel; Ivan departs.
3. The sister sends her brother for medicine; he departs.

[1] Antti A. Aarne warns against such an "error" in his *Leitfaden der vergleichenden Märchenforschung* (Hamina, 1913). [Propp]
[2] See Propp's *Morphology of the Folktale* (Austin, 1968) [Tr.]
[3] Russian equivalent of "Jack," as the standard name for the hero of a folktale.

he departs.

4. The stepmother sends her stepdaughter for fire; she departs.

5. The smith sends his apprentice for a cow; he departs.

The dispatch and the departure on a quest are constants. The dispatching and departing actors, the motivations behind the dispatch, and so forth, are variables. In later stages of the quest, obstacles impede the hero's progress; they, too, are essentially the same, but differ in the form of imagery. The function of the actors may be singled out. Fairy tales exhibit thirty-one functions, not all of which may be found in any one fairy tale; however, the absence of certain functions does not interfere with the order of appearance of the others. This aggregate constitutes one system, one composition. This system has proved to be extremely stable and widespread. The investigator, for example, can determine very accurately that both the ancient Egyptian fairy tale of the two brothers and the tale of the firebird, the tale of *Morozka*, the tale of the fisherman and the fish, as well as a number of myths follow the same general pattern. An analysis of the details bears this out. Thirty-one functions do not exhaust the system. Such a motif as "Baba-Jaga[4] gives Ivan a horse" contains four elements, of which only one represents a function, while the other three are of a static nature.

In all, the fairy tale knows about one hundred and fifty elements or constituents. Each of these elements can be labeled according to its bearing on the sequence of action. Thus, in the above example, Baba-Jaga is a donor, the word "gives" signals the moment of transmittal, Ivan is a recipient, and the horse is the gift. If the labels for all one hundred and fifty fairy tale elements are written down in the order dictated by the tales themselves, then, by definition, all fairy tales will fit such a table. Conversely, any tale which fits such a table is a fairy tale, and any tale which does not fit it belongs in another category. Every rubric is a constituent of the fairy tale, and reading the table vertically yields a series of basic forms and a series of derived forms. It is precisely these constituents which are subject to a comparison. This would correspond in zoology to a comparison of vertebra with vertebra, of tooth with tooth, etc. But there is a significant

[4] In Slavic folktales, a man-eating witch who lives in a hut that stands on chicken legs.

difference between organic formations and the fairy tale which makes our task easier. In the first instance, a change in a part or feature brings about a change in another feature, whereas each element of the fairy tale can change independently of the other elements. This has been noted by many investigators, although there have been so far no attempts to infer from it all the conclusions, methodological and otherwise.[5] Thus, Kaarle Krohn, in agreeing with Spiess on the question of constituent interchangeability, still considers it necessary to study the fairy tale in terms of entire structures rather than in terms of constituents. In so doing, Krohn does not (in keeping with the Finnish school) supply much in the way of evidence to support his stand. We conclude from this that the elements of the fairy tale may be studied independently of the plot they constitute. Studying the rubrics vertically reveals norms and types of transformations. What holds true for an isolated element also holds true for entire structures. This is owing to the mechanical manner in which the constituents are joined.

2

The present work does not claim to exhaust the problem. We will only indicate here certain basic guideposts which might subsequently form the basis of a broader theoretical investigation. Even in a brief presentation, however, it is necessary before examining the transformations themselves to establish the criteria which allow us to distinguish between basic and derived forms. The criteria may be expressed in two ways: in terms of general principles and in terms of special rules. First, the general principles. In order to establish these principles, the fairy tale has to be approached

[5] See F. Panzer, *Märchen, Sage und Dichtung* (Munich, 1905). "Seine Komposition ist eine Mosaikarbeit, die das schildernde Bild aus deutlich abgegrenzten Steinchen gefügt hat. Und diese Steinchen bleiben umso leichter auswechselbar, die einzelnen Motive können umso leichter variieren, als auch nirgends für eine Verbindung in die Tiefe gesorgt ist." (His composition is a mosaic that has fashioned the descriptive image of clearly delineated pieces. And these pieces are more readily interchangeable, the individual motifs can vary more easily, since at no time is there any provision made for an interconnection in depth.) This is clearly a denial of the theory of stable combinations or permanent ties. The same thought is expressed even more dramatically and in greater detail by K. Spiess in *Das deutsche Volksmärchen* (Leipzig, 1917). See also K. L. Krohn, *Die folkloristische Arbeitsmethode* (Oslo, 1926). [Propp]

from a standpoint of its environment, that is, the conditions under which it was created and exists. Life and, in the broad sense of the word, religion are most important for us here. The causes of transformations frequently lie outside the fairy tale, and we will not grasp the evolution of the tale unless we consider the environmental circumstances of the fairy tale.

The basic forms are those connected with the genesis of the fairy tale. Obviously, the tale is born out of life; however, the fairy tale reflects reality only weakly. Everything which derives from reality is of secondary formation. In order to determine the origins of the fairy tale, we must draw upon the broad cultural material of the past.

It turns out that the forms which, for one reason or another, are defined as basic are linked with religious concepts of the remote past. We can formulate the following premise: if the same form occurs both in a religious monument and in a fairy tale, the religious form is primary and the fairy tale form is secondary. This is particularly true of archaic religions. Any archaic religious phenomenon, dead today, is older than its artistic use in a current fairy tale. It is, of course, impossible to prove that here. Indeed, such a dependency in general cannot be *proved*; it can only be *shown* on the basis of a large range of material. Such is the first general principle, which is subject to further development. The second principle may be stated thus: if the same element has two variants, of which one derives from religious forms and the other from daily life, the religious formation is primary and the one drawn from life is secondary.

However, in applying these principles, we must observe reasonable caution. It would be an error to try to trace all basic forms back to religion and all derived ones to reality. To protect ourselves against such errors, we need to shed more light on the methods to be used in comparative studies of the fairy tale and religion and the fairy tale and life.

We can establish several types of relationships between the fairy tale and religion. The first is a direct genetic dependency, which in some cases is patently obvious, but which in other cases requires special historical research. Thus, if a serpent is encountered both in the fairy tale and in religion, it entered the fairy tale by way of religion, not the other way around.

However, the presence of such a link is not obligatory even in the case of very great similarity.

Its presence is probable only when we have access to direct cult and *ritual* material. Such ritual material must be distinguished from a combination of religious and *epic* material. In the first case, we can raise the question of a direct kinship along descending lines, analogous to the kinship line of fathers and children; in the second case we can speak only of parallel kinship or, to continue the analogy, the kinship of brothers. Thus the story of Samson and Delilah[6] cannot be considered the prototype of the fairy tale resembling their story: both the fairy tale and the Biblical text may well go back to a common source.

The primacy of cult material should likewise be asserted with a certain degree of caution. Nonetheless, there are instances when this primacy may be asserted with absolute confidence. True, evidence is frequently not found in the document itself but in the concepts which are reflected there and which underlie the fairy tale. But we are often able to form our judgment about the concepts only by means of the documents. For example, the Rig-Veda,[7] little studied by folklorists, belongs to such sources of the fairy tale. If it is true that the fairy tale knows approximately one hundred and fifty constituents, it is noteworthy that the Rig-Veda contains no fewer than sixty. True, their use is lyrical rather than epic, but it should not be forgotten that these are hymns of high priests, not of commoners. It is doubtless true that in the hands of the people (shepherds and peasants) this lyric took on features of the epic. If the hymn praises Indra as the serpent-slayer (in which case the details sometimes coincide perfectly with those of the fairy tale), the people were able in one form or another to *narrate* precisely how Indra killed the serpent.

Let us check this assertion with a more concrete example. We readily recognize Baba-Jaga and her hut in the following hymn:

> Mistress of the wood, mistress of the wood, whither do you vanish? Why do you not ask of the village? Are you afraid then?

> When the hue and cry of birds bursts forth, the mistress of the wood imagines herself a prince riding forth to the sound of cymbals.

[6]Judges 13–16.
[7]Oldest of the collections of Sanskrit hymns and lore (ca. 1000 B.C.E.).

Cattle seem to be grazing on the edge of the woods. Or is it a hut which stands darkly visible there? In the night is heard a squeaking and creaking as of a heavy cart. It is the mistress of the wood.

An unseen voice calls to the cattle. An ax rings out in the woods. A voice cries out sharply. So fancies the nocturnal guest of the mistress of the wood.

The mistress of the wood will do no harm unless alarmed. Feed on sweet fruits and peacefully sleep to full contentment.

Smelling of spices, fragrant, unsowing but ever having plenty, mother of the wild beasts, I praise the mistress of the wood.

We have certain fairy tale elements here: the hut in the woods, the reproach linked with inquiry (in the fairy tale it is normally couched in the form of direct address), a hospitable night's rest (she provides food, drink and shelter), a suggestion of the mistress of the wood's potential hostility, an indication that she is the mother of the wild beasts (in the fairy tale she calls them together); missing are the chicken legs of her hut as well as any indication of her external appearance, etc. One small detail presents a remarkable coincidence: wood is apparently being chopped for the person spending the night in the forest hut. In Afanásev (No. 99)[8] the father, after leaving his daughter in the hut, straps a boot last to the wheel of his cart. The last clacks loudly, and the girl says: *Se mij baten ka drovja rubæ* [Me pa be a-choppin' wood].

Furthermore, all of these coincidences are not accidental, for they are not the only ones. These are only a few out of a great many precise parallels between the fairy tale and the Rig-Veda.

The parallel mentioned cannot, of course, be viewed as proof that our Baba-Jaga goes back to the Rig-Veda. One can only stress that on the whole the line proceeds from religion to the fairy tale, not conversely, and that it is essential here to initiate accurate comparative studies.

However, everything said here is true only if religion and the fairy tale lie at a great chronological distance from each other, if, for example, the religion under consideration has already died out, and its origin is obscured by the prehistoric past. It is quite a different matter when we compare a living religion and a living fairy tale belonging to one and the same people. The reverse situation may occur, a dependency which is impossible in the case of a dead religion and a modern fairy tale. Christian elements in the fairy tale (the apostles as helpers, the devil as spoiler) are *younger* than the fairy tale, not older, as in the preceding example. In point of fact, we really ought not to call this relationship the reverse of the one in the preceding case. The fairy tale derives from ancient religions, but modern religions do not derive from the fairy tale. Modern religion does not create the fairy tale but merely *changes* its material. Yet there are probably isolated examples of a truly reversed dependency, that is, instances in which the elements of religion are derived from the fairy tale. A very interesting example is in the Western Church's canonization of the miracle of St. George the Dragon Slayer. This miracle was canonized much later than was St. George himself, and it occurred despite the stubborn resistance of the Church.[9] Because the battle with the serpent is a part of many pagan religions, we have to assume that it derives precisely from them. In the thirteenth century, however, there was no longer a living trace of these religions, only the epic tradition of the people could play the role of transmitter. The popularity of St. George on the one hand and his fight with the dragon on the other caused his image to merge with that of the dragon fight; the Church was forced to acknowledge the completed fusion and to canonize it.

Finally, we may find not only direct genetic dependency of the fairy tale on the religion, not only parallelism and reversed dependency, but also the complete absence of any link despite the outward similarity. Identical concepts may arise independently of one another. Thus the magic steed is comparable with the holy steeds of the Teutons and with the fiery horse Agni in the Rig-Veda. The former have nothing in common with Sivka-Burka, while the latter coincides with him in all respects. The analogy may be applied only if it is more or

---

[8] All references to Afanásev have been adjusted to the 1957 edition of *Naródnye rússkie skázki A. N. Afanásjeva* (Moscow, 1957). [Tr.] Alexander Nikolaievich Afanasyev (1826–1871) was a historian who in 1860 wrote the first systematic study of Russian folktales.

[9] J. B. Aufhauser, *Das Drachenwunder des heiligen Georg* (Leipzig, 1911). [Propp]

less complete. Heteronymous phenomena, however similar, must be excluded from such comparisons.

Thus the study of *basic* forms necessitates a comparison of the fairy tale with various religions.

Conversely, the study of *derived* forms in the fairy tale shows how it is linked with reality. A number of transformations may be explained as the intrusions of reality into the fairy tale. This forces us to clarify the problem concerning the methods to be used in studying the fairy tale's relationship to life.

In contrast to other types of tales (the anecdote, the novella, the fable, and so on), the fairy tale shows a comparatively sparse sprinkling of elements from real life. The role of daily existence in creating the fairy tale is often overrated. We can resolve the problem of the fairy tale's relationship to life only if we remember that artistic realism and the presence of elements from real life are two different concepts which do not always overlap. Scholars often make the mistake of searching for facts from real life to support a realistic narrative. Nikolai Lerner, for example, takes the following lines from Pushkin's "Bova":

This is really a golden Council,
No idle chatter here, but deep thought:
A long while the noble lords all thought.
Arzamor, old and experienced,
All but opened his mouth (to give counsel,
Perhaps, was the old greybeard's desire),
His throat he loudly cleared, but thought better
And in silence his tongue did bite
[All the council members keep silent and begin to
    drowse.]

and comments:

In depicting the council of bearded senility we may presume the poem to be a satire on the governmental forms of old Muscovite Russia. . . . We note that the satire might have been directed not only against Old Russia but against Pushkin's Russia as well. The entire assembly of snoring 'thinkers' could easily have been uncovered by the young genius in the society of his own day.

In actual fact, however, this is strictly a *fairy tale* motif. In Afanasev (for example, in No. 140) we find: "He asked once — the boyars were silent; a second time — they did not respond; a third time — not so much as half a word." We have here the customary scene in which the supplicant entreats aid, the entreaty usually occurring three times. It is first directed to the servants, then to the boyars (clerks, ministers), and third to the hero of the story. Each party in this triad may likewise be trebled in its own right. Thus we are not dealing with real life but with the amplification and specification (added names, etc.) of a folklore element. We would be making the same mistake if we were to consider the Homeric image of Penelope and the conduct of her suitors as corresponding to the facts of life in ancient Greece and to Greek connubial customs. Penelope's suitors are *false suitors,* a well-known device in epic poetry throughout the world. We should first isolate whatever is folkloric and only afterward raise the question as to the correspondence between specifically Homeric moments and factual life in ancient Greece.

Thus we see that the problem which deals with the fairy tale's relationship to real life is not a simple one. To draw conclusions about life directly from the fairy tale is inadmissible.

But, as we will see below, the role of real life in the *transformation* of the fairy tale is enormous. Life cannot destroy the overall structure of the fairy tale, but it does produce a wealth of younger material which replaces the old in a wide variety of ways.

3

The following are the principal and more precise criteria for distinguishing the basic form of a fairy tale element from a derived form:

1. A fantastical treatment of a constituent in the fairy tale is older than its rational treatment. Such a case is rather simple and does not require special development. If in one fairy tale Ivan receives a magical gift from Baba-Jaga and in another from an old woman passing by, the former is older than the latter. This viewpoint is theoretically based on the link between the fairy tale and religion. Such a viewpoint, however, may turn out to be invalid with respect to other types of tales (fables, etc.) which on the whole may be older than the fairy tale. The realism of such tales dates from time immemorial and cannot be traced back to religious concepts.

2. Heroic treatment is older than humorous treatment. This is essentially a frequent variant of the preceding case. Thus the idea of entering

4

By way of example we will go through all the possible changes of a single element — Baba-Jaga's hut. Morphologically, the hut represents the abode of the donor (that is, the actor who furnishes the hero with the magical tool). Consequently, we will direct attention not only to the hut but to the appearance of all the donor's abodes. We consider the basic Russian form of the abode to be the hut on chicken legs; it is in the forest, and it rotates. But since one element does not yield all the changes possible in a fairy tale, we will consider other examples as well.

1. *Reduction.* Instead of the full form, we may find the following types of changes:

i. The hut on chicken legs in the forest.
ii. The hut on chicken legs.
iii. The hut in the forest.
iv. The hut.
v. The pine forest (Afanas'ev No. 95).
vi. No mention of the abode.

Here the basic form is truncated. The chicken legs, the rotation, and the forest are omitted, and finally the very hut is dispensed with. Reduction may be termed an incomplete basic form. It is to be explained by a lapse of memory which in turn has more complex causes. Reduction points to the lack of agreement between the fairy tale and the whole tenor of the life surrounding it; reduction points to the low degree of relevance of the fairy tale to a given environment, to a given epoch, or to the reciter of the fairy tale.

2. *Expansion.* We turn now to the opposite phenomenon, by which the basic form is extended and broadened by the addition of extra detail. Here is an expanded form: The hut on chicken legs in the forest rests on pancakes and is shingled with cookies. More often than not, expansion is accompanied by reduction. Certain features are omitted, others are added. Expansion may be divided into categories according to origin (as is done below for substitutions). Some expanded forms derive from daily life; others represent an embellished detail from the fairy tale canon. This is illustrated by the preceding example. Examination reveals the donor to be a blend of hostile and hospitable qualities. Ivan is usually welcomed at the donor's

into mortal combat with a dragon precedes that of beating it in a card game.

3. A form used logically is older than a form used nonsensically.[10]

4. An international form is older than a national form.

Thus, if the dragon is encountered virtually the world over but is replaced in some fairy tales of the North by a bear or, in the South, by a lion, then the basic form is the dragon, while the lion and bear are derived forms.

Here we ought to say a few words concerning the methods of studying the fairy tale on an international scale. The material is so expansive that a single investigator cannot possibly study all the one hundred elements in the fairy tales of the entire world. He must first work through the fairy tales of one people, distinguishing between their basic and their derived forms. He must then repeat the same procedure for a second people, after which he may proceed to a comparative study.

In this connection, the thesis on international forms may be narrowed and stated thus: a broadly national form is older than a regional or provincial form. But, if we once start along this path, we cannot refute the following statement: a widespread form predates an isolated form. However, it is theoretically possible that a truly ancient form has survived only in isolated instances and that all other occurrences of it are younger. Therefore great caution must be exercised when applying the quantitative principle (the use of statistics); moreover, *qualitative* considerations of the material under study must be brought into play. An example: in the fairy tale "Pretty Vasilisa" (No. 104 in Afanasév) the figure of Baba-Jaga is accompanied by the appearance of three mounted riders who symbolize morning, day, and night. The question spontaneously arises: is this not a fundamental feature peculiar to Baba-Jaga, one which has been lost in the other fairy tales? Yet, after a rigorous examination of special considerations (which do not warrant mention at this point), this opinion must be rejected.

[10]For other examples, see I. V. Karnaukova in *Krest janskoe iskusstvo SSSR* [Peasant Art in the USSR] (Leningrad, 1927). [Propp]

abode. The forms this welcome may take are extremely varied. (She gave him food and drink. Ivan addresses the hut with the words: "We'd like to climb up and have a bite to eat." The hero sees in the hut a table laid, he samples all the food or eats his fill; he goes outside and slaughters some of the donor's cattle and chickens, etc.) This quality on the part of the donor is expressed by his very abode. In the German fairy tale *Hansel and Gretel,* this form is used somewhat differently, in conformance with the childlike nature of the story.

3. *Contamination.* In general, the fairy tale is in a state of decline today, and contamination is relatively frequent. Sometimes contaminated forms spread and take root. The idea that Baba-Jaga's hut turns continuously on its axis is an example of contamination. In the course of the action, the hut has a very specific purpose: it is a watchtower; the hero is tested to see whether or not he is worthy of receiving the magical tool. The hut greets Ivan with its closed side, and consequently it is sometimes called the "windowless, doorless hut." Its open side, that is, the side with the door, faces away from Ivan. It would appear that Ivan could very easily go around to the other side of the hut and enter through the door. But this Ivan cannot and in the fairy tale never does do. Instead, he utters the incantation: "Stand with your back to the forest and your front to me," or "Stand, as your mother stood you," and so on. The result was usually: "The hut turned." This "turned" became "spins," and the expression, "when it has to, it turns this way and that" became simply, "It turns this way and that." The expression thus lost its sense but was not deprived of a certain characteristic vividness.

4. *Inversion.* Often the basic form is reversed. Female members of the cast are replaced by males, and vice versa. This procedure may involve the huts as well. Instead of a closed and inaccessible hut, we sometimes get a hut with a wide-open door.

5–6. *Intensification and Attenuation.* These types of transformation only apply to the *actions* of the cast. Identical actions may occur at various degrees of intensity. One example of intensification: the hero is exiled instead of merely being sent on a quest. Dispatch is one of the constant elements of the fairy tale; this element occurs in such a variety of forms that all degrees of dispatch

intensity are demonstrable. The dispatch may be initiated in various ways. The hero is often asked to go and fetch some unusual thing. Sometimes the hero is given a task. ("Do me the service.") Often it is an order accompanied by threats, should he fail, and promises, should he succeed. Dispatch may also be a veiled form of exile: an evil sister sends her brother for the milk of a fierce animal in order to get rid of him; the master sends his helper to bring back a cow supposedly lost in the forest; a stepmother sends her stepdaughter to Baba-Jaga for fire. Finally, we have literal exile. These are the basic stages of dispatch, each of which allows a number of variations and transitional forms; they are especially important in examining fairy tales dealing with exiled characters. The order, accompanied by threats and promises, may be regarded as the basic form of dispatch. If the element of promise is omitted, such a reduction may be simultaneously considered an intensification — we are left with a dispatch *and* a threat. Omission of the threat will soften and weaken this form. Further attenuation consists in completely omitting the dispatch. As he prepares to leave, the son asks his parents for their blessing.

The six types of transformations discussed so far may be interpreted as very familiar *changes* in the basic form. There are, however, two other large groups of transformations: substitutions and assimilations. Both of them may be analyzed according to their origin.

7. *Internally Motivated Substitution.* Looking again at their donor's dwelling, we find the following forms:

   i. A palace.
   ii. A mountain alongside a fiery river.

These are not cases of either reduction or expansion, etc. They are not changes but substitutions. The indicated forms, however, are not drawn from without; they are drawn from the fairy tale's own reserves. A dislocation, a rearrangement of forms and material, has taken place. The palace (often of gold) is normally inhabited by a princess. Subsequently this dwelling is ascribed to the donor. Such dislocations in the fairy tale play a very important role. Each element has its own peculiar form. However, this form is not always exclusively bound to the given element. (The princess, for example, usually a sought member of the cast, may play the role of the donor, or that of the helper, etc.) One fairy tale image suppresses another; Baba-Jaga's daughter may appear as the princess. In the latter case, appropriately enough, Baba-Jaga does not live in her hut but in a palace, that is, the abode normally associated with a princess. Linked to this one are the palaces of copper, silver, and gold. The maidens living in such palaces are simultaneously donor and princess. The palaces possibly came about as the result of trebling the golden palace. Possibly they arose in complete independence, having, for example, no connection whatsoever with the idea of the Ages of Gold, Silver, and Iron, etc.

Similarly, the mountain alongside the fiery river is no other than the abode of the dragon, an abode which has been attributed to the donor. These dislocations play an enormous role in creating transformations. The majority of all transformations are substitutions or dislocations generated from within the fairy tale.

8. *Externally Motivated Substitutions.* If we have the forms:

i. An inn.
ii. A two-storied house.

it is apparent that the fantastic hut has been replaced by forms of dwelling normal to real life. The majority of such substitutions may be explained very easily, but there are substitutions which require a special ethnographic exegesis. Elements from life are always immediately obvious, and, more often than not, scholars center their attention upon them.

9. *Confessional Substitutions.* Current religion is also capable of suppressing old forms, replacing them with new ones. Here we are involved with instances in which the devil functions as a winged messenger, or an angel is the donor of the magical tool, or an act of penance replaces the performance of a difficult task (the donor tests the hero). Certain legends are basically fairy tales in which all elements have undergone supporting substitutions. Every people has its own confessional substitutions. Christianity, Islam, and Buddhism are reflected in the fairy tales of the corresponding peoples.

10. *Substitution by Superstition.* Obviously, superstition and local beliefs may likewise suppress the original material of a fairy tale. However,

we encounter this type of substitution much more rarely than we might expect at first glance (the errors of the mythological school). Pushkin was mistaken in saying that in the fairy tale:

Wonders abound, a wood-demon lurks,
Rusalka sits in the boughs.

If we encounter a wood-demon in the fairy tale, he almost always replaces Baba-Jaga. Water nymphs are met with but a single time in the entire Afanas'ev collection, and then only in an introductory flourish of dubious authenticity. In the collections by Onchukov, Zelinin, the Sokolovs, and others, there is not a single mention of Rusalka. The wood-demon only finds its way into the fairy tale because, as a creature of the forest, it resembles Baba-Jaga. The fairy tale accepts only those elements which can be readily accommodated in its construction.

11. *Archaic Substitutions.* We have already mentioned that the basic forms of the fairy tale go back to extinct religious concepts. Based on this fact, we can sometimes separate the basic forms from the derived ones. In certain unique instances, however, the basic form (more or less normal in the fairy tale epic) has been replaced by a form no less ancient which can likewise be traced back to a religious source, but whose occurrence is unique. For example, rather than the battle with the dragon in the fairy tale ''The Witch and the Sun's Sister'' (No. 93 in Afanas'ev), we have the following: the dragon's mate suggests to the prince, ''Let Prince Ivan come with me to the scales and we'll see who outweighs whom.'' The scales toss Ivan sky-high. Here we have traces of psychostasia (the weighing of souls). Where this form — well known in ancient Egypt — came from and how it came to be preserved in the fairy tale are questions which need study.

It is not always easy to distinguish between an archaic substitution and a substitution imposed by superstition. Both have their roots (sometimes) in deep antiquity. But if some item in the fairy tale is also found in a living faith, the substitution may be considered as a relatively new one (the wood-demon). A pagan religion may have two offshoots: one in the fairy tale and the other in a faith or custom. They may well have confronted each other in the course of centuries, and the one may have suppressed the other. Conversely, if a fairy tale element is not attested to in a living faith (the scales), the substitution has its origin in deep antiquity and may be considered archaic.

12. *Literary Substitutions.* Literary material shows the same low degree of likelihood of being accepted by the fairy tale that current superstition does. The fairy tale possesses such resistance that other genres shatter against it; they do not readily blend. If a clash takes place, the fairy tale wins. Of all the various literary genres, that of the fairy tale is the most likely to absorb elements from legend and epic. On rare occasions the novel provides a substitution; but even in such a case, it is only the chivalric romance which plays a certain role. The chivalric romance itself, however, is frequently a product of the fairy tale. The process occurs in stages: fairy tale → romance → fairy tale. Therefore, works such as "Eruslan Lazarevich" are among the "purest" of fairy tales in terms of construction, despite the bookish nature of individual elements. The *Schwank,* the novella, and other forms of popular prose are more flexible and more receptive to elements from other genres.

13. *Modification.* There are substitutions whose origin is not readily ascertainable. More often than not, these are imaginative substitutions which came into being through the teller's own resourcefulness. Such forms defy ethnographic or historical specification. We should note, however, that these substitutions play a greater role in animal tales and other types of tales than in fairy tales. (The bear is replaced by the wolf, one bird by another, etc.) Of course, they may occur in the fairy tale, too. Thus, as the winged messenger, we find an eagle, a falcon, a raven, geese, and others. As the sought-after marvel, we find a stag with antlers of gold, a steed with a mane of gold, a duck with feathers of gold, a pig with bristles of gold, and so on. Derived, secondary forms are generally those most likely to undergo modification. This may be shown by comparing a number of forms in which the sought wonder is simply a transformation of the sought princess with golden locks. If a comparison of the basic and the derived forms exhibits a certain descending line, a comparison of two derived forms reveals a certain parallelism. There are elements in the fairy tale having a particular variety of forms. One example is the "difficult task." If the task does not have a basic form, it makes little difference to the fairy tale, in terms of the unity of its construction, what kind of task is assigned. This phenomenon is even more apparent when we compare elements which have never belonged to a basic type of fairy tale. Motivation is one such element. But transformations sometimes create the need to motivate a certain act. As a result, we see a wide variety of motivations for one and the same act. Thus the hero's exile (exile is a secondary formation) is motivated by widely varied circumstances. On the other hand, the dragon's abduction of the maidens (a primary form) is hardly ever motivated externally but is motivated from within.

Certain features of the hut are also subject to modification. Instead of a hut on chicken legs, we encounter a hut on goat horns or on sheep legs.

14. *Substitutions of Unknown Origin.* We have been discussing substitutions from the point of view of their origin, but their origin is not always ascertainable; it does not always appear as a simple modification. Therefore we require a category for substitutions of unknown origin. For example, the little sister of the sun from the fairy tale "Little Sister" (Afanas'ev No. 93) plays the donor's role and may be considered a rudimentary form of the princess. She lives in the "solar rooms." We cannot know whether this reflects a sun cult, or the creative imagination of the narrator, or some suggestion by the collector asking the storyteller whether he knows any fairy tales dealing with a particular subject, or whether thus and so can be found; in such a case, the teller sometimes fabricates something to please the collector.

This places a limitation on substitutions. We could, of course, set up several more varieties which might be applied to a given isolated case. However, there is no need for that now. The substitutions specified here are meaningful throughout the entire breadth of fairy tale material; their application to isolated cases may be easily inferred and demonstrated by employing the transformational types cited.

Let us turn to another class of changes, that of assimilations. By assimilation we understand an incomplete suppression of one form by another, the two forms merging into a single form. Because assimilations follow the same classification scheme as the substitutions, they will be enumerated in brief.

15. *Internally Motivated Assimilations.* An example occurs in the forms:

i. A hut under a golden roof.

ii. A hut by a fiery river.

In a fairy tale we often meet with a palace under a golden roof. A hut plus a palace under a golden roof equals a hut under a golden roof. The same is true in the case of the hut by the fiery river.

The fairy tale "Fedor Vodovich and Ivan Vodovich" (Onchukov No. 4) provides a very interesting example. Two such very heterogeneous elements as the miraculous birth of the hero and his pursuit by the dragon's wives (sisters) have been drawn together by assimilation. The wives of the dragon, in pursuing the hero, usually turn into a well, a cloud, or a bed and situate themselves in Ivan's path. If he samples some fruit or takes a drink of water, etc., he is torn to pieces. For the miraculous birth, this motif is used in the follow-ing manner: the princess strolls about her father's courtyard, sees a well with a small cup, and by it a bed (the apple tree has been forgotten). She drinks a cupful and lies down on the bed to rest. From this she conceives and gives birth to two sons.

16. *Externally Motivated Assimilations.* Take the form:

i. A hut on the edge of the village.

ii. A cave in the woods.

Here we find that the imaginary hut has become a real hut and a real cave, but the solitude of its inhabitant has been preserved. Indeed, in the sec-ond instance, the forest element is also preserved. Fairy tale plus reality produces an assimilation which favors real life.

17. *Confessional Assimilations.* This process may be exemplified by the replacement of the dragon by the devil; however, the dragon, like the devil, dwells in a lake. The concept of evil beings of the deep does not necessarily have anything in common with the so-called lower mythology of the peasants; it is often explained as simply one type of transformation.

18. *Assimilation via Superstition.* This is a relatively rare phenomenon. The wood-demon living in a hut on chicken legs is an example.

19–20. *Literary and Archaic Assimilations.* These are encountered even more rarely.

Assimilations with the folk epic and legend are of some importance in the Russian fairy tale. Here, however, we are more likely to find sup-pression rather than the assimilation of one form by another, while the components of the fairy tale are preserved as such. Archaic assimilations require a detailed examination of each occur-rence. They do occur, but identifying them is possible only after highly specialized research.

Our survey of the transformation of types can end at this point. It is impossible to assert that absolutely all fairy tale forms will be accommo-dated by our classificatory scheme, but at any rate a significant number clearly are. It would have been possible to bring in still other types of transforma-tions, such as specification and generalization. In the first case, general phenomena become particularized (instead of the thrice-tenth kingdom, we find the city Khvalinsk); in the latter case, the opposite occurs (the thrice-tenth kingdom becomes simply a "dif-ferent, other' kingdom, etc.). But almost all types of specification may also be regarded as substitutions, and generalizations, as reductions. This is true, too, for rationalization (a winged steed becomes an earthbound horse) as well as for the conversion of the fairy tale into an anecdote, etc. A correct and consistent application of the types of transformation indicated will give a firmer foundation to the study of the fairy tale in the process of its development.

What is true for the individual elements of the fairy tale is also true for the fairy tale as a whole. If an extra element is added, we have amplification; in the reverse case, we have reduction, etc. Applying these methods to entire fairy tales is important for comparative studies on fairy tale plots.

One very important problem remains. If we write out all the occurrences (or at least a great many of them) of one element, not all the forms of one element can be traced back to some single basis. Let us suppose that we accept Baba-Jaga as the basic form of the donor. Such forms are a witch, Grannie-Behind-the-Door, Grandma-Widow, an old lady, an old man, a shepherd, a wood-demon, an angel, the devil, three maids, the king's daugh-ter, etc. — all may be satisfactorily explained as substitutions and other transformations of Baba-Jaga. But then we encounter a "fingernail-sized peasant with an elbow-length beard." Such a form for the donor does not come from Baba-Jaga. If such a form does occur in a religion, we have a form which has been coordinated with Baba-Jaga; if not, we have a substitution of unknown origin. Each element may have several basic forms, although the number of such parallel, coordinated forms is usually insignificant.

5

Our outline would be incomplete if we did not show a model for applying our observations. We will use more palpable material to exhibit a series of transformations; let us take the forms:

> The dragon abducts the king's daughter —
> the dragon tortures the king's daughter —
> the dragon demands the king's daughter.

From the point of view of the morphology of the fairy tale, we are dealing here with an element which we will call *basic harm*. Such harm usually serves as the start of the plot. In accordance with the principles proposed in this paper, we should compare not only abduction with abduction, etc., but also with all the various types of basic harm as one of the components of the fairy tale.

Caution demands that all three forms be regarded as coordinated forms, but it is possible to suggest that the first is still the basic form. In Egypt we find death conceived of as the abduction of the soul by a dragon. But this concept has been forgotten, whereas the idea that illness is a demon settled within the body lives on today. Finally, the dragon's demand for the princess as tribute reflects a shadowy archaism from real life. It is accompanied by the appearance of an army, which surrounds the city and threatens war. However, we cannot be certain. Be that as it may, all three forms are very old, and each allows a number of transformations.

Let us take the first form:

> The dragon abducts the king's daughter.

The dragon is viewed as the embodiment of evil. Confessional influence turns the dragon into a devil:

> Devils abduct the king's daughter.

The same influence affects the object of abduction:

> The devil abducts the priest's daughter.

The dragon figure has already become foreign to the village. It has been replaced by a dangerous animal that is better known (externally motivated substitution), the animal acquiring fantastic attributes (modifications):

> A bear with fur of iron carries off the king's children.

The villain merges with Baba-Jaga. One part of the fairy tale influences another part (internally motivated substitution). Baba-Jaga is the essence of the female sex, and, correspondingly, the person abducted is a male (inversion):

> A witch abducts the son of an old couple.

In one of the forms constantly complicating the fairy tale, the hero's brothers carry out a secondary abduction of their brother's prize. The intent to do harm has now been transferred to the hero's kin. This is a canonical form of complicating the action:

> His brothers abduct Ivan's bride.

The wicked brothers are replaced by other villainous relatives from reserve members of the fairy tale's cast (internally motivated substitution):

> The king (Ivan's father-in-law) abducts Ivan's wife.

The princess herself may take over the same function, and the fairy tale may assume more amusing forms. Here the figure of the villain has been reduced:

> The princess flees from her husband.

In all these cases, a human being was abducted, but, by way of example, the light of day may be abducted (an archaic substitution):

> The dragon abducts the light of the kingdom.

The dragon is replaced by other monstrous animals (modification); the object of abduction merges with the imagined life of the court:

> The mink-beast pilfers animals from the king's menagerie.

Talismans play a significant role in the fairy tale. They are often the only means by which Ivan can attain his goal. Hence it is understandable that they are often the object of abduction. If the action is thus complicated in the middle of the fairy tale, such an abduction is even obligatory as far as fairy tale canon is concerned. This middle moment in the fairy tale may be transferred to the beginning (internally motivated substitution). The abductor of the talisman is often a cheat, or a landowner, and so on (externally motivated substitution):

A shrewd lad abducts Ivan's talisman.

A landowner abducts the peasant's talisman.

The firebird fairy tale represents a transitional stage leading to other forms; here the stolen apples of gold are not talismans (cf. orpine apples). We should add that the theft of the talisman is not possible as a complication at the fairy tale's midpoint unless the talisman has already been acquired. The talisman can be made off with at the beginning only if its possession is properly motivated, however briefly. It is for this reason that the stolen items which appear at the beginning of the tale are not often talismans. The firebird found its way from the middle sectionof the tale back to the beginning. The bird is one of the basic forms of transporting Ivan to the three-tenth kingdom. Golden feathers and similar features are usually attributed to the animal life of the fairy tale:

The firebird steals the king's apples.

In every case the abduction is preserved. The disappearance of a bride, a daughter, a wife, etc., is ascribed to a mythic substratum in the fairy tale. However, this explanation of such a disappearance is alien to modern peasant life, therefore an alien, imported mythology is replaced by sorcery. Disappearance is ascribed to magic spells cast by evil sorcerers and sorceresses. The nature of the villainous deed changes, but its result is still the same: a disappearance entailing a quest (substitution via superstition):

A sorcerer abducts the king's daughter.

Nursie bewitches Ivan's bride and forces her to flee.

Again we see the activity transferred to wicked relatives:

Sisters force the girl's groom to flee.

Turning to the transformations of our second base form (a dragon tortures the king's daughter), we encounter transformations on the same patterns:

The devil tortures the king's daughter, etc.

Here the torture assumes the nature of seizure and vampirism, which can be fully explained ethnographically. Instead of the dragon and the devil, we see again another of the fairy tale's evil beings:

Baba-Jaga tortures the mistress of the knights.

A third variation of the basic form poses the threat of forced marriage:

The dragon demands the king's daughter.

This reveals a number of transformations:

A water sprite demands the king's son, etc.

This same form, morphologically speaking, may lead to a declaration of war without any of the king's offspring being demanded (reduction); a transfer of similar forms to relatives produces:

The sister, a witch, seeks to devour the king's son (her brother).

This case (Afanas'ev No. 93) is of special interest. Here the prince's sister is called a dragoness. Thus we have a classical example of internal assimilation. It points up the need for caution in studying kinship ties in the fairy tale. The marriage of brother and sister and other forms are not necessarily remnants of an old custom; rather, they may be the results of certain transformations, as the above case clearly shows.

The objection may be raised against all of the preceding that anything at all could be fitted into a single phrase having but two components. This is far from true. How would the start of the plot of the fairy tale "Frost, Sun and Wind" and many others fit into such a form? Second, the observed phenomena represent the same constructional element with respect to the overall composition. Although differently stated, they result in identical patterns in the progress of the plot's: a plea for help may be masked as a departure from home, as a meeting with a donor, etc. Not every fairy tale containing a theft produces this construction. If this construction does not follow, subsequent patterns, however similar, cannot be compared, for they are heteronymous. Otherwise, we have to admit that an element from the fairy tale has entered a construction foreign to the tale. Thus we return to the necessity of making juxtapositions on the basis of identical components and not external similarity.

Cleanth Brooks

1906–1994

To many minds, Cleanth Brooks is the archetypal New Critic, the man whose catch phrases, critical studies, and college textbooks epitomized New Critical ideas, practice, and pedagogy. Brooks was born in Kentucky, educated at Vanderbilt, Tulane, and Oxford (where he was a Rhodes scholar), and began his teaching career at Louisiana State University in 1932. From 1935 to 1942, Brooks and the poet Robert Penn Warren edited The Southern Review, *which promulgated the New Critical program; the two later collaborated on* Understanding Poetry *(1938) and* Understanding Fiction *(1943), textbooks which further advanced the New Critical cause. The year 1947 saw the publication of Brooks's classic of criticism,* The Well Wrought Urn, *and the beginning of his career at Yale, where he became a professor emeritus of rhetoric thirteen years later. Brooks's other works include two studies of William Faulkner (1963 and 1978),* Modern Poetry and the Tradition *(1939),* Literary Criticism: A Short History *(1957) with W. K. Wimsatt, and* A Shaping Joy: Studies in the Writer's Craft *(1972). "Irony as a Principle of Structure," from* Literary Opinion in America *(1951), edited by M. D. Zabel, is a revision of an article that first appeared in the February 1948 issue of* College English.

Irony as a Principle of Structure

One can sum up modern poetic technique by calling it the rediscovery of metaphor and the full commitment to metaphor. The poet can legitimately step out into the universal only by first going through the narrow door of the particular. The poet does not select an abstract theme and then embellish it with concrete details. On the contrary, he must establish the details, must abide by the details, and through his realization of the details attain to whatever general meaning he can attain. The meaning must issue from the particulars; it must not seem to be arbitrarily forced upon the particulars. Thus, our conventional habits of language have to be reversed when we come to deal with poetry. For here it is the tail that wags the dog. Better still, here it is the tail of the kite — the tail that makes the kite fly — the tail that renders the kite more than a frame of paper blown crazily down the wind.

The tail of the kite, it is true, seems to negate the kite's function: it weights down something made to rise; and in the same way, the concrete particulars with which the poet loads himself seem to deny the universal to which he aspires.

The poet wants to "say" something. Why, then, doesn't he say it directly and forthrightly? Why is he willing to say it only through his metaphors? Through his metaphors, he risks saying it partially and obscurely, and risks not saying it at all. But the risk must be taken, for direct statement leads to abstraction and threatens to take us out of poetry altogether.

The commitment to metaphor thus implies, with respect to general theme, a principle of indirection. With respect to particular images and statements, it implies a principle of organic relationship. That is, the poem is not a collection of beautiful or "poetic" images. If there really existed objects which were somehow intrinsically "poetic," still the mere assemblage of these would not give us a poem. For in that case, one might arrange bouquets of these poetic images and thus create poems by formula. But the elements of a poem are related to each other, not as blossoms juxtaposed in a bouquet, but as the blossoms are related to the other parts of a growing plant. The beauty of the poem is the flowering of the whole plant, and needs the stalk, the leaf, and the hidden roots.

If this figure seems somewhat highflown, let us borrow an analogy from another art: the poem is like a little drama. The total effect proceeds from all the elements in the drama, and in a good poem, as in a good drama, there is no waste motion and there are no superfluous parts.

In coming to see that the parts of a poem are related to each other organically, and related to the total theme indirectly, we have come to see the importance of *context*. The memorable verses in poetry — even those which seem intrinsically "poetic" — show on inspection that they derive their poetic quality from their relation to a particular context. We may, it is true, be tempted to say that Shakespeare's "Ripeness is all" is poetic because it is a sublime thought, or because it possesses simple eloquence; but that is to forget the context in which the passage appears. The proof that this is so becomes obvious when we contemplate such unpoetic lines as "vitality is all," "serenity is all," "maturity is all." — statements whose philosophical import in the abstract is about as defensible as that of "ripeness is all." Indeed, the commonplace word "never" repeated five times becomes one of the most poignant lines in *Lear*, but it becomes so because of the supporting context. Even the "meaning" of any particular item is modified by the context. For what is said in a particular situation and by a particular dramatic character.

The last instances adduced can be most properly regarded as instances of "loading" from the context. The context endows the particular word or image or statement with significance. Images so charged become symbols; statements so charged become dramatic utterances. But there is another way in which to look at the impact of the context upon the part. The part is modified by the pressure of the context.

Now the *obvious* warping of a statement by the context we characterize as "ironical." To take the simplest instance, we say "this is a fine state of affairs," and in certain contexts the statement means quite the opposite of what it purports to say literally. This is sarcasm, the most obvious kind of irony. Here a complete reversal of meaning is effected: effected by the context, and pointed, probably, by the tone of voice. But the modification can be most important even though it falls far short of sarcastic reversal, and it need not be underlined by

the tone of voice at all. The tone of irony can be effected by the skillful disposition of the context. Gray's *Elegy* will furnish an obvious example:

Can storied urn or animated bust
Back to its mansion call the fleeting breath?
Can Honour's voice provoke the silent dust,
Or Flatt'ry soothe the dull cold ear of death?

In its context, the question is obviously rhetorical. The answer has been implied in the characterization of the breath as fleeting and of the ear of death as dull and cold. The form is that of a question, but the manner in which the question has been asked shows that it is no true question at all.

These are obvious instances of irony, and even on this level, much more poetry is ironical than the reader may be disposed to think. Many of Hardy's poems and nearly all of Housman's, for example, reveal irony quite as definite and overt as this. Lest these examples, however, seem to specialize irony in the direction of the sardonic, the reader ought to be reminded that irony, even in its obvious and conventionally recognized forms, comprises a wide variety of modes: tragic irony, self-irony, playful, arch, mocking, or gentle irony, etc. The body of poetry which may be said to contain irony in the ordinary senses of the term stretches from *Lear*, on the one hand, to "Cupid and Campaspe Played," on the other.

What indeed would be a statement wholly devoid of an ironic potential — a statement that did not show any qualification of the context? One is forced to offer statements like "Two plus two equals four," or "The square on the hypotenuse of a right triangle is equal to the sum of the squares on the two sides." The meaning of these statements is unqualified by any context; if they are true, they are equally true in any possible context.[1]

This is not to say, of course, that such statements are not related to a particular "universe of discourse." They are indeed, as are all statements of whatever kind. But I distinguish here between "context" and "universe of discourse." "Two plus two equals four" is not dependent on a special dramatic context in the way in which a "statement" made in a poem is. Compare "Two plus two equals four" and the same "statement" as contained in Housman's poem:

— To think that two and two are four
And neither five nor three
The heart of man has long been sore
And long 'tis like to be.

[Brooks]

These statements are properly abstract, and their terms are pure denotations. (If "two" or "four" actually happened to have connotations for the fancifully minded, the connotations would be quite irrelevant: they do not participate in the meaningful structure of the statement.)

But connotations are important in poetry and do enter significantly into the structure of meaning which is the poem. Moreover, I should claim also — as a corollary of the foregoing proposition — that poems never contain abstract statements. That is, any "statement" made in the poem bears the pressure of the context and has its meaning modified by the context. In other words, the statements made — including those which appear to be philosophical generalizations — are to be read as if they were speeches in a drama. Their relevance, their propriety, their rhetorical force, even their meaning, cannot be divorced from the context in which they are imbedded.

The principle I state may seem a very obvious one, but I think that it is nonetheless very important. It may throw some light upon the importance of the term *irony* in modern criticism. As one who has certainly tended to overuse the term *irony* and perhaps, on occasion, has abused the term, I am closely concerned here. But I want to make quite clear what that concern is: it is not to justify the term *irony* as such, but rather to indicate why modern critics are so often tempted to use it. We have doubtless stretched the term too much, but it has been almost the only term available by which to point to a general and important aspect of poetry.

Consider this example: The speaker in Matthew Arnold's "Dover Beach" states that the world, "which seems to lie before us like a land of dreams . . . hath really neither joy nor love nor light. . . ." For some readers the statement will seem an obvious truism. (The hero of a typical Hemingway short story or novel, for example, will say this, though of course in a rather different idiom.) For other readers, however, the statement will seem false, or at least highly questionable. In any case, if we try to "prove" the proposition, we shall raise some very perplexing metaphysical questions, and in doing so, we shall certainly also move away from the problems of the poem and, finally, from a justification of the poem. For the lines are to be justified in the poem in terms of the context: the speaker is standing beside his loved one, looking out of the window on the calm sea, listening to the long withdrawing roar of the ebbing tide, and aware of the beautiful delusion of moonlight which "blanches" the whole scene. The "truth" of the statement, and of the poem itself, in which it is imbedded, will be validated, not by a majority report of the association of sociologists, or a committee of physical scientists, or of a congress of metaphysicians who are willing to stamp the statement as proved. How is the statement to be validated? We shall probably not be able to do better than to apply T. S. Eliot's test: does the statement seem to be that which the mind of the reader can accept as coherent, mature, and founded on the facts of experience? But when we raise such a question, we are driven to consider the poem as drama. We raise such further questions as these: Does the speaker seem carried away with his own emotions? Does he seem to oversimplify the situation? Or does he, on the other hand, seem to have won to a kind of detachment and objectivity? In other words, we are forced to raise the question as to whether the statement grows properly out of a context; whether it acknowledges the pressures of the context; whether it is "ironical" — or merely callow, glib, and sentimental.

I have suggested elsewhere that the poem which meets Eliot's test comes to the same thing as I. A. Richards's "poetry of synthesis" — that is, a poetry which does not leave out what is apparently hostile to its dominant tone, and which, because it is able to fuse the irrelevant and discordant, has come to terms with itself and is invulnerable to irony.[2] Irony, then, in this further sense, is not only an acknowledgment of the pressures of a context. Invulnerability to irony is the stability of a context in which the internal pressures balance and mutually support each other. The stability is like that of the arch: the very forces which are calculated to drag the stones to the ground actually provide the principle of support — a principle in which thrust and counterthrust become the means of stability.

In many poems the pressures of the context emerge in obvious ironies. Marvell's "To His Coy Mistress" or Raleigh's "Nymph's Reply" or even

[2]See I. A. Richards, *Principles of Literary Criticism* (New York: Harcourt Brace Jovanovich, 1924), pp. 774ff.

Gray's "Elegy" reveal themselves as ironical, even to readers who use irony strictly in the conventional sense.

But can other poems be subsumed under this general principle, and do they show a comparable basic structure? The test case would seem to be presented by the lyric, and particularly the simple lyric. Consider, for example, one of Shakespeare's songs:

Who is Silvia: what is she
That all our swains commend her?
Holy, fair, and wise is she;
The heavens such grace did lend her,
That she might admired be.

Is she kind as she is fair?
For beauty lives with kindness.
Love doth to her eyes repair,
To help him of his blindness,
And, being help'd, inhabits there.

Then to Silvia let us sing,
That Silvia is excelling;
She excels each mortal thing
Upon the dull earth dwelling:
To her let us garlands bring.

On one level the song attempts to answer the question "Who is Silvia?" and the answer given makes her something of an angel and something of a goddess. She excels each mortal thing "Upon the dull earth dwelling." Silvia herself, of course, dwells upon that dull earth, though it is presumably her own brightness which makes it dull by comparison. ("The dull earth," for example, yields bright garlands which the swains are bringing to her.) Why does she excel each mortal thing? Because of her virtues ("Holy, fair, and wise is she"), and these are a celestial gift. She is heaven's darling ("The heavens such grace did lend her"). Grace, I suppose, refers to grace of movement, and some readers will insist that we leave it at that. But since Silvia's other virtues include holiness and wisdom, and since her grace has been lent from above, I do not think that we can quite shut out the theological overtones. Shakespeare's audience would have found it even more difficult to do so. At any rate, it is interesting to see what happens if we are aware of these overtones. We get a delightful richness, and we also get something very close to irony.

The motive for the bestowal of grace — that she might admired be — is oddly untheological. But what follows is odder still, for the love that "doth to her eyes repair" is not, as we might expect, Christian "charity" but the little pagan god Cupid ("Love doth to her eyes repair, / To help him of his blindness.") But if Cupid lives in her eyes, then the second line of the stanza takes on another layer of meaning. "For beauty lives with kindness" becomes not merely a kind of charming platitude — actually often denied in human experience. (The Petrarchan lover, for example, as Shakespeare well knew, frequently found a beautiful and *cruel* mistress.) The second line, in this context, means also that the love god lives with the kind Silvia, and indeed has taken these eyes that sparkle with kindness for his own.

Is the mixture of pagan myth and Christian theology, then, an unthinking confusion into which the poet has blundered, or is it something wittily combined? It is certainly not a confusion, and if blundered into unconsciously, it is a happy mistake. But I do not mean to press the issue of the poet's self-consciousness (and with it, the implication of a kind of playful irony). Suffice it to say that the song is charming and delightful, and that the mingling of elements is proper to a poem which is a deft and light-fingered attempt to suggest the quality of divinity with which lovers perennially endow maidens who are finally mortal. The touch is light, there is a lyric grace, but the tone is complex, nonetheless.

I shall be prepared, however, to have this last example thrown out of court since Shakespeare, for all his universality, was a contemporary of the metaphysical poets, and may have incorporated more of their ironic complexity than is necessary or normal. One can draw more innocent and therefore more convincing examples from Wordsworth's Lucy poems:

She dwelt among the untrodden ways
Beside the springs of Dove,
A maid whom there were none to praise
And very few to love:

A violet by a mossy stone
Half hidden from the eye!
Fair as a star, when only one
Is shining in the sky.

She lived unknown, and few could know
 When Lucy ceased to be;
But she is in her grave, and, oh,
 The difference to me.

Which is Lucy really like — the violet or the star? The context in general seems to support the violet comparison. The violet, beautiful but almost unnoticed, already half hidden from the eye, is now, as the poem ends, completely hidden in its grave, with none but the poet to grieve for its loss. The star comparison may seem only vaguely relevant — a conventional and here a somewhat anomalous compliment. Actually, it is not difficult to justify the star comparison: to her lover's eyes, she is the solitary star. She has no rivals, nor would the idea of rivalry, in her unself-conscious simplicity, occur to her.

The violet and the star thus balance each other and between themselves define the situation: Lucy was, from the viewpoint of the great world, unnoticed, shy, modest, and half hidden from the eye, but from the standpoint of her lover, she is the single star, completely dominating that world, not arrogantly like the sun, but sweetly and modestly, like the star. The implicit contrast is that so often developed ironically by John Donne in his poems where the lovers, who amount to nothing in the eyes of the world, become, in their own eyes, each the other's world — as in "The Good-Morrow," where their love makes "one little room an everywhere," or as in "The Canonization," where the lovers drive into the mirrors of each other's eyes the "towns, countries, courts" — which make up the great world; and thus find that world in themselves. It is easy to imagine how Donne would have exploited the contrast between the violet and the star, accentuating it, developing the irony, showing how the violet was really like its antithesis, the star, etc.

Now one does not want to enter an Act of Uniformity against the poets. Wordsworth is entitled to his method of simple juxtaposition with no underscoring of the ironical contrast. But it is worth noting that the contrast with its ironic potential is there in his poem. It is there in nearly all of Wordsworth's successful lyrics. It is certainly to be found in "A slumber did my spirit seal."

A slumber did my spirit seal;
 I had no human fears:
She seemed a thing that could not feel
 The touch of earthly years.

No motion has she now, no force;
 She neither hears nor sees,
Rolled round in earth's diurnal course,
 With rocks, and stones, and trees.

The lover's insensitivity to the claims of mortality is interpreted as a lethargy of spirit — a strange slumber. Thus the "human fears" that he lacked are apparently the fears normal to human beings. But the phrase has a certain pliability. It could mean fears *for* the loved one as a mortal human being; and the lines that follow tend to warp the phrase in this direction: it does not occur to the lover that he needs to fear for one who cannot be touched by "earthly years." We need not ague that Wordsworth is consciously using a witty device, a purposed ambiguity; nor need we conclude that he is confused. It is enough to see that Wordsworth has developed, quite "normally," let us say, a context calculated to pull "human fears" in opposed directions, and that the slightest pressure of attention on the part of the reader precipitates an ironical effect.

As we move into the second stanza, the potential irony almost becomes overt. If the slumber has sealed the lover's spirit, a slumber, immersed in which he thought it impossible that his loved one could perish, so too a slumber has now definitely sealed *her* spirit: "No motion has she now, no force; / She neither hears nor sees." It is evident that it is her unnatural slumber that has waked him out of his. It is curious to speculate on what Donne or Marvell would have made of this.

Wordsworth, however, still does not choose to exploit the contrast as such. Instead, he attempts to suggest something of the lover's agonized shock at the loved one's present lack of motion — of his response to her utter and horrible inertness. And how shall he suggest this? He chooses to suggest it, not by saying that she lies as quiet as marble or as a lump of clay; on the contrary, he attempts to suggest it by imagining her in violent motion — violent, but imposed motion, the same motion indeed which the very stones share, whirled about as they are in earth's diurnal course. Why does the image convey so powerfully the sense of something inert and helpless? Part of the effect, of course, resides in the fact that a dead lifelessness is suggested more sharply by an object's being whirled about by something else than by an image of the object in repose. But there are other matters which are at work here: the sense of the girl's falling back into the clutter of things, companioned by things chained like a tree to one particular spot, or by things completely inanimate, like rocks and stones. Here, of course, the concluding figure leans upon the suggestion made in the first stanza, that the girl once seemed something not subject to earthly limitations at all. But surely, the image of the whirl itself is important in its suggestion of something meaningless — motion that mechanically repeats itself. And there is one further element: the girl, who to her lover seemed a thing that could not feel the touch of earthly years, is caught up helplessly into the empty whirl of the earth which measures and makes time. She is touched by and held by earthly time in its most powerful and horrible image. The last figure thus seems to me to summarize the poem — to offer in almost every facet of meaning suggested in the earlier lines a concurring and resolving image which meets and accepts and reduces each item to its place in the total unity.

Wordsworth, as we have observed above, does not choose to point up specifically the ironical contrast between the speaker's former slumber and the loved one's present slumber. But there is one ironical contrast which he does stress: this is the contrast between the two senses in which the girl becomes insulated against the "touch of earthly years." In the first stanza, she "could not feel / The touch of earthly years" because she seemed divine and immortal. But in the second stanza, now in her grave, she still does not "feel the touch of earthly years," for, like the rocks and stones, she feels nothing at all. It is true that Wordsworth does not repeat the verb "feels"; instead he writes "She neither *hears* nor *sees*." But the contrast, though not commented upon directly by any device of verbal wit, is there nonetheless, and is bound to make itself felt in any sensitive reading of the poem. The statement of the first stanza has been literally realized in the second, but its meaning has been ironically reversed.

Ought we, then, to apply the term *ironical* to Wordsworth's poem? Not necessarily. I am trying to account for my temptation to call such a poem ironical — not to justify my yielding to the temptation — least of all to insist that others so transgress. Moreover, Wordsworth's poem seems to be admirable, and I entertain no notion that it might have been more admirable still had John Donne written it rather than William Wordsworth. I shall be content if I can make a much more modest point: namely, that since both Wordsworth and Donne are poets, their work has at basis a similar structure, and that the dynamic structure — the pattern of thrust and counterthrust — which we associate with Donne has its counterpart in Wordsworth. In the work of both men, the relation between part and part is organic, which means that each part modifies and is modified by the whole.

Yet to intimate that there are potential ironies in Wordsworth's lyric may seem to distort it. After all, is it not simple and spontaneous? With these terms we encounter two of the critical catchwords of the nineteenth century, even as *ironical* is in danger of becoming a catchword of our own period. Are the terms *simple* and *ironical* mutually exclusive? What after all do we mean by *simple* or by *spontaneous*? We may mean that the poem came to the poet easily and even spontaneously: very complex poems may — indeed have — come just this way. Or the poem may seem in its effect on the reader a simple and spontaneous utterance: some poems of great complexity possess this quality. What is likely to cause trouble here is the intrusion of a special theory of composition. It is fairly represented as an intrusion since a theory as to how a poem is written is being allowed to dictate to us how the poem is to be read. There is no harm in thinking of Wordsworth's poem as simple and spontaneous unless these terms deny complexities that actually exist in the poem, and unless they justify us in reading the poem with only half our minds. A slumber ought not to seal the *reader's* spirit as he reads this poem, or any other poem.

I have argued that irony, taken as the acknowledgment of the pressures of context, is to be found in poetry of every period and even in simple lyrical poetry. But in the poetry of our own time, this pressure reveals itself strikingly.

A great deal of modern poetry does use irony as its special and perhaps its characteristic strategy. For this there are reasons, and compelling reasons. To cite only a few of these reasons: there is the breakdown of a common symbolism; there is the general scepticism as to universals; not least important, there is the depletion and corruption of the very language itself, by advertising and by the mass-produced arts of radio, the moving picture, and pulp fiction. The modern poet has the task of rehabilitating a tired and drained language so that it can convey meanings once more with force and with exactitude. This task of qualifying and modifying language is perennial; but it is imposed on the modern poet as a special burden. Those critics who attribute the use of ironic techniques to the poet's own bloodless sophistication and tired scepticism would be better advised to refer these vices to his potential readers, a public corrupted by Hollywood and the Book of the Month Club. For the modern poet is not addressing simple primitives but a public sophisticated by commercial art.

At any rate, to the honor of the modern poet be it said that he has frequently succeeded in using his ironic techniques to win through to clarity and passion. Randall Jarrell's "Eighth Air Force" represents a success of this sort.

> If, in an odd angle of the hutment,
> A puppy laps the water from a can
> Of flowers, and the drunk sergeant shaving
> Whistles *O Paradiso!* — shall I say that man
> Is not as men have said: a wolf to man?
>
> The other murderers troop in yawning;
> Three of them play Pitch, one sleeps, and one
> Lies counting missions, lies there sweating
> Till even his heart beats: One; One; One.
> *O murderers!* . . . Still, this is how it's done:
>
> This is a war. . . . But since these play, before they
>   die,
> Like puppies with their puppy; since, a man,
> I did as these have done, but did not die —
> I will content the people as I can
> And give up these to them: Behold the man!
>
> I have suffered, in a dream, because of him,
> Many things; for this last saviour, man,
> I have lied as I lie now. But what is lying?
> Men wash their hands, in blood, as best they can:
> I find no fault in this just man.

There are no superfluous parts, no dead or empty details. The airmen in their hutment are casual enough and honest enough to be convincing. The raw building is domesticated: there are the flowers in water from which the mascot, a puppy, laps. There is the drunken sergeant, whistling an opera aria as he shaves. These "murderers," as the poet is casually to call the airmen in the next stanza, display a touching regard for the human values. How, then, can one say that man is a wolf to man, since these men "play before they die, like puppies with their puppy." But the casual presence of the puppy in the hutment allows us to take the stanza both ways, for the dog is a kind of tamed and domesticated wolf, and his presence may prove on the contrary that the hutment is the wolf den. After all, the timber wolf plays with its puppies.

The second stanza takes the theme to a perfectly explicit conclusion. If three of the men play pitch, and one is asleep, at least one man is awake and counts himself and his companions murderers. But his unvoiced cry "O murderers" is met, countered, and dismissed with the next two lines: ". . . Still this is how it's done: / This is a war. . . ."

The note of casuistry and cynical apology prepares for a brilliant and rich resolving image, the image of Pontius Pilate, which is announced specifically in the third stanza:

> I will content the people as I can
> And give up these to them: behold the man!

Yet if Pilate, as he is first presented, is a jesting Pilate, who asks "What is truth?" it is a bitter and grieving Pilate who concludes the poem. It is the integrity of Man himself that is at stake. Is man a cruel animal, a wolf, or is he the last savior, the Christ of our secular religion of humanity?

The Pontius Pilate metaphor, as the poet uses it, becomes a device for tremendous concentration. For the speaker (presumably the young airman who cried "O murderers") is himself the confessed murderer under judgment, and also the Pilate who judges, and, at least as a representative of man, the savior whom the mob would condemn. He is even Pilate's better nature, his wife, for the lines "I have suffered, in a dream, because of him, / Many things" is merely a rearrangement of Matthew 27:19, the speech of Pilate's wife

It is easy at this point to misapprehend the function of irony. We can say that Jarrell's irony pares his theme down to acceptable dimensions. The theme of man's goodness has here been so qualified that the poet himself does not really believe in it. But this is not what I am trying to say. We do not ask a poet to bring his poem into line with our personal beliefs — still less to flatter our personal beliefs. What we do ask is that the poem dramatize the situation so accurately, so honestly, with such fidelity to the total situation that it is no longer a question of our beliefs, but of our participation in the poetic experience. At his best, Jarrell manages to bring us, by an act of imagination, to the most penetrating insight. Participating in that insight, we doubtless become better citizens. (One of the "uses" of poetry, I should agree, is to make us better citizens.) But poetry is not the eloquent rendition of the citizen's creed. It is not even the accurate rendition of his creed. Poetry must carry us beyond the abstract creed into the very matrix out of which, and from which, our creeds are abstracted. That is what "Eighth Air Force" does. That is what, I am convinced, all good poetry does.

For the theme in a genuine poem does not confront us as abstraction — that is, as one man's generalization from the relevant particulars. Finding its proper symbol, defined and refined by the participating metaphors, the theme becomes a part of the reality in which we live — an insight, rooted in and growing out of concrete experience, many-sided, three-dimensional. Even the resistance to generalization has its part in this process — even the drag of the particulars away from the universal — even the tension of opposing themes — play their parts. The kite properly loaded, tension maintained along the kite string, rises steadily *against* the thrust of the wind.

to her husband. But this last item is more than a reminiscence of the scriptural scene. It reinforces the speaker's present dilemma. The modern has had high hopes for man: are the hopes merely a dream? Is man incorrigible, merely a cruel beast? The speaker's present torture springs from that hope and from his reluctance to dismiss it as an empty dream. This Pilate is even harder-pressed than was the Roman magistrate. For he must convince himself of this last savior's innocence. But he has lied for him before. He will lie for him now.

Men wash their hands in blood, as best they can: I find no fault in this just man.

What is the meaning of "Men wash their hands in blood, as best they can"? It can mean: Since my own hands are bloody, I have no right to condemn the rest. It can mean: I know that man can love justice, even though his hands are bloody, for there is blood on mine. It can mean: Men are essentially decent; they try to keep their hands clean even if they have only blood in which to wash them. None of these meanings cancels out the others. All are relevant, and each meaning contributes to the total meaning. Indeed, there is not a facet of significance which does not receive illumination from the figure.

Some of Jarrell's weaker poems seem weak to me because they lean too heavily upon this concept of the goodness of man. In some of them, his approach to the theme is too direct. But in this poem, the affirmation of man's essential justness by a Pilate who contents the people as he washes his hands in blood seems to me to supply every qualification that is required. The sense of self-guilt, the yearning to believe in man's justness, the knowledge of the difficulty of so believing — all work to render accurately and dramatically the total situation.

R. S. Crane

1886–1967

Ronald Salmon Crane was the leader and moving spirit of the Chicago School of neo-Aristotelian criticism, one of the two major formalist movements in America. Crane was born in Michigan, took his A.B. from the University of Michigan, Ann Arbor (1908), and his doctorate at the University of Pennsylvania (1911). In 1911 he started teaching at Northwestern University in Illinois, then moved on in 1924 to the University of Chicago, where he became full professor in 1925 and head of the English department in 1935. Crane's interest in literary theory and his notion that criticism, rather than historical scholarship, was the preferred mode of teaching literature, began in the 1930s during the implementation of the innovative Hutchins curriculum. Crane's publications are primarily academic articles dense with thought, rather than critical books; the best and farthest reaching of his articles were collected in two volumes as The Idea of the Humanities and Other Essays Critical and Historical *(1967). His only theoretical treatise is* The Languages of Criticism and the Structure of Poetry *(1953). In* Critics and Criticism *(1952), Crane and his colleagues at Chicago presented their neo-Aristotelian system and analyzed the weaknesses of the rival formalism, the New Criticism. In the following selection, Crane takes aim at Cleanth Brooks for impoverishing criticism by reducing poetics to a simplistic analysis of language.*

From *The Critical Monism of Cleanth Brooks*

[W]hereas for Coleridge at least three sciences are necessary for criticism — grammar, logic, and psychology — Brooks finds it possible to get along with only one, namely, grammar; and with only one part of that, namely, its doctrine of qualification. His whole effort can be described not unfairly as an attempt to erect a theory of poetry by extending and analogizing from the simple proposition of grammar that the meaning of one word or group of words is modified by its juxtaposition in discourse with another word or group of words. The paradoxes and ironic oppositions and resolutions of discrepant "attitudes" which, in his system, distinguish poetry sharply from science and other nonpoetical modes of writing are merely the more striking forms which such qualification takes when it is considered, merely qua qualification of meaning by context, apart from, and in contrast with, what he takes to be the self-contained and "abstract" meaning, not dependent on any special context, of predications of fact or universal truth, such as "Two plus two equals four" or "The square on the hypotenuse of a right triangle is equal to the sum of the squares on the other two sides." To talk about the "prose-sense" of poems is to reduce them, or some part of them, to the status of assertions of this kind, and it is for the sake of eradicating this error — the source of "the heresy of paraphrase" — that he insists on finding the essence of poetry in its exclusive reliance on properties of speech which in earlier analyses of language were treated between the consideration of individual words and the consideration of linguistic wholes determined differently by the different ends of logic, dialectic, poetic, and rhetoric, as, for example, in Aristotle's discussions of ambiguity and equivocation; the modes of opposition or contrariety; the different senses of sameness and difference; the kinds of metaphor, including that which involves antithesis; amplification and depreciation in thought and words; the ways of making discourse lively and dramatic; the technique of the unexpected; and so on. Brooks has retained

So much for the manner in which Brooks constitutes the distinctive "language of poetry." His main interest, however, is in its distinctive "structure," and this would seem, on first thought, to be something requiring formulation in differ- ent, and even nongrammatical, terms. He tells us indeed, in his recent essay, that the statements made in a poem — including those which look like philosophical generalizations — "are to be read as if they were speeches in a drama," and in *The Well-Wrought Urn* he remarks that "the structure of a poem resembles that of a play." This sounds promising — and the analogy does, in fact, as we shall see, imply one idea which, if Brooks had worked it out, might have led to a more adequate theory than the one he gives us; but the promise is dimmed when we recollect that a "drama" is after all, when considered apart from the specific emotional quality of its plot, merely a grammatical entity, that is, a sequence of speeches with conflicting contexts.

Again, he has much to say about "unity," as when he remarks that the poet "must perforce dramatize the oneness of the experience, even though paying tribute to its diversity," and that the poet gives us "an insight which preserves the unity of experience," his final task being, indeed, "to unify experience." "He must return to us the unity of the experience itself as man knows it in his own experience." But this, too, is disappoint- ing, for it merely attributes to the poet the same necessity for "balancing and harmonizing conno- tations, attitudes, and meanings" which elsewhere in Brooks — and more typically — is said to follow from the nature of the linguistic instru- ment the poet uses, as contrasted with the fixed statement-making language of science. It is not, therefore, any special principle of unity derived from the nature of the "experience" or object represented in a given kind of poem that deter- mines poetical structure; rather it is the presence in poems of poetical structure — i.e., ironical opposition and resolution — that determines, and is the sign of, the unification of experience. And, as Brooks makes abundantly clear, the "structure of poetry" is a structure common to all poems. Only one alternative remains: to get the "struc- ture" of poems out of their linguistic elements or parts. And this is what Brooks tells us explicitly

very little of the complexity and precision of this old "grammatical" teaching, and he presents what remains of it as peculiarly relevant to poetry rather than as applicable generally to discourse, and, indeed, as constitutive by itself of the whole of poetic theory. For all his simplification and distortion of the ancient analyses, however, it is clear that the apparatus of terms and distinctions he brings to the study of poetry is a composite of elements that can be traced historically to the pre- propositional sections of logic and dialectic, the theory of diction, merely qua diction, of poetic, and the stylistic part of rhetoric.

His key concepts, "paradox" and "irony," reflect unmistakably their grammatical origin. They are terms that designate the mutual "quali- fication" — and especially one mode of it — that inevitably occurs when the meanings of individual words or sentences or passages are not fixed by prior definition but are determined immedi- ately, in the discourse itself, by the "contexts" in which they stand. "Irony," he says, "is the most general term that we have for the kind of quali- fication which the various elements in a context receive from the context. This kind of qualifi- cation . . . is of tremendous importance in any poem. Moreover, irony is our most general term for indicating that recognition of incon- gruities — which, again, pervades all poetry to a degree far beyond what our conventional criti- cism has been heretofore willing to allow." And "paradox" would seem to differ from "irony" only as it signifies "irony" especially in its narrower sense — not the general phenomenon of contextual qualification (the importance of which, Brooks tells us, we, or at least the "new critics," have at last come to see) but the special kind of qualification, so long neglected, which involves the resolution of opposites: in short, the antithetical metaphor of Aristotle, Johnson's "heterogeneous ideas yoked by violence together," and Coleridge's "imagination."[1]

[1]Aristotle discusses the special power of metaphor when it is combined with antithesis in the *Rhetoric* at 1412b; in a general discussion of the so-called "metaphysical poets" in his *Life of Donne*, published in *Lives of the Poets* (1783), Samuel Johnson speaks thus of their figures of speech; in his *Biographia Literaria*, ch. 14, Coleridge speaks of the imagi- nation as striving toward "the balance or reconciliation of opposite or discordant qualities" (see p. 226).

that he is doing. "The structure obviously is everywhere conditioned by the nature of the material which goes into the poem. The nature of the material sets the problem to be solved, and the solution is the ordering of the material." And again, and most plainly: "What is true of the poet's language in detail is true of the larger wholes of poetry." But what is true of the poet's language in detail, in Brooks's account of it, is that it is a language — "of paradox," as he says — which inevitably organizes itself, when two words are put together, into "organic" relations according to some pattern of ambiguity, metaphor, or ironic contrast. And nothing less, or more, than this can be said about the total organization of parts — that is to say, of lines and passages — in the poem as a whole. Brooks devotes a short paragraph in *The Well-Wrought Urn* to a familiar line of Gray's[2] *Elegy*:

> Grandeur is not to smile at the "short and simple annals of the poor." Properly speaking, of course, the poor do not have "annals." Kingdoms have annals, and so do kings, but the peasantry does not. The choice of the term is ironical, and yet the "short and simple" records of the poor are their "annals" — the important records for them.

Here is poetry, the whole of poetry, so far as its essence as "paradoxical" language is concerned, for here is ironic contrast and its resolution; and the only difference between this one line and the whole *Elegy* is merely a matter of the degree of complexity exhibited by the ironic interrelationships. We may speak, indeed, of partial "contexts" and of total "contexts," the latter being built up, as Brooks suggests in one place, out of the former; but the two are completely homogeneous in their elements and structure, and the relation between them is best described as that of microcosm to macrocosm.

The limiting consequences of this radical reduction of poetics to grammar become apparent

as soon as we consider what problems of criticism Brooks's system will not permit us to solve. Thus we cannot, by any legitimate extension of his principles, develop an apparatus for discriminating essentially and not solely in terms of accidents of subject matter or historical style — between poems so obviously different in the special kinds of pleasure they give us as are the *Odyssey* and *The Waste Land,* "Who Is Sylvia?" and "The Canonization," "Westminster Bridge" and Gray's *Elegy, The Rape of the Lock* and "Tears, Idle Tears."[3] What is revealed, if we stay with Brooks, is merely the ironical "structure" which all these, and other, poems have in common as contrasted with nonpoetical works or bad poems. But this is to shut our eyes to a whole range of questions, turning on specific differences in poetic ends and the means suitable for their realization, which are real problems for poets writing poems and hence, one would suppose, important problems for critics. For, literally speaking at any rate, a poet does not write poetry but individual poems. And these are inevitably, as finished wholes, instances of one or another poetic kind, differentiated not by any necessities of the linguistic instrument of poetry but primarily by the nature of the poet's conception, as finally embodied in his poem, of a particular form to be achieved through the representation, in speech used dramatically or otherwise, of some distinctive state of feeling, or moral choice, or action, complete in itself and productive of a certain emotion or complex of emotions in the reader. It is thus only relatively to the form of the poem, as the representation of a particularized human activity of a given emotional quality, that the poet can know whether his poem is too long or too short, whether the things to be said or left unsaid are properly chosen, whether the parts are rightly ordered and connected, or whether the words, metaphors, and "paradoxes" are appropriate or not to the thought, emotion, character, situation, or general effect. In other words, the principles of the poet's artistic reasoning (however

---

[2]Thomas Gray, English poet (1716–1771); his "Elegy Written in a Country Churchyard" (1751) is one of the best-known eighteenth-century poems. The full stanza from which the line is quoted runs:

Let not Ambition mock their useful toil,
Their homely joys, and destiny obscure;
Nor Grandeur hear with a disdainful smile
The short and simple annals of the Poor.

[3]The list, starting with "Who Is Sylvia?" and ending here, consists of texts Brooks analyzes in *The Well-Wrought Urn: Studies in the Structure of Poetry* (1947).

instinctive this may be) are always, and necessarily, ends or effects of some determinate sort to be accomplished in his poem, whether ultimately in the poem as a whole or mediately in some part of it; and the principles will differ, and along with them his decisions as to what must or can be done in constituting his action and its mode of representation, rendering his characters and their thoughts, and fashioning his diction, according as he is writing a simple lyric of feeling or a moral lyric of character, a tragedy or a mock-epic. A

sign of the adequacy to its subject of any theory of poetry which aims, as Brooks's theory does, to treat poetry as poetry and not another thing, is surely the extent to which it is able to cope, in specific terms, with problems of this nature. The construction of an adequate theory is not an impossible task, but it requires a basic analysis that will take account, as Brooks never does, of more than one among the several variable "parts" which are combined in different ways in each of the many distinguishable species of poetic works.

W. K. Wimsatt

1907–1975

Monroe C. Beardsley

1915–1985

Of the three important essays on which W. K. Wimsatt and Monroe C. Beardsley collaborated, "The Intentional Fallacy" (1946) is probably the most celebrated. The premier heresy hunter among the New Critics, William Kurtz Wimsatt was born in Washington, D.C., and educated at Georgetown University and at Yale, where he took his Ph.D. in 1939 and taught until his death. Yale published his dissertation, The Prose Style of Samuel Johnson, *in 1941. In addition to other works on Samuel Johnson and Alexander Pope, Wimsatt is also the author of* The Verbal Icon *(1954),* Literary Criticism: A Short History *(with Cleanth Brooks, 1957),* Hateful Contraries *(1965), and* The Day of the Leopards *(1976), a bitter response to contemporary trends in life and letters. Wimsatt argued for a "tensional" criticism that would avoid the intentional, affective, genetic, and stylistic "fallacies." Like Shelley, he found the value of poetry in its mystical incarnation, through metaphor, of relations and connections within reality. The formalist aesthetician Monroe Curtis Beardsley was born in Bridgeport, Connecticut, and educated at Yale (B.A., 1936; Ph.D., 1939). He taught philosophy there before moving on to Mt. Holyoke College (1944–46), Swarthmore College (1947–69), and finally Temple University. Beardsley's books include* Aesthetics from Classical Greece to the Present *(1966),* Aesthetic Inquiry *(1967), and* The Possibility of Criticism *(1970). The text of "The Intentional Fallacy" is taken from the version reprinted in* The Verbal Icon.

The Intentional Fallacy

I

The claim of the author's "intention" upon the critic's judgment has been challenged in a number of recent discussions, notably in the debate entitled *The Personal Heresy*, between Professors Lewis and Tillyard. But it seems doubtful if this claim and most of its romantic corollaries are as yet subject to any widespread questioning. The present writers, in a short article entitled "Intention"[1] for a *Dictionary* of literary criticism, raised the issue but were unable to pursue its implications at any length. We argued that the design or intention of the author is neither available

[1] *Dictionary of World Literature*, ed. Joseph T. Shipley (New York, 1942), pp. 326–29. [Wimsatt and Beardsley]

nor desirable as a standard for judging the success of a work of literary art, and it seems to us that this is a principle which goes deep into some differences in the history of critical attitudes. It is a principle which accepted or rejected points to the polar opposites of classical "imitation" and romantic expression. It entails many specific truths about inspiration, authenticity, biography, literary history and scholarship, and about some trends of contemporary poetry, especially its allusiveness. There is hardly a problem of literary criticism in which the critic's approach will not be qualified by his view of "intention."

"Intention," as we shall use the term, corresponds to *what he intended* in a formula which more or less explicitly has had wide acceptance.

"In order to judge the poet's performance, we must know what he intended." Intention is design or plan in the author's mind. Intention has obvious affinities for the author's attitude toward his work, the way he felt, what made him write.

We begin our discussion with a series of propositions summarized and abstracted to a degree where they seem to us axiomatic.

1. A poem does not come into existence by accident. The words of a poem, as Professor Stoll has remarked, come out of a head, not out of a hat. Yet to insist on the designing intellect as a cause of a poem is not to grant the design or intention as a standard by which the critic is to judge the worth of the poet's performance.

2. One must ask how a critic expects to get an answer to the question about intention. How is he to find out what the poet tried to do? If the poet succeeded in doing it, then the poem itself shows what he was trying to do. And if the poet did not succeed, then the poem is not adequate evidence, and the critic must go outside the poem — for evidence of an intention that did not become effective in the poem. "Only one caveat must be borne in mind," says an eminent intentionalist[2] in a moment when his theory repudiates itself; "the poet's aim must be judged at the moment of the creative act, that is to say, by the art of the poem itself."

3. Judging a poem is like judging a pudding or a machine. One demands that it work. It is only because an artifact works that we infer the intention of an artificer. "A poem should not mean but be."[3] A poem can be only through its meaning — since its medium is words — yet it is, simply is, in the sense that we have no excuse for inquiring what part is intended or meant. Poetry is a feat of style by which a complex of meaning is handled all at once. Poetry succeeds because all or most of what is said or implied is relevant; what is irrelevant has been excluded, like lumps from pudding and "bugs" from machinery. In this respect poetry differs from practical messages, which are successful if and only if we correctly infer the intention. They are more abstract than poetry.

[2] J. E. Spingarn, "The New Criticism," in Criticism in America (New York, 1924), pp. 24–25. [Wimsatt and Beardsley]

[3] Archibald MacLeish in "Ars Poetica."

4. The meaning of a poem may certainly be a personal one, in the sense that a poem expresses a personality or state of soul rather than a physical object like an apple. But even a short lyric poem is dramatic, the response of a speaker (no matter how abstractly conceived) to a situation (no matter how universalized). We ought to impute the thoughts and attitudes of the poem immediately to the dramatic speaker, and if to the author at all, only by an act of biographical inference.

5. There is a sense in which an author, by revision, may better achieve his original intention. But it is a very abstract sense. He intended to write a better work, or a better work of a certain kind, and now has done it. But it follows that his former concrete intention was not his intention. "He's the man we were in search of, that's true," says Hardy's rustic constable, "and yet he's not the man we were in search of. For the man we were in search of was not the man we wanted."

"Is not a critic," asks Professor Stoll, "a judge, who does not explore his own consciousness, but determines the author's meaning or intention, as if the poem were a will, a contract, or the constitution? The poem is not the critic's own." He has accurately diagnosed two forms of irresponsibility, one of which he prefers. Our view is yet different. The poem is not the critic's own and not the author's (it is detached from the author at birth and goes about the world beyond his power to intend about it or control it). The poem belongs to the public. It is embodied in language, the peculiar possession of the public, and it is about the human being, an object of public knowledge. What is said about the poem is subject to the same scrutiny as any statement in linguistics or in the general science of psychology.

A critic of our Dictionary article, Ananda K. Coomaraswamy, has argued[4] that there are two kinds of inquiry about a work of art: (1) whether the artist achieved his intentions; (2) whether the work of art "ought ever to have been undertaken at all" and so "whether it is worth preserving." Number (2), Coomaraswamy maintains, is not "criticism of any work of art qua work of art,"

[4] Ananda K. Coomaraswamy, "Intention," in American Bookman 1 (1944), pp. 41–48. [Wimsatt and Beardsley]

but is rather moral criticism; number (1) is artistic criticism. But we maintain that (2) need not be moral criticism: that there is another way of deciding whether works of art are worth preserving and whether, in a sense, they "ought" to have been undertaken, and this is the way of objective criticism of works of art as such, the way which enables us to distinguish between a skillful murder and a skillful poem. A skillful murder is an example which Coomaraswamy uses, and in his system the difference between the murder and the poem is simply a "moral" one, not an "artistic" one, since each if carried out according to plan is "artistically" successful. We maintain that (2) is an inquiry of more worth than (1), and since (2) and not (1) is capable of distinguishing poetry from murder, the name "artistic criticism" is properly given to (2).

II

It is not so much a historical statement as a definition to say that the intentional fallacy is a romantic one. When a rhetorician of the first century A.D. writes: "Sublimity is the echo of a great soul," or when he tells us that "Homer enters into the sublime actions of his heroes" and "shares the full inspiration of the combat," we shall not be surprised to find this rhetorician considered as a distant harbinger of romanticism and greeted in the warmest terms by Saintsbury.[5] One may wish to argue whether Longinus should be called romantic, but there can hardly be a doubt that in one important way he is.

Goethe's three questions for "constructive criticism" are "What did the author set out to do? Was his plan reasonable and sensible, and how far did he succeed in carrying it out?" If one leaves out the middle question, one has in effect the system of Croce — the culmination and crowning philosophic expression of romanticism. The beautiful is the successful intuition-expression, and the ugly is the unsuccessful; the intuition or private part of art is *the* aesthetic fact, and the medium or public part is not the subject of aesthetic at all.

> The Madonna of Cimabue is still in the Church of Santa Maria Novella; but does she speak to the visitor of to-day as to the Florentines of the thirteenth century?

[5] The rhetorician is Longinus; see "On the Sublime," p. 88.

> *Historical interpretation* labours . . . to reintegrate in us the psychological conditions which have changed in the course of history. It . . . enables us to see a work of art (a physical object) as its *author saw it* in the moment of production.[6]

The first italics are Croce's, the second ours. The upshot of Croce's system is an ambiguous emphasis on history. With such passages as a point of departure a critic may write a nice analysis of the meaning or "spirit" of a play by Shakespeare or Corneille — a process that involves close historical study but remains aesthetic criticism — or he may, with equal plausibility, produce an essay in sociology, biography, or other kinds of nonaesthetic history.

III

> I went to the poets; tragic, dithyrambic, and all sorts. . . . I took them some of the most elaborate passages in their own writings, and asked what was the meaning of them. . . . Will you believe me? . . . there is hardly a person present who would not have talked better about their poetry than they did themselves. Then I knew that not by wisdom do poets write poetry, but by a sort of genius and inspiration.[7]

That reiterated mistrust of the poets which we hear from Socrates may have been part of a rigorously ascetic view in which we hardly wish to participate, yet Plato's Socrates saw a truth about the poetic mind which the world no longer commonly sees — so much criticism, and that the most inspirational and most affectionately remembered, has proceeded from the poets themselves.

Certainly the poets have had something to say that the critic and professor could not say; their message has been more exciting: that poetry should come as naturally as leaves to a tree, that poetry is the lava of the imagination, or that it is emotion recollected in tranquillity.

[6] It is true that Croce himself in his *Ariosto, Shakespeare and Corneille* (London, 1920), chap. 7, "The Practical Personality and the Poetical Personality," and in his *Defense of Poetry* (Oxford, 1933), p. 24, and elsewhere, early and late, has delivered telling attacks on emotive geneticism, but the main drive of the *Aesthetic* is surely toward a kind of cognitive intentionalism. [Wimsatt and Beardsley]

[7] From Plato's *Apology*.

But it is necessary that we realize the character and authority of such testimony. There is only a fine shade of difference between such expressions and a kind of earnest advice that authors often give. Thus Edward Young, Carlyle, Walter Pater:

I know two golden rules from *ethics*, which are no less golden in *Composition*, than in life. 1. *Know thyself;* 2dly, *Reverence thyself.*

This is the grand secret for finding readers and retaining them: let him who would move and convince others, be first moved and convinced himself. Horace's rule, *Si vis me flere*, is applicable in a wider sense than the literal one. To every poet, to every writer, we might say: Be true, if you would be believed.

Truth! there can be no merit, no craft at all, without that. And further, all beauty is in the long run only *fineness* of truth, or what we call expression, the finer accommodation of speech to that vision within.

And Housman's little handbook to the poetic mind yields this illustration:

Having drunk a pint of beer at luncheon — beer is a sedative to the brain, and my afternoons are the least intellectual portion of my life — I would go out for a walk of two or three hours. As I went along, thinking of nothing in particular, only looking at things around me and following the progress of the seasons, there would flow into my mind, with sudden and unaccountable emotion, sometimes a line or two of verse, sometimes a whole stanza at once.

This is the logical terminus of the series already quoted. Here is a confession of how poems were written which would do as a definition of poetry just as well as "emotion recollected in tranquillity" — and which the young poet might equally well take to heart as a practical rule. Drink a pint of beer, relax, go walking, think on nothing in particular, look at things, surrender yourself to yourself, search for the truth in your own soul, listen to the sound of your own inside voice, discover and express the *vraie vérité.*[8]

It is probably true that all this is excellent advice for poets. The young imagination fired by Wordsworth and Carlyle is probably closer to the verge of producing a poem than the mind of the student who has been sobered by Aristotle or Richards. The art of inspiring poets, or at least of inciting something like poetry in young persons, has probably gone further in our day than ever before. Books of creative writing such as those issued from the Lincoln School are interesting evidence of what a child can do.[9] All this, however, would appear to belong to an art separate from criticism — to a psychological discipline, a system of self-development, a yoga, which the young poet perhaps does well to notice, but which is something different from the public art of evaluating poems.

Coleridge and Arnold were better critics than most poets have been, and if the critical tendency dried up the poetry in Arnold and perhaps in Coleridge, it is not inconsistent with our argument, which is that judgment of poems is different from the art of producing them. Coleridge has given us the classic "anodyne" story, and tells what he can about the genesis of a poem which he calls "psychological curiosity," but his definitions of poetry and of the poetic quality "imagination" are to be found elsewhere and in quite other terms.

It would be convenient if the passwords of the intentional school, "sincerity," "fidelity," "spontaneity," "authenticity," "genuineness," "originality," could be equated with the terms such as "integrity," "relevance," "unity," "function," "maturity," "subtlety," "adequacy," and other more precise terms of evaluation — in short, if "expression" always meant aesthetic achievement. But this is not so.

[8]True truth.

[9]See Hughes Mearns, *Creative Youth* (Garden City, 1925), esp. pp. 10, 27–29. The technique of inspiring poems has apparently been outdone more recently by the study of inspiration in successful poets and other artists. See, for instance, Rosamond E. M. Harding, *An Anatomy of Inspiration* (Cambridge, 1940); Julius Portnoy, *A Psychology of Art Creation* (Philadelphia, 1942); Rudolf Arnheim and others, *Poets at Work* (New York, 1947); Phyllis Bartlett, *Poems in Process* (New York, 1951); Brewster Ghiselin (ed.), *The Creative Process: A Symposium* (Berkeley and Los Angeles, 1952). [Wimsatt and Beardsley]

"Aesthetic" art, says Professor Curt Ducasse, an ingenious theorist of expression, is the conscious objectification of feelings, in which an intrinsic part is the critical moment. The artist corrects the objectification when it is not adequate. But this may mean that the earlier attempt was not successful in objectifying the self, or "it may also mean that it was a successful objectification of a self which, when it confronted us clearly, we disowned and repudiated in favor of another."[10] What is the standard by which we disown or accept the self? Professor Ducasse does not say. Whatever it may be, however, this standard is an element in the definition of art which will not reduce to terms of objectification. The evaluation of the work of art remains public; the work is measured against something outside the author.

IV

There is criticism of poetry and there is author psychology, which when applied to the present or future takes the form of inspirational promotion; but author psychology can be historical, too, and then we have literary biography, a legitimate and attractive study in itself, one approach, as Professor Tillyard would argue, to personality, the poem being only a parallel approach. Certainly it need not be with a derogatory purpose that one points out personal studies, as distinct from poetic studies, in the realm of literary scholarship. Yet there is danger of confusing personal and poetic studies; and there is the fault of writing the personal as if it were poetic.

There is a difference between internal and external evidence for the meaning of a poem. And the paradox is only verbal and superficial that what is (1) internal is also public: it is discovered through the semantics and syntax of a poem, through our habitual knowledge of the language, through grammars, dictionaries, and all the literature which is the source of dictionaries, in general through all that makes a language and culture; while what is (2) external is private or idiosyncratic; not a part of the work

as a linguistic fact: it consists of revelations (in journals, for example, or letters or reported conversations) about how or why the poet wrote the poem — to what lady, while sitting on what lawn, or at the death of what friend or brother. There is (3) an intermediate kind of evidence about the character of the author or about private or semiprivate meanings attached to words or topics by an author or by a coterie of which he is a member. The meaning of words is the history of words, and the biography of an author, his use of a word, and the associations which the word had for *him*, are part of the word's history and meaning.[11] But the three types of evidence, especially (2) and (3), shade into one another so subtly that it is not always easy to draw a line between examples, and hence arises the difficulty for criticism. The use of biographical evidence need not involve intentionalism, because while it may be evidence of what the author intended, it may also be evidence of the meaning of his words and the dramatic character of his utterance. On the other hand, it may not be all this. And a critic who is concerned with evidence of type (1) and moderately with that of type (3) will in the long run produce a different sort of comment from that of the critic who is concerned with (2) and with (3) where it shades into (2).

The whole glittering parade of Professor Lowes's *Road to Xanadu*, for instance, runs along the border between types (2) and (3) or boldly traverses the romantic region of (2). " 'Kubla Khan,'" says Professor Lowes, "is the fabric of a vision, but every image that rose up in its weaving had passed that way before. And it would seem that there is nothing haphazard or fortuitous in their return." This is not quite clear — not even when Professor Lowes explains that there were clusters of associations, like hooked atoms, which were drawn into complex relation with other clusters in the deep well of Coleridge's memory, and which then coalesced and issued forth as poems. If there was nothing "haphazard or fortuitous" in the way

---

[10]Curt Ducasse, *The Philosophy of Art* (New York, 1929), p. 116. [Wimsatt and Beardsley]

[11]And the history of words *after* a poem is written may contribute meanings which if relevant to the original pattern should not be ruled out by a scruple about intention. [Wimsatt and Beardsley.]

the images returned to the surface, that may mean (1) that Coleridge could not produce what he did not have, that he was limited in his creation by what he had read or otherwise experienced, or (2) that having received certain clusters of associations, he was bound to return them in just the way he did, and that the value of the poem may be described in terms of the experiences on which he had to draw. The latter pair of propositions (a sort of Hartleyan associationism which Coleridge himself repudiated in the *Biographia*) may not be assented to. There were certainly other combinations, other poems, worse or better, that might have been written by men who had read Bartram and Purchas and Bruce and Milton. And this will be true no matter how many times we are able to add to the brilliant complex of Coleridge's reading. In certain flourishes (such as the sentence we have quoted) and in chapter headings like "The Shaping Spirit," "The Magical Synthesis," "Imagination Creatrix," it may be that Professor Lowes pretends to say more about the actual poems than he does. There is a certain deceptive variation in these fancy chapter titles; one expects to pass on to a new stage in the argument, and one finds — more and more sources, more and more about "the streamy nature of association."[12]

"Wohin der Weg?" quotes Professor Lowes for the motto of his book. "Kein Weg! Ins Unbetretene."[13] Precisely because the way is *unbetreten*, we should say, it leads away from the poem. Bartram's *Travels* contains a good deal of the history of certain words and of certain romantic Floridian conceptions that appear in "Kubla Khan." And a good deal of that history has passed and was then passing into the very stuff of our language. Perhaps a person who has read Bartram appreciates the poem more than one who has not. Or, by looking up the vocabulary of "Kubla Khan" in the *Oxford English Dictionary*, or by reading some of the other books there quoted, a person may know the poem better. But it would seem to pertain little to the poem to know that *Coleridge* had read Bartram. There is a gross

body of life, of sensory and mental experience, which lies behind and in some sense causes every poem, but can never be and need not be known in the verbal and hence intellectual composition which is the poem. For all the objects of our manifold experience, for every unity, there is an action of the mind which cuts off roots, melts away context — or indeed we should never have objects or ideas or anything to talk about.

It is probable that there is nothing in Professor Lowes's vast book which could detract from anyone's appreciation of either *The Ancient Mariner* or "Kubla Khan." We next present a case where preoccupation with evidence of type (3) has gone so far as to distort a critic's view of a poem (yet a case not so obvious as those that abound in our critical journals).

In a well known poem by John Donne[14] appears this quatrain:

Moving of th' earth brings harmes and feares,
Men reckon what it did and meant,
But trepidation of the sphieares,
Though greater farre, is innocent.

A recent critic in an elaborate treatment of Donne's learning has written of this quatrain as follows:

He touches the emotional pulse of the situation by a skillful allusion to the new and the old astronomy. . . . Of the new astronomy, the "moving of the earth" is the most radical principle; of the old, the "trepidation of the spheres" is the motion of the greatest complexity. . . . The poet must exhort his love to quietness and calm upon his departure; and for this purpose the figure based upon the latter motion (trepidation), long absorbed into the traditional astronomy, fittingly suggests the "harmes and feares" implicit in the figure of the moving earth.[15]

The argument is plausible and rests on a well-substantiated thesis that Donne was deeply interested in the new astronomy and its repercussions in the theological realm. In various works Donne shows his familiarity with Kepler's *De Stella Nova*, with Galileo's *Siderius Nuncius*, with William Gilbert's

[12]Chaps. 8, "The Pattern," and 16, "The Known and Familiar Landscape," will be found of most help to the student of the poem. [Wimsatt and Beardsley]

[13]Goethe: "Whither leads the road? No road! Into the untraveled."

[14]"A Valediction, Forbidding Mourning."

[15]Charles M. Coffin, *John Donne and the New Philosophy* (New York, 1927), pp. 97-98. [Wimsatt and Beardsley]

De Magnete, and with Clavius's commentary on the *De Sphaera* of Sacrobosco. He refers to the new science in his Sermon at Paul's Cross and in a letter to Sir Henry Goodyer. In *The First Anniversary* he says the "new philosophy calls all in doubt." In the *Elegy on Prince Henry* he says that the "least moving of the center" makes "the world to shake."

It is difficult to answer argument like this, and impossible to answer it with evidence of like nature. There is no reason why Donne might not have written a stanza in which the two kinds of celestial motion stood for two sorts of emotion at parting. And if we become full of astronomical ideas and see Donne only against the background of the new science, we may believe that he did. But the text itself remains to be dealt with, the analyzable vehicle of a complicated metaphor. And one may observe: (1) that the movement of the earth according to the Copernican theory is a celestial motion, smooth and regular, and while it might cause religious or philosophic fears, it could not be associated with the crudity and earthiness of the kind of commotion which the speaker in the poem wishes to discourage; (2) that there is another moving of the earth, an earthquake, which has just these qualities and is to be associated with the tear-floods and sigh-tempests of the second stanza of the poem; (3) that "trepidation" is an appropriate opposite of earthquake, because each is a shaking or vibratory motion; and "trepidation of the spheres" is "greater far" than an earthquake, but not much greater (if two such motions can be compared as to greatness) than the annual motion of the earth; (4) that reckoning what it "did and meant" shows that the event has passed, like an earthquake, not like the incessant celestial movement of the earth. Perhaps a knowledge of Donne's interest in the new science may add another shade of meaning, an overtone to the stanza in question, though to say even this runs against the words. To make the geocentric and heliocentric antithesis the core of the metaphor is to disregard the English language, to prefer private evidence to public, external to internal.

V

If the distinction between kinds of evidence has implications for the historical critic, it has them no less for the contemporary poet and his critic.

Or, since every rule for a poet is but another side of a judgment by a critic, and since the past is the realm of the scholar and critic, and the future and present that of the poet and the critical leaders of taste, we may say that the problems arising in literary scholarship from the intentional fallacy are matched by others which arise in the world of progressive experiment.

The question of "allusiveness," for example, as acutely posed by the poetry of Eliot, is certainly one where a false judgment is likely to involve the intentional fallacy. The frequency and depth of literary allusion in the poetry of Eliot and others has driven so many in pursuit of full meanings to the *Golden Bough* and the Elizabethan drama that it has become a kind of commonplace to suppose that we do not know what a poet means unless we have traced him in his reading — a supposition redolent with intentional implications. The stand taken by F. O. Matthiessen is a sound one and partially forestalls the difficulty.

> If one reads these lines with an attentive ear and is sensitive to their sudden shifts in movement, the contrast between the actual Thames and the idealized vision of it during an age before it flowed through a megalopolis is sharply conveyed by that movement itself, whether or not one recognizes the refrain to be from Spenser.

Eliot's allusions work when we know them — and to a great extent even when we do not know them, through their suggestive power.

But sometimes we find allusions supported by notes, and it is a nice question whether the notes function more as guides to send us where we may be educated, or more as indications in themselves about the character of the allusions. "Nearly everything of importance . . . that is apposite to an appreciation of 'The Waste Land,' " writes Matthiessen of Miss Weston's book,[16] "has been incorporated into the structure of the poem itself, or into Eliot's Notes." And with such an admission it may begin to appear that it would not much matter if Eliot invented his sources (as Sir Walter Scott invented chapter epigraphs from "old plays" and "anonymous" authors, or as Coleridge wrote marginal

[16]Jessie Weston's *From Ritual to Romance* (1920), an influence on *The Waste Land*.

glosses for *The Ancient Mariner*). Allusions to Dante, Webster, Marvell, or Baudelaire doubtless gain something because these writers existed, but it is doubtful whether the same can be said for an allusion to an obscure Elizabethan:

The sound of horns and motors, which shall bring
Sweeney to Mrs. Porter in the spring.

"Cf. Day, *Parliament of Bees*," says Eliot,

When of a sudden, listening, you shall hear,
A noise of horns and hunting, which shall bring
Actaeon to Diana in the spring,
Where all shall see her naked skin.

The irony is completed by the quotation itself; had Eliot, as is quite conceivable, composed these lines to furnish his own background, there would be no loss of validity. The conviction may grow as one reads Eliot's next note: "I do not know the origin of the ballad from which these lines are taken: it was reported to me from Sydney, Australia." The important word in this note — on Mrs. Porter and her daughter who washed their feet in soda water — is "ballad." And if one should feel from the lines themselves their "ballad" quality, there would be little need for the note. Ultimately, the inquiry must focus on the integrity of such notes as parts of the poem, for where they constitute special information about the meaning of phrases in the poem, they ought to be subject to the same scrutiny as any of the other words in which it is written. Matthiessen believes that notes were the price Eliot "had to pay in order to avoid what he would have considered muffling the energy of his poem by extended connecting links in the text itself." But it may be questioned whether the notes and the need for them are not equally muffling. F. W. Bateson has plausibly argued that Tennyson's "The Sailor Boy" would be better if half the stanzas were omitted, and the best versions of ballads like "Sir Patrick Spens" owe their power to the very audacity with which the minstrel has taken for granted the story upon which he comments. What then if a poet finds he cannot take so much for granted in a more recondite context and rather than write informatively, supplies notes? It can be said in favor of this plan that at least the notes do

not pretend to be dramatic, as they would if written in verse. On the other hand, the notes may look like unassimilated material lying loose beside the poem, necessary for the meaning of the verbal symbol, but not integrated, so that the symbol stands incomplete.

We mean to suggest by the above analysis that whereas notes tend to seem to justify themselves as external indexes to the author's *intention*, yet they ought to be judged like any other parts of a composition (verbal arrangement special to a particular context), and when so judged their reality as parts of the poem, or their imaginative integration with the rest of the poem, may come into question. Matthiessen, for instance, sees that Eliot's titles for poems and his epigraphs are informative apparatus, like the notes. But while he is worried by some of the notes and thinks that Eliot "appears to be mocking himself for writing the note at the same time that he wants to convey something by it," Matthiessen believes that the "device" of epigraphs "is not at all open to the objection of not being sufficiently structural." "The *intention*," he says, "is to enable the poet to secure a condensed expression in the poem itself." "In each case the epigraph is *designed* to form an integral part of the effect of the poem." And Eliot himself, in his notes, has justified his poetic practice in terms of intention.

The Hanged Man, a member of the traditional pack, fits my purpose in two ways: because he is associated in my mind with the Hanged God of Frazer, and because I associate him with the hooded figure in the passage of the disciples to Emmaus in Part V.... The man with Three Staves (an authentic member of the Tarot pack) I associate, quite arbitrarily, with the Fisher King himself.

And perhaps he is to be taken more seriously here, when off guard in a note, than when in his Norton Lectures he comments on the difficulty of saying what a poem means and adds playfully that he thinks of prefixing to a second edition of *Ash Wednesday* some lines from *Don Juan*:

I don't pretend that I quite understand
My own meaning when I would be *very* fine;
But the fact is that I have nothing planned
Unless it were to be a moment merry.

If Eliot and other contemporary poets have any characteristic fault, it may be in *planning* too much.

Allusiveness in poetry is one of several critical issues by which we have illustrated the more abstract issue of intentionalism, but it may be for today the most important illustration. As a poetic practice allusiveness would appear to be in some recent poems an extreme corollary of the romantic intentionalist assumption, and as a critical issue it challenges and brings to light in a special way the basic premise of intentionalism. The following instance from the poetry of Eliot may serve to epitomize the practical implications of what we have been saying. In Eliot's "Love Song of J. Alfred Prufrock," toward the end, occurs the line: "I have heard the mermaids singing, each to each," and this bears a certain resemblance to a line in a Song by John Donne, "Teach me to heare Mermaides singing," so that for the reader acquainted to a certain degree with Donne's poetry, the critical question arises: Is Eliot's line an allusion to Donne's? Is Prufrock thinking about Donne? Is Eliot thinking about Donne? We suggest that there are two radically different ways of looking for an answer to this question. There is (1) the way of poetic analysis and exegesis, which inquires whether it makes any sense if Eliot-Prufrock *is* thinking about Donne. In an earlier part of the poem, when Prufrock asks, "Would it have been worth while, . . . To have squeezed the universe into a ball," his words take half their sadness and irony from certain energetic and passionate lines of Marvell "To His Coy Mistress." But the exegetical inquirer may wonder whether mermaids considered as "strange sights" (to hear them is in Donne's poem analogous to getting with child a mandrake root) have much to do with Prufrock's mermaids, which seem to be symbols of romance and dynamism, and which incidentally have literary authentication, if they need it, in a line of a sonnet by Gérard de Nerval. This method of inquiry may lead to the conclusion that the given resemblance between Eliot and Donne is without significance and is better not thought of, or the method may have the disadvantage of providing no certain conclusion. Nevertheless, we submit that this is the true and objective way of criticism, as contrasted to what the very uncertainty of exegesis might tempt a second kind of critic to undertake: (2) the way of biographical or genetic inquiry, in which, taking advantage of the fact that Eliot is still alive, and in the spirit of a man who would settle a bet, the critic writes to Eliot and asks what he meant, or if he had Donne in mind. We shall not here weigh the probabilities — whether Eliot would answer that he meant nothing at all, had nothing at all in mind — a sufficiently good answer to such a question — or in an unguarded moment might furnish a clear and, within its limits, irrefutable answer. Our point is that such an answer to such an inquiry would have nothing to do with the poem "Prufrock"; it would not be a critical inquiry. Critical inquiries, unlike bets, are not settled in this way. Critical inquiries are not settled by consulting the oracle.

2

STRUCTURALISM AND DECONSTRUCTION

No one disputes the principle of the arbitrary nature of the sign, but it is often easier to discover a truth than to assign to it its proper place. — FERDINAND DE SAUSSURE

What requires explanation is not the text itself so much as the possibility of reading and interpreting the text, the possibility of literary effects and literary communication. — JONATHAN CULLER

The passage beyond philosophy does not consist in turning the page of philosophy (which usually comes down to philosophizing badly), but in continuing to read philosophers in a certain way. — JACQUES DERRIDA

The author has disappeared. . . . God and man have died a common death. — MICHEL FOUCAULT

The special insight of the structuralist approach is that, though language may not be everything, practically everything we do that is specifically human is expressed in language. Most obviously we communicate with one another in hundreds of "natural" languages, whose conventions predate any human memory; and in recent decades we have become dependent upon computers, whose functioning is based on the creation of artificial languages for sorting and processing data, and for solving problems.

But most of the other activities of daily life, from the elegant to the homely, are equally dependent upon various codes. The performance of music requires a complex notation, as does the solution of mathematical problems. Our economic life rests upon the exchange of labor and goods for symbols, such as cash, checks, stock certificates, and various other documents that are more or less easily exchangeable for each other and for other people's labor and goods. The language of fashion is one we learn to speak with difficulty, and when we wonder if our tie is too loud or our dress too formal, we are considering whether our friends will be upset by the message our clothes convey. Social life depends on the meaningful gestures and signals of "body language" and revolves around the exchange of small, symbolic favors: drinks, parties, dinners. Family connections in patriarchal culture depend on the exchange — so momentous that it is difficult to think of it as symbolic — of a woman from one family group into another.

Merely noting that everything is language and cataloging the overwhelming variety of ways in which reality is structured in systems of signs and symbols does not get us very far. Structuralism required a method of analyzing systems of symbols, and this was provided by two developments. One was the theory of the nineteenth-century American philosopher Charles Sanders Peirce, which is termed *semiotics*. Peirce analyzed sign systems into three general types: (1) iconic signs, in which the signifier resembles the thing signified (such as the stick figures on washroom doors that signify "Men" or "Women"); (2) indexes, in which the signifier is a reliable indicator of the presence of the signified (like smoke and fire); and (3) true symbols, in which the signifier's relation to the thing signified is completely arbitrary and conventional (just as the sound /kat/ or the written word *cat* are conventional signs for the familiar feline).

The other development was the linguistic theory of Ferdinand de Saussure, who established that the special symbol systems of the natural languages are systems based on differences. In his lecture notes published posthumously as *Cours de linguistique générale* (1916), Saussure established the basic principles of structural linguistics and of structuralism more generally.[1] These principles rest on a number of technical distinctions:

1. *Langue* versus *parole*. A language is a system of constitutive rules — that is, the rules *are* the language in the same way that the rules of chess constitute the game of chess. (If we break the rules of chess by, say, taking two moves at a time, there is no penalty as there is when we break traffic laws or other normative rules; we just aren't playing chess any longer.) But the system of the language (*langue*) appears only in the behavior of its individual speakers, who produce instances of speech (*parole*). Speakers may or may not be aware of the rules of the language, but they usually know whether an individual instance is correct or deviant. The activity of the linguist is to infer the rules of the *langue* from the evidence of *parole*. American linguist Noam Chomsky's distinction between *competence* (ideal language ability) and *performance* (individual activity) is similar to that of *langue* and *parole*.

2. *Synchronic* versus *diachronic*. The system of a *langue* is complete at any one time, but languages, in their sound systems (phonology), their grammatical relationships (syntax), and their lexicons, change over time. In studying a language, one has to distinguish between a synchronic study, which attempts to display the *langue* at one particular time, and a *diachronic* investigation, which studies linguistic change.

3. *Paradigmata* and *syntagmata*. The two fundamental relationships of symbols are parataxis and syntaxis. An example of parataxis is the relationship of items in the same category on a menu: In ordering soup, one may choose the beef consommé *or* the lobster bisque *or* the clam chowder. The items are similar enough to belong to

---

[1]*Semiotics* and *structuralism* have been used here as though they were essentially similar terms, and certainly there was a great deal that connected the two movements. But semiotics takes off from Peirce — for whom language is one of numerous sign systems — and structuralism takes off from Saussure, for whom language was the sign system par excellence. As a result, semioticians discuss sign systems generically, while structuralists tend to use linguistic models exclusively — to speak of "the language of fashion" and so forth. A structuralist would compose a grammar of narrative, while a semiotician would analyze the multiple codes that relate expression to content, and so on.

one category (soups) yet different (in their ingredients). In a language, the consonants and vowels are paradigms on the phonological level, nouns and verbs are
paradigms on the grammatical level, and so on.

Syntax is the relationship of items from different categories in a meaningful
structure. Back in the restaurant, when we choose a soup, an appetizer, a main
course, and a dessert, we try to select a combination that will "go together" pleasantly. Or we try to pick items of clothing that will harmonize in color, texture, and
social tone when worn together. The rules of syntax in a natural language are far
more complex than the rules for wearing clothes or for ordering in a restaurant; it
takes several years of hard work, from the ages of two to four, to learn the most basic
relationships. But when we have succeeded, we comprehend subtle differences in
the syntax of sentences, even some that traditional grammar textbooks ignore.

In Noam Chomsky's famous pair of sentences, "John is eager to please" and
"John is easy to please," for example, the sentences appear to differ merely in one
lexical item: for the third word of each sentence, a different member of the paradigm class of adjectives has been selected. But any native speaker also intuitively
knows that the sentences also differ in their syntax. "John" is implicitly the *subject*
of "please" in the first sentence and the *object* of "please" in the second, despite the
fact that the sentences are apparently cut to the same pattern and that "John" is by
traditional standards the subject of the copula "is" in both.

4. The basic units, or *emes*. To return to paradigm classes, the problem is one
of identifying the basic categories in an unfamiliar language, where the categories
may not be the same as in one's native tongue. Saussure's basic principle was that
distinctions within categories depend on differences; the practical difficulty is figuring out which differences, of all those we can learn to distinguish, really make a
difference — which is not a simple matter.

Take the sound system of English. The letter *t* stands for the sound /t/ — but at
various positions in words /t/ is not a single sound but several different sounds. The
first sound in the word *tip* is not the same as the last sound in the word *pit*. The first
t is *aspirated* — pronounced with an explosion of air — while the second is not. To
complicate things further, the *t* sound in *bottle* is not the same as either of the other
two. But in English, these differences *do not* make a difference. If you pronounce
pit with an aspirated *t*, you have still said *pit*; no one will mistake which word you
have pronounced. Aspiration is a feature that does not make a basic difference in
English (though it does in Hindi and in several other languages). But voicing does
make a difference in English. Words like *tip* and *dip*, or *pit* or *bit*, differ according
to whether the initial consonant is *voiced* (pronounced with the vocal cords vibrat-
ing) or *unvoiced*. The point is that /t/ in all its various pronunciations (allophones)
is a single *phoneme* in English, a basic and minimal unit of the sound system. And
the phoneme /t/ differs from the phoneme /d/ because of the feature of voicing, and
from all the other phonemes of English because of various other sorts of differences.
If the basic minimal unit of a sound system is the phoneme, the basic minimal
unit of grammar is the *morpheme*. One example of a morpheme in English is the
plural, which is formed in a number of different ways, usually by adding /s/ or /z/
or /iz/ to the singular noun (as in bat/bats, pin/pins, church/churches, respectively),

but sometimes by changing the vowel (mouse/mice) or in other irregular ways. Languages other than English often have similar grammatical categories, but even languages with a common origin employ important variations (verbs in French have many more tenses; nouns in French always show gender). Some languages have grammatical categories and relationships that are totally distinct from those found in European languages. In each case it is important to locate the individual units of meaning as they occur, as spaces within a system made up of *differences.*

The impact of Saussure's general principles for discussing the structure of a language was felt first in linguistics. For several decades after Saussure's death, linguists and anthropologists trained in linguistics traveled to remote corners of the world, recording and analyzing the principles of hundreds of natural languages. But soon after the development of structural linguistics, the basic principles began to be generalized to other sorts of codes and structures, which could be analyzed in analogous fashion in terms of the combinations and permutations of various *emes* or basic elements. The smallest units or building blocks of stories were termed *mythemes* by Claude Lévi-Strauss; Julia Kristeva has called the irreducible atoms of social thought *ideologemes.*

As Roland Barthes said in "The Structuralist Activity" (1964), structuralism is not a set of beliefs, but two complementary practices: analysis and synthesis. The structuralist analyzes the products of human making into their smallest significant component parts, then tries to discover the principles of their articulation — how the parts fit together and function.[2] In this very broad sense, the first structuralist was Aristotle, and *Poetics* the first work of structuralist literary criticism. It would not be odd to consider formalist critics like R. S. Crane and Northrop Frye as structuralists. But today, the term is usually restricted to those whose practice of analysis and synthesis is performed using the tools, techniques, and terminology of linguistics.

Perhaps the chief human vector for the spread of structuralism was Roman Jakobson, one of the great linguists of the century. In his paper "Linguistics and Poetics" (translated in 1960), Jakobson presented the following model of the act of communication: A *sender,* having made *contact* with a *receiver,* sends a *message* about some external *context* using a *code.* These six factors — sender, contact, receiver, message, context, and code — define the six functions of communication. Most normal communication is *referential:* It emphasizes the context, the content that is to be conveyed. The *emotive* function of communication emphasizes the sender, while the *conative* emphasizes the receiver. The *phatic* function is that of establishing contact, like saying "hello" when we pick up the telephone. The *meta-linguistic* function is to investigate the code that sender and receiver are both using to clear up disagreements or ambiguities. Finally, there is the linguistic function that centers on the message qua message. This Jakobson defines as the *poetic* function.

Jakobson began as an ally of the Russian Formalists in the 1920s; migrated to Czechoslovakia, where he joined the Prague Linguistic Circle in the 1930s; and then traveled to New York, where he exerted a wide influence on numerous

[2]Roland Barthes, "The Structuralist Activity," in *Critical Essays,* trans. Richard Howard (New York: Farrar, Straus and Giroux, 1972).

intellectuals, including the ethnologist Claude Lévi-Strauss. They collaborated on literary essays, including an essay on Baudelaire's sonnet "The Cats" (1962),[3] but the most important product was Lévi-Strauss's integration of linguistics and myth in his book *Structural Anthropology* (1958), which changed the theory and practice of cultural studies around the world.

MYTH AND LANGUAGE

Claude Lévi-Strauss began his career with a dissertation on *The Elementary Structures of Kinship* (1949), which was a synthesis of the available data on the rules by which a vast number of cultures regulated marriage and kinship ties. Lévi-Strauss's method was to use language-data to verify social rules (for example, if a culture has a word for "mother's brother" that is *also* its word for "father-in-law," this correspondence strongly suggests that a boy is supposed to marry his maternal cross-cousin). In the course of his research, Lévi-Strauss developed a general theory of the way in which the exchange and circulation of women between families is used to knit cultures together.

But in the course of that study he recognized that another aspect of culture is used for exchange and circulation: language. As Lévi-Strauss began to theorize about the homologies between languages and kinship systems, it occurred to him that cultures with complex kinship structures, which gave the individual a small number of marital choices, tended to speak languages with complex syntax and a small lexicon, while cultures (like our own) with simple kinship structures, which give the individual a vast number of marital choices, tended to speak languages with simple syntax and a large lexicon.[4] We can see here a key feature of Lévi-Strauss's method: to try to construct revealing analogies between very different aspects of life and society by seeing each as a structural system of symbols. While the surface structure of the symbols might be very different, the way in which they are combined (syntaxis) might point to a similar deep structure.

Given this interest, Lévi-Strauss was attracted to the study of the richest source of symbols in anthropology: mythology. His four volumes of *Mythologiques* (*The Raw and the Cooked* [1964]; *From Honey to Ashes* [1967]; *The Origin of Table Manners* [1968]; and *L'Homme Nu* [1971]) present an elaborate survey of world myths to illustrate his basic thesis about mythic thinking: that myths are the way the "savage mind" — not the minds of savages, but the untamed mind within all of us — gives order to the world.

"The Structural Study of Myth" (1955), reprinted in part here, presents Lévi-Strauss's method in its purest form, as a way of reconstructing the *langue* of myth by the analysis of a particular *parole*. His analysis of the Oedipus myth demonstrates how he breaks down the chronological structure of the story in order to isolate the various elements (or *mythemes*) operating within the text. He next attempts to

[3]Roman Jakobson and Claude Lévi-Strauss, "Charles Baudelaire's 'The Cats'" (1962), in *Structuralism: A Reader*, ed. Michael Lane (London: Jonathan Cape, 1970).

[4]Claude Lévi-Strauss, "Language and the Analysis of Social Laws" (1951), in *Structural Anthropology* (New York: Basic Books, 1963), pp. 62–63.

understand the relation between the mythemes as members of paradigm classes separated from one another by the way they embody concrete differences. He then finds a way of generalizing the concrete issues of the story as a system of abstract binary terms. Finally, he interprets the interaction of the mythemes as giving order and structure to a significant spiritual conflict. In the case of Oedipus, the myth mediates between conflicting theories: that humanity is born out of the earth (autochthonous) or of the sexual union between man and woman.[5] Lévi-Strauss's point is that as long as the spiritual conflict continues (and if it is a genuine conflict, it can never be fully resolved), the myth will continue to be told, elaborated, varied, and retold in other forms that — structurally, at least — address the same issue.

STRUCTURALIST POETICS

One of the central texts of high structuralism in its most confident phase was the collaborative essay of Roman Jakobson and Lévi-Strauss on Baudelaire's sonnet, "The Cats." Their elaborate analysis of the geometrical symmetry of the grammatical structures within the sonnet showed what structuralism could do. But their conclusion — that the cats symbolize love cleansed of feminine impurity and knowledge cleansed of the sages' austerity — has, despite the seemingly scientific method, not won universal assent. As Michael Riffaterre has said, "the poem has been rebuilt by the two critics into a 'superpoem' inaccessible to the normal reader, and yet the structures described do not explain what establishes contact between poetry and reader. No grammatical analysis of a poem can give us more than the grammar of the poem."[6]

The difficulty is not with grammatical analysis as such (in fact, Riffaterre presents his own grammatical analysis of "Les Chats"). Stylistics, the linguistic analysis of literary effects, is a venerable and useful tool of criticism, but most linguists would begin with an impression of the poem's effect and then seek something in the syntax that might have caused that effect.[7] The problem arises from the hypothesis that, by checking successively into every symmetry of every grammatical category, the critic will stumble onto the secret of the poem. As Jonathan Culler attempted to show in the first half of *Structuralist Poetics* (1975), this hypothesis simply doesn't work: Structural analysis is not an effective discovery procedure. Or rather, it is too effective. Culler demonstrates that the elaborate syntactic symmetries that Jakobson and Lévi-Strauss found in the four strophes of "The Cats" can also be found in the first four prosy sentences of Jakobson's own "Postscriptum" to *Questions de poétique*.

In a long and useful pair of chapters, Culler goes on to discuss the poetics of the lyric poem in terms of the conventions through which we interpret its form and meaning and the operations we perform on the text in order to "naturalize" its language.

[5]Two further examples of the interpretation of myth, dealing with relatively unfamiliar American Indian tales, have been omitted.

[6]Michael Riffaterre, "Describing Poetic Structures: Two Approaches to Baudelaire's *Les Chats,*" in *Structuralism,* ed. Jacques Ehrmann (New York: Doubleday, 1970), pp. 201–02.

[7]As for example in David Richter, "Two Studies in Iconic Syntax: Alfred Lord Tennyson's 'Tears, Idle Tears' and William Carlos Williams's 'The Dance,' " *Language and Style* 18 (1985): 136–51.

(In effect, he suggests that to read a poem we have to *undo* the poet's defamiliar-ization of the material.) After giving a reading of a minimalist one-line poem by Apollinaire, Culler presents the universal principles underlying his performance:

Such an interpretation depends upon three general conventions — that a poem should be unified, that it should be thematically significant, and that this significance can take the form of reflection on poetry — and four general interpretive operations: that one should try to establish binary relations of opposition or equivalence, that one should look for and integrate puns and ambiguities, that items may be read as synecdoches (or metaphors, etc.) in order to attain the level of generality required, and that what a poem says can be related to the fact that it is a poem.[8]

When Culler wrote *Structuralist Poetics*, very little of the work of Umberto Eco had been translated from Italian; *The Role of the Reader* did not appear until 1979, although its constituent essays had been printed in various periodicals as early as 1962. "The Myth of Superman," one of the individual essays from *The Role of the Reader*, is typical of Eco's work in its combination of wit and intellectual rigor and in its immense range of reference, from revered texts like *Oedipus Rex* and *Finnegans Wake* to ephemera like Superman comics, Nero Wolfe detective stories, and the *Doctor Kildare* television series. The essay takes up only one very limited question within narrative poetics: the way narrative time needs to be handled in fiction that belongs to a series, which must therefore be designed to have an indefi-nite number of sequels. But *The Role of the Reader* as a whole has a much broader program: to understand the levels of discourse that occur within narratives (Eco's complex diagram lists ten such levels) and the interactions among them that give rise to interpretation. The result will be to reveal how each text produces the exact sort of Model Reader it needs to bring out its qualities — how "closed" texts elicit passively credulous and "open" texts actively suspicious readings.[9]

Perhaps the most influential theorist of narrative is Gérard Genette, whose tril-ogy *Figures* contains a series of arrestingly original and interconnected essays on the art of both fiction and poetry. As the overall title of the three volumes suggests, Genette's interest is in tropes, figures of speech; but he is far from being a naïve grammarian, interested only in classifying and regulating the use of tropes. Figures of speech are important because they introduce into the usual system of significa-tion a discontinuity requiring the reader's mediation. When we refer to "twenty sail" instead of "twenty ships" we use the figure of *synecdoche* — the part for the whole. As we interpret the figure, we note the presence of one signifier (sail) and the absence of another (ship). Thus, the working of the figure depends on something it cannot contain: the reader's sense of the absent signifier. Or, as Genette put it, "A figure is a gap in relation to usage, but a gap that is nevertheless a part of usage: that is the paradox of rhetoric."

[8] Jonathan Culler, "Poetics of the Lyric," in *Structuralist Poetics* (Ithaca: Cornell University Press, 1975), p. 177.

[9] These are not exhaustive categories. Eco finds a third sort of text, "an exclusive club whose chairman is probably *Tristram Shandy*," which is neither open nor closed but operates as a trap. It lures the reader into "an excess of cooperation and then punishes him for having overdone it."

THE PASSING OF STRUCTURALISM

Structuralism had slowly grown in influence from just after World War II until the middle of the 1960s, spreading from the anthropological studies of Lévi-Strauss to affect the study of literature, philosophy, history, mathematics, politics, economics — all the human sciences. There was a palpable sense at the time that a new method for the synthesis of knowledge was at hand, a method more powerful than the synthesis provided by Platonic dialectic in the ancient world or by Thomistic logic in the Middle Ages. The notion, barely glimpsed, that by using the tools of semiotics and linguistics, structuralism might manage to reunite the branches of knowledge that post-Renaissance specialization had severed, gave its adherents a messianic sense of mission. But in the late 1960s, as radical politics came and went leaving disillusion in its wake, the confident, broadly humanistic, universalizing mission of structuralism foundered as well.

The primary problem was the irresponsible promise of a synthesis of all human knowledge, a promise that was slow in bearing fruit. Many adherents expounded the principles of structuralism and made claims for what structuralism would surely do for the study of literature, but few produced concrete achievements that justified those claims. The claims may in fact have been implausible. One question we have already raised is whether the enabling assumption of structuralism — that everything is a language — is adequate. As James Phelan has suggested, literature is a *second-order* sign system built upon the *first-order* sign system of language. In effect, structuralism stands or falls on its assumption that a second-order system must reproduce the categories and relations of the first-order system. But we have no evidence that this must be the case, and natural science suggests the contrary: Biology, built on biochemistry, does not imitate its organization; nor does chemistry, built on molecular physics, reproduce its lower-order system.

Structuralism may also have lost momentum because it had shifted the focus of the study of literature from the exegesis of individual texts to the exploration of general conditions of the act of interpretation. Ironically, deconstruction, despite its implicit attack on the traditional values and bases of humanistic study, proceeds according to the techniques of close reading in which literary critics throughout the English-speaking world had already been trained under the dominance of New Criticism. In some ways, therefore, it was easier for American academics to follow deconstructionists such as Jacques Derrida and Paul de Man than to carry on the quest of Jakobson, Genette, and Eco.

But of course, in another sense, structuralism is not dead at all. Though it has had to relinquish its broadest assumptions together with its character as a world-historical movement, most of its original adherents — like Todorov and Eco, Genette and Riffaterre — have continued to pursue the study of systems of signs, and the results of their study have become, under the names semiotics, stylistics, and narratology, essential elements in the current battery of approaches to literature.

DERRIDA AND DECONSTRUCTION

One of the difficulties in reading Derrida is that there is no central document, no single, classic essay, like Sidney's *Apology for Poetry* or Kant's *Critique of Judgment*, that contains and expresses a body of systematic thought. In this, he is like some earlier philosophers, such as Hegel and Nietzsche, for whom no selection can give a sense of the whole. But what is unique to Derrida is that, while his rhetoric circles around the same themes, his terminology changes from essay to essay. (Even his principal term, *deconstruction*, is not fully stable. At one point, Derrida wanted to replace it with *desedimentation*, though that word never quite caught on.) This fluidity is entirely by design. Given his program, Derrida has tried to resist anything that would lead to setting up deconstruction as a *system of thought*.

Although it is risky to state that Derrida has a central issue, we can begin with his notion that all thought is necessarily inscribed in language, and that language itself is fraught with intractable paradoxes. We can repress or ignore these paradoxes, but we cannot escape from them or solve them. This is the burden of Derrida's most difficult work, *Of Grammatology*.

Derrida's basic concern is with how Western philosophy has built its metaphysics on a pervasive but fragile base, one that privileges the activity of *speech* over that of *writing*. Speech is opposed to writing and held to be logically prior as well as chronologically older. The valorization of speech begins in Plato's *Phaedrus*, in which Socrates condemns writing as a bastardized form of communication, separated from the Father (the moment of origin). Writing can easily mislead because the speaker is no longer there to explain what he had in mind. Socrates prefers speech because the speaker seems so immediately present in the voice. Meaning enters into sound, and sound as a real presence enters the listener and becomes meaning once more.

Derrida traces this position from Plato down through the centuries to philosophers such as Edmund Husserl and Martin Heidegger. Here we can discuss one classic example, that of the founder of structuralism. Ferdinand de Saussure treats writing as a means of representing speech; it remains an external accessory, however, a supplement that need not be fully taken into account in any philosophy of language. In fact, Saussure feels that writing is in a sense dangerous because it "disguises" language and "usurps" the role of speech (writing corrupts speech at times, as when people mispronounce words because of the way they are spelled). For all these reasons, writing is a *dangerous* supplement, which threatens the integrity of speech. The notion of the "dangerous supplement" is important to Derrida, for the very idea of a supplement challenges and calls into question the dichotomies and hierarchies on which philosophies are built. Like the appendix to a book, a supplement is part of and not part of the text at the same time: It seems to be adding something to what is already complete in itself, and the addition is thus implicitly a correction, even in a sense a recantation.

In Derrida's analysis of the writings of Jean-Jacques Rousseau, for example, he calls attention to Rousseau's characterization of education as a supplement to nature. As a supplement, education adds to something that is already supposedly complete in itself; at the same time, if education adds to nature, then nature must be something in itself — at least to the extent that one must be educated to know what is natural and what is not. Nature is the prior term, a presence that is there at the start. Yet the "supplement" of education reveals an inherent absence or lack within nature — and also an essential condition of its being.

At another point in the *Confessions,* Rousseau himself speaks of masturbation as a "dangerous supplement" to coital sexuality: a perverse addiction that can substitute for and take the place of sexual intercourse. But paradoxically, the fact that masturbation can act as a supplement shows that it shares in the nature of sexuality. Furthermore, what characterizes masturbation — the focus on an imagined sexual object, the impossibility of genuinely possessing what one desires — also characterizes sexual intercourse. One could thus turn the dichotomy upside down and claim that sexual intercourse is a more generalized version of masturbation.

To generalize Derrida's method from the last example: a dominant entity is defined by a form of presence (sexual intercourse) next to its supplement (masturbation), which is defined by a corresponding absence as inferior and marginal. But the distinguishing qualities of the marginal entity are in fact the defining qualities of the dominant. The result is that the rigid hierarchy of the dichotomy dissolves: As we consider the matter, it is no longer clear which is dominant and which marginal.

To come back now to where we began, with Derrida's analysis of the dichotomy of speech and writing, we valorize speech over writing because there, signifier and signified, sound and meaning, seem to be given together, fused for the moment. Form and meaning are simultaneously present. Voice appears as the direct manifestation of thought. In contrast, written words lack this presence; they are physical marks a reader must interpret and animate to supply meanings that do not seem to be *given.*

But in fact, the kind of absence that distinguishes writing from speech is the very condition of the existence of signs in the first place. As we showed above, the structural model of language presupposes absence in the sense that it is an elaborate system of presences and absences that allows signifiers to operate. The letter or phoneme /t/ exists only as part of a system of differences that distinguish it from /d/ or /f/ or any of the other letters or phonemes. The phoneme /t/ differs from /d/ by the quality of voicing (vibration of the vocal cords), which is absent in the former and present in the latter. But /t/ is not a defective /d/; there is only a relational meaning here, not a real presence.

Furthermore, for a token to be a sign, it must be iterable — repeatable. We learn the meaning of a sign by hearing the same sound in similar contexts. The difference between a sign and a mere noise is that one cannot repeat the latter (even if one clap of thunder were exactly like another, it would make no difference). In the case of a language-sign, one must be able to repeat it back, to quote it; but to quote a sign is to produce it as an example, to reproduce it in the absence of the original communicative intention. For a signifier to have value as a sign, therefore, it must be possible to counterfeit it, and when a sign is counterfeited or cited or produced as an example, it is without its original meaning. But this is *always* possible for *any* sign. Therefore the notion that a sign depends upon the presence conferred by voice cannot be maintained, and we cannot hold that speech is logically prior to writing. (Derrida is not denying, of course, that speech preceded writing historically.)

If speech is not prior to writing, then it does not make sense to treat writing as an auxiliary form of speech; indeed, Derrida suggests, we should treat speech as a form of writing — and refer both to an *archè-écriture* (from the Greek and French: "original-writing"). Rather than achieving meaning through the presence of voice, language strives toward meaning through the play of signifiers. This play occurs through the mechanism of what Derrida calls *différance* (a coinage that would be pronounced identically with the usual spelling difference reminding us that there are some things that writing can convey that sound cannot). Derrida's seminal essay of that title is difficult but rewarding. It's difficult because Derrida is trying to talk about precisely what eludes language, a system that operates (as Saussure showed) via formal differences that lack any content. The verb *différer* in French is ambiguous: it means both "to differ" and "to defer." A word, a letter, or a sound is known not through what it is but through its differences relative to other possibilities — the other possibilities that are not present but absent, existing only through the transient traces they leave on memory. Ultimate meaning, genuine presence, is always deferred — just as looking one word up in a dictionary leads to another and so on indefinitely. Between signifier and signified, therefore, there is not the rigid relation of container and contained. Rather, there is always "freeplay" (*jeu*), which suggests that language can never be pinned down to meaning, that it is always already indeterminate. In "Différance," Derrida intentionally repeats himself, going around the same circles more than once. Without marking itself off into separate sections, the essay runs through the paradoxes inherent to language and its representation of reality at least three times: The first time, Derrida focuses on language itself (using quotations from Saussure); the second time, with regard to consciousness and the paradoxes of the subject (using ideas in Freud); and the third, with regard to the nature of our knowledge of Being (using the phenomenology of Heidegger). In each case, *différance* is, so to speak, the black hole in the middle of the system of language, the principle of absence that makes things happen.

It is hard to overestimate the furor Derrida's theory of language provoked. He was not merely saying, like the New Critic William Empson, that poetry depends on seven types of ambiguity. He was claiming in effect that everything in the human sciences — history, political philosophy, psychology, and so on — was a species of poetry, invariably based on a terminology that was necessarily as indeterminate as the language in which it was written. But the real target of his notion of language was the structuralist attempt to synthesize all humanistic knowledge by using the tools of linguistics, for if there was freeplay in the signifier-signified relationship, there was no guarantee of even making sense. In the 1920s, the German mathematician Kurt Gödel put an end to the massive Russell-Whitehead project for systematizing mathematics by proving conclusively that any mathematical system complicated enough to be useful had either to contain contradictions or to be incomplete. Derrida's *Grammatology* was in effect the Gödel's Theorem for the human sciences in the late 1960s. It split the structuralist community down the middle, and even forty years later, the debate continues between those who accept and those who dispute the validity and the motivation of the deconstructive turn.

But there is more at stake than the apparently abstract question of whether or not there is freeplay between the signifier and the signified. For, in its most general sense, the activity of deconstruction involves the skeptical re-examination, not just of speech and writing, but of *all* the dialectical polarities that have formed the basis of Western culture, a re-examination searching for the point of privilege upon which standard hierarchies rest. We are used to arguing about various other presences and absences: art versus genius, culture versus nature, transcendence versus immanence, soul versus body, divine versus human, human versus animal, man versus woman, being versus becoming, and so on. In each case, the first term denotes the presence and the second the absence of something. Derrida uses the paradoxes involved in the logic of "supplements" in an effort to decenter the first term of each pair, to remove it from its privileged position relative to the second. Against the dominant metaphysics of presence, Derrida sets the countermetaphysics of absence. To the extent that these polarities are at the heart of Western culture, deconstruction attempts to expose the illusions upon which authority in Western culture is established. Where the conservative W. B. Yeats complained that "[t]hings fall apart. The center cannot hold," the anarchistic Derrida calls into question the very concept of a center. This is the argument of Derrida's most famous single essay, "Structure, Sign, and Play in the Discourse of the Human Sciences," reprinted here.

Invited to a conference on structuralism in 1966, Derrida proceeded to question the "whole history of the concept of structure" as the activity of naming and renaming in a succession of metaphors the center of the totality of existence: "the history of metaphysics, like the history of the West, is the history of these metaphors." Derrida then proceeded to deconstruct the concept of the center, beginning with the geometrical paradox that the center *defines* the circle but is not part of the line that *is* the circle. This center is, in effect, a transcendental point of absolute presence. So long as we can believe in a transcendental signified — a point of absolute meaning outside and above the world of discourse that gives significance to the whole — the center holds. But once we cease to have God and have only god-terms, once we accept that everything is a text and falls within the framework of discourse, then the very notion of a center must be challenged. And that, says Derrida, is where we currently stand: after the critiques of metaphysics by Nietzsche and Heidegger, after the critique of consciousness by Freud, the fundamental notions of being, truth, and self cannot be naively "centered" as they have been by the major philosophers from Plato through Hegel.

This brings Derrida to structuralism and its attempts to find a center through the science of signs. Most of "Structure, Sign, and Play" is devoted to a deconstruction of the opposition between nature and culture in the work of the founder of structuralism, Claude Lévi-Strauss. One must work out for oneself the chain of paradoxes, one within another, that Derrida finds in Lévi-Strauss's project in *Mythologiques* — for instance, that it is an empirical study that nevertheless rejects the principle of empiricism. Derrida concludes by exposing the ambivalence, the duality of Lévi-Strauss's attitudes. On the one hand, Lévi-Strauss accepts the presence of freeplay within the structure of myths and embraces the notion that mythography is itself a sort of mythical thinking; on the other hand, there is Lévi-Strauss's "ethic of presence, an ethic of nostalgia for origins, an ethic of archaic and natural innocence, of a purity of presence and self-presence in speech." Lévi-Strauss, and thus the structuralist activity in general, seems to be caught halfway between the old metaphysics, which "dreams of deciphering a truth or an origin," and the new revolutionary philosophy, like his own, that "tries to pass beyond man and humanism."

In his conclusion to "Structure, Sign, and Play," Derrida seems to be disclosing his attitudes toward the great precursors. In particular, he seems to be defining himself in opposition to Hegel and as a disciple of Nietzsche. Derrida circumvents Hegel's historical, progressive uses of dialectic; his oppositions always stay open, undecidable, untranscended. And like Nietzsche's philosophy, Derrida's attitudes toward political and social issues seem to be based on aesthetics rather than ethics; he revels in the sense of intellectual crisis and welcomes the coming transvaluation of all values.[10]

But what is more significant, Derrida's ironic gibe at "the nostalgia for the origin" is a slap directed at the existentialist philosopher Martin Heidegger, who influenced him deeply and against whom he reacted equally intensely. Although Heidegger, like Derrida, was an opponent of metaphysics, he did not go far enough for his disciple. As Christopher Norris has put it, Derrida questioned "Heidegger's own metaphysical motives, his quest for a grounding philosophy which would point the way back toward primordial Being. This nostalgic attachment to a lost or forgotten origin is, according to Derrida, the hallmark of all metaphysics."[11] Metaphysics, the abstract bugbear of twentieth-century philosophers from Wittgenstein onward, is like the "tar-baby" of the Uncle Remus stories: In combating it one inevitably gets involved in it. As Derrida states in "Structure, Sign, and Play," "There is no sense in doing without the concepts of metaphysics in order to attack metaphysics. We . . . cannot utter a single destructive proposition which has not already slipped into the form, the logic, and the implicit postulations of precisely what it seeks to contest." Derrida's strategy is to disrupt systematic thought, to wage a guerrilla campaign against it in constantly shifting terms, to stay on the margins of philosophy and avoid its central castle. "The passage beyond philosophy does not consist in turning the page of philosophy . . . but in continuing to read philosophers *in a certain way.*"

Exactly what Derrida meant by "in a certain way" becomes apparent in a passage from his lengthy essay, "Plato's Pharmacy," where he takes up the section of Plato's *Phaedrus* in which Socrates recites (or perhaps invents) a myth about the origin of writing. Derrida walks the reader carefully through this segment of the dialogue, attentive to the nuances and ambiguous usages of Greek nouns and verbs, searching out Plato's verbal play, his silent gliding between one sense and another. Plato's ostensible purpose here is an argument against mere rhetorical skill, a contention that language can be fashioned to be adequately descriptive of the real world, but as Derrida's reading demonstrates, the operations of Socrates' own rhetoric seem to deny the solidity of either discourse or reality.

10 See the introduction to Nietzsche (p. 279).
11 Christopher Norris, *The Deconstructive Turn* (London: Methuen, 1983), p. 24.

BARTHES AND FOUCAULT

As Derrida's message began its guerrilla war on the ends and assumptions of structuralism, a number of structuralism's leading figures became converts, including Roland Barthes, whose shifting aims and ideas are instructive. Barthes's interest, since his 1953 essay "Writing Degree Zero," has been in the immense tacit knowledge the reader must possess, over and above the syntax and basic semantics of a given language, to understand and interpret cultural systems of symbols. Barthes worked in *Mythologies* to demystify the complex languages and cultural systems represented by wrestling matches, striptease shows, advertisements, and other maps of popular culture. Later he attempted to codify the kind of knowledge structuralist analysis was and was not capable of providing, and how it related to other forms of semiotic analysis. The apex of Barthes's structuralist project appeared in the 1966 essay "Introduction to the Structural Analysis of Narratives," a densely written attempt to do complete justice to the *langue* of fiction. Though he is normally a supple and witty stylist, Barthes's tone here was dry and abstract, as though he were somewhat daunted by the complex task of analyzing into their separate components the elements (the *emes*) in the interpretation of narrative, and he characterized his essay, which was based on the previous work of Vladimir Propp, Claude Bremond, A. J. Greimas, and Tzvetan Todorov, as a "tentative effort" rather than a triumphant success.

In *S/Z* (1970), Barthes simplified and reduced these multiple integrative dimensions into a skein of five *codes,* to which the individual bits of text (*lexies*) each make their contribution. Barthes distinguished a *hermeneutic* code of enigmas and their solutions; a *semic* code of characteristics that go into the description of characters and places, a *proairetic* code of actions, a *symbolic* code of themes, and a *referential* code comprising the historical and cultural allusions within the text. The elaborate result was a 220-page commentary on "Sarrasine" (a minor story by Balzac) that — since it remained on the levels of "functions" and "actions" and was incomplete even there — was clearly only a mere sketch toward a full interpretation. *S/Z* was simultaneously the masterpiece and the reductio ad absurdum of Barthes's holistic approach to fiction, because it made clear that any genuinely complete analysis of a fictional text would be so long and complex as to be nearly unreadable. It was widely admired but never imitated, even by Barthes himself.

By the next year, Barthes had produced "From Work to Text," an account of the difference in the way the object of literary study is perceived by formal and structural criticism on the one hand and by poststructural criticism on the other. The essay is short, terse, informal, almost a set of jottings, but Barthes manages to characterize the stance of the deconstructive critic with lucidity and accuracy. Perhaps the most influential section of "From Work to Text" is the last, in which Barthes contrasts the emotional involvement of the reader before and after the deconstructive turn. The older, passive way of reading produced *plaisir* (pleasure), the consumer's enjoyment in being immersed in another's vision, actions, characters. The new way produces what Barthes terms *jouissance,* a nearly untranslatable word ("bliss" is the usual equivalent) that suggests both the joy and the sense of loss experienced in the sexual climax. Here and in later, more elaborate treatments of the phenomenology of reading, such as *The Pleasure of the Text*, Barthes's central contribution to Derrida's project was in clarifying its emotional as well as its intellectual appeal.

Whereas Barthes was a structuralist turned poststructuralist, Michel Foucault had never accepted the linguistic basis of structuralism. He had instead an independent poststructuralist framework of thought that is presented at greater length later in this book (see the introduction to New Historicism and Cultural Studies, p. 782, and the introduction to Gender Studies and Queer Theory, p. 956). Nevertheless, some of his influential essays contributed to the rejection of the structuralist model we have been exploring, and as an analyst of philosophical discourse he was as radical as Derrida. Like Derrida, Foucault was a disciple of the later Nietzsche and saw the will-to-power as dominant over any search for truth — as defining, in fact, the meaning and location of truth. As he puts it in his essay "Truth and Power":

Truth isn't outside power, or lacking in power: contrary to a myth whose history and functions would repay further study, truth isn't the reward of free spirits, the child of protracted solitude, nor the privilege of those who have succeeded in liberating themselves. Truth is a thing of this world: it is produced only by virtue of multiple forms of constraint. And it induces regular effects of power. Each society has its regime of truth, its "general politics" of truth: that is, the types of discourse which it accepts and makes function as true; the mechanisms and instances which enable one to distinguish true and false statements, the means by which each is sanctioned; the techniques and procedures accorded value in the acquisition of truth; the status of those who are charged with saying what is true.[12]

Today, Foucault goes on, the general politics confers truth on the form of scientific discourse; statements are true if and only if they have been the object of well-financed studies, and capitalism not only creates the studies but devotes other massive institutions (education, the media, and so on) to the diffusion and consumption of this form of truth. But though this might be true today, Foucault, like Derrida, became convinced that Western civilization was moving toward a new moment of crisis, a change in the dominant *episteme* (as Foucault called the historical modes of power/knowledge). His work is marked by an apocalyptic sense that it is in our interest — and our duty — to prepare the way for a new power and truth.

We can find some of these strains within Foucault's thought in his essay "What Is an Author?" included here. Foucault concentrates on the humanistic version of truth: authorship seen as a form of author-ity. Despite the apparent collapse of the Romantic conception of the author as incomprehensible genius and the advent of formalism and structuralism, which have successively substituted the central terms of *work* and of *écriture* (writing) for the romantic god-term of *author*, Foucault claims that authorship still retains its old power within advanced capitalism. While the author has been declared dead by some literary theorists, the author-function remains, "a certain functional principle by which, in our culture, one limits, excludes, and chooses; in short, by which one impedes the free circulation,

[12]Michel Foucault, "Truth and Power," in *The Foucault Reader*, ed. Paul Rabinow (New York: Pantheon Books, 1984), pp. 72–73.

the free manipulation, the free composition, decomposition, and recomposition of fiction. . . . The author is therefore the ideological figure by which one marks the manner in which we fear the proliferation of meaning." As long as literature belongs to the author, it cannot be truly ours. But Foucault looks forward to a moment of change in society when the "author-function will disappear." Foucault has no faith, however, that as author-ity fades, literature will belong to "us." He pessimistically foresees that it will instead be replaced by a new "system of constraint" yet to be understood or experienced. The old order changes, giving way to the new, but for Foucault, order is always a synonym for the prisons and asylums through which society controls thought. For Foucault, only a total breakdown of society could liberate us from the order of discourse.

DECONSTRUCTION AND CRITICISM

Like the structuralism it questions and attempts to supplant, deconstruction is not solely, or even primarily, a mode of literary criticism. As Derrida says in "Structure, Sign, and Play," he only wants "to read philosophers *in a certain way*." Indeed, deconstructionists like Rodolphe Gasché have suggested that the application of Derrida's methods to literary texts in search of new interpretations is paradoxical, almost perverse, since Derrida's revolutionary contribution was to treat philosophical texts as if they were bound by the same sorts of linguistic ambiguity and fluidity that had long been thought to characterize literature. (In effect Derrida constitutes the ultimate vindication of poetry against Plato's attack. For Derrida it is the poets, celebrating the freeplay of the signifier, who have had the right notion of language, and the philosophers, aiming for precision of terminology, who have been pursuing a will o' the wisp.)

Nevertheless, Derrida has had more impact in departments of English and French than in philosophy, as deconstruction has been applied less to Ayer or Sartre than to Yeats and Proust. To a large extent, the deconstruction of literature was made possible by the previous triumph of the New Criticism, which treated poetry as an especially complex mode of discourse, essentially dependent on tropes like irony or ambiguity, that led to the evocation of a set of propositions or attitudes toward the real world. If the ultimate purpose of poetry was to say something — in however complicated a form — then, like traditional philosophy and the other humane sciences, it was a discourse that sought "a truth and an origin." As such, it could also read "*in a certain way*." Furthermore, scholars trained in the New Criticism could easily adapt their methods to deconstruction; if once they sought paradox and ambiguity in pursuit of the meaning of texts, they could now seek it in the pursuit of the posited void at the center of meaning. In effect, the move from New Criticism to deconstruction principally involved abandoning the search for the balance and resolution that critics like Cleanth Brooks had sought behind the paradoxes and ambiguities of the text.

In America in the 1970s, the prime locus for this new mode of reading was Yale University, which had also become a haven for many of the New Critics in their last years. Professors Harold Bloom, Geoffrey Hartman, and J. Hillis Miller of the Yale

English Department and Paul de Man of the Department of French and Comparative Literature became known collectively as the "Gang of Four," in ironic token of the radicalism of their readings and their coherence as a group. With the death of de Man in 1983 and the departure of Miller for California a few years later, the group broke up, but not before it had succeeded in bringing deconstruction to America.

Actually, Bloom (see Ch. 4, Psychoanalytic Theory and Criticism) was never really a philosophically orthodox deconstructionist, though his notion that all reading was in fact creative misreading was not inconsistent with the Derridean notion of freeplay. With respect to the other three, it seems clear that the intellectual center and prime mover was de Man.

In his influential 1975 essay "Semiology and Rhetoric," de Man argued that meaning is not a dependable function of syntax. While this argument challenged a form of structuralism that had long ceased to be current, de Man's conclusion — that one does not deconstruct *texts* so much as show the means by which they deconstruct *themselves* — was crucially important. To use a metaphor derived from Roland Barthes, the deconstructionist finds the thread dangling from the sweater, pulls on it, and watches as the fabric of the garment unravels into the pile of yarn from which it was made.

As a mode of literary criticism, deconstruction became extremely influential in the late 1970s and early 1980s, when a second generation of theorist-critics, disciples of de Man and Derrida, such as Barbara Johnson, Cynthia Chase, Timothy Bahti, and Carol Jacobs, produced their most influential work, rereading important texts by Herman Melville, George Eliot, William Wordsworth, and so on. Despite the inventiveness of these readings, it became clear that regardless of the text ana-lyzed, the usual end product of deconstructive criticism was *aporia:* the intellectual vertigo caused by looking into an apparently endless hall of mirrors. This is an effect that, unfortunately, palls on repetition. Many scholars, initially struck by the power of deconstruction, found that, no matter how inventive the path, each venture led invariably to the same vista. Deconstruction nevertheless continued to be one of the most attractive modes of literary theory in the years following de Man's death from cancer in 1983.

But beginning in the summer of 1987, the news broke slowly over the literary world that Ortwin de Graef, a Belgian graduate student writing a thesis on de Man, had discovered over 100 articles by the critic published between 1940 and 1942 in Belgian newspapers sympathetic to the Nazi occupation, including essays espousing anti-Semitic and pro-Nazi sentiments. Even de Man's closest friends at Yale were clearly astonished to hear of this element from his past. De Man had not only kept silent about this episode but had actively misled acquaintances about where and how he had spent the wartime years. It was clear that de Man's posthumous reputation would be tarnished by his wartime collaboration, but it was not de Man's reputation alone that was at stake, but that of the theories of deconstruction with which he was indelibly associated.

When deconstruction began in France in the late 1960s, it had been associated with the leftist critical journal *Tel Quel,* and the politics of its founder, Jacques Derrida, which insofar as they were intelligible also leaned to the Left. But in the intense rivalry that developed in the 1970s between deconstruction and Marxist or New Historicist criticism, deconstruction was painted into the political right wing as a movement whose obsession with textuality blinded it to the significance of lived experience and historical change. American practitioners of deconstruction, in particular, feared that not only Marxists but liberals who (like the structuralist Tzvetan Todorov) had found de Man's theories antihumanistic might seek to find all deconstructionists guilty by association.

As journalists raked the scandal amid the atmosphere of a witch hunt, former students of de Man's, like Chase, colleagues like Hartman and Miller, and even Derrida himself, wrote elaborate and tormented defenses of de Man and, implicitly, of themselves. This controversy, a Dreyfus case in reverse, is fraught with paradoxes of the sort de Man himself would have approved: that many of de Man's defenders are Jews (including Derrida himself); that the focus of the scandal has been dead for over two decades; and that de Man's offenses around 1942 predated his adoption of deconstruction by over 25 years. It is difficult to make out any strong connection between de Man's collaboration with Nazi sympathizers and his literary theories, but if there is one it is most likely to be negative. De Man's deconstructionist theories seem a more rigorous extension of his attacks in the 1950s on "salvational poetics" — of which Nazi cultural imperialism would be one crude version. If this is so, then de Man's life as a critic and theorist might be viewed as a long atonement for his juvenile sins.

The fate of deconstruction after the de Man scandal has been somewhat similar to the fall of structuralism: While its messianic atmosphere has dissipated, its utility has persisted. The primary use of deconstruction today is as a tool for breaking down binarisms and problematizing fields of discourse with seemingly fixed categories. Gender theorists such as Judith Butler (see Ch. 8, Gender Studies and Queer Theory) for example, value the deconstructive turn as a way of overturning essentialist views on sexual orientation and identity. As a tool of analysis and discursive rhetoric, deconstruction, like semiotics, is very much alive.

Selected Bibliography

Abrams, M. H. "The Deconstructive Angel." *Critical Inquiry* 3 (1977): 425–38.
Angermüller, Johannes. "Derrida, Phenomenology, and Structuralism: Why American Critics Turned Deconstructionists." In *Pioneering North America: Mediators of European Culture and Literature*, ed. Klaus Martens and Andreas Hau. Würzburg, Germany: Königshausen & Neumann, 2000, pp. 163–70.
Arac, Jonathan, Wlad Godzich, and Wallace Martin, eds. *The Yale Critics: Deconstruction in America*. Minneapolis: University of Minnesota Press, 1983.
Bal, Mieke. *Narratology*. Paris: Klincksieck, 1977.
Barthes, Roland. *Writing Degree Zero*. 1953; New York: Beacon, 1970.
———. *Critical Essays*. 1964; Evanston: Northwestern University Press, 1970.
———. *Mythologies*. 1957; New York: Hill and Wang, 1972.
———. *S/Z*. 1970; New York: Hill and Wang, 1974.
———. *The Pleasure of the Text*. New York: Hill and Wang, 1975.
———. *Sade, Fourier, Loyola*. New York: Hill and Wang, 1976.

———. *Image, Music, Text.* New York: Hill and Wang, 1977.

———. *A Barthes Reader.* New York: Hill and Wang, 1982.

———. *The Responsibility of Forms: New Critical Essays on Music, Art and Representation.* New York: Hill and Wang, 1984.

———. *The Rustle of Language.* New York: Hill and Wang, 1986.

Benveniste, Emile. *Problems in General Linguistics.* Coral Gables: University of Miami Press, 1971.

Bloom, Harold, et al. *Deconstruction and Criticism.* New York: Seabury, 1979.

Bové, Paul. *Destructive Poetics: Heidegger and Modern American Poetry.* New York: Columbia University Press, 1980.

Cain, William E. "Deconstruction in America: The Recent Literary Criticism of J. Hillis Miller." *College English* 41 (1979): 367–82.

Cassirer, Ernst. "Structuralism in Modern Linguistics." *Word* 1 (1945): 99–120.

———. *Symbol, Myth and Culture.* New Haven: Yale University Press, 1979.

Caws, Peter. *Structuralism: The Art of the Intelligible.* Atlantic Highlands, NJ: Humanities, 1988.

Chase, Cynthia. "The Decomposition of the Elephants: Double-Reading *Daniel Deronda.*" *PMLA* 93 (1978): 215–27.

Chatman, Seymour, ed. *Essays on the Language of Literature.* Boston: Houghton Mifflin, 1967.

———. *Story and Discourse: Narrative Structure in Fiction and Film.* Ithaca: Cornell University Press, 1978.

Chomsky, Noam. *Syntactic Structures.* The Hague: Mouton, 1957.

———. *Aspects of the Theory of Syntax.* Cambridge: MIT Press, 1965.

Cohn, Dorrit. *Transparent Minds: Narrative Modes for Presenting Consciousness in Fiction.* Princeton: Princeton University Press, 1978.

Coward, Rosalind, and John Ellis. *Language and Materialism: Developments in Semiology and the Theory of the Subject.* London: Routledge and Kegan Paul, 1977.

Culler, Jonathan. *Structuralist Poetics.* Ithaca: Cornell University Press, 1975.

———. *The Pursuit of Signs: Semiotics, Literature, Deconstruction.* Ithaca: Cornell University Press, 1981.

———. *On Deconstruction: Theory and Criticism after Structuralism.* Ithaca: Cornell University Press, 1982.

———. *Roland Barthes.* New York: Oxford University Press, 1984.

———. *Ferdinand de Saussure.* Ithaca: Cornell University Press, 1986.

de Man, Paul. *Blindness and Insight.* New York: Oxford University Press, 1971.

———. *Allegories of Reading: Figural Language in Rousseau, Nietzsche, Rilke, and Proust.* New Haven: Yale University Press, 1979.

———. *The Rhetoric of Romanticism.* New York: Columbia University Press, 1984.

———. *The Resistance to Theory.* Minneapolis: University of Minnesota Press, 1986.

Derrida, Jacques. *Of Grammatology.* 1967; Baltimore: Johns Hopkins University Press, 1976.

———. *Writing and Difference.* 1967; Chicago: University of Chicago Press, 1978.

———. *Margins of Philosophy.* 1972; Chicago: University of Chicago Press, 1982.

———. *Positions.* trans. Alan Bass. 1972; Chicago: University of Chicago Press, 1981.

———. *Dissemination.* 1972; Chicago: University of Chicago Press, 1982.

———. *Speech and Phenomena, and Other Essays on Husserl's Theory of Signs.* 1973; Evanston: Northwestern University Press, 1978.

———. *Glas.* 1974; Lincoln: University of Nebraska Press, 1986.

———. *The Post Card: From Socrates to Freud and Beyond.* 1980; Chicago: University of Chicago Press, 1987.

———. "Like the Sound of the Sea Deep within a Shell: Paul de Man's War," trans. Peggy Kamuf. In *Responses on Paul de Man's Wartime Journalism,* ed. Werner Hamacher, Neil Hertz, and Thomas Kennan. Lincoln: University of Nebraska Press, 1988, pp. 127–64.

———. "Given Time: The Time of the King," trans. Peggy Kamuf. *Critical Inquiry* 18 (1992): 161–87.

———. "Shibboleth: For Paul Célan," trans. Joshua Wilner. In *Wordtraces: Readings of Paul Celan,* ed. Aris Fioretos. Baltimore: Johns Hopkins University Press, 1994, pp. 3–72.

———. *The Gift of Death.* Chicago: University Chicago Press, 1995.

———. *Acts of Religion.* New York: Routledge, 2001.

———. *On Cosmopolitanism and Forgiveness.* New York: Routledge, 2001.

———. *Negotiations: Interventions and Interviews 1971–2001.* Stanford: Stanford University Press, 2002.

Derrida, Jacques, Pascale-Anne Brault, and Michael Naas. *Adieu to Emmanuel Levinas.* Stanford: Stanford University Press, 1999.

Donoghue, Denis. *Ferocious Alphabets.* Boston: Little, Brown, 1981.

Dreyfus, Hubert L., and Paul Rabinow. *Michel Foucault: Beyond Structuralism and Hermeneutics,* 2nd ed. Chicago: University of Chicago Press, 1983.

Eco, Umberto. *A Theory of Semiotics.* Bloomington: Indiana University Press, 1975.

———. *The Role of the Reader: Explorations in the Semiotics of Texts.* Bloomington: Indiana University Press, 1979.

———. *Semiotics and the Philosophy of Language.* London: Macmillan, 1984.

Edelstein, Dan. "Between Myth and History: Michelet, Lévi-Strauss, Barthes, and the Structural Analysis of Myth." *CLIO* 32 (2003): 397–414.

Foucault, Michel. *The Order of Things: An Archaeology of the Human Sciences.* 1966; London: Tavistock, 1970.

———. *The Archeology of Knowledge.* 1969; New York: Pantheon, 1972.

———. *Language, Counter-Memory, Practice.* Ithaca: Cornell University Press, 1977.

———. *The Foucault Reader.* New York: Pantheon, 1984.

Gasché, Rodolphe. "The Scene of Writing: A Deferred Outset." *Glyph* 1 (1977): 150–71.

———. "Deconstruction as Criticism." *Glyph* 6 (1979): 177–216.

———. *Inventions of Difference: On Jacques Derrida.* Cambridge: Harvard University Press, 1994.

———. *The Wild Card of Reading: On Paul de Man.* Cambridge: Harvard University Press, 1998.

Genette, Gérard. *Narrative Discourse: An Essay in Method.* Ithaca: Cornell University Press, 1980.

———. *Figures of Literary Discourse.* New York: Columbia University Press, 1982.

Girard, René. *Deceit, Desire, and the Novel: The Self and Other in Literary Structure.* Baltimore: Johns Hopkins University Press, 1965.

———. *Violence and the Sacred.* Baltimore: Johns Hopkins University Press, 1977.

Graef, Ortwin de. *Serenity in Crisis: A Preface to Paul de Man 1939–1960.* Lincoln: University of Nebraska Press, 1993.

Greimas, A. J. *Structural Semantics: An Attempt at a Method.* Lincoln: University of Nebraska Press, 1984.

Harari, Josué. *Structuralists and Structuralisms.* Ithaca: Cornell University Press, 1971.

———. ed. *Textual Strategies: Perspectives in Post-Structuralist Criticism.* Ithaca: Cornell University Press, 1979.

Harris, Zellig. *Methods in Structural Linguistics.* Chicago: University of Chicago Press, 1951.

Hartman, Geoffrey H. *Beyond Formalism.* New Haven: Yale University Press, 1970.

——. *The Fate of Reading and Other Essays.* Chicago: University of Chicago Press, 1975.

——. *Criticism in the Wilderness.* New Haven: Yale University Press, 1980.

——. *Saving the Text: Literature/Derrida/Philosophy.* Baltimore: Johns Hopkins University Press, 1981.

Hawkes, Terence. *Structuralism and Semiotics.* Berkeley: University of California Press, 1977.

Herman, Luc, Kris Humbeeck, and Geert Lernout, eds. *(Dis)continuities: Essays on Paul de Man.* Amsterdam: Rodopi, 1989.

Hjelmslev, Louis. *Prolegomena to a Theory of Language.* Madison: University of Wisconsin Press, 1961.

Holland, Norman N. *The Critical I.* New York: Columbia University Press, 1992.

Husserl, Edmund. *The Idea of Phenomenology.* The Hague: Nijhoff, 1964.

Jakobson, Roman. *Selected Writings.* 8 vols. The Hague: Mouton, 1962–1985.

—— and Lawrence Jones. *Shakespeare's Verbal Art in ''Th' Expense of Spirit.''* The Hague: Mouton, 1970.

Jameson, Fredric. *The Prison House of Language: A Critical Account of Structuralism and Russian Formalism.* Princeton: Princeton University Press, 1971.

Johnson, Barbara. *The Critical Difference: Essays in the Contemporary Rhetoric of Reading.* Baltimore: Johns Hopkins University Press, 1980.

——. *A World of Difference.* Baltimore: Johns Hopkins University Press, 1987.

Kofman, Sarah. *Nietzsche et la scène philosophique.* Paris: Union générale d'éditions, 1979.

——. *Lectures de Derrida.* Paris: Éditions Galilée, 1984.

Kristeva, Julia. *Essays in Semiotics.* The Hague: Mouton, 1971.

Lane, Michael, ed. *Structuralism: A Reader.* London: Cape, 1970.

Leitch, Vincent. *Deconstructive Criticism: An Advanced Introduction.* New York: Columbia University Press, 1983.

Lévi-Strauss, Claude. *Structural Anthropology.* 1958; New York: Basic Books, 1963.

——. *The Savage Mind.* Chicago: University of Chicago Press, 1966.

——. *The Raw and the Cooked.* 1964; New York: Harper and Row, 1969.

——. *From Honey to Ashes.* 1966; London: Cape, 1973.

Lotman, Yuri. *Analysis of the Poetic Text.* Ann Arbor: Ardis, 1976.

Lyons, John. *Structural Semantics.* Oxford: Blackwell, 1973.

Macksey, Richard, and Eugenio Donato, eds. *The Languages of Criticism and the Sciences of Man.* Baltimore: Johns Hopkins University Press, 1970.

——. *The Structuralist Controversy: The Languages of Criticism and the Sciences of Man.* Baltimore: Johns Hopkins University Press, 1970.

Martin, Bill. *Humanism and Its Aftermath: The Shared Fate of Deconstruction and Politics.* Atlantic Highlands, NJ: Humanities, 1995.

McDonald, Christie V. ''Jacques Derrida's Reading of Rousseau.'' *The Eighteenth Century: Theory and Interpretation* 20 (1970): 82–95.

McQuillan, Martin. *Paul de Man.* London: Routledge, 2001.

Meyer, Michel, and Jacques Derrida. ''From Grammatology to Problematology.'' *Revue Internationale de Philosophie* 52 (1998): 359–65, 497–529.

Miller, J. Hillis. ''Ariadne's Thread: Repetition and the Narrative Line.'' *Critical Inquiry* 3 (1976): 57–78.

——. *Fiction and Repetition: Seven English Novels.* Cambridge: Harvard University Press, 1982.

————. *The Linguistic Moment: From Wordsworth to Stevens.* Princeton: Princeton University Press, 1985.

————. *The Ethics of Reading: Kant, de Man, Eliot, Trollope, James and Benjamin.* New York: Columbia University Press, 1987.

Murfin, Ross C. "Deconstruction and Derrida."In *Bram Stoker, Dracula,* ed. John Paul Riquelme. New York: Palgrave, 2002, pp. 538–59.

Nietzsche, Friedrich. *Complete Works.* 18 vols. Ed. Oscar Levy. New York: Russell and Russell, 1964.

Norris, Christopher. *The Deconstructive Turn: Essays in the Rhetoric of Philosophy.* New York: Methuen, 1984.

————. *The Contest of Faculties: Philosophy and Theory after Deconstruction.* New York: Methuen, 1985.

Patrick, Morag. *Derrida, Responsibility and Politics.* Aldershot, Eng.: Ashgate, 1997.

Piaget, Jean. *Structuralism.* New York: Basic Books, 1970.

Prince, Gerald. "Introduction à l'étude du narrataire." *Poétique* 14 (1963): 178–96.

Ricoeur, Paul. *The Conflict of Interpretations: Essays in Hermeneutics.* Evanston: Northwestern University Press, 1974.

————. *The Rule of Metaphor.* Toronto: University of Toronto Press, 1977.

————. *Time and Narrative.* Chicago: University of Chicago Press, 1984.

Riffaterre, Michael. *Semiotics of Poetry.* Bloomington: Indiana University Press, 1978.

————. *Text Production.* New York: Columbia University Press, 1983.

Robey, David, ed. *Structuralism: An Introduction.* London: Oxford University Press, 1973.

Rorty, Richard. "Philosophy as a Kind of Writing: An Essay on Derrida." *New Literary History* 10 (1978): 1411–60.

Royle, Nicholas. *After Derrida.* Manchester: Manchester University Press, 1995.

Ryan, Michael. *Marxism and Deconstruction.* Baltimore: Johns Hopkins University Press, 1982.

Saper, Craig J., and Laura Kipnis. *Artificial Mythologies: A Guide to Cultural Invention.* Minneapolis: University of Minnesota Press, 1997.

Saussure, Ferdinand de. *Course in General Linguistics.* 1923; New York: Philosophical Library, 1959.

Searle, John. *Speech Acts.* Cambridge: Cambridge University Press, 1969.

————. "Reiterating the Differences: A Reply to Derrida." *Glyph* 1 (1977): 198–208.

Sebeok, Thomas, ed. *Style in Language.* Cambridge: MIT Press, 1964.

————, ed. *Approaches to Semiotics.* The Hague: Mouton, 1964.

Silverman, Hugh J., and Gary E. Aylesworth, eds. *The Textual Sublime: Deconstruction and Its Differences.* Albany: State University of New York Press, 1990.

Smith, Barbara Herrnstein. *On the Margins of Discourse: The Relation of Literature to Language.* Chicago: University of Chicago Press, 1979.

Smith, Robert. *Derrida and Autobiography.* Cambridge: Cambridge University Press, 1995.

Sprinker, Michael. "Textual Politics: Foucault and Derrida." *Boundary* 28 (1980): 75–98.

Todorov, Tzvetan. *The Poetics of Prose.* Ithaca: Cornell University Press, 1977.

————. *Introduction to Poetics.* Minneapolis: University of Minnesota Press, 1981.

————. *Symbolism and Interpretation.* Ithaca: Cornell University Press, 1982.

————. *Theories of the Symbol.* Ithaca: Cornell University Press, 1982.

Ullmann, Stephen. *Language and Style.* Oxford: Blackwell, 1964.

Waters, Lindsay, and Wlad Godzich, eds. *Reading de Man Reading.* Minneapolis: University of Minnesota Press, 1988.

Ferdinand de Saussure

1857–1913

Ferdinand de Saussure was born in Geneva and educated at the University of Geneva and the University of Berlin before taking his Ph.D. at the University of Leipzig in 1880. The linguist and philologist taught at the École Pratique des Hautes Études in Paris before returning to his birthplace and a professorship at the University of Geneva, where he taught from 1891 to 1912. Saussure published specialized monographs in linguistics during his lifetime, such as his Memoir on the Primitive System of Vowels in the Indo-European Languages (1879). His current fame is based on the course in general linguistics that he gave in Geneva, which was posthumously recreated from lecture notes by his students and published in 1916 as Cours de linguistique générale (Course in General Linguistics), from which the following selections are taken.

Nature of the Linguistic Sign

1. SIGN, SIGNIFIED, SIGNIFIER

Some people regard language, when reduced to its elements, as a naming-process only — a list of words, each corresponding to the thing that it names. For example:

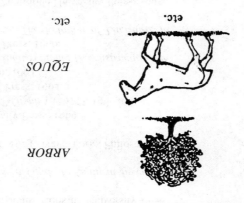

ARBOR

EQUOS

etc.

etc.

This conception is open to criticism at several points. It assumes that ready-made ideas exist before words; it does not tell us whether a name is vocal or psychological in nature (*arbor,* for instance, can be considered from either view-point); finally, it lets us assume that the linking of a name and a thing is a very simple operation — an assumption that is anything but true. But this rather naïve approach can bring us near the truth

by showing us that the linguistic unit is a double entity, one formed by the associating of two terms.

We have seen in considering the speaking-circuit that both terms involved in the linguistic sign are psychological and are united in the brain by an associative bond. This point must be emphasized.

The linguistic sign unites, not a thing and a name, but a concept and a sound-image.[1] The latter is not the material sound, a purely physical thing, but the psychological imprint of the sound, the impression that it makes on our senses. The sound-image is sensory, and if I happen to call it "material," it is only in that sense, and by way of opposing it to the other term of the association, the concept, which is generally more abstract.

Translated by Wade Baskin.

[1] The term sound-image may seem to be too restricted inasmuch as beside the representation of the sounds of a word there is also that of its articulation, the muscular image of the phonational act. But for F. de Saussure language is essentially a depository, a thing received from without. The sound-image is par excellence the natural representation of the word as a fact of potential language, outside any actual use of it in speaking. The motor side is thus implied or, in any event, occupies only a subordinate role with respect to the sound-image. [Bally and Séchehaye.] [Bally and Séchehaye redacted the lecture notes of Saussure's students into *Cours de linguistique générale.* [Tr.]

The psychological character of our sound-images becomes apparent when we observe our own speech. Without moving our lips or tongue, we can talk to ourselves or recite mentally a selection of verse. Because we regard the words of our language as sound-images, we must avoid speaking of the "phonemes" that make up the words. This term, which suggests vocal activity, is applicable to the spoken word only, to the realization of the inner image in discourse. We can avoid that misunderstanding by speaking of the *sounds* and *syllables* of a word provided we remember that the names refer to the sound-image.

The linguistic sign is then a two-sided psychological entity that can be represented by the drawing:

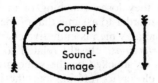

The two elements are intimately united, and each recalls the other. Whether we try to find the meaning of the Latin word *arbor* or the word that Latin uses to designate the concept "tree," it is clear that only the associations sanctioned by that language appear to us to conform to reality, and we disregard whatever others might be imagined.

Our definition of the linguistic sign poses an important question of terminology. I call the combination of a concept and a sound-image a *sign*, but in current usage the term generally designates only a sound-image, a word, for example (*arbor*, etc.). One tends to forget that *arbor* is called a sign only because it carries the concept "tree," with the result that the idea of the sensory part implies the idea of the whole.

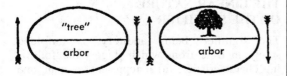

Ambiguity would disappear if the three notions involved here were designated by three names, each suggesting and opposing the others. I propose to retain the word *sign* [*signe*] to designate the whole and to replace *concept* and *sound-image* respectively by *signified* [*signifié*] and *signifier* [*signifiant*]; the last two terms have the advantage of indicating the opposition that separates them from each other and from the whole of which they are parts. As regards *sign,* if I am satisfied with it, this is simply because I do not know of any word to replace it, the ordinary language suggesting no other.

The linguistic sign, as defined, has two primordial characteristics. In enunciating them I am also positing the basic principles of any study of this type.

2. PRINCIPLE I: THE ARBITRARY NATURE OF THE SIGN

The bond between the signifier and the signified is arbitrary. Since I mean by sign the whole that results from the associating of the signifier with the signified, I can simply say: *the linguistic sign is arbitrary.*

The idea of "sister" is not linked by any inner relationship to the succession of sounds *s-ö-r* which serves as its signifier in French; that it could be represented equally by just any other sequence is proved by differences among languages and by the very existence of different languages: the signified "ox" has as its signifier *b-ö-f* on one side of the border and *o-k-s* (*Ochs*) on the other.

No one disputes the principle of the arbitrary nature of the sign, but it is often easier to discover a truth than to assign to it its proper place. Principle I dominates all the linguistics of language; its consequences are numberless. It is true that not all of them are equally obvious at first glance; only after many detours does one discover them, and with them the primordial importance of the principle.

One remark in passing: when semiology becomes organized as a science, the question will arise whether or not it properly includes modes of expression based on completely natural signs, such as pantomime. Supposing that the new science welcomes them, its main concern will still be the whole group of systems grounded on the arbitrariness of the sign. In fact, every means of expression used in society is based, in principle, on collective behavior or — what amounts to the same thing — on convention. Polite formulas, for instance, though often imbued with a certain natural expressiveness (as in the case of a Chinese who greets his emperor by bowing down to the ground nine times), are nonetheless fixed by rule; it is this rule and not the intrinsic value of the gestures that obliges one to use them. Signs that are wholly arbitrary realize better than the others the ideal of the semiological process; that is why language, the most complex and universal of all systems of expression, is also the most characteristic; in this sense linguistics can become the master-pattern for all branches of semiology although language is only one particular semiological system.

The word *symbol* has been used to designate the linguistic sign, or more specifically, what is here called the signifier. Principle I in particular weighs against the use of this term. One characteristic of the symbol is that it is never wholly arbitrary; it is not empty, for there is the rudiment of a natural bond between the signifier and the signified. The symbol of justice, a pair of scales, could not be replaced by just any other symbol, such as a chariot.

The word *arbitrary* also calls for comment. The term should not imply that the choice of the signifier is left entirely to the speaker (we shall see below that the individual does not have the power to change a sign in any way once it has become established in the linguistic community); I mean that it is unmotivated, i.e. arbitrary in that it actually has no natural connection with the signified.

In concluding let us consider two objections that might be raised to the establishment of Principle I:

1. *Onomatopoeia* might be used to prove that the choice of the signifier is not always arbitrary. But onomatopoeic formations are never organic elements of a linguistic system. Besides, their number is much smaller than is generally supposed. Words like French *fouet* "whip" or *glas* "knell" may strike certain ears with suggestive sonority, but to see that they have not always had this property we need only examine their Latin

²Cf. English *goodness!* and *zounds!* (from *God's wounds*). [Tr.]

forms (*fouet* is derived from *fāgus* "beech-tree," *glas* from *classicum* "sound of a trumpet"). The quality of their present sounds, or rather the quality that is attributed to them, is a fortuitous result of phonetic evolution.

As for authentic onomatopoeic words (e.g. *glug-glug, tick-tock,* etc.), not only are they limited in number, but also they are chosen somewhat arbitrarily, for they are only approximate and more or less conventional imitations of certain sounds (cf. English *bow-wow* and French *ouaoua*). In addition, once these words have been introduced into the language, they are to a certain extent subjected to the same evolution — phonetic, morphological, etc. — that other words undergo (cf. *pigeon,* ultimately from Vulgar Latin *pīpiō,* derived in turn from an onomatopoeic formation): obvious proof that they lose something of their original character in order to assume that of the linguistic sign in general, which is unmotivated.

2. *Interjections,* closely related to onomatopoeia, can be attacked on the same grounds and come no closer to refuting our thesis. One is tempted to see in them spontaneous expressions of reality dictated, so to speak, by natural forces. But for most interjections we can show that there is no fixed bond between their signified and their signifier. We need only compare two languages on this point to see how much such expressions differ from one language to the next (e.g. the English equivalent of French *aïe!* is *ouch!*). We know, moreover, that many interjections were once words with specific meanings (cf. French *diable!* "darn!" *mordieu!* "golly!" from *mort Dieu* "God's death," etc.).²

Onomatopoeic formations and interjections are of secondary importance, and their symbolic origin is in part open to dispute.

3. PRINCIPLE II: THE LINEAR NATURE OF THE SIGNIFIER

The signifier, being auditory, is unfolded solely in time from which it gets the following characteristics: (a) it represents a span, and

(b) the span is measurable in a single dimension; it is a line.

While Principle II is obvious, apparently linguists have always neglected to state it, doubtless because they found it too simple; nevertheless, it is fundamental, and its consequences are incalculable. Its importance equals that of Principle I; the whole mechanism of language depends upon it. In contrast to visual signifiers (nautical signals, etc.) which can offer simultaneous groupings in several dimensions, auditory signifiers have at their command only the dimension of time. Their elements are presented in succession; they form a chain. This feature becomes readily apparent when they are represented in writing and the spatial line of graphic marks is substituted for succession in time.

Sometimes the linear nature of the signifier is not obvious. When I accent a syllable, for instance, it seems that I am concentrating more than one significant element on the same point. But this is an illusion; the syllable and its accent constitute only one phonational act. There is no duality within the act but only different oppositions to what precedes and what follows.

[Binary Oppositions]

2. Linguistic Value from a Conceptual Viewpoint

When we speak of the value of a word, we generally think first of its property of standing for an idea, and this is in fact one side of linguistic value. But if this is true, how does *value* differ from *signification*? Might the two words be synonyms? I think not, although it is easy to confuse them, since the confusion results not so much from their similarity as from the subtlety of the distinction that they mark.

From a conceptual viewpoint, value is doubtless one element in signification, and it is difficult to see how signification can be dependent upon value and still be distinct from it. But we must clear up the issue or risk reducing language to a simple naming-process.

Let us first take signification as it is generally understood. . . . As the arrows in the drawing show, it is only the counterpart of the sound-image. Everything that occurs concerns only the sound-image and the concept when we look upon the word as independent and self-contained.

But here is the paradox: on the one hand the concept seems to be the counterpart of the sound-image, and on the other hand the sign itself is in turn the counterpart of the other signs of language.

Language is a system of interdependent terms in which the value of each term results solely from the simultaneous presence of the others, as in the diagram:

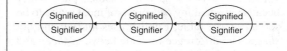

How, then, can value be confused with signification, i.e. the counterpart of the sound-image? It seems impossible to liken the relations represented here by horizontal arrows to those represented above by vertical arrows. Putting it another way — and again taking up the example of the sheet of paper that is cut in two — it is clear that the observable relation between the different pieces A, B, C, D etc. is distinct from the relation between the front and back of the same piece as in A/A′, B/B′, etc.

To resolve the issue, let us observe from the outset that even outside language all values are apparently governed by the same paradoxical principle. They are always composed:

(1) of a *dissimilar* thing that can be *exchanged* for the thing of which the value is to be determined; and

(2) of *similar* things that can be *compared* with the thing of which the value is to be determined.

Both factors are necessary for the existence of a value. To determine what a five-franc piece is worth one must therefore know: (1) that it can be exchanged for a fixed quantity of a different thing, e.g., bread; and (2) that it can be compared with a similar value of the same system, e.g., a one-franc piece, or with coins of another system (a dollar, etc.). In the same way a word can be exchanged for something dissimilar, an idea; besides, it can be compared with something of the same nature, another word. Its value is therefore not fixed so long as one simply states that it can be "exchanged" for a given concept, i.e., has this or that signification: one must also compare it with similar values, with other words that stand in opposition to it. Its content is really fixed only by the concurrence of everything that exists outside it. Being part of a system, it is endowed not only with a signification but also and especially with a value, and this is something quite different.

A few examples will show clearly that this is true. Modern French *mouton* can have the same signification as English *sheep* but not the same value, and this for several reasons, particularly because in speaking of a piece of meat ready to be served on the table, English uses *mutton* and not *sheep*. The difference in value between *sheep* and *mouton* is due to the fact that *sheep* has beside it a second term while the French word does not.

Within the same language, all words used to express related ideas limit each other reciprocally; synonyms like French *redouter* "dread," *craindre* "fear," and *avoir peur* "be afraid" have value only through their opposition: if *redouter* did not exist, all its content would go to its competitors. Conversely, some words are enriched through contact with others: e.g., the new element introduced in *décrépit* (un vieillard *décrépit*) results from the coexistence of *décrépi* (un mur *décrépi*). The value of just any term is accordingly determined by its environment; it is impossible

to fix even the value of the word signifying "sun" without first considering its surroundings: in some languages it is not possible to say "sit in the sun."

Everything said about words applies to any term of language, e.g., to grammatical entities. The value of a French plural does not coincide with that of a Sanskrit plural even though their signification is usually identical; Sanskrit has three numbers instead of two (*my eyes, my ears, my arms, my legs*, etc. are dual);[1] it would be wrong to attribute the same value to the plural in Sanskrit and in French; its value clearly depends on what is outside and around it.

If words stood for pre-existing concepts, they would all have exact equivalents in meaning from one language to the next; but this is not true. French uses *louer* (*une maison*) "let (a house)" indifferently to mean both "pay for" and "receive payment for," whereas German uses two words, *mieten* and *vermieten*; there is obviously no exact correspondence of values. The German verbs *schätzen* and *urteilen* share a number of significations, but that correspondence does not hold at several points.[2]

Inflection offers some particularly striking examples. Distinctions of time, which are so familiar to us, are unknown in certain languages. Hebrew does not recognize even the fundamental distinctions between the past, present, and future.[3] Proto-Germanic has no special form for the future; to say that the future is expressed by the present is wrong, for the value of the present is not the same in Germanic as in languages that have a future along with the present. The Slavic languages regularly single out two aspects of the

[1]The use of the comparative form for two and the superlative for more than two in English (e.g., *may the better boxer win: the best boxer in the world*) is probably a remnant of the old distinction between the dual [English has the remnants of a lost dual in archaic words like *eyne*] and the plural number. [Tr.]

[2]*Schätzen* means "to appraise" — to judge something's value; *urteilen* means "to judge generally."

[3]The biblical Hebrew verb has an immensely complicated mode and aspect system, but the tenses themselves are rudimentary, compared with French. In general Saussure's analysis of other languages is Francocentric (languages like German that use auxiliaries rather than inflecting the verb to convey the future tense are said not to have one).

verb: the perfective represents action as a point, complete in its totality; the imperfective represents it as taking place, and on the line of time. The categories are difficult for a Frenchman to understand, for they are unknown in French; if they were predetermined, this would not be true. Instead of pre-existing ideas then, we find in all the foregoing examples *values* emanating from the system. When they are said to correspond to concepts, it is understood that the concepts are purely differential and defined not by their positive content but negatively by their relations with the other terms of the system. Their most precise characteristic is in being what the others are not.

Now the real interpretation of the diagram of the signal becomes apparent. Thus

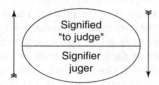

means that in French the concept "to judge" is linked to the sound-image *juger;* in short, it symbolizes signification. But it is quite clear that initially the concept is nothing, that is only a value determined by its relations with other similar values, and that without them the signification would not exist. If I state simply that a word signifies something when I have in mind the associating of a sound-image with a concept, I am making a statement that may suggest what actually happens, but by no means am I expressing the linguistic fact in its essence and fullness.

3. Linguistic Value from a Material Viewpoint

The conceptual side of value is made up solely of relations and differences with respect to the other terms of language, and the same can be said of its material side. The important thing in the word is not the sound alone but the phonic differences that make it possible to distinguish this word from all others, for differences carry signification.

This may seem surprising, but how indeed could the reverse be possible? Since one vocal image is no better suited than the next for what it is commissioned to express, it is evident, even *a priori*, that a segment of language can never in the final analysis be based on anything except its noncoincidence with the rest. *Arbitrary* and *differential* are two correlative qualities.

The alteration of linguistic signs clearly illustrates this. It is precisely because the terms *a* and *b* as such are radically incapable of reaching the level of consciousness — one is always conscious of only the *a/b* difference — that each term is free to change according to laws that are unrelated to its signifying function. No positive sign characterizes the genitive plural in Czech *žen*; still, the two forms *žena: žen* function as well as the earlier forms *žena: ženb; žen* has value only because it is different.

Here is another example that shows even more clearly the systematic role of phonic differences: in Greek, *éphēn* is an imperfect and *éstēn* an aorist[4] although both words are formed in the same way; the first belongs to the system of the present indicative of *phēmí* "I say," whereas there is no present *stēmi*;[5] now it is precisely the relation *phēmí: éphēn* that corresponds to the relation between the present and the imperfect (cf. *déiknūmi: edéiknūn,* etc.). Signs function, then, not through their intrinsic value but through their relative position.

In addition, it is impossible for sound alone, a material element, to belong to language. It is only a secondary thing, substance to be put to use. All our conventional values have the characteristic of not being confused with the tangible element which supports them. For instance, it is not the metal in a piece of money that fixes

---

[4]The imperfect and the aorist are two aspects of the verb in classical Greek. The aorist denotes a single past action; the imperfect denotes a process in the past. English usually uses the past vs. past + participle to convey the same distinction; e.g., "I ran"/"I was running." But some verbs do not have an imperfect and require an alternate verb to indicate process: e.g., "I saw a nightingale"/"I was looking at a nightingale" — not "I was seeing a nightingale."

[5]The asterisk means that there is no such Greek form; the first person singular present corresponding to *phemi* is *histemi*.

its value. A coin nominally worth five francs may contain less than half its worth in silver. Its value will vary according to the amount stamped upon it and according to its use inside or outside a political boundary. This is even more true of the linguistic signifier, which is not phonic but incorporeal — constituted not by its material substance but by the differences that separate its sound-image from all others.

The foregoing principle is so basic that it applies to all the material elements of language, including phonemes. Every language forms its words on the basis of a system of sonorous elements, each element being a clearly delimited unit and one of a fixed number of units. Phonemes are characterized not, as one might think, by their own positive quality but simply by the fact that they are distinct. Phonemes are above all else opposing, relative, and negative entities.

Proof of this is the latitude that speakers have between points of convergence in the pronunciation of distinct sounds. In French, for instance, general use of a dorsal *r* does not prevent many speakers from using a tongue-tip trill; language is not in the least disturbed by it; language requires only that the sound be different and not, as one might imagine, that it have an invariable quality. I can even pronounce the French *r* like German *ch* in *Bach, doch,* etc., but in German I could not use *r* instead of *ch,* for German gives recognition to both elements and must keep them apart. Similarly, in Russian there is no latitude for *t* in the direction of *t'* (palatalized[6] *t*), for the result would be the confusing of two sounds differentiated by the language (cf. *govorit* "speak" and *govorit* "he speaks"), but more freedom may be taken with respect to *th* (aspirated *t*) since this sound does not figure in the Russian system of phonemes.

Since an identical state of affairs is observable in writing, another system of signs, we shall use writing to draw some comparisons that will clarify the whole issue. In fact:

1) The signs used in writing are arbitrary; there is no connection, for example, between the letter *t* and the sound that it designates.

[6]With a bit of "ch" added, as in the "t," in nature.

2) The value of letters is purely negative and differential. The same person can write *t,* for instance, in different ways:

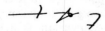

The only requirement is that the sign for *t* not be confused in his script with the signs used for *l, d,* etc.

3) Values in writing function only through reciprocal opposition within a fixed system that consists of a set number of letters. This third characteristic, though not identical to the second, is closely related to it, for both depend on the first. Since the graphic sign is arbitrary, its form matters little or rather matters only within the limitations imposed by the system.

4) The means by which the sign is produced is completely unimportant, for it does not affect the system (this also follows from characteristic 1). Whether I make the letters in white or black, raised or engraved, with pen or chisel — all this is of no importance with respect to their signification.

4. The Sign Considered in Its Totality

Everything that has been said up to this point boils down to this: in language there are only differences. Even more important: a difference generally implies positive terms between which the difference is set up; but in language there are only differences without *positive terms.* Whether we take the signified or the signifier, language has neither ideas nor sounds that existed before the linguistic system, but only conceptual and phonic differences that have issued from the system. The idea or phonic substance that a sign contains is of less importance than the other signs that surround it. Proof of this is that the value of a term may be modified without either its meaning or its sound being affected, solely because a neighboring term has been modified.

But the statement that everything in language is negative is true only if the signified and the signi-fer are considered separately; when we consider the sign in its totality, we have something that is positive in its own class. A linguistic system is a series of differences of sound combined with a series of differences of ideas; but the pairing of a certain number of acoustical signs with as many cuts made from the mass of thought engenders a system of values; and this system serves as the effective link between the phonic and psychological elements within each sign. Although both the signified and the signifier are purely differential and negative when considered separately, their combination is a positive fact; it is even the sole type of facts that language has, for maintaining the parallelism between the two classes of differences is the distinctive function of the linguistic institution.

Certain diachronic facts are typical in this respect. Take the countless instances where alteration of the signifier occasions a conceptual change and where it is obvious that the sum of the ideas distinguished corresponds in principle to the sum of the distinctive signs. When two words are confused through phonetic alteration (e.g., French *décrépit* from *dēcrepitus* and *décrépi* from *crispus*), the ideas that they express will also tend to become confused if only they have something in common.[7] Or a word may have different forms (cf. *chaise* "chair" and *chaire* "desk"[8]). Any nascent difference will tend invariably to become significant but without always succeeding or being successful on the first trial. Conversely, any conceptual difference perceived by the mind seeks to find expression through a distinct signifier, and two ideas that are no longer distinct in the mind tend to merge into the same signifier.

When we compare signs — positive terms — with each other, we can no longer speak of difference; the expression would not be fitting, for it applies only to the comparing of two sound-images, e.g. *father* and *mother*, or two ideas, e.g. the idea "father" and the idea "mother"; two signs, each having a signified and signifier, are not different but only distinct. Between them there is only *opposition*. The entire mechanism of language, with which we shall be concerned

later, is based on oppositions of this kind and on the phonic and conceptual differences that they imply.

What is true of value is true also of the unit. A unit is a segment of the spoken chain that corresponds to a certain concept; both are by nature purely differential.

Applied to units, the principle of differentiation can be stated in this way: *the characteristics of the unit blend with the unit itself.* In language, as in any semiological system, whatever distinguishes one sign from the others constitutes it. Difference makes characters just as it makes value and the unit.

Another rather paradoxical consequence of the same principle is this: in the last analysis what is commonly referred to as a "grammatical fact" fits the definition of the unit, for it always expresses an opposition of terms; it differs only in that the opposition is particularly significant (e.g. the formation of German plurals of the type *Nacht: Nächte*). Each term present in the grammatical fact (the singular without umlaut or final *e* in opposition to the plural with umlaut and –*e*) consists of the interplay of a number of oppositions within the system. When isolated, neither *Nacht* nor *Nächte* is anything: thus everything is opposition. Putting it another way, the *Nacht: Nächte* relation can be expressed by an algebraic formula *a/b* in which *a* and *b* are not simple terms but result from a set of relations. Language, in a manner of speaking, is a type of algebra consisting solely of complex terms. Some of its oppositions are more significant than others; but units and grammatical facts are only different names for designating diverse aspects of the same general fact: the functioning of linguistic oppositions. This statement is so true that we might very well approach the problem of units by starting from grammatical facts. Taking an opposition like *Nacht:Nächte*, we might ask what are the units involved in it. Are they only the two words, the whole series of similar words, *a* and *ä*, or all singulars and plurals, etc.?

Units and grammatical facts would not be confused if linguistic signs were made up of something besides differences. But language being what it is, we shall find nothing simple in it regardless of our approach; everywhere and

---

[7]Saussure's notion that *décrépi* comes from the Latin *crispus* (curled) is probably fanciful.

[8]*Chaire* is more accurately the pulpit from which a clergyman preaches or the lectern from which a professor lectures. It derives from the Latin *cathedra*.

the linguistic phenomenon must have substance.

CHAPTER V: SYNTAGMATIC AND ASSOCIATIVE RELATIONS

1. Definitions

In a language-state everything is based on rela-tions. How do they function?

Relations and differences between linguis-tic terms fall into two distinct groups, each of which generates a certain class of values. The opposition between the two classes gives a better understanding of the nature of each class. They correspond to two forms of our mental activity, both indispensable to the life of language.

In discourse, on the one hand, words acquire relations based on the linear nature of language because they are chained together. This rules out the possibility of pronouncing two elements simultaneously. The elements are arranged in sequence on the chain of speaking. Combinations supported by linearity are *syntagms*.[9] The syn-tagm is always composed of two or more consec-utive units (e.g., French *re-lire* "re-read," *contre tous* "against everyone," *la vie humaine* "human life," *Dieu est bon* "God is good," *s'il fait beau temps, nous sortirons* "if the weather is nice, we'll go out," etc.). In the syntagm a term acquires its value only because it stands in opposition to everything that precedes or follows it, or to both.

Outside discourse, on the other hand, words acquire relations of a different kind. Those that have something in common are associated in the memory, resulting in groups marked by diverse relations. For instance, the French word *enseignement* "teaching" will unconsciously call to mind a host of other words (*enseigner* "teach,"

renseigner "acquaint," etc.; or *armement* "arma-ment," *changement* "amendment," etc.; or *éduca-tion* "education," *apprentissage* "apprenticeship," etc.). All those words are related in some way.

We see that the co-ordinations formed outside discourse differ strikingly from those formed inside discourse. Those formed outside discourse are not supported by linearity. Their seat is in the brain; they are a part of the inner storehouse that makes up the language of each speaker. They are *associative relations*.

The syntagmatic relation is *in praesentia*. It is based on two or more terms that occur in an effective series. Against this, the associative relation unites terms *in absentia* in a potential mnemonic series.

From the associative and syntagmatic view-point a linguistic unit is like a fixed part of a building, e.g. a column. On the one hand, the column has a certain relation to the architrave that it supports; the arrangement of the two units in space suggests the syntagmatic relation. On the other hand, if the column is Doric, it sug-gests a mental comparison of this style with others (Ionic, Corinthian, etc.) although none of these elements is present in space: the relation is associative.

Each of the two classes of co-ordination calls for some specific remarks.

2. Syntagmatic Relations

The examples on pages [849–50] have already indicated that the notion of syntagm applies not only to words but to groups of words, to complex units of all lengths and types (compounds, deriva-tives, phrases, whole sentences).

It is not enough to consider the relation that ties together the different parts of syntagms (e.g., French *contre* "against" and *tous* "everyone" in *contre tous*, *contre* and *maître* "master" in *con-tremaître* "foreman");[10] one must also bear in mind the relation that links the whole to its parts (e.g., *contre tous* in opposition on the one hand to *contre* and on the other *tous*, or *contremaître* in opposition to *contre* and *maître*).

[9]It is scarcely necessary to point out that the study of *syntagms* is not to be confused with syntax. Syntax is only one part of the study of syntagms. [Bally and Séchehaye, eds.]

[10]Cf. English *head* and *waiter* in *headwaiter*. [Tr.]

An objection might be raised at this point. The sentence is the ideal type of syntagm. But it belongs to speaking, not to language. Does it not follow that the syntagm belongs to speaking? I do not think so. Speaking is characterized by freedom of combinations; one must therefore ask whether or not all syntagms are equally free.

It is obvious from the first that many expressions belong to language. These are the pat phrases in which any change is prohibited by usage, even if we can single out their meaningful elements (cf. *à quoi bon?* "what's the use?" *allons donc!* "nonsense!"). The same is true, though to a lesser degree, of expressions like *prendre la mouche* "take offense easily,"[11] *forcer la main à quelqu'un* "force someone's hand," *rompre une lance* "break a lance,"[12] or even *avoir mal (à la tête,* etc.) "have (a headache, etc.)," *à force de (soins,* etc.) "by dint of (care, etc.)," *que vous en semble?* "how do you feel about it?" *pas n'est besoin de . . .* "there's no need for . . .," etc., which are characterized by peculiarities of signification or syntax. These idiomatic twists cannot be improvised; they are furnished by tradition. There are also words which, while lending themselves perfectly to analysis, are characterized by some morphological anomaly that is kept solely by dint of usage (cf. *difficulté* "difficulty" beside *facilité* "facility," etc., and *mourrai* "[I] shall die" beside *dormirai* "[I] shall sleep").[13]

There are further proofs. To language rather than to speaking belong the syntagmatic types that are built upon regular forms. Indeed, since there is nothing abstract in language, the types exist only if language has registered a sufficient number of specimens. When a word like *indécorable* arises in speaking, its appearance supposes a fixed type, and this type is in turn possible only through remembrance of a sufficient number of similar words belonging to language (*impardonable* "unpardonable," *intolérable* "intolerable," *infatigable* "indefatigable," etc.). Exactly the same is true of sentences and groups of words built upon regular patterns. Combinations like *la terre tourne* "the world turns," *que vous dit-il?* "what does he say to you?" etc. correspond to general types that are in turn supported in the language by concrete remembrances.

But we must realize that in the syntagm there is no clear-cut boundary between the language fact, which is a sign of collective usage, and the fact that belongs to speaking and depends on individual freedom. In a great number of instances it is hard to class a combination of units because both forces have combined in producing it, and they have combined in indeterminable proportions.

3. Associative Relations

Mental association creates other groups besides those based on the comparing of terms that have something in common; through its grasp of the nature of the relations that bind the terms together, the mind creates as many associative series as there are diverse relations. For instance, in *enseignement* "teaching," *enseigner* "teach," *enseignons* "(we) teach," etc., one element, the radical, is common to every term; the same word may occur in a different series formed around another common element, the suffix (cf. *enseignement, armement, changement,* etc.); or the association may spring from the analogy of the concepts signified (*enseignement, instruction, apprentissage, éducation,* etc.); or again, simply from the similarity of the sound-images (e.g., *enseignement* and *justement* "precisely").[14] Thus there is at times a double similarity of meaning and form, at times similarity only of form or of meaning. A word can always evoke everything that can be associated with it in one way or another.

---

[11]Literally "take the fly." Cf. English *take the bull by the horns.* [Tr.]

[12]Cf. English *bury the hatchet.* [Tr.]

[13]The anomaly of the double *r* in the future forms of certain verbs in French may be compared to irregular plurals like *oxen* in English. [Tr.]

[14]The last case is rare and can be classed as abnormal, for the mind naturally discards associations that becloud the intelligibility of discourse. But its existence is proved by a lower category of puns based on the ridiculous confusions that can result from pure and simple homonomy like the French statement "Les musicians produisent les *sons* ["sounds, bran"] et les grainetiers les vendent" "musicians produce *sons* and seedsmen sell them." [Cf. Shakespeare's "Not on thy *sole,* but on thy *soul.*" (Tr.)] This is distinct from the case where an association, while fortuitous, is supported by a comparison of ideas (cf. French *ergot* "spur": *ergoter* "wrangle"; German *blau* "blue": *durchblauen* "thrash soundly"); the point is that one member of the pair has a new interpretation. Folk etymologies like these are of interest in the study of semantic evolution, but from the synchronic viewpoint they are in the same category as *enseigner: enseignement.* [Bally and Sèchenaye, eds.]

Whereas a syntagm immediately suggests an order of succession and a fixed number of elements, terms in an associative family occur neither in fixed numbers nor in a definite order. If we associate *painful, delightful, frightful*, etc. we are unable to predict the number of words that the memory will suggest or the order in which they will appear. A particular word is like the center of a constellation; it is the point of convergence of a indefinite number of co-ordinated terms.

But of the two characteristics of the associative series — indeterminate order and indefinite number — only the first can always be verified; the second may fail to meet the test. This happens in the case of inflectional paradigms, which are typical of associative groupings. Latin *dominus, domini, domino*, etc. is obviously an associative group formed around a common element, the noun theme *domin—*, but the series[15]

[15]Cf. English *education* and the corresponding associative series: *educate, educates*, etc.; *internship, training*, etc.; *vocation, devotion*, etc.; and *lotion, fashion*, etc. [Tr.]

is not indefinite as in the case of *enseigne-ment, changement*, etc.; the number of cases is definite. Against this, the words have no fixed order of succession, and it is by a purely arbitrary act that the grammarian groups them in one way rather than in another; in the mind of speakers the nominative case is by no means the first one in the declension, and the order in which terms are called depends on circumstances.

Claude Lévi-Strauss

1908–2009

Claude Lévi-Strauss, one of the major figures of social anthropology and of twentieth-century intellectual life generally, was born in Brussels and took degrees in philosophy and law at the University of Paris (1927–32). From 1934 to 1937, Lévi-Strauss served as a professor of sociology at the University of São Paulo in Brazil; his research among the Brazilian Indians informs the heart of his intellectual autobiography, Tristes tropiques *(1955). From 1941 to 1945 he was a visiting professor at the New School for Social Research in New York, where he came in contact with the ideas of Roman Jakobson. Made director of studies at the École Practique des Haute Études of the University of Paris in 1950, he was appointed in 1959 to the chair of social anthropology at the Collège de France. Lévi-Strauss's works include* The Elementary Structures of Kinship *(1949),* Structural Anthropology *(1958).* The Savage Mind *(1962), and the four volumes of* Mythologiques *(1964–71). His last books, published posthumously in 2011, were* L'Anthropologie face au problèmes du monde moderne *and* L'Autre face de la lune: Ecrits sur Japon. *"The Structural Study of Myth" first appeared in* Journal of American Folklore *78 (1955); this version is from the 1963 translation of* Structural Anthropology.

The Structural Study of Myth

It would seem that mythological worlds have been built up only to be shattered again, and that new worlds were built from the fragments.

— FRANZ BOAS[1]

Despite some recent attempts to renew them, it seems that during the past twenty years anthropology has increasingly turned from studies in the field of religion. At the same time, and precisely because the interest of professional anthropologists has withdrawn from primitive religion, all kinds of amateurs who claim to belong to other disciplines have seized this opportunity to move in, thereby turning into their private playground what we had left as a wasteland. The prospects for the scientific study of religion have thus been undermined in two ways.

The explanation for this situation lies to some extent in the fact that the anthropological study of religion was started by men like Tylor, Frazer, and Durkheim, who were psychologically oriented although not in a position to keep up with the progress of psychological research and theory. Their interpretations, therefore, soon became vitiated by the outmoded psychological approach which they used as their basis. Although they were undoubtedly right in giving their attention to intellectual processes, the way they handled these remained so crude that it discredited them altogether. This is much to be regretted, since, as Hocart so profoundly noted in his introduction to a posthumous book recently published,[2] psychological interpretations were withdrawn from the intellectual field only to be introduced again in the field of affectivity, thus adding to "the inherent defects of the psychological school . . . the mistake of deriving clear-cut ideas . . . from vague emotions." Instead of trying to enlarge the framework of our logic to include processes

Translated by Claire Jacobson and Brooke Grundfest Schoepf.

[1] In Boas's Introduction to James Teit, "Traditions of the Thompson River Indians of British Columbia," *Memoirs of the American Folklore Society,* VI (1898), p. 18. [Lévi-Strauss]

[2] A. M. Hocart, *Social Origins* (London: 1954), p. 7. [Lévi-Strauss]

Of all the chapters of religious anthropology probably none has tarried to the same extent as studies in the field of mythology. From a theoretical point of view the situation remains very much the same as it was fifty years ago, namely, chaotic. Myths are still widely interpreted in conflicting ways: as collective dreams, as the outcome of a kind of esthetic play, or as the basis of ritual. Mythological figures are considered as personified abstractions, divinized heroes, or fallen gods. Whatever the hypothesis, the choice amounts to reducing mythology either to idle play or to a crude kind of philosophic speculation.

In order to understand what a myth really is, must we choose between platitude and sophism? Some claim that human societies merely express, through their mythology, fundamental feelings common to the whole of mankind, such as love, hate, or revenge or that they try to provide some kind of explanations for phenomena which they cannot otherwise understand — astronomical, meteorological, and the like. But why should these societies do it in such elaborate and devious ways, when all of them are also acquainted with empirical explanations? On the other hand, psychoanalysts and many anthropologists have shifted the problems away from the natural or cosmological toward the sociological and psychological fields. But then the interpretation becomes too easy: If a given mythology confers prominence on a certain figure, let us say an evil grandmother, it will be claimed that in such a society grandmothers are actually evil and that mythology reflects the social structure and the social relations; but should the actual data be conflicting, it would be as readily claimed that the purpose of mythology is to provide an outlet for repressed feelings. Whatever the situation, a clever dialectic will always find a way to pretend that a meaning has been found.

Mythology confronts the student with a situation which at first sight appears contradictory. On the one hand it would seem that in the course of a myth anything is likely to happen. There is no logic, no continuity. Any characteristic can be attributed to any subject; every conceivable relation can be found. With myth, everything becomes possible. But on the other hand, this apparent arbitrariness is belied by the astounding similarity between myths collected in widely different regions. Therefore the problem: If the content of a myth is contingent, how are we going to explain the fact that myths throughout the world are so similar?

It is precisely this awareness of a basic antinomy pertaining to the nature of myth that may lead us toward its solution. For the contradiction which we face is very similar to that which in earlier times brought considerable worry to the first philosophers concerned with linguistic problems; linguistics could only begin to evolve as a science after this contradiction had been overcome. Ancient philosophers reasoned about language the way we do about mythology. On the one hand, they did notice that in a given language certain sequences of sounds were associated with definite meanings, and they earnestly aimed at discovering a reason for the linkage between those *sounds* and that *meaning.* Their attempt, however, was thwarted from the very beginning by the fact that the same sounds were equally present in other languages although the meaning they conveyed was entirely different. The contradiction was surmounted only by the discovery that it is the combination of sounds, not the sounds themselves, which provides the significant data.

It is easy to see, moreover, that some of the more recent interpretations of mythological thought originated from the same kind of misconception under which those early linguists were laboring. Let us consider, for instance, Jung's idea that a given mythological pattern — the so-called archetype — possesses a certain meaning. This is comparable to the long-supported error that a sound may possess a certain affinity with a meaning: for instance, the "liquid" semivowels with water, the open vowels with things that are big, large, loud, or heavy, etc., a theory which still has its supporters.[3] Whatever emendations

[3]See, for instance, Sir R. A. Paget, "The Origin of Language," *Journal of World History,* I, No. 2 (UNESCO, 1953). [Lévi-Strauss]

the original formulation may now call for,[4] everybody will agree that the Saussurean principle of the *arbitrary character of linguistic signs* was a prerequisite for the accession of linguistics to the scientific level.

To invite the mythologist to compare his precarious situation with that of the linguist in the prescientific stage is not enough. As a matter of fact we may thus be led only from one difficulty to another. There is a very good reason why myth cannot simply be treated as language if its specific problems are to be solved; myth *is* language: to be known, myth has to be told; it is a part of human speech. In order to preserve its specificity we must be able to show that it is both the same thing as language, and also something different from it. Here, too, the past experience of linguists may help us. For language itself can be analyzed into things which are at the same time similar and yet different. This is precisely what is expressed in Saussure's distinction between *langue* and *parole,* one being the structural side of language, the other the statistical aspect of it, *langue* belonging to a reversible time, *parole* being nonreversible. If those two levels already exist in language, then a third one can conceivably be isolated.

We have distinguished *langue* and *parole* by the different time referents which they use. Keeping this in mind, we may notice that myth uses a third referent which combines the properties of the first two. On the one hand, a myth always refers to events alleged to have taken place long ago. But what gives the myth an operational value is that the specific pattern described is timeless; it explains the present and the past as well as the future. This can be made clear through a comparison between myth and what appears to have largely replaced it in modern societies, namely, politics. When the historian refers to the French Revolution, it is always as a sequence of past happenings, a nonreversible series of events the remote consequences of which may still be felt at present. But to the French politician, as well as to his followers, the French Revolution is both a sequence belonging to the past — as to the historian — and a timeless pattern which can be detected in the contemporary French social structure and which provides a clue for its interpretation, a lead from which to infer future developments. Michelet, for instance, was a politically minded historian. He describes the French Revolution thus: "That day . . . everything was possible. . . . Future became present . . . that is, no more time, a glimpse of eternity."[5] It is that double structure, altogether historical and ahistorical, which explains how myth, while pertaining to the realm of *parole* and calling for an explanation as such, as well as to that of *langue* in which it is expressed, can also be an absolute entity on a third level which, though it remains linguistic by nature, is nevertheless distinct from the other two.

A remark can be introduced at this point which will help to show the originality of myth in relation to other linguistic phenomena. Myth is the part of language where the formula *traduttore, traditore*[6] reaches its lowest truth value. From that point of view it should be placed in the gamut of linguistic expressions at the end opposite to that of poetry, in spite of all the claims which have been made to prove the contrary. Poetry is a kind of speech which cannot be translated except at the cost of serious distortions; whereas the mythical value of the myth is preserved even through the worst translation. Whatever our ignorance of the language and the culture of the people where it originated, a myth is still felt as a myth by any reader anywhere in the world. Its substance does not lie in its style, its original music, or its syntax, but in the *story* which it tells. Myth is language, functioning on an especially high level where meaning succeeds practically at "taking off " from the linguistic ground on which it keeps on rolling.

To sum up the discussion at this point, we have so far made the following claims: (1) If there is a meaning to be found in mythology, it cannot reside in the isolated elements which enter into

<hr/>

[4] See Émile Benveniste, "Nature du signe linguistique," *Acta Linguistica,* I, No. 1 (1939); and Chapter V in *Structural Anthropology.* [Lévi-Strauss]

[5] Jules Michelet, *Histoire de la Révolution française,* IV, 1. I took this quotation from M. Merleau-Ponty, *Les Aventures de la dialectique* (Paris: 1955), p. 273. [Lévi-Strauss]

[6] To translate is to betray.

the composition of a myth, but only in the way those elements are combined. (2) Although myth belongs to the same category as language, being, as a matter of fact, only part of it, language in myth exhibits specific properties. (3) Those properties are only to be found *above* the ordinary linguistic level, that is, they exhibit more complex features than those which are to be found in any other kind of linguistic expression.

If the above three points are granted, at least as a working hypothesis, two consequences will follow: (1) Myth, like the rest of language, is made up of constituent units. (2) These constituent units presuppose the constituent units present in language when analyzed on other levels — namely, phonemes, morphemes, and sememes — but they, nevertheless, differ from the latter in the same way as the latter differ among themselves; they belong to a higher and more complex order. For this reason, we shall call them *gross constituent units*.

How shall we proceed in order to identify and isolate these gross constituent units or mythemes? We know that they cannot be found among phonemes, morphemes, or sememes, but only on a higher level; otherwise myth would become confused with any other kind of speech. Therefore, we should look for them on the sentence level. The only method we can suggest at this stage is to proceed tentatively, by trial and error, using as a check the principles which serve as a basis for any kind of structural analysis: economy of explanation; unity of solution; and ability to reconstruct the whole from a fragment, as well as later stages from previous ones.

The technique which has been applied so far by this writer consists in analyzing each myth individually, breaking down its story into the shortest possible sentences, and writing each sentence on an index card bearing a number corresponding to the unfolding of the story.

Practically each card will thus show that a certain function is, at a given time, linked to a given subject. Or, to put it otherwise, each gross constituent unit will consist of a *relation*.

However, the above definition remains highly unsatisfactory for two different reasons. First, it is well known to structural linguists that constituent units on all levels are made up of relations, and the true difference between our *gross* units

and the others remains unexplained: second, we still find ourselves in the realm of a nonreversible time, since the numbers of the cards correspond to the unfolding of the narrative. Thus the specific character of mythological time, which as we have seen is both reversible and nonreversible, synchronic and diachronic, remains unaccounted for. From this springs a new hypothesis, which constitutes the very core of our argument: The true constituent units of a myth are not the isolated relations but *bundles of such relations*, and it is only as bundles that these relations can be put to use and combined so as to produce a meaning. Relations pertaining to the same bundle may appear diachronically at remote intervals, but when we have succeeded in grouping them together we have reorganized our myth according to a time referent of a new nature, corresponding to the prerequisite of the initial hypothesis, namely a two-dimensional time referent which is simultaneously diachronic and synchronic, and which accordingly integrates the characteristics of *langue* on the one hand, and those of *parole* on the other. To put it in even more linguistic terms, it is as though a phoneme were always made up of all its variants.

Two comparisons may help to explain what we have in mind.

Let us first suppose that archaeologists of the future coming from another planet would one day, when all human life had disappeared from the earth, excavate one of our libraries. Even if they were at first ignorant of our writing, they might succeed in deciphering it — an undertaking which would require, at some early stage, the discovery that the alphabet, as we are in the habit of printing it, should be read from left to right and from top to bottom. However, they would soon discover that a whole category of books did not fit the usual pattern — these would be the orchestra scores on the shelves of the music division. But after trying, without success, to decipher the staffs one after the other, from the upper down to the lower, they would probably notice that the same patterns of notes recurred at intervals, either in full or in part, or that some patterns were strongly reminiscent of earlier ones. Hence the hypothesis: What if patterns showing affinity, instead of being considered in succession, were to be treated as one complex pattern and read as a whole? By getting at what we call *harmony*, they would then see that an orchestra score, to be meaningful, must be read diachronically along one axis — that is, page after page, and from left to right — and synchronically along the other axis, all the notes written vertically making up one gross constituent unit, that is, one bundle of relations.

The other comparison is somewhat different. Let us take an observer ignorant of our playing cards, sitting for a long time with a fortune-teller. He would know something of the visitors: sex, age, physical appearance, social situation, etc., in the same way as we know something of the different cultures whose myths we try to study. He would also listen to the séances and record them so as to be able to go over them and make comparisons — as we do when we listen to myth-telling and record it. Mathematicians to whom I have put the problem agree that if the man is bright and if the material available to him is sufficient, he may be able to reconstruct the nature of the deck of cards being used, that is, fifty-two or thirty-two cards according to the case, made up of four homologous sets consisting of the same units (the individual cards) with only one varying feature, the suit.

Now for a concrete example of the method we propose. We shall use the Oedipus myth, which is well known to everyone. I am well aware that the Oedipus myth has only reached us under late forms and through literary transmutations concerned more with esthetic and moral preoccupations than with religious or ritual ones, whatever these may have been. But we shall not interpret the Oedipus myth in literal terms, much less offer an explanation acceptable to the specialist. We simply wish to illustrate — and without reaching any conclusions with respect to it — a certain technique, whose use is probably not legitimate in this particular instance, owing to the problematic elements indicated above. The "demonstration" should therefore be conceived, not in terms of what the scientist means by this term, but at best in terms of what is meant by the street peddler, whose aim is not to achieve a concrete result, but to explain, as succinctly as possible, the functioning of the mechanical toy which he is trying to sell to the onlookers.

The myth will be treated as an orchestra score would be if it were unwittingly considered as a unilinear series; our task is to re-establish the correct arrangement. Say, for instance, we were confronted with a sequence of the type: 1,2,4,7,8, 2,3,4,6,8,1,4,5,7,8,1,2,5,7,3,4,5,6,8..., the assignment being to put all the 1's together, all the 2's, the 3's, etc.; the result is a chart:

1	2		4			7	8
	2	3	4		6		8
1			4	5		7	8
1	2			5		7	
		3	4	5	6		8

We shall attempt to perform the same kind of operation on the Oedipus myth, trying out several arrangements of the mythemes until we find one which is in harmony with the principles enumerated above. Let us suppose, for the sake of argument, that the best arrangement is as shown in Table 1 (although it might certainly be improved with the help of a specialist in Greek mythology).

We thus find ourselves confronted with four vertical columns, each of which includes several relations belonging to the same bundle. Were we to *tell* the myth, we would disregard the columns and read the rows from left to right and from top to bottom. But if we want to *understand* the myth, then we will have to disregard one half of the diachronic dimension (top to bottom) and read from left to right, column after column, each one being considered as a unit.

All the relations belonging to the same column exhibit one common feature which it is our task to discover. For instance, all the events grouped in the first column on the left have something to do with blood relations which are overemphasized, that is, are more intimate than they should be. Let us say, then, that the first column has as its common feature the *overrating of blood relations*. It is obvious that the second column expresses the same thing, but inverted: *underrating of blood relations*. The third column refers to monsters being slain. As to the fourth, a few words of clarification are needed. The remarkable connotation of the surnames in Oedipus' father-line has often been noticed. However, linguists usually disregard it, since to them the only way to define the meaning of a term is to investigate all the contexts in which it appears, and personal names, precisely because they are used as such, are not accompanied by any context. With the method we propose to follow the objection disappears, since the myth itself provides its own context. The significance is no longer to be sought in the eventual meaning of each name, but in the fact that all the names have a common feature: All the hypothetical meanings (which may well remain hypothetical) refer to *difficulties in walking straight and standing upright.*

What then is the relationship between the two columns on the right? Column three refers to monsters. The dragon is a chthonian[7] being which has to be killed in order that mankind be born from the Earth; the Sphinx is a monster unwilling to permit men to live. The last unit reproduces the first one, which has to do with the *autochthonous[8] origin* of mankind. Since the monsters are overcome by men, we may thus say that the common feature of the third column is *denial of the autochthonous origin of man.[9]*

This immediately helps us to understand the meaning of the fourth column. In mythology it

[7] Living within or under the earth.

[8] Born or sprung from the earth. Lévi-Strauss uses the term in a sense in opposition to "born from the sexual union of man and woman."

[9] We are not trying to become involved with specialists in an argument; this would be presumptuous and even meaningless on our part. Since the Oedipus myth is taken here merely as an example treated in arbitrary fashion, the chthonian nature ascribed to the Sphinx might seem surprising; we shall refer to the testimony of Marie Delcourt: "In the archaic legends, [she is] certainly born of the Earth itself.' (*Oedipe ou la légende du conquérant* [Liège: 1944], p. 108). No matter how remote from Delcourt's our method may be (and our conclusions would be, no doubt, if we were competent to deal with the problem in depth), it seems to us that she has convincingly established the nature of

Table 1

Cadmos seeks his sister Europa, ravished by Zeus			
		Cadmos kills the dragon	
	The Spartoi kill one another		
			Labdacos (Laios' father) = *lame (?)*
	Oedipus kills his father, Laios		
			Laios (Oedipus' father) = *left-sided (?)*
		Oedipus kills the Sphinx	
			Oedipus = *swollen-foot (?)*
Oedipus marries his mother, Jocasta			
	Eteocles kills his brother, Polynices		
Antigone buries her brother, Polynices, despite prohibition			

is a universal characteristic of men born from the Earth that at the moment they emerge from the depth they either cannot walk or they walk clumsily. This is the case of the chthonian beings in the mythology of the Pueblo: Muyingwu, who leads the emergence, and the chthonian Shumaikoli are lame ("bleeding-foot," "sore-foot"). The same happens to the Koskimo of the Kwakiutl after they have been swallowed by the chthonian monster, Tsiakish: When they returned to the surface of the earth "they limped forward or tripped sideways." Thus the common feature of the fourth column is *the persistence of the autochthonous origin of man.* It follows that column four is to column three as column one is to column two. The inability to connect two kinds of relationships is overcome (or rather replaced) by the assertion that contradictory relationships are identical inasmuch as they are both

the Sphinx in the archaic tradition, namely, that of a female monster who attacks and rapes young men; in other words, the personification of a female being with an inversion of the sign. This explains why, in the handsome iconography compiled by Delcourt at the end of her work, men and women are always found in an inverted "sky/earth" relationship.

As we shall point out below, we selected the Oedipus myth as our first example because of the striking analogies that seem to exist between certain aspects of archaic Greek thought and that of the Pueblo Indians, from whom we have borrowed the examples that follow. In this respect it should be noted that the figure of the Sphinx, as reconstructed by Delcourt, coincides with two figures of North American mythology (who probably merge into one). We are referring, on the one hand, to "the old hag," a repulsive witch whose physical appearance presents a "problem" to the young hero. If he "solves" this problem — that is, if he responds to the advances of the abject creature — he will find in his bed, upon awakening, a beautiful young woman who will confer power upon him (this is also a Celtic theme). The Sphinx, on the other hand, recalls even more "the child-protruding woman" of the Hopi Indians, that is, a phallic mother par excellence. This young woman was abandoned by her group in the course of a difficult migration, just as she was about to give birth. Henceforth she wanders in the desert as the "Mother of Animals," which she withholds from hunters. He who meets her in her bloody clothes "is so frightened that he has an erection," of which she takes advantage to rape him, after which she rewards him with unfailing success in hunting. See H. R. Voth, "The Oraibi Summer Snake Ceremony," *Field Columbian Museum,* Publication No. 83, Anthropological Series, Vol. III, No. 4 (Chicago: 1903), pp. 352–53 and p. 353, *n* 1. [Lévi-Strauss]

self-contradictory in a similar way. Although this is still a provisional formulation of the structure of mythical thought, it is sufficient at this stage.

Turning back to the Oedipus myth, we may now see what it means. The myth has to do with the inability, for a culture which holds the belief that mankind is autochthonous (see, for instance, Pausanias, VIII, xxix, 4: plants provide a *model* for humans), to find a satisfactory transition between this theory and the knowledge that human beings are actually born from the union of man and woman. Although the problem obviously cannot be solved, the Oedipus myth provides a kind of logical tool which relates the original problem — born from one or born from two? — to the derivative problem: born from different or born from same? By a correlation of this type, the overrating of blood relations is to the underrating of blood relations as the attempt to escape autochthony is to the impossibility to succeed in it. Although experience contradicts theory, social life validates cosmology by its similarity of structure. Hence cosmology is true.

Two remarks should be made at this stage.

In order to interpret the myth, we left aside a point which has worried the specialists until now, namely, that in the earlier (Homeric) versions of the Oedipus myth, some basic elements are lacking, such as Jocasta killing herself and Oedipus piercing his own eyes. These events do not alter the substance of the myth although they can easily be integrated, the first one as a new case of autodestruction (column three) and the second as another case of crippledness (column four). At the same time there is something significant in these additions, since the shift from foot to head is to be correlated with the shift from autochthonous origin to self-destruction.

Our method thus eliminates a problem which has, so far, been one of the main obstacles to the progress of mythological studies, namely, the quest for the *true* version, or the *earlier* one. On the contrary, we define the myth as consisting of all its versions; or to put it otherwise, a myth remains the same as long as it is felt as such. A striking example is offered by the fact that our interpretation may take into account the Freudian use of the Oedipus myth and is certainly applicable to it. Although the Freudian problem has ceased to be that of autochthony *versus* bisexual reproduction, it is still the problem of understanding how *one* can be born from *two:* How is it that we do not have only one procreator, but a mother plus a father? Therefore, not only Sophocles, but Freud himself, should be included among the recorded versions of the Oedipus myth on a par with earlier or seemingly more "authentic" versions.

An important consequence follows. If a myth is made up of all its variants, structural analysis should take all of them into account. After analyz- ing all the known variants of the Theban version, we should thus treat the others in the same way: first, the tales about Labdacos' collateral line including Agave, Pentheus, and Jocasta herself; the Theban variant about Lycos with Amphion and Zetos as the city founders; more remote vari- ants concerning Dionysus (Oedipus' matrilateral cousin); and Athenian legends where Cecrops take the place of Cadmos, etc. For each of them a similar chart should be drawn and then compared and reorganized according to the findings: Cecrops killing the serpent with the parallel episode of Cadmos; abandonment of Dionysus with abandon- ment of Oedipus; "Swollen Foot" with Dionysus' *loxias,* that is, walking obliquely; Europa's quest with Antiope's; the founding of Thebes by the Spartoi or by the brothers Amphion and Zetos; Zeus kidnapping Europa and Antiope and the same with Semele; the Theban Oedipus and the Argian Perseus, etc. We shall then have several two- dimensional charts, each dealing with a variant, to be organized in a three-dimensional order, as shown in Figure 1, so that three different readings become possible: left to right, top to bottom, front to back (or vice versa). All of these charts cannot be expected to be identical; but experience shows that any difference to be observed may be corre- lated with other differences, so that a logical treat- ment of the whole will allow simplifications, the final outcome being the structural law of the myth.

At this point the objection may be raised that the task is impossible to perform, since we can only work with known versions. Is it not possible that a new version might alter the picture? This is true enough if only one or two versions are avail- able, but the objection becomes theoretical as soon as a reasonably large number have been recorded. Let us make this point clear by a comparison. If the furniture of a room and its arrangement

Figure 1

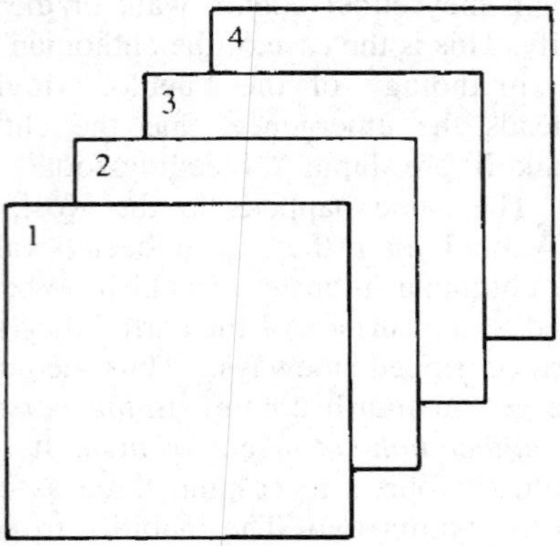

were known to us only through its reflection in two mirrors placed on opposite walls, we should theoretically dispose of an almost infinite number of mirror images which would provide us with a complete knowledge. However, should the two mirrors be obliquely set, the number of mirror images would become very small; neverthe- less, four or five such images would very likely give us, if not complete information, at least a sufficient coverage so that we would feel sure that no large piece of furniture is missing in our description.

On the other hand, it cannot be too strongly emphasized that all available variants should be taken into account. If Freudian comments on the Oedipus complex are a part of the Oedipus myth, then questions such as whether Cushing's version of the Zuni origin myth should be retained or dis- carded become irrelevant. There is no single "true" version of which all the others are but copies or distortions. Every version belongs to the myth.

The reason for the discouraging results in works on general mythology can finally be understood. They stem from two causes. First, comparative mythologists have selected preferred versions instead of using them all. Second, we have seen that the structural analysis of *one* variant of *one* myth belonging to *one* tribe (in some cases, even *one village*) already requires two dimensions.

When we use several variants of the same myth for the same tribe or village, the frame of reference becomes three-dimensional, and as soon as we try to enlarge the comparison, the number of dimensions required increases until it appears quite impossible to handle them intuitively. The confusions and platitudes which are the outcome of comparative mythology can be explained by the fact that multidimensional frames of reference are often ignored or are naïvely replaced by two- or three-dimensional ones. Indeed, progress in comparative mythology depends largely on the cooperation of mathematicians who would undertake to express in symbols multidimensional relations which cannot be handled otherwise.

Three final remarks may serve as conclusion.

First, the question has often been raised why myths, and more generally oral literature, are so much addicted to duplication, triplication, or quadruplication of the same sequence. If our hypotheses are accepted, the answer is obvious: The function of repetition is to render the structure of the myth apparent. For we have seen that the synchronic-diachronic structure of the myth permits us to organize it into diachronic sequences (the rows in our tables) which should be read synchronically (the columns). Thus, a myth exhibits a "slated" structure, which comes to the surface, so to speak, through the process of repetition.

However, the slates are not absolutely identical. And since the purpose of myth is to provide a logical model capable of overcoming a contradiction (an impossible achievement if, as it happens, the contradiction is real), a theoretically infinite number of slates will be generated, each one slightly different from the others. Thus, myth grows spiral-wise until the intellectual impulse which has produced it is exhausted. Its *growth* is a continuous process, whereas its *structure* remains discontinuous. If this is the case, we should assume that it closely corresponds, in the realm of the spoken word, to a crystal in the realm of physical matter. This analogy may help us to better understand the relationship of myth to both *langue* on the one hand and *parole* on the other. Myth is an intermediary entity between a statistical aggregate of molecules and the molecular structure itself.

Prevalent attempts to explain alleged differences between the so-called primitive mind and scientific thought have resorted to qualitative differences between the working processes of the mind in both cases, while assuming that the entities which they were studying remained very much the same. If our interpretation is correct, we are led toward a completely different view — namely, that the kind of logic in mythical thought is as rigorous as that of modern science, and that the difference lies, not in the quality of the intellectual process, but in the nature of the things to which it is applied. This is well in agreement with the situation known to prevail in the field of technology: What makes a steel ax superior to a stone ax is not that the first one is better made than the second. They are equally well made, but steel is quite different from stone. In the same way we may be able to show that the same logical processes operate in myth as in science, and that man has always been thinking equally well; the improvement lies, not in an alleged progress of man's mind, but in the discovery of new areas to which it may apply its unchanged and unchanging powers.

Roland Barthes

1915–1980

Before his untimely death in a traffic accident, the French critic and man of letters Roland Barthes was a prolific interpreter, disseminator, and reviser of most of the complex theoretical concepts that wound through his country's centers of learning from the 1950s on. Barthes's father, a naval officer, died in battle in the first year of his son's life. Barthes grew up in Bayonne, attended secondary school in Paris, and received degrees in classical letters (1939) and grammar and philosophy (1943) from the University of Paris. He taught French in Bucharest (1948–49) and Alexandria (1949–50). Although Barthes was director of the social sciences at the Ecole Pratique des Hautes Etudes in Paris from 1960 to 1977, there is the sense that he was more comfortable intellectually on the margins of the academy, carrying on guerrilla conversation with it. (On Racine [1963], for example, caused a juror among institutional classicists because of its nontraditional approach to the canonical playwright.) Barthes was elected to the chair of literary semiology at the Collège de France in 1976 and acknowledged as the leading critic of his generation in 1978. Barthes's works, many of which have been translated since his death, include Writing Degree Zero (1953), Mythologies (1957), Elements of Semiology (1964), Criticism and Truth (1966), S/Z (1970), Sade/Fourier/Loyola (1971), Critical Essays (1972), The Pleasure of the Text (1973), A Lover's Discourse: Fragments (1977), The Grain of the Voice (1981), The Responsibilities of Forms (1982), and The Rustle of Language (1984). "The Death of the Author" and "From Work to Text" are both from Image — Music — Text (1977).

From Work to Text

It is a fact that over the last few years a certain change has taken place (or is taking place) in our conception of language and, consequently, of the literary work which owes at least its phenomenal existence to this same language. The change is clearly connected with the current development of (amongst other disciplines) linguistics, anthropology, Marxism and psychoanalysis (the term "connection" is used here in a deliberately neutral way; one does not decide a determination, be it multiple and dialectical). What is new and which affects the idea of the work comes not necessarily from the internal recasting of each of these disciplines, but rather from their encounter in relation to an object which traditionally is the province of none of them. It is indeed as though the *interdisci-plinarity* which is today held up as a prime value

Translated by Richard Howard.

in research cannot be accomplished by the simple confrontation of specialist branches of knowledge. Interdisciplinarity is not the calm of an easy security; it begins *effectively* (as opposed to the mere expression of a pious wish) when the solidarity of the old disciplines breaks down — perhaps even violently, via the jolts of fashion — in the interests of a new object and a new language neither of which has a place in the field of the sciences that were to be brought peacefully together, this unease in classification being precisely the point from which it is possible to diagnose a certain mutation. The mutation in which the idea of the work seems to be gripped must not, however, be over-estimated: it is more in the nature of an epistemological slide than of a real break. The break, as is frequently stressed, is seen to have taken place in the last century with the appearance of Marxism and Freudianism; since then there has been no further break, so that in a way it can be said that for the last hundred years we have been living in repetition. What History, our History, allows us today is merely to slide, to vary, to exceed, to repudiate. Just as Einsteinian science demands that *the relativity of the frames of reference* be included in the object studied, so the combined action of Marxism, Freudianism and structuralism demands, in literature, the relativization of the relations of writer, reader and observer (critic). Over against the traditional notion of the *work,* for long — and still — conceived of in a, so to speak, Newtonian way, there is now the requirement of a new object, obtained by the sliding or overturning of former categories. That object is the *Text.* I know the word is fashionable (I am myself often led to use it) and therefore regarded by some with suspicion, but that is exactly why I should like to remind myself of the principal propositions at the intersection of which I see the Text as standing. The word "proposition" is to be understood more in a grammatical than in a logical sense: the following are not argumentations but enunciations, "touches," approaches that consent to remain metaphorical. Here then are these propositions; they concern method, genres, signs, plurality, filiation, reading and pleasure.

1. The Text is not to be thought of as an object that can be computed. It would be futile to try to separate out materially works from texts. In particular, the tendency must be avoided to say that the work is classic, the text avant-garde; it is not a question of drawing up a crude honours list in the name of modernity and declaring certain literary productions "in" and others "out" by virtue of their chronological situation: there may be "text" in a very ancient work, while many products of contemporary literature are in no way texts. The difference is this: the work is a fragment of substance, occupying a part of the space of books (in a library for example), the Text is a methodological field. The opposition may recall (without at all reproducing term for term) Lacan's distinction between "reality" and "the real": the one is displayed, the other demonstrated; likewise, the work can be seen (in bookshops, in catalogues, in exam syllabi), the text is a process of demonstration,

speaks according to certain rules (or against certain rules); the work can be held in the hand, the text is held in language, only exists in the movement of a discourse (or rather, it is Text for the very reason that it knows itself as text); the Text is not the decomposition of the work, it is the work that is the imaginary tail of the Text; or again, *the Text is experienced only in an activity of production.* It follows that the Text cannot stop (for example on a library shelf); its constitutive movement is that of cutting across (in particular, it can cut across the work, several works).

2. In the same way, the Text does not stop at (good) Literature; it cannot be contained in a hierarchy, even in a simple division of genres. What constitutes the Text is, on the contrary (or precisely), its subversive force in respect of the old classifications. How do you classify a writer like Georges Bataille? Novelist, poet, essayist, economist, philosopher, mystic? The answer is so difficult that the literary manuals generally prefer to forget about Bataille who, in fact, wrote texts, perhaps continuously one single text. If the Text poses problems of classification (which is furthermore one of its "social" functions), this is because it always involves a certain experience of limits (to take up an expression from Philippe Sollers). Thibaudet used already to talk — but in a very restricted sense — of limit-works (such as Chateaubriand's *Vie de Rancé,* which does indeed come through to us today as a "text"); the Text is that which goes to the limit of the rules of enunciation (rationality, readability, etc.). Nor is this a rhetorical idea, resorted to for some "heroic" effect: the Text tries to place itself very exactly *behind* the limit of the *doxa*[1] (is not general opinion — constitutive of our democratic societies and powerfully aided by mass communications — defined by its limits, the energy with which it excludes, its *censorship*?). Taking the word literally, it may be said that the Text is always *paradoxical.*

3. The Text can be approached, experienced, in reaction to the sign. The work closes on a signified. There are two modes of signification which can be attributed to this signified; either it is claimed to be evident and the work is then the

[1]Opinion.

object of a literal science, of philology, or else it is considered to be secret, ultimate, something to be sought out, and the work then falls under the scope of a hermeneutics, of an interpretation (Marxist, psychoanalytic, thematic, etc.): in short, the work itself functions as a general sign and it is normal that it should represent an institutional category of the civilization of the Sign. The Text, on the contrary, practices the infinite deferment of the signified, is dilatory; its field is that of the signifier and the signifier must not be conceived of as "the first stage of meaning," its material vestibule, but, in complete opposition to this, as its *deferred action*. Similarly, the *infinity* of the signifier refers not to some idea of the ineffable (the unnameable signified) but to that of a *playing*; the generation of the perpetual signifier (after the fashion of a perpetual calendar) in the field of the text (better, of which the text is the field) is realized not according to an organic progress of maturation or a hermeneutic course of deepening investigation, but, rather, according to a serial movement of disconnections, overlappings, variations. The logic regulating the Text is not comprehensive (define "what the work *means*") but metonymic; the activity of associations, contiguities, carryings-over coincides with a liberation of symbolic energy (lacking it, man would die); the work — in the best of cases — is *moderately* symbolic (its symbolic runs out, comes to a halt); the Text is *radically symbolic*: *a work conceived, perceived and received in its integrally symbolic nature is a text*. Thus is the Text restored to language; like language, it is structured but off-centred, without closure (note, in reply to the contemptuous suspicion of the "fashionable" sometimes directed at structuralism, that the epistemological privilege currently accorded to language stems precisely from the discovery there of a paradoxical idea of structure: a system with neither close nor centre).

4. The Text is plural. Which is not simply to say that it has several meanings, but that it accomplishes the very plural of meaning: an *irreducible* (and not merely an acceptable) plural. The Text is not a co-existence of meanings but a passage, an overcrossing; thus it answers not to an interpretation, even a liberal one, but to an explosion, a dissemination. The plural of the

Text depends, that is, not on the ambiguity of its contents but on what might be called the *stereographic plurality* of its weave of signifiers (etymologically, the text is a tissue, a woven fabric). The reader of the Text may be compared to someone at a loose end (someone slackened off from any imaginary): this passably empty subject strolls — it is what happened to the author of these lines, then it was that he had a vivid idea of the Text — on the side of a valley, a *oued*[2] flowing down below (*oued* is there to bear witness to a certain feeling of unfamiliarity): what he perceives is multiple, irreducible, coming from a disconnected, heterogeneous variety of substances and perspectives: lights, colours, vegetation, heat, air, slender explosions of noises, scant cries of birds, children's voices from over on the other side, passages, gestures, clothes of inhabitants near or far away. All these *incidents* are half-identifiable: they come from codes which are known but their combination is unique, founds the stroll in a difference repeatable only as difference. So the Text: it can be it only in its difference (which does not mean its individuality), its reading is semelfactive[3] (this rendering illusory any inductive-deductive science of texts — no "grammar" of the text) and nevertheless woven entirely with citations, references, echoes, cultural languages (what language is not?), antecedent or contemporary, which cut across it through and through in a vast stereophony. The intertextual in which every text is held, it itself being the text-between of another text, is not to be confused with some origin of the text: to try to find the "sources," the "influences" of a work, is to fall in with the myth of filiation[4]; the citations which go to make up a text are anonymous, untraceable, and yet *already read*: they are quotations without inverted commas. The work has nothing disturbing for any monistic philosophy (we know that there are opposing examples of these): for such a philosophy, plural is the Evil. Against the work, therefore, the text could well take as its motto the words of the man possessed by demons (*Mark 5:9*): "My name is Legion: for we are many." The plural or demoniacal

²A North African watercourse; a wadi.
³A nonce word made up from the Latin roots "semel" (half) and "factive" (creative).
⁴Descent, derivation.

texture which opposes text to work can bring with it fundamental changes in reading, and precisely in areas where monologism appears to be the Law: certain of the "texts" of Holy Scripture traditionally recuperated by theological monism (historical or anagogical) will perhaps offer themselves to a diffraction of meanings (finally, that is to say, to a materialist reading), while the Marxist interpretation of works, so far resolutely monistic, will be able to materialize itself more by pluralizing itself (if, however, the Marxist "institutions" allow it).

5. The work is caught up in a process of filiation. Are postulated: a *determination* of the work by the world (by race, then by History), a *consecution* of works amongst themselves, and a *conformity* of the work to the author. The author is reputed the father and the owner of his work: literary science therefore teaches *respect* for the manuscript and the author's declared intentions, while society asserts the legality of the relation of author to work (the *"droit d'auteur"* or "copyright," in fact of recent date since it was only really legalized at the time of the French Revolution). As for the Text, it reads without the inscription of the Father. Here again, the metaphor of the Text separates from that of the work: the latter refers to the image of an *organism* which grows by vital expansion, by "development" (a word which is significantly ambiguous, at once biological and rhetorical); the metaphor of the Text is that of the *network;* if the Text extends itself, it is as a result of a combinatory systematic (an image, moreover, close to current biological conceptions of the living being). Hence no vital "respect" is due to the Text: it can be *broken* (which is just what the Middle Ages did with two nevertheless authoritative texts — Holy Scripture and Aristotle); it can be read without the guarantee of its father, the restitution of the inter-text paradoxically abolishing any legacy. It is not that the Author may not "come back" in the Text, in his text, but he then does so as a "guest." If he is a novelist, he is inscribed in the novel like one of his characters, figured in the carpet; no longer privileged, paternal, aletheological,[5]

his inscription is ludic.[6] He becomes, as it were, a paper-author: his life is no longer the origin of his fictions but a fiction contributing to his work; there is a reversion of the work on to the life (and no longer the contrary); it is the work of Proust, of Genet which allows their lives to be read as a text. The word "bio-graphy" re-acquires a strong, etymological sense, at the same time as the sincerity of the enunciation — veritable "cross" borne by literary morality — becomes a false problem: the *I* which writes the text, it too, is never more than a paper-*I.*

6. The work is normally the object of a consumption; no demagogy is intended here in referring to the so-called consumer culture but it has to be recognized that today it is the "quality" of the work (which supposes finally an appreciation of "taste") and not the operation of reading itself which can differentiate between books: structurally, there is no difference between "cultured" reading and casual reading in trains. The Text (if only by its frequent "unreadability") decants the work (the work permitting) from its consumption and gathers it up as play, activity, production, practice. This means that the Text requires that one try to abolish (or at the very least to diminish) the distance between writing and reading, in no way by intensifying the projection of the reader into the work but by joining them in a single signifying practice. The distance separating reading from writing is historical. In the times of the greatest social division (before the setting up of democratic cultures), reading and writing were equally privileges of class. Rhetoric, the great literary code of those times, taught one to *write* (even if what was then normally produced were speeches, not texts). Significantly, the coming of democracy reversed the word of command: what the (secondary) School prides itself on is teaching to *read* (well) and no longer to write (consciousness of the deficiency is becoming fashionable again today: the teacher is called upon to teach pupils to "express themselves," which is a little like replacing a form of repression by a misconception). In fact, *reading,* in the sense of consuming, is far from *playing* with the

---

[5]A portmanteau word composed of *aletheia,* "truth," and *theological.*

[6]Playful.

text. "Playing" must be understood here in all its polysemy:[7] the text itself *plays* (like a door, like a machine with "play") and the reader plays the Text as one plays a game, looking for a practice which reproduces it, but, in order that that practice not be reduced to a passive, inner *mimesis* (the Text is precisely that which resists such a reduction), also playing the Text in the musical sense of the term. The history of music (as a practice, not as an "art") does indeed parallel that of the Text fairly closely: there was a period when practicing amateurs were numerous (at least within the confines of a certain class) and "playing" and "listening" formed a scarcely differentiated activity; then two roles appeared in succession, first that of the performer, the interpreter to whom the bourgeois public delegated its playing (though still itself able to play a little — the whole history of the piano) delegated its playing, then that of the (passive) amateur, who listens to music without being able to play (the gramophone record takes the place of the piano). We know that today post-serial music has radically altered the role of the "interpreter," who is called on to be in some sort the co-author of the score, completing it rather than giving it "expression." The Text is very much a score of this new kind: it asks of the reader a practical collaboration. Which is an important change, for who executes the work? (Mallarmé posed the question, wanting the audience to *produce* the book). Nowadays only the critic executes the work (accepting the play on words). The reduction of reading to a consumption is clearly responsible for the "boredom" experienced by many in the face of the modern ("unreadable") text, the avant-garde film or painting: to be bored means that one cannot produce the text, open it out, *set it going*.

7. This leads us to pose (to propose) a final approach to the Text, that of pleasure. I do not know whether there has ever been a hedonistic aesthetics (eudaemonist philosophies are themselves rare). Certainly there exists a pleasure of the work (of certain works): I can delight in reading and re-reading Proust, Flaubert, Balzac, even — why not? — Alexandre Dumas. But this pleasure, no matter how keen and even when free from all prejudice, remains in part (unless by some exceptional critical effort) a pleasure of consumption; for if I can read these authors, I also know that I cannot *re-write* them (that it is impossible today to write "like that") and this knowledge, depressing enough, suffices to cut me off from the production of these works, in the very moment their remoteness establishes my modernity (is not to be modern to know clearly what cannot be started over again?). As for the Text, it is bound to *jouissance*,[8] that is to a pleasure without separation. Order of the signifier, the Text participates in its own way in a social utopia; before History (supposing the latter does not opt for barbarism), the Text achieves, if not the transparence of social relations, that at least of language relations: the Text is that space where no language has a hold over any other, where languages circulate (keeping the circular sense of the term).

These few propositions, inevitably, do not constitute the articulations of a Theory of the Text and this is not simply the result of the failings of the person here presenting them (who in many respects has anyway done no more than pick up what is being developed round about him). It stems from the fact that a Theory of the Text cannot be satisfied by a metalinguistic exposition: the destruction of metalanguage, or at least (since it may be necessary provisionally to resort to metalanguage) its calling into doubt, is part of the theory itself: the discourse on the Text should itself be nothing other than text, research, textual activity, since the Text is that *social* space which leaves no language safe, outside, nor any subject of the enunciation in position as judge, master, analyst, confessor, decoder. The theory of the Text can coincide only with a practice of writing.

[7]Multiplicity of meaning.

[8]Joy, bliss. See the introduction to Structuralism and Deconstruction, p. 470.

The Death of the Author

In his story "Sarrasine" Balzac, describing a castrato disguised as a woman, writes the following sentence: *"This was woman herself, with her sudden fears, her irrational whims, her instinctive worries, her impetuous boldness, her fussings, and her delicious sensibility."* Who is speaking thus? Is it the hero of the story bent on remaining ignorant of the castrato hidden beneath the woman? Is it Balzac the individual, furnished by his personal experience with a philosophy of Woman? Is it Balzac the author professing "literary" ideas on femininity? Is it universal wisdom? Romantic psychology? We shall never know, for the good reason that writing is the destruction of every voice, of every point of origin. Writing is that neutral, composite, oblique space where our subject slips away, the negative where all identity is lost, starting with the very identity of the body writing.

No doubt it has always been that way. As soon as a fact is *narrated* no longer with a view to acting directly on reality but intransitively, that is to say, finally outside of any function other than that of the very practice of the symbol itself, this disconnection occurs, the voice loses its origin, the author enters into his own death, writing begins. The sense of this phenomenon, however, has varied; in ethnographic societies the responsibility for a narrative is never assumed by a person but by a mediator, shaman, or relator whose "performance" — the mastery of the narrative code — may possibly be admired but never his "genius." The author is a modern figure, a product of our society insofar as, emerging from the Middle Ages with English empiricism, French rationalism and the personal faith of the Reformation, it discovered the prestige of the individual, of, as it is more nobly put, the "human person." It is thus logical that in literature it should be this positivism, the epitome and culmination of capitalist ideology, which has attached the greatest importance to the "person" of the author. The *author* still reigns in histories of literature, biographies of writers, interviews, magazines,

Translated by Stephen Heath.

as in the very consciousness of men of letters anxious to unite their person and their work through diaries and memoirs. The image of literature to be found in ordinary culture is tyrannically centered on the author, his person, his life, his tastes, his passions, while criticism still consists for the most part in saying that Baudelaire's work is the failure of Baudelaire the man, van Gogh's his madness, Tchaikovsky's his vice. The *explanation* of a work is always sought in the man or woman who produced it, as if it were always in the end, through the more or less transparent allegory of the fiction, the voice of a single person, the *author* "confiding" in us.

Though the sway of the Author remains powerful (the New Criticism has often done no more than consolidate it), it goes without saying that certain writers have long since attempted to loosen it. In France, Mallarmé was doubtless the first to see and to foresee in its full extent the necessity to substitute language itself for the person who until then had been supposed to be its owner. For him, for us too, it is language which speaks, not the author; to write is, through a prerequisite impersonality (not at all to be confused with the castrating objectivity of the realist novelist), to reach that point where only language acts, "performs," and not "me." Mallarmé's entire poetics consists in suppressing the author in the interests of writing (which is, as will be seen, to restore the place of the reader). Valéry, encumbered by a psychology of the Ego, considerably diluted Mallarmé's theory, but his taste for classicism, leading him to turn to the lessons of rhetoric, he never stopped calling into question and deriding the Author; he stressed the linguistic and, as it were, "hazardous" nature of his activity, and throughout his prose works he militated in favor of the essentially verbal condition of literature, in the face of which all recourse to the writer's interiority seemed to him pure superstition. Proust himself, despite the apparently psychological character of what are called his *analyses*, was visibly concerned with the task of inexorably blurring, by an extreme subtilization, the relation between the writer and his characters; by making of the narrator not he who has seen and felt nor even he who is writing, but he who *is going to write* (the young man in the novel — but, in fact, how old is he and who is he? — wants to write but cannot; the novel ends when writing at last becomes possible), Proust gave modern writing its epic. By a radical reversal, instead of putting his life into his novel, as is so often maintained, he made of his very life a work for which his own book was the model; so that it is clear to us that Charlus does not imitate Montesquiou but that Montesquiou — in his anecdotal, historical reality — is no more than a secondary fragment, derived from Charlus.[1] Lastly, to go no further than this prehistory of modernity, Surrealism, though unable to accord language a supreme place (language being system and the aim of the movement being, romantically, a direct subversion of codes — itself moreover illusory: a code cannot be destroyed, only "played off"), contributed to the desacralization of the image of the Author by ceaselessly recommending the abrupt disappointment of expectations of meaning (the famous surrealist "jolt"), by entrusting the hand with the task of writing as quickly as possible what the head itself is unaware of (automatic writing), by accepting the principle and the experience of several people writing together. Leaving aside literature itself (such distinctions become really invalid), linguistics has recently provided the destruction of the Author with a valuable analytical tool by showing that the whole of the enunciation is an empty process, functioning perfectly without there being any need for it to be filled with the person of the interlocutors. Linguistically, the author is never more than the instance writing, just as I is nothing other than the instance saying I: language knows a "subject," not a "person," and this subject, empty outside of the very enunciation which defines it, suffices to make language "hold together," suffices, that is to say, to exhaust it.

The removal of the Author (one could talk here with Brecht of a veritable "distancing," the Author diminishing like a figurine at the far end of the literary stage),[2] is not merely an historical fact or an act of writing; it utterly transforms the modern text (or — which is the same thing — the

---

[1]Baron de Charlus, a character in Marcel Proust's *In Search of Lost Time* based largely on the dandy and esthete Comte Robert de Montesquiou.

[2]Barthes refers to German playwright Bertolt Brecht's doctrine of *Verfremdung* (or alienation), in which the spectators are emotionally distanced from the events represented on stage.

text is henceforth made and read in such a way that at all its levels the author is absent). The temporality is different. The Author, when believed in, is always conceived of as the past of his own book: book and author stand automatically on a single line divided into a *before* and an *after*. The Author is thought to *nourish* the book, which is to say that he exists before it, thinks, suffers, lives for it, is in the same relation of antecedence to his work as a father to his child. In complete contrast, the modern scriptor is born simultaneously with the text, is in no way equipped with a being preceding or exceeding the writing, is not the subject with the book as predicate; there is no other time than that of the enunciation and every text is eternally written *here and now*. The fact is (or, it follows) that *writing* can no longer designate an operation of recording, notation, representation, "depiction" (as the classics would say); rather, it designates exactly what linguists, referring to Oxford philosophy, call a performative,[3] a rare verbal form (exclusively given in the first person and in the present tense) in which the enunciation has no other content (contains no other proposition) than the act by which it is uttered — something like the *I declare* of kings or the *I sing* of very ancient poets. Having buried the Author, the modern scriptor can thus no longer believe, as according to the pathetic view of his predecessors, that this hand is too slow for his thought or passion and that consequently, making a law of necessity, he must emphasize this delay and indefinitely "polish" his form. For him, on the contrary, the hand, cut off from any voice, borne by a pure gesture of inscription (and not of expression), traces a field without origin — or which, at least, has no other origin than language itself, language which ceaselessly calls into question all origins.

We know now that a text is not a line of words releasing a single "theological" meaning (the "message" of the Author-God) but a multidimensional space in which a variety of writings, none of them original, blend and clash. The text is a tissue of quotations drawn from the innumerable centers of culture. Similar to Bouvard and Pécuchet,[4] those eternal

---

[3]Barthes refers to the speech-act theory of J. L. Austin, *How to Do Things with Words* (1962).

[4]Two copying clerks, soulmates who meet by chance, the protagonists of Gustave Flaubert's unfinished novel of that name published posthumously in 1881.

copyists, at once sublime and comic and whose profound ridiculousness indicates precisely the truth of writing, the writer can only imitate a gesture that is always anterior, never original. His only power is to mix writings, to counter the ones with the others, in such a way as never to rest on any one of them. Did he wish to *express himself*, he ought at least to know that the inner "thing" he thinks to "translate" is itself only a ready-formed dictionary, its words only explainable through other words, and so on indefinitely; something experienced in exemplary fashion by the young Thomas De Quincey, he who was so good at Greek that in order to translate absolutely modern ideas and images into that dead language, he had, so Baudelaire tells us (in *Paradis Artificiels*), "created for himself an unfailing dictionary, vastly more extensive and complex than those resulting from the ordinary patience of purely literary themes." Succeeding the Author, the scriptor no longer bears within him passions, humors, feelings, impressions, but rather this immense dictionary from which he draws a writing that can know no halt: life never does more than imitate the book, and the book itself is only a tissue of signs, an imitation that is lost, infinitely deferred.

Once the Author is removed, the claim to decipher a text becomes quite futile. To give a text an Author is to impose a limit on that text, to furnish it with a final signified, to close the writing. Such a conception suits criticism very well, the latter then allotting itself the important task of discovering the Author (or its hypostases: society, history, psyché, liberty) beneath the work: when the Author has been found, the text is "explained" — victory to the critic. Hence there is no surprise in the fact that, historically, the reign of the Author has also been that of the Critic, nor again in the fact that criticism (be it new) is today undermined along with the Author. In the multiplicity of writing, everything is to be *disentangled*, nothing *deciphered*; the structure can be followed, "run" (like the thread of a stocking) at every point and at every level, but there is nothing beneath: the space of writing is to be ranged over, not pierced; writing ceaselessly posits meaning ceaselessly to evaporate it, carrying out a systematic exemption of meaning. In precisely this way literature (it would be better from now on to say *writing*), by refusing to assign a "secret," an ultimate meaning, to the text (and to the world as text), liberates what may be called an antitheological activity, an activity that is truly revolutionary since to refuse to fix meaning is, in the end, to refuse God and his hypostases — reason, science, law.

Let us come back to the Balzac sentence. No one, no "person," says it: its source, its voice, is not the true place of the writing, which is reading. Another — very precise — example will help to make this clear: recent research (J.-P. Vernant[5]) has demonstrated the constitutively ambiguous nature of Greek tragedy, its texts being woven from words with double meanings that each character understands unilaterally (this perpetual misunderstanding is exactly the "tragic"); there is, however, someone who understands each word in its duplicity and who, in addition, hears the very deafness of the characters speaking in front of him — this someone being precisely the reader (or here, the listener). Thus is revealed the total existence of writing: a text is made of multiple writings, drawn from many cultures and entering into mutual relations to dialogue, parody, contestation, but there is one place where this multiplicity is focused and that place is the reader, not, as was hitherto said, the author. The reader is the space on which all the quotations that make up a writing are inscribed without any of them being lost; a text's unity lies not in its origin but in its destination. Yet this destination cannot any longer be personal: the reader is without history, biography, psychology; he is simply that *someone* who holds together in a single field all the traces by which the written text is constituted. Which is why it is derisory to condemn the new writing in the name of a humanism hypocritically turned champion of the reader's rights. Classic criticism has never paid any attention to the reader; for it, the writer is the only person in literature. We are now beginning to let ourselves be fooled no longer by the arrogant antiphrastical recriminations of good society in favor of the very thing it sets aside, ignores, smothers, or destroys; we know that to give writing its future, it is necessary to overthrow the myth: the birth of the reader must be at the cost of the death of the Author.

[5]Cf. Jean-Pierre Vernant (with Pierre Vidal-Naquet), *Mythe et tragédie en Grèce ancienne*, Paris 1972, esp. pp. 19–40, 99–131. [Barthes]

Michel Foucault

1926–1984

Michel Foucault, a major intellectual presence in France since the 1960s, was renowned for his writings, which attempted to erase the traditional boundaries between the disciplines of science, history, philosophy, and sociology. Born in Poitiers, the son of a doctor, Foucault was trained as a philosopher, but his earliest work, such as Madness and Civilization (1961), dealt with history — specifically, the history of attitudes toward mental illness and its treatment. Foucault taught at the University of Clermont-Ferrand between 1960 and 1968, spent two years at the University of Paris-Vincennes, and in 1970 was elevated to a professorship at the Collège de France — the highest position in the French academic system. He was also a visiting professor at a host of universities worldwide. In addition to Madness and Civilization, other works that have been translated into English include The Birth of the Clinic (1963), The Order of Things (1966), The Archaeology of Knowledge (1969), Discipline and Punish (1975), three volumes of The History of Sexuality (1976, 1985, 1986), and Power/Knowledge (1980). "What Is an Author?" originally appeared in the Bulletin de la Société Française de Philosophie in 1969.

What Is an Author?

The coming into being of the notion of "author" constitutes the privileged moment of *individualization* in the history of ideas, knowledge, literature, philosophy, and the sciences. Even today, when we reconstruct the history of a concept, literary genre, or school of philosophy, such categories seem relatively weak, secondary, and superimposed scansions in comparison with the solid and fundamental unit of the author and the work.

I shall not offer here a sociohistorical analysis of the author's persona. Certainly it would be worth examining how the author became individualized in a culture like ours, what status he has been given, at what moment studies of authenticity and attribution began, in what kind of system of valorization the author was involved, at what point we began to recount the lives of authors rather than of heroes, and how this fundamental category of "the-man-and-his-work criticism" began. For the moment, however, I want to deal solely with the relationship between text and author and with the manner in which the text points to this "figure" that, at least in appearance, is outside it and antecedes it.

Beckett nicely formulates the theme with which I would like to begin: "'What does it matter who is speaking,' someone said, 'what does it matter who is speaking.'" In this indifference appears one of the fundamental ethical principles of contemporary writing [*écriture*]. I say "ethical" because this indifference is not really a trait characterizing the manner in which one speaks and writes, but rather a kind of immanent rule, taken up over and over again, never fully applied, not designating writing as something completed, but dominating it as a practice. Since it is too familiar to require a lengthy analysis, this immanent rule can be adequately illustrated here by tracing two of its major themes.

First of all, we can say that today's writing has freed itself from the dimension of expression. Referring only to itself, but without being restricted to the confines of its interiority, writing is identified with its own unfolded exteriority. This means that it is an interplay of signs arranged less according to its signified content than according to the very nature of the signifier. Writing unfolds like a game

Translated by Josué Harari.

[*jeu*] that invariably goes beyond its own rules and transgresses its limits. In writing, the point is not to manifest or exalt the act of writing, nor is it to pin a subject within language; it is rather a question of creating a space into which the writing subject constantly disappears.

The second theme, writing's relationship with death, is even more familiar. This link subverts an old tradition exemplified by the Greek epic, which was intended to perpetuate the immortality of the hero: if he was willing to die young, it was so that his life, consecrated and magnified by death, might pass into immortality; the narrative then redeemed this accepted death. In another way, the motivation, as well as the theme and the pretext of Arabian narratives — such as *The Thousand and One Nights* — was also the eluding of death: one spoke, telling stories into the early morning, in order to forestall death, to postpone the day of reckoning that would silence the narrator. Scheherazade's narrative is an effort, renewed each night, to keep death outside the circle of life.

Our culture has metamorphosed this idea of narrative, or writing, as something designed to ward off death. Writing has become linked to sacrifice, even to the sacrifice of life: it is now a voluntary effacement which does not need to be represented in books, since it is brought about in the writer's very existence. The work, which once had the duty of providing immortality, now possesses the right to kill, to be its author's murderer, as in the cases of Flaubert, Proust, and Kafka. That is not all, however: this relationship between writing and death is also manifested in the effacement of the writing subject's individual characteristics. Using all the contrivances that he sets up between himself and what he writes, the writing subject cancels out the signs of his particular individuality. As a result, the mark of the writer is reduced to nothing more than the singularity of his absence; he must assume the role of the dead man in the game of writing.

None of this is recent; criticism and philosophy took note of the disappearance — or death — of the author some time ago. But the consequences of their discovery of it have not been sufficiently examined, nor has its import been accurately measured. A certain number of notions that are intended to replace the privileged position of the author actually seem to preserve that privilege and suppress the real meaning of his disappearance. I shall examine two of these notions, both of great importance today.

The first is the idea of the work. It is a very familiar thesis that the task of criticism is not to bring out the work's relationships with the author, not to reconstruct through the text a thought or experience, but rather, to analyze the work through its structure, its architecture, its intrinsic form, and the play of its internal relationships. At this point, however, a problem arises: "What is a work? What is this curious unity which we designate as a work? Of what elements is it composed? Is it not what an author has written?" Difficulties appear immediately. If an individual were not an author, could we say that what he wrote, said, left behind in his papers, or what has been collected of his remarks, could be called a "work"? When Sade was not considered an author, what was the status of his papers? Were they simply rolls of paper onto which he ceaselessly uncoiled his fantasies during his imprisonment?

Even when an individual has been accepted as an author, we must still ask whether everything that he wrote, said, or left behind is part of his work. The problem is both theoretical and technical. When undertaking the publication of Nietzsche's works, for example, where should one stop? Surely everything must be published, but what is "everything"? Everything that Nietzsche himself published, certainly. And what about the rough drafts for his works? Obviously. The plans for his aphorisms? Yes. The deleted passages and the notes at the bottom of the page? Yes. What if, within a workbook filled with aphorisms, one finds a reference, the notation of a meeting or of an address, or a laundry list: is it a work, or not? Why not? And so on, ad infinitum. How can one define a work amid the millions of traces left by someone after his death? A theory of the work does not exist, and the empirical task of those who naively undertake the editing of works often suffers in the absence of such a theory.

We could go even further: does *The Thousand and One Nights* constitute a work? What about Clement of Alexandria's *Miscellanies* or Diogenes Laertius' *Lives*? A multitude of questions arises with regard to this notion of the work.

Consequently, it is not enough to declare that we should do without the writer (the author) and study the work in itself. The word "work" and the unity that it designates are probably as problematic as the status of the author's individuality. Another notion which has hindered us from taking full measure of the author's disappearance, blurring and concealing the moment of this effacement and subtly preserving the author's existence, is the notion of writing [écriture]. When rigorously applied, this notion should allow us not only to circumvent references to the author, but also to situate his recent absence. The notion of writing, as currently employed, is concerned with neither the act of writing nor the indication — be it symptom or sign — of a meaning which someone might have wanted to express. We try, with great effort, to imagine the general condition of each text, the condition of both the space in which it is dispersed and the time in which it unfolds.

In current usage, however, the notion of writing seems to transpose the empirical characteristics of the author into a transcendental anonymity. We are content to efface the more visible marks of the author's empiricity by playing off, one against the other, two ways of characterizing writing, namely, the critical and the religious approaches. Giving writing a primal status seems to be a way of retranslating, in transcendental terms, both the theological affirmation of its sacred character and the critical affirmation of its creative character. To admit that writing is, because of the very history that it made possible, subject to the test of oblivion and repression, seems to represent, in transcendental terms, the religious principle of the hidden meaning (which requires interpretation) and the critical principle of implicit significations, silent determinations, and obscured contents (which gives rise to commentary). To imagine writing as absence seems to be a simple repetition, in transcendental terms, of both the religious principle of inalterable and yet never fulfilled tradition, and the aesthetic principle of the work's survival, its perpetuation beyond the author's death, and its enigmatic excess in relation to him.

This usage of the notion of writing runs the risk of maintaining the author's privileges under the protection of writing's a priori status: it keeps alive, in the grey light of neutralization, the interplay of those representations that formed a

particular image of the writer. The author's disappearance, which, since Mallarmé, has been a constantly recurring event, is subject to a series of transcendental barriers. There seems to be an important dividing line between those who believe that they can still locate today's discontinuities in the historico-transcendental tradition [ruptures] of the nineteenth century, and those who try to free themselves once and for all from that tradition.[1]

It is not enough, however, to repeat the empty affirmation that the author has disappeared. For the same reason, it is not enough to keep repeating (after Nietzsche) that God and man have died a common death. Instead, we must locate the space left empty by the author's disappearance, follow the distribution of gaps and breaches, and watch for the openings that this disappearance uncovers.

First, we need to clarify briefly the problems arising from the use of the author's name. What is an author's name? How does it function? Far from offering a solution, I shall only indicate some of the difficulties that it presents.

The author's name is a proper name, and therefore it raises the problems common to all proper names. (Here I refer to Searle's analyses, among others.[2]) Obviously, one cannot turn a proper name into a pure and simple reference. It has other than indicative functions: more than an indication, a gesture, a finger pointed at someone, it is the equivalent of a description. When one says "Aristotle," one employs a word that is the equivalent of one, or a series of, definite descriptions, such as "the author of the *Analytics*," "the founder of ontology," and so forth. One cannot stop there, however, because a proper name does not have just one signification. When we discover that Rimbaud did not write *La Chasse spirituelle*, we cannot pretend that the meaning of this proper name, or that of the author, has been altered. The proper name and the author's name are situated between the two poles of description and designation: they must have a certain link with what they

[1] For a discussion of the notions of discontinuity and historical tradition see Foucault's *Les Mots et les choses* (Paris: Gallimard, 1966), translated as *The Order of Things* (New York: Pantheon, 1971). [Tr.]

[2] John Searle, *Speech Acts: An Essay in the Philosophy of Language* (Cambridge: Cambridge University Press, 1969), pp. 162–74. [Tr.]

name, but one that is neither entirely in the mode of designation nor in that of description; it must be a *specific* link. However — and it is here that the particular difficulties of the author's name arise — the links between the proper name and the individual named and between the author's name and what it names are not isomorphic and do not function in the same way. There are several differences.

If, for example, Pierre Dupont does not have blue eyes, or was not born in Paris, or is not a doctor, the name Pierre Dupont will still always refer to the same person; such things do not modify the link of designation. The problems raised by the author's name are much more complex, however. If I discover that Shakespeare was not born in the house that we visit today, that is a modification which, obviously, will not alter the functioning of the author's name. But if we proved that Shakespeare did not write those sonnets which pass for his, that would constitute a significant change and affect the manner in which the author's name functions. If we proved that Shakespeare wrote Bacon's *Organon* by showing that the same author wrote both the works of Bacon and those of Shakespeare, that would be a third type of change which would entirely modify the functioning of the author's name. The author's name is not, therefore, just a proper name like the rest.

Many other facts point out the paradoxical singularity of the author's name. To say that Pierre Dupont does not exist is not at all the same as saying that Homer or Hermes Trismegistus did not exist. In the first case, it means that no one has the name Pierre Dupont; in the second, it means that several people were mixed together under one name, or that the true author had none of the traits traditionally ascribed to the personae of Homer or Hermes. To say that X's real name is actually Jacques Durand instead of Pierre Dupont is not the same as saying that Stendhal's name was Henri Beyle.[3] One could also question the meaning and functioning of propositions like "Bourbaki is so-and-so, so-and-so, etc."[4] and "Victor Eremita, Climacus, Anticlimacus, Frater Taciturnus, Constantine Constantius, all of these are Kierkegaard."

These differences may result from the fact that an author's name is not simply an element in a discourse (capable of being either subject or object, of being replaced by a pronoun, and the like); it performs a certain role with regard to narrative discourse, assuring a classificatory function. Such a name permits one to group together a certain number of texts, define them, differentiate them from and contrast them to others. In addition, it establishes a relationship among the texts. Hermes Trismegistus did not exist, nor did Hippocrates — in the sense that Balzac existed — but the fact that several texts have been placed under the same name indicates that there has been established among them a relationship of homogeneity, filiation,[5] authentification of some texts by the use of others, reciprocal explication, or concomitant utilization. The author's name serves to characterize a certain mode of being of discourse: the fact that the discourse has an author's name, that one can say "this was written by so-and-so" or "so-and-so is its author," shows that this discourse is not ordinary everyday speech that merely comes and goes, not something that is immediately consumable. On the contrary, it is a speech that must be received in a certain mode and that, in a given culture, must receive a certain status.

It would seem that the author's name, unlike other proper names, does not pass from the interior of a discourse to the real and exterior individual who produced it; instead, the name seems always to be present, marking off the edges of the text, revealing, or at least characterizing, its mode of being. The author's name manifests the appearance of a certain discursive set and indicates the status of this discourse within a society and a culture. It has no legal status, nor is it located in the fiction of the work; rather, it is located in the break that founds a certain discursive construct and its very particular mode of being. As a result, we could say that in a civilization like our own there are a certain number of discourses that are endowed with the "author-function," while others

---

[3]Marie-Henri Beyle wrote under the name of Stendhal.
[4]Bourbaki was the collective name of a group of French mathematicians.

[5]Descent, derivation.

Let us analyze this "author-function," as we have just described it. In our culture, how does one characterize a discourse containing the author-function? In what way is this discourse different from other discourses? If we limit our remarks to the author of a book or a text, we can isolate four different characteristics.

First of all, discourses are objects of appropriation. The form of ownership from which they spring is of a rather particular type; one that has been codified for many years. We should note that, historically, this type of ownership has always been subsequent to what one might call penal appropriation. Texts, books, and discourses really began to have authors (other than mythical, "sacralized" and "sacralizing" figures) to the extent that authors became subject to punishment, that is, to the extent that discourses could be transgressive. In our culture (and doubtless in many others), discourse was not originally a product, a thing, a kind of goods; it was essentially an act — an act placed in the bipolar field of the sacred and the profane, the licit and the illicit, the religious and the blasphemous. Historically, it was a gesture fraught with risks before becoming goods caught up in a circuit of ownership.

Once a system of ownership for texts came into being, once strict rules concerning author's rights, author-publisher relations, rights of reproduction, and related matters were enacted — at the end of the eighteenth and the beginning of the nineteenth century — the possibility of transgression attached to the act of writing took on, more and more, the form of an imperative peculiar to literature. It is as if the author, beginning with the moment at which he was placed in the system of property that characterizes our society, compensated for the status that he thus acquired by rediscovering the old bipolar field of discourse, systematically practicing transgression

and thereby restoring danger to a writing which was now guaranteed the benefits of ownership.

The author-function does not affect all discourses in a universal and constant way, however. This is its second characteristic. In our civilization, it has not always been the same types of texts which have required attribution to an author. There was a time when the texts that we today call "literary" (narratives, stories, epics, tragedies, comedies) were accepted, put into circulation, and valorized without any question about the identity of their author; their anonymity caused no difficulties since their ancientness, whether real or imagined, was regarded as a sufficient guarantee of their status. On the other hand, those texts that we would now call scientific — those dealing with cosmology and the heavens, medicine and illnesses, natural sciences and geography — were accepted in the Middle Ages, and accepted as "true," only when marked with the name of their author. "Hippocrates said," "Pliny recounts," were not really formulas of an argument based on authority; they were the markers inserted in discourses that were supposed to be received as statements of demonstrated truth.

A reversal occurred in the seventeenth or eighteenth century. Scientific discourses began to be received for themselves, in the anonymity of an established or always redemonstrable truth; their membership in a systematic ensemble, and not the reference to the individual who produced them, stood as their guarantee. The author-function faded away, and the inventor's name served only to christen a theorem, proposition, particular effect, property, body, group of elements, or pathological syndrome. By the same token, literary discourses came to be accepted only when endowed with the author-function. We now ask of each poetic or fictional text: from where does it come, who wrote it, when, under what circumstances, or beginning with what design? The meaning ascribed to it and the status or value accorded it depend upon the manner in which we answer these questions. And if a text should be discovered in a state of anonymity — whether as a consequence of an accident or the author's explicit wish — the game becomes one of redis-covering the author. Since literary anonymity is not tolerable, we can accept it only in the guise of an enigma. As a result, the author-function today plays an important role in our view of literary works. (These are obviously generalizations that would have to be refined insofar as recent critical practice is concerned.)

The third characteristic of this author-function is that it does not develop spontaneously as the attribution of a discourse to an individual. It is, rather, the result of a complex operation which constructs a certain rational being that we call "author." Critics doubtless try to give this intelligible being a realistic status, by discerning, in the individual, a "deep" motive, a "creative" power, or a "design," the milieu in which writing originates. Nevertheless, these aspects of an individual which we designate as making him an author are only a projection, in more or less psychologizing terms, of the operations that we force texts to undergo, the connections that we make, the traits that we establish as pertinent, the continuities that we recognize, or the exclusions that we practice. All these operations vary according to periods and types of discourse. We do not construct a "philosophical author" as we do a "poet," just as, in the eighteenth century, one did not construct a novelist as we do today. Still, we can find through the ages certain constants in the rules of author-construction.

It seems, for example, that the manner in which literary criticism once defined the author — or rather constructed the figure of the author beginning with existing texts and discourses — is directly derived from the manner in which Christian tradition authenticated (or rejected) the texts at its disposal. In order to "rediscover" an author in a work, modern criticism uses methods similar to those that Christian exegesis employed when trying to prove the value of a text by its author's saintliness. In *De viris illustribus,* Saint Jerome explains that homonymy is not sufficient to identify legitimately authors of more than one work: different individuals could have had the same name, or one man could have, illegitimately, borrowed another's patronymic. The name as an individual trademark is not enough when one works within a textual tradition.

How then can one attribute several discourses to one and the same author? How can one use the author-function to determine if one is dealing with one or several individuals? Saint Jerome proposes four criteria: (1) if among several books attributed to an author one is inferior to the others, it must be withdrawn from the list of the author's works (the author is therefore defined as a constant level of value); (2) the same should be done if certain texts contradict the doctrine expounded in the author's other works (the author is thus defined as a field of conceptual or theoretical coherence); (3) one must also exclude works that are written in a different style, containing words and expressions not ordinarily found in the writer's production (the author is here conceived as a stylistic unity); (4) finally, passages quoting statements that were made, or mentioning events that occurred after the author's death must be regarded as interpolated texts (the author is here seen as a historical figure at the crossroads of a certain number of events).

Modern literary criticism, even when — as is now customary — it is not concerned with questions of authentification, still defines the author the same way: the author provides the basis for explaining not only the presence of certain events in a work, but also their transformations, distortions, and diverse modifications (through his biography, the determination of his individual perspective, the analysis of his social position, and the revelation of his basic design). The author is also the principle of a certain unity of writing — all differences having to be resolved, at least in part, by the principles of evolution, maturation, or influence. The author also serves to neutralize the contradictions that may emerge in a series of texts: there must be — at a certain level of his thought or desire, of his consciousness or unconscious — a point where contradictions are resolved, where incompatible elements are at last tied together or organized around a fundamental or originating contradiction. Finally, the author is a particular source of expression that, in more or less completed forms, is manifested equally well, and with similar validity, in works, sketches, letters, fragments, and so on. Clearly, Saint Jerome's four criteria of authenticity (criteria which seem totally insufficient for today's exegetes) do define the four modalities according to which modern criticism brings the author-function into play.

But the author-function is not a pure and simple reconstruction made secondhand from a text given as passive material. The text always contains a certain number of signs referring to the author. These signs, well known to grammarians, are personal pronouns, adverbs of time and place, and verb conjugation. Such elements do not play the same role in discourses provided with the author-function as in those lacking it. In the latter, such "shifters" refer to the real speaker and to the spatio-temporal coordinates of his discourse (although certain modifications can occur, as in the operation of relating discourses in the first person). In the former, however, their role is more complex and variable. Everyone knows that, in a novel narrated in the first person, neither the first person pronoun, nor the present indicative refer exactly either to the writer or to the moment in which he writes, but rather to an alter ego whose distance from the author varies, often changing in the course of the work. It would be just as wrong to equate the author with the real writer as to equate him with the fictitious speaker; the author-function is carried out and operates in the scission itself, in this division and this distance.

One might object that this is a characteristic peculiar to novelistic or poetic discourse, a "game" in which only "quasi-discourses" participate. In fact, however, all discourses endowed with the author-function do possess this plurality of self. The self that speaks in the preface to a treatise on mathematics — and that indicates the circumstances of the treatise's composition — is identical neither in its position nor in its functioning to the self that speaks in the course of a demonstration, and that appears in the form of "I conclude" or "I suppose." In the first case, the "I" refers to an individual without an equivalent who, in a determined place and time, completed a certain task; in the second, the "I" indicates an instance and a level of demonstration which any individual could perform provided that he accept the same system of symbols, play of axioms, and set of previous demonstrations. We could also, in the same treatise, locate a third self, one that speaks to tell the work's meaning, the obstacles encountered, the results obtained, and the remaining problems; this self is situated in the field of already existing or yet-to-appear mathematical

discourses. The author-function is not assumed by the first of these selves at the expense of the other two, which would then be nothing more than a fictitious splitting in two of the first one. On the contrary, in these discourses the author-function operates so as to effect the dispersion of these three simultaneous selves.

No doubt analysis could discover still more characteristic traits of the author-function. I will limit myself to these four, however, because they seem both the most visible and the most important. They can be summarized as follows: (1) the author-function is linked to the juridical and institutional system that encompasses, determines, and articulates the universe of discourses; (2) it does not affect all discourses in the same way at all times and in all types of civilization; (3) it is not defined by the spontaneous attribution of a discourse to its producer, but rather by a series of specific and complex operations; (4) it does not refer purely and simply to a real individual, since it can give rise simultaneously to several selves, to several subjects — positions that can be occupied by different classes of individuals.

Up to this point I have unjustifiably limited my subject. Certainly the author-function in painting, music, and other arts should have been discussed, but even supposing that we remain within the world of discourse, as I want to do, I seem to have given the term "author" much too narrow a meaning. I have discussed the author only in the limited sense of a person to whom the production of a text, a book, or a work can be legitimately attributed. It is easy to see that in the sphere of discourse one can be the author of much more than a book — one can be the author of a theory, tradition, or discipline in which other books and authors will in their turn find a place. These authors are in a position which we shall call "transdiscursive." This is a recurring phenomenon — certainly as old as our civilization. Homer, Aristotle, and the Church Fathers, as well as the first mathematicians and the originators of the Hippocratic tradition, all played this role. Furthermore, in the course of the nineteenth century, there appeared in Europe another, more uncommon, kind of author, whom one should confuse with neither the "great" literary authors, nor the authors of religious texts, nor the founders of science. In a somewhat arbitrary way we shall call those who belong in this last group "founders of discursivity." They are unique in that they are not just the authors of their own works. They have produced something else: the possibilities and the rules for the formation of other texts. In this sense, they are very different, for example, from a novelist, who is, in fact, nothing more than the author of his own text. Freud is not just the author of *The Interpretation of Dreams* or *Jokes and Their Relation to the Unconscious;* Marx is not just the author of the *Communist Manifesto* or *Capital:* they both have established an endless possibility of discourse.

Obviously, it is easy to object. One might say that it is not true that the author of a novel is only the author of his own text; in a sense, he also, provided that he acquires some "importance," governs and commands more than that. To take a very simple example, one could say that Ann Radcliffe not only wrote *The Castles of Athlin and Dunbayne* and several other novels, but also made possible the appearance of the Gothic horror novel at the beginning of the nineteenth century; in that respect, her author-function exceeds her own work. But I think there is an answer to this objection. These founders of discursivity (I use Marx and Freud as examples, because I believe them to be both the first and the most important cases) make possible something altogether different from what a novelist makes possible. Ann Radcliffe's texts opened the way for a certain number of resemblances and analogies which have their model or principle in her work. The latter contains characteristic signs, figures, relationships, and structures which could be reused by others. In other words, to say that Ann Radcliffe founded the Gothic horror novel means that in the nineteenth-century gothic novel one will find, as in Ann Radcliffe's works, the theme of the heroine caught in the trap of her own innocence, the hidden castle, the character of the black, cursed hero devoted to making the world expiate the evil done to him, and all the rest of it.

On the other hand, when I speak of Marx or Freud as founders of discursivity, I mean that they made possible not only a certain number of analo-gies, but also (and equally important) a certain number of differences. They have created a possibility for something other than their discourse, yet something belonging to what they founded. To say that Freud founded psychoanalysis does not (simply) mean that we find the concept of the libido or the technique of dream analysis in the works of Karl Abraham or Melanie Klein; it means that Freud made possible a certain number of divergences — with respect to his own texts, concepts, and hypotheses — that all arise from the psychoanalytical discourse itself.

This would seem to present a new difficulty, however: is the above not true, after all, of any founder of a science, or of any author who has introduced some important transformation into a science? After all, Galileo made possible not only those discourses that repeated the laws that he had formulated, but also statements very different from what he himself had said. If Cuvier is the founder of biology or Saussure the founder of linguistics, it is not because they were imitated, nor because people have since taken up again the concept of organism or sign; it is because Cuvier made possible, to a certain extent, a theory of evolution diametrically opposed to his own fixism; it is because Saussure made possible a generative grammar radically different from his structural analyses. Superficially, then, the initiation of discursive practices appears similar to the founding of any scientific endeavor.

Still, there is a difference, and a notable one. In the case of a science, the act that founds it is on an equal footing with its future transformations; this act becomes in some respects part of the set of modifications that it makes possible. Of course, this belonging can take several forms. In the future development of a science, the founding act may appear as little more than a particular instance of a more general phenomenon which unveils itself in the process. It can also turn out to be marred by intuition and empirical bias; one must then reformulate it, making it the object of a certain number of supplementary theoretical operations which establish it more rigorously, etc. Finally, it can seem to be a hasty generalization which must be limited, and whose restricted domain of validity must be retraced. In other words, the founding act of a science can always be reintroduced within the machinery of those transformations that derive from it.

In contrast, the initiation of a discursive practice is heterogeneous to its subsequent transformations. To expand a type of discursivity, such as psychoanalysis as founded by Freud, is not to give it a formal generality that it would not have permitted at the outset, but rather to open it up to a certain number of possible applications. To limit psychoanalysis as a type of discursivity is, in reality, to try to isolate in the founding act an eventually restricted number of propositions or statements to which, alone, one grants a founding value, and in relation to which certain concepts or theories accepted by Freud might be considered as derived, secondary, and accessory. In addition, one does not declare certain propositions in the work of these founders to be false: instead, when trying to seize the act of founding, one sets aside those statements that are not pertinent, either because they are deemed inessential, or because they are considered "prehistoric" and derived from another type of discursivity. In other words, unlike the founding of a science, the initiation of a discursive practice does not participate in its later transformations.

As a result, one defines a proposition's theoretical validity in relation to the work of the founders — while, in the case of Galileo and Newton, it is in relation to what physics or cosmology is (in its intrinsic structure and "normativity") that one affirms the validity of any proposition that those men may have put forth. To phrase it very schematically: the work of initiators of discursivity is not situated in the space that science defines; rather, it is the science or the discursivity which refers back to their work as primary coordinates. In this way we can understand the inevitable necessity, within these fields of discursivity, for a "return to the origin." This return, which is part of the discursive field itself, never stops modifying it. The return is not a historical supplement which would be added to the discursivity, or merely an ornament; on the contrary, it constitutes an effective and necessary task of transforming the discursive practice itself. Re-examination of Galileo's text may well change our knowledge of the history of mechanics, but it will never be able

to change mechanics itself. On the other hand, re-examining Freud's texts modifies psychoanalysis itself just as a re-examination of Marx's would modify Marxism.[6]

What I have just outlined regarding the initiation of discursive practices is, of course, very schematic: this is true, in particular, of the opposition that I have tried to draw between discursive initiation and scientific founding. It is not always easy to distinguish between the two; moreover, nothing proves that they are two mutually exclusive procedures. I have attempted the distinction for only one reason: to show that the author-function, which is complex enough when one tries to situate it at the level of a book or a series of texts that carry a given signature, involves still more determining factors when one tries to analyze it in larger units, such as groups of works or entire disciplines.

To conclude, I would like to review the reasons why I attach a certain importance to what I have said.

First, there are theoretical reasons. On the one hand, an analysis in the direction that I have outlined might provide for an approach to a typology of discourse. It seems to me, at least at first glance, that such a typology cannot be constructed solely from the grammatical features, formal structures, and objects of discourse: more likely there exist properties or relationships peculiar to discourse (not reducible to the rules of grammar and logic), and one must use these to distinguish the major categories of discourse. The

6 To define these returns more clearly, one must also emphasize that they tend to reinforce the enigmatic link between an author and his works. A text has an inaugurative value precisely because it is the work of a particular author, and our returns are conditioned by this knowledge. As in the case of Galileo, there is no possibility that the rediscovery of an unknown text by Newton or Cantor will modify classical cosmology or set theory as we know them (at best, such an exhumation might modify our historical knowledge of their genesis). On the other hand, the discovery of a text like Freud's "Project for a Scientific Psychology" — insofar as it is a text by Freud — always threatens to modify not the historical knowledge of psychoanalysis, but its theoretical field, even if only by shifting the accentuation or the center of gravity. Through such returns, which are part of their make-up, these discursive practices maintain a relationship with regard to their "fundamental" and indirect author unlike that which an ordinary text entertains with its immediate author. [Tr.]

relationship (or nonrelationship) with an author, and the different forms this relationship takes, constitutes — in a quite visible manner — one of these discursive properties.

On the other hand, I believe that one could find here an introduction to the historical analysis of discourse. Perhaps it is time to study discourses not only in terms of their expressive value or formal transformations, but according to their modes of existence. The modes of circulation, valorization, attribution, and appropriation of discourses vary with each culture and are modified within each. The manner in which they are articulated according to social relationships can be more readily understood. I believe, in the activity of the author-function and in its modifications, than in the themes or concepts that discourses set in motion.

It would seem that one could also, beginning with analyses of this type, re-examine the privileges of the subject. I realize that in undertaking the internal and architectonic analysis of a work (be it a literary text, philosophical system, or scientific work), in setting aside biographical and psychological references, one has already called back into question the absolute character and founding role of the subject. Still, perhaps one must return to this question, not in order to re-establish the theme of an originating subject, but to grasp the subject's points of insertion, modes of functioning, and system of dependencies. Doing so means overturning the traditional problem, no longer raising the questions "How can a free subject penetrate the substance of things and give it meaning? How can it activate the rules of a language from within and thus give rise to the designs which are properly its own?" Instead, these questions will be raised: "How, under what conditions, and in what forms can something like a subject appear in the order of discourse? What place can it occupy in each type of discourse, what functions can it assume, and by obeying what rules?" In short, it is a matter of depriving the subject (or its substitute) of its role as originator, and of analyzing the subject as a variable and complex function of discourse.

Second, there are reasons dealing with the "ideological" status of the author. The question then becomes: How can one reduce the great peril, the great danger with which fiction threatens our world? The answer is: One can reduce it with the author. The author allows a limitation of the cancerous and dangerous proliferation of significations within a world where one is thrifty not only with one's resources and riches, but also with one's discourses and their significations. The author is the principle of thrift in the proliferation of meaning. As a result, we must entirely reverse the traditional idea of the author. We are accustomed, as we have seen earlier, to saying that the author is the genial creator of a work in which he deposits, with infinite wealth and generosity, an inexhaustible world of significations. We are used to thinking that the author is so different from all other men, and so transcendent with regard to all languages that, as soon as he speaks, meaning begins to proliferate, to proliferate indefinitely.

The truth is quite the contrary: the author is not an indefinite source of significations which fill a work; the author does not precede the works, he is a certain functional principle by which, in our culture, one limits, excludes, and chooses; in short, by which one impedes the free circulation, the free manipulation, the free composition, decomposition, and recomposition of fiction. In fact, if we are accustomed to presenting the author as a genius, as a perpetual surging of invention, it is because, in reality, we make him function in exactly the opposite fashion. One can say that the author is an ideological product, since we represent him as the opposite of his historically real function. (When a historically given function is represented in a figure that inverts it, one has an ideological production.) The author is therefore the ideological figure by which one marks the manner in which we fear the proliferation of meaning.

In saying this, I seem to call for a form of culture in which fiction would not be limited by the figure of the author. It would be pure romanticism, however, to imagine a culture in which the fictive would operate in an absolutely free state, in which fiction would be put at the disposal of everyone and would develop without passing through something like a necessary or constraining figure. Although, since the eighteenth century, the author has played the role of the regulator of the fictive, a role quite character-

istic of our era of industrial and bourgeois society, of individualism and private property, still,
given the historical modifications that are taking
place, it does not seem necessary that the author-
function remain constant in form, complexity,
and even in existence. I think that, as our society
changes, at the very moment when it is in the
process of changing, the author-function will
disappear, and in such a manner that fiction
and its polysemic texts will once again function
according to another mode, but still with a system
of constraint — one which will no longer be the
author, but which will have to be determined or,
perhaps, experienced.

All discourses, whatever their status, form,
value, and whatever the treatment to which they
will be subjected, would then develop in the
anonymity of a murmur. We would no longer
hear the questions that have been rehashed for
so long: ''Who really spoke? Is it really he and
not someone else? With what authenticity or
originality? And what part of his deepest self
did he express in his discourse?'' Instead, there
would be other questions, like these: ''What are
the modes of existence of this discourse? Where
has it been used, how can it circulate, and who
can appropriate it for himself? What are the places
in it where there is room for possible subjects?
Who can assume these various subject-functions?''
And behind all these questions, we would hear
hardly anything but the stirring of an indifference:
''What difference does it make who is speaking?''

Jacques Derrida

1930–2004

The prime mover of poststructuralism, Jacques Derrida was born in Algiers and educated in France. Trained as a philosopher — early in his career he published a study of Edmund Husserl, the founder of phenomenology — Derrida taught history of philosophy at the École des hautes études en sciences sociales and served as visiting professor at a dozen leading American universities. He died of cancer of the pancreas on October 8, 2004. His passing was marked both by glowing tributes (such as that in Le Monde*) and by unusually spiteful obituaries in liberal newspapers such as the* New York Times *and the London* Independent. *Derrida was very much the "bad boy" of the philosophic world, and his fame — or notoriety — in America can be traced to a talk he delivered at a structuralist conference at Johns Hopkins University in 1966. "Structure, Sign, and Play in the Discourse of the Human Sciences" confounded the structuralist enterprise and many of its adherents and precipitated the rise of post-structuralist theories. Derrida's publications were steadily translated into English; among them are* Speech and Phenomena *(1967),* Of Grammatology *(1967),* Writing and Difference *(1967),* Margins of Philosophy *(1972),* Positions *(1972),* Glas *(1974),* The Post Card *(1980),* Limited, Inc. *(1988),* Acts of Literature *(1991),* Cinders *(1991),* Memoirs of the Blind *(1993),* Aporias *(1993),* Specters of Marx *(1994),* On the Name *(1995),* The Gift of Death *(1995), and* Archive Fever: A Freudian Impression *(1996). This translation of "Structure, Sign, and Play in the Discourse of the Human Sciences" is from* The Structuralist Controversy *(1970), translated by Richard Macksey and Eugenio Donato; another version appears in* Writing and Difference *(1967; translated 1978 by Alan Bass).*

Structure, Sign, and Play in the Discourse of the Human Sciences

Perhaps something has occurred in the history of the concept of structure that could be called an "event," if this loaded word did not entail a meaning which it is precisely the function of structural — or structuralist — thought to reduce or to suspect. But let me use the term "event" anyway, employing it with caution and as if in quotation marks. In this sense, this event will have the exterior form of a *rupture* and a *redoubling.*

It would be easy enough to show that the concept of structure and even the word "structure" itself are as old as the *epistemé*[1] — that is to say, as old as western science and western philosophy — and that their roots thrust deep into the soil of ordinary language, into whose deepest recesses the *epistemé* plunges to gather them together once more, making them part of itself in a metaphorical displacement. Nevertheless, up until the event which I wish to mark out and define, structure — or rather the structurality of structure — although it has always been involved, has always been neutralized or reduced, and this by a process of giving it a center or referring it to a point of presence, a fixed origin. The function of this center was not only to orient, balance, and organize the structure — one cannot in fact conceive of an unorganized structure — but above all to make sure that the organizing principle of the structure would limit what we might call the

Translated by Richard Macksey and Eugenio Donato.
[1]System of thought and knowledge of a culture.

freeplay of the structure. No doubt that by orienting and organizing the coherence of the system, the center of a structure permits the freeplay of its elements inside the total form. And even today the notion of a structure lacking any center represents the unthinkable itself.

Nevertheless, the center also closes off the freeplay it opens up and makes possible. *Qua* center, it is the point at which the substitution of contents, elements, or terms is no longer possible. At the center, the permutation or the transformation of elements (which may of course be structures enclosed within a structure) is forbidden. At least this permutation has always remained *interdicted*[2] (I use this word deliberately). Thus it has always been thought that the center, which is by definition unique, constituted that very thing within a structure which governs the structure, while escaping structurality. This is why classical thought concerning structure could say that the center is, paradoxically, *within* the structure and *outside* it. The center is at the center of the totality, and yet, since the center does not belong to the totality (is not part of the totality), the totality *has its center elsewhere*. The center is not the center. The concept of centered structure — although it represents coherence itself, the condition of the *episteme* as philosophy or science — is contradictorily coherent. And, as always, coherence in contradiction expresses the force of a desire. The concept of centered structure is in fact the concept of a freeplay based on a fundamental ground, a freeplay which is constituted upon a fundamental immobility and a reassuring certitude, which is itself beyond the reach of the freeplay. With this certitude anxiety can be mastered, for anxiety is invariably the result of a certain mode of being implicated in the game, of being caught by the game, of being as it were from the very beginning at stake in the game.[3] From the basis of what we therefore call the center (and which, because it can be either inside or outside, is as readily called the origin as the

end, as readily *archè* as *telos*),[4] the repetitions, the substitutions, the transformations, and the permutations are always *taken* from a history of meaning [*sens*] — that is, a history, period — whose origin may always be revealed or whose end may always be anticipated in the form of presence. This is why one could perhaps say that the movement of any archeology, like that of any eschatology,[5] is an accomplice of this reduction of the structurality of structure and always attempts to conceive of structure from the basis of a full presence which is out of play.

If this is so, the whole history of the concept of structure, before the rupture I spoke of, must be thought of as a series of substitutions of center for center, as a linked chain of determinations of the center. Successively, and in a regulated fashion, the center receives different forms or names. The history of metaphysics, like the history of the West, is the history of these metaphors and metonymies. Its matrix — if you will pardon me for demonstrating so little and for being so elliptical in order to bring me more quickly to my principal theme — is the determination of being as *presence* in all the senses of this word. It would be possible to show that all the names related to fundamentals, to principles, or to the center have always designated the constant of a presence — *eidos, archè, telos, energeia, ousia* (essence, existence, substance, subject) *alètheia*,[6] transcendentality, consciousness, or conscience, God, man, and so forth.

The event I called a rupture, the disruption I alluded to at the beginning of this paper, would presumably have come about when the structurality of structure had to begin to be thought, that is to say, repeated, and this is why I said that this disruption was repetition in all of the senses of this word. From then on it became necessary to think the law which governed, as it were, the desire for the center in the constitution of structure and the process of signification prescribing its displacements and its substitutions for this law of the

---

2. *Interdite*: "forbidden," "disconcerted," "confounded," "speechless." [Tr.]

3. "... qui naît toujours d'une certaine manière d'être impliqué dans le jeu, d'être pris au jeu, d'être comme être d'entrée de jeu dans le jeu." [Tr.]

4. Beginning as end. *Telos* means "end" in the sense of "purpose."

5. Study of last things.

6. The six preceding Greek terms mean, respectively: form, origin, purpose, energy, being, and truth.

central presence — but a central presence which was never itself, which has always already been transported outside itself in its surrogate. The surrogate does not substitute itself for anything which has somehow pre-existed it. From then on it was probably necessary to begin to think that there was no center, that the center could not be thought in the form of a being-present, that the center had no natural locus, that it was not a fixed locus but a function, a sort of non-locus in which an infinite number of sign-substitutions came into play. This moment was that in which language invaded the universal problematic; that in which, in the absence of a center or origin, everything became discourse — provided we can agree on this word — that is to say, when everything became a system where the central signified, the original or transcendental signified, is never absolutely present outside a system of differences. The absence of the transcendental signified extends the domain and the interplay of signification *ad infinitum.*

Where and how does this decentering, this notion of the structurality of structure, occur? It would be somewhat naïve to refer to an event, a doctrine, or an author in order to designate this occurrence. It is no doubt part of the totality of an era, our own, but still it has already begun to proclaim itself and begun to *work.* Nevertheless, if I wished to give some sort of indication by choosing one or two "names," and by recalling those authors in whose discourses this occurrence has most nearly maintained its most radical formulation, I would probably cite the Nietzschean critique of metaphysics, the critique of the concepts of being and truth, for which were substituted the concepts of play, interpretation, and sign (sign without truth present); the Freudian critique of self-presence, that is, the critique of consciousness, of the subject, of self-identity and of self-proximity or self-possession; and, more radically, the Heideggerean destruction of metaphysics, of onto-theology, of the determination of being as presence. But all these destructive discourses and all their analogues are trapped in a sort of circle. This circle is unique. It describes the form of the relationship between the history of metaphysics and the destruction of the history of metaphysics. *There is no sense* in doing without the concepts of

metaphysics in order to attack metaphysics. We have no language — no syntax and no lexicon — which is alien to this history; we cannot utter a single destructive proposition which has not already slipped into the form, the logic, and the implicit postulations of precisely what it seeks to contest. To pick out one example from many: the metaphysics of presence is attacked with the help of the concept of the *sign.* But from the moment anyone wishes this to show, as I suggested a moment ago, that there is no transcendental or privileged signified and that the domain or the interplay of signification has, henceforth, no limit, he ought to extend his refusal to the concept and to the word sign itself — which is precisely what cannot be done. For the signification "sign" has always been comprehended and determined, in its sense, as sign-of, signifier referring to a signified, signifier different from its signified. If one erases the radical difference between signifier and signified, it is the word signifier itself which ought to be abandoned as a metaphysical concept. When Lévi-Strauss says in the preface to *The Raw and the Cooked*[7] that he has "sought to transcend the opposition between the sensible and the intelligible by placing [himself] from the very beginning at the level of signs," the necessity, the force, and the legitimacy of his act cannot make us forget that the concept of the sign cannot in itself surpass or bypass this opposition between the sensible and the intelligible. The concept of the sign is determined by this opposition: through and throughout the totality of its history and by its system. But we cannot do without the concept of the sign, we cannot give up this metaphysical complicity without also giving up the critique we are directing against this complicity, without the risk of erasing difference [altogether] in the self-identity of a signified reducing into itself its signifier, or, what amounts to the same thing, simply expelling it outside itself. For there are two heterogeneous ways of erasing the difference between the signifier and the signified: one, the classic way, consists in reducing or deriving the signifier, that is to say, ultimately in *submitting*

[7]*Le cru et le cuit* (Paris: Plon, 1964). [Tr.]

What is the relevance of this formal schema when we turn to what are called the "human sciences"? One of them perhaps occupies a privileged place — ethnology.[8] One can in fact assume that ethnology could have been born as a science only at the moment when a de-centering had come about: at the moment when European culture — and, in consequence, the history of metaphysics and of its concepts — had been *dislocated*, driven from its locus, and forced to stop considering itself as the culture of reference. This moment is not first and foremost a moment of philosophical or scientific discourse, it is also a moment which is political, economic, technical.

the sign to thought; the other, the one we are using here against the first one, consists in putting into question the system in which the preceding reduc-tion functioned: first and foremost, the opposition between the sensible and the intelligible. The *paradox* is that the metaphysical reduction of the sign needed the opposition it was reducing. The opposition is part of the system, along with the reduction. And what I am saying here about the sign can be extended to all the concepts and all the sentences of metaphysics, in particular to the discourse on "structure." But there are many ways of being caught in this circle. They are all more or less naïve, more or less empirical, more or less systematic, more or less close to the formulation or even to the formalization of this circle. It is these differences which explain the multiplicity of destructive discourses and the disagreement between those who make them. It was within concepts inherited from metaphysics that Nietzsche, Freud, and Heidegger worked, for example. Since these concepts are not elements or atoms and since they are taken from a syntax and a system, every particular borrowing drags along with it the whole of metaphysics. This is what allows these destroyers to destroy each other reciprocally — for example, Heidegger consider-ing Nietzsche, with as much lucidity and rigor as bad faith and misconstruction, as the last meta-physician, the last "Platonist." One could do the same for Heidegger himself, for Freud, or for a number of others. And today no exercise is more widespread.

and so forth. One can say in total assurance that there is nothing fortuitous about the fact that the critique of ethnocentrism — the very condition of ethnology — should be systematically and his-torically contemporaneous with the destruction of the history of metaphysics. Both belong to a single and same era.

Ethnology — like any science — comes about within the element of discourse. And it is primar-ily a European science employing traditional con-cepts, however much it may struggle against them. Consequently, whether he wants to or not — and this does not depend on a decision on his part — the ethnologist accepts into his discourse the premises of ethnocentrism at the very moment when he is employed in denouncing them. This necessity is irreducible; it is not a historical con-tingency. We ought to consider very carefully all its implications. But if nobody can escape this necessity, and if no one is therefore responsible for giving in to it, however little, this does not mean that all the ways of giving in to it are of an equal pertinence. The quality and the fecundity of a discourse are perhaps measured by the critical rigor with which this relationship to the history of metaphysics and to inherited concepts is thought. Here it is a question of a critical relationship to the language of the human sciences and a ques-tion of a critical responsibility of the discourse. It is a question of putting expressly and system-atically the problem of the status of a discourse which borrows from a heritage the resources necessary for the deconstruction of that heritage itself. A problem of *economy* and *strategy*.

If I now go on to employ an examination of the texts of Lévi-Strauss as an example, it is not only because of the privilege accorded to ethnol-ogy among the human sciences, nor yet because the thought of Lévi-Strauss weighs heavily on the contemporary theoretical situation. It is above all because a certain choice has made itself evident in the work of Lévi-Strauss and because a certain doctrine has been elaborated there, and precisely in a *more or less explicit manner*, in relation to this critique of language and to this critical lan-guage in the human sciences.

In order to follow this movement in the text of Lévi-Strauss, let me choose as one guiding thread among others the opposition between

[8] Cultural anthropology.

nature and culture. In spite of all its rejuvenations and its disguises, this opposition is congenital to philosophy. It is even older than Plato. It is at least as old as the Sophists. Since the statement of the opposition — *physis/nomos, physis/techne*[9] — it has been passed on to us by a whole historical chain which opposes "nature" to the law, to education, to art, to technics — and also to liberty, to the arbitrary, to history, to society, to the mind, and so on. From the beginnings of his quest and from his first book, *The Elementary Structures of Kinship,*[10] Lévi-Strauss has felt at one and the same time the necessity of utilizing this opposition and the impossibility of *making* it acceptable. In the *Elementary Structures,* he begins from this axiom or definition: that belongs to nature which is *universal* and spontaneous, not depending on any particular culture or on any determinate norm. That belongs to culture, on the other hand, which depends on a system of *norms* regulating society and is therefore capable of *varying* from one social structure to another. These two definitions are of the traditional type. But, in the very first pages of the *Elementary Structures,* Lévi-Strauss, who has begun to give these concepts an acceptable standing, encounters what he calls a *scandal,* that is to say, something which no longer tolerates the nature/culture opposition he has accepted and which seems to require *at one and the same time* the predicates of nature and those of culture. This scandal is the *incest-prohibition.* The incest-prohibition is universal; in this sense one could call it natural. But it is also a prohibition, a system of norms and interdicts; in this sense one could call it cultural.

> Let us assume therefore that everything universal in man derives from the order of nature and is characterized by spontaneity, that everything which is subject to a norm belongs to culture and presents the attributes of the relative and the particular. We then find ourselves confronted by a fact, or rather an ensemble of facts, which, in the light of the preceding definitions, is not far from appearing as a scandal: the prohibition of incest presents without the least equivocation, and indissolubly linked together,

the two characteristics in which we recognized the contradictory attributes of two exclusive orders. The prohibition of incest constitutes a rule, but a rule, alone of all the social rules, which possesses at the same time a universal character (p. 9).

Obviously there is no scandal except in the *interior* of a system of concepts sanctioning the difference between nature and culture. In beginning his work with the *factum*[11] of the incest-prohibition, Lévi-Strauss thus puts himself in a position entailing that this difference, which has always been assumed to be self-evident, becomes obliterated or disputed. For, from the moment that the incest-prohibition can no longer be conceived within the nature/culture opposition, it can no longer be said that it is a scandalous fact, a nucleus of opacity within a network of transparent significations. The incest-prohibition is no longer a scandal one meets with or comes up against in the domain of traditional concepts; it is something which escapes these concepts and certainly precedes them — probably as the condition of their possibility. It could perhaps be said that the whole of philosophical conceptualization, systematically relating itself to the nature/culture opposition, is designed to leave in the domain of the unthinkable the very thing that makes this conceptualization possible: the origin of the prohibition of incest.

I have dealt too cursorily with this example, only one among so many others, but the example nevertheless reveals that language bears within itself the necessity of its own critique. This critique may be undertaken along two tracks, in two "manners." Once the limit of nature/culture opposition makes itself felt, one might want to question systematically and rigorously the history of these concepts. This is a first action. Such a systematic and historic questioning would be neither a philological nor a philosophical action in the classic sense of these words. Concerning oneself with the founding concepts of the whole history of philosophy, de-constituting them, is not to undertake the task of the philologist or of the classic historian of philosophy. In spite of appearances, it is probably the most daring way of making the beginnings of a step outside of philosophy. The step "outside

[9]Nature vs. culture; nature vs. art.
[10]*Les structures élémentaires de la parenté* (Paris: Presses Universitaires de France, 1949). [Tr.]

[11]Given fact.

philosophy" is much more difficult to conceive than is generally imagined by those who think they made it long ago with cavalier ease, and who are in general swallowed up in metaphysics by the whole body of the discourse that they claim to have disengaged from it.

In order to avoid the possibly sterilizing effect of the first way, the other choice — which I feel corresponds more nearly to the way chosen by Lévi-Strauss — consists in conserving in the field of empirical discovery all these old concepts, while at the same time exposing here and there their limits, treating them as tools which can still be of use. No longer is any truth-value attributed to them; there is a readiness to abandon them if necessary if other instruments should appear more useful. In the meantime, their relative efficacy is exploited, and they are employed to destroy the old machinery to which they belong and of which they themselves are pieces. Thus it is that the language of the human sciences criticizes itself. Lévi-Strauss thinks that in this way he can separate method from truth, the instruments of the method and the objective significations aimed at by it. One could almost say that this is the primary affirmation of Lévi-Strauss; in any event, the first words of the Elementary Structures are: "One begins to understand that the distinction between state of nature and state of society (we would be more apt to say today: state of nature and state of culture), while lacking any acceptable historical signification, presents a value which fully justifies its use by modern society: its value as a methodological instrument." Lévi-Strauss will always remain faithful to this double intention: to preserve as an instrument that whose truth-value he criticizes.

On the one hand, he will continue in effect to contest the value of the nature/culture opposition. More than thirteen years after the Elementary Structures, The Savage Mind[12] faithfully echoes the text I have just quoted: "The opposition between nature and culture which I have previously insisted on seems today to offer a value which is above all methodological." And this methodological value is not affected by its "onto-logical" non-value (as could be said, if this notion

were not suspect here): "It would not be enough to have absorbed particular humanities into a general humanity; this first enterprise prepares the way for others . . . which belong to the natural and exact sciences: to reintegrate culture into nature, and finally, to reintegrate life into the totality of its physicochemical conditions" (p. 327).

On the other hand, still in The Savage Mind, what he presents as what he calls bricolage[13] what might be called the discourse of this method. The bricoleur, says Lévi-Strauss, is someone who uses "the means at hand," that is, the instruments he finds at his disposition around him, those which are already there, which had not been especially conceived with an eye to the operation for which they are to be used and to which one tries by trial and error to adapt them, not hesitating to change them whenever it appears necessary, or to try several of them at once, even if their form and their origin are heterogeneous — and so forth. There is therefore a critique of language in the form of bricolage, and it has even been possible to say that bricolage is the critical language itself. I am thinking in particular of the article by G[érard] Genette, "Structuralisme et Critique littéraire," published in homage to Lévi-Strauss in a special issue of L'Arc (no. 26, 1965), where it is stated that the analysis of bricolage could "be applied almost word for word" to criticism, and especially to "literary criticism."[14]

If one calls bricolage the necessity of borrowing one's concept from the text of a heritage which is more or less coherent or ruined, it must be said that every discourse is bricoleur. The engineer, whom Lévi-Strauss opposes to the bricoleur, should be one to construct the totality of his language, syntax, and lexicon. In this sense the engineer is a myth. A subject who would supposedly be the absolute origin of his own discourse and would supposedly construct it "out of nothing," "out of whole cloth," would be the creator of the verbe, the verbe itself. The notion of the engineer who had supposedly broken with all forms of bricolage is therefore a theological

[12]La pensée sauvage (Paris: Plon, 1962). [Tr.]

[13]A bricoleur is a jack-of-all-trades, someone who potters about with odds-and-ends, who puts things together out of bits and pieces. [Tr.]

[14]Reprinted in: G. Genette, Figures (Paris: Éditions du Seuil, 1966), p. 145. [Tr.]

idea; and since Lévi-Strauss tells us elsewhere that *bricolage* is mythopoetic, the odds are that the engineer is a myth produced by the *bricoleur.* From the moment that we cease to believe in such an engineer and in a discourse breaking with the received historical discourse, as soon as it is admitted that every finite discourse is bound by a certain *bricolage,* and that the engineer and the scientist are also species of *bricoleurs* then the very idea of *bricolage* is menaced and the difference in which it took on its meaning decomposes.

This brings out the second thread which might guide us in what is being unraveled here.

Lévi-Strauss describes *bricolage* not only as an intellectual activity but also as a mythopoetical activity. One reads in *The Savage Mind,* "Like *bricolage* on the technical level, mythical reflection can attain brilliant and unforeseen results on the intellectual level. Reciprocally, the mythopoetical character of *bricolage* has often been noted" (p. 26).

But the remarkable endeavor of Lévi-Strauss is not simply to put forward, notably in the most recent of his investigations, a structural science of knowledge of myths and of mythological activity. His endeavor also appears — I would say almost from the first — in the status which he accords to his own discourse on myths, to what he calls his "mythologicals." It is here that his discourse on the myth reflects on itself and criticizes itself. And this moment, this critical period, is evidently of concern to all the languages which share the field of the human sciences. What does Lévi-Strauss say of his "mythologicals"? It is here that we rediscover the mythopoetical virtue (power) of *bricolage.* In effect, what appears most fascinating in this critical search for a new status of the discourse is the stated abandonment of all reference to a *center,* to a *subject,* to a privileged *reference,* to an origin, or to an absolute *arché.* The theme of this decentering could be followed throughout the "Overture" to his last book, *The Raw and the Cooked.* I shall simply remark on a few key points.

1. From the very start, Lévi-Strauss recognizes that the Bororo myth which he employs in the book as the "reference-myth" does not merit this name and this treatment. The name is specious and the use of the myth improper. This myth deserves no more than any other its referential privilege:

> In fact the Bororo myth which will from now on be designated by the name *reference-myth* is, as I shall try to show, nothing other than a more or less forced transformation of other myths originating either in the same society or in societies more or less far removed. It would therefore have been legitimate to choose as my point of departure any representative of the group whatsoever. From this point of view, the interest of the reference-myth does not depend on its typical character, but rather on its irregular position in the midst of a group (p. 10).

2. There is no unity or absolute source of the myth. The focus or the source of the myth are always shadows and virtualities which are elusive, unactualizable, and nonexistent in the first place. Everything begins with the structure, the configuration, the relationship. The discourse on this acentric structure, the myth, that is, cannot itself have an absolute subject or an absolute center. In order not to shortchange the form and the movement of the myth, that violence which consists in centering a language which is describing an acentric structure must be avoided. In this context, therefore, it is necessary to forego scientific or philosophical discourse, to renounce the *epistemé* which absolutely requires, which is the absolute requirement that we go back to the source, to the center, to the founding basis, to the principle, and so on. In opposition to *epistémic* discourse, structural discourse on myths — *mythological* discourse — must itself be *mythomorphic.* It must have the form of that of which it speaks. This is what Lévi-Strauss says in *The Raw and the Cooked,* from which I would now like to quote a long and remarkable passage:

> In effect the study of myths poses a methodological problem by the fact that it cannot conform to the Cartesian principle of dividing the difficulty into as many parts as are necessary to resolve it. There exists no veritable end or term to mythical analysis, no secret unity which could be grasped at the end of the work of decomposition. The themes duplicate themselves to infinity. When we think we have disentangled them from each other and can hold them separate, it is only to realize that they are joining together again, in response to the attraction

of unforeseen affinities. In consequence, the unity of the myth is only tendential and projective; it never reflects a state or a moment of the myth. An imaginary phenomenon implied by the endeavor to interpret, its role is to give a synthetic form to the myth and to impede its dissolution into the confusion of contraries. It could therefore be said that the science or knowledge of myths is an *anaclastic*, taking this ancient term in the widest sense authorized by its etymology, a science which admits into its definition the study of the reflected rays along with that of the broken ones. But, unlike philosophical reflection, which claims to go all the way back to its source, the reflections in question here concern rays without any other than a virtual focus. . . . In wanting to imitate the spontaneous movement of mythical thought, my enterprise, itself too brief and too long, has had to yield to its demands and respect its rhythm. Thus is this book on myths itself and in its own way a myth."

This statement is repeated a little farther on (p. 20): "Since myths themselves rest on second-order codes (the first-order codes being those in which language consists), this book thus offers the rough draft of a third-order code, destined to insure the reciprocal possibility of translation of several myths. This is why it would not be wrong to consider it a myth: the myth of mythology, as it were." It is by this absence of any real and fixed center of the mythical or mythological discourse that the musical model chosen by Lévi-Strauss for the composition of his book is apparently justified. The absence of a center is here the absence of a subject and the absence of an author: "The myth and the musical work thus appear as orchestra conductors whose listeners are the silent performers. If it be asked where the real focus of the work is to be found, it must be replied that its determination is impossible. Music and mythology bring man face to face with virtual objects whose shadow alone is actual. . . . Myths have no authors" (p. 25). Thus it is at this point that ethnographic *brico-lage* deliberately assumes its mythopoetic function. But by the same token, this function makes the philosophical or epistemological requirement of a center appear as mythological, that is to say, as a historical illusion.

Nevertheless, even if one yields to the necessity of what Lévi-Strauss has done, one cannot ignore its risks. If the mythological is mythomorphic, are all discourses on myths equivalent? Shall we

have to abandon any epistemological requirement which permits us to distinguish between several qualities of discourse on the myth? A classic question, but inevitable. We cannot reply — and I do not believe Lévi-Strauss replies to it — as long as the problem of the relationships between the philosopheme or the theorem, on the one hand, and the mytheme or the mythopoem(e), on the other, has not been expressly posed. This is no small problem. For lack of expressly posing this problem, we condemn ourselves to transforming the claimed transgression of philosophy into an unperceived fault in the interior of the philosophical field. Empiricism would be the genus of which these faults would always be the species. Transphilosophical concepts would be transformed into philosophical naïvetés. One could give many examples to demonstrate this risk: the concepts of sign, history, truth, and so forth. What I want to emphasize is simply that the passage beyond philosophy does not consist in turning the page of philosophy (which usually comes down to philosophizing badly), but in continuing to read philosophers *in a certain way*. The risk I am speaking of is always assumed by Lévi-Strauss and it is the very price of his endeavor. I have said that empiricism is the matrix of all the faults menacing a discourse which continues, as with Lévi-Strauss in particular, to elect to be scientific. If we wanted to pose the problem of empiricism and *bricolage* in depth, we would probably end up very quickly with a number of propositions absolutely contradictory in relation to the status of discourse in structural ethnography. On the one hand, structuralism justly claims to be the critique of empiricism.[15] But at the same time there is not a single book or study by Lévi-Strauss which does not offer itself as an empirical essay which can always be completed or invalidated by new information. The structural schemata are always proposed as hypotheses resulting from a finite quantity of information and which are subjected to the proof of experience. Numerous texts could be used to demonstrate this double postulation.

[15]Because the aim of structuralism is to learn the constitutive rules of an activity, which are implicit in every instance of the activity, so that the massing of large quantities of data is unnecessary.

Let us turn once again to the "Overture" of *The Raw and the Cooked,* where it seems clear that if this postulation is double, it is because it is a question here of a language on language:

> Critics who might take me to task for not having begun by making an exhaustive inventory of South American myths before analyzing them would be making a serious mistake about the nature and the role of these documents. The totality of the myths of a people is of the order of the discourse. Provided that this people does not become physically or morally extinct, this totality is never closed. Such a criticism would therefore be equivalent to reproaching a linguist with writing the grammar of a language without having recorded the totality of the words which have been uttered since that language came into existence and without knowing the verbal exchanges which will take place as long as the language continues to exist. Experience proves that an absurdly small number of sentences . . . allows the linguist to elaborate a grammar of the language he is studying. And even a partial grammar or an outline of a grammar represents valuable acquisitions in the case of unknown languages. Syntax does not wait until it has been possible to enumerate a theoretically unlimited series of events before becoming manifest, because syntax consists in the body of rules which presides over the generation of these events. And it is precisely a syntax of South American mythology that I wanted to outline. Should new texts appear to enrich the mythical discourse, then this will provide an opportunity to check or modify the way in which certain grammatical laws have been formulated, an opportunity to discard certain of them and an opportunity to discover new ones. But in no instance can the requirement of a total mythical discourse be raised as an objection. For we have just seen that such a requirement has no meaning (pp. 15–16).

Totalization is therefore defined at one time as *useless,* at another time as *impossible.* This is no doubt the result of the fact that there are two ways of conceiving the limit of totalization. And I assert once again that these two determinations coexist implicitly in the discourses of Lévi-Strauss. Totalization can be judged impossible in the classical style: one then refers to the empirical endeavor of a subject or of a finite discourse in a vain and breathless quest of an infinite richness which it can never master. There is too much, more than one can say. But nontotalization can

also be determined in another way: not from the standpoint of the concept of finitude as assigning us to an empirical view, but from the standpoint of the concept of *freeplay.* If totalization no longer has any meaning, it is not because the infinity of a field cannot be covered by a finite glance or a finite discourse, but because the nature of the field — that is, language and a finite language — excludes totalization. This field is in fact that of *freeplay,* that is to say, a field of infinite substitutions in the closure of a finite ensemble. This field permits these infinite substitutions only because it is finite, that is to say, because instead of being an inexhaustible field, as in the classical hypothesis, instead of being too large, there is something missing from it: a center which arrests and grounds the freeplay of substitutions. One could say — rigorously using that word whose scandalous signification is always obliterated in French — that this movement of the freeplay, permitted by the lack, the absence of a center of origin, is the movement of *supplementarity.* One cannot determine the center, the sign which *supplements*[16] it, which takes its place in its absence — because this sign adds itself, occurs in addition, over and above, comes as a *supplement.*[17] The movement of signification adds something, which results in the fact that there is always more, but this addition is a floating one because it comes to perform a vicarious function, to supplement a lack on the part of the signified. Although Lévi-Strauss in his use of the word supplementary never emphasizes as I am doing here the two directions of meaning which are so strangely compounded within it, it is not by chance that he uses this word twice in his "Introduction to the Work of Marcel Mauss,"[18] at the point where he is speaking of the "superabundance

---

[16]The point being that the word, both in English and French, means "to supply a deficiency," on the one hand, and "to supply something additional," on the other. [Tr.] See pp. 477–479, on Derrida's antinomy of the supplement.

[17]". . . ce signe s'ajoute, vient en sus, en *supplément.*" [Tr.]

[18]"Introduction à l'oeuvre de Marcel Mauss," in: Marcel Mauss, *Sociologie et anthropologie* (Paris: Presses Universitaires de France, 1950). [Tr.] Marcel Mauss (1872–1950) was the French social anthropologist who wrote *The Gift* (1925).

of signifier, in relation to the signifieds to which this superabundance can refer:

In his endeavor to understand the world, man therefore always has at his disposition a surplus of signification (which he portions out amongst things according to the laws of symbolic thought — which it is the task of ethnologists and linguists to study). This distribution of a supplementary allowance [*ration supplémentaire*] — if it is permissible to put it that way — is absolutely necessary in order that on the whole the available signifier and the signified it aims at may remain in the relationship of complementarity which is the very condition of the use of symbolic thought (p. xlix).

(It could no doubt be demonstrated that this *ration supplémentaire* of signification is the origin of the *ratio* itself.) The word reappears a little farther on, after Lévi-Strauss has mentioned ''this floating signifier, which is the servitude of all finite thought'':

In other words — and taking as our guide Mauss's precept that all social phenomena can be assimilated to language — we see in *mana, Wakau, oranda* and other notions of the same type: the conscious expression of a semantic function, whose role it is to permit symbolic thought to operate in spite of the contradiction which is proper to it. In this way are explained the apparently insoluble antinomies attached to this notion. . . . At one and the same time force and action, quality and state, substantive and verb; abstract and concrete, omnipresent and localized — *mana* is in effect all these things. But is it not precisely because it is none of these things that *mana* is a simple form, or more exactly, a symbol in the pure state, and therefore capable of becoming charged with any sort of symbolic content whatever? In the system of symbols constituted by all cosmologies, *mana* would simply be a *valeur symbolique zéro*, that is to say, a sign marking the necessity of a symbolic content supplementary [my italics] to that with which the signified is already loaded, but which can take on any value required, provided only that this value still remains part of the available reserve and is not, as phonologists put it, a group-term.

Lévi-Strauss adds the note:

Linguists have already been led to formulate hypotheses of this type. For example: ''A zero phoneme is opposed to all the other phonemes in French in that it entails no differential characters and no constant phonetic value. On the contrary, the proper function of the zero phoneme is to be opposed to phoneme absence.'' (R. Jakobson and J. Lutz, ''Notes on the French Phonemic Pattern,'' *Word*, vol. 5, no. 2 [August, 1949], p. 155). Similarly, if we schematize the conception I am proposing here, it could almost be said that the function of notions like *mana* is to be opposed to the absence of signification, without entailing by itself any particular signification (p. l and note).

The *superabundance* of the signifier, its *supplementary* character, is thus the result of a finitude, that is to say, the result of a lack which must be supplemented.

It can now be understood why the concept of freeplay is important in Lévi-Strauss. His references to all sorts of games, notably to roulette, are very frequent, especially in his *Conversations*,[19] in *Race and History*,[20] and in *The Savage Mind*. This reference to the game or free-play is always caught up in a tension.

It is in tension with history, first of all. This is a classical problem, objections to which are now well worn or used up. I shall simply indicate what seems to me the formality of the problem: by reducing history, Lévi-Strauss has treated as it deserves a concept which has always been in complicity with a teleological and eschatological metaphysics, in other words, paradoxically, in complicity with that philosophy of presence to which it was believed history could be opposed. The thematic of historicity, although it seems to be a somewhat late arrival in philosophy, has always been required by the determination of being as presence. With or without etymology, and in spite of the classic antagonism which opposes these significations throughout all of classical thought, it could be shown that the concept of *episteme* has always called forth that of *historia*, if history is always the unity of a becoming, as tradition of truth or development of science or knowledge oriented toward the appropriation of truth in presence and self-presence, toward knowledge in

[19] Presumably: G. Charbonnier, *Entretiens avec Claude Lévi-Strauss* (Paris: Plon-Julliard, 1961). [Tr.]

[20] *Race and History* (Paris: UNESCO Publications, 1958). [Tr.]

consciousness-of-self.[21] History has always been conceived as the movement of a resumption of history, a diversion between two presences. But if it is legitimate to suspect this concept of history, there is a risk, if it is reduced without an express statement of the problem I am indicating here, of falling back into an ahistoricism of a classical type, that is to say, in a determinate moment of the history of metaphysics. Such is the algebraic formality of the problem as I see it. More concretely, in the work of Lévi-Strauss it must be recognized that the respect for structurality, for the internal originality of the structure, compels a neutralization of time and history. For example, the appearance of a new structure, of an original system, always comes about — and this is the very condition of its structural specificity — by a rupture with its past, its origin, and its cause. One can therefore describe what is peculiar to the structural organization only by not taking into account, in the very moment of this description, its past conditions: by failing to pose the problem of the passage from one structure to another, by putting history into parentheses. In this "structuralist" moment, the concepts of chance and discontinuity are indispensable. And Lévi-Strauss does in fact often appeal to them as he does, for instance, for that structure of structures, language, of which he says in the "Introduction to the Work of Marcel Mauss" that it "could only have been born in one fell swoop":

> Whatever may have been the moment and the circumstances of its appearance in the scale of animal life, language could only have been born in one fell swoop. Things could not have set about signifying progressively. Following a transformation the study of which is not the concern of the social sciences, but rather of biology and psychology, a crossing over came about from a stage where nothing had a meaning to another where everything possessed it (p. xlvi).

This standpoint does not prevent Lévi-Strauss from recognizing the slowness, the process of maturing, the continuous toil of factual transformations, history (for example, in *Race and History*). But, in accordance with an act which was also Rousseau's and Husserl's, he must "brush aside all the facts" at the moment when he wishes to recapture the specificity of a structure. Like Rousseau, he must always conceive of the origin of a new structure on the model of catastrophe — an overturning of nature in nature, a natural interruption of the natural sequence, a brushing aside *of* nature.

Besides the tension of freeplay with history, there is also the tension of freeplay with presence. Freeplay is the disruption of presence. The presence of an element is always a signifying and substitutive reference inscribed in a system of differences and the movement of a chin. Freeplay is always an interplay of absence and presence, but if it is to be radically conceived, freeplay must be conceived of before the alternative of presence and absence; being must be conceived of as presence or absence beginning with the possibility of freeplay and not the other way around. If Lévi-Strauss, better than any other, has brought to light the freeplay of repetition and the repetition of freeplay, one no less perceives in his work a sort of ethic presence, an ethic of nostalgia for origins, an ethic of archaic and natural innocence, of a purity of presence and self-presence in speech[22] — an ethic, nostalgia, and even remorse which he often presents as the motivation of the ethnological project when he moves toward archaic societies — exemplary societies in his eyes. These texts are well known.

As a turning toward the presence, lost or impossible, of the absent origin, this structuralist thematic of broken immediateness is thus the sad, *negative,* nostalgic, guilty, Rousseauist facet of the thinking of freeplay of which the Nietzschean *affirmation* — the joyous affirmation of the freeplay of the world and of the innocence of becoming, the affirmation of a world of signs without fault, without truth, without origin, offered to an active interpretation — would be the other side. *This affirmation then determines the non-center otherwise than as loss of the center. And it plays*

---

[21]." . . l'unité d'un devenir, comme tradition de la vérité dans la présence et la présence à soi, vers le savoir dans la conscience de soi." [Tr.]

[22]." . . de la présence à soi dans la parole." [Tr.]

the game without security. For there is a *sure* freeplay: that which is limited to the *substitution* of *given and existing, present,* pieces. In absolute chance, affirmation also surrenders itself to *genetic* indetermination, to the *seminal* adventure of the trace.[23]

There are thus two interpretations of interpretation, of structure, of sign, of freeplay. The one seeks to decipher, dreams of deciphering, a truth or an origin which is free from freeplay and from the order of the sign, and lives like an exile the necessity of interpretation. The other, which is no longer turned toward the origin, affirms freeplay and tries to pass beyond man and humanism, the name man being the name of that being who, throughout the history of metaphysics or of onto-theology — in other words, through the history of all of his history — has dreamed of full presence, the reassuring foundation, the origin and the end of the game. The second interpretation of interpretation, to which Nietzsche showed us the way, does not seek in ethnography, as Lévi-Strauss wished, the "inspiration of a new humanism."

There are more than enough indications today to suggest we might perceive that these two interpretations of interpretation — which are absolutely irreconcilable even if we live them simultaneously and reconcile them in an obscure economy — together share the field which we call, in such a problematic fashion, the human sciences.

For my part, although these two interpretations must acknowledge and accentuate their difference and define their irreducibility, I do not believe that today there is any question of *choosing* — in the first place because here we are in a region (let's say, provisionally, a region of historicity) where the category of choice seems particularly trivial; and in the second, because we must first try to conceive of the common ground, and the *dif-férance* of this irreducible difference.[24] Here there is a sort of question, call it historical, of which we are only glimpsing today the *conception, the formation, the gestation, the labor.* I employ these words, I admit, with a glance toward the business of childbearing — but also with a glance toward those who, in a company from which I do not exclude myself, turn their eyes away in the face of the as yet unnameable which is proclaiming itself and which can do so, as is necessary whenever a birth is in the offing, only under the species of the non-species, in the formless, mute, infant, and terrifying form of monstrosity.

23"Tournée vers la présence, perdue ou impossible, de l'origine absente, cette thématique structuraliste de l'immédiateté rompue est donc la face triste, *négative*, nostalgique, coupable, rousseauiste, de la pensée du jeu dont l'*affirmation* nietzschéenne, l'affirmation joyeuse du jeu du monde et de l'innocence du devenir, l'affirmation d'un monde de signes sans faute, sans vérité, sans origine, offert à une interprétation active, serait l'autre face. *Cette affirmation détermine alors le non-centre autrement que comme perte du centre. Et elle joue sans sécurité. Car il y a un jeu sûr:* celui qui se limite à la *substitution* de pièces *données et existantes, présentes.* Dans le hasard absolu, l'affirmation se livre aussi à l'indétermination *génétique, à l'aventure séminale de la trace.*" [Tr.] Derrida contrasts two methods of freeplay, Lévi-Strauss's and his own. The former is "sad" and "negative" in that it seeks a substitute for the absent center once provided by metaphysics; it is "nostalgic" for origins, "guilty" over European imperialism, "Rousseauist" in propounding a myth of the noble savage and privileging myth over rational thought. Its method of freeplay is "sure" in that its substitutions of one mytheme for another within the system create a closed system. On the contrary, Derrida's system of freeplay, like the philosophy of Nietzsche, is "joyful" in its affirmation of the power of the will to assign and alter all values. For Derrida, the lack of a center betokens freedom, not the loss of security. The Derridean is an adventurer who must abandon certainty for chance in following the "trace" — the chain of signifiers — wherever it leads.

24From *différer*, in the sense of "to postpone," "put off," "defer." Elsewhere Derrida uses the word as a synonym for the German *Aufschub*: "postponement," and relates it to the central Freudian concepts of *Verspätung, Nachträglichkeit*, and to the "*détours* to death" of *Beyond the Pleasure Principle* by Sigmund Freud (Standard Edition, ed. James Strachey, vol. XIX, London, 1961), Ch. V. [Tr.]

3

READER-RESPONSE THEORY

The literary work cannot be completely identical with the text, or with the [reader's] realization of the text, but in fact must lie halfway between the two. — WOLFGANG ISER

Interpretive communities are made up of those who share interpretive strategies not for reading (in the conventional sense) but for writing texts, for constituting their properties and assigning their intentions. — STANLEY FISH

It is . . . impossible to say from a text alone how people will respond to it. Only after we have understood how some specific individual responds, how the different parts of his individual personality re-create the different details of the text, can we begin to formulate general hypotheses about the way many or all readers respond. Only then — if then. — NORMAN N. HOLLAND

The critics grouped together here as reader-response theorists share a topic rather than a set of assumptions. They all have in common the conviction that the audience plays a vitally important role in shaping the literary experience and the desire to help to explain that role. But their interpretations of that role and their definitions of the literary experience vary enormously, in ways that dwarf the usual doctrinal distinctions even within diverse movements like formalism or semiotics.

Interest in the role of the reader goes back to the early classical period. Plato's Book X of *Republic* testifies to the philosopher's concern lest the audience be corrupted by texts that imitate falsely or concentrate the attention of the audience on unworthy matters; the *Ion,* while centrally involved with the question of creativity, suggests that the *enthousiasmós* the muse grants to the poet is transmitted, like magnetic force, through the performer to the spectator. In Aristotle's *Poetics,* tragedy is partially defined in terms of the emotional activity of the spectator, and the construction of the text is constantly subject to the question of how the audience will view the completed product. In Horace the audience becomes central. The chief criterion of excellence in *The Art of Poetry* is what will delight and instruct the reader or spectator, and the text is defined in operational terms as something whose language, incidents, and characters are to be judged as part of a literary (and in general, a cultural) scene. The legacy of Horace long endured: the rhetorical principle of criticism, based on an operational mode of thought, dominated Western literary criticism for nearly eighteen hundred years.

The displacement of the audience from the center of critical attention to its periphery is the result of Romanticism, which exalted the genius of the author at the expense of the critic (who might be considered the reader's better-paid persona). Most nineteenth- and early twentieth-century criticism centered on the author, and even the shift toward formalism at midcentury displaced the creator only to focus attention on the text itself. The New Critics may have paid greatest attention to the intentional fallacy, since the tendency of the historical scholars they had displaced was to read for authorial meaning. But Wimsatt and Beardsley also wrote a companion piece, "The Affective Fallacy," to defend the autonomous text against the encroachment of critics (primarily I. A. Richards) who might attempt to define the text in terms of the emotions it aroused in a real audience. The autonomous text of the New Criticism expressed feelings and attitudes to an ideal audience, and no evidence of how actual readers had reacted to it could possibly budge the critics' theory. While the once-controversial and experimental works of high modernism (the fiction of Joyce and Woolf, the poetry of Yeats and Eliot) were becoming canonical texts in the first two decades after World War II, the New Criticism was establishing theoretical strictures valorizing the objective textual surface and cultivating the tactic of ignoring the audience.

During the New Critical ascendancy works of audience-oriented theory, like Louise Rosenblatt's *Literature as Exploration* (1938), led a buried life, valued by the education establishment and used in pedagogy but ignored by literary theorists. But like Plato's banishment of the poets, the exile of the audience could not be enforced for long. The return of the reader to center stage was encouraged by one of the Chicago Aristotelians, Wayne C. Booth, with *The Rhetoric of Fiction* (1961). Booth's innovative ideas fit within the prevailing formalism, but in the following decades, other definably different modes of audience-centered criticism emerged. Within the structuralist movement, the audience became a central focus for theorists like Gerald Prince in addition to critics we have already discussed, like Gérard Genette, Jonathan Culler, and Umberto Eco (Ch. 2). A reader-oriented version of psychological criticism also developed, led by such theorists as David Bleich and Norman Holland. More recently, a phenomenological criticism of literature has arisen, which considers the reader as the performer of the text. And the reader has become a key topic in the feminist criticism of Judith Fetterley and Patrocinio Schweickart.

RHETORICAL CRITICISM

Probably the loosest of these groupings is the rhetorical approach, since it covers any perspective that treats the text as sending signals to the reader for interpretation. From Horace to Samuel Johnson, the principal variants in rhetorical theory have turned on two issues: the *object* communicated and the *character* of the audience addressed. On the first axis some critics, such as Dante, have emphasized the way literature communicates ethical and religious doctrine, while others, such as Horace, have concerned themselves chiefly with the pleasures enjoyed by the reader. On the other axis, critics such as Johnson have been concerned with what will be most generally pleasing to any audience, while others, such as Dryden, have assumed that texts are written to please and instruct a particular national group, or even a class within that group, and that the specific characteristics of the audience will dictate the rhetoric employed in the text. In a sense, the discrepancies in contemporary rhetorical criticism are most strongly marked along the axis of reader participation. The range runs from Wayne Booth, who emphasizes the way texts shape their audience into "proper" readers, through Susan Sontag, whose ideal condition would be the mutual transparency of text and reader, to Stanley Fish, who (in one phase of his work) views the text as being created by the reader's mental experience of it.

Booth's approach is both the most traditionally formalistic of the audience-centered modes and the one that has achieved the most widespread recognition. So thoroughly have its methods been embraced by contemporary practical critics that some textbook writers have taken it for a form of the New Criticism. In fact, Booth, like his mentor R. S. Crane, opposed New Critical doctrine on fiction and wrote *The Rhetoric of Fiction* partly to refute the ideas of New Critics like Allen Tate and Caroline Gordon. The prevailing doctrines, derived from the theory and practice of Henry James, valorized realistic stories told through a "natural," objective narrative technique that avoided authorial commentary and other overt signals of the creator behind the tale. Booth's book made it clear that such "natural" techniques of modernism were no less artificial, no less rhetorical, than the direct address to the reader practiced by Fielding and Sterne.

The real question was not *whether* the novelist should use rhetoric — it was impossible to avoid doing so — but what sort of rhetoric to use. Each of the author's technical decisions would shape in a particular way the reader's evaluation of the characters and the action, making some effects easy and others impossible. The axioms that arise from Booth's theory are less simple than those implicit in the New Criticism. They suggest that a reader's emotional distance from the characters in a narrative depends not only on the characters' values and beliefs but on the distance from the reader at which the narrative technique places them. Even relatively vicious characters can become sympathetic if readers are granted access to their consciousness and distanced from that of their victims.

The impact of *The Rhetoric of Fiction* was immense, not only in the development of theory but also in altering the canon of fiction. The popularity of eighteenth-century novelists like Defoe, Fielding, and Sterne, long muted by the disapproval of the New Critics, recovered, in part owing to Booth's debunking of modernist premises. In addition, Booth's terminology — such as "implied author" for the formal location of authorial values within a text, or "unreliable narrator" for a narrator (either personified or not within the text) whose values (intellectual, aesthetic, or ethical) depart from those of the implied author — has become the standard vocabulary in fiction courses.

Booth's concern with "implied authors" and "unreliable narrators," while presenting a view of literature as ineluctably rhetorical, largely focuses on the ways in which authors make texts that will engage or persuade their audiences: The focus, in other words, remains on the writer more than the reader and largely takes for granted the ways in which readers decode the symbols on the page. Booth's former student Peter Rabinowitz has reversed the emphasis. While Rabinowitz still deals with the literary text as a formal object, he focuses on the tacit knowledge the reader must possess to re-create its form.

Rabinowitz's most essential distinction is between the "narrative audience" and the "authorial audience": personifications of the two aspects of reading that all of us perform. As part of the "narrative audience," we follow the events of the narrative as if they were really happening; at the same time, as members of the "authorial audience," we read the text knowing that it is just a story created by an author with some sort of effect in mind.[1] The emotional power of a text depends on the success of the pretense that the events it portrays are real. Our sense of the shape of the narrative, our ability to predict what is going to happen, and our need to sympathize with some characters more than with others depends on our communion with the values and plans of the creating author. Ideally, that is. Actual readers may find it impossible to believe in the reality of a given narrative and may fail to capture an author's signals about the plot and values of a story, either because of the author's lack of artistry or because of conflict with their own ideas, values, and preconceptions. For Rabinowitz both the "narrative audience" and the "authorial audience" are virtual beings, a product of the text and of the rules for reading texts, rules we generally absorb while we are still too young to read on our own.

The first part of Rabinowitz's *Before Reading* (1987) consists of an analysis of some of the rules for reading texts that constitute the contemporary interpretive community: "rules of notice," which assign priority to certain kinds of details; "rules of signification," which help us interpret the meaning, symbolic and literal, of what we read; "rules of configuration," which give us a sense of completeness, closure and genre; and "rules of coherence" that allow us to harmonize and naturalize textual gaps or disjunctures. The second part, keyed to the book's subtitle, *Narrative Conventions and the Politics of Interpretation*, is an inquiry into the meaning of rules of reading as social texts, products of the ideology of the current age. Here Rabinowitz questions, for example, why we so often sympathize with irresponsible idealists when they are males (like Jay Gatsby) but find them lacking or contemptible when they are females (like Emma Bovary), and suggests that the rules of reading our society follows are implicitly sexist, racist, and bourgeois rather than working class in bias. He suggests that the first steps toward the formation of a just society should include understanding the ways in which we have been molded by our culture's implicit rules of reading. In this way, Rabinowitz's rhetorical mode of audience-oriented criticism shows links with some of the Marxists discussed in Chapter 5.

Whereas Booth views readers as being constructed by authors, and Rabinowitz hopes that readers can become aware of the ways in which they are manipulated by their culture's rules of reading, Stanley Fish argues that the text is completely malleable and that the all-powerful reader can interrogate it as he or she wishes. Fish began his career by advocating a method of interpretation that he called "affective

[1] For texts with narrators who present facts and values in a way so skewed that we need to allow for their distortions merely to reconstruct what is happening on the level of the text, Rabinowitz also distinguishes an "ideal narrative audience." This would contain the virtual audience for whom Jason Compson in Faulkner's *The Sound and the Fury*, or Whitey the Barber in Ring Lardner's "Haircut" is speaking.

stylistics," which could be seen as a special mode of the New Criticism. According to this method, the reader reads the text slowly, word by word, alive at each moment to the shifts in apparent position and direction. Texts that seemed to lead first to one conclusion, then another, Fish termed "self-consuming artifacts." The following passage from Sir Thomas Browne is an example:

> That Judas perished by hanging himself, there is no certainty in Scripture: though in one place it seems to affirm it, and by a doubtful word hath given occasion to translate it; yet in another place, in a more punctual description, it maketh it improbable, and seems to overthrow it.

Fish argues that Browne seems to commit himself to Judas's death by hanging up to the first comma, then gradually and *almost* entirely takes it all back: "The prose is continually opening, but then closing, on the possibility of verification in one direction or another."[2] (In a sense, this a variation on New Critic William Empson's sixth type of ambiguity, ambiguity of syntax.) But gradually Fish moved away from the idea that these features belonged primarily to the text, and insisted on their location within the reader. In effect, the text is not the words on the page, but the minutely detailed performance they elicit from the reader.

In his groundbreaking book *Is There a Text in This Class?*, Fish locates the text within the reader rather than in the words on the page. This is a bold procedure, since each reader is likely to come up with at least a slightly different "text." (Elsewhere, in *Self-Consuming Artifacts,* Fish blocks this objection by his appeal to the "informed reader.") Fish is willing to concede that the text-within-the-reader is unstable, but he attempts to demonstrate, as do Derrida and his followers, that the text-as-author's-words is equally unstable, although he does not base this radical skepticism about meaning on the Derridean metaphysics of absence. Instead, for each posited location of meaning within the so-called hermeneutic circle, Fish casts doubt by pushing the point of anchor back, one step at a time — from the words to the conventions for reading the words to the linguistic rules themselves, and so forth. But Fish does not give the full proof, and his argument assumes that readers either can complete it for themselves or trust it can be done.[3]

Whether the reader is convinced is not important, however, since Fish finally accounts for the *relative* stability of readers' sense of canonical texts of literature by appealing to the idea of *interpretive communities.* Interpretive communities have tacitly agreed to certain principles of textual interpretation, which authors must recognize as they write their poems or plays or novels. (In legal circles Fish's theory is seen as one way of accounting for the relationship between statute law and the "community" of judges whose profession it is to interpret that law.) In "How to Recognize a Poem When You See One" (reprinted on p. 596), Stanley Fish demonstrates that

---

[2]Stanley Fish, "Literature in the Reader," in *Is There a Text in This Class?* (Cambridge: Harvard University Press, 1980), p. 24.

[3]The "hermeneutic circle" (a vicious circle only when one is trying to think about it) refers to the difficulty of finding a stable point in the ascription of meaning to any text. Since any word has a large finite number of meanings, we are able to give a stable meaning to any word only from context, but the context itself consists of other words, with equally unstable meanings. Attempts to find a stable point by locating it in (for example) the speaker's intention, simply move the circularity elsewhere.

we can belong to different communities at the same time, via his story about writing a reading list for a morning class in linguistics on the blackboard:

Jacobs — Rosenbaum
Levin
Thorne
Hayes
Ohman (?)

The reading list was interpreted as a poem by the students in his subsequent class in seventeenth-century religious poetry, which met in the same room. The students had no trouble finding in the list a symbolic structure similar to the texts they had been studying. In "Jacobs" they found Jacob's ladder, traditionally moralized as the Christian's ascent to heaven. "Rosenbaum" — rose-tree in German — would then allude to the means of ascent, here no ladder but a tree (like the tree of life) whose character is given by the Rose (a traditional symbol for the Virgin Mary). And so it went: Even the shape of the assignment list was interpreted as being like an altar, since some seventeenth-century poets, like George Herbert, wrote "hieroglyphic" poetry in which the printed lines arranged themselves into angel's wings and other objects. It is easy to claim that Fish's students were reading more into the list than was legitimately there, but the moral of the story, as Fish draws it, is that "reading into" texts is never "just reading"; it is always "reading as." It always involves a "construction" of meaning by the reader in accordance with genre-specific conventions of interpretation established within a community. And it wasn't just the poetry students who were "reading as"; Fish's linguistics students had to construct the list of names as an "assignment" (with a different series of conventions) just as his poetry students had constructed it as a "poem."

Fish's arguments that textual genres (like "poem" or "assignment") in effect create texts by highlighting certain features of the words on the page and suppressing others have won general acceptance, as far as they go here. But is every hypothesis about a text plausible? Fish's denial that texts have any determinate structures independent of the strategies that readers deploy to interpret them has been received with much more skepticism. In "Data, Danda, and Disagreement," James Phelan used philosopher Stephen Pepper's distinction between *data* and *danda* (facts that are independent of, or dependent on, the viewpoint of the observer) to argue that hypotheses about texts can be evaluated in terms of how they account for the independent *data*, and that some hypotheses, on this text, may not be warrantable.[4]

THE STRUCTURALIST READER

The structuralist concern with the role of reader as the decoder of the text has already been discussed in Chapter 2. Umberto Eco's *The Role of the Reader* (1972) presented in theoretical and in practical terms how the central issues of semiotics have been applied to the audience. In *Structuralist Poetics*, Jonathan Culler argued more generally that structuralism had been led astray by its long search for syntactic

[4]*Diacritics* 13.2 (1983): 39–50

keys to authorial meaning and suggested that the movement would gain momentum if it concentrated its attention on the conventions that readers must learn and the procedures they must follow in interpreting the text. In a sense, this would dictate a search for rules and conventions.

The most "rhetorical" structuralist analyst of the reader's role is Gerald Prince. In "Introduction to the Study of the Narratee," Prince, taking off from Wayne Booth's differentiation between *real* and *implied* authors, distinguishes between the *reader,* the human being who peruses the text, and the *narratee* (in French, *narrataire*), whom the narrator explicitly or implicitly addresses within the text.[5] The narratee also differs from the *ideal reader* ("one who would understand perfectly and would approve entirely the least of his words, the most subtle of his intentions") and from the *virtual reader,* "a certain type of reader" on whom the author bestows "certain qualities, faculties and inclinations according to his opinion of men in general . . . and according to the obligations he feels should be respected."[6]

Prince's narratee may be a very well-defined individual, like the "you" to whom Jean-Baptiste Clamence speaks in Albert Camus's *The Fall,* who is defined explicitly as a French lawyer on holiday in Amsterdam. Or the narratee may be defined only by class, like the middle-class lady or gentleman reading Balzac's *Père Goriot:* "You who hold this book with a white hand, you who settle back in a well-padded arm-chair." At other times, the narratee is defined by very subtle signals indeed, such as what has to be explained and what does not. (The narratee of Hemingway's *The Sun Also Rises* does not know what sort of drink Pernod is or the order of events in a bullfight.) The narratee's various functions are outlined by Prince:

> He constitutes a relay between the narrator and the reader, he helps establish the narrative framework, he serves to characterize the narrator, he emphasizes certain themes, he contributes to the development of the plot, he becomes the spokesman for the moral of the work.

What links Prince with Genette, Culler, and Eco, and with other semioticians like Michael Riffaterre, is his confidence that the parameters of reading can be specified and codified. But on this point, other structuralists, like Roland Barthes, have been less sure. In his late study *The Pleasure of the Text* (1975), Barthes distinguishes between "*textes de plaisir,*" those readerly texts whose order can be uncovered, and "*textes de jouissance,*" or texts of bliss, those writerly texts, like the novels of Alain Robbe-Grillet, whose indefinite ambiguity frustrates the structuralist design.

THE PSYCHOLOGY AND SOCIOLOGY OF THE AUDIENCE

In both the formalist-rhetorical and the semiotic-structuralist versions of reader-oriented criticism, the reader considered is generally the reader constructed within the tale: either the posited or implied reader for whom the rhetoric is contrived, or the narratee located explicitly, like a half-realized character, within the narrative framework. The psychological and sociological versions of reader-oriented criticism

---

[5]In *Poétique,* no. 14 (1973): 177–96.
[6]See also Peter Rabinowitz, "Truth in Fiction: A Re-examination of Audiences," *Critical Inquiry* 4 (1977): 121–41.

introduce a different reader, the *actual* reader whom Prince distinguishes from the objects of his concern. Psychoanalytic critics like Norman Holland and social psy-chologists like David Bleich leave the ideal reader behind in favor of the quivering and unpredictable individual reader and his or her genuine but subjective response.

Shared by these theories is a relaxed acceptance of a fact most of us have observed: There are so many idiosyncratic differences between the response of one reader and that of another that, after listening to a group of people discussing a text, we some-times wonder if they have all read the same words.

One of the earliest of the psychological theorists was Louise Rosenblatt, whose *Literature as Exploration* (1938) pioneered the notion of reading as a *transaction* between text and reader. Rosenblatt conceived of the reading process in this way:

Through the medium of words, the text brings into the reader's consciousness certain con-cepts, certain sensuous experiences, certain images of things, people, actions, and scenes. The special meanings and, more particularly, the submerged associations that these words and images have for the individual reader will largely determine what the work commu-nicates to *him*. The reader brings to the work personality traits, memories of past events, present needs and preoccupations, a particular mood of the moment, and a particular physi-cal condition. These and many other elements in a never-to-be-duplicated combination determine his response to the peculiar contribution of the text.[7]

For Rosenblatt, each reading of a given text, even by a single individual, will be different, not because the text is inexhaustible but because each time we read it we are at least slightly different people. Despite this seemingly free-wheeling attitude, Rosenblatt retains the sense that though our response to the work of art is inevitably subjective, some sorts of subjectivity are preferable to others. Minimally, a reader's response should be to what is in the text, not to what is projected onto the text. At one point Rosenblatt warns that "an undistorted vision of the work of art requires a consciousness of one's own preconceptions and prejudices concerning the situations presented in the work, in contrast to the basic attitudes toward life assumed in the text." While it is useful to know what sorts of distortions one is likely to perpetrate on situations in literature and in life (psychologists call this "reality-testing"), the implication of Rosenblatt's warning is that it is possible to achieve an "undistorted" view of a text — something equivalent to an objective interpretation.

Rosenblatt presents the reader's subjective response in terms of the common-sense psychology of prejudices and preoccupations; Norman Holland arrived at his reader-oriented criticism by way of orthodox Freudianism (see the introduction to Psychoanalytic Theory, p. 627). His book *The Dynamics of Literary Response* (1968) presumed that the content of the text essentially determined the reader's response. Holland's text then had a manifest content (the story or poem, its events, its charac-ters, its language, its form) and a latent content of primitive fantasy (oral aggression, anal withholding) hedged about and hidden by defenses (like symbolization or subli-mation). In the reading transaction, the audience, in absorbing consciously the mani-fest content, would also be stimulated, under the table as it were, by the latent content.

[7]Louise Rosenblatt, *Literature as Exploration* (rev. ed.; London: Heinemann, 1968), pp. 30–31.

and the reader's own orality or anality would be gratified by the experience. In effect, the reader's experience would mirror the text's central fantasy and modes of defense.

As Holland explains in 5 *Readers Reading* (1975), this model gradually began to seem less and less satisfactory as it became clearer that the actual responses of self-aware individuals differed a great deal more than this approach could explain. In Holland's new model, the text still possesses manifest and latent content, but instead of assuming that all individuals will react to this content in much the same way, Holland suggests not only that different types of readers will react in different ways, but that even people with similar obsessions may react differently according to their individual styles of coping. In "UNITY IDENTITY TEXT SELF," Holland claims that "any individual shapes the materials the literary work offers him . . . to give him what he characteristically both wishes and fears, and . . . he also constructs his characteristic way of achieving what he wishes and defeating what he fears."

As an example, Holland invites us to imagine three readers responding to *Hamlet*, all of whom share a love–hate relationship with authority figures. The one whose characteristic defense against authority figures is to establish "alternatives in response to their demands" might find in the play "dualisms, split characters, the interplay of multiple plots." The one who reacts by "establishing limits and qualifications on authority" might stress "irony and occasional farce, Osric, Polonius, the gravediggers." The one who reacts with total compliance would respond "by seeking out and accepting, totally, uncritically, with a gee-gosh, the authority of its author."[8]

Holland would reject Rosenblatt's notion that an "undistorted" view of a text is possible; for Holland the solid ground upon which interpretation may be based is that of the individual personality itself. Texts may come and go, but the self, the personality style, the *identity theme* that determines the individual's repertoire of fantasies and defense mechanisms remains remarkably constant over time. What Holland suggests is that to the extent that a work of art threatens the reader's identity theme, the reader recomposes the text so that it replicates this theme. In effect, Holland substitutes the unity of the self for the unity of art. He usually speaks of the self as though it were more objectively knowable than texts are. As Holland admits from time to time, however, we can know others' selves only through our own (and thus the issue of counter-transference between the reader of the text and the observer of that reader cannot be evaded). Furthermore, Holland's idea of the self — his notion that one's identity does not change as the result of life experience — is debatable. Whether the defensive reading of the text replicates precisely the self that began to read or whether the self is not at least slightly altered by the experience are questions that cannot be defined out of existence.

David Bleich's theory of reading, as presented in *Readings and Feelings* (1975) and *Subjective Criticism* (1978), is closer to social psychology than to orthodox Freudianism. Bleich places the reading of texts in a social setting — the classroom — where knowledge about art and life is synthesized by a group. For Bleich, the text is a symbolic object upon which readers act, and the reader's initial and private response to a text is totally subjective, including all sorts of idiosyncratic associations and feelings. Within the social setting of the classroom, the private

---

[8]Norman Holland, "UNITY IDENTITY TEXT SELF," *PMLA* 90 (1975): 817–18.

response is "negotiated" into meaningful knowledge via the individual's sense of the group's purposes. In the course of articulating a response to a text under the social pressure of the group, the reader prunes away, or at least brackets off as private or irrelevant, those aspects of the response that may not apply to others or that are inconsistent with the aim of the class. The response to the text is generalized, placed within a context determined by the ideology of the group. Bleich feels that within the pedagogical setting, knowledge does not move from teacher to student but is constructed by students in accord with a sense of the group aim, which may be initially defined and articulated by a teacher. But Bleich's notions of reading apply beyond his posited pedagogical setting, since people often read or experience works of art within a social setting, with friends or family, and try to communicate a sense of the experience to others.

Any study of this process inevitably leads to the sociology of literature, a field in which one might expect the Marxists to have done a great deal of work. In practice, however, Marxist theorists have tended to shy away from empirical studies of the literary marketplace and how individuals and groups within social settings actually read texts. Two fine studies in literary sociology are Jeffrey Sammons's *Literary Sociology and Practical Criticism* (1977) and Janice Radway's *Reading the Romance: Women, Patriarchy, and Popular Literature* (1984). The former is a lucid overview of the major issues of literary sociology; the latter, a practical demonstration of what can be done in the field. Radway examines why women read popular romances, but instead of merely theorizing about the repressed American housewife and her need for escape, she uses interviews and questionnaires to study the responses of a community of romance readers. Radway's study is well grounded in reader-response theory, and her initial chapter presents an overview of literary reception.

A feminist approach to the reading process that is related to the work of both Bleich and Radway is contained in Judith Fetterley's *The Resisting Reader*, the introduction to which is reprinted in this chapter. Fetterley argues that the socialization produced by reading literature carries a special burden for the female reader. Because most canonical authors are male, their subjects, styles, modes of symbolism, desires, and images for those desires all presume a masculine attitude toward the world, which the female reader is forced to adopt in the course of reception. Just as sexist language (such as the use of "man" to include both men and women) denigrates women by implying that they are not to be taken into account, Fetterley believes the shape of desire in narratives written by men "immasculates" women by forcing them to internalize the values of the other sex.

This is particularly true of American literature, according to Fetterley, who draws on Nina Baym's essay, "Melodramas of Beset Manhood,"[9] which argues that once the westward expansion of the frontier came to be defined as the central experience of American history, the crucial moments of American literature came to be seen as those that showed men encountering Mother Nature at the edge of civilization in the wilderness. Fetterley sharply suggests that if Baym is correct, then "America is

[9]Nina Baym, "Melodramas of Beset Manhood: How Theories of American Literature Exclude Women Authors," *American Quarterly* 33, no. 2 (1981): 123–39.

female; to be American is to be male; and the quintessential American experience is betrayal by woman." Like Rabinowitz, Fetterley believes that the first step in contesting ideology is to make oneself aware of it, and she suggests that women become "resisting readers" of patriarchal texts, reading not passively with but actively against the grain of the masculine ideology that informs them.

While Fetterley argues cogently for the violence done to the female sensibility by the process of "immasculation," her own readings of male texts are sometimes not merely resistant but deeply obtuse. For example, her analysis reads Sherwood Anderson's "I Want To Know Why" as yet one more quintessential example of "betrayal by woman." In Fetterley's reading, the narrator, an adolescent boy mad for horses, feels the sting of disillusionment when he catches Jerry Tillford, a heroic jockey he idolizes, in the act of kissing a red-headed whore. What is lost in Fetterley's binary fixation on men and women is the polymorphous perversity of Anderson's tale: the way the narrator's libido attaches first to a powerful horse and then to the rider who can successfully control it; the way the tale's climax speaks less of betrayed ideals than of homosocial desire and sexual jealousy.

THE PHENOMENOLOGISTS

In effect, formalist/structuralist theories have staked out the reader within the text, while psycho/social theories have been based on the actual reader outside the text. To the extent that there can be a middle ground, it is occupied by the phenomenological approaches to literature, which focus on literature as it is experienced by the thinking subject, the "I" in the center of our conscious world. Two traditions occupy this territory — one represented by the French phenomenologists Jean-Paul Sartre and Georges Poulet, the other by the German critics of the school of Konstanz Wolfgang Iser and Hans Robert Jauss.

Although Jean-Paul Sartre has often been labeled a Marxist critic, his discussion of the role of the reader and the writer in *What Is Literature?* (1948) is thoroughly existentialist — and existentialism, as has often been observed, is the ethical and political branch of phenomenology. The reader of "Why Write?," the second essay in *What is Literature,* will find major similarities between it and the theories of Georges Poulet.

Poulet's discussion of the act of reading emphasizes the way reading transforms the book-as-object — the heavy, dead, material thing — into a subject, an intelligence, a mind to which we subordinate our own.

> Whenever I read, I mentally pronounce an *I,* yet the *I* which I pronounce is not myself. This is true even when the hero of a novel is presented in the third person, and even when there is no hero and nothing but reflections or propositions. . . . Another *I,* who has replaced my own, and who will continue to do so as long as I read. . . . A second self takes over, a self which thinks and feels for me.

For Poulet, the purpose of this abdication of the self is, paradoxically, the further realization of the self:

> The annexation of my consciousness by . . . the other which is the work . . . in no way implies that I am the victim of any deprivation of consciousness. Everything happens, on the

contrary, as though, from the moment I become a prey to what I read, I begin to share the use of my consciousness with . . . the conscious subject ensconced at the heart of the work.[10]

Poulet's characteristic images are close to those of Plato. The subjective consciousness of the text is *inbreathed* by the reader in a sort of passive inspiration, like the *enthousiasmós* of the *Ion* or the *Phaedrus*. For Iser and Jauss the relationship of author and reader is less like that of the demon and the human being it has possessed than that of the composer and the performer of a piece of music, a metaphor that suggests a new kind of connection between writer and reader. For the formalists and structuralists, the reader is essentially determined by the text. Fish's interpretive communities create the text themselves; the author's words are an indeterminate framework to which the community brings the meaning. Psychological critics like Holland view the text as fantasy material with which the reader copes, as with a disturbing dream. But Iser and Jauss perceive in the text the mutual dependence — the creative collaboration — of composer and performer. Although the composer is clearly the primary genius whose intentions must be respected, without the performer the composer would remain mute. Following the terminology of Roman Ingarden, Iser and Jauss speak of the text as being *concretized* by the reader: The vague and ideal word is in the reading process made flesh. The difference between Iser and Jauss is primarily one of perspective: Iser's interest is in the *act* of reading as it happens for each of us; Jauss's concern has been with the *history* of reading and the contribution a history of reception can make to the broader concerns of literary history.

For Iser, the reader's performative activity is called into play by the gaps that every text contains, since no text can be fully explicit about everything. In the process of reading, for example, we imagine what the hero and heroine look like in ways consistent with the descriptions we are given in the text; nevertheless, two readers' mental pictures of Tom Jones would be vastly different. (This, Iser says, is why film realizations of novels invariably make us say to ourselves, "That's not the way I pictured him.") But beyond filling in descriptions the text leaves indeterminate, the reader also imagines scenes the text leaves tacit, dialogue that is left unspoken, and so on. Furthermore, it is not just a matter of understanding and creating a full sense of illusion out of the words that are directly before the reader's eyes. In a novel, the reading process takes place within the flow of a narrative moving from a beginning through a middle to an end. As we read a given sentence, we may be forced to revise our understanding of what we have already read and processed, or to form expectations of what will happen in the future, expectations that may be fulfilled or shattered. Underlying this process, and guiding it, are "two main structural components within the text: first, a repertoire of familiar literary patterns and recurrent literary themes, together with allusions to familiar social and historical contexts; and second, techniques or strategies used to set the familiar against the unfamiliar." The text in any mature work of art, in other

[10]Georges Poulet, "Criticism and the Experience of Interiority," in Richard Macksey and Eugenio Donato, *The Structuralist Controversy: The Languages of Criticism and the Sciences of Man* (Baltimore: Johns Hopkins University Press, 1972), p. 56.

words, depends on the reader's prior understanding of the themes and conventions of story-telling, but it works *against* those conventions as much as it employs them in order to *defamiliarize* the reader, who would otherwise be bored by a predictable text.

During the last two hundred years, according to Iser's *The Implied Reader,* these general principles have been worked out in the English novel in very different ways. The reader in the eighteenth century was "guided — directly or indirectly, through affirmation or through negation — toward a conception of human nature and of reality." The nineteenth-century reader, by contrast, "was not told what part he was to play. Instead he had to discover the fact that society had imposed a part on him, the object being for him eventually to take up a critical attitude toward this imposition." Readers of the Victorian novel, therefore, were nudged into making the correct discoveries for themselves. Both of these modes depend upon the reader's capacity for subscribing to the illusion provoked by the text. The twentieth-century novel, in contrast, insists on rupturing these illusions and calling attention to its own use of technique — all this in order.

> to provoke the reader into establishing for himself the connections between perception and thought. . . . In this way he may then be given the chance of discovering himself, both in and through his constant involvement in "home-made" illusions and fictions.[11]

For Iser, the history of the novel is the history of the ways in which writers created gaps for their readers to fill, and to an extent, his ideas are easily assimilated to those of rhetorical critics like Peter Rabinowitz. For Hans Robert Jauss, on the other hand, literary history is as much the history of the reader as of the canonized authors or, to be more accurate, of the relationship between writing and the reading public that consumes and stimulates its production. These ideas are based on the philosophy of Hans-Georg Gadamer, whose theories of interpretation turn on the positive contributions made by our prejudices. Normally, "prejudice" has a negative connotation when it refers to one cause of our injustice to others, but for Gadamer and his pupils, these prejudices (in German, *Vorurteilungen*) are what allow us to understand the changing world at all. Our preunderstandings give us a settled context, a *horizon of expectations,* against which we can place and evaluate the new. And our horizon of expectations is constantly changing as our life experience adds to and alters our framework of vision.

In literary terms, there is a dialogical relation between the text and the reading public. The public reads the text from within its current horizon of expectations — that set of cultural, ethical, and aesthetic norms current at any given moment — and attempts to bring the work within those horizons. For some works, like popular literature meant for instant consumption, there will be no problem in fitting the text into such a horizon, but other works may challenge the audience's horizon of expectations along one or more fronts. Such works may succeed in changing the

---

[11]Wolfgang Iser, *The Implied Reader: Patterns of Communication in Prose Fiction from Bunyan to Beckett* (Baltimore: Johns Hopkins University Press, 1974), pp. xiii–xiv.

preunderstanding of the reading public, or a substantial portion of it, as was the case with Flaubert's *Madame Bovary*. On the other hand, such works may fail to engage the audience entirely and may be forgotten; or, like Melville's *Moby-Dick*, they may be read, but their most individual qualities may be ignored because they cannot be assimilated to the preunderstanding of the day. Forgotten or misread works, however, may be rediscovered by a later audience, when the horizon of expectations has, so to speak, caught up with them. Change in the horizon is produced partly by literary texts themselves, whose success creates a market and stimulates imitation by other authors, and partly by changes in economic, social, and political conditions, which make ideas and relations within texts more or less attractive.

For Jauss the writing of literary history would require that we recreate the horizon of expectations of the reading public for any given period. This we can piece together, partly from the texts themselves, and partly from the public and private responses of various levels of the reading public: other authors, publishers, critics, and private consumers. Creating the materials out of which a literary history might be written would require both synchronic and diachronic studies. One might begin with a synchronic study, in effect taking a "snapshot" of the literary world at a given date (Jauss himself has done a study of the horizon of expectations in France in 1857, the year of *Madame Bovary* and of Baudelaire's *Fleurs du Mal*), and by comparing such "snapshots" at various dates, put together a sense of how these horizons changed over time. In addition, diachronic studies, like histories of the reception of a given text from its publication to the present day, would be a useful supplement to the snapshots.

These "time-lapse photos" would give a stronger sense of how literary opinion shifts over the centuries (Jauss has produced a study over time of the reception of Baudelaire's "Spleen" poems). The end product will take a long time to produce, given the sheer amount of research into the reception of texts the method requires. But the result proposed is a literary history that goes beyond the "scissors-and-paste" histories detailing the lives and works of those authors that are currently valued. The history Jauss envisions would allow us to understand the evolution of textual production in relation to changes in the cultural scene that generated that evolution, including many factors we currently ignore, such as those evanescent productions whose popularity in one age were a passport to obscurity in the next.

As one might expect, the Marxists were most offended by Jauss's insistence that literary history needed to be reformed in order to include the participation of the readers who made up the market for literature. One might have thought them the group most concerned with the influence of the individual in a mass society, yet Jauss's competition with them exposed their neglect of the group they theoretically most favored. In fact, the publication of "Literary History as a Challenge to Literary Theory" provoked a decade of quarreling between the reception theorists of Constance and the Marxists across what was then the border with East Germany. By the 1980s, however, both parties saw that what they had in common dwarfed their area of contention, and indeed, some post-Althusserian Marxists (like the British Tony Bennett) have proposed programs for revamping literary history using methods that closely resemble Jauss's proposals. In addition to these quarrels with the

Marxists, Jauss's theories have also provoked a large number of scholars, not just in Germany but in England and North America as well, into undertaking reception studies, which are just beginning to produce the "snapshots" and "time-lapse photos" of the audience that will eventuate in the new literary history Jauss prophesied.

But as Jauss shows in "The Three Horizons of Reading," reprinted below, the process of historical reconstruction operates not just at the macro level but on the micro level each time we read a text and situate ourselves against it. In *Truth and Method*, Jauss's mentor, Hans-Georg Gadamer, described the process of reading as involving three stages that are distinct. *Understanding* is the basic hermeneutic process of uncovering what the poetic text means; *interpretation* involves uncovering how the poetic text works on us; *application* involves understanding the poet and oneself, the reader, in their historical relation to each other. These stages may actually occur simultaneously, and they influence each other, so Jauss is well aware that he is artificially separating them. All of them involve asking questions of a text and receiving answers. In understanding, for example, our immediate response to a text is to misunderstand it because we take the words in senses that are easy and familiar to us, but then as we project where the text is going, we are brought up short when it contradicts our expectations. We revise our sense and try again, and by trial and error arrive at an understanding that is consistent and coherent. The same process of dialogue of reader with text occurs in the other stages, which naturally affect one another: As we understand a text in terms of its era, we foreground verbal meanings that would be implausibly archaic in a contemporary text; as we come to understand a passage as metaphorical, interpretation is given something more to do. And, as Jauss shows, this complex hermeneutic process not only reveals the text, it reveals to us who *we* are as its interpreters.

COGNITIVE THEORY

The most recent of the reader-response approaches is that of cognitive theory. If one wishes, one can trace cognitive theory as far back as Plato, whose dialogues are as much about knowing as about being. But the contemporary discipline — which is about as *inter*disciplinary as such areas can be — probably got its start from Noam Chomsky, who around 1960 conjectured that natural languages are too similar in their deep structures to be the random product of culture, and are learned too quickly to be entirely the behaviorist result of the verbal stimuli children receive and their rewarded responses. Chomsky argued that children are born with a "Language Acquisition Device" hard-wired into their brains.

While his theory is still contested, the controversy sparked widespread investigations into the relationship of mind and brain, by which it became clear that, whether the tracks are hard-wired from birth or laid down by experience, the brain processes language in very specific sites. Neurologists examining patients with aphasias caused by brain lesions had long ago discovered that we store people's names in a different site from common nouns and that certain lesions prevented people from understanding metaphor and others, metonymy. Cognitive theory has progressed through advances in neuroscience that have enabled us, without creating

brain lesions in healthy subjects, to correlate specific thought processes with activity in specific areas of the brain by mapping which sites demand greater blood flow
or demonstrate greater electrical conductivity. We now know that we store short-
term memories in different places from long-term memories, and it is suspected that
the vivid dreams we experience while unconscious may be, *pace* Freud, an artifact
of the process of sorting and ''dumping'' the data of the previous day.

Another accelerant to cognitive theory has been the growth and ubiquity of computer data processing since 1970, since almost all of us use and many of us are able
to create programs — sets of instructions with feedback loops — that enable relatively simple machines based on silicon on/off switches to solve difficult mathematical problems or comb with enormous speed through a mass of data for the precise bit
of information we want. Our sense of how linear programming works has given us
some ideas about how that computer made of meat between our ears operates; it has
become reasonably clear that, given the slow speed of conductivity in the neurons of
our brain, we cannot possibly be operating by linear programming, that the human
brain instead performs more like a multitude of separate simple computers wired
together (''parallel processing'').

One consequence of the parallel development of neuroscience and cognitive
theory is that the relationship between nature and culture has, in some areas, become
murkier. We can think of metaphor and metonymy as tropes of purely literary interest to a Longinus or a Paul de Man, but cognitive psychologists view such verbal
analogues and connections as deeply enmeshed in the ways human beings learn their
world: They are the tools we think with. Telling stories artistically, as Homer and
Proust did, is a way to immortality, but basic narratives, telling each other stories
about predators or food supplies, seems to have been a major factor in why homo
sapiens succeeded in the struggle for existence.

The work of such contemporary critics as Elaine Scarry, Mark Turner, and
Lisa Zunshine, involves quite different applications of cognitive psychology to
literature, but each of these authors attempts to get inside the process of reading,
to understand how the brain processes literary texts. Most other reader-response
theory, whatever its philosophical base, has posited an opaque black box between
the literary text, on the one hand, and the response readers are able to verbalize after
reflecting on their experience. That is not true of Lisa Zunshine's essay ''Theory
of Mind and Experimental Reproductions of Fictional Consciousness,'' which is
included below. Lisa Zunshine's demonstration, in line with George Miller's experiments with short-term memory, investigates why and under what circumstances
certain kinds of high modernist narrative flirt with the limits of our ability to process
them. Cognitive theory, by thinking ''outside the box,'' is able, sometimes with surprising results, to get inside that box.

Interest in the reader is a late development in critical theory. As a topic for investigation, it has attracted each of the major schools of thought, from Marxism through
structuralism and feminism to deconstruction. It is likely that, following its neglect
in the wake of the ''affective fallacy,'' critical understanding of the audience — in
all its various manifestations — has changed more in the past thirty years than in the
previous two thousand.

Selected Bibliography

Altick, Richard. *The English Common Reader: A Social History of the Mass Reading Public, 1800–1900*. Chicago: University of Chicago Press, 1957.

Barthes, Roland. *The Pleasure of the Text*. New York: Hill and Wang, 1975.

Baym, Nina. "Melodramas of Beset Manhood: How Theories of American Literature Exclude Women Authors." *American Quarterly* 33 (1981): 123–39.

Bleich, David. *Readings and Feelings: An Introduction to Subjective Criticism*. Urbana, IL: National Council of Teachers of English, 1975.

———. *Subjective Criticism*. Baltimore: Johns Hopkins University Press, 1978.

Booth, Wayne C. *The Rhetoric of Fiction*. Chicago: University of Chicago Press, 1961; 2nd ed. 1983.

———. *A Rhetoric of Irony*. Chicago: University of Chicago Press, 1974.

———. *The Company We Keep: Ethical Criticism and the Ethics of Reading*. Berkeley: University of California Press, 1988.

Butte, George. *I Know That You Know That I Know: Narrating Subjects from Moll Flanders to Marnie*. Columbus: Ohio State University Press, 2004.

Carruthers, Peter, and Peter K. Smith, eds. *Theories of Theories of Mind*. Cambridge: Cambridge University Press, 1996.

Cruse, Amy. *The Englishman and His Books in the Early Nineteenth Century*. London: George G. Harrap, 1930.

Eco, Umberto. *The Role of the Reader: Explorations in the Semiotics of Texts*. Bloomington: Indiana University Press, 1979.

Escarpit, Robert. *Sociology of Literature*. Painesville, OH: Lake Erie College Press, 1965.

———. "The Sociology of Literature." *International Encyclopaedia of Social Science*, Vol. 9. New York: Macmillan, 1968, pp. 417–25.

Esrock, Ellen J. *The Reader's Eye: Visual Imaging as Reader Response*. Baltimore: Johns Hopkins University Press, 1994.

Fetterley, Judith. *The Resisting Reader: A Feminist Approach to American Fiction*. Bloomington: Indiana University Press, 1978.

———. "Reading about Reading: 'A Jury of Her Peers,' 'The Murders in the Rue Morgue,' and 'The Yellow Wallpaper.'" In *Gender and Reading: Essays on Readers, Texts, and Contexts*, ed. Elizabeth Flynn and Patrocinio Schweickart. Baltimore: Johns Hopkins University Press, 1986, pp. 147–64.

Fish, Stanley. *Self-Consuming Artifacts: The Experience of Seventeenth-Century Literature*. Berkeley: University of California Press, 1972.

———. *Is There a Text in This Class? The Authority of Interpretive Communities*. Cambridge: Harvard University Press, 1980.

———. *Doing What Comes Naturally: Change, Rhetoric, and the Practice of Theory in Literary and Legal Studies*. Durham: Duke University Press, 1989.

Flynn, Elizabeth A. "Gender and Reading." *College English* 45 (1983): 236–53.

Gadamer, Hans-Georg. *Truth and Method*. London: Sheed and Ward, 1975.

Harris, Paul L. *The Work of Imagination*. Oxford: Blackwell, 2001.

Hohendahl, Peter Uwe. "Introduction to Reception Aesthetics." *New German Critique* 10 (1977): 29–63.

Holland, Norman N. *The Dynamics of Literary Response*. New York: Oxford University Press, 1968.

———. *5 Readers Reading*. New Haven: Yale University Press, 1975.

———. "I-ing Film." *Critical Inquiry* 12 (1986): 654–71.

——. "'I-ing Lacan.'" In *Criticism and Dialogue on Language, Structure, and the Unconscious*, ed. Patrick C. Hogan and Lalita Pandit. Athens: University of Georgia Press, 1990, pp. 97–108.

——. *The Critical I.* New York: Columbia University Press, 1992.

Holub, Robert C. *Reception Theory: A Critical Introduction.* London: Methuen, 1984.

Ingarden, Roman. *The Cognition of the Literary Work of Art.* Evanston, IL: Northwestern University Press, 1973.

Iser, Wolfgang. *The Implied Reader: Patterns of Communication in Prose Fiction from Bunyan to Beckett.* Baltimore: Johns Hopkins University Press, 1974.

——. *The Act of Reading: A Theory of Aesthetic Response.* Baltimore: Johns Hopkins University Press, 1978.

——. "Towards a Literary Anthropology." In *The Future of Literary Theory*, ed. Ralph Cohen. New York: Routledge, 1989, pp. 208–28.

——. "Fictionalizing: The Anthropological Dimension of Literary Fictions." *New Literary History* 21 (1990): 939–55.

Jauss, Hans Robert. *Aesthetic Experience and Literary Hermeneutics.* Minneapolis: University of Minnesota Press, 1982.

——. *Toward an Aesthetics of Reception.* trans. Timothy Bahti. Minneapolis: University of Minnesota Press, 1982.

Johnson, Mark. *The Body in the Mind: The Bodily Basis of Meaning, Imagination and Reason.* Chicago: University of Chicago Press, 1987.

Kavanagh, Thomas M., ed. *The Limits of Theory.* Stanford: Stanford University Press, 1989.

Koelb, Clayton. *The Incredulous Reader: Literature and the Function of Disbelief.* Ithaca: Cornell University Press, 1984.

Leavis, Q. D. *Fiction and the Reading Public.* London: Chatto and Windus, 1932.

Lesser, Simon O. *Fiction and the Unconscious.* Boston: Vintage, 1957.

Mailloux, Steven J. *Interpretive Conventions.* Ithaca: Cornell University Press, 1982.

Miles, David H. "Literary Sociology: Some Introductory Notes." *German Quarterly* 48 (1975): 20–45.

Miller, Owen J. "Reading as a Process of Reconstruction: A Critique of Recent Structuralist Formulations." In *Interpretation of Narrative*, ed. Mario J. Valdés and Owen J. Miller. Toronto: University of Toronto Press, 1978, pp. 19–27.

Naumann, Manfred. "Literary Production and Reception." *New Literary History* 8 (1976): 107–26.

Ortony, Andrew, ed. *Metaphor and Thought.* Cambridge: Cambridge University Press, 1993.

Phelan, James. *Reading People, Reading Plots: Character, Progression, and the Interpretation of Narrative.* Chicago: University of Chicago Press, 1989.

——. *Living to Tell about It: A Rhetoric and Ethics of Character Narration.* Ithaca: Cornell University Press, 2005.

Poulet, Georges. "Criticism and the Experience of Interiority." In *The Structuralist Controversy: The Languages of Criticism and the Sciences of Man*, ed. Richard Macksey and Eugenio Donato. Baltimore: Johns Hopkins University Press, 1972.

Preston, John. *The Created Self: The Reader's Role in Eighteenth-Century Fiction.* New York: Barnes and Noble, 1970.

Prince, Gerald. "Introduction to the Study of the Narratee." *Poétique* 14 (1973): 177–96.

Rabinowitz, Peter. "Truth in Fiction: A Reexamination of Audiences." *Critical Inquiry* 4 (1977): 121–41.

——. *Before Reading.* Ithaca: Cornell University Press, 1987.

——. "Readings of Narrative, 1937–1987." *PMLA* 108 (1993): 410–532.

————. "'Betraying the Sender': The Rhetoric and Ethics of Fragile Texts." *Narrative* 2 (1994): 201–13.

Radway, Janice A. *Reading the Romance: Women, Patriarchy, and Popular Literature.* Chapel Hill: University of North Carolina Press, 1984.

Reichert, John. *Making Sense of Literature.* Chicago: University of Chicago Press, 1977.

Richards, I. A. *Practical Criticism: A Study of Literary Judgment.* New York: Harcourt, Brace, 1935.

Richardson, Alan, and Francis F. Steen, eds. *Literature and the Cognitive Revolution.* A special issue. *Poetics Today* 23 (2002).

Richter, David H. "The Reader as Ironic Victim." *Novel* 14 (1981): 135–51.

————. "The Reception of the Gothic Novel in the 1790's." In *The Idea of the Novel in the Eighteenth Century,* ed. Robert Uphaus. East Lansing, MI: Colleagues Press, 1988.

————. "The Unguarded Prison: Reception Theory, Structural Marxism, and the Structure of Literary History." *The Eighteenth Century: Theory and Interpretation* 30 (1989): 1–17.

Rosenblatt, Louise. *The Reader, the Text, the Poem: The Transactional Theory of the Literary Work.* Carbondale: Southern Illinois University Press, 1978.

————. *Literature as Exploration.* New York: Modern Language Association, 1983.

Sammons, Jeffrey. *Literary Sociology and Practical Criticism.* Bloomington: Indiana University Press, 1977.

Sartre, Jean-Paul. *What Is Literature?* New York: Philosophical Library, 1966.

Scarry, Elaine. *Dreaming by the Book.* New York: Farrar, Straus & Giroux, 1999.

Schücking, L. L. *The Sociology of Literary Taste,* 3rd ed. Chicago: University of Chicago Press, 1966.

Spolsky, Ellen. *Gaps in Nature: Literary Interpretation and the Modular Mind.* Albany: State University of New York Press, 1993.

Stockwell, Peter. *Cognitive Poetics: An Introduction.* London: Routledge, 2002.

Suleiman, Susan, and Inge Crosman, eds. *The Reader in the Text: Essays on Audience and Interpretation.* Princeton: Princeton University Press, 1980.

Turner, Mark. *Death Is the Mother of Beauty: Mind, Metaphors, and Criticism.* Chicago: University of Chicago Press, 1987.

————. *Reading Minds: The Study of English in the Age of Cognitive Science.* Princeton: Princeton University Press, 1991.

————. *The Literary Mind.* New York: Oxford University Press, 1996.

Tompkins, Jane P., ed. *Reader-Response Criticism: From Formalism to Post-Structuralism.* Baltimore: Johns Hopkins University Press, 1980.

Weimann, Robert. "'Reception Aesthetics' and the Crisis of Literary History." *Clio* 5 (1975): 3–33.

Zunshine, Lisa. *Why We Read Fiction: An Explanation from Cognitive Theory.* Columbus: Ohio State University Press, 2006.

Hans Robert Jauss

1921–1997

Hans Robert Jauss has been acknowledged the leader and principal theorist of the movement termed "reception aesthetics," which views literary history as formed, at least in part, by the readings and assessments that texts have received throughout the past. Jauss was born in 1921 and served on the Eastern front in the Waffen-SS throughout World War II. He completed his Ph.D. at the University of Heidelberg and taught there, and at Münster and Giessen, before joining the faculty at Konstanz, where he was professor of Romance languages and literature from 1967 until his death. He held visiting professorships at the Sorbonne, Columbia, Yale, Berkeley, and UCLA. Jauss's prodigious scholarly output (which also comprises over 75 articles, in addition to editions and translations) includes Zeit und Erinnerung in Marcel Proust's A la recherche du temps perdu (Time and Memory in Marcel Proust's In Search of Lost Time, 1955); Untersuchungen zu mittelalterlichen Tierdichtung (Researches into Medieval Beast Literature, 1959); La génèse de la poésie allegorique française au Moyen-Age (The Origin of Medieval French Allegory, 1962); Literaturgeschichte als Provokation der Literaturwissenschaft (Literary History as a Challenge to Literary Theory, 1967); Kleine Apologie der ästhetischen Erfahrung (Short Defense of Aesthetic Experience, 1972); Alterität und Modernität der mittelalterischen Literatur (Ancientness and Modernity in Medieval Literature, 1977); and Ästhetische Erfahrung und literarische Hermeneutik (Aesthetic Experience and Literary Hermeneutics, 1977). Jauss's major essays have been translated into English and are collected in Toward an Aesthetics of Reception (1978), Aesthetic Experience and Literary Hermeneutics (1982), and Question and Answer: Forms of Dialogic Understanding (1989). "The Three Horizons of Reading" is excerpted from "The Poetic Text within the Change of Horizons of Reading: The Example of Baudelaire's 'Spleen II,'" which in turn appeared in Toward an Aesthetics of Reception.

[The Three Horizons of Reading]
from Toward an Aesthetics of Reception

I. THE DISTINGUISHING OF VARIOUS HORIZONS OF READING AS A PROBLEM FOR LITERARY HERMENEUTICS

The following study has the character of an experiment. I will attempt to distinguish method-ologically into three stages of interpretation that which normally remains undistinguished in the interpretive practice of philological commentary as well as textual analysis. If it is the case there that understanding and interpretation as well as immediate reception and reflective exegesis of a

literary text are at once blended in the course of interpretation, then here the horizon of a first, aes-thetically perceptual reading will be distinguished from that of a second, retrospectively interpre-tive reading. To this I will add a third, historical reading that begins with the reconstruction of the horizon of expectations in which the poem "Spleen" inscribed itself with the appearance of the *Fleurs du mal,* and that then will follow the history of its reception or "readings," up to the most recent one, that is, my own.

The three steps of my interpretation — no methodological innovation of mine — are grounded in the theory that the hermeneutic process is to be conceived as a unity of the three moments of understanding (*intelligere*), interpretation (*interpretare*), and application (*applicare*). Hans-Georg Gadamer deserves the credit for having brought the significance of this triadic unity of the hermeneutic process back to light.[1] This unity has determined, in a manner more or less one-sidedly realized, all textual interpretation from time immemorial; it was explicitly formulated by pietistic hermeneutics during the Enlightenment as the doctrine of the three *subtilitates*; it became discredited with the victory of the historicist and positivist ideal of scholarship; and it took center stage in the development of theory with the renewal of theological and juridical hermeneutics.[2] The obvious backwardness of literary hermeneutics is explainable by the facts that here the hermeneutic process reduces to interpretation alone, that no theory of understanding has been developed for texts of an aesthetic character, and that the question of "application" has been relegated to book reviewers' criticism as an unscholarly one. Gadamer's suggestion, "to redefine the hermeneutics of the human studies from the perspective of the hermeneutics of jurisprudence and theology," is thus an opportunity for literary hermeneutics,[3] for the sake of which I ask the question whether and how the hermeneutic unity of all three moments realizes itself in the interpretation of a poetic text.

I direct my hermeneutic experiment at this problem by dividing into three steps the interpretation of a poem that already has a history of reception. The steps might be described phenomenologically as three successive readings. In dividing the hermeneutic process into three steps, the distinction between the three readings must be fabricated to a certain degree; yet only in this manner is it possible to demonstrate what kind of understanding, interpretation, and

application might be proper to a text of aesthetic character. If there is to be an autonomous literary hermeneutics, it must prove itself in the fact — as Peter Szondi correctly demanded — "that it does not just consider the aesthetic character of the text to be interpreted in an appreciation that only follows upon the interpretation, but rather that makes the aesthetic character the premise of the interpretation itself."[4] This premise cannot be fulfilled with the methods of traditional stylistics (in the sense of Leo Spitzer's "critique des beautés"),[5] linguistic poetics, and "textual analysis" alone. Whatever may be recognized in the final texture of the text, in the closed whole of its structure, as a verbal function bearing significance or as aesthetic equivalency, always presupposes something provisionally understood. That which the poetic text, thanks to its aesthetic character, provisionally offers to understanding proceeds from its processlike effect; for this reason it cannot be directly deduced from a description of its final structure as "artifact," however comprehensively this might have construed its "levels" and its aesthetic equivalencies. Today, the structural description of texts can and should be grounded hermeneutically in an analysis of the process of reception: the debate between Roman Jakobson and Claude Lévi-Strauss, and Michael Riffaterre teaches as much.[6] The poetic

---

[4]*Einführung in die literarische Hermeneutik* (Frankfurt, 1975), p. 13. [Jauss]

[5]The term *critique des beautés* is from the French critic Chateaubriand (1768–1848), who counseled commentators on literature to discuss the good points of a text rather than (as had been traditional) enumerate its faults. Leo Spitzer (1887–1960), a founder of the post–World War II comparative literature movement, attempted to use the analytic methods of linguistics to isolate moments of stylistic excellence. Jauss's snarky reference to Spitzer suggests his dissatisfaction with locating linguistic structures "out there" in the text rather than in how the text is performed by a reader.

[6]R. Posner drew this conclusion from the debate: "Obviously, neither the prosody nor the semantics of the poem can be revealed through the mere description of the written text — to say nothing of the aesthetic code of the poem that above all makes use of these textual levels. Similarly to how one can get the prosodic indicators right only by beginning with their acoustic realization, one also can only describe the semantics adequately if one begins with a text that is already fully received and understood." See his "Strukturalismus in der Gedichtsinterpretation," *Sprache im technischen Zietalter* 29 (1969), pp. 27–58, esp. p. 47. [Jauss]

Translated by Timothy Bahti.

[1]*Wahrheit und Methode* (Tübingen, 1960), pp. 290 ff. Available in English as *Truth and Method*, translation edited by Garrett Barden and John Cumming (New York, 1975). [Jauss]

[2]Jauss is reminding us that interpretive method was codified first for the interpretation of the Bible and of legal codes.

[3]Ibid., p. 294. [Jauss]

text can be disclosed in its aesthetic function only when the poetic structures that are read out of the finished aesthetic object as its characteristics are retranslated, from out of the objectification of the description, back into the process of the experience of the text that allows the reader to take part in the genesis of the aesthetic object. Put another way, and using the formulation with which Michael Riffaterre in 1962 introduced the turn from the structural description to the analysis of the reception of the poetic text: the text, which structural poetics described as the endpoint and sum of the devices actualized in it, must from now on be considered as the point of departure for its aesthetic effect; and this must be investigated in the succession of the pregiven elements of the reception that govern the process of aesthetic perception, and thereby also limit the arbitrariness of readings that are supposedly merely subjective.[7]

With the experiment begun here, I go further and in another direction than Riffaterre, who recently developed his structural stylistics into a *Semiotics of Poetry* (1978), which is more interested in the pregiven elements of reception and in the "rules of actualization" than in the aesthetic activity of the reader who takes up or receives the text.[8] I, on the other hand, seek to divide this activity into the two hermeneutic acts, understanding and interpretation, in that I distinguish reflective interpretation as the phase of a second reading from immediate understanding within aesthetic perception as the phase of the first reading. This distinction was necessitated by my interest in making, once and for all, the aesthetic character of the poetic text expressly and demonstrably into the premise of its interpretation. To recognize how the poetic text, thanks to its aesthetic character, allows us to initially perceive and understand something, the analysis

cannot begin with the question of the significance of the particular within the achieved form of the whole; rather, it must pursue the significance still left open in the process of perception that the text, like a "score," indicates for the reader. The investigation of the aesthetic character proper to the poetic text, in distinction to the theological, the juridical, or even the philosophical one, must follow the orientation given to aesthetic perception through the construction of the text, the suggestion of its rhythm, and the gradual achievement of its form.

In the poetic text, aesthetic understanding is primarily directed at the process of perception; therefore it is hermeneutically related to the horizon of expectations of the first reading — which often, especially with historically distant texts or with hermetic[9] lyrics, can only be made visible in its shaped coherence and its fullness of significance through repeated readings. The explicit interpretation in the second and in each further reading also remains related to the horizon of expectations of the first, i.e., perceptual reading — as long as the interpreter claims to make concrete a specific coherence of significance from out of the horizon of meaning of this text, and would not, for example, exercise the license of allegories to translate the meaning of the text into a foreign context, that is, to give it a significance transcending the horizon of meaning and thereby the intentionality of the text.[10] The interpretation of a poetic text always presupposes aesthetic perception as its pre-understanding; it may only concretize significances that appeared or could have appeared possible to the interpreter within the horizon of his preceding reading. Gadamer's dictum, "To understand means to understand something as an answer,"[11] must therefore be limited in regard to the poetic text. Here it can only concern the secondary act of *interpretive understanding* insofar as this concretizes a specific

---

[7] Now in *Essais de stylistique structurale* (Paris, 1971), pp. 307 ff.; cf. his "The Reader's Perception of Narrative," in *Interpretation of Narrative* (Toronto, 1978). [Jauss]

[8] Ibid., p. 29: "Instead of only looking for rules regulating narrative structures, I propose that we look for rules regulating actualization of such structures in the text, that is, regulating the very performance of literature as communication." On his "reader-reception modes," see *Semiotics of Poetry* (Bloomington, Indiana, 1978), pp. 115 ff. [Jauss]

[9] Mystical or private.

[10] Jauss hints here at the temptation to "creatively misread" difficult texts by turning their private symbols into an allegory we manufacture out of whole cloth.

[11] In a still unpublished lecture on literary hermeneutics, Dubrovnik, 1978. [Jauss]

significance as an answer to a question; it may not, however, concern the primary act of *perceptual* understanding that introduces and constitutes the aesthetic experience of the poetic text. To be sure, aesthetic perception also always already includes understanding. For as is well known, the poetic text as an aesthetic object makes possible, in contrast to everyday perception that degenerates into a norm, a mode of perception at once more complex and more meaningful, which as aesthetic pleasure is able to rejuvenate cognitive vision or visual recognition (*aisthesis*).[12] Yet this accomplishment of aisthesis, capable of meaningful understanding, is not already in need of interpretation, and thus it also does not necessarily have the character of an answer to an implicit or explicit question. If it should hold for the reception of a poetic text that here — as Gadamer himself, following Husserl, has formulated it — "the eidetic reduction is spontaneously achieved in aesthetic experience,"[13] then the understanding within the act of aesthetic perception may not be assigned to an interpretation that — by the very fact that something is understood as an answer — reduces the surplus of meaning of the poetic text to one of its possible utterances. In the eidetic reduction of aesthetic perception, the reflective reduction on the part of the interpretation that would understand the text as an answer to an implicit question, can for the time being remain suspended, while at the same time an understanding can be at work allowing the reader to experience language in its power and, thereby, the world in its fullness of significance.

The distinguishing of reflective interpretation from the perceptual understanding of a poetic text is thus not as artificial as it might at first have seemed. It is made possible throughout the self-evident horizonal structure of the experience of rereading. Every reader is familiar with the experience that the significance of a poem often discloses itself only on rereading, after returning from the end to the beginning. Here the experience of the first reading becomes the horizon of the second one: what the reader received in the progressive horizon of interpretation. If one adds that the interpretation itself may in turn become the foundation for an application — more precisely, that a text from the past is of interest not only in reference to its primary context, but that it is also interpreted to disclose a possible significance for the contemporary situation — then what comes to light is that the triadic unity of understanding, interpretation, and application (such as it is accomplished in the hermeneutic process) corresponds to the three horizons of relevance — thematic, interpretive, and motivational — the mutual relation of which, according to Alfred Schütz, determines the constitution of the subjective experience of the life-world [*Lebenswelt*].[14]

In executing the experiment of a repeated reading that will seek to identify thematically the three acts of the hermeneutic process, I may take up and develop further notions that Michael Riffaterre, Wolfgang Iser, and Roland Barthes have introduced into the analysis of the processes of reception. Riffaterre analyzes the course of the reception of a poem as the play of anticipation and correction conditioned through the categories of equivalence of tension, surprise, disappointment, irony, and comedy. An "over-determination" is common to these categories that demands attention through the respective correction of an expectation, thereby steering the reader's course of reception and, consequently, progressively determining the meaning of the text to be interpreted. In my experience, Riffaterre's categories are more appropriate to narrative texts than to lyric ones: the reading of a poem awakens not so much tension regarding its continuation, as the expectation of what I would like to call lyrical consistency — the expectation that the lyrical movement will allow one to grasp verse by verse a coherence at first hidden, and thus allow

---

[12]On this, see my *Ästhetische Erfahrung und literarische Hermeneutik* (Munich, 1979), p. 62 and chapter A 6. This book is forthcoming in the English translation of Michael Shaw from the University of Minnesota Press. [Jauss]

[13]The Dubrovnik lecturer (see note [12]). *Wahrheit und Methode*, p. 291, touches on my qualification that in aesthetic perception understanding certainly implies interpretation, but does not at the same time have to articulate it as a theme. "Interpretation is not an act that occasionally and retrospectively attaches to understanding; rather, understanding is always interpretation, and interpretation therefore the explicit form of understanding." [Jauss]

[14]*Das Problem der Relevanz* (Frankfurt, 1971). [Jauss]

the spectacle of the world to arise anew from a particular situation. Innovation and recognition become complementary in lyrical aisthesis, so that the positive category of satisfied expectation may be placed alongside Riffaterre's negative categories of surprise and disappointment, in which he speaks of satisfied expectation only pejoratively, as if it were equivalent to the effect of a cliché.15,16

Finally, his model for the reception of a poem presupposes the ideal reader ("superreader,") who is not only equipped with the sum total of literary historical knowledge available today, but also is capable of consciously registering every aesthetic impression and referring it back to the text's structure of effect. Thus the interpreting competence overshadows the analysis of perceptual understanding, even though Riffaterre interprets within the open horizon of the syntagmatic unfolding and correction of the system. To escape this dilemma, I have not fabricated something like a "naive reader," but rather have transposed myself into the role of a reader with the educational horizon of our contemporary present. The role of this historical reader should presuppose that one is experienced in one's associations with lyrics, but that one can initially suspend one's literary historical or linguistic competence, and put in its place the capacity occasionally to wonder during the course of the reading, and to express this wonder in the form of questions. Beside this historical reader from 1979, I have placed a commentator with scholarly competence, who deepens the aesthetic impressions of the reader whose understanding takes the form of pleasure, and who refers back to the text's structures of effect as much as possible. (In what follows, this commentary is indicated through indentation.)

Since I still do not yet suffer from not having become an empiricist, I can calmly put up with the fact that my solution does not yet provide the model for the overdue empirical research into

15 *Essais de stylistique structurale*, p. 340. [Jauss]

16 Jauss suggests that the aesthetic appreciation of lyric poetry is heightened when expectations are fulfilled, when things fall into place so that we see a completed design, whereas with narrative the direct fulfillment of expectations usually makes for a dull story.

reception. I will probably bring upon myself the reproach of not being typical enough as a reader, and not being sufficiently versed in linguistics or semiotics as an analyst; and yet I hope to have tested practically the theoretical postulate of combining structural and semiotic analysis with phenomenological interpretation and hermeneutic reflection. To find a methodological starting-point capable of further development, it was for me above all a matter of separating more sharply than has been done before the levels of aesthetic perception and reflective interpretation in the interpretation of poetic texts. An initial methodological advance may already result from this separation, namely that with the help of the question-answer relationship, the textual signals may now be specified within their syntagmatic coherence as the givens of the course of the reception that establish consistency. The "structures-of-appeal," "offers-of-identification," and "absences of meaning" [*Appellstrukturen, Identifikationsangebote, und Sinnlücken*] that Wolfgang Iser has conceived as categories in his theory of aesthetic effect are most easily made concrete in the course of the reception as inducements toward the constitution of meaning when one describes the effective factors of the poetic text as expectations, and transposes them into questions that the text in such passages either produces, leaves open, or answers.17 If Iser, in *The Act of Reading* — in contrast to Riffaterre, who views the process of reception under the dominant category of overdetermination and interprets it *noles volens*18 — has rehabilitated the aesthetic character of fictional texts under the dominant category of "indeterminacy" (and "redeterminability"), it nonetheless remained to me to describe the course of the reception in the first, perceptual reading as an experience of accumulating evidence that is also aesthetically more convincing, which, in turn, as the pregiven horizon for a second, interpretive reading, at once opens up and delimits the space for possible concretizations.

Accordingly, the change of horizons between the first and the second readings may be described as follows: the reader — who performs the "score" of the text in the course of the reception of verse

17 *Der Akt des Lesens* (Munich, 1976). [Jauss]

18 Latin for "willy-nilly."

after verse, and who is led toward the ending in a perceptual act of anticipation, from the particular toward the possible whole of form and meaning — becomes aware of the fulfilled form of the poem, but not yet of its fulfilled significance, let alone of its "whole meaning." Whoever acknowledges the hermeneutic premise that the meaningful whole of a lyric work is no longer to be understood as if substantial, as if its meaning were pregiven and timeless; rather it is to be understood as a meaning to be performed — whoever acknowledges this premise awaits from the reader the recognition that from now on he may, in the act of interpretive understanding, hypostasize one among other possible significations of the poem, the relevance of which for him does not exclude the worth of others for discussion. From now on, the reader will seek and establish the still unfulfilled significance retrospectively, through a new reading from the perspective of the fulfilled form, in a return from the end to the beginning, from the whole to the particular. Whatever initially resisted understanding manifests itself in the questions that the first going-through has left open. In answering them, one may expect that from the particular elements of significance — in various respects still indeterminate — a fulfilled whole may be established on the level of meaning through the labor of interpretation, which whole is every bit as much on the level of meaning as on the level of form. This meaningful whole can be found only through a selective taking of perspectives and cannot be attained through a supposedly objective description — this falls under the hermeneutic premise of partiality. With this, the question of the historical horizon is posed, the horizon that conditioned the genesis and effect of the work and that once again delimits the present reader's interpretation. To investigate it is now the task of a third, historical reading.

This third step, insofar as it concerns the interpretation of a work from the premises of its time and genesis, is the one most familiar to historical-philological hermeneutics. Yet there the historically reconstructive reading is traditionally the first step, to which historicism adds the injunction that the interpreter has to ignore himself and his standpoint to be able to take up ever more purely the "objective meaning" of the text. Under the spell of this scholarly ideal, the objectivistic illusions of which are evident to almost everyone today, the hermeneutics of the classical and modern philologies sought to privilege historical understanding over the aesthetic appreciation, which, for its part, was rarely attempted at all. Such historicism failed to recognize that the aesthetic character of its texts — as a hermeneutic bridge denied to other disciplines — is that which makes possible the historical understanding of art across the distance in time in the first place, and which therefore must be integrated into the execution of the interpretation as a hermeneutic premise. But inversely, aesthetic understanding and interpretation also remain in reference to the controlling function of the historicist-reconstructive reading. It prevents the text from the past from being naively assimilated to the prejudices and expectations of meaning of the present, and thereby — through explicitly distinguishing the past horizon from the present — allows the poetic text to be seen in its alterity. The investigation of the "otherness," the unique distance, within the contemporaneity of the literary text, demands a reconstructive reading that can begin by seeking out the questions (most often inexplicit ones) to which the text was the response in its time. An interpretation of a literary text as a response should include two things: its response to expectations of a formal kind, such as the literary tradition prescribed for it before its appearance; and its response to questions of meaning such as they could have posed themselves within the historical life-world of its first readers.[19] The reconstruction of the original horizon of expectations would nonetheless fall back into historicism if the historical interpretation could not in turn serve to transform the question, "What did the text say?" into the question, "What does the text say to me, and what do I say to it?" If, like theological or juridical hermeneutics, literary hermeneutics is to

[19]In illustration of Jauss's point that literary texts are often responses to other literary texts that are "alive" for the writer, one could point to Pope's *Essay on Man*, which proposes to "vindicate the ways of God to man," clearly situating itself as a response to Milton's *Paradise Lost*. Jauss is arguing also that the issues such texts are raising for their first readers — in this case, about whether the world reflects a benevolent and omniscient God — are ones that the poet's contemporaries are still asking, unsatisfied by the earlier text's answers.

move from understanding, through interpretation, to application, then application here certainly cannot dissolve into practical action, but rather instead can satisfy the no less legitimate interest of using literary communication with the past to measure and to broaden the horizon of one's own experience vis-à-vis the experience of the other.

The omission of the distinguishing of horizons can have consequences such as may be indicated with the analysis of the reception of a Poe story by Roland Barthes.[20] Its strength lies in the demonstration of how the structuralist description of the narrative principle — which explains the text as a variant of a pregiven model — can be transformed into the textual analysis of "signifi-cance" that allows one to understand the text as a process, as an ongoing production of meaning or more precisely, of possibilities of meaning or forms, the codes according to which meanings are possible").[21] Its weakness lies in a naive fus-ing of horizons: according to its own intention, the reading is supposed to be unmediated and ahistorical ("we will take up the text as it is, as it is when we read it"[22]), and yet this reading only comes about through a "superreader" who brings a comprehensive knowledge of the nineteenth century into play and who, in the course of the reception, notes those passages above all where cultural and linguistic codes can be recalled or associated. One cannot speak of a joining of the interpretation to the process of aesthetic percep-tion, for this, as the "code of the 'actants'" in combination with the "symbolic code or field," can itself be one more code among others (the "scientific, rhetorical, chronological, destina-tory code," etc.).[23] Thus, a reading arises that is neither historical nor aesthetic, but rather is as subjective as it is impressionistic, and yet is sup-posed to ground the theory that each particular text is a tissue of texts — the interminable play of a free-floating intertextuality in "the struggle between man and signs."[24]

Literary hermeneutics, which Barthes not acci-dentally views as a (for him) "enigmatic code," is on the contrary surely no longer interested today in interpreting the text as the revelation of the single truth concealed within it.[25] Against the theory of the "plural text," with its notion of "intertextuality" as a limitless and arbitrary pro-duction of possibilities of meaning and of no less arbitrary interpretations, literary hermeneutics poses the hypothesis that the concretization of the meaning of literary works progresses histori-cally and follows a certain "logic" that precipi-tates in the formation and transformation of the aesthetic canon. Furthermore, it postulates that in the change of horizons of the interpretations, one may distinguish absolutely between arbitrary interpretations and those available to a consensus, between those that are merely original and those that are formative of a norm. The fundamental aspect that supports this hypothesis can lie only in the aesthetic character of the texts: as a regula-tive principle, it allows for there being a series of interpretations, but that are also capable of being reintegrated with respect to the meaning made concrete. Here I may recall the attempt at a pluralistic interpretation of Apollinaire's poem "L'arbre," undertaken at the second colloquium of the *Poetik und hermeneutik* group. On the one hand, the distance vis-à-vis the poem adopted by each reader itself allowed for a different aesthetic perception to arise, and each specific concretiza-tion of the significance necessarily had to ignore other, no less plausible interpretations. And yet, the surprising confirmation that the individual interpretations did not contradict one another despite their differences led to the conclusion that even this "pluralistic text" can provide a unifying aesthetic orientation for perceptual understanding within the horizon of the first reading.[26]

[20]"Analyse textuelle d'un conte d'Edgar Poe," in *Sémiotique narrative et textuelle*, ed. Claude Chabrol (Paris, 1973), pp. 29–54. [Jauss]

[21]Ibid., p. 30. [Jauss]

[22]Ibid., p. 32. [Jauss]

[23]Ibid., p. 51. [Jauss]

[24]Ibid., pp. 30 and 52. [Jauss]

[25]Ibid., p. 30. [Jauss]

[26]*Immanente Ästhetik — Ästhetische Reflexion: Poetik und Hermeneutik II*, ed. Wolfgang Iser (Munich, 1966), pp. 461–84, esp. pp. 473 and 480: "For a concrete interpretation and for a judgment of the quality of the poem, it is not enough to provide its structural principle and to describe Apollinaire's poetic technique. A series of ambiguities is not yet a compel-ling whole. If this whole provokes an ever newer interpreta-tion on the basis of the technique in which it is unfolded, then

To be sure, one may object that, after Baudelaire, a modern poem cannot furnish the reader with this evidence of a compelling whole after only the first reading, but rather only in rereading. And one may object that, mutatis mutandis,[27] a poem from an older tradition or from another culture often only discloses itself for aesthetic understanding when historicist understanding has removed the obstacles to its reception and rendered possible an aesthetic perception of the formerly unenjoyable text. I am also thoroughly of this opinion,[28] so that I can use these objections for precisely one last point.

The priority of aesthetic perception within the triad of literary hermeneutics has need of the *horizon*, but not the temporal priority, of the first reading; this horizon of aesthetic understanding may also be gained only in the course of rereading or with the help of historicist understanding.[29] Aesthetic perception is no universal code with timeless validity, but rather — like all aesthetic experience — is intertwined with historical experience. Thus, for the interpretation of texts from other cultures, the aesthetic character of poetic texts from the western tradition can only offer heuristic advantages. Literary interpretation must compensate with the three achievements of the hermeneutic process for the fact that aesthetic perception itself is subject to historical exchange. It thereby gains the opportunity of broadening historicist knowledge through aesthetic understanding, and perhaps of constituting, through its unconstrained kind of application, a corrective to other applications that are subject to situational pressures and the compulsions of decision-making.

---

this interpretation is neither accidental in its details nor free from a fundamental orientation that is compellingly provided through the construction of the text. The first reading provides this compulsion through the suggestion of the rhythm. The interpretation must give itself over to this medium in which the poem moves" (Dieter Henrich). This interpretation is translated as "Group Interpretation of Apollinaire's 'Arbre,'" in *New Perspectives in German Literary Criticism*, ed. Richard E. Amacher and Victor Lange (Princeton, 1979), pp. 182–207. [Jauss]

[27]Latin for "when necessary changes have been made."

[28]On this, see my *Alterität und Modernität der mittelalterlichen Literatur* (Munich, 1977), esp. p. 10 ff. [Jauss]

[29]Jauss's point is that the order of the three horizons of reading is not temporal: readers may not be able to appreciate a text aesthetically till they have grounded themselves in the history of its period.

Wayne C. Booth

1921–2005

His 1971 Quantrell Prize for undergraduate teaching at the University of Chicago is one indication that Wayne Clayson Booth has been the most effective teacher — in the most far-reaching sense — of the neo-Aristotelians. He was born in American Fork, Utah, and educated at Brigham Young University, where he received his B.A. in 1944. After serving in the infantry during World War II, Booth completed his M.A. and Ph.D. at the University of Chicago, where his mentor was R. S. Crane (see Ch. 1). He taught at Haverford and at Earlham College, where he became professor and chairman of the department of English before returning to a named chair at Chicago in 1962. Booth has received fellowships from the Ford Foundation (1952), the Guggenheim Foundation (1956–57 and 1969–70), and the National Endowment for the Humanities (1975–76). He served as dean of the college of the University of Chicago from 1964 to 1969, and as president of the Modern Language Association in 1982. Booth's meteoric success began with the publication of The Rhetoric of Fiction (1961; second ed., 1983), which shifted from the formalism of Crane to the explicit consideration of the audience and the ways in which texts make the readers they require. Other works have included A Rhetoric of Irony (1974), Modern Dogma and the Rhetoric of Assent (1974), and his most ambitious work, a pluralistic guide to the variety of pluralisms, Critical Understanding (1979). The Company We Keep: Ethical Criticism and the Ethics of Reading (1988) is a long-considered effort to clarify some of the controversy excited by Booth's hint, in The Rhetoric of Fiction, at the potentially injurious effect of narratives by Céline and Nabokov. Booth's most recent books include For the Love of It: Amateuring and Its Rivals (1999), a meditation on amateur musicianship and the healing and enrichment it has brought to his life, and his final work, the manifesto The Rhetoric of Rhetoric: The Quest for Effective Communication (2004).

Control of Distance in *Jane Austen's Emma*

Jane Austen was instinctive and charming. . . . For signal examples of what composition, distribution, arrangement can do, of how they intensify the life of a work of art, we have to go elsewhere.

— HENRY JAMES

A heroine whom no one but myself will much like.

— JANE AUSTEN *describing* EMMA

SYMPATHY AND JUDGMENT IN "EMMA"

Henry James once described Jane Austen as an instinctive novelist whose effects, some of which are admittedly fine, can best be explained as "part of her unconsciousness." It is as if she "fell-a-musing" over her work-basket, he said, lapsed into "wool-gathering," and afterward picked up "her dropped stitches," as "little masterstrokes of imagination."¹

---

¹'The Lesson of Balzac.' *The Question of Our Speech* (Cambridge, 1905), p. 63. A fuller quotation can be found in R. W. Chapman's indispensable *Jane Austen: A Critical Bibliography* (Oxford, 1955). Some important Austen items published too late to be included by Chapman are: (1) Ian Watt, *The Rise of the Novel* (Berkeley, Calif., 1957); (2) Stuart M. Tave, review of Marvin Mudrick's *Jane Austen: Irony as Defense and Discovery* (Princeton, N.J., 1952) in *Philological Quarterly* 32 (July 1953): 256–57; (3) Andrew H. Wright, *Jane Austen's Novels: A Study in Structure* (London, 1953), pp. 36–82; (4) Christopher Gillie, "*Sense and Sensibility,* An Assessment," *Essays in Criticism* 9 (January 1959): 1–9, esp. 5–6; (5) Edgar F. Shannon, Jr., "*Emma:* Character and Construction," *PMLA* 71 (September 1956): 637–50. [Booth]

The amiable accusation has been repeated in various forms, most recently as a claim that Jane Austen creates characters toward whom we cannot react as she consciously intends.[2]

Although we cannot hope to decide whether Jane Austen was entirely conscious of her own artistry, a careful look at the technique of any of her novels reveals a rather different picture from that of the unconscious spinster with her knitting needles. In *Emma* especially, where the chances for technical failure are great indeed, we find at work one of the unquestionable masters of the rhetoric of narration.

At the beginning of *Emma*, the young heroine has every requirement for deserved happiness but one. She has intelligence, wit, beauty, wealth, and position, and she has the love of those around her. Indeed, she thinks herself completely happy. The only threat to her happiness, a threat of which she is unaware, is herself: charming as she is, she can neither see her own excessive pride honestly nor resist imposing herself on the lives of others. She is deficient both in generosity and in self-knowledge. She discovers and corrects her faults only after she has almost ruined herself and her closest friends. But with the reform in her character, she is ready for marriage with the man she loves, the man who throughout the book has stood in the reader's mind for what she lacks.

It is clear that with a general plot of this kind Jane Austen gave herself difficulties of high order. Though Emma's faults are comic, they constantly threaten to produce serious harm. Yet she must remain sympathetic or the reader will not wish for and delight sufficiently in her reform.

Obviously, the problem with a plot like this is to find some way to allow the reader to laugh at the mistakes committed by the heroine and at her punishment, without reducing the desire to see her reform and thus earn happiness. In *Tom Jones* this double attitude is achieved . . . partly through the invention of episodes producing sympathy and relieving any serious anxiety we might have, and partly through the direct and sympathetic commentary. In *Emma*, since most of the episodes must illustrate the heroine's faults and thus increase either our emotional distance or our anxiety, a different method is required. If we fail to see Emma's faults as revealed in the ironic texture from line to line, we cannot savor to the full the comedy as it is prepared for us. On the other hand, if we fail to love her, as Jane Austen herself predicted we would[3] — if we fail to love her more and more as the book progresses — we can neither hope for the conclusion, a happy and deserved marriage with Knightley following upon her reform, nor accept it as an honest one when it comes.[4] Any attempt to solve the problem by reducing either the love or the clear view of her faults would have been fatal.

SYMPATHY THROUGH CONTROL OF INSIDE VIEWS

The solution to the problem of maintaining sympathy despite almost crippling faults was primarily to use the heroine herself as a kind of narrator, though in third person, reporting on her own experience. So far as we know, Jane Austen never formulated any theory to cover her own practice; she invented no term like James's "central intelligence" or "lucid reflector" to describe her method of viewing the world of the book primarily through Emma's own eyes. We can thus never know for sure to what extent James's accusation of "unconsciousness" was right. But whether she was inclined to speculate about her method scarcely matters; her solution was clearly a brilliant one. By showing most of the story through Emma's eyes, the author insures that we shall travel with Emma rather than stand against her. It is not simply that Emma provides, in the

---

[2]See, for example, Mudrick, pp. 91, 165; Frank O'Connor, *The Mirror in the Roadway* (London, 1957), p. 30. [Booth]

[3]"A heroine whom no one but myself will much like" (James Edward Austen-Leigh, *Memoir of His Aunt* [London, 1870; Oxford, 1926], p. 157). [Booth]

[4]The best discussion of this problem is Reginald Farrer's "Jane Austen," *Quarterly Review* 228 (July 1917): 1–30; reprinted in William Heath's *Discussion of Jane Austen* (Boston, 1961). For one critic the book fails because the problem was never recognized by Jane Austen herself: Mr. E. N. Hayes, in what may well be the least sympathetic discussion of *Emma* yet written, explains the whole book as the author's failure to see Emma's faults. "Evidently Jane Austen wished to protect Emma . . . The author is therefore in the ambiguous position of both loving and scorning the heroine" ("'Emma': A Dissenting Opinion," *Nineteenth-Century Fiction* 4 [June 1949]: 18, 19. [Booth]

unimpeachable evidence of her own conscience, proof that she has many redeeming qualities that do not appear on the surface; such evidence could be given with authorial commentary, though perhaps not with such force and conviction. Much more important, the sustained inside view leads the reader to hope for good fortune for the character with whom he travels, quite independently of the qualities revealed.

Seen from the outside, Emma would be an unpleasant person, unless, like Mr. Woodhouse and Knightley, we knew her well enough to infer her true worth. Though we might easily be led to laugh at her, we could never be made to laugh sympathetically. While the final unmasking of her faults and her humiliation would make artistic sense to an unsympathetic reader, her marriage with Knightley would become irrelevant if not meaningless. Unless we desire Emma's happiness and her reform which alone can make that happiness possible, a good third of this book will seem irredeemably dull.

Yet sympathetic laughter is never easily achieved. It is much easier to set up a separate fool for comic effects and to preserve your heroine for finer things. Sympathetic laughter is especially difficult with characters whose faults do not spring from sympathetic virtues. The grasping but witty Volpone can keep us on his side so long as his victims are more grasping and less witty than he, but as soon as the innocent victims, Celia and Bonario, come on stage, the quality of the humor changes; we no longer delight unambiguously in his triumphs. In contrast to this, the great sympathetic comic heroes often are comic largely because their faults, like Uncle Toby's sentimentality, spring from an excess of some virtue. Don Quixote's madness is partly caused by an excess of idealism, an excess of loving concern for the unfortunate. Every crazy gesture he makes gives further reason for loving the well-meaning old fool, and we can thus laugh at him in somewhat the same spirit in which we laugh at our own faults — in a benign, forgiving spirit. We may be contemptible for doing so; to persons without a sense of humor such laughter often seems a wicked escape. But self-love being what it is, we laugh at ourselves in a thoroughly forgiving way, and we laugh in the same way at Don Quixote:

we are convinced that his heart, like ours, is in the right place.

Nothing in Emma's comic misunderstandings can serve for the same effect. Her faults are not excesses of virtue. She attempts to manipulate Harriet not from an excess of kindness but from a desire for power and admiration. She flirts with Frank Churchill out of vanity and irresponsibility. She mistreats Jane Fairfax because of Jane's *good* qualities. She abuses Miss Bates because of her own essential lack of "tenderness" and "good will."

We have only to think of what Emma's story would be if seen through Jane Fairfax's or Mrs. Elton's or Robert Martin's eyes to recognize how little our sympathy springs from any natural view, and to see how inescapable is the decision to use Emma's mind as a reflector of events — however beclouded her vision must be. To Jane Fairfax, who embodies throughout the book most of the values which Emma discovers only at the end, the early Emma is intolerable.

But Jane Austen never lets us forget that Emma is not what she might appear to be. For every section devoted to her misdeeds — and even they are seen for the most part through her own eyes — there is a section devoted to her self-reproach. We see her rudeness to poor foolish Miss Bates, and we see it vividly. But her remorse and act of penance in visiting Miss Bates after Knightley's rebuke are experienced even more vividly. We see her successive attempts to mislead Harriet, but we see at great length and in high color her self-castigation (Chs. 16, 17, 48). We see her boasting proudly that she does not need marriage, boasting almost as blatantly of her "resources" as does Mrs. Elton (Ch. 10). But we know her too intimately to take her conscious thoughts at face value. And we see her, thirty-eight chapters later, chastened to an admission of what we have known all along to be her true human need for love. 'If all took place that might take place among the circle of her friends, Hartfield must be comparatively deserted; and she left to cheer her father with the spirits only of ruined happiness. The child to be born at Randalls must be a tie there even dearer than herself; and Mrs. Weston's heart and time would be occupied by it. . . . All that were good would be withdrawn' (Ch. 48).

Perhaps the most delightful effects from our sustained inside view of a very confused and very charming young woman come from her frequent thoughts about Knightley. She is basically right all along about his pre-eminent wisdom and virtue, and she is our chief authority for taking *his* authority so seriously. And yet in every thought about him she is misled. Knightley rebukes her; the reader knows that Knightley is in the right. But Emma?

> Emma made no answer, and tried to look cheerfully unconcerned, but was really feeling uncomfortable, and wanting him very much to be gone. She did not repeat what she had done; she still thought herself a better judge of such a point of female right and refinement than he could be; but yet she had a sort of habitual respect for his judgment in general, which made her dislike having it so loudly against her; and to have him sitting just opposite to her in an angry state, was very disagreeable [Ch. 8].

Even more striking is the lack of self-knowledge shown when Mrs. Weston suggests that Knightley might marry Jane Fairfax.

> Her objections to Mr. Knightley's marrying did not in the least subside. She could see nothing but evil in it. It would be a great disappointment to Mr. John Knightley [Knightley's brother]; consequently to Isabella. A real injury to the children — a most mortifying change, and material loss to them all; — a very great deduction from her father's daily comfort — and, as to herself, she could not at all endure the idea of Jane Fairfax at Donwell Abbey. A Mrs. Knightley for them all to give way to! — No, Mr. Knightley must never marry. Little Henry must remain the heir of Donwell [Ch. 26].

Self-deception could hardly be carried further, at least in a person of high intelligence and sensitivity.

Yet the effect of all this is what our tolerance for our own faults produces in our own lives. While only immature readers ever really identify with any character, losing all sense of distance and hence all chance of an artistic experience, our emotional reaction to every event concerning Emma tends to become like her own. When she feels anxiety or shame, we feel analogous emotions. Our modern awareness that such "feelings" are not identical with those we feel in our own lives in similar circumstances has tended to blind us to the fact that aesthetic form can be built out of patterned emotions as well as out of other materials. It is absurd to pretend that because our emotions and desires in responding to fiction are in a very real sense disinterested, they do not or should not exist. Jane Austen, in developing the sustained use of a sympathetic inside view, has mastered one of the most successful of all devices for including a parallel emotional response between the deficient heroine and the reader.

Sympathy for Emma can be heightened by withholding inside views of others as well as by granting them of her. The author knew, for example, that it would be fatal to grant any extended inside view of Jane Fairfax. The inadequacies of impressionistic criticism are nowhere revealed more clearly than in the suggestion often made about such minor characters that their authors would have liked to make them vivid but didn't know how.[5] Jane Austen knew perfectly well how to make such a character vivid; Anne in *Persuasion* is a kind of Jane Fairfax turned into heroine. But in *Emma*, Emma must shine supreme. It is not only that the slightest glance inside Jane's mind would be fatal to all of the author's plans for mystification about Frank Churchill, though this is important. The major problem is that any extended view of her would reveal her as a more sympathetic person than Emma herself. Jane is superior to Emma in most respects except the stroke of good fortune that made Emma the heroine of the book. In matters of taste and ability, of head and of heart, she is Emma's superior, and Jane Austen, always in danger of losing our sympathy for Emma, cannot risk any degree of distraction. Jane could, it is true, be granted fewer virtues, and then made more vivid. But to do so would greatly weaken the force of Emma's mistakes of heart and head in her treatment of the almost faultless Jane.

---

[5] A. C. Bradley, for example, once argued that Jane Austen intended Jane Fairfax to be as interesting throughout as she becomes at the end, but "the moralist in Jane Austen stood for once in her way. The secret engagement is, for her, so serious an offence, that she is afraid to win our hearts for Jane until it has led to great unhappiness" ("Jane Austen," in *Essays and Studies, by Members of the English Association*, II [Oxford, 1911], p. 23). [Booth]

But the very effectiveness of the rhetoric designed to produce sympathy might in itself lead to a serious misreading of the book. In reducing the emotional distance, the natural tendency is to reduce — willy-nilly — moral and intellectual distance as well. In reacting to Emma's faults from the inside out, as if they were our own, we may very well not only forgive them but overlook them.[6] There is, of course, no danger that readers who persist to the end will overlook Emma's serious mistakes; since she sees and reports those mistakes, everything becomes crystal clear at the end. The real danger inherent in the experiment is that readers will overlook the mistakes as they are committed and thus miss much of the comedy that depends on Emma's distorted view from page to page. If readers who dislike Emma cannot enjoy the preparation for the marriage to Knightley, readers who do not recognize her faults with absolute precision cannot enjoy the details of the preparation for the comic abasement which must precede that marriage.

It might be argued that there is no real problem, since the conventions of her time allowed for reliable commentary whenever it was needed to place Emma's faults precisely. But Jane Austen is not operating according to the conventions, most of which she had long since parodied and outgrown:

[6] I know of only one full-scale attempt to deal with the "tension between sympathy and judgment" in modern literature, Robert Langbaum's *The Poetry of Experience* (London, 1957). Langbaum argues that in the dramatic monologue, with which he is primarily concerned, the sympathy engendered by the direct portrayal of internal experience leads the reader to suspend his moral judgment. Thus, in reading Browning's portraits of moral degeneration — e.g., the duke in "My Last Duchess" or the monk in "Soliloquy of a Spanish Cloister" — our moral judgment is overwhelmed "because we prefer to participate in the duke's power and freedom, in his hard core of character fiercely loyal to itself. Moral judgment is in fact important as the thing to be suspended, as a measure of the price we pay for the privilege of appreciating to the full this extraordinary man" (p. 83). While I think that Langbaum seriously underplays the extent to which moral judgment remains even after psychological vividness has done its work, and while he perhaps defines "morality" too narrowly when he excludes from it such things as power and freedom and fierce loyalty to one's own character, his book is a stimulating introduction to the problems raised by the internal portraiture of flawed characters. [Booth]

CONTROL OF JUDGMENT

her technique is determined by the needs of the novel she is writing. We can see this clearly by contrasting the manner of *Emma* with that of *Persuasion*, the next and last-completed work. In *Emma* there are many breaks in the point of view, because Emma's beclouded mind cannot do the whole job. In *Persuasion*, where the heroine's viewpoint is faulty only in her ignorance of Captain Wentworth's love, there are very few. Anne Elliot's consciousness is sufficient, as Emma's is not, for most of the needs of the novel which she dominates. Once the ethical and intellectual framework has been established by the narrator's introduction, we enter Anne's consciousness and remain bound to it much more rigorously than we are bound to Emma's. It is still true that whenever something must be shown that Anne's consciousness cannot show, we move to another center; but since her consciousness can do much more for us than Emma's, there need be few departures from it.

The most notable shift for rhetorical purposes in *persuasion* comes fairly early. When Anne first meets Captain Wentworth after their years of separation that follow her refusal to marry him, she is convinced that he is indifferent. The major movement of *Persuasion* is toward her final discovery that he still loves her; *her* suspense is thus strong and inevitable from the beginning. The reader, however, is likely to believe that Wentworth is still interested. All the conventions of art favor such a belief: the emphasis is clearly on Anne and her unhappiness; the lover has returned; we have only to wait, perhaps with some tedium, for the inevitable outcome. Anne learns (Ch. 7) that he has spoken of her as so altered "he should not have known her again!" "These were words which could not but dwell with her. Yet she soon began to rejoice that she had heard them. They were of sobering tendency; they allayed agitation; they composed, and consequently must make her happier." And suddenly we enter Wentworth's mind for one time only: "Frederick Wentworth had used such words, or something like them, but without an idea that they would be carried round to her. He had thought her wretchedly altered, and, in the first moment of appeal, had spoken as he felt. He had not forgiven Anne Elliot. She had used him ill." — and so he goes on, for five more paragraphs. The necessary point, the fact that

Frederick believes himself to be indifferent, has been made, and it could not have been made without some kind of shift from Anne's consciousness.

At the end of the novel, we learn that Wentworth was himself deceived in this momentary inside view: "He had meant to forget her, and believed it to be done. He had imagined himself indifferent, when he had only been angry." We may want to protest against the earlier suppression as unfair, but we can hardly believe it to be what Miss Lascelles calls "an oversight."[7] It is deliberate manipulation of inside views in order to destroy our conventional security. We are thus made ready to go along with Anne in her long and painful road to the discovery that Frederick loves her after all.

The only other important breaks in the angle of vision of *Persuasion* come at the beginning and at the end. Chapter one is an excellent example of how a skillful novelist can, by the use of his own direct voice, accomplish in a few pages what even the best novelist must take chapters to do if he uses nothing but dramatized action. Again at the conclusion the author enters with a resounding reaffirmation that the Wentworth-Elliot marriage is as good a thing as we have felt it to be from the beginning.

> Who can be in doubt of what followed? When any two young people take it into their heads to marry, they are pretty sure by perseverance to carry their point, be they ever so poor, or ever so imprudent, or ever so little likely to be necessary to each other's ultimate comfort. This may be bad morality to conclude with, but I believe it to be truth; and if such parties succeed, how should a Captain Wentworth and an Anne Elliot, with the advantage of maturity of mind, consciousness of right, and one independent fortune between them, fail of bearing down every opposition?[8]

[7] *Jane Austen and Her Art* (Oxford, 1939), p. 204. [Booth]
[8] It seems to be difficult for some modern critics, accustomed to ferreting values out from an impersonal or ironic context without the aid of the author's voice, to make use of reliable commentary like this when it is provided. Even a highly perceptive reader like Mark Schorer, for example, finds himself doing unnecessary acrobatics with the question of style, and particularly metaphor, as clues to the norms against which the author judges her characters. In reading *Persuasion* he finds these clues among the metaphors "from commerce and property, the counting house and the inherited estate" with which it abounds ("Fiction and the Matrix of Analogy," *Kenyon Review* [Autumn 1949]: 540). No one would deny that the novel is packed with such metaphors, although Schorer is

Except for these few intrusions and one in Chapter 19, Anne's own mind is sufficient in *Persuasion*, but we can never rely completely on Emma. It is hardly surprising that Jane Austen has provided many correctives to insure our placing her errors with precision.

The chief corrective is Knightley. His commentary on Emma's errors is a natural expression of his love; he can tell the reader and Emma at the same time precisely how she is mistaken. Thus, nothing Knightley says can be beside the point. Each affirmation of a value, each accusation of error is in itself an action in the plot. When he rebukes Emma for manipulating Harriet, when he attacks her for being "insolent" and "unfeeling" in her treatment of Miss Bates, we have Jane Austen's judgment on Emma, rendered dramatically. But it has come from someone who is essentially sympathetic toward Emma, so that his judgments against her are presumed to be temporary. His sympathy reinforces ours even as he criticizes, and her respect for his opinion, shown in her self-abasement after he has criticized, is one of our main reasons for expecting her to reform.

If Henry James had tried to write a novel about Emma, and had cogitated at length on the problem of getting her story told dramatically, he could not have done better than this. It is possible, of course, to think of *Emma* without Knightley as *raisonneur*, just as it is possible to think of *The Golden Bowl*, say, without the Assinghams as

---

somewhat overingenious in marshaling to his cause certain dead metaphors that Austen could not have avoided without awkward circumlocution (esp. p. 542). But the crucial question surely is: What precisely are these metaphors of the countinghouse doing in the novel? Whose values are they supposed to reveal? Accustomed to reading modern fiction in which the novelist very likely provides no direct assistance in answering this question, Schorer leaves it really unanswered; at times he seems almost to imply that Jane Austen is unconsciously giving herself away in her use of them (e.g., p. 543).

But the novel is really very clear about it all. The introduction, coming directly from the wholly reliable narrator, establishes unequivocally and without "analogy" the conflict between the world of the Elliots, depending for its values on selfishness, stupidity, and pride — and the world of Anne, a world where "elegance of mind and sweetness of character" are the supreme values. The commercial values stressed by Schorer are only a selection from what is actually a rich group of evils. And Anne's own expressed views again and again provide direct guidance to the reader. [Booth]

ficelles to reflect something not seen by the prince or princess. But Knightley, though he receives less independent space than the Assinghams and is almost never seen in an inside view, is clearly more useful for Jane Austen's purposes than any realistically limited *ficelle* could possibly be. By combining the role of commentator with the role of hero, Jane Austen has worked more economically than James, and though economy is as dangerous as any other criterion when applied universally, even James might have profited from a closer study of the economies that a character like Knightley can be made to achieve. It is as if James had dared to make one of the four main characters, say the Prince, into a thoroughly good, wise, perceptive man, a thoroughly clear rather than a partly confused "reflector."

Since Knightley is established early as completely reliable, we need no views of his secret thoughts. He has no secret thoughts, except for the unacknowledged depths of his love for Emma and his jealousy of Frank Churchill. The other main characters have more to hide, and Jane Austen moves in and out of minds with great freedom, choosing for her own purposes what to reveal and what to withhold. Always the seeming violation of consistency is in the consistent service of the particular needs of Emma's story. Sometimes a shift is made simply to direct our suspense, as when Mrs. Weston suggests a possible union of Emma and Frank Churchill, at the end of her conversation with Knightley about the harmful effects of Emma's friendship with Harriet (Ch. 5). "Part of her meaning was to conceal some favourite thoughts of her own and Mr. Weston's on the subject, as much as possible. There were wishes at Randalls respecting Emma's destiny, but it was not desirable to have them suspected."

One objection to this selective dipping into whatever mind best serves our immediate purposes is that it suggests mere trickery and inevitably spoils the illusion of reality. If Jane Austen can tell us what Mrs. Weston is thinking, why not what Frank Churchill and Jane Fairfax are thinking? Obviously, because she chooses to build a mystery, and to do so she must refuse, arbitrarily and obtrusively, to grant the privilege of an inside view to characters whose minds would reveal

too much. But is not the mystery purchased at the price of shaking the reader's faith in Jane Austen's integrity? If she simply withholds until later what she might as well relate now — if her procedure is not dictated by the very nature of her materials — why should we take her seriously? If a natural surface were required in all fiction, then this objection would hold. But if we want to read *Emma* in its own terms, the real question about these shifts cannot be answered by an easy appeal to general principles. Every author withholds until later what he "might as well" relate now. The question is always one of desired effects, and the choice of any one effect always bans innumerable other effects. There is, indeed, a question to be raised about the use of mystery in *Emma*, but the conflict is not between an abstract end that Jane Austen never worried about and a shoddy mystification that she allowed to betray her. The conflict is between two effects both of which she cares about a good deal. On the one hand she cares about maintaining some sense of mystery as long as she can. On the other, she works at all points to heighten the reader's sense of dramatic irony, usually in the form of a contrast between what Emma knows and what the reader knows.

As in most novels, whatever steps are taken to mystify inevitably decrease the dramatic irony, and, whenever dramatic irony is increased by telling the reader secrets the characters have not yet suspected, mystery is inevitably destroyed. The longer we are in doubt about Frank Churchill, the weaker our sense of ironic contrast between Emma's views and the truth. The sooner we see through Frank Churchill's secret plot, the greater our pleasure in observing Emma's innumerable misreadings of his behavior and the less interest we have in the mere mystery of the situation. And we all find that on second reading we discover new intensities of dramatic irony resulting from the complete loss of mystery; knowing what abysses of error Emma is preparing for herself, even those of us who may on first reading have deciphered nearly all the details of the Churchill mystery find additional ironies.

But it is obvious that these ironies could have been offered even on a first reading, if Austen had been willing to sacrifice her mystery. A single phrase in her own name — "his secret engagement to Jane Fairfax" — or a short inside view of either of the lovers could have made us aware of every ironic touch.

The author must, then, choose whether to purchase mystery at the expense of irony. For many of us Jane Austen's choice here is perhaps the weakest aspect of this novel. It is a commonplace of our criticism that significant literature arouses suspense not about the "what" but about the "how." Mere mystification has been mastered by so many second-rate writers that her efforts at mystification seem second-rate.

But again we must ask whether criticism can be conducted effectively by balancing one abstract quality against another. Is there a norm of dramatic irony for all works, or even for all works of a given kind? Has anyone ever formulated a "law of first and second readings" that will tell us just how many of our pleasures on page one should depend on our knowledge of what happens on page the last? We quite properly ask that the books we call great be able to stand up under repeated reading, but we need not ask that they yield identical pleasures on each reading. The modern works whose authors pride themselves on the fact that they can never be read but only re-read may be very good indeed, but they are not made good by the fact that their secret pleasures can only be wrested from them by repeated readings.

In any case, even if one accepted the criticism of Jane Austen's efforts at mystification, the larger service of the inside views is clear: the crosslights thrown by other minds prevent our being blinded by Emma's radiance.

THE RELIABLE NARRATOR AND THE NORMS OF "EMMA"

If mere intellectual clarity about Emma were the goal in this work, we should be forced to say that the manipulation of inside views and the extensive commentary of the reliable Knightley are more than is necessary. But for maximum intensity of the comedy and romance, even these are not enough. The "author herself" — not necessarily the real Jane Austen but an implied author, represented in this book by a reliable narrator — heightens the effects by directing

our intellectual, moral, and emotional progress. She performs, of course, most of the functions described in Chapter 7. But her most important role is to reinforce both aspects of the double vision that operates throughout the book: our inside view of Emma's worth and our objective view of her great faults.

The narrator opens *Emma* with a masterful simultaneous presentation of Emma and of the values against which she must be judged: "Emma Woodhouse, handsome, clever, and rich, with a comfortable home and happy disposition, seemed to unite some of the best blessings of existence; and had lived nearly twenty-one years in the world with very little to distress or vex her." This "seemed" is immediately reinforced by more directly stated reservations. "The real evils of Emma's situation were the power of having rather too much her own way, and a disposition to think a little too well of herself; these were the disadvantages which threatened alloy to her many enjoyments. The danger, however, was at present so unperceived, that they did not by any means rank as misfortunes with her."

None of this could have been said by Emma, and if shown through her consciousness, it could not be accepted, as it must be, without question. Like most of the first three chapters, it is non-dramatic summary, building up, through the ostensible business of getting the characters introduced, to Emma's initial blunder with Harriet and Mr. Elton. Throughout these chapters, we learn much of what we must know from the narrator, but she turns over more and more of the job of summary to Emma as she feels more and more sure of our seeing precisely to what degree Emma is to be trusted. Whenever we leave the "real evils" we have been warned against in Emma, the narrator's and Emma's views coincide: we cannot tell which of them, for example, offers the judgment on Mr. Woodhouse that "his talents could not have recommended him at any time," or the judgment on Mr. Knightley that he is "a sensible man," "always welcome" at Hartfield, or even that "Mr. Knightley, in fact, was one of the few people who could see faults in Emma Woodhouse, and the only one who ever told her of them."

But there are times when Emma and her author are far apart, and the author's direct guidance aids the reader in his own break with Emma. The beautiful irony of the first description of Harriet, given through Emma's eyes (Ch. 3) could no doubt be grasped intellectually by many read-ers without all of the preliminary commentary. But even for the most perceptive its effect is heightened, surely, by the sense of standing with the author and observing with her precisely how Emma's judgment is going astray. Perhaps more important, we ordinary, less perceptive readers have by now been raised to a level suited to grasp the ironies. Certainly, most readers would over-look some of the barbs directed against Emma if the novel began, as a serious modern novelist might well begin it, with this description:

[Emma] was not struck by any thing remarkably clever in Miss Smith's conversation, but she found her altogether very engaging — not inconveniently shy, not unwilling to talk — and yet so far from pushing, shewing so proper and becoming a def-erence, seeming so pleasantly grateful for being admitted to Hartfield, and so artlessly impressed by the appearance of every thing in so superior a style to what she had been used to, that she must have good sense and deserve encouragement. Encouragement should be given. Those soft blue eyes . . . should not be wasted on the inferior society of Highbury. . . .

And so Emma goes on, giving herself away with every word, pouring out her own sense of her own beneficence and general value. Harriet's past friends, "though very good sort of people, must be doing her harm." Without knowing them, Emma knows that they "must be the coarse and unpolished, and very unfit to be the intimates of a girl who wanted only a little more knowledge and elegance to be quite perfect." And she concludes with a beautiful burst of egotism: "She would notice her; she would improve her; she would detach her from her bad acquaintance, and intro-duce her into good society; she would form her opinions and her manners. It would be an interest-ing, and certainly a very kind undertaking; highly becoming her own situation in life, her leisure, and powers." Even the most skilful reader might not easily plot an absolutely true course through these ironies without the prior direct assistance we have been given. Emma's views are not so outlandish that they could never have been held

by a female novelist writing in her time. They cannot serve effectively as signs of her character unless they are clearly disavowed as signs of Jane Austen's views. Emma's unconscious catalogue of her egotistical uses for Harriet, given under the pretense of listing the services she will perform, is thus given its full force by being framed explic-itly in a world of values which Emma herself cannot discover until the conclusion of the book. The full importance of the author's direct imposition of an elaborate scale of norms can be seen by considering that conclusion. The sequence of events is a simple one: Emma's faults and mistakes are brought home to her in a rapid and humiliating chain of rebukes from Knightley and blows from hard fact. These blows to her self-esteem produce at last a genuine reform (for example, she brings herself to apolo-gize to Miss Bates, something she could never have done earlier in the novel). The change in her character removes the only obstacle in the way of Knightley's proposal, and the marriage fol-lows. "The wishes, the hopes, the confidence, the predictions of the small band of true friends who witnessed the ceremony, were fully answered in the perfect happiness of the union."

It may be that if we look at Emma and Knightley as real people, this ending will seem false. G. B. Stern laments, in *Speaking of Jane Austen*, "Oh, Miss Austen, it was not a good solution; it was a bad solution, an unhappy end-ing, could we see beyond the last pages of the book." Edmund Wilson predicts that Emma will find a new protégée like Harriet, since she has not been cured of her inclination to "infatua-tions with women." Marvin Mudrick even more emphatically rejects Jane Austen's explicit rheto-ric; he believes that Emma is still a "confirmed exploiter," and for him the ending must be read as ironic.[9]

But it is precisely because this ending is nei-ther life itself nor a simple bit of literary irony that it can serve so well to heighten our sense of a complete and indeed perfect resolution to all that has gone before. If we look at the values that

[9] The first two quotations are from Wilson's "A Long Talk about Jane Austen," *A Literary Chronicle: 1920–1950* (New York, 1952). The third is from Mudrick, *Jane Austen*, p. 206. [Booth]

have been realized in this marriage and compare them with those realized in conventional marriage plots, we see that Jane Austen means what she says: this will be a happy marriage because there is simply nothing left to make it anything less than perfectly happy. It fulfills every value embodied in the world of the book — with the possible exception that Emma may never learn to apply herself as she ought to her reading and her piano! It is a union of intelligence: of "reason," of "sense," of "judgment." It is a union of virtue: of "good will," of generosity, of unselfishness. It is a union of feeling: of "taste," "tenderness," "love," "beauty."[10]

In a general way, then, this plot offers us an experience superficially like that offered by most tragicomedy as well as by much of the cheapest popular art: we are made to desire certain good things for certain good characters, and then our desires are gratified. If we depended on general criteria derived from our justified boredom with such works, we should reject this one. But the critical difference lies in the precise quality of the values appealed to and the precise quality of the characters who violate or realize them. All of the cheap marriage plots in the world should not lead us to be embarrassed about our pleasure in Emma and Knightley's marriage. It is more than just the marriage: it is the *rightness* of *this* marriage, as a conclusion to all of the comic wrongness that has gone before. The good for Emma includes both her necessary reform and the resulting marriage. Marriage to an intelligent, amiable, good, and attractive man is the best thing that can happen to this heroine, and the readers who do not experience it as such are, I am convinced, far from knowing what Jane Austen is

about — whatever they may say about the "bitter spinster's" attitude toward marriage.

Our modern sensibilities are likely to be rasped by any such formulation. We do not ordinarily like to encounter perfect endings in our novels — even in the sense of "perfectedness" or completion, the sense obviously intended by Jane Austen. We refuse to accept it when we see it: witness the many attempts to deny Dostoevski's success with Alyosha and Father Zossima in *The Brothers Karamazov*. Many of us find it embarrassing to talk of emotions based on moral judgment at all, particularly when the emotions have any kind of affirmative cast. Emma herself is something of a "modern" in this regard throughout most of the book. Her self-deception about marriage is as great as about most other important matters. Emma boasts to Harriet of her indifference to marriage, at the same time unconsciously betraying her totally inadequate view of the sources of human happiness.

> If I know myself, Harriet, mine is an active, busy mind, with a great many independent resources; and I do not perceive why I should be more in want of employment at forty or fifty than one-and-twenty. Women's usual occupations of eye and hand and mind will be as open to me then, as they are now; or with no important variation. If I draw less, I shall read more; if I give up music, I shall take to carpet-work.

Emma at carpet-work! If she knows herself indeed.

> And as for objects of interest, objects for the affections, which is, in truth, the great point of inferiority, the want of which is really the great evil to be avoided in *not* marrying [a magnificent concession, this] I shall be very well off, with all the children of a sister I love so much, to care about. There will be enough of them, in all probability, to supply every sort of sensation that declining life can need. There will be enough for every hope and every fear; and though my attachment to none can equal that of a parent, it suits my ideas of comfort better than what is warmer and blinder. My nephews and nieces! — I shall often have a niece with me [Ch. 10].

Without growing solemn about it — it is wonderfully comic — we can recognize that the humor springs here from very deep sources indeed. It can be fully enjoyed, in fact, only by the reader who

[10]It has lately been fashionable to underplay the value of tenderness and good will in Jane Austen, in reaction to an earlier generation that overdid the picture of "gentle Jane." The trend seems to have begun in earnest with D. W. Harding's "Regulated Hatred: An Aspect of the Work of Jane Austen," *Scrutiny* 8 (March 1940): 346–62. While I do not feel as strongly aroused against this school of readers as does R. W. Chapman (see his *A Critical Bibliography*, p. 52, and his review of Mudrick's work in the *T. L. S.* [September 19, 1952]), it seems to me that another swing of the pendulum is called for: when Jane Austen praises the "relenting heart," she means that praise, though she is the same author who can lash the unrelenting heart with "regulated hatred." [Booth]

has attained to a vision of human felicity far more profound than Emma's "comfort" and "want" and "need." It is a vision that includes not simply marriage, but a kind of loving converse not based, as is Emma's here, on whether the "loved" person will serve one's irreducible needs.

The comic effect of this repudiation of marriage is considerably increased by the fact that Emma always thinks of marriage for others as *their* highest good, and in fact unconsciously encourages her friend Harriet to fall in love with the very man she herself loves without knowing it. The delightful denouement is thus what we want not only because it is a supremely good thing for Emma, but because it is a supremely comic outcome of Emma's profound misunderstanding of herself and of the human condition. In the schematic language of chapter 5, it satisfies both our practical desire for Emma's well-being and our appetite for the qualities proper to these artistic materials. It is thus a more resounding resolution than either of these elements separately could provide. The other major resolution of the work — Harriet's marriage with her farmer — reinforces this interpretation. Emma's sin against Harriet has been something far worse than the mere meddling of a busy-body. To destroy Harriet's chances for happiness — chances that depend entirely on her marriage — is as close to viciousness as any author could dare to take a heroine designed to be loved. We can laugh with Emma at this mistake (Ch. 54). We only because Harriet's chance for happiness is restored.

Other values, like money, blood, and "consequence," are real enough in *Emma*, but only as they contribute to or are mastered by good taste, good judgment, and good morality. Money alone can make a Mrs. Churchill, but a man or woman "is silly to marry without it." Consequence untouched by sense can make a very inconsequential Mr. Woodhouse; untouched by sense or virtue it can make the much more contemptible Mr. and Miss Elliot of *Persuasion*. But it is a pleasant thing to have, and it does no harm unless, like the early Emma, one takes it too seriously. Charm and elegance without sufficient moral force can make a Frank Churchill; unschooled by morality it can lead to the baseness of Henry Crawford in *Mansfield*

Park or Wickham in *Pride and Prejudice*. Even the supreme virtues are inadequate in isolation: good will alone will make a comic Miss Bates or a Mr. Weston, judgment with insufficient good will a comic Mr. John Knightley, and so on.

I am willing to risk the commonplace in such a listing because it is only thus that the full force of Jane Austen's comprehensive view can be seen. There is clearly at work here a much more detailed ordering of values than any conventional public philosophy of her time could provide. Obviously, few readers in her own time, and far fewer in our own, have ever approached this novel in full and detailed agreement with the author's norms. But they were led to join her as they read, and so are we.

EXPLICIT JUDGMENTS ON EMMA WOODHOUSE

We have said in passing almost enough of the other side of the coin — the judgment of particular actions as they relate to the general norms. But something must be said of the detailed "placing" of Emma, by direct commentary, in the hierarchy of values established by the novel. I must be convinced, for example, not only that tenderness for other people's feelings is an important trait but also that Emma's particular behavior violates the true standards of tenderness, if I am to savor the full the episode of Emma's insult to Miss Bates and Knightley's reproach which follow. If I refuse to blame Emma, I may discover a kind of intellectual enjoyment in the episode, and I will probably think that any critic who talks of "belief" in tenderness as operating in such a context is taking things too seriously. But I can never enjoy the episode in its full intensity or grasp its formal coherence. Similarly, I must agree not only that to be dreadfully boring is a minor fault compared with the major virtue of "good will," but also that Miss Bates's exemplification of this fault and of this virtue entitle her to the respect which Emma denies. If I do not — while yet being able to laugh at Miss Bates — I can hardly understand, let alone enjoy, Emma's mistreatment of her.

But these negative judgments must be counteracted by a larger approval, and, as we would expect, the novel is full of direct apologies for

Emma. Her chief fault, lack of good will or tenderness, must be read not only in relationship to the code of values provided by the book as a whole — a code which judges her as seriously deficient; it must also be judged in relationship to the harsh facts of the world around her, a world made up of human beings ranging in degree of selfishness and egotism from Knightley, who lapses from perfection when he tries to judge frank Churchill, his rival, down to Mrs. Elton, who has most of Emma's faults and none of her virtues. In such a setting, Emma is easily forgiven. When she insults Miss Bates, for example, we remember that Miss Bates lives in a world where many others are insensitive and cruel. "Miss Bates, neither young, handsome, rich, nor married, stood in the very worst predicament in the world for having much of the public favour; and she had no intellectual superiority to make atonement to herself, or frighten those who might hate her, into outward respect." While it would be a mistake to see only this "regulated hatred" in Jane Austen's world, overlooking the tenderness and generosity, the hatred of viciousness is there, and there is enough vice in evidence to make Emma almost shine by comparison.

Often, Jane Austen makes this apology-by-comparison explicit. When Emma lies to Knightley about Harriet, very close to the end of the book, she is excused with a generalization about human nature: "Seldom, very seldom, does complete truth belong to any human disclosure; seldom can it happen that something is not a little disguised, or a little mistaken; but where, as in this case, though the conduct is mistaken, the feelings are not, it may not be very material. — Mr. Knightley could not impute to Emma a more relenting heart than she possessed, or a heart more disposed to accept of his."

THE IMPLIED AUTHOR AS FRIEND AND GUIDE

With all of this said about the masterful use of the narrator in *Emma,* there remain some "intrusions" unaccounted for by strict service to the story itself. "What did she say?" the narrator asks, at the crucial moment in the major love scene. "Just what she ought, of course. A lady always does. — She said enough to show there need not be despair — and to invite him to say more himself." To some readers this has seemed to demonstrate the author's inability to write a love scene, since it sacrifices "the illusion of reality."[11] But who has ever read this far in *Emma* under the delusion that he is reading a realistic portrayal which is suddenly shattered by the unnatural appearance of the narrator? If the narrator's superabundant wit is destructive of the kind of illusion proper to this work, the novel has been ruined long before.

But we should now be in a position to see precisely why the narrator's wit is not in the least out of place at the emotional climax of the novel. We have seen how the inside views of the characters and the author's commentary have been used from the beginning to get the values straight and to keep them straight and to help direct our reactions to Emma. But we also see here a beautiful case of the dramatized author as friend and guide. "Jane Austen," like "Henry Fielding," is a paragon of wit, wisdom, and virtue. She does not talk about her qualities; unlike Fielding she does not in *Emma* call direct attention to her artistic skill. But we are seldom allowed to forget about her for all that. When we read this novel we accept her as representing everything we admire most. She is as generous and wise as Knightley; in fact, she is a shade more penetrating in her judgment. She is as subtle and witty as Emma would like to think herself. Without being sentimental she is in favor of tenderness. She is able to put an adequate but not excessive value on wealth and rank. She recognizes a fool when she sees one, but unlike Emma she knows that it is both immoral and foolish to be rude to fools. She is, in short, a perfect human being, within the concept of perfection established by the book she writes; she even recognizes that human perfection of the kind *she* exemplifies is not quite attainable in real life. The process of her domination is of course circular; her character establishes the values for us according to which her character is then found to be perfect. But this circularity does not affect the success of her endeavor; in fact it insures it.

[11]Edd Winfield Parks, "Exegesis in Austen's Novels," *The South Atlantic Quarterly* 2. (January 1952): 117. [Booth]

Her "omniscience" is thus a much more remarkable thing than is ordinarily implied by the term. All good novelists know all about their characters — all that they need to know. And the question of how their narrators are to find out all that *they* need to know, the question of "authority," is a relatively simple one. The real choice is much more profound than this would imply. It is a choice of the moral, not merely the technical, angle of vision from which the story is to be told.

Unlike the central intelligences of James and his successors, "Jane Austen" has learned nothing at the end of the novel that she did not know at the beginning. She needed to learn nothing. She knew everything of importance already. We have been privileged to watch with her as she observes her favorite character climb from a considerably lower platform to join the exalted company of Knightley, "Jane Austen," and those of us readers who are wise enough, good enough, and perceptive enough to belong up there too. As Katherine Mansfield says, "the truth is that every true admirer of the novels cherishes the happy thought that he alone — reading between the lines — has

become the secret friend of their author."12 Those who love "gentle Jane" as a secret friend may undervalue the irony and with those who see her in effect as the greatest of Shaw's heroines, flashing about her with the weapons of irony, may undervalue the emphasis on tenderness and good will. But only a very few can resist her.

The dramatic illusion of her presence as a character is thus fully as important as any other element in the story. When she intrudes, the illusion is not shattered. The only illusion we care about, the illusion of traveling intimately with a hardy little band of readers whose heads are screwed on tight and whose hearts are in the right place, is actually strengthened when we are refused the romantic love scenes. Like the author herself, we don't care about the love scenes. We can find love scenes in almost any novelist's works, but only here can we find a mind and heart that can give us clarity without oversimplification, sympathy and romance without sentimentality, and biting irony without cynicism.

12*Novels and Novelists*, ed. J. Middleton Murry (London, 1930), p. 304. [Booth]

Wolfgang Iser

1926–2007

Partly because his method involves critical analysis rather than historical scholarship and partly because he works on well-known British fiction, Wolfgang Iser is more familiar to North American critics than his phenomenologist colleague, Hans Robert Jauss. Iser was born in Marienberg, Germany, in 1926, and received his Ph.D. from the University of Heidelberg in 1957. His published books include Die Weltanschauungs Henry Fieldings (Henry Fielding's World View, 1952), Walter Pater — Die Autonomie des Ästhetischen *(1960; translated as* Walter Pater: The Aesthetic Moment), Die Appelstruktur der Texte (The Affective Structure of the Text, *1970), and* Spensers Arkadien: Fiktion und Geschichte in der Englische Renaissance (Spenser's Arcadia: Fiction and History in the English Renaissance, *1970). In North America, his most influential works are the two theoretical treatises based on the hermeneutics of Hans-Georg Gadamer and Roman Ingarden,* Der Implizite Leser *(1972; translated as* The Implied Reader*) and* Der Akte des Lesens *(1976; translated as* The Act of Reading*). Starting in the mid-1980s, Iser's work turned from purely phenomenological research to what he called "literary anthropology," a study of the cultural uses of literature. His work along that line is contained in* Prospecting: From Reader Response to Literary Anthropology *(1989);* The Fictive and the Imaginary: Charting Literary Anthropology *(1993); and* Staging Politics: The Lasting Impact of Shakespeare's Historical Plays *(1993). Iser was professor of English literature at the University of Konstanz in Germany and a permanent visiting professor at the University of California at Irvine. Iser's Wellek Library lecture series,* The Range of Interpretation, *was published in 2000; his final published book was* How to Do Theory *(Blackwell, 2005).*

The Reading Process: A Phenomenological Approach

I

The phenomenological theory of art lays full stress on the idea that, in considering a literary work, one must take into account not only the actual text but also, and in equal measure, the actions involved in responding to that text. Thus Roman Ingarden confronts the structure of the literary text with the ways in which it can be *konkretisiert* (realized).[1] The text as such offers different "schematised views"[2] through which the subject matter of the work can come to light, but the actual bringing to light is an action of *Konkretisation*. If this is so, then the literary work has two poles, which we might call the artistic and the esthetic: the artistic refers to the text created by the author, and the esthetic to the realization accomplished by the reader. From this polarity it follows that the literary work cannot be completely identical with the text, or with the realization of the text, but in fact must lie halfway between the two. The work is more than the text, for the text only takes on life when it is realized, and furthermore the realization is by no means independent of the individual disposition of the reader — though this in turn is acted upon by the different patterns of the text. The convergence of text and reader brings the literary work

[1] Cf. Roman Ingarden, *Vom Erkennen des literarischen Kunstwerks* (Tübingen, 1968), pp. 49 ff. [Iser]

[2] For a detailed discussion of this term see Roman Ingarden, *Das literarische Kunstwerk* (Tübingen, 1960), pp. 270 ff. [Iser]

into existence, and this convergence can never be precisely pinpointed, but must always remain virtual, as it is not to be identified either with the reality of the text or with the individual disposition of the reader.

It is the virtuality of the work that gives rise to its dynamic nature, and this in turn is the precondition for the effects that the work calls forth. As the reader uses the various perspectives offered him by the text in order to relate the patterns and the "schematised views" to one another, he sets the work in motion, and this very process results ultimately in the awakening of responses within himself. Thus, reading causes the literary work to unfold its inherently dynamic character. That this is no new discovery is apparent from references made even in the early days of the novel. Laurence Sterne remarks in *Tristram Shandy*: ". . . no author, who understands the just boundaries of decorum and good-breeding, would presume to think all: The truest respect which you can pay to the reader's understanding, is to halve this matter amicably, and leave him something to imagine, in his turn, as well as yourself. For my own part, I am eternally paying him compliments of this kind, and do all that lies in my power to keep his imagination as busy as my own."[3] Sterne's conception of a literary text is that it is something like an arena in which reader and author participate in a game of the imagination. If the reader were given the whole story, and there were nothing left for him to do, then his imagination would never enter the field, the result would be the boredom which inevitably arises when everything is laid out cut and dried before us. A literary text must therefore be conceived in such a way that it will engage the reader's imagination in the task of working things out for himself, for reading is only a pleasure when it is active and creative. In this process of creativity, the text may either not go far enough, or may go too far, so we may say that boredom and overstrain form the boundaries beyond which the reader will leave the field of play.

The extent to which the "unwritten" part of a text stimulates the reader's creative participation is

brought out by an observation of Virginia Woolf's in her study of Jane Austen:

Jane Austen is thus a mistress of much deeper emotion than appears upon the surface. She stimulates us to supply what is not there. What she offers is, apparently, a trifle, yet is composed of something that expands in the reader's mind and endows with the most enduring form of life scenes which are outwardly trivial. Always the stress is laid upon character. . . . The turns and twists of the dialogue keep us on the tenterhooks of suspense. Our attention is half upon the present moment, half upon the future. Here, indeed, in this unfinished and in the main inferior story, are all the elements of Jane Austen's greatness.[4]

The unwritten aspects of apparently trivial scenes and the unspoken dialogue within the "turns and twists" not only draw the reader into the action but also lead him to shade in the many outlines suggested by the given situations, so that these take on a reality of their own. But as the reader's imagination animates these "outlines," they in turn will influence the effect of the written part of the text. Thus there begins a whole dynamic process: the written text imposes certain limits on its unwritten implications in order to prevent these from becoming too blurred and hazy, but at the same time these implications, worked out by the reader's imagination, set the given situation against a background which endows it with far greater significance than it might have seemed to possess on its own. In this way, trivial scenes suddenly take on the shape of an "enduring form of life." What constitutes this form is never named, let alone explained in the text, although in fact it is the end product of the interaction between text and reader.

II

The question now arises as to how far such a process can be adequately described. For this purpose a phenomenological analysis recommends itself, especially since the somewhat sparse observations hitherto made of the psychology of reading

[3]Laurence Sterne, *Tristram Shandy* (London, 1956), II, 11: 79. [Iser]

[4]Virginia Woolf, *The Common Reader*, First Series (London, 1957), p. 174. [Iser]

tend mainly to be psychoanalytical, and so are restricted to the illustration of predetermined ideas concerning the unconscious. We shall, however, take a closer look later at some worthwhile psychological observations.

As a starting point for a phenomenological analysis we might examine the way in which sequent sentences act upon one another. This is of especial importance in literary texts in view of the fact that they do not correspond to any objective reality outside themselves. The world presented by literary texts is constructed out of what Ingarden has called *intentionale Satzkorrelate* (intentional sentence correlatives):

> Sentences link up in different ways to form more complex units of meaning that reveal a very varied structure giving rise to such entities as a short story, a novel, a dialogue, a drama, a scientific theory. . . . In the final analysis, there arises a particular world, with component parts determined in this way or that, and with all the variations that may occur within these parts — all this as a purely intentional correlative of a complex of sentences. If this complex finally forms a literary work, I call the whole sum of sequent intentional sentence correlatives the "world presented" in the work.[5]

This world, however, does not pass before the reader's eyes like a film. The sentences are "component parts" insofar as they make statements, claims, or observations, or convey information, and so establish various perspectives in the text. But they remain only "component parts" — they are not the sum total of the text itself. For the intentional correlatives disclose subtle connections which individually are less concrete than the statements, claims, and observations, even though these only take on their real meaningfulness through the interaction of their correlatives.

How is one to conceive the connection between the correlatives? It marks those points at which the reader is able to "climb aboard" the text. He has to accept certain given perspectives, but in doing so he inevitably causes them to interact. When Ingarden speaks of intentional sentence correlatives in literature, the statements made or information conveyed in the sentence is already in a certain sense qualified: the sentence does not consist solely of a statement — which, after all, would be absurd, as one can only make statements about things that exist — but aims at something beyond what it actually says. This is true of all sentences in literary works, and it is through the interaction of these sentences that their common aim is fulfilled. This is what gives them their own special quality in literary texts. In their capacity as statements, observations, purveyors of information, etc., they are always indications of something that is to come, the structure of which is foreshadowed by their specific content.

They set in motion a process out of which emerges the actual content of the text itself. In describing man's inner consciousness of time, Husserl once remarked: "Every originally constructive process is inspired by pre-intentions, which construct and collect the seed of what is to come, as such, and bring it to fruition."[6] For this bringing to fruition, the literary text needs the reader's imagination, which gives shape to the interaction of correlatives foreshadowed in structure by the sequence of the sentences. Husserl's observation draws our attention to a point that plays a not insignificant part in the process of reading. The individual sentences not only work together to shade in what is to come; they also form an expectation in this regard. Husserl calls this expectation "preintentions." As this structure is characteristic of *all* sentence correlatives, the interaction of these correlatives will not be a fulfillment of the expectation so much as a continual modification of it.

For this reason, expectations are scarcely ever fulfilled in truly literary texts. If they were, then such texts would be confined to the individualization of a given expectation, and one would inevitably ask what such an intention was supposed to achieve. Strangely enough, we feel that any confirmative effect — such as we implicitly demand of expository texts, as we refer to the objects they are meant to present — is a defect in a literary text. For the more a text individualizes

[5]Ingarden, *Vom Erkennen des literarischen Kunstwerks*, p. 29. [Iser]

[6]Edmund Husserl, *Zur Phänomenologie des inneren Zeitbewusstseins, Gesammelte Werke* (The Hague, 1966), 10:52. [Iser]

or confirms an expectation it has initially aroused. the more aware we become of its didactic purpose, so that at best we can only accept or reject the thesis forced upon us. More often than not, the very clarity of such texts will make us want to free ourselves from their clutches. But generally the sentence correlatives of literary texts do not develop in this rigid way, for the expectations they evoke tend to encroach on one another in such a manner that they are continually modified as one reads. One might simplify by saying that each intentional sentence correlative opens up a particular horizon, which is modified, if not completely changed, by succeeding sentences. While these expectations arouse interest in what is to come, the subsequent modification of them will also have a retrospective effect on what has already been read. This may now take on a different significance from that which it had at the moment of reading.

Whatever we have read sinks into our memory and is foreshortened. It may later be evoked again and set against a different background with the result that the reader is enabled to develop hitherto unforeseeable connections. The memory evoked, however, can never reassume its original shape, for this would mean that memory and perception were identical, which is manifestly not so. The new background brings to light new aspects of what we had committed to memory; conversely these, in turn, shed their light on the new background, thus arousing more complex anticipations. Thus, the reader, in establishing these interrelationships between past, present and future, actually causes the text to reveal its potential multiplicity of connections. These connections are the product of the reader's mind working on the raw material of the text, though they are not the text itself — for this consists just of sentences, statements, information, etc.

This is why the reader often feels involved in events which, at the time of reading, seem real to him, even though in fact they are very far from his own reality. The fact that completely different readers can be differently affected by the "reality" of a particular text is ample evidence of the degree to which literary texts transform reading into a creative process that is far above mere perception of what is written. The literary text activates our own faculties, enabling us to recreate the world it presents. The product of this creative activity is what we might call the virtual dimension of the text, which endows it with its reality. This virtual dimension is not the text itself, nor is it the imagination of the reader: it is the coming together of text and imagination.

As we have seen, the activity of reading can be characterized as a sort of kaleidoscope of perspectives, preintentions, recollections. Every sentence contains a preview of the next and forms a kind of viewfinder for what is to come; and this in turn changes the "preview" and so becomes a "viewfinder" for what has been read. This whole process represents the fulfillment of the potential, unexpressed reality of the text, but it is to be seen only as a framework for a great variety of means by which the virtual dimension may be brought into being. The process of anticipation and retrospection itself does not by any means develop in a smooth flow. Ingarden has already drawn attention to this fact and ascribes a quite remarkable significance to it:

> Once we are immersed in the flow of Satzdenken (sentence-thought), we are ready, after completing the thought of one sentence, to think out the "continuation," also in the form of a sentence — and that is, in the form of a sentence that connects up with the sentence we have just thought through. In this way the process of reading goes effortlessly forward. But if by chance the following sentence has no tangible connection whatever with the sentence we have just thought through, there then comes a blockage in the stream of thought. This hiatus is linked with a more or less active surprise, or with indignation. This blockage must be overcome if the reading is to flow once more.[7]

The hiatus that blocks the flow of sentences is, in Ingarden's eyes, the product of chance, and is to be regarded as a flaw; this is typical of his adherence to the classical idea of art. If one regards the sentence sequence as a continual flow, this implies that the anticipation aroused by one sentence will generally be realized by the next, and the frustration of one's expectations will arouse feelings of exasperation. And yet literary texts are full of unexpected twists and turns, and

[7]Ingarden, *Vom Erkennen des literarischen Kunstwerks,* p. 32. [Iser]

frustration of expectations. Even in the simplest story there is bound to be some kind of blockage, if only because no tale can ever be told in its entirety. Indeed, it is only through inevitable omissions that a story gains its dynamism. Thus whenever the flow is interrupted and we are led off in unexpected directions, the opportunity is given to us to bring into play our own faculty for establishing connections — for filling in the gaps left by the text itself.[8]

These gaps have a different effect on the process of anticipation and retrospection, and thus on the "gestalt" of the virtual dimension, for they may be filled in different ways. For this reason, one text is potentially capable of several different realizations, and no reading can ever exhaust the full potential, for each individual reader will fill in the gaps in his own way, thereby excluding the various other possibilities; as he reads, he will make his own decision as to how the gap is to be filled. In this very act the dynamics of reading are revealed. By making his decision he implicitly acknowledges the inexhaustibility of the text; at the same time it is this very inexhaustibility that forces him to make his decision. With "traditional" texts this process was more or less unconscious, but modern texts frequently exploit it quite deliberately. They are often so fragmentary that one's attention is almost exclusively occupied with the search for connections between the fragments; the object of this is not to complicate the "spectrum" of connections, so much as to make us aware of the nature of our own capacity for providing links. In such cases, the text refers back directly to our own preconceptions — which are revealed by the act of interpretation that is a basic element of the reading process. With all literary texts, then, we may say that the reading process is selective, and the potential text is infinitely richer than any of its individual realizations. This is borne out by the fact that a second reading of a piece of literature often produces a different impression from the first. The reasons for this may lie in the reader's own change of circumstances, still, the text must be such as to allow this variation. On a second reading familiar occurrences now tend to appear in a new light and seem to be at times corrected, at times enriched.

In every text there is a potential time sequence which the reader must inevitably realize, as it is impossible to absorb even a short text in a single moment. Thus the reading process always involves viewing the text through a perspective that is continually on the move, linking up the different phases, and so constructing what we have called the virtual dimension. This dimension, of course, varies all the time we are reading. However, when we have finished the text, and read it again, clearly our extra knowledge will result in a different time sequence; we shall tend to establish connections by referring to our awareness of what is to come, and so certain aspects of the text will assume a significance we did not attach to them on a first reading, while others will recede into the background. It is a common enough experience for a person to say that on a second reading he noticed things he had missed when he read the book for the first time, but this is scarcely surprising in view of the fact that the second time he is looking at the text from a different perspective. The time sequence that he realized on his first reading cannot possibly be repeated on a second reading, and this unrepeatability is bound to result in modifications of his reading experience. This is not to say that the second reading is "truer" than the first — they are, quite simply, different: the reader establishes the virtual dimension of the text by realizing a new time sequence. Thus even on repeated viewings a text allows and, indeed, induces innovative reading.

In whatever way, and under whatever circumstances the reader may link the different phases of the text together, it will always be the process of anticipation and retrospection that leads to the formation of the virtual dimension, which in turn transforms the text into an experience for the reader. The way in which this experience comes about through a process of continual modification is closely akin to the way in which we gather experience in life. And thus the "reality" of the reading experience can illuminate basic patterns of real experience:

We have the experience of a world, not understood as a system of relations which wholly determine each event, but as an open totality the synthesis of

[8]For a more detailed discussion of the function of "gaps" in literary texts see Wolfgang Iser, "Indeterminacy and the Reader's Response in Prose Fiction," *Aspects of Narrative* (English Institute Essays), ed. J. Hillis Miller (New York, 1971), pp. 1–45. [Iser]

which is inexhaustible. . . . From the moment that experience — that is, the opening on to our *de facto* world — is recognized as the beginning of knowledge, there is no longer any way of distinguishing a level of *a priori* truths and one of factual ones, what the world must necessarily be and what it actually is.[9]

The manner in which the reader experiences the text will reflect his own disposition, and in this respect the literary text acts as a kind of mirror; but at the same time, the reality which this process helps to create is one that will be *different* from his own (since, normally, we tend to be bored by texts that present us with things we already know perfectly well ourselves). Thus we have the apparently paradoxical situation in which the reader is forced to reveal aspects of himself in order to experience a reality which is different from his own. The impact this reality makes on him will depend largely on the extent to which he himself actively provides the unwritten part of the text, and yet in supplying all the missing links, he must think in terms of experiences different from his own; indeed, it is only by leaving behind the familiar world of his own experience that the reader can truly participate in the adventure the literary text offers him.

III

We have seen that, during the process of reading, there is an active interweaving of anticipation and retrospection, which on a second reading may turn into a kind of advance retrospection. The impressions that arise as a result of this process will vary from individual to individual, but only within the limits imposed by the written as opposed to the unwritten text. In the same way, two people gazing at the night sky may both be looking at the same collection of stars, but one will see the image of a plough, and the other will make out a dipper. The ''stars'' in a literary text are fixed; the lines that join them are variable. The author of the text may, of course, exert plenty of influence on the reader's imagination — he has the whole panoply of narrative techniques at his disposal — but no author worth

⁹M. Merleau-Ponty, *Phenomenology of Perception*, trans. Colin Smith (New York, 1962), pp. 219, 221. [Iser]

his salt will ever attempt to set the *whole* picture before his reader's eyes. If he does, he will very quickly lose his reader, for it is only by activating the reader's imagination that the author can hope to involve him and so realize the intentions of his text.

Gilbert Ryle, in his analysis of imagination, asks: ''How can a person fancy that he sees something, without realizing that he is not seeing it?'' He answers as follows:

Seeing Helvellyn [the name of a mountain] in one's mind's eye does not entail, what seeing Helvellyn and seeing snapshots of Helvellyn entail, the having of visual sensations. It does involve the thought of having a view of Helvellyn and it is therefore a more sophisticated operation than that of having a view of Helvellyn. It is one utilization among others of the knowledge of how Helvellyn should look, or, in one sense of the verb, it is thinking how it should look. The expectations which are fulfilled in the recognition at sight of Helvellyn are not indeed fulfilled in picturing it, but the picturing of it is something like a rehearsal of getting them fulfilled. So far from picturing involving the having of faint sensations, or wraiths of sensations, it involves missing just what one would be due to get, if one were seeing the mountain.[10]

If one sees the mountain, then of course one can no longer imagine it, and so the act of picturing the mountain presupposes its absence. Similarly, with a literary text we can only picture things which are not there: the written part of the text gives us the knowledge, but it is the unwritten part that gives us the opportunity to picture things; indeed without the elements of indeterminacy, the gaps in the text, we should not be able to use our imagination.[11]

The truth of this observation is borne out by the experience many people have on seeing, for instance, the film of a novel. While reading *Tom Jones*, they may never have had a clear conception of what the hero actually looks like, but on seeing the film, some may say, ''That's not how I imagined him.'' The point here is that the reader of *Tom Jones* is able to visualize the hero virtually for himself, and so his imagination senses the

¹⁰Gilbert Ryle, *The Concept of Mind* (Harmondsworth, 1968), p. 255. [Iser]

¹¹Cf. Iser, ''Indeterminacy,'' pp. 11 ff., 42 ff. [Iser]

vast number of possibilities; the moment these possibilities are narrowed down to one complete and immutable picture, the imagination is put out of action, and we feel we have somehow been cheated. This may perhaps be an oversimplification of the process, but it does illustrate plainly the vital richness of potential that arises out of the fact that the hero in the novel must be pictured and cannot be seen. With the novel the reader must use his imagination to synthesize the information given him, and so his perception is simultaneously richer and more private; with the film he is confined merely to physical perception, and so whatever he remembers of the world he had pictured is brutally cancelled out.

IV

The "picturing" that is done by our imagination is only one of the activities through which we form the "gestalt" of a literary text. We have already discussed the process of anticipation and retrospection, and to this we must add the process of grouping together all the different aspects of a text to form the consistency that the reader will always be in search of. While expectations may be continually modified, and images continually expanded, the reader will still strive, even if unconsciously, to fit everything together in a consistent pattern. "In the reading of images, as in the hearing of speech, it is always hard to distinguish what is given to us from what we supplement in the process of projection which is triggered off by recognition . . . it is the guess of the beholder that tests the medley of forms and colours for coherent meaning, crystallizing it into shape when a consistent interpretation has been found."[12] By grouping together the written parts of the text, we enable them to interact, we observe the direction in which they are leading us, and we project onto them the consistency which we, as readers, require. This "gestalt" must inevitably be colored by our own characteristic selection process. For it is not given by the text itself; it arises from the meeting between the written text and the individual mind of the reader with its own particular

history of experience, its own consciousness, its own outlook. The "gestalt" is not the true meaning of the text; at best it is a configurative meaning; " . . . comprehension is an individual act of seeing-things-together, and only that."[13] With a literary text such comprehension is inseparable from the reader's expectations, and where we have expectations, there too we have one of the most potent weapons in the writer's armory — illusion.

Whenever "consistent reading suggests itself . . . illusion takes over."[14] Illusion, says Northrop Frye, is "fixed or definable, and reality is best understood as its negation."[15] The "gestalt" of a text normally takes on (or, rather, is given) this fixed or definable outline, as this is essential to our own understanding, but on the other hand, if reading were to consist of nothing but an uninterrupted building up of illusions, it would be a suspect, if not downright dangerous, process: instead of bringing us into contact with reality, it would wean us away from realities. Of course, there is an element of "escapism" in all literature, resulting from this very creation of illusion, but there are some texts which offer nothing but a harmonious world, purified of all contradiction and deliberately excluding anything that might disturb the illusion once established, and these are the texts that we generally do not like to classify as literary. Women's magazines and the brasher forms of the detective story might be cited as examples.

However, even if an overdose of illusion may lead to triviality, this does not mean that the process of illusion-building should ideally be dispensed with altogether. On the contrary, even in texts that appear to resist the formation of illusion, thus drawing our attention to the cause of this resistance, we still need the abiding illusion that the resistance itself is the consistent pattern underlying the text. This is especially true of modern texts, in which it is the very precision of the written details which increases the proportion of indeterminacy; one detail appears to contradict another, and so simultaneously stimulates and frustrates our desire to "picture," thus continually causing our imposed "gestalt" of the test

[12]E. H. Gombrich, *Art and Illusion* (London, 1962), p. 204. [Iser]

[13]Louis O. Mink, "History and Fiction as Modes of Comprehension," *New Literary History* I (1970): 553. [Iser]
[14]Gombrich, *Art and Illusion*, p. 278. [Iser.]
[15]Northrop Frye, *Anatomy of Criticism* (New York, 1967), pp. 169 f. [Iser]

to disintegrate. Without the formation of illusions, the unfamiliar world of the text would remain unfa-miliar; through the illusions, the experience offered by the text becomes accessible to us, for it is only the illusion, on its different levels of consistency, that makes the experience "readable." If we cannot find (or impose) this consistency, sooner or later we will put the text down. The process is virtually hermeneutic. The text provokes certain expecta-tions which in turn we project onto the text in such a way that we reduce the polysemantic possi-bilities to a single interpretation in keeping with the expectations aroused, thus extracting an individual, configurative meaning. The polysemantic nature of the text and the illusion-making of the reader are opposed factors. If the illusion were complete, the polysemantic nature would vanish; if the polyse-mantic nature were all-powerful, the illusion would be totally destroyed. Both extremes are conceiv-able, but in the individual literary text we always find some form of balance between the two con-flicting tendencies. The formation of illusions, therefore, can never be total, but it is this very incompleteness that in fact gives it its productive value.

With regard to the experience of reading, Walter Pater once observed: "For to the grave reader words too are grave; and the ornamental word, the figure, the accessory form or colour or reference, is rarely content to die to thought precisely at the right moment, but will inevitably linger awhile, stirring a long 'brainwave' behind it of perhaps quite alien associations."[16] Even while the reader is seeking a consistent pattern in the text, he is also uncovering other impulses which cannot be immediately integrated or will even resist final integration. Thus the semantic possibilities of the text will always remain far richer than any configurative meaning formed while reading. But this impression is, of course, only to be gained through reading the text. Thus the configurative meaning can be nothing but a *pars pro toto*[17] fulfillment of the text, and yet this fulfillment gives rise to the very richness which it seeks to restrict, and indeed in some modern

[16]Walter Pater, *Appreciations* (London, 1920), p. 18. [Iser]

[17]Partial.

texts, our awareness of this richness takes prece-dence over any configurative meaning.

This fact has several consequences which, for the purpose of analysis, may be dealt with separately, though in the reading process they will all be working together. As we have seen, a con-sistent, configurative meaning is essential for the apprehension of an unfamiliar experience, which through the process of illusion-building we can incorporate in our own imaginative world. At the same time, this consistency conflicts with the many other possibilities of fulfillment it seeks to exclude, with the result that the configurative meaning is always accompanied by "alien associations" that do not fit in with the illusions formed. The first consequence, then, is the fact that in forming our illusions, we also produce at the same time a latent disturbance of these illusions. Strangely enough, this also applies to texts in which our expectations are actually fulfilled — though one would have thought that the fulfillment of expectations would help to complete the illusion. "Illusion wears off once the expectation is stepped up; we take it for granted and want more."[18]

The experiments in gestalt psychology referred to by Gombrich in *Art and Illusion* make one thing clear: ". . . though we may be intellectually aware of the fact that any given experience *must* be an illusion, we cannot, strictly speaking, watch ourselves having an illusion."[19] Now, if illusion were not a transitory state, this would mean that we could be, as it were, permanently caught up in it. And if reading were exclusively a matter of producing illusion — necessary though this is for the understanding of an unfamiliar experience — we should run the risk of falling victim to a gross deception. But it is precisely during our read-ing that the transitory nature of the illusion is revealed to the full.

As the formation of illusions is constantly accompanied by "alien associations" which cannot be made consistent with the illusions, the reader constantly has to lift the restrictions he places on the "meaning" of the text. Since it is he who builds the illusions, he oscillates between involvement in and observation of those illusions; he opens himself

[18]Gombrich, *Art and Illusion*, p. 54. [Iser]

[19]Ibid., p. 5. [Iser]

to the unfamiliar world without being imprisoned in it. Through this process the reader moves into the presence of the fictional world and so experiences the realities of the text as they happen.

In the oscillation between consistency and "alien associations," between involvement in and observation of the illusion, the reader is bound to conduct his own balancing operation, and it is this that forms the esthetic experience offered by the literary text. However, if the reader were to achieve a balance, obviously he would then no longer be engaged in the process of establishing and disrupting consistency. And since it is this very process that gives rise to the balancing operation, we may say that the inherent nonachievement of balance is a prerequisite for the very dynamism of the operation. In seeking the balance we inevitably have to start out with certain expectations, the shattering of which is integral to the esthetic experience.

> Furthermore, to say merely that "our expectations are satisfied" is to be guilty of another serious ambiguity. At first sight such a statement seems to deny the obvious fact that much of our enjoyment is derived from surprises, from betrayals of our expectations. The solution to this paradox is to find some ground for a distinction between "surprise" and "frustration." Roughly, the distinction can be made in terms of the effects which the two kinds of experiences have upon us. Frustration blocks or checks activity. It necessitates new orientation for our activity, if we are to escape the *cul de sac.* Consequently, we abandon the frustrating object and return to blind impulse activity. On the other hand, surprise merely causes a temporary cessation of the exploratory phase of the experience, and a recourse to intense contemplation and scrutiny. In the latter phase the surprising elements are seen in their connection with what has gone before, with the whole drift of the experience, and the enjoyment of these values is then extremely intense. Finally, it appears that there must always be some degree of novelty or surprise in all these values if there is to be a progressive specification of the direction of the total act . . . and any aesthetic experience tends to exhibit a continuous interplay between "deductive" and "inductive" operations.[20]

[20]B. Ritchie, "The Formal Structure of the Aesthetic Object," in *The Problems of Aesthetics,* ed. Eliseo Vivas and Murray Krieger (New York, 1965), pp. 230 f. [Iser]

It is this interplay between "deduction" and "induction" that gives rise to the configurative meaning of the text, and not the individual expectations, surprises, or frustrations arising from the different perspectives. Since this interplay obviously does not take place in the text itself, but can only come into being through the process of reading, we may conclude that this process formulates something that is unformulated in the text and yet represents its "intention." Thus, by reading we uncover the unformulated part of the text, and this very indeterminacy is the force that drives us to work out a configurative meaning while at the same time giving us the necessary degree of freedom to do so.

As we work out a consistent pattern in the text, we will find our "interpretation" threatened, as it were, by the presence of other possibilities of "interpretation," and so there arise new areas of indeterminacy (though we may only be dimly aware of them, if at all, as we are continually making "decisions" which will exclude them). In the course of a novel, for instance, we sometimes find that characters, events, and backgrounds seem to change their significance; what really happens is that the other "possibilities" begin to emerge more strongly, so that we become more directly aware of them. Indeed, it is this very shifting of perspectives that makes us feel that a novel is much more "true-to-life." Since it is we ourselves who establish the levels of interpretation and switch from one to another as we conduct our balancing operation, we ourselves impart to the text the dynamic lifelikeness which, in turn, enables us to absorb an unfamiliar experience into our personal world.

As we read, we oscillate to a greater or lesser degree between the building and the breaking of illusions. In a process of trial and error, we organize and reorganize the various data offered us by the text. These are the given factors, the fixed points on which we base our "interpretation," trying to fit them together in the way we think the author meant them to be fitted. "For to perceive, a beholder must *create* his own experience. And his creation must include relations comparable to those which the original producer underwent. They are not the same in any literal sense. But with the perceiver, as with the artist, there must be an ordering of the elements of the whole that is in form, although not in details, the same as the process of organization the creator of the work consciously experienced. Without an act of recreation the object is not perceived as a work of art."[21]

The act of recreation is not a smooth or continuous process, but one which, in its essence, relies on *interruptions* of the flow to render it efficacious. We look forward, we look back, we decide, we change our decisions, we form expectations, we are shocked by their nonfulfillment, we question, we muse, we accept, we reject; this is the dynamic process of recreation. This process is steered by two main structural components within the text: first, a repertoire of familiar literary patterns and recurrent literary themes, together with allusions to familiar social and historical contexts; second, techniques or strategies used to set the familiar against the unfamiliar. Elements of the repertoire are continually backgrounded or foregrounded with a resultant strategic overmagnification, trivialization, or even annihilation of the allusion. This defamiliarization of what the reader thought he recognized is bound to create a tension that will intensify his expectations as well as his distrust of those expectations. Similarly, we may be confronted by narrative techniques that establish links between things we find difficult to connect, so that we are forced to reconsider data we at first held to be perfectly straightforward. One need only mention the very simple trick, so often employed by novelists, whereby the author himself takes part in the narrative, thus establishing perspectives which would not have arisen out of the mere narration of the events described. Wayne Booth once called this the technique of the "unreliable narrator,"[22] to show the extent to which a literary device can counter expectations arising out of the literary text. The figure of the narrator may act in permanent opposition to the impressions we might otherwise form. The question then arises as to whether this strategy, opposing the formation of illusions, may be integrated into a consistent

[21] John Dewey, *Art as Experience* (New York, 1958), p. 54. [Iser]

[22] Cf. Wayne C. Booth, *The Rhetoric of Fiction* (Chicago, 1961), pp. 211 ff., 339 ff. [Iser]

pattern, lying, as it were, a level deeper than our original impressions. We may find that our narrator, by opposing us, in fact turns us against him and thereby strengthens the illusion he appears to be out to destroy; alternatively, we may be so much in doubt that we begin to question all the processes that lead us to make interpretative decisions. Whatever the cause may be, we will find ourselves subjected to this same interplay of illusion-forming and illusion-breaking that makes reading essentially a recreative process.

We might take, as a simple illustration of this complex process, the incident in Joyce's *Ulysses* in which Bloom's cigar alludes to Ulysses's spear. The context (Bloom's cigar) summons up a particular element of the repertoire (Ulysses's spear); the narrative technique relates them to one another as if they were identical. How are we to "organize" these divergent elements, which, through the very fact that they are put together, separate one element so clearly from the other? What are the prospects here for a consistent pattern? We might say that it is ironic — at least that is how many renowned Joyce readers have understood it.[23] In this case, irony would be the form of organization that integrates the material. But if this is so, what is the object of the irony? Ulysses's spear, or Bloom's cigar? The uncertainty surrounding this simple question already puts a strain on the consistency we have established and, indeed, begins to puncture it, especially when other problems make themselves felt as regards the remarkable conjunction of spear and cigar. Various alternatives come to mind, but the variety alone is sufficient to leave one with the impression that the consistent pattern has been shattered. And even if, after all, one can still believe that irony holds the key to the mystery, this irony must be of a very strange nature; for the formulated text does not merely mean the opposite of what has been formulated. It may even mean something that cannot be formulated at all. The moment we try to impose a consistent pattern on the text, discrepancies are bound to arise. These are, as it were, the reverse side of the interpretative

[23] Richard Ellmann, "*Ulysses*: The Divine Nobody," in *Twelve Original Essays on Great English Novels*, ed. Charles Shapiro (Detroit, 1960), p. 247, classified this particular allusion as "mock-heroic." [Iser]

coin, an involuntary product of the process that creates discrepancies by trying to avoid them. And it is their very presence that draws us into the text, compelling us to conduct a creative examination not only of the text but also of ourselves.

This entanglement of the reader is, of course, vital to any kind of text, but in the literary text we have the strange situation that the reader cannot know what his participation actually entails. We know that we share in certain experiences, but we do not know what happens to us in the course of this process. This is why, when we have been particularly impressed by a book, we feel the need to talk about it; we do not want to get away from it by talking about it — we simply want to understand more clearly what it is in which we have been entangled. We have undergone an experience, and now we want to know consciously *what* we have experienced. Perhaps this is the prime usefulness of literary criticism — it helps to make conscious those aspects of the text which would otherwise remain concealed in the subconscious; it satisfies (or helps to satisfy) our desire to talk about what we have read.

The efficacy of a literary text is brought about by the apparent evocation and subsequent negation of the familiar. What at first seemed to be an affirmation of our assumptions leads to our own rejection of them, thus tending to prepare us for a re-orientation. And it is only when we have outstripped our preconceptions and left the shelter of the familiar that we are in a position to gather new experiences. As the literary text involves the reader in the formation of illusion and the simultaneous formation of the means whereby the illusion is punctured, reading reflects the process by which we gain experience. Once the reader is entangled, his own preconceptions are continually overtaken, so that the text becomes his "present" while his own ideas fade into the "past"; as soon as this happens he is open to the immediate experience of the text, which was impossible so long as his preconceptions were his "present."

V

In our analysis of the reading process so far, we have observed three important aspects that form the basis of the relationship between reader and text: the process of anticipation and retrospection, the consequent unfolding of the text as a living event, and the resultant impression of lifelikeness.

Any "living event" must, to a greater or lesser degree, remain open. In reading, this obliges the reader to seek continually for consistency, because only then can he close up situations and comprehend the unfamiliar. But consistency-building is itself a living process in which one is constantly forced to make selective decisions — and these decisions in their turn give a reality to the possibilities which they exclude, insofar as they may take effect as a latent disturbance of the consistency established. This is what causes the reader to be entangled in the text-"gestalt" that he himself has produced.

Through this entanglement the reader is bound to open himself up to the workings of the text and so leave behind his own preconceptions. This gives him the chance to have an experience in the way George Bernard Shaw once described it: "You have learnt something. That always feels at first as if you had lost something."[24] Reading reflects the structure of experience to the extent that we must suspend the ideas and attitudes that shape our own personality before we can experience the unfamiliar world of the literary text. But during this process, something happens to us.

This "something" needs to be looked at in detail, especially as the incorporation of the unfamiliar into our own range of experience has been to a certain extent obscured by an idea very common in literary discussion: namely, that the process of absorbing the unfamiliar is labeled as the *identification* of the reader with what he reads. Often the term "identification" is used as if it were an explanation, whereas in actual fact it is nothing more than a description. What is normally meant by "identification" is the establishment of affinities between oneself and someone outside oneself — a familiar ground on which we are able to experience the unfamiliar. The author's aim, though, is to convey the experience and, above all, an attitude toward that experience. Consequently, "identification" is not an end in

[24]G. B. Shaw, *Major Barbara* (London, 1964), p. 316. [Iser]

itself, but a stratagem by means of which the author stimulates attitudes in the reader.

This of course is not to deny that there does arise a form of participation as one reads; one is certainly drawn into the text in such a way that one has the feeling that there is no distance between oneself and the events described. This involvement is well summed up by the reaction of a critic to reading Charlotte Brontë's *Jane Eyre:* "We took up *Jane Eyre* one writer's evening, somewhat piqued at the extravagant commendations we had heard, and sternly resolved to be as critical as Croker. But as we read on we forgot both commendations and criticism, identified ourselves with Jane in all her troubles, and finally married Mr. Rochester about four in the morning."[25] The question is how and why did the critic identify himself with Jane?

In order to understand this "experience," it is well worth considering Georges Poulet's observations on the reading process. He says that books only take on their full existence in the reader.[26] It is true that they consist of ideas thought out by someone else, but in reading the reader becomes the subject that does the thinking. Thus there disappears the subject-object division that otherwise is a prerequisite for all knowledge and all observation, and the removal of this division puts reading in an apparently unique position as regards the possible absorption of new experiences. This may well be the reason why relations with the world of the literary text have so often been misinterpreted as identification. From the idea that in reading we must think the thoughts of someone else, Poulet draws the following conclusion: "'Whatever I think is a part of *my* mental world. And yet here I am thinking a thought which manifestly belongs to another mental world, which is being thought in me just as though I did not exist. Already the notion is inconceivable and seems even more so if I reflect that, since every thought must have a subject to think it, this *thought* which is alien to me and yet in me, must also have in me a *subject* which is alien to me. . . . Whenever

I read, I mentally pronounce an *I,* and yet the *I* which I pronounce is not myself."[27]

But for Poulet this idea is only part of the story. The strange subject that thinks the strange thought in the reader indicates the potential presence of the author, whose ideas can be "internalized" by the reader: "Such is the characteristic condition of every work which I summon back into existence by placing my consciousness at its disposal. I give it not only existence, but awareness of existence."[28] This would mean that consciousness forms the point at which author and reader converge, and at the same time it would result in the cessation of the temporary self-alienation that occurs to the reader when his consciousness brings to life the ideas formulated by the author. This process gives rise to a form of communication which, however, according to Poulet, is dependent on two conditions: the life-story of the author must be shut out of the work and the individual disposition of the reader must be shut out of the act of reading. Only then can the thoughts of the author take place subjectively in the reader, who thinks what he is not. It follows that the work itself must be thought of as a consciousness, because only in this way is there an adequate basis for the author-reader relationship — a relationship that can only come about through the negation of the author's own life-story and the reader's own disposition. This conclusion is actually drawn by Poulet when he describes the work as the self-presentation or materialization of consciousness: "And so I ought not to hesitate to recognize that so long as it is animated by this vital inbreathing inspired by the act of reading, a work of literature becomes (at the expense of the reader whose own life it suspends) a sort of human being, that it is a mind conscious of itself and constituting itself in me as the subject of its own objects."[29] Even though it is difficult to follow such a substantialist conception of the consciousness that constitutes itself in the literary work, there are, nevertheless, certain points in Poulet's argument that are worth holding onto. But they should be developed along somewhat different lines.

[25]William George Clark, *Fraser's* (December, 1849): 692, quoted by Kathleen Tillotson, *Novels of the Eighteen-Forties* (Oxford, 1961), p. 19 f. [Iser]
[26]Cf. Georges Poulet, "Phenomenology of Reading," *New Literary History* I (1969): 54. [Iser]

[27]Ibid., p. 56. [Iser]
[28]Ibid., p. 59. [Iser]
[29]Ibid. [Iser]

If reading removes the subject-object division that constitutes all perception, it follows that the reader will be "occupied" by the thoughts of the author, and these in turn will cause the drawing of new "boundaries." Text and reader no longer confront each other as object and subject, but instead the "division" takes place within the reader himself. In thinking the thoughts of another, his own individuality temporarily recedes into the background, since it is supplanted by these alien thoughts, which now become the theme on which his attention is focused. As we read, there occurs an artificial division of our personality, because we take as a theme for ourselves something that we are not. Consequently when reading we operate on different levels. For although we may be thinking the thoughts of someone else, what we are will not disappear completely — it will merely remain a more or less powerful virtual force. Thus, in reading there are these two levels — the alien "me" and the real, virtual "me" — which are never completely cut off from each other. Indeed, we can only make someone else's thoughts into an absorbing theme for ourselves, provided the virtual background of our own personality can adapt to it. Every text we read draws a different boundary within our personality, so that the virtual background (the real "me") will take on a different form, according to the theme of the text concerned. This is inevitable, if only for the fact that the relationship between alien theme and virtual background is what makes it possible for the unfamiliar to be understood.

In this context there is a revealing remark made by D. W. Harding, arguing against the idea of identification with what is read: "What is sometimes called wish-fulfilment in novels and plays can . . . more plausibly be described as wish-formulation or the definition of desires. The cultural levels at which it works may vary widely;

the process is the same. . . . It seems nearer the truth . . . to say that fictions contribute to defining the reader's or spectator's values, and perhaps stimulating his desires, rather than to suppose that they gratify desire by some mechanism of vicarious experience."[30] In the act of reading, having to think something that we have not yet experienced does not mean only being in a position to conceive or even understand it; it also means that such acts of conception are possible and successful to the degree that they lead to something being formulated in us. For someone else's thoughts can only take a form in our consciousness if, in the process, our unformulated faculty for deciphering those thoughts is brought into play — a faculty which, in the act of deciphering, also formulates itself. Now since this formulation is carried out on terms set by someone else, whose thoughts are the theme of our reading, it follows that the formulation of our faculty for deciphering cannot be along our own lines of orientation.

Herein lies the dialectical structure of reading. The need to decipher gives us the chance to formulate our own deciphering capacity — i.e., we bring to the fore an element of our being of which we are not directly conscious. The production of the meaning of literary texts — which we discussed in connection with forming the "gestalt" of the text — does not merely entail the discovery of the unformulated, which can then be taken over by the active imagination of the reader; it also entails the possibility that we may formulate ourselves and so discover what had previously seemed to elude our consciousness. These are the ways in which reading literature gives us the chance to formulate the unformulated.

[30]D. W. Harding, "Psychological Processes in the Reading of Fiction," in *Aesthetics in the Modern World,* ed. Harold Osborne (London, 1968), p. 313 f. [Iser]

Stanley Fish
b. 1938

The agent provocateur of contemporary literary theory, Stanley Fish was born in Providence, Rhode Island, and raised in Philadelphia. He received his A.B. at Penn (1959) and his A.M. and Ph.D. (1962) at Yale, which published his dissertation on John Skelton. Fish taught at Berkeley, becoming a full professor in that year. In 1974, Fish moved to Johns Hopkins as Kenan professor, and in 1986, as both professor of law and as chairman of the English department, to Duke University, where he has attracted a stellar group of theorists, including Fredric Jameson (Ch. 5) and Barbara Herrnstein Smith (Part One). Fish left Duke to become Dean of Arts and Sciences at the University of Illinois at Chicago, and in 2005 became Davidson-Kahn Distinguished Professor of Humanities and Law at Florida International University. He is currently Floresheimer Distinguished Visiting Professor of Law at the Benjamin N. Cardozo School of Law at Yeshiva University. In his most recent metatheoretical work, Fish has attacked theory as pointless, impotent to constrain the will-to-power of interpretation, whereas formerly, he had restricted his rhetorical assaults to individual theorists like Wolfgang Iser or to fields like linguistics and stylistics. Fish's career as a gadfly began with his second book, Surprised by Sin: The Reader in Paradise Lost (1967), which transgressed with both feet the "affective fallacy" by which the New Criticism had eliminated the study of the audience. The object of Fish's concern has shifted from the implied reader immanent within the text in Self-Consuming Artifacts: The Experience of Seventeenth-Century Literature (1972), to the experience of actual readers and interpretive communities of readers in Is There a Text in This Class? (1980). Most recently, Fish has generalized his pragmatic approach to rhetoric and the reader beyond literary concerns; his social and political essays appear in Doing What Comes Naturally: Change, Rhetoric, and the Practice of Theory in Literary and Legal Studies (1989), There's No Such Thing As Free Speech: And It's a Good Thing, Too (1994), Professional Correctness: Literary Studies and Political Change (1995), and The Trouble with Principle (1999). His latest books are How to Write a Sentence and How to Read One (2011) and Versions of Academic Freedom: From Professionalism to Revolution (2014). Fish has also revisited and revised his Paradise Lost interpretation in How Milton Works (2001). "How to Recognize a Poem When You See One" first appeared in Is There a Text in This Class? (1980).

How to Recognize a Poem When You See One

Last time I sketched out an argument by which meanings are the property neither of fixed and stable texts nor of free and independent readers but of interpretive communities that are responsible both for the shape of a reader's activities and for the texts those activities produce. In this lecture I propose to extend that argument so as to account not only for the meanings a poem might be said to have but for the fact of its being recognized as a poem in the first place. And once again I would like to begin with an anecdote.

In the summer of 1971 I was teaching two courses under the joint auspices of the Linguistic Institute of America and the English Department of the State University of New York at Buffalo. I taught these courses in the morning and in the same room. At 9:30 I would meet a group of students who were interested in the relationship between linguistics and literary criticism. Our nominal subject was stylistics but our concerns were finally theoretical and extended to the presuppositions and assumptions which underlie both linguistic and literary practice. At 11:00 these students were replaced by another group whose concerns were exclusively literary and were in fact confined to English religious poetry of the seventeenth century. These students had been learning how to identify Christian symbols and how to recognize typological patterns and how to move from the observation of these symbols and patterns to the specification of the poetic intention that was usually didactic or homiletic. On the day I am thinking about, the only connection between the two classes was an assignment given to the first which was still on the blackboard at the beginning of the second. It read:

Jacobs — Rosenbaum
Levin
Thorne
Hayes
Ohman (?)

I am sure that many of you will already have recognized the names on this list, but for the sake of the record, allow me to identify them. Roderick Jacobs and Peter Rosenbaum are two linguists who have coauthored a number of textbooks and coedited a number of anthologies. Samuel Levin is a linguist who was one of the first to apply the operations of transformational grammar to literary texts. J. P. Thorne is a linguist at Edinburgh who, like Levin, was attempting to extend the rules of transformational grammar to the notorious irregularities of poetic language. Curtis Hayes is a linguist who was then using transformational grammar in order to establish an objective basis for his intuitive impression that the language of Gibbon's *Decline and Fall of the Roman Empire* is more complex than the language of Hemingway's novels. And Richard Ohmann is the literary critic who, more than any other, was responsible for introducing the

vocabulary of transformational grammar to the literary community. Ohmann's name was spelled as you see it here because I could not remember whether it contained one or two *n*'s. In other words, the question mark in parenthesis signified nothing more than a faulty memory and desire on my part to appear scrupulous. The fact that the names appeared in a list that was arranged vertically, and that Levin, Thorne, and Hayes formed a column that was more or less centered in relation to the paired names of Jacobs and Rosenbaum, was similarly accidental and was evidence only of a certain compulsiveness if, indeed, it was evidence of anything at all.

In the time between the two classes I made only one change. I drew a frame around the assignment and wrote on the top of that frame "p. 43." When the members of the second class filed in I told them that what they saw on the blackboard was a religious poem of the kind they had been studying and I asked them to interpret it. Immediately they began to perform in a manner that, for reasons which will become clear, was more or less predictable. The first student to speak pointed out that the poem was probably a hieroglyph,[1] although he was not sure whether it was in the shape of a cross or an altar. This question was set aside as the other students, following his lead, began to concentrate on individual words, interrupting each other with suggestions that came so quickly that they seemed spontaneous. The first line of the poem (the very order of events assumed the already constituted status of the object) received the most attention: Jacobs was explicated as a reference to Jacob's ladder, traditionally allegorized as a figure for the Christian ascent to heaven. In this poem, however, or so my students told me, the means of ascent is not a ladder but a tree, a rose tree or rosenbaum. This was seen to be an obvious reference to the Virgin Mary who was often characterized as a rose without thorns, itself an emblem of the immaculate conception. At this point the poem appeared to the students to be operating in the familiar manner of an iconographic riddle. It

[1]A poem whose shape on the printed page carries symbolic meaning, such as George Herbert's "Easter Wings." Older texts of this sort are often called *emblems*, modern ones, *concrete poetry*.

at once posed the question, "How is it that a man can climb to heaven by means of a rose tree?" and directed the reader to the inevitable answer: by the fruit of that tree, the fruit of Mary's womb, Jesus. Once this interpretation was established it received support from, and conferred significance on, the word "thorne," which could only be an allusion to the crown of thorns, a symbol of the trial suffered by Jesus and of the price he paid to save us all. It was only a short step (really no step at all) from this insight to the recognition of Levin as a double reference, first to the tribe of Levi, of whose priestly function Christ was the fulfillment, and second to the unleavened bread carried by the children of Israel on their exodus from Egypt, the place of sin, and in response to the call of Moses, perhaps the most familiar of the old testament types of Christ. The final word of the poem was given at least three complementary readings: it could be "omen," especially since so much of the poem is concerned with foreshadowing and prophecy; it could be Oh Man, since it is man's story as it intersects with the divine plan that is the poem's subject; and it could, of course, be simply "amen," the proper conclusion to a poem celebrating the love and mercy shown by a God who gave his only begotten son so that we may live.

In addition to specifying significances for the words of the poem and relating those significances to one another, the students began to discern larger structural patterns. It was noted that of the six names in the poem three — Jacobs, Rosenbaum, and Levin — are Hebrew, two — Thorne and Hayes — are Christian, and one — Ohman — is ambiguous, the ambiguity being marked in the poem itself (as the phrase goes) by the question mark in parenthesis. This division was seen as a reflection of the basic distinction between the old dispensation and the new, the law of sin and the law of love. That distinction, however, is blurred and finally dissolved by the typological perspective which invests the old testament events and heroes with new testament meanings. The structure of the poem, my students concluded, is therefore a double one, establishing and undermining its basic pattern (Hebrew vs. Christian) at the same time. In this context there is finally no pressure to resolve the ambiguity of Ohman since the two

possible readings — the name is Hebrew, the name is Christian — are both authorized by the reconciling presence in the poem of Jesus Christ. Finally, I must report that one student took to counting letters and found, to no one's surprise, that the most prominent letters in the poem were S. O. N.

Some of you will have noticed that I have not yet said anything about Hayes. This is because of all the words in the poem it proved the most recalcitrant to interpretation, a fact not without consequence, but one which I will set aside for the moment since I am less interested in the details of the exercise than in the ability of my students to perform it. What is the source of that ability? How is it that they were able to do what they did? What is it that they did? These questions are important because they bear directly on a question often asked in literary theory. What are the distinguishing features of literary language? Or, to put the matter more colloquially, How do you recognize a poem when you see one? The commonsense answer, to which many literary critics and linguists are committed, is that the act of recognition is triggered by the observable presence of distinguishing features. That is, you know a poem when you see one because its language displays the characteristics that you know to be proper to poems. This, however, is a model that quite obviously does not fit the present example. My students did not proceed from the noting of distinguishing features to the recognition that they were confronted by a poem; rather, it was the act of recognition that came first — they knew in advance that they were dealing with a poem — and the distinguishing features then followed.

In other words, acts of recognition, rather than being triggered by formal characteristics, are their source. It is not that the presence of poetic qualities compels a certain kind of attention but that the paying of a certain kind of attention results in the emergence of poetic qualities. As soon as my students were aware that it was poetry they were seeing, they began to look with poetry-seeing eyes, that is, with eyes that saw everything in relation to the properties they knew poems to possess. They knew, for example (because they were told by their teachers), that poems are (or are supposed to be) more densely and intricately organized than ordinary communications; and that knowledge translated itself into a willingness — one might even say a determination — to see connections between one word and another and between every word and the poem's central insight. Moreover, the assumption that there *is* a central insight is itself poetry-specific, and presided over its own realization. Having assumed that the collection of words before them was unified by an informing purpose (because unifying purposes are what poems have), my students proceeded to find one and to formulate it. It was in the light of that purpose (now assumed) that significances for the individual words began to suggest themselves, significances which then fleshed out the assumption that had generated them in the first place. Thus the meanings of the words and the interpretation in which those words were seen to be embedded emerged together, as a consequence of the operations my students began to perform once they were told that this was a poem.

It was almost as if they were following a recipe — if it's a poem do this, if it's a poem, see it that way — and indeed definitions of poetry *are* recipes, for by directing readers as to what to look for in a poem, they instruct them in ways of looking that will produce what they expect to see. If your definition of poetry tells you that the language of poetry is complex, you will scrutinize the language of something identified as a poem in such a way as to bring out the complexity you know to be "there." You will, for example, be on the look-out for latent ambiguities; you will attend to the presence of alliterative and consonantal patterns (there will always be some), and you will try to make something of them (you will always succeed); you will search for meanings that subvert, or exist in a tension with the meanings that first present themselves; and if these operations fail to produce the anticipated complexity, you will even propose a significance for the words that are *not* there, because, as everyone knows, everything about a poem, including its omissions, is significant. Nor, as you do these things, will you have any sense of performing in a willful manner, for you will only be doing what you learned to do in the course of becoming a skilled reader of poetry. Skilled reading is usually thought to be a matter of discerning what is there, but if the example of my students can be generalized, it is a matter of knowing how to *produce* what can thereafter be said to be there. Interpretation is not the art of construing but the art of constructing. Interpreters do not decode poems; they make them.

To many, this will be a distressing conclusion, and there are a number of arguments that could be mounted in order to forestall it. One might point out that the circumstances of my students' performance were special. After all, they had been concerned exclusively with religious poetry for some weeks, and therefore would be uniquely vulnerable to the deception I had practiced on them and uniquely equipped to impose religious themes and patterns on words innocent of either. I must report, however, that I have duplicated this experiment any number of times at nine or ten universities in three countries, and the results are always the same, even when the participants know from the beginning that what they are looking at was originally an assignment. Of course this very fact could itself be turned into an objection: doesn't the reproducibility of the exercise prove that there is something about these words that leads everyone to perform in the same way? Isn't it just a happy accident that names like Thorne and Jacobs have counterparts or near counterparts in biblical names and symbols? And wouldn't my students have been unable to do what they did if the assignment I gave to the first class had been made up of different names? The answer to all of these questions is no. Given a firm belief that they were confronted by a religious poem, my students would have been able to turn any list of names into the kind of poem we have before us now, because they would have read the names within the assumption that they were informed with Christian significance. (This is nothing more than a literary analogue to Augustine's rule of faith.[2]) You can test this assertion by replacing Jacobs-Rosenbaum, Levin, Thorne, Hayes, and Ohman with names drawn from the faculty of Kenyon College — Temple, Jordan, Seymour,

---

[2]A reference to *Confessions* 6:4, in which St. Augustine recommends reading the less edifying biblical narratives from the Old Testament as sacred allegory, a practice extended by Aquinas and Dante to secular literature as well.

Daniels, Star, Church. I will not exhaust my time or your patience by performing a full-dress analysis, which would involve, of course, the relation between those who saw the River Jordan and those who saw *more* by seeing the Star of Bethlehem, thus fulfilling the prophecy by which the temple of Jerusalem was replaced by the inner temple or church built up in the heart of every Christian. Suffice it to say that it could easily be done (you can take the poem home and do it yourself) and that the shape of its doing would be constrained not by the names but by the interpretive assumptions that gave them a significance even before they were seen. This would be true even if there were no names on the list, if the paper or blackboard were blank; the blankness would present no problem to the interpreter, who would immediately see in it the void out of which God created the earth, or the abyss into which unregenerate sinners fall, or, in the best of all possible poems, both.

Even so, one might reply, all you've done is demonstrate how an interpretation, if it is prosecuted with sufficient vigor, can impose itself on material which has its own proper shape. Basically, at the ground level, in the first place, when all is said and done, "Jacobs-Rosenbaum Levin Thorne Hayes Ohman (?)" is an assignment, it is only a trick that allows you to transform it into poem, and when the effects to the trick have worn off, it will return to its natural form and be seen as an assignment once again. This is a powerful argument because it seems at once to give interpretation its due (as an act of the will) and to maintain the independence of that on which interpretation works. It allows us, in short, to preserve our commonsense intuition that interpretation must be interpretation of *something*. Unfortunately, the argument will not hold because the assignment we all see is no less the product of interpretation than the poem into which it was turned. That is, it requires just as much work, and work of the same kind, to see this as an assignment as it does to see it as a poem. If this seems counterintuitive, it is only because the work required to see it as an assignment is work we have already done, in the course of acquiring the huge amount of background knowledge that enables you and me to function in the academic world. In order to know what an assignment is, that is, in order to know what to do with something identified as an assignment, you must first know what a class is (know that it isn't an economic grouping) and know that classes meet at specified times for so many weeks, and that one's performance in a class is largely a matter of performing between classes.

Think for a moment of how you would explain this last to someone who did not already know it. "Well," you might say, "a class is a group situation in which a number of people are instructed by an informed person in a particular subject." (Of course the notion of "subject" will itself require explication.) "An assignment is something you do when you're not in class." "Oh, I see," your interlocutor might respond, "an assignment is something you do to take your mind off what you've been doing in class." "No, an assignment is a part of a class." "But how can that be if you only do it when the class is not meeting?" Now it would be possible, finally, to answer that question, but only by enlarging the horizons of your explanation to include the very concept of a university, what it is one might be doing there, why one might be doing it instead of doing a thousand other things, and so on. For most of us these matters do not require explanation, and indeed, it is hard for us to imagine someone for whom they do; but that is because our tacit knowledge of what it means to move around in academic life was acquired so gradually and so long ago that it doesn't seem like knowledge at all (and therefore something someone else might *not* know) but a part of the world. You might think that when you're on campus (a phrase that itself requires volumes) that you are simply walking around on the two legs God gave you; but your walking is informed by an internalized awareness of institutional goals and practices, of norms of behavior, of lists of do's and don't's, of invisible lines and the dangers of crossing them; and, as a result, you see everything as *already* organized in relation to those same goals and practices. It would never occur to you, for example, to wonder if the people pouring out of that building are fleeing from a fire; you *know* that they are exiting from a class (what could be more obvious?) and you know that because your perception of their action occurs within a knowledge of what people in a university could possibly be doing and the reasons they could have for doing it (going to the next class, going back to the dorm, meeting someone in the student union). It is within that same knowledge that an assignment becomes intelligible so that it appears to you immediately as an obligation, as a set of directions, as something with parts, some of which may be more significant than others. That is, it is a proper question to ask of an assignment whether some of its parts might be omitted or slighted, whereas readers of poetry know that no part of a poem can be slighted (the rule is "everything counts") and they do not rest until every part has been given a significance.

In a way this amounts to no more than saying what everyone already knows: poems and assignments are different, but my point is that the differences are a result of the different interpretive operations we perform and not of something inherent in one or the other. An assignment no more compels its own recognition than does a poem; rather, as in the case of a poem, the shape of an assignment emerges when someone looks at something identified as one with assignment-seeing eyes, that is, with eyes which are capable of seeing the words as already embedded within the institutional structure that makes it possible for assignments to have a sense. The ability to see, and therefore to make, an assignment is no less a learned ability than the ability to see, and therefore to make, a poem. Both are constructed artifacts, the products and not the producers of interpretation, and while the differences between them are real, they are interpretive and do not have their source in some bedrock level of objectivity.

Of course one might want to argue that there is a bedrock level at which these names constitute neither an assignment nor a poem but are merely a list. But that argument too fails because a list is no more a natural object — one that wears its meaning on its face and can be recognized by anyone — than an assignment or a poem. In order to see a list, one must already be equipped with the concepts of seriality, hierarchy, subordination, and so on, and while these are by no means esoteric concepts and seem available to almost everyone, they are nonetheless learned, and if there were someone who had not learned them, he or she would not be able to see a list. The next recourse is to descend still lower (in the direction of atoms) and to claim objectivity for letters, paper, graphite, black marks on white spaces, and so on; but these entities too have palpability and shape only because of the assumption of some or other system of intelligibility, and they are therefore just as available to a deconstructive dissolution as are poems, assignments, and lists.

The conclusion, therefore, is that all objects are made and not found, and that they are made by the interpretive strategies we set in motion. This does not, however, commit me to subjectivity because the means by which they are made are social and conventional. That is, the "you" who does the interpretative work that puts poems and assignments and lists into the world is a communal you and not an isolated individual. No one of us wakes up in the morning and (in French fashion) reinvents poetry or thinks up a new educational system or decides to reject seriality in favor of some other, wholly original, form of organization. We do not do these things because we could not do them, because the mental operations we can perform are limited by the institutions in which we are *already* embedded. These institutions precede us, and it is only by inhabiting them, or being inhabited by them, that we have access to the public and conventional senses they make. Thus while it is true to say that we create poetry (and assignments and lists), we create it through interpretive strategies that are finally not our own but have their source in a publicly available system of intelligibility. Insofar as the system (in this case a literary system) constrains us, it also fashions us, furnishing us with categories of understanding, with which we in turn fashion the entities to which we can then point. In short, to the list of made or constructed objects we must add ourselves, for we no less than the poems and assignments we see are the products of social and cultural patterns of thought.

To put the matter in this way is to see that the opposition between objectivity and subjectivity is a false one because neither exists in the pure form that would give the opposition its point. This is precisely illustrated by my anecdote in which we do *not* have free-standing readers in a relationship of perceptual adequacy or inadequacy to an equally free-standing text. Rather, we have readers whose consciousnesses are constituted by a set of conventional notions which when put into operation constitute in turn a conventional, and convention-ally seen, object. My students could do what they did, and do it in unison, because as members of a literary community they knew what a poem was (their knowledge was public), and that knowledge led them to look in such a way as to populate the landscape with what they knew to be poems.

Of course poems are not the only objects that are constituted in unison by shared ways of see-ing. Every object or event that becomes available within an institutional setting can be so character-ized. I am thinking, for example, of something that happened in my classroom just the other day. While I was in the course of vigorously making a point, one of my students, William Newlin by name, was just as vigorously waving his hand. When I asked the other members of the class what it was that Mr. Newlin was doing, they all answered that he was seeking permission to speak. I then asked them how they knew that. The imme-diate reply was that it was obvious; what else could he be thought to be doing? The meaning of his gesture, in other words, was right there on its sur-face, available for reading by anyone who had eyes to see. That meaning, however, would not have been available to someone without any knowledge of what was involved in being a student. Such a person might have thought that Mr. Newlin was pointing to the fluorescent lights hanging from the ceiling, or calling our attention to some subject that was about to fall (''the sky is falling,'' ''the sky is falling''). And if the someone in question were a child of elementary or middle-school age, Mr. Newlin might well have been seen as seeking permission not to speak but to go to the bathroom, an interpretation or reading that would never occur to a student at Johns Hopkins or any other institution of ''higher learning'' (and how would we explain to the uninitiated the meaning of that phrase).

The point is the one I have made so many times before: it is neither the case that the significance of Mr. Newlin's gesture is imprinted on its surface where it need only be read off, or that the construc-tion put on the gesture by everyone in the room was individual and idiosyncratic. Rather, the source of our interpretive unanimity was a structure of inter-ests and understood goals, a structure whose cate-gories so filled our individual consciousnesses that they were rendered as one, immediately investing phenomena with the significance they *must* have, given the already-in-place assumption about what someone could possibly be intending (by word or gesture) in a classroom. By seeing Mr. Newlin's raised hand with a single shaping eye, we were demonstrating what Harvey Sacks has character-ized as ''the fine power of a culture. It does not, so to speak, merely fill brains in roughly the same way, it fills them so that they are alike in fine detail.''[3] The occasion of Sacks's observation was the ability of his hearers to understand a sequence of two sentences — ''The baby cried. The mommy picked it up.'' — exactly as he did (assuming, for example that ''the mommy'' who picks up the 'baby' is the mommy of that baby''), despite the fact that alternative ways of understanding were demonstrably possible. That is, the mommy of the second sentence could well have been the mommy of the some other baby, and it need not even have been a baby that this ''floating'' mommy was picking up. One is tempted to say that in the absence of a specific context we are authorized to take the words literally, which is what Sacks's hearers do; but as Sacks's observes, it is within the assumption of a context — one so deeply assumed that we are unaware of it — that the words acquire what seems to be their literal meaning. There is nothing *in the words* that tells Sacks and his hear-ers how to relate the mommy and the baby of this story, just as there is nothing *in the form* of Mr. Newlin's gesture that tells his fellow students how to determine its significance. In both cases the determination (of relation and significance) is the work of categories of organization — the fam-ily, being a student — that are from the very first giving shape and value to what is heard and seen. Indeed, these categories are the very shape of seeing itself, in that we are not to imagine a perceptual ground more basic than the one they afford. That is, we are not to imagine a moment when my students ''simply see'' a physical con-figuration of atoms and *then* assign the configura-tion a significance, according to the situation they happen to be in. To be in the situation (this or any other) is to ''see'' with the eyes of its interests, its goals, its understood practices, values, and

3''On the Analysability of Stories by Children,'' in *Ethnomethodology*, ed. Roy Turner (Baltimore: Penguin, 1974), p. 218. [Fish]

norms, and so to be conferring significance *by* seeing, not after it. The categories of my students' vision are the categories by which they understand themselves to be functioning as students (what Sacks might term "doing studenting"), and objects will appear to them in forms related to that way of functioning rather than in some objective or preinterpretive form. (This is true even when an object is seen as not related, since nonrelation is not a pure but a differential category — the specification of something by enumerating what it is not; in short, nonrelation is merely one form of relation, and its perception is always situation-specific.)

Of course, if someone who was not functioning as a student was to walk into my classroom, he might very well see Mr. Newlin's raised hand (and "raised hand" is already an interpretation-laden description) in some other way, as evidence of a disease, as the salute of a political follower, as a muscle-improving exercise, as an attempt to kill flies, but he would always see it in *some* way, and never as purely physical data waiting for his interpretation. And, moreover, the way of seeing, whatever it was, would never be individual or idiosyncratic, since its source would always be the institutional structure of which the "see-er" was an extending agent. This is what Sacks means when he says that a culture fills brains "so that they are alike in fine detail"; it fills them so that no one's interpretive acts are exclusively his own but fall to him by virtue of his position in some socially organized environment and are therefore always shared and public. It follows, then, that the fear of solipsism, of the imposition by the unconstrained self of its own prejudices, is unfounded because the self does not exist apart from the communal or conventional categories of thought that enable its operations (of thinking, seeing, reading). Once one realizes that the conceptions that fill consciousness, including any conception of its own status, are culturally derived, the very notion of an unconstrained self, of a consciousness wholly and dangerously free, becomes incomprehensible.

But without the notion of the unconstrained self, the arguments of Hirsch, Abrams, and the other proponents of objective interpretation are deprived of their urgency. They are afraid that in the absence of the controls afforded by a normative system of meanings, the self will simply substitute its own meanings for the meanings (usually identified with the intentions of the author) that texts bring with them, the meanings that texts *"have"*; however, if the self is conceived of not as an independent entity but as a social construct whose operations are delimited by the systems of intelligibility that inform it, then the meanings it confers on texts are not its own but have their source in the interpretive community (or communities) of which it is a function. Moreover, these meanings will be neither subjective nor objective, at least in the terms assumed by those who argue within the traditional framework: they will not be objective because they will always have been the product of a point of view rather than having been simply "read off"; and they will not be subjective because that point of view will always be social or institutional. Or by the same reasoning one could say that they are *both* subjective and objective: they are subjective because they inhere in a particular point of view and are therefore not universal; and they are objective because the point of view that delivers them is public and conventional rather than individual or unique.

To put the matter in either way is to see how unhelpful the terms "subjective" and "objective" finally are. Rather than facilitating inquiry, they close it down, by deciding in advance what shape inquiry can possibly take. Specifically, they assume, without being aware that it is an assumption and therefore open to challenge, the very distinction I have been putting into question, the distinction between interpreters and the objects they interpret. That distinction in turn assumes that interpreters and their objects are two different kinds of *a*contextual entities, and within these twin assumptions the issue can only be one of control: will texts be allowed to constrain their own interpretation or will irresponsible interpreters be allowed to obscure and overwhelm texts. In the spectacle that ensues, the spectacle of Anglo-American critical controversy, texts and selves fight it out in the persons of their respective champions, Abrams, Hirsch, Reichert, Graff on the one hand, Holland, Bleich, Slatoff, and (in some characterizations of him) Barthes on the other. But if selves are constituted by the ways of thinking and seeing that inhere in social organizations, and if these constituted selves in turn constitute texts according to these same ways, then there can be no adversary relationship between text and self because they are the necessarily related products of the same cognitive possibilities. A text cannot be overwhelmed by an irresponsible reader and one need not worry about protecting the purity of a text from a reader's idiosyncrasies. It is only the distinction between subject and object that gives rise to these urgencies, and once the distinction is blurred they simply fall away. One can respond with a cheerful yes to the question "Do readers make meanings?" and commit oneself to very little because it would be equally true to say that meanings, in the form of culturally derived interpretive categories, make readers.

Indeed, many things look rather different once the subject-object dichotomy is eliminated as the assumed framework within which critical discussion occurs. Problems disappear, not because they have been solved but because they are shown never to have been problems in the first place. Abrams, for example, wonders how, in the absence of a norma-tive system of stable meanings, two people could ever agree on the interpretation of a work or even of a sentence; but the difficulty is only a difficulty if the two (or more) people are thought of as isolated individuals whose agreement must be compelled by something external to them. (There is something of the police state in Abrams's vision, complete with posted rules and boundaries, watchdogs to enforce them, procedures for identifying their violators as criminals.) But if the understandings of the people in question are informed by the same notions of what counts as a fact, of what is central, perhaps, and worthy of being noticed — in short, by the same interpretive principles — then agreement between them will be assured, and its source will not be a text that enforces its own perception but a way of perceiving that results in the emergence to those who share it (or those whom it shares) of the same text. That text might be a poem, as it was in the case of those who first "saw" "Jacobs-Rosenbaum Levin Hayes Thorne Ohman (?)," or a hand, as it is every day in a thousand classrooms; but whatever it is, the shape and meaning it appears immediately to have will be the "ongoing accom-plishment"[4] of those who agree to produce it.

[4] A phrase used by the ethnomethodologists to characterize the interpretive activities that create and maintain the features of everyday life. See, for example, Don H. Zimmerman, "Fact as a Practical Accomplishment," in Ethnomethodology, pp. 128–43. [Fish]

Judith Fetterley

b. 1938

Judith Fetterley was born in New York City but was raised in Toronto until the age of ten, when her family moved to Franklin, Indiana. Fetterley's special interest and slant on U.S. culture comes from this complex position as both insider and outsider. Fetterley took her A.B. from Swarthmore in 1960, then worked for the Harvard Business School and the American Friends Service Committee before returning to graduate school at Indiana University, where she received her Ph.D. in 1969. Fetterley taught at the University of Pennsylvania from 1967 to 1973, then moved to the State University of New York at Albany, where she is currently Distinguished Teaching Professor Emerita of English. Fetterley's scholarly and theoretical work includes The Resisting Reader: A Feminist Approach to American Fiction *(1978) along with numerous articles on nineteenth- and twentieth-century American writers. She also founded and is general editor for the Rutgers University Press American Women Writers reprint series. Fetterley has edited* Provisions: A Reader from Nineteenth-Century American Women Writers *(1985) and (with Marjorie Pryse) the* Norton Anthology of American Women Regionalists, 1850–1910 *(1995).*

Introduction to
The Resisting Reader

I

Literature is political. It is painful to have to insist on this fact, but the necessity of such insistence indicates the dimensions of the problem. John Keats once objected to poetry "that has a palpable design upon us."[1] The major works of American fiction constitute a series of designs on the female reader, all the more potent in their effect because they are "impalpable." One of the main things that keeps the design of our literature unavailable to the consciousness of the woman reader, and hence impalpable, is the very posture of the apolitical, the pretense that literature speaks universal truths through forms from which all the merely personal, the purely subjective, has been burned away or at least transformed through the medium of art into the representative. When only one reality is

encouraged, legitimized, and transmitted and when that limited vision endlessly insists on its comprehensiveness, then we have the conditions necessary for that confusion of consciousness in which impalpability flourishes. it is the purpose of this book to give voice to a different reality and different vision, to bring a different subjectivity to bear on the old "universality." To examine American fictions in light of how attitudes toward women shape their form and content is to make available to consciousness that which has been largely left unconscious and thus to change our understanding of these fictions, our relation to them, and their effect on us. It is to make palpable their designs.

American literature is male. To read the canon of what is currently considered classic American literature is perforce to identify as male. Though exceptions to this generalization can be found here and there — a Dickinson poem, a Wharton novel — these exceptions usually function to obscure the argument and confuse the issue: American literature is male. Our literature neither

---

[1] From Keats's letter to John Hamilton Reynolds of February 3, 1818. Keats goes on to say that "Poetry should be great & unobtrusive, a thing which enters into one's soul, and does not startle or amaze it with itself but with its subject."

leaves women alone nor allows them to participate. It insists on its universality at the same time that it defines that universality in specifically male terms. "Rip Van Winkle" is paradigmatic of this phenomenon. While the desire to avoid work, escape authority, and sleep through the major decisions of one's life is obviously applicable to both men and women, in Irving's story this "universal" desire is made specifically male. Work, authority, and decision-making are symbolized by Dame Van Winkle, and the longing for flight is defined against her. She is what one must escape from, and the "one" is necessarily male. In Mailer's *An American Dream*, the fantasy of eliminating all one's ills through the ritual of scapegoating is equally male: the sacrificial scapegoat is the woman/wife and the cleansed survivor is the husband/male. In such fictions the female reader is co-opted into participation in an experience from which she is explicitly excluded; she is asked to identify with a selfhood that defines itself in opposition to her; she is required to identify herself.

The woman reader's relation to American literature is made even more problematic by the fact that our literature is frequently dedicated to defining what is peculiarly American about experience and identity. Given the pervasive male bias of this literature, it is not surprising that in it the experience of being American is equated with the experience of being male. In Fitzgerald's *The Great Gatsby*, the background for the experience of disillusionment and betrayal revealed in the novel is the discovery of America, and Daisy's failure of Gatsby is symbolic of the failure of America to live up to the expectations in the imagination of the men who "discovered" it, America is female; to be American is male; and the quintessential American experience is betrayal by woman. Henry James certainly defined our literature, if not our culture, when he picked the situation of women as the subject of *The Bostonians*, his very American tale. Power is the issue in the politics of literature, as it is in the politics of anything else. To be excluded from a literature that claims to define one's identity is to experience a peculiar form of powerlessness — not simply the powerlessness which derives from not seeing one's experience articulated, clarified, and legitimized in art, but more significantly the powerlessness which results

from the endless division of self against self, the consequence of the invocation to identify as male while being reminded that to be male — to be universal, to be American — is to be *not female*. Not only does powerlessness characterize woman's experience of reading, it also describes the content of what is read. Each of the works chosen for this study presents a version and an enactment of the drama of men's power over women. The final irony, and indignity, of the woman reader's relation to American literature, then, is that she is required to dissociate herself from the very experience the literature engenders. Powerlessness is the subject and powerlessness the experience, and the design insists that Rip Van Winkle/Frederic Henry/ Nick Carraway/Stephen Rojack speak for us all.

The drama of power in our literature is often disguised. In "Rip Van Winkle," Rip poses as powerless, the hen-pecked husband cowering before his termagant Dame. Yet, when Rip returns from the mountains, armed by the drama of female deposition witnessed there, to discover that his wife is dead and he is free to enjoy what he has always wanted, the "Shucks, Ma'am, I don't mean no harm" posture dissolves. In Sherwood Anderson's "I Want to Know Why," the issue of power is refracted through the trauma of a young boy's discovery of what it means to be male in a culture that gives white men power over women, horses, and niggers. More sympathetic and honest than "Rip," Anderson's story nevertheless exposes both the imaginative limits of our literature and the reasons for those limits. Storytelling and art can do no more than lament the inevitable — boys must grow up to be men; it can provide no alternative vision of being male. Bathed in nostalgia, "I Want to Know Why" is infused with the perspective it abhors, because finally to disavow that perspective would be to relinquish power. The lament is self-indulgent; it offers the luxury of feeling bad without the responsibility of change. And it is completely male-centered, registering the tragedy of sexism through its cost to men. At the end we cry for the boy and not for the whores he will eventually make use of.

In Hawthorne's "The Birthmark," the subject of power is more explicit. The fact of men's power over women and the full implications of that fact are the crux of the story. Aylmer is free to experiment on Georgiana, to the point of death, because she is both woman and wife. Hawthorne indicates the attractiveness of the power that marriage puts in the hands of men through his description of Aylmer's reluctance to leave his laboratory and through his portrayal of Aylmer's inherent discomfort with women and sex. And why does Aylmer want this power badly enough to overcome his initial reluctance and resistance? Hitherto Aylmer has failed in all his efforts to achieve a power equal to that of "Mother" nature. Georgiana provides an opportunity for him to outdo nature by remaking her creation. And if he fails, he still will have won because he will have destroyed the earthly embodiment and representative of his adversary. Hawthorne intends his character to be seen as duplicitous, and he maneuvers Aylmer through the poses of lover, husband, and scientist to show us how Aylmer attempts to gain power and to use that power to salve his sense of inadequacy. But even so, Hawthorne, like Anderson, is unwilling to do more with the sickness than call it sick. He obscures the issue of sexual politics behind a haze of "universals" and clothes the murder of wife by husband in the language of idealism.

Though the grotesque may serve Faulkner as a disguise in the same way that the ideal serves Hawthorne, "A Rose for Emily" goes farther than "The Birthmark" in making the power of men over women an overt subject. Emily's life is shaped by her father's absolute control over her; her murder of Homer Barron is *re*action, not action. Though Emily exercises the power the myths of sexism make available to her, that power is minimal; her retaliation is no alternative to the patriarchy which oppresses her. Yet Faulkner, like Anderson and Hawthorne, ultimately protects himself and short-circuits the implications of his analysis, not simply through the use of the grotesque, which makes Emily eccentric rather than central, but also through his choice of her victim. In having Emily murder Homer Barron, a northern day-laborer, rather than Judge Stevens, the southern patriarch, Faulkner indicates how far he is willing to go in imagining even the minimal reversal of power involved in retaliation. The elimination of Homer Barron is no real threat to the system Judge Stevens represents. Indeed, a few day-laborers may have to be sacrificed here and there to keep that system going.

In *A Farewell to Arms,* the issue of power is thoroughly obscured by the mythology, language, and structure of romantic love and by the invocation of an abstract, though spiteful, "they" whose goal it is to break the good, the beautiful, and the brave. Yet the brave who is broken is Catherine; at the end of the novel Catherine is dead, Frederic is alive, and the resemblance to "Rip Van Winkle" and "The Birthmark" is unmistakable. Though the scene in the hospital is reminiscent of Aylmer's last visit to Georgiana in her chambers, Hemingway, unlike Hawthorne, separates his protagonist from the source of his heroine's death, locating the agency of Catherine's demise not simply in "them" but in her biology. Frederic survives several years of war, massive injuries, the dangers of a desperate retreat, and the threat of execution by his own army; Catherine dies in her first pregnancy. Clearly, biology is destiny. Yet, Catherine is as much a scapegoat as Dame Van Winkle, Georgiana, Daisy Fay, and Deborah Rojack. For Frederic to survive, free of the intolerable burdens of marriage, family, and fatherhood, yet with his vision of himself as the heroic victim of cosmic antagonism intact, Catherine must die. Frederic's necessities determine Catherine's fate. He is, indeed, the agent of her death.

In its passionate attraction to the phenomenon of wealth, *The Great Gatsby* reveals its author's consuming interest in the issue of power. In the quintessentially male drama of poor boy's becoming rich boy, ownership of women is invoked as the index of power: he who possesses Daisy Fay is the most powerful boy. But when the rich boy, fearing finally for his territory, repossesses the girl and, by asking "Who is he," strips the poor boy of his presumed power, the resultant animus is directed not against the rich boy but against the girl, whose rejection of him exposes the poor boy's powerlessness. The struggle for power between men is deflected into safer and more certain channels, and the consequence is the familiar demonstration of male power over women. This demonstration, however, is not simply the result of a greater safety in directing anger at women than at men. It derives as well from the fact that even the poorest male gains something from a system in which all women are at some level his subjects. Rather than attack the men who represent and manifest that system, he identifies with them and acquires his sense of power through superiority to women. It is not surprising, therefore, that the drama of *The Great Gatsby* involves an attack on Daisy, whose systematic reduction from the glamorous object of Gatsby's romantic longings to the casual killer of Myrtle Wilson provides an accurate measure of the power available to the most "powerless" male.

By his choice of scene, context, and situation, Henry James in *The Bostonians* directly confronts the hostile nature of the relations between men and women and sees in that war the defining characteristics of American culture. His honesty provides the opportunity for a clarification rather than a confusion of consciousness and offers a welcome relief from the deceptions of other writers. Yet the drama, while correctly labeled, is still the same. *The Bostonians* is an unrelenting demonstration of the extent, and an incisive analysis of the sources, of the power of men as a class over women as a class. Yet, though James laments women's oppression, and laments it because of its effects *on women,* he nevertheless sees it as inevitable. *The Bostonians* represents a kind of end point in the literary exploration of sex/class power; it would be impossible to see more clearly and feel more deeply and still remain convinced that patriarchy is inevitable. Indeed, there is revolution latent in James's novel, and, while he would be articulating and romanticizing the tragic elements in women's powerlessness, *The Bostonians* provides the material for that analysis of American social reality which is the beginning of change.

Norman Mailer's *An American Dream* represents another kind of end point. Mailer is thoroughly enthralled by the possibility of power that sexism makes available to men, absolutely convinced that he is in danger of losing it, and completely dedicated to maintaining it, at whatever cost. It is impossible to imagine a more frenzied commitment to the maintenance of male power than Mailer's. In *An American Dream* all content has been reduced to the enactment of men's power over women, and to the development and legitimization of that act Mailer brings every strategy he can muster the least of which is an extended elaboration of the mythology of female power. In Mailer's work the effort to obscure the issue, disguise reality, and confuse consciousness is so frantic that the antitheses he provides to protect his thesis become in fact his message and his confusions shed a lurid illumination. If *The Bostonians* induces one to rearrange James's conceptual framework and so to make evitable his inevitable, *An American Dream* induces a desire to eliminate Mailer's conceptual framework altogether and start over. Beyond his frenzy is only utter nausea and weariness of spirit and a profound willingness to give up an exhausted, sick, and sickening struggle. In Mailer, the drama of power comes full circle; at once the most sexist writer, he is also the most freeing, and out of him it may be possible to create anew.

II

But what have I to say of *Sexual Politics* itself? Millett has undertaken a task which I find particularly worthwhile: the consideration of certain events or works of literature from an unexpected, even startling point of view. Millett never suggests that hers is a sufficient analysis of any of the works she discusses. Her aim is to wrench the reader from the vantage point he has long occupied, and force him to look at life and letters from a new coign.[2] Hers is not meant to be the last word on any writer, but a wholly new word, little heard before and strange. For the first time we have been asked to look at literature as women; we, men, women and Ph.D.'s, have always read it as men. Who cannot point to a certain overemphasis in the way Millett reads Lawrence or Stalin or Euripides. What matter? We are rooted in our vantage points and require transplanting which, always dangerous, involves violence and the possibility of death.

— CAROLYN HEILBRUN[3]

The method that is required is not one of correlation but of *liberation.* Even the term "method" must be reinterpreted and in fact wrenched out of its usual semantic field, for the emerging creativity in women

[2]Vantage point.

[3]Carolyn Heilbrun, "Millett's *Sexual Politics:* A Year Later," *Aphra* 2 (Summer 1971), 39. [Fetterley]

is by no means a merely cerebral process. In order to understand the implications of this process it is necessary to grasp the fundamental fact that women have had the power of *naming* stolen from us. We have not been free to use our own power to name ourselves, the world, or God. The old naming was not the product of dialogue — a fact inadvertently admitted in the Genesis story of Adam's naming the animals and the woman. Women are now realizing that the universal imposing of names by men has been false because partial. That is, inadequate words have been taken as adequate.   — MARY DALY[4]

Re-vision — the act of looking back, of seeing with fresh eyes, of entering an old text from a new critical direction — is for us more than a chapter in cultural history: it is an act of survival. Until we can understand the assumptions in which we are drenched we cannot know ourselves. And this drive to self-knowledge, for woman, is more than a search for identity: it is part of her refusal of the self-destructiveness of male-dominated society. A radical critique of literature, feminist in its impulse, would take the work first of all as a clue to how we live, how we have been living, how we have been led to imagine ourselves, how our language has trapped as well as liberated us; and how we can begin to see — and therefore live — afresh.

— ADRIENNE RICH[5]

A culture which does not allow itself to look clearly at the obvious through the universal accessibility of art is a culture of tragic delusion, hardly viable.   — CYNTHIA OZICK[6]

When a system of power is thoroughly in command, it has scarcely need to speak itself aloud; when its workings are exposed and questioned, it becomes not only subject to discussion, but even to change.   — KATE MILLETT[7]

Consciousness is power. To create a new understanding of our literature is to make possible a new effect of that literature on us. And to make possible a new effect is in turn to provide the conditions for changing the culture that the literature reflects. To expose and question that complex of ideas and mythologies about women and men which exist in our society and are confirmed in our literature is to make the system of power embodied in the literature open not only to discussion but even to change. Such questioning and exposure can, of course, be carried on only by a consciousness radically different from the one that informs the literature. Such a closed system cannot be opened up from within but only from without. It must be entered into from a point of view which questions its values and assumptions and which has its investment in making available to consciousness precisely that which the literature wishes to keep hidden. Feminist criticism provides that point of view and embodies that consciousness.

In "A Woman's Map of Lyric Poetry," Elizabeth Hampsten, after quoting in full Thomas Campion's "My Sweetest Lesbia," asks, "And Lesbia, what's in it for her?"[8] The answer to this question is the subject of Hampsten's essay and the answer is, of course, nothing. But implicit in her question is another answer — a great deal, for someone. As Lillian Robinson reminds us, "and, always, *cui bono* — who profits?"[9] The questions of who profits, and how, are crucial because the attempt to answer them leads directly to an understanding of the function of literary sexual politics. Function is often best known by effect. Though one of the most persistent of literary stereotypes is the castrating bitch, the cultural reality is not the emasculation of men by women but the *immasculation* of women by men. As readers and teachers and scholars, women are taught to think as men, to identify with a male point of view, and to accept as normal and legitimate a male system of values, one of whose central principles is misogyny.

One of the earliest statements of the phenomenon of immasculation, serving indeed as a

[4]Mary Daly, *Beyond God the Father: Toward a Philosophy of Women's Liberation* (Boston: Beacon, 1973), p. 8. [Fetterley]

[5]Adrienne Rich, "When We Dead Awaken: Writing as Re-Vision," *College English* 34 (1972), 18. [Fetterley]

[6]Cynthia Ozick, "Women and Creativity: The Demise of the Dancing Dog," *Motive* 29 (1969); reprinted in *Woman in Sexist Society,* eds. Vivian Gornick and Barbara Moran (New York: Signet-New American Library, 1972), p. 450. [Fetterley]

[7]Kate Millett, *Sexual Politics* (Garden City: Doubleday, 1970), p. 58. [Fetterley]

[8]*College English* 34 (1973), 1075. [Fetterley]

[9]"Dwelling in Decencies: Radical Criticism and the Feminist Perspective," *College English* 32 (1971), 887; reprinted in *Sex, Class, and Culture* (Bloomington: Indiana University Press, 1978), p. 16. [Fetterley]

position paper, is Elaine Showalter's "Women and the Literary Curriculum." In the opening part of her article, Showalter imaginatively recreates the literary curriculum the average young woman entering college confronts:

In her freshman year she would probably study literature and composition, and the texts in her course would be selected for their timeliness, or their relevance, or their power to involve the reader, rather than for their absolute standing in the literary canon. Thus she might be assigned any one of the texts which have recently been advertised for Freshman English: an anthology of essays, perhaps such as *The Responsible Man,* "for the student who wants literature relevant to the world in which he lives," or *Conditions of Men,* or *Man in Crisis: Perspectives on The Individual and His World,* or again, *Representative Men: Cult Heroes of Our Time,* in which thirty-three men represent such categories of heroism as the writer, the poet, the dramatist, the artist, and the guru, and the only two women included are the Actress Elizabeth Taylor and The Existential Heroine Jacqueline Onassis. . . . By the end of her freshman year, a woman student would have learned something about intellectual neutrality; she would be learning, in fact, how to think like a man.[10]

Showalter's analysis of the process of immasculation raises a central question: "What are the effects of this long apprenticeship in negative capability[11] on the self-image and the self-confidence of women students?" And the answer is self-hatred and self-doubt: "Women are estranged from their own experience and unable to perceive its shape and authenticity; . . . they are expected to identify as readers with a masculine experience and perspective, which is presented as the human one. . . . Since they have no faith in the validity of their own perceptions and experiences, rarely seeing them confirmed in literature, or accepted in criticism, can we wonder that women students are so often timid, cautious, and insecure when we exhort them to 'think for themselves'?"[12]

The experience of immasculation is also the focus of Lee Edwards' article, "Women, Energy, and *Middlemarch.*" Summarizing her experience, Edwards concludes:

Thus, like most women, I have gone through my entire education — as both student and teacher — as a schizophrenic, and I do not use this term lightly, for madness is the bizarre but logical conclusion of our education. Imagining myself male, I attempted to create myself male. Although I knew the case was otherwise, it seemed I could do nothing to make this other critically real.

Edwards extends her analysis by linking this condition to the effects of the stereotypical presentation of women in literature:

I said simply, and for the most part silently that, since neither those women nor any women whose acquaintances I had made in fiction had much to do with the life I led or wanted to lead, I was not female. Alien from the women I saw most frequently imagined, I mentally arranged them in rows labeled respectively insipid heroines, sexy survivors, and demonic destroyers. As organizer I stood somewhere else, alone perhaps, but hopefully above them.[13]

Intellectually male, sexually female, one is in effect no one, nowhere, immasculated.

Clearly, then, the first act of the feminist critic must be to become a resisting rather than an assenting reader and, by this refusal to assent, to begin the process of exorcizing the male mind that has been implanted in us. The consequence of this exorcism is the capacity for what Adrienne Rich describes as re-vision — "the act of looking back, of seeing with fresh eyes, of entering an old text from a new critical direction." And the consequence, in turn, of this re-vision is that books will no longer be read as they have been read and thus will lose their power to bind us unknowingly to their designs. While women obviously cannot rewrite literary works so that they become ours by virtue of reflecting our reality, we can accurately name the reality they do reflect and so change literary criticism from a closed conversation to an active dialogue. In making available to women this power of naming reality, feminist criticism is revolutionary.

10 *College English* 32 (1971), 855. [Fetterley]

11 Showalter means something like "self-abnegation," not the prelude to creativity postulated by Keats.

12 Ibid., 856–57. [Fetterley]

13 *Massachusetts Review* 13 (1972), 226, 227. [Fetterley]

The significance of such power is evident if one considers the strength of the taboos against it:

> I permit no woman to teach ... she is to keep silent. — St. Paul

> By Talmudic law a man could divorce a wife whose voice could be heard next door. From there to Shakespeare: "Her voice was ever soft, / Gentle, and low — an excellent thing in woman." And to Yeats: "The women that I picked spoke sweet and low / And yet gave tongue." And to Samuel Beckett, guessing at the last torture, The Worst: "a woman's voice perhaps, I hadn't thought of that, they might engage a soprano."
>
> — Mary Ellmann[14]

> The experience of the class in which I voiced my discontent still haunts my nightmares. Until my face froze and my brain congealed, I was called prude and, worse yet, insensitive, since I willfully misread the play in the interest of proving a point false both to the work and in itself.
>
> — Lee Edwards[15]

The experience Edwards describes of attempting to communicate her reading of the character of Shakespeare's Cleopatra is a common memory for most of us who have become feminist critics. Many of us never spoke; those of us who did speak were usually quickly silenced. The need to keep certain things from being thought and said reveals to us their importance. Feminist criticism represents the discovery/recovery of a voice, a unique and uniquely powerful voice capable of canceling out those other voices, so movingly described in Sylvia Plath's *The Bell Jar*, which spoke about us and to us and at us but never for us.

III

The eight works analyzed in this book were chosen for their individual significance, their representative value, and their collective potential. They are interconnected in the ways that they comment on and illuminate each other, and they form a dramatic whole whose meaning transcends the mere sum of the parts. These eight are

meant to stand for a much larger body of literature; their individual and collective designs can be found elsewhere repeatedly.

The four short stories form a unit, as do the four novels. These units are subdivided into pairs. "Rip Van Winkle" and "I Want to Know Why" are companion pieces whose focus is the fear of and resistance to growing up. The value of Anderson's story lies mainly in the light it sheds on Irving's, making explicit the fear of sexuality only implied in "Rip" and focusing attention on the strategy of deflecting hostility away from men and onto women. "The Birthmark" and "A Rose for Emily" are richly related studies of the consequences of growing up and, by implication, of the reasons for the resistance to it. In both stories sexual desire leads to death. More significantly, they are brilliant companion analyses of that sex/class hostility that is the essence of patriarchal culture and that underlies the adult identity Anderson's boy recoils from assuming. "The Birthmark" is the story of how to murder your wife and get away with it; "A Rose for Emily" is the story of how the system which allows you to murder your wife makes it possible for your wife to murder you.

Both *A Farewell to Arms* and *The Great Gatsby* are love stories; together they demonstrate the multiple uses of the mythology of romantic love in the maintenance of male power. In addition they elaborate on the function of scapegoating evident in "Rip Van Winkle" and "The Birthmark." In its more obvious connection of the themes of love and power, *The Great Gatsby* brings closer to consciousness the hostility which *A Farewell to Arms* seeks to disguise and bury. *The Bostonians* and *An American Dream* form the most unlikely and perhaps the most fascinating of the pairs. In both, the obfuscation of romantic love has been cleared away and the issue of power directly joined. James's novel describes a social reality — male power, female powerlessness — which Mailer's denies by creating a social mythology — female power, male powerlessness — that inverts that reality. Yet finally, the intention of Mailer's mythology is to maintain the reality it denies. *The Bostonians* forces the strategies of *An American Dream* into the open by its massive documentation of women's oppression, and *An American Dream*

---

[14]*Thinking About Women* (New York: Harcourt Brace Jovanovich, 1968), pp. 149–50. [Fetterley]

[15]Edwards, p. 230. [Fetterley]

provides the political answer to *The Bostonians'* inevitability by its massive, though unintended, demonstration of the fact that women's oppression grows not out of biology but out of men's need to oppress.

The sequence of both the stories and the novels is generated by a scale of increasing complexity, increasing consciousness, and increasing "feminist" sympathy and insight. Thus, the movement of the stories is from the black and white of "Rip Van Winkle," with its postulation of good guy and villain and its formulation in terms of innocent fable, to the complexity of "A Rose for Emily," whose action forces sexual violence into consciousness and demands understanding for the erstwhile villain. The movement of the novels is similar. *A Farewell to Arms* is as simplistic and disguised and hostile as "Rip Van Winkle"; indeed, the two have many affinities, not the least of which is the similarity of their sleep-centered protagonists who believe that women are a bad dream that will go away if you just stay in bed long enough. The sympathy and

complexity of consciousness in *The Bostonians* is even larger than that in "A Rose for Emily," and is exceeded only by the imagination of *An American Dream*, which is "feminist" not by design but by default. Yet the decision to end with *An American Dream* comes not simply from its position on the incremental scale. *An American Dream* is "Rip Van Winkle" one hundred and fifty years later, intensified to be sure, but *exactly the same story*. Thus, the complete trajectory of the immasculating imagination of American literature is described by the movement from "Rip Van Winkle" to *An American Dream*, and that movement is finally circular. This juxtaposition of beginning and end provides the sharpest possible exposure of that circular quality in the design of our literature, apparent in the movements within and between works, which defines its imaginative limits. Like the race horse so loved by Anderson's boy, the imagination which informs our "classic" American literature runs endlessly round a single track, unable because unwilling to get out of the race.

Lisa Zunshine

b. 1968

Lisa Zunshine was born in 1968 in what was then Soviet Russia and came to the United States as a refugee in 1990. In 2000, she received a Ph.D. in eighteenth-century British Literature at the University of California and was hired by the University of Kentucky where she is currently Bush-Holbrook Professor of English. Her books include Bastards and Foundlings: Illegitimacy in Eighteenth-Century Britain *(2005)* Why We Read Fiction: An Explanation from Cognitive Theory *(2006), and* Getting Inside Your Head, What Cognitive Science Can Tell Us About Popular Culture *(2012), as well as edited volumes:* Nabokov at the Limits: Redrawing Critical Boundaries *(1999),* Philanthropy and Fiction in Eighteenth-Century England *(2006), and* Approaches to Teaching the Novels of Samuel Richardson *(2006, co-edited with Jocelyn Harris). Her essays have appeared in* Narrative, Poetics Today, Philosophy and Literature, Modern Philology, The Eighteenth-Century: Theory and Interpretation, Eighteenth-Century Life, The Eighteenth-Century Novel, *and a variety of edited collections. The following essay appeared in slightly different form in* Narrative *(2003).*

Theory of Mind and Experimental Representations of Fictional Consciousness

Let me begin with a seemingly nonsensical question.[1] When Peter Walsh unexpectedly comes to see Clarissa Dalloway "at eleven o'clock on the morning of the day she [is] giving a party," and, "positively trembling," asks her how she is, "taking both her hands; kissing both her hands," thinking that "she's grown older," and deciding that he "shan't tell her anything about it . . . for she's grown older" (40), how do we know that his "trembling" is to be accounted for by his excitement at seeing his Clarissa again after all these years, and not, for instance, by his progressing Parkinson's disease?

[1] I am grateful to James Phelan for his thoughtful suggestions and comments. The original version of this essay, published in *Narrative* in 2003, contained a discussion of the implications of research on autism and theory of mind for the study of literature. I have eliminated this discussion from the present version because given what I have been learning about autism, I consider my earlier generalization about autism and fiction incorrect. For a further discussion, see Savarese and Zunshine, "The Critic as Neurocosmopolite."

Assuming that you are a particularly good-natured reader of *Mrs. Dalloway*, you could patiently explain to me that if Walsh's trembling were occasioned by an illness, Woolf would tell us so. She wouldn't leave us long under the impression that Walsh's body language betrays his agitation, his joy, and his embarrassment, and that the meeting has instantaneously and miraculously brought back the old days when Clarissa and Peter had "this queer power of communicating without words" because, reflecting Walsh's "trembling," Clarissa herself is "so surprised, . . . so glad, so shy, so utterly taken aback to have [him] come to her unexpectedly in the morning!" (40). Too much, you would point out, hinges on our getting the emotional undertones of the scene right for Woolf to withhold from us a crucial piece of information about Walsh's health.

I then would ask you why it is that were Walsh's trembling caused by an illness, Woolf would have to explicitly tell us so, but as it is not,

she can simply take for granted that we will interpret it as being caused by his emotions. In other
words, what allows Woolf to assume that we will
automatically read a character's body language as
indicative of his thoughts and feelings?

She assumes this because of our collective
past history as readers, you perhaps would say.
Writers have been using descriptions of their
characters' behaviors to inform us about their
feelings since time immemorial, and we expect
authors to do so when we open the book. We all
learn, whether consciously or not, that the default
interpretation of behavior reflects the character's
state of mind, and every fictional story that we
read reinforces our tendency to make that kind of
interpretation first.[2]

Had this imaginary conversation about readers'
automatic assumptions taken place twenty years
ago, it would have ended here. Or it would have
never happened — not even in this hypothetical
form — because the answers to my naive questions
would have seemed so obvious. Today, however,
this conversation has to continue because recent
research in cognitive psychology and anthropology
may explain just why we see the default meaning
of a character's behavior in the character's mental
state. To understand what enables most of us to
constrain the range of possible interpretations, we
may have to go beyond the explanation that evokes
our personal reading histories and admit some evidence from our evolutionary history.

In what follows, then, I attempt to make a
broader case for introducing the recent findings
of cognitive scientists into literary studies by
showing how their research into our ability to
explain behavior in terms of the underlying states
of mind — or our *mind-reading* ability — can
furnish us with a series of surprising insights into
our interaction with literary texts. I begin by arguing that theory of mind is a cognitive capacity that
makes literature, as we know it, possible. I then

consider the potentially controversial issue of the
"effortlessness" with which we thus read other
people's — including literary characters' —
minds. To explore one specific aspect of the
role played by such mind-reading in fictional
representations of consciousness, I then return to
Mrs. Dalloway. Here I describe a series of recent
experiments exploring our capacity for imagining serially embedded representations of mental
states (that is, "representations of representations
of representations" of mental states[3]) and suggest that Woolf's prose pushes this particular
capacity beyond its everyday "zone of comfort,"
a realization that may account partially for the
trepidation that Woolf's writing tends to provoke
in some of her readers. I conclude by discussing
the relationship between cognitive analysis and
the more traditional literary-historical analysis
of Woolf, thus addressing the interdisciplinary
potential of the new field of cognitive approaches
to literature.

I. FICTION AND THEORY OF MIND

Mind-reading is a term used by cognitive psychologists to describe our ability to explain people's behavior in terms of their thoughts, feelings,
beliefs, and desires; for example, "Lucy *reached*
for the chocolate because she *wanted* something
sweet," or "Peter Walsh was *trembling* because
he was *excited* to see Clarissa again." They also
call this ability our theory of mind, and I will use
the two terms interchangeably throughout this
essay.

Most scholars working with theory of mind
agree that this adaptation must have developed
during the "massive neurocognitive evolution"
which took place during the Pleistocene, when
our brain increased threefold in size. The determining factor behind the increase in brain size
was the social nature of our species (which we
share with other primates).[4] The emergence of a

3. For a related analysis of "representations of representations" or "metarepresentations," see Zunshine, "Eighteenth-
Century Print Culture." [Zunshine]

4. On the social intelligence of nonhuman primates, see Byrne
and Whiten, *Machiavellian Intelligence* and "The Emergence
of Metarepresentation"; Gomez, "Visual Behavior"; Premack
and Dasser, "Perceptual Origins." [Zunshine]

2. Like Hermione Lee, we could ground it in Woolf's position as a "pioneer of reader-response theory." Woolf, she
writes, "was extremely interested in the two-way dialogue
between readers and writers. Books change their readers:
they teach you how to read them. But readers also change
books. 'Undoubtedly,' Woolf herself had written, 'all writers are immensely influenced by the people who read them'"
("Virginia Woolf's Essays" 91). [Zunshine]

theory of mind adaptation was evolution's answer to the "staggeringly complex" challenge faced by our ancestors, who needed to make sense of the behavior of other people in their group, which could include up to two hundred individuals. As cognitive psychologist Simon Baron-Cohen points out, "attributing mental states to a complex system (such as a human being) is by far the easiest way of understanding it," that is, of "coming up with an explanation of the complex system's behavior and predicting what it will do next" (21).[5] Thus our tendency to explain observed behavior in terms of underlying mental states seems to be so effortless and automatic because our evolved cognitive architecture "prods" us toward learning and practicing mind-reading daily, from the beginning of awareness. (This is not to say, however, that our actual interpretations of other people's mental states are always correct — far from it!)

It is possible, moreover, that the cognitive adaptations that evolved to process information about human thoughts and feelings are constantly on the alert, checking out their environment for cues that fit their input conditions.[6] On some level, then, works of fiction manage to "cheat" these adaptations into "believing" that they are in the presence of material that they were "designed" to process, i.e., that they are in the presence of agents endowed with a potential for a rich array of intentional stances. Literature pervasively capitalizes on and stimulates theory of mind mechanisms that evolved to deal with real people, even as readers remain aware on some level that fictive characters are not real people at all.[7]

Thus one preliminary implication of applying what we know about theory of mind to our study of fiction is that theory of mind makes literature as we know it possible. The very process of making sense of what we read appears to be grounded in our ability to invest the flimsy verbal constructions that we generously call "characters" with a potential for a variety of thoughts, feelings, and desires, and then to look for the "cues" that allow us to guess at their feelings and thus to predict their actions.[8] (The illusion is complete: like Erich Auerbach, we are convinced that "the people whose story the author is telling experience much more than [the author] can ever hope to tell" [549].)

II. "EFFORTLESS" MIND-READING

As we discuss mind-reading as an evolved cognitive capacity enabling both our interaction with each other and our ability to make sense of fiction, we have to be aware of the definitional differences between the terminology used by cognitive scientists and literary critics. Cognitive psychologists and philosophers of mind investigating our theory of mind ask such questions as: what is the evolutionary history of this adaptation, i.e., in response to what environmental challenges did it evolve? At what age and in what forms does it begin to manifest itself? What are its neurological foundations? They focus on the ways "in which mind-reading [plays] an essential part in *successful* communication" (Baron-Cohen 29, emphasis mine). When cognitive scientists turn to literary (or, as in the case below, cinematic) examples to illustrate our ability for investing fictional characters with minds of their own and reading those minds, they stress the "effortlessness" with which we do so. As Dennett observes, "watching a film with a highly original and unstereotyped plot, we see the hero smile at the villain and we all swiftly and effortlessly arrive at the same complex theoretical diagnosis: 'Aha!' we conclude (but perhaps not consciously), 'He

---

[5]For a discussion of alternatives to the Theory of Mind approach, see Dennett, *The Intentional Stance*. [Zunshine]

[6]By using the word "mechanism," I am not trying to smuggle the outdated "body as a machine" metaphor into literary studies. Tainted as this word is by its previous history, it can still function as a convenient shorthand designation for extremely complex cognitive processes. [Zunshine]

[7]For a discussion, see Leslie 120–25; Carruthers, "Autism as Mind-Blindness" 262–63; Hernadi 58; and Spolsky, "Why and How." [Zunshine]

[8]The scale of such investment emerges as truly staggering if we attempt to spell out the host of unspoken assumptions that make it possible (for a discussion, see Zunshine, "Richardson's *Clarissa*"). This realization lends new support to what theorists of narrative view as the essential underdetermination or "undertelling" of fiction, its "interior nonrepresentation" (Sternberg 119). [Zunshine]

wants her to think he doesn't know she intends to defraud her brother!" (48). Readers out-side the cognitive science community may find this emphasis on "effortlessness" and "success" unhelpful. Literary critics, in particular, know that the process of attributing thoughts, beliefs, and desires to other people may lead to *misinter-preting* those thoughts, beliefs, and desires. Thus, they would rightly resist any notion that we could effortlessly — that is, correctly and unambigu-ously, nearly telepathically — figure out what the person whose behavior we are trying to explain is thinking. It is important to underscore here that cognitive scientists and lay readers (here includ-ing literary critics) bring very different frames of reference to measuring the relative "success" of mind-reading. For the lay reader, the example of a glaring failure in mind-reading and communica-tion might be a person's interpreting her friend's tears of joy as tears of grief and reacting accord-ingly. For a cognitive psychologist, this misinter-pretation would still be a fully actualized (hence, successful) mind-reading because it would be the result of the relevant cognitive architecture hav-ing narrowed the range of possible interpretive possibilities and restricted them, in this particular case, to the domain of emotions.

Consequently, one of the crucial insights offered by cognitive psychologists is that by thus parsing the world and narrowing the scope of relevant interpretations of a given phenomenon, our cognitive adaptations enable us to contem-plate an infinitely rich array of interpretations *within* that scope. As Nancy Easterlin puts it, "without the inborn tendency to organize infor-mation in specific ways, we would not be able to experience choice in our responses" ("Making Knowledge" 137).[9] "Constraints," N. Katherine Hayles observes in a different context, "oper-ate constructively by restricting the sphere of possibilities" (145).[10] In other words, our theory of mind allows us to connect Peter Walsh's trem-bling to his emotional state (in the absence of any additional information that could account for his

body language in a different way), thus usefully constraining our interpretive domain and enabling us to start considering endlessly nuanced choices *within that domain.* The context of the episode would then constrain our interpretation even further: we could decide, for instance, that it is unlikely that Peter is trembling because of a barely concealed hatred and begin to explore the compli-cated gamut of his bittersweet feelings. Any addi-tional information that we would bring to bear upon our reading of the passage — biographical, sociohistorical, literary-historical — would alert us to new shades in its meaning, and could, in principle, lead us to some startling conjectures about Walsh's state of mind. Note too, that the description of Walsh's "trembling" may connect to something in my personal experience that will induce me to give significantly more weight to one detail of the text and to ignore others, which means that you and I may wind up with wildly different readings of Peter's and Clarissa's emo-tions "at eleven o'clock on the morning of the day she [is] giving a party." None of this can happen, however, before we have first eliminated a whole range of other explanations, such as explanations evoking various physical forces (for instance, a disease) acting upon the body, and have focused instead solely on the mind of the character.

This elimination of irrelevant interpretations can happen so fast as to be practically impercep-tible. Consider an example from Stanley Fish's famous essay, "How to Recognize a Poem."[11] To demonstrate his point that our mental opera-tions are "limited by institutions in which we are already embedded," Fish reports the following classroom experiment:

> While I was in the course of vigorously making a point, one of my students, William Newlin by name, was just as vigorously waving his hand. When I asked the other members of the class what it was that [he] was doing, they all answered that he was seeking permission to speak. I then asked them how they knew that. The immediate reply was that it was obvious: what else could he be thought of doing? The meaning of his gesture, in other words, was right there on its surface, available for reading by anyone who had the eyes to see. That meaning,

[9]For a qualification of the term "inborn" in relation to the processing of incoming data, see Spolsky, *Satisfying Skepticism* 164. [Zunshine]

[10]For an important recent discussion of "constraints," see Spolsky, "Cognitive Literary Historicism." [Zunshine]

[11]See p. 596.

however, would not have been available to someone without any knowledge of what was involved in being a student. Such a person might have thought that Mr. Newlin was pointing to the fluorescent lights hanging from the ceiling, or calling our attention to some object that was about to fall ("the sky is falling," "the sky is falling"). And if the someone in question were a child of elementary or middle-school age, Mr. Newlin might well have been seen as seeking permission not to speak but to go to the bathroom, an interpretation or reading that would never have occurred to a student at Johns Hopkins or any other institution of "higher learning." (110–11)

Fish's point that "it is only by inhabiting . . . the institutions [that] precede us [here, the college setting] that we have access to the public and conventional senses they make [here, the raised hand means the person seeks permission to speak]" (110) is well taken. Yet note that all of his patently "wrong" explanations (e.g., Mr. Newlin thought that the sky was falling; he wanted to go to the bathroom, etc.) are "correct" in the sense that they call on a theory of mind; that is, they explain the student's behavior in terms of his underlying thoughts, beliefs, and desires. As Fish puts it, "what else could he be *thought* of doing?" (emphasis mine). Nobody ventured to suggest, for example, that there was a thin, practically invisible string threaded through the loop in the classroom's ceiling, one end of which was attached to Mr. Newlin's sleeve and another held by a person sitting behind him who could pull the string any time and produce the corresponding movement of Mr. Newlin's hand. Absurd, we should say, especially since nobody could observe any string hovering over Mr. Newlin's head. Is it not equally absurd, however, to explain a behavior in terms of a mental state that is completely unobservable? Yet we do it automatically, and the only reason that no "normal" (i.e., non-autistic) person would think of a "mechanistic" explanation (such as the string pulling on the sleeve) is that we have cognitive adaptations that prompt us to "see bodies as animated by minds."

But then, by the very logic of Fish's essay, which urges us not to take for granted our complex *institutional* embedment that allows us to make sense of the world, shouldn't we inquire with equal vigor into our *cognitive* embedment that — as I hope I have demonstrated in the example above — profoundly informs the institutional one? Given the suggestively constrained range of the "wrong" interpretations offered by Fish (that is, all his interpretations connect the behavior to a mental state), shouldn't we qualify his assertion that unless we read Mr. Newlin's raised hand in the context of his being a student, "there is nothing *in the form* of [his] gesture that tells his fellow students how to determine its significance" (112)? Surely the *form* of the gesture — staying with the word that Fish himself has emphasized — is quite informative because its very deliberateness seems to delimit the range of possible "wrong" interpretations. That is, had Mr. Newlin unexpectedly jerked his hand instead of "waving" it "vigorously," some mechanical explanation such as a physiological spasm or someone pushing his elbow, perhaps even a wire attached to his sleeve, would seem far less absurd.

To return, then, to the potentially problematic issue of the effortlessness with which we "read" minds: a flagrantly "wrong," from lay readers' perspective, interpretation, such as taking tears of grief for tears of joy or thinking that Mr. Newlin raises his hand to point out that the sky is falling, is still "effortless" from the point of view of cognitive psychologists because of the ease with which we correlate tears with an emotional state or the raised hand with a certain underlying desire/intention. Mind-reading is thus effortless in the sense that we "intuitively" connect people's behavior to their mental states — as in the example involving Walsh's "trembling" — although our subsequent description of their mental states could run a broad gamut of mistaken or disputed meanings. For any description is, as Fish reminds us on a different occasion, "always and already interpretation," a "text," a story reflecting the personal history, biases, and desires of the reader.[12]

---

[12]For a discussion, see Fish, *Is There a Text in this Class?* [Zunshine]

III. CAN COGNITIVE SCIENCE TELL US WHY WE ARE AFRAID OF MRS. DALLOWAY?

How much prompting do we need to begin to attribute a mind of her own to a fictional character? Very little, it seems, since any indication that we are dealing with a self-propelled entity (e.g., "Peter Walsh has come back") leads us to assume that this entity possesses thoughts, feelings, and desires, at least some of which we could intuit, interpret, and, frequently, misinterpret. Writers exploit our constant readiness to posit a mind whenever we observe behavior when they experiment with the amount and kind of interpretation of the characters' mental states that they supply themselves and that they expect their readers to supply. When Woolf shows Clarissa observing Peter's body language (Clarissa notices that he is "positively trembling"), she has an option of providing us with a representation of either Clarissa's mind that would make sense of Peter's physical action (something to the effect of "how excited must he be to see her again!") or of Peter's own mind (as in "so excited was he to see his Clarissa again!"). Instead she tells us, first, that Peter is thinking that Clarissa has grown older and, second, that Clarissa is thinking that Peter looks "exactly the same: . . . the same queer look; the same check suit" (40). Peter's "trembling" still feels like an integral part of this scene, but we make no mistake: we, the readers, are called on to supply the missing bit of information (such as "he must be excited to see her again") that makes the narrative emotionally cohesive.

Hemingway famously made it his trademark to underrepresent his protagonists' feelings by forcing the majority of his characters' physical actions to stand in for mental states (for example, as in the ending of *A Farewell to Arms*: "After a while I went out and left the hospital and walked back to the hotel in the rain" [314]). Hemingway could afford such a deliberate, and in its own way highly elaborate, undertelling for the same reason that Woolf could afford to let Peter's trembling "speak for itself": our evolved cognitive tendency to assume that there *must be* a mental stance behind each physical action and our striving to represent to ourselves that possible mental stance even when the author has left us

with the absolute minimum of necessary cues for constructing such a representation.

It is thus when we start to inquire into how writers of fiction *experiment* with our mind-reading ability, and perhaps even push it further, that the insights offered by cognitive scientists become particularly pertinent. Although cognitive scientists' investigation of theory of mind is very much a project-in-progress, literary scholars have enough carefully documented research already available to them to begin asking such questions as: is it possible that literary narrative trains our capacity for mind-reading and also tests its limits? How do different cultural-historical milieus encourage different literary explorations of this capacity? How do different genres? Speculative and tentative as the answers to these questions could only be at this point, they mark the possibility of a genuine interaction between cognitive psychology and literary studies, with both fields having much to offer to each other.

This section's tongue-in-cheek title refers to my attempt to apply a series of recent experiments conducted by cognitive psychologists studying theory of mind to *Mrs. Dalloway*. I find the results of such an application both exciting and unnerving. On the one hand, I can argue now with a reasonable degree of confidence that certain aspects of Woolf's prose do place extraordinarily high demands on our mind-reading ability and that this could account, *at least in part,* for the fact that many readers feel challenged by that novel. On the other hand, I have come to be "afraid" of *Mrs. Dalloway* — and, indeed, other novels — in a different fashion, realizing that any initial inquiry into the ways fiction teases our theory of mind immediately raises more questions about theory of mind and fiction than we are currently able to answer. My ambivalence, in other words, stems from the realization that theory of mind underlies our interaction with literary texts in such profound and complex ways that any endeavor to isolate one particular aspect of such an interaction feels like carving the text at joints that are fundamentally, paradigmatically absent.

This proviso should be kept in mind as we turn to the experiments investigating one particular aspect of theory of mind, namely, our ability to navigate multiple levels of intentionality present in a narrative. Although theory of mind is formally defined as a second-order intentionality, as in the statements "I believe that you desire X" or "Peter Walsh thinks that Clarissa 'would think [him] a failure'" (43), the levels of intentionality can "recurse" further back, for example, to the fourth level, as in a statement like "I believe that you think that she believes that he thinks that X." Dennett, who first discussed this recursiveness of the levels of intentionality in 1983, thought it could be, in principle, infinite. A recent series of striking experiments reported by Robin Dunbar and his colleagues have suggested, however, that our cognitive architecture may discourage the proliferation of cultural narratives that involve "infinite" levels of intentionality.

In those experiments, subjects were given two types of stories — one that involved a "simple account of a sequence of events in which 'A gave rise to B, which resulted in C, which in turn caused D, etc.'" and another that introduced "short vignettes on everyday experiences (someone wanting to date another person, someone wanting to persuade her boss to award a pay raise), . . . [all of which] contained between three and five levels of embedded intentionality." Subjects were then asked to complete a "series of questions graded by the levels of intentionality present in the story," including some factual questions "designed to check that any failures of intentionality questions were not simply due to failure to remember the material facts of the story." The results of the study were revealing: "Subjects had little problem with the factual causal reasoning story: error rates were approximately 5% across six levels of causal sequencing. Error rates on the mind-reading tasks were similar (5–10%) up to and including fourth-level intentionality, but rose dramatically to nearly 60% on fifth-order tasks." Cognitive scientists knew that this "failure on the mind-reading tasks [was] not simply a consequence of forgetting what happened, because subjects performed well on the memory-for-facts tasks embedded into the mind-reading questions" (Dunbar 241). The results thus suggest that people have marked difficulties processing stories that involve mind-reading above the fourth level.

An important point that should not be lost in the discussion of these experiments is that it is the *content* of the information in question that makes the navigation of multiply-embedded data either relatively easy or difficult. Cognitive evolutionary psychologists suggest the following reason for the relative ease with which we can process long sequences such as "A gave rise to B, which resulted in C, which in turn caused D, which led to E, which made possible F, which eventually brought about G, etc.," as opposed to similarly long sequences that require attribution of states of mind, such as "A wants B to believe that C thinks that D wanted E to consider F's feelings about G." It is likely that cognitive adaptations that underwrite the attribution of states of mind differ in functionally important ways from the adaptations that underwrite reasoning that does not involve such an attribution, a difference possibly predicated on the respective evolutionary histories of both types of adaptations.[13] A representation of a mind as represented by a mind as represented by yet another mind will thus be supported by cognitive processes distinct (to a degree which remains a subject of debate) from cognitive processes supporting a mental representation, for example, of events related to each other as a series of causes and effects or of a representation of a Russian doll nested within another doll nested within another doll. The cognitive process of representing depends crucially on *what* is being represented.

Consider now a randomly selected passage roughly halfway into Woolf's *Mrs. Dalloway*, in which Richard Dalloway and Hugh Whitbread come to Lady Bruton to write a letter to the *Times*, and in which, to understand what is going on, we have to confront a series of multiply embedded states of mind:

> And Miss Brush went out, came back; laid papers on the table; and Hugh produced his fountain pen; his silver fountain pen, which had done twenty years' service, he said, unscrewing the cap. It was still in perfect order; he had shown it to the makers; there was no reason, they said, why it should ever wear out; which was somehow to Hugh's credit,

[13]For a discussion, see Carey and Spelke and Cosmides and Tooby on domain specificity. For a recent application of the theory of domain specificity to the study of literature, see Zunshine, "Rhetoric, Cognition, and Ideology." [Zunshine]

and to the credit of the sentiments which his pen expressed (so Richard Dalloway felt) as Hugh began carefully writing capital letters with rings round them in the margin, and thus marvelously reduced Lady Bruton's tangles to sense, to grammar such as the editor of the *Times*, Lady Bruton felt, watching the marvelous transformation, must respect. (110)

What is going on in this passage? We are seemingly invited to deduce the excellence of Millicent Bruton's civic ideas — put on paper by Hugh — first from the resilience of the pen that he uses, and then from the beauty of his "capital letters with rings around them on the margins." Of course, this reduction of lofty sentiments and superior analytic skills to mere artifacts, such as writing utensils and calligraphy, achieves just the opposite effect. By the end of the paragraph, we are ready to accept Richard Dalloway's view of the resulting epistle as "all stuffing and bunkum," but a harmless bunkum at that. Its inoffensiveness and futility are underscored by the tongue-in-cheek phallic description of the silver pen (should "silver" bring to our mind "gray"?) that has served Hugh for twenty years but that is still "in perfect order" — or so Hugh thinks — once he's done "unscrewing the cap."

There are several ways to map this passage out in terms of the nested levels of intentionality. I will start by listing the smallest irreducible units of embedded intentionality and gradually move up to those that capture as much of the whole narrative gestalt of the described scene as possible:

1. The makers of the pen *think* that it will never wear out. (First level)
2. Hugh *says* that the makers of the pen *think* it will never wear out. (Second level)
3. Lady Bruton *wants* the editor of the *Times* to *respect* and publish her ideas. (Second level)
4. Hugh *wants* Lady Bruton and Richard to *believe* that because the makers of the pen *think* that it will never wear out, the editor of the *Times* will *respect* and publish the ideas recorded by this pen. (Fourth level)
5. Richard *is aware* that Hugh *wants* Lady Bruton and Richard Dalloway to *believe*

that because the makers of the pen *think* that it will never wear out, the editor of the *Times* will *respect* and publish the ideas recorded by this pen. (Fifth level)
6. Richard *suspects* that Lady Bruton indeed *believes* that because, as Hugh *says*, the makers of the pen *think* that it will never wear out, the editor of the *Times* will *respect* and publish the ideas recorded by this pen. (Fifth level)
7. By inserting a parenthetical observation ("so Richard Dalloway felt"), Woolf *intends us to recognize* that Richard *is aware* that Hugh *wants* Lady Bruton and Richard to *think* that because the makers of the pen *believe* that it will never wear out, the editor of the *Times* will *respect* and publish the ideas recorded by this pen. (Sixth level)

It could be argued, of course, that in the process of reading we automatically cut through Woolf's stylistic pyrotechnics to come up with a series of more comprehensible, first-, second-, and third-level attributions of states of mind, such as "Richard does not particularly like Hugh"; "Lady Bruton thinks that Hugh is writing a marvelous letter"; "Richard feels that Lady Bruton thinks that Hugh is writing a marvelous letter"; and so on. Such abbreviated attributions may seem destructive since the effect that they have on Woolf's prose is equivalent to the effect of paraphrasing on poetry, but they do, in fact, convey some general sense of what is going on in the paragraph. The main problem with them, however, is that to arrive at such simplified descriptions of Richard's and Lady Bruton's states of mind, we have to grasp the full meaning of this passage, and to do that, we first have to process several sequences that embed at least five levels of intentionality. Moreover, we have to do it on the spot, unaided by pen and paper and not forewarned that the number of levels of intentionality that we are about to encounter is considered by cognitive scientists to create "a very significant load on most people's cognitive abilities" (Dunbar 240).

Note that in this particular passage, Woolf not only "demands" that we process a string of fifth- and sixth-level intentionalities but she also introduces such embedded intentionalities through descriptions of body language that in some ways approach those of Hemingway in their emotional blandness. No more telling "trembling," as in the earlier scene featuring Peter and Clarissa. Instead, we get Richard watching Lady Bruton watching Hugh producing his pen, unscrewing the cap, and beginning to write. True, Woolf offers us two emotionally colored words ("carefully" and "marvelously"), but what they signal is that Hugh cares a great deal about his writing and that Lady Bruton admires the letter that he produces — two snapshots of the states of mind that only skim the surface of the complex affective undertow of this episode.

Because Woolf has depicted physical actions relatively lacking in immediate emotional content, here, in striking contrast to the scene in Clarissa's drawing-room, she hastens to provide an authoritative interpretation of each character's mental state. We are told what Lady Bruton feels as she watches Hugh (she feels that the editor of the *Times* will respect so beautifully written a letter); we are told what Hugh thinks as he unscrews the cap (he thinks that the pen will never wear out and that its longevity contributes to the worth of the sentiments it produces); we are told what Richard feels as he watches Hugh, his capital letters, and Lady Bruton (he is amused both by Hugh's exalted view of himself and by Lady Bruton's readiness to take Hugh's self-importance at its face value). The apparently unswerving linear hierarchy of the scene — Richard can represent the minds of both Hugh and Lady Bruton, but Hugh and Lady Bruton cannot represent Richard's representations of their minds — seems to enforce the impression that each mind is represented fully and correctly.

Of course, Woolf is able to imply that her representations of Hugh's, Lady Bruton's, and Richard's minds are exhaustive and correct because, creatures with a theory of mind that we are, we *just know* that there *must be* mental states behind the emotionally opaque body language of the protagonists. The paucity of textual cues that could allow us to imagine those mental states ourselves leaves us no choice but to accept the representations provided by the author. We have to work hard for them, of course, for sifting through all those levels of embedded intentionality tends to push the boundaries of our mind-reading ability to its furthest limits.

When we try to articulate our perception of the cognitive challenge induced by this task of processing fifth- and sixth-level intentionality, we may say that Woolf's writing is difficult or even refuse to continue reading her novels. The personal aesthetics of individual readers thus could be grounded *at least in part* in the nuances of their individual mind-reading capacities. By saying this I do not mean to imply that if somebody "loves" or "hates" Woolf, it should tell us something about that person's general mind-reading "sophistication" — a cognitive literary analysis does not support such misguided value judgments. The nuances of each person's mind-reading profile are unique to that person, just as, for example, we all have the capacity for developing memories (unless that capacity has been clinically impaired), but each individual's actual memories are unique. My combination of memories serves me, and it would be meaningless to claim that it somehow serves me "better" than my friend's combination of memories serves her. At the same time, I see no particular value in celebrating the person's dislike of Woolf as the manifestation of his or her individual cognitive make-up. My teaching experience has shown that if we alert our students to the fact that Woolf tends to play this particular kind of cognitive "mind game" with her readers, it significantly eases their anxiety about "not getting" her prose and actually helps them to start enjoying her style.[14]

[14]Thus bringing the findings of cognitive scientists to bear upon the literary text does not diminish its aesthetic value. As Scarry has argued in response to the fear that science would "unweave the rainbow" of artistic creation, "the fact of the matter is that when we actually look at the nature of artistic creation and composition, understanding it does not mean doing it less well. To become a dancer, for example, one must do the small steps again and again and understand them, if one is to achieve virtuosity. Right now we need virtuosity, not only within each discipline, but across the disciplines as well" ("Panel Discussion" 253). [Zunshine]

IV. COGNITIVE LITERARY ANALYSIS OF MRS. DALLOWAY

It is now time to return to the imaginary conversation that opened my essay. Some versions of that exchange did take place at several scholarly forums where I have presented my research on theory of mind and literature. Once, for instance, after I described the immediate pedagogical payoffs of counting the levels of intentionality in *Mrs. Dalloway* with my undergraduates, I was asked if I could foresee the time when such a cognitive reading would supersede and render redundant the majority of other, more traditional approaches to Woolf.[15] My immediate answer was, and still remains, an unqualified no, but since then I have had the opportunity to consider several of that question's implications that are important for those of us wishing cognitive approaches to literature to thrive.

First of all, counting the levels of intentionality in *Mrs. Dalloway* does not constitute *the* cognitive approach to Woolf. It merely begins to explore one particular way — among numerous others — in which Woolf builds on and experiments with our theory of mind, and — to cast the net broader — in which fiction builds on and experiments with our cognitive propensities.[16] Many of these propensities, I feel safe saying in spite of remarkable advances in the cognitive sciences during the last two decades, still remain unknown to us.

However, the current state of cognitive approaches to literature already testifies to the spectacular diversity of venues offered by the parent fields of cognitive neuroscience, artificial intelligence, philosophy of mind, cognitive linguistics, evolutionary biology, cognitive psychology, and cognitive anthropology. Literary critics have begun to investigate the ways in which recent research in these areas opens new avenues in gender studies (F. Elizabeth Hart); feminism (Elizabeth Grosz);

cultural materialism (Mary Thomas Crane, Alan Richardson); deconstruction (Ellen Spolsky); literary aesthetics (Elaine Scarry, Gabrielle Starr); history of moral philosophy (Blakey Vermeule); ecocriticism (Nancy Easterlin); and narrative theory (Porter Abbott, David Herman, Paul Hernadi).

What these scholars' publications show is that far from displacing the traditional approaches or rendering them redundant, a cognitive approach ensures their viability as it builds on, strengthens, and develops their insights.

Second, the ongoing dialogue with, for instance, cultural historicism or feminism is not simply a matter of choice for scholars of literature interested in cognitive approaches. There is no such thing as a cognitive ability, such as theory of mind, free-floating "out there" in isolation from its human embodiment and its historically and culturally concrete expression. Evolved cognitive predispositions, to borrow Patrick Colm Hogan's characterization of literary universals, "are instantiated variously, particularized in specific circumstances" (226).[17] *Everything* that we learn about Woolf's life and about the literary, cultural, and sociohistorical contexts of *Mrs. Dalloway* is thus potentially crucial for understanding why this particular woman, at this particular historical juncture, seeing herself as working both within and against a particular set of literary traditions, began to push beyond the boundaries of her readers' cognitive "zone of comfort" (that is, beyond the fourth level of intentionality).

At the same time, to paraphrase David Herman ("Regrounding"), the particular combination of these personal, literary, and historical contexts, in all their untold complexity, is a "necessary though not a sufficient condition" for understanding why Woolf wrote the way she did. No matter how much we learn about the writer herself and her multiple environments, and no matter how much we find out about the cognitive endowments of our species that, "particularized in specific circumstances," make fictional narratives possible, we can only go so far in our cause-and-effect analysis. As George Butte puts it, "accounts of material circumstances can

---

[15] For a discussion, see Easterlin, "Voyages in the Verbal Universe." [Zunshine]

[16] As Blakely Vermeule observes, "literature-fiction-writing is so powerful because it eats theories for breakfast, including cognitive/evolutionary approaches" (personal communication, 20 November 2002). [Zunshine]

[17] For a discussion of embodied cognition, see also Hart. [Zunshine]

describe changes in gender systems and economic privileges, but they cannot explain why *this* bankrupt merchant wrote *Moll Flanders*, or why *this* genteelly-impoverished clergyman's daughter wrote *Jane Eyre*." There will always remain a gap between our ever-increasing store of knowledge and the phenomenon of Woolf's prose — or, for that matter, Defoe's, Austen's, Brontë's, and Hemingway's prose.

Yet to consider just one example of how crucial our "other" knowledges are for our cognitive inquiry into *Mrs. Dalloway*, let us situate Woolf's experimentation with multiple levels of intentionality within the history of the evolution of the means of textual reproduction. It appears that a written culture is, on the whole, more able than an oral culture to support elaborately nested intentionality simply because a paragraph with six levels of intentional embedment does not yield itself easily to memorization and subsequent oral transmission. It is thus highly unlikely that we would find many passages that require us to go beyond the fourth level of intentionality in oral epics such as *Gilgamesh* or *The Iliad*. Walter Benjamin captures the broad point of this difference when he observes that the "listener's naïve relationship to the storyteller is controlled by his interest in retaining what he is told. The cardinal point for the unaffected listener is to assure himself of the possibility of reproducing the story" (97). The availability of the means of written transmission, such as print, enables the writer "to carry the incommensurable to extremes in representations of human life,"[18] and by so doing, to explore (or shall we actually say "develop," thus drawing upon Paul Hernadi's recent argument about the evolutionary origins of literature?)[19] the hitherto quiescent cognitive spaces.

[18]For a related discussion, see Hogan 242–43. [Zunshine]

[19]Hernadi argues that "literature, whether encountered in live performance or in textual and electronic recording, can challenge and thus enhance our brains' vital capacities for expression, communication, representation, and signification." He further connects the fictional text's capacity for developing our minds to the evolutionary history of the literary endeavor. He points out that, "the protoliterary experiences of some early humans could, other things being equal, enable them to outdo their less imaginative rivals in the biological competition for becoming the ancestors of later men and women" (56). [Zunshine]

Of course, for a variety of aesthetic, personal, and financial reasons, not every author writing under the conditions of print will venture into such cognitive unknown. Even a cursory look through the best-selling mainstream fiction, from Belva Plain to Danielle Steel, confirms the continuous broad popular appeal of narratives dwelling under the fourth level of intentional embedment.[20] It is, then, the personal histories of individuals (here, individual writers and their audiences) that insure that, as Alan Richardson and Francis Steen observe, the history of cognitive structures "is neither identical to nor separate from the culture they make possible" (3).

In the case of Woolf, scholars agree that severing ties with the Duckworth — the press that had brought forth her first two novels and was geared toward an audience that was "Victorian, conventional, anti-experimentation" (*Diary* 1:261) — "liberated [her] experimentalism" (Whitworth 150). Having her own publishing house, the Hogarth Press, meant that she was "able to do what" she "like[d] — no editors, or publishers, and only people to read who more or less like that sort of thing" (*Letters* 167). Another factor possibly informing the cognitive extremes of *Mrs. Dalloway* was Woolf's acute awareness of the passing of time: "my theory is that at 40 one either increases the pace or slows down" (*Diary* 2:259). Woolf wanted to *increase* the pace of her explorations, to be able to "embody, at last," as she would write several years later, "the exact shapes my brain holds" (*Diary* 4:53). Having struggled in her previous novels with the narrator "chocked with observations" (*Jacob's Room* 67), she discovered in the process of working on *Mrs. Dalloway* how to "dig out beautiful caves behind [her] characters; . . . The idea is that the caves shall connect, and each comes to daylight at the present moment" (*Diary* 2:263). Embodying the "exact shapes" of Woolf's brain thus meant, among other things, shifting "the focus from the mind of the narrator to the minds of the characters" and "from the external world to the minds of the characters perceiving it" (Dick 51, 52), a technique that would eventually prompt

[20]For the most recent rethinking of this argument, see Zunshine, "From the Social to the Literary."

Auerbach to inquire in exasperation, "Who is speaking in this paragraph?" (531).[21] Woolf's meditations on her writing remind us of yet another reason that simply counting levels of intentionality in *Mrs. Dalloway* will never super-sede other forms of critical inquiry into the novel. When Woolf explains that she wants to construct a "present moment" as a delicate "connection" among the "caves" dug behind each character, the emerging image overlaps suggestively with Dennett's image of the infinitely recursive levels of intentionality. ("Aha," concludes the delighted cognitive literary critic, "Woolf had some sort of proto-theory of recursive mind-reading!") But with her vivid description of the catacomb-like subjectivity of the shared present moment,[22] Woolf also manages to do something else — and that "something else" proceeds to quietly burrow into our (and her) cognitive theorizing.

This brings us to a seemingly counterintuitive but important point underlying cognitive literary analysis. Even as I map the passage featuring Richard Dalloway and Hugh Whitbread at Lady Bruton's as a linear series of embedded inten-tionalities, I expect that something else present in that passage will complicate that linearity and re-pose Auerbach's question, albeit with a difference. Will it be the phallic overtones of the description of Hugh's pen? Or the intrusion of rhetoric of economic exchange — "credit," "makers," "produce," "capital," "margin"? Or the vexed gender contexts of the "ventrilo-quism" implied by the image of Millicent Bruton spouting political platitudes in Hugh's voice?[23] Or the equally vexed social class contexts of the "seating arrangements" that hierarchize the mind-reading that goes on in the passage? (After all, Woolf must have "seated" Lady Bruton's secre-tary, Miss Brush, too far from the desk to be able to see the shape of Hugh's letters so as not to add yet another level of mental embedment by having Miss Brush watch Richard watching Lady Bruton watching Hugh.) Cognitive *literary* analysis thus continues beyond the line drawn by cognitive scientists — with the reintroduction of something else, a "noise," if you will, that is usually care-fully controlled for and excised, whenever pos-sible, from the laboratory settings. [. . .]

[21]Strictly speaking, Auerbach's question refers to *To the Lighthouse*, but it is equally pertinent for our discussion of *Mrs. Dalloway*. [Zunshine]

[22]George Butte's study, *I Know That You Know That I Know: Narrating Subjects from Moll Flanders to Marnie*, offers a fascinating perspective on a writer's interest in constructing a "present moment" as a delicate "connec-tion" among the characters' subjectivities. Applying Maurice Merleau-Ponty's analysis of interlocking consciousnesses (*Phenomenology of Perception*) to a broad selection of eighteenth- and nineteenth-century novels, as well as to the films of Hitchcock, Hawks, and Woody Allen, Butte argues compellingly that something had changed in the narrative representation of consciousness at the time of Jane Austen: writers became able to represent the "deep intersubjectivity" of their characters, portraying them as aware of each other's per-ceptions of themselves and as responding to such perceptions with body language observable by their interlocutors, which generated a further series of mutual perceptions and reactions. Although Butte does not refer in his work to cognitive science or the Theory of Mind, his argument is in many respects com-patible with the literary criticism that does. [Zunshine]

[23]On Woolf's definition of narrative ventriloquism, see DiBattista 132. [Zunshine]

Works Cited

Abbott, Porter. "Humanists, Scientists and Cultural Surplus." *Substance* 94/95; 30 (2001): 203–17.

Auerbach, Erich. *Mimesis*. Princeton: Princeton Univ. Press, 1991.

Baron-Cohen, Simon. *Mindblindness: An Essay on Autism and Theory of Mind*. Cambridge: MIT Press, 1995.

Benjamin, Walter. *Illuminations*. New York: Harcourt, Brace & World, 1955.

Brook, Andrew, and Don Ross. *Daniel Dennett*. Cambridge: Cambridge Univ. Press, 2002.

Butte, George. *I Know That You Know That I Know: Narrating Subjects from Moll Flanders to Marnie*. Columbus: The Ohio State Univ. Press, 2004.

Byrne, Richard W., and Andrew Whiten. "The Emergence of Metarepresentation in Human Ontogeny and Primate Phylogeny." In *Natural Theories of Mind: Evolution, Development, and Simulation of Everyday Mindreading*, edited by Andrew Whiten, 267–82. Oxford: Basil Blackwell, 1991.

————. *Machiavellian Intelligence: Social Expertise and the Evolution of Intellect in Monkeys, Apes, and Humans.* Oxford: Oxford Univ. Press, 1988.

Carey, Susan, and Elizabeth Spelke. "Domain-Specific Knowledge and Conceptual Change." In *Mapping the Mind: Domain Specificity in Cognition and Culture*, edited by Lawrence A. Hirschfeld and Susan A. Gelman, 169–200. New York: Cambridge Univ. Press, 1994.

Cosmides, Leda, and John Tooby. "Origins of Domain Specificity: The Evolution of Functional Organization." In *Mapping the Mind: Domain Specificity in Cognition and Culture*, edited by Lawrence A. Hirschfeld and Susan A. Gelman, 85–116. New York: Cambridge Univ. Press, 1994.

Crane, Mary Thomas. *Shakespeare's Brain: Reading with Cognitive Theory.* Princeton: Princeton Univ. Press, 2001.

Dennett, Daniel. *The Intentional Stance.* Cambridge: MIT Press, 1987.

DiBattista, Maria. "Virginia Woolf and the Language of Authorship." In *The Cambridge Companion to Virginia Woolf*, edited by Sue Roe and Susan Sellers, 127–45. Cambridge: Cambridge Univ. Press, 2000.

Dick, Susan. "Literary Realism in *Mrs. Dalloway, To the Lighthouse, Orlando* and *The Waves*." In *The Cambridge Companion to Virginia Woolf*, edited by Sue Roe and Susan Sellers, 50–71. Cambridge: Cambridge Univ. Press, 2000.

Dunbar, Robin. "On the Origin of the Human Mind." In *Evolution and the Human Mind: Modularity, Language, and Meta-Cognition*, edited by Peter Carruthers and Andrew Chamberlain, 238–53. Cambridge: Cambridge Univ. Press, 2000.

Easterlin, Nancy. "Making Knowledge: Bioepistemology and the Foundations of Literary Theory." *Mosaic* 32 (1999): 131–47.

————. "Voyages in the Verbal Universe: The Role of Speculation in Darwinian Literary Criticism." *Interdisciplinary Literary Studies: A Journal of Criticism and Theory* 2, no. 2 (Spring 2001): 59–73.

Fish, Stanley. "How to Recognize a Poem When You See One." In *American Criticism in the Poststructuralist Age*, edited by Ira Konigsberg, 102–15. Ann Arbor: Univ. of Michigan Press, 1981.

————. *Is There a Text in This Class?* Cambridge: Cambridge Univ. Press, 1980.

Gomez, Juan C. "Visual Behavior as a Window for Reading the Mind of Others in Primates." In *Natural Theories of Mind: Evolution, Development, and Simulation of Everyday Mindreading*, edited by Andrew Whiten, 195–208. Oxford: Basil Blackwell, 1991.

Grosz, Elizabeth. "Feminist Futures?" *Tulsa Studies in Women's Literature* 21, no. 1 (Spring 2002): 13–20.

Harris, Paul L. *The Work of Imagination.* Oxford: Blackwell Publishers, 2001.

Hart, F. Elizabeth. "The Epistemology of Cognitive Literary Studies." *Philosophy and Literature* 25 (2002): 314–34.

Hayles, N. Katherine. "Desiring Agency: Limiting Metaphors and Enabling Constraints in Dawkins and Deleuze/Guattari." *Substance* 94/95: 30 (2001): 144–59.

Hemingway, Ernest. *A Farewell to Arms.* New York: Charles Scribner's Sons, 1929.

Herman, David. "Regrounding Narratology: The Study of Narratively Organized Systems for Thinking." In *What Is Narratology?* edited by Jan-Christoph Meister, Tom Kindt, and Hans-Harald Müller. Berlin: de Gruyter, 2003.

————. "Scripts, Sequences, and Stories: Elements of a Postclassical Narratology." *PMLA* 112 (1997): 1046–59.

Hernadi, Paul. "Literature and Evolution." *Substance* 94/95: 30 (2001): 55–71.

Hogan, Patrick Colm. "Literary Universals." *Poetics Today* 18 (1997): 223–49.

Hughes, Claire, and Robert Plomin. "Individual Differences in Early Understanding of Mind: Genes, Non-Shared Environment and Modularity." In *Evolution and the Human Mind: Modularity, Language, and Meta-Cognition*, edited by Peter Carruthers and Andrew Chamberlain, 47–61. Cambridge: Cambridge Univ. Press, 2000.

Lee, Hermione. *Virginia Woolf.* New York: Alfred A. Knopf, 1997.

————. "Virginia Woolf's Essays." In *The Cambridge Companion to Virginia Woolf*, edited by Sue Roe and Susan Sellers, 91–108. Cambridge: Cambridge Univ. Press, 2000.

Leslie, Alan. "ToMM, ToBY, and Agency: Core Architecture and Domain Specificity." In *Mapping the Mind: Domain Specificity in Cognition and Culture*, edited by Lawrence Hirschfeld and Susan Gelman, 119–48. New York: Cambridge Univ. Press, 1994.

Pinker, Steven. *The Blank Slate: The Modern Denial of Human Nature.* New York: Viking, 2002.

Premack, David, and Verena Dasser. "Perceptual Origins and Conceptual Evidence for Theory of Mind in Apes and Children." In *Natural Theories of Mind: Evolution, Development, and Simulation of Everyday Mindreading,* edited by Andrew Whiten, 253–66. Oxford: Basil Blackwell, 1991.

Richardson, Alan. *British Romanticism and the Science of Mind.* Cambridge: Cambridge Univ. Press, 2001.

Richardson, Alan, and Francis Steen. "Literature and the Cognitive Revolution: An Introduction." *Poetics Today* 23 (2002): 1–8.

Savarese, Ralph James, and Lisa Zunshine. "The Critic as Neurocosmopolite; Or, What Cognitive Approaches to Literature Can Learn from Disability Studies: Lisa Zunshine in Conversation with Ralph James Savarese." *Narrative* 22.1 (January 2014), 17–44

Scarry, Elaine. *Dreaming by the Book.* New York: Farrar, Straus, Giroux, 1999.

——. "Panel Discussion: Science, Culture, Meaning Values." In *Unity of Knowledge: The Convergence of Natural and Human Science,* 233–57. New York: The New York Academy of Sciences, 2001.

Spolsky, Ellen. "Cognitive Literary Historicism: A Response to Adler and Gross." *Poetics Today,* forthcoming.

——. *Satisfying Skepticism: Embodied Knowledge in the Early Modern World.* Aldershot: Ashgate, 2001.

——. "Why and How to Take the Wheat and Leave the Chaff." *Substance* 94/95; 30, nos. 1–2 (2001): 178–98.

Starr, Gabrielle G. "Ethics, Meaning, and the Work of Beauty." *Eighteenth-Century Studies* 35 (2002): 361–78.

Sternberg, Meir. "How Narrativity Makes a Difference." *Narrative* 9 (2001): 115–22.

Turner, Mark. *The Literary Mind.* New York: Oxford Univ. Press, 1996.

Vermeule, Blakey. *The Party of Humanity: Writing Moral Psychology in Eighteenth-Century Britain.* Baltimore: The Johns Hopkins Univ. Press, 2000.

Whitworth, Michael. "Virginia Woolf and Modernism." In *The Cambridge Companion to Virginia Woolf,* edited by Sue Roe and Susan Sellers, 146–63. Cambridge: Cambridge Univ. Press, 2000.

Woolf, Virginia. *The Diary of Virginia Woolf.* 5 vols. Edited by Anne Olivier Bell. London: Penguin, 1977–84.

——. *Jacob's Room.* London: Hogarth, 1976.

——. *The Letters of Virginia Woolf.* Vol. 2. Edited by Nigel Nicholson. London: Hogarth Press, 1975–80.

——. *Mrs. Dalloway.* San Diego: Harcourt Brace, 1981.

Zunshine, Lisa. "Eighteenth-Century Print Culture and the 'Truth' of Fictional Narrative." *Philosophy and Literature* 25 (2001): 215–32.

——. "From the Social to the Literary: Approaching Cao Xueqin's *The Story of the Stone* (紅樓夢) from a Cognitive Perspective." In *The Oxford Handbook of Cognitive Literary Studies,* edited by Lisa Zunshine, 176–198. New York: Oxford University Press, 2015.

——. "Rhetoric, Cognition, and Ideology in Anna Laetitia Barbauld's 1781 *Hymns in Prose for Children.*" *Poetics Today* 23 (2001): 231–59.

——. *Why We Read Fiction: Theory of Mind and the Novel.* Columbus: The Ohio State University Press, 2006.

4

PSYCHOANALYTIC THEORY AND CRITICISM

The Unconscious is structured like a language. — JACQUES LACAN

Oedipus, blind, was on the path to oracular godhood, and the strong poets have followed him by transforming their blindness towards their precursors into the revisionary insights of their own work. — HAROLD BLOOM

The analyst . . . accepts the text and puts all his effort and desire, his passion and personal virtuosity, into reciting it, while remaining indifferent to the events that he enacts. This "indifference," called "benevolent neutrality," is the modest toga with which we cover our interpretive desire. Yet by shedding it, by implicating ourselves, we bring to life, to meaning, the dead discourses . . . which summon us. — JULIA KRISTEVA

Because Sigmund Freud once acknowledged that most of his discoveries about the unconscious mind had been anticipated by the poets and artists of the past, it should not be surprising that the light of depth psychology has long been trained upon literature in an effort to explain its origins, character, and effects. While Freud's own reflections on literature are included in Part One of this book, this chapter contains essays by followers of Freud who, like Peter Brooks, have discovered new ways of using Freudian theory to understand the psychological significance of literary form. It also contains essays by Jacques Lacan, the French psychoanalyst whose recasting of Freud's ideas in a new semiotic form has done so much to revitalize our thinking about language and the mind, and by followers and revisers of Lacan, like Laura Mulvey and Slavoj Žižek, who can help us to understand both the powers of Lacan's thought and its limitations.

Freud's ideas originated not in the ivory tower of theory but in his Vienna consulting room, where he practiced as a neurologist specializing in the treatment of hysteria. Only after experimenting with various physical cures did Freud come to believe that many of his patients' symptoms were caused by something less tangible. At first he hypothesized that hysteria was always a delayed psychosomatic reaction to a real trauma, like childhood rape or incest; eventually, however, he concluded that the cause was the patient's own incestuous desires, desires so unacceptable that they could not be admitted to consciousness but were instead repressed and held in the unconscious, emerging as symptoms in later life.

In Freud's original scheme, the unconscious was part of a system consisting of (1) the conscious mind; (2) the preconscious mind, which included anything on which attention was not currently focused, including forgotten memories and thoughts that could with effort be brought back up into consciousness; and (3) the unconscious itself, whose workings were not directly available to consciousness. The evidence for the existence of the unconscious, as well as the sense of its contents, comes from dreams and fantasies and from *parapraxes* (meaningful mistakes) — slips of the tongue, pen, or memory — that also reveal repressed desires and fears. In the original formulation, the unconscious was a realm of energies, generated by the instincts or drives, focusing and binding onto objects (*cathexis*), and being diverted from their goals. Two major drives function in the unconscious: the sexual drive (*libido*), which aims at pleasure, and the aggressive drive, which aims at destruction. These drives are generally fused, and often the term *libido* is used for both.

In the course of infancy and childhood, the libido is focused on different parts of the body (*erogenous zones*), starting with the mouth in early infancy and shifting to the anus around the second year and the genitals in the third year. These are the oral, anal, and phallic phases of what is termed *infantile sexuality*, and whether or not it feels appropriate to use the term *sexual* for the pleasure infants get from sucking on their thumbs (or adults from smoking), it is clearly a drive, and one that has to do with pleasure rather than with nourishment or any other obviously physi-ological mechanism.

As Freud elaborated his notion of a mind within the mind, the unconscious was transformed from a simple, dark cave of repression into a complex transactional world. In his later, "topographical" formulation of the unconscious (1923), Freud theorized a polity inhabited in earliest infancy only by the *id* (the location of the drives). As the infant becomes socialized, however, the direct satisfaction of the drives is no longer possible. Most of us gradually learn to eat and eliminate wastes at socially appro-priate times and to refrain from grabbing the man or woman we want and forcibly eliminating our rivals. Thus the unconscious develops as the battleground between the pleasure principle — the desire to gratify impulses immediately — and the reality principle, which controls these impulses for the sake of higher social values. Part of this learning takes the form of the suppression or redirection of our unconscious drives: The libido is opposed by alternative energies or shifted to a more appropriate object or aim or occasion. These shiftings of the libido are called *defenses*, and their operation is the function of a differentiated part of the uncon-scious, the *ego*. One of the major defenses against the power of the drives is *repres-sion*, which Freud discovered in his patients, but there are many others as well. Among those most often occurring in literature are *projection* (ascribing an impulse of one's own to someone else) and *symbolization* (shifting the object of a drive to something else that can stand as a metaphorical or metonymic substitute for it).

Freud used the term "primary process" to refer to the direct work of libido-energy within the unconscious — primary because it is how psychic energy functions before the development of the ego. It is characterized by the instantaneous gratification of impulses or their rapid rechanneling into other, similar activities. The person who cannot express anger at work but shouts at his or her spouse at home is engaging in *primary process thinking*. The term *secondary process* denotes the working of the mature ego, which might channel the energy of inexpressible anger at the boss into doing a better job at work — or finding a more satisfying career.

The third part of the unconscious is called the *superego*, which begins to form during childhood as a result of the Oedipus complex, one of the most powerfully determinative elements in the growth of the child. The Oedipus complex begins in a late phase of infantile sexuality, between the child's third and sixth year, and it takes a different form in males than it does in females. Boys and girls together begin life relating more powerfully to the mother than to the father, and both sexes wish to possess the mother exclusively. They also begin to sense that their claim to exclusive attention is thwarted by the mother's attention to the father, and already in the phallic stage in which the genitals have become an erogenous zone, they connect that attention to the sexual activities that mother and father participate in and from which they are excluded. The result is a murderous rage against the father (and any other siblings who may be potential competitors) and a desire to possess the mother. (There is also a rage against the mother for permitting the primacy of the father.) Many things keep this rage from being acted out, including feelings of love for the father, dependency on him, and fear of loss of approval or retaliation for aggressive behavior.

Where the Oedipus complex differs in boys and girls is in the functioning of the related *castration complex*. Boys know from observing their own bodies and those of their fathers that they have a penis but that some people (including their mother) do not. Freud theorized that during the Oedipal rivalry, boys fantasize that punishment for their rage will take the form of the loss of the penis. Fear of this leads the boy to repress his rage and desire. In a successful Oedipal outcome, the boy learns to identify with the father in the hope of someday possessing a woman like his mother. In girls, the castration complex does not take the form of *anxiety*, because their lack of a penis suggests that the dreaded castration has already occurred, as it has to the desired mother as well. The result is a frustrated rage in which the girl shifts her sexual desire from the mother to the father (who possesses the penis she wants), and then, when her sexual advances to the father are opposed, begins to identify with the mother in order eventually to possess another man like the father.

The process, as Freud theorized it, is like so many love affairs, long and painful; it involves not only frustration and repression of desires but the turning of desire against itself in the form of self-criticism, self-punishment, and even self-hatred. The conflict generates the moralist of the unconscious, the superego, which is itself divided into the ego-ideal, the repository of images of perfection against which the child (and later the adult) will unhappily compare him- or herself, and the conscience, where approval and disapproval of one's actions are registered. It must be remembered, of course, that Freud's conscience is part of the unconscious, and its work of judgment and self-punishment takes the form of irrational feelings of guilt and unworthiness, and neurotic behavior against which the ego must make defenses as surely as it does against the id.

The final topographical configuration of the unconscious as id, superego, and ego may seem rather like Plato's tripartite soul, mythologized in the *Phaedrus* as Evil Horse, Good Horse, and Charioteer, which may reflect Plato's intuitive sense of the unconscious as well as Freud's own classical education.

STYLES OF FREUDIAN CRITICISM

Traditionally, there have been three stages at which psychoanalysis may enter the study of the literary work: We can examine the mind of the author, the minds of the author's characters, and our own minds as we read the text. Though Freud concludes his essay on "Creative Writers and Daydreaming" (see p. 312) with the suggestion that artistic works allow the audience to revel in their own forbidden fantasies, his focus is primarily on the text as the fantasy-construct of the artist. And there is a long tradition of Freudian criticism that seeks in the text for the buried motives and hidden neurotic conflicts that generated the writer's art. One widely admired study of this sort is Frederick C. Crews's *The Sins of the Fathers: Hawthorne's Psychological Themes* (1966), which examines the tales of the 1840s for the different ways in which they embody the unresolved Oedipus complex suggested by what we know of Hawthorne's youth and manhood. Hawthorne provided a great deal of material for such a study in his private diaries, and biographers began their work soon after his death. The hazards of doing psychoanalytic criticism in this mode are inversely proportional to the amount of material available on the author's life and private thoughts. It is never completely safe to guess at the psychic significance of a work of art, even that of a candid living author, and for some major writers (like Chaucer and Shakespeare), we have only the most minimal sense of what their private lives may have been like, so that psychoanalytic criticism in this mode must be mere speculation.

After the author, we can analyze the characters. This has also been a popular mode of criticism, beginning with *Hamlet and Oedipus* by Freud's disciple and biographer, Ernest Jones, who interpreted Hamlet's problematic hesitation to slay Claudius as stemming from an identification with his uncle, since Hamlet, too, wished to kill the elder Hamlet and marry Gertrude. It is tempting to analyze characters whom we see rendered with telling truth both internally and externally, but, in fact, the hazards of speculation about characters are even greater than about authors. Although Hamlet's actions and language reveal a great deal about him, all we will ever know is contained in the four thousand lines of Shakespeare's play.

Another problem stems from the fact that characters are both more and less than real persons. While some aspects of characters have a *mimetic* function (the representation of human action and motivation), others have primarily *textual* functions (the revelation — or concealment — of information to an audience), which has no precise parallel in life.[1] The contradictions in Hamlet's character may result from the psychic complexities Shakespeare imagined, but they also result from the

[1]One should remember that though literary characters are not the same as real persons, real persons in the masks they present to the world often resemble literary characters.

fact that Hamlet is an agent in a tragic drama with a highly developed system of conventions. An additional problem of psychoanalytic interpretation is whether a character's degree of self-awareness is to be seen as a psychological "fact" or an unintended consequence of the character's textual function. One might raise this question about James Bryan's discussion of J. D. Salinger's *The Catcher in the Rye* (1974), in which Holden Caulfield's maladjustment is ascribed to his repressed incestuous desires for his prepubescent sister Phoebe. The material on which Bryan bases his interpretation comes directly from Holden, whose only mildly embarrassed awareness of his sister's sexiness argues against rather than for Bryan's diagnosis of neurotic repression.[2]

It is tempting to seek in psychoanalysis the secret of a text, but it can be more illuminating to reverse the explanation and to look to literature, as Freud himself did, for clarifications of psychology. Such an approach is exemplified in Samuel Alexander's discussion (1939) of the *Henry IV* plays, which claims that they portray the growth of the ego (Prince Hal), resisting the id's blandishments of immediate gratification (Falstaff), rejecting also the superego's repression (the Chief Justice), mastering phallic desire (Hotspur), and reconciling his rivalry with the father (King Henry) before assuming the crown of adulthood.

Since authors may not provide much material for the would-be analyst, and since characters are not real persons, it would seem that the safest form of psychoanalytic criticism is the analysis of the audience. The readers' gaze into their own unconscious responses to literature is limited only by their insight into their own psychic processes. In the hands of Norman Holland and David Bleich, this has produced a reader-response mode of analytic criticism (see the introduction to Reader-Response Theory, p. 543). The questions that tend to be raised about methods like those of Holland and Bleich have less to do with the tact and accuracy of their findings than with their subjectivity. If readers find anal imagery in a poem, are they revealing its author's fixations or only their own? Two possible answers result, depending on whether the analytic critic believes in the objective existence of a "text" to be analyzed. Those who do believe, like David Bleich or Norman Holland in his early phase, have replied that in the first place, *all* criticism is necessarily subjective, and the personal character of analytic criticism is only more honestly and explicitly so; and that in the second place, idiosyncratic readings can be identified and corrected by the usual forms of reality-testing, through self-examination and self-analysis and through exposure to debate with others. Those who do not believe, like Holland in his later phase (5 *Readers Reading* [1975] and thereafter), would reply that the question, in the form in which it was posed, is meaningless. The text has no meaning before it is read, and there can be no distinction between what is "in" the text and what is "in" the reader.

Author, character, and audience usually exhaust the spectrum of Freudian criticism. A fourth alternative has been proposed by Peter Brooks in *Reading for the Plot* (1984). In its central chapter, "Freud's Masterplot" reprinted in this chapter,

---

[2]James Bryan, "The Psychological Structure of *The Catcher in the Rye*," *PMLA* 89 (1974): 1065–74.

Brooks discusses *Beyond the Pleasure Principle* (1920), that ambiguous late treatise in which Freud examines the *repetition-compulsion*, a neurotic form of behavior that substitutes repetition for remembrance when a memory is too distressing for repression to overcome. Freud finds that he cannot account for the excruciating manifestations of the repetition-compulsion on the basis of the pleasure principle. He is forced to theorize that it is the product of a death-drive, which balances the life-drive of libido. For Brooks, the repetition-compulsion is the central motif of literature. Repetition not only sets the conditions of narrative (one thinks of fairy tales, in which the same situation recurs three times), but it is also basic, through rhyme, refrains, and thematic devices, to poetry. Brooks reads *Beyond the Pleasure Principle* "as a text about textuality" in which "plot mediates meanings within the contradictory human world of the eternal and the mortal, Freud's masterplot speaks of the temporality of desire, and speaks to our very desire for fictional plots."

A more metaphorical variety of Freudian criticism is that of Harold Bloom. In *The Anxiety of Influence* (1973), Bloom begins with the notion that literary influence is analogous to paternity. Weak poets may merely copy their forebears, but for strong poets of the post-Romantic era, Bloom expects an Oedipal rivalry between the younger "ephebe" and the earlier strong poet he has chosen as his artistic "father." The "son" needs metaphorically to kill or castrate the "father" to make room for his own adult life, and he does so by creatively *misreading* his predecessor in ways that necessitate his own corrective labors. Bloom's theory is not simple, and he posits a vast repertoire of ways in which the younger "ephebe" can perform this liberating act of misprision. Bloom's work has not only proved influential in itself, it has also inspired imitation and challenge. In *The Madwoman in the Attic* (1979), Sandra Gilbert and Susan Gubar have appropriated Bloom's method for their feminist purposes. In effect, they discuss how Bloom's question must be adapted when talking of *women* writers and the Fathers who would seem to exclude them from the succession by reason of their sex, and the special anxiety of authorship women suffer, which can be overcome, at least in part, by participation in the powerful sisterhood of the female literary tradition (see Feminist Criticism, p. 871).

LACAN

The revisions to Freudian theory of Jacques Lacan, the French psychoanalyst whose thought has had such a broad influence on literary theory since the 1960s through seminars attended by Parisian intellectuals — including Louis Althusser, Michel Foucault, Paul Ricoeur, Roland Barthes, and Julia Kristeva — can only be discussed briefly. His ideas are still unfamiliar to many practicing American psychoanalysts, perhaps because Lacan largely jettisoned the therapeutic model of psychoanalysis leading to the cure of symptoms, considering it a branch more of philosophy than of medicine. Of course, while Lacan deviated from the mainstream of psychoanalytic thought and was expelled from the International Psychoanalytic Association, he believed himself to be returning to Freud rather than departing from him.

Where Freud views the mechanisms of the unconscious as generated by libido (sexual energy) in a transactional system resembling that of thermodynamics, Lacan centers the theory of the unconscious on the sense within us of something *absent*.[3] The sense of absence can take the form of mere lack (*manque*) or need (*besoin*), which force the psyche to make demands, or it can take the higher form of desire (*désir*). It is in the true desire — for an object that is itself conscious and can desire us in return — that the higher forms of self-consciousness arise. (This dialectic of desire Lacan took not from Freud but from Hegel's *Phenomenology of Spirit*, 1807.) Lacan's term for the universal symbol or signifier of desire is the *Phallus*. It is important not to confuse the Phallus in this sense with the male sexual organ, the penis. *Both* sexes experience the absence of and desire for the Phallus — which may be one reason Lacan's restructuring of Freud has appealed to feminists like Hélène Cixous and Luce Irigaray.

This revision of Freud shifts the description of mental processes from a purely biological model to a semiotic one. Freud, for instance, discusses the first phase of childhood as the oral phase, in which the child's pleasure come largely from suckling; the anal phase follows, when the child learns to control and to enjoy controlling the elimination of feces. In Lacan, the analogue of the oral phase is the Mirror-Stage, from six to eighteen months, in which the child's image of its bodily self changes from mere formlessness and fragmentation to a jubilant identification with the unified shape it can see in the mirror. During this development, the child experiences itself as "le Désir de la Mère," the desire of the mother in both senses. The baby not only knows it needs its mother but also feels itself to be what completes and fulfills the mother (the Phallus). Within this phase of development there is no unconscious, because there is nothing to repress and no way to repress it. From this phase Lacan derives the psychic field of the Imaginary, which continues into adult life, where the sense of reality is grasped purely as images and fantasies of the fulfillment of desire.

Repression and the unconscious arrive together with the insertion of the child into language, around eighteen months, when Freud's anal stage begins. As the child learns the names of things, its desires are no longer met automatically; the child finds that it must ask for what it wants and that it can no longer ask for things that do not have names. As the child learns to ask for a signified by pronouncing a signifier, it learns that one thing can symbolize another. As Muller and Richardson have put it, "from this point on the child's desire, like an endless quest for a lost paradise, must be channelled like an underground river through the subterranean passageways of the symbolic order, which make it possible that things be present in their absence in some ways through words."[4] Now desires can be repressed, and the child can ask for something that metaphorically or metonymically replaces the desired object. Lacan punningly called this stage of development "le Nom-du-Père": "the Name-of-the-Father," which, in French, is pronounced like "the no-of-the-Father"; for language is only the first of the negations and subjections to law that will now begin to affect the child. The child has entered what Lacan calls the field of the Symbolic.

---

[3]Like the deconstructionist Jacques Derrida and the Marxist Louis Althusser, whom he influenced, Lacan subscribes to a metaphysic based on *absence* rather than one based on *presence*.

[4]John P. Muller and William J. Richardson, *Lacan and Language: A Reader's Guide to Écrits* (New York: International Universities Press, 1982), p. 23.

A third Lacanian field, less discussed in his writings than the others, is that of the Real. By this Lacan seems to mean those incomprehensible aspects of experience that exist beyond the grasp of images and symbols through which we think and constitute our reality. The Real functions rather like the noumena in Kant (see pp. 218–19). Lacan recognizes that adult humans are always inscribed within language, but he does not suggest that language must thereby constitute the ultimate reality.

Since in Lacan's dialectic of desire one object may symbolize another, which is a substitute for still another, Lacan has said that "the unconscious is structured like a language." Lacan derives his ideas of language and the unconscious not from Freud but from one of the fathers of semiotics, Ferdinand de Saussure, as he was interpreted by the structuralist anthropologist Claude Lévi-Strauss. Lévi-Strauss considered the unconscious not as "the repository of a unique history which makes each of us an irreplaceable being" but rather as "reducible to a function — the symbolic function," which in turn was merely "the aggregate of the laws" of language.[5]

The primary laws of language in structural linguistics are those of the selection and combination of primary basic elements.[6] Metaphor is a mode of symbolization in which one thing is signified by another that is like it, that is part of the same paradigmatic class. And Lacan saw metaphor as equivalent to the Freudian defense of condensation (in which one symbol becomes the substitute for a whole series of associations). Metonymy is a mode of symbolization in which one thing is signified by another that is associated with it but not of the same class — a syntagmatic relationship — which Lacan regarded as equivalent to Freudian displacement. Because most of the Freudian defenses could be read as versions either of condensation or displacement, it appears that unconscious psychic mechanisms operate like linguistic tropes. On the other hand, we should not look within Lacan's linguistic psychology for anything like the hierarchical structure imposed on the elements of language by a syntax.[7]

If the unconscious is like a language, it is one characterized as a foreign tongue: "the discourse of the Other." What Lacan means by this is not clear or simple. Since in Lacan's thought the original Other is the father, the unconscious is Other in its origins — in the *Nom-du-Père*. But the unconscious is also the residence of alterity and alienation within ourselves, the Other to whom we must speak and whom we hear speaking in our internal dialogue. In treating the unconscious as a language rather than a polity, Lacan eliminates the notion of the ego as a homunculus inside ourselves, constantly defending itself against the depredations of the id. What he

[5] Claude Lévi-Strauss, "The Effectiveness of Symbols," in *Structural Anthropology* (New York: Anchor Books, 1967), p. 198.

[6] Technically these are called paradigmatic and syntagmatic relationships and are discussed at greater length in the introduction to Chapter 2, Structuralism, Semiotics, and Deconstruction.

[7] This gap may betoken a blind spot in Lacan's use of linguistics. Much of the French theory that is ultimately based on Saussure (Lacan, Derrida, Althusser) seems trapped in the limitations of structural linguistics, a rigid schema of polarized differences that was better able to explain the phonology and morphology of words than the hierarchical reorderings of grammar. If Lacan regretted that Freud's conception of language had been impoverished by the state of linguistics in his time, we may regret that Lacan was not exposed to the revolution in syntactic theory that began with Zellig Harris and Noam Chomsky.

leaves in its place is far less solid and reified. The ego is an Imaginary construct, a false image of identity and wholeness; but the ego is less important to Lacan than the subject, and the subject is simply the fluid position from which an "I" speaks and the signification of desire takes place. The subject is not entirely effaced, but it is decentered from a privileged spot to that of a function of language.

Like Freud, Lacan approached literature primarily as material that, properly interpreted, illustrated the major concepts of his psychology. He gave seminars on "Desire and the Interpretation of Desire in *Hamlet*"[8]; and the somewhat more accessible "Seminar on 'The Purloined Letter.'"[9] The latter essay takes off from a strictly Freudian account of Poe's "The Purloined Letter" by the analyst Marie Bonaparte, who, noting the resemblances between the detective Dupin and his quarry, the Minister D., suggested that the latter was a father figure and analyzed the story as an Oedipal triangle in which Dupin succeeds in destroying the father/minister for the sake of the mother/queen. Lacan finds that the resemblances and repetitions, once he starts to look, go much further than this, and involve the author — and the reader — in the Lacanian dialectic of desire.

Lacan's indirect influence on criticism has been considerable, primarily because his psychology has affected the philosophy and literary theory of the many French intellectuals who attended his seminars (and at a further remove, British and American scholars influenced by the French, as Fredric Jameson has been influenced by Althusser). But a strain of direct Lacanian criticism also began to appear in the 1980s, in separate essays and in collections such as those edited by Shoshana Felman (1981) and Robert Con Davis (1983). Many of these works have taken the form of interpenetrative readings of Lacan and a literary text, which inevitably find the basic themes of Lacan's psychology within the text. Perhaps this is a workable compromise while Lacan's ideas are still relatively unfamiliar, but one suspects that, like Lacanian analysis itself, Lacanian criticism will be centered intensively on the Word and the chains of association that are developed within the text.

Two complete selections from Lacan are reprinted in this chapter. "The Mirror Stage," already alluded to above, presents Lacan's meditations on the epoch-making moment when the developing child experiences the Aha! moment, recognizing that whole, complete individual in the mirror as itself. More occurs than the inception of the Imaginary realm of psychic experience. For without that moment, Lacan suggests, we would tumble into the terrifying world of psychasthenia, where psychotics who have lost their ontological anchors, who do not know who or where they are, experience physical space as a devouring threat. On the other side, however, Lacan would have us recollect that this recognition is, like so many developmental moves, a *méconnaissance*, a misrecognition. For the truth is that, despite the wholeness that the mirror promises, we are not unitary selves, nor are we conscious of everything

[8]Published 1977 in *Yale French Studies* 55/56, and reprinted in Shoshana Felman's *Literature and Psychoanalysis: The Question of Reading: Otherwise* (Baltimore: Johns Hopkins University Press, 1981).
[9]Published in the French edition of *Écrits* and translated by Jeffrey Mehlman in *Yale French Studies* 47/48 (1966).

going on in our interior lives. "The Mirror Stage" thus concludes with a series of swipes at Jean-Paul Sartre, and other existentialists, whose arguments about the *Pour-Soi* and the *En-Soi* (see p. 395) presume that human selves are Real rather than Imaginary constructs.

The second selection is "The Meaning of the Phallus," which is Lacan's attempt to straighten out the confusion he feels has been caused by a grotesquely overliteral misreading of Freud's view of the castration complex. This, more than anything else, along with the notion of "penis envy," led feminists to dismiss Freud as insulting to women. Indeed, it may seem insulting to both sexes to argue that children catch sight of their nude mother and come to the conclusion that she has been castrated. In the first place, Lacan clearly differentiates here between the penis, which men but not women possess, and which functions within the order of the Real, and the Phallus, which functions within the Symbolic order as the signifier of Desire, a unique transcendental signifier lacking any corresponding signified. In the first stage of the castration com- plex, children of both sexes respond in the same way to the realization that the Mother is incomplete in herself, that she does not possess the Phallus, since she is the subject of Desire as well as the object of the child's desires. In the second stage, however, sexual differentiation occurs, as the male child, through another *méconnaissance* (mistaken recognition), mistakes his penis for the Phallus. Realizing, however, that he only appears to possess the Phallus but does not, his sexual desire will take the form of an intense desire to recuperate his loss, to *have* the Phallus. In the female child, by contrast, the dialectic of Desire is shaped by disappointment and Lack, into a desire to *be* the Phallus.[10] The distinction between having and being, as Lacan demonstrates, leads to an understanding of the differences between male and female sexuality, their characteristic responses to inadequacy and *aphanisis* (loss of sexual pleasure), as well of the different origins of male and female homosexuality. As we shall see in later chapters, feminism has been deeply ambivalent about Lacan and his reformulation of Freud's explanations of the Oedipus complex. Some have found the elimination of the anatomical basis of development enormously appealing, since anatomy, while not entirely eliminated as a factor, certainly is not destiny. Others have argued that Lacan's "phallologocentrism," with its valorization of the Phallus as transcendental signifier, along with its association of masculinity with reason and discourse and femininity with imagination, is as deeply flawed in the same old way as Freud.

LACAN WITH A DIFFERENCE

One feminist revision of Lacan is that of Julia Kristeva. Kristeva, born in Bulgaria, moved to Paris during the cultural thaw of 1966, where she was mentored by Roland Barthes. Kristeva takes off from Lacan's notion of field of the Imaginary; in Lacan's

10 The difference between wanting to have and to be the Phallus might be illustrated by what would be typical masculine and feminine reactions, according to Lacan, to an attractive man and woman walk- ing by. A man observing them would simply desire the beautiful woman, whereas a woman, instead of simply desiring the handsome man, would want to have whatever the attractive woman had to make her the object of that man's desire. But as Lacan immediately admits, anatomy is not destiny here either, and either sex can practice masculine and feminine modes of desire.

terms, the Imaginary is the realm of the wordless image, informed by desire (*le désir de la mère*), and thus characterized by Lacan as feminine; whereas the field of the Symbolic, the realm of the word informed by the *nom-du-père*, is characterized as masculine, although both are obviously operative in individuals of both sexes. Nevertheless, for Lacanians literature as a Symbolic product is implicitly marked as a masculine domain.

Kristeva's feminist revision of Lacan involves substituting what she calls the Semiotic for the Imaginary. She posits that prior to its insertion into language, the infant is the site of drives (pulsions) and primary processes: "Discrete quantities of energy move through the body of the subject who is not yet constituted as such."[11] These quanta of energy operate according to regulated bodily rhythms whose articulations are, like language, a signifying process, though they do not constitute a symbol system. Kristeva calls the "nonexpressive totality formed by the drives and their stases" the *chora*, after Plato's term for "an invisible and formless being which receives all things and mysteriously participates in the intelligible, and which is most incomprehensible."[12] For the child to learn language at all, the chora must be repressed. But as Terry Eagleton has put it, "The repression . . . is not total: for the semiotic can still be discerned as a kind of pulsional pressure within language itself, in tone, rhythm, the bodily and material qualities of language, but also in contradiction, meaninglessness, disruption, silence and absence."[13]

In all language, but particularly within poetic language (with its emphasis on sonority and on tropes), one may discern the irruption of the chora: Like all productions of the subject, poetic discourse is split between the pre-Oedipal Semiotic and the Oedipal Symbolic: "The very practice of art necessitates reinvesting the maternal chora so that it transgresses the symbolic order."[14] The "revolution" to which Kristeva's title refers has to do with this "transgression": The semiotic always subverts the symbolic and sometimes, especially in poetic discourse, the semiotic manages to overrun the symbolic and to rule the signifying process.

The key difference is that where Lacan conceives of the Imaginary and the Symbolic as gendered binaries — the former non-linguistic and feminine, the latter linguistic and masculine — Kristeva's terms are not stark dichotomies. Her Semiotic field is not mute image but rather operates as a continual pressure upon language; nor is it gendered exclusively as feminine either. As Toril Moi puts it, the image of the pre-Oedipal mother, with whom Kristeva locates the semiotic field, "looms as large for baby boys as for baby girls" and thus "cannot be reduced to an example of 'femininity' for the simple reason that the opposition between feminine and masculine does not exist in pre-Oedipality."[15] Indeed, Kristeva's applications of her theory about the literary operations of the "semiotic" in *La Révolution du langage poétique* were texts by male poets, such as Lautréamont, Mallarmé, and Artaud.

[11] Julia Kristeva, *Revolution in Poetic Language* (New York: Columbia University Press, 1984), p. 25.
[12] Plato, *Timaeus* 51 a-b (Cornford translation), in *Plato: Collected Dialogues*, ed. Edith Hamilton and Huntington Cairns (New York: Pantheon Books, 1961), p. 1178.
[13] Terry Eagleton, *Literary Theory: An Introduction* (Minneapolis: University of Minnesota Press, 1983), p. 188.
[14] Kristeva, *Revolution in Poetic Language*, p. 102.
[15] Toril Moi, *Sexual/Textual Politics* (New York: Methuen, 1985), p. 165.

Kristeva's later study, *Pouvoirs de l'horreur* (1980; translated as *Powers of Horror: An Essay on Abjection*, 1982), centers on the concept of abjection, an affect that includes physical disgust, spiritual repulsion, and religious renunciation. For Kristeva, the origin of abjection is coterminous with the origin of the self when the infant separates as an individual from the pre-Oedipal mother. It is the obverse side of the pleasure the infant takes in fusion with the mother's body; in this moment of abjection Kristeva discovers the sources of fetish and taboo, and, more generally, of language and culture. She explores the social ramifications of abjection in Eastern and Western societies, but her primary interest is the place of women — as objects of disgust and of religious taboo. Kristeva's psychoanalytic approach — Lacanian with a difference — also informs her feminist theory, such as the essay "Women's Time," which appears in full in Chapter 7.

GENDERING THE GAZE

But it is possible to write Lacanian criticism that is feminist without necessarily revising Lacan. One feminist critic who uses Lacanian psychoanalysis to expose the patriarchal basis of Hollywood cinema is Laura Mulvey, whose famous essay "Visual Pleasure and Narrative Cinema" (1975), reprinted here, has inspired not only an entire school of film theory, but an approach to literature in which narrative point of view, the seeing eye of the text and its reader, is substituted for the gaze of the camera and the spectator. In a sense the issues raised by such reader-oriented feminists as Judith Fetterley and Patrocinio Schweickart connect with Mulvey's analysis of the psychology of the reader as split between identification with the (usu-ally female) object of the gaze and desire and identification with the (usually male) subject who functions as the protagonist of the narrative.[16]

Mulvey believes that the split psychodynamics between the male subject and female object is intractable within narrative film, whose drive from beginning through middle to end must turn on an erotics of desire and frustration.[17] She recommends as the only envisageable feminist solution the rejection of narrative itself. Her feminist heroes, like Chantal Akerman, are independent filmmakers who follow an aesthetic — pioneered by Bertolt Brecht in the theater and Jean-Luc Godard in film — of breaking the spectator's engagement with protagonists within plots and making discovery rather than pleasure the object of the film experience. Such an asceticism inevitably leads to a division between the commercial movies

[16]Judith Fetterley has given the name "immasculation" to the process whereby female readers are forced to identify with male authors and characters, and thus with patriarchal ideology; she suggests that one answer is to become a "resisting reader": to read against the grain of the text when it asks one to reject one's own femininity (see pp. 610–11). Patrocinio Schweickart in "Reading Ourselves" gives some support to this strategy but argues that it may go too far, since at least some androcentric texts contain what Fredric Jameson calls a "utopian moment" that can be recuperated for women by (mentally) reversing the sexes, giving the role of Subject to the female. See "Reading Ourselves: Toward a Feminist Theory of Reading," in *Gender and Reading: Essays on Readers Texts and Contexts*, ed. Elizabeth Flynn and Patrocinio P. Schweickart (Baltimore: Johns Hopkins University Press, 1986), pp. 1–62.

[17]For a fuller explanation of this erotics of plot, see Peter Brooks's "Freud's Masterplot," p. 656.

that define contemporary culture and an avant-garde cinema of ideas whose major audience, ironically, comprises the academics and intellectuals already converted to those ideas. Teresa de Lauretis, in *Alice Doesn't* (1984), rejects the hopelessness of Mulvey's conclusion, and explicates how women might "construct the terms of reference of another measure of desire and the conditions of visibility for another social subject" (155). Mulvey, too, has had second thoughts about the use being made of her work.

One also wonders, with a distance of more than forty years from Mulvey's groundbreaking essay, whether her distinction between male as subject and female as passive object of the gaze may have been based too exclusively on the "classic cinema" of directors like Hitchcock and von Sternberg, who were notoriously obsessed with their leading ladies. The blockbuster films of the 1990s continued to show objects of voyeurism, but the viewer's gaze in these films is often focused on male actors such as Arnold Schwartzenegger and Bruce Willis rather than on female icons comparable to Marlene Dietrich and Kim Novak. Did the postfeminist nineties create a new female-oriented cinema where the erotic gaze of desire shifted to sweaty leading men? Or did popular culture merely find new female objects of the gaze, such as the supermodel, who can inspire desire without narrative? Minimally, it would seem that the classic split between the male subject and female object of the gaze has broken down within contemporary popular film, and that now *either* a Demi Moore *or* a Bruce Willis can be either the *subject* or the *object* of the gaze. The Oedipal agon continues to be the basic fantasy underlying film plots, but the male version of the conflict is featured less exclusively than it used to be, and where it is present, it can often operate unencumbered by obsessive heterosexual erotics.[18]

ŽIŽEK: LACAN MEETS LENIN

Perhaps the most approachable, certainly the most enjoyable, practitioner of the Lacanian approach to literature and culture is Slavoj Žižek, a Slovenian theorist who writes all his books (and he has written dozens, at this point) in a racy colloquial English, and who has a genuine gift for explaining difficult psychoanalytical concepts by finding a startling and illuminating metaphor from ordinary experience. He illustrates the Lacanian *objet petit a*, for example, by comparing it with the little toy inside those chocolate eggs one buys for children, and imagining the child saying to the egg: "I love you, but inexplicably I love something inside of you more than you, and therefore I destroy you." Žižek's books tend to be readings of texts rather than

---

[18]More is going on here than the traditional split between subject and object of the gaze. The close relationships between oddly matched "buddies" in contemporary action films (such as Bruce Willis and Samuel L. Jackson in *Die Hard with a Vengeance* or Sean Connery and Nicolas Cage in *The Rock*) are often triangulated through their mutual concern about one or both men's relationships with a woman (wife, girlfriend, daughter) who is either kept offscreen or relegated to a bit part. Eve Kosofsky Sedgwick's discussion of male homosocial desire and how it can be handled so as to defuse its erotic potential clearly applies to more than the nineteenth-century narratives she treats in *Between Men*. See the discussion of Sedgwick, p. 1020.

philosophical tomes, and the texts are usually films and popular literature, includ-ing the Sherlock Holmes detective stories, although he knows the canon of world literature as well as anyone else writing today, and his readings are genuinely filled with surprises, like those chocolate eggs.

A democratic liberal, with an anarchistic streak, Žižek finds himself deeply depressed by the universal triumph of global capitalism because it has robbed humanity, all over the world, of any sense that political progress and change is pos-sible. When offered a government post just after Slovenia became an independent state, Žižek refused to be minister of culture or education, but offered, perhaps seri-ously, to become head of the secret police. This is because Žižek combines Lacanian theory with his own brand of Marxism, one that includes a certain nostalgia for the totalitarian state. For Žižek, a repressive government focuses people's lives and gives them hope, even if it is only the hope of overthrowing it. With the downfall of the Soviet state and the decay of Marxist governments worldwide, Žižek, a lifelong atheist, has turned in the direction of Christianity, which interests him as yet another vision demanding absolute obedience. For Žižek, any belief system that provides mankind with a Sublime Object of Ideology is better than none.

Selected Bibliography

Bersani, Leo. *The Freudian Body: Psychoanalysis and Art.* New York: Columbia University Press, 1985.

Bloom, Harold. *The Anxiety of Influence.* New York: Oxford University Press, 1975.
———. *A Map of Misreading.* Oxford and New York: Oxford University Press, 1980.
———. *Agon: Toward a Theory of Revisionism.* Oxford and New York: Oxford University Press, 1982.

Bonaparte, Marie. *The Life and Works of Edgar Allan Poe.* 1933; London: Imago, 1949.

Boothby, Richard. *Death and Desire: Psychoanalytic Theory in Lacan's Return to Freud.* New York: Routledge, 1991.

Bowie, Malcolm. *Freud, Proust, and Lacan: Theory as Fiction.* New York: Cambridge University Press, 1987.
———. *Lacan.* Cambridge: Harvard University Press, 1991.

Brennan, Teresa. *History after Lacan.* New York: Routledge, 1991.
———. *The Interpretation of the Flesh: Freud and Femininity.* New York: Routledge, 1994.

Brenner, Charles. *An Elementary Textbook of Psychoanalysis.* New York: Anchor Books, 1974.

Brooks, Peter. *Reading for the Plot.* New York: Knopf, 1984.

Burgoyne, Bernard. *The Klein-Lacan Dialogue.* New York: Other Press, 1999.

Clément, Catherine. *The Lives and Legends of Jacques Lacan.* New York: Columbia University Press, 1983.

Crews, Frederick. *The Sins of the Fathers: Hawthorne's Psychological Themes.* New York: Oxford University Press, 1966.
———. *Out of My System: Psychology, Ideology and Critical Method.* New York: Oxford University Press, 1976.

Davis, Robert Con, ed. *Lacan and Narration: The Psychoanalytic Difference in Narrative Theory.* Baltimore: Johns Hopkins University Press, 1983.

Deleuze, Gilles, and Félix Guattari. *Anti-Oedipus: Capitalism and Schizophrenia,* trans. Robert Hurley, Mark Seem, and Helen R. Lane. Preface by Michel Foucault. Minneapolis: University of Minnesota Press, 1983.

———. *Kafka: Towards a Minor Literature.* Minneapolis: University of Minnesota Press, 1985.

Derrida, Jacques. "The Purveyor of Truth." *Yale French Studies* 52 (1975): 31–113.

Elliott, Anthony, and Stephen Frosh, eds. *Psychoanalysis in Contexts: Paths between Theory and Modern Culture.* New York: Routledge, 1995.

Felman, Shoshana. "Turning the Screw of Interpretation." *Yale French Studies* 55/56 (1977): 94–207.

———, ed. *Literature and Psychoanalysis: The Question of Reading: Otherwise.* Baltimore: Johns Hopkins University Press, 1981.

———. "Rereading Femininity." *Yale French Studies* 62 (1981): 19–44.

Freud, Anna. *The Ego and the Mechanisms of Defense.* 1936; New York: International Universities Press, 1966.

Freud, Sigmund. *The Standard Edition of the Complete Psychological Works.* 24 vols. 1940–68; London: Hogarth Press and the Institute of Psychoanalysis, 1953.

Gallop, Jane. *The Daughter's Seduction: Feminism and Psychoanalysis.* Ithaca: Cornell University Press, 1982.

———. *Reading Lacan.* Ithaca: Cornell University Press, 1984.

Gilman, Sander L., ed. *Introducing Psychoanalytic Theory.* New York: Brunner/Mazel, 1982.

Grosz, Elizabeth. *Jacques Lacan: A Feminist Introduction.* New York: Routledge, 1990.

Hartman, Geoffrey H., ed. *Psychoanalysis and the Question of the Text: Selected Papers from the English Institute.* Baltimore: Johns Hopkins University Press, 1979.

Holland, Norman N. *The Dynamics of Literary Response.* New York: Oxford University Press, 1968.

———. *Poems in Persons.* New York: Norton, 1975.

———. *5 Readers Reading.* New Haven: Yale University Press, 1975.

Johnson, Barbara. "The Frame of Reference: Poe, Lacan, Derrida." *Yale French Studies* 55/56 (1977): 457–505.

Jones, Ernest. *Hamlet and Oedipus.* New York: Doubleday, 1949.

Jung, Carl Gustav. *Complete Works.* 17 vols. Ed. Herbert Read, Michael Fordham, and Gerhard Adler. New York: Pantheon, 1953–.

Kris, Ernst. *Psychoanalytic Explorations in Art.* 1952; New York: Schocken Books, 1964.

Kristeva, Julia. *Desire in Language.* New York: Columbia University Press, 1980.

Kurzweil, Edith, and William Phillips, eds. *Literature and Psychoanalysis.* New York: Columbia University Press, 1983.

Lacan, Jacques. "The Seminar on 'The Purloined Letter.'" *Yale French Studies* 48 (1972): 39–72.

———. *Écrits: A Selection.* New York: Norton, 1977.

———. *The Seminar of Jacques Lacan*, ed. Jacques-Alain Miller. *Book I: Freud's Papers on Technique* 1953–1954, trans. John Forrester. New York and London: Norton, 1988.

———. *The Seminar of Jacques Lacan*, ed. Jacques-Alain Miller. *Book II: The Ego in Freud's Theory and in the Technique of Psychoanalysis* 1954–1955, trans. Sylvana Tomaselli. New York and London: Norton, 1988.

———. *The Seminar of Jacques Lacan*, ed. Jacques-Alain Miller. *Book III: The Psychoses* 1955–1956, trans. Russell Grigg. New York and London: Norton, 1993.

Laplanche, Jean, and Jean-Baptiste Pontalis. *The Language of Psychoanalysis*. London: Hogarth Press, 1973.

Lawrence, D. H. *Studies in Classical American Literature*. New York: Penguin, 1977.

Leader, Darian, and Judy Groves. *Introducing Lacan*. London: Icon Books, 2000.

Lesser, Simon O. *Fiction and the Unconscious*. Chicago: University of Chicago Press, 1957.

MacCannell, Juliet Flower. *Figuring Lacan: Criticism and the Cultural Unconscious*. Beckenham: Croon Helm, 1986.

Muller, John P., and William J. Richardson. *Lacan and Language: A Reader's Guide to Écrits*. New York: International Universities Press, 1982.

Mulvey, Laura. *Visual and Other Pleasures*. Basingstoke, Eng.: Macmillan, 1989.

—— . *Fetishism and Curiosity*. Bloomington: Indiana University Press, 1996.

Nancy, J.-L., and P. Lacoue-Labarthe (1973). *The Title of the Letter: A Reading of Lacan*, trans. F. Raffoul and D. Pettigrew. Albany: State University of New York Press, 1992.

Rabaté, Jean-Michel, ed. *The Cambridge Companion to Lacan*. Cambridge: Cambridge University Press, 2003.

Roudinesco, Elisabeth, and Barbara Bray. *Jacques Lacan: Outline of a life, History of a System of Thought*. New York: Columbia University Press, 1997.

Shamdasani, Sonu, and Michael Munchow, eds. *Speculations after Freud: Psychoanalysis, Philosophy and Culture*. New York: Routledge, 1994.

Skura, Meredith Anne. *The Literary Use of the Psychoanalytic Process*. New Haven: Yale University Press, 1981.

Smith, Joseph H., and William Kerrigan, eds. *Interpreting Lacan*. New Haven and London: Yale University Press, 1983.

Trilling, Lionel. "Art and Neurosis" and "Freud and Literature." *The Liberal Imagination*. New York: Doubleday, 1947.

Turkle, Sherry. *Psychoanalytic Politics: Freud's French Revolution*. New York: Basic Books, 1978.

Wilden, Anthony. *The Language of the Self: The Function of Language in Psychoanalysis*. New York: Dell, 1968.

Wright, Elizabeth. *Psychoanalytic Criticism: Theory in Practice*. New York and London: Methuen, 1984.

Zizek, Slavoj. *The Sublime Object of Ideology*. New York: Verso, 1989.

—— . *Looking Awry: An Introduction to Jacques Lacan through Popular Culture*. Cambridge: MIT Press, 1991.

—— . *Enjoy Your Symptom! Jacques Lacan in Hollywood and Out*. New York: Routledge, 1992.

—— . *The Metastases of Enjoyment*. New York: Verso, 1994.

—— . *The Ticklish Subject: The Absent Center of Political Ontology*. London: Verso, 1999.

—— . *The Puppet and the Dwarf: The Perverse Core of Christianity*. Cambridge: MIT Press, 2003.

Zupancic, Alenka. *Kant and Lacan: Ethics of the Real*. London: Verso, 2000.

Jacques Lacan

1901–1981

Probably the most controversial figure in French psychiatry, Jacques Marie Émile Lacan dedicated himself to getting strictly back to Freud by way of structural linguistics. An admirer of the surrealists, Lacan published his doctoral thesis on paranoid psychosis (1932). Expelled in 1953 from the International Psychoanalytic Association for unorthodox analytical practices, Lacan with Daniel Lagache, another analyst, created the Société Française de Psychoanalyse. As his theoretical positions continued to develop, Lacan and his followers went on to found the École Freudienne in Paris in 1964. The publication of his Écrits (1966) gained Lacan international attention. Leading intellectuals flocked to his seminars, and he exercised a cryptic but powerful influence on the French cultural scene of the 1970s. Concerned that the École was losing its integrity, Lacan unilaterally dissolved it in 1980. His intention to begin a new one was unfulfilled at the time of his death from cancer the next year. Editions of Lacan available in English include selections from Écrits *(1977);* The Language of the Self *(1968, translated and with a commentary by Anthony Wilden);* The Four Fundamental Concepts of Psychoanalysis *(1977);* Feminine Sexuality *(1982); and twenty volumes of* The Seminar of Jacques Lacan, *edited by Jacques-Alain Miller:* Freud's Writings on Technique 1953–1954 *(1988),* The Ego in Freud's Theory and in the Technique of Psychoanalysis 1954–55 *(1988), and* The Psychoses 1955–1956 *(1993). "The Mirror Stage as Formative of the Function of the I as Revealed in Psychoanalytic Experience," translated by Alan Sheridan, is from* Écrits: A Selection; *it was originally delivered as a lecture on July 17, 1949, to the 16th International Congress of Psychoanalysis. "The Meaning of the Phallus," translated by Jacqueline Rose, is from* Feminine Sexuality: Jacques Lacan and the École Freudienne; *it was originally delivered as a lecture, in German, at the Max Planck Institute in Munich in 1958.*

The Mirror Stage as Formative of the Function of the I as Revealed in Psychoanalytic Experience

The conception of the mirror stage that I introduced at our last congress, thirteen years ago, has since become more or less established in the practice of the French group. However, I think it worthwhile to bring it again to your attention, especially today, for the light it sheds on the formation of the *I*[1] as we experience it in psychoanalysis. It is an experience that leads us to oppose any philosophy directly issuing from the *Cogito*.[2]

Some of you may recall that this conception originated in a feature of human behavior illuminated by a fact of comparative psychology. The child, at an age when he is for a time, however

Translated by Alan Sheridan.

[1]Standard Freudian translations usually Latinize Freud's German terms (*der Ich, das Es*, literally "the I" and "the It") into "the ego" and "the id." Lacan prefers to peel off this distancing artifact of translation.

[2]Shorthand for "cogito ergo sum," Latin for "I think, therefore I am," French philosopher René Descartes's phrase summing up his position that we have absolute knowledge of our own identity because thinking implies a thinker. Lacan's essay interrogates this relation between thinking and being.

short, outdone by the chimpanzee in instrumental intelligence, can nevertheless already recognize as such his own image in a mirror. This recognition is indicated in the illuminative mimicry of the *Aha-Erlebnis*,[3] which Köhler sees as the expression of situational apperception, an essential stage of the act of intelligence.

This act, far from exhausting itself, as in the case of the monkey, once the image has been mastered and found empty, immediately rebounds in the case of the child in a series of gestures in which he experiences in play the relation between the movements assumed in the image and the reflected environment, and between this virtual complex and the reality it reduplicates — the child's own body, and the persons and things, around him.

This event can take place, as we have known since Baldwin, from the age of six months, and its repetition has often made me reflect upon the startling spectacle of the infant in front of the mirror. Unable as yet to walk, or even to stand up, and held tightly as he is by some support (what, in France, we call a "*trotte-bébé*"[4]), he nevertheless overcomes, in a flutter of jubilant activity, the obstructions of his support and, fixing his attitude in a slightly leaning-forward position, in order to hold it in his gaze, brings back an instantaneous aspect of the image.

For me, this activity retains the meaning I have given it up to the age of eighteen months. This meaning discloses a libidinal dynamism,[5] which has hitherto remained problematic, as well as an ontological structure of the human world that accords with my reflections on paranoiac knowledge.

We have only to understand the mirror stage as an identification,[6] in the full sense that analysis

gives to the term: namely, the transformation that takes place in the subject when he assumes an image — whose predestination to this phase-effect is sufficiently indicated by the use, in analytic theory, of the ancient term *imago*.[7]

This jubilant assumption of his specular image by the child at the *infans*[8] stage, still sunk in his motor incapacity and nursling dependence, would seem to exhibit in an exemplary situation the symbolic matrix in which the *I* is precipitated in a primordial form, before it is objectified in the dialectic of identification with the other, and before language restores to it, in the universal, its function as subject.

This form would have to be called the Ideal-I,[9] if we wished to incorporate it into our usual register, in the sense that it will also be the source of secondary identifications, under which term I would place the functions of libidinal normalization. But the important point is that this form situates the agency of the ego, before its social determination, in a fictional direction, which will always remain irreducible for the individual alone, or rather, which will only rejoin the coming-into-being (*le devenir*) of the subject asymptotically,[10] whatever the success of the dialectical syntheses by which he must resolve as *I* his discordance with his own reality.

[3] German for "aha! experience." Term used by the psychologist Wolfgang Köhler (1887–1967), known for his experiments with dogs and monkeys on animal intelligence, for the moment of insight when the mind bridges a cognitive gap.

[4] A walker.

[5] An operation of the pleasure principle.

[6] Normally this term is used for an ego-defense, in which one identifies with someone other than oneself, but Lacan is using it for a stage in the formation of the self.

[7] Freud uses the term *imago* (Latin for image or statue) for the mental picture of a beloved parent that becomes the pattern on which the individual's loving object relations are based ("On the Universal Tendency to Debasement in the Sphere of Love"). Jung uses the term to refer to internal archetypes (such as the Anima) with whom the individual identifies. As before, Lacan applies the term to the image of the self.

[8] The Latin word means "unable to speak." Lacan is pointing to the fact that this occurs before the development of language.

[9] Throughout this article I leave in its peculiarity the translation I have adopted for Freud's *Ideal-Ich* [i.e., "je-idéal"], without further comment, other than to say that I have not maintained it since. [Lacan] The usual English term is "Ego Ideal," which in Freudian terminology forms part of the Superego.

[10] In mathematics an asymptote is a line that a curve approaches but never touches. Lacan's point is that the imaginary sense of self created in the Mirror Stage approximates but is never identical with the Ego that is formed later through the Oedipal struggle, alluded to later in the same sentence.

The fact is that the total form of the body by which the subject anticipates in a mirage the maturation of his power is given to him only as *Gestalt*,[11] that is to say, in an exteriority in which this form is certainly more constituent than constituted, but in which it appears to him above all in a contrasting size (*un relief de stature*) that fixes it and in a symmetry that inverts it, in contrast with the turbulent movements that the subject feels are animating him. Thus, this *Gestalt* — whose pregnancy should be regarded as bound up with the species, though its motor style remains scarcely recognizable — by these two aspects of its appearance, symbolizes the mental permanence of the *I*, at the same time as it prefigures its alienating destination; it is still pregnant with the correspondences that unite the *I* with the statue in which man projects himself, with the phantoms that dominate him, or with the automaton in which, in an ambiguous relation, the world of his own making tends to find completion.

Indeed, for the *imagos* — whose veiled faces it is our privilege to see in outline in our daily experience and in the penumbra of symbolic efficacity[12] — the mirror-image would seem to be the threshold of the visible world, if we go by the mirror disposition that the *imago of one's own body* presents in hallucinations or dreams, whether it concerns its individual features, or even its infirmities, or its object-projections; or if we observe the role of the mirror apparatus in the appearances of the *double*, in which psychical realities, however heterogeneous, are manifested.

That a *Gestalt* should be capable of formative effects in the organism is attested by a piece of biological experimentation that is itself so alien to the idea of psychical causality that it cannot bring itself to formulate its results in these terms. It nevertheless recognizes that it is a necessary condition for the maturation of the gonad of the female pigeon that it should see another member of its species, of either sex; so sufficient in itself is this condition that the desired effect may be obtained merely by placing the individual within reach of the field of reflection of a mirror. Similarly, in the case of the migratory locust, the transition within a generation from the solitary to the gregarious form can be obtained by exposing the individual, at a certain stage, to the exclusively visual action of a similar image, provided it is animated by movements of a style sufficiently close to that characteristic of the species. Such facts are inscribed in an order of homeomorphic[13] identification that would itself fall within the larger question of the meaning of beauty as both formative and erogenic.[14]

But the facts of mimicry are no less instructive when conceived as cases of heteromorphic identification, in as much as they raise the problem of the signification of space for the living organism — psychological concepts hardly seem less appropriate for shedding light on these matters than ridiculous attempts to reduce them to the supposedly supreme law of adaptation. We have only to recall how Roger Caillois (who was then very young, and still fresh from his breach with the sociological school[15] in which he was trained) illuminated the subject by using the term "*legendary psychasthenia*"[16] to classify morphological mimicry as an obsession with space in its derealizing effect.

---

[11]German for pattern.

[12]Cf. Claude Lévi-Strauss, *Structural Anthropology*, Chapter X. [Lacan] Lacan refers to the chapter ("The Effectiveness of Symbols") in which Lévi-Strauss explicitly compares psychoanalysis with the way in which a shaman, inducing a patient to re-experience the cause of her illness, cures her of it.

[13]Of the same form, opposed to "heteromorphic," of different form.

[14]Giving rise to sexual desire.

[15]The "sociological school" Caillois broke with was that of the Surrealists, led by André Breton, whose ultimate goal was resistance to Fascism through the liberation of the mind which would be achieved via the externalization of images from the individual unconscious.

[16]The issue Lacan is referring to here is that some psychological disturbances take the symptomatic form of a terrifying sense of dislocation, not knowing where one is, because one has disappeared into one's surroundings, like animals (e.g., chameleons, octopi) who can alter their appearance for camouflage. In "Mimicry and Legendary Psychasthenia" (*Minatoure* 7 [1935]), anthropologist Roger Caillois (1913–1978) wrote: "from the moment when it can no longer be a process of defense, mimicry can be nothing else but [a disturbance in the perception of space]. . . . There can be no doubt that the perception of space is a complex phenomenon. . . . The feeling

I have myself shown in the social dialectic that structures human knowledge as paranoiac[17] why human knowledge has greater autonomy than animal knowledge in relation to the field of force of desire, but also why human knowledge is determined in that "little reality" (ce peu de réalité), which the Surrealists, in their restless way, saw as its limitation. These reflections lead me to recognize in the spatial captation manifested in the mirror-stage, even before the social dialectic, the effect in man of an organic insufficiency in his natural reality — in so far as any meaning can be given to the word "nature."

I am led, therefore, to regard the function of the mirror-stage as a particular case of the function of the imago, which is to establish a relation between the organism and its reality — or, as they say, between the Innenwelt and the Umwelt.[18]

In man, however, this relation to nature is altered by a certain dehiscence[19] at the heart of the organism, a primordial Discord betrayed by the signs of uneasiness and motor unco-ordination of the neo-natal months. The objective notion of the anatomical incompleteness of the pyramidal system[20] and likewise the

---

of personality, considered as the organism's feeling of disjunction from its surroundings, of the connection between consciousness and a particular point in space, cannot fail under these conditions to be seriously undermined; one then enters into the psychology of psychasthenia, and more specifically of legendary psychasthenia, if we agree to use this name for the disturbance in the above relations between personality and space. [Schizophrenics are] dispossessed souls [for whom] space seems to be a devouring force. Space pursues them, encircles them, digests them. . . . It ends by replacing them. . . . He tries to look at himself from any point whatever in space. He feels himself becoming space, dark space where things cannot be put. . . . All these expressions shed light on a single process: depersonalization by assimilation to space, i.e., what mimicry achieves morphologically in certain animal species. The magical hold (one can truly call it so without doing violence to the language) of night and obscurity, the fear of the dark, probably also has its roots in the peril in which it puts the opposition between the organism and the milieu."

[17] Cf. "Aggressivity in Psychoanalysis," p. 8 and Écrits, p. 180. [Lacan]

[18] Innenwelt is German for inner world; Umwelt means outer world.

[19] Natural splitting.

[20] Part of the central nervous system involved in voluntary movement.

presence of certain humoral residues of the maternal organism confirm the view I have formulated as the fact of a real specific prematurity of birth in man.

It is worth noting, incidentally, that this is a fact recognized as such by embryologists, by the term foetalization, which determines the prevalence of the so-called superior apparatus of the neurax,[21] and especially of the cortex, which psycho-surgical operations lead us to regard as the intra-organic mirror.[22]

This development is experienced as a temporal dialectic that decisively projects the formation of the individual into history. The mirror stage is a drama whose internal thrust is precipitated from insufficiency to anticipation — and which manufactures for the subject, caught up in the lure of spatial identification, the succession of fantasies that extends from a fragmented body-image to a form of its totality that I shall call orthopedic[23] — and, lastly, to the assumption of the armor of an alienating identity, which will mark with its rigid structure the subject's entire mental development. Thus, to break out of the circle of the Innenwelt into the Umwelt generates the inexhaustible quadrature of the ego's verifications.[24]

This fragmented body — which term I have also introduced into our system of theoretical references — usually manifests itself in dreams when the movement of the analysis encounters a certain level of aggressive disintegration in the individual. It then appears in the form of disjointed limbs, or of those organs represented in exoscopy,[25] growing wings and taking up arms for intestinal persecutions — the very same that

[21] Nervous system.

[22] Lacan refers to surgical experiments that allowed neurologists to "map" areas of the cerebral cortex corresponding to the different parts of the physical human body.

[23] From Greek roots meaning "straight," and "child"; Lacan is suggesting that the mirror stage enables the child to develop properly.

[24] Lacan's point is that the "reality testing" by which the ego attempts to ascertain what is appropriate relative to what is "out there," involves an impossible feat (quadrature = squaring the circle), because the mind can never actually get outside itself.

[25] Viewed from outside.

the visionary Hieronymus Bosch[26] has fixed, for all time, in painting, in their ascent from the fifteenth century to the imaginary zenith of modern man. But this form is even tangibly revealed at the organic level, in the lines of "fragilization" that define the anatomy of fantasy, as exhibited in the schizoid and spasmodic symptoms of hysteria.

Correlatively, the formation of the *I* is symbolized in dreams by a fortress, or a stadium — its inner arena and enclosure, surrounded by marshes and rubbish-tips, dividing it into two opposed fields of contest where the subject flounders in quest of the lofty, remote inner castle whose form (sometimes juxtaposed in the same scenario) symbolizes the id in a quite startling way. Similarly, on the mental plane, we find realized the structures of fortified works, the metaphor of which arises spontaneously, as if issuing from the symptoms themselves, to designate the mechanisms of obsessional neurosis — inversion, isolation, reduplication, cancellation and displacement.[27]

But if we were to build on these subjective givens alone — however little we free them from the condition of experience that makes us see them as partaking of the nature of a linguistic technique — our theoretical attempts would remain exposed to the charge of projecting themselves into the unthinkable of an absolute subject. This is why I have sought in the present hypothesis, grounded in a conjunction of objective data, the guiding grid for a *method of symbolic reduction*.

It establishes in the *defences of the ego* a genetic order, in accordance with the wish formulated by Miss Anna Freud, in the first part of her great work,[28] and situates (as against a frequently expressed prejudice) hysterical repression and its returns at a more archaic stage than obsessional inversion and its isolating processes, and the latter in turn as preliminary to paranoid alienation, which dates from the deflection of the specular *I* into the social *I*.

This moment in which the mirror-stage comes to an end inaugurates, by the identification with the *imago* of the counterpart and the drama of primordial jealousy (so well brought out by the school of Charlotte Bühler in the phenomenon of infantile *transitivism*[29]), the dialectic that will henceforth link the *I* to socially elaborated situations.

It is this moment that decisively tips the whole of human knowledge into mediatization through the desire of the other, constitutes its objects in an abstract equivalence by the co-operation of others, and turns the *I* into that apparatus for which every instinctual thrust constitutes a danger, even though it should correspond to a natural maturation — the very normalization of this maturation being henceforth dependent, in man, on a cultural mediation as exemplified, in the case of the sexual object, by the Oedipus complex.[30]

In the light of this conception, the term primary narcissism,[31] by which analytic doctrine designates the libidinal investment characteristic of that moment, reveals in those who invented it the most profound awareness of semantic latencies. But it also throws light on the dynamic opposition between this libido and the sexual libido, which the first analysts tried to define when they invoked destructive and, indeed, death instincts, in order to explain the evident connection between the narcissistic libido and the alienating function of the *I*, the aggressivity it releases in any relation to the other, even in a relation involving the most Samaritan of aid.[32]

---

[29]Psychologist Charlotte Bühler (1893–1974) observed and called by this name a behavior whereby a child does not distinguish between its own experience and that of another (e.g., crying when another child has been hurt).

[30]Lacan's point is that the "I" formed by the mirror stage is always already an Other (seen as a specular whole from the outside), and all the other Others through normal development, including the specular Father and Mother of the Oedipal struggle, take their shape by virtue of this formation.

[31]Freud's term for the exclusive investment of a small child in its own pleasures and needs. Primary narcissism is healthy, but those who do not outgrow it (in the narcissistic character disorder) direct libido exclusively toward representations of themselves.

[32]Alluding to the parable of the Good Samaritan (Luke 10:30–37), in which the Samaritan aids someone Other, an Israelite, Lacan suggests that the motive for altruism is narcissistic, in the sense that it promotes an aggrandized sense of self.

[26]Flemish painter, born Jeroen van Aken (1450–1516), whose work, like the "Hell" panel from *The Garden of Earthly Delights*, includes surrealistic imagery including animated body parts, such as Lacan has alluded to.

[27]Lacan is listing ego defenses, for which see the discussion of Freud, p. 628.

[28]*The Ego and the Mechanisms of Defense* (1935) by Anna Freud (1895–1982).

In fact, they were encountering that existential negativity whose reality is so vigorously proclaimed by the contemporary philosophy of being and nothingness.[33]

But unfortunately that philosophy grasps negativity only within the limits of a self-sufficiency of consciousness, which, as one of its premises, links to the *méconnaissances*[34] that constitute the ego, the illusion of autonomy to which it entrusts itself. This flight of fancy, for all that it draws, to an unusual extent, on borrowings from psychoanalytic experience, culminates in the pretension of providing an existential psychoanalysis.

At the culmination of the historical effort of a society to refuse to recognize that it has any function other than the utilitarian one, and in the anxiety of the individual confronting the "concentrational"[35] form of the social bond that seems to arise to crown this effort, existentialism must be judged by the explanations it gives of the subjective impasses that have indeed resulted from it: a freedom that is never more authentic than when it is within the walls of a prison; a demand for commitment, expressing the impotence of a pure consciousness to master any situation; a voyeuristic–sadistic idealization of the sexual relation; a personality that realizes itself only in suicide; a consciousness of the other that can be satisfied only by Hegelian murder.[36]

[33]Citing the title of Jean-Paul Sartre's *L'Être et le néant*, Lacan goes on to critique existentialist philosophy, which posits a self that is always present to itself, always self-aware. (Lacan, to the contrary, has all along been suggesting that the monadic "self" we are aware of is an imaginary product of the Mirror Stage.)

[34]Mistaken recognitions (here, of the image in the mirror with the "self").

[35]"Concentrationnaire," an adjective coined after World War II (this article was written in 1949) to describe the life of the concentration camp. In the hands of certain writers it became, by extension, applicable to many aspects of "modern" life. [Tr.]

[36]This paragraph arranges a series of critiques of existentialism, alluding successively to Jean-Paul Sartre's story "Le Mur," his novel *La Nausée*, to *L'Âge de raison*, the first volume of his trilogy *Les Chemins de la liberté*, and to Albert Camus's *L'Étranger* (in which the protagonist murders an Arab to assert his existential freedom).

These propositions are opposed by all our experience, in so far as it teaches us not to regard the ego as centered on the *perception-consciousness system*,[37] or as organized by the "reality principle" — a principle that is the expression of a scientific prejudice most hostile to the dialectic of knowledge. Our experience shows that we should start instead from the *function of méconnaissance* that characterizes the ego in all its structures, so markedly articulated by Miss Anna Freud. For, if the *Verneinung*[38] represents the patent form of that function, its effects will, for the most part, remain latent, so long as they are not illuminated by some light reflected on to the level of fatality, which is where the id manifests itself.

We can thus understand the inertia characteristic of the formations of the *I*, and find there the most extensive definition of neurosis — just as the captation[39] of the subject by the situation gives us the most general formula for madness, not only the madness that lies behind the walls of asylums, but also the madness that deafens the world with its sound and fury.

The sufferings of neurosis and psychosis are for us a schooling in the passions of the soul, just as the beam of the psychoanalytic scales, when we calculate the tilt of its threat to entire communities, provides us with an indication of the deadening of the passions in society.

At this junction of nature and culture, so persistently examined by modern anthropology,[40] psychoanalysis alone recognizes this knot of imaginary servitude that love must always undo again, or sever.

[37]Freud's phrase for the conscious mind, which was only a part, and not the most important one for psychic functioning.

[38]German for denial (one of Freud's ego defenses).

[39]"Literally," "seizure." The captation of the "subject by the situation" suggests the fragility of the "I" — as with the schizophrenic in Caillois's description, who fades into the surroundings. But Lacan means to imply that societies too can become psychotic in this way, murdering others through a "deadening of the passions."

[40]Anthropologist Claude Lévi-Strauss had posited that the incest taboo (and hence the Oedipal struggle) lies at the boundary of nature and culture (see p. 475).

For such a task, we place no trust in altruistic feeling, we who lay bare the aggressivity that underlies the activity of the philanthropist, the idealist, the pedagogue, and even the reformer.

In the recourse of subject to subject that we preserve, psychoanalysis may accompany the patient to the ecstatic limit of the *"Thou art that,"*[41] in which is revealed to him the cipher of his mortal destiny, but it is not in our mere power as practitioners to bring him to that point where the real journey begins.

[41] The knowledge of one's own mortality. Lacan alludes to the skull often in the foreground of paintings of idyllic pastoral beauty; "thou art that" is what the skull says to the viewer.

The Meaning of the Phallus

What follows is the unaltered text of a paper delivered in German on 9 May 1958, at the Max Planck Institute of Munich where Professor Paul Matussek had invited me to speak.

The vaguest idea of the state of mind then prevailing in circles, not for the most part uninformed, will give some measure of the impact of terms such as "the other scene," to take one example used here, which I was the first to extract from Freud's work.

If "deferred action" (*Nachtrag*), to rescue another such term from its current affectation, makes this effort unfeasible, it should be realized that they were unheard of at that time.

We know that the unconscious castration complex[1] has the function of a knot:

1. in the dynamic structuring of symptoms in the analytic sense of the term, meaning that which can be analyzed in neuroses, perversions and psychoses;

2. as the regulator of development giving its *ratio*[2] to this first role: that is, by installing in the subject an unconscious position without which he would be unable to identify with the ideal type of his sex, or to respond without grave risk to the needs of his partner in the sexual relation, or even to receive adequately the needs of the child thus procreated.

What we are dealing with is an antinomy internal to the assumption by man (*Mensch*)[3] of his sex: why must he take up its attributes only by means of a threat, or even in the guise of a privation? As we know, in *Civilization and Its Discontents*, Freud went so far as to suggest not a contingent, but an essential disturbance of human sexuality, and one of his last articles[4] turns on the irreducibility for any finite (*endliche*) analysis of the effects following from the castration complex in the masculine unconscious and from *penisneid* [penis envy] in the unconscious of the woman.

This is not the only point of uncertainty, but it is the first that the Freudian experience and its resulting metapsychology introduced into our experience of man. It cannot be solved by any reduction to biological factors, as the mere necessity of the myth underlying the structuring of the Oedipus complex makes sufficiently clear.

Any recourse to an hereditary amnesic given would in this instance be mere artifice, not only because such a factor is in itself disputable, but because it leaves the problem untouched, namely, the link between the murder of the father and the pact of the primordial law, given that it is included in that law that castration should be the punishment for incest.

Only on the basis of the clinical facts can there be any fruitful discussion. These facts go to show that the relation of the subject to the phallus is set up regardless of the anatomical difference between the sexes, which is what makes its interpretation particularly intractable in the case of the

Translated by Jacqueline Rose.
[1] See Freud, p. 309.
[2] Reason, rationale.
[3] In German a neuter term for a person of either sex.

[4] Lacan is referring to Freud's *Analysis Terminable and Interminable* (1937).

woman and in relationship to her, specifically on the four following counts:

1. as to why the little girl herself considers, if only for a moment, that she is castrated, in the sense of being deprived of the phallus, at the hand of someone who is in the first instance her mother, an important point, and who then becomes her father, but in such a way that we must recognize in this transition a transference in the analytic sense of the term;

2. as to why, at a more primordial level, the mother is for both sexes considered as provided with a phallus, that is, as a phallic mother;

3. as to why, correlatively, the meaning of castration only acquires its full (clinically manifest) weight as regards symptom formation when it is discovered as castration of the mother;

4. these three problems culminate in the question of the reason for the phallic phase[5] in development. We know that Freud used this term to specify the earliest genital maturation — as on the one hand characterized by the imaginary predominance of the phallic attribute and masturbatory pleasure, and on the other by a localizing of this pleasure for the woman in the clitoris, which is thereby raised to the function of the phallus. This would seem to rule out for both sexes, until the end of this phase, that is, until the dissolution of the Oedipus complex, any instinctual awareness of the vagina as the place of genital penetration.

This ignorance smacks of mis-recognition [méconnaissance] in the technical sense of the term, especially as it is on occasions disproved. All it agrees with, surely, is Longus's fable in which he depicts the initiation of Daphnis and Chloé as dependent on the revelations of an old woman.[6]

It is for this reason that certain authors have been led to regard the phallic phase as an effect of repression, and the function assumed in it by the phallic object as a symptom. The difficulty starts when we need to know which symptom? Phobia, according to one, perversion according to

[5] See Freud, p. 309.

[6] In *Daphnis and Chloé*, a pastoral romance in Greek by Longus (probably early third century C.E.), the titular characters do not know how to consummate their love until it is explained to Daphnis by Lycanion, an old woman.

another — or, indeed, to the same one. In this last case, it's not worth speculating: not that interesting transmutations of the object from phobia into fetish do not occur, but their interest resides precisely in the different place which they occupy in the structure. There would be no point in asking these authors to formulate this difference from the perspective of object relations which is currently in favor. This being for lack of any reference on the matter other than the loose notion of the part object,[7] uncriticized since Karl Abraham[8] first introduced it, which is more the pity in view of the easy option which it provides today.

The fact remains that, if one goes back to the surviving texts of the years 1928-32, the now abandoned debate on the phallic phase is a refreshing example of a passion for doctrine, which has been given an additional note of nostalgia by the degradation of psychoanalysis consequent on its American transplantation.[9]

A mere summary of the debate could only distort the genuine diversity of the positions taken by figures such as Helene Deutsch, Karen Horney and Ernest Jones, to mention only the most eminent.

The series of three articles which Jones devoted to the subject is especially suggestive: if only for the starting premise on which he constructs his argument, signalled by the term *aphanisis*,[10] which he himself coined. For by correctly posing the problem of the relationship between castration and desire, he reveals such a proximity to what he cannot quite grasp that the term which will later provide us with the key to the problem seems to emerge out of his very failure.

The amusing thing is the way he manages, on the authority of the very letter of Freud's text, to formulate a position which is directly opposed to it: a true model in a difficult genre.

[7] Fetishistic feelings that attach not to an entire person but to a single body part (e.g., the mother's breast).

[8] Karl Abraham (1877–1925) was one of Freud's early disciples, known principally for having set up the institution of analytic training which gives practitioners of psychoanalysis their credential of expertise.

[9] This and the next four paragraphs involve Lacan's attack on American psychoanalysts (Deutsch, Horney, and Jones) whom he accuses of distorting Freud's doctrines, muddleheadedly evading the key issue of the castration complex.

[10] Jones's term for loss of sexual desire.

The problem, however, refuses to go away, seeming to subvert Jones's own case for a re-establishment of the equality of natural rights (which surely gets the better of him in the Biblical "Man and woman God created them" with which he concludes). What does he actually gain by normalizing the function of the phallus as part object if he has to invoke its presence in the mother's body as internal object, a term which is a function of the fantasies uncovered by Melanie Klein,[11] and if he cannot therefore separate himself from her doctrine which sees these fantasies as a recurrence of the Oedipal formation which is located right back in earliest infancy.

We will not go far wrong if we re-open the question by asking what could have imposed on Freud the obvious paradox of his position. For one has to allow that he was better guided than anyone else in his recognition of the order of unconscious phenomena, which order he had discovered, and that for want of an adequate articulation of the nature of these phenomena his followers were bound to go more or less astray.

It is on the basis of such a wager — laid down by me as the principle of a commentary of Freud's work which I have been pursuing for seven years — that I have been led to certain conclusions: above all, to argue, as necessary to any articulation of analytic phenomena, for the notion of the signifier, in the sense in which it is opposed to that of the signified in modern linguistic analysis.[12] The latter, born since Freud, could not be taken into account by him, but it is my contention that Freud's discovery stands out precisely for having had to anticipate its formulas, even while setting out from a domain in which one could hardly expect to recognize its sway. Conversely, it is Freud's discovery that gives to the opposition of signifier to signified the full weight which it should imply: namely, that the signifier has an active function in determining the effects in which the signifiable appears as submitting to its mark, becoming through that passion the signified.

This passion of the signifier then becomes a new dimension of the human condition, in that it is not only man who speaks, but in man and through man that it [ça] speaks,[13] that his nature is woven by effects in which we can find the structure of language, whose material he becomes, and that consequently there resounds in him, beyond anything ever conceived of by the psychology of ideas, the relation of speech.

It is in this sense that one can say that the consequences of the discovery of the unconscious have not been so much as glimpsed in the theory, although its repercussions have been felt in the praxis to a much greater extent than we are as yet aware of, even if only translated into effects of retreat.

Let me make clear that to argue for man's relation to the signifier as such has nothing to do with a "culturalist" position in the ordinary sense of the term, such as that which Karen Horney found herself anticipating in the dispute over the phallus and which Freud himself characterized as feminist.[14] The issue is not man's relation to language as a social phenomenon, since the question does not even arise of anything resembling that all too familiar ideological psychogenesis, not superseded by a peremptory recourse to the entirely metaphysical notion, underlying the mandatory appeal to the concrete, which is so pathetically conveyed by the term "affect."

It is a question of rediscovering in the laws governing that other scene (*eine andere Schauplatz*) which Freud designated, in relation to dreams, as that of the unconscious, the effects discovered at the level of the materially unstable elements which constitute the chain of language: effects determined by the double play of combination and substitution in the signifier, along the two axes of metaphor and metonymy which generate the signified; effects which are determinant in the

---

[11]English psychoanalyst (1882–1960) who disagreed with Freud's notion that the superego develops as a result of the Oedipal struggle (among many other things); for Klein it occurs at the age of two or three. Lacan assumes that any American psychoanalyst who bases his theories on Klein must be at best misguided.

[12]See the Introduction to Structuralism and Deconstruction, p. 470.

[13]"It" here means the Freudian *id*.

[14]Karen Horney (1885–1952) disputed the universality of penis envy among females and suggested that males feel "womb envy." Lacan intends for his explanation of the phallus as a signifier to cut through the "culturalist" issues of patriarchy and feminism.

institution of the subject. What emerges from this attempt is a topology in the mathematical sense of the term,[15] without which, as soon becomes clear, it is impossible even to register the structure of a symptom in the analytic sense of the term.

It speaks in the Other,[16] I say, designating by this Other the very place called upon by a recourse to speech in any relation where it intervenes. If it speaks in the Other, whether or not the subject hears it with his own ears, it is because it is there that the subject, according to a logic prior to any awakening of the signified, finds his signifying place. The discovery of what he articulates in that place, that is, in the unconscious, enables us to grasp the price of the division (*Spaltung*)[17] through which he is thus constituted.

The phallus is elucidated in its function here. In Freudian doctrine, the phallus is not a fantasy, if what is understood by that is an imaginary effect. Nor is it as such an object (part, internal, good, bad, etc. . . .) in so far as this term tends to accentuate the reality involved in a relationship. It is even less the organ, penis or clitoris, which it symbolizes. And it is not incidental that Freud took his reference for it from the simulacrum which it represented for the Ancients.

For the phallus is a signifier, a signifier whose function in the intrasubjective economy of analysis might lift the veil from that which it served in the mysteries. For it is to this signified that it is given to designate as a whole the effect of there being a signified, inasmuch as it conditions any such effect by its presence as signifier.

Let us examine, then, the effects of this presence. First they follow from the deviations of man's needs by the fact that he speaks, in the sense that as long as his needs are subjected to

demand they return to him alienated. This is not the effect of his real dependency (one should not expect to find here the parasitic conception represented by the notion of dependency in the theory of neuroses) but precisely of the putting into signifying form as such and of the fact that it is from the place of the Other that his message is emitted.[18]

What is thus alienated in needs constitutes an *Urverdrängung* (primal repression) because it cannot, by definition, be articulated in demand. But it reappears in a residue which then presents itself in man as desire (*das Begehren*). The phenomenology which emerges from analytic experience is certainly such as to demonstrate the paradoxical, deviant, erratic, eccentric and even scandalous character by which desire is distinguished from need. A fact too strongly attested not to have always won the recognition of moralists worthy of the name. It does seem that early Freudianism had to give this fact its due status. Yet paradoxically psychoanalysis finds itself at the head of an age-old obscurantism, all the more wearisome for its denial of the fact through the ideal of a theoretical and practical reduction of desire to need.

Hence the necessity for us to articulate that status here, starting with demand whose proper characteristics are eluded in the notion of frustration (which was never employed by Freud). Demand in itself bears on something other than the satisfactions which it calls for. It is demand for a presence or an absence. This is manifest in the primordial relation to the mother, pregnant as it is with that Other to be situated *some way short of* any needs which it might gratify. Demand constitutes this Other as already possessing the "privilege" of satisfying needs, that is, the power

[15] In the "mathematical sense," topology is the study of what properties of geometrical objects remain constant under deformation.

[16] Phrases like "It speaks in the Other," which recur for the next few pages, need to be translated into the Lacanian terminology those attending his seminar would already have internalized. Here "It" is the Freudian id, the site of the drives, and the Other is the Symbolic realm of language-signs ("the very place called on by a recourse to speech").

[17] German for cleavage or splitting. Freud used this term for those who simultaneously know something and refuse to acknowledge it.

[18] Lacan is demonstrating, here and in what follows, the distortions (or knots) that follow from the expression of need in language. To demand something in a love relationship is implicitly to imply that the other person has power over one and that one is not getting what one has demanded, or that one is getting it, but only as a result of having asked, which devalues the gift. The Hegelian dialectic of desire (see the Introduction to this chapter) also leads to knots here, where what one wants is to be what the other person most desires, but whatever is given can no longer be desired (since one can desire only what one lacks).

to deprive them of the one thing by which they are satisfied. This privilege of the Other thus sketches out the radical form of the gift of something which it does not have, namely, what is called its love.

Hence it is that demand cancels out (*aufhebt*) the particularity of anything which might be granted by transmuting it into a proof of love, and the very satisfactions of need which it obtains are degraded (*sich erniedrigt*) as being no more than a crushing of the demand for love (all of which is palpable in the psychology of early child-care to which our nurse-analysts are so dedicated).

There is, then, a necessity for the particularity thus abolished to reappear *beyond* demand. Where it does indeed reappear, but preserving the structure harboring within the unconditional character of the demand for love. In a reversal which is not a simple negation of negation, the force of pure loss arises from the relic of an obliteration. In place of the unconditional aspect of demand, desire substitutes the "absolute" condition: in effect this condition releases that part of the proof of love which is resistant to the satisfaction of a need. Thus desire is neither the appetite for satisfaction, nor the demand for love, but the difference resulting from the subtraction of the first from the second, the very phenomenon of their splitting (*Spaltung*).

One can see how the sexual relation occupies this closed field of desire in which it will come to play out its fate. For this field is constituted so as to produce the enigma which this relation provokes in the subject, by "signifying" it to him twice over: as a return of the demand it arouses in the form of a demand made on the subject of need, and as an ambiguity cast onto the Other who is involved, in the proof of love demanded. The gap in this enigma betrays what determines it, conveyed at its simplest in this formula: that for each partner in the relation, the subject and the Other, it is not enough to be the subjects of need, nor objects of love, but they must stand as the cause of desire.

This truth is at the heart of all the mishaps of sexual life which belong in the field of psychoanalysis.

It is also the precondition in analysis for the subject's happiness: and to disguise this gap by relying on the virtue of the "genital" to resolve it through the maturation of tenderness (that is by a recourse to the Other solely as reality), however piously intended, is none the less a fraud. Admittedly it was French psychoanalysts with their hypocritical notion of genital oblativity[19] who started up the moralizing trend which, to the tune of Salvationist choirs, is now followed everywhere.

In any case man cannot aim at being whole (the "total personality" being another premise where modern psychotherapy goes off course) once the play of displacement and condensation, to which he is committed in the exercise of his functions, marks his relation as subject to the signifier.

The phallus is the privileged signifier of that mark where the share of the logos is wedded to the advent of desire. One might say that this signifier is chosen as what stands out as most easily seized upon in the real of sexual copulation, and also as the most symbolic in the literal (typographical) sense of the term, since it is the equivalent in that relation of the (logical) copula. One might also say that by virtue of its turgidity, it is the image of the vital flow as it is transmitted in generation.

All these propositions merely veil over the fact that the phallus can only play its role as veiled, that is, as in itself the sign of the latency with which everything signifiable is struck as soon as it is raised (*aufgehoben*) to the function of signifier.

The phallus is the signifier of this *Aufhebung* itself which it inaugurates (initiates) by its own disappearance. This is why the demon of Αἰδώς [*Scham*, shame] in the ancient mysteries rises up exactly at the moment when the phallus is unveiled (cf. the famous painting of the Villa of Pompei).[20]

It then becomes the bar which, at the hands of this demon, strikes the signified, branding it as the bastard offspring of its signifying concatenation.

In this way a condition of complementarity is produced by the signifier in the founding of the subject: which explains his *Spaltung* as well as

---

[19]Self-sacrifice.
[20]At the House of the Vettii in Pompeii is a mural depicting the god Priapus weighing his enormous penis in a pair of scales against a sack of gold.

the intervening movement through which this is effected. Namely:

1. that the subject designates his being only by crossing through everything which it signifies, as can be seen in the fact that he wishes to be loved for himself, a mirage not dispelled merely by being denounced as grammatical (since it abolishes discourse);

2. that the living part of that being in the *urver-drängt* [primary repressed] finds its signifier by receiving the mark of the *Verdrängung* [repression] of the phallus (whereby the unconscious is language).

The phallus as signifier gives the ratio of desire (in the musical sense of the term as the "mean and extreme" ratio of harmonic division).

It is, therefore, as an algorithm that I am going to use it now, relying — necessarily if I am to avoid drawing out my account indefinitely — on the echoes of the experience which unites us to give you the sense of this usage.

If the phallus is a signifier then it is in the place of the Other that the subject gains access to it. But in that the signifier is only there veiled and as the ratio of the Other's desire, so it is this desire of the Other as such which the subject has to recognize, meaning, the Other as itself a subject divided by the signifying *Spaltung*.

What can be seen to emerge in psychological genesis confirms this signifying function of the phallus.

Thus, to begin with, we can formulate more correctly the Kleinian fact that the child appre-hends from the outset that the mother "contains" the phallus.

But it is the dialectic of the demand for love and the test of desire which dictates the order of development.

The demand for love can only suffer from a desire whose signifier is alien to it. If the desire of the mother *is* the phallus, then the child wishes to be the phallus so as to satisfy this desire. Thus the division immanent to desire already makes itself felt in the desire of the Other, since it stops the subject from being satisfied with presenting to the Other anything real it might *have* which corresponds to this phallus — what he has being

worth no more than what he does not have as far as his demand for love is concerned, which requires that he *be* the phallus.

Clinical practice demonstrates that this test of the desire of the Other is not decisive in the sense that the subject learns from it whether or not he has a real phallus, but insomuch as he learns that the mother does not.[21] This is the moment of expe-rience without which no symptomatic or structural consequence (that is, phobia or *penisneid*) refer-ring to the castration complex can take effect. It is here that the conjunction is signed between desire, in so far as the phallic signifier is its mark, and the threat or the nostalgia of lack-in-having.

It is, of course, the law introduced into this sequence by the father which will decide its future.

But simply by keeping to the function of the phallus, we can pinpoint the structures which will govern the relations between the sexes.

Let us say that these relations will revolve around a being and a having which, because they refer to a signifier, the phallus, have the contra-dictory effect of on the one hand lending reality to the subject in that signifier, and on the other making unreal the relations to be signified.

This follows from the intervention of an "appearing" which gets substituted for the "hav-ing" so as to protect it on one side and to mask its lack on the other, with the effect that the ideal or typical manifestations of behavior in both sexes, up to and including the act of sexual copulation, are entirely propelled into comedy.

These ideals gain new strength from the demand which it is in their power to satisfy, which is always the demand for love,[22] with its complement of reducing desire to demand.

[21]Lacan has arrived at the point where the Freudian castra-tion complex is restated in its symbolic meaning. It isn't that little boys and girls think their mother has been castrated in any physical sense, it is that they have worked out that, since they as children are *le désir de la mère*, the object of maternal desire, and since the phallus is the signifier of desire and since one cannot desire what one already has, the mother must lack the phallus. (The "phallic mother" of early object relations is the image of the spectacularly powerful figure before the child works that out.)

[22]The sexes differ over the issue of being and having, and Lacan's paradoxical formulation is that women want to *be* the phallus, whereas men want to *have* the phallus.

Paradoxical as this formulation might seem, I would say that it is in order to be the phallus, that is to say, the signifier of the desire of the Other, that the woman will reject an essential part of her femininity, notably all its attributes through masquerade. It is for what she is not that she expects to be desired as well as loved. But she finds the signifier of her own desire in the body of the one to whom she addresses her demand for love. Certainly we should not forget that the organ actually invested with this signifying function takes on the value of a fetish. But for the woman the result is still a convergence onto the same object of an experience of love which as such (cf. above) ideally deprives her of that which it gives, and a desire which finds in that same experience its signifier. Which is why it can be observed that the lack of satisfaction proper to sexual need, in other words, frigidity, is relatively well tolerated in women, whereas the *Verdrängung* inherent to desire is lesser in her case than in the case of the man.

In men, on the other hand, the dialectic of demand and desire gives rise to effects, whose exact point of connection Freud situated with a sureness which we must once again admire, under the rubric of a specific depreciation (*Erniedrigung*) of love.[23]

If it is the case that the man manages to satisfy his demand for love in his relationship to the woman to the extent that the signifier of the phallus constitutes her precisely as giving in love what she does not have — conversely, his own desire for the phallus will throw up its signifier in the form of a persistent divergence towards

"another woman" who can signify this phallus under various guises, whether as a virgin or a prostitute. The result is a centrifugal tendency of the genital drive in the sexual life of the man which makes impotence much harder for him to bear, at the same time as the *Verdrängung* inherent to desire is greater.

We should not, however, think that the type of infidelity which then appears to be constitutive of the masculine function is exclusive to the man. For if one looks more closely, the same redoubling is to be found in the woman, except that in her case, the Other of love as such, that is to say, the Other as deprived of that which he gives, is hard to perceive in the withdrawal whereby it is substituted for the being of the man whose attributes she cherishes.

One might add here that masculine homosexuality, in accordance with the phallic mark which constitutes desire, is constituted on its axis, whereas the orientation of feminine homosexuality, as observation shows, follows from a disappointment which reinforces the side of the demand for love. These remarks should be qualified by going back to the function of the mask inasmuch as this function dominates the identifications through which refusals of love are resolved.

The fact that femininity takes refuge in this mask, because of the *Verdrängung* inherent to the phallic mark of desire, has the strange consequence that, in the human being, virile display itself appears as feminine.

Correlatively, one can glimpse the reason for a feature which has never been elucidated and which again gives a measure of the depth of Freud's intuition: namely, why he advances the view that there is only one libido, his text clearly indicating that he conceives of it as masculine in nature. The function of the signifier here touches on its most profound relation: by way of which the Ancients embodied in it both the *Νοῦς* [*Nous*, sense] and the *Λογὸς* [*Logos*, reason].

---

[23]Lacan alludes to the Groucho Marx paradox, that one wouldn't want to join a club that would be willing to have one as a member. Once a woman becomes, in the realm of the signifier, the phallus the man wants, he ceases to want it, and is drawn to other women. Similarly, though, for the woman, the gift of the phallus deprives the man of what he has, and thereby diminishes her desire. One sees why Lacan refers to the relations between the sexes as a comedy. . .

Peter Brooks

b. 1938

Peter Preston Brooks was born in New York City and educated at Harvard University, where he received his Ph.D. in French in 1965. He has taught French, comparative literature, and law at Yale, the University of Virginia, and Princeton. He is currently Sterling Professor Emeritus of Comparative Literature at Yale, and the Andrew W. Mellon Foundation Scholar at Princeton. His publications include The Novel of Worldliness (1969), The Child's Part (1972), and The Melodramatic Imagination (1975). Recent essays have analyzed works by Balzac, Flaubert, Maupassant, Zola, and Henry James. His most influential book, a classic manifesto on the relationship between literature and modern French psychoanalysis, is Reading for the Plot: Design and Intention in Narrative (1984; second edition, 1990), from which the following selection is excerpted. His most recent books are Body Work: Objects of Desire in Modern Narrative (1993), Psychoanalysis and Storytelling (1994), Law's Stories: Narrative and Rhetoric in the Law (1996), Troubling Confessions: Speaking Guilt in Law and Literature (2000), Realist Visions (2005), and Enigmas of Identity (2011). Brooks has also written a novel, World Elsewhere (1999).

Freud's Masterplot

As if they would confine th' Interminable,
And tie him to his own prescript.[1]

In one of his best essays in "narratology," where he is working toward a greater formalization of principles advanced by Vladimir Propp and Viktor Shklovsky,[2] Tzvetan Todorov elaborates a model of narrative transformation whereby narrative plot (*le récit*) is constituted in the tension of two formal categories, difference and resemblance.[3] Transformation — a change in a predicate term common to beginning and end — represents a synthesis of difference and resemblance: it is, we might say, the same-but-different. Now "the same-but-different" is a common (and if inadequate, not altogether false) definition of metaphor. If Aristotle affirmed that the master of metaphor must have an eye for resemblances,[4] modern treatments of the subject have affirmed equally the importance of difference included within the operation of resemblance, the chief value of the metaphor residing in its "tension." Narrative operates as metaphor in its affirmation of resemblance, in that it brings into relation different actions, combines them through perceived similarities (Todorov's common predicate term), appropriates them to a common plot, which implies the rejection of merely contingent (or unassimilable) incident or action. The plotting of meaning cannot do without metaphor, for meaning in plot is the structure of

I wish at the outset of this essay to express my debt to two colleagues whose thinking has helped to clarify my own: Andrea Bertolini and David A. Miller. It is to the latter that I owe the term "the narratable." [Brooks]

[1] From Milton, *Samson Agonistes*, lines 307–08.

[2] See the introduction to Formalism, p. 411.

[3] Tzvetan Todorov, "Les Transformations narratives," in *Poétique de la prose* (Paris: Seuil, 1971), p. 240. Todorov's terms *récit* and *histoire* correspond to the Russian Formalist distinction between *sjužet* and *fabula*. In English, we might use with the same sense of distinctions: narrative plot and story. [Brooks]

[4] See Aristotle, *Poetics*, p. 50.

action in closed and legible wholes. Metaphor is in this sense totalizing. Yet it is equally apparent that the key figure of narrative must in some sense be not metaphor but metonymy: the figure of contiguity and combination, the figure of syntagmatic relations.[5] The description of narrative needs metonymy as the figure of movement, of linkage in the signifying chain, of the slippage of the signified under the signifier. That Jacques Lacan has equated metonymy and desire[6] is of the utmost pertinence, since desire must be considered the very motor of narrative, its dynamic principle.

The problem with "the same-but-different" as a definition of narrative would be the implication of simultaneity and stasis in the formulation. The postulation of a static model indeed is the central deficiency of most formalist and structuralist work on narrative, which has sought to make manifest the structures of narrative in spatial and atemporal terms, as versions of Lévi-Strauss's "atemporal matrix structure."[7] Todorov is an exception in that, faithful to Propp, he recognizes the need to consider sequence and succession as well as the paradigmatic matrix. He supplements his definition with the remark: "Rather than a 'coin with two faces,' [transformation] is an operation in two directions: it affirms at once resemblance and difference; it puts time into

motion and suspends it, in a single movement; it allows discourse to acquire a meaning without this meaning becoming pure information; in a word, it makes narrative possible and reveals its very definition."[8] The image of a double operation upon time has the value of returning us to the evident but frequently eluded fact that narrative meanings are developed in time, that any narrative partakes more or less of what Proust called "un jeu formidable . . . avec le Temps," and that this game of time is not merely in the world of reference (or in the *fabula*) but as well in the narrative, in the *sjužet,* be it only that the meanings developed by narrative *take time:* the time of reading.[9] If at the end of a narrative we can suspend time in a moment where past and present hold together in a metaphor which may be the very recognition which, said Aristotle, every good plot should bring,[10] that moment does not abolish the movement, the slidings, the errors and partial recognitions of the middle. As Roland Barthes points out, in what so far must be counted our most satisfactory dynamic analysis of plot, the proairetic and hermeneutic codes — code of actions, code of enigmas and answers — are irreversible: their interpretation is determined linearly, in sequence, in one direction.[11]

Ultimately — Barthes writes elsewhere — the passion that animates us as readers of narrative is the passion for (of) meaning.[12] Since for Barthes meaning (in the "classical" or "readable" text) resides in full predication, completion of the codes in a "plenitude" of signification, this passion appears to be finally a desire for the end. It is at the end — for Barthes as for Aristotle — that

---

[5]See Roman Jakobson, "Two Types of Language and Two Types of Aphasic Disturbances," in Jakobson and Halle, *Fundamentals of Language* (The Hague: Mouton, 1956). Todorov in a later article adds to "transformation" the term "succession," and sees the pair as definitional of narrative. He discusses the possible equation of these terms with Jakobson's "metaphor" and "metonymy," to conclude that "the connection is possible but does not seem necessary." (Todorov, "The Two Principles of Narrative," *Diacritics,* Fall, 1971, p. 42.) But there seem to be good reasons to maintain Jakobson's terms as "master tropes" referring to two aspects of virtually any text. [Brooks]

[6]See Jacques Lacan, "The Mirror Stage, as Formative of the Function of the I as Revealed in Psychoanalytic Experience" (1977). See p. 643.

[7]See Claude Lévi-Strauss, "La Structure et la forme," *Cahiers de l'Institut de science économique appliquée,* 99, série M, no. 7 (1960), p. 29. This term is cited with approval by A. J. Greimas in *Sémantique structurale* (Paris: Larousse, 1966) and Roland Barthes, in "Introduction à l'analyse structurale des récits," *Communications* 8 (1966). [Brooks]

[8]Todorov, "Les Transformations narratives," *Poétique de la prose,* p. 240. Translations from the French, here and elsewhere, are my own. [Brooks]

[9]Proust's phrase is cited by Gérard Genette in "Discours du récit," *Figures III* (Paris: Seuil, 1972), p. 182. Whereas Barthes maintains in "Introduction à l'analyse structurale des récits" that time belongs only to the referent of narrative, Genette gives attention to the time of reading and its necessary linearity. See pp. 77–78. [Brooks]

[10]See Aristotle, *Poetics,* p. 50.

[11]See Roland Barthes, *S/Z* (Paris: Seuil, 1970), p. 37. [Brooks]

[12]"Introduction à l'analyse structurale des récits," p. 27. [Brooks]

recognition brings its illumination, which then can shed retrospective light. The function of the end, whether considered syntactically (as in Todorov and Barthes) or ethically (as in Aristotle) or as formal or cosmological closure (as in Barbara H. Smith or Frank Kermode)[13] continues to fascinate and to baffle. One of the strongest statements of its determinative position in narrative plots comes in a passage from Sartre's *La Nausée* which bears quotation once again. Roquentin is reflecting on the meaning of "adventure" and the difference between living and narrating. When you narrate, you appear to start with a beginning. You say, "It was a fine autumn evening in 1922. I was a notary's clerk in Marommes." But, says Roquentin:

In reality you have started at the end. It was there, invisible and present, it is what gives these few words the pomp and value of a beginning. "I was out walking, I had left the town without realizing it, I was thinking about my money troubles." This sentence, taken simply for what it is, means that the man was absorbed, morose, a hundred miles from an adventure, exactly in a mood to let things happen without noticing them. But the end is there, transforming everything. For us, the man is already the hero of the story. His moroseness, his money troubles are much more precious than ours, they are all gilded by the light of future passions. And the story goes on in the reverse: instants have stopped piling themselves up by the end of the story which draws them and each one in its turn draws another, they are caught up by the end of the story the instant preceding it; "It was night, the street was deserted." The sentence is thrown out negligently, it seems superfluous; but we don't let ourselves be duped, we put it aside: this is a piece of information whose value we will understand later on. And we feel that the hero has lived all the details of this night as annunciations, as promises, or even that he has lived only those that were promises, blind and deaf to all that did not herald adventure. We forget that the future wasn't yet there; the man was walking in a night without premonitions, which offered him in disorderly fashion its monotonous riches, and he did not choose.[14]

The beginning in fact presupposes the end. The very possibility of meaning plotted through time depends on the anticipated structuring force of the ending: the interminable would be the meaningless. We read the incidents of narration as "promises and annunciations" of final coherence: the metaphor reached through the chain of metonymies. As Roquentin further suggests, we read only those incidents and signs which can be construed as promise and annunciation, enchained toward a construction of significance — those signs which, as in the detective story, appear to be *clues* to the underlying intentionality of event. The sense of beginning, then, is determined by the sense of an ending. And if we inquire further into the nature of the ending, we no doubt find that it eventually has to do with the human end, with death. In *Les Mots*, Sartre pushes further his reflection on ends. He describes how in order to escape contingency and the sense of being unjustified he had to imagine himself as one of the children in *L'Enfance des hommes illustres*, determined, as promise and annunciation, by what he would become for posterity. He began to live his life retrospectively, in terms of the death that alone would confer meaning and necessity on existence. As he succinctly puts it, "I became my own obituary."[15] All narration is obituary in that life acquires definable meaning only at, and through, death. In an independent but convergent argument, Walter Benjamin has claimed that life assumes transmissible form only at the moment of death. For Benjamin, this death is the very "authority" of narrative: we seek in fictions the knowledge of death, which in our own lives is denied to us. Death — which may be figural but in the classic instances of the genre is so often literal — quickens meaning: it is the "flame," says Benjamin, at which we warm our "shivering" lives.[16]

We need to know more about this deathlike ending which is nonetheless animating of meaning in relation to initiatory desire, and about how the

[13] Barbara Herrnstein Smith's *Poetic Closure* (1968) analyzed "formal closure"; Frank Kermode's *The Sense of an Ending* (1967) invoked the concept of cosmological closure.

[14] Jean-Paul Sartre, *La Nausée* (Paris: Livre de Poche, 1957), pp. 62–63. [Brooks]

[15] Sartre, *Les Mots* (Paris: Gallimard, 1968), p. 171. [Brooks]

[16] Walter Benjamin, "The Storyteller," in *Illuminations*, translated by Harry Zohn (New York: Schocken Books, 1969), p. 101. [Brooks]

interrelationship of the two determines, shapes, necessitates the middle — Barthes's "dilatory space" of retard, postponement — and the kinds of vacillation between illumination and blindness that we find there. If the end is recognition which retrospectively illuminates beginning and middle, it is not the exclusive truth of the text, which must include the processes along the way — the processes of "transformation" — in their metonymical complexity. If beginning is desire, and is ultimately desire for the end, between lies a process we feel to be necessary (plots, Aristotle tells us, must be of "a certain length")[17] but whose relation to originating desire and to end remains problematic. It is here that Freud's most ambitious investigation of ends in relation to beginnings may be of help — and may suggest a contribution to a properly dynamic model of plot.

We undertake, then, to read *Beyond the Pleasure Principle* as an essay about the dynamic interrelationship of ends and beginnings, and the kind of processes that constitute the middle. The enterprise may find a general sort of legitimation in the fact that *Beyond the Pleasure Principle* is in some sense Freud's own masterplot, the text in which he most fully lays out a total scheme of how life proceeds from beginning to end, and how each individual life in its own way repeats the masterplot. Of Freud's various intentions in this text, the boldest — and most mysterious — may be to provide a theory of comprehension of the dynamic of the life-span, its necessary duration and its necessary end, hence, implicitly, a theory of the very narratability of life. In his pursuit of his "beyond," Freud is forced to follow the implications of argument — "to throw oneself into a line of thought and follow it wherever it leads," as he says late in the essay — to ends that he had not originally or consciously conceived.[18] *Beyond the Pleasure Principle* shows the very plotting of a masterplot made necessary by the structural demands of Freud's thought, and it is in this sense that we shall attempt to read it as a model for narrative plot.

Narrative always makes the implicit claim to be in a state of repetition, as a going over again of a ground already covered: a *sjužet* repeating the *fabula,* as the detective retraces the tracks of the criminal.[19] This claim to an act of repetition — "I sing," "I tell" — appears to be initiatory of narrative. It is equally initiatory of *Beyond the Pleasure Principle;* it is the first problem and clue that Freud confronts. Evidence of a "beyond" that does not fit neatly into the functioning of the pleasure principle comes first in the dreams of patients suffering from war neuroses, or from the traumatic neuroses of peace: dreams which return to the moment of trauma, to relive its pain in apparent contradiction of the wish-fulfillment theory of dreams. This "dark and dismal" example is superseded by an example from "normal" life, and we have the celebrated moment of child's play: the toy thrown away, the reel on the string thrown out of the crib and pulled back, to the alternate exclamation of *fort* and *da.*[20] When he has established the equivalence between making the toy disappear and the child's mother's disappearance, Freud is faced with a set of possible interpretations. Why does the child repeat an unpleasurable experience? It may be answered that by staging his mother's disappearance and return, the child is compensating for his instinctual renunciation. Yet the child has also staged disappearance alone, without reappearance, as a game. This may make one want to argue that the essential experience involved is the movement from a passive to an active role in regard to his mother's disappearance, claiming mastery in a situation which he has been compelled to submit to.

Repetition as the movement from passivity to mastery reminds us of "The Theme of the Three Caskets," where Freud, considering Bassanio's choice of the lead casket in *The Merchant of Venice* — the correct choice in the suit of

---

[17]See Aristotle, *Poetics,* p. 50.

[18]Sigmund Freud, "Beyond the Pleasure Principle" (1920), in *The Standard Edition of the Complete Psychological Works of Sigmund Freud,* ed. James Strachey (London: Hogarth Press, 1955), 18, 59. Subsequent page references will be given between parentheses in the text. [Brooks]

[19]J. Hillis Miller, in *Ariadne's Thread: Story Lines* (1995), notes that the term *diegesis* suggests that narrative is a retracing of a journey already made. On the detective story, see Tzvetan Todorov, "Typologie du roman policier," *Poétique de la prose,* pp. 58–59. [Brooks]

[20]"Gone" and "here."

Portia — decides that the choice of the right maiden in man's literary play is also the choice of death; by this choice, he asserts an active mastery of what he must in fact endure. "Choice stands in the place of necessity, of destiny. In this way man overcomes death, which he has recognized intellectually."[21] If repetition is mastery, movement from the passive to the active; and if mastery is an assertion of control over what man must in fact submit to — choice, we might say, of an imposed end — we have already a suggestive comment on the grammar of plot, where repetition, taking us back again over the same ground, could have to do with the choice of ends.

But other possibilities suggest themselves to Freud at this point. The repetition of unpleasant experience — the mother's disappearance — might be explained by the motive of revenge, which would yield its own pleasure. The uncertainty which Freud faces here is whether repetition can be considered a primary event, independent of the pleasure principle, or whether there is always some direct yield of pleasure of another sort involved. The pursuit of this doubt takes Freud into the analytic experience, to his discovery of patients' need to repeat, rather than simply remember, repressed material: the need to reproduce and to "work through" painful material from the past as if it were present. The analyst can detect a "compulsion to repeat," ascribed to the unconscious repressed, particularly discernible in the transference, where it can take "ingenious" forms. The compulsion to repeat gives patients a sense of being fatefully subject to a "perpetual recurrence of the same thing"; it suggests to them pursuit by a daemonic power. We know also, from Freud's essay on "The Uncanny," that this feeling of the daemonic, arising from involuntary repetition, is a particular attribute of the literature of the uncanny.[22]

Thus in analytic work (as also in literary texts) there is slim but real evidence of a compulsion to repeat which can override the pleasure principle, and which seems "more primitive, more

[21] Freud, "The Theme of the Three Caskets" (1913), Standard Edition, 12, 299. [Brooks]

[22] See Freud, "The Uncanny" (Das Unheimliche) (1919), in Standard Edition, 17, 219–52. [Brooks].

elementary, more instinctual than the pleasure principle which it overrides" (23). We might note at this point that the transference itself is a metaphor, a substitutive relationship for the patient's infantile experiences, and thus approximates the status of a text. Now repetition is so basic to our experience of literary texts that one is simultaneously tempted to say all and to say nothing on the subject. To state the matter baldly: rhyme, alliteration, assonance, meter, refrain, all the mnemonic elements of fictions and indeed most of its tropes are in some manner repetitions which take us back in the text, which allow the ear, the eye, the mind to make connections between different textual moments, to see past and present as related and as establishing a future which will be noticeable as some variation in the pattern. Todorov's "same but different" depends on repetition. If we think of the trebling characteristic of the folk tale, and of all formulaic literature, we may consider that the repetition by three constitutes the minimal repetition to the perception of series, which would make it the minimal intentional structure of action, the minimum plot. Narrative must ever present itself as a repetition of events that have already happened, and within this postulate of a generalized repetition it must make use of specific, perceptible repetitions in order to create plot, that is, to show us a significant interconnection of events. Event gains meaning by repeating (with variation) other events. Repetition is a return in the text, a doubling back. We cannot say whether this return is a return *to* or a return *of*: for instance, a return to origins or a return of the repressed. Repetition through this ambiguity appears to suspend temporal process, or rather, to subject it to an indeterminate shuttling or oscillation which binds different moments together as a middle which might turn forward or back. This inescapable middle is suggestive of the daemonic. The relation of narrative plot to story may indeed appear to partake of the daemonic, as a kind of tantalizing play with the primitive and the instinctual, the magic and the curse of reproduction or "representation." But in order to know more precisely the operations of repetition, we need to read further in Freud's text.

"What follows is speculation" (24). With this gesture, Freud, in the manner of Rousseau's dismissal of the facts in the *Discourse on the Origins of Inequality,* begins the fourth chapter and his sketch of the economic and energetic model of the mental apparatus: the system Pcpt-Cs and Ucs,[23] the role of the outer layer as shield against excitations, and the definition of trauma as the breaching of the shield, producing a flood of stimuli which knocks the pleasure principle out of operation. Given this situation, the repetition of traumatic experiences in the dreams of neurotics can be seen to have the function of seeking retrospectively to master the flood of stimuli, to perform a mastery or binding of mobile energy through developing the anxiety whose omission was the cause of the traumatic neurosis. Thus the repetition compulsion is carrying out a task that must be accomplished *before* the dominance of the pleasure principle can begin. Repetition is hence a primary event, independent of the pleasure principle and more primitive. Freud now moves into an exploration of the theory of the instincts.[24] The instinctual is the realm of freely mobile, "unbound" energy: the "primary process," where energy seeks immediate discharge, where no postponement of gratification is tolerated. It appears that it must be "the task of the higher strata of the mental apparatus to bind the instinctual excitation reaching the primary process" before the pleasure principle can assert its dominance over the psychic economy (34–35). We may say that at this point in the essay we have moved from a postulate of repetition as the assertion of mastery (as in the passage from passivity to activity in the child's game) to a conception whereby repetition works as a process of *binding* toward the creation of an energetic constant-state situation which will permit the emergence of mastery, and the possibility of postponement.

[23]Standard abbreviations for "perceptual-conscious" and "unconscious."

[24]I shall use the term "instinct" since it is the translation of *Trieb* given throughout the Standard Edition. But we should realize that "instinct" is inadequate and somewhat misleading, since it loses the sense of "drive" associated with the word *Trieb.* The currently accepted French translation, *pulsion,* is more to our purposes: the model that interests me here might indeed be called "pulsional." [Brooks]

That Freud at this point evokes once again the daemonic and the uncanny nature of repetition, and refers us not only to children's play but as well to their demand for exact repetition in storytelling, points our way back to literature. Repetition in all its literary manifestations may in fact work as a "binding," a binding of textual energies that allows them to be mastered by putting them into serviceable form within the energetic economy of the narrative. Serviceable form must in this case mean perceptible form: repetition, repeat, recall, symmetry, all these journeys back in the text, returns to and returns of, that allow us to bind one textual moment to another in terms of similarity or substitution rather than mere contiguity. Textual energy, all that is aroused into expectancy and possibility in a text — the term will need more definition, but corresponds well enough to our experience of reading — can become usable by plot only when it has been bound or formalized. It cannot otherwise be plotted in a course to significant discharge, which is what the pleasure principle is charged with doing. To speak of "binding" in a literary text is thus to speak of any of the formalizations (which, like binding, may be painful, retarding) that force us to recognize sameness within difference, or the very emergence of a *sjužet* from the material of *fabula.*

We need at present to follow Freud into his closer inquiry concerning the relation between the compulsion to repeat and the instinctual. The answer lies in "a universal attribute of instincts and perhaps of organic life in general," that *"an instinct is an urge inherent in organic life to restore an earlier state of things"* (36). Instincts, which we tend to think of as a drive toward change, may rather be an expression of "the conservative nature of living things." The organism has no wish to change; if its conditions remained the same, it would constantly repeat the very same course of life. Modifications are the effect of external stimuli, and these modifications are in turn stored up for further repetition, so that, while the instincts may give the appearance of tending toward change, they "are merely seeking to reach an ancient goal by paths alike old and new" (38). Hence Freud is able to proffer, with a certain bravado, the formulation: *"the aim of all life is death."* We are given an evolutionary image of the organism in which the tension created by external influences has forced living substance to "diverge ever more widely from its original course of life and to make ever more complicated *détours* before reaching its aim of death" (38–39). In this view, the self-preservative instincts function to assure that the organism shall follow its own path to death, to ward off any ways of returning to the inorganic which are not immanent to the organism itself. In other words, "the organism wishes to die only in its own fashion." It must struggle against events (dangers) which would help it to achieve its goal too rapidly — by a kind of short-circuit.

We are here somewhere near the heart of Freud's masterplot for organic life, and it generates a certain analytic force in its superimposition on fictional plots. What operates in the text through repetition is the death instinct, the drive toward the end. Beyond and under the domination of the pleasure principle is this baseline of plot, its basic "pulsation," sensible or audible through the repetitions which take us back in the text. Repetition can take us both backwards and forwards because these terms have become reversible: the end is a time before the beginning. Between these two moments of quiescence, plot itself stands as a kind of divergence or deviance, a postponement in the discharge which leads back to the inanimate. For plot starts (must give the illusion of starting) from that moment at which story, or "life," is stimulated from quiescence into a state of narratability, into a tension, a kind of irritation, which demands narration. Any reflection on novelistic beginnings shows the beginning as an awakening, an arousal, the birth of an appetency, ambition, desire or intention.[25] To say this is of course to say — perhaps more pertinently — that beginnings are the arousal of an intention in reading, stimulation into a tension. (The specifically erotic nature of the

tension of writing and its rehearsal in reading could be demonstrated through a number of exemplary texts, notably Rousseau's account, in *The Confessions*, of how his novel *La Nouvelle Héloïse* was born of a masturbatory reverie and its necessary fictions, or the very similar opening of Jean Genet's *Notre-Dame des fleurs*; but of course the sublimated forms of the tension are just as pertinent.) The ensuing narrative — the Aristotelian "middle" — is maintained in a state of tension, as a prolonged deviance from the quiescence of the "normal" — which is to say, the unnarratable — until it reaches the terminal quiescence of the end. The development of a narrative shows that the tension is maintained as an ever more complicated postponement or *détour* leading back to the goal of quiescence. As Sartre and Benjamin compellingly argued, the narrative must tend toward its end, seek illumination in its own death. Yet this must be the right death, the correct end. The complication of the *détour* is related to the danger of short-circuit: the danger of reaching the end too quickly, of achieving the improper death. The improper end indeed lurks throughout narrative, frequently as the wrong choice: choice of the wrong casket, misapprehension of the magical agent, false erotic object-choice. The development of the subplot in the classical novel usually suggests (as William Empson has intimated) a different solution to the problems worked through by the main plot, and often illustrates the danger of short-circuit.[26] The subplot stands as one means of warding off the danger of short-circuit, assuring that the main plot will continue through to the right end. The desire of the text (the desire of reading) is hence desire for the end, but desire reached only through the complicated *détour*, the at least minimally complicated *détour*, the intentional deviance, in tension, which is the plot of narrative.

Deviance, *détour*, an intention which is irritation: these are characteristics of the narratable, of "life" as it is the material of narrative.

[25]On the beginning as intention, see Edward Said, *Beginnings: Intention and Method* (New York: Basic Books, 1975). It occurs to me that the exemplary narrative beginning might be that of Kafka's *Metamorphosis:* waking up to find oneself transformed into a monstrous vermin. [Brooks]

[26]See William Empson, "Double Plots," in *Some Versions of Pastoral* (New York: New Directions, 1960), pp. 25–84. [Brooks]

of *fabula* become *sjužet*. Plot is a kind of arabesque or squiggle toward the end. It is like Corporal Trim's arabesque with his stick, in *Tristram Shandy*, retraced by Balzac at the start of *La Peau de chagrin* to indicate the arbitrary, transgressive, gratuitous line of narrative, its deviance from the straight line, the shortest distance between beginning and end — which would be the collapse of one into the other, of life into immediate death. Freud's text will in a moment take us closer to understanding of the formal organization of this deviance toward the end. But it also at this point offers further suggestions about the beginning. For when he has identified both the death instincts and the life (sexual) instincts as conservative, tending toward the restoration of an earlier state of things, Freud feels obliged to deconstruct the will to believe in a human drive toward perfection, an impulsion forward and upward: a force which — he here quotes *Faust* as the classic text of man's forward striving — "*ungebändigt immer vorwärts dringt.*"[27] The illusion of the striving toward perfection is to be explained by instinctual repression and the persisting tension of the repressed instinct, and the resulting difference between the pleasure of satisfaction *demanded* and that which is *achieved,* a difference which "provides the driving factor which will permit of no halting at any position attained" (36). This process of subtraction reappears in modified form in the work of Lacan, where it is the difference between *need* (the infant's need for the breast) and *demand* (which is always demand for recognition) that gives as its result *desire,* which is precisely the driving power, of plot certainly, since desire for Lacan is a metonymy, the forward movement of the signifying chain. If Roman Jakobson is able, in his celebrated essay, to associate the metonymic pole with prose fiction (particularly the nineteenth-century novel) — as the metaphoric pole is associated with lyric poetry — it would seem to be because the meanings peculiar to narrative inhere (or, as Lacan would say, "insist") in the

metonymic chain, in the drive of desire toward meaning in time.[28]

The next-to-last chapter of *Beyond the Pleasure Principle* cannot here be rehearsed in detail. In brief, it leads Freud twice into the findings of biology, first on the track of the origins of death, to find out whether it is a necessary or merely a contingent alternative to interminability, then in pursuit of the origins of sexuality, to see whether it satisfies the description of the instinctual as conservative. Biology can offer no sure answer to either investigation, but it offers at least metaphorical confirmation of the necessary dualism of Freud's thought, and encouragement to reformulate his earlier opposition of ego instincts to sexual instincts as one between life instincts and death instincts, a shift in the grouping of oppositional forces which then allows him to reformulate the libidinal instincts themselves as the Eros "of the poets and philosophers" which holds all living things together, and which seeks to combine things in ever greater living wholes. Desire would then seem to be totalizing in intent, a process tending toward combination in new unities: metonymy in the search to become metaphor. But for the symmetry of Freud's opposition to be complete, he needs to be able to ascribe to Eros, as to the death instinct, the characteristic of a need to restore an earlier state of things. Since biology will not answer, Freud, in a remarkable gesture, turns toward myth, to come up with Plato's Androgyne, which precisely ascribes Eros to a search to recover a lost primal unity which was split asunder.[29] Freud's apologetic tone in this last twist to his argument is partly disingenuous, for we detect a contentment to have formulated the forces of the human masterplot as "philosopher and poet." The apology is coupled with a reflection that much of the obscurity of the

[27]"Unhampered always moves forwards."

[28]See Jakobson, "Two Types of Language . . . ." See, in Lacan's work, especially "Le Stade du miroir" and "L'Instance de la lettre dans l'inconscient," in *Écrits* (Paris: Seuil, 1966). [Brooks] For Lacan's essay, see p. 643.

[29]In Plato's *Symposium,* Aristophanes explains the nature of love in the form of a fable. Humanity was originally designed to be androgynous, but a mischievous demiurge split the double-sexed creature in half. The result is that we are all incomplete, seeking in Eros for our missing halves.

processes Freud has been considering "is merely due to our being obliged to operate with the scientific terms, that is to say with the figurative language, peculiar to psychology" (60). *Beyond the Pleasure Principle*, we are to understand, is not merely metapsychology, it is also mythopoesis, necessarily resembling "an equation with two unknown quantities" (57), or, we might say, a formal dynamic the terms of which are not substantial but purely relational. We perceive that *Beyond the Pleasure Principle* is itself a plot which has formulated that dynamic necessary to its own *détour*.

The last chapter of Freud's text recapitulates, but not without difference. He returns to the problem of the relationship between the instinctual processes of repetition and the dominance of the pleasure principle. One of the earliest and most important functions of the mental apparatus is to bind the instinctual impulses which impinge upon it, to convert freely mobile energy into a quiescent cathexis. This is a preparatory act on behalf of the pleasure principle, which permits its dominance. Sharpening his distinction between a *function* and a *tendency*, Freud argues that the pleasure principle is a "tendency" operating in the service of a function whose business it is to free the mental apparatus from excitation or to keep the amount of excitation in it constant or to keep it as low as possible" (62). This function is concerned "with the most universal endeavour of all living substance — namely to return to the quiescence of the inorganic world." Hence one can consider "binding" to be a preliminary function which prepares the excitation for its final elimination in the pleasure of discharge. In this manner, we could say that the repetition compulsion and the death instinct serve the pleasure principle; in a larger sense, the pleasure principle keeping watch on the invasion of stimuli from without and especially from within, seeking their discharge, serves the death instinct, making sure that the organism is permitted to return to quiescence. The whole evolution of the mental apparatus appears as a taming of the instincts so that the pleasure principle — itself tamed, displaced — can appear to dominate in the complicated *détour* called life which leads back to death. In fact, Freud seems here at the very end to

imply that the two antagonistic instincts serve one another in a dynamic interaction which is a perfect and self-regulatory economy which makes both end and *détour* perfectly necessary and interdependent. The organism must live in order to die in the proper manner, to die the right death. We must have the arabesque of plot in order to reach the end. We must have metonymy in order to reach metaphor.

We emerge from reading *Beyond the Pleasure Principle* with a dynamic model which effectively structures ends (death, quiescence, non-narratability) against beginnings (Eros, stimulation into tension, the desire of narrative) in a manner that necessitates the middle as *détour*, as struggle toward the end and under the compulsion of imposed delay, as arabesque in the dilatory space of the text. We detect some illumination of the necessary distance between beginning and end, the drives which connect them but which prevent the one collapsing back into the other: the way in which metonymy and metaphor serve one another, the necessary temporality of the same-but-different which to Todorov constitutes the narrative transformation. The model suggests further that along the way of the path from beginning to end — in the middle — we have repetitions serving to bind the energy of the text in order to make its final discharge more effective. In fictional plots, these bindings are a system of repetitions which are returns to and returns of, confounding the movement forward to the end with a movement back to origins, reversing meaning within forward-moving time, serving to formalize the system of textual energies, offering the possibility (or the illusion) of "meaning" wrested from "life."

As a dynamic-energetic model of narrative plot, then, *Beyond the Pleasure Principle* gives an image of how "life," or the *fabula*, is stimulated into the condition of narrative, becomes *sjužet*: enters into a state of deviance and *détour* (ambition, quest, the pose of a mask) in which it is maintained for a certain time, through an at least minimally complex extravagance, before returning to the quiescence of the non-narratable. The energy generated by deviance, extravagance, excess — an energy which belongs to the textual hero's career and to the reader's expectation, his desire of and for the text — maintains the plot in its movement through the vacillating play of the middle, where repetition as binding works toward the generation of significance, toward recognition and the retrospective illumination which will allow us to grasp the text as total metaphor, but not therefore to discount the metonymies that have led to it. The desire of the text is ultimately the desire for the end, for that recognition which is the moment of the death of the reader in the text. Yet recognition cannot abolish textuality, does not annul the middle which, in its oscillation between blindness and recognition, between origin and endings, is the truth of the narrative text.

It is characteristic of textual energy in narrative that it should always be on the verge of premature discharge, of short-circuit. The reader experiences the fear — and excitation — of the improper end, which is symmetrical to — but far more immediate and present than — the fear of endlessness. The possibility of short-circuit can of course be represented in all manner of threats to the protagonist or to any of the functional logics which demand completion; it most commonly takes the form of temptation to the mistaken erotic object choice, who may be of the "Belle Dame sans merci" variety, or may be the too-perfect and hence annihilatory bride. Throughout the Romantic tradition, it is perhaps most notably the image of incest (of the fraternal-sororal variety) which hovers as the sign of a passion interdicted because its fulfillment would be too perfect, a discharge indistinguishable from death, the very cessation of narrative movement. Narrative is in a state of temptation to oversameness, and where we have no literal threat of incest (as in Chateaubriand, or Faulkner), lovers choose to turn the beloved into a soul-sister so that possession will be either impossible or mortal: Werther and Lotte, for instance, or, at the inception of the tradition, Rousseau's *La Nouvelle Héloïse,* where Saint-Preux's letter to Julie following their night of love begins: "Mourons, ô ma douce amie." Incest is only the exemplary version of a temptation of short-circuit from which the protagonist and the text must be led away, into *détour,* into the cure which prolongs narrative.

It may finally be in the logic of our argument that repetition speaks in the text of a return which ultimately subverts the very notion of beginning and end, suggesting that the idea of beginning presupposes the end, that the end is a time before the beginning, and hence that the interminable never can be finally bound in a plot. Analysis, Freud would eventually discover, is inherently interminable, since the dynamics of resistance and the transference can always generate new beginnings in relation to any possible end.[30] It is the role of fictional plots to impose an end which yet suggests a return, a new beginning: a rereading. A narrative, that is, wants at its end to refer us back to its middle, to the web of the text: to recapture us in its doomed energies.

One ought at this point to make a new beginning, and to sketch the possible operation of the model in the study of the plot of a fiction. One could, for instance, take Dickens's *Great Expectations.* One would have to show how the energy released in the text by its liminary "primal scene" — Pip's terrifying meeting with Magwitch in the graveyard — is subsequently bound in a number of desired but unsatisfactory ways (including Pip's "being bound" as apprentice, the "dream" plot of Satis House, the apparent intent of the "expectations"), and simultaneously in censored but ultimately more satisfying ways (through all the returns of the repressed identification of Pip and his convict). The most salient device of this novel's "middle" is literally the journey back — from London to Pip's home town — a repeated return to apparent origins which is also a return of the repressed, of what Pip calls "that old spell of my childhood." It would be interesting to demonstrate that each of Pip's choices in the novel, while consciously life-furthering, forward oriented, in fact leads back, to the insoluble question of origins, to the palindrome of his name, so that the end of the narrative — its "discharge" — appears as the image of a "life" cured of "plot," as celibate clerk for Clarrikers.

Pip's story, while ostensibly the search for progress, ascension, and metamorphosis, may

[30]See Freud, "Analysis Terminable and Interminable" (1937), in *Standard Edition,* 23, 216–53. [Brooks]

after all be the narrative of an attempted home-coming: of the effort to reach an assertion of origin through ending, to find the same in the different, the time before in the time after. Most of the great nineteenth-century novels tell this same tale. Georg Lukács has called the novel "the literary form of the transcendent homelessness of the idea," and argued that it is in the discrepancy between idea and the organic that time, the process of duration, becomes constitutive of the novel as of no other genre:

Only in the novel, whose very matter is seeking and failing to find the essence, is time posited together with the form: time is the resistance of the organic — which possesses a mere semblance of life — to the present meaning, the will of life to remain within its own completely enclosed immanence. . . . In the novel, meaning is separated from life, and hence the essential from the temporal; we might almost say that the entire inner action of the novel is nothing but a struggle against the power of time.[31]

The understanding of time, says Lukács, the transformation of the struggle against time into a process full of interest, is the work of memory — or more precisely, we could say with Freud, of "remembering, repeating, working through." Repetition, remembering, reenactment are the ways in which we replay time, so that it may not be lost. We are thus always trying to work back through time to that transcendent home, knowing of course that we cannot. All we can do is subvert or, perhaps better, pervert time: which is what narrative does.[32]

[31]Georg Lukács, *The Theory of the Novel*, trans. Anna Bostock (Cambridge, Mass.: MIT Press, 1971), p. 122. [Brooks]

[32]Genette discusses Proust's "perversion" of time in "Discours du récit," p. 182. "Remembering, Repeating, and Working Through" (*Erinnern, Wiederholen und Durcharbeiten*, 1914) is the subject of one of Freud's papers on technique. See *Standard Edition* 12, 145–56. [Brooks]

To forgo any true demonstration on a novel, and to bring a semblance of conclusion, we may return to the assertion, by Barthes and Todorov, that narrative is essentially the articulation of a set of verbs. These verbs are no doubt ultimately all versions of desire. Desire is the wish for the end, for fulfillment, but fulfillment delayed so that we can understand it in relation to origin, and to desire itself. The story of Scheherazade is doubtless the story of stories. This suggests that the tale as read is inhabited by the reader's desire, and that further analysis should be directed to that desire, not (in the manner of Norman Holland) his individual desire and its origins in his own personality, but his transindividual and intertextually determined desire as a reader. Because it concerns in relation to beginnings and the forces that animate the middle in between, Freud's model is suggestive of what a reader engages when he responds to plot. It images that engagement as essentially dynamic, an interaction with a system of energy which the reader activates. This in turn suggests why we can read *Beyond the Pleasure Principle* as a text concerning textuality, and conceive that there can be psychoanalytic criticism of the text itself that does not become — as has usually been the case — a study of the psychogenesis of the text (the author's unconscious), the dynamics of literary response (the reader's unconscious), or the occult motivations of the characters (postulating an "unconscious" for them). It is rather the superimposition of the model of the functioning of the mental apparatus on the functioning of the text that offers the possibility of a psychoanalytic criticism. And here the superimposition of Freud's psychic masterplot on the plots of fiction seems a valid and useful maneuver. Plot mediates meanings with the contradictory human world of the eternal and the mortal. Freud's masterplot of the temporality of desire, and speaks to our very desire for fictional plots.

Laura Mulvey
b. 1941

Laura Mulvey was born in Oxford, England, and studied history at St. Hilda's College, Oxford, before embarking on a dual career as a film director and a film theorist. Her films, co-directed with her husband Peter Wollen, include Penthesilea *(1974),* Riddles of the Sphinx *(1978),* Amyl *(1980),* Crystal Gazing *(1981),* The Bad Sister *(1983), and* 23 August 2008 *(2013). Her film* Disgraced Monuments *(1996) was a solo project. Her books on the gaze in cinema and photography include* Visual and Other Pleasures *(1989),* Citizen Kane *(1993),* Mary Kelly *(1998), and* Fetishism and Curiosity: Cinema and the Mind's Eye *(new edition, 2013). She currently teaches film and media studies at Birkbeck College, University of London. "Visual Pleasure and Narrative Cinema" written in 1973, was published in* Screen *in 1975. In a piece entitled "Afterthoughts on Visual Pleasure and Narrative Cinema," published in* Framework *in 1981, Mulvey reflects on her famous essay.*

Visual Pleasure and Narrative Cinema

I. INTRODUCTION

(a) A Political Use of Psychoanalysis

This paper intends to use psychoanalysis to discover where and how the fascination of film is reinforced by pre-existing patterns of fascination already at work within the individual subject and the social formations that have moulded him. It takes as its starting-point the way film reflects, reveals and even plays on the straight, socially established interpretation of sexual difference which controls images, erotic ways of looking and spectacle. It is helpful to understand what the cinema has been, how its magic has worked in the past, while attempting a theory and a practice which will challenge this cinema of the past. Psychoanalytic theory is thus appropriated here as a political weapon, demonstrating the way the unconscious of patriarchal society has structured film form.

The paradox of phallocentrism[1] in all its manifestations is that it depends on the image of the castrated woman to give order and meaning to its world. An idea of woman stands as linchpin to the system: it is her lack that produces the phallus as a symbolic presence, it is her desire to make good the lack that the phallus signifies. Recent writing in *Screen* about psychoanalysis and the cinema has not sufficiently brought out the importance of the representation of the female form in a symbolic order in which, in the last resort, it speaks castration and nothing else. To summarise briefly: the function of woman in forming the patriarchal unconscious is twofold: she firstly symbolises the castration threat by her real lack of a penis and secondly thereby raises her child into the symbolic. Once this has been achieved, her meaning in the process is at an end. It does not last into the world of law and language except as a memory, which oscillates between memory of maternal plentitude and

---

[1]*Phallocentrism* refers to the organization of the symbolic order, specifically, the binary opposition in which the phallus represents the positive principle of presence as a masculine entity, as opposed to a "castrated" feminine entity (see introduction to Gender Studies, p. 953.) Mulvey's terminology here — the *phallus* as the signifier of desire, the *imaginary* and *symbolic* orders as the sites of image and word, the dialectical relation between *lack, need,* and *desire* — derives from Jacques Lacan; see the introduction to Psychoanalytic Theory, p. 627.

memory of lack. Both are posited on nature (or on anatomy in Freud's famous phrase).[2] Woman's desire is subjugated to her image as bearer of the bleeding wound; she can exist only in relation to castration and cannot transcend it. She turns her child into the signifier of her own desire to possess a penis (the condition, she imagines, of entry into the symbolic). Either she must gracefully give way to the word, the name of the father and the law, or else struggle to keep her child down with her in the half-light of the imaginary. Woman then stands in patriarchal culture as a signifier for the male other, bound by a symbolic order in which man can live out his fantasies and obsessions through linguistic command by imposing them on the silent image of woman still tied to her place as bearer, not maker, of meaning.

There is an obvious interest in this analysis for feminists, a beauty in its exact rendering of the frustration experienced under the phallocentric order. It gets us nearer to the roots of our oppression, it brings closer an articulation of the problem, it faces us with the ultimate challenge: how to fight the unconscious structured like a language (formed critically at the moment of arrival of language) while still caught within the language of the patriarchy? There is no way in which we can produce an alternative out of the blue, but we can begin to make a break by examining patriarchy with the tools it provides, of which psychoanalysis is not the only but an important one. We are still separated by a great gap from important issues for the female unconscious which are scarcely relevant to phallocentric theory: the sexing of the female infant and her relationship to the symbolic, the sexually mature woman as non-mother, maternity outside the signification of the phallus, the vagina. But, at this point, psychoanalytic theory as it now stands can at least advance our understanding of the status quo, of the patriarchal order in which we are caught.

(b) Destruction of Pleasure as a Radical Weapon

As an advanced representation system, the cinema poses questions about the ways the unconscious (formed by the dominant order) structures ways of seeing and pleasure in looking. Cinema has changed over the last few decades. It is no longer the monolithic system based on large capital investment exemplified at its best by Hollywood in the 1930s, 1940s and 1950s. Technological advances (16mm and so on) have changed the economic conditions of cinematic production, which can now be artisanal as well as capitalist.[3] Thus it has been possible for an alternative cinema to develop. However self-conscious and ironic Hollywood managed to be, it always restricted itself to a formal *mise en scène*[4] reflecting the dominant ideological concept of the cinema. The alternative cinema provides a space for the birth of a cinema which is radical in both a political and an aesthetic sense and challenges the basic assumptions of the mainstream film. This is not to reject the latter moralistically, but to highlight the ways in which its formal preoccupations reflect the psychical obsessions of the society which produced it and, further, to stress that the alternative cinema must start specifically by reacting against these obsessions and assumptions. A politically and aesthetically avant-garde cinema is now possible, but it can still only exist as a counterpoint.

The magic of the Hollywood style at its best (and of all the cinema which fell within its sphere of influence) arose, not exclusively, but in one important aspect, from its skilled and satisfying manipulation of visual pleasure. Unchallenged, mainstream film coded the erotic into the language of the dominant patriarchal order. In the highly developed Hollywood cinema it was only through these codes that the alienated subject, torn in his imaginary memory by a sense of loss, by the terror of potential lack in fantasy, came near to finding a glimpse of satisfaction: through its formal beauty and its play on his own formative obsessions. This article will discuss the interweaving of that erotic pleasure in film, its meaning and, in particular, the central place of the image of woman. It is said that analysing pleasure, or beauty, destroys it. That is the intention of this

[2]Freud's famous phrase is "Anatomy is destiny."

[3]The 35mm film used by Hollywood was too expensive to permit very extensive use by those outside the studios; the advent of 16mm film in the 1960s allowed an alternative cinema to develop and proliferate.

[4]Staging.

article. The satisfaction and reinforcement of the ego that represent the high point of film history hitherto must be attacked. Not in favour of a reconstructed new pleasure, which cannot exist in the abstract, nor of intellectualised unpleasure, but to make way for a total negation of the ease and plenitude of the narrative fiction film. The alternative is the thrill that comes from leaving the past behind without simply rejecting it, transcending outworn or oppressive forms, and daring to break with normal pleasurable expectations in order to conceive a new language of desire.

II. PLEASURE IN LOOKING/ FASCINATION WITH THE HUMAN FORM

A. The cinema offers a number of possible pleasures. One is scopophilia (pleasure in looking). There are circumstances in which looking itself is a source of pleasure, just as, in the reverse formation, there is pleasure in being looked at. Originally, in his *Three Essays on Sexuality,*[5] Freud isolated scopophilia as one of the component instincts of sexuality which exist as drives quite independently of the erotogenic zones. At this point he associated scopophilia with taking other people as objects, subjecting them to a controlling and curious gaze. His particular examples centre on the voyeuristic activities of children, their desire to see and make sure of the private and forbidden (curiosity about other people's genital and bodily functions, about the presence or absence of the penis and, retrospectively, about the primal scene). In this analysis scopophilia is essentially active. (Later, in "Instincts and Their Vicissitudes," Freud developed his theory of scopophilia further, attaching it initially to pregenital auto-eroticism, after which, by analogy, the pleasure of the look is transferred to others. There is a close working here of the relationship between the active instinct and its further development in a narcissistic form.) Although the instinct is modified by other factors, in particular the constitution of the ego, it continues to exist as the erotic basis for pleasure in looking at another person as object. At the extreme, it can become fixated

[5]Sigmund Freud published *Three Essays on the Theory of Sexuality* in 1905, "Instincts and Their Vicissitudes" in 1915.

into a perversion, producing obsessive voyeurs and Peeping Toms whose only sexual satisfaction can come from watching, in an active controlling sense, an objectified other.

At first glance, the cinema would seem to be remote from the undercover world of the surreptitious observation of an unknowing and unwilling victim. What is seen on the screen is so manifestly shown. But the mass of mainstream film, and the conventions within which it has consciously evolved, portray a hermetically sealed world which unwinds magically, indifferent to the presence of the audience, producing for them a sense of separation and playing on their voyeuristic fantasy. Moreover the extreme contrast between the darkness in the auditorium (which also isolates the spectators from one another) and the brilliance of the shifting patterns of light and shade on the screen helps to promote the illusion of voyeuristic separation. Although the film is really being shown, is there to be seen, conditions of screening and narrative conventions give the spectator an illusion of looking in on a private world. Among other things, the position of the spectators in the cinema is blatantly one of repression of their exhibitionism and projection of the repressed desire onto the performer.

B. The cinema satisfies a primordial wish for pleasurable looking, but it also goes further, developing scopophilia in its narcissistic aspect. The conventions of mainstream film focus attention on the human form. Scale, space, stories are all anthropomorphic. Here, curiosity and the wish to look intermingle with a fascination with likeness and recognition: the human face, the human body, the relationship between the human form and its surroundings, the visible presence of the person in the world. Jacques Lacan has described how the moment when a child recognises its own image in the mirror is crucial for the constitution of the ego. Several aspects of this analysis are relevant here. The mirror phase occurs at a time when children's physical ambitions outstrip their motor capacity, with the result that their recognition of themselves is joyous in that they imagine their mirror image to be more complete, more perfect than they experience in their own body. Recognition is thus overlaid with misrecognition: the image recognised is conceived as the reflected body of the self, but its misrecognition as superior projects this body outside itself as an ideal ego, the alienated subject which, reintrojected as an ego ideal, prepares the way for identification with others in the future. This mirror moment predates language for the child.[6]

Important for this article is the fact that it is an image that constitutes the matrix of the imaginary, of recognition/misrecognition and identification, and hence of the first articulation of the I, of subjectivity. This is a moment when an older fascination with looking (at the mother's face, for an obvious example) collides with the initial inklings of self-awareness. Hence it is the birth of the long love affair/despair between image and self-image which has found such intensity of expression in film and such joyous recognition in the cinema audience. Quite apart from the extraneous similarities between screen and mirror (the framing of the human form in its surroundings, for instance), the cinema has structures of fascination strong enough to allow temporary loss of ego while simultaneously reinforcing it. The sense of forgetting the world as the ego has come to perceive it (I forgot who I am and where I was) is nostalgically reminiscent of that pre-subjective moment of image recognition. While at the same time, the cinema has distinguished itself in the production of ego ideals, through the star system where they act out a complex process of likeness and difference (the glamorous impersonates the ordinary).

C. Sections A and B have set out two contradictory aspects of the pleasurable structures of looking in the conventional cinematic situation. The first, scopophilic, arises from pleasure in using another person as an object of sexual stimulation through sight. The second, developed through narcissism and the constitution of the ego, comes from identification with the image seen. Thus, in film terms, one implies a separation of the erotic identity of the subject from the object on the screen (active scopophilia), the

other demands identification of the ego with the object on the screen through the spectator's fascination with and recognition of his like. The first is a function of the sexual instincts, the second of ego libido. This dichotomy was crucial for Freud. Although he saw the two as interacting and overlaying each other, the tension between instinctual drives and self-preservation polarises in terms of pleasure. But both are formative structures, mechanisms without intrinsic meaning. In themselves they have no signification, unless attached to an idealisation. Both pursue aims in indifference to perceptual reality, and motivate eroticised phantasmagoria that affect the subject's perception of the world to make a mockery of empirical objectivity.

During its history, the cinema seems to have evolved a particular illusion of reality in which this contradiction between libido and ego has found a beautifully complementary fantasy world. In *reality* the fantasy world of the screen is subject to the law which produces it. Sexual instincts and identification processes have a meaning within the symbolic order which articulates desire. Desire, born with language, allows the possibility of transcending the instinctual and the imaginary, but its point of reference continually returns to the traumatic moment of its birth: the castration complex. Hence the look, pleasurable in form, can be threatening in content, and it is woman as representation/image that crystallises this paradox.

III. WOMAN AS IMAGE, MAN AS BEARER OF THE LOOK

A. In a world ordered by sexual imbalance, pleasure in looking has been split between active/passive and male/female. The determining male gaze projects its fantasy onto the female figure, which is styled accordingly. In their traditional exhibitionist role women are simultaneously looked at and displayed, with their appearance coded for strong visual and erotic impact so that they can be said to connote *to-be-looked-at-ness*. Woman displayed as sexual object is the *leitmotif* of erotic spectacle: from pin-ups to strip-tease,

[6]See Jacques Lacan, "The Mirror Stage as Formative of the Function of the I as Revealed in Psychoanalytic Experience," p. 643.

[7]Recurring theme.

from Ziegfeld to Busby Berkeley,[8] she holds the look, and plays to and signifies male desire. Mainstream film neatly combines spectacle and narrative. (Note, however, how, in the musical, song-and-dance numbers interrupt the flow of the diegesis.[9]) The presence of woman is an indispensable element of spectacle in normal narrative film, yet her visual presence tends to work against the development of a story-line, to freeze the flow of action in moments of erotic contemplation. This alien presence then has to be integrated into cohesion with the narrative. As Budd Boetticher has put it:

> What counts is what the heroine provokes, or rather what she represents. She is the one, or rather the love or fear she inspires in the hero, or else the concern he feels for her, who makes him act the way he does. In herself the woman has not the slightest importance.

(A recent tendency in narrative film has been to dispense with this problem altogether; hence the development of what Molly Haskell has called the "buddy movie," in which the active homosexual eroticism of the central male figures can carry the story without distraction.) Traditionally, the woman displayed has functioned on two levels: as erotic object for the characters within the screen story, and as erotic object for the spectator within the auditorium, with a shifting tension between the looks on either side of the screen. For instance, the device of the show-girl allows the two looks to be unified technically without any apparent break in the diegesis. A woman performs within the narrative; the gaze of the spectator and that of the male characters in the film are neatly combined without breaking narrative verisimilitude. For a moment the sexual impact of the performing woman takes the film into a no man's land outside its own time and space. Thus Marilyn Monroe's first appearance in *The*

River of No Return and Lauren Bacall's songs in *To Have and Have Not.* Similarly, conventional close-ups of legs (Dietrich, for instance) or a face (Garbo) integrate into the narrative a different mode of eroticism. One part of a fragmented body destroys the Renaissance space, the illusion of depth demanded by the narrative; it gives flatness, the quality of a cut-out or icon, rather than verisimilitude, to the screen.

B. An active/passive heterosexual division of labour has similarly controlled narrative structure. According to the principles of the ruling ideology and the psychical structures that back it up, the male figure cannot bear the burden of sexual objectification. Man is reluctant to gaze at his exhibitionist like. Hence the split between spectacle and narrative supports the man's role as the active one of advancing the story, making things happen. The man controls the film fantasy and also emerges as the representative of power in a further sense: as the bearer of the look of the spectator, transferring it behind the screen to neutralise the extradiegetic tendencies represented by woman as spectacle. This is made possible through the processes set in motion by structuring the film around a main controlling figure with whom the spectator can identify. As the spectator identifies with the main male protagonist, he projects his look onto that of his like, his screen surrogate, so that the power of the male protagonist as he controls events coincides with the active power of the erotic look, both giving a satisfying sense of omnipotence. A male movie star's glamorous characteristics are thus not those of the erotic object of the gaze, but those of the more perfect, more complete, more powerful ideal ego conceived in the original moment of recognition in front of the mirror. The character in the story can make things happen and control events better than the subjects/spectator, just as the image in the mirror was more in control of motor co-ordination.

In contrast to woman as icon, the active male figure (the ego ideal of the identification process) demands a three-dimensional space corresponding to that of the mirror recognition, in which the alienated subject internalised his own representation of his imaginary existence. He is a figure in a landscape. Here the function of film is to

[8]Florenz Ziegfeld (1867–1932) was the producer, from 1907, of the *Ziegfeld Follies,* an annual musical revue staged in New York, featuring beautiful, often scantily clad, chorus girls. Busby Berkeley (1895–1976) was the director and choreographer of numerous films, beginning with *42nd Street* (1933); he created geometrically elaborate dance numbers featuring hundreds of nearly identical starlets.

[9]The act of telling a story (as opposed to the story that is told).

reproduce as accurately as possible the so-called natural conditions of human perception. Camera technology (as exemplified by deep focus in particular) and camera movements (determined by the action of the protagonist), combined with invisible editing (demanded by realism), all tend to blur the limits of screen space. The male protagonist is free to command the stage, a stage of spatial illusion in which he articulates the look and creates the action. (There are films with a woman as main protagonist, of course. To analyse this phenomenon seriously here would take me too far afield. Pam Cook and Claire Johnston's study of *The Revolt of Mamie Stover* in Phil Hardy [ed.], *Raoul Walsh* [Edinburgh, 1974], shows in a striking case how the strength of this female protagonist is more apparent than real.)

C1. Sections III A and B have set out a tension between a mode of representation of woman in film and conventions surrounding the diegesis. Each is associated with a look: that of the spectator in direct scopophilic contact with the female form displayed for his enjoyment (connoting male fantasy) and that of the spectator fascinated with the image of his like set in an illusion of natural space, and through him gaining control and possession of the woman within the diegesis. (This tension and the shift from one pole to the other can structure a single text. Thus both in *Only Angels Have Wings* and in *To Have and Have Not*, the film opens with the woman as object of the combined gaze of spectator and all the male protagonists in the film. She is isolated, glamorous, on display, sexualised. But as the narrative progresses she falls in love with the main male protagonist and becomes his property, losing her outward glamorous characteristics, her generalised sexuality, her show-girl connotations; her eroticism is subjected to the male star alone. By means of identification with him, through participation in his power, the spectator can indirectly possess her too.)

But in psychoanalytic terms, the female figure poses a deeper problem. She also connotes something that the look continually circles around but disavows: her lack of a penis, implying a threat of castration and hence unpleasure. Ultimately, the meaning of woman is sexual difference, the visually ascertainable absence

of the penis, the material evidence on which is based the castration complex essential for the organisation of entrance to the symbolic order and the law of the father. Thus the woman as icon, displayed for the gaze and enjoyment of men, the active controllers of the look, always threatens to evoke the anxiety it originally signified. The male unconscious has two avenues of escape from this castration anxiety: preoccupation with the re-enactment of the original trauma (investigating the woman, demystifying her mystery), counterbalanced by the devaluation, punishment or saving of the guilty object (an avenue typified by the concerns of the *film noir*[10]); or else complete disavowal of castration by the substitution of a fetish object or turning the represented figure itself into a fetish so that it becomes reassuring rather than dangerous (hence overvaluation, the cult of the female star).

This second avenue, fetishistic scopophilia, builds up the physical beauty of the object, transforming it into something satisfying in itself. The first avenue, voyeurism, on the contrary, has associations with sadism: pleasure lies in ascertaining guilt (immediately associated with castration), asserting control and subjugating the guilty person through punishment or forgiveness. This sadistic side fits in well with narrative. Sadism demands a story, depends on making something happen, forcing a change in another person, a battle of will and strength, victory/defeat, all occurring in a linear time with a beginning and an end. Fetishistic scopophilia, on the other hand, can exist outside linear time as the erotic instinct is focused on the look alone. These contradictions and ambiguities can be illustrated more simply by using works by Hitchcock and Sternberg, both of whom take the look almost as the content or subject matter of many of their films. Hitchcock is the more complex, as he uses both mechanisms. Sternberg's work, on the other hand, provides many pure examples of fetishistic scopophilia.

[10]The term *film noir*, literally "black cinema," refers to genre movies of the 1940s and early 1950s portraying the underside of a corrupt society with seductive female villains and cynical heroes. Well-known examples include Michael Curtiz's *Casablanca*, Howard Hawks's *The Big Sleep*, and Billy Wilder's *Sunset Boulevard*.

C2. Sternberg once said he would welcome his films being projected upside-down so that the story and character involvement would not interfere with the spectator's undiluted appreciation of the screen image. This statement is revealing but ingenuous: ingenuous in that his films do demand that the figure of the woman (Dietrich, in the cycle of films with her, as the ultimate example) should be identifiable; but revealing in that it emphasises the fact that for him the pictorial space enclosed by the frame is paramount, rather than narrative or identification processes. While Hitchcock goes into the investigative side of voyeurism, Sternberg produces the ultimate fetish, taking it to the point where the powerful look of the male protagonist (characteristic of traditional narrative film) is broken in favour of the image in direct erotic rapport with the spectator. The beauty of the woman as object and the screen space coalesce; she is no longer the bearer of guilt but a perfect product, whose body, stylised and fragmented by close-ups, is the content of the film and the direct recipient of the spectator's look.

Sternberg plays down the illusion of screen depth; his screen tends to be one-dimensional, as light and shade, lace, steam, foliage, net, streamers and so on reduce the visual field. There is little or no mediation of the look through the eyes of the main male protagonist. On the contrary, shadowy presences like La Bessière in *Morocco* act as surrogates for the director, detached as they are from audience identification. Despite Sternberg's insistence that his stories are irrelevant, it is significant that they are concerned with situation, not suspense, and cyclical rather than linear time, while plot complications revolve around misunderstanding rather than conflict. The most important absence is that of the controlling male gaze within the screen scene. The high point of emotional drama in the most typical Dietrich films, her supreme moments of erotic meaning, take place in the absence of the man she loves in the fiction. There are other witnesses, other spectators watching her on the screen, their gaze is one with, not standing in for, that of the audience. At the end of *Morocco*, Tom Brown has already disappeared into the desert when Amy Jolly kicks off her gold sandals and walks after him. At the end of *Dishonoured,* Kranau is indifferent to the fate of Magda. In both cases, the erotic impact, sanctified by death, is displayed as a spectacle for the audience. The male hero misunderstands and, above all, does not see.

In Hitchcock, by contrast, the male hero does see precisely what the audience sees. However, although fascination with an image through scopophilic eroticism can be the subject of the film, it is the role of the hero to portray the contradictions and tensions experienced by the spectator. In *Vertigo* in particular, but also in *Marnie* and *Rear Window,* the look is central to the plot, oscillating between voyeurism and fetishistic fascination. Hitchcock has never concealed his interest in voyeurism, cinematic and non-cinematic. His heroes are exemplary of the symbolic order and the law — a policeman *(Vertigo),* a dominant male possessing money and power *(Marnie)* — but their erotic drives lead them into compromised situations. The power to subject another person to the will sadistically or to the gaze voyeuristically is turned onto the woman as the object of both. Power is backed by a certainty of legal right and the established guilt of the woman (evoking castration, psychoanalytically speaking). True perversion is barely concealed under a shallow mask of ideological correctness — the man is on the right side of the law, the woman on the wrong. Hitchcock's skilful use of identification processes and liberal use of subjective camera from the point of view of the male protagonist draw the spectators deeply into his position, making them share his uneasy gaze. The spectator is absorbed into a voyeuristic situation within the screen scene and diegesis, which parodies his own in the cinema.

In an analysis of *Rear Window,* Douchet takes the film as a metaphor for the cinema. Jeffries is the audience, the events in the apartment block opposite correspond to the screen. As he watches, an erotic dimension is added to his look, a central image to the drama. His girlfriend Lisa had been of little sexual interest to him, more or less a drag, so long as she remained on the spectator side. When she crosses the barrier between his room and the block opposite, their relationship is reborn erotically. He does not merely watch her through his lens, as a distant meaningful image, he also sees her as a guilty intruder exposed by a dangerous man threatening her with punishment, and thus finally giving him the opportunity to save her. Lisa's exhibitionism has already been established by her obsessive interest in dress and style, in being a passive image of visual perfection; Jeffries's voyeurism and activity have also been established through his work as a photo-journalist, a maker of stories and captor of images. However, his enforced inactivity,[11] binding him to his seat as a spectator, puts him squarely in the fantasy position of the cinema audience.

In *Vertigo*, subjective camera predominates. Apart from one flashback from Judy's point of view, the narrative is woven around what Scottie sees or fails to see. The audience follows the growth of his erotic obsession and subsequent despair precisely from his point of view. Scottie's voyeurism is blatant: he falls in love with a woman he follows and spies on without speaking to. Its sadistic side is equally blatant: he has chosen (and freely chosen, for he had been a successful lawyer[12]) to be a policeman, with all the attendant possibilities of pursuit and investigation. As a result, he follows, watches and falls in love with a perfect image of female beauty and mystery. Once he actually confronts her, his erotic drive is to break her down and force her to *tell* by persistent cross-questioning.

In the second part of the film, he re-enacts his obsessive involvement with the image he loved to watch secretly. He reconstructs Judy as Madeleine, forces her to conform in every detail to the actual physical appearance of his fetish. Her exhibitionism, her masochism, make her an ideal passive counterpart to Scottie's active sadistic voyeurism. She knows her part is to perform, and only by playing it through and then replaying it can she keep Scottie's erotic interest. But in the repetition he does break her down and succeeds in exposing her guilt. His curiosity wins through; she is punished.

[11] The hero of *Rear Window* is housebound with a broken leg as the story begins.

[12] Mulvey may be thinking about Flavières, the protagonist of the novel (*D'entre les morts*, by Boileau and Narcejac) on which *Vertigo* was based, who was a lawyer before he became a detective; there's no indication of that in the screenplay of Hitchcock's *Vertigo*.

Thus, in *Vertigo*, erotic involvement with the look boomerangs: the spectator's own fascination is revealed as illicit voyeurism as the narrative content enacts the processes and pleasures that he is himself exercising and enjoying. The Hitchcock hero here is firmly placed within the symbolic order, in narrative terms. He has all the attributes of the patriarchal superego. Hence the spectator, lulled into a false sense of security by the apparent legality of his surrogate, sees through his look and finds himself exposed as complicit, caught in the moral ambiguity of looking. Far from being simply an aside on the perversion of the police, *Vertigo* focuses on the implications of the active/looking, passive/looked-at split in terms of sexual difference and the power of the male symbolic encapsulated in the hero. *Marnie*, too, performs for Mark Rutland's gaze and masquerades as the perfect to-be-looked-at image. He, too, is on the side of the law until, drawn in by obsession with her guilt, her secret, he longs to see her in the act of committing a crime, make her confess and thus save her. So he, too, becomes complicit as he acts out the implications of his power. He controls money and words; he can have his cake and eat it.

IV. SUMMARY

The psychoanalytic background that has been discussed in this article is relevant to the pleasure and unpleasure offered by traditional narrative film. The scopophilic instinct (pleasure in looking at another person as an erotic object) and, in contradistinction, ego libido (forming identification processes) act as formations, mechanisms, which mould this cinema's formal attributes. The actual image of woman as (passive) raw material for the (active) gaze of man takes the argument a step further into the content and structure of representation, adding a further layer of ideological significance demanded by the patriarchal order in its favourite cinematic form — illusionistic narrative film. The argument must return again to the psychoanalytic background: women in representation can signify castration, and activate voyeuristic or fetishistic mechanisms to circumvent this threat. Although none of these interacting layers is intrinsic to film, it is only in the film form that they can reach a perfect and beautiful contradiction, thanks to the possibility in the cinema of shifting the emphasis of the look. The place of the look defines cinema, the possibility of varying it and exposing it. This is what makes cinema quite different in its voyeuristic potential from, say, strip-tease, theatre, shows and so on. Going far beyond highlighting a woman's to-be-looked-at-ness, cinema builds the way she is to be looked at into the spectacle itself. Playing on the tension between film as controlling the dimension of time (editing, narrative) and film as controlling the dimension of space (changes in distance, editing), cinematic codes create a gaze, a world and an object, thereby producing an illusion cut to the measure of desire. It is these cinematic codes and their relationship to formative external structures that must be broken down before mainstream film and the pleasure it provides can be challenged.

To begin with (as an ending), the voyeuristic — scopophilic look that is a crucial part of traditional filmic pleasure can itself be broken down. There are three different looks associated with cinema: that of the camera as it records the pro-filmic event, that of the audience as it watches the final product, and that of the characters at each other within the screen illusion. The conventions of narrative film deny the first two and subordinate them to the third, the conscious aim being always to eliminate intrusive camera presence and prevent a distancing awareness in the audience. Without these two absences (the material existence of the recording process, the critical reading of the spectator), fictional drama cannot achieve reality, obviousness and truth. Nevertheless, as this article has argued, the structure of looking in narrative fiction film contains a contradiction in its own premises: the female image as a castration threat constantly endangers the unity of the diegesis and bursts through the world of illusion as an intrusive, static, one-dimensional fetish. Thus the two looks materially present in time and space are obsessively subordinated to the neurotic needs of the male ego. The camera becomes the mechanism for producing an illusion of Renaissance space, flowing movements compatible with the human eye, an ideology of representation that revolves around the perception of the subject; the camera's look is disavowed in order to create a convincing world in which the spectator's surrogate can perform with verisimilitude. Simultaneously, the look of the audience is denied an intrinsic force: as soon as fetishistic representation of the female image threatens to break the spell of illusion, and the erotic image on the screen appears directly (without mediation) to the spectator, the fact of fetishisation, concealing as it does castration fear, freezes the look, fixates the spectator and prevents him from achieving any distance from the image in front of him.

This complex interaction of looks is specific to film. The first blow against the monolithic accumulation of traditional film conventions (already undertaken by radical film-makers) is to free the look of the camera into its materiality in time and space and the look of the audience into dialectics and passionate detachment. There is no doubt that this destroys the satisfaction, pleasure and privilege of the "invisible guest," and highlights the way film has depended on voyeuristic active/passive mechanisms. Women, whose image has continually been stolen and used for this end, cannot view the decline of the traditional film form with anything much more than sentimental regret.

Slavoj Žižek
b. 1949

Slavoj Žižek was born in Ljubljana, Slovenia, where he has remained to this day, aside from having lectured at dozens of universities around the world. He received his B.A., M.A., and D.A. in philosophy at the University of Ljubljana, where he is currently a professor. He also received a D.A. in psychoanalysis at the Université Paris-VIII in 1985. Žižek was analyzed by Jacques-Alain Miller, Jacques Lacan's son-in-law, and is deeply invested in a post-Lacanian view of politics and popular culture, but is also influenced by Schelling and Hegel. Žižek analyzes the various metaphors of contemporary culture, representing everything from gender and religion to film and popular music, in order to extrapolate conclusions about the nature of symbols themselves as representations of the impossible, which he sees as fundamental to desire. Žižek's political interests are more than just scholarly; he ran for president of the Republic of Slovenia in 1990 in the nation's first multiparty election. Žižek is known for the mischievous nature of his scholarship, which includes a highly polemical proposal to re-actualize Leninist communism, in "Repeating Lenin" (1997), and the text for an Abercrombie & Fitch catalog, a commercial periodical known for its transgressive, idealized representations of teenage sexuality. His first book, The Sublime Object of Ideology (1989), has been followed by too many to list here. They include Looking Awry: An Introduction to Jacques Lacan through Popular Culture (1991), Enjoy Your Symptom! Jacques Lacan in Hollywood and Out (1992), Everything You Always Wanted to Know about Lacan (But Were Afraid to Ask Hitchcock) (1992), The Ticklish Subject: The Absent Centre of Political Ontology (1999), The Fragile Absolute: Or Why the Christian Legacy Is Worth Fighting For (2000), Did Someone Say Totalitarianism?: Four Interventions in the Misuse of a Notion (2001), Organs without Bodies (2003), The Puppet and the Dwarf (2003), Iraq: The Borrowed Kettle (2004), First as History, Then as Farce (2009), Living in the End Times (2011), and, most recently, Event: A Philosophical Journey Through a Concept (2014). This essay, "Courtly Love, or, Woman as Thing," was originally printed in The Metastases of Enjoyment: Six Essays on Woman and Causality (1994).

Courtly Love; or, Woman as Thing

Why talk about courtly love [*l'amour courtois*] today, in an age of permissiveness when the sexual encounter is often nothing more than a "quickie" in some dark corner of an office? The impression that courtly love is out of date, long superseded by modern manners, is a lure blinding us as to how the logic of courtly love still defines the parameters within which the two sexes relate to each other. This claim, however, in no way implies an evolutionary model

through which courtly love would provide the elementary matrix out of which we generate its later, more complex variations. Our thesis is, instead, that history has to be read retroactively: the anatomy of man offers the key to the anatomy of the ape, as Marx put it. It is only with the emergence of masochism, of the masochist couple, towards the end of the last century that we can now grasp the libidinal economy of courtly love.

THE MASOCHISTIC THEATER OF COURTLY LOVE

The first trap to be avoided apropos of courtly love is the erroneous notion of the Lady as the sublime object[1]: as a rule, one evokes here the process of spiritualization, the shift from raw sensual coveting to elevated spiritual longing. The Lady is thus perceived as a kind of spiritual guide into the higher sphere of religious ecstasy, in the sense of Dante's Beatrice.[2] In contrast to this notion, Lacan emphasizes a series of features which belie such a spiritualization: true, the Lady in courtly love loses concrete features and is addressed as an abstract ideal, so that "writers have noted that all the poets seem to be addressing the same person. . . . In this poetic field the feminine object is emptied of all real substance."[3] However, this abstract character of the Lady has nothing to do with spiritual purification; rather, it points towards the abstraction that pertains to a cold, distanced, inhuman partner — the Lady is by no means a warm, compassionate, understanding fellow-creature:

> By means of a form of sublimation specific to art, poetic creation consists in positing an object I can only describe as terrifying, an inhuman partner.
>
> The Lady is never characterized for any of her real, concrete virtues, for her wisdom, her prudence, or even her competence. If she is described as wise it is only because she embodies an immaterial wisdom or because she represents its functions more than she exercises them. On the contrary, she is as arbitrary as possible in the tests she imposes on her servant.[4]

The knight's relationship to the Lady is thus the relationship of the subject-bondsman, vassal, to his feudal Master-Sovereign who subjects him to senseless, outrageous, impossible, arbitrary, capricious ordeals. It is precisely in order to emphasize the non-spiritual nature of these ordeals that Lacan quotes a poem about a Lady who demanded that her servant literally lick her arse: the poem consists of the poet's complaints about the bad smells that await him down there (one knows the sad state of personal hygiene in the Middle Ages), about the imminent danger that, as he is fulfilling his duty, the Lady will urinate on his head. . . . The Lady is thus as far as possible from any kind of purified spirituality: she functions as an inhuman partner in the sense of a radical Otherness which is wholly incommensurable with our needs and desires; as such, she is simultaneously a kind of automaton, a machine which utters meaningless demands at random.

This coincidence of absolute, inscrutable Otherness and pure machine is what confers on the Lady her uncanny, monstrous character — the Lady is the Other which is not our "fellow creature"; that is to say, she is someone with whom no relationship of empathy is possible. This traumatic Otherness is what Lacan designates by means of the Freudian term *das Ding*,[5] the Thing — the Real that "always returns to its place,"[6] the hard kernel that resists

---

[1]The aesthetics of the sublime are discussed in Longinus and in Kant; see pp. 86 and 165, respectively. Kant in particular is interested in the terror invested in the sublime object. Elsewhere, Žižek writes about Madeleine, the central female character in Hitchcock's *Vertigo*, as a "sublime object."

[2]Based on the real Beatrice Portinari, whom Dante Alighieri glimpsed in the streets of Florence as a boy of twelve, Beatrice is the saint who takes over from Virgil and guides the pilgrim Dante through Paradise.

[3]Jacques Lacan, *The Ethics of Psychoanalysis* (London: Routledge, 1992), p. 149. [Žižek]

[4]Ibid., p. 150; translation modified. [Žižek]

[5]Literally "the thing." Freud's term for the originary lost object against which all other losses are measured. Lacan elsewhere notes that there are two German words for "thing," *Ding* and *Sache*, and that Freud uses *Sache* for things that can be symbolized, reserving *Ding* for the missing object that can be neither imagined nor spoken of, which lives in Lacan's realm of the Real — for which see the introduction to Psychoanalytic Theory and Criticism, p. 627. See also Lacan's "The Freudian Thing" in *Ecrits: A Selection*, p. 114.

[6]Is not Lacan's definition of the Real as that which always returns to its place "pre-Einsteinian" and, as such, de-valorized by the relativization of space with regard to the observer's point of view — that is, by the cancellation of the notion of absolute space and time? However, the theory of relativity involves its own absolute constant; the space-time interval between two events is an absolute that never varies. Space–time interval is defined as the hypotenuse of a right-angled triangle whose legs are the time and space distance between the two events. One observer may be in a state of motion such that for him there is a time and a distance involved between the two events; another may be in a state of motion such that his measuring devices indicate a different distance and a different time between the events, but the space-time interval between them does not vary. *This* constant is the Lacanian Real that "remains the same in all possible universes." [Žižek]

symbolization. The idealization of the Lady, her elevation to a spiritual, ethereal Ideal, is therefore to be conceived of as a strictly secondary phenomenon: it is a narcissistic projection whose function is to render her traumatic dimension invisible. In this precise and limited sense, Lacan concedes that "the element of idealizing exaltation that is expressly sought out in the ideology of courtly love has certainly been demonstrated; it is fundamentally narcissistic in character."[7] Deprived of every real substance, the Lady functions as a mirror on to which the subject projects his narcissistic ideal. In other words — those of Christina Rossetti, whose sonnet "In an Artist's Studio" speaks of Dante Gabriel Rossetti's relationship to Elizabeth Siddal,[8] his Lady — the Lady appears "not as she is, but as she fills his dream."[9] For Lacan, however, the crucial accent lies elsewhere:

The mirror may on occasion imply the mechanisms of narcissism, and especially the dimension of destruction or aggression that we will encounter subsequently. But it also fulfills another role, a role as limit. It is that which cannot be crossed. And the only organization in which it participates is that of the inaccessibility of the object.[10]

Thus, before we embrace the commonplaces about how the Lady in courtly love has nothing to do with actual women, how she stands for

the man's narcissistic projection which involves the mortification of the flesh-and-blood woman, we have to answer this question: where does that empty surface come from, that cold, neutral screen which opens up the space for possible projections? That is to say, if men are to project on to the mirror their narcissistic ideal, the mute mirror-surface must already be there. This surface functions as a kind of "black hole" in reality, as a limit whose Beyond is inaccessible.

The next crucial feature of courtly love is that it is thoroughly a matter of courtesy and etiquette; it has nothing to do with some elementary passion overflowing all barriers, immune to all social rules. We are dealing with a strict fictional formula, with a social game of "as if," where a man pretends that his sweetheart is the inaccessible Lady. And it is precisely this feature which enables us to establish a link between courtly love and a phenomenon which, at first, seems to have nothing whatsoever to do with it: namely, masochism, as a specific form of perversion articulated for the first time in the middle of the last century in the literary works and life-practice of Sacher-Masoch.[11] In his celebrated study of masochism,[12] Gilles Deleuze demonstrates that masochism is not to be conceived of as a simple symmetrical inversion of sadism. The sadist and his victim never form a complementary "sado-masochist" couple. Among those features evoked by Deleuze to prove the asymmetry between sadism and masochism, the crucial one is the opposition of the modalities of negation. In sadism we encounter direct negation, violent destruction and tormenting, whereas in masochism negation assumes the form of disavowal — that is, of feigning, of an "as if," which suspends reality.

Closely depending on this first opposition is the opposition of institution and contract. Sadism follows the logic of institution, of institutional power tormenting its victim and taking pleasure in the victim's helpless resistance. More precisely, sadism is at work in the obscene.

[7]Lacan, The Ethics of Psychoanalysis, p. 151. [Žižek]

[8]Lizzie Siddal (1829–1862) was a model of working-class English origins who posed for most of the important pre-Raphaelite painters, including Millais and Holman Hunt, as well as Dante Gabriel Rossetti, who married her in 1860, and who painted her as Dante's Beatrice both before and after her death from an overdose of laudanum.

[9]It is clear, therefore, that it would be a fateful mistake to identify the Lady in courtly love, this unconditional Ideal of the Woman, with woman in so far as she is not submitted to phallic enjoyment: the opposition of everyday, "tamed" woman, with whom sexual relationship may appear possible, and the Lady qua "inhuman partner," has nothing whatsoever to do with the opposition of woman submitted to phallic signifier and woman qua bearer of the Other enjoyment. The Lady is the projection of man's narcissistic Ideal; her figure emerges as the result of the masochistic pact by way of which woman accepts the role of dominatrix in the theater staged by man. For that reason, Rossetti's Beata Beatrix, for example, is not to be perceived as the figuration of the Other enjoyment: as with Isolde's love death in Wagner's Tristan, we are dealing with man's fantasy. [Žižek]

[10]Lacan, The Ethics of Psychoanalysis, p. 151. [Žižek]

[11]Leopold von Sacher-Masoch (1836–1895), author of Venus in Furs (1869), a novel consisting of fantasies of domination. The eponym "masochism" was coined by Richard von Krafft-Ebing in Psychopathia Sexualis (1886).

[12]Gilles Deleuze, "Coldness and Cruelty," in Masochism (New York: Zone Press, 1991). [Žižek]

superego underside that necessarily redoubles and accompanies, as its shadow, the "public" law. Masochism, on the contrary, is made to the measure of the victim: it is the victim (the servant in the masochistic relationship) who initiates a contract with the Master (woman), authorizing her to humiliate him in any way she considers appropriate (within the terms defined by the contract) and binding himself to act "according to the whims of the sovereign Lady," as Sacher-Masoch put it. It is the servant, therefore, who writes the screenplay — that is, who actually pulls the strings and dictates the activity of the woman [*dominatrix*]: he stages his own servitude.[13] One further differential feature is that masochism, in contrast to sadism, is inherently theatrical: violence is for the most part feigned, and even when it is "real," it functions as a component of a scene, as a part of a theatrical performance. Furthermore, violence is never carried out, brought to its conclusion; it always remains suspended, as the endless repeating of an interrupted gesture.

It is precisely this logic of disavowal which enables us to grasp the fundamental paradox of the masochistic attitude. That is to say, how does the typical masochistic scene look? The man-servant establishes in a cold, businesslike way the terms of the contract of the woman-master: what she is to do to him, what scene is to be rehearsed endlessly, what dress she is to wear, how far she is to go in the direction of the real, physical torture (how severely she is to whip him, in what precise way she is to enchain him, where she is to stamp him with the tips of her high heels, etc.). When they finally pass over to the masochistic game proper, the masochist constantly maintains a kind of reflective distance; he never really gives way to his feelings or fully abandons himself to the game; in the midst of the game, he can suddenly assume the stance of a stage director, giving precise instructions (put more pressure on that point, repeat that movement . . .), *without thereby in the least "destroying the illusion."*

[13]For that reason lesbian sadomasochism is far more subversive than the usual "soft" lesbianism, which elevates tender relationships between women in contrast to aggressive-phallic male penetration: although the content of lesbian sadomasochism imitates "aggressive" phallic heterosexuality, this content is subverted by the very contractual form. [Žižek]

Once the game is over, the masochist again adopts the attitude of a respectful bourgeois and starts to talk with the Sovereign Lady in a matter-of-fact, businesslike way: "Thank you for your favor. Same time next week?" and so on. What is of crucial importance here is the total self-externalization of the masochist's most intimate passion: the most intimate desires become objects of contract and composed negotiation. The nature of the masochistic theater is therefore thoroughly "non-psychological": the surrealistic passionate masochistic game, which suspends social reality, none the less fits easily into that everyday reality.[14]

For this reason, the phenomenon of masochism exemplifies in its purest form what Lacan had in mind when he insisted again and again that psychoanalysis is not psychology. Masochism confronts us with the paradox of the symbolic order *qua* the order of "fictions": there is more truth in the mask we wear, in the game we play, in the "fiction" we obey and follow, than in what is concealed beneath the mask. The very kernel of the masochist's being is externalized in the staged game towards which he maintains his constant distance. And the Real of violence breaks out precisely when the masochist is hystericized — when the subject refuses the role of an object-instrument of the enjoyment of his Other, when he is horrified at the prospect of being reduced in the eyes of the Other to *objet a*;[15] in order to escape this deadlock, he resorts to *passage à l'acte*,[16] to the "irrational" violence aimed at the other. Towards the end of P. D. James's *A Taste for*

[14]Here the logic is the same as in the "non-psychological" universe of *Twin Peaks*, in which we encounter two main types of people: "normal," everyday people (based on soap-opera clichés) and "crazy" eccentrics (the lady with a log, etc); the uncanny quality of the *Twin Peaks* universe hinges on the fact that the relationship between these two groups follows the rules of "normal" communication: "normal" people are not at all amazed or outraged by the strange behavior of the eccentrics; they accept them as part of their daily routine. [Žižek]

[15]Also *objet petit a* where *a* stands for *autre* [other] to distinguish it from the capitalized Other/Autre. In Lacan's system, it may refer to any individual loved object, but is frequently used in a more limited sense, as a sexual fetish.

[16]In French law, the term denotes a stage, often involving psychological dissociation, between a criminal's departure from ordinary behavior and the violent act itself.

Death, the murderer describes the circumstances of the crime, and lets it be known that the factor which resolved his indecision and pushed him towards the act (the murder) was the attitude of the victim (Sir Paul Berowne):

> He wanted to die, God rot him, he wanted it! He practically asked for it. He could have tried to stop me, pleaded, argued, put up a fight. He could have begged for mercy, "No, please don't do it, Please!" That's all I wanted from him. Just that one word. . . . He looked at me with such contempt. . . . He knew then. Of course he knew. And I wouldn't have done it, not if he'd spoken to me as if I were even half-human.[17]
>
> He didn't even look surprised. He was supposed to be terrified. He was supposed to prevent it from happening. . . . He just looked at me as if he were saying "So it's you. How strange it has to be you." As if I had no choice. Just an instrument. Mindless. But I did have a choice. And so did he, Christ, he could have stopped me. Why didn't he stop me?[18]

Several days before his death, Sir Paul Berowne experienced an "inner breakdown" resembling symbolic death: he stepped down as a government Minister and cut all his principal "human ties," assuming thereby the "excremental" position of a saint, of *objet petit a*, which precludes any intersubjective relationship of empathy. This attitude was what the murderer found unbearable: he approached his victim as $, a split subject — that is to say, he wanted to kill him, yet he was simultaneously waiting for a sign of fear, of resistance, from the victim, a sign which would prevent the murderer from accomplishing the act. The victim, however, did not give any such sign, which would have subjectivized the murderer, acknowledging him as a (divided) subject, Sir Paul's attitude of non-resistance, of indifferent provocation, objectivized the murderer, reducing him to an instrument of the Other's will, and so left him with no choice. In short, what compelled the murderer to act was the experience of having his desire to kill the victim coincide with the victim's death drive. This coincidence recalls the way a male hysterical "sadist" justifies his beating of a woman:

> "Why does she make me do it? She really wants me to hurt her, she compels me to beat her so that she can enjoy it — *so I'll beat her black and blue and teach her what it really means to provoke me?* What we encounter here is a kind of loop in which the (mis)perceived effect of the brutal act upon the victim retroactively legitimizes the act: I set out to beat a woman and when, at the very point where I think that I thoroughly dominate her, I notice that I am actually her slave — since she wants the beating and provoked me to deliver it — I get really mad and beat her. . . .[19]

THE COURTLY "IMP OF THE PERVERSE"

How, on closer examination, are we to conceptualize the inaccessibility of the Lady-Object in courtly love? The principal mistake to avoid is reducing this inaccessibility to the simple dialectic of desire and prohibition according to which we covet the forbidden fruit precisely in so far

17P. D. James, *A Taste for Death* (London and Boston, MA: Faber & Faber 1986) p. 439. [Žižek]

18Ibid., p. 440. [Žižek]

19An exemplary case of the inverse constellation — of the gaze *qua objet a* hystericizing the other — is provided by Robert Montgomery's *Lady in the Lake*, a film whose interest consists in its very failure. The point of view of the hard-boiled detective to which we are confined via a continuous subjective camera in no way arouses in us, the spectators, the impression that we are actually watching the events through the eyes of the person shown by the camera in the prologue or the epilogue (the only "objective" shots" in the film) or when it confronts a mirror. Even Marlowe "sees" himself in the mirror," the spectator does not accept that the face he sees, the eyes on it, is the point of view of the camera. When the camera drags on in its clumsy, slow way it seems, rather, that the point of view is that of a living dead from Romero's *Night of the Living Dead* (the same association is further encouraged by the Christmas choral music, very unusual for a *film noir*). More precisely, it is as if the camera is positioned next to or closely behind Marlowe and somehow looks over his back, imitating the virtual gaze of his shadow, of his "undead" sublime double. There is no double to be seen next to Marlowe, since this double, what is in Marlowe "more than himself," is the gaze itself as the Lacanian *objet petit a* that does not have a specular image. (The voice that runs a commentary on the story belongs to this gaze, not to Marlowe *qua* diegetic person.) This object-gaze is the cause of the desire of women who, all the time, turn towards it (i.e. look into the camera): it lays them bare in an obscene way — or, in other words, it hystericizes them by simultaneously attracting and repelling them. It is on account of this objectivization of the gaze that *The Lady in the Lake* is not a *film noir*: the essential feature of a *film noir* proper is that the point of view of the narration is that of a subject. [Žižek]

as it is forbidden — or, to quote Freud's classic formulation:

> . . . the psychical value of erotic needs is reduced as soon as their satisfaction becomes easy. An obstacle is required in order to heighten libido; and where natural resistances to satisfaction have not been sufficient men have at all times erected conventional ones so as to be able to enjoy love.[20]

Within this perspective, courtly love appears as simply the most radical strategy for elevating the value of the object by putting up conventional obstacles to its attainability. When, in his seminar *Encore*, Lacan provides the most succinct formulation of the paradox of courtly love, he says something that is apparently similar, yet fundamentally different: "A very refined manner to supplant the absence of the sexual relationship is by feigning that it is us who put the obstacle in its way."[21] The point, therefore, is not simply that we set up additional conventional hindrances in order to heighten the value of the object: *external hindrances that thwart our access to the object are there precisely to create the illusion that without them, the object would be directly accessible* — what such hindrances thereby conceal is the inherent impossibility of attaining the object. The place of the Lady-Thing is originally empty: she functions as a kind of "black hole" around which the subject's desire is structured. The space of desire is bent like space in the theory of relativity; the only way to reach the Object-Lady is indirectly, in a devious, meandering way — proceeding straight on ensures that we miss the target. This is what Lacan has in mind when, apropos of courtly love, he evokes "the meaning we must attribute to the negotiation of the detour in the psychic economy":

> The detour in the psyche isn't always designed to regulate the commerce between whatever is organized in the domain of the pleasure principle and whatever presents itself as the structure of reality. There are also detours and obstacles which are organized so as to make the domain of the vacuole stand out as such. . . . The techniques involved in courtly love — and they are precise enough to allow us to perceive what might on occasion become fact, what is properly speaking of the sexual order in the inspiration of this eroticism — are techniques of holding back, of suspension, of *amor interruptus*. The stages courtly love lays down previous to what is mysteriously referred to as *le don de merci*, "the gift of mercy" — although we don't know exactly what it meant — are expressed more or less in terms that Freud uses in his *Three Essays* as belonging to the sphere of foreplay.[22]

For that reason, Lacan accentuates the motif of anamorphosis[23] (in his Seminar on the Ethics of Psychoanalysis, the title of the chapter on courtly love is "Courtly Love as Anamorphosis"): the Object can be perceived only when it is viewed from the side, in a partial, distorted form, as its own shadow — if we cast a direct glance at it we see nothing, a mere void. In a homologous way, we could speak of temporal anamorphosis: the Object is attainable only by way of an incessant postponement, as its absent point of reference. The Object, therefore, is literally something that is created — whose place is encircled — through a network of detours, approximations and nearmisses. It is here that *sublimation* sets in — sublimation in the lacanian sense of the elevation of an object into the dignity of the Thing: "sublimation" occurs when an object, part of everyday reality, finds itself at the place of the impossible Thing. Herein resides the function of those artificial obstacles that suddenly hinder our access to some ordinary object: they elevate the object into a stand-in for the Thing. This is how the impossible changes into the prohibited: by way of the short circuit between the Thing and some positive object rendered inaccessible through artificial obstacles.

The tradition of Lady as the inaccessible object is alive and well in our century — in surrealism, for example. Suffice it to recall Luis Buñuel's *That Obscure Object of Desire*, in

[20]Sigmund Freud, "On the Universal Tendency to Debasement in the Sphere of Love" (1912), in James Strachey, ed., *The Standard Edition of the Complete Psychological Works of Sigmund Freud*, vol. 11 (London: Hogarth Press, 1986) p. 187. [Žižek]

[21]Jacques Lacan, *Le séminaire, livre XX: Encore* (Paris: Éditions du Seuil, 1975) p. 65. [Žižek]

[22]Lacan, *The Ethics of Psychoanalysis*, p. 152. [Žižek]

[23]An image distorted in such a way that it looks "normal" from a particular viewing angle; one example is Hans Holbein's painting *The Ambassadors,* in the National Gallery, London, which includes an anamorphic skull in the foreground that pops out at the viewer who encounters the painting from below and to the right (coming upstairs, for example).

that assumes a sublime quality the moment it occupies the place of Thing.[24]

What the paradox of the Lady in courtly love ultimately amounts to is thus the paradox of *detour*: our "official" desire is that we want to sleep with the Lady; whereas in truth, there is nothing we fear more than a Lady who might generously yield to this wish of ours — what we truly expect and want from the Lady is simply yet another new ordeal, yet one more postponement. In his *Critique of Practical Reason*, Kant offers a parable about a libertine who claims that he cannot resist the temptation to gratify his illicit sexual desire, yet when he is informed that the gallows now await him as the price to be paid for his adultery, he suddenly discovers that he can resist the temptation after all (proof, for Kant, of the pathological nature of sexual desire — Lacan opposes Kant by claiming that a man of true amorous passion would be even more aroused by the prospect of the gallows . . .). But for the faithful servant of a Lady the choice is structured in a totally different way: perhaps he would even prefer the gallows to an immediate gratification of his desire for the Lady. The Lady therefore functions as a unique short circuit in which the Object of desire itself coincides with the force *that prevents its attainment* — in a way, the object "is," its own withdrawal, its own retraction.

It is against this background that one must conceive of the often mentioned, yet no less often misunderstood, "phallic" value of the woman in Lacan — his equation Woman = Phallus. That is to say, precisely the same paradox characterizes the phallic signifier *qua* signifier of castration. "Castration means that *jouissance* must be refused, so that it can be reached on the inverted ladder of the Law of desire."[25] How is this "economic"

which a woman, through a series of absurd tricks, postpones again and again the final moment of sexual re-union with her aged lover (when, for example, the man finally gets her into bed, he discovers beneath her nightgown an old-fashioned corset with numerous buckles which are impossible to undo . . .). The charm of the film lies in this very nonsensical short circuit between the fundamental, metaphysical Limit and some trivial empirical impediment. Here we find the logic of courtly love and of sublimation at its purest: some common, everyday object or act becomes inaccessible or impossible to accomplish once it finds itself in the position of the Thing — although the thing should be easily within reach, the entire universe has somehow been adjusted to produce, again and again, an unfathomable contingency blocking access to the object. Buñuel himself was quite aware of this paradoxical logic: in his autobiography he speaks of "the non-explainable impossibility of the fulfillment of a simple desire," and a whole series of films offers variations on this motif: in *The Criminal Life of Archibaldo de la Cruz* the hero wants to accomplish a simple murder, but all his attempts fail; in *The Exterminating Angel,* after a party, a group of rich people cannot cross the threshold and leave the house; in *The Discreet Charm of the Bourgeoisie* two couples want to dine together, but unexpected complications always prevent the fulfillment of this simple wish . . .

It should be clear, now, what determines the difference with regard to the usual dialectic of desire and prohibition: the aim of the prohibition is not to "raise the price" of an object by rendering access to it more difficult, but to raise this object itself to the level of the Thing, of the "black hole," around which desire is organized. For that reason, Lacan is quite justified in inverting the usual formula of sublimation, which involves shifting the libido from an object that satisfies some concrete, material need to an object that has no apparent connection to this need: for example, destructive literary criticism becomes sublimated aggressivity, scientific research into the human body becomes sublimated voyeurism, and so on. What Lacan means by sublimation, on the contrary, is shifting the libido from the void of the "unserviceable" Thing to some concrete, material object of need

[24] ". . . [P]ar une inversion de l'usage du terme de sublimation, j'ai le droit de dire que nous voyons ici la déviation quant au but se faire en sens inverse de l'objet d'un besoin" (Jacques Lacan, *Le séminaire, livre VIII, Le transfert* [Paris: Éditions du Seuil, 1991] p. 250). The same goes for every object which functions as a sign of love: its use is suspended, it changes into a means of the articulation of the demand for love. [Žižek]

[25] Jacques Lacan, *Écrits: A Selection* (New York: Norton, 1977) p. 324. The first to formulate this "economic paradox of castration" in the domain of philosophy was Kant. One of the standard reproaches to Kant is that he was a contradictory

paradox" feasible, how can the machinery of desire be "set in motion" — that is to say, how can the subject be made to renounce enjoyment not for another, higher Cause but simply in order to gain access to it? Or — to quote Hegel's formulation of the same paradox — how is it that we can attain identity only by losing it? There is only one solution to this problem: the phallus, the signifier of enjoyment, had simultaneously to be the signifier of "castration," that is to say, *one and the same signifier had to signify enjoyment as well as its loss*. In this way, it becomes possible that the very agency which entices us to search for enjoyment induces us to renounce it.[26]

Back to the Lady: are we, therefore, justified in conceiving of the Lady as the personification of the Western metaphysical passion, as an exorbitant, almost parodical example of metaphysical *hubris,* of the elevation of a particular entity or feature into the Ground of all being? On closer examination, what constitutes this metaphysical or simply philosophical *hubris?* Let us take what might appear to be a surprising example. In Marx, the specifically *philosophical* dimension is at work when he points out that production, one of the four moments of the totality of production, distribution, exchange and consumption, is simultaneously the encompassing totality of the four moments, conferring its specific color on that totality. (Hegel made the same point in asserting that every genus has two species, itself and its species — that is to say, the genus is always one of its own species.) The "philosophical" or "metaphysical" is this very "absolutization," this elevation of a particular moment of the totality into its Ground, this *hubris* which "disrupts" the harmony of a balanced Whole.

Let us mention two approaches to language: that of John L. Austin[27] and that of Oswald Ducrot.[28] Why is it legitimate to treat their work as "philosophy"? Austin's division of all verbs into performatives and constatives is not yet philosophy proper: we enter the domain of philosophy with his "unbalanced," "excessive" hypothesis that every proposition, including a constative, *already is a performative* — that

---

thinker who got stuck halfway: on the one hand *already* within the new universe of democratic rights (*égaliberté*, to use Étienne Balibar's term), on the other hand *still* caught in the paradigm of man's subordination to some superior Law (imperative). However, Lacan's formula of fetishism (a fraction with *a* above minus phi of castration) enables us to grasp the co-dependence of these two allegedly opposed aspects. The crucial feature that distinguishes the democratic field of *égaliberté* from the pre-bourgeois field of traditional authority is the potential *infinity* of rights: rights are never fully realized or even explicitly formulated, since we are dealing with an unending process of continually articulating new rights. On that account, the status of rights in the modern democratic universe is that of *objet petit a,* of an evasive object-cause of desire. Where does this feature come from? Only one consistent answer is possible: *rights are (potentially) infinite because the renunciation upon which they are based is also infinite.* The notion of a radical, "infinite" renunciation as the price the individual must pay for his entry into the social-symbolic universe — that is to say, the notion of a "discontent in civilization," of an irreducible antagonism between man's "true nature" and the social order — emerged only with the modern democratic universe. Previously, within the field of traditional authority, "sociability," a propensity for subordination to authority and for aligning oneself with some community, was conceived of as an integral part of the very "nature" of man *qua zōon politikon.* (This, of course, does not mean that this renunciation — "symbolic castration," in psychoanalytic terms — was not, implicitly, at work from the very beginning: we are dealing here with the logic of retroactivity where things "become what they always-already were": the modern bourgeois universe of Rights made visible a renunciation that was *always-already* there.) And the infinite domain of rights arises precisely as a kind of "compensation": it is what we *get in exchange* for the infinite renunciation as the price we had to pay for our entry into society. [Žižek]

[26]This paradox of castration also offers the key to the function of perversion, to its constitutive loop: the pervert is a subject who directly assumes the paradox of desire and inflicts pain in order to enable enjoyment, who introduces schism in

order to enable reunion, and so on. And, incidentally, theology resorts to obscure talk about the "inscrutable divine mystery" precisely at the point where it would otherwise be compelled to acknowledge the perverse nature of God: "the ways of the Lord are mysterious," which usually means that when misfortune pursues us everywhere, we must presuppose that He plunged us into misery in order to force us to take the opportunity to achieve spiritual salvation. . . . [Žižek]

[27]J. L. Austin was a central figure of the "ordinary language" school of philosophy. He is known primarily for the development of speech-act theory, which he presented as the William James lectures at Harvard in 1955. These lectures were posthumously published in 1962 as *How to Do Things with Words.*

[28]Perhaps best known as the editor, with Tzvetan Todorov, of the *Encyclopedic Dictionary of the Sciences of Language,* Oswald Ducrot is a French linguist who teaches at EHESS (École des Hautes Etudes en Sciences Sociales).

the performative, as one of the two moments of the Whole, simultaneously *is* the Whole. The same goes for Oswald Ducrot's thesis that every predicate possesses, over and above its informative value, an argumentative value. We remain within the domain of positive science as long as we simply endeavor to discern in each predicate the level of information and the level of argumentation — that is, the specific modality of how certain information ''fits'' some argumentative attitude. We enter philosophy with the ''excessive'' hypothesis that the predicate as such, including its informative content, is nothing but a condensed argumentative attitude, so that we can never ''distil'' from it its ''pure'' informative content, untainted by some argumentative attitude. Here, of course, we encounter the paradox of ''non-all'': the fact that ''no aspect of a predicate's content remains unaffected by some argumentative attitude'' does not authorize us to draw the seemingly obvious universal conclusion that ''the entire content of a predicate is argumentative'' — the elusive surplus that persists, although it cannot be pinned down anywhere, is the Lacanian Real.

This, perhaps, offers another way of considering Heidegger's ''ontological difference'': as the distance that always yawns between the (specific feature, elevated into the) Ground of the totality and the Real which eludes this Ground, which itself cannot be ''Grounded'' in it. That is to say, ''non-metaphysical'' is not a ''balanced'' totality devoid of any *hubris*, a totality (or, in more Heideggerian terms: the Whole of entities) in which no particular aspect or entity is elevated into its Ground. The domain of entities gains its consistency from its sup-posited Ground, so that ''non-metaphysics'' can only be an insight into the difference between Ground and the elusive Real which — although its positive content (''reality'') is grounded in the Ground — none the less eludes and undermines the reign of the Ground.

And now, back to the Lady again: this is why the Lady is *not* another name for the metaphysical Ground but, on the contrary, one of the names for the self-retracting Real which, in a way, grounds the Ground itself. And in so far as one of the names for the metaphysical Ground of all entities is ''supreme Good,'' the Lady *qua* Thing can also be designated as the embodiment of radical Evil, of the Evil that Edgar Allan Poe, in two of his stories, ''The Black Cat'' and ''The Imp of the Perverse,'' called the ''spirit of perverseness':

Of this spirit philosophy takes no account. Yet I am not more sure that my soul lives, than I am that perverseness is one of the primitive impulses of the human heart? Who has not, a hundred times, found himself committing a vile or a stupid action, for no other reason than because he knows he should *not?* Have we not a perpetual inclination, in the teeth of our best judgment, to violate that which is Law, merely because we understand it to be such? (''The Black Cat'')

. . . it is, in fact, a *mobile* without motive, a motive not *motiviert.* Through its promptings we act without comprehensible object; or, if this shall be understood as a contradiction in terms, we may so far modify the proposition as to say, that through its promptings we act, for the reason that we should *not.* In theory, no reason can be more unreasonable; but, in fact, there is none more strong. . . . I am not more certain that I breathe, than that the assurance of the wrong or error of any action is often the one unconquerable *force* which impels us, and alone impels us to its prosecution. Nor will this overwhelming tendency to do wrong for the wrong's sake, admit of analysis, or resolution into ulterior elements. It is a radical, a primitive impulse — elementary. (''The Imp of the Perverse'')

The affinity of crime as an unmotivated *acte gratuit* to art is a standard topic of Romantic theory (the Romantic cult of the artist comprises the notion of the artist *qua* criminal): it is deeply significant that Poe's formulas (''a *mobile* without motive, a motive not *motiviert''*) immediately recall Kant's determinations of the aesthetic experience (''purposefulness without purpose,'' etc.). What we must not overlook here is the crucial fact that this command — ''You must because you are not allowed to!'' that is to say, a purely negative grounding of an act accomplished only because it is prohibited — is possible only within the differential symbolic order in which negative determination as such has a positive reach — in which the very *absence* of a feature functions as a *positive feature.* Poe's ''imp of the perverse'' therefore marks the point at which the motivation of an act, as it were, cuts off its external link to empirical objects and grounds itself solely in the immanent circle of self-reference — in short, Poe's "imp" corresponds to the point of freedom in the strict Kantian sense.

This reference to Kant is far from accidental. According to Kant, the faculty of desiring does not possess a transcendental status, since it is wholly dependent upon pathological objects and motivations. Lacan, on the contrary, aims to demonstrate the transcendental status of this faculty — that is, the possibility of formulating a motivation for our desire that is totally independent of pathology (such a non-pathological object-cause of desire is the Lacanian *objet petit a*). Poe's "imp of the perverse" offers us an immediate example of such a pure motivation: when I accomplish an act "only because it is prohibited," I remain within the universal-symbolic domain, without reference to any empirical-contingent object — that is to say, I accomplish what is *stricto sensu* a non-pathological act. Here, then, Kant miscalculated his wager: by cleansing the domain of ethics of pathological motivations, he wanted to extirpate the very possibility of doing Evil in the guise of Good; what he actually did was to open up a new domain of Evil far more uncanny than the usual "pathological" Evil.

EXEMPLIFICATIONS

From the thirteenth century to modern times, we encounter numerous variations on this matrix of courtly love. In *Les Liaisons dangereuses*,[29] for example, the relationship between the Marquise de Montreuil and Valmont is clearly the relationship between a capricious Lady and her servant. The paradox here turns on the nature of the task the servant must perform in order to earn the promised gesture of Mercy: he must seduce other ladies. His Ordeal requires that, even at the height of passion, he maintain a cold distance towards his victims: in the very moment of triumph, he must humiliate them by abandoning them without reason, thereby proving his fidelity to the Lady. Things get complicated when Valmont

falls in love with one of his victims (Présidente de Tourvel) and thereby "betrays his Duty": the Marquise is quite justified in dismissing his excuse (the famous "'c'est pas ma faute" : it's beyond my control, it's the way things are . . .) as beneath Valmont's dignity, as a miserable recourse to a "pathological" state of things (in the Kantian sense of the term).

The Marquise's reaction to Valmont's "betrayal" is thus strictly ethical: Valmont's excuse is exactly the same as the excuse invoked by moral weaklings when they fail to perform their duty — "I just couldn't help it, such is my nature, I'm simply not strong enough. . . ." Her message to Valmont recalls Kant's motto "Du kannst, denn du sollst! [You can, because you must!]." For that reason, the punishment imposed by the Marquise on Valmont is quite appropriate: in renouncing the Présidente de Tourvel, he must have recourse to exactly the same words — that is, he must compose a letter to her, explaining to her that "it's not his fault" if his passion for her has expired, it's simply the way things are. . . .

Another variation on the matrix of courtly love emerges in the story of Cyrano de Bergerac[30] and Roxane. Ashamed of his obscene natural deformity (his too-long nose), Cyrano has not dared to confess his love to the beautiful Roxane; so he interposes between himself and her a good-looking young soldier, conferring on him the role of proxy through whom he expresses his desire. As befits a capricious Lady, Roxane demands that her lover articulate his love in elegant poetic terms; the unfortunate simple-minded young soldier is not up to the task, so Cyrano hastens to his assistance, writing passionate love letters for the soldier from the battlefield. The dénouement takes place in two stages, tragic and melodramatic. Roxane tells the soldier that she does not love his beautiful body alone; she loves his refined soul even more: she is so deeply moved by his letters that she would continue to love him even if his body were to become mutilated and ugly. The soldier shudders at these words: he realizes that Roxane does not love him as he

---

[29]Epistolary novel (1782) by Pierre Choderlos de Laclos (1741–1803), filmed by Stephen Frears in 1988.

[30]Žižek refers to the Romantic drama (1897) by Edmond Rostand (1869–1918). It was filmed by Jean-Paul Rappeneau in 1993.

really is but as the author of his letters — in other words, she unknowingly loves Cyrano. Unable to endure this humiliation, he rushes suicidally into an attack and dies. Roxane enters a clois- ter, where she has regular visits from Cyrano, who keeps her informed about the social life of Paris. During one of these visits Roxane asks him to read aloud the last letter of her dead lover. The melodramatic moment now sets in: Roxane suddenly notices that Cyrano does not read the letter, he recites it — thereby proving that he is its true author. Deeply shaken, she recognizes in this crippled merrymaker her true love. But it is already too late: Cyrano has come to this meeting mortally wounded.

One of the most painful and troubling scenes from David Lynch's *Wild at Heart*[31] is also comprehensible only against the matrix of the logic of suspension that characterizes courtly love. In a lonely motel room, Willem Dafoe exerts a rude pressure on Laura Dern: he touches and squeezes her, invading the space of her intimacy and repeating in a threatening way "Say fuck me!" that is, extorting from her a word that would signal her consent to a sexual act. The ugly, unpleasant scene drags itself on, and when, finally, the exhausted Laura Dern utters a barely audible "Fuck me!" Dafoe abruptly steps away, assumes a nice, friendly smile and cheerfully retorts: "No thanks, I don't have time today; but on another occasion I would do it gladly. . . ." He has attained what he really wanted: not the act itself, just her consent to it, her symbolic humiliation. What intervenes here is the function of the big Other, the trans-subjective symbolic order: by means of his intrusive pressure, Dafoe wants to extort the inscription, the "registration," of her consent in the field of the big Other.

The reverse variation on the same motif is at work in a short love scene from Truffaut's *La Nuit américaine*[32] (*Day for Night*). When, on the drive from the hotel to the studio, a car tire blows, the assistant cameraman and the script-girl find themselves alone on a lake shore. The assistant,

who has pursued the girl for a long time, seizes the opportunity and bursts into a pathetic speech about how much he desires her and how much it would mean to him if, now that they are alone, she were to consent to a quick sexual encounter: the girl simply says "Yes, why not?" and starts to unbutton her trousers. . . . This non-sublime gesture, of course, totally bewilders the seducer, who conceived of her as the unattainable Lady: he can only stammer "How do you mean? Just like that?" What this scene has in common with the scene from *Wild at Heart* (and what sets it within the matrix of courtly love) is the unex- pected gesture of refusal: the man's response to the woman's "Yes!" obtained by long, arduous effort, is to refuse the act.

We encounter a more refined variation on the matrix of courtly love in Eric Rohmer's *Ma nuit chez Maud*:[33] courtly love provides the only logic that can account for the hero's lie at the end. The central part of the film depicts the night that the hero and his friend Maud spend together; they talk long into the small hours and even sleep in the same bed, but the sexual act does not take place, owing to the hero's indecision — he is unable to seize the opportunity, obsessed as he is by the mysteri- ous blonde woman whom he saw the evening before in a church. Although he does not yet know who she is, he has already decided to marry her (i.e. the blonde is his Lady). The final scene takes place several years later. The hero, now happily married to the blonde, encounters Maud on a beach; when his wife asks him who this unknown woman is, the hero tells a lie — apparently to his detriment: he informs his wife that Maud was his last love adventure before marriage. Why this lie? Because the truth could have aroused the suspicion that Maud also occupied the place of the Lady, with whom a brief, noncommittal sexual encounter is not possible — precisely by telling a lie to his wife, by claiming that he did have sex with Maud, he assures her that Maud was not his Lady, but just a passing friend.

---

[31]Released in 1990, based on a novel of the same title by Barry Gifford.

[32]Released in 1973, based on a screenplay by Suzanne Schiffman.

[33]The film (*My Night at Maud's*, 1969) is the fourth in Rohmer's series *Six contes moraux* (*Six Moral Tales*).

The definitive version of courtly love in recent decades, of course, arrives in the figure of the *femme fatale* in *film noir*:[34] the traumatic Woman-Thing who, through her greedy and capricious demands, brings ruin to the *hard-boiled* hero. The key role is played here by the third person (as a rule the gangster boss) to whom the *femme fatale* "legally" belongs: his presence renders her inaccessible and thus confers on the hero's relationship with her the mark of transgression. By means of his involvement with her, the hero betrays the paternal figure who is also his boss (in *The Glass Key, The Killers, Criss-Cross, Out of the Past,*[35] etc.).

This link between the courtly Lady and the *femme fatale* from the *noir* universe may appear surprising: is not the *femme fatale* in *film noir* the very opposite of the noble sovereign Lady to whom the knight vows service? Is not the hard-boiled hero ashamed of the attraction he feels for her; doesn't he hate her (and himself) for loving her; doesn't he experience his love for her as a betrayal of his true self? However, if we bear in mind the original traumatic impact of the Lady, not its secondary idealization, the connection is clear: like the Lady, the *femme fatale* is an "inhuman partner," a traumatic Object with whom no relationship is possible, an apathetic void imposing senseless, arbitrary ordeals.[36]

[34]A movie genre so named by French film critics Raymond Borde and Étienne Chaumeton in 1946. Popular during and just after World War II (and successfully revived recently), the genre features a disillusioned, alienated protagonist, a seductress whose charms are often fatal both to the protagonist and to herself, and a film technique that emphasizes night shots and strange angles. Recent examples of film noir are Lawrence Kasdan's *Body Heat,* Alex Proyas's *Dark City,* Andy and Larry Wachowski's *Bound,* and John Dahl's *The Last Seduction.*

[35]There were two versions of *The Glass Key* made within a few years of each other from the same Dashiell Hammett novel of 1931, but probably Žižek is referring to the more familiar Stuart Heisler version (1942) starring Alan Ladd, rather than the Frank Tuttle version (1935) starring George Raft. The film noir version of *The Killers* is by Robert Siodmak (1946) from Hemingway's 1927 short story. Siodmak also made *Criss-Cross* (1949); both films starred Burt Lancaster. *Out of the Past* (1947) by Jacques Tourneur, from a Daniel Mainwaring novel, starred Robert Mitchum.

[36]Films that transpose the *noir* matrix into another genre (science fiction, musical comedy, etc.) often exhibit some

FROM THE COURTLY GAME TO *THE CRYING GAME*[37]

The key to the extraordinary and unexpected success of Neil Jordan's *The Crying Game* is perhaps the ultimate variation that it delivers on the motif of courtly love. Let us recall the outlines of the story: Fergus, a member of the IRA guarding a captured black British soldier, develops friendly links with him; the soldier asks him, in the event of his liquidation, to pay a visit to his girlfriend, Dil, a hairdresser in a London suburb, and to give her his last regards. After the death of the soldier, Fergus withdraws from the IRA, moves to London, finds a job as a bricklayer and pays a visit to the soldier's love, a beautiful black woman. He falls in love with her, but Dil maintains an ambiguous ironic, sovereign distance towards him. Finally, she gives way to his advances; but before they go to bed together she leaves for a brief moment, returning in a transparent nightgown; while casting a covetous glance at her body, Fergus suddenly perceives her penis — "she" is a transvestite. Sickened, he crudely pushes her away. Shaken and wet with tears, Dil tells him that she thought he knew all the time how things stood (in his obsession with her, the hero — as well as the public — did not notice a host of telltale details, including the fact that the bar where they usually met was a meeting-place for transvestites). This scene of the failed sexual encounter is structured as the exact inversion of the scene referred to by Freud as the primordial trauma of fetishism: the child's gaze, sliding down the naked female body towards the sexual organ, is shocked to find nothing where one expects to see something (a penis) — in the case of *The Crying Game,* the shock is caused when the eye finds *something* where it expected *nothing.*

After this painful revelation, the relationship between the two is reversed: now it turns out that Dil is passionately in love with Fergus, although

crucial ingredient of the *noir* universe more patently than the *noir* proper. When, for example, in *Who Framed Roger Rabbit?,* Jessica Rabbit, a cartoon character, answers the reproach of her corruption with "I'm not bad, I was just drawn that way!," she thereby displays the truth about *femme fatale* as a male fantasy — that is, as a creature whose contours are drawn by man. [Žižek]

[37]Released in 1992, original screenplay by Neil Jordan.

she knows her love is impossible. From a capricious and ironic sovereign Lady she changes into the pathetic figure of a delicate, sensitive boy who is desperately in love. It is only at this point that true love emerges, love as a metaphor in the precise Lacanian sense:[38] we witness the sublime moment when *eromenos* (the loved one) changes into *erastes* (the loving one) by stretching out her hand and "returning love." This moment designates the "miracle" of love, the moment of the "answer of the Real"; as such, it perhaps enables us to grasp what Lacan has in mind when he insists that the subject itself has the status of an "answer of the Real." That is to say, up to this reversal the loved one has the status of an object: he is loved on account of something that is "in him more than himself" and that he is unaware of — I can never answer the question "What am I as an object for the other? What does the other see in me that causes his love?" We thus confront an asymmetry — not only the asymmetry between subject and object, but asymmetry in a far more radical sense of a discord between what the lover sees in the loved one and what the loved one knows himself to be.

Here we find the inescapable deadlock that defines the position of the loved one: the other sees something in me and wants something from me, but I cannot give him what I do not possess — or, as Lacan puts it, there is no relationship between what the loved one possesses and what the loving one lacks. The only way for the loved one to escape this deadlock is to stretch out his hand towards the loving one and to "return love" — that is, to exchange, in a metaphorical gesture, his status as the loved one for the status of the loving one. This reversal designates the point of subjectivization: the object of love changes into the subject the moment it answers the call of love. And it is only by way of this reversal that a genuine love emerges: I am truly in love not when I am simply fascinated by the *agalma*[39] in the other, but when I experience the other, the object of love, as

[38]See Chapters 3 and 4 of Lacan, *Le séminaire, livre VIII, Le transfert* (1960–61). [Žižek]

[39]Greek for votive offering. Lacan used the term in Seminar VIII to denote the mystical, supremely beautiful thing in the Other that provokes one's desire. (Lacan also uses it to signify the treasure that is pursued by means of psychoanalysis.)

frail and lost, as lacking "it," and my love none the less survives this loss.

We must be especially attentive here so that we do not miss the point of this reversal: although we now have two loving subjects instead of the loving one and the loved one, the asymmetry persists, since it was the object itself that, as it were, confessed to its lack by means of its subjectivization. Something deeply embarrassing and truly scandalous abides in this reversal by means of which the mysterious, fascinating, elusive object of love discloses its deadlock, and thus acquires the status of another subject.

We encounter the same reversal in horror stories: is not the most sublime moment in Mary Shelley's *Frankenstein* the moment of the monster's subjectivization — the moment when the monster-object (who has been continually described as a ruthless killing machine) starts talking in the first person, revealing his miserable, pitiful existence? It is deeply symptomatic that all the films based on Shelley's *Frankenstein* have avoided this gesture of subjectivization. And perhaps, in courtly love itself, the long-awaited moment of highest fulfillment, when the Lady renders *Gnade*, mercy, to her servant, is not the Lady's surrender, her consent to the sexual act, nor some mysterious rite of initiation, but simply a sign of love on the part of the Lady, the "miracle" that the Object answered, stretching its hand out towards the supplicant.[40]

[40]This moment when the object of fascination subjectivizes itself and stretches out its hand is the magical moment of crossing the frontier that separates the fantasy-space from "ordinary" reality: it is as if, at this moment, the object that otherwise belongs to another, sublime space intervenes in "ordinary" reality. Suffice it to recall a scene from *Possessed*, Clarence Brown's early Hollywood melodrama with Joan Crawford. Crawford, a poor small-town girl, stares amazed at the luxurious private train that slowly passes in front of her at the local railway station; through the windows of the carriages she sees the rich life going on in the illuminated inside — dancing couples, cooks preparing dinner, and so on. The crucial feature of the scene is that we, the spectators, together with Crawford, perceive the train as a magic, immaterial apparition from another world. When the last carriage passes by, the train comes to a halt and we see on the observation deck a good-natured drunkard with a glass of champagne in his hand, which stretches over the railing towards Crawford — as if, for a brief moment, the fantasy-space intervened in reality. . . . [Žižek]

So, back to *The Crying Game*: Dil is now ready to do anything for Fergus, and he is more and more moved and fascinated by the absolute, unconditional character of her love for him, so that he overcomes his aversion and continues to console her. At the end, when the IRA again tries to involve him in a terrorist act, he even sacrifices himself for Dil and assumes responsibility for a killing she committed. The last scene of the film takes place in the prison where she visits him, again dressed up as a provocatively seductive woman, so that every man in the visiting room is aroused by her looks. Although Fergus has to endure more than four thousand days of prison — they count them up together — she cheerfully pledges to wait for him and visit him regularly. . . . The external impediment — the glass-partition in the prison preventing any physical contact — is here the exact equivalent to the obstacle in courtly love that renders the object inaccessible; it thereby accounts for the absolute, unconditional character of this love in spite of its inherent impossibility — that is, in spite of the fact that their love will never be consummated, since he is a "straight" heterosexual and she is a homosexual transvestite. In his Introduction to the published screenplay, Jordan points out that

> the story ended with a kind of happiness. I say a kind of happiness, because it involved the separation of a prison cell and other more profound separations, of racial, national, and sexual identity. But for the lovers, it was the irony of what divided them that allowed them to smile. So perhaps there is hope for our divisions yet.[41]

Is not the division — the unsurmountable barrier — that allows for a smile the most concise mechanism of courtly love? What we have here is an "impossible" love which will never be consummated, which can be realized only as a feigned spectacle intended to fascinate the gaze of the spectators present, or as an endlessly postponed expectation; this love is absolute precisely in so far as it transgresses not only the barriers of class, religion and race, but also the ultimate barrier of sexual orientation, of sexual identification. Herein resides the film's paradox and, at the same time, its irresistible charm: far from denouncing heterosexual love as a product of male repression, it renders the precise circumstances in which this love can today retain its absolute, unconditional character.

THE CRYING GAME GOES EAST

This reading of *The Crying Game* immediately brings to mind one of the standard reproaches to Lacanian theory: in all his talk about feminine inconsistency, and so on, Lacan speaks about woman only as she appears or is mirrored in male discourse, about her distorted reflection in a medium that is foreign to her, never about woman as she is in herself: to Lacan, as earlier to Freud, feminine sexuality remains a "dark continent." In answer to this reproach, we must emphatically assert that if the fundamental Hegelian paradox of reflexivity remains in force anywhere, it is here: the remove, the step back, from woman-in-herself to how woman *qua* absent Cause distorts male discourse brings us much closer to the "feminine essence" than a direct approach. That is to say, is not "woman" ultimately just the name for a distortion or inflection of the male discourse? Is not the specter of "woman-in-herself," far from being the active cause of this distortion, rather its reified-fetishized effect.

All these questions are implicitly addressed by *M. Butterfly* (directed by David Cronenberg, script by David Henry Hwang from his own play), a film whose subtitle could well have been *"The Crying Game" Goes to China*. The first feature of this film that strikes the eye is the utter "improbability" of its narrative: without the information (given in the credits) that the story is based on true events, nobody

---

[41] *A Neil Jordan Reader* (New York: Vintage Books, 1993), pp. xii–xiii. The question to be raised here is also that of inserting *The Crying Game* into the series of Jordan's other films: are not the earlier *Mona Lisa* and *Miracle* variations on the same motif? In all three cases, the relationship between the hero and the enigmatic woman he is obsessed with is doomed to fail — because she is a lesbian, because she is the hero's mother, because she is not a "she" at all but a transvestite. Jordan thus provides a veritable matrix of the impossibilities of sexual relationship. [Žižek]

would take it seriously.[42] During the Great Cultural Revolution, a minor French diplomat in Beijing (Jeremy Irons) falls in love with a Chinese opera singer who sings some Puccini arias at a reception for foreigners (John Lone). His courting leads to a lasting love relationship; the singer, who is to him the fatal love object (with reference to Puccini's opera, he affectionately calls her "my butterfly"), apparently becomes pregnant, and produces a child. While their affair is going on she induces him to spy for China, claiming that this is the only way the Chinese authorities will tolerate their association. After a professional failure the diplomat is transferred to Paris, where he is assigned to the minor post of diplomatic courier. Soon afterwards, his love joins him there and tells him that if he will carry on spying for China, the Chinese authorities will allow "their" child to join them. When, finally, French security discovers his spying activities and they are both arrested, it turns out that "she" is not a woman at all, but a man — in his Eurocentric ignorance, the hero did not know that in Chinese opera, female roles are sung by men.

It is here that the story stretches the limits of our credulity: how was it that the hero, in their long years of consummated love, did not see that he was dealing with a man? The singer incessantly evoked the Chinese sense of shame, s/he never undressed, they had (unbeknownst to him, anal) sex discreetly, s/he sitting on his lap. . . in short, what he mistook for the shyness of the Oriental woman was, on "her" side, a défi

[42]Bernard Boursicot (b. 1944), a French diplomat stationed in Beijing, met Shi Peipu (b. 1940), a composer and former Beijing opera star, in 1964. In real life Boursicot met Shi in male attire but Boursicot got the idea that Shi was actually a woman who had been raised as a boy because of his family's fixation on male heirs. (Shi denies having misled Boursicot.) They became lovers, Boursicot unaware of Shi's sex, and in 1965 Shi claimed to be pregnant and produced, months later, a son, whom they named Bertrand. During the Cultural Revolution, Boursicot passed documents to China, purportedly in order to keep Shi and Bertrand out of prison, and in 1982 got them out of China. In 1983, in France, both Shi and Boursicot were arrested for espionage, and Shi's sex was revealed to Boursicot, who attempted, unsuccessfully, to commit suicide by cutting his throat. Both went to prison in 1986.

manipulation destined to conceal the fact that "she" was not a woman at all. The choice of the music that obsesses the hero is crucial here: the famous aria "Un bel di, vedremo" from Madama Butterfly, perhaps the most expressive example of Puccini's gesture that is the very opposite of bashful self-concealment — the obscenely candid self-exposure of the (feminine) subject that always borders upon kitsch. The subject pathetically professes what she is and what she wants, she lays bare her most intimate and frail dreams — a confession which, of course, reaches its apogee in the desire to die (in "Un bel di, vedremo," Madama Butterfly imagines the scene of Pinkerton's return: at first, she will not answer his call, "in part for fun and in part not to die at the first encounter [per non morir al primo incontro]").

From what we have just said, it may seem that the hero's tragic blunder consists in projecting his fantasy-image on to an inadequate object — that is to say, in mistaking a real person for his fantasy-image of the love object, the Oriental woman of the Madama Butterfly type. However, things are definitely more complex. The key scene of the film occurs after the trial, when the hero and his Chinese partner, now in an Ordinary man's suit, find themselves alone in the closed compartment of a police car on their way to prison. The Chinese takes off his clothes and offers himself naked to the hero, desperately proclaiming his availability: "Here I am, your butterfly!" He proposes himself as what he is outside the hero's fantasy-frame of a mysterious Oriental woman. At this crucial moment, the hero retracts: he avoids his lover's eyes and rejects the offer. It is here that he gives up his desire and is thereby marked by an indelible guilt: he betrays the true love that aims at the real kernel of the object beneath the phantasmic layers. That is to say, the paradox resides in the fact that although he loved the Chinese without any underhand thoughts, while the Chinese manipulated his love on behalf of the Chinese secret service, it now becomes obvious that the Chinese's love was in some sense purer and far more authentic. Or, as John le Carré put it in A Perfect Spy: "Love is whatever you can still betray."

As every reader of "true" spy adventures knows very well, a large number of cases in which a woman has seduced a man out of duty, in order to extract from him some vital piece of information (or vice versa) end with a happy marriage — far from dispelling the mirage of love, the disclosure of the deceitful manipulation that brought the lovers together only strengthened their bond. To put it in Deleuzian terms: we are dealing here with a split between the "depth" of reality, the intermixture of bodies in which the other is the instrument I mercilessly exploit, in which love itself and sexuality are reduced to means manipulated for politico-military purposes, and the level of love *qua* pure surface event. Manipulation at the level of bodily reality renders all the more manifest love *qua* surface event, *qua* effect irreducible to its bodily support.[43]

The painful final scene of the film conveys the hero's full recognition of his guilt.[44] In prison, the hero stages a performance for his vulgar and noisy fellow-prisoners: dressed as Madama Butterfly (a Japanese kimono, heavily made-up face) and accompanied by excerpts from Puccini's opera, he retells his story; at the very climax of "Un bel di, vedremo," he cuts his throat with a razor and collapses dead. This scene of a man performing public suicide dressed as a woman has a long and respectable history: suffice it to mention Hitchcock's *Murder* (1930), in which the murderer Handel Fane, dressed as a female trapeze artist, hangs himself in front of a packed house after finishing his number. In *M. Butterfly*, as in *Murder*, this act is of a strictly ethical nature: in both cases the hero stages a psychotic identification with his love object, with his *sinthome* (synthetic formation of the nonexistent woman, "Butterfly") — that is, he "regresses" from the object-choice to an immediate identification with the object; the only way out of the insoluble

deadlock of this identification is suicide *qua* the ultimate *passage à l'acte*. By his suicidal act the hero makes up for his guilt, for his rejection of the object when the object was offered to him outside the fantasy-frame.

Here, of course, the old objection again awaits us: ultimately, does not *M. Butterfly* offer a tragicomic confused bundle of male fantasies about women, not a true relationship with a woman? The entire action of the film takes place among men. Does not the grotesque incredibility of the plot simultaneously mask and point towards the fact that what we are dealing with is a case of homosexual love for the transvestite? The film is simply dishonest, and refuses to acknowledge this obvious fact. This "elucidation," however, fails to address the true enigma of *M. Butterfly* (and of *the Crying Game*): how can a hopeless love between the hero and his partner, a man dressed up as a woman, realize the notion of heterosexual love far more "authentically" than a "normal" relationship with a woman?

How, then, are we to interpret this perseverance of the matrix of courtly love? It bears witness to a certain deadlock in contemporary feminism. True, the courtly image of man serving his Lady is a semblance that conceals the actuality of male domination; true, the masochist's theater is a private *mise en scène* designed to recompense the guilt contracted by man's social domination; true, the elevation of woman to the sublime object of love equals her debasement into the passive stuff or screen for the narcissistic projection of the male ego-ideal, and so on. Lacan himself points out how, in the very epoch of courtly love, the actual social standing of women as objects of exchange in male power-plays was probably at its lowest. However, this very semblance of man serving his Lady provides women with the fantasy-substance of their identity whose effects are real: it provides them with all the features that constitute so-called "femininity" and define woman not as she is in her *jouissance féminine*, but as she refers to herself with regard to her (potential) relationship to man, as an object of his desire. From this fantasy-structure springs the near-panic

---

[43]As for this Deleuzian opposition of surface event and bodily depth, see Chapter 5 below. [Žižek]

[44]At this point the film differs from "reality": the "true" hero is still alive and rotting in a French prison. [Žižek] Boursicot and Shi actually served only one year, and were released in 1987. Shi passed away in Paris on 2009, the "son" Bertrand (a.k.a. Shi Dudu) has three children of his own, and Boursicot has "come out of the closet" and is living with a partner.

reaction — not only of men, but also of many a woman — to a feminism that wants to deprive woman of her very "femininity." By opposing "patriarchal domination," women simultaneously undermine the fantasy-support of their own "feminine" identity.

The problem is that once the relationship between the two sexes is conceived of as a symmetrical, reciprocal, voluntary partnership or contract, the fantasy matrix which first emerged in courtly love remains in power. Why? In so far as sexual difference is a Real that resists symbolization, the sexual relationship is condemned to remain an asymmetrical non-relationship in which the Other, our partner, prior to being a subject, is a Thing, an "inhuman partner"; as such, the sexual relationship cannot be transposed into a symmetrical relationship between pure subjects. The bourgeois principle of contract between equal subjects can be applied to sexuality only in the form of the *perverse* — masochistic — contract in which, paradoxically, the very form of balanced contract serves to establish a relationship of domination. It is no accident that in the so-called alternative sexual practices ("sadomasochistic" lesbian and gay couples) the Master-and-Slave relationship re-emerges with a vengeance, including all the ingredients

of the masochistic theater. In other words, we are far from inventing a new "formula" capable of replacing the matrix of courtly love.

For that reason, it is misleading to read *The Crying Game* as an anti-political tale of escape into privacy — that is to say, as a variation on the theme of a revolutionary who, disillusioned by the cruelty of the political power-play, discovers sexual love as the sole field of personal realization, of authentic existential fulfillment. Politically, the film remains faithful to the Irish cause, which functions as its inherent background. The paradox is that in the very sphere of privacy where the hero hoped to find a safe haven, he is compelled to accomplish an even more vertiginous revolution in his most intimate personal attitudes. Thus *The Crying Game* eludes the usual ideological dilemma of "privacy as the island of authenticity, exempt from political power-play" versus "sexuality as yet another domain of political activity": it renders visible the *antagonistic* complicity between public political and personal sexual subversion, the antagonism that is already at work in Sade, who demanded a sexual revolution as the ultimate accomplishment of the political revolution. In short, the subtitle of *The Crying Game* could have been "Irishmen, yet another effort, if you want to become republicans!"

5

MARXIST CRITICISM

Not least among the tasks now confronting thought is that of placing all the reactionary arguments against Western culture in the service of progressive enlightenment.
— Theodor W. Adorno

It is the view of the world, the ideology or weltanschauung *underlying a writer's work, that counts. And it is the writer's attempt to reproduce this view of the world which constitutes his "intention" and is the formative principle underlying the style of a given piece of writing.*
— Georg Lukács

The socialist critic does not see literature in terms of ideology and class-struggle because they happen to be his or her political interests, arbitrarily projected onto literary works. Such matters are the very stuff of history, and in so far as literature is a historical phenomenon, they are the very stuff of literature too.
— Terry Eagleton

Always historicize!
— Fredric Jameson

Like Sigmund Freud, Karl Marx not only created an immense, subtle, and complex body of research but inspired an entire discourse written by his followers, a world of diverse social theory that speaks for itself but speaks, at the same time, in Marx's name. American philosophy and literary criticism have only recently become leavened by Marxist social theory, for reasons that have to do with the gyrations of twentieth-century history and politics. For American workers in the 1920s and 1930s, Marx was a hero who had proclaimed a new world of equality and meaningful work, whose followers set up schools to educate the proletariat of the future. But for many of those who grew up in the 1950s and 1960s, an era dominated by a Cold War between the Marxist-Leninist Soviet Union and the capitalist United States, Marxism carried a whiff of sulfur with it, as a dangerous and unpatriotic credo, a philosophy of the Other. After the purges and show trials of the 1930s, after the Hitler-Stalin pact, after the revelations of the Gulag, Marx became the "God that failed" even to many former socialists who had believed. It is no accident that so many of the important works of British and American historical scholarship written from the 1940s to the 1970s (with notable exceptions, like Christopher Hill's

Milton and the English Revolution) proceeded in deliberate disregard of Marx and his theories of history and culture. During the 1960s European Marxists like Herbert Marcuse were read and discussed widely, at least within the counterculture. Today, with the Soviet Union no longer standing as a grim parody of the workers' state Marx had envisioned, it is possible for those of all political stripes to view Marx and the richly complex European traditions that he spawned as the key tools for viewing literature as a social text and as the product of history.

Marx's historicism was a product of the later Enlightenment, when historical change first began to be viewed as a source of explanation of changing social and cultural moves. While Philip Sidney viewed history as a source of ethical exempla, Samuel Johnson's criticism marks the beginnings of literature seen as a social text; he treated Shakespeare and the major English authors of the seventeenth century as men who must be judged (where morals were not concerned) by the standards of their own day rather than by those of his, Johnson's friend, Thomas Warton, was to write the first *History of English Poetry* (1774–81), operating on the then-novel assumption that an appreciation of the classics of one's own language had to be mediated by an understanding of the manners and concerns of earlier times. Their Scottish contemporary Adam Smith authored not only the great apologia for capitalism, *The Wealth of Nations* (1776), but a treatise on moral philosophy that presented human societies as advancing unevenly through successive stages of social and political development driven by the motor of economic change. Walter Scott, who absorbed Smith's lessons at the University of Edinburgh, used them to construct in *Waverley* (1814) and *Old Mortality* (1816) fables of the Jacobite risings where a still feudal Scotland, savage and hierarchical, bravely confronts at a hopeless disadvantage the more advanced commercial nation of England. And Marx may have derived his sense of how history works in practice as much from Scott, the novelist he most loved, as from his teacher, the philosopher Hegel.

Marx's social theories are more fully explicated in the introduction to Marx (see p. 241), and they are reviewed in Raymond Williams's discussion of "Base and Superstructure" (see p. 747). Briefly, however, Marx was a dialectical materialist. He was a materialist in the sense that he believed, unlike Hegel, that what drives historical change are the material realities of the economic base of society (*Grundlage*), rather than the ideological superstructure (*Überbau*) of politics, law, philosophy, religion, and art that is built upon that economic base. Like Hegel, Marx believed that change comes about through dialectical oppositions within a given state of society. Apparently stable societies develop sites of resistance: contradictions built into the social system that ultimately lead to social revolution and the development of a new society upon the ruins of the old. These contradictions are resolved by the structural shift to a new level of operation that in turn generates other contradictions, new tensions, further revolutions.

Beyond these basic assumptions, however, Marxist theory and the application of Marxist theory to literature have taken a dizzying variety of forms, depending, among other things, on how the literary text is positioned relative to material reality and to ideology.[1] Wide discrepancies were inevitable in part because Marxism is primarily a political and economic philosophy rather than a guide to the explication of literary texts. The few comments Marx and Engels addressed to matters of art and literature left many of the most important questions of method open. Differences also arise because Marxism is, as we have hinted, not only a philosophy but a movement with a conflicted history of its own, where ideas, including ideas about art, have had fateful political consequences. For example, Georg Lukács's attack on naturalism was also a covert attack on Soviet Realist art, which used naturalist premises, and therefore on its political sponsor, Joseph Stalin. Because of this conflicted history, there are many Marxist critics but no single Marxist school of criticism in the usual sense, and we will have to mention many more representatives of the tradition Marx began than we can include in this chapter.

THE AMERICAN LIBERALS

Largely because of the long-standing fear of the Soviet Union, there has been no strong American tradition of socialism since the Bolshevik revolution, and only the briefest of periods — in the mid-1930s — when the Communist party attracted any share of intellectuals. To the extent that American criticism was touched directly by this movement (as in the writings of Granville Hicks), it was of a form usually termed (not without reason) "vulgar Marxism," which featured the adulation of the proletariat: works written by proletarians themselves and works celebrating proletarian characters, denouncing capitalism, and forecasting the revolution. Leon Trotsky had himself written with contempt (in *Literature and Revolution,* 1923) of such efforts to force literature to serve politics directly. Yet Raymond Williams has

---

[1]The Marxist term "ideology" is an essentially contested concept. The notion of ideology presented in the introduction to Marx (see p. 247), as "a culture's collective consciousness of its own being," is one of several currently used in Marxist circles, but there are many others, often in direct contradiction to it. My definition is close to a sense in which Marx uses the term in the following famous passage from *A Contribution to a Critique of Political Economy* (1859): "A distinction should always be made between the material transformation of the economic conditions of production . . . and the legal, political, religious, aesthetic, or philosophic — in short, ideological — forms in which men become conscious of this conflict and fight it out" (see p. 410). But if here "ideology" means any representation of consciousness, the most common use of "ideology" in Marx and Engels is the pejorative one of "false consciousness," a set of illusions fostered by the dominant class in order to assure social stability — and its own continued dominance (Letter to Mehring, 1893). Ideology in this sense is expected to wither away and vanish in the Marxist utopia of the dictatorship of the proletariat. Louis Althusser's often quoted dictum, "Ideology has no history," would seem to contradict this view, since it implies that ideology will retain a function forever — and thus even in the workers' state. But Althusser's definition of ideology ("the 'lived' relation between men and their world, or a reflected form of this unconscious relation") is closer to the unpejorative usage of Marx in the *Critique of Political Economy.* See Raymond Williams, *Keywords: A Vocabulary of Culture and Society* (London: Oxford University Press, 1976), pp. 126–30; and Louis Althusser, *For Marx* (New York: Pantheon, 1969), p. 252.

Another worrisome ambiguity lurking in the word *ideology* arises from the relative concreteness with which it is represented to the consciousness. While most Marxist thinkers view "ideology" as something explicit and official, like a body of laws, a political doctrine, or a philosophy, other Marxists (or the same ones, in other circumstances) use the term to denote something more vague and implicit, even unconscious: a way of understanding, a worldview.

conceded that, although such a position is ''crude and reductionist . . . no Marxist . . . can wholly give it up without abandoning the Marxist tradition.''[2]

''Vulgar Marxism'' as such did not become an important American tradition, but a group of New York intellectuals, associated with the Left magazine *Partisan Review*, had flirted with Communism during the Spanish Civil War and had become disillusioned with Stalinist Russia but not with the utopian ideals that Marxism represented. The most broadly learned among them was Edmund Wilson, whose journalistic essays and books introduced European writers and ideas to what even in the 1930s and 1940s was a largely provincial America. Their leading literary critic, Lionel Trilling, was instrumental in turning the college of Columbia University into a training camp for ideas on culture and society. Important followers and contemporaries included Philip Rahv, Alfred Kazin, and Irving Howe. Neither Wilson nor Trilling should be credited with fashioning a significant critical methodology or a doctrinally pure way of reading Marx. Indeed, it may be going too far to call them Marxists, since both were influenced almost as heavily by Freud, and they avoided using most conventional Marxist terminology. They wrote, instead, in an Arnoldian tradition of cultural commentary, committed to literature as an expression of culture, and concerned primarily with expressing in their writings both the tension within their own responses to literature and the broadest and most complex views of life.

REFLECTION THEORIES: TROTSKY, LUKÁCS, AND BRECHT

At least two major theories derive from the notion that literature consists of an imitation of social reality. The first, which can be traced to Marx but is best expressed by Leon Trotsky, Georgii Plekhanov, and other writers of the Third International (an organization founded in Moscow in 1919 to support the Bolshevik revolution), equates mimesis with a pure ''slice of life'' and considers it unimportant that writers take a radical stance toward the reality they portray. The royalist reactionary Balzac is thus a more valuable writer in his accurate portraits of society than a less perceptive writer of doctrinally correct (i.e., socialist) tendencies.

A second, more complex version of reflection theory is found in the criticism of Georg Lukács. Lukács held that writers must do more than reflect the mere surface features of their society: They must also portray the various forces acting on that society that eventuate in social change. Lukács despised the naturalists (like Emile Zola and Theodore Dreiser) who were satisfied to present characters typical of the social order. In ''The Ideology of Modernism'' (1956), Lukács pours equal scorn on the modernists' exaltation of the subjective and the psychological at the expense of any portrayal of the dynamic movements underlying social change. To either naturalism or modernism, Lukács prefers the realism — less sophisticated though it be — of Walter Scott. Scott's Edward Waverley is not the typical English gentleman of his time, nor is he invested with much psychological depth; nevertheless, in *Waverley*, whose relationships and loyalties position him between the mercantile

2 Raymond Williams, ''Marxism, Structuralism, and Literary Analysis'' in *New Left Review* 129 (1981): 51–66.

English and the still feudal Highland Scots on the eve of the 1745 rebellion, Scott created a character who embodies the social and political conflicts of his epoch.

A third version of Marxist reflection aesthetics is to be found in Bertolt Brecht's essays on the theater. Like Lukács, Brecht had little sympathy for aesthetic regimes enforced by commissars, like the Socialist Realism approved by Stalin's hand-picked minister of culture, Andrei Zhdanov. He envisioned the masses as intelligent and aggressive, too feisty to be satisfied with naturalistic texts that depict circumstances as overwhelming to the individual or collective will, and with minds too nimble to be satisfied by derivative or hackneyed stories or plays. German workers of 1930 responded, he found, to his *Threepenny Opera*, despite its being set in eighteenth-century London among beggars and thieves: They were able to abstract the social truth it embodied as long as the story avoided the narcotic of cheap feelings, as long as it was presented with wit and humor, in a way that made them think. Realism, for Brecht, is a question of the social truth embodied within and beneath the surface representation; the latter can be as abstract or concrete, as familiar or deeply alien, as the dramatist wishes, so long as it does not lull the audience into a slumber where thought becomes impossible.

FORMS OF MEDIATION THEORY: BENJAMIN AND ADORNO

Just as there have been various forms of Marxian "reflection" so have there also been different versions of the principle of "mediation" — the notion that ideology establishes relationships between the two levels of Marxist dialectic, between the base and the superstructure, between the relations of production and the work of art. These versions arose in part because of the aesthetic inadequacy of the concept of reflection. "Reflection" was a useful term for discussing the novel, but most other modes of literature and art could not incorporate, as a novel could, a view of an entire society. At times the term "mediation" has been used merely to denote the more subtle versions of mimesis — like that of Lukács — but it more properly describes theories like Walter Benjamin's notion of correspondences.

One would not say that, for example, the poetry of Baudelaire reflects his society, in the sense that it depicts an image of it. But as Benjamin noted, industrialization had produced changes in the city and its crowds that resulted in a new version of both the individual and the individual's attitude toward himself, which connected with aspects of Baudelaire's poetry. Benjamin describes Baudelaire's notion of the *correspondance* as "an experience which seeks to establish itself in crisis-proof form." It is the artist's reaction to the impermanence of post-industrial urban life, typified in the shock and abrasion of the crowded streets. Benjamin viewed Baudelaire as nostalgic about the decline of that mystical quality of art Benjamin called "aura" — that spiritual quality, a relic of the human attachment to ritual and magic, which gives a work of art an almost animate sensibility: "To perceive the aura of an object means to invest it with the ability to look at us in return."

In "The Work of Art in the Age of Mechanical Reproduction" (1936), reprinted below, Benjamin examines the central fact of industrialism's relation to art in the twentieth century: that, for the first time, a painting or sculpture can be infinitely replicated. On the one hand there is the genuine possibility of art for the masses, not simply because anyone can possess a copy of Botticelli's *Birth of Venus* but also because of the evolution of film, a medium intended for mass audiences. On the other hand, the mystical aura, the cult value of the art object, is simultaneously beginning to disappear. As a socialist, Benjamin ought to be applauding this trend, but the essay is caught up in emotional ambiguity because of his own nostalgia for the cult of memory. Although the preface bravely declares that his theses "brush aside a number of outmoded concepts, such as creativity and genius, eternal value and mystery," the tone of the later sections seems at odds with this intent. When Benjamin contrasts the stage actor, engaged both in acting as an art and in a particular role, with the alienated film actor, who is at best an "exile" and at worst a "stage prop," or when he notes that aura survives in film in the obscene adulation paid to film stars, or when he observes that film is the art uniquely suited to the "distracted" and "absent-minded" specta-tor, a reader may infer that the proletarianization of art progressively dehumanizes both participants and spectators. Reading Benjamin, one may feel trapped within his ironies, but perhaps Benjamin was trapped in them himself. Although he knew well that socialism meant industrialization, mechanical reproduction, and the death of the cult value of art, he nevertheless felt intensely the loss of that value.

Benjamin was willing to allow for Baudelairean correspondences, for the media-tion of ideology, at the level of content. Other members of the so-called Frankfurt school, like Theodor W. Adorno, were not so willing. For Adorno, the Frankfurt school's principal aesthetician, the relationship between art and society operated on the formal level and could easily be located even in nonreferential art such as music. Thus, in *Philosophy of Modern Music* (1949), Adorno suggested that the rootless chaos and tragic ambiguity of Arnold Schönberg's musical harmonies, together with his drive to mechanize and systematize composition, served as a correspon-dence with the dominant ideology of the early twentieth century. (Adorno judged Schönberg to be a more authentic artist than Igor Stravinsky, whose shifting formal allegiances — from neoclassicism to primitivism — were either ideologically reac-tionary or attempts to evade history altogether.)

As one might expect, Adorno took the opposite position from Lukács on the issue of modernism in literature and defended the bleak vision of novelists like Kafka. While Adorno agrees with Lukács that modern fiction is morbidly subjective and obsessed with the torture of the individual consciousness, he claimed that the mod-ern novel "a critical posture towards social reality by means of its style . . . not by its 'content' or view of the world."[3] In a sense, modernist fiction exemplifies "negative dialectic" — Adorno's term for criticism that operates without reproduc-ing the conceptual features of what it criticizes — a necessary feature in capitalist society, where, according to Adorno, concepts distort and mask social realities.

The way modern mass culture distorts its representation of social reality — the oppo-site side of the "negative dialectic" — can be seen in "The Culture Industry: Enlight-enment as Mass Deception," by Adorno in collaboration with his Frankfurt School colleague, Max Horkheimer. In this chapter from *Dialectic of Enlightenment* (1944),

[3]Gillian Rose, *The "Melancholy Science": An Introduction to the Thought of Theodor W. Adorno* (London: Macmillan, 1978), p. 124.

a selection from which is reprinted below, Horkheimer and Adorno portray with the steely logic of a nightmare Benjamin's vision of a postindustrial culture. Benjamin had been ambivalent about mechanical reproduction, partly because of the lure of cultural aura, partly because of his fear that mass culture could be used to support Fascism. But Horkheimer and Adorno, writing at a time when European Fascism had, to all intents and purposes, been defeated, view contemporary popular culture as a political tool of American capitalism. The workers have been subjugated by technology, but resistance is impossible because the technology that enslaves them also keeps them entertained, at a shallow level, with cheap films and nearly free music from the radio; every moment of their leisure time is occupied, because so long as the people are fed mindless pleasures they cannot think, cannot relate to one another, cannot form any sense of the system they serve.

People differ, of course, in the kinds of entertainments they find absorbing, but the culture industry caters to differences: For the more refined soul there are symphony programs and higher-toned dramatic films; for the less educated there are pseudo jazz and cowboy movies. What is important is that no one be left out, so that no one is left to question the system of domination. The fact that most of the film actors and musicians lack any real talent allows the audience to have fantasies of social mobility, because they feel that they too, had they been chosen, could have been movie stars or teen idols. The product of the culture industry, in other words, is ideology in the sense of "false consciousness." The films and the music provoke a phony sense of community, since the community one belongs to is that of the passive consumer of culture: The audience can talk to one another about a particular film star or musical performer, but they lack any real sense of solidarity. Most of all, however the audience talks, the system never allows anyone to talk back. Horkheimer and Adorno are writing in the days before television network broadcasting — during the brief interval between the invention of the technology and its exploitation — but they were well aware that the ultimate medium of ideology was about to be rolled out for an ever more passive mass audience. Their idea that the mass media were creating a pseudo public sphere that was being used to legitimate political decisions made by the power of money was equally prophetic — and inspired, as we shall see, their disciple Jürgen Habermas.

Reading "The Culture Industry" today, one may feel that its authors had chosen a cushy spot — sunny California — from which to critique the vast wasteland of American culture, at a time — 1944 — when their fellow socialists lay dead in German concentration camps or on the battlefields of the Eastern Front. One needs to remember that Horkheimer and Adorno had seen their own liberal society, that of the Weimar Republic, turn quickly into a Fascist regime that used culture for ideological purposes, and that, as European socialists, they discovered in the Roosevelt New Deal a mere travesty of the just society of which they dreamed.

GENETIC STRUCTURALISM:
LUCIEN GOLDMANN AND RAYMOND WILLIAMS

Between the mediation theories of the Frankfurt school and the structural Marxism of the Althusserians, there are transitional modes of Marxist criticism. One of the most important was that practiced by Lucien Goldmann, who called himself a "genetic" structuralist because the structures he was concerned about were derived from the work's genesis in the ideology of its times. Like Adorno, Goldmann believed that the correspondences between a work and an age would be correspondences of form rather than content. But unlike most Marxist critics, who would claim that the ideology of an age is invariably present in all of its products, Goldmann felt that only the greatest works of an age contain its deepest consciousness.

Goldmann's analysis of seventeenth-century France in *The Hidden God* (1955) presents *homologies* — analogies of function rather than content — between literary and ideological structures, which during that period take the form of tragic dilemmas. The seventeenth-century Jansenists were torn between obedience to a silent God and participation in the new rationalism: the "nobility of the robe" (the gentry deriving from the legal profession) were torn between the authority of the king and the new spirit of commercial enterprise. Similarly, in the plays of Racine, who was both a Jansenist and a scion of the *noblesse de robe*, the protagonists (such as Hippolytus and Andromache) must choose between service to a hidden God and the pleasures and duties of the world — and are damned no matter which they choose.

The most distinguished English practitioner of genetic structuralism was probably Raymond Williams. The son of working-class parents from the border country of Wales, Williams brought to his readings of literature a proletarian background highly unusual in a Marxist critic, few of whom have had any close acquaintance with hard manual labor. Instead of Benjamin's more abstract and aestheticized term "correspondences," Williams spoke of the "complex forms of feeling" within which literature and ideology find common ground. In Williams's *The Country and the City* (1973), for example, his thought about the Industrial Revolution is filtered through his personal sense of what alienation from the countryside might have meant to the poets of the eighteenth and early nineteenth centuries. As with Goldmann, the structures of feeling Williams found in poetry exhibit homologies with elements in the nonaesthetic segments of the superstructure or the relations of production in the base.

In fact, Williams talks of seeking "structures of feeling" in art instead of "ideology," as such; the novel phase differentiates the concrete, lived experience represented in art ("social experiences in *solution*," as he calls it) from the "precipitated" manner in which social relationships are likely to be characterized in an expository text, a treatise, or a newspaper article.

It would be misleading to characterize Williams as merely a follower of Goldmann, however. Williams was a rather protean social and historical critic whose work shifted rapidly through a number of phases. He began his career rejecting the revolutionary doctrines of Marxism, particularly its concept of the masses, and went through a left-Leavisite phase of cultural criticism that kept what Williams himself termed "a certain conscious distance" from Marxism. After *Culture and Society* (1958), however, Williams converged with Marxist thought. Following his "genetic structuralist" phase, Williams became what he called a "cultural material-ist," influenced primarily by the Italian Marxist Antonio Gramsci and his concept of hegemony.

To Gramsci, power is expressed partly through the direct means of control (*dominio:* rule) and partly through something at once less formal and conscious and yet more total (*egemonia:* hegemony). As Williams says in *Marxism and Literature* (1977), from which the selection in this chapter is taken:

> Hegemony is . . . a lived system of meanings and values — constitutive and constituting — which, as they are experienced as practices appear as reciprocally confirming. It thus constitutes a sense of reality for most people in the society . . . beyond which it is very difficult for most members of the society to move. . . . It is . . . in the strongest sense a "culture" but a culture which has also to be seen as the lived dominance and subordination of particular classes. (See p. 753)

Williams finds this conception attractive because it allows for the notion of *alternative* hegemonies centered in the working class and for revolutionary activity in the shape of cultural rather than political action. The implication is that hegemonies may be relatively successful, but they are never complete. Instead of a single ruling class, there are interpenetrating hegemonic groups; and instead of a single catastrophic revolution, there are dominant, emergent, and residual elements of culture belonging to classes whose power has peaked or is increasing or declining. This concept of hegemony modifies the rigid base/superstructure formula of Marxist thought, a modification Williams had already sought in the homologies of Goldmann. In general, Williams seems to have sought a more fluid and responsive Marxism — also an aim of Louis Althusser.

LOUIS ALTHUSSER AND STRUCTURAL MARXISM

The newest development of Marxist thought — post-Althusserian Marxism — originates in the structural thought of the mature Marx as interpreted by Louis Althusser and in the theories of the signifier developed by Jacques Lacan (see Ch. 4), which were later to influence Jacques Derrida (Ch. 2). In *Reading Capital,* Althusser questions the traditional portrait of Marx as a Hegelian humanist; for Althusser there were two Marxes: a young Marx (up to the year 1845), whose ideas roughly corresponded with the usual view of dialectical materialism, and a mature Marx (from 1857 onward), whose way of thinking was radically different. For Althusser, the older Marx, author of *Capital,* had evolved a form of dialectic that was different from Hegel's — not just an inversion of it — and no longer held to the simple deterministic relation of base and superstructure. Economics is determinative but only *"in the last instance."*[4] But Althusser's most important shift is in his vision of history. Earlier writers on Marx had assumed that history is a real force, concrete, univocal, and ineluctable. In Althusser's reading of Marx, history has become a myth, or perhaps more properly, a text, in that it is a symbolic structure, produced by discourse. We cannot evade history any more than we can think without our faculty for symbolization, but neither can we view history from outside that subjective faculty.

In Althusser's interpretation, Marx becomes a canny reader of his own chosen texts, those of his predecessors, the classical economists; in quoting Marx, Althusser

---

[4]Louis Althusser, "Contradiction and Overdetermination," in *For Marx,* trans. Ben Brewster (New York: Pantheon, 1969), pp. 84–114.

presents him as aware of their oversights, their subtle shifts in point of view. Althusser's point is that these writers' areas of blindness are as significant as their areas of insight, for the gaps and incoherencies that a critical reading of the texts reveals are the signs of what the writers are unconsciously hiding from themselves. This is not the personal, Freudian repression of individuals, but blind spots left by what the ideology of their age is unable to talk about.

Pierre Macherey's *A Theory of Literary Production* (1966) presents a literary-critical version of these ideas. In "Jules Verne: The Faulty Narrative," Macherey shows how Verne's plans for his novels went awry. *The Mysterious Island*, for example, originated in Verne's wish to rewrite *Robinson Crusoe* more rigorously. Unlike Defoe, who had provided Crusoe with a shipload of modern equipment and tools, Verne would demonstrate how castaways with a knowledge of science man-age to recreate modern technology out of nothing on an empty island. The novel begins thus, but halfway along Verne reveals that the castaways are not alone on the island: he introduces Captain Nemo and his crew, who give the castaways a crate of tools. Most readers would interpret this as a mere lapse on Verne's part, a melodramatic corruption of his plan. For Macherey, there are no mistakes, and Verne's introduction of Nemo betokens his attempt to *evade* what he knows: that science cannot be pure knowledge, as he would wish, but relies on the technological capacity of a capitalistic society to bring it into being. Furthermore, Verne's book implicitly acknowledges that there are no empty lands, only those whose aborigi-nes are rendered invisible by imperialist ideology, just as technology cannot arise purely from scientific knowledge but must in fact emerge from a technological social organization. Macherey argues that the rifts in Verne's plot are there because of preexisting rifts in the ideology of bourgeois capitalism and that the novel itself, as an aesthetic practice whose raw materials are ideology, tends to widen these rifts as it foregrounds them, making them visible to the reader.

By reifying the flat notions of ideology in the roundness of a narrative, the artist unwittingly exposes their incoherencies to the view of a critical reader. This version of Marxism is practiced by Raymond Williams's disciple, Terry Eagleton, and by Althusser's most important American disciple, Fredric Jameson. Jameson's highly acclaimed *The Political Unconscious* (1981) presents a theory of interpretation in which Althusser's politics and Lacan's theory of the unconscious intersect.

EAGLETON

Terry Eagleton did not begin as a post-Althusserian Marxist but as a Christian humanist of working-class origins, studying literature at Cambridge under Raymond Williams. His post-Althusserian phase began in the mid-1970s, when he broke decisively with the humanist-socialist position he had inherited from Williams, just as Williams himself was refashioning a rigorous and dialectical Marxism based on the ideas of the Italian thinker Antonio Gramsci. In *Marxism and Literary Criticism* (1976), Eagleton surveys Marxist aesthetics from Marx's and Engels's own essays and letters to the continental neo-Marxists of the 1960s, portraying this history as a long decline from the insights of the original master until its post-Althusserian renaissance in his own day. He attacked not only the antiartistic repressions of Stalin and Zhdanov but also the British Marxists of the 1930s, like Christopher Caudwell and Arnold Kettle, and contrasted the broad world-historical issues favored by Georg Lukács (for Eagleton a "stiff-necked Stalinist") with the more subtle questions about the social determinants of art which post-Althusserian Marxists like Pierre Macherey were able to ask.

Eagleton went on in *Criticism and Ideology* (1976) to provide a fuller explanation of post-Althusserian literary theory as well as some practical criticism based on that theory. This work contains Eagleton's declaration of independence from Raymond Williams, whose shifting allegiances Eagleton subjects to the same sort of sharp but ultimately generous scrutiny that many well-adjusted post-adolescents apply to their fathers. For readers trying to learn how to read or write neo-Marxist criticism, the most important sections, however, are the second and third chapters. Here Eagleton presents the literary work as determined not solely by the "economic base," as in classical Marxism, but by a large number of interrelated factors, including the "literary mode of production" — whether the text is transmitted orally, through handwritten manuscripts, printed books, periodicals, etc. — the "general ideology," the "aesthetic ideology" of the time, and the "authorial ideology" — the writer's particular slant on the social conflicts of his or her day. In addition, Eagleton presents the Althusserian thesis that ideology, far from being a coherent and unified mode of social consciousness (as Lukács, for example, had conceived of it), is actually fragmented and inconsistent. The artistic work, as a production of ideology, foregrounds such incoherencies and makes them visible to the reader. Thus, art can have revolutionary effects, regardless of the social views of the artist.

Ultimately, Eagleton came to see his attempt to create a "science of the text" as too sterile. During the Thatcher years, when the gains of the workers under the Labour Party quickly evaporated, this working-class theorist decided that criticism would have to do more than analyze literature. He espoused what he called a "revolutionary criticism," for which he claimed practical as well as intellectual aims:

> What seemed important when I wrote [*Criticism and Ideology*], at a time when "Marxist criticism" had little anchorage in Britain, was to examine its prehistory and to systematize the categories essential for a "science of the text." [This] is perhaps no longer the focal concern of Marxist cultural studies. Partly under the pressure of global capitalist crisis, partly under the influence of new themes and forces within socialism, the centre of such studies is shifting from narrowly textual or conceptual analysis to problems of cultural production and the political use of artefacts. . . . This shift in direction was in turn obscurely related to certain deep-seated changes in my own personal and political life. . . .[5]

One index to these "deep-seated changes" may be Eagleton's dedication of his book on Walter Benjamin to the poststructuralist feminist critic Toril Moi, whose intellectual influence he gratefully acknowledges. Moi's influence may be seen in Eagleton's vision of a "revolutionary criticism" based primarily on the "paradigm" of "feminist criticism." Like those contemporary feminist critics who attempt to make patriarchy visible in order to dismantle it, Eagleton proposes to "dismantle the

---

[5]Terry Eagleton, *Walter Benjamin, or Towards a Revolutionary Criticism* (London: Verso, 1981), p. xii.

ruling concepts of 'literature,' reinserting 'literary' texts into the whole field of cultural practices." He proposes further to "deconstruct the received hierarchies of 'literature,'" to reevaluate the canon, and to reveal the role of literature "in the ideological construction of the subject."[6] In effect, Eagleton is calling for a new political criticism that would apply to class issues the lessons that feminists have learned in their approach to gender. His books on subjects from Shakespeare to Richardson to Brontë to Wilde have come out at a rate of nearly one per year, but it remains an open question whether Eagleton has succeeded in fulfilling the promise of his theoretical manifesto.

JAMESON AND THE POLITICAL UNCONSCIOUS

Fredric Jameson came to Marxism through his dissertation on Sartre, and his position as the foremost American Marxist critic solidified after the publication of *Marxism and Form* (1971). Like Eagleton, Jameson was at pains to jettison the tedious and tendentious forms of Russian Marxism, and he championed the more Hegelian Marxism of Lukács, Benjamin, and Adorno. What was most original in *Marxism and Form* was Jameson's final chapter, "Towards Dialectical Criticism," in which he sets forth his own ideas of what a genuine dialectical-materialist criticism would be like. The most important of these is his notion of criticism as "metacommentary" that must always "include a commentary on its own intellectual instruments as part of its own working structure."[7] Jameson would argue that while for a formalist like Wayne Booth the concept of "point of view" is a neutral tool of analysis without historical content — after all, any narrative, whenever written, must be told from some point of view — in fact, the notion of "point of view" is not timeless at all; it reflects the specific historical situation of Henry James (who invented the term) and the "lived experience" of the middle class in the late nineteenth century; "seeing life from the relatively restricted vision of our own monad."[8] For Jameson, a genuinely dialectical criticism would be self-conscious about the terms and structures that it assumes and would attempt to understand these tools in their historical contexts.

The last part of "Towards Dialectical Criticism" presents a complex "allegorical" vision of literary interpretation based on Jameson's notion of the interconvertability of form and content. For Jameson, in addition to the usual "form" and "content" of any literary text, there is the "form of the content" and the "content of the form." Jameson claims that the "content" of a literary work "never really is initially formless . . . but is rather already meaningful from the outset, being . . . the very components of our concrete social life itself: words, thoughts, objects, desires, people, places, activities."[9] It is the lived experience of the social world. On the other side "form" itself has its "content": styles and plots encode ideas about the material world. One obvious example would be the love sonnet of the Renaissance, whose importance underscores the dynastic or commercial character of the marital bond in that era. (In our own era, men and women who can marry for love as a matter

---

6Ibid., p. 98.

7Fredric Jameson, *Marxism and Form: Twentieth-Century Dialectical Theories of Literature* (Princeton, NJ: Princeton University Press, 1971), p. 336.

8Ibid., p. 355.

9Ibid., pp. 402–03.

of course do not need to create such formal objectifications of feeling.) Sometimes the "content of the form" operates in surprising ways. For example, Jameson views the surface violence and anxiety of science fiction movies of the 1950s not merely as a covert reference to the terror of nuclear annihilation during a period of escalation in the Cold War, but as also encoding a collective wish-fulfillment fantasy on the part of postwar society, a utopian fantasy about genuinely gratifying work that is personified in the ubiquitous scientist hero whose activity — empowering, untrammeled by routine, rewarded by deep self-satisfactions rather than by cash — suggests "a return to older modes of work organization, the more personal and psychologically satisfying world of the guilds."[10] In *Marxism and Form* Jameson presents his vision of a new dialectical criticism that would interpret literature in such a way as to penetrate to the repressed collective political desires of the society in which it was produced: He would show that criticism in action ten years later in *The Political Unconscious* (1981).

The title of *The Political Unconscious* refers to the ideas of Althusser and Macherey discussed previously: that society represses its internal contradictions by means of ideology but that by carefully reading literary texts we are often able to witness the "return of the repressed," the surfacing of the fissures in the ideology of a society. For Jameson, literary texts are allegorical, encoding both the "false consciousness" of their age and its "utopian" dreams. This encoding takes place within the three "concentric frameworks" of *politics* (the plotting of particular events), *society* (the tensions operating between groups), and *history* (the succession of social formations within the larger vision of social change). For Jameson, these three frameworks point also to three moments in the act of interpretation that he calls the three "horizons" of the text. In the first horizon, it is within the boundaries of the text itself that the symbolic tensions of the political unconscious are set forth; in the second, the text is seen as an ideological utterance within a system of discourse, an example of *parole* within a *langue*. Finally the text is viewed as a field of force within which artifacts deriving from sign-systems dominant in successive social formations can be simultaneously viewed. Jameson aligns these three horizons with "phases" in Northrop Frye's *Anatomy of Criticism* that themselves derive roughly from the literal, the allegorical, and the anagogical modes of medieval interpretation.

In addition, Jameson employs two other methodological tropes. One is the "rectangle" of the structural linguist A. J. Greimas, which structures the themes of a narrative text into a synchronic system through various modes of equivalence and opposition. The other is what he calls the "molecular" and "molar" aspects of the allegorical representation of ideology in narrative. Generally, Marxist critics have dealt with the large-scale features of a text, its plot and themes, to the exclusion of its fine structure. Jameson calls this the "molar" level (in chemistry, a "mole" is 6.2×10^{19} molecules of a substance). But Jameson believes that the political thematics of narratives can also be found at the "molecular" level of the structure of individual sentences, and demonstrates, in passages from Balzac's "La Vieille Fille," Dreiser's *Sister Carrie,* and Conrad's *Lord Jim* and *Nostromo,* how the political unconscious operates at the stylistic level of the text.

[10]Ibid., p. 405.

It was *The Political Unconscious* that made Jameson one of the critics most frequently quoted in literary circles. However, some Marxists were less enthusiastic about this text. Terry Eagleton, already in his "revolutionary" phase, suggested that Jameson's subtle analyses of the "utopian moment" in various nineteenth-century texts, while transcending the tendentious arguments of "vulgar Marxism," seemed also to have transcended its revolutionary spirit and its identification with the oppressed: "'[T]he question irresistibly raised for the Marxist reader of Jameson is simply this: how is a Marxist-Structuralist critique of a minor novel of Balzac to help shake the foundations of capitalism?'"[11]

It is hard to know whether or not Jameson was stung by Eagleton's imputation of right-wing deviationism, but in the years since the publication of *The Political Unconscious*, Jameson has become more a cultural than a literary critic, and the "texts" upon which he works are much more likely to be films or buildings than novels or stories. His magisterial book on postmodernism depicts our contemporary world as suffering from a continuous and unresolved crisis in which our cultural representations parody and subvert themselves. The ultimate cause of these cultural and psychological phenomena is what Jameson calls "late capitalism," with its unfathomable bureaucratic web and fragmented social system. The individual today is even more alienated from any vision of supportive community and rewarding work than the nineteenth-century wage-slave of the Industrial Revolution. In the post-industrial West, factories themselves have often been moved by multinational corporations to developing countries, where wages are low, leaving behind the service industries and the large-scale corporate activities of finance and marketing. At the same time, the traditional Marxist distinction between economic base and cultural superstructure begins to dissolve in late capitalism, as the primary business of the developed world becomes the creation of culture for everyone, via designs for manufactured objects, architectural planning, media programming, and the computer and information systems. In general, Jameson's cultural criticism has continued to explore the political unconscious of artistic representations: the truth behind the false consciousness of ideology that is allegorically expressed in these fictions, and their utopian fantasy rooted in eternal human desire.

JÜRGEN HABERMAS AND PUBLIC DISCOURSE

Unlike Eagleton and Jameson, but like Marx himself, Jürgen Habermas is primarily a social philosopher rather than a literary and cultural critic. He is usually considered the premier thinker of the second generation of the Frankfurt school, whose first generation included Herbert Marcuse, Walter Benjamin, Max Horkheimer, and Habermas's teacher and chief influence, Theodor W. Adorno. Like any good Marxist, however, Habermas's goal has been not merely to extend the cultural critique of the Frankfurt school but to transcend it. The Frankfurt school had itself been a continuation and transcendence of Marx's philosophy. Whereas Marx had embraced scientific rationalism as an antidote

11Terry Eagleton, "The Idealism of American Criticism," Review of *The Political Unconscious*, by Fredric Jameson. *New Left Review* 127 (1981): 65.

to the religious idealism of Hegel and his followers, by the 1930s capitalism had advanced to the point where science and technology appeared to be simultaneously the means of creating a just society and a major obstacle to social equality. The bureaucratic organizations that needed to produce scientific knowledge and use it for practical ends were producing a society organized from the top down, destructive of all dialogue, while the cult of scientific fact and the notion of a split between "hard" facts and "soft" values stifled any communal discussion of social justice. The Frankfurt school rejected the scientistic Marxism coming out of the Soviet Union in favor of an analysis of the social formation and mentalities produced by capitalism, eventuating in, as one can see in the work of Adorno, a grimly pessimistic critique in which artists like Kafka and Schönberg were seen as protesting — by means of literary or musical form — the inhuman societies developing around them.

Habermas saw Adorno's critique of culture as a blind alley leading only to alienation and quietism. He framed the need to heal the split between socioeconomic study and cultural critique, between fact and value, as a problem of the breakdown of public discourse, seeking a way to recuperate the Enlightenment ideal of a just and rational society within the context of late capitalism. For Habermas, the aim of society must be "the end of coercion and the attainment of autonomy through reason, the end of alienation through a consensual harmony of interests, and the end of injustice and poverty through the rational administration of justice."[12] As one might expect given his historical position as a philosopher, writing at a time when rhetoric and discourse are seen as the constituents of reality rather than as verbal veils of deeper material or spiritual truths, Habermas envisions progress as coming not just from material and organizational reform, but from a purification of public discourse.

Habermas's analysis of discourse owes a great deal to Wittgenstein, to Gadamer, and to the speech-act theorists,[13] whose ideas he adopted and against whom he reacted. His theory presumes that social dialogue occurs within a framework that makes certain idealizing assumptions (he calls them "validity claims") about real-life utterances: that what we say is understandable, that its objective propositional content is true, that the speaker is sincere, and that it is appropriate for the speaker to be performing the speech-act. Obviously these assumptions do not hold for all, or even most, real-life utterances, so that we often need to problematize one or another of these validity

---

[12]Jane Braaten, *Habermas's Critical Theory of Society* (Albany: State University of New York Press, 1991), p. 111.

[13]Speech-act theory relates to the branch of linguistics called "pragmatics," which operates above the level of the sentence to analyze the ways sentences are construed as part of a social situation. One pioneering volume is that of philosopher of language J. L. Austin (1921–1960), whose *How to Do Things with Words* (Cambridge: Harvard University Press, 1962) contrasts "constative" language, which states facts (e.g., "The distance between New York and Chicago is 713 miles"), with "performative" language by which people promise, or threaten, or perform other acts (e.g., "I sentence you to be hanged by the neck until you are dead"). Austin suggests that "felicity conditions" need to be observed for performatives: The last example will not "work" as a performative unless the speaker is a judge, the recipient of the utterance is a person who has been found guilty of a capital crime, the scene is a courtroom, and so on. Ultimately Austin was dissatisfied with the distinction between constatives and performatives, and speech-act theory gradually shifted to distinguishing between "locutionary," "illocutionary," and "perlocutionary" speech-acts (in the first one would "say" something; in the second "argue" something to someone; in the third "convince" someone of something). See also John R. Searle, *Speech Acts* (Cambridge, Cambridge University Press, 1969).

claims, questioning the speaker's truth or sincerity, say, and rising to a meta-level of discourse in our critique. Nonetheless, conversation and dialogue and the attainment of any consensus needed for action depend on these validity claims.[14] Genuine consensus can be built provided all the participants in a dialogue have a fair share in the discourse, are allowed freely to assert or question any claim that is made, and are able to express attitudes, feelings, and intentions, without being dominated, materially or ideologically, by another speaker. In such a dialogue people attempt to persuade one another not by authority or by false claims of scientific rationality but by the force of the better argument. Habermas knows that such a situation is counterfactual, that contemporary society throws up hundreds of barriers to the production of what he calls "legitimate" consensus, but he holds up the ideal of a society in which the actors attempt to persuade each other on rational grounds. The conditions he envisions as a prerequisite for the attainment of such a consensus of intersubjective truth are the conditions of the just society of which Marx and Adorno dreamed.

Given his melioristic general program for social discourse and social organization, it is clear that neither postmodernism nor poststructural thought has any positive place in Habermas's thought. The fragmented bricolage of postmodernism implicitly presumes that what successive generations each in turn called the "modern" project of progress and enlightenment is over, that the fragmentation of an instrumentalist social system has left modern humanity in an alienation beyond remedy. And the anarchistic rhetoric of Jacques Derrida and Michel Foucault, derived from Heidegger and the later Nietzsche, is equally poisonous to Habermas's project, as it denies both the "validity claims" needed for communicative competence and the possibility of the social conditions needed for legitimate consensus. Habermas argues that the poststructuralist versions of rhetoric held by Richard Rorty and Derrida essentially cheat, in that they employ logic and reason against the values of logic and reason, use the terms of metaphysics in order to destroy metaphysics, and require our consent to reasoned argument without recuperating any new mode of consensus discourse at some meta-level of reason. Habermas explores equally basic contradictions within the thought of Foucault, a philosopher whose empirical investigations of madness, disease, and criminal behavior operate within a system that denies empiricism, whose rebarbative truths operate within a system that portrays truth as merely a function of power. Habermas's ultimate point is that "the radical critique of reason exacts a high price for taking leave of modernity."[15] It leaves us with a hopeless solipsism, when what is needed for taking on the alienating conditions of late capitalism and the power of the interventionist state is a discourse that can build toward legitimate consensus, not to "pass beyond man and humanism" as Derrida put it (see p. 542), but to redeem the as-yet unrealized ideal of a liberal society. like poststructuralism, postmodernism strikes Habermas as a premature revolutionary movement, one that would give back the gains of the enlightenment before they had been fully realized.

14 Thomas McCarthy, Translator's Introduction to Jürgen Habermas, *Legitimation Crisis* (Boston: Beacon, 1975), p. xiv.

15 Jürgen Habermas, *The Philosophical Discourse of Modernity: Twelve Lectures*, trans. Frederick G. Lawrence (Cambridge: MIT Press, 1990), p. 336.

Selected Bibliography

Adorno, Theodor. *Prisms: Cultural Criticism and Society.* 1955; London: Neville Spearman, 1967.

———. *Minima Moralia: Reflections from Damaged Life,* trans. E. F. Jephcott. New York: Norton, 1985.

———. *Notes to Literature,* trans. Shierry W. Nicholsen. New York: Columbia University Press, 1991.

———. *Aesthetic Theory,* trans. Rolf Tiedemann. Minneapolis: University of Minnesota Press, 1996.

Althusser, Louis. *For Marx.* New York: Pantheon, 1969.

———. *Lenin and Philosophy and Other Essays.* London: New Left Books, 1971.

Althusser, Louis, and Etienne Balibar. *Reading Capital.* New York: Pantheon, 1970.

Aronson, Ronald, *After Marxism.* New York: Guilford Press, 1995.

Bakhtin, Mikhail. *Between Phenomenology and Marxism.* New York: Cambridge University Press, 1995.

Barker, Francis, Peter Hulme, and Margaret Iverson, eds. *The Uses of History: Marxism, Postmodernism and the Renaissance.* New York: St. Martin's Press, 1991.

Benjamin, Walter. *Illuminations.* New York: Harcourt Brace & World, 1968.

———. *Charles Baudelaire: A Lyric Poet in the Era of High Capitalism.* London: New Left Books, 1973.

———. *Reflections: Essays, Aphorisms, Autobiographical Writings,* ed. Peter Demetz. New York: Harcourt Brace Jovanovich, 1978.

———. *Correspondence of Walter Benjamin.* Chicago: University of Chicago Press, 1994.

Bennett, Tony. *Formalism and Marxism.* London: Methuen, 1979.

Benton, Ted, ed. *The Greening of Marxism.* New York: Guilford Press, 1996.

Brecht, Bertolt. *Brecht on Theatre: The Development of an Aesthetic*, ed. and trans. John Willett. New York: Hill and Wang, 1978.

Caudwell, Christopher. *Illusion and Reality: A Study of the Sources of Poetry.* New York: International Publishers, 1963.

Cohen, Naomi. *Feminism and Marxism in the Nineties: A Revolutionary Women's Agenda.* New York: World View Forum, 1993.

Cook, Deborah. *The Culture Industry Revisited: Theodor W. Adorno on Mass Culture.* Lanham, MD: Rowman & Littlefield, 1996.

Coward, Rosemary, and John Ellis. *Language and Materialism: Developments in Semiology and the Theory of the Subject.* London: Routledge and Kegan Paul, 1977.

Demetz, Peter. *Marx, Engels and the Poets: Origins of Marxist Literary Criticism.* Chicago: University of Chicago Press, 1967.

Dowling, William. *Jameson, Althusser, Marx: An Introduction to the Political Unconscious.* Ithaca: Cornell University Press, 1984.

Eagleton, Terry. *Criticism and Ideology: A Study in Marxist Literary Theory.* London: New Left Books, 1976.

———. *Marxism and Literary Criticism.* Berkeley: University of California Press, 1976.

———. *Criticism and Ideology: A Study in Marxist Theory.* New York: Norton, 1978.

———. *Saint Oscar.* London: Faber and Faber, 1990.

———. *The Ideology of the Aesthetic.* London: Blackwell, 1994.

———. *Ideology.* White Plains: Longman Publishing Group, 1995.

———. *Heathcliff and the Great Hunger.* New York: Norton, 1995.

———. *The Illusions of Postmodernism.* London: Blackwell, 1996.

————. *The Idea of Culture*. Oxford: Blackwell, 2000.

————. *After Theory*. New York: Basic Books, 2003.

Eagleton, Terry, and Drew Milne, eds. *Marxist Literary Theory: A Reader*. Oxford: Blackwell, 1996.

Fekete, John. *The Critical Twilight*. Boston: Routledge and Kegan Paul, 1976.

Fokkema, Douwe W., and Elrud Ibsch. *Theories of Literature in the Twentieth Century: Structuralism, Marxism, Aesthetics of Reception, Semiotics,* 2nd ed. New York: St. Martin's Press, 1995.

Foley, Barbara. *Telling the Truth: The Theory and Practice of Documentary Fiction*. Ithaca: Cornell University Press, 1986.

Freedman, Carl Howard. *The Incomplete Projects: Marxism, Modernity, and the Politics of Culture*. Middletown: Wesleyan University Press, 2002.

Frow, John. *Marxism and Literary History*. Ithaca: Cornell University Press, 1986.

Goldmann, Lucien. *The Hidden God: A Study of the Tragic Vision in the Pensées of Pascal and the Tragedies of Racine*. 1955; London: Routledge and Kegan Paul, 1964.

————. "Marxist Criticism." In *The Philosophy of the Enlightenment*. Cambridge: MIT Press, 1973, pp. 86–97.

Gramsci, Antonio. *The Modern Prince and Other Writings*. London: Lawrence and Wishart, 1957.

————. *Selections from the Prison Notebooks*. London: Lawrence and Wishart, 1971.

Habermas, Jürgen. *The Philosophical Discourse of Modernity: Twelve Lectures,* trans. Frederick G. Lawrence. Cambridge: MIT Press, 1990.

————. *Jürgen Habermas on Society and Politics: A Reader,* trans. Steven Seidman. Boston: Beacon Press, 1989.

————. *The Structural Transformation of the Public Sphere: An Inquiry into a Category of Bourgeois Society*. Cambridge: MIT Press, 1989.

————. *The Theory of Communicative Action, Vol. I: Reason and the Rationalization of Society,* trans. Thomas McCarthy. Boston: Beacon Press, 1985.

————. *The Theory of Communicative Action, Vol. II: Lifeworld and System: A Critique of Functionalist Reason,* trans. Thomas McCarthy. Boston: Beacon Press, 1989.

————. *The Future of Human Nature*. Malden, MA: Blackwell, 2003.

————. *Truth and Justification*, ed. and trans. Barbara Fultner. Cambridge: MIT Press, 2003.

Hartley, George. *The Abyss of Representation: Marxism and the Postmodern Sublime*. Durham: Duke University Press, 2003.

Hawthorn, Jeremy. *Cunning Passages: New Historicism, Cultural Materialism, and Marxism in the Contemporary Literary Debate*. New York: Routledge, 1996.

Hicks, Granville. *The Great Tradition: An Interpretation of American Literature Since the Civil War*. 1933; Chicago: Quadrangle Books, 1969.

Hohendahl, Peter Uwe. "Prolegomena to a History of Literary Criticism." *New German Critique* 11 (1977): 151–63.

Horkheimer, Max. *Eclipse of Reason*. New York: Continuum, 1992.

Horkheimer, Max, and Theodor W. Adorno. *Dialectic of Enlightenment*, trans. John Cumming. New York: Continuum, 1998.

Jameson, Fredric. *Marxism and Form: Twentieth Century Dialectical Theories of Literature*. Princeton: Princeton University Press, 1971.

————. *The Prison-House of Language: A Critical Account of Structuralism and Russian Formalism*. Princeton: Princeton University Press, 1972.

————. *The Political Unconscious: Studies in the Ideology of Form*. Ithaca: Cornell University Press, 1981.

———. *Late Marxism: Adorno or the Persistence of the Dialectic.* New York: Norton, 1990.

———. *Postmodernism, or, the Cultural Logic of Late Capitalism.* Durham: Duke University Press, 1991.

———. *The Seeds of Time.* New York: Columbia University Press, 1996.

———. *Brecht and Method.* London: Verso, 1998.

———. *A Singular Modernity.* London: Verso, 2002.

Kellner, Douglas. *Critical Theory, Marxism, and Modernity.* Baltimore: Johns Hopkins University Press, 1989.

Kettle, Arnold. *Introduction to the English Novel.* 2 vols. 1951; New York: Harper and Row, 1960.

Lifshitz, Mikail. *The Philosophy of Art of Karl Marx.* 1933; London: Pluto Press, 1973.

Lukács, Georg. *Realism in Our Time: Literature and the Class Struggle.* 1957; New York: Harper and Row, 1964.

———. *The Historical Novel.* London: Merlin Press, 1962.

———. *The Theory of the Novel: A Historico-Philosophical Essay on the Forms of Great Epic Literature.* 1920; London: Merlin Press, 1971.

Macherey, Pierre. *A Theory of Literary Production.* 1966; Boston: Routledge and Kegan Paul, 1978.

Marcuse, Herbert. *The Aesthetic Dimension: Toward a Critique of Marxist Aesthetics.* Boston: Beacon Press, 1978.

Marx, Karl, and Friedrich Engels. *Marx and Engels on Literature and Art.* St. Louis: Telos Press, 1973.

Morris, William. *On Art and Socialism.* London: Lehmann, 1947.

Ohmann, Richard. *English in America: A Radical View of the Profession.* New York: Oxford University Press, 1976.

Orwell, George. *Critical Essays.* London: Secker and Warberg, 1946.

Robinson, Lillian S. *Sex, Class, and Culture.* Bloomington: Indiana University Press, 1978.

Rose, Gillian. *The "Melancholy Science": An Introduction to the Thought of Theodor W. Adorno.* London: Macmillan, 1978.

Sartre, Jean-Paul. *What Is Literature?* New York: Harper and Row, 1965.

———. *Between Existentialism and Marxism.* New York: Pantheon, 1974.

Sherman, Howard J. *Reinventing Marxism.* Baltimore: Johns Hopkins University Press, 1995.

Smith, Steven B. *Reading Althusser.* Ithaca: Cornell University Press, 1984.

Trotsky, Leon. *Literature and Revolution.* 1924; Ann Arbor: University of Michigan Press, 1960.

Weimann, Robert. *Structure and Society in Literary History.* Charlottesville: University Press of Virginia, 1976.

Williams, Raymond. *Culture and Society, 1780–1950.* London: Chatto and Windus, 1958.

———. *The Country and the City.* New York: Oxford University Press, 1973.

———. *Marxism and Literature.* New York: Oxford University Press, 1977.

———. *The Sociology of Culture.* Chicago: University of Chicago Press, 1995.

———. *The Politics of Modernism: Against the New Conformists.* London: Verso, 1996.

Wilson, Edmund. *Axel's Castle.* 1931; New York: Scribner's, 1961.

———. *The Triple Thinkers.* 1938; New York: Oxford University Press, 1948.

Wood, Ellen Meiksins, and John Bellamy Foster, eds. *In Defense of History: Marxism and the Postmodern Agenda.* New York: Monthly Review Press, 1997.

Walter Benjamin 1892–1940

It is said that Walter Benjamin, one of the most influential cultural theorists in the Marxist tradition, did not look into Marx's writings until the final decade of his tragically abbreviated life. Benjamin was born in Berlin to a wealthy Jewish family. His studies at Freiburg, Munich, Berlin, and Berne resulted in a doctorate in 1919, but his dissertation on German tragic drama — a brilliant but unorthodox performance completed when he was thirty-three — was rejected by the University of Frankfurt. With a university career closed to him, Benjamin appears to have turned to journalism. From 1925 to 1933 Benjamin made his living mainly with his pen and became friendly with a number of left-wing intellectuals, including Bertolt Brecht. His visit to Moscow in the winter of 1926–27 affirmed his sympathy with the Soviet state, although he never joined the Communist party. When the Nazi seizure of power drove him from Berlin — he emigrated to Paris in 1933 — commissions from the Frankfurt Institute for Social Research enabled him to eke out a living. During these years of exile, he wrote some of his most admired work, including "The Work of Art in the Age of Mechanical Reproduction" (1936). In 1940, Benjamin committed suicide in Port Bou, Spain, in the mistaken belief that his plan to emigrate to America had been thwarted and that he would have to return to Nazi-occupied France. The translation of "The Work of Art in the Age of Mechanical Reproduction" is from the collection Illuminations (1969).

The Work of Art in the Age of Mechanical Reproduction

Our fine arts were developed, their types and uses were established, in times very different from the present, by men whose power of action upon things was insignificant in comparison with ours. But the amazing growth of our techniques, the adaptability and precision they have attained, the ideas and habits they are creating, make it a certainty that profound changes are impending in the ancient craft of the Beautiful. In all the arts there is a physical component which can no longer be considered or treated as it used to be, which cannot remain unaffected by our modern knowledge and power. For the last twenty years neither matter nor space nor time has been what it was from time immemorial. We must expect great innovations to transform the entire technique of the arts, thereby affecting artistic invention itself and perhaps even bringing about an amazing change in our very notion of art.[1]

—PAUL VALÉRY, *Pièces sur l'art,*
"La Conquête de l'ubiquité," Paris

PREFACE

When Marx undertook his critique of the capitalistic mode of production, this mode was in its infancy. Marx directed his efforts in such a way

Translated by Harry Zohn.

[1]Quoted from Paul Valéry, "The Conquest of Ubiquity," *Aesthetics,* trans. Ralph Manheim (New York: Pantheon Books, Bollingen Series, 1964), p. 225. [Tr.]

as to give them prognostic value. He went back to the basic conditions underlying capitalistic production and through his presentation showed what could be expected of capitalism in the future. The result was that one could expect it not only to exploit the proletariat with increasing intensity, but ultimately to create conditions which would make it possible to abolish capitalism itself.

The transformation of the superstructure, which takes place far more slowly than that of the substructure, has taken more than half a century to manifest in all areas of culture the change in the conditions of production. Only today can it be indicated what form this has taken. Certain prognostic requirements should be met by these statements. However, theses about the art of the proletariat after its assumption of power or about the art of a classless society would have less bearing on these demands than theses about the developmental tendencies of art under present conditions of production. Their dialectic is no less noticeable in the superstructure than in the economy. It would therefore be wrong to underestimate the value of such theses as a weapon. They brush aside a number of outmoded concepts, such as creativity and genius, eternal value and mystery — concepts whose uncontrolled (and at present almost uncontrollable) application would lead to a processing of data in the Fascist sense. The concepts which are introduced into the theory of art in what follows differ from the more familiar terms in that they are completely useless for the purposes of Fascism. They are, on the other hand, useful for the formulation of revolutionary demands in the politics of art.

I

In principle a work of art has always been reproducible. Manmade artifacts could always be imitated by men. Replicas were made by pupils in practice of their craft, by masters for diffusing their works, and, finally, by third parties in the pursuit of gain. Mechanical reproduction of a work of art, however, represents something new. Historically, it advanced intermittently and in leaps at long intervals, but with accelerated intensity. The Greeks knew only two procedures of technically reproducing works of art: founding and stamping. Bronzes, terra cottas, and coins were the only art works which they could produce in quantity. All others were unique and could not be mechanically reproduced. With the woodcut, graphic art became mechanically reproducible for the first time, long before script became reproducible by print. The enormous changes which printing, the mechanical reproduction of writing, has brought about in literature are a familiar story. However, within the phenomenon which we are here examining from the perspective of world history, print is merely a special, though particularly important, case. During the Middle Ages engraving and etching were added to the woodcut; at the beginning of the nineteenth century lithography made its appearance.

With lithography the technique of reproduction reached an essentially new stage. This much more direct process was distinguished by the tracing of the design of a stone rather than its incision on a block of wood or its etching on a copperplate and permitted graphic art for the first time to put its products on the market, not only in large numbers as hitherto, but also in daily changing forms. Lithography enabled graphic art to illustrate everyday life, and it began to keep pace with printing. But only a few decades after its invention, lithography was surpassed by photography. For the first time in the process of pictorial reproduction, photography freed the hand of the most important artistic functions which henceforth devolved only upon the eye looking into a lens. Since the eye perceives more swiftly than the hand can draw, the process of pictorial reproduction was accelerated so enormously that it could keep pace with speech. A film operator shooting a scene in the studio captures the images at the speed of an actor's speech. Just as lithography virtually implied the illustrated newspaper, so did photography foreshadow the sound film. The technical reproduction of sound was tackled at the end of the last century. These convergent endeavors made predictable a situation which Paul Valéry pointed up in this sentence: "Just as water, gas, and electricity are brought into our houses from far off to satisfy our needs in response to a minimal effort, so we shall be supplied with visual or auditory images, which will appear and disappear at a simple movement of the hand, hardly more than a sign." Around 1900 technical reproduction had reached a standard that not only permitted it to reproduce all transmitted works of art and thus to cause the most profound change in their impact upon the public; it also had captured a place of its own among the artistic processes. For the study of this standard nothing is more revealing than the nature of the repercussions that these two different manifestations — the reproduction of works of art and the art of the film — have had on art in its traditional form.

II

Even the most perfect reproduction of a work of art is lacking in one element: its presence in time and space, its unique existence at the place where it happens to be. This unique existence of the work of art determined the history to which it was subject throughout the time of its existence. This includes the changes which it may have suffered in physical condition over the years as well as the various changes in its ownership.[2] The traces of the first can be revealed only by chemical or physical analyses which it is impossible to perform on a reproduction; changes of ownership are subject to a tradition which must be traced from the situation of the original.

The presence of the original is the prerequisite to the concept of authenticity. Chemical analyses of the patina of a bronze can help to establish this, as does the proof that a given manuscript of the Middle Ages stems from an archive of the fifteenth century. The whole sphere of authentic-ity is outside technical — and, of course, not only technical — reproducibility.[3] Confronted with its

[2]Of course, the history of a work of art encompasses more than this. The history of the Mona Lisa, for instance, encompasses the kind and number of its copies made in the seventeenth, eighteenth, and nineteenth centuries. [Benjamin]

[3]Precisely because authenticity is not reproducible, the intensive penetration of certain (mechanical) processes of reproduction was instrumental in differentiating and grading authenticity. To develop such differentiations was an impor-tant function to the trade in works of art. The invention of the woodcut may be said to have struck at the root of the quality of authenticity even before its late flowering. To be sure, at the time of its origin a medieval picture of the Madonna could not yet be said to be "authentic." It became "authentic" only during the succeeding centuries and perhaps most strikingly so during the last one. [Benjamin]

manual reproduction, which was usually branded as a forgery, the original preserved all its authority; not so *vis à vis* technical reproduction. The reason is twofold. First, process reproduction is more inde-pendent of the original than manual reproduction. For example, in photography, process reproduction can bring out those aspects of the original that are unattainable to the naked eye yet accessible to the lens, which is adjustable and chooses its angle at will. And photographic reproduction, with the aid of certain processes, such as enlargement or slow motion, can capture images which escape natural vision. Secondly, technical reproduction can put the copy of the original into situations which would be out of reach for the original itself. Above all, it enables the original to meet the beholder halfway, be it in the form of a photograph or a phonograph record. The cathedral leaves its locale to be received in the studio of a lover of art; the choral produc-tion, performed in an auditorium or in the open air, resounds in the drawing room.

The situations into which the product of mechanical reproduction can be brought may not touch the actual work of art, yet the quality of its presence is always depreciated. This holds not only for the art work but also, for instance, for a landscape which passes in review before the spectator in a movie. In the case of the art object, a most sensitive nucleus — namely, its authenticity — is interfered with whereas no natural object is vulnerable on that score. The authenticity of a thing is the essence of all that is transmissible from its beginning, ranging from its substantive duration to its testimony to the history which it has experienced. Since the his-torical testimony rests on the authenticity, the former too, is jeopardized by reproduction when substantive duration ceases to matter. And what is really jeopardized when the historical testimony is affected is the authority of the object.[4]

One might subsume the eliminated element in the term "aura" and go on to say: that which withers

[4]The poorest provincial staging of *Faust* is superior to a *Faust* film in that, ideally, it competes with the first performance at Weimar. Before the screen it is unprofit-able to remember traditional contents which might come to mind before the stage — for instance, that Goethe's friend Johann Heinrich Merck is hidden in Mephisto, and the like. [Benjamin]

in the age of mechanical reproduction is the aura of the work of art. This is a symptomatic process whose significance points beyond the realm of art. One might generalize by saying: the technique of reproduction detaches the reproduced object from the domain of tradition. By making many reproductions it substitutes a plurality of copies for a unique existence. And in permitting the reproduction to meet the beholder or listener in his own particular situation, it reactivates the object reproduced. These two processes lead to a tremendous shattering of tradition which is the obverse of the contemporary crisis and renewal of mankind. Both processes are intimately connected with the contemporary mass movements. Their most powerful agent is the film. Its social significance, particularly in its most positive form, is inconceivable without its destructive, cathartic aspect, that is, the liquidation of the traditional value of the cultural heritage. This phenomenon is most palpable in the great historical films. It extends to ever new positions. In 1927 Abel Gance exclaimed enthusiastically: "Shakespeare, Rembrandt, Beethoven will make films . . . all legends, all mythologies and all myths, all founders of religion, and the very religions . . . await their exposed resurrection, and the heroes crowd each other at the gate."[5] Presumably without intending it, he issued an invitation to a far-reaching liquidation.

III

During long periods of history, the mode of human sense perception changes with humanity's entire mode of existence. The manner in which human sense perception is organized, the medium in which it is accomplished, is determined not only by nature but by historical circumstances as well. The fifth century, with its great shifts of population, saw the birth of the late Roman art industry and the Vienna Genesis, and there developed not only an art different from that of antiquity but also a new kind of perception. The scholars of the Viennese school, Riegl and Wickhoff, who resisted the weight of classical tradition under which these later art forms had been buried, were the first to draw conclusions from them concerning the organization of perception at the time. However far-reaching their insight, these scholars limited themselves to showing the significant, formal hallmark which characterized perception in late Roman times. They did not attempt — and, perhaps, saw no way — to show the social transformations expressed by these changes of perception. The conditions for an analogous insight are more favorable in the present. And if changes in the medium of contemporary perception can be comprehended as decay of the aura, it is possible to show its social causes.

The concept of aura which was proposed above with reference to historical objects may usefully be illustrated with reference to the aura of natural ones. We define the aura of the latter as the unique phenomenon of a distance, however close it may be. If, while resting on a summer afternoon, you follow with your eyes a mountain range on the horizon or a branch which casts its shadows over you, you experience the aura of those mountains, of that branch. This image makes it easy to comprehend the social bases of the contemporary decay of the aura. It rests on two circumstances, both of which are related to the increasing significance of the masses in contemporary life. Namely, the desire of contemporary masses to bring things "closer" spatially and humanly, which is just as ardent as their bent toward overcoming the uniqueness of every reality by accepting its reproduction.[6] Every day the urge grows stronger to get hold of an object at very close range by way of its likeness, its reproduction. Unmistakably, reproduction as offered by picture magazines and newsreels differs from the image seen by the unarmed eye. Uniqueness and permanence are as closely linked in the latter as are transitoriness and reproducibility in the former. To pry an object from its shell, to destroy

[5]Abel Gance, "Le Temps de l'image est venu," *L'Art Cinématographique* 2 (Paris, 1927): 94–95. [Tr.] Gance was the director of the epic film *Napoleon* (1927).

[6]To satisfy the human interest of the masses may mean to have one's social function removed from the field of vision. Nothing guarantees that a portraitist of today, when painting a famous surgeon at the breakfast table in the midst of his family, depicts his social function more precisely than a painter of the seventeenth century who portrayed his medical doctors as representing this profession, like Rembrandt in his *Anatomy Lesson*. [Benjamin]

its aura, is the mark of a perception whose "sense of the universal equality of things" has increased to such a degree that it extracts it even from a unique object by means of reproduction. Thus is manifested in the field of perception what in the theoretical sphere is noticeable in the increasing importance of statistics. The adjustment of reality to the masses and of the masses to reality is a process of unlimited scope, as much for thinking as for perception.

IV

The uniqueness of a work of art is inseparable from its being imbedded in the fabric of tradition. This tradition itself is thoroughly alive and extremely changeable. An ancient statue of Venus, for example, stood in a different traditional context with the Greeks, who made it an object of veneration, than with the clerics of the Middle Ages, who viewed it as an ominous idol. Both of them, however, were equally confronted with its uniqueness, that is, its aura. Originally the contextual integration of art in tradition found its expression in the cult. We know that the earliest art works originated in the service of a ritual — first the magical, then the religious kind. It is significant that the existence of the work of art with reference to its aura is never entirely separated from its ritual function.[7] In other words, the unique value of the "authentic" work of art has its basis in ritual, the location of its original use value. This ritualistic basis, however remote, is still recognizable as secularized ritual even in the most profane forms of the cult of beauty.[8] The secular cult of beauty, developed during the

---

[7] The definition of the aura as a "unique phenomenon of a distance however close it may be" represents nothing but the formulation of the cult value of the work of art in categories of space and time perception. Distance is the opposite of closeness. The essentially distant object is the unapproachable one. Unapproachability is indeed a major quality of the cult image. True to its nature, it remains "distant, however close it may be." The closeness which one may gain from its subject matter does not impair the distance which it retains in its appearance. [Benjamin]

[8] To the extent to which the cult value of the painting is secularized, the ideas of its fundamental uniqueness lose distinctness. In the imagination of the beholder the uniqueness of the phenomena which hold sway in the cult image is more and more displaced by the empirical uniqueness of the creator or

Renaissance and prevailing for three centuries, clearly showed that ritualistic basis in its decline and the first deep crisis which befell it. With the advent of the first truly revolutionary means of reproduction, photography, simultaneously with the rise of socialism, art sensed the approaching crisis which has become evident a century later. At the time, art reacted with the doctrine of *l'art pour l'art*,[9] that is, with a theology of art. This gave rise to what might be called a negative theology in the form of the idea of "pure" art, which not only denied any social function of art but also any categorizing by subject matter. (In poetry, Mallarmé was the first to take this position.)

An analysis of art in the age of mechanical reproduction must do justice to these relationships, for they lead us to an all-important insight: for the first time in world history, mechanical reproduction emancipates the work of art from its parasitical dependence on ritual. To an ever greater degree the work of art reproduced becomes the work of art designed for reproducibility.[10] From a photographic negative, for example, one can make any number of prints; to ask for the "authentic" print makes no sense. But the instant the criterion of authenticity ceases to

---

[9] Art for art's sake. [Benjamin]

[10] In the case of films, mechanical reproduction is not, as with literature and painting, an external condition for mass distribution. Mechanical reproduction is inherent in the very technique of film production. This technique not only permits in the most direct way but virtually causes mass distribution. It enforces distribution because the production of a film is so expensive that an individual who, for instance, might afford to buy a painting no longer can afford to buy a film. In 1927 it was calculated that a major film, in order to pay its way, had to reach an audience of nine million. With the sound film, to be sure, a setback in its international distribution occurred at first: audiences became limited by language barriers. This coincided with the Fascist emphasis on national interests. It is more important to focus on this connection with Fascism than on this setback, which was soon minimized by synchronization. The simultaneity of both phenomena is attributable to the depression. The same disturbances which, on a larger scale, led to an attempt to maintain the existing property structure

be applicable to artistic production, the total function of art is reversed. Instead of being based on ritual, it begins to be based on another practice — politics.

V

Works of art are received and valued on different planes. Two polar types stand out: with one, the accent is on the cult value; with the other, on the exhibition value of the work.[11] Artistic production begins with ceremonial objects destined to serve in a cult. One may assume that what mattered was their existence, not their being on view. The elk portrayed by the man of the Stone Age on the walls of his cave was an instrument of magic. He did expose it to his fellow men, but in

the main it was meant for the spirits. Today the cult value would seem to demand that the work of art remain hidden. Certain statues of gods are accessible only to the priest in the cella;[12] certain Madonnas remain covered nearly all year round; certain sculptures on medieval cathedrals are invisible to the spectator on ground level. With the emancipation of the various art practices from ritual go increasing opportunities for the exhibition of their products. It is easier to exhibit a portrait bust that can be sent here and there than to exhibit the statue of divinity that has its fixed place in the interior of a temple. The same holds for the painting as against the mosaic or fresco that preceded it. And even though the public presentability of a mass originally may have been just as great as that of a symphony, the latter originated at the moment when its public presentability promised to surpass that of the mass.

With the different methods of technical reproduction of a work of art, its fitness for exhibition increased to such an extent that the quantitative shift between its two poles turned into a qualitative transformation of its nature. This is comparable to the situation of the work of art in prehistoric times when, by the absolute emphasis

---

by sheer force led the endangered film capital to speed up the development of the sound film. The introduction of the sound film brought about a temporary relief, not only because it again brought the masses into the theaters but also because it merged new capital from the electrical industry with that of the film industry. Thus, viewed from the outside, the sound film promoted national interests, but seen from the inside it helped to internationalize film production even more than previously. [Benjamin]

[11]This polarity cannot come into its own in the aesthetics of Idealism. Its idea of beauty comprises these polar opposites without differentiating between them and consequently excludes their polarity. Yet in Hegel this polarity announces itself as clearly as possible within the limits of Idealism. We quote from his *Philosophy of History:*

> Images were known of old. Piety at an early time required them for worship, but it could do without *beautiful* images. These might even be disturbing. In every beautiful painting there is also something nonspiritual, merely external, but its spirit speaks to man through its beauty. Worshipping, conversely, is concerned with the work as an object, for it is but a spiritless stupor of the soul. . . . Fine art has arisen . . . in the church . . . , although it has already gone beyond its principle as art.

Likewise, the following passage from *The Philosophy of Fine Art* indicates that Hegel sensed a problem here.

> We are beyond the stage of reverence for works of art as divine and objects deserving our worship. The impression they produce is one of a more reflective kind, and the emotions they arouse require a higher test. . . . —
> G. W. F. Hegel, *The Philosophy of Fine Arts,* trans., with notes, by F. P. B. Osmaston, vol. 1 (London, 1920), p. 12.

The transition from the first kind of artistic reception to the second characterizes the history of artistic reception in general. Apart from that, a certain oscillation between these two polar modes of reception can be demonstrated for each work

of art. Take the Sistine Madonna. Since Hubert Grimme's research it has been known that the Madonna originally was painted for the purpose of exhibition. Grimme's research was inspired by the question: What is the purpose of the molding in the foreground of the painting which the two cupids lean upon? How, Grimme asked further, did Raphael come to furnish the sky with two draperies? Research proved that the Madonna had been commissioned for the public lying-in-state of Pope Sixtus. The Popes lay in state in a certain side chapel of St. Peter's. On that occasion Raphael's picture had been fastened in a nichelike background of the chapel, supported by the coffin. In this picture Raphael portrays the Madonna approaching the papal coffin in clouds from the background of the niche, which was demarcated by green drapes. At the obsequies of Sixtus a preeminent exhibition value of Raphael's picture was taken advantage of. Some time later it was placed on the high altar in the church of the Black Friars at Piacenza. The reason for this exile is to be found in the Roman rites which forbid the use of paintings exhibited at obsequies as cult objects on the high altar. This regulation devalued Raphael's picture to some degree. In order to obtain an adequate price nevertheless, the Papal See resolved to add to the bargain the tacit toleration of the picture above the high altar. To avoid attention the picture was given to the monks of the far-off provincial town. [Benjamin]

[12]Cell (prison or monastic).

on its cult value, it was, first and foremost, an instrument of magic. Only later did it come to be recognized as a work of art. In the same way today, by the absolute emphasis on its exhibition value the work of art becomes a creation with entirely new functions, among which the one we are conscious of, the artistic function, later may be recognized as incidental.[13] This much is certain: today photography and the film are the most serviceable exemplifications of this new function.

VI

In photography, exhibition value begins to displace cult value all along the line. But cult value does not give way without resistance. It retires into an ultimate retrenchment: the human countenance. It is no accident that the portrait was the focal point of early photography. The cult of remembrance of loved ones, absent or dead, offers a last refuge for the cult value of the picture. For the last time the aura emanates from the early photographs in the fleeting expression of a human face. This is what constitutes their melancholy, incomparable beauty. But as man withdraws from the photographic image, the exhibition value for the first time shows its superiority to the ritual value. To have pinpointed this new stage constitutes the incomparable significance of Atget,[14] who, around 1900, took photographs of deserted Paris streets. It has quite justly been said of him that he photographed them like scenes of crime. The scene of a crime, too, is deserted; it is photographed for the purpose of establishing evidence. With Atget, photographs become standard evidence for historical occurrences, and acquire

[13]Bertolt Brecht, on a different level, engaged in analogous reflections: "If the concept of 'work of art' can no longer be applied to the thing that emerges once the work is transformed into a commodity, we have to eliminate this concept with cautious care but without fear, lest we liquidate the function of the very thing as well. For it has to go through this phase without mental reservation, and not as noncommittal deviation from the straight path; rather, what happens here with the work of art will change it fundamentally and erase its past to such an extent that should the old concept be taken up again — and it will, why not? — it will no longer stir any memory of the thing it once designated." [Benjamin]

[14]Jean-Eugène-Auguste Atget (1857–1927), Parisian photographer.

a hidden political significance. They demand a specific kind of approach; free-floating contemplation is not appropriate to them. They stir the viewer; he feels challenged by them in a new way. At the same time picture magazines begin to put up signposts for him, right ones or wrong ones, no matter. For the first time, captions have become obligatory. And it is clear that they have an altogether different character than the title of a painting. The directives which the captions give to those looking at pictures in illustrated magazines soon become even more explicit and more imperative in the film where the meaning of each single picture appears to be prescribed by the sequence of all preceding ones.

VII

The nineteenth-century dispute as to the artistic value of painting versus photography today seems devious and confused. This does not diminish its importance, however; if anything, it underlines it. The dispute was, in fact, the symptom of a historical transformation the universal impact of which was not realized by either of the rivals. When the age of mechanical reproduction separated art from its basis in cult, the semblance of its autonomy disappeared forever. The resulting change in the function of art transcended the perspective of the century; for a long time it even escaped that of the twentieth century, which experienced the development of the film.

Earlier much futile thought had been devoted to the question of whether photography is an art. The primary question — whether the very invention of photography had not transformed the entire nature of art — was not raised. Soon the film theoreticians asked the same ill-considered question with regard to the film. But the difficulties which photography caused traditional aesthetics were mere child's play as compared to those raised by the film. Whence the insensitive and forced character of early theories of the film. Abel Gance, for instance, compares the film with hieroglyphs: "Here, by a remarkable regression, we have come back to the level of expression of the Egyptians. ... Pictorial language has not yet matured because our eyes have not yet adjusted to it. There is as yet insufficient respect for, insufficient cult of, what it expresses."[15] Or, in the words of Séverin-Mars: "What art has been granted a dream more poetical and more real at the same time! Approached in this fashion the film might represent an incomparable means of expression. Only the most high-minded persons, in the most perfect and mysterious moments of their lives, should be allowed to enter its ambience."[16] Alexandre Arnoux concludes his fantasy about the silent film with the question: "Do not all the bold descriptions we have given amount to the definition of prayer?"[17] It is instructive to note how their desire to class the film among the "arts" forces these theoreticians to read ritual elements into it — with a striking lack of discretion. Yet when these speculations were published, films like *L'Opinion publique* and *The Gold Rush* had already appeared. This, however, did not keep Abel Gance from adducing hieroglyphs for purposes of comparison, nor Séverin-Mars from speaking of the film as one might speak of paintings by Fra Angelico. Characteristically, even today ultrareactionary authors give the film a similar contextual significance — if not an outright sacred one, then at least a supernatural one. Commenting on Max Reinhardt's film version of *A Midsummer Night's Dream,* Werfel states that undoubtedly it was the sterile copying of the exterior world with its streets, interiors, railroad stations, restaurants, motorcars, and beaches which until now had obstructed the elevation of the film to the realm of art. "The film has not yet realized its true meaning, its real possibilities . . . these consist in its unique faculty to express by natural means and with incomparable persuasiveness all that is fairylike, marvelous, supernatural."[18]

VIII

The artistic performance of a stage actor is definitely presented to the public by the actor in person; that of the screen actor, however, is presented by a camera, with a twofold consequence. The camera that presents the performance of the film actor to the public need not respect the performance as an integral whole. Guided by the cameraman, the camera continually changes its position with respect to the performance. The sequence of positional views which the editor composes from the material supplied him constitutes the completed film. It comprises certain factors of movement which are in reality those of the camera, not to mention special camera angles, close-ups, etc. Hence, the performance of the actor is subjected to a series of optical tests. This is the first consequence of the fact that the actor's performance is presented by means of a camera. Also, the film actor lacks the opportunity of the stage actor to adjust to the audience during his performance, since he does not present his performance to the audience in person. This permits the audience to take the position of a critic, without experiencing any personal contact with the actor. The audience's identification with the actor is really an identification with the camera. Consequently the audience takes the position of the camera; its approach is that of testing.[19] This is not the approach to which cult values may be exposed.

IX

For the film, what matters primarily is that the actor represents himself to the public before the camera, rather than representing someone else. One of the first to sense the actor's metamorphosis by this form of testing was Pirandello. Though his remarks on the subject in his novel *Si Gira* were limited to the negative aspects of the question and to the silent film only, this hardly impairs their validity.

[15]Abel Gance, pp. 100–101. [Tr.]
[16]Séverin-Mars, quoted by Abel Gance, p. 100. [Tr.]
[17]Alexandre Arnoux, *Cinéma pris* (1929), p. 28. [Tr.]
[18]Franz Werfel, "Ein Sommersnachtstraum, Ein Film von Shakespeare und Reinhardt," *Neues Wiener Journal,* cited in *Lu* (November 1935). [Tr.]

[19]"The film . . . provides — or could provide — useful insight into the details of human actions. . . . Character is never used as a source of motivation; the inner life of the persons never supplies the principal cause of the plot and seldom is its main result." (Bertolt Brecht, "Der Dreigroschenprozess," *Versuche,* p. 268.) The expansion of the field of the testable which mechanical equipment brings about for the actor corresponds to the extraordinary expansion of the field of the testable brought about for the individual through economic conditions. Thus, vocational aptitude tests become constantly more important. What matters in these tests are segmental performances of the individual. The film shot and the vocational aptitude test are taken before a committee of experts. The camera director in the studio occupies a place identical with that of the examiner during aptitude tests. [Benjamin]

For in this respect, the sound film did not change anything essential. What matters is that the part is acted not for an audience but for a mechanical contrivance — in the case of the sound film, for two of them. "The film actor," wrote Pirandello, "feels as if in exile — exiled not only from the stage but also from himself. With a vague sense of discomfort he feels inexplicable emptiness: his body loses its corporeality, it evaporates, it is deprived of reality, life, voice, and the noises caused by his moving about, in order to be changed into a mute image, flickering an instant on the screen, then vanishing into silence. . . . The projector will play with his shadow before the public, and he himself must be content to play before the camera."[20] This situation might also be characterized as follows: for the first time — and this is the effect of the film — man has to operate with his whole living person, yet forgoing its aura. For aura is tied to his presence; there can be no replica of it. The aura which, on the stage, emanates from Macbeth, cannot be separated for the spectators from that of the actor. However, the singularity of the shot in the studio is that the camera is substituted for the public. Consequently, the aura that envelops the actor vanishes, and with it the aura of the figure he portrays.

It is not surprising that it should be a dramatist such as Pirandello who, in characterizing the film, inadvertently touches on the very crisis in which we see the theater. Any thorough study proves that there is indeed no greater contrast than that of the stage play to a work of art that is completely subject to, or, like the film, founded in, mechanical reproduction. Experts have long recognized that in the film "the greatest effects are almost always obtained by 'acting' as little as possible. . . ." In 1932 Rudolf Arnheim saw "the latest trend . . . in treating the actor as a stage prop chosen for its characteristics and . . . inserted at the proper place."[21] With this idea something else is closely connected. The stage actor identifies

himself with the character of his role. The film actor very often is denied this opportunity. His creation is by no means all of a piece; it is composed of many separate performances. Besides certain fortuitous considerations, such as cost of studio, availability of fellow players, décor, etc., there are elementary necessities of equipment that split the actor's work into a series of mountable episodes. In particular, lighting and its installation require the presentation of an event that, on the screen, unfolds as a rapid and unified scene, in a sequence of separate shootings which may take hours at the studio; not to mention more obvious montage. Thus a jump from the window can be shot in the studio as a jump from a scaffold, and the ensuing flight, if need be, can be shot weeks later when outdoor scenes are taken. Far more paradoxical cases can easily be construed. Let us assume that an actor is supposed to be startled by a knock at the door. If his reaction is not satisfactory, the director can resort to an expedient: when the actor happens to be at the studio again he has a shot fired behind him without his being forewarned of it. The frightened reaction can be shot now and be cut into the screen version. Nothing more strikingly shows that art has left the realm of the "beautiful"

---

20 Luigi Pirandello, Si Gira, quoted by Léon Pierre-Quint, "Signification du cinéma," L'Art cinématographique, pp. 14–15. [Tr.]

21 Rudolf Arnheim, Film als Kunst (Berlin, 1932), pp. 176 f. In this context certain seemingly unimportant details in which the film director deviates from stage practices gain in interest. Such is the attempt to let the actor play without makeup, as made among others by Dreyer in his Jeanne d'Arc.

Dreyer spent months seeking the forty actors who constitute the Inquisitors' tribunal. The search for these actors resembled that for stage properties that are hard to come by. Dreyer made every effort to avoid resemblances of age, build, and physiognomy. If the actor thus becomes a stage property, this latter, on the other hand, frequently functions as actor. At least it is not unusual for the film to assign a role to the stage property. Instead of choosing at random from a great wealth of examples, let us concentrate on a particularly convincing one. A clock that is working will always be a disturbance on the stage. There it cannot be permitted its function of measuring time. Even in a naturalistic play, astronomical time would clash with theatrical time. Under these circumstances, it is highly revealing that the film can, wherever appropriate, use time as measured by a clock. From this more than from many other touches it may clearly be recognized that under certain circumstances each and every prop in a film may assume important functions. From here it is but one step to Pudovkin's statement that "the playing of an actor which is connected with an object and is built around it . . . is always one of the strongest methods of cinematic construction." (W. Pudovkin, Filmregie und Filmmanuskript [Berlin, 1928], p. 126.) The film is the first art form capable of demonstrating how matter plays tricks on man. Hence, films can be an excellent means of materialistic representation. [Benjamin]

semblance" which, so far, had been taken to be the only sphere where art could thrive.

X

The feeling of strangeness that overcomes the actor before the camera, as Pirandello describes it, is basically of the same kind as the estrangement felt before one's own image in the mirror. But now the reflected image has become separable, transportable. And where is it transported? Before the public.[22] Never for a moment does the screen actor cease to be conscious of this fact. While facing the camera he knows that ultimately he will face the public, the consumers who constitute the market. This market, where he offers not only his labor but also his whole self, his heart and soul, is beyond his reach. During the shooting he has as little contact with it as any article made in a factory. This may contribute to that oppression, that new anxiety which, according to Pirandello, grips the actor before the camera. The film responds to the shriveling of the aura with an artificial build-up of the "personality" outside the studio. The cult of the movie star, fostered by the money of the film industry, preserves not the unique aura of the person but the "spell of the personality," the phony spell of a commodity. So long as the movie-makers' capital sets the fashion, as a rule no other revolutionary merit can be accredited to today's film than the promotion of a revolutionary criticism of traditional concepts of art. We do not deny that in some cases today's films can also promote revolutionary criticism of social conditions, even of the distribution of property. However, our present study is no more specifically concerned with this than is the film production of Western Europe.

It is inherent in the technique of the film as well as that of sports that everybody who witnesses its accomplishments is somewhat of an expert. This is obvious to anyone listening to a group of newspaper boys leaning on their bicycles and discussing the outcome of a bicycle race. It is not for nothing that newspaper publishers arrange races for their delivery boys. These arouse great interest among the participants, for the victor has an opportunity to rise from delivery boy to professional racer. Similarly, the newsreel offers everyone the opportunity to rise from passer-by to movie extra. In this way any man might even find himself part of a work of art, as witness Vertoff's *Three Songs About Lenin* or Ivens's *Borinage*. Any man today can lay claim to being filmed. This claim can best be elucidated by a comparative look at the historical situation of contemporary literature.

For centuries a small number of writers were confronted by many thousands of readers. This changed toward the end of the last century. With the increasing extension of the press, which kept placing new political, religious, scientific, professional, and local organs before the readers, an increasing number of readers became writers — at first, occasional ones. It began with the daily press opening to its readers space for "letters to the editor." And today there is hardly a gainfully employed European who could not, in principle, find an opportunity to publish somewhere or other comments on his work, grievances, documentary reports, or that sort of thing. Thus, the distinction between author and public is about to lose its basic character. The difference becomes merely functional; it may vary from case to case. At any moment the reader is ready to turn into a writer. As expert, which he had to become willy-nilly in an extremely specialized work process, even if only in some minor respect, the

[22]The change noted here in the method of exhibition caused by mechanical reproduction applies to politics as well. The present crisis of the bourgeois democracies comprises a crisis of the conditions which determine the public presentation of the rulers. Democracies exhibit a member of government directly and personally before the nation's representatives. Parliament is his public. Since the innovations of camera and recording equipment make it possible for the orator to become audible and visible to an unlimited number of persons, the presentation of the man of politics before camera and recording equipment becomes paramount. Parliaments, as much as theaters, are deserted. Radio and film not only affect the function of the professional actor but likewise the function of those who also exhibit themselves before this mechanical equipment, those who govern. Though their tasks may be different, the change affects equally the actor and the ruler. The trend is toward establishing controllable and transferrable skills under certain social conditions. This results in a new selection, a selection before the equipment from which the star and the dictator emerge victorious. [Benjamin]

reader gains access to authorship. In the Soviet Union work itself is given a voice. To present it verbally is part of a man's ability to perform the work. Literary license is now founded on polytechnic rather than specialized training and thus becomes common property.[23]

All this can easily be applied to the film, where transitions that in literature took centuries

[23]The privileged character of the respective techniques is lost. Aldous Huxley writes:

> Advances in technology have led . . . to vulgarity. . . . Process reproduction and the rotary press have made possible the indefinite multiplication of writing and pic- tures. Universal education and relatively high wages have created an enormous public who know how to read and can afford to buy reading and pictorial matter. A great industry has been called into existence in order to sup- ply these commodities. Now, artistic talent is a very rare phenomenon; whence it follows . . . that, at every epoch and in all countries, most art has been bad. But the pro- portion of trash in the total artistic output is greater now than at any other period. That it must be so is a matter of simple arithmetic. The population of Western Europe has a little more than doubled during the last century. But the amount of reading — and seeing — matter has increased, I should imagine, at least twenty and possibly fifty or even a hundred times. If there were a men of talent in a popu- lation of x millions, there will presumably be 2n men of talent among 2x millions. The situation may be summed up thus. For every page of print and pictures published a century ago, twenty or perhaps even a hundred pages are published today. But for every man of talent then liv- ing, there are now only two men of talent. It may be of course that, thanks to universal education, many potential talents which in the past would have been stillborn are now enabled to realize themselves. Let us assume, then, that there are now three or even four men of talent to every one of earlier times. It still remains true to say that the consumption of reading — and seeing — matter has far outstripped the natural production of gifted writers and draughtsmen. It is the same with hearing-matter. Prosperity, the gramophone and the radio have created an audience of hearers who consume an amount of hearing- matter that has increased out of all proportion to the increase of population and the consequent natural increase of talented musicians. It follows from all this that in all the arts the output of trash is both absolutely and relatively greater than it was in the past; and that it must remain greater for just so long as the world continues to consume the present inordinate quantities of reading-matter, seeing- matter, and hearing-matter. — Aldous Huxley, *Beyond the Mexique Bay: A Traveller's Journal* (London, 1949), pp. 274 ff. First published in 1934.
>
> This mode of observation is obviously not progressive. [Benjamin]

have come about in a decade. In cinematic practice, particularly in Russia, this changeover has partially become established reality. Some of the players whom we meet in Russian films are not actors in our sense but people who por- tray *themselves* — and primarily in their own work process. In Western Europe the capitalistic exploitation of the film denies consideration to modern man's legitimate claim to being repro- duced. Under these circumstances the film indus- try is trying hard to spur the interest of the masses through illusion-promoting spectacles and dubi- ous speculations.

XI

The shooting of a film, especially of a sound film, affords a spectacle unimaginable anywhere at any time before this. It presents as process in which it is impossible to assign to a spectator a viewpoint which would exclude from the actual scene such extraneous accessories as camera equipment, lighting machinery, staff assistants, etc. — unless his eye were on a line parallel with the lens. This circumstance, more than any other, renders superficial and insignificant any possible simi- larity between a scene in the studio and one on the stage. In the theater one is well aware of the place from which the play cannot immediately be detected as illusionary. There is no such place for the movie scene that is being shot. Its illusionary nature is that of the second degree, the result of cutting. That is to say, in the studio the mechani- cal equipment has penetrated so deeply into reality that its pure aspect freed from the foreign substance of equipment is the result of a special procedure, namely, the shooting by the specially adjusted camera and the mounting of the shot together with other similar ones. The equipment- free aspect of reality here has become the height of artifice; the sight of immediate reality has become an orchid in the land of technology.

Even more revealing is the comparison of these circumstances, which differ so much from those of the theater, with the situation in painting. Here the question is: How does the cameraman compare with the painter? To answer this we take recourse to an analogy with a surgical operation. The surgeon represents the polar opposite of the magician. The magician heals a sick person by the laying on of hands; the surgeon cuts into the patient's body. The magician maintains the natural distance between the patient and himself; though he reduces it very slightly by the laying on of hands, he greatly increases it by virtue of his authority. The surgeon does exactly the reverse; he greatly diminishes the distance between himself and the patient by penetrating into the patient's body, and increases it but little by the caution with which his hand moves among the organs. In short, in contrast to the magician — who is still hidden in the medical practitioner — the surgeon at the decisive moment abstains from facing the patient man to man; rather, it is through the operation that he penetrates into him.

Magician and surgeon compare to painter and cameraman. The painter maintains in his work a natural distance from reality, the cameraman penetrates deeply into its web.[24] There is a tremendous difference between the pictures they obtain. That of the painter is a total one, that of the cameraman consists of multiple fragments which are assembled under a new law. Thus, for contemporary man the representation of reality by the film is incomparably more significant than that of the painter, since it offers, precisely because of the thoroughgoing permeation of reality with mechanical equipment, as aspect of reality which is free of all equipment. And that is what one is entitled to ask from a work of art.

XII

Mechanical reproduction of art changes the reaction of the masses toward art. The reactionary

[24]The boldness of the cameraman is indeed comparable to that of the surgeon. Luc Durtain lists among specific technical sleights of hand those "which are required in surgery in the case of certain difficult operations. I choose as an example a case from oto-rhino-laryngology; . . . the so-called endonasal perspective procedure; or I refer to the acrobatic tricks of larynx surgery which have to be performed following the reversed picture in the laryngoscope. I might also speak of ear surgery which suggests the precision work of watchmakers. What range of the most subtle muscular acrobatics is required from the man who wants to repair or save the human body! We have only to think of the couching of a cataract where there is virtually a debate of steel with nearly fluid tissue, or of the major abdominal operations (laparotomy)." — Luc Durtain. [Benjamin]

attitude toward a Picasso painting changes into the progressive reaction toward a Chaplin movie. The progressive reaction is characterized by the direct, intimate fusion of visual and emotional enjoyment with the orientation of the expert. Such fusion is of great social significance. The greater the decrease in the social significance of an art form, the sharper the distinction between criticism and enjoyment by the public. The conventional is uncritically enjoyed, and the truly new is criticized with aversion. With regard to the screen, the critical and the receptive attitudes of the public coincide. The decisive reason for this is that individual reactions are predetermined by the mass audience response they are about to produce, and this is nowhere more pronounced than in the film. The moment these responses become manifest they control each other. Again, the comparison with painting is fruitful. A painting has always had an excellent chance to be viewed by one person or by a few. The simultaneous contemplation of paintings by a large public, such as developed in the nineteenth century, is an early symptom of the crisis of painting, a crisis which was by no means occasioned exclusively by photography but rather in a relatively independent manner by the appeal of art works to the masses.

Painting simply is in no position to present an object for simultaneous collective experience, as it was possible for architecture at all times, for the epic poem in the past, and for the movie today. Although this circumstance in itself should not lead one to conclusions about the social role of painting, it does constitute a serious threat as soon as painting, under special conditions and, as it were, against its nature, is confronted directly by the masses. In the churches and monasteries of the Middle Ages and at the princely courts up to the end of the eighteenth century, a collective reception of paintings did not occur simultaneously, but by graduated and hierarchized mediation. The change that has come about is an expression of the particular conflict in which painting was implicated by the mechanical reproducibility of paintings. Although paintings began to be publicly exhibited in galleries and salons, there was no way for the masses to organize and control themselves in their reception.[25] Thus the same public which responds in a progressive manner toward a grotesque film is bound to respond in a reactionary manner to surrealism.

XIII

The characteristics of the film lie not only in the manner in which man presents himself to mechanical equipment but also in the manner in which, by means of this apparatus, man can represent his environment. A glance at occupational psychology illustrates the testing capacity of the equipment. Psychoanalysis illustrates it in a different perspective. The film has enriched our field of perception with methods which can be illustrated by those of Freudian theory. Fifty years ago, a slip of the tongue passed more or less unnoticed. Only exceptionally may such a slip have revealed dimensions of depth in a conversation which had seemed to be taking its course on the surface. Since the *Psychopathology of Everyday Life* things have changed. This book isolated and made analyzable things which had heretofore floated along unnoticed in the broad stream of perception. For the entire spectrum of optical, and now also acoustical, perception the film has brought about a similar deepening of apperception. It is only an obverse of this fact that behavior items shown in a movie can be analyzed much more precisely and from more points of view than those presented on paintings or on the stage. As compared with painting, filmed behavior lends itself more readily to analysis because of its incomparably more precise statements of the situation. In comparison with the stage scene, the filmed behavior item lends itself more readily to analysis because it can be isolated more easily. This circumstance derives its chief importance from its tendency to promote the mutual penetration of art and science. Actually, of a screened behavior item which is neatly brought out in a certain situation,

[25]This mode of observation may seem crude, but as the great theoretician Leonardo has shown, crude modes of observation may at times be usefully adduced. Leonardo compares painting and music as follows: "Painting is superior to music because, unlike unfortunate music, it does not have to die as soon as it is born. . . . Music which is consumed in the very act of its birth is inferior to painting which the use of varnish has rendered eternal." (Tratalo I, 29.) [Benjamin]

like a muscle of a body, *it is difficult to say which* is more fascinating, its artistic value or its value for science. To demonstrate the identity of the artistic and scientific uses of photography which heretofore usually were separated will be one of the revolutionary functions of the film.[26]

By close-ups of the things around us, by focusing on hidden details of familiar objects, by exploring commonplace milieus under the ingenious guidance of the camera, the film, on the one hand, extends our comprehension of the necessities which rule our lives; on the other hand, it manages to assure us of an immense and unexpected field of action. Our taverns and our metropolitan streets, our offices and furnished rooms, our railroad stations and our factories appeared to have us locked up hopelessly. Then came the film and burst this prison-world asunder by the dynamite of the tenth of a second, so that now, in the midst of its far-flung ruins and debris, we calmly and adventurously go traveling. With the close-up, space expands; with slow motion, movement is extended. The enlargement of a snapshot does not simply render more precise what in any case was visible, though unclear: it reveals entirely new structural formations of the subject. So, too, slow motion not only presents familiar qualities of movement but reveals in them entirely unknown ones "which, far from looking like retarded rapid movements, give the effect of singularly gliding, floating, supernatural motions."[27] Evidently a different nature opens itself to the camera than opens to the naked eye — if only because an unconsciously penetrated space is substituted for a space consciously explored by man. Even if one has a general knowledge of the way people walk,

[26]Renaissance painting offers a revealing analogy to this situation. The incomparable development of this art and its significance rested not least on the integration of a number of new sciences, or at least of new scientific data. Renaissance painting made use of anatomy and perspective, of mathematics, meteorology, and chromatology. Valéry writes: "What could be further from us than the strange claim of a Leonardo to whom painting was a supreme goal and the ultimate demonstration of knowledge? Leonardo was convinced that painting demanded universal knowledge, and he did not even shrink from a theoretical analysis which to us is stunning because of its very depth and precision. . . ." — Paul Valéry, "Autour de Corot," *Pièces sur l'art* (Paris), p. 191. [Benjamin]

[27]Rudolf Arnheim, p. 138. [Tr.]

one knows nothing of a person's posture during the fractional second of a stride. The act of reaching for a lighter or a spoon is familiar routine, yet we hardly know what really goes on between hand and metal, not to mention how this fluctuates with our moods. Here the camera intervenes with the resources of its lowerings and liftings, its interruptions and isolations, its extensions and accelerations, its enlargements and reductions. The camera introduces us to unconscious optics as does psychoanalysis to unconscious impulses.

XIV

One of the foremost tasks of art has always been the creation of a demand which could be fully satisfied only later.[28] The history of every art form shows critical epochs in which a certain art form aspires to effects which could be fully obtained only with a changed technical standard, that is

---

[28]"The work of art," says André Breton, "is valuable only insofar as it is vibrated by the reflexes of the future." Indeed, every developed art form intersects three lines of development. Technology works toward a certain form of art. Before the advent of the film there were photo booklets with pictures which flitted by the onlooker upon pressure of the thumb, thus portraying a boxing bout or a tennis match. Then there were the slot machines in bazaars; their picture sequences were produced by the turning of a crank.

Secondly, the traditional art forms in certain phases of their development strenuously work toward effects which later are effortlessly attained by the new ones. Before the rise of the movie the Dadaists' performances tried to create an audience reaction which Chaplin later evoked in a more natural way.

Thirdly, unspectacular social changes often promote a change in receptivity which will benefit the new art form. Before the movie had begun to create its public, pictures that were no longer immobile captivated an assembled audience in the so-called *Kaiserpanorama*. Here the public assembled before a screen into which stereoscopes were mounted, one to each beholder. By a mechanical process individual pictures appeared briefly before the stereoscopes, then made way for others. Edison still had to use similar devices in presenting the first movie strip before the film screen and projection were known. This strip was presented to a small public which stared into the apparatus in which the succession of pictures was reeling off. Incidentally, the institution of the *Kaiserpanorama* shows very clearly a dialectic of the development. Shortly before the movie turned the reception of pictures into a collective one, the individual viewing of pictures in these swiftly outmoded establishments came into play once more with an intensity comparable to that of the ancient priest beholding the statue of a divinity in the cella. [Benjamin]

---

to say, in a new art form. The extravagances and crudities of art which thus appear, particularly in the so-called decadent epochs, actually arise from the nucleus of its richest historical energies. In recent years, such barbarisms were abundant in Dadaism.[29] It is only now that its impulse becomes discernible: Dadaism attempted to create by pictorial — and literary — means the effects which the public today seeks in the film.

Every fundamentally new, pioneering creation of demands will carry beyond its goal. Dadaism did so to the extent that it sacrificed the market values which are so characteristic of the film in favor of higher ambitions — though of course it was not conscious of such intentions as here described. The Dadaists attached much less importance to the sales value of their work than to its uselessness for contemplative immersion. The studied degradation of their material was not the least of their means to achieve this uselessness. Their poems are "word salad" containing obscenities and every imaginable waste product of language. The same is true of their paintings, on which they mounted buttons and tickets. What they intended and achieved was a relentless destruction of the aura of their creations, which they branded as reproductions with the very means of production. Before a painting of Arp's or a poem by August Stramm it is impossible to take time for contemplation and evaluation as one would like before a canvas of Derain's or a poem by Rilke. In the decline of middle-class society, contemplation became a school for asocial behavior; it was countered by distraction as a variant of social conduct.[30] Dadaistic activities actually assured a rather vehement distraction by making works of art the center of scandal. One requirement was foremost: to outrage the public.

---

[29]Movement in the 1920s in both poetry and graphic art characterized by a parodistic treatment of mechanized society and an outrageous assault on the viewer. Major works of Dada include the Buñuel-Dali film *Un Chien Andalou* and Alfred Jarry's play *Ubu roi;* its principal theorist was André Breton.

[30]The theological archetype of this contemplation is the awareness of being alone with one's God. Such awareness, in the heyday of the bourgeoisie, went to strengthen the freedom to shake off clerical tutelage. During the decline of the bourgeoisie this awareness had to take into account the hidden tendency to withdraw from public affairs those forces which the individual draws upon in his communion with God. [Benjamin]

From an alluring appearance or persuasive structure of sound the work of art of the Dadaists became an instrument of ballistics. It hit the spectator like a bullet, it happened to him, thus acquiring a tactile quality. It promoted a demand for the film, the distracting element of which is also primarily tactile, being based on changes of place and focus which periodically assail the spectator. Let us compare the screen on which a film unfolds with the canvas of a painting. The painting invites the spectator to contemplation; before it the spectator can abandon himself to his associations. Before the movie frame he cannot do so. No sooner has his eye grasped a scene than it is already changed. It cannot be arrested. Duhamel, who detests the film and knows nothing of its significance, though something of its structure, notes this circumstance as follows: "I can no longer think what I want to think. My thoughts have been replaced by moving images."[31] The spectator's process of association in view of these images is indeed interrupted by their constant, sudden change. This constitutes the shock effect of the film, which, like all shocks, should be cushioned by heightened presence of mind.[32] By means of its technical structure, the film has taken the physical shock effect out of the wrappers in which Dadaism had, as it were, kept it inside the moral shock effect.[33]

[31]Georges Duhamel, *Scènes de la vie future* (Paris, 1930), p. 52. [Tr.]

[32]The film is the art form that is in keeping with the increased threat to his life which modern man has to face. Man's need to expose himself to shock effects is his adjustment to the dangers threatening him. The film corresponds to profound changes in the apperceptive apparatus — changes that are experienced on an individual scale by the man in the street in big-city traffic, on a historical scale by every present-day citizen. [Benjamin]

[33]As for Dadaism, insights important for Cubism and Futurism are to be gained from the movie. Both appear as deficient attempts of art to accommodate the pervasion of reality by the apparatus. In contrast to the film, these schools did not try to use the apparatus as such for the artistic presentation of reality, but aimed at some sort of alloy in the joint presentation of reality and apparatus. In Cubism, the premonition that this apparatus will be structurally based on optics plays a dominant part; in Futurism, it is the premonition of the effects of this apparatus which are brought out by the rapid sequence of the film strip. [Benjamin]

XV

The mass is a matrix from which all traditional behavior toward works of art issues today in a new form. Quantity has been transmuted into quality. The greatly increased mass of participants has produced a change in the mode of participation. The fact that the new mode of participation first appeared in a disreputable form must not confuse the spectator. Yet some people have launched spirited attacks against precisely this superficial aspect. Among these, Duhamel has expressed himself in the most radical manner. What he objects to most is the kind of participation which the movie elicits from the masses. Duhamel calls the movie "a pastime for helots,[34] a diversion for uneducated, wretched, worn-out creatures who are consumed by their worries . . . , a spectacle which requires no concentration and presupposes no intelligence . . . , which kindles no light in the heart and awakens no hope other than the ridiculous one of somebody becoming a 'star' in Los Angeles."[35] Clearly, this is at bottom the same ancient lament that the masses seek distraction whereas art demands concentration. That is a commonplace. The question remains whether it provides a platform for the analysis of the film. A closer look is needed here. Distraction and concentration form polar opposites which may be stated as follows: A man who concentrates before a work of art is absorbed by it. He enters into this work of art the way legend tells of the Chinese painter when he viewed his finished painting. In contrast, the distracted mass absorbs the work of art. This is most obvious with regard to buildings. Architecture has always represented the prototype of a work of art the reception of which is consummated by a collectivity in a state of distraction. The laws of its reception are most instructive.

Buildings have been man's companions since primeval times. Many art forms have developed and perished. Tragedy begins with the Greeks, is extinguished with them, and after centuries its "rules" only are revived. The epic poem, which had its origin in the youth of nations, expires in

[34]Slaves.

[35]Duhamel, p. 58. [Tr.]

Europe at the end of the Renaissance. Panel painting is a creation of the Middle Ages, and nothing guarantees its uninterrupted existence. But the human need for shelter is lasting. Architecture has never been idle. Its history is more ancient than that of any other art, and its claim to being a living force has significance in every attempt to comprehend the relationship of the masses to art. Buildings are appropriated in a twofold manner: by use and by perception — or rather, by touch and sight. Such appropriation cannot be understood in terms of the attentive concentration of a tourist before a famous building. On the tactile side there is no counterpart to contemplation on the optical side. Tactile appropriation is accomplished not so much by attention as by habit. As regards architecture, habit determines to a large extent even optical reception. The latter, too, occurs much less through rapt attention than by noticing the object in incidental fashion. This mode of appropriation, developed with reference to architecture, in certain circumstances acquires canonical value. For the tasks which face the human apparatus of perception at the turning points of history cannot be solved by optical means, that is, by contemplation, alone. They are mastered gradually by habit, under the guidance of tactile appropriation.

The distracted person, too, can form habits. More, the ability to master certain tasks in a state of distraction proves that their solution has become a matter of habit. Distraction as provided by art presents a covert control of the extent to which new tasks have become soluble by apperception. Since, moreover, individuals are tempted to avoid such tasks, art will tackle the most difficult and most important ones where it is able to mobilize the masses. Today it does so in the film. Reception in a state of distraction, which is increasing noticeably in all fields of art and is symptomatic of profound changes in apperception, finds in the film its true means of exercise. The film with its shock effect meets this mode of reception halfway. The film makes the cult value recede into the background not only by putting the public in the position of the critic, but also by the fact that at the movies this position requires no attention. The public is an examiner, but an absent-minded one.

EPILOGUE

The growing proletarianization of modern man and the increasing formation of masses are two aspects of the same process. Fascism attempts to organize the newly created proletarian masses without affecting the property structure which the masses strive to eliminate. Fascism sees its salvation in giving these masses not their right, but instead a chance to express themselves.[36] The masses have a right to change property relations; Fascism seeks to give them an expression while preserving property. The logical result of Fascism is the introduction of aesthetics into political life. The violation of the masses, whom Fascism, with its *Führer* cult, forces to their knees, has its counterpart in the violation of an apparatus which is pressed into the production of ritual values.

All efforts to render politics aesthetic culminate in one thing: war. War and war only can set a goal for mass movements on the largest scale while respecting the traditional property system. This is the political formula for the situation. The technological formula may be stated as follows: Only war makes it possible to mobilize all of today's technical resources while maintaining the property system. It goes without saying that the Fascist apotheosis of war does not employ such arguments. Still, Marinetti[37] says in his manifesto

---

[36]One technical feature is significant here, especially with regard to newsreels, the propagandist importance of which can hardly be overestimated. Mass reproduction is aided especially by the reproduction of masses. In big parades and monster rallies, in sports events, and in war, all of which nowadays are captured by camera and sound recording, the masses are brought face to face with themselves. This process, whose significance need not be stressed, is intimately connected with the development of the techniques of reproduction and photography. Mass movements are usually discerned more clearly by a camera than by the naked eye. A bird's-eye view best captures gatherings of hundreds of thousands. And even though such a view may be as accessible to the human eye as it is to the camera, the image received by the eye cannot be enlarged the way a negative is enlarged. This means that mass movements, including war, constitute a form of human behavior which particularly favors mechanical equipment. [Benjamin]

[37]Italian-French futurist writer and enthusiastic backer of Mussolini (1876–1944), author of *Guerra sola igiene del mundo* (*War — Sole Hygiene of the World*, 1915).

on the Ethiopian colonial war: "For twenty-seven years we Futurists have rebelled against the branding of war as antiaesthetic.... Accordingly we state: ... War is beautiful because it establishes man's dominion over the subjugated machinery by means of gas masks, terrifying megaphones, flame throwers, and small tanks. War is beautiful because it initiates the dreamt-of metalization of the human body. War is beautiful because it enriches a flowering meadow with the fiery orchids of machine guns. War is beautiful because it combines the gunfire, the cannonades, the cease-fire, the scents, and the stench of putrefaction into a symphony. War is beautiful because it creates new architecture, like that of the big tanks, the geometrical formation flights, the smoke spirals from burning villages, and many others.... Poets and artists of Futurism! ... remember these principles of an aesthetics of war so that your struggle for a new literature and a new graphic art ... may be illumined by them!"

This manifesto has the virtue of clarity. Its formulations deserve to be accepted by dialecticians. To the latter, the aesthetics of today's war appears as follows: If the natural utilization of productive forces is impeded by the property system, the increase in technical devices, in speed, and in the sources of energy will press for an unnatural utilization, and this is found in war. The destructiveness of war furnishes proof that society has been mature enough to incorporate technology as its organ, that technology has not been sufficiently developed to cope with the elemental forces of society. The horrible features of imperialistic warfare are attributable to the discrepancy between the tremendous means of production and their inadequate utilization in the process of production — in other words, to unemployment and the lack of markets. Imperialistic war is a rebellion of technology which collects, in the form of "human material," the claims to which society has denied its natural material. Instead of draining rivers, society directs a human stream into a bed of trenches; instead of dropping seeds from airplanes, it drops incendiary bombs over cities; and through gas warfare the aura is abolished in a new way.

"Fiat ars — pereat mundus,"[38] says Fascism, and, as Marinetti admits, expect war to supply the artistic gratification of a sense perception that has been changed by technology. This is evidently the consummation of "l'art pour l'art." Mankind, which in Homer's time was an object of contemplation for the Olympian gods, now is one for itself. Its self-alienation has reached such a degree that it can experience its own destruction as an aesthetic pleasure of the first order. This is the situation of politics which Fascism is rendering aesthetic. Communism responds by politicizing art.

[38]Let art exist, let the world perish.

Max Horkheimer
1895–1977

Max Horkheimer was born in 1895 in Stuttgart to assimilated Jewish parents. His family pressured him not to pursue academics, but to leave school at sixteen to work in his father's factory. After World War I, he finally began his studies in philosophy and psychology at Munich. When he moved to Frankfurt am Main to study under Hans Cornelius, he met Theodor Adorno, who would become his great friend and collaborator in forming the Frankfurt School of critical theory. In 1930, just five years after receiving his Ph.D., Horkheimer was named the director of the Institute for Social Research. As its first openly Marxist director, he worked with Herbert Marcuse, Erich Fromm, Walter Benjamin, and Adorno. The Institute was active and fruitful until the Nazi government closed it in 1933. Exiled first to Switzerland, Horkheimer was invited to bring the Institute to Columbia University, where the Institute's journal could continue to be published. During this time, he published his first major work, Authority and the Family *(1936). In 1940 Horkheimer became a U.S. citizen and moved to Berkeley, where he and Adorno would publish* Dialectic of Enlightenment *(1947), from which the following essay, "The Culture Industry: Enlightenment as Mass Deception," is excerpted. In this work, Adorno and Horkheimer argued that society's uncritical reception of scientific rationality would lead to the perversion of "reason" that had occurred under the Nazis in Germany. Although Adorno was a much more prolific writer, Horkheimer did continue to publish other works, such as 1967's* Eclipse of Reason. *Influenced by Schopenhauer, Horkheimer became increasingly pessimistic about the erosion of Enlightenment ideals under twentieth-century capitalism. In 1949 Horkheimer moved the Institute back to Frankfurt, where he became Rector of the University. After a five-year stint at the University of Chicago (1954–59), Horkheimer retired from university life, though he continued to write and publish. He died in Nuremberg in 1977.*

Theodor W. Adorno
1903–1969

Theodor Wiesengrund Adorno was born to middle-class parents in Frankfurt, Germany, where he studied psychology, sociology, and music, and took his Ph.D. in philosophy in 1924. He went to Vienna to study composition with the serial composer Alban Berg in 1925, then came back to Frankfurt for post-doctoral study in 1928. Strongly influenced by the Hegelian Marxism of Georg Lukács, he founded with Max Horkheimer the Institute for Social Research that was the nucleus of what became known as the Frankfurt school, a group that also included Herbert Marcuse, Walter Benjamin, and, in the next generation, Jürgen Habermas. In the waning days of the Weimar Republic, Adorno left for England, then spent the war years in America. In 1949 he returned to the University of Frankfurt, where he served as professor of sociology and philosophy, and where he became assistant director of the Institute in 1949, and sole director from 1958 until his death. Adorno's works include The Dialectic of Enlightenment *(1944, with Max Horkheimer; translated 1972);* The Philosophy of Modern Music *(1949; translated 1973);* Minima Moralia: Reflections from Damaged Life *(1951; translated 1974);* Prisms *(1955; translated 1967);* Introduction to the Sociology of Music *(1962; translated 1976);* Negative Dialectics *(1966; translated 1973); and the posthumous* Aesthetic Theory *(1970; translated 1996).*

From *The Culture Industry: Enlightenment as Mass Deception*

Translated by John Cumming.

The sociological theory that the loss of the support of objectively established religion, the dissolution of the last remnants of precapitalism, together with technological and social differentiation or specialization, have led to cultural chaos is disproved every day; for culture now impresses the same stamp on everything. Films, radio and magazines make up a system which is uniform as a whole and in every part. Even the aesthetic activities of political opposites are one in their enthusiastic obedience to the rhythm of the iron system. The decorative industrial management buildings and exhibition centers in authoritarian countries are much the same as anywhere else. The huge gleaming towers that shoot up every-where are outward signs of the ingenious plan-ning of international concerns, toward which the unleashed entrepreneurial system (whose monu-ments are a mass of gloomy houses and business premises in grimy, spiritless cities) was already hastening. Even now the older houses just outside the concrete city centers look like slums, and the new bungalows on the outskirts are at one with the flimsy structures of world fairs in their praise of technical progress and their built-in demand to be discarded after a short while like empty food cans. Yet the city housing projects designed to perpetuate the individual as a supposedly independent unit in a small hygienic dwelling make him all the more subservient to his adver-sary — the absolute power of capitalism. Because the inhabitants, as producers and as consumers, are drawn into the center in search of work and pleasure, all the living units crystallize into well-organized complexes. The striking unity of micro-cosm and macrocosm presents men with a model of their culture: the false identity of the general and the particular. Under monopoly all mass culture is identical, and the lines of its artificial framework begin to show through. The people at the top are no longer so interested in concealing monopoly: as its violence becomes more open, so its power grows. Movies and radio need no longer pretend to be art. The truth that they are just busi-ness is made into an ideology in order to justify the rubbish they deliberately produce. They call themselves industries; and when their directors' incomes are published, any doubt about the social utility of the finished products is removed.

Interested parties explain the culture industry in technological terms. It is alleged that because millions participate in it, certain reproduction processes are necessary that inevitably require identical needs in innumerable places to be satis-fied with identical goods. The technical contrast between the few production centers and the large number of widely dispersed consumption points is said to demand organization and planning by management. Furthermore, it is claimed that standards were based in the first place on con-sumers' needs, and for that reason were accepted with so little resistance. The result is the circle of manipulation and retroactive need in which the unity of the system grows ever stronger. No men-tion is made of the fact that the basis on which technology acquires power over society is the power of those whose economic hold over society is greatest. A technological rationale is the ratio-nale of domination itself. It is the coercive nature of society alienated from itself. Automobiles, bombs, and movies keep the whole thing together until their leveling element shows its strength in the very wrong which it furthered. It has made the technology of the culture industry no more than the achievement of standardization and mass production, sacrificing whatever involved a dis-tinction between the logic of the work and that of the social system. This is the result not of a law of movement in technology as such but of its func-tion in today's economy. The need which might resist central control has already been suppressed by the control of the individual consciousness. The step from the telephone to the radio has clearly distinguished the roles. The former still allowed the subscriber to play the role of subject, and was liberal. The latter is democratic: it turns all participants into listeners and authoritatively subjects them to broadcast programs which are all exactly the same. No machinery of rejoinder has been devised, and private broadcasters are denied any freedom. They are confined to the apocryphal field of the "amateur," and also have to accept organization from above. But any trace of spontaneity from the public in official broadcasting is controlled and absorbed by talent scouts, studio competitions and official programs of every kind selected by professionals. Talented performers belong to the industry long before it displays them; otherwise they would not be so eager to fit in. The attitude of the public, which ostensibly and actually favors the system of the culture industry, is a part of the system and not an excuse for it. If one branch of art follows the same formula as one with a very different medium and content; if the dramatic intrigue of broadcast soap operas becomes no more than useful material for showing how to master technical problems at both ends of the scale of musical experience — real jazz or a cheap imitation; or if a movement from a Beethoven symphony is crudely "adapted" for a film soundtrack in the same way as a Tolstoy novel is garbled in a film script: then the claim that this is done to satisfy the spontaneous wishes of the public is no more than hot air. We are closer to the facts if we explain these phenomena as inherent in the technical and personnel apparatus which, down to its last cog, itself forms part of the economic mechanism of selection. In addition there is the agreement — or at least the determination — of all executive authorities not to produce or sanction anything that in any way differs from their own rules, their own ideas about consumers, or above all themselves.

In our age the objective social tendency is incarnate in the hidden subjective purposes of company directors, the foremost among whom are in the most powerful sectors of industry — steel, petroleum, electricity, and chemicals. Culture monopolies are weak and dependent in comparison. They cannot afford to neglect their appeasement of the real holders of power if their sphere of activity in mass society (a sphere producing a specific type of commodity which anyhow is still too closely bound up with easygoing liberalism and Jewish intellectuals) is not to undergo a series of purges. The dependence of the most powerful broadcasting company on the electrical industry, or of the motion picture industry on the banks, is characteristic of the whole sphere, whose individual branches are themselves economically interwoven. All are in such close contact that the extreme concentration of mental forces allows demarcation lines between different firms and technical branches to be ignored. The ruthless unity in the culture industry is evidence of what will happen in politics. Marked differentiations such as those of A and B films,[1] or of stories in magazines in different price ranges, depend not so much on subject matter as on classifying, organizing, and labeling consumers. Something is provided for all so that none may escape; the distinctions are emphasized and extended. The public is catered for with a hierarchical range of mass-produced products of varying quality, thus advancing the rule of complete quantification. Everybody must behave (as if spontaneously) in accordance with his previously determined and indexed level, and choose the category of mass product turned out for his type. Consumers appear as statistics on research organization charts, and are divided by income groups into red, green, and blue areas; the technique is that used for any type of propaganda.

How formalized the procedure is can be seen when the mechanically differentiated products prove to be all alike in the end. That the difference between the Chrysler range and General Motors products is basically illusory strikes every child with a keen interest in varieties. What connoisseurs discuss as good or bad points serve only to perpetuate the semblance of competition and range of choice. The same applies to the Warner Brothers and Metro Goldwyn Mayer productions.

[1]During the 1930s, as the Depression took hold, movie attendance diminished and film studios responded by directing the movie theaters they owned and operated to show double features, consisting of an "A" movie (with important film stars and better scripts) and a "B" movie (often a genre film about gangsters or cowboys, with lesser actors). In 1948 a Supreme Court decision required studios to divest themselves of their theaters, and both the A/B system and the double feature slowly but eventually came to an end.

But even the differences between the more expensive and cheaper models put out by the same firm steadily diminish: for automobiles, there are such differences as the number of cylinders, cubic capacity, details of patented gadgets; and for films there are the number of stars, the extravagant use of technology, labor, and equipment, and the introduction of the latest psychological formulas. The universal criterion of merit is the amount of "conspicuous production," of blatant cash investment. The varying budgets in the culture industry do not bear the slightest relation to factual values, to the meaning of the products themselves. Even the technical media are relentlessly forced into uniformity. Television aims at a synthesis of radio and film, and is held up only because the interested parties have not yet reached agreement, but its consequences will be quite enormous and promise to intensify the impoverishment of aesthetic matter so drastically, that by tomorrow the thinly veiled identity of all industrial culture products can come triumphantly out into the open, derisively fulfilling the Wagnerian dream of the *Gesamtkunstwerk* — the fusion of all the arts in one work.[2] The alliance of word, image, and music is all the more perfect then in *Tristan* because the sensuous elements which all approvingly reflect the surface of social reality are in principle embodied in the same technical process, the unity of which becomes its distinctive content. This process integrates all the elements of the production, from the novel (shaped with an eye to the film) to the last sound effect. It is the triumph of invested capital, whose title as absolute master is etched deep into the hearts of the dispossessed in the employment line; it is the meaningful content of every film, whatever plot the production team may have selected.

The man with leisure has to accept what the culture manufacturers offer him. Kant's formalism still expected a contribution from the individual, who was thought to relate the varied experiences of the senses to fundamental concepts; but industry robs the individual of his function. Its prime

service to the customer is to do his schematizing for him. Kant said that there was a secret mechanism in the soul which prepared direct intuitions in such a way that they could be fitted into the system of pure reason.[3] But today that secret has been deciphered. While the mechanism is to all appearances planned by those who serve up the data of experience, that is, by the culture industry, it is in fact forced upon the latter by the power of society, which remains irrational, however we may try to rationalize it; and this inescapable force is processed by commercial agencies so that they give an artificial impression of being in command. There is nothing left for the consumer to classify. Producers have done it for him. Art for the masses has destroyed the dream but still conforms to the tenets of that dreaming idealism which critical idealism balked at. Everything derives from consciousness: for Malebranche and Berkeley,[4] from the consciousness of God; in mass art, from the consciousness of the production team. Not only are the hit songs, stars, and soap operas cyclically recurrent and rigidly invariable types, but the specific content of the entertainment itself is derived from them and only appears to change. The details are interchangeable. The short interval sequence which was effective in a hit song, the hero's momentary fall from grace (which he accepts as good sport), the rough treatment which the beloved gets from the male star, the latter's rugged defiance of the spoilt heiress, are, like all the other details, ready-made clichés to be slotted in anywhere; they never do anything more than fulfil the purpose allotted them in the overall plan. Their whole *raison d'être* is to confirm it by being its constituent parts. As soon as the film begins, it is quite clear how it will end, and who will be rewarded, punished, or forgotten. In light music, once the trained ear has heard the first notes of the hit song, it can guess what is coming and feel flattered

[2]Composer Richard Wagner (1813–1883), in *The Artwork of the Future* (1849) held up as the ideal the work of art that would combine music, poetry, and scenic beauty to appeal to all the senses at once. His opera *Tristan und Isolde* (produced 1865) is mentioned in the next sentence as an example.

[3]Kant argued that the process of perception involved an active synthesis of sense data on the part of the perceiver: see above, pp. 218-19.

[4]Nicholas Malebranche (1638–1715) argued that our knowledge of external reality comes from seeing "everything" within God. George Berkeley (1685–1753) argued that being requires perception, but that material things continue to exist even when unobserved by humans because they are always perceived by the mind of God.

when it does come. The average length of the short story has to be rigidly adhered to. Even gags, effects, and jokes are calculated like the setting in which they are placed. They are the responsibility of special experts and their narrow range makes it easy for them to be apportioned in the office. The development of the culture industry has led to the predominance of the effect, the obvious touch, and the technical detail over the work itself — which once expressed an idea, but was liquidated together with the idea. When the detail won its freedom, it became rebellious and, in the period from Romanticism to Expressionism, asserted itself as free expression, as a vehicle of protest against the organization. In music the single harmonic effect obliterated the awareness of form as a whole; in painting the individual color was stressed at the expense of pictorial composition; and in the novel psychology became more important than structure.[5] The totality of the culture industry has put an end to this. Though concerned exclusively with effects, it crushes their insubordination and makes them subserve the formula, which replaces the work. The same fate is inflicted on whole and parts alike. The whole inevitably bears no relation to the details — just like the career of a successful man into which everything is made to fit as an illustration or a proof, whereas it is nothing more than the sum of all those idiotic events. The so-called dominant idea is like a file which ensures order but not coherence. The whole and the parts are alike; there is no antithesis and no connection. Their prearranged harmony is a mockery of what had to be striven after in the great bourgeois works of art. In Germany the graveyard stillness of the dictatorship already hung over the gayest films of the democratic era.

The whole world is made to pass through the filter of the culture industry. The old experience of the moviegoer, who sees the world outside as an extension of the film he has just left (because the latter is intent upon reproducing the world of everyday perceptions), is now the producer's guideline. The more intensely and flawlessly his techniques duplicate empirical objects, the easier it is today for the illusion to prevail that the outside world is the straightforward continuation of that presented on the screen. This purpose has been furthered by mechanical reproduction since the lightning takeover by the sound film.

Real life is becoming indistinguishable from the movies. The sound film, far surpassing the theater of illusion, leaves no room for imagination or reflection on the part of the audience, who is unable to respond within the structure of the film, yet deviate from its precise detail without losing the thread of the story; hence the film forces its victims to equate it directly with reality. The stunting of the mass-media consumer's powers of imagination and spontaneity does not have to be traced back to any psychological mechanisms; he must ascribe the loss of those attributes to the objective nature of the products themselves, especially to the most characteristic of them, the sound film. They are so designed that quickness, powers of observation, and experience are undeniably needed to apprehend them at all; yet sustained thought is out of the question if the spectator is not to miss the relentless rush of facts. Even though the effort required for his response is semi-automatic, no scope is left for the imagination. Those who are so absorbed by the world of the movie — by its images, gestures, and words — that they are unable to supply what really makes it a world, do not have to dwell on particular points of its mechanics during a screening. All the other films and products of the entertainment industry which they have seen have taught them what to expect; they react automatically. The might of industrial society is lodged in men's minds. The entertainments manufacturers know that their products will be consumed with alertness even when the customer is distraught, for each of them is a model of the huge economic machinery which has always sustained the masses, whether at work or at leisure — which is akin to work. From every sound film and every broadcast program the social effect can be inferred which is exclusive to none but is shared by all alike. The culture industry as a whole has molded men as a type unfailingly reproduced in every product. All the agents of this process, from the producer to the women's clubs, take good care that the simple reproduction of this mental state is not nuanced or extended in any way.

[5]Here the authors bring up salient features of modernism in music, painting, and prose fiction.

The art historians and guardians of culture who complain of the extinction in the West of a basic style-determining power are wrong. The stereotyped appropriation of everything, even the inchoate, for the purposes of mechanical reproduction surpasses the rigor and general currency of any "real style," in the sense in which cultural cognoscenti celebrate the organic precapitalist past.[6] No Palestrina[7] could be more of a purist in eliminating every unprepared and unresolved discord than the jazz arranger in suppressing any development which does not conform to the jargon. When jazzing up Mozart he changes him not only when he is too serious or too difficult but when he harmonizes the melody in a different way, perhaps more simply, than is customary now. No medieval builder can have scrutinized the subjects for church windows and sculptures more suspiciously than the studio hierarchy scrutinizes a work by Balzac or Hugo before finally approving it. No medieval theologian could have determined the degree of the torment to be suffered by the damned in accordance with the ordo of divine love[8] more meticulously than the producers of shoddy epics calculate the torture to be undergone by the hero or the exact point to which the leading lady's hemline shall be raised. The explicit and implicit, exoteric and esoteric catalog of the forbidden and tolerated is so extensive that it not only defines the area of freedom but is all-powerful inside it. Everything down to the last detail is shaped accordingly. . . .

[6]Adorno in particular had seen the progression of styles in painting, music, and literature as obeying a historical law. But after the triumphant modernism of the 1920s and 1930s, the progression seemed to come to a halt. Here the authors explain that halt in terms of the ownership of the culture industry and the intention of the owners.

[7]Giovanni Perluigi di Palestrina (1525–1594), Renaissance composer of liturgical music. The authors' suggestion of censorship may refer to a legend that the Council of Trent had threatened to ban polyphonic music, on the ground that the liturgical text became incomprehensible, but that Palestrina composed a mass, the *Missa Papae Marcelli*, that reconciled the authorities to this style.

[8]*Ordo* is Latin for "order." The allusion is to Dante's *Divine Comedy*, where Dante finds written on the gates of Hell that they were built by "divina potestate / la somma sapienza e il primo Amore" — divine power, the highest wisdom, and primal love.

Whenever Orson Welles[9] offends against the tricks of the trade, he is forgiven because his departures from the norm are regarded as calculated mutations which serve all the more strongly to confirm the validity of the system. The constraint of the technically-conditioned idiom which stars and directors have to produce as "nature," so that the people can appropriate it, extends to such fine nuances that they almost attain the subtlety of the devices of an avant-garde work as against those of truth. The rare capacity minutely to fulfill the obligations of the natural idiom in all branches of the culture industry becomes the criterion of efficiency. What and how they say it must be measurable by everyday language, as in logical positivism. The producers are experts. The idiom demands an astounding productive power, which it absorbs and squanders. In a diabolical way it has overreached the culturally conservative distinction between genuine and artificial style. A style might be called artificial which is imposed from without on the refractory impulses of a form. But in the culture industry every element of the subject matter has its origin in the same apparatus as that jargon whose stamp it bears. The quarrels in which the artistic experts become involved with sponsor and censor about a lie going beyond the bounds of credibility are evidence not so much of an inner aesthetic tension as of a divergence of interests. The reputation of the specialist, in which a last remnant of objective independence sometimes finds refuge, conflicts with the business politics of the Church, or the concern which is manufacturing the cultural commodity. But the thing itself has been essentially objectified and made viable before the established authorities began to argue about it. Even before Zanuck acquired her, Saint Bernadette was regarded by her latter-day hagiographer as brilliant propaganda for all interested parties.[10] That is what became of the emotions

[9]Orson Welles (1915–1985), maverick Hollywood director of *Citizen Kane* (1941).

[10]Darryl F. Zanuck was the studio head of Twentieth-Century Fox, which made *The Song of Bernadette* (1943), a film that won four Oscars and was nominated for eight others, based on the play by the authors' compatriot and fellow exile Franz Werfel.

of the character. Hence the style of the culture industry, which no longer has to test itself against any refractory material, is also the negation of style. The reconciliation of the general and particular, of the rule and the specific demands of the subject matter, the achievement of which alone gives essential, meaningful content to style, is futile because there has ceased to be the slightest tension between opposite poles: these concordant extremes are dismally identical; the general can replace the particular, and vice versa.

Nevertheless, this caricature of style does not amount to something beyond the genuine style of the past. In the culture industry the notion of genuine style is seen to be the aesthetic equivalent of domination. Style considered as mere aesthetic regularity is a romantic dream of the past. The unity of style not only of the Christian Middle Ages but of the Renaissance expresses in each case the different structure of social power, and not the obscure experience of the oppressed in which the general was enclosed. The great artists were never those who embodied a wholly flawless and perfect style, but those who used style as a way of hardening themselves against the chaotic expression of suffering, as a negative truth. The style of their works gave what was expressed that force without which life flows away unheard. Those very art forms which are known as classical, such as Mozart's music, contain objective trends which represent something different to the style which they incarnate. As late as Schönberg and Picasso, the great artists have retained a mistrust of style, and at crucial points have subordinated it to the logic of the matter. What Dadaists and Expressionists called the untruth of style as such triumphs today in the sung jargon of a crooner, in the carefully contrived elegance of a film star, and even in the admirable expertise of a photograph of a peasant's squalid hut. Style represents a promise in every work of art. That which is expressed is subsumed through style into the dominant forms of generality, into the language of music, painting, or words, in the hope that it will be reconciled thus with the idea of true generality. This promise held out by the work of art that it will create truth by lending new shape to the conventional social forms is as necessary as it is hypocritical. It unconditionally posits the real forms of life as it is by suggesting that fulfillment lies in their aesthetic derivatives. To this extent the claim of art is always ideology too. However, only in this confrontation with tradition of which style is the record can art express suffering. That factor in a work of art which enables it to transcend reality certainly cannot be detached from style; but it does not consist of the harmony actually realized, of any doubtful unity of form and content, within and without, of individual and society; it is to be found in those features in which discrepancy appears: in the necessary failure of the passionate striving for identity. Instead of exposing itself to this failure in which the style of the great work of art has always achieved self-negation, the inferior work has always relied on its similarity with others — on a surrogate identity.

In the culture industry this imitation finally becomes absolute. Having ceased to be anything but style, it reveals the latter's secret: obedience to the social hierarchy. Today aesthetic barbarity completes what has threatened the creations of the spirit since they were gathered together as culture and neutralized. To speak of culture was always contrary to culture. Culture as a common denominator already contains in embryo that schematization and process of cataloguing and classification which bring culture within the sphere of administration. And it is precisely the industrialized, the consequent, subsumption which entirely accords with this notion of culture. By subordinating in the same way and to the same end all areas of intellectual creation, by occupying men's senses from the time they leave the factory in the evening to the time they clock in again the next morning with matter that bears the impress of the labor process they themselves have to sustain throughout the day, this subsumption mockingly satisfies the concept of a unified culture which the philosophers of personality contrasted with mass culture.

And so the culture industry, the most rigid of all styles, proves to be the goal of liberalism, which is reproached for its lack of style. Not only do its categories and contents derive from liberalism — domesticated naturalism as well as operetta and revue — but the modern culture monopolies form the economic area in which, together with the corresponding entrepreneurial types, for the time being some part of its sphere of operation survives, despite the process of disintegration elsewhere. It is still possible to make one's way in entertainment, if one is not too obstinate about one's own concerns, and proves appropriately pliable. Anyone who resists can only survive by fitting in. Once his particular brand of deviation from the norm has been noted by the industry, he belongs to it as does the land-reformer to capitalism. Realistic dissidence is the trademark of anyone who has a new idea in business. In the public voice of modern society accusations are seldom audible; if they are, the perceptive can already detect signs that the dissident will soon be reconciled. The more immeasurable the gap between chorus and leaders, the more certainly there is room at the top for everybody who demonstrates his superiority by well-planned originality. Hence, in the culture industry, too, the liberal tendency to give full scope to its able men survives. To do this for the efficient today is still the function of the market, which is otherwise proficiently controlled; as for the market's freedom, in the high period of art as elsewhere, it was freedom for the stupid to starve. Significantly, the system of the culture industry comes from the more liberal industrial nations, and all its characteristic media, such as movies, radio, jazz, and magazines, flourish there. Its progress, to be sure, had its origin in the general laws of capital. Gaumont and Pathé, Ullstein and Hugenberg[11] followed the international trend with some success; Europe's economic dependence on the United States after war and inflation was a contributory factor. The belief that the barbarity of the culture industry is a result of "cultural lag," of the fact that the American consciousness did not keep up with the growth of technology, is quite wrong. It was pre-Fascist Europe which did not keep up with the trend toward the culture monopoly. But it was this very lag which left intellect and creativity

some degree of independence and enabled its last representatives to exist — however dismally. In Germany[12] the failure of democratic control to permeate life had led to a paradoxical situation. Many things were exempt from the market mechanism. The German educational system, universities, theaters with artistic standards, great orchestras, and museums enjoyed protection. The political powers, state and municipalities, which had inherited such institutions from absolutism, had left them with a measure of the freedom from the forces of power which dominates the market, just as princes and feudal lords had done up to the nineteenth century. This strengthened art in this late phase against the verdict of supply and demand, and increased its resistance far beyond the actual degree of protection. In the market itself the tribute of a quality for which no use had been found was turned into purchasing power; in this way, respectable literary and music publishers could help authors who yielded little more in the way of profit than the respect of the connoisseur. But what completely fettered the artist was the pressure (and the accompanying drastic threats), always to fit into business life as an aesthetic expert. Formerly, like Kant and Hume, they signed their letters "Your most humble and obedient servant," and undermined the foundations of throne and altar. Today they address heads of government by their first names, yet in every artistic activity they are subject to their illiterate masters. The analysis Tocqueville[13] offered a century ago has in the meantime proved wholly accurate. Under the private culture monopoly it is a fact that "tyranny leaves the body free and directs its attack at the soul. The ruler no longer says: You must think as I do or die. He says: You are free not to think as I do; your life, your property, everything shall remain yours, but from this day on you are a stranger among us." Not to

---

[11]French and German film studios.

[12]The authors are speaking of the Weimar Republic — "pre-Fascist" post-Imperial Germany between 1918 and 1933.

[13]Alexis de Tocqueville (1805–1859) wrote De la Démocratie en Amérique (Democracy in America), a sociological analysis of the United States in 1835–40, which stressed that the tyranny of the majority had supplanted the tyranny of nobility.

conform means to be rendered powerless, economically and therefore spiritually — to be "self-employed." When the outsider is excluded from the concern, he can only too easily be accused of incompetence. Whereas today in material production the mechanism of supply and demand is disintegrating,[14] in the superstructure it still operates as a check in the rulers' favor. The consumers are the workers and employees, the farmers and lower middle class. Capitalist production so confines them, body and soul, that they fall helpless victims to what is offered them. As naturally as the ruled always took the morality imposed upon them more seriously than did the rulers themselves, the deceived masses are today captivated by the myth of success even more than the successful are. Immovably, they insist on the very ideology which enslaves them. The misplaced love of the common people for the wrong which is done them is a greater force than the cunning of the authorities. It is stronger even than the rigorism of the Hays Office,[15] just as in certain great times in history it has inflamed greater forces that were turned against it, namely, the terror of the tribunals. It calls for Mickey Rooney in preference to the tragic Garbo, for Donald Duck instead of Betty Boop.[16] The industry submits to the vote which it has itself inspired. What is a loss for the firm which cannot fully exploit a contract with a declining star is a legitimate expense for the system as a whole. By craftily sanctioning the demand for rubbish it inaugurates total harmony. The connoisseur and the expert are despised for

their pretentious claim to know better than the others, even though culture is democratic and distributes its privileges to all. In view of the ideological truce, the conformism of the buyers and the effrontery of the producers who supply them prevail. The result is a constant reproduction of the same thing. A constant sameness governs the relationship to the past as well. What is new about the phase of mass culture compared with the late liberal stage is the exclusion of the new. The machine rotates on the same spot. While determining consumption it excludes the untried as a risk. The movie-makers distrust any manuscript which is not reassuringly backed by a bestseller. Yet for this very reason there is never-ending talk of ideas, novelty, and surprise, of what is taken for granted but has never existed. Tempo and dynamics serve this trend. Nothing remains as of old; everything has to run incessantly, to keep moving. For only the universal triumph of the rhythm of mechanical production and reproduction promises that nothing changes, and nothing unsuitable will appear. Any additions to the well-proven culture inventory are too much of a speculation. The ossified forms — such as the sketch, short story, problem film, or hit song — are the standardized average of late liberal taste, dictated with threats from above. The people at the top in the culture agencies, who work in harmony as only one manager can with another, whether he comes from the rag trade[17] or from college, have long since reorganized and rationalized the objective spirit. One might think that an omnipresent authority had sifted the material and drawn up an official catalog of cultural commodities to provide a smooth supply of available mass-produced lines. The ideas are written in the cultural firmament where they had already been numbered by Plato — and were indeed numbers, incapable of increase and immutable.

[14]This was written during World War II, when the authors were aware of the fact that many Americans not fighting overseas had plenty of money but no consumer goods to buy, whereas the government bought its needs (military equipment) at dictated prices.

[15]A censorship board set up by the film studios in 1934 under Will Hays, the postmaster general, which for twenty years dictated strictly what could not be said or shown in studio films.

[16]Sexy female cartoon character created by Max and Dave Fleischer in 1932; the Hays Production Code forced the "flapper" to wear longer skirts and hide her cleavage, and the character was retired in 1939 (aside from recent nostalgic revivals).

[17]Garment manufacture. The authors may be alluding to the studio head of MGM, Sam Goldwyn (1882–1974), who had succeeded in the garment industry before moving on to movies.

Louis Althusser

1918-1990

The controversial French Marxist Louis Althusser was born in 1918 in Birmandreis, Algeria, and educated at a lycée in Lyons. While awaiting placement into the higher education system in 1939, he was drafted into the French army; he spent five years as a prisoner of the Third Reich. In 1945 Althusser began attending the prestigious École Normale Supérieure in Paris, where he completed his doctorate, and where he taught philosophy for the rest of his active career. He is best known for the two books he published in 1965, For Marx and Reading "Capital," in which he re-interprets Marxist theory in a way similar to the way Lacan re-interpreted Freud, arguing that he was recovering Marx's original meaning. And just as Lacan viewed the "self" as an imaginary construct produced by the child's observation of himself in a mirror, Althusser viewed the individual subject as an equally imaginary construct, produced by ideology, which "interpellates" or addresses us as occupying a particular position. In Lenin and Philosophy (1969), Althusser argued that one class rules another not through repressive measures but rather through its hegemony over "ideological state apparatuses," like the church or school system. Such institutions not only mold beliefs but reproduce their ruling cadres, as loyal laymen become priests, or loyal students become teachers. Althusser also claimed that philosophy should not be considered a science, as it has no object and no history, but should be viewed as "the class struggle within theory." While some have accused Althusser of mystification, and of distorting Marx by reading him selectively, Fredric Jameson has praised his work for battling the tradition of empiricism. Pierre Macherey has transferred Althusser's concept of "symptomatic reading" to the field of literary criticism, and Maurice Godelier has found his social theories applicable to anthropological studies of the development of capitalist societies. Louis Althusser suffered from manic depression throughout most of his life, and in 1976 he married sociologist Hélène Legotier, who thereafter served as his private nurse. In November 1980, he strangled her to death. Due to his well-documented mental instability, he was judged unfit for trial, and locked up in the Centre Hospitalier Sainte Anne, a psychiatric hospital in Paris, for three years. He died in 1990. The selection below, taken from "Ideology and Ideological State Apparatuses," was published in Lenin and Philosophy.

From *Ideology and Ideological State Apparatuses*

IDEOLOGY IS A "REPRESENTATION" OF THE IMAGINARY RELATIONSHIP OF INDIVIDUALS TO THEIR REAL CONDITIONS OF EXISTENCE

In order to approach my central thesis on the structure and functioning of ideology, I shall first present two theses, one negative, the other positive. The first concerns the object which is "represented" in the imaginary form of ideology, the second concerns the materiality of ideology.

THESIS I: Ideology represents the imaginary relationship of individuals to their real conditions of existence.

We commonly call religious ideology, ethical ideology, legal ideology, political ideology, etc., so many "world outlooks." Of course, assuming that we do not live in one of these ideologies as the

Translated by Ben Brewster.

truth (e.g. "believe" in God, Duty, Justice, etc. . . .), we admit that the ideology we are discussing from a critical point of view, examining it as the ethnologist examines the myths of a "primitive society," that these "world outlooks" are largely imaginary, i.e. do not "correspond to reality."

However, while admitting that they do not correspond to reality, i.e. that they constitute an illusion, we admit that they do make allusion to reality, and that they need only be "interpreted" to discover the reality of the world behind their imaginary representation of that world (ideology = *illusion/allusion*).

There are different types of interpretation, the most famous of which are the *mechanistic* type, current in the eighteenth century (God is the imaginary representation of the real King), and the *"hermeneutic"* interpretation, inaugurated by the earliest Church Fathers, and revived by Feuerbach[1] and the theologico-philosophical school which descends from him, e.g. the theologian Barth[2] (to Feuerbach, for example, God is the essence of real Man). The essential point is that on condition that we interpret the imaginary transposition (and inversion) of ideology we arrive at the conclusion that in ideology "men represent their real conditions of existence to themselves in an imaginary form."

Unfortunately, this interpretation leaves one small problem unsettled: why do men "need" this imaginary transposition of their real conditions of existence in order to "represent to themselves" their real conditions of existence?

The first answer (that of the eighteenth century) proposes a simple solution: Priests or Despots are responsible. They "forged" the Beautiful Lies so that, in the belief that they were obeying God, men would in fact obey the Priests and Despots, who are usually in alliance in their imposture, the Priests acting in the interests of the Despots or *vice versa*, according to the political positions of the "theoreticians" concerned. There is therefore a cause for the imaginary transposition of the real conditions of existence: that cause is the existence of a small number of cynical men who base their domination and exploitation of the "people" on a falsified representation of the world which they have imagined in order to enslave other minds by dominating their imaginations.

The second answer (that of Feuerbach, taken over word for word by Marx in his Early Works) is more "profound," i.e. just as false. It, too, seeks and finds a cause for the imaginary transposition and distortion of men's real conditions of existence, in short, for the alienation in the imaginary of the representation of men's conditions of existence. This cause is no longer Priests or Despots, nor their active imagination and the passive imagination of their victims. This cause is the material alienation which reigns in the conditions of existence of men themselves. This is how, in *The Jewish Question* and elsewhere, Marx defends the Feuerbachian idea that men make themselves an alienated (= imaginary) representation of their conditions of existence because these conditions of existence are themselves alienating (in the 1844 *Manuscripts*: because these conditions are dominated by the essence of alienated society — *"alienated labor"*).[3]

All these interpretations thus take literally the thesis which they presuppose, and on which they depend, i.e. that what is reflected in the imaginary representation of the world found in an ideology is the conditions of existence of men, i.e. their real world.

Now I can return to a thesis which I have already advanced: it is not their real conditions of existence, their real world, that "men" "represent to themselves" in ideology, but above all it is their relation to those conditions of existence which is represented to them there. It is this relation which is at the center of every ideological, i.e. imaginary, representation of the real world. It is this relation that contains the "cause" which has to explain the imaginary distortion of the ideological representation of the real world. Or rather, to leave aside the language of causality it is necessary to advance the thesis that it is the *imaginary nature of this relation* which underlies all the imaginary distortion that

[1]Ludwig Feuerbach (1804–1872), philosopher and theologian, to whose materialist interpretation of religion Marx responded in 1845.

[2]Karl Barth (1886–1968), theologian.

[3]See Marx, . . . *The Alienation of Labor*, p. 250.

we can observe (if we do not live in its truth) in all ideology.

To speak in a Marxist language, if it is true that the representation of the real conditions of existence of the individuals occupying the posts of agents of production, exploitation, repression, ideologization and scientific practice, does in the last analysis arise from the relations of production, and from relations deriving from the relations of production, we can say the following: all ideology represents in its necessarily imaginary distortion not the existing relations of production (and the other relations that derive from them), but above all the (imaginary) relationship of individuals to the relations of production and the relations that derive from them. What is represented in ideology is therefore not the system of the real relations which govern the existence of individuals, but the imaginary relation of those individuals to the real relations in which they live.

If this is the case, the question of the "cause" of the imaginary distortion of the real relations in ideology disappears and must be replaced by a different question: why is the representation given to individuals of their (individual) relation to the social relations which govern their conditions of existence and their collective and individual life necessarily an imaginary relation? And what is the nature of this imaginariness? Posed in this way, the question explodes the solution by a "clique,"[4] by a group of individuals (Priests or Despots) who are the authors of the great ideological mystification, just as it explodes the solution by the alienated character of the real world. We shall see why later in my exposition. For the moment I shall go no further.

THESIS II: Ideology has a material existence.

I have already touched on this thesis by saying that the "ideas" or "representations," etc., which seem to make up ideology do not have an ideal (idéale or idéelle)[5] or spiritual existence, but a material existence. I even suggested that the ideal

(idéale, idéelle) and spiritual existence of "ideas" arises exclusively in an ideology of the "idea" and of ideology, and let me add, in an ideology of what seems to have "founded" this conception since the emergence of the sciences, i.e. what the practitioners of the sciences represent to themselves in their spontaneous ideology as "ideas," true or false. Of course, presented in affirmative form, this thesis is unproven. I simply ask that the reader be favorably disposed towards it, say, in the name of materialism. A long series of arguments would be necessary to prove it.

This hypothetical thesis of the not spiritual but material existence of "ideas" or other "representations" is indeed necessary if we are to advance in our analysis of the nature of ideology. Or rather, it is merely useful to us in order the better to reveal what every at all serious analysis of any ideology will immediately and empirically show to every observer, however critical.

While discussing the ideological State apparatuses and their practices, I said that each of them was the realization of an ideology (the unity of these different regional ideologies — religious, ethical, legal, political, aesthetic, etc. — being assured by their subjection to the ruling ideology). I now return to this thesis: an ideology always exists in an apparatus, and its practice, or practices. This existence is material.

Of course, the material existence of the ideology in an apparatus and its practices does not have the same modality as the material existence of a paving-stone or a rifle. But, at the risk of being taken for a Neo-Aristotelian[6] (NB Marx had a very high regard for Aristotle), I shall say that "matter" is discussed in many senses," or rather that it exists in different modalities, all rooted in the last instance in "physical" matter.

Having said this, let me move straight on and see what happens to the "individuals" who live in ideology, i.e. in a determinate (religious, ethical, etc.) representation of the world whose imaginary distortion depends on their imaginary relation to

[4] I use this very modern term deliberately. For even in Communist circles, unfortunately, it is a commonplace to "explain" some political deviation (left or right opportunism) by the action of a "clique." [Althusser]

[5] Idéale means "ideal"; idéelle means "ideational," the production or generation of ideas.

[6] Not in the literary-critical sense (e.g., a follower of R. S. Crane), but a materialist in the sense that Aristotle was, excluding ideal essences, but seeing reality as embodied in actions, processes, practices, and habits. See Introduction to Aristotle, p. 46.

their conditions of existence, in other words, in the last instance, to the relations of production and to class relations (ideology = an imaginary relation to real relations). I shall say that this imaginary relation is itself endowed with a material existence.

Now I observe the following.

An individual believes in God, or Duty, or Justice, etc. This belief derives (for everyone, i.e. for all those who live in an ideological representation of ideology, which reduces ideology to ideas endowed by definition with a spiritual existence) from the ideas of the individual concerned, i.e. from him as a subject with a consciousness which contains the ideas of his belief. In this way, i.e. by means of the absolutely ideological "conceptual" device (*dispositif*) thus set up (a subject endowed with a consciousness in which he freely forms or freely recognizes ideas in which he believes), the (material) attitude of the subject concerned naturally follows.

The individual in question behaves in such and such a way, adopts such and such a practical attitude, and, what is more, participates in certain regular practices which are those of the ideological apparatus on which "depend" the ideas which he has in all consciousness freely chosen as a subject. If he believes in God, he goes to Church to attend Mass, kneels, prays, confesses, does penance (once it was material in the ordinary sense of the term) and naturally repents and so on. If he believes in Duty, he will have the corresponding attitudes, inscribed in ritual practices "according to the correct principles." If he believes in Justice, he will submit unconditionally to the rules of the Law, and may even protest when they are violated, sign petitions, take part in a demonstration, etc.

Throughout this schema we observe that the ideological representation of ideology is itself forced to recognize that every "subject" endowed with a "consciousness" and believing in the "ideas" that his "consciousness" inspires in him and freely accepts, must "*act* according to his ideas," must therefore inscribe his own ideas as a free subject in the actions of his material practice. If he does not do so, "that is wicked."

Indeed, if he does not do what he ought to do as a function of what he believes, it is because he does something else, which, still as a function of the same idealist scheme, implies that he has other ideas in his head as well as those he proclaims, and that he acts according to these other ideas, as a man who is either "inconsistent" ("no one is willingly evil") or cynical, or perverse.

In every case, the ideology of ideology thus recognizes, despite its imaginary distortion, that the "ideas" of a human subject exist in his actions, or ought to exist in his actions, and if that is not the case, it lends him other ideas corresponding to the actions (however perverse) that he does perform. This ideology talks of actions: I shall talk of actions inserted into *practices*. And I shall point out that these practices are governed by the *rituals* in which these practices are inscribed, within the *material existence of an ideological apparatus*, be it only a small part of that apparatus: a small mass in a small church, a funeral, a minor match at a sports club, a school day, a political party meeting, etc.

Besides, we are indebted to Pascal's defensive "dialectic" for the wonderful formula which will enable us to invert the order of the notional schema of ideology. Pascal says more or less: "Kneel down, move your lips in prayer, and you will believe." He thus scandalously inverts the order of things, bringing, like Christ, not peace but strife, and in addition something hardly Christian (for woe to him who brings scandal into the world!) — scandal itself. A fortunate scandal which makes him stick with Jansenist defiance to a language that directly names the reality.[7]

I will be allowed to leave Pascal to the arguments of his ideological struggle with the religious ideological State apparatus of his day. And I shall be expected to use a more directly Marxist vocabulary, if that is possible, for we are advancing in still poorly explored domains.

I shall therefore say that, where only a single subject (such and such an individual) is concerned, the existence of the ideas of his belief is material in that *his ideas are his material*

---

[7]Althusser is comparing his view, that actions within social practices shape the subject of ideology, to the advice of Blaise Pascal (1623–1662) that the Christian should go through the motions of prayer in order to bring about faith. Pascal was one of the most notable Jansenists (i.e., a follower of Cornelius Jansen [1585–1638], whose view of grace and predestination was declared heretical by the Catholic Church).

actions inserted into material practices gov-erned by material rituals which are themselves defined by the material ideological apparatus from which derive the ideas of that subject. Naturally, the four inscriptions of the adjective "material" in my proposition must be affected by different modalities: the materialities of a displacement for going to mass, of kneeling down, of the gesture of the sign of the cross, or of the mea culpa, of a sentence, of a prayer, of an act of contrition, of a penitence, of a gaze, of a hand-shake, of an external verbal discourse or an "internal" verbal discourse (conscious-ness), are not one and the same materiality. I shall leave on one side the problem of a theory of the differences between the modalities of materiality.

It remains that in this inverted presentation of things, we are not dealing with an "inversion" at all, since it is clear that certain notions have purely and simply disappeared from our presenta-tion, whereas others on the contrary survive, and new terms appear.

Disappeared: the term *ideas.*

Survive: the terms *subject, consciousness, belief, actions.*

Appear: the terms *practices, rituals, ideologi-cal apparatus.*

It is therefore not an inversion or overturning (except in the sense in which one might say a government or a glass is overturned), but a reshuf-ffle (of a non-ministerial type), a rather strange reshuffle, since we obtain the following result.

Ideas have disappeared as such (insofar as they are endowed with an ideal or spiritual exis-tence), to the precise extent that it has emerged that their existence is inscribed in the actions of practices governed by rituals defined in the last instance by an ideological apparatus. It there-fore appears that the subject acts insofar as he is acted by the following system (set out in the order of its real determination): ideology existing in a material ideological apparatus, prescribing material practices governed by a material ritual, which practices exist in the material actions of a subject acting in all consciousness according to his belief.

But this very presentation reveals that we have retained the following notions: subject, consciousness, belief, actions. From this series I shall immediately extract the decisive central term on which everything else depends: the notion of the subject.

And I shall immediately set down two conjoint theses:

1. there is no practice except by and in an ideology;
2. there is no ideology except by the subject and for subjects.

I can now come to my central thesis.

IDEOLOGY INTERPELLATES[8] INDIVIDUALS AS SUBJECTS

This thesis is simply a matter of making my last proposition explicit: there is no ideology except by the subject and for subjects. Meaning, there is no ideology except for concrete subjects, and this destination for ideology is only made possible by the subject: meaning, by the category of the subject and its functioning.

By this I mean that, even if it only appears under this name (the subject) with the rise of bourgeois ideology, above all with the rise of legal ideology,[9] the category of the subject (which may function under other names: e.g., as the soul in Plato, as God, etc.) is the constitutive category of all ideology, whatever its determina-tion (regional or class) and whatever its historical date — since ideology has no history.

I say: the category of the subject is constitu-tive of all ideology, but at the same time and immediately I add that *the category of the subject is only constitutive of all ideology insofar as all ideology has the function (which defines it) of "constituting" concrete individuals as subjects.* In the interaction of this double constitution exists the functioning of all ideology, ideology being nothing but its functioning in the material forms of existence of that functioning.

In order to grasp what follows, it is essential to realize that both he who is writing these lines and

[8]To interpellate is to hail someone in a way that defines one's identity.

[9]Which borrowed the legal category of "subject in law" to make an ideological notion: man is by nature a subject. [Althusser]

the reader who reads them are themselves subjects, and therefore ideological subjects (a tautological proposition), i.e. that the author and the reader of these lines both live "spontaneously" or "naturally" in ideology in the sense in which I have said that "man is an ideological animal by nature."

That the author, insofar as he writes the lines of a discourse which claims to be scientific, is completely absent as a "subject" from "his" scientific discourse (for all scientific discourse is by definition a subject-less discourse, there is no "subject of science" except in an ideology of science) is a different question which I shall leave on one side for the moment.

As St. Paul admirably put it, it is in the "Logos," meaning in ideology, that we "live, move and have our being." It follows that, for you and for me, the category of the subject is a primary "obviousness" (obviousnesses are always primary): it is clear that you and I are subjects (free, ethical, etc. . . .). Like all obviousnesses, including those that make a word "name a thing" or "have a meaning" (therefore including the obviousness of the "transparency" of language), the "obviousness" that you and I are subjects — and that that does not cause any problems — is an ideological effect, the elementary ideological effect.[10] It is indeed a peculiarity of ideology that it imposes (without appearing to do so, since these are "obviousnesses") obviousnesses as obviousnesses, which we cannot *fail to recognize* and before which we have the inevitable and natural reaction of crying out (aloud or in the "still, small voice of conscience"): "That's obvious! That's right! That's true!"

At work in this reaction is the ideological *recognition* function which is one of the two functions of ideology as such (its inverse being the function of *misrecognition — méconnaissance*).[11]

To take a highly "concrete" example, we all have friends who, when they knock on our door and we ask, through the door, the question "Who's there?" answer (since "it's obvious") "It's me." And we recognize that "it is him," or "her." We open the door, and "it's true, it really was she who was there." To take another example, when we recognize somebody of our (previous) acquaintance ((re)-connaissance) in the street, we show him that we have recognized him (and have recognized that he has recognized us) by saying to him "Hello, my friend," and shaking his hand (a material ritual practice of ideological recognition in everyday life — in France, at least; elsewhere, there are other rituals).

In this preliminary remark and these concrete illustrations, I only wish to point out that you and I are *always already* subjects, and as such constantly practice the rituals of ideological recognition, which guarantee for us that we are indeed concrete, individual, distinguishable and (naturally) irreplaceable subjects. The writing I am currently executing and the reading you are currently[12] performing are also in this respect rituals of ideological recognition, including the "obviousness" with which the "truth" or "error" of my reflections may impose itself on you.

But to recognize that we are subjects and that we function in the practical rituals of the most elementary everyday life (the hand-shake, the fact of calling you by your name, the fact of knowing, even if I do not know what it is, that you "have" a name of your own, which means that you are recognized as a unique subject, etc.) — this recognition only gives us the "consciousness" of our incessant (eternal) practice of ideological recognition — its consciousness, i.e. its *recognition* — but in no sense does it give us the (scientific) *knowledge* of the mechanism of this recognition. Now it is this knowledge that we have to reach, if you will, while speaking in ideology, and from within ideology we have to outline a discourse which tries to break with ideology, in

[10]Linguists and those who appeal to linguistics for various purposes often run up against difficulties which arise because they ignore the action of the ideological effects in all discourses — including even scientific discourses. [Althusser]

[11]Althusser uses Lacan's term (mis-recognition) here, because his notion of how the subject is constituted by ideology, as an imaginary relation of the individual to his material circumstances, is parallel to Lacan's Mirror Stage, in which the Imaginary self-image of the individual as a coherent totality is formed by the same process of *méconnaissance*.

[12]NB: this double "currently" is one more proof of the fact that ideology is eternal, since these two "currentlys" are separated by an indefinite interval; I am writing these lines on 6 April 1969, you may read them at any subsequent time. [Althusser]

order to dare to be the beginning of a scientific (i.e. subjectless) discourse on ideology.

Thus in order to represent why the category of the "subject" is constitutive of ideology, which only exists by constituting concrete subjects as subjects, I shall employ a special mode of exposition: "concrete" enough to be recognized, but abstract enough to be thinkable and thought, giving rise to a knowledge.

As a first formulation I shall say: *all ideology hails or interpellates concrete individuals as concrete subjects*, by the functioning of the category of the subject.

This is a proposition which entails that we distinguish for the moment between concrete individuals on the one hand and concrete subjects on the other, although at this level concrete subjects only exist insofar as they are supported by a concrete individual.

I shall then suggest that ideology "acts" or "functions" in such a way that it "recruits" subjects among the individuals (it recruits them all), or "transforms" the individuals into subjects (it transforms them all) by that very precise operation which I have called *interpellation* or hailing, and which can be imagined along the lines of the most commonplace everyday police (or other) hailing: "Hey, you there!"[13]

Assuming that the theoretical scene I have imagined takes place in the street, the hailed individual will turn round. By this mere one-hundred-and-eighty-degree physical conversion, he becomes a *subject*. Why? Because he has recognized that the hail was "really" addressed to him, and that "it *was really him* who was hailed" (and not someone else). Experience shows that the practical telecommunication of hailings is such that they hardly ever miss their man: verbal call or whistle, the one hailed always recognizes that it is really him who is being hailed. And yet it is a strange phenomenon, and one which cannot be explained solely by "guilt feelings," despite the large numbers who "have something on their consciences."

13 Hailing as an everyday practice subject to a precise ritual takes a quite "special" form in the policeman's practice of "hailing" which concerns the hailing of "suspects." [Althusser]

Naturally for the convenience and clarity of my little theoretical theater I have had to present things in the form of a sequence, with a before and an after, and thus in the form of a temporal succession.

There are individuals walking along. Somewhere (usually behind them) the hail rings out: "Hey, you there!" One individual (nine times out of ten it is the right one) turns round, believing/suspecting/knowing that it is for him, i.e. recognizing that "it really is he" who is meant by the hailing. But in reality these things happen without any succession. The existence of ideology and the hailing or interpellation of individuals as subjects are one and the same thing.

I might add: what thus seems to take place outside ideology (to be precise, in the street), in reality takes place in ideology. What really takes place in ideology seems therefore to take place outside it. That is why those who are in ideology believe themselves by definition outside ideology: one of the effects of ideology is the practical *denegation* of the ideological character of ideology by ideology: ideology never says, "I am ideological." It is necessary to be outside ideology, i.e. in scientific knowledge, to be able to say: I am in ideology (a quite exceptional case) or (the general case): I was in ideology. As is well known, the accusation of being in ideology only applies to others, never to one-self (unless one is really a Spinozist or a Marxist, which, in this matter, is to be exactly the same thing). Which amounts to saying that ideology has *no outside* (for itself), but at the same time that it is *nothing but outside* (for science and reality).

Spinoza explained this completely two centuries before Marx, who practiced it but without explaining it in detail. But let us leave this point, although it is heavy with consequences, consequences which are not just theoretical, but also directly political, since, for example, the whole theory of criticism and self-criticism, the golden rule of the Marxist-Leninist practice of the class struggle, depends on it.

Thus ideology hails or interpellates individuals as subjects. As ideology is eternal, I must now suppress the temporal form in which I have presented the functioning of ideology, and say: ideology has always-already interpellated individuals as subjects, which amounts to making it clear that individuals are always-already interpellated by ideology as subjects, which necessarily leads us to one last proposition: *individuals are always-already subjects*. Hence individuals are "abstract" with respect to the subjects which they always-already are. This proposition might seem paradoxical.

That an individual is always-already a subject, even before he is born, is nevertheless the plain reality, accessible to everyone and not a paradox at all. Freud shows that individuals are always "abstract" with respect to the subjects they always-already are, simply by noting the ideological ritual that surrounds the expectation of a "birth," that "happy event." Everyone knows how much and in what way an unborn child is expected. Which amounts to saying, very prosaically, if we agree to drop the "sentiments," i.e. the forms of family ideology (paternal/maternal/conjugal/fraternal) in which the unborn child is expected: it is certain in advance that it will bear its Father's Name, and will therefore have an identity and be irreplaceable. Before its birth, the child is therefore always-already a subject, appointed as a subject in and by the specific familial ideological configuration in which it is "expected" once it has been conceived. I hardly need add that this familial ideological configuration is, in its uniqueness, highly structured, and that it is in this implacable and more or less "pathological" (presupposing that any meaning can be assigned to that term) structure that the former subject-to-be will have to "find" "its" place, i.e. "become" the sexual subject (boy or girl) which it already is in advance. It is clear that this ideological constraint and pre-appointment, and all the rituals of rearing and then education in the family, have some relationship with what Freud studied in the forms of the pre-genital and genital "stages" of sexuality, i.e. in the "grip" of what Freud registered by its effects as being the unconscious. But let us leave this point, too, on one side.

Let me go one step further. What I shall now turn my attention to is the way the "actors" in this *mise en scène* of interpellation, and their respective roles, are reflected in the very structure of all ideology.

AN EXAMPLE: THE CHRISTIAN RELIGIOUS IDEOLOGY

As the formal structure of all ideology is always the same, I shall restrict my analysis to a single example, one accessible to everyone, that of religious ideology, with the proviso that the same demonstration can be produced for ethical, legal, political, aesthetic ideology, etc.

Let us therefore consider the Christian religious ideology. I shall use a rhetorical figure and "make it speak," i.e. collect into a fictional discourse what it "says" not only in its two Testaments, its Theologians, Sermons, but also in its practices, its rituals, its ceremonies and its sacraments. The Christian religious ideology says something like this:

It says: I address myself to you, a human individual called Peter (every individual is called by his name, in the passive sense, it is never he who provides his own name), in order to tell you that God exists and that you are answerable to Him. It adds: God addresses himself to you through my voice (Scripture having collected the Word of God, Tradition having transmitted it, Papal Infallibility fixing it for ever on "nice" points). It says: this is who you are: you are Peter! This is your origin, you were created by God for all eternity, although you were born in the 1920th year of Our Lord! This is your place in the world! This is what you must do! By these means, if you observe the "law of love" you will be saved, you, Peter, and will become part of the Glorious Body of Christ! Etc. . . .

Now this is quite a familiar and banal discourse, but at the same time quite a surprising one. . . .

Let me summarize what we have discovered about ideology in general.

The duplicate mirror-structure of ideology ensures simultaneously:

1. the interpellation of "individuals" as subjects;

2. their subjection to the Subject;

3. the mutual recognition of subjects and Subject, the subjects' recognition of each other, and finally the subject's recognition of himself;[14]

---

[14]Hegel is (unknowingly) an admirable "theoretician" of ideology insofar as he is a "theoretician" of Universal Recognition who unfortunately ends up in the ideology of Absolute Knowledge. Feuerbach is an astonishing "theoretician" of the mirror connection, who unfortunately ends up in the ideology of the Human Essence. To find the material with which to construct a theory of the guarantee, we must turn to Spinoza. [Althusser]

4. the absolute guarantee that everything really is so, and that on condition that the subjects recognize what they are and behave accordingly, everything will be all right: Amen — *"So be it."*

Result: caught in this quadruple system of interpellation as subjects, of subjection to the Subject, of universal recognition and of absolute guarantee, the subjects "work," they "work by themselves" in the vast majority of cases, with the exception of the "bad subjects" who on occasion provoke the intervention of one of the detachments of the (repressive) State apparatus. But the vast majority of (good) subjects work all right "all by themselves," i.e. by ideology (whose concrete forms are realized in the Ideological State Apparatuses). They are inserted into practices governed by the rituals of the ISAs. They "recognize" the existing state of affairs (*das Bestehende*), that "it really is true that it is so and not otherwise," and that they must be obedient to God, to their conscience, to the priest, to de Gaulle,[15] to the boss, to the engineer, that thou shalt "love thy neighbor as thyself," etc. Their concrete, material behavior is simply the inscription in life of the admirable words of the prayer: "Amen — *So be it.*"

Yes, the subjects "work by themselves." The whole mystery of this effect lies in the first two moments of the quadruple system I have just discussed, or, if you prefer, in the ambiguity of the term *subject.* In the ordinary use of the term, *subject* in fact means: (1) a free subjectivity, a center of initiatives, author of and responsible for its actions; (2) a subjected being, who submits to a higher authority, and is therefore stripped

of all freedom except that of freely accepting his submission. This last note gives us the meaning of this ambiguity, which is merely a reflection of the effect which produces it: the individual is interpellated as a (free) subject in order that he shall submit freely to the commandments of the Subject, i.e. in order that he shall (freely) accept his subjection, i.e. in order that he shall make the gestures and actions of his subjection "all by himself." *There are no subjects except by and for their subjection.* That is why they "work all by themselves."

"*So be it!. . .*" This phrase which registers the effect to be obtained proves that it is not "naturally" so ("naturally": outside the prayer, i.e. outside the ideological intervention). This phrase proves that it *has* to be so if things are to be what they must be, and let us let the words slip: if the reproduction of the relations of production is to be assured, even in the processes of production and circulation, every day, in the "consciousness," i.e. in the attitudes of the individual-subjects occupying the posts which the socio-technical division of labor assigns to them in production, exploitation, repression, ideologization, scientific practice, etc. Indeed, what is really in question in this mechanism of the mirror recognition of the Subject and of the individuals interpellated as subjects, and of the guarantee given by the Subject to the subjects if they freely accept their subjection to the Subject's "commandments"? The reality in question in this mechanism, the reality which is necessarily *ignored* (*méconnue*) in the very forms of recognition (ideology = misrecognition/ignorance) is indeed, in the last resort, the reproduction of the relations of production and of the relations deriving from them.

[15]Charles de Gaulle (1890–1970), President of France at the time this essay was written.

Raymond Williams

1921–1988

Born to working-class parents in a Welsh border village, Raymond Williams was that rare creature, a Marxist intellectual with genuine proletarian roots. After serving in the British army from 1941 until the close of the war, Williams earned his M.A. from Trinity College, Cambridge, in 1946, and then attended Oxford, where he worked his way up the ladder of appointments. A professor of drama at Jesus College, Cambridge, until 1983, he was considered by many to be the preeminent Marxist literary critic and theorist of postwar Britain. In addition to his landmark study Culture and Society, 1780–1950 *(1958), and his masterpiece* The Country and the City *(1973), Williams wrote more than a dozen other books, including* The Long Revolution *(1961),* Drama from Ibsen to Brecht *(1969),* The English Novel from Dickens to Lawrence *(1970),* Keywords: A Vocabulary of Culture and Society *(1976),* Marxism and Literature *(1977),* The Sociology of Culture *(1982),* Writing in Society *(1983), and* Politics of Modernism *(1989), which was published in the year following his death. The following selection is from Williams's primer on Marxist concepts,* Marxism and Literature *(1977).*

From *Marxism and Literature*

1. BASE AND SUPERSTRUCTURE

Any modern approach to a Marxist theory of culture must begin by considering the proposition of a determining base and a determined superstructure. From a strictly theoretical point of view this is not, in fact, where we might choose to begin. It would be in many ways preferable if we could begin from a proposition which originally was equally central, equally authentic: namely the proposition that social being determines consciousness. It is not that the two propositions necessarily deny each other or are in contradiction. But the proposition of base and superstructure, with its figurative element and with its suggestion of a fixed and definite spatial relationship, constitutes, at least in certain hands, a very specialized and at times unacceptable version of the other proposition. Yet in the transition from Marx to Marxism, and in the development of mainstream Marxism itself, the proposition of the determining base and the determined superstructure has been commonly held to be the key to Marxist cultural analysis.

The source of this proposition is commonly taken to be a well-known passage in Marx's 1859 Preface to *A Contribution to the Critique of Political Economy:*

> In the social production of their life, men enter into definite relations that are indispensable and independent of their will, relations of production which correspond to a definite stage of development of their material productive forces. The sum total of these relations of production constitutes the economic structure of society, the real foundation, on which rises a legal and political superstructure and to which correspond definite forms of social consciousness. The mode of production of material life conditions the social, political and intellectual life process in general. It is not the consciousness of men that determines their being, but, on the contrary, their social being that determines their consciousness. At a certain stage of their development, the material productive forces of society come in conflict with the existing relations of production or — what is but a legal expression for the same thing — with the property relations within which they have been at work hitherto. From forms of development of the productive forces these relations turn into their fetters. Then begins an

epoch of social revolution. With the change of the eco-nomic foundation the entire immense superstructure is more or less rapidly transformed. In considering such transformations a distinction should always be made between the material transformation of the eco-nomic conditions of production, which can be deter-mined with the precision of natural science, and the legal, political, religious, aesthetic or philosophic — in short, ideological — forms in which men become conscious of this conflict and fight it out.[1]

This is hardly an obvious starting-point for any cultural theory. It is part of an exposition of his-torical materialist method in the understanding of legal relations and forms of state. The first use of the term "superstructure" is explicitly qualified as "legal and political." (It should incidentally be noted that the English translation in most common use has a plural — "legal and political superstructures" — for Marx's singular "juris-tischer und politischer Überbau.") "Definite forms of social consciousness" are further said to "cor-respond" to it (entsprechen). Transformation of the "entire immense superstructure," in the social revolution which begins from the altered relations of productive forces and relations of production, is a process in which "men become conscious of this conflict and fight it out" in "ideologi-cal forms" which now include the "religious, aesthetic, or philosophic" as well as the legal and political. Much has been deduced from this formulation, but the real context is inevitably lim-ited. Thus it would be possible, simply from this passage, to define "cultural" ("religious, aesthetic or philosophic") forms in which "men become conscious of this conflict," without necessarily supposing that these specific forms are the whole of "cultural" activity.

There is at least one earlier use, by Marx, of the term "superstructure." It is in *The Eighteenth Brumaire of Louis Napoleon*, 1851–2:

Upon the several forms of property, upon the social conditions of existence, a whole superstructure is reared of various and peculiarly shaped feelings (Empfindungen), illusions, habits of thought and conceptions of life. The whole class produces and shapes these out of its material foundation and out

of the corresponding social conditions. The indi-vidual unit to whom they flow through tradition and education may fancy that they constitute the true reasons for and premises of his conduct.[2]

This is an evidently different use. The "super-structure" is here the whole "ideology" of the class: its "form of consciousness"; its constitutive ways of seeing itself in the world. It would be possible, from this and the later use, to see three senses of "superstructure" emerging: (a) legal and political forms which express existing real relations of production; (b) forms of conscious-ness which express a particular class view of the world; (c) a process in which, over a whole range of activities, men become conscious of a funda-mental economic conflict and fight it out. These three senses would direct our attention, respec-tively, to (a) institutions; (b) forms of conscious-ness; (c) political and cultural practices.

It is clear that these three areas are related and must, in analysis, be interrelated. But on just this crucial question of interrelation the term itself is of little assistance, just because it is variably applied to each area in turn. Nor is this at all surprising, since the use is not primarily con-ceptual, in any precise way, but metaphorical. What it primarily expresses is the important sense of a visible and formal "superstructure" which might be analysed on its own but which cannot be understood without seeing that it rests on a "foundation." The same point must be made of the corresponding metaphorical term. In the use of 1851–2 it is absent, and the origins of a par-ticular form of class consciousness are specified as "forms of property" and "social conditions of existence." In the use of 1859 it appears in almost conscious metaphor: "the real structure of society — the real foundation (die reale Basis), on which rises (erhebt) a legal and political superstructure (Überbau)." It is replaced, later in the argument, by "the economic foundation" (ökonomische Grundlage). The continuity of meaning is relatively clear, but the variation of terms for one part of the relationship ("forms of property, social conditions of existence"; "real economic structure of society"; "real basis"; "real"

---

[1] Karl Marx and Friedrich Engels, *Selected Works*, vol. 1 (London, 1962), pp. 362–64. (See also Marx, p. 247.)

[2] *Ibid.*, pp. 272–73.

foundation"; *Basis; Grundlage*) is not matched by explicit variation of the other term of the relationship, though the actual signification of this term (*Überbau;* superstructure) is, as we have seen, variable. It is part of the complexity of the subsequent argument that the term rendered in English explication (probably first by Engels) as "base" is rendered in other languages in significant variations (in French usually as *infrastructure,* in Italian as *struttura,* and so on, with some complicating effects on the substance of the argument).

In the transition from Marx to Marxism, and then in the development of expository and didactic formulations, the words used in the original arguments were projected, first, as if they were precise concepts, and second, as if they were descriptive terms for observable "areas" of social life. The main sense of the words in the original arguments had been relational, but the popularity of the terms tended to indicate either (a) relatively enclosed categories or (b) relatively enclosed areas of activity. These were then correlated either temporally (first material production, then consciousness, then politics and culture), or in effect, forcing the metaphor, spatially (visible and distinguishable "levels" or "layers" — politics and culture, then forms of consciousness, and so on down to "the base"). The serious practical problems of method, which the original words had indicated, were then usually in effect bypassed by methods derived from a confidence, rooted in the popularity of the terms, in the relative enclosure of categories or areas expressed as "the base," "the superstructure."

It is then ironic to remember that the force of Marx's original criticism had been mainly directed against the *separation* of "areas" of thought and activity (as in the separation of consciousness from material production) and against the related evacuation of specific content — real human activities — by the imposition of abstract categories. The common abstraction of "the base" and "the superstructure" is thus a radical persistence of the modes of thought which he attacked. That in the course of other arguments he gave some warrant for this, within the intrinsic difficulties of any such formulation, is certainly true. But it is significant that when he came to any sustained analysis, or to a realization of the

need for such analysis, he was at once specific and flexible in his use of his own terms. He had already observed, in the formulation of 1859, a distinction between analysing "the economic conditions of production, which can be determined with the precision of natural science" and the analysis of "ideological forms," for which methods were evidently less precise. In 1857 he had noted:

> As regards art, it is well known that some of its peaks by no means correspond to the general development of society; nor do they therefore to the material substructure, the skeleton as it were of its organization.

His solution of the problem he then discusses, that of Greek art, is hardly convincing, but the "by no means correspond" is a characteristic practical recognition of the complexity of real relations. Engels, in his essay *Feuerbach and the End of Classical German Philosophy,* still argued specifically, showing how the "economic basis" of a political struggle could be dulled in consciousness or altogether lost sight of, and how a legal system could be projected as independent of its economic content, in the course of its professional development. Then:

> Still higher ideologies, that is, such as are still further removed from the material, economic basis, take the form of philosophy and religion. Hence the interconnection between conceptions and their material conditions of existence becomes more and more complicated, more and more obscured by intermediate links. But the interconnection exists.

This relational emphasis, including not only complexity but recognition of the ways in which some connections are lost to consciousness, is of course very far from the abstract categories (though it supports the implication of separate areas) of "superstructure" and "base."

In all serious Marxist analysis the categories are of course not used abstractly. But they may have their effect none the less. It is significant that the first phase of the recognition of practical complexities stressed what are really *quantitative* relations. By the end of the nineteenth century it was common to recognize what can best be described as disturbances, or special difficulties, of an otherwise regular relationship. This is true of the idea of "lags" in time, which had been developed from Marx's observation that some of the "peaks" of art "by no means correspond to the general development of society." This could be expressed (though Marx's own "solution" to this problem had not been of this kind) as a matter of *temporal* "delay" or "unevenness." The same basic model is evident in Engels's notion of the *relative distance* ("still further removed") of the "higher ideologies." Or consider Engels's letter to Bloch of September 1890:

According to the materialist conception of history, the *ultimately* determining element in history is the production and reproduction of real life. More than this neither Marx nor I have ever asserted. Hence if somebody twists this into saying that the economic element is the *only* determining one, he transforms that proposition into a meaningless, abstract, senseless phrase. The economic situation is the basis, but the various elements of the super-structure — political forms of the class struggle and its results, to wit: constitutions established by the victorious class after a successful battle, etc., juridical forms, and even the reflexes of all these actual struggles in the brains of the participants, political, juristic, philosophical theories, religious views and their further development into systems of dogma — also exercise their influence upon the course of the historical struggles and in many cases preponderate in determining their *form*. There is an interaction of all these elements in which, amid all the endless host of accidents (that is, of things and events whose inner interconnection is so remote or so impossible of proof that we can regard it as non-existent, as negligible), the economic movement finally asserts itself as necessary. Otherwise the application of the theory to any period of history would be easier than the solution of a simple equa-tion of the first degree.

This is a vital acknowledgement of real and meth-odological complexities. It is particularly relevant to the idea of "determination," which will be separately discussed, and to the decisive problem of consciousness as "reflexes" or "reflection." But within the vigour of his contrast between real history and a "meaningless, abstract, senseless phrase," and alongside his recognition of a new (and theoretically significant) exception — "the endless host of accidents" — Engels does not

so much revise the enclosed categories — "the basis" ("the economic element," "the economic situation," "the economic movement") and "the various elements" (political, juridical, theoreti-cal) of "the superstructure" — as reiterate the categories and instance certain exceptions, indi-rectnesses, and irregularities which obscure their otherwise regular relation. What is fundamentally lacking, in the theoretical formulations of this important period, is any adequate recognition of the indissoluble connections between material production, political and cultural institutions and activity, and consciousness. The classic sum-mary of "the relationship between the base and the superstructure" is Plekhanov's[3] distinction of "five sequential elements: (i) the state of productive forces; (ii) the economic conditions; (iii) the socio-political regime; (iv) the psyche of social man; (v) various ideologies reflecting the properties of this psyche" (*Fundamental Problems of Marxism*, Moscow, 1922, 76). This is better than the bare projection of "a base" and "a superstructure," which has been so common. But what is wrong with it is its description of these "elements" as "sequential," when they are in practice indissoluble: not in the sense that they cannot be distinguished for purposes of analysis, but in the decisive sense that these are not separate "areas" or "elements" but the whole, specific activities and products of real men. That is to say, the analytic categories, as so often in idealist thought, have, almost unnoticed, become substantive descriptions, which then take habitual priority over the whole social process to which, as analytic categories, they are attempting to speak. Orthodox analysts began to think of "the base" and "the superstructure" as if they were separable concrete entities. In doing so they lost sight of the very processes — not abstract relations but constitutive processes — which it should have been the special function of historical material-ism to emphasize. I shall be discussing later the major theoretical response to this loss: the attempt to reconstitute such processes by the idea of "mediation."

[3]Gyorgi Valentinovich Plekhanov (1857-1918), Russian revolutionary and political philosopher.

A persistent dissatisfaction, within Marxism, about the proposition of "base and superstructure," has been most often expressed by an attempted refinement and revaluation of "the superstructure." Apologists have emphasized its complexity, substance, and "autonomy" or autonomous value. Yet most of the difficulty still lies in the original extension of metaphorical terms for a relationship into abstract categories or concrete areas *between* which connections are looked for and complexities or relative autonomies emphasized. It is actually more important to observe the character of this extension in the case of "the base" than in the case of the always more varied and variable "superstructure." By extension and by habit, "the base" has come to be considered virtually as an object (a particular and reductive version of "material existence"). Or, in specification, "the base" is given very general and apparently uniform properties. "The base" is the real social existence of man. "The base" is the real relations of production corresponding to a stage of the development of material productive forces. "The base" is a mode of production at a particular stage of its development. Of course these are, in practice, different propositions. Yet each is also very different from Marx's central emphasis on productive *activities.* He had himself made the point against reduction of "the base" to a category:

> In order to study the connexion between intellectual and material production it is above all essential to conceive the latter in its determined historical form and not as a general category. For example, there corresponds to the capitalist mode of production a type of intellectual production quite different from that which corresponded to the medieval mode of production. Unless material production itself is understood in its specific historical form, it is impossible to grasp the characteristics of the intellectual production which corresponds to it or the reciprocal action between the two. (*Theorien über den Mehrwert,* cit. Bottomore and Rubel, 96–97.)

We can add that while a particular stage of "real social existence," or of "relations of production," or of a "mode of production," can be discovered and made precise by analysis, it is never, as a body of activities, either uniform or static. It is one of the central propositions of Marx's sense of history, for example, that in actual development there are deep contradictions in the relationships of production

and in the consequent social relationships. There is therefore the continual possibility of the dynamic variation of these forces. The "variations" of the superstructure might be deduced from this fact alone, were it not that the "objective" implications of "the base" reduce all such variations to secondary consequences. It is only when we realize that "the base," to which it is habitual to *refer* variations, is itself a dynamic and internally contradictory process — the specific activities and modes of activity, over a range from association to antagonism, of real men and classes of men — that we can begin to free ourselves from the notion of an "area" or a "category" with certain fixed properties for deduction to the variable processes of a "superstructure." The physical fixity of the terms exerts a constant pressure against just this realization.

Thus, contrary to a development in Marxism, it is not "the base" and "the superstructure" that need to be studied, but specific and indissoluble real processes, within which the decisive relationship, from a Marxist point of view, is that expressed by the complex idea of "determination."

6. HEGEMONY

The traditional definition of "hegemony" is political rule or domination, especially in relations between states. Marxism extended the definition of rule or domination to relations between social classes, and especially to definitions of a *ruling class.* "Hegemony" then acquired a further significant sense in the work of Antonio Gramsci, carried out under great difficulties in a Fascist prison between 1927 and 1935. Much is still uncertain in Gramsci's use of the concept, but his work is one of the major turning-points in Marxist cultural theory.

Gramsci made a distinction between "rule" *(dominio)* and "hegemony." "Rule" is expressed in directly political forms and in times of crisis by direct or effective coercion. But the more normal situation is a complex interlocking of political, social, and cultural forces, and "hegemony," according to different interpretations, is either this or the active social and cultural forces which are its necessary elements. Whatever the implications of the concept for Marxist political theory (which has still to recognize many kinds of direct political control, social class control, and economic control, as well as this more general formation), the effects on cultural theory are immediate. For "hegemony" is a concept which at once includes and goes beyond two powerful earlier concepts: that of "culture" as a "whole social process," in which men define and shape their whole lives; and that of "ideology," in any of its Marxist senses, in which a system of meanings and values is the expression or projection of a particular class interest.

"Hegemony" goes beyond "culture," as previously defined, in its insistence on relating the "whole social process" to specific distributions of power and influence. To say that "men" define and shape their whole lives is true only in abstraction. In any actual society there are specific inequalities in means and therefore in capacity to realize this process. In a class society these are primarily inequalities between classes. Gramsci therefore introduced the necessary recognition of dominance and subordination in what has still, however, to be recognized as a whole process.

It is in just this recognition of the *wholeness* of the process that the concept of "hegemony" goes beyond "ideology." What is decisive is not only the conscious system of ideas and beliefs, but the whole lived social process as practically organized by specific and dominant meanings and values. Ideology, in its normal senses, is a relatively formal and articulated system of meanings, values, and beliefs, of a kind that can be abstracted as a "world-view" or a "class outlook." This explains its popularity as a concept in retrospective analysis (in base–superstructure models or in homology), since a *system* of ideas can be abstracted from that once living social process and represented, usually by the selection of "leading" or typical "ideologists" or "ideological features," as the decisive form in which consciousness was at once expressed and controlled (or, as in Althusser, was in effect unconscious, as an imposed structure). The relatively mixed, confused, incomplete, or inarticulate consciousness of actual men in that period and society is thus overridden in the name of this decisive generalized system, and indeed of this structural homology is procedurally excluded as peripheral or ephemeral. It is the fully articulate and systematic forms which are recognizable as ideology, and there is a corresponding tendency

in the analysis of art to look only for similarly fully articulate and systematic expressions of this ideology in the content (base–superstructure) or form (homology) of actual works. In less selective procedures, less dependent on the inherent classicism of the definition of form as fully articulate and systematic, the tendency is to consider works as variants of, or as variably affected by, the decisive abstracted ideology.

More generally, this sense of "an ideology" is applied in abstract ways to the actual consciousness of both dominant and subordinated classes. A dominant class "has" this ideology in relatively pure and simple forms. A subordinate class has, in one version, *nothing but* this ideology as its consciousness (since the production of all ideas is, by axiomatic definition, in the hands of those who control the primary means of production) or, in another version, has this ideology imposed on its otherwise different consciousness, which it must struggle to sustain or develop against "ruling-class ideology."

The concept of hegemony often, in practice, resembles these definitions, but it is distinct in its refusal to equate consciousness with the articulate formal system which can be and ordinarily is abstracted as "ideology." It of course does not exclude the articulate and formal meanings, values and beliefs which a dominant class develops and propagates. But it does not equate these with consciousness, or rather it does not reduce consciousness to them. Instead it sees the relations of domination and subordination, in their forms as practical consciousness, as in effect a saturation of the whole process of living — not only of political and economic activity, nor only of manifest social activity, but of the whole substance of lived identities and relationships, to such a depth that the pressures and limits of what can ultimately be seen as a specific economic, political, and cultural system seem to most of us the pressures and limits of simple experience and common sense. Hegemony is then not only the articulate upper level of "ideology," nor are its forms of control only those ordinarily seen as "manipulation" or "indoctrination." It is a whole body of practices and expectations, over the whole of living: our senses and assignments of energy, our shaping perceptions of ourselves and our world. It is a lived system of meanings and values — constitutive and constituting — which as they are experienced as practices appear as reciprocally confirming. It thus constitutes a sense of reality for most people in the society, a sense of absolute because experienced reality beyond which it is very difficult for most members of the society to move, in most areas of their lives. It is, that is to say, in the strongest sense a "culture," but a culture which has also to be seen as the lived dominance and subordination of particular classes.

There are two immediate advantages in this concept of hegemony. First, its forms of domination and subordination correspond much more closely to the normal processes of social organization and control in developed societies than the more familiar projections from the idea of a ruling class, which are usually based on much earlier and simpler historical phases. It can speak, for example, to the realities of electoral democracy, and to the significant modern areas of "leisure" and "private life," more specifically and more actively than older ideas of domination, with their trivializing explanations of simple "manipulation," "corruption," and "betrayal." If the pressures and limits of a given form of domination are to this extent experienced *and in practice internalized,* the whole question of class rule, and of opposition to it, is transformed. Gramsci's emphasis on the creation of an alternative hegemony, by the practical connection of many different forms of struggle, including those not easily recognizable as and indeed not primarily "political" and "economic," thus leads to a much more profound and more active sense of revolutionary activity in a highly developed society than the persistently abstract models derived from very different historical situations. The sources of any alternative hegemony are indeed difficult to define. For Gramsci they spring from the working class, but not this class as an ideal or abstract construction. What he sees, rather, is a working people which has, precisely, to become a class, and a potentially hegemonic class, against the pressures and limits of an existing and powerful hegemony.

Second, and more immediately in this context, there is a whole different way of seeing cultural activity, both as tradition and as practice. Cultural work and activity are not now, in any ordinary sense, a superstructure: not only because of the depth and thoroughness at which any cultural hegemony is lived, but because cultural tradition and practice are seen as much more than superstructural expressions — reflections, mediations, or typifications — of a formed social and economic structure. On the contrary, they are among the basic processes of the formation itself and, further, related to a much wider area of reality than the abstractions of "social" and "economic" experience. People seeing themselves and each other in directly personal relationships; people seeing the natural world and themselves in it; people using their physical and material resources for what one kind of society specializes to "leisure" and "entertainment" and "art": all these active experiences and practices, which make up so much of the reality of a culture and its cultural production can be seen as they are, without reduction to other categories of content, and without the characteristic straining to fit them (directly as reflection, indirectly as mediation or typification or analogy) to other and determining manifest economic and political relationships. Yet they can still be seen as elements of a hegemony: an inclusive social and cultural formation which indeed to be effective has to extend to and include, indeed to form and be formed from, this whole area of lived experience.

Many difficulties then arise, both theoretically and practically, but it is important to recognize how many blind alleys we may now be saved from entering. If any lived culture is necessarily so extensive, the problems of domination and subordination on the one hand, and of the extraordinary complexity of any actual cultural tradition and practice on the other, can at last be directly approached.

There is of course the difficulty that domination and subordination, as effective descriptions of cultural formation, will, by many, be refused; that the alternative language of co-operative shaping, of common contribution, which the traditional concept of "culture" so notably expressed, will be found preferable. In this fundamental choice there is no alternative, from any socialist position, to recognition and emphasis of the massive historical and immediate experience of class domination and subordination, in all their different forms. This becomes, very quickly, a matter of specific experience and argument. But there is a closely related problem within the concept of "hegemony" itself. In some uses, though not I think in Gramsci, the totalizing tendency of the concept, which is significant and indeed crucial, is converted into an abstract totalization, and in this form it is readily compatible with sophisticated senses of "the superstructure" or even "ideology." The hegemony, that is, can be seen as more uniform, more static, and more abstract than in practice, if it is really understood, it can ever actually be. Like any other Marxist concept it is particularly susceptible to epochal as distinct from historical definition, and to categorical as distinct from substantial description. Any isolation of its "organizing principles," or of its "determining features," which have indeed to be grasped in experience and by analysis, can lead very quickly to a totalizing abstraction. And then the problems of the reality of domination and subordination, and of their relations to co-operative shaping and common contribution, can be quite falsely posed.

A lived hegemony is always a process. It is not, except analytically, a system or a structure. It is a realized complex of experiences, relationships, and activities, with specific and changing pressures and limits. In practice, that is, hegemony can never be singular. Its internal structures are highly complex, as can readily be seen in any concrete analysis. Moreover (and this is crucial, reminding us of the necessary thrust of the concept), it does not just passively exist as a form of dominance. It has continually to be renewed, recreated, defended, and modified. It is also continually resisted, limited, altered, challenged by pressures not at all its own. We have then to add to the concept of hegemony the concepts of counter-hegemony and alternative hegemony, which are real and persistent elements of practice.

One way of expressing the necessary distinction between practical and abstract senses within the concept is to speak of "the hegemonic" rather than "the hegemony," and of "the dominant" rather than simple "domination." The reality of any hegemony, in the extended political and cultural sense, is that, while by definition it is always dominant, it is never either total or exclusive. At any time, forms of alternative or directly oppositional politics and culture exist as significant

elements in the society. We shall need to explore their conditions and their limits, but their active presence is decisive, not only because they have to be included in any historical (as distinct from epochal) analysis, but as forms which have had significant effect on the hegemonic process itself. That is to say, alternative political and cultural emphases, and the many forms of opposition and struggle, are important not only in themselves but as indicative features of what the hegemonic process has in practice had to work to control. A static hegemony, of the kind which is indicated by abstract totalizing definitions of a dominant "ideology" or "world-view," can ignore or isolate such alternatives and opposition, but to the extent that they are significant the decisive hegemonic function is to control or transform or even incorporate them. In this active process the hegemonic has to be seen as more than the simple transmission of an (unchanging) dominance. On the contrary, any hegemonic process must be especially alert and responsible to the alternatives and opposition which question or threaten its dominance. The reality of cultural process must then always include the efforts and contributions of those who are in one way or another outside or at the edge of the terms of the specific hegemony.

Thus it is misleading, as a general method, to reduce all political and cultural initiatives and contributions to the terms of the hegemony. That is the reductive consequence of the radically different concept of "superstructure." The specific functions of "the hegemonic," "the dominant," have always to be stressed, but not in ways which suggest any a priori totality. The most interesting and difficult part of any cultural analysis, in complex societies, is that which seeks to grasp the hegemonic in its active and formative but also its transformational processes. Works of art, by their substantial and general character, are often especially important as sources of this complex evidence.

The major theoretical problem, with immediate effect on methods of analysis, is to distinguish between alternative and oppositional initiatives and contributions which are made within or against a specific hegemony (which then sets certain limits to them or which can succeed in neutralizing, changing or actually incorporating them) and other kinds of initiative and contribution which are irreducible to the terms of the original or the adaptive hegemony, and are in that sense independent. It can be persuasively argued that all or nearly all initiatives and contributions, even when they take on manifestly alternative or oppositional forms, are in practice tied to the hegemonic: that the dominant culture, so to say, at once produces and limits its own forms of counter-culture. There is more evidence for this view (for example in the case of the Romantic critique of industrial civilization) than we usually admit. But there is evident variation in specific kinds of social order and in the character of the consequent alternative and oppositional formations. It would be wrong to overlook the importance of works and ideas which, while clearly affected by hegemonic limits and pressures, are at least in part significant breaks beyond them, which may again in part be neutralized, reduced, or incorporated, but which in their most active elements nevertheless come through as independent and original.

Thus cultural process must not be assumed to be merely adaptive, extensive, and incorporative. Authentic breaks within and beyond it, in specific social conditions which can vary from extreme isolation to pre-revolutionary breakdowns and actual revolutionary activity, have often in fact occurred. And we are better able to see this, alongside more general recognition of the insistent pressures and limits of the hegemonic, if we develop modes of analysis which instead of reducing works to finished products, and activities to fixed positions, are capable of discerning, in good faith, the finite but significant openness of many actual initiatives and contributions. The finite but significant openness of many works of art, as signifying forms making possible but also requiring persistent and variable signifying responses, is then especially relevant.

7. TRADITIONS, INSTITUTIONS, AND FORMATIONS

Hegemony is always an active process, but this does not mean that it is simply a complex of dominant features and elements. On the contrary, it is always a more or less adequate organization and interconnection of otherwise separated and even disparate meanings, values, and practices, which it specifically incorporates in a significant culture and an effective social order. These are themselves living resolutions — in the broadest sense, political resolutions — of specific economic realities. This process of incorporation is of major cultural importance. To understand it, but also to understand the material on which it must work, we need to distinguish three aspects of any cultural process, which we can call traditions, institutions, and formations.

The concept of tradition has been radically neglected in Marxist cultural thought. It is usually seen as at best a secondary factor, which may at most modify other and more decisive historical processes. This is not only because it is ordinarily diagnosed as superstructure, but also because "tradition" has been commonly understood as a relatively inert, historicized segment of a social structure: tradition as the surviving past. But this version of tradition is weak at the very point where the incorporating sense of tradition is strong: where it is seen, in fact, as an actively shaping force. For tradition is in practice the most evident expression of the dominant and hegemonic pressures and limits. It is always more than an inert historicized segment; indeed it is the most powerful practical means of incorporation. What we have to see is not just "a tradition" but a *selective tradition:* an intentionally selective version of a shaping past and pre-shaped present, which is then powerfully operative in the process of social and cultural definition and identification.

It is usually not difficult to show this empirically. Most versions of "tradition" can be quickly shown to be radically selective. From a whole possible area of past and present, in a particular culture, certain meanings and practices are selected for emphasis and certain other meanings and practices are neglected or excluded. Yet, within a particular hegemony, and as one of its decisive processes, this selection is presented and usually successfully passed off as "the tradition," "the significant past." What has then to be said about any tradition is that it is in this sense an aspect of *contemporary* social and cultural organization, in the interest of the dominance of a specific class. It is a version of the past which is intended to connect with and ratify the present. What it offers in practice is a sense of *predisposed continuity*.

There are, it is true, weaker senses of "tradition," in explicit contrast to "innovation" and "the contemporary." These are often points of retreat for groups in the society which have been left stranded by some particular hegemonic development. All that is now left to them is the retrospective affirmation of "traditional values." Or, from an opposite position, "traditional habits" are isolated, by some current hegemonic development, as elements of the past which have now to be discarded. Much of the overt argument about tradition is conducted between representatives of these two positions. But at a deeper level the hegemonic sense of tradition is always the most active: a deliberately selective and connecting process which offers a historical and cultural ratification of a contemporary order.

It is a very powerful process, since it is tied to many practical continuities — families, places, institutions, a language — which are indeed directly experienced. It is also, at any time, a vulnerable process, since it has in practice to discard whole areas of significance, or reinterpret or dilute them, or convert them into forms which support or at least do not contradict the really important elements of the current hegemony. It is significant that much of the most accessible and influential work of the counter-hegemony is historical: the recovery of discarded areas, or the redress of selective and reductive interpretations. But this in turn has little effect unless the lines to the present, in the actual process of the selective tradition, are clearly and actively traced. Otherwise any recovery can be simply residual or marginal. It is at the vital points of *connection*, where a version of the past is used to ratify the present and to indicate directions for the future, that a selective tradition is at once powerful and vulnerable. Powerful because it is so skilled in making active selective connections, dismissing those it does not want as "out of date" or "nostalgic," attacking those it cannot incorporate as "unprecedented" or "alien." Vulnerable because the real record is effectively recoverable, and many of the alternative or opposing practical continuities are still available. Vulnerable also because the selective version of "a living tradition"

is always tied, though often in complex and hidden ways, to explicit contemporary pressures and limits. Its practical inclusions and exclusions are selectively encouraged or discouraged, often so effectively that the deliberate selection is made to verify itself in practice. Yet its selective privileges and interests, material in substance but often ideal in form, including complex elements of style and tone and of basic method, can still be recognized, demonstrated, and broken. This struggle for and against selective traditions is understandably a major part of all contemporary cultural activity.

It is true that the effective establishment of a selective tradition can be said to depend on identifiable institutions. But it is an understatement of the process to suppose that it depends on institutions alone. The relations between cultural, political, and economic institutions are themselves very complex, and the substance of these relations is a direct indication of the character of the culture in the wider sense. But it is never only a question of formally identifiable institutions. It is also a question of *formations:* those effective movements and tendencies, in intellectual and artistic life, which have significant and sometimes decisive influence on the active development of a culture, and which have a variable and often oblique relation to formal institutions.

Formal institutions, evidently, have a profound influence on the active social process. What is abstracted in orthodox sociology as "socialization" is in practice, in any actual society, a specific kind of incorporation. Its description as "socialization," the universal abstract process on which all human beings can be said to depend, is a way of avoiding the specific content and intention. Any process of socialization of course includes things that all human beings have to learn, but any specific process ties this necessary learning to a selected range of meanings, values, and practices which, in the very closeness of their association with necessary learning, constitute the real foundations of the hegemonic. In a family children are cared for and taught to care for themselves, but within this necessary process fundamental and selective attitudes to self, to others, to a social order, and to the material world are both consciously and unconsciously taught. Education transmits necessary knowledge and skills, but always by a particular selection from the whole available range, and with intrinsic attitudes, both to learning and social relations, which are in practice virtually inextricable. Institutions such as churches are explicitly incorporative. Specific communities and specific places of work, exerting powerful and immediate pressures on the conditions of living and of making a living, teach, confirm, and in most cases finally enforce selected meanings, values, and activities. To describe the effect of all institutions of these kinds is to arrive at an important but still incomplete understanding of incorporation. In modern societies we have to add the major communications systems. These materialize selected news and opinion, and a wide range of selected perceptions and attitudes.

Yet it can still not be supposed that the sum of all these institutions is an organic hegemony. On the contrary, just because it is not "socialization" but a specific and complex hegemonic process, it is in practice full of contradictions and of unresolved conflicts. This is why it must not be reduced to the activities of an "ideological state apparatus." Such apparatus exists, although variably, but the whole process is much wider, and is in some important respects self-generating. By selection it is possible to identify common features in family, school, community, work, and communications, and these are important. But just because they are specific processes, with variable particular purposes, and with variable but always effective relations with what must in any case, in the short term, be done, the practical consequence is as often confusion and conflict between what are experienced as different purposes and different values, as it is crude incorporation of a theoretical kind. An effective incorporation is usually in practice achieved; indeed to establish and maintain a class society it must be achieved. But no mere training or pressure is truly hegemonic. The true condition of hegemony is effective *self-identification* with the hegemonic forms: a specific and internalized "socialization" which is expected to be positive but which, if that is not possible, will rest on a (resigned) recognition of the inevitable and the necessary. An effective culture, in this sense, is always more than the sum of its institutions: not only because these can be seen, in analysis, to derive much of their character from it, but mainly because it is at the level of a whole culture that the crucial *interrelations,* including confusions and conflicts, are really negotiated.

This is why, in any analysis, we have also to include *formations.* These are most recognizable as conscious movements and tendencies (literary, artistic, philosophical or scientific) which can usually be readily discerned after their formative productions. Often, when we look further, we find that these are articulations of much wider effective formations, which can by no means be wholly identified with formal institutions, or their formal meanings and values, and which can sometimes even be positively contrasted with them. This factor is of the greatest importance for the understanding of what is habitually specialized as intellectual and artistic life. In this fundamental relation between the institutions and formations of a culture there is great historical variability, but it is generally characteristic of developed complex societies that formations, as distinct from institutions, play an increasingly important role. Moreover, since such formations relate, inevitably, to real social structures, and yet have highly variable and often oblique relations with formally discernible social institutions, any social and cultural analysis of them requires procedures radically different from those developed for institutions. What is really being analysed, in each case, is a mode of specialized practice. Moreover, within an apparent hegemony, which can be readily described in generalizing ways, there are not only alternative and oppositional formations (some of them, at certain historical stages, having become or in the process of becoming alternative and oppositional institutions) but, within what can be recognized as the dominant, effectively varying formations which resist any simple reduction to some generalized hegemonic function.

It is at this point, normally, that many of those in real contact with such formations and their work retreat to an indifferent emphasis on the complexity of cultural activity. Others altogether deny (even theoretically) the relation of such formations and such work to the social process and especially the material social process. Others again, when the historical reality of the formations is grasped, render this back to ideal constructions — national traditions, literary and artistic traditions, histories of ideas, psychologi-cal types, spiritual archetypes — which indeed acknowledge and define formations, often much more substantially than the usual generalizing accounts of explicit social derivation or super-structural function, but only by radically displac-ing them from the immediate cultural process. As a result of this displacement, the formations and their work are not seen as the active social and cultural substance that they quite invariably are. In our own culture, this form of displacement, made temporarily or comparatively convincing by the failures of derivative and superstructural inter-pretation, is itself, and quite centrally, hegemonic.

8. DOMINANT, RESIDUAL, AND EMERGENT

The complexity of a culture is to be found not only in its variable processes and their social definitions — traditions, institutions, and formations — but also in the dynamic interrelations, at every point in the process, of historically varied and variable elements. In what I have called "epochal" analysis, a cultural process is seized as a cultural system, with determinate dominant features: feudal culture or bourgeois culture or a transition from one to the other. This emphasis on dominant and definitive lineaments and features is important and often, in practice, effective. But it then often happens that its methodology is preserved for the very different function of historical analysis, in which a sense of movement within what is ordi-narily abstracted as a system is crucially necessary, especially if it is to connect with the future as well as with the past. In authentic historical analysis it is necessary at every point to recognize the complex interrelations between movements and tendencies both within and beyond a specific and effective dominance. It is necessary to examine how these relate to the whole cultural process rather than only to the selected and abstracted dominant system. Thus "bourgeois culture" is a significant general-izing description and hypothesis, expressed within epochal analysis by fundamental comparisons with "feudal culture" or "socialist culture." However, as a description of cultural process, over four or five centuries and in scores of different societ-ies, it requires immediate historical and internally

comparative differentiation. Moreover, even if this is acknowledged or practically carried out, the "epochal" definition can exert its pressure as a static type against which all real cultural process is measured, either to show "stages" or "variations" of the type (which is still historical analysis) or, at its worst, to select supporting and exclude "mar-ginal" or "incidental" or "secondary" evidence.

Such errors are avoidable if, while retaining the epochal hypothesis, we can find terms which recognize not only "stages" and "variations" but the internal dynamic relations of any actual pro-cess. We have certainly still to speak of the "domi-nant" and the "effective," and in these senses of the hegemonic. But we find that we have also to speak, and indeed with further differentiation of each, of the "residual" and the "emergent," which in any real process, and at any moment in the process, are significant both in themselves and in what they reveal of the characteristics of the "dominant."

By "residual" I mean something different from the "archaic," though in practice these are often very difficult to distinguish. Any culture includes available elements of its past, but their place in the contemporary cultural process is profoundly variable. I would call the "archaic" that which is wholly recognized as an element of the past, to be observed, to be examined, or even on occasion to be consciously "revived," in a deliberately special-izing way. What I mean by the "residual" is very different. The residual, by definition, has been effectively formed in the past, but it is still active in the cultural process, not only and often not at all as an element of the past, but as an effective element of the present. Thus certain experiences, meanings, and values which cannot be expressed or substan-tially verified in terms of the dominant culture, are nevertheless lived and practised on the basis of the residue — cultural as well as social — of some previous social and cultural institution or forma-tion. It is crucial to distinguish this aspect of the residual, which may have an alternative or even oppositional relation to the dominant culture, from that active manifestation of the residual (this being its distinction from the archaic) which has been wholly or largely incorporated into the dominant culture. In three characteristic cases in contempo-rary English culture this distinction can become a precise term of analysis. Thus organized religion is predominantly residual, but within this there is a significant difference between some practically alternative and oppositional meanings and values (absolute brotherhood, service to others without reward) and a larger body of incorporated meanings and values (official morality, or the social order of which the other-worldly is a separated neutralizing or ratifying component). Again, the idea of rural community is predominantly residual, but is in some limited respects alternative or oppositional to urban industrial capitalism, though for the most part it is incorporated, as idealization or fantasy, or as an exotic — residential or escape — leisure function of the dominant order itself. Again, in monarchy, there is virtually nothing that is actively residual (alternative or oppositional), but, with a heavy and deliberate additional use of the archaic, a residual function has been wholly incorporated as a specific political and cultural function — marking the limits as well as the methods — of a form of capitalist democracy.

A residual cultural element is usually at some distance from the effective dominant culture, but some part of it, some version of it — and especially if the residue is from some major area of the past — will in most cases have had to be incorporated if the effective dominant culture is to make sense in these areas. Moreover, at certain points the dominant culture cannot allow too much residual experience and practice outside itself, at least without risk. It is in the incorporation of the actively residual — by reinterpretation, dilution, projection, discriminating inclusion and exclusion — that the work of the selective tradition is especially evident. This is very notable in the case of versions of "the literary tradition," passing through selective versions of the character of literature to connecting and incorporated definitions of what literature now is and should be. This is one among several crucial areas, since it is in some alternative or even oppositional versions of what literature is (has been) and what literary experience (and in one common derivation, other significant experience) is and must be, that, against the pressures of incorporation, actively residual meanings and values are sustained.

By "emergent" I mean, first, that new meanings and values, new practices, new relationships and kinds of relationship are continually being created. But it is exceptionally difficult to distinguish between those which are really elements of some new phase of the dominant culture (and in this sense "species-specific") and those which are substantially alternative or oppositional to it: emergent in the strict sense, rather than merely novel. Since we are always considering relations within a cultural process, definitions of the emergent, as of the residual, can be made only in relation to a full sense of the dominant. Yet the social location of the residual is always easier to understand, since a large part of it (though not all) relates to earlier social formations and phases of the cultural process, in which certain real meanings and values were generated. In the subsequent default of a particular phase of a dominant culture there is then a reaching back to those meanings and values which were created in actual societies and actual situations in the past, and which still seem to have significance because they represent areas of human experience, aspiration, and achievement which the dominant culture neglects, undervalues, opposes, represses, or even cannot recognize.

The case of the emergent is radically different. It is true that in the structure of any actual society, and especially in its class structure, there is always a social basis for elements of the cultural process that are alternative or oppositional to the dominant elements. One kind of basis has been valuably described in the central body of Marxist theory: the formation of a new class, the coming to consciousness of a new class, and within this, in actual process, the (often uneven) emergence of elements of a new cultural formation. Thus the emergence of the working class as a class was immediately evident (for example, in nineteenth-century England) in the cultural process. But there was extreme unevenness of contribution in different parts of the process. The making of new social values and institutions far outpaced the making of strictly cultural institutions, while specific cultural contributions, though significant, were less vigorous and autonomous than either general or institutional innovation. A new class is always a source of emergent cultural practice, but while it is still, as a class, relatively subordinate, this is always likely to be uneven and is certain to be incomplete. For new practice is not, of course, an isolated process. To the degree that it emerges, and especially to the degree that it is oppositional rather than alternative,

the process of attempted incorporation signif-
cantly begins. This can be seen, in the same period
in England, in the emergence and then the effective
incorporation of a radical popular press. It can be
seen in the emergence and incorporation of working-class writing, where the fundamental problem
of emergence is clearly revealed, since the basis
of incorporation, in such cases, is the effective
predominance of received literary forms — an
incorporation, so to say, which already conditions
and limits the emergence. But the development
is always uneven. Straight incorporation is most
directly attempted against the visibly alternative
and oppositional class elements: trade unions,
working-class political parties, working-class life
styles (as incorporated into "popular" journalism,
advertising, and commercial entertainment). The
process of emergence, in such conditions, is then
a constantly repeated, an always renewable, move
beyond a phase of practical incorporation: usually
made much more difficult by the fact that much
incorporation looks like recognition, acknowledgement, and thus a form of *acceptance*. In this
complex process there is indeed regular confusion
between the locally residual (as a form of resistance to incorporation) and the generally emergent.

Cultural emergence in relation to the emergence and growing strength of a class is then
always of major importance, and always complex.
But we have also to see that it is not the only kind
of emergence. This recognition is very difficult,
theoretically, though the practical evidence is
abundant. What has really to be said, as a way of
defining important elements of both the residual
and the emergent, and as a way of understanding
the character of the dominant, is that *no mode of
production and therefore no dominant social order
and therefore no dominant culture ever in reality
includes or exhausts all human practice, human
energy, and human intention*. This is not merely
a negative proposition, allowing us to account for
significant things which happen outside or against
the dominant mode. On the contrary it is a fact
about the modes of domination, that they select
from and consequently exclude the full range of
human practice. What they exclude may often be
seen as the personal or the private, or as the natural
or even the metaphysical. Indeed it is usually in
one or other of these terms that the excluded area is

expressed, since what the dominant has effectively
seized is indeed the ruling definition of the social.
It is this seizure that has especially to be resisted.
For there is always, though in varying degrees,
practical consciousness, in specific relationships,
specific skills, specific perceptions, that is unquestionably social and that a specifically dominant
social order neglects, excludes, represses, or simply fails to recognize. A distinctive and comparative feature of any dominant social order is how
far it reaches into the whole range of practices
and experiences in an attempt at incorporation.
There can be areas of experience it is willing to
ignore or dispense with: to assign as private or to
specialize as aesthetic or to generalize as natural.
Moreover, as a social order changes, in terms of its
own developing needs, these relations are variable.
Thus in advanced capitalism, because of changes
in the social character of labour, in the social
character of communications, and in the social
character of decision-making, the dominant culture
reaches much further than ever before in capitalist society into hitherto "reserved" or "resigned"
areas of experience and practice and meaning. The
area of effective penetration of the dominant order
into the whole social and cultural process is thus
now significantly greater. This in turn makes the
problem of emergence especially acute, and narrows the gap between alternative and oppositional
elements. The alternative, especially in areas that
impinge on significant areas of the dominant,
is often seen as oppositional and, by pressure,
often converted into it. Yet even here there can
be spheres of practice and meaning which, almost
by definition from its own limited character, or in
its profound deformation, the dominant culture is
unable in any real terms to recognize. Elements of
emergence may indeed be incorporated, but just as
often the incorporated forms are merely facsimiles
of the genuinely emergent cultural practice. Any
significant emergence, beyond or against a dominant mode, is very difficult under these conditions;
in itself and in its repeated confusion with the
facsimiles and novelties of the incorporated phase.
Yet, in our own period as in others, the fact of
emergent cultural practice is still undeniable, and
together with the fact of actively residual practice is a necessary complication of the would-be
dominant culture.

This complex process can still in part be described in class terms. But there is always other social being and consciousness which is neglected and excluded: alternative perceptions of others, in immediate relationships; new perceptions and practices of the material world. In practice these are different in quality from the developing and articulated interests of a rising class. The relations between these two sources of the emergent — the class and the excluded social (human) area — are by no means necessarily contradictory. At times they can be very close and on the relations between them much in political practice depends. But culturally and as a matter of theory the areas can be seen as distinct.

What matters, finally, in understanding emergent culture, as distinct from both the dominant and the residual, is that it is never only a matter of immediate practice; indeed it depends crucially on finding new forms or adaptations of form. Again and again what we have to observe is in effect a *pre-emergence,* active and pressing but not yet fully articulated, rather than the evident emergence which could be more confidently named. It is to understand more closely this condition of pre-emergence, as well as the more evident forms of the emergent, the residual, and the dominant, that we need to explore the concept of structures of feeling.

9. STRUCTURES OF FEELING

In most description and analysis, culture and society are expressed in an habitual past tense. The strongest barrier to the recognition of human cultural activity is this immediate and regular conversion of experience into finished products. What is defensible as a procedure in conscious history, where on certain assumptions many actions can be definitively taken as having ended, is habitually projected, not only into the always moving substance of the past, but into contemporary life, in which relationships, institutions and formations in which we are still actively involved are converted, by this procedural mode, into formed wholes rather than forming and formative processes. Analysis is then centred on relations between these produced institutions, formations, and experiences, so that now, as in that produced past, only the fixed explicit forms exist, and living presence is always, by definition, receding.

When we begin to grasp the dominance of this procedure, to look into its centre and if possible past its edges, we can understand, in new ways, that separation of the social from the personal which is so powerful and directive a cultural mode. If the social is always past, in the sense that it is always formed, we have indeed to find other terms for the undeniable experience of the present: not only the temporal present, the realization of this and this instant, but the specificity of present being, the inalienably physical, within which we may indeed discern and acknowledge institutions, formations, positions, but not always as fixed products, defining products. And then if the social is the fixed and explicit — the known relationships, institutions, formations, positions — all that is present and moving, all that escapes or seems to escape from the fixed and the explicit and the known, is grasped and defined as the personal: this, here, now, alive, active, "subjective."

There is another related distinction. As thought is described, in the same habitual past tense, it is indeed so different, in its explicit and finished forms, from much or even anything that we can presently recognize as thinking, that we set against it more active, more flexible, less singular terms — consciousness, experience, feeling — and then watch even these drawn towards fixed, finite, receding forms. The point is especially relevant to works of art, which really are, in one sense, explicit and finished forms — actual objects in the visual arts, objectified conventions and notations (semantic figures) in literature. But it is not only that, to complete their inherent process, we have to make them present, in specifically active "readings." It is also that the making of art is never itself in the past tense. It is always a formative process, within a specific present. At different moments in history, and significantly different ways, the reality and even the primacy of such presences and such processes, such diverse and yet specific actualities, have been powerfully asserted and reclaimed, as in practice of course they are all the time lived. But they are then often asserted as forms themselves, in contention with other known forms: the subjective as distinct from the objective; experience from belief; feeling from thought; the immediate from the general; the personal from the social. The undeniable power of two great modern ideological systems — the "aesthetic" and the "psychological" — is, ironically, systematically derived from these senses of instance and process, where experience, immediate feeling, and then subjectivity and personality are newly generalized and assembled. Against these 'personal' forms, the ideological systems of fixed social generality, of categorical products, of absolute formations, are relatively powerless, within their specific dimension. Of one dominant strain in Marxism, with its habitual abuse of the "subjective" and the "personal," this is especially true.

Yet it is the reduction of the social to fixed forms that remains the basic error. Marx often said this, and some Marxists quote him, in fixed ways, before returning to fixed forms. The mistake, as so often, is in taking terms of analysis as terms of substance. Thus we speak of a world-view or of a prevailing ideology or of a class outlook, often with adequate evidence, but in this regular slide towards a past tense and a fixed form suppose, or even do not know that we have to suppose, that these exist and are lived specifically and definitively, in singular and developing forms. Perhaps the dead can be reduced to fixed forms, though their surviving records are against it. But the living will not be reduced, at least in the first person; living third persons may be different. All the known complexities, the experienced tensions, shifts, and uncertainties, are against the terms of the reduction and soon, by extension, against social analysis itself. Social forms are then often admitted for generalities but debarred, contemptuously, from any possible relevance to this immediate and actual significance of being. And from the abstractions formed in their turn by this act of debarring — the "human imagination," the "human psyche," the "unconscious," with their "functions" in art and in myth and in dream — new and displaced forms of social analysis and categorization, overriding all specific social conditions, are then more or less rapidly developed.

Social forms are evidently more recognizable when they are articulate and explicit. We have seen this in the range from institutions to formations and traditions. We can see it again in the range from dominant systems of belief and education to influential systems of explanation and argument. All these have effective presence. Many are formed and deliberate, and some are quite fixed. But when they have all been identified they are not a whole inventory of social consciousness in its simplest sense. For they become social consciousness only when they are lived, actively, in real relationships, and moreover in relationships which are more than systematic exchanges between fixed units. Indeed just because all consciousness is social, its processes occur not only between but within the relationship and the related. And this practical consciousness is always more than a handling of fixed forms and units. There is frequent tension between the received interpretation and practical experience. Where this tension can be made direct and explicit, or where some alternative interpretation is available, we are still within a dimension of relatively fixed forms. But the tension is as often an unease, a stress, a displacement, a latency: the moment of conscious comparison not yet come, often not even coming. And comparison is by no means the only process, though it is powerful and important. There are the experiences to which the fixed forms do not speak at all, which indeed they do not recognize. There are important mixed experiences, where the available meaning would convert part to all, or all to part. And even where form and response can be found to agree, without apparent difficulty, there can be qualifications, reservations, indications elsewhere: what the agreement seemed to settle but still sounding elsewhere. Practical consciousness is almost always different from official consciousness, and this is not only a matter of relative freedom or control. For practical consciousness is what is actually being lived, and not only what it is thought is being lived. Yet the actual alternative to the received and produced fixed forms is not silence: not the absence, the unconscious, which bourgeois culture has mythicized. It is a kind of feeling and thinking which is indeed social and material, but each in an embryonic phase before it can become fully articulate and defined exchange. Its relations with the already articulate and defined are then exceptionally complex.

This process can be directly observed in the history of a language. In spite of substantial and at some levels decisive continuities in grammar and vocabulary, no generation speaks quite the same language as its predecessors. The difference can be defined in terms of additions, deletions, and modifications, but these do not exhaust it. What really changes is something quite general, over a wide range, and the description that often fits the change best is the literary term "style." It is a general change, rather than a set of deliberate choices, yet choices can be deduced from it, as well as effects. Similar kinds of change can be observed in manners, dress, building, and other similar forms of social life. It is an open question — that is to say, a set of specific historical questions — whether in any of these changes this or that group has been dominant or influential, or whether they are the result of much more general interaction. For what we are defining is a particular quality of social experience and relationship, historically distinct from other particular qualities, which gives the sense of a generation or of a period. The relations between this quality and the other specifying historical marks of changing institutions, formations, and beliefs, and beyond these the changing social and economic relations between and within classes, are again an open question: that is to say, a set of specific historical questions. The methodological consequence of such a definition, however, is that the specific qualitative changes are not *assumed* to be epiphenomena of changed institutions, formations, and beliefs, or merely secondary evidence of changed social and economic relations between and within classes. At the same time they are from the beginning taken as *social* experience, rather than as "personal" experience or as the merely superficial or incidental "small change" of society. They are social in two ways that distinguish them from reduced senses of the social as the institutional and the formal: first, in that they are *changes of presence* (while they are being lived this is obvious; when they have been lived it is still their substantial characteristic); second, in that although they are emergent or pre-emergent, they do not have to await definition, classification, or rationalization before they exert palpable pressures and set effective limits on experience and on action.

Such changes can be defined as changes in *structures of feeling.* The term is difficult, but "feeling" is chosen to emphasize a distinction from more formal concepts of "world-view" or "ideology." It is not only that we must go beyond formally held and systematic beliefs, though of course we have always to include them. It is that we are concerned with meanings and values as they are actively lived and felt, and the relations between these and formal or systematic beliefs are in practice variable (including historically variable), over a range from formal assent with private dissent to the more nuanced interaction between selected and interpreted beliefs and acted and justified experiences. An alternative definition would be structures of *experience:* in one sense the better and wider word, but with the difficulty that one of its senses has that past tense which is the most important obstacle to recognition of the area of social experience which is being defined. We are talking about characteristic elements of impulse, restraint, and tone; specifically affective elements of consciousness and relationships: not feeling against thought, but thought as felt and feeling as thought: practical consciousness of a present kind, in a living and interrelating continuity. We are then defining these elements as a "structure": as a set, with specific internal relations, at once interlocking and in tension. Yet we are also defining a social experience which is still *in process,* often indeed not yet recognized as social but taken to be private, idiosyncratic, and even isolating, but which in analysis (though rarely otherwise) has its emergent, connecting, and dominant characteristics, indeed its specific hierarchies. These are often more recognizable at a later stage, when they have been (as often happens) formalized, classified, and in many cases built into institutions and formations. By that time the case is different; a new structure of feeling will usually already have begun to form, in the true social present.

Methodologically, then, a "structure of feeling" is a cultural hypothesis, actually derived from attempts to understand such elements and their connections in a generation or period, and needing always to be returned, interactively, to such evidence. It is initially less simple than more formally structured hypotheses of the social, but it is more adequate to the actual range of cultural evidence: historically certainly, but even more (where it matters more) in our present cultural process. The hypothesis has a special relevance to art and literature, where the true social content is in a significant number of cases of this present and affective kind, which cannot without loss be reduced to belief-systems, institutions, or explicit general relationships, though it may include all these as lived and experienced, with or without tension, as it also evidently includes elements of social and material (physical or natural) experience which may lie beyond, or be uncovered or imperfectly covered by, the elsewhere recognizable systematic elements. The unmistakable presence of certain elements in art which are not covered by (though in one mode they may be reduced to) other formal systems is the true source of the specializing categories of "the aesthetic," "the arts," and "imaginative literature." We need, on the one hand, to acknowledge (and welcome) the specificity of these elements — specific feelings, specific rhythms — and yet to find ways of recognizing their specific kinds of sociality, thus preventing that extraction from social experience which is conceivable only when social experience itself has been categorically (and at root historically) reduced. We are then not only concerned with the restoration of social content in its full sense, that of a generative immediacy. The idea of a structure of feeling can be specifically related to the evidence of forms and conventions — semantic figures — which, in art and literature, are often among the very first indications that such a new structure is forming. These relations will be discussed in more detail in subsequent chapters, but as a matter of cultural theory this is a way of defining forms and conventions in art and literature as inalienable elements of a social material process: not by derivation from other social forms and pre-forms, but as social formation of a specific kind which may in turn be seen as the articulation (often the only fully available articulation) of structures of feeling which as living processes are much more widely experienced.

For structures of feeling can be defined as social experiences *in solution*, as distinct from other social semantic formations which have been *precipitated* and are more evidently and more immediately available. Not all art, by any means, relates to a contemporary structure of feeling. The effective formations of most actual art relate to already manifest social formations, dominant or residual, and it is primarily to emergent formations (though often in the form of modification or disturbance in older forms) that the structure of feeling, *as solution*, relates. Yet this specific solution is never mere flux. It is a structured formation which, because it is at the very edge of semantic availability, has many of the characteristics of a pre-formation, until specific articulations — new semantic figures — are discovered in material practice: often, as it happens, in relatively isolated ways, which are only later seen to compose a significant (often in fact minority) generation; this often, in turn, the generation that substantially connects to its successors. It is thus a specific structure of particular linkages, particular emphases and suppressions, and, in what are often its most recognizable forms, particular deep starting-points and conclusions. Early Victorian ideology, for example, specified the exposure caused by poverty or by debt or by illegitimacy as social failure or deviation; the contemporary structure of feeling, meanwhile, in the new semantic figures of Dickens, of Emily Brontë, and others, specified exposure and isolation as a *general* condition, and poverty, debt, or illegitimacy as its connecting instances. An alternative ideology, relating such exposure to the nature of the social order, was only later generally formed: offering explanations but at now a reduced tension: the social explanation fully admitted, the intensity of experienced fear and shame now dispersed and generalized.

The example reminds us, finally, of the complex relation of differentiated structures of feeling to differentiated classes. This is historically very variable. In England between 1660 and 1690, for example, two structures of feeling (among the defeated Puritans and in the restored Court) can be readily distinguished, though neither, in its literature and elsewhere, is reducible to the ideologies of these groups or to their formal (in fact complex) class relations. At times the emergence of a new structure of feeling is best related to the rise of a class (England, 1700–60): at other times to contradiction, fracture, or mutation within a class (England, 1780–1830 or 1890–1930), when a formation appears to break away from its class norms, though it retains its substantial affiliation, and the tension is at once lived and articulated in radically new semantic figures. Any of these examples requires detailed substantiation, but what is now in question, theoretically, is the hypothesis of a mode of social formation, explicit and recognizable in specific kinds of art, which is distinguishable from other social and semantic formations by its articulation of *presence*.

Fredric Jameson

b. 1934

Without doubt the foremost Marxist literary critic in America today, Fredric R. Jameson was born in Cleveland, Ohio, raised in New Jersey, and educated at Haverford College and Yale University, where he received his Ph.D. in 1960. He has taught at Harvard University (1959–67), the University of California at San Diego (1967–76), Yale University (1976–83), and the University of California at Santa Cruz (1983–85), and since 1986 he has been Lane Professor of Comparative Literature at Duke University. In addition to studies of Jean-Paul Sartre (1961) and Wyndham Lewis (1979), his major works include Marxism and Form: Twentieth Century Dialectical Theories of Literature *(1971),* The Prison-House of Language: A Critical Account of Russian Formalism and Structuralism *(1972), and* The Political Unconscious: Narrative as a Socially Symbolic Act *(1981); two volumes of collected essays entitled* The Ideologies of Theory *(1988) and* Modernism and Imperialism *(1988); a book of film criticism entitled* Signatures of the Visible *(1990); and* Late Marxism: Adorno or the Persistence of the Dialectic *(1990),* Postmodernism, or, The Cultural Logic of Late Capitalism *(1991),* The Geopolitical Aesthetic: Cinema and Space in the World System *(1992), the Wellek lecture series published as* The Seeds of Time *(1994), and* A Singular Modernity: Notes on the Ontology of the Present *(2002). His most recent works are* The Modernist Papers *(2007),* Valences of the Dialectic *(2009),* The Hegel Variations: On the Phenomenology of the Spirit *(2010),* Representing Capital: A Reading of Volume One *(2011),* The Antinomies of Realism *(2013), and* The Ancients and the Postmoderns: On the Historicity of Forms *(2015). The following selection is from the introductory chapter of* The Political Unconscious.

From *The Political Unconscious*

III

At this point it might seem appropriate to juxtapose a Marxist method of literary and cultural interpretation with those just outlined,[1] and to document its claims to greater adequacy and validity. For better or for worse, however, as I warned in the Preface, this obvious next step is not the strategy projected by the present book, which rather seeks to argue the perspectives of Marxism as necessary preconditions for adequate literary comprehension. Marxist critical insights will therefore here be defended as something like

an ultimate *semantic* precondition for the intelligibility of literary and cultural texts. Even this argument, however, needs a certain specification: in particular we will suggest that such semantic enrichment and enlargement of the inert givens and materials of a particular text must take place within three concentric frameworks, which mark a widening out of the sense of the social ground of a text through the notions, first, of political history, in the narrow sense of punctual event and a chroniclelike sequence of happenings in time; then of society, in the now already less diachronic and time-bound sense of a constitutive tension and struggle between social classes; and, ultimately, of history now conceived in its vastest sense of the sequence of modes of production and

[1]Jameson has just discussed psychoanalytic criticism and the myth criticism of Northrop Frye.

the succession and destiny of the various human social formations, from prehistoric life to what-ever far future history has in store for us.[2]

These distinct semantic horizons are, to be sure, also distinct moments of the process of interpretation, and may in that sense be understood as dialectical equivalents of what Frye has called the successive "phases" in our reinterpretation — our rereading and rewrit-ing — of the literary text. What we must also note, however, is that each phase or horizon governs a distinct reconstruction of its object, and construes the very structure of what can now only in a general sense be called "the text" in a different way.

Thus, within the narrower limits of our first, narrowly political or historical, horizon, the "text," the object of study, is still more or less construed as coinciding with the individual liter-ary work or utterance. The difference between the perspective enforced and enabled by this horizon, however, and that of ordinary explica-tion de texte, or individual exegesis, is that here the individual work is grasped essentially as a symbolic act.

When we pass into the second phase, and find that the semantic horizon within which we grasp a cultural object has widened to include the social order, we will find that the very object of our analysis has itself been thereby dialectically transformed, and that it is no longer construed as an individual "text" or work in the narrow sense, but has been reconstituted in the form of the great collective and class discourses of which a text is little more than an individual parole or utterance. Within this new horizon, then, our object of study will prove to be the ideologeme, that is, the smallest intelligible unit of the essen-tially antagonistic collective discourses of social classes.

When finally, even the passions and values of a particular social formation find themselves placed in a new and seemingly relativized per-spective by the ultimate horizon of human his-tory as a whole, and by their respective positions in the whole complex sequence of the modes of production, both the individual text and its ide-ologemes know a final transformation, and must be read in terms of what I will call the ideology of form, that is, the symbolic messages transmitted to us by the coexistence of various sign systems which are themselves traces or anticipations of modes of production.

The general movement through these three progressively wider horizons will largely coin-cide with the shifts in focus of the final chapters in this book, and will be felt, although not nar-rowly and programmatically underscored, in the methodological transformations determined by the historical transformations of their textual objects, from Balzac to Gissing to Conrad.[3]

We must now briefly characterize each of these semantic or interpretive horizons. We have suggested that it is only in the first nar-rowly political horizon — in which history is reduced to a series of punctual events and crises in time, to the diachronic agitation of the year-to-year, the chroniclelike annals of the rise and fall of political regimes and social fashions, and the passionate immediacy of struggles between historical individuals — that the "text" or object of study will tend to coincide with the individual

---

[2] A useful discussion of the phenomenological concept of "horizon" may be found in Hans-Georg Gadamer, Truth and Method, trans. G. Barden and J. Cumming (New York: Seabury, 1975), pp. 216–20, 267–74. It will become clear in the course of my subsequent discussion that a Marxian conception of our relationship to the past requires a sense of our radical difference from earlier cultures which is not adequately allowed for in Gadamer's influential notion of Horizontverschmelzung (fusion of horizons). This is perhaps also the moment to add that from the perspective of Marxism as an "absolute historicism," the stark antithesis proposed by E. D. Hirsch, Jr., between Gadamer's historicist "relativism" and Hirsch's own conception of a more absolute interpre-tive validity, will no longer seem particularly irreconcilable. Hirsch's distinction between Sinn and Bedeutung, between the scientific analysis of a text's intrinsic "meaning" and what he is pleased to call our "ethical" evaluation of its "significance" (see, for example, The Aims of Interpretation [Chicago: University of Chicago Press, 1976]), corresponds to the tra-ditional Marxist distinction between science and ideology, particularly as it has been retheorized by the Althusserians. It is surely a useful working distinction, although in the light of current revisions of the idea of science one should probably make no longer theoretical claims for it than this operative one. [Jameson]

[3] In later chapters of The Political Unconscious, Jameson analyzes texts by these three authors, viewed as typical of real-ist, naturalist, and modernist eras in fiction.

literary work or cultural artifact. Yet to specify this individual text as a symbolic act is already fundamentally to transform the categories with which traditional *explication de texte* (whether narrative or poetic) operated and largely still operates.

The model for such an interpretive operation remains the readings of myth and aesthetic structure of Claude Lévi-Strauss as they are codified in his fundamental essay "The Structural Study of Myth."[4] These suggestive, often sheerly occasional, readings and speculative glosses immediately impose a basic analytical or interpretive principle: the individual narrative, or the individual formal structure is to be grasped as the imaginary resolution of a real contradiction. Thus, to take only the most dramatic of Lévi-Strauss's analyses — the "interpretation" of the unique facial decorations of the Caduveo Indians — the starting point will be an immanent description of the formal and structural peculiarities of this body art; yet it must be a description already preprepared and oriented toward transcending the purely formalistic, a movement which is achieved not by abandoning the formal level for something extrinsic to it — such as some inertly social "content" — but rather immanently, by construing purely formal patterns as a symbolic enactment of the social within the formal and the aesthetic. Such symbolic functions are, however, rarely found by an aimless enumeration of random formal and stylistic features; our discovery of a text's symbolic efficacity must be oriented by a formal description which seeks to grasp it as a determinate structure of still properly formal *contradictions*. Thus, Lévi-Strauss orients his still purely visual analysis of Caduveo facial decorations toward this climactic account of their contradictory dynamic: "the use

of a design which is symmetrical but yet lies across an oblique axis . . . a complicated situation based upon two contradictory forms of duality, and resulting in a compromise brought about by a secondary opposition between the ideal axis of the object itself [the human face] and the ideal axis of the figure which it represents."[5] Already on the purely formal level, then, this visual text has been grasped as a contradiction by way of the curiously provisional and asymmetrical resolution it proposes for that contradiction.

Lévi-Strauss's "interpretation" of this formal phenomenon may now, perhaps overhastily, be specified. Caduveo are a hierarchical society, organized in three endogamous groups or castes. In their social development, as in that of their neighbors, this nascent hierarchy is already the place of the emergence, if not of political power in the strict sense, then at least of relations of domination: the inferior status of women, the subordination of youth to elders, and the development of a hereditary aristocracy. Yet whereas this latent power structure is, among the neighboring Guana and Bororo, masked by a division into moieties which cuts across the three castes, and whose exogamous exchange appears to function in a nonhierarchical, essentially egalitarian way, it is openly present in Caduveo life, as surface inequality and conflict. The social institutions of the Guana and Bororo, on the other hand, provide a realm of appearance, in which real hierarchy and inequality are dissimulated by the reciprocity of the moieties, and in which, therefore, "asymmetry of class is balanced . . . by symmetry of 'moieties.'"

As for the Caduveo,

> they were never lucky enough to resolve their contradictions, or to disguise them with the help of institutions artfully devised for that purpose. On the social level, the remedy was lacking . . . but it was never completely out of their grasp. It was within them, never objectively formulated, but present as a source of confusion and disquiet. Yet since they were unable to conceptualize or to live this solution directly, they began to dream it, to project it into the imaginary. . . . We must therefore interpret the

---

[4]Claude Lévi-Strauss, *Structural Anthropology,* trans. C. Jacobson and B. G. Schoepf (New York: Basic, 1963), pp. 206–31. The later four-volume *Mythologiques* reverses the perspective of this analysis: where the earlier essay focused on the individual mythic *parole* or utterance, the later series models the entire system or *langue* in terms of which the various individual myths are related to each other. *Mythologiques* should therefore rather be used as suggestive material on the historical difference between the narrative mode of production of primitive societies and that of our own: in this sense, the later work would find its place in the third and final horizon of interpretation. [Jameson] See p. 503.

[5]Claude Lévi-Strauss, *Tristes Tropiques,* trans. John Russell (New York: Atheneum, 1971), p. 176. [Jameson]

graphic art of Caduveo women, and explain its mysterious charm as well as its apparently gratuitous complication, as the fantasy production of a society seeking passionately to give symbolic expression to the institutions it might have had in reality, had not interest and superstition stood in the way.[6]

In this fashion, then, the visual text of Caduveo facial art constitutes a symbolic act, whereby real social contradictions, insurmountable in their own terms, find a purely formal resolution in the aesthetic realm.

This interpretive model thus allows us a first specification of the relationship between ideology and cultural texts or artifacts: a specification still conditioned by the limits of the first, narrowly historical or political horizon in which it is made. We may suggest that from this perspective, ideology is not something which informs or invests symbolic production; rather the aesthetic act is itself ideological, and the production of aesthetic or narrative form is to be seen as an ideological act in its own right, with the function of inventing imaginary or formal "solutions" to unresolvable social contradictions.

Lévi-Strauss's work also suggests a more general defense of the proposition of a political unconscious than we have hitherto been able to present, insofar as it offers the spectacle of so-called primitive peoples perplexed enough by the dynamics and contradictions of their still relatively simple forms of tribal organization to project decorative or mythic resolutions of issues that they are unable to articulate conceptually. But if this is the case for precapitalist and even pre-political societies, then how much more must it be true for the citizen of the modern *Gesellschaft*,[7] faced with the great constitutional options of the revolutionary period, and with the corrosive and tradition-annihilating effects of the spread of a money and market economy, with the changing cast of collective characters which oppose the bourgeoisie, now to an embattled aristocracy, now to an urban proletariat, with the great fantasms of the various nationalisms, now themselves virtual "subjects of history" of a rather different kind, with the social homogenization and psychic constriction

of the rise of the industrial city and its "masses," the sudden appearance of the great transnational forces of communism and fascism, followed by the advent of the superstates and the onset of that great ideological rivalry between capitalism and communism, which, no less passionate and obsessive than that which, at the dawn of modern times, seethed through the wars of religion, marks the final tension of our now global village? It does not, indeed, seem particularly farfetched to suggest that these texts of history, with their fantasmatic collective "actants," their narrative organization, and their immense charge of anxiety and libidinal investment, are lived by the contemporary subject as a genuine politico-historical *pensée sauvage*[8] which necessarily informs all of our cultural artifacts, from the literary institutions of high modernism all the way to the products of mass culture. Under these circumstances, Lévi-Strauss's work suggests that the proposition whereby all cultural artifacts are to be read as symbolic resolutions of real political and social contradictions deserves serious exploration and systematic experimental verification. It will become clear in later chapters of this book that the most readily accessible formal articulation of the operations of a political *pensée sauvage* of this kind will be found in what we will call the structure of a properly political *allegory*, as it develops from networks of topical allusion in Spenser or Milton or Swift to the symbolic narratives of class representatives or "types" in novels like those of Balzac. With political allegory, then, a sometimes repressed ur-narrative[9] or master fantasy about the interaction of collective subjects, we have moved to the very borders of our second horizon, in which what we formerly regarded as individual texts are grasped as "utterances" in an essentially collective or class discourse.

We cannot cross those borders, however, without some final account of the critical operations involved in our first interpretive phase. We have implied that in order to be consequent, the will to read literary or cultural texts as symbolic acts must necessarily grasp them as resolutions of determinate contradictions; and it is clear

Society.

[6]Ibid., pp. 179–80. [Jameson]

[8]Literally "savage mind"; Lévi-Strauss's term for the part of the mind that thinks using myth.

[9]Original narrative.

that the notion of contradiction is central to any Marxist cultural analysis, just as it will remain central in our two subsequent horizons, although it will there take rather different forms. The methodological requirement to articulate a text's fundamental contradiction may then be seen as a test of the completeness of the analysis: this is why, for example, the conventional sociology of literature or culture, which modestly limits itself to the identification of class motifs or values in a given text, and feels that its work is done when it shows how a given artifact "reflects" its social background, is utterly unacceptable. Meanwhile, Kenneth Burke's play of emphases, in which a symbolic act is on the one hand affirmed as a genuine *act,* albeit on the symbolic level, while on the other it is registered as an act which is "merely" symbolic, its resolutions imaginary ones that leave the real untouched, suitably dramatizes the ambiguous status of art and culture.[10]

Still, we need to say a little more about the status of this external reality, of which it will otherwise be thought that it is little more than the traditional notion of "context" familiar in older social or historical criticism. The type of interpretation here proposed is more satisfactorily grasped as the rewriting of the literary text in such a way that the latter may itself be seen as the rewriting or restructuration of a prior historical or ideological *subtext,* it being always understood that that "subtext" is not immediately present as such, not some common-sense external reality, nor even the conventional narratives of history manuals, but rather must itself always be (re)constructed after the fact. The literary or aesthetic act therefore always entertains some active relationship with the Real;[11] yet in order to do so, it cannot simply allow "reality" to persevere inertly in its own being, outside the text and at distance. It must rather draw the Real into its own texture, and the ultimate paradoxes and false problems of linguistics, and most notably of semantics, are to be traced back to this process, whereby language manages to carry the Real within itself as its own

intrinsic or immanent subtext. Insofar, in other words, as symbolic action — what Burke will map as "dream," "prayer," or "chart"[12] — is a way of doing something to the world, to that degree what we are calling "world" must inhere within it, as the content it has to take up into itself in order to submit it to the transformations of form. The symbolic act therefore begins by generating and producing its own context in the same moment of emergence in which it steps back from it, taking its measure with a view toward its own projects of transformation. The whole paradox of what we have here called the subtext may be summed up in this, that the literary work or cultural object, as though for the first time, brings into being that very situation to which it is also, at one and the same time, a reaction. It articulates its own situation and textualizes it, thereby encouraging and perpetuating the illusion that the situation itself did not exist before it, that there is nothing but a text, that there never was any extra- or con-textual reality before the text itself generated it in the form of a mirage. One does not have to argue the reality of history: necessity, like Dr. Johnson's stone, does that for us.[13] That history — Althusser's "absent cause," Lacan's "Real" — is *not* a text, for it is fundamentally non-narrative and nonrepresentational; what can be added, however, is the proviso that history is inaccessible to us except in textual form, or in other words, that it can be approached only by way of prior (re)textualization. Thus, to insist on either of the two inseparable yet incommensurable dimensions of the symbolic act without the other: to overemphasize the active way in which the text reorganizes its subtext (in order, presumably, to reach the triumphant conclusion that the "referent" does not exist); or on the other hand to stress the imaginary status of the symbolic act so completely as to reify its social ground, now no longer understood as a subtext but merely as some inert given that the text passively or fantasmatically

[10]See the introduction to Burke, p. 385.

[11]Jameson is alluding to the Lacanian field of the Real; see the introduction to Psychoanalytic Theory, p. 627. Later in The Political Unconscious Jameson will define the Real as "what hurts."

[12]Kenneth Burke, *The Philosophy of Literary Form* (Berkeley: University of California Press, 1973), pp. 5–6; and see also my "Symbolic Inference; or Kenneth Burke and Ideological Analysis," *Critical Inquiry,* 4 (Spring, 1978), 507–23. [Jameson]

[13]Samuel Johnson, when told that Bishop George Berkeley denied the existence of corporeal reality, kicked a stone, saying, "Thus I refute Berkeley."

"reflects" — to overstress either of these functions of the symbolic act at the expense of the other is surely to produce sheer ideology, whether it be, as in the first alternative, the ideology of structuralism, or, in the second, that of vulgar materialism. Still, this view of the place of the "referent" will be neither complete nor methodologically usable unless we specify a supplementary distinction between several types of subtext to be (re)constructed. We have implied, indeed, that the social contradiction addressed and "resolved" by the formal prestidigitation of narrative must, however reconstructed, remain an absent cause, which cannot be directly or immediately conceptualized by the text. It seems useful, therefore, to distinguish, from this ultimate subtext which is the place of social contradiction, a secondary one, which is more properly the place of ideology, and which takes the form of the *aporia* or the *antinomy:* what can in the former be resolved only through the intervention of praxis here comes before the purely contemplative mind as logical scandal or double bind, the unthinkable and the conceptually paradoxical, that which cannot be unknotted by the operation of pure thought, and which must therefore generate a whole more properly narrative apparatus — the text itself — to square its circles and to dispel, through narrative movement, its intolerable closure. Such a distinction, positing a system of antinomies as the symptomatic expression and conceptual reflex of something quite different, namely a social contradiction, will now allow us to reformulate that coordination between a semiotic and a dialectical method, which was evoked in the preceding section. The operational validity of semiotic analysis, and in particular of the Greimassian semiotic rectangle,[14] derives, as was suggested there, not from its adequacy to nature or being, nor even from its capacity to map all forms of thinking or language, but rather from its vocation specifically to model ideological closure and to articulate the workings of binary oppositions, here the privileged form of what we have called the antinomy. A dialectical reevaluation of the findings of semiotics intervenes, however, at the moment in which this entire system of ideological closure is taken as the symptomatic projection of something quite different, namely of social contradiction.

We may now leave this first textual or interpretive model behind, and pass over into the second horizon, that of the social. The latter becomes visible, and individual phenomena are revealed as social facts and institutions, only at the moment in which the organizing categories of analysis become those of social class. I have in another place described the dynamics of ideology in its constituted form as a function of social class:[15] suffice it to recall here that for Marxism classes must always be apprehended relationally, and that the ultimate (or ideal) form of class relationship and class struggle is always dichotomous. The constitutive form of class relationships is always that between a dominant and a laboring

---

[14] Jameson explains later that Greimas's "semiotic rectangle . . ." is the representation of a binary opposition of two contraries (S and −S) along with the simple negations or contradictories of both terms (the so-called subcontraries −S and S): significant slots are constituted by the various possible combinations of these terms, most notably the "complex" term (or ideal synthesis of the two contraries) and the "neutral" term (or ideal synthesis of the two subcontraries). See A. J. Greimas and François Rastier, 'The Interaction of Semiotic Constraints.' *Yale French Studies* No. 41 (1968), pp. 86–105.

(*The Political Unconscious*, p. 166). For Jameson, the fascination of the "semiotic rectangle" is that a "static analytical scheme" can work in his dialectical criticism "as the very locus and model of ideological closure" (p. 47).

For example, Jameson analyzes the ideology of the "character system" of Conrad's *Lord Jim* in terms of the expansion of a binary opposition between activity and value. The "semiotic rectangle" presents four points (activity, value, not-activity, not-value) which then define the position of the various agents: Lord Jim himself represents the synthesis of activity and value; Gentleman Brown, of activity and not-value; the pilgrims on the Patna, of value and not-activity; the "desk-chair sailors" of not-value and not-activity (p. 256). This arrangement, for Jameson, represents the deep structure of the ideological work Conrad's novel was expected to perform.

[15]*Marxism and Form*, pp. 376–82; and see below, pp. 288–91. The most authoritative contemporary Marxist statement of this view of social class is to be found in E. P. Thompson, *The Making of the English Working Classes* (New York: Vintage, 1966), pp. 9–11: in *The Poverty of Theory*, Thompson has argued that his view of classes is incompatible with "structural" Marxism, for which classes are not "subjects" but rather "positions" within the social totality (see, for the Althusserian position, Nicos Poulantzas, *Political Power and Social Classes*). [Jameson]

class: and it is only in terms of this axis that class fractions (for example, the petty bourgeoisie) or ec-centric or dependent classes (such as the peasantry) are positioned. To define class in this way is sharply to differentiate the Marxian model of classes from the conventional sociological analysis of society into strata, subgroups, professional elites and the like, each of which can presumably be studied in isolation from one another in such a way that the analysis of their "values" or their "cultural space" folds back into separate and independent *Weltanschauungen,*[16] each of which inertly reflects its particular "stratum." For Marxism, however, the very content of a class ideology is relational, in the sense that its "values" are always actively in situation with respect to the opposing class, and defined against the latter: normally, a ruling class ideology will explore various strategies of the *legitimation* of its own power position, while an oppositional culture or ideology will, often in covert and disguised strategies, seek to contest and to undermine the dominant "value system."

This is the sense in which we will say, following Mikhail Bakhtin, that within this horizon class discourse — the categories in terms of which individual texts and cultural phenomena are now rewritten — is essentially *dialogical* in its structure.[17] As Bakhtin's (and Voloshinov's) own work in this field is relatively specialized, focusing primarily on the heterogeneous and explosive pluralism of moments of carnival or festival (moments, for example, such as the immense resurfacing of the whole spectrum of the religious or political sects in the English 1640s or the Soviet 1920s) it will be necessary to add the qualification that the normal form of the dialogical is essentially an *antagonistic* one, and that the dialogue of class struggle is one in which

two opposing discourses fight it out within the general unity of a shared code. Thus, for instance, the shared master code of religion becomes in the 1640s in England the place in which the dominant formulations of a hegemonic theology are reappropriated and polemically modified.[18]

Within this new horizon, then, the basic formal requirement of dialectical analysis is maintained, and its elements are still restructured in terms of *contradiction* (this is essentially, as we have said, what distinguishes the relationality of a Marxist class analysis from static analysis of the sociological type). Where the contradiction of the earlier horizon was univocal, however, and limited to the situation of the individual text, to the place of a purely individual symbolic resolution, contradiction here appears in the form of the dialogical as the irreconcilable demands and positions of antagonistic classes. Here again, then, the requirement to prolong interpretation to the point at which this ultimate contradiction begins to appear offers a criterion for the completeness or insufficiency of the analysis.

Yet to rewrite the individual text, the individual cultural artifact, in terms of the antagonistic dialogue of class voices is to perform a rather different operation from the one we have ascribed to our first horizon. Now the individual text will be refocused as a *parole,* or individual utterance, of that vaster system, or *langue,* of class discourse. The individual text retains its formal structure as a symbolic act: yet the value and character of such symbolic action are now significantly modified and enlarged. On this rewriting, the individual utterance or text is grasped as a symbolic move in an essentially polemic and strategic ideological confrontation between the classes, and to describe it in these terms (or to reveal it in this form) demands a whole set of different instruments.

For one thing, the illusion or appearance of isolation or autonomy which a printed text projects must now be systematically undermined. Indeed, since by definition the cultural monuments and masterworks that have survived tend necessarily to perpetuate only a single voice in this class

[16]World-pictures.

[17]Mikhail Bakhtin, *Problems of Dostoyevsky's Poetics,* trans. R. W. Rotsel (Ann Arbor: Ardis, 1973), pp. 153–69. See also Bakhtin's important book on linguistics, written under the name of V. N. Voloshinov, *Marxism and the Philosophy of Language,* trans. L. Matejka and I. R. Titunik (New York: Seminar Press, 1973), pp. 83–98; and Bakhtin's posthumous collection, *Esthétique et théorie du roman,* trans. Daria Olivier (Paris: Gallimard, 1978), esp. pp. 152–82. [Jameson] See the introduction to Bakhtin, p. 349.

[18]See Christopher Hill, *The World Turned Upside Down* (London: Temple Smith, 1972). [Jameson]

dialogue, the voice of a hegemonic class, they cannot be properly assigned their relational place in a dialogical system without the restoration or artificial reconstruction of the voice to which they were initially opposed, a voice for the most part stifled and reduced to silence, marginalized, its own utterances scattered to the winds, or reappropriated in their turn by the hegemonic culture. This is the framework in which the reconstruction of so-called popular cultures must properly take place — most notably, from the fragments of essentially peasant cultures: folk songs, fairy tales, popular festivals, occult or oppositional systems of belief such as magic and witchcraft. Such reconstruction is of a piece with the reaffirmation of the existence of marginalized or oppositional cultures in our own time, and the reaudition of the oppositional voices of black or ethnic cultures, women's and gay literature, "naïve" or marginalized folk art, and the like. But once again, the affirmation of such nonhegemonic cultural voices remains ineffective if it is limited to the merely "sociological" perspective of the pluralistic rediscovery of other isolated social groups: only an ultimate rewriting of these utterances in terms of their essentially polemic and subversive strategies restores them to their proper place in the dialogical system of the social classes. Thus, for instance, Bloch's reading of the fairy tale, with its magical wish-fulfillments and its Utopian fantasies of plenty and the *pays de Cocagne*,[19] restores the dialogical and antagonistic content of this "form" by exhibiting it as a systematic deconstruction and undermining of the hegemonic aristocratic form of the epic, with its somber ideology of heroism and baleful destiny; thus also the work of Eugene Genovese on black religion restores the vitality of these utterances by reading them, not as the replication of imposed beliefs, but rather as a process whereby the hegemonic Christianity of the slave-owners is appropriated, secretly emptied of its content and subverted to the transmission of quite different oppositional and coded messages.[20]

[19]Ernst Bloch, "Zerstörung, Rettung des Mythos durch Licht," in *Verfremdungen I* (Frankfurt: Suhrkamp, 1963), pp. 152–62. [Jameson]

[20]Eugene Genovese, *Roll Jordan Roll* (New York: Vintage, 1976), pp. 161–284. [Jameson]

Moreover, the stress on the dialogical then allows us to reread or rewrite the hegemonic forms themselves; they also can be grasped as a process of the reappropriation and neutralization, the cooptation and class transformation, the cultural universalization, of forms which originally expressed the situation of "popular," subordinate, or dominated groups. So the slave religion of Christianity is transformed into the hegemonic ideological apparatus of the medieval system; while folk music and peasant dance find themselves transmuted into the forms of aristocratic or court festivity and into the cultural visions of the pastoral; and popular narrative from time immemorial — romance, adventure story, melodrama, and the like — is ceaselessly drawn on to restore vitality to an enfeebled and asphyxiating "high culture." Just so, in our own time, the vernacular and its still vital sources of production (as in black language) are reappropriated by the exhausted and media-standardized speech of a hegemonic middle class. In the aesthetic realm, indeed, the process of cultural "universalization" (which implies the repression of the oppositional voice, and the illusion that there is only one genuine "culture") is the specific form taken by what can be called the process of legitimation in the realm of ideology and conceptual systems.

Still, this operation of rewriting and of the restoration of an essentially dialogical or class horizon will not be complete until we specify the "units" of this larger system. The linguistic metaphor (rewriting texts in terms of the opposition of a *parole* to a *langue*) cannot, in other words, be particularly fruitful until we are able to convey something of the dynamics proper to a class *langue* itself, which is evidently, in Saussure's sense, something like an ideal construct that is never wholly visible and never fully present in any one of its individual utterances. This larger class discourse can be said to be organized around minimal "units" which we will call *ideologemes*. The advantage of this formulation lies in its capacity to mediate between conceptions of ideology as abstract opinion, class value, and the like, and the narrative materials with which we will be working here. The ideologeme is an amphibious formation, whose essential structural characteristic may be described as its possibility to manifest itself either as a pseudoidea — a conceptual or belief system, an abstract value, an opinion or prejudice — or as a protonarrative, a kind of ultimate class fantasy about the "collective characters" which are the classes in opposition. This duality means that the basic requirement for the full description of the ideologeme is already given in advance: as a construct it must be susceptible to both a conceptual description and a narrative manifestation all at once. The ideologeme can of course be elaborated in either of these directions, taking on the finished appearance of a philosophical system on the one hand, or that of a cultural text on the other; but the ideological analysis of these finished cultural products requires us to demonstrate each one as a complex work of transformation on that ultimate raw material which is the ideologeme in question. The analyst's work is thus first that of the identification of the ideologeme, and, in many cases, of its initial naming in instances where for whatever reason it had not yet been registered as such. The immense preparatory task of identifying and inventorying such ideologemes has scarcely even begun, and to it the present book will make but the most modest contribution: most notably in its isolation of that fundamental nineteenth-century ideologeme which is the "theory" of *ressentiment*,[21] and in its "unmasking" of ethics and the ethical binary opposition of good and evil as one of the fundamental forms of ideological thought in Western culture. However, our stress here and throughout on the fundamentally narrative character of such ideologemes (even where they seem to be articulated only as abstract conceptual beliefs or values) will offer the advantage of restoring the complexity of the transactions between opinion and protonarrative or libidinal fantasy. Thus we will observe, in the case of Balzac, the generation of an overt and constituted ideological and political "value system" out of the operation of an essentially narrative and fantasy dynamic; the chapter on Gissing, on the other hand, will show how an already constituted "narrative paradigm" emits an ideological message in its own right without the mediation of authorial intervention.

[21]Literally, rancor; Nietzsche's term for the hatred felt by the weak for the strong.

This focus or horizon, that of class struggle and its antagonistic discourses, is, as we have already suggested, not the ultimate form a Marxist analysis of culture can take. The example just alluded to — that of the seventeenth-century English revolution, in which the various classes and class fractions found themselves obliged to articulate their ideological struggles through the shared medium of a religious master code — can serve to dramatize the shift whereby these objects of study are reconstituted into a structurally distinct "text" specific to this final enlargement of the analytical frame. For the possibility of a displacement in emphasis is already given in this example: we have suggested that within the apparent unity of the theological code, the fundamental difference of antagonistic class positions can be made to emerge. In that case, the inverse move is also possible, and such concrete semantic differences can on the contrary be focused in such a way that what emerges is rather the all-embracing unity of a single code which they must share and which thus characterizes the larger unity of the social system. This new object — code, sign system, or system of the production of signs and codes — thus becomes an index of an entity of study which greatly transcends those earlier ones of the narrowly political (the symbolic act), and the social (class discourse and the ideologeme), and which we have proposed to term the historical in the larger sense of this word. Here the organizing unity will be what the Marxian tradition designates as a *mode of production*.

I have already observed that the "problematic" of modes of production is the most vital new area of Marxist theory in all the disciplines today; not paradoxically, it is also one of the most traditional, and we must therefore, in a brief preliminary way, sketch in the "sequence" of modes of production as classical Marxism, from Marx and Engels to Stalin, tended to enumerate them.[22] These modes, or "stages" of human society, have traditionally

[22]The "classical" texts on modes of production, besides Lewis Henry Morgan's *Ancient Society* (1877), are Karl Marx, *Pre-Capitalist Economic Formations,* a section of the *Grundrisse* (1857–58) published separately by Eric Hobsbawm (New York: International, 1965), and Friedrich Engels, *The Family, Private Property, and the State* (1884). Important recent contributions to the mode of production "debate" include Etienne Balibar's contribution to Althusser's

included the following: primitive communism or tribal society (the horde), the *gens* or hierarchical kinship societies (neolithic society), the Asiatic mode of production (so-called Oriental despotism), the *polis* or an oligarchical slaveholding society (the ancient mode of production), feudalism, capitalism, and communism (with a good deal of debate as to whether the "transitional" stage between these last — sometimes called "socialism" — is a genuine mode of production in its own right or not). What is more significant in the present context is that even this schematic or mechanical conception of historical "stages" (what the Althusserians have systematically criticized under the term "historicism") includes the notion of a cultural dominant or form of ideological coding specific to each mode of production. Following the same order these have generally been conceived as magic and mythic narrative, kinship, religion or the sacred, "politics" according to the narrower category of citizenship in the ancient city state, relations of personal domination, commodity reification, and (presumably) original and as yet nowhere fully developed forms of collective or communal association.

Before we can determine the cultural "text" or object of study specific to the horizon of modes of production, however, we must make two preliminary remarks about the methodological problems it raises. The first will bear on whether the concept of "mode of production" is a synchronic one, while the second will address the temptation to use the various modes of production for a classifying or typological operation, in which cultural texts are simply dropped into so many separate compartments.

Indeed, a number of theorists have been disturbed by the apparent convergence between the properly Marxian notion of an all-embracing and all-structuring mode of production (which assigns everything within itself — culture, ideological production, class articulation, technology — a specific and unique place), and non-Marxist

visions of a "total system" in which the various elements or levels of social life are programmed in some increasingly constricting way, Weber's dramatic notion of the "iron cage" of an increasingly bureaucratic society,[23] Foucault's image of the gridwork of an ever more pervasive "political technology of the body,"[24] but also more traditional "synchronic" accounts of the cultural programming of a given historical "moment," such as those that have variously been proposed from Vico and Hegel to Spengler and Deleuze — all such monolithic models of the cultural unity of a given historical period have tended to confirm the suspicions of a dialectical tradition about the dangers of an emergent "synchronic" thought, in which change and development are relegated to the marginalized category of the merely "diachronic," the contingent or the rigorously nonmeaningful (and this, even where, as with Althusser, such models of cultural unity are attacked as forms of a more properly Hegelian and idealistic "expressive causality"). This theoretical foreboding about the limits of synchronic thought can perhaps be most immediately grasped in the political area, where the model of the "total system" would seem slowly and inexorably to eliminate any possibility of the *negative* as such, and to reintegrate the place of an oppositional or even merely "critical" practice and resistance back into the system as the latter's mere inversion. In particular, everything about class struggle that was anticipatory in the older dialectical framework, and seen as an emergent space for

collective volume, *Reading Capital*; Emmanuel Terray, *Marxism and "Primitive" Societies*, trans. M. Klopper (New York: Monthly Review, 1972); Maurice Godelier, *Horizon: trajets marxistes en anthropologie* (Paris: Maspéro, 1973); J. Chesneaux, ed., *Sur le "mode de production asiatique"* (Paris: Editions Sociales, 1969); and Barry Hindess and Paul Hirst, *Pre-Capitalist Modes of Production* (London: Routledge & Kegan Paul, 1975). [Jameson]

23"The Puritan wanted to work in a calling; we are forced to do so. For when asceticism was carried out of monastic cells into everyday life, and began to dominate worldly morality, it did its part in building the tremendous cosmos of the modern economic order. This order is now bound to the technical and economic conditions of machine production which today determine the lives of all the individuals who are born into this mechanism, not only those directly concerned with economic acquisition, with irresistible force. Perhaps it will so determine them until the last ton of fossilized coal is burnt. In Baxter's view the care for external goods should only lie on the shoulders of the saint 'like a light cloak, which can be thrown aside at any moment.' But fate decreed that the cloak should become an iron cage." *The Protestant Ethic and the Spirit of Capitalism*, trans. T. Parsons (New York: Scribner's, 1958), p. 181. [Jameson]

24Michel Foucault, *Surveiller et punir* (Paris: Gallimard, 1975), pp. 27–28 and passim. [Jameson]

radically new social relations, would seem, in the synchronic model, to reduce itself to practices that in fact tend to reinforce the very system that foresaw and dictated their specific limits. This is the sense in which Jean Baudrillard has suggested that the "total-system" view of contemporary society reduces the options of resistance to anarchist gestures, to the sole remaining ultimate protests of the wildcat strike, terrorism, and death. Meanwhile, in the framework of the analysis of culture also, the latter's integration into a synchronic model would seem to empty cultural production of all its antisystemic capacities, and to "unmask" even the works of an overtly oppositional or political stance as instruments ultimately programmed by the system itself.

It is, however, precisely the notion of a series of enlarging theoretical horizons proposed here that can assign these disturbing synchronic frameworks their appropriate analytical places and dictate their proper use. This notion projects a long view of history which is inconsistent with concrete political action and class struggle only if the specificity of the horizons is not respected; thus, even if the concept of a mode of production is to be considered a synchronic one (and we will see in a moment that things are somewhat more complicated than this), at the level of historical abstraction at which such a concept is properly to be used, the lesson of the "vision" of a total system is for the short run one of the structural limits imposed on praxis rather than the latter's impossibility.

The theoretical problem with the synchronic systems enumerated above lies elsewhere, and less in their analytical framework than in what in a Marxist perspective might be called their infrastructural regrounding. Historically, such systems have tended to fall into two general groups, which one might term respectively the hard and soft visions of the total system. The first group projects a fantasy future of a "totalitarian" type in which the mechanisms of domination — whether these are understood as part of the more general process of bureaucratization, or on the other hand derive more immediately from the deployment of physical and ideological force — are grasped as irrevocable and increasingly pervasive tendencies whose mission is to colonize the last remnants and survivals of human freedom — to occupy and organize, in other words, what still persists of Nature objectively and subjectively (very schematically, the Third World and the Unconscious).

This group of theories can perhaps hastily be associated with the central names of Weber and Foucault; the second group may then be associated with names such as those of Jean Baudrillard and the American theorists of a "post-industrial society."[25] For this second group, the characteristics of the total system of contemporary world society are less those of political domination than those of cultural programming and penetration: not the iron cage, but rather the *société de consommation*[26] with its consumption of images and simulacra, its free-floating signifiers and its effacement of the older structures of social class and traditional ideological hegemony. For both groups, world capitalism is in evolution toward a system which is not socialist in any classical sense, on the one hand the nightmare of total control and on the other the polymorphous or schizophrenic intensities of some ultimate counterculture (which may be no less disturbing for some than the overtly threatening characteristics of the first vision). What one must add is that neither kind of analysis respects the Marxian injunction of the "ultimately determining instance" of economic organization and tendencies: for both, indeed, economics (or political economy) of that type is in the new total system of the contemporary world at an end, and the economic finds itself in both reassigned to a secondary and nondeterminant position beneath the new dominant of political power or of cultural production, respectively.

There exist, however, within Marxism itself precise equivalents to these two non-Marxian visions of the contemporary total system: rewritings, if one likes, of both in specifically Marxian and "economic" terms. These are the analyses of

[25]Jean Baudrillard, *Le Système des objets* (Paris: Gallimard, 1968); *La Société de consommation* (Paris: Denöel, 1970); *Pour une économie politique du signe* (Paris: Gallimard, 1972). The most influential statement of the American version of this "end of ideology"/consumer society position is, of course, that of Daniel Bell: see his *Coming of Post-Industrial Society* (New York: Basic, 1973) and *The Cultural Contradictions of Capitalism* (New York: Basic, 1976). [Jameson]

[26]Consumer society typical of late capitalism.

late capitalism in terms of *capitalogic*,[27] and of *disaccumulation*,[28] respectively; and while this book is clearly not the place to discuss such theories at any length, it must be observed here that both, seeing the originality of the contemporary situation, reassert the theoretical priority of the organizing concept of the mode of production within capitalism, which we have been concerned to argue.

We must therefore now turn to the second related problem about this third and ultimate horizon, and deal briefly with the objection that cultural analysis pursued within it will tend toward a purely typological or classificatory operation, in which we are called upon to "decide," such issues as whether Milton is to be read within a "precapitalist" or a nascent capitalist context, and so forth. I have insisted elsewhere on the sterility of such classificatory procedures, which may always, it seems to me, be taken as symptoms and indices of the repression of a more genuinely dialectical or historical practice of cultural analysis. This diagnosis may now be expanded to cover all three horizons at issue here, where the practice of homology, that of a merely "sociological"

[27]See, for a review and critique of the basic literature, Stanley Aronowitz, "Marx, Braverman, and the Logic of Capital," *Insurgent Sociologist*, VIII, No. 2/3 (Fall, 1978), pp. 126–46; and see also Hans-George Backhaus, "Zur Dialektik der Wertform," in A. Schmidt, ed., *Beiträge zur marxistischen Erkenntnistheorie* (Frankfurt: Suhrkamp, 1969), pp. 128–52; and Helmut Reichelt, *Zur logischen Struktur des Kapitalbegriffs bei Karl Marx* (Frankfurt: Europäische Verlagsanstalt, 1970). For the Capitallogicians, the "material-ist kernel" of Hegel is revealed by grasping the concrete or objective reality of Absolute Spirit (the Notion in-and-for-itself) as none other than capital (Reichelt, pp. 77–78). This tends, however, to force them into the post-Marxist position for which the dialectic is seen as the thought-mode proper only to capitalism (Backhaus, pp. 140–41): in that case, of course, the dialectic would become unnecessary and anach-ronistic in a society that had abolished the commodity form. [Jameson]

[28]The basic texts on "disaccumulation theory" are Martin J. Sklar, "On the Proletarian Revolution and the End of Political-Economic Society," *Radical America*, III, No. 3 (May–June, 1969), pp. 1–41; Jim O'Connor, "Productive and Unproductive Labor," *Politics and Society*, 5 (1975), pp. 297–336; Fred Block and Larry Hirschhorn, "New Productive Forces and the Contradictions of Contemporary Capitalism," *Theory and Society*, 7 (1979), 363–95; and Stanley Arono-witz, "The End of Political Economy," *Social Text*, No. 2 (1980), pp. 3–52. [Jameson]

search for some social or class equivalent, and that, finally, of the use of some typology of social and cultural systems, respectively, may stand as examples of the misuse of these three frame-works. Furthermore, just as in our discussion of the first two we have stressed the centrality of the category of contradiction for any Marxist analysis (seen, within the first horizon, as that which the cultural and ideological artifact tries to "resolve," and in the second as the nature of the social and class conflict within which a given work is one act or gesture), so too here we can effectively validate the horizon of the mode of production by showing the form contradiction takes on this level, and the relationship of the cultural object to it.

Before we do so, we must take note of more recent objections to the very concept of the mode of production. The traditional schema of the various modes of production as so many historical "stages" has generally been felt to be unsatisfactory, not least because it encourages the kind of typologizing criticized above, in political quite as much as in cultural analysis. (The form taken in political analysis is evidently the pro-cedure which consists in "deciding" whether a given conjuncture is to be assigned to a moment within feudalism — the result being a demand for bourgeois and parliamentary rights — or within capitalism — with the accompanying "reformist" strategy — or, on the contrary, a genuine "revo-lutionary" moment — in which case the appropri-ate revolutionary strategy is then deduced.)

On the other hand, it has become increasingly clear to a number of contemporary theorists that such classification of "empirical" materials within this or that abstract category is impermis-sible in large part because of the level of abstrac-tion of the concept of a mode of production: no historical society has ever "embodied" a mode of production in any pure state (nor is *Capital* the description of a historical society, but rather the construction of the abstract concept of capital-ism). This has led certain contemporary theorists, most notably Nicos Poulantzas,[29] to insist on the distinction between a "mode of production" as

[29]Poulantzas, *Political Power and Social Classes*, pp. 13–16. [Jameson]

a purely theoretical construction and a "social formation" that would involve the description of some historical society at a certain moment of its development. This distinction seems inadequate and even misleading, to the degree that it encourages the very empirical thinking which it was concerned to denounce, in other words, subsuming a particular or an empirical "fact" under this or that corresponding "abstraction." Yet one feature of Poulantzas' discussion of the "social formation" may be retained: his suggestion that every social formation or historically existing society has in fact consisted in the overlay and structural coexistence of *several* modes of production all at once, including vestiges and survivals of older modes of production, now relegated to structurally dependent positions within the new, as well as anticipatory tendencies which are potentially inconsistent with the existing system but have not yet generated an autonomous space of their own.

But if this suggestion is valid, then the problems of the "synchronic" system and of the typological temptation are both solved at one stroke. What is synchronic is the "concept" of the mode of production; the moment of the historical coexistence of several modes of production is not synchronic in this sense, but open to history in a dialectical way. The temptation to classify texts according to the appropriate mode of production is thereby removed, since the texts emerge in a space in which we may expect them to be crisscrossed and intersected by a variety of impulses from contradictory modes of cultural production all at once.

Yet we have still not characterized the specific object of study which is constructed by this new and final horizon. It cannot, as we have shown, consist in the concept of an individual mode of production (any more than, in our second horizon, the specific object of study could consist in a particular social class in isolation from the others). We will therefore suggest that this new and ultimate object may be designated, drawing on recent historical experience, as *cultural revolution,* that moment in which the coexistence of various modes of production becomes visibly antagonistic, their contradictions moving to the very center of political, social, and historical life. The incomplete

Chinese experiment with a "proletarian" cultural revolution may be invoked in support of the proposition that previous history has known a whole range of equivalents for similar processes to which the term may legitimately be extended. So the Western Enlightenment may be grasped as part of a properly bourgeois cultural revolution, in which the values and the discourses, the habits and the daily space, of the *ancien régime* were systematically dismantled so that in their place could be set the new conceptualities, habits and life forms, and value systems of a capitalist market society. This process clearly involved a vaster historical rhythm than such punctual historical events as the French Revolution or the Industrial Revolution, and includes in its *longue durée* such phenomena as those described by Weber in *The Protestant Ethic and the Spirit of Capitalism* — a work that can now in its turn be read as a contribution to the study of the bourgeois cultural revolution, just as the corpus of work on romanticism is now repositioned as the study of a significant and ambiguous moment in the resistance to this particular "great transformation," alongside the more specifically "popular" (precapitalist as well as working-class) forms of cultural resistance.

But if this is the case, then we must go further and suggest that all previous modes of production have been accompanied by cultural revolutions specific to them of which the neolithic "cultural revolution," say, the triumph of patriarchy over the older matriarchal or tribal forms, or the victory of Hellenic "justice" and the new legality of the *polis* over the vendetta system are only the most dramatic manifestations. The concept of cultural revolution, then — or more precisely, the reconstruction of the materials of cultural and literary history in the form of this new "text" or object of study which is cultural revolution — may be expected to project a whole new framework for the humanities, in which the study of culture in the widest sense could be placed on a materialist basis.

This description is, however, misleading to the degree to which it suggests that "cultural revolution" is a phenomenon limited to so-called "transitional" periods, during which social formations dominated by one mode of production undergo a radical restructuration in the course of which a different "dominant" emerges. The problem of such "transitions" is a traditional crux of the Marxian problematic of modes of production, nor can it be said that any of the solutions proposed, from Marx's own fragmentary discussions to the recent model of Etienne Balibar, are altogether satisfactory, since in all of them the inconsistency between a "synchronic" description of a given system and a "diachronic" account of the passage from one system to another seems to return with undiminished intensity. But our own discussion began with the idea that a given social formation consisted in the coexistence of various synchronic systems or modes of production, each with its own dynamic or time scheme — a kind of metasynchronicity, if one likes — while we have now shifted to a description of cultural revolution which has been couched in the more diachronic language of systemic transformation. I will therefore suggest that these two apparently inconsistent accounts are simply the twin perspectives which our thinking (and our presentation or *Darstellung* of that thinking) can take on this same vast historical object, just as overt revolution is no punctual event either, but brings to the surface the innumerable daily struggles and forms of class polarization which are at work in the whole course of social life that precedes it, and which are therefore latent and implicit in "prerevolutionary" social experience, made visible as the latter's deep structure only in such "moments of truth" — so also the overtly "transitional" moments of cultural revolution are themselves but the passage to the surface of a permanent process in human societies, of a permanent struggle between the various coexisting modes of production. The triumphant moment in which a new systemic dominant gains ascendency is therefore only the diachronic manifestation of a constant struggle for the perpetuation and reproduction of its dominance, a struggle which must continue throughout its life course, accompanied at all moments by the systemic or structural antagonism of those older and newer modes of production that resist assimilation or seek deliverance from it. The task of cultural

and social analysis thus construed within this final horizon will then clearly be the rewriting of its materials in such a way that this perpetual cultural revolution can be apprehended and read as the deeper and more permanent constitutive structure in which the empirical textual objects know intelligibility.

Cultural revolution thus conceived may be said to be beyond the opposition between synchrony and diachrony, and to correspond roughly to what Ernst Bloch has called the *Ungleichzeitigkeit* (or "nonsynchronous development") of cultural and social life.[30] Such a view imposes a new use of concepts of periodization, and in particular of that older schema of the "linear" stages which is here preserved and canceled all at once. We will deal more fully with the specific problems of periodization in the next chapter: suffice it to say at this point that such categories are produced within an initial diachronic or narrative framework, but become usable only when that initial framework has been annulled, allowing us now to coordinate or articulate categories of diachronic origin (the

[30]Ernst Bloch, "Nonsynchronism and Dialectics," *New German Critique*, No. 11 (Spring, 1977), pp. 22–38; or *Erbschaft dieser Zeit* (Frankfurt: Suhrkamp, 1973). The "nonsynchronous" use of the concept of mode of production outlined above is in my opinion the only way to fulfill Marx's well-known program for dialectical knowledge "of rising from the abstract to the concrete" (1857 Introduction, *Grundrisse*, p. 101). Marx there distinguished three stages of knowledge: (1) the notation of the particular (this would correspond to something like empirical history, the collection of data and descriptive materials on the variety of human societies); (2) the conquest of abstraction, the coming into being of a properly "bourgeois" science or of what Hegel called the categories of the Understanding (this moment, that of the construction of a static and purely classificatory concept of "modes of production," is what Hindess and Hirst quite properly criticize in *Precapitalist Modes of Production*); (3) the transcendence of abstraction by the dialectic, the "rise to the concrete," the setting in motion of hitherto static and typologizing categories by their reinsertion in a concrete historical situation (in the present context, this is achieved by moving from a classificatory use of the categories of modes of production to a perception of their dynamic and contradictory coexistence in a given cultural moment). Althusser's own epistemology, incidentally — *Generalities* I, II, and III (*Pour Marx* [Paris: Maspero, 1965], pp. 187–90) — is a gloss on this same fundamental passage of the 1857 Introduction, but one which succeeds only too well in eliminating its dialectical spirit.

[Jameson]

various distinct modes of production) in what is now a synchronic or metasynchronic way.

We have, however, not yet specified the nature of the textual object which is constructed by this third horizon of cultural revolution, and which would be the equivalent within this dialectically new framework of the objects of our first two horizons — the symbolic act, and the ideologeme or dialogical organization of class discourse. I will suggest that within this final horizon the individual text or cultural artifact (with its appearance of autonomy which was dissolved in specific and original ways within the first two horizons as well) is here restructured as a field of force in which the dynamics of sign systems of several distinct modes of production can be registered and apprehended. These dynamics — the newly constituted "text" of our third horizon — make up what can be termed *the ideology of form,* that is, the determinate contradiction of the specific messages emitted by the varied sign systems which coexist in a given artistic process as well as in its general social formation.

What must now be stressed is that at this level "form" is apprehended as content. The study of the ideology of form is no doubt grounded on a technical and formalistic analysis in the narrower sense, even though, unlike much traditional formal analysis, it seeks to reveal the active presence within the text of a number of discontinuous and heterogeneous formal processes. But at the level of analysis in question here, a dialectical reversal has taken place in which it has become possible to grasp such formal processes as sedimented content in their own right, as carrying ideological messages of their own, distinct from the ostensible or manifest content of the works; it has become possible, in other words, to display such formal operations from the standpoint of what Louis Hjelmslev[31] will call the "content of form" rather than the latter's "expression," which is generally the object of the various more narrowly formalizing approaches. The simplest and most accessible demonstration of this reversal may be found in the area of literary genre. Our next chapter, indeed, will model the process

whereby generic specification and description can, in a given historical text, be transformed into the detection of a host of distinct generic messages — some of them objectified survivals from older modes of cultural production, some anticipatory, but all together projecting a formal conjuncture through which the "conjuncture" of coexisting modes of production at a given historical moment can be detected and allegorically articulated.

Meanwhile, that what we have called the ideology of form is something other than a retreat from social and historical questions into the more narrowly formal may be suggested by the relevance of this final perspective to more overtly political and theoretical concerns; we may take the much debated relation of Marxism to feminism as a particularly revealing illustration. The notion of overlapping modes of production outlined above has indeed the advantage of allowing us to short-circuit the false problem of the priority of the economic over the sexual, or of sexual oppression over that of social class. In our present perspective, it becomes clear that sexism and the patriarchal are to be grasped as the sedimentation and the virulent survival of forms of alienation specific to the oldest mode of production of human history, with its division of labor between men and women, and its division of power between youth and elder. The analysis of the ideology of form, properly completed, should reveal the formal persistence of such archaic structures of alienation — and the sign systems specific to them — beneath the overlay of all the more recent and historically original types of alienation — such as political domination and commodity reification — which have become the dominants of that most complex of all culturalrevolutions, late capitalism, in which all the earlier modes of production in one way or anotherstructurally coexist. The affirmation of radical feminism, therefore, that to annul the patriarchal is the most *radical* political act — insofar as it includes and subsumes more partial demands, such as the liberation from the commodity form — is thus perfectly consistent with an expanded Marxian framework, for which the transformation of our own dominant mode of production must be accompanied and completed

---

[31]Danish linguist, author of *Prolegomena to a Theory of Language* (Ann Arbor: University of Wisconsin Press, 1961).

by an equally radical restructuration of all the more archaic modes of production with which it structurally coexists.

With this final horizon, then, we emerge into a space in which History itself becomes the ultimate ground as well as the untranscendable limit of our understanding in general and our textual interpretations in particular. This is, of course, also the moment in which the whole problem of interpretive priorities returns with a vengeance, and in which the practitioners of alternate or rival interpretive codes — far from having been persuaded that History is an interpretive code that includes and transcends all the others — will again assert "History!" as simply one more code among others, with no particularly privileged status. This is most succinctly achieved when the critics of Marxist interpretation, borrowing its own traditional terminology, suggest that the Marxian interpretive operation involves a thematization and a reification of "History!" which is not markedly different from the process whereby the other interpretive codes produce their own forms of thematic closure and offer themselves as absolute methods.

It should by now be clear that nothing is to be gained by opposing one reified theme — History — by another — Language — in a polemic debate as to ultimate priority of one over the other. The influential forms this debate has taken in recent years — as in Jürgen Habermas' attempt to subsume the "Marxist" model of production beneath a more all-embracing model of "communication" or of "intersubjectivity,"[32] or in Umberto Eco's assertion of the priority of the Symbolic in general over the technological and productive systems which it must organize as *signs* before they can be used as *tools*[33] — are based on the misconception that the Marxian category of a "mode of production" is a form of technological or "productionist" determinism.

It would seem therefore more useful to ask ourselves, in conclusion, how History as a ground and as an absent cause can be conceived in such a way as to resist such thematization or

[32]See Jürgen Habermas, *Knowledge and Human Interests*, trans. J. Shapiro (Boston: Beacon, 1971), esp. Part I. [Jameson]

[33]Umberto Eco, *A Theory of Semiotics* (Bloomington: Indiana University Press, 1976), pp. 21–26. [Jameson]

reification, such transformation back into one optional code among others. We may suggest such a possibility obliquely by attention to what the Aristotelians would call the generic satisfaction specific to the form of the great monuments of historiography, or what the semioticians might call the "history-effect" of such narrative texts. Whatever the raw material on which historiographic form works (and we will here only touch on that most widespread type of material which is the sheer chronology of fact as it is produced by the rote-drill of the history manual), the "emotion" of great historiographic form can then always be seen as the radical restructuration of that inert material, in this instance the powerful reorganization of otherwise inert chronological and "linear" data in the form of Necessity; why what happened (at first received as "empirical" fact) had to happen the way it did. From this perspective, then, causality is only one of the possible tropes by which this formal restructuration can be achieved, although it has obviously been a privileged and historically significant one. Meanwhile, should it be objected that Marxism is rather a "comic" or "romance" paradigm, one which sees history in the salvational perspective of some ultimate liberation, we must observe that the most powerful realizations of a Marxist historiography — from Marx's own narratives of the 1848 revolution through the rich and varied canonical studies of the dynamics of the Revolution of 1789 all the way to Charles Bettelheim's study of the Soviet revolutionary experience — remain visions of historical Necessity in the sense evoked above. But Necessity is here represented in the form of the inexorable logic involved in the determinate failure of all the revolutions that have taken place in human history: the ultimate Marxian presupposition — that socialist revolution can only be a total and worldwide process (and that this in turn presupposes the completion of the capitalist "revolution" and of the process of commodification on a global scale) — is the perspective in which the failure or the blockage, the contradictory reversal or functional inversion, of this or that local revolutionary process is grasped as "inevitable," and as the operation of objective limits.

History is therefore the experience of Necessity, and it is this alone which can forestall its thematization or reification as a mere object of representation or as one master code among many others. Necessity is not in that sense a type of content, but rather the inexorable *form* of events; it is therefore a narrative category in the enlarged sense of some properly narrative political unconscious which has been argued here, a retextualization of History which does not propose the latter as some new representation or "vision," some new content, but as the formal effects of what Althusser, following Spinoza, calls an "absent cause." Conceived in this sense, History is what hurts, it is what refuses desire and sets inexorable limits to individual as well as collective praxis, which its "ruses" turn into grisly and ironic revsersals of their overt intention. But this History can be apprehended only through its effects, and never directly as some reified force. This is indeed the ultimate sense in which History as ground and untranscendable horizon needs no particular theoretical justification: we may be sure that its alienating necessities will not forget us, however much we might prefer to ignore them.

9

NEW HISTORICISM AND CULTURAL STUDIES

To understand the practices of writers and artists, and not least their products, entails under-standing that they are the result of the meeting of two histories: the history of the positions they occupy and the history of their dispositions.

— PIERRE BOURDIEU

As in more familiar exercises in close reading, one can start anywhere in a culture's reper-toire of forms and end up anywhere else . . . But whatever the level at which one operates, and however intricately, the guiding principle is the same: societies, like lives, contain their own interpretations. One has only to learn how to gain access to them.

— CLIFFORD GEERTZ

Modern thought and experience have taught us to be sensitive to what is involved in repre-sentation, in studying the Other, in racial thinking, in unthinking and uncritical acceptance of authority and authoritative ideas, in the sociopolitical role of intellectuals, in the great value of a skeptical critical consciousness. Perhaps if we remember that the study of human experience usually has an ethical, to say nothing of a political, consequence . . . we will not be indifferent to what we do as scholars.

— EDWARD W. SAID

THE NEW HISTORICISM: THEORIES AND PRACTICES

Born around 1982, the New Historicism quickly became one of the most vital modes of literary study in the 1980s. The name the brilliant young Renaissance scholar Stephen Greenblatt gave to the approach he pioneered was conferred in haste. Asked for a title for a special issue of the journal *Genre* in which his own essays and those of colleagues were appearing, Greenblatt carelessly threw out the title "New Historicism." Greenblatt has tried ever since to rename what he does "cultural poet-ics," in order to avoid the connotations of historical inevitability implicit in the word *historicism* and to more clearly label his practice as a literary version of cultural anthropology. But, alas, in vain: The name has stuck fast.

Greenblatt correctly insists that New Historicism is not a theory or a set of doctrines but a practice.[1] However, it is a practice that has developed out of contemporary theory, particularly the structuralist realization that all human systems are symbolic and subject to the rules of language, and the deconstructive realization that there is no way of positioning oneself as an observer outside the closed circle of textuality. What sort of practice New Historicism is and what its motives are is suggested by Michael Warner's fast-and-dirty positioning of it in relation to other critical practices current in the mid-1980s:

> New Historicism is a label that historians don't like much because they understand something different by historicism. But nobody's asking historians; the people the New Historicists are reacting against are the New Critics, and historicism seems an important term for that purpose because it emphasizes that meaning is established in concrete historical situations. . . . If the "Historicism" in the New Historicism is to distinguish it from the New Critics and their idea that a text means what it means regardless of what your cultural situation is, the "New" in New Historicism is to distinguish it from the somewhat dreary and encyclopedic historical work that the philologists used to do. . . . While critics have realized on the one hand that language and the symbolic are never essential and timeless but always contingent on cultural politics, on the other hand they have realized that cultural politics is always symbolic. New Historicism has a motto: "The text is historical, and history is textual." The first part means that meaning does not transcend context but is produced within it; the second part means that human actions and institutions and relations, while certainly hard facts, are not hard facts as distinguished from language. They are themselves symbolic representations, though this is not to say, as so many old historicists might conclude, that they are not real.[2]

Warner's characterization seems reasonably fair to the New Critics, who were deeply uncomfortable with the notion that the author's and reader's ways of construing a text might diverge with the passage of time. It is less fair to the philologists and historians, whose "dreary" labors give us whatever picture we possess of past ages, and who were far less naive about the way language is used in writing history than Warner suggests. The philosopher of history R. G. Collingwood made it clear several decades before the advent of the New Historicism that historians are politically and culturally implicated in the history they write, that their work tells us as much about them as the period they investigate and explore.[3]

What is new about the New Historicism might be seen in Stephen Greenblatt's "*King Lear* and Harsnett's 'Devil-Fiction,'" reprinted below. Samuel Harsnett's *Declaration of Egregious Popish Impostures* (printed in 1603), exposes the impostures of Catholic exorcists, who would pretend to drive out devils from "possessed" individuals, shills of theirs, as a way of demonstrating their power and that of the Roman Catholic Church. Greenblatt did not discover Harsnett's text, which had long been recognized as one of the books Shakespeare must have read while composing *King Lear* since it contains names of the devils Edgar cites in the "Poor Tom" scenes

[1]See Stephen Greenblatt, "Toward a Poetics of Culture," in *The New Historicism*, ed. H. Aram Veeser (New York: Routledge, 1989), p. 1.
[2]Michael Warner, "Literary Studies and the History of the Book," *The Book* 12 (1987): 5.
[3]See, for example, Collingwood's *Essays in the Philosophy of History*, ed. William Debbins (New York and London: Garland, 1985).

on the heath. However, Greenblatt's essay is not a conventional source study; his take on the two texts is to compare the unlicensed, forbidden theatrical performances of the Catholic exorcists in Protestant England with the licensed, permitted theatrical performances conducted on the stage of Shakespeare's Globe, in order to view Shakespeare's play as "a secular version of the ritual of exorcism" and to show how the state benefits from a transgression that can be represented but contained within the wooden "O" of the theater.

While the New Historicists are not, by and large, theorists, their work grew out of three or four advances in theory in radically disconnected fields. From Michel Foucault, the historical philosopher, the New Historicists developed the notion that texts within a particular period are linked by a broad totalizing cultural formation (the *episteme*), in which the workings of power and knowledge and their interrelationships can be defined. From Clifford Geertz, the cultural anthropologist, they absorbed a sense of how both primitive and advanced cultures operate through symbolic representation and ritual enactment of conflict, and they incorporated Geertz's ideal of the "thick description" of a culture that can come only from genuine immersion in its ways. From Hayden White, the philosopher of history, they took the notion that figural relationships — the tropes, or figures of speech used by a writer — can be clues to the way historians think and the way their representations of the past are filtered and shifted through the language of history. Finally, from French philosophical sociologists like Pierre Bourdieu and Michel de Certeau, new historical practice appropriated theories of intellectual practice aimed at understanding how the structure of learned professions alters the way knowledge and the power associated with it are originated and distributed.

CULTURAL STUDIES: THE WORLD AS SOCIAL TEXT

All five of the theorists just mentioned have been appropriated equally by the allied practice of cultural studies.[4] Cultural studies, though, is much harder to pin down than the New Historicism. It is not even clear whether cultural studies is older as a practice than the New Historicism or younger, since it depends on what one wants to count as examples of cultural studies. Books addressing cultural studies by name did not begin to appear until the early 1990s. Nevertheless, Simon During, the British editor of *The Cultural Studies Reader* (1993), views the key player as Richard Hoggart, who began the Center for Cultural Studies at the University of Birmingham in the 1950s, and who inspired, along with Raymond Williams, the media studies

[4]There is no consensus concerning the intellectual substructures of New Historicism and cultural studies. Other historians of criticism have portrayed New Historicism as being influenced by the work of Karl Marx, Raymond Williams, the Italian Marxist Antonio Gramsci, Mikhail Bakhtin, philosopher of science Thomas Kuhn, Walter Benjamin, and dozens of others, including American Marxists such as Fredric Jameson and Frank Lentricchia who have ferociously attacked the New Historicists. The variety of influence on cultural studies is literally unbounded, given the wide range of subject matter analyzed. My principle for choosing exemplars in this chapter has been to avoid duplication while focusing on those influences that seem widest and most significant.

work of Stuart Hall.[5] In addition to the cultural materialism of British working-class Marxism, During locates an alternate, "structuralist" side to cultural studies arising from Althusserian Marxism and Lacanian psychoanalysis (for a description of these schools see the introductions to Chs. 5 and 4, respectively). The story is probably even more complicated than this, however. Many contemporary scholars would agree that continental criticism such as Theodor Adorno's *Philosophy of Modern Music* (1949), which compares the compositional practices of Schönberg and Stravinsky in terms of their responses to modernity, and Roland Barthes's essays on fashion, restaurant menus, and wrestling matches in *Mythologies* (1957) were engaged in practices not much different from Meaghan Morris's brilliant study of shopping centers, or Ien Ang's approach to watching television, which date from the late 1980s and early 1990s.[6] Given its inchoate nature, trying to date cultural studies precisely is impossible, but it would be fair to claim that its origins long preceded its current vogue, which started in the late 1980s.

Stuart Hall's "Cultural Studies: Two Paradigms" (1980) is a careful tracing of the ideological affiliations of the Birmingham group begun by Richard Hoggart in the twin directions of British Marxism and French structuralism. Hall's British Marxist forebears are Raymond Williams and E. P. Thompson, who were not dialecticians so much as students of the culture of the English past. Williams, in fact, was a historian of "forms of feeling," which he is reluctant to ascribe to anything so doctrinaire as ideology, until he was stimulated by Thompson's questioning to take on a harder line and accept the historical motor for change provided by materialist dialectic. The other structuralist side, for Hall, is represented by Claude Lévi-Strauss, whom Hall locates in the tradition of Emile Durkheim and Marcel Mauss. Hall chronicles the nebulous attachments Lévi-Strauss made with Marxism, although he finds clearer connections between the two paradigms with Louis Althusser and Lucien Goldmann. For Hall the virtue of structuralism is its ability to view the human condition as determined, indeed overdetermined, by symbolic networks operating at different levels and its comprehension of the lived relationships of society as a totality.

Hall concludes with a paean to Michel Foucault and Antonio Gramsci, who he claims "between them account for most of the most productive work on *concrete analysis* now being undertaken in the field." Of course Gramsci was a somewhat unorthodox Marxist, and Foucault was never a believer in the structuralist synthesis of knowledge, and the two are strangely matched, Gramsci's concept of hegemony (see p. 701) granting the oppressed classes areas of autonomy that Foucault's disciplinary systems would rigorously deny. Indeed, from a different point of view, Marxism and structuralism might be seen as an oddly matched couple, the former insisting on a dialectical framework for thought, with progress emerging from conflict, the latter an operational schema, reducing every object of analysis to its

[5]See *The Cultural Studies Reader*, ed. Simon During (London: Routledge, 1993); Richard Hoggart, *The Uses of Literacy* (London: Penguin, 1957); and Stuart Hall and Paddy Whannel, *The Popular Arts* (London: Hutchinson, 1964).

[6]See Meaghan Morris, "Things to Do with Shopping Centers" in *Grafts* (London: Verso, 1988) and Ien Ang, *Watching Television* (London: Routledge, 1991).

smallest functional parts, understanding totalities as syntactic structures built out of these atoms.

Cultural studies involves viewing and analyzing practically any recorded phenomenon, present or past, as a social text. The "texts" analyzed include such evanescent events as music videos, comic books, letters from summer camp, and radio talk shows: Madonna Studies at one point threatened to become a major subfield. In addition, they include phenomena that are not usually thought of as texts at all, such as government regulations, embroidery, surgical operations, meatpacking, and mapmaking. Since canonical literary works and their formal elements are also viewed as social texts, one could in theory write "cultural studies" about Alexander Pope's pastorals. But, in practice, the tendency has been to seek out subjects disdained by the traditional hierarchies of aesthetic value, or ones that in their exoticism stand outside the older canon.

To some extent, the New Historicism has also focused on nonliterary texts. For example, Richard McCoy has written about the ritual order and physical arrangements of Elizabeth Tudor's coronation, which, as he demonstrates, were composed with as assiduous an eye to metaphor and symbol as any epic poem; he has also studied Henrician and Elizabethan tournaments as performance art, as ritual, and as political act.[7] But McCoy also discusses Sidney and Spenser in the light of the rituals of chivalry, so, in his work there is certainly nothing like the absolute breach with literary texts and the literary canon that one finds in much of cultural studies.[8]

Like the New Historicism, cultural studies is not a theory as such or even a combination of theories; it is not even a single coherent practice, but rather a disparate set of related practices. Some practitioners of cultural studies relate easily to Gramscian or Althusserian Marxism, while others like Michel Foucault himself and his numerous fellow travelers are loath to situate cultural power principally as a byproduct of economics. Even if they do not present a single, consistent social philosophy,[9] essays in cultural studies must situate themselves in relation to *some* literary and social theory to make the questions they raise, the texts they choose, and the methods they follow comprehensible. More eclectic even than New Historicism, cultural studies draws on structuralism, deconstruction, Lacanian psychology, post-Althusserian Marxism, reception theory, feminism, and gender studies; to fully

[7] See Richard McCoy, *The Rites of Knighthood: The Literature and Politics of Elizabethan Chivalry* (New York: Cambridge University Press, 1989).

[8] I am not sure precisely how to characterize my own reading, in the introduction to *True Crime in Nineteenth-Century Literature* (2011), of the idea of "identity" (the concept of a sense of self that might be discarded, refashioned, stolen, or feigned) as a cultural phenomenon of England in the 1860s. This *mentalité* was stimulated by Wilkie Collins's sensational novel *The Woman in White* (1860), which sensitized English readers to the idea that one's identity might be stolen by a clever criminal, and clearly had taken hold ten years later, as is shown by the real-life case of the Tichborne claimant, an Australian rogue falsely claiming to be an English baronet, whose struggle in court to get his "rights" absorbed aristocrat and commoner alike for several years. Is the analysis of how England developed a fixation on identity a form of New Historicism or cultural studies?

[9] It is probably a safe guess that most practitioners of both the New Historicism and cultural studies would locate themselves well to the left of the ostensibly left-leaning "New Labour" Party in the UK or the Democratic Party in the United States.

understand its intellectual basis would require reading virtually this entire book. The placement of cultural studies in the same chapter as the New Historicism marks the fact that they share many key influences, including Foucault's social and sexual theories, Geertz's ideal of "thick description," and Bourdieu's analysis of cultural power and capital.

FOUCAULT: ARCHAEOLOGIES AND GENEALOGIES, POWER AND KNOWLEDGE

It is hard to know how to characterize Foucault. He refused to be termed a philosopher, though for a time he held the chair in philosophy at the Collège de France. He was certainly not a literary critic. Most of his works are in the field of social history. *Folie et déraison: Histoire de la folie à l'âge classique* (1961; translated as *Madness and Civilization*, 1973) is a history of the forms of treatment for insanity since the Renaissance. *Surveillir et punir: Naissance de la prison* (1975; translated as *Discipline and Punish*, 1977) deals with the treatment of crime and delinquency over the same period. *The History of Sexuality* (1976), a projected six-volume treatise left unfinished at Foucault's death in 1984, examines moral attitudes toward sexual desire beginning with the ancient Greeks (see the introduction to Gender Studies and Queer Theory, p. 956). Nevertheless, Foucault stood aloof from the social historians of the *Annales* school (including Fernand Braudel, Phillipe Ariès, and Emmanuel Leroi-Ladurie) who were working on the sort of "local knowledge" prized by Clifford Geertz, and Foucault was pilloried by social historians both in France and abroad for his cavalier use of facts and documents, and for his tendency to create universal generalizations based on slim and sometimes unrepresentative bits of evidence.

It was as a philosopher of history that Foucault was most influential, both on the New Historicists and on the larger and more diverse group of cultural studies scholars. But he was a philosopher of history who preached the obsolescence of history as it had been practiced. For Foucault, history was certainly not the working out of a single plotted idea, as it was for Hegel or Marx. Foucault believed that not only are there no ideas governing reality but that we cannot even know the reality of the past, as we have access only to representations purporting to map the real. Nor is there a unitary self doing this mapping, only a subject constituted by society as an effect of its repressive social and economic structures.

Furthermore, in addition to viewing history as a mode of knowledge that is obsolescent, tied to the modern *epistemé* that he felt was on its way out, Foucault believed history constitutes a method of repression. For Foucault, history embodies

> the various . . . aspects of the will to knowledge [*vouloir-savoir*]: instinct, passion, the inquisitor's devotion, cruel subtlety, and malice. It discovers the violence of a position that sides with those who are happy in their ignorance, against the effective illusions by which humanity protects itself, a position that encourages the dangers of research and delights in disturbing discoveries. The historical analysis of the rancorous will to knowledge reveals that all knowledge rests upon injustice (that there is no right, not even in

the act of knowing, to truth or a foundation for truth) and that the instinct for knowledge is malicious.[10]

For obsolescent history, Foucault wishes to substitute "genealogy" in Nietzsche's sense of a study of "emergences" that "rejects the metahistorical deployment of ideal significations and indefinite teleologies," that "opposes itself to the search for 'origins.'" (140).

The key text for Foucault's vision of history is *Les mots et les choses* (1966; translated as *The Order of Things: An Archaeology of the Human Sciences*, 1970). Though Foucault is a philosophical nominalist, no Platonist could be more rigidly totalizing in his periodization. The four epochs into which Foucault divides Western history — conventionally called the Renaissance, the Enlightenment, the modern age, and the postmodern future — are each separated by what he refers to as a *cou-pure*, or rupture, that forces a complete break with the mode of thought of the past. For Foucault, these epochs are entirely discontinuous, like an archeological dig in which the culture of one era is separated by fault lines from what precedes and fol-lows it. Each band of culture is integrated by what Foucault calls an *episteme* a mode of power/knowledge with its own discursive practices: methods of expression that are also methods of oppression.

In the Renaissance, the connections between facts, their ordering and hierar-chies, were expressed in terms of similitudes and sympathies, natural metaphors and metonymies that anyone could read in God's creation. In the Enlightenment, such connections were based on classifications, types and their tokens, ordered like grammars or taxonomies. In the modern age, history itself, with its emphasis on the narrative, has become the master mode of organization. For example, Marx presents his ideas about economics and the social and political relations that emerge from economics not in the form of charts and tables but as a master narrative of human-ity's history from the Bronze Age through the Industrial Revolution that culminates in his prophecy of the decline and violent overthrow of capitalism and the creation of a worker's state. Similarly, Freud presents his idea of the drives and defenses that make people so complex in terms of a developmental narrative in which the individ-ual passes through oral, anal, and phallic phases of pregenital sexuality and emerges from the Oedipal crisis of adolescence before attaining adulthood. To argue against Marx and Freud, one has to attack not just their principles but their narratives — as their revisers have in fact done. This mode of argumentation belongs to the modern age, which in Foucault's view is passing with the coming of postmodernism, which will engender some new *episteme* or way of organizing knowledge, that will make the historical, or narrative mode obsolete.

Foucault's "archaeological" method, as presented in *The Order of Things*, is essentially synchronic, presenting history as a series of sedimentary layers separated by fault lines. In contrast, his separate studies of madness, illness, crime, and sex are "genealogical," diachronic studies that link various discursive practices with one another — often through similitudes and catachreses — "in order to establish those

[10]Michel Foucault, "Nietzsche, Genealogy, History," in *Language, Counter-memory, Practice* (Oxford: Basil Blackwell, 1977), pp. 162–63.

diverse converging, and sometimes divergent, but never autonomous series that enable us to circumscribe the 'locus' of an event, the limits to its fluidity and the conditions of its emergence."[11] Within each of Foucault's genealogies — his stories of the emergence of new methods of punishment, new modes of treatment for mental illness, or new attitudes toward the body and sexuality — his treatment of historical change is more or less coherent.

A self-contradiction appears, however, when one places the various genealogies against one another. Then it becomes evident that although changes in each of the discursive formations are supposed to occur within a *coupure*, a fissure between *epistemés* the changes in one area of social regulation do not occur simultaneously with changes in other areas, as one would think they should. The beginning of the regulation of the lives of imprisoned criminals by timetables and rules, for example, starts about a century after one might expect, given Foucault's general vision of the Enlightenment with its fascination with types and taxonomies. Foucault does not attempt to disguise this fact. As he says in *The Archaeology of Knowledge,* "We must not imagine that rupture is a sort of great drift that carries with it all discursive formations at once. . . . The idea of a single break suddenly, at a given moment, dividing all discursive formations, interrupting them in a single moment and reconstituting them in accordance with the same rules — such an idea cannot be sustained. The contemporaneity of several transformations does not mean their exact chronological coincidence: each transformation may have its own particular index of temporal 'viscosity'" (175). But if discursive formations may linger for more than a century because of their "temporal viscosity," the notion of an *epistemé* as a coherent historical formation begins to seem empty.

Another hollowness is Foucault's notion of causality. Unlike most social historians, Foucault has no interest in what made things happen, in baring the nexus of conditionality and contingency, of what is necessary and what sufficient for one state of affairs to transmute itself into another. As he says,

> The old questions of the traditional analysis (What link should be made between disparate events? How can a causal succession be established between them? What continuity or overall significance do they possess? Is it possible to define a totality, or must one be content with reconstitution of connexions?) are now being replaced by questions of another type: which strata should be isolated from others? What types of series should be established? What system of relations . . . may be established between them? What series of series may be established? And in what large-scale chronological table may distinct series of events be determined?[12]

For many a historian, such questions represent an evasion of history rather than its fulfillment. Nevertheless, Foucault's notions of historical periodization and of discursive practices of power/knowledge have been highly influential both on New Historicists and practitioners of cultural studies.

[11]Michel Foucault, "The Discourse on Language," in *The Archaeology of Knowledge and the Discourse on Language* (New York: Pantheon, 1971), p. 230.
[12]Ibid., pp. 3–4.

For example, Stephen Greenblatt's discussion of the relationship between the bounded (and thereby licensed) representation of transgression within the theater of the English Renaissance and the remorseless persecution of similar transgressors (Catholics, witches, transvestites) in the society at large derives straight from Foucault, who uses it, among other places, in his *History of Sexuality.* Greenblatt also explicitly rejects the notion of causality as a principal focus of genealogical investigation. In the course of relating Shakespeare's theatrical representations of women who dress up as boys (like Viola in *Twelfth Night*) to a story of cross-dressing by Martin le Marcis in Montaigne's *Travel Journal,* to Jacques Duval's story of a woman married to a hermaphrodite (*De Hermaphroditis,* 1603), and to Galen's and Paré's various misconceptions about the male and female sexual organs (ca. 130 and ca. 1575, respectively), Greenblatt hastens to assure us that he realizes that it is unlikely that Shakespeare had studied Galen and Paré, and almost inconceivable that he had heard about the cases of cross-dressing and hermaphroditism mentioned by Montaigne and Duval. These are not sources but intertexts. "The relation I wish to establish between medical and theatrical practice is not one of cause and effect or source and literary realization. We are dealing rather with a shared code, a set of interlocking tropes and similitudes that function not only as the objects but as the conditions of the representation."[13] There is nothing dishonest at all going on here, but Greenblatt appears less defensive when the cultural text against which he reads Shakespeare is, like Samuel Harsnett's *Declaration of Egregious Popish Impostures,* a book Shakespeare is likely to have read while writing *King Lear,* or like William Strachey's account of storm and shipwreck near Bermuda, a text Shakespeare probably saw in manuscript while working on *The Tempest.*

GENDER AND THEORY

What Foucault shares with the practitioners of the *Annales* school in France and the various "history from the bottom up" movements in English-speaking countries is a central focus on social history rather than political history: history "without the king," centering on institutions like the family, the trades, and professions, as well as the ways in which societies deal with individuals and groups that are transgressive (heretics, criminals, sexual deviates) or "other" in less obvious ways, such as infants and the aged. Ironically, one charge leveled against the New Historicism in the late 1980s was that it had ignored issues of sex and gender. Judith Lowder Newton complained in "History as Usual? Feminism and the 'New Historicism'" (1988) that while the king had been gotten rid of, the patriarch seemed to hold full sway. Newton argued that while many of her female colleagues were engaged with the New Historicism, historians of the critical practice tended to ignore their work on changing gender roles. In particular, she wanted these histories to take account of such feminist scholarship as Catherine Gallagher's *The Industrial Reformation of English Fiction: Social Discourse and Narrative Form, 1832–1867* (1985),

[13]Stephen Greenblatt, *Shakespearean Negotiations: The Circulation of Social Energy in Renaissance England* (Oxford: Clarendon Press, 1988), p. 86.

Mary Poovey's *Uneven Developments: The Ideological Work of Gender in Mid-Victorian England* (1988), and Nancy Armstrong's *Desire and Domestic Fiction: A Political History of the Novel* (1987).

Armstrong, influenced by the cultural materialism of Raymond Williams as well as by Foucault, has researched the ways in which institutions like the domestic household were created and reshaped by texts of domesticity — courtesy manuals, cookery books, and the domestic novel — written about and often by women with a conscious eye toward the changing structure of the family. Armstrong's notions that changes in society and the role of women are not on the fringes of politics but at its center, expressed in "Some Call It Fiction: On the Politics of Domesticity" (reprinted here), would find an echo in other feminist thinkers and gender theorists. Her placement in this chapter reminds us that both the New Historicism and cultural studies have begun to move gender roles and the changes they have undergone to the center of the agenda.

WHITE: HISTORY AS DISCOURSE

Greenblatt's sense that common "tropes and similitudes" of representation are key indications of historical linkage is indebted to Foucault but also to Hayden White's study of historiography. White's first book, *Metahistory* (1974), was in effect an inside-out version of New Historicism, a demonstration of the textuality of history centering on the ways in which various Enlightenment and post-Romantic historians (including Gibbon, Macaulay, and Burckhardt) were "literary" in the strongest sense of the word. White argued that these historians' imaginative conceptions of the Roman Empire, or the Glorious Revolution, or the Civilization of the Renaissance in Italy were shaped in accordance with the four primary literary genres (tragedy, comedy, romance, and satire) and conveyed their visions of truth through language mediated by the four "master tropes" of metaphor (analogy), metonymy (association), synecdoche (the part for the whole), and irony (reversal).

In analyzing the rhetoric of a particular historian, White sometimes finds that a sequence of tropes works to signify the development of consciousness. In his analysis of E. P. Thompson's classic history, *The Making of the English Working Class* (1963), White argues that Thompson's rhetoric presents the "awakening" of working-class consciousness in the eighteenth century in an analogical, or "metaphorical" mode of thought. White categorizes Thompson's later account of labor in the early nineteenth century as "metonymic," because Thompson emphasizes the ways in which working-class consciousness became defined in terms of the "distinctive kinds" of work into which labor was transformed. White views Thompson's description of laborers after the Peterloo Massacre of 1819 as"synecdochic," since Thompson presents the workers as viewing themselves as parts of one whole. Finally, White argues that Thompson's presentation of the class-consciousness of the workers as developing, around 1835, into a form of *self*-consciousness falls into the mode of irony, from which we would correctly predict "the fatal fracturing of the working-class movement itself."[14]

---

[14]Hayden White, *Tropics of Discourse: Essays in Cultural Criticism* (Baltimore: Johns Hopkins University Press, 1978), pp. 16–20.

In "The Historical Text as Literary Artifact" (1974), reprinted here, White theorizes the basis of his project for making history textual, locating his vision of history in relation to predecessors like Robin Collingwood, Northrop Frye, and, on the distant horizon, Aristotle. In each case, White performs an act of misprision, misreading his predecessors in order to create space for his sense of historical writing. Collingwood, an idealist philosopher in the tradition of Croce, had seen the historian's task as forming a constructive intuition, a sense of the shaping form of the human events of his chronicle. White takes this conception of the historian's task, but redefines it in terms of his requirement that the intuition take shape in terms of the tropes of literary language and in the form of a literary genre. The genres themselves are wrested from Northrop Frye's myths of spring, summer, autumn, and winter, although Frye himself did not view historical writing as a form of literature. And finally White defines his poetics of historiography in contrast with Aristotle's poetics, although any historical text written in accord with White's literary vision would have easily qualified for Aristotle as a form of poetry. Within this fascinat-ing essay White makes what may at the time have seemed a strange detour, a long paragraph relating the historian's task of decoding and recoding the past to what happens in psychoanalysis, as a process in which the patient discards the old story about himself he has internalized and re-assembles the fragments of his past into a new and different narrative. It seems no coincidence that in the last four decades an entirely new field of psychoanalysis has sprung up, narrative psychotherapy, based on ideas strikingly similar to White's.

GEERTZ: LOCAL KNOWLEDGE AND THICK DESCRIPTION

Clifford Geertz is no more a literary critic than Foucault or White; he is a cultural anthropologist, and his immense influence on both the New Historicism and cultural studies stems from his "semiotic" view of culture. Like Claude Lévi-Strauss, Geertz reads cultures as systems of signs in which relationships in one social arena stand in for others, but unlike Lévi-Strauss, who argues that kinship patterns within a culture can always be extracted from the interrelationships of myth, Geertz carries no meta-physical baggage and has no preconceived sense of the way in which cultures are constructed. He stands in the central tradition of the field anthropologists who, from the time of Bronislaw Malinowski (1884–1942), went out to see exotic peoples for themselves. However, in contrast to the positivistic ethos of classical anthropology, Geertz displays the postmodern sense that the observer cannot be detached from what is observed.

In the opening chapter of The Interpretation of Cultures, Geertz insists that, to understand a society, one cannot stand aloof from it, observing behaviors and glean-ing information from informants; instead, one needs to be immersed in a culture's relationships to bring out a credible report of what events mean to their participants. Such a credible report Geertz calls a "thick description," borrowing a term from the English philosopher Gilbert Ryle, who contrasted "thin" descriptions of exter-nal behavior (which are unable to distinguish a wink from a facial tic) with the "thick" descriptions that include the significance of events. A tic is an involuntary behavior, whereas a wink is a message, one that, as Geertz puts it, communicates "(1) deliberately, (2) to someone in particular, (3) to impart a particular message, (4) according to a socially established code, (5) without the cognizance of the rest of the company."[15] And of course things can get even more complicated: Winks can be feigned, or parodied, or performed to show how one winks.

Different observers of a culture will bring back different reports, of course, particularly because of their individual preconceptions and partly because of the different ways in which each individual will relate to an exotic culture (and will be related to the culture's members). This means that anthropology cannot be a precise science, any more than history can, because the meaning found in cultural activities is ultimately constructed by the anthropologist. The inevitable contradictions between anthropologists' reports cannot be mediated by any "objective" observer (since no observer can be objective), and in the last analysis the proof of an anthropologist's account rests on the conviction that the rhetoric of "thick description" can convey.

Geertz's influential article "Deep Play: Notes on the Balinese Cockfight" (1992) presents a concrete example of "thick description" focused on an aspect of Balinese society that other observers had ignored as trivial. Geertz's theoretical coda modestly insists that no "close reading" of the sort he has performed can reveal more than a single facet of a complete culture. But if "the culture of a people is an ensemble of texts," then each "reading" of social semiotics brings us closer to an understanding of a society. Cultural theorists have read our own contemporary society through the semiotics of the texts of television series and the layout of shopping centers, just as New Historicists have produced "readings" of Henrician and Elizabethan jousting scorecards, and enriched our sense of the literature as well as the life of the times.

CERTEAU AND BOURDIEU: CULTURAL FREEDOM, CULTURAL POWER

A fourth major influence on both New Historicism and cultural studies has been French sociology, the Lacan-inflected sociology of Michel de Certeau and the Marxian sociology of Pierre Bourdieu.

Certeau turned the lens of linguistic analysis on to ordinary human behavior, looking for the underlying rules by which ordinary people go about their everyday rituals of shopping, cooking, going to work, negotiating the spaces of the city and the transportation networks. By looking at practices, he hoped to discover the laws by which we live. As Certeau put it in his introduction to *The Practice of Everyday Life* (1974), which was translated into English in 1984, just two years before his death, "An investigation analogous to Chomsky's study of the oral uses of language must seek to restore to everyday practices their logical and cultural legitimacy, at least in the sectors — still very limited — in which we have at our disposal the instruments necessary to account for them. This kind of research is complicated by the fact that these practices themselves alternately exacerbate and disrupt our logics. Its regrets

---

[15]Clifford Geertz, "Local Knowledge," in *The Interpretation of Cultures* (New York: Basic Books, 1973), p. 6.

are like those of the poet, and like him, it struggles against oblivion." The dark specter lurking behind the thought of Certeau is the Foucault of *Discipline and Punish,* ever seeking in the grid of the city a way for the eye of power to see and exert control over everyone. Certeau is moved by this vision to oppose it; he does not deny the possibility of totalitarian control but seeks to elude it by an inquiry "analogous and contrary" to Foucault's: "If it is true that the grid of 'discipline' is everywhere becoming clearer and more extensive, it is all the more urgent to discover how an entire society resists being reduced to it, what popular procedures (also 'minuscule' and quotidian) manipulate the mechanisms of discipline and conform to them only in order to evade them, and finally, what 'ways of operating' form the counterpart, on the consumer's . . . side, of the mute processes that organize the establishment of socioeconomic order." Again and again Certeau relies on the concept of *bricolage* (improvisational engineering, patching things together with whatever materials are at hand) as a metaphor for the unpredictable ways people operate in asserting their freedom.

Pierre Bourdieu, beginning in the early 1970s, had his own original way of looking at practices and power relationships. First of all, he divided society into a series of fields (such as the economic, the political, the cultural, and the educational) within which relationships occur. Although he did not want to reinstate the romantic notion of the "self," Bourdieu also rejected the poststructuralist "subject position," with its vision of actions without agents. Instead, he put forward the notion of a "habitus," which he defined as a "system of dispositions," the social equivalent of "linguistic competence" (Noam Chomsky's term for the sum of all the tacit knowledge one has to possess to speak a language with native fluency; see p. 557). Randal Johnson defines "habitus" not as a set of rules but rather as "the feel for the game" that one possesses for life, that one passes on to other players in the course of playing.[16] Bourdieu viewed "habitus" as class related: Persons of the same class were likely, he found, to adopt a similar habitus across different social fields.

For the New Historicism and cultural studies, the main contribution of Bourdieu has been his provision of a way of thinking about culture that complicates the Marxist notion of superstructure (see the introduction to Marx, p. 247). For Bourdieu the field of cultural production depends in part on the fields of political power and large-scale economic production, but it also obeys rules of its own that are dictated by its relation to other fields such as education. "The Market in Symbolic Goods" (1971) starts out with the notion that what Bourdieu calls "goods of restricted production" (objects of art and highly skilled craft) were for much of human history financed by the patronage of the aristocracy and the church. A shift toward relative autonomy occurred with the development of mercantile capitalism during the Renaissance, as cultural production came to be regulated primarily by the market, as opposed to the patronage system. The cultural market operates not only on goods being produced at any given moment (contemporary paintings, music, literature, fine porcelains, and such) but on the goods of the past which are simultaneously in circulation. Bourdieu

[16]Randal Johnson, "Introduction" to Pierre Bourdieu, *The Field of Cultural Production* (New York: Columbia University Press, 1993), p. 6.

points out that the social value of such symbolic goods, their worth in the cultural field, rests not merely in their rarity (as with gold and gemstones), but in the cultural "capital" derived from the education that needs to be invested to appreciate them. What this means is that the popular art of one era (Elizabethan drama, for example) may subsequently become the highly valued masterpiece of another.

In *Distinction* (1979), Bourdieu applied his theory of habitus and cultural capital to aesthetic taste, arguing — against the aesthetic theory of Kant — that tastes and predispositions, both in matters of bodily taste and art of various kinds, not only are far from universal, but are one of the chief means whereby social distinctions are enforced in a capitalist economy that makes money easier to come by than class. Bourdieu did not merely theorize about taste; he took elaborate surveys of preferences, both in provincial Lille and in Paris, using subjects from different social backgrounds, economic ranges, and educational achievements. He discovered that education and income goes some distance to overcome the disadvantages of working-class origins, particularly in areas covered in the educational curriculum. One might learn that way to prefer a fugue from Bach's "Well-Tempered Clavier" to Strauss's "Blue Danube Waltz." But educational background would be less likely to help one to make the approved aristocratic choice in extracurricular matters like popular music or cinema, where those of good family would be likely to choose a song by Leo Ferré[17] over a ballad by Petula Clark, or a genre film like The *Big Sleep* by Howard Hawks over a middlebrow drama like *Mrs. Miniver*. Bourdieu's argument is that two centuries after the Revolution, the court of Versailles still holds sway, insubstantially, in the way those who truly belong show that they do by subtle choices in the art on their walls, the music coming out of their speakers, what they read, eat, and drink.

GUILLORY AND CULTURAL CAPITAL

One application of Pierre Bourdieu's post-Marxist analysis of culture and class is John Guillory's *Cultural Capital: The Problem of Literary Canon Formation* (1993), reprinted in part below. Guillory insists, in the first place, that the function of the school as institution is not peripheral but central to the class structure of capitalist society. Schools not only train the young in the specific information and skills they need to operate in a utilitarian society under capitalism, they also reproduce the structure of that society by creating young heirs to take their places within the social hierarchy. The class basis of culture requires the reproduction of cultural capital: From one generation to the next, in a society based on inequalities, the distribution of such capital must be unequal. Some people must get more than others. The acquisition of a certain quantity of cultural capital is needed to produce the vision and discourse of a member of the ruling class and to distinguish him or her from social inferiors. There is no rule that allows one to predict precisely which forms of cultural capital will be valued in a particular time and place: The mandarins of the Ming Dynasty were required to know literary classics from the previous millennium; the aristocrats

---

[17]Anarchist poet/singer (1911–1993) revered in France but relatively unknown in the English-speaking world — one needs to imagine a Bob Dylan who was fifty-two rather than twenty-seven in 1968.

of the Enlightenment were required to be able to compose Latin and Greek verses; and the upper bourgeoisie of the nineteenth century were required to know and revere the classics of Western literature from Homer and Virgil through the early modern period. Needless to say, things are different now. Guillory writes that

> At the present moment, the nation-state still requires a relatively homogeneous language to administer its citizenry, but it no longer requires that a distinctive practice of that language identify a culturally homogeneous bourgeoisie. That class has long since been replaced by a culturally heterogeneous New Class, which has in turn been fully integrated into mass culture, a media culture mediating the desires of every class and group. In this new phase of civilization, the historical function of the literary curriculum — to produce at the lower levels of the educational system a practice of Standard English and at the higher levels a more refined bourgeois language, a *literary English* — is no longer important to the social order. (263)

The "crisis of the humanities," which is the name journalism has given to the flight of young men and women in the universities away from specializing in literature, history, and other traditional liberal arts subjects, is thus a purely utilitarian reaction. Students' future employers will want them to calculate market shares and perform multiple regressions, so the less time they spend developing an expertise in the liberal arts, the better. Professors of literature experience themselves as power-less, Guillory argues, precisely because they have become functionless. The allusive literary language that was once the possession of every successful businessman and bureaucrat is no longer a prerequisite for success. The one thing English departments do that still has genuine value for contemporary capitalism is training the university's students in composition and rhetoric. The art of incisive expository writing with "proper" diction and syntax, almost universally neglected at the primary and secondary levels of schooling, is still a necessary component of the education of the professional-managerial elite, one that in fact differentiates those who will rise to executive management positions from those who will stay at the lower sales and technical levels of the corporate structure. One irony is that, in the last three decades, composition training has itself become a specialization within the English faculty, rather than a natural and unspoken part of the expertise of any teacher of literature. Another is that most of the composition training at universities since the 1990s is done by underpaid graduate assistants serving apprenticeships to become professors of literature, who hope, if they are successful in their pursuit, to do less and less of what their society actually values.

The warfare over the canon represents, for Guillory, the thrashing about of a profession whose central preoccupation, literature, no longer has the significance for society it once did. The humanities faculty imagines that it could reclaim its useful-ness within the educational system if it could only redefine the canon, or replace it with other objects of study. But the problem, Guillory argues, is that the noncanoni-cal texts that multiculturalists want to substitute for the Western canon do not in fact constitute a different form of cultural capital.

Meanwhile the revolution in the social order has made theory itself, rather than the canon, the center of the study of the humanities. Literary study, in order to be viewed as equivalent in value to the scientific and economic studies that are actually useful within the technical and bureaucratic culture of the current ruling class, had to be made more difficult and technical than heretofore, more rigorous, less a matter of genteel improvisation than the close readings that characterized the New Criticism. Just as the discipline of economics has become ever more pervasively mathematical, providing a factitious precision to its descriptions of the workings of society, literary studies has become wed to the technical rigor of rhetoric and philosophy. At the same time, theory itself has been routinized. As Guillory notes in *Cultural Capital*,

> Those authors or texts designated as theoretical are now increasingly capable of being introduced to students in traditional routinized forms, even by anthologies. It is difficult to imagine how graduate education could proceed at the present moment without recourse to a relatively standardized set of theoretical texts, which are employed not only in the context of application to works of literature but also in the seminar on theory. (260)

The logic of the structural shift of the ruling class in capitalism has driven the task of the humanities from the comprehension and reproduction of the canon of Western literature to the understanding and reproduction of the canon of literary theory, of what one might call the critical tradition. The book you hold in your hands is evidence of this sea change in the structure of the class system, the school, and the humanities, and we are all, I am afraid — students and teachers alike — in on this together.

CULTURE MEETS NATURE: ECOCRITICISM

The skein of influences on New Historicism and cultural studies extends, by no means strangely, to one of the newer movements within theory, ecocriticism, which we could call "nature studies" by way of distinction, except that it is culture that determines our view of nature.

Cheryll Glotfelty and Harold Fromm, editors of *The Ecocriticism Reader,* argue that the "world" posited by theorists is generally confined to the social world, and needs to be opened out to ask questions about the earth and the rest of the physical universe — but naturally the primary issues they raise are about how nature is represented within cultural frameworks, including traditional literary texts. The questions Glotfelty and Fromm present include:

> How is nature represented in this sonnet? . . . Are the values expressed in this play consistent with ecological wisdom? How do our metaphors of the land influence the way we treat it? How can we characterize nature writing as a genre? In addition to race, class, and gender, should *place* become a new critical category? Do men write about nature differently than women do? In what ways has literacy itself affected humankind's relationship to the natural world? How has the concept of wilderness changed over time? In what ways and to what effect is the environmental crisis seeping into contemporary literature and popular culture? What view of nature informs U.S. Government reports, corporate advertising, and televised nature documentaries, and to what rhetorical effect? What bearing might the science of ecology have on literary studies? . . . What cross-fertilization is possible between literary studies and environmental discourse in related disciplines such as history, philosophy, psychology, art history, and ethics? (xviii –xix.)

These questions are not open-ended; they are, as Lawrence Buell puts it in *Writing for an Endangered World* (2001), "issue-driven," framed by a sense of "environmental crisis,' created by a conspiracy between American government, industry, and a public that refuses to be fully aware of the price that will ultimately be exacted for its selfish wastefulness. The conspiracy to despoil nature has been going on for a long time: the protest against it in literature goes back to Fenimore Cooper, back to Goldsmith certainly, perhaps back to Chaucer. And Buell's "insurgency" is united only in opposition to its enemy: Their multifarious critical methods and ideological allegiances, other than to the environment, defy easy identification.

THE INEVITABILITY OF CULTURAL STUDIES

Cultural studies is the "hegemonic" critical discourse at the moment, one that contains the humanities and social sciences' collective response to what we might call the Era of Grand Theory, the two decades beginning with the structuralist revolution in the 1960s. The Era of Grand Theory produced a vital set of competing ideas about literature, society, and the mind but failed to coalesce in any single new rationale for textual and literary study. The New Criticism had been displaced and decentered, but nothing had taken its place. In its enormous variety and eclecticism, cultural studies is not a new paradigm of knowledge so much as a way of making do temporarily without a paradigm. Or as Vincent Leitch puts it, cultural studies "aspired to be a new discipline but served as an unstable meeting point for various interdisciplinary feminists, Marxists, literary and media critics, postmodern theorists, social semioticians, rhetoricians, fine arts specialists, and sociologists and historians of culture."[18]

The eclecticism of Leitch's list is not an anomaly. As of this writing, the "Cultural Studies" webpage of the internet "Voice of the Shuttle" resource file describes itself as "the intersection between cultural criticism/theory and selective resources in sociology, media studies, postcolonial studies, economics, literature, and other fields." The "special topics" elaborately listed and linked include Body/Corporeality Theory, Cybercensorship, Generation Wars, Globalism, Millennial Studies, Postcolonial Studies, and Post-Industrial Business Theory.

Besides its eclecticism, what is most obvious about this list of topics is its topicality: Cultural studies is about whatever is happening at the moment rather than about a body of texts created in the past. "Happening" topics, generally speaking, are the mass media themselves, which, in a postmodern culture, dominate the cultural lives of its inhabitants, or topics that have been valorized by the mass media. One of the great virtues of cultural studies is in fact its relentlessly critical attitude toward journalism, publishing, cinema, television, and other forms of mass media, whose seemingly transparent windows through which we view "reality" probably constitute the most blatant and pervasive mode of false consciousness of our era. But though some cultural critics would deny it, their bias toward what is "happening" tends to valorize mass culture at the expense of the more local, private, and reclusive formations whose study would require the rigorous methods of field anthropology. In a

[18]See Vincent Leitch, "Cultural Studies," in *The Johns Hopkins Guide to Literary Criticism and Theory*, ed. Michael Groden and Michael Kreiswirth (Baltimore: Johns Hopkins University Press, 1994), p. 188.

sense this is as much a bias toward an easier object of study as was the restriction of literary "history," in the era before the New Historicism, to the relations among a small body of canonical texts.

Cultural studies is willing to question the cultural significance of the canon wars in the sense of analyzing what might be at stake for partisans on both sides. However, rather than entering the fray, it has questioned all attempts at canon formation, particularly attempts to valorize the classic Western canon. This negative bias of cultural studies toward canonical literature can be seen as an inevitable result of what Pierre Bourdieu calls the devaluation of canonical literature as part of the cultural capital needed for membership in the ruling class of late capitalist society. Investment bankers were once expected to read Jane Austen and be able to quote Shakespeare; today's managers of mutual funds need only know whether revenues from Kenneth Branagh's *Hamlet* surpassed Mel Gibson's at the box office. Writing still holds a key to power, but not critically acclaimed writing. Even those who still aspire to write canonical literature, to become the next Faulkner, are aware that writing the Great American Novel can guarantee one a living only if the novel gets optioned as the basis for a movie or turned into a successful television series.[19] Young theorists are trained in the doctrine that everything is some sort of text, analyzable through the structuralist principles that underlie most contemporary theory. It isn't strange that they should find it hard to resist the urge to study the objects and practices contemporary culture actually values rather than those it merely enshrines. The oppositional stance of cultural studies toward the methods and products of contemporary corporate America thus veils what might otherwise be taken as worship of its success. Beyoncé Studies, anyone?

Selected Bibliography

Ang, Ien. *Watching Television.* New York: Routledge, 1991.

Armstrong, Nancy. *Desire and Domestic Fiction.* New York: Oxford University Press, 1987.

Ashcroft, Bill, Gareth Griffiths, and Helen Tiffin, eds. *The Post-Colonial Studies Reader.* New York: Routledge, 1995.

Barthes, Roland. *Mythologies.* 1957; New York: Farrar, Straus and Giroux, 1972.

Belsey, Catherine. *Critical Practice.* New York: Methuen, 1980.

Berubé, Michael, ed. *Aesthetics and Cultural Studies.* Malden: Blackwell, 2004.

Bourdieu, Pierre. *Outline of a Theory of Practice.* Cambridge: Cambridge University Press, 1977.

———. *Distinction: A Social Critique of the Judgment of Taste.* Cambridge: Harvard University Press, 1984.

———. *Homo Academicus.* 1984; Stanford: Stanford University Press, 1988.

———. *The Field of Cultural Production.* New York: Columbia University Press, 1993.

———. *Practical Reason: On the Theory of Action.* Stanford: Stanford University Press, 1998.

———. *Masculine Domination.* Stanford: Stanford University Press, 2001.

[19]Even half a century ago, Faulkner wrote screenplays in Hollywood for projects like *Land of the Pharaohs* to finance the whiskey he needed to write *Absalom, Absalom!*

Branch, Michael P., ed. *The ISLE Reader: Ecocriticism 1993–2003.* Athens: University of Georgia Press, 2003.

Brannigan, John. *New Historicism and Cultural Materialism.* New York: St. Martin's Press, 1998.

Brantlinger, Patrick. *Crusoe's Footprints: Cultural Studies in Britain and America.* New York: Routledge, 1990.

Buell, Lawrence. *Writing for an Endangered World.* Cambridge: Harvard University Press, 2001.

Certeau, Michel de. *The Practice of Everyday Life.* Berkeley: University of California Press, 1984.

Clifford, James. *The Predicament of Culture.* Cambridge: Harvard University Press, 1988.

———. *Culture in the Plural.* Minneapolis: University of Minnesota Press, 1997.

———. *The Writing of History.* New York: Columbia University Press, 1988.

Dollimore, Jonathan. *Radical Tragedy: Religion, Ideology and Power in the Drama of Shakespeare and His Contemporaries.* Brighton, Eng.: Harvester, 1984.

During, Simon, ed. *The Cultural Studies Reader.* New York: Routledge, 1993.

———. *The Cultural Studies Reader.* 2nd edition. New York: Routledge, 1999.

Foucault, Michel. *Madness and Civilization: A History of Insanity in the Age of Reason.* 1961; New York: Pantheon, 1973.

———. *The Birth of the Clinic: An Archaeology of Medical Perception.* 1963; New York: Pantheon, 1973.

———. *The Order of Things: An Archaeology of the Human Sciences.* 1966; New York: Vintage, 1973.

———. *The Archaeology of Knowledge and the Discourse on Language.* 1969; New York: Pantheon, 1972.

———. *Discipline and Punish: The Birth of the Prison.* 1975; New York: Pantheon, 1977.

———. *Language, Counter-Memory, Practice.* Ithaca: Cornell University Press, 1977.

———. *The Foucault Reader.* New York: Pantheon, 1984.

Fuery, Patrick, and Nick Mansfield. *Cultural Studies and the New Humanities.* New York: Oxford University Press, 1997.

Gallagher, Catherine. *The Industrial Reformation of English Fiction: Social Discourse and Narrative Form, 1832–1867.* Chicago: University of Chicago Press, 1985.

Gallagher, Catherine, and Stephen Greenblatt. *Practicing New Historicism.* Chicago: University of Chicago Press, 2000.

Garrard, Greg. *Ecocriticism.* New York: Routledge, 2004.

Geertz, Clifford. *The Interpretation of Cultures: Selected Essays.* New York: Basic Books, 1973.

———. *Local Knowledge.* New York: Basic Books, 1985.

———. *Works and Lives: The Anthropologist as Author.* Stanford: Stanford University Press, 1988.

———. *Available Light.* Princeton: Princeton University Press, 2000.

Goldberg, Jonathan. *James I and the Politics of Literature.* Baltimore: Johns Hopkins University Press, 1983.

Gramsci, Antonio. *Selections from Cultural Writings.* London: Lawrence and Wishart, 1985.

Greenblatt, Stephen. *Renaissance Self-Fashioning: From More to Shakespeare.* Chicago: University of Chicago Press, 1980.

———. *Shakespearean Negotiations.* Berkeley: University of California Press, 1988.

———. *Will in the World: How Shakespeare Became Shakespeare.* New York: Norton, 2004.

————, ed. *Representing the English Renaissance*. Berkeley: University of California Press, 1988.

Grossberg, Lawrence, Cary Nelson, and Paula Treichler, eds. *Cultural Studies*. New York: Routledge, 1992.

Guillory, John. *Cultural Capital*. Chicago: University of Chicago Press, 1993.

Hall, Stuart, and Paddy Whannel. *The Popular Arts*. London: Hutchinson, 1964.

Hall, Stuart, ed. *Representation: Cultural Representations and Signifying Practices*. London: Sage, 1997.

Hartley, John. *A Short History of Cultural Studies*. London: Sage, 2003.

Hebdige, Dick. *Subculture: The Meaning of Style*. London: Methuen, 1979.

Hoggart, Richard. *The Uses of Literacy: Changing Patterns in English Mass Culture*. Harmondsworth, Eng.: Penguin, 1957.

Howard, Jean E., and Marion F. O'Connor, eds. *Shakespeare Reproduced: The Text in History and Ideology*. New York: Methuen, 1987.

Hutcheon, Linda. *The Politics of Postmodernism*. London: Routledge, 1989.

JanMohammed, Abdul, and David Lloyd. "Introduction: Toward a Theory of Minority Discourse." *Cultural Critique* 6 (1987): 5–12.

Kipnis, Laura. *Bound and Gagged: Pornography and the Politics of Fantasy in America*. New York: Grove, 1996.

LaCapra, Dominick. *History and Criticism*. Ithaca: Cornell University Press, 1985.

Laclau, Ernesto, and Chantal Mouffe. "Postmarxism without Apologies." *New Left Review* 166 (1987): 79–106.

Lentricchia, Frank. *Ariel and the Police*. Madison: University of Wisconsin Press, 1988.

Lindenberger, Herbert. *Historical Drama: The Relation of Literature and Reality*. Chicago: University of Chicago Press, 1975.

————, ed. *History in Literature: On Value, Genre, Institutions*. New York: Columbia University Press, 1990.

Lyotard, Jean-François. *The Post-Modern Condition: A Report on Knowledge*. Minneapolis: University of Minnesota Press, 1984.

McCoy, Richard. *The Rites of Knighthood: The Literature and Politics of Elizabethan Chivalry*. Berkeley: University of California Press, 1989.

McGann, Jerome. *The Beauty of Inflections: Literary Investigations in Historical Method and Theory*. Oxford: Clarendon Press, 1985.

————, ed. *Historical Studies and Literary Criticism*. Madison: University of Wisconsin Press, 1985.

Michaels, Walter Benn. *The Gold Standard and the Logic of Naturalism*. Berkeley: University of California Press, 1987.

Montrose, Louis. "Renaissance Literary Studies and the Subject of History." *English Literary Renaissance* 16 (1986): 3–21.

Morris, Meaghan. "Things to Do with Shopping Centres." In *Grafts: Feminist Cultural Criticism*, ed. Susan Sheridan. London: Verso, 1988.

————. *Too Soon Too Late: History in Popular Culture*. Bloomington: Indiana University Press, 1998.

Newton, Judith. "History as Usual?: Feminism and the 'New Historicism.'" *Cultural Critique* 8 (1988): 87–121.

Poovey, Mary. *Uneven Developments: The Ideological Work of Gender in Mid-Victorian England*. Chicago: University of Chicago Press, 1988.

Richter, David H. *The Progress of Romance: Literary Historiography and the Gothic Novel*. Columbus: Ohio State University Press, 1996.

Ricoeur, Paul. *Time and Narrative*. Chicago: University of Chicago Press, 1984.

Rosendale, Steven. *The Greening of Literary Scholarship*. Iowa City: University of Iowa Press, 2002.

Ryan, Kiernan, ed. *New Historicism and Cultural Materialism: A Reader*. New York: St. Martin's Press, 1996.

Storey, John. *Cultural Studies and the Study of Popular Culture*. Athens: University of Georgia Press, 2003.

———, ed. *What Is Cultural Studies?* New York: St. Martin's Press, 1996.

Tennenhouse, Leonard. *Power on Display: The Politics of Shakespeare's Genres*. New York: Methuen, 1986.

Thomas, Brook. *The New Historicism and Other Old-Fashioned Topics*. Princeton: Princeton University Press, 1991.

Veeser, H. Aram, ed. *The New Historicism*. New York: Routledge, 1989.

———. *The New Historicism Reader*. New York: Routledge, 1994.

White, Hayden. *Metahistory: The Historical Imagination in Nineteenth-Century Europe*. Baltimore: Johns Hopkins University Press, 1974.

———. *Tropics of Discourse: Essays in Cultural Criticism*. Baltimore: Johns Hopkins University Press, 1978.

———. *The Content of the Form*. Baltimore: Johns Hopkins University Press, 1988.

Williams, Raymond. *The Country and the City*. New York: Oxford University Press, 1973.

Hayden White

b. 1928

While many of us had long suspected that our history books were fiction, it took Hayden White to demonstrate that they were actually poetry, imbued with metaphor, metonymy, and irony. White was born in Martin, Tennessee, and attended Wayne State University before taking his masters and doctoral degrees at the University of Michigan. He began teaching at Wayne State but soon moved to the University of Rochester, where he rose to full professor and chair of the department. From 1973 to 1977 he directed the Center for the Humanities at Wesleyan University and from 1976–78 was Kenan Professor of History there. In 1978 he moved to the University of California at Santa Cruz, where he became Professor of the History of Consciousness. He is now Professor Emeritus at the University of California at Santa Cruz (History of Consciousness Program), having retired from his most recent position as Professor of Comparative Literature at Stanford University. White has published almost a dozen books, but it was Metahistory: The Historical Imagination in Nineteenth-Century Europe *(1973) that established his indispensability to the New Historicism, with its readings of history as both rhetoric and poetry. His other major books are* Tropics of Discourse: Essays in Cultural Criticism *(1978),* The Content of the Form: Narrative Discourse and Historical Representation *(1987), and* Figural Realism: Studies in the Mimesis Effect *(1999). His most recent publication is* The Practical Past *(2014). "The Historical Text as Literary Artifact" was originally a lecture given at Yale in 1974; it first appeared in print in* Clio *3, no. 3 (June 1974): 277–303. The present version is taken from* Tropics of Discourse *(1978).*

The Historical Text as Literary Artifact[1]

One of the ways that a scholarly field takes stock of itself is by considering its history. Yet it is difficult to get an objective history of a scholarly discipline, because if the historian is himself a practitioner of it, he is likely to be a devotee of one or another of its sects and hence biased; and if he is not a practitioner, he is unlikely to have the expertise necessary to distinguish between the significant and the insignificant events of the field's development. One might think that these difficulties would not arise in the field of history itself, but they do and not only for the reasons

---

[1]This essay is a revised version of a lecture given before the Comparative Literature Colloquium of Yale University on 24 January, 1974. In it I have tried to elaborate some of the themes that I originally discussed in an article, "The Structure of Historical Narrative," CLIO I (1972): 5–20. I have also drawn upon the materials of my book *Metahistory: The Historical Imagination in Nineteenth-Century Europe* (Baltimore, 1973), especially the introduction, entitled "The Poetics of History." The essay profited from conversations with Michael Holquist and Geoffrey Hartman, both of Yale University and both experts in the theory of narrative. The quotations from Claude Lévi-Strauss are taken from his *Savage Mind* (London, 1966) and "Overture to *Le Cru et le cuit*," in *Structuralism*, ed. Jacques Ehrmann (New York, 1966). The remarks on the iconic nature of metaphor draw upon Paul Henle, *Language, Thought, and Culture* (Ann Arbor, 1966). Jakobson's notions of the tropological nature of style are in "Linguistics and Poetics," in *Style and Language*, ed. Thomas A. Sebeok (New York and London,

mentioned above. In order to write the history of any given scholarly discipline or even of a science, one must be prepared to ask questions *about* it of a sort that do not have to be asked in the practice *of* it. One must try to get behind or beneath the presuppositions which sustain a given type of inquiry and ask the questions that can be begged in its practice in the interest of determining why this type of inquiry has been designed to solve the problems it characteristically tries to solve. This is what metahistory seeks to do. It addresses itself to such questions as, What is the structure of a peculiarly *historical* consciousness? What is the epistemological status of historical *explanations*, as compared with other kinds of explanations that might be offered to account for the materials with which historians ordinarily deal? What are the possible *forms* of historical representation and what are their bases? What authority can historical accounts claim as contributions to a secured knowledge of reality in general and to the human sciences in particular?

Now, many of these questions have been dealt with quite competently over the last quarter-century by philosophers concerned to define history's relationships to other disciplines, especially the physical and social sciences, and by historians interested in assessing the success of their discipline in mapping the past and determining the relationship of that past to the present. But there is one problem that neither philosophers nor historians have looked at very seriously and to which literary theorists have given only passing attention. This question has to do with the status of the historical narrative, considered purely as a verbal artifact purporting to be a model of structures and processes long past and therefore not subject to either experimental or observational controls. This is not to say that historians and philosophers of history have failed to take notice of the essentially provisional and

continent nature of historical representations and of their susceptibility to infinite revision in the light of new evidence or more sophisticated conceptualization of problems. One of the marks of a good professional historian is the consistency with which he reminds his readers of the purely provisional nature of his characterizations of events, agents, and agencies found in the always incomplete historical record. Nor is it to say that literary theorists have *never* studied the structure of historical narratives. But in general there has been a reluctance to consider historical narratives as what they most manifestly are: verbal fictions, the contents of which are as much *invented* as *found* and the forms of which have more in common with their counterparts in literature than they have with those in the sciences.[2]

Now, it is obvious that this conflation of mythic and historical consciousness will offend some historians and disturb those literary theorists whose conception of literature presupposes a radical opposition of history to fiction or of fact to fancy. As Northrop Frye has remarked, "In a sense the historical is the opposite of the mythical, and to tell the historian that what gives shape to his book is a myth would sound to him vaguely insulting."[3] Yet Frye grants that "when a historian's scheme gets to a certain point of comprehensiveness it becomes mythical in shape, and so approaches the poetic in its structure." He even speaks of different kinds of historical myths: Romantic myths "based on a quest or pilgrimage to a City of God or classless society"; Comic "myths of progress through evolution or revolution"; Tragic myths of "decline and fall," like the works of Gibbon and Spengler";[4] and Ironic "myths of recurrence or casual catastrophe."

1960). In addition to Northrop Frye's *Anatomy of Criticism* (Princeton, 1957); see also his essay on philosophy of history, "New Directions from Old," in *Fables of Identity* (New York, 1963). On story and plot in historical narrative in R. G. Collingwood's thought, see, of course, *The Idea of History* (Oxford, 1956). [White]

2White's observation is anticipated by Catherine Morland, the heroine of Austen's *Northanger Abbey* (1817), who thinks it "odd that [history] should be so dull, for a great deal of it must be invention. The speeches that are put into the heroes' mouths, their thoughts and designs — the chief of all this must be invention, and invention is what delights me in other books" (chapter 14).

3From Northrop Frye, *Anatomy of Criticism* (1957).

4*The Decline and Fall of the Roman Empire* by British historian Edward Gibbon (1737–1794) began to appear in 1776; German historian Oswald Spengler (1880–1936) wrote *The Decline of the West* (1918).

But Frye appears to believe that these myths are operative only in such victims of what might be called the "poetic fallacy" as Hegel, Marx, Nietzsche, Spengler, Toynbee, and Sartre — historians whose fascination with the "constructive" capacity of human thought has deadened their responsibility to the "found" data. "The historian works inductively," he says, "collecting his facts and trying to avoid any informing patterns except those he sees, or is honestly convinced he sees, in the facts themselves." He does not work "from" a "unifying form," as the poet does, but "toward" it; and it therefore follows that the historian, like any writer of discursive prose, is to be judged "by the truth of what he says, or by the adequacy of his verbal reproduction of his external model," whether that external model be the actions of past men or the historian's own thought about such actions.

What Frye says is true enough as a statement of the *ideal* that has inspired historical writing since the time of the Greeks, but that ideal presupposes an opposition between myth and history that is as problematical as it is venerable. It serves Frye's purposes very well, since it permits him to locate the specifically "fictive" in the space between the two concepts of the "mythic" and the "historical." As readers of Frye's *Anatomy of Criticism* will remember, Frye conceives fictions to consist in part of sublimates of archetypal myth-structures. These structures have been displaced to the interior of verbal artifacts in such a way as to serve as their latent meanings. The fundamental meanings of all fictions, their thematic content, consist, in Frye's view, of the "pre-generic plot-structures" or *mythoi* derived from the corpora of Classical and Judaeo-Christian religious literature. According to this theory, we understand *why* a particular story has "turned out" as it has when we have identified the archetypal myth, or pregeneric plot structure, of which the story is an exemplification. And we see the "point" of a story when we have identified its theme (Frye's translation of *dianoia*),[5] which makes of it a "parable or illustrative fable." "Every work

of literature," Frye insists, "has both a fictional and a thematic aspect," but as we move from "fictional projection" toward the overt articulation of theme, the writing tends to take on the aspect of "direct address, or straight discursive writing and cease[s] to be literature." And in Frye's view, as we have seen, history (or at least "proper history") belongs to the category of "discursive writing," so that when the fictional element — or mythic plot structure — is *obviously* present in it, it ceases to be history altogether and becomes a bastard genre, product of an unholy, though not unnatural, union between history and poetry.

Yet, I would argue, histories gain part of their explanatory effect by their success in making stories out of *mere* chronicles; and stories in turn are made out of chronicles by an operation which I have elsewhere called "emplotment." And by emplotment I mean simply the encoding of the facts contained in the chronicle as components of specific *kinds* of plot structures, in precisely the way that Frye has suggested is the case with "fictions" in general.

The late R. G. Collingwood[6] insisted that the historian was above all a story teller and suggested that historical sensibility was manifested in the capacity to make a plausible story out of a congeries of "facts" which, in their unprocessed form, made no sense at all. In their efforts to make sense of the historical record, which is fragmentary and always incomplete, historians have to make use of what Collingwood called "the constructive imagination," which told the historian — as it tells the competent detective — what "must have been the case" given the available evidence and the formal properties it displayed to the consciousness capable of putting the right question to it. This constructive imagination functions in much the same way that Kant supposed the *a priori* imagination functions when it tells us that even though we cannot perceive both sides of a tabletop simultaneously, we can be certain it has *two* sides if it has one, because the very concept of *one side* entails at least *one other*. Collingwood suggested that

[5]The usual translation would be "thought."

[6]Robin George Collingwood (1889–1943), British philosopher of history.

historians come to their evidence endowed with a sense of the *possible* forms that different kinds of recognizably human situations *can* take. He called this sense the nose for the "story," contained in the evidence or for the "true" story that was buried in or hidden behind the "apparent" story. And he concluded that historians provide plausible explanations for bodies of historical evidence when they succeed in discovering the story or complex of stories implicitly contained within them.

What Collingwood failed to see was that no given set of casually recorded historical events can in itself constitute a story;[7] the most it might offer to the historian are story *elements*. The events are *made* into a story by the suppression or subordination of certain of them and the highlighting of others, by characterization, motific repetition, variation of tone and point of view, alternative descriptive strategies, and the like — in short, all of the techniques that we would normally expect to find in the emplotment of a novel or a play. For example, no historical event is *intrinsically tragic*; it can only be conceived as such from a particular point of view or from within the context of a structured set of events of which it is an element enjoying a privileged place. For in history what is tragic from one perspective is comic from another, just as in society what appears to be tragic from the standpoint of one class may be, as Marx purported to show of the 18th Brumaire of Louis Bonaparte, only a farce from that of another class.[8] Considered as potential elements of a story, historical events are value-neutral. Whether they find their place finally in a story that is tragic, comic, romantic or ironic—to use Frye's categories—depends upon the historian's decision to *configure* them according to the imperatives of one plot structure or mythos rather than another. The same set of events can serve as components of a story that is tragic *or* comic, as the case may be, depending on the historian's choice of the plot structure that he considers most appropriate for ordering events of that kind so as to make them into a comprehensible story.

This suggests that what the historian brings to his consideration of the historical record is a notion of the *types* of configurations of events that can be recognized as stories by the audience for which he is writing. True, he can misfire. I do not suppose that anyone would accept the emplotment of the life of President Kennedy as comedy, but whether it ought to be emplotted romantically, tragically, or satirically is an open question. The important point is that most historical sequences can be emplotted in a number of different ways, so as to provide different interpretations of those events and to endow them with different meanings. Thus, for example, what Michelet in his great history of the French Revolution construed as a drama of Romantic transcendence, his contemporary Tocqueville emplotted as an ironic Tragedy.[9] Neither can be said to have had more knowledge of the "facts" contained in the record; they simply had different notions of the kind of story that best fitted the facts they knew. Nor should it be thought that they told different stories of the Revolution because they had discovered different *kinds* of facts, political on the one hand, social on the other. They sought out different kinds of facts because they had different kinds of stories to tell. But why did these alternative, not to say mutually exclusive, representations of what was substantially the same set of events appear equally plausible to their respective audiences? Simply because the historians shared with their audiences certain preconceptions about how the Revolution might be emplotted, in response to imperatives that were generally extra historical, ideological, aesthetic, or mythical.

Collingwood once remarked that you could never explicate a tragedy to anyone who was not already acquainted with the kinds of situations that are regarded as "tragic" in our culture.

---

[7]Collingwood was not quite as dim as White suggests. As an idealist philosopher, he saw the constructive act in the historian's intuition of the shape of events, not in the practical act of turning that intuition into a written text.

[8]White alludes to Marx's notorious remark in *The Eighteenth Brumaire of Louis Napoleon* (1852) that history always repeats itself, "the first time as tragedy, the second time as farce."

[9]Jules Michelet's *History of the French Revolution* came out 1847–53; Alexis de Tocqueville's *The Old Regime and the French Revolution* in 1856.

Anyone who has taught or taken one of those omnibus courses usually entitled Western Civilization or Introduction to the Classics of Western Literature will know what Collingwood had in mind. Unless you have some idea of the generic attributes of tragic, comic, romantic, or ironic situations, you will be unable to recognize them as such when you come upon them in a literary text. But historical situations do not have built into them intrinsic meanings in the way that literary texts do. Historical situations are not *inherently* tragic, comic or romantic. They may all be inherently ironic, but they need not be emplotted that way. All the historian needs to do to transform a tragic into a comic situation is to shift his point of view or change the scope of his perceptions. Anyway, we only think of situations as tragic or comic because these concepts are part of our generally cultural and specifically literary heritage. *How* a given historical situation is to be configured depends on the historian's subtlety in matching up a specific plot structure with the set of historical events that he wishes to endow with a meaning of a particular kind. This is essentially a literary, that is to say fiction-making, operation. And to call it that in no way detracts from the status of historical narratives as providing a kind of knowledge. For not only are the pregeneric plot structures by which sets of events can be constituted as stories of a particular kind limited in number, as Frye and other archetypal critics suggest; but the encodation of events in terms of such plot structures is one of the ways that a culture has of making sense of both personal and public pasts.

We can make sense of sets of events in a number of different ways. One of the ways is to subsume the events under the causal laws which may have governed their concatenation in order to produce the particular configuration that the events appear to assume when considered as "effects" of mechanical forces. This is the way of scientific explanation. Another way we make sense of a set of events which appears strange, enigmatic, or mysterious in its immediate manifestations is to encode the set in terms of culturally provided categories, such as metaphysical concepts, religious beliefs, or story forms. The effect of such encodations is to familiarize the

unfamiliar; and in general this is the way of historiography, whose "data" are always immediately strange, not to say exotic, simply by virtue of their distance from us in time and their origin in a way of life different from our own.

The historian shares with his audience *general notions* of the *forms* that significant human situations *must* take by virtue of his participation in the specific processes of sense-making which identify him as a member of one cultural endowment rather than another. In the process of studying a given complex of events, he begins to perceive the *possible* story form that such events *may* figure. In his narrative account of how this set of events took on the shape which he perceives to inhere within it, he emplots his account as a story of a particular kind. The reader, in the process of following the historian's account of those events, gradually comes to realize that the story he is reading is of one kind rather than another: romance, tragedy, comedy, satire, epic, or what have you. And when he has perceived the class or type to which the story that he is reading belongs, he experiences the effect of having the events in the story explained to him. He has at this point not only successfully *followed* the story; he has grasped the point of it, *understood* it as well. The original strangeness, mystery, or exoticism of the events is dispelled, and they take on a familiar aspect, not in their details, but in their functions as elements of a familiar kind of configuration. They are rendered comprehensible by being subsumed under the categories of the plot structure in which they are encoded as a story of a particular kind. They are familiarized, not only because the reader now has more *information* about the events, but also because he has been shown how the data conform to an *icon* of a comprehensible finished process, a plot structure with which he is familiar as a part of his cultural endowment.

This is not unlike what happens, or is supposed to happen, in psychotherapy. The sets of events in the patient's past which are the presumed cause of his distress, manifested in the neurotic syndrome, have been defamiliarized, rendered strange, mysterious, and threatening and have assumed a meaning that he can neither accept nor effectively reject. It is not that the patient does not *know* what those events were, does not know the facts; for if he did not in some sense know the facts, he would be unable to recognize them and repress them whenever they arise in his consciousness. On the contrary, he knows them all too well. He knows them so well, in fact, that he lives with them constantly and in such a way as to make it impossible for him to see any other facts except through the coloration that the set of events in question gives to his perception of the world. We might say that, according to the theory of psychoanalysis, the patient has overemplotted these events, has charged them with a meaning so intense that, whether real or merely imagined, they continue to shape both his perceptions and his responses to the world long after they should have become "past history." The therapist's problem, then, is not to hold up before the patient the "real facts" of the matter, the "truth" as against the "fantasy" that obsesses him. Nor is it to give him a short course in psychoanalytical theory by which to enlighten him as to the true nature of his distress by cataloguing it as a manifestation of some "complex." This is what the analyst might do in relating the patient's case to a third party, and especially to another analyst. But psychoanalytic theory recognizes that the patient will resist both of these tactics in the same way that he resists the intrusion into consciousness of the traumatized memory traces in the *form* that he obsessively remembers them. The problem is to get the patient to "reemplot" his whole life history in such a way as to change the *meaning* of those events for him and their *significance* for the whole set of events that make up his life. As thus envisaged, the therapeutic process is an exercise in the refamiliarization of events that have been defamiliarized, rendered alienated from the patient's life-history, by virtue of their over-determination as causal forces. And we might say that the events are detraumatized by being removed from the plot structure in which they have a dominant place and inserted in another in which they have a subordinate or simply ordinary function as elements of a life shared with all other men.[10]

Now, I am not interested in forcing the analogy between psychotherapy and historiography; I use the example merely to illustrate a point about the fictive component in historical narratives. Historians seek to refamiliarize us with events which have been forgotten through either accident, neglect, or repression. Moreover, the greatest historians have always dealt with those events in the histories of their cultures which are "traumatic" in nature and the meaning of which is either problematical or overdetermined in the significance that they still have for current life, events such as revolutions, civil wars, large-scale processes such as industrialization and urbanization, or institutions which have lost their original function in a society but continue to play an important role on the current social scene. In looking at the ways in which such structures took shape or evolved, historians *refamiliarize* them, not only by providing more information about them, but also by showing how their development conformed to one or another of the story types that we conventionally invoke to make sense of our own life-histories.

Now, if any of this is plausible as a characterization of the explanatory effect of historical narrative, it tells us something important about the *mimetic* aspect of historical narratives. It is generally maintained — as Frye said — that a history is a verbal model of a set of events external to the mind of the historian. But it is wrong to think of a history as a model similar to a scale model of an airplane or ship, a map, or a photograph. For we can check the adequacy of this latter kind of model by going and looking at the original and, by applying the necessary rules of translation, seeing in what respect the model has actually succeeded in reproducing aspects of the original. But historical structures and processes are not like these originals, we cannot go and look at them in order

[10]White's explanation here correlates with the ideas of Donald Spence, *Narrative Truth and Historical Truth: Meaning and Interpretation in Psychoanalysis* (1982), and Roy Schafer, *A New Language for Psychoanalysis* (1976): an entire field of narrative psychotherapy has since grown up dedicated to changing the way individuals emplot their personal stories.

to see if the historian has adequately reproduced them in his narrative. Nor should we want to, even if we could, for after all it was the very strangeness of the original as it appeared in the documents that inspired the historian's efforts to make a model of it in the first place. If the historian only did that for us, we should be in the same situation as the patient whose analyst merely told him, on the basis of interviews with his parents, siblings, and childhood friends, what the "true facts" of the patient's early life were. We would have no reason to think that anything at all had been *explained* to us.

This is what leads me to think that historical narratives are not only models of past events and processes, but also metaphorical statements which suggest a relation of similitude between such events and processes and the story types that we conventionally use to endow the events of our lives with culturally sanctioned meanings. Viewed in a purely formal way, a historical narrative is not only a *reproduction* of the events reported in it, but also a *complex of symbols* which gives us directions for finding an *icon* of the structure of those events in our literary tradition.

I am here, of course, invoking the distinctions between sign, symbol, and icon which C. S. Peirce developed in his philosophy of language.[11] I think that these distinctions will help us to understand what is fictive in all putatively realistic representations of the world and what is realistic in all manifestly fictive ones. They help us, in short, to answer the question, What are historical representations *representations of*? It seems to me that we must say of histories what Frye seems to think is true only of poetry or philosophies of history, namely that, considered as a system of signs, the historical narrative points in two directions simultaneously: *toward* the events described in the narrative and *toward* the story type or mythos which the historian has chosen to serve as the icon of the structure of the events. The narrative itself is not the icon; what it does is *describe* events in the historical record in such a ways as to inform the reader *what to take as an icon* of the events so as to render them "familiar"

to him. The historical narrative thus mediates between the events reported in it on the one side and pregeneric plot structures conventionally used in our culture to endow unfamiliar events and situations with meanings, on the other.

The evasion of the implications of the fictive nature of historical narrative is in part a consequence of the utility of the concept "history" for the definition of other types of discourse. "History" can be set over against "science" by virtue of its want of conceptual rigor and failure to produce the kinds of universal laws that the sciences characteristically seek to produce. Similarly, "history" can be set over against "literature" by virtue of its interest in the "actual" rather than the "possible," which is supposedly the object of representation of "literary" works. Thus, within a long and distinguished critical tradition that has sought to determine what is "real" and what is "imagined" in the novel, history has served as a kind of archetype of the "realistic" pole of representation. I am thinking of Frye, Auerbach, Booth, Scholes and Kellogg, and others.[12] Nor is it unusual for literary theorists, when they are speaking about the "context" of a literary work, to suppose that this context — the "historical milieu" — has a concreteness and an accessibility that the work itself can never have, as if it were easier to perceive the reality of a past world put together from a thousand historical documents than it is to probe the depths of a single literary work that is present to the critic studying it. But the presumed concreteness and accessibility of historical milieux, these contexts of the texts that literary scholars study, are themselves products of the fictive capability of the historians who have studied those contexts. The historical documents are not less opaque than the texts studied by the literary critic. Nor is the world those documents figure more accessible. The one is no more "given" than the other. In fact, the opaqueness of the world figured in historical documents is, if anything, increased by

---

[11]For Peirce's distinctions among icons, indexes, and symbols, see the introduction to Structuralism and Deconstruction, p. 470.

[12]White is listing narrative theorists. Northrop Frye wrote *The Anatomy of Criticism* (1957); Eric Auerbach wrote *Mimesis: The Representation of Reality in Western Literature* (1953); for Booth, see p. 570. Robert Scholes and Robert Kellogg were co-authors of *The Nature of Narrative* (1966).

the production of historical narratives. Each new historical work only adds to the number of possible texts that have to be interpreted if a full and accurate picture of a given historical milieu is to be faithfully drawn. The relationship between the past to be analyzed and historical works produced by analysis of the documents is paradoxical: the *more* we know about the past, the more difficult it is to generalize about it.

But if the increase in our knowledge of the past makes it more difficult to generalize about it, it should make it easier for us to generalize about the forms in which that knowledge is transmitted to us. Our knowledge of the past may increase incrementally, but our understanding of it does not. Nor does our understanding of the past progress by the kind of revolutionary breakthroughs that we associate with the development of the physical sciences. Like literature, history progresses by the production of classics, the nature of which is such that they cannot be disconfirmed or negated, in the way that the principal conceptual schemata of the sciences are. And it is their nondisconfirmability that testifies to the essentially *literary* nature of historical classics. There is something in a historical masterpiece that cannot be negated, and this nonnegatable element is its form, the form which is its fiction.

It is frequently forgotten or, when remembered, denied that no given set of events attested by the historical record comprises a *story* manifestly finished and complete. This is as true as the events that comprise the life of an individual as it is of an institution, a nation, or a whole people. We do not *live* stories, even if we give our lives meaning by retrospectively casting them in the form of stories. And so too with nations or whole cultures. In an essay on the "mythical" nature of historiography, Lévi-Strauss remarks on the astonishment that a visitor from another planet would feel if confronted by the thousands of histories written about the French Revolution. For in those works, the "authors do not always make use of the same incidents; when they do, the incidents are revealed in different lights. And yet these are variations which have to do with the same country, the same period, and the same events — events whose reality is scattered across every level of a multilayered structure." He

goes on to suggest that the criterion of validity by which historical accounts might be assessed cannot depend on their elements" — that is to say — their putative factual content. On the contrary, he notes, "pursued in isolation, each element shows itself to be beyond grasp. But certain of them derive consistency from the fact that they can be integrated into a system whose terms are more or less credible when set against the overall coherence of the series."[13] But his "coherence of the series" cannot be the coherence of the *chronological* series, that sequence of "facts" organized into the temporal order of their original occurrence. For the "chronicle" of events, out of which the historian fashions his story of "what really happened," already comes precoded. There are "hot" and "cold" chronologies, chronologies in which more or fewer dates appear to demand inclusion in a full chronicle of what happened. Moreover, the dates themselves come to us already grouped into classes of dates, classes which are constitutive of putative domains of the historical field, domains which appear as problems for the historian to solve if he is to give a full and culturally responsible account of the past.

All this suggests to Lévi-Strauss that, when it is a matter of working up a comprehensive account of the various domains of the historical record in the form of a story, the "alleged historical continuities" that the historian purports to find in the record are "secured only by dint of fraudulent outlines" imposed by the historian on the record. These "fraudulent outlines" are, in his view, a product of "abstraction" and a means of escape from the "threat of an infinite regress" that always lurks at the interior of every complex set of historical "facts." We can construct a comprehensible story of the past, Lévi-Strauss insists, only by a decision to "give up" one or more of the domains of facts offering themselves for inclusion in our accounts. *Our explanations* of historical structures and processes are thus determined more by what we leave out of our representations than by what we put in. For it is in

[13]As in Lévi-Strauss's spatial reinterpretation of the Oedipus myth, p. 503. The specific sources of White's quotations can be found in note 1.

this brutal capacity to exclude certain facts in the interest of constituting others as components of comprehensible stories that the historian displays his tact as well as his understanding. The "overall coherence" of any given "series" of historical facts is the coherence of story, but this coherence is achieved only by a tailoring of the "facts" to the requirements of the story form. And thus Lévi-Strauss concludes: "In spite of worthy and indispensable efforts to bring another moment in history alive and to possess it, a clairvoyant history should admit that it never completely escapes from the nature of myth."

It is this mediative function that permits us to speak of a historical narrative as an extended metaphor. As a symbolic structure, the historical narrative does not *reproduce* the events it describes; it tells us in what direction to think about the events and charges our thought about the events with different emotional valences. The historical narrative does not *image* the things it indicates; it *calls to mind* images of the things it indicates, in the same way that a metaphor does. When a given concourse of events is emplotted as a "tragedy," this simply means that the historian has so described the events as to *remind us* of that form of fiction which we associate with the concept "tragic." Properly understood, histories ought never to be read as unambiguous signs of the events they report, but rather as symbolic structures, extended metaphors, that "liken" the events reported in them to some form with which we have already become familiar in our literary culture.

Perhaps I should indicate briefly what is meant by the *symbolic* and *iconic* aspects of a metaphor. The hackneyed phrase "My love, a rose" is not, obviously, intended to be understood as suggesting that the loved one is *actually* a rose. It is not even meant to suggest that the loved one has the specific attributes of a rose — that is to say, that the loved one is red, yellow, orange, or black, is a plant, has thorns, needs sunlight, should be sprayed regularly with insecticides, and so on. It is meant to be understood as indicating that the beloved shares the *qualities* which the rose has come to *symbolize* in the customary linguistic usages of Western culture. That is to say, considered as a message, the metaphor gives directions for finding an entity that will evoke the images associated *with loved ones and roses alike* in our culture. The metaphor does not *image* the thing it seeks to characterize, *it gives directions* for finding the set of images that are intended to be associated with that thing. It functions as a symbol, rather than as a sign: which is to say that it does not give us either a *description* or an *icon* of the thing it represents, but *tells us* what images to look for in our culturally encoded experience in order to determine how we *should feel* about the thing represented.

So too for historical narratives. They succeed in endowing sets of past events with meanings, over and above whatever comprehension they provide by appeal to putative causal laws, by exploiting the metaphorical similarities between sets of real events and the conventional structures of our fictions. By the very constitution of a set of events in such a way as to make a comprehensible story out of them, the historian charges those events with the symbolic significance of a comprehensible plot structure. Historians may not like to think of their works as translations of fact into fictions; but this is one of the effects of their works. By suggesting alternative emplotments of a given sequence of historical events, historians provide historical events with all of the possible meanings with which the literary art of their culture is capable of endowing them. The real dispute between the proper historian and the philosopher of history has to do with the latter's insistence that events can be emplotted in one and only one story form. History-writing thrives on the discovery of all the possible plot structures that might be invoked to endow sets of events with different meanings. And our understanding of the past increases precisely in the degree to which we succeed in determining how far that past conforms to the strategies of sense-making that are contained in their purest forms in literary art.

Conceiving historical narratives in this way may give us some insight into the crisis in historical thinking which has been under way since the beginning of our century. Let us imagine that the problem of the historian is to make sense of a hypothetical *set* of events by arranging them in a *series* that is at once chronologically *and* syntactically structured, in the way that any discourse from a sentence all the way up to a novel is structured. We can see immediately that the imperatives of chronological arrangement of the events constituting the set must exist in tension with the imperatives of the syntactical strategies alluded to, whether the latter are conceived as those of logic (the syllogism) or those of narrative (the plot structure).

Thus, we have a set of events

1.   *a, b, c, d, e* . . . . *n,*

ordered chronologically but requiring description and characterization as elements of plot or argument by which to give them meaning. Now, the series can be emplotted in a number of different ways and thereby endowed with different meanings without violating the imperatives of the chronological arrangement at all. We may briefly characterize some of these emplotments in the following ways:

2.   *A, b, c, d, e* . . . . *n*
3.   *a, B, c, d, e* . . . . *n*
4.   *a, b, C, d, e* . . . . *n*
5.   *a, b, c, D, e* . . . . *n*

And so on.

The capitalized letters indicate the privileged status given to certain events or sets of events in the series by which they are endowed with explanatory force, either as causes explaining the structure of the whole series or as symbols of the plot structure of the series considered as a story of a specific kind. We might say that any history which putatively endows any event (*a*) with the status of a decisive factor (*A*) in the structuration of the whole series of events following after it is "determinstic." The emplotments of the history of "society," by Rousseau in his *Second Discourse,* Marx in the *Manifesto,* and Freud in *Totem and Taboo* would fall into this category. So too, any history which endows the last event in the series (*e*), whether real or only speculatively projected, with the force of full explanatory power (*E*) is of the type of all eschatological or apocalyptical histories. St. Augustine's *City of God* and the various

versions of the Joachite[14] notion of the advent of a millennium, Hegel's *Philosophy of History,* and, in general, all idealist histories are of this sort. In between we would have the various forms of historiography which appeal to plot structures of a distinctively "fictional" sort (Romance, Comedy, Tragedy, and Satire) by which to endow the series with a perceivable form and a conceivable "meaning."

If the series were simply recorded in the order in which the events originally occurred, under the assumption that the ordering of the events in their temporal sequence itself provided a kind of explanation of why they occurred when and where they did, we would have the pure form of the *chronicle.* This would be a "naïve" form of chronicle, however, inasmuch as the categories of time and space alone served as the informing interpretative principles. Over against the naïve form of chronicle we could postulate as a logical possibility its "sentimental" counterpart, the ironic denial that historical series have any kind of larger significance or describe any imaginable plot structure or indeed can even be construed as a story with a discernible beginning, middle, and end. We could conceive such accounts of history as intending to serve as antidotes to their false or overemplotted counterparts (nos. 2, 3, 4, and 5 above) and could represent them as an ironic return to mere chronicle as constituting the only sense which any cognitively responsible history could take. We could characterize such histories thus:

6.   "*a, b, c, d, e* . . . . *n*"

with the quotation marks indicating the conscious interpretation of the events as having nothing other than seriality as their meaning.

This schema is of course highly abstract and does not do justice to the possible mixtures of and variations within the types that it is meant to

[14]Referring to the followers of Gioacchino da Fiore (1135–1202), who believed that the world would have three ages, an age of the Father (corresponding to the Old Testament period), an age of the Son (beginning with the birth of Jesus and ending around 1260), and an age of the Holy Spirit (which would quickly lead to the end of Time and the beginning of Eternity).

distinguish. But it helps us, I think, to conceive how events might be emplotted in different ways without violating the imperatives of the chronological order of the events (however they are construed) so as to yield alternative, mutually exclusive, and yet, equally plausible interpretations of the set. I have tried to show in *Metahistory* how such mixtures and variations occur in the writings of the master historians of the nineteenth century; and I have suggested in that book that classic historical accounts always represent attempts both to emplot the historical series adequately and implicitly to come to terms with other plausible emplotments. It is this dialectical tension between two or more possible emplotments that signals the element of critical self-consciousness present in any historian of recognizably classical stature.

Histories, then, are not only about events but also about the possible sets of relationships that those events can be demonstrated to figure. These sets of relationships are not, however, immanent in the events themselves; they exist only in the mind of the historian reflecting on them. Here they are present as the modes of relationships conceptualized in the myth, fable, and folklore, scientific knowledge, religion, and literary art, of the historian's own culture. But more importantly, they are, I suggest, immanent in the very language which the historian must use to *describe* events prior to a scientific analysis of them or a fictional emplotment of them. For if the historian's aim is to familiarize us with the unfamiliar, he must use figurative, rather than technical, language. Technical languages are familiarizing only *to* those who have been indoctrinated in their uses and only *of* those sets of events which the practitioners of a discipline have agreed to describe in a uniform terminology. History possesses no such generally accepted technical specific subject matter. The historian's characteristic instrument of encodation, communication, and exchange is ordinary educated speech. This implies that the only instrument that he has for endowing his data with meaning, of rendering the strange familiar, and of rendering the mysterious past comprehensible, are the techniques of *figurative* language. All historical narratives presuppose figurative characterizations of the events they purport to represent and explain. And this means that historical narratives, considered purely as verbal artifacts, can be characterized by the mode of figurative discourse in which they are cast.

If this is the case, then it may well be that the kind of emplotment that the historian decides to use to give meaning to a set of historical events is dictated by the dominant figurative mode to the language he has used to *describe* the elements of his account *prior* to his composition of a narrative. Geoffrey Hartman once remarked in my hearing, at a conference on literary history, that he was not sure that he knew what historians of literature might want to do, but he did know that to write a history meant to place an event within a context, by relating it as a part to some conceivable whole. He went on to suggest that as far as he knew, there were only two ways of relating parts to wholes, by metonymy and by synecdoche.[15] Having been engaged for some time in the study of the thought of Giambattista Vico,[16] I was much taken with this thought, because it conformed to Vico's notion that the "logic" of all "poetic wisdom" was contained in the relationships which language itself provided in the four principal modes of figurative representation: metaphor, metonymy, synecdoche, and irony. My own hunch — and it is a hunch which I find confirmed in Hegel's reflections on the nature of nonscientific discourse — is that in any field of study which, like history, has not yet become disciplinized to the point of constructing a formal terminological system for describing its objects, in the way that physics and chemistry have, it is the types of figurative discourse that dictate the fundamental forms of the data to be studied. This means that the *shape* of the *relationships* which will appear to be inherent in the objects inhabiting the field will in reality have been imposed on the field by the investigator

[15]Synecdoche (a figure of speech where the part is used for the whole, or the species for the genus) is usually thought of as a specific form of metonymy (where one word is used for another associated word).

[16]Italian rhetorician and philosopher (1668–1744), author of *La Scienza nuova* (1725, 1744), which contains a vision of successive stages through which nations pass. The notion influenced both Peacock and Shelley.

in the very act of *identifying and describing* the objects that he finds there. The implication is that historians *constitute* their subjects as possible objects of narrative representation by the very language they use to *describe* them. And if this is the case, it means that the different kinds of historical interpretations that we have of the same set of events, such as the French Revolution as interpreted by Michelet, Tocqueville, Taine, and others, are little more than projections of the linguistic protocols that these historians used to *pre*-figure that set of events prior to writing their narratives of it. It is only a hypothesis, but it seems possible that the conviction of the histo-rian that he has "found" the form of his narrative in the events themselves, rather than imposed it upon them, in the way the poet does, is a result of a certain lack of linguistic self-consciousness which obscures the extent to which descriptions of events *already* constitute interpretations of their nature. As thus envisaged, the difference between Michelet's and Tocqueville's accounts of the Revolution does not reside only in the fact that the former emplotted his story in the modal-ity of a Romance and the latter his in the modal-ity of Tragedy; it resides as well in the tropological mode — metaphorical and metonymic, respec-tively — with each brought to his apprehension of the facts as they appeared in the documents.

I do not have the space to try to demonstrate the plausibility of this hypothesis, which is the inform-ing principle of my book *Metahistory*. But I hope that this essay may serve to suggest an approach to the study of such discursive prose forms as historiography, an approach that is as old as the study of rhetoric and as new as modern linguis-tics. Such a study would proceed along the lines laid out by Roman Jakobson in a paper entitled "Linguistics and Poetics,"[17] in which he charac-terized the difference between Romantic poetry and the various forms of nineteenth-century Realistic prose as residing in the essentially meta-phorical nature of the former and the essentially metonymical nature of the latter. I think that this characterization of the difference between poetry and prose is too narrow, because it presupposes

that complex macrostructural narratives such as the novel are little more than projections of the "selective" (i.e., phonemic) axis of all speech acts. Poetry, and especially Romantic poetry, is then characterized by Jakobson as a projection of the "combinatory" (i.e., morphemic) axis of language. Such a binary theory pushes the analyst toward a dualistic opposition between poetry and prose which appears to rule out the possibility of a metonymical poetry and a metaphorical prose. But the fruitfulness of Jakobson's theory lies in its suggestion that the various forms of both poetry and prose, all of which have their counter-parts in narrative in general and therefore in his-toriography too, can be characterized in terms of the dominant trope which serves as the paradigm, provided by language itself, of all significant relationships conceived to exist in the world by anyone wishing to represent those relationships in language.

Narrative, or the syntagmatic dispersion of events across a temporal series presented as a prose discourse, in such a way as to display their progressive elaboration as a comprehensible form, would represent the "inward turn" that discourse takes when it tries to *show* the reader the true form of things existing behind a merely apparent formlessness. Narrative *style*, in history as well as in the novel, would then be construed as the modality of the movement from a representa-tion of some original state of affairs to some sub-sequent state. The primary *meaning* of a narrative would then consist of the destructuration of a set of events (real or imagined) originally encoded in one tropological mode and the progressive restructuration of the set in another tropological mode. As thus envisaged, narrative would be a process of decodation and recodation in which an original perception is clarified by being cast in a figurative mode different from that in which it has come encoded by convention, authority, or custom. And the explanatory force of the narra-tive would then depend on the contrast between the original encodation and the later one.

For example, let us suppose that a set of experiences comes to us as a grotesque, i.e., as unclassified and unclassifiable. Our problem is to identify the modality of the relationships that bind the discernible elements of the formless

[17] See the introduction to Structuralism and Deconstruction. p. 473.

totality together in such a way as to make of it a whole of some sort. If we stress the similarities among the elements, we are working in the mode of metaphor; if we stress the differences among them, we are working in the mode of metonymy. Of course, in order to make sense of any set of experiences, we must obviously identify both the parts of a thing that appear to make it up and the nature of the shared aspects of the parts that make them identifiable as a totality. This implies that all original characterizations of anything must utilize *both* metaphor and metonymy in order to "fix" it as something about which we can meaningfully discourse.

In the case of historiography, the attempts of commentators to make sense of the French Revolution are instructive. Burke decodes the events of the Revolution which his contemporaries experience as a grotesque by recoding it in the mode of irony;[18] Michelet recodes these events in the mode of synecdoche; Tocqueville recodes them in the mode of metonymy. In each case, however, the movement from code to recode is narratively described, i.e., laid out on a time-line in such a way as to make the interpretation of the events that made up the "Revolution" a kind of drama that we can recognize as Satirical, Romantic, and Tragic, respectively. This drama can be followed by the reader of the narrative in such a way as to be experienced as a progressive revelation of what the *true* nature of the events consists of. The revelation is not experienced, however, as a restructuring of perceptions so much as an illumination of a field of occurrence. But actually what has happened is that a set of events originally encoded in one way is simply being decoded by being recoded in another. The events themselves are not substantially changed from one account to another. That is to say, the data that are to be analyzed are not significantly different in the different accounts. What is different are the modalities of their relationships. These modalities, in turn, although they *may* appear to the reader to be based on different theories of the nature of society, politics, and history, ultimately have their origin in the figurative characterizations of the whole set of events as representing wholes of fundamentally different sorts. It is for this reason that, when it is a matter of setting different interpretations of the same set of historical phenomena over against one another in an attempt to decide which is the best or most convincing, we are often driven to confusion or ambiguity. This is not to say that we cannot distinguish between good and bad historiography, since we can always fall back on such criteria as responsibility to the rules of evidence, the relative fullness of narrative detail, logical consistency, and the like to determine this issue. But it is to say that the effort to distinguish between good and bad interpretations of a historical event such as the Revolution is not as easy as it might at first appear when it is a matter of dealing with alternative interpretations produced by historians of relatively equal learning and conceptual sophistication. After all, a great historical classic cannot be disconfirmed or nullified either by the discovery of some new datum that might call a specific explanation of some element of the whole account into question or by the generation of new methods of analysis which permit us to deal with questions that earlier historians might not have taken under consideration. And it is precisely because great historical classics, such as works by Gibbon, Michelet, Thucydides, Mommsen, Ranke, Burckhardt, Bancroft, and so on, cannot be definitely disconfirmed that we must look to the specifically literary aspects of their work as crucial, and not merely subsidiary, elements in their historiographical technique.

What all this points to is the necessity of revising the distinction conventionally drawn between poetic and prose discourse in discussion of such narrative forms as historiography and recognizing that the distinction, as old as Aristotle,[19] between history and poetry obscures as much as it illuminates about both. If there is an element of the historical in all poetry, there is an element of poetry in every historical account of the world.

[18]White is referring to *Reflections on the Revolution in France* (1791) by Edmund Burke (1729–1797), Irish literary figure and parliamentarian.

[19]See Aristotle, *Poetics*, chapter 9, p. 59. Since the kind of history White is considering limits itself to discussing events that are "necessary or probable" with respect to the historian's literary schema, this form of history would certainly be poetry in Aristotle's sense.

And this because in our account of the historical world we are dependent, in ways perhaps that we are not in the natural sciences, on the techniques of *figurative language* both for our *characterization* of the objects of our narrative representations and for the *strategies* by which to constitute narrative accounts of the transformations of those objects in time. And this because history has no stipulatable subject matter uniquely its own; it is always written as part of a contest between contending poetic figurations of what the past *might* consist of.

The older distinction between fiction and history, in which fiction is conceived as the representation of the imaginable and history as the representation of the actual, must give place to the recognition that we can only know the *actual* by contrasting it with or likening it to the *imaginable*. As thus conceived, historical narratives are complex structures in which a world of experience is imagined to exist under at least two modes, one of which is encoded as "real," the other of which is "revealed" to have been illusory in the course of the narrative. Of course, it is a fiction of the historian that the various states of affairs which he constitutes as the beginning, the middle, and the end of a course of development are all "actual" or "real" and that he has merely recorded "what happened" in the transition from the inaugural to the terminal phase. But both the beginning state of affairs and the ending one are inevitably poetic constructions, and as such, dependent upon the modality of the figurative language used to give them the aspect of coherence. This implies that all narrative is not simply a recording of "what happened" in the transition from one state of affairs to another, but a progressive *redescription* of sets of events in such a way as to dismantle a structure encoded in one verbal mode in the beginning so as to justify a recoding of it in another mode at the end. This is what the "middle" of all narratives consists of.

All of this is highly schematic, and I know that this insistence on the fictive element in all historical narratives is certain to arouse the ire of historians who believe that they are doing something fundamentally different from the novelist, by virtue of the fact that they deal with "real," while the novelist deals with "imagined," events.

But neither the form nor the explanatory power of narrative derives from the different contents it is presumed to be able to accommodate. In point of fact, history — the real world as it evolves in time — is made sense of in the same way that the poet or novelist tries to make sense of it, i.e., by endowing what originally appears to be problematical and mysterious with the aspect of a recognizable, because it is a familiar, form. It does not matter whether the world is conceived to be real or only imagined; the manner of making sense of it is the same.

So too, to say that we make sense of the real world by imposing upon it the formal coherency that we customarily associate with the products of writers of fiction in no way detracts from the status as knowledge which we ascribe to historiography. It would only detract from it if we were to believe that literature did not teach us anything about reality, but was a product of an imagination which was not of this world but of some other, inhuman one. In my view, we experience the "fictionalization" of history as an "explanation" for the same reason that we experience great fiction as an illumination of a world that we inhabit along with the author. In both we recognize the forms by which consciousness both constitutes and colonizes the world it seeks to inhabit comfortably.

Finally, it may be observed that if historians were to recognize the fictive element in their narratives, this would not mean the degradation of historiography to the status of ideology or propaganda. In fact, the recognition would serve as a potent antidote to the tendency of historians to become captive of ideological preconceptions which they do not recognize as such but honor as the "correct" perception of "the way things *really* are."[20] By drawing historiography nearer to its origins in literary sensibility, we should be able to identify the ideological, because it is the fictive, element in our own discourse. We are always able to see the fictive element in those historians with whose interpretations of a given set of events we disagree; we seldom perceive that element in our

[20]White alludes to the famous statement by historian Leopold von Ranke (1795–1886) in "The Purpose of a Historian": The purpose, he said, was to show "wie es eigentlich gewesen." — how things really happened.

own prose. So, too, if we recognized the literary or fictive element in every historical account, we would be able to move the teaching of historiography onto a higher level of self-consciousness than it currently occupies.

What teacher has not lamented his inability to give instruction to apprentices in the *writing* of history? What graduate student of history has not despaired at trying to comprehend and imitate the model which his instructors *appear* to honor but the principles of which remain uncharted? If we recognize that there is a fictive element in all historical narrative, we would find in the theory of language and narrative itself the basis for a more subtle presentation of what historiography consists of than that which simply tells the student to go and "find out the facts" and write them up in such a way as to tell "what really happened."

In my view, history as a discipline is in bad shape today because it has lost sight of its origins in the literary imagination. In the interest of *appearing* scientific and objective, it has repressed and denied to itself its own greatest source of strength and renewal. By drawing historiography back once more to an intimate connection with its literary basis, we should not only be putting ourselves on guard against *merely* ideological distortions; we should be by way of arriving at that "theory" of history without which it cannot pass for a "discipline" at all.

Pierre Bourdieu
1930–2002

It is no surprise that academics should find interesting the man who attempted to demystify their own mysterious behaviors and affiliations, applying a mordant Marxist sociology to the culture of culture. Pierre Bourdieu was born in Denguin, France, and educated at the elite École Normale Supérieure where he took his Agrégé in philosophy in 1954. Bourdieu taught philosophy in the provincial lycée at Moulins, then accepted a position at the University of Algiers in the closing days of French colonial possession. He moved back to Paris in 1960, becoming director of studies at the École des Hautes Études in 1964 and professor of sociology at the Collège de France in 1982. Bourdieu's many works include Outline of a Theory of Practice (1977), Reproduction in Education, Society and Culture (1977; revised 1990), Distinction: A Social Critique of the Judgment of Taste (1987), Homo Academicus (1988), The Logic of Practice (1990), Language and Symbolic Power (1991), The Field of Cultural Production: Essays on Art and Literature (1993), Free Exchange (1995), The Rules of Art: Genesis and Structure of the Literary Field (1995), The State Nobility: Elite Schools and the Field of Power (1996), On Television (1998), Practical Reason: On the Theory of Action (1998), The Weight of the World: Social Suffering in Contemporary Society (1999, with Alain Accardo), Masculine Domination (2001), The Social Structures of the Economy (2003), and The Science of Science and Reflexivity (2004). Bourdieu has himself been analyzed in Bourdieu: Critical Perspectives, edited by Craig Calhoun, Edward LiPuma, and Moishe Postone (1993). The selection reprinted is the introduction to Distinction: A Social Critique of the Judgment of Taste, translated by Richard Nice.

From Distinction: A Social Critique of the Judgment of Taste

INTRODUCTION

*You said it, my good knight! There ought to be
laws to protect the body of acquired knowledge.*

*Take one of our good pupils, for example: modest
and diligent, from his earliest grammar classes
he's kept a little notebook full of phrases.*

*After hanging on the lips of his teachers for twenty
years, he's managed to build up an intellectual
stock in trade; doesn't it belong to him as if it
were a house, or money?* — PAUL CLAUDEL, *Le
soulier de satin,* DAY III, SCENE ii[1]

Translated by Richard Nice.

[1]*The Satin Slipper* (1930) is a lengthy play (running time of 11 hours at its revival at the 2004 Edinburgh Festival) by religious poet and dramatist Paul Claudel (1868–1955).

There is an economy of cultural goods, but it has a specific logic. Sociology endeavors to establish the conditions in which the consumers of cultural goods, and their taste for them, are produced, and at the same time to describe the different ways of appropriating such of these objects as are regarded at a particular moment as works of art, and the social conditions of the constitution of the mode of appropriation that is considered legitimate. But one cannot fully understand cultural practices unless "culture," in the restricted, normative sense of ordinary usage, is brought back into "culture" in the anthropological sense, and the elaborated taste for the most refined objects is reconnected with the elementary taste for the flavors of food.

Whereas the ideology of charisma regards taste in legitimate culture as a gift of nature, scientific observation shows that cultural needs are the product of upbringing and education: surveys establish that all cultural practices (museum visits, concert-going, reading etc.), and preferences in literature, painting or music, are closely linked to educational level (measured by qualifications or length of schooling) and secondarily to social origin.[2] The relative weight of home background and of formal education (the effectiveness and duration of which are closely dependent on social origin) varies according to the extent to which the different cultural practices are recognized and taught by the educational system, and the influence of social origin is strongest — other things being equal — in "extra-curricular" and avant-garde culture. To the socially recognized hierarchy of the arts, and within each of them, of genres, schools or periods, corresponds a social hierarchy of the consumers. This predisposes tastes to function as markers of "class." The manner in which culture has been acquired lives on in the manner of using it: the importance attached to manners can be understood once it is seen that it is these imponderables of practice which distinguish the different — and ranked — modes of culture acquisition, early or late, domestic or scholastic, and the classes of individuals which they characterize (such as "pedants" and *mondains*).[3] Culture also has its titles ofnobility — awarded by the educational system — and its pedigrees, measured by seniority in admission to the nobility.

The definition of cultural nobility is the stake in a struggle which has gone on unceasingly, from the seventeenth century to the present day, between groups differing in their ideas of culture and of the legitimate relation to culture and to works of art, and therefore differing in the conditions of acquisition of which these dispositions are the product.[4] Even in the classroom, the dominant definition of the legitimate way of appropriating culture and works of art favors those who have had early access to legitimate culture, in a cultured household, outside of scholastic disciplines, since even within the educational system it devalues scholarly knowledge and interpretation as "scholastic" or even "pedantic" in favor of direct experience and simple delight.

The logic of what is sometimes called, in typically "pedantic" language, the "reading" of a work of art, offers an objective basis for this opposition. Consumption is, in this case, a stage in a process of communication, that is, an act of deciphering, decoding, which presupposes practical or explicit mastery of a cipher or code. In a sense, one can say that the capacity to see (*voir*) is a function of the knowledge (*savoir*), or concepts, that is, the words, that are available to name visible things, and which are, as it were, programs for perception. A work of art has meaning and interest only for someone who possesses the cultural competence, that is, the code, into which it is encoded. The conscious or unconscious implementation of explicit or implicit schemes of perception and appreciation which constitutes pictorial or musical culture is the hidden condition for recognizing the styles characteristic of a period, a school or an author, and, more generally, for the familiarity with the internal logic of works that aesthetic enjoyment presupposes. A beholder who lacks the specific code feels lost in a chaos of sounds and rhythms, colors and lines, without rhyme or reason. Not having learnt to adopt the adequate disposition, he stops short at what Erwin Panofsky calls the "sensible properties," perceiving a skin as downy or lace-work as delicate, or at the emotional resonances aroused by these properties, referring to "austere" colors or a "joyful" melody. He cannot move from the "primary stratum of the meaning

---

[2]Bourdieu et al., *Un art moyen: essai sur les usages sociaux de la photographie* (Paris: Ed. de Minuit, 1965); P. bourdieu and A. Darbel, *L'Amour de l'art: les musées et leur public* (Paris, Ed. de Minuit, 1966). [Bourdieu]

[3]Worldly, sophisticated people.

[4]The word *disposition* seems particularly suited to express what is covered by the concept of habitus (defined as a system of dispositions) — used later in this chapter. It expresses first the *result of an organizing action*, with a meaning close to that of words such as structure; it also designates a way of being, a habitual state (especially of the body) and, in particular, a *predisposition, tendency, propensity* or *inclination*. [The semantic cluster of "disposition" is rather wider in French than in English, but as this note—translated literally— shows, the equivalence is adequate. Translator.] P. Bourdieu, *Outline of a Theory of Practice* (Cambridge: Cambridge University Press, 1977), p. 214, n. 1. [Bourdieu]

we can grasp on the basis of our ordinary experience" to the "stratum of secondary meanings," i.e., the "level" of the meaning of what is signified," unless he possesses the concepts which go beyond the sensible properties and which identify the specifically stylistic properties of the work.[5] Thus the encounter with a work of art is not "love at first sight" as is generally supposed, and the act of empathy, *Einfühlung*, which is the art-lover's pleasure, presupposes an act of cognition, a decoding operation, which implies the implementation of a cognitive acquirement, a cultural code.[6] This typically intellectualist theory of artistic perception directly contradicts the experience of the art-lovers closest to the legitimate definition; acquisition of legitimate culture by insensible familiarization within the family circle tends to favor an enchanted experience of culture which implies forgetting the acquisition.[7] The "eye" is

[5]E. Panofsky, "Iconography and Iconology: An Introduction to the Study of Renaissance Art," *Meaning in the Visual Arts* (New York: Doubleday, 1955), p. 28. [Bourdieu]

[6]It will be seen that this internalized code called culture functions as cultural capital owing to the fact that, being unequally distributed, it secures profits of distinction. [Bourdieu]

[7]The sense of familiarity in no way excludes the ethnocentric misunderstanding which results from applying the wrong code. Thus, Michael Baxandall's work in historical ethnology enables us to measure all that separates the perceptual schemes that now tend to be applied to Quattrocento paintings and those which their immediate addressees applied. The "moral and spiritual eye" of Quattrocento man, that is, the set of cognitive and evaluative dispositions which were the basis of his perception of the world and his perception of pictorial representation of the world, differs radically from the "pure" gaze (purified, first of all, of reference to economic value) with which the modern cultivated spectator looks at works of art. As the contracts show, the clients of Filippo Lippi, Domenico Ghirlandaio or Piero della Francesca were concerned to get "value for money." They approached works of art with the mercantile dispositions of a businessman who can calculate quantities and prices at a glance, and they applied some surprising criteria of appreciation, such as the expense of the colors, which sets gold and ultramarine at the top of the hierarchy. The artists, who shared this world view, were led to include arithmetical and geometrical devices in their compositions so as to flatter this taste for measurement and calculation; and they tended to exhibit the technical virtuosity which, in this context, is the most visible evidence of the quantity and quality of the labor provided. M. Baxandall, *Painting and Experience in Fifteenth-Century Italy: A Primer in the Social History of Pictorial Style* (Oxford: Oxford University Press, 1972). [Bourdieu] Quattrocento is Italian for fifteenth century. The three mentioned painters were all of this era.

a product of history reproduced by education. This is true of the mode of artistic perception now accepted as legitimate, that is, the aesthetic disposition, the capacity to consider in and for themselves, as form rather than function, not only the works designated for such apprehension, i.e., legitimate works of art, but everything in the world, including cultural objects which are not yet consecrated — such as, at one time, primitive arts, or, nowadays, popular photography or kitsch[8] — and natural objects. The "pure" gaze is a historical invention linked to the emergence of an autonomous field of artistic production, that is, a field capable of imposing its own norms on both the production and the consumption of its products.[9] An art which, like all Post-Impressionist painting, is the product of an artistic intention which asserts the primacy of the mode of representation over the object of representation demands categorically an attention to form which previous art only demanded conditionally.

The pure intention of the artist is that of a producer who aims to be autonomous, that is, entirely the master of his product, who tends to reject not only the "programs" imposed a priori by scholars and scribes, but also—following the old hierarchy of doing and saying — the interpretations superimposed a posteriori on his work. The production of an "open work," intrinsically and deliberately polysemic, can thus be understood as the final stage in the conquest of artistic autonomy by poets and, following in their footsteps, by painters, who had long been reliant on writers and their work of "showing" and "illustrating." To assert the autonomy of production is to give primacy to that of which the artist is master, i.e., form, manner, style, rather than the "subject," the external referent, which involves subordination to functions — even if only the most elementary one, that of representing, signifying, saying something. It also means a refusal to recognize any necessity other than that inscribed in the specific tradition of the artistic discipline in question: the shift from an art which

[8]Art that is pretentiously worthless.

[9]See P. Bourdieu, "Le marché des biens symboliques," *L'Année Sociologique*, 22 (1973), 49–126; and "Outline of a Sociological Theory of Art Perception," *International Social Science Journal*, 20 (Winter 1968), 589–612. [Bourdieu]

imitates nature to an art which imitates art, deriving from its own history the exclusive source of its experiments and even of its breaks with tradition. An art which ever increasingly contains reference to its own history demands to be perceived historically; it asks to be referred not to an external referent, the represented or designated "reality," but to the universe of past and present works of art. Like artistic production, in that it is generated in a field, aesthetic perception is necessarily historical, inasmuch as it is differential, relational, attentive to the deviations (*écarts*) which make styles. Like the so-called naive painter who, operating outside the field and its specific traditions, remains external to the history of the art, the "naive" spectator cannot attain a specific grasp of works of art which only have meaning — or value — in relation to the specific history of an artistic tradition. The aesthetic disposition demanded by the products of a highly autonomous field of production is inseparable from a specific cultural competence. This historical culture functions as a principle of pertinence which enables one to identify, among the elements offered to the gaze, all the distinctive features and only these, by referring them, consciously or unconsciously, to the universe of possible alternatives. This mastery is, for the most part, acquired simply by contact with works of art — that is, through an implicit learning analogous to that which makes it possible to recognize familiar faces without explicit rules or criteria — and it generally remains at a practical level; it is what makes it possible to identify styles, i.e., modes of expression characteristic of a period, a civilization or a school, without having to distinguish clearly, or state explicitly, the features which constitute their originality. Everything seems to suggest that even among professional valuers, the criteria which define the stylistic properties of the "typical works" on which all their judgements are based usually remain implicit.

The pure gaze implies a break with the ordinary attitude towards the world, which, given the conditions in which it is performed, is also a social separation. Ortega y Gasset[10] can be believed when he attributes to modern art a systematic refusal of all that is "human," i.e., generic, common — as

opposed to distinctive, or distinguished — namely, the passions, emotions and feelings which "ordinary" people invest in their "ordinary" lives. It is as if the "popular aesthetic" (the quotation marks are there to indicate that this is an aesthetic "in itself" not "for itself")[11] were based on the affirmation of the continuity between art and life, which implies the subordination of form to function. This is seen clearly in the case of the novel and especially the theater, where the working-class audience refuses any sort of formal experimentation and all the effects which, by introducing a distance from the accepted conventions (as regards scenery, plot etc.), tend to distance the spectator, preventing him from getting involved and fully identifying with the characters (I am thinking of Brechtian "alienation"[12] or the disruption of plot in the *nouveau roman*).[13] In contrast to the detachment and disinterestedness which aesthetic theory regards as the only way of recognizing the work of art for what it is, i.e., autonomous, *selbständig*, the "popular aesthetic" ignores or refuses the refusal of "facile" involvement and "vulgar" enjoyment, a refusal which is the basis of the taste for formal experiment. And popular judgements of paintings or photographs spring from an "aesthetic" (in fact it is an ethos) which is the exact opposite of the Kantian aesthetic. Whereas, in order to grasp the specificity of the aesthetic judgement, Kant strove to distinguish that which pleases from that which gratifies and, more generally, to distinguish disinterestedness, the sole guarantor of the specifically aesthetic quality of contemplation,[14] from the interest of reason which defines the Good, working-class people expect every image to explicitly perform a function, if only that of a sign, and their judgements make reference, often explicitly, to the norms of morality or agreeableness. Whether rejecting or praising, their appreciation always has an ethical basis.

Popular taste applies the schemes of the ethos, which pertain in the ordinary circumstances of life,

---

[10]José Ortega y Gasset (1883–1955), Spanish philosopher.

[11]Bourdieu alludes ironically to the existential philosophy of Jean-Paul Sartre, where the "en soi" characterizes material things, the "pour soi" transcendent consciousness.

[12]See the introduction to Marxist Criticism, p. 697.

[13]Postmodern fiction by Alain Robbe-Grillet, Michel Butor, and others.

[14]See Kant, p. 165.

to legitimate works of art, and so performs a sys-tematic reduction of the things of art to the things of life. The very seriousness (or naivety) which this taste invests in fictions and representations demonstrates a contrario that pure taste performs a suspension of "naïve" involvement which is one dimension of a "quasi-ludic" relationship with the necessities of the world. Intellectuals could be said to believe in the representation — litera-ture, theater, painting — more than in the things represented, whereas the people chiefly expect representations and the conventions which gov-ern them to allow them to believe "naïvely," in the things represented. The pure aesthetic is rooted in an ethic, or rather, an ethos of elective distance from the necessities of the natural and social world, which may take the form of moral agnosti-cism (visible when ethical transgression becomes an artistic *parti pris*)[15] or of an aestheticism which presents the aesthetic disposition as a uni-versally valid principle and takes the bourgeois denial of the social world to its limit. The detach-ment of the pure gaze cannot be dissociated from a general disposition towards the world which is the paradoxical product of conditioning by negative economic necessities — a life of ease — that tends to induce an active distance from necessity.

Although art obviously offers the greatest scope to the aesthetic disposition, there is no area of practice in which the aim of purifying, refining and sublimating primary needs and impulses can-not assert itself, no area in which the stylization of life, that is, the primacy of forms over func-tion, of manner over matter, does not produce the same effects. And nothing is more distinctive, more distinguished, than the capacity to confer aesthetic status on objects that are banal or even "common" (because the "common" people make them their own, especially for aesthetic pur-poses), or the ability to apply the principles of a "pure" aesthetic to the most everyday choices of everyday life, e.g., in cooking, clothing or decora-tion, completely reversing the popular disposition which annexes aesthetics to ethics.

In fact, through the economic and social con-ditions which they presuppose, the different ways

[15]Inclination, disposition.

of relating to realities and fictions, of believing in fictions and the realities they simulate, with more or less distance and detachment, are very closely linked to the different possible positions in social space and, consequently, bound up with the systems of dispositions (habitus) character-istic of the different classes and class fractions. Taste classifies, and it classifies the classifier. Social subjects, classified by their classifications, distinguish themselves by the distinctions they make, between the beautiful and the ugly, the distinguished and the vulgar, in which their posi-tion in the objective classifications is expressed or betrayed. And statistical analysis does indeed show that oppositions similar in structure to those found in cultural practices also appear in eating habits. The antithesis between quantity and quality, substance and form, corresponds to the opposition — linked to different distances from necessity — between the taste of neces-sity, which favors the most "filling" and most economical foods, and the taste of liberty — or luxury — which shifts the emphasis to the man-ner (of presenting, serving, eating etc.) and tends to use stylized forms to deny function.

The science of taste and of cultural consump-tion begins with a transgression that is in no way aesthetic: it has to abolish the sacred frontier which makes legitimate culture a separate uni-verse, in order to discover the intelligible rela-tions which unite apparently incommensurable "choices," such as preferences in music and food, painting and sport, literature and hairstyle. This barbarous reintegration of aesthetic consumption into the world of ordinary consumption abol-ishes the opposition, which has been the basis of high aesthetics since Kant, between the "taste of sense" and the "taste of reflection," and between facile pleasure, pleasure reduced to a pleasure of the senses, and pure pleasure, pleasure purified of pleasure, which is predisposed to become a symbol of moral excellence and a measure of the capacity for sublimation which defines the truly human man. The culture which results from this magical division is sacred. Cultural consecration does indeed confer on the objects, persons and situations it touches, a sort of ontological promo-tion akin to a transsubstantiation. Proof enough of this is found in the two following quotations, which might almost have been written for the delight of the sociologist:

"What struck me most is this: nothing could be obscene on the stage of our premier theater, and the ballerinas of the Opera, even as naked dancers, sylphs, sprites or Bacchae, retain an inviolable purity."[16]

"There are obscene postures: the simulated intercourse which offends the eye. Clearly, it is impossible to approve, although the interpolation of such gestures in dance routines does give them a symbolic and aesthetic quality which is absent from the intimate scenes the cinema daily flaunts before its spectators' eyes. . . . As for the nude scene, what can one say, except that it is brief and theatrically not very effective? I will not say it is chaste or innocent, for nothing commercial can be so described. Let us say it is not shocking, and that the chief objection is that it serves as a box-office gimmick. . . . In *Hair*, the nakedness fails to be symbolic."[17]

The denial of lower, coarse, vulgar, venal, servile — in a word, natural — enjoyment, which constitutes the sacred sphere of culture, implies an affirmation of the superiority of those who can be satisfied with the sublimated, refined, disinterested, gratuitous, distinguished pleasures forever closed to the profane. That is why art and cultural consumption are predisposed, consciously and deliberately or not, to fulfil a social function of legitimating social differences.

---

[16]O. Merlin, "Mlle. Thibon dans la vision de Marguerite," *Le Monde*, 9 December 1965. [Bourdieu]

[17]F. Chenique, "*Hair* est-il immoral?" *Le Monde*, 28 January 1970. [Bourdieu]

Stuart Hall
1932–2014

One of the most important figures in the development of contemporary cultural studies as a discipline, Stuart Hall was born in Kingston, Jamaica, in 1932. He moved to Bristol with his mother at age nineteen and became a Rhodes scholar at Oxford University. He received his M.A. from Merton College. With E. P. Thompson, Raphael Samuel, Ralph Miliband, and Raymond Williams, Hall launched two radical leftist journals, The New Reasoner and New Left Review, where he would publish many innovative essays that helped to guide the future of British cultural studies. In 1964, he co-authored The Popular Arts, a work that attracted the attention of Richard Hoggart, who invited Hall to direct the Centre for Contemporary Cultural Studies at the University of Birmingham. During this fruitful period, he wrote Situating Marx: Evaluations and Departures (1972), Encoding and Decoding in the Television Discourse (1973), Reading of Marx's 1857 Introduction to the Grundrisse (1973) and Policing the Crisis (1978). A post-Gramscian cultural theorist, Hall was a developer of reception theory, which views the audience of a text as complicit in interpretation, rather than a passive recipient. Although Hall agrees with other cultural theorists that mass media's signification system most often reflects the ideologies of the ruling class, he argues that it is also important to study the active, interpretive responses of the people who receive these media. In 1979, Hall became a professor of sociology at the Open University, where he remained until his retirement in 1997. His later works include The Hard Road to Renewal (1988), Resistance Through Rituals (1989), Modernity and Its Future (1992), The Formation of Modernity (1992), Questions of Cultural Identity (1996), Cultural Representations and Signifying Practices (1997), and Visual Cultural (1999). From 1997–2000, Hall served on the Runnymede Trust's commission on the future of multiethnic Britain. Hall spent the last decade of his life involved in the movement for black artists in Britain and across Europe. This work is the subject of John Akomfrah's film, The Stuart Hall Project (2013). The following article, "Cultural Studies: Two Paradigms" was originally published in the journal Media, Culture, and Society in 1980.

Cultural Studies: Two Paradigms

In serious, critical intellectual work, there are no "absolute beginnings" and few unbroken continuities. Neither the endless unwinding of "tradition," so beloved in the History of Ideas, nor the absolutism of the "epistemological rupture," punctuating Thought into its "false" and "correct" parts, once favored by the Althusserans,[1] will do. What we find, instead, is an untidy but characteristic unevenness of development. What is important are the significant *breaks* — where old lines of thought are disrupted, older constellations displaced, and elements, old and new, are regrouped around a different set of premises and themes. Changes in a problematic[2] do significantly transform the nature of the questions asked, the forms in which they are proposed, and the manner in which they can be adequately answered. Such shifts in perspective reflect not only the results of an internal

[1] See p. 738.

[2] Here (and elsewhere) this word is an anglicization of the French noun *problematique*, which means "the complex of issues associated with a topic, considered collectively."

intellectual labor, but the manner in which real historical developments and transformations are appropriated in thought, and provide Thought, not with its guarantee of "correctness" but with its fundamental orientations, its conditions of existence. It is because of this complex articulation between thinking and historical reality, reflected in the social categories of thought, and the continuous dialectic between "knowledge" and "power," that the breaks are worth recording.

Cultural Studies, as a distinctive problematic, emerges from one such moment, in the mid-1950s. It was certainly not the first time that its characteristic questions had been put on the table. Quite the contrary. The two books which helped to stake out the new terrain — [Richard] Hoggart's *Uses of Literacy* [1957] and [Raymond] Williams's *Culture and Society* [1958] — were both, in different ways, works (in part) of recovery. Hoggart's book took its reference from the "cultural debate," long sustained in the arguments around "mass society" and in the tradition of work identified with [F. R.] Leavis and *Scrutiny*. *Culture and Society* reconstructed a long tradition which Williams defined as consisting, in sum, of "a record of a number of important and continuing reactions to . . . changes in our social, economic and political life" and offering "a special kind of map by means of which the nature of the changes can be explored" (p.16). The books looked, at first, simply like updating of these earlier concerns, with reference to the post-war world. Retrospectively, their "breaks" with the traditions of thinking in which they were situated seem as important, if not more so, than their continuity with them. The *Uses of Literacy* did set out — much in the spirit of "practical criticism" — to "read" working-class culture for the values and meanings embodied in its patterns and arrangements: as if they were certain kinds of "texts." But the application of this method to a living culture, and the rejection of the terms of the "cultural debate" (polarized around the high/low culture distinction) was a thoroughgoing departure. *Culture and Society* — in one and the same movement — constituted a tradition (*the* "culture-and-society" tradition), defined its "unity" (not in terms of common positions but in its characteristic concerns and the idiom

of its inquiry), itself made a distinctive modern contribution to it — *and* wrote its epitaph. The Williams book which succeeded it — *The Long Revolution* — clearly indicated that the "culture-and-society" mode of reflection could only be completed and developed by moving somewhere else — to a significantly different kind of analysis. The very difficulty of some of the writing in *The Long Revolution* — with its attempt to "theorize" on the back of a tradition resolutely empirical and particularist in its idiom of thought, the experiential "thickness" of its concepts, and the generalizing movement of argument in it — stems, in part, from this determination to *move on* (Williams's work, right through to the most recent *Politics and Letters*, is exemplary precisely in its sustained developmentalism). The "good" and the "bad" parts of *The Long Revolution* both arise from its status as a work "of the break." The same could be said of E. P. Thompson's *Making of the English Working Class*, which belongs decisively to this "moment," even though, chronologically, it appeared somewhat later [1963]. It, too, had been "thought" within certain distinctive historical traditions: English Marxist historiography, economic and "labor" history. But in its foregrounding of the questions of culture consciousness and experience, and its accent on agency, it also made a decisive break: with a certain kind of technological evolutionism, with a reductive economism and an organizational determinism. Between them, these three books constituted the caesura out of which — among other things — "Cultural Studies" emerged.

They were, of course, seminal and formative texts. They were not, in any sense, "textbooks" for the founding of a new academic subdiscipline: nothing could have been further from their intrinsic impulse. Whether historical or contemporary in focus, they were, themselves, focused *by*, organized through and constituted responses to, the immediate pressures of the time and society in which they were written. They not only took "culture" seriously — as a dimension without which historical transformations, past and present, simply could not adequately be thought. They were, themselves, "cultural" in the *Culture and Society* sense. They forced on their readers' attention the proposition that "concentrated in the word *culture* are questions directly raised by the great historical changes which the changes in industry, democracy, and class, in their own way, represent, and to which the changes in art are a closely related response" (p. 16). This was a question for the 1960s and 70s as well as the 1860s and 70s. And this is perhaps the point to note that this line of thinking was roughly coterminous with what has been called the "agenda" of the early New Left, to which these writers, in one sense or another, belonged, and whose texts these were. This connection placed the "politics of intellectual work" squarely at the center of Cultural Studies from the beginning — a concern from which, fortunately, it has never been, and can never be, freed, in a deep sense, the "setting of accounts" in *Culture and Society*, the first part of *The Long Revolution*, Hoggart's densely particular, concrete study of some aspects of working-class culture and Thompson's historical reconstruction of the formation of a class culture and popular traditions in the 1790–1830 period formed, between them, the break, and defined the space from which a new area of study and practice opened. In terms of intellectual bearings and emphases, this was — if ever such a thing can be found — Cultural Studies' moment of "refounding." The institutionalization of Cultural Studies — first, in the Centre at Birmingham, and then in courses and publications from a variety of sources and places — with its characteristic gains and losses, belongs to the 1960s and later.

"Culture" was the site of the convergence. But what definitions of this core concept emerged from this body of work? And, since this line of thinking has decisively shaped Cultural Studies, and represents the most formative *indigenous* or "native" tradition, around what space were its concerns and concepts unified? The fact is that no single, unproblematic definition of "culture" is to be found here. The concept remains a complex one — a site of convergent interests, rather than a logically or conceptually clarified idea. This "richness" is an area of continuing tension and difficulty in the field. It might be useful, therefore, briefly to resume the characteristic stresses and emphases through which the concept has arrived at its present state of (in)-determinacy.

(The characterizations which follow are, necessarily crude and over-simplified, synthesizing rather than carefully analytic.) Two main problematics only are discussed. Two rather different ways of conceptualizing "culture" can be drawn out of the many suggestive formulations in Raymond Williams's *Long Revolution*. The first relates "culture" to the sum of the available descriptions through which societies make sense of and reflect their common experiences. This definition takes up the earlier stress on "ideas," but subjects it to a thorough reworking. The conception of "culture" is itself democratized and socialized. It no longer consists of the sum of the "best that has been thought and said," regarded as the summits of an achieved civilization — that ideal of perfection to which, in earlier usage, all aspired. Even "art" — assigned in the earlier framework a privileged position, as touchstone of the highest values of civilization — is now redefined as only one, special form of a general social process: the giving and taking of meanings, and the slow development of "common" meanings — a common culture: "culture," in this special sense, "is ordinary" (to borrow the title of one of Williams's earlier attempts to make his general position more widely accessible). If even the highest, most refined of descriptions offered in works of literature are also "part of the general process which creates conventions and institutions, through which the meanings that are valued by the community are shared and made active" (p. 55), then there is no way in which this process can be hived off or distinguished or set apart from the other practices of the historical process: "Since our way of seeing things is literally our way of living, the process of communication is in fact the process of community: the sharing of common meanings, and thence common activities and purposes; the offering, reception and comparison of new meanings, leading to tensions and achievements of growth and change" (p. 55). Accordingly, there is no way in which the communication of descriptions, understood in this way, can be set aside and compared externally with other things. "If the art is part of society, there is no solid whole, outside it, to which, by the form of our question, we concede priority. The art is there, as an activity, with the production, the trading, the politics, the raising of families. To study the relations adequately we must study them actively, seeing all activities as particular and contemporary forms of human energy."

If this first emphasis takes up and reworks the connotation of the term "culture" with the domain of "ideas," the second emphasis is more deliberately anthropological, and emphasizes that aspect of "culture" which refers to social *practices*. It is from this second emphasis that the somewhat simplified definition — "culture is a whole way of life" — has been rather too neatly abstracted. Williams did relate this aspect of the concept to the more "documentary" — that is, descriptive, even ethnographic — usage of the term. But the earlier definition seems to me the more central one, into which "way of life" is integrated. The important point in the argument rests on the active and indissoluble relationships between elements or social practices normally separated out. It is in *this* context that the "theory of culture" is defined as "the study of relationships between elements in a whole way of life." "Culture" is not *a* practice; nor is it simply the descriptive sum of the "mores and folkways" of societies — as it tended to become in certain kinds of anthropology. It is threaded through *all* social practices, and is the sum of their interrelationship. The question of what, then, is studied, and how, resolves itself. The "culture" is those patterns of organization, those characteristic forms of human energy which can be discovered as revealing themselves — in "unexpected identities and correspondence" as well as in "discontinuities of an unexpected kind" (p. 63) — within or underlying *all* social practices. The analysis of culture is, then, "the attempt to discover the nature of the organization which is the complex of these relationships." It begins with "the discovery of patterns of a characteristic kind." One will discover them, not in the art, production, trading, politics, the raising of families, treated as separate activities, but through "studying a general organization in a particular example" (p. 61). Analytically, one must study "the relationships between these patterns." The purpose of the analysis is to grasp how the interactions between all these practices and patterns are lived and experienced as a whole, in any particular period. This is its "structure of feeling."

It is easier to see what Williams was getting at, and why he was pushed along this path, if we understand what were the problems he addressed, and what pitfalls he was trying to avoid. This is particularly necessary because *The Long Revolution* (like much of Williams's work) carries on a submerged, almost "silent" dialogue with alternative positions, which are not always as clearly identified as one would wish. There is a clear engagement with the "idealist" and "civilizing" definitions of culture — both the equation of "culture" with *ideas*, in the idealist tradition; and the assimilation of culture to an *ideal*, prevalent in the elitist terms of the "cultural debate." But there is also a more extended engagement with certain kinds of Marxism, against which Williams's definitions are consciously pitched. He is arguing against the literal operations of the base-superstructure metaphor, which in classical Marxism ascribed the domain of ideas and of meanings to the "superstructures," themselves conceived as merely reflective of and determined in some simple fashion by "the base," without a social effectivity of their own. That is to say, his argument is constructed against a vulgar materialism and an economic determinism. He offers, instead, a radical interactionism: in effect, the interaction of all practices in and with one another, skirting the problem of determinacy. The distinction between practices is overcome by seeing them all as variant forms of *praxis* — of a general human activity and energy. The underlying patterns which distinguish the complex of practices in any specific society at any specific time are the characteristic "forms of its organization" which underlie them all, and which can therefore be traced in each.

There have been several, radical revisions of this early position: and each has contributed much to the redefinition of what Cultural Studies is and should be. We have acknowledged already the exemplary nature of Williams's project, in constantly rethinking and revising older arguments — in going on thinking. Nevertheless, one is struck by a marked line of continuity through these seminal revisions. One such moment is the occasion of his recognition of

Lucien Goldmann's work,[3] and through him, of the array of Marxist thinkers who had given particular attention to superstructural forms and whose work began, for the first time, to appear in English translation in the mid-1960s. The contrast between the alternative Marxist traditions which sustained writers like Goldmann and Lukács, as compared with Williams's isolated position and the impoverished Marxist tradition he had to draw on, is sharply delineated. But the points of convergence — both what they are against, and what they are about — are identified in ways which are not altogether out of line with his earlier arguments. Here is the negative, which he sees as linking his work to Goldmann's: "I came to believe that I had to give up, or at least to leave aside, what I knew as the Marxist tradition: to attempt to develop a theory of social totality; to see the study of culture as the study of relations between elements in a whole way of life; to find ways of studying structure . . . which could stay in touch with and illuminate particular artworks and forms, but also forms and relations of more general social life; to replace the formula of base and superstructure with the more active idea of a field of mutually if also unevenly determining forces" (*NLR* [*New Left Review*] 67, May–June 1971). And here is the positive — the point where the convergence is marked between Williams's "structure of feeling" and Goldmann's "genetic structuralism": "I found in my own work that I had to develop the idea of a structure of feeling . . . But then I found Goldmann beginning . . . from a concept of structure which contained, in itself, a relation between social and literary facts. This relation, he insisted, was not a matter of content, but of mental structures: categories which simultaneously organize the empirical consciousness of a particular social group, and the imaginative world created by the writer." By definition, these structures are not individually but collectively created." The stress there on the interactivity of practices and on the underlying totalities, and the homologies between them, is characteristic and significant. "A correspondence of content between a writer and his world is less

significant than this correspondence of organization, of structure."

A second such "moment" is the point where Williams really takes on board E. P. Thompson's critique of *The Long Revolution* (cf. the review in *NLR* 9 and 10) — that no "whole way of life" is without its dimension of struggle and confrontation between opposed *ways* of life — and attempts to rethink the key issues of determination and domination via Gramsci's concept of "hegemony." This essay ("Base and Superstructure," *NLR* 82 1973) is a seminal one, especially in its elaboration of dominant, residual and emergent cultural practices, and its return to the problematic of determinacy as "limits and pressures."[4] Nonetheless, the earlier emphases recur, with force: "we cannot separate literature and art from other kinds of social practice, in such a way as to make them subject to quite special and distinct laws." And, "no mode of production, and therefore no dominant society or order of society, and therefore no dominant culture, in reality exhausts human practice, human energy, human intention." And this note is carried forward — indeed, it is radically accented — in Williams's most sustained and succinct recent statement of his position: the masterly condensations of *Marxism and Literature*. Against the structuralist emphasis on the specificity and 'autonomy' of practices, and their analytic separation of societies into their discrete instances, Williams's stress is on 'constitutive activity' in general, on 'sensuous activity' in general, on 'sensuous human activity, as practice,' from Marx's first 'thesis" on Feuerbach; on different practices conceived as a "whole indissoluble practice'; on totality.[5] "Thus, contrary to one development in Marxism, it is not 'the base' and the 'super-structure' that need to be studied, but specific and indissoluble real processes, within which the decisive relationship, from a Marxist point

[3]See the introduction to Marxist Criticism where "genetic structuralism" is discussed, p. 699.

[4]See Raymond Williams, p. 747.

[5]Marx's first "Thesis on Feuerbach" (1845) runs, in part: "The chief defect of all hitherto existing materialism (that of Feuerbach included) is that the thing, reality, sensuousness, is conceived only in the form of the object or of contemplation, but not as sensuous human activity, practice, not subjectively. Hence, in contradistinction to materialism, the active side was developed abstractly by idealism — which, of course, does not know real, sensuous activity as such."

of view, is that expressed by the complex idea of 'determination'"(*M & L*, pp. 30–31, 82).

At one level, Williams's and Thompson's work can only be said to converge around the terms of the same problematic through the operation of a violent and schematically dichotomous theorization. The organizing terrain of Thompson's work — classes as relations, popular struggle, and historical forms of consciousness, class cultures in their historical particularity — is foreign to the more reflective and "generalizing" mode in which Williams typically works. And the dialogue between them begins with a very sharp encounter. The review of *The Long Revolution*, which Thompson undertook, took Williams sharply to task for the evolutionary way in which culture as a "whole way of life" had been conceptualized; for his tendency to absorb conflicts between class cultures into the terms of an extended "conversation"; for his impersonal tone — above the contending classes, as it were; and for the imperializing sweep of his concept of "culture" (which, heterogeneously, swept everything into its orbit because it was the study of the interrelationships between the forms of energy and organization underlying *all* practices. But wasn't this — Thompson asked — where History came in?). Progressively, we can see how Williams has persistently rethought the terms of his original paradigm to take these criticisms into account — though this is accomplished (as it so frequently is in Williams) obliquely: via a particular appropriation of Gramsci, rather than in a more direct modification.

Thompson also operates with a more "classical" distinction than Williams, between "social being" and "social consciousness" (the terms he infinitely prefers, from Marx, to the more fashionable "base and superstructure"). Thus, where Williams insists on the absorption of all practices into the totality of "real, indissoluble practice," Thompson does deploy an older distinction between what is "culture" and what is "not culture." "Any theory of culture must include the concept of the dialectical interaction between culture and something that is *not* culture." Yet the definition of culture is not, after all, so far removed from Williams's: "We must suppose the raw material of life experience to be at one pole,

and all the infinitely complex human disciplines and systems, articulate and inarticulate, formalized in institutions or dispersed in the least formal ways, which 'handle,' transmit or distort this raw material to be at the other." Similarly, with respect to the commonality of "practice" which underlies all the distinct practices: "It is the active process — which is at the same time the process through which men make their history — that I am insisting upon" (*NLR* 9, p. 33, 1961). And the two positions come close together around — again — certain distinctive negatives and positives. Negatively, against the "base/superstructure" metaphor, and a reductionist or "economistic" definition of determinacy. On the first: "The dialectical intercourse between social being and social consciousness — or between 'culture' and intercourse between social being and social consciousness — or between 'culture' and '*not* culture' — is at the heart of any comprehension of the historical process within the Marxist tradition. . . . The tradition inherits a dialectic that is right, but the particular mechanical metaphor through which it is expressed is wrong. This metaphor from constructional engineering . . . must in any case be inadequate to describe the flux of conflict, the dialectic of a changing social process. . . . All the metaphors which are commonly offered have a tendency to lead the mind into schematic modes and away from the interaction of being-consciousness." And on "reductionism": "Reductionism is a lapse in historical logic by which political or cultural events are 'explained' in terms of the class affiliations of the actors. . . . But the mediation between 'interest' and 'belief' was not through Nairn's 'complex of superstructures' but through the people themselves" ("Peculiarities of the English," *Social Register*, 1965, pp. 351–352). And, more positively — a simple statement which may be taken as defining virtually the whole of Thompson's historical work, from *The Making* to *Whigs and Hunters*, *The Poverty of Theory* and beyond — "capitalist society was founded upon forms of exploitation which are simultaneously economic, moral and cultural. Take up the essential defining productive relationship . . . and turn it round, and it reveals itself now in one aspect (wage-labor), now in another (an acquisitive ethos), and now in another (the alienation of such intellectual faculties as are not required by the worker in his productive role)" (ibid., p. 356).

Here, then, despite the many significant differences, is the outline of one significant line of thinking in Cultural Studies — some would say, *the dominant paradigm*. It stands opposed to the residual and merely reflective role assigned to "the cultural." In its different ways, it conceptu- alizes culture as interwoven with all social prac- tices; and those practices, in turn, as a common form of human activity: sensuous human praxis, the activity through which men and women make history. It is opposed to the base-superstructure way of formulating the relationship between ideal and material forces, especially where the "base" is defined as the determination by "the economic" in any simple sense. It prefers the wider formulation — the dialectic between social being and social consciousness: neither separable into its distinct poles (in some alterna- tive formulations, the dialectic between "cul- ture" and "non-culture"). It defines "culture" as *both* the meanings and values which arise amongst distinctive social groups and classes, on the basis of their given historical conditions and relationships, through which they "handle" and respond to the conditions of existence; *and* as the lived traditions and practices through which those "understandings" are expressed and in which they are embodied. Williams brings together these two aspects — definitions and ways of life — around the concept of "culture" itself. Thompson brings the two elements — consciousness and conditions — around the con- cept of "experience." Both positions entail cer- tain difficult fluctuations around these key terms. Williams so totally absorbs "definitions of expe- rience" into our "ways of living," and both into an indissoluble real material practice-in-general, as to obviate any distinction between "culture" and "not-culture." Thompson sometimes uses "experience" in the more usual sense of con- sciousness, as the collective ways in which men "handle, transmit or distort" their given condi- tions, the raw materials of life; sometimes as the domain of the "lived," the mid-term between "conditions" and "culture"; and sometimes as against the objective conditions themselves —

which particular modes of consciousness are counterposed. But, whatever the terms, both positions tend to read structures of relations in terms of how they are "lived" and "experienced." Williams's "structure of feeling" — with its deliberate condensation of apparently incompat- ible elements — is characteristic. But the same is true of Thompson, despite his far fuller histori- cal grasp of the "given-ness" or structuredness of the relations and conditions into which men and women necessarily and involuntarily enter, and his clearer attention to the determinacy of productive and exploitative relations under capitalism. This is a consequence of giving culture-consciousness and experience so pivotal a place in analysis. The *experiential pull* in this paradigm, and the emphasis on the creative and on historical agency, constitute the two key elements in the *humanism* of the position outlined. Each consequently accords "experi- ence" an authenticating position in any cultural analysis. It is, ultimately, where and how people experience their conditions of life, define them and respond to them, which, for Thompson defines why every mode of production is also a culture, and every struggle between classes is always also a struggle between cultural modali- ties; and which, for Williams, is what a "cultural analysis," in the final instance, should deliver. In "experience," all the different practices inter- sect — within "culture" the different practices interact — even if on an uneven and mutu- ally determining basis. This sense of cultural totality — of *the whole* historical process — overrides any effort to keep the instances and ele- ments distinct. Their real interconnection, under given historical conditions, must be matched by a totalizing movement "in thought," in the analysis. It establishes for both the strongest protocols against any form of analytic abstrac- tion which distinguishes practices, or which sets out to test the "actual historical movement" in all its intertwined complexity and particularity by any more sustained logical or analytical opera- tion. These positions, especially in their more concrete historical rendering (*The Making, The Country and the City*) are the very opposite of a Hegelian search for underlying Essences. Yet, in their tendency to reduce practices to *praxis* and to find common and homologous "forms" underlying the most apparently differentiated areas, their movement is "essentializing." They have a particular way of understanding the totality — though it is with a small "t," concrete and historically determinate, uneven in its correspondences. They understand it "expressively." And since they constantly inflect the more traditional analysis towards the experiential level, or read the other structures and relations downwards from the vantage point of how they are "lived," they are properly (even if not adequately or fully) characterized as "culturalist" in their emphasis: even when all the caveats and qualifications against a too rapid "dichotomous theorizing" have been entered. (Cf. for "culturalism," Richard Johnson's two seminal articles on the operation of the paradigm: in "Histories of Culture/Theories of Ideology," *Ideology and Cultural Production*, eds. M. Barrett, P. Corrigan et al., Croom Helm, 1979; and "Three Problematics" in *Working Class Culture*, Clarke, Critcher and Johnson, Hutchinsons and CCCS, 1979. For the dangers in "dichotomous theorizing," cf. the Introduction, "Representaion and Cultural Production," to Barrett, Corrigan et al.)

The "culturalist" strand in Cultural Studies was interrupted by the arrival on the intellectual scene of the "structuralisms." These, possibly more varied than the "culturalisms," nevertheless shared certain positions and orientations in common which makes their designation under a single title not altogether misleading. It has been remarked that whereas the "culturalist" paradigm can be defined without requiring a conceptual reference to the term "ideology" (the *word*, of course, does appear: but it is not a key concept), the "structuralist" interventions have been largely articulated around the concept of "ideology": in keeping with its more impeccably Marxist lineage, "culture" does not figure so prominently. Whilst this may be true of the Marxist structuralists, it is at best less than half the truth about the structuralist enterprise as such. But it is now a common error to condense the latter exclusively around the impact of Althusser and all that has followed in the wake of his interventions — where "ideology" has played a seminal, but modulated role: and to omit the

significance of Lévi-Strauss.[6] Yet, in strict historical terms, it was Lévi-Strauss, and the early semiotics, which made the first break. And though the Marxist structuralisms have superseded the latter, they owed, and continue to owe, an immense theoretical debt (often fended off or downgraded into footnotes, in the search for a retrospective orthodoxy) to his work. It was Lévi-Strauss's structuralism which, in its appropriation of the linguistic paradigm, after Saussure, offered the promise to the "human sciences of culture" of a paradigm capable of rendering them scientific and rigorous in a thoroughly new way. And when, in Althusser's work, the more classical Marxist themes were recovered, it remained the case that Marx was "read" — and reconstituted — through the terms of the linguistic paradigm. In *Reading Capital*, for example, the case is made that the mode of production — to coin a phrase — could best be understood as if "structured like a language" (through the selective combination of invariant elements).[7] The a-historical and synchronic stress, against the historical emphases of "culturalism," derived from a similar source. So did a preoccupation with "the social, *sui generis*" — used not adjectivally but substantively: a usage Lévi-Strauss derived, not from Marx, but from Durkheim (the Durkheim who analyzed the social categories of thought — e.g. in *Primitive Classification* — rather than the Durkheim of *The Division of Labour*, who became the founding father of American structural-functionalism).[8]

Lévi-Strauss did, on occasion, toy with certain Marxist formulations. Thus, "Marxism, if not Marx himself, has too commonly reasoned as

[6]See the introduction to Structuralism and Deconstruction, p. 470.

[7]Hall's "structured like a language" is a quotation from Jacques Lacan; his point is that the structural Marxist Louis Althusser in effect reads Marx through Lacan. See the introduction to Psychoanalytic Theory and Criticism, p. 627, and the introduction to Marxist Criticism, p. 693.

[8]Emile Durkheim (1858–1917) was a French philosopher, not an American, and is usually spoken of as the father of sociology as a discipline. *Primitive Classification* is a collaborative work with Marcel Mausss, "De quelques formes primitives de classification: contribution à l'étude des représentations collectives." *Année sociologique* 6 (1903): 1–72. *The Division of Labor in Society* was published in 1893.

though practices followed directly from praxis. Without questioning the undoubted primacy of infrastructures, I believe that there is always a mediator between praxis and practices, namely, the conceptual scheme by the operation of which matter and form, neither with any independent existence, are realized as structures, that is as entities which are both empirical and intelligible." But this — to coin another phrase — was largely "gestural." This structuralism shared with cultur-alism a radical break with the terms of the base/superstructure metaphor, as derived from the sim-pler parts of the *German Ideology*.[9] And, though "It is to this theory of the superstructures, scarcely touched on by Marx" to which Lévi-Strauss aspired to contribute, his contribution was such as to break in a radical way with [all its] terms of reference, as finally and irrevocably as the "cultur-alists" did. Here — and we must include Althusser in this characterization—culturalists and struc-turalists alike ascribed to the domains hitherto defined as "superstructural," a specificity and effectivity, a constitutive primacy, which pushed them beyond the terms of reference of "base" and "superstructure." Lévi-Strauss and Althusser, too, were anti-reductionist and anti-economist in their very cast of thought, and critically attacked that transitive causality which, for so long, had passed itself off as "classical Marxism."

Lévi-Strauss worked consistently with the term "culture." He regarded "ideologies" as of much lesser importance; mere "secondary rationalization." Like Williams and Goldmann, he worked, not at the level of correspondences between the *content* of a practice, but at the level of their forms and structures. But the manner in which these were conceptualized was altogether at variance with either the "culturalism" of Williams or Goldmann's "genetic structural-ism." This divergence can be identified in three distinct ways. First, he conceptualized "culture" as the categories and frameworks in thought and language through which different societies clas-sified out their conditions of existence — above all (since Lévi-Strauss was an anthropologist), the relations between the human and the natural worlds. Second, he thought of the manner and

[9]See Marx, p. 247.

practice through which these categories and mental frameworks were produced and trans-formed, largely on an analogy with the ways in which language itself — the principal medium of "culture" — operated. He identified what was specific to them and their operation as the "pro-duction of meaning": they were, above all, *signi-fying* practices. Third, after some early flirtations with Durkheim and Mauss's social categories of thought, he largely gave up the question of the relation *between* signifying and non-signifying practices — between "culture" and "not-culture," to use other terms — for the sake of concentration on the *internal* relations within signifying practices by means of which the categories of meaning were produced. This left the question of determinacy, of totality, largely in abeyance. This causal logic of determinacy was abandoned in favor of a structuralist causal-ity — a logic of *arrangement*, of internal rela-tions, of articulation of parts within a structure. Each of these aspects is also positively present in Althusser's work and that of the Marxist structuralists, even when the terms of reference had been regrounded in Marx's "immense theo-retical revolution." In one of Althusser's seminal formulations about ideology — defined as the themes, concepts and representations through which men and women "live," in an imaginary relation, their relation to their real conditions of existence — we can see the skeleton outline of Lévi-Strauss's "conceptual schemes between praxis and practices." "Ideologies" are here being conceptualized, not as the contents and surface forms of ideas, but as the unconscious categories through which conditions are repre-sented and lived. We have already commented on the active presence in Althusser's thinking of the linguistic paradigm — the second element identified above. And though, in the concept of "over-determination" — one of his most seminal and fruitful contributions — Althusser did return to the problems of the relations *between* prac-tices and the question of determinacy (propos-ing, incidentally, a thoroughly novel and highly suggestive reformulation, which has received far too little subsequent attention), he did tend to reinforce the "relative autonomy" of differ-ent practices, and their internal specificities, conditions and effects at the expense of an "expressive" conception of the totality, with its typical homologies and correspondences.

Aside from the wholly distinct intellectual and conceptual universes within which these alternative paradigms developed, there were certain points where, despite their apparent overlaps, culturalism and structuralism were starkly counterposed. We can identify this counterposition at one of its sharpest points precisely around the concept of "experience," and the role the term played in each perspective. Whereas, in "culturalism," experience was the ground — the terrain of "the lived" — where consciousness and conditions intersected, structuralism insisted that "experience" could not, by definition, be the ground of anything, since one could only "live" and experience one's conditions *in and through* the categories, classifications and frameworks of the culture. These categories, however, did not arise from or in experience: rather, experience was their "effect." The culturalists had defined the forms of consciousness and culture as collective. But they had stopped far short of the radical proposition that, in culture and in language, the subject was "spoken by" the categories of culture in which he/she thought, rather than individual productions: they were *unconscious* structures. That is why, though Lévi-Strauss spoke only of "Culture," his concept provided the basis for an easy translation, by Althusser, into the conceptual framework of ideology: "Ideology is indeed a system of 'representations,' but in the majority of these cases these representations have nothing to do with 'consciousness': . . . it is above all as structures that they impose on the vast majority of men, not via their 'consciousness' . . . it is within this ideological unconsciousness that men succeed in altering the 'lived' relation between them and the world and acquiring that new form of specific unconsciousness called 'consciousness'" (*For Marx,* p. 233). It was, in this sense, that "experience" was conceived, not as an authenticating source but as an effect: not as a reflection of the real but as an "imaginary relation." It was only a short step — the one which separates *For Marx* from the "Ideological State Apparatuses" essay — to the development of an account of how this "imaginary relation" served,

not simply the dominance of a ruling class over a dominated one, but (through the reproduction of the relations of production, and the constitution of labor-power in a form fit for capitalist exploitation) the expanded reproduction of the mode of production itself. Many of the other lines of divergence between the two paradigms flow from this point: the conception of "men" as bearers of the structures that speak and place them, rather than as active agents in the making of their own history; the emphasis on a structural rather than a historical "logic"; the preoccupation with the constitution — in "theory" — of a nonideological, scientific discourse; and hence the privileging of conceptual work and of Theory as guaranteed; the recasting of history as a march of the structures (cf. passim, *The Poverty of Theory*[10]): the structuralist "machine. . . ."

There is no space in which to follow through the many ramifications which have followed from the development of one or [an]other of these "master paradigms" in Cultural Studies. Though they by no means account for all, or even nearly all, of the many strategies adopted, it is fair to say that, between them, they have defined the principal lines of development in the field. The seminal debates have been polarized around their thematics; some of the best concrete work has flowed from the efforts to set one or [an]other of these paradigms to work on particular problems and materials. Characteristically — the sectarian and self-righteous climate of critical intellectual work in England being what it is, and its dependency being so marked — the arguments and debates have most frequently been over-polarized into their extremes. At these extremities, they frequently appear only as mirror-reflections or inversions of one another. Here, the broad typologies we have been working with — for the sake of convenient exposition — become the prison-house of thought.

Without suggesting that there can be any easy synthesis between them, it might usefully be said at this point that neither "culturalism" nor "structuralism" is, in its present manifestation, adequate to the task of constructing the study of culture as a conceptually clarified and theoretically informed

[10]Book by E. P. Thompson (1978).

The great strength of the structuralisms is their stress on "determinate conditions." They remind us that, unless the dialectic really can be held, in any particular analysis, between both halves of the proposition — that "men make history . . ." on the basis of conditions which are not of their making" — the result will inevitably be a naive humanism, with its necessary consequence: a voluntarist and populist political practice. The fact that "men" can become conscious of their conditions, organize to struggle against them and in fact transform them — without which no active politics can even be conceived, let alone practiced — must not be allowed to override the awareness of the fact that, in capitalist relations, men and women are placed and positioned in relations which constitute them as agents. "Pessimism of the intellect, optimism of the will" is a better starting point than a simple heroic affirmation. Structuralism does enable us to begin to think — as Marx insisted — of the *relations* of a structure on the basis of something other than their reduction to relationships between "people." This was Marx's privileged level of abstraction: that which enabled him to break with the obvious but incorrect starting point of "political economy," — bare individuals.

But this connects with a second strength: the recognition by structuralism not only of the necessity of abstraction as the instrument of thought through which "real relations" are appropriated, but also of the presence, in Marx's work, of a continuous and complex move-ment *between different levels of abstraction.* It is, of course, the case — as "culturalism" argues — that, in historical reality, practices do not appear neatly distinguished out into their respective instances. However, to think about or to analyze the complexity of the real, the act or practice of thinking is required; and this neces-sitates the use of the power of abstraction and analysis, the formation of concepts with which to cut into the complexity of the real, in order precisely to reveal and bring to light relation-ships and structures which cannot be visible to the naive naked eye, and which can neither

present nor authenticate themselves: "In the analysis of economic forms, neither micro-scopes nor chemical reagents are of assistance. The power of abstraction must replace both." Of course, structuralism has frequently taken this proposition to its extreme. Because thought is impossible without "the power of abstrac-tion," it has confused this with giving an abso-lute primacy to the level of the formation of concepts — and at the highest, most abstract level of abstraction only: Theory with a capital "T" then becomes judge and jury. But this is pre-cisely to lose the insight just won from Marx's own practice. For it is clear in, for example, *Capital,* that the *method* — whilst, of course, taking place "in thought" (as Marx asked in the 1857 Introduction, where else?) — rests, not on the simple exercise of abstraction but on the movement and relations which the argument is constantly establishing between *different levels* of abstraction: at each, the premises in play must be distinguished from those which — for the sake of the argument — have to be held constant. The movement to another level of magnification (to deploy the microscope meta-phor) requires the specifying of further condi-tions of existence not supplied at a previous, more abstract level: in this way, by succes-sive abstractions of different magnitudes, to *move towards* the constitution, the *reproduc-tion,* of "the concrete in thought" as an effect of a certain kind of thinking. This method is adequately represented in *neither* the absolut-ism of Theoretical Practice, in structuralism, nor in the anti-abstraction "Poverty of Theory" position into which, in reaction, culturalism appears to have been driven or driven itself. Nevertheless it is intrinsically *theoretical,* and must be. Here, structuralism's insistence that thought does not reflect reality, but is articu-lated on and appropriates it, is a necessary starting point. An adequate *working through of* the consequences of this argument might begin to produce a method which takes us outside the permanent oscillations between abstraction/ anti-abstraction and the false dichotomies of Theoreticism vs. Empiricism which have both marked and disfigured the structuralism-culturalism encounter to date.

Stucturalism has another strength, in its conception of "the whole." There is a sense in which, though culturalism constantly insists on the radical particularity of its practices, its mode of conceptualizing the "totality" has something of the complex simplicity of an expressive totality behind it. Its complexity is constituted by the fluidity with which practices move into and out of one another: but this complexity is reducible, conceptually, to the "simplicity" of praxis — human activity, as such — in which the same contradictions constantly appear, homologously reflected in each. Structuralism goes too far in erecting the machine of a "Structure," with its self-generating propensities (a "Spinozean eternity," whose function is only the sum of its effects: a truly structural*ist* deviation), equipped with its distinctive instances. Yet it represents an advance over culturalism in the conception it has of the necessary *complexity* of the unity of a structure (over-determination being a more successful way of thinking this complexity than the combinatory invariance of structuralist causality). Moreover, it has the conceptual ability to think of a unity which is constructed through the *differences* between, rather than the homology of, practices. Here, again, it has won a critical insight about Marx's method: one thinks of the complex passages of the 1857 Introduction to the *Grundrisse* where Marx demonstrates how it is possible to think of the "unity" of a social formation as constructed, not out of identity but out of *difference*.[11] Of course, the stress on difference can — and has — led the structuralisms into a fundamental conceptual heterogeneity, in which all sense of structure and totality is lost. Foucault and other post-Althussereans have taken this devious path into the absolute, not the relative, autonomy of practices, via their necessary heterogeneity and "necessary non-correspondence." But the emphasis on unity-in-difference, on complex unity — Marx's concrete as the "unity of many determinations" — can be worked in another, and ultimately more fruitful,

direction: towards the problematic of relative autonomy and "over-determination," and the study of *articulation*. Again, articulation contains the danger of a high formalism. But it also has the considerable advantage of enabling us to think of how specific practices (articulated around contradictions which do not all arise in the same way, at the same point, in the same moment), can nevertheless be thought *together*. The structuralist paradigm thus does — if properly developed — enable us to begin really to *conceptualize* the specificity of different practices (analytically distinguished, abstracted out), without losing its grip on the ensemble which they constitute. Culturalism constantly affirms the specificity of different practices — "culture" must not be absorbed into "the economic": but it lacks an adequate way of establishing this specificity theoretically.

The third strength which structuralism exhibits lies in its decentering of "experience" and its seminal work in elaborating the neglected category of "ideology." It is difficult to conceive of a Cultural Studies thought within a Marxist paradigm which is innocent of the category of "ideology." Of course, culturalism constantly makes reference to this concept: but it does not in fact lie at the center of its conceptual universe. The authenticating power and reference of "experience" imposes a barrier between culturalism and a proper conception of "ideology." Yet, without it, the effectivity of "culture" for the reproduction of a particular mode of production cannot be grasped. It is true that there is a marked tendency in the more recent structuralist conceptualizations of "ideology" to give it a functionalist reading — as the necessary cement of the social formation. From this position, it is indeed impossible — as culturalism would correctly argue — to conceive either of ideologies which are not, by definition, "dominant": or of the concept of struggle (the latter's appearance in Althusser's famous ISA's[12] article being — to coin yet another phrase — largely "gestural"). Nevertheless, work is already being done which suggests ways in which the field of ideology may be adequately conceptualized as a

[11]Hall may be thinking of this sentence from the *Grundrisse*: "The conclusion we reach is not that production, distribution, exchange and consumption are identical, but that they all form the members of a totality, distinctions within a unity."

[12]Hall refers to Althusser's article, "Ideology and Ideological State Apparatuses"; see p. 738.

terrain of struggle (through the work of Gramsci, and more recently, of Laclau),[13] and these have structuralist rather than culturalist bearings.

Culturalism's strengths can almost be derived from the weaknesses of the structuralism posi-tion already noted, and from the latter's strategic absences and silences. It has insisted, correctly, on the affirmative moment of the development of conscious struggle and organization as a neces-sary element in the analysis of history, ideology and consciousness: against its persistent down-grading in the structuralist paradigm. Here, again, it is largely Gramsci who has provided us with a set of more refined terms through which to link the largely 'unconscious' and given cultural cat-egories of 'common sense' with the formation of more active and organic ideologies, which have the capacity to intervene in the ground of com-mon sense and popular traditions and, through such interventions, to organize masses of men and women. In this sense, culturalism properly restores the dialectic between the unconscious-ness of cultural categories and the moment of conscious organization: even if, in its character-istic movement, it has tended to match structur-alism's over-emphasis on 'conditions' with an altogether too-inclusive emphasis on 'conscious-ness.' It therefore not only recovers — as the necessary moment of any analysis — the process by means of which classes-in-themselves, defined primarily by the way in which economic rela-tions position 'men' as agents — become active historical and political forces — for themselves: it also — against its own anti-theoretical good sense — *requires* that, when properly developed, each moment must be understood in terms of the level of abstraction at which the analysis is oper-ating. Again, Gramsci has begun to point a way through this false polarization in his discussion of 'the passage between the structure and the sphere of the complex superstructures,' and its distinct forms and moments.

We have concentrated in this argument largely on a characterization of what seem to us to be the two seminal paradigms at work in Cultural

[13]Ernesto Laclau, Argentine political theorist, author of *Politics and Ideology in Marxist Theory* (1977), well-known today for his collaborative work with Chantal Mouffe.

Studies. Of course, they are by no means the only active ones. New developments and lines of think-ing are by no means adequately netted with refer-ence to them. Nevertheless, these paradigms can, in a sense, be deployed to measure what appear to us to be the radical weaknesses or inadequacies of those which offer themselves as alternative rallying-points. Here, briefly, we identify three.

The first is that which follows on from Lévi-Strauss, early semiotics and the terms of the linguistic paradigm, and the centering on 'signi-fying practices,' moving by way of psychoana-lytic concepts and Lacan to a radical recentering of virtually the whole terrain of Cultural Studies around the terms 'discourse' and 'the subject.' One way of understanding this line of thinking is to see it as an attempt to fill that empty space in early structuralism (of both the Marxist and non-Marxist varieties) where, in earlier discourses, 'the subject' and subjectivity might have been expected to appear but did not. This is, of course, precisely one of the key points where culturalism brings its pointed criticisms to bear on structural-ism's 'process without a subject.' The difference is that, whereas culturalism would correct for the hyper-structuralism of earlier models by restor-ing the unified subject (collective or individual) of consciousness at the center of 'the Structure,' discourse theory, by way of the Freudian con-cepts of the unconscious and the Lacanian con-cepts of how subjects are constituted in language (through the entry into the Symbolic and the Law of Culture), restores the *decentered* subject, the contradictory subject, as a set of positions in language and knowledge, from which culture can appear to be enunciated. This approach clearly identifies a gap, not only in structuralism but in Marxism itself. The problem is that the manner in which this 'subject' of culture is conceptualized is of a transhistorical and 'universal' character: it addresses the subject-in-general, not historically determinate social subjects, or socially determi-nate particular languages. Thus it is incapable, so far, of moving its in-general propositions to the level of concrete historical analysis. The second difficulty is that the processes of contradiction and struggle — lodged by early structuralism wholly at the level of 'the structure,' — are now, by one of those persistent mirror-inversions, lodged exclusively at the level of the unconscious processes of the subject. It may be, as culturalism often argues, that the "subjective" is a necessary moment of any such analysis. But this is a very different proposition from dismantling the whole of the social processes of particular modes of production and social formations, and reconstituting them exclusively at the level of unconscious psychoanalytic processes. Though important work has been done, both within this paradigm and to define and develop it, its claims to have replaced *all* the terms of the earlier paradigms with a more adequate set of concepts seems wildly over-ambitious. Its claims to have integrated Marxism into a more adequate materialism is, largely, a semantic rather than a conceptual claim.

A second development is the attempt to return to the terms of a moral classical "political economy" of culture. This position argues that the concentration on the cultural and ideological aspects has been wildly overdone. It would restore the older terms of "base/superstructure," finding, in the last-instance determination of the cultural-ideological by the economic, that hierarchy of determinations which both alternatives appear to lack. This position insists that the economic processes and structures of cultural production are more significant than their cultural-ideological aspect; and that these are quite adequately caught in the more classical terminology of profit, exploitation, surplus-value and the analysis of culture as commodity. It retains a notion of ideology as "false consciousness."

There is, of course, some strength to the claim that both structuralism and culturalism, in their different ways, have neglected the economic analysis of cultural and ideological production. All the same, with the return to this more "classical" terrain, many of the problems which originally beset it also reappear. The specificity of the effect of the cultural and ideological dimension once more tends to disappear. It tends to conceive the economic level as not only a "necessary" but a "sufficient" explanation of cultural and ideological effects. Its focus on the analysis of the commodity form, similarly, blurs all the carefully established distinctions between different practices, since it is the most *generic* aspects of the commodity-form which attract attention. Its deductions are therefore, largely, confined to an epochal level of abstraction: the generalizations about the commodity-form hold true throughout the capitalist epoch as a whole. Very little by way of concrete and conjunctural analysis can be derived at this high-level "logic of capital" form of abstraction. It also tends to its own kind of functionalism — a functionalism of "logic" rather than of "structure" or history. This approach, too, has insights which are well worth following through. But it sacrifices too much of what has been painfully secured, without a compensating gain in explanatory power.

The third position is closely related to the structuralist enterprise, but has followed the path of "difference" through into a radical heterogeneity. Foucault's work — currently enjoying another of those uncritical periods of discipleship through which British intellectuals reproduce today their dependency on yesterday's French ideas — has had an exceedingly positive effect: above all because in suspending the nearly-insoluble problems of determination Foucault has made possible a welcome return to the concrete analysis of particular ideological and discursive formations, and the sites of their elaboration. Foucault and Gramsci between them account for much of the most productive work on *concrete analysis* now being undertaken in the field: thereby reinforcing and — paradoxically — supporting the sense of the concrete historical instance which has always been one of culturalism's principal strengths. But, again, Foucault's example is positive only if his general epistemological position is not swallowed whole. For in fact Foucault so resolutely suspends judgment, and adopts so thoroughgoing a skepticism about any determinacy or relationship between practices, other than the largely contingent, that we are entitled to see him, not as an agnostic on these questions but as deeply committed to the necessary non-correspondence of all practices to one another. From such a position neither a social formation, nor the State can be adequately thought. And indeed Foucault is constantly falling into the pit which he has dug for himself. For when — against his well-defended epistemological positions — he stumbles across certain "correspondences" (for example, the simple fact that all the major moments of transition he has traced in each of his studies — on the prison, sexuality, medicine, the asylum, language and political economy — all appear to converge around exactly that point where industrial capitalism and the bourgeoisie make their fateful, historical rendezvous), he lapses into a vulgar reductionism, which thoroughly belies the sophisticated positions he has elsewhere advanced.[14]

I have said enough to indicate that, in my view, the line in Cultural Studies which has attempted to *think forward* from the best elements in the structuralist and culturalist enterprises, by way of some of the concepts elaborated in Gramsci's work, comes closest to meeting the requirements of the field of study. And the reason for that should by now also be obvious. Though neither structuralism nor culturalism will do, as self-sufficient paradigms of study, they have a centrality to the field which all the other contenders lack because (in their divergences as well as their convergences) they address what must be the *core problem* of Cultural Studies. They constantly return us to the

terrain marked out by those strongly coupled but not mutually exclusive concepts culture/ideology. They pose, together, the problems consequent on trying to think *both* the specificity of different practices and the forms of the articulated unity they constitute. They make a constant, if flawed return to the base/superstructure metaphor. They are correct in insisting that this question — which resumes all the problems of a nonreductive determinacy — is the heart of the matter: and that, on the solution of this problem will turn the capacity of Cultural Studies to supersede the endless oscillations between idealism and reductionism they confront — even if in radically opposed ways — the dialectic between conditions and consciousness. At another level, they pose the question of the relation between the logic of thinking and the "logic" of historical process. They continue to hold out the promise of a properly materialist theory of culture. In their sustained and mutually reinforcing antagonisms they hold out no promise of an easy synthesis. But, between them, they define where, if at all, is the space, and what are the limits, within which such a synthesis might be constituted. In Cultural Studies, theirs are the "names of the game."

[14]He is quite capable of wheeling in through the back door the classes he recently expelled from the front. [Hall]

Nancy Armstrong

b. 1938

The American scholar who has perhaps done the most to breach the barrier between feminism and cultural studies, Nancy Armstrong attended Wellesley College for two years, had three children in rapid succession, completed her B.A. at the State University of New York at Buffalo, and left, children in tow, for the Ph.D. program at the University of Wisconsin–Madison in 1967. Before receiving her doctorate in 1977, she taught on a Fulbright Fellowship in Portugal at the University of Coimbra, where she tries to return every two or three years. Since then, she has taught at Wayne State University, the State University of New York at Buffalo, the University of Minnesota, and Yale, Wesleyan, and Brown Universities. She is currently Gilbert, Louis, and Edward Lehrman Professor of English at Duke University. Her books include two collections of essays edited with Leonard Tennenhouse: The Ideology of Conduct: Essays on Literature and the History of Sexuality *(1986) and* The Violence of Representation *(1989);* Desire and Domestic Fiction: A Political History of the Novel *(1987),* The Imaginary Puritan: Literature, Intellectual Labor, and the Origins of Personal Life *(with Leonard Tennenhouse, 1992);* Fiction in the Age of Photography *(1997) and* How Novels Think: The Limits of British Individualism 1719–1900 *(2005). "Some Call It Fiction" was originally presented to the Focused Research Program in Gender and Women's Studies at the University of California at Irvine during 1985–88, before being published in Juliet Flower MacCannell's collection of papers from that program,* The Other Perspective in Gender and Culture *(1990).*

Some Call It Fiction: On the Politics of Domesticity

It is queer how out of touch with truth women are. They live in a world of their own, and there has never been anything like it, and never can be.
— JOSEPH CONRAD, *Heart of Darkness*

For some years now, American scholars have been puzzling out the relationship between literature and history. Apparently the right connections were not made when literary histories were first compiled. Yet in turning to the question of how some of the most famous British novelists were linked to their moment in time, I have found I must begin at step one, with extremely powerful conventions of representation. Though old and utterly familiar, nothing new has taken their place. Their potency has not diminished in this country despite the theory revolution and the calls for a new literary history that came in its wake. The conventions to which I refer are many and various indeed, but all reinforce the assumption that history consists of economic or political events, as if these were essentially different from other cultural events. Some of us — a distinct minority, to be sure — feel that to proceed on this assumption is to brush aside most of the activities composing everyday life and so shrink the category of "the political" down to a very limited set of cultural practices. And then, having classified most of our symbolic activities as "personal," "social," or "cultural" (it is all much the same), traditional histories would have us place them in a secondary relationship either to the economy or to the official institu- tions of state. This essay is written in opposi- tion to models of history that confine political practices to activities directly concerned with the marketplace, the official institutions of the state, or else resistance to these. I write as one who feels that such models have not provided an ade- quate basis for understanding the formation of a modern bureaucratic culture or for our place, as intellectuals, within it. More than that, I regard any model that places personal life in a separate sphere and that grants literature a secondary and passive role in political history as unconsciously sexist. I believe such models necessarily fail to account for the formation of a modern bureau- cratic culture because they fail to account for the place of women within it.

Some of our best theorizers of fiction's relation- ship to history — Raymond Williams in England and Edward Said[1] in the United States — have done much to tear down the barrier between culture and state. They demonstrate that the middle-class hegemony succeeded in part because it constructed separate historical narratives for self and society, family and factory, literature and his- tory. They suggest that by maintaining these divi- sions within culture, liberal intellectuals continue to sanitize certain areas of culture — namely, the personal, domestic, and literary. The practices that go by these names consequently appear to be benignly progressive, in their analyses, to provide a place of escape from the political world, and even to offer forms of resistance. Still, I would argue, such efforts as those of Williams and Said will be only partially successful so long as they continue to ignore *the sexual division of labor* that underwrites and naturalizes the difference between culture and politics.

THE LIMITS OF POLITICAL HISTORY

To put some life into all these abstractions, let me now turn to domestic fiction and the difficulties that scholars encounter when they try to place writing of this kind in history. Ian Watt convincingly describes the socioeconomic

[1] See Williams, p. 747, and Said, p. 1066.

character of the new readership for whom Defoe, Richardson, and Fielding wrote, a readership whose rise in turn gave rise to the novel. But Watt has no similar explanation for Austen. Her popularity he ascribes to her talent, and her talent, to nature. And so he concludes that nature must have given Austen a good eye for detail.[2] Although Williams moves well beyond such reflection theories in his ground-breaking account of the information revolution, his model of history ultimately serves us no better than Watt's when it comes to explaining domestic fiction. His *Long Revolution* regards intellectual labor as a political force in its own right without which capitalism could not have unfolded as smoothly and completely as it appears to have done. But however much power Williams grants this domain, it belongs to culture and, as such, exists in a secondary relationship with political history. To historicize writing, he feels com- pelled to give it a source in events outside of and prior to writing. He does not entertain the pos- sibility that the classic unfolding of capitalism was predicated on writing, much less on writing by women or writing that appealed to the inter- ests of a female readership.[3] For Williams as for

[2] Ian Watt, *The Rise of the Novel* (Berkeley: University of California Press, 1957), p. 57. [Armstrong]

[3] In *The Long Revolution* (New York: Columbia University Press, 1961), Williams sets out to show how the "creative" or cultural dimension of social experience opposed exist- ing forms of political authority during the seventeenth and eighteenth centuries and won. Part one of his book indeed gives culture priority over the official institutions of state (as it must during the eighteenth century), claiming that cultural history "is more than a department, a special area of change. In this creative area the changes and conflicts of the whole way of life are necessarily involved" (p. 122). But latent in this promise to extend the category of "the political" broadly to include "the whole way of life" is the contradictory sug- gestion that political practices are also a special category of "the whole." The second notion of politics emerges in part two, where Williams describes such historical processes as the growth of the reading public, of the popular press, and of standard English through which the new middle classes con- verted the power of language into economic power. Here the narrow definition of political events, as those which take place in the houses of government, the courts, and the marketplace, assumes control over the "creative" cultural dimension of social experience. For example, Williams writes, "as 1688 is a significant political date, so 1695 is significant in the history of the press. For in that year Parliament declined to renew

Watt, historical events take place in the official institutions of state or else through resistance to these institutions, and both forms of power are exercised primarily through men.

I have found Watt and Williams especially helpful for establishing links between the history of fiction and the rise of the new middle classes in England. At the same time, I am perplexed to find that, in establishing a relationship between writing and political history, these otherwise conscientious scholars completely neglect to account for the most obvious fact of all, namely, that sometime during the eighteenth century, in the words of Virginia Woolf, "the middle class woman began to write."[4] If, as Watt and Williams say, the rise of the novel was directly related to the rise of the new middle classes, then some of our best literary evidence suggests that the rise of the novel was related to the emergence of women's writing as well. In drawing this equation, of course, I have doubled the difficulties entailed in historicizing fiction, for I have suggested that to historicize fiction we must politicize not only intellectual labor but female labor as well. Much of British fiction exists at the intersection of these two definitively modern subsets of culture and is thereby twice removed from the mainstream of political history.

The writing I call domestic fiction is gender-inflected writing. Unlike the work of earlier women of letters, it comes to us as women's writing. In designating certain forms of writing as feminine, it designates other writing as masculine. The enclosure that marks a Jane Austen novel does not simply distinguish her "world" from that of a Shakespeare, a Blake, a Dickens, or a Yeats. The boundaries it constructs between inside and outside are personal in a far more wide-reaching and historically significant way.

They mark the difference between the world over which women novelists have authority — the domain of the personal — and that which is ruled by men and their politics. In doing this, Austen makes Richardson the father of the novel, for, like him, she identifies the work of the novelist with the writing of women as well as with other forms of labor that are suitably feminine.[5] To move beyond the impasse that prevents us from situating this work in history, we have, it seems to me, to toss out the idea that the gendering of vast areas of culture was a consequence of political events over which men had control. To consider gender itself as a political formation over which modern cultures gave women authority, we will have to invert these priorities. Having done so, one comes face to face with the possibility that a revolution in the home preceded the spread of the factory system and all that hinged

[5]For an account of the early eighteenth-century tradition that links the novel to criminal culture, see Lennard Davis, *Factual Fictions: The Origins of the English Novel* (New York: Columbia University Press, 1983), pp. 123–37. For the objection to novels because of their quasi-erotic appeal, see John Richetti, *Popular Fiction Before Richardson's Narrative Patterns, 1700–1734* (Oxford: Clarendon, 1969). In an issue of Addison's *Spectator,* for example, Mr. Spectator warns readers about the perils of May, advising that women "be in a particular Manner how they meddle with Romances, Chocolates, Novels, and the like inflamers, which I look upon to be very dangerous to be made use of during this great Carnival of Nature," quoted in *Four Before Richardson: Selected English Novels, 1720–1727,* William H. McBurney, ed. (Lincoln: University of Nebraska Press, 1963), p. ix. Toward the end of the eighteenth century, however, one discovers a good number of pedagogical treatises echo Austen's *Northanger Abbey* in advocating certain works of fiction as the fitting way to occupy leisure time. The fiction that was supposed to have a salutary effect on young women was either produced by lady novelists that gained currency during the age of Burney and the other lady novelists or else by earlier novelists who celebrated the same domestic virtues and saw the same form of domestic happiness as the ultimate reward for demonstrating these virtues. It was during this time, as Homer O. Brown explains, that certain novels were published under the editorship of Scott and Barbauld and marked as polite reading, and on the basis of this limited and anomalous body of works, a history of the novel was constructed backward in time (from his book in progress, *Institutions of the English Novel in the Eighteenth Century*). [Armstrong.] See Homer Obed Brown, *Institutions of the English Novel from Defoe to Scott* (Philadelphia: University of Pennsylvania Press, 1997).

---

the 1662 Licensing Act, and the stage for expansion was now fully set" (p. 180). Had Williams actually gathered data that would compose the record of "the whole" of life, he might have broken out of this circle. But, in producing cultural histories, he invariably bows to tradition and stops before entering into the female domain. [Armstrong]

[4]Virginia Woolf, *A Room of One's Own* (New York: Harcourt, Brace and World, 1975), p. 69. [Armstrong] See Woolf in this text, p. 370.

upon its becoming the means of distributing the wealth of the nation.[6]

To deal with this possibility, I begin with the proposition Marx put forth in *The German Ideology* and Gramsci[7] later developed into the concept of "hegemony" in his essays on the formation of intellectuals and the organization of culture and education: no political revolution is complete without a cultural revolution. To dominate, the dominant group must offer to one and all a view that makes their form of domination seem true and necessary if not desirable and right. Gramsci developed the contradiction inherent in Marx's notion of labor — that labor was not only a commodity, but also a social practice — into a theory that stressed the double-sidedness of middle-class power: it controlled not only the physical dimension of production but also the social dimension. During the twentieth century, moreover, Gramsci could see that a form of power that worked through spatial location, supervision, and individuals' relationship with machines was giving way to something more ubiquitous — bureaucratic control that divided and hierarchized individuals so as to place their labor on separate social planes. And indeed, as the wage was generalized to include members of this and other bureaucracies, those who performed productive labor shrank in number and importance.

More recently, therefore, a number of us who work in the humanities and social sciences have begun to feel theories of resistance which depend upon an essentialized class or, for that matter, any other essentialized group will no longer do. Once taken up by theory, such essentialisms quickly cease to represent the possibility of power coalescing outside a pluralistic society. Rather, they identify contradictory positions within that system and, in so doing, only supply more differences in a differential system that exists on an abstract plane of ideas. The system to which I refer is no system in the abstract, however, but the disciplinary institution itself. Slouching by way of homology from one cultural site to another, it has achieved the status of a paradigm. In its atomizing structure, political issues get lost. Everything matters. All truths are equivalent — only some are more complex and, in this respect alone, more satisfying than others. In the maze of differences, the difference between positive and negative has all but disappeared, and the paradise of liberalism seems near at hand.[8]

[6]A number of social historians have suggested that the factory system, and with it the economic domination of the new middle classes, was stalled until the beginning of the nineteenth century. In *The Making of the English Working Class* (New York: Random House, 1966) p. 198, E. P. Thompson suggests that fear of Jacobinism produced a new alignment between landowners and industrialists that divided the traditional resistance to industrialization. In *The Machinery Question and the Making of Political Economy* (Cambridge: Cambridge University Press, 1980), Maxine Berg explains how the development of political economy as a problem-solving logic at the end of the eighteenth century helped to make industrialization seem like an answer rather than a problem to be avoided at all costs. It was under such conditions that various authors first saw how many people had economic interests in common with the industrialists and described them as a class. In *Desire and Domestic Fiction: A Political History of the Novel* (New York: Oxford University Press, 1987), I carry this argument further by suggesting that well before they felt they had economic interests in common, numerous social groups ranging between the lower gentry and skilled workers were persuaded, in large part by authors unknown to us today, to buy into a single notion of personal life that centered around the kind of woman one desired to marry and the sort of happiness she would provide (pp. 59–95). [Armstrong]

[7]See the introduction to Marxist Criticism, p. 693.

[8]In discussing Feuerbach, Marx not only stresses that the "ruling ideas" of an epoch are the ideas of a ruling class who "regulate the production and distribution of ideas of their age" (p. 64). He also speculates that during the modern epoch, the production and distribution of ideas (i.e., the production of consciousness) will become increasingly important to the preservation of the bourgeois "state" and to its eventual disintegration or overthrow. *The German Ideology*, Part One, C. J. Arthur, ed. (New York: International Publishers, 1985). Without sliding back into the idealist philosophy from which Marx sought to rescue "the production of ideas," Gramsci applies the contradiction inherent in Marx's notion of labor to intellectual labor. The intellectual does not necessarily identify with the ruling class by reproducing the ideas inherited from the past but at certain moments may expand their political horizon by lending unity and coherence to the view of an emergent group, *The Modern Prince and Other Writings* (New York: International Publishers, 1957). In *Hegemony and Socialist Strategy*, Winston Moore and Paul Cammack, trs. (London: Verso, 1985), Ernesto Laclau and Chantal Mouffe update this principle for a postmodern society by broadening Gramsci's notions of both power and resistance. Where the

So perceiving *her* historical moment, one can consider in a radically materialist light the Foucauldian propositions that the modern state was called into being in writing, exists mainly as a state of mind, and perpetuates itself through the well orchestrated collection, regulation, and dissemination of information. The idea of order that Foucault sometimes calls "discourse" or "power" and at other times names "sexuality" or "discipline" is indeed a ruling idea. But in a world that is ruled more surely by ideas than by physical or economic means, one has to be especially careful not to hypothesize some corresponding "reality" as their source. We cannot grant these ideas the autonomy, universality, and mystic interconnection that they have achieved, but neither can we seek out some more primary truth behind or below them. Rather, we must understand them, as Foucault suggests, as the self-conception of a class that has achieved hegemony. And hegemony in the case of modern post-industrial societies, depends on self-conceptions capable of swallowing up all opposition in a single system of micro-differences.

The power of the system depends upon the production of a particular form of consciousness that is at once unique and standardizing. In place of what he calls the "repressive hypothesis," the assumption that culture either "suppresses" or "imposes itself on" the individual's desire, Foucault offers a productive hypothesis that turns this commonplace on its ear. The first volume of *The History of Sexuality* argues that the very forms of subjectivity we consider most essential to ourselves as selves had no existence prior to their symbolization, that the deepest and most private recesses of our being are culturally produced.[9] His *Discipline and Punish* mounts a detailed historical argument to show that the truth of the modern individual existed first as writing, before she or he was transformed successively into speech, thought, and unconscious desire.[10] Thus Foucault enables us to see the European Enlightenment as a revolution in words, which gave writing a new and awesome power over the world of objects as it shaped the individuals who established a relationship with that world through reading. In England, I would like to suggest, this cultural revolution was the only kind of revolution to occur during the eighteenth century, because in England the revolution in words took a form that prevented popular revolution.[11]

Having torn down the conceptual barrier between writing and political history, we have cleared the way to see the intellectual labor of women as part of the mainstream of political events. Foucault will not help us achieve this particular step, however. His *History of Sexuality* is not concerned with the history of gender. Nor does it deal with the role that writing for, by, and about women played in the history of sexuality. For this reason, his procedures cannot identify the decisive events that detached family life from politics, and these are the very events that tie the formation of a domestic domain to the development of an institutional culture in England. Foucault's *Discipline and Punish* overlooks the

[9] Michel Foucault, *The History of Sexuality*, vol. 1, *An Introduction*, Robert Hurley, tr. (New York: Pantheon, 1978). [Armstrong] See Foucault in this text, p. 972.

[10] *Discipline and Punish: The Birth of the Prison*. Alan Sheridan, tr. (New York: Vintage, 1979). All citations are to this edition. [Armstrong]

[11] In *The Imaginary Puritan: Literature and the Origins of Personal Life* (forthcoming), Leonard Tennenhouse and I explain at length how the English Revolution failed to produce the base transformations that mark political revolution. We argue for a more adequate definition of the political, showing that while political change, in the narrow sense of the term, failed to occur, cultural change was profound and lasting. Before the modern middle classes gained economic control, and well before they gained control of the Houses of Parliament, a new class of intellectuals gained hegemony over aristocratic culture as it translated puritanism into the secular practices composing modern domesticity and personal life. [Armstrong] See *The Imaginary Puritan: Literature, Intellectual Labor, and the Origins of Personal Life* (Berkeley: University of California Press, 1992).

difference between production in the traditional sense and the production of information has virtually disappeared, the antagonism between worker and owner is likewise dispersed. Where such polarities could once be taken for granted, then, it becomes extremely difficult to create polarities along political lines. Laclau and Mouffe find it necessary to depart from Gramsci's reliance on the emergence of labor in conflict with capital and to turn instead to the intellectual labor of negativities and positivities out of the contemporary swamp of equivalences. For another important analysis of power in post-modern society, see Bonaventura de Sousa Santos, "Law and Community: The Changing Nature of State Power in Late Capitalism," *International Journal of the Sociology of the Law* (1980), 8: 379–97. [Armstrong]

fact that the modern household served as the groundbreaking prototype of modern institutions. His *History of Sexuality* neglects to theorize the power of that prototype as it spills over from this account of modern personal life into his account of institutional power to saturate and make intelligible the theory of discipline. Despite the anti-Cartesian thrust of his work, Foucault does not finally break through the barrier that separates his position as theorizer of the sexual subject in *The History of Sexuality* from the one he takes up in order to theorize the political subject in *Discipline and Punish*. Yet not only does he use the same figure to think out the two; he also gives the strategies producing the sexual subject (those organizing the home) priority in his thinking over the strategies that subject the individual to the state (those of disciplinary institutions).

Central to the central chapter on "Panopticism" in *Discipline and Punish* is Foucault's figure of the city under plague. In contrast with leprosy, which calls for exclusionary strategies more consistent with the aristocratic imagination of power, the plague, as he plays with the figure, seems to require inclusion and enclosure as preconditions for a modern system of surveillance. The division of the population into progressively smaller subdivisions of which the household is the basic module, is followed by the ritual purification of each and every household:

Five or six days after the beginning of the quarantine, the process of purifying the houses one by one is begun. All the inhabitants are made to leave; in each room "the furniture and goods" are raised from the ground or suspended from the air; perfume is poured around the room; after carefully sealing the windows, doors and even the keyholes with wax, the perfume is set alight. Finally, the entire house is closed while the perfume is consumed; those who have carried out the work are searched, as they were on entry, "in the presence of the residents of the house, to see that they did not have something on their persons as they left that they did not have on entering." Four hours later, the residents are allowed to re-enter their homes. (p. 197)

Such enclosure and purification of the house produces a new household free from the taint of any unregulated intercourse with the world, its membrane permeable only to certain kinds of information. Reading this account of the plague, I am struck by the difference between its place in the modern imagination and its use by Boccaccio, who imagined a small aristocratic community safely ensconced in the country to pass the time free from the infection of the city.[12] In this early modern world, those who remain in the city are to be regarded as a different social body altogether, behaving much like the riotous and grotesquely permeable body celebrated by Bakhtin.[13] How significant, then, that Foucault, in contrast with Bakhtin, imagines a city purified from the inside out by the production of hygienically pure domestic spaces within the body politic! In this attempt to fantasize the present from the position of the past, households serve as magical spaces where people go to die in order that they may be reborn as modern individuals — enclosed and self-regulating.

Having pursued the internal logic of his figure thus far, Foucault extends it outward from the newly enclosed domestic world — as from a new source of power — into the cultural and political domains, and from there into history. First, he notes how a "whole literary fiction of the festival grew up around the plague: suspended laws, lifted prohibitions, the frenzy of passing time, bodies mingling together without respect, individuals unmasked, abandoning their statutory identity and the figure under which they had been recognized, allowing a quite different truth to appear. But," he continues, "there was also a political dream of the plague, which was exactly its reverse: not the collective festival, but strict divisions; not laws transgressed, but the penetration of regulation into even the smallest details of everyday life . . . ; not masks that were put on and taken off, but the assignment to each individual of his 'true' name, his 'true' place, his 'true' disease" (pp. 197–198). On the metaphor of the city under plague thus rests Foucault's entire theory of the development of modern institutions: "If it is true that the leper gave rise to rituals of exclusion, which to a certain extent provided the model for and general form of the Great Confinement, then the plague gave rise to disciplinary projects"

12 In the *Decameron* (1353).
13 In *Rabelais and His World* (1965).

(p. 198). Metaphorical use of disease allows him to declare the eighteenth-century hospital with its anatomy theater as the historical prototype for the modern prison.

And to be sure, I *like* Foucault for transgressing the boundary between the therapeutic and the punitive to demonstrate how much they have in common. But this, to my mind, is also a way of avoiding the full implications of his chosen metaphor, the city under plague, implications that would destroy the differences between sexual subject and political subject, and between these and the subject's material body, all of which rest upon preserving the line that divvies up cultural information according to gender. This is the line between inside and outside that is implanted in his metaphor from the beginning to distinguish personal from political life. This is the first division of the conceptual zygote, the line without which the fantasy of an entire political world cannot develop its inexorable symmetry, a symmetry that cuts beneath and through particular features that culture manifests at one site rather than another. While he opens the category of political power considerably by including institutions other than those officially charged to distribute wealth and power, Foucault extends the cultural scope of discipline only so far as institutions that, in becoming institutions, came to be dominated by men. Thus if power does not originate in the minds of individual men or in the bodies of men collectively, it arises from the cultural patterns that make men think of themselves as certain kinds of men and exercise power accordingly.

But if one pursues the implications of Foucault's chosen metaphor for modern power, his city under plague, in contrast with a Boccaccian remedy, contains a certain form of household that is the perfect and obvious answer to the indiscriminate mingling of bodies spreading the infection. When we expand our concept of the political further even than Foucault's, we discover grounds on which to argue that the modern household rather than the clinic provided the proto-institutional setting where government through relentless supervision first appeared, and appeared in its most benevolent guise. Foucault never takes note of these continuities between home and state even though they are as plain as the words on his page. More curious still is his failure to acknowledge the fact that a home espoused by various subgroups aspiring for the status of "respectability," a home overseen by a woman, actually preceded the formation of other social institutions by at least fifty years. There is little to suggest this household took root in practice much before the beginning of the nineteenth century, even though it frequently appeared in the literature and political argumentation of the previous century. From writing, it can be argued, the new family passed into the realm of common sense, where it came to justify the distribution of national wealth through wages paid to men. Indeed, it remains extremely powerful to this day as both metaphor and metonymy, the unacknowledged model and source of middle-class power.[14]

THE POWER OF DOMESTICITY

It is at this point in my argument that a feminist perspective must be invoked, but it cannot be a feminism that sinks comfortably into the rhetoric of victimization. It has to be thoroughly politicized. By this I mean we must be willing to accept the idea that, as middle-class women, we are empowered, although we are not empowered in traditionally masculine ways. We have to acknowledge that as middle-class intellectuals we are not critical mirrors of a separate and more primary process orchestrated by others — be they politicians, bureaucrats, captains of industry, or simply men. As women intellectuals we are doubly implicated in the process of reproducing the state of mind upon which other openly and avowedly political institutions depend. It is on this basis that I reject the notion that women's writing exists in a domain of experience outside of political history. I can no longer accept what conventional histories assume — that such writing occupies the secondary status of a "reflection" or "consequence" of changes within more

[14]I have argued this at length in *Desire and Domestic Fiction*. This essay began as an early version of the introduction and later developed into a theoretical investigation of my argument with literature, history, and academic feminism. I refer readers to the book for evidence supporting the necessarily brief outline of the events in the history of modern sexuality which composes part of this essay. [Armstrong]

primary social institutions — the army, hospital, prison, or factory. To the contrary, my evidence reveals domestic fiction actively disentangled the language of sexual relations from that of political economy. The rhetoric of this fiction (in Wayne Booth's sense of the term[15]) laid out a new cultural logic that would eventually become common sense, sensibility, and public opinion. In this way, female knowledge successfully combatted one kind of power, based on title, wealth, and physical force, with another, based on the control of literacy. By equating good reading with what was good for women readers, a new standard for reading laid down the semantic ground for a new common sense and established the narrative conventions structuring public opinion. The new standard of literacy helped to bring a new class of people into existence. This class laid claim to the right to privacy on behalf of each individual. Yet this class set in motion the systematic invasion of private life by surveillance, observation, evaluation, and remediation. In a word, it ruled, still rules, through countless microtechniques of socialization, all of which may be lumped together under the heading of education.[16] During the second half of the nineteenth century, institutions were created to perform these operations upon masses of people in much the same way as domestic fiction did upon characters.

Those of us who have grown up within an institutional culture consequently carry around a voice much like that of a fictional narrator in his or her head. Sensitive to the least sign of disorder — a foul word, a piece of clothing undone, some food sliding off one's fork, or, worse still, some loss of control over bodily functions — the presence of this voice, now nearly two hundred years old, more surely keeps us in line than fear of the police or the military. For the unofficial forms of power have a terrible advantage over those which are openly and avowedly regulatory. They

[15] See the introduction to Reader-Response Theory, p. 543.

[16] In "'The Mother Made Conscious': The Historical Development of a Primary School Pedagogy," *History Workshop* (1985), vol. 20, Carolyn Steedman has researched the rationale and analyzed the process by which the techniques of mothering were extended beyond the household and through the establishment of a national educational system, became the gentle but unyielding girders of a new institutional culture. [Armstrong]

make us afraid of ourselves. They operate on the supposition that we harbor desires dangerous to the general good. Believing in the presence of a self that is essentially subversive, we keep watch over ourselves — in mirrors, on clocks, on scales, through medical exams, and by means of any number of other such practices. Thus we internalize a state that is founded on the conflict between self and state interests, and we feel perfectly justified in enacting its power — which is, after all, only good for oneself — upon others.

Convinced that power exerted in and through the female domain is at least as powerful as the more conventional forms of power associated with the male, I want to sketch out the relationship between the two during the modern period. I will suggest that modern institutional cultures depend upon the separation of "the political" from "the personal" and that they produce and maintain this separation on the basis of gender — the formation of masculine and feminine domains of culture. For, I will argue, even as certain forms of cultural information were separated into these two opposing fields, they were brought together as an intricate set of pressures that operated on the subject's body and mind to induce self-regulation. We can observe this peculiarly effective collaboration of the official and unofficial forms of power perhaps most clearly in the formation of a national education system during the Victorian period and in the whole constellation of efforts that went on simultaneously to appropriate leisure time.[17] British fiction participates in both efforts and therefore demonstrates the modes of collaboration between them.

To introduce their highly influential *Practical Education* in 1801, Maria Edgeworth and her father announce their break with the curriculum that reinforced traditional political distinctions: "On religion and politics we have been silent because we have no ambition to gain partisans, or to make proselytes, and because we do not

[17] See, for example, Peter Stallybrass and Allon White, *The Politics and Poetics of Transgression* (London: Methuen, 1986); Peter Clark, *The English Alehouse: A Social History, 1200–1830* (London: Longman, 1983); Thomas Walter Laqueur, *Religion and Respectability: Sunday Schools and Working Class Culture, 1780–1850* (New Haven: Yale University Press, 1976). [Armstrong]

address ourselves to any sect or party."[18] In virtually the same breath, they assure readers, "With respect to what is commonly called the education of the heart, we have endeavored to suggest the easiest means of inducing useful and agreeable habits, well regulated sympathy and benevolent affections" (p. viii). Their program substitutes abstract terms of emotion and behavior for those of one's specific socioeconomic identity. Rooting identity in the very subjective qualities that earlier curricula had sought to inculcate in young women alone, the Edgeworths' program gives priority to the schoolroom and parlor over the church and courts for purposes of regulating human behavior. In doing this, their educational program promises to suppress the political signs of human identity (which is of course a powerful political gesture in its own right). Perfectly aware of the power to be exercised through education, the Edgeworths justify their curriculum for cultivating the heart on grounds that it offered a new and more effective method of policing. In their words, "It is the business of education to prevent crimes, and to prevent all those habitual propensities which necessarily lead to their commission" (p. 354).

To accomplish their ambitious political goal, the Edgeworths invoke an economy of pleasure which cannot in fact be understood apart from the novel and the criticism that was produced both to censor and to foster it. First, the Edgeworths accept the view prevailing during the eighteenth century which said that fiction was sure to mislead female desire:

> With respect to sentimental stories, and books of mere entertainment, we must remark, that they should be sparingly used, especially in the education of girls. This species of reading cultivates what is called the heart prematurely, lowers the tone of the mind, and induces indifference for those common pleasures and occupations which . . . constitute by far the greatest portion of our daily happiness. (p. 105)

But the same turn of mind could as easily recognize the practical value of pleasure when it is harnessed and aimed at the right goals.

Convinced that "the pleasures of literature" acted upon the reader in much the same way as a child's "taste for sugar-plums" (p. 80), forward-thinking educators began to endorse the reading of fiction, so long as it was governed by principles that made conformity seem desirable.

In formulating a theory of mass education in which fiction had a deceptively marginal role to play, the Edgeworths and their colleagues were adopting a rhetoric which earlier reformers had used to level charges of violence and corruption against the old aristocracy. They placed themselves in the tradition of radical Protestant dissent going back to the sixteenth century, a tradition which had always argued that political authority should be based on moral superiority. Sexual relations so often provided the terms for making this claim that no representation of the household could be considered politically neutral. To contest that notion of the state which depended upon inherited power, puritan treatises on marriage and household governance represented the family as a self-enclosed social unit into whose affairs the state had no right to intervene. Against genealogy they posited domesticity. But in claiming sovereignty for the natural father over his household, these treatises were not proposing a new distribution of political power. They were simply trying to limit the monarch's power. To understand the social transformation that was achieved by the English Revolution (according to Christopher Hill, not achieved until more than a century later), we have to turn away from what we consider to be the political themes of the puritan argument and consider instead what happens to gender.[19]

---

[18]Maria Edgeworth and Robert L. Edgeworth, *Practical Education* (London, 1801), 2: ix. Citations in the text are to this edition. [Armstrong]

[19]For a discussion of the paternalism that emerged in opposition to patriarchy in seventeenth-century puritan writing, see Leonard Tennenhouse, *Power on Display: The Politics of Shakespeare's Genres* (New York: Methuen, 1986), especially the chapter entitled "Family Rites." In describing the alternative to patriarchy that arose at the end of the seventeenth and beginning of the eighteenth century in aristocratic families, Randolph Trumbach opposes the term "patriarchal" to the term "domesticity," by which he refers to the modern household. This social formation is authorized by internal relations of gender and generation rather than by way of analogy to external power relations between monarch and subject or between God and man, *The Rise of the Egalitarian Family* (New York: Academic Press, 1978), pp. 119–63. [Armstrong]

According to Kathleen M. Davis, the puritan doctrine of equality insisted upon the difference of sexual roles, in which the female was certainly subordinate to the male, and not upon the equality of the woman in kind. "The result of this partnership," she explains, "was a definition of mutual and complementary duties and characteristics." Gender was so clearly understood in these oppositional terms that it could be graphically represented:[20]

Husband	Wife
Get goods	Gather them together and save them
Travel, seek a living	Keep the house
Get money and provisions	Do not vainly spend it
Deal with many men	Talk with few
Be "entertaining"	Be solitary and withdrawn
Be skillful in talk	Boast of silence
Be a giver	Be a saver
Apparel yourself as you may	Apparel yourself as it becomes you
Dispatch all things outdoors	Oversee and give order within

In so representing the household as the opposition of complementary genders, the authors of countless puritan tracts asked readers to imagine the household as a self-enclosed social unit. But if these authors wanted to define the family as an independent source of authority, their moment did not arrive. The puritan household consisted of a male and a female who were structurally identical, positive and negative versions of the same thing. The authority of the housewife described above could not yet be imagined as a positive thing in its own right. Until she took up her vigil and began to order personal life, a single understanding of power reigned, and men fought to determine the balance among its various parts. Unlike the authors of seventeenth-century marriage manuals and domestic economies, the

educational reformers of nineteenth-century England could look back on a substantial body of writing whose main purpose was to produce a historically new woman. During the centuries between the English Revolution and the present day, this woman was inscribed with values which appealed to a whole range of competing interest groups, and, through her, these groups seized authority over domestic relations and personal life. In this way, I believe, they created a need for the kind of surveillance which modern institutions provide. Indeed, the last two decades of the seventeenth century saw an explosion of writing aimed at educating the daughters of the numerous aspiring social groups. The new curriculum promised to educate these women in such a way as to make them more desirable than women who had only their own rank and fortune to recommend them. This curriculum exalted a woman whose value resided chiefly in her femaleness rather than in the traditional signs of status, a woman who possessed emotional depth rather than a physically stimulating surface. In other words, excelled in the very qualities that differentiated her from the male. As gender was redefined in these terms, the woman exalted by an aristocratic tradition of letters ceased to appear so desirable. In becoming the other side of this new sexual coin, she represented surface rather than depth, embodied material as opposed to moral value, and displayed idle sensuality instead of unflagging concern for the well-being of others. So conceived, the aristocratic woman no longer defined what was truly and most desirably female. But it was not until the mid-nineteenth-century that the project of defining people on the basis of gender began to acquire some of the immense political influence it still exercises today. Around the 1830s, one can see the discourse of sexuality relax its critical gaze on the aristocracy as the newly forming working classes became a more obvious target of moral reform. Authors suddenly took notice of social elements who had hardly mattered before. These reformers and men of letters discovered that rebellious artisans and urban laborers, for example, lacked the kind of motivation that supposedly characterized normal individuals. Numerous writers sought out the source of poverty, illiteracy,

[20] Kathleen M. Davis, "The Sacred Condition of Equality — How Original Were Puritan Doctrines of Marriage?" *Social History* (1977), 5: 570. Davis quotes this list from John Dod and Robert Cleaver, *A Godly Forme of Householde Government* (London, 1614). [Armstrong]

and demographic change in these underdeveloped individuals, whose behavior was generally found to be not only promiscuous but also ambiguously gendered. Once they succeeded in translating an overwhelming economic problem into a sexual scandal, middle-class intellectuals could step forward and offer themselves, their technology, their supervisory skills, and their institutions of education and social welfare as the appropriate remedy for growing political resistance.

In all fairness, as Foucault notes, the middle classes rarely applied institutional procedures to others without first trying them out on themselves. When putting together a national curriculum, the government officials and educators in charge adopted one modeled on the educational theory that grew up around the Edgeworths and their intellectual circle, the heirs of the dissenting tradition.[21] This was basically the same as the curriculum proposed by eighteenth-century pedagogues and reformers as the best way of producing a marriageable daughter. By the end of the eighteenth century, the Edgeworths were among those who had already determined that the program aimed at producing the ideal woman could be applied to boys just as well as to girls. And by the mid-nineteenth century, one can see the government figuring out how to administer much the same program on a mass basis. In providing the conceptual foundation for a national curriculum, a particular idea of the self thus became commonplace, and as gendered forms of identity determined how people thought of themselves as well as others, that self became the dominant social reality.

Such an abbreviated history cannot do justice to the fierce controversies punctuating the institution of a national education system in England. I simply call attention to this material as a site where political history obviously converged with the history of sexuality as well as with that of the novel to produce a specific kind of individual. I do this to suggest the political implications of representing these as separate narratives. As it began to deny its political and religious bias and to present itself instead as a moral and psychological truth, the rhetoric of reform obviously severed its ties with an aristocratic past and took up a new role in history. It no longer constituted a form of resistance but enclosed a specialized domain of culture apart from political relations where apolitical truths could be told. The novel's literary status hinged upon this event. Henceforth fiction would deny the political basis for its meaning and refer instead to the private regions of the self or to the specialized world of art but never to the use of words that created and still maintains these distinctions so basic to our culture. Favored among kinds of fiction were novels that best performed the rhetorical operations of division and self-containment and thus turned existing political information into the discourse of sexuality. These works of fiction gave novels a good name, a name free of politics, and often the name of a woman such as Pamela, Evelina, Emma, or Jane Eyre.[22] Then, with the translation of human identity into sexual identity came widespread repression of the political literacy characterizing an earlier culture, and with it, too, mass forgetting that there was a history of sexuality to tell.

THE POLITICS OF DOMESTIC FICTION

Let me offer a detailed example of the exchange between reader and literary text to provide a sense of how the power of domesticity works through such an exchange. Charlotte Brontë flaunted this very power in writing her novel *Shirley*.[23] The novel contains an otherwise gratuitous scene where Shakespeare's *Coriolanus* is read aloud and critiqued, as if to give the reader precise rules for reading, rules that should fascinate literary historians. They are not Brontë's own but rules developed during the preceding century by countless authors of ladies' conduct books and educational treatises. These authors proposed the first curriculum to include native

[21]See Brian Simon, *Studies in the History of Education, 1780–1870* (London: Lawrence and Wishart, 1960), pp. 1–62. [Armstrong]

[22]Eponymous heroines of novels by Samuel Richardson (1740), Frances Burney (1778), Jane Austen (1816), and Charlotte Brontë (1847).
[23]Published in 1849.

British literature. Around the time Brontë sat down to write *Shirley*, a new generation of writers had taken up the question of how to distinguish good reading from bad. Their efforts swelled the growing number of Victorian magazines. Whether or not girls should read novels was the concern that shaped the debates over a curriculum for women during the eighteenth century, then nineteenth-century pedagogical theory developed around the question of how to make fiction useful for teaching foreigners and working-class people as well as women and children. Rules for reading developed along with the national standard curriculum that extended a curriculum originally meant only for girls of the literate classes to young Englishmen and women at various levels and their counterparts throughout the colonies. It is much the same theory of education that informs our educational system today. By using this example from *Shirley* to illustrate the rationale and procedures by which Victorian intellectuals extended what had been regarded as a female form of literacy to male education, I also want to mark an important difference between Charlotte Brontë's understanding of this process and our own. She was, I believe, far more aware of the politics of literary interpretation than we are.

One of her least colorful heroines, Carolyn Helstone, uses Shakespeare to while away an evening of leisure with her beloved cousin and future husband Robert Moore, a surly manufacturer, whose authoritarian way of dealing with factory hands is earning him threats of Luddite[24] reprisals. During this, their one intimate moment together until the end of the novel, they reject all the pastimes available to lovers in an Austen novel in favor of reading Shakespeare's *Coriolanus*. Far more detailed than any such exchange in earlier fiction, this act of reading spells out the procedures by which reading literature was thought to produce a form of knowledge that was also a form of social control. Robert Moore

is half Belgian, half English. It is through reading Shakespeare that, according to Carolyn, he "shall be entirely English."[25] For, as she patiently explains to him, "Your French forefathers don't speak so sweetly, not so solemnly, nor so impressively as your English ancestors, Robert." But being English does not identify a set of political affiliations — as it would in Shakespeare's time. It refers instead to essential qualities of human mind. Carolyn has selected a part for Robert to read aloud that, in her words, "is toned with something in you. It shall waken your nature, fill your mind with music; it shall pass like a skillful hand over your heart. . . . Let glorious William come near and touch it; you will see how he will draw the English power and melody out of its chords."

I have called this relationship between reader and text an exchange in order to stress the fact that writing cannot be turned to the task of constituting readers without giving up old features and acquiring new ones of its own; to dwell on the reader is to explain but one half of the transformational logic of this exchange. Just as Robert, the rude Belgian, becomes a gentle Englishman by reading Shakespeare, so, too, the Jacobean playwright is transformed by the domestic setting in which he is read. Carolyn urges Robert to receive the English of another historical moment as the voice of an ancestor speaking to him across time and cultural boundaries. To no one's surprise, the written Shakespeare, thus resurrected, has acquired the yearnings and anxieties of an early nineteenth-century factory owner. And as we observe the Bard becoming the nineteenth-century man, we also witness an early version of our own literary training. Here, extending through the educated middle-class female to the male and, through him, acquiring universal application, we can see how voices that speak from positions vastly different in social space and time quickly translate into aspects of modern consciousness.

[24]Named after the semilegendary Ned Lud, who in a fit had smashed stocking frames in 1779, the Luddites were organized groups of laborers who destroyed industrial machinery in the British midlands and northern counties during the years 1811–16.

[25]Charlotte Brontë, *Shirley*, Andrew and Judith Hook, eds. (Harmondsworth: Penguin, 1974), p. 114. Citations of the text are to this edition. [Armstrong]

Thus Shakespeare becomes the means of reproducing specifically modern states of mind within the reader. Reading Shakespeare is supposed "to stir you," Carolyn explains, "to give you new sensations. It is to make you feel your life strongly, not only your virtues, but your vicious, perverse points. Discover by the feeling the reading will give you at once how high and how low you are" (p. 115). If Shakespeare loses the very turns of mind that would identify him with his moment in history, then Robert loses features of a similar kind in Brontë's representation of the scene of reading. And this, of course, is the point. Reading Shakespeare translates Robert's political attitudes into essential features of mind. It simultaneously objectifies those features and subjects them to evaluation. The "English power" that Robert acquires by reading literature is simply the power of observing himself through the lens of liberal humanism — as a self flushed with the grandiosity of an ordinariness that has been totally liberated from historical bias and political commitment. For it is through this lens that the novel has us perceive the transformations that come over Robert as he reads *Coriolanus* under the gentle tutelage of Carolyn Helstone: "stepping out of the narrow line of private prejudices, he began to revel in the large picture of human nature, to feel the reality stamped upon the characters who were speaking from that page before him" (p. 116).

Her tutoring induces Robert to renounce one mode of power — which Carolyn associates with the imperiously patriarchal nature of *Coriolanus* — and to adopt another — which she identifies as a benevolent form of paternalism. As it is administered by a woman and used to mediate a sexual exchange, *Coriolanus* becomes the means for effecting historical change: *Coriolanus* becomes Carolyn. Performed as writing and reading, that is, the play becomes the means of internalizing a form of authority identified with the female. The political implications of feminizing the reader are clear as Carolyn gives Robert a moral to "tack to the play: . . . you must not be proud to your workpeople; you must not neglect chances of soothing them, and you must not be of an inflexible nature, uttering a request

as austerely as if it were a command" (p. 114). Brontë is less than subtle in dramatizing the process by which reading rids Robert of the foreign devil. She seems to know exactly what political objective is fulfilled as he fills the mold of the Englishman and benevolent father. Brontë also puts the woman in charge of this process even though she gives her heroine the less imperious passages to read. Retiring, feminine, and thoroughly benign, Carolyn's power is hardly visible as such. Yet she is clearly the one who declares that reading has the power "to stir you; to give you new sensations. It is to make you feel your life strongly, not only your virtues, but your vicious, perverse points" (p. 115). And when Robert has finished reading, she is the one to ask, "Now, have you felt Shakespeare?" (p. 117). She suppresses all that belongs to the past as so much noise in her effort to being under examination the grand currents of emotion that run straight from Shakespeare to the modern day reader, a reader who is thoroughly English. In thus guiding his reading with her smiles and admonitions, Carolyn executes a set of delicate procedures capable of translating any and all cultural information into shades of modern middle-class consciousness and the substance of a literary text. Although its setting — during the Luddite rebellions — makes *Shirley* anachronistic by about thirty years, the solution it proposes for the problem of political resistance, through the production of a new ruling-class mentality, marks this novel as utterly Victorian — perhaps even ahead of its time.

As similar textualizing strategies were deployed here and elsewhere throughout Victorian culture, an intricate system of psychological differences completely triumphed over a long-standing tradition of overtly political signs to usher in a new form of state power. This power — the power of representation over the thing represented — wrested authority from the old aristocracy on grounds that a government was morally obliged to rehabilitate deviant individuals rather than subdue them by force. The Peterloo Massacre of 1819 made it clear that the state's capacity for violence had become a source of embarrassment to the state. Overt displays of force worked against legitimate authority just as they did against subversive factions.[26] If acts of open rebellion had justified intervention in areas of society that government had not had to deal with before, then the government's use of force gave credence to the workers' charges of government oppression. The power of surveillance came into dominance at precisely this moment in English history, displacing traditional displays of violence. Remarkably like the form of vigilance that insured an orderly household, this power did not create equality so much as trivialize the material signs of difference by translating all such signs into differences in the quality, intensity, direction, and self-regulatory capability of an individual's desire.

In saying this, I am not suggesting that we should use British fiction to identify forms of repression or to perform acts of liberation, although my project has a definite political goal. I simply want to represent the discourse of sexuality as deeply implicated in — if not directly responsible for — the shape of the novel, and to show the novel's implication, at the same time, in producing a subject who knew herself and saw that self in relation to others according to the same feminizing strategies that had shaped fiction. I regard fiction, in other words, both as a document and as an agency of cultural history. I believe it helped to formulate the ordered space we now recognize as the household, that it made that space totally functional and used it as the context for representing normal behavior. In doing all this, fiction contested alternative bases for human relationships. As the history of this female domain is figured into political history, then, it will outline boldly the telling cultural move upon which, I believe, the supremacy of middle-class culture ultimately hinged. That is, it will reenact the moment when writing invaded,

[26] E. P. Thompson, pp. 680–85. [Armstrong] What became known as the "Peterloo Massacre" was the Fifteenth Hussars' attack on a peaceful and well-organized demonstration of over sixty thousand workers massed at St. Peter's Fields outside Manchester, England, in 1819; they had been protesting against the Corn Laws and in favor of Parliamentary reform. Eleven workers were killed and many hundreds seriously injured by sabre cuts and flying hooves.

revised, and contained the household according to strategies that distinguished private from social life and thus detached sexuality from political history.

Where others have isolated rhetorical strategies that naturalize the subordination of female to male, no one has thoroughly examined the figure that differentiates the sexes as it links them together by sexual desire. And if no one asks why, how, and when gender differentiation became the root of human identity, no degree of theoretical sophistication can help us understand the totalizing power of this figure and the very real interests such power inevitably serves. So basic are the terms "male" and "female" to the semiotics of modern life that no one can use them without to some degree performing the very reifying gesture whose operations we need to understand and whose power we want to historicize. Whenever we cast our political lot in the dyadic formation of gender, we place ourselves in a classic double bind, which confines us to alternatives that are not really alternatives at all. That is to say, any political position founded primarily on sexual identity ultimately confirms the limited choices offered by such a dyadic model. Once one thinks within such a structure, sexual relationships appear as the model for all power relationships. This makes it possible to see the female as representative of all subjection and to use her subjectivity as if it were a form of resistance. Having inscribed social conflict within a domestic configuration, however, one loses sight of all the various contrary political affiliations for which any given individual provides the site. This power of sexuality to appropriate the voice of the victim works as surely through inversion, of course, as by strict adherence to the internal organization of the model.

Still, there is a way in which I owe everything to the very academic feminism I seem to critique, for unless it were now acceptable to read women's texts as women's texts, there would be no call to historicize this area of culture. In view of the fact that women writers have been taken up by the Norton Anthology as part of the standard survey of British literature and also as a collection all of their own, and in view of the fact that we now have male feminists straining to hop on the bandwagon, I feel it is simply time to take stock. It is time to consider why literary criticism presently feels so comfortable with a kind of criticism that began as a critique both of the traditional canon and of the interpretive procedures the canon called forth. This should tell us that by carving out a separate domain for women within literary criticism, feminist criticism has yet to destabilize the reigning metaphysics of sexuality. Literary historians continue to remain aloof from but still firmly anchored in a narrow masculinist notion of politics as more and more areas within literary studies have given ground to the thematics of sexuality promoted by academic feminism. Indeed, a sexual division of labor threatens to reproduce itself within the academy whereby women scholars interpret literature as the expression of the sexual subject while male scholars attend to matters of history and politics. To subvert this process, I believe we must read fiction not as literature but as the history of gender differences and a means by which we have reproduced a class and culture specific form of consciousness.

Stephen Greenblatt
b. 1943

Renaissance scholar Stephen Greenblatt is in the vanguard of academics responsible for the rise of New Historicist studies in the United States. Greenblatt was born in Cambridge, Massachusetts; he took a B.A. (1964), an M.Phil. (1968), and a Ph.D. (1969) in English at Yale, and an A.B. (1966) and M.A. (1968) at Pembroke College, Cambridge University. Starting in 1969 Greenblatt taught at the University of California at Berkeley, becoming a full professor in 1980. Since 1997 Greenblatt has taught at Harvard University, where he is now John Cogan University Professor of the Humanities. Among Greenblatt's honors are a Fulbright scholarship (1964–66), a Guggenheim fellowship (1975), and a visiting professorship at the University of Peking (1982). His books include Sir Walter Raleigh: The Renaissance Man and His Roles (1973), Allegory and Representation (1979), Renaissance Self-Fashioning: From More to Shakespeare (1980), Representing the English Renaissance (1988), Shakespearean Negotiations: The Circulation of Social Energy in Renaissance England (1988), Learning to Curse: Essays in Early Modern Culture (1990), Marvelous Possessions: The Wonder of the New World (1991), Re-Drawing the Boundaries: The Transformation of English and American Literary Studies (1992, ed., with Giles Gunn), New World Encounters (1992), Practicing New Historicism (1999, with Catherine Gallagher), Hamlet in Purgatory (2001), and his best-selling biography of Shakespeare, Will in the World (2004). His most recent books are Cultural Mobility (2010), Shakespeare's Freedom (2010), and The Swerve: How the World Became Modern (2011). Greenblatt is also the editor of Representations, a Berkeley-based journal in which New Historicist articles regularly appear. The selections here are from a special issue of Genre (Spring/Summer 1982), titled The Power of Forms in the English Renaissance. In the Introduction, Greenblatt makes reference to some of the other essays in the volume but not to his own "King Lear and Harsnett's 'Devil-Fiction.'"

Introduction to *The Power of Forms in the English Renaissance*

"I am Richard II. Know ye not that?" exclaimed Queen Elizabeth on August 4, 1601, in the wake of the abortive Essex rising. On the day before the rising, someone had paid the Lord Chamberlain's Men forty shillings to revive their old play about the deposing and killing of Richard II. As far as we know, the play — almost certainly Shakespeare's — was performed only once at the Globe, but in Elizabeth's bitter recollection the performance has metastasized: "this tragedy was played 40tie times in open streets and houses."[1] The Queen enjoyed and protected the theater; against moralists who charged that it was a corrupting and seditious force, she evidently

[1] Elizabeth was speaking to William Lambarde the antiquary; see the Arden edition of Shakespeare's *King Richard II*, ed. Peter Ure (Cambridge: Harvard University Press, 1956), pp. lvii–lxii. [Greenblatt]

sided with those who replied that it released social tensions, inculcated valuable moral lessons, and occupied with harmless diversion those who might otherwise conspire against legitimate authority. But there were some in the Essex faction who saw in the theater the power to subvert, or rather the power to wrest legitimation from the established ruler and confer it on another. This power, notwithstanding royal protection, censorship, and the players' professions of unswerving loyalty, could be purchased for forty shillings.

The story of Richard II was obviously a highly charged one in a society where political discussion was conducted, as in parts of the world today, with Aesopian indirection. Clearly it is not the text alone — over which the censor had some control — that bears the full significance of Shakespeare's play, or of any version of the story. It is rather the story's full situation — the genre it is thought to embody, the circumstances of its performance, the imaginings of its audience — that governs its shifting meanings. "40tie times in open streets and houses": for the Queen the repeatability of the tragedy, and hence the numbers of people who have been exposed to its infection, is part of the danger, along with the fact (or rather her conviction) that the play had broken out of the boundaries of the playhouse, where such stories are clearly marked as powerful illusions, and moved into the more volatile zone — the zone she calls "open" — of the streets. In the streets the story begins to lose the conventional containment of the playhouse, where audiences are kept at a safe distance both from the action on stage and from the world beyond the walls. And in the wake of this subversive deregulation, the terms that mark the distinction between the lucid and the real become themselves problematic: are the "houses" to which Elizabeth refers public theaters or private dwellings where her enemies plot her overthrow? can "tragedy" be a strictly literary term when the Queen's own life is endangered by the play?[2]

Modern historical scholarship has assured Elizabeth that she had nothing to worry about: Richard II is not at all subversive but rather a hymn to Tudor order. The play, far from encouraging thoughts of rebellion, regards the deposition of the legitimate king as a "sacrilegious" act that drags the country down into "the abyss of chaos"; "that Shakespeare and his audience regarded Bolingbroke as a usurper," declares J. Dover Wilson, "is incontestable."[3] But in 1601 neither Queen Elizabeth nor the Earl of Essex were so sure: after all, someone on the eve of a rebellion thought the play sufficiently seditious to warrant squandering two pounds on the players, and the Queen understood the performance as a threat. Moreover, even before the Essex rising, the actual deposition scene (IV.i.154–318 in the Arden edition) was carefully omitted from the first three quartos of Shakespeare's play and appears for the first time only after Elizabeth's death.

How can we account for the discrepancy between Dover Wilson's historical reconstruction and the anxious response of the figures whose history he purports to have accurately reconstructed? The answer lies at least in part in the difference between a conception of art that has no respect whatsoever for the integrity of the text ("I am Richard II. Know ye not that?") and one that hopes to find, through historical research, a stable core of meaning within the text, a core that united disparate and even contradictory parts into an organic whole. That whole may provide a perfectly orthodox celebration of legitimacy and order, as measured by homilies, royal pronouncements, and official propaganda, but the Queen is clearly responding to something else: to the presence of *any* representation of deposition, whether regarded as sacrilegious or not; to the choice of this particular story at this particular time; to the place of the performance; to her own identity as it is present in the public sphere and as it fuses with the figure of the murdered king. Dover Wilson is

---

[2]The ambiguity is intensified by the Queen's preceding comment, according to Lambarde: "*Her Majestie.* 'He that will forget God, will also forget his benefactors; this tragedy was played 40tie times in open streets and houses'" (Ure, p. lix). [Greenblatt]

[3]John Dover Wilson, "The Political Background of Shakespeare's *Richard II* and *Henry IV*," *Shakespeare-Jahrbuch,* 75 (1939), 47. The condemnation of Bolingbroke is "evident," we are told, "from the whole tone and emphasis of *Richard II*" (p. 48). I am grateful to Patricia Allen for the reference to this essay. [Greenblatt]

response.

Dover Wilson's work is a distinguished example of the characteristic assumptions and methods of the mainstream literary history practiced in the first half of our century, and a further glance at these may help us to bring into focus the distinctive assumptions and methods exemplified in the essays collected in this volume. To be sure, these essays are quite diverse in their concerns and represent no single critical practice; a comparative glance, for example, at the brilliant pieces by Franco Moretti and John Traugott will suggest at once how various this work is. Yet diverse as they are, many of the present essays give voice, I think, to what we may call the new historicism, set apart from both the dominant historical scholarship of the past and the formalist criticism that partially displaced this scholarship in the decades after World War Two. The earlier historicism tends to be monological; that is, it is concerned with discovering a single political vision, usually identical to that said to be held by the entire literate class or indeed the entire population ("In the eyes of the later middle ages," writes Dover Wilson, Richard II "represented the type and exemplar of royal martyrdom" [p. 50]). This vision, most often presumed to be internally coherent and consistent, though occasionally analyzed as the fusion of two or more elements, has the status of an historical fact. It is not thought to be the product of the historian's interpretation, nor even of the particular interests of a given social group in conflict with other groups. Protected then from interpretation and conflict, this vision can serve as a stable point of reference, beyond contingency, to which literary interpretation can securely refer. Literature is conceived to mirror the period's beliefs, but to mirror them, as it were, from a safe distance.

The new historicism erodes the firm ground of both criticism and literature. It tends to ask questions about its own methodological assumptions and those of others: in the present case, for example, it might encourage us to examine the ideological situation not only of *Richard II* but of Dover Wilson on *Richard II*. The lecture from which I have quoted — "The Political Background of Shakespeare's *Richard II* and *Henry IV*" — was delivered before the German Shakespearean Society, at Weimar, in 1939. We might, in a full discussion of the critical issues at stake here, look closely at the relation between Dover Wilson's reading of *Richard II* — a reading that discovers Shakespeare's fears of chaos and his consequent support for legitimate if weak authority over the claims of ruthless usurpers — and the eerie occasion of his lecture ("these plays," he concludes, "should be of particular interest to German students at this moment of that everlasting adventure which we call history" [p. 51]).

Moreover, recent criticism has been less concerned to establish the organic unity of literary works and more open to such works as fields of force, places of dissension and shifting interests, occasions for the jostling of orthodox and subversive impulses. "The Elizabeth playhouse, playwright, and player," writes Louis Adrian Montrose in a brilliant recent essay, "exemplify the contradictions of Elizabethan society and make those contradictions their subject. If the world is a theatre and the theatre is an image of the world, then by reflecting upon its own artifice, the drama is holding the mirror up to nature."4 As the problematizing of the mirror metaphor suggests, Renaissance literary works are no longer regarded either as a fixed set of texts that are set apart from all other forms of expression and that contain their own determinate meanings or as a stable set of reflections of historical facts that lie beyond them. The critical practice represented in [*The Power of Forms in the English Renaissance*] challenges the assumptions that guarantee a secure distinction between "literary foreground" and "political background" or, more generally, between artistic production and other kinds of social production. Such distinctions do in fact exist, but they are

4. "The Purpose of Playing: Reflections on a Shakespearean Anthropology," *Helios*, n.s. 7 (1980), 57. [Greenblatt]

not intrinsic to the texts; rather they are made up and constantly redrawn by artists, audiences, and readers. These collective social constructions on the one hand define the range of aesthetic possibilities within a given representational mode and, on the other, link that mode to the complex network of institutions, practices, and beliefs that constitute the culture as a whole. In this light, the study of genre is an exploration of the poetics of culture.

King Lear *and Harsnett's "Devil-Fiction"*

Modern critics tend to assume that Shakespearean self-consciousness and irony lead to a radical transcendence of the network of social conditions, paradigms, and practices in the plays. I would submit, by contrast, that Renaissance theatrical representation itself is fully implicated in this network and that Shakespeare's self-consciousness is in significant ways bound up with the institutions and the symbology of power it anatomizes.

To grasp this we might consider *King Lear*. We happen to know one of the books that Shakespeare had been reading and seems indeed to have had open before him as he revised the old play of *King Leir*. The book, printed in 1603, is by Samuel Harsnett, then chaplain to the Bishop of London, and is entitled *A Declaration of Egregious Popish Impostures, to with-draw the harts of her Majesties Subjects from their allegeance, and from the truth of Christian Religion professed in England, under the pretense of casting out devils. Practised by Edmunds, alias Weston a Jesuit, and divers Romish Priests his wicked associates. Where-unto are annexed the Copies of the Confessions and Examinations of the parties themselves, which were pretended to be possessed, and dispossessed, taken upon oath before her Majesties Commissioners for Causes Ecclesiasticall.*[1] From this remarkable book — a scathing account of a series of spectacular exorcisms conducted between the spring of 1585 and the summer of 1586 principally in the house of a recusant gentleman, Sir George Peckham of Denham, Buckinghamshire — Shakespeare took many small details, especially for the demonology Edgar exhibits in his disguise as the possessed Poor Tom. My interest here is not in these details which have been noted since the eighteenth century, but in the broader institutional implications of Harsnett's text and of the uses to which Shakespeare puts it.

The *Declaration* is a semi-official attack on exorcism as practiced by Jesuits secretly residing in England (and under constant threat of capture and execution), but the charges are not limited to Catholicism, since Harsnett had earlier written against the Puritan exorcist John Darrell. Like other spokesmen for the Anglican establishment, Harsnett concedes that at some distant time exorcism was a legitimate practice (as, of course, it is in the Bible), but miracles have ceased and corporeal possession by demons is no longer possible. What has taken its place, he writes, is fraud, and, more precisely, theater: exorcisms are stage plays written by cunning clerical dramatists and performed by skilled actors. To be sure, not all the participants are professionals, but the priests, as Harsnett depicts them, run what is in effect an acting school. They begin by talking about the

---

[1] On Harsnett, see D. P. Walker, *Unclean Spirits: Possession and Exorcism in France and England in the Late Sixteenth and Early Seventeenth Centuries* (Philadelphia: University of Pennsylvania Press, 1981), pp. 43–49; Keith Thomas, *Religion and the Decline of Magic* (London: Weidenfeld and Nicolson, 1971), pp. 477–92. On Harsnett and *Lear,* see Kenneth Muir, "Samuel Harsnett and *King Lear,*" *RES,* New Series 2 (1951), 11–21; William Elton, *King Lear and the Gods* (San Marino, CA: Huntington Library, 1966). [Greenblatt]

way successful exorcisms abroad had taken place and describe in lurid detail the precise symptoms of the possessed; then the young "scholers," as Harsnett calls those whom the priests have chosen to manipulate, "frame themselves jumpe and fit unto the Priests humors, to mop, mow, jest, raile, rave, roare, commend & discommend, and as the priest would have them, upon fitting occasions (according to the difference of times, places, and commers in) in all things to play the devils accordingle" (p. 38).

Harsnett's *Declaration* then is a massive document of disenchantment; the solemn ceremony of exorcism is, as the attack on Darrell puts it, "now discovered to be but a pure play," and the reverence and fear that the performance inspires are nothing but "miserable shifts to helpe [the exorcist] off the stage, that he might not be hissed at of all the world."[2] The Jesuits and their retinue are not a holy band driven by religious persecution to move from place to place but closely resemble "vagabond players," that coast from Towne to Towne with a trusse and a cast of fiddles, to carry in theyr consort, broken queanes, and *Ganimedes*, as well for their night pleasance, as their dayes pastime" (p. 149). The power this sleazy crew possesses is the power of the theater. If the end of a comedy, Harsnett notes, is applause for the author and actors, while the end of a tragedy is the "moving of affection, and passion in the spectators," our "*Daemonopoiia*, or devil-fiction, is *Tragico-comoedia*," for it elicits both exclamations of admiration — "*O that all the Protestans* (sic) *in England did see the power of the Catholick Church*" — and tears (p. 50).

The spectators, of course, do not know that they are merely responding to an effective if tawdry play; they believe that they are celebrants at a moving and sanctified communal ritual. "The devil speakes treason . . . so aptly, distinctly, and elegantly on the stage, that it enchaunted the harts, and affections of the poore bewitched people, and chained them to the Pope" (p. 154); the lowest estimate of the conversions achieved "by this well acted tragedie" is five hundred, and Harsnett states that "devil-tragedians" themselves

claim four to five thousand converts. To impress these large crowds, the exorcists, led by Father Edmunds, invoke the vast forces of heaven and hell, call forth by name whole legions of devils, and drive them from the bodies of the possessed by means of powerful amulets and charms. The performance is spectacular, with the writhing demoniac bound in a chair and tortured until the devils are compelled to depart. But the devils, says Harsnett, are tattered figures from the old Church plays, their names grotesque forgeries, and the hallowed vestments and holy objects contemptible stage properties. As for the possessed themselves, they are either histrionic scoundrels like Robert Mayne or servant girls like the sisters Sara and Friswood Williams, whose position of social dependency made them susceptible to the powers of suggestion, intimidation, and torture.

Harsnett's detailed identification of exorcism as theater, a conception that is elaborated through almost three hundred pages, is more than a satirical analogy; it is a polemical institutional analysis whose purpose is not only to expose the fraudulence of exorcism but to link that practice to the pervasive theatricality of the Catholic Church (or, as Harsnett elsewhere terms it, "the Pope's playhouse").[3] Priests do not actually believe in their "charmes, and consecrate attire," but only "act, fashion, and play them" in order to gull the ignorant (p. 88); the Mass itself is nothing but "a pageant of moppes, mowes, elevations, crouches, and ridiculous gesticulations" (p. 158). Theatricality here is not so much the consequence of the Church's deviation from the truth as the very essence of that deviation and hence the explanatory key to the entire institution: Catholicism is a "Mimick superstition (it being the onely religion to catch fooles, children, and women, by reason it is naught else, save a conceited pageant of Puppits, and gaudes" (p. 20). Now *King Lear* at once stages a version of these disenchanted perceptions — most notably in the representation of Edgar's histrionic and fraudulent demonic possession, complete with names drawn directly from the *Declaration* — and insinuates itself paradoxically into the place made vacant by Harsnett's attack: that is, where

[2] Samuel Harsnett, *A Discovery of the Fraudulent Practices of John Darrel* (London, 1599), p. A3ʳ. [Greenblatt]

[3] Harsnett, *Discovery*, p. A3ʳ. [Greenblatt]

Harsnett had condemned exorcism as a stage play, Shakespeare's play is itself a secular version of the ritual of exorcism. What exactly is being exorcised? Harsnett would say, in effect, that the question is misguided: what matters is the theatrical experience, the power of the performance to persuade the audience that it has heard the voices of radical evil and witnessed the violent expulsion of the agents of Darkness.

The ritual in this staged form is acceptable because the institution it serves is not a theatrical church but a public, state-supervised theater, and the on-lookers are induced to pay homage (and the price of admission) not to a competing religious authority but to professional entertainers safely circumscribed by the wooden walls of the playhouse. Within these walls, the force of Shakespeare's theatrical improvisation is to appropriate the power of the traditional, quasi-magical practice and of the newer, rationalized analysis and then, with this convergent power, to raise questions about the production of the enabling distinctions between supernatural and secular evil, real and theatrical ritual, authority and madness, belief and illusion. Such disturbing questions are at once licensed and contained by the aesthetic, economic, and physical demarcation of playing companies in a play space. Hence the ideological and historical situation of *King Lear* produces the oscillation, the simultaneous affirmation and negation, the constant undermining of its own assertions and questioning of its own practices — in short, the supreme aesthetic self-consciousness — that lead us to celebrate its universality, its literariness, and its transcendence of all ideology.

John Guillory

b. 1952

Born in New Orleans, Louisiana, Guillory was educated first at Tulane and then at Yale University, where he received his Ph.D. in 1979. He taught at Yale until 1989, then at Johns Hopkins and Harvard, and since 1999 has been Julius Silver Professor of English at New York University, where he is currently department chair. His first book, Poetic Authority: Spenser, Milton, and Literary History, was published in 1983. His second book, Cultural Capital: The Problem of Literary Canon Formation, was published by the University of Chicago Press in 1993 and won the René Wellek Prize of the American Comparative Literature Association. Guillory is currently working on a book entitled Literary Study in the Age of Professionalism, a disciplinary history of literary study in the context of the professionalization of science and scholarship in the new American university of the later nineteenth century.

The following selection is from Cultural Capital.

From Cultural Capital: The Problem of Literary Canon Formation

MULTICULTURAL INTERLUDE: THE QUESTION OF A CORE CURRICULUM

Every relationship of "hegemony" is an educational relationship.

— GRAMSCI, *Prison Notebooks*

While the debate over the canon concerns what texts should be taught in the schools, what remains invisible within this debate — too large to be seen at all — is the school itself. The absence of reflection on the school as an institution is the condition for the most deluded assumption of the debate, that the school is the vehicle of transmission for something like a national culture. What is transmitted by the school is, to be sure, a kind of culture; but it is the *culture of the school*. School culture does not unify the nation cultur- ally so much as it projects out of a curriculum of artifact-based knowledge an imaginary cultural unity never actually coincident with the culture of the nation-state. In this way the left hand of the educational system — the dissemination of a supposedly national culture — remains ignorant of what the right hand is doing — the differential tracking of students according to class or the possession of cultural capital. If the structure of the system, its multiple levels and its division between public and private institutions, divides the population in this way, the culture the *univer- sity* produces (as opposed to other kinds or levels of school), can only be "national" for that plural- ity which acquires this level of education. What this group may learn to think of as a national cul- ture is always a specific *relation* to the knowledge defined by the university curriculum.[1]

The extraordinary effects of confusing school culture with national culture are most conspicu- ous when the national culture is made to swal- low whole the even larger fish called "Western

[1]Bourdieu makes this point in his essay "Systems of Education and Systems of Thought." *International Social Science Journal* 19 (1967), 349: "An individual's contact with his culture depends basically on the circumstances in which he has acquired it, among other things because the act whereby culture is communicated is, as such, the exemplary expression of a certain type of relation to the culture." [Guillory] See Bourdieu, p. 818.

culture," and in such a way as to produce an image of the American nation as the telos[2] of Western cultural evolution. Here we may adduce William Bennett's complacent version of this narrative in "To Reclaim a Legacy":

> We are a part and a product of Western civilization. That our society was founded upon such principles as justice, liberty, government with the consent of the governed, and equality under the law is the result of ideas descended directly from great epochs of Western civilization — Enlightenment England and France, Renaissance Florence, and Periclean Athens. These ideas, so revolutionary in their times yet so taken for granted now, are the glue that binds together our pluralistic nation. The fact that we as Americans — whether black or white, Asian or Hispanic, rich or poor — share these beliefs aligns us with other cultures of the Western tradition.[3]

The interesting point about this argument is not the typically American chauvinism Bennett immediately denies ("It is not ethnocentric or chauvinistic to acknowledge this"), or the dubious assimilation of Western thinkers to democratic political principles many or even most of them would not in fact have endorsed. What remains interesting and consequential in Bennett's statement is a confusion which, as we shall see, characterizes both Bennett and his opponents in the canon debate: the slippage between *culture* and *civilization*. The semantic burden of the latter term obliquely recognizes what the concept of the national culture denies — the necessity of defining that culture largely by reference to the High Cultural artifacts to which access is provided in the schools. Bennett admits as much, without drawing any adverse conclusion from this point: "No student of our civilization should be denied access to the best that tradition has to offer." Is "our civilization," then, the same as "our culture"? One may reasonably question what necessary *cultural* relation a university-trained suburban manager or technocrat has to Plato or Homer by virtue of his or her American citizenship — no more, in fact, than an educationally disadvantaged dweller in the most impoverished urban ghetto. The suburban technocrat and the ghetto dweller

on the other hand have very much more in common culturally with each other than either of them ever need have with the great writers of Western civilization. If "Western" civilization — defined by a collection of cultural artifacts — can imaginarily displace the real cultural continuities that obtain at the national level, such an exemplary expression of the social imaginary is the effect of a crucial ambiguity in the concept of culture itself, an ambiguity familiar enough in the history of the concept as the distinction between culture in the sense of refinement — in this case, familiarity with the great works of "civilization" — and in the ethnographic sense of common beliefs, behaviors, attitudes — what a "national culture" would really have to mean.[4] The attempt to make the first sense of culture *stand for* the second names a certain project for the university, but one which it seems less well suited to undertake than ever (for reasons I will consider presently). The apparent failure of the university's cultural project of constituting a national culture elicits from the New Right the clamorous demand for a return to what was after all the *bourgeois* school, the institution enabling the old bourgeoisie to identify itself culturally by acquiring the cultural capital formerly restricted to the aristocratic or clerical estates. This capital consisted of nothing other than the "great works" of Western civilization.

If the national cultural project of the school is no longer a real possibility (it was always a class project anyway), the canon debate has nevertheless decisively problematized the notion of culture in its controversial language. The absence, however, of any concept of a specific *school* culture in the debate has meant that the perceived monolith of Western culture has had to be contested by the assertion of an antithetical "multiculturalism" as the basis of a politically progressive curriculum. Multiculturalism defines Western culture as its political antagonist, and vice versa. Yet the rather

---

[2]End product.
[3]William Bennett, "To Reclaim a Legacy," 21. [Guillory]

[4]See the entry for "culture" in Raymond Williams's *Keywords: A Vocabulary of Culture and Society,* revised edition (New York: Oxford University Press, 1976, 1983), 87–93, for a lucid account of what is at stake in the different meanings of "culture" historically. We might sum up the difference between our national culture and our school culture by acknowledging that for national culture "Nike" is the name of an athletic shoe, for school culture a Greek goddess. [Guillory]

too neat polarization of these terms elides the question of what school culture really is, that is, what *relation to culture* is produced by the formal study of cultural artifacts. Whatever other effects the introduction of multicultural curricula may have, the *theory* of multiculturalism perpetuates the confusion of culture as the study of preserved artifacts with the sense of culture as common beliefs, behaviors, attitudes. It is by no means the case that the study of cultural works simply operates as the agency of cultural transmission in the second sense — although school culture, as Bourdieu has shown, does its part to install a *class habitus*[5] in the subjects of its pedagogy. This habitus is defined not by the content of cultural works (Plato is not really part of "our culture"), but by the relation to culture inculcated by the school, the relation named precisely by Bennett's "legacy" — a relation of *ownership*. It is not the ideas expressed in the great works that account for their status in arguments such as Bennett's, but the fact that these works are appropriated as the cultural capital of a dominant fraction. That appropriation is in turn justified by representing the ideational content of the great works as an expression of the same ideas which are realized in the current social order, with its current distribution of cultural goods.

In order to accomplish the cultural task of appropriation, however, the school must traverse the heavily mined terrain of a certain alienation produced by the formal study of cultural works. We should not forget that the effects of this alienation are sometimes permanent, and that it is precisely "one's own" culture which sometimes fails to survive the culture of the school (that is to say, the school sometimes produces despite its acculturative function, dissident intellectuals). Similarly the formal study of cultural works produced within minority cultures is not a means of reproducing minority culture (in the ethnographic sense). If the formal study of Latin-American

novels in the university does not really transmit or reproduce Latino culture, it follows that the relation of even Latino students to these artifacts will not be entirely unlike the relation of "American" students to the works of "Western" (American or European) culture. The question is what this relation should be.

One conclusion to be drawn immediately from this argument is that there is no ground of commensuration between Western cultural artifacts on the one hand, if examples of these are the *Odyssey* or the Parthenon; and Latino culture on the other, if the latter means the totality of a living culture, and not just its artifacts. Insofar as it is only the *works* of Western or Latino culture to which one has direct access in the school, these works will ultimately be constructed and legitimated as objects of study *in the same way*, by a process of deracination from the actual cultural circumstances of their production and consumption.[6] If works by Afro-American, Latin-American, or postcolonial writers are read now in formal programs of university study, this fact may be the immediate result of a political project of inclusion, or the affirmation of cultural diversity. But the survival of these works in future school curricula will be seen otherwise, as a consequence of their status as interesting and important cultural works that no intellectually responsible program of study can ignore. The current project of affirming

[5] Bourdieu defines *habitus* as a "system of dispositions," the social equivalent of "linguistic competence" (Noam Chomsky's term for the sum of all the tacit knowledge one has to possess to speak a natural language), or the feel a skilled player has for a game. Bourdieu viewed *habitus* as class-related: Persons of the same class were likely, he found, to adopt a similar habitus across different social fields.

[6] Bourdieu, "Systems of Education and Systems of Thought," *International Social Science Journal* 19 (1967), 351, points to an analogous confusion when the concept of culture is made to refer indifferently both to popular culture and to school culture: "Just as Basil Bernstein contrasts the 'public language' of the working classes, employing descriptive rather than analytical concepts, with a more complex 'formal language,' more conducive to verbal elaboration and abstract thought, we might contrast an academic culture, confined to those who have been long subjected to the disciplines of the school, with a 'popular' culture, peculiar to those who have been excluded from it, were it not that, by using the same concept of culture in both cases, we should be in danger of concealing that these two systems of patterns of perception, language, thought, action and appreciation are separated by an essential difference. This is that only the system of patterns cultivated by the school, i.e. academic culture (in the subjective sense of personal cultivation or *Bildung* in German), is organized primarily by reference to a system of works embodying that culture, by which it is both supported and expressed." [Guillory]

cultures themselves through the legitimation of cultural works in university curricula is enabled by the very conflation between the senses of culture to which I have drawn attention. The very intensity of our "symbolic struggle" reduces cultural conditions of extreme complexity to an allegorical conflict between a Western cultural Goliath and its Davidic multicultural antagonists. Hence it is never really Greek culture, or French culture, or Roman culture, that is compared with Latino culture or Afro-American culture, but always "Western" culture. Multiculturalism finds itself in the position of having to credit both the reality and the homogeneity of that fictional cultural entity, which achieves its spurious self-identity only by consisting of *nothing but* cultural artifacts.[7]

If the fiction of the cultural homogeneity of the West is nevertheless a very powerful one (because it is ideological), perhaps the better strategy for resisting its domination-effect may be to expose the relation between the "culture" it pretends to embody and the institution which is its support in reality. It is just by suppressing culture in the ethnographic sense — or reserving that sense of culture for non-"Western" artifacts — that the traditional curriculum can appropriate the "great works" of Western civilization for the purpose of constituting an imaginary cultural unity such as Bennett or Hirsch[8] envisions. The deracination of the text tradition thus forces us to define

the intertextual relation, say, between Aquinas and Aristotle as evidence of the continuity of Western culture, but it allows us to set aside the fact that Aristotle and Aquinas have almost nothing in common *culturally*. It should be remarked here also that the construction of Western culture depends more upon a body of philosophical than literary texts. If the canon debate originated in university literature departments, the defenders of the canon extended the debate to the question of the humanities curriculum as a whole — the "core" curriculum — by resurrecting the philosophical text tradition as the basis for that core curriculum. This text tradition can be invoked more easily than national vernacular literatures to maintain the fiction of a profound evolution or destiny of Western thought extending from the pre-Socratics to the present.[9] Yet the fact remains that this continuity was always the historical support for *nationalist* agendas. The schools in the early modern nation-states provided an instrument by means of which the state could dissolve the residually feudal bonds of local sovereignty and reattach personal loyalty to itself. Nationalism is, as we have seen, entirely on the surface in Bennett's document. In the early modern period, the great vernacular literary works of the nation-states were taught in such a way as to constitute retroactively a pre-national "West" (usually classical rather than medieval), a continuity intended to cover over the traumatic break of early modern societies with traditional feudal cultures. The "West" was always the creation of

---

[7]This argument should not be taken to deny the fact that the "West" is a real politico-economic entity, even though its cultural homogeneity lags far behind the unity of its politico-economic system. The *image* of that cultural unity remains the ideological support for the real unity of the West in its imperial relations with the Third World, or in its militarist competition with what was formerly the Eastern Bloc. The collapse of the Soviet Union as a result of that competition, and the consolidation of a Western alliance in the Persian Gulf War are sufficient evidence of what was and is at stake in maintaining the fiction of the cultural unity of the West. Finally, do we need to be reminded that it is Coca-Cola and not Plato which signifies Western culture in the realm of what Immanuel Wallerstein calls "geo-culture"? On this subject, see John Tomlinson, *Cultural Imperialism: A Critical Introduction* (Baltimore: Johns Hopkins University Press, 1991). [Guillory]

[8]Eric Donald Hirsch (b. 1928), formerly professor of English at the University of Virginia, argued in his best-selling book, *Cultural Literacy: What Every American Needs to Know* (1987), that the deficiencies of American primary and secondary education were owing partly to the

systematic neglect of geographical, historical, and scientific facts, without which students were unable to make sense of political and cultural ideas. Hirsch's book concluded with a list of facts with which he thought every citizen ought to be familiar. While Guillory admits that Hirsch's agenda is not quite so simplistic as those of right-wing pundits like Bennett, he argues elsewhere that the "handy finiteness" of Hirsch's list of significant facts conferring cultural literacy "is the ideological denial of the heterogeneity" of Western culture (p. 354).

[9]This is the argument of Joan Shelley Rubin, *The Making of Middlebrow Culture* (Chapel Hill: University of North Carolina Press, 1992). Discussing John Erskine's original idea for a "great books" program at Columbia University, Rubin notes: "[B]y contending that 'great books' portrayed timeless, universal human situations [Erskine] permitted the conclusion that the classics of Western literature *were* the American heritage" (173). [Guillory]

nationalism, and that is why one observes that the assertion of the continuity of Western tradition exactly corresponds in its intensity to the assertion of nationalism itself.[10]

The homogenizing textual effects of deracination are even more obvious when we consider the fact that, for us, Plato and Aristotle, Virgil and Dante, are great works of literature *in English*. The translation of the "classics" into one's own vernacular is a powerful institutional buttress of imaginary cultural continuities; it confirms the nationalist agenda by permitting the easy appropriation of texts in foreign languages. Yet the device of translation should not be regarded as extraordinary or atypical of school culture, for translation is only a more explicit version of the same technique of deracination by which all cultural works are constructed as objects of study. This point may clarify the otherwise confusing status of "oral literature," which has become a favored site for the contestation of Western culture's hegemony. It is not a mere contingency that oral works must become "written" in order to be brought into the arena of curricular conflict as "noncanonical" works, excluded or devalued by the Western text tradition. In fact, oral works *cannot* otherwise enter the institutional field, since orality as a cultural condition can only be studied at all ethnographically, as the "writing of culture." When the condition of oral production is on the other hand ignored in the context of interpreting or evaluating these works (by treating oral works as though they were other written works), the real difference between school culture and the culture which gives rise to works disappears from view. By suppressing the context of a cultural work's production and consumption, the school produces the illusion that "our" culture (or the culture of the "other") is transmitted simply by contact with the works themselves. But a text tradition is not sufficient in itself either to constitute or to transmit a culture, and thus school culture can never be more than a part of a total process of acculturation which, for societies with schools, is always complex and has many other institutional sites.

The function imposed upon schools of acculturating students in "our" culture often thus requires that texts be read "out of context," as signs of cultural continuity, or cultural unity. We need not deny that the text tradition can sustain intertextual dialogue over centuries and millennia, however, in order to insist that what is revealed by the historical context of this dialogue is cultural discontinuity and heterogeneity.[11] A rather different pedagogy, one that emphasizes historical contextualization, would at the very least inhibit the assimilation of cultural works to the agenda of constituting a national culture, or the Western culture which is its ideological support.[12] For the very same reason, only the simplest countercultural pedagogy can make the works of the multicultural curriculum stand in a "subversive"

[10]The example of Heidegger almost goes without saying, but not quite. Heidegger's belief in the deep affinity between the Greek and German languages, supposedly the only truly philosophical languages, forces us to recall that the text tradition which is the support of the notion of the West is itself supported in modern European thought both by philological and racial concepts of continuity. [Guillory]

[11]Bourdieu, "Systems of Education and Systems of Thought": "Because of its own inertia, the school carries along categories and patterns of thought belonging to different ages. In the observance of the rules of the dissertation in three points, for example, French schoolchildren are still contemporaries of Saint Thomas. The feeling of the 'unity' of European culture' is probably due to the fact that the school brings together and reconciles — as it must for the purposes of teaching — types of thought belonging to very different periods" (352). What I have been calling a "text tradition" is obviously the site of critical judgment, in the sense that the entire domain of intertextuality, or response to earlier by later writers. Nevertheless I have consistently argued for locating the site of canon formation in the school, for the reason implied by Bourdieu in the passage just quoted. The point of the sociological argument, for both Bourdieu and myself, is that authors learn whom to read and how to judge in the schools, and that even the judgment of recent but uncanonized work must eventually be validated in the passage of writers into school curricula in order for one to speak of canonicity. One should not forget that literary history is filled with the names of writers whose high standing with other, more famous authors was still insufficient to insure their canonicity. [Guillory]

[12]Schools do not always have to acknowledge the fact of deracination, nor do they necessarily have to employ historicizing strategies of recontextualization in classroom practice. Precisely to the extent that they deny the former and decline the latter, they can realize the objective of merely reproducing culture as dogma, as in the case of religious schools. The operation of culture as dogma will be taken up in Chapter 3, Ideology and Canonical Form. [Guillory]

relation to Western culture. The historicization of these works too will have to confront the mutual influence and interrelation between dominant Western and dominated non-Western cultures (in the case of postcolonial works, for example, the fact that "Western culture" appears as a cultural unity *only* through the lens of the colonial educational system, and that postcolonial literatures are in constant dialogue with the works taught in that system). While there exists a multiplicity of sites of cultural production, then, this multiplicity can never really be equated with the multiplicity of cultures, as though every cultural work were only the organic expression of a discrete and autonomous culture.[13] The fact that we now expect the curriculum to reflect as a principle of its organization the very distinctness of cultures, Western or non-Western, canonical or noncanonical, points to a certain insistent error of culturalist politics, its elision of the difference the school itself makes in the supposed transmission of culture.

From the perspective of long-term developments in the educational system, the canon debate itself may seem oddly beside the point. Bennett and his associates already acknowledged in their 1984 document that the "crisis of the humanities" refers to the fact that fewer undergraduates choose to major in traditional humanities than in the past. One has the impression in surveying the musings of the right-wing pundits that this fact is the result of nothing less than abdication by the professors of their duty to teach the traditional texts.[14] Nothing could be further from the truth — these texts still constitute the vastly greater part of the humanities curriculum — and in that sense the complaint of the New Right is simply fraudulent. A welcome reality check is provided by Patrick Brantlinger in his analysis of the "crisis":

> Tradition gives the humanities an importance that current funding and research priorities belie. At giant public "multiversities" like the Big Ten schools, humanities courses are taken by many students only as requirements — a sort of force-feeding in writing skills, history, great books, and appropriate "values" before they select the chutes labeled "preprofessional" — pre-med, pre-law, and so forth. . . . Clearly, one doesn't need to blame the radical sixties for the current marginalization and sense of irrelevance that pervades the humanities today.[15]

The crisis of the humanities is the result not of university professors' unwillingness to teach great works (the idea is an insult especially to those teachers and graduate students who could not find employment in the recessions of the 70s and 80s) but of the decisions students themselves make in the face of economic realities. Granted the fact that the crisis is not the result of curricular decisions by humanities teachers, why is the content of the curriculum the site of such controversy? The canon debate will not go away, and it is likely to intensify as the positions of the right and of the multiculturalists are further polarized. The very strength of the reactionary backlash, its success in acquiring access to the national media and funding for its agitprop, suggests that the symptomatic importance of the debate is related in some as yet obscurely discerned way to the failure of the contestants to give an account of the general decline in the significance of the humanities in the educational system. It has proven to be much easier to quarrel about the content of the curriculum than to confront the implications of a fully emergent professional-managerial class which no longer requires the cultural capital of the old bourgeoisie. The decline of the humanities was never the result of newer noncanonical courses or texts, but of a large-scale "capital flight" in the domain of culture. The debate over what amounts to the supplementation (or modernization) of the traditional curriculum is thus a misplaced response

[13]This point has been eloquently argued by Kwame Anthony Appiah in the context of the production and consumption of African cultural works: "If there is a lesson in the broad shape of this circulation of cultures, it is surely that we are all already contaminated by each other, that there is no longer a fully autochthonous *echt*-African culture awaiting salvage by our artists (just as there is, of course, no American culture without African roots). And there is a clear sense in some postcolonial writing that the postulation of a unitary Africa over against a monolithic West — the binarism of Self and Other — is the last of the shibboleths of the modernizers that we must learn to live without." "Is the Post- in Postmodernism the Post- in Postcolonial?" *Critical Inquiry* 17 (1991), 354. [Guillory]

[14]See Allan Bloom, *The Closing of the American Mind* (New York: Simon and Schuster, 1987), p. 352. [Guillory]

[15]Patrick Brantlinger, *Crusoe's Footprints: Cultural Studies in Britain and America* (New York: Routledge, 1990), p. 7. [Guillory]

to that capital flight, and as such the debate has been conducted largely in the realm of the pedagogic imaginary, I would propose, then, that the division now characterizing the humanities syllabus — between Western and multicultural, canonical and noncanonical, hegemonic and non-hegemonic works — is the symptom of a more historically significant split between two kinds of cultural capital, one of which is "traditional," the other organic to the constitution of the professional-managerial class.

In this larger socioeconomic context, the polarization of the debate into a conflict between Western culture and multiculturalism has proven to be a political misstep for the left. For both the reactionary scapegoating of the noncanonical syllabus as the cause of the crisis of the humanities, and multiculturalism's reduction of canonical works to the ideology of a monolithic Western culture fail to recognize the real relations between the humanities curriculum and the social forces which operate on it. If the debate is ever to acknowledge the presence of these forces, it will have to move beyond the curricular distinction between the canonical and the noncanonical; it will have to raise the much larger question of what is at stake in the relation between the kinds of cultural capital. Since both canonical and noncanonical works constitute at base, despite their apparent conflict, the same *kind* of cultural capital, the social forces displacing this kind of capital will sooner or later strand the participants in the canon debate on an ever shrinking island within the university itself.

What needs urgently to be recognized now is that the polarization of the curriculum into canonical and noncanonical works is very much more in the interest of the right than of the left. The investment of the right in the great works of Western civilization — a "core" curriculum — is in extreme bad faith. For Bennett has already decided that what Bloom calls the "big questions" have been given definitive answers in the American social and political system, which rests on the unshakeable foundation of the *free market*. Yet it is the market itself which produces the effect of cultural capital flight. The professional-managerial class has made the correct assessment that, so far as its future profit is concerned, the reading of great works is not worth the investment of very much time or money. The perceived devaluation of the humanities curriculum is in reality a decline in its *market* value. If the liberal arts curriculum still survives as the preferred course of study in some elite institutions, this fact has everything to do with the class constituency of these institutions. With few exceptions, it is only those students who belong to the financially secure upper classes who do not feel compelled to acquire professional or technical knowledge as undergraduates. The professional-managerial class, on the other hand, many of whose members have only recently attained to middle and upper middle-class status, depends entirely on the acquisition of technical knowledge in order to maintain its status, or to become upwardly mobile. The challenge posed to a class analysis of culture by the professional-managerial class has been well described by Gouldner in his *The Future of Intellectuals and the Rise of the New Class:* "What is needed for the systematic analysis of the old and new class is a *general theory of capital* in which moneyed capital is seen as part of the whole, as a special case of capital. Conversely, what is required for the understanding of culture as capital is nothing less than a political economy of culture."[16] Whether such a political economy of culture has been successfully elaborated in the work of Gouldner or Bourdieu, it is entirely indicative of the conceptual limits of the curriculum debate that it could be carried on for over a decade virtually without reference to either figure.

[16]Alvin W. Gouldner, *The Future of Intellectuals and the Rise of the New Class* (New York: Oxford University Press, 1979), p. 21. Gouldner argues persuasively that "An investment in education is not simply a consumable. Something is left over, which produces a subsequent flow of income. It is *cultural capital,* the economic basis of the New Class" (27). On the other hand, I am not convinced that the problem-solving orientation of the New Class constitutes what Gouldner calls a "culture of critical discourse." This is not to say that the professional-managerial class has not produced some forms of social criticism — it has — but that this criticism is seldom systemic (it is usually anti-state but not anti-capital). I am also aware that arguments *against* systemic critique have been made on certain "post-Marxist" grounds. Foucault's concept of the "specific intellectual" might in this context be compared to Gouldner's concept of the New Class intellectual. My own argument follows Bourdieu, however, in his version of systemic critique. [Guillory]

In this context the right-wing design of purging noncanonical works from the curriculum has as one of its evident objectives the revaluation of the cultural capital of canonical works by associating them with currently popular nationalist and xenophobic sentiments. Mary Louise Pratt is surely correct in identifying the aim of this polemic as the creation of "a narrowly specific cultural capital that will be the normative *referent* for everyone, but will remain the *property* of a small and powerful caste that is linguistically and ethnically unified."[17] The crucial question, however, is not how "narrowly specific" this cultural capital is to be, but how it is to produce the effect of unifying a "caste." Because this unity is not preexistent in American society — capital itself is dispersed now among a number of ethnicities, genders, and even linguistic groups — it must be constituted in the university *after the fact,* as a new project for that institution. This circumstance explains why the right's agenda for the university always makes room for *some* members of minority groups, because the right believes these self-made individuals can be assimilated to the "caste" of all those with an interest in preserving the rights and privileges of their acquired capital. Such assimilation will leave (and has left) the grossly inequitable social structure more or less unchallenged. It is not quite the case, then, that the New Right wishes to purge the university of all linguistic or ethnic others, but that it sets the university the project of unifying the new possessors of cultural capital by cultural means, by means of a "common" curriculum which will identify them as (justly) privileged. In this way Bennett's "legacy" can be reclaimed for its proper inheritors, those who leave the university possessed of capital, of whatever kind. The cultural legacy so probated will present an image to a somewhat more ethnically heterogeneous propertied class of its unified cultural identity as the inheritors of cultural capital.

If this analysis is correct it does not seem the most effective strategy for the left to cede to the right the *definition* of cultural capital; but this is

exactly what a multiculturalism does when it yields canonical works to the right, when it accepts the right's characterization of the canonical syllabus as constitutive of a unified and monolithic Western culture. Basing its agenda upon such assumptions, a left politics of representation seems to have no other choice than to institutionalize alternative syllabi as representative images of non-Western or "counter"-cultures. This is finally why the project of legitimizing noncanonical works in the university produces an irresolvable contradiction between the presentation of these works as equal in cultural value to canonical works, and at the same time as the embodiment of countercultural values which by their very definition are intended to delegitimize the cultural values embodied in canonical works. The polarization of the debate into Western culturalism versus multiculturalism must then be seen not as a simple conflict between regressive and progressive pedagogies but as the symptom of the transformation of cultural capital in response to social conditions not yet recognized as the real and ultimately determining context of the canon debate. Both the right-wing attempt to shore up the cultural capital of the "great works" by advocating a return to a core curriculum, and the pluralist advocacy of multiculturalism respond to the same demographic circumstances, the heterogeneous constituency of the university. But neither version of culturalist politics responds to the heterogenous constitution of cultural capital, and hence both movements are condemned to register this condition symptomatically, as a false perception of the mutual (cultural) exclusivity of canonical and noncanonical works.

It is chastening to recall that a leftist analysis of the heterogeneity of cultural capital was available long before Bourdieu or Gouldner, in the work of Antonio Gramsci. In his prescient notes on the subject of education, Gramsci recognized that the displacement of the classical curriculum by professional and technical knowledge would have the effect of precipitating the "humanist" curriculum into what seems to be a permanent state of crisis:

The basic division of schools into classical (i.e. grammar) and trade schools was a rational scheme: trade schools for the instrumental classes, classical

---

[17]Pratt, "Humanities for the Future: Reflections on the Western Culture Debate at Stanford," *South Atlantic Quarterly* 89 (1990): 9. [Guillory]

schools for the ruling classes and intellectuals. The development of the industrial base in both town and country led to a growing need for a new type of urban intellectual: alongside the classical school there developed the technical school (professional but not manual), and this brought into question the very principle of the concrete orientation of general culture based on the Greco-Roman tradition. This orientation, once brought into question was in fact doomed, since its formative capacity was largely based on the general and traditionally indisputable prestige of a particular form of civilization.[18]

Gramsci expresses in his notes what may seem to the present liberal academy a surprising conservatism on curricular issues. Without arguing for the retention of the classical curriculum — Gramsci allows that it had to be replaced — he was concerned to point out the paradoxical social effects of the "new type of school" which, while it "appears and is advocated as being democratic" is actually "destined not merely to perpetuate social differences but to crystallize them in Chinese complexities".[19] The apparently conservative tenor of his remarks should not be confused, then, with the usual complaint about "specialization," which expresses nostalgia for the even less democratic educational system of the past (Gramsci insists that the older system was always "intended for the new generation of the ruling class"). The question is not whether technical or professional knowledges will or should be taught, but whether there exists a body of knowledge to which *everyone* should have access in the schools. Gramsci's solution to the emergence of a "crisis of the humanities" was to propose the formation of a "single, humanistic, formative, primary school of general culture which will correctly balance the development of ability for manual (technical, industrial) work with the development of ability for intellectual work.".[20] Gramsci's proposal may seem, at this date, uncritical of the content of such a curriculum, since he

did not have to consider his own society as in our sense "pluralist"; but we should remember that his sense of a politically strategic educational practice is supported by what is perhaps the most powerful theory of intellectual labor in the Marxist tradition, as well as by the very concept of hegemony that is invoked in virtually all forms of current cultural criticism. For these reasons a serious consideration of Gramsci's analysis may be in order.

What Gramsci called the "unitary school" was supposed to "break [the] pattern" of the traditional educational system, in which "each group has its own type of school, intended to perpetuate a specific traditional function, ruling or subordinate."[21] The new technical and professional schools reinstated the division of society "into juridically fixed and crystallized estates rather than moving towards the transcendence of class divisions." The issue here is not only class division but the conditions of possibility for democratic self-government, since Gramsci rightly sees the schools as providing the means for participating in government: "But democracy, by definition, cannot mean merely that an unskilled worker can become skilled. It must mean that every 'citizen' can 'govern' and that society places him, even if only abstractly, in a general condition to achieve this" (318). This is of course an old theme, but the simultaneous and not unrelated decline of both public education and participatory democracy in the United States should confirm its continued pertinence. For reasons too obvious to belabor, Gramsci's "unitary school" was never a goal in this country; but since our concern is with the American educational system, we can at least note that the very limited "democratization" of that system has been accompanied by the gradual displacement upwards to the university level of the curriculum Gramsci conceived as the basis of a "unitary school." This arrangement accomplishes the effect of class fractioning by tracking most students into the work force at the end of their primary or secondary schooling (an effect reinforced also by the distinction between public and private schools). Given the social pressure to enforce vocational tracking at the lower levels of the educational system, and to dispense more

[18] Antonio Gramsci, *The Modern Prince and Other Writings* (New York: International Publishers, 1957), 126. [Guillory]

[19] Antonio Gramsci, *The Antonio Gramsci Reader: Selected Writings 1916–1935*, ed. David Forgas (New York: Schocken Books, 1988), 317. [Guillory]

[20] Gramsci, *The Modern Prince*, 127. [Guillory]

[21] Gramsci, *The Antonio Gramsci Reader*, 318. [Guillory]

highly valued professional and technical knowledge at the university level, the slot into which the humanities curriculum is confined is very small — as we know, the first two years of college study. In the absence of a "unitary school" at the primary or secondary levels, the possibility of installing a core curriculum of philosophical or literary works exists only during this brief period. Many colleges, of course, have always had some form of a core curriculum, but the important point is that the formal study of a set list of "great works" is condemned to have something of a remedial status for those students who have not read literary or philosophical works, either historical or contemporary, at the lower levels of the system, and who will not continue to study them after their sophomore year. It is only by first recognizing the remedial status of the first two years of college study that we can then pose the question of what Gramsci's analysis may have to offer the present debate.

It will first be necessary to exit the social imaginary by acknowledging that there is no question of producing a *national* culture by means of a *university* curriculum. Or conversely of producing a national multiculturalist ethos by the same means. The question is rather what social effects are produced by the knowledges disseminated in the university, and by the manner of their dissemination. It should not be the business of the university to produce a "common culture" even if the educational system inevitably produces a school culture, a specific relation to knowledge among its subjects. The objective of political integration is not to be confused with the altogether questionable objective of cultural assimilation. Gramsci's analysis suggests that a necessary social condition of democracy is the general exercise of a certain kind of intellectual labor, and that a specific body of knowledge (by which is meant neither *information* in Hirsch's sense, nor *culture* in Bennett's) is the necessary medium in the schools for the exercise of this intellectual labor. The point of the unitary school is that it is a school for everyone; by definition it is not the university. A necessary objective of a Gramscian reconsideration of the curriculum debate would thus be the rearticulation of that debate in the context of the educational system *as* a system. In this context, we can recognize that the constraints upon the university curriculum at its present moment and in its present form account for the fact that the project of a core curriculum is so easily annexed to a socially regressive agenda. Time is one such constraint, since it intensifies the effect of deracination to the point of reducing the study of "great works" to a shallow rehearsal of contextless ideas; such "ideas" turn out unsurprisingly to be nothing more than the clichés of right-wing ideology.[22] It has been all too easy as a consequence for the left/liberal professoriate to identify the only respectable adversarial stance with opposition to a core curriculum. The institutionalization of the distinction between canonical and noncanonical works thus emerges as the necessary response to any attempt to reinstitute an exclusively traditional curriculum. As an expression of the same culturalist politics which confuses school culture with culture in general, this adversarial position unfortunately also deprives the teaching of canonical works of an adequate progressive rationale.

[22]There is reason to believe that the inevitable brevity and shallowness of the great-books tour are not so undesirable to the New Right. For they are less interested finally in inquiring closely into historical complexities or discursive ambiguities than in making sure that students come away from their experience of reading great works with the *right ideas*. This objective is quite openly acknowledged by the classicist Donald Kagan, who has been celebrated in the right-wing media for using his position as the dean of Yale College as a bully pulpit for what he calls "common studies." Mindful of the liberal persuasion of many of his faculty, however, the dean has expressed some doubt about their suitability to teach these works in the *right way:* "Consider what a core constructed by the current faculty would look like, and the consequences that would ensue if they also had the responsibility of teaching it." See Donald Kagan, "Yale University: Testing the Limits," *Academic Questions* 4 (1991), 33. On the historical origins of the idea of "great books" in American society, and the tendency toward the "superficial" assimilation of the books, see Rubin, *The Making of Middlebrow Culture,* 192ff. Rubin demonstrates persuasively that Mortimer Adler's transformation of John Erskine's notion of a great-books program into the Encyclopaedia Britannica's *Great Books of the Western World* produced nothing less than a monument of middlebrow culture. The almost exclusive emphasis on philosophical rather than literary works in the Britannica project called forth the famous "Syntopicon" of "Great Ideas," which virtually assured that no one would ever have to read the books themselves. [Guillory]

It is perhaps time for progressive teachers to take back the humanities curriculum — all of it — as an integrated program of study. Such a program will be severely limited by the narrow stratum of the educational system which it is forced to inhabit, but until we can begin to think and speak about education as a system of interrelated levels, these limits will continue to function subliminally, beyond analysis or intervention. In the meantime, we can imagine that an integrated curriculum would supersede the distinction between canonical and noncanonical works in the recognition that a syllabus of study always enacts a negotiation between *historical* works and *modern* works. There is no question now, nor has there even been, of the inevitability of curricular change: the latter-day curriculum is the archaeological evidence of its own sedimented history. When we read Plato or Homer or Virgil in a humanities course, then, we are reading what *remains* of the classical curriculum after the vernacular revolutions of the early modern period. The fact that we no longer read these works in Greek or Latin, or that we read far fewer classical Greek or Latin works than students of premodern school systems, represents a real loss; but this loss must be reckoned as the price of the *integration* of these works into a modern curriculum. The inevitable loss of older works in any humanities curriculum, even one hypothetically much larger than current programs tend to be, is the result, as we have observed, of the *absolute* accumulation of cultural works. The reactionary defense of the traditional "canon" thus betrays itself as ignorant of the cultural history sedimented in the very syllabus it desires to fix. On the other hand it should no longer be necessary to present certain other works, "noncanonical" works, as intrinsically opposed to a hegemonic principle of canonicity, as this is likewise to forget the history sedimented in any syllabus of study.

An alternative theoretical formulation of the curriculum problem will thus have to repudiate the practice of fetishizing the curriculum, of locating the politics of pedagogy in the anxious drawing up of a list of representative names. The *particular* names matter even less at the university level, since the number of historical and modern works worth studying is vastly greater than any (remedial) course of study could begin to consider. The syllabus should rather be conceived as the means of providing *access* to cultural works, both historical and modern (the contrary assumption — that works not on the syllabus will never be read — is an entirely disreputable assumption for teachers to make). Since noncanonical works are in every case either historical works (the objects of research or revaluation) or modern works (the objects of legitimation for the first time as cultural capital), they are in fact what all canonical works once were. To contend otherwise is to commit oneself to the notion that some works are intrinsically canonical, simply expressive of the dominant ideology, and other works intrinsically noncanonical, utterly unassimilable to hegemonic culture. If that were true, what would the struggle to legitimize new works as objects of study be *for?* Hegemony, in Gramsci's sense, is to be fought for; it is something that is continually won and lost by struggles which take place at the specific sites of social practice.

What difference would such a reformulation of terms make? First, that current research programs such as women's studies, or Afro-American studies be recognized as such, as research programs and not as the institution of separate curricula for separate constituencies. But even more important, the humanities curriculum should be presented as an integrated program of study in which the written works studied constitute a certain kind of cultural capital, and in which works therefore cannot be allegorized as intrinsically canonical or intrinsically noncanonical, intrinsically hegemonic or intrinsically antihegemonic. No cultural work of any interest at all is simple enough to be credibly allegorized in this way, because any cultural work will *objectify* in its very form and content the same social conflicts that the canon debate allegorizes by means of a divided curriculum. Further, a conception of an integrated curriculum would make it impossible to forget that what one internalizes in the school is not one's own culture but the culture of the school (which has in turn a certain relation, but not a relation of identity, to culture in the ethnographic sense). The school produces a culture, then, neither unambiguously good or bad, but it does not simply reproduce a given culture, hegemonic or antihegemonic, through the *content* of the curriculum. If it is a defensible objective of the school to disseminate knowledge about the "multicultural" diversity of the nation (defensible because the nation *is* so diverse), it follows from this very objective that it is just as important for majority students to study the cultural products of minority cultures as it is for minority students to be able to study the cultural works of their own cultures. Hence when works by minority writers are legitimized as cultural capital by becoming objects of study in the university, it will follow that everyone will have a right of access to them.

Especially in the wake of a reactionary backlash which indicts the liberal critique of the canon for the abandonment of all standards of judgment, it is no longer politically strategic to argue for the necessity of teaching certain "noncanonical" works solely on the grounds that these works represent social minorities. It is on the contrary much more strategic to argue that the school has the social obligation of providing access to these works, *because they are important and significant cultural works.* In this way we will disabuse ourselves and our students of the idea that canonical or noncanonical syllabi have natural constituencies, the members of dominant or subordinate cultures respectively. The latter notion operates tacitly in the canon debate as the illegitimate displacement of liberal concepts of representation to a site — the school — where democratic objectives are better served by the modestly coercive structure of (in Gramsci's terms) a "unitary" curriculum. Extrapolating from Gramsci's analysis of the relation between the school and democracy, we can predict that different curricula for different constituencies will produce the same effects of social stratification as different schools for different classes. There is not, and should not be, one national culture, but there is, and there should be, one educational system.

But here we return to the fundamental point: pluralism has been able to affirm different cultures but not the fact that cultures are inescapably interdependent both at the moment of a cultural work's production and at that of its consumption. The question is whether or not the school is to acknowledge this "postmodern" condition. It is certainly acknowledged in the domain of

mass culture, where cultural products are very often produced for particular constituencies, but where their circulation "interculturally" is virtually assured by the restless promiscuity of commodity exchange. These conditions need not be denied in the university but rather made the occasion of what Christopher Miller, in responding to Hirsch's notion of a national culture, has called "intercultural literacy": "Intercultural literacy would consist of a mode of inquiry that respects the accumulation of shared symbols (thus the term *literacy*) but also invites research into the processes by which cultures are formed and particularly encourages analysis of how cultures constitute themselves *by reference to each other.*"[23]

An integrated curriculum would imply a second, pragmatic assumption: It is just as important for both minority and nonminority students to study historical works as it is for both groups to study modern works. The study of historical works need not be justified as an apotropaic[24] exercise — because these works are supposed to embody hegemonic values — but because they *are* historical works. The cultures which give rise to them are as other to all of us as minority cultures are to some of us. Here we can take leave of another fetish of the canon debate, namely, the exclusive emphasis on cultural artifacts as representative of cultures, in the absence of real knowledge about the history of these cultures. The relative lack of reference to history in the curriculum debate is symptomatic of how the concept of culture is deformed in the mirror of the pedagogic imaginary, all the more so since this deformation fails to account for the immanent historicity of even the most recent works. No program of multiculturalism will succeed in producing more than a kind of favorable media-image of minority cultures if it is not supported at every point by an understanding of the historical relations between cultures. At the same time one must insist that it is no longer intellectually

---

[23]Christopher L. Miller, "Literary Studies and African Literature: The Challenge of Intercultural Literacy," in *Africa and the Disciplines: Contributions of Research in Africa to the Social Sciences and Humanities,* ed. Robert H. Bates et al. (Chicago: University of Chicago Press, 1983). [Guillory]
[24]Intended to avert evil.

alone, because it is an effect of the educational *system*, of which the university is only a part. Does this mean that curricular reform is pointless, or that it has no social consequences? On the con-trary, the university curriculum is at this moment a privileged site for raising questions about the educational system as a whole, just because it is the site at which a "crisis" of cultural capital (or the "humanities") has occurred. The claim of the present argument is that an analysis of this crisis in terms of the distribution of cultural capital will produce a more strategic theory of curricular reform than will a pluralist critique.

If progressive teachers have a considerable stake in disseminating the kind of knowledge (the study of cultural works as a practice of read-ing and writing) that is the vehicle for critical thinking, this knowledge is nevertheless only the vehicle for critical thought, not its realization. As cultural capital it is always also the object of appropriation by the dominant classes. The pluralist strategy of institutionalizing the cat-egory of the noncanonical is incapable of grasp-ing this essential ambiguity of the school as an institution. For the same reason that a syllabus of canonical works cannot reproduce a culture of the dominant outside a certain total struc-turation of the educational system, no syllabus of noncanonical works can function ipso facto as the embodiment of that system's critique. To demand that critical thinking be institutional-ized entails an obvious contradiction, but the desire for the institutionalization of a pluralist cri-tique is what drives the current form of curricular revision. We can at most, however, institutional-ize the *conditions* of critical thought, in this case a curriculum that makes possible the maximum dissemination of the practices of reading and writing. Inasmuch as the study of cultural works in historical context constitutes a good condition for these practices, no curricular intervention which does not *reaffirm* the cultural capital of these works can ensure the viability of that condi-tion. In the present regime of capital distribu-tion, the school will remain both the agency for the reproduction of unequal social relations and a necessary site for the critique of that system.

defensible to equate historical knowledge with "Western history." It has always been the case (if not always acknowledged) that Western history is the history of the *global* relations of Western states, societies, and cultures; and even more that it is only as a consequence of its global relations that the "West" could conceive or write its own history. If the curriculum is to produce intercul-tural literacy, in recognition of the imbricated[25] sites of cultural production, we must assume that the context of cultural production is nothing *less* than global.

Were the left/liberal academy to reappropriate the "humanities," that is, to take back the author-ity to define the cultural capital embodied in its curriculum of study, it would have to devise a rationale for an integrated curriculum of textual/historical study exceeding the laudable objective of affirming cultural diversity. A left rationale for an integrated curriculum would have to present all of the cultural works in that curriculum, whatever their provenance, as a species of cultural capital constitutively different from the capital embodied in technical and professional knowledge. This difference can be defined by the proposition that *everyone* has a right of access to cultural works, to the means of both their production and their consumption. The dissemination of these means produces at every level of the educational system a form of "literacy," or what we would otherwise recognize as the practices of *reading* and *writing*. It would make an immense social difference if the knowledge designated by the latter terms were the property of everyone; but we are speaking here of what may be called "socialized" educa-tion, that is, of something that does not exist in this country. If the current educational institution does indeed (like every other social institution) reproduce social inequities, it achieves this effect by the unequal distribution of cultural capital, or by presenting cultural works in the classroom as the organic expression of the dominant classes' entitlement to those works. This effect cannot be undone by changing the university curriculum

25 Composed of overlapping parts.

7

FEMINIST CRITICISM

*The madwoman in literature by women is not, as she might be in male literature, an antago-
nist or foil to the heroine. Rather she is usually in some sense the author's double, an image
of her own anxiety and rage.* — SANDRA GILBERT AND SUSAN GUBAR

*To write chapters decrying the sexual stereotyping of women in our literature while closing
our eyes to the sexual harassment of our women students and colleagues . . . destroys both
the spirit and meaning of what we are about.* — ANNETTE KOLODNY

*The existence of a feminist movement was an essential precondition to the growth of feminist
literature. . . . The fact that a parallel Black feminist movement has been much slower in
evolving cannot help but have impact upon the situation of Black women writers and artists
and explains in part why . . . we have been so ignored.* — BARBARA SMITH

*Feminist criticism is currently so appealing to male theorists that some feminists are begin-
ning to regard the development with some suspicion.* — ELAINE SHOWALTER

What is feminist criticism and what is not? To begin, feminist criticism does not
include all literary criticism written by women, since some commentators on literature, from Anna Laetitia Barbauld to Camille Paglia, do not seem to meet their
own era's definition of feminism or ours. Nor does it include all criticism written
by feminists. The late Eve Sedgwick considered herself a feminist, but her book on
male homosocial desire, *Between Men,* whose introduction forms part of Chapter 8,
explores a subject whose relation to feminism is tangential. The characteristic common to the essays grouped here is their concern for how being a woman affects both
reading and writing: how men write about women; how women read both men's
and women's writing; how the sexes differ in their use of language and the roots of
their creativity.

This chapter primarily explores a particular tradition of Anglo-American feminist
literary criticism, a particular set of stages in the evolution of thinking about sex
and writing. Chronicles presenting a history of feminist criticism, such as those of
K. K. Ruthven and Toril Moi, or in Elaine Showalter's essay "Toward a Feminist
Poetics," usually present a standard evolutionary sequence. It begins with a critique

of patriarchal culture. In the field of literary criticism, this critique strives to expose the explicit and implicit misogyny in male writing about women. This phase would also include, as a corrective, a presentation of the very different ways in which women read male writers — and each other. The second phase might be character-ized by a concern about the place of female writers within a canon largely shaped by male publishers, reviewers, and academic critics. The third phase (which Showalter calls "gynocritics" as a translation of the French *gynocritique*) consists of a search for the conditions of women's language and creativity, for modes of textuality based in gender.

This is the evolutionary history, or a part of it, of feminist literary criticism in England and America in the 1970s and 1980s. It should be remembered, however, that each of the phases continues to inspire significant work: none of the suc-cessive stages of feminist criticism has been ousted from its evolutionary niche by its successors. But both the evolutionary history and the issues of concern to successive stages of feminist criticism look somewhat different when one turns to France, where patriarchy has taken a different form than in Anglophone cultures. In "Women's Time" (1979), reprinted below, Julia Kristeva distinguishes between three "generations" of feminists. The first, which she identifies with women who came to feminism before the radicalizing moment of May 1968 (when students and workers united in a strike intended to bring on a new French revolution), was concerned to reform patriarchy and to achieve liberal political goals—abortion, contraception, equal pay, professional recognition, and so on. This process of reform, Kristeva states, is transforming the world, but does not represent a revolu-tion in values, for women are only attempting to appropriate the things men had formerly kept for themselves. The second, post-1968 generation, that of Hélène Cixous, proposes a radical shift in values: the valorization of "feminine" over "masculine" characteristics, a revaluation that Kristeva rejects as a mere inver-sion of the dialectic of patriarchy. Like René Girard, Kristeva reads patriarchy as a political institution that channels sacred violence against scapegoats for the sake of social order. If women have been throughout recorded time the usual sym-bolic sacrifices, as they have, Kristeva sees no improvement to the social order if they change places with men. The third generation, according to Kristeva, in the process of formation in the late 1970s, was a generation for whom "the very dichotomy man/woman as an opposition between two rival entities" is coming to be understood as "belonging to metaphysics." In effect Kristeva heralds the deconstruction of the premises of both patriarchy and feminism in a move that today might be called "post-feminism." In a different sense, Kristeva also anticipates the work of Judith Butler and other gender theorists we shall meet in Chapter 8, Gender Studies and Queer Theory.

Patriarchal misogyny, the canon, and women's writing are key issues for the crit-ics represented in this chapter, but it is important to note that the feminist criticism of the 1970s and 1980s had important forebears, some of whose representatives appear in Part One of this book. Christine de Pisan in the Middle Ages and Aphra Behn in the Restoration were concerned to counter misogyny and the claim that women could not be effective and creative writers. Germaine de Staël in eighteenth-century

France had a strong sense of what literary tasks women writers could perform more effectively than men. Simone de Beauvoir explicated the ways in which Woman becomes the site of Alterity for men — always an Object, never allowed to attain the status of Subject on her own. And many of the concerns addressed in this chapter were raised as long ago as 1929 in Virginia Woolf's *A Room of One's Own.* Woolf's ironic commentary, set in the British Museum and one of the new women's colleges at Oxford, on how women have been traditionally denigrated by male scholars and teachers, long predates the work of both de Beauvoir and images-of-women critics such as Kate Millett and Mary Ellmann. Woolf's analysis of the women novelists of the nineteenth century — how Austen succeeded in devising a "feminine" sentence that allowed her to say just what she needed to, while the adoption of a "masculine" prose by Charlotte Brontë and George Eliot hampered their expressiveness — anticipates more recent research on women's language and writing. And Woolf's emphatic endorsement of Coleridge's claim that a great mind is naturally androgynous takes a stand on an issue that moves us beyond the concerns of the current chapter into those of the next.

WOMEN READING MEN READING WOMEN

Woolf's groundbreaking exploration of the major issues precipitated no immediate outpouring of feminist studies. Feminist criticism is a cultural outgrowth of the women's movement in general, and the 1930s and 1940s, owing to the Depression, the rise of fascism, and World War II, were not favorable times for feminist politics. After the war, however, feminist criticism revived and focused on the ways in which male authors present women — distorted by their own masculine prejudices and needs. The precursor text here is Simone de Beauvoir's *The Second Sex* (1949), in which de Beauvoir analyzes sexism in most of its cultural forms (see p. 394 for a detailed discussion). De Beauvoir recognizes that even the greatest poets and writers, and even those who were most favorably disposed toward women, like Stendhal, created Women either subtly or grossly as the Other they required.

Although *The Second Sex* was published in North America in 1953, Beauvoir did not become an iconic figure here until the 1970s, when the American feminist movement began to gather steam. By that time, two other important American works, Mary Ellmann's *Thinking about Women* (1968) and Kate Millett's *Sexual Politics* (1970), had launched the feminist critique of male writing. Ellmann's *Thinking about Women* is an ironic work, concerned less about the way male writers talk about women than about the way male reviewers talk about women *writers;* the result is a "phallic criticism" that emphasizes the writers' figurative "bust, waist, and hip measurements" rather than their literary qualities. Kate Millett's book proclaimed the general thesis that, if the century from 1830 to 1930 had been one of sexual revolution, the succeeding three decades had been years of counterrevolution. In the earlier period, women gained the right to education, the right to work, and the right to vote, and generally achieved the capacity for political existence independent of men; in the more recent period, ideologies from Freudian psychology to Marxism to fascism had conspired to keep women in their place. In literary terms, Millett's critique of the new patriarchy operates through readings of Henry Miller, Norman Mailer, and D. H. Lawrence. By the standards of today's feminist writers, Millet's readings of texts can often seem simplistic and reductive; her passages for analysis, however, are aptly chosen for the polemical points she makes.

WOMEN READING

In the 1960s Millett and Ellmann were primarily concerned with how men read women: in the 1970s women began to read men — and each other — in new and theoretically interesting ways. Perhaps the most sophisticated of the reader-response feminist critics is Annette Kolodny, whose "Some Notes on Defining a 'Feminist Literary Criticism'" (1975), explored problems of methodology, aiming to prove to prejudiced males that feminist questions required serious thought. Kolodny's position was empiricist. While women's experience in the past and present differed from men's, it would be unsafe to claim that women's literature was distinctive until this could be demonstrated directly. Kolodny appears to be skeptical about contemporary claims, like those of Showalter, for a distinctively female kind of writing. The case she makes out is that women read differently from men: they read both life and literature from the perspective of a disparate personal experience.[1] Kolodny's "A Map for Rereading" (1980) discusses two issues: how the differing interpretive modes of men and women appear within two stories (Charlotte Perkins Gilman's "The Yellow Wallpaper" and Susan Keating Glaspell's "A Jury of Her Peers"); and how the discrepancy between male and female ways of apprehending the world was mirrored in the fate of these two stories in the male-dominated literary marketplace. Kolodny has been more concerned than most feminist critics with finding a rhetoric to counter male opposition to feminism. In "Dancing Through the Minefield" (reprinted in this chapter), Kolodny presents her feminist theses so "that current hostilities might be transformed into a true dialogue with our critics."

Kolodny's theoretical perspective on the differences between male and female ways of reading the codes of literature and life is echoed in the practical criticism of Judith Fetterley. Fetterley's book *The Resisting Reader* (1978; see p. 605) begins by dismantling the assumption that texts — in her case, the primary texts of American fiction — are written for a universal audience. In fact, Fetterley states, "To read the canon of what is currently considered classic American literature is perforce to identify as male. . . . It insists on its universality at the same time that it defines that universality in specifically male terms" (p. xii). Traditionally, women have allowed themselves to be "immasculated" — inscribed within masculinity — in reading these texts, but they do so at the heavy price of internalizing self-hatred or at least self-doubt. Today, that price is too high. "The first act of the feminist critic must be to become a resisting rather than an assenting reader, to begin the process of exorcising the male mind that has been implanted in us" (p. xxii).

[1] "Some Notes on Defining a 'Feminist Literary Criticism,'" *Critical Inquiry* 2 (1975): 75–92.

Jonathan Culler's "Reading as a Woman," a section from his book *On Deconstruction* (1983), takes a somewhat different slant on the issue of feminist reading. It would be easy to mistake Culler's analysis of the different ways women read men, and each other, for a careful exposition of theorists discussed elsewhere in this introduction (Ellmann, Millett, and Showalter) or discussed in other chapters (such as Judith Fetterley, discussed in Chapter 3 as a reader-response critic, or Luce Irigaray, discussed in the Introduction to Chapter 8). It is only after presenting three modes or moments of feminist reading that Culler's own ideas come to the fore:

> From these varied writings, a general structure emerges. In the first moment or mode, where woman's experience is treated as a firm ground for interpretation, one swiftly discovers that this experience is not the sequence of thoughts present to the reader's consciousness as she moves through the text but a reading or interpretation of "woman's experience" — her own and others' — which can be set in a vital and productive relation to the text. In the second mode, the problem is how to make it possible to read as a woman: the possibility of this fundamental experience induces an attempt to produce it. In the third mode, the appeal to experience is veiled but still there, as a reference to maternal rather than paternal relations or to woman's situation and experience of marginality, which may give rise to an altered mode of reading. The appeal to the experience of the reader provides leverage for displacing or undoing the system of concepts or procedures of male criticism, but "experience" always has this divided, duplicitous character: it has always already occurred and yet is still to be produced — an indispensable point of reference, yet never simply there. . . . For a woman to read as a woman is not to repeat an identity or an experience but to play a role she constructs with reference to her identity as a woman, which is also a construct, so that the series can continue: a woman reading as a woman reading as a woman. . . .

Culler is in effect deconstructing the idea of "woman's experience" in terms of the role it plays in feminist reading, always receding from the point of reference it is given. When it is appealed to as a natural fact, that only uncovers its cultural construction; appealed to as a cultural construct, we come to wonder how a phallocentric culture can construct something as foreign to it as "woman's experience." Woman must know who she is in order to read as she does, but only learns who she is in the course of reading. This is not by any means a vicious circle, but it gives one much to ponder.

WOMEN TALKING

One of the more intriguing questions feminist criticism has broached is whether there is a special "women's language" that is different from that spoken by men. One would expect that inscription within patriarchy would have its effects on the way women speak, and this notion has been firmly endorsed by the pioneering studies of linguist Robin Lakoff in *Language and Woman's Place* (1975). Lakoff suggests that more is involved in "talking like a lady" than mere vocabulary (e.g., the use of adjectives like "adorable" or "divine" and of color-words like "mauve"; the avoidance of scatological terms). Lakoff considers some syntactic constructions as typically female, like the "tag-question," which seeks agreement rather than aggressively taking a stand (e.g., "Mozart is a wonderful composer, isn't he?"). She suggests that women's traditional powerlessness is reflected in their greater use of indirect utterances but that such usages also reinforce current sex roles.

While Lakoff was developing the concept of "genderlect" — dialectical differences owing to gender — she tended to believe that sexist usages were unalterably
fixed in language. She doubted that it was possible to dislodge the generic use of
man to include women or of *he* as the neutral pronoun; but she was equally uncertain
that these forms were seriously sexist and was inclined to consider them innocuous
asymmetries. But are they innocuous? In an empirical study (1980), Jeanette Silveira
found that respondents often did not understand that females were included in the
generic *man or he*, and that this was true of female as well as male subjects.[2] On the
issue of change, Lakoff's conservatism seemed justified at the time by the long and
futile history — going back to 1850 — of attempts at pronoun reform (the use of
constructed neuter pronouns like *thon* or *hiser*). But since 1975 an effective series of
guidelines for using sex-neutral language has been adopted by most publishers. Not
only has the generic masculine been dropped but also phrases suggesting that certain
jobs are gender-oriented, either by direct implication ("fireman" or "policeman") or
by marking the less common gender (e.g., "lady lawyer" or "male nurse"). Another
sexist practice noted by Lakoff, that of referring to a female author by both first and
last names (Jane Austen, Emily Dickinson) but to a male author by last name alone
(Dickens, Lawrence), seems to be passing. Similarly "Ms," as the marriage-neutral
form of address for women has become common if not universal. In effect, Lakoff's
work has dated because society has become sensitive to sexist language and has
made some significant attempts at reform.

Lakoff's work has dated in another sense, too: Some of its assertions have been
questioned by later empirical studies. For example, her claim that women use tag
questions more often than men do was supported by two experiments and refuted by
three others. It now appears that social setting may be more important than gender
in determining whether speakers produce tag questions; even powerful males tend
to use many tag questions when they are running meetings. In general, theories of
"genderlect" are less popular than they were in the 1970s, as researchers recognize
that the variations in speech patterns *within* each gender are greater than the differences *between* genders.

Feminist linguists have focused instead on sociolinguistic issues, such as the
frequency with which women are addressed in familiar terms ("dear," or "honey,")
by people they do not know, the relative frequency with which women and men
interrupt each other and allow themselves to be interrupted,[3] the large number of
pejorative terms for women as opposed to those for men,[4] and the unexamined
assumptions that women will take their father's name at birth and their husband's
name upon marriage. (Feminist linguists sensitive to this issue have changed or

---

[2]Jeanette Silveira, "Generic Masculine Words and Thinking," in *The Voices and Words of Women and
Men*, ed. Cheris Kramarae (Oxford: Pergamon Press, 1980), pp. 165–78.

[3]Candice West and Don H. Zimmerman, "Small Insults: A Study of Interruptions in Cross-sex
Conversations between Unacquainted Persons," in *Language, Gender, and Society*, ed. Barrie Thorne
et al. (Rowley, MA: Newbury House, 1983), pp. 103–18.

[4]Julia Penelope Stanley found 220 terms for a sexually promiscuous woman, only 22 for a man.
See "Paradigmatic Woman: The Prostitute," in *Papers in Language Variation*, ed. David Shores
(Birmingham: University of Alabama Press, 1977).

reinvented their names: e.g., Cheris Kramarae previously published as Chris Kramer, Julia Penelope Stanley is now Julia Penelope.)

More recently, the work of Deborah Tannen, another sociolinguist and a former collaborator of Robin Lakoff, has enjoyed extraordinary popular success. Tannen's *You Just Don't Understand: Women and Men in Conversation* (1990) explicates the mutual misprisions of men and women in terms of the differences between their customary purposes of dialogue: Males make "report talk," presenting facts evaluable with hierarchal logic, while females make "rapport talk" to create alliances and cement relationships. Whether these generalizations are any more defensible than Lakoff's, the success of *You Just Don't Understand,* which stayed on the *New York Times* bestseller list for over four years, was immense, partly because the book was interpreted as an important tool for corporate management techniques. Tannen has followed up *You Just Don't Understand* with further discussions of gender styles, including *That's Not What I Meant* (1992) and *Talking Nine to Five: Men and Women in the Workplace: Language, Sex and Power* (1995). Her earlier scholarly articles on such psycholinguistic issues as interruption, origination of topics, and ethnic styles of conversation are collected in *Gender and Discourse* (1994).

WOMEN WRITING

Perhaps the least controversial aspect of recent feminist studies has been its attempt to locate and expand a female tradition of writing. Some authors (from Christine de Pisan to Kate Chopin) have been exhumed from near oblivion and raised to the status of classics; others (like Anne Bradstreet and Mary Shelley), never really lost to sight, have been reinterpreted as central to the literary canon rather than as marginal, if well-known, figures. As in all efforts to expand the canon, more candidates will inevitably be proposed than will eventually find a place within. And if some writers now receiving general attention are those like Charlotte Perkins Gilman, who enrich and deepen feminists' sense of their own history, others, like Mary Shelley and Anna Laetitia Barbauld, espoused conservative attitudes toward "woman's place," which their present-day readers would be loath to adopt.

If the criterion is whether literature by women is taught in colleges and universities, the effort to expand the canon has been successful. But much of this success has occurred within special "women's studies" programs and in special courses within traditional programs, so that one may wonder whether women have truly been included within the traditional canon or whether a counter-canon of literature by women has been advanced to parallel the former canon defined primarily by men. And feminist critics like Nina Baym have questioned whether the canon has been created in a gender-neutral fashion or whether the books have been cooked.

Nina Baym's historical research in "Melodramas of Beset Manhood" (1981), reprinted below, reveals that women authors such as Susannah Rowson dominated the American fiction market in the decades before 1800, and that many women including Harriet Beecher Stowe and Emma D. E. N. Southworth, were among the most widely read novelists in the nineteenth century. How did it happen, Baym asks, that by 1977 the canon "did not contain any women novelists"? Bracketing the simplistic hypotheses that women wrote nothing but sensational trash and that American literary historians were simply misogynistic bigots hostile to women's writing, Baym explores the way the formation of an American canon was influenced by an emerging idea of America. Texts were not evaluated according to an ostensibly pure aesthetic: Instead, the best American literature was believed to be that which most clearly reflected the current consensus as to what was quintessentially American. Various formulations of the essence of American culture were in competition in the early years of the twentieth century, but eventually a consensus formed around the myth "that in this new land, untrammeled by history and social accident, a person will be able to achieve complete self-definition. . . . Society exerts an unmitigatedly destructive pressure on individuality. . . . Thus . . . the essential quality of America comes to reside in its unsettled wilderness and the opportunities that such a wilderness offers to the individual as the medium on which he may inscribe, unhindered, his own destiny and his own nature."

One likely foundation for this vision of the essence of American culture is Frederick Jackson Turner's enormously influential historical study, *The Frontier in American History* (1920), with its nostalgic vision of the uniqueness of the American experiment until the closing of the Western frontier at the end of the nineteenth century. Although Baym does not specifically mention Turner's book, it was republished in 1947, and all of the books she accuses of peddling the American myth of the individual versus society (by Lionel Trilling, Henry Nash Smith, Charles Feidelson, R. W. B. Lewis, Richard Chase, and Daniel Hoffman) appeared within the following decade. Whether the origin of the myth is Turner or, as Baym thinks, Trilling, is immaterial: The result was that works in touch with this myth, like James Fenimore Cooper's *Leatherstocking Tales* (1823–41) and Nathaniel Hawthorne's *The Scarlet Letter* (1850), or ones that operated in some ironic relation to it, like Mark Twain's *Huckleberry Finn* (1885) and F. Scott Fitzgerald's *The Great Gatsby* (1925), were canonized at the expense of works, many of them by women, that centered on the discontents of civilization rather than the romance of the wilderness. In a sense, the issue is not purely a feminist one, since Baym argues that writers like William Dean Howells and Henry James also posed a "continual challenge to the masculinist bias of American critical theory."

One question that remains is how to understand the body of literature by women, and whether it forms a tradition on its own that can be understood apart from the body of literature by men. Most critics are likely to identify the three major texts of the second phase of feminist criticism, the analysis of women's writing, as Ellen Moers's *Literary Women* (1976), Elaine Showalter's *A Literature of Their Own* (1977), and Sandra Gilbert and Susan Gubar's *The Madwoman in the Attic* (1979). As Toril Moi's survey of feminist criticism puts it, "Taken together, these three books represent the coming-of-age of Anglo-American feminist criticism."⁵ Moers's *Literary Women* is subtitled "*The Great Writers,*" as if to establish its relationship to F. R. Leavis's *The Great Tradition* (1948), and there is indeed

⁵Toril Moi, *Sexual/Textual Politics: Feminist Literary Theory* (New York: Methuen, 1985), p. 52.

something Leavisite about its socially oriented survey of centuries of female creativity. Moers focuses on those aspects of women writers that derive from the central fact of their being women and ignores the rest as far as possible. Thus, Moers interprets Mary Shelley's *Frankenstein* as a myth of birth, in which the newborn is "at once monstrous agent of destruction and piteous victim of parental abandonment," a myth she sees as the product of Shelley's personal history — as an unwed mother at the time of its writing and as an infant whose birth occasioned her mother's death. Moers's method, if it can be called that, is impressionistic and biographical; in calling up her most admired heroine, George Sand, she asks the reader to picture "her typical country evening at Nohant. At the center sits Madame Sand with the needlework she loved in her hands, surrounded by a houseful of friends, children, lovers, guests, neighbors. Nohant was a messy household, full of laughter and games and theatricals and family arguments and good intellectual talk and tobacco smoke and music — just like yours and mine." Later critics were to avoid her chattiness and decry her insistence on biographical explanations, but feminist criticism was advanced by her wide-ranging discussion of the canon of women's literature and the central place of women's experience in forming that canon.

Elaine Showalter's book *A Literature of Their Own* has been more influential than Moers's. In addition to establishing a complex relationship to Woolf's *A Room of One's Own,* Showalter's title alludes ironically to John Stuart Mill, who in *The Subjection of Women* (1869) stated that "[i]f women lived in a different country from men and had never read any of their writings, they would have a literature of their own." As things stood, Mill thought, they did not: "[A] much longer time is necessary . . . before [women's literature] can emancipate itself from the influence of accepted models, and guide itself by its own impulses." Showalter would not claim that the body of texts produced by women has the coherent character of a national literature that can be studied entirely apart from the texts produced by men, and she suspects that the hypothesis of a distinctive "female imagination" will encourage the stereotyped images of women that feminists have been so eager to dispel. Nevertheless, Showalter claims that women, as a subculture within English society, have produced something definable as a "female literary tradition" in the English novel from the generation of the Brontës to the present.

Showalter's analysis of nineteenth-century English fiction by women presents an evolutionary theory of the development of women's writing, which she argues ran parallel to that by blacks, Jews, and other groups outside the white Christian male power elite:

> In looking at literary subcultures . . . we can see that they all go through three major phases. First, there is a prolonged phase of *imitation* of the prevailing modes of the dominant tradition, and *internalization* of its standards of art and its views on social roles. Second, there is a phase of *protest* against these standards and values, and *advocacy* of minority rights and values, including a demand for autonomy. Finally, there is a phase of *self-discovery,* a turning inward freed from some of the dependency of opposition, a search for identity. An appropriate terminology for women writers is to call these stages *Feminine, Feminist,* and *Female.* These are obviously not rigid categories. . . . The phases overlap. . . . One might . . . find all three phases in the career of a single novelist.

but entering a new stage of self-awareness about 1960. (p. 13).

Nonetheless, it seems useful to point to periods of crisis when a shift of literary values occurred. In this book I identify the Feminine phase as the period from the appearance of the male pseudonym in the 1840s to the death of George Eliot in 1880; the Feminist phase as 1880 to 1920, or the winning of the vote; and the Female phase as 1920 to the present,

Obviously in Showalter's program there is some danger of overestimating the extent to which the female tradition and the male tradition are separable and (as Kenneth Ruthven has put it) of feminist critics' "repeating exactly the same mistake for which they take male critics to task, namely an exclusive preoccupation with the writings of one sex."[6] This is a problem, however, of which Showalter is well aware. What seems less guarded is her bias against that version of feminism represented by Virginia Woolf — a foremother whom she attacks with fury. Showalter consid- ers Woolf's idealization of androgyny a mere flight from any genuine femininity and terms her vision of womanhood "as deadly as it is disembodied" (p. 289). Showalter's arguments against an androgynous ideal seem *ad feminam* (so to speak), and she does not understand the appeal of androgyny even to women (like Mary Shelley) who loved men and were devoted to their children.

Whatever the controversies surrounding Showalter's attitudes toward nineteenth- and twentieth-century fiction by women, her methodology is simple and straight- forward. *The Madwoman in the Attic*, by Sandra Gilbert and Susan Gubar, brought to the female tradition some less traditional ways of reading, similar to those we associate with Yale (which eventually published their study). In particular, Gilbert and Gubar take off from the poetics of Harold Bloom's *Anxiety of Influence*. But where Bloom was concerned with the Oedipal relation between the "strong" poet and the forebear he has chosen as his ghostly "father," whose works he must misread to make room for his own, Gilbert and Gubar are concerned with the female half of the equation, with the woman writer who, defined always by men, is uncomfortable defining herself, who, lacking a pen/penis, is anxious about whether she can create at all. Whatever women's lesser disabilities today, women writers in the nineteenth century eventually "overcame their 'anxiety of authorship,' repudiated debilitating patriarchal prescriptions, and recovered or remembered the lost female foremothers who could help them find their distinctive female power" (p. 59).

But within a patriarchy, women's writing cannot fully express itself; as a result, women writers (consciously or unconsciously) revised their own meanings to make them acceptable to their culture. "Women from Jane Austen and Mary Shelley to Emily Brontë and Emily Dickinson produced literary works . . . whose surface designs conceal or obscure deeper, less accessible (and less socially acceptable) lev- els of meaning" (p. 73). Women authors used a "cover story" — coded messages dis- guising their intent. They often created villainesses, in Gilbert and Gubar's readings of the novels, who speak powerfully for the values they were forced to repress. Under the surface, Bertha Mason Rochester, the titular Madwoman in the Attic, is

[6]K. K. Ruthven, *Feminist Literary Studies: An Introduction* (Cambridge: Cambridge University Press, 1984), p. 125.

the true heroine of *Jane Eyre*. Her frank impulsiveness and sensuality underlie what the reader values in Jane herself.

The Madwoman in the Attic gave an enormous new impetus to feminist criticism, yet there were skeptics, largely among Gilbert and Gubar's fellow feminists. In her review of *Madwoman* in *Signs*, Mary Jacobus attacked the book's "unstated complicity with the autobiographical 'phallacy,' whereby male critics hold that women's writing is somehow closer to their own experience than men's, that the female text *is* the author."[7] Toril Moi has a different problem with *The Madwoman in the Attic*. In fact, as one can see from her discussion of Gilbert and Gubar in *Sexual/Textual Politics* (1985), she has an interlocking set of problems.[8] Moi is a poststructuralist theorist whose allegiances, like Kristeva's, reach out to both Marx and Freud as reinterpreted by contemporary theory. As a neo-Marxist, Moi sees patriarchy as a production of ideology, but rejects the way Gilbert and Gubar characterize it as a relentless and all-pervasive force. If it were that, Moi asks, how did women manage to write at all? Moi suggests that Gilbert and Gubar need to think about ideology the way Althusser does, as fragmentary and contradictory, and not as irresistibly coherent. Moi is critical as well of Gilbert and Gubar's suggestion that women have been "fragmented" by patriarchy and long to become whole and complete. Wholeness and completeness of the self, for a psychoanalytic thinker like Moi, is an illusion, an obsession that belongs to the Lacanian Imaginary, as a product of the "mirror stage" (see p. 635). Gilbert and Gubar should be deconstructing this sort of "phallic" thinking, which Moi argues underlies patriarchy, rather than reproducing it with feminist overtones.

WOMEN ON THE MARGINS

In *A Literature of Their Own,* Elaine Showalter's attempt to describe female writing as a variant of the experience of minority cultures searching for a place within the mainstream implicitly suggests that women's writing belongs to the white, male, Protestant, and British or American traditions with one exception: that of gender. While this was true of the British writers Showalter discussed, obviously some women may be multiply marginalized, not only as women but as African Americans, Chicanos, Asian Americans, Caribbean Islanders, or as lesbians on the margin of the heterosexual majority.

The marginalization of the African American female writer has become a significant issue as writers such as Phillis Wheatley and Zora Neale Hurston, Alice Walker and Toni Morrison, Gwendolyn Brooks and Nikki Giovanni are entering the canon, either in courses in American literature or through their success as popular best-sellers. In a number of ways, the issues of black feminist criticism overlap with those of white feminism. But African American women have long felt excluded from white feminist politics, and some of the central texts of women's studies ignore women who are not white. In her manifesto, "Toward a Black Feminist Criticism," Barbara Smith expresses outrage at this failure to recognize

---

[7] *Signs* 6 (1981): 520.
[8] Toril Moi, *Sexual, Textual Politics* (New York: Methuen, 1985), pp. 57–69.

that "Black and female identity ever coexist, specifically in a group of Black women writers." Smith attacks as "barely disguised cultural imperialism" Showalter's pro-posal to build a feminist scholarship on the model of "black American novelists." Smith also notes that most studies of women writers written by white women tend to ignore African Americans and other minorities — Moers's *Literary Women* "includes the names of four Black and one Puertorriqueña writer in her seventy pages of bibliographical notes" — and that other feminist writers show a "suspiciously selective" ignorance of the existence of black women writers. The feminists are not the only target here, however, for Smith sees both black and white male scholars of black writing as even more distortive of the creative achievements of black women. Deborah McDowell, in her essay "New Directions for Black Feminist Criticism," while entirely sympathetic to the sense of marginality against which earlier black feminists reacted, seeks to escape the divisiveness of black versus white, women vs. men, lesbian vs. het-erosexual, that organizes Smith's manifesto.[9] For McDowell black feminist criticism is less a cause than a task, for which one must go beyond politics and slogans. Whereas ear-lier black feminists had simply equated their race and sex with a special use of language, McDowell calls instead for concrete investigations into the content of black female poetics using contemporary methodologies. Like Kolodny, McDowell considers the walls of separation between male and female, black and white, at best a mixed bless-ing. She quotes the Nigerian playwright Wole Soyinka on the creative asphyxiation that accompanies too exclusive an attention to ideology, fearing that a separatist black feminist criticism could become a narrower and less vital enterprise than it has the potential to be.

Lesbian feminist literary criticism centers on a different sort of marginality. Just as black women writers and critics have felt excluded from white feminist studies, so lesbian writers and critics have been excluded by feminist attempts to seek a specifically heterosexual female identity. Bonnie Zimmerman points out the homophobia of both Moers's *Literary Women* and Patricia Meyer Spacks's *The Female Imagination*: "Spacks claims that Gertrude Stein, 'whose life lack[ed] real attachments' (a surprise to Alice B. Toklas) also 'denied whatever is special to women' (which lesbianism is not?)."[10] Lesbian feminist criticism confronts some of the same difficulties as heterosexual feminism, such as whether lesbian writing has a historical continuity apart from the writing of women and, indeed, of men, and whether it encounters unique difficulties of its own. For example, establishing the canon of lesbian writers involves first establishing writers' sexual orientation, which may be ambiguous or simply indecipherable owing to lack of evidence. Lesbian literature itself is difficult to define: Adrienne Rich defines lesbianism so inclusively as to embrace all female bonding and most female creativity, yet the lesbian canon might also be restricted to texts by exclusively homosexual women.

The expansion of the feminist dialogue to take into account various groups pre-viously marginalized within the women's movement is only one version, perhaps,

[9]Deborah E. McDowell, "New Directions for Black Feminist Criticism," *Black American Literature Forum* 14, 1980, pp. 153–59.

[10]Bonnie Zimmerman, "'What Has Never Been: An Overview of Lesbian Feminist Literary Criticism," in *The New Feminist Criticism*, ed. Elaine Showalter (New York: Pantheon, 1985), p. 203.

of the tendency of women's studies to expand its boundaries and to address areas traditionally dominated by men. It is impossible to do justice to the breadth of the movement here, but no study of feminist criticism can be complete without at least mentioning the connections between feminism and psychoanalysis (drawn by writers such as Jane Gallop and Mary Jacobus), between feminism and deconstruction (Peggy Kamuf and Nancy K. Miller), and between feminism and Marxism (Juliet Mitchell and Michèle Barrett).

Like Marxism, feminism was a social and political movement long before it was a mode of literary criticism, but also like Marxism, the cultural wing of the ideology has naturally attracted many of the brightest and most energetic minds. This poses a problem to the movement as a whole. Just as Terry Eagleton scoffed at the idea that Jameson's analyses of Balzac were going to shake the foundations of capitalism, so some feminists have wondered how analyzing Charlotte Brontë would alter the fact that women's pay is only seventy-nine percent of men's.

It is obviously necessary for women to understand their past and the accomplishments that their forebears have achieved against heavy odds. But there is at least a slight edge of irony about the success of feminist criticism as an academic career choice. Lillian Robinson has been concerned that feminist critics be feminists first and critics second. "Some people are trying to make an honest woman out of the feminist critic, to claim that every 'worthwhile' department should stock one. I am not terribly interested in whether feminism becomes a respectable part of academic criticism. I am very much concerned that feminist critics become a useful part of the women's movement. . . . Marx's note about philosophers may apply to cultural critics as well: that up to now they have interpreted the world and the real point is to change it." [11]

THE FATE OF ANGLO-AMERICAN FEMINISM

Most scholars would agree that the essays reproduced in this chapter represent a particular phase of Anglo-American feminism, one whose theoretical constitution was essentially complete before 1985. This does not mean that the movement has died out or even lost its steam. On the contrary, all the projects promoted by that constitution are continuing with great vigor. For example, Showalter's argument, elaborated in *A Literature of Their Own,* that there was a long and healthy tradition of women's writing all through the nineteenth century, has been extended backwards by many other hands, and extraordinary efforts are under way to rediscover women's writing from all periods and to make it available to readers. The advent of computers and the internet has assisted enormously in this endeavor, because poetry and fiction by women that commercial publishers might deem too marginal in popular interest to warrant republication in book form can now be circulated as text files or hard copy to interested readers using electronic media. Thus the Women's Collective at Brown University, to take only one example, has made available to scholars literally hundreds of seventeenth- and eighteenth-century British novels

[11]Lillian S. Robinson, *Sex, Class, and Culture* (Bloomington: Indiana University Press, 1978), pp. 19–20.

by women that would otherwise have to be sought in rare book collections.[12]

While scholars of my generation merely learned of the existence of popular women novelists at the time of Defoe, such as Eliza Haywood and Delariviere Manley, scholars today can read their works and come directly to terms with their concerns and those of their readership. Similar efforts are under way to unearth unsung and underappreciated American women writers, and, as Deborah McDowell predicted, women writers of color are reaping gains as well. Where twenty years ago college reading lists were incomplete without Kate Chopin's *The Awakening* (1899), today the most assigned novels by women writers are probably Toni Morrison's *Beloved* (1987) and Zora Neale Hurston's *Their Eyes Were Watching God* (1937). And while Judith Fetterley recommended "resistant reading" to women threatened with "immasculation" by canonical male texts (see p. 605), a good deal of interesting research has gone on, in ways hinted at by Annette Kolodny in "Dancing Through the Minefield," into how women actually read. Both Susan Sniader Lanser and Peter Rabinowitz have suggested that women may be decoding texts in ways that men would not.[13]

But while the projects of Anglo-American feminism continue, the 1980s saw the development of a rift in American feminist criticism between adherents of the Anglo-American tradition and a new generation of feminist theorists interested both in considering the implications of deconstructivist, psychoanalytic, Marxist, and New Historical theory for their studies of gender difference and in opening up such originally androcentric movements to a consideration of gender.[14] There was a reluctance on the part of some of the most important Anglo-American feminists to problematize the concept of gender and to theorize about the relationship between femaleness and femininity. Showalter's edited collection, *The New Feminist Criticism*, published in 1985, was designed to showcase the best that had been known and thought in the feminist world, but it pointedly sidelined the theorizing about gender that had been going on in France for at least a decade. A single short and rather lukewarm essay by Ann Rosalind Jones, positioned at the end of the volume, briefly summarized some of the positions of Julia Kristeva, Hélène Cixous, Luce Irigaray, and Monique Wittig, without presenting the Lacanian psychoanalytic theory that would have allowed the reader to make sense of them.[15] Showalter's own

12When I was a young scholar, for example, the major poetical romance by Lady Mary Wroth, *The Countess of Montgomery's Urania* (1621), was an obscure work mentioned in literary histories and available only in one of the rare copies held at the North Library of the British Museum. About twenty years ago, with the rapid growth of Wroth's reputation as one of the major poets of the seventeenth century, it became possible to read the *Urania* using the computer text version made available by the Women's Collective. Today it is possible to consult a hardbound scholarly edition edited by the late Josephine Roberts, and a 280-page abridgement edited by Mary Ellen Lamb is available in paperback.

13See Susan Sniader Lanser: *Fictions of Authority: Women Writers and Narrative Voice* (Ithaca: Cornell University Press, 1992); and Peter Rabinowitz, "End Sinister: Neat Closure as Disruptive Force," in *Reading Narrative: Form, Ethics, Ideology* (Columbus: Ohio State University Press, 1989).

14See, for example, the work of Nancy Armstrong, p. 839.

15Ann Rosalind Jones, "Writing the Body: Toward an Understanding of l'Écriture Féminine," in *The New Feminist Criticism: Women, Literature, Theory,* ed. Elaine Showalter (New York: Pantheon, 1985), pp. 361–77. Showalter's volume also sidelines reader-response feminist theory, presenting the central strand as what she calls "gynocritics," the analysis of female creativity.

treatment of the French feminists in her introduction was less than lukewarm, dourly arguing that "Anglo-American feminist poetics must insist on an analysis of specific cultural contexts rather than merely relying on an idealized and abstract view of the feminine" (p. 15).

It is not clear exactly what motivated the refusal to admit theorizing about gender into the big tent of Anglo-American feminism, but the reason may have been academic politics. The world of literary scholarship was deeply split in the early 1980s between traditional scholars who could make no sense of the theoretical revolution that had been building for at least a decade and theorists who were using the new Marxism, psychoanalysis, semiotics, and deconstruction to produce radically new work, who saw no sense at all in continuing the old practices. Showalter's stand in favor of "specific cultural contexts" may have been a way of stationing feminism as a mode of traditional criticism that should be supported by old-style scholars for its conservative methodology as well as by radical theorists taken with its political program. But the genie of gender theory was already out of the bottle, and the ideas and movements that are currently reshaping our understanding of the relationship between sex, gender, and literature are considered in Chapter 8.

Selected Bibliography

Abel, Elizabeth, ed. *Writing and Sexual Difference.* Chicago: University of Chicago Press, 1982.

Auerbach, Nina. *Woman and the Demon: The Life of a Victorian Myth.* Cambridge: Harvard University Press, 1982.

Baym, Nina. *Woman's Fiction: A Guide to Novels by and about Women in America.* Ithaca: Cornell University Press, 1978.

———. *Feminism and American Literary History.* New Brunswick: Rutgers University Press, 1992.

Beauvoir, Simone de. *Le Deuxième sexe.* Paris: Gallimard, *1949.* Trans. H. M. Parshley as *The Second Sex.* New York: Knopf, 1972.

Belsey, Catherine. *Critical Practice.* London: Methuen, 1980.

Blau Duplessis, Rachel. *Writing Beyond the Ending: Narrative Strategies of Twentieth-Century Women Writers.* Bloomington: Indiana University Press, 1985.

Brownstein, Rachel. *Becoming a Heroine: Reading about Women in Novels.* New York: Viking, 1982.

Cameron, Deborah. *Feminism in Linguistic Theory.* London: Macmillan, 1992.

Chodorow, Nancy. *The Reproduction of Mothering: Psychoanalysis and the Sociology of Gender.* Berkeley: University of California Press, 1978.

———. *Feminism and Psychoanalytic Theory.* New Haven: Yale University Press, 1989.

De Lauretis, Teresa. *Alice Doesn't: Feminism, Semiotics, Cinema.* Bloomington: Indiana University Press, 1984.

Delany, Sheila. *Writing Women: Women Writers and Women in Literature, Medieval to Modern.* New York: Schocken, 1984.

Donovan, Josephine, ed. *Feminist Literary Criticism: Explorations in Theory.* Lexington: University Press of Kentucky, 1975.

Douglas, Ann. *The Feminization of American Culture.* New York: Knopf, 1978.

Ellmann, Mary. *Thinking about Women.* New York: Harcourt Brace Jovanovich, 1968.

Felman, Shoshana. "Rereading Femininity." *Yale French Studies* 62 (1981): 19–44.

Fetterley, Judith. *The Resisting Reader: A Feminist Approach to American Fiction.* Bloomington: Indiana University Press, 1978.

Firestone, Shulamith. *The Dialectic of Sex: The Case for Feminist Revolution.* London: Women's Press, 1979.

Flynn, Elizabeth A., and Patrocinio P. Schweickart. *Gender and Reading: Essays on Readers, Texts and Contexts.* Baltimore: Johns Hopkins University Press, 1986.

Gallop, Jane. *The Daughter's Seduction: Feminism and Psychoanalysis.* Ithaca: Cornell University Press, 1982.

Gates, Henry Louis, Jr., ed. *Reading Black, Reading Feminist: A Critical Anthology.* New York: Meridian, 1990.

Gilbert, Sandra M., and Susan Gubar. *The Madwoman in the Attic: The Woman Writer and the Nineteenth-Century Literary Imagination.* New Haven: Yale University Press, 1979.

Greer, Germaine. *The Female Eunuch.* London: McGibbon and Kee, 1970.

hooks, bell [Gloria Watkins]. *Ain't I a Woman? Black Women and Feminism.* Boston: South End Press, 1981.

Jacobus, Mary. *Women's Writing and Writing about Women.* New York: Barnes and Noble, 1979.

Jehlen, Myra. "Archimedes and the Paradox of Feminist Criticism." *Signs* 6 (1981): 575–601.

Kahn, Coppélia, and Gayle Greene, eds. *Making a Difference: Feminist Literary Criticism.* New York: Methuen, 1985.

Kamuf, Peggy. "Replacing Feminist Criticism." *Diacritics* 12 (1982): 42–47.

Kolodny, Annette. "Some Notes on Defining a 'Feminist Literary Criticism.'" *Critical Inquiry* 2 (1975): 75–92.

———. "Dancing Through the Minefield: Some Observations on the Theory, Practice and Politics of a Feminist Literary Criticism." *Feminist Studies* 6 (1980): 1–25.

———. *The Land Before Her: Fantasy and Experience of the American Frontiers, 1630–1860.* Chapel Hill: University of North Carolina Press, 1984.

Kowaleski-Wallace, Elizabeth, ed. *Encyclopedia of Feminist Literary Theory.* New York: Garland, 1997.

Kramarae, Cheris. *Women and Men Speaking: Frameworks for Analysis.* Rowley, MA: Newbury House, 1981.

Kristeva, Julia. *About Chinese Women.* New York: Urizen Books, 1977.

———. "Women's Time." *Signs* 7 (1981): 13–35.

Lakoff, Robin. *Language and Women's Place.* New York: Harper and Row, 1975.

Leavy, Barbara. *In Search of the Swan Maiden: A Narrative on Folklore and Gender.* New York: New York University Press, 1994.

Looser, Devoney, and E. Ann Kaplan, eds. *Generations: Academic Feminists in Dialogue.* Minneapolis: University of Minnesota Press, 1995.

McConnell-Ginet, Sally, Ruth Borker, and Nelly Furman, eds. *Women and Language in Literature and Society.* New York: Praeger, 1980.

Marks, Elaine, and Isabelle de Courtivron, eds. *New French Feminisms: An Anthology.* Amherst: University of Massachusetts Press, 1980.

Martin, Wendy. *An American Triptych: Anne Bradstreet, Emily Dickinson, and Adrienne Rich.* Chapel Hill: University of North Carolina Press, 1984.

Miller, Nancy K. "The Text's Heroine: A Feminist Critic and Her Fictions." *Diacritics* 12 (1982): 48–53.

Millett, Kate. *Sexual Politics.* New York: Avon Books, 1970.

Mitchell, Juliet. *Psychoanalysis and Feminism.* New York: Pantheon, 1974.

———. *Women's Estate.* New York: Vintage Books, 1971.

———. *The Longest Revolution.* New York: Pantheon, 1984.

Moers, Ellen. *Literary Women.* New York: Doubleday, 1976.

Moi, Toril. *Sexual/Textual Politics: Feminist Literary Theory.* New York: Methuen, 1985.

Newton, Judith Lowder. *Women, Power, and Subversion: Social Strategies in British Fiction, 1778–1860.* Athens: University of Georgia Press, 1981.

———, and Deborah Rosenfelt, eds. *Feminist Criticism and Social Change.* New York: Methuen, 1985.

Nicholson, Linda, ed. *The Second Wave: A Reader in Feminist Theory.* New York: Routledge, 1997.

Poovey, Mary. *The Proper Lady and the Woman Writer: Ideology as Style in the Works of Mary Wollstonecraft, Mary Shelley, and Jane Austen.* Chicago: University of Chicago Press, 1984.

Rich, Adrienne. *On Lies, Secrets and Silence.* New York: Norton, 1979.

Robinson, Lillian. *Sex, Class and Culture.* Bloomington: Indiana University Press, 1978.

Rogers, Katherine M. *The Troublesome Helpmate: A History of Misogyny in Literature.* Seattle: University of Washington Press, 1966.

Ruthven, Kenneth K. *Feminist Literary Studies: An Introduction.* Cambridge: Cambridge University Press, 1984.

Showalter, Elaine. *A Literature of Their Own: British Women Novelists from Brontë to Lessing.* Princeton: Princeton University Press, 1977.

———, ed. *The New Feminist Criticism: Essays on Women, Literature, Theory.* New York: Pantheon, 1985.

———. *Sexual Anarchy: Gender and Culture at the Fin de Siècle.* New York: Viking, 1990.

Spacks, Patricia Meyer. *The Female Imagination.* New York: Knopf, 1975.

Spender, Dale. *Man Made Language.* London: Routledge and Kegan Paul, 1980.

Spivak, Gayatri Chakravorty. *In Other Worlds: Essays in Cultural Politics.* New York: Methuen, 1987.

Thorne, Barrie, Cheris Kramarae, and Nancy Henley, eds. *Language, Gender, and Society.* Rowley, MA: Newbury House, 1983.

Walker, Alice. *In Search of Our Mother's Gardens.* New York: Harcourt Brace Jovanovich, 1983.

Warhol, Robyn R., and Diane Price Herndl. *Feminisms: An Anthology of Literary Theory and Criticism,* 2nd ed. New York: Routledge, 1997.

Washington, Mary Helen. *Midnight Birds: Stories of Contemporary Black Women Writers.* Garden City, NY: Anchor Books, 1980.

Whelehan, Imelda, ed. *Modern Feminist Thought.* New York: NYU Press, 1995.

Zimmerman, Bonnie. "What Has Never Been: An Overview of Lesbian Feminist Literary Criticism." *Feminist Studies* 7 (1981): 451–75.

Nina Baym

b. 1936

Nina Baym's work has been instrumental in bringing about academic recognition of women's studies across the United States. Born in Princeton, New Jersey, Baym received her B.A. from Cornell University (1957) and her M.A. (1958) and Ph.D. (1963) in English from Harvard University. After receiving her doctorate, Baym taught English and American literature at the University of Illinois at Urbana-Champaign, where she became a full professor in 1972 and Director of the School of Humanities in 1976. Retired, she is now professor emerita at the University of Illinois at Urbana-Champaign. Baym has been a Guggenheim fellow (1975–76) and a fellow of the National Endowment for the Humanities (1982–83). She has served on the editorial boards of several major journals, including American Quarterly, New England Quarterly, and American Literature, and is the general editor of The Norton Anthology of American Literature. Her publications include The Shape of Hawthorne's Career (1976), Woman's Fiction: A Guide to Novels by and about Women in America (1820–1870) (1978), Nathaniel Hawthorne and His Mother (1982), Novels, Readers, and Reviewers: Responses to Fiction in Antebellum America (1984), Feminism and American Literary History (1992), American Women of Letters and the Nineteenth-Century Sciences (2002) and Women Writers of the American West, 1833–1927 (2011).

Melodramas of Beset Manhood

"Melodramas of Beset Manhood" is reprinted from American Quarterly 33 (1981).

How Theories of American Fiction Exclude Women Authors

This paper is about American literary criticism rather than American literature. It proceeds from the assumption that we have never read American literature directly or freely, but always through the perspective allowed by theories. Theories account for the inclusion and exclusion of texts in anthologies, and theories account for the way we read them. My concern is with the fact that the theories controlling our reading of American literature have led to the exclusion of women authors from the canon.

Let me use my own practice as a case in point. In 1977 there was published a collection of essays on images of women in major British and American literature, to which I contributed.[1]

[1] Marlene Springer, ed., *What Manner of Woman: Essays on English and American Life and Literature* (New York: New York University Press, 1977). [Baym]

The American field was divided chronologically among six critics, with four essays covering literature written prior to World War II. Taking seriously the charge that we were to focus only on the major figures, the four of us — working quite independently of each other — selected altogether only four women writers. Three of these were from the earliest period, a period which predates the novel: the poet Anne Bradstreet and the two diarists Mary Rowlandson and Sarah Kemble Knight. The fourth was Emily Dickinson. For the period between 1865 and 1940 no women were cited at all. The message that we — who were taking women as our subject — conveyed was clear: there have been almost no major women writers in America; the major novelists have all been men.

Now, when we wrote our essays we were not undertaking to reread all American literature and make our own decisions as to who the major authors were. That is the point: we accepted the going canon of major authors. As late as 1977, that canon did not include any women novelists. Yet, the critic who goes beyond what is accepted and tries to look at the totality of literary production in America quickly discovers that women authors have been active since the earliest days of settlement. Commercially and numerically they have probably dominated American literature since the middle of the nineteenth century. As long ago as 1854, Nathaniel Hawthorne complained to his publisher about the "damned mob of scribbling women" whose writings — he fondly imagined — were diverting the public from his own.

Names and figures help make this dominance clear. In the years between 1774 and 1799 — from the calling of the First Continental Congress to the close of the eighteenth century — a total of thirty-eight original works of fiction were published in this country.[2] Nine of these, appearing pseudonymously or anonymously, have not yet been attributed to any author. The remaining twenty-nine are the work of eighteen individuals, of whom four are women. One of these women, Susannah Rowson, wrote six of them, or more than a fifth of the total. Her most popular work, *Charlotte* (also known as *Charlotte Temple*), was printed three times in the decade it was published, nineteen times between 1800 and 1810, and eighty times by the middle of the nineteenth century. A novel by a second of the four women, Hannah Foster, was called *The Coquette* and had thirty editions by mid-nineteenth century. *Uncle Tom's Cabin*, by a woman, is probably the all-time biggest seller in American history. A woman, Mrs. E.D.E.N. Southworth, was probably the most widely read novelist in the nineteenth century. How is it possible for a critic or historian of American literature to leave these books, and these authors, out of the picture?

I see three partial explanations for the critical invisibility of the many active women authors in America. The first is simple bias. The critic does not like the idea of women as writers, does not believe that women can be writers, and hence does not see them even when they are right before his eyes. His theory or his standards may well be

[2]See Lyle H. Wright, *American Fiction: A Contribution Towards a Bibliography*, vol. 1, 1774–1850, 2d ed. (San Marino, Calif.: Huntington Library Press, 1969). [Baym]

nonsexist but his practice is not. Certainly, an *a priori* resistance to recognizing women authors as serious writers has functioned powerfully in the mind-set of a number of influential critics. One can amusingly demonstrate the inconsistencies between standard and practice in such critics, show how their minds slip out of gear when they are confronted with a woman author. But this is only a partial explanation.

A second possibility is that, in fact, women have not written the kind of work that we call "excellent," for reasons that are connected with their gender although separable from it. This is a serious possibility. For example, suppose we required a dense texture of classical allusion in all works that we called excellent. Then, the restriction of a formal classical education to men would have the effect of restricting authorship of excellent literature to men. Women would not have written excellent literature because social conditions hindered them. The reason, though gender-connected, would not be gender per se.

The point here is that the notion of the artist, or of excellence, has efficacy in a given time and reflects social realities. The idea of "good" literature is not only a personal preference, it is also a cultural preference. We can all think of species of women's literature that do not aim in any way to achieve literary excellence as society defines it: for example, the "Harlequin Romances." Until recently, only a tiny proportion of literary women aspired to artistry and literary excellence in the terms defined by their own culture. There tended to be a sort of immediacy in the ambitions of literary women leading them to professionalism rather than artistry, by choice as well as by social pressure and opportunity. The gender-related restrictions were really operative, and the responsible critic cannot ignore them. But again, these restrictions are only partly explanatory.

There are, finally, I believe, gender-related restrictions that do not arise out of cultural realities contemporary with the writing woman, but out of later critical theories. These theories may follow naturally from cultural realities pertinent to their own time, but they impose their concerns anachronistically, after the fact, on an earlier period. If one accepts current theories of American literature, one accepts as a consequence — perhaps not deliberately but nevertheless inevitably — a literature that is essentially male. This is the partial explanation that I shall now develop.

Let us begin where the earliest theories of American literature begin, with the hypothesis that American literature is to be judged less by its form than by its content. Traditionally, one ascertains literary excellence by comparing a writer's work with standards of performance that have been established by earlier authors, where formal mastery and innovation are paramount. But from its historical beginnings, American literary criticism has assumed that literature produced in this nation would have to be groundbreaking, equal to the challenge of the new nation, and completely original. Therefore, it could not be judged by referring it back to earlier achievements. The earliest American literary critics began to talk about the "most American" work rather than the "best" work because they knew no way to find out the best other than by comparing American with British writing. Such a criticism struck them as both unfair and unpatriotic. We had thrown off the political shackles of England; it would not do for us to be servile in our literature. Until American literature developed its own inherent forms, the early critic looked for a standard of Americanness rather than a standard of excellence. Inevitably, perhaps, it came to seem that the quality of "Americanness," whatever it might be, constituted literary excellence for American authors. Beginning as a nationalistic enterprise, American literary criticism and theory has retained a nationalist orientation to this day.

Of course, the idea of Americanness is even more vulnerable to subjectivity than the idea of the best. When they speak of "most American," critics seldom mean the statistically most representative or most typical, the most read or the most sold. They have some qualitative essence in mind, and frequently their work develops as an explanation of this idea of "American" rather than a description and evaluation of selected authors. The predictable recurrence of the term "America" or "American" in works of literary criticism treating a dozen or fewer authors indicates that the critic has chosen his authors on the basis of their conformity to his idea of what is truly American.

For examples: *American Renaissance, The Romance in America, Symbolism and American Literature, Form and Fable in American Fiction, The American Adam, The American Novel and Its Tradition, The Place of Style in American Literature* (a subtitle), *The Poetics of American Fiction* (another subtitle). But an idea of what is American is no more than an idea, needing demonstration. The critic all too frequently ends up using his chosen authors as demonstrations of Americanness, arguing through them to his definition.

So Marius Bewley explains in *The Eccentric Design* that "for the American artist there was no social surface responsive to his touch. The scene was crude, even beyond successful satire," but later, in a concluding chapter titled "The Americanness of the American Novel," he agrees that "this 'tradition' as I have set it up here has no room for the so-called realists and naturalists."[3] F. O. Matthiessen, whose *American Renaissance* enshrines five authors, explains that "the one common denominator of my five writers, uniting even Hawthorne and Whitman, was their devotion to the possibilities of democracy."[4] The jointly written *Literary History of the United States* proclaims in its "address to the reader" that American literary history "will be a history of the books of the great and the near-great writers in a literature which is most revealing when studied as a by-product of American experience."[5] And Joel Porte announces confidently in *The Romance in America* that "students of American literature . . . have provided a solid theoretical basis for establishing that the rise and growth of fiction in this country is dominated by our authors' conscious adherence to a tradition of non-realistic romance sharply at variance with the broadly novelistic mainstream of English writing. When there has been disagreement among recent critics as to the contours of American fiction, it has usually disputed.

[3]Marius Bewley, *The Eccentric Design: Form in the Classic American Novel* (New York: Columbia University Press, 1963), pp. 15, 291. [Baym]

[4]F. O. Matthiessen, *American Renaissance* (New York: Oxford University Press, 1941), p. ix. [Baym]

[5]Robert E. Spiller et al., eds., *Literary History of the United States* (New York: Macmillan, 1959), p. xix. [Baym]

not the existence per se of a romance tradition, but rather the question of which authors, themes, and stylistic strategies *deserve* to be placed with certainty at the heart of that tradition" (emphasis added).[6]

Before he is through, the critic has had to insist that some works in America are much more American than others, and he is as busy excluding certain writers as "un-American" as he is including others. Such a proceeding in the political arena would be extremely suspect, but in criticism it has been the method of choice. Its final result goes far beyond the conclusion that only a handful of American works are very good. *That* statement is one we could agree with, since very good work is rare in any field. But it is odd indeed to argue that only a handful of American works are really American.[7]

Despite the theoretical room for an infinite number of definitions of Americanness, critics have generally agreed on it — although the shifting canon suggests that agreement may be a matter of fad rather than fixed objective qualities.[8] First, America as a nation must be the ultimate subject of the work. The author must be writing about aspects of experience and character that are American only, setting Americans off from other people and the country from other nations. The author must be writing his story specifically to display these aspects, to meditate on them, and to derive from them some generalizations and conclusions about "the" American experience. To Matthiessen the topic is the possibilities of democracy; Sacvan Bercovitch (in *The Puritan Origins of the American Self*) finds it in American identity. Such content excludes, at one extreme, stories about universals, aspects of experience common to people in a variety of times and places — mutability,

mortality, love, childhood, family, betrayal, loss. Innocence versus experience is an admissible theme *only* if innocence is the essence of the American character, for example.

But at the other extreme, the call for an overview of America means that detailed, circumstantial portrayals of some aspect of American life are also, peculiarly, inappropriate: stories of wealthy New Yorkers, Yugoslavian immigrants, Southern rustics. Jay B. Hubbell rather ingratiatingly admits as much when he writes, "in both my teaching and my research I had a special interest in literature as a reflection of American life and thought. This circumstance may explain in part why I found it difficult to appreciate the merits of the expatriates and why I was slow in doing justice to some of the New Critics. I was repelled by the sordid subject matter found in some of the novels written by Dreiser, Dos Passos, Faulkner, and some others."[9] Richard Poirier writes that "the books which in my view constitute a distinctive American tradition ... resist within their pages forces of environment that otherwise dominate the world," and he distinguishes this kind from "the fiction of Mrs. Wharton, Dreiser, or Howells."[10] The *Literary History of the United States* explains that "historically, [Edith Wharton] is likely to survive as the memorialist of a dying aristocracy."[11] And so on. These exclusions abound in all the works which form the stable core of American literary criticism at this time.

Along with Matthiessen, the most influential exponent of this exclusive Americanness is Lionel Trilling, and his work has particular applicability because it concentrates on the novel form. Here is a famous passage from his 1940 essay, "Reality in America," in which Trilling is criticizing Vernon Parrington's selection of authors in *Main Currents in American Thought*:

> A culture is not a flow, nor even a confluence: the form of its existence is struggle — or at least debate — it is nothing if not a dialectic. And in

[6]Joel Porte, *The Romance in America: Studies in Cooper, Poe, Hawthorne, Melville, and James* (Middletown, Conn.: Wesleyan University Press, 1969), p. ix. [Baym]

[7]A good essay on this topic is William C. Spengemann's "What Is American Literature?" *Centennial Review* 22 (Spring 1978): 119–38. [Baym]

[8]See Jay B. Hubbell, *Who Are the Major American Authors?* (Durham, N.C.: Duke University Press, 1972). [Baym]

[9]Ibid., pp. 335–36. [Baym]

[10]Richard Poirier, *A World Elsewhere: The Place of Style in American Literature* (New York: Oxford University Press, 1966), p. 5. [Baym]

[11]Spiller et al., *Literary History of the United States*, p. 1211. [Baym]

any culture there are likely to be certain artists who contain a large part of the dialectic within themselves, their meaning and power lying in their contradictions; they contain within themselves, it may be said, the very essence of the culture. To throw out Poe because he cannot be conveniently fitted into a theory of American culture . . . to find his gloom to be merely personal and eccentric . . . as Hawthorne's was . . . to judge Melville's response to American life to be less noble than that of Bryant or of Greeley, to speak of Henry James as an escapist . . . this is not merely to be mistaken in aesthetic judgment. Rather it is to examine without attention and from the point of view of a limited and essentially arrogant conception of reality the documents which are in some respects the most suggestive testimony to what America was and is, and of course to get no answer from them.[12]

Trilling's immediate purpose is to exclude Greeley and Bryant from the list of major authors and to include Poe, Melville, Hawthorne, and James. We probably share Trilling's aesthetic judgment. But note that he does not base his judgment on aesthetic grounds; indeed, he dismisses aesthetic judgment with the word "merely." He argues that Parrington has picked the wrong artists because he doesn't understand the culture. Culture is his real concern.

But what makes Trilling's notion of culture more valid than Parrington's? Trilling really has no argument; he resorts to such value-laden rhetoric as "a limited and essentially arrogant conception of reality" precisely because he cannot objectively establish his version of culture over Parrington's. For the moment, there are two significant conclusions to draw from this quotation. First, the disagreement is over the nature of our culture. Second, there is no disagreement over the value of literature — it is valued as a set of "documents" which provide "suggestive testimony to what America was and is."

One might think that an approach like this which is subjective, circular, and in some sense nonliterary or even antiliterary would not have had much effect. But clearly Trilling was simply carrying on a longstanding tradition of searching

for cultural essence, and his essays gave the search a decided and influential direction toward the notion of cultural essence as some sort of tension. Trilling succeeded in getting rid of Bryant and Greeley, and his choice of authors is still dominant. They all turn out — and not by accident — to be white, middle-class, male, of Anglo-Saxon derivation or at least from an ancestry which had settled in this country before the big waves of immigration which began around the middle of the nineteenth century. In every case, however, the decision made by these men to become professional authors pushed them slightly to one side of the group to which they belonged. This slight alienation permitted them to belong, and yet not to belong, to the so-called "mainstream." These two aspects of their situation — their membership in the dominant middle-class white Anglo-Saxon group, and their modest alienation from it — defined their boundaries, enabling them to "contain within themselves" the "contradictions" that, in Trilling's view, constitute the "very essence of the culture." I will call the literature they produced, which Trilling assesses so highly, a "consensus criticism of the consensus."

This idea plainly excludes many groups but it might not seem necessarily to exclude women. In fact, nineteenth-century women authors were overwhelmingly white, middle-class, and Anglo-Saxon in origin. Something more than what is overtly stated by Trilling (and others cited below) is added to exclude them. What critics have done is to assume, for reasons shortly to be expounded, that the women writers invariably represented the consensus, rather than the criticism of it; to assume that their gender made them part of the consensus in a way that prevented them from partaking in the criticism. The presence of these women and their works is acknowledged in literary theory and history as an impediment and obstacle, that which the essential American literature had to criticize as its chief task.

So, in his lively and influential book of 1960, *Love and Death in the American Novel*, Leslie Fiedler describes women authors as creators of the "flagrantly bad best-seller" against which "our best fictionists" — all male — have had to struggle for "their integrity and their

[12] Lionel Trilling, *The Liberal Imagination* (Garden City, N.Y.: Anchor Books, 1950), pp. 7–9. [Baym]

livelihoods."[13] And, in a 1978 reader's introduction to an edition of Charles Brockden Brown's *Wieland*, Sydney J. Krause and S. W. Reid write as follows:

> What it meant for Brown personally, and belles lettres in America historically, that he should have decided to write professionally is a story unto itself. Americans simply had no great appetite for serious literature in the early decades of the Republic — certainly nothing of the sort with which they devoured ... the ubiquitous melodramas of beset womanhood, "tales of truth," like Susanna Rowson's *Charlotte Temple* and Hannah Foster's *The Coquette*.[14]

There you see what has happened to the woman writer. She has entered literary history as the enemy. The phrase "tales of truth" is put in quotes by the critics, as though to cast doubt on the very notion that a "melodrama of beset womanhood" could be either true or important. At the same time, ironically, they are proposing for our serious consideration, as a candidate for intellectually engaging literature, a highly melodramatic novel with an improbable plot, inconsistent characterizations, and excesses of style that have posed tremendous problems for all students of Charles Brockden Brown. But by this strategy it becomes possible to begin major American fiction historically with male rather than female authors. The certainty here that stories about women could not contain the essence of American culture means that the matter of American experience is inherently male. And this makes it highly unlikely that American women would write fiction encompassing such experience. I would suggest that the theoretical model of a story which may become the vehicle of cultural essence is: "a melodrama of beset manhood." This melodrama is presented in a fiction which, as we will later see, can be taken as representative of the author's literary experience, his struggle for integrity and livelihood against flagrantly bad best-sellers written by women. Personally beset in a way that epitomizes the tensions of our culture, the male author produces his melodramatic testimony to our culture's essence — so the theory goes.

Remember that the search for cultural essence demands a relatively uncircumstantial kind of fiction, one which concentrates on national universals (if I may be pardoned the paradox). This search has identified a sort of nonrealistic narrative, a romance, a story free to catch an essential, idealized American character, to intensify his essence and convey his experience in a way that ignores details of an actual social milieu. This nonrealistic or antisocial aspect of American fiction is noted — as a fault — by Trilling in a 1947 essay, "Manners, Morals, and the Novel." Curiously, Trilling here attacks the same group of writers he had rescued from Parrington in "Reality in America." But, never doubting that his selection represents "the" American authors, he goes ahead with the task that really interests him — criticizing the culture through its representative authors:

> The novel in America diverges from its classic [i.e., British] intention which ... is the investigation of the problem of reality beginning in the social field. The fact is that American writers of genius have not turned their minds to society. Poe and Melville were quite apart from it; the reality they sought was only tangential to society. Hawthorne was acute when he insisted that he did not write novels but romances — he thus expressed his awareness of the lack of social texture in his work. . . . In America in the nineteenth century, Henry James was alone in knowing that to scale the moral and aesthetic heights in the novel one had to use the ladder of social observation.[15]

Within a few years after publication of Trilling's essay, a group of Americanists took its rather disapproving description of American novelists and found in this nonrealism or romanticism the essentially American quality they had been seeking. The idea of essential Americanness then developed in such influential works of criticism as *Virgin Land* by Henry Nash Smith (1950), *Symbolism and American Literature* by Charles Feidelson (1953), *The American Adam*

[13]Leslie Fiedler, *Love and Death in the American Novel* (New York: Criterion Books, 1960), p. 93. [Baym]

[14]Charles Brockden Brown, *Wieland*, ed. Sydney J. Krause and S. W. Reid (Kent, Ohio: Kent State University Press, 1978), p. xii. [Baym]

[15]Trilling, *The Liberal Imagination*, p. 206. [Baym]

by R. W. B. Lewis (1955), *The American Novel and Its Tradition* by Richard Chase (1957), and *Form and Fable in American Fiction* by Daniel G. Hoffman (1961). These works, and others like them, were of sufficiently high critical quality, and sufficiently like each other, to compel assent to the picture of American literature that they presented. They used sophisticated New Critical close-reading techniques to identify a myth of America which had nothing to do with the classical fictionist's task of chronicling probable people in recognizable social situations.

The myth narrates a confrontation of the American individual, the pure American self divorced from specific social circumstances, with the promise offered by the idea of America. This promise is the deeply romantic one that in this new land, untrammeled by history and social accident, a person will be able to achieve complete self-definition. Behind this promise is the assurance that individuals come before society, that they exist in some meaningful sense prior to, and apart from, societies in which they happen to find themselves. The myth also holds that, as something artificial and secondary to human nature, society exerts an unmitigatedly destructive pressure on individuality. To depict it at any length would be a waste of artistic time; and there is only one way to relate it to the individual — as an adversary.

One may believe all this and yet look in vain for a way to tell a believable story that could free the protagonist from society or offer the promise of such freedom, because nowhere on earth do individuals live apart from social groups. But in America, given the original reality of large tracts of wilderness, the idea seems less a fantasy, more possible in reality or at least more believable in literary treatment. Thus it is that the essential quality of America comes to reside in its unsettled wilderness and the opportunities that such a wilderness offers to the individual as the medium on which he may inscribe, unhindered, his own destiny and his own nature.

As the nineteenth century wore on, and settlements spread across the wilderness, the struggle of the individual against society became more and more central to the myth; where, let's say, Thoreau could leave in chapter 1 of *Walden*, Huckleberry

Finn has still not made his break by the end of chapter 42 (the conclusion) of the book that bears his name. Yet one finds a struggle against society as early as the earliest Leatherstocking tale (*The Pioneers*, 1823). In a sense, this supposed promise of America has always been known to be delusory. Certainly by the twentieth century the myth has been transmuted into an avowedly hopeless quest for unencumbered space (*On the Road*), or the evocation of flight for its own sake (*Rabbit, Run* and *Henderson the Rain King*), or as pathetic acknowledgment of loss — for example, the close of *The Great Gatsby* where the narrator Nick Carraway summons up "the old island here that flowered once for Dutch sailors' eyes — a fresh, green breast of the new world . . . the last and greatest of all human dreams" where man is "face to face for the last time in history with something commensurate to his capacity for wonder."

We are all very familiar with this myth of America in its various fashionings, and owing to the selective vision that has presented this myth to us as the whole story, many of us are unaware of how much besides it has been created by literary Americans. Keeping our eyes on this myth, we need to ask whether anything about it puts it outside women's reach. In one sense, and on one level, the answer is no. The subject of this myth is supposed to stand for human nature, and if men and women share a common human nature, then all can respond to its values, its promises, and its frustrations. And in fact, as a teacher I find women students responsive to the myth insofar as its protagonist is concerned. It is true, of course, that in order to represent some kind of believable flight into the wilderness, one must select a protagonist with a certain believable mobility, and mobility has until recently been a male prerogative in our society. Nevertheless, relatively few men are actually mobile to the extent demanded by the story, and hence the story is really not much more vicarious, in this regard, for women than for men. The problem is thus not to be located in the protagonist or his gender per se; the problem is with the other participants in his story — the entrammeling society and the promising landscape. For both of these are depicted in unmistakably feminine terms, and this gives a sexual character to the protagonist's story which does, indeed, limit its applicability to women. And this sexual definition has melodramatic, misogynist implications.

In these stories, the encroaching, constricting, destroying society is represented with particular urgency in the figure of one or more women. There are several possible reasons why this might be so. It seems to be a fact of life that we all — women and men alike — experience social conventions and responsibilities and obligations first in the persons of women, since women are entrusted by society with the task of rearing young children. Not until he reaches mid-adolescence does the male connect up with other males whose primary task is socialization; but at about this time — if he is heterosexual — his lovers and spouses become the agents of a permanent socialization and domestication. Thus, although women are not the source of social power, they are experienced as such. And although not all women are engaged in socializing the young, the young do not encounter women who are not. So from the point of view of the young man, the only kind of women who exist are entrappers and domesticators.

For heterosexual man, these socializing women are also the locus of powerful attraction. First, because everybody has social and conventional instincts: second, because his deepest emotional attachments are to women. This attraction gives urgency and depth to the protagonist's rejection of society. To do it, he must project onto the woman those attractions that he feels, and cast her in the melodramatic role of temptress, antagonist, obstacle — a character whose mission in life seems to be to ensnare him and deflect him from life's important purposes of self-discovery and self-assertion. (A Puritan would have said: from communion with Divinity.) As Richard Chase writes in *The American Novel and Its Tradition,* "The myth requires celibacy." It is partly against his own sexual urges that the male must struggle, and so he perceives the socializing and domesticating woman as a doubly powerful threat; for this reason, Chase goes on to state, neither Cooper nor "any other American novelist until the age of James and Edith Wharton" could imagine "a fully developed woman of sexual age."[16] Yet in making this statement, Chase is talking about his myth rather than Cooper's. (One should add that, for a homosexual male, the demands of society that he link himself for life to a woman make for a particularly misogynist version of this aspect of the American myth, for the hero is propelled not by a rejected attraction but by true revulsion.) Both heterosexual and homosexual versions of the myth cooperate with the hero's perceptions and validate the notion of woman as threat.

Such a portrayal of women is likely to be uncongenial, if not basically incomprehensible, to a woman. It is not likely that women will write books in which women play this part; and it is by no means the case that most novels by American men reproduce such a scheme. Even major male authors prominent in the canon have other ways of depicting women: for example, Cooper's *Pathfinder* and *The Pioneers,* Hemingway's *For Whom the Bell Tolls,* Fitzgerald's *The Beautiful and Damned.* The novels of Henry James and William Dean Howells pose a continual challenge to the masculinist bias of American critical theory. And in one work — *The Scarlet Letter* — a "fully developed woman of sexual age" who is the novel's protagonist has been admitted into the canon, but only by virtue of strenuous critical revisions of the text that remove Hester Prynne from the center of the novel and make her subordinate to Arthur Dimmesdale.

So Leslie Fiedler, in *Love and Death in the American Novel,* writes this of *The Scarlet Letter:*

> It is certainly true, in terms of the plot, that Chillingworth drives the minister toward confession and penance, while Hester would have lured him to evasion and flight. But this means, for all of Hawthorne's equivocations, that the eternal feminine does not draw us on toward grace, rather that the woman promises only madness and damnation. . . . [Hester] is the female temptress of Puritan mythology, but also, though sullied, the secular madonna of sentimental Protestantism.[17]

---

[16]Richard Chase, *The American Novel and Its Tradition* (Garden City, N.Y.: Anchor Books, 1957), pp. 55, 64. [Baym]
[17]Fiedler, *Love and Death in the American Novel,* p. 236. [Baym]

In the rhetorical "us" Fiedler presumes that all readers are men, that the novel is an act of communication among and about males. His characterization of Hester as one or another myth or image makes it impossible for the novel to be in any way about Hester as a human being. Giving the novel so highly specific a gender reference, Fiedler makes it inaccessible to women and limits its reference to men in comparison to the issues that Hawthorne was treating in the story. Not the least of these issues was, precisely, the human reference of a woman's tale.

Amusingly, then, since he has produced this warped reading, Fiedler goes on to condemn the novel for its sexual immaturity. *The Scarlet Letter* is integrated into Fiedler's general exposure of the inadequacies of the American male — inadequacies which, as his treatment of Hester shows, he holds women responsible for. The melodrama here is not Hawthorne's but Fiedler's — the American critic's melodrama of beset manhood. Of course, women authors as major writers are notable and inevitably absent from Fiedler's chronicle.

In fact, many books by women — including such major authors as Edith Wharton, Ellen Glasgow, and Willa Cather — project a version of the particular myth we are speaking of but cast the main character as a woman. When a woman takes the central role, it follows naturally that the socializer and domesticator will be a man. This is the situation in *The Scarlet Letter*. Hester is beset by the male reigning oligarchy and by Dimmesdale, who passively tempts her and is responsible for fathering her child. Thereafter, Hester (as the myth requires) elects celibacy, as do many heroines in versions of this myth by women: Thea in Cather's *The Song of the Lark*, Dorinda in Glasgow's *Barren Ground*, Anna Leath in Wharton's *The Reef*. But what is written in the criticism about these celibate women? They are said to be untrue to the imperatives of their gender, which require marriage, childbearing, domesticity. Instead of being read as a woman's version of the myth, such novels are read as stories of the frustration of female nature. Stories of female frustration are not perceived as commenting on, or containing, the essence of our culture, and so we do not find them in the canon.

So the role of entrapper and impediment in the melodrama of beset manhood is reserved for women. Also, the role of the beckoning wilderness, the attractive landscape, is given a deeply feminine quality. Landscape is deeply imbued with female qualities, as society is; but where society is menacing and destructive, landscape is compliant and supportive. It has the attributes simultaneously of a virginal bride and a nonthreatening mother: its female qualities are articulated with respect to a male angle of vision: what can nature do for me, asks the hero, what can it give me?

Of course, nature has been feminine and maternal from time immemorial, and Henry Nash Smith's *Virgin Land* picks up a timeless archetype in its title. The basic nature of the image leads one to forget about its potential for imbuing with sexual meanings any story in which it is used, and the gender implications of a female landscape have only recently begun to be studied. Recently, Annette Kolodny has studied the traditional canon from this approach.[18] She theorizes that the hero, fleeing a society that has been imagined as feminine, then imposes on nature some ideas of women which, no longer subject to the correcting influence of real-life experience, become more and more fantastic. The fantasies are infantile, concerned with power, mastery, and total gratification: the all-nurturing mother, the all-passive bride. Whether one accepts all the Freudian or Jungian implications of her argument, one cannot deny the way in which heroes of American myth turn to nature as sweetheart and nurture, anticipating the satisfaction of all desires through her and including among these the desires for mastery and power. A familiar passage that captures these ideas is one already quoted: Carraway's evocation of the "fresh green breast" of the New World. The fresh greenness is the virginity that offers itself to the sailors, but the breast promises maternal solace and delight. *The Great Gatsby* contains our two images of women: while Carraway evokes the impossible dream of a maternal landscape, he blames a nonmaternal

[18] Annette Kolodny, *The Lay of the Land: Metaphor As Experience and History in American Life and Letters* (Chapel Hill: University of North Carolina Press, 1975). [Baym]

woman, the socialite Daisy, for her failure to satisfy Gatsby's desires. The true adversary, of course, is Tom Buchanan, but he is hidden, as it were, behind Daisy's skirts.

I have said that women are not likely to cast themselves as antagonists in a man's story; they are even less likely, I suggest, to cast themselves as virgin land. The lack of fit between their own experience and the fictional role assigned to them is even greater in the second instance than in the first. If women portray themselves as brides or mothers it will not be in terms of the mythic landscape. If a woman puts a female construction on nature — as she certainly must from time to time, given the archetypal female resonance of the image — she is likely to write of it as more active, or to stress its destruction or violation. On the other hand, she might adjust the heroic myth to her own psyche by making nature out to be male — as, for example, Willa Cather seems to do in *O Pioneers!* But a violated landscape or a male nature does not fit the essential American pattern as critics have defined it, and hence these literary images occur in an obscurity that criticism cannot see. Thus, one has an almost classic example of the double bind. When the woman writer creates a story that conforms to the expected myth, it is not recognized for what it is because of a superfluous sexual specialization in the myth as it is entertained in the critics' minds. (Needless to say, many male novelists also entertain this version of the myth, and do not find the masculinist bias with which they imbue it to be superfluous. It is possible that some of these novelists, especially those who write in an era in which literary criticism is a powerful influence, have formed their ideas from their reading in criticism.) But if she does not conform to the myth, she is understood to be writing minor or trivial literature.

Two remaining points can be treated much more briefly. The description of the artist and of the act of writing which emerges when the critic uses the basic American story as his starting point contains many attributes of the basic story itself. This description raises the exclusion of women to a more abstract, theoretical — and perhaps more pernicious — level. Fundamentally, the idea is that the artist writing a story of this essential American kind is engaging in a task very much like the one performed by his mythic hero. In effect, the artist writing his narrative is imitating the mythic encounter of hero and possibility in the safe confines of his study; or, reversing the temporal order, one might see the mythic encounter of hero and possibility as a projection of the artist's situation.

Although this idea is greatly in vogue at the moment, it has a history. Here, for example, is Richard Chase representing the activity of writing in metaphors of discovery and exploration, as though the writer were a hero in the landscape: "The American novel has usually seemed content to explore . . . the remarkable and in some ways unexampled territories of life in the New World and to reflect its anomalies and dilemmas. It has . . . wanted . . . to discover a new place and a new state of mind."[19] Richard Poirier takes the idea further:

> The most interesting American books are an image of the creation of America itself. . . . They carry the metaphoric burden of a great dream of freedom — of the expansion of national consciousness into the vast spaces of a continent and the absorption of those spaces into ourselves. . . . The classic American writers try through style temporarily to free the hero (and the reader) from systems, to free them from the pressures of time, biology, economics, and from the social forces which are ultimately the undoing of American heroes and quite often of their creators. . . . The strangeness of American fiction has . . . to do . . . with the environment [the novelist] tries to create for his hero, usually his surrogate.[20]

The implicit union of creator and protagonist is made specific and overt at the end of Poirier's passage here. The ideas of Poirier and Chase, and others like them, are summed up in an anthology called *Theories of American Literature*, edited by Donald M. Kartiganer and Malcolm A. Griffith. The editors write, "It is as if with each new work our writers feel they must invent again the complete world of a literary form." (Yet, the true subject is not what the writers feel, but what the critics think they feel.) "Such a condition of nearly absolute freedom to create has appeared to our authors both as possibility and liability, an

[19]Chase, *American Novel*, p. 5. [Baym]
[20]Poirier, *A World Elsewhere*, pp. 3, 5, 9. [Baym]

utter openness suggesting limitless opportunity for the imagination, or an enormous vacancy in which they create from nothing. For some it has meant an opportunity to play Adam, to assume the role of an original namer of experience.[21]

One can see in this passage the transference of the American myth from the Adamic hero *in* the story to the Adamic creator *of* the story, and the reinterpretation of the American myth as a metaphor for the American artist's situation.

This myth of artistic creation, assimilating the act of writing novels to the Adamic myth, imposes on artistic creation all the gender-based restrictions that we have already examined in that myth. The key to identifying an "Adamic writer" is the formal appearance, or, more precisely, the *informal* appearance, of his novel. The unconventionality is interpreted as a direct representation of the open-ended experience of exploring and taming the wilderness, as well as a rejection of "society" as it is incorporated in conventional literary forms. There is no place for a woman author in this scheme. Her roles in the drama of creation are those allotted to her in a male melodrama: either she is to be silent, like nature, or she is the creator of conventional works, the spokesperson of society. What she might do as an innovator in her own right is not to be perceived.

In recent years, some refinements of critical theory coming from the Yale and Johns Hopkins and Columbia schools have added a new variant to the idea of creation as a male province. I quote from a 1979 book entitled *Home as Found* by Eric Sundquist. The author takes the idea that in writing a novel the artist is really writing a narrative about himself and proposes this addition:

Writing a narrative about oneself may represent an extremity of Oedipal usurpation or identification, a bizarre act of self fathering. . . . American authors have been particularly obsessed with *fathering* a tradition of their own, with becoming their "own sires." . . . The struggle . . . is central to the crisis of representation, and hence of style, that allows American authors to find in their own fantasies

those of a nation and to make of those fantasies a compelling and instructive literature.[22]

These remarks derive clearly from the work of such critics as Harold Bloom. The point for our purpose is the facile translation of the verb "to author" into the verb "to father," with the profound gender restrictions of that translation unacknowledged. According to this formulation, insofar as the author writes about a character who is his surrogate — which, apparently, he always does — he is trying to become his own father.

We can scarcely deny that men think a good deal about, and are profoundly affected by, relations with their fathers. The theme of fathers and sons is perennial in world literature. Somewhat more spaciously, we recognize that intergenerational conflict, usually perceived from the point of view of the young, is a recurrent literary theme, especially in egalitarian cultures. Certainly, this idea involves the question of authority, and "authority" is a notion related to that of "the author." And there is some gender-specific significance involved since authority in most cultures that we know tends to be invested in adult males. But the theory has built from these useful and true observations to a restriction of literary creation to a sort of therapeutic act that can only be performed by men. If literature is the attempt to *father* oneself by the author, then every act of writing by a woman is both perverse and absurd. And, of course, it is bound to fail.

Since this particular theory of the act of writing is drawn from psychological assumptions that are not specific to American literature, it may be argued that there is no need to confine it to American authors. In fact, Harold Bloom's *Anxiety of Influence*, defining literature as a struggle between fathers and sons, or the struggle of sons to escape from their fathers, is about British literature. And so is Edward Said's book *Beginnings*, which chronicles the history of the nineteenth-century British novel as exemplification of what he

[21]Donald M. Kartiganer and Malcolm A. Griffith, eds. *Theories of American Literature: The Critical Perspective* (New York: Macmillan, 1962), pp. 4–5. [Baym]

[22]Eric J. Sundquist, *Home as Found: Authority and Genealogy in Nineteenth-Century American Literature* (Baltimore: Johns Hopkins University Press, 1979), pp. xviii–xix. [Baym]

calls "filiation." His discussion omits Jane Austen, George Eliot, all three Brontë sisters, Mrs. Gaskell, Mrs. Humphrey Ward — not a sign of a woman author is found in his treatment of Victorian fiction. The result is a revisionist approach to British fiction that recasts it in the accepted image of the American myth. Ironically, just at the time that feminist critics are discovering more and more important women, the critical theorists have seized upon a theory that allows the women less and less presence. This observation points up just how significantly the critic is engaged in the act of *creating* literature.

Ironically, then, one concludes that in pushing the theory of American fiction to this extreme, critics have "deconstructed" it by creating a tool with no particular American reference. In pursuit of the uniquely American, they have arrived at a place where Americanness has vanished into the depths of what is alleged to be the universal male psyche. The theory of American fiction has boiled down to the phrase in my title: a melodrama of beset manhood. What a reduction this is of the enormous variety of fiction written in this country, by both women and men! And, ironically, nothing could be further removed from Trilling's idea of the artist as embodiment of a culture. As in the working out of all theories, its weakest link has found it out and broken the chain.

Sandra M. Gilbert

b. 1936

Susan Gubar

b. 1944

Sandra M. Gilbert and Susan Gubar are best known for their collaborative explorations of women's literary tradition. They have co-authored The Madwoman in the Attic: The Woman Writer and the Nineteenth-Century Literary Imagination *(1979) and have extended their tracing of the special characteristics of women's writing into the twentieth century in a three-volume sequel collectively entitled* No Man's Land, *the volumes of which are separately titled* The War of the Words *(1988),* Sexchanges *(1991), and* Letters from the Front *(1994). They have also coedited* Shakespeare's Sisters: Feminist Essays on Women Poets *(1979) and* The Norton Anthology of Literature by Women, *third edition (2007), which provides canonical treatment of literature by women in English for college courses, and have coauthored* Masterpiece Theatre: An Academic Melodrama *(1995). Both Gilbert and Gubar were born in New York City. Sandra Mortola Gilbert took a B.A. at Cornell (1957), an M.A. at New York University (1961), and a Ph.D. at Columbia (1968). After appointments at Indiana University and Princeton, she is now Professor of English Emerita at the University of California at Davis. Throughout her career Gilbert has written poetry of her own; her most recent volumes are* Inventions of Farewell *(2001),* The Italian Collection: Poems of Heritage *(2003),* Belongings *(2006), and* Aftermath *(2011). Susan David Gubar, Distinguished Professor Emerita of English and Women's Studies at Indiana University at Bloomington, received her B.A. from City College of New York (1965), her M.A. from the University of Michigan (1968), and her Ph.D. from the University of Iowa (1972). Gubar's career includes a Guggenheim fellowship (1983–84) and teaching at the University of Illinois and at Tufts. Gubar has written numerous essays on eighteenth-century literature, science fiction and fantasy, and contemporary women's writing. Gubar's recent solo books have been* Racechanges: White Skin Black Face in American Culture *(1997),* Critical Condition: Feminism at the Turn of the Century *(2000),* Poetry after Auschwitz *(2003),* Rooms of Our Own *(2006),* Judas: A Biography *(2009), and* Memoir of a Debulked Woman: Enduring Ovarian Cancer *(2012). "Infection in the Sentence" is the second chapter of* The Madwoman in the Attic.

From *Infection in the Sentence:*
The Woman Writer and the
Anxiety of Authorship

The man who does not know sick women does not know women. — S. WEIR MITCHELL

I try to describe this long limitation, hoping that with such power as is now mine, and such use of language as is within that power, this will convince any one who cares about it that this "living" of mine had been done under a heavy handicap. . . . — CHARLOTTE PERKINS GILMAN

A Word dropped careless on a Page
May stimulate an eye
When folded in perpetual seam
The Wrinkled Maker lie

Infection in the sentence breeds
We may inhale Despair
At distances of Centuries
From the Malaria — — EMILY DICKINSON

I stand in the ring
in the dead city
and tie on the red shoes

. . . .

They are not mine,
they are my mother's,
her mother's before,
handed down like an heirloom
but hidden like shameful letters.

— ANNE SEXTON

What does it mean to be a woman writer in a culture whose fundamental definitions of literary authority are, as we have seen, both overtly and covertly patriarchal? If the vexed and vexing polarities of angel and monster, sweet dumb Snow White and fierce mad Queen, are major images literary tradition offers women, how does such imagery influence the ways in which women attempt the pen? If the Queen's looking glass speaks with the King's voice, how do its perpetual kingly admonitions affect the Queen's own voice? Since his is the chief voice she hears, does the Queen try to sound like the King, imitating his tone, his inflections, his phrasing, his point of view? Or does she "talk back" to him in her own vocabulary, her own timbre, insisting on her own viewpoint? We believe these are basic questions feminist literary criticism — both theoretical and practical — must answer, and consequently they are questions to which we shall turn again and again, not only in this chapter but in all our readings of nineteenth-century literature by women.

Dis-eased and infected by the sentences of patriarchy, yet unable to deny the urgency of that "poet-fire"[1] she felt within herself, what strategies did the woman writer develop for overcoming her anxiety of authorship? How did she dance out of the looking glass of the male text into a tradition that enabled her to create her own authority? Denied the economic, social, and psychological status ordinarily essential to creativity; denied the right, skill, and education to tell their own stories with confidence, women who did not retreat into angelic silence seem at first to have had very limited opinions. On the one hand, they could accept the "parsley wreath"[2] of self-denial, writing in "lesser" genres — children's books, letters, diaries — or limiting their readership to "mere" women like themselves and producing what George Eliot called "Silly Novels by Lady Novelists."[3] On the other hand, they could become males *manqués,* mimics who disguised their identities and, denying themselves, produced most frequently a literature of bad faith and inauthenticity. Given such weak solutions to what appears to have been an overwhelming problem, how could there be a great tradition of literature by women? Yet, as we shall show, there is just such a tradition, a tradition especially encompassing the works

[1]Gilbert and Gubar allude to Elizabeth Barrett Browning's sonnet to George Sand.
[2]As opposed to the laurel wreath traditionally given to (male) poets of distinction.
[3]See George Eliot, "Silly Novels by Lady Novelists," *Westminster Review* 64 (1856): 442–61. [Gilbert and Gubar]

of nineteenth-century women writers who found viable ways of circumventing the problematic strategies we have just outlined.

Inappropriate as male-devised genres must always have seemed, some women have always managed to work seriously in them. Indeed, when we examine the great works written by nineteenth-century women poets and novelists, we soon notice two striking facts. First, an extraordinary number of literary women either eschewed or grew beyond both female "modesty" and male mimicry. From Austen to Dickinson, these female artists all dealt with central female experiences from a specifically female perspective. But this distinctively feminine aspect of their art has been generally ignored by critics because the most successful women writers often seem to have channeled their female concerns into secret or at least obscure corners. In effect, such women have created submerged meanings, meanings hidden within or behind the more accessible, "public" content of their works, so that their literature could be read and appreciated even when its vital concern with female dispossession and disease was ignored. Second, the writing of these women often seems "odd" in relation to the predominantly male literary history defined by the standards of what we have called patriarchal poetics. Neither Augustans nor Romantics, neither Victorian sages nor Pre-Raphaelite sensualists, many of the most distinguished late eighteenth-century and nineteenth-century English and American women writers do not seem to "fit" into any of those categories to which our literary historians have accustomed us. Indeed, to many critics and scholars, some of these literary women look like isolated eccentrics.

We may legitimately wonder, however, if the second striking fact about nineteenth-century literature by women may not in some sense be a function of the first. Could the "oddity" of this work be associated with women's secret but insistent struggle to transcend their anxiety of authorship? Could the "isolation" and apparent "eccentricity" of these women really represent their common female struggle to solve the problem of what Anne Finch[4] called the literary woman's

[4]The Countess of Winchilsea (1661–1720), a poet whose Miscellanies was published in 1713.

"fall," as well as their common female search for an aesthetic that would yield a healthy space in an overwhelmingly male "Palace of Art"? Certainly when we consider the "oddity" of women's writing in relation to its submerged content, it begins to seem that when women did not turn into male mimics or accept the "parsley wreath" they may have attempted to transcend their anxiety of authorship by revising male genres, using them to record their own dreams and their own stories in disguise. Such writers, therefore, both participated in and — to use one of Harold Bloom's key terms[5] — "swerved" from the central sequences of male literary history, enacting a uniquely female process of revision and redefinition that necessarily caused them to seem "odd." At the same time, while they achieved essential authority by telling their own stories, these writers allayed their distinctively female anxieties of authorship by following Emily Dickinson's famous (and characteristically female) advice to "Tell all the Truth but tell it slant — ."[6] In short, like the twentieth-century American poet H. D., who declared her aesthetic strategy by entitling one of her novels Palimpsest,[7] women from Jane Austen and Mary Shelley to Emily Brontë and Emily Dickinson produced literary works that are in some sense palimpsestic, works whose surface designs conceal or obscure deeper, less accessible (and less socially acceptable) levels of meaning. Thus these authors managed the difficult task of achieving true female literary authority by simultaneously conforming to and subverting patriarchal literary standards.

Of course, as the allegorical figure of Duessa[8] suggests, men have always accused women of the duplicity that is essential to the literary strategies we are describing here. In part, at least, such accusations are well founded, both in life and in art. As in the white-black relationship,

[5]See Bloom in the introduction to Psychoanalytic Theory and Criticism, p. 63a.

[6]J, 1129, The Complete Poems of Emily Dickinson, 3 vols., ed. Thomas H. Johnson (Cambridge, MA: The Belknap Press of Harvard University Press, 1955). [Gilbert and Gubar]

[7]A palimpsest is a manuscript that has been erased and written over.

[8]In Spenser's Faerie Queene, Duessa is the daughter of Falsehood and Shame.

the dominant group in the male-female relationship rightly fears and suspects that the docility of the subordinate caste masks rebellious passions. Moreover, just as blacks did in the master-slave relationships of the American South, women in patriarchy have traditionally cultivated accents of acquiescence in order to gain freedom to live their lives on their own terms, if only in the privacy of their own thoughts. Interestingly, indeed, several feminist critics have recently used Frantz Fanon's model of colonialism to describe the relationship between male (parent) culture and female (colonized) literature.[9] But with only one language at their disposal, women writers in England and America had to be even more adept at doubletalk than their colonized counterparts. We shall see, therefore, that in publicly presenting acceptable facades for private and dangerous visions women writers have long used a wide range of tactics to obscure but not obliterate their most subversive impulses. Along with the twentieth-century American painter Judy Chicago, any one of these artists might have noted that "formal issues" were often "something that my content had to be hidden behind in order for my work to be taken seriously." And with Judy Chicago, too, any one of these women might have confessed that "Because of this duplicity, there always appeared to be something 'not quite right' about my pieces according to the prevailing aesthetic."[10]

To be sure, male writers also "swerve" from their predecessors, and they too produce literary texts whose revolutionary messages are concealed behind stylized facades. The most original male writers, moreover, sometimes seem "not quite right" to those readers we have recently come to call "establishment" critics. As Bloom's theory of the anxiety of influence implies, however, and as our analysis of the metaphor of literary paternity also suggests, there are powerful paradigms of male intellectual struggle which enable the male writer to explain his rebelliousness,

his "swerving," and his "originality" both to himself and to the world, no matter how many readers think him "not quite right." In a sense, therefore, he conceals his revolutionary energies only so that he may more powerfully reveal them, and swerves or rebels so that he may triumph by founding a new order, since his struggle against his precursor is a "battle of strong equals."

For the woman writer, however, concealment is not a military gesture but a strategy born of fear and dis-ease. Similarly, a literary "swerve" is not a motion by which the writer prepares for a victorious accession to power but a necessary evasion. Locked into structures created by and for men, eighteenth- and nineteenth-century women writers did not so much rebel against the prevailing aesthetic as feel guilty about their inability to conform to it. With little sense of a viable female culture, such women were plainly much troubled by the fact that they needed to communicate truths which other (i.e. male) writers apparently never felt or expressed. Conditioned to doubt their own authority anyway, women writers who wanted to describe what, in Dickinson's phrase, is "not brayed of tongue"[11] would find it easier to doubt themselves than the censorious voices of society. The evasions and concealments of their art are therefore far more elaborate than those of most male writers. For, given the patriarchal biases of nineteenth-century literary culture, the literary woman did have something crucial to hide.

Because so many of the lost or concealed truths of female culture have recently been retrieved by feminist scholars, women readers in particular have lately become aware that nineteenth-century literary women felt they had things to hide. Many feminist critics, therefore, have begun to write about these phenomena of evasion and concealment in women's writing. In *The Female Imagination,* for instance, Patricia Meyer Spacks repeatedly describes the ways in which women's novels are marked by "subterranean challenges" to truths that the writers of such works appear on the surface to accept. Similarly, Carolyn Heilbrun and Catharine Stimpson discuss "the presence of absence" in literature by women, the "hollows,

---

[9]See, for instance, Barbara Charlesworth Gelpi, "A Common Language: The American Woman Poet," in *Shakespeare's Sisters,* ed. Gilbert and Gubar, pp. 269–79. [Gilbert and Gubar]

[10]Judy Chicago, *Through the Flower: My Struggle as a Woman Artist* (New York: Doubleday, 1977), p. 40. [Gilbert and Gubar]

[11]Dickinson, *Poems,* J. 512 ("The Soul has Bandaged moments —"). [Gilbert and Gubar]

centers, caverns within the work — places where activity that one might expect is missing . . . or deceptively coded." Perhaps most trenchantly, Elaine Showalter has recently pointed out that feminist criticism, with its emphasis on the woman writer's inevitable consciousness of her own gender, has allowed us to "see meaning in what has previously been empty space. The orthodox plot recedes, and another plot, hitherto submerged in the anonymity of the background, stands out in bold relief like a thumbprint."[12]

But what is this other plot? Is there any one other plot? What is the secret message of literature by women, if there is a single secret message? What, in other words, have women got to say? Most obviously, of course, if we return to the angelic figure of Makarie[13] — that ideal of "contemplative purity" who no doubt had headaches precisely because her author inflicted upon her a life that seemed to have "no story," — what literary women have hidden or disguised is what each writer knows is in some sense her own story. Because, as Simone de Beauvoir puts it, women "still dream through the dreams of men,"

internalizing the structures that the Queen's looking glass utters in its kingly voice, the message or story that has been hidden is "merely," in Carolyn Kizer's bitter words, "the private lives of one half of humanity."[14] More specifically, however, the one plot that seems to be concealed in most of the nineteenth-century literature by women which will concern us here is in some sense a story of the woman writer's quest for her own story; it is the story, in other words, of the woman's quest for self-definition. Like the speaker of Mary Elizabeth Coleridge's[15] "The Other Side of a Mirror," the literary woman frequently finds herself staring with horror at a fearful image of herself that has been mysteriously inscribed on the surface of the glass, and she tries to guess the truth that cannot be uttered by the wounded and bleeding mouth, the truth behind the "leaping fire / Of jealousy and fierce revenge," the truth "of hard unsanctified distress." Uneasily aware that, like Sylvia Plath, she is "inhabited by a cry," she secretly seeks to unify herself by coming to terms with her own fragmentation. Yet even though, with Mary Elizabeth Coleridge, she strives to "set the crystal surface" of the mirror free from frightful images, she continually feels, as May Sarton puts it, that she has been "broken in two / By sheer definition."[16] The story," she may guess," therefore, is the story of her own attempt to make herself whole by healing her own infections and diseases.

To heal herself, however, the woman writer must exorcise the sentences which bred her infection in the first place; she must overtly or covertly free herself of the despair she inhaled from some "Wrinkled Maker," and she can only do this by revising the Maker's texts. Or, to put the matter in terms of a different metaphor, to "set the crystal surface free," a literary woman must shatter the mirror that has so long reflected

[12]Patricia Meyer Spacks, *The Female Imagination* (New York: Knopf, 1975), p. 317; Carolyn Heilbrun and Catharine Stimpson, "Theories of Feminist Criticism: A Dialogue," in Josephine Donovan, ed., *Feminist Literary Criticism* (Lexington: The University Press of Kentucky, 1975), p. 62; Elaine Showalter, "Review Essay," *Signs* 1, no. 2 (Winter 1975): 435. See also Annis V. Pratt, "The New Feminist Criticism: Exploring the History of the New Space," in *Beyond Intellectual Sexism: A New Woman, A New Reality*, ed. Joan I. Roberts (New York: David McKay, 1976). On p. 183 Pratt describes what she calls her "drowning theory," which "comes from a phenomenon in black culture: You have a little black church black in the marsh and you're going to sing 'Go Down Moses' [but] Every now and then the members of the congregation want to break loose and sing 'Oh Freedom.' . . . Whenever they sing that, they've got this big old black pot in the vestibule, and as they sing they pound the pot. That way, no white folks are going to hear. The drowning effect, this banging on the pot to drown out what they are actually saying about feminism, came in with the first woman's novel and hasn't gone out yet. Many women novelists have even succeeded in hiding the covert or implicit feminism in their books from themselves. . . . As a result we get explicit cultural norms superimposed upon an authentic creative mind in the form of all kinds of feints, ploys, masks and disguises embedded in the plot structure and characterization." [Gilbert and Gubar]

[13]Makarie is a character in *Wilhelm Meisters Wanderjahre* (1821–29) by Johann Wolfgang von Goethe (1749–1832).

[14]De Beauvoir, *The Second Sex* (New York: Knopf, 1973), p. 132; Kizer, "Three," from "Pro Femina," in *No More Masks!*, ed. Florence Howe and Ellen Bass (New York: Doubleday, 1973), p. 175. [Gilbert and Gubar]

[15]English poet (1861–1907), author of *Fancy's Following* (1896) and *Fancy's Guerdon* (1897).

[16]Plath, "Elm," *Ariel* (New York: Harper & Row, 1966), p. 16; Sarton, "Birthday on the Acropolis," *A Private Mythology* (New York: Norton, 1966), p. 48. [Gilbert and Gubar]

what every woman was supposed to be. For these reasons, then, women writers in England and America, throughout the nineteenth century and on into the twentieth, have been especially concerned with assaulting and revising, deconstructing and reconstructing those images of women inherited from male literature, especially, as we noted in our discussion of the Queen's looking glass, the paradigmatic polarities of angel and monster. Examining and attacking such images, however, literary women have inevitably had consciously or unconsciously to reject the values and assumptions of the society that created these fearsome paradigms. Thus, even when they do not overtly criticize patriarchal institutions or conventions (and most of the nineteenth-century women we shall be studying do *not* overtly do so), these writers almost obsessively create characters who enact their own, covert authorial anger. With Charlotte Brontë, they may feel that there are "evils" of which it is advisable "not too often to think." With George Eliot, they may declare that the "woman question" seems "to overhang abysses, of which even prostitution is not the worst."[17] But over and over again they project what seems to be the energy of their own despair into passionate, even melodramatic characters who act out the subversive impulses every woman inevitably feels when she contemplates the "deep-rooted" evils of patriarchy.

It is significant, then, that when the speaker of "The Other Side of a Mirror" looks into her glass the woman that she sees is a madwoman, "wild / With more than womanly despair," the monster that she fears she really is rather than the angel she has pretended to be. What the heroine of George Eliot's verse-drama *Armgart* calls "basely feigned content, the placid mask / Of woman's misery" *is* merely a mask, and Mary Elizabeth Coleridge, like so many of her contemporaries, records the emergence from behind the mask of a figure whose rage "once no man on earth could guess."[18] Repudiating "basely feigned

content," this figure arises like a bad dream, bloody, envious, enraged, as if the very process of writing had itself liberated a madwoman, a crazy and angry woman, from a silence in which neither she nor her author can continue to acquiesce. Thus although Coleridge's mirrored madwoman is an emblem of "speechless woe" because she has "no voice to speak her dread," the poet ultimately speaks *for* her when she whispers "I am she!" More, she speaks for her in writing the poem that narrates her emergence from behind the placid mask, "the aspects glad and gay, / That erst were found reflected there."

As we explore nineteenth-century literature, we will find that this madwoman emerges over and over again from the mirrors women writers hold up both to their own natures and to their own visions of nature. Even the most apparently conservative and decorous women writers obsessively create fiercely independent characters who seek to destroy all the patriarchal structures which both their authors and their authors' submissive heroines seem to accept as inevitable. Of course, by projecting their rebellious impulses not into their heroines but into mad or monstrous women (who are suitably punished in the course of the novel or poem), female authors dramatize their own self-division, their desire both to accept the strictures of patriarchal society and to reject them. What this means, however, is that the madwoman in literature by women is not merely, as she might be in male literature, an antagonist or foil to the heroine. Rather, she is usually in some sense the *author's* double, an image of her own anxiety and rage. Indeed, much of the poetry and fiction written by women conjures up this mad creature so that female authors can come to terms with their own uniquely female feelings of fragmentation, their own keen sense of the discrepancies between what they are and what they are supposed to be.

We shall see, then, that the mad double is as crucial to the aggressively sane novels of Jane Austen and George Eliot as she is in the more obviously rebellious stories told by Charlotte and Emily Brontë. Both gothic and anti-gothic writers represent themselves as split like Emily Dickinson between the elected nun and the damned witch, or like Mary Shelley between

---

[17] *The George Eliot Letters*, 7 vols., ed. Gordon S. Haight (New Haven: Yale University Press, 1954–55), 5:58. [Gilbert and Gubar]

[18] Eliot, *Poems*, 2 vols. (New York: Croscup, 1896), p. 124. [Gilbert and Gubar]

the noble, censorious scientist and his enraged, childish monster. In fact, so important is this female schizophrenia of authorship that, as we hope to show, it links these nineteenth-century writers with such twentieth-century descendants as Virginia Woolf (who projects herself into both ladylike Mrs. Dalloway and crazed Septimus Warren Smith), Doris Lessing (who divides herself between sane Martha Hesse and mad Lynda Coldridge), and Sylvia Plath (who sees herself as both a plaster saint and a dangerous "old yellow" monster).

To be sure, in the works of all these artists — both nineteenth- and twentieth-century — the mad character is sometimes created only to be destroyed: Septimus Warren Smith and Bertha Mason Rochester are both good examples of such characters, as is Victor Frankenstein's monster. Yet even when a figure of rage seems to function only as a monitory image, her (or his) fury must be acknowledged not only by the angelic protagonist to whom s/he is opposed, but, significantly, *by the reader as well*. With his usual perceptiveness, Geoffrey Chaucer anticipated the dynamics of this situation in the *Canterbury Tales*. When he gave the Wife of Bath a tale of her own, he portrayed her projecting her subversive vision of patriarchal institutions into the story of a furious hag who demands supreme power over her own life and that of her husband: only when she gains his complete acceptance of her authority does this witch transform herself into a modest and docile beauty. Five centuries later, the threat of the hag, the monster, the witch, the madwoman, still lurks behind the compliant paragon of women's stories.

To mention witches, however, is to be reminded once again of the traditional (patriarchally defined) association between creative women and monsters. In projecting their anger and dis-ease into dreadful figures, creating dark doubles for themselves and their heroines, women writers are both identifying with and revising the self-definitions patriarchal culture has imposed on them. All the nineteenth- and twentieth-century literary women who evoke the female monster in their novels and poems alter her meaning by virtue of their own identification with her. For it is usually because she is in some sense imbued with

interiority that the witch-monster-madwoman becomes so crucial an avatar of the writer's own self. From a male point of view, women who reject the submissive silences of domesticity have been seen as terrible objects — Gorgons, Sirens, Scyllas, serpent-Lamias, Mothers of Death or Goddesses of Night. But from a female point of view the monster woman is simply a woman who seeks the power of self-articulation, and therefore, like Mary Shelley giving the first-person story of a monster who seemed to his creator to be merely a "filthy mass that moves and talks," she presents this figure for the first time from the inside out. Such a radical misreading of patriarchal poetics frees the woman artist to imply her criticism of the literary conventions she has inherited even as it allows her to express her ambiguous relationship to a culture that has not only defined her gender but shaped her mind. In a sense, as a famous poem by Muriel Rukeyser implies, all these women ultimately embrace the role of that most mythic of female monsters, the Sphinx, whose indecipherable message is the key to existence, because they know that the secret wisdom so long hidden from men is precisely *their point of view*.[19]

There is a sense, then, in which the female literary tradition we have been defining participates on all levels in the same duality or duplicity that necessitates the generation of such doubles as monster characters who shadow angelic authors and mad anti-heroines who complicate the lives of sane heroines. Parody, for instance, is another one of the key strategies through which this female duplicity reveals itself. As we have noted, nineteenth-century women writers frequently both use and misuse (or subvert) a common male tradition or genre. Consequently, we shall see over and over again that a "complex vibration" occurs between stylized generic gestures and unexpected deviations from such obvious gestures, a vibration that undercuts and ridicules the genre being employed. Some of the best-known recent poetry by women openly uses such parody in the cause of feminism: traditional figures of patriarchal

[19]Rukeyser, "Myth," *Breaking Open* (New York: Random House, 1973), p. 20. [Gilbert and Gubar]

mythology like Circe, Leda, Cassandra, Medusa, Helen, and Persephone have all lately been reinvented in the images of their female creators, and each poem devoted to one of these figures is a reading that reinvents her original story.[20] But though nineteenth-century women did not employ this kind of parody so openly and angrily, they too deployed it to give contextual force to their revisionary attempts at self-definition. Jane Austen's novels of sense and sensibility, for instance, suggest a revolt against both those standards of female excellence. Similarly, Charlotte Brontë's critical revision of *Pilgrim's Progress* questions the patriarchal ideal of female submissiveness by substituting a questing Everywoman for Bunyan's questing Christian. In addition, as we shall show in detail in later chapters, Mary Shelley, Emily Brontë, and George Eliot covertly reappraise and repudiate the misogyny implicit in Milton's mythology by misreading and revising Milton's story of woman's fall. Parodic, duplicitous, extraordinarily sophisticated, all this female writing is both revisionary and revolutionary, even when it is produced by writers we usually think of as models of angelic resignation.

To summarize this point, it is helpful to examine a work by the woman who seems to be the most modest and gentle of the three Brontë sisters. Anne Brontë's *The Tenant of Wildfell Hall* (1848) is generally considered conservative in its espousal of Christian values, but it tells what is in fact a story of woman's liberation. Specifically, it describes a woman's escape from the prisonhouse of a bad marriage, and her subsequent attempts to achieve independence by establishing herself in a career as an artist. Since Helen Graham, the novel's protagonist, must remain incognito in order to elude her husband, she signs with false initials the landscapes she produces when she becomes a professional artist, and she titles the

works in such a way as to hide her whereabouts. In short, she uses her art both to express and to camouflage herself. But this functionally ambiguous aesthetic is not merely a result of her flight from home and husband. For even earlier in the novel, when we encounter Helen before her marriage, her use of art is duplicitous. Her painting and drawing seem at first simply to be genteel social accomplishments, but when she shows one of her paintings to her future husband, he discovers a pencil sketch of his own face on the back of the canvas. Helen has been using the reverse side of her paintings to express her secret desires, and although she has remembered to rub out all the other sketches, this one remains, eventually calling his attention to the dim traces on the backs of all the others.

In the figure of Helen Graham, Anne Brontë has given us a wonderfully useful paradigm of the female artist. Whether Helen covertly uses a supposedly modest young lady's "accomplishments" for unladylike self-expression or publicly flaunts her professionalism and independence, she must in some sense deny or conceal her own art, or at least deny the self-assertion implicit in her art. In other words, there is an essential ambiguity involved in her career as an artist. When, as a girl, she draws on the backs of her paintings, she must make the paintings themselves work as public masks to hide her private dreams, and only behind such masks does she feel free to choose her own subjects. Thus she produces a public art which she herself rejects as inadequate but which she secretly uses to discover a new aesthetic space for herself. In addition, she subverts her genteelly "feminine" works with personal representations which endure only in tracings, since her guilt about the impropriety of self-expression has caused her to efface her private drawings just as it has led her to efface herself.

It is significant, moreover, that the sketch on the other side of Helen's canvas depicts the face of the Byronically brooding, sensual Arthur Huntingdon, the man she finally decides to marry. Fatally attracted by the energy and freedom that she desires as an escape from the constraints of her own life, Helen pays for her initial attraction by watching her husband metamorphose from a fallen angel into a fiend, as he relentlessly and

---

[20]For "complex vibration," see Elaine Showalter, "Review Essay," p. 435. For reinventions of mythology, see Mona Van Duyn, "Leda" and "Leda Reconsidered," in *No More Masks!*, pp. 129–32, and Margaret Atwood, "Circe/Mud Poems," in *You Are Happy* (New York: Harper & Row, 1974), pp. 71–94. A poet like H. D. continually reinvents Persephone, Medusa, and Helen in her uniquely female epics, for example in *Helen in Egypt* (New York: New Directions, 1961). [Gilbert and Gubar]

self-destructively pursues a diabolical career of gaming, whoring, and drinking. In this respect, too, Helen is prototypical, since we shall see that women artists are repeatedly attracted to the Satanic/Byronic hero even while they try to resist the sexual submission exacted by this oppressive younger son who seems, at first, so like a brother or a double. From Jane Austen, who almost obsessively rejected this figure, to Mary Shelley, the Brontës, and George Eliot, all of whom iden- tified with his fierce presumption, women writers develop a subversive tradition that has a unique relationship to the Romantic ethos of revolt.

What distinguishes Helen Graham (and all the women authors who resemble her) from male Romantics, however, is precisely her anxiety about her own artistry, together with the duplic- ity that anxiety necessitates. Even when she becomes a professional artist, Helen continues to fear the social implications of her vocation. Associating female creativity with freedom from male domination, and dreading the misogynistic censure of her community, she produces art that at least partly hides her experience of her actual place in the world. Because her audience poten- tially includes the man from whom she is trying to escape, she must balance her need to paint her own condition against her need to circumvent detection. Her strained relationship to her art is thus determined almost entirely by her gender, so that from both her anxieties and her strategies for overcoming them we can extrapolate a number of the crucial ways in which women's art has been radically qualified by their femaleness.

As we shall see, Charlotte Brontë's sister Anne depicts similar anxieties and similar strategies for overcoming anxiety in the careers of all the female artists who appear in her novels. From timid Frances Henri to demure Jane Eyre, from mysteri- ous Lucia to flamboyant Vashti, Brontë's women artists withdraw behind their art even while they assert themselves through it, as if deliberately adopting Helen Graham's duplicitous techniques of self-expression. For the great women writers of the past two centuries are linked by the ingenuity with which all, while no one was really looking, danced out of the debilitating looking glass of the male text into the health of female author- ity. Tracing subversive pictures behind socially

acceptable facades, they managed to appear to dis- sociate themselves from their own revolutionary impulses even while passionately enacting such impulses. Articulating the "private lives of one half of humanity," their fiction and poetry both records and transcends the struggle of what Marge Piercy has called "Unlearning to not speak."[21]

We must not forget, however, that to hide behind the facade of art, even for so crucial a process as "Unlearning to not speak," is still to be hidden, to be confined: to be secret is to be secreted. In a poignant and perceptive poem to Emily Dickinson, Adrienne Rich has noted that in her "half-cracked way" Dickinson chose "silence for entertainment, / chose to have it out at last / on [her] own premises."[22] This is what Jane Austen, too, chose to do when she ironically defined her work-space as two inches of ivory, what Emily Brontë chose to do when she hid her poems in kitchen cabinets (and perhaps destroyed her Gondal stories), what Christina Rossetti chose when she elected an art that glorified the reli- gious constrictions of the "convent threshold." Rich's crucial pun on the word *premises* returns us, therefore, to the confinement of these women, a confinement that was inescapable for them even at their moments of greatest triumph, a confinement that was implicit in their secretiveness. This confinement was both literal and figurative. Literally, women like Dickinson, Brontë, and Rossetti were imprisoned in their homes, their father's houses; indeed, almost all nineteenth- century women were in some sense imprisoned in men's houses. Figuratively, such women were, as we have seen, locked into male texts, texts from which they could escape only through ingenuity and indirection. It is not surprising, then, that spa- tial imagery of enclosure and escape, elaborated with what frequently becomes obsessive inten- sity, characterizes much of their writing.

In fact, anxieties about space sometimes seem to dominate the literature of both nineteenth-century women and their twentieth-century descendants.

[21]Marge Piercy, "Unlearning to not speak," *To Be Of Use* (New York: Doubleday, 1973), p. 38. [Gilbert and Gubar]

[22]"I am in danger — sir — ," *Adrienne Rich's Poetry*, ed. Barbara Charlesworth Gelpi and Albert Gelpi (New York: Norton, 1975), pp. 30–31. [Gilbert and Gubar]

In the genre Ellen Moers has recently called "female Gothic,"[23] for instance, heroines who characteristically inhabit mysteriously intricate or uncomfortably stifling houses are often seen as captured, fettered, trapped, even buried alive. But other kinds of works by women — novels of manners, domestic tales, lyric poems — also show the same concern with spatial constrictions. From Ann Radcliffe's melodramatic dungeons to Jane Austen's mirrored parlors, from Charlotte Brontë's haunted garrets to Emily Brontë's coffin-shaped beds, imagery of enclosure reflects the woman writer's own discomfort, her sense of powerlessness, her fear that she inhabits alien and incomprehensible places. Indeed, it reflects her growing suspicion that what the nineteenth century called "woman's place" is itself irrational and strange. Moreover, from Emily Dickinson's haunted chambers to H. D.'s tightly shut sea-shells and Sylvia Plath's grave-caves, imagery of entrapment expresses the woman writer's sense that she has been dispossessed precisely because she is so thoroughly possessed — and possessed in every sense of the word.

The opening stanzas of Charlotte Perkins Gilman's punningly titled "In Duty Bound" show how inevitable it was for a female artist to translate into spatial terms her despair at the spiritual constrictions of what Gilman ironically called "home comfort."

> In duty bound, a life hemmed in,
>   Whichever way the spirit turns to look;
> No chance of breaking out, except by sin;
>   Not even room to shirk —
>   Simply to live, and work.
>
> An obligation preimposed, unsought,
>   Yet binding with the force of natural law;
> The pressure of antagonistic thought;
>   Aching within, each hour,
>   A sense of wasting power.
>
> A house with roof so darkly low
>   The heavy rafters shut the sunlight out;
> One cannot stand erect without a blow;
>   Until the soul inside
>   Cries for a grave — more wide.[24]

Literally confined to the house, figuratively confined to a single "place," enclosed in parlors and encased in texts, imprisoned in kitchens and enshrined in stanzas, women artists naturally found themselves describing dark interiors and confusing their sense that they were house-bound with their rebellion against being duty bound. The same connections Gilman's poem made in the nineteenth century had after all been made by Anne Finch in the eighteenth, when she complained that women who wanted to write poetry were scornfully told that "the dull mannage of a servile house" was their "outmost art and use." Inevitably, then, since they were trapped in so many ways in the architecture — both the houses and the institutions — of patriarchy, women expressed their anxiety of authorship by comparing their "presumptuous" literary ambitions with the domestic accomplishments that had been prescribed for them. Inevitably, too, they expressed their claustrophobic rage by enacting rebellious escapes.

Dramatizations of imprisonment and escape are so all-pervasive in nineteenth-century literature by women that we believe they represent a uniquely female tradition in this period. Interestingly, though works in this tradition generally begin by using houses as primary symbols of female imprisonment, they also use much of the other paraphernalia of "woman's place" to enact their central symbolic drama of enclosure and escape. Ladylike veils and costumes, mirrors, paintings, statues, locked cabinets, drawers, trunks, strong-boxes, and other domestic furnishings appear and reappear in female novels and poems throughout the nineteenth century and on into the twentieth to signify the woman writer's sense that, as Emily Dickinson put it, her "life" has been "shaven and fitted to a frame," a confinement she can only tolerate by believing that "the soul has moments of escape / When bursting all the doors / She dances like a bomb abroad."[25] Significantly, too, the explosive violence of these "moments of escape" that women writers continually imagine for themselves returns us to the phenomenon of the mad double so many of these women have projected into their works. For it is, after all, through the violence of the double that the female author enacts

[23]Ellen Moers, *Literary Women* (New York: Doubleday, 1976), pp. 90–112. [Gilbert and Gubar]

[24]*The Living of Charlotte Perkins Gilman* (1935; New York: Harper & Row, 1975), p. 77. [Gilbert and Gubar]

[25]Dickinson, *Poems,* J. 512 ("The Soul has Bandaged moments — "). [Gilbert and Gubar]

her own raging desire to escape male houses and male texts, while at the same time it is through the double's violence that this anxious author articulates for herself the costly destructiveness of anger repressed until it can no longer be contained.

As we shall see, therefore, infection continually breeds in the sentences of women whose writing obsessively enacts this drama of enclosure and escape. Specifically, what we have called the distinctively female diseases of anorexia and agoraphobia are closely associated with this dramatic/thematic pattern. Defining themselves as prisoners of their own gender, for instance, women frequently create characters who attempt to escape, if only into nothingness, through the suicidal self-starvation of anorexia. Similarly, in a metaphorical elaboration of bulimia, the disease of overeating which is anorexia's complement and mirror-image (as Marlene Boskind-Lodahl has recently shown),[26] women writers often envision an "outbreak" that transforms their characters into huge and powerful monsters. More obviously, agoraphobia and its complementary opposite, claustrophobia, are by definition associated with the spatial imagery through which these poets and novelists express their feelings of social confinement and their yearning for spiritual escape. The paradigmatic female story, therefore — the story such angels in the house of literature as Goethe's Makarie and Patmore's Honoria[27] were in effect "forbidden" to tell — is frequently an arrangement of the elements most readers will readily remember from Charlotte Brontë's *Jane Eyre*. Examining the psychosocial implications of a "haunted" ancestral mansion, such a tale explores the tension between parlor and attic, the psychic split between the lady who submits to male dicta and the lunatic who rebels. But in examining these matters the paradigmatic female story inevitably considers also the equally uncomfortable spatial options of expulsion into the cold outside or suffocation in the hot indoors,

[26]Boskind-Lodahl, "Cinderella's Step-Sisters: A Feminist Perspective on Anorexia Nervosa and Bulimia," *Signs* 2, no. 2 (1976): 342–56. [Gilbert and Gubar]

[27]*The Angel in the House* (1854–63) was the lyric sequence by Coventry Patmore (1823–90) extolling his own marriage.

and in addition it often embodies an obsessive anxiety both about starvation to the point of disappearance and about monstrous inhabitation.

Many nineteenth-century male writers also, of course, used imagery of enclosure and escape to make deeply felt points about the relationship of the individual and society. Dickens and Poe, for instance, on opposite sides of the Atlantic, wrote of prisons, cages, tombs, and cellars in similar ways and for similar reasons. Still, the male writer is so much more comfortable with his literary role that he can usually elaborate upon his visionary theme more consciously and objectively than the female writer can. The distinction between male and female images of imprisonment is — and always has been — a distinction between, on the one hand, that which is both metaphysical and metaphorical, and on the other hand, that which is social and actual. Sleeping in his coffin, the seventeenth-century poet John Donne was piously rehearsing the constraints of the grave in advance, but the nineteenth-century poet Emily Dickinson, in purdah in her white dress, was anxiously living those constraints in the present. Imagining himself buried alive in tombs and cellars, Edgar Allan Poe was letting his mind poetically wander into the deepest recesses of his own psyche, but Dickinson, reporting that "I do not cross my Father's ground to any house in town," was recording a real, self-willed, self-burial. Similarly, when Byron's Prisoner of Chillon notes that "my very chains and I grew friends," the poet himself is making an epistemological point about the nature of the human mind, as well as a political point about the tyranny of the state. But when Rose Yorke in *Shirley* describes Caroline Helstone as living the life of a toad enclosed in a block of marble, Charlotte Brontë is speaking through her about her own deprived and constricted life, and its real conditions.[28]

[28]Dickinson, *The Letters of Emily Dickinson*, 3 vols., ed. Thomas H. Johnson (Cambridge, MA: The Belknap Press of Harvard University Press, 1958), 2:460. Byron, "The Prisoner of Chillon," lines 389–92; Brontë, *Shirley* (New York: Dutton, 1970), p. 316; see also Brontë to W. S. Williams, 26 July 1849. [Gilbert and Gubar]

Thus, though most male metaphors of imprisonment have obvious implications in common (and many can be traced back to traditional images used by, say, Shakespeare and Plato), such metaphors may have very different aesthetic functions and philosophical messages in different male literary works. Wordsworth's prison-house in the "Intimations" ode serves a purpose quite unlike that served by the jails in Dickens's novels. Coleridge's twice-five miles of visionary greenery ought not to be confused with Keats's vale of soul-making, and the escape of Tennyson's Art from her Palace should not be identified with the resurrection of Poe's Ligeia. Women authors, however, reflect the literal reality of their own confinement in the constraints they depict, and so all at least begin with the same unconscious or conscious purpose in employing such spatial imagery. Recording their own distinctively female experience, they are secretly working through and within the conventions of literary texts to define their own lives.

While some male authors also use such imagery for implicitly or explicitly confessional projects, women seem forced to live more intimately with the metaphors they have created to solve the "problem" of their fall. At least one critic does deal not only with such images but with their psychological meaning as they accrue around houses. Noting in *The Poetics of Space* that "the house image would appear to have become the topography of our inmost being," Gaston Bachelard shows the ways in which houses, nests, shells, and wardrobes are in us as much as we are in them.[29] What is significant from our point of view, however, is the extraordinary discrepancy between the almost consistently "felicitous space" he discusses and the negative space we have found. Clearly, for Bachelard the protective asylum of the house is closely associated with its maternal features, and to this extent he is following the work done on dream symbolism by Freud and on female inner space by Erikson. It seems clear too, however, that such symbolism must inevitably have very different implications for male critics and for female authors.

Women themselves have often, of course, been described or imagined as houses. Most recently Erik Erikson advanced his controversial theory of female "inner space" in an effort to account for little girls' interest in domestic enclosures. But in medieval times, as if to anticipate Erikson, statues of the Madonna were made to open up and reveal the holy family hidden in the Virgin's inner space. The female womb has certainly, always and everywhere, been a child's first and most satisfying house, a source of food and dark security, and therefore a mythic paradise imaged over and over again in sacred caves, secret shrines, consecrated huts. Yet for many a woman writer these ancient associations of house and self seem mainly to have strengthened the anxiety about enclosure which she projected into her art. Disturbed by the real physiological prospect of enclosing an unknown part of herself that is somehow also not herself, the female artist may, like Mary Shelley, conflate anxieties about maternity with anxieties about literary creativity. Alternatively, troubled by the anatomical "emptiness" of spinsterhood, she may, like Emily Dickinson, fear the inhabitations of nothingness and death, the transformation of womb into tomb. Moreover, conditioned to believe that as a house she is herself owned (and ought to be inhabited) by a man, she may once again but for yet another reason see herself as inescapably an object. In other words, even if she does not experience her womb as a kind of tomb or perceive her child's occupation of her house/body as depersonalizing, she may recognize that in an essential way she has been defined simply by her purely biological usefulness to her species.

To become literally a house, after all, is to be denied the hope of that spiritual transcendence of the body which, as Simone de Beauvoir has argued, is what makes humanity distinctively human. Thus, to be confined in childbirth (and significantly "confinement" was the key nineteenth-century term for what we would now, just as significantly, call "delivery") is in a way just as problematical as to be confined in a house or prison. Indeed, it might well seem to the literary woman that, just as ontogeny may be said to

[29]Gaston Bachelard, *The Poetics of Space,* trans. Maria Jolas (Boston: Beacon, 1970), p. xxxii. [Gilbert and Gubar]

recapitulate phylogeny, the confinement of pregnancy replicates the confinement of society. For
even if she is only metaphorically denied transcendence, the woman writer who perceives the
implications of the house/body equation must
unconsciously realize that such a trope does not
just "place" her in a glass coffin, it transforms her
into a version of the glass coffin herself. There is
a sense, therefore, in which, confined in such a
network of metaphors, what Adrienne Rich has
called a "thinking woman" might inevitably feel
that now she has been imprisoned within her own
alien and loathsome body.[30] Once again, in other
words, she has become not only a prisoner but a
monster.

As if to comment on the unity of all these
points — on, that is, the anxiety-inducing connections between what women writers tend to see
as their parallel confinements in texts, houses,
and maternal female bodies — Charlotte Perkins
Gilman brought them all together in 1890 in a
striking story of female confinement and escape,
a paradigmatic tale which (like *Jane Eyre*) seems
to tell *the* story that all literary women would tell
if they could speak their "speechless woe." "The
Yellow Wallpaper," which Gilman herself called
"a description of a case of nervous breakdown,"
recounts in the first person the experiences of a
woman who is evidently suffering from a severe
postpartum psychosis.[31] Her husband, a censorious and paternalistic physician, is treating her
according to methods by which S. Weir Mitchell,
a famous "nerve specialist," treated Gilman herself for a similar problem. He has confined her to
a large garret room in an "ancestral hall" he has
rented, and he has forbidden her to touch pen to
paper until she is well again, for he feels, says
the narrator, "that with my imaginative power
and habit of story-making, a nervous weakness
like mine is sure to lead to all manner of excited
fancies, and that I ought to use my will and good
sense to check the tendency" (15–16).

The cure, of course, is worse than the disease,
for the sick woman's mental condition deterio-
rates rapidly. "I think sometimes that if I were
only well enough to write a little it would relieve
the press of ideas and rest me," she remarks, but
literally confined in a room she thinks is a one-
time nursery because it has "rings and things" in
the walls, she is literally locked away from creativity. The "rings and things," although reminiscent of children's gymnastic equipment, are really
the paraphernalia of confinement, like the gate at
the head of the stairs, instruments that definitively
indicate her imprisonment. Even more tormenting, however, is the room's wallpaper: a sulphu-
rous yellow paper, torn off in spots, and patterned
with "lame uncertain curves" that "plunge off at
outrageous angles" and "destroy themselves in
unheard of contradictions." Ancient, smolder-
ing, "unclean" as the oppressive structures of
the society in which she finds herself, this paper
surrounds the narrator like an inexplicable text,
censorious and overwhelming as her physician
husband, haunting as the "hereditary estate" in
which she is trying to survive. Inevitably she
studies its suicidal implications — and inevitably, because of her "imaginative power and habit
of story-making," she revises it, projecting her
own passion for escape into its otherwise incomprehensible hieroglyphics. "This wall-paper," she
decides, at a key point in her story,

has a kind of sub-pattern in a different shade, a
particularly irritating one, for you can only see it in
certain lights, and not clearly then.

But in the places where it isn't faded and where
the sun is just so — I can see a strange, provoking,
formless sort of figure, that seems to skulk about
behind that silly and conspicuous front design. [18]

As time passes, this figure concealed behind
what corresponds (in terms of what we have
been discussing) to the facade of the patriarchal
text becomes clearer and clearer. By moonlight
the pattern of the wallpaper "becomes bars! The
outside pattern I mean, and the woman behind it
is as plain as can be." And eventually, as the narrator sinks more deeply into what the world calls
madness, the terrifying implications of both the
paper and the figure imprisoned behind the paper
begin to permeate — that is, to *haunt* — the

---

30 *Adrienne Rich's Poetry*, p. 12: "A thinking woman
sleeps with monsters. / The beak that grips her, she becomes."
("Snapshots of a Daughter-in-Law," #3). [Gilbert and Gubar]

31 Charlotte Perkins Gilman, *The Yellow Wallpaper* (Old
Westbury: The Feminist Press, 1973). All references in the
text will be to page numbers in this edition. [Gilbert and
Gubar]

rented ancestral mansion in which she and her husband are immured. The "yellow smell" of the paper "creeps all over the house," drenching every room in its subtle aroma of decay. And the woman creeps too — through the house, in the house, and out of the house, in the garden and "on that long road under the trees." Sometimes, indeed, the narrator confesses, "I think there are a great many women" both behind the paper and creeping in the garden,

> and sometimes only one, and she crawls around fast, and her crawling shakes [the paper] all over.... And she is all the time trying to climb through. But nobody could climb through that pattern — it strangles so; I think that is why it has so many heads. [30]

Eventually it becomes obvious to both reader and narrator that the figure creeping through and behind the wallpaper is both the narrator and the narrator's double. By the end of the story, moreover, the narrator has enabled this double to escape from her textual/architectural confinement: "I pulled and she shook, I shook and she pulled, and before morning we had peeled off yards of that paper." Is the message of the tale's conclusion mere madness? Certainly the righteous Doctor John — whose name links him to the anti-hero of Charlotte Brontë's *Villette*[32] — has been temporarily defeated, or at least momentarily stunned. "Now why should that man have fainted?" the narrator ironically asks as she creeps around her attic. But John's unmasculine swoon of surprise is the least of the triumphs Gilman imagines for her madwoman. More significant are the madwoman's own imaginings and creations, mirages of health and freedom with which her author endows her like a fairy godmother showering gold on a sleeping heroine. The woman from behind the wallpaper creeps away, for instance, creeps fast and far on the long road, in broad daylight. "I have watched her sometimes away off in the open country," says the narrator, "creeping as fast as a cloud shadow in a high wind."

Indistinct and yet rapid, barely perceptible but inexorable, the progress of that cloud shadow is not unlike the progress of nineteenth-century literary women out of the texts defined by patriarchal poetics into the open spaces of their own authority. That such an escape from the numb world behind the patterned walls of the text was a flight from dis-ease into health was quite clear to Gilman herself. When "The Yellow Wallpaper" was published she sent it to Weir Mitchell, whose strictures had kept her from attempting the pen during her own breakdown, thereby aggravating her illness, and she was delighted to learn, years later, that "he had changed his treatment of nervous prostration since reading" her story. "If that is a fact," she declared, "I have not lived in vain."[33] Because she was a rebellious feminist besides being a medical iconoclast, we can be sure that Gilman did not think of this triumph of hers in narrowly therapeutic terms. Because she knew, with Emily Dickinson, that "Infection in the sentence breeds," she knew that the cure for female despair must be spiritual as well as physical, aesthetic as well as social. What "The Yellow Wallpaper" shows she knew, too, is that even when a supposedly "mad" woman has been sentenced to imprisonment in the "infected" house of her own body, she may discover that, as Sylvia Plath was to put it seventy years later, she has "a self to recover, a queen."[34]

---

[32]John Bretton is the doctor for the school where Lucy Snowe works in Charlotte Brontë's *Villette*.

[33]*The Living of Charlotte Perkins Gilman*, p. 121. [Gilbert and Gubar]

[34]"Stings," *Ariel*, p. 62. [Gilbert and Gubar]

Annette Kolodny

b. 1941

Annette Kolodny's career is an exemplary combination of feminist scholarship and political activism. Born in New York City, Kolodny was briefly on the editorial staff of Newsweek before attending the University of California at Berkeley, where she received her M.A. and Ph.D. In 1969–70, she taught at Yale before moving to Canada with her husband, who had been denied conscientious objector status and faced conscription into the military. At the University of British Columbia in 1970–74, Kolodny designed Western Canada's first accredited, multidisciplinary women's studies program. On her return to the United States in 1974, Kolodny organized a women's studies program at the University of New Hampshire. Her first book, The Lay of the Land, appeared in 1975. When Kolodny was denied promotion and tenure, she filed an anti-Semitism and sexism suit against the university and in 1980 was awarded a landmark out-of-court settlement, a portion of which she used to set up a legal fund and a task force against discrimination. Kolodny stayed in New Hampshire to complete The Land Before Her (1984) before joining the faculty at Rensselaer Polytechnic Institute. She is currently College of Humanities Professor Emerita of American Literature and Culture at the University of Arizona, where she taught for many years and served as dean of the College of Humanities. Kolodny's experiences as a feminist in higher education administration are detailed in Failing the Future: A Dean Looks at Higher Education in the Twenty-first Century (1998). Her most recent work has been in Native American studies, and in 2012 she published In Search of First Contact: The Vikings of Vinland, the Peoples of the Dawnland, and the Anglo-American Anxiety of Discovery. The following selection is excerpted from her prize-winning article of the same title, which was originally published in Feminist Studies 6 (1980).

Dancing through the Minefield: Some Observations on the Theory, Practice, and Politics of a Feminist Literary Criticism

Had anyone the prescience, ten years ago, to pose the question of defining a "feminist" literary criticism, she might have been told, in the wake of Mary Ellmann's *Thinking About Women*,[1] that it involved exposing the sexual stereotyping of women in both our literature and our literary criticism and, as well, demonstrating the inadequacy of established critical schools and methods to deal fairly or sensitively with works written by women. In broad outline, such a prediction would have stood well the test of time, and, in fact, Ellmann's book continues to be widely read and to point us in useful directions. What could not have been anticipated in 1969, however, was the catalyzing force of an ideology that, for many of us, helped to bridge the gap between the world as we found it and the world as we wanted it to be. For those of us who studied literature, a previously unspoken sense of exclusion from authorship, and a painfully personal distress at discovering whores, bitches, muses, and heroines dead in childbirth where we had once hoped to discover ourselves, could — for the

[1]Mary Ellmann, *Thinking About Women* (New York: Harcourt Brace Jovanovich, Harvest, 1968). [Kolodny]

first time — begin to be understood as more than "a set of disconnected, unrealized private emotions."[2] With a renewed courage to make public our otherwise private discontents, what had once been "felt individually as personal insecurity" came at last to be "viewed collectively as structural inconsistency"[3] within the very disciplines we studied. Following unflinchingly the full implications of Ellmann's percipient observations, and emboldened by the liberating energy of feminist ideology — in all its various forms and guises — feminist criticism very quickly moved beyond merely "expos[ing] sexism in one work of literature after another,"[4] and promised, instead, that we might at last "begin to record new choices in a new literary history."[5] So powerful was that impulse that we experienced it, along with Adrienne Rich, as much "more than a chapter in cultural history": it became, rather, "an act of survival."[6] What was at stake was not so much literature or criticism as such, but the historical, social, and ethical consequences of women's participation in, or exclusion from, either enterprise.

The pace of inquiry these last ten years has been fast and furious — especially after Kate Millett's 1970 analysis of the sexual politics of literature[7] added a note of urgency to what had earlier been Ellmann's sardonic anger — while the diversity of that inquiry easily outstripped all efforts to define feminist literary criticism as either a coherent system or a unified set of methodologies. Under its wide umbrella, everything has been thrown into question: our established canons, our aesthetic criteria, our interpretative strategies, our reading habits, and, most of all, ourselves as critics and as teachers. To delineate its full scope would require nothing less than a book — a book that would be outdated even as it was being composed.

To have attempted so many difficult questions and to have accomplished so much — even acknowledging the inevitable false starts, overlapping, and repetition — in so short a time, should certainly have secured feminist literary criticism an honored berth on that ongoing intellectual journey which we loosely term in academia, "critical analysis." Instead of being welcomed onto the train, however, we've been forced to negotiate a minefield. The very energy and diversity of our enterprise have rendered us vulnerable to attack on the grounds that we lack both definition and coherence; while our particular attentiveness to the ways in which literature encodes and disseminates cultural value systems calls down upon us imprecations echoing those heaped upon the Marxist critics of an earlier generation. If we are scholars dedicated to rediscovering a lost body of writings by women, then our finds are questioned on aesthetic grounds. And if we are critics, determined to practice revisionist readings, it is claimed that our focus is too narrow, and our results are only distortions or, worse still, polemical misreadings.

The very vehemence of the outcry, coupled with our total dismissal in some quarters,[8] suggests not our deficiencies, however, but the potential magnitude of our challenge. For what we are asking be scrutinized are nothing less than shared cultural assumptions so deeply rooted and so long ingrained that, for the most part, our critical colleagues have ceased to recognize

[2]See Clifford Geertz, "Ideology as a Cultural System," in his *The Interpretation of Cultures: Selected Essays* (New York: Basic Books, 1973), p. 232. [Kolodny]

[3]Ibid., p. 204. [Kolodny]

[4]Lillian S. Robinson, "Cultural Criticism and the *Horror Vacui,*" *College English* 33, no. 1 (1972); reprinted as "The Critical Task" in her *Sex, Class, and Culture* (Bloomington: Indiana University Press, 1978), p. 51. [Kolodny]

[5]Elaine Showalter, *A Literature of Their Own: British Women Novelists from Brontë to Lessing* (Princeton: Princeton University Press, 1977), p. 36. [Kolodny]

[6]Adrienne Rich, "When We Dead Awaken: Writing as Re-Vision," *College English* 34, no. 1 (October 1972); reprinted in *Adrienne Rich's Poetry,* ed. Barbara Charlesworth Gelpi and Albert Gelpi (New York: W. W. Norton Co., 1975), p. 90. [Kolodny]

[7]Kate Millett, *Sexual Politics* (Garden City, N.Y.: Doubleday and Co., 1970). [Kolodny]

[8]Consider, for example, Robert Boyers's reductive and inaccurate generalization that "what distinguishes ordinary books and articles about women from feminist writing is the feminist insistence on asking the same questions of every work and demanding ideologically satisfactory answers to those questions as a means of evaluating it," in his "A Case Against Feminist Criticism," *Partisan Review* 43, no. 4 (1976): 602. It is partly as a result of such misconceptions, that we have the paucity of feminist critics who are granted a place in English departments which otherwise pride themselves on the variety of their critical orientations. [Kolodny]

for the truly radicalizing premises that lie at the theoretical core of all we have so far accomplished. It may be time, therefore, to redirect discussion, forcing our adversaries to deal with the substantive issues and pushing ourselves into a clearer articulation of what, in fact, we are about. Up until now, I fear, we have only piecemeal dealt with the difficulties inherent in challenging the authority of established canons and then justifying the excellence of women's traditions, sometimes in accord with standards to which they have no intrinsic relation.

At the very point at which we must perforce enter the discourse — that is, claiming excellence or importance for our "finds" — all discussion has already, we discover, long ago been closed. "If Kate Chopin were *really* worth reading," an Oxford-trained colleague once assured me, "she'd have lasted — like Shakespeare"; and he then proceeded to vote against the English department's crediting a women's studies seminar I was offering in American women writers. The canon, for him, conferred excellence; Chopin's exclusion demonstrated only her lesser worth. As far as he was concerned, I could no more justify giving the English department credit for the study of Chopin than I could dare publicly to question Shakespeare's genius. Through hindsight, I've now come to view that discussion as not only having posed fruitless oppositions, but also as having entirely evaded the much more profound problem lurking just beneath the surface of our disagreement. That is, that the fact of canonization puts any work beyond questions of establishing its merit and, instead, invites students to offer only increasingly more ingenious readings and interpretations, the purpose of which is to validate the greatness already imputed by canonization.

Had I only understood it for what it was then, into this circular and self-serving set of assumptions I might have interjected some statement of my right to question why *any* text is revered and my need to know what it tells us about. "how we live, how we have been living, how we have been led to imagine ourselves, [and] how our language has trapped as well as liberated us."[12] The very fact of our critical training within the strictures

[12] Rich, "When We Dead Awaken," p. 90. [Kolodny]

them as such. In other words, what is really being bewailed in the claims that we distort texts or threaten the disappearance of the great Western literary tradition itself[9] is not so much the disappearance of either text or tradition but, instead, the eclipse of that particular *form* of the text, and that particular *shape* of the canon, which previously reified male readers' sense of power and significance in the world. Analogously, by asking whether, as readers, we ought to be "really satisfied by the marriage of Dorothea Brooke to Will Ladislaw? of Shirley Keeldar to Louis Moore?"[10] or whether, as Jean Kennard suggests, we must reckon with the ways in which "the qualities we have been invited to admire in these heroines [have] been sacrificed to structural neatness,"[11] is to raise difficult and profoundly perplexing questions about the ethical implications of our otherwise unquestioned aesthetic pleasures. It is, after all, an imposition of high order to ask the viewer to attend to Ophelia's sufferings in a scene where, before, he'd always so comfortably kept his eye fixed firmly on Hamlet. To understand all this, then, as the real nature of the challenge we have offered and, in consequence, as the motivation for the often overt hostility we've aroused, should help us learn to negotiate the minefield, if not with grace, then with at least a clearer comprehension of its underlying patterns.

The ways in which objections to our work are usually posed, of course, serve to obscure their deeper motivations. But this may, in part, be due to our own reticence at taking full responsibility

[9] Ambivalent though he is about the literary continuity that begins with Homer, Harold Bloom nonetheless somewhat ominously prophesies "that the first true break . . . will be brought about in generations to come, if the burgeoning religion of Liberated Woman spreads from its clusters of enthusiasts to dominate the West," in his *A Map of Misreading* (New York: Oxford University Press, 1975), p. 33. On p. 36, he acknowledges that while something "as violent [as] a quarrel would ensue if I expressed my judgment" on Robert Lowell and Norman Mailer, "it would lead to something more intense than quarrels if I expressed my judgment upon . . . the 'literature of Women's Liberation.'" [Kolodny]

[10] Dorothea Brooke and Will Ladislaw marry in the dénouement of George Eliot's novel, *Middlemarch* (1871–72), Shirley Keeldar and Louis Moore in that of Charlotte Brontë's *Shirley* (1849). [Kolodny]

[11] Jean E. Kennard, *Victims of Convention* (Hamden, Conn.: Archon Books, 1978), p. 14. [Kolodny]

imposed by an established canon of major works and authors, however, repeatedly deflects us from such questions. Instead, we find ourselves endlessly responding to the *riposte* that the overwhelmingly male presence among canonical authors was only an accident of history — and never intentionally sexist — coupled with claims to the "obvious" aesthetic merit of those canonized texts. It is, as I say, a fruitless exchange, serving more to obscure than to expose the territory being protected and dragging us, again and again, through the minefield.

It is my contention that current hostilities might be transformed into a true dialogue with our critics if we at last make explicit what appear, to this observer, to constitute the three crucial propositions to which our special interests inevitably give rise. They are, moreover, propositions which, if handled with care and intelligence, could breathe new life into now moribund areas of our profession: (1) Literary history (and, with that, the historicity of literature) is a fiction; (2) insofar as we are taught how to read, what we engage are not texts but paradigms; and, finally, (3) that since the grounds upon which we assign aesthetic value to texts are never infallible, unchangeable, or universal, we must reexamine not only our aesthetics but, as well, the inherent biases and assumptions informing the critical methods which (in part) shape our aesthetic responses. For the sake of brevity, I won't attempt to offer the full arguments for each but, rather, only sufficient elaboration to demonstrate what I see as their intrinsic relation to the potential scope of and present challenge implied by feminist literary study.

1. *Literary history (and, with that, the historicity of literature) is a fiction.* To begin with, an established canon functions as a model by which to chart the continuities and discontinuities, as well as the influences upon and the interconnections between works, genres, and authors. That model we tend to forget, however, is of our own making. It will take a very different shape, and explain its inclusions and exclusions in very different ways, if the reigning critical ideology believes that new literary forms result from some kind of ongoing internal dialectic within preexisting styles and traditions or if, by contrast, the

ideology declares that literary change is dependent upon societal development and thereby determined by upheavals in the social and economic organization of the culture at large.[13] Indeed, whenever in the previous century of English and American literary scholarship one alternative replaced the other, we saw dramatic alterations in canonical "wisdom."

This suggests, then, that our sense of a "literary history" and, by extension, our confidence in a "historical" canon, is rooted not so much in any definitive understanding of the past, as it is in our need to call up and utilize the past on behalf of a better understanding of the present. Thus, to paraphrase David Couzens Hoy, it becomes "necessary to point out that the understanding of art and literature is such an essential aspect of the present's self-understanding that this self-understanding conditions what even gets taken" as comprising that artistic and literary past. To quote Hoy fully, "this continual reinterpretation of the past goes hand in hand with the continual reinterpretation by the present of itself."[14] In our own time, uncertain as to which, if any, model truly accounts for our canonical choices or accurately explains literary history, and pressured further by the feminists' call for some justification of the criteria by which women's writings were largely excluded from both that canon and history, we suffer what Harold Bloom has called "a remarkable dimming" of "our mutual sense of canonical standards."[15]

Into this apparent impasse, feminist literary theorists implicitly introduce the observation that our choices and evaluations of current literature have the effect either of solidifying or of reshaping our sense of the past. The authority of any established canon, after all, is reified by our perception that current work seems to grow, almost inevitably, out of it (even in opposition or rebellion), and is called into question when what

---

[13]The first is a proposition currently expressed by some structuralists and formalist critics; the best statement of the second probably appears in Georg Lukács, *Writer and Critic* (New York: Grosset and Dunlap, 1970), p. 119. [Kolodny]

[14]David Couzens Hoy, "Hermeneutic Circularity, Indeterminacy, and Incommensurability," *New Literary History* 10, no. 1 (Autumn 1978): 166–67. [Kolodny]

[15]Bloom, *Map of Misreading*, p. 36. [Kolodny]

we read appears to have little or no relation to what we recognize as coming before. So, were the larger critical community to begin to seriously attend to the recent outpouring of fine literature by women, this would surely be accompanied by a concomitant researching of the past, by literary historians, in order to account for the present phenomenon. In that process, literary history would itself be altered: works by seventeenth-, eighteenth-, or nineteenth-century women, to which we had not previously attended, might be given new importance as "precursors," or as prior influences upon present-day authors; while selected male writers might also be granted new prominence as figures whom the women today, or even yesterday, needed to reject. I am arguing, in other words, that the choices we make in the present inevitably alter our sense of the past that led to them.

Related to this is the feminist challenge to that patently mendacious critical fallacy that we read the "classics" in order to reconstruct the past "the way it really was," and that we read Shakespeare and Milton in order to apprehend the meanings that they intended. Short of time machines or miraculous resurrections, there is simply no way to know, precisely or surely, what "really was," what Homer intended when he sang, or Milton when he dictated. Critics more acute than I have already pointed out the impossibility of grounding a reading in the imputation of authorial intention because the further removed the author is from us, so too must be her or his systems of knowledge and belief, points of view, and structures of vision (artistic and otherwise).[16] (I omit here the difficulty of finally either proving or disproving the imputation of intentionality because, inescapably,

[16]John Dewey offered precisely this argument in 1934 when he insisted that a work of art "is recreated every time it is esthetically experienced... It is absurd to ask what an artist 'really' meant by his product: he himself would find different meanings in it at different days and hours and in different stages of his own development." Further, he explained, "It is simply an impossibility that any one today should experience the Parthenon as the devout Athenian contemporary citizen experienced it, any more than the religious statuary of the twelfth century can mean, esthetically, even to a good Catholic today just what it meant to the worshipers of the old period," in Art as Experience (New York: Capricorn Books, 1958), pp. 108–09. [Kolodny]

the only appropriate authority is unavailable: deceased.) What we have really come to mean when we speak of competence in reading historical texts, therefore, is the ability to recognize literary conventions which have survived through time — so as to remain operational in the mind of the reader — and, where these are lacking, the ability to translate (or perhaps transform?) the text's ciphers into more current and recognizable shapes. But we never really reconstruct the past in its own terms. What we gain when we read the "classics," then, is neither Homer's Greece nor George Eliot's England as they knew it but, rather, an approximation of an already actively imputed past made available, through our interpretive strategies, for present concerns. Only by understanding this can we put to rest that recurrent delusion that the "continuing relevance" of the classics serves as "testimony to perennial features of human experience."[17] The only "perennial feature" to which our ability to read and reread texts written in previous centuries testifies is our inventiveness — in the sense that all of literary history is a fiction which we daily recreate as we reread it. What distinguishes feminists in this regard is their desire to alter and extend what we take as historically relevant from out of that vast storehouse of our literary inheritance and, further, feminists' recognition of the storehouse for what it really is: a resource for remodeling our literary history, past, present, and future.

2. *Insofar as we are taught how to read, what we engage are not texts but paradigms.* To pursue the logical consequences of the first proposition leads, however uncomfortably, to the conclusion that we appropriate meaning from a text according to what we need (or desire) or, in other words, according to the critical assumptions or predispositions (conscious or not) that we bring to it. And we appropriate different meanings, or report different gleanings, at different times — even from the same text — according to our changed assumptions, circumstances, and requirements. This, in essence, constitutes the heart of the second proposition. For insofar as literature is itself

[17]Charles Altieri, "The Hermeneutics of Literary Indeterminacy: A Dissent from the New Orthodoxy," New Literary History 10, no. 1 (Autumn 1978): 90. [Kolodny]

a social institution, so, too, reading is a highly socialized — or learned — activity. What makes it so exciting, of course, is that it can be constantly relearned and refined, so as to provide either an individual or an entire reading community, over time, with infinite variations of the same text. It *can* provide that, but, I must add, too often it does not. Frequently our reading habits become fixed, so that each successive reading experience functions, in effect, normatively, with one particular kind of novel stylizing our expectations of those to follow, the stylistic devices of any favorite author (or group of authors) alerting us to the presence or absence of those devices in the works of others, and so on. "Once one has read his first poem," Murray Krieger has observed, "he turns to his second and to the others that will follow thereafter with an increasing series of preconceptions about the sort of activity in which he is indulging. In matters of literary experience, as in other experiences," Krieger concludes, "one is a virgin but once."[18]

For most readers, this is a fairly unconscious process, and not unnaturally, what we are taught to read well and with pleasure, when we are young, predisposes us to certain specific kinds of adult reading tastes. For the professional literary critic, the process may be no different, but it is at least more conscious. Graduate schools, at their best, are training grounds for competing interpretive paradigms or reading techniques: affective stylistics, structuralism, and semiotic analysis, to name only a few of the more recent entries. The delight we learn to take in the mastery of these interpretive strategies is then often mistakenly construed as our delight in reading specific texts, especially in the case of works that would otherwise be unavailable or even offensive to us. In my own graduate career, for example, with superb teachers to guide me, I learned to take great pleasure in *Paradise Lost,* even though as both a Jew and a feminist, I can subscribe neither to its theology nor to its hierarchy of sexual valuation. If, within its own terms (as I have been taught to understand them), the text manipulates my sensibilities and moves me to pleasure — as I will affirm it does — then, at least in part, that must be because, in spite of my real-world alienation from many of its basic tenets, I have been able to enter that text through interpretive strategies which allow me to displace less comfortable observations with others to which I have been taught pleasurably to attend. Though some of my teachers may have called this process "learning to read the text properly," I have now come to see it as learning to effectively manipulate the critical strategies which they taught me so well. Knowing, for example, the poem's debt to epic conventions, I am able to discover in it echoes and reworkings of both lines and situations from Virgil and Homer; placing it within the ongoing Christian debate between Good and Evil, I comprehend both the philosophic and the stylistic significance of Satan's ornate rhetoric as compared to God's majestic simplicity in Book III. But, in each case, an interpretative model, already assumed, had guided my discovery of the evidence for it.[19]

When we consider the implications of these observations for the processes of canon formation and for the assignment of aesthetic value, we find ourselves locked in a chicken-and-egg dilemma, unable easily to distinguish as primary the importance of *what* we read as opposed to *how* we have learned to read it. For, simply put, we read well, and with pleasure, what we already know how to read; and what we know how to read is to a large extent dependent upon what we have already read (works from which we've developed our expectations and learned our interpretive strategies). What we then choose to read — and, by extension, teach and thereby "canonize" — usually follows upon our previous reading. Radical breaks are tiring, demanding, uncomfortable, and sometimes wholly beyond our comprehension.

Though the argument is not usually couched in precisely these terms, a considerable segment of the most recent feminist rereadings of women

[18]Murray Krieger, *Theory of Criticism: A Tradition and Its System* (Baltimore: The Johns Hopkins University Press, 1976), p. 6. [Kolodny]

[19]See Stanley E. Fish, "Normal Circumstances, Literal Language, Direct Speech Acts, the Ordinary, the Everyday, the Obvious, What Goes without Saying, and Other Special Cases," *Critical Inquiry* 4, no. 4 (Summer 1978): 627–28. [Kolodny]

writers allows the conclusion that, where those authors have dropped out of sight, the reason may be due not to any lack of merit in the work but, instead, to an incapacity of predominantly male readers to properly interpret and appreciate women's texts — due, in large part, to a lack of prior acquaintance. The fictions which women compose about the worlds they inhabit may owe a debt to prior, influential works by other women or, simply enough, to the daily experience of the writer herself or, more usually, to some combina-tion of the two. The reader coming upon such fiction, with knowledge of neither its informing literary traditions nor its real-world contexts, will thereby find himself hard-pressed, though he may recognize the words on the page, to compe-tently decipher its intended meanings. And this is what makes the recent studies by Patricia Meyer Spacks, Ellen Moers, Elaine Showalter, Sandra Gilbert and Susan Gubar, and others so crucial. For, by attempting to delineate the connections and interrelations that make for a female liter-ary tradition, they provide us invaluable aids for recognizing and understanding the unique literary traditions and sex-related contexts out of which women write.

The (usually male) reader who, both by expe-rience and by reading, has never made acquain-tance with those contexts — historically, the lying-in room, the parlor, the nursery, the kitchen, the laundry, and so on — will necessarily lack the capacity to fully interpret the dialogue or action embedded therein; for, as every good novelist knows, the meaning of any character's action or statement is inescapably a function of the specific situation in which it is embed-ded.[20] Virginia Woolf therefore quite properly anticipated the male reader's disposition to write off what he could not understand, abandoning women's writings as offering "not merely a dif-ference of view, but a view that is weak, or trivial, or sentimental because it differs from his own." In her 1929 essay, "Women and Fiction," Woolf grappled most obviously with the ways in which male writers and male subject matter had already preempted the language of literature. Yet she was also tacitly commenting on the problem of (male)

audience and conventional reading expectations when she speculated that the woman writer might well 'find that she is perpetually wishing to alter the established values [in literature]' — to make serious what appears insignificant to a man, and trivial what is to him important.'"[21] "The com-petence necessary for understanding [a] literary message ... depends upon a great number of codices," after all, as Cesare Segre has pointed out, to be competent, a reader must either share or at least be familiar with, "in addition to the code language ... the codes of custom, of society, and of conceptions of the world"[22] (what Woolf meant by "values"). Males ignorant of women's "values" or conceptions of the world will neces-sarily, thereby, be poor readers of works that in any sense recapitulate their codes.

The problem is further exacerbated when the language of the literary text is largely dependent upon figuration. For it can be argued, as Ted Cohen has shown, that while "in general, and with some obvious qualifications ... all literal use of language is accessible to all whose lan-guage it is ... figurative use can be inaccessible to all but those who share information about one another's knowledge, beliefs, intentions, and attitudes."[23] There was nothing fortuitous, for example, in Charlotte Perkins Gilman's decision to situate the progressive mental breakdown and increasing incapacity of the protagonist of *The Yellow Wallpaper* in an upstairs room that had once served as a nursery (with barred windows, no less). But the reader unacquainted with the ways in which women traditionally inhabited a household might not have taken the initial description of the setting as semantically rel-evant; and the progressive infantilization of the adult protagonist would thereby lose some of its symbolic implications. Analogously, the contem-porary poet who declares, along with Adrienne Rich, the need for 'a whole new poetry begin-ning here' is acknowledging that the materials

[20]Ibid., p. 643. [Kolodny]

[21]Virginia Woolf, "Women and Fiction," *Granite and Rainbow: Essays* (London: Hogarth, 1958), p. 81. [Kolodny]

[22]Cesare Segre, "Narrative Structures and Literary History," *Critical Inquiry* 3, no. 2 (Winter 1976): 271–73. [Kolodny]

[23]Ted Cohen, "Metaphor and the Cultivation of Intimacy," *Critical Inquiry* 5, no. 1 (Autumn 1978): 9. [Kolodny]

available for symbolization and figuration from women's contexts will necessarily differ from those that men have traditionally utilized:

Vision begins to happen in such a life
as if a woman quietly walked away
from the argument and jargon in a room
and sitting down in the kitchen, began turning in
    her lap
bits of yarn, calico and velvet scraps,
....
pulling the tenets of a life together
with no mere will to mastery,
only care for the many-lived, unending
forms in which she finds herself.[24]

What, then, is the fate of the woman writer whose competent reading community is composed only of members of her own sex? And what, then, the response of the male critic who, on first looking into Virginia Woolf or Doris Lessing, finds all of the interpretative strategies at his command inadequate to a full and pleasurable deciphering of their pages? Historically, the result has been the diminished status of women's products and their consequent absence from major canons. Nowadays, however, by pointing out that the act of "interpreting language is no more sexually neutral than language use or the language system itself," feminist students of language, like Nelly Furman, help us better understand the crucial linkage between our gender and our interpretive, or reading, strategies. Insisting upon "the contribution of the . . . reader [in] the active attribution of significance to formal signifiers,"[25] Furman and others promise to shake us all — female and male alike — out of our canonized and conventional aesthetic assumptions.

3. *Since the grounds upon which we assign aesthetic value to texts are never infallible, unchangeable, or universal, we must reexamine not only our aesthetics but, as well, the inherent biases and assumptions informing the critical methods which (in part) shape our aesthetic responses.* I am, on the one hand, arguing that men will be better readers, or appreciators, of women's books when they have read more of them (as women have always been taught to become astute readers of men's texts). On the other hand, it will be noted, the emphasis of my remarks shifts the act of critical judgment from assigning aesthetic valuations to texts and directs it, instead, to ascertaining the adequacy of any interpretive paradigm to a full reading of both female and male writing. My third proposition — and, I admit, perhaps the most controversial — thus calls into question that recurrent tendency in criticism to establish norms for the evaluation of literary works when we might better serve the cause of literature by developing standards for evaluating the adequacy of our critical methods.[26] This does not mean that I wish to discard aesthetic valuation. The choice, as I see it, is not between retaining or discarding aesthetic values; rather, the choice is between having some awareness of what constitutes (at least in part) the bases of our aesthetic responses and going without such an awareness. For it is my view that insofar as aesthetic responsiveness continues to be an integral aspect of our human response system — in part spontaneous, in part learned and educated — we will inevitably develop theories to help explain, formalize, or even initiate those responses.

In challenging the adequacy of received critical opinion or the imputed excellence of established canons, feminist literary critics are essentially seeking to discover how aesthetic value is assigned in the first place, where it resides (in the text or in the reader), and, most importantly, what validity may really be claimed by our aesthetic "judgments." What ends do those judgments serve, the feminist asks; and what conceptions of the world or ideological stances do they (even if unwittingly) help to perpetuate? In so doing, she points out, among other things, that any response labeled "aesthetic" may as easily designate some immediately experienced

[24]From Adrienne Rich's "Transcendental Etude" in her *The Dream of a Common Language: Poems* 1974–1977 (New York: W. W. Norton and Co., 1978), pp. 76–77. [Kolodny]

[25]Furman, "The Study of Women and Language, Nelly: Comment on Vol. 3, no. 3" in *Signs* 4, no. 1 (Autumn 1978), p. 184. [Kolodny]

[26]"A recurrent tendency in criticism is the establishment of false norms for the evaluation of literary works," notes Robert Scholes in his *Structuralism in Literature: An Introduction* (New Haven: Yale University Press, 1974), p. 131. [Kolodny]

moment or event as it may designate a species of nostalgia, a yearning for the components of a simpler past, when the world seemed known or at least understandable. Thus the value accorded a Shakespeare play may well reside in the viewer's immediate viewing pleasure, or it may reside in the play's nostalgic evocation of a once-comprehensible and ordered world. At the same time, the feminist confronts, for example, the reader who cannot simply entertain the possibility that women's worlds are symbolically rich, the reader who, like the male characters in Susan Glaspell's 1917 short story, "A Jury of Her Peers," has already assumed the innate "insignificance of kitchen things."[27] Such a reader, she knows, will prove himself unable to assign significance to fictions that attend to "kitchen things" and will, instead, judge such fictions as trivial and as aesthetically wanting. For her to take useful issue with such a reader, she must make clear that what appears to be a dispute about aesthetic merit is, in reality, a dispute about the *contexts of judgment*; and what is at issue, then, is the adequacy of the prior assumptions and reading habits brought to bear on the text. To put it bluntly: we have had enough pronouncements of aesthetic valuation for a time; it is now our task to evaluate the imputed norms and normative reading patterns that, in part, led to those pronouncements.

By and large, I think I've made my point. Only to clarify it do I add this coda: when feminists turn their attention to the works of male authors which have traditionally been accorded high aesthetic value and, where warranted, follow Tillie Olsen's advice that we assert our "right to say: this is surface, this falsifies reality, this degrades."[28] such statements do not necessarily mean that we will end up with a diminished canon. To question the source of the aesthetic pleasures we've gained from reading Spenser, Shakespeare, Milton, and so on,

[27]For a full discussion of the Glaspell short story which takes this problem into account, please see my "A Map for Re-Reading; Or, Gender and the Interpretation of Literary Texts," forthcoming in a Special Issue on Narrative, *New Literary History* (1980). [Kolodny]

[28]Tillie Olsen, *Silences* (New York: Delacorte Press/ Seymour Lawrence, 1978), p. 45. [Kolodny]

does not imply that we must deny those pleasures. It means only that aesthetic response is once more invested with epistemological, ethical, and moral concerns. It means, in other words, that readings of *Paradise Lost* which analyze its complex hierarchal structures but fail to note the implications of gender within that hierarchy; or which insist upon the inherent (or even inspired) perfection of Milton's figurative language but fail to note the consequences, for Eve, of her specifically gender-marked weakness, which, like the flowers to which she attends, requires "propping up"; or which concentrate on the poem's thematic reworking of classical notions of martial and epic prowess into Christian (moral) heroism but fail to note that Eve is stylistically edited out of that process — all such readings, however useful, will no longer be deemed wholly adequate. The pleasures we had earlier learned to take in the poem will not be diminished thereby, but they will become part of an altered reading attentiveness.

These three propositions I believe to be at the theoretical core of most current feminist literary criticism, whether acknowledged as such or not. If I am correct in this, then that criticism represents more than a profoundly skeptical stance toward all other preexisting and contemporaneous schools and methods, and more than an impassioned demand that the variety and variability of women's literary expression be taken into full account, rather than written off as caprice and exception, the irregularity in an otherwise regular design. It represents that locus in literary study where, in unceasing effort, female self-consciousness turns in upon itself, attempting to grasp the deepest conditions of its own unique and multiplicitous realities, in the hope, eventually, of altering the very forms through which the culture perceives, expresses, and knows itself. For, if what the larger women's movement looks for in the future is a transformation of the structures of primarily male power which now order our society, then the feminist literary critic demands that we understand the ways in which those structures have been — and continue to be — reified by our literature and by our literary criticism. Thus, along with other "radical" critics and critical schools, though our focus remains the power of the word to both structure and mirror human experience, our overriding commitment is to a radical alteration — an improvement, we hope — in the nature of that experience.

What distinguishes our work from those similarly oriented "social consciousness" critiques, it is said, is its lack of systematic coherence. Pitted against, for example, psychoanalytic or Marxist readings, which owe a decisive share of their persuasiveness to their apparent internal consistency as a system, the aggregate of feminist literary criticism appears woefully deficient in system, and painfully lacking in program. It is, in fact, from all quarters, the most telling defect alleged against us, the most explosive threat in the minefield. And my own earlier observation that, as of 1976, feminist literary criticism appeared "more like a set of interchangeable strategies than any coherent school or shared goal orientation," has been taken by some as an indictment, by others as a statement of impatience. Neither was intended. I felt then, as I do now, that this would "prove both its strength *and* its weakness,"[29] in the sense that the apparent disarray would leave us vulnerable to the kind of objection I've just alluded to; while the fact of our diversity would finally place us securely where, all along, we should have been: camped out, on the far side of the minefield, with the other pluralists and pluralisms.

In our heart of hearts, of course, most critics are really structuralists (whether or not they accept the label) because what we are seeking are patterns (or structures) that can order and explain the otherwise inchoate; thus, we invent, or believe we discover, relational patternings in the texts we read which promise transcendence from difficulty and perplexity to clarity and coherence. But, as I've tried to argue in these pages, to the imputed "truth" or "accuracy" of these findings, the feminist must oppose the painfully obvious truism that what is attended to in a literary work, and hence what is reported about it, is often determined not so much by the work itself as by the critical technique or aesthetic criteria through which it is filtered or, rather, read and decoded. All the feminist is asserting, then, is her own equivalent right to liberate new (and perhaps different) significances from these same texts; and, at the same time, her right to choose which features of a text she takes as relevant because she is, after all, asking new and different questions of it. In the process, she claims neither definitiveness nor structural completeness for her different readings and reading systems, but only their usefulness in recognizing the particular achievements of woman-as-author and their applicability in conscientiously decoding woman-as-sign.

That these alternate foci of critical attentiveness will result in alternate readings or interpretations of the same text — even among feminists — should be no cause for alarm. Such developments illustrate only the pluralist contention that, "in approaching a text of any complexity . . . the reader must choose to emphasize certain aspects which seem to him crucial" and that, "in fact, the variety of readings which we have for many works is a function of the selection of crucial aspects made by the variety of readers." Robert Scholes, from whom I've been quoting, goes so far as to assert that "there is no single 'right' reading for any complex literary work," and, following the Russian formalist school, he observes that "we do not speak of readings that are simply true or false, but of readings that are more or less rich, strategies that are more or less appropriate."[30] Because those who share the term "feminist" nonetheless practice a diversity of critical strategies, leading, in some cases, to quite different readings, we must acknowledge among ourselves that sister critics, "having chosen to tell a different story, may in their interpretation identify different aspects of the meanings conveyed by the same passage."[31]

[29]Annette Kolodny, "Literary Criticism," Review Essay in *Signs* 2, no. 2 (Winter 1976): 420. [Kolodny]

[30]Scholes, *Structuralism in Literature,* pp. 144–45. These comments appear within his explication of Tzvetan Todorov's theory of reading. [Kolodny]

[31]I borrow this concise phrasing of pluralistic modesty from M. H. Abrams's "The Deconstructive Angel," *Critical Inquiry* 3, no. 3 (Spring 1977): 427. Indications of the pluralism that was to mark feminist inquiry were to be found in the diversity of essays collected by Susan Koppelman Cornillon for her early and ground-breaking anthology, *Images of Women in Fiction: Feminist Perspectives* (Bowling Green, Ohio: Bowling Green University Popular Press, 1972). [Kolodny]

Adopting a ''pluralist'' label does not mean, however, that we cease to disagree; it means only that we entertain the possibility that different readings, even of the same text, may be differently useful, even illuminating, within different contexts of inquiry. It means, in effect, that we enter a dialectical process of examining, testing, even trying out the contexts — be they prior critical assumptions or explicitly stated ideological stances (or some combination of the two) — that led to the disparate readings. Not all will be equally acceptable to every one of us, of course, and even those prior assumptions or ideologies that are acceptable may call for further refinement and/or clarification. But, at the very least, because we will have grappled with the assumptions that led to it, we will be better able to articulate why we find a particular reading or interpretation adequate or inadequate. This kind of dialectical process, moreover, not only makes us more fully aware of what criticism is, and how it functions; it also gives us access to its future possibilities, making us conscious, as R. P. Blackmur put it, ''of what we have done,'' ''of what can be done next, or done again,''[32] or, I would add, of what can be done differently. To put it still another way: just because we will no longer tolerate the specifically sexist omissions and oversights of earlier critical schools and methods does not mean that, in their stead, we must establish our own ''party line.''

In my view, our purpose is not and should not be the formulation of any single reading method or potentially procrustean set of critical procedures nor, even less, the generation of prescriptive categories for some dreamed-of nonexist literary canon.[33] Instead, as I see it, our task is to initiate nothing less than a playful pluralism, responsive to the possibilities of multiple critical schools and methods, but captive of none, recognizing that the many tools needed for our analysis will necessarily be largely inherited and only partly of our own making. Only by employing a plurality of methods will we protect ourselves from the temptation of so oversimplifying any text — and especially those particularly offensive to us — that we render ourselves unresponsive to what Scholes has called ''its various systems of meaning and their interaction.''[34] Any text we deem worthy of our critical attention is usually, after all, a locus of many and varied kinds of (personal, thematic, stylistic, structural, rhetorical, etc.) relationships. So, whether we tend to treat a text as a *mimesis*, in which words are taken to be recreating or representing viable worlds; or whether we prefer to treat a text as a kind of equation of communication, in which decipherable messages are passed from writers to readers; and whether we locate meaning as inherent in the text, the act of reading, or in some collaboration between reader and text — whatever our predilection, let us not generate from it a straitjacket that limits the scope of possible analysis. Rather, let us generate an ongoing dialogue of competing potential possibilities — among feminists and, as well, between feminist and nonfeminist critics.

The difficulty of what I describe does not escape me. The very idea of pluralism seems to threaten a kind of chaos for the future of literary inquiry while, at the same time, it seems to deny the hope of establishing some basic conceptual model which can organize all data — the hope which always begins any analytical exercise. My effort here, however, has been to demonstrate the essential delusions that inform such objections: If literary inquiry has historically escaped chaos by establishing canons, then it has only substituted one mode of arbitrary action for another — and, in this case, at the expense of half the population. And if feminists openly acknowledge ourselves as pluralists, then we do not give up the search for patterns of opposition and connection — probably the basis of thinking itself; what we give up is simply the arrogance of claiming that our work is either exhaustive or definitive. (It is, after all, the identical arrogance we are asking our nonfeminist colleagues to abandon.) If this kind of pluralism appears to threaten both the

---

32 R. P. Blackmur, ''A Burden for Critics,'' *The Hudson Review* 1 (1948): 171. Blackmur, of course, was referring to the way in which criticism makes us unconscious of how art functions; I use his wording here because I am arguing that that same awareness must also be focused on the critical act itself. ''Consciousness,'' he avers, ''is the way we feel the critic's burden.'' [Kolodny]

33 I have earlier elaborated my objection to prescriptive categories for literature in ''The Feminist as Literary Critic,'' Critical Response in *Critical Inquiry* 2, no. 4 (Summer 1976): 827–28. [Kolodny]

34 Scholes, *Structuralism in Literature*, pp. 151–52. [Kolodny]

present coherence of and the inherited aesthetic criteria for a canon of "greats," then, as I have earlier argued, it is precisely that threat which, alone, can free us from the prejudices, the strictures, and the blind spots of the past. In feminist hands, I would add, it is less a threat than a promise.

What unites and repeatedly invigorates feminist literary criticism, then, is neither dogma nor method but, as I have indicated earlier, an acute and impassioned *attentiveness* to the ways in which primarily male structures of power are inscribed (or encoded) within our literary inheritance; the consequences of that encoding for women — as characters, as readers, and as writers; and, with that, a shared analytic *concern* for the implications of that encoding not only for a better understanding of the past, but also for an improved reordering of the present and future as well. If that *concern* identifies feminist literary criticism as one of the many academic arms of the larger women's movement, then that *attentiveness,* within the halls of academe, poses no less a challenge for change, generating, as it does, the three propositions explored here. The critical pluralism that inevitably follows upon those three propositions, however, bears little resemblance to what Lillian Robinson has called "the greatest bourgeois theme of all, the myth of pluralism, with its consequent rejection of ideological commitment as 'too simple' to embrace the (necessarily complex) truth."[35] Only ideological commitment could have gotten us to enter the minefield, putting in jeopardy our careers and our livelihood. Only the power of ideology to transform our conceptual worlds, and the inspiration of that ideology to liberate long-suppressed energies and emotions, can account for our willingness to take on critical tasks that, in an earlier decade, would have been "abandoned in despair or apathy."[36] The fact of differences among us proves only that, despite our shared commitments, we have nonetheless refused to shy away from complexity, preferring rather to openly disagree than to give up either intellectual honesty or hard-won insights.

Finally, I would argue, pluralism informs feminist literary inquiry not simply as a description of what already exists but, more importantly, as the only critical stance consistent with the current status of the larger women's movement. Segmented and variously focused, the different women's organizations neither espouse any single system of analysis nor, as a result, express any wholly shared, consistently articulated ideology. The ensuing loss in effective organization and political clout is a serious one, but it has not been paralyzing; in spite of our differences, we have united to *act* in areas of clear mutual concern (the push for the Equal Rights Amendment is probably the most obvious example). The trade-off, as I see it, has made possible an ongoing and educative dialectic of analysis and proffered solutions, protecting us thereby from the inviting traps of reductionism and dogma. And so long as this dialogue remains active, both our politics and our criticism will be free of dogma — but never, I hope, of feminist ideology, in all its variety. For, "whatever else ideologies may be — projections of unacknowledged fears, disguises for ulterior motives, phatic expressions of group solidarity" (and the women's movement, to date, has certainly been all of these, and more) — whatever ideologies express, they are, as Clifford Geertz astutely observes, "most distinctively, maps of problematic social reality and matrices for the creation of collective conscience." And despite the fact that "ideological advocates ... tend as much to obscure as to clarify the true nature of the problems involved," as Geertz notes, "they at least call attention to their existence and, by polarizing issues, make continued neglect more difficult. Without Marxist attack, there would have been no labor reform; without Black Nationalists, no deliberate speed."[37] Without Seneca Falls, I would add, no enfranchisement of women, and without "consciousness raising," no feminist literary criticism nor, even less, women's studies.

---

[35]Lillian Robinson, "Dwelling in Decencies: Radical Criticism and the Feminist Perspective," *College English* 32, no. 8 (May 1971); reprinted in *Sex, Class, and Culture,* p. 11. [Kolodny]

[36]"Ideology bridges the emotional gap between things as they are and as one would have them be, thus insuring the performance of roles that might otherwise be abandoned in despair or apathy," comments Geertz in "Ideology as a Cultural System," p. 205. [Kolodny]

[37]Ibid., pp. 220, 205. [Kolodny]

Ideology, however, only truly manifests its power by ordering the *sum* of our actions.[38] If feminist criticism calls anything into question, it must be that dog-eared myth of intellectual neutrality. For, what I take to be the underlying spirit, or message, of any consciously ideologically premised criticism — that is, that ideas are important *because* they determine the ways we live, or want to live, in the world — is vitiated by confining those ideas to the study, the classroom, or the pages of our books. To write chapters decrying the sexual stereotyping of women in our literature, while closing our eyes to the sexual harassment of our women students and colleagues; to display Katherine Hepburn and Rosalind Russell in our courses on "The Image of the Independent Career Women in Film," while managing not to notice the paucity of female

[38]I here follow Fredric Jameson's view in *The Prison-House of Language: A Critical Account of Structuralism and Russian Formalism* (Princeton: Princeton University Press, 1974), p. 107, that: "Ideology would seem to be that grillwork of form, convention, and belief which orders our actions."

[Kolodny]

administrators on our own campus; to study the women who helped make universal enfranchisement a political reality, while keeping silent about our activist colleagues who are denied promotion or tenure; to include segments on "Women in the Labor Movement" in our American studies or women's studies courses, while remaining willfully ignorant of the department secretary fired for her efforts to organize a clerical workers' union; to glory in the delusions of "merit," "privilege," and "status" which accompany campus life in order to insulate ourselves from the millions of women who labor in poverty — all this is not merely hypocritical; it destroys both the spirit and the meaning of what we are about. It puts us, however unwittingly, in the service of those who laid the minefield in the first place. In my view, it is a fine thing for many of us, individually, to have traversed the minefield; but that happy circumstance will only prove of lasting importance if, together, we expose it for what it is (the male fear of sharing power and significance with women) and deactivate its components, so that others, after us, may literally dance through the minefield.

Julia Kristeva

b. 1941

Born in Bulgaria, Julia Kristeva took a degree from the Literary Institute of Sofia before going to Paris in 1966 and submitting a troisième cycle doctoral thesis and then a thesis for the Doctorat d'État. *A tenured professor at the University of Paris, she was an early contributor to the influential avant-garde journal* Tel Quel, *an officer of the International Association of Semiotics, and an editor of the review* Sémiotica. *She is also a "Lacanian" psychoanalyst, which is not to suggest that Kristeva is merely an epigone or follower of Jacques Lacan or of the other imposing figures she has studied under, such as Lucien Goldmann and Claude Lévi-Strauss. Rather, Kristeva has persistently contributed to the development of structuralist and poststructuralist thought, at once helping shape emerging ideas and incorporating them as they emerge into her own eclectic, ever-evolving body of thought. Her* Σημειωτιχὴ *(1969), for example, is a critique of structuralism that pointed in the direction of the notion of "semanalysis" — a semiotic/psychoanalytical approach to texts for which Kristeva is perhaps best known. Her other works include* The Text of the Novel *(1970),* About Chinese Women *(1974),* Revolution in Poetic Language *(1974),* Powers of Horror: An Essay on Abjection *(1980),* Desire in Language: A Semiotic Approach to Literature and Art *(1980),* In the Beginning Was Love: Psychoanalysis and Faith *(1985),* Black Sun: Depression and Melancholia *(1987),* Language: The Unknown *(1989),* Nations without Nationalism *(1993),* Proust and the Sense of Time *(1993),* Time and Sense: Proust and the Experience of Literature *(1996),* Hannah Arendt *(2001),* Intimate Revolt *(2002),* Colette *(2004),* The Incredible Need to Believe *(2009),* Hatred and Forgiveness *(2010),* The Severed Head: Capital Visions *(2011), and* Teresa My Love: An Imagined Life of the Saint of Avila *(2014). She has also published four novels. "Women's Time" was originally published as "Le Temps des femmes" in* Cahiers de recherche de sciences des textes et documents, *no. 5 (Winter 1979), and is reprinted from its first English translation, by Alice Jardine and Harry Blake, in* Signs *(1981).*

Women's Time

The nation — dream and reality of the nineteenth century — seems to have reached both its apogee and its limits when the 1929 crash and the National-Socialist apocalypse demolished the pillars that, according to Marx, were its essence: economic homogeneity, historical tradition, and linguistic unity.[1] It could indeed be demonstrated that World War II, though fought in the name of national values (in the above sense of the term), brought an end to the nation as a reality: It was turned into a mere illusion which, from that point forward, would be preserved only for ideological or strictly political purposes, its social and philosophical coherence having collapsed. To move quickly toward the specific problematic that will occupy us in this article, let us say that the chimera of economic *homogeneity* gave way to *interdependence* (when not submission to the economic superpowers), while *historical* tradition and *linguistic* unity were recast as a broader and deeper determinant: what might be called a *symbolic denominator*, defined as the cultural and religious memory forged by the interweaving of history and geography. The variants of this memory produce social territories which then

---

Translated by Alice Jardine and Harry Blake.

[1] The following discussion emphasizes Europe in a way which may seem superfluous to some American readers given the overall emphasis on deterritorialization. It is, however, essential to the movement of an article that is above all devoted to the necessity of paying attention to the place from which we speak. [Tr.]

redistribute the cutting up into political parties which is still in use but losing strength. At the same time, this memory or symbolic denominator, common to them all, reveals beyond economic globalization and/or uniformization certain characteristics transcending the nation that sometimes embrace an entire continent. A new social ensemble superior to the nation has thus been constituted,[2] within which the nation, far from losing its own traits, rediscovers and accentuates them in a strange temporality, in a kind of "future perfect," where the most deeply repressed past gives a distinctive character to a logical and sociological distribution of the most modern type. For this memory or symbolic common denominator concerns the response that human groupings, united in space and time, have given not to the problems of the production of material goods (i.e., the domain of the economy and of the human relationships it implies, politics, etc.) but, rather, to those of *reproduction*, survival of the species, life and death, the body, sex, and symbol. If it is true, for example, that Europe is representative of such a sociocultural ensemble, it seems to me that its existence is based more on this "symbolic denominator," which its art, philosophy, and religions manifest, than on its economic profile, which is certainly interwoven with collective memory but whose traits change rather rapidly under pressure from its partners.

It is clear that a social ensemble thus constituted possesses both a *solidity* rooted in a particular mode of reproduction and its representations through which the biological species is connected to its humanity, which is a tributary of time; as well as a certain *fragility* as a result of the fact that, through its universality, the symbolic common denominator is necessarily echoed in the corresponding symbolic denominator of another sociocultural ensemble. Thus, barely constituted as such, Europe finds itself being asked to compare itself with, or even to recognize itself in, the cultural, artistic, philosophical, and religious constructions belonging to other supranational

[2]Kristeva is perhaps gesturing, in her discussion of nationalism becoming transcendentally absorbed into something larger, toward the European Union: the first direct elections for the European Parliament were held in the year she wrote this (1979).

sociocultural ensembles. This seems natural when the entities involved were linked by history (e.g., Europe and North America, or Europe and Latin America), but the phenomenon also occurs when the universality of this denominator we have called symbolic juxtaposes modes of production and reproduction apparently opposed in both the past and the present (e.g., Europe and India, or Europe and China). In short, with sociocultural ensembles of the European type, we are constantly faced with a double problematic: that of their *identity* constituted by historical sedimentation, and that of their *loss of identity* which is produced by this connection of memories which escape from history only to encounter anthropology. In other words, we confront two temporal dimensions: the time of linear history, or *cursive time* (as Nietzsche called it),[3] and the time of another history, thus another time, *monumental time* (again according to Nietzsche), which englobes these supranational, sociocultural ensembles within even larger entities.

I should like to draw attention to certain formations which seem to me to summarize the dynamics of a sociocultural organism of this type. The question is one of sociocultural groups, that is, groups defined according to their place in production, but especially according to their role in the mode of reproduction and its representations, which, while bearing the specific sociocultural traits of the formation in question, are *diagonal* to it and connect it to other sociocultural formations. I am thinking in particular of sociocultural groups which are usually defined as age groups (e.g., "young people in Europe"), as sexual divisions (e.g., "European women"), and so forth. While it is obvious that "young people" or "women" in Europe have their own particularity, it is nonetheless just as obvious that what defines them as "young people," or as "women" places them in a diagonal relationship to their European "origin" and links them to similar categories in North

[3]Nietzsche discusses "monumental history" and its alternatives (antiquarian history, critical history) in the essay "On the Use and Abuse of History for Life" published in *Untimely Meditations* (1874); in section VII, he contrasts what he considers culturally unhealthy attempts at objectivity, on the part of "monumental" historians, with what he envisions, a new form of history written as narrative art.

America or in China, among others. That is, insofar as they also belong to "monumental history," they will not be only European "young people" or "women" of Europe but will echo in a most specific way the universal traits of their structural place in reproduction and its representations.

Consequently, the reader will find in the following pages, first, an attempt to situate the problematic of women in Europe within an inquiry on time: that time which the feminist movement both inherits and modifies. Second, I will attempt to distinguish two phases or two generations of women which, while immediately universalist and cosmopolitan in their demands, can nonetheless be differentiated by the fact that the first generation is more determined by the implications of a national problematic (in the sense suggested above), while the second, more determined by its place within the "symbolic denominator," is European *and* trans-European. Finally, I will try, both through the problems approached and through the type of analysis I propose, to present what I consider a viable stance for a European — or at least a European woman — within a domain which is henceforth worldwide in scope.

WHICH TIME?

"Father's time, mother's species," as Joyce put it;[4] and, indeed, when evoking the name and destiny of women, one thinks more of the *space* generating and forming the human species than of *time*, becoming, or history. The modern sciences of subjectivity, of its genealogy and accidents, confirm in their own way this intuition, which is perhaps itself the result of a sociohistorical conjuncture. Freud, listening to the dreams and fantasies of his patients, thought that "hysteria was linked to place."[5] Subsequent studies on the acquisition of the symbolic function by children show that the permanence and quality of maternal love condition the appearance of the first spatial references

which induce the child's laugh and then induce the entire range of symbolic manifestations which lead eventually to sign and syntax.[6] Moreover, antipsychiatry and psychoanalysis as applied to the treatment of psychoses, before attributing the capacity for transference and communication to the patient, proceed to the arrangement of new places, gratifying substitutes that repair old deficiencies in the maternal space. I could go on giving examples. But they all converge on the problematic of space, which innumerable religions of matriarchal (re)appearance attribute to "woman," and which Plato, recapitulating in his own system the atomists of antiquity, designated by the aporia of the *chora*,[7] matrix space, nourishing, unnameable, anterior to the One, to God and, consequently, defying metaphysics.[8]

As for time, female[9] subjectivity would seem to provide a specific measure that essentially retains *repetition* and *eternity* from among the multiple modalities of time known through the

[4]In *Finnegans Wake* (1939); Kristeva will continue to juxtapose time and space against the paternal and maternal principles.

[5]Sigmund Freud and Carl G. Jung, *Correspondance* (Paris: Gallimard, 1975), 1:87. [Kristeva]

[6]R. Spitz, *La Première année de la vie de l'enfant* [First year of life: a psychoanalytic study of normal and deviant development of object relations] (Paris: PUF, 1958); D. Winnicott, *Jeu et réalité* [Playing and Reality] (Paris: Gallimard, 1975); Julia Kristeva, "Noms de lieu" in *Polylogue* (Paris: Editions du Seuil, 1977), translated as "Place Names" in Julia Kristeva, *Desire in Language: A Semiotic Approach to Literature and Art,* ed. Leon S. Roudiez, trans. Thomas Gora, Alice Jardine, and Leon Roudiez (New York: Columbia University Press, 1980) (hereafter cited as *Desire in Language*). [Kristeva]

[7]For Kristeva's revision of Lacan, see the introduction to Psychoanalytic Theory and Criticism, p. 636.

[8]Plato *Timeus* 52: "Indefinitely a place; it cannot be destroyed, but provides a ground for all that can come into being; itself being perceptible, outside of all sensation, by means of a sort of bastard reasoning; barely assuming credibility, it is precisely that which makes us dream when we perceive it, and affirm that all that exists must be somewhere, in a determined place . . ." (author's translation). [Kristeva]

[9]As most readers of recent French theory in translation know, *le féminin* does not have the same pejorative connotations it has come to have in English. It is a term used to speak about women in general, but, as used most often in this article, it probably comes closest to our "female" as defined by Elaine Showalter in *A Literature of Their Own* (Princeton, N.J.: Princeton University Press, 1977). I have therefore used either "women" or "female" according to the context (cf. also n. 9 in "Introduction to Julia Kristeva's 'Women's Time'" [this issue; hereafter cited as "Introduction"]). "Subjectivity" here refers to the state of being "a thinking, speaking, acting, doing or writing agent" and never, e.g., as opposed to "objectivity" (see the glossary in *Desire in Language*). [Tr.]

history of civilizations. On the one hand, there are cycles, gestation, the eternal recurrence of a bio-logical rhythm which conforms to that of nature and imposes a temporality whose stereotyping may shock, but whose regularity and unison with what is experienced as extrasubjective time, cosmic time, occasion vertiginous visions and unnameable *jouissance*.[10] On the other hand, and perhaps as a consequence, there is the massive presence of a monumental temporality, without cleavage or escape, which has so little to do with linear time (which passes) that the very word "temporality" hardly fits: All-encompassing and infinite like imaginary space, this temporality reminds one of Kronos in Hesiod's mythol-ogy, the incestuous son whose massive presence covered all of Gea in order to separate her from Ouranos, the father.[11] Or one is reminded of the various myths of resurrection which, in all reli-gious beliefs, perpetuate the vestige of an anterior or concomitant maternal cult, right up to its most recent elaboration, Christianity, in which the body of the Virgin Mother does not die but moves from one spatiality to another within the same time via dormition (according to the Orthodox faith) or via assumption (the Catholic faith).[12] The fact that these two types of temporal-ity (cyclical and monumental) are traditionally linked to female subjectivity insofar as the lat-ter is thought of as necessarily maternal should not make us forget that this repetition and this eternity are found to be the fundamental, if not the sole, conceptions of time in numerous civi-lizations and experiences, particularly mystical ones.[13] The fact that certain currents of modern feminism recognize themselves here does not render them fundamentally incompatible with "masculine" values.

[10] I have retained *jouissance* — that word for pleasure which defies translation — as it is rapidly becoming a "believ-able neologism" in English (see the glossary in *Desire in Language*). [Tr.]

[11] This particular mythology has important implications — equal only to those of the oedipal myth — for current French thought. [Tr.]

[12] See Julia Kristeva, "Héretique de l'amour," *Tel quel*, no. 74 (1977), pp. 30–49. [Kristeva]

[13] See H. C. Puech, *La Gnose et la temps* (Paris: Gallimard, 1977). [Kristeva]

In return, female subjectivity as it gives itself up to intuition becomes a problem with respect to a certain conception of time: time as project, teleology, linear and prospective unfolding; time as departure, progression, and arrival — in other words, the time of history.[14] It has already been abundantly demonstrated that this kind of tem-porality is inherent in the logical and ontological values of any given civilization, that this temporal-ity renders explicit a rupture, an expectation, or an anguish which other temporalities work to conceal. It might also be added that this linear time is that of language considered as the enunciation of sentences (noun + verb; topic-comment; beginning-ending), and that this time rests on its own stumbling block, which is also the stumbling block of that enun-ciation — death. A psychoanalyst would call this "obsessional time," recognizing in the mastery of time the true structure of the slave. The hysteric (either male or female) who suffers from reminis-cences would, rather, recognize his or her self in the anterior temporal modalities: cyclical or monu-mental. This antinomy, one perhaps embedded in psychic structures, becomes, nonetheless, within a given civilization, an antinomy among social groups and ideologies in which the radical posi-tions of certain feminists would rejoin the discourse of marginal groups of spiritual or mystical inspira-tion and, strangely enough, rejoin recent scientific preoccupations. Is it not true that the problematic of a time indissociable from space, of a space-time in infinite expansion, or rhythmed by accidents or catastrophes, preoccupies both space science and genetics?[15] And, at another level, is it not true that the contemporary media revolution,[16] which is manifest in the storage and reproduction of infor-mation, implies an idea of time as frozen or explod-ing according to the vagaries of demand, returning to its source but uncontrollable, utterly bypassing

[14] See "Introduction." [Tr.]

[15] Kristeva gestures toward the conflict among astronomers between the "steady state" and "big bang" theories explaining the expansion of the universe and the conflict among biolo-gists between the "gradualist" and "punctuated equilibrium" theories of evolution.

[16] Kristeva gestures toward the centralization of informa-tion on digital computers, which at the date of writing were still large institutional machines controlled and programmed by specialists.

its subject and leaving only two preoccupations to those who approve of it: Who is to have power over the origin (the programming) and over the end (the use)?

It is for two precise reasons, within the framework of this article, that I have allowed myself this rapid excursion into a problematic of unheard of complexity. The reader will undoubtedly have been struck by a fluctuation in the term of reference: mother, woman, hysteric. . . . I think that the apparent coherence which the term "woman" assumes in contemporary ideology, apart from its "mass" or "shock" effect for activist purposes, essentially has the negative effect of effacing the differences among the diverse functions or structures which operate beneath this word. Indeed, the time has perhaps come to emphasize the multiplicity of female expressions and preoccupations so that from the intersection of these differences there might arise, more precisely, less commercially, and more truthfully, the real *fundamental difference* between the two sexes: a difference that feminism has had the enormous merit of rendering painful, that is, productive of surprises and of symbolic life in a civilization which, outside the stock exchange and wars, is bored to death.

It is obvious, moreover, that one cannot speak of Europe or of "women in Europe" without suggesting the time in which this sociocultural distribution is situated. If it is true that a female sensibility emerged a century ago, the chances are great that by introducing *its own* notion of time, this sensibility is not in agreement with the idea of an "eternal Europe" and perhaps not even with that of a "modern Europe." Rather, through and with the European past and present, as through and with the ensemble of "Europe," which is the repository of memory, this sensibility seeks its own transEuropean temporality. There are, in any case, three attitudes on the part of European feminist movements toward this conception of linear temporality, which is readily labeled masculine and which is at once both civilizational and obsessional.

TWO GENERATIONS

In its beginnings, the women's movement, as the struggle of suffragists and of existential feminists, aspired to gain a place in linear time as the time of project and history. In this sense, the movement, while immediately universalist, is also deeply rooted in the sociopolitical life of nations. The political demands of women; the struggles for equal pay for equal work, for taking power in social institutions on an equal footing with men; the rejection, when necessary, of the attributes traditionally considered feminine or maternal insofar as they are deemed incompatible with insertion in that history — all are part of the *logic of identification*[17] with certain values: not with the ideological (these are combated, and rightly so, as reactionary) but, rather, with the logical and ontological values of a rationality dominant in the nation-state. Here it is unnecessary to enumerate the benefits which this logic of identification and the ensuing struggle have achieved and continue to achieve for women (abortion, contraception, equal pay, professional recognition, etc.); these have already had or will soon have effects even more important than those of the Industrial Revolution. Universalist in its approach, this current in feminism *globalizes* the problems of women of different milieux, ages, civilizations, or simply of varying psychic structures, under the label "Universal Woman." A consideration of *generations* of women can only be conceived of in this global way as a succession, as a progression in the accomplishment of the initial program mapped out by its founders.

In a second phase, linked, on the one hand, to the younger women who came to feminism after May 1968 and, on the other, to women who had an aesthetic of psychoanalytic experience, linear temporality has been almost totally refused, and as a consequence there has arisen an exacerbated

---

[17]The term "identification" belongs to a wide semantic field ranging from everyday language to philosophy and psychoanalysis. While Kristeva is certainly referring in principle to its elaboration in Freudian and Lacanian psychoanalysis, it can be understood here, as a logic, in its most general sense (see the entry on "identification" in Jean LaPlanche and J. B. Pontalis, *Vocabulaire de la psychanalyse* [The language of psychoanalysis] [Paris: Presses Universitaires de France, 1967; rev. ed., 1976]). [Tr.] It is also possible that Kristeva may be referring to the projective ego defense of "identification with the aggressor" (as Freud characterizes the mechanism operating in masochistic women attracted to narcissistic men). In the first phase of feminism, women want to become identical to men, by getting what men already have.

distrust of the entire political dimension. If it is true that this more recent current of feminism refers to its predecessors and that the struggle for sociocultural recognition of women is necessarily its main concern, this current seems to think of itself as belonging to another generation — qualitatively different from the first one — in its conception of its own identity and, consequently, of its temporality as such. Essentially interested in the specificity of female psychology and its symbolic realizations, these women seek to give a language to the intrasubjective and corporeal experiences left mute by culture in the past. Either as artists or writers, they have undertaken a veritable exploration of the *dynamic of signs*, an exploration which relates this tendency, at least at the level of its aspirations, to all major projects of aesthetic and religious upheaval. Ascribing this experience to a new generation does not only mean that other, more subtle problems have been added to the demands for sociopolitical identification made in the beginning. It also means that, by demanding recognition of an irreducible identity, without equal in the opposite sex and, as such, exploded, plural, fluid, in a certain way nonidentical, this feminism situates itself outside the linear time of identities which communicate through projection and revindication. Such a feminism rejoins, on the one hand, the archaic (mythical) memory and, on the other, the cyclical or monumental temporality of marginal movements. It is certainly not by chance that the European and trans-European problematic has been posited as such at the same time as this new phase of feminism.

Finally, it is the mixture of the two attitudes — *insertion into history* and the radical *refusal* of the subjective limitations imposed by this history's time on an experiment carried out in the name of the irreducible difference — that seems to have broken loose over the past few years in European feminist movements, particularly in France and in Italy.

If we accept this meaning of the expression "a new generation of women," two kinds of questions might then be posed. What sociopolitical processes or events have provoked this mutation? What are its problems; its contributions as well as dangers?

SOCIALISM AND FREUDIANISM

One could hypothesize that if this new generation of women shows itself to be more diffuse and perhaps less conscious in the United States and more massive in Western Europe, this is because of a veritable split in social relations and mentalities, a split produced by socialism and Freudianism. I mean by *socialism* that egalitarian doctrine which is increasingly broadly disseminated and accepted as based on common sense, as well as that social practice adopted by governments and political parties in democratic regimes which are forced to extend the zone of egalitarianism to include the distribution of goods as well as access to culture. By *Freudianism* I mean that lever, inside this egalitarian and socializing field, which once again poses the question of sexual difference and of the difference among subjects who themselves are not reducible one to the other.

Western socialism, shaken in its very beginnings by the egalitarian or differential demands of its women (e.g., Flora Tristan[18]), quickly got rid of those women who aspired to recognition of a specificity of the female role in society and culture, only retaining from them, in the egalitarian and universalistic spirit of Enlightenment Humanism, the idea of a necessary identification between the two sexes as the only and unique means for liberating the "second sex." I shall not develop here the fact that this "ideal" is far from being applied in practice by these socialist-inspired movements and parties and that it was in part from the revolt against this situation that the new generation of women in Western Europe was born after May 1968. Let us just say that in theory, and as put into practice in Eastern Europe, socialist ideology, based on a conception of the human being as determined by its place in *production* and the *relations of production*, did not take into consideration this same human being being according to its place in *reproduction*, on the one hand, or in the *symbolic order*, on the other. Consequently, the specific character of women could only appear as nonessential or even nonexistent

---

[18] Flora Tristan (Flore-Celestine-Thérèse-Henriette Tristan-Moscoso, 1803–1844) was a socialist writer and activist whose ideas bore fruit only after her death, in the revolutions of 1848.

to the totalizing and even totalitarian spirit of this ideology.[19] We begin to see that this same egalitarian and in fact censuring treatment has been imposed, from Enlightenment Humanism through socialism, on religious specificities and, in particular, on Jews.[20]

What has been achieved by this attitude remains nonetheless of capital importance for women, and I shall take as an example the change in the destiny of women in the socialist countries of Eastern Europe. It could be said, with only slight exaggeration, that the demands of the suffragists and existential feminists have, to a great extent, been met in these countries, since three of the main egalitarian demands of early feminism have been or are now being implemented despite vagaries and blunders: economic, political, and professional equality. The fourth, sexual equality, which implies permissiveness in sexual relations (including homosexual relations), abortion, and contraception, remains stricken by taboo in Marxian ethics as well as for reasons of state. It is, then, this fourth equality which is the problem and which therefore appears *essential* in the struggle of a new generation. But simultaneously and as a consequence of these socialist accomplishments — which are in fact a total deception[21] — the struggle is no longer concerned with the quest for equality but, rather, with difference and specificity. It is precisely at this point that the new generation encounters what might be called the *symbolic* question.[22] Sexual difference — which is at once biological, physiological, and relative

to reproduction — is translated by and translates a difference in the relationship of subjects to the symbolic contract which *is* the social contract: a difference, then, in the relationship to power, language, and meaning. The sharpest and most subtle point of feminist subversion brought about by the new generation will henceforth be situated on the terrain of the inseparable conjunction of the sexual and the symbolic, in order to try to discover, first, the specificity of the female, and then, in the end, that of each individual woman.

A certain saturation of socialist ideology, a certain exhaustion of its potential as a program for a new social contract (it is obvious that the effective realization of this program is far from being accomplished, and I am here treating only its system of thought) makes way for . . . Freudianism. I am, of course, aware that this term and this practice are somewhat shocking to the American intellectual consciousness (which rightly reacts to a muddled and normatizing form of psychoanalysis) and, above all, to the feminist consciousness. To restrict my remarks to the latter: Is it not true that Freud has been seen only as a denigrator or even an exploiter of women? as an irritating phallocrat in a Vienna which was at once Puritan and decadent — a man who fantasized women as sub-men, castrated men?

CASTRATED AND/OR SUBJECT TO LANGUAGE

Before going beyond Freud to propose a more just or more modern vision of women, let us try, first, to understand his notion of castration. It is, first of all, a question of an *anguish* or *fear* of castration, or of correlative penis *envy*; a question, therefore, of *imaginary* formations readily perceivable in the *discourse* of neurotics of both sexes, men and women. But, above all, a careful reading of Freud, going beyond his biologism and his mechanism, both characteristic of his time, brings out two things. First, as presupposition for the "primal scene," the castration fantasy and its correlative (penis envy) are hypotheses, a priori suppositions intrinsic to the theory itself, in the sense that these are not the ideological fantasies of their inventor but, rather, logical necessities to be placed at the "origin" in order to explain what unceasingly

[19]See D. Desanti, "L'Autre Sexe des bolcheviks," *Tel quel*, no. 76 (1978); Julia Kristeva, *Des Chinoises* (Paris: Editions des femmes, 1975), translated as *On Chinese Women*, trans. Anita Barrows (New York: Urizen Press, 1977). [Kristeva]

[20]See Arthur Hertzberg, *The French Enlightenment and the Jews* (New York: Columbia University Press, 1968); *Les Juifs et la révolution française*, ed. B. Blumenkranz and A. Seboul (Paris: Edition Privat, 1976). [Kristeva]

[21]The French word *deception* can also be translated "disappointment."

[22]Here, "symbolic" is being more strictly used in terms of that function defined by Kristeva in opposition to the semiotic: "it involves the thetic phase, the identification of subject and its distinction from objects, and the establishment of a sign system" (see the glossary in *Desire in Language*, and Alice Jardine, "Theories of the Feminine: Kristeva," *Enclitic*, *Enclitic* 4, ii (1980)). [Tr.]

functions in neurotic discourse. In other words, neurotic discourse, in man and woman, can only be understood in terms of its own logic when its fundamental causes are admitted as the fantasies of the damental causes are admitted as the fantasies of the primal scene and castration, even if (as may be the case) nothing renders them present in reality itself. Stated in still other terms, the reality of castration is no more real than the hypothesis of an explosion which, according to modern astrophysics, is at the origin of the universe: Nothing proves it, in a sense it is an article of faith, the only difference being that numerous phenomena of life in this "big-bang" universe are explicable only through this initial hypothesis. But one is infinitely more jolted when this kind of intellectual method concerns inanimate matter than when it is applied to our own subjectivity and thus, perhaps, to the fundamental mechanism of our epistemophilic thought.

Moreover, certain texts written by Freud (*The Interpretation of Dreams*, but especially those of the second topic, in particular the *Metapsychology*) and their recent extensions (notably by Lacan),[23] imply that castration is, in sum, the imaginary construction of a radical operation which constitutes the symbolic field and all beings inscribed therein. This operation constitutes signs and syntax; that is, language, as a *separation* from a presumed state of nature, of pleasure fused with nature so that the introduction of an articulated network of differences, which refers to objects henceforth and only in this way separated from a subject, may constitute *meaning*. This logical operation of separation (confirmed by all psycholinguistic and child psychology) which preconditions the binding of language which is already syntactical, is therefore the common destiny of the two sexes, men and women. That certain biofamilial conditions and relationships cause women (and notably hysterics) to deny this separation and the language which ensues from it, whereas men (notably obsessionals) magnify it both and, terrified, attempt to master them — this is what Freud's discovery has to tell us on this issue.[24]

[23]See, in general, Jacques Lacan, *Écrits* (Paris: Éditions du Seuil, 1966) and, in particular, Jacques Lacan, *Le Séminaire XX: Encore* (Paris: Éditions du Seuil, 1975). [Tr.]

[24]Kristeva's rapid summary of Lacan's revision of Freud's theory of the castration complex; for an expanded version, see p. 649-55.

The analytic situation indeed shows that it is the penis which, becoming the major referent in this operation of separation, gives full meaning to the *lack* or to the *desire* which constitutes the subject during his or her insertion into the order of language. I should only like to indicate here that, in order for this operation constitutive of the symbolic and the social to appear in its full truth and for it to be understood by both sexes, it would be just to emphasize its extension to all that is privation of fulfillment and of totality; exclusion of a pleasing, natural, and sound state: in short, the break indispensable to the advent of the symbolic.

It can now be seen how women, starting with this theoretical apparatus, might try to understand their sexual and symbolic difference in the framework of social, cultural, and professional realization, in order to try, by seeing their position therein, either to fulfil their own experience to a maximum or — but always starting from this point — to go further and call into question the very apparatus itself.

LIVING THE SACRIFICE

In any case, and for women in Europe today, whether or not they are conscious of the various mutations (socialist and Freudian) which have produced or simply accompanied their coming into their own, the urgent question on our agenda might be formulated as follows: *What can be our place in the symbolic contract?* If the social contract, far from being that of equal men, is based on an essentially sacrificial relationship of separation and articulation of differences which in this way produces communicable meaning, what is our place in this order of sacrifice and/or of language? No longer wishing to be excluded or no longer content with the function which has always been demanded of us (to maintain, arrange, and perpetuate this sociosymbolic contract as mothers, wives, nurses, doctors, teachers . . .), how can we reveal our place, first as it is bequeathed to us by tradition, and then as we want to transform it?

It is difficult to evaluate what in the relationship of women to the symbolic as it reveals itself now arises from a sociohistorical conjuncture (patriarchal ideology, whether Christian, humanist, socialist or so forth), and what arises from a structure. We can speak only about a structure observed in a sociohistorical context, which is that of Christian, Western civilization and its lay ramifications. In this sense of psychosymbolic structure, women, "we" (is it necessary to recall the warnings we issued at the beginning of this article concerning the totalizing use of this plural?) seem to feel that they are the casualties, that they have been left out of the sociosymbolic contract, of language as the fundamental social bond. They find no affect there, no more than they find the fluid and infinitesimal significations of their relationships with the nature of their own bodies, that of the child, another woman, or a man. This frustration, which to a certain extent belongs to men also, is being voiced today principally by women, to the point of becoming the essence of the new feminist ideology. A therefore difficult, if not impossible, identification with the sacrificial logic of separation and syntactical sequence at the foundation of language and the social code leads to the rejection of the symbolic — lived as the rejection of the paternal function and ultimately generating psychoses.

But this limit, rarely reached as such, produces two types of counterinvestment of what we have termed the sociosymbolic contract. On the one hand, there are attempts to take hold of this contract, to possess it in order to enjoy it as such or to subvert it. How? The answer remains difficult to formulate (since, precisely, any formulation is deemed frustrating, mutilating, sacrificial) or else is in fact formulated using stereotypes taken from extremist and often deadly ideologies. On the other hand, another attitude is more lucid from the beginning, more self-analytical which — without refusing or sidestepping this sociosymbolic order — consists in trying to explore the constitution and functioning of this contract, starting less from the knowledge accumulated about it (anthropology, psychoanalysis, linguistics) than from the very personal affect experienced when facing it as subject and as a woman. This leads to the active research,[25]

still rare, undoubtedly hesitant but always dissident, being carried out by women in the human sciences; particularly those attempts, in the wake of contemporary art, to break the code, to shatter language, to find a specific discourse closer to the body and emotions, to the unnameable repressed by the social contract. I am not speaking here of a "woman's language," whose (at least syntactical) existence is highly problematical and whose apparent lexical specificity is perhaps more the product of a social marginality than of a sexual-symbolic difference.[26]

Nor am I speaking of the aesthetic quality of productions by women, most of which — with a few exceptions (but has this not always been the case with both sexes?) — are a reiteration of a more or less euphoric or depressed romanticism and always an explosion of an ego lacking narcissistic gratification.[27] What I should like to retain, nonetheless, as a mark of collective aspiration, as an undoubtedly vague and unimplemented intention, but one which is intense and which has been deeply revealing these past few years, is this: The new generation of women is showing that its major social concern has become the sociosymbolic contract as a sacrificial contract. If anthropologists and psychologists, for at least a century, have not stopped insisting on this in

[25]This work is periodically published in various academic women's journals, one of the most prestigious being *Signs: Journal of Women in Culture and Society*, University of Chicago Press. Also of note are the special issues: "Ecriture, féminité, féminisme," *La Revue des sciences humaines* (Lille III), no. 4 (1977); and "Les Femmes et la philosophie," *Le Doctrinal de sapience* (Editions Solin), no. 3 (1977). [Kristeva]

[26]See linguistic research on "female language": Robin Lakoff, *Language and Women's Place* (New York: Harper & Row, 1974); Mary R. Key, *Male/Female Language* (Metuchen, N.J.: Scarecrow Press, 1973); A. M. Houdebine, "Les Femmes et la langue," *Tel quel*, no. 74 (1977), pp. 84–95. The contrast between these "empirical" investigations of women's "speech acts" and much of the research in France on the conceptual bases for a "female language" must be emphasized here. It is somewhat helpful, if ultimately inaccurate, to think of the former as an "external" study of language and the latter as an "internal" exploration of the process of signification. For further contrast, see, e.g., "Part II: Contemporary Feminist Thought in France: Translating Difference" in *The Future of Difference*, ed. Hester Eisenstein and Alice Jardine (Boston: G. K. Hall & Co., 1980); the "Introductions" to *New French Feminisms*, ed. Elaine Marks and Isabelle de Courtivron (Amherst: University of Massachusetts Press, 1980); and for a very helpful overview of the problem of "difference and language" in France, see Stephen Heath, "Difference" in *Screen* 19 no. 3 (Autumn 1978): 51–112. [Tr.]

[27]This is one of the more explicit references to the mass marketing of "écriture féminine" in Paris over the last ten years. [Tr.]

their attention to "savage thought," wars, the discourse of dreams, or writers, women are today affirming — and we consequently face a mass phenomenon — that they are forced to experience this sacrificial contract against their will.[28] Based on this, they are attempting a revolt which they see as a resurrection but which society as a whole understands as murder. This attempt can lead us to a not less and sometimes more deadly violence. Or to a cultural innovation. Probably to both at once. But that is precisely where the stakes are, and they are of epochal significance.

THE TERROR OF POWER OR THE POWER OF TERRORISM

First in socialist countries (such as the USSR and China) and increasingly in Western democracies, under pressure from feminist movements, women are being promoted to leadership positions in government, industry, and culture. Inequalities, devalorizations, underestimations, even persecution of women at this level continue to hold sway in vain. The struggle against them is a struggle against archaisms. The cause has nonetheless been understood, the principle has been accepted.[29] What remains is to break down the resistance to change. In this sense, this struggle, while still one of the main concerns of the new generation, is not, strictly speaking, its problem. In relationship to *power*, *its* problem might rather be summarized as follows: What happens when women come into power and identify with it? What happens when, on the contrary, they refuse power and create a parallel society, a counterpower which then takes on aspects ranging from a club of ideas to a group of terrorist commandos?[30]

The assumption by women of executive, industrial, and cultural power has not, up to the present time, radically changed the nature of this power. This can be clearly seen in the East, where women promoted to decision-making positions suddenly obtain the economic as well as the narcissistic advantages refused them for thousands of years and become the pillars of the existing governments, guardians of the status quo, the most zealous protectors of the established order.[31] This identification by women with the very power structures previously considered as frustrating, oppressive, or inaccessible has often been used in modern times by totalitarian regimes: the German National-Socialists and the Chilean junta are examples of this.[32] The fact that this is a paranoid type of counterinvestment in an initially denied symbolic order can perhaps explain this troubling phenomenon; but an explanation does not prevent its massive propagation around the globe, perhaps in less dramatic forms than the totalitarian ones mentioned above, but all moving toward leveling, stabilization, conformism, at the cost of crushing exceptions, experiments, chance occurrences.

Some will regret that the rise of a libertarian movement such as feminism ends, in some of its aspects, in the consolidation of conformism; others will rejoice and profit from this fact. Electoral campaigns, the very life of political parties, continue to bet on this latter tendency. Experience proves that too quickly even the protest or innovative initiatives on the part of women inhaled by power systems (when they do not submit to them right off) are soon credited to the system's account; and that the long-awaited

[28]The expression *à leur corps défendant* translates as "against their will," but here the emphasis is on women's bodies: literally, "against their bodies." I have retained the former expression in English, partly because of its obvious intertextuality with Susan Brownmiller's *Against Our Will* (New York: Simon & Schuster, 1975). Women are increasingly describing their experience of the violence of the symbolic contact as a form of rape. [Tr.]

[29]Many women in the West who are once again finding all doors closed to them above a certain level of employment, especially in the current economic chaos, may find this statement, even qualified, troubling, to say the least. It is accurate, however, *in principle:* whether that of infinite capitalist recuperation or increasing socialist expansion — within both economies, our integration functions as a kind of operative illusion. [Tr.]

[30]The very real existence and autonomous activities of both of these versions of women's groups in Europe may seem a less urgent problem in the United States where feminist groups are often absorbed by the academy and/or are forced to remain financially dependent on para-academic/government agencies. [Tr.]

[31]See *Des Chinoises.* [Kristeva]

[32]See M.A. Macciocchi, *Eléments pour une analyse du fascisme* (Paris: 10/18, 1976); Michèle Mattelart, "Le Coup d'état au féminin," *Les Temps modernes* (January 1975). [Kristeva]

democratization of institutions as a result of the entry of women most often comes down to fabricating a few "chiefs" among them. The difficulty presented by this logic of integrating the second sex into a value system experienced as foreign and therefore counterinvested is how to avoid the centralization of power, how to detach women from it, and how then to proceed, through their critical, differential, and autonomous interventions, to render decision-making institutions more flexible.

Then there are the more radical feminist currents which, refusing homologation to any role of identification with existing power no matter what the power may be, make of the second sex a *countersociety*. A "female society" is then constituted as a sort of alter ego of the official society, in which all real or fantasized possibilities for *jouissance* take refuge. Against the sociosymbolic contract, both sacrificial and frustrating, this countersociety is imagined as harmonious, without prohibitions, free and fulfilling. In our modern societies which have no hereafter or, at least, which are caught up in a transcendency either reduced to this side of the world (Protestantism) or crumbling (Catholicism and its current challenges), the countersociety remains the only refuge for fulfillment since it is precisely an a-topia, a place outside the law, utopia's floodgate.

As with any society, the countersociety is based on the expulsion of an excluded element, a scapegoat charged with the evil of which the community duly constituted can then purge itself;[33] a purge which will finally exonerate that community of any future criticism. Modern protest movements have often reiterated this logic, locating the guilty one — in order to fend off

criticism — in the foreign, in capital alone, in the other religion, in the other sex. Does not feminism become a kind of inverted sexism when this logic is followed to its conclusion? The various forms of marginalism — according to sex, age, religion, or ideology — represent in the modern world this refuge for *jouissance*, a sort of laicized transcendence. But with women, and insofar as the number of those feeling concerned by this problem has increased, although in less spectacular forms than a few years ago, the problem of the countersociety is becoming massive: It occupies no more and no less than "half of the sky."

It has, therefore, become clear, because of the particular radicalization of the second generation, that these protest movements, including feminism, are not "initially libertarian" movements which only later, through internal deviations or external chance manipulations, fall back into the old ruts of the initially combated archetypes. Rather, the very logic of counterpower and of countersociety necessarily generates, by its very structure, its essence as a simulacrum of the combated society or of power. In this sense and from a viewpoint undoubtedly too Hegelian, modern feminism has only been but a moment in the interminable process of coming to consciousness about the implacable violence (separation, castration, etc.) which constitutes any symbolic contract.

Thus the identification with power in order to consolidate it or the constitution of a fetishist counterpower — restorer of the crises of the self and provider of a *jouissance* which is always already a transgression — seem to be the two social forms which the face-off between the new generation of women and the social contract can take. That one also finds the problem of terrorism there is structurally related.

The large number of women in terrorist groups (Palestinian commandos, the Baader-Meinhoff Gang, Red Brigades, etc.[34]) has already been

---

[33]the principles of a "sacrificial anthropology" are developed by René Girard in *La Violence et le sacré* [Violence and the sacred] (Paris: Grasset, 1972) and esp. in *Des choses cachées depuis la fondation du monde* (Paris: Grasset, 1978). [Kristeva] There Girard argues, on the basis of the myths of various nations, that human societies all over the world channeled impulses that might otherwise break out into a general violence of each against all into a ritual sacrifice of surrogate victims. Even when human sacrifice is no longer practiced, societies create scapegoats to give the rest of the society cohesion. Kristeva's allusion to Girard is by way of critique of second-generation feminists who in valorizing the feminine are scapegoating the masculine, and thus buying into the "sacrificial economy" she (and Girard) hope humanity can transcend.

[34]The Baader-Meinhoff Gang was a terrorist group based in Germany that began by firebombing a Frankfurt department store in 1968. It was led by Andreas Baader and his lover Gudrun Ensslin; another leader was Ulrike Meinhof, a journalist who helped Baader escape from custody. By 1977 the key members of the group were all dead, primarily

pointed out, either violently or prudently according to the source of information. The exploitation of women is still too great and the traditional prejudices against them too violent for one to be able to envision this phenomenon with sufficient distance. It can, however, be said from now on that this is the inevitable product of what we have called a denial of the sociosymbolic contract and its counterinvestment as the only means of self-defense in the struggle to safeguard an identity. This paranoid-type mechanism is at the base of any political involvement. It may produce different civilizing attitudes in the sense that these attitudes allow a more or less flexible reabsorption of violence and death. But when a subject is too brutally excluded from this sociosymbolic stratum; when, for example, a woman feels her affective life as a woman or her condition as a social being too brutally ignored by existing discourse or power (from her family to social institutions); she may, by counterinvesting the violence she has endured, make of herself a 'possessed' agent of this violence in order to combat what was experienced as frustration — with arms which may seem disproportional, but which are not so in comparison with the subjective or more precisely narcissistic suffering from which they originate. Necessarily opposed to the bourgeois democratic regimes in power, this terrorist violence offers as a program of liberation an order which is even more oppressive, more sacrificial than those it combats. Strangely enough, it is not against totalitarian regimes that these terrorist groups with women participants unleash themselves but, rather, against liberal systems, whose essence is, of course, exploitative, but whose expanding democratic legality guarantees relative tolerance. Each time, the mobilization takes place in the name of a nation, of an oppressed group, of a human essence imagined as good and sound; in

the name, then, of a kind of fantasy of archaic fulfillment which an arbitrary, abstract, and thus even bad and ultimately discriminatory order has come to disrupt. While that order is accused of being oppressive, is it not actually being reproached with being too weak, with not measuring up to this pure and good, but henceforth lost, substance? Anthropology has shown that the social order is sacrificial, but sacrifice orders violence, binds it, tames it. Refusal of the social order exposes one to the risk that the so-called good substance, once it is unchained, will explode, without curbs, without law or right, to become an absolute arbitrariness.

Following the crisis of monotheism, the revolutions of the past two centuries, and more recently fascism and Stalinism, have tragically set in action this logic of the oppressed goodwill which leads to massacres. Are women more apt than other social categories, notably the exploited classes, to invest in this implacable machine of terrorism? No categorical response, either positive or negative, can currently be given to this question. It must be pointed out, however, that since the dawn of feminism, and certainly before, the political activity of exceptional women, and thus in a certain sense of liberated women, has taken the form of murder, conspiracy, and crime. Finally, there is also the connivance of the young girl with her mother, her greater difficulty than the boy in detaching herself from the mother in order to accede to the order of signs as invested by the absence and separation constitutive of the paternal function. A girl will never be able to reestablish this contact with her mother — a contact which the boy may possibly rediscover through his relationship with the opposite sex — except by becoming a mother herself, through a child, or through a homosexuality which is in itself extremely difficult and judged as suspect by society; and, what is more, why and in the name of what dubious symbolic benefit would she want to make this detachment so as to conform to a symbolic system which remains foreign to her? In sum, all of these considerations — her eternal debt to the woman-mother — make a woman more vulnerable within the symbolic order, more fragile when she suffers within it, more virulent when she protects herself from it. If the archetype of the belief in a good and pure substance, that of utopias, is the belief in the omnipotence of an

by suicide while in prison. The "Red Brigades" are Italian terrorist groups who, beginning around 1972, assassinated government and business leaders, financing their operations through kidnappings. They were responsible for the kidnap/murder of former Italian prime minister Aldo Moro in 1978; in the wake of this crime they were repressed with ferocity by the Italian police, although remnants of these groups reportedly still exist.

archaic, full, total, englobing mother with no frustration, no separation, with no break-producing symbolism (with no castration, in other words), then it becomes evident that we will never be able to defuse the violences mobilized through the counterinvestment necessary to carrying out this phantasm, unless one challenges precisely this myth of the archaic mother. It is in this way that we can understand the warnings against the recent invasion of the women's movements by paranoia,[35] as in Lacan's scandalous sentence "There is no such thing as Woman."[36] Indeed, she does *not* exist with a capital "W," possessor of some mythical unity — a supreme power, on which is based the terror of power and terrorism as the desire for power. But what an unbelievable force for subversion in the modern world! And, at the same time, what playing with fire!

CREATURES AND CREATRESSES

The desire to be a mother, considered alienating and even reactionary by the preceding generation of feminists, has obviously not become a standard for the present generation. But we have seen in the past few years an increasing number of women who not only consider their maternity compatible with their professional life or their feminist involvement (certain improvements in the quality of life are also at the origin of this: an increase in the number of day-care centers and nursery schools, more active participation of men in child care and domestic life, etc.) but also find it indispensable to their discovery, not of the plenitude, but of the complexity of the female experience, with all that this complexity comprises in joy and pain. This tendency has its extreme: in the refusal of the paternal function by lesbian and single mothers can be seen one of the most violent forms taken by the rejection of the symbolic

[35]Cf. Micheline Enriquez, "Fantasmes paranoiaques: différences des sexes, homosexualité, loi du père," *Topiques*, no. 13 (1974). [Kristeva]

[36]See Jacques Lacan, "Dieu et la jouissance de la femme" in *Encore* (Paris: Editions du Seuil, 1975), pp. 61–71, esp. p. 68. This seminar has remained a primary critical and polemical focus for multiple tendencies in the French women's movement. For a brief discussion of the seminar in English, see Heath (n. 26 above). [Tr.]

outlined above, as well as one of the most fervent divinizations of maternal power — all of which cannot help but trouble an entire legal and moral order without, however, proposing an alternative to it. Let us remember here that Hegel distinguished between female right (familial and religious) and male law (civil and political). If our societies know well the uses and abuses of male law, it must also be recognized that female right is designated, for the moment, by a blank. And if these practices of maternity, among others, were to be generalized, women themselves would be responsible for elaborating the appropriate legislation to check the violence to which, otherwise, both their children and men would be subject. But are they capable of doing so? This is one of the important questions that the new generation of women encounters, especially when the members of this new generation refuse to ask those questions, seized by the same rage with which the dominant order originally victimized them.

Faced with this situation, it seems obvious — and feminist groups become more aware of this when they attempt to broaden their audience — that the refusal of maternity cannot be a mass policy and that the majority of women today see the possibility for fulfillment, if not entirely at least to a large degree, in bringing a child into the world. What does this desire for motherhood correspond to? This is one of the new questions for the new generation, a question the preceding generation had foreclosed. For want of an answer to this question, feminist ideology leaves the door open to the return of religion, whose discourse, tried and proved over thousands of years, provides the necessary ingredients for satisfying the anguish, the suffering, and the hopes of mothers. If Freud's affirmation — that the desire for a child is the desire for a penis and, in this sense, a substitute for phallic and symbolic dominion — can be only partially accepted, what modern women have to say about this experience should nonetheless be listened to attentively. Pregnancy seems to be experienced as the radical ordeal of the splitting of the subject:[37] redoubling up of the body,

[37]The "split subject" (from *Spaltung* as both "splitting" and "cleavage"), as used in Freudian psychoanalysis, here refers directly to Kristeva's "subject in process / in question / on trial" as opposed to the unity of the transcendental ego (see n. 14 in "Introduction"). [Tr.]

separation and coexistence of the self and of an other, of nature and consciousness, of physiology and speech. This fundamental challenge to identity is then accompanied by a fantasy of totality — narcissistic completeness — a sort of instituted, socialized, natural psychosis. The arrival of the child, on the other hand, leads the mother into the labyrinths of an experience that, without the child, she would only rarely encounter: love for an other. Not for herself, nor for an identical being, and still less for another person with whom ''I'' fuse (love or sexual passion). But the slow, difficult, and delightful apprenticeship in attentiveness, gentleness, forgetting oneself. The ability to succeed in this path without masochism and without annihilating one's affective, intellectual, and professional personality — such would seem to be the stakes to be won through guiltless maternity. It then becomes a creation in the strong sense of the term. For this moment, utopian?

On the other hand, it is in the aspiration toward artistic and, in particular, literary creation that woman's desire for affirmation now manifests itself. Why literature?

Is it because, faced with social norms, literature reveals a certain knowledge and sometimes the truth itself about an otherwise repressed, nocturnal, secret, and unconscious universe? Because it thus redoubles the social contract by exposing the unsaid, the uncanny? And because it makes a game, a space of fantasy and pleasure, out of the abstract and frustrating order of social signs, the words of everyday communication? Flaubert said, ''Madame Bovary, c'est moi.'' Today many women imagine, ''Flaubert, c'est moi.'' This identification with the potency of the imaginary is not only an identification, an imaginary potency (a fetish, a belief in the maternal penis maintained at all costs), as a far too normative view of the social and symbolic relationship would have it. This identification also bears witness to women's desire to lift the weight of what is sacrificial in the social contract from their shoulders, to nourish our societies with a more flexible and free discourse, one able to name what has thus far never been an object of circulation in the community: the enigmas of the body, the dreams, secret joys, shames, hatreds of the second sex.

It is understandable from this that women's writing has lately attracted the maximum attention of both ''specialists'' and the media.[38] The pitfalls encountered along the way, however, are not to be minimized: For example, does one not read there a relentless belittling of male writers whose books, nevertheless, often serve as ''models'' for countless productions by women? Thanks to the feminist label, does one not sell numerous works whose naive whining or market-place romanticism would otherwise have been rejected as anachronistic? And does one not find the pen of many a female writer being devoted to phantasmic attacks against Language and Sign as the ultimate supports of phallocratic power, in the name of a semi-aphonic corporality whose truth can only be found in that which is ''gestural'' or ''tonal''? And yet, no matter how dubious the results of these recent productions by women, the symptom is there — women are writing, and the air is heavy with expectation: What will they write that is new?

IN THE NAME OF THE FATHER, THE SON . . . AND THE WOMAN?

These few elements of the manifestations by the new generation of women in Europe seem to me to demonstrate that, beyond the sociopolitical level where it is generally inscribed (or inscribes itself), the women's movement — in its present stage, less aggressive but more artful — is situated within the very framework of the religious crisis of our civilization. I call ''religion'' this phantasmic necessity on the part of speaking beings to provide themselves with a representation (animal, female, male, parental, etc.) in place of what constitutes them as such, in other words, symbolization — the double articulation and syntactic sequence of language, as well as its preconditions or substitutes (thoughts, affects, etc.). The elements of the current practice of feminism that we have just brought to light seem precisely to constitute such a representation which makes up for the frustrations imposed on

[38]Again a reference to *écriture féminine* as generically labeled in France over the past few years and not to women's writing in general. [Tr.]

women by the anterior code (Christianity or its lay humanist variant). The fact that this new ideology has affinities, often revindicated by its creators, with so-called matriarchal beliefs (in other words, those beliefs characterizing matrilinear societies) should not overshadow its radical novelty. This ideology seems to me to be part of the broader antisacrificial current which is animating our culture and which, in its protest against the constraints of the sociosymbolic contract, is no less exposed to the risks of violence and terrorism. At this level of radicalism, it is the very principle of sociality which is challenged.

Certain contemporary thinkers consider, as is well known, that modernity is characterized as the first epoch in human history in which human beings attempt to live without religion. In its present form, is not feminism in the process of becoming one?

Or is it, on the contrary and as avant-grade feminists hope, that having started with the idea of difference, feminism will be able to break free of its belief in Woman, Her power, Her writing, so as to channel this demand for difference into each and every element of the female whole, and, finally, to bring out the singularity of each woman, and beyond this, her multiplicities, her plural languages, beyond the horizon, beyond sight, beyond faith itself?

A factor for ultimate mobilization? Or a factor for analysis?

Imaginary support in a technocratic era where all narcissism is frustrated? Or instruments fitted to these times in which the cosmos, atoms, and cells — our true contemporaries — call for the constitution of a fluid and free subjectivity?

The question has been posed. Is to pose it already to answer it?

ANOTHER GENERATION IS ANOTHER SPACE

If the preceding can be *said* — the question whether all this is *true* belongs to a different register — it is undoubtedly because it is now possible to gain some distance on these two preceding generations of women. This implies, of course, that a *third* generation is now forming, at least in Europe. I am not speaking of a new group of young women (though its importance should not be underestimated) or of another "mass feminist movement" taking the torch passed on from the second generation. My usage of the word "generation" implies less a chronology than a *signifying space*, a both corporeal and desiring mental space. So it can be argued that as of now a third attitude is possible, thus a third generation, which does not exclude — quite to the contrary — the *parallel* existence of all three in the same historical time, or even that they be interwoven one with the other.

In this third attitude, which I strongly advocate — which I imagine? — the very dichotomy man/woman as an opposition between two rival entities may be understood as belonging to *metaphysics*.[39] what can "identity," even "sexual identity," mean in a new theoretical and scientific space where the very notion of identity is challenged?[40] I am not simply suggesting a very hypothetical bisexuality which, even if it existed, would only, in fact, be the aspiration toward the totality of one of the sexes and thus an effacing of difference. What I mean is, first of all, the demassification of the problematic of *difference*, which would imply, in a first phase, an apparent de-dramatization of the "fight to the death" between rival groups and thus between the sexes. And this not in the name of some reconciliation — feminism has at least had the merit of showing what is irreducible and even deadly in the social contract — but in order that the struggle, the implacable difference, the violence be conceived in the very place where it operates with the maximum intransigence, in other words, in personal and sexual identity itself, so as to make it disintegrate in its very nucleus.

It necessarily follows that this involves risks not only for what we understand today as "personal equilibrium" but also for social equilibrium itself, made up as it now is of the counterbalancing of aggressive and murderous forces massed in social, national, religious, and political groups.

[39]By this point in theoretical discourse, to say that a distinction belongs to metaphysics is implicitly to deconstruct it; see Derrida, p. 533.
[40]See Seminar on *Identity* directed by Lévi-Strauss (Paris: Grasset & Fasquelle, 1977). [Kristeva]

But is it not the insupportable situation of tension and explosive risk that the existing "equilibrium" presupposes which leads some of those who suffer from it to divest it of its economy, to detach themselves from it, and to seek another means of regulating difference?

To restrict myself here to a personal level, as related to the question of women, I see arising, under the cover of a relative indifference toward the militance of the first and second generations, an attitude of retreat from sexism (male as well as female) and, gradually, from any kind of anthropomorphism. The fact that this might quickly become another form of spiritualism turning its back on social problems, or else a form of repression[41] ready to support all status quos, should not hide the radicalness of the process. This process could be summarized as an *interiorization of the founding separation of the sociosymbolic contract*, as an introduction of its cutting edge into the very interior of every identity whether subjective, sexual, ideological, or so forth. This in such a way that the habitual and increasingly explicit attempt to fabricate a scapegoat victim as foundress of a society or a countersociety may be replaced by the analysis of the potentialities of *victim/executioner* which characterize each identity, each subject, each sex.

What discourse, if not that of a religion, would be able to support this adventure which surfaces as a real possibility, after both the achievements and the impasses of the present ideological reworkings, in which feminism has participated? It seems to me that the role of what is usually called "aesthetic practices" must increase not only to counterbalance the storage and uniformity of information by present-day mass media, data-bank systems, and,

in particular, modern communications technology, but also to demystify the identity of the symbolic bond itself, to demystify, therefore, the *community* of language as a universal and unifying tool, one which totalizes and equalizes. In order to bring out — along with the *singularity* of each person and, even more, along with the multiplicity of every person's possible identifications (with atoms, e.g., stretching from the family to the stars) — the *relativity of his/her symbolic as well as biological existence*, according to the variation in his/her specific symbolic capacities. And in order to emphasize the *responsibility* which all will immediately face of putting this fluidity into play against the threats of death which are unavoidable whenever an inside and an outside, a self and an other, one group and another, are constituted. At this level of interiorization with its social as well as individual stakes, what I have called "aesthetic practices" are undoubtedly nothing other than the modern reply to the eternal question of morality. At least, this is how we might understand an ethics which, conscious of the fact that its order is sacrificial, reserves part of the burden for each of its adherents, therefore declaring them guilty while immediately affording them the possibility for *jouissance*, for various productions, for a life made up of both challenges and differences.

Spinoza's question can be taken up again here: Are women subject to ethics? If not to that ethics defined by classical philosophy — in relationship to which the ups and downs of feminist generations seem dangerously precarious — are women not already participating in the rapid dismantling that our age is experiencing at various levels (from wars to drugs to artificial insemination) and which poses the *demand* for a new ethics? The answer to Spinoza's question can be affirmative only at the cost of considering feminism as but a *moment* in the thought of that anthropomorphic identity which currently blocks the horizon of the discursive and scientific adventure of our species.

[41]Repression (*le refoulement* or *Verdrängung*) as distinguished from the foreclosure (*la forclusion* or *Verwerfung*) evoked earlier in the article (see LaPlanche and Pontalis). [Tr.]

Barbara Smith

b. 1946

Since the 1970s, Barbara Smith has been a writer, a teacher, and a black feminist leader. Born in Cleveland, Smith was educated at Mount Holyoke College and at the University of Pittsburgh. She has taught English and women's studies at the University of Massachusetts, Barnard College, and New York University, and has been a visiting professor at the University of Minnesota and at Hobart and William Smith colleges. In 1974, she was co-founder of the Combahee River Collective, a black feminist group in Boston, which she helped direct until 1980. In 1982 she co-edited All the Women Are White, All the Blacks Are Men, but Some of Us Are Brave, *the title of which reflects Smith's feeling that black women have frequently been excluded from both feminist and African American studies. In 1983 Smith edited* Home Girls, *a black feminist anthology highlighting the relationships between race, gender, sexual orientation, and class that became a major influence on the current renaissance of African American women writers. Her latest book is* The Truth That Never Hurts: Writings on Race, Gender, and Freedom *(1998). A short story writer as well as a feminist theorist, Smith has been artist-in-residence at the Hambridge Center for the Arts, the Millay Colony, Yaddo, and the Blue Mountain Center. As a result of her many activities, Smith was presented with the Outstanding Woman of Color award for 1982 and the Women Educator's Curriculum Award for 1983. The recently published* Ain't Gonna Let Nobody Turn Me Around: Forty Years of Activism with Barbara Smith *(2014), edited by Alethia Jones and Virginia Eubanks in collaboration with Smith, brings together interviews with Smith conducted by fellow activists. The following piece was published as a pamphlet in 1977, and reprinted in* Some of Us Are Brave.

Toward a Black Feminist Criticism

For all my sisters, especially Beverly and Demita

I do not know where to begin. Long before I tried to write this I realized that I was attempting something unprecedented, something dangerous merely by writing about Black women writers from a feminist perspective and about Black lesbian writers from any perspective at all. These things have not been done. Not by white male critics, expectedly. Not by Black male critics. Not by white women critics who think of themselves as feminists. And most crucially not by Black women critics who, although they pay the most attention to Black women writers as a group, seldom use a consistent feminist analysis or write about Black lesbian literature. All segments of the literary world — whether establishment, progressive, Black, female, or lesbian — do not know, or at least act as if they do not know, that Black women writers and Black lesbian writers exist.

For whites, this specialized lack of knowledge is inextricably connected to their not knowing in any concrete or politically transforming way that Black women of any description dwell in this place. Black women's existence, experience, and culture and the brutally complex systems of oppression which shape these are in the "real world" of white and/or male consciousness beneath consideration, invisible, unknown.

This invisibility, which goes beyond anything that either Black men or white women experience and tell about in their writing, is one reason it is so difficult for me to know where to start. It seems overwhelming to break such a massive silence. Even more numbing, however, is the realization that so many of the women who will read this have not yet noticed us missing either from their reading matter, their politics, or their lives. It is galling that ostensible feminists and acknowledged lesbians have been so blinded to the implications of any womanhood that is not white womanhood and that they have yet to struggle with the deep racism in themselves that is at the source of this blindness.

I think of the thousands and thousands of books, magazines, and articles which have been devoted, by this time, to the subject of women's writing and I am filled with rage at the fraction of those pages that mention Black and other Third World women. I finally do not know how to begin because in 1977 I want to be writing this for a Black feminist publication, for Black women who know and love these writers as I do and who, if they do not yet know their names, have at least profoundly felt the pain of their absence.

The conditions that coalesce into the impossibilities of this essay have as much to do with politics as with the practice of literature. Any discussion of Afro-American writers can rightfully begin with the fact that for most of the time we have been in this country we have been categorically denied not only literacy, but the most minimal possibility of a decent human life. In her landmark essay, "In Search of Our Mothers' Gardens," Alice Walker discloses how the political, economic, and social restrictions of slavery and racism have historically stunted the creative lives of Black women.[1]

At the present time I feel that the politics of feminism have a direct relationship to the state of Black women's literature. A viable, autonomous Black feminist movement in this country would open up the space needed for the exploration of Black women's lives and the creation of consciously Black woman-identified art. At the same time a redefinition of the goals and strategies of the white feminist movement would lead to much needed change in the focus and content of what is now generally accepted as women's culture.

I want to make in this essay some connections between the politics of Black women's lives, what we write about, and our situation as artists. In order to do this I will look at how Black women have been viewed critically by outsiders, demonstrate the necessity for Black feminist criticism, and try to understand what the existence or nonexistence of Black lesbian writing reveals about the state of Black women's culture and the intensity of all Black women's oppression.

The role that criticism plays in making a body of literature recognizable and real hardly needs to be explained here. The necessity for nonhostile and perceptive analysis of works written by persons outside the "mainstream" of white/male cultural rule has been proven by the Black cultural resurgence of the 1960s and '70s and by the even more recent growth of feminist literary scholarship. For books to be read and remembered they have to be talked about. For books to be understood they must be examined in such a way that the basic intentions of the writers are at least considered. Because of racism Black literature has usually been viewed as a discrete subcategory of American literature and there have been Black critics of Black literature who did much to keep it alive long before it caught the attention of whites. Before the advent of specifically feminist criticism in this decade, books by white women, on the other hand, were not clearly perceived as the cultural manifestation of an oppressed people. It took the surfacing of the second wave of the North American feminist movement to expose the fact that these works contain a stunningly accurate record of the impact of patriarchal values and practice upon the lives of women and more significantly that literature by women provides essential insights into female experience.

In speaking about the current situation of Black women writers, it is important to remember that the existence of a feminist movement was an essential precondition to the growth of feminist literature, criticism, and women's studies, which focused at the beginning almost entirely upon investigations of literature. The fact that a parallel Black feminist movement has been much slower in evolving cannot help but have impact upon the situation of Black women writers and

[1]Alice Walker, "In Search of Our Mothers' Gardens," in *Ms.* (May 1974) and in *Southern Exposure* 4: 4, *Generations: Women in the South* (Winter 1977): 60–64. [Smith]

explains in part why during this very same period we have been so ignored.

There is no political movement to give power or support to those who want to examine Black women's experience through studying our history, literature, and culture. There is no political presence that demands a minimal level of consciousness and respect from those who write or talk about our lives. Finally, there is not a developed body of Black feminist political theory whose assumptions could be used in the study of Black women's art. When Black women's books are dealt with at all, it is usually in the context of Black literature which largely ignores the implications of sexual politics. When white women look at Black women's works they are of course ill-equipped to deal with the subtleties of racial politics. A Black feminist approach to literature that embodies the realization that the politics of sex as well as the politics of race and class are crucially interlocking factors in the works of Black women writers is an absolute necessity. Until a Black feminist criticism exists we will not even know what these writers mean. The citations from a variety of critics which follow prove that without a Black feminist critical perspective not only are books by Black women misunderstood, they are destroyed in the process.

Jerry H. Bryant, the *Nation's* white male reviewer of Alice Walker's *In Love & Trouble: Stories of Black Women,* wrote in 1973:

> The subtitle of the collection, "Stories of Black Women," is probably an attempt by the publisher to exploit not only black subjects but feminine ones. There is nothing feminist but these stories, however.[2]

Blackness and feminism are to his mind mutually exclusive and peripheral to the act of writing fiction. Bryant of course does not consider that Walker might have titled the work herself, nor did he apparently read the book which unequivocally reveals the author's feminist consciousness.

In *The Negro Novel in America,* a book that Black critics recognize as one of the worst examples of white racist pseudoscholarship, Robert Bone cavalierly dismisses Ann Petry's classic,

The Street. He perceives it to be ". . . a superficial social analysis" of how slums victimize their Black inhabitants.[3] He further objects that:

> It is an attempt to interpret slum life in terms of *Negro* experience, when a larger frame of reference is required. As Alain Locke has observed, "*Knock on Any Door* is superior to *The Street* because it designates class and environment, rather than mere race and environment, as its antagonist."[4]

Neither Robert Bone nor Alain Locke, the Black male critic he cites, can recognize that *The Street* is one of the best delineations in literature of how sex, race, *and* class interact to oppress Black women.

In her review of Toni Morrison's *Sula* for *The New York Times Book Review* in 1973, putative feminist Sara Blackburn makes similarly racist comments. She writes:

> . . . Toni Morrison is far too talented to remain only a marvelous recorder of the black side of provincial American life. If she is to maintain the large and serious audience she deserves, she is going to have to address a riskier contemporary reality than this beautiful but nevertheless distanced novel. *And if she does this, it seems to me that she might easily transcend that early and unintentionally limiting classification "black woman writer" and take her place among the most serious, important and talented American novelists now working.*[5] [Italics mine.]

Recognizing Morrison's exquisite gift, Blackburn unashamedly asserts that Morrison is "too talented" to deal with mere Black folk, particularly those double nonentities, Black women. In order to be accepted as "serious," "important," "talented," and "American," she must obviously focus her efforts upon chronicling the doings of white men.

The mishandling of Black women writers by whites is paralleled more often by their not being handled at all, particularly in feminist criticism. Although Elaine Showalter in her review essay on literary criticism for *Signs* states that: "The best work being produced today [in feminist criticism]

[2]Jerry H. Bryant, "The Outskirts of a New City," in the *Nation* 12 (November 1973): 502. [Smith]

[3]Robert Bone, *The Negro Novel in America* (New Haven: Yale University Press, 1958), p. 180. [Smith]
[4]Idem. (*Knock on Any Door* is a novel by Black writer Willard Motley.) [Smith]
[5]Sara Blackburn, "You Still Can't Go Home Again," in *The New York Times Book Review,* 30 December 1973, p. 3. [Smith]

is exacting and cosmopolitan," her essay is neither.[6] If it were, she would not have failed to
mention a single Black or Third World woman
writer, whether "major" or "minor," to cite
her questionable categories. That she also does
not even hint that lesbian writers of any color
exist renders her purported overview virtually
meaningless. Showalter obviously thinks that the
identities of being Black and female are mutually
exclusive, as this statement illustrates:

Furthermore, there are other literary subcultures
(black American novelists, for example) whose
history offers a precedent for feminist scholarship
to use.[7]

The idea of critics like Showalter using Black
literature is chilling, a case of barely disguised
cultural imperialism. The final insult is that she
footnotes the preceding remark by pointing readers to works on Black literature by white males
Robert Bone and Roger Rosenblatt!

Two recent works by white women, Ellen
Moers's Literary Women: The Great Writers and
Patricia Meyer Spacks's The Female Imagination,
evidence the same racist flaw.[8] Moers includes
the names of four Black and one Puertorriqueña
writer in her seventy pages of bibliographical
notes and does not deal at all with Third World
women in the body of her book. Spacks refers to
a comparison between Negroes (sic) and women
in Mary Ellmann's Thinking About Women under
the index entry, "blacks, women and." "Black
Boy (Wright)" is the preceding entry. Nothing
follows. Again there is absolutely no recognition that Black and female identity ever coexist,
specifically in a group of Black women writers.
Perhaps one can assume that these women do not
know who Black women writers are, that they
have little opportunity like most Americans to
learn about them. Perhaps their ignorance seems
suspiciously selective, however, particularly in
the light of the dozens of truly obscure white
women writers they are able to unearth. Spacks
was herself employed at Wellesley College at the
same time that Alice Walker was there teaching
one of the first courses on Black women writers
in the country.

I am not trying to encourage racist criticism of
Black women writers like that of Sara Blackburn,
to cite only one example. As a beginning I would
at least like to see in print white women's acknowledgment of the contradictions of who and what are
being left out of their research and writing.[9]

Black male critics can also act as if they do not
know that Black women writers exist and are, of
course, hampered by an inability to comprehend
Black women's experience in sexual as well as
racial terms. Unfortunately there are also those
who are as virulently sexist in their treatment of
Black women writers as their white male counterparts. Darwin Turner's discussion of Zora Neale
Hurston in his In a Minor Chord: Three Afro-
American Writers and Their Search for Identity is
a frightening example of the near assassination of
a great Black woman writer.[10] His descriptions of
her and her work as "artful," "coy," "irrational,"
"superficial," and "shallow" bear no relationship
to the actual quality of her achievements. Turner
is completely insensitive to the sexual political
dynamics of Hurston's life and writing.

In a recent interview the notoriously misogynist writer, Ishmael Reed, comments in this way
upon the low sales of his newest novel:

. . . but the book only sold 8000 copies. I don't
mind giving out the figure: 8000. Maybe if I was
one of those young female Afro-American writers that are so hot now, I'd sell more. You know,
fill my books with ghetto women who can do no
wrong. . . . But come on, I think I could have sold
8000 copies by myself.[11]

[6]Elaine Showalter, "Review Essay: Literary Criticism,"
Signs 2 (Winter 1975): 460. [Smith]

[7]Ibid., p. 445. [Smith].

[8]Ellen Moers, Literary Women: The Great Writers
(Garden City, N.Y.: Anchor Books, 1977); Patricia Meyer
Spacks, The Female Imagination (New York: Avon Books,
1976). [Smith].

[9]An article by Nancy Hoffman, "White Women, Black
Women: Inventing an Adequate Pedagogy," in the Women's
Studies Newsletter 5: 1 & 2 (Spring 1977): 21–24, gives valuable insights into how white women can approach the writing
of Black women. [Smith]

[10]Darwin T. Turner, In a Minor Chord: Three Afro-
American Writers and Their Search for Identity (Carbondale
and Edwardsville: Southern Illinois University Press, 1971).
[Smith].

[11]John Domini, "Roots and Racism: An Interview with
Ishmael Reed," in The Boston Phoenix, 5 April 1977, p. 20.
[Smith].

The politics of the situation of Black women are glaringly illuminated by this statement. Neither Reed nor his white male interviewer has the slightest compunction about attacking Black women in print. They need not fear widespread public denunciation since Reed's statement is in perfect agreement with the values of a society that hates Black people, women, and Black women. Finally the two of them feel free to base their actions on the premise that Black women are powerless to alter either their political or cultural oppression.

In her introduction to "A Bibliography of Works Written by American Black Women" Ora Williams quotes some of the reactions of her colleagues toward her efforts to do research on Black women. She writes:

> Others have reacted negatively with such statements as, "I really don't think you are going to find very much written," "Have 'they' written anything that is any good?" and, "I wouldn't go overboard with this woman's lib thing." When discussions touched on the possibility of teaching a course in which emphasis would be on the literature by Black women, one response was, "Ha, ha. That will certainly be the most nothing course ever offered!"[12]

A remark by Alice Walker capsulizes what all the preceding examples indicate about the position of Black women writers and the reasons for the damaging criticism about them. She responds to her interviewer's question, "Why do you think that the black woman writer has been so ignored in America? Does she have even more difficulty than the black male writer, who perhaps has just begun to gain recognition?" Walker replies:

> There are two reasons why the black woman writer is not taken as seriously as the black male writer. One is that she's a woman. Critics seem unusually ill-equipped to intelligently discuss and analyze the works of black women. Generally, they do not even make the attempt; they prefer, rather, to talk about the lives of black women writers, not about

what they write. And, since black women writers are not — it would seem — very likable — until recently they were the least willing worshippers of male supremacy — comments about them tend to be cruel.[13]

A convincing case for Black feminist criticism can obviously be built solely upon the basis of the negativity of what already exists. It is far more gratifying, however, to demonstrate its necessity by showing how it can serve to reveal for the first time the profound subtleties of this particular body of literature.

Before suggesting how a Black feminist approach might be used to examine a specific work I will outline some of the principles that I think a Black feminist critic could use. Beginning with a primary commitment to exploring how both sexual and racial politics and Black and female identity are inextricable elements in Black women's writings, she would also work from the assumption that Black women writers constitute an identifiable literary tradition. The breadth of her familiarity with these writers would have shown her that not only is theirs a verifiable historical tradition that parallels in time the tradition of Black men and white women writing in this country, but that thematically, stylistically, aesthetically, and conceptually Black women writers manifest common approaches to the act of creating literature as a direct result of the specific political, social, and economic experience they have been obliged to share. The way, for example, that Zora Neale Hurston, Margaret Walker, Toni Morrison, and Alice Walker incorporate the traditional Black female activities of rootworking, herbal medicine, conjure, and midwifery into the fabric of their stories is not mere coincidence, nor is their use of specifically Black female language to express their own and their characters' thoughts accidental. The use of Black women's language and cultural experience in books *by* Black women *about* Black women results in a miraculously rich coalescing of form and content and also takes their writing far beyond the confines of white/male literary structures. The Black

---

[12]Ora Williams, "A Bibliography of Works Written by American Black Women," in *College Language Association Journal* 15:3 (March 1972): 355. There is an expanded book-length version of this bibliography: *American Black Women in the Arts and Social Sciences: A Bibliographic Survey* (Metuchen, N.J.: The Scarecrow Press, 1973; rev. and expanded ed., 1978). [Smith]

[13]John O'Brien, ed., *Interviews with Black Writers* (New York: Liveright, 1973), p. 201. [Smith]

Feminist critic would find innumerable common-alities in works by Black women.

Another principle which grows out of the con-cept of a tradition and which would also help to strengthen this tradition would be for the critic to look first for precedents and insights in interpre-tation within the works of other Black women. In other words she would think and write out of her own identity and not try to graft the ideas or methodology of white/male literary thought upon the precious materials of Black women's art. Black feminist criticism would by definition be highly innovative, embodying the daring spirit of the works themselves. The Black feminist critic would be constantly aware of the political implica-tions of her work and would assert the connections between it and the political situation of all Black women. Logically developed, Black feminist criti-cism would owe its existence to a Black feminist movement while at the same time contributing ideas that women in the movement could use.

Black feminist criticism applied to a particular work can overturn previous assumptions about it and expose for the first time its actual dimensions. At the "Lesbians and Literature" discussion at the 1976 Modern Language Association convention Bertha Harris suggested that if in a woman writer's work a sentence refuses to do what it is supposed to do, if there are strong images of women and if there is a refusal to be linear, the result is innately lesbian literature. As usual, I wanted to see if these ideas might be applied to the Black women writers that I know and quickly realized that many of their works were, in Harris's sense, lesbian. Not because women are "lovers," but because they are the central figures, are positively portrayed and have pivotal relationships with one another. The form and language of these works are also nothing like what white patriarchal culture requires or expects. I was particularly struck by the way in which Toni Morrison's novels *The Bluest Eye* and *Sula* could be explored from this new perspective.[14] In both works the relationships between girls and women are essential, yet at the same time physi-cal sexuality is overtly expressed only between

men and women. Despite the apparent hetero-sexuality of the female characters I discovered in re-reading *Sula* that it works as a lesbian novel not only because of the passionate friendship between Sula and Nel, but because of Morrison's consistently critical stance toward the hetero-sexual institutions of male/female relationships, marriage, and the family. Consciously or not, Morrison's work poses both lesbian and feminist questions about Black women's autonomy and their impact upon each other's lives.

Sula and Nel find each other in 1922 when each of them is twelve, on the brink of puberty and the discovery of boys. Even as awakening sexuality "clotted their dreams," each girl desires "a someone," obviously female with whom to share her feelings. Morrison writes:

. . . for it was in dreams that the two girls had met. Long before Edna Finch's Mellow House met, even before they marched through the chocolate halls of Garfield Primary School . . . they had already made each other's acquaintance in the delirium of their noon dreams. They were solitary little girls whose loneliness was so profound it intoxicated them and sent them stumbling into Technicolored visions that always included a pres-ence, a someone who, quite like the dreamer, shared the delight of the dream. When Nel, an only child, sat on the steps of her back porch surrounded by the high silence of her mother's incredibly orderly house, feeling the neatness pointing at her back, she studied the poplars and fell easily into a picture of herself lying on a flower bed, tangled in her own hair, waiting for some fiery prince. He approached but never quite arrived. But always, watching the dream along with her, were some smiling sympa-thetic eyes. Someone as interested as she herself in the flow of her imagined hair, the thickness of the mattress of flowers, the voile sleeves that closed below her elbows in gold-threaded cuffs.

Similarly, Sula, also an only child, but wedged into a household of throbbing disorder constantly awry with things, people, voices and the slamming of doors, spent hours in the attic behind a roll of linoleum galloping through her own mind on a gray-and-white horse tasting sugar and smelling roses in full view of someone who shared both the taste and the speed.

So when they met, first in those chocolate halls and next through the ropes of the swing, they felt the ease and comfort of old friends. Because each

[14]Toni Morrison, *The Bluest Eye* (New York: Pocket Books, 1972, orig. 1970) and *Sula* (New York: Alfred A. Knopf, 1974). All subsequent references to this work will be designated in the text. [Smith]

had discovered years before that they were neither white nor male, and that all freedom and triumph was forbidden to them, they had set about creating something else to be. Their meeting was fortunate, for it let them use each other to grow on. Daughters of distant mothers and incomprehensible fathers (Sula's because he was dead; Nel's because he wasn't), they found in each other's eyes the intimacy they were looking for. (51–52)

As this beautiful passage shows, their relationship, from the very beginning, is suffused with an erotic romanticism. The dreams in which they are initially drawn to each other are actually complementary aspects of the same sensuous fairytale. Nel imagines a "fiery prince" who never quite arrives while Sula gallops like a prince "on a gray-and-white horse."[15] The "real world" of patriarchy requires, however, that they channel this energy away from each other to the opposite sex. Lorraine Bethel explains this dynamic in her essay "Conversations With Ourselves: Black Female Relationships in Toni Cade Bambara's *Gorilla, My Love* and Toni Morrison's *Sula*." She writes:

> I am not suggesting that Sula and Nel are being consciously sexual, or that their relationship has an overt lesbian nature. I am suggesting, however, that there is a certain sensuality in their interactions that is reinforced by the mirror-like nature of their relationship. Sexual exploration and coming of age is a natural part of adolescence. Sula and Nel discover men together, and though their flirtations with males are an important part of their sexual exploration, the sensuality that they experience in each other's company is equally important.[16]

Sula and Nel must also struggle with the constrictions of racism upon their lives. The knowledge that "they were neither white nor male" is the inherent explanation of their need for each other. Morrison depicts in literature the necessary bonding that has always taken place between Black women for the sake of barest survival. Together

the two girls can find the courage to create themselves.

Their relationship is severed only when Nel marries Jude, an unexceptional young man who thinks of her as "the hem — the tuck and fold that hid his raveling edges" (83). Sula's inventive wildness cannot overcome social pressure or the influence of Nel's parents who "had succeeded in rubbing down to a dull glow any sparkle or splutter she had" (83). Nel falls prey to convention while Sula escapes it. Yet at the wedding which ends the first phase of their relationship, Nel's final action is to look past her husband toward Sula:

> . . . a slim figure in blue, gliding, with just a hint of a strut, down the path towards the road. . . . Even from the rear Nel could tell that it was Sula and that she was smiling; that something deep down in that litheness was amused. (85)

When Sula returns ten years later, her rebelliousness full-blown, a major source of the town's suspicions stems from the fact that although she is almost thirty, she is still unmarried. Sula's grandmother, Eva, does not hesitate to bring up the matter as soon as she arrives. She asks:

> "When you gone to get married? You need to have some babies. It'll settle you. . . . Ain't no woman got no business floatin' around without no man." (92)

Sula replies: "I don't want to make somebody else. I want to make myself" (92). Self-definition is a dangerous activity for any woman to engage in, especially a Black one, and it expectedly earns Sula pariah status in Medallion.

Morrison clearly points out that it is the fact that Sula has not been tamed or broken by the exigencies of heterosexual family life which most galls the others. She writes:

> Among the weighty evidence piling up was the fact that Sula did not look her age. She was near thirty and, unlike them, had lost no teeth, suffered no bruises, developed no ring of fat at the waist or pocket at the back of her neck. (115)

In other words she is not a domestic serf, a woman run down by obligatory childbearing or a victim of battering. Sula also sleeps with the husbands of the town once and then discards them,

---

[15]My sister, Beverly Smith, pointed out this connection to me. [Smith]

[16]Lorraine Bethel, "Conversations With Ourselves: Black Female Relationships in Toni Cade Bambara's *Gorilla, My Love* and Toni Morrison's *Sula*," unpublished paper written at Yale, 1976, 47 pp. (Bethel has worked from a premise similar to mine in a much more developed treatment of the novel.) [Smith]

needing them even less than her own mother did, for sexual gratification and affection. The town reacts to her disavowal of patriarchal values by becoming fanatically serious about their own family obligations, as if in this way they might counteract Sula's radical criticism of their lives. Sula's presence in her community functions much like the presence of lesbians everywhere to expose the contradictions of supposedly "normal" life. The opening paragraph of the essay "Woman Identified Woman" has amazing relevance as an explanation of Sula's position and character in the novel. It asks:

What is a lesbian? A lesbian is the rage of all women condensed to the point of explosion. She is the woman who, often beginning at an extremely early age, acts in accordance with her inner compulsion to be a more complete and freer human being than her society — perhaps then, but cer- tainly later — cares to allow her. These needs and actions, over a period of years, bring her into pain- ful conflict with people, situations, the accepted ways of thinking, feeling and behaving, until she is in a state of continual war with everything around her, and usually with herself. She may not be fully conscious of the political implications of what for her began as personal necessity, but on some level she has not been able to accept the limitations and oppression laid on her by the most basic role of her society — the female role.[17]

The limitations of the Black female role are even greater in a racist and sexist society as is the amount of courage it takes to challenge them. It is no wonder that the townspeople see Sula's independence as imminently dangerous.

Morrison is also careful to show the reader that despite their years of separation and their oppos- ing paths, Nel and Sula's relationship retains its primacy for each of them. Nell feels transformed when Sula returns and thinks:

It was like getting the use of an eye back, having a cataract removed. Her old friend had come home. Sula. Who made her laugh, who made her see old things with new eyes, in whose presence she felt clever, gentle and a little raunchy. (95)

[17]New York Radicalesbians, "Woman Identified Woman," in Lesbians Speak Out (Oakland: Women's Press Collective, 1974), p. 87. [Smith]

Laughing together in the familiar "rib-scraping" way, Nel feels "new, soft and new" (98). Morrison uses here the visual imagery which symbolizes the women's closeness throughout the novel.

Sula fractures this closeness, however, by sleeping with Nel's husband, an act of little import according to her system of values. Nel, of course, cannot understand. Sula thinks ruefully:

Nel was the one person who had wanted nothing from her, who had accepted all aspects of her. Now she wanted everything, and all because of that. Nel was the first person who had been real to her, whose name she knew, who had seen as she had the slant of life that made it possible to stretch it to its limits. Now Nel was one of them. (119–20)

Sula also thinks at the realization of losing Nel about how unsatisfactory her relationships with men have been and admits:

She had been looking all along for a friend, and it took her a while to discover that a lover was not a comrade and could never be — for a woman. (121)

The nearest that Sula comes to actually loving a man is in a brief affair with Ajax and what she values most about him is the intellectual compan- ionship he provides, the brilliance he "allows" her to show.

Sula's feelings about sex with men are also consistent with a lesbian interpretation of the novel, Morrison writes:

She went to bed with men as frequently as she could. It was the only place where she could find what she was looking for: *misery and the ability to feel deep sorrow.* . . . During the lovemaking she found and needed to find the cutting edge. When she left off cooperating with her body and began to assert herself in the act, particles of strength gathered in her like steel shavings drawn to a spa- cious magnetic center, forming a tight cluster that nothing, it seemed, could break. *And there was utmost irony and outrage in lying under someone, in a position of surrender, feeling her own abiding strength and limitless power.* . . . When her partner disengaged himself, she looked up at him in wonder trying to recall his name . . . waiting impatiently for him to turn away . . . *leaving her to the postco- ital privateness in which she met herself, welcomed herself, and joined herself in matchless harmony.* (122–23) [Italics mine.]

Sula uses men for sex which results not in communion with them, but in her further delving into self.

Ultimately the deepest communion and communication in the novel occurs between two women who love each other. After their last painful meeting, which does not bring reconciliation, Sula thinks as Nel leaves her:

> "So she will walk on down that road, her back so straight in that old green coat ... thinking how much I have cost her and never remember the days when we were two throats and one eye and we had no price." (147)

It is difficult to imagine a more evocative metaphor for what women can be to each other, the "pricelessness" they achieve in refusing to sell themselves for male approval, the total worth that they can only find in each other's eyes.

Decades later the novel concludes with Nel's final comprehension of the source of the grief that has plagued her from the time her husband walked out. Morrison writes:

> "All that time, all that time, I thought I was missing Jude." And the loss pressed down on her chest and came up into her throat. "We was girls together," she said as though explaining something. "O Lord, Sula," she cried, "girl, girl, girlgirlgirl."
>
> It was a fine cry — loud and long — but it had no bottom and it had no top, just circles and circles of sorrow. (174)

Again Morrison exquisitely conveys what women, Black women, mean to each other. This final passage verifies the depth of Sula and Nel's relationship and its centrality to an accurate interpretation of the work.

Sula is an exceedingly lesbian novel in the emotions expressed, in the definition of female character, and in the way that the politics of heterosexuality are portrayed. The very meaning of lesbianism is being expanded in literature, just as it is being redefined through politics. The confusion that many readers have felt about *Sula* may well have a lesbian explanation. If one sees Sula's inexplicable "evil" and nonconformity as the evil of not being male-identified, many elements in the novel become clear. The work might be clearer still if Morrison had approached her subject with the consciousness that a lesbian

relationship was at least a possibility for her characters. Obviously Morrison did not *intend* the reader to perceive Sula and Nel's relationship as inherently lesbian. However, this lack of intention only shows the way in which heterosexist assumptions can veil what may logically be expected to occur in a work. What I have tried to do here is not to prove that Morrison wrote something that she did not, but to point out how a Black feminist critical perspective at least allows consideration of this level of the novel's meaning.

In her interview in *Conditions: One* Adrienne Rich talks about unconsummated relationships and the need to re-evaluate the meaning of intense yet supposedly non-erotic connections between women. She asserts:

> We need a lot more documentation about what actually happened: I think we can also imagine it, because we know it happened — we know it out of our own lives.[18]

Black women are still in the position of having to "imagine," discover, and verify Black lesbian literature because so little has been written from an avowedly lesbian perspective. The near non-existence of Black lesbian literature which other Black lesbians and I so deeply feel has everything to do with the politics of our lives, the total suppression of identity that all Black women, lesbian or not, must face. This literary silence is again intensified by the unavailability of an autonomous Black feminist movement through which we could fight our oppression and also begin to name ourselves.

In a speech, "The Autonomy of Black Lesbian Women," Wilmette Brown comments upon the connection between our political reality and the literature we must invent:

> Because the isolation of Black lesbian women, given that we are superfreaks, given that our lesbianism defies both the sexual identity that capital gives us and the racial identity that capital gives us, the isolation of Black lesbian women from heterosexual Black women is very profound. Very profound. I have searched throughout Black history, Black literature, whatever, looking for some women that I could see were somehow lesbian. Now I know

[18]Elly Bulkin, "An Interview With Adrienne Rich: Part I," in *Conditions: One,* Vol. 1, no. 1 (April 1977), p. 62. [Smith]

that in a certain sense they were all lesbian. But that was a very painful search.[19]

Heterosexual privilege is usually the only privilege that Black women have. None of us have racial or sexual privilege, almost none of us have class privilege, maintaining "straightness" is our last resort. Being out, particularly out in print, is the final renunciation of any claim to the crumbs of "tolerance" that nonthreatening "ladylike" Black women are sometimes fed. I am convinced that it is our lack of privilege and power in every other sphere that allows so few Black women to make the leap that many white women, particularly writers, have been able to make in this decade, not merely because they are white or have economic leverage, but because they have had the strength and support of a movement behind them.

As Black lesbians we must be out not only in white society, but in the Black community as well, which is at least as homophobic. That the sanctions against Black lesbians are extremely high is well illustrated in this comment by Black male writer Ishmael Reed. Speaking about the inroads that whites make into Black culture, he asserts:

In Manhattan you find people actively trying to impede intellectual debate among Afro-Americans. The powerful "liberal/radical/existentialist" influences of the Manhattan literary and drama establishment speak through tokens, like for example that ancient notion of the *one* black ideologue (who's usually a Communist), the *one* black poetess (who's usually a feminist lesbian).[20]

To Reed, "feminist" and "lesbian" are the most pejorative terms he can hurl at a Black woman and totally invalidate anything she might say, regardless of her actual politics or sexual identity. Such accusations are quite effective for keeping Black women writers who are writing with integrity and strength from any conceivable perspective in line, but especially ones who are actually feminist and lesbian. Unfortunately Reed's reactionary attitude is all too typical. A community which has not confronted sexism, because a widespread Black feminist movement has not required it to, has likewise not been challenged to examine its heterosexism. Even at this moment I am not convinced that one can write explicitly as a Black lesbian and live to tell about it.

Yet there are a handful of Black women who have risked everything for truth. Audre Lorde, Pat Parker, and Ann Allen Shockley have at least broken ground in the vast wilderness of works that do not exist.[21] Black feminist criticism will again have an essential role not only in creating a climate in which Black lesbian writers can survive, but in undertaking the total reassessment of Black literature and literary history needed to reveal the Black woman-identified-women that Wilmette Brown and so many of us are looking for.

Although I have concentrated here upon what does not exist and what needs to be done, a few Black feminist critics have already begun this work. Gloria T. Hull at the University of Delaware has discovered in her research on Black women poets of the Harlem Renaissance that many of the women who are considered "minor" writers of the period were in constant contact with each other and provided both intellectual stimulation and psychological support for each other's work. At least one of these writers, Angelina Weld Grimké, wrote many unpublished love poems to women. Lorraine Bethel, a recent graduate of Yale College, has done substantial work on Black women writers, particularly in her senior essay, "This Infinity of Conscious Pain: Blues Lyricism and Hurston's Black Female Folk Aesthetic and Cultural Sensibility in *Their Eyes Were Watching God*," in which she brilliantly defines and uses the principles of Black feminist

[19]Wilmette Brown, "The Autonomy of Black Lesbian Women," ms. of speech delivered July 24, 1976, Toronto, Canada, p. 7. [Smith]

[20]Domini, op. cit., p. 18. [Smith]

[21]Audre Lorde, *New York Head Shop and Museum* (Detroit: Broadside, 1974); *Coal* (New York: W. W. Norton, 1976); *Between Our Selves* (Point Reyes, Calif.: Eidolon Editions, 1976); *The Black Unicorn* (New York: W. W. Norton, 1978); Pat Parker, *Child of Myself* (Oakland: Women's Press Collective, 1972 and 1974); *Pit Stop* (Oakland: Women's Press Collective, 1973); *Womanslaughter* (Oakland: Diana Press, 1978); *Movement in Black* (Oakland: Diana Press, 1978); Ann Allen Shockley, *Loving Her* (Indianapolis: Bobbs-Merrill, 1974). [Smith]

There is at least one Black lesbian writers' collective, Jemima, in New York. They do public readings and have available a collection of their poems. They can be contacted c/o Boyce, 41-11 Parsons Blvd., Flushing, NY 11355. [Smith]

criticism. Elaine Scott at the State University of New York at Old Westbury is also involved in highly creative and politically resonant research on Hurston and other writers.

The fact that these critics are young and, except for Hull, unpublished merely indicates the impediments we face. Undoubtedly there are other women working and writing whom I do not even know, simply because there is no place to read them. As Michele Wallace states in her article, "A Black Feminist's Search for Sisterhood":

> We exist as women who are Black who are feminists, each stranded for the moment, working independently because there is not yet an environment in this society remotely congenial to our struggle — [or our thoughts].[22]

I only hope that this essay is one way of breaking our silence and our isolation, of helping us to know each other.

Just as I did not know where to start I am not sure how to end. I feel that I have tried to say too much and at the same time have left too much unsaid. What I want this essay to do is lead everyone who reads it to examine *everything* that they have ever thought and believed about feminist culture and to ask themselves how their thoughts connect to the reality of Black women's writing and lives. I want to encourage in white women, as a first step, a sane accountability to all the women who write and live on this soil. I want most of all for Black women and Black lesbians somehow not to be so alone. This last will require the most expansive of revolutions as well as many new words to tell us how to make this revolution real. I finally want to express how much easier both my waking and my sleeping hours would be if there were one book in existence that would tell me something specific about my life. One book based in Black feminist and Black lesbian experience, fiction or nonfiction. Just one work to reflect the reality that I and the Black women whom I love are trying to create. When such a book exists then each of us will not only know better how to live, but how to dream.

---

[22]Michele Wallace, "A Black Feminist's Search for Sisterhood," in *The Village Voice,* 28 July 1975, p. 7. [Smith]

8

GENDER STUDIES AND QUEER THEORY[1]

> *It is the nature of power — particularly the kind of power that operates in our society — to be repressive, and to be especially careful in repressing useless energies, the intensity of pleasures, and irregular modes of behavior.*
>
> — MICHEL FOUCAULT

> *Woman . . . is only a more or less complacent facilitator for the working out of man's fantasies. It is possible, and even certain, that she experiences vicarious pleasure there, but this pleasure is above all a masochistic prostitution of her body to a desire that is not her own. . . .*
>
> — LUCE IRIGARAY

> *Gender is not a performance that a prior subject elects to do, but gender is performative. . . . It is a compulsory performance in the sense that acting out of line with heterosexual norms brings with it ostracism, punishment, and violence, not to mention the transgressive pleasures produced by those very prohibitions.*
>
> — JUDITH BUTLER

GENDER STUDIES AND FEMINISM

From the words themselves one might expect that *feminism* is a political movement and *gender studies* a research project. There is some truth to this, but in a more important sense it was the ease with which certain forms of feminism within the academy had become co-opted politically into a series of research projects in

[1]The term *queer theory* was popularized by Teresa de Lauretis in a special "Queer Theory" issue of the journal *Differences* (vol. 3, no. 2, 1992). One of de Lauretis's motives was to link up the theoretical activities of academics with the activist politics of the gay and lesbian rights group Queer Nation. The "in your face" quality of the term *queer* appeals to such groups because it forces straight people using or hearing the term to confront their own feelings about homosexuals and homosexuality. De Lauretis's other motive was to distinguish the theorists presented in her special issue, who were questioning and problematizing issues of gender identity and sexual orientation, from other researchers in gay and lesbian studies who were happy with the notion of stable gender identity. In the years since the publication of the "Queer Theory" issue of *Differences*, that distinction has muddied. While some gay and lesbian gender theorists may still resist the term *queer theory*, most on both sides of the gender identity issue have embraced it because of its defiant political implications.

women's studies, with the usual rewards for the top players, that gave rise to the new field of gender studies. Much of the most praised feminist research in the 1980s took the form of new editions of women writers, proposals to add such writers to the existing literary canon, and analyses of the work of patriarchy in keeping males in the front ranks. Effective as this work was in changing what teachers taught and what students read, there was a sense on the part of some feminist critics that though the expansion team was successfully playing the game, it was still the old game that was being played, when what was needed was a new game entirely. The argument posed was that in order to counter patriarchy, it was necessary not merely to think about new texts, but to think about them in radically new ways.

The problem was not that male chauvinists held the named chairs at Princeton — feminists of stature would in their turn be appointed to those professorships — or that males got most of the pages in the Norton Anthologies, but that academic discourse about gender and the gender system was being conducted within a language and a logic, a discursive system, that had been fashioned by male supremacy and reproduced that unconscious ideology at every step. Contemporary feminists might note the prevalence of that ideology in my own figure of speech in the previous paragraph, where male team sports (only the all-male professional leagues have expansion teams) are used as a metaphor for gender politics. But how does one change a discursive system from within, when we can only speak with words that have already been tainted by ideology?

The first step is to recognize the need for a change. The work of Gilbert and Gubar, in revising for the female tradition Bloom's crypto-Freudian analysis of the male poet's impetus to originality, had obviously not gone far enough. Freud viewed women as inherently lacking, warped by the sense that they had already been castrated. In representing this metaphoric wound as the site of female creativity and resistance, Gilbert and Gubar had in effect reinforced Freud's demeaning psychological discourse. For the pioneers of what has come to be known as gender studies, a way to avoid this double bind was to recuperate Freud with a difference, to find a way of reading psychology that could turn the tables on patriarchy. The key to doing this was the work of French psychologist Jacques Lacan.[2] Lacan's postmodern reading of Freud replaced the Viennese doctor's thermodynamic metaphors (about energies, drives, and transferences) with linguistic metaphors: The unconscious was structured not like an infernal machine but like a language. Although Lacan was often given to misogynistic remarks, his recasting of Freud's conception of the physical penis (a fleshly organ for women to envy) into the privileged signifier of the Phallus, a symbol with which both sexes identify as *le désir de la Mère* and from which both sexes feel alienated after the fall into language, was a major step toward feminist revisions of Freud.

THE FEMALE (AS) TEXT: IRIGARAY AND CIXOUS

One of the most influential of the French theorists, Luce Irigaray, is a disciple of Lacan. Irigaray's difficult, learned, ironically allusive thesis, *Speculum of the Other*

---

[2]See Lacan in the introduction to Psychoanalytic Theory and Criticism, p. 632, and Lacan readings, pp. 643, and 649.

Woman (1974), undertakes a re-examination of Plato, Freud, and a dozen thinkers in between. Like Simone de Beauvoir, Irigaray is outraged about the way women have been seen as an Other by men, spoken about and spoken for, but never allowed to speak themselves.[3] Her critique of Freud is largely of his theories of sexual differences (like the notions of penis envy and the castration complex), theories that falter, according to Irigaray, on Freud's failure to perceive that men and women actually *are* different, rather than more or less adequate versions of the same (male) norm. Quoting Freud against himself, Irigaray demonstrates the incoherence of his theories of femininity.

Despite Irigaray's training as a Lacanian psychoanalyst, her own version of femininity seems to have a biological basis that harks back to the source of the errors she exposes in Freud. In her most famous essay, "This Sex Which Is Not One" (1977), she characterizes both males and females as essentially like their primary genitalia: men, like the phallus, are single (-minded), hard, simple, direct; women, like the two lips of the vulva and their sensations, are multiple, diffuse, soft, indirect. Similarly, Irigaray's notion of women's writing takes off from this genital analogy of the labia, which always touch each other:

This "style" or "writing" of women tends to put the torch to fetish words, proper terms, well-constructed forms. This "style" does not privilege sight; instead, it takes each figure back to its source, which is among other things *tactile*. It comes back in touch with itself in that origin without ever constituting itself in it, as some sort of unity. *Simultaneity* is its "proper" aspect — a property that is never fixed in the possible identity-to-self of some form or other. It is always *fluid*, without neglecting the characteristics of fluids that are difficult to idealize: those rubbings between two infinitely near neighbors that create a dynamics. Its "style" resists and explodes every firmly established form, figure, idea, or concept. Which does not mean that it lacks style . . . but its "style" cannot be upheld as a thesis, cannot be the object of a position.[4]

Despite the abstract tenor of this characterization, the general traits Irigaray posits for women's discourse — inconsistency, fluidity, incoherence, tactility — are the very ones men have used to denigrate the female intellect. Irigaray's position seems a jumping-off point for a separatist feminism that renounces for women whatever has been tainted by masculinity — logic, coherence, power.

Hélène Cixous is a more difficult writer than Irigaray, but the problems of reading her are somewhat different. Where Irigaray is learned, detached, abstract, and so ambiguously ironical that her meaning is often in danger of being misunderstood, Cixous speaks primarily through images and metaphors. The intense poetic quality of her prose is part of what has caused her essay "The Laugh of the Medusa" to become the central manifesto of French feminism. Cixous's difficulty is intentional and programmatic: Feeling that the major modes of conceptual analysis themselves are anti-female, she writes in a way that resists dialectic. To show this, Cixous (following Derrida in *Of Grammatology*) sets up a series of binary

[3]See de Beauvoir, p. 394.

[4]Luce Irigaray, "The Power of Discourse," in *This Sex Which Is Not One* (Ithaca: Cornell University Press, 1985), p. 79.

oppositions (active/passive, sun/moon, culture/nature, day/night, father/mother, logos/pathos). Each pair can be analyzed as a hierarchy in which the former term represents the positive and masculine and the latter the negative and feminine principle. Nor can the terms live in harmony: Cixous suggests that, in each case, the masculine term is forced to "kill" the feminine one. This for her is the deadly "phallocentric" principle that she derives from Derrida's critique of logocentrism. Cixous rejects the idea of "feminine writing," as "a dangerous and stylish expression full of traps. . . . My work in fact aims at getting rid of words like 'feminine and masculine,' even 'man' and 'woman.'. . ."[5]

One might think Cixous, like Virginia Woolf, would be an exponent of androgyny; in fact Cixous attacks androgyny as an annulment of differences, and supports instead what she calls "the *other bisexuality*," which involves the "multiplication of the effects of the inscription of desire, over all parts of my body and the other body, indeed, this *other bisexuality* doesn't annul differences, but stirs them up, pursues them, increases them" ("The Laugh of the Medusa"). For Cixous, woman is bisexual; man, unwilling to give up the phallus, is monosexual. This is the point at which the binary polarities, having been kicked out the door, creep back in through the window, and they return upside down, with the female terms on top. At one point Cixous speaks "of a decipherable libidinal femininity which can be read in a writing produced by a male or a female." But as she later explains "libidinal femininity," she ends up attributing it almost exclusively to biological females. She finds its essential, moist, life-giving properties, for example, in the work of women writers like Clarice Lispector, while the work of a male writer like Maurice Blanchot is "a text that goes toward the drying up." (She finds a feminine sensibility in one male writer, Heinrich von Kleist, but that, as she says, is "highly exceptional.") Female sexuality is "giving," where the male is retentive, avaricious; female sexuality achieves full genitality, while male sexuality is fixated in oral dominance or anal "exchange."[6] Where Derrida presented the standard polarities of Western culture in order to dismantle and discredit dialectical thinking, it seems that Cixous has adopted Derridean terminology for a philosophically different program that simply inverts the standard pairings.

BORN A WOMAN

For other gender theorists, Lacan is not the answer. Instead one can attempt to analyze the system of gender down to its roots, to see where it comes from and how it is implicated in the material and familial relationships of our society. One of the key texts in that analysis is Gayle Rubin's "The Traffic in Women," reproduced in part below. Like Monique Wittig, Rubin takes her approach from Simone de Beauvoir's line "One is not born a woman." One is indeed born female, Rubin admits, but the oppression of women is something that happens because of the way society is constituted. Rubin begins by analyzing patriarchy within capitalist society using Marxist

[5]Interview with Cixous in Verena Andermatt Conley, *Hélène Cixous: Writing the Feminine* (Lincoln and London: University of Nebraska Press, 1984), p. 129.
[6]Conley, 129–33.

terminology to understand relationships that Marx and Engels tended to avoid. If capitalism works by extracting as much surplus value from the worker as possible, there are limits to the exploitation: the worker may be a wage slave, but after work-ing all day he needs to show up at the job site in shape to do his next day's work. To keep the system going, women who are not a direct part of the wage system themselves must become in effect the slaves of the slaves, subordinates employed to prepare food and do other forms of housework (including raising the next generation of wage slaves and houseworkers).

If this were all, gender oppression would disappear after a socialist revolution. But Rubin, a trained anthropologist, is well aware that Western capitalism is only one economic system among many, and that patriarchy — the current term for a sex/gender system that generates gender oppression under capitalism[7] — is only the most recent and developed of a great variety of such systems. Rubin investigates the different systems in primitive societies as described by Evans-Pritchard and Lévi-Strauss, most of which involve the acquisition of power through alliances that depend on the exchange of women between men. This exchange, in turn, depends on compulsory heterosexuality and on women being sexually passive. When women are pawns in relationships between men, it helps if "the woman in question did not have too many ideas of her own about whom she might want to sleep with."

The material position of women is only half of the problem with the sex/gender system; psychology accounts for the rest. As presented in the introduction to Freud and to psychoanalytical theory (Chapter 4), gender takes shape in the Oedipal crisis. Before the crisis, both boys and girls relate primarily to their mothers, whom they love and with whom they identify. Girls are feminized when they realize that their anatomy is like their mother's but that this anatomy is defective: The person she loves, her heterosexual mother, is attracted, not to another woman, someone who looks like her, but rather the father, who has a different anatomy. In a "successful" resolution of the castration complex, the girl continues to identify with her mother but devalues her (and also herself) as she shifts her desire to someone with the penis she lacks. Boys have it considerably easier: They need to shift their identification from the mother to the father, but can continue to desire their mother. This puts them in conflict with their father, but only temporarily, since in the long run, as Rubin puts it, "the social contract guarantees their rights to a woman of their own." Rubin presents our sex/gender system, whereby heterosexual parents reproduce themselves as heterosexual children, and where women are mere pawns in a system of alliances between men, as having a mutually reinforcing stability. That suggests that only a very radical change of society could produce a semblance of equality between the sexes: one where heterosexuality is not compulsory and where childrearing is shared (so that children of both sexes identify with both parents).

What Rubin presents through elaborate analysis — that the sex/gender system cannot be made just, that it would need to be utterly uprooted or destroyed — is

[7]Rubin is unhappy with *patriarchy* as a term for the current sex/gender system because its biblical origin (the "patriarchs" are Abraham, Isaac, and Jacob) suggests its relationship between a pastoral and nomadic, rather than urban and capitalistic social system.

presupposed in Monique Wittig's refreshingly brutal essay "One Is Not Born a Woman," reprinted here. To be a lesbian, and to form a lesbian society, is the only possible form of liberation from a gender system in which a woman is, by her defined position within the social system, a slave to men. "Lesbians are not women" was in fact the triumphant conclusion of her MLA presentation later published as "The Straight Mind." Because lesbians, as opposed to women, do not define themselves vis-à-vis men, they have liberated themselves; they can consequently work outside the system for a revolution that will liberate females as an oppressed class, a revolution that will destroy "woman" as a category. Indeed, women's liberation — the program of Anglo-American feminism — is to Wittig a contradiction in terms, and even the androgynous vision of Cixous strikes Wittig as a mediocre half measure, an accommodation with the enemy. Wittig's forte is her ability to imagine a society wiped clean of the sex/gender system: in her novels, such as *Les Guérrillères*, even the gender inherent in the French language (where normally every noun or pronoun is inflected as masculine or feminine) has been jettisoned.

BINARIES AND TALK ABOUT BINARIES

It is difficult to talk about "heterosexuality" without raising the question of its binary opposite, "homosexuality." And just as the impulse of gender theory began with an effort to destabilize the customary boundaries of "masculinity" and "femininity," to clear the way for a different sort of discourse that could subvert the entrenched language of patriarchy, the next stage for gender theory was to take on the issues of sexual orientation and sexual identity.

While our society portrays binary oppositions like "masculine" and "feminine" or "straight" and "gay" as elementary "natural" categories, the rules have little to do with nature and everything to do with culture. The word *homosexual* has an astonishingly short history, dating from the last quarter of the nineteenth century, and *heterosexual* is an even newer term, apparently coined in opposition to *homosexual*. It is not clear that "sexual identity" had the binary structure it does today much before the coining of these terms, and even today many people perform sexual acts that do not accord with the label they would apply to themselves. Precisely which sexual acts are "normal" and accepted and for whom depends upon the society in which one lives. For example, among the upper classes in Periclean Athens, it was considered normal for mature men to play the active sexual role with women, with both male and female slaves, and with male adolescents of their own class; and it was normal for male adolescents to take the passive sexual role with an adult mentor. But Athenian society thought it abnormal for men to continue to prefer the passive sexual role after coming to mature years and shameful to be the slave of sexual desire at any age.

Nor do the various binary oppositions hold their shape under close inspection. "Homosexuality" and "heterosexuality" cover not two but many forms of identity and map an enormous range of overlapping behaviors. The readers of Dr. Alfred Kinsey's pioneering surveys of sexual behavior in American men and women (1948 and 1953) were shocked to learn that men and women who considered themselves heterosexual had, more often than not, a history of experimentation with homosex-ual activities, and that it was unusual for homosexuals not to have tried heterosexual acts. Today we are no longer shocked: Indeed, we tend to think that every man, how-ever masculine, has his feminine side (and vice versa), and that being too "manly" to stay in touch with one's inner woman is a defect rather than a virtue. In this sense we are all bisexual, to one degree or another: Our "sexual orientation" is merely a bias to one side or the other. Adrienne Rich speaks of the "lesbian continuum" as a way of suggesting the range of activities by which women bond to each other, not confined to "consciously desired genital sexual experience with another woman," activities including "the sharing of a rich inner life, the bonding against male tyranny, the giv-ing and receiving of practical and political support."[8]

Similarly, the distinction between "masculine" and "feminine" activities and behaviors is constantly changing, so that women who wear baseball caps and fatigues, pump iron, and smoke cigars (at the appropriate times and seasons) can be perceived as more piquantly sexy by some heterosexual men than those women who wear white frocks and gloves and look down demurely. (Needless to say, the sexual orientation of the observer makes a difference: What most lesbians find appealing in a woman may differ from what attracts most heterosexual men.) One needs to ques-tion, too, whether such change simply involves crossing borders: Is the drag queen appropriating onto his male body the signifiers of feminine gender (makeup, wigs, gowns, high heels), or does the drag queen represent a separate form of sexuality? Even the physical dualism of sexual genetic structures and bodily parts breaks down when one considers those instances — the XXY syndromes, natural sexual bimor-phisms, as well as surgical transsexuals — that defy attempts at binary classification. However, the real question for all the theorists represented in this chapter is not about the physical signifiers of sexuality but about its psychology and its discourse.

SEX AND POLITICS

If none of this is late-breaking news, much of the credit goes to contemporary gender theorists, who have been researching the historical parameters of sex and gender for the past thirty years. But while theirs is a research project, mostly financed by the universities, it is a politically committed research project, more an Arnoldian "criticism of life" than a disinterested investigation of literary texts. Toward the end of his essay "Homographesis," Lee Edelman becomes momentarily defensive about drawing conclusions that could be seen as leading merely to newer and more subtle readings of literary texts, and feels compelled to insist that his analysis of the rhetoric of gender is not "an apolitical formalism" but the grounding of an effective political critique of the patriarchal, homophobic ideology of gender.

The political movement, comparable to suffragist feminism, that aims to overturn the homophobic constructions of contemporary American discourse and the legal penalties gay men and lesbians endure was given a powerful impetus nearly fifty

[8] Adrienne Rich, "Compulsory Heterosexuality" (1980), in *The Lesbian and Gay Studies Reader*, ed. Henry Abelove et al. (New York: Routledge, 1993), p. 227.

years ago with the legendary Stonewall rebellion of 1969 in New York City, which occurred in reaction to an illegal police raid on a gay bar. A more militant "gay liberation" program has been the unspoken motivation of much of gender studies since that time. The force, even stridency, of such political critique has much to do with conditions in America, where gays and lesbians are among the few minorities still suffering under *legal* discrimination, discrimination that is not merely a threat to dignity and peace of mind but which can have serious consequences.

Although most European countries had long decriminalized all sexual activities between consenting adults, it was not until 2003, in *Lawrence v. Texas*, that the Supreme Court invalidated "sodomy" laws in thirteen U.S. states. And although many gay men served with conspicuous bravery in the U.S. military throughout its history, openly acknowledging one's homosexual orientation constituted grounds for dishonorable discharge from the armed services until 2011. Same-sex marriage, already available throughout most of Western Europe, was in 2015 made a "fundamental right" in all 50 states by the Supreme Court in *Obergefell v. Hodges*.

These positive legal changes have followed in the train of increasingly tolerant social attitudes toward homosexuality, which in turn has followed a post-Stonewall move by homosexuals out of the "closet" and toward the expression of gay pride. Overt bigotry against gays and lesbians is no longer tolerated in most circles, and a 2013 poll stated that less than a third of Americans still think that homosexuality "should not be accepted by society."

Nevertheless gay and lesbian couples still may find it hard to adopt children: Only nine states prohibit discrimination against them in placement. And there is no federal law protecting against housing or employment discrimination based on sexual orientation. There is only a patchwork of regulations in a minority of states, and even in some of these states, gays and lesbians are protected, but not transsexuals.

Such discrimination is all the more irrational since it has become clear that sexual preference and gender identity is not a life-style decision one intentionally makes.

Recent biological research has begun to suggest that a person's gender identity and attraction to one's own or the opposite sex is governed, at least in part, by complex genetic codes. However, gay liberationists are not entirely happy about the prospect of isolating a "gay gene." While it might help dissolve some people's prejudices to think of homosexuality as a genetically determined trait, it could also encourage homophobic parents to abort fetuses carrying the gene and would allow societies more repressive than ours to discover gays in even the darkest closet. More important to the issues raised by the theorists collected here, the notion of biological determinism reifies and essentializes homosexuality as a genetic outcome rather than encouraging us to understand it as a social practice or a discourse.

FOUCAULT AND THE HISTORICIZATION OF SEXUALITY

That homosexuality should be thought of preeminently as a "discourse" rather than as an action that can be studied by positivistic scientific method, or thoughts and feelings that can be analyzed by the polls of social science, is a sign of the pervasive influence on gay studies of Michel Foucault.[9] When it appeared in 1976, Foucault's *Le Volonté de savoir* (*The Will to Knowledge*), Volume I of *The History of Sexuality*, seemed to promise an appropriate sequel to his historical studies of madhouses (*Folie et Deraison* [*Madness and Civilization*], 1961), hospitals (*Le Naissance du Clinique* [*The Birth of the Clinic*], 1963), and prisons (*Surveiller et Punir* [*Discipline and Punish*], 1975) as the sites in which society isolates and punishes deviation.

While the popular view of the Victorian era is that it was a unique period of sexual repression preceded and followed by eras of greater personal liberty and sexual candor, Foucault suggests that in fact a variety of different forms of repression had succeeded one another in the centuries before, during, and after the nineteenth century. Though Foucault was gay, the gay male is not the sole or even the principal focus of *The History of Sexuality*, but only one of four categories he suggests as sites of study. (The others are the hysterical female, the masturbating child, and the Malthusian couple.) Foucault planned to analyze the transformations of power and knowledge from the early modern era to the present in relation to each of these categories.

Foucault's first volume is an extended meditation, without very much in the way of specific data, on the way he intends to approach sexuality as a site of what he had come to call *pouvoir/savoir* ("power/knowledge"). For Foucault, knowledge confers power, just as having power allows one to define what counts as knowledge. But, for Foucault, power is not necessarily the centralized power of the monarch or the ruling class; it is not a system imposed from above, like the juridical system of law. Foucault conceives of power as a field of forces operating in all directions in private as well as public life. Foucault uses this conception of power to analyze the different ways in which the human body, conceived as a type of machine from the seventeenth century onward, was "improved" in its operation by what he calls a "technology" of sex that was directed by experts of various sorts — priests, lawyers, doctors, scientists, educators, therapists — and operated both through and outside the family structure. The specific forms of repression, prohibition, and blockage of sexual desires operate differently in different areas and at different times (genuine liberation for the individual being a hopeless ideal beyond the reach of any social system Foucault is capable of envisioning). In the early twentieth century, for example, an unhappy and rebellious adolescent might have been diagnosed by educators as suffering from excessive masturbation, which was presumed to cause insanity; today, however, he or she might be treated by therapists who would interview the parents about their own sexual problems, which would be presumed to be responsible for those of their children.

Foucault had apparently prepared to spend the rest of what promised to be a long life researching the changing social practices and discourses of various forms of sexuality. But during a stay at the University of California at Berkeley, he decided to shift his project from exterior questions concerning the impact of power and knowledge on the individual to the more psychological issue of how individuals come "to recognize themselves as subjects of a 'sexuality'" through the "hermeneutics of

[9] For more on Foucault, see the introductions to Structuralism and Deconstruction and New Historicism and Cultural Studies, pp. 470 and 782, respectively.

desire" (*Uses of Pleasure,* 4–6). Foucault, in other words, shifted his study toward the production of a history of sexual identity rather than a history of sexual practices. The second volume of the *History of Sexuality, The Uses of Pleasure* (1984; translated 1985), which takes up the place of sexuality and desire in ancient Greece, and the third volume, *The Care of the Self* (1984; translated 1986), which covers the first two centuries of the Roman empire, bear the marks of this shift in Foucault's program. These volumes, obviously meant to be continued, were also written under the pressure of time, as Foucault was diagnosed with AIDS in the early 1980s. Both volumes were published after Foucault's death in 1984.

QUEER THEORY AND HOMOSEXUAL PANIC

The history of sexuality has continued to be a subject of theorizing and research since Foucault, and perhaps the most celebrated American contributor to this field has been Eve Kosofsky Sedgwick. Her groundbreaking *Between Men: English Literature and Male Homosocial Desire* (1985) theorized that the strong and close personal relationships between men needed for success in nineteenth-century Britain placed Victorian males in a state of continual homosexual panic, a panic that was often assuaged by triangulating the relationship through a woman. David Copperfield's relation to Steerforth via Little Em'ly is an obvious fictional representation of this, but such triangulated relationships also appear, as one might expect, in literary biography and other non-fiction narratives of the age. One recalls, for example, that Arthur Henry Hallam was not only Tennyson's closest friend at the time of his death, but had become his sister's fiancé. Sedgwick's *Epistemology of the Closet* (1990) advances her study to the end of World War I, with discussions of Melville, Wilde, James, and Proust. It also makes explicit the antihomophobic politics on which it is founded. Indeed, Sedgwick insists that homosexuality is everyone's issue, as heterosexual males define their own identity in opposition to — and thus in terms of — that of the gay Other, and maneuver in significant ways to obscure their own objects of desire.

The issue of gay identity as such dominates the work of Judith Butler. Butler's book *Gender Trouble* (1990) uses a deconstructive rhetoric to subvert the binarisms of male/female, masculine/feminine, and gay/straight. While many gay liberationists have attempted to construct positive models of gay identity as a way of resisting a homophobic society, to Butler the entire issue of gender identity is political poison. The essentialization of categories like "gay" and "straight" or "female" and "male," is inherently restrictive. Just as the 1970s feminist project of creating a positive image of Woman implicitly defined an ideal for every woman to live up to, depriving each individual of the right to be whoever and whatever she was, the creation of fixed images of gay and lesbian identity can result in the "regulatory imperative" to be a "proper" gay or lesbian individual.

In "Imitation and Gender Insubordination" (1991), Butler confesses that she "suffered for a long time from being told that what I 'am' is a copy, an imitation, a derivative example, a shadow of the real." For those who essentialize sexuality, biological sex defines one's gender, and gender defines one's sexual orientation.

Heterosexuals define themselves by oppressing those who transgress, whose signifiers don't line up. And just as the notion of a platonic ideal of Woman has been used to oppress lesbians, the image of the Ideal Lesbian can be used to oppress those who do not come up to whatever mark the politics of the group has set forth. In good Derridean fashion, Butler deconstructs the binary of original versus copy, questioning not merely which is the real and which the imitation, but whether our entire concept of gender is not in fact based on imitations for which no real essences exist. Both homosexuals and heterosexuals seem to want to buy into this destructive mythic logic, in which gender is "an imitation that performatively constitutes itself as the original." But to perform something is to play at something; to play at something is not *to be* that something. Just as Derrida insisted on recognizing language as a freeplay of signifiers lacking a stable center, Butler suggests that we would spare ourselves a great deal of misery by recognizing that there are no fixed sexual identities that shape our actions and thoughts, that gender is something we "put on" or perform. What we do, our performances from moment to moment, driven by strong inner imperatives, are all we are or can be.

Martha Nussbaum, also by training a philosopher, whose central interest is ethics as it can be taught by the experience of imaginative literature took issue with Butler's position on gender in her 1999 review of Butler's *Excitable Speech* for the *New Republic*. To Nussbaum, the error of essentializing sexual preferences is comparatively trivial by comparison with the distance that Butler opens up between what oppressors can do and what the oppressed can do about it. To view gender as an "insubordinate" performative act that deconstructs and parodies the cultural clichés that underlie sexism or homophobia is implicitly to suggest that there is nothing concrete that can be done about them. Nussbaum suggests that, in following Foucault's logic, Butler finds herself in a position where she cannot recommend social action because she is incapable of imagining a favorable outcome, a change whose structure of power would leave us more free and happy than we were before.

GAY LIVES, GAY TEXTS

The work of such theorists as Judith Halberstam, Lauren Berlant, and Michael Warner is primarily about gay identities and practices and their relation to the heterosexual world within which those identities take shape. As such, it is informed, inevitably, by the theories of Foucault, Sedgwick, and Butler. In terms of the varieties of sexual preferences outlined by Sedgwick in *Epistemology of the Closet*, Judith Halberstam (also known as "Jack") is a transgendered female. Her sexual identity is masculine — she desires women — but her body is female and, unlike transsexuals, she has no plan or wish to acquire a male anatomy. The history of gender theory has, to an extent, orphaned those in her category. From the beginning, vastly more attention has been paid to the question of what femininity is all about than to the multiple forms of masculinity. The varieties of masculinity, particularly as they are inflected by race and ethnicity, have only recently begun to be studied, but in a sense transgendered females like Halberstam offer an opportunity to study masculinity in an especially pure form, in the absence of maleness.

Halberstam likes to stress the asymetrical aspects of gender identification. As she stated in an interview, "Since femininity signifies in general as the effect of artifice, as the essence of 'performativity' . . . , we have an easier time understanding it as transferable, mobile, fluid. But masculinity has an altogether different relation to performance, the real and the natural, and it appears to be far more difficult to pry masculinity and maleness apart than femininity and femaleness."[10] Alluding to Butler's view of performativity here, Halberstam suggests that performing masculinity involves not performing, or at least not appearing to perform: It is the impassivity of male icons like Clint Eastwood that conveys their masculinity. Halberstam would argue that the dominance of male over female in Western culture has made masculinity the "default" position. It takes far more effort for a man to cross-dress and look feminine than for a woman to cross-dress and look masculine. Social mores arrange other asymmetries, such as those of the public toilet. A masculine woman may well be tempted to use the "wrong" toilet in the airport, because in the Ladies' Room she is likely to be noticed and to have to explain her presence, or even demonstrate her femaleness to a security guard. She would be less likely to arouse suspicion in a Men's Room, where men are, or pretend to be, oblivious of each other's appearance and of the fact that others are present for private functions. On the other hand, there might be violent consequences to being caught.[11] Given Halberstam's concern with the details of performing gender, one has little sense that she considers her gender something she merely acts out. She seems to consider her identity as a masculine woman as something innate. She was a tomboy who — unlike Frankie Adams, in *The Member of the Wedding* — refused at adolescence to conform herself to the standard of enacted femininity demanded of females by her society.

That standard is just one part of "heteronormativity" which is the central topic of Berlant and Warner's 1998 *Critical Inquiry* essay "Sex in Public." At stake are "the radical aspirations of queer culture building" — and *radical* is the key word. As the authors define it, heteronormativity is the "institutions, structures of understanding, and practical orientations that make heterosexuality seem not only coherent . . . but privileged."[12] A very small part of their issue is that heterosexuality itself is the presumed or "unmarked" position: People who are gay have to make that clear to the people getting to know them, whereas people who are straight don't have to do anything. And attitudes held by heterosexuals are considered the norm for everyone. For example, while it is certainly considered heteronormal to date and experiment widely at the outset of sexual activity, it is presumed that variety loses its spice, and that an optimum life history will involve episodes of lengthy intimacy, marriage, and the cares of raising a family. Gays who "settle down" into long-term partnerships, whether or not they choose to have or adopt children, have in effect been co-opted

[10]"Masculinity without Men," *Genders* 29 (1999).
[11]Halberstam does not mention in her book the case of Brandon Teena, the female-to-male transgender from Falls River, Nebraska, who was raped and then murdered in 1993 by two young men who had discovered her secret. Teena was the subject of a documentary film in 1998 and the 1999 feature film *Boys Don't Cry*, for which Hilary Swank won her first Academy Award.
[12]Lauren Berlant and Michael Warner, "Sex in Public," *Critical Inquiry* 24 (1998): 547–66.

into this aspect of heteronormativity.[13] Berlant and Warner argue that "queer social practices like sex and theory" should "try to unsettle" the hegemonic force of heteronormativity. The "outlaw" aspects of queer sex, of which sex toys and leather bars are only two examples, have a value to Berlant and Warner, not merely in themselves, but in the way they serve to destabilize the deadening culture that accepts "differ-ence" in the abstract but doesn't really want to be challenged by it. That the hetero-sexual population — in the liberal cities at least — has come to accept most elements of the gay lifestyle as desirable or indifferent aspects of urban life is a sign of how far and how quickly the center of the culture has moved from the standard homophobia of my own childhood fifty years ago. Have we arrived here at a post–queer theory, where the key danger to gay and lesbian culture is what Herbert Marcuse once called "repressive tolerance"?[14] Maybe not quite yet: Berlant and Warner seem to relish the "queer outlaw" role in theory, but are also upset that an anti-pornography zoning statute might banish gay sex clubs with live performances to lonely streets near the New York City waterfront, where patrons would have a greater likelihood of being mugged than their former locations in the better patrolled parts of Greenwich Village. Perhaps homoradicalism can be as incoherent an ideology as heteronormativity.

RESISTING THE FREUDIAN MATRIX

Butler and Sedgwick are engaged in one side of the theoretical task of gay libera-tion, that of liberating the movement from its recapitulation of the same binarism and exclusionary politics that characterize patriarchal ideology and that, as we have seen, continue to characterize some schools of feminist thought. The other side of the theoretical task is that of accomplishing for gays what Cixous and Irigaray achieved for women in their rereadings of Freud and Lacan: the recuperation of the psychoanalytical discourse of gender as a language that heals rather than wounds the spirit. This is not an easy task, as Freud's view of homosexuality was that it stems from a wrong turning, a regression to an earlier stage of development caused by failure to make a necessary leap. According to Freud, the individual progresses through a series of stages, from early infantile sexuality, an autoeroticism that seeks pleasure purely in the self, to a primary narcissism in which one loves oneself in undifferentiated unity with the parent, to the conflicts of the Oedipal crisis, in which genuine object relations develop that lead to desire for the opposite sex. In the case of the homosexual, Freud argues that some crushing of the self-image occurs in the

[13]The way the wedge issue of same-sex marriage played out in the years before the Supreme Court settled the matter in 2015 shows that "heteronormativity" is not always coherent. Religious conservatives were appalled by the possibility of what they would consider a parody of the sacred institution, which they define as taking place between one man and one woman. Liberal heterosexuals, on the other hand, were likely to favor gay marriage because it would help bring queer culture into line with heteronor-mativity. Berlant and Warner might well find both positions repugnant since, for both conservative and liberal heterosexuals, same-sex marriage would be "about" their own views on life rather than those of the people most directly concerned.

[14]See "Repressive Tolerance" (1965) in Robert Paul Wolff, Barrington Moore, Jr., and Herbert Marcuse, A Critique of Pure Tolerance (Boston: Beacon Press, 1969), 95–137. Marcuse, a former mem-ber of the Frankfurt School with Horkheimer and Adorno, argued that the liberal ideology of toleration of dissent makes it more difficult to radically reform the capitalist world.

course of development that leads the child to choose as a sexual object a figure of the same sex, embodying the ideal elements the child feels to be missing from himself.

In his response to Freud, *Homosexual Desire*, Guy Hocquenghem may have become the first of the queer theorists, since his 1972 essay appeared in French four years before *La Volonté de savoir*, the first volume of Foucault's *History of Sexuality*. Foucault may in fact have been responding to Hocquenghem, since they knew each other and since Hocquenghem was certainly responding to the early Foucault of *Madness and Civilization,* with its vision of medical science creating classes of people who, for the sake of decency, had to be locked up:

> Homosexuality is a manufactured product of the normal world. . . . What is manufactured is a psychologically repressive category, "homosexuality": an abstract division of desire which allows even those who escape to be dominated, inscribing within the law what is outside the law. The category under discussion, as well as the term indicating it, is a fairly recent invention. The growing imperialism of a society seeking to attribute a social status to everything, even to the unclassifiable, created this particular form of disequilibrium: up to the end of the eighteenth century, people who denied the existence of God, who could not speak, or who practised sodomy, were locked up in the same prisons. Just as the advent of psychiatry and mental hospitals demonstrates society's ability to invent specific means for classifying the unclassifiable (see Foucault's *Histoire de la folie à l'âge classique*), so modern thought creates a new disease, homosexuality. According to Havelock Ellis, the word "homosexual" was invented in 1869 by a German doctor. Dividing in order to rule, psychiatry's modern pseudo-scientific thought has turned barbarous intolerance into civilised intolerance. (50–51)

In *Homosexual Desire*, Hocquenghem's analysis of the medical regime, unless I am mistaking its tone, takes the form of brisk satire. It brushes aside any explanation of homosexuality, such as Hirschfeld's "third sex" theory, that might make sense to real people who have experienced homosexual desire. Hocquenghem lavishes his analysis instead on the theories of Freud and his disciple Sandor Ferenczi, showing how they continually turn each category into a set of binaries that mimic and thus map onto the basic binary of male and female. There must be object-homosexuals and subject-homosexuals, perverts and inverts, masochists and sadists. Homosexual desire as such cannot exist because it would create a third entity or, even worse, dissolve the entire system of binaries by suggesting that sexual desire — homo, hetero, whatever — is a single indivisible force. That was precisely what Hocquenghem believed: "Homosexual desire: the expression is meaningless. There is no subdivision of desire . . ." (49). To counterbalance the binary gymnastics of the psychoanalysts, Hocquenghem opposes the imaginative truth of Robert Musil's novella, *Young Törless*, whose confused protagonist knows more about desire than his sophisticated friends or his schoolmasters.

While queer theory and gender studies have become areas of theory that are distinct from feminist criticism and women's studies, it would be misleading to ignore the connections among these schools. Gender studies became possible as a result of the projects of feminist criticism, and queer theory has drawn both energies and insights from feminist thinkers. In their first books, both Butler and Sedgwick defined their work as feminist, and Butler, especially, is still very sensitive to the connections between gender theory and feminism. Which is more important: likeness or difference? The contradictions inherent in identity politics inevitably generate dual impulses to split off and to merge, as gay males, lesbians, bisexuals, transsexuals, and cross-dressers sense how different their cultural situations and concerns are from those of "mainstream" feminists but simultaneously understand the political consequences of isolation and the advantages of a combined resistance to patriarchy.

Selected Bibliography

Abelove, Henry, Michèle Aina Barale, and David M. Halperin, eds. *The Lesbian and Gay Studies Reader*. New York: Routledge, 1993.

Belsey, Catherine. *Critical Practice*. New York: Methuen, 1980.

Bersani, Leo. "Is the Rectum a Grave?" *October* 43 (1987): 197–222.

Boone, Joseph Allen. *Tradition Counter Tradition: Love and the Form of Fiction*. Chicago: University of Chicago Press, 1987.

Boone, Joseph Allen, and Michael Cadden, eds. *Engendering Men: The Question of Male Feminist Criticism*. New York: Routledge, 1990.

Boswell, John. *Christianity, Social Tolerance, and Homosexuality: Gay People in Western Europe from the Beginning of the Christian Era to the Fourteenth Century*. Chicago: University of Chicago Press, 1980.

Bray, Alan. *Homosexuality in Renaissance England*. London: Gay Men's Press, 1982.

Burger, Glenn, and Steven F. Kruger, eds. *Queering the Middle Ages*. Minneapolis: University of Minnesota Press, 2001.

Butler, Judith. *Gender Trouble: Feminism and the Subversion of Identity*. New York and London: Routledge, 1990.

Butters, Ronald R., John M. Clum, and Michael Moon, eds. *Displacing Homophobia: Gay Male Perspectives in Literature and Culture*. Durham: Duke University Press, 1989.

Castle, Terry. *The Apparitional Lesbian: Female Homosexuality and Modern Culture*. New York: Columbia University Press, 1993.

Cixous, Hélène. "Le Rire de la Méduse." *L'Arc* 61 (1975): 39–54. Trans. Keith and Paula Cohen as "The Laugh of the Medusa." *Signs* 1 (1976): 875–99.

——. *La Jeune née* (with Catherine Clément). Paris: UGE Press, 1975. Trans. Betsy Wing as *The Newly Born Woman*. Minneapolis: University of Minnesota Press, 1986.

De Lauretis, Teresa. *Alice Doesn't: Feminism, Semiotics, Cinema*. Bloomington: Indiana University Press, 1984.

——, ed. *The Practice of Love: Lesbian Sexualities and Perverse Desire*. Bloomington: Indiana University Press, 1994.

Edelman, Lee. *Homographesis: Essays in Gay Literary and Cultural Theory*. New York and London: Routledge, 1994.

Foucault, Michel. *The History of Sexuality*, Volume I: *The Will to Knowledge*, trans. Robert Hurley. New York: Random House, 1980.

——. Volume II: *The Uses of Pleasure*, trans. Robert Hurley. New York: Pantheon, 1985.

——. Volume III: *The Care of the Self*, trans. Robert Hurley. New York: Pantheon, 1986.

Fuss, Diana, ed. *Inside/Out: Lesbian Theories, Gay Theories*. New York: Routledge, 1991.

Garber, Marjorie. *Vested Interests: Cross-dressing and Cultural Anxiety*. New York: Routledge, 1991.

Goldberg, Jonathan, ed. *Queering the Renaissance*. Durham: Duke University Press, 1994.

Haggerty, George E., and Bonnie Zimmerman. *Professions of Desire: Lesbian and Gay Studies in Literature*. New York: MLA Press, 1995.

Halperin, David. *One Hundred Years of Homosexuality and Other Essays on Greek Love.* New York: Routledge, 1990.

Hocquenghem, Guy. *Homosexual Desire* (1972), trans. Daniella Dangoor. London: Allison and Busby, 1978.

Irigaray, Luce. *Spéculum de l'autre femme.* Paris: Minuit, 1974. Trans. Gillian C. Gill as *The Speculum of the Other Woman.* Ithaca: Cornell University Press, 1985.

———. *Ce sexe qui n'en est pas un.* Paris: Minuit, 1977. Trans. Catharine Porter with Carolyn Burke as *This Sex Which Is Not One.* Ithaca: Cornell University Press, 1985.

Jagose, Annamarie. *Queer Theory.* Victoria: Melbourne University Press, 1996.

Jardine, Alice. *Gynesis: Configurations of Woman and Modernity.* Ithaca: Cornell University Press, 1985.

Jay, Karla, and Allen Young, eds. *Out of the Closets: Voices of Gay Liberation* (1972). New York: NYU Press, 1992.

Kauffman, Linda, ed. *Gender and Theory: Dialogues on Feminist Criticism.* New York: Blackwell, 1985.

Keohane, Nannerl, Michelle Z. Rosaldo, and Barbara C. Gelpi, eds. *Feminist Theory: A Critique of Ideology.* Chicago: University of Chicago Press, 1982.

Koestenbaum, Wayne. *The Queen's Throat: Opera, Homosexuality and the Mystery of Desire.* New York: Poseidon Press, 1993.

Kruger, Steven. *AIDS Narratives.* New York: Garland, 1996.

Marks, Elaine, and Isabelle de Courtivron, eds. *New French Feminisms: An Anthology.* Amherst: University of Massachusetts Press, 1980.

Miller, D. A. *The Novel and the Police.* Berkeley: University of California Press, 1988.

Miller, Nancy K., ed. *The Poetics of Gender.* New York: Columbia University Press, 1986.

Mulvey, Laura. *Visual and Other Pleasures.* Basingstoke, Eng.: Macmillan, 1989.

Norton, Rictor. *The Myth of the Modern Homosexual: Queer History and the Search for Cultural Unity.* London: Cassell, 1997.

Reid-Pharr, Robert. *Black Gay Man.* New York: NYU Press, 2001.

Rich, Adrienne. "Compulsory Heterosexuality and Lesbian Existence." In *Women, Sex and Sexuality,* ed. Catharine Stimpson and Ethel Spector Person. Chicago: University of Chicago Press, 1980, pp. 62–91.

Rosario, Vernon A., ed. *Science and Homosexualities.* New York: Routledge, 1997.

Rubin, Gayle. "Thinking Sex: Notes for a Radical Theory of the Politics of Sexuality." In *Pleasure and Danger: Exploring Female Sexuality,* ed. Carol A. Vance. New York: Routledge, 1984, pp. 267–319.

Sedgwick, Eve Kosofsky. *Between Men: English Literature and Male Homosocial Desire.* New York: Columbia University Press, 1985.

———. *Epistemology of the Closet.* Berkeley: University of California Press, 1990.

Seidman, Steven. *Queer Theory/Sociology.* Cambridge: Blackwell, 1996.

Warner, Michael, ed. *Fear of a Queer Planet: Queer Politics and Social Theory.* Minneapolis: University of Minnesota Press, 1993.

Watney, Simon. *Policing Desire: Pornography, AIDS and the Media.* Minneapolis: University of Minnesota Press, 1987.

Weeks, Jeffrey. *Sex, Politics and Society: The Regulation of Sexuality Since 1800.* New York: Longman, 1981.

———. *Sexuality and Its Discontents: Meanings, Myths and Modern Sexualities.* London: Routledge, 1985.

Wittig, Monique. *The Straight Mind.* Boston: Beacon, 1992.

Michel Foucault

1926–1984

The following selection is taken from Robert Hurley's translation of Le Volonté de savoir *(The Will to Knowledge),* Volume 1 of Foucault's History of Sexuality *(1980). (For biographical information, see the introduction to Foucault, p. 520.)*

From *The History of Sexuality*

1. OBJECTIVE

. . . This history of sexuality, or rather this series of studies concerning the historical relationships of power and the discourse on sex, is, I realize, a circular project in the sense that it involves two endeavors that refer back to one another. We shall try to rid ourselves of a juridical and negative representation of power, and cease to conceive of it in terms of law, prohibition, liberty, and sovereignty. But how then do we analyze what has occurred in recent history with regard to this thing — seemingly one of the most forbidden areas of our lives and bodies — that is sex? How, if not by way of prohibition and blockage, does power gain access to it? Through which mechanisms, or tactics, or devices? But let us assume in turn that a somewhat careful scrutiny will show that power in modern societies has not in fact governed sexuality through law and sovereignty; let us suppose that historical analysis has revealed the presence of a veritable "technology" of sex, one that is much more complex and above all much more positive than the mere effect of a "defense" could be: this being the case, does this example — which can only be considered a privileged one, since power seemed in this instance, more than anywhere else, to function as prohibition — not compel one to discover principles for analyzing power which do not derive from the system of right and the form of

Translated by Robert Hurley.

2. METHOD

Hence the objective is to analyze a certain form of knowledge regarding sex, not in terms of repression or law, but in terms of power. But the word *power* is apt to lead to a number of misunderstandings — misunderstandings with respect to its nature, its form, and its unity. By power, I do not mean "Power" as a group of institutions and mechanisms that ensure the subservience of the citizens of a given state. By power, I do not mean, either, a mode of subjugation which, in contrast to violence, has the form of the rule. Finally, I do not have in mind a general system of domination exerted by one group over another, a system whose effects, through successive derivations, pervade the entire social body. The analysis, made in terms of power, must not assume that the sovereignty of the state, the form of the law, or the over-all unity of a domination are given at the outset; rather, these are only the terminal forms power takes. It seems to me that power must be understood in the first instance as the multiplicity of force relations immanent in the

law? Hence it is a question of forming a different grid of historical decipherment by starting from a different theory of power; and, at the same time, of advancing little by little toward a different conception of power through a closer examination of an entire historical material. We must at the same time conceive of sex without the law, and power without the king.

sphere in which they operate and which constitute their own organization; as the process which, through ceaseless struggles and confrontations, transforms, strengthens, or reverses them; as the support which these force relations find in one another, thus forming a chain or a system, or on the contrary, the disjunctions and contradictions which isolate them from one another; and lastly, as the strategies in which they take effect, whose general design or institutional crystallization is embodied in the state apparatus, in the formulation of the law, in the various social hegemonies. Power's condition of possibility, or in any case the viewpoint which permits one to understand its exercise, even in its more "peripheral" effects, and which also makes it possible to use its mechanisms as a grid of intelligibility of the social order, must not be sought in the primary existence of a central point, in a unique source of sovereignty from which secondary and descendent forms would emanate; it is the moving substrate of force relations which, by virtue of their inequality, constantly engender states of power, but the latter are always local and unstable. The omnipresence of power: not because it has the privilege of consolidating everything under its invincible unity, but because it is produced from one moment to the next, at every point, or rather in every relation from one point to another. Power is everywhere; not because it embraces everything, but because it comes from everywhere. And "Power," insofar as it is permanent, repetitious, inert, and self-reproducing, is simply the over-all effect that emerges from all these mobilities, the concatenation that rests on each of them and seeks in turn to arrest their movement. One needs to be nominalistic, no doubt: power is not an institution, and not a structure; neither is it a certain strength we are endowed with; it is the name that one attributes to a complex strategical situation in a particular society.

Should we turn the expression around, then, and say that politics is war pursued by other means?[1] If we still wish to maintain a separation between war and politics, perhaps we should postulate rather that this multiplicity of force relations can be coded — in part but never totally — either in the form of "war," or in the form of "politics"; this would imply two different strategies (but the one always liable to switch into the other) for integrating these unbalanced, heterogeneous, unstable, and tense force relations.

Continuing this line of discussion, we can advance a certain number of propositions:

Power is not something that is acquired, seized, or shared, something that one holds on to or allows to slip away; power is exercised from innumerable points, in the inter-play of nonegalitarian and mobile relations.

Relations of power are not in a position of exteriority with respect to other types of relationships (economic processes, knowledge relationships, sexual relations), but are immanent in the latter; they are the immediate effects of the divisions, inequalities, and disequilibriums which occur in the latter, and conversely they are the internal conditions of these differentiations; relations of power are not in the superstructural[2] positions, with merely a role of prohibition or accompaniment; they have a directly productive role, wherever they come into play.

Power comes from below; that is, there is no binary and all-encompassing opposition between rulers and ruled at the root of power relations, and serving as a general matrix — no such duality extending from the top down and reacting on more and more limited groups to the very depths of the social body. One must suppose rather that the manifold relationships of force that take shape and come into play in the machinery of production, in families, limited groups, and institutions, are the basis for wide-ranging effects of cleavage that run through the social body as a whole. These then form a general line of force that traverses the local oppositions and links them together;

[1]Foucault is alluding to the famous definition of Prussian General Karl von Clausewitz (1780–1831) in *On War* (1832): "War is the continuation of politics by other means."

[2]Although no Marxist, Foucault is here making use of Marx's distinction between base and superstructure. In the two paragraphs following this one, he refers to Gramsci's notion of hegemony and Althusser's notion of "ideological state apparatuses." See the introduction to Marxist Criticism, p. 693.

to be sure, they also bring about redistributions, realignments, homogenizations, serial arrangements, and convergences of the force relations. Major dominations are the hegemonic effects that are sustained by all these confrontations.

Power relations are both intentional and non-subjective. If in fact they are intelligible, this is not because they are the effect of another instance that "explains" them, but rather because they are imbued, through and through, with calculation: there is no power that is exercised without a series of aims and objectives. But this does not mean that it results from the choice or decision of an individual subject; let us not look for the headquarters that presides over its rationality; neither the caste which governs, nor the groups which control the state apparatus, nor those who make the most important economic decisions direct the entire network of power that functions in a society (and makes it function): the rationality of power is characterized by tactics that are often quite explicit at the restricted level where they are inscribed (the local cynicism of power), tactics which, becoming connected to one another, attracting and propagating one another, but finding their base of support and their condition elsewhere, end by forming comprehensive systems: the logic is perfectly clear, the aims decipherable, and yet it is often the case that no one is there to have invented them, and few who can be said to have formulated them: an implicit characteristic of the great anonymous, almost unspoken strategies which coordinate the loquacious tactics whose "inventors" or decision makers are often without hypocrisy.

Where there is power, there is resistance, and yet, or rather consequently, this resistance is never in a position of exteriority in relation to power. Should it be said that one is always "inside" power, there is no "escaping" it, there is no absolute outside where it is concerned, because one is subject to the law in any case? Or that, history being the ruse of reason, power is the ruse of history, always emerging the winner? This would be to misunderstand the strictly relational character of power relationships. Their existence depends on a multiplicity of points of resistance:

these play the role of adversary, target, support, or handle in power relations. These points of resistance are present everywhere in the power network. Hence there is no single locus of great Refusal, no soul of revolt, source of all rebellions, or pure law of the revolutionary. Instead there is a plurality of resistances, each of them a special case: resistances that are possible, necessary, improbable; others that are spontaneous, savage, solitary, concerted, rampant, or violent; still others that are quick to compromise, interested, or sacrificial; by definition, they can only exist in the strategic field of power relations. But this does not mean that they are only a reaction or rebound, forming with respect to the basic domination an underside that is in the end always passive, doomed to perpetual defeat. Resistances do not derive from a few heterogeneous principles; but neither are they a lure or a promise that is of necessity betrayed. They are the odd term in relations of power; they are inscribed in the latter as an irreducible opposite. Hence they too are distributed in irregular fashion: the points, knots, or focuses of resistance are spread over time and space at varying densities, at times mobilizing groups or individuals in a definitive way, inflaming certain points of the body, certain moments in life, certain types of behavior. Are there no great radical ruptures, massive binary divisions, then? Occasionally, yes. But more often one is dealing with mobile and transitory points of resistance, producing cleavages in a society that shift about, fracturing unities and effecting regroupings, furrowing across individuals themselves, cutting them up and remolding them, marking off irreducible regions in them, in their bodies and minds. Just as the network of power relations ends by forming a dense web that passes through apparatuses and institutions, without being exactly localized in them, so too the swarm of points of resistance traverses social stratifications and individual unities. And it is doubtless the strategic codification of these points of resistance that makes a revolution possible, somewhat similar to the way in which the state relies on the institutional integration of power relationships.

It is in this sphere of force relations that we must try to analyze the mechanisms of power.

In this way we will escape from the system of Law-and-Sovereign which has captivated political thought for such a long time. And if it is true that Machiavelli was among the few — and this no doubt was the scandal of his "cynicism" — who conceived the power of the Prince in terms of force relationships, perhaps we need to go one step further, do without the persona of the Prince, and decipher power mechanisms on the basis of a strategy that is immanent in force relationships.

To return to sex and the discourses of truth that have taken charge of it, the question that we must address, then, is not: Given a specific state structure, how and why is it that power needs to establish a knowledge of sex? Neither is the question: What over-all domination was served by the concern, evidenced since the eighteenth century, to produce true discourses on sex? Nor is it: What law presided over both the regularity of sexual behavior and the conformity of what was said about it? It is rather: In a specific type of discourse on sex, in a specific form of extortion of truth, appearing historically and in specific places (around the child's body, apropos of women's sex, in connection with practices restricting births, and so on), what were the most immediate, the most local power relations at work? How did they make possible these kinds of discourses, and conversely, how were these discourses used to support power relations? How was the action of these power relations modified by their very exercise, entailing a strengthening of some terms and a weakening of others, with effects of resistance and counterinvestments, so that there has never existed one type of stable subjugation, given once and for all? How were these power relations linked to one another according to the logic of a great strategy, which in retrospect takes on the aspect of a unitary and voluntarist politics of sex? In general terms: rather than referring all the infinitesimal violences that are exerted on sex, all the anxious gazes that are directed at it, and all the hiding places whose discovery is made into an impossible task, to the unique form of a great Power, we must immerse the expanding production of discourses on sex in the field of multiple and mobile power relations.

Which leads us to advance, in a preliminary way, four rules to follow. But these are not intended as methodological imperatives; at most they are cautionary prescriptions.

1. Rule of Immanence

One must not suppose that there exists a certain sphere of sexuality that would be the legitimate concern of a free and disinterested scientific inquiry were it not the object of mechanisms of prohibition brought to bear by the economic or ideological requirements of power. If sexuality was constituted as an area of investigation, this was only because relations of power had established it as a possible object; and conversely, if power was able to take it as a target, this was because techniques of knowledge and procedures of discourse were capable of investing it. Between techniques of knowledge and strategies of power, there is no exteriority, even if they have specific roles and are linked together on the basis of their difference. We will start, therefore, from what might be called "local centers" of power-knowledge: for example, the relations that obtain between penitents and confessors, or the faithful and their directors of conscience. Here, guided by the theme of the "flesh" that must be mastered, different forms of discourse — self-examination, questionings, admissions, interpretations, interviews — were the vehicle of a kind of incessant back-and-forth movement of forms of subjugation and schemas of knowledge. Similarly, the body of the child, under surveillance, surrounded in his cradle, his bed, or his room by an entire watch-crew of parents, nurses, servants, educators, and doctors, all attentive to the least manifestations of his sex, has constituted, particularly since the eighteenth century, another "local center" of power-knowledge.

2. Rules of Continual Variations

We must not look for who has the power in the order of sexuality (men, adults, parents, doctors) and who is deprived of it (women, adolescents, children, patients); nor for who has the right to know and who is forced to remain ignorant. We must seek rather the pattern of the modifications which the relationships of force imply by the very nature of their process. The "distributions for the Malthusian control of the birthrate,[3] for the populationist incitements, for the medical-ization of sex and the psychiatrization of its nongenital forms.

4. Rule of the Tactical Polyvalence of Discourses

What is said about sex must not be analyzed simply as the surface of projection of these power mechanisms. Indeed, it is in discourse that power and knowledge are joined together. And for this very reason, we must conceive discourse as a series of discontinuous segments whose tactical function is neither uniform nor stable. To be more precise, we must not imagine a world of discourse divided between accepted discourse and excluded discourse, or between the dominant discourse and the dominated one; but as a multiplicity of discursive elements that can come into play in various strategies. It is this distribution that we must reconstruct, with the things said and those concealed, the enunciations required and those forbidden, that it comprises; with the variants and different effects — according to who is speaking, his position of power, the institutional context in which he happens to be situated — that it implies; and with the shifts and reutilizations of identi-cal formulas for contrary objectives that it also includes. Discourses are not once and for all sub-servient to power or raised up against it, any more than silences are. We must make allowance for the complex and unstable process whereby discourse can be both an instrument and an effect of power, but also a hindrance, a stumbling-block, a point of resistance and a starting point for an oppos-ing strategy. Discourse transmits and produces power; it reinforces it, but also undermines and exposes it, renders it fragile and makes it possible to thwart it. In like manner, silence and secrecy are a shelter for power, anchoring its prohibi-tions; but they also loosen its holds and provide for relatively obscure areas of tolerance. Consider

[3] In *An Essay on the Principle of Population* (1798), British economist Thomas Robert Malthus (1766–1834), observing that population increased geometrically while consumer goods increased arithmetically, recommended sexual restraint as an alternative to the otherwise inevitable conse-quences of poverty and starvation.

of power" and the "appropriations of knowl-edge" never represent only instantaneous slices taken from processes involving, for example, a cumulative reinforcement of the strongest fac-tor, or a reversal of relationship, or again, a simultaneous increase of two terms. Relations of power-knowledge are not static forms of distribu-tion, they are "matrices of transformations." The nineteenth-century grouping made up of the father, the mother, the educator, and the doctor, around the child and his sex, was subjected to constant modifications, continual shifts. One of the more spectacular results of the latter was a strange reversal: whereas to begin with the child's sexual-ity had been problematized within the relationship established between doctor and parents (in the form of advice, or recommendations to keep the child under observation, or warnings of future dangers), ultimately it was in the relationship of the psychiatrist to the child that the sexuality of adults themselves was called into question.

3. Rule of Double Conditioning

No "local center," no "pattern of transformation" could function if, through a series of sequences, it did not eventually enter into an over-all strat-egy. And inversely, no strategy could achieve comprehensive effects if it did not gain support from precise and tenuous relations serving, not as its point of application or final outcome, but as its prop and anchor point. There is no discontinu-ity between them, as if one were dealing with two different levels (one microscopic and the other macroscopic); but neither is there homogeneity (as if the one were only the enlarged projection or the miniaturization of the other); rather, one must conceive of the double conditioning of a strategy by the specificity of possible tactics, and of tactics by the strategic envelope that makes them work. Thus the father in the family is not the "representative" of the sovereign or the state; and the latter are not projections of the father on a different scale. The family does not duplicate society, just as society does not imitate the fam-ily. But the family organization, precisely to the extent that it was insular and heteromorphous with respect to the other power mechanisms, was used to support the great "maneuvers" employed

for example the history of what was once "the" great sin against nature. The extreme discretion of the texts dealing with sodomy — that utterly confused category — and the nearly universal reticence in talking about it made possible a twofold operation: on the one hand, there was an extreme severity (punishment by fire was meted out well into the eighteenth century, without there being any substantial protest expressed before the middle of the century), and on the other hand, a tolerance that must have been widespread (which one can deduce indirectly from the infrequency of judicial sentences, and which one glimpses more directly through certain statements concerning societies of men that were thought to exist in the army or in the courts). There is no question that the appearance in nineteenth-century psychiatry, jurisprudence, and literature of a whole series of discourses on the species and subspecies of homosexuality, inversion, pederasty, and "psychic hermaphrodism" made possible a strong advance of social controls into this area of "perversity"; but it also made possible the formation of a "reverse" discourse: homosexuality began to speak in its own behalf, to demand that its legitimacy or "naturality" be acknowledged, often in the same vocabulary, using the same categories by which it was medically disqualified. There is not, on the one side, a discourse of power, and opposite it, another discourse that runs counter to it. Discourses are tactical elements or blocks operating in the field of force relations; there can exist different and even contradictory discourses within the same strategy; they can, on the contrary, circulate without changing their form from one strategy to another, opposing strategy. We must not expect the discourses on sex to tell us, above all, what strategy they derive from, or what moral divisions they accompany, or what ideology — dominant or dominated — they represent; rather we must question them on the two levels of their tactical productivity (what reciprocal effects of power and knowledge they ensure) and their strategical integration (what conjunction and what force relationship make their utilization necessary in a given episode of the various confrontations that occur).

In short, it is a question of orienting ourselves to a conception of power which replaces the privilege of the law with the viewpoint of the objective, the privilege of prohibition with the viewpoint of tactical efficacy, the privilege of sovereignty with the analysis of a multiple and mobile field of force relations, wherein far-reaching, but never completely stable, effects of domination are produced. The strategical model, rather than the model based on law. And this, not out of a speculative choice or theoretical preference, but because in fact it is one of the essential traits of Western societies that the force relationships which for a long time had found expression in war, in every form of warfare, gradually became invested in the order of political power.

3. DOMAIN

Sexuality must not be described as a stubborn drive, by nature alien and of necessity disobedient to a power which exhausts itself trying to subdue it and often fails to control it entirely. It appears rather as an especially dense transfer point for relations of power: between men and women, young people and old people, parents and offspring, teachers and students, priests and laity, an administration and a population. Sexuality is not the most intractable element in power relations, but rather one of those endowed with the greatest instrumentality: useful for the greatest number of maneuvers and capable of serving as a point of support, as a linchpin, for the most varied strategies.

There is no single, all-encompassing strategy, valid for all of society and uniformly bearing on all the manifestations of sex. For example, the idea that there have been repeated attempts, by various means, to reduce all of sex to its reproductive function, its heterosexual and adult form, and its matrimonial legitimacy fails to take into account the manifold objectives aimed for, the manifold means employed in the different sexual politics concerned with the two sexes, the different age groups and social classes.

In a first approach to the problem, it seems that we can distinguish four great strategic unities which, beginning in the eighteenth century, formed specific mechanisms of knowledge and power centering on sex. These did not come into being fully developed at that time; but it was then that they took on a consistency and gained an effectiveness in the order of power, as well as a productivity in the order of knowledge, so that it is possible to describe them in their relative autonomy.

1. *A hysterization of women's bodies:* a threefold process whereby the feminine body was analyzed — qualified and disqualified — as being thoroughly saturated with sexuality; whereby it was integrated into the sphere of medical practices, by reason of a pathology intrinsic to it; whereby, finally, it was placed in organic communication with the social body (whose regulated fecundity it was supposed to ensure), the family space (of which it had to be a substantial and functional element), and the life of children (which it produced and had to guarantee, by virtue of a biologico-moral responsibility lasting through the entire period of the children's education): the Mother, with her negative image of "nervous woman," constituted the most visible form of this hysterization.

2. *A pedagogization of children's sex:* a double assertion that practically all children indulge or are prone to indulge in sexual activity; and that, being unwarranted, at the same time "natural" and "contrary to nature," this sexual activity posed physical and moral, individual and collective dangers; children were defined as "preliminary" sexual beings, on this side of sex, yet within it, astride a dangerous dividing line. Parents, families, educators, doctors, and eventually psychologists would have to take charge, in a continuous way, of this precious and perilous, dangerous and endangered sexual potential: this pedagogization was especially evident in the war against onanism, which in the West lasted nearly two centuries.

3. *A socialization of procreative behavior:* an economic socialization via all the incitements and restrictions, the "social" and fiscal measures brought to bear on the fertility of couples; a political socialization achieved through the "responsibilization" of couples with regard to the social body as a whole (which had to be limited or on the contrary reinvigorated), and a medical socialization carried out by attributing a pathogenic value — for the individual and the species — to birth-control practices.

4. *A psychiatrization of perverse pleasure:* the sexual instinct was isolated as a separate biological and psychical instinct; a clinical analysis was made of all the forms of anomalies by which it could be afflicted; it was assigned a role of normalization or pathologization with respect to all behavior; and finally, a corrective technology was sought for these anomalies.

Four figures emerged from this preoccupation with sex, which mounted throughout the nineteenth century — four privileged objects of knowledge, which were also targets and anchorage points for the ventures of knowledge: the hysterical woman, the masturbating child, the Malthusian couple, and the perverse adult. Each of them corresponded to one of these strategies which, each in its own way, invested and made use of the sex of women, children, and men.

What was at issue in these strategies? A struggle against sexuality? Or were they part of an effort to gain control of it? An attempt to regulate it more effectively and mask its more indiscreet, conspicuous, and intractable aspects? A way of formulating only that measure of knowledge about it that was acceptable or useful? In actual fact, what was involved, rather, was the very production of sexuality. Sexuality must not be thought of as a kind of natural given which power tries to hold in check, or as an obscure domain which knowledge tries gradually to uncover. It is the name that can be given to a historical construct: not a furtive reality that is difficult to grasp, but a great surface network in which the stimulation of bodies, the intensification of pleasures, the incitement to discourse, the formation of special knowledges, the strengthening of controls and resistances, are linked to one another, in accordance with a few major strategies of knowledge and power.

It will be granted no doubt that relations of sex gave rise, in every society, to a *deployment of alliance:* a system of marriage, of fixation and development of kinship ties, of transmission of names and possessions. This deployment of alliance, with the mechanisms of constraint that ensured its existence and the complex knowledge it often required, lost some of its importance as economic processes and political structures could no longer rely on it as an adequate instrument or sufficient support. Particularly from the eighteenth century onward, Western societies created and deployed a new apparatus which was superimposed on the previous one, and which, without completely supplanting the latter, helped to reduce its importance. I am speaking of the *deployment of sexuality:* like the *deployment of alliance,* it connects up with the circuit of sexual partners, but in a completely different way. The two systems can be contrasted term by term. The deployment of alliance is built around a system of rules defining the permitted and the forbidden, the licit and the illicit, whereas the deployment of sexuality operates according to mobile, polymorphous, and contingent techniques of power. The deployment of alliance has as one of its chief objectives to reproduce the interplay of relations and maintain the law that governs them; the deployment of sexuality, on the other hand, engenders a continual extension of areas and forms of control. For the first, what is pertinent is the link between partners and definite statutes; the second is concerned with the sensations of the body, the quality of pleasures, and the nature of impressions, however tenuous or imperceptible these may be. Lastly, if the deployment of alliance is firmly tied to the economy due to the role it can play in the transmission or circulation of wealth, the deployment of sexuality is linked to the economy through numerous and subtle relays, the main one of which, however, is the body — the body that produces and consumes. In a word, the deployment of alliance is attuned to a homeostasis of the social body, which it has the function of maintaining; whence its privileged link with the law; whence too the fact that the important phase for it is "reproduction." The deployment of sexuality has its reason for being, not in reproducing itself, but in proliferating, innovating, annexing, creating, and penetrating bodies in an increasingly detailed way, and in controlling populations in an increasingly comprehensive way. We are compelled, then, to accept three or four hypotheses which run counter to the one on which the theme of a sexuality repressed by the modern forms of society is based: sexuality is tied to recent devices of power; it has been expanding at an increasing rate since the seventeenth century; the arrangement that has sustained it is not governed by reproduction; it has been linked from the outset

with an intensification of the body — with its exploitation as an object of knowledge and an element in relations of power.

It is not exact to say that the deployment of sexuality supplanted the deployment of alliance. One can imagine that one day it will have replaced it. But as things stand at present, while it does tend to cover up the deployment of alliance, it has neither obliterated the latter nor rendered it useless. Moreover, historically it was around and on the basis of the deployment of alliance that the deployment of sexuality was constructed. First the practice of penance, then that of the examination of conscience and spiritual direction, was the formative nucleus: as we have seen, what was at issue to begin with at the tribunal of penance was sex insofar as it was the basis of relations; the questions posed had to do with the commerce allowed or forbidden (adultery, extramarital relations, relations with a person prohibited by blood or statute, the legitimate or illegitimate character of the act of sexual congress); then, coinciding with the new pastoral[4] and its application in seminaries, secondary schools, and convents, there was a gradual progression away from the problematic of relations toward a problematic of the "flesh," that is, of the body, sensation, the nature of pleasure, the more secret forms of enjoyment or acquiescence. "Sexuality" was taking shape, born of a technology of power that was originally focused on alliance. Since then, it has not ceased to operate in conjunction with a system of alliance on which it has depended for support. The family cell, in the form in which it came to be valued in the course of the eighteenth century, made it possible for the main elements of the deployment of sexuality (the feminine body, infantile precocity, the regulation of births, and to a lesser extent no doubt, the specification of the perverted) to develop along its two primary dimensions: the husband-wife axis and the parents-children axis. The family, in its contemporary form, must not be understood as a social, economic, and political structure of alliance that excludes or at least restrains sexuality, that diminishes it as much as possible, preserving only its useful functions. On the contrary, its role is to

[4]Pastoral refers to the duties of priests.

anchor sexuality and provide it with a permanent support. It ensures the production of a sexuality that is not homogeneous with the privileges of alliance, while making it possible for the systems of alliance to be imbued with a new tactic of power which they would otherwise be impervious to. The family is the interchange of sexuality and alliance: it conveys the law and the juridical dimension in the deployment of sexuality; and it conveys the economy of pleasure and the intensity of sensations in the regime of alliance.

This interpenetration of the deployment of alliance and that of sexuality in the form of the family allows us to understand a number of facts: that since the eighteenth century the family has become an obligatory locus of affects, feelings, love; that sexuality has its privileged point of development in the family; that for this reason sexuality is "incestuous" from the start. It may be that in societies where the mechanisms of alliance predominate, prohibition of incest is a functionally indispensable rule. But in a society such as ours, where the family is the most active site of sexuality, and where it is doubtless the exigencies of the latter which maintain and prolong its existence, incest — for different reasons altogether and in a completely different way — occupies a central place; it is constantly being solicited and refused; it is an object of obsession and attraction, a dreadful secret and an indispensable pivot. It is manifested as a thing that is strictly forbidden in the family insofar as the latter functions as a deployment of alliance; but it is also a thing that is continuously demanded in order for the family to be a hotbed of constant sexual incitement. If for more than a century the West has displayed such a strong interest in the prohibition of incest, if more or less by common accord it has been seen as a social universal and one of the points through which every society is obliged to pass on the way to becoming a culture, perhaps this is because it was found to be a means of self-defense, not against an incestuous desire, but against the expansion and the implications of this deployment of sexuality which had been set up, but which, among its many benefits, had the disadvantage of ignoring the laws and juridical forms of alliance. By asserting that all societies without exception, and consequently our own, were subject to this

rule of rules, one guaranteed that this deployment of sexuality, whose strange effects were beginning to be felt — among them, the affective intensification of the family space — would not be able to escape from the grand and ancient system of alliance.[5] Thus the law would be secure, even in the new mechanics of power. For this is the paradox of a society which, from the eighteenth century to the present, has created so many technologies of power that are foreign to the concept of law: it fears the effects and proliferations of those technologies and attempts to recode them in forms of law. If one considers the threshold of all culture to be prohibited incest, then sexuality has been, from the dawn of time, under the sway of law and right. By devoting so much effort to an endless reworking of the transcultural theory of the incest taboo, anthropology has proved worthy of the whole modern deployment of sexuality and the theoretical discourses it generates.

What has taken place since the seventeenth century can be interpreted in the following manner: the deployment of sexuality which first developed on the fringes of familial institutions (in the direction of conscience and pedagogy, for example) gradually became focused on the family: the alien, irreducible, and even perilous effects it held in store for the deployment of alliance (an awareness of this danger was evidenced in the criticism often directed at the indiscretion of the directors, and in the entire controversy, which occurred somewhat later, over the private or public, institutional or familial education of children[6]) were absorbed by the family, a family that was reorganized, restricted no doubt, and in any case intensified in comparison with the functions it formerly exercised in the deployment of alliance. In the family, parents and relatives became the chief agents of a deployment of sexuality which drew its outside support from

[5] Foucault refers to the theory of anthropologist Claude Lévi-Strauss that the incest-taboo is universal within human cultures, indeed defines human culture. See Lévi-Strauss, p. 859.

[6] Molière's *Tartuffe* and Jakob Michael Lenz's *Tutor*, separated by more than a century, both depict the interference of the deployment of sexuality in the family organization, of the deployment of spiritual direction in *Tartuffe* and education in *The Tutor*. [Foucault]

doctors, educators, and later psychiatrists, and which began by competing with the relations of alliance but soon "psychologized" or "psychiatrized" the latter. Then these new personages made their appearance: the nervous woman, the frigid wife, the indifferent mother — or worse, the mother beset by murderous obsessions — the impotent, sadistic, perverse husband, the hysterical or neurasthenic girl, the precocious and already exhausted child, and the young homosexual who rejects marriage or neglects his wife. These were the combined figures of an alliance gone bad and an abnormal sexuality; they were the means by which the disturbing factors of the latter were brought into the former; and yet they also provided an opportunity for the alliance system to assert its prerogatives in the order of sexuality. Then a pressing demand emanated from the family: a plea for help in reconciling these unfortunate conflicts between sexuality and alliance; and, caught in the grip of this deployment of sexuality which had invested it from without, contributing to its solidification into its modern form, the family broadcast the long complaint of its sexual suffering to doctors, educators, psychiatrists, priests, and pastors, to all the "experts" who would listen. It was as if it had suddenly discovered the dreadful secret of what had always been hinted at and inculcated in it: the family, the keystone of alliance, was the germ of all the misfortunes of sex. And lo and behold, from the mid-nineteenth century onward, the family engaged in searching out the slightest traces of sexuality in its midst, wrenching from itself the most difficult confessions, soliciting an audience with everyone who might know something about the matter, and opening itself unreservedly to endless examination. The family was the crystal in the deployment of sexuality: it seemed to be the source of a sexuality which it actually only reflected and diffracted. By virtue of its permeability, and through that process of reflections to the outside, it became one of the most valuable tactical components of the deployment.

Monique Wittig
1935–2003

Born in Dannemarie in southern Alsace, the daughter of the poet Henri Dubois, Monique attended the Sorbonne at the University Paris, earning a degree in Oriental languages. She was one of the found-ers of the Mouvement de Libération Féminine, and like many of her generation, her revolutionary politics were formed by the utopian dreams of May 1968 (when students and workers united in a strike intended to bring on a new French revolution). Wittig began by writing experimental novels, such as The Opoponax (1964), Les Guérillères (1969), The Lesbian Body (1975), and Across the Acheron (1987). In each of these works, the grammar and syntax of narrative is broken down and reconstructed in ways that reflect the sexual and social reconstructions performed by the characters. Each text depicts a patriarchal society whose norms are violently rejected by female characters, who re-create society so that the power and language infrastructures allow for feminine/homosexual participation. Wittig received her Ph.D. from the École des Hautes Études en Sciences Sociales in Paris, where she studied under Gérard Genette. After publishing Lesbian Peoples: Material for a Dictionary (with her partner, Sande Zeig, 1976), Wittig emigrated to the United States, where she lectured at many univer-sities, including Berkeley, Duke, New York University, and Vassar, until she took her final position in 1990 as a professor of French and Women's Studies at the University of Arizona. She died of a sudden heart attack in January 2003. The following essay, "One Is Not Born a Woman," takes its title from Simone de Beauvoir (with whom Wittig collaborated on the periodical Questions Féministes), and was originally published in Feminist Issues 1, no. 2 (1981).

One Is Not Born a Woman

A materialist feminist[1] approach to women's oppression destroys the idea that women are a "natural group": "a racial group of a special kind, a group perceived as *natural*, a group of men considered as materially specific in their bodies."[2] What the analysis accomplishes on the level of ideas, practice makes actual at the level of facts: by its very existence, lesbian society destroys the artificial (social) fact constituting women as a "natural group." A lesbian society[3] pragmatically reveals that the division from men of which women have been the object is a political one and shows that we have been ideologically rebuilt into a "natural group." In the case of women, ideology goes far since our bodies as well as our minds are the product of this manipulation. We have been compelled in our bodies and in our minds to correspond, feature by feature, with the *idea* of nature that has been established for us. Distorted to such an extent that our deformed body is what they call "natural," what is supposed

---

[1]Christine Delphy, "Pour un féminisme matérialiste," *L'Arc* 61 (1975). Translated as "For a Materialist Feminism," *Feminist Issues* 1, no. 2 (Winter 1981). [Wittig]

[2]Colette Guillaumin, "Race et nature: système des marques, idée de groupe naturel et rapports sociaux," *Pluriel* 11 (1977). Translated as "Race and Nature: The System of Marks: The Idea of a Natural Group and Social Relationships," *Feminist Issues* 8, no. 2 (Fall 1988). [Wittig]

[3]I use the word *society* with an extended anthropological meaning; strictly speaking, it does not refer to societies, in that lesbian societies do not exist completely autonomously from heterosexual social systems. [Wittig]

to exist as such before oppression. Distorted to such an extent that in the end oppression seems to be a consequence of this "nature" within ourselves (a nature which is only an *idea*). What a materialist analysis does by reasoning, a lesbian society accomplishes practically: not only is there no natural group "women" (we lesbians are living proof of it), but as individuals as well we question "woman," which for us, as for Simone de Beauvoir, is only a myth. She said: "One is not born, but becomes a woman. No biological, psychological, or economic fate determines the figure that the human female presents in society: it is civilization as a whole that produces this creature, intermediate between male and eunuch, which is described as feminine."[4]

However, most of the feminists and lesbian-feminists in America and elsewhere still believe that the basis of women's oppression *is biological as well as* historical. Some of them even claim to find their sources in Simone de Beauvoir.[5] The belief in mother right and in a "prehistory" when women created civilization (because of a biological predisposition) while the coarse and brutal men hunted (because of a biological predisposition) is symmetrical with the biologizing interpretation of history produced up to now by the class of men. It is still the same method of finding in women and men a biological explanation of their division, outside of social facts. For me this could never constitute a lesbian approach to women's oppression, since it assumes that the basis of society or the beginning of society lies in heterosexuality. Matriarchy is no less heterosexual than patriarchy: it is only the sex of the oppressor that changes. Furthermore, not only is this conception still imprisoned in the categories of sex (woman and man), but it holds onto the idea that the capacity to give birth (biology) is what defines a woman. Although practical facts and ways of living contradict this theory in lesbian society, there are lesbians who affirm that "women and men are different species or races (the words are used interchangeably): men are biologically inferior to women; male violence is a biological inevitability . . ."[6] By doing this, by admitting that there is a "natural" division between women and men, we naturalize history, we assume that "men" and "women" have always existed and will always exist. Not only do we naturalize history, but also consequently we naturalize the social phenomena which express our oppression, making change impossible. For example, instead of seeing giving birth as a forced production, we see it as a "natural," "biological" process, forgetting that in our societies births are planned (demography), forgetting that we ourselves are programmed to produce children, while this is the only social activity "short of war"[7] that presents such a great danger of death. Thus, as long as we will be "unable to abandon by will or impulse a lifelong and centuries-old commitment to childbearing as *the* female creative act,"[8] gaining control of the production of children will mean much more than the mere control of the material means of this production: women will have to abstract themselves from the definition "woman" which is imposed upon them.

A materialist feminist approach shows that what we take for the cause or origin of oppression is in fact only the *mark*[9] imposed by the oppressor: the "myth of woman,"[10] plus its material effects and manifestations in the appropriated consciousness and bodies of women. Thus, this mark does not predate oppression: Colette Guillaumin has shown that before the socioeconomic reality of black slavery, the concept of race did not exist, at least not in its modern meaning, since it was applied to the lineage of families. However, now, race, exactly like sex, is taken as an "immediate given," a "sensible given," "physical features," belonging to a natural order. But what we believe to be a physical and direct perception is only a sophisticated and mythic construction, an

---

[4]Simone de Beauvoir, *The Second Sex* (New York: Bantam, 1952): 249. [Wittig] See de Beauvoir, p. 394.

[5][Kathie Sarahchild, ed.] *Feminist Revolution: Redstockings of the Women's Liberation Movement* (New York: Random House, 1978): 18. [Wittig]

[6]Andrea Dworkin, "Biological Superiority: The World's Most Dangerous and Deadly Idea," *Heresies* 6 (1989): 46. [Wittig]

[7]Ti-Grace Atkinson, *Amazon Odyssey* (New York: Links, 1974): 15. [Wittig]

[8]Dworkin, op. cit. [Wittig]

[9]Guillaumin, op. cit. [Wittig]

[10]Beauvoir, op. cit. [Wittig]

"imaginary formation,"[11] which reinterprets physical features (in themselves as neutral as any others but marked by the social system) through the network of relationships in which they are perceived. (They are seen as *black*, therefore they *are* black; they are seen as *women*, therefore, they *are* women. But before being *seen* that way, they first had to be *made* that way.) Lesbians should always remember and acknowledge how "unnatural," compelling, totally oppressive, and destructive being "woman" was for us in the old days before the women's liberation movement. It was a political constraint, and those who resisted it were accused of not being "real" women. But then we were proud of it, since in the accusation there was already something like a shadow of victory: the avowal by the oppressor that "woman" is not something that goes without saying, since to be one, one has to be a "real" one. We were at the same time accused of wanting to be men. Today this double accusation has been taken up again with enthusiasm in the context of the women's liberation movement by some feminists and also, alas, by some lesbians whose political goal seems somehow to be becoming more and more "feminine." To refuse to be a woman, however, does not mean that one has to become a man. Besides, if we take as an example the perfect "butch," the classic example which provokes the most horror, whom Proust would have called a woman/man, how is her alienation different from that of someone who wants to become a woman? Tweedledum and Tweedledee.[12] At least for a woman, wanting to become a man proves that she has escaped her initial programming. But even if she would like to, with all her strength, she cannot become a man. For becoming a man would demand from a woman not only an external appearance but his consciousness as well, that is, the consciousness of one who disposes by right of at least two "natural" slaves during his life span. This is impossible, and one feature of lesbian oppression consists precisely of making women out of reach for us, since women belong to men. Thus

[11] Guillaumin, op. cit. [Wittig]

[12] Identical twins in Lewis Carroll's *Through the Looking Glass* (1872).

a lesbian *has to* be something else, a not-woman, a not-man, a product of society, not a product of nature, for there is no nature in society.

The refusal to become (or to remain) heterosexual always meant to refuse to become a man or a woman, consciously or not. For a lesbian this goes further than the refusal of the *role* "woman." It is the refusal of the economic, ideological, and political power of a man. This, we lesbians, and nonlesbians as well, knew before the beginning of the lesbian and feminist movement. However, as Andrea Dworkin emphasizes, many lesbians recently "have increasingly tried to transform the very ideology that has enslaved us into a dynamic, religious, psychologically compelling celebration of female biological potential."[13] Thus, some avenues of the feminist and lesbian movement lead us back to the myth of woman which was created by men especially for us, and with it we sink back into a natural group. Having stood up to fight for a sexless society,[14] we now find ourselves entrapped in the familiar deadlock of "woman is wonderful." Simone de Beauvoir underlined particularly the false consciousness which consists of selecting among the features of the myth (that women are different from men) those which look good and using them as a definition for women. What the concept "woman" is wonderful" accomplishes is that it retains for defining women the best features (best according to whom?) which oppression has granted us, and it does not radically question the categories "man" and "woman," which are political categories and not natural givens. It puts us in a position of fighting within the class "women," not as the other classes do, for the disappearance of our class, but for the defense of "woman" and its reinforcement. It leads us to develop with complacency "new" theories about our specificity: thus, we call our passivity "nonviolence," when the main and emergent point for us is to fight our passivity (our fear, rather, a justified one). The ambiguity of the term "feminist" sums up the whole situation. What does "feminist" mean? Feminist is formed

[13] Dworkin, op. cit. [Wittig]

[14] Atkinson, p. 6: "If feminism has any logic at all, it must be working for a sexless society." [Wittig]

with the word "femme," "woman," and means: someone who fights for women. For many of us it means someone who fights for women as a class and for the disappearance of this class. For many others it means someone who fights for woman and her defense — for the myth, then, and its reenforcement. But why was the word "feminist" chosen if it retains the least ambiguity? We chose to call ourselves "feminists" ten years ago, not in order to support or reenforce the myth of woman, nor to identify ourselves with the oppressor's definition of us, but rather to affirm that our movement had a history and to emphasize the political link with the old feminist movement.

It is, then, this movement that we can put in question for the meaning that it gave to feminism. It so happens that feminism in the last century could never resolve its contradictions on the subject of nature/culture, woman/society. Women started to fight for themselves as a group and rightly considered that they shared common features as a result of oppression. But for them these features were natural and biological rather than social. They went so far as to adopt the Darwinist theory of evolution. They did not believe like Darwin, however, "that women were less evolved than men, but they did believe that male and female natures had diverged in the course of evolutionary development and that society at large reflected this polarization."[15] "The failure of early feminism was that it only attacked the Darwinist charge of female inferiority, while accepting the foundations of this charge — namely, the view of woman as 'unique.'"[16] And finally it was women scholars — and not feminists — who scientifically destroyed this theory. But the early feminists had failed to regard history as a dynamic process which develops from conflicts of interests. Furthermore, they still believed as men do that the cause (origin) of their oppression lay within themselves. And therefore after some astonishing victories the feminists of this first front found themselves at an impasse out of a lack of reasons to fight. They upheld the illogical principle of "equality in difference," an idea now being born

again. They fell back into the trap which threatens us once again: the myth of woman.

Thus it is our historical task, and only ours, to define what we call oppression in materialist terms, to make it evident that women are a class, which is to say that the category "woman" as well as the category "man" are political and economic categories not eternal ones. Our fight aims to suppress men as a class, not through a genocidal, but a political struggle. Once the class "men" disappears, "women" as a class will disappear as well, for there are no slaves without masters. Our first task, it seems, is to always thoroughly dissociate "women" (the class within which we fight) and "woman," the myth. For "woman" does not exist for us: it is only an imaginary formation,[17] while "women" is the product of a social relationship. We felt this strongly when everywhere we refused to be called a *"woman's* liberation movement." Furthermore, we have to destroy the myth inside and outside ourselves. "Woman" is not each one of us, but the political and ideological formation which negates "women" (the product of a relation of exploitation). "Woman" is there to confuse us, to hide the reality "women." In order to be aware of being a class and to become a class we first have to kill the myth of "woman" including its most seductive aspects (I think about Virginia Woolf when she said the first task of a woman writer is to kill "the angel in the house").[18] But to become a class we do not have to suppress our individual selves, and since no individual can be reduced to her/his oppression we are also confronted with the historical necessity of constituting ourselves as the individual subjects of our history as well. I believe this is the reason why all these attempts at "new" definitions of woman are blossoming now. What is at stake (and of course not only for women) is an individual definition as well as a class definition. For once one has acknowledged oppression, one needs to know and

[15]Rosalind Rosenberg, "In Search of Women's Nature," *Feminist Studies* 3, nos. 1–2 (1975): 144. [Wittig]

[16]Rosenberg, 146. [Wittig]

[17]Wittig suggests that "woman" as a concept or myth is like the unitary "self" in Lacan's "mirror stage," a wish-fulfilling product of the field of the Imaginary. See Lacan, p. 643.

[18]"The angel in the house" is a personification of Victorian womanhood, as in the 1854 poem of the same name by Coventry Patmore (1823–1896); Woolf's attack on the concept appears in her essay "Professions for Women" (1942).

experience the fact that one can constitute oneself as a subject (as opposed to an object of oppression), that one can become *someone* in spite of oppression, that one has one's own identity. There is no possible fight for someone deprived of an identity, no internal motivation for fighting, since, although I can fight only with others, first I fight for myself.

The question of the individual subject is historically a difficult one for everybody. Marxism, the last avatar of materialism, the science which has politically formed us, does not want to hear anything about a "subject." Marxism has rejected the transcendental subject, the subject as constitutive of knowledge, the "pure" consciousness. All that thinks per se, before all experience, has ended up in the garbage can of history, because it claimed to exist outside matter, prior to matter, and needed God, spirit, or soul to exist in such a way. This is what is called "idealism." As for individuals, they are only the product of social relations, therefore their consciousness can only be "alienated." (Marx, in *The German Ideology*,[19] says precisely that individuals of the dominating class are also alienated, although they are the direct producers of the ideas that alienate the classes oppressed by them. But since they draw visible advantages from their own alienation they can bear it without too much suffering.) There exists such a thing as class consciousness, but a consciousness which does not refer to a particular subject, except as participating in general conditions of exploitation at the same time as the other subjects of their class, all sharing the same consciousness. As for the practical class problem — outside of the class problems as traditionally defined — that one could encounter (for example, sexual problems), they were considered "bourgeois" problems that would disappear with the final victory of the class struggle. "Individualistic," "subjectivist," "petit bourgeois," these were the labels given to any person who had shown problems which could not be reduced to the "class struggle" itself.

Thus Marxism has denied the members of oppressed classes the attribute of being a subject. In doing this, Marxism, because of the ideological and political power this "revolutionary"

19 See Marx, p. 247.

science" immediately exercised upon the workers' movement and all other political groups, has prevented all categories of oppressed peoples from constituting themselves historically as subjects (subjects of their struggle, for example). This means that the "masses" did not fight for themselves but for *the* party or its organizations. And when an economic transformation took place (end of private property, constitution of the socialist state), no revolutionary change took place within the new society, because the people themselves did not change.

For women, Marxism had two results. It prevented them from being aware that they are a class and therefore from constituting themselves as a class for a very long time, by leaving the relation "women/men" outside the social order, by turning it into a natural relation, doubtless for Marxists the only one, along with the relation of mothers to children, to be seen this way, and by hiding the class conflict between men and women behind a natural division of labor (*The German Ideology*). This concerns the theoretical (ideological) level. On the practical level, Lenin, *the* party, all the communist parties up to now, including all the most radical political groups, have always reacted to any attempt on the part of women to reflect and form groups based on their own class problem with an accusation of divisiveness. By uniting, we women are dividing the strength of the people. This means that for the Marxists women *belong* either to the bourgeois class or to the proletariat class, in other words, to the men of these classes. In addition, Marxist theory does not allow women any more than other classes of oppressed people to constitute themselves as historical subjects, because Marxism does not take into account the fact that a class also consists of individuals one by one. Class consciousness is not enough. We must try to understand philosophically (politically) these concepts of "subject" and "class consciousness" and how they work in relation to our history. When we discover that women are the objects of oppression and appropriation, at the very moment that we become able to perceive this, we become subjects in the sense of cognitive subjects, through an operation of abstraction. Consciousness of oppression is not only a reaction to (fight against) oppression. It is also the whole conceptual revaluation of the social world, its whole reorganization with new concepts, from the point of view of oppression. It is what I would call the science of oppression created by the oppressed. This operation of understanding reality has to be undertaken by every one of us: call it a subjective, cognitive practice. The movement back and forth between the levels of reality (the conceptual reality and the material reality of oppression, which are both social realities) is accomplished through language.

It is we who historically must undertake the task of defining the individual subject in materialist terms. This certainly seems to be an impossibility since materialism and subjectivity have always been mutually exclusive. Nevertheless, and rather than despairing of ever understanding, we must recognize the *need* to reach subjectivity in the abandonment by many of us to the myth "woman" (the myth of woman being only a snare that holds us up). This real necessity for everyone to exist as an individual, as well as a member of a class, is perhaps the first condition for the accomplishment of a revolution, without which there can be no real fight or transformation. But the opposite is also true; without class and class consciousness there are no real subjects, only alienated individuals. For women to answer the question of the individual subject in materialist terms is first to show, as the lesbians and feminists did, that supposedly "subjective," "individual," "private" problems are in fact social problems, class problems; that sexuality is not for women an individual and subjective expression, but a social institution of violence. But once we have shown that all so-called personal problems are in fact class problems, we will still be left with the question of the subject of each singular woman — not the myth, but each one of us. At this point, let us say that a new personal and subjective definition for all humankind can only be found beyond the categories of sex (woman and man) and that the advent of individual

subjects demands first destroying the categories of sex, ending the use of them, and rejecting all sciences which still use these categories as their fundamentals (practically all social sciences).

To destroy "woman" does not mean that we aim, short of physical destruction, to destroy lesbianism simultaneously with the categories of sex, because lesbianism provides for the moment the only social form in which we can live freely. Lesbian is the only concept I know of which is beyond the categories of sex (woman and man), because the designated subject (lesbian) is *not* a woman, either economically, or politically, or ideologically. For what makes a woman is a specific social relation to a man, a relation that we have previously called servitude,[20] a relation which implies personal and physical obligation as well as economic obligation ("forced residence,"[21] domestic corvée,[22] conjugal duties, unlimited production of children, etc.), a relation which lesbians escape by refusing to become or to stay heterosexual. We are escapees from our class in the same way as the American runaway slaves were when escaping slavery and becoming free. For us this is an absolute necessity; our survival demands that we contribute all our strength to the destruction of the class of women within which men appropriate women. This can be accomplished only by the destruction of heterosexuality as a social system which is based on the oppression of women by men and which produces the doctrine of the difference between the sexes to justify this oppression.

[20]In an article published in *L'Idiot international* (May 1970), whose original title was "Pour un mouvement de libération des femmes." [Wittig]
[21]Christiane Rochefort, *Les Stances à Sophie* (Paris: Grasset, 1963). [Wittig]
[22]A tax under the French monarchy exacted in terms of forced labor on public works; here it refers to housework assigned to wives, even those who work outside the home.

Hélène Cixous

b. 1937

Hélène Cixous, one of the most versatile and radical voices in contemporary French feminism, was born in Oran, Algeria. A brilliant student, she received her agrégation in English in 1959 and her Docteur en lettres in 1968, the year that also saw her participation in the May student uprisings. Cixous taught at the University of Bordeaux (1962), the Sorbonne (1965–67), Nanterre (1967), and the University of Paris VIII-Vincennes (now at Saint-Denis), where she is a professor of English literature. In 1970, with Gérard Genette and Tzvetan Todorov, she founded the structuralist journal Poétique, and in 1974 established a center for women's studies at the University of Paris VIII. The work of Shakespeare and James Joyce (about whom she wrote her doctoral thesis), Heinrich von Kleist and Franz Kafka, Arthur Rimbaud and the Brazilian writer Clarice Lispector, Jacques Derrida and Jacques Lacan, has been particularly important to her. Cixous has written short stories (Le Prénom de Dieu, 1966), novels (Dedans, 1969, which won the Prix Médicis), and a great deal of literary and cultural criticism. Some of her other writings are Portrait of Dora (1976), The Newly Born Woman (1975; with Catherine Clément), and La Venue à l'écriture (1977; with Annie LeClerc and Madeleine Gagnon). Her most recent fiction includes La Jour où je n'étais pas là (2000), Benjamin à Montaigne: Il ne faut pas le dire (2001), Rêve je te dis (2003), and Neuter (2004). Her most recent criticism and theory in English include Writing Differences: Readings from the Seminar of Hélène Cixous (1988), Readings: The Poetics of Blanchot, Joyce, Kafka, Kleist, Lispector and Tsvetayeva (1991), Coming to Writing and Other Essays (1994), The Hélène Cixous Reader (1994), Manna (1994), Stigmata: Escaping Texts (1998), Portrait of Jacques Derrida as a Young, Jewish Saint (2004), Dream I Tell You (2006), Insister of Jacques Derrida (2008). "The Laugh of the Medusa," first published in L'Arc in 1975, was translated for the first volume of the feminist journal Signs (1976).

The Laugh of the Medusa

I shall speak about women's writing: *about what it will do.* Woman must write her self: must write about women and bring women to writing, from which they have been driven away as violently as from their bodies — for the same reasons, by the same law, with the same fatal goal. Woman must put herself into the text — as into the world and into history — by her own movement.

The future must no longer be determined by the past. I do not deny that the effects of the past are still with us. But I refuse to strengthen them by repeating them, to confer upon them an ire-movability the equivalent of destiny, to confuse the biological and the cultural. Anticipation is imperative.

Since these reflections are taking shape in an area just on the point of being discovered, they necessarily bear the mark of our time — a time during which the new breaks away from the old, and, more precisely, the (feminine) new from the old (*la nouvelle de l'ancien*). Thus, as there are no grounds for establishing a discourse, but rather an arid millennial ground to break, what I say has at least two sides and two aims: to break

Translated by Keith Cohen and Paula Cohen. The essay's title alludes to Freud's speculation about the head of Medusa, p. 317.

up, to destroy; and to foresee the unforeseeable, to project.

I write this as a woman, toward women. When I say "woman," I'm speaking of woman in her inevitable struggle against conventional man; and of a universal woman subject who must bring women to their senses and to their meaning in history. But first it must be said that in spite of the enormity of the repression that has kept them in the "dark" — that dark which people have been trying to make them accept as their attribute — there is, at this time, no general woman, no one typical woman. What they have *in common* I will say. But what strikes me is the infinite richness of their individual constitutions: you can't talk about *a* female sexuality, uniform, homogeneous, classifiable into codes — any more than you can talk about one unconscious resembling another. Women's imaginary[1] is inexhaustible, like music, painting, writing: their stream of phantasms is incredible.

I have been amazed more than once by a description a woman gave me of a world all her own which she had been secretly haunting since early childhood. A world of searching, the elaboration of a knowledge, on the basis of a systematic experimentation with the bodily functions, a passionate and precise interrogation of her erotogeneity. This practice, extraordinarily rich and inventive, in particular as concerns masturbation, is prolonged or accompanied by a production of forms, a veritable aesthetic activity, each stage of rapture inscribing a resonant vision, a composition, something beautiful. Beauty will no longer be forbidden.

I wished that that woman would write and proclaim this unique empire so that other women, other unacknowledged sovereigns, might exclaim: I, too, overflow; my desires have invented new desires, my body knows unheard-of songs. Time and again, I, too, have felt so full of luminous torrents that I could burst — burst with forms much more beautiful than those which are put up in frames and sold for a stinking fortune. And I,

too, said nothing, showed nothing; I didn't open my mouth, I didn't repaint my half of the world. I was ashamed. I was afraid, and I swallowed my shame and my fear. I said to myself: You are mad! What's the meaning of these waves, these floods, these outbursts? Where is the ebullient, infinite woman who, immersed as she was in her naiveté, kept in the dark about herself, led into self-disdain by the great arm of parental-conjugal phallocentrism, hasn't been ashamed of her strength? Who, surprised and horrified by the fantastic tumult of her drives (for she was made to believe that a well-adjusted normal woman has a . . . divine composure), hasn't accused herself of being a monster? Who, feeling a funny desire stirring inside her (to sing, to write, to dare to speak, in short, to bring out something new), hasn't thought she was sick? Well, her shameful sickness is that she resists death, that she makes trouble.

And why don't you write? Write! Writing is for you, you are for you; your body is yours, take it. I know why you haven't written. (And why I didn't write before the age of twenty-seven.) Because writing is at once too high, too great for you, it's reserved for the great — that is, for "great men"; and it's "silly." Besides, you've written a little, but in secret. And it wasn't good, because it was in secret, and because you punished yourself for writing, because you didn't go all the way; or because you wrote, irresistibly, as when we would masturbate in secret, not to go further, but to attenuate the tension a bit, just enough to take the edge off. And then as soon as we come, we go and make ourselves feel guilty — so as to be forgiven; or to forget, to bury it until the next time.

Write, let no one hold you back, let nothing stop you; not man; not the imbecilic capitalist machinery, in which publishing houses are the crafty, obsequious relayers of imperatives handed down by an economy that works against us and off our backs; and not *yourself.* Smug-faced readers, managing editors, and big bosses don't like the true texts of women — female-sexed texts. That kind scares them.

I write woman: woman must write woman. And man, man. So only an oblique consideration will be found here of man; it's up to him to say

---

[1]The imaginary is a "field" in the psychology of Jacques Lacan. Cixous refers later to the other Lacanian field, the symbolic, and to Lack (*manque*), the sense of absence that is the basis of unconscious desire. See the introduction to Psychoanalytic Theory and Criticism, p. 627.

where his masculinity and femininity are at; this will concern us once men have opened their eyes and seen themselves clearly.[2]

Now women return from afar, from always: from "without," from the heath where witches are kept alive; from below, from beyond "culture"; from their childhood which men have been trying desperately to make them forget, condemning it to "eternal rest." The little girls and their "ill-mannered" bodies immured, well-preserved, intact unto themselves, in the mirror. Frigidified. But are they ever seething underneath! What an effort it takes — there's no end to it — for the sex cops to bar their threatening return. Such a display of forces on both sides that the struggle has for centuries been immobilized in the trembling equilibrium of a deadlock.

Here they are, returning, arriving over and again, because the unconscious is impregnable. They have wandered around in circles, confined to the narrow room in which they've been given a deadly brainwashing. You can incarcerate them, slow them down, get away with the old Apartheid routine, but for a time only. As soon as they begin to speak, at the same time as they're taught their name, they can be taught that their territory is black: because you are Africa, you are black. Your continent is dark. Dark is dangerous. You can't see anything in the dark, you're afraid. Don't move, you might fall. Most of all, don't go into the forest. And so we have internalized this horror of the dark.

Men have committed the greatest crime against women. Insidiously, violently, they have

[2] Men still have everything to say about their sexuality, and everything to write. For what they have said so far, for the most part, stems from the opposition activity/passivity, from the power relation between a fantasized obligatory virility meant to invade, to colonize, and the consequential phantasm of woman as a "dark continent" to penetrate and to "pacify." (We know what "pacify" means in terms of scotomizing the other and misrecognizing the self.) Conquering her, they've made haste to depart from her borders, to get out of sight, out of body. The way man has of getting out of himself and into her whom he takes not for the other but for his own, deprives him, he knows, of his own bodily territory. One can understand how man, confusing himself with his penis and rushing in for the attack, might feel resentment and fear of being "taken" by the woman, of being lost in her, absorbed, or alone. [Cixous]

led them to hate women, to be their own enemies, to mobilize their immense strength against themselves, to be the executants of their virile needs. They have made for women an antinarcissism! A narcissism which loves itself only to be loved for what women haven't got! They have constructed the infamous logic of antilove.

We the precocious, we the repressed of culture, our lovely mouths gagged with pollen, our wind knocked out of us, we the labyrinths, the ladders, the trampled spaces, the bevies — we are black and we are beautiful.

We're stormy, and that which is ours breaks loose from us without our fearing any debilitation. Our glances, our smiles, are spent; laughs exude from all our mouths; our blood flows and we extend ourselves without ever reaching an end; we never hold back our thoughts, our signs, our writing; and we're not afraid of lacking.

What happiness for us who are omitted, brushed aside at the scene of inheritances; we inspire ourselves and we expire without running out of breath, we are everywhere!

From now on, who, if we say so, can say no to us? We've come back from always.

It is time to liberate the New Woman from the Old by coming to know her — by loving her for getting by, for getting beyond the Old without delay, by going out ahead of what the New Woman will be, as an arrow quits the bow with a movement that gathers and separates the vibrations musically, in order to be more than her self.

I say that we must, for, with a few rare exceptions, there has not yet been any writing that inscribes femininity; exceptions so rare, in fact, that, after plowing through literature across languages, cultures, and ages,[3] one can only be startled at this vain scouting mission. It is well known that the number of women writers (while having increased very slightly from the nineteenth century on) has always been ridiculously small. This is a useless and deceptive fact unless from their species of female writers we do not first deduct the immense majority whose workmanship is in no way different from male

[3] I am speaking here only of the place "reserved" for women by the Western world. [Cixous]

writing, and which either obscures women or reproduces the classic representations of women (as sensitive — intuitive — dreamy, etc.).[4]

Let me insert here a parenthetical remark. I mean it when I speak of male writing. I maintain unequivocally that there is such a thing as *marked* writing; that, until now, far more extensively and repressively than is ever suspected or admitted, writing has been run by a libidinal and cultural — hence political, typically masculine — economy; that this is a locus where the repression of women has been perpetuated, over and over, more or less consciously, and in a manner that's frightening since it's often hidden or adorned with the mystifying charms of fiction; that this locus has grossly exaggerated all the signs of sexual opposition (and not sexual difference), where woman has never *her* turn to speak — this being all the more serious and unpardonable in that writing is precisely *the very possibility of change*, the space that can serve as a springboard for subversive thought, the precursory movement of a transformation of social and cultural structures.

Nearly the entire history of writing is confounded with the history of reason, of which it is at once the effect, the support, and one of the privileged alibis. It has been one with the phallocentric tradition. It is indeed that same self-admiring, self-stimulating, self-congratulatory phallocentrism.

With some exceptions, for there have been failures — and if it weren't for them, I wouldn't be writing (I-woman, escapee) — in that enormous machine that has been operating and turning out its "truth" for centuries. There have been poets who would go to any lengths to slip something by at odds with tradition — men capable of loving love and hence capable of

loving others and of wanting them, of imagining the woman who would hold out against oppression and constitute herself as a superb, equal, hence "impossible" subject, untenable in a real social framework. Such a woman the poet could desire only by breaking the codes that negate her. Her appearance would necessarily bring on, if not revolution — for the bastion was supposed to be immutable — at least harrowing explosions. At times it is in the fissure caused by an earthquake, through that radical mutation of things brought on by a material upheaval when every structure is for a moment thrown off balance and an ephemeral wildness sweeps order away, that the poet slips something by, for a brief span, of woman. Thus did Kleist expend himself in his yearning for the existence of sister-lovers, maternal daughters, mother-sisters, who never hung their heads in shame. Once the palace of magistrates is restored, it's time to pay: immediate bloody death to the uncontrollable elements.

But only the poets — not the novelists, allies of representationalism. Because poetry involves gaining strength through the unconscious and because the unconscious, that other limitless country, is the place where the repressed manage to survive: women, or as Hoffmann would say, fairies.

She must write her self, because this is the invention of a *new insurgent* writing which, when the moment of her liberation has come, will allow her to carry out the indispensable ruptures and transformations in her history, first at two levels that cannot be separated.

1. Individually. By writing her self, woman will return to the body which has been more than confiscated from her, which has been turned into the uncanny stranger on display — the ailing or dead figure, which so often turns out to be the nasty companion, the cause and location of inhibitions. Censor the body and you censor breath and speech at the same time.

Write your self. Your body must be heard. Only then will the immense resources of the unconscious spring forth. Our naphtha will spread, throughout the world, without dollars — black or gold — nonassessed values that will change the rules of the old game.

[4]Which works, then, might be called feminine? I'll just point out some examples: one would have to give them full readings to bring out what is pervasively feminine in their significance. Which I shall do elsewhere. In France (have you noted our infinite poverty in this field? — the Anglo-Saxon countries have shown resources of distinctly greater consequence), leafing through what's come out of the twentieth-century — and it's not much — the only inscriptions of femininity that I have seen were by Colette, Marguerite Duras, . . . and Jean Genêt. [Cixous]

To write. An act which will not only "realize" the decensored relation of woman to her sexuality, giving her access to her native strength; it will give her back her goods, her pleasures, her organs, her immense bodily territories which have been kept under seal; it will tear her away from the superegoized structure in which she has always occupied the place reserved for the guilty (guilty of every-thing, guilty at every turn: for having desires, for not having any; for being frigid, for being "too hot"; for not being both at once; for being too motherly and not enough; for having children and for not having any; for nursing and for not nursing . . .) — tear her away by means of this research, this job of analysis and illumination, this emancipation of the marvelous text of her self that she must urgently learn to speak. A woman without a body, dumb, blind, can't pos-sibly be a good fighter. She is reduced to being the servant of the militant male, his shadow. We must kill the false woman who is preventing the live one from breathing. Inscribe the breath of the whole woman.

2. An act that will also be marked by woman's *seizing* the occasion to *speak*, hence her shattering entry into history, which has always been based *on her suppression*. To write and thus to forge for herself the antilogos weapon. To become *at will* the taker and initiator, for her own right, in every symbolic system, in every political process.

It is time for women to start scoring their feats in written and oral language.

Every woman has known the torment of getting up to speak. Her heart racing, at times entirely lost for words, ground and language slip-ping away — that's how daring a feat, how great a transgression it is for a woman to speak — even just open her mouth — in public. A double dis-tress, for even if she transgresses, her words fall almost always upon the deaf male ear, which hears in language only that which speaks in the masculine.

It is by writing, from and toward women, and by taking up the challenge of speech which has been governed by the phallus, that women will confirm women in a place other than that which is reserved in and by the symbolic, that is, in a place other than silence. Women should break out of the snare of silence. They shouldn't be conned into accepting a domain which is the margin or the harem.

Listen to a woman speak at a public gather-ing (if she hasn't painfully lost her wind). She doesn't "speak," she throws her trembling body forward; she lets go of herself, she flies; all of her passes into her voice, and it's with her body that she vitally supports the "logic" of her speech. Her flesh speaks true. She lays herself bare. In fact, she physically materializes what she's thinking; she signifies it with her body. In a certain way she *inscribes* what she's saying, because she doesn't deny her drives the intractable and impassioned part they have in speaking. Her speech, even when "theoretical" or political, is never simple or linear or "objectified," generalized: she draws her story into history.

There is not that scission, that division made by the common man between the logic of oral speech and the logic of the text, bound as he is by his antiquated relation — servile, calculating — to mastery. From which proceeds the niggardly lip service which engages only the tiniest part of the body, plus the mask.

In women's speech, as in their writing, that element which never stops resonating, which, once we've been permeated by it, profoundly and imperceptibly touched by it, retains the power of moving us — that element is the song: first music from the first voice of love which is alive in every woman. Why this privileged relationship with the voice? Because no woman stockpiles as many defenses for countering the drives as does a man. You don't build walls around yourself, you don't forego pleasure as "wisely" as he. Even if phallic mystification has generally contaminated good relationships, a woman is never far from "mother" (I mean out-side her role functions: the "mother" as noname and as source of goods). There is always within her at least a little of that good mother's milk. She writes in white ink.

Woman for women. — There always remains in woman that force which produces/is produced by the other — in particular, the other woman. *In* her, matrix, cradler; herself giver as her mother and child; she is her own sister-daughter.

You might object, "What about she who is the hysterical offspring of a bad mother?" Everything will be changed once woman gives woman to the other woman. There is hidden and always ready in woman the source; the locus for the other. The mother, too, is a metaphor. It is necessary and sufficient that the best of herself be given to woman by another woman for her to be able to love herself and return in love the body that was "born" to her. Touch me, caress me, you the living no-name, give me my self as myself. The relation to the "mother," in terms of intense pleasure and violence, is curtailed no more than the relation to childhood (the child that she was, that she is, that she makes, remakes, undoes, there at the point where, the same, she others herself). Text: my body — shot through with streams of song; I don't mean the overbearing, clutchy "mother" but, rather, what touches you, the equivoice that affects you, fills your breast with an urge to come to language and launches your force; the rhythm that laughs you; the intimate recipient who makes all metaphors possible and desirable; body (body? bodies?), no more describable than god, the soul, or the Other; that part of you that leaves a space between yourself and urges you to inscribe in language your woman's style. In women there is always more or less of the mother who makes everything all right, who nourishes, and who stands up against separation; a force that will not be cut off but will knock the wind out of the codes. We will rethink womankind beginning with every form and every period of her body. The Americans remind us, "We are all Lesbians"; that is, don't denigrate woman, don't make of her what men have made of you.

Because the "economy" of her drives is prodigious, she cannot fail, in seizing the occasion to speak, to transform directly and indirectly *all* systems of exchange based on masculine thrift. Her libido will produce far more radical effects of political and social change than some might like to think.

Because she arrives, vibrant, over and again, we are at the beginning of a new history, or rather of a process of becoming in which several histories intersect with one another. As subject for history, woman always occurs simultaneously in several places. Woman un-thinks[5] the unifying, regulating history that homogenizes and channels forces, herding contradictions into a single battlefield. In woman, personal history blends together with the history of all women, as well as national and world history. As a militant, she is an integral part of all liberations. She must be farsighted, not limited to a blow-by-blow interaction. She foresees that her liberation will do more than modify power relations or toss the ball over to the other camp; she will bring about a mutation in human relations, in thought, in all praxis: hers is not simply a class struggle, which she carries forward into a much vaster movement. Not that in order to be a woman-in-struggle(s) you have to leave the class struggle or repudiate it; but you have to split it open, spread it out, push it forward, fill it with the fundamental struggle so as to prevent the class struggle, or any other struggle for the liberation of a class or people, from operating as a form of repression, pretext for postponing the inevitable, the staggering alteration in power relations and in the production of individualities. This alteration is already upon us — in the United States, for example, where millions of night crawlers are in the process of undermining the family and disintegrating the whole of American sociality.

The new history is coming; it's not a dream, though it does extend beyond men's imagination, and for good reason. It's going to deprive them of their conceptual orthopedics, beginning with the destruction of their enticement machine.

It is impossible to *define* a feminine practice of writing, and this is an impossibility that will remain, for this practice can never be theorized, enclosed, coded — which doesn't mean that it doesn't exist. But it will always surpass the discourse that regulates the phallocentric system; it does and will take place in areas other than those subordinated to philosophico-theoretical domination. It will be conceived of only by subjects who are breakers of automatisms, by peripheral figures that no authority can ever subjugate.

Hence the necessity to affirm the flourishes of this writing, to give form to its movement, its near

---

[5]"*Dé-pense*," a neologism formed on the verb *penser*, hence "unthinks," but also "spends" (from *dépenser*). [Tr.]

and distant byways. Bear in mind to begin with (1) that sexual opposition, which has always worked for man's profit to the point of reducing writing, too, to his laws, is only a historico-cultural limit. There is, there will be more and more rapidly pervasive now, a fiction that produces irreducible effects of femininity. (2) That it is through ignorance that most readers, critics, and writers of both sexes hesitate to admit or deny outright the possibility or the pertinence of a distinction between feminine and masculine writing. It will usually be said, thus disposing of sexual difference: either that all writing, to the extent that it materializes, is feminine; or, inversely — but it comes to the same thing — that the act of writing is equivalent to masculine masturbation (and so the woman who writes herself out a paper penis); or that writing is bisexual, hence neuter, which again does away with differentiation. To admit that writing is precisely working (in) the in-between, inspecting the process of the same and of the other without which nothing can live, undoing the work of death — to admit this is first to want the two, as well as both, the ensemble of the one and the other, not fixed in sequences of struggle and expulsion or some other form of death but infinitely dynamized by an incessant process of exchange from one subject to another. A process of different subjects knowing one another and beginning one another anew only from the living boundaries of the other: a multiple and inexhaustible course with millions of encounters and transformations of the same into the other and into the in-between, from which woman takes her forms (and man, in his turn; but that's his other history).

In saying "bisexual, hence neuter," I am referring to the classic conception of bisexuality, which, squashed under the emblem of castration fear and along with the fantasy of a "total" being (though composed of two halves), would do away with the difference experienced as an operation incurring loss, as the mark of dreaded sectility.

To this self-effacing, merger-type bisexuality, which would conjure away castration (the writer who puts up his sign: "bisexual written here, come and see," when the odds are good that it's neither one nor the other), I oppose the *other bisexuality* on which every subject not enclosed in the false

theater of phallocentric representationalism has founded his/her erotic universe. Bisexuality: that is, each one's location in self (*repérage en soi*) of the presence — variously manifest and insistent according to each person, male or female — of both sexes, nonexclusion either of the difference or of one sex, and, from this "self-permission," multiplication of the effects of the inscription of desire, over all parts of my body and the other body.

Now it happens that at present, for historico-cultural reasons, it is women who are opening up to and benefiting from this vatic bisexuality which doesn't annul differences but stirs them up, pursues them, increases their number. In a certain way, "woman is bisexual"; man — it's a secret to no one — being poised to keep glorious phallic monosexuality in view. By virtue of affirming the primacy of the phallus and of bringing it into play, phallocratic ideology has claimed more than one victim. As a woman, I've been clouded over by the great shadow of the scepter and been told: idolize it, that which you cannot brandish. But at the same time, man has been handed that grotesque and scarcely enviable destiny (just imagine) of being reduced to a single idol with clay balls. And consumed, as Freud and his followers note, by a fear of being a woman! For, if psychoanalysis was constituted from woman, to repress femininity (and not so successful a repression at that — men have made it clear), its account of masculine sexuality is now hardly refutable; as with all the "human" sciences, it reproduces the masculine view, of which it is one of the effects.

Here we encounter the inevitable man-with-rock, standing erect in his old Freudian realm, in the way that, to take the figure back to the point where linguistics is conceptualizing it "anew," Lacan preserves it in the sanctuary of the phallos (φ) "sheltered" from *castration's lack!* Their "symbolic" exists, it holds power — we, the sowers of disorder, know it only too well. But we are in no way obliged to deposit our lives in their banks of lack, to consider the constitution of the subject in terms of a drama manglingly restaged, to reinstate again and again the religion of the father. Because we don't want that. We don't fawn around the supreme hole. We have no wom-an's reason to pledge allegiance to the negative.

The feminine (as the poets suspected) affirms: ". . . And yes," says Molly, carrying *Ulysses* off beyond any book and toward the new writing; "I said yes, I will Yes."

The Dark Continent is neither dark nor unexplorable. — It is still unexplored only because we've been made to believe that it was too dark to be explorable. And because they want to make us believe that what interests us is the white continent, with its monuments to Lack. And we believed. They riveted us between two horrifying myths: between the Medusa and the abyss. That would be enough to set half the world laughing, except that it's still going on. For the phallologocentric sublation[6] is with us, and it's militant, regenerating the old patterns, anchored in the dogma of castration. They haven't changed a thing: they've theorized their desire for reality! Let the priests tremble, we're going to show them our sexts!

Too bad for them if they fall apart upon discovering that women aren't men, or that the mother doesn't have one. But isn't this fear convenient for them? Wouldn't the worst be, isn't the worst, in truth, that women aren't castrated, that they have only to stop listening to the Sirens (for the Sirens were men) for history to change its meaning? You only have to look at the Medusa straight on to see her. And she's not deadly. She's beautiful and she's laughing.

Men say that there are two unrepresentable things: death and the feminine sex. That's because they need femininity to be associated with death; it's the jitters that gives them a hard-on! for themselves! They need to be afraid of us. Look at the trembling Perseuses moving backward toward us, clad in apotropes.[7] What lovely backs! Not another minute to lose. Let's get out of here.

Let's hurry: the continent is not impenetrably dark. I've been there often. I was overjoyed one day to run into Jean Genêt. It was in *Pompes funèbres*.[8] He had come there led by his Jean. There are some men (all too few) who aren't afraid of femininity.

---

[6]Standard English term for the Hegelian *Aufhebung*, the French *la relève*. [Tr.]

[7]A coinage from two Greek roots meaning "to turn away."

[8]Jean Genêt, *Pompes funèbres* (Paris, 1948), p. 185. [Cixous]

Almost everything is yet to be written by women about femininity: about their sexuality, that is, its infinite and mobile complexity, about their eroticization, sudden turn-ons of a certain minuscule-immense area of their bodies; not about destiny, but about the adventure of such and such a drive, about trips, crossings, trudges, abrupt and gradual awakenings, discoveries of a zone at one time timorous and soon to be forthright. A woman's body, with its thousand and one thresholds of ardor — once, by smashing yokes and censors, she lets it articulate the profusion of meanings that run through it in every direction — will make the old single-grooved mother tongue reverberate with more than one language.

We've been turned away from our bodies, shamefully taught to ignore them, to strike them with that stupid sexual modesty; we've been made victims of the old fool's game: each one will love the other sex. I'll give you your body and you'll give me mine. But who are the men who give women the body that women blindly yield to them? Why so few texts? Because so few women have as yet won back their body. Women must write through their bodies, they must invent the impregnable language that will wreck partitions, classes, and rhetorics, regulations and codes, they must submerge, cut through, get beyond the ultimate reserve-discourse, including the one that laughs at the very idea of pronouncing the word "silence," the one that, aiming for the impossible, stops short before the word "impossible" and writes it as "the end."

Such is the strength of women that, sweeping away syntax, breaking that famous thread (just a tiny little thread, they say) which acts for men as a surrogate umbilical cord, assuring them — otherwise they couldn't come — that the old lady is always right behind them, watching them make phallus, women will go right up to the impossible.

When the "repressed" of their culture and their society returns, it's an explosive, *utterly* destructive, staggering return, with a force never yet unleashed and equal to the most forbidding of suppressions. For when the Phallic period comes to an end, women will have been either annihilated or borne up to the highest and most violent incandescence. Muffled throughout their history, they have lived in dreams, in bodies (though muted), in silences, in aphonic revolts. And with such force in their fragility; a fragility, a vulnerability, equal to their incomparable intensity. Fortunately, they haven't sublimated; they've saved their skin, their energy. They haven't worked at liquidating the impasse of lives without futures. They have furiously inhabited these sumptuous bodies: admirable hysterics who made Freud succumb to many voluptuous moments impossible to confess, bombarding his Mosaic statue with their carnal and passionate body words, haunting him with their unaudible and thundering denunciations, dazzling, more than naked underneath the seven veils of modesty. Those who, with a single word of the body, have inscribed the vertiginous immensity of a history which is sprung like an arrow from the whole history of men and from biblico-capitalist society, are the women, the supplicants of yesterday, who come as forebears of the new women, after whom no intersubjective relation will ever be the same. You, Dora,[9] you the indomitable, the poetic body, you are the true "mistress" of the Signifier. Before long your speech efficacity will be seen at work when your speech is no longer suppressed, its point turned in against your breast, but written out over against the other.

In body. — More so than men who are coaxed toward social success, toward sublimation, women are body. More body, hence more writing. For a long time it has been in body that women have responded to persecution, to the familial-conjugal enterprise of domestication, to the repeated attempts at castrating them. Those who have turned their tongues 10,000 times seven times before not speaking are either dead from it or more familiar with their tongues and their mouths than anyone else. Now, I-woman am going to blow up the Law: an explosion henceforth possible and ineluctable; let it be done, right now, *in* language.

Let us not be trapped by an analysis still encumbered with the old automatisms. It's not to be feared that language conceals an invincible adversary, because it's the language of men and

⁹The female subject of Freud's first case study in hysteria.

their grammar. We mustn't leave them a single place that's any more theirs alone than we are.

If woman has always functioned "within" the discourse of man, a signifier that has always referred back to the opposite signifier which annihilates its specific energy and diminishes or stifles its very different sounds, it is time for her to dislocate this "within," to explode it, turn it around, and seize it; to make it hers, containing it, taking it in her own mouth, biting that tongue with her very own teeth to invent for herself a language to get inside of. And you'll see with what ease she will spring forth from that "within" — the "within" where once she so drowsily crouched — to overflow at the lips she will cover the foam.

Nor is the point to appropriate their instruments, their concepts, their places, or to begrudge them their position of mastery. Just because there's a risk of identification doesn't mean that we'll succumb. Let's leave it to the worriers, to masculine anxiety and its obsession with how to dominate the way things work — knowing "how it works" in order to "make it work." For us the point is not to take possession in order to internalize or manipulate, but rather to dash through and to "fly."[10]

Flying is woman's gesture — flying in language and making it fly. We have all learned the art of flying and its numerous techniques; for centuries we've been able to possess anything only by flying; we've lived in flight, stealing away, finding, when desired, narrow passageways, hidden crossovers. It's no accident that *voler* has a double meaning, that it plays on each of them and thus throws off the agents of sense. It's no accident: women take after birds and robbers just as robbers take after women and birds. They *(elles)*[11] go by, fly by the coop, take pleasure in jumbling the order of space, in disorienting it, in changing around the furniture, dislocating things and values, breaking them all up, emptying structures, and turning propriety upside down.

¹⁰"*Also,*" "to steal." Both meanings of the verb *voler* are played on, as the text itself explains in the following paragraph. [Tr.]

¹¹*Illes* is a fusion of the masculine pronoun *ils,* which refers back to birds and robbers, with the feminine pronoun *elles,* which refers to women. [Tr.]

What woman hasn't flown/stolen? Who hasn't felt, dreamt, performed the gesture that jams sociality? Who hasn't crumbled, held up to ridicule, the bar of separation? Who hasn't inscribed with her body the differential, punctured the system of couples and opposition? Who, by some act of transgression, hasn't overthrown successiveness, connection, the wall of circumfusion?

A feminine text cannot fail to be more than subversive. It is volcanic; as it is written it brings about an upheaval of the old property crust, carrier of masculine investments; there's no other way. There's no room for her if she's not a he. If she's a her-she, it's in order to smash everything, to shatter the framework of institutions, to blow up the law, to break up the "truth" with laughter.

For once she blazes *her* trail in the symbolic, she cannot fail to make of it the chaosmos of the "personal" — in her pronouns, her nouns, and her clique of referents. And for good reason. There will have been the long history of gynocide. This is known by the colonized peoples of yesterday, the workers, the nations, the species off whose backs the history of men has made its gold; those who have known the ignominy of persecution derive from it an obstinate future desire for grandeur; those who are locked up know better than their jailers the taste of free air. Thanks to their history, women today know (how to do and want) what men will be able to conceive of only much later. I say woman overturns the "personal," for if, by means of laws, lies, blackmail, and marriage, her right to herself has been extorted at the same time as her name, she has been able, through the very movement of mortal alienation, to see more closely the inanity of "propriety," the reductive stinginess of the masculine-conjugal subjective economy, which she doubly resists. On the one hand she has constituted herself necessarily as that "person" capable of losing a part of herself without losing her integrity. But secretly, silently, deep down inside, she grows and multiplies, for, on the other hand, she knows far more about living and about the relation between the economy of the drives and the management of the ego than any man. Unlike man, who holds so dearly to his title and his titles, his pouches of value, his cap, crown, and everything connected with his head, woman couldn't care less about the

fear of decapitation (or castration), adventuring, without the masculine temerity, into anonymity, which she can merge with without annihilating herself: because she's a giver.

I shall have a great deal to say about the whole deceptive problematic of the gift. Woman is obviously not that woman Nietzsche dreamed of who gives only in order to.[12] Who could ever think of the gift as a gift-that-takes? Who else but man, precisely the one who would like to take everything?

If there is a "propriety of woman," it is paradoxically her capacity to depropriate unselfishly: body without end, without appendage, without principal "parts." If she is a whole, it's a whole composed of parts that are wholes, not simple partial objects but a moving, limitlessly changing ensemble, a cosmos tirelessly traversed by Eros, an immense astral space not organized around any one sun that's any more of a star than the others.

This doesn't mean that she's an undifferentiated magma, but that she doesn't lord it over her body or her desire. Though masculine sexuality gravitates around the penis, engendering that centralized body (in political anatomy) under the dictatorship of its parts, woman does not bring about the same regionalization which serves the couple head/genitals and which is inscribed only within boundaries. Her libido is cosmic, just as her unconscious is worldwide. Her writing can only keep going, without ever inscribing or discerning contours, daring to make these vertiginous crossing of the other(s) ephemeral and passionate sojourns in him, her, them, whom she inhabits long enough to look at from the point closest to their unconscious from the moment they awaken, to love them at the point closest to their drives; and then further, impregnated through and through with these brief, identificatory embraces, she goes and passes into infinity. She alone dares and wishes to know from within, where she, the outcast, has never ceased to hear the resonance of fore-language. She lets

[12]Reread Derrida's text, "Le Style de la femme," in *Nietzsche aujourd'hui* (Paris: Union Générale d'Editions, Coll. 10/18), where the philosopher can be seen operating an *Aufhebung* of all philosophy in its systematic reducing of woman to the place of seduction: she appears as the one who is taken for; the bait in person, all veils unfurled, the one who doesn't give but who gives only in order to (take). [Cixous]

the other language speak — the language of 1,000 tongues which knows neither enclosure nor death. To life she refuses nothing. Her language does not contain, it carries; it does not hold back, it makes possible. When id is ambiguously uttered — the wonder of being several — she doesn't defend herself against these unknown women whom she's surprised at becoming, but derives pleasure from this gift of alterability. I am spacious, singing flesh, on which is grafted no one knows which I, more or less human, but alive because of transformation. Write! and your self-seeking text will know itself better than flesh and blood, rising, insurrectionary dough kneading itself, with sonorous, perfumed ingredients, a lively combination of flying colors, leaves, and rivers plunging into the sea we feed. ''Ah, there's her sea,'' he will say as he holds out to me a basin full of water from the little phallic mother from whom he's inseparable. But look, our seas are what we make of them, full of fish or not, opaque or transparent, red or black, high or smooth, narrow or bankless; and we are ourselves sea, sand, coral, seaweed, beaches, tides, swimmers, children, waves. . . . More or less wavily sea, earth, sky — what matter would rebuff us? We know how how to speak them all.

Heterogeneous, yes. For her joyous benefit she is erogenous; she is the erotogeneity of the heterogeneous: airborne swimmer, in flight, she does not cling to herself; she is dispersible, prodigious, stunning, desirous and capable of others, of the other woman that she will be, of the other woman she isn't, of him, of you.

Woman be unafraid of any other place, of any same, or any other. My eyes, my tongue, my ears, my nose, my skin, my mouth, my body-for-(the)-other — not that I long for it in order to fill up a hole, to provide against some defect of mine, or because, as fate would have it, I'm spurred on by feminine ''jealousy''; not because I've been dragged into the whole chain of substitutions that brings that which is substituted back to its ultimate object. That sort of thing you would expect to come straight out of ''Tom Thumb,'' out of the *Penisneid*[13] whispered to us by old grandmother ogresses, servants to their father-sons.

[13]Penis-envy.

If they believe, in order to muster up some self-importance, if they really need to believe that we're dying of desire, that we are this hole fringed with desire for their penis — that's their immemorial business. Undeniably (we verify it at our own expense — but also to our amusement), it's their business to let us know they're getting a hard-on, so that we'll assure them (we the maternal mistresses of their little pocket signifier) that they still can, that it's still there — that men structure themselves only by being fitted with a feather. In the child it's not the penis that the woman desires, it's not that famous bit of skin around which every man gravitates. Pregnancy cannot be traced back, except within the historical limits of the ancients, to some form of fate, to those mechanical substitutions brought about by the unconscious of some eternal ''jealous woman''; not to penis envies; and not to narcissism or to some sort of homosexuality linked to the everpresent mother! Begetting a child doesn't mean that the woman or the man must ineluctably fall into patterns or must recharge the circuit of reproduction. If there's a risk there's not an inevitable trap: may women be spared the pressure, under the guise of consciousness-raising, of a supplement of interdictions. Either you want a kid or you don't — *that's your business.* Let nobody threaten you; in satisfying your desire, let not the fear of becoming the accomplice to a sociality succeed the old-time fear of being ''taken.'' And man, are you still going to bank on everyone's blindness and passivity, afraid lest the child make a father and, consequently, that in having a kid the woman land herself more than one bad deal by engendering all at once child — mother — father — family? No; it's up to you to break the old circuits. It will be up to man and woman to render obsolete the former relationship and all its consequences, to consider the launching of a brand-new subject, alive, with defamilialization. Let us demater-paternalize rather than deny woman, in an effort to avoid the co-optation of procreation, a thrilling era of the body. Let us defetishize. Let's get away from the dialectic which has it that the only good father is a dead one, or that the child is the death of his parents. The child is the other, but the other without violence, bypassing loss, struggle. We're fed up with the reuniting of bonds forever to be severed, with the litany of castration that's handed down and genealogized. We won't advance backward anymore; we're not going to repress something so simple as the desire for life. Oral drive, anal drive, vocal drive — all these drives are our strengths, and among them is the gestation drive — just like the desire to write: a desire to live self from within, a desire for the swollen belly, for language, for blood. We are not going to refuse, if it should happen to strike our fancy, the unsurpassed pleasures of pregnancy which have actually been always exaggerated or conjured away — or cursed — in the classic texts. For if there's one thing that's been repressed here's just the place to find it: in the taboo of the pregnant woman. This says a lot about the power she seems invested with at the time, because it has always been suspected, that, when pregnant, the woman not only doubles her market value, but — what's more important — takes on intrinsic value as a woman in her own eyes and, undeniably, acquires body and sex.

There are thousands of ways of living one's pregnancy; to have or not to have with that still invisible other a relationship of another intensity. And if you don't have that particular yearning, it doesn't mean that you're in any way lacking. Each body distributes in its own special way, without model or norm, the nonfinite and changing totality of its desires. Decide for yourself on your position in the arena of contradictions, where pleasure and reality embrace. Bring the other to life. Women know how to live detachment; giving birth is neither losing nor increasing. It's adding to life an other. Am I dreaming? Am I mis-recognizing? You, the defenders of "theory," the sacrosanct yes-men of Concept, enthroners of the phallus (but not of the penis):

Once more you'll say that all this smacks of "idealism," or what's worse, you'll splutter that I'm a "mystic."

And what about the libido? Haven't I read the "Signification of the Phallus"? And what about separation, what about that bit of self for which, to be born, you undergo an ablation — an ablation, so they say, to be forever commemorated by your desire?

Besides, isn't it evident that the penis gets around in my texts, that I give it a place and appeal? Of course I do. I want all. I want all of me with all of him. Why should I deprive myself of a part of us? I want all of us. Woman of course has a desire for a "loving desire" and not a jealous one. But not because she is gelded; not because she's deprived and needs to be filled out, like some wounded person who wants to console herself or seek vengeance: I don't want a penis to decorate my body with. But I do desire the other for the other, whole and entire, male or female; because living means wanting everything that is, everything that lives, and wanting it alive. Castration? Let others toy with it. What's a desire originating from a lack? A pretty meager desire.

The woman who still allows herself to be threatened by the big dick, who's still impressed by the commotion of the phallic stance, who still leads a loyal master to the beat of the drum: that's the woman of yesterday. They still exist, easy and numerous victims of the oldest of farces: either they're cast in the original silent version in which, as titanesses lying under the mountains they make with their quivering, they never see erected that theoretic monument to the golden phallus looming, in the old manner, over their bodies. Or, coming today out of their *infans*[14] period and into the second, "enlightened" version of their virtuous debasement, they see themselves suddenly assaulted by the builders of the analytic empire and, as soon as they've begun to formulate the new desire, naked, nameless, so happy at making an appearance, they're taken in their bath by the new old men, and then, whoops! Luring them with flashy signifiers, the demon of interpretation — oblique, decked out in modernity — sells them the same old handcuffs, baubles, and chains. Which castration do you prefer? Whose degrading do you like better, the father's or the mother's? Oh, what pwetty eyes, you pwetty little girl. Here, buy my glasses and you'll see the Truth-Me-Myself tell you everything you should know. Put them on your nose and take a fetishist's look (you are me, the other analyst — that's what I'm telling you) at your body and the body of the other. You see? No? Wait, you'll have everything explained to you, and you'll know at last which sort of neurosis you're related to. Hold still, we're

[14]Mute.

going to do your portrait, so that you can begin looking like it right away.

Yes, the naives to the first and second degree are still legion. If the New Women, arriving now, dare to create outside the theoretical, they're called in by the cops of the signifier, finger-printed, remonstrated, and brought into the line of order that they are supposed to know; assigned by force of trickery to a precise place in the chain that's always formed for the benefit of a privileged signifier. We are pieced back to the string which leads back, if not to the Name-of-the-Father, then, for a new twist, to the place of the phallic-mother.

Beware, my friend, of the signifier that would take you back to the authority of a signified! Beware of diagnoses that would reduce your generative powers. ''Common'' nouns are also proper nouns that disparage your singularity by classifying it into species. Break out of the circles; don't remain within the psychoanalytic closure. Take a look around, then cut through!

And if we are legion, it's because the war of liberation has only made as yet a tiny breakthrough. But women are thronging to it. I've seen them, those who will be neither dupe nor domestic; those who will not fear the risk of being a woman; will not fear any risk, any desire, any space still explored in themselves, among themselves and others or anywhere else. They do not fetishize, they do not deny, they do not hate. They observe, they approach, they try to see the other woman, the child, the lover — not to strengthen their own narcissism or verify the solidity or weakness of the master, but to make love better, to invent.

Other love. — In the beginning are our differences. The new love dares for the other, wants the other, makes dizzying, precipitous flights between knowledge and invention. The woman arriving over and over again does not stand still: she's everywhere, she exchanges, she is the desire-that-gives. (Not enclosed in the paradox of the gift that takes nor under the illusion of unitary fusion. We're past that.) She comes in, comes-in-between herself me and you, between the other me where one is always infinitely more

than one and more than me, without the fear of ever reaching a limit; she thrills in our becoming. And we'll keep on becoming! She cuts through defensive loves, moorages, and devourations: beyond selfish narcissism, in the moving, open, transitional space, she runs her risks. Beyond the struggle-to-the-death that's been removed to the bed, beyond the love-battle that claims to represent exchange, she scorns at an Eros dynamic that would be fed by hatred. Hatred: a heritage, again, a remainder, a duping subservience to the phallus. To love, to watch-think-seek the other in the other, to despecularize, to unhoard. Does this seem difficult? It's not impossible, and this is what nourishes life — a love that has no commerce with the apprehensive desire that provides against the lack and stultifies the strange; a love that rejoices in the exchange that multiplies. Wherever history still unfolds as the history of death, she does not tread. Opposition, hierarchizing exchange, the struggle for mastery which can end only in at least one death (one master — one slave, or two nonmasters ≠ two dead) — all that comes from a period in time governed by phallocentric values. The fact that this period extends into the present doesn't prevent woman from starting the history of life somewhere else. Elsewhere, she gives. She doesn't ''know'' what she's giving, she doesn't measure it; she gives, though, neither a counterfeit impression nor something she hasn't got. She gives more, with no assurance that she'll get back even some unexpected profit from what she puts out. She gives that there may be life, thought, transformation. This is an ''economy'' that can no longer be put in economic terms. Wherever she loves, all the old concepts of management are left behind. At the end of a more or less conscious computation, she finds not her sum but her differences. I am for you what you want me to be at the moment you look at me in a way you've never seen me before: at every instant. When I write, it's everything that we don't know we can be that is written out of me, without exclusions, without stipulation, and everything we will be calls us to the unflagging, intoxicating, unappeasable search for love. In one another we will never be lacking.

Gayle Rubin

b. 1949

Gayle Rubin grew up in a small, segregated Southern town in one of the few local pro-integration families. When she began college at the University of Michigan in 1966, she saw a similar kind of unequal segregation between male and female students and led a student revolt against the sexist rules about dress and personal freedoms. Interested in the connections between gender and politics, Rubin helped to start the university's women's studies program. In 1971, while a graduate student in anthropology in Ann Arbor, Rubin gathered a coalition of activists that became the Radicalesbians group. She is now professor of anthropology and women's studies at the University of Michigan, where she received her Ph.D. in 1994 for her groundbreaking dissertation, "The Valley of the Kings: Leathermen in San Francisco, 1960–1990." From 1996 to 1998, Rubin served as a visiting lecturer of women's studies at the University of California, Santa Cruz. Using the methods of Claude Lévi-Strauss, her work continues to explore the most marginalized sexual practices, especially in urban centers where communities arise to assist members in determining their sexual roles. Following Foucault's arguments about the constructed nature of gender and its source in the infrastructure of power, Rubin theorizes that the prohibition of certain sexual practices is a method of political control, and that all sex, especially that viewed as "deviant," is inherently a declaration of political dissent. A collection of her essays, Deviations: A Gayle Rubin Reader, *was published in 2011. The following article, "The Traffic in Women: Notes on the 'Political Economy' of Sex," was originally printed in the 1975 volume,* Toward an Anthropology of Women.

From *The Traffic in Women: Notes on the "Political Economy" of Sex*

The literature on women — both feminist and anti-feminist — is a long rumination on the question of the nature and genesis of women's

Acknowledgements are an inadequate expression of how much this paper, like most, is the product of many minds. They are also necessary to free others of the responsibility for what is ultimately a personal vision of a collective conversation. I want to free and thank the following persons: Tom Anderson and Arlene Gorelick, with whom I co-authored the paper from which this one evolved; Rayna Reiter, Larry Shields, Ray Kelly, Peggy White, Norma Diamond, Randy Reiter, Frederick Wyatt, Anne Locksley, Juliet Mitchell, and Susan Harding, for countless conversations and ideas; Marshall Sahlins, for the revelation of anthropology; Lynn Eden, for sardonic editing; the members of Women's Studies 340/004, for my initiation into teaching; Sally Brenner, for heroic typing; Susan Lowes, for incredible patience; and Emma Goldman, for the title. [Rubin]

oppression and social subordination. The question is not a trivial one, since the answers given it determine our visions of the future, and our evaluation of whether or not it is realistic to hope for a sexually egalitarian society. More importantly, the analysis of the causes of women's oppression forms the basis for any assessment of just what would have to be changed in order to achieve a society without gender hierarchy. Thus, if innate male aggression and dominance are at the root of female oppression, then the feminist program would logically require either the extermination of the offending sex, or else a eugenics project to modify its character. If sexism is a by-product of capitalism's relentless appetite for profit, then sexism would wither away in the advent of a successful socialist revolution. If the world historical defeat of women occurred at the hands of an armed patriarchal revolt, then it is time for Amazon guerrillas to start training in the Adirondacks.

It lies outside the scope of this paper to conduct a sustained critique of some of the currently popular explanations of the genesis of sexual inequality — theories such as the popular evolution exemplified by *The Imperial Animal*,[1] the alleged overthrow of prehistoric matriarchies, or the attempt to extract all of the phenomena of social subordination from the first volume of *Capital*.[2] Instead, I want to sketch some elements of an alternate explanation of the problem.

Marx once asked: ''What is a Negro slave?'' A man of the black race. The one explanation is as good as the other. A Negro is a Negro. He only becomes a slave in certain relations. A cotton spinning jenny is a machine for spinning cotton. It becomes *capital* only in certain relations. Torn from these relationships it is no more capital than gold in itself is money or sugar is the price of sugar'' (Marx, 28).[3] One might paraphrase: What is a domesticated woman? A female of the species. The one explanation is as good as the other. A woman is a woman. She only becomes a domestic, a wife, a chattel, a playboy bunny, a prostitute, or a human dictaphone[4] in certain relations. Torn from these relationships, she is no more the helpmate of man than gold in itself is money . . . etc. What then are these relationships by which a female becomes an oppressed woman? The place to begin to unravel the system of relationships by which women become the prey of men is in the overlapping works of Claude Lévi-Strauss and Sigmund Freud.[5] The domestication of women, under other names, is discussed at length in both of their *oeuvres*. In reading through these works, one begins to have a sense of a systematic

social apparatus which takes up females as raw materials and fashions domesticated women as products. Neither Freud nor Lévi-Strauss sees his work in this light, and certainly neither turns a critical glance upon the processes he describes. Their analyses and descriptions must be read, therefore, in something like the way in which Marx read the classical political economists who preceded him. Freud and Lévi-Strauss are in some sense analogous to Ricardo and Smith:[6] They see neither the implications of what they are saying, nor the implicit critique which their work can generate when subjected to a feminist eye. Nevertheless, they provide conceptual tools with which one can build descriptions of the part of social life which is the locus of the oppression of women, of sexual minorities, and of certain aspects of human personality within individuals. I call that part of social life the ''sex/gender system,'' for lack of a more elegant term. As a preliminary definition, a ''sex/gender system'' is the set of arrangements by which a society transforms biological sexuality into products of human activity, and in which these transformed sexual needs are satisfied.

The purpose of this essay is to arrive at a more fully developed definition of the sex/gender system, by way of a somewhat idiosyncratic and exegetical reading of Lévi-Strauss and Freud. I use the word ''exegetical'' deliberately. The dictionary defines ''exegesis'' as a ''critical explanatory or interpretive interpretation of the Scriptures.'' At times, my reading of Lévi-Strauss and Freud is freely interpretive, moving from the explicit content of a text to its presuppositions and implications. My reading of certain psychoanalytic texts is filtered through a lens provided by Jacques Lacan, whose own interpretation of the Freudian scripture has been heavily influenced by Lévi-Strauss.[7]

---

[1]Book by sociobiologists Lionel Tiger and Robin Fox (1971) based on studies of baboons and macaques, arguing that hierarchical male-dominant social systems are natural to primates (including man).

[2]See the introduction to Marx, p. 247.

[3]Karl Marx, *Wage-Labor and Capital*. New York: International, 1971.

[4]Business machine like a tape recorder once used by secretaries to type letters dictated by their employers.

[5]For Lévi-Strauss, see p. 503; for Freud, see p. 309.

[6]David Ricardo (1772–1823), author of *Principles of Political Economy and Taxation* (1817), and Adam Smith (1723–1790), author of *The Wealth of Nations* (1776), are the classical economists of whose work Marx's *Capital* is an ''implicit critique.''

[7]Moving between Marxism, structuralism, and psychoanalysis produces a certain clash of epistemologies. In particular, structuralism is a can from which worms crawl out all over the epistemological map. Rather than trying to cope with this problem, I have more or less ignored the fact that Lacan

I will return later to a refinement of the definition of a sex/gender system. First, however, I will try to demonstrate the need for such a concept by discussing the failure of classical Marxism to fully express or conceptualize sex oppression. This failure results from the fact that Marxism, as a theory of social life, is relatively unconcerned with sex. In Marx's map of the social world, human beings are workers, peasants, or capitalists; that they are also men and women is not seen as very significant. By contrast, in the maps of social reality drawn by Freud and Lévi-Strauss, there is a deep recognition of the place of sexuality in society, and of the profound differences between the social experience of men and women.

MARX

There is no theory which accounts for the oppression of women — in its endless variety and monotonous similarity, cross-culturally and throughout history — with anything like the explanatory power of the Marxist theory of class oppression. Therefore, it is not surprising that there have been numerous attempts to apply Marxist analysis to the question of women. There are many ways of doing this. It has been argued that women are a reserve labor force for capitalism, that women's generally lower wages provide extra surplus to a capitalist employer, that women serve the ends of capitalist consumerism in their roles as administrators of family consumption, and so forth.

However, a number of articles have tried to do something much more ambitious — to locate the oppression of women in the heart of the capitalist dynamic by pointing to the relationship between housework and the reproduction of labor. To do this is to place women squarely in the definition of capitalism, the process in which capital is produced by the extraction of surplus value from labor by capital.

Briefly, Marx argued that capitalism is distinguished from all other modes of production by its unique aim: the creation and expansion of capital. Whereas other modes of production might find their purpose in making useful things to satisfy human needs, or in producing a surplus for a ruling nobility, or in producing to insure sufficient sacrifice for the edification of the gods, capitalism produces capital. Capitalism is a set of social relations — forms of property, and so forth — in which production takes the form of turning money, things, and people into capital. And capital is a quantity of goods or money which, when exchanged for labor, reproduces and augments itself by extracting unpaid labor, or surplus value, from labor and into itself.

> The result of the capitalist production process is neither a mere product (use-value) nor a *commodity*, that is, a use-value which has exchange value. Its result, its product, is the creation of *surplus-value* for capital, and consequently the actual *transformation* of money or commodity into capital. . . ." (Marx, 399; italics in the original)[8]

The exchange between capital and labor which produces surplus value, and hence capital, is highly specific. The worker gets a wage; the capitalist gets the things the worker has made during his or her time of employment. If the total value of the things the worker has made exceeds the value of his or her wage, the aim of capitalism has been achieved. The capitalist gets back the cost of the wage, plus an increment — surplus value. This can occur because the wage is determined not by the value of what the laborer makes, but by the value of what it takes to keep him or her going — to reproduce him or her from day to day, and to reproduce the entire work force from one generation to the next. Thus, surplus value is the difference between what the laboring class produces as a whole, and the amount of that total which is recycled into maintaining the laboring class.

> The capital given in exchange for labour power is converted into necessaries, by the consumption of which the muscles, nerves, bones, and brains of existing labourers are reproduced, and new labourers

---

and Lévi-Strauss are among the foremost living ancestors of the contemporary French intellectual revolution (see Foucault, *The Order of Things*. New York: Pantheon, 1970). It would be fun, interesting, and, if this were France, essential, to start my argument from the center of the structuralist maze and work my way out from there, along the lines of a "dialectical theory of signifying practices" (see Hefner "The *Tel Quel* Order of Things," *SubStance* 8 [1974], 127–38). [Rubin]

[8]Karl Marx, *Theories of Surplus Value*. Moscow: Progress, 1969.

> are begotten . . . the individual consumption of the labourer, whether it be part of the process of production or not, forms therefore a factor of the production and reproduction of capital, just as cleaning machinery does. . . . (Marx, 572)[9]

> Given the individual, the production of labour-power consists in his reproduction of himself or his maintenance. For his maintenance he requires a given quantity of the means of subsistence. . . . Labour-power sets itself in action only by working. But thereby a definite quantity of human muscle, brain, nerve, etc., is wasted, and these require to be restored. . . . (Ibid.:171)

The amount of the difference between the reproduction of labor power and its products depends, therefore, on the determination of what it takes to reproduce that labor power. Marx tends to make that determination on the basis of the quantity of commodities — food, clothing, housing, fuel — which would be necessary to maintain the health, life, and strength of a worker. But these commodities must be consumed before they can be sustenance, and they are not immediately in consumable form when they are purchased by the wage. Additional labor must be performed upon these things before they can be turned into people. Food must be cooked, clothes cleaned, beds made, wood chopped, etc. Housework is therefore a key element in the process of the reproduction of the laborer from whom surplus value is taken. Since it is usually women who do housework, it has been observed that it is through the reproduction of labor power that women are articulated into the surplus value nexus which is the *sine qua non*[10] of capitalism.[11] It can be further argued that since no

[9]Karl Marx, *Capital*. New York: International, 1972.

[10]Necessary element.

[11]A lot of the debate on women and housework has centered around the question of whether or not housework is "productive" labor. Strictly speaking, housework is not ordinarily "productive" in the technical sense of the term (Ian Gough, "Marx and Reproductive Labour," *New Left Review* 76 [1972]: 47–72; Marx, *Theories of Surplus Value*, 387–413). But this distinction is irrelevant to the main line of the argument. Housework may not be "productive," in the sense of directly producing surplus value and capital, and yet be a crucial element in the production of surplus value and capital.[Rubin]

wage is paid for housework, the labor of women in the home contributes to the ultimate quantity of surplus value realized by the capitalist. But to explain women's usefulness to capitalism is one thing. To argue that this usefulness explains the genesis of the oppression of women is quite another. It is precisely at this point that the analysis of capitalism ceases to explain very much about women and the oppression of women.

Women are oppressed in societies which can by no stretch of the imagination be described as capitalist. In the Amazon valley and the New Guinea highlands, women are frequently kept in their place by gang rape when the ordinary mechanisms of masculine intimidation prove insufficient. "We tame our women with the banana," said one Mundurucu man (Murphy, 195).[12] The ethnographic record is littered with practices whose effect is to keep women "in their place." — men's cults, secret initiations, arcane male knowledge, etc. And pre-capitalist, feudal Europe was hardly a society in which there was no sexism. Capitalism has taken over, and rewired, notions of male and female which predate it by centuries. No analysis of the reproduction of labor power under capitalism can explain foot-binding, chastity belts, or any of the incredible array of Byzantine, fetishized indignities, let alone the more ordinary ones, which have been inflicted upon women in various times and places. The analysis of the reproduction of labor power does not even explain why it is usually women who do domestic work in the home, rather than men.

In this light it is interesting to return to Marx's discussion of the reproduction of labor. What is necessary to reproduce the worker is determined in part by the biological needs of the human organism, in part by the physical conditions of the place in which it lives, and in part by cultural tradition. Marx observed that beer is necessary for the reproduction of the English working class, and wine necessary for the French.

> . . . the number and extent of his [the worker's] so-called necessary wants, as also the modes of satisfying them, are themselves the product of

[12]Robert Murphy, "Social Structure and Sex Antagonism," *Southwestern Journal of Anthropology* 15.1 (1959): 18–96.

historical development, and depend therefore to great extent on the degree of civilization of a country, moreparticularly on the conditions under which, and consequently on the habits and degree of comfort in which, the class of free labourers has been formed. *In contradistinction therefore to the case of other commodities, there enters into the determination of the value of labour-power a historical and moral element.* . . . (Marx, *Capital*, 171, my italics)

It is precisely this "historical and moral element" which determines that a "wife" is among the necessities of a worker, that women rather than men do housework, and that capitalism is heir to a long tradition in which women do not inherit, in which women do not lead, and in which women do not talk to god. It is this "historical and moral element" which presented capitalism with a cultural heritage of forms of masculinity and femininity. It is within this "historical and moral element" that the entire domain of sex, sexuality, and sex oppression is subsumed. And the briefness of Marx's comment only serves to emphasize the vast area of social life which it covers and leaves unexamined. Only by subjecting this "historical and moral element" to analysis can the structure of sex oppression be delineated.

ENGELS

In *The Origin of the Family, Private Property, and the State* (1884), Engels sees sex oppression as part of capitalism's heritage from prior social forms. Moreover, Engels integrates sex and sexuality into his theory of society. *Origin* is a frustrating book. Like the nineteenth-century tomes on the history of marriage and the family which it echoes, the state of the evidence in *Origin* renders it quaint to a reader familiar with more recent developments in anthropology. Nevertheless, it is a book whose considerable insight should not be overshadowed by its limitations. The idea that the "relations of sexuality" can and should be distinguished from the "relations of production" is not the least of Engels' intuitions:

According to the materialistic conception, the determining factor in history is, in the final instance, the production and reproduction of immediate life. *This again, is of a twofold character: on the one hand, the production of the means of existence, of food, clothing, and shelter and the tools necessary for that production; on the other side, the production of human beings themselves*, the propagation of the species. The social organization under which the people of a particular historical epoch and a particular country live is determined by both kinds of production: by the stage of development of labor on the one hand, and of the family on the other . . . (Engels, 71–72; my italics)[13]

This passage indicates an important recognition — that a human group must do more than apply its activity to reshaping the natural world in order to clothe, feed, and warm itself. We usually call the system by which elements of the natural world are transformed into objects of human consumption the "economy." But the needs which are satisfied by economic activity even in the richest, Marxian sense, do not exhaust fundamental human requirements. A human group must also reproduce itself from generation to generation. The needs of sexuality and procreation must be satisfied as much as the need to eat, and one of the most obvious deductions which can be made from the data of anthropology is that these needs are hardly ever satisfied in any "natural" form, any more than are the needs for food. Hunger is hunger, but what counts as food is culturally determined and obtained. Every society has some form of organized economic activity. Sex is sex, but what counts as sex is equally culturally determined and obtained. Every society also has a sex/gender system — a set of arrangements by which the biological raw material of human sex and procreation is shaped by human, social intervention and satisfied in a conventional manner, no matter how bizarre some of the conventions may be.[14]

---

[13]Friedrich Engels, *The Origin of the Family, Private Property, and the State*. Ed. Eleanor Leacock. New York: International, 1972.

[14]That some of them are pretty bizarre, from our point of view, only demonstrates the point that sexuality is expressed through the intervention of culture (see Ford and Beach, 1972). Some examples may be chosen from among the exotica in which anthropologists delight.

Among the Banaro, marriage involves several socially sanctioned sexual partnerships. When a woman is married, she is initiated into intercourse by the sib-friend of her groom's father. After bearing a child by this man, she begins to have intercourse with her husband. She also has an institutionalized partnership with the sib-friend of her husband. A man's partners include his wife, the wife of his sib-friend, and the wife of his sib-friend's son (Thurnwald, 1916). Multiple intercourse is a more pronounced custom among the Marind Anim. At the time of marriage, the bride has intercourse with all of the members of the groom's clan, the groom coming last. Every major festival is accompanied by a practice known as *otiv-bombari*, in which semen is collected for ritual purposes. A few women have intercourse with many men, and the resulting semen is collected in coconut-shell buckets. A Marind male is subjected to multiple homosexual intercourse during initiation. Among the Etoro, heterosexual intercourse is taboo for between 205 and 260 days a year. In much of New Guinea, men fear copulation and think that it will kill them if they engage in it without magical precautions. Usually, such ideas of feminine pollution express the subordination of women. But symbolic systems contain internal contradictions, whose logical extensions sometimes lead to inversions of the propositions on which a system is based. In New Britain, men's fear of sex is so extreme that rape appears to be feared by men rather than women. Women run after the men, who flee from them, women are the sexual aggressors, and it is bridegrooms who are reluctant. [Rubin]

The realm of human sex, gender, and pro-creation has been subjected to, and changed by, relentless social activity for millennia. Sex as we know it — gender identity, sexual desire and fantasy, concepts of childhood — is itself a social product. We need to understand the relations of its production, and forget, for awhile, about food, clothing, automobiles, and transistor radios. In most Marxist tradition, and even in Engels' book, the concept of the "second aspect of material life" has tended to fade into the background, or to be incorporated into the usual notions of "material life." Engels' suggestion has never been followed up and subjected to the refinement which it needs. But he does indicate the existence and importance of the domain of social life which I want to call the sex/gender system.

Other names have been proposed for the sex/gender system. The most common alternatives are "mode of reproduction" and "patriarchy." It may be foolish to quibble about terms, but both of these can lead to confusion. All three proposals have been made in order to introduce a distinction between "economic" systems and "sexual" systems, and to indicate that sexual systems have a certain autonomy and cannot always be explained in terms of economic forces. "Mode of reproduction," for instance, has been proposed in opposition to the more familiar "mode of

production." But this terminology links the "economy" to production, and the sexual system to "reproduction." It reduces the richness of either system, since "productions" and "reproductions" take place in both. Every mode of production involves reproduction — of tools, labor, and social relations. We cannot relegate all of the multi-faceted aspects of social reproduction to the sex system. Replacement of machinery is an example of reproduction in the economy. On the other hand, we cannot limit the sex system to "reproduction" in either the social or biological sense of the term. A sex/gender system is not simply the reproductive moment of a "mode of production." The formation of gender identity is an example of production in the realm of the sexual system. And a sex/gender system involves more than the "relations of procreation," reproduction in the biological sense.

The term "patriarchy" was introduced to distinguish the forces maintaining sexism from other social forces, such as capitalism. But the use of "patriarchy" obscures other distinctions. Its use is analogous to using capitalism to refer to all modes of production, whereas the usefulness of the term "capitalism" lies precisely in that it distinguishes between the different systems by which societies are provisioned and organized. Any society will have some system of "political economy." Such a system may be egalitarian or socialist. It may be class stratified, in which case the oppressed class may consist of serfs, peasants, or slaves. The oppressed class may consist of wage laborers, in which case the system is properly labeled "capitalist." The power of the term lies in its implication that, in fact, there are alternatives to capitalism.

Similarly, any society will have some systematic ways to deal with sex, gender, and babies. Such a system may be sexually egalitarian, at least in theory, or it may be "gender stratified," as seems to be the case for most or all of the known examples. But it is important — even in the face of a depressing history — to maintain a distinction between the human capacity and necessity to create a sexual world, and the empirically oppressive ways in which sexual worlds have been organized. Patriarchy subsumes both meanings into the same term. Sex/gender system, on the other hand, is a neutral term which refers to the domain and indicates that oppression is not inevitable in that domain, but is the product of the specific social relations which organize it.

Finally, there are gender-stratified systems which are not adequately described as patriarchal. Many New Guinea societies (Enga, Maring, Bena Bena, Huli, Melpa, Kuma, Gahuku-Gama, Fore, Marind Anim, ad nauseum) are viciously oppressive to women. But the power of males in these groups is not founded on their roles as fathers or patriarchs, but on their collective adult maleness, embodied in secret cults, men's houses, warfare, exchange networks, ritual knowledge, and various initiation procedures. Patriarchy is a specific form of male dominance, and the use of the term ought to be confined to the Old Testament-type pastoral nomads from whom the term comes, or groups like them. Abraham was a Patriarch — one old man whose absolute power over wives, children, herds, and dependents was an aspect of the institution of fatherhood, as defined in the social group in which he lived.

Whichever term we use, what is important is to develop concepts to adequately describe the social organization of sexuality and the reproduction of the conventions of sex and gender. We need to pursue the project Engels abandoned when he located the subordination of women in a development within the mode of production.[15] To do this, we can imitate Engels in his method rather than in his results. Engels approached the task of analyzing the "second aspect of material life" by way of an examination of a theory of kinship systems. Kinship systems are and do many things. But they are made up of, and reproduce, concrete forms of socially organized

sexuality. Kinship systems are observable and empirical forms of sex/gender systems.

KINSHIP

(On the part played by sexuality in the transition from ape to "man")

To an anthropologist, a kinship system is not a list of biological relatives. It is a system of categories and statuses which often contradict actual genetic relationships. There are dozens of examples in which socially defined kinship statuses take precedence over biology. The Nuer custom of "woman marriage" is a case in point. The Nuer define the status of fatherhood as belonging to the person in whose name cattle bridewealth is given for the mother. Thus, a woman can be married to another woman, and be husband to the wife and father of her children, despite the fact that she is not the inseminator (Evans-Pritchard, 107–09).[16]

In pre-state societies, kinship is the idiom of social interaction, organizing economic, political, and ceremonial, as well as sexual, activity. One's duties, responsibilities, and privileges vis-à-vis others are defined in terms of mutual kinship or lack thereof. The exchange of goods and services, production and distribution, hostility and solidarity, ritual and ceremony, all take place within the organizational structure of kinship. The ubiquity and adaptive effectiveness of kinship has led many anthropologists to consider its invention, along with the invention of language, to have been the developments which decisively marked the discontinuity between semi-human hominids and human beings.

While the idea of the importance of kinship enjoys the status of a first principle in anthropology, the internal workings of kinship systems have long been a focus for intense controversy. Kinship systems vary wildly from one culture to the next. They contain all sorts of bewildering rules which govern whom one may or may not marry. Their internal complexity is dazzling. Kinship systems have for decades provoked the anthropological imagination into trying to explain incest taboos,

[15]Engels thought that men acquired wealth in the form of herds and, wanting to pass this wealth to their own children, overthrew "mother right" in favor of patrilineal inheritance. "The overthrow of mother right was the *world historical defeat of the female sex.* The man took command in the home also; the woman was degraded and reduced to servitude; she became the slave of his lust and a mere instrument for the production of children" (Engels, *Origin,* 1972, 120–21, italics in original). As has been often pointed out, women do not necessarily have significant social authority in societies practicing matrilineal inheritance. (David Schneider and Kathleen Gough, eds., *Matrilineal Kinship.* Berkeley: U California P, 1961). [Rubin]

[16]E. E. Evans-Pritchard, *Kinship and Marriage Among the Nuer.* London: Oxford UP, 1951.

cross-cousin marriage, terms of descent, relationships of avoidance or forced intimacy, clans and sections, taboos on names — the diverse array of items found in descriptions of actual kinship systems. In the nineteenth century, several thinkers attempted to write comprehensive accounts of the nature and history of human sexual systems. One of these was *Ancient Society*, by Lewis Henry Morgan. It was this book which inspired Engels to write *The Origin of the Family, Private Property, and the State*. Engels' theory is based upon Morgan's account of kinship and marriage.

In taking up Engels' project of extracting a theory of sex oppression from the study of kinship, we have the advantage of the maturation of ethnology since the nineteenth century. We also have the advantage of a peculiar and particularly appropriate book, Lévi-Strauss' *The Elementary Structures of Kinship*. This is the boldest twentieth-century version of the nineteenth-century project to understand human marriage. It is a book in which kinship is explicitly conceived of as an imposition of cultural organization upon the facts of biological procreation. It is permeated with an awareness of the importance of sexuality in human society. It is a description of society which does not assume an abstract, genderless human subject. On the contrary, the human subject in Lévi-Strauss' work is always either male or female, and the divergent social destinies of the two sexes can therefore be traced. Since Lévi-Strauss sees the essence of kinship systems to lie in an exchange of women between men, he constructs an implicit theory of sex oppression. Aptly, the book is dedicated to the memory of Lewis Henry Morgan.

"Vile and precious merchandise" — Monique Wittig

The Elementary Structures of Kinship is a grand statement on the origin and nature of human society. It is a treatise on the kinship systems of approximately one-third of the ethnographic globe. Most fundamentally, it is an attempt to discern the structural principles of kinship. Lévi-Strauss argues that the application of these principles (summarized in the last chapter of *Elementary Structures*) to kinship data reveals an

intelligible logic to the taboos and marriage rules which have perplexed and mystified Western anthropologists. He constructs a chess game of such complexity that it cannot be recapitulated here. But two of his chess pieces are particularly relevant to women — the "gift" and the incest taboo, whose dual articulation adds up to his concept of the exchange of women.

The Elementary Structures is in part a radical gloss on another famous theory of primitive social organization, Mauss' *Essay on the Gift*. It was Mauss who first theorized as to the significance of one of the most striking features of primitive societies: the extent to which giving, receiving, and reciprocating gifts dominates social intercourse. In such societies, all sorts of things circulate in exchange — food, spells, rituals, words, names, ornaments, tools, and powers.

Your own mother, your own sister, your own pigs, your own yams that you have piled up, you may not eat. Other people's mothers, other people's sister, other people's pigs, other people's yams that they have piled up, you may eat. (Arapesh, cited in Lévi-Strauss, 27)[17]

In a typical gift transaction, neither party gains anything. In the Trobriand Islands, each household maintains a garden of yams and each household eats yams. But the yams a household grows and the yams it eats are not the same. At harvest time, a man sends the yams he has cultivated to the household of his sister; the household in which he lives is provisioned by his wife's brother (Malinowski).[18] Since such a procedure appears to be a useless one from the point of view of accumulation or trade, its logic has been sought elsewhere. Mauss proposed that the significance of gift giving is that it expresses, affirms, or creates a social link between the partners of an exchange. Gift giving confers upon its participants a special relationship of trust, solidarity, and mutual aid. One can solicit a friendly relationship in the offer of a gift; acceptance implies a willingness to return a gift and a confirmation of the relationship. Gift

[17] Claude Lévi-Strauss, *The Elementary Structures of Kinship*. Boston: Beacon, 1969.

[18] Bronislaw Malinowski, *The Sexual Life of Savages*. London: Routledge, 1929.

exchange may also be the idiom of competition and rivalry. There are many examples in which one person humiliates another by giving more than can be reciprocated. Some political systems, such as the Big Man systems of Highland New Guinea, are based on exchange which is unequal on the material plane. An aspiring Big Man wants to give away more goods than can be reciprocated. He gets his return in political prestige.

Although both Mauss and Lévi-Strauss emphasize the solidary[19] aspects of gift exchange, the other purposes served by gift giving only strengthen the point that it is an ubiquitous means of social commerce. Mauss proposed that gifts were the threads of social discourse, the means by which such societies were held together in the absence of specialized governmental institutions. "The gift is the primitive way of achieving the peace that in civil society is secured by the state. . . . Composing society, the gift was the liberation of culture" (Sahlins, 169, 175).[20]

Lévi-Strauss adds to the theory of primitive reciprocity the idea that marriages are a most basic form of gift exchange, in which it is women who are the most precious of gifts. He argues that the incest taboo should best be understood as a mechanism to insure that such exchanges take place between families and between groups. Since the existence of incest taboos is universal, but the content of their prohibitions variable, they cannot be explained as having the aim of preventing the occurrence of genetically close matings. Rather, the incest taboo imposes the social aim of exogamy and alliance upon the biological events of sex and procreation. The incest taboo divides the universe of sexual choice into categories of permitted and prohibited sexual partners. Specifically, by forbidding unions within a group it enjoins marital exchange between groups.

> The prohibition on the sexual use of a daughter or a sister compels them to be given in marriage to another man, and at the same time it establishes a right to the daughter or sister of this other man. . . . The woman whom one does not take is, for that very reason, offered up. (Lévi-Strauss, *Elementary Structures*, 51)

[19]Stemming from communal interests.
[20]Marshall Sahlins, *Stone Age Economics*. Chicago: Aldine, 1972.

> The prohibition of incest is less a rule prohibiting marriage with the mother, sister, or daughter, than a rule obliging the mother, sister, or daughter to be given to others. It is the supreme rule of the gift. . . . (Ibid.: 481)

The result of a gift of women is more profound than the result of other gift transactions, because the relationship thus established is not just one of reciprocity, but one of kinship. The exchange partners have become affines, and their descendents will be related by blood: "Two people may meet in friendship and exchange gifts and yet quarrel and fight in later times, but intermarriage connects them in a permanent manner" (Best, cited in Lévi-Strauss, *Elementary Structures*, 481). As is the case with other gift giving, marriages are not always so simply activities to make peace. Marriages may be highly competitive, and there are plenty of affines who fight each other. Nevertheless, in a general sense the argument is that the taboo on incest results in a wide network of relations, a set of people whose connections with one another are a kinship structure. All other levels, amounts, and directions of exchange — including hostile ones — are ordered by this structure. The marriage ceremonies recorded in the ethnographic literature are moments in a ceaseless and ordered procession in which women, children, shells, words, cattle names, fish, ancestors, whale's teeth, pigs, yams, spells, dances, mats, etc., pass from hand to hand, leaving as their tracks the ties that bind. Kinship is organization, and organization gives power. But who is organized?

If it is women who are being transacted, then it is the men who give and take them who are linked, the woman being a conduit of a relationship rather than a partner to it.[21] The exchange of women does not necessarily imply that women are objectified, in the modern sense, since objects in the primitive world are imbued with highly personal qualities. But it does imply a distinction

[21]"What, would you like to marry your sister? What is the matter with you? Don't you want a brother-in-law? Don't you realize that if you marry another man's sister and another man marries your sister, you will have at least two brothers-in-law, while if you marry your own sister you will have none? With whom will you hunt, with whom will you garden, whom will you go visit?" (Arapesh, cited in Lévi-Strauss, *Elementary Structures*, 485). [Rubin]

The ''exchange of women'' is a seductive and powerful concept. It is attractive in that it places the oppression of women within social systems, rather than in biology. Moreover, it suggests that we look for the ultimate locus of women's oppression within the traffic in women, rather than within the traffic in merchandise. It is certainly not difficult to find ethnographic and historical examples of trafficking in women. Women are given in marriage, taken in battle, exchanged for favors, sent as tribute, traded, bought, and sold. Far from being confined to the ''primitive'' world, these practices seem only to become more pronounced and commercialized in more ''civilized'' societies. Men are of course also trafficked — but as slaves, hustlers, athletic stars, serfs, or as some other catastrophic social status, rather than as men. Women are transacted as slaves, serfs, and prostitutes, but also simply as women. And if men have been sexual subjects — exchangers — and women sexual semi-objects — gifts — for much of human history, then manycustoms, clichés, and personality traits seem to make a great deal of sense (among others, the curious custom by which a father gives away the bride).

The ''exchange of women'' is also a problematic concept. Since Lévi-Strauss argues that the incest taboo and the results of its application constitute the origin of culture, it can be deduced that the world historical defeat of women occurred with the origin of culture, and is a prerequisite of culture. If his analysis is adopted in its pure form, the feminist program must include a task even more onerous than the extermination of men: it must attempt to get rid of culture and substitute some entirely new phenomena on the face of the earth. However, it would be a dubious proposition at best to argue that if there were no exchange of women there would be no culture, if for no other reason than that culture is, by definition, inventive. It is even debatable that ''exchange of women'' adequately describes all of the empirical evidence of kinship systems. Some cultures, such as the Lele and the Luma, exchange women explicitly and overtly. In other cultures, the exchange of women can be inferred. In some — particularly those hunters and gatherers excluded from Lévi-Strauss's sample — the efficacy of the concept becomes altogether questionable. What are

between gift and giver. If women are the gifts, then it is men who are the exchange partners. And it is the partners, not the presents, upon whom reciprocal exchange confers its quasi-mystical power of social linkage. The relations of such a system are such that women are in no position to realize the benefits of their own circulation. As long as the relations specify that men exchange women, it is men who are the beneficiaries of the product of such exchanges — social organization.

The total relationship of exchange which constitutes marriage is not established between a man and a woman, but between two groups of men, and the woman figures only as one of the objects in the exchange, not as one of the partners. . . . This remains true even when the girl's feelings are taken into consideration, as, moreover, is usually the case. In acquiescing to the proposed union, she precipitates or allows the exchange to take place, she cannot alter its nature. . . . (Lévi-Strauss in ibid.: 115)[22]

To enter into a gift exchange as a partner, one must have something to give. If women are for men to dispose of, they are in no position to give themselves away.

''What woman,'' mused a young Northern Melpa man, ''is ever strong enough to get up and say, 'Let us make moka, let us find wives and pigs, let us give our daughters to men, let us wage war, let us kill our enemies!' No indeed not!.. they are little rubbish things who stay at home simply, don't you see?'' (Strathern, 161)[23]

What women indeed! The Melpa women of whom the young man spoke can't get wives, they are wives, and what they get are husbands, an entirely different matter. The Melpa women can't give their daughters to men, because they do not have the same rights in their daughters that their male kin have, rights of bestowal (although not of ownership).

[22]This analysis of society as based on bonds between men by means of women makes the separatist responses of the women's movement thoroughly intelligible. Separatism can be seen as a mutation in social structure, as an attempt to form social groups based on unmediated bonds between women. It can also be seen as a radical denial of men's ''rights'' in women, and as a claim by women of rights in themselves. [Rubin]

[23]Marilyn Strathern, Women in Between. New York: Seminar, 1972.

we to make of a concept which seems so useful and yet so difficult?

The "exchange of women" is neither a definition of culture nor a system in and of itself. The concept is an acute, but condensed, apprehension of certain aspects of the social relations of sex and gender. A kinship system is an imposition of social ends upon a part of the natural world. It is therefore "production" in the most general sense of the term: a molding, a transformation of objects (in this case, people) to and by a subjective purpose (for this sense of production, see Marx, 80–99).[24] It has its own relations of production, distribution, and exchange, which include certain "property" forms in people. These forms are not exclusive, private property rights, but rather different sorts of rights that various people have in other people. Marriage transactions — the gifts and material which circulate in the ceremonies marking a marriage — are a rich source of data for determining exactly who has which rights in whom. It is not difficult to deduce from such transactions that in most cases women's rights are considerably more residual than those of men.

Kinship systems do not merely exchange women. They exchange sexual access, genealogical statuses, lineage names and ancestors, rights and *people* — men, women and children — in concrete systems of social relationships. These relationships always include certain rights for men, others for women. "Exchange of women" is a shorthand for expressing that the social relations of a kinship system specify that men have certain rights in their female kin, and that women do not have the same rights either to themselves or to their male kin. In this sense, the exchange of women is a profound perception of a system in which women do not have full rights to themselves. The exchange of women becomes an obfuscation if it is seen as cultural necessity, and when it is used as the single tool with which an analysis of a particular kinship system is approached.

If Lévi-Strauss is correct in seeing the exchange of women as a fundamental principle of kinship, the subordination of women can be seen as a product of the relationships by which sex and gender are organized and produced. The economic oppression of women is derivative and secondary. But there is an "economics" of sex and gender, and what we need is a political economy of sexual systems. We need to study each society to determine the exact mechanisms by which particular conventions of sexuality are produced and maintained. The "exchange of women" is an initial step toward building an arsenal of concepts with which sexual systems can be described.

DEEPER INTO THE LABYRINTH

More concepts can be derived from an essay by Lévi-Strauss, "The Family," in which he introduces other considerations into his analysis of kinship. In *The Elementary Structures of Kinship*, he describes rules and systems of sexual combination. In "The Family," he raises the issue of the preconditions necessary for marriage systems to operate. He asks what sort of "people" are required by kinship systems, by way of an analysis of the sexual division of labor.

Although every society has some sort of division of tasks by sex, the assignment of any particular task to one sex or the other varies enormously. In some groups, agriculture is the work of women, in others, the work of men. Women carry the heavy burdens in some societies, men in others. There are even examples of female hunters and warriors, and of men performing child-care tasks. Lévi-Strauss concludes from a survey of the division of labor by sex that it is not a biological specialization, but must have some other purpose. This purpose, he argues, is to insure the union of men and women by making the smallest viable economic unit contain at least one man and one woman.

> The very fact that it [the sexual division of labor] varies endlessly according to the society selected for consideration shows that . . . it is the mere fact of its existence which is mysteriously required, the form under which it comes to exist being utterly irrelevant, at least from the point of view of any natural necessity . . . the sexual division of labor is nothing else than a device to institute a reciprocal state of dependency between the sexes. (Lévi-Strauss, 347–48)[25]

[24]Karl Marx, *Pre-Capitalist Economic Formations*. New York: International, 1971.

[25]Claude Lévi-Strauss, "The Family," in H. Shapiro, ed., *Man, Culture, and Society*. London: Oxford UP, 1971.

The division of labor by sex can therefore be seen as a "taboo": a taboo against the sameness of men and women, a taboo dividing the sexes into two mutually exclusive categories, a taboo which exacerbates the biological differences between the sexes and thereby *creates* gender. The division of labor can also be seen as a taboo against sexual arrangements other than those containing at least one man and one woman, thereby enjoining heterosexual marriage.

The argument in "The Family" displays a radical questioning of all human sexual arrangements, in which no aspect of sexuality is taken for granted as "natural" (Hertz constructs a similar argument for a thoroughly cultural explanation of the denigration of left-handedness).[26] Rather, all manifest forms of sex and gender are seen as being constituted by the imperatives of social systems. From such a perspective, even *The Elementary Structures of Kinship* can be seen to assume certain preconditions. In purely logical terms, a rule forbidding some marriages and commanding others presupposes a rule enjoining marriage. And marriage presupposes individuals who are disposed to marry.

It is of interest to carry this kind of deductive enterprise even further than Lévi-Strauss does, and to explicate the logical structure which underlies his entire analysis of kinship. At the most general level, the social organization of sex rests upon gender, obligatory heterosexuality, and the constraint of female sexuality.

Gender is a socially imposed division of the sexes. It is a product of the social relations of sexuality. Kinship systems rest upon marriage. They therefore transform males and females into "men" and "women," each an incomplete half which can only find wholeness when united with the other. Men and women are, of course, different. But they are not as different as day and night, earth and sky, yin and yang, life and death. In fact, from the standpoint of nature, men and women are closer to each other than either is to anything else — for instance, mountains, kangaroos, or coconut palms. The idea that men and women are more different from one another

[26]Robert Hertz, *Death and the Right Hand*. Glencoe, IL: Free Press, 1960.

than either is from anything else must come from somewhere other than nature. Furthermore, although there is an average difference between males and females on a variety of traits, the range of variation of those traits shows considerable overlap. There will always be some women who are taller than some men, for instance, even though men are on the average taller than women. But the idea that men and women are two mutually exclusive categories must arise out of something other than a nonexistent "natural" opposition.[27] Far from being an expression of natural differences, exclusive gender identity is the suppression of natural similarities. It requires repression: in men, of whatever is the local version of "feminine" traits; in women, of the local definition of "masculine" traits. The division of the sexes has the effect of repressing some of the personality characteristics of virtually everyone, men and women. The same social system which oppresses women in its relations of exchange, oppresses everyone in its insistence upon a rigid division of personality.

Furthermore, individuals are engendered in order that marriage be guaranteed. Lévi-Strauss comes dangerously close to saying that hetero-sexuality is an instituted process. If biological and hormonal imperatives were as overwhelm-ing as popular mythology would have them, it would hardly be necessary to insure heterosexual unions by means of economic interdependency. Moreover, the incest taboo presupposes a prior, less articulate taboo on homosexuality. A prohi-bition against *some* heterosexual unions assumes a taboo against *non*-heterosexual unions. Gender is not only an identification with one sex; it also entails that sexual desire be directed toward the other sex. The sexual division of labor is implicated in both aspects of gender — male and female — it creates them, and it creates them heterosexual. The suppression of the homosexual component of human sexuality, and by corollary, the oppression of homosexuals, is therefore a product of the same system whose rules and rela-tions oppress women.

[27]"The woman shall not wear that which pertaineth unto a man, neither shall a man put on a woman's garment: for all that do so *are* abominated unto the LORD thy God" (Deuteron-omy, 22:5; emphasis not mine). [Rubin]

In fact, the situation is not so simple, as is obvious when we move from the level of generalities to the analysis of specific sexual systems. Kinship systems do not merely encourage heterosexuality to the detriment of homosexuality. In the first place, specific forms of heterosexuality may be required. For instance, some marriage systems have a rule of obligatory cross-cousin[28] marriage. A person in such a system is not only heterosexual, but "cross-cousin-sexual." If the rule of marriage further specifies matrilateral cross-cousin marriage, then a man will be "mother's-brother's-daughter-sexual" and a woman will be "father's-sister's-son-sexual."

On the other hand, the very complexities of a kinship system may result in particular forms of institutionalized homosexuality. In many New Guinea groups, men and women are considered to be so inimical to one another that the period spent by a male child *in utero* negates his maleness. Since male life force is thought to reside in semen, the boy can overcome the malevolent effects of his fetal history by obtaining and consuming semen. He does so through a homosexual partnership with an older male kinsman.

In kinship systems where bridewealth determines the statuses of husband and wife, the simple prerequisites of marriage and gender may be overridden. Among the Azande, women are monopolized by older men. A young man of means may, however, take a boy as wife while he waits to come of age. He simply pays a bridewealth (in spears) for the boy, who is thereby turned into a wife (Evans-Pritchard).[29] In Dahomey, a woman could turn herself into a husband if she possessed the necessary bridewealth (Herskovitz, 1937).[30]

The institutionalized "transvesticism" of the Mohave permitted a person to change from one sex to the other. An anatomical man could become a woman by means of a special ceremony, and an anatomical woman could in the same way become a man. The transvestite then took a wife or husband of her/his own anatomical sex and opposite social sex. These marriages, which we would label homosexual, were heterosexual ones by Mohave standards, unions of opposite socially defined sexes. By comparison with our society, this whole arrangement permitted a great deal of freedom. However, a person was not permitted to be some of both genders — he/she could be either male or female, but not a little of each.

In all of the above examples, the rules of gender division and obligatory heterosexuality are present even in their transformations. These two rules apply equally to the constraint of both male and female behavior and personality. Kinship systems dictate some sculpting of the sexuality of both sexes. But it can be deduced from *The Elementary Structures of Kinship* that more constraint is applied to females when they are pressed into the service of kinship than to males. If women are exchanged, in whatever sense we take the term, marital debts are reckoned in female flesh. A woman must become the sexual partner of some man to whom she is owed as return on a previous marriage. If a girl is promised in infancy, her refusal to participate as an adult would disrupt the flow of debts and promises. It would be in the interests of the smooth and continuous operation of such a system if the woman in question did not have too many ideas of her own about whom she might want to sleep with. From the standpoint of the system, the preferred female sexuality would be one which responded to the desire of others, rather than one which actively desired and sought a response.

This generality, like the ones about gender and heterosexuality, is also subject to considerable variation and free play in actual systems. The Lele and the Kuma provide two of the clearest ethnographic examples of the exchange of women. Men in both cultures are perpetually engaged in schemes which necessitate that they have full control over the sexual destinies of their female kinswomen. Much of the drama in both societies consists in female attempts to evade the sexual control of their kinsmen. Nevertheless, female resistance in both cases is severely circumscribed.

One last generality could be predicted as a consequence of the exchange of women under a system in which rights to women are held by men. What would happen if our hypothetical

---

[28]Child of one's mother's brother or father's sister (the child of one's father's brother or mother's sister is an ortho cousin).

[29]E. E. Evans-Pritchard, "Sexual Inversion among the Azande," *American Anthropologist* 72 (1970): 1428–34.

[30]Melville Herskovitz, "A Note on 'Woman-Marriage' in Dahomey," *Africa* 10.3 (1937): 335–41.

woman not only refused the man to whom she was promised, but asked for a woman instead? If a single refusal were disruptive, a double refusal would be insurrectionary. If each woman is promised to some man, neither has a right to dispose of herself. If two women managed to extricate themselves from the debt nexus, two other women would have to be found to replace them. As long as men have rights in women which women do not have in themselves, it would be sensible to expect that homosexuality in women would be subject to more suppression than in men.

In summary, some basic generalities about the organization of human sexuality can be derived from an exegesis of Lévi-Strauss's theories of kinship. These are the incest taboo, obligatory heterosexuality, and an asymmetric division of the sexes. The asymmetry of gender — the difference between exchanger and exchanged — entails the constraint of female sexuality. Concrete kinship systems will have more specific conventions, and these convention vary a great deal. While particular socio-sexual systems vary, each one is specific, and individuals within it will have to conform to a finite set of possibilities. Each new generation must learn and become its sexual destiny, each person must be encoded with its appropriate status within the system. It would be extraordinary for one of us to calmly assume that we would conventionally marry a mother's brother's daughter, or a father's sister's son. Yet there are groups in which such a marital future is taken for granted.

Anthropology, and descriptions of kinship systems, do not explain the mechanisms by which children are engraved with the conventions of sex and gender. Psychoanalysis, on the other hand, is a theory about the reproduction of kinship. Psychoanalysis describes the residue left within individuals by their confrontation with the rules and regulations of sexuality of the societies to which they are born.

PSYCHOANALYSIS AND ITS DISCONTENTS

The battle between psychoanalysis and the women's and gay movements has become legendary. In part, this confrontation between sexual revolutionaries and the clinical establishment has been due to the evolution of psychoanalysis in the United States, where clinical tradition has fetishized anatomy. The child is thought to travel through its organismic stages until it reaches its anatomical destiny and the missionary position. Clinical practice has often seen its mission as the repair of individuals who somehow have become derailed en route to their "biological" aim. Transforming moral law into scientific law, clinical practice has acted to enforce sexual convention upon unruly participants. In this sense, psychoanalysis has often become more than a theory of the mechanisms of the reproduction of sexual arrangements; it has been one of those mechanisms. Since the aim of the feminist and gay revolts is to dismantle the apparatus of sexual enforcement, a critique of psychoanalysis has been in order.

But the rejection of Freud by the women's and gay movements has deeper roots in the rejection by psychoanalysis of its own insights. Nowhere are the effects on women of male-dominated social systems better documented than within the clinical literature. According to the Freudian orthodoxy, the attainment of "normal" femininity extracts severe costs from women. The theory of gender acquisition could have been the basis of a critique of sex roles. Instead, the radical implications of Freud's theory have been radically repressed. This tendency is evident even in the original formulations of the theory, but it has been exacerbated over time until the potential for a critical psychoanalytic theory of gender is visible only in the symptomatology of its denial — an intricate rationalization of sex roles as they are. It is not the purpose of this paper to conduct a psychoanalysis of the psychoanalytic unconscious; but I do hope to demonstrate that it exists. Moreover, the salvage of psychoanalysis from its own motivated repression is not for the sake of Freud's good name. Psychoanalysis contains a unique set of concepts for understanding men, women, and sexuality. It is a theory of sexuality in human society. Most importantly, psychoanalysis provides a decryption of the mechanisms by which the sexes are divided and deformed, of how bisexual, androgynous infants are transformed into boys and girls.[31] Psychoanalysis is a feminist theory *manqué*. . . .

WOMEN UNITE TO OFF THE OEDIPAL RESIDUE OF CULTURE

The precision of the fit between Freud and Lévi-Strauss is striking. Kinship systems require a division of the sexes. The Oedipal phase divides the sexes. Kinship systems include sets of rules governing sexuality. The Oedipal crisis is the assimilation of these rules and taboos. Compulsory heterosexuality is the product of kinship. The Oedipal phase constitutes heterosexual desire. Kinship rests on a radical difference between the rights of men and women. The Oedipal complex confers male rights upon the boy, and forces the girl to accommodate herself to her lesser rights.

This fit between Lévi-Strauss and Freud is by implication an argument that our sex/gender system is still organized by the principles outlined by Lévi-Strauss, despite the entirely nonmodern character of his data base. The more recent data on which Freud bases his theories testifies to the endurance of these sexual structures. If my reading of Freud and Lévi-Strauss is accurate, it suggests that the feminist movement must attempt to resolve the Oedipal crisis of culture by reorganizing the domain of sex and gender in such a way that each individual's Oedipal experience would be less destructive. The dimensions of such a task are difficult to imagine, but at least certain conditions would have to be met.

Several elements of the Oedipal crisis would have to be altered in order that the phase not have

such disastrous effects on the young female ego. The Oedipal phase institutes a contradiction in the girl by placing irreconcilable demands upon her. On the one hand, the girl's love for the mother is induced by the mother's job of child care. The girl is then forced to abandon this love because of the female sex role — to belong to a man. If the sexual division of labor were such that adults of both sexes cared for children equally, primary object choice would be bisexual. If heterosexuality were not obligatory, this early love would not have to be suppressed, and the penis would not be overvalued. If the sexual property system were reorganized in such a way that men did not have overriding rights in women (if there was no exchange of women) and if there were no gender, the entire Oedipal drama would be a relic. In short, feminism must call for a revolution in kinship.

The organization of sex and gender once had functions other than itself — it organized society. Now, it only organizes and reproduces itself. The kinds of relationships of sexuality established in the dim human past still dominate our sexual lives, our ideas about men and women, and the ways we raise our children. But they lack the functional load they once carried. One of the most conspicuous features of kinship is that it has been systematically stripped of its functions — political, economic, educational, and organizational. It has been reduced to its barest bones — *sex and gender*.

Human sexual life will always be subject to convention and human intervention. It will never be completely "natural," if only because our species is social, cultural, and articulate. The wild profusion of infantile sexuality will always be tamed. The confrontation between immature and helpless infants and the developed social life of their elders will probably always leave some residue of disturbance. But the mechanisms and aims of this process need not be largely independent of conscious choice. Cultural evolution provides us with the opportunity to seize control of the means of sexuality, reproduction, and socialization, and to make conscious decisions to liberate human sexual life from the archaic relationships which deform it. Ultimately, a thoroughgoing feminist revolution would liberate more than women. It would liberate forms of

[31]"In studying women we cannot neglect the methods of a science of the mind, a theory that attempts to explain how women become women and men, men. The borderline between the biological and the social which finds expression in the family is the land psychoanalysis sets out to chart, the land where sexual distinction originates." (Juliet Mitchell, *Women's Estate*. New York: Vintage, 1971, 167)

"What is the object of psychoanalysis? . . . but the '*effects*,' prolonged into the surviving adult, of the extraordinary adventure which from birth the liquidation of the Oedipal phase transforms a small animal conceived by a man and a woman into a small human child . . . the 'effects' still present in the survivors of the forced 'humanization' of the small human animal into a *man* or a *woman*. . . ." (Louis Althusser, "Freud and Lacan," *New Left Review* 55 (1971): 57, 59; italics in original) [Rubin]

sexual expression, and it would liberate human personality from the straitjacket of gender.

"Daddy, daddy, you bastard, I'm through." — Sylvia Plath

In the course of this essay I have tried to construct a theory of women's oppression by borrowing concepts from anthropology and psychoanalysis. But Lévi-Strauss and Freud write within an intellectual tradition produced by a culture in which women are oppressed. The danger in my enterprise is that the sexism in the tradition of which they are a part tends to be dragged in with each borrowing. "We cannot utter a single destructive proposition which has not already slipped into the form, the logic, and the implicit postulations of precisely what it seeks to contest" (Derrida, 1972:250).[32] And what slips in is formidable. Both psychoanalysis and structural anthropology are, in one sense, the most sophisticated ideologies of sexism around.[33]

For instance, Lévi-Strauss sees women as being like words, which are misused when they are not "communicated" and exchanged. On the last page of a very long book, he observes that this creates something of a contradiction in women, since women are at the same time "speakers" and

[32] See p. 531 (Derrida, "Structure, Sign, and Play," originally published in *The Structuralist Controversy: The Languages of Criticism and the Science of Man*. Baltimore: Johns Hopkins, 1972).

[33] Parts of Wittig's *Les Guérillères* (1973) appear to be tirades against Lévi-Strauss and Lacan. For instance:

Has he not indeed written, power and the possession of women, leisure and the enjoyment of women? He writes that you are currency, an item of exchange. He writes, barter, possession and acquisition of women and merchandise. Better for you to see your guts in the sun and utter the death rattle than to live a life that anyone can appropriate. What belongs to you on this earth? Only death. No power on earth can take that away from you. And — consider explain tell yourself — if happiness consists in the possession of something, then hold fast to this sovereign happiness — to die. (Monique Wittig, *Les Guérillères*, New York: Avon, 1973:115–16; see also 106–07; 113–14; 134)

The awareness of French feminists of Lévi-Strauss and Lacan is most clearly evident in a group called "Psychoanalyse et Politique" which defined its task as a feminist use and critique of Lacanian psychoanalysis. [Rubin]

"spoken." His only comment on this contradiction is this:

But woman could never become just a sign and nothing more, since even in a man's world she is still a person, and since insofar as she is defined as a sign she must be recognized as a generator of signs. In the matrimonial dialogue of men, woman is never purely what is spoken about; for if women in general represent a certain category of signs, destined to a certain kind of communication, each woman preserves a particular value arising from her talent, before and after marriage, for taking her part in a duel. In contrast to words, which have wholly become signs, woman has remained at once a sign and a value. *This explains why the relations between the sexes have preserved that affective richness, ardour and mystery which doubtless originally permeated the entire universe of human communications.* (Lévi-Strauss, *Elementary Structures*, 496; my italics)

This is an extraordinary statement. Why is he not, at this point, denouncing what kinship systems do to women, instead of presenting one of the greatest rip-offs of all time as the root of romance? A similar insensitivity is revealed within psychoanalysis by the inconsistency with which it assimilates the critical implications of its own theory. For instance, Freud did not hesitate to recognize that his findings posed a challenge to conventional morality:

We cannot avoid observing with critical eyes, and we have found that it is impossible to give our support to conventional sexual morality or to approve highly of the means by which society attempts to arrange the practical problems of sexuality in life. *We can demonstrate with ease that what the world calls its code of morals demands more sacrifices than it is worth,* and that its behavior is neither dictated by honesty nor instituted with wisdom. (Freud, 376–77; my emphasis)[34]

Nevertheless, when psychoanalysis demonstrates with equal facility that the ordinary components of feminine personality are masochism, self-hatred, and passivity,[35] a similar judgment is not made. Instead, a double standard of interpretation

[34] Sigmund Freud, *A General Introduction to Psychoanalysis*. Garden City, NY, 1943.

[35] "Every woman adores a fascist." — Sylvia Plath. [Rubin]

is employed. Masochism is bad for men, essential to women. Adequate narcissism is necessary for men, impossible for women. Passivity is tragic in man, while lack of passivity is tragic in a woman.

It is this double standard which enables clinicians to try to accommodate women to a role whose destructiveness is so lucidly detailed in their own theories. It is the same inconsistent attitude which permits therapists to consider lesbianism as a problem to be cured, rather than as the resistance to a bad situation that their own theory suggests.[36]

There are points within the analytic discussions of femininity where one might say, "This is oppression of women," or "We can demonstrate with ease that what the world calls femininity demands more sacrifices than it is worth." It is precisely at such points that the implications of the theory are ignored, and are replaced with formulations whose purpose is to keep those implications firmly lodged in the theoretical unconscious. It is at these points that all sorts of mysterious chemical substances, joys in pain, and biological aims are substituted for a critical assessment of the costs of femininity. These substitutions are the symptoms of theoretical repression, in that they are not consistent with the usual canons of psychoanalytic argument. The extent to which these rationalizations of femininity go against the grain of psychoanalytic logic is strong evidence for the extent of the need to suppress the radical and feminist implications of the theory of femininity

[36]One clinician, Charlotte Wolff (*Love Between Women.* New York: St. Martin's, 1971) has taken the psychoanalytic theory of womanhood to its logical extreme and proposed that lesbianism is a healthy response to female socialization.

> Women who do not rebel against the status of object have declared themselves defeated as persons in their own right. (Wolff, 65)

> The lesbian girl is the one who, by all means at her disposal, will try to find a place of safety inside and outside the family, through her fight for equality with the male. She will not, like other women, play up to him: indeed, she despises the very idea of it. (Ibid.:59)

> The lesbian was and is unquestionably in the avant-garde of the fight for equality of the sexes, and for the psychical liberation of women. (Ibid.:66)

It is revealing to compare Wolff's discussion with the articles on lesbianism in Marmor, 1965. [Rubin]

(Deutsch's[37] discussions are excellent examples of this process of substitution and repression).

The argument which must be woven in order to assimilate Lévi-Strauss and Freud into feminist theory is somewhat tortuous. I have engaged it for several reasons. First, while neither Lévi-Strauss nor Freud questions the undoubted sexism endemic to the systems they describe, the questions which ought to be posed are blindingly obvious. Secondly, their work enables us to isolate sex and gender from "mode of production," and to counter a certain tendency to explain sex oppression as a reflex of economic forces. Their work provides a framework in which the full weight of sexuality and marriage can be incorporated into an analysis of sex oppression. It suggests a conception of the women's movement as analogous to, rather than isomorphic with, the working-class movement, each addressing a different source of human discontent. In Marx's vision, the working-class movement would do more than throw off the burden of its own exploitation. It also had the potential to change society, to liberate humanity, to create a classless society. Perhaps the women's movement has the task of effecting the same kind of social change for a system of which Marx had only an imperfect apperception. Something of this sort is implicit in Wittig (1973) — the dictatorship of the Amazon *guérillères* is a temporary means for achieving a genderless society.

The sex/gender system is not immutably oppressive and has lost much of its traditional function. Nevertheless, it will not wither away in the absence of opposition. It still carries the social burden of sex and gender, of socializing the young, and of providing ultimate propositions about the nature of human beings themselves. And it serves economic and political ends other than those it was originally designed to further. The sex/gender system must be reorganized through political action.

Finally, the exegesis of Lévi-Strauss and Freud suggests a certain vision of feminist politics and the feminist utopia. It suggests that we should not aim for the elimination of men, but for the elimination of the social system that creates

[37]Helene Deutsch (1884–1982), American psychoanalyst, author of *The Psychology of Women* (1944).

sexism and gender. I personally find a vision of an Amazon matriarchate, in which men are reduced to servitude or oblivion (depending on the possibilities for parthenogenetic reproduction), distasteful and inadequate. Such a vision maintains gender and the division of the sexes. It is a vision which simply inverts the arguments of those who base their case for inevitable male dominance on ineradicable and significant biological differences between the sexes. But we are not only oppressed *as* women, we are oppressed by having to *be* women, or men as the case may be. I personally feel that the feminist movement must dream of even more than the elimination of the oppression of women. It must dream of the elimination of obligatory sexualities and sex roles. The dream I find most compelling is one of an androgynous and genderless (though not sexless) society, in which one's sexual anatomy is irrelevant to who one is, what one does, and with whom one makes love.

THE POLITICAL ECONOMY OF SEX

It would be nice to be able to conclude here with the implications for feminism and gay liberation of the overlap between Freud and Lévi-Strauss. But I must suggest, tentatively, a next step on the agenda: a Marxist analysis of sex/gender systems. Sex/gender systems are not ahistorical emanations of the human mind; they are products of historical human activity.

We need, for instance, an analysis of the evolution of sexual exchange along the lines of Marx's discussion in *Capital* of the evolution of money and commodities. There is an economics and a politics to sex/gender systems which is obscured by the concept of "exchange of women." For instance, a system in which women are exchangeable only for one another has different effects on women than one in which there is a commodity equivalent for women.

That marriage in simple societies involves an "exchange" is a somewhat vague notion that has often confused the analysis of social systems. The extreme case is the exchange of "sisters," formerly practiced in parts of Australia and Africa. Here the term has the precise dictionary meaning of "to be received as an equivalent for," "to give and receive."

reciprocally." From quite a different standpoint the virtually universal incest prohibition means that marriage systems necessarily involve "exchanging" siblings for spouses, giving rise to a reciprocity that is purely notational. But in most societies marriage is mediated by a set of intermediary transactions. If we see these transactions as simply implying immediate or long-term reciprocity, then the analysis is likely to be blurred. . . . The analysis is further limited if one regards the passage of property simply as a symbol of the transfer of rights, for then the nature of the objects handed over . . . is of little importance. . . . Neither of these approaches is wrong; both are inadequate. (Goody and Tambiah, 1973:2)[38]

There are systems in which there is no equivalent for a woman. To get a wife, a man must have a daughter, a sister, or other female kinswoman in whom he has a right of bestowal. He must have control over some female flesh. The Lele and Kuma are cases in point. Lele men scheme constantly in order to stake claims in some as yet unborn girl, and scheme further to make good their claims. A Kuma girl's marriage is determined by an intricate web of debts, and she has little say in choosing her husband. A girl is usually married against her will, and her groom shoots an arrow into her thigh to symbolically prevent her from running away. The young wives almost always do run away, only to be returned to their new husbands by an elaborate conspiracy enacted by their kin and affines.

In other societies, there is an equivalent for women. A woman can be converted into bridewealth,[39] and bridewealth can be in turn converted into a woman. The dynamics of such systems vary accordingly, as does the specific kind of pressure exerted upon women. The marriage of a Melpa woman is not a return for a previous debt. Each transaction is self-contained, in that the payment of a bridewealth in pigs and shells will cancel the debt. The Melpa woman therefore has more latitude in choosing her husband than does her Kuma counterpart. On the other hand, her destiny is linked to bridewealth.

[38] Jack Goody and S. J. Tambiah, *Bridewealth and Dowry.* Cambridge: Cambridge UP, 1973.

[39] Property that must be given in exchange for a woman (opposite of dowry, property which is given together with a woman).

If her husband's kin are slow to pay, her kin may encourage her to leave him. On the other hand, if her consanguineal kin are satisfied with the balance of payments, they may refuse to back her in the event that she wants to leave her husband. Moreover, her male kinsmen use the bridewealth for their own purposes, in *moka* exchange and for their own marriages. If a woman leaves her husband, some or all of the bridewealth will have to be returned. If, as is usually the case, the pigs and shells have been distributed or promised, her kin will be reluctant to back her in the event of marital discord. And each time a woman divorces and remarries, her value in bridewealth tends to depreciate. On the whole, her male consanguines will lose in the event of a divorce, unless the groom has been delinquent in his payments. While the Melpa woman is freer as a new bride than a Kuma woman, the bridewealth system makes divorce difficult or impossible (Strathern, *Women in Between,* 1972).

In some societies, like the Nuer, bridewealth can only be converted into brides. In others, bridewealth can be converted into something else, like political prestige. In this case, a woman's marriage is implicated in a political system. In the Big Man systems of Highland New Guinea, the material which circulates for women also circulates in the exchanges on which political power is based. Within the political system, men are in constant need of valuables to disburse, and they are dependent upon input. They depend not only upon their immediate partners, but upon the partners of their partners, to several degrees of remove. If a man has to return some bridewealth he may not be able to give it to someone who planned to give it to someone else who intended to use it to give a feast upon which his status depends. Big Men are therefore concerned with the domestic affairs of others, whose relationship with them may be extremely indirect. There are cases in which headmen intervene in marital disputes involving indirect trading partners in order that *moka* exchanges not be disrupted. The weight of this entire system may come to rest upon one woman kept in a miserable marriage.

In short, there are other questions to ask of a marriage system than whether or not it exchanges women. Is the woman traded for a woman, or is there an equivalent? Is this equivalent only for women, or can it be turned into something else? If it can be turned into something else, is it turned into political power or wealth? On the other hand, can bridewealth be obtained only in marital exchange, or can it be obtained from elsewhere? Can women be accumulated through amassing wealth? Can wealth be accumulated by disposing of women? Is a marriage system part of a system of stratification?[40]

These last questions point to another task for a political economy of sex. Kinship and marriage are always parts of total social systems, and are always tied into economic and political arrangements.

> Lévi-Strauss . . . rightly argues that the structural implications of a marriage can only be understood if we think of it as one item in a whole series of transactions between kin groups. So far, so good. But in none of the examples which he provides in his book does he carry this principle far enough. The reciprocities of kinship obligation are not merely symbols of alliance; they are also economic transactions, political transactions, charters to rights of domicile and land use. No useful picture of "how a kinship system works" can be provided unless these several aspects or implications of the kinship organization are considered simultaneously. (Leach, 90)[41]

Among the Kachin, the relationship of a tenant to a landlord is also a relationship between a son-in-law and a father-in-law. "The procedure for acquiring land rights of any kind is in almost all cases tantamount to marrying a woman from the lineage of the lord" (ibid.: 88). In the Kachin system, bridewealth moves from commoners to aristocrats, women moving in the opposite direction.

> From an economic aspect the effect of matrilateral cross-cousin marriage is that, on balance, the headman's lineage constantly pays wealth to the chief's lineage in the form of bridewealth. The payment can also, from an analytical point of view, be regarded as a rent paid to the senior landlord by the tenant. The most important part of this payment is in the form of consumer goods — namely cattle. The

[40]Another line of inquiry would compare bridewealth systems to dowry systems. Many of these questions are treated in Goody and Tambiah, 1973. [Rubin]

[41]Edmund Leach, *Rethinking Anthropology.* New York: Humanities, 1971.

chief converts this perishable wealth into imperishable prestige through the medium of spectacular feasting. The ultimate consumers of the goods are in this way original producers, namely, the commoners who attend the feast. (Ibid.: 89)

In another example, it is traditional in the Trobriands for a man to send a harvest gift — *urigubu* — of yams to his sister's household. For the commoners, this amounts to a simple circulation of yams. But the chief is polygamous, and marries a woman from each subdistrict within his domain. Each of these subdistricts therefore sends *urigubu* to the chief, providing him with a bulging storehouse out of which he finances feasts, craft production, and *kula* expeditions. This "fund of power" underwrites the political system and forms the basis for chiefly power (Malinowski).[42]

In some systems, position in a political hierarchy and position in a marriage system are intimately linked. In traditional Tonga, women married up in rank. Thus, low-ranking lineages would send women to higher ranking lineages. Women of the highest lineage were married into the "house of Fiji," a lineage defined as outside the political system. If the highest ranking chief gave his sister to a lineage other than one which had no part in the ranking system, he would no longer be the highest ranking chief. Rather, the lineage of his sister's son would outrank his own. In times of political rearrangement, the demotion of the previous high-ranking lineage was formalized when it gave a wife to a lineage which it had formerly outranked. In traditional Hawaii, the situation was the reverse. Women married down, and the dominant lineage gave wives to junior lines. A paramount[43] would either marry a sister or obtain a wife from Tonga. When a junior lineage usurped its position by giving a wife to its former senior line.

There is even some tantalizing data suggesting that marriage systems may be implicated in the evolution of social strata, and perhaps in the development of early states. The first round of the

political consolidation which resulted in the formation of a state in Madagascar occurred when one chief obtained title to several autonomous districts through the vagaries of marriage and inheritance (Henry Wright, personal communication). In Samoa, legends place the origin of the paramount title — the *Tafa'ifa* — as a result of intermarriage between ranking members of four major lineages. My thoughts are too speculative, my data too sketchy, to say much on this subject. But a search ought to be undertaken for data which might demonstrate how marriage systems intersect with large-scale political processes like state-making. Marriage systems might be implicated in a number of ways: in the accumulation of wealth and the maintenance of differential access to political and economic resources; in the building of alliances; in the consolidation of high-ranking persons into a single closed stratum of endogamous[44] kin.

These examples — like the Kachin and the Trobriand ones — indicate that sexual systems cannot, in the final analysis, be understood in complete isolation. A full-bodied analysis of women in a single society, or throughout history, must take *everything* into account: the evolution of commodity forms in women, systems of land tenure, political arrangements, subsistence technology, etc. Equally important, economic and political analyses are incomplete if they do not consider women, marriage, and sexuality. Traditional concerns of anthropology and social science — such as the evolution of social stratification and the origin of the state — must be reworked to include the implications of matrilateral cross-cousin marriages, the surplus extracted in the form of daughters, the conversion of female labor into male wealth, the conversion of female lives into marriage alliances, the contribution of marriage to political power, and the transformations which all of these varied aspects of society have undergone in the course of time.

This sort of endeavor is, in the final analysis, exactly what Engels tried to do in his effort to weave a coherent analysis of so many of the diverse aspects of social life. He tried to relate

[40]Overlord.

[42]Bronislaw Malinowski, "The Primitive Economics of the Trobriand Islanders," in T. Harding and B. Wallace, eds. *Cultures of the Pacific.* New York: Free Press, 1970.

[44]Marrying within a lineage to a close relative.

men and women, town and country, kinship and state, forms of property, systems of land tenure, convertibility of wealth, forms of exchange, the technology of food production, and forms of trade, to name a few, into a systematic historical account. Eventually someone will have to write a new version of *The Origin of the Family, Private Property and the State*, recognizing the mutual interdependence of sexuality, economics, and politics without underestimating the full significance of each in human society.

Eve Kosofsky Sedgwick

1950–2009

Few would have guessed from Eve Kosofsky Sedgwick's 1975 doctoral dissertation, published as The Coherence of Gothic Conventions *in 1980, that she was to be one of the founders of gay and lesbian studies in America, nor that her 1989 MLA talk "Jane Austen and the Masturbating Girl" (published in 1991 in Critical Inquiry) would be singled out for attack by right-wing columnist Roger Kimball as a prime example of "tenured radicalism." Eve Sedgwick was born in Dayton, Ohio, and educated at Cornell and Yale. Her strikingly original work on homosocial desire began from lectures she gave while teaching women's studies at Boston University. Sedgwick writes: "When I began work on* Between Men: English Literature and Male Homosocial Desire *(1986), I saw myself as working mainly in the context of feminist literary criticism and theory. By the time I published* Epistemology of the Closet *in 1990, it was unmistakably clear that lesbian/gay criticism was a going concern in its own right. I see my work as being strongly marked by a queer politics that is at once antiseparatist and antiassimilationist; by a methodology that draws on deconstruction among other techniques; and by writerly experimentation." A poet as well as a critic, Sedgwick taught writing and literature at Hamilton College, Boston University, Amherst College, Duke University, and the Graduate Center of the City University of New York. Her recent books include* Tendencies *(1993),* Fat Art, Thin Art *(1994),* Novel Gazing: Queer Readings in Fiction *(1997),* A Dialogue on Love *(1999), and* Touching Feeling: Affect, Pedagogy, Performativity *(2003). In 2009, Sedgwick died of metastatic breast cancer. In the last decade of her life, she was working toward a book on Proust, and the posthumously published* The Weather in Proust *(2011), edited by Jonathan Goldberg and Michael Moon, is a collection of her essays and lectures. The following selections are from the introductions to* Between Men *and* Epistemology of the Closet.

From *Between Men*

INTRODUCTION

i. Homosocial Desire

The subject of this book is a relatively short, recent, and accessible passage of English culture, chiefly as embodied in the mid-eighteenth- to mid-nineteenth-century novel. The attraction of the period to theorists of many disciplines is obvious: condensed, self-reflective, and widely influential change in economic, ideological, and gender arrangements, I will be arguing that concomitant changes in the structure of the continuum of male "homosocial desire" were tightly, often causally bound up with the other more visible changes; that the emerging pattern of male

"Male homosocial desire": the phrase in the title of this study is intended to mark both discriminations and paradoxes. "Homosocial desire," to begin with, is a kind of oxymoron. "Homosocial" is a word occasionally used in history and the social sciences, where it describes social bonds between persons of the same sex; it is a neologism, obviously formed by analogy with "homosexual," and just as obviously meant

friendship, mentorship, entitlement, rivalry, and hetero- and homosexuality was in an intimate and shifting relation to class; and that no element of that pattern can be understood outside of its relation to women and the gender system as a whole.

to be distinguished from "homosexual." In fact, it is applied to such activities as "male bonding," which may, as in our society, be characterized by intense homophobia, fear and hatred of homosexuality.[1] To draw the "homosocial" back into the orbit of "desire," of the potentially erotic, then, is to hypothesize the potential unbrokenness of a continuum between homosocial and homosexual — a continuum whose visibility, for men, in our society, is radically disrupted. It will become clear, in the course of my argument, that my hypothesis of the unbrokenness of this continuum is not a *genetic* one — I do not mean to discuss genital homosexual desire as "at the root of" other forms of male homosociality — but rather a strategy for making generalizations about, and marking historical differences in, the *structure* of men's relations with other men. "Male homosocial desire" is the name this book will give to the entire continuum.

I have chosen the word "desire" rather than "love" to mark the erotic emphasis because, in literary critical and related discourse, "love" is more easily used to name a particular emotion, and "desire" to name a structure; in this study, a series of arguments about the structural permutations of social impulses fuels the critical dialectic. For the most part, I will be using "desire"

in a way analogous to the psychoanalytic use of "libido" — not for a particular affective state or emotion, but for the affective or social force, the glue, even when its manifestation is hostility or hatred or something less emotively charged, that shapes an important relationship. how far this force is properly sexual (what, historically, it means for something to be "sexual") will be an active question.

The title is specific about *male* homosocial desire partly in order to acknowledge from the beginning (and stress the seriousness of) a limitation of my subject; but there is a more positive and substantial reason, as well. It is one of the main projects of this study to explore the ways in which the shapes of sexuality, and what *counts* as sexuality, both depend on and affect historical power relationships.[2] A corollary is that in a society where men and women differ in their access to power, there will be important gender differences, as well, in the structure and constitution of sexuality.

For instance, the diacritical opposition between the "homosocial" and the "homosexual" seems to be much less thorough and dichotomous for women, in our society, than for men. At this particular historical moment, an intelligible continuum of aims, emotions, and valuations links lesbianism with the other forms of women's attention to women: the bond of mother and daughter, for instance, the bond of sister and sister, women's friendship, "networking," and the active struggles of feminism.[3] the continuum is crisscrossed with deep discontinuities — with much homophobia, with conflicts of race and class — but its intelligibility seems now a matter of simple common sense. However agonistic the politics, however conflicted the feelings, it seems at this moment to make an obvious kind of sense to say that women in our society who love women, women who teach, study, nurture, suckle,

[1] The notion of "homophobia" is itself fraught with difficulties. To begin with, the word is etymologically nonsensical. A more serious problem is that the linking of fear and hatred in the "-phobia" suffix, and in the word's usage, does tend to prejudge the question of the cause of homosexual oppression: it is attributed to fear, as opposed to (for example) a desire for power, privilege, or material goods. An alternative term that is more suggestive of collective, structurally inscribed, perhaps materially based oppression is "heterosexism." This study will, however, continue to use "homophobia," for three reasons. First, it will be an important concern here to question, rather than to reinforce, the presumptively symmetrical opposition between homo- and heterosexuality, which seems to be implicit in the term "heterosexism." Second, the etiology of individual people's attitudes toward male homosexuality will not be a focus of discussion. And third, the ideological and thematic treatments of male homosexuality to be discussed from the late eighteenth century onward do combine fear and hatred in a way that is appropriately called phobic. For a good summary of social science research on the concept of homophobia, see [Stephen M.] Morin and [Ellen] Garfinkle, "Male Homophobia" [in *Gayspeak: Gay Male and Lesbian Communication.* Ed. James W. Chesebro. New York: Pilgrim Press, 1981, pp. 117–29]. [Sedgwick]

[2] For a good survey of the background to this assertion, see Jeffrey Weeks, *Sex, Politics and Society: The Regulation of Sexuality since* 1800 (London: Longman, 1981), pp. 1–18. [Sedgwick]

[3] Adrienne Rich describes these bonds as forming a "lesbian continuum," in her essay, "Compulsory Heterosexuality and Lesbian Existence," in Catherine R. Stimpson and Ethel Spector Person, eds., *Women, Sex and Sexuality*, (Chicago: U Chicago P, 1980), pp. 62–91; especially pp. 79–82. [Sedgwick]

write about, march for, vote for, give jobs to, or otherwise promote the interests of other women, are pursuing congruent and closely related activities. Thus the adjective "homosocial," as applied to women's bonds (by, for example, historian Carroll Smith-Rosenberg)[4] need not be pointedly dichotomized as against "homosexual"; it can intelligibly denominate the entire continuum.

The apparent simplicity — the unity — of the continuum between "women loving women" and "women promoting the interests of women," extending over the erotic, social, familial, economic, and political realms, would not be so striking if it were not in strong contrast to the arrangement among males. When Ronald Reagan and Jesse Helms get down to serious logrolling on "family policy," they are men promoting men's interests. (In fact, they embody Heidi Hartmann's definition of patriarchy: "relations between men, which have a material base, and which, though hierarchical, establish or create interdependence and solidarity among men that enable them to dominate women.")[5] Is their bond in any way congruent with the bond of a loving gay male couple? Reagan and Helms would say no — disgustedly. Most gay couples would say no — disgustedly. But why not? Doesn't the continuum between "men-loving-men" and "men-promoting-the-interests-of-men" have the same intuitive force that it has for women?

Quite the contrary: much of the most useful recent writing about patriarchal structures suggests that "obligatory heterosexuality" is built into male-dominated kinship systems, or that homophobia is a *necessary* consequence of such patriarchal institutions as heterosexual marriage.[6] Clearly, however convenient it might be to group together all the bonds that link males

to males, and by which males enhance the status of males — usefully symmetrical as it would be, that grouping meets with a prohibitive structural obstacle. From the vantage point of our own society, at any rate, it has apparently been impossible to imagine a form of patriarchy that was not homophobic. Gayle Rubin writes, for instance, "The suppression of the homosexual component of human sexuality, and by corollary, the oppression of homosexuals, is . . . a product of the same system whose rules and relations oppress women."[7]

The historical manifestations of this patriarchal oppression of homosexuals have been savage and nearly endless. Louis Crompton makes a detailed case for describing the history as genocidal.[8] Our own society is brutally homophobic; and the homophobia directed against both males and females is not arbitrary or gratuitous, but tightly knit into the texture of family, gender, age, class, and race relations. Our society could not cease to be homophobic and have its economic and political structures remain unchanged.

Nevertheless, it has yet to be demonstrated that, because most patriarchies structurally include homophobia, therefore patriarchy structurally *requires* homophobia. K. J. Dover's recent study, *Greek Homosexuality*, seems to give a strong counter example in classical Greece. Male homosexuality, according to Dover's evidence, was a widespread, licit, and very influential part of the culture. Highly structured along lines of class, and within the citizen class along lines of age, the pursuit of the adolescent boy by the older man was described by stereotypes that we associate with romantic heterosexual love (conquest, surrender, the "cruel fair," the absence of desire in the love object), with the passive part going to the boy. At the same time, however, because the boy was destined in turn to grow into manhood, the assignment of roles was not permanent.[9] Thus the

[4]"The Female World of Love and Ritual," in [Nancy F.] Cott and [Elizabeth] Pleck, eds., *A Heritage of Their Own*, New Haven: Yale UP, 1977, pp. 311–42; the usage appears on, e.g., pp. 316, 317. [Sedgwick]

[5]"The Unhappy Marriage of Marxism and Feminism: Towards a More Progressive Union," in Lydia Sargent, ed., *Women and Revolution* (Boston: South End Press, 1981), pp. 1–41; quotation is from p. 14. [Sedgwick]

[6]See, for example, Gayle Rubin, "The Traffic in Women," in Reyna Reiter, ed., *Toward an Anthropology of Women* (New York: Monthly Review Press, 1975), pp. 182–83. [Sedgwick] See p. 1664.

[7]See Rubin, p. 180. [Sedgwick] See p. 1012.

[8]Louis Crompton, "Gay Genocide: From Leviticus to Hitler" in *The Gay Academic*, ed. Louie Crew (Palm Springs, CA: ETC Publications, 1978) 67–91; but see chapter 5 for a discussion of the limitations of "genocide" as an understanding of the fate of homosexual men. [Sedgwick]

[9]On this, see Jean Baker Miller, *Towards a New Psychology of Women* (Boston: Beacon Press, 1976), ch. 1. [Sedgwick]

love relationship, while temporarily oppressive to the object, had a strongly educational functions; Dover quotes Pausanias in Plato's *Symposium* as saying "that it would be right for him [the boy] to perform any service for one who improves him in mind and character."[10] Along with its erotic component, then, this was a bond of mentorship; the boys were apprentices in the ways and virtues of Athenian citizenship, whose privileges they inherited. These privileges included the power to command the labor of slaves of both sexes, and of women of any class including their own. "Women and slaves belonged and lived together," Hannah Arendt writes. The system of sharp class and gender subordination was a necessary part of what the male culture valued most in itself: "Contempt for laboring originally [arose] out of a passionate striving for freedom from necessity and a no less passionate impatience with every effort that left no trace, no monument, no great work worthy of remembrance";[11] so the contemptible labor was left to women and slaves.

The example of the Greeks demonstrates, I think, that while heterosexuality is necessary for the maintenance of any patriarchy, homophobia, against males at any rate, is not. In fact, for the Greeks, the continuum between "men loving men" and "men promoting the interests of men" appears to have been quite seamless. It is as if, in our terms, there were no perceived discontinuity between the male bonds at the Continental Baths and the male bonds at the Bohemian Grove[12] or in the board room or Senate cloakroom.

[10]K. J. Dover, *Greek Homosexuality* (New York: Random House, 1980), p. 91. [Sedgwick]

[11]Hannah Arendt, *The Human Condition* (Chicago: U Chicago P, 1958), p. 83, quoted in Adrienne Rich, *On Lies, Secrets and Silence* (New York: Norton, 1979) p. 206. [Sedgwick]

[12]On the Bohemian Grove, an all male summer camp for American ruling-class men, see G. William Domhoff, *The Bohemian Grove and Other Retreats* (New York: Harper and Row, 1974); and a more vivid, although homophobic, account,

It is clear, then, that there is an asymmetry in our present society between, on the one hand, the relatively continuous relation of female homosocial and homosexual bonds, and, on the other hand, the radically discontinuous relation of male homosocial and homosexual bonds. The example of the Greeks (and of other, tribal cultures, such as the New Guinea "Sambia" studied by G. H. Herdt) shows, in addition, that the structure of homosocial continuums is culturally contingent, not an innate feature of either "maleness" or "femaleness." Indeed, closely tied though it obviously is to questions of male vs. female power, the explanation will require a more exact mode of historical categorization than "patriarchy," as well, since patriarchal power structures (in Hartmann's sense) characterize both Athenian and American societies. Nevertheless, we may take as an explicit axiom that the historically differential shapes of male and female homosociality — much as they themselves may vary over time — will always be articulations and mechanisms of the enduring inequality of power between women and men.

Why should the different shapes of the homosocial continuum be an interesting question? Why should it be a *literary* question? Its importance for the practical politics of the gay movement as a minority rights movement is already obvious from the recent history of strategic and philosophical differences between lesbians and gay men. In addition, it is theoretically interesting partly as a way of approaching a larger question of "sexual politics": what does it mean — what difference does it make — when a social or political relationship is sexualized? if the relation of homosocial to homosexual bonds is so shifty, then what theoretical framework do we have for drawing any links between sexual and power relationships?

John van der Zee, *The Greatest Men's Party on Earth: Inside the Bohemian Grove* (New York: Harcourt, 1974). [Sedgwick]

AXIOM 6: THE RELATION OF GAY STUDIES TO DEBATES ON THE LITERARY CANON IS, AND HAD BEST BE, TORTUOUS.

Early on in the work on *Epistemology of the Closet*, in trying to settle on a literary text that would provide a first example for the kind of argument I meant the book to enable, I found myself circling around a text of 1891, a narrative that in spite of its relative brevity has proved a durable and potent centerpiece of gay male intertextuality and indeed has provided a durable and potent physical icon for gay male desire. It tells the story of a young Englishman famous for an extreme beauty of face and figure that seems to betray his aristocratic origin — an origin marked, however, also by mystery and class misalliance. If the gorgeous youth gives his name to the book and stamps his bodily image on it, the narrative is nonetheless more properly the story of a male triangle: a second, older man is tortured by a desire for the youth for which he can find no direct mode of expression, and a third man, emblem of suavity and the world, presides over the dispensation of discursive authority as the beautiful youth murders the tortured lover and is himself, in turn, by the novel's end ritually killed.

But maybe, I thought, one such text would offer an insufficient basis for cultural hypothesis. Might I pick two? It isn't yet commonplace to read *Dorian Gray* and *Billy Budd* by one another's light, but that can only be a testimony to the power of accepted English and American literary canons to insulate and deform the reading of politically important texts. In any gay male canon the two contemporaneous experimental works must be yoked together as overarching gateway texts of our modern period, and the conventionally obvious differences between them of style, literary positioning, national origin, class ethos, structure, and the thematics must cease to be taken for granted and must instead become newly salient in the context of their startling erotic congruence. The book of the beautiful male

English body foregrounded on an international canvas: the book of its inscription and evocation through a trio of male figures — the lovely boy, the tormented desirer, the deft master of the rules of their discourse; the story in which the lover is murdered by the boy and the boy is himself sacrificed; the deftly magisterial recounting that finally frames, preserves, exploits, and desublimates the male bodily image: *Dorian Gray* and *Billy Budd* are both that book.

The year 1891 is a good moment to which to look for a cross section of the inaugural discourses of modern homo/heterosexuality — in medicine and psychiatry, in language and law, in the crisis of female status, in the career of imperialism. *Billy Budd* and *Dorian Gray* are among the texts that have set the terms for a modern homosexual identity. And in the Euro-American culture of this past century it has been notable that foundational texts of modern gay culture — *A la recherche du temps perdu* and *Death in Venice*, for instance, along with *Dorian Gray* and *Billy Budd* — have often been the identical texts that mobilized and promulgated the most potent images and categories for (what is now visible as) the canon of homophobic mastery.

Neither *Dorian Gray* nor *Billy Budd* is in the least an obscure text. Both are available in numerous paperback editions, for instance; and, both con-veniently short, each differently canonical within a different national narrative. As what they are taught, however, and as what canon-ized, comes so close to disciplining the reading permitted of each that even the contemporaneity of the two texts (*Dorian Gray* was published as a book the year *Billy Budd* was written) may startle. That every major character in the archetypal American "allegory of good and evil" is English; that the archetypal English fin-de-siècle "alle-gory of art and life" was a sufficiently American event to appear in a Philadelphia publisher's magazine nine months before it became a London book — the canonic regimentation that effaces these international bonds has how much the more scope to efface the intertext and the intersexed. How may the strategy of a new canon operate in this space?

Contemporary discussions of the question of the literary canon tend to be structured either around the possibility of change, of rearrangement and reassignment of texts, within one overarching master-canon of literature — the strategy of adding Mary Shelley to the Norton Anthology — or, more theoretically defensible at the moment, around a vision of an exploding master-canon whose fracture would produce, or at least leave room for, a potentially infinite plurality of mini-canons, each specified as to its thematic or structural or authorial coverage: francophone Canadian or Inuit canons, for instance; clusters of magical realism or national allegory; the blues tradition; working-class narrative; canons of the sublime or the self-reflexive; Afro-Caribbean canons; canons of Anglo-American women's writing.

In fact, though, the most productive canon effects that have been taking place in recent literary studies have occurred, not from within the mechanism either of the master-canon or of a postfractural plurality of canons, but through an interaction between these two models of the canon. In this interaction the new pluralized mini-canons have largely failed to dislodge the master-canon from its empirical centrality in such institutional practices as publishing and teaching, although they have made certain specific works and authors newly available for inclusion in the master-canon. Their more important effect, however, has been to challenge, if not the empirical centrality, then the conceptual anonymity of the master-canon. The most notorious instance of this has occurred with feminist studies in literature, which by on the one hand confronting the master-canon with alternative canons of women's literature, and on the other hand reading rebelliously within the master-canon, has not only somewhat rearranged the table of contents for the master-canon but, more important, given it a title. If it is still in important respects *the* master-canon it nevertheless cannot now escape naming itself with every syllable also *a* particular canon, a canon of mastery, in this case of men's mastery over, and over against, women. Perhaps never again need women — need, one hopes, anybody — feel greeted by the Norton Anthology of mostly white men's Literature with the implied insolent salutation, "I'm nobody. Who are you?"

This is an encouraging story of female canon-formation, working in a sort of pincers movement with a process of feminist canon-*naming,* that has been in various forms a good deal told by now. How much the cheering clarity of this story is indebted, however, to the scarifying coarseness and visibility with which women and men are, in most if not all societies, distinguished publicly and once and for all from one another emerges only when attempts are made to apply the same model to that very differently structured though closely related form of oppression, modern homophobia. It is, as we have seen, only recently — and, I am arguing, only very incompletely and raggedly, although to that extent violently and brutally — that a combination of discursive forces have carved out, for women and for men, a possible though intensively proscribed homosexual identity in Euro-American culture. To the extent that such an identity is traceable, there is clearly the possibility, now being realized within literary criticism, for assembling alternative canons of lesbian and gay male writing *as* minority canons, as a literature of oppression and resistance and survival and heroic making. This modern view of lesbians and gay men as a distinctive minority population is of course importantly anachronistic in relation to earlier writing, however; and even in relation to modern writing it seems to falter in important ways in the implicit analysis it offers of the mechanisms of homophobia and of same-sex desire. It is with these complications that the relation between lesbian and gay literature as a minority canon, and the process of making salient the homosocial, homosexual, and homophobic strains and torsions in the already existing master-canon, becomes especially revealing.

It's revealing only, however, for those of us for whom relations within and among canons are active relations of thought. From the keepers of a dead canon we hear a rhetorical question — that is to say, a question posed with the arrogant intent of maintaining ignorance. Is there, as Saul Bellow put it, a Tolstoi of the Zulus? Has there been, ask the defenders of a monocultural curriculum, not intending to stay for an answer, has there ever yet been a Socrates of the Orient, an African American

Proust, a female Shakespeare? However assaultive or fatuous, in the context of the current debate the question has not been unproductive. To answer it in good faith has been to broach inquiries across a variety of critical fronts: into the canonical or indeed world-historic texts of non–Euro-American cultures, to begin with, but also into the nonuniversal functions of literacy and the literary, into the contingent and uneven secularization and sacralization of an aesthetic realm, into the relations of public to private in the ranking of genres, into the cult of the individual author and the organization of liberal arts education as an expensive form of masterpiece theatre.

Moreover, the flat insolent question teases by the very difference of its resonance with different projects of inquiry: it stimulates or irritates or reveals differently in the context of oral or writ-ten cultures; of the colonized or the colonizing, or cultures that have had both experiences; of peoples concentrated or in diaspora; of traditions partially internal or largely external to a dominant culture of the latter twentieth century.

From the point of view of this relatively new and inchoate academic presence, then, the gay studies movement, what distinctive soundings are to be reached by posing the question our way — and staying for an answer? Let's see how it sounds.

Has there ever been a gay Socrates?
Has there ever been a gay Shakespeare?
Has there ever been a gay Proust?

Does the Pope wear a dress? If these questions startle, it is not least as tautologies. A short answer, though a very incomplete one, might be that not only have there been a gay Socrates, Shakespeare, and Proust but that their names are Socrates, Shakespeare, Proust; and, beyond that, legion — dozens or hundreds of the most cen-trally canonic figures in what the monoculturalists are pleased to consider "our" culture, as indeed, always in different forms and senses, in every other.

What's now in place, in contrast, in most scholarship and most curricula is an even briefer response to questions like these: Don't ask. Or, less laconically: You shouldn't know. The

vast preponderance of scholarship and teaching, accordingly, even among liberal academics, does simply neither ask nor know. At the most expan-sive, there is a series of dismissals of such ques-tions on the grounds that:

1. Passionate language of same-sex attraction was extremely common during whatever period is under discussion — and there-fore must have been completely meaning-less. Or

2. Same-sex genital relations may have been perfectly common during the period under discussion — but since there was no lan-guage about them, *they* must have been completely meaningless. Or

3. Attitudes about homosexuality were intol-erant back then, unlike now — so people probably didn't do anything. Or

4. Prohibitions against homosexuality didn't exist back then, unlike now — so if people did anything, it was completely meaning-less. Or

5. The word "homosexuality" wasn't coined until 1869 — so everyone before then was heterosexual. (Of course, heterosexuality has always existed.) Or

6. The author under discussion is certified or rumored to have had an attachment to someone of the other sex — so their feel-ings about people of their own sex must have been completely meaningless. Or (under a perhaps somewhat different rule of admissible evidence)

7. There is no actual proof of homosexual-ity, such as sperm taken from the body of another man or a nude photograph with another *woman* — so the author may be assumed to have been ardently and exclu-sively heterosexual. Or (as a last resort)

8. The author or the author's important attachments may very well have been homosexual — but it would be provincial to let so insignificant a fact make any dif-ference at all to our understanding of any serious project of life, writing, or thought.

These responses reflect, as we have already seen, some real questions of sexual definition and historicity. But they only reflect them and don't reflect *on* them: the family resemblance among this group of extremely common responses comes from their closeness to the core grammar of *Don't ask; You shouldn't know*. It didn't happen; it doesn't make any difference; it didn't mean anything; it doesn't have interpretive consequences. Stop asking just here; stop asking just now; we know in advance the kind of difference that would be made by the invocation of *this* difference; it makes no difference; it doesn't mean. The most openly repressive project of censorship, such as William Bennett's[1] literally murderous opposition to serious AIDS education in schools on the grounds that it would communicate a tolerance for the lives of homosexuals, are, through this mobilization of the powerful mechanism of the open secret, made perfectly congruent with the smooth, dismissive knowingness of the urbane and the pseudo-urbane.

And yet the absolute canonical centrality of the list of authors about whom one might think to ask these questions — What was the structure, function, historical surround of same-sex love in and for Homer or Plato or Sappho? What, then, about Euripides or Virgil? If a gay Marlowe, what about Spenser or Milton? Shakespeare? Byron? But what about Shelley? Montaigne, Leopardi . . . ? Leonardo, Michelangelo, but . . . ? Beethoven? Whitman, Thoreau, Dickinson (Dickinson?), Tennyson, Wilde, Woolf, Hopkins, but Brontë? Wittgenstein, but . . . Nietzsche? Proust, Musil, Kafka, Cather, but . . . Mann? James, but . . . Lawrence? Eliot? but . . . Joyce? The very centrality of this list and its seemingly almost infinite elasticity suggest that no one *can* know *in advance* where the limits of a gay-centered inquiry are to be drawn, or where a gay theorizing of and through even the hegemonic high culture of the Euro-American tradition may need or be able to lead. The emergence, even within the last year or two, of nascent but ambitious programs and courses in gay and lesbian studies, at schools including those of the Ivy League, may now make it possible for the first time to ask these difficult questions from within the very heart of the empowered cultural institutions to which they pertain, as well as from the marginal and endangered institutional positions from which, for so long, the most courageous work in this area has emanated.

Furthermore, as I have been suggesting, the violently contradictory and volatile energies that every morning's newspaper proves to us are circulating even at this moment, in our society, around the issues of homo/heterosexual definition show over and over again how preposterous is anybody's urbane pretense at having a clear, simple story to tell about the outlines and meanings of what and who are homosexual and heterosexual. To be gay, or to be potentially classifiable as gay — that is to say, *to be sexed or gendered* — in this system is to come under the radically overlapping aegises of a universalizing discourse of acts or bonds and at the same time of a minoritizing discourse of kinds of persons. Because of the double binds implicit in the space overlapped by universalizing and minoritizing models, the stakes in matters of definitional control are extremely high.

Obviously, this analysis suggests as one indispensable approach to the traditional Euro-American canon a pedagogy that could treat it neither as something quite exploded nor as something quite stable. A canon seen to be genuinely unified by the maintenance of a particular tension of homo/heterosexual definition can scarcely be dismantled; but neither can it ever be treated as the repository of reassuring "traditional" truths that could be made matter for any settled consolidation or congratulation. Insofar as the problematics of homo-heterosexual definition, in an intensely homophobic culture, are seen to be precisely internal to the central nexuses of that culture, this canon must always be treated as a loaded one. Considerations of the canon, it becomes clear, while vital in themselves cannot take the place of questions of pedagogic relations within and around the canon. Canonicity itself then seems the necessary wadding of pious obliviousness that allows for the transmission from one generation to another of texts that have the potential to dismantle the impacted foundations upon which a given culture rests.

[1]William Bennett was secretary of education in the George H. W. Bush administration (1988–1992).

Judith Butler

b. 1956

Judith Butler's first training in philosophy took place in the synagogue in her hometown of Cleveland, Ohio. She attended Bennington College and then Yale University, where she received her B.A. in philosophy in 1978 and her Ph.D. in 1984. She taught at Wesleyan and at Johns Hopkins Universities before becoming Maxine Elliot Professor in the Department of Comparative Literature and Program of Critical Theory at the University of California at Berkeley. Butler has written extensively on questions of identity politics, gender, and sexuality. Her books include Subjects of Desire (1987), Gender Trouble: Feminism and the Subversion of Identity (1989), Bodies That Matter: On the Discursive Limits of "Sex" (1993), The Psychic Life of Power: Theories in Subjection (1997), Precarious Life: The Powers of Mourning and Violence (2004), Undoing Gender (2004), Who Sings the Nation-State?: Language, Politics, Belonging (with Gayatri Spivak in 2008), Frames of War: When is Life Grievable? (2009), and Senses of the Subject (2015). Her Wellek Library lectures have been published as Antigone's Claim: Kinship Between Life and Death (2000); her Spinoza lectures have been published as Giving an Account of Oneself: A Critique of Ethical Violence (2003). Originally given as a lecture in 1989 at a conference on homosexuality at Yale, "Imitation and Gender Insubordination" is reprinted from Inside/Out: Lesbian Theories, Gay Theories, edited by Diana Fuss (New York: Routledge, 1991).

Imitation and Gender Insubordination

So what is this divided being introduced into language through gender? It is an impossible being, it is a being that does not exist, an ontological joke.

— MONIQUE WITTIG[1]

Beyond physical repetition and the psychical or metaphysical repetition, is there an ontological repetition? . . . This ultimate repetition, this ultimate theatre, gathers everything in a certain way; and in another way, it destroys everything; and in yet another way, it selects from everything.

— GILLES DELEUZE[2]

TO THEORIZE AS A LESBIAN?

At first I considered writing a different sort of essay, one with a philosophical tone: the "being" of being homosexual. The prospect of being anything, even for pay, has always produced in me a certain anxiety, for "to be" gay, "to be" lesbian seems to be more than a simple injunction to become who or what I already am. And in no way does it settle the anxiety for me to say that this is "part" of what I am. To write or speak as a *lesbian* appears a paradoxical appearance of this "I," one which feels neither true nor false. For it is a production, usually in response to a request, to come out or write in the name of an identity which, once produced, sometimes functions as a politically efficacious phantasm. I'm not at ease with "lesbian theories, gay theories," for as I've argued elsewhere,[3] identity categories tend to be instruments of regulatory regimes, whether as the normalizing categories of oppressive structures or as the rallying points for a liberatory contestation of that very oppression. This is not to say that I will not appear at political occasions

1."The Mark of Gender," *Feminist Issues* 5 no. 2 (1985): 6. [Butler]

2.*Différence et répétition* (Paris: PUF, 1986), 374; my translation. [Butler]

3.*Gender Trouble: Feminism and the Subversion of Identity* (New York and London: Routledge, 1990). [Butler]

under the sign of lesbian, but that I would like to have it permanently unclear what precisely that sign signifies. So it is unclear how it is that I can contribute to this book and appear under its title, for it announces a set of terms that I propose to contest. One risk I take is to be recolonized by the sign under which I write, and so it is this risk that I seek to thematize. To propose that the invocation of identity is always a risk does not imply that resistance to it is always or only symptomatic of a self-inflicted homophobia. Indeed, a Foucaultian perspective might argue that the affirmation of "homosexuality" is itself an extension of a homophobic discourse. And yet "discourse," he writes on the same page, "can be both an instrument and an effect of power, but also a hindrance, a stumbling-block, a point of resistance and a starting point for an opposing strategy."[4]

So I am skeptical about how the "I" is determined as it operates under the title of the lesbian sign, and I am no more comfortable with its homophobic determination than with those normative definitions offered by other members of the "gay or lesbian community." I'm permanently troubled by identity categories, consider them to be invariable stumbling-blocks, and understand them, even promote them, as sites of necessary trouble. In fact, if the category were to offer no trouble, it would cease to be interesting to me: it is precisely the *pleasure* produced by the instability of those categories which sustains the various erotic practices that make me a candidate for the category to begin with. To install myself within the terms of an identity category would be to turn against the sexuality that the category purports to describe; and this might be true for any identity category which seeks to control the very eroticism that it claims to describe and authorize, much less "liberate."

And what's worse, I do not understand the notion of "theory," and am hardly interested in being cast as its defender, much less in being signified as part of an elite gay/lesbian theory crowd that seeks to establish the legitimacy and domestication of gay/lesbian studies within the academy. Is there a pregiven distinction between theory, politics, culture, media? How do those

divisions operate to quell a certain intertextual writing that might well generate wholly different epistemic maps? But I am writing here now: is it too late? Can this writing, can any writing, refuse the terms by which it is appropriated even as, to some extent, that very colonizing discourse enables or produces this stumbling block, this resistance? How do I relate the paradoxical situation of this dependency and refusal?

If the political task is to show that theory is never merely *theoria,* in the sense of disengaged contemplation, and to insist that it is fully political (*phronesis*[5] or even *praxis*), then why not simply call this operation *politics,* or some necessary permutation of it?

I have begun with confessions of trepidation and a series of disclaimers, but perhaps it will become clear that *disclaiming,* which is no simple activity, will be what I have to offer as a form of affirmative resistance to a certain regulatory operation of homophobia. The discourse of "coming out" has clearly served its purposes, but what are its risks? And here I am not speaking of unemployment or public attack or violence, which are quite clearly and widely on the increase against those who are perceived as "out" whether or not of their own design. Is the "subject" who is "out" free of its subjection and finally in the clear? Or could it be that the subjection that subjectivates the gay or lesbian subject in some ways continues to oppress, or oppresses most insidiously, once "outness" is claimed? What or who is it that is "out," made manifest and fully disclosed, when and if I reveal myself as lesbian? What is it that is now known, anything? What remains permanently concealed by the very linguistic act that offers up the promise of a transparent revelation of sexuality? Can sexuality even remain sexuality once it submits to a criterion of transparency and disclosure, or does it perhaps cease to be sexuality precisely when the semblance of full explicitness is achieved?[6] Is sexuality of any kind even possible without that

[5]Practical understanding.

[6]Here I would doubtless differ from the very fine analysis of Hitchcock's *Rope* offered by D. A. Miller in this volume. [Butler] See D. A. Miller, "Anal Rope." *Inside/Out: Lesbian Theories, Gay Theories,* ed. Diana Fuss (New York: Routledge, 1991), pp. 119–41.

[4]Michel Foucault, *The History of Sexuality, Vol. I,* trans. Robert Hurley (New York: Random House, 1980), 101. [Butler]

opacity designated by the unconscious, which means simply that the conscious "I" who would reveal its sexuality is perhaps the last to know the meaning of what it says?

To claim that this is what I *am* is to suggest a provisional totalization of this "I." But if the I so determine itself, then that which it excludes in order to make that determination remains consti-tutive of the determination itself. In other words, such a statement presupposes that the "I" exceeds its determination, and even produces that very excess in and by the act which seeks to exhaust the semantic field of that "I." In the act which would disclose the true and full content of that "I," a certain radical *concealment* is thereby produced. For it is always finally unclear what is meant by invoking the lesbian-signifier, since its significa-tion is always to some degree out of one's control, but also because its *specificity* can only be demar-cated by exclusions that return to disrupt its claim to coherence. What, if anything, can lesbians be said to share? And who will decide this ques-tion, and in the name of whom? If I claim to be a lesbian, I "come out" only to produce a new and different "closet." The "you" to whom I come out now has access to a different region of opacity. Indeed, the locus of opacity has simply shifted: before, you did not know whether I "am," but now you do not know what that means, which is to say that the copula[7] is empty, that it cannot be substi-tuted for with a set of descriptions.[8] And perhaps that is a situation to be valued. Conventionally, one comes out *of* the closet (and yet, how often is it the case that we are "outed" when we are young and without resources?); so we are out of the closet, but into what? what new unbounded spatiality?[7] the room, the den, the attic, the base-ment, the house, the bar, the university, some new enclosure whose door, like Kafka's door,[9] pro-duces the expectation of a fresh air and a light of

[7]Refers to the verb "to be," used with a predicate noun or adjective.

[8]For an example of "coming out" that is strictly unconfes-sional and which, finally, offers no content for the category of lesbian, see Barbara Johnson's deftly constructed "Sula Passing: No Passing" presentation at UCLA, May 1990. [Butler]

[9]Butler refers to the parable of the law in *The Trial* by Franz Kafka.

illumination that never arrives? Curiously, it is the figure of the closet that produces this expectation, and which guarantees its dissatisfaction. For being "out" always depends to some extent on being "in"; it gains its meaning only within that polarity. Hence, being "out" must produce the closet again and again in order to maintain itself as "out." In this sense, *outness* can only produce a new opacity; and *the closet* produces the promise of a disclosure that can, by definition, never come. Is this infinite postponement of the disclosure of "gayness," produced by the very act of "coming out," to be lamented? Or is this very deferral of the signified *to be valued*, a site for the production of values, precisely because the term now takes on a life that cannot be, can never be, permanently controlled?

It is possible to argue that whereas no trans-parent or full revelation is afforded by "lesbian" and "gay," there remains a political imperative to use these necessary errors or category mis-takes, as it were (what Gayatri Spivak might call "catachrestic"[10] operations: to use a proper name improperly[11]), to rally and represent an oppressed political constituency. Clearly, I am not legislating against the use of the term. My question is simply: which use will be legislated, and what play will there be between legisla-tion and use such that the instrumental uses of "identity" do not become regulatory imperatives? If it is already true that "lesbians" and "gay men" have been traditionally designated as impossible identities, errors of classification, unnatural disas-ters within juridico-medical discourses, or, what perhaps amounts to the same, the very paradigm of what calls to be classified, regulated, and controlled, then perhaps these sites of disruption, error, confusion, and trouble can be the very ral-lying points for a certain resistance to classifica-tion and to identity as such.

The question is not one of *avowing* or *dis-avowing* the category of lesbian or gay, but, rather, why it is that the category becomes the site of this "ethical" choice? What does it mean

[10]Rhetorical term for an outrageous play on words.

[11]Gayatri Chakravorty Spivak, "Displacement and the Discourse of Woman." In *Displacement: Derrida and After*, ed. Mark Krupnick (Bloomington: Indiana University Press, 1983). [Butler]

to *avow* a category that can only maintain its specificity and coherence by performing a prior set of *disavowals?* Does this make "coming out" into the avowal of disavowal, that is, a return to the closet under the guise of an escape? And it is not something like heterosexuality or bisexuality that is disavowed by the category, but a set of identificatory and practical crossings between these categories that renders the discreteness of each equally suspect. Is it not possible to maintain and pursue heterosexual identifications and aims within homosexual practice, and homosexual identifications and aims within heterosexual practices? If a sexuality is to be disclosed, what will be taken as the true determinant of its meaning: the phantasy structure, the act, the orifice, the gender, the anatomy? And if the practice engages a complex interplay of all of those, which one of these erotic dimensions will come to stand for the sexuality that requires them all? Is it the *specificity* of a lesbian experience or lesbian desire or lesbian sexuality that lesbian theory needs to elucidate? Those efforts have only and always produced a set of contests and refusals which should by now make it clear that there is no necessarily common element among lesbians, except perhaps that we all know something about how homophobia works against women — although, even then, the language and the analysis we use will differ.

To argue that there might be a *specificity* to lesbian sexuality has seemed a necessary counterpoint to the claim that lesbian sexuality is just heterosexuality once removed, or that it is derived, or that it does not exist. But perhaps the claim of specificity, on the one hand, and the claim of derivativeness or non-existence, on the other, are not as contradictory as they seem. Is it not possible that lesbian sexuality is a process that reinscribes the power domains that it resists, that it is constituted in part from the very heterosexual matrix that it seeks to displace, and that its specificity is to be established, not *outside* or *beyond* that reinscription or reiteration, but in the very modality and effects of that reinscription. In other words, the negative constructions of lesbianism as a fake or a bad copy can be occupied and reworked to call into question the claims of heterosexual priority. In a sense I hope to make clear in what follows, lesbian sexuality can be understood to redeploy its "derivativeness" in the service of displacing hegemonic heterosexual norms. Understood in this way, the political problem is not to establish the specificity of lesbian sexuality over and against its derivativeness, but to turn the homophobic construction of the bad copy against the framework that privileges heterosexuality as origin, and so "derive" the former from the latter. This description requires a reconsideration of imitation, drag, and other forms of sexual crossing that affirm the internal complexity of a lesbian sexuality constituted in part within the very matrix of power that it is compelled both to reiterate and to oppose.

ON THE BEING OF GAYNESS AS NECESSARY DRAG

The professionalization of gayness requires a certain performance and production of a "self," which is the *constituted effect* of a discourse that nevertheless claims to "represent" that self as a prior truth. When I spoke at the conference on homosexuality in 1989,[12,13] I found myself telling my friends beforehand that I was off to Yale to

[12] The conference on homosexuality at Yale, at which this essay was given as an oral presentation in somewhat different form.

[13] Let me take this occasion to apologize to the social worker at that conference who asked a question about how to deal with those clients with AIDS who turned to Bernie Segal and others for the purposes of psychic healing. At the time, I understood this questioner to be suggesting that such clients were full of self-hatred because they were trying to find the causes of AIDS in their own selves. The questioner and I appear to agree that any effort to locate the responsibility for AIDS in those who suffer from it is politically and ethically wrong. I thought the questioner, however, was prepared to tell his clients that they were self-hating, and I reacted strongly (too strongly) to the paternalistic prospect that this person was going to pass judgment on someone who was clearly not only suffering, but already passing judgment on him or herself. To call another person self-hating is itself an act of power that calls for some kind of scrutiny, and I think in response to someone who is already dealing with AIDS, that is perhaps the last thing one needs to hear. I also happened to have a friend who sought out advice from Bernie Segal, not with the belief that there is an exclusive or even primary psychic cause or solution for AIDS, but that there might be a psychic contribution to be made to surviving with AIDS. Unfortunately, I reacted quickly to this questioner, and with some anger. And I regret now that I didn't have my wits about me to discuss the distinctions with him that I have just laid out.

be a lesbian, which of course didn't mean that I wasn't one before, but that somehow then, as I spoke in that context, I *was* one in some more thorough and totalizing way, at least for the time being. So I *am* one, and my qualifications are even fairly unambiguous. Since I was sixteen, being a lesbian is what I've been. So what's the anxiety, the discomfort? Well, it has something to do with that redoubling, the way I can say, I'm going to Yale to be a lesbian; a lesbian is what I've been being for so long. How is it that I can both "be" one, and yet endeavor to be one at the same time? When and where does my being a lesbian come into play, when and where does this playing a lesbian constitute something like what I am? To say that I "play" at being one is not to say that I am not one "really"; rather, how and where I play at being one is the way in which that "being" gets established, instituted, circulated, and confirmed. This is not a performance from which I can take radical distance, for this is deep-seated play, psychically entrenched play, and this *"I" does not play its lesbianism as a role.* Rather, it is through the repeated play of this sexuality that the "I" is insistently reconstituted as a lesbian "I"; paradoxically, it is precisely the *repetition* of "I"; paradoxically, it is precisely the *repetition* of that play that establishes as well the *instability* of the very category that it constitutes. For if the "I" is a site of repetition, that is, if the "I" only achieves the semblance of identity through a certain repetition of itself, then the I is always displaced by the very repetition that sustains it. In other words, does or can the "I" ever repeat itself, cite itself, faithfully, or is there always a displacement from its former moment that establishes the permanently non-self-identical status of that "I" or its "being lesbian"? What "performs" does not

---

Curiously, this incident was invoked at a CLAGS (Center for Lesbian and Gay Studies) meeting at CUNY sometime in December of 1989 and, according to those who told me about it, my angry denunciation of the social worker was taken to be symptomatic of the political insensitivity of a "theorist" in dealing with someone who is actively engaged in AIDS work. That attribution implies that I do not do AIDS work, that I am not politically engaged, and that the social worker in question does not read theory. Needless to say, I was reacting angrily on behalf of an absent friend with AIDS who sought out Bernie Segal and company. So as I offer this apology to the CLAGS member who misunderstood me will offer me one in turn. [Butler]

exhaust the "I"; it does not lay out in visible terms the comprehensive content of that "I," for if the performance is "repeated," there is always the question of what differentiates from each other the moments of identity that are repeated. And if the "I" is the effect of a certain repetition, one which produces the semblance of a continuity or coherence, then there is no "I" that precedes the gender that it is said to perform; the repetition, and the failure to repeat, produce a string of performances that constitute and contest the coherence of that "I."

But *politically*, we might argue, isn't it quite crucial to insist on lesbian and gay identities precisely because they are being threatened with erasure and obliteration from homophobic quarters? Isn't the above theory *complicitous* with those political forces that would obliterate the possibility of gay and lesbian identity? Isn't it "no accident" that such theoretical contestations of identity emerge within a political climate that is performing a set of similar obliterations of homosexual identities through legal and political means? The question I want to raise in return is this: ought such threats of obliteration dictate the terms of the political resistance to them, and if they do, do such homophobic efforts to that extent win the battle from the start? There is no question that gays and lesbians are threatened by the violence of public erasure, but the decision to counter that violence must be careful not to reinstall another in its place. Which version of lesbian or gay ought to be rendered visible, and which internal exclusions will that rendering visible institute? Can the visibility of identity *suffice* as a political strategy, or can it only be the starting point for a strategic intervention which calls for a transformation of policy? Is it not a sign of despair over public policy when identity becomes its own policy, bringing with it those who would "police" it from various sides? And this is not a call to return to silence or invisibility, but, rather, to make use of a category that can be called into question, made to account for what it excludes. That any consolidation of identity requires some set of differentiations and exclusions seems clear. But which ones ought to be valorized? That the identity-sign I use now has its purposes seems right, but there is no way to predict or control the political uses to which that sign will be put in the future. And perhaps this is a kind of openness, regardless of its risks, that ought to be safeguarded for political reasons. If the rendering visible of lesbian/gay identity now presupposes a set of exclusions, then perhaps part of what is necessarily excluded is *the future uses of the sign.* There is a political necessity to use some sign now, and we do, but how to use it in such a way that its futural significations are not *foreclosed?* How to use the sign and avow its temporal contingency at once?

In avowing the sign's strategic provisionality (rather than its strategic essentialism), that identity can become a site of contest and revision, indeed, take on a future set of significations that those of us who use it now may not be able to foresee. It is in the safeguarding of the future of the political signifiers — preserving the signifier as a site of rearticulation — that Laclau and Mouffe discern its democratic promise.

Within contemporary U.S. politics, there are a vast number of ways in which lesbianism in particular is understood as precisely that which cannot or dare not *be.* In a sense, Jesse Helms's attack on the NEA for sanctioning representations of "homoeroticism" focuses various homophobic fantasies of what gay men are and do on the work of Robert Mapplethorpe.[14] In a sense, for Helms, gay men exist as objects of prohibition; they are, in his twisted fantasy, sadomasochistic exploiters of children, the paradigmatic exemplars of "obscenity"; in a sense, the lesbian is not even produced within this discourse as a prohibited object. Here it becomes important to recognize that oppression works not merely through acts of overt prohibition, but covertly, through the constitution of viable subjects and through the corollary constitution of a domain of unviable (un)subjects — *abjects,* we might call them — who are neither named nor prohibited within the economy of the law. Here oppression works through the production of a domain of unthinkability and unnameability. Lesbianism is not explicitly prohibited in part because it has not even made its way into the thinkable, the imaginable, that grid of cultural intelligibility that regulates the real and the nameable. How, then, to "be" a lesbian in a political context in which the lesbian does not exist? That is, in a political discourse that wages its violence against lesbianism in part by excluding lesbianism from discourse itself? To be prohibited explicitly is to occupy a discursive site from which something like a reverse-discourse can be articulated; to be implicitly proscribed is not even to qualify as an object of prohibition.[15] And though homosexualities of all kinds in this present climate are being erased, reduced, and (then) reconstituted as sites of radical homophobic fantasy, it is important to retrace the different routes by which the unthinkability of homosexuality is being constituted time and again.

It is one thing to be erased from discourse, and yet another to be present within discourse as an abiding falsehood. Hence, there is a political imperative to render lesbianism visible, but how is that to be done outside or through existing regulatory regimes? Can the exclusion from ontology itself become a rallying point for resistance?

Here is something like a confession which is meant merely to thematize the impossibility of confession: As a young person, I suffered for a long time, and I suspect many people have, from being told, explicitly or implicitly, that what I "am" is a copy, an imitation, a derivative example, a shadow of the real. Compulsory heterosexuality sets itself up as the original, the true, the authentic; the norm that determines the real implies that "being" lesbian is always a kind of miming, a vain effort to participate in the phantasmatic plenitude of naturalized heterosexuality which will always and only fail.[16] And yet, I remember quite distinctly when I first read in Esther Newton's *Mother Camp: Female*

---

[14]See my "The Force of Fantasy: Feminism, Mapplethorpe, and Discursive Excess," *Differences* 2, no. 2 (Summer 1990). Since the writing of this essay, lesbian artists and representations have also come under attack. [Butler]

[15]It is this particular ruse of erasure which Foucault for the most part fails to take account of in his analysis of power. He almost always presumes that power takes place through discourse as its instrument, and that oppression is linked with subjection and subjectivation, that is, that it is installed as the formative principle of the identity of subjects. [Butler]

[16]Although miming suggests that there is a prior model which is being copied, it can have the effect of exposing that prior model as purely phantasmatic. In Jacques Derrida's "The Double Session" in *Dissemination,* trans. Barbara Johnson (Chicago: University of Chicago Press, 1981),

Impersonators in America[17] that drag is not an imitation or a copy of some prior and true gender; according to Newton, drag enacts the very structure of impersonation by which any gender is assumed. Drag is not the putting on of a gender that belongs properly to some other group, i.e. an act of *expropriation* or *appropriation* that assumes that gender is the rightful property of sex, that "masculine" belongs to "male" and "feminine" belongs to "female." There is no "proper" gender, a gender proper to one sex rather than another, which is in some sense that sex's cultural property. Where that notion of the "proper" operates, it is always and only *improperly* installed as the effect of a compulsory system. Drag constitutes the mundane way in which genders are appropriated, theatricalized, worn, and done; it implies that all gendering is a kind of impersonation and approximation. If this is true, it seems, there is no original or primary gender that drag imitates, but *gender is a kind of imitation for which there is no original;* in fact, it is a kind of imitation that produces the very notion of the original as an *effect* and consequence of the imitation itself. In other words, the naturalistic effects of heterosexualized genders are produced through imitative strategies; what they imitate is a phantasmatic ideal of heterosexual identity, one that is produced by the imitation as its effect. In this sense, the "reality" of heterosexual identities is performatively constituted through an imitation that sets itself up as the origin and the ground of all imitations. In other words, heterosexuality is always in the process of imitating and approximating its own phantasmatic idealization of itself — *and failing.* Precisely because it is bound to fail, and yet endeavors to succeed, the project of heterosexual identity is propelled into an endless repetition of itself. Indeed, in its efforts to naturalize itself as the original, heterosexuality must be understood as a compulsive and compulsory repetition that can only produce the *effect* of its own originality; in other words, compulsory heterosexual identities, those ontologically consolidated phantasms of "man" and "woman," are theatrically produced effects that posture as grounds, origins, the normative measure of the real.[18]

Reconsider then the homophobic charge that queens and butches and femmes are imitations of the heterosexual real. Here "imitation" carries the meaning of "derivative" or "secondary," a copy of an origin which is itself the ground of all copies, but which is itself a copy of nothing. Logically, this notion of an "origin" is suspect, for how can something operate as an origin if there are no secondary consequences which retrospectively confirm the originality of that origin? The origin requires its derivations in order to affirm itself as an origin,

---

he considers the textual effect of the mime in Mallarmé's "Mimique." There Derrida argues that the mime does not imitate or copy some prior phenomenon, idea, or figure, but constitutes — some might say *performatively* — the phantasm of the original in and through the mime:

He represents nothing, imitates nothing, does not have to conform to any prior referent with the aim of achieving adequation or verisimilitude. One can here foresee an objection: since the mime imitates nothing, reproduces nothing, opens up in its origin the very thing he is tracing out, presenting, or producing, he must be the very movement of truth. Not, of course, truth in the form of adequation between the representation and the present of the thing itself, or between the imitator and the imitated, but truth as the present unveiling of the present . . . But this is not the case . . . We are faced then with mimicry imitating nothing; faced, so to speak, with a double that couples no simple, a double that nothing anticipates, nothing. This speculum reflects no reality; it produces mere "reality-effects." . . . In this speculum with no reality, in this mirror of a mirror, a difference or dyad does exist, since there are mimes and phantoms. But it is a difference without reference, or rather reference without a referent, without any first or last unit, a ghost that is the phantom of no flesh . . . (206). [Butler]

[17]Esther Newton, *Mother Camp: Female Impersonators in America* (Chicago: University of Chicago Press, 1972). [Butler]

[18]In a sense, one might offer a redescription of the above in Lacanian terms. The sexual "positions" of heterosexually differentiated "man" and "woman" are part of the *Symbolic,* that is, an ideal embodiment of the Law of sexual difference which constitutes the object of imaginary pursuits, but which is always thwarted by the "real." These symbolic positions for Lacan are by definition impossible to occupy even as they are impossible to resist as the structuring telos of desire. I accept the former point, and reject the latter one. The imputation of universal necessity to such positions simply encodes compulsory heterosexuality at the level of the Symbolic, and the "failure" to achieve it is implicitly lamented as a source of heterosexual pathos. [Butler] See the introduction to Psychoanalytic Theory and Criticism, p. 632.

for origins only make sense to the extent that they are differentiated from that which they produce as derivatives. Hence, if it were not for the notion of the homosexual *as* copy, there would be no construct of heterosexuality *as* origin. Heterosexuality here presupposes homosexuality. And if the homosexual *as* copy *precedes* the heterosexual as *origin,* then it seems only fair to concede that the copy comes before the origin, and that homosexuality is thus the origin, and heterosexuality the copy.

But simple inversions are not really possible. For it is only *as* a copy that homosexuality can be argued to *precede* heterosexuality as the origin. In other words, the entire framework of copy and origin proves radically unstable as each position inverts into the other and confounds the possibility of any stable way to locate the temporal or logical priority of either term.

But let us then consider this problematic inversion from a psychic/political perspective. If the structure of gender imitation is such that the imitat*ed* is to some degree produced — or, rather, *re*produced — by imitation (see again Derrida's inversion and displacement of mimesis in "The Double Session"), then to claim that gay and lesbian identities are implicated in heterosexual norms or in hegemonic culture generally is not to *derive* gayness from straightness. On the contrary, *imitation* does not copy that which is prior, but produces and *inverts* the very terms of priority and derivativeness. Hence, if gay identities are implicated in heterosexuality, that is not the same as claiming that they are determined or derived from heterosexuality, and it is not the same as claiming that that heterosexuality is the only cultural network in which they are implicated. These are, quite literally, *inverted* imitations, ones which invert the order of imitated and imitation, and which, in the process, expose the fundamental dependency of "the origin" on that which it claims to produce as its secondary effect.

What follows if we concede from the start that gay identities as derivative inversions are in part defined in terms of the very heterosexual identities from which they are differentiated? If heterosexuality is an impossible imitation of itself, an imitation that performatively constitutes itself as the original, then the imitative parody of "heterosexuality" — when and where it exists in gay cultures — is always and only an imitation of an imitation, a copy of a copy, for which there is no original. Put in yet a different way, the parodic or imitative effect of gay identities works neither to copy nor to emulate heterosexuality, but rather, to expose heterosexuality as an incessant and *panicked* imitation of its own naturalized idealization. That heterosexuality is always in the act of elaborating itself is evidence that it is perpetually at risk, that is, that it "knows" its own possibility of becoming undone: hence, its compulsion to repeat which is at once a foreclosure of that which threatens its coherence. That it can never eradicate that risk attests to its profound dependency upon the homosexuality that it seeks fully to eradicate and never can or that it seeks to make second, but which is always already there as a prior possibility.[19] Although this failure of naturalized heterosexuality might constitute a source of pathos for heterosexuality itself — what its theorists often refer to as its constitutive malaise — it can become an occasion for a subversive and proliferating parody of gender norms in which the very claim to originality and to the real is shown to be the effect of a certain kind of naturalized gender mime.

It is important to recognize the ways in which heterosexual norms reappear within gay identities, to affirm that gay and lesbian identities are not only structured in part by dominant heterosexual frames, but that they are *not* for that reason *determined* by them. They are running commentaries on those naturalized positions as well, parodic replays and resignifications of precisely those heterosexual structures that would consign gay life to discursive domains of unreality and unthinkability. But to be constituted or structured in part by the very heterosexual norms by which gay people are oppressed is not, I repeat, to be claimed or determined by those structures. And it is not necessary to think of such heterosexual constructs as the pernicious intrusion of "the straight mind," one that must be rooted out in its entirety. In a way, the presence of heterosexual constructs and positionalities in whatever form

[19]Of course, it is Eve Kosofsky Sedgwick's *Epistemology of the Closet* (Berkeley: University of California Press, 1990) which traces the subtleties of this kind of panic in Western heterosexual epistemes. [Butler] See Sedgwick p.1026.

in gay and lesbian identities presuppose that there is a gay and lesbian repetition of straightness — a recapitulation of straightness — which is itself a repetition and recapitulation of its own ideality — within its own terms, a site in which all sorts of resignifying and parodic repetitions become possible. The parodic replication and resignification of heterosexual constructs within non-heterosexual frames brings into relief the utterly constructed status of the so-called original, but it shows that heterosexuality only constitutes itself as the original through a convincing act of repetition. The more that "act" is expropriated, the more the heterosexual claim to originality is exposed as illusory.

Although I have concentrated in the above on the reality-effects of gender practices, performances, repetitions, and mimes, I do not mean to suggest that drag is a "role" that can be taken on or taken off at will. There is no volitional subject behind the mime who decides, as it were, which gender it will be today. On the contrary, the very possibility of becoming a viable subject requires that a certain gender mime be already under way. The "being" of the subject is no more self-identical than the "being" of any gender; in fact, coherent gender, achieved through an apparent repetition of the same, produces as its *effect* the illusion of a prior and volitional subject. In this sense, gender is not a performance that a prior subject elects to do, but gender is *performative* in the sense that it constitutes as an effect the very subject it appears to express. It is a *compulsory* performance in the sense that acting out of line with heterosexual norms brings with it ostracism, punishment, and violence, not to mention the transgressive pleasures produced by those very prohibitions.

To claim that there is no performer prior to the performed, that the performance is performative, that the performance constitutes the appearance of a "subject" as its effect is difficult to accept. This difficulty is the result of a predisposition to think of sexuality and gender as "expressing" in some indirect or direct way a psychic reality that precedes it. The denial of the *priority* of the subject, however, is not the denial of the subject; in fact, the refusal to conflate the subject with the psyche marks the psychic as that which exceeds the domain of the conscious subject. This psychic excess is precisely what is being systematically denied by the notion of a volitional "subject" who elects at will which gender and/or sexuality to be at any given time and place. It is this excess which erupts within the intervals of those repeated gestures and acts that construct the apparent uniformity of heterosexual positionalities, indeed which compels the repetition itself, and which guarantees its perpetual failure. In this sense, it is this excess which, within the heterosexual economy, implicitly includes homosexuality, that perpetual threat of a disruption which is quelled through a reenforced repetition of the same. And yet, if repetition is the way in which power works to construct the illusion of a seamless heterosexual identity, if heterosexuality is compelled to *repeat itself* in order to establish the illusion of its own uniformity and identity, then this is an identity permanently at risk, for what if it fails to repeat, or if the very exercise of repetition is redeployed for a very different performative purpose? If there is, as it were, always a compulsion to repeat, repetition never fully accomplishes identity. That there is a need for a repetition at all is a sign that identity is not self-identical. It requires to be instituted again and again, which is to say that it runs the risk of becoming *de*-instituted at every interval.

So what is this psychic excess, and what will constitute a subversive or *de*-instituting repetition? First, it is necessary to consider that sexuality always exceeds any given performance, presentation, or narrative which is why it is not possible to derive or read off a sexuality from any given gender presentation. And sexuality may be said to exceed any definitive narrativization. Sexuality is never fully "expressed" in a performance or practice; there will be passive and butchy femmes, femmy and aggressive butches, and both of those, and more, will turn out to describe more or less anatomically stable "males" and "females." There are no direct expressive or causal lines between sex, gender, gender presentation, sexual practice, fantasy and sexuality. None of those terms captures or determines the rest. Part of what constitutes sexuality is precisely that which does not appear and that which, to some degree, can never appear. This is perhaps the most fundamental reason why sexuality is to some degree always closeted, especially to the one who would express it through acts of self-disclosure. That which is excluded for a given gender presentation to "succeed" may be precisely what is played out sexually, that is, an "inverted" relation, as it were, between gender and gender presentation, and gender presentation and sexuality. On the other hand, both gender presentation and sexual practices may corollate such that it appears that the former "expresses" the latter, and yet both are jointly constituted by the very sexual possibilities that they exclude.

This logic of inversion gets played out interestingly in versions of lesbian butch and femme gender stylization. For a butch can present herself as capable, forceful, and all-providing, and a stone butch may well seek to constitute her lover as the exclusive site of erotic attention and pleasure. And yet, this "providing" butch who seems *at first* to replicate a certain husband-like role, can find herself caught in a logic of inversion whereby that "providingness" turns to a self-sacrifice, which implicates her in the most ancient trap of feminine self-abnegation. She may well find herself in a situation of radical need, which is precisely what she sought to locate, find, and fulfill in her femme lover. In effect, the butch inverts into the femme or remains caught up in the specter of that inversion, or takes pleasure in it.[20] On the other hand, the femme who, as Amber Hollibaugh has argued, "orchestrates" sexual exchange,[21] may well eroticize a certain dependency only to learn that the very power to orchestrate that dependency exposes her own incontrovertible power, at which point she inverts into a butch or becomes caught up in the specter of that inversion, or perhaps delights in it.

[20]Butler's argument here recapitulates Hegel's paradox of the master and the slave, in which the master, in his dependency, becomes in effect the slave to his slaves.

[21]Amber Hollibaugh and Cherríe Moraga, "What We're Rollin Around in Bed With: Sexual Silences in Feminism," in *Powers of Desire: The Politics of Sexuality,* ed. Ann Snitow, Christine Stansell, and Sharon Thompson (New York: Monthly Review Press, 1983), 394–405. [Butler]

PSYCHIC MIMESIS

What stylizes or forms an erotic style and/or a gender presentation — and that which makes such categories inherently unstable — is a set of *psychic identifications* that are not simple to describe. Some psychoanalytic theories tend to construe identification and desire as two mutually exclusive relations to love objects that have been lost through prohibition and/or separation. Any intense emotional attachment thus divides into either wanting to have someone or wanting to be that someone, but never both at once. It is important to consider that identification and desire can coexist, and that their formulation in terms of mutually exclusive oppositions serves a heterosexual matrix. But I would like to focus attention on yet a different construal of that scenario, namely, that "wanting to be" and "wanting to have" can operate to differentiate mutually exclusive positionalities internal to lesbian erotic exchange. Consider that identifications are always made in response to loss of some kind, and that they involve a certain *mimetic practice* that seeks to incorporate the lost love within the very "identity" of the one who remains. This was Freud's thesis in "Mourning and Melancholia" in 1917 and continues to inform contemporary psychoanalytic discussions of identification.[22]

For psychoanalytic theorists Mikkel Borch-Jacobsen and Ruth Leys, however, identification and, in particular, identificatory mimetism, *precedes* "identity" and constitutes identity as that which is fundamentally "other to itself." The notion of this Other *in* the self, as it were, implies that the self/Other distinction is *not* primarily external (a powerful critique of ego psychology follows from this); the self is from the start radically implicated in the "Other." This theory of primary mimetism differs from Freud's account of melancholic incorporation. In Freud's view, which I continue to find useful, incorporation — a kind of psychic miming — is a response to, and refusal of, *loss*. Gender as the site of such psychic mimes is thus constituted by the variously gendered Others who have been loved and lost, where the loss is

[22]Mikkel Borch-Jacobsen, *The Freudian Subject* (Stanford: Stanford University Press, 1988); for citations of Ruth Leys's work, see the following two notes. [Butler]

suspended through a melancholic and imaginary incorporation (and preservation) of those Others into the psyche. Over and against this account of the psyche, the theory of primary mimetism argues an even stronger position in favor of the non-self-identity of the psychic subject. Mimetism is not motivated by a drama of loss and wishful recovery, but appears to precede and constitute desire (and motivation) itself; in this sense, mimetism would be prior to the possibility of loss and the disappointments of love.

Whether loss or mimetism is primary (perhaps an undecidable problem), the psychic subject is nevertheless constituted internally by differentially gendered Others and is, therefore, never, as a gender, self-identical.

In my view, the self only becomes a self on the condition that it has suffered a separation (grammar fails us here, for the "it" only becomes differentiated through that separation), a loss which is suspended and provisionally resolved through a melancholic incorporation of some "Other." That "Other" installed in the self thus establishes the permanent incapacity of that "self" to achieve self-identity; it is as it were always already disrupted by that Other; the disruption of the Other at the heart of the self is the very condition of that self's possibility.[23]

Such a consideration of psychic identification would vitiate the possibility of any stable set of typologies that explain or describe something like gay or lesbian identities. And any effort to supply one — as evidenced in Kaja Silverman's recent

[23]For a very fine analysis of primary mimetism with direct implications for gender formation, see Ruth Leys, "The Real Miss Beauchamp: The History and Sexual Politics of the Multiple Personality Concept," in *Feminists Theorize the Political*, eds. Judith Butler and Joan W. Scott (New York and London: Routledge, 1992). For Leys, a primary mimetism or suggestibility requires that the "self" from the start is constituted by its incorporations; the effort to differentiate oneself from that by which one is constituted is, of course, impossible, but it does entail a certain "incorporative violence," to use her term. The violence of identification is in this way in the service of an effort at differentiation, to take the place of the Other who is, as it were, installed at the foundation of the self. That this replacement, which seeks to be a displacement, fails, and must repeat itself endlessly, becomes the trajectory of one's psychic career. [Butler]

inquiries into male homosexuality — suffer from simplification, and conform, with alarming ease, to the regulatory requirements of diagnostic epistemic regimes. If incorporation in Freud's sense in 1914 is an effort to *preserve* a lost and loved object and to refuse or postpone the recognition of loss and, hence, of grief, then to become *like* one's mother or father or sibling or other early "lovers" may be an act of love and/or a hateful effort to replace or displace. How would we "typologize" the ambivalence at the heart of mimetic incorporations such as these?[24]

How does this consideration of psychic identification return us to the question, what constitutes a subversive repetition? How are troublesome identifications apparent in cultural practices? Well, consider the way in which heterosexuality naturalizes itself through setting up certain illusions of continuity between sex, gender, and desire. When Aretha Franklin sings, "you make me feel like a natural woman," she seems at first to suggest that some natural potential of her biological sex is actualized by her participation in the cultural position of "woman" as object of heterosexual recognition. Something in her "sex" is thus expressed by her "gender" which is then fully known and consecrated within the heterosexual scene. There is no breakage, no discontinuity between "sex" as biological facticity and essence, or between gender and sexuality. Although Aretha appears to be all too glad to have her naturalness confirmed, she also seems fully and paradoxically mindful that that confirmation is never guaranteed, that the effect of natural-ness is only achieved as a consequence of that moment of heterosexual recognition. After all, Aretha sings, you make me feel *like* a natural woman, suggesting that this is a kind of metaphorical substitution, an act of imposture, a kind of sublime and momentary participation in an ontological illusion produced by the mundane operation of heterosexual drag.

[24]Here again, I think it is the work of Ruth Leys which will clarify some of the complex questions of gender constitution that emerge from a close psychoanalytic consideration of imitation and identification. Her forthcoming book manuscript will doubtless galvanize this field: *The Subject of Imitation.* [Butler]

But what if Aretha were singing to me? Or what if she were singing to a drag queen whose performance somehow confirmed her own?

How do we take account of these kinds of identifications? It's not that there is some kind of *sex* that exists in hazy biological form that is somehow *expressed* in the gait, the posture, the gesture; and that some sexuality then expresses both that apparent gender or that more or less magical sex. If gender is drag, and if it is an imitation that regularly produces the ideal it attempts to approximate, then gender is a performance that *produces* the illusion of an inner sex or essence or psychic gender core; it *produces* on the skin, through the gesture, the move, the gait (that array of corporeal theatrics understood as gender presentation), the illusion of an inner depth. In effect, one way that gender gets naturalized is through being constructed as an inner psychic or physical *necessity*. And yet, it is always a surface sign, a signification on and with the public body that produces this illusion of an inner depth, necessity or essence that is somehow magically, causally expressed.

To dispute the psyche as *inner depth*, however, is not to refuse the psyche altogether. On the contrary, the psyche calls to be rethought precisely as a compulsive repetition, as that which conditions and disables the repetitive performance of identity. If every performance repeats itself to institute the effect of identity, then every repetition requires an interval between the acts, as it were, in which risk and excess threaten to disrupt the identity being constituted. The unconscious is this excess that enables and contests every performance, and which never fully appears within the performance itself. The psyche is not "in" the body, but in the very signifying process through which that body comes to appear; it is the lapse in repetition as well as its compulsion, precisely what the performance seeks to deny, and that which compels it from the start.

To locate the psyche within this signifying chain as the instability of all iterability[25] is not the same as claiming that it is inner core that is awaiting its full and liberatory expression. On the contrary, the psyche is the permanent failure of expression, a failure that has its values, for it impels repetition and so reinstates the possibility of disruption. What then does it mean to pursue disruptive repetition within compulsory heterosexuality?

Although compulsory heterosexuality often presumes that there is first a sex that is expressed through a gender and then through a sexuality, it may now be necessary fully to invert and displace that operation of thought. If a regime of sexuality mandates a compulsory performance of sex, then it may be only through that performance that the binary system of gender and the binary system of sex come to have intelligibility at all. It may be that the very categories of sex, of sexual identity, of gender are produced or maintained in the *effects* of this compulsory performance, effects which are disingenuously renamed as causes, origins, disingenuously lined up within a causal or expressive sequence that the heterosexual norm produces to legitimate itself as the origin of all sex. How then to expose the causal lines as retrospectively and performatively produced fabrications, and to engage gender itself as an inevitable fabrication, to fabricate gender in terms which reveal every claim to the origin, the inner, the true, and the real as nothing other than the effects of *drag,* whose subversive possibilities ought to be played and replayed to make the "sex" of gender into a site of insistent political play? Perhaps this will be a matter of working sexuality *against* identity, even against gender, and of letting that which cannot fully appear in any performance persist in its disruptive promise.

[25]See the introduction to Structuralism and Deconstruction, p. 479.

6

POSTCOLONIALISM AND ETHNIC STUDIES

This chapter links together postcolonial and ethnic studies, two key theoretical positions. Postcolonialism deals with the contemporary literatures and cultures of nations today that once formed part of overseas European empires; ethnic studies addresses the literatures and cultures of minority groups such as African Americans, Latinos, Asians, and others operating within a majority culture whose leaders are primarily whites of European origin. We will be analyzing the relations of power and knowledge, politics and aesthetics, among these groups, groups that in both cases are marked for race, nationality, or ethnicity. In both postcolonial and ethnic studies, the same theorists — Marx and Gramsci, Foucault and Derrida — will provide our foundations. In both cases we will consider the way we form imaginary communities to which we are ourselves attached, or create in our imagination for those whom we exclude from our own community. And in both areas of study parallel questions have emerged: whether the use of the metropolitan language/white dialect robs the subaltern/black of his or her culture, and whether literary theory itself, with its origins in European thought, is too "white" to be useful in the cultural struggles in which ethnic and postcolonial scholars are engaged.

This is not a mere marriage of convenience, then, and indeed, it may be hard to distinguish postcolonial writing from that of minority groups inhabiting European countries, who may be primarily citizens from these former colonies or their descendants.[1] The most significant minority groups living in the United States may not, as in Europe, have been connected with overseas colonies; instead, they are likely to have become American citizens by an analogous process of internal colonization which proceeded through absorption or immigration. Native Americans, French Creoles, and Mexicans were absorbed as their vast territories were annexed to the expanding nation, while Africans and Europeans immigrated (by brute force in the case of African slaves, or compelled by starvation and persecution in the case of

---

[1]Similar distinctions between the periphery and the metropolis can be significant within areas that were never colonies as such, such as Scotland's position within the United Kingdom.

most European ethnics). Nationality interacts with ethnicity, so there will be differences between the cultural stance of Jamaicans of African origin living in Jamaica, where they form the majority, and those living as minorities in Brixton, South London, or in the borough of Queens in New York. All three groups, however, may consider themselves as living in the African diaspora.[2]

IMPERIALISM AND DECOLONIZATION

Imperialism as a military adventure began at the dawn of human history, or even perhaps before it, since the very first recorded annals speak of how the rulers of Egypt, Mesopotamia, and China extended their power by conquest over neighboring peoples. The Bible records Israel both as an imperial state and as a colony, a conquering nation under David, whose empire was later conquered by Babylon, and then for good measure by Persia, Greece, and Rome. Rome, whose Mediterranean empire may have seemed universal, split in two and then fell in its turn, replaced in Europe by a Holy Roman Empire, and in Asia successively by the Caliphate of the Arabs, the Khanate of the Moguls, and the Sultanate of the Ottomans. Off the stage of the Eurasian land mass, we are more dimly aware of how the Aztecs wiped out the Mayas in the Americas, or how Songhai displaced Mali in Central Africa. Some of these conquerors left subjected peoples with their own rulers and cultures, appointing a military garrison and a tax-gatherer as the only oppressive forces; others imposed new laws and religions, in effect a new culture; still others pursued wars of annihilation, holocausts of long ago.

But what most of us mean by the Age of Imperialism began around 1500 as European sailors after voyages of discovery laid claim to huge inhabited territories in Asia and the Americas, despoiling the aboriginal peoples of their wealth, infecting them with virulent diseases, enslaving them, or forcing their escape into the hinterland. Portugal and Spain were the first world powers to succeed at this strategy, though by the seventeenth century they shared the stage with rival powers — Holland, France, and Great Britain — and began to decline. The eighteenth century saw wars primarily fought to obtain by conquest lucrative overseas possessions, although by this point the primary advantage of empire was in securing wealth through trade, as colonies produced raw materials and became captive markets for manufactured goods produced at the seat of empire. In the nineteenth century the great European powers scrambled to divide up Africa, with England and France taking the vast heart of the continent, with smaller pieces for Portugal and Spain, Belgium, Italy, and Germany. At its height around 1900,

---

[2]Exactly what status a group needs to have in order to constitute a recognized "minority" worth studying seems to be a question of local interests and politics. Programs in "African American Studies" exist on many campuses throughout the country, but at Queens College, where I teach, most students of color are descended not from American slaves but are rather immigrants from former colonies in the Caribbean, and our program marks that difference by being called "Africana Studies." (Similarly, we have a "Latin American Area Studies" program rather than one in Chicano Studies because the Spanish-speaking groups in the borough are not primarily from Mexico.) Queens College also has an old and well-funded program in Italian Studies, reflecting, among other things, its founders' wish to counter the tendency of ethnic Italians to enter manual trades rather than the learned professions, and more recently has added institutes studying Asian American and modern Greek cultures.

the British Empire, with possessions nearly everywhere, counted over 400 million subjects of the Crown living on about 25 percent of the earth's landmass, compared with the 35 million inhabitants of the British Isles who lived on less than 0.2 percent. Although some colonies separated by an ocean from the seat of empire broke away through insurgencies and wars of liberation and became independent nations as early as the eighteenth century, it was not until the twentieth century that the great European empires broke up and worldwide decolonization occurred. After World War I, the losers, particularly the Ottoman and Austrian empires, were chopped up into smaller states, whose governance was often given "in trust" to one or another of the victorious countries (e.g., Lebanon and Syria to France, Palestine and Iraq to Great Britain). But after World War II, even the victors gave up the vast majority of their colonies, sometimes voluntarily, sometimes after bloody wars of insurgency, with the result that the United Nations organization, formed in 1945 by 51 states, grew to the nearly 200 states it is today.[3] Whether the new nations formed by decolonization then became truly independent is a debatable point, though, particularly because of the polarization of the world through the second half of the twentieth century toward either the United States or the Soviet Union, the two nuclear superpowers. The "Cold War" was fought not only through the buildup of huge arsenals, but through hot stretches of proxy war between the superpowers fought out primarily between or within these new states. It was often hard to distinguish between this kind of proxy war and a war of national liberation fought against a Western democracy with the aid of tactical support by communist powers.[4] One classic example was the civil war that broke out in Angola, after it had achieved independence from Portugal in 1974, between factions allied with the Soviet Union and those with the West, although one should remember that, in this and other "proxy" wars, the nations or factions involved have their own interests at stake and may not think of themselves as proxies for the Great Powers.

For as long as the Cold War lasted, about half a century, the West spoke of a "Free World" of allied industrialized nations including the United States and Canada, the European democracies, and Japan; and a "Communist World" of industrial nations allied with Soviet Russia and mainland China. Decolonization produced a "Third World" of unaligned "developing" nations in Central and South America, Africa, and Asia, many of them former European colonies. Around 1990, at the end of the Cold War era, which coincidentally was also the end of the era of grand theory, the distinctions between the three worlds began to dissolve as victorious global capitalism stretched its tentacles everywhere (for a discussion of the era of

---

[3] A few dozen colonies, mainly small islands, still exist, and a classic colonial war between rival claimants of territory occurred as recently as 1982 between Britain and Argentina over the ownership of the Falkland Islands (called Las Malvinas by Argentina).

[4] The classic case of this category mistake was Vietnam, whose insurgency against the colonial power of France was taken by American leaders to be a strategic move by China in the Cold War, one that would inevitably lead by a "domino effect" to the loss to the Western alliance, one after another, of its neighboring countries. Failing to understand the deep hostility of the Vietnamese to China, which for millennia had been the hegemonic power in the region, the United States intervened, prolonging the war by a decade, escalating the bloodshed, and directly or indirectly causing millions of deaths not only in Vietnam but in neighboring Laos and Cambodia.

grand theory, see above, p. vi). Global communism ceased to be a coherent force as the Soviet Union itself splintered into over a dozen separate states, while its satellite nations joined Europe and even NATO. Meanwhile the economic split between "developed" countries pursuing manufactures and "developing" nations supplying agricultural products and other raw materials has been at least partly effaced. Over the past two decades, Europe and America have come to support fewer industrial jobs, which have moved to countries such as Mexico, India, and Singapore, where a worker's pay is a fraction of what it is in the West, and recently it has become possible to "outsource" to other countries the jobs of knowledge workers (such as computer technicians and radiologists). Today it seems to be multinational corporations, capable of moving capital and creating jobs anywhere in the world, that are calling the shots, rather than the imperial nation-states that began to compete with each other for power and wealth over five hundred years ago.

Having come thus far with this familiar narrative, one needs to reflect on its characteristic pitfalls. One is that it takes a particular subject position: that of the imperialists, the colonial Powers That Were. It is their motives, their agency, that form the basis of the narrative, rather than those of the peoples whom they ruled. We have viewed the situation from the perspective of those making voyages of discovery and conquest, not of those on whose shores they landed. Each of the peoples who lived on each of those shores has another story to tell, though, and it is a story that reads very differently. Those of us who have read Chinua Achebe's *Things Fall Apart* often become aware that the story of how the lives of men and women of Nigeria are affected by the invasion of English Christian culture is both unfamiliar and too familiar — unfamiliar because we are unused to the perspective; too familiar because it is the obverse of Joseph Conrad's *Heart of Darkness*.

Another unexamined assumption of the conventional narrative is that political independence marks the end of colonial status. For most former colonies, independence may be only the beginning of the end, since colonial structures — political, economic, and cultural — usually continue long after the European viceroy closes down his office and departs. To perpetuate these structures is to perpetuate one's subaltern status, but to tear them down before others have been readied is to invite chaos. As Ama Ata Adoo put it, "Applied to Africa, India, and some other parts of the world, [the concept of the] 'postcolonial' is not only a fiction but a most pernicious fiction, a cover-up of a dangerous period in our people's lives."[5]

Another dangerous assumption is the limitation of colonialism to a single standard scenario, like that of the British Raj, in which a European power sends military force and a bureaucracy to take over and administer an extraterritorial land. In this sense the United States has been a colonial power very briefly and only in very limited areas. But in another sense the expansion of the United States, from the colonies

---

[5]Quoted in Padmini Mongia ed., *Contemporary Postcolonial Theory: A Reader* (London: Arnold, 1997), p. 1. One needs to add that some overseas former colonies have not sought independence but rather have been annexed to the mother country, such as French Guyana, which is legally part of France, an extraterritorial department where the euro is the official currency. Similarly, the Hawaiian islands, once a colony of the United States, were admitted to the union as the fiftieth state. Puerto Rico, perhaps the most culturally significant of the remaining colonies of the United States, seems for the present to have rejected both statehood and separation as an independent nation.

originally implanted by Britain on the Atlantic seaboard to its present compass, including most of the fertile lands on the North American continent, has taken place by a sort of internal colonization, annexing by war or by purchase lands inhabited by Native Americans, by French Creoles in Louisiana, and by Spanish colonialists in Florida and the southwest from Texas to California. In these territories no movement of decolonization seems likely to occur.[6]

Furthermore, one needs to take account of another analogue of colonization that occurs through forced migrations, particularly the transfer of millions of Africans as slaves to the colonies in the Americas and the Caribbean. Migrations can be "forced" by economic conditions as easily as by brute physical power, and it may be useful to extend the analogy beyond internal colonization to immigrant groups with a different coherent culture. Here might be considered, among others, the Irish, Italian, German, and Eastern Europeans who populated the American cities and hinterland beginning in the 1840s; the vast numbers of middle class East Indian immigrants who migrated to work in the infrastructure of Caribbean and African colonies under the British Empire, most of whom remained after decolonization; and the former colonials from the Maghreb, Central Africa, or Southeast Asia who have migrated to France, or the Caribbean Islanders, Africans, and South Asians who have migrated to England. The large communities of guest workers from Turkey and other Islamic countries in present-day Germany are a related example.

In terms of this history, "postcolonial" literature and culture might be defined as the literature of the countries that in the nineteenth and twentieth centuries were administered by the United States, Great Britain, France, and other European countries, particularly on the Indian subcontinent, in northern and central Africa, southeast Asia, and Central and South America. Postcolonial criticism has focused on both the literatures developed by these nations, which are sometimes — as in the case of the works of Chinua Achebe, Salman Rushdie, and Naguib Mahfouz — written in European languages and sometimes not, and on white European responses to colonialism in texts by such familiar authors as Rudyard Kipling, Joseph Conrad, E. M. Forster, George Orwell, and Albert Camus.[7] However, like other cultural critics, postcolonial theorists enjoy examining texts outside the standard literary genres, and frequently examine phenomena that are analogically related to those encountered in former European colonies. These include the writings and cultural productions of aboriginal groups (such as the Native Americans or the Maoris in New Zealand), marginalized groups that have been included within a nation as the result of its border wars (such as Latinos who became citizens of the United States as a result of its

[6] A similar internal colonization of Eurasian lands annexed by Russia occurred over roughly the same period, with decolonization occurring rapidly after 1989. The insurgency in Chechnya seems to have been a war of liberation conducted by a people whose attempt to set up their own state was opposed rather than encouraged by the new Russian government, as it did with Georgia and Armenia.

[7] These writers are all white Europeans, but in addition one needs to consider the agonistic relationship of different colonial populations with one another. The novelist V. S. Naipaul, for example, is not a white European, being descended from Indians imported by Great Britain to form a middle-class infrastructure in Caribbean islands. But Naipaul is so much less sympathetic to the ruling cadres of African and Asian former colonies than most white writers are that postcolonial scholars tend to lump him with patronizing Europeans like Conrad. See in particular *A Bend in the River*.

wars and treaties with Mexico), and immigrant groups, willing or otherwise (including African American descendants of slaves in the Unites States and guest workers in Europe). It should go without saying that the histories, legal status, and cultural relations of these groups with the dominant culture differ from one another and that it is dangerous to import ideas taken from a cultural study of one group into that of another without carefully examining their applicability. But the theoretical questions that animate postcolonial studies are nevertheless very much a part of the discourse of African American studies, Latino/a studies, Asian studies, and other ethnically oriented components of the cultural studies movements.

THEORIZING NATIONALITY AND ETHNICITY: BENEDICT ANDERSON

All the groups and formations of which the theorists in this chapter will speak are versions of what the anthropologist Benedict Anderson has called "imagined communities." There are real communities of limited size and scope — the people of a village who all know one another, your classmates and colleagues, your fellow congregants at your church — but races, ethnic groups, nations, are all communities that, despite their tremendous hold on us, exist only in our minds. Anderson cites the French philosopher Ernest Renan, who ironically remarked that "it is of the essence of a nation that all its individuals have lots of things in common that they have forgotten."[8] As a particular form of imagined community, the nation is limited and sovereign. The nation

is imagined as *limited* because even the largest of them encompassing perhaps a billion living human beings, has finite, if elastic boundaries, beyond which lie other nations. No nation imagines itself coterminous with mankind. . . . It is imagined as *sovereign* because the concept was born in an age in which Enlightenment and Revolution were destroying the legitimacy of the divinely-ordained, hierarchical dynastic realm. Coming to maturity at a stage of human history when even the most devout adherents of any universal religion were inescapably confronted with the living pluralism of such religions, and the allomorphism between each faith's ontological claims and territorial stretch, nations dream of being free, and, if under God, directly so. The gage and emblem of this freedom is the sovereign state. Finally, it is imagined as a *community*, because, regardless of the actual inequality and exploitation that may prevail in each, the nation is always conceived as a deep, horizontal comradeship. Ultimately it is this fraternity that makes it possible, over the past two centuries, for so many millions of people, not so much to kill, as willingly to die for such limited imaginings.

The chapter from *Imagined Communities* that we have included is "The Origins of National Consciousness," in which Anderson speculates about the connection between the age of print culture, which began in the middle of the eighteenth century throughout Europe, and what he considers its two political consequences: the development of the "idea of the nation" within the individual Frenchman or Britisher, and the beginnings of the development of European empires whose common languages would extend the reach of the imagined national community.

[8] Renan's 1882 lecture, "Qu'est-ce qu'une nation?" ["What Is a Nation?"].

THE PREHISTORY OF POSTCOLONIALISM

The resistance to colonialism began centuries ago, as one might expect, with colonialism itself, long before postcolonial theory became a recognized academic discipline. And the writings of popular resistance leaders like Mohandas K. Gandhi and Kwame Nkrumah were naturally inspirational to their followers in India and Africa. The period after World War II provoked many intellectuals who had been born in colonies just achieving their freedom to try to understand the political and psychological burdens of emerging nations, of whom three of the most important are Albert Memmi, Aimé Césaire, and Frantz Fanon.

Albert Memmi was born in 1920 in Tunis in Jewish Arabic-speaking parents. Memmi fought in World War II and was imprisoned during 1943–45 in a labor camp. He later taught at a lycée in Tunis. Following the decolonization of Tunisia, he moved to France, where he married, got his doctorate, and had a career as novelist and psychologist; he became a professor at the University of Paris/Nanterre. His major work in this field is *The Colonizer and the Colonized* (1957), which came out one year after the decolonization of Tunisia and during the tremendous violence of the Algerian war of independence. It featured Memmi's unique cultural perspective, which was neither Arab nor entirely French. Although most of the Jews of Tunis generally assimilated culturally to the dominant French, Memmi himself joined the decolonization movement of the Arabs. Memmi's book is about the social and psychological consequences of colonialism for both the natives and the European colonizers. The Arabs of Tunisia were tempted to assimilate culturally to France, as a way of rising in the world (only as far as the colonizers would allow, of course). Those who do not assimilate are even worse off. All the colonized are excluded from real politics; they may become apathetic or may find a source of self-esteem in religion or in revolutionary politics, or in some combination. Revolt, according to Memmi, is not a final solution: Even decolonization is only a stage in the evolution of the alienation of the colonized. The colonizers have their own problems. Psychologically they consider themselves exiles, although there is nothing preventing them from returning to their homeland. The exile is purely positional: In the colony they may have achieved a position of importance, whereas back in France they would return to mediocrity; in the colony their salaries are high and prices are low, and a return to France would lower their financial status. Most important of all is self-esteem: The colonizers are of the top caste when in North Africa, with servants to bully, feeling above any member of the majority Arab population, no matter how accomplished.

Aimé Césaire (1913–2008) was born in Martinique and was educated there and at the prestigious Lycée Louis-le-Grand in Paris, where he came under the influence of Leopold Senghor, founder of the négritude movement, whose purpose was to bolster the cultural self-image of Africans everywhere. After founding a journal for students of African descent, Césaire returned to Martinique, where he taught school along with his wife. After World War II, Martinique and the other French colonies in the Americas — Guyane, Guadeloupe — were not made independent countries but were instead converted into *departements* of France, the equivalent of statehood. Césaire, a member of the Communist party, was in 1945 elected mayor of Fort-de-France, the capital of Martinique, and a delegate in the representative assembly. In 1950 he published his "Discourse on Colonialism," which compares colonialism with Nazism as a racist ideology. Césaire is perhaps most famous for his play *Une Tempête* (1968), a take-off on Shakespeare's *Tempest* in which Caliban accuses Prospero of forcing him to believe in his own monstrosity as a result of the wizard's lies and spells.

Like Césaire, Frantz Fanon (1925–1961) was born in Martinique and, after fighting with the Free French army during 1943–45, was educated in France in medicine and psychiatry. His experience with racism in France led him to write *Black Skin, White Masks* (1952), which lays out the idea of cultural binarism, explicating the way white French identity is constituted by contrast with the black- and brown-skinned peoples who have come to France from the colonies. For Fanon, the pervasive racism comes from the culture as a whole, and particularly from the language, which equates blackness with evil. Thus in striving to succeed in Francophone society, the black colonial needs to internalize a sign-system that alienates him from himself. Fanon moved to Algeria in the early 1950s, becoming the head of psychiatry at the hospital at Blida-Joinville, where his patients included both Arab revolutionaries and the French colonial officials who fought against, and often tortured, those revolutionaries. Fanon resigned his post in 1956 in order to work actively for the Algerian revolution, which succeeded in ousting France but whose outcome disappointed Fanon. In 1961, as he lay dying of leukemia, Fanon published his most influential book, *The Wretched of the Earth*, which is a critique both of colonialism and of the emergent nationalism that generally followed decolonization. For Fanon, the irony of decolonization was that, for the most part, the lot of the peasants who were most deeply oppressed during the imperial period, and who shed their blood during the insurgency, was not materially improved by decolonization. The underclass were encouraged to focus their feelings on nationalist enthusiasm by the real winners of the revolution, those bourgeois Arabs and blacks who most closely identified with the culture of the European oppressors. Fanon felt that the revolutions that had freed Africa from its European overlords would be incomplete until the new nations were led by *fellahin* (peasants) from the lower depths of the class structure, and he counseled "total revolution," uncompromising violence, until that end could be achieved.

THEORIZING THE COLONIAL: SAID, SPIVAK, BHABHA

The book that is generally considered to have launched the growing field of postcolonial theory is Edward Said's *Orientalism* (1978). Said takes off from Michel Foucault's position that as knowledge is in itself a way of exercising power, so discourses become a weapon of imperial and international politics. In this light Said presents the Western study of the Orient in the nineteenth century (limiting himself almost exclusively to the Near East here) as one of the ways Europe found to dominate that region. Said treats the scholarship into Near Eastern languages, cultures, and social structures as an archive that he mines for the Western ways of "knowing" the East that become a way of asserting the superiority of the West. For example,

Edward Lane's 1836 book on the manners and customs of the Egyptians of his own day presents that culture in the form of descriptions that are "sadomasochistic colossal tidbits: the self-mutilation of dervishes, the cruelty of judges, the blending of religion with licentiousness among Muslims, the excess of libidinous passions, and so on" (162). Even fields that might seem utterly neutral, the comparative study of language, can be used to disparage the culture of the Near East. Said shows how Ernest Renan's philological treatise on the evolution of human languages takes the "organic" development of the Indo-European languages as the norm, with each new language — Sanskrit, Greek, Latin, French — developing new energies as it buds off from its predecessor. By contrast the Oriental Semitic languages (Hebrew, Aramaic, Arabic) are seen as "inorganic, essentially unregenerative . . . , ossified" (143). In effect the vital, energetic West is contrasted with the played-out and regressive East. In particular, Said witheringly critiques the Western image of the Oriental as "irrational, depraved (fallen), childlike, 'different,'" which has allowed the West to define itself as "rational, virtuous, mature, 'normal'" (40). Western students of Oriental literature and culture, from artists to professors of language and history, have helped to create this self-affirming vision, which in turn has been used to justify the domination of the Arab and other Asian peoples by European governments, the marginalization of their languages and cultures, and the uprooting of their institutions. For Said, the cultural practices and forms of knowledge typical of Orientalism have not vanished with the official colonial regimes. As a Palestinian theorist, Said views his own attempt to understand the cultural work of Orientalism as a site of resistance to the hegemony of Western values and ideas.

Said's argument in *Orientalism* also has the defects of its virtues. Even more than Foucault's own "archeological" investigations into prisons and madhouses, Said presents Orientalism as a historical phenomenon tied causally to European imperialism, but his examples widen out so far as to contradict his conclusion. In the first place, Orientalism seems to have always existed: Said cites Aeschylus's representation of the Persians as effeminate and depraved, or Dante's placement of Mohammed in the *Inferno* not among the prophets of God but among the Christian heretics. Examples so many centuries removed from the European imperialist enterprise seem less connected with the British and French takeover of Arab lands than part of a timeless universal ethnocentrism in which cultures treat their antagonists as "others" who represent lower forms of life. An anti-Said could certainly collect from Eastern writings equivalent examples of "Occidentalism."

In the second place, Orientalism, as an unchanging ideology held over several centuries throughout the West, fails to explain why the policy of the British Raj became increasingly repressive of Indian culture during the nineteenth century[9] or why the extensive Orientalist research by German scholars was never connected with any political move toward empire in the Near East. In general Said's notion of a "latent" Orientalism, universal within Western culture, expands to become the

[9]For a recent account of this, see Gauri Viswanathan, *Masks of Conquest* (New York: Columbia University Press, 1989). Other specific problems with Said's historical understanding are outlined in Moore-Gilbert, p. 45ff.

disparaging basis not only for imperialism but for the occasional resistance within the West to the project of imperialism. This would include not only Arabophile scholarship like that of Sir Richard Burton but also narratives by Kipling, Conrad, Orwell, and Forster that sometimes attack or satirize the blind stupidity and cruelty of the imperial administration. This comfortless vision may leave no one a place to stand, not even, perhaps, the Western-educated Said himself.

The notion of postcolonial studies as constituting a site of resistance appears as well in theorists who are less taken with Foucault's methodology of cultural study than Said is. Gayatri Chakravorti Spivak, born in Calcutta, did a dissertation on Yeats under Paul de Man and found fame as the first English translator of Jacques Derrida's *Of Grammatology* (1967, translated 1976). Spivak's version of postcolonialism prefers the deconstructive mode as a way of questioning the binarisms and exposing the misunderstandings of language and signification set up within colonial discourse. She has called herself a "gadfly," and her chosen mode of discourse is critique. Her tendency when she looks at a piece of discourse is to ask in effect, "What gets left out, what is silenced, when we look at things *this* way?" Spivak sees herself as a Marxist and as a feminist, but is usually found to be boring away from within at the blind spots of these theories. In the introduction it was shown how Spivak's analysis of "subaltern studies," as practiced by Marxist social historians in India, silences or occludes the female subject by shaping the question in terms of a dialogue between (male-dominated) Western and (male-dominated) Asian characterizations of social institutions. This works the other way round as well: Giving the female voice may silence the subaltern.

In "Three Women's Texts and a Critique of Imperialism," included in this chapter, Spivak trains the lens of deconstructive analysis on women's writing, and finds that giving voice to the feminine indeed entails the silencing or occlusion of the colonized subject. *Jane Eyre*, which Spivak calls a "cult text of feminism," empowers Brontë's titular heroine at the expense of her "dark double" Bertha Mason, who, though specified as being from a wealthy Creole family, is staged as the colonial Caliban, mute except for a horrid laugh, on the borderline between the human and the animal. On the other side, Brontë's feminism sponsors the imperialist mission Jane considered for herself before heeding the preternatural call of Rochester; the life of "active goodness" of which she dreamed looking out from Thornfield took the form of attending upon the missionary St. John Rivers and going forth to the East to convert the heathen in Calcutta. Jean Rhys's *Wide Sargasso Sea*, a reinscription of *Jane Eyre*, gets a little closer to the silenced colonized subject by placing at the center the white Creole woman, called Antoinette in the text, through whom we can understand what it feels like to become the colonial Caliban, even as she finds reflections of herself in the darker natives of her own sex, her black friend Tia and her maid Christophine.

Spivak finds the strongest critique of imperialism in Mary Shelley's *Frankenstein*, which may seem strange since on a literal level (as Spivak herself points out), the narrative approves of bringing Western civilization to the East: Victor's admired friend Clerval is presented as studying Eastern languages in order to take up the white man's burden where Arabic or Persian are spoken. There is even a passive colonial subject in the Arabian girl Safie. To get her reading, Spivak is forced to allegorize the central story through the metaphorical lens of colonialism. In this reading the Monster, whose speech and literacy are accidental developments, becomes the colonial Caliban, the occluded subject whom Frankenstein creates just as the colonial governors seek to create the empire's colonized subjects, but from whose demands for companionship and autonomy the master recoils with fear and horror. What seems to Spivak most honest about this vision is how uncompromising it is: The Monster and Frankenstein cannot be reconciled; neither can absorb the other into his vision of the self, so that the Caliban and the Prospero can only destroy each other.

Bombay-born Homi Bhabha, like Spivak, is interested in probing and problematizing Said's binaries of East/West using the deconstructive tools of Derrida and Lacan. For Bhabha, the problem with Said's analysis is the way in which it restricts itself to analyzing the consciousness of Europeans vis-à-vis the Orient, with little attention to the way in which colonized peoples are implicated in this relationship. Bhabha sees the experience of colonial peoples as creating a hybridity of perspective, a split consciousness in which the individual identifies simultaneously with his or her own people and with the colonial power. This hybridity or liminality (existing on the borderline) is not necessarily an undesirable state: It is, as Bhabha sees it, part of the postmodern condition. It is the situation not only of the colonial subject but of minority groups like African Americans and, to one extent or another, of every inhabitant of the globe. Bhabha's *Locations of Culture* presents his view of the connections between minority and postcolonial literature as sites of resistance. While W. E. B. Du Bois a century ago had understood "double consciousness" to be an inevitable condition of the souls of black folk, Bhabha understands it as inevitable for us all.

The complexities of the doubled relationships of the imperialist and the colonized subaltern, whose mimicry of the imperialist includes both flattery and a kind of mockery, are central to Bhabha's breakthrough essay "Signs Taken for Wonders." The title of the essay itself contains a dry mock of the phrase "signs and wonders," which appears many times in the Hebrew Bible in terms of the mighty acts God performed for the liberation of the Israelites in Egypt. Bhabha's scene of signs outside Delhi in 1817 is all about the opposite of liberation: it is about enslavement, particularly how the technologies of imperialism can be used to remake the colonial subject in the image of the English ruler by importing the English book. The hope, as Macaulay would later put it explicitly, is that cheap or free Bibles imparting the English language and the spiritual comforts of Christianity will ultimately undermine native Indian languages and religions. Using missionary records, Bhabha portrays an Indian convert, Anund Messeh, bringing the Gospel (which God "gave long ago to the Sahibs") to his countrymen. His audience, apparently respectful and ingratiating, compete to be the quickest to learn and the best teachers of this Word, but in copying the Sahibs they very much remain themselves. They insist on their own customs, including the separation of castes, and refuse the very notion of taking communion because when the Word is made flesh it becomes abhorrent, since "the Europeans eat cow's flesh and this will never do for us."

Bhabha juxtaposes to this scene a pair of other scenes later in the history of imperialism. The first is of Conrad's Marlow, going up the Congo toward the heart of darkness, where he questions his faith in the Western mission, finding relief from his spiritual vertigo when he comes upon another sort of "bible" devoted to the Western technology of imperialism, a book on navigation (Towson's *Seamanship*). The second is of the postcolonial Caribbean/Indian writer V. S. Naipaul, who, during his own voyage to England to take up the life of an expatriate writer, discovers that another English book, in his case Conrad's *Heart of Darkness*, sets a high bar for any performance of his own: "Conrad . . . had been everywhere before me." Messeh, Marlow, Naipaul: All turn away from the messy, mocking, imitative colonial world toward the enlightened truth of the Western Bible, Western Science, Western Literature.

As Bhabha sums it up:

> The discovery of the English book establishes both a measure of mimesis and a mode of civil authority and order. If these scenes, as I have narrated them, suggest the triumph of the writ of colonialist power, then it must be conceded that the wily letter of the law inscribes a much more ambivalent text of authority. For it is in between the edict of Englishness and the assault of the dark unruly spaces of the earth, through an act of repetition, that the colonial text emerges uncertainly. . . . The colonial presence is always ambivalent, split between its appearance as original and authoritative and its articulation as repetition and difference.

THEORIZING MINORITY LITERATURE: DELEUZE AND GUATTARI

Disadvantaged minority groups perforce write what French critics Gilles Deleuze and Felix Guattari call "minor literature." In "What Is a Minor Literature?" Deleuze and Guattari take time from their study of novelist Franz Kafka to theorize about the special character his writing derived from his being a Jew in Prague, writing not in Yiddish or Hebrew (the languages of his ethnic group) nor in Czech (the language of a majority of the natives of Prague) but in German (the language of the Austro-Hungarian elite who ruled the province of Bohemia). This language, when used by a Prague Jew, is "deterritorialized" — it speaks not for a country or province but rather for people of a diaspora living as an Other in a land not their own. Within such minor literatures "everything . . . is political" and "everything takes on a collective value" as every observation speaks about the hegemonic society from the perspective of the silenced members of the minority.[10] Deleuze and Guattari conclude paradoxically that there is no major literature except minor literature, for poetic value resides precisely in the tensions inherent in using the language of the oppressors to speak for the oppressed. Deleuze and Guattari explicitly compare Kafka's Prague German with "what blacks in America today are able to do with the English language."

---

[10] Gilles Deleuze and Felix Guattari, *Kafka: Toward a Minor Literature* (Minneapolis, University of Minnesota Press, 1986), p. 17.

AFRICANISM: RACISM HERE AND ABROAD

Just as Edward Said coined the term "Orientalism" to refer to the ways in which darker colonial people are characterized as the Other in the works of European writers, Toni Morrison in *Playing in the Dark: Whiteness and the Literary Imagination* (1992) uses the term "Africanism" in a parallel way to refer to the literal and figurative "black-ness" whites found in the new world, and the ways they represented that "blackness." Morrison sees Africanism as pervasive: It appears not only in texts like *Uncle Tom's Cabin* and *Huckleberry Finn* that feature important black characters, but in texts that have only minor roles for blacks or none at all, even texts in which race and slavery are never mentioned.[11] Morrison feels that every major work of American literature was shaped in part by the fact that, in the midst of a republic dedicated to freedom, there was a large population held in total subjection. The motif of the Forest in a work like *The Scarlet Letter*, for example, brings up the dialectic between savagery and civilization. Morrison is in effect asking whether Hawthorne's vision of the Savage could avoid being affected by the idea of the Savage that whites pro-jected onto blacks, an idea that was derived in part from their own savage treatment of their human property. In fact it is Morrison's contention that all the major themes in which critics have sought the unity of American literature, "individualism, mas-culinity, the conflict between social engagement and historical isolation, an acute and ambiguous moral problematics, the juxtaposition of innocence with figures representing death and hell" draw their mythic strength from the dark Other within the American body politic. Africanism is thus to be found everywhere in white pub-lic discourse: "encoded or overt, the linguistic responses to an Africanistic presence complicate the texts, sometimes contradicting them entirely."

Morrison's method of reading can be enormously revealing, but it may need to be employed with some tact. Africans were surely not the only group constituted as "Other" in American society and represented as the "Other" in American literature. European colonists had encountered the Native Americans as friendly or hostile cohabitants of the continent long before African slavery was institutionalized, and it has been well documented how the encounter with the Native American reshaped the imagination of Europe and of those Europeans who had migrated to America. And from the mid-nineteenth century, the new migrant (from Europe or Asia) began to serve as a representation of the Other to native-born Americans a few generations removed from their own immigration.

Within British (as opposed to American) literature, ethnic and racial otherness operates with similar complexities. Within medieval and early modern literature, the English defined themselves predominantly against outsiders like Jews or Moors, peoples that loomed large in the English imagination given their tiny popula-tions in English society.[12] From the eighteenth century, as England was taking its

[11]At the same time, Morrison is painfully aware that the blackness of some of the most important African characters in American literature — including Ahab's servant Pip in Melville's *Moby-Dick*, the slave girl Nancy Till in Willa Cather's *Sapphira and the Slave Girl*, Melanctha in Gertrude Stein's *Three Women* — appears to be a subject taboo to the polite practitioners of literary criticism.

[12]It would be a mistake to leave out the Irish as the Other within British Literature, usually seen as comically feckless rather than sinister, from a colony England acquired long before India.

pre-eminent place in the colonization of Africa and South Asia, the racial Other became African or Indian, often portrayed as the childlike object of European benevolence and Enlightenment rationality, or as the female object of forbidden desire, a dark body constructed by masculine fantasy.

A British version of Morrison's "Africanism" inspires the Nigerian novelist Chinua Achebe's resistant reading of Conrad's *Heart of Darkness*.[13] This is a text often celebrated by white readers for its liberal exposure of the hideous face under the benevolent mask of colonialism, as it portrays Kurtz, the apostle of European enlightenment, degenerating into a mad, genocidal tyrant. Achebe finds it hard to concur, arguing that, whatever its liberal political position on the imperial mission, Conrad denies to the Africans that he portrays the humanity — well-intentioned or self-centered — that he accords even the slimiest of the Europeans. The natives of the Congo are a mere exotic spectacle, appearing out of or disappearing into the bush, yelling like savages or dying silently but picturesquely near the coastal forts. But they are not imagined as people, for which reason Achebe feels that *Heart of Darkness* is an "offensive and deplorable book" and Conrad himself "a bloody racist." Achebe is expressing here the bitterness with which the African views the white liberal position on British imperialism, which allowed England to deprive hundreds of millions of darker-skinned men and women of their political and economic freedom so long as that imperial rule was just and humane by European standards.

But is that an inevitable position? Wilson Harris, another colonial novelist of African descent (from Guyana) argues that Conrad was writing, not out of Enlightenment optimism, as Achebe suggested, but rather out of a profound despair arising from his sense that the "sacred human" order "may come to shelter the greatest evil." Harris calls *Heart of Darkness* a "frontier novel," by which he means one that interprets and translates between the European societies that had been transformed by their imperialist mission and the African, Asian, and American societies that had become hybrid mixtures of native and European social and mental structures. Harris is deeply aware of the way black Caribbean writers like himself and African writers like Wole Soyinka have used Conrad, along with other European texts, in generating a fertile postcolonial literature. And he hints that Achebe has a deep need to misread Conrad in order to make imaginative space for himself, a site of resistance from which he can speak.

THE MASTER'S LANGUAGE, THE MASTER'S TOOLS

One key political question that troubles postcolonial theory is about the language in which postcolonial literature should be written. There are in Africa dozens, perhaps hundreds, of indigenous languages, as opposed to the handful of "metropolitan" languages of the imperialists, including English, French, and Arabic. Can African writers be truly African, can they be true to their ethnic identities, while using the languages of imperialism? "Is it right that a man should abandon his mother tongue for someone else's? It looks like a dreadful betrayal."

[13]Chinua Achebe, "An Image of Africa: Racism in Conrad's *Heart of Darkness*," *Massachusetts Review* 18 (1977): 782–94.

That question was Chinua Achebe's, but finally Achebe concluded that, despite the fact that no one uses a second language as well as the native tongue, there is no other practical solution. He himself does not have the time to learn the other six or seven ethnic languages in his own native Nigeria, much less all the other languages of Africa, so that if there is to be an African literature that can be read all over Africa and the rest of the world, it can be written only in the metropolitan languages. Achebe suggests, though, that Africans writing in English will — because they have something new to say — change English into something that is at least partly African: "The price a world language must pay is submission to many kinds of use. . . . The English language will be able to carry the weight of my African experience. But it will have to be a new English, still in full communion with its ancestral home but altered to suit its new African surroundings."[14]

After writing and publishing his first important works in English, the Kenyan novelist Ngũgĩ wa Thiong'o eventually came down on the other side from Achebe, and around 1976 began to write his fiction in his native Gikuyu instead. In "Europhonism, Universities, and the Magic Fountain," a lecture delivered at Cambridge University in May 1999, Ngũgĩ presented the most complex and far-reaching arguments for his personal decision, although ultimately it rests upon an organic theory of culture. For Ngũgĩ, the soil and the people of Africa can be the only basis for African culture, and an educational system that explicitly ignores and implicitly disparages the ethnic languages of Africa's villagers is one that cuts Africa's intellectuals off from their culture, leaving them rootless, incapable of understanding each other or themselves. And although he finds much to admire in the literature Africans have written in English, Ngũgĩ has a sense that too much energy has gone into imitating European models — an energy that he feels invigorates European languages and cultures without giving anything back to Africa. Worse: It is a Europhone literature, and not a genuinely African literature.

What inspires Ngũgĩ most intensely now, one suspects, forty years after he began writing in Gikuyu, is the threat of spiritual death from the homogenized universal commercial culture that derives from globalism — what Benjamin Barber has called "McWorld" — which threatens by its very ubiquity to engulf and destroy every vestige of local culture. Ngũgĩ's increasingly desperate appeal to African writers is to return to the languages of their childhood as the "magic fountain" of an authentic cultural life. To a theorist like Bhabha, of course, this crucial "debate" between Achebe and Ngũgĩ would be only more evidence of "liminality"; the way postcolonial writers negotiate the threshold between two worlds.[15] Similar linguistic issues come up within ethnic studies: Chicana writers like Sandra Cisneros have to decide whether to write in English or in their own regional dialect of American Spanish, or

[14]Chinua Achebe, "The African Writer and the English Language," from *Morning Yet on Creation Day* (New York: Doubleday, 1975), pp. 91–103.

[15]It may seem obvious that it would be more "politically correct" to use a native language than a Europhone language, but that may depend on precisely which native language one speaks. In *The Great Railway Bazaar* (1975), Paul Theroux encounters on a train a group of Tamil speakers from the south-ernmost tip of India who resent being addressed in Hindi, the local language of New Delhi, the capital far to the north. They insist on using English, because the language of the former oppressor has the virtue of equalizing the status of their province and the capital.

in both, and African American writers need to decide just how intensely they want to evoke the special qualities of African American vernacular.

The special liminality of Chicano/Chicana culture is evoked brilliantly in the late Gloria Anzaldúa's "La conciencia de la mestiza: Towards a New Consciousness"; the essay is written in a mixture of English and Spanish, which monolingual readers should try to penetrate as well as they can without recourse to the supplied notes, at least at first, to get a sense of the way her language expresses the continuous movement of her discourse across the permeable borderlands. Anzaldúa portrays herself as a *nahual* — a magical shape-shifter who can transform herself into "a tree, a coyote, another person." A *mestiza* is literally a half-breed: Anzaldúa not only finds herself on the boundary between languages, she feels simultaneously the pull of the different races that have gone into her gene pool: the native Americans of Mexico, the Spaniards, the African slaves with whom they intermarried, the "gringo" Americans stemming from Northern Europe. Her spiritual vision reflects all these roots: She recognizes from Africa "Eshu, Yoruba god of indeterminacy," sees the Aztec mother goddess Coatlapopeuh blend in with the Virgin of Guadalupe. If all these elements could live together in peace, the consciousness of the *mestiza* would be richer and fuller than any pure-blood culture, but there is an internal quarrel that leaves her alienated within herself: "[C]ommonly held beliefs of the white culture attack commonly held beliefs of the Mexican culture, and both attack commonly held beliefs of the indigenous culture." And the attack is not only internal: Everywhere the half-breed is despised by the pureblood, and since Anzaldúa is a lesbian as well, she has a sense of being an outcast by sexuality as well as race. Despite this sense of alienation, similar to what Fanon described in North African culture, Anzaldúa's stance is an attempt at inclusiveness and balance. She understands the pull of violence but for her the "proudly defiant" attitude of the "counterstance" defines one in terms of what one is against, and she does not want an identity merely borrowed from the oppressor; she wants "to act and not react." In the long run, the conflict might lead to violence, or to a withdrawal from the dominant culture, or there might be some more complex accommodation that will occur, when we realize that no one is pure, that we are all complex mixtures, that we all share the consciousness of the *mestiza: el dia de la Chicana.*

DIALOGUE: JAMESON AND AHMAD ON THIRD WORLD LITERATURE

An even more complex dilemma appears in a dialogue between Fredric Jameson and Aijaz Ahmad on Third World literature that took place in the pages of *Social Text* between 1986 and 1987. Jameson begins the exchange by addressing the debate at the time over the Western literary canon and the extent to which it could and should be opened to include previously ignored writing by women and ethnic minorities. He argues that one problem with gaining equivalent traction for contemporary Third World writing is that its insistent social realism reminds Western readers of writers of over a century ago, like Dreiser and Zola, and its production today suggests that it is being written not for them at all but for another kind of reader, a naive Third

World reader not yet ready for modernist, much less postmodernist texts. The other problem is that the Third World novel, by taking the literary form of national alle-gory, transgresses the Western split between the political and the personal: "*The story of the private individual destiny is always an allegory of the embattled situ-ation of the public third world culture and society.*"[16] (italics Jameson's). Jameson may have solved, to his satisfaction, the question of the resistance of the West to Third World writing, but for Ahmad — who is like Jameson a Marxist theorist indebted to Gramsci and the Frankfurt School — there is a different sort of resis-tance and in fact a personal as well as a theoretical problem here: "I realized that what was being theorized was, among many other things, myself. . . ."

But Ahmad's response is not merely personal: What he wants to point out is the way Jameson is essentializing the Third World as the Other of the West — a sophis-ticated equivalent of saying "All you darkies look alike to us." As Ahmad points out, they don't look alike to each other because they aren't alike: Each new nation has had a different history with a different relationship to metropolitan cultures, so there is no single "public third world culture" and no single "embattled situation." Ahmad wants to get rid of the entire "three worlds" metaphor, in fact. Because if we are all living in one world today, not a hierarchy of three where it can be taken for granted that it is the aesthetic sensibility of the West that matters, then the question Jameson starts with can be turned on its head. Perhaps we should be asking how the Western canon of literature looks in the eyes of traditional Urdu aesthetics.

In the final response of Jameson to Ahmad, there is a bit of backpedaling — he has a sense, probably unusual for Jameson, of having missed some of the complexity of the questions he raised. But Jameson insists on the perhaps deplorable fact that living in one world does not make us all equal: Western power (the power of finance more than the power of its weaponry) is going to skew inevitably whose vision of humanity and society becomes dominant and whose aesthetics dominate that arena. It does not seem an accident that the most influential writers of the Third World, like Gabriel Garcia Marquez, Chinua Achebe, and Salman Rushdie, are those modernists or postmodernists whose aesthetic is closest to our own. But it also doesn't seem an accident that it is Jameson, the Marxist born in the West, who calls attention to that fact, or that Jameson and Ahmad seem divided less by ideology than by location.

DIALOGUE: BAKER ON GATES

The response of Houston Baker Jr. to the early work of Henry Louis Gates Jr. was also an intercine quarrel, but here the quarreling family consisted of theorists of African American literature, and the quarrel was quite a bit like that of theorists in general about whether to emphasize the language of literature or its social basis. Gates arrived on the scene as the scholar whose mission it was to adapt the fashion-able theories of structuralism and deconstruction to the study of African American literature. Where Saussure and the structuralists had stressed the arbitrary relation

[16]Frederick Jameson, Essay "World Literature in an Age of Multinational Capitalism", p. 69.

of the signifier and the signified, where Derrida had stressed the free play of the signifier, Gates stressed "signifying" — an African American locution for language at play, what might be called free play, as it was developed by the enslaved and the formerly enslaved to ensnare the listener, to speak truth to power, or to trick the more mighty opponent. Gates published his credo emphasizing the semiotic issues in African American writing as "Preface to Blackness: Texts and Pretexts" in the important Dexter Fisher/Robert B. Stepto collection, *Afro-American Literature: The Reconstruction of Instruction* (1979). As Gates was to put it in "Criticism in de Jungle" (1981), "The challenge of black literary criticism is to derive principles of literary criticism from the black tradition itself, as defined in the idiom of critical theory but also in the idiom which constitutes the 'language of blackness,' the signifyin(g) difference which makes the black tradition our very own."

This emphasis on the free play of the signifier struck other African American literary theorists, like Houston Baker, as a way to cut literary forms off from the specific social origins that produce human consciousness, a consciousness that can create such forms and respond to them. In *Blues, Ideology and Afro-American Literature* (1984), Baker quoted Gates and responded from his Marxist perspective: Literature, as a form of ideology, can have no history that can be cut off or isolated from the history of the social formation that produces it.

Many quarrels within literary theory are dialogues of the deaf, but the one between Baker and Gates was not. Instead of digging in their heels, each responded by narrowing the distance between their two stances. As Theodore Mason has put it, "While Gates could be seen as moving from theory towards literary nationalism (to put it crudely), Baker could be seen as moving from a profoundly nationalistic cultural base toward a revision of that position complicated by an engagement with language and with theory. Consequently, by the end of the [twentieth century], both Gates and Baker, for all their differences, early and late, could be seen as occupying relatively similar positions" (Michael Groden, Martin Kreiswirth, and Imre Szeman, ed., *Johns Hopkins Guide to Literary Theory and Criticism*, 2005, p. 18).

How similar may appear from the selection in this chapter, "Writing, 'Race,' and the Difference It Makes." In this essay, Gates examines the history of doubt, expressed by freeborn Englishmen and slaveowners, as to whether people of African origin were truly human (that is, possessed of reason, the Enlightenment criterion of humanity) and able to be subjects as well as objects of discourse. Some seventeenth-century philosophers held that the "Negro" was not human at all, while Hume and Kant placed the African at the bottom of the human scale on the Great Chain of Being. The poems of Phillis Wheatley, a young African girl whose master had taught her to read and write both English and Latin, offended Thomas Jefferson's prejudice that blacks should be unable to write poetry, though it is not clear whether his contemptuous opinion — "the compositions published under her name are below the dignity of criticism" — was meant to dismiss the poems on the ground of quality, Wheatley's authorship, or both. To keep them from establishing their humanity through participation in the world of letters, slaves were forbidden to learn to write or read. Thus the slave narratives of African Americans, such as

their transgressive existence as subjects.

Frederick Douglass, William Wells Brown, and dozens of others, were assertions of

But Gates argues that "black people . . . have not been 'liberated' from racism by their writings. . . . Black writing . . . served not to obliterate the difference
of 'race,' . . . rather, the inscription of the black voice in Western literatures has
preserved those very cultural differences to be imitated and revised in a separate
Western literary tradition, a tradition of black difference." For Gates, the African
American writer is torn between two traditions: the written tradition of Western
European culture into which African slaves were forcibly transplanted, and what
he calls the "talking book" or the "speakerly text," the oral tradition of Africa that
survives in the songs, legends, and stories of the people. In creating in 1996 his prestigious *Norton Anthology of African American Literature*, Gates not only included
work songs and blues, legends and stories, but a cassette tape as well so that the
"reader" can listen to the texts as performed.

One might ask, though, whether Gates may have come too far toward Baker,
whether he may be slanting the African American canon by privileging texts with
the strongest roots in the African oral traditions at the expense of those that, written in an English indistinguishable from that of the oppressor, exploit the "double
consciousness" that W. E. B. Du Bois felt was the inevitable lot of the African
American. Should we prefer Paul Laurence Dunbar's dialect poems, such as "Little
Brown Baby" and "When Malindy Sings," as Howells[17] did, or his poems written
in standard English, like "We Wear the Mask"? It seems clear that Gates values the
"speakerly text" derived from the oral tradition, over a dense and "writerly" tradition
of African American literature, represented by James Baldwin and Ralph Ellison,
that pays allegiance to one particular white master — Henry James. When a minority group is identified with a particular mode of writing, it inevitably marginalizes
those in that minority who write otherwise. This may be the key danger inherent in
the attempt to essentialize some particular version of "blackness" as the core of the
African American tradition.

DIALOGUE: IS THEORY WHITE?

The same sort of issue underlies Barbara Christian's provocation piece, "The Race
for Theory," and the responses that it evoked. Published in 1988 in an issue of
Feminist Studies devoted to feminism and deconstruction, Christian's disturbingly
heartfelt discourse expresses the pain of a scholar and critic who had devoted her
life to elucidating and promoting the status of literature by African American women
and who views her life's work as marginalized by a change in fashion within the
academy. The theoretical revolution that broke over departments of literature starting in the late 1970s produced, along with a great deal of stimulating discourse,
considerable acrimony, particularly among professors for whom "close reading"
of poetic texts was the beginning and end of literary study, and among traditional

---

scholars pursuing answers to literary-historical questions. The academy is a hierarchy in which status is based on the presumed importance of one's work, and to the extent that prestige was being conferred on theorists, together with the perquisites that went with prestige — fellowships, professorial chairs, the chance to train the best students — less would be left for traditional scholars and critics. It may not be exactly a zero-sum game, where one person's winnings must be another's losses, but it is close.[18] Theory could be a real threat to one's research projects.

Christian's narrative makes it clear that her early work had been energized by the attention that was newly being paid both to feminism and to the African American studies movement, but that attention had shifted to applications of "high theory," particularly interpretive theory based on poststructuralist thinkers like Derrida and de Man, and French feminist thinkers about gender whose ideas are based on neo-Freudian analysts like Lacan. Christian does not name specific names of those applying high theory to African American literature, but it would be surprising if she did not have male theorists like Houston Baker Jr. in mind, or white theorists like Barbara Johnson who applied Lacan to Zora Neale Hurston. The name that seems most clearly unspoken, perhaps, is that of Henry Louis Gates Jr., who after unearthing in 1981 the first novel published by an African American woman — *Our Nig* (1859), by Harriet E. Wilson — rocketed to fame within white academia by becoming the first African American scholar to apply high theory to black literature.

Part of the problem, Christian argues, is that she finds theory "prescriptive." Here she clearly is worried about repeating her own history with the "Black Arts Movement" of the 1960s, which attempted to judge texts by African Americans according to their participation in a posited essence of blackness, an essence that tended to exclude works by black women. But she never explains why French poststructuralist theory should be prescriptive in the same way the highly political Black Arts group had been, and the reader may come away thinking, ironically, that it is Christian who has become politically prescriptive, because for her the problem with theory is that it is too white and too male, even when practiced by women and persons of color.

Christian's attack on theory drew a wide range of responses, including Michael Awkward's "Appropriative Gestures" (2000), which argued that African American scholars and critics would do their work best if they took over whatever tools were needed to do their job, regardless of the color, gender, and nationality of the inventors. Awkward approves of Christian's efforts to move the literary work of African American women closer to the center of the canon, where they will affect the lives of their readers, but he argues that this end will be poorly served by isolating such texts from contemporary theoretical methods. "If the literature of black women is . . . to gain the respect it doubtlessly deserves as an ideologically and aesthetically complex, analytically rich literary tradition within an increasingly theoretical academy, it

[18]Possibly worse than a zero-sum game, if, as Louis Menand has shown, federal and state governments since 1975 have been cutting the funds available for higher education, with the cuts disproportionately centered in the arts and humanities. As the flow of grant money dried up, the academy became more and more competitive, which increased the desperation for ambitious scholars to become affiliated to whatever movement was the "flavor of the month."

will require that its critics . . . master the discourse of contemporary literary theory," And as African American critics become prominent in the canon of theory, theory itself will cease to be "white."

Deborah E. McDowell's response to this controversy in her essay "Recycling" (1992) is fascinating, particularly because McDowell is *herself* one of the foremost African American scholars doing theory within the academy. Her much earlier essay, "New Directions for Black Feminist Criticism," although sympathetic to the sense of marginalization that provoked critics like Barbara Smith and Barbara Christian, sought to escape the divisiveness of the standard binaries: black versus white, women versus men, lesbian versus heterosexual, and it urged black scholars to approach their tasks using any and all available methodologies. In "Recycling," McDowell seems to have circled back to a more defensive posture against the reach of poststructural- ist theory. She does not take the view that "theory is white" as such — she knows that black theorists are using it without losing touch with their own identities or the cultural significance of the texts they treat. But she is troubled by the way the move to valorize texts by black female authors seems always to take place under the aegis of white men (Marx, Derrida, Lacan, and the other usual suspects) and to evade the particulars of black female experience. McDowell's "counterhistory" suggests that poststructural theory, with its proclamations of the loss of stable meaning and the death of the author, may be liberating when it destabilizes ancient and unquestioned dogmas about literature and culture, the "great tradition" of dead white males, but to the extent that it installs a different "great tradition" of white male theorists, it can have the unintended result of undermining the best efforts of black feminist scholar- ship today. And she quotes Rey Chow — whom we shall discuss shortly — to the effect that the very same kind of undermining takes place with respect to the litera- ture of the Third World as well.

The fact is that African American feminist criticism is by no means the only one that senses a rivalry with theory: The same kind of conflict exists between practitioners of postcolonial studies and practitioners of postcolonial theory. Bart Moore-Gilbert's excellent study, *Postcolonial Theory: Contexts, Practices, Politics*, spends the first chapter outlining the deep divisions — divisions that he thinks can ultimately be bridged — between the high theorists with which this chapter began and scholars of postcolonial literatures. Some of the causes of the conflict are fairly superficial, like the annoyance with the arcane vocabulary of poststructural theory, and some may primarily reflect resentment over the academic success of theorists like Said and Spivak. But other issues are harder to dismiss: Scholars like Stephen Slemon and Helen Tiffin argue that theorists like Bhabha evade "the real politics of the postcolonial predicament as a consequence of their obsession with 'a set of philosophical questions whose cultural and historical specificity within postmodern Anglo-American culture is rarely admitted.'"[19] Aijaz Ahmad, from his own Marxist perspective, views postcolonial theory as aloof and hyperintellectual, preferring a

[19]Stephen Slemon and Helen Tiffin, Introduction to *After Europe*, xi, quoted in Moore-Gilbert, pp. 20–21.

textual to a material engagement with the forces of repression, and isolated from the struggles for liberation still going on in the poorest of the former colonies.[20] To the extent that this is an ethical challenge to the theorists, it can often be answered with biography: Edward Said was, until his recent death from leukemia, a tireless advocate of the Palestinian people in their quest for autonomy and statehood, and Gayatri Spivak, for at least the last ten years, has been involved in creating and training "barefoot schools" for the women of rural India. Nevertheless, one could claim that there is a split between theory and practice here, between the Foucauldian theorist of Orientalism and the Palestinian advocate, between the deconstructor of subaltern studies and the benefactor of Indian women. So in postcolonial studies, as with ethnic studies, the question remains: Is theory white?

Rey Chow's difficult but rewarding essay "The Interruption of Referentiality," takes the blunt question "Is theory white?" to what are probably its sublimest heights. At the outset of her argument, Chow very abstractly delineates a certain rhetorical move that, at this point, should be rather familiar to us. A critic studying a "particular group, identity, or ethnic culture" gestures toward Western theory in order to reject it. You can call the identity group "African American women," if you like, but because it really doesn't matter which group, Chow abstractly calls it X. But what Chow means by Western theory isn't just any old theory: Chow specifically excludes historical, sociological, anthropological theories that quickly get down to cases: She is talking about poststructuralist theories such as those of Lacan, Foucault, and Derrida, which tend to question the nature of meaning as referentiality (in which a signifier points to a signified) and instead refer meaning to differences in a chain of signifiers. Deconstructive theory destabilizes the standard Western hierarchies valorizing "man" over "woman," "white" over "black," "heterosexual" over "homosexual," and so on, which is why those who study marginalized identity groups want to gesture toward theory. But by destabilizing meaning as reference, theory also calls into question the stability of the identity group, which is why they want to resist or reject theory.

> In the face of the practical struggles that go on daily against different forms of social injustice, it is, for many, unacceptable to declare, in accordance with poststructuralist theoretical logic, that these versions of X do not exist. Yet the alternative — the insistence that they are real . . . , that their empirical existence is absolutely incontestable, and that they are thus a core from which to stage resistance to the virtual claims of high theory — is equally untenable because it is theoretically naive.

The dizzying paradox into which Chow's logic draws us explains why critics studying X keep making that same rhetorical move and also why that move somehow always fails to work. It explains how come all the "new projects of articulating alternative identities, cultures, and group formations often seem so predictable in the end" with their endless talk of ambivalence, hybridity, disruptiveness, resistance: The rhetoric of poststructuralism homogenizes all cultural differences into a mishmash of *différance*.

---

[20]Aijaz Ahmad, Introduction to *In Theory*, p. 3.

Selected Bibliography

Achebe, Chinua. *Hopes and Impediments*. London: Doubleday, 1988.

———. "The African Writer and the English Language." *Morning Yet on Creation Day*.
     New York: Doubleday, 1975.

Ahmad, [Mohammed] Aijaz. *In Theory: Classes, Nations, Literatures*. London: Verso, 1992.

Anderson, Benedict. *Imagined Communities: Reflections on the Origin and Spread of
     Nationalism*. New York: Verso, 1983.

Anzaldúa, Gloria. *Borderlands/La Frontera*. San Francisco: Aunt Lute, 1999.

Appiah, Kwame Anthony. *In My Father's House: Africa in the Philosophy of Culture*.
     London: Methuen, 1992.

Ashcroft, Bill, Gareth Griffiths, and Helen Tiffin, eds. *The Empire Writes Back: Theory and
     Practice in Post-Colonial Literatures*. London: Routledge, 1989.

Awkward, Michael. *Negotiating Difference: Race, Gender, and the Politics of Positionality*.
     Chicago: University of Chicago Press, 1995.

Bahri, Deepika. *Coming to Terms with the "Postcolonial": Between the Lines*. Philadelphia:
     Temple University Press, 1996.

Baker, Houston A., Jr. *Blues, Ideology, and Afro-American Literature: A Vernacular Theory*.
     Chicago: University of Chicago Press, 1984.

Baker, Houston A., Jr., and Patricia Redmond, eds. *Afro-American Literary Study in the
     1990s*. Chicago: University of Chicago Press, 1989.

Bhabha, Homi K. *The Location of Culture*. New York: Routledge, 1994.

———, ed. *Nation and Narration*. New York: Routledge, 1990.

Brantlinger, Patrick. *Rule of Darkness: British Literature and Imperialism, 1830–1914*.
     Ithaca: Cornell University Press, 1988.

Césaire, Aimé. *Un tempête*. Paris: Seuil, 1969.

Chow, Rey. *Writing Diaspora: Tactics of Intervention in Contemporary Cultural Studies*.
     Bloomington: Indiana University Press, 1993.

Christian, Barbara. *Black Feminist Criticism*. New York: Pergamon, 1985.

Deleuze, Gilles, and Félix Guattari. *Kafka: Toward a Minor Literature*. Minneapolis:
     University of Minnesota Press, 1986.

Fanon, Frantz. *Black Skin, White Masks*. New York: Grove Press, 1967.

———. *The Wretched of the Earth*. New York: Grove Press, 1961.

Gates, Henry Louis. *Black Literature and Literary Theory*. New York: Methuen, 1984.

———. *Loose Canons: Notes on the Culture Wars*. New York: Oxford University Press,
     1992.

———. *The Signifying Monkey: A Theory of African-American Literary Criticism*. New
     York: Oxford University Press, 1988.

———, ed. *"Race," Writing, and Difference*. Chicago: University of Chicago Press, 1986.

Gilroy, Paul. *The Black Atlantic: Modernity and Double Consciousness*. Cambridge: Harvard
     University Press, 1993.

Harris, Wilson. *Selected Essays*. New York: Routledge, 1999.

Jameson, Fredric. *The Geopolitical Aesthetic: Cinema and Space in the World System*.
     Bloomington: Indiana University Press, 1992.

———. "Third World Literature in the Era of Multinational Capitalism." *Social Text* 15
     (1986): 65–88.

Jameson, Fredric, and Masao Miyoshi, eds. *The Cultures of Globalization*. Durham: Duke
     University Press, 1998.

Loomba, Ania, ed. *Colonialism/Postcolonialism*. New York: Routledge, 1998.

McDowell, Deborah. *The Changing Same: Black Women's Literature, Criticism, and Theory*. Bloomington: Indiana University Press, 1995.

Memmi, Albert. *The Colonizer and the Colonized*. Boston: Beacon Press, 1965.

Menand, Louis. "What Are Universities For?" *Harper's* 283 (December 1991): 47–56.

Mohanty, Chandra Talpade, Ann Russo, and Lourdes Torres, eds. *Third World Women and the Politics of Feminism*. Bloomington: Indiana University Press, 1991.

Mongia, Padmini, ed. *Contemporary Postcolonial Theory: A Reader*. London: Arnold, 1997.

Moore-Gilbert, Bart, Gareth Stanton, and Willy Maley, eds. *Postcolonial Criticism*. London: Longman, 1997.

Morrison, Toni. *Playing in the Dark: Whiteness and the Literary Imagination*. Cambridge: Harvard University Press, 1992.

Naipaul, V. S. *The Middle Passage*. London: Deutsch, 1962.

Ngugi wa Thiong'o. *Decolonising the Mind: The Politics of Language*. London: James Currey, 1989.

———. *Moving the Centre: The Struggle for Cultural Freedom*. London: James Currey, 1993.

———. *Penpoints, Gunpoints, and Dreams: Towards a Critical Theory of the Arts and the State in Africa*. New York: Oxford University Press, 1998.

Riquelme, John P. "Location and Home in Beckett, Bhabha, Fanon, and Heidegger." *Centennial Review* 42, no. 3 (1998): 541–68.

Rushdie, Salman. *Imaginary Homelands: Essays and Criticism, 1981–1991*. London: Penguin, 1991.

Said, Edward. *Orientalism*. New York: Vintage, 1979.

———. *The World, the Text, and the Critic*. Cambridge: Harvard University Press, 1983.

———. *Culture and Imperialism*. New York: Vintage, 1994.

Sharpe, Jenny. "Is the United States Postcolonial? Transnationalism, Immigration, and Race." *Diaspora* 4, no. 2 (Fall 1995): 181–99.

Slemon, Stephen, and Helen Tiffin, eds. *After Europe: Critical Theory and Post-Colonial Writing*. Mundelstrup: Dangaroo Press, 1990.

Soyinka, Wole. *Myth, Literature and the African World*. Cambridge: Cambridge University Press, 1990.

Spillers, Hortense J. "Who Cuts the Borders? Some Readings on 'America.'" In *Comparative American Identities: Race, Sex, and Nationality in the Modern Text*, ed. Hortense J. Spillers. New York: Routledge, 1991.

Spivak, Gayatri Chakravorti. *In Other Worlds: Essays in Cultural Politics*. London: Methuen, 1987.

———. "Can the Subaltern Speak?" *Marxism and the Interpretation of Culture*, ed. Cary Nelson and Lawrence Grossberg. Urbana: University of Illinois Press, 1988.

———. *A Critique of Post-Colonial Reason: Toward a History of the Vanishing Present*. Cambridge: Harvard University Press, 1999.

Trinh, T. Minh-Ha, *Woman, Native, Other: Writing Postcoloniality and Feminism*. Bloomington: Indiana University Press, 1989.

West, Cornel. *Race Matters*. Boston: Beacon Press, 1993.

Williams, Patrick, and Laura Chrisman, eds. *Colonial Discourse and Post-Colonial Theory*. New York: Harvester Wheatsheaf, 1993.

Edward W. Said

1935–2003

Although his early writings focused on the usefulness of Continental philosophy and interdisciplinary approaches to literary studies, Edward W. Said's work increasingly dealt with questions of the relation of literary criticism to international politics. Said was born in 1935 in Jerusalem, and attended Western schools in Jerusalem, Cairo, and Massachusetts before receiving degrees at Princeton and Harvard. Beginning in 1963 he was a professor of English and comparative literature at Columbia University and a visiting professor at Yale, Stanford, Harvard, and Johns Hopkins Universities. From the late 1980s until his death, Said often appeared on news programs as a moderate and articulate spokesman for the Palestinian people. His book Orientalism (1978) was a runner-up for a National Book Award for criticism. His other books include Joseph Conrad and the Fiction of Autobiography (1966), Beginnings: Intention and Method (1975), The Question of Palestine (1979), The World, the Text, and the Critic (1983), After the Last Sky: Palestinian Lives (1986), Blaming the Victims (1988), Culture and Imperialism (1993), Peace and Its Discontents (1996), Covering Islam (1997), Reflections on Exile (2000), Parallels and Paradoxes (2002, with Daniel Barenboim), and Humanism and Democratic Criticism and From Oslo to Iraq (both published posthumously in 2004). The following selection is from the introduction to Orientalism.

From the Introduction to *Orientalism*

II

I have begun with the assumption that the Orient is not an inert fact of nature. It is not merely *there*, just as the Occident itself is not just *there* either. We must take seriously Vico's[1] great observation that men make their own history, that what they can know is what they have made, and extend it to geography: as both geographical and cultural entities — to say nothing of historical entities — such locales, regions, geographical sectors as "Orient" and "Occident" are manmade. Therefore as much as the West itself, the Orient is an idea that has a history and a tradition of thought, imagery, and vocabulary that have given it reality and presence in and for the West. The two geographical entities thus support and to an extent reflect each other.

Having said that, one must go on to state a number of reasonable qualifications. In the first place, it would be wrong to conclude that the Orient was *essentially* an idea, or a creation with no corresponding reality. When Disraeli said in his novel *Tancred* that the East was a career,[2] he meant that to be interested in the East was something that bright young Westerners would find to be an all-consuming passion; he should not be interpreted as saying that the East was *only* a career for Westerners. There were — and are — cultures and nations whose location is in the East, and their lives, histories, and customs have a brute reality obviously greater than anything that could be said about them in the West. About that fact this study of Orientalism has very little to contribute, except to acknowledge it tacitly. But the

[1] The *Scienza nuova* (1725) of Italian philosopher Giambattista Vico (1668–1744) presented a theory of historical evolution of cultures.

[2] British prime minister and novelist Benjamin Disraeli (1804–1871) wrote *Tancred* as part of his Condition of England trilogy in 1847.

phenomenon of Orientalism as I study it here deals principally, not with a correspondence between Orientalism and Orient, but with the internal consistency of Orientalism and its ideas about the Orient (the East as career) despite or beyond any correspondence, or lack thereof, with a "real" Orient. My point is that Disraeli's statement about the East refers mainly to that created consistency, that regular constellation of ideas as that pre-eminent thing about the Orient, and not to its mere being, as Wallace Stevens's phrase has it.[3]

A second qualification is that ideas, cultures, and histories cannot seriously be understood or studied without their force, or more precisely their configurations of power, also being studied. To believe that the Orient was created — or, as I call it, "Orientalized" — and to believe that such things happen simply as a necessity of the imagination, is to be disingenuous. The relationship between Occident and Orient is a relationship of power, of domination, of varying degrees of a complex hegemony, and is quite accurately indicated in the title of K. M. Panikkar's classic *Asia and Western Dominance*.[4] The Orient was Orientalized not only because it was discovered to be "Oriental" in all those ways considered commonplace by an average nineteenth-century European, but also because it *could be* — that is, submitted to being — *made* Oriental. There is very little consent to be found, for example, in the fact that Flaubert's encounter with an Egyptian courtesan produced a widely influential model of the Oriental woman; she never spoke of herself, she never represented her emotions, presence, or history. *He* spoke for and represented her. He was foreign, comparatively wealthy, male, and these were historical facts of domination that allowed him not only to posses Kuchuk Hanem physically but to speak for her and tell his readers in what way she was "typically Oriental." My argument is that Flaubert's situation of strength in relation to Kuchuk Hanem was not an isolated instance. It fairly stands for the pattern of relative strength between East and West, and the discourse about the Orient that it enabled.[5]

This brings us to a third qualification. One ought never to assume that the structure of Orientalism is nothing more than a structure of lies or of myths which, were the truth about them to be told, would simply blow away. I myself believe that Orientalism is more particularly valuable as a sign of European-Atlantic power over the Orient than it is as a veridic discourse about the Orient (which is what, in its academic or scholarly form, it claims to be). Nevertheless, what we must respect and try to grasp is the sheer knitted-together strength of Orientalist discourse, its very close ties to the enabling socio-economic and political institutions, and its redoubtable durability. After all, any system of ideas that can remain unchanged as teachable wisdom (in academies, books, congresses, universities, foreign-service institutes) from the period of Ernest Renan[6] in the late 1840s until the present in the United States must be something more formidable than a mere collection of lies. Orientalism, therefore, is not an airy European fantasy about the Orient, but a created body of theory and practice in which, for many generations, there has been a considerable material investment. Continued investment made Orientalism, as a system of knowledge about the Orient, an accepted grid for filtering through the Orient into Western consciousness, just as that same investment multiplied — indeed, made truly productive — the statements proliferating out from Orientalism into the general culture.

Gramsci[7] has made the useful analytic distinction between civil and political society in which the former is made up of voluntary (or at least rational and noncoercive) affiliations like schools, families, and unions, the latter of state institutions

---

[3]The author is referring to Wallace Stevens's poem "Of Mere Being" (1955).

[4]K. M. Panikkar, *Asia and Western Dominance* (London: George Allen & Unwin, 1959). [Said]

[5]As Said explains later, Hanem was an Egyptian dancer and courtesan with whom Gustave Flaubert slept during his 1859 tour of Greece and the Middle East. Said argues that the experience influenced Flaubert's portraits of oriental women like Salammbô and Salomé as visions of escapist sexual fantasy.

[6]Ernest Renan (1823–1892) won the Prix Volney for his 1847 *General History of the Semitic Languages*, a work Said characterizes as racist and reductive.

[7]See the introduction to Marxist Criticism, p. 701.

(the army, the police, the central bureaucracy) whose role in the polity is direct domination. Culture, of course, is to be found operating within civil society, where the influence of ideas, of institutions, and of other persons works not through domination but by what Gramsci calls consent. In any society not totalitarian, then, certain cultural forms predominate over others, just as certain ideas are more influential than others; the form of this cultural leadership is what Gramsci has identified as *hegemony*, an indispensable concept for any understanding of cultural life in the industrial West. It is hegemony, or rather the result of cultural hegemony at work, that gives Orientalism the durability and the strength I have been speaking about so far. Orientalism is never far from what Denys Hay has called the idea of Europe,[8] a collective notion identifying "us" Europeans as against all "those" non-Europeans, and indeed it can be argued that the major component in European culture is precisely what made that culture hegemonic both in and outside Europe: the idea of European identity as a superior one in comparison with all the non-European peoples and cultures. There is in addition the hegemony of European ideas about the Orient, themselves reiterating European superiority over Oriental backwardness, usually overriding the possibility that a more independent, or more skeptical, thinker might have had different views on the matter.

In a quite constant way, Orientalism depends for its strategy on this flexible *positional superiority*, which puts the Westerner in a whole series of possible relationships with the Orient without ever losing him the relative upper hand. And why should it have been otherwise, especially during the period of extraordinary European ascendancy from the late Renaissance to the present? The scientist, the scholar, the missionary, the trader, or the soldier was in, or thought about, the Orient because he *could be there*, or could think about it, with very little resistance on the Orient's part. Under the general heading of knowledge of the Orient, and within the umbrella of Western hegemony over the Orient during the period from the end of the eighteenth century, there emerged a

[8]Denys Hay, *Europe: The Emergence of an Idea*, 2nd ed. (Edinburgh): Edinburgh University Press, 1968). [Said]

complex Orient suitable for study in the academy, for display in the museum, for reconstruction in the colonial office, for theoretical illustration in anthropological, biological, linguistic, racial, and historical theses about mankind and the universe, for instances of economic and sociological theories of development, revolution, cultural personality, national or religious character. Additionally, the imaginative examination of things Oriental was based more or less exclusively upon a sovereign Western consciousness out of whose unchallenged centrality an Oriental world emerged, first according to general ideas about who or what was an Oriental, then according to a detailed logic governed not simply by empirical reality but by a battery of desires, repressions, investments, and projections. If we can point to great Orientalist works of genuine scholarship like Silvestre de Sacy's *Chrestomathie arabe* or Edward William Lane's *Account of the Manners and Customs of the Modern Egyptians*,[9] we need also to note that Renan's and Gobineau's[10] racial ideas came out of the same impulse, as did a great many Victorian pornographic novels (see the analysis by Steven Marcus of "The Lustful Turk").[11]

And yet, one must repeatedly ask oneself whether what matters in Orientalism is the general group of ideas overriding the mass of material — about which who could deny that they were shot through with doctrines of European superiority, various kinds of racism, imperialism, and the like, dogmatic views of "the Oriental" as a kind of ideal and unchanging abstraction? — or the much more varied work produced by almost uncountable individual writers, whom one would

[9]Baron Antoine Isaac Silvestre de Sacy (1758–1838), French Arabist, published his influential anthology *Chrestomathie arabe* (3 Vols.) in 1806. Edward William Lane (1801–1876), scholar of oriental languages, published his *Account of the Manners and Customs of the Modern Egyptians* in 1836.

[10]Joseph Arthur, comte de Gobineau (1816–1882), was a French sociologist, whose most important work, *The Moral and Intellectual Diversity of Races* (1854), stated the thesis of Nordic racial superiority espoused by composer Richard Wagner and adopted by Adolf Hitler.

[11]Steven Marcus, *The Other Victorians: A Study of Sexuality and Pornography in Mid-Nineteenth Century England* (1966; reprint ed., New York: Bantam Books, 1967), pp. 200–19. [Said]

take up as individual instances of authors dealing with the Orient. In a sense the two alternatives, general and particular, are really two perspectives on the same material: in both instances one would have to deal with pioneers in the field like William Jones, with great artists like Nerval or Flaubert.[12] And why would it not be possible to employ both perspectives together, or one after the other? Isn't there an obvious danger of distortion (of precisely the kind that academic Orientalism has always been prone to) if either too general or too specific a level of description is maintained systematically?

My two fears are distortion and inaccuracy, or rather the kind of inaccuracy produced by too dogmatic a generality and too positivistic a localized focus. In trying to deal with these problems I have tried to deal with three main aspects of my own contemporary reality that seem to me to point the way out of the methodological or perspectival difficulties I have been discussing, difficulties that might force one, in the first instance, into writing a coarse polemic on so unacceptably general a level of description as not to be worth the effort, or in the second instance, into writing so detailed and atomistic a series of analyses as to lose all track of the general lines of force informing the field, giving it its special cogency. How then to recognize individuality and to reconcile it with its intelligent, and by no means passive or merely dictatorial, general and hegemonic context?

III

I mentioned three aspects of my contemporary reality: I must explain and briefly discuss them now, so that it can be seen how I was led to a particular course of research and writing.

I. *The distinction between pure and political knowledge.* It is very easy to argue that knowledge about Shakespeare or Wordsworth is not political whereas knowledge about contemporary China or the Soviet Union is. My own formal and professional designation is that of "humanist," a title which indicates the humanities as my field and therefore the unlikely eventuality that there might be anything political about what I do in that field. Of course, all these labels and terms are quite unnuanced as I use them here, but the general truth of what I am pointing to is, I think, widely held. One reason for saying that a humanist who writes about Wordsworth, or an editor whose specialty is Keats, is not involved in anything political is that what he does seems to have no direct political effect upon reality in the everyday sense. A scholar whose field is Soviet economics works in a highly charged area where there is much government interest, and what he might produce in the way of studies or proposals will be taken up by policymakers, government officials, institutional economists, intelligence experts. The distinction between "humanists" and persons whose work has policy implications, or political significance, can be broadened further by saying that the former's ideological color is a matter of incidental importance to politics (although possibly of great moment to his colleagues in the field, who may object to his Stalinism or fascism or too easy liberalism), whereas the ideology of the latter is woven directly into his material — indeed, economics, politics, and sociology in the modern academy are ideological sciences — and therefore taken for granted as being "political."

Nevertheless the determining impingement on most knowledge produced in the contemporary West (and here I speak mainly about the United States) is that it be nonpolitical, that is, scholarly, academic, impartial, above partisan or small-minded doctrinal belief. One can have no quarrel with such an ambition in theory, perhaps, but in practice the reality is much more problematic. No one has ever devised a method for detaching the scholar from the circumstances of life, from the fact of his involvement (conscious or unconscious) with a class, a set of beliefs, a social position, or from the mere activity of being a member of a society. These continue to bear on what he does professionally, even though naturally enough his research and its fruits do attempt to reach a level of relative freedom from the

---

[12]Sir William Jones (1746–1794) translated Arabic and Sanskrit poetry in the 1780s and 1790s. Gérard de Nerval (1808–1855) was a French symbolist poet who wrote *Le Voyage en orient* in 1851.

inhibitions and the restrictions of brute, everyday reality. For there is such a thing as knowledge that is less, rather than more, partial than the individual (with his entangling and distracting life circumstances) who produces it. Yet this knowledge is not therefore automatically nonpolitical.

Whether discussions of literature or of classical philology are fraught with — or have unmediated — political significance is a very large question that I have tried to treat in some detail elsewhere.[13] What I am interested in doing now is suggesting how the general liberal consensus that "true" knowledge is fundamentally nonpolitical (and conversely, that overtly political knowledge is not "true") obscures the highly if obscurely organized political circumstances obtaining when knowledge is produced. No one is helped in understanding this today when the adjective "political" is used as a label to discredit any work for daring to violate the protocol of pretended suprapolitical objectivity. We may say, first, that civil society recognizes a gradation of political importance in the various fields of knowledge. To some extent the political importance given a field comes from the possibility of its direct translation into economic terms; but to a greater extent political importance comes from the closeness of a field to ascertainable sources of power in political society. Thus an economic study of long-term Soviet energy potential and its effect on military capability is likely to be commissioned by the Defense Department, and thereafter to acquire a kind of political status impossible for a study of Tolstoi's early fiction financed in part by a foundation. Yet both works belong in what civil society acknowledges to be a similar field, Russian studies, even though one work may be done by a very conservative economist, the other by a radical literary historian. My point here is that "Russia" as a general subject matter has political priority over nicer distinctions such as "economics" and "literary history," because political society in Gramsci's sense reaches into such realms of civil society as the

academy and saturates them with significance of direct concern to it.

I do not want to press all this any further on general theoretical grounds: it seems to me that the value and credibility of my case can be demonstrated by being much more specific, in the way, for example, Noam Chomsky has studied the instrumental connection between the Vietnam War and the notion of objective scholarship as it was applied to cover state-sponsored military research.[14] Now because Britain, France, and recently the United States are imperial powers, their political societies impart to their civil societies a sense of urgency, a direct political infusion as it were, where and whenever matters pertaining to their imperial interests abroad are concerned. I doubt that it is controversial, for example, to say that an Englishman in India or Egypt in the later nineteenth century took an interest in those countries that was never far from their status in his mind as British colonies. To say this may seem quite different from saying that all academic knowledge about India and Egypt is somehow tinged and impressed with, violated by, the gross political fact — and yet that is what I am saying in this study of Orientalism. For if it is true that no production of knowledge in the human sciences can ever ignore or disclaim its author's involvement as a human subject in his own circumstances, then it must also be true that for a European or American studying the Orient there can be no disclaiming the main circumstances of his actuality: that he comes up against the Orient as a European or American first, as an individual second. And to be a European or an American in such a situation is by no means an inert fact. It meant and means being aware, however dimly, that one belongs to a power with definite interests in the Orient, and more important, that one belongs to a part of the earth with a definite history of involvement in the Orient almost since the time of Homer.

Put in this way, these political actualities are still too undefined and general to be really

13See my book *The World, the Text, and the Critic* (Cambridge, Mass.: Harvard University Press, 1983). [Said]

14Principally in his *American Power and the New Mandarins: Historical and Political Essays* (New York: Pantheon Books, 1969) and *For Reasons of State* (New York: Pantheon Books, 1973). [Said]

interesting. Anyone would agree to them without necessarily agreeing also that they mattered very much, for instance, to Flaubert as he wrote *Salammbô*, or to H. A. R. Gibb as he wrote *Modern Trends in Islam*.[15] The trouble is that there is too great a distance between the big dominating fact, as I have described it, and the details of everyday life that govern the minute discipline of a novel or a scholarly text as each is being written. Yet if we eliminate from the start any notion that "big" facts like imperial domination can be applied mechanically and deterministically to such complex matters as culture and ideas, then we will begin to approach an interesting kind of study. My idea is that European and then American interest in the Orient was political according to some of the obvious historical accounts of it that I have given here, but that it was the culture that created that interest, that acted dynamically along with brute political, economic, and military rationales to make the Orient the varied and complicated place that it obviously was in the field I call Orientalism.

Therefore, Orientalism is not a mere political subject matter or field that is reflected passively by culture, scholarship, or institutions; nor is it a large and diffuse collection of texts about the Orient; nor is it representative and expressive of some nefarious "Western" imperialist plot to hold down the "Oriental" world. It is rather a *distribution* of geopolitical awareness into aesthetic, scholarly, economic, sociological, historical, and philological texts; it is an *elaboration* not only of a basic geographical distinction (the world is made up of two unequal halves, Orient and Occident) but also of a whole series of "interests" which, by such means as scholarly discovery, philological reconstruction, psychological analysis, landscape and sociological description, it not only creates but also maintains; it *is*, rather than expresses, a certain *will* or *intention* to understand, in some cases to control, manipulate, even to incorporate, what is a mainfestly different (or alternative and novel)

world; it is, above all, a discourse that is by no means in direct, corresponding relationship with political power in the raw, but rather is produced and exists in an uneven exchange with various kinds of power, shaped to a degree by the exchange with power political (as with a colonial or imperial establishment), power intellectual (as with reigning sciences like comparative linguistics or anatomy, or any of the modern policy sciences), power cultural (as with orthodoxies and canons of taste, texts, values), power moral (as with ideas about what "we" do and what "they" cannot do or understand as "we" do). Indeed, my real argument is that Orientalism is — and does not simply represent — a considerable dimension of modern political-intellectual culture, and as such has less to do with the Orient than it does with "our" world.

Because Orientalism is a cultural and a political fact, then, it does not exist in some archival vacuum; quite the contrary, I think it can be shown that what is thought, said, or even done about the Orient follows (perhaps occurs within) certain distinct and intellectually knowable lines. Here too a considerable degree of nuance and elaboration can be seen working as between the broad superstructural pressures and the details of composition, the facts of textuality. Most humanistic scholars are, I think, perfectly happy with the notion that texts exist in contexts, that there is such a thing as intertextuality, that the pressures of conventions, predecessors, and rhetorical styles limit what Walter Benjamin once called the "overtaxing of the productive person in the name of . . . the principle of 'creativity,'" in which the poet is believed on his own, and out of his pure mind, to have brought forth his work.[16] Yet there is a reluctance to allow that political, institutional, and ideological constraints act in the same manner on the individual author. A humanist will believe it to be an interesting fact to any interpreter of Balzac that he was influenced in the *Comédie humaine*

---

[15]In this 1947 text Sir Hamilton Gibb wrote of the Muslim "rejection of rationalist modes of thought."

[16]Walter Benjamin, *Charles Baudelaire: A Lyric Poet in the Era of High Capitalism*, trans. Harry Zohn (London: New Left Books, 1973), p. 71. [Said]

by the conflict between Geoffroy Saint-Hilaire and Cuvier,[17] but the same sort of pressure on Balzac of deeply reactionary monarchism is felt in some vague way to demean his literary "genius" and therefore to be less worth serious study. Similarly — as Harry Bracken has been tirelessly showing — philosophers will conduct their discussions of Locke, Hume, and empiricism without ever taking into account that there is an explicit connection in these classic writers between their "philosophic" doctrines and racial theory, justifications of slavery, or arguments for colonial exploitation.[18] These are common enough ways by which contemporary scholarship keeps itself pure.

Perhaps it is true that most attempts to rub culture's nose in the mud of politics have been crudely iconoclastic; perhaps also the social interpretation of literature in my own field has simply not kept up with the enormous technical advances in detailed textual analysis. But there is no getting away from the fact that literary studies in general, and American Marxist theorists in particular, have avoided the effort of seriously bridging the gap between the superstructural and the base levels in textual, historical scholarship.[19] on another occasion I have gone so far as to say that the literary-cultural establishment as a whole has declared the serious study of imperialism and culture off limits.[20] For Orientalism brings one up directly against that political question — that is, to realizing that political question governs an entire field of study,

imagination, and scholarly institutions — in such a way as to make its avoidance an intellectual and historical impossibility. Yet there will always remain the perennial escape mechanism of saying that a literary scholar and a philosopher, for example, are trained in literature and philosophy respectively, not in politics or ideological analysis. In other words, the specialist argument can work quite effectively to block the larger and, in my opinion, the more intellectually serious perspective.

Here it seems to me there is a simple two-part answer to be given, at least so far as the study of imperialism and culture (or Orientalism) is concerned. In the first place, nearly every nineteenth-century writer (and the same is true enough of writers in earlier periods) was extraordinarily well aware of the fact of empire: this is a subject not very well studied, but it will not take a modern Victorian specialist long to admit that liberal cultural heroes like John Stuart Mill, Arnold, Carlyle, Newman, Macaulay, Ruskin, George Eliot, and even Dickens had definite views on race and imperialism, which are quite easily to be found at work in their writing. So even a specialist must deal with the knowledge that Mill, for example, made it clear in *On Liberty* and *Representative Government* that his views there could not be applied to India (he was an India Office functionary for a good deal of his life, after all) because the Indians were civilizationally, if not racially, inferior. The same kind of paradox is to be found in Marx, as I try to show in this book. In the second place, to believe that politics in the form of imperialism bears upon the production of literature, scholarship, social theory, and history writing is by no means equivalent to saying that culture is therefore a demeaned or denigrated thing. Quite the contrary: my whole point is to say that we can better understand the persistence and the durability of saturating hegemonic systems like culture when we realize that their internal constraints upon writers and thinkers were *productive*, not unilaterally inhibiting. It is this idea that Gramsci, certainly, and Foucault and Raymond Williams in their very different ways have been trying to illustrate. Even one or two pages by Williams on "the uses of the Empire" in *The Long Revolution* tell us more about

17Étienne Geoffroy Saint-Hilaire (1772–1844), French naturalist, collaborated with paleontologist Baron Georges Cuvier (1769–1832) on five works of natural history published in the first decade of the nineteenth century. The two later quarrelled furiously over biological principle. Cuvier was a functionalist who believed that invariant species were specialized by nature for their ecological niches. Saint-Hilaire, on the contrary, thought that all organisms stemmed from one original structure, and that there were many rudimentary organs that betrayed a long-term evolution of organisms from one mode of functioning to another.

18Harry Bracken, "Essence, Accident and Race," *Hermathena* 116 (Winter 1973): 81–96. [Said]

19See Raymond Williams on base and superstructure, pp. 747.

20In an interview published in *Diacritics* 6, no. 3 (Fall 1976): 38. [Said]

nineteenth-century cultural richness than many volumes of hermetic textual analyses.[21]

Therefore I study Orientalism as a dynamic exchange between individual authors and the large political concerns shaped by the three great empires — British, French, American — in whose intellectual and imaginative territory the writing was produced. What interests me most as a scholar is not the gross political verity but the detail, as indeed what interests us in someone like Lane or Flaubert or Renan is not the (to him) indisputable truth that Occidentals are superior to Orientals, but the profoundly worked over and modulated evidence of his detailed work within the very wide space opened up by that truth. One need only remember that Lane's *Manners and Customs of the Modern Egyptians* is a classic of historical and anthropological observation because of its style, its enormously intelligent and brilliant details, not because of its simple reflection of racial superiority, to understand what I am saying here.

The kind of political questions raised by Orientalism, then, are as follows; What other sorts of intellectual, aesthetic, scholarly, and cultural energies went into the making of an imperialist tradition like the Orientalist one? How did philology, lexicography, history, biology, political and economic theory, novel-writing, and lyric poetry come to the service of Orientalism's broadly imperialist view of the world? What changes, modulations, refinements, even revolutions take place within Orientalism? What is the meaning of originality, of continuity, of individuality, in this context? How does Orientalism transmit or reproduce itself from one epoch to another? In fine, how can we treat the cultural, historical phenomenon of Orientalism as a kind of *willed human work* — not of mere unconditioned ratiocination — in all its historical complexity, detail, and worth without at the same time losing sight of the alliance between cultural work, political tendencies, the state, and the specific realities of domination? Governed by such concerns a humanistic study can responsibly address itself to politics *and* culture. But this is not to say that such a study establishes a hard-and-fast rule

about the relationship between knowledge and politics. My argument is that each humanistic investigation must formulate the nature of that connection in the specific context of the study, the subject matter, and its historical circumstances.

2. *The methodological question.* In a previous book I gave a good deal of thought and analysis to the methodological importance for work in the human sciences of finding and formulating a first step, a point of departure, a beginning principle.[22] A major lesson I learned and tried to present was that there is no such thing as a merely given, or simply available, starting point: beginnings have to be made for each project in such a way as to *enable* what follows from them. Nowhere in my experience has the difficulty of this lesson been more consciously lived (with what success — or failure — I cannot really say) than in this study of Orientalism. The idea of beginning, indeed the act of beginning, necessarily involves an act of delimitation by which something is cut out of a great mass of material, separated from the mass, and made to stand for, as well as be, a starting point, a beginning; for the student of texts one such notion of inaugural delimitation is Louis Althusser's idea of the *problematic*, a specific determinate unity of a text, or group of texts, which is something given rise to by analysis.[23] Yet in the case of Orientalism (as opposed to the case of Marx's texts, which is what Althusser studies) there is not simply the problem of finding a point of departure, or problematic, but also the question of designating which texts, authors, and periods are the ones best suited for study.

It has seemed to me foolish to attempt an encyclopedic narrative history of Orientalism, first of all because if my guiding principle was to be "the European idea of the Orient" there would be virtually no limit to the material I would have had to deal with; second, because the narrative model itself did not suit my descriptive and political interests; third, because in such books as Raymond Schwab's *La Renaissance orientale*, Johann Fück's *Die Arabischen Studien in Europa bis*

---

[21]Raymond Williams, *The Long Revolution* (London: Chatto & Windus, 1961), pp. 66–7. [Said]

[22]In my *Beginnings: Intention and Method* (New York: Basic Books, 1975). [Said.]
[23]Louis Althusser, *For Marx*, trans. Ben Brewster (New York: Pantheon Books, 1969), pp. 65–7. [Said]

in den Anfang des 20. Jahrhunderts, and more recently, Dorothee Metlitzki's *The Matter of Araby in Medieval England*[24] there already exist encyclopedic works on certain aspects of the European-Oriental encounter such as make the critic's job, in the general political and intellectual context I sketched above, a different one.

There still remained the problem of cutting down a very fat archive to manageable dimensions, and more important, outlining something in the nature of an intellectual order within that group of texts without at the same time following a mindlessly chronological order. My starting point therefore has been the British, French, and American experience of the Orient taken as a unit, what made that experience possible by way of historical and intellectual background, what the quality and character of the experience has been. For reasons I shall discuss presently I limited that already limited (but still inordinately large) set of questions to the Anglo-French-American experience of the Arabs and Islam, which for almost a thousand years stood together for the Orient. Immediately upon doing that, a large part of the Orient seemed to have been eliminated — India, Japan, China, and other sections of the Far East — not because these regions were not important (they obviously have been) but because one could discuss Europe's experience of the Near Orient, or of Islam, apart from its experience of the Far Orient. Yet at certain moments of that general European history of interest in the East, particular parts of the Orient like Egypt, Syria, and Arabia cannot be discussed without also studying Europe's involvement in the more distant parts, of which Persia and India are the most important; a notable case in point is the connection between Egypt and India so far as eighteenth- and nineteenth-century Britain was concerned. Similarly the French role in deciphering the Zend-Avesta,[25] the pre-eminence

of Paris as a center of Sanskrit studies during the first decade of the nineteenth century, the fact that Napoleon's interest in the Orient was contingent upon his sense of the British role in India: all these Far Eastern interests directly influenced French interest in the Near East, Islam, and the Arabs.

Britain and France dominated the Eastern Mediterranean from about the end of the seventeenth century on. Yet my discussion of that domination and systematic interest does not do justice to (a) the important contributions to Orientalism of Germany, Italy, Russia, Spain, and Portugal and (b) the fact that one of the important impulses toward the study of the Orient in the eighteenth century was the revolution in Biblical studies[26] stimulated by such variously interesting pioneers as Bishop Lowth, Eichhorn, Herder, and Michaelis. In the first place, I had to focus rigorously upon the British-French and later the American material because it seemed inescapably true not only that Britain and France were the pioneer nations in the Orient and in Oriental studies, but that these vanguard positions were held by virtue of the two greatest colonial networks in pre-twentieth-century history; the American Oriental position since World War II has fit — I think, quite self-consciously — in the places excavated by the two earlier European powers. Then, too, I believe that the sheer quality, consistency, and mass of British, French, and American writing on the Orient lifts it above the doubtless crucial work done in Germany, Italy, Russia, and elsewhere. But I think it is also true that the major steps in Oriental scholarship were first taken in either Britain and France, then elaborated upon by Germans, Silvestre de Sacy, for example, was not only the first modern and institutional European Orientalist, who worked on Islam, Arabic literature, the Druze religion,

25 The ''bible'' of the Zoroastrian religion, sacred to the Parsees.

24 Raymond Schwab, *La Renaissance orientale* (Paris: Payot, 1950); Johann W. Flück, *Die Arabischen Studien in Europa bis in den Anfang des 20. Jahrhunderts* (Leipzig: Otto Harrassowitz, 1955); Dorothee Metlitzki, *The Matter of Araby in Medieval England* (New Haven, Conn.: Yale University Press, 1977). [Said]

26 Said alludes to the ''higher criticism'' of the late eighteenth and nineteenth centuries which, taking the Bible as created by men (however inspired) rather than by God, sought to understand the biblical texts as products of the near eastern societies of the first millennium B.C.E. and the two subsequent centuries. This in turn led to intense study of near eastern languages, customs, geography, and history as a means of illuminating the chief documents of Western European religion.

and Sassanid Persia; he was also the teacher of Champollion[27] and of Franz Bopp, the founder of German comparative linguistics. A similar claim of priority and subsequent pre-eminence can be made for William Jones and Edward William Lane.

In the second place — and here the failings of my study of Orientalism are amply made up for — there has been some important recent work on the background in Biblical scholarship to the rise of what I have called modern Orientalism. The best and the most illuminatingly relevant is E. S. Shaffer's impressive *"Kubla Khan" and The Fall of Jerusalem*,[28] an indispensable study of the origins of Romanticism, and of the intellectual activity underpinning a great deal of what goes on in Coleridge, Browning, and George Eliot. To some degree Shaffer's work refines upon the outlines provided in Schwab, by articulating the material of relevance to be found in the German Biblical scholars and using that material to read, in an intelligent and always interesting way, the work of three major British writers. Yet what is missing in the book is some sense of the political as well as ideological edge given the Oriental material by the British and French writers I am principally concerned with; in addition, unlike Shaffer I attempt to elucidate subsequent developments in academic as well as literary Orientalism that bear on the connection between British and French Orientalism on the one hand and the rise of an explicitly colonial-minded imperialism on the other. Then too, I wish to show how all these earlier matters are reproduced more or less in American Orientalism after the Second World War.

Nevertheless there is a possibly misleading aspect to my study, where, aside from an occasional reference, I do not exhaustively discuss the German developments after the inaugural period dominated by Sacy. Any work that seeks to provide an understanding of academic Orientalism and pays little attention to scholars like Steinthal, Müller, Becker, Goldziher, Brockelmann, Nöldeke — to mention only a handful — needs to be reproached, and I freely reproach myself. I particularly regret not taking more account of the great scientific prestige that accrued to German scholarship by the middle of the nineteenth century, whose neglect was made into a denunciation of insular British scholars by George Eliot. I have in mind Eliot's unforgettable portrait of Mr. Casaubon in *Middlemarch*. One reason Casaubon cannot finish his Key to All Mythologies is, according to his young cousin Will Ladislaw, that he is unacquainted with German scholarship. For not only has Casaubon chosen a subject "as changing as chemistry: new discoveries are constantly making new points of view": he is undertaking a job similar to a refutation of Paracelsus because "he is not an Orientalist, you know."[29]

Eliot was not wrong in implying that by about 1830, which is when *Middlemarch* is set, German scholarship had fully attained its European pre-eminence. Yet at no time in German scholarship during the first two-thirds of the nineteenth century could a close partnership have developed between Orientalists and a protracted, sustained *national* interest in the Orient. There was nothing in Germany to correspond to the Anglo-French presence in India, the Levant, North Africa. Moreover, the German Orient was almost exclusively a scholarly, or at least a classical, Orient: it was made the subject of lyrics, fantasies, and even novels, but it was never actual, the way Egypt and Syria were actual for Chauteaubriand, Lane, Lamartine, Burton, Disraeli, or Nerval. There is some significance in the fact that the two most renowned German works on the Orient, Goethe's *Westöstlicher Diwan* and Friedrich Schlegel's *Über die Sprache*

---

[27]Jean François Champollion (1790–1832) was a French archaeologist who worked out the grammar and lexicon of the ancient Egyptian hieroglyphic language by deciphering the Rosetta Stone. The stone is a black basalt slab discovered by Napoleon's troops in 1799; about two thousand years earlier, it had been inscribed with a royal decree in three scripts: hieroglyphic and demotic Egyptian and Greek.

[28]E. S. Shaffer, *"Kubla Khan" and The Fall of Jerusalem: The Mythological School in Biblical Criticism and Secular Literature, 1770–1880* (Cambridge: Cambridge University Press, 1975). [Said]

[29]George Eliot, *Middlemarch: A Study of Provincial Life* (1872; reprint ed., Boston: Houghton Mifflin Co., 1956), p. 164. [Said]

und Weisheit der Indier,[30] were based respectively on a Rhine journey and on hours spent in Paris libraries. What German Oriental scholarship did was to refine and elaborate techniques whose application was to texts, myths, ideas, and languages almost literally gathered from the Orient by imperial Britain and France.

Yet what German Orientalism had in common with Anglo-French and later American Orientalism was a kind of intellectual *authority* over the Orient within Western culture. This authority must in large part be the subject of any description of Orientalism, and it is so in this study. Even the name *Orientalism* suggests a serious, perhaps ponderous style of expertise; when I apply it to modern American social scientists (since they do not call themselves Orientalists, my use of the word is anomalous), it is to draw attention to the way Middle East experts can still draw on the vestiges of Orientalism's intellectual position in nineteenth-century Europe.

There is nothing mysterious or natural about authority. It is formed, irradiated, disseminated; it is instrumental, it is persuasive; it has status, it establishes canons of taste and value; it is virtually indistinguishable from certain ideas it dignifies as true, and from traditions, perceptions, and judgments it forms, transmits, reproduces. Above all, authority can, indeed must, be analyzed. All these attributes of authority apply to Orientalism, and much of what I do in this study is to describe both the historical authority in and the personal authorities of Orientalism.

My principal methodological devices for studying authority here are what can be called *strategic location*, which is a way of describing the author's position in a text with regard to the Oriental material he writes about, and *strategic formation*, which is a way of analyzing the relationship between texts and the way in which groups of texts, types of texts, even textual genres, acquire mass, density, and referential

[30]Goethe's *Westöstliche Diwan* (1819; the title is untranslatable: the first word is German for "Western/Eastern," the second is Persian for the audience-chamber where the Sultan meets with his court) consists of lyrics imitated from the fourteenth-century Persian poet Hafiz; it is not a scientific treatise like the younger Schlegel's *On the Languages and Learning of India* (1808).

power among themselves and thereafter in the culture at large. I use the notion of strategy simply to identify the problem every writer on the Orient has faced: how to get hold of it, how to approach it, how not to be defeated or overwhelmed by its sublimity, its scope, its awful dimensions. Everyone who writes about the Orient must locate himself vis-à-vis the Orient; translated into his text, this location includes the kind of narrative voice he adopts, the type of structure he builds, the kinds of images, themes, motifs that circulate in his text — all of which add up to deliberate ways of addressing the reader, containing the Orient, and finally, representing it or speaking in its behalf. None of this takes place in the abstract, however. Every writer on the Orient (and this is true even of Homer) assumes some Oriental precedent, some previous knowledge of the Orient, to which he refers and on which he relies. Additionally, each work on the Orient *affiliates* itself with other works, with audiences, with institutions, with the Orient itself. The ensemble of relationships between works, audiences, and some particular aspects of the Orient therefore constitutes an analyzable formation — for example, that of philological studies, of anthologies of extracts from Oriental literature, of travel books, of Oriental fantasies — whose presence in time, in discourse, in institutions (schools, libraries, foreign services) gives it strength and authority.

It is clear, I hope, that my concern with authority does not entail analysis of what lies hidden in the Orientalist text, but analysis rather of the text's surface, its exteriority to what it describes. I do not think that this idea can be overemphasized. Orientalism is premised upon exteriority, that is, on the fact that the Orientalist, poet or scholar, makes the Orient speak, describes the Orient, renders its mysteries plain for and to the West. He is never concerned with the Orient except as the first cause of what he says. What he says and writes, by virtue of the fact that it is said or written, is meant to indicate that the Orientalist is outside the Orient, both as an existential and as a moral fact. The principal product of this exteriority is of course representation: as early as Aeschylus's play *The Persians* the Orient is transformed from a very far distant and often threatening

Otherness into figures that are relatively familiar (in Aeschylus's case, grieving Asiatic women). The dramatic immediacy of representation in *The Persians* obscures the fact that the audience is watching a highly artificial enactment of what a non-Oriental has made into a symbol for the whole Orient. My analysis of the Orientalist text therefore places emphasis on the evidence, which is by no means invisible, for such representations *as representations*, not as "natural" depictions of the Orient. This evidence is found just as prominently in the so-called truthful text (histories, philological analyses, political treatises) as in the avowedly artistic (i.e., openly imaginative) text. The things to look at are style, figures of speech, setting, narrative devices, historical and social circumstances, *not* the correctness of the representation nor its fidelity to some great original. The exteriority of the representation is always governed by some version of the truism that if the Orient could represent itself, it would; since it cannot, the representation does the job, for the West, and *faute de mieux*,[31] for the poor Orient. "Sie können sich nicht vertreten, sie müssen vertreten werden," as Marx wrote in *The Eighteenth Brumaire of Louis Bonaparte*.[32]

Another reason for insisting upon exteriority is that I believe it needs to be made clear about cultural discourse and exchange within a culture that what is commonly circulated by it is not "truth" but representations. It hardly needs to be demonstrated again that language itself is a highly organized and encoded system, which employs many devices to express, indicate, exchange messages and information, represent, and so forth. In any instance of at least written language, there is no such thing as a delivered presence, but a *re-presence*, or a representation. The value, efficacy, strength, apparent veracity of a written statement about the Orient therefore relies very little, and cannot instrumentally depend, on the Orient as such. On the contrary, the written statement is a presence to the reader by virtue of its having excluded, displaced, made supererogatory any such *real thing* as "the Orient." Thus all of Orientalism stands forth and away from the Orient: that Orientalism makes sense at all depends more on the West than on the Orient, and this sense is directly indebted to various Western techniques of representation that make the Orient visible, clear, "there" in discourse about it. And these representations rely upon institutions, traditions, conventions, agreed-upon codes of understanding for their effects, not upon a distant and amorphous Orient.

The difference between representations of the Orient before the last third of the eighteenth century and those after it (that is, those belonging to what I call modern Orientalism) is that the range of representation expanded enormously in the later period. It is true that after William Jones and Anquetil-Duperron,[33] and after Napoleon's Egyptian expedition, Europe came to know the Orient more scientifically, to live in it with greater authority and discipline than ever before. But what mattered to Europe was the expanded scope and the much greater refinement given its techniques for receiving the Orient. When around the turn of the eighteenth century the Orient definitively revealed the age of its languages — thus outdating Hebrew's divine pedigree — it was a group of Europeans who made the discovery, passed it on to other scholars, and preserved the discovery in the new science of Indo-European philology. A new powerful science for viewing the linguistic Orient was born, and with it, as Foucault has shown in *The Order of Things*, a whole web of related scientific interests. Similarly William Beckford,[34] Byron, Goethe, and Hugo restructured the Orient by their art and made its colors, lights, and people visible through their images, rhythms, and motifs. At most, the "real" Orient provoked a writer to his vision; it very rarely guided it.

---

[31]For want of better.

[32]"They cannot represent themselves: they must be represented." Marx's statement about the class of small peasant proprietors in *The Eighteenth Brumaire of Louis Bonaparte*.

[33]Abraham Hyacinthe Anquetil-Duperron (1731–1805), French orientalist, author of *Zend-Avesta* (1771, 3 vols.), a life of Zoroaster and a collection of Zoroastrian writings.

[34]William Beckford (1760–1844), English author of *The History of the Caliph Vathek* (1782 in French, translated in 1786), an oriental-Gothic tale.

Orientalism responded more to the culture that produced it than to its putative object, which was also produced by the West. Thus the history of Orientalism has both an internal consistency and a highly articulated set of relationships to the dominant culture surrounding it. My analyses consequently try to show the field's shape and internal organization, its pioneers, patriarchal authorities, canonical texts, doxological ideas, exemplary figures, its followers, elaborators, and new authorities; I try also to explain how Orientalism borrowed and was frequently informed by "strong" ideas, doctrines, and trends ruling the culture. Thus there was (and is) a linguistic Orient, a Freudian Orient, a Spenglerian Orient, a Darwinian Orient, a racist Orient — and so on. Yet never has there been such a thing as a pure, or unconditional, Orient; similarly, never has there been a nonmaterial form of Orientalism, much less something so innocent as an "idea" of the Orient. In this underlying conviction and in its ensuing methodological consequences do I differ from scholars who study the history of ideas. For the emphases and the executive form, above all the material effectiveness, of statements made by Orientalist discourse are possible in ways that any hermetic history of ideas tends completely to scant. Without those emphases and that material effectiveness Orientalism would be just another idea, whereas it is and was much more than that. Therefore I set out to examine not only scholarly works but also works of literature, political tracts, journalistic texts, travel books, religious and philological studies. In other words, my hybrid perspective is broadly historical and "anthropological," given that I believe all texts to be worldly and circumstantial in (of course) ways that vary from genre to genre, and from historical period to historical period.

Yet unlike Michel Foucault, to whose work I am greatly indebted, I do believe in the determining imprint of individual writers upon the otherwise anonymous collective body of texts constituting a discursive formation like Orientalism. The unity of the large ensemble of texts I analyze is due in part to the fact that they frequently refer to each other: Orientalism is after all a system for citing works and authors. Edward William Lane's *Manners and Customs*

of the Modern Egyptians was read and cited by such diverse figures as Nerval, Flaubert, and Richard Burton.[35] He was an authority whose use was an imperative for anyone writing or thinking about the Orient, not just about Egypt: when Nerval borrows passages verbatim from *Modern Egyptians* it is to use Lane's authority to assist him in describing village scenes in Syria, not Egypt. Lane's authority and the opportunities provided for citing him discriminately as well as indiscriminately were there because Orientalism could give his text the kind of distributive currency that he acquired. There is no way, however, of understanding Lane's currency without also understanding the peculiar features of his text; this is equally true of Renan, Sacy, Lamartine, Schlegel, and a group of other influential writers. Foucault believes that in general the individual text or author counts for very little; empirically, in the case of Orientalism (and perhaps nowhere else) I find this not to be so. Accordingly my analyses employ close textual readings whose goal is to reveal the dialectic between individual text or writer and the complex collective formation to which his work is a contribution.

Yet even though it includes an ample selection of writers, this book is still far from a complete history or general account of Orientalism. Of this failing I am very conscious. The fabric of as thick a discourse as Orientalism has survived and functioned in Western society because of its richness: all I have done is to describe parts of that fabric at certain moments, and merely to suggest the existence of a larger whole, detailed, interesting, dotted with fascinating figures, texts, and events. I have consoled myself with believing that this book is one installment of several, and hope there are scholars and critics who might want to write others. There is still a general essay to be written on imperialism and culture; other studies would go more deeply into the connection between Orientalism and pedagogy, or into Italian, Dutch, German, and Swiss Orientalism, or into the dynamic between scholarship and imaginative

[35] Sir Richard Francis Burton (1821–1890), known for his African explorations as well as his sixteen-volume translation of *The Arabian Nights* (1885–88).

writing, or into the relationship between administrative ideas and intellectual discipline. Perhaps the most important task of all would be to undertake studies in contemporary alternatives to Orientalism, to ask how one can study other cultures and peoples from a libertarian, or a non-repressive and nonmanipulative, perspective. But then one would have to rethink the whole complex problem of knowledge and power. These are all tasks left embarrassingly incomplete in this study.

The last, perhaps self-flattering, observation on method that I want to make here is that I have written this study with several audiences in mind. For students of literature and criticism, Orientalism offers a marvelous instance of the interrelations between society, history, and textuality; moreover, the cultural role played by the Orient in the West connects Orientalism with ideology, politics, and the logic of power, matters of relevance, I think, to the literary community. For contemporary students of the Orient, from university scholars to policymakers, I have written with two ends in mind: one, to present their intellectual genealogy to them in a way that has not been done; two, to criticize — with the hope of stirring discussion — the often unquestioned assumptions on which their work for the most part depends. For the general reader, this study deals with matters that always compel attention, all of them connected not only with Western conceptions and treatments of the Other but also with the singularly important role played by Western culture in what Vico called the world of nations. Lastly, for readers in the so-called Third World, this study proposes itself as a step towards an understanding not so much of Western politics and of the non-Western world in those politics as of the *strength* of Western cultural discourse, a strength too often mistaken as merely decorative or "superstructural." My hope is to illustrate the formidable structure of cultural domination and, specifically for formerly colonized peoples, the dangers and temptations of employing this structure upon themselves or upon others.[36]

[36]Said's third aspect "of my contemporary reality" (see p. 1804), omitted in this selection, is "the personal dimension," his own experience as "a child growing up in two British colonies."

Benedict Anderson

b. 1936

Benedict Richard O'Gorman Anderson was born in Kunming, China, to James O'Gorman, an officer in the Imperial Maritime Customs, and Veronica Beatrice Mary Anderson. He began school in 1941 in California. He received his B.A. in classics at Cambridge University in England before pursuing a Ph.D. in Indonesian studies in the government department at Cornell University, where he taught political science. During this time, his studies led him to Jakarta in 1961. In 1966, he published a report about the previous year's coup and massacres that indicated the uprising was instigated not by the communists, but by disgruntled army officers. This report, known as the "Cornell Paper," caused Anderson to be barred indefinitely from Indonesia. He was exiled to Thailand, where he spent a few years before returning to Cornell, where he is Aaron L. Binenkort Professor Emeritus of International Studies, Government, and Asian Studies. Based on observations of southeastern Asia and of the development of the United Nations, Anderson theorizes that the nation itself is an "imagined political community that is imagined as both inherently limited and sovereign." He argues that Creole states (New World nations) were the first to develop a concept of nationhood because the shared language and customs with their parent countries forced a conceptualization of national boundaries beyond the racial or linguistic. His books include Imagined Communities *(1972),* Java in a Time of Revolution *(1972), Reflections on the Origin and Spread of Nationalism (1983), Literature and Politics in Siam in the American Era (1986), Language and Power: Exploring Political Cultures in Indonesia (1990), The Spectre of Comparisons (1998), The Fate of Rural Hell: Asceticism and Desire in Buddhist Thailand (2012), and The Age of Globalization: Anarchists and the Anti-Colonial Imagination (2013). The following selection is excerpted from* Imagined Communities.

The Origins of National Consciousness

If the development of print-as-commodity is the key to the generation of wholly new ideas of simultaneity, still, we are simply at the point where communities of the type "horizontal-secular, transverse-time" become possible. Why, within that type, did the nation become so popular? The factors involved are obviously complex and various. But a strong case can be made for the primacy of capitalism.

As already noted, at least 20,000,000 books had already been printed by 1500,[1] signalling the

onset of Benjamin's "age of mechanical reproduction."[2] If manuscript knowledge was scarce and arcane lore, print knowledge lived by reproducibility and dissemination.[3] If, as [Lucien Paul Victor] Febvre and [Henri-Jean] Martin believe, possibly as many as 200,000,000 volumes had been manufactured by 1600, it is no wonder that

[1] The population of that Europe where print was then known was about 100,000,000. Lucien Febvre and Henri-Jean Martin, *The Coming of the Book,* (New Left, 1976), pp. 248–49. [Anderson]

[2] Emblematic is Marco Polo's *Travels,* which remained largely unknown till its first printing in 1559. *The Travels of Marco Polo,* trans. and ed. William Marsden (London and New York: Everyman, 1945), p. xiii. [Anderson]

[3] See Walter Benjamin's *The Work of Art in an Age of Mechanical Reproduction,* p. 712.

Francis Bacon believed that print had changed "the appearance and state of the world."[4]

One of the earlier forms of capitalist enterprise, book-publishing, felt all of capitalism's restless search for markets. The early printers established branches all over Europe: "in this way a veritable 'international' of publishing houses, which ignored national [sic] frontiers, was created."[5] And since the years 1500–1550 were a period of exceptional European prosperity, publishing shared in the general boom. "More than at any other time" it was "a great industry under the control of wealthy capitalists."[6] Naturally, "booksellers were primarily concerned to make a profit and to sell their products, and consequently they sought out first and foremost those works which were of interest to the largest possible number of their contemporaries."[7]

The initial market was literate Europe, a wide but thin stratum of Latin-readers. Saturation of this market took about a hundred and fifty years. The determinative fact about Latin — aside from its sacrality — was that it was a language of bilinguals. Relatively few were born to speak it and even fewer, one imagines, dreamed in it. In the sixteenth century the proportion of bilinguals within the total population of Europe was quite small; very likely no larger than the proportion in the world's population today, and — proletarian internationalism notwithstanding — in the centuries to come. Then and now the bulk of mankind is monoglot. The logic of capitalism thus meant

that once the elite Latin market was saturated, the potentially huge markets represented by the monoglot masses would beckon. To be sure, the Counter-Reformation encouraged a temporary resurgence of Latin-publishing, but by the mid-seventeenth century the movement was in decay, and fervently Catholic libraries replete. Meantime, a Europe-wide shortage of money made printers think more and more of peddling cheap editions in the vernaculars.[8]

The revolutionary vernacularizing thrust of capitalism was given further impetus by three extraneous factors, two of which contributed directly to the rise of national consciousness. The first, and ultimately the least important, was a change in the character of Latin itself. Thanks to the labors of the Humanists in reviving the broad literature of pre-Christian antiquity and spreading it through the print-market, a new appreciation of the sophisticated stylistic achievements of the ancients was apparent among the trans-European intelligentsia. The Latin they now aspired to write became more and more Ciceronian, and, by the same token, increasingly removed from ecclesiastical and everyday life. In this way it acquired an esoteric quality quite different from that of Church Latin in medieval times. For the older Latin was not arcane because of its subject matter or style, but simply because it was written at all, i.e. because of its status as *text*. Now it became arcane because of what was written, because of the language-in-itself.

Second was the impact of the Reformation, which, at the same time, owed much of its success to print-capitalism. Before the age of print, Rome easily won every war against heresy in Western Europe because it always had better internal lines of communication than its challengers. But when in 1517 Martin Luther nailed his theses to the chapel-door in Wittenberg, they were printed up in German translation, and "within 15 days [had been] seen in every part of the country."[9] In the two decades 1520–1540 three times as many books were published in German as in the period 1500–1520, an astonishing transformation to which Luther was absolutely central. His

[4]Quoted in Elizabeth Eisenstein, "Some Conjectures about the Impact of Printing on Western Society and Thought: A Preliminary Report," *Journal of Modern History* 40 (1968): 56. [Anderson] It was in *Novum Organum* (1620) that Bacon said that "printing, gunpowder, and the magnetic compass" had changed the world.

[5]Febvre and Martin, *The Coming of the Book*, p. 122. (The original text, however, speaks simply of "par-dessus les frontières." *L'Apparition du livre*, [Paris: Michel, 1958], p. 184.) [Anderson]

[6]Ibid., p. 187. The original text speaks of "puissants" (powerful) rather than "wealthy" capitalists. *L'Apparition*, p. 281. [Anderson]

[7]"Hence the introduction of printing was in this respect a stage on the road to our present society of mass consumption and standardisation." Ibid., pp. 259–60. (The original text has "une civilisation de masse et de standardisation," which may be better rendered "standardised, mass civilization." *L'Apparition*, p. 394). [Anderson]

[8]Ibid., p. 195. [Anderson]

[9]Ibid., pp. 289–90. [Anderson]

works represented no less than one third of *all* German-language books sold between 1518 and 1525. Between 1522 and 1546, a total of 430 editions (whole or partial) of his Biblical translations appeared. "We have here for the first time a truly mass readership and a popular literature within everybody's reach."[10] In effect, Luther became the first best-selling author *so known*. Or, to put it another way, the first writer who could "sell" his *new* books on the basis of his name.[11]

Where Luther led, others quickly followed, opening the colossal religious propaganda war that raged across Europe for the next century. In this titanic "battle for men's minds," Protestantism was always fundamentally on the offensive, precisely because it knew how to make use of the expanding vernacular print-market being created by capitalism, while the Counter-Reformation defended the citadel of Latin. The emblem for this is the Vatican's *Index Librorum Prohibitorum* — to which there was no Protestant counterpart — a novel catalogue made necessary by the sheer volume of printed subversion. Nothing gives a better sense of this siege mentality than François I's panicked 1535 ban on the printing of *any* books in his realm — on pain of death by hanging! The reason for both the ban and its unenforceability was that by then his realm's eastern borders were ringed with Protestant states and cities producing a massive stream of smugglable print. To take Calvin's Geneva alone: between 1533 and 1540 only 42 editions were published there, but the numbers swelled to 527 between 1550 and 1564, by which latter date no less than 40 separate printing-presses were working overtime.[12]

The coalition between Protestantism and print-capitalism, exploiting cheap popular editions, quickly created large new reading publics — not least among merchants and women, who typically knew little or no Latin — and simultaneously

[10]Ibid., pp. 291–95. [Anderson]

[11]From this point it was only a step to the situation in seventeenth-century France where Corneille, Molière, and La Fontaine could sell their manuscript tragedies and comedies directly to publishers, who bought them as excellent investments in view of their authors' market reputations. Ibid., p. 161. [Anderson]

[12]Ibid., pp. 310–15. [Anderson]

mobilized them for politico-religious purposes. Inevitably, it was not merely the Church that was shaken to its core. The same earthquake produced Europe's first important non-dynastic, non-city states in the Dutch Republic and the Commonwealth of the Puritans. (François I's panic was as much political as religious.)

Third was the slow, geographically uneven, spread of particular vernaculars as instruments of administrative centralization by certain well-positioned would-be absolutist monarchs. Here it is useful to remember that the universality of Latin in medieval Western Europe never corresponded to a universal political system. The contrast with Imperial China, where the reach of the mandarinal bureaucracy and of painted characters largely coincided, is instructive. In effect, the political fragmentation of Western Europe after the collapse of the Western Empire meant that no sovereign could monopolize Latin and make it his-and-only-his language-of-state, and thus Latin's religious authority never had a true political analogue.

The birth of administrative vernaculars predated both print and the religious upheaval of the sixteenth century, and must therefore be regarded (at least initially) as an independent factor in the erosion of the sacred imagined community. At the same time, nothing suggests that any deep-seated ideological, let alone proto-national, impulses underlay this vernacularization where it occurred. The case of "England" — on the northwestern periphery of Latin Europe — is here especially enlightening. Prior to the Norman Conquest, the language of the court, literary and administrative, was Anglo-Saxon. For the next century and a half virtually all royal documents were composed in Latin. Between about 1200 and 1350 this state-Latin was superseded by Norman French. In the meantime, a slow fusion between this language of a foreign ruling class and the Anglo-Saxon of the subject population produced Early English. The fusion made it possible for the new language to take its turn, after 1362, as the language of the courts — and for the opening of Parliament. Wycliffe's vernacular manuscript Bible followed in 1382.[13] It is essential to bear in

[13]Seton-Watson, *Nations and States*, pp. 28–29; Bloch, *Feudal Society*, I, p. 25. [Anderson]

mind that this sequence was a series of "state," not "national," languages; and that the state concerned covered at various times not only today's England and Wales, but also portions of Ireland, Scotland *and France*. Obviously, huge elements of the subject populations knew little or nothing of Latin, Norman French, or Early English.[14] Not till almost a century *after* Early English's political enthronement was London's power swept out of "France."

On the Seine, a similar movement took place, if at a slower pace. As Bloch wryly puts it, "French, that is to say a language which, since it was regarded as merely a corrupt form of Latin, took several centuries to raise itself to literary dignity,"[15] only became the official language of the courts of justice in 1539, when François I issued the Edict of Villers-Cotterêts.[16] In other dynastic realms Latin survived much longer — under the Habsburgs well into the nineteenth century. In still others, "foreign" vernaculars took over: in the eighteenth century the languages of the Romanov court were French and German.[17]

In every instance, the "choice" of language appears as a gradual, unselfconscious, pragmatic, not to say haphazard development. As such, it was utterly different from the selfconscious language policies pursued by nineteenth-century dynasts confronted with the rise of hostile popular linguistic-nationalisms. One clear sign of the difference is that the old administrative languages were *just that*: languages used by and for officialdoms for their own inner convenience. There was no idea of systematically imposing the language on the dynasts' various subject populations.[18] Nonetheless, the elevation of these vernaculars to the status of languages-of-power, where, in one sense, they were competitors with Latin (French in Paris, [Early] English in London), made its own contribution to the decline of the imagined community of Christendom.

At bottom, it is likely that the esotericization of Latin, the Reformation, and the haphazard development of administrative vernaculars are significant, in the present context, primarily in a negative sense — in their contributions to the dethronement of Latin. It is quite possible to conceive of the emergence of the new imagined national communities without any one, perhaps all, of them being present. What, in a positive sense, made the new communities imaginable was a half-fortuitous, but explosive, interaction between a system of production and productive relations (capitalism), a technology of communications (print), and the fatality of human linguistic diversity.[19]

The element of fatality is essential. For whatever superhuman feats capitalism was capable of, it found in death and languages two tenacious adversaries.[20] Particular languages can die or be wiped out, but there was and is no possibility of humankind's general linguistic unification. Yet this mutual incomprehensibility was historically of only slight importance until capitalism and print created monoglot mass reading publics.

While it is essential to keep in mind an idea of fatality, in the sense of a *general* condition of irremediable linguistic diversity, it would be a

---

[14]We should not assume that administrative vernacular unification was immediately or fully achieved. It is unlikely that the Guyenne ruled from London was ever primarily administered in Early English. [Anderson]

[15]Marc Bloch, *Feudal Society*, I (Chicago: U Chicago P, 1961), p. 98. [Anderson]

[16]Hugh Seton-Watson, *Nations and States: An Enquiry into the Origins of Nations and the Politics of Nationalism* (Boulder: Westview, 1977), p. 48. [Anderson]

[17]Ibid., p. 83. [Anderson]

[18]An agreeable confirmation of this point is provided by François I, who, as we have seen, banned all printing of books in 1535 and made French the language of his courts four years later! [Anderson]

[19]It was not the first "accident" of its kind. Febvre and Martin note that while a visible bourgeoisie already existed in Europe by the late thirteenth century, paper did not come into general use until the end of the fourteenth. Only paper's smooth plane surface made the mass reproduction of texts and pictures possible — and this did not occur for still another seventy-five years. But paper was not a European invention. It floated in from another history — China's — through the Islamic world. *The Coming of the Book*, pp. 22, 30, and 45. [Anderson]

[20]We still have no giant multinationals in the world of publishing. [Anderson] True in 1983 but true no longer: multinationals dominate book publishing today. Bertelsmann A.G., based in Germany, owns the American group Random House, Inc.; Rupert Murdoch's News Corp owns the international HarperCollins, based in the U.S.A. and the U.K., and much else; the book you hold, published by Bedford/St.Martin's is a division of Von Holtzbrinck of Stuttgart, Germany, an honor it shares with Farrar, Straus and Giroux and Henry Holt.

mistake to equate this fatality with that common element in nationalist ideologies which stresses the primordial fatality of *particular* languages and their association with *particular* territorial units. The essential thing is the *interplay* between fatality, technology, and capitalism. In pre-print Europe, and, of course, elsewhere in the world, the diversity of spoken languages, those languages that for their speakers were (and are) the warp and woof of their lives, was immense; so immense, indeed, that had print-capitalism sought to exploit each potential oral vernacular market, it would have remained a capitalism of petty proportions. But these varied idiolects were capable of being assembled, within definite limits, into print-languages far fewer in number. The very arbitrariness of any system of signs for sounds facilitated the assembling process.[21] (At the same time, the more ideographic[22] the signs, the vaster the potential assembling zone. One can detect a sort of descending hierarchy here from algebra through Chinese and English, to the regular syllabaries of French or Indonesian.) Nothing served to "assemble" related vernaculars more than capitalism, which, within the limits imposed by grammars and syntaxes, created mechanically reproduced print-languages capable of dissemination through the market.[23]

These print-languages laid the bases for national consciousnesses in three distinct ways. First and foremost, they created unified fields of exchange and communication below Latin and

[21] For a useful discussion of this point, see S. H. Steinberg, *Five Hundred Years of Printing*, chapter 5. That the sign *ough* is pronounced differently in the words although, bough, lough, rough, cough, and hiccough, shows both the idiolectic variety out of which the now-standard spelling of English emerged, and the ideographic quality of the final product. [Anderson]

[22] An ideograph is a single character symbolizing an idea, as in Chinese.

[23] I say "nothing served . . . more than capitalism" advisedly. Both Steinberg and Eisenstein come close to theomorphizing "print," *qua* print as the genius of modern history. Febvre and Martin never forget that behind print stand printers and publishing firms. It is worth remembering in this context that although printing was invented first in China, possibly 500 years before its appearance in Europe, it had no major, let alone revolutionary impact — precisely because of the absence of capitalism there. [Anderson]

above the spoken vernaculars. Speakers of the huge variety of Frenches, Englishes, or Spanishes, who might find it difficult or even impossible to understand one another in conversation, became capable of comprehending one another via print and paper. In the process, they gradually became aware of the hundreds of thousands, even millions, of people in their particular language-field, and at the same time that *only those* hundreds of thousands, or millions, so belonged. These fellow-readers, to whom they were connected through print, formed, in their secular, particular, visible invisibility, the embryo of the nationally imagined community.

Second, print-capitalism gave a new fixity to language, which in the long run helped to build that image of antiquity so central to the subjective idea of the nation. As Febvre and Martin remind us, the printed book kept a permanent form, capable of virtually infinite reproduction, temporally and spatially. It was no longer subject to the individualizing and "unconsciously modernizing" habits of monastic scribes. Thus, while twelfth-century French differed markedly from that written by Villon[24] in the fifteenth, the rate of change slowed decisively in the sixteenth. "By the 17th century languages in Europe had generally assumed their modern forms."[25] To put it another way, for three centuries now these stabilized print-languages have been gathering a darkening varnish; the words of our seventeenth-century forebears are accessible to us in a way that to Villon his twelfth-century ancestors were not.

Third, print-capitalism created languages-of-power of a kind different from the older administrative vernaculars. Certain dialects inevitably were "closer" to each print-language and dominated their final forms. Their disadvantaged cousins, still assimilable to the emerging print-language, lost caste, above all because they were unsuccessful (or only relatively

[24] François Villon (1431–1465?), the best known French poet of the Middle Ages (*The Legacy*, 1456; *The Testament*, 1461).

[25] *The Coming of the Book*, p. 319. Cf. *L'Apparition*, p. 477: "Au XVIIe siècle, les langues nationales apparaissent un peu partout cristallisées." [Anderson]

successful) in insisting on their own print-form. "Northwestern German" became Platt Deutsch, a largely spoken, thus sub-standard, German, because it was assimilable to print-German in a way that Bohemian spoken-Czech was not. High German, the King's English, and, later, Central Thai, were correspondingly elevated to a new politico-cultural eminence. (Hence the struggles in late-twentieth-century Europe by certain "sub-"nationalities to change their subordinate status by breaking firmly into print — and radio.)

It remains only to emphasize that in their origins, the fixing of print-languages and the differentiation of status between them were largely unselfconscious processes resulting from the explosive interaction between capitalism, technology and human linguistic diversity. But as with so much else in the history of nationalism, once "there," they could become formal models to be imitated, and, where expedient, consciously exploited in a Machiavellian spirit. Today, the Thai government actively discourages attempts by foreign missionaries to provide its hill-tribe minorities with their own transcription-systems and to develop publications in their own languages: the same government is largely indifferent to what these minorities *speak*. The fate of the Turkic-speaking peoples in the zones incorporated into today's Turkey, Iran, Iraq, and the USSR is especially exemplary.[26] A family of spoken languages, once everywhere assemblable, thus comprehensible, within an Arabic orthography, has lost that unity as a result of conscious manipulations. To heighten Turkish-Turkey's national consciousness at the expense of any wider Islamic identification, Atatürk imposed compulsory romanization.[27] The Soviet authorities followed suit, first with an anti-Islamic, anti-Persian compulsory romanization, then, in Stalin's 1930s, with a Russifying compulsory Cyrillicization.[28]

We can summarize the conclusions to be drawn from the argument thus far by saying that the convergence of capitalism and print technology on the fatal diversity of human language created the possibility of a new form of imagined community, which in its basic morphology set the stage for the modern nation. The potential stretch of these communities was inherently limited, and, at the same time, bore none but the most fortuitous relationship to existing political boundaries (which were, on the whole, the highwater marks of dynastic expansionisms).

Yet it is obvious that while today almost all modern self-conceived nations — and also nation-states — have "national print-languages," many of them have these languages in common, and in others only a tiny fraction of the population "uses" the national language in conversationor on paper. The nation-states of Spanish America or those of the "Anglo-Saxon family" are conspicuous examples of the first outcome; many ex-colonial states, particularly in Africa, of the second. In other words, the concrete formation of contemporary nation-states is by no means isomorphic with the determinate reach of particular print-languages. To account for the discontinuity-in-connectedness between print-languages, national consciousness, and nation-states, it is necessary to turn to the large cluster of new political entities that sprang up in the Western hemisphere between 1776 and 1838, all of which self-consciously defined themselves as nations, and, with the interesting exception of Brazil, as (non-dynastic) republics. For not only were they historically the first such states to emerge on the world stage, and therefore inevitably provided the first real models of what such states should "look like," but their numbers and contemporary births offer fruitful ground for comparative enquiry.

[26]With the breakup of the Soviet Union, these Turkic-speaking peoples of Central Asia are located today in the new nations of Uzbekistan, Turkmenistan, Tajikistan, Kyrgyzstan, and Kazakhstan. Their Turkic languages were originally written in Arabic script, then the Cyrillic alphabet used for Russian; today the Latin alphabet is coming into fashion as these nations break ties with Russia and look west toward Europe.

[27]Hans Kohn, *The Age of Nationalism: The First Era of Global History* (New York: Harper; 1962), p. 108. It is probably only fair to add that Kemal also hoped thereby to align Turkish nationalism with the modern, romanized civilization of Western Europe. [Anderson]

[28]Seton-Watson, *Nations and States*, p. 317. [Anderson]

Gayatri Chakravorty Spivak
b. 1942

The chief spokesperson for "subaltern studies," Gayatri Chakravorty Spivak was born in Calcutta and educated at the University of Calcutta and at Cornell University. Her translation of and introduction to Jacques Derrida's Of Grammatology (1967) made her a national figure, and her critical method continues to feature the deconstructive turn. But she is even more widely known today as a postcolonial theorist from a global feminist Marxist perspective. Her social commitments are not merely theoretical: Professor Spivak is active in rural literacy teacher training on the grassroots level in India and Bangladesh. Spivak was the Andrew W. Mellon Professor of English at the University of Pittsburgh before becoming Avalon Professor at Columbia University in 1991. Spivak's books include Myself I Must Remake: The Life and Poetry of W. B. Yeats (1974), In Other Worlds: Essays in Cultural Politics (1988), Selected Subaltern Studies (ed., 1988), The Post-Colonial Critic (1990), Outside in the Teaching Machine (1993), A Critique of Postcolonial Reason: Toward a History of the Vanishing Present (1999), Death of a Discipline (2003), An Aesthetic Education in the Era of Globalization (2012), and Readings (2014). Her work in progress includes a book on W. E. B. DuBois and the General Strike. The present selection, originally published in Critical Inquiry 12 (Autumn 1985), is here included because of its important place in the history of postcolonial theory. Over the twenty years since it was first published, however, Spivak has changed her position on many of the issues she raised here, and the interested reader must be referred to the revised version, which appears in her Critique of Postcolonial Reason (1999), pp. 112–48.

Three Women's Texts and a Critique of Imperialism

It should not be possible to read nineteenth-century British literature without remembering that imperialism, understood as England's social mission, was a crucial part of the cultural representation of England to the English. The role of literature in the production of cultural representation should not be ignored. These two obvious "facts" continue to be disregarded in the reading of nineteenth-century British literature. This itself attests to the continuing success of the imperialist project, displaced and dispersed into more modern forms.

If these "facts" were remembered, not only in the study of British literature but in the study of the literatures of the European colonizing cultures of the great age of imperialism, we would produce a narrative, in literary history, of the "worlding" of what is now called "the Third World." To consider the Third World as distant cultures, exploited but with rich intact literary heritages waiting to be recovered, interpreted, and curricularized in English translation fosters the emergence of "the Third World" as a signifier that allows us to forget that "worlding," even as it expands the empire of the literary discipline.[1]

It seems particularly unfortunate when the emergent perspective of feminist criticism reproduces the axioms of imperialism. A basically isolationist admiration for the literature of the

[1] My notion of the "worlding" of a "world" upon what must be assumed to be uninscribed earth is a vulgarization of Martin Heidegger's idea; see "The Origin of the Work of Art," *Poetry, Language, Thought*, trans. Albert Hofstadter (New York, 1977), pp. 17–87. [Spivak]

female subject in Europe and Anglo-America establishes the high feminist norm. It is supported and operated by an information-retrieval approach to "Third-World" literature which often employs a deliberately "non-theoretical" methodology with self-conscious rectitude.

In this essay, I will attempt to examine the operation of the "worlding" of what is today "the Third World" by what has become a cult text of feminism: *Jane Eyre*.[2] I plot the novel's reach and grasp, and locate its structural motors. I read *Wide Sargasso Sea* as *Jane Eyre's* reinscription and *Frankenstein* as an analysis — even a deconstruction — of a "worlding" such as *Jane Eyre's*.[3]

I need hardly mention that the object of my investigation is the printed book, not its "author." To make such a distinction is, of course, to ignore the lessons of deconstruction. A deconstructive critical approach would loosen the binding of the book, undo the opposition between verbal text and the biography of the named subject "Charlotte Brontë," and see the two as each other's "scene of writing." In such a reading, the life that writes itself as "my life" is as much a production in psychosocial space (other names can be found) as the book that is written by the holder of that named life — a book that is then consigned to what *is* most often recognized as genuinely "social": the world of publication and distribution.[4] To touch Brontë's "life" in such a way, however, would be too risky here. We must rather strategically take shelter in an essentialism which, not wishing to lose the important advantages won by U.S. mainstream feminism, will continue to honor the suspect binary oppositions — book and author, individual and history — and start with an assurance

of the following sort: my readings here do not seek to undermine the excellence of the individual artist. If even minimally successful, the readings will incite a degree of rage against the imperialist narrativization of history, that it should produce so abject a script for her. I provide these assurances to allow myself some room to situate feminist individualism in its historical determination rather than simply to canonize it as feminism as such.

Sympathetic U.S. feminists have remarked that I do not do justice to Jane Eyre's subjectivity. A word of explanation is perhaps in order. The broad strokes of my presuppositions are that what is at stake, for feminist individualism in the age of imperialism, is precisely the making of human beings, the constitution and "interpellation" of the subject not only as individual but as "individualist."[5] This stake is represented on two registers: childbearing and soul making. The first is domestic-society-through-sexual-reproduction cathected[6] as "companionate love"; the second is the imperialist project cathected as civil-society-through-social-mission. As the female individualist, not-quite/not-male, articulates herself in shifting relationship to what is at stake, the "native female" as such (*within* discourse, *as* a signifier) is excluded from any share in this emerging norm.[7] If we read this account from

[2]See Charlotte Brontë, *Jane Eyre* (New York, 1960); all further references to this work, abbreviated *JE*, will be included in the text. [Spivak]

[3]See Jean Rhys, *Wide Sargasso Sea* (Harmondsworth, 1996); all further references to this work, abbreviated *WSS*, will be included in the text. And see Mary Shelley, *Frankenstein; or, the Modern Prometheus* (New York, 1965); all further references to this work, abbreviated *F*, will be included in the text. [Spivak]

[4]I have tried to do this in my essay "Unmaking and Making in *To the Lighthouse*," in *Women and Language in Literature and Society*, ed. Sally McConnell-Ginet, Ruth Borker, and Nelly Furman (New York, 1980), pp. 310–27. [Spivak]

[5]As always, I take my formula from Louis Althusser, "Ideology and Ideological State Apparatuses (Notes towards an Investigation)," *Lenin and Philosophy and Other Essays*, trans. Ben Brewster (New York, 1971), pp. 127–86. For an acute differentiation between the individual and individualism, see V. N. Vološinov, *Marxism and the Philosophy of Language*, trans. Ladislav Matejka and I. R. Titunik, *Studies in Language*, vol. 1 (New York, 1973), pp. 93–94 and 152–53. For a "straight" analysis of the roots and ramifications of English "individualism," see C. B. MacPherson, *The Political Theory of Possessive Individualism: Hobbes to Locke* (Oxford, 1962). I am grateful to Jonathan Rée for bringing this book to my attention and for giving a careful reading of all but the very end of the present essay. [Spivak] For Althusser, see p. 738.

[6]In Freudian terminology, to cathect is to invest emotional energy (libido) in some way.

[7]I am constructing an analogy with Homi Bhabha's powerful notion of "not-quite/not white" in his "Of Mimicry and Man: The Ambiguity of Colonial Discourse," *October* 28 (Spring 1984): 132. I should also add that I use the word "native" here in reaction to the term "Third-World Woman." It cannot, of course, apply with equal historical justice to both the West Indian and the Indian contexts nor to contexts of imperialism by transportation. [Spivak]

To develop further the notion that my stance need not be an accusing one, I will refer to a passage from Roberto Fernández Retamar's "Caliban."[8] José Enrique Rodó had argued in 1900 that the model for the Latin American intellectual in relationship to Europe could be Shakespeare's Ariel.[9] In 1971 Retamar, denying the possibility of an identifiable "Latin American Culture," recast the model as Caliban. Not surprisingly, this powerful exchange still excludes any specific consideration of the civilizations of the Maya, the Aztecs, the Incas, or the smaller nations of what is now called Latin America. Let us note carefully that, at this stage of my argument, this "conversation" between Europe and Latin America (without a specific consideration of the political economy of the "worlding" of the "native") provides a sufficient thematic description of our attempt to confront the ethnocentric and reverse-ethnocentric benevolent double bind (that is, considering the "native" as object for enthusiastic information-retrieval and thus denying its own "worlding") that I sketched in my opening paragraphs.

In a moving passage in "Caliban," Retamar locates both Caliban and Ariel in the postcolonial intellectual:

There is no real Ariel–Caliban polarity: both are slaves in the hands of Prospero, the foreign magician. But Caliban is the rude and unconquer-able master of the island, while Ariel, a creature of the air, although also a child of the isle, is the intellectual.

The deformed Caliban — enslaved, robbed of his island, and taught the language by Prospero — rebukes

him thus: "You taught me language, and my profit on't/ Is, I know how to curse." ["C," pp. 28, 11]

As we attempt to unlearn our so-called privilege as Ariel and "seek from [a certain] Caliban the honor of a place in his rebellious and glorious ranks," we do not ask that our students and colleagues should emulate us but that they should attend to us ("C," p. 72). If, however, we are driven by a nostalgia for lost origins, we too run the risk of effacing the "native" and stepping forth as "the real Caliban," of forgetting that he is a name in a play, an inaccessible blankness circumscribed by an interpretable text.[10] The stagings of Caliban work alongside the narrativization of history: claiming to be Caliban legitimizes the very individualism that we must persistently attempt to undermine from within.

Elizabeth Fox-Genovese, in an article on history and women's history, shows us how to define the historical moment of feminism in the West in terms of female access to individualism.[11] The battle for female individualism plays itself out within the larger theater of the establishment of meritocratic individualism, indexed in the aesthetic field by the ideology of "the creative imagination." Fox-Genovese's presupposition will guide us into the beautifully orchestrated opening of *Jane Eyre*.

It is a scene of the marginalization and privatization of the protagonist: "There was no possibility of taking a walk that day. . . . Out-door exercise was now out of the question, I was glad of it." Brontë writes (*JE*, p. 9). The movement continues as Jane breaks the rules of the appropriate topography of withdrawal. The family at the center withdraws into the sanctioned architectural space of the withdrawing room or drawing room; Jane inserts herself — "I slipped in" — into the margin — "A small breakfast-room *adjoined* the drawing room" (*JE*, p. 9; my emphasis).

[8]See Roberto Fernández Retamar, "Caliban: Notes towards a Discussion of Culture in Our America," trans. Lynn Garafola, David Arthur McMurray, and Robert Márquez, *Massachusetts Review* 15 (Winter–Spring 1974): 7–72; all further references to this work, abbreviated "C," will be included in the text. [Spivak]

[9]See José Enrique Rodó, *Ariel*, ed. Gordon Brotherston (Cambridge, 1967). [Spivak]

[10]For an elaboration of "an inaccessible blankness circumscribed by an interpretable text," see my "Can the Subaltern Speak?" *Interpretation of Culture*, eds. Cary Nelson and Lawrence Grossberg (Urbana, Ill., 1988). [Spivak]

[11]See Elizabeth Fox-Genovese, "Placing Women's History in History," *New Left Review* 133 (May–June 1982): 5–29. [Spivak]

The manipulation of the domestic inscription of space within the upwardly mobilizing currents of the eighteenth- and nineteenth-century bourgeoisie in England and France is well known. It seems fitting that the place to which Jane withdraws is not only not the withdrawing room but also not the dining room, the sanctioned place of family meals. Nor is it the library, the appropriate place for reading. The breakfast room "contained a book-case" (*JE*, p. 9). As Rudolph Ackerman wrote in his *Repository* (1823), one of the many manuals of taste in circulation in nineteenth-century England, these low book-cases and stands were designed to "contain all the books that may be desired for a sitting-room without reference to the library."[12] Even in this already triply off-center place, "having drawn the red moreen curtain nearly close, I [Jane] was shrined in double retirement" (*JE*, pp. 9–10).

Here in Jane's self-marginalized uniqueness, the reader becomes her accomplice: the reader and Jane are united — both are reading. Yet Jane still preserves her odd privilege, for she continues never quite doing the proper thing in its proper place. She cares little for reading what is *meant* to be read: the "letter-press." *She* reads the pictures. The power of this singular hermeneutics[13] is precisely that it can make the outside inside. "At intervals, while turning over the leaves of my book, I studied the aspect of that winter afternoon." Under "the clear panes of glass," the rain no longer penetrates, "the drear November day" is rather a one-dimensional "aspect" to be "studied," not decoded like the "letter-press" but, like pictures, deciphered by the unique creative imagination of the marginal individualist (*JE*, p. 10).

Before following the track of this unique imagination, let us consider the suggestion that the progress of *Jane Eyre* can be charted through a sequential arrangement of the family/counter-family dyad. In the novel, we encounter, first, the Reeds as the legal family and Jane, the late Mr. Reed's sister's daughter, as the representative of a near incestuous counter-family; second, the

Brocklehursts, who run the school Jane is sent to, as the legal family and Jane, Miss Temple, and Helen Burns as a counter-family that falls short because it is only a community of women; third, Rochester and the mad Mrs. Rochester as the legal family and Jane and Rochester as the illicit counter-family. Other items may be added to the thematic chain in this sequence: Rochester and Céline Varens as structurally functional counter-family; Rochester and Blanche Ingram as dissimulation of legality — and so on. It is during this sequence that Jane is moved from the counter-family to the family-in-law. In the next sequence, it is Jane who restores full family status to the as-yet-incomplete community of siblings, the Riverses. The final sequence of the book is a *community of families*, with Jane, Rochester, and their children at the center.

In terms of the narrative energy of the novel, how is Jane moved from the place of the counter-family to the family-in-law? It is the active ideology of imperialism that provides the discursive field.

(My working definition of "discursive field" must assume the existence of discrete "systems of signs" at hand in the socius,[14] each based on a specific axiomatics. I am identifying these systems as discursive fields. "Imperialism as social mission" generates the possibility of one such axiomatics. How the individual artist taps the discursive field at hand with a sure touch, if not with transhistorical clairvoyance, in order to make the narrative structure move I hope to demonstrate through the following example. It is crucial that we extend our analysis of this example beyond the minimal diagnosis of "racism.")

Let us consider the figure of Bertha Mason, a figure produced by the axiomatics of imperialism. Through Bertha Mason, the white Jamaican Creole, Brontë renders the human/animal frontier as acceptably indeterminate, so that a good greater than the letter of the Law can be broached. Here is the celebrated passage, given in the voice of Jane:

> In the deep shade, at the further end of the room, a figure ran backwards and forwards. What it

[12]Rudolph Ackerman, *The Repository of Arts, Literature, Commerce, Manufactures, Fashions, and Politics* (London, 1823), p. 310. [Spivak]

[13]Mode of interpretation.

[14]Individual considered as a unit of society.

was, whether beast or human being, one could not . . . tell: it grovelled, seemingly, on all fours; it snatched and growled like some strange wild animal: but it was covered with clothing, and a quantity of dark, grizzled hair, wild as a mane, hid its head and face. [*JE*, p. 295]

In a matching passage, given in the voice of Rochester speaking *to* Jane, Brontë presents the imperative for a shift beyond the Law as divine injunction rather than human motive. In the terms of my essay, we might say that this is the register not of mere marriage or sexual reproduction but of Europe and its not-yet-human Other, of soul making. The field of imperial conquest is here inscribed as Hell:

'One night I had been awakened by her yells . . . it was a fiery West Indian night. . . .

'"This life," said I at last, "is hell! — this is the air — those are the sounds of the bottomless pit! I *have a right to deliver myself from it if I can.* . . . Let me break away, and go home to God!" . . .

'"A wind fresh from Europe blew over the ocean and rushed through the open casement: the storm broke, streamed, thundered, blazed, and the air grew pure. . . . It was true Wisdom that consoled me in that hour, and showed me the right path. . . .

'"The sweet wind from Europe was still whispering in the refreshed leaves, and the Atlantic was thundering in glorious liberty. . . .

'"Go," said Hope, "and live again in Europe. . . . You have done all that God and Humanity require of you."' [*JE*, pp. 310–11; my emphasis]

It is the unquestioned ideology of imperialist axiomatics, then, that conditions Jane's move from the counter-family set to the set of the family-in-law. Marxist critics such as Terry Eagleton have seen this only in terms of the ambiguous *class* position of the governess.[15] Sandra Gilbert and Susan Gubar, on the other hand, have seen Bertha Mason only in psychological terms, as Jane's dark double.[16]

I will not enter the critical debates that offer themselves here. Instead, I will develop the suggestion that nineteenth-century feminist individualism

could conceive of a "greater" project than access to the closed circle of the nuclear family. This is the project of soul making beyond "mere" sexual reproduction. Here the native "subject" is not almost an animal but rather the object of what might be termed the terrorism of the categorical imperative.

I am using "Kant" in this essay as a metonym for the most flexible ethical moment in the European eighteenth century. Kant words the categorical imperative, conceived as the universal moral law given by pure reason, in this way: "In all creation every thing one chooses and over which one has any power, may be used *merely as means*; man alone, and with him every rational creature, *is an end in himself.*" It is thus a moving displacement of Christian ethics from religion to philosophy. As Kant writes: "With this agrees very well the possibility of such a command as: *Love God above everything, and thy neighbor as thyself.* For as a command it requires respect for a law which commands *love* and does not leave it to our own arbitrary choice to make this our principle."[17]

The "categorical" in Kant cannot be adequately represented in determinately grounded action. The dangerous transformative power of philosophy, however, is that its formal subtlety can be travestied in the service of the state. Such a travesty in the case of the categorical imperative can justify the imperialist project by producing the following formula: *make* the heathen into a human so that he can be treated as an end in himself.[18] This project

[15] See Terry Eagleton, *Myths of Power: A Marxist Study of the Brontës* (London, 1975): this is one of the general presuppositions of his book. [Spivak]

[16] See Sandra M. Gilbert and Susan Gubar, *The Madwoman in the Attic: The Woman Writer and the Nineteenth-Century Literary Imagination* (New Haven, Conn., 1979), pp. 360–62. [Spivak] For Gilbert and Gubar, see p. 902.

[17] Immanuel Kant, *Critique of Practical Reason, The "Critique of Pure Reason," the "Critique of Practical Reason" and Other Ethical Treatises, the "Critique of Judgement,"* trans. J. M. D. Meiklejohn et al. (Chicago, 1952), pp. 328, 326. [Spivak]

[18] I have tried to justify the reduction of sociohistorical problems to formulas or propositions in my essay "Can the Subaltern Speak?" The "travesty" I speak of does not befall the Kantian ethic in its purity as an accident but rather exists within its lineaments as a possible supplement. On the register of the human being as child rather than heathen, my formula can be found, for example, in "What Is Enlightenment?" in Kant, *"Foundations of the Metaphysics of Morals," "What Is Enlightenment?" and a Passage from "The Metaphysics of Morals,"* trans. and ed. Lewis White Beck (Chicago, 1950). I have profited from discussing Kant with Jonathan Rée. [Spivak]

is presented as a sort of tangent in *Jane Eyre*, a tangent that escapes the closed circle of the *narrative* conclusion. The tangent narrative is the story of St. John Rivers, who is granted the important task of concluding the *text*.

At the novel's end, the *allegorical* language of Christian psychobiography — rather than the textually constituted and seemingly *private* grammar of the creative imagination which we noted in the novel's opening — marks the inaccessibility of the imperialist project as such to the nascent "feminist" scenario. The concluding passage of *Jane Eyre* places St. John Rivers within the fold of *Pilgrim's Progress*.[19] Eagleton pays no attention to this but accepts the novel's ideological lexicon, which establishes St. John Rivers' heroism by identifying a life in Calcutta with an unquestioning choice of death. Gilbert and Gubar, by calling *Jane Eyre* "Plain Jane's Progress," see the novel as simply replacing the male protagonist with the female. They do not notice the distance between sexual reproduction and soul making, both actualized by the unquestioned idiom of imperialist presuppositions evident in the last part of *Jane Eyre*:

> Firm, faithful, and devoted, full of energy, and zeal, and truth, [St. John Rivers] labours for his race. . . . His is the sternness of the warrior Greatheart, who guards his pilgrim convoy from the onslaught of Apollyon. . . . His is the ambition of the high master-spirit[s] . . . who stand without fault before the throne of God; who share the last mighty victories of the Lamb; who are called, and chosen, and faithful. [*JE*, p. 455]

Earlier in the novel, St. John Rivers himself justifies the project: "My vocation? My great work? . . . My hopes of being numbered in the band who have merged all ambitions in the glorious one of bettering their race — of carrying knowledge into the realms of ignorance — of substituting peace for war — freedom for bondage — religion for superstition — the hope of heaven for the fear of hell?" (*JE*, p. 376). Imperialism and its territorial and subject-constituting project are a violent deconstruction of these oppositions.

When Jean Rhys, born on the Caribbean island of Dominica, read *Jane Eyre* as a child, she was moved by Bertha Mason: "I thought I'd try to write her a life."[20] *Wide Sargasso Sea*, the slim novel published in 1965, at the end of Rhys' long career, is that "life."

I have suggested that Bertha's function in *Jane Eyre* is to render indeterminate the boundary between human and animal and thereby to weaken her entitlement under the spirit if not the letter of the Law. When Rhys rewrites the scene in *Jane Eyre* where Jane hears "a snarling, snatching sound, almost like a dog quarrelling" and then encounters a bleeding Richard Mason (*JE*, p. 210), she keeps Bertha's humanity, indeed her sanity as critic of imperialism, intact. Grace Poole, another character originally in *Jane Eyre*, describes the incident to Bertha in *Wide Sargasso Sea*: "So you don't remember that you attacked this gentleman with a knife? . . . I didn't hear all he said except 'I cannot interfere legally between yourself and your husband.' It was when he said 'legally' that you flew at him'" (*WSS*, p. 150). In Rhys' retelling, it is the dissimulation that Bertha discerns in the word "legally" — not an innate bestiality — that prompts her violent *re*action.

In the figure of Antoinette, whom in *Wide Sargasso Sea* Rochester violently renames Bertha, Rhys suggests that so intimate a thing as personal and human identity might be determined by the politics of imperialism. Antoinette, as a white Creole child growing up at the time of emancipation in Jamaica,[21] is caught between the English imperialist and the black native. In recounting Antoinette's development, Rhys reinscribes some thematics of Narcissus.

There are, noticeably, many images of mirroring in the text. I will quote one from the first section. In this passage, Tia is the little black servant girl who is Antoinette's close companion: "We had eaten the same food, slept side by side, bathed in the same river. As I ran, I thought, I will live with Tia and I will be like her. . . . When I was close I saw the jagged stone in her hand but I did

[19]The inset quotation from *Jane Eyre* below alludes to Part II of Bunyan's *Pilgrim's Progress* (1684), the sequel in which Christian's wife, Christiana, follows in her husband's path.

[20]Jean Rhys, in an interview with Elizabeth Vreeland, quoted in Nancy Harrison, *Jean Rhys and the Novel as Women's Text* (Chapel Hill: University of North Carolina P, 1988). This is an excellent, detailed study of Rhys. [Spivak]

[21]Jamaica's slaves were emancipated in 1834.

not see her throw it. . . . We stared at each other, blood on my face, tears on hers. It was as if I saw myself. Like in a looking glass" (*WSS*, p. 38).

A progressive sequence of dreams reinforces this mirror imagery. In its second occurrence, the dream is partially set in a *hortus conclusus*, or "enclosed garden" — Rhys uses the phrase (*WSS*, p. 50) — a Romance rewriting of the Narcissus topos as the place of encounter with Love.[22] In the enclosed garden, Antoinette encounters not Love but a strange threatening voice that says merely "in here," inviting her into a prison which masquerades as the legalization of love (*WSS*, p. 50). In Ovid's *Metamorphoses*, Narcissus' madness is disclosed when he recognizes his Other as his self: "Iste ego sum."[23] Rhys makes Antoinette see her *self* as her Other, Brontë's Bertha. In the last section of *Wide Sargasso Sea*, Antoinette acts out *Jane Eyre*'s conclusion and recognizes herself as the so-called ghost in Thornfield Hall: "I went into the hall again with the tall candle in my hand. It was then that I saw her — the ghost. The woman with streaming hair. She was surrounded by a gilt frame but I knew her" (*WSS*, p. 154). The gilt frame encloses a mirror: as Narcissus' pool reflects the selfed Other, so this "pool" reflects the Othered self. Here the dream sequence ends, with an invocation of none other than Tia, the Other that could not be selfed, because the fracture of imperialism rather than the Ovidian pool intervened. (I will return to this difficult point.) "That was the third time I had my dream, and it ended. . . . I called 'Tia' and jumped and woke" (*WSS*, p. 155). It is now, at the very end of the book, that Antoinette/Bertha can say: "Now at last I know why I was brought here and what I have to do" (*WSS*, pp. 155–56). We can read this as her having been brought into the England of Brontë's novel: "This cardboard house" — a book between cardboard covers — "where I walk at night is not England" (*WSS*, p. 148). In this fictive England, she must play out her role, act

out the transformation of her "self" into that fictive Other, set fire to the house and kill herself, so that Jane Eyre can become the feminist individualist heroine of British fiction. I must read this as an allegory of the general epistemic violence of imperialism, the construction of a self-immolating colonial subject for the glorification of the social mission of the colonizer. At least Rhys sees to it that the woman from the colonies is not sacrificed as an insane animal for her sister's consolidation.

Critics have remarked that *Wide Sargasso Sea* treats the Rochester character with understanding and sympathy.[24] Indeed, he narrates the entire middle section of the book. Rhys makes it clear that he is a victim of the patriarchal inheritance law of entailment rather than of a father's natural preference for the firstborn: in *Wide Sargasso Sea*, Rochester's situation is clearly that of a younger son dispatched to the colonies to buy an heiress. If in the case of Antoinette and her identity, Rhys utilizes the thematics of Narcissus, in the case of Rochester and his patrimony, she touches on the thematics of Oedipus. (In this she has her finger on our "historical moment." If, in the nineteenth century, subject-constitution is represented as childbearing and soul making, in the twentieth century psychoanalysis allows the West to plot the itinerary of the subject from Narcissus [the "imaginary"] to Oedipus [the "symbolic"]. This subject, however, is the normative male subject. In Rhys' reinscription of these themes, divided between the female and the male protagonist, feminism and a critique of imperialism become complicit.)

In place of the "wind from Europe" scene, Rhys substitutes the scenario of a suppressed letter to a father, a letter which would be the "correct" explanation of the tragedy of the book.[25] "I thought about the letter which should

[22] See Louise Vinge, *The Narcissus Theme in Western European Literature Up to the Early Nineteenth Century*, trans. Robert Dewsnap et al. (Lund, 1967), chap. 5. [Spivak]

[23] For a detailed study of this text, see John Brenkman, "Narcissus in the Text," *Georgia Review* 30 (Summer 1976): 293–327. [Spivak] *Iste ego sum* is Latin for 'I am that man.' The phrase is from Ovid, *Metamorphoses* 3: 463.

[24] See, e.g., Thomas F. Staley, *Jean Rhys: A Critical Study* (Austin, Tex., 1979), pp. 108–16; it is interesting to note Staley's masculinist discomfort with this and his consequent dissatisfaction with Rhys' novel. [Spivak]

[25] I have tried to relate castration and suppressed letters in my "The Letter As Cutting Edge," in *Literature and Psychoanalysis: The Question of Reading: Otherwise*, ed. Shoshana Felman (New Haven, Conn., 1981), pp. 208–26. [Spivak]

have been written to England a week ago. Dear Father . . ." (*WSS*, p. 57). This is the first instance: the letter not written. Shortly afterward:

> Dear Father. The thirty thousand pounds have been paid to me without question or condition. No provision made for her (that must be seen to). . . . I will never be a disgrace to you or to my dear brother the son you love. No begging letters, no mean requests. None of the furtive shabby manoeuvres of a younger son. I have sold my soul or you have sold it, and after all is it such a bad bargain? The girl is thought to be beautiful, she is beautiful. And yet . . . [*WSS*, p. 59]

This is the second instance: the letter not sent. The formal letter is uninteresting; I will quote only a part of it:

> Dear Father, we have arrived from Jamaica after an uncomfortable few days. This little estate in the Windward Islands is part of the family property and Antoinette is much attached to it. . . . All is well and has gone according to your plans and wishes. I dealt of course with Richard Mason. . . . He seemed to become attached to me and trusted me completely. This place is very beautiful but my illness has left me too exhausted to appreciate it fully. I will write again in a few days' time. [*WSS*, p. 63]

And so on.

Rhys' version of the Oedipal exchange is ironic, not a closed circle. We cannot know if the letter actually reaches its destination. "I wondered how they got their letters posted," the Rochester figures muses. "I folded mine and put it into a drawer of the desk. . . . There are blanks in my mind that cannot be filled up" (*WSS*, p. 64). It is as if the text presses us to note the analogy between letter and mind.

Rhys denies to Brontë's Rochester the one thing that is supposed to be secured in the Oedipal relay: the Name of the Father, or the patronymic. In *Wide Sargasso Sea*, the character corresponding to Rochester has no name. His writing of the final version of the letter to his father is supervised, in fact, by an image of the *loss* of the patronymic: "There was a crude bookshelf made of three shingles strung together over the desk and I looked at the books, Byron's poems, novels by Sir Walter Scott, *Confessions of an Opium*

Eater . . . and on the last shelf, *Life and Letters of* . . . The rest was eaten away" (*WSS*, p. 63).

Wide Sargasso Sea marks with uncanny clarity the limits of its own discourse in Christophine, Antoinette's black nurse. We may perhaps surmise the distance between *Jane Eyre* and *Wide Sargasso Sea* by remarking that Christophine's unfinished story is the tangent to the latter narrative, as St. John Rivers' story is to the former. Christophine is not a native of Jamaica; she is from Martinique. Taxonomically, she belongs to the category of the good servant rather than that of the pure native. But within these borders, Rhys creates a powerfully suggestive figure.

Christophine is the first interpreter and named speaking subject in the text. "The Jamaican ladies had never approved of my mother, 'because she pretty like pretty self' Christophine said," we read in the book's opening paragraph (*WSS*, p. 15). I have taught this book five times, once in France, once to students who had worked on the book with the well-known Caribbean novelist Wilson Harris, and once at a prestigious institute where the majority of the students were faculty from other universities. It is part of the political argument I am making that all these students blithely stepped over this paragraph without asking or knowing what Christophine's patois, so-called incorrect English, might mean.

Christophine is, of course, a commodified person. "She was your father's wedding present to me" explains Antoinette's mother, "one of his presents" (*WSS*, p. 18). Yet Rhys assigns her some crucial functions in the text. It is Christophine who judges that black ritual practices are culture-specific and cannot be used by whites as cheap remedies for social evils, such as Rochester's lack of love for Antoinette. Most important, it is Christophine alone whom Rhys allows to offer a hard analysis of Rochester's actions, to challenge him in a face-to-face encounter. The entire extended passage is worthy of comment. I quote a brief extract:

> "She is Creole girl, and she have the sun in her. Tell the truth now. She don't come to your house in this place England they tell me about, she don't come to your beautiful house to beg you to marry with her. No, it's you come all the long way to her house — it's you beg her to marry. And she love

you and she give you all she have. Now you say you don't love her and you break her up. What you do with her money, eh?'' [And then Rochester, the white man, comments silently to himself] Her voice was still quiet but with a hiss in it when she said ''money,'' (WSS, p. 130].

Her analysis is powerful enough for the white man to be afraid: ''I no longer felt dazed, tired, half hypnotized, but alert and wary, ready to defend myself'' (WSS, p. 130).

Rhys does not, however, romanticize indi-vidual heroics on the part of the oppressed. When the Man refers to the forces of Law and Order, Christophine recognizes their power. This exposure of civil inequality is emphasized by the fact that, just before the Man's successful threat, Christophine had invoked the emancipation of slaves in Jamaica by proclaiming: ''No chain gang, no tread machine, no dark jail either. This is free country and I am free woman'' (WSS, p. 131).

As I mentioned above, Christophine is tan-gential to this narrative. She cannot be contained by a novel which rewrites a canonical English text within the European novelistic tradition in the interest of the white Creole rather than the native. No perspective critical of imperi-alism can turn the Other into a self, because the project of imperialism has always already historically refracted what might have been the absolutely Other into a domesticated Other that consolidates the imperialist self.[26] The Caliban of Retamar, caught between Europe and Latin America, reflects this predicament. We can read Rhys' reinscription of Narcissus as a thematiza-tion of the same problematic.

Of course, we cannot know Jean Rhys' feel-ings in the matter. We can, however, look at the scene of Christophine's inscription in the text. Immediately after the exchange between her and the Man, well before the conclusion, she is simply driven out of the story, with neither narrative nor characterological explanation or justice. ''Read and write I don't know. Other things I know.' She walked away without looking back'' (WSS, p. 133).

[26]This is the main argument of my ''Can the Subaltern Speak?'' [Spivak].

Indeed, if Rhys rewrites the madwoman's attack on the Man by underlining of the misuse of ''legality,'' she cannot deal with the passage that corresponds to St. John Rivers' own justifica-tion of his martyrdom, for it has been displaced into the current idiom of modernization and development. Attempts to construct the ''Third-World Woman'' as a signifier remind us that the hegemonic definition of literature is itself caught within the history of imperialism. A full literary reinscription cannot easily flourish in the impe-rialist fracture or discontinuity, covered over by an alien legal system masquerading as Law as such, an alien ideology established as only Truth, and a set of human sciences busy establishing the ''native'' as self-consolidating Other.

In the Indian case at least, it would be dif-ficult to find an ideological clue to the planned epistemic violence of imperialism merely by rearranging curricula or syllabi within existing norms of literary pedagogy. For a later period of imperialism — when the constituted colonial subject has firmly taken hold — straightforward experiments of comparison can be undertaken, say, between the functionally witless India of Mrs. Dalloway, on the one hand, and literary texts produced in India in the 1920s, on the other. But the first half of the nineteenth century resists questioning through literature or literary criticism in the narrow sense, because both are implicated in the project of producing Ariel. To reopen the fracture without succumbing to a nostalgia for lost origins, the literary critic must turn to the archives of imperial governance.

In conclusion, I shall look briefly at Mary Shelley's Frankenstein, a text of nascent femi-nism that remains cryptic, I think, simply because it does not speak the language of femi-nist individualism which we have come to hail as the language of high feminism within English literature. It is interesting that Barbara Johnson's brief study tries to rescue this recalcitrant text for the service of feminist autobiography.[27] Alternatively, George Levine reads Frankenstein in the context of the creative imagination and the

[27]See Barbara Johnson, ''My Monster/My Self,'' Diacritics 12 (Summer 1982): 2–10. [Spivak]

nature of the hero. He sees the novel as a book about its own writing and about writing itself, a Romantic allegory of reading within which Jane Eyre as unself-conscious critic would fit quite nicely.[28]

I propose to take *Frankenstein* out of this arena and focus on it in terms of that sense of English cultural identity which I invoked at the opening of this essay. Within that focus we are obliged to admit that, although *Frankenstein* is ostensibly about the origin and evolution of man in our society, it does not deploy the axiomatics of imperialism.

Let me say at once that there is plenty of incidental imperialist sentiment in *Frankenstein*. My point, within the argument of this essay, is that the discursive field of imperialism does not produce unquestioned ideological correlatives for the narrative structuring of the book. The discourse of imperialism surfaces in a curiously powerful way in Shelley's novel, and I will later discuss the moment at which it emerges.

Frankenstein is not a battleground of male and female individualism articulated in terms of sexual reproduction (family and female) and social subject-production (race and male). That binary opposition is undone in Victor Frankenstein's laboratory — an artificial womb where both projects are undertaken simultaneously, though the terms are never openly spelled out. Frankenstein's apparent antagonist is God himself as Maker of Man, but this real competitor is also woman as the maker of children. It is not just that his dream of the death of mother and bride and the actual death of his bride are associated with the visit of his monstrous homoerotic "son" to his bed. On a much more overt level, the monster is a bodied "corpse," unnatural because bereft of a determinable childhood: "No father had watched my infant days, no mother had blessed me with smiles and caresses; or if they had, all my past was now a blot, a blind vacancy in which I distinguished nothing" (*F*, pp. 57, 115). It is Frankenstein's own ambiguous and miscued understanding of the real motive for the monster's vengefulness

that reveals his own competition with woman as maker:

> I created a rational creature and was bound towards him to assure, as far as was in my power, his happiness and well-being. This was my duty, but there was another still paramount to that. My duties towards the beings of my own species had greater claims to my attention because they included a greater proportion of happiness or misery. Urged by this view, I refused, and I did right in refusing, to create a companion for the first creature. [*F*, p. 206]

It is impossible not to notice the accents of transgression inflecting Frankenstein's demolition of his experiment to create the future Eve. Even in the laboratory, the woman-in-the-making is not a bodied corpse but " a human being." The (il)logic of the metaphor bestows on her a prior existence which Frankenstein aborts, rather than an anterior death which he reembodies: "The remains of the half-finished creature, whom I had destroyed, lay scattered on the floor, and I almost felt as if I had mangled the living flesh of a human being" (*F*, p. *163*).

In Shelley's view, man's hubris as soul maker both usurps the place of God and attempts — vainly — to sublate woman's physiological prerogative.[29] Indeed, indulging a Freudian fantasy here, I could urge that, if to give and withhold to/from the mother a phallus is *the* male fetish, then to give and withhold to/from the man a womb might be the female fetish.[30] The icon of the sublimated womb in man is surely his productive brain, the box in the head.

In the judgment of classical psychoanalysis, the phallic mother exists only by virtue of the

[29]Consult the publications of the Feminist International Network for the best overview of the current debate on reproductive technology. [Spivak]

[30]For the male fetish, see Sigmund Freud, "Fetishism," *The Standard Edition of the Complete Psychological Works of Sigmund Freud*, ed. and trans. James Strachey et al., 24 vols. (London, 1953–74), 21: 152–57. For a more "serious" Freudian study of *Frankenstein*, see Mary Jacobus, "Is There a Woman in This Text?" *New Literary History* 14 (Autumn 1982): 117–41. My "fantasy" would of course be disproved by the "fact" that it is more difficult for a woman to assume the position of fetishist than for a man; see Mary Ann Doane, "Film and the Masquerade: Theorising the Female Spectator," *Screen* 23 (Sept./Oct. 1982): 74–87. [Spivak]

[28]See George Levine, *The Realistic Imagination: English Fiction from Frankenstein to Lady Chatterley* (Chicago, 1981), pp. 23–35. [Spivak]

castration-anxious son: in *Frankenstein's* judgment, the hysteric father (Victor Frankenstein gifted with his laboratory — the womb of theoretical reason) cannot produce a daughter. Here the language of racism — the dark side of imperialism understood as social mission — combines with the hysteria of masculinism into the idiom of (the withdrawal of) sexual reproduction rather than subject-constitution. The roles of masculine and feminine individualists are hence reversed and displaced. Frankenstein cannot produce a "daughter" because "she might become ten thousand times more malignant than her mate ... [and because] one of the first results of those sympathies for which the demon thirsted would be children, and a race of devils would be propagated upon the earth who might make the very existence of the species of man a condition precarious and full of terror" (*F*, p. 158). This particular narrative strand also launches a thoroughgoing critique of the eighteenth-century European discourses on the origin of society through (Western Christian) man.[31] Should I mention that, much like Jean-Jacques Rousseau's remark in his *Confessions*, Frankenstein declares himself to be "by birth a Genevese" (*F*, p. 31)?

In this overtly didactic text, Shelley's point is that social engineering should not be based on pure, theoretical, or natural-scientific reason alone, which is her implicit critique of the utilitarian vision of an engineered society. To this end, she presents in the first part of her deliberately schematic story three characters, childhood friends, who seem to represent Kant's three-part conception of the human subject: Victor Frankenstein, the forces of theoretical reason or "natural philosophy"; Henry Clerval, the forces of practical reason or "the moral relations of things"; and Elizabeth Lavenza, that aesthetic judgment — "the aerial creation of the poets" — which, according to Kant, is "a suitable mediating link connecting the realm of the concept of nature and that of the concept of

freedom ... (which) promotes ... *moral feeling*" (*F*, pp. 37, 36).[32]

This three-part subject does not operate harmoniously in *Frankenstein*. That Henry Clerval, associated as he is with practical reason, should have as his "design ... to visit India, in the belief that he had in his knowledge of its various languages, and in the views he had taken of its society, the means of materially assisting the progress of European colonization and trade" is proof of this, as well as part of the incidental imperialist sentiment that I speak of above (*F*, pp. 151–52). I should perhaps point out that the language here is entrepreneurial rather than missionary:

He came to the university with the design of making himself complete master of the Oriental languages, as thus he should open a field for the plan of life he had marked out for himself. Resolved to pursue no inglorious career, he turned his eyes towards the East as affording scope for his spirit of enterprise. The Persian, Arabic, and Sanskrit languages engaged his attention. [*F*, pp. 66–67]

But it is of course Victor Frankenstein, with his strange itinerary of obsession with natural philosophy, who offers the strongest demonstration that the multiple perspectives of the three-part Kantian subject cannot cooperate harmoniously. Frankenstein creates a putative human subject out of natural philosophy alone. According to his own miscued summation: "In a fit of enthusiastic madness I created a rational creature" (*F*, p. 206). It is not at all farfetched to say that Kant's categorical imperative can most easily be mistaken for the hypothetical imperative — a command to ground in cognitive comprehension what can be apprehended only by moral will — by putting natural philosophy in the place of practical reason.

I should hasten to add here that just as readings such as this one do not necessarily accuse Charlotte Brontë the named individual of harboring imperialist sentiments, so also they do not necessarily commend Mary Shelley the named individual for writing a successful Kantian allegory. The most I can say is that it is possible to

[31]Spivak is gesturing at the relationship between the "state of nature" argument in Rousseau's *Social Contract* and Frankenstein's imagined state of war between the races of men and monsters.

[32]Kant, *Critique of Judgement*, trans. J. H. Bernard (New York, 1951), p. 39. [Spivak]

read these texts, within the frame of imperialism and the Kantian ethical moment, in a politically useful way. Such an approach presupposes that a "disinterested" reading attempts to render transparent the interests of the hegemonic readership. (Other "political" readings — for instance, that the monster is the nascent working class — can also be advanced.)

Frankenstein is built in the established epistolary tradition of multiple frames. At the heart of the multiple frames, the narrative of the monster (as reported by Frankenstein to Robert Walton, who then recounts it in a letter to his sister) is of his almost learning, clandestinely, to be human. It is invariably noticed that the monster reads *Paradise Lost* as true history. What is not so often noticed is that he also reads Plutarch's *Lives*, "the histories of the first founders of the ancient republics," which he compares to "the patriarchal lives of my protectors" (*F*, pp. 123, 124). And his *education* comes through "Volney's *Ruins of Empires*," which he purported to be a prefiguration of the French Revolution, published after the event and after the author had rounded off his theory with practice (*F*, p. 113). It is an attempt at an enlightened universal secular, rather than a Eurocentric Christian, history, written from the perspective of a narrator "from below," somewhat like the attempts of Eric Wolf or Peter Worsley in our own time.[33]

This Caliban's education in (universal secular) humanity takes place through the monster's eavesdropping on the instruction of an Ariel — Safie, the Christianized "Arabian" to whom "a residence in Turkey was abhorrent" (*F*, p. 121). In depicting Safie, Shelley uses some commonplaces of eighteenth-century liberalism that are shared by many today: Safie's Muslim father was a victim of (bad) Christian religious prejudice and yet was himself a wily and ungrateful man not as morally refined as her (good) Christian mother. Having tasted the emancipation of woman, Safie could not go home. The confusion between "Turk" and "Arab" has its counterpart in present-day confusion about Turkey and Iran as "Middle Eastern" but not "Arab."

Although we are a far cry here from the unexamined and covert axiomatics of imperialism in *Jane Eyre*, we will gain nothing by celebrating the time-bound pieties that Shelley, as the daughter of two antievangelicals, produces. It is more interesting for us that Shelley differentiates the Other, works at the Caliban/Ariel distinction, and *cannot* make the monster identical with the proper recipient of these lessons. Although he had "heard of the discovery of the American hemisphere and *wept with Safie* over the helpless fate of its original inhabitants," Safie cannot reciprocate his attachment. When she first catches sight of him, "Safie, unable to attend to her friend [Agatha], rushed out of the cottage" (*F*, pp. 114, [my emphasis], 129).

In the taxonomy of characters, the Muslim-Christian Safie belongs with Rhys' Antoinette/Bertha. And indeed, like Christophine the good servant, the subject created by the fiat of natural philosophy is the tangential unresolved moment in *Frankenstein*. The simple suggestion that the monster is human inside but monstrous outside and only provoked into vengefulness is clearly not enough to bear the burden of so great a historical dilemma.

At one moment, in fact, Shelley's Frankenstein does try to tame the monster, to humanize him by bringing him within the circuit of the Law. He "repair[s] to a criminal judge in the town and . . . relate[s his] history briefly but with firmness" — the first and disinterested version of the narrative of Frankenstein — "marking the dates with accuracy and never deviating into invective or exclamation. . . . When I had concluded my narration I said, 'This is the being whom I accuse

[33]See [Constantin François Chasseboeuf de Volney], *The Ruins; or, Meditations on the Revolutions of Empires*, trans. pub. (London, 1811). Johannes Fabian has shown us the manipulation of time in "new" secular histories of a similar kind; see *Time and the Other: How Anthropology Makes Its Object* (New York, 1983). See also Eric R. Wolf, *Europe and the People without History* (Berkeley and Los Angeles, 1982), and Peter Worsley, *The Third World*, 2d ed. (Chicago, 1973); I am grateful to Dennis Dworkin for bringing the latter book to my attention. The most striking ignoring of the monster's education through Volney is in Gilbert's otherwise brilliant "Horror's Twin: Mary Shelley's Monstrous Eve," *Feminist Studies* 4 (June 1980): 48–73. Gilbert's essay reflects the absence of race-determinations in a certain sort of feminism. Her present work has most convincingly filled in this gap; see, e.g., her recent piece on H. Rider Haggard's *She* ("Rider Haggard's Heart of Darkness," *Partisan Review* 50, no. 3 [1983]: 444–53. [Spivak]

and for whose seizure and punishment I call upon you to exert your whole power. It is in your duty as a magistrate" (*F.*, pp. 189, 190). The sheer social reasonableness of the mundane voice of Shelley's "Genevan magistrate" reminds us that the absolutely Other cannot be selfed, that the monster has "properties" which will not be contained by "proper" measures:

"'I will exert myself [he says], and if it is in my power to seize the monster, be assured that he shall suffer punishment proportionate to his crimes. But I fear, from what you have yourself described to be his properties, that this will prove impracticable; and thus, while every proper measure is pursued, you should make up your mind to disappointment.'" [*F.*, p. 190]

In the end, as is obvious to most readers, distinctions of human individuality themselves seem to fall away from the novel. Monster, Frankenstein, and Walton seem to become each others' relays. Frankenstein's story comes to an end in death; Walton concludes his own story within the frame of his function as letter writer. In the *narrative* conclusion, he is the natural philosopher who learns from Frankenstein's example. At the end of the *text*, the monster, having confessed his guilt toward his maker and ostensibly intending to immolate himself, is borne away on an ice raft. We do not see the conflagration of his funeral pile — the self-immolation is not consummated in the text: he too cannot be contained by the text. In terms of narrative logic, he is "lost in darkness and distance" (*F.*, p. 211) — these are the last words of the novel — into an existential temporality that is coherent with neither the territorializing individual imagination (as in the opening of *Jane Eyre*) nor the authoritative scenario of Christian psychobiography (as at the end of Brontë's work). The very relationship between sexual reproduction and social subject-production — the dynamic nineteenth-century topos of feminism-in-imperialism — remains problematic within the limits of Shelley's text and, paradoxically, constitutes its strength.

Earlier, I offered a reading of woman as womb holder in *Frankenstein*. I would now suggest that there is a framing woman in the book who is neither tangential, nor encircled, nor yet encircling. "Mrs. Saville," "excellent Margaret," "beloved Sister" are her address and kinship inscriptions (*F.*, pp. 15, 16, 22). She is the occasion, though not the protagonist, of the novel. She is the feminine *subject* rather than the female individualist: she is the irreducible *recipient-function* of the letters that constitute *Frankenstein*. I have commented on the singular appropriative hermeneutics of the reader reading with Jane in the opening pages of *Jane Eyre*. Here the reader must read with Margaret Saville in the crucial sense that she must *intercept* the recipient-function, read the letters *as* recipient, in order for the novel to exist.[34] Margaret Saville does not respond to close the text as frame. The frame is thus simultaneously not a frame, and the monster can step "beyond the text" and be "lost in darkness." Within the allegory of our reading, the place of both the English lady and the unnameable monster are left open by this great flawed text. It is satisfying for a postcolonial reader to consider this a noble resolution for a nineteenth-century English novel. This is all the more striking because, on the anecdotal level, Shelley herself abundantly "identifies" with Victor Frankenstein.[35]

I must myself close with an idea that I cannot establish within the limits of this essay. Earlier I contended that *Wide Sargasso Sea* is necessarily bound by the reach of the European novel. I suggested that, in contradistinction, to reopen

[34] "A letter is always and *a priori* intercepted, . . . the 'subjects' are neither the senders nor the receivers of messages. . . . The letter is constituted . . . by its interception" (Jacques Derrida, "Discussion," after Claude Rabant, "Il n'a aucune chance de l'entendre," in *Affranchissement: Du transfert et de la lettre*, ed. René Major [Paris, 1981], p. 106; my translation). Margaret Saville is not made to appropriate the reader's "subject" into the signature of her own "individuality." [Spivak]

[35] The most striking "internal evidence" is the admission in the "Author's Introduction" that, after dreaming of the yet-unnamed Victor Frankenstein figure and being terrified (through, yet not quite through, him) by the monster in a scene she later reproduced in Frankenstein's story, Shelley began her tale "on the morrow . . . with the words 'It was on a dreary night of November'" (*F.*, p. xi). Those are the opening words of chapter 5 of the finished book, where Frankenstein begins to recount the actual making of his monster (see *F.*, p. 56). [Spivak]

the epistemic fracture of imperialism without succumbing to a nostalgia for lost origins, the critic must turn to the archives of imperialist governance. I have not turned to those archives in these pages. In my current work, by way of a modest and inexpert "reading" of "archives," I try to extend, outside the reach of the European novelistic tradition, the most powerful suggestion in *Wide Sargasso Sea*: that *Jane Eyre* can be read as the orchestration and staging of the self-immolation of Bertha Mason as "good wife." The power of that suggestion remains unclear if we remain insufficiently knowledgeable about the history of the legal manipulation of widow-sacrifice in the entitlement of the British government in India. I would hope that an informed critique of imperialism, granted some attention from readers in the First World, will at least expand the frontiers of the politics of reading.

Gloria Anzaldúa   1942–2004

Gloria Anzaldúa was born in 1942 in Jesus Maria of the Valley, Texas, to a family of Mexican immigrants. The only person from her neighborhood to achieve a college degree, a B.A. from Pan American University, she went on to receive an M.A. in English and education from the University of Texas. Anzaldúa began teaching a bilingual preschool program for the children of migrant farm workers and then taught mentally and emotionally handicapped students. At the University of Texas at Austin, Vermont College of Norwich University, and San Francisco State University, she taught courses in feminism, Chicano Studies, and creative writing. Her book Borderlands/La Frontera: The New Mestiza (1987) was a radical combination of Spanish and English poetry, memoir, and historical analysis, and became the basis for academic attention to Chicano literature, language, and culture. As a lesbian feminist and the bilingual daughter of Mexican parents, Anzaldúa theorizes the necessity of self-fashioning and finding new identities separate from those offered by society. She edited the collections Making Face, Making Soul/Haciendo Caras: Creative and Critical Perspectives by Feminists of Color (1989) and This Bridge We Call Home: Radical Visions for Transformation (2002, with Analouise Keating), and wrote La Prieta (1997) and a number of books for children. She died in 2004 from a diabetes-related illness, just weeks from completing her Ph.D. at the University of California at Santa Cruz. The following essay, "La conciencia de la mestiza: Towards a New Consciousness," appears in Borderlands/La Frontera.

La conciencia de la mestiza: Towards a New Consciousness

Por la mujer de mi raza
hablará el espíritu.[1]

Jose Vasconcelos, Mexican philosopher, envisaged *una raza mestiza, una mezcla de razas afines, una raza de color* — *la primera raza síntesis del globo.* He called it a cosmic race, *la raza cósmica,* a fifth race embracing the four major races of the world.[2] Opposite to the theory of the pure Aryan, and to the policy of racial purity that white America practices, his theory is one of inclusivity. At the confluence of two or more genetic streams, with chromosomes constantly "crossing over," this mixture of races, rather than resulting in an inferior being, provides hybrid progeny, a mutable, more malleable species with a rich gene pool. From this racial, ideological, cultural and biological cross-pollinization, an "alien" consciousness is presently in the making — a new *mestiza* consciousness, *una conciencia de mujer.* It is a consciousness of the Borderlands.

UNA LUCHA DE FRONTERAS / A STRUGGLE OF BORDERS

Because I, a *mestiza,*
continually walk out of one culture
and into another,
because I am in all cultures at the same time,

---

[1] This is my own "take-off" on Jose Vasconcelos' idea. Jose Vasconcelos, *La Raza Cósmica: Misión de la Raza Ibero-Americana* (México: Aguilar S. A. de Ediciones, 1961). [Anzaldúa]

[2] Vasconcelos. [Anzaldúa]

alma entre dos mundos, tres, cuatro,
me zumba la cabeza con lo contradictorio.
Estoy norteada por todas las voces que me hablan
simultáneamente.

The ambivalence from the clash of voices results in mental and emotional states of perplexity. Internal strife results in insecurity and indecisiveness. The *mestiza*'s dual or multiple personality is plagued by psychic restlessness.

In a constant state of mental nepantilism, an Aztec word meaning torn between ways, *la mestiza* is a product of the transfer of the cultural and spiritual values of one group to another. Being tricultural, monolingual, bilingual or multilingual, speaking a patois, and in a state of perpetual transition, the *mestiza* faces the dilemma of the mixed breed: which collectivity does the daughter of a darkskinned mother listen to?

El choque de un alma atrapado entre el mundo del espíritu y el mundo de la técnica a veces la deja entullada. Cradled in one culture, sandwiched between two cultures, straddling all three cultures and their value systems, *la mestiza* undergoes a struggle of flesh, a struggle of borders, an inner war. Like all people, we perceive the version of reality that our culture communicates. Like others having or living in more than one culture, we get multiple, often opposing messages. The coming together of two self-consistent but habitually incompatible frames of reference[3] causes *un choque*, a cultural collision.

Within us and within *la cultura chicana*, commonly held beliefs of the white culture attack commonly held beliefs of the Mexican culture, and both attack commonly held beliefs of the indigenous culture. Subconsciously, we see an attack on ourselves and our beliefs as a threat and we attempt to block with a counterstance.

But it is not enough to stand on the opposite river bank, shouting questions, challenging patriarchical, white conventions. A counterstance locks one into a duel of oppressor and oppressed; locked in mortal combat, like the cop and the criminal,

both are reduced to a common denominator of violence. The counterstance refutes the dominant culture's views and beliefs, and, for this, it is proudly defiant. All reaction is limited by, and dependent on, what it is reacting against. Because the counterstance stems from a problem with authority — outer as well as inner — it's a step towards liberation from cultural domination. But it is not a way of life. At some point, on our way to a new consciousness, we will have to leave the opposite bank, the split between the two mortal combatants somehow healed so that we are on both shores at once and, at once, see through serpent and eagle eyes. Or perhaps we will decide to disengage from the dominant culture, write it off altogether as a lost cause, and cross the border into a wholly new and separate territory. Or we might go another route. The possibilities are numerous once we decide to act and not react.

A TOLERANCE FOR AMBIGUITY

These numerous possibilities leave *la mestiza* floundering in uncharted seas. In perceiving conflicting information and points of view, she is subjected to a swamping of her psychological borders. She has discovered that she can't hold concepts or ideas in rigid boundaries. The borders and walls that are supposed to keep the undesirable ideas out are entrenched habits and patterns of behavior; these habits and patterns are the enemy within. Rigidity means death. Only by remaining flexible is she able to stretch the psyche horizontally and vertically. *La mestiza* constantly has to shift out of habitual formations; from convergent thinking, analytical reasoning that tends to use rationality to move toward a single goal (a Western mode), to divergent thinking,[4] characterized by movement away from set patterns and goals and toward a more whole perspective, one that includes rather than excludes.

The new *mestiza* copes by developing a tolerance for contradictions, a tolerance for ambiguity. She learns to be an Indian in Mexican culture, to be Mexican from an Anglo point of

---

[3]Arthur Koestler termed this "bisociation." Albert Rothenberg, *The Creative Process in Art, Science, and Other Fields* (Chicago, IL: University of Chicago Press, 1979), 12. [Anzaldúa]

[4]In part, I derive my definitions for "convergent" and "divergent" thinking from Rothenberg, 12–13. [Anzaldúa]

view. She learns to juggle cultures. She has a plural personality, she operates in a pluralistic mode — nothing is thrust out, the good, the bad and the ugly, nothing rejected, nothing abandoned. Not only does she sustain contradictions, she turns the ambivalence into something else.

She can be jarred out of ambivalence by an intense, and often painful, emotional event which inverts or resolves the ambivalence. I'm not sure exactly how. The work takes place underground — subconsciously. It is work that the soul performs. That focal point or fulcrum, that juncture where the *mestiza* stands, is where phenomena tend to collide. It is where the possibility of uniting all that is separate occurs. This assembly is not one where severed or separated pieces merely come together. Nor is it a balancing out of opposing powers. In attempting to work out a synthesis, the self has added a third element which is greater than the sum of its severed parts. That third element is a new consciousness — a *mestiza* consciousness — and though it is a source of intense pain, its energy comes from a continual creative motion that keeps breaking down the unitary aspect of each new paradigm.

En unas pocas centurias, the future will belong to the *mestiza.* Because the future depends on the breaking down of paradigms, it depends on the straddling of two or more cultures. By creating a new mythos — that is, a change in the way we perceive reality, the way we see ourselves and the ways we behave — *la mestiza* creates a new consciousness.

The work of *mestiza* consciousness is to break down the subject-object duality that keeps her a prisoner and to show in the flesh and through the images in her work how duality is transcended. The answer to the problem between the white race and the colored, between males and females, lies in healing the split that origi-nates in the very foundation of our lives, our culture, our languages, our thoughts. A massive uprooting of dualistic thinking in the individual and collective consciousness is the beginning of a long struggle, but one that could, in our best hopes, bring us to the end of rape, of violence, of war.

LA ENCRUCIJADA/THE CROSSROADS

A chicken is being sacrificed
at a crossroads, a simple mound of earth
a mud shrine for Eshu,
Yoruba god of indeterminacy,
who blesses her choice of path.
She begins her journey.

Su cuerpo es una bocacalle. La mestiza has gone from being the sacrificial goat to becoming the officiating priestess at the crossroads.

As a *mestiza* I have no country, my homeland cast me out; yet all countries are mine because I am every woman's sister or potential lover. (As a lesbian I have no race, my own people disclaim me; but I am all races because there is the queer of me in all races.) I am cultureless because, as a feminist, I challenge the collective cultural/religious male-derived beliefs of Indo-Hispanics and Anglos; yet I am cultured because I am participating in the creation of yet another culture, a new story to explain the world and our participation in it, a new value system with images and symbols that connect us to each other and to the planet. *Soy un amasamiento,* I am an act of kneading, of uniting and joining that not only has produced both a creature of darkness and a creature of light, but also a creature that questions the definitions of light and dark and gives them new meanings.

We are the people who leap in the dark, we are the people on the knees of the gods. In our flesh, (r)evolution works out the clash of cultures. It makes us crazy constantly, but if the center holds, we've made some kind of evolutionary step forward. *Nuestra alma el trabajo,* the opus, the great alchemical work; spiritual *mestizaje,* a "morphogenesis,"[5] an inevitable unfolding. We have become the quickening serpent movement.

[5]"To borrow chemist Ilya Prigogine's theory of "dissipative structures." Prigogine discovered that substances interact not in predictable ways as it was taught in science, but in different and fluctuating ways to produce new and more complex structures, a kind of birth he called "morphogenesis," which created unpredictable innovations. Harold Gilliam, "Searching for a New World View," *This World* (January, 1981), 23. [Anzaldúa]

Indigenous like corn, like corn, the *mestiza* is a product of crossbreeding, designed for preservation under a variety of conditions. Like an ear of corn — a female seed-bearing organ — the *mestiza* is tenacious, tightly wrapped in the husks of her culture. Like kernels she clings to the cob; with thick stalks and strong brace roots, she holds tight to the earth — she will survive the crossroads.

Lavando y remojando el maíz en agua de cal, despojando el pellejo. Moliendo, mixteando, amasando, haciendo tortillas de masa.[6] She steeps the corn in lime, it swells, softens. With stone roller on *metate*, she grinds the corn, then grinds again. She kneads and moulds the dough, pats the round balls into *tortillas*.

We are the porous rock in the stone *metate*
squatting on the ground.
We are the rolling pin, *el maíz y agua*,
la masa harina. Somos el amasijo.
Somos lo molido en el metate.
We are the *comal* sizzling hot,
the hot *tortilla*, the hungry mouth.
We are the coarse rock.
We are the grinding motion,
the mixed potion, *somos el molcajete.*
We are the pestle, the *comino, ajo, pimienta,*
We are the *chile colorado*,
the green shoot that cracks the rock.
We will abide.

EL CAMINO DE LA MESTIZA/ THE *MESTIZA* WAY

Caught between the sudden contraction, the breath sucked in and the endless space, the brown woman stands still, looks at the sky. She decides to go down, digging her way along the roots of trees. Sifting through the bones, she shakes them to see if there is any marrow in them. Then, touching the dirt to her forehead, to her tongue, she takes a few bones, leaves the rest in their burial place.

She goes through her backpack, keeps her journal and address book, throws away the muni-bart

[6]Corn tortillas are of two types, the smooth uniform ones made in a tortilla press and usually bought at a tortilla factory or supermarket, and *gorditas*, made by mixing *masa* with lard or shortening or butter (my mother sometimes puts in bits of bacon or *chicharrones*). [Anzaldúa]

metromaps. The coins are heavy and they go next, then the greenbacks flutter through the air. She keeps her knife, can opener and eyebrow pencil. She puts bones, pieces of bark, *hierbas*, eagle feather, snakeskin, tape recorder, the rattle and drum in her pack and she sets out to become the complete *tolteca*.

Her first step is to take inventory. *Despojando, desgranando, quitando paja.* Just what did she inherit from her ancestors? This weight on her back — which is the baggage from the Indian mother, which the baggage from the Spanish father, which the baggage from the Anglo?

Pero es difícil differentiating between *lo heredado, lo adquirido, lo impuesto.* She puts history through a sieve, winnows out the lies, looks at the forces that we as a race, as women, have been a part of. *Luego bota lo que no vale, los desmientos, los desencuentos, el embrutecimiento. Aguarda el juicio, hondo y enraízado, de la gente antigua.* This step is a conscious rupture with all oppressive traditions of all cultures and religions. She communicates that rupture, documents the struggle. She reinterprets history and, using new symbols, she shapes new myths. She adopts new perspectives toward the darkskinned, women and queers. She strengthens her tolerance (and intolerance) for ambiguity. She is willing to share, to make herself vulnerable to foreign ways of seeing and thinking. She surrenders all notions of safety, of the familiar. Deconstruct, construct. She becomes a *nahual*, able to transform herself into a tree, a coyote, into another person. She learns to transform the small "I" into the total Self. *Se hace moldeadora de su alma. Según la concepción que tiene de sí misma, así será.*

QUE NO SE NOS OLVIDE LOS HOMBRES

"Tú no sirves pa' nada —
you're good for nothing.
Eres pura vieja."

"You're nothing but a woman" means you are defective. Its opposite is to be *un macho*. The modern meaning of the word "machismo," as well as the concept, is actually an Anglo invention. For men like my father, being "macho" meant being strong enough to protect and support my mother and us, yet being able to show love.

Today's macho has doubts about his ability to feed and protect his family. His "machismo" is an adaptation to oppression and poverty and low self-esteem. It is the result of hierarchical male dominance. The Anglo, feeling inadequate and inferior and powerless, displaces or transfers these feelings to the Chicano by shaming him. In the Gringo world, the Chicano suffers from excessive humility and self-effacement, shame of self and self-depreciation. Around Latinos he suffers from a sense of language inadequacy and its accompanying discomfort; with Native Americans he suffers from a racial amnesia which ignores our common blood, and from guilt because the Spanish part of him took their land and oppressed them. He has an excessive compensatory hubris when around Mexicans from the other side. It overlays a deep sense of racial shame.

The loss of a sense of dignity and respect in the macho breeds a false machismo which leads him to put down women and even to brutalize them. Coexisting with his sexist behavior is a love for the mother which takes precedence over that of all others. Devoted son, macho pig. To wash down the shame of his acts, of his very being, and to handle the brute in the mirror, he takes to the bottle, the snort, the needle, and the fist.

Though we "understand" the root causes of male hatred and fear, and the subsequent wounding of women, we do not excuse, we do not condone and we will no longer put up with it. From the men of our race, we demand the admission/acknowledgement/disclosure/testimony that they wound us, violate us, are afraid of us and of our power. We need them to say they will begin to eliminate their hurtful put-down ways. But more than the words, we demand acts. We say to them: we will develop equal power with you and those who have shamed us.

It is imperative that *mestizas* support each other in changing the sexist elements in the Mexican-Indian culture. As long as woman is put down, the Indian and the Black in all of us is put down. The struggle of the *mestiza* is above all a feminist one. As long as *los hombres* think they have to *chingar mujeres* and each other to be men, as long as men are taught that they are superior and therefore culturally favored over *la mujer*, as long as to be a *vieja* is a thing of derision, there can be no real healing of our psyches. We're halfway there — we have such love of the Mother, the good mother. The first step is to unlearn the *puta/virgen* dichotomy and to see *Coatlapopeuh* — *Coatlicue* in the Mother, *Guadalupe*.

Tenderness, a sign of vulnerability, is so feared that it is showered on women with verbal abuse and blows. Men, even more than women, are fettered to gender roles. Women at least have had the guts to break out of bondage. Only gay men have had the courage to expose themselves to the woman inside them and to challenge the current masculinity. I've encountered a few scattered and isolated gentle straight men, the beginnings of a new breed, but they are confused, and entangled with sexist behaviors that they have not been able to eradicate. We need a new masculinity and the new man needs a movement.

Lumping the males who deviate from the general norm with man, the oppressor, is a gross injustice. *Asombra pensar que nos hemos quedado en ese pozo oscuro donde el mundo encierra a las lesbianas. Asombra pensar que hemos, como femenistas y lesbianas, cerrado nuestros corazones a los hombres, a nuestros hermanos los jotos, desheredados y marginales como nosotros.* Being the supreme crossers of cultures, homosexuals have strong bonds with the queer white, Black, Asian, Native American, Latino and with the queer in Italy, Australia and the rest of the planet. We come from all colors, all classes, all races, all time periods. Our role is to link people with each other — the Blacks with Jews with Indians with Asians with whites with extraterrestrials. It is to transfer ideas and information from one culture to another. Colored homosexuals have more knowledge of other cultures; have always been at the forefront (although sometimes in the closet) of all liberation struggles in this country; have suffered more injustices and have survived them despite all odds. Chicanos need to acknowledge the political and artistic contributions of their queer. People, listen to what your *jotería* is saying.

The *mestizo* and the queer exist at this time and point on the evolutionary continuum for a purpose. We are a blending that proves that all blood is intricately woven together, and that we are spawned out of similar souls.

SOMOS UNA GENTA

> *Hay tantísimas fronteras*
> que dividen a la gente,
> pero por cada frontera
> existe también un puente. — GINA VALDÉS[7]

Divided Loyalties

Many women and men of color do not want to have any dealings with white people. It takes too much time and energy to explain to the downwardly mobile, white middle-class women that it's okay for us to want to own "possessions," never having had any nice furniture on our dirt floors or "luxuries" like washing machines. Many feel that whites should help their own people rid themselves of race hatred and fear first. I, for one, choose to use some of my energy to serve as mediator. I, think we need to allow whites to be our allies. Through our literature, art, *corridos* and folktales we must share our history with them so when they set up committees to help Big Mountain Navajos or the Chicano farmworkers or *los Nicaragüenses* they won't turn people away because of their racial fears and ignorances. They will come to see that they are not helping us but following our lead.

Individually, but also as a racial entity, we need to voice our needs. We need to say to white society: we need you to accept the fact that Chicanos are different, to acknowledge your rejection and negation of us. We need you to own the fact that you looked upon us as less than human, that you stole our lands, our personhood, our self-respect. We need you to make public restitution: to say that, to compensate for your own sense of defectiveness, you strive for power over us, you erase our history and our experience because it makes you feel guilty — you'd rather forget your brutish

acts. To say you've split yourself from minority groups, that you disown us, that your dual consciousness splits off parts of yourself, transferring the "negative" parts onto us. (Where there is persecution of minorities, there is shadow projection. Where there is violence and war, there is repression of shadow.) To say that you are afraid of us, that to put distance between us, you wear the mask of contempt. Admit that Mexico is your double, that she exists in the shadow of this country, that we are irrevocably tied to her. Gringo, accept the doppelganger in your psyche. By taking back your collective shadow the intracultural split will heal. And finally, tell us what you need from us.

BY YOUR TRUE FACES WE WILL KNOW YOU

I am visible — see this Indian face — yet I am invisible. I both blind them with my beak nose and am their blind spot. But I exist, we exist. They'd like to think I have melted in the pot. But I haven't, we haven't.

The dominant white culture is killing us slowly with its ignorance. By taking away our self-determination, it has made us weak and empty. As a people we have resisted and we have taken expedient positions, but we have never been allowed to develop unencumbered — we have never been allowed to be fully ourselves. The whites in power want us people of color to barricade ourselves behind our separate tribal walls so they can pick us off one at a time with their hidden weapons; so they can whitewash and distort history. Ignorance splits people, creates prejudices. A misinformed people is a subjugated people.

Before the Chicano and the undocumented worker and the Mexican from the other side can come together, before the Chicano can have unity with Native Americans and other groups, we need to know the history of their struggle and they need to know ours. Our mothers, our sisters and brothers, the guys who hang out on street corners, the children in the playgrounds, each of us must know our Indian lineage, our afro-*mestisaje*, our history of resistance.

To the immigrant *mexicano* and the recent arrivals we must teach our history. The 80 million

[7]Gina Valdés, *Puentes y Fronteras: Coplas Chicanas* (Los Angeles, CA: Castle Lithograph, 1982), 2. [Anzaldúa]

mexicanos and the Latinos from Central and South America must know of our struggles. Each one of us must know basic facts about Nicaragua, Chile and the rest of Latin America. The Latinoist movement (Chicanos, Puerto Ricans, Cubans and other Spanish-speaking people working together to combat racial discrimination in the market place) is good but it is not enough. Other than a common culture we will have nothing to hold us together. We need to meet on a broader communal ground.

The struggle is inner: Chicano, *indio*, American Indian, *mojado*, *mexicano*, immigrant Latino, Anglo in power, working class Anglo, Black, Asian — our psyches resemble the border-towns and are populated by the same people. The struggle has always been inner, and is played out in the outer terrains. Awareness of our situation must come before inner changes, which in turn come before changes in society. Nothing happens in the "real" world unless it first happens in the images in our heads.

El día de la Chicana

I will not be shamed again
Nor will I shame myself.

I am possessed by a vision: that we Chicanas and Chicanos have taken back or uncovered our true faces, our dignity and self-respect. It's a validation vision.

Seeing the Chicana anew in light of her history. I seek an exoneration, a seeing through the fictions of white supremacy, a seeing of ourselves in our true guises and not as the false racial personality that has been given to us and that we have given to ourselves. I seek our true faces, I seek the positive and the negative seen clearly, free of the tainted biases of male dominance. I seek new images of identity, new beliefs about ourselves, our humanity and worth no longer in question.

Estamos viviendo en la noche de la Raza, un tiempo cuando el trabajo se hace a lo quieto, en el oscuro. El día cuando aceptamos tal y como somos y para en donde vamos y porque — ese día será el día de la Raza. Yo tengo el compromiso de

expresar mi visión, mi sensibilidad, mi percepción de la revalidación de la gente mexicana, su mérito, estimación, honra, aprecio y validez.

On December 2nd and when my sun goes into my first house, I celebrate *el día de la Chicana y el Chicano*. On that day I clean my altars, light my *Coatlalopeuh* candle, burn sage and copal, take *el baño para espantar basura*, sweep my house. On that day I bare my soul, make myself vulnerable to friends and family by expressing my feelings. On that day I affirm who we are.

On that day I look inside our conflicts and our basic introverted racial temperament. I identify our needs, voice them. I acknowledge that the self and the race have been wounded. I recognize the need to take care of our personhood, of our racial self. On that day I gather the splintered and disowned parts of *la gente mexicana* and hold them in my arms. *Todas las partes de nosotros valen.*

On that day I say, "Yes, all you people wound us when you reject us. Rejection strips us of self-worth; our vulnerability exposes us to shame. It is our innate identity you find wanting. We are ashamed that we need your good opinion, that we need your acceptance. We can no longer camouflage our needs, can no longer let defenses and fences sprout around us. We can no longer withdraw. To rage and look upon you with contempt is to rage and be contemptuous of ourselves. We can no longer blame you, nor disown the white parts, the male parts, the pathological parts, the queer parts, the vulnerable parts. Here we are weaponless with open arms, with only our magic. Let's try it our way, the *mestiza* way, the Chicana way, the woman way.

On that day, I search for our essential dignity as a people, a people with a sense of purpose — to belong and contribute to something greater than our *pueblo*. On that day I seek to recover and reshape my spiritual identity. *¡Anímate! Raza, a celebrar el día de la Chicana.*

El retorno

All movements are accomplished in six stages,
and the seventh brings return. — I CHING[8]

[8]Richard Wilhelm, *The I Ching or Book of Changes*, trans. Cary F. Baynes (Princeton, NJ: Princeton University Press, 1950), 98. [Anzaldúa]

Tanto tiempo sin verte casa mía,
mi cuna, mi hondo nido de la huerta.
— "SOLEDAD"[9]

I stand at the river, watch the curving, twisting serpent, a serpent nailed to the fence where the mouth of the Rio Grande empties into the Gulf.

I have come back. *Tanto dolor me costó el ale-jamiento.* I shade my eyes and look up. The bone beak of a hawk slowly circling over me, checking me out as potential carrion. In its wake a little bird flickering its wings, swimming sporadically like a fish. In the distance the expressway and the slough of traffic like an irritated sow. The sudden pull in my gut, *la tierra, los aguaceros.* My land, *el viento soplando la arena, el lagartijo debajo de un nopalito. Me acuerdo como era antes. Una región desértica de vasta llanuras, costeras de baja altura, de escasa lluvia, de chaparrales formados por mesquites y huizaches.* If I look real hard I can almost see the Spanish fathers who were called "the cavalry of Christ" enter this valley riding their burros, see the clash of cultures commence.

Tierra natal. This is home, the small towns in the Valley, *los pueblitos* with chicken pens and goats picketed to mesquite shrubs. *En las colo-nias* on the other side of the tracks, junk cars line the front yards of hot pink and lavender-trimmed houses — Chicano architecture we call it, self-consciously. I have missed the TV shows where hosts speak in half and half, and where awards are given in the category of Tex-Mex music. I have missed the Mexican cemeteries blooming with artificial flowers, the fields of aloe vera and red pepper, rows of sugar cane, of corn hanging on the stalks, the cloud of *polvareda* in the dirt roads behind a speeding truck, *el sabor de tamales de rez y venado.* I have missed *la yequa colorada* gnawing the wooden gate of her stall, the smell of horse flesh from Carito's corrals. *He hecho menos las noches calientes sin aire, noches de linternas y lechuzas* making holes in the night.

I still feel the old despair when I look at the unpainted, dilapidated, scrap lumber houses

consisting mostly of corrugated aluminum. Some of the poorest people in the U.S. live in the Lower Rio Grande Valley, an arid and semi-arid land of irrigated farming, intense sunlight and heat, citrus groves next to chaparral and cactus. I walk through the elementary school I attended so long ago, that remained segregated until recently. I remember how the white teachers used to punish us for being Mexican.

How I love this tragic valley of South Texas, as Ricardo Sánchez calls it; this borderland between the Nueces and the Rio Grande. This land has survived possession and ill-use by five countries: Spain, Mexico, the Republic of Texas, the Confederacy, and the U.S. again. It has survived Anglo-Mexican blood feuds, lynchings, burnings, rapes, pillage.

Today I see the Valley still struggling to survive. Whether it does or not, it will never be as I remember it. The borderlands depression that was set off by the 1982 peso devaluation in Mexico resulted in the closure of hundreds of Valley businesses. Many people lost their homes, cars, land. Prior to 1982, U.S. store owners thrived on retail sales to Mexicans who came across the borders for groceries and clothes and appliances. While goods on the U.S. side have become 10, 100, 1000 times more expensive for Mexican buyers, goods on the Mexican side have become 10, 100, 1000 times cheaper for Americans. Because the Valley is heavily dependent on agriculture and Mexican retail trade, it has the highest unemployment rates along the entire border region; it is the Valley that has been hardest hit.[10]

"It's been a bad year for corn," my brother, Nune, says. As he talks, I remember my father scanning the sky for a rain that would end the drought, looking up into the sky, day after day, while the corn withered on its stalk. My father has been dead for 29 years, having worked himself to death. The life span of a Mexican farm laborer is

---

[9]"Soledad" is sung by the group Haciendo Punto en Otro Son. [Anzaldúa]

[10]Out of the twenty-two border counties in the four border states, Hidalgo County (named for Father Hidalgo who was shot in 1810 after instigating Mexico's revolt against Spanish rule under the banner of *la Virgen de Guadalupe*) is the most poverty-stricken county in the nation as well as the largest home base (along with Imperial in California) for migrant farmworkers. It was here that I was born and raised, I am amazed that both it and I have survived. [Anzaldúa]

56 — he lived to be 38. It shocks me that I am older than he. I, too, search the sky for rain. Like the ancients, I worship the rain god and the maize goddess, but unlike my father I have recovered their names. Now for rain (irrigation) one offers not a sacrifice of blood, but of money.

"Farming is in a bad way," my brother says. "Two to three thousand small and big farmers went bankrupt in this country last year. Six years ago the price of corn was $8.00 per hundred pounds," he goes on. "This year it is $3.90 per hundred pounds." And, I think to myself, after taking inflation into account, not planting anything puts you ahead.

I walk out to the back yard, stare at *los rosales de mamá.* She wants me to help her prune the rose bushes, dig out the carpet grass that is chok-ing them. *Mamagrande Ramona también tenía rosales.* Here every Mexican grows flowers. If they don't have a piece of dirt, they use car tires, jars, cans, shoe boxes. Roses are the Mexican's favorite flower. I think, how symbolic — thorns and all.

Yes, the Chicano and Chicana have always taken care of growing things and the land. Again I see the four of us kids getting off the school bus, changing into our work clothes, walking into the field with Papi and Mami, all six of us bending to the ground. Below our feet, under the earth lie the watermelon seeds. We cover them with paper plates, putting *terremotes* on top of the plates to keep them from being blown away by the wind. The paper plates keep the freeze away. Next day or the next, we remove the plates, bare the tiny green shoots to the elements. They survive and grow, give fruit hundreds of times the size of the seed. We water them and hoe them. We har-vest them. The vines dry, rot, are plowed under. Growth, death, decay, birth. The soil prepared again and again, impregnated, worked on. A constant changing of forms, *renacimientos de la tierra madre.*

This land was Mexican once
was Indian always
and is.
And will be again.

Barbara Christian

1943–2000

Born on St. Thomas in the U.S. Virgin Islands in 1943, Barbara Christian was educated at Marquette University and did her doctoral work at Columbia. During the 1960s, while teaching at City College in New York, Christian was deeply involved in the Black Liberation movement and the opposition to the Vietnam War. In 1971, Christian took a position at the University of California at Berkeley. Christian called academic attention to African American women like Zora Neale Hurston, Alice Walker, and Toni Morrison, moving them from special-interest status to a more central position within academic and popular circles of readership in America. Works by these authors had been criticized according to the rubrics of Eurocentric masculinist literary analysis, according to Christian, who helped to develop a Black Feminist Criticism that could understand this literature on its own terms. Christian died of cancer in 2000 at the age of fifty-six. Her books include Black Women Novelists: The Development of a Tradition, 1892–1976 *(1980),* Black Feminist Criticism: Perspectives on Black Women Writers *(1985),* From the Inside Out: Afro-American Women's Literary Tradition and the State *(1987), and* Alice Walker's "The Color Purple" and Other Works: A Critical Commentary *(1988).*

In the following essay, "The Race for Theory," excerpted from Gender and Theory: Dialogues on Feminist Criticism *(1989), Christian argues that the academic race to theorize African American women's writing has often eclipsed the theoretical implications of the literature itself. Her argument that theory was "white" created a controversy within the African American academy.*

The Race for Theory

I have seized this occasion to break the silence among those of us, critics, as we are now called, who have been intimidated, devalued by what I call the race for theory. I have become convinced that there has been a takeover in the literary world by Western philosophers from the old literary élite, the neutral humanists. Philosophers have been able to effect such a takeover because so much of the literature of the West has become pallid, laden with despair, self-indulgent, and disconnected. The New Philosophers, eager to understand a world that is today fast escaping their political control, have redefined literature so that the distinctions implied by that term, that is, the distinctions between everything written and those things written to evoke feeling as well as to express thought, have been blurred. They have changed literary critical language to suit their own purposes as philosophers, and they have reinvented the meaning of theory.

My first response to this realization was to ignore it. Perhaps, in spite of the egocentrism of this trend, some good might come of it. I had, I felt, more pressing and interesting things to do, such as reading and studying the history and literature of black women, a history that had been totally ignored, a contemporary literature bursting with originality, passion, insight, and beauty. But unfortunately it is difficult to ignore this new takeover, since theory has become a commodity which helps determine whether we are hired or promoted in academic institutions — worse, whether we are heard at all. Due to this new orientation, works (a word which evokes labor) have become texts. Critics are no longer concerned with literature, but with other critics' texts, for the critic yearning for attention has displaced the writer and has conceived of himself as the center. Interestingly in the first part of this century, at least in England and America, the critic was usually also a writer of poetry, plays, or novels. But today, as a new generation of professionals develops, he or she is increasingly an academic. Activities such as teaching or writing one's response to specific works of literature have, among this group, become subordinated to one primary thrust, that moment when one creates a theory, thus fixing a constellation of ideas for a time at least, a fixing which no doubt will be replaced in another month or so by somebody else's competing theory as the race accelerates. Perhaps because those who have effected the takeover have the power (although they deny it) first of all to be published, and thereby to determine the ideas which are deemed valuable, some of our most daring and potentially radical critics (and by *our* I mean black, women, third world) have been influenced, even co-opted, into speaking a language and defining their discussion in terms alien to and opposed to our needs and orientation. At least so far, the creative writers I study have resisted this language.

For people of color have always theorized — but in forms quite different from the Western form of abstract logic. And I am inclined to say that our theorizing (and I intentionally use the verb rather than the noun) is often in narrative forms, in the stories we create, in riddles and proverbs, in the play with language, since dynamic rather than fixed ideas seem more to our liking. How else have we managed to survive with such spiritedness the assault on our bodies, social institutions, countries, our very humanity? And women, at least the women I grew up around, continuously speculated about the nature of life through pithy language that unmasked the power relations of their world. It is this language, and the grace and pleasure with which they played with it, that I find celebrated, refined, critiqued in the works of writers like Morrison and Walker. My folk, in other words, have always been in a race for theory — though more in the form of the hieroglyph, a written figure which is both

sensual and abstract, both beautiful and communicative. In my own work I try to illuminate and explain these hieroglyphs, which is, I think, an activity quite different from the creating of the hieroglyphs themselves. As the Buddhists would say, the finger pointing at the moon is not the moon.

In this discussion, however, I am more concerned with the issue raised by my first use of the term, the race for theory, in relation to its academic hegemony, and possibly of its inappropriateness to the energetic emerging literatures in the world today. The pervasiveness of this academic hegemony is an issue continually spoken about — but usually in hidden groups, lest we, who are disturbed by it, appear ignorant to the reigning academic elite. Among the folk who speak in muted tones are people of color, feminists, radical critics, creative writers, who have struggled for much longer than a decade to make their voices, their various voices, heard, and for whom literature is not an occasion for discourse among critics but is necessary nourishment for their people and one way by which they come to understand their lives better. Clichéd though this may be, it bears, I think, repeating here.

The race for theory, with its linguistic jargon, its emphasis on quoting its prophets, its tendency towards "Biblical" exegesis, its refusal even to mention specific works of creative writers, far less contemporary ones, its preoccupations with mechanical analyses of language, graphs, algebraic equations, its gross generalizations about culture, has silenced many of us to the extent that some of us feel we can no longer discuss our own literature, while others have developed intense writing blocks and are puzzled by the incomprehensibility of the language set adrift in literary circles. There have been, in the last year, any number of occasions on which I had to convince literary critics who have pioneered entire new areas of critical inquiry that they did have something to say. Some of us are continually harassed to invent wholesale theories regardless of the complexity of the literature we study. I, for one, am tired of being asked to produce a black feminist literary theory as if I were a mechanical man. For I believe such theory is prescriptive — it ought to have some relationship to practice. Since

I can count on one hand the number of people attempting to be black feminist literary critics in the world today, I consider it presumptuous of me to invent a theory of how we ought to read. Instead, I think we need to read the works of our writers in our various ways and remain open to the intricacies of the intersection of language, class, race, and gender in the literature. And it would help if we share our process, that is, our practice, as much as possible since, finally, our work is a collective endeavor.

The insidious quality of this race for theory is symbolized for me by the very name of this special issue — Minority Discourse — a label which is borrowed from the reigning theory of the day and is untrue to the literatures being produced by our writers, for many of our literatures (certainly Afro-American literature) are central, not minor, and by the titles of many of the articles, which illuminate language as an assault on the other, rather than as possible communication, and play with, or even affirmation of another. I have used the passive voice in my last sentence construction, contrary to the rules of Black English, which like all languages has a particular value system, since I have not placed responsibility on any particular person or group. But that is precisely because this new ideology has become so prevalent among us that it behaves like so many of the other ideologies with which we have had to contend. It appears to have neither head nor center. At the least, though, we can say that the terms "minority" and "discourse" are located firmly in a Western dualistic or "binary" frame which sees the rest of the world as minor, and tries to convince the rest of the world that it *is* major, usually through force and then through language, even as it claims many of the ideas that we, its "historical" other, have known and spoken about for so long. For many of us have never conceived of ourselves only as somebody's *other*.

Let me not give the impression that by objecting to the race for theory I ally myself with or agree with the neutral humanists who see literature as pure expression and will not admit to the obvious control of its production, value, and distribution by those who have power, who deny, in other words, that literature is, of necessity, political. I am studying an entire body of literature that has been denigrated for centuries by such terms as *political*. For an entire century Afro-American writers, from Charles Chesnutt in the nineteenth century through Richard Wright in the 1930s, Imamu Baraka in the 1960s, Alice Walker in the 1970s, have protested the literary hierarchy of dominance which declares when literature is literature, when literature is great, depending on what it thinks is to its advantage. The Black Arts Movement of the 1960s, out of which Black Studies, the Feminist Literary Movement of the 1970s, and Women's Studies grew, articulated precisely those issues, which came *not* from the declarations of the New Western philosophers but from these groups' reflections on their own lives. That Western scholars have long believed their ideas to be universal has been strongly opposed by many such groups. Some of my colleagues do not see black critical writers of previous decades as eloquent enough. Clearly they have not read Wright's "Blueprint for Negro Writing," Ellison's *Shadow and Act*, Chesnutt's resignation from being a writer, or Alice Walker's "In Search of Zora Neale Hurston." There are two reasons for this general ignorance of what our writer-critics have said. One is that black writing has been generally ignored in this country. Since we, as Toni Morrison has put it, are seen as a discredited people, it is no surprise, then, that our creations are also discredited, but this is also due to the fact that until recently dominant critics in the Western World have also been creative writers who have had access to the upper middle class institutions of education and until recently our writers have decidedly been excluded from these institutions and in fact have often been opposed to them. Because of the academic world's general ignorance about the literature of black people and of women, whose work too has been discredited, it is not surprising that so many of our critics think that the position arguing that literature is political begins with these New Philosophers. Unfortunately, many of our young critics do not investigate the reasons *why* that statement — literature is political — is now acceptable when before it was not; nor do we look to our own antecedents for the sophisticated arguments upon which we can build in order to change the tendency of any established Western idea to become hegemonic.

For I feel that the new emphasis on literary critical theory is as hegemonic as the world which it attacks. I see the language it creates as one which mystifies rather than clarifies our condition, making it possible for a few people who know that particular language to control the critical scene — that language surfaced, interestingly enough, just when the literature of peoples of color, of black women, or Latin Americans, of Africans began to move to "the center." Such words as *center* and *periphery* are themselves instructive. *Discourse, canon, texts*, words as latinate as the tradition from which they come, are quite familiar to me. Because I went to a Catholic Mission school in the West Indies I must confess that I cannot hear the word "canon" without smelling incense, that the word "text" immediately brings back agonizing memories of Biblical exegesis, that "discourse" reeks for me of metaphysics forced down my throat in those courses that traced *world* philosophy from Aristotle through Thomas Aquinas to Heidegger. "Periphery," too is a word I heard throughout my childhood, for if anything was seen as being at the periphery, it was those small Caribbean islands which had neither land mass nor military power. Still I noted how intensely important this periphery was, for U.S. troops were continually invading one island or another if any change in political control even seemed to be occurring. As I lived among folk for whom language was an absolutely necessary way of validating our existence, I was told that the minds of the world lived only in the small continent of Europe. The metaphysical language of the New Philosophy, then, I must admit, is repulsive to me and is one reason why I raced from philosophy to literature, since the latter seemed to me to have the possibilities of rendering the world as large and as complicated as I experienced it, as sensual as I knew it was. In literature I sensed the possibility of the integration of feeling/knowledge, rather than the split between the abstract and the emotional in which Western philosophy inevitably indulged.

Now I am being told that philosophers are the ones who write literature, that authors are dead, irrelevant, mere vessels through which their narratives ooze, that they do or do not work nor have they the faintest idea what they are doing; rather they produce texts as disembodied as the angels. I am frankly astonished that scholars who call themselves Marxists or post-Marxists could seriously use such metaphysical language even as they attempt to deconstruct the philosophical tradition from which their language comes. And as a student of literature, I am appalled by the sheer ugliness of the language, its lack of clarity, its unnecessarily complicated sentence construction, its lack of pleasurableness, its alienating quality. It is the kind of writing for which composition teachers would give a freshman a resounding F.

Because I am a curious person, however, I postponed readings of black women writers I was working on and read some of the prophets of this new literary orientation. These writers did announce their dissatisfaction with some of the cornerstone ideas of their own tradition, a dissatisfaction with which I was born. But in their attempt to change the orientation of Western scholarship, they, as usual, concentrated on themselves and were not in the slightest interested in the worlds they had ignored or controlled. Again I was supposed to know *them*, while they were not at all interested in knowing *me*. Instead they sought to "deconstruct" the tradition to which they belonged even as they used the same forms, style, language of that tradition, forms which necessarily embody its values. And increasingly as I read them and saw their substitution of their philosophical writings for literary ones, I began to have the uneasy feeling that their folk were not producing any literature worth mentioning. For they always harkened back to the masterpieces of the past, again reifying the very texts they said they were deconstructing. Increasingly, as *their* way, *their* terms, *their* approaches remained central and became the means by which one defined literary critics, many of my own peers who had previously been concentrating on dealing with the other side of the equation, the reclamation and discussion of past and *present* third world literatures, were diverted into continually discussing the new literary theory.

From my point of view as a critic of contemporary Afro-American women's writing, this orientation is extremely problematic. In attempting to find the deep structures in the literary tradition, a major preoccupation of the new New Criticism, many of us have become obsessed with the nature of reading itself to the extent that we have stopped writing about literature being written today. Since I am slightly paranoid, it has begun to occur to me that the literature being produced *is* precisely one of the reasons why this new philosophical-literary-critical theory of relativity is so prominent. In other words, the literature of blacks, women of South America and Africa, etc., as overtly "political" literature was being preempted by a new Western concept which proclaimed that reality does not exist, that everything is relative, and that every text is silent about something — which indeed it must necessarily be.

There is, of course, much to be learned from exploring how we know what we know, how we read what we read, an exploration which, of necessity, can have no end. But there also has to be a "what," and that "what," when it is even mentioned by the new philosophers, are texts of the past, primarily Western male texts, whose norms are again being transferred onto third world, female texts as theories of reading proliferate. Inevitably a hierarchy has now developed between what is called theoretical criticism and practical criticism, as mind is deemed superior to matter. I have no quarrel with those who wish to philosophize about how we know what we know. But I do resent the fact that this particular orientation is so privileged and has diverted so many of us from doing the first readings of the literature being written today as well as of past works about which nothing has been written. I note, for example, that there is little work done on Gloria Naylor, that most of Alice Walker's works have not been commented on — despite the rage around *The Color Purple* — that there has yet to be an in-depth study of Frances Harper, the nineteenth-century abolitionist poet and novelist. If our emphasis on theoretical criticism continues, critics of the future may have to reclaim the writers we are now ignoring, that is, if they are even aware these artists exist.

I am particularly perturbed by the movement to exalt theory, as well, because of my own adult history. I was an active member of the Black Arts Movement of the sixties and know how dangerous theory can become. Many today may not be aware of this, but the Black Arts Movement tried to create Black Literary Theory and in doing so became prescriptive. My fear is that when Theory is not rooted in practice, it becomes prescriptive, exclusive, élitish.

An example of this prescriptiveness is the approach the Black Arts Movement took towards language. For it, blackness resided in the use of black talk which they defined as hip urban language. So that when Nikki Giovanni reviewed Paule Marshall's *Chosen Place, Timeless People*, she criticized the novel on the grounds that it was not black, for the language was too elegant, too white. Blacks, she said, did not speak that way. Having come from the West Indies where we do, some of the time, speak that way, I was amazed by the narrowness of her vision. The emphasis on *one way* to be black resulted in the works of Southern writers being seen as non-black since the black talk of Georgia does not sound like the black talk of Philadelphia. Because the ideologues, like Baraka, come from the urban centers they tended to privilege their way of speaking, thinking, writing, and to condemn other kinds of writing as not being black enough. Whole areas of the canon were assessed according to the dictum of the Black Arts Nationalist point of view, as in Addison Gayle's *The Way of the New World*, while other works were ignored because they did not fit the scheme of cultural nationalism. Older writers like Ellison and Baldwin were condemned because they saw that the intersection of Western and African influences resulted in a new Afro-American culture, a position with which many of the Black Nationalist ideologues disagreed. Writers were told that writing love poems was not being black. Further examples abound.

It is true that the Black Arts Movement resulted in a necessary and important critique both of previous Afro-American literature and of the white-established literary world. But in attempting to take over power, it, as Ishmael Reed satirizes so well in *Mumbo Jumbo*, became much like its opponent, monolithic and downright repressive.

It is this tendency towards the monolithic, monotheistic, etc., which worries me about the race for theory. Constructs like the *center* and the *periphery* reveal that tendency to want to make the world less complex by organizing it according to one principle, to fix it through an idea which is really an ideal. Many of us are particularly sensitive to monolithism since one major element of ideologies of dominance, such as sexism and racism, is to dehumanize people by stereotyping them, by denying them their variousness and complexity. Inevitably, monolithism becomes a metasystem, in which there is a controlling ideal, especially in relation to pleasure. Language as one form of pleasure is immediately restricted, and becomes heavy, abstract, prescriptive, monotonous.

Variety, multiplicity, eroticism are difficult to control. And it may very well be that these are the reasons why writers are often seen as *persona non grata* by political states, whatever form they take, since writers/artists have a tendency to refuse to give up their way of seeing the world and of playing with possibilities; in fact, their very expression relies on that insistence. Perhaps that is why creative literature, even when written by politically reactionary people, can be so freeing, for in having to embody ideas and recreate the world, writers cannot merely produce "one way."

The characteristics of the Black Arts Movement are, I am afraid, being repeated again today, certainly in the other area to which I am especially tuned. In the race for theory, feminists, eager to enter the halls of power, have attempted their own prescriptions. So often I have read books on feminist literary theory that restrict the definition of what *feminist* means and overgeneralize about so much of the world that most women as well as men are excluded. Nor seldom do feminist theorists take into account the complexity of life — that women are of many races and ethnic backgrounds with different histories and cultures and that as a rule women belong to different classes that have different concerns. Seldom do they note these distinctions, because if they did they could not articulate a theory. Often as a way of clearing themselves they do acknowledge that women of color, for example, do exist, then go on to do what they were going to do anyway, which is to invent a theory that has little relevance for us. That tendency towards monolithism is precisely how I see the French feminist theorists. They concentrate on the female body as the means to creating a female language, since language

they say, is male and necessarily conceives of woman as other. Clearly many of them have been irritated by the theories of Lacan for whom language is phallic. But suppose there are peoples in the world whose language was invented primarily in relation to women, who after all are the ones who relate to children and teach language? Some Native American languages, for example, use female pronouns when speaking about non-gender specific activity. Who knows who, according to gender, created languages. Further, by positing the body as the source of everything French feminists return to the old myth that biology determines everything and ignore the fact that gender is a social rather than a biological construct.

I could go on critiquing the positions of French feminists who are themselves more various in their points of view than the label which is used to describe them, but that is not my point. What I am concerned about is the authority this school now has in feminist scholarship — the way it has become *authoritative discourse*, monologic, which occurs precisely because it does have access to the means of promulgating its ideas. The Black Arts Movement was able to do this for a time because of the political movements of the 1960s — so too with the French feminists who could not be inventing "theory" if a space had not been created by the Women's Movement. In both cases, both groups posited a theory that excluded many of the people who made that space possible. Hence one of the reasons for the surge of Afro-American women's writing during the 1970s and its emphasis on sexism in the black community is precisely that when the ideologues of the 1960s said *black*, they meant *black male*. I and many of my sisters do not see the world as being so simple. And perhaps that is why we have not rushed to create abstract theories. For we know there are countless women of color, both in America and in the rest of the world to whom our singular ideas would be applied. There is, therefore, a caution we feel about pronouncing black feminist theory that might be seen as a decisive statement about Third World women. This is not to say we are not theorizing. Certainly our literature is an indication of the ways in which our theorizing, of necessity, is based on our multiplicity of experiences.

There is at least one other lesson I learned from the Black Arts Movement. One reason for its monolithic approach had to do with its desire to destroy the power which controlled black people, but it was a power which many of its ideologues wished to achieve. The nature of our context today is such that an approach which desires power singlemindedly must of necessity become like that which it wishes to destroy. Rather than wanting to change the whole model, many of us want to be at the center. It is this point of view that writers like June Jordan and Audre Lorde continually critique even as they call for empowerment, as they emphasize the fear of difference among us and our need for leaders rather than a reliance on ourselves.

For one must distinguish the desire for power from the need to become empowered — that is, seeing oneself as capable of and having the right to determine one's life. Such empowerment is partially derived from a knowledge of history. The Black Arts Movement did result in the creation of Afro-American Studies as a concept, thus giving it a place in the university where one might engage in the reclamation of Afro-American history and culture and pass it on to others. I am particularly concerned that institutions such as Black Studies and Women's Studies, fought for with such vigor and at some sacrifice, are not often seen as important by many of our black or women scholars precisely because the old hierarchy of traditional departments is seen as superior to these "marginal" groups. Yet, it is in this context that many others of us are discovering the extent of our complexity, the interrelationships of different areas of knowledge in relation to a distinctly Afro-American or female experience. Rather than having to view our world as subordinate to others, or rather than having to work as if we were hybrids, we can pursue ourselves as subjects.

My major objection to the race for theory, as some readers have probably guessed by now, really hinges on the question, "for whom are we doing what we are doing when we do literary criticism?" It is, I think, the central question today especially for the few of us who have infiltrated the academy enough to be wooed by it. The answer to that question determines what orientation we take in our work, the language we use, the purposes for which it is intended.

I can only speak for myself. But what I write and how I write is done in order to save my own life. And I mean that literally. For me literature is a way of knowing that I am not hallucinating, that whatever I feel/know *is*. It is an affirmation that sensuality is intelligence, that sensual language is language that makes sense. My response, then, is directed to those who write what I read and to those who read what I read — put concretely — to Toni Morrison and to people who read Toni Morrison (among whom I would count few academics). That number is increasing, as is the readership of Walker and Marshall. But in no way is the literature Morrison, Marshall, or Walker create supported by the academic world. Nor given the political context of our society, do I expect that to change soon. For there is no reason, given who controls these institutions, for them to be anything other than threatened by these writers.

My readings do presuppose a need, a desire among folk who like me also want to save their own lives. My concern, then, is a passionate one, for the literature of people who are not in power has always been in danger of extinction or of co-optation, not because we do not theorize, but because what we can even imagine, far less who we can reach, is constantly limited by societal structures. For me, literary criticism is promotion as well as understanding, a response to the writer to whom there is often no response, to folk who need the writing as much as they need anything. I know, from literary history, that writing disappears unless there is a response to it. Because I write about writers who are now writing, I hope to help ensure that their tradition has continuity and survives.

So my "method," to use a new "lit. crit." word, is not fixed but relates to what I read and to the historical context of the writers I read *and* to the many critical activities in which I am engaged, which may or may not involve writing. It is a learning from the language of creative writers, which is one of surprise, so that I might discover what language I might use. For my language is very much based on what I read and how it affects me, that is, on the surprise that comes from reading something that compels you to read differently, as I believe literature does. I, therefore, have no set method, another prerequisite of the new theory, since for me every work suggests a new approach. As risky as that might seem, it is, I believe, what intelligence means — a tuned sensitivity to that which is alive and therefore cannot be known until it is known. Audre Lorde puts it in a far more succinct and sensual way in her essay "Poetry Is Not a Luxury":

> As they become known to and accepted by us, our feelings and the honest exploration of them become sanctuaries and spawning grounds for the most radical and daring of ideas. They become a safe-house for that difference so necessary to change and the conceptualization of any meaningful action. Right

now, I could name at least ten ideas I would have found intolerable or incomprehensible and frightening, except as they came after dreams and poems. This is not idle fantasy, but a disciplined attention to the true meaning of "it feels right to me." We can train ourselves to respect our feelings and to transpose them into a language so they can be shared. And where that language does not yet exist, it is our poetry which helps to fashion it. Poetry is not only dream and vision; it is the skeleton architecture of our lives. It lays the foundations for a future of change, a bridge across our fears of what has never been before.[1]

[1]Audre Lord, *Sister Outsider* (Trumansburg, N.Y.: The Crossing Press, 1984), 37.

Homi K. Bhabha

b. 1949

Homi Bhabha was born into the Parsi community of Bombay and grew up in the shade of the Fire Temple. Bhabha received a B.A. from Bombay University, and an M.A., M.Phil., and D.Phil. from Christ Church, Oxford University. Bhabha has taught at the University of Sussex, Princeton University, the University of Pennsylvania, Dartmouth College, and the University of Chicago. He is currently Anne F. Rothenberg Professor of English and American Literature at Harvard University. Bhabha has edited the essay collection Nation and Narration *(1990) and is the author of* The Location of Culture *(1994), along with many articles and interviews. The following selection, "Signs Taken for Wonders," originally appeared in* Critical Inquiry *in 1985 and was reprinted in* The Location of Culture.

Signs Taken for Wonders:[1] Questions of Ambivalence and Authority under a Tree Outside Delhi, May 1817

A remarkable peculiarity is that they (the English) always write the personal pronoun I with a capital letter. May we not consider this Great I as an unintended proof how much an Englishman thinks of his own consequence?
— ROBERT SOUTHEY, *Letters from England*

I would like to thank Stephan Feuchtwang for his sustaining advice, Gayatri Spivak for suggesting that I should further develop my concept of colonial mimicry; Parveen Adams for her impeccable critique of the text; and Jacqueline Bhabha, whose political engagement with the discriminatory nature of British immigration and nationality law has convinced me of the modesty of the theoretical enterprise. [Bhabha]

[1]Bhabha's title duplicates the title of a 1983 book by comparatist Franco Moretti, but given that the "English book" is the Bible, it seems rather to point to a biblical phrase, "signs and wonders" (probably a hendiadys for "wondrous signs") that appears about thirty times throughout the Old and New Testaments. Hendiadys (Greek for "one by means of two") is a figure of speech in which two words, joined by "and," are actually joined in a more intimate way (one of the nouns, usually the second, is secretly being used as an adjective). As when Edmund says to Edgar in *King Lear*: "I have told

There is a scene in the cultural writings of English colonialism which repeats so insistently after the early nineteenth century — and, through that repetition, so triumphantly *inaugurates* a literature of empire — that I am bound to repeat it once more. It is the scenario, played out in the wild and wordless wastes of colonial India, Africa, the Caribbean, of the sudden, fortuitous discovery of the English book. It is, like all myths of origin, memorable for its balance between epiphany and enunciation. The discovery of the book is, at once, a moment of originality and authority, as well as a process of displacement that, paradoxically, makes the presence of the book wondrous to the extent to which it is repeated, translated, misread, displaced. It is with the emblem of the English book — "signs taken for wonders" — as an insignia of colonial authority and a signifier of colonial desire and discipline, that I want to begin this essay.

you what I have seen and heard but faintly, nothing like the image and horror of it." (where "image and horror" = "horrible image"). Or Lady Macbeth: "To be the same in thine own act and valour/As thou art in desire." (act and valor = valorous act.)

In the first week of May 1817, Anund Messeh, one of the earliest Indian catechists, made a hurried and excited journey from his mission in Meerut to a grove of trees just outside Delhi.

He found about 500 people, men, women and children, seated under the shade of the trees, and employed, as had been related to him, in reading and conversation. He went up to an elderly looking man, and accosted him, and the following conversa-tion passed.

'Pray who are all these people? and whence come they?' 'We are poor and lowly, and we read and love this book.' — 'What is that book?'

'The book of God!' — 'Let me look at it, if you please.' Anund, on opening the book, perceived it to be the Gospel of our Lord, translated into the Hindoostanee Tongue, many copies of which seemed to be in the possession of the party: some were PRINTED, others WRITTEN by themselves from the printed ones. Anund pointed to the name of Jesus, and asked, 'Who is that?' 'That is God! He gave us this book.' — 'Where did you obtain it?' 'An Angel from heaven gave it us, at Hurdwar fair.' — 'An Angel?' 'Yes, to us he was God's Angel; but he was a man, a learned Pundit.'[2] (Doubtless these translated Gospels must have been the books distributed, five or six years ago, at Hurdwar by the Missionary.) 'The written cop-ies we write ourselves, having no other means of obtaining more of this blessed word.' — 'These books,' said Anund, 'teach the religion of the European Sahibs. It is THEIR book; and they printed it in our language, for our use.' 'Ah! no,' replied the stranger, 'that cannot be, for they eat flesh.' — 'Jesus Christ,' said Anund, 'teaches that it does not signify what a man eats or drinks. EATING is nothing before God. *Not that which entereth into a man's mouth defileth him, but that which cometh out of the mouth, this defileth a man: for vile things come forth from the heart. Out of the heart proceed evil thoughts, murders, adulteries, fornications, thefts; and these are the things that defile.*'[3]

'That is true; but how can it be the European Book, when we believe that it is God's gift to us? He sent it to us at Hurdwar.' 'God gave it to us long ago to the Sahibs, and THEY sent it to us.' . . . The ignorance and simplicity of many are very striking, never having heard of a printed book before; and its very appearance was to them miraculous. A great stir was excited by the gradual increasing informa-tion hereby obtained, and all united to acknowledge the superiority of the doctrines of this Holy Book to every thing which they had hitherto heard or known. An indifference to the distinctions of Caste soon manifested itself; and the interference and tyrannical authority of the Brahmins became more offensive and contemptible. At last, it was deter-mined to separate themselves from the rest of their Hindoo Brethren; and to establish a party of their own choosing, four or five, who could read the best, to be the public teachers from this newly-acquired Book. . . . Anund asked them, 'Why are you all dressed in white?' 'The people of God should wear white raiment,' was the reply, 'as a sign that they are clean, and rid of their sins.' — Anund observed, 'You ought to be BAPTIZED, in the name of the Father, and of the Son, and of the Holy Ghost. Come to Meerut: there is a Christian Padre there; and he will shew you what you ought to do.' They answered, 'Now we must go home to the harvest; but, as we mean to meet once a year, perhaps the next year we may come to Meerut.' . . . I explained to them the nature of the Sacrament and of Baptism; in answer to which, they replied, 'We are willing to be baptized, but we will never take the Sacrament. To all the other customs of Christians we are willing to conform, but not to the Sacrament, because the Europeans eat cow's flesh, and this will never do for us.' To this I answered, 'This WORD is of God, and not of men; and when HE makes your hearts to understand, then you will PROPERLY comprehend it.' They replied, 'If all our country will receive this Sacrament, then will we.' I then observed, 'The time is at hand, when all the countries will receive this word!' They replied, 'True!'[4]

Almost a hundred years later, in 1902, Joseph Conrad's Marlow, traveling in the Congo, in the night of the first ages, without a sign and no memories, cut off from the comprehension of his surroundings, desperately in need of a deliber-ate belief, comes upon Towson's (or Towser's) *Inquiry into Some Points of Seamanship*.

[2]The original meaning, which arrives in English in the seventeenth century, is a Hindu learned in Sanskrit.

[3]The Biblical quotation is from Mark 7: 15–23. Since upper-caste Hindus (Brahmins) are vegetarians, Jesus's thesis about the unimportance of dietary laws is as revolutionary to the Indians as it was to the Jews of his own day.

[4]*Missionary Register*, Church Missionary Society, London, Jan. 1818, pp. 18–19; all further references to this work, abbreviated *MR*, will be included in the text, with dates and page numbers in parentheses. [Bhabha]

Not a very enthralling book; but at the first glance you could see there a singleness of intention, an honest concern for the right way of going to work, which made these humble pages, thought out so many years ago, luminous with another than a professional light. . . . I assure you to leave off reading was like tearing myself away from the shelter of an old and solid friendship. . . .

"It must be this miserable trader — this intruder," exclaimed the manager, looking back malevolently at the place we had left. "He must be English," I said.[5]

Half a century later, a young Trinidadian discovers that same volume of Towson's in that very passage from Conrad and draws from it a vision of literature and a lesson of history. "The scene," writes V. S. Naipaul,[6]

answered some of the political panic I was beginning to feel.

To be a colonial was to know a kind of security; it was to inhabit a fixed world. And I suppose that in my fantasy I had seen myself coming to England as to some purely literary region, where, untrammeled by the accidents of history or background, I could make a romantic career for myself as a writer. But in the new world I felt that ground move below me. . . . Conrad . . . had been everywhere before me. Not as a man with a cause, but a man offering . . . a vision of the world's half-made societies . . . where always "something inherent in the necessities of successful action . . . carried with it the moral degradation of the idea." Dismal but deeply felt: a kind of truth and half a consolation.[7]

Written as they are in the name of the father and the author, these texts of the civilizing mission immediately suggest the triumph of the colonialist moment in early English Evangelism and modern English literature. The discovery of the book installs the sign of appropriate representation: the word of God, truth, art creates the conditions for a beginning, a practice of history and narrative. But the institution of the Word in the wilds is also an *Entstellung*,[8] a process of displacement, distortion, dislocation, repetition[9] — the dazzling light of literature sheds only areas of darkness. Still the idea of the English book is presented as universally adequate: like the "metaphoric writing of the West," it communicates "the immediate vision of the thing, freed from the discourse that accompanied it, or even encumbered it."[10]

Shortly before the discovery of the book, Marlow interrogates the odd, inappropriate, "colonial" transformation of a textile into an uncertain textual sign, possibly a fetish:

Why? Where did he get it? Was it a badge — an ornament — a charm — a propitiatory act? Was there any idea at all connected with it? It looked startling round his black neck, this bit of white thread from beyond the seas.[11]

Such questions of the historical act of enunciation, which carry a political intent, are lost, a few pages later, in the myth of origins and discovery. The immediate vision of the book figures those ideological correlatives of the Western sign — empiricism, idealism, mimeticism, monoculturalism (to use Edward Said's term) — that sustain a tradition of English "national" authority. It is, significantly, a normalizing

[5]Joseph Conrad, *Heart of Darkness*, ed. Paul O'Prey (Harmondsworth, 1983), pp. 71, 72. [Bhabha] Bhabha is later to refer to Conrad's international origins: "a Polish émigré, deeply influenced by Gustave Flaubert, writing about Africa, produces an English classic."

[6]Vidiadhar Surajprasad Naipaul (b. 1932) was born on Trinidad, where his father had come as an indentured servant, was educated at Oxford, and has had a four-decade career as a novelist and writer, culminating in the Nobel Prize for literature in 2001. Because of his defense of Western, particularly British, institutions over those that evolved in former colonies after decolonization, Naipaul is a frequent target of postcolonial theorists.

[7]V. S. Naipaul, "Conrad's Darkness," *The Return of Eva Perón* (New York, 1974), p. 233. [Bhabha]

[8]Freud's word for an ego defense, usually translated "displacement."

[9]Overall effect of the dream-work: the latent thoughts are transformed into a manifest formation in which they are not easily recognizable. They are not only transposed, as it were, into another key, but *they are also distorted in such a fashion that only an effort of interpretation can reconstitute them*" (J. Laplanche and J. B. Pontalis, *The Language of PsychoAnalysis*, trans. Donald Nicholson-Smith [London, 1980], p. 124; my emphasis). See also Samuel Weber's excellent chapter "Metapsychology Set Apart," *The Legend of Freud* (Minneapolis, 1982), pp. 32–60. [Bhabha]

[10]Jacques Derrida, *Dissemination*, trans. Barbara Johnson (Chicago, 1981), pp. 189–90; all further references to this work, abbreviated *D*, will be included in the text. [Bhabha]

[11]Conrad, *Heart of Darkness*, p. 45. [Bhabha]

myth whose organic and revisionary narrative is also the history of that nationalist discipline of Commonwealth history and its equally expansionist epigone, Commonwealth literature. Their versions of traditional, academicist wisdom moralize the conflictual moment of colonialist intervention into that constitutive chain of exemplum and imitation, what Friedrich Nietzsche describes as the monumental history beloved of "gifted egoists and visionary scoundrels."[12] For despite first appearances, a repetition of the episodes of the book reveals that they represent important moments in the historical transformation and discursive transfiguration of the colonial text and context.

Anund Messeh's riposte to the natives who refuse the sacrament — "the time is at hand when all countries *will* receive this WORD" (my emphasis) — is both firmly and timely spoken in 1817. For it represents a shift away from the "orientalist" educational practice of, say, Warren Hastings[13] and the much more interventionist and "interpellative" ambition of Charles Grant[14] for a culturally and linguistically homogeneous English India. It was with Grant's election to the board of the East India Company in 1794 and to Parliament in 1802, and through his energetic espousal of the Evangelical ideals of the Clapham sect, that the East India Company reintroduced a "pious clause" into its charter for 1813. By 1817 the Church Missionary Society ran sixty-one schools, and in 1818 it commissioned the Burdwan Plan, a central plan of education for instruction in the English language. The aim of the plan anticipates, almost to the word, Thomas Macaulay's infamous 1835 "Minute on Education": "to form a body of well instructed labourers, competent in their proficiency in English to act as Teachers,"

Translators, and Compilers of useful works for the masses of the people."[15] Anund Messeh's lifeless repetition of chapter and verse, his artless technique of translation, participate in one of the most artful technologies of colonial power.

In the same month that Anund Messeh discovered the miraculous effects of the book outside Delhi — May 1817 — a correspondent of the Church Missionary Society wrote to London describing the method of English education at Father John's mission in Tranquebar:

The principal method of teaching them the English language would be by giving them English phrases and sentences, with a translation for them to commit to memory. These sentences might be so arranged as to teach them whatever sentiments the instructor should choose. They would become, in short, attached to the Mission; and though first put into the school from worldly motives alone, they might soon be converted, accustomed as they are to the language, manners and climate of the country, they might soon be prepared for a great usefulness in the cause of religion. . . . In this way the Heathens themselves might be made the instruments of pulling down their own religion, and of erecting in its ruins the standards of the Cross. [MR, May 1817, p. 187]

Marlow's ruminative closing statement, "He must be English," acknowledges at the heart of darkness, in Conrad's *fin de siècle*[16] malaise which Ian Watt so thoroughly describes, the particular debt that both Marlow and Conrad owe to the ideals of English "liberty" and its liberal-conservative culture.[17] Caught as he is — between the madness of "prehistoric" Africa and the unconscious desire to repeat the traumatic intervention of modern colonialism within the compass of a seaman's yarn — Towson's manual provides Marlow with a singleness of intention. It is the book of work that turns delirium into the discourse of civil address. For the ethic of work, as Conrad was to exemplify in "Tradition"

12 Friedrich Nietzsche, *Untimely Meditations*, trans. R. J. Hollingdale (Cambridge, 1983), p. 71. [Bhabha]

13 Hastings (1732–1818) was the first governor-general of India (1773–86), who respected the Hindu scriptures and employed learned Brahmins to shape the law that would apply to the British Raj.

14 Grant (1746–1823) was a merchant working in India 1763–90 (contemporary with Hastings); on his return to Britain he rose within the East India Corporation to chairman of the board, and forcefully promoted evangelical missionary activity in India.

15 Thomas Babington Macaulay, "Minute on Education," quoted in Elmer H. Cutts, "The Background of Macaulay's Minute," *American Historical Review* 58 (July 1953): 839. [Bhabha]

16 French for "end of the [nineteenth] century." [Bhabha]

17 See Ian Watt, *Conrad in the Nineteenth Century* (Berkeley and Los Angeles, 1979), chap. 4, pt. 1. [Bhabha]

(1918), provides a sense of right conduct and honor achievable only through the acceptance of those "customary" norms which are the signs of culturally cohesive "civil" communities.[18] These aims of the civilizing mission, endorsed in the "idea" of British imperialism and enacted on the red sections of the map,[19] speak with a peculiarly English authority based upon the *customary practice* on which both English common law and the English national language rely for their effectivity and appeal.[20] It is the ideal of English civil discourse that permits Conrad to entertain the ideological ambivalences that riddle his narratives. It is under its watchful eye that he allows the fraught text of late nineteenth-century imperialism to implode within the practices of early modernism. The devastating effects of such an encounter are not only contained in an (un)common yarn; they are concealed in the propriety of a civil "lie" told to the Intended (the complicity of the customary?): "The horror! The horror!" must not be repeated in the drawing-rooms of Europe.

It is to preserve the peculiar sensibility of what he understands as a tradition of civility that Naipaul "translates" Conrad, from Africa to the Caribbean, in order to transform the despair of postcolonial history into an appeal for the autonomy of art. The more fiercely he believes that "the wisdom of the heart ha[s] no concern with the erection or demolition of theories," the more convinced he becomes of the unmediated nature of the Western book — "the words it pronounces have the value of acts of integrity."[21] The values that such a perspective generates for his own work, and for the once colonized world it chooses to represent and evaluate, are visible in the hideous panorama that some of his titles provide: *The Loss of El Dorado, The Mimic Men,* *An Area of Darkness, A Wounded Civilization, The Overcrowded Barracoon.*

The discovery of the English book establishes both a measure of mimesis and a mode of civil authority and order. If these scenes, as I've narrated them, suggest the triumph of the writ of colonialist power, then it must be conceded that the wily letter of the law inscribes a much more ambivalent text of authority. For it is in between the edict of Englishness and the assault of the dark unruly spaces of the earth, through an act of repetition, that the colonial text emerges uncertainly. Anund Messeh disavows the natives' disturbing questions as he returns to repeat the now questionable "authority" of Evangelical dicta; Marlow turns away from the African jungle to recognize, in retrospect, the peculiarly "English" quality of the discovery of the book; Naipaul turns his back on the hybrid half-made colonial world to fix his eye on the universal domain of English literature. What we witness is neither an untroubled, innocent dream of England nor a "secondary revision" of the nightmare of India, Africa, the Caribbean. What is "English" in these discourses of colonial power cannot be represented as a plenitude or a "full" presence; it is determined by its belatedness. As a signifier of authority, the English book acquires its meaning *after* the traumatic scenario of colonial difference, cultural or racial, returns the eye of power to some prior, archaic image or identity. Paradoxically, however, such an image can neither be "original" — by virtue of the act of repetition that constructs it — nor "identical" — by virtue of the difference that defines it. Consequently, the colonial presence is always ambivalent, split between its appearance as original and authoritative and its articulation as repetition and difference.

It is this ambivalence that makes the boundaries of colonial "positionality" — the division of self/other — and the question of colonial power — the differentiation of colonizer/colonized — different from both the Hegelian master/slave dialectic[22] or the phenomenological projection of Otherness. It is a *différance*[23]

---

[18]See Conrad, "Tradition," *Notes on Life and Letters* (London, 1925), pp. 194–201. [Bhabha]

[19]In the first half of the twentieth century, maps conventionally colored red the United Kingdom and all the countries that formed part of the British Empire or Commonwealth.

[20]See John Barrell's excellent chapter "The Language Properly So-called: The Authority of Common Usage," *English Literature in History, 1730–1780: An Equal Wide Survey* (New York, 1983), pp. 110–75. [Bhabha]

[21]Conrad, quoted in Naipaul, "Conrad's Darkness," p. 236. [Bhabha]

[22]See Butler, p. 1039, n. 20.

[23]Bhabha is alluding to Jacques Derrida's essay "Differance."

produced within the act of enunciation as a specifically colonial articulation of those two disproportionate sites of colonial discourse and power: the colonial scene as the invention of his-toricity, mastery, mimesis or as the "other scene" of *Entstellung*, displacement, fantasy, psychic defence, and an "open" textuality. Such a display of difference produces a mode of authority that is agonistic (rather than antagonistic). Its discrimi-natory effects are visible in those split subjects of the racist stereotype — the simian Negro, the effeminate Asiatic male — which ambivalently fix identity as the fantasy of difference.[24] To recognize the *différance* of the colonial pres-ence is to realize that the colonial text occupies that space of double inscription, hallowed — no, hollowed — by Jacques Derrida:

whenever any writing both marks and goes back over its mark with an undecidable stroke . . . [this] double mark escapes the pertinence or authority of truth: it does not overturn it but rather inscribes it within its play as one of its functions or parts. This displacement does not take place, has not taken place once as an *event*. It does not occupy a simple place. It does not take place *in writing*. This dislocation (is what) writes/is (what) [*D*, p. 193]

How can the question of authority, the power and presence of the English, be posed in the interstices of a double inscription? I have no wish to replace an idealist myth — the metaphoric English book — with a historicist one — the colonialist project of English civility. Such a reductive reading would deny what is obvi-ous, that the representation of colonial authority depends less on a universal symbol of English identity than on its productivity as a sign of dif-ference. Yet in my use of "English" there is a "transparency" of reference that registers a certain obvious presence: the Bible translated into Hindi, propagated by Dutch or native catechists, is still the English book; a Polish émigré, deeply influ-enced by Gustave Flaubert, writing about Africa, produces an English classic. What is there about such a process of visibility and recognition that

24 See my "The Other Question — The Stereotype and Colonial Discourse." *Screen* 24 (Nov.–Dec. 1983): 18–36.

[Bhabha]

never fails to be an authoritative acknowledge-ment without ceasing to be a "spacing between desire and fulfillment, between perpetuation and its recollection . . . [a] medium [which] has noth-ing to do with a center" (*D*, p. 212)?

This question demands a departure from Derrida's objectives in "The Double Session"; a turning away from the vicissitudes of interpreta-tion in the mimetic act of reading to the question of the effects of power, the inscription of strate-gies of individuation and domination in those "dividing practices" which construct the colonial space — a departure from Derrida which is also a return to those moments in his essay when he acknowledges the problematic of "presence" as a certain quality of discursive transparency which he describes as "the production of *mere* reality-effects" or "the effect of content" or as the problematic relation between the "medium of writing and the determination of each textual unit." In the rich ruses and rebukes with which he shows up the "false appearance of the pres-ent," Derrida fails to decipher the specific and determinate system of *address* (not referent) that is signified by the "effect of content" (see *D*, pp. 173–85). It is precisely such a strategy of address — the *immediate presence* of the English — that engages the questions of authority that I want to raise. When the ocular metaphors of presence refer to the process by which content is fixed as an "effect of the present," we encounter not plenitude but the structured gaze of power whose objective is authority, whose "subjects" are historical.

The reality effect constructs a mode of address in which a complementarity of meaning — not a correspondential notion of truth, as anti-real-ists insist — produces the moment of discursive transparency. It is the moment when, "under the false appearance of the present," the semantic seems to prevail over the syntactic, the signified over the signifier. Contrary to current avant-garde orthodoxy, however, the transparent is neither simply the triumph of the "imaginary" capture of the subject in realist narrative nor the ultimate interpellation of the individual by ideology. It is not a proposal that you cannot positively refuse. It is better described, I suggest, as a form of the *disposal* of those discursive signs of presence/

the present within the strategies that articulate the range of meanings from "dispose to disposition." Transparency is the action of the distribution and arrangement of differential spaces, positions, knowledges in relation to each other, relative to a differential, not inherent, sense of order. This effects a regulation of spaces and places that is authoritatively assigned; it puts the addressee into the proper frame or condition for some action or result. Such a mode of governance addresses itself to a form of conduct that is achieved through a reality effect that equivocates between the sense of disposal, as the bestowal of a frame of reference, and disposition, as mental inclination, a frame of mind. Such equivocation allows neither an equivalence of the two sites of disposal nor their division as self/other, subject/object. Transparency achieves an effect of authority in the present (and an authoritative presence) through a process similar to what Michel Foucault describes as "an effect of finalisation, relative to an objective." Without its necessary attribution to a subject that makes a prohibitory law, thou shalt or thou shalt not.[25]

The place of difference and otherness, or the space of the adversarial, within such a system of "disposal" as I've proposed, is never entirely on the outside or implacably oppositional. It is a pressure, and a presence, that acts constantly, if unevenly, along the entire boundary of authorization, that is, on the surface between what I've called disposal-as-bestowal and disposition-as-inclination. The contour of difference is agonistic, shifting, splitting, rather like Freud's description of the system of consciousness which occupies a position in space lying on the borderline between outside and inside, a surface of protection, reception, and projection.[26] The power play of presence is lost if its transparency is treated naively as the nostalgia for plenitude that should be flung repeatedly into the abyss — *mise en abîme* — from which its desire is born. Such theoreticist anarchism cannot intervene in the agonistic space of authority where

> the true and the false are separated and specific effects of power [are] attached to the true, it being understood also that it is not a matter of a battle "on behalf" of the truth, but of a battle about the status of truth and the economic and political role it plays.[27]

It is precisely to intervene in such a battle for the *status* of the truth that it becomes crucial to examine the *presence* of the English book. For it is this *surface* that stabilizes the agonistic colonial space; it is its *appearance* that regulates the ambivalence between origin and *Entstellung*, discipline and desire, mimesis and repetition.

Despite appearances, the text of transparency inscribes a double vision: the field of the "true" emerges as a visible effect of knowledge/power only after the regulatory and displacing division of the true and the false. From this point of view, discursive "transparency" is best read in the photographic sense in which a transparency is also always a negative, processed into visibility through the technologies of reversal, enlargement, lighting, editing, projection, not a source but a re-source of light. Such a bringing to light is never a prevision; it is always a question of the provision of visibility as a capacity, a strategy, an agency but also in the sense in which the prefix pro(vision) might indicate an elision of sight, delegation, substitution, contiguity, in place of . . . what?

This is the question that brings us to the ambivalence of the presence of authority, peculiarly visible in its colonial articulation. For if transparency signifies discursive closure — intention, image, author — it does so through a disclosure of its *rules of recognition* — those social texts of epistemic, ethnocentric, nationalist intelligibility which cohere in the address of authority as the "present," the voice of modernity. The acknowledgement of authority depends upon the immediate — unmediated — visibility of its rules of recognition as the unmistakable referent

[25]Michel Foucault, "The Confession of the Flesh," *Power/Knowledge: Selected Interviews and Other Writings*, 1972–1977, ed. Colin Gordon, trans. Gordon et al. (New York, 1980), p. 204. [Bhabha]

[26]See Sigmund Freud, *Beyond the Pleasure Principle*, trans. and ed. James Strachey (London, 1974), pp. 18–25. [Bhabha]

[27]Foucault, "Truth and Power," *Power/Knowledge*, p. 132. [Bhabha]

of historical necessity. In the doubly inscribed space of colonial representation where the presence of authority — the English book — is also a question of its repetition and displacement, where transparency is *techné*,[28] the immediate visibility of such a régime of recognition is resisted. Resistance is not necessarily an oppositional act of political intention, nor is it the simple negation or exclusion of the "content" of an other culture, as a difference once perceived. It is the effect of an ambivalence produced within the rules of recognition of dominating discourses as they articulate the signs of cultural difference and reimplicate them within the deferential relations of colonial power — hierarchy, normalization, marginalization, and so forth. For domination is achieved through a process of disavowal that denies the *différance* of colonialist power — the chaos of its intervention as *Entstellung*, its dislocatory presence — in order to preserve the authority of its identity in the universalist narrative of nineteenth-century historical and political evolutionism.

The exercise of colonialist authority, however, requires the production of differentiations, individuations, identity effects through which discriminatory practices can map out subject populations that are tarred with the visible and transparent mark of power. Such a mode of subjection is distinct from what Foucault describes as "power through transparency": the reign of opinion, after the late eighteenth century, which could not tolerate areas of darkness and sought to exercise power through the mere fact of things being known and people seen in an immediate, collective gaze.[29] What radically differentiates the exercise of colonial power is the unsuitability of the Enlightenment assumption of collectivity and the eye that beholds it. For Jeremy Bentham[30] (as Michel Perrot[31] points out), the small group

is representative of the whole society — the part is *already* the whole. Colonial authority requires modes of discrimination (cultural, racial, administrative . . .) that disallow a stable unitary assumption of collectivity. The "part" (which must be the colonialist foreign body) must be representative of the "whole" (conquered country), but the right of representation is based on its radical difference. Such doublethink is made viable only through the strategy of disavowal just described, which requires a theory of the "hybridization" of discourse and power that is ignored by Western post-structuralists who engage in the battle for "power" as the purists of difference.

The discriminatory effects of the discourse of cultural colonialism, for instance, do not simply refer to a "person," or to a dialectical power struggle between self and Other, or to a discrimination between mother culture and alien cultures. Produced through the strategy of disavowal, the *reference* of discrimination is always to a process of splitting as the condition of subjection: a discrimination between the mother culture and its bastards, the self and its doubles, where the trace of what is disavowed is not repressed but repeated as something *different* — a mutation, a hybrid. It is such a partial and double force that is more than the mimetic but less than the symbolic, that disturbs the visibility of the colonial presence and makes the recognition of its authority problematic. To be authoritative, its rules of recognition must reflect consensual knowledge or opinion; to be powerful, these rules of recognition must be breached in order to represent the exorbitant objects of discrimination that lie beyond its purview. Consequently, if the unitary (and essentialist) reference to race, nation, or cultural tradition is essential to preserve the presence of authority as an immediate mimetic effect, such essentialism must be exceeded in the articulation of "differentiatory," discriminatory identities.

To demonstrate such an "excess" is not merely to celebrate the joyous power of the signifier. Hybridity is the sign of the productivity of colonial power, its shifting forces and fixities; it is the name for the strategic reversal of the process of domination through disavowal (that is, the production of discriminatory identities that

28 Greek for "art."

29 Foucault, "The Eye of Power," *Power/Knowledge*, p. 154; and see pp. 152-56. [Bhabha]

30 English utilitarian philosopher (1748-1832).

31 Probably Bhabha means Michelle Perrot, French cultural historian of the Annales school, author of "L'Inspecteur Bentham" and editor of *Le Panoptique* (1977), a French edition of Bentham's writings on the model prison, the Panopticon, that he proposed in 1787.

secure the "pure" and original identity of authority). Hybridity is the revaluation of the assumption of colonial identity through the repetition of discriminatory identity effects. It displays the necessary deformation and displacement of all sites of discrimination and domination. It unsettles the mimetic or narcissistic demands of colonial power but reimplicates its identifications in strategies of subversion that turn the gaze of the discriminated back upon the eye of power. For the colonial hybrid is the articulation of the ambivalent space where the rite of power is enacted on the site of desire, making its objects at once disciplinary and disseminatory — or, in my mixed metaphor, a negative transparency. If discriminatory effects enable the authorities to keep an eye on them, their proliferating difference evades that eye, escapes that surveillance. Those discriminated against may be instantly recognized, but they also force a recognition of the immediacy and articulacy of authority — a disturbing effect that is familiar in the repeated hesitancy afflicting the colonialist discourse when it contemplates its discriminated subjects: the *inscrutability* of the Chinese, the *unspeakable* rites of the Indians, the *indescribable* habits of the Hottentots. It is not that the voice of authority is at a loss for words. It is, rather, that the colonial discourse has reached that point when, faced with the hybridity of its objects, the *presence* of power is revealed as something other than what its rules of recognition assert.

If the effect of colonial power is seen to be the *production* of hybridization rather than the noisy command of colonialist authority or the silent repression of native traditions, then an important change of perspective occurs. It reveals the ambivalence at the source of traditional discourses on authority and enables a form of subversion, founded on that uncertainty, that turns the discursive conditions of dominance into the grounds of intervention. It is traditional academic wisdom that the presence of authority is properly established through the nonexercise of private judgment and the exclusion of reasons, in conflict with the authoritative reason. The recognition of authority, however, requires a validation of its source that must be immediately, even intuitively, apparent — "You have that in your countenance which I would fain call master"[32] — and held in common (rules of recognition). What is left unacknowledged is the paradox of such a demand for proof and the resulting ambivalence for positions of authority. If, as Steven Lukes rightly says, the acceptance of authority excludes any evaluation of the content of an utterance, and if its source, which must be acknowledged, disavows both conflicting reasons and personal judgment, then can the "signs" or "marks" of authority be anything more than "empty" presences of strategic devices?[33] Need they be any the less effective because of that? Not less effective but effective in a different form, would be our answer.

Tom Nairn reveals a basic ambivalence between the symbols of English imperialism which could not help "looking universal" and a "hollowness [that] sounds through the English imperialist mind in a thousand forms: in Rider Haggard's necrophilia, in Kipling's moments of gloomy doubt, . . . in the gloomy cosmic truth of Forster's Marabar caves."[34] Nairn explains this "imperial delirium" as the disproportion between the grandiose rhetoric of English imperialism and the *real* economic and political situation of late Victorian England. I would like to suggest that these crucial moments in English literature are not simply crises of England's own making. They are also the signs of a discontinuous history, an estrangement of the English book. They mark the disturbance of its authoritative representations by the uncanny forces of race, sexuality, violence, cultural and even climatic differences which emerge in the colonial discourse as the mixed and split texts of hybridity. If the appearance of the English book is read as a production of colonial hybridity, then it no longer simply commands authority. It gives rise to a series of *questions of authority* that, in my bastardized repetition, must sound strangely familiar:

> Was it a badge — an ornament — a charm — a propitiatory act? Was there any idea at all connected with it? It looked startling in this black neck of the woods, this bit of white writing from beyond the seas.

[32] Alludes to Kent's line spoken to Lear in *King Lear* I.iv.
[33] See Steven Lukes, "Power and Authority," in *A History of Sociological Analysis*, ed. Tom Bottomore and Robert Nisbet (New York, 1978), pp. 633–76. [Bhabha]
[34] Tom Nairn, *The Break-Up of Britain: Crisis and Neo-Nationalism* (London, 1981), p. 265. [Bhabha]

In repeating the scenario of the English book, I hope I have succeeded in representing a colonial difference: it is the effect of uncertainty that afflicts the discourse of power, an uncertainty that estranges the familiar symbol of English "national" authority and emerges from its colonial appropriation as the sign of its difference. Hybridity is the name of this displacement of value from symbol to sign that causes the dominant discourse to split along the axis of its power to be representative, authoritative. Hybridity represents that ambivalent "turn" of the discriminated subject into the terrifying, exorbitant object of paranoid classification — a disturbing questioning of the images and presences of authority. To grasp the ambivalence of hybridity, it must be distinguished from an inversion that would suggest that the originary is, really, only the "effect" of an *Entstellung*. Hybridity has no such perspective of depth or truth to provide: it is not a third term that resolves the tension between two cultures, or the two scenes of the book, in a dialectical play of "recognition." The displacement from symbol to sign creates a crisis for any concept of authority based on a system of recognition: colonial specularity, doubly inscribed, does not produce a mirror where the self apprehends itself; it is always the split screen of the self and its doubling, the hybrid.

These metaphors are very much to the point, because they suggest that colonial hybridity is not a *problem* of genealogy or identity between two *different* cultures which can then be resolved as an issue of cultural relativism. Hybridity is a *problematic* of colonial representation and individuation that reverses the effects of the colonialist disavowal, so that other "denied" knowledges enter upon the dominant discourse and estrange the basis of its authority — its rules of recognition. Again, it must be stressed, it is not simply the *content* of disavowed knowledges — be they forms of cultural Otherness or traditions of colonialist treachery — that return to be acknowledged as counterauthorities. For the resolution of conflicts between authorities, civil discourse always maintains an adjudicative procedure. What is irremediably estranging in the presence of the hybrid — in the revaluation of the symbol of national authority as the sign of colonial difference — is that the difference of cultures can no longer be identified or evaluated as objects of epistemological or moral contemplation: they are not simply *there* to be seen or appropriated.

Hybridity reverses the *formal* process of disavowal so that the violent dislocation the *Entstellung* of the act of colonization, becomes the *conditionality* of colonial discourse. The presence of colonialist authority is no longer immediately visible: its discriminatory identifications no longer have their authoritative reference to this culture's cannibalism or that people's perfidy. As an articulation of displacement and dislocation, it is now possible to identify "the cultural" as a disposal of power, a negative transparency that comes to be agonistically constructed *on the boundary* between frame of reference/ frame of mind. It is crucial to remember that the colonial construction of the cultural (the site of the civilizing mission) through the process of disavowal is authoritative to the extent to which it is structured around the ambivalence of splitting, denial, repetition — strategies of defence that mobilize culture as an open-textured, warlike strategy whose aim "is rather a continued agony than a total disappearance of the pre-existing culture."[35] To see the cultural not as the *source* of conflict — *different* cultures — but as the *effect* of discriminatory practices — the production of cultural *differentiation* as signs of authority — changes its value and its rules of recognition. What is preserved is the visible surfaces of its artefacts — the mere *visibility* of the symbol, as a fleeting immediacy. Hybridity intervenes in the exercise of authority not merely to indicate the impossibility of its identity but to represent the unpredictability of its presence. The book retains its presence, but it is no longer a representation of an essence; it is now a partial presence, a (strategic) device in a specific colonial engagement, an appurtenance of authority.

This partializing process of hybridity is best described as a metonymy of presence. It shares Sigmund Freud's valuable insight into the strategy of disavowal as the persistence of the narcissistic demand in the acknowledgement of

[35]Frantz Fanon, *Toward the African Revolution*, trans. Haakon Chevalier (Harmondsworth, 1967), p. 44. [Bhabha]

difference.[36] This, however, exacts a price, for the existence of two contradictory knowledges (multiple beliefs) splits the ego (or the discourse) into two psychical attitudes, and forms of knowledge, toward the external world. The first of these takes reality into consideration while the second replaces it with a product of desire. What is remarkable is that these two contradictory objectives always represent a "partiality" in the construction of the fetish object, at once a substitute for the phallus and a mark of its absence. There is an important difference between fetishism and hybridity. The fetish reacts to the change in the value of the phallus by fixing on an object *prior to the perception of difference*, an object that can metaphorically substitute for its presence while registering the difference. So long as it fulfills the fetishistic ritual, the object can look like anything (or nothing!). The hybrid object, however, retains the actual semblance of the authoritative symbol but revalues its presence by resisting it as the signifier of *Entstellung — after the intervention of difference*. It is the power of this strange metonymy of presence to so disturb the systematic (and systemic) construction of discriminatory knowledges that the cultural, once recognized as the medium of authority, becomes virtually unrecognizable. Culture, as a colonial space of intervention and agonism, as the trace of the displacement of symbol to sign, can be transformed by the unpredictable and partial desire of hybridity. Deprived of their full presence, the knowledges of cultural authority may be articulated with forms of "native" knowledges or faced with those discriminated subjects that they must rule but can no longer represent. This may lead, as in the case of the natives outside Delhi, to questions of authority that the authorities — the Bible included — cannot answer. Such a process is not the deconstruction of a cultural system from the margins of its own aporia nor, as in Derrida's "Double Session," the mime that haunts mimesis. The display of hybridity — its peculiar "replication" — terrorizes authority with the *ruse* of recognition, its mimicry, its mockery.

Such a reading of colonial authority profoundly unsettles the demand that figures at the center of the originary myth of colonialist power. It is the demand that *the space it occupies be unbounded*, its reality *coincident* with the emergence of an imperialist narrative and history, its discourse *nondialogic*, its enunciation *unitary*, unmarked by the trace of difference — a demand that is recognizable in a range of justificatory Western "civil" discourses where the presence of the "colony" often alienates its own language of liberty and reveals its universalist concepts of labor and property as particular, post-Enlightenment ideological and technological practices. Consider, for example: Locke's notion of the wasteland of Carolina — "Thus in the beginning all the World was *America*"; Montesquieu's emblem of the wasteful and disorderly life and labor in despotic societies — "When the savages of Louisiana are desirous of fruit, they cut the tree to the root, and gather the fruit"; Grant's belief in the impossibility of law and history in Muslim and Hindu India — "where treasons and revolutions are continual; by which the insolent and abject frequently change places"; or the contemporary Zionist myth of the neglect of Palestine — "of a *whole* territory," Said writes, "essentially unused, unappreciated, misunderstood . . . *to be made* useful, appreciated, understandable."[37]

What renders this demand of colonial power impossible is precisely the point at which the question of authority emerges. For the unitary voice of command is interrupted by questions that arise from these heterogeneous sites and circuits of power which, though momentarily "fixed" in the authoritative alignment of subjects, must continually be represented in the production of terror or fear — the paranoid threat from the hybrid is finally uncontainable because it breaks down the symmetry and duality of self/Other, inside/outside. In the productivity of power, the

---

[36]See Freud, *An Outline of Psycho-Analysis*, trans. and ed. Strachey (London, 1973), pp. 59–61. [Bhabha]

[37]John Locke, "The Second Treatise of Government," *Two Treatises of Government* (New York, 1965), p. 343, par. 49; Baron de Montesquieu, *The Spirit of the Laws*, trans. Thomas Nugent (New York, 1949), p. 57; Charles Grant, "Observations on the State of Society among the Asiatic Subjects of Great Britain," *Sessional Papers of the East India Company* 10, no. 282 (1812–13): 70; Edward W. Said, *The Question of Palestine* (New York, 1979), p. 85. [Bhabha]

boundaries of authority — its reality effects — are always besieged by "the other scene" of fixations and phantoms. We can now understand the link between the psychic and political that is suggested in Frantz Fanon's figure of speech: the colon[38] is an exhibitionist, because his *preoccupation* with security makes him "remind the native out loud that there he alone is master."[39] The native, caught in the chains of colonialist command, achieves a "pseudo-petrification" which further incites and excites him, thus making the settler-native bound-ary an anxious and ambivalent one. What then presents itself as the subject of authority in the discourse of colonial power is, in fact, a desire that so exceeds the original authority of the book and the immediate visibility of its metaphoric writing that we are bound to ask: What does colonial power want? My answer is only partially in agreement with Lacan's *vel*[40] or Derrida's veil or hymen. For the desire of colonial discourse is a splitting of hybridity that is *less than one and double*; and if that sounds enigmatic, it is because its explanation has to wait upon the authority of those canny questions that the natives put, so insistently, to the English book.

The native questions quite literally turn the origin of the book into an enigma. First: *How can the word of God come from the flesh-eating mouths of the English?* — a question that faces the unitary and universalist assumption of author-ity with the cultural difference of its historical moment of enunciation. And later: *How can it be the European Book, when we believe that it is*

[38] French for "colonialist."

[39] Fanon, *The Wretched of the Earth*, trans. Constance Farrington (Harmondsworth, 1969), p. 42. [Bhabha]

[40] *Vel* is Latin for an exclusive "or": A or B, and never both. In *The Four Fundamental Concepts of Psychoanalysis*, Lacan introduces the concept of the "*vel*" as the choice by which the subject is alienated from the self. At the fall into language, the subject has to choose between meaning (the big Other, language) and being (the subject): The choice splits the subject: when one chooses being, the subject disappears into non-meaning; when one chooses meaning, the part of meaning that corresponds to the subject disappears into the unconscious. Later Bhabha will allude to Seminar XI, in which Lacan illustrates the *vel* with the highwayman's line, "Your money or your life." Choosing your money doesn't mean you get to live to spend your money, but no matter what you choose, you don't get to keep everything. So the fall into language is always accompanied by a sense of loss.

God's gift to us? He sent it to Hurdwar. This is not merely an illustration of what Foucault would call the capillary effects of the microtechnics of power. It reveals the penetrative power — *both* psychic and social — of the technology of the printed word in early nineteenth-century rural India. Imagine the scene: the Bible, perhaps trans-lated into a North Indian dialect like Brighbasha, handed out free or for one rupee within a culture where usually only caste Hindus would possess a copy of the Scriptures, and received in awe by the natives as both a novelty and a household deity. Contemporary missionary records reveal that, in Middle India alone, by 1815 we could have wit-nessed the spectacle of the Gospel "doing its own work," as the Evangelicals put it, in at least eight languages and dialects, with a first edition of between one thousand and ten thousand copies in each translation (see *MR*, May 1816, pp. 181–82). It is the force of these colonialist practices that produces that discursive tension between Anund Messeh, whose address *assumes* its authority, and the natives who question the English presence and seek a culturally differentiated, "colonial" authority *to* address.

The subversive character of the native ques-tions will be realized only once we recognize the strategic disavowal of cultural/historical differ-ence in Anund Messeh's Evangelical discourse. Having introduced the *presence* of the English and their *intercession* — "God gave [the Book] long ago to the Sahibs, and THEY sent it to us" — he then disavows that political/linguistic "imposition" by attributing the intervention of the Church to the power of God and the received authority of chapter and verse. What is being dis-avowed is not entirely visible in Anund Messeh's avowal "What he, as well as the English "enounced." What he, at the level of the contradictory statements, must conceal are their particu-lar enunciatory conditions — that is, the design of the Burdwan Plan to deploy "natives" to destroy native culture and religion. This is done through the repeated production of a teleological narrative of Evangelical witness: eager conversions, bereft Brahmins, and Christian gatherings. The descent from God to the English is both linear and circu-lar: "This WORD is of God, and not of men; and when HE makes your hearts to understand, then you will PROPERLY comprehend." The historical "evidence" of Christianity is plain for all to see, Indian Evangelists would have argued, with the help of William Paley's *Evidences of Christianity* (1791), the most important missionary manual throughout the nineteenth century. The miraculous authority of colonial Christianity, they would have held, lies precisely in its being both English and universal, empirical and uncanny, for "ought we not rather to expect that such a Being on occasions of peculiar importance, may interrupt the order which he had appointed?"[41] The Word, no less theocratic than logocentric, would have certainly borne absolute witness to the gospel of Hurdwar had it not been for the rather tasteless fact that most Hindus were vegetarian!

By taking their stand on the grounds of dietary law, the natives resist the miraculous equivalence of God and the English. They introduce the practice of colonial cultural differentiation *as* an indispensable *enunciative function* in the discourse of authority — a function Foucault describes as linked to "a 'referential' that . . . forms the place, the condition, the field of emergence, the *authority to differentiate* between individuals or objects, states of things and relations that are brought into play by the statement itself; it defines the possibilities of appearance and delimitation."[42] Through the natives' strange questions, it is possible to see, with historical hindsight, what they resisted in questioning the presence of the English — as religious mediation and as a cultural and linguistic medium. What is the value of English in the offering of the Hindi Bible? It is the creation of a print technology calculated to produce a visual effect that will not "look like the work of foreigners"; it is the decision to produce simple, abridged tracts of the plainest narrative that may inculcate the habit of "private, solitary reading," as a missionary wrote in 1816, so that the natives may resist the Brahmin's "monopoly of knowledge" and lessen their dependence on their own religious and cultural traditions; it is the

opinion of the Reverend Donald Corrie that "on learning English they acquire ideas quite new, and of the first importance, respecting God and his government" (*MR*, July 1816, p. 193; Nov. 1816, pp. 444–45; Mar. 1816, pp. 106–7). It is the shrewd view of an unknown native, in 1819:

> For instance, I take a book of yours and read it awhile and whether I become a Christian or not, I leave the book in my family: after my death, my son, conceiving that I would leave nothing useless or bad in my house, will look into the book, understand its contents, consider that his father left him that book, and become a Christian. [*MR*, Jan. 1819, p. 27]

When the natives demand an Indianized Gospel, they are using the powers of hybridity to resist baptism and to put the project of conversion in an impossible position. Any adaptation of the Bible was forbidden by the evidences of Christianity, for, as the bishop of Calcutta preached in his Christmas sermon in 1815: "I mean that it is a Historical Religion: the History of the whole dispensation is before us from the creation of the world to the present hour: and it is throughout consistent with itself and with the attributes of God" (*MR*, Jan. 1817, p. 31). Their stipulation that only mass conversion would persuade them to take the sacrament touches on a tension between missionary zeal and the East India Company Statutes for 1814 which strongly advised against such proselytizing. When they make these intercultural, hybrid demands, the natives are both challenging the boundaries of discourse and subtly changing its terms by setting up another specifically colonial space of power/ knowledge. And they do this under the eye of authority, through the production of "partial" knowledges and positionalities in keeping with my earlier, more general explanation of hybridity. Such objects of knowledges make the signifiers of authority enigmatic in a way that is "less than one and double." They change their conditions of recognition while maintaining their visibility; they introduce a lack that is then represented as a doubling or mimicry. This mode of discursive disturbance is a sharp practice, rather like that of the perfidious barbers in the bazaars of Bombay who do not mug their customers with the blunt Lacanian *vel* "Your money or your life," leaving

---

[41]William Paley, quoted in D. L. LeMahieu, *The Mind of William Paley: A Philosopher and His Age* (Lincoln, Nebr., 1976), p. 97. [Bhabha]

[42]Foucault, *The Archaeology of Knowledge*, trans. A. M. Sheridan Smith (London, 1972), p. 91; my emphasis. [Bhabha]

them with nothing. No, these wily oriental thieves, with far greater skill, pick their clients' pockets and cry out, "How the master's face shines!" and then, in a whisper, "But he's lost his mettle!"

And this traveler's tale, told by a native, is an emblem of that form of splitting — less than one and double — that I have suggested for the reading of the ambivalence of colonial cultural texts. In estranging the word of God from the English medium, the natives' questions dispense the logical order of the discourse of authority — "These books . . . teach the religion of the European Sahibs. It is their Book; and they printed it in our language, for our use." The natives expel the copula, or middle term, of the Evangelical "power = knowledge" equation, which then disarticulates the structure of the God-Englishman equivalence. Such a crisis in the positionality and propositionality of colonial-ist authority destabilizes the sign of authority. For by alienating "English," as the middle term, the presence of authority is freed of a range of ideological correlates — for instance, intentional-ity, originality, authenticity, cultural normativity. The Bible is now ready for a specific colonial appropriation. On the one hand, its paradigmatic presence as the Word of God is assiduously pre-served: it is only to the direct quotations from the Bible that the natives give their unquestion-ing approval — "True!" The expulsion of the copula, however, empties the presence of its syntagmatic supports — codes, connotations, and cultural associations that give it contiguity and continuity — that make its presence culturally and politically authoritative.

In this sense, then, it may be said that the *presence* of the book has acceded to the logic of the signifier and has been "separated," in Lacan's use of the term, from "itself." If, on one side, its authority, or some symbol or meaning of it, is maintained — willy-nilly, *less than one* — then, on the other, it fades. It is at the point of its fading that the signifier of presence gets caught up in an alienating strategy of doubling or repetition. Doubling repeats the fixed and empty presence of authority by articulating it syntagmatically with a range of differential knowledges and posi-tionalities that both estrange its "identity" and produce new forms of knowledge, new modes

of differentiation, new sites of power. In the case of the colonial discourse, these syntagmatic appropriations of presence confront it with those contradictory and threatening differences of its enunciative function that had been disavowed. In their repetition, these disavowed knowledges return to make the presence of authority uncertain. This may take the form of multiple or contradic-tory beliefs, as in some forms of native knowl-edges: "We are willing to be baptized, but we will never take the Sacrament." Or they may be forms of mythic explanation that refuse to acknowledge the agency of the Evangelicals: "An Angel from heaven gave it [the Bible] us at Hurdwar fair." Or they may be the fetishistic repetition of litany in the face of an unanswerable challenge to author-ity: for instance, Anund Messeh's "*Not that which entereth into a man's mouth defileth him, but that which cometh out of the mouth.*"

In each of these cases we see a colonial doubling which I've described as a strategic displacement of value through a process of the metonymy of presence. It is through this partial process, repre-sented in its enigmatic, inappropriate signifiers — stereotypes, jokes, multiple and contradictory beliefs, the "native" Bible — that we begin to get a sense of a specific space of cultural colonial discourse. It is a "separate" space, a space of *separation* — less than one and double — which has been systematically denied by both colonial-ists and nationalists who have sought authority in the authenticity of "origins." It is precisely as a separation from origins and essences that this colonial space is constructed. It is separate, in the sense in which the French psychoanalyst Victor Smirnoff describes the separateness of the fetish as a "separateness that makes the fetish easily available, so that the subject can make use of it in his own way and establish it in an order of things that frees it from any subordination."[43]

The metonymic strategy produces the signifier of colonial *mimicry* as the affect of hybridity — at once a mode of appropriation and of resis-tance, from the disciplined to the desiring. As the discriminated object, the metonym of presence

[43]Victor N. Smirnoff, "The Fetishistic Transaction," in *Psychoanalysis in France*, ed. Serge Leboivici and Daniel Widlöcher (New York, 1980), p. 307. [Bhabha]

becomes the support of an authoritarian voyeurism, all the better to exhibit the eye of power. Then, as discrimination turns into the assertion of the hybrid, the insignia of authority becomes a mask, a mockery. After our experience of the native interrogation, it is difficult to agree entirely with Fanon that the psychic choice is to "turn white or disappear."[44] There is the more ambivalent, third choice: camouflage, mimicry, black skins/white masks. "Mimicry reveals something in so far as it is distinct from what might be called an *itself* that is behind. The effect of mimicry," writes Lacan, "is camouflage, in the strictly technical sense. It is not a question of harmonizing with the background but, against a mottled background, of being mottled — exactly like the technique of camouflage practiced in human warfare."[45]

Read as a masque of mimicry, Anund Messeh's tale emerges as a *question* of colonial authority, an agonistic space. To the extent to which discourse is a form of defensive warfare, mimicry marks those moments of civil disobedience within the discipline of civility: signs of spectacular resistance. When the words of the master become the site of hybridity — the warlike sign of the native — then we may not only read between the lines but even seek to change the often coercive reality that they so lucidly contain. It is with the strange sense of a hybrid history that I want to end.

Despite Anund Messeh's miraculous evidence, "native Christians were never more than vain phantoms" as J. A. Dubois wrote in 1815, after twenty-five years in Madras. Their parlous partial state caused him particular anxiety,

> for in embracing the Christian religion they never entirely renounce their superstitions towards which they always keep a secret bent . . . there is no *unfeigned, undisguised* Christian among these Indians. [*MR*, Nov. 1816, p. 212]

And what of the native discourse? Who can tell?

The Reverend Mr. Corrie, the most eminent of the Indian evangelists, warned that

> till they came under the English Government, they have not been accustomed to assert the nose upon their face their own. . . . This temper prevails, more or less, in the converted. [*MR*, Mar. 1816, pp. 106–7]

Archdeacon Potts, in handing over charge to the Reverend J. P. Sperschneider in July 1818, was a good deal more worried:

> If you urge them with their gross and unworthy misconceptions of the nature and will of God or the monstrous follies of their fabulous theology, they will turn it off with a sly civility perhaps, or with a popular and careless proverb. [*MR*, Sept. 1818, p. 375]

Was it in the spirit of such sly civility that the native Christians parried so long with Anund Messeh and then, at the mention of baptism, politely excused themselves: "Now we must go home to the harvest. . . . perhaps the next year we may come to Meerut."

And what is the significance of the Bible? Who knows?

Three years before the native Christians received the Bible at Hurdwar, a schoolmaster named Sandappan wrote from southern India, asking for a Bible:

> Rev. Fr. Have mercy upon me. I am amongst so many craving beggars for the Holy Scriptures the chief craving beggar. The bounty of the bestowers of this treasure is so great I understand, that even this book is read in rice and salt-markets. [*MR*, June 1813, pp. 221–22]

But, in the same year — 1817 — as the miracle outside Delhi, a much-tried missionary wrote in some considerable rage:

> Still everyone would gladly receive a Bible. And why? That he may store it up as a curiosity; sell it for a few pice; or use it for waste paper. . . . Some have been bartered in the markets. . . . If these remarks are at all warranted then an indiscriminate distribution of the scriptures, to everyone who may say he wants a Bible, can be little less than a waste of time, a waste of money and a waste of expectations. For while the public are hearing of so many Bibles distributed, they expect to hear soon of a correspondent number of conversions. [*MR*, May 1817, p. 186]

[44]See Fanon, "The Negro and Psychopathology," *Black Skin, White Masks*, trans. Charles Lam Markmann (New York, 1967). [Bhabha]

[45]Jacques Lacan, *The Four Fundamental Concepts of Psycho-analysis*, ed. Jacques-Alain Miller, trans. Alan Sheridan (New York, 1978), p. 99. [Bhabha]

Henry Louis Gates Jr.
b. 1950

Henry Louis Gates Jr. was born in Keyser, West Virginia, and received his bachelor's degree in history from Yale University. At age twenty, he hitchhiked through Africa on a Carnegie Foundation fellowship. In 1973 Gates studied at Clare College, Cambridge University, where his tutor, the African writer Wole Soyinka, shifted Gates's interests from history to literature, particularly to the ways in which African mythology and folktales inform the literature of Africa and the American diaspora. Upon completing his Ph.D. in English literature at Cambridge in 1979, Gates was appointed to a professorship at Yale, where he had been teaching since 1976. Gates's initial groundbreaking publication was the reprinting in 1983 of the first novel by a black woman, Harriet Wilson's Our Nig (1859). Gates has continued his recovery of "lost" texts by black Americans in the Schomberg Library of Nineteenth-Century Black Women's Writings, of which he is series editor. In 1987 he published two books, Figures in Black: Words, Signs, and the Racial Self, and The Signifying Monkey: Towards a Theory of Afro-American Literature, which together established his reputation as one of the premier black theorists in the country, but also attracted animated response from those whose work stressed material culture rather than semiotics and style. Drawing on his work with Soyinka in African mythology, Gates's poststructuralist approach to African American literature defines its particular way of "signifying" as being based on an inherited oral tradition. His work is equally concerned with the continuities between African and African American modes of reader-response and interpretation. Gates has taught at Yale, Cornell, and Duke Universities, and is currently Alphonse Fletcher Professor and Director of the Hutchins Center for African American Research at Harvard University. His recent books include Loose Canons: Notes on the Culture Wars (1992), Speaking of Race, Speaking of Sex: Hate Speech, Civil Rights, and Civil Liberties (1994), The Future of the Race (with Cornel West, 1996), The Norton Anthology of African American Literature (general editor, with Nelly Y. McKay, 1996; second edition 2004), Thirteen Ways of Looking at a Black Man (1997), The African American Century (2000), The Trials of Phillis Wheatley (2003), America Behind the Color Line (2004), In Search of Our Roots (2009), Tradition and the Black Atlantic: Critical Theory in the African Diaspora (2010), Faces of America (2010), and Life Upon These Shores: Looking at African American History 1513–2008 (2011). His autobiography is Colored People: A Memoir (1994). The present selection, which was first published in Critical Inquiry in 1985, is reprinted from Loose Canons.

Writing, "Race," and the
Difference It Makes

The truth is that, with the fading of the Renaissance ideal through progressive stages of specialism, leading to intellectual emptiness, we are left with a potentially suicidal movement among "leaders of the profession," while, at the same time, the profession sprawls, without its old center, in helpless disarray.

One quickly cited example is the professional organization, the Modern Language Association. . . . A glance at its thick program for its last meeting shows a massive increase and fragmentation into more than 500 categories! I cite a few examples. . . . "The Trickster Figure in Chicano and Black Literature". . . . Naturally, the progressive trivialization of topics has made these meetings a laughingstock in the national press.

— W. JACKSON BATE

... language, for the individual consciousness, lies on the borderline between oneself and the other. The word in language is half someone else's. It becomes "one's own" only when the speaker populates it with his own intention, his own accent, when he appropriates the word, adapting it to his own semantic and expressive intention. Prior to this moment of appropriation, the word does not exist in a neutral and impersonal language (it is not, after all, out of a dictionary that the speaker gets his words!), but rather it exists in other people's mouths, in other people's contexts, serving other people's intentions: it is from there that one must take the word, and make it "one's own."

— MIKHAIL BAKHTIN

They cannot represent themselves; they must be represented.

— MARX

I

Of what import is "race" as a meaningful category in the study of literature and the shaping of critical theory? If we attempt to answer this question by examining the history of Western literature and its criticism, our initial response would ostensibly be "nothing," or at the very least, "nothing explicitly." Indeed, until the past decade or so, even the most subtle and sensitive literary critics would most probably have argued that, except for aberrant moments in the history of criticism, "race" has been brought to bear upon the study of literature in no apparent way. The Western literary tradition, after all, and the canonical texts that comprise this splendid tradition, has been defined since Eliot as a more-or-less closed set of works that somehow speak to, or respond to, the "human condition" and to each other in formal patterns of repetition and revision.[1] And while judgment is subject to the moment and indeed does reflect temporal-specific presuppositions, certain works seem to transcend value judgments of the moment, speaking irresistibly to

the "human condition." The question of the place of texts written by "the Other" (be that odd metaphor defined as African, Arabic, Chinese, Latin American, female, or Yiddish authors) in the proper study of "literature," "Western literature," or "comparative literature" has, until recently, remained an unasked question, suspended or silenced by a discourse in which the "canonical" and the "noncanonical" stand as the ultimate opposition. "Race," in much of the thinking about the proper study of literature in this century, has been an invisible quality, present implicitly at best.

This was not always the case, of course. By the middle of the nineteenth century, "national spirit" and "historical period" had become widely accepted metaphors within theories of the nature and function of literature which argued that the principal value in a "great" work of literary art resided in the extent to which these categories were *reflected* in that work of art. Montesquieu's *Esprit des lois* had made a culture's formal social institution the repository of its "guiding spirit," while Vico's *Principii d'una scienza nuova* had read literature against a complex pattern of historical cycles.[2] The two Schlegels managed rather deftly to bring to bear upon the interpretation of literature "both national spirit and historical period," as Walter Jackson Bate has shown.[3] But it was Taine who made the implicit explicit by postulating "race, moment, and *milieu*" as positivistic criteria through which any work could be read, and which, by definition, any work reflected. Taine's *History of English Literature* is the great foundation upon which subsequent nineteenth-century notions of "national literatures" would be constructed.[4]

[1]Gates alludes to T. S. Eliot's "Tradition and the Individual Talent"; see p. 321.

[2]Charles-Louis de Secondat Montesquieu (1689–1755), a French philosopher, wrote *De l'esprit des lois (On the Spirit of the Laws)* in 1749. Giambattista Vico (1668–1744), an Italian philosopher, wrote *Principii d'una scienza nuova intorno alla natura delle nazioni (Principles of a New Science of Nations)*, proposing a cyclical theory of history in 1725; the work is generally referred to as the *Scienza nuova*.

[3]August Wilhelm (1767–1845) and Friedrich von Schlegel (1772–1829) were German philologists, theorists of the Romantic movement.

[4]The *Histoire de la littérature anglaise* (1863) of Hippolyte Taine (1828–1893) accounted for national literatures in terms of a scheme involving ethnicity, environment, and history: *race, milieu, moment.*

What Taine called "race" was the source of all structures of feeling. To "track the root of man," he wrote, "is to consider the race itself. . . . the structure of his character and mind, his general processes of thought and feeling, . . . the irregularity and revolutions of his conception, which arrest in him the birth of fair dispositions and harmonious forms, the disdain of appearances, the desire for truth, the attachment for bare and abstract ideas, which develop in him conscience, at the expense of all else." In "race," Taine concluded, was predetermined "a particularity inseparable from all the motions of his intellect and his heart. Here lie the grand causes, for they are the universal and permanent causes. . . . indestructible, and finally infallibly supreme." "Poetries," as Taine put it, and all other forms of social expression, "are in fact only the imprints stamped by their seal."

"Race," for Taine was "the first and richest source of these master faculties from which historical events take their rise;" it was a "community of blood and intellect which to this day binds its off-shoots together." Lest we misunderstand the *naturally* determining role of "race," Taine concluded that it "is no simple spring but a kind of lake, a deep reservoir wherein other springs have, for a multitude of centuries, discharged their several streams."

Taine's originality lay not in these ideas about the nature and role of race, but in their almost "scientific" application to the history of literature. These ideas about race were received from the Enlightenment, if not from the Renaissance. By midpoint in the nineteenth century, ideas of irresistible racial differences were commonly held: when Abraham Lincoln invited a small group of black leaders to the White House in 1862 to share with them his ideas about returning all blacks in America to Africa, his argument turned upon these "natural" differences. "You and we are different races," he said. "We have between us a broader difference than exists between any other two races." Since this sense of difference was never to be bridged, Lincoln concluded, the slaves and the ex-slaves should be returned to their own. The growth of canonical "national" literatures was coterminous with the shared assumption among intellectuals that

"race" was a "thing," an ineffaceable quantity, which irresistibly determined the shape and contour of thought and feelings as surely as it did the shape and contour of human anatomy.

How did the great movement away from "race, moment, and *milieu*" and toward the language of the text in the 1920s and 1930s in the Practical Criticism movement at Cambridge[5] and the New Criticism movement at Yale affect this category of "race" in the reading of literature? Race, along with all sorts of other unseemly or untoward notions about the composition of the literary work of art, was bracketed or suspended. Race, within these theories of literature to which we are all heir, was rendered *implicit* in the elevation of ideas of canonical *cultural* texts that comprise the Western tradition in Eliot's simultaneous order, with a simultaneous existence. History, *milieu*, and even moment were brought to bear upon the interpretation of literature through philology and etymology: the dictionary — in the Anglo-American tradition, the *Oxford English Dictionary* — was the castle in which Taine's criteria took refuge. Once the concept of value became encased in the belief in a canon of texts whose authors purportedly shared a "common culture" inherited from *both* the Greco-Roman and the Judeo-Christian traditions, no one need speak of matters of "race," since "the race" of these authors was "the same." One not heir to these traditions was, by definition, of another "race." This logic was impenetrable.

Despite their beliefs in the unassailable primacy of language in the estimation of a work of literature, however, both I. A. Richards and Allen Tate,[6] in separate prefaces to books of poems by black authors, paused to wonder aloud about the black faces of the authors, and the import this had upon the reading of their texts. The often claimed

5 The "Practical Criticism movement at Cambridge" refers to the British branch of New Criticism pioneered by I. A. Richards and William Empson. See the introduction to Formalisms, p. 416.

6 John Orley Allen Tate (1899–1979) was a Kentucky-born poet and critic whose *Reason in Madness* (1941) allied him with the group of other Southern critics (including Cleanth Brooks, Robert Penn Warren, John Crowe Ransom) who led the American wing of "New Criticism." See the introduction to Formalisms, p. 416.

"racism" of the Southern Agrarians,[7] while an easily identifiable target, was only an explicit manifestation of presuppositions that formed a large segment of the foundation upon which formalism was built. The citizens of the republic of literature, in other words, were all white, and mostly male. Difference, if difference obtained at all, was a difference obliterated by the "simultaneity" of Eliot's "tradition." Eliot's fiction of tradition, for the writer of a culture of color, was the literary equivalent of the "grandfather clause." So, in response to Robert Penn Warren's statement in "Pondy Woods" — "Nigger, your breed ain't metaphysical" — Sterling A. Brown wrote, "Cracker, your breed ain't exegetical." The Signifyin(g) pun deconstructed the "racialism" inherent in these claims of tradition.

II

"Race" as a meaningful criterion within the biological sciences has long been recognized to be a fiction. When we speak of the "white race" or the "black race," the "Jewish race" or the "Aryan race," we speak in misnomers, biologically, and in metaphors, more generally. Nevertheless, our conversations are replete with usages of *race* which have their sources in the dubious pseudoscience of the eighteenth and nineteenth centuries. One need only flip through the pages of the *New York Times* to find headlines such as "Brown University President Sees School Racial Problems," or "Sensing Racism, Thousands March in Paris." In a lead editorial of its March 29, 1985, number, "The Lost White Tribe," the *Times* notes that while "racism is not unique to South Africa," we must condemn that society because "Betraying the religious tenets underlying Western culture, it has made race the touchstone of political rights." Eliot's "dissociation of sensibility," caused in large part by the "fraternal" atrocities of World War I, and then by the inexplicable and insane murder of European Jews two decades later, the *Times* editorial echoes. (For millions of people who originated outside Europe, however, this dissociation of sensibility had its origins in colonialism and human slavery.) *Race*, in these usages, pretends to be an objective term of classification, when in fact it is a trope.[8]

The sense of difference defined in popular usages of the term *race* has been used both to describe and *inscribe* differences of language, belief system, artistic tradition, "gene pool," and all sorts of supposedly "natural" attributes such as rhythm, athletic ability, cerebration, usury, and fidelity. The relation between "racial character" and these sorts of "characteristics" has been inscribed through tropes of race, lending to even supposedly "innocent" descriptions of cultural tendencies and differences the sanction of God, biology, or the natural order. "Race consciousness," Zora Neale Hurston wrote, "is a deadly explosive on the tongues of men." I even heard a member of the House of Lords in 1973 describe the differences between Irish Protestants and Catholics in terms of their "distinct and clearly definable differences of race."

"You mean to say that you can tell them apart?" I asked incredulously.

"Of course," responded the lord. "Any Englishman can."

Race has become a trope of ultimate, irreducible difference between cultures, linguistic groups, or practitioners of specific belief systems, who more often than not have fundamentally opposed economic interests. Race is the ultimate trope of difference because it is so very arbitrary in its application. The sanction of biology contained in sexual difference, simply put, does not and can never obtain when one is speaking of "racial difference." Yet, we carelessly use language in such a way as to *will* this sense of *natural* difference into our formulations. To do so is to engage in a pernicious act of language, one which exacerbates the complex problem of cultural or "ethnic" difference, rather than assuages or redresses it. This is especially the case at a time when racism has become fashionable, once again. That, literally every day, scores of people

[7]Social philosophy of the 1930s, hostile to both Marxism and corporate capitalism, espoused primarily by Southern intellectuals. Tate contributed an essay, "Remarks on the Southern Religion" to *I'll Take My Stand: The South and the Agrarian Tradition by Twelve Southerners* (1930).

[8]Gates may be alluding to the fact that the word "race" originates with the Latin *radix*, "root."

are killed in the name of differences ascribed to "race," only makes even more imperative this gesture to "deconstruct," if you will, the ideas of difference inscribed in the trope of race, to take discourse itself as our common subject to be explicated to reveal the latent relations of power and knowledge inherent in popular and academic usages of "race." When twenty-five thousand people feel compelled to gather on the Rue de Rivoli in support of the antiracist "Ne touche pas à mon pote" movement,[9] when thousands of people willingly accept arrest to protest apartheid, when Iran and Iraq feel justified in murdering the other's citizens because of their "race," when Beirut stands as a museum of shards and pieces reflecting degrees of horror impossible to comprehend, the gesture that we make here seems local and tiny.

There is a curious dialectic between formal language use and the inscription of metaphorical "racial" differences. At times, as Nancy Stepan expertly shows in *The Idea of Race in Science*, these metaphors have sought a universal and transcendent sanction in biological science. Western writers in French, Spanish, German, Portuguese, and English have sought to make literal these rhetorical figures of "race," to make them natural, absolute, essential. In doing so, they have *inscribed* these differences as fixed and finite categories which they merely report or draw upon for authority. But it takes little reflection to recognize that these pseudoscientific categories are themselves figures of thought. Who has seen a black or red person, a white, yellow, or brown? These terms are arbitrary constructs, not reports of reality. But language is not only the medium of this often pernicious tendency, it is its *sign*. Language use signifies the difference between cultures and their possession of power, spelling the difference between subordinate and superordinate, between bondsman and lord. Its call into use is simultaneous with the shaping of an economic order in which the cultures of color have been dominated in several important senses by Western Judeo-Christian, Greco-Hellenic cultures

[9]The slogan of an antiracist movement founded in Paris in the 1980s by Harlem Désir was "Touche pas à mon pote," colloquial French for "Don't touch my pal."

and their traditions. To use contemporary theories of criticism to explicate these modes of inscription is to demystify large and obscure ideological relations and indeed theory itself. It would be useful here to consider a signal example of the black tradition's confinement and delimitation by the commodity of writing. For literacy, as I hope to demonstrate, could be the most pervasive emblem of capitalist commodity functions.

III

Where better to test this thesis than in the example of the black tradition's first poet in English, the African slave girl Phillis Wheatley. Let us imagine a scene:

One bright morning in the spring of 1772, a young African girl walked demurely into the courthouse at Boston, to undergo an oral examination, the results of which would determine the direction of her life and work. Perhaps she was shocked upon entering the appointed room. For there, gathered in a semicircle, sat eighteen of Boston's most notable citizens. Among them was John Erving, a prominent Boston merchant; the Reverend Charles Chauncey, pastor of the Tenth Congregational Church and a son of Cotton Mather; and John Hancock, who would later gain fame for his signature on the Declaration of Independence. At the center of this group would have sat His Excellency, Thomas Hutchinson, governor of the colony, with Andrew Oliver, his lieutenant governor, close by his side.

Why had this august group been assembled? Why had it seen fit to summon this young African girl, scarcely eighteen years old, before it? This group of "the most respectable characters in Boston," as it would later define itself, had assembled to question the African adolescent closely on the slender sheaf of poems that the young woman claimed to have written by herself. We can only speculate on the nature of the questions posed to the fledgling poet. Perhaps they asked her to explain for all to hear exactly who were the Greek and Latin gods and poets alluded to so frequently in her work. Or perhaps they asked her to conjugate a verb in Latin, or even to translate randomly selected passages from the Latin, which she and her master, John Wheatley, claimed that she "had made some progress in." Or perhaps they asked her to recite from memory key passages from the texts of Milton and Pope, the two poets by whom the African claimed to be most directly influenced. We do not know.

We do know, however, that the African poet's responses were more than sufficient to prompt the eighteen august gentlemen to compose, sign, and publish a two-paragraph "Attestation," an open letter "To the Publick" that prefaces Phillis Wheatley's book, and which reads in part:

> We whose Names are underwritten, do assure the World, that the poems specified in the following Page, were (as we verily believe) written by Phillis, a young Negro Girl, who was but a few Years since, brought an uncultivated Barbarian from *Africa*, and has ever since been, and now is, under the Disadvantage of serving as a Slave in a Family in this Town. She has been examined by some of the best judges, and is thought qualified to write them.

So important was this document in securing a publisher for Phillis's poems that it forms the signal element in the prefatory matter printed in the opening pages of her *Poems on Various Subjects, Religious and Moral*, published at London in 1773.

Without the published "Attestation," Wheatley's publisher claimed, few would believe that an African could possibly have written poetry all by herself. As the eighteen put the matter clearly in their letter, "Numbers would be ready to suspect they were not really the Writings of Phillis." Phillis's master, John Wheatley, and Phillis had attempted to publish a similar volume in 1770 at Boston, but Boston publishers had been incredulous. Three years later, "Attestation" in hand, Phillis and her mistress's son, Nathaniel Wheatley, sailed for England, where they completed arrangements for the publication of a volume of her poems, with the aid of the Countess of Huntington and the Earl of Dartmouth.

This curious anecdote, surely one of the oddest oral examinations on record, is only a tiny part of a larger, and even more curious, episode in the eighteenth century's Enlightenment. At least since 1600, Europeans had wondered aloud whether or not the African "species of men," as they most commonly put it, *could* ever create

formal literature, could ever master the "arts and sciences." If they could, the argument ran, then the African variety of humanity and the European variety were fundamentally related. If not, then it seemed clear that the African was destined by nature to be a slave.

Determined to discover the answer to this crucial quandary, several Europeans and Americans undertook experiments in which young African slaves were tutored and trained along with white children. Phillis Wheatley was merely one result of such an experiment. Francis Williams, a Jamaican who took the B.A. at the University of Cambridge before 1730; Jacobus Capitein, who earned several degrees in Holland; Wilheim Amo, who took the doctorate degree in philosophy at Halle; and Ignatius Sancho, who became a friend of Sterne's and who published a volume of letters in 1782 — these were just a few of the black subjects of such "experiments." The published writings of these black men and one woman, who wrote in Latin, Dutch, German, and English, were seized upon both by pro- and antislavery proponents as proof that their arguments were sound.

So widespread was the debate over "the nature of the African" between 1730 and 1830 that not until the Harlem Renaissance would the work of black writers be as extensively reviewed as it was in the eighteenth century. Phillis Wheatley's list of reviewers includes Voltaire, Thomas Jefferson, George Washington, Samuel Rush, and James Beatty, to name only a few.[10] Francis Williams's work was analyzed by no less than David Hume and Immanuel Kant. Hegel, writing in the *Philosophy of History* in 1813, used the writings of these Africans as the sign of their innate inferiority. The list of commentators is extensive, amounting to a "Who's Who" of the French, English, and American Enlightenment.

Why was the *creative writing* of the African of such importance to the eighteenth century's debate over slavery? I can briefly outline one thesis: After Descartes, *reason* was privileged,

[10]"Samuel Rush" may be Benjamin Rush (1745–1813), Pennsylvania-born scientist and abolitionist; "James Beatty" may be James Beattie (1735–1803), Scottish poet and philosopher.

or valorized, among all other human characteristics. Writing, especially after the printing press became so widespread, was taken to be the *visible* sign of reason. Blacks were "reasonable," and hence "men," if — and only if — they demonstrated mastery of the "arts and sciences," the eighteenth century's formula for writing. So, while the Enlightenment is famous for establishing its existence upon the human ability to reason, it simultaneously used the absence and presence of "reason" to delimit and circumscribe the very humanity of the cultures and people of color which Europeans had been "discovering" since the Renaissance. The urge toward the systematization of all human knowledge, by which we characterize the Enlightenment, led directly to the relegation of black people to a lower rung on the Great Chain of Being, an eighteenth-century construct that arranged all of creation on a vertical scale from animals and plants and insects through humans to the angels and God himself.

By 1750, the chain had become individualized; the human scale slid from "the lowliest Hottentot" (black south Africans) to "glorious Milton and Newton." If blacks could write and publish imaginative literature, then they could, in effect, take a few Giant Steps up the Chain of Being, in a pernicious game of "Mother, May I?" As the Reverend James W. C. Pennington, an ex-slave who wrote a slave narrative and who was a prominent black abolitionist, summarized this curious idea in his prefatory note "To the Reader" that authorized Ann Plato's 1841 book of essays, biographies, and poems: "The history of the arts and sciences is the history of individuals, of individual nations." Only by publishing books such as Plato's, he argued, could blacks demonstrate *"the fallacy of that stupid theory, that nature has done nothing but fit us for slaves, and that art cannot unfit us for slavery?"*

IV

The relation between what, for lack of a better term, I shall call the "nonwhite" writer and the French, Portuguese, Spanish, and English languages and literatures manifests itself in at least two ways of interest to theorists of literature and literary history. I am thinking here of what in psychoanalytic criticism is sometimes called "the other," and more especially of this "other" as the subject and object in literature. What I mean by citing these two overworked terms is precisely this: how blacks are figures in literature, and also how blacks *figure*, as it were, literature of their own making.

These two poles of a received opposition have been formed, at least since the early seventeenth century, by an extraordinary *subdiscourse* of the European philosophies of aesthetic theory and language. The two subjects, often in marginal ways, have addressed directly the supposed relation among "race," defined variously as language use and "place in nature." Human beings wrote books. Beautiful books were reflections of sublime genius. Sublime genius was the province of the European. Blacks, and other people of color, could not "write." "Writing," these writers argued, stood alone among the fine arts as the most salient repository of "genius," the visible sign of reason itself. In this subordinate role, however, "writing," although secondary to "reason," was nevertheless the *medium* of reason's expression. *They knew* reason by its writing, by its representations. This representation could assume the spoken or the written form. And while several superb scholars gave priority to the spoken as the privileged of the pair, in their writings about blacks, at least, Europeans privileged *writing* as the principal measure of Africans' "humanity," their "capacity for progress," their very place in "the great chain of being."

This system of signs is arbitrary. Key words, such as *capacity*, which became a metaphor for cranial size, reflect the predominance of "scientific" discourse in metaphysics. That "reason," moreover, could be seen to be "natural" was the key third term of a homology which, in practice, was put to pernicious uses. The transformation of writing from an activity of mind into a commodity not only reflects larger mercantile relations between Africa and Europe but is also the subject I wish to explore here. Let me retrace, in brief, the history of this idea, of the relationship of the absence of "writing" and the absence of "humanity" in European letters of 1600.

We must understand this correlation of use and *presence* in language if we are to begin to learn how to read, the slave's narrative within what Geoffrey H. Hartman calls its "text-milieu." The slave narratives, taken together, represent the attempt of blacks to *write themselves into being*. What a curious idea: Through the mastery of formal Western languages, the presupposition went, a black person could posit a full and sufficient self, as an act of self-creation through the medium of language. Accused of having no collective history by Hegel, blacks effectively responded by publishing hundreds of individual histories which functioned as the part standing for the whole. As Ralph Ellison defined this relation, "We tell ourselves our individual stories so as to become aware of our *general* story."

Writing as the visible sign of Reason, at least since the Renaissance in Europe, had been consistently invoked in Western aesthetic theory in the discussion of the enslavement and status of the black. The origin of this received association of political salvation and artistic genius can be traced at least to the seventeenth century. What we arrive at by extracting a rather black and slender thread from among the philosophical discourses of the Enlightenment is a reading of another side of the philosophy of enlightenment, indeed its nether side. Writing in *The New Organon* in 1620, Sir Francis Bacon, confronted with the problem of classifying the people of color which a seafaring Renaissance Europe had "discovered," turned to the arts as the ultimate measure of a race's place in nature. "Again," he wrote, "let a man only consider what a difference there is between the life of men in the most civilized province of Europe, and in the wildest and most barbarous districts of New India; he will feel it be great enough to justify the saying that 'man is a god to man,' not only in regard to aid and benefit, but also by comparison of condition. And this difference comes not from soil, not from climate, not from race, but from the arts." Eleven years later, Peter Heylyn, in his *Little Description of the Great World*, used Bacon's formulation to relegate the blacks to a subhuman status: Black Africans, he wrote, lacked completely "the use of Reason which is peculiar unto man; [they are] of little Wit; and destitute of all arts and sciences; prone to luxury, and for the greatest part Idolators." All subsequent commentaries on the matter were elaborations upon Heylyn's position.

By 1680, Heylyn's key words, *reason* and *wit*, had been reduced to "reading and writing," as Morgan Godwyn's summary of received opinion attests:

> [A] disingenuous and unmanly *Position* had been formed; and privately (and as it were *in the dark*) handed to and again, which is this, That the Negro's though in their figure they carry some resemblances of manhood, yet are indeed *no* men. . . . the consideration of the shape and figure of our Negro's Bodies, their Limbs and members; their Voice and Countenance, in all things according with other mens; together with their *Risibility* and *Discourse* (man's Peculiar Faculties) should be sufficient Conviction. How should they otherwise be capable of *Trades*, and other no less manly imployments; as also of *Reading and Writing*, or show so much Discretion in management of Business; . . . but wherein (we know) that many of our own People are *deficient*, were they not truly Men?

Such a direct correlation of political rights and literacy helps us to understand both the transformation of writing into a commodity and the sheer burden of received opinion that motivated the black slave to seek his or her text. As well, it defined the "frame" against which each black text would be read. The following 1740 South Carolina statute was concerned to make it impossible for black literacy mastery even to occur:

> *And whereas* the having of slaves taught to write, or suffering them to be employed in writing, may be attending with great inconveniences;
>
> *Be it enacted*, that all and every person and persons whatsoever, who shall hereafter teach, or cause any slave or slaves to be taught to write, or shall use or employ any slave as a scribe in any manner of writing whatsoever, hereafter taught to write; every such person or persons shall, for every offense, forfeit the sum of one hundred pounds current money.

Learning to read and to write, then, was not only difficult, it was a violation of a law. That Frederick Douglass, Thomas Smallwood, William Wells Brown, Moses Grandy, James Pennington, and John Thompson, among numerous others,[11] all

---

[11]Frederick Douglass and the rest were authors of slave narratives.

rendered statements about the direct relation between freedom and discourse not only as central scenes of instruction but also as repeated fundamental structures of their very rhetorical strategies only emphasizes the dialectical relation of black texts to a "context," defined here as "*other*," racist texts, against which the slave's narrative, by definition, was forced to react.

By 1705, a Dutch explorer, William Bosman, had encased Peter Heylyn's bias into a myth which the Africans he had "discovered" had purportedly related to him. It is curious insofar as it justifies human slavery. According to Bosman, the blacks 'tell us that in the beginning God created Black as well as White men; thereby giving the Blacks the first Election, who chose Gold, and left the Knowledge of Letters to the White. God granted their request, but being incensed at their Avarice, resolved that the Whites should ever be their masters, and they obliged to wait on them as their slaves." Bosman's fabrication, of course, was a myth of origins designed to sanction through mythology a political order created by Europeans. It was David Hume, writing at midpoint in the eighteenth century, who gave to Bosman's myth the sanction of Enlightenment philosophical reasoning.

In a major essay, "Of National Characters" (1748), Hume discussed the "characteristics" of the world's major division of human beings. In a footnote added to his original text in 1753 (the margins of his discourse), Hume posited with all of the authority of philosophy the fundamental identity of complexion, character, and intellectual capacity. "I am apt to suspect the negroes," he wrote,

and in general all the other species of men (for there are four or five different kinds) to be naturally inferior to the whites. There never was a civilized nation of any other complexion than white, nor even any individual eminent either in action or speculation. No ingenious manufacturers amongst them, *no arts, no sciences.*...Such a uniform and constant difference could not happen, in so many countries and ages, if *nature* had not made our original distinction betwixt these breeds of men. Not to mention our colonies, there are Negroe slaves dispersed all over Europe, of which none ever discovered any symptoms of ingenuity....In Jamaica, indeed they

talk of one negroe as a man of parts and learning [Francis Williams, the Cambridge-educated poet who wrote verse in Latin]; but 'tis likely he is admired for very slender accomplishments, like a parrot who speaks a few words plainly.

Hume's opinion on the subject, as we might expect, became prescriptive.

Writing in 1764, in his *Observations on the Feelings of the Beautiful and the Sublime,* Immanuel Kant elaborated upon Hume's essay in a fourth section entitled "Of National Characteristics, as far as They Depend upon the Distinct Feeling of the Beautiful and the Sublime." Kant first claimed that "So fundamental is the difference between [the black and white] races of man, and it appears to be as great in regard to mental capacities as in color." Kant, moreover, was one of the earliest major European philosophers to conflate "color" with "intelligence," a determining relation he posited with dictatorial surety. The excerpt bears citation:

...Father Labat reports that a Negro carpenter, whom he reproached for haughty treatment toward his wives, answered: "You whites are indeed fools, for first you make great concessions to your wives, and afterward you complain when they drive you mad." And it might be that there were something in this which perhaps deserved to be considered; but in short, this fellow was *quite black* from head to foot, a clear proof that what he said was stupid. (emphasis added)

The correlation of "blackness" and "stupidity" Kant posited as if self-evident.

Writing in "Query XIV" of *Notes on the State of Virginia,* Thomas Jefferson maintained that "Never yet could I find that a black had uttered a thought above the level of plain narration, never see even an elementary trait of painting or sculpture." Of Wheatley, the first black person to publish a book of poetry in England, Jefferson wrote, "Misery is often the parent of the most affecting touches in poetry. Among the blacks is misery enough, God knows, but not poetry.... The compositions published under her name are below the dignity of criticism."

In that same year (1785), Kant, basing his observations on the absence of published writing among blacks, noted as if simply obvious that "Americans [Indians] and blacks are lower in their mental capacities than all other races." Again, Hegel, echoing Hume and Kant, noted the absence of history among black people and derided them for failing to develop indigenous African scripts, or even to master the art of writing in modern languages.

Hegel's strictures on the African about the absence of "history" presume a crucial role of *memory* — a collective, cultural memory — in the estimation of civilization. Metaphors of the "childlike" nature of the slaves, of the masked, puppetlike "personality" of the black, all share this assumption about the absence of memory. Mary Langdon, in her 1855 novel *Ida May: A Story of Things Actual and Possible*, wrote that "but then they *are* mere children. . . . You seldom hear them say much about anything that's past, if they only get enough to eat and drink at the present moment." Without writing, there could exist no *repeatable* sign of the workings of reason, of mind. Without memory or mind, there could exist no history. Without history, there could exist no "humanity," as defined consistently from Vico to Hegel. As William Gilmore Simms[12] argued at the middle of the nineteenth century:

> [If one can establish] that the negro intellect is fully equal to that of the white race . . . you not only take away the best argument for keeping him in subjection, but you take away the possibility of doing so. *Prima facie*, however, the fact that he *is* a slave, is conclusive against the argument for his freedom, as it is against his equality of claim in respect of intellect. . . . Whenever the negro shall be fully fit for freedom, he will make himself free, and no power on earth can prevent him.

V

Ironically, Anglo-African writing arose as a response to allegations of its absence. Black people responded to these profoundly serious allegations about their "nature" as directly as they

[12]Gilmore Simms (1806–1870) is best known as the author of *The Yemasee* (1835), a romance influenced by Walter Scott about the conflict between the Carolina colonists and the native Yemasee tribe.

could: they wrote books, poetry, autobiographical narratives. Political and philosophical discourse were the predominant forms of writing. Among these, autobiographical "deliverance" narratives were the most common, and the most accomplished. Accused of lacking a formal and collective history, blacks published individual histories which, taken together, were intended to narrate, in segments, the larger yet fragmented history of blacks in Africa, now dispersed throughout a cold New World. The narrated, descriptive "eye" was put into service as a literary form to posit both the individual "I" of the black author and the collective "I" of the race. Text created author, and black authors, it was hoped, would create, or re-create, the image of the race in European discourse. The very *face* of the race, representations of the features of which are common in all sorts of writings about blacks at this time, was contingent upon the recording of the black *voice*. Voice presupposes a face but also seems to have been thought to determine the contours of the black face.

The recording of an "authentic" black voice, a voice of deliverance from the deafening discursive silence which an enlightened Europe cited as proof of the absence of the African's humanity, was the millennial instrument of transformation through which the African would become the European, the slave become the ex-slave, the brute animal become the human being. So central was this idea to the birth of the black literary tradition in the eighteenth century that five of the earliest slave narratives draw upon the figure of the voice in the text as crucial "scenes of instruction" in the development of the slave on the road to freedom. James Gronniosaw in 1770, John Marrant in 1785, Ottobah Cugoano in 1787, Olaudah Equiano in 1789, and John Jea in 1815 — all drew upon the trope of the talking book. Gronniosaw's usage bears citing here especially because it repeats Kant's correlation of physical — and, as it were, metaphysical — characteristics:

> My master used to read prayers in public to the ship's crew every Sabbath day; and when I first saw him read, I was never so surprised in my life, as when I saw the book talk to my master, for I thought it did, as I observed him to look upon it, and move his lips. I wished it would do so with

me. As soon as my master had done reading, I followed him to the place where he put the book, being mightily delighted with it, and when nobody saw me, I opened it, and put my ear down close upon it, in great hope that it would say something to me; but I was very sorry, and greatly disappointed, when I found that it would not speak. This thought immediately presented itself to me, that every body and every thing despised me because I was black.

Even for this black author, his own mask of black humanity was a negation, a sign of absence. Gronniosaw accepted his role as a nonspeaking would-be subject and the absence of his common humanity with the European.

That the figure of the talking book recurs in these five black eighteenth-century texts says much about the degree of presupposition and intertextuality in early black letters, more than we heretofore thought. Equally important, however, this figure itself underscores the received correlation between silence and blackness which we have been tracing, as well as the urgent need to make the text speak, the process by which the slave marked his distance from the master. The voice in the text was truly a millennial voice for the African person of letters in the eighteenth century, for it was that very voice of deliverance and of redemption which would signify a new order for the black.

These narrators, linked by revision of a trope into the very first black chain of signifiers, implicitly signify upon another "chain," the meta-phorical Great Chain of Being. Blacks were most commonly represented on the chain either as the "lowest" of the human races, or as first cousin to the ape. Since writing, according to Hume, was the ultimate sign of difference between animal and human, these writers implicitly were Signifying(g) upon the figure of the chain itself, simply by publishing autobiographies that were indictments of the received order of Western culture, of which slavery, to them, by definition stood as the most salient sign. The writings of Gronniosaw, Marrant, Equiano, Cugoano, and Jea served as a critique of the sign of the Chain of Being and the black person's "place" on the chain. This chain of black signifiers, regardless of their intent or desire, made the first

political gesture in the Anglo-African literary tra-dition "simply" by the act of writing, a collective act that gave birth to the black literary tradition and defined it as the "other's chain," the chain of black being as black people themselves would have it. Making the book speak, then, constituted a motivated, and political, engagement with and condemnation of Europe's fundamental figure of domination, the Great Chain of Being.

The trope of the talking book is not a trope of the presence of voice at all, but of its absence. To speak of a "silent voice" is to speak in an oxymoron. There is no such thing as a silent voice. Furthermore, as Juliet Mitchell has put the matter, there is something untenable about the attempt to represent what is not there, to repre-sent that which is *missing* or absent. Given that this is what these five black authors sought to do, we are justified in wondering aloud if the sort of subjectivity that they sought could be realized through a process that was so very ironic from the outset. Indeed, how can the black subject posit a full and sufficient self in a language in which blackness is a sign of absence? Can writing, the very "difference" it makes and marks, mask the blackness of the black face that addresses the text of Western letters, in a voice that "speaks English" in an idiom that contains the irreducible element of cultural difference that shall always separate the white voice from the black? Black people, we know, have not been "liberated" from racism by their writings, and they accepted a false premise by assuming that racism would be destroyed once white racists became convinced that we were human, too. Writing stood as a complex "certificate of humanity," as Paulin J. Hountondji put it. Black writing, and especially the literature of the slave, served not to obliterate the difference of "race," as a would-be white man such as Gronniosaw so ardently desired; rather, the inscription of the black voice in Western literatures has preserved those very cultural dif-ferences to be imitated and revised in a separate Western literary tradition, a tradition of black difference.

Blacks, as we have seen, tried to write them-selves out of slavery, a slavery even more pro-found than mere physical bondage. Accepting the challenge of the great white Western tradition, black writers wrote as if their lives depended upon it — and, in a curious sense, their lives did, the "life" of "the race" in Western discourse. But if blacks accepted this challenge, we also accepted its premises, premises in which perhaps lay concealed a trap. What trap might this be? Let us recall the curious case of M. Edmond Laforest.

In 1915, Edmond Laforest, a prominent member of the Haitian literary movement called La Ronde, made of his death a symbolic, if ironic, statement of the curious relation of the "non-Western" writer to the act of writing in a modern language. M. Laforest, with an inimitable, if fatal, flair for the grand gesture, stood upon a bridge, calmly tied a Larousse dictionary[13] around his neck, then proceeded to leap to his death by drowning. While other black writers, before and after M. Laforest, have suffocated as artists beneath the weight of various modern languages, Laforest chose to make his death an emblem of this relation of indenture.

It is the challenge of the black tradition to critique this relation of indenture, an indenture that obtains for our writers and for our critics. We must master, as Derrida wrote, "how to speak the other's language without renouncing (our) own." When we attempt to appropriate, by inversion, *race* as a term for an essence, as did the Negritude movement, for example ("We feel, therefore we are," as Senghor argued of the African), we yield too much, such as the basis of a shared humanity. Such gestures, as Anthony Appiah has observed, are futile and dangerous because of their further inscription of new and bizarre stereotypes. How do we meet Derrida's challenge in the discourse of criticism? The Western critical tradition has a canon, just as does the Western literary tradition. Whereas I once thought it our most important gesture to *master* the canon of criticism, to *imitate* and *apply* it, I now believe that we must turn to the black tradition itself to arrive at theories of criticism indigenous to our literatures. Alice Walker's revision of a parable of white interpretation written in 1836 by Rebecca Cox Jackson,

a Shaker eldress and black visionary, makes this point most tellingly. Jackson, who like John Jea claimed to have been taught to read by the Lord, wrote in her autobiography that she dreamed that a "white man" came to her house to teach her how to *interpret* and "understand" the word of God, now that God had taught her to read:

> A white man took me by my right hand and led me on the north side of the room, where sat a square table. On it lay a book open. And he said to me, "Thou shall be instructed in this book, from Genesis to Revelations." And then he took me on the west side, where stood a table. And it looked like the first. And said, "Yea, thou shall be instructed from the beginning of creation to the end of time." And then he took me on the east side of the room also, where stood a table and book like the two first, and said, "I will instruct thee — yea, thou shall be instructed from the beginning of all things to the end of all things. Yea, thou shall be well instructed. I will instruct."

> And then I awoke, and I saw him as plain as I did in my dream. And after that he taught me daily. And when I would be reading and come to a hard word, I would see him standing by my side and he would teach me the word right. And often, when I would be in meditation and looking into things which was hard to understand, I would find him by me, teaching and giving me understanding. And oh, his labor and care which he had with me often caused me to weep bitterly, when I would see my great ignorance and the great trouble he had to make me understand eternal things. For I was so buried in the depth of the tradition of my forefathers, that it did seem as if I never could be dug up.

In response to Jackson's relation of interpretive indenture to a "white man," Alice Walker, writing in *The Color Purple*, records an exchange between Celie and Shug about turning away from "the old white man," which soon turns into a conversation about the elimination of "man" as a mediator between a woman and "everything":

> . . . You have to git man off your eyeball, before you can see anything a'tall.

> Man corrupt everything, say Shug. He on your box of grits, in your head, and all over the radio. He try to make you think he everywhere. Soon as you think he everywhere, you think he God. But he ain't. Whenever you trying to pray, and man plot

---

[13]The Larousse is the standard French dictionary-encyclopedia.

racial differences generate and structure literary texts by us *and* about us; we must determine how critical methods can effectively disclose the traces of racial difference in literature; but we must also understand how certain forms of difference and the *languages* we employ to define those supposed "differences" not only reinforce each other but tend to create and maintain each other. Similarly, and as importantly, we must analyze the language of contemporary criticism itself, recognizing that hermeneutical systems, especially, are not "universal," "color-blind," or "apolitical," or "neutral." Whereas some critics wonder aloud, as Appiah notes, about such matters as whether or not "a structuralist poetics is inapplicable in Africa because structuralism is Europeon," the concern of the "Third World" critic should properly be to understand the ideological subtext which any critical theory reflects and embodies, and what relation this subtext bears to the production of meaning. No critical theory — be that Marxism, feminism, poststructuralism, Nkrumah's consciencism, or whatever — escapes the specificity of value and ideology, no matter how mediated these may be. To attempt to appropriate our own discourses using Western critical theory "uncritically" is to substitute one mode of neocolonialism for another. To begin to do this in my own tradition, theorists have turned to the black vernacular tradition — to paraphrase Rebecca Cox Jackson, to dig into the depths of the tradition of our foreparents — to isolate the signifying black difference through which to theorize about the so-called Discourse of the Other.

himself on the other end of it, tell him to git lost, say Shug.

Celie and Shug's omnipresent "man," of course, echoes the black tradition's epithet for the white power structure, "the man."

For non-Western, so-called noncanonical critics, getting the "man off your eyeball" means using the most sophisticated critical theories and methods generated by the Western tradition to reappropriate and to define our own "colonial" discourses. We must use these theories and methods insofar as these are relevant and applicable to the study of our own literatures. The danger in doing so, however, is best put, again by Anthony Appiah in his definition of what he calls the "Naipaul fallacy"[14]: "It is not necessary to show that African literature is fundamentally the same as European literature in order to show that it can be treated with the same tools. . . . Nor should we endorse a more sinister line . . . : the post-colonial legacy which requires us to show that African literature is worthy of study precisely (but only) because it is fundamentally the same as European literature." *We must not*, Appiah concludes, "ask the reader to understand Africa by embedding it in European culture."

We must, of course, analyze the ways in which writing relates to "race," how attitudes toward

[14]V[idiadhar] S[urajprasad] Naipaul (b. 1932), a Trinidad-born, Oxford-educated novelist and journalist whose works chronicle racism, corruption, and violence in the new nations of Africa and the Caribbean ruled by blacks, is a favorite object of odium to Africanist cultural critics such as Gates and Appiah.

Rey Chow
b. 1957

Born in Hong Kong and educated at British colonial and American institutions, Rey Chow received her Ph.D. in modern thought and literature from Stanford University. She taught at the University of Minnesota, the University of California at Irvine, and Brown University before becoming Anne Firor Scott Professor of Literature at Duke University. Her many publications, which have been widely anthologized and translated into major Asian and European languages, include Woman and Chinese Modernity: The Politics of Reading between West and East *(1991),* Writing Diaspora: Tactics of Intervention in Contemporary Cultural Studies *(1993),* Primitive Passions: Visuality, Sexuality, Ethnography, and Contemporary Chinese Cinema *(1995),* Ethics After Idealism: Theory-Culture-Ethnicity-Reading *(1998),* The Protestant Ethic and the Spirit of Capitalism *(2002),* The Age of the World Target: Self-Referentiality in War, Theory, and Comparative Work *(2006),* Sentimental Fabulations, Contemporary Chinese Films: Attachment in the Age of Global Visibility *(2007), and* Entanglements, or Transmedial Thinking about Capture *(2012). She is also the editor of the collection* Modern Chinese Literary and Cultural Studies in the Age of Theory: Reimagining a Field *(2001). The following essay, "The Interruption of Referentiality: Poststructuralism and the Conundrum of Critical Multiculturalism," was originally published in the winter 2002 issue of* The South Atlantic Quarterly.

The Interruption of Referentiality: Poststructuralism and the Conundrum of Critical Multiculturalism

In the increasingly globalized realm of theoretical discourse, a habitual move may be readily discerned in critical discussions regarding marginalized groups and non-Western cultures: the critic makes a gesture toward Western theory, but only in such a way as to advance the point that such theory is inadequate, negligent, and Eurocentric. As a consequence, what legitimates concern for the particular group, identity, or ethnic culture under discussion (which for the purposes of this essay I will simply call X) is its historical, cultural, gendered difference, which becomes, in terms of the theoretical strategies involved, the basis for the claim of opposition and resistance. Epistemologically, what is specific to X — that is, local, history-bound, culturally unique — is imagined to pose a certain challenge to Western

theory; hence the frequent adoption of the vocabulary of contestation, disruption, critique, and so forth. I refrain from references to particular authors whose works fall into such critical patterns because the point is not to show individuals up for their theoretical shortcomings.[1] Rather, it would be more productive to delineate a general picture of the predicament we face collectively as scholars whose intellectual lives have been deeply affected both by the presence of theory and by the reactions to theory in the past few decades.

I use the term *theory* to mark the paradigm shift introduced by poststructuralism, whereby the study of language, literature, and cultural

[1]Barbara Christian's "The Race for Theory" (see p. 1109) and its responses are in this tradition.

forms becomes irrevocably obligated to attend to the semiotic operations involved in the production of meanings, meanings that can no longer be assumed to be natural. Obviously there are other types of theories that have had great impact on large numbers of academic intellectuals — one thinks of the cultural writings of the Frankfurt School critics, various forms of historicisms, or sociological and anthropological theories, for instance — but it is arguably poststructuralism, with its tenacious attention to the materiality of human signification, that has generated some of the most far-reaching ramifications for the ways we approach questions of objectivity and ques-tions of subjectivity alike.

The one indisputable accomplishment of post-structuralist theory in the past several decades has been its systematic unsettling of the stability of meaning, its interruption of referentiality. If such meaning had never been entirely stable even in pretheory days, what poststructuralist theory provides is a metalanguage in which it (meaning) can now be defined anew as a repetitive effect produced in the chain of signification in the form of an exact but illusory correspondence between signifier and signified. While referentiality as such may continue to exist, for the new metalan-guage it is the movements in the realm of signifi-cation that matter, that command critical interest as the (shifting) basis for meaning. Henceforth, *meaning* is a term that occurs within scare quotes. With the emphasis on material signifiers comes the determining function of difference — to be further differentiated as both differing and deferring — which would from now on take the place of sameness and identity as the condition for signification. Ferdinand de Saussure's sum-mary statements may be conveniently recalled here: "In language there are only differences. Even more important: a difference generally implies positive terms between which the differ-ence is set up; but in language there are only dif-ferences without positive terms." "*Language is a form and not a substance.*"[2] The foregrounding of

[2]Ferdinand de Saussure, *Course in General Linguistics*, intro. Jonathan Culler, ed. Charles Bally and Albert Sechehaye in collaboration with Albert Reidlinger, trans. Wade Baskin (Glasgow: Collins, 1974), 120, 122; emphases in the original. [Chow] For Saussure, see p. 841.

differencing means that it is no longer possible to speak casually about any anchorage for mean-ing. If intelligibility itself is now understood as the effect of a movement of differencing, a movement that always involves delays and deferrals, then no longer can the old-fashioned belief in epistemological groundedness hold. In its stead the conception of (linguistic) identity becomes structurally defined, with (linguistic) signifiers mutually dependent on one another for the generation of what makes sense. Rather than being that which follows identity, difference now precedes identity. It is difference that creates an object of study.

It is necessary, in any consideration of the vicissitudes of theory, to acknowledge the sub-stantial impact made by poststructuralism's land-mark demotion and refusal of referentiality. The exercise of bracketing referentiality is enor-mously useful because adherence to referentiality has often led to a conservative clinging to a "real-ity" that is presumed to exist, in some unchanging manner, independently of language and significa-tion. This a priori real world is, moreover, often given the authority of what authenticates, of what bestows the value of transcendental truth on lan-guage and signification. The dismantling of such a metaphysics of presence is hence most effective in disciplines in which the presumption of a fac-tographic form of knowing has traditionally gone uncontested (as in some practices of history, for instance), but it is groundbreaking also in areas in which the naturalness of an object of knowl-edge — such as literature, for instance — has seldom been put into question. By intensifying our awareness of (linguistic) signification as first and foremost *self-referential*, poststructuralist theory opens a way for the ingrained ideological presuppositions behind such practices of knowl-edge production to be rethought.

From these fundamental revelations of post-structuralism, many critics have gone on prag-matically to explore differencing and its liberating egalitarianism in various social and historical contexts. They do so, for instance, by translat-ing the open-endedness of linguistic signification into the fluidity of the human subject. When transplanted into the tradition of individualism, significatory differencing quite logically means the multiplication of selves. Nowadays, what is commonly referred to as identity politics typically takes as its point of departure the problematizing and critiquing of essentialist notions that are attached to personhood, subjectivity, and identity formation.[3] Such branching off from high theory into democratic investigations of selfhood (through a thematization of differencing) is in many cases justifiable, but it has also left certain problems intact. In this regard I think it is important not simply to practice antiessentialist differencing ad infinitum but also to reconsider such a practice in conjunction with the rejection of referentiality that lies at the origins of poststructuralism. Exactly what is being thrown out when referentiality is theoretically rejected? I hope the significance of this point will become clear as I move through my arguments, for it bears on what I think is the conundrum in the critical study of marginalized groups and non-Western cultures today.

To begin, let me briefly revisit the question of how poststructuralist theory has methodologically radicalized the very production not only of the subject but also of the notion of an object of study. Albeit discussed much less frequently these days (simply because objectivity itself, it is assumed, can no longer be assumed), the issues that surround this topic remain instructive.

Consider the discipline of literature, for which one ongoing concern on which poststructuralist theory has helped to shed light is the problem of literariness, of what is specific to literature. At one level, this is of course precisely a question about referentiality. What is literature all about? To what does it refer? What reality does it represent? Old-fashioned though it may sound, such a preoccupation with literariness has surprising affinities with the contemporary cultural politics that clusters around identity. Let us retrace some of the well-known attempts at approaching this problem.

Marx's and Engels's discussion of literary writing and aesthetic representation provides a good instance of this because it is contextualized in their more general concern for social revolution and radical political practice. In their exchanges with authors seeking advice on writing fiction, Marx and Engels, we remember, made some rather startling statements.[4] Albeit theoretically forward looking, they were careful to warn these writers against turning literature into socialist propaganda in which fictional characters simply become mouthpieces for revolutionary doctrines. "The solution of the problem," writes Engels, "must become manifest from the situation and the action themselves without being expressly pointed out and . . . the author is not obliged to serve the reader on a platter the future historical resolution of the social conflicts which he describes."[5] Embedded in these brief remarks is an intuitive sense that theoretical and literary discourses are distinguished from each other by an essential articulatory difference, and that literary discourse, which specializes in indirection, can only become dull and mediocre should one turn it into a platform for direct proletarian pronouncements. Even where the subject matter cries out for justice to be done on some people's behalf, literary writing, they suggest, tends to accomplish its task more effectively when it does not explicitly solicit the reader's sympathy as such. In literature, the modus operandi is not to speak about something expressly even when one feels one must, in a manner quite opposite the clarity and forthrightness of theoretical argumentation. "The more the opinions of the author

---

[3]The greatly influential work of Judith Butler is exemplary in this regard. [Chow] See Butler, p. 1030.

[4]For useful discussions of the problematic of (aesthetic) reflection in Marxist theory, see, for instance, Pierre Macherey, *A Theory of Literary Production*, trans. Geoffrey Wall (London: Routledge, 1978), and Terry Eagleton, *Criticism and Ideology* (London: Verso, 1978). For related discussions, see Henri Arvon, *Marxist Esthetics*, trans. Helen R. Lane, intro. Fredric Jameson (Ithaca: Cornell University Press, 1973); *Marxism and Art: Essays Classic and Contemporary*, selected and with historical and critical commentary by Maynard Solomon (New York: Knopf, 1973); and Theodor Adorno, Walter Benjamin, Ernst Bloch, Bertolt Brecht, and Georg Lukács, *Aesthetics and Politics*, afterword by Fredric Jameson, trans. Ronald Taylor (London: Verso, 1980), as well as the essays in David Craig, ed., *Marxists on Literature: An Anthology* (New York: Penguin, 1975). [Chow]

[5]Friedrich Engels, "Letter to Minna Kautsky," in Craig, *Marxists on Literature*, 268. See also chaps. 8, 9 (Marx's and Engels's letters to Lasalle), and 13 (Engels's letter to Margaret Harkness), all reprinted from Karl Marx and Friedrich Engels, *Selected Correspondence* (Moscow: n.p., n.d.). [Chow]

remain hidden, the better for the work of art."[6] In other words, a very different kind of power for producing change is in play. David Craig summarizes this point succinctly: "Surely, if literature affects action or changes someone's life, it is not by handing out a recipe for the applying but rather by disturbing us emotionally, mentally, because it *finds* us . . . , so that, after a series of such experiences and along with others that work with it, we feel an urge to 'do something,' or at least to ask ourselves the question (the great question put by Chernyshevsky, Lenin, and Silone): 'What is to be done?'"[7]

What remains illuminating in these discussions is a perception of the work of indirection that seemed, to Marx and Engels at least, to be the unique characteristic of literary discourse; this is remarkable especially in light of their political belief in asserting the necessity to reform and revolutionize society, a belief that, in discursive terms, would be more in line with direct, straightforward, clear-cut expression — the very antithesis of their observations about literary writing. As political theorists, Marx and Engels nonetheless recognized that literary production could not be reduced to a mechanical mirroring of some reality out there, and that whatever literature is "about," such referentiality occurs, by definition, in a refracted manner rather than by straightforward declaration.[8]

In subsequent debates it was the critics who were overtly concerned with form (rather than with politics) who would continue the elaboration of this observation of literature-as-indirection, even though indirection was now theorized in different terms. For instance, the Russian Formalists' effort in defining the defamiliarizing capacity of art and literature — of art's capacity for presenting something familiar in such a manner as to call attention to its "artfulness," or its

capacity for taking readers by surprise through the process of de-formation — can in retrospect be understood as an attempt to identify, perhaps to construct, a kind of rupture and distance from within a conventional discourse, so that the shock and alienating effect produced can be described as what is specific to art and literary expression.[9] Such shock and alienation, again, are not a matter of direct expression but, rather, of a sensitively perceived differential — the more implicitly the perceived differential — the more implicitly the differential is grasped, the greater the effect of artfulness and literariness — so much so that the art object itself takes on only secondary importance.

In the Anglo-American world the literary-theoretical avant-garde of the twentieth century was represented by New Criticism, which specializes in the discernment of a literary work's specificity through close reading.[10] The contradiction between the aim and the practice of New Criticism has been well noted. Between the nostalgic desire to produce a complete, intrinsic reading that would exemplify the literary work as a self-sufficient world with rules that apply only to itself,[11] on the one hand, and the ambiguous open-endedness of meaning that results ironically from such desire-in-practice, on the other, lies the aporia that becomes, for a deconstructive critic such as Paul de Man, New Criticism's unwitting self-undoing. De Man demonstrates this by reinforcing the dimension of temporality — hence of postponements, deferrals, and belatedness — in the process of coming to terms with literary discourse: "The temporal factor, so persistently forgotten, should remind us that the form is never anything but a process on its way to completion."[12] Whereas New Criticism is still

---

[6]Engels, "Letter to Margaret Harkness," in Craig, *Marxists on Literature*, 270. [Chow]

[7]David Craig, introduction to Craig, *Marxists on Literature*, 22. [Chow]

[8]Pierre Macherey's discussion of Lenin's reading of Leo Tolstoy (and the question of reflection in Tolstoy's works) remains one of the most illuminating accounts in this regard. See Macherey, *Theory of Literary Production*, 105–35, 299–323. [Chow]

[9]See Shklovsky, p. 426.

[10]For New Criticism, see p. 411.

[11]See John Bender and David E. Wellbery, "Rhetoricality," On the Modernist Return of Rhetoric," in *The Ends of Rhetoric: History, Theory, Practice*, ed. John Bender and David E. Wellbery (Stanford, Calif.: Stanford University Press, 1990), 3–39. The authors see modernist rhetoricality, with its emphasis on the groundlessness of truth, as a legacy of Friedrich Nietzsche. [Chow]

[12]Paul de Man, "Form and Intent in the American New Criticism," "The Rhetoric of Temporality," and "The Dead-End of Formalist Criticism," in *Blindness and Insight:*

invested in a kind of time-less reading of the work of literature, a reading that circumvents temporality by the ideological projection of the work's organic wholeness, deconstruction would distinguish its comparable interest in literary specificity by underscoring the effects of time as manifested through the negative momentum of language. In de Man's hands, the previous attempts to get at literature's indirectness culminate in a sophisticated reformulation by way of the originary constitutive role of temporal difference, one that consistently undermines textual presence and plenitude.[13] If literature is indirect, defamiliarizing, ambiguous, ironic, allegorical, and so forth — if, in other words, it is never straightforwardly referential — it is because human linguistic signification itself is always already mediated by the slow but indismissible labor of temporality.

But the perception of time alone does not necessarily account for the derailing of reference. One is reminded of the great humanist literary critic Erich Auerbach, for instance, for whom the noticeable temporal shifts in modernist literary representation, shifts he describes with animation and verve, nonetheless do not challenge the basic idea that there exists something common to all of our lives even in the midst of diversities.[14] From a poststructuralist, difference-oriented perspective, this statement from the end of Auerbach's *Mimesis* is quite astonishing, particularly in view of the sensitive close readings he has performed:

> The more it is exploited, the more the elementary things which our lives have in common come to light. The more numerous, varied, and simple the

people are who appear as subjects of such random moments, the more effectively must what they have in common shine forth. In this unprejudiced and exploratory type of representation we cannot but see to what an extent — below the surface conflicts — the differences between men's ways of life and forms of thought have already lessened. The strata of societies and their different ways of life have become inextricably mingled. There are no longer even exotic peoples. A century ago (in Mérimée for example), Corsicans or Spaniards were still exotic; today the term would be quite unsuitable for Pearl Buck's Chinese peasants.[15]

In spite of his grasp of the changes in literary, representational time, referentiality itself is not a problem for Auerbach because he remains convinced of a universal something called human reality. Mimesis is simply a way of accessing it; accessibility itself is not an issue.

The contribution made by poststructuralist theory, then, lies not merely in its articulation of temporality but also in its insistence that time does not coincide with itself. This recurrent slippage and intrinsic irreconcilability — between speaking and writing, between sign and meaning, and between fiction and reality — allows deconstructionist critics to assert that deconstruction is a rigorously historical process. As Geoff Bennington writes, "Deconstruction, insofar as it insists on the necessary non-coincidence of the present with itself, is in fact in some senses the most historical of discourses imaginable."[16] For Marian Hobson, the point of deconstruction-as-history is precisely that identity is never possible and that such impossibility is itself plural: "It is trace, track, which makes identity impossible. But this impossibility is itself plural, not simple. It is not a straight negative — not simple, identical, non-identity. Trace, lack of self-coincidence, is on the contrary a plurality of impossibilities, a disjunction of negatives."[17] If conventional practices of history may

Essays in the Rhetoric of Contemporary Criticism, 2d ed., rev., intro. Wlad Godzich (Minneapolis: University of Minnesota Press, 1983), 20–35, 187–228, 299–45. The quotation is on p. 31. [Chow]

[13] See the introduction to Structuralism and Deconstruction, p. 485.

[14] Erich Auerbach, *Mimesis: The Representation of Reality in Western Literature*, trans. Willard R. Trask (Princeton, N.J.: Princeton University Press, 1953). See especially his perceptive discussion of Virginia Woolf, in whose work, as he notes, external events often have only the vaguest contours while the rich and sensitively registered internal time of the characters has led to the abdication of authorial objectivity and hegemony. [Chow]

[15] Ibid., 552. [Chow]

[16] Geoff Bennington, "Demanding History," in *Post-structuralism and the Question of History*, ed. Derek Attridge, Geoff Bennington, and Robert Young (New York: Cambridge University Press, 1987), 17. [Chow]

[17] Marian Hobson, "History Traces," in Attridge, Bennington, and Young, *Post-structuralism and the Question of History*, 102–3. [Chow]

be criticized on the basis of a premature projec-tion of the referent, deconstruction's response is that history resides, rather, in the permanently self-undermining process of differentiation, a process that, by the sheer force of its logic, need not have an end in sight.

This potential alliance between the lack of (temporal and ontological) self-presence and differentiation-as-historicity is one major reason poststructuralism has left such indelible imprints on those areas of knowledge production that do not at first seem to have much to do with semi-otics or, for that matter, with the revamping of metalanguages, but that are intimately linked to empirical issues such as culture and group identity. It is not difficult to see that the basic tenets of structuralist linguistics and semiotics — difference, identity, value, arbitrariness, con-vention, and systematicity — carry within them connotations that have resonances well beyond the terrain of a narrow sense of language. With the bracketing of the object of knowledge and the foregrounding of the process of signifi-cation, as introduced by poststructuralism, it is inevitable that the certitude of the identi-ties involved — epistemological, subjective, or collective — can no longer be safely taken for granted. It is not surprising, therefore, that one of the most prevalent uses of the poststructural-ist metalanguage of differencing is to be found in areas in which existential identity is most at stake: multiculturalism, postcoloniality, and ethnicity.[18]

If this is the case, how is it that in these areas of study there is currently also a persistent refrain that non-Western subjects and subject matters are "oppositional" and "resistant" to Western theory? About fifteen to twenty years ago, even though the same ambivalent gesture toward the West might have been made, theory itself was not an issue. Nowadays, as can be surmised from journals, conferences, antholo-gies, and single-author publications, not only are more trendy topics such as transgender politics,

Asian pop music, Third World urban geography, or cultural translation obligated to gesture toward one kind of Western theory or another; even the study of ancient ethnic poems and narratives must, in order to argue the case of their unique-ness, their beyond-comparison status, somehow demonstrate an awareness of the background of Western theoretical issues. If all this is testimony to the hegemony enjoyed by Western theory, why are claims of resistance and opposition at the same time so adamant?

If the exploration of literary difference was in order to ground literary specificity — that is, to define literature as an object with its essential attributes, attributes that make literature definitively unlike anything else — then one of the consequences of such exploration is, ironi-cally, the dissipation of this "object" altogether. From the nineteenth-century perception of its essence (in Marx and Engels) as indirection to the late-twentieth-century assertion (by deconstruc-tionist critics) of its noncoincidence with itself, the object of literariness seems to have become theoretically unsustainable exactly at the moment of its concrete definition: it "is" what it always is not. If the ongoing efforts to define the literary difference have brought to light all that has been repressed, neglected, or ignored, such efforts have also shown how literature does not and can-not stop at the mere restoration or redemption of such difference. Inevitably, difference as such will continue to fragment and dismantle what-ever specificity that may have been established through it, once again rendering the goal of stable objectification impossible.

Permanent differentiation and permanent impermanence: these are the key features of poststructuralist theoretical practice as we find it today. The example of literature has simply demonstrated the Pyrrhic victory[19] of the scien-tific or social scientific attempt to produce an object of knowledge by way of differencing. If literariness is that which tends to disappear into something else at the moment of its being objec-tified, then literature is, ultimately, a historically mobile, changing relationship (of writing) rather

[18] I discuss this in greater detail in "The Secrets of Ethnic Abjection," in *Traces 2* (2001): 53–77. A few passages from that essay have been incorporated with modifications into the present one. [Chow]

[19] An apparent victory that is actually a defeat.

than a concrete essence. Might this lesson about literariness be extended beyond the discipline of literature?

Consider now the study of X, those areas that, as I mentioned at the beginning, often attain visibility by gesturing toward and resisting Western theory at the same time. As in the case of literariness, we may set out to define X as an object with certain attributes. But we already know from the example of literariness that such an attempt at discovering the specificity of X will lead first to the process of differencing and eventually to the dissipation of X itself as a stable referent. Should we then say that, ultimately, X as such does not exist, that X, like literariness, is a permanently shifting, non-self-identical relationship? What might be the implications of proclaiming, let us say, that African American, Asian American, and gay and lesbian specificities do not exist? Such proclamations are, to be sure, intolerable to many, but it is perhaps less because these "people" really do exist than because the theoretical claim for their existence is inseparable from the hierarchical politics of race, class, gender, and ethnicity that structure Western and non-Western societies alike. In the face of the practical struggles that go on daily against different forms of social injustice, it is, for many, unacceptable to declare, in accordance with poststructuralist theoretical logic, that these versions of X do not exist. Yet the alternative — the insistence that they are real, that they are out there, that their empirical existence is absolutely incontestable, and that they are thus a core from which to stage resistance to the virtual claims of high theory — is equally untenable because it is theoretically naive.

The conundrum we face today in the wake of theory may thus be described as follows: In their attempts to argue the specificity of their objects of study, critics of marginalized historical areas often must rhetorically assert their resistance to or distrust of Western theory. But what exactly is the nature of that which they are resisting and distrusting? As these critics try to defend the viability of their proposed objects, they are compelled, against their own proclaimed beliefs, to set into motion precisely the poststructuralist operation of differencing, of making essentialist categories of identity disintegrate. Indeed,

differencing is often the very weapon with which they mount their criticisms of Western theory. While they criticize Western theory, then, these critics are meanwhile implementing the bracketing of anchored, referential meanings that constitutes one of contemporary Western theory's most profound influences. Since there is nothing inherent in the methodological mechanism of structural differentiation that calls for resistance or differentiation at a level beyond the chain of signification, the objects to which these critics cling — in resistance — inevitably dissipate over time in a manner similar to that in which the object of literariness dissipates. To truly argue for resistance, they would in fact need to go against or abandon altogether the very theoretical premises (of poststructuralist differencing) on which they make their criticisms in the first place.[20]

Put in a different way, the attempt to argue the specificity of X as such, even as it discredits Western theory, tends to reproduce the very terms — and the very problems — that once surrounded the theoretical investigation of literariness. Like literature, X is often constructed (negatively) as what defamiliarizes, what departs from conventional expectations, what disrupts the norm, and so forth, terms that are invested in constructing specificity by way of differentiation. Like the attempt to define literariness also, the attempt to define X seems doomed to destroy its own object in the process of objectification. More disturbing still, if representation of X as such is recognizable in these similar theoretical terms, does it not mean that there is no essential difference between X and high theory — that the articulation of X, however historically specific it may be, is somehow already *within* the trajectory mapped out by high theory?

This is the juncture at which a rethinking of poststructuralist theory is in order, not once again by way of temporal differencing but, more significantly, by way of reexamining theory's interruption of referentiality. By bracketing referentiality,

[20]For a succinct critique of the contradictions that accompany poststructuralist theory and that have had a profound impact on the multiculturalist trends in the humanities, see Masao Miyoshi, "Ivory Tower in Escrow," *boundary* 2 27.1 (2000), in particular 39–50. [Chow]

separating it from the signified, and making the signified part of the chain of signification and an effect produced by the play of signifiers, poststructuralism has devised an epistemological framework in which what lies "outside" can be recoded as what is inside. There is hence no outside to the text. At the same time, however, this also means that poststructuralism really does not offer a way of thinking about any outside except by reprogramming it into part of an ongoing interior (chain) condition. This is not exactly the same as saying that poststructuralism is a closed system of permutations; rather, it is simply that its mechanism of motility, which provides a set of terms that redefines referentiality effectively as the illusion produced by the play of temporal differences, also tends to preclude any other way of getting at the outside than by directing it inward. My point, then, is this: rather than systematicity per se (which was the problem characteristic of structuralism), the problem here is perhaps none other than temporality rendered as nonpresence.

Although it is arguably what constitutes what is poststructuralism's most radical intervention in European thought, the notion of time's noncoincidence with itself may nevertheless have a substantially contrary set of reverberations once we go beyond the parameters of Europe. Where otherness stands as an empirical and a cultural as well as a theoretical issue, the assertion of temporal disjunction as such (as an absolute force that structures all signification) may coincide, or become complicit, with the anthropological problematic that Johannes Fabian has called, in his well-known phrase, the denial of coevalness — *"a persistent and systematic tendency to place the referent(s) of anthropology in a Time other than the present of the producer of anthropological discourse."*[21] In other words, whereas the insistence on the noncoincidence of the present with itself may indeed be a revolutionary charge within the philo-sophical and epistemological terrains from which

poststructuralism stems, such an insistence, when seen in light of Europe's history with its colo-nized others, may turn out to be no more than another current of what Fabian calls allochronic discourse, in which other peoples who are our contemporaries are discursively confined each to their culture gardens/ethnic ghettos, in the name, precisely, of difference. Be it temporal, onto-logical, linguistic, or identitarian, noncoincidence can hardly be considered groundbreaking in the global circuits of colonialism and imperialism because the non-Western others are already, by definition, classified as noncoincident, discon-tinuous, and fundamentally different (from popu-lations in the West, from the times and languages of Western ethnographers). To emphasize nonco-incidence as such is thus merely to reify and raise to the level of metalanguage a rather conven-tional anthropological attitude toward the other's otherness — which is often unproblematically upheld as a fact — without actually confront-ing the conditions that enable such assumptions of noncoincidence to stand in the first place. Referring to the relevance of Fabian's work for the study of colonial America, for instance, Carlos Alonso comments on one such manifesta-tion of the (principle of) noncoincidence inherent to the rhetoric of temporality — the expression of amazement: "Europe's rhetoric of amazement vis-à-vis America . . . necessitates the ceaseless deferral of total cognitive mastery. But rather than being deployed in order to maintain an irre-ducible alterity, the European figuration of the New World as new posited a continuity between itself and the new territories that made possible European appropriation of the recently discov-ered lands while simultaneously affirming their exoticism."[22]

Let me push my point one step further: the definition of time as non-coincidental with itself, I would like to suggest, means that poststructur-alism ultimately does not offer any viable way of thinking about an act of exclusion except by recoding it as a (passive) condition of exterior-ity. Once recoded (in the form of an "always

[21]Johannes Fabian, *Time and the Other: How Anthropology Makes Its Object* (New York: Columbia University Press, 1983), 31; emphasis in the original. [Chow] To put Fabian's point crudely, anthropologists' discourse about "primitive" peoples implicitly suggests that they somehow belong to a time earlier than that of the observer.

[22]Carlos J. Alonso, *The Burden of Modernity: The Rhetoric of Cultural Discourse in Spanish America* (New York: Oxford University Press, 1998), 7. [Chow]

already"), this condition is channeled into an existing interior in such a manner as to become part of this interior's infinite series of differentiations over time, always open ended and incomplete, always ready for further differentiation to be sure, yet never again directed at the primary, originary moment involving the as yet unresolved outside. At the level of metalanguage, this outside, or what has been banished there, is none other than referentiality, which must henceforth live the life of the exiled, the exotic, and the exorcised — that which is barred once and for all from entering, from migrating into the interior of, the chain of signification.

It follows that when one is dealing with sexual, cultural, and ethnic others, it is always considered premature in poststructuralist theory to name and identify such references as such; instead, deconstruction's preferred benevolent gesture is to displace and postpone these others to a utopian, unrealizable realm, to a spectral dimension whose radicalness lies precisely in its spectrality, the fact that it cannot materialize *in the present*. Again, Alonso's observations about the discursive place occupied by America in the European imagination during the colonial epoch are pointedly on the mark. From being perceived as novel, he writes, America gradually shifted into the position of the future:

> Almost imperceptibly, the coevalness that the narrative of newness required was replaced by a narrative paradigm in which America occupied a position of *futurity* vis-à-vis the Old World. This transformation from novelty to futurity was significant because, among other things, it created the conditions for a permanent exoticization of the New World — the sort that cannot be undermined or dissolved by actual experience or objective analysis: safely ensconced in an always postponed future, America could become the object of a ceaselessly regenerating discourse of mystification and perpetual promise.[23]

This inability to deal with the other except by temporal displacement returns us to the scenario with which I began this essay. When scholars of marginalized groups and non-Western subjects rely on notions of resistance and opposition (to

Western theory) in their attempts to argue the specificity of X, they are unwittingly reproducing the epistemological conundrum by which the specificity of an object of study is conceived of in terms of a differential — a differential, moreover, that has to be included in the chain of signification in order to be recognized. However, by virtue of its mechanism of postponement and displacement, this kind of logic implies the eventual dissolution of the object without being able to address *how X* presents not just a condition (exteriority) that has always already existed but more importantly an active politics of exclusion and discrimination. Within the bounds of this logic, the more resistive and oppositional (that is, on the outside) X is proclaimed to be, the more inevitably it is to lose its specificity (that is, become incorporated) in the larger framework of the systematic production of differences, while the circumstances that make this logic possible (that is, that enable it to unfold and progress as a self-regulating interior) remain unchallenged. This is one reason why so many new projects of articulating alternative identities, cultures, and group formations often seem so predictable in the end. Whether the topic under discussion is a particular ethnic work or the identity of an ethnic person, what has become predictable is precisely the invocation of "ambivalence," "multiplicity," "hybridity," "heterogeneity," "disruptiveness," "resistance," and the like, and no matter how new an object of study may appear to be, it is bound to lose its novelty once the play of temporal difference is set into motion. The moves permitted by the rules of the originary exclusion — the difference that makes the difference, as it were — have already been exhausted, and critics dealing with X can only repeatedly run up against the incommensurability between the experience of temporality as self-deconstruction (with its radical theoretical nuances) and the experience of temporality as allochronism (with its racialist anthropological ramifications).

In sum, contemporary uses of poststructuralist theory have tended to adopt poststructuralism's solution, differencing, without sufficiently reflecting on its flip side, its circumvention of exclusion. Yet contemporary issues of identity and cultural conflict almost invariably involve the

[23]Ibid., 8; emphasis in the original. [Chow]

that is not pure difference but difference thor-oughly immersed in and corrupted by the errors and delusions of history.

For similar reasons, an awareness of historical asymmetries of power, aggression, social antago-nism, inequality of representation, and their like cannot simply be accomplished through an adher-ence to the nebulous concept of resistance and opposition. That concept itself is often constituted with the logic of differentiation — of disruption and departure — within a theoretical framework whose success lies precisely in its perennial capacity for including and absorbing that which is on the outside. Resistance that imagines itself as purely premised on the outside is thus a futile exercise in the wake of poststructuralist theory. In its stead, it would be more productive to let referentiality interrupt, to reopen the poststruc-turalist closure on this issue, to acknowledge the inevitability of reference even in the most avant-garde of theoretical undertakings, and to demand a thorough reassessment of an originary act of repudiation/exclusion in terms that can begin to address the "scandal of domination and exploita-tion of one part of mankind by another."[24]

[24]Fabian, *Time and the Other*, x. In Miyoshi's terms, this would mean restoring the hitherto discredited function of so-called metanarratives: "The academics' work in this marketized world . . . is to learn and watch problems in as many sites as they can keep track of, not in any specific areas, nations, races, ages, genders, or cultures, but in all areas, nations, races, ages, genders, and cultures. In other words, far from abandoning the master narratives, the critics and scholars in the humanities must restore the public rigor of the metanarratives" ("Ivory Tower in Escrow," 49). [Chow]

politics of exclusion. Can these mutually incom-patible states of affairs be reconciled with each other? How can they be reconciled? Can specific-ity be imagined in terms other than a naturalized differential, an automatized discontinuity? Are there perhaps forms of closure, limits, and refer-ences that should not be prematurely disavowed, because the act of disavowing them inevitably becomes a self-contradictory move, leading only to a theoretical impasse? (That is, the act of reprogramming everything as part of an interior inevitably becomes an act to exclude, with what is excluded being, first and foremost, the asser-tion of the violence of exclusion itself.)

The reference that is social injustice — itself a type of differential but a differential hierarchized with value — cannot be as easily postponed or displaced, because the mechanisms of postpone-ment and displacement do not by themselves address the hierarchical or discriminatory nature of the differential involved. As a result, however permanently the issue may be deferred, the origi-nary differential of inequality will not and cannot go away. The kind of theoretical mechanism that works by dissolving specificities into differences is therefore incapable of addressing the concerns implied here, because there is nothing inher-ent in such a mechanism that would necessitate the recognition of the inequality and injustice that may indeed, for lack of a better term, be "out there," yet that may not be immediately or entirely incorporable into the chain of significa-tion. Referentiality, reformulated in this manner, may in the end require us to accept it precisely as the limit, the imperfect, irreducible difference

Index

Alternative cinema, 669

Alternative hegemony: in Jameson, 776; in Williams, 759–61

Althusser, Louis, 13, 556, 632–35, 695, 701–03, 705, 756, 770, 773, 778, 785–86, 824, 831–33, 835, 883, 1015, 1073, 1087; biography, 738; *Ideology and Ideological State Apparatuses,* **738–46;** *Reading Capital,* 701

Altieri, Charles, 920

Ambiguity, 403, 549; in Anzaldua, 1101; in Aristotle, 72; in Peter Brooks, 660; in Dante, 102; in Empson, 417, 419; in Fish, 547; in New Criticism, 412; in Pope, 147

Amo, Wilhelm, 1137

Anacreon, 226

Anagogy: in Dante, 103

Anal phase: in Freud, 628, 631, 633

Analysis: in Arnold, 267; in Coleridge, 225; in Freud, 630; in Shelley, 228, 230

Anamorphosis: in Lacan, 682

Anderson, Benedict, 1047; biography, 1080, **"The Origins of National Consciousness,"** **1080–85**

Anderson, Sherwood: "I Want to Know Why," 553, 607–08, 612

Andrewes, Lancelot, 320

Androgyny, 959: in Cixous, 961, 994; in Showalter, 882; in Woolf, 372, 882

Angel in the house: in Gilbert and Gubar, 907. *See also* Patmore

Anglo-American feminist literary criticism. *See* Feminist literary criticism

Anima: in Jung, 331–37, 339, 644

Animus: in Jung, 331–32, 334–37

Annales school, 787, 790

Anquetil-Duperron, Abraham Hyacinthe, 1077

Anticipation: in Iser, 587–90, 594

Antonioni, Michelangelo, 408

Anxiety of authorship, 882, 904; in Gilbert and Gubar, 903–14

Anxiety of influence: in Bloom, 632, 905; in Eliot, 321; in Gilbert and Gubar, 632

Anxiety, spatial: in Gilbert and Gubar, 910–15

Anzaldúa, Gloria, 1064; and liminality, 1057; biography, 1100; **"La conciencia de la mestiza: Towards a New Consciousness,"** **1100–1108**

Aphanisis, 650; in Lacan, 636

Apollinaire, Guillaume, 476, 568

Apollo: in Nietzsche, 282–86, 291

Aporia, 486, 774; and deconstruction, 486

Appiah, Kwame Anthony, 864, 1143–44

Application: as horizon; in Jauss, 565

Appreciation: aesthetic; in Jauss, 567

Apuleius, 137

Aquinas, St. Thomas, 101, 601, 1112

Archaeology: in Foucault, 788; in Levi-Strauss, 506

Archaic (cultural formation): in Williams, 762

Arché-écriture: in Derrida, 480

Archetypes: 6; anima, 328; animus, 328; in Baym, 898; in Jung, 327, 331–39, 504; mask, 328; quest, 328; shadow, 328; spirit, 328. *See also* specific archetypes: Anima, Animus, Night-sea-journey; Shadow, Spirit

Archilochus, 39, 40, 78, 96, 98, 288, 289

Architectonic: in Sidney, 114, 121

Architecture: in Benjamin, 729

Arendt, Hannah, 1025

Aries, Philippe, 787

Ariosto, Ludovico, 240, 313; *Orlando Furioso,* 119, 241, 244

Aristophanes, 53

Aristotle, 2, 5, 7–9, 12–13, 26, 47–50, 74–75, 87, 112–14, 136, 138, 150, 152, 157, 160, 166, 212, 263, 351, 404, 421–22, 457–58, 464, 473, 515, 522, 526, 658, 744, 792, 815, 864, 1112; biography, 46; materialism, 47; *Metaphysics,* 102, 104; *Nicomachean Ethics,* 126; ***Poetics,*** **50–72**,120–21, 124, 126, 129–30, 134, 263, 291, 543, 656–59, 816; *Politics,* 50; *Posterior Analytics* 48; problematic method, 47; *Rhetoric,* 65; style, 68

Armstrong, Nancy, 791, 886; biography, 839; *Desire and Domestic Fiction,* 791, 841; development of female domain, 846–50; female discourse as site of power, 850–53; **"Some Call It Fiction: On the Politics of Domesticity,"** **839–53**; theory of culture and discourse, 840

Arnheim, Rudolf, 723, 727

Arnold, Matthew, 2, 88, 464, 962, 1072; biography, 263; *Culture and Anarchy,* 263; "Dover Beach," 451; elitism, 264; *Essays in Criticism,* 263; **"The Function of Criticism at the Present Time,"** **265–78**; holistic method, 264

Aronowitz, Stanley, 780

Arrian, 93

Art: in Arnold, 263; in Benjamin, 713–14, 720, 726; in Coleridge, 227; in Du Bois, 342, 344, 347–49; in Freud, 630; in Horace, 82, 84; in James, 300, 304; in Johnson, 164; in Kant, 166–68, 183, 190;

in Longinus, 87–88, 90, 92; in Marx, 249–250, 254, 261–62; in Nietzsche, 280, 282, 290; in Plato, 2, 40, 46; in Plotinus, 5; in Pope, 148–50, 153; in Potebnya, 413; in Shklovsky, 427; in Sidney, 125, 136; in Williams, 765; popular, 8; powers, 2; properties, 2; rules, 3; sources, 2; uses, 2; value, 5, 28

Artaud, Antonin, 402, 637

Artisanal production: in Mulvey, 669. *See also* Author, Poet

Artist, 2, 3, 8; in Baym, 899, 901; in Eliot, 322; in Freud, 630; in James, 301, 309; in Kant, 169; in Longinus, 88; in Nietzsche, 284; in Sidney, 115

Artistic autonomy: in Bourdieu, 820

Assimilation, 1048

Associationism, 220–21

Astell, Mary, 142

Atget, Eugène, 720

Audience, 3–4, 6–9, 543; in Aristotle, 8, 60, 62, 64, 543; in Benjamin, 714, 717, 720, 722, 726, 729; in Bleich, 544, 551; in Booth, 554; in Culler, 544, 548; in Eco, 544, 548; in Fish, 554; in Freud, 311, 317, 630–31; in Genette, 544; in Greenblatt, 857, 859; in Holland, 544, 550, 554; in Horace, 74, 78, 80–81, 543; in Horkheimer and Adorno, 741; in Hume, 168; in Iser, 554; in James, 300; in Jauss, 554, 557; in Johnson, 160, 162; in Kant, 168; in Kolodny, 876; in Longinus, 87, 89, 92; in Mulvey, 670, 672, 676; national, 6; in New Criticism, 417, 544; in Nietzsche, 290; in Plato, 42, 543; in Poulet, 553; in rhetorical theory, 6; in Richards, 544; in Rosenblatt, 550; in Said, 1076; in structuralism, 544, 548; universal, 6. *See also* Reader

Auerbach, Erich, 616, 625, 809, 1149

Aura (Benjamin), 697, 714–15, 723–24, 732

Austen, Jane, 309, 372, 375, 377–78, 381, 585, 625, 799, 840–41, 850, 875, 882, 901, 904, 907, 909–11; *Emma*, 570–582, 849; *Mansfield Park*, 581; *Northanger Abbey*, 804, 841; *Persuasion*, 574–75, 581

Austin, J. L., 351, 519, 684, 707

Authenticity (Benjamin), 714, 717

Author: in Bakhtin, 363; in Coleridge, 226; in Foucault, 520, 521, 522, 523, 524, 525, 527, 529; in Freud, 630; in Horace, 80; in James, 301; in Longinus, 87; in McDowell, 1062; in Rabinowitz, 546; in Said, 1076; in Wimsatt and Beardsley, 462, 465; death of, in Barthes, 514–519; in Foucault, 484; determined by history, 9

Author-function (Foucault), 484, 523–24, 526, 528, 530

Authorial audience (Rabinowitz), 546

Authorial commentary (Booth), 545

Authorial ideology (Eagleton), 703

Authoritative discourse (Bakhtin), 355–357, 360

Authority: in Baym, 900; in Benjamin, 726; in Burke, 387; in Cixous, 1000; in Gilbert and Gubar, 903; in Greenblatt, 859; in Said, 1076

Auto-eroticism, 670

Autonomy: in Greenblatt, 856; in Williams, 755

Avant-garde, 669

Avenarius, Richard, 428

Awkward, Michael, 1061

Ayer, A.J., 485

Baader-Meinhoff Gang, 939

Babbitt, Irving, 319

Bach, Johann Sebastian, 167

Bachelard, Gaston: *Poetics of Space*, 913

Bacon, Sir Francis, 232–33, 243, 245, 523, 1081, 1139

Bahti, Timothy, 486

Baker, Houston, 1058–59, 1061

Bakhtin, Mikhail Mikhailovich, 16–18, 21–23, 87–88, 350–353, 775, 784, 844, 1133; biography, 350–51, **"Heteroglossia in the Novel,"** 362–68; *Problems in Dostoevsky's Poetics*, **368–69**; *Rabelais and His World*, 350, 844 **"The Topic of the Speaking Person,"** 352–61

Baldwin, James, 1060, 1113

Balibar, Etienne, 684, 782

Balzac, Honoré de, 381, 483, 516–17, 519, 523, 705, 770, 772, 777, 1072; *La Peau de chagrin*, 664; *Le Père Goriot*, 549

Bambara, Toni Cade, 951

Baraka, Imamu Amiri (aka Leroi Jones), 1111, 1113

Barbauld, Anna Laetitia, 841, 873, 879

Barber, Benjamin, 1056

Barth, Karl, 743

Barthes, Roland, 402, 409, 473, 483–84, 486, 488–89, 512, 519, 565, 604, 632, 637, 657, 659, 667; biography, 512; **"The Death of the Author,"** 517–19; **"From Work to Text,"** 512–17; *Mythologies*, 483, 785; *The Pleasure of the Text, S/Z*, 483; 484, 549

Base (*Grundlage*): in Foucault, 973; in Marx, 694, 701, 703, 713, 753–56; in Said, 1072; in Williams, 751, 827. *See also* Superstructure (*Überbau*)

Bataille, George, 513

Brecht, Bertolt, 518, 638, 712, 720, 821, 1147

Bremond, Claude, 483

Bresson, Robert, 409

Breton, André, 399–400, 645, 728

Bricolage: in Certeau, 794; in Lévi-Strauss, 536, 538

Brontë, Anne, 901; *The Tenant of Wildfell Hall*, 909

Brontë: Charlotte, 372, 377–78, 381, 595, 875, 901, 907, 1029, 1051, 1087–93, 1095, 1097–99; *Jane Eyre*, 372–73, 595, 624, 849, 881–83, 909, 912, 1088; *Shirley*, 850–53, 912, 918; *Villette*, 915

Brontë, Emily, 372, 375, 377, 704, 768, 881–82, 901,904, 907, 909–11; *Wuthering Heights*, 378, 909

Brooks, Cleanth, 386, 403, 416, 418, 420–21; 457–60, 485, 1134; biography, 449; **"Irony as a Principle of Structure," 449–56**

Brooks, Gwendolyn, 883

Brooks, Peter, 311, 403, 627, 631–32, 656; biography, 656; Freud's Masterplot, 639; **"Freud's Masterplot," 656–66**

Brown, Charles Brockden, 895

Brown, Homer Obed, 841

Brown, Richard Lonsdale, 347

Brown, Sterling A., 1135

Brown, William Wells, 1060, 1139

Brown, Wilmette, 953, 954

Browne, Sir Thomas, 381, 547

Browning, Elizabeth Barrett, 903

Browning, Robert, 320, 346, 574, 1075

Brownmiller, Susan, 938

Bruns, Gerald, 16

Bryan, James, 631

Bryant, William Cullen, 894

Brydges, Sir Egerton, 381

Buell, Lawrence, 797

Buñuel, Luis: *The Criminal Life of Archibaldo de la Cruz*, 683; *The Discreet Charm of the Bourgeoisie*, 683; *The Exterminating Angel*, 683; *That Obscure Object of Desire*, 682

Bunyan, John: *Pilgrim's Progress*, 909, 1091

Burckhardt, Jakob, 791, 815

Burke, Edmund, 87–88, 194, 270; *Reflections on the Revolution in France*, 194, 815

Burke, Kenneth, 13, 773; A Grammar of Motives, 389; Attitudes toward History, 387; biography, 386; critical method, 389; Language as Symbolic Action, 388; **"Literature as Equipment for Living," 388–93**; theory of symbols, 386

Burney, Frances, 841; *Evelina*, 849

Burton, Sir Richard, 1051, 1075, 1078

Butch (masculine lesbian): in Butler, 1036–37,1039; in Wittig, 984

Butler, Judith, 487, 874, 956, 965–69, 1147; biography, 1030; **"Imitation and Gender Insubordination," 1030–41**

Butor, Michel, 822

Butte, George, 625

Byron, George Gordon, Lord, 268–69, 912, 1029, 1077, 1093; *Childe Harold's Pilgrimage*, 263, 415

Caecilius, 89

Caillois, Roger, 645, 648

Calderón de la Barca, Pedro, 236, 240, 243

Caliban (symbol of colonized subject), 1049, 1051–52, 1088, 1094, 1097

Calvin, John, 1082

Cambridge Platonists, 26

Campion, Thomas: "My Sweetest Lesbia," 610

Camus, Albert, 648, 1046; *The Fall*, 549

Canon, 7, 11, 786, 796–97, 799, 860–61, 863, 865–67, 870–71, 874, 879–80, 884, 890, 897–98, 918–19, 957, 1134, 1143; in Armstrong, 853; in Baym, 890, 893–98; in Booth, 545; in Eliot, 321; in Fetterley, 606; in Guillory, 796, 872; in Kolodny, 898, 918–19, 921; in Pope, 151; Sedgwick, 1026–29; Western, 1057–58

Cantor, Georg, 528

Capitalism, 778, 783; and print culture, 1082–84; in Benjamin, 713; in Marx, 249; in Mulvey, 669; in Rubin, 1004–06; in Adam Smith, 694; in Williams, 763–64

Capitein, Jacobus, 1137

Carlyle, Thomas, 274, 376, 464,1072

Carnivalization (Bakhtin), 351

Casablanca (Michael Curtiz), 673

Castelvetro, Lodovico, 50

Castration anxiety, 673; in Spivak, 1092

Castration complex, 649, 654, 673, 958; in Cixous, 997; in Freud, 312, 318, 629, 636, 654; in Kristeva, 935–36; in Lacan, 683–84; in Mulvey, 669; in Žižek, 684

Categorical imperative (Kant), 1090

Categories: in Kant, 167

Catharsis, 5; in Aristotle, 49–50, 55, 60

Cather, Willa, 898, 1029; *O Pioneers*, 899; *Sapphira and the Slave Girl*, 1054; *Song of the Lark*, 898

Cathexis (Freud), 313

Catullus, Caius Valerius, 207, 238

Caudwell, Christopher, 703

Conrad, Joseph, 770, 839, 1046, 1120; *Heart of Darkness*, 1045, 1055, 1118, 1120; *Lord Jim*, 705, 774; *Nostromo*, 705

Conscious mind: in Freud, 628; in Jung, 335

Consciousness: in Althusser, 745; in Derrida, 532; in Freud, 533; in Hegel, 12; in Iser, 586, 590, 596; in Marx, 248–50, 255, 257–61; in Nietzsche, 281; in Williams, 752; in Wimsatt and Beardsley, 462

Constatives (J. L. Austin), 684, 707. *See also* Performatives

Constitutive rules, 471

Constraints on interpretation: in Zunshine, 615, 617

Consumer culture: in Barthes, 515; in Bourdieu, 819; in Jameson, 779

Content: in Cleanth Brooks, 419; in Jameson 704, 783; latent and manifest, 403; in Horkheimer and Adorno, 739; in Russian formalism, 414; in Sontag, 404–09

Context: in Cleanth Brooks, 450, 451, 454

Conventions, 921: in Fish, 602; in Horace, 75, 80; in Johnson, 160;

Coomaraswamy, Ananda K., 462

Cooper, James Fenimore, 798, 880, 896–97; *Last of the Mohicans*, 328

Corneille, Pierre, 463, 1082

Correspondences: in Adorno, 698; in Benjamin, 697–98; in Goldmann, 700; in Williams, 700

Counterculture, 759, 779

Coupure (Foucault), 788–89

Courtly love: 677–93

Cowley, Abraham, 207

Craig, David, 1148

Crane, Ronald Salmon, 10, 11, 418, 421, 457, 479, 744; **"The Critical Monism of Cleanth Brooks,"** **457–60**

Creativity, 3, 7–8; in Aristotle, 49, 263; in Arnold, 266, 267, 268, 271, 279; in Baym, 899; in Bely, 429; in Benjamin, 713; in Coleridge, 221; in Foucault, 522; in Freud, 313, 315–17; 630; in Iser, 585; in Kant, 168, 190; in Longinus, 89; in mimetic theories, 4; in Nietzsche, 290; in Pope, 148; in Rich, 884; in Shelley, 243; in Shklovsky, 429; in Sidney, 119; in Wordsworth, 211, 266

Crews, Frederick C.: *The Sins of the Fathers: Hawthorne's Psychological Themes*, 630

Critical practice: in New Criticism, 417

Criticism: archetypal, 8, 10; biographical, 8, 10; cultural, 412; deconstructionist, 421; ethical, 10; evolution of, 7; expressive, 3, 5–6, 8, 10; feminist, 421, 632, 875; formalist, 4, 7–9, 657, 856; Freudian, 403, 630; historical, 10, 411; history of, 3; in Arnold, 263, 266–68, 271–79; in Baym, 899; in Benjamin, 726; in Burke, 393; in Eliot, 323; in Greenblatt, 856; in Horace, 85; in James, 299; in Sontag, 403; in Wordsworth, 266; Lacanian, 635; Marxist, 9, 403, 421; mimetic, 3, 7,10; objective, 5; psychoanalytic, 8, 10, 407, 630–31, 667; reader-response, 11, 631; rhetorical, 3–4, 6, 9–10, 87; sociological, 8, 10; structuralist, 412, 657; thematic, 419

Criticism of life: in Arnold, 264

Critique des beautés: in Chateaubriand, 563

Croce, Benedetto, 418, 463, 792

Cronenberg, David: *M. Butterfly*, 690–92

Cross-dressing, 115, 962, 970, 1033. *See also* Drag

Cugoano, Ottobah, 1141–42

Cullen, Countee, 341, 346

Culler, Jonathan, 470, 475, 476, 488, 877

Cult value: in Benjamin, 719, 722, 731

Cultural capital, 861, 872; in Bourdieu, 795, 799, 820; in Guillory, 796, 865

Cultural field (Bourdieu): 794

Cultural formation: in Williams, 761. *See also* Dominant, Emergent, Residual

Cultural materialism, 700, 785; in Williams, 791

Cultural poetics. *See* New Historicism

Cultural production, 864; in Bourdieu, 794; in Guillory, 872; in Williams, 757

Cultural revolution: in Armstrong, 843; in Jameson, 781

Cultural studies, 9, **782–872**, 825–26, 830, 1047; and Marxism, 824–31; and structuralism, 831–37

Culture: 792, in Anzaldua, 1101; in Arnold, 263, 265, 275; in Baym, 891; in Burke, 393; in Foucault, 520, 523, 529; in Greenblatt, 857; in Guillory, 796, 860–870; in Horkheimer and Adorno, 699, 734–40; in Lévi-Strauss, 535–36; in Nietzsche, 292, 295; in Said, 1072; in Sontag, 402, 408; in Trilling, 894; in Williams, 752, 827; in Wimsatt and Beardsley, 465; Latino, 862; minority, 862; postcolonial, 1046

Cuvier, Georges, 527, 1072

Cyberculture, 798

Dadaism, 728, 729, 739

Dante Alighieri, 6, 117, 125, 140, 229, 232–33, 240–43, 264, 294, 325, 409, 468, 544, 601, 678, 738, 864; biography, 101; *Inferno*, 240, 325, 1050; **Letter to Can Grande della Scala, 101–03**, 405; *Paradiso*, 240; *Purgatorio*, 435

Darwin, Charles, 265, 985, 1078

Davies, Sarah Emily, 377, 384

Davis, Kathleen, 848

Davis, Lennard, 841

Davis, Robert Con, 635

Davis, Walter, 12

Day, Thomas: *Sandford and Merton*, 196

De Graef, Ortwin, 486

De Man, Paul, 13, 477, 486–91, 558, 1051, 1061, 1148–49; and salvational poetics, 487; wartime collaboration, 486, 487

De Quincey, Thomas, 381; *Confessions of an English Opium Eater*, 1093;

Death instinct: in Freud, 663, 665; in Lacan, 647

Decolonization, 1046, 1048–49, 1119; economic effects, 1045; history, 1044; political effects, 1044

Deconstruction, 18, 20–22, 470–91, 495, 497, 499, 501, 504, 506–07, 510, 512–13, 515, 519, 558, 623, 786, 886, 965, 1058, 1060, 1087, 1091, 1112, 1127, 1149–50, 1153; and binaries, 1063; and politics, 486; and literature, 485; and New Criticism, 485; and politics, 486–87; and referentiality, 1149; as critical toolkit, 487; as mode of close reading, 477; at Yale, 486; in Baym, 901; in Bhabha, 1121–22; in Butler, 966, 1034, 1036; in Chow, 1148–50; in Cixous, 959; in Culler, 877; in De Man, 486; in Derrida, 534; in Freud, 664; in Gates, 1136; in Spivak, 1087

Decorum: in Horace, 77, 80–81; in Johnson, 160; in Sidney, 115, 137

Defamiliarization: in Culler, 476; in Iser, 593; in Russian formalism, 413; in Shklovsky, 413, 430–34

Defense mechanisms, 10, 403, 550; in Freud, 628–30

Defoe, Daniel, 142, 545, 702, 840; *Moll Flanders*, 624

Deleuze, Gilles, 692, 778, 1030, 1053, 1064

Delight: in Horace, 75, 83; in Kant, 167, 172; in Nietzsche, 294; in Pope, 151; in rhetorical theory, 6; in Shelley, 228, 235; in Sidney, 114, 120–21, 127, 130, 133, 137, 139; in Wordsworth, 205, 216

Democritus, 82

Demosthenes, 90, 96–98, 138

Dennett, Daniel, 616, 620, 625–26

Dennis, John, 152, 156

Denotation: in Cleanth Brooks, 451

Denouement: in Booth, 580–81; in Peter Brooks, 658, 660, 663–65,667; in Kermode, 658

Deracination: in Guillory, 864

Derrida, Jacques, 13, 470, 477–91, 531, 542, 633–34, 701,708,943,958–59,966,988,997,1016,1037,1042,

1051–52, 1061–63, 1086, 1098, 1119, 1122, 1124, 1127–28, 1142–43; biography, 531; *Of Grammatology*, 478, 958; **"Structure, Sign and Play in the Discourse of the Human Sciences," 531–42**

Derzhavin, Gavrila, 435

Descartes, René, 13, 643, 844

Description: in James, 304

Desire, 631; in Booth, 580; in Cixous, 989, 999; in Derrida, 532; in Freud, 628; in Kant, 168, 170, 177, 184; in Lacan, 633, 635, 650, 653, 657, 663–68; in Mulvey, 638, 670; in Nietzsche, 280; in Peter Brooks, 632, 659, 663, 666–67

Deterritorialization (Deleuze and Guattari), 1053

Deus ex machina: in Aristotle, 62; in Horace, 80

Deutsch, Helene, 650, 1017

Dewey, John, 12–13, 593, 920

Diachronic: in Saussure, 499

Dialectic: in Derrida, 481, 482; in Hegel, 482; in Iser, 596; in Jameson, 778; in Lacan, 634–35; in Marx, 248, 694. 697, 701; in Nietzsche, 291; method, 13

Dialects: in Bakhtin, 367

Dialogism: in Bakhtin, 351–52, 354, 358–61, 776; in Jauss, 555

Diaspora culture, 1043

Dickens, Charles, 17, 298, 309, 363–64, 366–67, 370, 381, 409, 768, 841, 912–13, 1072; *David Copperfield*, 302, 965; *Great Expectations*, 666

Dickinson, Emily, 15–18, 21–22, 161, 606, 882, 890, 904–05, 907, 910–13, 915, 1029

Diction: in Aristotle, 48, 55–56, 65, 71; in Longinus, 88, 90, 92, 96; in Sidney, 138; in Wordsworth, 204–05, 210, 214

Didacticism: in James, 308; in Johnson, 159, 160

Diegesis: in Mulvey, 672

Dietrich, Marlene, 639, 672, 674

Différance: in Bhabha, 1121, 1124; in Chow, 1063; in Derrida, 480, 530, 533, 542

Difference: in Derrida, 533; in Saussure, 496, 499; in Todorov, 656

Ding (Freudian "Thing"): in Lacan, 678; in Žižek, 682

Diogenes Laertius, 521

Dionysius of Halicarnassus, 157

Dionysus: in Aristotle, 41; in Nietzsche, 282, 284–85, 287, 289, 291, 295

Discourse, 12–13; in Aristotle, 66; in Bakhtin, 354, 358, 360–62; in Derrida, 534, 539; in Foucault, 523–24, 526–28, 530, 843, 976; in operationalism, 13; in Said, 1067, 1071

Empedocles, 52, 85

Empire. *See* Colonialism, Imperialism

Empiricism, 1119; in Aristotle, 48; in Levi-Strauss, 481

Emplotment: in White, 805

Empson, William, 102, 386, 416–17, 419–20, 547, 663, 1134; *Seven Types of Ambiguity*, 417

Ending. *See* Denouement

Engels, Friedrich, 248, 251, 695, 702, 753–54, 777, 960, 1005–08, 1020, 1147, 1150

Enlightenment, 563, 788, 843, 861, 1047, 1055, 1059, 1124, 1127, 1137–39

Ennius, 81

Enthousiasmós: in Plato, 28, 41–42, 46. *See also* Inspiration

Enthusiasm: in Wordsworth, 211

Epic, 87, 229, 233, 415, 460; in Aristotle, 51, 54, 63–64, 68–69, 73; in Bakhtin, 363–66; in Benjamin, 730; in Nietzsche, 289; in Propp, 439, 445; in Sidney, 129

Epictetus, 360

Epistemé: in Derrida, 531, 540; in Foucault, 484, 520, 784, 787–89; in Lévi-Strauss, 537

Epistemology: in Plato, 28

Equiano, Olaudah, 1141–42

Erasmus, Desiderius, 130, 157

Erikson, Erik, 913

Erlich, Victor, 412

Erotic identity: in Mulvey, 671–74, 1031. *See also* Sexual identity

Essentialism, 1030, 1058; in Christian, 1061

Estrangement: in Benjamin, 724; in Marx, 251–56

Etherege, George, 141

Ethics and literature, 12, 13; in Bakhtin, 357; in Behn, 144; in Booth, 574, 580, 582–83; in Christine de Pisan, 108–12, 109; in Dante, 104; in James, 297, 300, 308; in Jung, 332; in Kant, 167, 173, 178; in Nietzsche, 295; in Pope, 156; in Johnson, 162–63; in Shelley, 235, 236, 245; in Sidney, 119, 121, 124; in Wimsatt and Beardsley, 463; in Wordsworth, 208, 216, 218

Ethnic studies, 1042; African American, 1047; Asian, 1043, 1047; Chicano, 1043; Greek, 1043; Italian, 1043; Latino, 1047

Ethnicity, 1042–43, 1150; in Chow, 1151

Ethnocentrism: in Spivak, 1088

Euripides, 41, 60, 63–64, 68, 71, 134, 137, 235, 281, 291, 609, 1029; *Bacchae*, 289; *Electra*, 100; *Iphigenia at Aulis*, 61–62; *Iphigenia at Tauris*, 59, 61–63; *Medea*, 60, 62, 72; *Orestes*, 61, 72

Europhonism (Ngugi), 1056

Evaluation: in Baym, 892; in Booth, 545; in James, 305

Evans-Pritchard, E. E., 960, 1007, 1013

Evidence: external, 465, 467; internal, 465, 467

Evolution, literary: in Russian formalism, 416

Exchange of women, 471; in Rubin, 960, 1008–11, 1013, 1015, 1018, 1020

Exegesis. *See* Interpretation

Exhibition value: in Benjamin, 719–20

Existentialism, 636, 648; in Beauvoir, 395; in Sartre, 553

Expectations: in Iser, 566, 586, 590, 592

Experience: in Iser, 590–92, 594, 596; in Kant, 180

Explication: in Jameson, 770; in New Criticism, 416, 419

Expression, 9, 404, 465; in Croce, 463; in Eliot, 322; in Foucault, 520, 525; in Freud, 316, in James, 303–04, 306; in Pope, 153; in Wimsatt and Beardsley, 461, 464; in Woolf, 381

Expressionism, 737, 739

Fabian, Johannes, 1097, 1152, 1154

Fable: in Shklovsky, 430; in Sidney, 134

Fabula, 656; in Peter Brooks, 659, 661, 664–65; in Shklovsky, 413. *See also Sjužet*

Fairy tale, 437, 442

Fame: in Horace, 77, 83; in Longinus, 98

Family: in Foucault, 976, 980–81

Fancy: in Coleridge, 221–23, 227; in Johnson, 160; in Sidney, 132; in Wordsworth, 205. *See also* Imagination

Fanon, Frantz, 905, 1048, 1057, 1064–65, 1126, 1128, 1131; *Black Skins, White Masks*, 1131; cultural binarism, 1049

Fantasies, 10, 669, 956, 1035; in Freud, 310–17; in Holland, 550

Fascism, 699, 713, 717, 731–32, 772

Faulkner, William, 608, 666, 799, 893; "A Rose for Emily," 608, 612; *The Sound and the Fury*, 546

Fauset, Jessie, 346

Febvre, Lucien Paul Victor, 1080

Feelings: in Eliot, 325; in Jung, 337; in New Criticism, 417; in Richards, 416; in Russian formalism, 414; in Wordsworth, 205, 208, 212, 215, 217–18. *See also* Emotions

Feidelson, Charles, 880, 895

Felman, Shoshana, 635

Female domain as site of power: in Armstrong, 846–50

Female language, 937

Female monster: in Gilbert and Gubar, 907–08

Female reader: in Fetterley, 606

Femininity, 958–59, 961, 966–67, 990–91, 994–95; in Cixous, 990, 994–95; in Freud, 958; in Kristeva, 931

Feminism (social movement), 557–58, 623, 633, 638, 669, 783, 786, 798, 874–75, 882, 956–58, 962, 969, 988, 1023, 1051, 1060–61, 1087–88, 1092, 1094, 1097–1100, 1111, 1143–44; and deconstruction, 885; and homophobia, 945–50; and Lacan, 636; and Marxism, 885; and psychoanalysis, 885; and racism, 945–50; black, 1062; in Armstrong, 845, 852–53; in Beauvoir, 395–400; in Behn, 142, 145; in Christine de Pisan, 106; in Kolodny, 917, 924, 927; in Kristeva, 634, 637–38, 936–39, 941–43; in Rubin, 1018; in Sedgwick, 1027; in Spivak, 1087–88, 1090; in Wittig, 982–85; in Woolf, 371; lesbian, 884

Feminist literary criticism, 544, **873–955**, 969, 1114; and gender theory, 885; definitions, 873; evolution, 874

Femme (feminine lesbian): in Butler, 1039

Femme fatale, 688

Ferenczi, Sandor, 318, 969

Fetishism, 655, 673–76, 958

Fetterley, Judith, 552, 553, 605, 638, 876–77, 886; biography, 605; *The Resisting Reader 605–12*

Feudalism, 778

Feuerbach, Ludwig, 743, 749, 753

Fiction: in Armstrong, 840; in Baym, 901; in Coleridge, 222; in Foucault, 529; in Freud, 311; in James, 304, 306; in Johnson, 161, 163; in Sidney, 132; in Sontag, 408

Fiedler, Leslie, 894, 897

Field: in Bourdieu. *See* Cultural field, Economic field, etc.; in Lacan. *See* Imaginary, Real, Symbolic

Fielding, Henry, 363, 367, 545, 582, 584, 840; *Tom Jones*, 159, 589

Figures of speech: in Longinus, 88, 92; in New Criticism, 412; in Pope, 152; in Sidney, 138; in White, 813; in Wordsworth, 209–10. *See also* Tropes; and individual figures such as Metaphor, Metonymy, etc.

Filiation: in Barthes, 514–15; in Russian Formalism, 416

Film, 638–39; in Benjamin, 717, 720, 723–26, 728–29, 731; in Mulvey, 667–675

Film noir, 673, 681, 688

Finch, Anne, Countess of Winchilsea, 904, 911

Fish, Stanley, 543, 546, 617–18, 922; biography, 597; **"How to Recognize a Poem When You See One,"** **596–604**; legal applications, 547; self-consuming artifacts, 547

Fitzgerald, Edward, 375

Fitzgerald, F. Scott: *The Beautiful and Damned*, 897; *The Great Gatsby*, 546, 607–09, 612, 880, 898

Flaubert, Gustave, 305, 309, 376, 516, 518, 521, 556, 942, 1067, 1069, 1073, 1078; *Madame Bovary*, 392, 546; *Salammbo*, 1071

Fletcher, John, 207

Foley, Barbara, 421

Folk tale, 414–15; in Peter Brooks, 660

Forces of production: in Benjamin, 732. *See also* Base

Form, 7–8, 10; in Aristotle, 7, 54, 263; in Arnold, 263; in Cleanth Brooks, 419; in Peter Brooks, 661; in Coleridge, 221, 225, 416; in Dante, 103; in Derrida, 479; in Freud, 630; in Holland, 550; in Horkheimer and Adorno, 737, 739; in James, 297, 300–01; in Jameson, 704; in Kant, 177, 179, 181–82; in Mulvey, 668; in Neo-Aristotelianism, 422; in New Criticism, 403, 417–18; in Nietzsche, 283; in Propp, 439, 441; in Russian formalism, 414; in Shelley, 233, 237; in Sontag, 404, 408–09; in Williams, 756

Formalism, 8, 388, **411–469**, 484, 543–44, 656, 783

Forster, E. M., 1046, 1051, 1125

Forty-Second Street (Busby Berkeley), 671

Foster, Hannah, 891, 895

Foucault, Michel, 470, 484, 485, 489, 491, 520, 632, 708, 778–79, 784–92, 800, 835, 837, 843–45, 849, 867, 956, 963–66, 969, 1003, 1031, 1042, 1049–51, 1063, 1072, 1077–78, 1123–24, 1128–29; and structuralism, 484; as disciple of Nietzsche, 484; biography, 520; *Birth of the Clinic*, 964; *Discipline and Punish*, 787, 794, 843–44, 964; *History of Sexuality*, 787, 790, 843, 964, **972–81**; *Madness and Civilization*, 787, 964; *The Order of Things*, 788, 1077; plague as metaphor 840; truth and power, 484, **"What Is an Author?"** **520–30**

Fox-Genovese, Elizabeth, 1088

Frankfurt school, 698–700, 706–07, 733

Frazer, Sir James, 467–68, 503; *The Golden Bough*, 327

Frederick the Great, 191

Free play. *See* Play

Freedom: in Kant, 178, 181; in Sartre, 648

French Revolution, 194, 781, 784

Freud, Anna, 647

Horace (Quintus Horatius Flaccus), 6, 8, 87, 114–15, 124, 131, 140, 147, 149, 157–59, 238, 245–46, 351, 374, 464, 544; **The Art of Poetry, 75–85,** 104, 117, 120, 123, 137, 151, 161; biography, 74; *Epistles,* 128–29, 148, 162; maxims in, 74; *Satires,* 133; occasion, 74; organization, 74; reputation, 74

Horizon: in Gadamer, 555; in Jauss, 555, 562, 564, 567–68

Horkheimer, Max, 698–99, 706, 710, 968; biography, 729; **"The Culture Industry: Enlightenment as Mass Deception,"** 730–37

Horney, Karen, 650, 651

Hountondji, Paulin J., 1142

Housman, A. E., 450, 464

Howe, Irving, 696

Howells, William Dean, 880, 893, 897, 1060

Hoy, David Couzens, 919

Hubbell, Jay, 893

Hughes, Langston, 346

Hugo, Victor, 1077

Hull, Gloria T., 954

Hulme, T. E., 412

Human nature: in Arnold, 273; in Nietzsche, 280; in Shelley, 233, 241; in Wordsworth, 207, 211, 213

Humanism: in Barthes, 519

Humanities, curriculum and crisis; in Guillory, 796, 870

Hume, David, 6, 148, 167–68, 220, 243, 251, 740, 1072, 1137, 1140, 1142

Humours: in Shelley, 237

Hurston, Zora Neale, 883, 948–49, 954, 1061, 1109, 1111, 1135; *Their Eyes Were Watching God,* 886

Husserl, Edmond, 478, 488, 490, 531, 541, 565, 586

Huxley, Aldous, 725

Hybridity, 1063, 1125, 1126, 1131; in Anzaldua, 1100; in Bhabha, 1052, 1124–30; in Chow, 1153

Hysteria, 647, 932–33; hysterical subject, in Foucault, 964, 978, 981

I (Lacanian subject): in Butler, 1031–32, 1034; in Lacan, 643–45, 647–48, 657, 671. *See also* Ego, Subject

Iconic signs, 471

Id: in Freud, 628–29, 634, 643; in Lacan, 647, 651

Idea: in Kant, 169; in Sidney, 124

Idealism, 1119; in Plato, 5, 26–27, 29; in Plotinus, 5; in Shelley, 228, 229

Ideas: in Kant, 185

Identification: in Iser, 594; in Lacan, 644; in Mulvey, 672; in Poulet, 595

Identity: categories, 1030–32, 1151; effects: in Bhabha, 1124–25

identity politics, 970, 1153; in Berlant and Warner, 966; in Butler, 1034; in Chow, 1145–47,1151; in Halberstam, 966; in Smith, 945–50

Identity theme: in Holland, 551

Ideologeme, 473, 777; in Jameson, 770, 776, 783

Ideological State apparatuses: in Althusser, 744; in Williams, 761

Ideology, 7, 756, 766–67, 774–75, 957; collective consciousness, 695; false consciousness, 695, 699; in Althusser, 742–43, 748–49; in Arnold, 264; in Baker, 1059; in Bakhtin, 353, 355, 357, 359; in Fetterley, 553; in Foucault, 529, 977; in Gilbert and Gubar, 883; in Goldmann, 700; in Greenblatt, 856, 859; in Guillory, 869; in Hall, 831; in Horkheimer and Adorno, 734, 739, 741; in Jameson, 770, 783; in Kolodny, 927; in Marx, 249–50, 260; in Marxist criticism, 697, 702; in Rabinowitz, 546; in Williams, 752, 756; in Wittig, 982; in Žižek, 640; Marxist concept, 695; religious, 749

Illocutionary utterance (Austin): 707

Image, 94, 412; in Baym, 898; in Burke, 389; in Eliot, 325; in Heilman, 420; in James, 303; in Lacan, 633–34; in Nietzsche, 281; in Potebnya, 426; in Shklovsky, 426–28, 432

Imagery: archetypal, 6; in Longinus, 90; in Pope, 147; in Johnson, 164; in Shelley, 233; in Sidney, 124, 129; in Wordsworth, 214

Imaginary (Lacanian field), 635, 636, 644, 648, 652, 668, 743; in Bhabha, 1122; in Butler, 1040; in Cixous, 989; in Guillory, 869; in Jameson, 773; in Lacan, 633, 635, 637; in Mulvey, 668–69, 671–72; in Spivak, 1092; in Wittig, 984–85

Imagination, 6, 8; and gender, 881; in Benjamin, 717; in Cixous, 993; in Coleridge, 219, 221–23, 227, 416, 464; in Collingwood, 805; in Freud, 313–17; in Horkheimer and Adorno, 737; in Iser, 584, 586–87, 589–90, 596; in James, 302; in Johnson, 162, 164; in Jung, 337; in Kant, 168, 170, 178, 180, 182–83, 185–87, 190–92, 220; in Marx, 257, 260, 262; in New Criticism, 418; in Nietzsche, 284; in Pope, 149; in Shelley, 228, 230–32, 235, 238, 244; in Sidney, 124, 131; in Spivak, 1098; in Wimsatt and Beardsley, 464; in Woolf, 375, 380; in Wordsworth, 205, 207, 216; primary, 221, 223; productive, 221; secondary, 221, 223. *See also* Fancy, Genius

Imago: in Freud, 644; in Lacan, 644, 647

Jardine, Alice, 929, 931, 935, 937

Jarrell, Randall: "Eighth Air Force," 455–56

Jarry, Alfred, 728

Jauss, Hans Robert, 553, 584; biography, 562, **"The Three Horizons of Reading," 562–69**

Jea, John, 1141–43

Jean de Meun, 106–07

Jean Paul (Johann Paul Friedrich Richter), 363, 368–69

Jefferson, Thomas, 1059, 1137, 1140

Jews, 87, 94

Joan of Arc, 106

Johnson, Barbara, 486, 1061, 1094

Johnson, Samuel, 6–7, 204–05, 217, 266, 299, 381, 413; 694, 773; biography, 159; *Irene*, 266; *Lives of the Poets*, 266; "London", 416; moralism, 159; "Preface to Shakespeare," 115, 264; *Rambler #4*, **160–63**; *Rasselas*, **163–64**; rhetorical principles, 159; tragic vision, 160; universalizing perspective, 160; "Vanity of Human Wishes", 416

Jones, Ann Rosalind, 886

Jones, Ernest, 650; *Hamlet and Oedipus*, 630

Jones, Sir William, 1069, 1075, 1077

Jonson, Ben, 142, 145, 321; *The Alchemist*, 145; *Every Man out of His Humour*, 153; *Volpone*, 573

Jordan, June, 1115

Jordan, Neil: *The Crying Game*, 688, 690–93

Jouissance, 483, 692; in Barthes, 483, 516, 549; in Kristeva, 932; in Lacan, 683

Joyce, James, 297, 544, 1029; *Finnegans Wake*, 476, 931; *Ulysses*, 593, 995

Judgment: critical, 10; in Arnold, 278; in Baym, 891; in Booth, 574–75; in Eliot, 323; in Kant, 166, 168, 170–71, 173–75, 177–78, 180–82, 184, 187–89; in Pope, 149, 151, 154, 156; in Wimsatt and Beardsley, 464

Jung, Carl Gustav, 6, 10, 310–11, 504, 644; biography, 327; **"The Principal Archetypes," 328–38**

Juvenal, 246; *Satires*, 135, 138

Kafka, Franz, 406, 521, 698, 707, 1029, 1053, 1064; *The Metamorphosis*, 663; *The Trial*, 1032

Kamuf, Peggy, 885

Kant, Immanuel, 88, 148, 200, 219–20, 228, 295, 330, 634, 683–85, 736, 740, 795, 805, 821–22, 1059, 1090, 1096, 1137, 1139–41; biography, 166; *Critique of Judgment*, **169–92**, 477, 685, 686; *Critique of Practical Reason*, 177, 683; *Critique of Pure Reason*, 166, 219; *Metaphysic of Morals*, 178

Kazin, Alfred, 696

Keast, William Rea, 421

Keats, John, 325, 376, 606, 611, 1069; "Ode on a Grecian Urn," 389

Kellogg, Robert, 809

Kennard, Jean, 918

Kepler, Johannes, 466

Kermode, Frank, 658

Kerouac, Jack, 896

Kettle, Arnold, 703

Kierkegaard, Søren, 523

King, Martin Luther, 340, 342

Kinsey, Alfred, 961

Kinship systems: in Rubin, 1007–09, 1011, 1013–14, 1016; in Sedgwick, 1024

Kipling, Rudyard, 384, 1046, 1051, 1125

Kipnis, Laura, 801

Kitsch, 820

Klein, Melanie, 527, 651, 654

Kleist, Heinrich von, 959, 991

Knight, Sarah Kemble, 890

Knot (Lacan), 648–49, 652

Knowledge: in Longinus, 92; in Plato, 5, 32, 39, 43–44, 46; in Pope, 157; in Sidney, 133; in Wordsworth, 213. *See also* Power/knowledge: Foucault

Koestler, Arthur, 1101

Kohler, Wolfgang, 644

Kolodny, Annette, 873; 884, 886; biography, 916; **"Dancing Through the Minefield," 916–28**; misprisions of feminist criticism, 916–18; theses on literary history, 919–26

Kramarae, Cheris, 879

Krieger, Murray, 416, 921

Kristeva, Julia, 627, 632, 637, 873, 886; biography, 929; feminism and national politics, 929–31; feminism and socialism, 934–35; feminism and time, 931–33; feminism's second phase, 933; generations within feminism, 931; *Revolution in Poetic Language*, 637; **"Women's Time," 874, 929–44**

Kuchuk Hanem, 1067

Kuhn, Thomas, 7, 784

La Fontaine, Jean de, 1082

Labor: in Marx, 248–49, 251–59, women's, 1004

Lacan, Jacques, 13, 513, 627, 632, 634, 637–38, 664, 668–69, 677–78, 680, 682, 701, 742, 747, 773, 785, 836, 886, 929, 931, 936, 941, 957–59, 968, 985, 988–89, 994, 1003, 1016, 1052, 1061–63, 1114, 1128–31; and Kristeva, 931; and Žižek, 684; biography, 643; **"The Meaning of the Phallus," 649–55**; **"The Mirror Stage," 643–49**, 657, 670–71

Psalms of David, 118

Pseudostatements: in Cleanth Brooks, 451; in New Criticism, 403, in Richards, 416

Psychic censor: in Freud, 310–11

Psychoanalysis, 13, 504, 528, 637, 643, 648, 650, 652, 727, 792, 942, 957; and feminism, 885, and gender, 968; in Barthes, 512; in Kristeva, 931; in Lacan, 680; in Rubin, 1002, 1014; political uses, 668

Psychoanalytic criticism, 627–92; 886, 925; in Jameson, 769

Psychology: in Jung, 329–30; in Kant, 166, 168

Public sphere: in Habermas, 699

Publication: in Horace, 75

Publishing industry: effect on literary scene, 8

Purposiveness without purpose (Kant), 167, 176–79, 183–84

Pushkin, Alexander, 21, 441; *Eugene Onegin*, 359, 435

Pythagoras, 33, 117

Qualitative criticism: in Longinus, 87

Quality: in Kant, 167, 170

Queer culture: in Anzaldua, 1105; in Berlant and Warner, 967

Queer theory, 787, 874, **956–1041**; 965, 969; in Hocquenghem, 969; origins of the term, 956

Querelle de la Rose, 106–13

Quintilian, 147, 157

Quintilius, 85

Rabelais, Francois, 351, 367, 368, 369; *Gargantua and Pantagruel*, 318

Rabinowitz, Peter, 421, 546, 549, 886

Race, 1134, 1042, 1151; and gender, 883–884, 983; in Anzaldua, 1104–05, in Bhabha, 1122; in Du Bois, 342, in Gates, 1133, 1138; in Rubin, 1002; in Taine, 1134; in Wittig, 984

Racine, Jean, 512, 700

Racism, 945, 951, 1068–69, 1089, 1096, 1114, 1134, 1142–43; and Fanon, 1049; in Enlightenment Europe, 1141; in white feminist critics, 947–48

Radcliffe, Ann, 527, 911

Rader, Ralph, 421–22

Radway, Janice, 552

Rahv, Philip, 696

Raleigh, Sir Walter, 451

Raleigh, Walter Alexander, 384

Ransom, John Crowe, 387, 416–20, 1134

Reader, 9, 543–44; actual, 550; as performer, 566; gendered, 2, 850, 924; ideal, 9, 549; implied, 549; in Armstrong, 850; in Bakhtin, 357; in Barthes, 483, 515, 519, 568, 657; in Behn, 143; in Benjamin, 724; in Booth, 545, 577, 579; in Peter Brooks, 667; in Burke, 392; in cognitive science, 558; in Derrida, 479; in Dryden, 545; in Fetterley, 544; in Fish, 545, 547, 597, 602, 605; in Genette, 476; in Horace, 544; in Iser, 584–86, 588–90, 592, 594, 596; in Johnson, 544–45; in Kolodny, 876; in Mulvey, 638; in Neo-Aristotelianism, 422; in New Criticism, 417; in rhetorical criticism, 544; in Richards, 416; in Schweickart, 544; in Sontag, 402, 545; in Spivak, 1098; in Wordsworth, 205, 216, 218; real, 549; social, 552; virtual, 549. *See also* Audience, Narrative audience, Authorial audience

Reading public, 8

Real (Lacanian field), 634, 636, 653, 678, 680, 685, 689, 693; in Jameson, 773

Realism: in Booth, 582; in Burke, 392; in James, 297, 299–300, 303; in Lukács, 696; in Johnson, 161

Reality: in Benjamin, 725; in James, 302; in Propp, 439, 446

Reality-effect: in Bhabha, 1122, 1123

Reality principle: in Freud, 628

Reality-testing: in Lacan, 646

Realization: in Iser, 584

Rear Window (Alfred Hitchcock), 674

Reason: in Kant, 172–73, 179, 186; in Plato, 35–36; in Pope, 151; in Shelley, 228, 230

Reception, 786: in Benjamin, 728–29, 731; in Iser, 564, 566; in Jauss, 556, 562, 566; in Kant, 168; in Radway, 552; in Riffaterre, 565; in Sontag, 402

Recognition (*anagnorisis*): in Aristotle, 58, 62, 69, 658; in Barthes, 658; in Peter Brooks, 666

Reed, Ishmael, 948, 954, 1113

Referentiality: in Auerbach, 1149; in Chow, 1146–47, 1151, 1153–54; in Richards, 416

Reflection theory, 840; in Lukács, 696–97; in Marxist criticism, 696, 697

Reichert, John, 604

Relations of production: in Marxist criticism, 697, 700

Religion, 12; in Arnold, 275; in New Criticism, 419; in Propp, 440

Rembrandt van Rijn, 715

Renaissance, 113, 115, 147, 294, 417, 717, 727, 731, 788, 856

Renan, Ernest, 1047, 1050, 1067–68, 1073, 1078

Renoir, Jean, 409

Repertoire: in Iser, 593

axiomatics of imperialism: in Spivak, 1089, 1095, 1097; biography, 1086; **"Three Women's Texts and a Critique of Imperialism,"** 1086–99

Springer, Mary Doyle, 421

St. Augustine, 101, 112, 360, 600; *The City of God,* 812

St. Jerome, 525

St. Paul, 112

Staël, Germaine de, 874

Stalin, Joseph, 412, 609, 703

State apparatus: in Althusser, 973; in Foucault, 973–74

Stein, Gertrude, 884; *Three Women,* 1054

Stendhal (Marie-Henri Beyle), 397, 399–400, 523, 875

Stepan, Nancy, 1136

Stephen, Leslie, 371

Sternberg, Josef von, 639, 673–74

Sterne, Laurence, 220, 363, 367–69, 381, 545, 1137; *Tristram Shandy,* 413, 476, 573, 584–85, 664

Stevens, Wallace: *Of Mere Being,* 1067

Stevenson, Robert Louis: *Treasure Island,* 307

Stimpson, Catharine, 905

Stoll, Edgar, 462

Stowe, Harriet Beecher, 879; *Uncle Tom 's Cabin,* 347, 891, 1054

Strachey, William, 790

Stramm, August, 728

Strauss, David Friedrich, 265, 276

Stravinsky, Igor, 698, 785

Structural linguistics, 471, 473, 634; in Levi-Strauss, 506

Structural Marxism, 700

Structuralism, 7, 9, 415, **470–542,** 544, 548, 557–58, 564, 566, 568, 599, 651, 774, 786, 798, 921, 929, 1058, 1143, 1150, 1152; and anthropology, 474; as activity, 473; decline, 477; in Barthes, 483; in Kolodny, 925; in Lévi-Strauss, 538; in Rubin, 1002; logistic method, 785

Structure: in Cleanth Brooks, 454; in Peter Brooks, 656, 660; in Coleridge, 222; in Derrida, 531–32, 534, 541; in Foucault, 521; in Greenblatt, 856; in Lévi-Strauss, 511, 537; in Propp, 437; in Ransom, 419

Structures of feeling (Williams), 765–68

Strunk, Janet, 115

Style: feminine, 958; in Aristotle, 67–69, 72; in Booth, 575; in Dante, 104; in Horace, 83, 87; in Longinus, 87, 91–92, 95; in Pope, 152; in Johnson, 165; in Wordsworth, 204, 207, 209, 215; literary, 7

Style systems: in Horkheimer and Adorno, 738–39

Stylistics, 475, 563–64, 597–98

Subaltern Studies, 18–20, 22, 1042, 1045, 1051–52, 1063, 1086

Subject: 794; in Althusser, 745, 746; in Foucault, 521, 526, 529, 787; in James, 297, 305; in Jung, 338; in Kant, 166, 170–71, 173, 177; in Lacan, 635, 647, 652, 654; in Lévi-Strauss, 538; in Nietzsche, 281, 288, 290

Subjectivity: in Kant, 175

Sublimation: in Lacan, 683

Sublime: in Arnold, 264; in Cleanth Brooks, 450; in Dante, 104; in Eliot, 325; in Kant, 168, 182–83, 185–89; in Longinus, 88– 90, 92–98

Sublime object: in Žižek, 640

Subordination, 701, 756–58, 771

Suffering: in Aristotle, 59–60

Sundquist, Eric, 900

Sunset Boulevard (Billy Wilder), 673

Superego, 631; in Freud, 312, 629, 644, 651

Superreader (Barthes), 568

Superstructure (*Überbau*), 700–01; in Marx, 713, 752–56, 758; in Said, 1071–72, in Williams, 751

Supplement: in Derrida, 481, 539; in Lévi-Strauss, 539

Surplus value: in Marx, 960, 1003

Surrealism, 645

Surrey, Henry Howard, Earl of, 136

Surveillance: in Foucault, 975

Swift, Jonathan, 163, 772

Symbol, 407, 412, 470–71, 474, 483, 511; in Blackmur, 420; in Cleanth Brooks, 450, 456; in Greenblatt, 857; in Jung, 333; in Lacan, 633; in Robert Penn Warren, 420; in Wimsatt and Beardsley, 468

Symbolic (Lacanian field), 633–34, 636–37, 652, 668–69, 671, 674–75; in Butler, 1037; in Cixous, 989, 992, 994, 997; in Mulvey, 668–69, 673, 675; in Spivak, 1092; in Žižek, 687

Symbolic action: in Burke, 386, 392, 773; in Jameson, 770, 773, 777, 783

Symbolism (literary), 427; Freudian, 407; in Cleanth Brooks, 455; in Nietzsche, 280; in Sontag, 408

Symbolization (defense mechanism): in Freud, 628; in Lacan, 634

Synchronic and diachronic: in Jauss, 556; in Levi-Strauss, 506, 511

Synecdoche, 476, 813; in White, 791

81–82; in Longinus, 90; in Nietzsche, 280–82, 285, 288, 290–91, 294–95; in Plato, 32, 35; in Johnson, 160; in Shelley, 236–37, 243; in Sidney, 115, 120, 127–28, 136–37; in White, 791

Tragicomedy: in Booth, 580; in Sidney, 137

Traherne, Thomas, 320

Transaction: in Holland, 550

Transference: in Lacan, 650

Transformation: in Propp, 438, 443–48

Transformational grammar (Chomsky), 598

Transgender, 962, 966; in Rubin, 1013

Trevelyan, George Macaulay, 375

Trilling, Lionel, 2, 386, 402, 696, 880, 893–95, 901

Trollope, Anthony, 299–300

Tropes, 791; in Peter Brooks, 660. *See also* Figures of speech, Metaphor, Metonymy, etc.

Trotsky, Leon: *Literature and Revolution*, 695–96

Truffaut, François, 408; *Day for Night*, 687

Truth: in Aristotle, 49; in Arnold, 275; in Coleridge, 226; in James, 300, 309; in Plato, 49; in Shelley, 229, 233; in Sidney, 131–32

Turgenev, Ivan Sergeievich, 305, 430

Turner, Frederick Jackson, 880

Turner, Mark, 558, 615

Twain, Mark (Samuel Clemens): *Huckleberry Finn*, 880, 1054

Tynyanov, Yuri, 351, 414, 416

Types and tokens: in Derrida, 479

Typology: Biblical, 598

Tyutchev, Fyodor, 427

Überbau. See Superstructure

Uncanny: in Freud, 311–12; in Žižek, 660–61, 678, 681, 686

Unconscious, 627, 1032; collective, 6; in Freud, 310–11, 316, 318, 628–29, 632, 651; in Jung, 327, 329, 333–34, 337–38; in Lacan, 627, 633–34. *See also* Political unconscious

Understanding: aesthetic, 567; as horizon: in Jauss, 565; historical: in Coleridge, 227; in Jauss, 564, 567; in Kant, 170, 181–82, 186, 191–92

Unities of drama: in Pope, 152; in Johnson, 160

Unity, 464; in Aristotle, 56, 69, 73; in Bakhtin, 353; in Cleanth Brooks, 458; in Coleridge, 227; in Foucault, 525; in Horace, 79; in Kant, 188; in Neo-Aristotelianism, 422

Unity of action: in Behn, 145; in Sidney, 115

Unity of place: in Behn, 145; in Sidney, 115, 136

Unity of time: in Aristotle, 54; in Behn, 145; in Johnson, 160; in Sidney, 115, 136–37

Universality: in Aristotle, 57; in Kant, 167, 174–76, 182; in Johnson, 160; in Sidney, 124

Unpacking, 14

Unpleasure (Mulvey), 670, 673, 675

Unreliable narrator (Booth), 545, 593–94

Updike, John, 14; *Rabbit, Run*, 896

Utility: in Horace, 77; in Kant, 167

Valéry, Paul, 517, 712–13, 727

Value of poetry: in Plato, 35; in Sidney, 129

Values: in Booth, 545, 580–82

Vasconcelos, José, 1100

Velazquez, Diego, 167; *Las Meninas*, 788

Verisimilitude: in Iser, 594. *See also* Realism, Truth

Verne, Jules, 702

Verse, 121; in Sidney, 130; in Wordsworth, 207. *See also* Poetry

Vertigo (Alfred Hitchcock), 674–75

Veselovsky, Alexander, 413, 428

Vico, Giambattista, 229, 778, 813, 1066, 1079, 1141; *La Scienza nuova*, 1133

Vida, Marco Girolamo, 157

Villon, François, 264, 1084

Virgil (Publius Vergilius Maro), 74, 77, 119–20, 131, 136, 140, 148–50, 158, 226, 230, 238, 241, 245–46, 294, 374, 678, 796, 864, 870, 921, 1029; *Aeneid*, 118, 123–24, 126, 135, 153, 263; *Eclogues*, 127, 278

Virtual dimension: in Iser, 587–88

Virtue: in Kant, 173

Viscosity: in Foucault, 789

Viswanathan, Gauri, 1050

Volney, Constantin François, Comte de: *Ruins of Empire*, 1097

Voloshinov, Valentin Nikolaievich, 351, 775, 1087

Voltaire, 243, 269, 276, 1137

Vouloir-savoir (will to knowledge): in Foucault, 787. *See also* Power/knowledge

Voyeurism: in Mulvey, 670, 673–76

Vulgar Marxism, 695–96

Wagner, Richard, 281, 295, 1068; *Die Meistersinger*, 283; *Parsifal*, 281; *Tristan und Isolde*, 281, 679, 736

Walker, Alice, 883, 948–49, 1109–11, 1113, 1115, 1143; *The Color Purple*, 1143; *In Search of Our Mothers' Gardens*, 946

Excitable Speech

Excitable Speech

A Politics of
the Performative

Judith Butler

Routledge
New York & London

Published in 1997 by
Routledge
29 West 35th Street
New York, NY 10001

Published in Great Britain by
Routledge
11 New Fetter Lane
London EC4P 4EE

Library of Congress Cataloging-in-Publication Data

Butler, Judith P.
Excitable speech: a politics of the performative / Judith Butler
p.   cm.
Includes bibliographical references and index.
ISBN 0-415-91587-2 (hc.) — ISBN 0-415-91588-0 (pbk.)
1. Oral communication—Social aspects. 2. Hate speech. 3. Speech acts (Linguistics).
4. Language and languages—Political aspects. I. Title.
P95.54.B88 1996
302.2'242—dc21   96-33054
                                                                            CIP

for Maureen

/Contents/

/Acknowledgments/

This project could not have been completed
without the generous support of the University
of California Humanities Research Institute
located on the Irvine campus, and a Faculty
Research Grant from the Humanities Division at the
University of California at Berkeley. I also thank Wendy
Brown, Robert Gooding-Williams, Joan W. Scott, Diana
Fuss, Hayden White, Morris Kaplan, Homi Bhabha, Janet
Halley, Robert Post, and Drucilla Cornell for responding
with useful comments to parts of the manuscript in process.
I alone remain responsible for not heeding all their important
suggestions. I also thank Dave Wittenberg, Valerie Ross, Jane

Malmo, and Gayle Salamon for their research assistance. As always, I thank Maureen MacGrogan for her versatile and generous editorial guidance.

Most of all, I thank my students at UC–Berkeley and at the Dartmouth School for Criticism and Theory during the summer of 1995 for indulging my thinking and showing me directions to take I otherwise would not have seen.

Chapter One appeared in *Critical Inquiry* 23:2 (Winter: 1997), and Chapter Two appeared first in *Deconstruction is/in America: A New Sense of the Political*, ed. Anselm Haverkamp (New York: New York University Press, 1995) and was reprinted in *Performativity and Performance*, eds. Eve Kosofsky Sedgwick and Andrew Parker (New York: Routledge, 1995).

"Infelicity is an ill to which *all* acts are heir which have the general character of ritual or ceremonial, all *conventional* acts."

"There are more ways of outraging speech than contradiction merely."

J.L. AUSTIN

Introduction / ON LINGUISTIC VULNERABILITY

When we claim to have been injured by language, what kind of claim do we make? We ascribe an agency to language, a power to injure, and position ourselves as the objects of its injurious trajectory. We claim that language acts, and acts against us, and the claim we make is a further instance of language, one which seeks to arrest the force of the prior instance. Thus, we exercise the force of language even as we seek to counter its force, caught up in a bind that no act of censorship can undo.

Could language injure us if we were not, in some sense, linguistic beings, beings who require language in

order to be? Is our vulnerability to language a consequence of our being constituted within its terms? If we are formed in language, then that formative power precedes and conditions any decision we might make about it, insulting us from the start, as it were, by its prior power.

//

The insult, however, assumes its specific proportion in time. To be called a name is one of the first forms of linguistic injury that one learns. But not all name-calling is injurious. Being called a name is also one of the conditions by which a subject is constituted in language; indeed, it is one of the examples Althusser supplies for an understanding of "interpellation."[1] Does the power of language to injure follow from its interpellative power? And how, if at all, does linguistic agency emerge from this scene of enabling vulnerability?

The problem of injurious speech raises the question of which words wound, which representations offend, suggesting that we focus on those parts of language that are uttered, utterable, and explicit. And yet, linguistic injury appears to be the effect not only of the words by which one is addressed but the mode of address itself, a mode—a disposition or conventional bearing—that interpellates and constitutes a subject.

One is not simply fixed by the name that one is called. In being called an injurious name, one is derogated and demeaned. But the name holds out another possibility as well: by being called a name, one is also, paradoxically, given a certain possibility for social existence, initiated into a temporal life of language that exceeds the prior purposes that animate that call. Thus the injurious address may appear to fix or paralyze the one it hails, but it may also produce an unexpected and enabling response. If to be addressed is to be interpellated, then the offensive call runs the risk of inaugurating a subject in speech who comes to use language to counter the offensive call. When the address is injurious, it works its force upon the one it injures. What is this force, and how might we come to understand its faultlines?

J. L. Austin proposed that to know what makes the force of an utterance effective, what establishes its performative character, one

must first locate the utterance within a "total speech situation."[2] There is, however, no easy way to decide on how best to delimit that totality. An examination of Austin's own view furnishes at least one reason for such difficulty. Austin distinguishes "illocutionary" from "perlocution-ary" speech acts: the former are speech acts that, in saying do what they say, and do it in the moment of that saying; the latter are speech acts that produce certain effects as their consequence; by saying some-thing, a certain effect follows. The illocutionary speech act is itself the deed that it effects; the perlocutionary merely leads to certain effects that are not the same as the speech act itself.

Any delimitation of the total speech act in such illocutionary cases would doubtless include an understanding of how certain conventions are invoked at the moment of utterance, whether the person who invokes them is authorized, whether the circumstances of the invoca-tion are right. But how does one go about delimiting the kind of "con-vention" that illocutionary utterances presume? Such utterances do what they say on the occasion of the saying; they are not only conven-tional, but in Austin's words, "ritual or ceremonial." As utterances, they work to the extent that they are given in the form of a ritual, that is, repeated in time, and, hence, maintain a sphere of operation that is not restricted to the moment of the utterance itself.[3] The illocutionary speech act performs its deed *at the moment* of the utterance, and yet to the extent that the moment is ritualized, it is never merely a single moment. The "moment" in ritual is a condensed historicity: it exceeds itself in past and future directions, an effect of prior and future invoca-tions that constitute and escape the instance of utterance.

Austin's claim, then, that to know the force of the illocution is only possible once the "total situation" of the speech act can be identified is beset by a constitutive difficulty. If the temporality of linguistic con-vention, considered as ritual, exceeds the instance of its utterance, and that excess is not fully capturable or identifiable (the past and future of the utterance cannot be narrated with any certainty), then it seems that part of what constitutes the "total speech situation" is a failure to achieve a totalized form in any of its given instances.

In this sense, it is not enough to find the appropriate context for the speech act in question, in order to know how best to judge its

effects. The speech situation is thus not a simple sort of context, one that might be defined easily by spatial and temporal boundaries. To be injured by speech is to suffer a loss of context, that is, not to know where you are. Indeed, it may be that what is *unanticipated* about the injurious speech act is what constitutes its injury, the sense of putting its addressee out of control. The capacity to circumscribe the situation of the speech act is jeopardized at the moment of injurious address. To be addressed injuriously is not only to be open to an unknown future, but not to know the time and place of injury, and to suffer the disorientation of one's situation as the effect of such speech. Exposed at the moment of such a shattering is precisely the volatility of one's "place" within the community of speakers; one can be "put in one's place" by such speech, but such a place may be no place.

"Linguistic survival" implies that a certain kind of surviving takes place in language. Indeed, the discourse on hate speech continually makes such references. To claim that language injures or, to cite the phrase used by Richard Delgado and Mari Matsuda, that "words wound" is to combine linguistic and physical vocabularies.[4] The use of a term such as "wound" suggests that language can act in ways that parallel the infliction of physical pain and injury. Charles R. Lawrence III refers to racist speech as a "verbal assault," underscoring that the effect of racial invective is "like receiving a slap in the face. The injury is instantaneous".(68) Some forms of racial invective also "produce physical symptoms that temporarily disable the victim. . . ."(68) These formulations suggest that linguistic injury acts like physical injury, but the use of the simile suggests that this is, after all, a comparison of unlike things. Consider, though, that the comparison might just as well imply that the two can be compared only metaphorically. Indeed, it appears that there is no language specific to the problem of linguistic injury, which is, as it were, forced to draw its vocabulary from physical injury. In this sense, it appears that the metaphorical connection between physical and linguistic vulnerability is essential to the description of linguistic vulnerability itself. On the one hand, that there appears to be no description that is "proper" to linguistic injury makes it more difficult to identify the specificity of linguistic vulnerability over and against physical vulnerability. On the other hand, that physical meta-

phors seize upon nearly every occasion to describe linguistic injury suggests that this somatic dimension may be important to the understanding of linguistic pain. Certain words or certain forms of address not only operate as threats to one's physical well-being, but there is a strong sense in which the body is alternately sustained and threatened through modes of address.

Language sustains the body not by bringing it into being or feeding it in a literal way; rather, it is by being interpellated within the terms of language that a certain social existence of the body first becomes possible. To understand this, one must imagine an impossible scene, that of a body that has not yet been given social definition, a body that is, strictly speaking, not accessible to us, that nevertheless becomes accessible on the occasion of an address, a call, an interpellation that does not "discover" this body, but constitutes it fundamentally. We may think that to be addressed one must first be recognized, but here the Althusserian reversal of Hegel seems appropriate: the address constitutes a being within the possible circuit of recognition and, accordingly, outside of it, in abjection.

/ 5

We may think that the situation is more ordinary: certain already constituted bodily subjects happen to be called this or that. But why do the names that the subject is called appear to instill the fear of death and the question of whether or not one will survive? Why should a merely linguistic address produce such a response of fear? Is it not, in part, because the contemporary address recalls and reenacts the formative ones that gave and give existence? Thus, to be addressed is not merely to be recognized for what one already is, but to have the very term conferred by which the recognition of existence becomes possible. One comes to "exist" by virtue of this fundamental dependency on the address of the Other. One "exists" not only by virtue of being recognized, but, in a prior sense, by being *recognizable*.[5] The terms that facilitate recognition are themselves conventional, the effects and instruments of a social ritual that decide, often through exclusion and violence, the linguistic conditions of survivable subjects.

If language can sustain the body, it can also threaten its existence. Thus, the question of the specific ways that language threatens violence seems bound up with the primary dependency that any speaking

being has by virtue of the interpellative or constitutive address of the Other. In *The Body in Pain*, Elaine Scarry makes the point that the threat of violence is a threat *to* language, its world-making and sense-making possibility.[6] Her formulation tends to set violence and language in opposition, as the inverse of each other. What if language has within it its own possibilities for violence and for world-shattering? For Scarry, the body is not only anterior to language, but she argues persuasively that the body's pain is inexpressible in language, that pain shatters language, and that language can counter pain even as it cannot capture it. She shows that the morally imperative endeavor to represent the body in pain is confounded (but not rendered impossible) by the unrepresentability of the pain that it seeks to represent. One of the injurious consequences of torture, in her view, is that the one tortured loses the ability to document in language the event of torture; thus, one of the effects of torture is to efface its own witness. Scarry also shows how certain discursive forms, such as interrogation, aid and abet the process of torture. Here, however, language assists violence, but appears not to wield *its own* violence. This raises the following question: if certain kinds of violence disable language, how do we account for the specific kind of injury that language itself performs?

Toni Morrison refers specifically to "the violence of representation" in the 1993 Nobel Lecture in Literature. "Oppressive language," she writes, "does more than represent violence; it is violence." (16) Morrison offers a parable in which language itself is figured as a "living thing," where this figure is not false or unreal, but indicates something true about language. In the parable, young children play a cruel joke and ask a blind woman to guess whether the bird that is in their hands is living or dead. The blind woman responds by refusing and displacing the question: "I don't know . . . but what I do know is that it is in your hands. It is in your hands." (11)

Morrison then elects to read the woman in the parable as a practiced writer, and the bird, as language, and she conjectures on how this practiced woman writer thinks of language: "she thinks of language partly as a system, partly as a living thing over which one has control, but mostly as agency—as an act with consequences. So the question

that the children put to her, 'Is it living or dead?,' is not unreal, because she thinks of language as susceptible to death, erasure. . . ." (13)

Here Morrison writes in a conjectural way what the practiced woman writer conjectures, a speculation both in and about language and its conjectural possibilities. Remaining within a figural frame, Morrison announces the "reality" of that frame from within its own terms. The woman thinks of language as living: Morrison gives us the performance of this act of substitution, this simile by which language is figured as life. The "life" of language is thus exemplified by this very enactment of simile. But what sort of enactment is this?

Language is thought of "mostly as agency—an act with conse-quences," an extended doing, a performance with effects. This is some-thing short of a definition. Language is, after all, "thought of," that is, posited or constituted as "agency." Yet it is *as* agency that it is thought; a *figural* substitution makes the thinking of the agency of language possible. Because this very formulation is offered *in* language, the "agency" of language is not only the theme of the formulation, but its very action. This positing as well as this figuring appear to exemplify the agency at issue. / 7

We might be tempted to think that attributing agency to language is not quite right, that only subjects do things with language, and that agency has its origins in the subject. But is the agency of language the same as the agency of the subject? Is there a way to distinguish between the two? Morrison not only offers agency as a figure for lan-guage, but language as a figure for agency, one whose "reality" is incontestible. She writes: "We die. That may be the meaning of life. But we *do* language. That may be the measure of our lives." (22) She does not state: "language is agency," for that kind of assertion would deprive language of the agency she means to convey. In refusing to answer the children's cruel question, the blind woman, according to Morrison, "shifts attention away from the assertions of power to the instrument through which that power is exercised." (12) Similarly, Morrison refuses to offer dogmatic assertions on what language is, for that would obscure how the "instrument" of that assertion participates in that very being of language; the irreducibility of any assertion to its

instrument is precisely what establishes language as self-divided. The failure of language to rid itself of its own instrumentality or, indeed, rhetoricity, is precisely the inability of language to annul itself in the telling of a tale, in the reference to what exists or in the volatile scenes of interlocution.

Significantly, for Morrison, "agency" is not the same as "control"; neither is it a function of the systematicity of language. It seems that we cannot first give an account of human agency and then specify the kind of agency that humans have in language. "We *do* language. That may be the measure of our lives."

We do things with language, produce effects with language, and we do things to language, but language is also the thing that we do. Language is a name for our doing: both "what" we do (the name for the action that we characteristically perform) and that which we effect, the act and its consequences.

In the parable that Morrison offers, the blind woman is analogized to a practiced writer, suggesting that writing is to some extent blind, that it cannot know the hands into which it will fall, how it will be read and used, or the ultimate sources from which it is derived. The scene in the parable is an interlocution, where the children exploit the blindness of the woman in order to force her to make a choice she cannot make, and where the force of that address is what the woman reads, exercising an agency that the address had meant to deny her. She does not make the choice, but calls attention to "the instrument through which power is exercised," establishing that the choice is in the hands of the interlocutors she cannot see. She cannot know, according to Morrison's interpretation, whether language will live or die in the hands of those who use speech with the force of cruelty. In both the parable and in the reading that Morrison provides, the question of responsibility is central, figured as "the hands" of the children or, indeed, those who inherit the responsibility for whether language will live or die. The writer is blind to the future of the language in which she writes. Thus language is thought of "mostly as agency," distinguished from forms of mastery or control, on the one hand, and by the closure of system on the other.

Morrison's analogy suggests that language lives or dies as a living

thing might live or die, and that the question of survival is central to the question of how language is used. She claims that "oppressive language . . . *is* violence," not merely a representation of it. Oppressive language is not a substitute for the experience of violence. It enacts its own kind of violence. Language remains alive when it refuses to "encapsulate" (20) or "capture" (21) the events and lives it describes. But when it seeks to effect that capture, language not only loses its vitality, but acquires its own violent force, one that Morrison throughout the lecture associates with statist language and censorship. She writes, "the vitality of language lies in its ability to limn the actual, imagined and possible lives of its speakers, readers, writers. Although its poise is sometimes in displacing experience, it is not a substitute for it. It arcs toward the place where meaning may lie." (20) And later: "its force, its felicity, is in its reach toward the ineffable." (21) The violence of language consists in its effort to capture the ineffable and, hence, to destroy it, to seize hold of that which must remain elusive for language to operate as a living thing.

The children's question is cruel not because it is certain that they have killed the bird, but because the use of language to force the choice from the blind woman is itself a seizing hold of language, one whose force is drawn from the conjured destruction of the bird. The hate speech that the children perform seeks to capture the blind woman in the moment of humiliation, but also to transfer the violence done to the bird to the woman herself, a transfer that belongs to the particular temporality of the threat. In a sense, the threat begins the performance of that which it threatens to perform; but in not quite fully performing it, seeks to establish, through language, the certitude of that future in which it will be performed.

Although the threat is not quite the act that it portends, it is still an act, a speech act, one that not only announces the act to come, but registers a certain force in language, a force that both presages and inaugurates a subsequent force. Whereas the threat tends to produce an expectation, the threat of violence destroys the very possibility of expectation: it initiates a temporality in which one expects the destruction of expectation and, hence, cannot expect it at all.

Whereas the threat prefigures the act, it would be a mistake to

/ 9

conclude that whereas the threat takes place merely in language, the threatened act takes place in a material instance fully beyond language, between and among bodies. Implicit in the notion of a threat is that what is spoken in language may prefigure what the body might do; the act referred to in the threat is the act that one might actually perform. But this view fails to take into account that *speaking is itself a bodily act.*

In Shoshana Felman's book, *The Literary Speech Act: Don Juan with J. L. Austin, or Seduction in Two Languages*[7], she reminds us that the relation between speech and the body is a scandalous one, "a relation consisting at once of incongruity and of inseparability . . . the scandal consists in the fact that the act cannot know what it is doing." (96) Felman thus suggests that the speech act, as the act of a speaking body, is always to some extent unknowing about what it performs, that it always says something that it does not intend, and that it is not the emblem of mastery or control that it sometimes purports to be. She calls attention to the way in which a speaking body signifies in ways that are not reducible to what such a body "says." In this sense, the speaker is "blind" in much the same way that, for Morrison, the practiced woman writer is "blind": the utterance performs meanings that are not precisely the ones that are stated or, indeed, capable of being stated at all. Whereas Morrison calls attention to the "instrument through which [assertions] are made," Felman identifies that instrument as the body from which speech is uttered. That body becomes a sign of unknowingness precisely because its actions are never fully consciously directed or volitional. For Felman, what remains unconscious in a bodily action such as speech might be construed as the "instrument" through which the assertion is made. Similarly, that unknowing body marks the limit of intentionality in the speech act. The speech act says more, or says differently, than it means to say.

For Felman, however, this does not mean that speech and the body are radically separable, only that the idea of a fully intentional speech act is perpetually subverted by that in speech which subverts intentionality. Felman writes, "If the problem of the human act consists in the relation between language and the body, it is because the act is conceived—by performative analysis as well as by psychoanalysis—as

that which problematizes at one and the same time the separation and opposition between the two. The act, an enigmatic and problematic production of the *speaking body*, destroys from its inception the metaphysical dichotomy between the domain of the 'mental' and the domain of the 'physical,' breaks down the opposition between body and spirit, between matter and language."[8]

For Felman, however, this breakdown of the opposition between matter and language does not entail a simple unity of these terms. They remain incongruously interrelated. In speaking, the act that the body is performing is never fully understood; the body is the blindspot of speech, that which acts in excess of what is said, but which also acts in and through what is said. That the speech act is a bodily act means that the act is redoubled in the moment of speech: there is what is said, and then there is a kind of saying that the bodily "instrument" of the utterance performs.

Thus a statement may be made that, on the basis of a grammatical analysis alone, appears to be no threat. But the threat emerges precisely through the act that the body performs in the speaking the act. Or the threat emerges as the apparent effect of a performative act only to be rendered harmless through the bodily demeanor of the act (any theory of acting knows this). The threat prefigures or, indeed, promises a bodily act, and yet is already a bodily act, thus establishing in its very gesture the contours of the act to come. The act of threat and the threatened act are, of course, distinct, but they are related as a chiasmus. Although not identical, they are both bodily acts: the first act, the threat, only makes sense in terms of the act that it prefigures. The threat begins a temporal horizon within which the organizing aim is the act that is threatened; the threat begins the action by which the fulfillment of the threatened act might be achieved. And yet, a threat can be derailed, defused, can fail to furnish the act that it threatens. The threat states the impending certitude of another, forthcoming act, but the statement itself cannot produce that forthcoming act as one of its necessary effects. This failure to deliver on the threat does not call into question the status of the speech act as a threat—it merely questions its efficacy. The self-conceit that empowers the threat, however,

is that the speech act that is the threat will fully materialize that act threatened by the speech. Such speech is, however, vulnerable to failure, and it is that vulnerability that must be exploited to counter the threat.

For the threat to work, it requires certain kinds of circumstances, and it requires a venue of power by which its performative effects might be materialized. The teleology of action conjured by the threat is disruptible by various kinds of infelicities. Nevertheless, the fantasy of sovereign action that structures the threat is that a certain kind of saying is at once the performance of the act referred to in that saying; this would be an illocutionary performative, in Austin's view, one that immediately does what it says. The threat may well solicit a response, however, that it never anticipated, losing its own sovereign sense of expectation in the face of a resistance it advertently helped to produce. Instead of obliterating the possibility of response, paralyzing the addressee with fear, the threat may well be countered by a different kind of performative act, one that exploits the redoubled action of the threat (what is intentionally and non-intentionally performed in any speaking), to turn one part of that speaking against the other, confounding the performative power of the threat.

Because the threat is a speech act that is at once a bodily act, it is already, in part, out of its own control. Morrison makes this point: the blind woman returns the implicit threat delivered by the children by referring to "the hands" of the one who holds the bird, to expose the body of the one who speaks, to counter the act with an act that exposes what is most unknown to the ones who deliver the threat, illuminating the blindness that motivates their speech act, the question of what they will do, in a bodily sense, given what they have already done, bodily, in speaking as they have.

The notion that speech wounds appears to rely on this inseparable and incongruous relation between body and speech, but also, consequently, between speech and its effects. If the speaker addresses his or her body to the one addressed, then it is not merely the body of the speaker that comes into play: it is the body of the addressee as well. Is the one speaking merely speaking, or is the one speaking comporting her or his body toward the other, exposing the body of the other as

12/

vulnerable to address. As an "instrument" of a violent rhetoricity, the body of the speaker exceeds the words that are spoken, exposing the addressed body as no longer (and not ever fully) in its own control.

UNEXPECTED CALLS

To decide the matter of what is a threat or, indeed, what is a word that wounds, no simple inspection of words will suffice. We may think that an elaboration of the institutional conditions of utterance is necessary to identify the probability that certain kinds of words will wound under such circumstances. But the circumstances alone do not make the words wound. Or we may be compelled to claim that any word can be a word that wounds, that it depends on its deployment, and that the deployment of words is not reducible to the circumstances of their utterance. This last makes sense, but such a view cannot tell us why certain words wound in the way that they do, or why it is more difficult to separate certain words from their power to wound.

Indeed, recent efforts to establish the incontrovertibly wounding power of certain words seem to founder on the question of who does the interpreting of what such words mean and what they perform. The recent regulations governing lesbian and gay self-definition in the military or, indeed, the recent controversies over rap music suggest that no clear consensus is possible on the question of whether there is a clear link between the words that are uttered and their putative power to injure.[9] To argue, on the one hand, that the offensive effect of such words is fully contextual, and that a shift of context can exacerbate or minimize that offensiveness, is still not to give an account of the power that such words are said to exercise. To claim, on the other hand, that some utterances are always offensive, regardless of context, that they carry their contexts with them in ways that are too difficult to shed, is still not to offer a way to understand how context is invoked and restaged at the moment of utterance.

Neither view can account for the restaging and resignifying of offensive utterance, deployments of linguistic power that seek at once to expose and counter the offensive exercise of speech. I will consider these at greater length in the chapters to come, but consider for a

/ 13

moment how often such terms are subject to resignification. Such a redoubling of injurious speech takes place not only in rap music and in various forms of political parody and satire, but in the political and social critique of such speech, where "mentioning"[10] those very terms is crucial to the arguments at hand, and even in the legal arguments that make the call for censorship, in which the rhetoric that is deplored is invariably proliferated within the context of legal speech. Paradoxically, the explicit legal and political arguments that seek to tie such speech to certain contexts fail to note that even in their own discourse, such speech has become citational, breaking with the prior contexts of its utterance and acquiring new contexts for which it was not intended. The critical and legal discourse on hate speech is itself a restaging of the performance of hate speech. The present discourse breaks with the prior ones, but not in any absolute sense. On the contrary, the present context and its apparent "break" with the past are themselves legible only in terms of the past from which it breaks. The present context does, however, elaborate a new context for such speech, a future context, not yet delineable and, hence, not yet precisely a context.

14/

The arguments in favor of a counter-appropriation or restaging of offensive speech are clearly undercut by the position that the offensive effect of the speech act is *necessarily* linked to the speech act, its originating or enduring context or, indeed, its animating intentions or original deployments. The revaluation of terms such as "queer" suggest that speech can be "returned" to its speaker in a different form, that it can be cited against its originary purposes, and perform a reversal of effects. More generally, then, this suggests that the changeable power of such terms marks a kind of discursive performativity that is not a discrete series of speech acts, but a ritual chain of resignifications whose origin and end remain unfixed and unfixable. In this sense, an "act" is not a momentary happening, but a certain nexus of temporal horizons, the condensation of an iterability that exceeds the moment it occasions. The possibility for a speech act to resignify a prior context depends, in part, upon the gap between the originating context or intention by which an utterance is animated and the effects it produces. For the threat, for instance, to have a future it never intended, for it to be returned to its speaker in a different form, and defused through that

return, the meanings the speech act acquires and the effects it performs must exceed those by which it was intended, and the contexts it assumes must not be quite the same as the ones in which it originates (if such an origin is to be found).

Those who seek to fix with certainty the link between certain speech acts and their injurious effects will surely lament the open temporality of the speech act. That no speech act *has* to perform injury as its effect means that no simple elaboration of speech acts will provide a standard by which the injuries of speech might be effectively adjudicated. Such a loosening of the link between act and injury, however, opens up the possibility for a counter-speech, a kind of talking back, that would be foreclosed by the tightening of that link. Thus, the gap that separates the speech act from its future effects has its auspicious implications: it begins a theory of linguistic agency that provides an alternative to the relentless search for legal remedy. The interval between instances of utterance not only makes the repetition and resignification of the utterance possible, but shows how words might, through time, become disjoined from their power to injure and recontextualized in more affirmative modes. I hope to make clear that by affirmative, I mean "opening up the possibility of agency," where agency is not the restoration of a sovereign autonomy in speech, a replication of conventional notions of mastery.

/ 15

The main concerns of *Excitable Speech* are both rhetorical and political. In the law, "excitable" utterances are those made under duress, usually confessions that cannot be used in court because they do not reflect the balanced mental state of the utterer. My presumption is that speech is always in some ways out of our control. In a formulation that anticipates Felman's reading of the speech act, Austin writes that "actions in general (not all) are liable, for example, to be done under duress, or by accident, or owing to this or that variety of mistake, say, or otherwise unintentionally." (21) Austin then takes the occasion to delink the speech act from the subject in some instances: "in many such cases we are certainly unwilling to say of some such act simply that it was done or that he did it." (21) Untethering the speech act from the sovereign subject founds an alternative notion of agency and, ultimately, of responsibility, one that more fully acknowledges the way in

which the subject is constituted in language, how what it creates is also what it derives from elsewhere. Whereas some critics mistake the critique of sovereignty for the demolition of agency, I propose that agency begins where sovereignty wanes. The one who acts (who is not the same as the sovereign subject) acts precisely to the extent that he or she is constituted as an actor and, hence, operating within a linguistic field of enabling constraints from the outset.

The sovereign conceit emerges in hate speech discourse in several ways. The one who speaks hate speech is imagined to wield sovereign power, to do what he or she says when it is said. Similarly, the "speech" of the state often takes a sovereign form, whereby the speaking of declarations are, often literally, "acts" of law. The effort to locate such illocutionary instances of speech, however, posed difficulties for Austin, and led him to devise a series of provisos and new distinctions to take account of the complexity of the performative terrain. Not all utterances that have the form of the performative, whether illocutionary or perlocutionary, actually work. This insight has important consequences for the consideration of the putative efficacy of hate speech.

16 /

Rhetorically, the assertion that some speech not only communicates hate, but constitutes an injurious act, presumes not only that language acts, but that it acts *upon* its addressee in an injurious way. These are, however, two importantly different claims, and not all speech acts are the kinds of acts that act upon another with such force. For instance, I may well utter a speech act, indeed, one that is illocutionary in Austin's sense, when I say, "I condemn you," but if I am not in a position to have my words considered as binding, then I may well have uttered a speech act, but the act is, in Austin's sense, unhappy or infelicitous: you escape unscathed. Thus, many such speech acts are "conduct" in a narrow sense, but not all of them have the power to produce the effects or initiate a set of consequences; indeed, many of them are quite comic in this regard, and one might read Austin's tract, *How to Do Things with Words*, as an amusing catalogue of such failed performatives.

A speech act can be an act without necessarily being an efficacious act. If I utter a failed performative, that is, I make a command and no

one hears or obeys, I make a vow, and there is no one to whom or before whom the vow might be made, I still perform an act, but I perform an act with no or little effect (or, at least, not with the effect that is figured by the act). A felicitous performative is one in which I not only perform the act, but some set of effects follows from the fact that I perform it. To act linguistically is not necessarily to produce effects, and in this sense, a speech act is not always an efficacious action. To say that there is an equivocation, then, between speech and action is not necessarily to say that speech acts efficaciously.

Austin offers a tentative typology of the kinds of locutions that are performative. The illocutionary act is one in which in saying something, one is at the same time doing something; the judge who says, "I sentence you" does not state an intention to do something or describe what he is doing: his saying is itself a kind of doing. Illocutionary speech acts produce effects. They are supported, Austin tells us, by linguistic and social conventions. Perlocutionary acts, on the other hand, are those utterances that initiate a set of consequences: in a perlocutionary speech act, "saying something will produce certain consequences," but the saying and the consequences produced are temporally distinct; those consequences are not the same as the act of speech, but are, rather, "what we bring about or achieve by saying something."(109) Whereas illocutionary acts proceed by way of conventions (107), perlocutionary acts proceed by way of consequences. Implicit in this distinction is the notion that illocutionary speech acts produce effects without any lapse of time, that the saying is itself the doing, and that they are one another simultaneously.

/ 17

Austin remarks as well that some consequences of a perlocution may be unintentional, and the example he offers is the unintentional insult, thus locating verbal injury within the orbit of the perlocution. Thus, Austin suggests that injury does not inhere in the conventions that a given speech act invokes, but in the specific consequences that a speech act produces.

Austin's work has been cited recently by legal scholars and philosophers (Catharine MacKinnon, Rae Langton, among others[11]) in order to argue that pornographic representations are performative, that is,

they do not state a point of view or report on a reality, but constitute a certain kind of conduct. These scholars further claim that the conduct "silences" those who are depicted in a subordinate fashion within pornographic representations.

These arguments will be considered at length in subsequent chapters, but for introductory purposes, it is important to note that pornography is construed as a kind of hate speech, and that its performative force is described as illocutionary. Significantly, MacKinnon's argument against pornography has moved from a conceptual reliance on a perlocutionary model to an illocutionary one.[12] In the work of Mari Matsuda, hate speech is understood not only to *act upon* its listener (a perlocutionary scene), but to contribute to the social constitution of the one addressed (and, hence, to become part of a process of social interpellation).[13] The listener is understood to occupy a social position or to have become synonymous with that position, and social positions themselves are understood to be situated in a static and hierarchical relation to one another. By virtue of the social position he or she occupies, then, the listener is injured as a consequence of that utterance. The utterance also enjoins the subject to reoccupy a subordinate social position. According to this view, such speech reinvokes and reinscribes a structural relation of domination, and constitutes the linguistic occasion for the reconstitution of that structural domination. Although sometimes this view on hate speech enumerates a set of consequences that such speech produces (a perlocutionary view of the matter), there are other formulations of this position where the force of the performative is secured through conventional means (an illocutionary model). In Mari Matsuda's formulation, for instance, speech does not merely *reflect* a relation of social domination; speech *enacts* domination, becoming the vehicle through which that social structure is reinstated. According to this illocutionary model, hate speech *constitutes* its addressee at the moment of its utterance; it does not describe an injury or produce one as a consequence; it is, in the very speaking of such speech, the performance of the injury itself, where the injury is understood as social subordination.[14]

What hate speech does, then, is to constitute the subject in a subordinate position. But what gives hate speech the power to constitute the

subject with such efficacy? Is hate speech as felicitous as it appears in this account, or are there faultlines that make its constituting power less felicitous than the above description would imply?

I wish to question for the moment the presumption that hate speech always works, not to minimize the pain that is suffered as a consequence of hate speech, but to leave open the possibility that its failure is the condition of a critical response. If the account of the injury of hate speech forecloses the possibility of a critical response to that injury, the account confirms the totalizing effects of such an injury. Such arguments are often useful in legal contexts, but are counter-productive for the thinking of nonstate-centered forms of agency and resistance.

Even if hate speech works to constitute a subject through discursive means, is that constitution necessarily final and effective? Is there a possibility of disrupting and subverting the effects produced by such speech, a faultline exposed that leads to the undoing of this process of discursive constitution? What kind of power is *attributed to* speech such that speech is figured as having the power to constitute the subject with such success? / 19

Matsuda's argument presumes that a social structure is enunciated at the moment of the hateful utterance; hate speech reinvokes the position of dominance, and reconsolidates it at the moment of utterance. As the linguistic rearticulation of social domination, hate speech becomes, for Matsuda, the site for the mechanical and predictable reproduction of power. In some ways, the question of mechanical breakdown or "misfire" and of the unpredictability of speech is precisely what Austin repeatedly emphasizes when he focuses on the various ways in which a speech act can go wrong. More generally, however, there are reasons to question whether a static notion of "social structure" is reduplicated in hate speech, or whether such structures suffer destructuration through being reiterated, repeated, and rearticulated. Might the speech act of hate speech be understood as less efficacious, more prone to innovation and subversion, if we were to take into account the temporal life of the "structure" it is said to enunciate? If such a structure is dependent upon its enunciation for its continuation, then it is at the site of enunciation that the question of its continuity is to be posed. Can

there be an enunciation that discontinues that structure, or one that subverts that structure through its repetition in speech? As an invocation, hate speech is an act that recalls prior acts, requiring a future repetition to endure. Is there a repetition that might disjoin the speech act from its supporting conventions such that its repetition confounds rather than consolidates its injurious efficacy?

SCENES OF UTTERANCE

It would be a mistake to think that working out the theoretical problems of the speech act will offer a set of clarifying solutions to the contemporary political operation of the speech act. The relation between theory and politics tends to work the other way. Theoretical positions are always appropriated and deployed in political contexts that expose something of the strategic value of such theories. A cursory review of the political instances in which the speech act makes an appearance show that there is significant disagreement on which speech acts, if any, should be viewed as conduct rather than "speech" in the legal sense. Broadly considered arguments in favor of the collapse of the speech/conduct distinction tend to strengthen the case for state regulation and to suspend reference to the first Amendment. Arguments that insist that speech acts are speech rather than conduct, on the other hand, tend to work in favor of suspending state intervention. In Chapter One, "Burning Acts," I note that a majority opinion on the Supreme Court in *R.A.V. v. St. Paul* struck down a local ordinance which would have construed the burning of a cross in the front of a black family's house as "fighting words" and questioned whether that kind of "speech" simply "communicates a message" and expresses "a viewpoint"—even as that "viewpoint" was also held to be "reprehensible." [15] The Court clearly discounted a more recent legal argument that the burning cross is *both* speech and conduct, that is, the communication of a message of inferiority as well as an act of discrimination (in the sense that a sign, "whites only," both expresses an idea and constitutes in itself discriminatory conduct.)

In MacKinnon's recent work, *Only Words*, pornography is construed as both speech and conduct, indeed, as "performative utter-

20 /

ance," and is understood not only to "act on" women in injurious ways (a perlocutionary claim), but to constitute, through representation, the class of women as an inferior class (an illocutionary claim). The burning cross is understood to be analogous to the pornographic utterance to the extent that both of them represent and enact an injury. But can the illocutionary claim be made about pornography as easily as it can about the burning cross? The theory of representation and, indeed, the theory of performativity at work differs in each of these cases. I will argue that, taken generically, the visual text of pornography cannot "threaten" or "demean" or "debase" in the same way that the burning cross can. To suggest that both examples instantiate the same kind of verbal conduct is not only a mistake in judgment, but the exploitation of the sign of racial violence for the purposes of enhancing, through a metonymical slippage, the putatively injurious power of pornography.

We have heard recently about speech that "incites" certain kinds of action. The Israeli press devoted much attention to the incendiary rhetoric of the rightwing in Israel and whether that rhetoric could be held responsible for the slaying of Yitzhak Rabin. How is it in such cases that we imagine utterance to have insinuated itself into action: how do we imagine that speech is heard, taken up as motivation, mechanically or contagiously inducing the listener to act? "Pro-life" activists have argued with limited legislative success that terms such as "abortion" that appear on the Internet are themselves "obscenity," and I recently saw an airplane movie in which the word "abortion" was "bleeped" in the course of its utterance. The utterance is understood not merely to offend a set of sensibilities, but to constitute an injury, as if the word performed the act, and the injured party were the defenseless "unborn." The ascription of such magical efficacy to words emerges in the context of the U.S. military in which the declaration that one is a homosexual is understood to communicate something of homosexuality and, hence, to be a homosexual act of some kind.

Significantly, this magical view of the performative does not operate in those political instances in which speech is, as it were, violently separated from conduct. The Court's willingness to treat the burning cross in *R.A.V. v. St. Paul* as potentially protected "speech" suggests that the nonperformative view of speech can be extended to defend

/ 21

certain kinds of racist conduct, a defense that manipulates the distinction between speech and conduct in order to achieve certain political aims. Similarly, MacKinnon's appeal to the state to construe pornography as performative speech and, hence, as the injurious conduct of representation, does not settle the theoretical question of the relation between representation and conduct, but collapses the distinction in order to enhance the power of state intervention over graphic sexual representation.

In many ways, this very extension of state power, however, comes to represent one of the greatest threats to the discursive operation of lesbian and gay politics. Central to such politics are a number of "speech acts" that can be, and have been, construed as offensive and, indeed, injurious conduct: *graphic self-representation*, as in Mapplethorpe's photography; *explicit self-declaration*, such as that which takes place in the practice of coming out; and *explicit sexual education*, as in AIDS education. In these three instances, it is important to note that to represent homosexuality is not exactly the same as performing it, even when the representation has a significantly performative dimension to it. When one declares that one is a homosexual, the declaration is the performative act—not the homosexuality, unless we want to claim that homosexuality *is* itself nothing but a kind of declaration, which would be an odd move to make. Similarly, it seems crucial and right to argue that to represent sexual practices in AIDS education is not to circulate AIDS nor to incite certain kinds of sexuality (unless we understand the incitation to safe sex as one of the aims of such an education). In a related way, when conservative critics suggest that gangsta rap is responsible for urban crime and the degradation of women, they construe representation not merely as performative, but as causative. In calling for public opposition to gangsta rap, William Bennett and C. Delores Tucker[16] did not seek state intervention against the corporations financing the music, but they did circulate the view that such music (and lyrics) have perlocutionary effects, and they represented representation itself as inducing criminal violence. The collapse of speech and conduct thus works to localize the "cause" of urban violence, and perhaps, as in the Israeli concern with incendiary rhetoric, to silence a discussion of the broader institutional conditions

22 /

that produce right-wing violence. In the United States, the turn against the lyrics of gangsta rap may also operate as a deflection from a more fundamental analysis on race, poverty and rage, and how those conditions are graphically registered in urban African-American popular musical genres.[17]

Unfortunately, it seems that some appropriations of the hate speech argument tend to minimize the effects of racial injury while expanding the possible field of sexual injury; and in the conservative attack on rap, feminist arguments against injurious representation appear to be tacitly appropriated. New standards of "decency" require that certain urban conditions of violence not be represented. At the same time, sexual injury to women is to be understood through racial tropes: the dignity of women is understood to be under attack not by the weakening of rights to reproductive freedom and the widespread loss of public assistance, but primarily by African-American men who sing.

There are views that subscribe to the efficacious model of the performative in both its illocutionary and perlocutionary forms that are feminist and anti-feminist, racist and anti-racist, homophobic and anti-homophobic. Thus there is no simple way to correlate views on the efficacy of the speech act with political views in general or, more specifically, with a view on the appropriate jurisdiction of the first Amendment. Nevertheless, it seems clear that legal precedents for the curtailment of "speech," broadly construed, are supported by the use of the illocutionary model of hate speech. The firmer the link is made between speech and conduct, however, and the more fully occluded the distinction between felicitous and infelicitous acts, the stronger the grounds for claiming that speech not only produces injury as one of its consequences, but constitutes an injury in itself, thus becoming an unequivocal form of conduct. The collapse of speech into conduct, and the concomitant occlusion of the gap between them, tends to support the case for state intervention, for if "speech" in any of the above cases can be fully subsumed under conduct, then the first Amendment is circumvented. To insist on the gap between speech and conduct, however, is to lend support for the role of nonjuridical forms of opposition, ways of restaging and resignifying speech in contexts that exceed those determined by the courts. Strategies devised on the part of progressive

legal and social movements thus run the risk of being turned against those very movements by virtue of extending state power, specifically legal power, over the issues in question. Whether by expanding the scope of obscenity or attempting the implementation of the fighting words doctrine (unsuccessful so far) or extending anti-discrimination law to include speech as discriminatory conduct, such strategies tend to enhance state regulation over the issues in question, potentially empowering the state to invoke such precedents against the very social movements that pushed for their acceptance as legal doctrine.

SPEECH ACTS AS INTERPELLATION

If hate speech acts in an illocutionary way, injuring in and through the moment of speech, and constituting the subject through that injury, then hate speech exercises an interpellative function.[18] At first, it appears that the Austinian notion of an illocutionary utterance is incompatible with an Althusserian notion of interpellation. For Austin, the subject who speaks precedes the speech in question. For Althusser, the speech act that brings the subject into linguistic existence precedes the subject in question. Indeed, the interpellation that precedes and forms the subject in Althusser appears to constitute the prior condition of those subject-centered speech acts that populate Austin's domain of analysis. Austin, however, makes clear that he does not think the workings of the performative always depend on the intention of the speaker. He refutes forms of psychologism that would require that "fictitious inward acts" (10) accompany the promise, one of the first speech acts he considers, in order to validate that act. Although a good intention may well make a promise felicitous, an intention not to perform the act does not deprive the speech act of its status as a promise; the promise is still performed (11). The force of the speech act is separable from its meaning, and illocutionary force is secured through convention.[19] Just as for Austin the convention governing the institution of promise-making is verbally honored even in the case of a promise that no one intends to fulfill, so for Althusser one is entered into the "ritual" of ideology regardless of whether there is a prior and authenticating belief in that ideology.

Austin's view that the illocutionary speech act is conditioned by its conventional, that is, "ritual" or "ceremonial" dimension, finds a counterpart in Althusser's insistence that ideology has a "ritual" form, and that ritual constitutes "the material existence of an ideological apparatus." (168) Ritual is material to the extent that it is productive, that is, it produces the belief that appears to be "behind" it. Thus Althusser scandalously invokes Pascal on religious belief at the moment he is called upon to explain the ritual dimension of ideology: "Pascal says more or less: 'Kneel down, move your lips in prayer, and you will believe.'" The hollow gesture becomes filled in time, and ideation is produced in the course of this ritualized repetition of convention. "Ideas," for Althusser, do not *precede* such actions, but have their "existence . . . inscribed in the actions of practices governed by rituals. . ." (170). In the famous scene of interpellation that Althusser provides, the policeman hails the passerby with "hey you there" and the one who recognizes himself and turns around (nearly everyone) to answer the call does not, strictly speaking, preexist the call. Althusser's scene is, therefore, fabulous, but what could it mean? The passerby turns precisely to acquire a certain identity, one purchased, as it were, with the price of guilt. The act of recognition becomes an act of constitution: the address animates the subject into existence.

/ 25

Neither the Austinian promise nor the Althusserian prayer require a preexisting mental state to "perform" in the way that they do. But where Austin assumes a subject who speaks, Althusser, in the scene in which the policeman hails the pedestrian, postulates a voice that brings that subject into being. The Austinian subject speaks *conventionally*, that is, it speaks in a voice that is never fully singular. That subject invokes a formula (which is not quite the same as following a rule), and this may be done with no or little reflection on the conventional character of what is being said. The ritual dimension of convention implies that the moment of utterance is informed by the prior and, indeed, future moments that are occluded by the moment itself. Who speaks when convention speaks? In what time does convention speak? In some sense, it is an inherited set of voices, an echo of others who speak as the "I." [20]

To bridge the Austinian and Althusserian views, one would need

to offer an account of how the subject constituted through the address of the Other becomes then a subject capable of addressing others. In such a case, the subject is neither a sovereign agent with a purely instrumental relation to language, nor a mere effect whose agency is pure complicity with prior operations of power. The vulnerability to the Other constituted by that prior address is never overcome in the assumption of agency (one reason that "agency" is not the same as "mastery").

The argument that hate speech is illocutionary, that it produces the subject in a position of subordination, approximates the view that the subject is interpellated by an anterior voice, one that exercises a ritual form. In hate speech, the ritual in question appears to be that of subordination. Indeed, one of the strongest arguments in favor of the state regulation of hate speech is that certain kinds of utterances, when delivered by those in positions of power against those who are already subordinated, have the effect of resubordinating those to whom such utterances are addressed.

For such a view to become persuasive, it is necessary to distinguish between kinds of injury that are socially contingent and avoidable, and kinds of subordination that are, as it were, the constitutive condition of the subject. This distinction is difficult to make, though not impossible, because it seems that the former kind of speech exploits the prior possibility of the latter. Hate speech exposes a prior vulnerability to language, one that we have by virtue of being interpellated kinds of beings, dependent on the address of the Other in order to be. That one comes to "be" through a dependency on the Other—an Hegelian and, indeed, Freudian postulation—must be recast in linguistic terms to the extent that the terms by which recognition is regulated, allocated, and refused are part of larger social rituals of interpellation. There is no way to protect against that primary vulnerability and susceptibility to the call of recognition that solicits existence, to that primary dependency on a language we never made in order to acquire a tentative ontological status. Thus we sometimes cling to the terms that pain us because, at a minimum, they offer us some form of social and discursive existence.[21] The address that inaugurates the possibility of agency, in a single stroke, forecloses the possibility of radical autonomy. In this sense,

an "injury" is performed by the very act of interpellation, the one that rules out the possibility of the subject's autogenesis (and gives rise to that very fantasy). It is therefore impossible to regulate fully the potentially injurious effect of language without destroying something fundamental about language and, more specifically, about the subject's constitution in language. On the other hand, a critical perspective on the kinds of language that govern the regulation and constitution of subjects becomes all the more imperative once we realize how inevitable is our dependency on the ways we are addressed in order to exercise any agency at all.

The utterances of hate speech are part of the continuous and uninterrupted process to which we are subjected, an on-going subjection (*assujetissement*) that is the very operation of interpellation, that continually repeated action of discourse by which subjects are formed in subjugation. Those offensive terms that mark out a discursive place of violation precede and occasion the utterance by which they are enacted; the utterance is the occasion for the renewal of that interpellating operation; indeed, that operation is only instanced by the "verbal conduct," / 27 but the operation of interpellation happens with or without such conduct. Indeed, one can be interpellated, put in place, given a place, through silence, through not being addressed, and this becomes painfully clear when we find ourselves preferring the occasion of being derogated to the one of not being addressed at all.

We might be tempted to understand the existence of injurious language as posing an ethical question on the order of: what kind of language ought we to use? How does the language we use affect others? If hate speech is citational, does that mean that the one who uses it is not responsible for that usage? Can one say that someone else made up this speech that one simply finds oneself using and thereby absolve oneself of all responsibility? I would argue that the citationality of discourse can work to enhance and intensify our sense of responsibility for it. The one who utters hate speech is responsible for the manner in which such speech is repeated, for reinvigorating such speech, for reestablishing contexts of hate and injury. The responsibility of the speaker does not consist of remaking language ex nihilo, but rather of negotiating the legacies of usage that constrain and enable that speaker's speech.

To understand this sense of responsibility, one afflicted with impurity from the start, requires that we understand the speaker as formed in the language that he or she also uses. This paradox intimates an ethical dilemma brewing at the inception of speech.

The question of how best to use speech is an explicit ethical question that can emerge only later. It presupposes a prior set of questions: who are "we" such that without language we cannot be, and what does it mean "to be" within language? How is it that injurious language strikes at this very condition of possibility, of linguistic persistence and survival? If the subject who speaks is also constituted by the language that she or he speaks, then language is the condition of possibility for the speaking subject, and not merely its instrument of expression. This means that the subject has its own "existence" implicated in a language that precedes and exceeds the subject, a language whose historicity includes a past and future that exceeds that of the subject who speaks. And yet, this "excess" is what makes possible the speech of the subject.

Foucault refers to this loss of control over language when he writes, "discourse is not life; its time is not yours."[22] By this statement, Foucault appears to mean that one's life is not reducible to the discourse that one speaks or to the sphere of discourse that animates one's life. What he fails to emphasize, however, is that the time of discourse, even in its radical incommensurability with the time of the subject, *makes possible* the speaking time of the subject. That linguistic domain over which the subject has no control becomes the condition of possibility for whatever domain of control is exercised by the speaking subject. Autonomy in speech, to the extent that it exists, is conditioned by a radical and originary dependency on a language whose historicity exceeds in all directions the history of the speaking subject. And this excessive historicity and structure makes possible that subject's linguistic survival as well as, potentially, that subject's linguistic death.

THE INJURIOUS ACTION OF NAMES

Although some injurious language depends on the use of names, calling another a name, other forms seem to rely on descriptions or even silences. And yet, we may understand something of linguistic vulnera-

bility through a consideration of the power of the name. Lacan writes that, "the name is the time of the object." But it is also the time of the Other. One is, as it were, brought into social location and time through being named. And one is dependent upon another for one's name, for the designation that is supposed to confer singularity. Whether the name is shared by others, the name, as a convention, has a generality and a historicity that is in no sense radically singular, even though it is understood to exercise the power of conferring singularity. At least, this is the general understanding of the *proper name*. But do other kinds of names, descriptions, linguistic bearings (including silence) borrow and derive some of the constituting power of the proper name? Do they also confer a spatial and temporal specificity, inaugurating a time of the subject that is not the same as the time of language, enforcing the sense of the subject's finitude that follows from that incommensurability?

Consider for a moment the more general conditions of naming. First, a name is offered, given, imposed by someone or by some set of someones, and it is attributed to someone else. It requires an intersubjective context, but also *a mode of address*, for the name emerges as the *addressing of a coinage to another, and in that address, a rendering of that coinage proper.* The scene of naming appears then first as a unilateral action: there are those who address their speech to others, who borrow, amalgamate, and coin a name, deriving it from available linguistic convention, and establish that derivation as *proper* in the act of naming. And yet, the one who names, who works within language to find a name for another, is presumed to be already named, positioned within language as one who is already subject to that founding or inaugurating address. This suggests that such a subject in language is positioned as both addressed and addressing, and that the very possibility of naming another requires that one first be named. The subject of speech who is named becomes, potentially, one who might well name another in time.

Although we might think of this action first and foremost as conferring a proper name, it does not necessarily take that form. The jarring, even terrible, power of naming appears to recall this initial power of the name to inaugurate and sustain linguistic existence, to confer

singularity in location and time. After having received the proper name, one is subject to being named again. In this sense, the vulnerability to being named constitutes a constant condition of the speaking subject. And what if one were to compile all the names that one has ever been called? Would they not present a quandary for identity? Would some of them cancel the effect of others? Would one find oneself fundamentally dependent upon a competing array of names to derive a sense of oneself? Would one find oneself alienated in language, finding oneself, as it were, in the names addressed from elsewhere? Thus, as Benveniste has shown, the very conditions of the possibility for becoming an "I" in language remain indifferent to the "I" that one becomes. The more one seeks oneself in language, the more one loses oneself precisely there where one is sought.

Positioned as both addressed and addressing, taking its bearings within that crossed vector of power, the subject is not only founded by the other, requiring an address in order to be, but its power is derived from the structure of address as both linguistic vulnerability and exercise. If one comes to be through address, can we imagine a subject apart from his or her linguistic bearing? We cannot imagine them or they could not be what they are, apart from the constitutive possibility of addressing others and being addressed by others. If these subjects could not be who they are without this linguistic bearing toward one another, then it seems that this linguistic bearing might well qualify as something essential to who these subjects are, something without which they could not be said to exist; their linguistic bearing toward one another, their linguistic vulnerability toward one another, is not something simply added on to their social relations to one another. It is one of the primary forms that this social relation takes.[23]

The linguistic scene we have been considering is one in which there are subjects who stand in a relation of addressing and being addressed, where the capacity to address appears to be derived from having been addressed, where a certain subjectivation in language is constituted by this reversibility. The presumption of a dyadic relation, however, need not constrain our understanding of interpellation.

Consider the situation in which one is named without knowing

that one is named, which is, after all, the condition of all of us at the beginning and even, sometimes, prior to the beginning. The name constitutes one socially, but one's social constitution takes place without one's knowing. Indeed, one may well imagine oneself in ways that are quite to the contrary of how one is socially constituted; one may, as it were, meet that socially constituted self by surprise, with alarm or pleasure, even with shock. And such an encounter underscores the way in which the name wields a linguistic power of constitution in ways that are indifferent to the one who bears the name. One need not know about or register a way of being constituted for that constitution to work in an efficacious way. For the measure of that constitution is not to be found in a reflexive appropriation of that constitution, but, rather, in a chain of signification that exceeds the circuit of self-knowledge. The time of discourse is not the time of the subject.

In this sense, Althusser's view of interpellation requires revision. The subject need not always turn around in order to be constituted as a subject, and the discourse that inaugurates the subject need not take the form of a voice at all.

/ 31

In "Ideology and Ideological State Apparatuses," Althusser attempts to describe the subject-constituting power of ideology through recourse to the figure of a divine voice that names, and in naming brings its subjects into being. The divine name makes what it names, but it also subordinates what it makes. In claiming that social ideology operates in an analogous way to the divine voice, Althusser inadvertently assimilates social interpellation to the divine performative. The example of religion thus assumes the status of a paradigm for thinking ideology as such: the authority of the "voice" of ideology, the "voice" of interpellation, is figured as a voice almost impossible to refuse. The force of interpellation in Althusser is derived from notable examples: God's voice in the naming of Peter (and Moses) and its secularization in the postulated voice of the representative of state authority; the policeman's voice in the hailing of the wayward pedestrian with "Hey you there!"

In other words, the divine power of naming structures the theory of interpellation that accounts for the ideological constitution of the

subject. God names "Peter," and this address establishes God as the origin of Peter (177); the name remains attached to Peter permanently by virtue of the implied and continuous presence residing in the name of the one who names him. Within the terms of Althusser's examples, however, this naming cannot be accomplished without a certain readiness or anticipatory desire on the part of the one addressed. To the extent that the naming is an address, there is already an addressee, prior to the address; but given that the address is a name which creates what it names, there appears to be no "Peter" without the name, "Peter." Indeed, "Peter" does not exist without the name that supplies that linguistic guarantee of existence. In this sense, as a prior and essential condition of the formation of the subject, there is a certain readiness to be compelled by the authoritative interpellation, a readiness that suggests that one is, as it were, already in a binding relation to the divine voice before one succumbs to its call. In other words, one is already claimed by the voice that calls the name, already subordinate to the authority to which one subsequently yields.

32 /   As useful as it is, Althusser's scheme restricts the notion of interpellation to the action of a voice, attributing a creative power to the voice that recalls and reconsolidates the figure of the divine voice in its ability to bring about what it names. Interpellation must be dissociated from the figure of the voice in order to become the instrument and mechanism of discourses whose efficacy is irreducible to their moment of enunciation. Consider the efficacy of written or reproduced language in the production of social effects and, in particular, the constitution of subjects. But perhaps most important to consider is that the voice is implicated in a notion of *sovereign* power, power figured as emanating from a subject, activated in a voice, whose effects appear to be the magical effects of that voice. In other words, power is understood on the model of the divine power of naming, where to utter is to create the effect uttered. Human speech rarely mimes that divine effect except in the cases where the speech is backed by state power, that of a judge, the immigration authority, or the police, and even then there does sometimes exist recourse to refute that power. If we concede that the one who speaks powerfully, who makes happen what she

or he says, is enabled in his/her speech by first having been addressed and, hence, initiated into linguistic competence through the address, then it follows that the power of the speaking subject will always, to some degree, be derivative, that it will not have its source in the speaking subject.

The policeman who hails the person on the street is enabled to make that call through the force of reiterated convention. This is one of the speech acts that police perform, and the temporality of the act exceeds the time of the utterance in question. In a sense, the police *cite* the convention of hailing, participate in an utterance that is indifferent to the one who speaks it. The act "works" in part because of the citational dimension of the speech act, the historicity of convention that exceeds and enables the moment of its enunciation. For Althusser, there must be a one who turns around, who reflexively appropriates the term by which one is hailed; only once this appropriative gesture takes place does hailing become interpellation. But if we accept the notion that the linguistic constitution of the subject can take place without that subject's knowing, as when one is constituted out of earshot, as, say, the referent of a third-person discourse, then interpellation can function without the "turning around," without anyone ever saying, "Here I am."

/ 33

Imagine the quite plausible scene in which one is called by a name and one turns around only to protest the name: "That is not me, you must be mistaken!" And then imagine that the name continues to force itself upon you, to delineate the space you occupy, to construct a social positionality. Indifferent to your protests, the force of interpellation continues to work. One is still constituted by discourse, but at a distance from oneself. Interpellation is an address that regularly misses its mark, it requires the recognition of an authority at the same time that it confers identity through successfully compelling that recognition. Identity is a function of that circuit, but does not preexist it. The mark interpellation makes is not descriptive, but inaugurative. It seeks to introduce a reality rather than report on an existing one; it accomplishes this introduction through a citation of existing convention. Interpellation is an act of speech whose "content" is neither true nor

false: it does not have description as its primary task. Its purpose is to indicate and establish a subject in subjection, to produce its social contours in space and time. Its reiterative operation has the effect of sedimenting its "positionality" over time.

The interpellative name may arrive without a speaker—on bureaucratic forms, the census, adoption papers, employment applications. Who utters such words? The bureaucratic and disciplinary diffusion of sovereign power produces a terrain of discursive power that operates without a subject, but that constitutes the subject in the course of its operation. This does not mean that there are no individuals who write and distribute the forms. It means only that they are not the originators of the discourse they convey and that their intentions, however strong, are not finally what control the meaning of that discourse.

Although the subject surely speaks, and there is no speaking without a subject, the subject does not exercise sovereign power over what it says. As a result, interpellation after the diffusion of sovereign power has an origin that is as unclear as its end. From whom does the address emerge, and to whom is it addressed? If the one who delivers it does not author it, and the one who is marked by it is not described by it, then the workings of interpellative power exceed the subjects constituted by its terms, and the subjects so constituted exceed the interpellation by which they are animated.

The workings of interpellation may well be necessary, but they are not for that reason mechanical or fully predictable. The power of a name to injure is distinct from the efficacy with which that power is exercised. Indeed, power is not as easy to identify or to localize as some speech act theory appears to imply.[24] The subject who speaks hate speech is clearly responsible for such speech, but that subject is rarely the originator of that speech. Racist speech works through the invocation of convention; it circulates, and though it requires the subject for its speaking, it neither begins nor ends with the subject who speaks or with the specific name that is used.

Foucault counsels against the effort to localize the conceptualization of power, and his theory of power has implications for the attempt to locate power in the name. His remarks have less to do with the

power of the name than with *the name of power*, and with the nominalistic presuppositions that go along with construing power as if it were a name.

He writes, (HS, 93): "One needs to be nominalistic, no doubt: power is not an institution, and not a structure; neither is it a certain strength we are endowed with; *it is the name that one attributes to a complex strategical situation* in a particular society" (my emphasis). It is the name that one attributes to a complexity which is not easily named. Power does not arrive in the form of a name; its structures and its institutions are not such that the name seems perfectly suited to whatever power is. A name tends to fix, to freeze, to delimit, to render substantial, indeed, it appears to recall a metaphysics of substance, of discrete and singular kinds of beings; a name is not the same as an undifferentiated temporal process or the complex convergence of relations that go under the rubric of "a situation." But power is the name that one attributes to this complexity, a name that substitutes for that complexity, a name that renders manageable what might be otherwise too unwieldy or complex, and what, in its complexity, might defy the limiting and substantializing ontology presupposed by the name. Of course, when Foucault claims that "power is the name that one attributes to a strategical situation," then it appears that power is but the name that one attributes, that the name is an arbitrary or abbreviated version of what power is but then Foucault offers a description: "a strategical situation in a particular society," and the question emerges: is this description any less arbitrary or abbreviated than the name by which it is replaced, the name which stands as a substitution for this description? In other words, is the description any less of a substitute than the name?

What is power in this view? If it is not a certain strength with which we are endowed, is it perhaps a certain strength with which language is endowed? If it is neither, that is, if power cannot be said to inhere in every subject as an "endowed strength" or, for that matter, to inhere in any set of names as an "endowed strength," then how might we account for those occasions in which power comes to appear precisely as that with which a subject is endowed *or* as that with which a name is endowed.

Power works through dissimulation: it comes to appear as something other than itself, indeed, it comes to appear as *a name*. "Power" Foucault writes, placing the term in quotation marks; power so-called; power, as people say. Power, the name, is, among other things, the over-all effect that emerges from all these mobilities, "the concatenation that rests on each of these ["mobilities"] *and seeks to arrest their movement."* (HS, 93) It is movement, it is a concatenation, a concatenation that rests on them, but which is in a sense derived from them, a concatenation derived from them which turns against them, which seeks to arrest movement itself. Is the "name" perhaps one way in which that arrest is performed? A strange way to think about power, as the arrest of movement, as a movement which comes to a halt or arrests itself—through nominalization. The name carries within itself the movement of a history that it arrests.

Clearly, injurious names have a history, one that is invoked and reconsolidated at the moment of utterance, but not explicitly told. This is not simply a history of how they have been used, in what contexts, and for what purposes; it is the way such histories are installed and arrested in and by the name. The name has, thus, a *historicity*, what might be understood as the history which has become internal to a name, has come to constitute the contemporary meaning of a name: the sedimentation of its usages as they have become part of the very name, a sedimentation, a repetition that congeals, that gives the name its force.[25]

If we understand the force of the name to be an effect of its historicity, then that force is not the mere causal effect of a an inflicted blow, but works in part through an encoded memory or a trauma, one that lives in language and is carried in language. The force of the name depends not only on its iterability, but on a form of repetition that is linked to trauma, on what is, strictly speaking, not remembered, but relived, and relived in and through the linguistic substitution for the traumatic event. The traumatic event is an extended experience that defies and propagates representation at once.[26] Social trauma takes the form, not of a structure that repeats mechanically, but rather of an ongoing subjugation, the restaging of injury through signs that both

occlude and reenact the scene. Can repetition be both the way that trauma is repeated but also the way in which it breaks with the historicity to which it is in thrall? What makes for a reverse citation in the scene of trauma, how can hate speech be cited against itself?

The proposals to regulate hate speech invariably end up citing such speech at length, offering lengthy lists of examples, codifying such speech for regulatory purposes, or rehearsing in a pedagogical mode the injuries that have been delivered through such speech. It seems that the repetition is inevitable, and that the strategic question remains, what best use is to be made of repetition? This is not an exercise of agency at a distance, but precisely a struggle from within the constraints of compulsion. In the case of hate speech, there appears to be no way to ameliorate its effects except through its recirculation, even if that recirculation takes place in the context of a public discourse that calls for the censorship of such speech: the censor is compelled to repeat the speech that the censor would prohibit. No matter how vehement the opposition to such speech is, its recirculation inevitably reproduces trauma as well. There is no way to invoke examples of racist speech, for instance, in a classroom without invoking the sensibility of racism, the trauma and, for some, the excitement. / 37

I found through a difficult experience in the summer 1995 at the Dartmouth School for Criticism and Theory that to offer examples of such language is in some instances to incite their usage. A student, apparently responding to the course content, sent hateful letters to various students in the class, offering "knowing" speculation on their ethnicity and sexuality; she or he wrote the letters with no name attached: nameless, calling names, attempting to distill the operation of interpellation into a unilateral address according to which the letter-writer can only address others, but cannot be addressed in return. Hence, the trauma of the example returned, as it were, in the trauma of the unsigned letter. Afterwards, in the class, the trauma was reiterated again for pedagogical purposes. The incitement of discourse about the trauma, though, did not work to ameliorate it, although there was a way in which the affectless scrutiny of the terms did something to ameliorate the rush of excitement that, for some, went along with the

utterance. The liberal capacity to refer to such terms as if one were merely mentioning them, not making use of them, can support the structure of disavowal that permits for their hurtful circulation. The words are uttered and disavowed at the moment of the utterance, and the critical discourse on them becomes precisely the instrument of their perpetration.

This story underscores the limits and risks of resignification as a strategy of opposition. I will not propose that the pedagogical recirculation of examples of hate speech always defeats the project of opposing and defusing such speech, but I want to underscore the fact that such terms carry connotations that exceed the purposes for which they may be intended and can thus work to afflict and defeat discursive efforts to oppose such speech. Keeping such terms unsaid and unsayable can also work to lock them in place, preserving their power to injure, and arresting the possibility of a reworking that might shift their context and purpose.

That such language carries trauma is not a reason to forbid its use. There is no purifying language of its traumatic residue, and no way to work through trauma except through the arduous effort it takes to direct the course of its repetition. It may be that trauma constitutes a strange kind of resource, and repetition, its vexed but promising instrument. After all, to be named by another is traumatic: it is an act that precedes my will, an act that brings me into a linguistic world in which I might then begin to exercise agency at all. A founding subordination, and yet the scene of agency, is repeated in the ongoing interpellations of social life. This is what I have been called. Because I have been called something, I have been entered into linguistic life, refer to myself through the language given by the Other, but perhaps never quite in the same terms that my language mimes. The terms by which we are hailed are rarely the ones we choose (and even when we try to impose protocols on how we are to be named, they usually fail); but these terms we never really choose are the occasion for something we might still call agency, the repetition of an originary subordination for another purpose, one whose future is partially open.

SCHEMA

If agency is not derived from the sovereignty of the speaker, then the force of the speech act is not sovereign force. The "force" of the speech act is, however incongruously, related to the body whose force is deflected and conveyed through speech. As excitable, such speech is at once the deliberate and undeliberate effect of a speaker. The one who speaks is not the originator of such speech, for that subject is produced in language through a prior performative exercise of speech: interpellation. Moreover, the language the subject speaks is conventional and, to that degree, citational. The legal effort to curb injurious speech tends to isolate the "speaker" as the culpable agent, as if the speaker were at the origin of such speech. The responsibility of the speaker is thus misconstrued. The speaker assumes responsibility precisely through the citational character of speech. The speaker renews the linguistic tokens of a community, reissuing and reinvigorating such speech. Responsibility is thus linked with speech as repetition, not as origination.

/ 39

If the performativity of injurious speech is considered perlocutionary (speech leads to effects, but is not itself the effect), then such speech works its injurious effect only to the extent that it produces a set of non-necessary effects. Only if other effects may follow from the utterance does appropriating, reversing, and recontextualizing such utterances become possible. To the extent that some legal approaches assume the illocutionary status of hate speech (speech is the immediate and necessary exercise of injurious effects), the possibility of defusing the force of that speech through counter-speech is ruled out. Significantly, the legal discourse in which the status of the performativity of hate speech takes place is its own performative exercise. In the current U.S. political climate, the law that decides the question of hate speech tends to be applied inconsistently in order to further reactionary political aims: the action of speech is considered unequivocally to be injurious conduct (an illocutionary view of the speech act) in those instances in which the graphic representation of sexuality is at issue. Gay and lesbian self-declaration in the military is one such example. The relation

between speech and conduct is considered equivocal, if not undecidable, by the courts in instances of racist speech.

My view is that efforts to argue that speech is conduct are taken
up by conservative courts to endorse the view that sexual speech is a
sexual act; the courts tend to dispute the conflation of speech and conduct, however, in matters pertaning to racist language. This becomes
painfully clear in those cases in which racial minorities come to stand
for the source or origin of sexually injurious representation (as in rap)
or where that very pornographic debasement is exercised by the state
itself when the speech of Anita Hill, rendered as a sexualized racial
spectacle, is deprived of credibility. The transposition of the hate
speech model from race to sex thus fails to work without producing
a series of politically problematic consequences. Racial tropes are
exploited to make false analogies with sex, and the intersection
between the two remains critically uninterrogated.

As much as this text seeks to understand the particulars of recent
arguments concerning hate speech, it also seeks to outline a more general theory of the performativity of political discourse. The point is not
to enumerate the political consequences of a theory of the performative, but rather to show how a theory of the performative is already at
work in the exercise of political discourse (theory can work in implicit
and fugitive ways). Understanding performativity as a renewable
action without clear origin or end suggests that speech is finally constrained neither by its specific speaker nor its originating context. Not
only defined by social context, such speech is also marked by its capacity to break with context. Thus, performativity has its own social temporality in which it remains enabled precisely by the contexts from
which it breaks. This ambivalent structure at the heart of performativity implies that, within political discourse, the very terms of resistance
and insurgency are spawned in part by the powers they oppose (which
is not to say that the latter are reducible to the former or always already
coopted by them in advance).

The political possibility of reworking the force of the speech act
against the force of injury consists in misappropriating the force of
speech from those prior contexts. The language that counters the
injuries of speech, however, must repeat those injuries without pre-

cisely reenacting them. Such a strategy affirms that hate speech does not destroy the agency required for a critical response. Those who argue that hate speech produces a "victim class" deny critical agency and tend to support an intervention in which agency is fully assumed by the state. In the place of state-sponsored censorship, a social and cultural struggle of language takes place in which agency is derived from injury, and injury countered through that very derivation.

Misappropriating the force of injurious language to counter its injurious operations constitutes a strategy that resists the solution of state-sponsored censorship, on the one hand, and the return to an impossible notion of the sovereign freedom of the individual, on the other. The subject is constituted (interpellated) in language through a selective process in which the terms of legible and intelligible subjecthood are regulated. The subject is called a name, but "who" the subject is depends as much on the names that he or she is never called: the possibilities for linguistic life are both inaugurated and foreclosed through the name.

Thus, language constitutes the subject in part through foreclosure, ⁄ 41 a kind of unofficial censorship or primary restriction in speech that constitutes the possibility of agency in speech. The kind of speaking that takes place on the border of the unsayable promises to expose the vacillating boundaries of legitimacy in speech. As a further marking of the limit to sovereignty, this view suggests that agency is derived from limitations in language, and that limitation is not fully negative in its implications.

Indeed, as we think about worlds that might one day become thinkable, sayable, legible, the opening up of the foreclosed and the saying of the unspeakable become part of the very "offense" that must be committed in order to expand the domain of linguistic survival. The resigni-fication of speech requires opening new contexts, speaking in ways that have never yet been legitimated, and hence producing legitimation in new and future forms.

1 / BURNING ACTS, INJURIOUS SPEECH

The title of J. L. Austin's *How to Do Things with Words* poses the question of performativity as what it means to say that "things might be done with words." The problem of performativity is thus immediately bound up with a question of transitivity. What does it mean for a word not only to name, but also in some sense to perform and, in particular, to perform what it names? On the one hand, it may seem that the word—for the moment we do not know which word or which kind of word—enacts what it names; where the "what" of "what it names" remains distinct from the name itself and the performance of that "what."

After all, Austin's title questions how to do things *with* words, suggesting that words are instrumentalized in getting things done. Austin, of course, distinguishes between illocutionary and perlocutionary acts of speech, between actions that are performed by virtue of words, and those that are performed as a consequence of words. The distinction is tricky, and not always stable. According to the perlocutionary view, words are instrumental to the accomplishment of actions, but they are not themselves the actions which they help to accomplish. This form of the performative suggests that the words and the things done are in no sense the same. But according to his view of the illocutionary speech act, the name performs *itself*, and in the course of that performing becomes a thing done; the pronouncement is the act of speech at the same time that it is the speaking of an act. Of such an act, one cannot reasonably ask for a "referent," since the effect of the act of speech is not to refer beyond itself, but to perform itself, producing a strange enactment of linguistic immanence.

The title of Austin's manual, *How to Do Things With Words*, suggests that there is a perlocutionary kind of doing, a domain of things done, and then an instrumental field of "words," indeed, that there is also a deliberation that precedes that doing, and that the words will be distinct from the things that they do.

But what happens if we read that title with an emphasis on the illocutionary form of speech, asking instead what it might mean for a word "to do" a thing, where the doing is less instrumental than it is transitive. Indeed, what would it mean for a thing to be "done by" a word or, for that matter, for a thing to be "done in" by a word? When and where, in such a case, would such a thing become disentangled from the word by which it is done or done in, and where and when would that conjunction between word and thing appear indissoluble? If a word in this sense might be said to "do" a thing, then it appears that the word not only signifies a thing, but that this signification will also be an enactment of the thing. It seems here that the meaning of a performative act is to be found in this apparent coincidence of signifying and enacting.

And yet it seems that this "act-like" quality of the performative is itself an achievement of a different order, and that de Man was clearly

on to something when he asked whether a trope is not animated at the moment when we claim that language "acts," that language posits itself in a series of distinct acts, and that its primary function might be understood as this kind of periodic acting. Significantly, I think, the common translation of Nietzsche's account of the metaleptic relation between doer and deed rests on a certain confusion about the status of the "deed." For even there, Nietzsche will claim that certain forms of morality require a subject and institute a subject as the consequence of that requirement. This subject will be installed as prior to the deed in order to assign blame and accountability for the painful effects of a certain action. A being is hurt, and the vocabulary that emerges to moralize that pain is one which isolates a subject as the intentional originator of an injurious deed; Nietzsche understands this, first, as the moralization by which pain and injury are rendered equivalent and, second, as the production of a domain of painful effects suffused with conjectured intention. At such a moment the subject is not only fabricated as the prior and causal origin of a painful effect that is recast as an injury, but the action whose effects are injurious is no longer an action, the continuous present of "a doing," but is reduced to a "singular act."

/ 45

The following citation from *On the Genealogy of Morals* is usually read with an emphasis on the retroactive positing of the doer prior to the deed; but note that simultaneous with this retroactive positing is a moral resolution of a continuous "doing" into a periodic "deed": "there is no 'being' behind the doing, effecting, becoming: 'the doer' is merely a fiction added to the deed—the deed is everything." ". . . es gibt kein 'Sein' hinter dem Tun, Wirken, Werden; 'der Täter' ist zum Tun blos hinzugedichtet—das Tun ist alles." In the German, there is no reference to an "act"—*die Tat*—but only to a "doing"—*das Tun*, and to the word for a culprit or wrong-doer, *der Täter*, which translates merely as a "doer."[1] Here the very terms by which "doing" is retroactively fictionalized (*hinzugedichtet*) as the intentional effect of a "subject," establishes the notion of a "doer" primarily as a wrong-doer. Furthermore, in order to attribute accountability to a subject, an origin of action in that subject is fictively secured. In the place of a "doing" there appears the grammatical and juridical constraint on thought by which a subject is produced first and foremost as the accountable originator of

an injurious deed. A moral causality is thus set up between the subject and its act such that both terms are separated off from a more temporally expansive "doing" that appears to be prior and oblivious to these moral requirements.

For Nietzsche, the subject appears only as a consequence of a demand for accountability; a set of painful effects is taken up by a moral framework that seeks to isolate the "cause" of those effects in a singular and intentional agent, a moral framework that operates through a certain economy of paranoid fabrication and efficiency. *The question, then, of who is accountable for a given injury precedes and initiates the subject, and the subject itself is formed through being nominated to inhabit that grammatical and juridical site.*

In a sense, for Nietzsche, the subject comes to be only within the requirements of a moral discourse of accountability. The requirements of blame figure the subject as the "cause" of an act. In this sense, there can be no subject without a blameworthy act, and there can be no "act" apart from a discourse of accountability and, according to Nietzsche, without an institution of punishment.

But here it seems that Nietzsche's account of subject-formation in *On the Genealogy of Morals* exposes something of its own impossibility. For if the "subject" is first animated through accusation, conjured as the origin of an injurious action, then it would appear that the accusation has to come *from* an interpellating performative that precedes the subject, one that presupposes the prior operation of an efficacious speaking. Who delivers that formative judgment? If there is an institution of punishment within which the subject is formed, is there not also a figure of the law who performatively sentences the subject into being? Is this not, in some sense, the conjecturing by Nietzsche of a prior and more powerful subject? Nietzsche's own language elides this problem by claiming that the "der Täter ist zum Tun blos hinzugedichtet." This passive verb formation, hinzugedichtet," poetically or fictively added on to, appended, or applied, leaves unclear who or what executes this fairly consequential formation.

If, on the occasion of pain, a subject is belatedly attributed to the act as its origin, and the act then attributed to the subject as its effect, this double attribution is confounded by a third, namely, the attribution

of an injurious consequence to the subject and its act. In order to establish injurious consequence within the domain of accountability, is it necessary to install a subject, and to establish the singularity and discreteness of the act itself as well as the efficacy of the act to produce injury? If the injury can be traced to a specifiable act, it qualifies as an object of prosecution: it can be brought to court and held accountable. Does tracing the injury to the act of a subject and privileging of the juridical domain as the site to negotiate social injury not unwittingly stall the analysis of how precisely discourse produces injury by taking the subject and its spoken deed as the proper place of departure? And when it is words that wound, to borrow Richard Delgado's phrase, how are we to understand the relation between the word and the wound? If it is not a causal relation, and not the materialization of an intention, is it perhaps a kind of discursive transitivity that needs to be specified in its historicity and its violence? What is the relation between this transitivity and the power to injure?

In Robert Cover's impressive essay, "Violence and the Word," he elaborates the violence of legal interpretation as "the violence that *judges* deploy as instruments of a modern nation-state."[2] "Judges," he contends, "deal pain and death," "for as the judge interprets, using the concept of punishment, she also acts—through others—to restrain, hurt, render helpless, even kill the prisoner" [note the unfortunate implication of liberal feminism when it decides to legislate the feminine as the universal]. Cover's analysis is relevant to the question of prosecuting hate speech precisely because it underscores the power of the *judiciary* to enact violence through speech. Defenders of hate speech prosecution have had to shift the analysis to acknowledge that agents other than governments and branches of government wield the power to injure through words. Indeed, an analogy is set up between state action and citizen action such that both kinds of actions are understood to have the power to deny rights and liberties protected by the Equal Protection Clause of the Constitution. Consequently, one obstacle to contemporary efforts to legislate against hate speech is that the "state action doctrine" qualifies recourse to the Equal Protection Clause in such instances, presuming as it does that only governments can be the agents of harmful treatment that results in a deprivation of

rights and liberties.[3] To argue that citizens can effectively deprive *each other* of such rights and liberties through words that wound requires overcoming the restrictions imposed by the state action doctrine.[4]

Whereas Cover emphasizes the *juridical* power to inflict pain through language, recent jurisprudence has shifted the terms away from the interpretive violence enacted by nation-states and toward the violence enacted by citizen-subjects toward members of minority groups. In this shift, it is not simply that citizens are said to act like states, but the power of the state is refigured as a power wielded by a citizen-subject. By "suspending" the state action doctrine, proponents of hate speech prosecution may also suspend a critical understanding of state power, relocating that power as the agency and effect of the citizen-subject. Indeed, if hate speech prosecution will be adjudicated by the state, in the form of the judiciary, the state is tacitly figured as a neutral instrument of legal enforcement. Hence, the "suspension" of the state action doctrine may involve both a suspension of critical insight into state power and state violence in Cover's sense, but also a displacement of that power onto the citizen and the citizenry, figured as sovereigns whose speech now carries a power that operates like state power to deprive other "sovereigns" of fundamental rights and liberties.[5]

In shifting the emphasis from the harm done by the state to the harm done by citizens and non-state institutions against citizens, a reassessment of how power operates in and through discourse is also at work. When the words that wound are not the actions of the nation-state—indeed, when the nation-state and its judiciary are appealed to as the arbiter of such claims made by citizens against one another—how does the analysis of the violence of the word change? Is the violence perpetrated by the courts unwittingly backgrounded in favor of a politics that presumes the fairness and efficacy of the courts in adjudicating matters of hate speech? And to what extent does the potential for state violence become greater to the degree that the state action doctrine is suspended?

The subject as sovereign is presumed in the Austinian account of performativity: the figure for the one who speaks and, in speaking performs what she/he speaks, as the judge or some other representative of

the law. A judge pronounces a sentence and the pronouncement is the act by which the sentence first becomes binding, as long as the judge is a legitimate judge and the conditions of felicity are properly met. The one who speaks the performative effectively is understood to operate according to uncontested power. The doctor who receives the child and pronounces—"It's a girl"—begins that long string of interpellations by which the girl is transitively girled: gender is ritualistically repeated, whereby the repetition occasions both the risk of failure and the congealed effect of sedimentation. Kendall Thomas makes a similar argument that the subject is always "raced," transitively racialized by regulatory agencies from its inception.[6] The power to "race" and, indeed, the power to gender, precedes the "one" who speaks such power, and yet the one who speaks nevertheless appears to have that power.

If performativity requires a power to effect or enact what one names, then who will be the "one" with such a power, and how will such a power be thought? How might we account for *the injurious word* within such a framework, the word that not only names a social subject, but constructs that subject in the naming, and constructs that subject through a violating interpellation? Is it the power of a "one" to effect such an injury through the wielding of the injurious name, or is that a power accrued through time which is concealed at the moment that a single subject utters its injurious terms? Does the "one" who speaks the term *cite* the term, thereby establishing him or herself as the author while at the same time establishing the derivative status of that authorship? Is a community and history of such speakers not magically invoked at the moment in which that utterance is spoken? And if and when that utterance brings injury, is it the utterance or the utterer who is the cause of the injury, or does that utterance perform its injury through a transitivity that cannot be reduced to a causal or intentional process originating in a singular subject?

Indeed, is iterability or citationality not precisely this: *the operation of that metalepsis by which the subject who "cites" the performative is temporarily produced as the belated and fictive origin of the performative itself?* The subject who utters the socially injurious words is mobilized by that long string of injurious interpellations: the subject achieves a temporary sta-

tus in the citing of that utterance, in performing itself as the origin of that utterance. That subject-effect, however, is the consequence of that very citation; it is derivative, the effect of a belated metalepsis by which that invoked legacy of interpellations is dissimulated as the subject and the "origin" of its utterance. If the utterance is to be prosecuted, where and when would that prosecution begin, and where and when would it end? Would this not be something like the effort to prosecute a history that, by its very temporality, cannot be called to trial? If the function of the subject as fictive origin is to occlude the genealogy by which that subject is formed, the subject is also installed in order to assume the burden of responsibility for the very history that subject dissimulates; the juridicalization of history, then, is achieved precisely through the search for subjects to prosecute who might be held accountable and, hence, temporarily resolve the problem of a fundamentally unprosecutable history.

This is not to say that subjects ought not to be prosecuted for their injurious speech; I think that there are probably occasions when they should. But what is precisely being prosecuted when the injurious word comes to trial and is it finally or fully prosecutable?

That words wound seems incontestably true, and that hateful, racist, misogynist, homophobic speech should be vehemently countered seems incontrovertibly right. But does understanding from where speech derives its power to wound alter our conception of what it might mean to counter that wounding power? Do we accept the notion that injurious speech is attributable to a singular subject and act? If we accept such a juridical constraint on thought—the grammatical requirements of accountability—as a point of departure, what is lost from the political analysis of injury? Indeed, when political discourse is fully collapsed into juridical discourse, the meaning of political opposition runs the risk of being reduced to the act of prosecution.

How is the analysis of the discursive historicity of power unwittingly restricted when the subject is presumed as the point of departure for such an analysis? A clearly theological construction, the postulation of the subject as the causal origin of the performative act is understood to generate that which it names; indeed, this divinely empowered subject is one for whom the name itself is generative. According to the

biblical rendition of the performative, "Let there be light!," it appears that by virtue of *the power of a subject or its will* a phenomenon is named into being. Although the sentence is delivered in the subjunctive, it qualifies as a "masquerading" performative in the Austinian sense. In a critical reformulation of the performative, Derrida makes clear in relation to Austin that this power is not the function of an originating will but is always derivative:

> Could a performative utterance succeed if its formulation did not repeat a "coded" or iterable utterance, or in other words, if the formula I pronounce in order to open a meeting, launch a ship or a marriage were not identifiable as conforming with an iterable model, if it were not then identifiable in some way as a "citation"? . . . [I]n such a typology, the category of intention will not disappear; it will have its place, but from that place it will no longer be able to govern the entire scene and system of utterance [*l'énonciation*].[7]

To what extent does discourse gain the authority to bring about / 51 what it names through citing the linguistic conventions of authority, conventions that are themselves legacies of citation? Does a subject appear as the author of its discursive effects to the extent that the citational practice by which he/she is conditioned and mobilized remains unmarked? Indeed, could it be that the production of the subject as originator of his/her effects is precisely a consequence of this dissimulated citationality?

If a performative provisionally succeeds (and I will suggest that "success" is always and only provisional), then it is not because an intention successfully governs the action of speech, but only because that action echoes prior actions, and *accumulates the force of authority through the repetition or citation of a prior and authoritative set of practices*. It is not simply that the speech act takes place *within* a practice, but that the act is itself a ritualized practice. What this means, then, is that a performative "works" to the extent that *it draws on and covers over* the constitutive conventions by which it is mobilized. In this sense, no term or statement can function performatively without the accumulating and dissimulating historicity of force.

When the injurious term injures (and let me make clear that I think it does), it works its injury precisely through the accumulation and dissimulation of its force. The speaker who utters the racial slur is thus citing that slur, making linguistic community with a history of speakers. What this might mean, then, is that precisely the iterability by which a performative enacts its injury establishes a permanent difficulty in locating final accountability for that injury in a singular subject and its act.

/ /

In two recent cases, the Supreme Court has reconsidered the distinction between protected and unprotected speech in relation to the phenomenon of "hate speech." Are certain forms of invidious speech to be construed as "fighting words," and if so, are they appropriately considered to be a kind of speech unprotected by the first Amendment? In the first case, *R.A.V. v. St. Paul,* 112 S. Ct. 2538, 120 L. Ed. 2d 305 (1992), the ordinance in question was one passed by the St. Paul City Council in 1990, and read in part as follows:

> Whoever places on public or private property a symbol, object, appellation, characterization or graffiti, including, but not limited to, a burning cross or Nazi swastika, which one knows or has reasonable grounds to know arouses anger, alarm, or resentment in others, on the basis of race, color, creed, religion or gender commits disorderly conduct and shall be guilty of a misdemeanor.[8]

A white teenager was charged under this ordinance after burning a cross in front of a black family's house. The charge was dismissed by the trial court but reinstated by the Minnesota State Supreme Court; at stake was the question whether the ordinance itself was "substantially overbroad and impermissably content based." The defense contended that the burning of the cross in front of the black family's house was to be construed as an example of protected speech. The State Supreme Court overturned the decision of the trial court, arguing first that the burning of the cross could not be construed as protected speech because it constituted "fighting words" as defined in *Chaplinsky v. New*

Hampshire, 315 U.S. 568, 572 (1942), and second, that the reach of the ordinance was permissible considering the "compelling government interest in protecting the community against bias-motivated threats to public safety and order." *In Re Welfare of R.A.V.,* 464 N.W.2 507, 510 (Minn. 1991).

The United States Supreme Court reversed the State Supreme Court decision, reasoning first that the burning cross was not an instance of "fighting words," but a "viewpoint" within the "free marketplace of ideas" and that such "viewpoints" are categorically protected by the first Amendment."[9] The majority on the High Court (Scalia, Rehnquist, Kennedy, Souter, Thomas) then offered a *second* reason for declaring the ordinance unconstitutional, a judicially activist contribution which took many jurists by surprise: the justices severely restricted the possible doctrinal scope of "fighting words" by claiming it unconstitutional to impose prohibitions on speech solely on the basis of the "content" or "subjects addressed" in that speech. In order to determine whether words are fighting words, there can be no decisive recourse to the content and the subject matter of what is said. /53

One conclusion on which the justices appear to concur is that the ordinance imposed overbroad restrictions on speech, given that forms of speech *not* considered to fall within the parameters of fighting words would nonetheless be banned by the ordinance. But while the Minnesota ordinance proved too broad for all the justices, Scalia, Thomas, Rehnquist, Kennedy, and Souter took the opportunity of this review to severely restrict any future application of the fighting words doctrine. At stake in the majority opinion is not only when and where "speech" constitutes some component of an injurious act such that it loses its protected status under the first Amendment, but what constitutes the domain of "speech" itself.

According to a rhetorical reading of this decision—distinguished from a reading that follows established conventions of legal interpretation—the court might be understood as asserting its state-sanctioned linguistic power to determine what will and will not count as "speech" and, in the process, enacting a potentially injurious form of juridical speech. What follows, then, is a reading which considers not only the account that the Court gives of how and when speech becomes injuri-

ous, but considers as well the injurious potential of the account itself as "speech" considered in a broad sense. Recalling Cover's claim that legal decisions can engage the nexus of language and violence, consider that the adjudication of what will and will not count as protected speech will itself be a kind of speech, one which implicates the state in the very problem of discursive power with which it is invested to regulate, sanction, and restrict such speech.

In the following, then, I will read the "speech" in which the decision is articulated against the version of "speech" officially circumscribed as protected content in the decision. The point of this kind of reading is not only to expose a contradictory set of rhetorical strategies at work in the decision, but to consider the power of that discursive domain which not only produces what will and will not count as "speech," but which regulates the political field of contestation through the tactical manipulation of that very distinction. Furthermore, I want to argue that the very reasons that account for the injuriousness of such acts, construed as speech in a broad sense, are precisely what render difficult the prosecution of such acts. Lastly, I want to suggest that the court's speech carries with it its *own* violence, and that the very institution that is invested with the authority to adjudicate the problem of hate speech recirculates and redirects that hatred in and as its own highly consequential speech, often by coopting the very language that it seeks to adjudicate.

The majority opinion, written by Scalia, begins with the construction of the act, the burning of the cross; and one question at issue is whether or not this act constitutes an injury, whether it can be construed as "fighting words" or whether it communicates a content which is, for better or worse, protected by first Amendment precedent. The figure of burning will be repeated throughout the opinion, first in the context in which the burning cross is construed as the free expression of a viewpoint within the marketplace of ideas, and, second, in the example of the burning of the flag, which could be held illegal were it to violate an ordinance prohibiting outside fires, but which could not be held to be illegal if it were the expression of an idea. Later Scalia will close the argument through recourse to yet another fire: "Let there be no mistake about our belief that burning a cross in someone's front yard

is reprehensible." "But," Scalia continued, "St. Paul has sufficient means at its disposal to prevent such behavior without adding the first Amendment to the fire." *R.A.V. v. St. Paul*, 112 S. Ct. at 2550, 120 L. Ed. 2d at 326.

Significantly, Scalia here aligns the act of cross-burning with those who defend the ordinance, since both are producing fires, but whereas the cross-burner's fire is constitutionally protected speech, the ordinance-maker's language is figured as the incineration of free speech. The analogy suggests that the ordinance is itself a kind of cross-burning, and Scalia then draws on the very destructive implications of cross-burning to underscore his point that the ordinance itself is destructive. The figure thus affirms the destructiveness of the cross-burning that the decision itself effectively denies, the destructiveness of the act that it has just elevated to the status of protected verbal currency within the marketplace of ideas.

The Court thus transposes the place of the ordinance and the place of the cross-burning, but also figures the first Amendment in an analogous relation to the black family and its home which in the course of the writing has become reduced to "someone's front yard." The stripping of blackness and family from the figure of the complainant is significant, for it refuses the dimension of social power that constructs the so-called speaker and the addressee of the speech act in question, the burning cross. And it refuses as well the racist history of the convention of cross-burning by the Ku Klux Klan which marked, targeted, and, hence, portended a further violence against a given addressee. Scalia thus figures himself as quenching the fire which the ordinance has lit, and which is being stoked with the first Amendment, apparently in its totality. Indeed, compared with the admittedly "reprehensible" act of burning a cross in "someone's" front yard, the ordinance itself appears to conflagrate in much greater dimensions, threatening to burn the book which it is Scalia's duty to uphold; Scalia thus champions himself as an opponent of those who would set the constitution on fire, cross-burners of a more dangerous order.[10]

The lawyers arguing for the legality of the ordinance based their appeal on the fighting words doctrine. This doctrine, formulated in *Chaplinsky v. New Hampshire*, 315 U.S. 568, 572 (1942), argued that

speech acts unprotected by the Constitution are those which are not essential to the communication of ideas: "such utterances are no essential part of any exposition of ideas, and are of such slight social value as a step to truth that any benefit that may be derived from them is clearly outweighed by the social interest in order and morality." Scalia takes this phrasing to legitimate the following claim: "the unprotected features of the words are, despite their verbal character, essentially a 'non-speech' element of communication." *R.A.V. v. St. Paul*, 112 S. Ct. at 2545, 120 L. Ed. 2d at 319. In his efforts to protect all contents of communication from proscription, Scalia establishes a distinction between the content and the vehicle of that expression; it is the latter which is proscribable, and the former which is not. He continues, "fighting words are thus analogous to a noisy sound truck." *Id.* What is injurious, then, is the sound, but not the message, indeed, "the government may not regulate use based on hostility—or favoritism—towards the underlying message expressed." *Id.*

The connection between the signifying power of the burning cross and Scalia's regressive new critical distinction between what is and is not a speech element in communication is nowhere marked in the text.[11] Scalia assumes that the burning cross is a message, an expression of a viewpoint, a discussion of a "subject" or "content": in short, that the act of burning the cross is fully and exhaustively translatable into a *constative* act of speech; the burning of the cross which is, after all, on the black family's lawn, is thus made strictly analogous—and morally equivalent—to an individual speaking in public on whether or not there ought to be a fifty-cent tax on gasoline. Significantly, Scalia does not tell us what the cross would say if the cross could speak, but he does insist that what the burning cross is doing is expressing a viewpoint, discoursing on a content which is, admittedly, controversial, but for that very reason, ought not to be proscribed. Thus the defense of cross-burning as free speech rests on an unarticulated analogy between that act and a public constation. This speech is not a doing, an action or an injury, even as it is the enunciation of a set of "contents" that might offend.[12] The injury is thus construed as one that is registered at the level of sensibility, which is to say that it is an offense that is one of the risks of free speech.

That the cross burns and thus constitutes an incendiary destruction is not considered as a sign of the intention to reproduce that incendiary destruction at the site of the house or the family; the historical correlation between cross-burning and marking a community, a family, or an individual for further violence is also ignored. How much of that burning is translatable into a declarative or constative proposition? And how would one know exactly what constative claim is being made by the burning cross? If the cross is the expression of a viewpoint, is it a declaration as in, "I am of the opinion that black people ought not to live in this neighborhood" or even, "I am of the opinion that violence ought to be perpetrated against black people," or is it a perlocutionary performative, as in imperatives and commands which take the form of "Burn!" or "Die!"? Is it an injunction that works its power metonymically not only in the sense that the fire recalls prior burnings which have served to mark black people as targets for violence, but also in the sense that the fire is understood to be transferable from the cross to the target that is marked by the cross? The relation between cross-burning and torchings of both persons and properties is historically established. Hence, from this perspective, the burning cross assumes the status of a direct address and a *threat* and, as such, is construed either as the incipient moment of injurious action *or* as the statement of an intention to injure.[13]

Although Justice Stevens agreed with the decision to strike down the Minnesota ordinance, he takes the occasion to rebuke Scalia for restricting the fighting words doctrine. Stevens reviews special cases in which conduct may be prohibited by special rules. Note in the following quotation how the cross-burning is nowhere mentioned, but the displacements of the figure of fire appear in a series of examples which effectively transfer the need for protection *from racist speech* to the need for protection *from public protest against racism*. Even within Stevens's defense of proscribing conduct, a phantasmatic figure of a menacing riot emerges:

> Lighting a fire near an ammunition dump or a gasoline storage tank is especially dangerous; such behavior may be punished more severely than burning trash in a vacant lot. Threatening someone

because of her race or religious beliefs may cause particularly severe trauma or touch off a riot, and threatening a high public official may cause substantial social disruptions; such threats may be punished more severely than threats against someone based on, say, his support of a particular athletic team. *R.A.V. v. St. Paul*, 112 S. Ct. at 2561, 120 L Ed. 2d at 340.

Absent from the list of fires above is the burning of the cross in question. In the place of that prior scene, we are asked first to imagine someone who would light a fire near a gas tank, and then to imagine a more innocuous fire in a vacant lot. But with the vacant lot, we enter the metaphor of poverty and property, which appears to effect the unstated transition to the matter of blackness[14] introduced by the next line, "threatening someone because of her race or religious beliefs . . .": *because* of her race is not the same as "on the basis of" her race and leaves open the possibility that the race causally induces the threat. The threat appears to shift mid-sentence as Stevens continues to elaborate a second causality: this threat "may cause particularly severe trauma or touch off a riot" at which point it is no longer clear whether the threat which warrants the prohibition on conduct refers to the "threatening someone because of her race or religious beliefs" or to the riot that might result therefrom. What immediately follows suggests that the limitations on rioters has suddenly become more urgent to authorize than the limitation on those who would threaten this "her" "because of her race. . . ." After "or touch off a riot," the sentence continues, "and threatening a high official may cause substantial social disruption . . . ," as if the racially marked trauma had already led to a riot and an attack on high officials.

This sudden implication of the justices themselves might be construed as a paranoid inversion of the original cross-burning narrative. That original narrative is nowhere mentioned, but its elements have been redistributed throughout the examples; the fire which was the original "threat" against the black family is relocated first as an incendiary move against industry, then as a location in a vacant lot, and then reappears tacitly in the riot which now appears to follow from the trauma and threaten public officials. The fire which initially consti-

58/

tuted the threat against the black family becomes metaphorically transfigured as the threat that blacks in trauma now wield against high officials. And though Stevens is on record as endorsing a construction of "fighting words" that would include cross-burning as *un*protected speech, the language in which he articulates this view deflects the question to that of the state's right to circumscribe conduct to protect itself against a racially motivated riot.[15]

The circumscription of content explicitly discussed in the decision appears to emerge through a production of semantic excess in and through the metonymic chain of anxious figuration. The separability of content from sound, for instance, or of content from context, is exemplified and illustrated through figures which signify in excess of the thesis which they are meant to support. Indeed, to the extent that, in the Scalia analysis, "content" is circumscribed and purified to establish its protected status, that content is secured through the production and proliferation of "dangers" from which it calls to be protected. Hence, the question of whether or not the black family in Minnesota is entitled to protection from public displays such as cross-burnings is displaced onto the question of whether or not the "content" of free speech is to be protected from those who would burn it. The fire is thus displaced from the cross to the legal instrument wielded by those who would protect the family from the fire, but then to the black family itself, to blackness, to the vacant lot, to rioters in Los Angeles who explicitly oppose the decision of a court and who now represent the incendiary power of the traumatized rage of black people who would burn the judiciary itself. But, of course, that construal is already a reversal of the narrative in which a court delivers a decision of acquittal for the four policemen indicted for the brutal beating of Rodney King, a decision that might be said to "spark" a riot which calls into question whether the claim of having been injured can be heard and countenanced by a jury and a judge who are extremely susceptible to the suggestion that a black person is always and only endangering, but never endangered. And so the high Court might be understood in its decision of June 22, 1992, to be taking its revenge on Rodney King, protecting itself against the riots in Los Angeles and elsewhere which appeared to be attacking the system of justice itself. Hence, the justices

/ 59

identify with the black family who sees the cross burning and takes it as a threat, but they substitute themselves for that family, and reposition blackness as the agency behind the threat itself.[16]

The decision enacts a set of metonymic displacements which might well be read as anxious deflections and reversals of the injurious action at hand; indeed, the original scene is successively reversed in the metonymic relation between figures such that the fire is lit by the ordinance, carried out by traumatized rioters on the streets of Los Angeles, and threatens to engulf the justices themselves.

Mari Matsuda and Charles Lawrence also write of this text as enacting a rhetorical reversal of crime and punishment: "The cross burners are portrayed as an unpopular minority that the Supreme Court must defend against the power of the state. The injury to the Jones family is appropriated and the cross burner is cast as the injured victim. The reality of ongoing racism and exclusion is erased and bigotry is redefined as majoritarian condemnation of racist views."[17]

Significantly, the justices revisited *R.A.V. v. St. Paul* in a more recent decision, *Wisconsin v. Mitchell*, 113 S. Ct. 2194, 14 L. Ed. 2d 436 (1993), in which the court unanimously decided that racist speech could be included as evidence that a victim of a crime was intentionally selected because of his/her race and could constitute one of the factors that come into play in determining whether an enhanced penalty for the crime is in order. *Wisconsin v. Mitchell* did not address whether racist speech is injurious, but only whether speech that indicates that the victim was selected on the basis of race could be brought to bear in determining penalty enhancement for a crime which is itself not a crime of speech, as it were. Oddly, the case at hand involved a group of young black men, including Todd Mitchell who had just left the film, *Mississippi Burning*. They decided to "move on" some white people, and proceeded to beat a young white man who had approached them on the street. Rehnquist is quick to note that these young men were discussing a scene from the film, one in which "a white man beat a young black boy who was praying." Rehnquist then goes on to quote Mitchell whose speech will become consequential in the decision: "Do you all feel hyped up to move on some white people" and later, "You all want to fuck somebody up? There goes a white boy; go get him."

Wisconsin v. Mitchell, 113 S. Ct. at 2196-7, 120 L. Ed. 2d at 442 (citing Brief for Petitioner). Now, the irony of this event, it seems, is that the film narrates the story of three civil rights workers (two white and one black) who are murdered by Klansmen who regularly threaten with burning crosses and firebombs any townspeople who appear to help the Justice Department in their search for the bodies of the slain civil rights activists and then their murderers. The court system is first figured within the film as sympathetic to the Klan, refusing to imprison the murdering Klansmen, and then as setting improper restraints on the interrogation. Indeed, the Justice Department official is able to entrap the Klansman only by acting against the law, freely brutalizing those he interrogates. This official is largely regarded as rehabilitating masculinity on the side of what is right over and against a liberal "effeminization" represented by judicial due process. But perhaps most important, while the effective official acts in the name of the law, he also acts against the law, and purports to show that his unlawfulness is the only efficacious way to fight racism. The film thus appeals to a widespread lack of faith in the law and its proceduralism, reconstructing a lawless white masculinity even as it purports to curb its excesses.

／61

In some ways, the film shows that violence is the consequence of the law's failure to protect its citizens, and in this way allegorizes the reception of the judicial decisions. For if the film shows that the court will fail to guarantee the rights and liberties of its citizens, and only violence can counter racism, then the street violence that literally follows the film reverses the order of that allegory. The black men who leave the film and embark upon violence in the street find themselves in a court that not only goes out of its way to indict the film—which is, after all, an indictment of the courts—but implicitly goes on to link the street violence to the offending representation, and effectively to link the one through the other.

The court seeks to decide whether or not the selection of the target of violence is a racially motivated one by quoting Todd Mitchell's speech. This speech is then taken to be the consequence of having watched the film, indeed, to be the very extension of the speech that constitutes the text of the film. But the Court itself is implicated in the

extended text of the film, "indicted" by the film as complicit with racial violence. Hence, the punishment of Mitchell and his friends—and the attribution of racially selective motives to them—reverses the "charges" that the film makes against the Court. In *R.A.V. v. St. Paul*, the Court makes a cameo appearance in the decision as well, reversing the agency of the action, substituting the injured for the injurer, and figuring itself as a site of vulnerability.

In each of these cases, the Court's speech exercises the power to injure precisely by virtue of being invested with the authority to adjudicate the injurious power of speech. The reversal and displacement of injury in the name of "adjudication" underscores the particular violence of the "decision," one which becomes both dissimulated and enshrined once it becomes word of law. It may be said that all legal language engages this potential power to injure, but that insight supports only the argument that it will be all the more important to gain a reflective understanding of the specificities of that violence. It will be necessary to distinguish between those kinds of violence that are the necessary conditions of the binding character of legal language, and those kinds which exploit that very necessity in order to redouble that injury in the service of injustice.

The arbitrary use of this power is evidenced in the contrary use of precedents on hate speech to promote conservative political goals and thwart progressive efforts. Here it is clear that what is needed is not a better understanding of speech acts or the injurious power of speech, but the strategic and contradictory uses to which the Court puts these various formulations. For instance, this same Court has been willing to countenance the expansion of definitions of obscenity, and to use the very rationale proposed by some arguments in favor of hate-crime legislation to augment its case to exclude obscenity from protected speech.[18] Scalia refers to *Miller v. California* (1973) as the case which installs obscenity as an exception to the categorical protection of content through recourse to what is "patently offensive," and then remarks that in a later case, *New York v. Ferber*, 458 U.S. 747 (1982), in exempting child pornography from protection, there was no "question here of censoring a particular literary theme," *R.A.V. v. St. Paul*, 112 S. Ct at 2543, 120 L. Ed. 2d at 318. What constitutes the "literary" is thus cir-

cumscribed in such a way that child pornography is excluded from both the literary and the thematic. Although it seems that one must be able to recognize the genre of child pornography, to identify and delimit it in order to exempt it from the categorical protection of content, the identifying marks of such a product can be neither literary nor thematic. Indeed, the Court appears in one part of its discussion to accept the controversial position of Catharine MacKinnon, which claims that certain verbal expressions constitute sex discrimination, when it says "sexually derogatory 'fighting words' . . . may produce a violation of Title VII's general prohibition against sexual discrimination in employment practices" *Id.* at 2546, 120 L. Ed. 2d at 321. But here the court is clear that it does not prohibit such expressions on the basis of their content, but only on the basis of the effects that such expressions entail.

I would suggest that the contemporary conservative sensibility exemplified by the court and right-wing members of Congress is also exemplified in the willingness to expand the domain of obscenity and, to that end, to enlarge the category of the pornographic and to claim the unprotected status of both, and so, potentially, to position obscenity to become a species of "fighting words," that is, to accept that graphic sexual representation is injurious. This is underscored by the rationale used in *Miller v. California* in which the notion of "appealing to prurience" is counterposed to the notion of "literary, artistic, political, or scientific value." Here the representation that is deemed immediately and unobjectionably injurious is excluded from the thematic and the valuable and, hence, from protected status.

This same rationale has been taken up by Jesse Helms and others to argue that the National Endowment for the Arts is under no obligation to fund obscene materials, and then to argue that various lesbian performers and gay male photographers produce work that is obscene and lacking in literary value. Significantly, it seems, the willingness to accept the nonthematic and unobjectionably injurious quality of graphic sexual representations, when these representations cannot be said to leave the page or to "act" in some obvious way, must be read against the unwillingness to countenance the injuriousness of the burning cross in front of the black family's house. That the graphic depiction

/ 63

of homosexuality, say, can be construed as nonthematic or simply prurient, figured as a sensuousness void of meaning, whereas the burning of the cross, to the extent that it communicates a message of racial hatred, might be construed as a sanctioned point in a public debate over admittedly controversial issues, suggest that the rationale for expanding the fighting words doctrine to include unconventional depictions of sexuality within its purview has been strengthened, but that the rationale for invoking fighting words to outlaw racist threats is accordingly weakened. This is perhaps a way in which a heightened sexual conservatism works in tandem with an increasing governmental sanction for racist violence, but in such a way that whereas the "injury" claimed by the viewer of graphic sexual representation is honored as fighting words, the injury sustained by the black family with the burning cross out front, like the injury of Rodney King, proves too ambiguous, too hypothetical to abrogate the ostensible sanctity of the first Amendment.[19] And it is not simply that prohibitions against graphic sexual representation will be supported by this kind of legal reasoning, whereas racist injury will be dignified as protected speech, but that racially marked depictions of sexuality will be most susceptible to prosecution, and those representations that threaten the pieties and purities of race and sexuality will become most vulnerable.

Two remarks of qualification: first, some critical race theorists such as Charles Lawrence will argue that cross burning is speech, but that not all speech is to be protected, indeed, not all speech *is* protected, and that racist speech conflicts with the Equal Protection Clause because it hinders the addressed subject from exercising his/her rights and liberties. Other legal scholars in critical race studies, such as Richard Delgado, will argue for expanding the domain of the fighting words restriction on first Amendment rights. Matsuda and MacKinnon, following the example of sex discrimination jurisprudence, will argue that it is impossible to distinguish between conduct and speech, that hateful remarks are injurious actions. Oddly enough, this last kind of reasoning has reappeared in the recent policy issued on gays in the military, where the statement "I am a homosexual" is considered to be a "homosexual act." I will consider that conflation of speech and conduct in Chapter Three. According to this policy, the act

of coming out is implicitly construed as fighting words. Here it seems that one must be reminded that the prosecution of hate speech in a court runs the risk of giving that court the opportunity to impose a further violence of its own. And if the court begins to decide what is and is not violating speech, that decision runs the risk of constituting the most binding of violations.

For, as in the case with the burning cross, it was not merely a question of whether the court knows how to read the threat contained in the burning cross, but whether the court itself signifies along a parallel logic. For this has been a court that can only imagine the fire engulfing the first Amendment, sparking the riot which will fray its own authority. And so it protects itself against the imagined threat of that fire by protecting the burning cross, allying itself with those who would seek legal protection from a spectre wrought from their own fantasy. Thus the court protects the burning cross as free speech, figuring those it injures as the site of the true threat, elevating the burning cross as a deputy for the court, the local protector and token of free speech: with so much protection, what do we have to fear?

/ 65

FROM HATE SPEECH TO PORNOGRAPHY

MacKinnon herself understands this risk of invoking state power, but in her recent book, *Only Words* (1993), she argues that state power is on the side of the pornographic industry; and that the construction of women within pornography in subordinate positions is, effectively, a state-sanctioned construction. A fuller discussion of her position takes place in the following chapter, but I offer an analysis of the putative performativity of pornography here to show how the construal of the visual image as illocutionary speech effectively sidesteps the first Amendment by claiming that pornography is sovereign conduct.

MacKinnon has argued that pornography is a kind of hate speech, and that the argument in favor of restricting hate speech ought to be based on the argument in favor of restricting pornography. This analogy rests upon the assumption that the visual image in pornography operates as an imperative, and that this imperative has the power to realize that which it dictates. The problem, for MacKinnon, is *not* that

pornography reflects or expresses a social structure of misogyny, but that it is an institution with the performative power to bring about that which it depicts. She writes that pornography not only substitutes for social reality, but that that substitution is one which creates a social reality of its own, the social reality of pornography. This self-fulfilling capacity of pornography is, for her, what gives sense to the claim that pornography *is* its own social context. She writes,

> Pornography does not simply express or interpret experience; it substitutes for it. Beyond bringing a message from reality, it stands in for reality. . . . To make visual pornography, and to live up to its imperatives, the world, namely women, must do what the pornographers want to 'say.' Pornography brings its conditions of production to the consumer. . . . Pornography makes the world a pornographic place through its making and use, establishing what women are said to exist as, are seen as, are treated as, constructing the social reality of what a woman is and can be in terms of what can be done to her, and what a man is in terms of doing it. (25)

66 /

In the first instance, pornography substitutes for experience, implying that there is an experience which is supplanted, and supplanted thoroughly, through pornography. Hence, pornography takes the place of an experience and thoroughly constitutes a new experience understood as a totality; by the second line this second-order experience is rendered synonymous with a second order "reality," which suggests that in this universe of pornography there is no distinction between an experience of reality and reality. MacKinnon herself makes clear that this systemic conflation of the two takes place within a reality which is itself a mere substitution for another reality, one which is figured as more original, perhaps one which furnishes the normative or utopian measure by which she judges the pornographic reality that has taken its place. This visual field is then figured as speaking, indeed, as delivering imperatives, at which point the visual field operates as a subject with the power to bring into being what it names, to wield an efficacious power analogous to the divine performative. The reduction of that visual field to a speaking figure, an authoritarian speaker, rhetorically effects a different substitution than the one that Mac-

Kinnon describes. She substitutes a set of linguistic imperatives for the visual field, implying not only a full transposition of the visual into the linguistic, but a full transposition of visual depiction into an efficacious performative.

When pornography is then described as "constructing the social reality of what a woman is," the sense of "construction" needs to be read in light of the above two transpositions. That construction can be said to work, that is, "to produce the social reality of what a woman is," only if the visual can be transposed into the linguistically efficacious in the way that she suggests. Similarly, the analogy between pornography and hate speech works to the extent that the pornographic image can be transposed into a set of efficacious spoken imperatives. In MacKinnon's paraphrase of how the pornographic image speaks, she insists that the image says, "do this," where the commanded act is an act of sexual subordination, and where, in the doing of that act, the social reality of woman is constructed precisely as the position of the sexually subordinate. Here "construction" is not simply the doing of the act—which remains, of course, highly ambiguous in order perhaps to ward off the question of an equivocal set of readings—but *the depiction* of that doing, where the depiction is understood as the dissimulation and fulfillment of the verbal imperative, "do this." For MacKinnon, no one needs to speak such words because the speaking of such words already functions as the frame and the compulsory scripting of the act; in a sense, to the extent that the frame orchestrates the act, it wields a performative power; it is conceived by MacKinnon as encoding the will of a masculine authority, and compelling a compliance with its command.

But does the frame impart the will of a preexisting subject, or is the frame something like the derealization of will, the production and orchestration of a phantasmatic scene of willfulness and submission? I don't mean to suggest a strict distinction between the phantasmatic and the domain of reality, but I do mean to ask, to what extent does the operation of the phantasmatic within the construction of social reality render that construction more frail and less determinative than MacKinnon would suggest? In fact, although one might well agree that a good deal of pornography is offensive, it does not follow that its

/ 67

offensiveness consists in its putative power to construct (unilaterally, exhaustively) the social reality of what a woman is. To return for a moment to MacKinnon's own language, consider the way in which the hypothetical insists itself into the formulation of the imperative, as if the force of her own assertions about the force of pornographic representation tends toward its own undoing: "pornography establish[es] . . . what women are said to exist, *are seen as*, are treated *as* . . ." Then, the sentence continues: "constructing the social reality of what a woman is": here to be treated as a sexual subordinate is to be constructed as one, and to have a social reality constituted in which that is precisely and only what one is. But if the "as" is read as the assertion of a likeness, it is not for that reason that assertion of a metaphorical collapse into identity. Through what means does the "as" turn into a "is," and is this the doing of pornography, or is it the doing of the very *depiction* of pornography that MacKinnon provides? For the "as" could also be read a "as if," "as if one were," which suggests that pornography neither represents nor constitutes what women are, but offers an allegory of masculine willfulness and feminine submission (although these are clearly not its only themes), one which repeatedly and anxiously rehearses its own *un*realizability. Indeed, one might argue that pornography depicts impossible and uninhabitable positions, compensatory fantasies that continually reproduce a rift between those positions and the ones that belong to the domain of social reality. Indeed, one might suggest that pornography is the text of gender's unreality, the impossible norms by which it is compelled, and in the face of which it perpetually fails. The imperative "do this" is less delivered. than "depicted," and if what is depicted is a set of compensatory ideals, hyperbolic gender norms, then pornography charts a domain of unrealizable positions that hold sway over the social reality of gender positions, but do not, strictly speaking, constitute that reality; indeed, it is their failure to constitute it that gives the pornographic image the phantasmatic power that it has. In this sense, to the extent that an imperative is "depicted" and not "delivered," it fails to wield the power to construct the social reality of what a woman is. This failure, however, is the occasion for an allegory of such an imperative, one that concedes the unrealizability of that imperative from the start, and which, finally, cannot

68 /

overcome the unreality that is its condition and its lure. My call, as it were, is for a feminist reading of pornography that resists the literalization of this imaginary scene, one which reads it instead for the incommensurabilities between gender norms and practices that it seems compelled to repeat without resolution.

In this sense, it makes little sense to figure the visual field of pornography as a subject who speaks and, in speaking, brings about what it names; its authority is decidedly less divine; its power, less efficacious. It only makes sense to figure the pornographic test as the injurious act of a speaker if we seek to locate accountability at the prosecutable site of the subject. Otherwise our work is more difficult, for what pornography delivers is what it recites and exaggerates from the resources of compensatory gender norms, a text of insistent and faulty imaginary relations that will not disappear with the abolition of the offending text, the text that remains for feminist criticism relentlessly to read. To read such texts against themselves is to concede that the performativity of the text is not under sovereign control. On the contrary, if the text acts once, it can act again, and possibly against its prior act. This raises the possibility of *re*signification as an alternative reading of performativity and of politics.

/ 69

2 / SOVEREIGN PERFORMATIVES

Recent proposals to regulate hate speech on campus, in the workplace, and in other public domains have spawned a set of ambivalent political consequences. The sphere of language has become a privileged domain in which to interrogate the cause and effects of social injury. Whereas earlier moments in the civil rights movement or in feminist activism were primarily concerned with documenting and seeking redress for various forms of discrimination, the current political concern with hate speech emphasizes the linguistic form that discriminatory conduct assumes,

seeking to establish verbal conduct as discriminatory action.[1] But what is verbal conduct? Clearly, the law has definitions to offer and those definitions often institutionalize catachrestic extensions of ordinary understandings of speech; hence, the burning of a flag or even a cross may be construed as "speech" for legal purposes. Recently, however, jurisprudence has sought the counsel of rhetorical and philosophical accounts of language in order to account for hate speech in terms of a more general theory of linguistic performativity. Strict adherents of First Amendment absolutism subscribe to the view that freedom of speech has priority over other constitutionally protected rights and liberties and is, in fact, presupposed by the exercise of other rights and liberties. They also tend to include all "content-based" utterances as protected speech and consider forms of threatening verbal conduct as subject to the question of whether such threats remain "speech" or whether they have wandered over into the domain of "conduct." Only in the latter case is the "speech" in question proscribable. In the context of hate speech controversies, a recent view of speech is emerging that troubles any recourse to such a strict distinction; that view holds that the very "content" of certain kinds of speech can be understood only in terms of *the action that the speech performs*. In other words, racist epithets not only relay a message of racial inferiority, but that "relaying" is the verbal institutionalization of that very subordination. Thus, hate speech is understood not only to communicate an offensive idea or set of ideas but also to enact the very message it communicates: the very communication is at once a form of conduct.[2]

I propose to review some of the senses in which "verbal conduct" is thought in the proposed hate speech regulation, and to offer an alternative view of how one might at once affirm that language does act, even injuriously, while insisting that it does not directly or causatively "act on" the addressee in quite the way that proponents of hate speech legislation tend to describe. Indeed, the act-like character of certain offensive utterances may be precisely what keeps them from saying what they mean to say or doing what it is they say.

The legal scholars and activists who have contributed to the volume *Words that Wound*, tend to expand and complicate the legal parameters of "speech" to provide a rationale for the regulation of hate

speech. This is accomplished in part by conceptualizing utterances as both "expressive" of ideas and as forms of "conduct" in themselves: racist speech in particular both proclaims the inferiority of the race to whom it is addressed, and effects the subordination of that race through the utterance itself.[3] To the extent that the utterance enjoys first Amendment "protection," it is viewed, by Matsuda and others, as enjoying the backing of the state. The failure of the state to intervene is, in her view, tantamount to an endorsement by the state: "the chilling sight of avowed racists in threatening regalia marching through our neighborhood with full police protection is a statement of state authorization." (49) The utterance thus has the power to effect the subordination that it either depicts or promotes precisely through its free operation within the public sphere unimpeded by state intervention. Effectively, for Matsuda, the state allows for the injury of its citizens, and, she concludes, the "victim [of hate speech] becomes a stateless person." (25)

Relying on recently proposed hate speech regulation, Catharine MacKinnon makes a similar argument concerning pornography. In *Only Words* (1993) pornography ought to be construed as a kind of "wound," according to MacKinnon, because it proclaims and effects the subordinated status of women.[4] Thus, MacKinnon invokes the constitutional principle of equality (the Fourteenth Amendment, in particular) and argues that pornography is a form of unequal treatment; she takes this discriminatory action to be more serious and severe than any spurious exercise of "liberty" or "free expression" on the part of the pornographic industry. That exercise of "freedom," she argues, takes place at the expense of other citizens' rights to equal participation and the equal exercise of fundamental rights and liberties. In Matsuda's view, there are certain forms of harassing speech that qualify as discriminatory action, and those forms of racially and sexually based hate speech may undermine the social conditions for the exercise of fundamental rights and liberties on the part of those who are addressed through such speech.

I propose to focus here on the power attributed to the pornographic text to effect the subordinated status of women not to ascertain whether the text does effect that subordination in the way that she

/ 73

describes, but rather to discover what version of the performative is at work in the claim that it does. MacKinnon's use of the performative engages a figure of the performative, a figure of sovereign power that governs how a speech act is said to act—as efficacious, unilateral, transitive, generative. Finally, I read the figure of sovereignty as it emerges within the contemporary discourse on the performative in terms of the Foucaultian view that contemporary power is no longer sovereign in character. Does the figure of the sovereign performative compensate for a lost sense of power, and how might that loss become the condition for a revised sense of the performative?

The interest in this figure of the performative follows from a conviction that a similar way of regarding speech as conduct is at work in several political spheres at the same time and for political purposes that are not always reconcilable with one another. Utterance itself is regarded in inflated and highly efficacious ways, no longer as a representation of power or its verbal epiphenomenon, but as the *modus vivendi* of power itself.

74 / We might regard this overdetermination of the performative as the "linguistification" of the political field (one for which discourse theory is hardly responsible, but which it might be said to "register" in some important ways). Consider, then, the paradoxical emergence of a similar figure of the efficacious utterance in recent political contexts that would appear to be inimical to those just mentioned. One is the U.S. military, to be considered in the following chapter, in which certain kinds of *utterances*, namely, "I am a homosexual," are, within the recently contested policy, now considered to be "offensive conduct."[5] Similarly—but not identically—certain kinds of sexually graphic aesthetic representations, such as those produced and performed by the rap groups, 2 Live Crew or Salt n Pepa, are debated in legal contexts on the question of whether they fall under the rubric of "obscenity" as defined by *Miller v. California* (1973). Is the recirculation of injurious epithets in the context of the performance (where "performance" and "recirculation" are importantly equivocal) substantially different from the use of such epithets on campus, in the workplace, or in other spheres of public life? The question is not simply whether such works participate in recognizable genres of literary or artistic value, as if that

would suffice to guarantee their protected status. The controversy here, as Henry Louis Gates, Jr. has shown, is more complicated. Appropriating and recirculating established African-American genres of folk art, "signifying" being one central genre, such artistic productions participate in genres that may not be recognizable to the court. Paradoxically and poignantly, when the courts become the ones who are invested with the power to regulate such expressions, new occasions for discrimination are produced in which the courts discount African-American cultural production as well as lesbian and gay self-representation as such through the arbitrary and tactical use of obscenity law.[6]

It may seem at first that these various instances of "speech as conduct" are not at all commensurate with one another, and I do not propose to argue that they are. In each case the figure of the efficacious utterance emerges in a consequentially different scene of address. In Matsuda's discussion, harassing and injurious speech is figured as an address from one citizen to another, or from an employer or manager to a worker, or from a teacher to a student. The effect of the speech is, in Matsuda's view, to degrade or demean; it may "hit the gut" (23) of the addressee; it may undermine the addressee's capacity to work, to study or, in the public sphere, to exercise his or her constitutionally guaranteed rights and liberties: "the victim becomes a stateless person" (25). If the speech in question has undermined this capacity of the addressee to participate in the constitutionally protected sphere of action and expression, the injurious utterance may be said to have violated, or to have precipitated the violation of, the Equal Protection Clause that guarantees full and equal access to constitutionally protected rights and liberties. Matsuda's assumption is that calling someone a name or, more specifically, being addressed in an injurious way establishes that person's social subordination and, moreover, has the effect of depriving the addressee of the capacity to exercise commonly accepted rights and liberties within either a specific context (education or employment) or within the more generalized context of the national public sphere. Although some arguments in favor of the regulation of speech are context-specific, restricting the regulation to specific workplaces or educational environments, Matsuda seems prepared to claim that the na-

/ 75

tional public sphere in its totality is a proper frame of reference for hate speech regulation. To the extent that certain groups have been "historically subordinated," hate speech directed towards such groups consists in a ratification and extension of that "structural subordination." For Matsuda, it appears that certain historical forms of subordination have assumed a "structural" status, so that this generalized history and structure constitutes "the context" in which hate speech proves to be efficacious.

In the case of the U.S. military, there is some public quarrel over the question of whether stating publicly that one is a homosexual is the same as stating an intention to perform the act, and it appears that if the intention is stated, then the statement itself is offensive. In an early version of the policy, the military found offensive not the intention to act, but *the statement of the intention*. Here an act of speech in which a sexual intention is stated or implied becomes oddly indissociable from a sexual action. Indeed, the two can be rendered separable, it appears, only by an explicit disclaimer of that prior statement and the articulation of a further intention, namely, an intention *not* to act on one's desire. As in the example of pornographic "speech," a certain sexualization of speech is at issue, one in which the verbal reference to or depiction of sexuality is considered tantamount to a sexual act. As difficult and painful as it is to imagine, could the military have targeted this form of utterance as a codifiable offense without the precedent of sexual harassment law and its extension into the areas of pornography and hate speech?[7] In any case, in the revised guidelines to the policy, still in dispute in the courts, it is now possible to say, "I am a homosexual" and to add to that statement "and I have no intention or propensity to act on that desire." By disclaiming the action, the statement returns to a constative or merely descriptive claim, and we arrive at President Clinton's distinction between a protected status—"I am"—and unprotected conduct—"I do" or "I will do."

I consider the logic of this policy in the next chapter, and I propose to return to that figure of efficacious and offensive utterance toward the end of this one. In the interim, however, I aim to consider the construal of hate speech as offensive conduct, the effort to construe pornography as hate speech, and the concomitant effort to seek re-

course to the state to remedy the injuries allegedly caused by hate speech. What happens when we seek recourse to the state to regulate such speech? In particular, how is the regulatory power of the state enhanced through such an appeal? This is, perhaps, a familiar argument that I hope to make in a less than familiar way. My concern is not only with the protection of civil liberties against the incursion of the state, but with the peculiar *discursive power* given over to the state through the process of legal redress.

I would like to suggest a formulation for the problem that might seem paradoxical, but which I think, even in its hyperbolic mode, might shed some light on the problem that regulating hate speech poses. That formulation is this: *the state produces hate speech*, and by this I do not mean that the state is accountable for the various slurs, epithets, and forms of invective that currently circulate throughout the population. I mean only that the category cannot exist without the state's ratification, and this power of the state's judicial language to establish and maintain the domain of what will be publicly speakable suggests that the state plays much more than a limiting function in such decisions; in fact, the state actively produces the domain of publically acceptable speech, demarcating the line between the domains of the speakable and the unspeakable, and retaining the power to make and sustain that consequential line of demarcation. The inflated and efficacious utterance attributed to hate speech in some of the politicized contexts discussed above is itself modeled on the speech of a sovereign state, understood as a sovereign speech act, a speech act with the power to do what it says. This sovereign power is attributed to hate speech when it is said to "deprive" us of rights and liberties. The power attributed to hate speech is a power of absolute and efficacious agency, performativity and transitivity at once (it does what it says and it does what it says it will do to the one addressed by the speech). Precisely this power of *legal* language is that to which we refer when we call upon the state to effect the regulation of offensive speech. The problem, then, is not that the force of the sovereign performative is wrong, but when used by citizens it is wrong, and when intervened upon by the state, it is, in these contexts, right.

The same kind of force, however, is attributed to the performative

in both instances, and that version of performative power is never brought into question by those who pursue heightened regulation. What is this power? And how are we to account for its sustained production within hate speech discourse, as well as its continuing allure?

Before venturing an answer to these questions, it seems worth noting that this invocation of the sovereign performative takes place against the background of a political situation in which power is no longer constrained within the sovereign form of the state. Diffused throughout disparate and competing domains of the state apparatus, and through civil society in diffuse forms as well, power cannot be easily or definitively traced to a single subject who is its "speaker," to a sovereign representative of the state. To the extent that Foucault is right to describe contemporary relations of power as emanating from a number of possible sites, power is no longer constrained by the parameters of sovereignty. The difficulty of describing power as a sovereign formation, however, in no way precludes fantasizing or figuring power in precisely that way; to the contrary, the historical loss of the sovereign organization of power appears to occasion the fantasy of its return—a return, I want to argue, that takes place in language, in the figure of the performative. The emphasis on the performative phantasmatically resurrects the performative in language, establishing language as a displaced site of politics and specifying that displacement as driven by a wish to return to a simpler and more reassuring map of power, one in which the assumption of sovereignty remains secure.

If power is no longer constrained by models of sovereignty, if it emanates from any number of "centers," how are we to find the origin and cause of that act of power by which injury is done? The constraints of legal language emerge to put an end to this particular historical anxiety, for the law requires that we resituate power in the language of injury, that we accord injury the status of an act and trace that act to the specific conduct of a subject. Thus, the law requires and facilitates a conceptualization of injury in relation to a culpable subject, resurrecting "the subject" (which could just as well be a corporate or group entity as an individual) in response to the demand to seek accountability for injury. Is such a location of the subject as the "origin" and "cause" of racist structures, much less of racist speech, justified?

Foucault argues that "sovereignty," as a dominant mode for thinking power, restricts our view of power to prevailing conceptions of the
subject, making us unable to think about the problem of domination.[8]
His view of domination, however, is in marked contrast with
Matsuda's: "domination" is not "that solid and global kind of domination that one person exercises over others, or one group over another,
but the manifold forms of domination that can be exercised within
society," (96) ones that require neither the sovereign representative of
the state, i.e., the king, nor his "subjects" as its sole or primary sites of
exercise. On the contrary, Foucault writes, "one should try to locate
power at the extreme of its exercise, where it is always less legal in
character" (97).[9] The subject, for Foucault, is precisely *not* the extreme
of power's exercise. In an anti-voluntarist account of power, Foucault
writes,

> the analysis [of power] should not attempt to consider power from
> its internal point of view and . . . should refrain from posing the
> labyrinthine and unanswerable question: 'Who then has power
> and what has he in mind? What is the aim of someone who pos-
> sesses power?' Instead, it is a case of studying power at the point
> where its intention, if it has one, is completely invested in its real
> and effective practices.(97)

/ 79

This shift from the subject of power to a set of practices in which
power is actualized in its effects signals, for Foucault, a departure from
the conceptual model of sovereignty that, he claims, dominates thinking on politics, law, and the question of right. Among the very practices that Foucault counters to that of the subject are those that seek to
account for the formation of the subject itself: "let us ask . . . how things
work at the level of on-going subjugation, at the level of those continuous and uninterrupted processes which subject our bodies, govern our
gestures, dictate our behaviours, etc. . . . we should try to discover how
it is that subjects are gradually, progressively, really and materially constituted through a multiplicity of organisms, forces, energies, materials,
desires, thoughts, etc. We should try *to grasp subjection in its material instance as a constitution of subjects*" (97, emphasis mine).

When the scene of racism is reduced to a single speaker and his or

her audience, the political problem is cast as the tracing of the harm as it travels from the speaker to the psychic/somatic constitution of the one who hears the term or to whom it is directed. The elaborate institutional structures of racism as well as sexism are suddenly reduced to the scene of utterance, and utterance, no longer the sedimentation of prior institution and use, is invested with the power to establish and maintain the subordination of the group addressed. Does this theoretical move not constitute an overdetermination of the scene of utterance, one in which the injuries of racism become reducible to the injuries produced in language?[10] And does this not lead to a view of the power of the subject who speaks and, hence, of his/her culpability, in which the subject is prematurely identified as the "cause" of the problem of racism?

By locating the cause of our injury in a speaking subject and the power of that injury in the power of speech, we set ourselves free, as it were, to seek recourse to the law—now set against power and imagined as neutral—in order to control that onslaught of hateful words. This phantasmatic production of the culpable speaking subject, spawned from the constraints of legal language, casts subjects as the only agents of power. Such a reduction of the agency of power to the actions of the subject may well seek to compensate for the difficulties and anxieties produced in the course of living in a contemporary cultural predicament in which neither the law nor hate speech are uttered exclusively by a singular subject. The racial slur is always cited from elsewhere, and in the speaking of it, one chimes in with a chorus of racists, producing at that moment the linguistic occasion for an imagined relation to an historically transmitted community of racists. In this sense, racist speech does not originate with the subject, even if it requires the subject for its efficacy, as it surely does. Indeed, racist speech could not act as racist speech if it were not *a citation of itself*; only because we already know its force from its prior instances do we know it to be so offensive now, and we brace ourselves against its future invocations. The iterability of hate speech is effectively dissimulated by the "subject" who speaks the speech of hate.

To the extent that the speaker of hate speech is understood to effect the subordinating message that he or she relays, that speaker is

figured as wielding the sovereign power to do what he or she says, one for whom speaking is immediately acting. Examples of such illocutionary performatives in J. L. Austin's *How to Do Things With Words* are very often culled from legal instances: "I sentence you," "I pronounce you": these are words of the state that perform the very action that they enunciate. As a sign of a certain displacement from the law, this very performative power is attributed now to the one who utters hate speech—thus constituting his or her agency, efficaciousness, and likelihood of being prosecuted. The one who speaks hate speech exercises a performative in which subordination is effected, however "masquerading"[11] that performative may be. As a performative, hate speech also deprives the one addressed of precisely *this* performative power, a performative power that some see as a linguistic condition of citizenship. The ability to use words efficaciously in this way is considered to be the necessary condition for the normative operation of the speaker and the political actor in the public domain.

But what kind of speech is attributed to the citizen in such a view, and how does such an account draw the line between the performativity that is hate speech and the performativity that is the linguistic condition of citizenship? If hate speech is a kind of speech that no citizen ought to exercise, then how might its power be specified, if it can be? And how are both the proper speech of citizens and the improper hate speech of citizens to be distinguished from yet a third level of performative power, that which belongs to the state? / 81

This last seems crucial to interrogate if only because hate speech is itself described through the sovereign trope derived from state discourse (and discourse on the state). Figuring hate speech as an exercise of sovereign power implicitly performs a catachresis by which the one who is charged with breaking the law (the one who utters hate speech) is nevertheless invested with the sovereign power of law. What the law says, it does, but so, too, the speaker of hate. The performative power of hate speech is figured as the performative power of state-sanctioned legal language, and the contest between hate speech and the law becomes staged, paradoxically, as a battle between two sovereign powers.

Does the one who "utters" hate speech act like the law in the sense

that one has the power to make happen what one says (as a judge backed by law in a relatively stable political order has the power to do); and do we attribute to the illocutionary force of that utterance imaginary state power, backed by the police?

This idealization of the speech act as sovereign action (whether positive or negative) appears linked with the idealization of sovereign state power or, rather, with the imagined and forceful voice of that power. It is as if the proper power of the state has been expropriated, delegated to its citizens, and the state then reemerges as a neutral instrument to which we seek recourse to protect us from other citizens, who have become revived emblems of a (lost) sovereign power.

MACKINNON AND THE LOGIC OF THE PORNOGRAPHIC UTTERANCE

MacKinnon's recent arguments are as compelling as they are problematic. The class of people, mainly women, who are subordinated and degraded through their depiction in pornography, the class to whom pornography addresses its imperative of subordination, are the ones who lose their voice, as it were, as the consequence of having been addressed and discredited by the voice of pornography. Understood as hate speech, pornography deprives the addressee (the one depicted who is at once presumed to be the one to whom pornography is addressed) of the power to speak. The speech of the addressee is deprived of what Austin called its "illocutionary force." The speech of the addressee no longer has the power to do what it says, but always to do something other than what it says (a doing distinct from the doing that would be consonant with its saying) or to mean precisely the opposite of what it intends to mean.[12]

MacKinnon invokes Anita Hill to illustrate this expropriation and deformation of speech performed by pornography. The very act by which Anita Hill gave testimony, one intended to establish that an injury was done to her, was taken up by the Senate hearings—itself a pornographic scene—as a confession of her shame and, hence, her guilt. In that reappropriative reception by which testimony is taken as confession, the speaker's words are no longer taken as communicating or performing what they appear to be doing (exemplifying the illocution-

ary force of utterance); they are, rather, a display or enactment of sexual guilt. As Hill utters the sexualized discourse, she is sexualized by it,
and that very sexualization undercuts her effort to represent sexualization itself as a kind of injury. After all, in speaking it, she assumes it,
furthers it, produces it; her speaking appears as an active appropriation
of the sexualization she seeks to counter. Within pornography, there is
no countering of this sexualization without having that very countering become a sexualized act. The pornographic is marked precisely by
this power of sexual appropriation.

Yet MacKinnon uses Hill as the "example" of such sexualization
without considering the relation between racialization and exemplification. In other words, it is not only that Hill is doubly oppressed,
as African-American and as a woman, but that race becomes a way to
represent sexuality pornographically. Just as the racialized scene of
Thomas and Hill allows for the externalization of sexual degradation,
so it permits for a purification in prurience for the white imaginary.
African-American status permits for a spectacularization of sexuality
and a recasting of whites as outside the fray, witnesses and watchers   / 83
who have circuited their own sexual anxieties through the publicized
bodies of blacks.

Pornography almost always works through inversions of various
sorts, but these inversions have a life and power that exceeds the domain of the pornographic. Consider, then, that in the account of Mac-
Kinnon's view I have just rendered—which I hope is a fair one—the
problem with pornography is precisely that it *recontextualizes* the intended meaning of an act of speech, where that act of speech intends a
"no"—or is figured as intending a "no"—and that recontextualization
takes the specific form of a *reversal* in which the "no" is taken as, read
as, a "yes." The resistance to sexuality is thus refigured as the peculiar
venue for its affirmation and recirculation.

This very sexualization takes place in and as the act of speech. In
speaking, Hill displays her agency; in speaking of sexuality, she displays
her sexual agency; hence, any claim made against the sexualization of
discourse from that position of the active sexualization of discourse is
rhetorically refuted by the act of speech itself or, rather, by the act-like
character of speech and the fictive "agency" presumed at work in the

act of speaking. This is what some would call a performative contradiction: an act of speech that in its very acting produces a meaning that undercuts the one it purports to make. To the extent that she speaks, she displays her agency, for speech is taken to be a sign of agency, and the notion that we might speak, utter words, without voluntary intention (much less *unconsciously*) is regularly foreclosed by this construal of pornography. Paradoxically, the problem with the pornographic construal of her speech is that it sets her words against her intentions, and so presumes that the two are not only severable, but able to be posed against one another. Precisely through this display of linguistic agency, her meaning becomes reversed and discounted. The more she speaks, the less she is believed, the less her meaning is taken to be the one she intends. But this remains true only as long as the meaning she intends is consonant with the sexualization of her utterance, and the one she does not intend is in opposition to that very sexualization.

This pornographic recontextualization of Anita Hill's act of speech is taken by MacKinnon to be paradigmatic of the kind of reversal of meanings that pornography systematically performs. And, for MacKinnon, this power of pornographic recontextualization means that whenever a woman says "no" within a pornographic context, that "no" is presumed to be a "yes." Pornography, like the Freudian unconscious, knows no negation. This account of the "structure" of pornography, however, cannot account for the context of Hill's speech act; it is not regarded as communicative, but a racialized sexual spectacle. She is the "example" of pornography because, as black, she becomes the spectacle for the projection and living out of white sexual anxiety.

But MacKinnon's concern is of another order. She presupposes that one ought to be in a position to utter words in such a way that the meaning of those words coincides with the intention with which they are uttered, and that the performative dimension of that uttering works to support and further that intended meaning. Hence, one of the problems with pornography is that it creates a scene in which the performative dimension of discourse runs counter to its semantic or communicative functioning. Presupposed by this conception of the utterance is a normative view of a person with the ability and power to exercise speech in a straightforward way; this view is elaborated by the

philosopher Rae Langton in an essay that seeks to give logical force to MacKinnon's largely rhetorical claims.[13] This power to exercise speech such that the performance and the reception are governed and reconciled by a single and controlling intention is conceived by Langton as essential to the operation and agency of a rights-bearing person, one who is socially capable of exercising fundamental rights and liberties such as those guaranteed under the Equal Protection Clause of the Fourteenth Amendment.

Significantly and paradoxically, the argument against pornography seeks to limit the first Amendment rights of pornographers but also to expand the sphere of first Amendment protection for those depicted and (hence, ostensibly) "addressed" by pornography: pornographic representation discredits and degrades those whom it depicts—mainly women—such that the effect of that degradation is to cast doubt on whether the speech uttered by those depicted can ever be taken to mean what it says. In other words, just as Hill's testimony was converted within the Senate chambers into a confession of her complicity or, indeed, her powers of sexual fantasy, so the speech of the class of persons depicted by pornography, namely women, is converted into its opposite; it is speech that means one thing even as it intends to mean another, or it is speech that knows not what it means, or it is speech as display, confession, and evidence, but not as communicative vehicle, having been deprived of its capacity to make truthful claims. Indeed, the act of speech, though it signifies agency, undoes itself precisely because it does not say what it means; the act of speech implicates an always already active and choosing being, indeed, a consenting subject whose "no" is always undercut by her implied "yes." Although this attribution of a reversed intention effectively violates the sovereignty of the speaking subject, it seems equally true that this account of pornography also exploits a certain notion of liberal sovereignty to further its own aims, insisting that consent always and only constitutes the subject.

This critique of the effect of pornography on speech, of how, in particular, it may be said to *silence* speech, is motivated by an effort to reverse the threat to the sovereign performed by the pornographic depiction. As an effort to retether the utterance to the sovereign inten-

/ 85

tion, the antipornography stance opposes the state of disarray into which the utterance has apparently fallen: the utterance risks meaning in ways that are not intended or never intended; it becomes a sexualized act, evidencing itself as seduction (hence, as perlocutionary) rather than as truth-based (hence, as constative). (Pornography debases the utterance to the status of rhetoric, and exposes its limits as philosophy.)

CONTESTATIONS OF UNIVERSALITY

If pornography performs a deformation of speech, what is presumed to be the proper form of speech? What is the notion of nonpornographic speech that conditions this critique of pornography? Langton writes that "the ability to perform speech acts can be a measure of political power" (314) and of "authority" (315) and "one mark of powerlessness is an inability to perform speech acts that one might otherwise like to perform." (314) In having a speech act silenced, one cannot effectively use the performative. When the "no" is taken as "yes," the capacity to make use of the speech act is undermined. But what might guarantee a communicative situation in which no one's speech disables or silences another's speech in this way? This seems to be the very project in which Habermas and others are engaged—an effort to devise a communicative speech situation in which speech acts are grounded in consensus where no speech act is permissible that performatively refutes another's ability to consent through speech. Indeed, although neither Langton nor MacKinnon consults Habermas, their projects seem to be structured by similar cultural desires. The reversal or deformation of speech by pornography—as described by MacKinnon and Langton— would seem to be an example of precisely the kind of degraded speech situation that the Habermasian theory of speech seeks to criticize and invalidate.

The ideal of consent, however, makes sense only to the degree that the terms in question submit to a consensually established meaning. Terms that mean in equivocal ways are thus a threat to the ideal of consensus. Thus, Habermas insists that reaching consensus requires that words be correlated with univocal meanings: "the productivity of the process of understanding remains unproblematic only as long as all par-

ticipants stick to the reference point of possibly achieving a mutual understanding in which the *same* utterances are assigned the same meaning."[14] But are we, whoever "we" are, the kind of community in which such meanings could be established once and for all? Is there not a permanent diversity within the semantic field that constitutes an irreversible situation for political theorizing? Who stands above the interpretive fray in a position to "assign" the same utterances the same meanings? And why is it that the threat posed by such an authority is deemed less serious than the one posed by equivocal interpretation left unconstrained?

If utterances bear equivocal meanings, then their power is, in principle, less unilateral and sure than it appears. Indeed, the equivocity of the utterance means that it might not always mean in the same way, that its meaning might be turned or derailed in some significant way and, most importantly, that the very words that seek to injure might well miss their mark and produce an effect counter to the one intended. The disjuncture between utterance and meaning is the condition of possibility for revising the performative, of the performative as the repetition of its prior instance, a repetition that is at once a reformulation. Indeed, testimony would not be possible without *citing* the injury for which one seeks compensation. And Anita Hill's speech must recite the words spoken to her in order to display their injurious power. They are not originally "her" words, as it were, but their citation constitutes the condition of possibility for her agency in the law, even as, as we all saw in this case, they were taken up precisely to discount her agency. The citationality of the performative produces that possibility for agency and expropriation at the same time.

The political advantages to be derived from insisting on such a disjuncture are starkly different from those supposedly gained by following Habermas's notion of consensus. For if one always risks meaning something other than what one thinks one utters, then one is, as it were, vulnerable in a specifically linguistic sense to a social life of language that exceeds the purview of the subject who speaks. This risk and vulnerability are proper to democratic process in the sense that one cannot know in advance the meaning that the other will assign to one's utterance, what conflict of interpretation may well arise, and how best

/ 87

to adjudicate that difference. The effort to come to terms is not one that can be resolved in anticipation but only through a concrete struggle of translation, one whose success has no guarantees.

Habermas, however, insists that a guarantee might be found in the anticipation of consensus, that there are "idealizing suppositions" (198) that constrain in advance the kinds of interpretations to which utterances are subject: ". . . language games only work because they presuppose idealizations that transcend any particular language game; as a necessary condition of possibly reaching understanding, these idealizations give rise to the perspective of an agreement that is open to criticism on the basis of validity claims." (199) Matsuda's arguments appear to coincide with this view as well, since one of the arguments she makes against racist speech is that it implicitly makes a claim of racial inferiority rejected and invalidated by the international community. Hence, there is no reason for the Constitution to protect such speech, given that such speech conflicts with the commitments to universal equality that are fundamental to the Constitution. In arguing to "protect" such expressions, the judicial representatives of the Constitution would be working against one of the fundamental tenets of that founding text.

This last claim is significant, for more is at stake than might appear. According to this view, not only does racist speech contradict the universalist premise of the Constitution, but any speech that actively contests the founding premise of the Constitution ought not for that reason to be protected by the Constitution. To protect such speech would be to engage in a performative contradiction. Implicit to this argument is the claim that the only speech that ought to be protected by the Constitution is speech grounded in its universalist premises.

Taken as a positive criterion for establishing protected speech, this last is a controversial and ambitious claim. The domain of speakability is to be governed by prevailing and accepted versions of universality. We are no longer considering what constitutes hate speech, but, rather, the broader category of what constitutes a reasonable criteria by which protected speech is to be distinguished from unprotected speech. Moreover, at stake in the delineation of protected speech is the question: What will constitute the domain of the legally and legitimately

speakable? Is the normative notion of legitimate speech presupposed by Matsuda's analysis one in which any speaker is constrained by *existing* notions of universality? How would we reconcile such a view with that of Etienne Balibar, for instance, who argues that racism informs our current notions of universality?[15] How might we continue to insist upon more expansive reformulations of universality, if we commit ourselves to honoring only the provisional and parochial versions of universality currently encoded in international law? Clearly, such precedents are enormously useful for political arguments in international contexts, but it would be a mistake to think that such already established formulations exhaust the possibilities of what might be meant by the universal. To say that a convention of consensus has been achieved is not to acknowledge that the temporal life of convention exceeds its past. Are we to expect that we will know in advance the meaning to be assigned to the utterance of universality, or is this utterance the occasion for a meaning that is not to be fully or concretely anticipated?

Indeed, it seems important to consider that standards of universality are historically articulated and that exposing the parochial and exclusionary character of a given historical articulation of universality is part of the project of extending and rendering substantive the notion of universality itself. Racist speech, to be sure, contests current standards governing the universal reach of political enfranchisement. But there are other sorts of speech that constitute valuable contestations crucial to the continuing elaboration of the universal itself, and it would be a mistake to foreclose them. Consider, for example, that situation in which subjects who have been excluded from enfranchisement by existing conventions governing the exclusionary definition of the universal seize the language of enfranchisement and set into motion a "performative contradiction," claiming to be covered by that universal, thereby exposing the contradictory character of previous conventional formulations of the universal. This kind of speech appears at first to be impossible or contradictory, but it constitutes one way to expose the limits of current notions of universality, and to constitute a challenge to those existing standards to become more expansive and inclusive. In this sense, being able to utter the performative contradiction is hardly a self-defeating enterprise; on the contrary, performative contradiction is

crucial to the continuing revision and elaboration of historical standards of universality proper to the futural movement of democracy itself. To claim that the universal has not yet been articulated is to insist
that the "not yet" is proper to an understanding of the universal itself:
that which remains "unrealized" by the universal constitutes it essentially. The universal begins to become articulated precisely through
challenges to its *existing* formulation, and this challenge emerges from
those who are not covered by it, who have no entitlement to occupy
the place of the "who," but who, nevertheless, demand that the universal as such ought to be inclusive of them. The excluded, in this sense,
constitute the contingent limit of universalization. And the "universal,"
far from being commensurate with its conventional formulation,
emerges as a postulated and open-ended *ideal* that has not been adequately encoded by any given set of legal conventions.[16] If existing and
accepted conventions of universality *constrain* the domain of the speakable, this constraint produces the speakable, marking a border of demarcation between the speakable and the unspeakable.

90 /   The border that produces the speakable by excluding certain
forms of speech becomes an operation of censorship exercised by the
very postulation of the universal. Does every postulation of the universal as an existent, as a given, not codify the exclusions by which that
postulation of universality proceeds? In this instance and through this
strategy of relying on *established conventions of universality*, do we unwittingly stall the process of universalization within the bounds of established convention, naturalizing its exclusions, and preempting the possibility of its radicalization? The universal can only be articulated in
response to a challenge from (its own) outside. As we call for the regulation of injurious speech on the basis of "universally" accepted presuppositions, do we reiterate practices of exclusion and abjection? What
constitutes the community that might qualify as a legitimate community that debates and agrees upon this universality? If that very community is constituted through racist exclusions, how shall we trust it to
deliberate on the question of racist speech?

At stake in this definition of universality is the distinction between
an idealizing supposition of consensus that is in some ways already
there and one that is yet to be articulated, defying the conventions that

govern our anticipatory imaginings. This last is something other than a nonconventional idealization (Habermas) conceived as always already there, or as one encoded in given international law (Matsuda) and thus equating present and ultimate accomplishments. The anticipated universality, for which we have no ready concept, is one whose articulations will only follow, if they do, from a contestation of universality at its already imagined borders.

The notion of "consensus" presupposed by either of the first two views proves to be a prelapsarian contention, one which short-circuits the necessarily difficult task of forging a universal consensus from various locations of culture, to borrow Homi Bhabha's title and phrase, and the difficult practice of translation among the various languages in which universality makes its varied and contending appearances. The task of cultural translation is one that is necessitated precisely by that performative contradiction that takes place when one with no authorization to speak within and as the universal nevertheless lays claim to the term. Or, perhaps more appropriately phrased, one who is excluded from the universal, and yet belongs to it nevertheless, speaks from a split situation of being at once authorized and deauthorized (so much for delineating a neat "site of enunciation"). That speaking is not a simple assimilation to an existing norm, for that norm is predicated on the exclusion of the one who speaks, and whose speech calls into question the foundation of the universal itself. Speaking and exposing the alterity within the norm (the alterity without which the norm would not "know itself") exposes the failure of the norm to effect the universal reach for which it stands, exposes what we might underscore as *the promising ambivalence of the norm.*

/91

The failure of the norm is exposed by the performative contradiction enacted by one who speaks in its name even as the name is not yet said to designate the one who nevertheless insinuates his or her way into the name enough to speak "in" it all the same. Such double-speaking is precisely the temporalized map of universality's future, the task of a postlapsarian translation whose future remains unpredictable. The contemporary scene of cultural translation emerges with the presupposition that the utterance does not have the same meaning everywhere, indeed, that the utterance has become a scene of conflict (to

such a degree, in fact, that we seek to prosecute the utterance in order, finally, to "fix" its meaning). The translation that takes place at this scene of conflict is one in which the meaning intended is no more determinative of a "final" reading than the one that is received, and no final adjudication of conflicting positions can emerge. That lack of finality is precisely the interpretive dilemma to be valued, for it suspends the need for final judgment in favor of an affirmation of a certain linguistic vulnerability to reappropriation. This vulnerability marks the way that a postsovereign democratic demand makes itself felt in the contemporary scene of the utterance.[17]

The argument that seeks to regulate hate speech on the grounds that it contradicts both the *sovereign* status of the speaker (MacKinnon's argument concerning the effect of pornography) or the *universal* basis for its speech (Matsuda's argument) attempts to revitalize the ideal of a sovereign speaker who not only says what he means, but whose utterance is singular and universal at once. The normative conception of the political speaker, as outlined in Langton's essay, and the objection to the "silencing" effects of hate speech and pornography, as argued by MacKinnon and Matsuda, both contend that political participation requires the ability not only to represent one's intention in speech but to actualize one's intention through the act of speech.

The problem is not simply that, from a theoretical point of view, it makes no sense to assume that intentions are always properly materialized in utterances, and utterances materialized in deeds, but that the insight into those sometimes disjunctive relations constitutes an alternative view of the linguistic field of politics. Does the assertion of a potential incommensurability between intention and utterance (not saying what one means), utterance and action (not doing what one says), and intention and action (not doing what one meant), threaten the very linguistic condition for political participation, or do such disjunctures produce the possibility for a politically consequential renegotiation of language that exploits the undetermined character of these relations? Could the concept of universality become exposed to revision without the presumption of such a disjuncture?

Consider the situation in which racist speech is contested to the point that it does not have the power to effect the subordination that it

espouses and recommends; the undetermined relation between saying and doing is successfully exploited in depriving the saying of its projected performative power. And if that same speech is taken up by the one to whom it is addressed, and turned, becoming the occasion of a speaking back and a speaking through, is that racist speech, to some extent, unmoored from its racist origins? The effort to guarantee a kind of efficacious speaking in which intentions materialize in the deeds they have "in mind," and interpretations are controlled in advance by intention itself, constitutes a wishful effort to return to a sovereign picture of language that is no longer true, and that might never have been true, one that, for political reasons, one might rejoice over not being true. That the utterance can be turned, untethered from its origin, is one way to shift the locus of authority in relation to the utterance. And though we might lament that others have this power with our language, consider the perils of not having that power of interruption and redirection with respect to others. The recent appropriation of "civil rights" discourse to oppose affirmative action in California is such a perilous expropriation, one which can only now be countered by an / 93 aggressive reappropriation.

I am not arguing that one always says what one does not mean, that saying defeats meaning, or that words never perform what they claim to perform. Rendering such a disjuncture necessary to all speech is as suspect as legislating lines of necessary continuity among intention, utterance, and deed. Although Langton presupposes that political agency and citizenship in particular requires such a continuity, contemporary forms of political agency, especially those unauthorized by prior conventions or by reigning prerogatives of citizenship, tend to derive political agency from the failures in the performative apparatus of power, turning the universal against itself, redeploying equality against its existing formulations, retrieving freedom from its contemporary conservative valence.[18]

Is this political possibility for reappropriation distinguishable from pornographic appropriation opposed by MacKinnon? Or is the risk of appropriation one that accompanies all performative acts, marking the limits of the putative sovereignty of such acts? The Foucaultian argument is familiar: the more one insists that sexuality

is repressed, the more one speaks about sexuality, the more sexuality becomes a confessional sort of speech. Sexuality thus appropriates unexpected discourses. The repressive "no" traced by psychoanalytic doctrine is converted to a strange sort of "yes" (a thesis that is not inconsistent with psychoanalysis and with its insistence that there is no negation in the unconscious). On the surface, his account appears paradoxically similar to MacKinnon's, but where the "no" in her view is issued as a refusal to consent, for Foucault, it is performed by the repressive law against the sexual subject who, we are left to surmise, might otherwise say yes. For Foucault, as for pornography, the very terms by which sexuality is said to be negated become, inadvertently but inexorably, the site and instrument of a new sexualization. The putative repression of sexuality becomes the sexualization of repression.[19]

Recontextualizing the law—prohibition, in this case—occasions a reversal in which the sexuality prohibited becomes the sexuality produced. The discursive occasion for a prohibition—renunciation, interdiction, confession—become precisely the new incitement to sexuality, an incitement to discourse as well. That discourse itself proliferates as the repeated enunciation of the prohibitive law suggests that its productive power depends upon its break with an originating context and intention, and that its recirculation is not within the control of any given subject.

MacKinnon and Langton have both argued that the recontextualization of an utterance or, more specifically, a sexualized recontextualization in which an original "no" is reversed into a derivative "yes," constitutes the very silencing effects of pornography; the performance of an utterance within the pornographic context necessarily reverses in the direction of sexualization the very meaning that the utterance is said to communicate: this is the measure of the pornographic. Indeed, one might consider the uncontrollable effects of resignification and recontextualization, understood as the mundane appropriative work of sexuality, as continually inciting antipornographic agitation. For MacKinnon, the recontextualization takes the form of attributing falsely an assent to becoming sexualized to the one sexualized by a given depiction, the turning of a "no" into a "yes." The disjunctive re-

lation between affirmation and negation discounts the erotic logic of ambivalence in which the "yes" can accompany the "no" without exactly negating it. The domain of the phantasmatic is precisely *suspended* action, neither fully affirmed nor fully denied, and most often structured in some form of ambivalent pleasure ("yes" and "no" at once).

MacKinnon insists that a woman's "consent" is depicted by the pornographic text, and that depiction at once overrides her consent. This thesis is necessary to sustain and extend the analogy between the pornographic text and acts of harassment and rape. If, on the other hand, questions of consent and action are suspended through the pornographic text, then the text does not override consent, but produces a visual field of sexuality that is in some sense prior to consent and, indeed, prior to the constitution of the willing subject itself. As a cultural reserve of a sexually overdetermined visual field, the pornographic is precisely what circulates without our consent, but not for that reason against it. The insistence that consent precedes sexuality in all instances signals a return to a pre-Freudian notion of liberal individualism in which "consent" is constitutive of personhood.

For Anita Hill to make her claim against Thomas and against the Senate hearings, she will have to testify again, and that testimony will have to repeat the injury, record it, say it again, and thus open itself to a misappropriation. To distinguish the testimony from the events it records, one would have to mark off the repetition of injury that testimony performs from the performance of injury to which it refers. But if testimony must repeat the injury to make its claim, and that repetition is taken as a sign of agency, then the misconstrual of testimony as a confession of complicity appears to be a risk that no amount of marking off can safeguard against.

More generally, the circulation of the pornographic resists the possibility of being effectively patrolled, and if it could be, the mechanism of patrol would simply become incorporated into a pornographic thematic as one of its more savory plots concerning the law and its transgression. The effort to stop such a circulation is an effort to stop the sexualized field of discourse, and to reassert the capacity of the intentional subject over and against this field.

STATE SPEECH/HATE SPEECH

Hate speech is a kind of speech that acts, but it is also *referred* to as a kind of speech that acts and, hence, as an item and object of discourse. Although hate speech may be a saying that is a kind of doing or a kind of conduct, it can be established as such only through a language that authoritatively describes this doing for us; thus, the speech act is always delivered twice-removed, that is, through *a theory of the speech act* that has its own performative power (and that is, by definition, in the business of *producing* speech acts, thus redoubling the performativity it seeks to analyze). The description of this act of speech is a doing or a kind of conduct of an equally discursive and equally consequential kind. This is, I think, made nowhere more clearly than in the consideration of how the judgement as legal utterance determines hate speech in highly specific ways.

Considered as discriminatory action, hate speech is a matter for the courts to decide, and so "hate speech" is not deemed hateful or discriminatory until the courts decide that it is. There is no hate speech in the full sense of that term until and unless there is a court that decides that there is.[20] Indeed, the petition to call something hate speech, and to argue that it is also conduct, efficacious in its effects, consequentially and significantly privative of rights and liberties, is not yet to have made the case. The case is made only when it is "decided." In this sense, it is the decision of the state, the sanctioned utterance of the state, which produces the act of hate speech—produces, but does not cause. Here the temporal relation in which the utterance of hate speech precedes the utterance of the court is precisely the reverse of the logical relation in which there is no hate speech prior to the decision of the court. Although the hate speech which is not yet hate speech precedes the judicial consideration of that utterance, it is only upon the affirmative decision of the court that the speech in question becomes hate speech. The adjudication of hate speech is thus a matter for the state or, more particularly, its judiciary branch. A determination made by the state, hate speech becomes a determination made by yet another "act of speech"—the speech of the law. This odd dependency of the very existence of the hateful utterance on the voice-over of the court means that

the hateful utterance is not finally distinguishable from the speech of the state by which it is decided.

I am *not* trying to claim that the speech of the state in the moment of decision is *the same as* the racial or sexual slur it seeks to adjudicate. I am suggesting, however, that they are indissociable in a specific and consequential way. Consider as misnomer the claim that an instance of hate speech is submitted to the court for adjudication, since what is at stake in such an adjudication is whether the speech in question is hateful. And here I don't mean hateful in any sense, but in the legally precise senses which Matsuda, Delgado, and Lawrence explicate. The process of adjudication—which presumes that the injury precedes the judgment of the court—is an effect of that judgment, a production of that judgment. Thus hate speech is produced by the law, and constitutes one of its most savory productions; it becomes the legal instrument through which to produce and further a discourse on race and sexuality under the rubric of combatting racism and sexism. By such a formulation, I do not mean to suggest that the law causes or incites hate speech, but only that the decision to select which of the various acts of speech will be covered under the rubric of hate speech will be decided by the courts. Thus, the rubric is a legal norm to be augmented or restricted by the judiciary in the ways that it deems fit.

This last impresses me as particularly important considering that hate speech arguments have been invoked against minority groups, that is, in those contexts in which homosexuality is rendered graphic (Mapplethorpe) or verbally explicit (the U.S. military) and those in which African-American vernacular, especially in rap music, recirculates the terms of social injury and is thereby held responsible for such terms. Those efforts at regulation are inadvertently strengthened by the enhanced power of the state to enforce the distinction between publicly protected and unprotected speech. Thus Justice Scalia asked in *R.A.V. v. St. Paul* whether a burning cross, though "reprehensible," may not be communicating a message that is protected within the free marketplace of ideas. In each of these cases, the state not only constrains speech, but in the very act of constraining, produces legally consequential speech: not only does the state curb homosexual speech, but produces as well—through its decisions—a public notion of the self-cen-

/ 97

soring homosexual; similarly, it produces a public picture of an obscene black sexuality, even as it claims to be curbing obscenity; and it produces the burning cross as an emblem of intelligible and protected speech.

The state's exercise of this productive discursive function is underestimated in the writings that favor of hate speech legislation. Indeed, they minimize the possibility of a misappropriation by the law in favor of a view of the law as politically neutral and malleable. Matsuda argues that law, though formed in racism, can be redirected against racism. She figures the law as a set of "ratchet" tools, describing it in purely instrumental terms, and discounting the productive misappropriations by which it proceeds. This view invests all power and agency in the subject who would use such an instrument. However reactionary its history, this instrument can be put in the service of a progressive vision, thus "defying the habit of neutral principles to entrench existing power." Later she writes: "nothing inherent in law ties our hands," (50) approving of a method of doctrinal *reconstruction*. In other words, legal language is precisely the kind of language that can be cited into a reverse meaning, where the reversal takes a law with a reactionary history and turns it into a law with a progressive aim.

There are at least two remarks to be made about this faith in the resignifying capacities of legal discourse. First, the kind of citational reversal that the law is said to perform is exactly the opposite of the citational reversal attributed to pornography. The reconstructive doctrine allows the once reactionary legal apparatus to become progressive, regardless of the originating intentions that animate the law. Pornography's insistence on recontextualizing the original or intended meaning of an utterance is supposed to be its pernicious power. And yet, even MacKinnon's act of advocacy in which she represents a woman's "yes" and "no" depends upon a recontextualization and a textual violence of sorts, one that Matsuda, in the case of the law, elevates to the level of legal method under the rubric of doctrinal reconstruction. In both cases, the utterance is uncontrollable, appropriable, and able to signify otherwise and in excess of its animating intentions.

The second point is this: although the law, however reactionary its formation, is understood as a resignifying practice, hate speech,

however reactionary its formation, is not deemed to be susceptible to a significant resignification in the same way. This is the unlucky moment in which the willingness of the courts to discount the literary value of "signifying" as it operates in rap converges with the claim made by the proponents of hate speech regulation that hate speech *cannot* be resignified. Although Matsuda makes an exception for "satire and stereotyping," this exception holds only to the extent that such utterances do not make use of "persecutory language." It would be difficult to understand how satire works if it did not recontextualize persecutory language.

The defusing power of this kind of resignification of hate speech, however, appears to have no place within Matsuda's view. And yet, the speech of the law is considered to be resignifiable beyond any limit: the law has no single or essential meaning; it can be redirected, reserviced, and reconstructed; its language, though harmful in some contexts, is not necessarily harmful, and can be turned and redirected in the service of progressive politics. Hate speech, however, is not recontextualizable or open to a resignification in the way that legal language is. Indeed, although all sorts of historically and potentially injurious words are recirculated in rap, in film, even as calligrammatic emblems in photography and painting, it seems that such recontextualizations are not to be construed as aesthetic reenactments worthy of legal protection.

An aesthetic enactment of an injurious word may both *use* the word and *mention* it, that is, make use of it to produce certain effects but also at the same time make reference to that very use, calling attention to it as a citation, situating that use within a citational legacy, making that use into an explicit discursive item to be reflected on rather than a taken for granted operation of ordinary language. Or, it may be that an aesthetic reenactment *uses* that word, but also *displays* it, points to it, outlines it as the arbitrary material instance of language that is exploited to produce certain kinds of effects. In this sense, the word as a material signifier is foregrounded as semantically empty in itself, but as that empty moment in language that can become the site of semantically compounded legacy and effect. This is not to say that the word loses its power to injure, but that we are given the word in such a way

that we can begin to ask: how does a word become the site for the power to injure? Such use renders the term as a textual object to be thought about and read, even as it also implicates us in a relation of knowingness about its conventional force and meaning. The aggressive reappropriation of injurious speech in the rap of, say, Ice T becomes a site for a traumatic reenactment of injury, but one in which the terms not only mean or communicate in a conventional way, but are themselves set forth as discursive items, in their very linguistic conventionality and, hence, as both forceful and arbitrary, recalcitrant and open to reuse.

This view, however, would be strongly countered, I think, by some who favor hate speech regulation and argue that recontextualization and the reversal of meaning is limited when it comes to certain words. Richard Delgado writes, "Words such as 'nigger' and 'spick' are badges of degradation even when used between friends: *these words have no other connotation.*" And yet, this very statement, whether written in his text or cited here, has another connotation; he has just used the word in a significantly different way. Even if we concede—as I think we must—that the injurious connotation is inevitably *retained* in Delgado's use, indeed, that it is difficult to utter those words or, indeed, to write them here, because they unwittingly recirculate that degradation, it does not follow that such words can have *no other connotation.* Indeed, their repetition is necessary (in court, as testimony; in psychoanalysis, as traumatic emblems; in aesthetic modes, as a cultural working-through) in order to enter them as objects of another discourse. Paradoxically, their status as "act" is precisely what undermines the claim that they evidence and actualize the degradation that they intend. As acts, these words become phenomenal; they become a kind of linguistic display that does not overcome their degrading meanings, but that reproduces them as public text and that, in being reproduced, displays them as reproducible and resignifiable terms. The possibility of decontextualizing and recontextualizing such terms through radical acts of public misappropriation constitutes the basis of an ironic hopefulness that the conventional relation between word and wound might become tenuous and even broken over time. Such words do wound,

and yet, as even Derrick Bell has remarked: "racist structures are vulnerable." I take this to apply to racist linguistic structures as well.

I do not mean to subscribe to a simple opposition between the aesthetic and juridical domains, for what is at stake in many of these controversies is precisely the power of the state to define what will count as aesthetic representation. The aesthetic sphere, considered as "protected," still exists as a dispensation of the state. The legal domain of the state clearly has its own "aesthetic" moments as well, some of which we have considered here: dramatic rearticulation and reenactment, the production of sovereign speech, the replaying of phantasmatic scenes.

When the task of reappropriation, however, is taken up within the domain of protected public discourse, the consequences seem more promising and more democratic than when the task of adjudicating the injury of speech is given over to the law. The state resignifies only and always its own law, and that resignification constitutes an extension of its jurisdiction and its discourse. Consider that hate speech is not only a production of the state, as I have tried to argue, but that the very intentions that animate the legislation are inevitably misappropriated by the state. To give the task of adjudicating hate speech to the state is to give that task of misappropriation to the state. It will not simply be a legal discourse on racial and sexual slurring, but it will also reiterate and restage those slurs, reproduce them this time as state-sanctioned speech. Given that the state retains the power to create and maintain certain forms of injurious speech as its own, the political neutrality of legal language is highly dubious.

/ 101

Hate speech regulations that are not state-centered, such as those that have restricted jurisdiction within a university, for instance, are clearly less worrisome in this regard. But here I would suggest that such regulations must remain restricted to hate speech as a perlocutionary scene, that is, one in which the effects of such speech must be shown, in which the burden of evidence must be assumed. If certain kinds of verbal conduct on the part of a professor undermine a student's capacity to work, then it seems crucial to show a pattern of verbal conduct and make a persuasive case that such conduct has had the debilitating effects on the student that it has. If we accept that hate speech is il-

locutionary, we accept as well that words perform injury immediately and automatically, that the social map of power makes it so, and we are under no obligation to detail the concrete effects that hate speech does produce. The saying is not itself the doing, but it can lead to the doing of harm that must be countered. Maintaining the gap between saying and doing, no matter how difficult, means that there is always a story to tell about how and why speech does the harm that it does.

In this sense, I am not opposed to any and all regulations, but I am skeptical about the value of those accounts of hate speech that maintain its illocutionary status and thus conflate speech and conduct completely. But I do think that the ritual chain of hateful speech cannot be effectively countered by means of censorship. Hate speech is repeatable speech, and it will continue to repeat itself as long as it is hateful. Its hate is a function of its repeatability. Given that the slur is always cited from elsewhere, that it is taken up from already established linguistic conventions and reiterated and furthered in its contemporary invocations, the question will be whether the state or public discourse will take up that practice of reenactment. We are beginning to see how the state produces and reproduces hate speech, finding it in the homosexual utterance of identity and desire, in the graphic representation of sexuality, of sexual and bodily fluids, in the various graphic efforts to repeat and overcome the forces of sexual shame and racial degradation. That speech is a kind of act does not necessarily mean that it does what it says; it can mean that it displays or enacts what it says at the same time that it says it or, indeed, rather than saying it at all. The public display of injury is also a repetition, but it is not simply that, for what is displayed is never quite the same as what is meant, and in that lucky incommensurability resides the linguistic occasion for change. No one has ever worked through an injury without repeating it: its repetition is both the continuation of the trauma and that which marks a self-distance within the very structure of trauma, its constitutive possibility of being otherwise. There is no possibility of *not* repeating. The only question that remains is: How will that repetition occur, at what site, juridical or nonjuridical, and with what pain and promise?

3 / CONTAGIOUS WORD

PARANOIA AND "HOMOSEXUALITY" IN THE MILITARY

The question of whether citizenship requires the repression of homosexuality is not new, but the recent efforts to regulate the self-declaration of homosexuality within the military repose this question in a different light. After all, military personnel enjoy some of the rights and obligations of citizenship, but not all of them. The military is thus already a zone of partial citizenship, a domain in which selected features of citizenship are preserved, and others are suspended. Recent efforts of the U.S. military to impose sanctions on homosexual speech have undergone a series of revisions[1] and at the time of this writ-

ing, continue to be contested in court. In the first version of these regulations proposed by the Department of Defense, the term "homosexual" was disallowed as part of a self-ascription or self-definition on the part of military personnel. The term itself was not banished, but only its utterance within the context of self-definition. The very regulation in question, must utter the term in order to perform the circumscription of its usage. The occasion for the formulation of this regulation was, of course, one in which the term "homosexual" already proliferated in military, state, and media discourse. Thus, it is apparently not a problem, within the terms of the regulation, to utter the word: as a consequence of the regulation, in fact, it appears that public discourse on homosexuality has dramatically increased. Indeed, the regulations might be held accountable, paradoxically, for the appa-rent fact that the word has become more speakable rather than less. And yet the proliferation of public sites in which it has become speakable seems directly tied to the proposal to make it unspeakable in the military as a term that might be taken to describe oneself. The regulations propose the term as unspeakable within the context of self-definition, but they still can only do this by repeatedly proposing the term. Thus, the regulations bring the term into public discourse, rhetorically enunciating the term, performing the circumscription by which—and through which—the term becomes speakable. But the regulations insist as well that there are conditions under which the term is *not* to be insisted on at all, that is, in the service of self-definition. The regulation must conjure one who defines him or herself as a homosexual in order to make plain that no such self-definition is permissible within the military.

The regulation of the term is thus no simple act of censorship or silencing; on the contrary, the regulation redoubles the term it seeks to constrain, and can only effect this constraint through this paradoxical redoubling. The term not only appears in the regulation as that discourse to be regulated, but reappears in the public debate over its fairness and value, specifically as the conjured or imagined act of self-ascription that is explicitly prohibited by the regulation, a prohibition that cannot take place without a conjuring of the very act. We might conclude that the state and the military are merely concerned *to retain*

control over what the term will mean, the conditions under which it may be uttered by a speaking subject, restricting that speaking to precisely and exclusively those subjects who are not described by the term they utter. The term is to remain a term used to describe others, but the term is not to be used by those who might use it for the purposes of self-description; to describe oneself by the term is to be prohibited from its use, except in order to deny or qualify the description. The term "homosexual" thus comes to describe a class of persons who are to remain prohibited from defining themselves; the term is to be attributed always from elsewhere. And this is, in some ways, the very definition of the homosexual that the military and the Congress provide. A homosexual is one whose definition is to be left to others, one who is denied the act of self-definition with respect to his or her sexuality, one whose self-denial is a prerequisite for military service.

What could account for such a strange regulation of homosexual locution, one that seems bound to redouble the term at the site of its prohibition? How do we understand this simultaneous production and restriction of the term? What is it about the speaking of the term in the context of self-description that seems more threatening to military morale than the tacit operation of the sexual practice itself? /105

The military suspends certain rights for its own personnel that are accorded to civilians, but that very suspension offers an opportunity to interrogate what is perhaps most uneasily anchored in, and most easily jettisoned from, the zone of citizenship. In this sense, one might consider gays in the military as overlapping with other retractable zones of citizenship: recent immigration law and the suspended zone of citizenship for immigrants, the various degrees of suspension accorded to different immigrant statuses, not only legal and illegal, but degrees of legality as well. Such comparisons might well be considered in relation to Giorgio Agamben's recent thesis that the state itself has become a protracted "state of emergency," one in which the claims of citizenship are more or less permanently suspended.[2]

The revisions of the policy on gay speech in the military make clear how rights based on the first Amendment, privacy claims, or the Equal Protection Clause have been systematically suspended. Whereas

Clinton proposed that homosexuals ought only to be excluded from military service to the extent that they engaged in conduct, and not on the basis of their "status," it became clear in subsequent clarifications of the policy that stating that one is a homosexual, that is, making reference to one's status is reasonably construed as homosexual conduct itself. In the Department of Defense Policy, statements are themselves conduct: according to the more recent Congressional Statute, statements present evidence of a homosexual "propensity" that poses an unacceptable risk for the military.

It seems clear, as Janet Halley has shown, that arguments that seek to restrict the prosecution of homosexuality to either status or conduct are bound to produce ambiguities that threaten the coherence of either legal basis. In the most recent version of the policy, Halley argues, the question of whether a reasonable person would surmise that another person has a "propensity" to engage in homosexual conduct constitutes the standard by which interrogations proceed. Halley rightly points out that the "reasonable person" is, in this instance, the one who embodies homophobic cultural norms. I would add that this reasonable person is also pervasively paranoid, externalizing a homosexuality that "endangers" the reasonable person from within. It is no longer the case that a statement making reference to one's homosexuality is sufficient to infer the "propensity" to engage in homosexuality: there may be other "signs" —affiliations, gestures, nuances, all of which equally point in the same direction. The "propensity" clause appears to ascribe a natural teleology to homosexual status, whereby we are asked to understand such status as always almost culminating in an act. And yet, this "propensity," though attributed to homosexual status as its natural inclination to express itself, is attributed by the "reasonable" person, and thus remains a figment of the homophobic imaginary.

Although the military now suspects all kinds of signs as indices of "propensity," I will be concentrating on the view of explicit gay self-declaration that the military seeks to prevent, and which it takes to be equivalent to homosexual conduct itself.

The act by which the Department of Defense seeks to circumscribe this act of speech is one that depends on a fabrication of the

speech act to be constrained, one in which the fabrication already begins to perform the work of constraint.

In the recent military regulations on homosexual conduct, homosexual self-definition is explicitly construed as contagious and offensive conduct. The words, "I am a homosexual," do not merely describe; they are figured as performing what they describe, not only in the sense that they constitute the speaker as a homosexual, but that they constitute the speech as homosexual conduct. In what follows, I hope to show that the regulation describes as performative the self-ascription of homosexuality, doing precisely that which it says. In describing the power of such acts of utterance, the regulations produce such utterances for us, exercising a performativity that remains the tacit and enabling condition for the delineation of "I am a homosexual" as a performative utterance. Only within that regulatory discourse is the performative power of homosexual self-ascription performatively produced. In this sense, the regulations conjure the spectre of a performative homosexual utterance—an utterance that does the deed—that it seeks to censor, engaging in a circularity of fabrication and censorship that will be specified as paranoid.

/ 107

If, however, the military can be said to produce a paranoid construal of homosexual utterance as contagious and offensive action, as performing or constituting that to which such utterances refer, how is this attributed performativity to be distinguished from the kind of performativity that is explicitly owned by the movement to authorize greater homosexual publicity, the clear aim of queer politics? According to this latter movement, coming out and acting out are part of the cultural and political meaning of what it is to be homosexual; speaking one's desire, the public display of desire, is essential to the desire itself, the desire cannot be sustained without such speaking and display, and the discursive practice of homosexuality is indissociable from homosexuality itself.

Toward the end of this chapter, I will return to this issue, if only to pose the question of whether homosexuality is not the kind of term that constantly threatens—or promises—to become its own referent, that is, to constitute the very sexuality to which it refers. I hope to sug-

gest that the term cannot fully or exhaustively perform its referent, that no term can, and that "it's a good thing, too." The political benefits to be derived from this incommensurability between performativity and referentiality have to do with setting limits on authoritative constructions of homosexuality and keeping the signifiers of "homosexuality," "gayness," or "queerness," as well as host of related terms, alive for a future linguistic life. Over and against the commonly stated worry that if homosexuality has no referent, there can be no effective gay and lesbian politics, I would suggest that the absence of a final referent for the term keeps the term from ever being quite as performative as the military imagines that it is. The term gestures toward a referent it cannot capture. Moreover, that lack of capture constitutes the linguistic possibility of a radical democratic contestation, one that opens the term to future rearticulations.[3]

//

108 /   In what sense are the military regulations symptomatic of a paranoia that forms the possibility of military citizenship? The specific performativity attributed to homosexual utterance is not simply that the utterance performs the sexuality of which it speaks, but that it transmits sexuality through speech: the utterance is figured as a site of contagion, a figure that precipitates a return to Freud's *Totem and Taboo* in which the speaking of prohibited names becomes the occasion for an uncontrollable communication. Through recourse to Freud's view of conscience, in which the repression of male homosexuality becomes the prerequisite for constituting manhood, the analysis of the military regulations can be read as producing a notion of the "man" as a self-denying homosexual. Against a psychological reductionism that might locate military acts as acts of individual psyches, I propose to turn to psychoanalysis as a way of reading the text of a highly symptomatic regulation of military citizenship.[4]

Psychoanalysis not only sheds theoretical light on the tensions between homosexuality and citizenship, but psychoanalytic discourse is itself a textual allegory for how the production of the citizen takes place through the rejection and transmutation of an always imagined homo-

sexuality. Indeed, I hope to show that the peculiar form of imagining against oneself which is paranoia constitutes homosexuality not only as a form of inversion, but as the exemplary model for the action of conscience, the turning against oneself that involves the inversion and idealization of the sexual aim. In this sense, Freud's text proves to be as much diagnosis as symptom, and though I propose to read his text psychoanalytically (and, hence, not merely as the enunciation of psychoanalytic practice), I will also be proposing a way to read psychoanalysis allegorically.[5] What this means, more simply, is that Freud will appear to tell us a story about how citizenship and social feeling emerge from the sublimation of homosexuality, but his discourse will be, in the course of this narration, implicated in the very sublimation it describes.[6]

To understand the act of homosexual self-definition as an offense, it seems reasonable to ask, what set of relations or bonds are potentially offended or threatened by such an utterance? It makes sense to turn to Freud's text, "On the Mechanism of Paranoia," in which he links the suppression of homosexual drives to the production of social feeling. At the end of that essay, he remarks that "homosexual drives" help to constitute "the social instincts, thus contributing an erotic factor to friendship and comradeship, to *esprit de corps* and to the love of mankind in general." (31) And at the close of the essay "On Narcissism," he might be read as specifying the logic whereby this production of social feeling takes place. The "ego-ideal," he writes, has a social side: "it is also the common ideal of a family, a class or a nation. It not only binds the narcissistic libido, but also a considerable amount of the person's homosexual libido, which in this way becomes turned back into the ego. The dissatisfaction due to the non-fulfillment of the ideal liberates homosexual libido, which is transformed into sense of guilt (dread of the community)." (81) This transformation of homosexuality into guilt and, therefore, into the basis of social feeling, takes place when the fear of parental punishment becomes generalized as the dread of losing the love of fellow men. Paranoia is the way in which that love is consistently reimagined as always almost withdrawn, and it is, paradoxically, the fear of losing that love that motivates the sublimation or introversion of homosexuality. Indeed, this sublimation is not quite as instrumental as it may sound, for it is not that one disavows homosexuality in

order to gain the love of fellow men, but that it is precisely a certain homosexuality that can be achieved and contained only *through and as* this disavowal.

In Freud's discussion of the formation of conscience in *Civilization and its Discontents*, the very prohibition against homosexuality that conscience is said to enact or articulate is precisely what founds and constitutes conscience itself as a psychic phenomenon. The prohibition against the desire is the desire as it turns back upon itself, and this turning back upon itself becomes the very inception of what is later called "conscience." Hence, what the noun form of "conscience" suggests as a psychic entity, is nothing other than an habituated reflexive activity, the turning back upon oneself, a routing of desire against desire, such that the prohibition becomes the site and satisfaction of desire. That repeated practice of introversion constitutes the misnomer of "conscience" as a mental faculty.

The restrictions on homosexual self-definition suggest that the very circuit of self-prohibition necessary for the production and maintenance of social feeling can no longer be guaranteed by conscience, that conscience is no longer in the service of social regulation. If the military represents a fairly explicit extreme of this regulatory production of homoerotic sociality, it seems that this circuit by which homosexuality is enjoined to turn back on itself again and again has failed to close. This paradox was articulated perhaps most obviously in the claim that social cohesion in the military requires the prohibition on homosexuality, where that cohesion was then described as a magical *je ne sais quoi* that kept military men glued together. The formulation might read: *we must not have our homosexuality in order to have our homosexuality: please take it / don't take it away from us.*

The prohibition that seeks to restrict the outbreak of homosexuality from within this circle of collective introversion figures the very word as a contagious substance, a dangerous fluid. Contagion will be important here, as I will try to show, for homosexuality will be figured implicitly on the model of AIDS, and will be said to "communicate" along the lines of a disease.

The text is overtly one which seeks to regulate homosexual behav-

110 /

ior, but as regulatory, it is also incessantly productive. What is conjured in this text is a kind of homosexuality that acts through the magical efficacy of words: to declare that one is a homosexual becomes, within the terms of this law, not merely the representation of conduct, offensive conduct, but offensive conduct itself.

> Sexual orientation will not be a bar to service unless manifested by homosexual conduct. The military will discharge members who engage in homosexual conduct, which is defined as a homosexual act, a statement that the member is homosexual or bisexual, or a marriage or attempted marriage to someone of the same gender.[7]

The statement begins by making a distinction between orientation and conduct, restricting the military to discharging only those who engage in homosexual conduct. But then homosexual conduct is defined through a set of appositions which, rather than delimit the barriers of homosexual conduct, proliferate the possibilities of homosexuality. Homosexual conduct includes "a homosexual act"—even in the singular, which is to say that it is not yet a practice, a repeated or ritual affair. And though subsequent clarifications have made clear that a one-time act, if disavowed as a mistake, will be pardoned, the language of the policy maintains the one-time requirement, insisting on a conflation of "act" and "conduct." What is perhaps more properly an *inflation* of act *into* conduct is significant, for it tacitly and actively imagines the singularity of the event as a series of events, a regular practice, and so imagines a certain force of homosexuality to drive the one-time practitioner into a compulsive or regular repetition. If the act is already conduct, then it has repeated itself before it has any chance to repeat; it is, as it were, always already repeating, a figure for a repetition—compulsion with the force to undermine all sorts of social morale.

Let us return to the phrasing in order to read this passage as an articulation of a homophobic phantasmatic:

The military will discharge members who engage in homosexual

/ 111

conduct, which is defined as a homosexual act, a statement that the member is homosexual or bisexual, or a marriage or attempted marriage to someone of the same gender.

Homosexual conduct, defined as "a statement that the member is homosexual or bisexual"; in this definition the "statement" is a form of "conduct," and new meaning is given to MacKinnon's reference to "only words." If the statement is conduct, and it is homosexual conduct, then the statement that one is a homosexual is construed as acting homosexually on the person to whom or before whom it is uttered. The statement is in some sense not only an act, but a form of conduct, a ritualistic form of speech that wields the power to *be* what it *says*, not a re-presentation of a homosexuality, but a homosexual act and, hence, an offense. Under what conditions does an utterance that represents a disposition or a practice become that very disposition and practice, a becoming, a transitivity, that depends on and institutes the collapse of the distinction between speech and conduct? This is not to say that an absolute distinction between speech and conduct might be drawn. On the contrary, that a statement is a kind of act, a speech act, is true enough, but that is not the same as claiming that the statement perforce enacts what it says or constitutes the referent to which it refers. Many speech acts are "conduct" in a narrow sense, but not all of them are felicitous in the sense that Austin maintains. That is, not all of these acts have the power to produce effects or initiate a set of consequences.

The utterance which claims or proclaims homosexual identity is construed as offensive conduct only if we concede that something about the very speaking of homosexuality in the context of self-definition is disruptive. But what gives such words the disruptive power they are presumed to wield? Does such a presumption not imply that the one who hears the utterance imagines him/herself to be solicited by the statement? In a sense, the reception traces the Foucaultian formulation in reverse: if Foucault thought that there were first homosexual "acts" and only later did homosexuality emerge as an "identity," then the military takes every ascription of identity as equivalent to the doing of an act. It is important to distinguish, however, between two ways of rethinking identity as act: where one might say

that what I mean by saying that "I am a homosexual" is that "I perform homosexual acts, or engage in homosexual practices or relationships," I would still be referring to those acts, but not, strictly speaking, performing them and certainly not performing them through the act of speaking. The military reading of the claim, however, appears to be of another order. That reading takes the claim, "I am a homosexual" to be one of the very acts of homosexuality, not a reporting on the happening of acts, but the discursive happening of the act itself.

In what sense is the act "conduct"? Surely, one might claim that any locution is "conduct", and Austin concedes that all utterance is in some sense an "act." But even if every utterance can be construed as an act, it does not follow that all utterance *acts upon* its listener in a prescribed or mechanical way; the problem of "uptake" in Austin underscores the contingent dimension of all such appropriation regarding perlocutionary performatives. But are there situations in which the contingency, the interpretive diversity, and potential failure of "uptake" appears to be determined by the force of the utterance? And is the proclamation, "I am a homosexual," an instance of such a determining utterance? / 113

The problem of uptake is displaced from view when the performative force attributed to the utterance becomes overdetermined in fantasy. Such an overdetermination takes place in the paranoid fantasy by which the military construes homosexual utterance to take place. The statement, then, "I am a homosexual," is fabulously misconstrued as, "I want you sexually." A claim that is, in the first instance, reflexive, that attributes a status only to oneself, is taken to be solicitous, that is, a claim that announces availability or desire, the intention to act, the act itself: the verbal vehicle of seduction. In effect, a desirous intention is attributed to the statement *or* the statement is itself invested with the *contagious* power of the magical word, whereby to hear the utterance is to "contract" the sexuality to which it refers. The presumption here is that when and if the term, "homosexual," is claimed for oneself, it is in the service not only of a statement of desire, but becomes the discursive condition and vehicle of the desire, transferring that desire, arousing that desire. This is a statement construed as a solicitation; a constative taken as an interrogative; a self-ascription taken as an address.

Presumed in the military construal of the self-defining statement as offensive action is that the speakability of the term breaks a taboo within public discourse, the floodgates open, and expressions of desire become uncontrollable. Hence, the one before whom the desire under taboo is spoken becomes immediately afflicted by the desire borne by the word; to speak the word before such a person is to implicate that person in unspeakable desire. The word—and the desire—is caught in precisely the way in which a disease is said to be caught. Within contemporary military discourse, the taboo status of homosexuality is intensified by the phobic reduction of homosexual relations to the communication of AIDS, intensifying the sense of homosexual proclamations as contagious acts.

Indeed, consider the salience of the metaphor of contagion for Freud's discussion of taboo in *Totem and Taboo*:

> taboo is a . . . prohibition imposed (by some authority) from outside, and directed against the most powerful longings to which human beings are subject. The desire to violate it persists in their unconscious; those who obey the taboo have an ambivalent attitude to what the taboo prohibits. The magical power that is attributed to taboo is based on the capacity for arousing temptation; and it acts like a contagion because examples are contagious and because the prohibited desire in the unconscious shifts from one thing to another.(35)

In this last remark, Freud makes clear that the prohibited desire in the unconscious shifts from one thing to another, is itself an uncontrollably transferable desire, subject to a metonymic logic that is not yet constrained by the law. Indeed, it is the incessant transferability of this desire that is instituted by the taboo, and that informs the logic of contagion by which the desire under taboo enters into discourse as a highly communicable name. If I say, "I am a homosexual," in front of you, then you become implicated in the "homosexuality" that I utter; the utterance is presumed to establish a relationship between the speaker and the audience, and if the speaker is proclaiming homosexuality, then that discursive relationship becomes constituted by virtue of that utterance, and that very homosexuality is communicated in the

114/

transitive sense. The utterance appears both to communicate and transfer that homosexuality (becomes itself the vehicle for a displacement
onto the addressee) according to a metonymic rush which is, by
definition, beyond conscious control. Indeed, the sign of its *unconscious*
status is precisely that it "communicates" or "transfers" between
speaker and audience in precisely that uncontrollable way.

Earlier in this same text, Freud refers to "dangerous attributes"
applied indifferently and simultaneously to persons, their states, their
acts; the attribute not only shifts between these registers, but it
becomes tempting and terrifying precisely by virtue of this shiftiness:
"Anyone who has violated a taboo becomes taboo himself because he
possesses the dangerous quality of tempting others to follow his example: why should *he* be allowed to do what is forbidden to others?
Thus he is truly contagious in that every example encourages imitation. . . ."(32) Freud distinguishes between those kinds of taboos
invested with contagious power that "produce temptation and encourage imitation" and another in which the transmissability of a taboo is
its displacement onto material objects.(34) These two forms converge
later, however, when he refers to taboo *names* as that material instance
of language that carries both the desire and its prohibition, that is, that
becomes the discursive site for the displacement of ambivalence. The
"transmissability of taboo" is a function of metonymic displacement,
"the tendency . . . for the unconscious instinct . . . to shift constantly
along associative paths on to new objects."(34)

The question that emerges in trying to read the logic of contagion
as it operates within the military ban on homosexual statements and
acts is how a name and the act of self-naming in particular becomes
precisely such a material/discursive carrier for this displacement and
"transmissability." The sign uttered in the service of a prohibition carries that prohibition and becomes speakable only in the service of that
prohibition. The breaking of the prohibition through the uttering of
the sign becomes, then, a disjoining of that sign from its prohibitive
function, and an unconscious transfer of the desire that the sign has,
until this resignification, kept in check. The name, "homosexual," is
not merely a sign of desire, but becomes the means by which desire is
absorbed into and carried by the sign itself. The sign, in the service of

prohibition, has substituted for the desire it represents, but also has acquired a "carrier" function that links homosexuality with contagion. It is, of course, not difficult to imagine which one. How are we to account for this symbolic conflation of the fluidity of the sign and "dangerous fluids"? Homosexuality, within this paranoid metonymy, has become a paradigm for contagion. The self-descriptive utterance of "homosexuality" becomes the very act of dangerous communication which, participating in a contemporary revaluation of that sacred scene, infects its listener—immaculately—through the ear.

Freud concludes his remarks with the reminder that the taboo can be reinstalled only through the speech act that *renounces* desire: "The fact that the violation of a taboo can be atoned for by a renunciation shows that renunciation lies at the basis of obedience to taboo." (35) In a corollary move, the military makes provisions for those who would recant their indiscretion; the only way to counter the public force and threat of a public act of self-definition as a homosexual is through an equally public self-renunciation. In remarks intended to clarify how the policy would be implemented, the military makes clear that to assert one is a homosexual presents a "rebuttable presumption" that one will act in a homosexual way. In other words, one may now say, "I am a homosexual and I intend not to act on my desire," and in such a case, the first clause, "I am a homosexual," loses its performative force; its constative status is restored through the addition of the second clause. In Freud, the renunciation takes the form of regret and atonement, but it makes no claims to having annihilated the desire; indeed, within renunciation, the desire is kept intact, and there is a strange and important way in which prohibition might be said to *preserve* desire.

In *Civilization and its Discontents*, the repression of the libido is itself a libidinally-invested repression. The libido is not absolutely negated through repression, but rather becomes the instrument of its own subjection. The repressive law is not external to the libido that it represses, but the repressive law represses to the extent that repression becomes a libidinal activity.[8] Further, moral interdictions, especially those that are turned against the body, are themselves sustained by the very bodily activity that they seek to curb:

An idea . . . which belongs entirely to psychoanalysis and which is foreign to people's ordinary way of thinking . . . it tells us that conscience (or more correctly, the anxiety which later becomes conscience) is indeed the cause of instinctual renunciation to begin with, but that later that relationship is reversed. Every renunciation of instinct now becomes a dynamic source of conscience and every fresh renunciation increases the latter's severity and intolerance. (CD,84)

According to Freud the self-imposed imperatives that characterize the circular route of conscience are pursued and applied precisely because they become the site of the very satisfaction they seek to prohibit. In other words, prohibition becomes the displaced site of satisfaction for the "instinct" or desire that is prohibited, an occasion for the reliving of the instinct under the rubric of the condemning law. This is of course the source of that form of comedy in which the bearer of the moral law turns out to be the most serious transgressor of its precepts. And precisely because this displaced satisfaction is experienced through the application of the law, that application is reinvigorated and intensified with the emergence of every prohibited desire. The prohibition does not seek the obliteration of prohibited desire; on the contrary, prohibition pursues the reproduction of prohibited desire and becomes itself intensified through the renunciations it effects. The afterlife of prohibited desire takes place through the prohibition itself, where the prohibition not only sustains, but is *sustained by*, the desire that it forces into renunciation. In this sense, then, renunciation takes place *through* the very desire that is renounced, which is to say that the desire is *never* renounced, but becomes preserved and reasserted in the very structure of renunciation. The renunciation by which the military citizen is purged of his sin and reestablished in his or her place, then, becomes the act by which the prohibition at once denies and concedes homosexual desire; it is not, strictly speaking, *un*speakable, but is, more generally, retained in the speaking of the prohibition. In the case of the homosexual who claims to be one, but insists that he or she will not act on his or her desire, the homosexuality persists in and as the application

/ 117

of that prohibition to oneself. This is, interestingly, how Paul Ricouer once described the psychic circuit of hell: a vicious circle of desire and interdiction. And it may be that the military "regulation" is an intensified cultural site for the continuing theological force of that interdiction.

But consider how it is that a term or the proclamation of an identity might be understood discursively to carry or cause an injury. What is the theory of causation in this instance, and is this a "cause" established in paranoia? Freud offers the following account of how it is that paranoia is *caused*, but not in the analysis of how the causal account of paranoia slides into the paranoid account of causation: He writes, "paranoia is a disorder in which a sexual aetiology is by no means obvious; on the contrary, the strikingly prominent features in the causation of paranoia, especially among males, are social humiliations and slights. . . ." So far Freud appears to be substituting a true for a false cause of paranoia: it appears that what causes paranoia are slights and injuries, but what truly causes paranoia is a sexual wish subject to an introversion; the imagined punishment by others is the idealized and exteriorized effect of a prohibition against one's desire that is at the origin of that idealization and exteriorization. The agency of that prohibition is in some sense displaced, and the reasons for the beratement have already become illegible. Freud then continues, claiming that if we go into the matter "more deeply," we shall see that "the really operative factor in these social injuries lies in the part played in them by the homosexual components of affective life." (30)

It is this last phrase that introduces ambiguity into Freud's account. For how are we to understand how "homosexual components of affective life play a part in these social injuries." To feel slighted or injured, to imagine oneself slighted or injured, how precisely is this to be read as a permutation of homosexuality? Is the slight, the injury, the imagined external form that the prohibition against homosexuality takes, and is one being slighted and injured by virtue of one's homosexual desires? Or is this being slighted and injured an imagining of the social injury to which an exposed homosexual might very well be subject? The uncertainty appears to be this: is the prohibition a social one which might be said to become diffuse and generalized, or is it a psy-

chic and internal one which becomes externalized and generalized in the course of paranoia?

In the first instance, it is the social vulnerability of the homosexual to injury which is projected onto a more generalized sense of others as berating and slighting in their behavior; but in the latter case, it is the psychic sublimation of homosexuality which creates the very notion of the social, the notion of Others as regulating, watching, and judging, an imaginary scenario which becomes what is known as "conscience" and prepares the subject for that social feeling that supports citizenship. The two possible sequences differ dramatically in their consequences. The second view postulates a homosexual desire which turns against itself, and then produces a notion of the social as a consequence of that turning back against itself: social feeling, understood here as coextensive with social regulation, is a consequence of sublimated homosexuality, the projection and generalization of a set of judging and watching Others. This is a formulation that postulates homosexuality as the outside to the social, as the presocial, and derives the social, understood as a primarily regulatory domain, from the self-suppression of this sexuality.

/ 119

But how are we to understand this self-suppression apart from the social regulations by which homosexuality is itself cast as the asocial, the presocial, the impossibility of the social within the social? If the two versions of prohibition (psychic and social) cannot be dissociated from one another, how are they to be thought together? The slights and injuries experienced within what is called paranoia are the psychic traces of existing social regulations, even as those traces have become estranged from the regulations from which they are derived. The slights and injuries are not only the effects of a desire turned back on itself, and the subsequent projection of those turned back desires onto the judgments of others (Indeed a blending of super-egoic functions with social ones); rather, it is the coincidence of the judgment of Others and that turning back upon oneself that produces the imaginary scenario in which the condemned and unlived desire registers psychically as the imagined slights and injuries performed by Others.

Thus, the turn to Freud is not an effort to read Freud as the truth of homosexuality, but, rather, as a way to exemplify or allegorize the

circularity in the account of paranoia, a circularity that comes to afflict Freud's own account. For instance, in "On the Mechanism of Paranoia," he writes approvingly of the way in which homosexual feelings are necessary to the love of mankind, how they euphemistically "combine" with the instincts for self-preservation to produce "man" in the "proper sense" of that term. If, to use his terms, homosexual tendencies "combine with" ego-instincts, where ego-instincts are defined as self-preservative, then it becomes part of the project of "man's" self-preservation—the preservation of "man, properly speaking"—to deflect, and preserve in deflection, his homosexuality.(69) Hence, the etiology that Freud offers us is already within the normative and regulatory domain of the social for which he seeks to give an account. It is not that there are first homosexual feelings which then combine with self-preservative instincts, but that, according to the social norms that govern the conditions of self-preservation *as a man*, homosexuality must remain a permanently deflected possibility. Hence, it is not man's homosexuality that helps to constitute his social instincts, and his general mindfulness of others, but, rather, the repression or deflection of the ostensible narcissism of homosexuality that is construed as the condition for altruism, understood as one of the benefits of an accomplished heterosexuality. In this sense, the desexualization and externalization of homosexuality makes for a "man"—properly speaking—who will always feel slights and injuries in the place where homosexual desire might have lived, and for whom this transposition of desire into imagined injury will become the basis of social feeling and citizenship. Note that this unacted homosexuality becomes the condition for sociality and the love of mankind in general.

It is not simply that homosexuality must remain unacted and deflected such that man in his self-preserving and proper sense may live, but that the very notion of the "ego-ideal"—the imaginary measure by which citizenship is psychically regulated—is itself composed of this unacted and deflected homosexuality. The ego-ideal is formed through the withdrawal of large quantities of homosexual cathexis.[9] This homosexuality, however, is neither simply withdrawn nor simply deflected or repressed, but, rather turned back on itself, and this turning back on itself is not a simple self-cancellation; on the contrary, it is

the condition for the fabrication of the ego-ideal in which homosexuality and its prohibition "combine" in the figure of the heterosexual citizen, one whose guilt will be more or less permanent. Indeed Freud will say that homosexual libido is "transformed into sense of guilt" and citizenship itself—the attachment to and embodiment of the law—will be derived from this guilt.

How, then, do we return to the problem that emerges within the military, where the military is at once a zone of suspended citizenship, and one which, by virtue of this suspended status, articulates in graphic terms the production of the masculinist citizen through the prohibition on homosexuality. Although the military regulations appear to figure homosexuality in masculinist terms, it is clear that lesbians are targeted as well, but that, paradoxically, the interrogations into their personal life often take the form of sexual harassment. In other words, women cannot speak their homosexuality because that would be to threaten the heterosexual axis along which gender subordination is secured. And if men speak their homosexuality, that speaking threatens to bring into explicitness and, hence, destroy, the homosociality by which the class of men coheres. / 121

The line that demarcates the speakable from the unspeakable instates the current boundaries of the social. Could the uttering of the word constitute a slight, an injury, indeed, an offense, if the word did not carry the sedimented history of its own suppression? In this sense, the word becomes an "act" precisely to the extent that its unspeakability circumscribes the social. The speaking of the word outside its prohibition calls into question the integrity and the ground of the social as such. In this way, the word contests the boundaries of the social, the repressive ground of the citizen subject by naming the relation that must be assumed for that sociality to emerge, but which can only produce that sociality by remaining unnamed. Unwittingly, it seems, the military introduces that word into its contagious circuit precisely through the prohibition which is supposed to secure its unspeakability. And it is in this way that the military speaks its desire again and again at the very moment, through the very terms, by which it seeks its suppression.

In fact, it is crucial to consider that the military does not merely

confront the homosexual as a problem to be regulated and contained, but it actively produces this figure of the homosexual, insisting that this homosexual be deprived of the power of self-ascription, remaining named and animated by the state and its powers of interpellation. In its military dimension, the state insists on the codification of homosexuality. The homosexual subject is brought into being through a discourse that at once names that "homosexuality" and produces and defines this identity as an infraction against the social. But where it names this subject compulsively, it denies to this subject the power to name itself; thus the state seeks to curb not merely homosexual actions, but the excessive power of the name when it becomes unshackled from the prohibitions by which it is spawned. What and who will the name describe on the occasion when it no longer serves the disciplinary aims of military nomination?

How, then, do we think about the situation in which the self-ascription, the reflexive statement, "I am a homosexual," is misconstrued as a seduction or an assault, one in which a desire is not merely described but, in being described, is understood to be enacted and conveyed? In the first instance, I think we must read this construal of homosexuality and homosexual acts as assault and/or disease as an effort to circumscribe homosexuality within that pathologizing set of figurations. This is not simply an account of how the words of homosexuals performatively produce homosexuality, but, as state-sanctioned figure, a restrictive definition of homosexuality as an assaultive and contagious action. Hence, the performativity attributed to the homosexual utterance can only be established through the performativity of a state discourse that makes this very attribution. The figuring of homosexual utterance as contagion is a performative sort of figuring, a performativity that belongs to regulatory discourse. Does the statement reveal the performative power of homosexual utterance, or does it merely underscore the productive or performative power of those who exercise the power to define homosexuality in these terms?

This discursive power to enforce a definition of the homosexual is one that finally belongs neither to the military nor to those who oppose it. After all, I have just produced the military production for you and entered into the chain of performativity that I've been chart-

122 /

ing, implicating myself in the reproduction of the term, with far less power, admittedly, than those whose acts I describe. Is anything like homosexuality being described in this chain of performativity? Perhaps it is a mistake to claim that we might have the power to produce an authoritative or affirmative notion of homosexuality when we go about naming it, naming ourselves, defining its terms. The problem is not merely that homophobic witnesses to self-proclaiming homosexuals hallucinate the speaking of the word as the doing of the deed, but that even those who oppose the military are willing to accept the notion that naming is performative, that to some extent it brings into linguistic being that which it names. There does seem to be a sense in which speech acts and speech, more generally, might be said to constitute conduct, and that the discourse produced about homosexuality is part of the social constitution of homosexuality as we know it. Conven-tional distinctions between speech and conduct do collapse when, for instance, what we might loosely call representation *is* coextensive with, say, being "out" as a cultural practice of gayness and queerness, between cultural representations that express homosexuality and homosexuality "itself". It would, after all, be somewhat reductive to claim that homosexuality is only sexual behavior in some very restricted sense, and that there is then, superadded to this behavior, a set of representations of homosexuality that, strictly speaking, *are not* homosexuality proper. Or are they?

/ 123

Many would want to argue that homosexuality and its cultural representation are *not* dissociable, that representation does not follow sexuality as its dim reflection, but that representation has a constitutive function, and that, if anything, sexuality follows representation as one of its effects: this appears to be the presumption in the claim that public conventions organize and make possible "sexuality" and that the acts, and the cultural practices that orchestrate and sustain the acts, as it were, cannot be strictly distinguished. To construe sexuality as an "act" is already to abstract from a cultural practice, a reiterative ritual, in which it takes place and of which it is an instance. Indeed, the very notion of a sexual practice is precisely that which overrides the distinction between "act" and "representation."

To insist, however, that discourse on homosexuality, including the

discursive act of "coming out," is part of what is understood, culturally, as "homosexuality" is not quite the same as claiming that saying one is homosexual is itself a homosexual act, much less a homosexual offense. Although I think we can imagine queer activists who would claim that the self-appellation is a sexual act in some broadly interpreted sense of that term, there is a certain comedy that emerges when "queer" becomes so utterly disjoined from sexual practice that every well-meaning heterosexual takes on the term. But we surely need to take seriously the contention that "coming out" is intended as a contagious example, that it is supposed to set a precedent and incite a series of similarly structured acts in public discourse. The military may be responding precisely to the felicitous perlocutionary consequences of coming out, the way in which the example has spawned a rash of coming outs throughout the public sphere, proliferating itself as if it were a certain kind of linguistic contagion—a contagion, we might conjecture, that is meant in part to counter the force of that other contagion, namely, AIDS. What, then, is the difference between the logic that governs the military policy and the one which governs queer activism?

124 /

One way of understanding this, I think, is to note the way in which paranoid military listening consistently closes the gap between the speaking of a desire and the desire that is being spoken. The one appears to communicate the other directly in moments of seduction (but even there we know through painful examples that the communication is not always interpreted in quite the right way); in paranoia, though, the desire that the speaking elicits is imagined as emerging wholly and without solicitation from the one who speaks it. It comes from the outside, as an assault, or as a disease, and becomes registered as injury and/or contamination. Hence, the desire is already figured as assault or disease, and can be received in one form or the other, or both. How is that figuration to be understood as different from the production of a discourse about homosexuality, which might work against this pathological reduction and constitute a socially affirmative meaning for homosexuality?

Here is where I want to argue for the notion that a discursive production of homosexuality, a talking about, a writing about, and institu-

tional recognition of, homosexuality, is not exactly the same as the desire of which it speaks. Whereas the discursive apparatus of homosexuality constitutes its social reality, it does not constitute it fully. The declaration that is "coming out" is certainly a kind of act, but it does not fully constitute the referent to which it refers; indeed, *it renders homosexuality discursive, but it does not render discourse referential.* This is not to say that desire is a referent that we might describe in some other or better way; on the contrary, it is a referent that sets a certain limit to referential description in general, one that nevertheless compels the chain of performativity by which it is never quite captured. In an effort to preserve this sense of desire as a limit to referentiality, it is important not to close the gap between the performative and the referential and to think that by proclaiming homosexuality, homosexuality itself becomes nothing other than the proclamation by which it is asserted. Although Foucault might claim that discourse becomes sexualized through such an act, it may be that discourse is precisely what desexualizes homosexuality in this instance.[11] My sense is that this kind of account of the discursive production of homosexuality makes the mistake of substituting the name for what it names, and though that referent cannot be finally named, it must be kept separate from what is nameable, if only to guarantee that no name claims finally to exhaust the meaning of what we are and what we do, an event that would foreclose the possibility of becoming more and different than what we have already become, in short, foreclose the future of our life within language, a future in which the signifier remains a site of contest, available to democratic rearticulation.

/ 125

In this sense, I would argue that the discourse about homosexual desire is not, strictly speaking, the same as the desire that it speaks, and when we think that we are acting homosexually when we speak about homosexuality we are, I think, making a bit of a mistake. For one of the tasks of a critical production of alternative homosexualities will be to disjoin homosexuality from the figures by which it is conveyed in dominant discourse, especially when they take the form of either assault or disease. Indeed, as much as it is necessary to produce other figures, to continue the future of performativity and, hence, of homo-

sexuality, it will be the distance between something called "homosexuality" and that which cannot be fully interpellated through such a call that will undermine the power of any figure to be the last word on homosexuality. And it is that last word, I think, that is most important to forestall.

Yes, speech is a species of action. Yes, there are some acts that only speech can perform. But there are some acts that speech alone cannot accomplish. You cannot heal the sick by pronouncing them well. You cannot uplift the poor by declaring them to be rich.

HENRY LOUIS GATES, JR.

4 / IMPLICIT CENSORSHIP AND DISCURSIVE AGENCY

To argue that certain speech acts are more properly construed as conduct rather than speech sidesteps the question of censorship. Censorship appears to be the restriction of speech, and if hate speech or pornography or gay self-declaration is no longer understood as "speech," then the restriction on any of those activities would no longer appear to be censorship. Indeed, MacKinnon has argued that the ordinances against pornography that she has devised and supported are not censorship, that they are rather concerned with extending the scope of the Equal Protection Clause of the Constitution.[1] What might have been

considered a free speech issue is now to be construed as a question of substantive equality.

If we do not remain restricted to the legal definition of censorship, we are in a position to ask how the very regulation of the distinction between speech and conduct works in the service of a more implicit form of censorship. To claim that certain speech is not speech and, therefore, not subject to censorship is already to have exercised the censor. Indeed, this particular exercise of censorship exceeds the bounds of legal definition even as it deploys the law as one of its instruments.[2]

COUNTERING THE CENSOR

Conventional accounts of censorship presume that it is exercised by the state against those who are less powerful. Conventional defenses of those less powerful argue that it is their freedom that is being constrained and sometimes, more particularly, their freedom of speech.

128 / Censorship is most often referred to as that which is directed against persons or against the content of their speech. If censorship, however, is a way of *producing* speech, constraining in advance what will and will not become acceptable speech, then it cannot be understood exclusively in terms of juridical power. In the conventional view, censorship appears to follow the utterance of offensive speech: speech has already become offensive, and then some recourse to a regulatory agency is made. But in the view that suggests that censorship *produces* speech, that temporal relation is inverted. Censorship precedes the text (by which I include "speech" and other cultural expressions), and is in some sense responsible for its production.

At a recent conference, I heard two apparently opposite views voiced on the topic. One view maintained that "uncensoring a text is necessarily incomplete."[3] This claim appears to suggest that no text can remain a text, that is, remain readable, without first being subjected to some kind of censorship. This view presupposes that censorship precedes the text in question, and that for a text to become readable, it must be produced through a process of selection that rules out certain possibilities, and realizes others. The process of selection appears to pre-

suppose a decision, one made by the author of the text. And yet, the author does not create the rules according to which that selection is made; those rules that govern the intelligibility of speech are "decided" prior to any individual decision. A more radical view would be that those rules, "decided" prior to any individual decision, are precisely the constraining conditions which *make possible* any given decision. Thus, there is an ambiguity of agency at the site of this decision. The speaking subject makes his or her decision only in the context of an already circumscribed field of linguistic possibilities. One decides on the condition of an already decided field of language, but this repetition does not constitute the decision of the speaking subject as a redundancy. The gap between redundancy and repetition is the space of agency.

The second view was that "censoring a text is necessarily incomplete." This view maintains that a text always escapes the acts by which it is censored, and that censorship is always and only an attempted or partial action. Here, it seems, something about the text under censorship exceeds the reach of the censor, suggesting that some account is required of this "excessive" dimension of speech. One might appeal to a generalized theory of textuality to suggest ways in which the effort to constrain speech cannot fully target or capture the polysemy of language. Similarly, one might argue that the communicative sphere of language necessarily posits a realm of obscenity that it seeks, with always partial success, to keep rigorously excluded from its own operation.[4] This attempt to purify the sphere of public discourse by institutionalizing the norms that establish what ought properly to be included there operates as a preemptive censor. Such efforts not only labor under a fear of contamination, but they are also compelled to restage in the spectacles of public denunciations they perform the very utterances they seek to banish from public life. Language that is compelled to repeat what it seeks to constrain invariably reproduces and restages the very speech that it seeks to shut down. In this way, speech exceeds the censor by which it is constrained.

The generalizable character of both of these explanations is useful but limited: they cannot tell us when and why certain kinds of censorship are, in fact, more complete than others, why some operations of censorship seem to capture the offensive speech, and others seem quite

/ 129

helpless to effect any capture at all. What accounts for the efficacy and vulnerability to failure that characterizes different operations of censorship? Never fully separable from that which it seeks to censor, censorship is implicated in its own repudiated material in ways that produce paradoxical consequences. If censoring a text is always in some sense incomplete, that may be partly because the text in question takes on new life as part of the very discourse produced by the mechanism of censorship.[5]

This paradoxical production of speech by censorship works in implicit and inadvertent ways. Thus, it becomes important to distinguish between explicit and implicit censorship. The latter refers to implicit operations of power that rule out in unspoken ways what will remain unspeakable. In such cases, no explicit regulation is needed in which to articulate this constraint. The operation of implicit and powerful forms of censorship suggests that the power of the censor is not exhausted by explicit state policy or regulation. Such implicit forms of censorship may be, in fact, more efficacious than explicit forms in enforcing a limit on speakability. Explicit forms of censorship are exposed to a certain vulnerability precisely through being more readily legible. The regulation that *states what it does not want stated* thwarts its own desire, conducting a performative contradiction that throws into question that regulation's capacity to mean and do what it says, that is, its sovereign pretension. Such regulations introduce the censored speech into public discourse, thereby establishing it as a site of contestation, that is, as the scene of public utterance that it sought to preempt.

A case in point was discussed in the previous chapter: the congressional statute passed in October of 1994 put into law the "don't ask, don't tell" policy on homosexual self-declaration in the military. The statute did not constrain reference to homosexuality in the military, but proliferated such references in its own supporting documentation and in the public debates fostered on the issue. The point of the statute was not only to limit the "coming out" of military personnel, but to establish that such self-ascriptive speech constitutes either a form of homosexual conduct or a sign that a propensity to engage in homosexual conduct is likely.[6] The military thus engaged in a rather protracted discussion on the matter of what is to be considered "homosexual" and

130/

how speech and conduct is to be distinguished, and whether it can or should be. The regulation of the term "homosexual" is thus no simple act of censorship or silencing. The regulation *redoubles* the term it seeks to constrain, and can only effect this constraint through this paradoxical redoubling. The term is not itself unspeakable, but only becomes unspeakable in those contexts in which one uses it to describe oneself, and fails to make an adequate or convincing distinction between that ascription of a status and the intention to engage in homosexual conduct.

Thus, the effort to constrain the term culminates in its very proliferation—an unintended rhetorical effect of legal discourse. The term not only appears in the regulation as that discourse to be regulated, but reappears in the public debate over its fairness and value specifically as the conjured or imagined act of self-ascription that is explicitly prohibited by the regulation. The prohibition thus conjures the speech act that it seeks to constrain, and becomes caught up in a circular, imaginary production of its own making. This uttering of the utterance that the military seeks to censor also enacts the fulfillment of the desire to establish itself as the author-origin of all the utterances that take place within its domain. The regulation, as it were, will speak the part of the one censored as well as the censoring voice itself, assimilating the drama as one way to establish control over the utterance. / 131

I elaborate upon this example because it illustrates the way in which the mechanism of censorship is engaged in the production of a figure of homosexuality, a figure that is, as it were, backed by the state. The regulations that determine whether homosexuals will be allowed to enter or remain in the military does not simply constrain the speech of those it regulates; it appears to be about certain kinds of speech, but it is also concerned *to establish a norm by which military subjectification proceeds*. In relationship to the masculine military subject, this means that the norms governing masculinity will be those that require the denial of homosexuality. For women, the self-denial requires either a return to an apparent heterosexuality or to an asexuality (sometimes linked together within dominant conceptions of female heterosexuality) that suits the military's notion of unit cohesion.

Thus, the mechanism of censorship is not only actively engaged in

the production of subjects, but also in circumscribing the social parameters of speakable discourse, of what will and will not be admissible in public discourse.[7] The failure of censorship to effect a complete censoring of the speech under question has everything to do with (a) the failure to institute a complete or total subjectification through legal means and (b) the failure to circumscribe effectively the social domain of speakable discourse.

Clearly, the military's effort to regulate speech is not paradigmatic of all kinds of censorship. It does, however, introduce at least two "productive" modalities of power that contrast with the conventional view of censorship as juridical power. By "productive" I do not mean positive or beneficial, but rather, a view of power as formative and constitutive, that is, not conceived exclusively as an external exertion of control or as the deprivation of liberties.[8] According to this view, censorship is not merely restrictive and privative, that is, active in depriving subjects of the freedom to express themselves in certain ways, but also formative of subjects and the legitimate boundaries of speech. This notion of a productive or formative power is not reducible to the tutelary function of the state, that is, the moral instruction of its citizens, but operates to make certain kinds of citizens possible and others impossible. Some who take this point of view make clear that censorship is not primarily about speech, that it is exercised in the service of other kinds of social aims, and that the restriction of speech is instrumental to the achievements of other, often unstated, social and state goals. One example of this includes a conception of censorship as a necessary part of the process of nation-building, where censorship can be exercised by marginalized groups who seek to achieve cultural control over their own representation and narrativization. A similar, but distinct kind of argument, however, is also made typically on behalf of a dominant power that seeks to control any challenges posed to its own legitimacy. Another related example is the use of censorship in an effort to build (or rebuild) consensus within an institution, such as the military, or within a nation; another example is the use of censorship in the codification of memory, as in state control over monument preservation and building, or in the insistence that certain kinds of historical events only be narrated one way.

The view of censorship as "productive," however, is not always coextensive with views that hold that censorship is always *instrumental* to the achievement of other social aims. Consider that in the examples I have just suggested, censorship is not primarily concerned with speech, and that the control or regulation of speech is incidental to the achievement of other kinds of social aims (strengthening particular views of legitimacy, consensus, cultural autonomy, national memory). In the most extreme version of this kind of instrumentalism, speech is cast as wholly incidental to the aims of censorship or, rather, speech works as a cover for the real political aims of censorship, ones that have nothing or little to do with speech.

Censorship is a productive form of power: it is not merely privative, but formative as well. I propose that censorship seeks to produce subjects according to explicit and implicit norms, and that the production of the subject has everything to do with the regulation of speech. The subject's production takes place not only through the regulation of that subject's speech, but through the regulation of the social domain of speakable discourse. The question is not what it is I will be able to say, but what will constitute the domain of the sayable within which I begin to speak at all. To become a subject means to be subjected to a set of implicit and explicit norms that govern the kind of speech that will be legible as the speech of a subject.[9]

Here the question is not whether certain kinds of speech uttered by a subject are censored, but how a certain operation of censorship determines who will be a subject depending on whether the speech of such a candidate for subjecthood obeys certain norms governing what is speakable and what is not. *To move outside of the domain of speakability is to risk one's status as a subject. To embody the norms that govern speakability in one's speech is to consummate one's status as a subject of speech.* "Impossible speech" would be precisely the ramblings of the asocial, the rantings of the "psychotic" that the rules that govern the domain of speakability produce, and by which they are continually haunted.[10]

Some would argue that no text can be fully freed from the shackles of censorship because every text or expression is in part structured through a process of selection that is determined in part by the decisions of an author or speaker and in part by a language that operates

/ 133

according to selective and differential rules that no individual speaker ever made (that may well be collectively forged, but not traceable to a single author, except in specific cases of grammatical revision and coinage). A highly generalized thesis, it appears to apply to *any* and *all* language. And though it may well be true and valid, I think that in its generalized form, it does not directly translate into a political consideration of censorship or a normative view on how best to decide issues of censorship. Indeed, taken in its most generalized form, one normative implication of such a view is the following: because all expression is always already censored to some degree, it makes no sense to try to oppose censorship, for that would be to oppose the conditions of intelligibility (and, thus, to oppose the very terms by which the opposition is articulated).

The view that I am proposing, however, revises this more generalized thesis in the following direction: the conditions of intelligibility are themselves formulated in and by power, and this normative exercise of power is rarely acknowledged as an operation of power at all. Indeed, we may classify it among the most implicit forms of power, one that works precisely through its illegibility: it escapes the terms of legibility that it occasions. That power continues to act in illegible ways is one source of its relative invulnerability.

The one who speaks according to the norms that govern speakability is not necessarily following a rule in a conscious way. One speaks according to a tacit set of norms that are not always explicitly coded as rules. Charles Taylor argues that our understanding of these rules cannot be reduced to having a self-conscious representation of them: "it is carried in patterns of appropriate action." [11] A "background understanding . . . underlies our ability to grasp directions and follow rules," and this background understanding is not only embodied, but embodied as a shared social sense: one does not follow a rule alone. In *Language and Symbolic Power*, Pierre Bourdieu cautions against the reduction of such a bodily understanding, or *habitus*, to the practice of self-consciously following a rule:

> All symbolic domination presupposes, on the part of those who submit to it, a form of complicity which is neither passive submis-

sion to external constraint nor a free adherence to values. The recognition of the legitimacy of the official language has nothing in common with an explicitly professed, deliberate and revocable belief, or with an intentional act of accepting a 'norm.'(50–51)

To understand how the social understanding of such "rules" is an embodied activity, let us distinguish more precisely between that operation of censorship that tacitly forms the subject of speech and that action of censorship subsequently imposed on that subject. If censorship produces the parameters of the subject, how do those norms come to inhabit the bodily life of the subject? Finally, we shall ask how the tacit operation of censorship, understood as a kind of foreclosure, constitutes the violent inauguration of the bodily life of the speaking subject, the incongruity of that body's speech, a speaking whose rhetoricity confounds its normativity.

If a subject becomes a subject by entering the normativity of language, then in some important ways, these rules precede and orchestrate the very formation of the subject. Although the subject enters the normativity of language, the subject exists only as a grammatical fiction prior to that very entrance. Moreover, as Lacan and Lacanians have argued, that entrance into language comes at a price: the norms that govern the inception of the speaking subject differentiate the subject from the unspeakable, that is, produce an unspeakability as the condition of subject formation.

Although psychoanalysis refers to this inception of the subject as taking place in infancy, this primary relation to speech, the subject's entry into language by way of the originary "bar" is reinvoked in political life when the question of being able to speak is once again a condition of the subject's survival. The question of the "cost" of this survival is not simply that an unconscious is produced that cannot be fully assimilated to the ego, or that a "real" is produced that can never be presented within language. The condition for the subject's survival is precisely the foreclosure of what threatens the subject most fundamentally; thus, the "bar" produces the threat and defends against it at the same time. Such a primary foreclosure is approximated by those traumatic political occasions in which the subject who would speak is con-

/ 135

strained precisely by the power that seeks to protect the subject from its own dissolution.

This doubled dimension of the Lacanian "bar," however, is to be thought not merely as a structure that once inaugurated the subject, but as a continuing dynamic in the life of the subject. The rules that constrain the intelligibility of the subject continue to structure the subject throughout his or her life. And this structuring is never fully complete. Acting one's place in language continues the subject's viability, where that viability is held in place by a threat both produced and defended against, the threat of a certain dissolution of the subject. If the subject speaks impossibly, speaks in ways that cannot be regarded as speech or as the speech of a subject, then that speech is discounted and the viability of the subject called into question. The consequences of such an irruption of the unspeakable may range from a sense that one is "falling apart" to the intervention of the state to secure criminal or psychiatric incarceration.

The link between survival and speakability is delineated in the speech that constitutes the inauguration of the self-denying and repentant homosexual into military ranks: I am not what you suspect me to be, but my not being that is precisely what I have now become, thus, determined by my denial, my new self-definition. Or consider the situation that Saidiya Hartman has outlined in which the emancipation from slavery into citizenship requires the bartering of one's labor power, the translation of one's value into a commodity form and, hence, a new form of subjection.[12] The discourse of freedom in which one makes the claim of emancipation suppresses the very energies it purports to unleash. Or note the predicament in which litigating against domestic sexual abuse requires that a woman offer a version of herself that vitiates any doubt as to her sexual purity, her ability to coincide before the law with an idealized and desexualized version of feminine heterosexuality. When we ask what it means to qualify to petition before the law, we note the belated repetition of foreclosure that orchestrates and makes possible a speaking subject with such a claim.[13]

In cultural contexts where there is no necessary or obvious link to the law, forms of "compulsory discursivity"[14] still govern the conditions under which a political claim can be made. Regimes of confes-

sional discourse structure the way in which policy issues are framed; in reference to drugs, for instance, a story about abuse and healing becomes central to the way the topic is addressed in policy; in reference to anti-affirmative action approaches to meritocracy (evidenced in the University of California resolution),[15] narratives of individuals who heroically overcome adverse circumstances to triumph over any analysis of systematic institutional discrimination in education. Such "forced" narratives, as Wendy Brown explains, impose a discursive form on politicization that not only determines (a) under what discursive form a claim becomes legible as political but, more importantly, (b) consolidates *politics as a production of discourse*, and establishes "silence" as a site of potential resistance to such discursive regimes and their normalizing effects.[16]

The view of censorship as one in which a centralized or even sovereign power unilaterally represses speech suggests that the subject of speech is burdened by the exteriority of power. The subject is not quite as victimized in the view that asserts that citizens wield the power to deprive each other of the freedom of speech. When that subject, through its derogatory remarks or representations, works to "censor" another subject, that form of censorship is regarded as "silencing" (Langton). In that form, the citizen addressed by such speech is effectively deprived of the power to respond, deauthorized by the derogatory speech act by which that citizen is ostensibly addressed. Silence is the performative effect of a certain kind of speech, where that speech is an address that has as its object the deauthorization of the speech of the one to whom the speech act is addressed. It is the subject who now is said to wield such power, and not the state or some other centralized institution, although institutional power is presupposed and invoked by the one who delivers the words that silence. Indeed, the subject is described on the model of state power, and though the *locus* of power has shifted from the state to the subject, the unilateral action of power remains the same. Power is exerted by a subject on a subject; its exertion culminates in a deprivation of speech.

It is one thing for certain kinds of speech to be censored, and quite another for censorship to operate on a level prior to speech, namely, as the constituting norm by which the speakable is differentiated from

the unspeakable. The psychoanalysts Jean Laplanche and J.-B. Pontalis have distinguished the censorious act of repression from a preemptive operation of a norm, and offered the term "foreclosure" as a way of designating preemptive action, one that is not performed *by* a subject, but, rather, whose operation makes possible the formation of the subject.[17] Apart from the use of the term in real estate matters to refer to legally barring the redemption of a mortgage for value, "foreclosure" means, according to the Oxford English Dictionary, "to bar, exclude, shut out completely."

As an action, it appears to presuppose a subject, but that presupposition may well be nothing more than a seduction of grammar. Indeed, psychoanalytically considered, foreclosure is not a singular action, but the reiterated effect of a structure. Something is barred, but no subject bars it; the subject emerges as the result of the bar itself. That barring is an action that is not exactly performed *on* a pregiven subject, but performed in such a way that the subject him/herself is performatively produced as a result of this primary cut. The remainder or what is cut out constitutes the unperformable in all performativity.

138 /

Before the bar is what can be known only through an imagining of that "before," one that is pervaded by the belatedness of the imaginary itself, its thwarted nostalgia. In asking what or who performs the bar, we ask for a grammatical expectation to be fulfilled: that we can ask the question at all appears to presuppose that the question is answerable. But what grammar has produced the possibility of the question, and how was that grammar produced? If the very grammatical position of the subject is the result of foreclosure, then any explanation of foreclosure we might give within such a grammar will always be the effect of that which it seeks to explain. Hence, we ask for the state of affairs prior to such a grammar to be explained within the terms of a grammar that, by definition, postdates the scene. The question thus exposes the limiting condition of the grammar that makes the question possible.

Although the psychoanalytic use of foreclosure is richly complicated, I propose that we actively misappropriate the term for other purposes, transpose its proper meaning into an improper one, for the task of rethinking the way in which censorship acts as a "productive" form

of power. I suggest this not simply because I think such a transposition might be interesting, but because I think that the action of foreclosure does not simply happen once, that it continues to happen, and that what is reinvoked by its continued action is precisely that primary scene in which the formation of the subject is tied to the circumscribed production of the domain of the speakable. This accounts for the sense of a subject at risk when the possibility of speech is foreclosed.

The operation of foreclosure is tacitly referenced in those instances in which we ask: what must remain unspeakable for contemporary regimes of discourse to continue to exercise their power? How is the "subject" before the law produced through the exclusion of other possible sites of enunciation within the law? To the extent that such a constitutive exclusion provides the condition of possibility for any act of speech, it follows that "uncensoring a text is necessarily incomplete." On the assumption that no speech is permissible without some other speech becoming *im*permissible, censorship is what permits speech by enforcing the very distinction between permissible and impermissible speech. Understood as foreclosure, censorship produces discursive regimes through the production of the unspeakable. / 139

Although the one who speaks is an effect of such a foreclosure, the subject is never fully or exhaustively reduced to such an effect. A subject who speaks at the border of the speakable takes the risk of redrawing the distinction between what is and is not speakable, the risk of being cast out into the unspeakable. Because the agency of the subject is not a property of the subject, an inherent will or freedom, but an effect of power, it is constrained but not determined in advance. If the subject is produced in speech through a set of foreclosures, then this founding and formative limitation sets the scene for the agency of the subject. Agency becomes possible on the condition of such a foreclosure. This is not the agency of the sovereign subject, one who only and always exercises power instrumentally on another. As the agency of a post-sovereign subject, its discursive operation is delimited in advance but also open to a further and unexpected delimitation. Because the action of foreclosure does not take place once and for all, it must be repeated to reconsolidate its power and efficacy. A structure only remains a structure through being reinstated as one.[18] Thus, the subject who

speaks within the sphere of the speakable implicitly reinvokes the foreclosure on which it depends and, thus, depends on it again. This reinvocation, however, is neither mechanical nor deliberate. Indeed, the
subject does not stand at an instrumental distance from this foreclosure; what is reinvoked is also that which grounds the possibility of the
reinvocation, even as the form that the reinvocation takes is not
reducible to its presupposed form. One speaks a language that is never
fully one's own, but that language only persists through repeated occasions of that invocation. That language gains its temporal life only in
and through the utterances that reinvoke and restructure the conditions of its own possibility.

The critical task is not simply to speak "against" the law, as if the
law were external to speech, and speech the privileged venue for freedom. If speech depends upon censorship, then the principle that one
might seek to oppose is at once the formative principle of oppositional
speech. There is no opposition to the lines drawn by foreclosure except
through the redrawing of those very lines. This is, however, not a
dead-end for agency, but the temporal dynamic and promise of its
peculiar bind. The possibility remains to exploit the presuppositions of
speech to produce a future of language that is nowhere implied by
those presuppositions.

Such a view of censorship, broadly construed, as engaged in forming the subject of speech does not tell us how best to decide questions
of censorship. It does not furnish criteria by which one might distinguish invidious from non-invidious instances of censorship. It offers,
however, an analysis of a set of presuppositions on which any such cri-
terial discussion depends. It is important to know what one means by
"censorship" (indeed, what has become "censored" in the definition of
censorship) in order to understand the limits of its eradicability as well
as the bounds within which such normative appeals might plausibly be
made. Moreover, what we mean by "normative" necessarily alters
once we recognize that the very field of speech is structured and
framed through norms that precede the possibility of description. We
are accustomed to claiming that we first offer a description of various
practices of censorship and then decide among them through recourse
to normative principles. But if our descriptions are themselves norma-

tively structured in advance, through a foreclosure that establishes the domain of the speakable (and, within that, the describable), then to view censorship in this way means rethinking where and how we understand the powers of normativity.

Any decision on what to do will be implicated in a process of censorship that it cannot fully oppose or eradicate. In this sense, censorship is at once the condition for agency and its necessary limit. This paradox does not refute the possibility of decision, but merely suggests that agency is implicated in power; decision becomes possible only on the condition of a decided field, one that is not decided once and for all. This prior decision performed by no one does not foreclose agency, but constitutes the foreclosure that first makes agency possible.

SPEECH ACTS POLITICALLY

The implicit operation of censorship is, by definition, difficult to describe. If it operates within a bodily understanding, as Taylor and Bourdieu suggest, how do we understand the bodily operation of such a linguistic understanding? If censorship is the condition of agency, how do we best understand linguistic agency? In what does the "force" of the performative consist, and how can it be understood as part of politics? Bourdieu argues that the "force" of the performative is the effect of social power, and social power is to be undertood through established contexts of authority and their instruments of censorship. Opposed to this social account of performative force, Derrida argues that the breaking of the utternace from prior, established contexts consitutes the "force" of the utterance.

In the introduction I maintained that the speech act is a bodily act, and that the "force" of the performative is never fully separable from bodily force: this constituted the chiasm of the "threat" as a speech act at once bodily and linguistic. Felman's contribution to speech act theory underscores that speech, precisely because it is a bodily act, is not always "knowing" about what it says. In other words, the bodily effects of speech exceed the intentions of the speaker, raising the question of the speech act itself as a nexus of bodily and psychic forces. In the preceding discussion, I noted that foreclosure, in its revised sense, inaugu-

rates or forms the subject, delimiting the limits of speakable discourse as the viable limits of the subject. Foreclosure implies that the normative production of the subject takes place prior to an overt act of censoring a subject. and ought to be undertood as a modality of productive power in Foucault's sense. The question now emerges: how is it that the norms that govern speech come to inhabit the body? Moreover, how do the norms that produce and regulate the subject of speech also seek to inhabit and craft the embodied life of the subject?

Pierre Bourdieu offers one account of how norms become embodied, suggesting that they craft and cultivate the *habitus* of the body, the cultural style of gesture and bearing. In the final discussion, then, I hope to show how Bourdieu offers a promising account of the way in which non-intentional and non-deliberate incorporation of norms takes place. What Bourdieu fails to understand, however, is how what is bodily in speech resists and confounds the very norms by which it is regulated. Moreover, he offers an account of the performativity of political discourse that neglects the tacit performativity of bodily "speech," the performativity of the *habitus*. His conservative account of the speech act presumes that the conventions that will authorize the performative are already in place, thus failing to account for the Derridean "break" with context that utterances perform. His view fails to consider the crisis in convention that speaking the unspeakable produces, the insurrectionary "force" of censored speech as it emerges into "official discourse" and opens the performative to an unpredictable future.

Pierre Bourdieu writes that "modalities of practices . . . are powerful and hard to resist precisely because they are silent and insidious, insistent and insinuating." He makes clear what he means by this in a number of works, but perhaps most precisely in his essay, "Censorship and the Imposition of Form." [19] There he writes of specialized languages, indeed, the specialized languages of the academy, and suggests that they are not only based on censorship, but also on a sedimentation and skewing of everyday linguistic usage—"strategies of euphemization," to use his phrase. Focusing on the work of Heidegger, Bourdieu argues that Heidegger's language consistently engages strategies that produce the illusion that it has broken with ordinary language. Codes

of legitimacy are established precisely through the invocation of non-ordinary words in ways that appear to have a systematic relation to one another. "Once transformed and transfigured in this way," Bourdieu writes, "the word loses its social identity and its ordinary meaning in order to assume a distorted meaning." (142) "Every word, " he writes, "carries the indelible trace of the *break* which separates the authentically ontological sense from the ordinary and vulgar one. . . ." (144) He suggests not only that such philosophical discourse depends upon the distinction between sacred and profane knowledge, but that the codification of that distinction must itself be an instance of its sacred exercise.

Bourdieu's task, however, is not simply to return us to a world of ordinary locutions. Indeed, he offers us a theoretical reconstruction of the split that Heidegger's discourse is said to institutionalize, and refuses to treat ordinary language as primary and irreducible. Ordinary language, in his view, is "moulded politically": "the objectively political principles of opposition (between social groups) are recorded and preserved in ordinary language."

/ 143

According to Bourdieu, then, a philosophical discourse apparently opposes itself to ordinary language, and an ordinary language is structured by political and sociological oppositions between groups, and the latter are structured in part by what he calls the market, understood as an objective field. Ordinary language records and preserves social oppositions, and yet it does so in a way that is not readily transparent. Those oppositions are sedimented within ordinary language and a theoretical reconstruction of that very process of sedimentation is necessary in order to understand them at all. A philosophical discourse such as Heidegger's thus distances itself from both ordinary language and the possibility of theoretically reconstructing the ways in which social oppositions have become sedimented there. Moreover, philosophical discourse recapitulates a class opposition, but in a deflected way; opposed to ordinary language, philosophy participates in a hierarchical set of oppositions that obscurely reenacts the very social oppositions sedimented in, and occluded by, ordinary language.

Bourdieu argues in favor of a theoretical reconstruction of this very split between ordinary and philosophical usage. In this sense, he

opposes a hyper-intellectualism that fails to acknowledge the break from ordinary language that it performs, but he opposes as well an anti-intellectualism that fails to give a theoretical account of the split between the ordinary and the philosophical that he outlines.

Several kinds of views have been offered within recent American cultural politics to the effect that it makes sense to throw off the shackles of the censor and return to a more immediate and direct form of discourse. Within literary and cultural studies recently, we have witnessed not merely a turn to the personal voice, but a nearly compulsory production of exorbitant affect as the sign of proof that the forces of censorship are being actively and insistently countered. That these expressions quickly become generic and predictable suggests that a more insidious form of censorship operates at the site of their production, and that the failure to approximate a putatively rule-breaking emotionality is precisely a failure to conform to certain implicit rules, ones that govern the "liberatory" possibilities of cultural life.

When anti-intellectualism becomes the counter to anti-censorship, and academic language seeks to dissolve itself in an effort to approximate the ordinary, the bodily, and the intimate, then the rituals of codification at work in such renderings become more insidious and less legible. The substitution of a notion of ordinary language, often romanticized and hypostacized, for an apparently evasive intellectual language becomes the alternative to censorship, fails to take account of the formative power of censorship, as well as its subversive effects. The "break" with ordinary discourse that intellectual language performs does not have to be complete for a certain decontextualization and denaturalization of discourse to take place, one with potentially salutary consequences. The play between the ordinary and non-ordinary is crucial to the process of reelaborating and reworking the constraints that maintain the limits of speakability and, consequently, the viability of the subject.

The effects of catachresis in political discourse are possible only when terms that have traditionally signified in certain ways are misappropriated for other kinds of purposes.[20] When, for instance, the term "subject" appears to be too bound up with presumptions of sovereignty and epistemological transparency, arguments are made that such a term

can no longer be used. And yet, it seems that the reuse of such a term in, say, a post-sovereign context, rattles the otherwise firm sense of context that such a term invokes. Derrida refers to this possibility as reinscription. The key terms of modernity are vulnerable to such reinscriptions as well, a paradox to which I will return toward the end of this chapter. Briefly, though, my point is this: precisely the capacity of such terms to acquire non-ordinary meanings constitutes their continuing political promise. Indeed, I would suggest that the insurrectionary potential of such invocations consists precisely in the break that they produce between an ordinary and an extraordinary sense. I propose to borrow and depart from Bourdieu's view of the speech act as a rite of institution to show that there are invocations of speech that are insurrectionary acts.

To account for such speech acts, however, one must understand language not as a static and closed system whose utterances are functionally secured in advance by the "social positions" to which they are mimetically related. The force and meaning of an utterance are not exclusively determined by prior contexts or "positions"; an utterance /145 may gain its force precisely by virtue of the break with context that it performs. Such breaks with prior context or, indeed, with ordinary usage, are crucial to the political operation of the performative. Language takes on a non-ordinary meaning in order precisely to contest what has become sedimented in and as the ordinary.

Bourdieu insists that a certain intellectualism, taking place under the rubric of "literary semiology" or "linguistic formalism," misconstrues its own theoretical construction as a valid description of social reality. Such an intellectual enterprise, according to Bourdieu, not only misunderstands the positions of social power that it occupies within the institutions of the legitimate academy, but it fails to discern the critical difference between the *linguistic* and *social* dimensions of the very textual practices it attends. Although Bourdieu does not elaborate on whose intellectual positions he is criticizing under the rubric of "literary semiology," he appears to be engaged in a tacit struggle with Jacques Derrida's reading in "Signature, Event, Context" of Austin's theory of the performative.

Both Bourdieu and Derrida read Austin in order to delineate more

clearly the "force" of the performative utterance, of what gives a linguistic utterance the force to do what it says, or to facilitate a set of effects as a result of what it says. Austin makes clear that the illocutionary performative derives its forcefulness or efficacy through recourse to established conventions. Once a convention is set, and the performative participates in a conventional formula—and all the circumstances are appropriate—then the word becomes the deed: the baptism is performed, the alleged criminal arrested, the straight couple marries. For Austin, conventions appear to be stable, and that stability is mirrored in a stable social context in which those conventions have become sedimented over time. The thinness of this "theory" of social context is criticized by Bourdieu precisely because it presumes without elaborating an account of the power of social institutions, including but not limited to language itself. In an effort to counter the incipient formalism of Austin's account, Bourdieu writes of "the essence of the error which is expressed in its most accomplished form by Austin (and after him, Habermas)":

146 /

he thinks that he has found in discourse itself—in the specifically linguistic substance of speech, as it were—the key to the efficacy of speech. By trying to understand the power of linguistic manifestations linguistically, by looking at language for the principle underlying the logic and effectiveness of the language of institutions, one forgets that authority comes to language from outside. . . . Language at most *represents* this authority, manifests and symbolizes it. (109)

For Bourdieu, then, the distinction between performatives that work and those that fail has everything to do with the social power of the one who speaks: the one who is invested with legitimate power makes language act; the one who is not invested may recite the same formula, but produces no effects. The former is legitimate, and the latter, an imposter.

But is there a sure way of distinguishing between the imposter and the real authority? And are there moments in which the utterance forces a blurring between the two, where the utterance calls into question the established grounds of legitimacy, where the utterance, in fact,

performatively produces a shift in the terms of legitimacy as an *eff ect* of the utterance itself? Bourdieu offers the example of liturgical ritual, and offers several examples of the conditions of its utterance and the alterations in its formulae that render the liturgy false. His judgment, however, on what is a right and wrong ritual assumes that the legitimate forms of liturgical ritual have already been established, and that new forms of legitimate invocation will not come to transform and supplant the old. In fact, the ritual that performs an infringement of the liturgy may still be the liturgy, the liturgy in its futural form.

Bourdieu's example is significant because his theory fails to recognize that a certain performative force results from the rehearsal of the conventional formulae in non-conventional ways. The possibility of a resignification of that ritual is based on the prior possibility that a formula can break with its originary context, assuming meanings and functions for which it was never intended. In making social institutions static, Bourdieu fails to grasp the logic of iterability that governs the possibility of social transformation. By understanding the false or wrong invocations as *reiterations*, we see how the form of social institu- ⁄ 147 tions undergoes change and alteration and how an invocation that has no prior legitimacy can have the effect of challenging existing forms of legitimacy, breaking open the possibility of future forms. When Rosa Parks sat in the front of the bus, she had no prior right to do so guaranteed by any of the segregationist conventions of the South. And yet, in laying claim to the right for which she had no *prior* authorization, she endowed a certain authority on the act, and began the insurrectionary process of overthrowing those established codes of legitimacy.

Significantly, the very iterability of the performative that Bourdieu fails to see is what preoccupies the reading of Austin that Derrida provides. For Derrida, the force of the performative is derived precisely from its decontextualization, from its break with a prior context and its capacity to assume new contexts. Indeed, he argues that a performative, to the extent that it is conventional, must be repeated in order to work. And this repetition presupposes that the formula itself continues to work in successive contexts, that it is bound to no context in particular even as, I would add, it is always found in some context or another. The "illimitability" of context simply means that any delin-

eation of a context that one might perform is itself subject to a further contextualization, and that contexts are not given in unitary forms. This does not mean, and never meant, that one should cease any effort to delineate a context; it means only that any such delineation is subject to a potentially infinite revision.

If Bourdieu fails to theorize the particular force produced by the utterance as it breaks with prior context, enacting the logic of iterability, Derrida focuses on those ostensibly "structural" features of the performative that persist quite apart from any and all social contexts, and all considerations of semantics. Performative utterances operate according to the same logic as written marks, according to Derrida, which, as signs, carry "a force that breaks with its context . . . the breaking force (*force de rupture*) is not an accidental predicate but the very structure of the written text. . . ." (9) Later on that same page, Derrida links the force of rupture to spacing, or the problem of the interval that iterability introduces. The sign, as iterable, is a differential mark cut off from its putative production or origin. Whether the mark is "cut off" from its origin, as Derrida contends, or loosely tethered to it raises the question of whether the function of the sign is essentially related to the sedimentation of its usages, or essentially free of its historicity.

Derrida's account tends to accentuate the relative autonomy of the structural operation of the sign, identifying the "force" of the performative as a structural feature of any sign that must break with its prior contexts in order to sustain its iterability as a sign. The force of the performative is thus not inherited from prior usage, but issues forth precisely from its break with any and all prior usage. That break, that force of rupture, is the force of the performative, beyond all question of truth or meaning. Derrida opposes the structural dimension of language to the semantic and describes an autonomous operation of the structural apparently purified of social residue. In writing that a performative is "repetitive or citational in its structure," (17) he clearly opposes the Austinian account of repeatability as a function of language as social convention. For Derrida, the iterability proper to convention has a structural status that appears separable from any consideration of the social. That "dissemination is irreducible to polysemy" means that

the dissemination of the sign, as a graphematic mark, is not reducible to the sign's capacity to bear multiple meanings; the dissemination takes place at a structural rather than semantic level.

In response to Austin's claim that "infelicity is an ill to which *all* acts are heir which have the general character of ritual or ceremonial, all *conventional* acts," Derrida responds with the following reformulation of the performative (enacting the repetition of the formula with a difference):

> Austin, at this juncture, appears to consider solely the conventionality constituting the *circumstance* of the utterance (*énoncé*), its contextual surroundings, and not a certain conventionality intrinsic to what constitutes the speech act (*locution*) itself, all that might be summarized rapidly under the problematical rubric of 'the arbitrary nature of the sign,' which extends, aggravates, and radicalizes the difficulty. 'Ritual' is not a possible occurrence (*éventualité*), but rather, *as* iterability, a structural characteristic of every mark. (15)

If iterability is a structural characteristic of every mark, then there is no mark without its own proper iterability; that is, for a mark to be a mark, it must be repeatable, and have that repeatability as a necessary and constitutive feature of itself. Earlier in this same essay, Derrida suggests that "communicating, in the case of the performative. . . would be tantamount to communicating a force through the impetus (*impulsion*) of a mark." (13) This force is associated with the break from context, the scene in which, through repetition, the formula establishes its structural independence from any of the specific contexts in which it appears. The "force" is not derived from conditions that are outside of language, as Bourdieu suggests, but results from the iterability of the graphematic sign.

/ 149

Noting that performative effects are linked with a force that is distinct from questions of meaning or truth, Derrida remarks that "the semantic horizon that habitually governs the notion of communication is exceeded or split by the intervention of writing. . . ." He then adds the phrase that we considered briefly above: ". . . by a *dissemination* irreducible to *polysemy.*" (20) In this formulation, the semantic and the structural appear to work always and only at cross-purposes. How is

this "always and only" to be defended? What guarantees the permanence of this crossed and vexed relation in which the structural exceeds and opposes the semantic, and the semantic is always crossed and defeated by the structural? Is there a structural necessity for that relationship of confounding, a structure that founds this structure or, perhaps, a semantics?

The question seems important if one takes seriously the demand to think through the logic of iterability as a social logic. Approaching the question of the performative from a variety of political scenes—hate speech, burning crosses, pornography, gay self-declaration—compels a reading of the speech act that does more than universalize its operation on the basis of its putatively formal structure. If the break from context that a performative can or, in Derridean terms, *must* perform is something that every "mark" performs by virtue of its graphematic structure, then all marks and utterances are equally afflicted by such failure, and it makes no sense to ask how it is that certain utterances break from prior contexts with more ease than others or why certain utterances come to carry the force to wound that they do, whereas others fail to exercise such force at all. Whereas Bourdieu fails to take account of the way in which a performative can break with existing context and assume new contexts, refiguring the terms of legitimate utterance themselves, Derrida appears to install the break as a structurally necessary feature of every utterance and every codifiable written mark, thus paralyzing the social analysis of forceful utterance. We have yet to arrive at an account of the social iterability of the utterance.

When Austin wrote that all conventional acts are subject to infelicity and "all conventional acts are exposed to failure," he sought to isolate the conditions of failure, in part, as circumstantial. Derrida, however, argues that there is a conventionality and a risk of failure proper to the speech act itself (15)—a failure that is the equivalent of the arbitrariness of the sign. The sense of convention in Austin, augmented by the terms "ritual" and "ceremonial," is fully transmuted into linguistic iterability in Derrida. The socially complex notion of ritual, which also appears in Althusser's definitions of ideology as a "ritual," is rendered void of all social meaning; its repetitive function is abstracted from its

150

social operation and established as a inherent structural feature of any and all marks.

Bourdieu, on the other hand, will seek to expand the "ritual" sense of "convention" and exclude any consideration of the temporality or logic of performativity. Indeed, he will contextualize ritual within the social field of the "market" in order more radically to exteriorize the source of linguistic power.

The Austinian "infelicities" to which performatives are liable are thus conceived very differently: performatives fail either because, for Derrida, they must fail as a condition of their iterability or, for Bourdieu, they are not backed by the appropriate expressions of social power. Derrida claims that the failure of the performative is the condition of its possibility, "the very force and law of its emergence." (17) That performative utterances can go wrong, be misapplied or misinvoked, is essential to their "proper" functioning: such instances exemplify a more general citationality that can always go awry, and which is exploited by the "imposture" performed by the mimetic arts. Indeed, all performativity rests on the credible production of "authority" and is, thus, not only a repetition of its own prior instance and, hence, a loss of the originary instance, but its citationality assumes the form of a mimesis without end. The imposture of the performative is thus central to its "legitimate" working: every credible production must be produced according to the norms of legitimacy and, hence, fail to be identical with those norms and remain at a distance from the norm itself. The performance of legitimacy is the credible production of the legitimate, the one that apparently closes the gap which makes it possible.

/ 151

Bourdieu argues that every misfire or misapplication highlights the social conditions by which a performative operates, and gives us a way of articulating those conditions. Bourdieu charges Derrida under the rubric of "literary semiology" with offering an excessively formal interpretation of the performative, and yet Bourdieu amplifies the social dimension of the performative at the expense of its transformability. In this way, paradoxically, Derrida's formulation offers a way to think performativity in relation to transformation, to the break with

prior contexts, with the possibility of inaugurating contexts yet to come.

The question of what constitutes the "force" of the performative, however, can be adequately answered by neither formulation, although both views, taken together, gesture toward a theory of the social iterability of the speech act. It makes sense to remember that the "force" of the speech act, as it was articulated by both Toni Morrison and Shoshana Felman, has everything to do with the status of speech as a bodily act. That speech is not the same as writing seems clear, not because the body is present in speech in a way that it is not in writing, but because the oblique relation of the body to speech is itself performed by the utterance, deflected yet carried by the performance itself. To argue that the body is equally absent in speech and writing is true only to the extent that neither speech nor writing makes the body immediately present. But the ways in which the body obliquely appears in speech is, of necessity, different from the way it appears in writing. Although both are bodily acts, it is the mark of the body, as it were, that is read in the written text. Whose body it is can remain permanently unclear. The speech act, however, is performed bodily, and though it does not instate the absolute or immediate presence of the body, the simultaneity of the production and delivery of the expression communicates not merely what is said, but the bearing of the body as the rhetorical instrument of expression. This makes plain the incongruous interrelatedness of body and speech to which Felman refers, the excess in speech that must be read along with, and often against, the propositional content of what is said.

Bourdieu offers a theory of bodily knowingness in his notion of the *habitus*, but he does not relate this discussion of the body to the theory of the performative. The *habitus* refers to those embodied rituals of everydayness by which a given culture produces and sustains belief in its own "obviousness".[21] In this way, Bourdieu underscores the place of the body, its gestures, its stylistics, its unconscious "knowingness" as the site for the reconstitution of a practical sense without which social reality would not be constituted as such. The practical sense is carried by the body, where the body is not a mere positive datum, but the repository or the site of an incorporated history.[22]

The body is not only the site of such a history, but also the instrument through which the belief in contemporary obviousness is reconstituted. Thus, it operates magically, but in the same sense that Bourdieu reserves for the operation of the performative. Bourdieu invokes the phenomenon of "social magic" to characterize the productive force of performative speech acts, those "officialization strategies" by which those in power use language to produce certain kinds of binding social effects. This same term, however, might just as well apply to the *habitus*, his notion of "the bodily hexis," and the social effects that this embodied practice produces. Interestingly, the generative or productive domain of the *habitus* is *not* linked to the problem of performativity that Bourdieu elaborates in relation to the problem of intellectualism and linguistic formalism. In these latter contexts, Bourdieu rethinks the meaning of performative speech acts in a direction counter to Austin's in order to establish the dual and separate workings of social and linguistic elements in constituting what makes certain kinds of speech acts into "social magic," that is, what gives certain speech acts the efficacious force of authority.

To what extent is the *habitus* structured by a kind of performativity, admittedly one that is less explicit and juridical than the examples drawn from the operation of state power, i.e. marriage, declarations, pronouncements of various kinds? Indeed, if we consider that the *habitus* operates according to a performativity, then it would appear that the theoretical distinction between the social and the linguistic is difficult, if not impossible, to sustain. The social life of the body is produced through an interpellation that is at once linguistic and productive. The way in which that interpellative call continues to call, to take form in a bodily stylistics that, in turn, performs its own social magic constitutes the tacit and corporeal operation of performativity.

Interpellations that "hail" a subject into being, that is, social performatives that are ritualized and sedimented through time, are central to the very process of subject-formation as well as the embodied, participatory *habitus*. To be hailed or addressed by a social interpellation is to be constituted discursively and socially at once. This interpellation need not take on an explicit or official form in order to be socially efficacious and formative in the formation of the subject. Considered

in this way, the interpellation as performative establishes the discursive constitution of the subject as inextricably bound to the social constitution of the subject. Although Althusser's own account of interpellation does not suffice to account for the discursive constitution of the subject, it sets the scene for the misappropriation of interpellating performatives that is central to any project of the subversive territorialization and resignification of dominant social orders.

In *Outline of a Theory of Practice*, Bourdieu writes of the relation between "Belief and the Body"[23]: "The body believes in what it plays at: it weeps if it mimes grief. It does not represent what it performs, it does not memorize the past, it *enacts* the past, bringing it back to life." Bourdieu here makes clear that the body does not merely act in accordance with certain regularized or ritualized practices; it *is* this sedimented ritual activity; its action, in this sense, is a kind of incorporated memory.[24] Here the apparent materiality of the body is recast as a kind of practical activity, undeliberate and yet to some degree improvisational. But this bodily *habitus* is generated by the tacit normativity that governs the social game in which the embodied subject acts. In this sense, the body appropriates the rule-like character of the habitus through playing by those rules in the context of a given social field. Its participation in the game is the precondition for a mimesis or, more precisely, a mimetic identification, that acquires the habitus precisely through a practical conformity to its conventions. "The process of acquisition," Bourdieu writes, is "a practical *mimesis* (or mimeticism) which implies an overall relation of identification and has nothing in common with an *imitation* that would presuppose a conscious effort to reproduce a gesture, an utterance or an object explicitly constituted as a model."[25] This acquisition is historical to the extent that the "rules of the game"[26] are, quite literally, *incorporated*, made into a second nature, constituted as a prevailing *doxa*. Neither the subject nor its body forms a representation of this conventional activity, for the body is itself formed in the *hexis*[27] of this mimetic and acquisitive activity. The body is, thus, not a purely subjective phenomenon that houses memories of its participation in the conventional games of the social field; its participatory competence is itself dependent on the incorporation of that cultural memory and its knowingness. In this sense, one can hear

strong echoes of Merleau-Ponty on the sedimented or habituated "knowingness" of the body, indeed, on the indissociability of thought and body: "Thought and expression . . . are simultaneously constituted, when our cultural store is put at the service of this unknown law, as our body suddenly lends itself to some new gesture in the formation of habit."[28] But one hears as well Althusser's invocation of Pascal in the explaining of ideology: one kneels in prayer, and only later acquires belief.

To the extent that Bourdieu acknowledges that this *habitus* is formed over time, and that its formation gives rise to a strengthened belief in the "reality" of the social field in which it operates, he understands social conventions as animating the bodies which, in turn, reproduce and ritualize those conventions as practices. In this sense, the *habitus* is formed, but it is also *formative*: it is in this sense that the bodily *habitus* constitutes a tacit form of performativity, a citational chain lived and believed at the level of the body. The *habitus* is not only a site for the reproduction of the belief in the reality of a given social field—a belief by which that field is sustained—but it also generates *dispositions* which "incline" the social subject to act in relative conformity with the ostensibly objective demands of the field.[29]   / 155

The body, however, is not simply the sedimentation of speech acts by which it has been constituted. If that constitution fails, a resistance meets interpellation at the moment it exerts its demand; then something exceeds the interpellation, and this excess is lived as the outside of intelligibility. This becomes clear in the way the body rhetorically exceeds the speech act it also performs. This excess is what Bourdieu's account appears to miss or, perhaps, to suppress: the abiding incongruity of the speaking body, the way in which it exceeds its interpellation, and remains uncontained by any of its acts of speech.

For Felman, the body that speaks is a scandal precisely because its speech is not fully governed by intention. No act of speech can fully control or determine the rhetorical effects of the body which speaks. It is scandalous as well because the bodily action of speech is not predictable in any mechanical way. That the speech act is a bodily act does not mean that the body is fully present in its speech. The relationship between speech and the body is that of a chiasmus. Speech is bodily,

but the body exceeds the speech it occasions; and speech remains irreducible to the bodily means of its enunciation.

Bourdieu's view, however, presupposes that the body is formed by the repetition and acculturation of norms, and that this forming is effective. What breaks down in the course of interpellation, opening up the possibility of a derailment from within, remains unaccounted for. Bodies are formed by social norms, but the process of that formation runs its risk. Thus, the situation of constrained contingency that governs the discursive and social formation of the body and its (re)productions remains unacknowledged by Bourdieu. This oversight has consequences for his account of the condition and possibility of discursive agency. By claiming that performative utterances are only effective when they are spoken by those who are (already) in a position of social power to exercise words as deeds, Bourdieu inadvertently forecloses the possibility of an agency that emerges from the margins of power. His main concern, however, is that the formal account of performative force be replaced by a social one; in the process, he opposes the putative playfulness of deconstruction with an account of social power that remains structurally committed to the status quo.

In Bourdieu's account of performative speech acts, the subject who utters the performative is positioned on a map of social power in a fairly fixed way, and this performative will or will not work depending on whether the subject who performs the utterance is already authorized to make it work by the position of social power she or he occupies. In other words, a speaker who declares a war or performs a wedding ceremony, and pronounces into being that which he declares to be true, will be able to animate the "social magic" of the performative *to the extent* that the subject is already authorized or, in Bourdieu's terms, *delegated* to perform such binding speech acts.[30] Although Bourdieu is clearly right that not all performatives "work" and that not all speakers can participate in the apparently divine authorization by which the performative works its social magic and compels collective recognition of its authority, he fails to take account of the way in which social positions are themselves constructed through a more tacit operation of performativity. Indeed, not only is the act of "delegation" a performative, that is, a naming which is at once the action of entitlement,

but authorization more generally is to a strong degree a matter of being addressed or interpellated by prevailing forms of social power. Moreover, this tacit and performative operation of authorization and entitlement is not always initiated by a subject or by a representative of a state apparatus. For example, the racialization of the subject or its gendering or, indeed, its social abjection more generally is performatively induced from various and diffuse quarters that do not always operate as "official" discourse.

What happens in linguistic practices reflects or mirrors what happens in social orders conceived as external to discourse itself. Hence, in Bourdieu's effort to elaborate Saussure's paradox of a "social heterogeneity inherent in language," he construes a mimetic relation between the linguistic and the social, rehabilitating the base/superstructure model whereby the linguistic becomes epiphenomenal:

> the social uses of language owe their specifically social value to the fact that they tend to be organized in systems of difference . . . which reproduce . . . the system of social difference. . . . To speak is to appropriate one or another of the expressive styles already constituted in and through usage and objectively marked by their position in a hierarchy of styles which expresses the hierarchy of corresponding social groups.(54)

/ 157

Referring to the "generative capacities of language [to] produce statements that are *formally* impeccable but semantically empty," he proceeds to claim that "rituals are the limiting case of situations of *imposition* in which, through the exercise of a technical competence which may be very imperfect, a social competence is exercised—namely, that of the legitimate speaker, authorized to speak, and to speak with authority." (41) Of interest here is the equivalence posited between "being authorized to speak" and "speaking with authority," for it is clearly possible to speak with authority *without* being authorized to speak.

Indeed, I would argue that it is precisely the *expropriability* of the dominant, "authorized" discourse that constitutes one potential site of its subversive resignification. What happens, for instance, when those who have been denied the social power to claim "freedom" or "democ-

racy" appropriate those terms from the dominant discourse and rework or resignify those highly cathected terms to rally a political movement?[31] If the performative must compel collective recognition in order to work, must it compel only those kinds of recognition that are *already* institutionalized, or can it also compel a critical perspective on existing institutions? What is the performative power of claiming an entitlement to those terms—"justice", "democracy"—that have been articulated to exclude the ones who now claim that entitlement? What is the performative power of calling for freedom or the end to racism precisely when the one or the "we" who calls has been radically *dis*enfranchised from making such a call, when the "we" who makes the call reterritorializes the term from its operation within dominant discourse precisely in order to counter the effects of that group's marginalization? Or, equally important, what is the performative power of appropriating the very terms by which one has been abused in order to deplete the term of its degradation or to derive an affirmation from that degradation, rallying under the sign of "queer" or revaluing affirmatively the category of "black" or of "women"?

158

The question here is whether the improper use of the performative can succeed in producing the effect of authority where there is no recourse to a prior authorization; indeed, whether the misappropriation or expropriation of the performative might not be the very occasion for the exposure of prevailing forms of authority and the exclusions by which they proceed.

If one argues that language itself can only act to the extent that it is "backed" by existing social power, then one needs to supply a theory of how it is that social power "backs" language in this way. If language only represents the larger, institutional conditions that give it its force, then what is that relationship of "representation" that accounts for institutions being represented in language? Is the mimetic relationship ascribed to language and the prior institutions of social power not itself a relationship of signification, that is, how language comes to signify social power? It seems that such a relationship can only be explained through a further theory of language and signification.

Performatives do not merely reflect prior social conditions, but produce a set of social effects, and though they are not always the

effects of "official" discourse, they nevertheless work their social power not only to regulate bodies, but to form them as well. Indeed, the efforts of performative discourse exceed and confound the authorizing contexts from which they emerge. Performatives cannot always be retethered to their moment of utterance, but they carry the mnemic trace of the body in the force that they exercise. One need only consider the way in which the history of having been called an injurious name is embodied, how the words enter the limbs, craft the gesture, bend the spine. One need only consider how racial or gendered slurs live and thrive in and as the flesh of the addressee, and how these slurs accumulate over time, dissimulating their history, taking on the semblance of the natural, configuring and restricting the *doxa* that counts as "reality." In such bodily productions resides the sedimented history of the performative, the ways in which sedimented usage comes to compose, without determining, the cultural sense of the body, and how the body comes to disorient that cultural sense in the moment of expropriating the discursive means of its own production. The appropriation of such norms to oppose their historically sedimented effect   / 159 constitutes the insurrectionary moment of that history, the moment that founds a future through a break with that past.

THE TACIT PERFORMATIVITY OF POWER

The performative needs to be rethought not only as an act that an official language-user wields in order to implement already authorized effects, but precisely as social ritual, as one of the very "modalities of practices [that] are powerful and hard to resist precisely because they are silent and insidious, insistent and insinuating." When we say that an insult strikes like a blow, we imply that our bodies are injured by such speech. And they surely are, but not in the same way as a purely physical injury takes place. Just as physical injury implicates the psyche, so psychic injury effects the bodily *doxa*, that lived and corporeally registered set of beliefs that constitute social reality. The "constructive" power of the tacit performative is precisely its ability to establish a practical sense for the body, not only a sense of what the body is, but how it can or cannot negotiate space, its "location" in terms of prevail-

ing cultural coordinates. The performative is not a singular act used by an already established subject, but one of the powerful and insidious ways in which subjects are called into social being from diffuse social quarters, inaugurated into sociality by a variety of diffuse and powerful interpellations. In this sense the social performative is a crucial part not only of subject *formation*, but of the ongoing political contestation and reformulation of the subject as well. The performative is not only a ritual practice: it is one of the influential rituals by which subjects are formed and reformulated.

This point seems to me to be a crucial one, and raises again the possibility of a speech act as an insurrectionary act. The argument that a speech act exercises authority to the extent that it is *already* authorized suggests that the authorizing contexts for such acts are already in place, and that speech acts do not work to transform the contexts by which they are or are not authorized. If hate speech constitutes the kind of act that seeks to silence the one to whom it is addressed, but which might revive within the vocabulary of the silenced as its unexpected rejoinder, then the response to hate speech constitutes the "deofficialization" of the performative, its expropriation for non-ordinary means. Within the political sphere, performativity can work in precisely such counter-hegemonic ways. That moment in which a speech act without prior authorization nevertheless assumes authorization in the course of its performance may anticipate and instate altered contexts for its future reception.[32]

With respect to the political discourse of modernity, it is possible to say that its basic terms are all tainted, and that to use such terms is to reinvoke the contexts of oppression in which they were previously used. Paul Gilroy points out, for instance, that terms such as universality have been premised on the exclusion of women, of people of color, that they are wrought along class lines and with strong colonial interests. But he adds, crucially, that the struggles against those very exclusions end up *reappropriating* those very terms from modernity in order to configure a different future. A term like "freedom" may come to signify what it never signified before, may come to embrace interests and subjects who have been excluded from its jurisdiction; "justice" may also come to embrace precisely what could not be contained

under its description. "Equality" has certainly turned out to be a term with a kind of reach that is difficult, if not impossible, to have predicted on the basis of its prior articulations.

Such reappropriations illustrate the vulnerability of these sullied terms to an unexpected innocence; such terms are not property; they assume a life and a purpose for which they were never intended. They are not to be seen as merely tainted goods, too bound up with the history of oppression, but neither are they to be regarded as having a pure meaning that might be distilled from their various usages in political contexts. The task, it seems, is to compel the terms of modernity to embrace those they have traditionally excluded, and to know that such an embrace cannot be easy; it would wrack and unsettle the polity that makes such an embrace. This is not a simple assimilation and accommodation of what has been excluded into existing terms, but, rather, the admission of a sense of difference and futurity into modernity that establishes for that time an unknown future, one that can only produce anxiety in those who seek to patrol its conventional boundaries. If there can be a modernity without foundationalism (and perhaps this is / 161 what is meant by the postmodern), then it will be one in which the key terms of its operation are not fully secured in advance, one that assumes a futural form for politics that cannot be fully anticipated: and this will be a politics of both hope and anxiety, what Foucault termed "a politics of discomfort."

I would agree with Bourdieu's critique of some deconstructive positions that argue that the speech act, by virtue of its internal powers, breaks with every context from which it emerges. That is simply not the case, and it is clear to me, especially in the example of hate speech, that contexts inhere in certain speech acts in ways that are very difficult to shake. On the other hand, I would insist that the speech act, as a rite of institution, is one whose contexts are never fully determined in advance, and that the possibility for the speech act to take on a non-ordinary meaning, to function in contexts where it has not belonged, is precisely the political promise of the performative, one that positions the performative at the center of a politics of hegemony, one that offers an unanticipated political future for deconstructive thinking.

The opening up of unknown contexts, however, is clearly a source

of anxiety for some. The desire not to have an open future can be strong. In political calculations, it is important not to underestimate the force of the desire to foreclose futurity. This is one reason that asking certain questions is considered dangerous, and why we live in a time in which intellectual work is demeaned in public life, and anti-intellectualism marks a substantial part of the climate within the academy. Imagine the situation that a student of mine reports, that of reading a book and thinking, I cannot ask the questions that are posed here because to ask them is to introduce doubt into my political convictions, and to introduce doubt into my political convictions could lead to the dissolution of those convictions. At such a moment, the fear of thinking, indeed, the fear of the question, becomes a moralized defense of politics, and the work of intellectual life and the work of politics are sundered from one another. Politics becomes that which requires a certain anti-intellectualism. To remain unwilling to rethink one's politics on the basis of questions posed is to opt for a dogmatic stand at the cost of both life and thought.

162 /   Such dogmatism appears as well in the effort to circumscribe speech that injures, excites, threatens, and offends. Whether it is the censorship of particular kinds of representation or the circumscription of the domain of public discourse itself, the effort to tighten the reins on speech undercuts those political impulses to exploit speech itself for its insurrectionary effects. The intellectual opposition to questions that destabilize a sense of reality seems a mundane academic case in point.

To question a term, a term like "the subject" or "universality," is to ask how it plays, what investments it bears, what aims it achieves, what alterations it undergoes. The changeable life of that term does not preclude the possibility of its use. If a term becomes questionable, does that mean it cannot be used any longer, and that we can only use terms that we *already know how to master*? Why is it that posing a question about a term is considered the same as effecting a prohibition against its use? Why is it that we sometimes do feel that if a term is dislodged from its prior and known contexts, that we will not be able to live, to survive, to use language, to speak for ourselves? What kind of guarantee does this effort to refer the speech act back to its originating con-

text exercise, and what sort of terror does it forestall? Is it that in the ordinary mode, terms are assumed, terms like "the subject" and "universality," and the sense in which they "must" be assumed is a *moral* one, taking the form of an imperative, and like some moral interdictions, a defense against what terrifies us most? Are we not paralyzed by a fear of the unknown future of words that keeps us from interrogating the terms that we need to live, and of taking the risk of living the terms that we keep in question?

We began by noting that hate speech calls into question linguistic survival, that being called a name can be the site of injury, and conclude by noting that this name-calling may be the initiating moment of a counter-mobilization. The name one is called both subordinates and enables, producing a scene of agency from ambivalence, a set of effects that exceed the animating intentions of the call. To take up the name that one is called is no simple submission to prior authority, for the name is already unmoored from prior context, and entered into the labor of self-definition. The word that wounds becomes an instrument of resistance in the redeployment that destroys the prior territory of / 163 its operation. Such a redeployment means speaking words without prior authorization and putting into risk the security of linguistic life, the sense of one's place in language, that one's words do as one says. That risk, however, has already arrived with injurious language as it calls into question the linguistic survival of the one addressed. Insurrectionary speech becomes the necessary response to injurious language, a risk taken in response to being put at risk, a repetition in language that forces change.

/ Notes /

INTRODUCTION

1. Louis Althusser, "Ideology and Ideological State Apparatuses," in *Lenin and Philosophy*, tr. Ben Brewster, (New York and London: Monthly Review Press, 1971), pp. 170–86.

2. J. L. Austin, *How to Do Things With Words*, (Cambridge, Mass.: Harvard University Press, 1962), p. 52.

3. Whereas Pierre Bourdieu emphasizes the ritual dimension of the conventions that support the speech act in Austin, Derrida substitutes the term "iterability" for ritual, thus establishing a structural account of repetition in the place of a more semantically compounded sense of social ritual. The final chapter of this book will attempt to negotiate between these posi-

tions and offer an account of the social power of the speech act that takes into account its specific social iterability and the social temporality. See Pierre Bourdieu, *Language and Symbolic Power*, (Cambridge, Mass.: Harvard University Press, 1991), Part II, pp. 105–62. See Jacques Derrida, "Signature Event Context" in *Limited Inc*, tr. Samuel Weber and Jeffrey Mehlman, ed. Gerald Graff, (Evanston: Northwestern University Press, 1988), pp. 1–23.

4. Matsuda writes of the "deadly violence that accompanies the persistent verbal degradation of those subordinated. . ." and later remarks that "Racist hate messages, threats, slurs, epithets, and disparagement all hit the gut of those in the target group." *Words that Wound: Critical Race Theory, Assaultive Speech, and the First Amendment*, eds. Mari J. Matsuda, Charles R. Lawrence, III, Richard Delgado, and Kimberlé Williams Crenshaw (Boulder: Westview Press, 1993), p. 23.

5. For a fuller discussion of this point, see my *The Psychic Life of Power: Theories in Subjection*, (Stanford: Stanford University Press, 1997).

6. Elaine Scarry, *The Body in Pain: The Making and Unmaking of the World*, (New York: Oxford University Press, 1985), pp. 2–27.

7. Shoshana Felman, *The Literary Speech Act: Don Juan with J. L. Austin, or Seduction in Two Languages*, tr. Catherine Porter, (Ithaca: Cornell University Press, 1983). This text is originally published as *Le Scandale du corps parlant* (Éditions du Seuil, 1980).

8. Shoshana Felman, *The Literary Speech Act*, p. 94. Felman provides a marvelous reading of Austin's humor and irony, showing how the reiterated problem of performative "misfire" reveals how the performative is always beset by a failure it cannot explain. The performative performs in ways that no convention fully governs, and which no conscious intention can fully determine. This unconscious dimension of every act surfaces in Austin's text as the tragi-comedy of performative misfire. At one point, she quotes Lacan: "Failure (misfire) can be defined as what is sexual in every human act." (110)

9. For a thorough cultural analysis of rap music that complicates its relation to violence, see Tricia Rose, *Black Noise: Rap Music and Black Culture in Contemporary America*, (Hanover, NH: New England Universities Press, 1994). For a fine account of how the censorship of rap is an effort to regulate and destroy cultural memory, see George Lipsitz, "Censorship of Commercial Culture: Silencing Social Memory and Suppressing Social Theory," on file with the author. This piece was presented at the Getty Center Conference on "Censorship and Silencing" in Los Angeles, December, 1995.

10. Gottlob Frege argued for the distinction between the use and mention of certain terms, suggesting that one might be able to refer to a term, that

is, mention it, without precisely using it. This distinction does not quite hold with hate speech, for the examples in which it is "mentioned" continue to be a kind of use. See "On Sense and Reference," in *Translations from the Philosophical Writings of Gottlob Frege*, eds., Peter Geach and Max Black, tr. Max Black, (Oxford: Oxford University Press, 1952).

11. See Catharine MacKinnon, *Only Words*, (Cambridge, Mass.: Harvard University Press, 1993) and Rae Langton, "Speech Acts and Unspeakable Acts," *Philosophy and Public Affairs*, vol. 22: no. 4 (Fall, 1993), pp. 293–330.

12. Catharine MacKinnon, *Only Words*, p. 21.

13. See Matsuda's introduction to *Words that Wound: Critical Race Theory, Assaultive Speech and the First Amendment*, eds. Mari Matsuda, Richard Delgado, Charles Lawrence III, and Kimberlè Crenshaw, (Boulder: Westview Press, 1993).

14. See the arguments put forth by Patricia Williams on the constructivist power of racist speech acts in *The Alchemy of Race and Rights*, (Cambridge, Mass.: Harvard University Press, 1991), p. 236.

15. For a thorough discussion of "fighting words" and an interesting argument on the First Amendment, see Kent Greenawalt, *Fighting Words: Individual, Communities, and Liberties of Speech*, (Princeton: Princeton University Press, 1995).

16. Op-Ed, *New York Times*, June 2, 1995.

17. See George Lipsitz, "Censorship of Commericial Culture. . .".

18. For a fuller account of Althusser's theory of interpellation, see my "Conscience Doth Make Subjects of Us All" which appeared first in *Yale French Studies*, #88, (Winter, 1995), pp. 6–26 and reprinted in my *The Psychic Life of Power*, forthcoming.

19. For an excellent overview of current debates on the status of linguistic convention, see *Rules and Conventions: Literature, Philosophy, Social Theory*, ed. Mette Hjort, (Baltimore: Johns Hopkins University Press, 1992). In particular, see "The Temporality of Convention: Convention Theory and Romanticism" by Claudia Brodsky Lacour in that volume. Central to nearly every post-Austinian analytic discussion of convention is David K. Lewis' *Convention: A Philosophical Study*, (Cambridge, Mass.: Harvard University Press, 1986). Stanley Cavell makes a convincing case for extending Austin's view of language in a Wittgensteinian direction, implicitly expanding the notion of "convention" in a broader conception of ordinary language. He also defends Austin against those who would oppose Austin's view of language to literary language. See Cavell, "What Did Derrida Want of Austin?" in *Philosophical Passages: The Bucknell Lectures in Literary Theory* (Cambridge, UK: Basil Black-

well, 1995), pp. 42–65. See as well Cavell's similar discussion in "Counter-Philosophy and the Pawn of Voice" in *A Pitch of Philosophy: Autobiographical Exercises* (Cambridge, Mass.: Harvard University Press, 1994) pp. 53–128.

20. This feature of Austinian iteration leads Shoshana Felman to compare Austin's work with that of Lacan. See Felman, *The Literary Speech Act*, Chapter IV. Also on this very indifference of linguistic convention to the "I" that it enables, see Felman's discussion of Emile Benveniste, pp. 13–22.

21. For a similar view that emphasizes "the imperfect character of verbal statements which renders them answerable and human communication possible," see J.G.A. Pocock, "Verbalizing a Political Act: Towards a Politics of Speech" in Michael J. Shapiro, *Language and Politics*, (New York: New York University Press, 1984), pp. 25–43.

22. Michel Foucault, "Politics and the Study of Discourse," in *The Foucault Effect: Studies in Governmentality*, ed. Graham Burchell, Colin Gordon, and Peter Miller, (Chicago: University of Chicago Press, 1991), p. 71

23. Of course, Habermas and others will extrapolate from this fundamentally Heideggerian point to make the claim that we participate in a universal community of sorts by virtue of what is commonly presupposed in every speech act, but this is I think quite a stretch from our current consideration. A more limited and plausible claim is that social context comes to inhere in language. For an excellent essay on how social contexts come to inhere in the literal use of language and the speech act, see William F. Hanks, "Notes on Semantics in Linguistic Practice," in *Bourdieu: Critical Perspectives*, eds. Craig Calhoun, Edward LiPuma, and Moishe Postone, (Chicago: University of Chicago Press, 1993), pp. 139–54.

24. The work of Stanley Cavell on J.L. Austin appears to be an important exception to this rule. Cavell argues that the attempt to attribute a determining intention to the speech act misses Austin's point that intentions are not as important as the conventions that give an illocutionary act its binding power.

For a fuller elaboration of this view, as well as a keen set of suggestions on how to read Austin on the question of seriousness, see Stanley Cavell, *A Pitch of Philosophy*, cited above.

25. Heidegger writes that historicity is not only the immanent operation of history, but its essential operation as well, and cautions against a reduction of historicity to the summation of moments: "Dasein does not exist as the sum of the momentary actualities of Experiences which come along successively and disappear. . . . Dasein does not fill up a track or stretch 'of life' . . . with its momentary actualities. It stretches *itself* along in such a way that its own Being is constituted in advance as a stretching-along," Martin Heidegger, *Being and Time*, ed. John Macquarrie and Edward Robinson, (New York: Harper &

Row, 1962), p. 426. Hans-Georg Gadamer emphasizes that this historicity is not bound to the moment in which it appears to inhere. Revising Heidegger, he writes, "the historical movement of human life consists in the fact that it is never utterly bound to any one standpoint, and hence can never have a truly closed horizon," *Truth and Method* (New York: Seabury Press, 1991), p. 235.

26. Cathy Caruth writes that "trauma is not experienced as a mere repression or defense, but as a temporal delay that carries the individual beyond the shock of the first moment. The trauma is the repeated suffering of the event," "Psychoanalysis, Culture, and Trauma," *American Imago, 48.1* (Spring, 1991), p. 6. See also Shoshana Felman and Dori Laub, M.D., *Testimony: Crisis of Witnessing in Literature, Psychoanalysis, and History*, (New York: Routledge, 1992).

CHAPTER 1

1. I greatly appreciate the thoughtful readings given to this chapter in an earlier form by Wendy Brown, Robert Gooding-Williams, Morris Kaplan, Robert Post, and Hayden White. Any inaccuracies and all misreadings are, of course, my responsibility alone. I thank Jane Malmo for help with preparing the manuscript. ⁄169

2. This criminal sense of an actor is to be distinguished both from the commercial and theatrical terms (*Händlerin* and *Schauspielerin*, respectively).

3. Robert M. Cover, "Violence and the Word," 96 *Yale Law Journal* 1595, 1601 n I (1986).

4. "The [state action] doctrine holds that although someone may have suffered harmful treatment of a kind that one might ordinarily describe as a deprivation of liberty or a denial of equal protection of the laws, that occurrence excites no constitutional concern unless the proximate active perpetrators of the harm include persons exercising the special authority or power of the government of a state." Frank Michelman, "Conceptions of Democracy in American Constitutional Argument: The Case of Pornography Regulation," 56 *Tennessee Law Review* 291, 306 (1989).

5. Charles Lawrence III, "If He Hollers Let Him Go: Regulating Racist Speech on Campus," in *Words that Wound: Critical Race Theory, Assaultive Speech and the First Amendment*, ed. Mari J. Matsuda, Charles R. Lawrence III, Richard Delgado, and Kimberlé Williams Crenshaw (Boulder: Westview Press, 1993), p. 65.

6. I thank Robert Post for this last analogy, suggested to me in conversation.

7. Kendall Thomas, "The Eclipse of Reason: A Rhetorical Reading of

'Bowers v. Hardwick'," 79 *Virginia Law Review*, 1805–1832 (Oct. 1993).

8. Jacques Derrida, "Signature, Event, Context," in *Limited Inc.*, ed. Gerald Graff, tr. Samuel Weber and Jeffrey Mehlman (Evanston, 1988), p. 18.

9. St. Paul Bias Motivated Crime Ordinance, Section 292.02 Minn. Legis. Code (1990).

10. Charles R. Lawrence III argues that "it is not just the prevalence and strength of the idea of racism that make the unregulated marketplace of ideas an untenable paradigm for those individuals who seek full and equal personhood for all. The real problem is that the idea of the racial inferiority of nonwhites infects, skews, and disables the operation of a market" in "If He Hollers Let Him Go: Regulating Racist Speech on Campus," in *Words That Wound*, p. 77.

11. The lawyers defending the application of the ordinance to the cross burning episode made the following argument:

> . . . we ask the Court to reflect on the 'content' of the 'expressive conduct' represented by a 'burning cross.' It is no less than the first step in an act of racial violence. It was and unfortunately still is the equivalent of [the] waving of a knife before the thrust, the pointing of a gun before it is fired, the lighting of the match before the reason, the hanging of the noose before the lynching. It is not a political statement, or even a cowardly statement of hatred. It is the first step in an act of assault. It can be no more protected than holding a gun to a victim['s] head. It is perhaps the ultimate expression of 'fighting words.'

R.A.V. v. St. Paul, 112 S. Ct. at 2569–70, fn. 8, 120 L. Ed. 2d at 320 (App. to Brief for Petitioner).

12. The new critical assumption to which I refer is that of the separable and fully formal unity that is said to characterize a given text.

13. All of the Justices concur that the St. Paul ordinance is overbroad because it isolates "subject-matter" as offensive, and (a) potentially prohibits discussion of such subject-matters even by those whose political sympathies are with the ordinance, and (b) fails to distinguish between the subject-matter's injuriousness and the context in which it is enunciated.

14. Justice Stevens, in a decision offered separately from the argument offered by the majority, suggests that the burning cross is precisely a threat, and that whether a given "expression" is a threat can only be determined *contextually*. Stevens bases his conclusion on *Chaplinsky*, which argued that one of the characteristics that justifies the constitutional status of fighting words is that such words "by their very utterance inflict injury or tend to incite an

immediate breach of the peace." *Chaplinsky v. New Hampshire*, 315 U.S. 568,572 (1942).

Here Stevens argues, first, that certain kinds of contents have always been proscribable, and, second, that the fighting words doctrine has depended for its very implementation on the capacity to discriminate among kinds of contents (i.e., political speech is more fully protected than obscene speech, etc.)., but also, third, that fighting words that are construed as a threat are in themselves injurious, and that it is this injurious character of speech, and not a separable "context" that is at issue. As he continues, however, Stevens is quick to point out that whether or not an expression is injurious is a matter of determining the force of an expression within a given context. This determination will never be fully predictable, precisely because, one assumes, contexts are also not firmly delimitable. Indeed, if one considers not only historical circumstance, but the historicity of the utterance itself, it follows that the demarcation of relevant context will be as fraught as the demarcation of injurious content.

Stevens links content, injurious performativity, and context together when he claims, objecting to both Scalia and White, that there can be no categorical approach to the question of proscribability: "few dividing lines in First Amendment laws are straight and unwavering, and efforts at categorization inevitably give rise only to fuzzy boundaries . . . the quest for doctrinal certainty through the definition of categories and subcategories is, in my opinion, destined to fail." *R.A.V. v. St. Paul*, 112 S. Ct. at 2561, 120 L. Ed. 2d, at 346. Furthermore, he argues, "the meaning of any expression and the legitimacy of its regulation can only be determined in context." *Id.*

At this point in his analysis, Stevens cites a metaphoric description of "the word" by Justice Holmes, a term which stands synecdochally for "expression" as it is broadly construed within First Amendment jurisprudence: the citation from Holmes runs as follows: "a word is not a crystal, transparent and unchanged, it is the skin of a living through and may vary greatly in color and content according to the circumstances and the time in which it is used" 11–12). We might consider this figure not only as a racial metaphor which describes the "word" as a "skin" that varies in "color," but also in terms of the theory of semantics it invokes. Although Stevens believes that he is citing a figure which will affirm the historically changing nature of an "expression's" semantic "content," denoted by a "skin" that changes in color and content according to the historical circumstance of its use, it is equally clear that the epidermal metaphor suggests a living and disembodied thought which remains dephenomenalized, the noumenal quality of life, the living spirit in

its skinless form. Skin and its changing color and content thus denote what is historically changing, but they also are, as it were, the signifiers of historical change. The racial signifier comes to stand not only for changing historical circumstances in the abstract, but for the specific historical changes marked by explosive racial relations.

15. Toni Morrison remarks that poverty is often the language in which black people are spoken about.

16. The above reading raises a series of questions about the rhetorical status of the decision itself. Kendall Thomas and others have argued that the figures and examples used in judicial decisions are as central to its semantic content as the explicit propositional claims that are delivered as the conclusions of the argumentation. In a sense, I am raising two kinds of rhetorical questions here, one has to do with the "content" of the decision, and the other with the way in which the majority ruling, written by Scalia, itself delimits what will and will not qualify as the content of a given public expression in light of the new restrictions imposed on fighting words. In asking, then, after the rhetorical status of the decision itself, we are led to ask how the rhetorical status of the decision presupposes a theory of semantics that undermines or works against the explicit theory of semantics argued for and in the decision itself.

172 /

Specifically, it seems, the decision itself draws on a distinction between the verbal and non-verbal parts of speech, those which Scalia appears to specify as "message" and "sound." *R.A.V. v. St. Paul*, 120 L. Ed. 2d 305, 319–21. For Scalia, only the sound of speech is proscribable or, analogously, that sensuous aspect of speech deemed inessential to the alleged ideality of semantic content. Although Justice Stevens rejects what he calls this kind of "absolutism," arguing instead that the proscribability of content can only be determined in context, he nevertheless preserves a strict distinction between the semantic properties of an expression and the context, including historical circumstance, but also conditions of address. For both Scalia and Stevens, then, the "content" is understood in its separability from both the non-verbal and the historical, although in the latter case, determined in relation to it.

17. The decision made in the trial of the policemen in Simi Valley relied on a similar kind of reversal of position, whereby the jury came to believe that the policemen, in spite of their graphic beating of King, were themselves the endangered party in the case.

18. Matsuda and Lawrence, "Epilogue," *Words that Wound*, p. 135.

19. *Chaplinsky* makes room for this ambiguity by stipulating that some speech loses its protected status when it constitutes "no essential part of any exposition of ideas." This notion of an inessential part of such an exposition

forms the basis of a 1973 ruling, *Miller v. California*, 413 U.S. 15, extending the unprotected status of obscenity. In that ruling the picture of a model sporting a political tattoo, constructed by the court as "anti-government speech," is taken as *un*protected precisely because it is said, "taken as a whole to lack serious literary, artistic, political, or scientific value." Such a representation, then, is taken to be "no essential part of any exposition of ideas." But here, you will note that "no essential part" of such an exposition has become "no valuable part." Consider then Scalia's earlier example of what remains unprotected in speech, that is, the noisy sound truck, the semantically void part of speech which, he claims, is the "nonspeech element of communication." Here he claims that only the semantically empty part of speech, its pure sound, is unprotected, but that the "ideas" which are sounded in speech most definitely are protected. This loud street noise, then, forms no essential part of any exposition but, perhaps more poignantly, forms no valuable part. Indeed, we might speculate that whatever form of speech is unprotected will be reduced by the justices to the semantically empty sounding title of "pure noise." Hence, the film clip of the ostensibly nude model sporting an anti-government tattoo would be nothing but pure noise, not a message, not an idea, but the valueless soundings of street noise.

20. Kimberlé Crenshaw marks this ambivalence in the law in a different way, suggesting that the courts will discount African-American forms of artistic expression as artistic expression and subject such expression to censorship precisely because of racist presumptions about what counts as artistic. On the other hand, she finds the representation of women in these expressions to be repellant, and so feels herself to be "torn" between the two positions. See "Beyond Racism and Misogyny: Black Feminism and 2 Live Crew," in *Words That Wound*.

21. Note the subsumption of the declaration that one is a homosexual under the rubric of offensive conduct: "Sexual orientation will not be a bar to service unless manifested by homosexual conduct. The military will discharge members who engage in homosexual conduct, which is defined as a homosexual act, a statement that the member is homosexual or bisexual, or a marriage or attempted marriage to someone of the same gender." "The Pentagon's New Policy Guidelines on Homosexuals in the Military," *The New York Times* (July 20, 1993), p. A14.

CHAPTER 2

1. Catharine MacKinnon writes in *Only Words* that "group defamation is the verbal form inequality takes." (99)

2. First Amendment jurisprudence has always allowed for the view that some speech is not protected, and has included in that category libel, threats, fraudulent advertising. Mari Matsuda writes, "there is much speech that is close to action. Conspiratorial speech, inciting speech, fraudulent speech, obscene phone calls, and defamatory speech. . ." (32).

3. Mari Matsuda, *Words that Wound*, 35–40.

4. "Whatever damage is done through such words is done not only through their context but through their content, in the sense that if they did not contain what they contain, and convey the meanings and feelings and thoughts that they convey, they would not evidence or actualize the discrimination that they do." Catharine MacKinnon, *Only Words*, (14); or "crossburning is nothing but an act, yet it is pure expression, doing the harm it does solely through the message it conveys." (33).

5. One of the most recent ruling *as* of this writing has struck down the new policy on the grounds that homosexuals ought not to be held responsible for "exciting the prejudices" of those who object to their homosexuality.

6. See Henry Louis Gates, Jr., "An Album is Judged Obscene; Rap, Slick, Violent, Nasty and, Maybe Helpful." *New York Times,* June 17, 1990, p. 1. Gates argues that the African-American genre of "signifying" is misunderstood by the court, and that such genres ought properly to be recognized as works of literary and cultural value.

7. For an excellent discussion of the "speech act component" of lesbian and gay self-identification, and its dependence on First Amendment protection, see William B. Rubenstein, "The 'Hate Speech' Debate from a Lesbian/Gay Perspective," in *Speaking of Race, Speaking of Sex: Hate Speech, Civil Rights, and Civil Liberties*, eds. Henry Louis Gates, Jr. et al, (New York: New York University Press, 1994), pp. 280–99.

8. Michel Foucault, *Power/Knowledge*, ed. Colin Gordon. "Two Lectures."

9. Earlier in the same lecture, Foucault offers a slightly more expanded formulation of this view: "the analysis in question . . . should be concerned with power at its extremities, in its ultimate destinations, with those points where becomes capillary, that is, in its more regional and local forms and institutions. Its paramount concern, in fact, should be with the point where power surmounts the rules of right which organize and delimit it and extends itself beyond them. . . ." (96)

10. This abstraction of the communicative scene of utterance appears to be the effect, in part, of a First Amendment jurisprudence organized in relation to the "Spence Test," formulated in *Spence v. Washington* 418 U.S. 405

(1974). For a very interesting effort within First Amendment jurisprudence to counter this move toward abstract communicative events with a situating of speech within social structure, see Robert Post, "Recuperating First Amendment Doctrine," *Stanford Law Review*, vol. 47, no. 6 (July, 1995) pp. 1249–1281.

11. See J.L. Austin, *How to Do Things With Words* on the "masquerading" forms of the performative (4). A performative does not have to assume an explicit grammatical form in order to operate as a performative. Indeed, a command might be as efficaciously enacted through silence as it is through its explicit verbal formulation. I gather that even a silent bearing would qualify as a linguistic performative to the extent that we understand silence as a constitutive dimension of speech.

12. It is important to note that Austin understood all performatives to be subject to misuse and misfire and to a relative impurity; this "failure" of felicity is generalized into a condition of performativity itself for Jacques Derrida and Shoshana Felman.

13. Rae Langton, "Speech Acts and Unspeakable Acts," *Philosophy and Public Affairs*, vol. 22: no. 4, (Fall, 1993), pp. 293–330.

14. Jürgen Habermas, *The Philosophical Discourse of Modernity*, tr. Frederick Lawrence, (Cambridge, Mass.: MIT Press, 1987), p. 198.

/175

15. Etienne Balibar, "Racism as Universalism," in *Masses, Classes, and Ideas*, trans. James Swenson, (NewYork: Routledge, 1994).

16. See the comparable views of ideals and idealization in Drucilla Cornell, *The Imaginary Domain* (NewYork: Routledge, 1995) and Owen Fiss, *The Irony of Free Speech*, (Cambridge, Mass.: Harvard University Press, 1996).

17. On the paradoxical efforts to invoke universal rights by French feminists both included and excluded from its domain, see Joan W. Scott, *Only Paradoxes to Offer: French Feminists and the Rights of "Man"* , Cambridge: Harvard University Press, forthcoming.

18. For an effort to retrieve freedom from conservative political discourse, see the introductory chapter of Wendy Brown's *States of Injury*, (Princeton, N.J.: Princeton University Press, 1995).

19. Although he makes this argument against psychoanalysis, it is, I would insist, a psychoanalytic argument all the same, and one can see this in a variety of texts in which Freud articulates the erotic economy of "conscience" for instance or in which the super-ego is understood to be, at least in part, wrought from the sexualization of a prohibition and only secondarily becomes the prohibition of sexuality.

20. This is, of course, not the case in those instances in which hate speech regulations are implemented within universities or other such institutions that retain ultimate authority over their jurisdiction.

CHAPTER 3

1. The Pentagon announced its "New Policy Guidelines on Homosexuals in the Military" on July 19, 1993, which included the following "discharge" policy: "Sexual orientation will not be a bar to service unless manifested by homosexual conduct. The military will discharge members who engage in homosexual conduct, which is defined as a homosexual act, a statement that the member is homosexual or bisexual, or a marriage or attempted marriage to someone of the same gender." After discussions in Congress on the policy, the Department of Defense on December 22, 1993 issued a set of new regulations seeking to clarify problems concerning implementation of the policy. One of the key issues to be clarified was whether a "statement" to the effect that one is a homosexual can be taken not only as "conduct" but as sufficient grounds for dismissal from the military. The clarification offered by the Department of Defense made clear that "statements that can be a basis for discharge are those which demonstrate a propensity or intent to engage in acts." Over and against those who claim that statements of the desire or intentions of an individual are not the same as conduct, the Department of Defense insisted that what they now have is "a conduct-based policy", on that is based on "the likelihood that the person would act." They explain, "a statement creates a rebuttable presumption a person will engage in acts, but the service member then has an opportunity to rebut. . . ."

Here, the "statement" that one is a homosexual presents the occasion to rebut the presumption, but later in this same presentation, the spokesperson from the Department of Defense appears to suggest the opposite: "Associational activities, like going to a gay parade or reading a magazine—in and of themselves—are not credible information [bearing on the conduct of the individual in question], and only rise to that level if they are such that a reasonable person would believe that *the conduct was intended to make a statement, intended to tell other people that the person is a homosexual*" (my emphasis). Here the question appears no longer to be whether the statement presents a rebuttable presumption that the person will engage in conduct, but whether conduct, of an associational kind, is sufficient to establish that a statement is being made. Whether the basis for dismissal is statement or conduct remains effectively open (July 20, 1993; Dec.22, 1993, *New York Times*).

In addition to the former and current Department of Defense policy, Congress entered the fray by introducing legislation of its own: The National Defense Authorization Act for Fiscal Year 1994. This binding statute emphasizes the problem of homosexual "propensity," and states that persons who demonstrate a propensity to act homosexually are deemed incompatible with military service. The statute also shows leniency for those who commit such acts on an occasion, but who repent or claim it was an accident. It also reintroduces the obligation of military officers "to ask" servicemen about their orientation. Whereas it does not accept statements regarding one's own homosexuality as tantamount to homosexual acts, it does regard such statements as *evidence of a propensity* that poses a rebuttable presumption of homosexuality.

Recent rulings on the new policy have split on the question of whether First Amendment rights are denied by the policy (suits concerning the "old policy" continue to be litigated as well, with mixed results). For a thorough and incisive review of this litigation, one on which I heavily rely in this discussion, see Janet Halley, "The Status/Conduct Distinction in the 1993 Revisions to Military Anti-Gay Policy" in *GLQ*, Winter, 1996.

2. Giorgio Agamben, "States of Emergency," lecture at the University of California at Berkeley, November, 1995.

3. Ernesto Laclau and Chantal Mouffe, *Hegemony and Socialist Strategy*, (London: Verso, 1986). /177

4. The following texts by Sigmund Freud are cited in this chapter: "On the Mechanism of Paranoia," (1911) and "On Narcissism: An Introduction" (1914), from *General Psychological Theory: Papers on Metapsychology*, (New York: MacMillan, 1963) pp. 29–48 and pp. 56–82, respectively; *Civilization and its Discontents*, tr. James Strachey, (New York: Norton, 1961; and *Totem and Taboo*, tr. James Strachey, (New York: Norton, 1950).

5. By allegory, I mean a kind of narrative in which, most generally, one speaks otherwise than one appears to speak, where one offers a sequential narrative ordering for something which cannot be described sequentially, and where the apparent referent of the allegory becomes the very action of elaboration that allegorical narrative performs.

6. For an interesting and relevant account of allegory, see Craig Owens, *Beyond Recognition: Representation, Power, and Culture*, ed. Scott Bryson, (Berkeley: University of California Press, 1992).

7. "The Pentagon's New Policy Guidelines on Homosexuals in the Military," *The New York Times*, July 20, 1993, p. A14.

8. Here one can see that Foucault's critique of Freud in *The History of Sexuality, Volume I* is partially wrong.

9. Sigmund Freud, "On Narcissism: An Introduction," *Standard Edition* Vol. XIV, (London: Hogarth Press, 1957), p. 96.

10. This would be a way to both confirm and deny the recent suggestions by Leo Bersani in *Homos* (Cambridge, Mass: Harvard University Press, 1995) that asserting a stable identity is a precondition of gay activism and that the intellectual skepticism directed at the success of that speech act are complicitous with a desexualization of gayness. To come out is still to perform a linguistic act and, hence, not necessarily to have sex or be sexual, except in that discursive way that may constitute a further instance of the linguistic sublimation of sex that Bersani laments.

CHAPTER 4

1. For a defense of MacKinnon along these lines, see Francis Ferguson, "Pornography: The Theory," in *Critical Inquiry*, summer, 1995.

2. For a strong defense of First Amendment "values" over and against hate speech regulation, see Robert Post, "Racist Speech, Democracy, and the First Amendment," in *Speaking Sex, Speaking Race*.

3. I am indebted on this point to insights offered in Richard Burt's wide-ranging work on censorship: "Uncensoring in Detail," presented at the Getty Center in December, 1995, as well as *Licensed by Authority: Ben Johnson and the Discourses of Censorship*, (Ithaca: Cornell University Press, 1993), and *The Administration of Aesthetics: Censorship, Political Criticism, and the Public Sphere*, ed. Richard Burt, (Minneapolis: University of Minnesota Press, 1994).

4. Ellen Burt has made this argument in "An Immediate Taste for Truth": Censoring History in Baudelaire's 'Les Bijoux'," in *Censorship and Silencing*, ed. Robert Post, (New York: Oxford University Press), forthcoming.

5. I take up this issue briefly in "The Force of Fantasy: Mapplethorpe, Feminism, and Discursive Excess," in *differences*, 2:2, (Fall, 1990).

6. For a thorough and insightful discussion of the statute and the "propensity" clause, see Janet E. Halley, "Achieving Military Discharge: the 1993 Revisions to Military Anti-Gay Policy" *GLQ: A Journal of Lesbian and Gay Studies*, 1996.

7. See Robert Post's "Racist Speech. . ." for a fuller discussion of public discourse.

8. This is a distinction that Michel Foucault offers in the second volume of *The History of Sexuality* in his effort to counter disciplinary form of power to sovereign power. He distinguishes between power conceived as "repressive," and power, as "productive."

9. This may seem like a convoluted formulation, but consider that political theorists from Aristotle to Arendt have made the claim that it is as *linguistic* that humans become political kinds of beings. My reflections constitute an extension of such a claim. Arendt cites Aristotle's definition of "man as a *zoon logon ekhon*," one for whom exists the possibility of ". . .a way of life in which speech and only speech made sense . . ." in *The Human Condition* (Chicago: University of Chicago Press, 1985) p. 27. See pages 25–27 for Arendt's interpretation of Aristotle on the political animal as a speaking being.

10. A further elaboration of this view can be found in Dina Al-Kassim's dissertation on "ranting" written for the Department of Comparative Literature at Berkeley: "On Pain of Speech: Fantasies of the First Order and the Literary Rant."

11. Charles Taylor, "To Follow a Rule. . . ," in *Bourdieu: Critical Perspectives*, eds. Craig Calhoun, Edward LiPuma, and Moishe Postone, (Chicago: University of Chicago Press, 1993), p. 51.

12. See Saidiya Hartman, *Scenes of Subjection*, (New York: Oxford University Press), forthcoming.

13. Vicki Schultz, "Women 'Before the Law'" in *Feminists Theorize the Political*, eds. Butler and Scott, (New York: Routledge, 1993).

14. Wendy Brown, "Freedom's Silences" in *Censorship and Silencing*, ed. /179 Robert Post (New York: Oxford University Press), forthcoming.

15. On July 20, 1995, the Board of Regents of the University of California passed two resolutions, SP-1 and SP-2, which ban the use of "race, religion, sex, color, ethnicity, or national origin as criteria for admission to the University or to any program of study" as well as in employment and contracting by the University.

In Section 4 of this document, the Regents make clear that they are willing to make exceptions for some individuals who have heroically overcome adversity: "consideration shall be given to individuals who, despite having suffered disadvantage economically or in terms of their social environment (such as abusive or otherwise dysfunctional home or a neighborhood of unwholesome or antisocial influences), but have nonetheless demonstrated sufficient character and determination in overcoming obstacles to warrant confidence. . . ."

16. Wendy Brown, "Freedom's Silences."

17. Lacan's word is "forclusion" and is introduced as the French translation of Freud's term, "Verwerfung." "Verwerfung" in Freud is generally translated into English as repudiation or rejection. In the *Vocabulaire de la psychanalyse*, Jean Laplanche and J.-B Pontalis refer to foreclosure as a primordial rejection

of that which remains outside of the symbolic universe of the subject. This definition makes use of a specific sense of the "outside," however, one that is close to the notion of the "constitutive outside" as used by Jacques Derrida. This "outside" is the defining limit or exteriority to a given symbolic universe, one which, were it imported into that universe, would destroy its integrity and coherence. In other words, what is set outside or repudiated from the symbolic universe in question is precisely what binds that universe together *through its exclusion.*

Laplanche and Pontalis argue that what is foreclosed is to be distinguished from what is repressed (*refoulement* in French, and *Verdrängung* in German). What is foreclosed is not integrated into the unconscious of the subject; it cannot be recalled or remembered and brought into consciousness. It does not belong to the realm of neurosis, but to that of psychosis; indeed, its entry into the symbolic universe threatens psychosis, which is to say that its exclusion guarantees symbolic coherence. Freud makes reference to "Verwerfung" in relation to the fear of castration in both "The Three Essays on the Theory of Sexuality" (*SE, VII*, 227) and "The History of an Infantile Neurosis" (*SE, XVII*, 85). Whereas Freud occasionally attempts to define a form of repression that corresponds to psychosis, Lacan introduces "foreclosure" to specify that form of repression.

18. Here I take my cue from Derrida's influential early essay, "Structure, Sign, and Play in the Discourse of the Human Sciences," in *Writing and Difference,* tr. Alan Bass, (Chicago: University of Chicago Press, 1978), pp. 278–294.

19. Pierre Bourdieu, *Language and Symbolic Power,* ed. John B. Thompson, tr. Gino Raymond and Matthew Adamson, (Cambridge, Mass: Harvard University Press), 1991, pp. 137–62.

20. See Gayatri Chakravorty Spivak, "In a Word. Interview" with Ellen Rooney, in *differences: A Journal of Feminist Cultural Studies,* vol. 1: no.2, (summer, 1989), pp. 124–56.

21. Bourdieu's notion of the *habitus* might well be read as a reformulation of Althusser's notion of ideology. Whereas Althusser will write that ideology constitutes the "obviousness" of the subject, but that this obviousness is the effect of a *dispositif.* That same term reemerges in Bourdieu to describe the way in which a *habitus* generates certain beliefs. Dispositions are generative and transposable. Note in Althusser's "Ideology and Ideological State Apparatuses" the inception of this latter reappropriation:

> "An individual believes in God, or Duty, or Justice, etc. This belief derives (for everyone, i.e. for all those who live in an ideological representation of ideology, which reduces ideology to ideas endowed by

definition with a spiritual existence) from the ideas of the individual concerned, i.e. from him as a subject with a consciousness which contains the ideas of his belief. In this way, i.e. by means of the absolutely ideological 'conceptual' device (*dispositif*) thus set up (a subject endowed with a consciousness in which he freely forms or freely recognizes ideas in which he believes), the (material) attitude of the subject concerned naturally follows." (167)

22. See editor's introduction, *Language and Symbolic Action*, p. 13.

23. *The Logic of Practice*, p. 73.

24. Bourdieu argues in a vein highly reminiscent of Henri Bergson's argument in *Matter and Memory* that the body acts as a repository for the entirety of its history. Bourdieu writes, "the *habitus*—embodied history, internalized as a second nature and so forgotten as history—is the active presence of the whole past of which it is the product." (56). The metaphorics of the body as "depository" or "repository" recalls Bergson (and Plato's discussion of the *chora*, that famous receptacle in the *Timaeus*). But the presumption that the entirety of memory is preserved or "acted" in the present characterizes the temporal dimension of the body's materiality for Bergson: " . . . memory itself, with the totality of our past, is continually pressing forward, so as to insert the largest possible part of itself into our present action." (168). Earlier in *Matter and Memory*, he writes, "Habit rather than memory, it acts our past experience but does not call up its image" (151).

25. *The Logic of Practice*, p. 73.

26. *Ibid.*, p. 66.

27. *Ibid.*, p. 69.

28. Maurice, Merleau-Ponty, *The Phenomenology of Perception* tr. Colin Smith, (London: Routledge & Kegan Paul, 1962), p. 183.

29. For an interesting and thoughtful consideration of the paradoxes produced by Bourdieu's theory of "inclination" and "motivation", see Theodore Richard Schatzki, "Overdue Analysis of Bourdieu's Theory of Practice", *Inquiry*, 30, (March: 1987), pp. 113–135.

30. Bourdieu also argues that this magic is to be understood as the power to produce collective recognition of the authority of the performative, and that the performative cannot succeed without this collective recognition: "One should never forget that language, by virtue of the infinite generative but also originative capacity—in the Kantian sense—which it derives from its power to produce existence by producing the collectively recognized, and thus realized, representation of existence, is no doubt the principal support of the dream of absolute power." *Language and Symbolic Power*, p. 42.

31. For a relevant discussion of the phantasmatic promise of the performative, see Slavoj Žižek, *The Sublime Object of Ideology*, (Verso, 1989), pp. 94–120.

32. Here it is clear that Derrida's notion of the performative as a speech act that must break with prior contexts if it is to remain a performative, that is, governed by an iterable code, offers an important counterpoint to functionalist social theory. One sees as well the specific social meaning of Derridean iterability in the context of this discussion of expropriation and resignification.

Index /

DATE DUE

CHANGING VISIONS

Human Cognitive Maps:
Past, Present, and Future

Ervin Laszlo, Robert Artigiani
Allan Combs, Vilmos Csányi

PRAEGER

Westport, Connecticut

Published in the United States and Canada by Praeger Publishers
88 Post Road West, Westport, CT 06881
An imprint of Greenwood Publishing Group, Inc.

Printed in the United States of America

The paper used in this book complies with the
Permanent Paper Standard issued by the National
Information Standards Organization (Z39.48–1984).

10 9 8 7 6 5 4 3 2 1

English language edition, except the United States and Canada,
published by Adamantine Press Limited, 3 Henrietta Street, Covent
Garden, London WC2E 8LU England.

First published in 1996

Library of Congress Cataloging-in-Publication Data

Changing visions : human cognitive maps : past, present, and future /
    Ervin Laszlo . . . [et al.] ; edited by Allan Combs.
        p.   cm.—(Praeger studies on the 21st century, ISSN
    1076–1850)
    Includes bibliographical references and index.
    ISBN 0–275–95676–8 (alk. paper)—ISBN 0–275–95677–6 (pbk. :
alk. paper)
    1. Cognitive maps.   2. Cognitive maps—Social aspects.   3. Schemas
(Psychology)   4. Human information processing.   5. Psychology,
Comparative.   I. Laszlo, Ervin, 1932–   .   II. Combs, Allan, 1942–
    BF314.C43   1996
    153—dc20   96–15309

Library of Congress Catalog Card Number: 96–15309
ISBN: 0–275–95676–8   Cloth
        0–275–95677–6   Paperback

Copyright © 1996 by Adamantine Press Limited

Contents

Notes on the Authors

Professor Robert Artigiani teaches courses in the History and Philosophy of Science. A founding member of both the General Evolution Research Group and the Washington Evolutionary Systems Society (WESS), he is President of the editorial board of *World Futures: The Journal of General Evolution* and Vice President of WESS.

Professor Artigiani has lectured at many European, American, and Indian universities. He was among the first to perceive the social implications of contemporary scientific paradigms and has organized several conferences for discussing ways to reconcile the sciences and humanities.

He has published articles in several scholarly journals as well as in books edited by, among others, Ervin Laszlo.

Professor Allan Combs is a neuropsychologist and systems theorist at the University of North Carolina at Asheville and Saybrook Institute in San Francisco. Author of over fifty articles, chapters, and books on consciousness and the brain, he is co-founder of the Society for Chaos Theory in Psychology and a member of the General Evolution Research Group and the Club of Budapest.

His books include *Synchronicity: Science, Myth and the Trickster*, with Mark Holland; *Chaos Theory in Psychology and the Life Sciences*, edited with Robin Robertson; and *The Radiance of Being: Complexity, Chaos, and the Evolutions of Consciousness*.

Dr Combs has Psychology degrees from the Ohio State University and the University of Florida, and holds a doctorate in BioPsychology from the University of Georgia. He is Book Review Editor of the journal *World Futures*.

Vilmos Csányi is Professor of Ethology at the Lorand Eötvös, University of Budapest, Hungary, and the founder and Director of the Department of Ethology there. He is the author of more than one hundred research articles, twelve books, and many popular articles on various biological topics.

Ervin Laszlo, Ph.D. is editor of the journal *World Futures* and the author or editor of forty-nine books, including *The Choice* and *Goals for Human Society: A Report to the Club of Rome on the New Horizons of Global Community.*

Dr Laszlo was Professor of Philosophy at the State University of New York, and has taught Systems Science, Futures Studies, World Order Studies, and Aesthetics at Portland State University, the University of Houston, Princeton, and Indiana University.

As well as being President of the newly formed Club of Budapest and of the International Society for the Systems Sciences, he is a prominent member of the Club of Rome, and advisor to the Director-General of Unesco.

Introduction

Everybody carries a picture of the world in his head, said mathematician Henri Poincaré. Neither he, nor anyone else would add, however, that this picture must necessarily be correct. There is indeed such a thing as a "cognitive map" of the world we experience, but this map need not be a faithful representation of that world. Indeed, it is likely to be partial, and to contain illusory and mistaken elements. Faulty maps, however, prompt erroneous behaviors, giving rise to various kinds and degrees of shocks and surprises.

Shocks and surprises are not entirely avoidable, for the world is not knowable in its entirety (and, even if it were knowable in its entirety, it might still not be predictable in its entirety). However, beyond some margin of tolerance, shocks and surprises begin to eat into one's chances of well-being—even of survival. It is in everyone's interest, therefore, to make the picture that he or she carries in his or her head as faithful as possible to the world in which he or she actually lives.

Cognitive maps are held by individuals, but the set of cognitive maps of individuals produces a collective kind of construction that constitutes a *social* cognitive map. Such a map, once evolved, takes on a life of its own; it cannot be reduced or disaggregated to the particular maps held by individuals. Since we are guided both by our own individual cognitive map and by that of our society, attention must be paid to both. In this study we review the origins and development of individual and social cognitive maps.

The origin of cognitive maps in the animal kingdom provides a useful insight into the nature and function of the maps held by individuals, though it does not follow that human cognitive maps are nothing but animal maps in a refined form. The evolution of human cognitive maps in the course of history has further lessons: it shows how individuals interact with the cognitive maps of others in their historical time and

place and evolve the map typical of their society. Reviewing the developmental background can help us better to understand our own situation here and now. The crucial question is how the cognitive maps held in our own brain–mind came about, and how they are being shaped today—above all, whether they are good enough to assure the goals of our own existence, and that of our peers.

Aside from such metaphysical questions as "is our map an assuredly true mapping of the reality that surrounds us?" we can ask more modest and pragmatic questions, such as "is our cognitive map faithful enough to the world around us to guide our steps without creating shocks and surprises that impair our well-being and threaten our survival?" Such questions are no longer matters of merely theoretical interest. We shall not survive either as individuals or as a species if our maps fail to reflect the nature of the world that surrounds us—a world with which we constantly interact and that, in some measure, we also create, albeit without necessarily recognizing what it is that we interact with and what it is that we create.

Making our own cognitive map an adequately faithful representation of the world around us does not require us to be scientists. Indeed, a scientist, being a specialist in a particular field, cannot help but have a narrow map, corresponding to his or her research specialty. Though such a map may be more exact than commonsense maps, it will not be of great assistance in guiding everyday behavior if it deals with nuclear processes on Gamma Centauri, or with any other topic typical of the highly focused attention of contemporary natural scientists. The human and social sciences, of course, come closer to promoting the formation of faithful maps of lived reality, but such maps may still be what psychologist Edward Tolman (1948) called "strip maps," rather than basically adequate representations. Religion, common sense, even art can fill in and sharpen one's world-picture, but only a realization that such pictures are fluid and adaptable, and come from many streams and dimensions of experiences can enable people constantly to update and adapt their cognitive maps and make them into functional guides for their action and behavior.

It is our hope that reviewing the origins, development, and current changes in individual and social cognitive maps will prompt the reader to become more conscious of the nature and role of his or her own map, and better able to adapt it to the exigencies of our changing world. The exercise, if undertaken with sincerity and attention, cannot but benefit both the individuals who undertake it and the human and social world in which they live.

The Cognitive Maps of Individuals

Cognitive maps are mental representations of the worlds in which we live. They are built of our individual experiences, recorded as memories and tested against the unceasing demands of reality. These maps, however, do not simply represent the worlds of our experience in a passive and unchanging way. They are, in fact, dynamic models of the environments in which we carry out our daily lives, and as such determine much of what we expect, and even what we see. Thus, they represent and at the same time participate in the creation of our individual realities. These ideas will be explored in the following pages, beginning with the creation of cognitive maps in the brain, then proceeding to the role of such maps in the creation of our experience of reality itself. From there we will move beyond the individual to the social fabric of reality, woven of individual cognitive maps, which ultimately form tapestries that have realities entirely of their own.

The idea of cognitive maps was developed in the early decades of this century by the American psychologist Edward Tolman (1886–1959). Like many psychologists of his day, he was interested in how laboratory rats learned to navigate mazes, but unlike his colleagues, he believed that the rats acquired a figural, or gestalt-like, knowledge of each entire maze. This amounted to a mental road map that the rat could use to find its way to food at the end of the run. Most psychologists of that era preferred more objective explanations of behavior, holding that rats simply learned to connect particular responses to particular stimuli. Tolman disagreed with this reductionistic view, according to which, in his words, the rats "helplessly" responded "to a succession of external stimuli—sights, sounds, smells, pressures, etc." (Tolman 1948: 190). He argued for the presence of internal representations of the environment that included parts of the maze well beyond what could be seen from any single location.

Many informal observations avowed the presence of cognitive maps. One rat, for instance, escaped from the start chamber and ran straight across the top of the maze to the finish box. In terms of systematic research, Tolman's most convincing demonstrations involved the process of *latent learning*. To demonstrate latent learning, the experimenter would place a rat in a maze and let it walk around and explore at leisure. No food or other reward was placed in the maze at this time. Later, however, when the same rat was trained to run the maze for food, it would perform better than a rat that did not have the benefit of previous experience with the maze. Evidently, in simply exploring the maze with no particular incentive to find its way through, the rat had learned something about the lay of the land. This learning was latent in the sense that it was not visible until the rat was later required to use the learning to find food. Tolman maintained that the rat had actually constructed an internal representation, a cognitive map, of the maze.

Tolman, of course, was interested in more than just rats, and intended the idea of cognitive maps to apply to other organisms as well, including human beings. Working with rats, however, he discovered that some cognitive maps are broad and comprehensive, while others, which he called "strip maps," are narrow and confining, causing the rat to restrict its searches to a small portion of the entire maze. He observed that strip maps can result from a number of factors, including too much training in a single runway, too few environmental cues, and strongly motivating or frustrating conditions. He felt that the latter produced what amounted to a state of anxiety, and believed that strip maps, or their equivalents in human beings, are at the root of many forms of behavioral pathology.

The Creation of Cognitive Maps

The extent to which the complex brain of the human being creates its own reality is a question that is still open (Anderson 1990). Among those who ponder such matters, all but a few agree that a substantial portion of our experience of "reality" is self-created. At the level of perception alone, it seems that the world does not simply present itself to us finished, as if our eyes were merely windows that allowed images to enter and pass on, unchanged, into the brain. As we move about in space, retinal images undergo fluid alterations in size, shape, brightness, and color that do not at all resemble the fixed landscapes we actually experience. The constancy of the perceived visual world bears witness

to the active role played by the eye and the brain in interpreting the optical display that arrives at the retina. It seems that, as organisms, we are better suited to dealing with a universe of fixed and reliable properties than a more primary one of energy flux and transformation.

In recent years, the active role of the human in interpreting the raw data of the senses has come to be recognized as so profound that more than a few perceptual psychologists have found themselves tipping over into the field of cognitive psychology, which studies the active involvement of the mind in organizing and defining the world. One such psychologist is Ulric Neisser. In the 1960s, Neisser became interested in how retinal images are identified as familiar objects such as cups, shoes, airplanes, and pencils (Neisser 1976).

Neisser observed that a logical analysis of this problem suggests two general types of solution. One is that the brain acts like a computer, and sorts through all the objects represented in its memory to compare each with that represented in the retinal image. The search continues until a favorable match is obtained. This is called a *bottom-up* approach. Its computational cost, however, is enormous. The brain must be prepared to review virtually everything represented in its entire memory. In other words, it must check every known object against the one in front of it. Even for large computers such a task is too time-consuming to be practical unless the size of the search is artificially narrowed. The human brain, however, is not a computer but a biological organ. It is not designed to carry out multiple operations in the space of nanoseconds, and so is evidently not designed to enact computational programs that rely on speed for success.

The other type of solution is somehow to anticipate the type of object most likely to be represented by the retinal image, and then conduct a narrow search within the anticipated category. This strategy, termed a *top-down* approach, still requires some searching, but narrows it to the objects most likely to be seen. Suppose, for instance, that one sees an object on the kitchen counter. Here, the context of the kitchen immediately narrows the search to objects such as a butter knife, can opener, or pie pan. Such objects will be more quickly recognized than a screwdriver or a pipe wrench. The bottom-up approach requires that the brain (or computer) have a certain amount of knowledge about how the world works, in this case about what kinds of object are commonly found in various locations about the house, in kitchens, workshops, bathrooms, and so forth. Neisser called such patterns of information *anticipatory schemata.*

Based on such considerations and the results of much research,

Neisser developed the *perceptual cycle* model, according to which activity moves, or cycles, between these two modes. Confronted with an object on the kitchen counter, a pipe wrench for instance, one would first expect it to be something commonly found in the kitchen. Failing to recognize the object, one momentarily flounders before entertaining comparisons from other schemata, such as the one that identifies objects found in the bathroom or workshop.

All of this, of course, concerns the act of recognition. However, the ability of the eye and brain to produce a solid visual experience despite the continuous fluctuation of the retinal image hints at a deeper enigma. This is the question of how, out of the mercurial flux of energies that continually rain down on the sensory organs of the body, the nervous system constructs the experience of a solid world in the first place. And beyond this, to what extent, if any, does that construction represent some "real," objective world beyond the senses?

In a classic study of the evolution of the nervous system, Jerison (1973) showed that one of the brain's central problems is to coordinate sensory input as it arrives on a number of diverse channels—touch, taste, smell, hearing, and vision. He pointed out that the most efficient mechanism for bringing about a complete integration of these disparate channels is to project—in a word, *create*—a unified external reality within which sensory features can be located. It is easier for the brain to deal with a solid living tiger than to consider separately the implications of its odor, its stripes, its roar, and so on!

Jerison argued that the mode of sensory integration developed by mammals is essentially visual. Its beginnings go back to the late Triassic period, about 200 million years ago, when mammals first appeared as nocturnal "reptiles" in whom audition came to replace vision as the primary distance sense. Neurologically, the transition from vision to audition was accomplished by the remapping of auditory input onto previously established reptilian visual networks, which, like the retina itself, represented vision in a spatially distributed fashion. In time, the mammalian forebrain became the center in which virtually all the external senses are mapped into a visually structured world. Thus the mammalian brain became a world-maker. In Jerison's words:

"Reality" or a "real world" is a construction of the nervous system. It is, in fact, a model of a possible world which enables the nervous system to process the mass of incoming and outgoing information in a consistent way. It is a trick, as it were, to enable an organism with a large nervous system to handle almost inconceivably large amounts of information that are usually thought of as nerve impulses or states of membranes of single cells. (1973: 410)

In other words, from a neurologically informed perspective, the experienced world is a map.

It is of interest that recent research has provided substantial support for an understanding of the brain that views it as taking in frequency information—sound frequency, visuospatial frequency, and so on—and, by processes analogous to those of holography, using this information to create a unified perceptual world (Globus 1987a; Pribram 1991).

Just how much flexibility is allowed in this process of world formation is anyone's guess (Anderson 1990). It is apparent from both anthropology and history that different cultures have survived admirably well using widely disparate maps of reality. On the other hand, a visit to the local psychiatric hospital, or an attempt to build a simple electric circuit at home, will demonstrate that there are limits to improvisation.

At the most conservative extreme, the prominent psychologist J. J. Gibson started a school of perceptual psychology that champions the idea that the visual display arriving at the eye carries pre-packaged within itself all the relationships that characterize external reality (Gibson 1966). These are simply picked up, or at best interpreted, and there is no need for internal representations along the lines of a cognitive map—certainly not at the sensory level. Such realism, however, is considered a little naive by most scientists. At the other extreme neuropsychiatrist Gordon Globus (1987a) argues that, in its enormous complexity and flexibility, the human brain is capable of creating and projecting a virtually unlimited number of entire worlds. He states that "the brain in its unsurpassed complexity generates its own holoplenum of *possibilia*—a virtual holoworld of possible worlds" (p. 378). From the evidence of altered states of consciousness, shamanism, and the experience of ordinary dreams, he concludes that "human beings have the capacity to constitute *de novo* perfectly authentic worlds . . . worlds which have never previously been experienced" (p. 382). Surely the answer falls somewhere between the poles represented by these two opinions. It is certain, however, that if we do not create the universe *ex nihilo*, we actively participate in molding our experience of it.

A startling observation that emerges from all of the above is that the maps that the nervous system spins of reality are, for the person concerned, no less than reality itself. In a sense that is not trivial—and contrary to the famous words of Count Alfred Korzybski (1958)—the map *is* the territory. What is more, such mapmaking (reality-spinning) is not limited to sensory perception, but extends to virtually all levels of experience. Not only do we see the pipe wrench on the kitchen

counter as a solid object with fixed features—despite fluctuations in lighting, distance, and angle subtended at the eye—but the fact that it presents itself to us as a pipe wrench and not a hammer, paperweight, tomahawk, or the jawbone of a god, that it is owned by a particular person and is not communal property, and that it is out of place in the kitchen, all attest to the character of the cognitive maps (reality) by which we appraise it.

It seems that maintaining highly consistent cognitive maps is a passion, indeed an obsession, of human beings. Neuropsychologist Michael Gazzaniga (1985) has in fact postulated the existence of a left-hemispheric brain process called the *interpreter*, the job of which is to monitor everything coming out of other brain processes, such as those concerned with memory, emotion, and the senses, in order to come up with a coherent picture (map) of the individual's immediate situation. It might observe, for instance, "My memory tells me that I haven't eaten for several hours, I notice that my stomach feels hollow and that my mouth is watering, and I am experiencing fantasies of food. I interpret all this to mean I am hungry." This example is too literal because it assumes the interpreter to be conscious of its own operation—and apparently it is not—but it captures the basic idea of how it works.

The dramatic thing about this interpreter is that it seems impelled to conceive a single interpretation of reality, a unitary mapping of the events of the moment, and then stick to it tenaciously, even when the product is patently distorted. For example, Gazzaniga (1985) tells of a woman who was hospitalized at the Memorial Sloan-Kettering hospital in New York City with damage to her right parietal lobe. She was charming, witty, and in all ways intelligent, except that she insisted she was at her home in Freeport, Maine! No one could convince her otherwise. In desperation, Gazzaniga pointed to the big hospital elevator doors just outside her room and asked, "What are those things over there?" "Those," she responded, "are elevators. Do you have any idea what it cost me to have them put in my house?"

According to Gazzaniga, the problem with this woman was that whatever brain mechanism is responsible for keeping track of real-time location was producing dramatically distorted output, while other brain systems continued to function as usual, oblivious to the error. It seemed simply to be beyond the capability of this otherwise intelligent woman to recognize the distortion in her map that located her in Freeport, Maine.

It would appear that as human beings each of us stands at the center of a multitude of self-created maps of reality, each of which charts some

dimension of our experience. Some maps, such as the one gone wrong for the lady in the Memorial Sloan-Kettering hospital, graph our physical landscapes, plotting our location and movement in space and time. Others map overlapping classes of information useful in different spheres of our daily lives, while still others chart value systems. The class of information needed to visit a restaurant, for instance, includes rules for how to interact with the waiter and the maître d', when and where to leave the tip, how to eat in a mannerly fashion, and so on. These rules, of course, differ somewhat from restaurant to restaurant, depending on variables such as social class and ethnic orientation. Since classes of information such as that needed for proper restaurant behavior seem to form recognizable patterns, they are often understood by cognitive scientists as *schemata*, not unlike Neisser's perceptual schemata, which provided information about a particular visual situation. These terms are similar to our use of the term *map*.

Such maps, or schemata, turn out to be surprisingly complex. A couple of decades ago, when artificial intelligence experts first began to program computers to simulate simple human behaviors, it was discovered, much to the consternation of the programmers, that without exquisitely elaborate programs, computers made unbelievably stupid errors. A simulation of a restaurant scene, for instance, might find the patrons entering by walking directly through the walls, whereupon they might seat themselves on the floor (exactly where the computer probably has the waiter serve the food) and eventually tip the cook before leaving. To get this scene right, the programmer must supply the computer with an enormous amount of commonsense information of the kind that makes up the basic cognitive maps that guide human behavior.

The human "restaurant map," as we will call it, overlaps with larger maps that represent general rules for how to behave in public. If we know these larger maps well, we are unlikely to go too far afield in our restaurant behavior. Maps that carry information about our professions, as well those that govern our relationships with members of our immediate families, are more general than the restaurant map. On the other hand, they are more limited than those governing public behavior in general. Moreover, the information contained in these various maps is highly redundant. Thus, it is perhaps not surprising that damage to particular regions of the brain rarely destroys entire cognitive maps. Brain injury patients rarely loose their entire sense of social protocol, or their entire knowledge of where things are in space. On the other hand, more limited maps are vulnerable. Thus, we read of seemingly

bizarre cases in which a stroke victim has lost his ability to recall the names of garden flowers, say, or vegetables.

The notion of maps, like that of schemata, implies a connected world of experience. Maps can vary in breadth as well as in detail. Among cartographers there is the further understanding that each map utilizes some particular *projection*, or coordinate system, that is laid out in a specific fashion. Flat maps representing the sphere of the Earth, for instance, have strikingly different appearances depending on the nature of the projection used. If the metaphor of projections can be carried over to cognitive maps, then different projection systems would be equivalent to different ways of organizing reality. Here we are not speaking of the actual content displayed by the maps. Rather, it is a matter of how the content is represented. All projections of the Earth exhibit the same continents, but their appearance differs according to the nature of the projection. The bottom line is that each projection system is the equivalent of a unique experienced world.

Cognitive Maps in Animals

Before proceeding further in our examination of cognitive maps in humans, let us trace the origins of cognitive maps in the animal kingdom. This will provide us with a wider perspective from which to further our understanding of cognitive maps. Animals have developed such organs as the nervous system and the brain for perceiving, understanding, and influencing the external world in the interests of their own survival. But the brains of animals can never grasp the surrounding world in its totality. They focus, rather, on those aspects of the environment that are essential for their own survival and reproduction. We will refer to these aspects as *environmental information.*

Information about the environment influences animals in at least two ways. On the one hand it affects their immediate behavior. On the other hand—and this is equally important—it takes part in events leading to the evolution of entirely new behavior patterns.

Every animal species has a special food-acquiring behavior pattern. The blue tit, for example, searches for insects in the cracks of bark on trees—an activity that presupposes an appropriate bill, good sight, and a brain that is able to process the perceived stimuli very quickly. The techniques for acquiring food can be very sophisticated, including the use of traps, radio-location, electricity, and an extremely refined mind. The food-getting activities of animals are controlled by the best kind

of "computer" in the world, the nervous system. In lower invertebrates, the nervous system is only slightly "programmable," so these kinds of animal do not learn much during their life. The technique for acquiring their food is a genetic heritage, stored in the "genetic memory." The way spiders spin nets or catch and kill their prey is entirely determined by genetic programs.

If a food-getting technique were analyzed in order to find the simplest units of behavioral instruction (called algorithms in computer language), we would find these algorithms stored mainly in genetic memory. In the course of its development, the animal's nervous system has been programmed for the proper algorithms by the genetic memory. Whenever it is necessary, the programs are activated automatically by information from the environment and the animal fulfills these instructions exactly. Instructions are not rigid; they are able to evolve. Natural selection ensures that the behavioral algorithms are always nearly perfect. For example, if a spider is born without the ability to spin nets, owing to some genetic or developmental defect, it will not be able to catch its food and, therefore, to produce offspring. Thus the wrong program cannot be transmitted to the next generation. However, occasionally a slight transformation of the original program in the genetic material slightly improves the behavioral algorithm. In this case, the transformation can survive in the offspring and it is this which forms the basis for the evolution of behavior. As a consequence of natural selection, the food-getting behavior of an animal is exactly that which enables it to obtain food within the natural environment.

The higher vertebrates are not only supported by their genetic memory—although a great variety of instructions are also fixed in it—but are also provided with a neural memory, developed during the course of various learning processes and permitting a more sophisticated adaptation compared to the genetic memory. Mammals, particularly, have a highly developed memory of this kind, as the young benefit from a long period of parental guidance—something that provides the opportunity for the young to acquire the most appropriate behavioral algorithms. The two kinds of memory are not separated rigorously but combine subtly during the life of the animal. Predatory mammals hold instructions in their genetic memory such as "chase everything that moves." This is a general instruction and we can observe it very well in the behavior of juvenile predators. As soon as they are able to move, they chase any moving object, including their litter-mates, their mother (or her tail), fallen leaves whirled along by the wind, but mostly any living creatures that move. The special function of neural memory is

to make the general instruction more specific, to "fill it up" according to the actual life-circumstances of the animal, which must realize that not every moving object represents prey. In the course of the fine-tuning of the neural memory, the animal has many chances to learn mechanisms used by its own parents, or it can discover new tricks for acquiring food more efficiently.

All of the special mechanisms of the nervous system serve to acquire relevant information, interpreted to the animal's own benefit. In other words, the nervous system acts like a huge filter, neglecting and excluding effects that are presumably not needed by the animal. Therefore, the world which is seen, heard, or perceived by animals differs widely from the (presumed) real one. From the external environment, the animals are affected continuously by various events. Some of these events—which we call *stimuli*—have special importance regarding the survival of the animals, but others do not. Only environmental factors that influence the nervous system become information perceived by the receptors. This further narrows the set of stimuli processed by the brain. It is very important, therefore, for all animals to respond only to essential aspects of their environment. Their nervous systems have the ability to choose the aspects to be responded to. Different mechanisms of the nervous system serve this function; some of them do so by way of the receptors of the sense organs (these are the sensory stimulus-filters), while others influence central information-processing (the central stimulus-filters).

Some kind of stimulus-filtering is provided by various sense organs as a result of the limits of their sensitivity and capacity. The human ear cannot hear sounds above a frequency of 20 kilohertz and the human eye cannot see ultraviolet and infrared light waves, whereas certain other animals can perceive these very well. An interesting example of the selectivity of sense organs was discovered in a tree frog (*Eleuthero-dactylus coqui*). This frog was named after the male's characteristic croaking, which sounds something like "co-qui." The male's croaking frightens other males but is attractive to females. The reason is that the males perceive only the "co" sound from the whole croaking, while the females perceive only the "qui" calling them. The basis of this selectivity is the different tuning of the ear membrane in the male and female frogs (McFarland 1985).

Frog vision is restricted in a special way by the receptor cells of the retina, as has been shown in the leopard frog (*Rana pipiens*). H. R. Maturana and his co-workers (1960) detected five kinds of sensory neuron in the retina of the frog, which fire when receiving quite dif-

ferent stimuli. One of these types is stimulated if the light is switched on or off, or if the illumination is decreasing or increasing. This type will fire if an object passes through the field of vision, but only in cases where the edge of the object is within the field of the given neuron. (There is normally no reaction to an object that is constantly present in the visual field, except when the object's illumination changes.) This type of neuron is called a contrast-detector. The second type, not sensitive to changes in illumination but reacting to passing clear edges, is called a contour-detector. The third type reacts to decreasing illumination independently of any motion; the fourth type reacts when illumination increases. These receptors continuously measure the increase or decrease in light intensity. But the most interesting is the fifth type of neuron, which Maturana called a bug-detector. This type begins to fire with great intensity if a small (compared to the visual field) and dark (compared to the background) object crosses the visual field. The retina of the frog represents a very effective filter mechanism; any information reaching the brain is already selected according to the subsequent actions of feeding or flight. In the first case, a small object moves, which could be snatched and swallowed; in the other case, there is a big and dark object that it is better to avoid.

Some moth species from the genus *Catocala*, which are hunted by bats, have a special "ear," the so-called *tympanal organ*. This consists of a membrane that is able to oscillate and a small air pocket behind it (Roeder and Treat 1961). The oscillations of the membrane are sensed by neurons and transmitted to the moth's central nervous system. Using the tympanal organ, the moth is able to detect the ultrasound of approaching bats and tries to avoid them with the appropriate movements. Based on Roeder and Treat's studies we know that significant stimulus-filtering occurs in the tympanal organ. Thin electrodes were implanted into the axons of the two types of neuron (A1, A2) that are in contact with the tympanal membrane to investigate how each type reacts when different kinds of sound are generated near the moth. It turned out that neither of the neurons reacts specifically to the frequency of the sounds, which indicates that the moths are unable to detect the bats by this means. In fact, it is the intensity of the sounds that is of real importance; if it is low, only the A1 neurons fire, but if the sounds are strong both A1 and A2 neurons start firing and, additionally, the rate of A1 firing increases significantly. Thus, of the various sound parameters reaching the moth during flight, the nervous system is interested solely in the perception of the intensity of the sounds. This peculiar behavior of the two kinds of neuron provides the

moth with sufficient information to survive. The limits of perception are ensured by genetic factors.

Generally speaking, insects look at, listen to, smell, or taste only that which is especially important for them, while higher animals usually have less selective, more universal sensors. For example, humans can distinguish a large variety of odors because the olfactory receptors are not highly specific. On the other hand, the male silk moth shows a very specific and sensitive reaction to a single scent compound, bombykol, secreted by a special abdominal gland in the female. The male is able to perceive this scent even if the female is several kilometers away because the neurons of the olfactory receptors begin to fire as soon as a single molecule of bombykol reaches a sensory cell (Payne 1974). This is the maximum sensitivity that is theoretically possible. However, these receptors do not show any reaction to other scents.

It is not only the particular selectivity of the sense organs that acts as a filter on the environmental effects recognized by animals; there is also an efficient processing of information in the central nervous system directed by genetic memory. The two important ethological concepts concerning the central stimulus-filters are the key-stimulus and the releasing mechanism. Lack (1939) was the first to observe that male robins (*Erithacus rubecula*) attack other males of the same species that have red feathers on their breast if they happen to enter their territory during the breeding period. The birds also vigorously attack a stuffed robin, but only if it has red feathers on its breast. A stuffed bird with the red feathers painted black is ignored. Lack also showed that robins even attack a bunch of red feathers as if these were another aggressive male. The conclusion is unambiguous: territorial defense is triggered by the sight of red feathers in spite of the fact that the bird is apparently able to perceive other features of the species members. Thus, the filtering of stimuli is not performed by the sensory receptors but is based on a central processing of information; that is, a central selection occurs. Stimuli playing a role in situations such as the above are called *key-stimuli* in ethology.

Key-stimuli may also change according to the internal state of the animal. The herring gull (*Larus argentatus*) often steals and eats the eggs of other birds nesting in the same colony. It has been shown by Tinbergen (1960) that when stealing eggs the gull recognizes them according to their shape, but when its own eggs roll out of the nest, their size and color pattern become the key-stimuli, and it pulls them back with characteristic movements. However, when it returns to the eggs to continue brooding, shape becomes significant again through tactile

sensation. If the pulled-in objects are not round it does not remain sitting on them. Thus, the gull's egg, through three different groups of stimuli, activates three different actions (Tinbergen 1960). Based on these and similar events, it is possible to make a distinction between perceived stimuli (acting on the receptors and activating them) and effective stimuli (triggering a typical activity).

Another animal that demonstrates this difference is the diving beetle. The beetle often hunts tadpoles, but if a tadpole is placed in a glass tube, the diving beetle will not try to catch it. On the other hand, it will chase a plug of cotton wool wildly if there is a tiny piece of meat inside. This means that the triggering key-stimulus for capturing behavior is of a chemical nature (Eibl-Eibesfeldt 1970).

The female turkey recognizes her chicks by their sound, and can be made to brood a stuffed polecat if turkey-chick peeping is heard through a tiny loud-speaker inside. If a brooding turkey has been deafened before the first hatching, she will kill her chicks because she does not hear the sounds. However, if the mother turkey has already had a chance to brood before the operation, she will accept her chicks in spite of her deafness (Schleidt, Schleidt, and Magg 1960). This means that, through learning, visual stimuli might be substituted for the important key-stimulus, sound. Thus, in some cases, genetic and neural memories can substitute for one another.

Ethologists assume that there is a central, innate releasing mechanism (RM) belonging to each of the key-stimuli, a special part of the nervous system where the key-stimulus is recognized and a behavioral instruction is initiated to perform the proper reaction. It was also originally supposed that in the absence of the key-stimulus (also called a *releaser*), responses are inhibited by the releasing mechanism; that is, the neural action-centers are always ready to fire but the specific RMs inhibit their manifestation. In fact, it turned out that the early theory of RMs is not as generally applicable as was supposed. Although in many cases it has been possible to demonstrate the existence of RMs by neuro-physiological experiments, in other cases it has become clear that the responses given to particular stimuli emerge from the interaction of different parts of the brain. Whatever the correct description, the model of key-stimulus and releasing mechanism is a current and important explanatory idea in ethology.

The key-stimulus is often complex, and the real releaser is a particular relationship between the stimulus components. This type of key-stimulus is called a *configurational stimulus*. The young of the black-bird (*Turdus merula*) perform an intense gaping reaction when presented

with even a very simplified dummy of the adult bird, consisting of two connected black disks, differing in size. The young gape in the direction of the smaller disk as if it were the head of a parent. In this case the key-stimulus is the size relation of the two disks. If a "two-headed" dummy is shown, the young gape at only one of the heads, chosen on the basis of the size relations (Eibl-Eibesfeldt 1970).

It often happens that the same behavior is elicited by several, different key-stimuli, the effects of which are more or less additive. The red abdomen of male sticklebacks elicits aggression in other males of the same species. During fighting, the males keep themselves in a perpendicular position, "standing on their head," because the head-down position is also a strong key-stimulus that triggers fighting. If a territory-seeking male is presented with a dummy of a stickleback, it will accept only these two key-stimuli. The most intensive attack can be triggered by a red-bellied dummy in the head-down position, although a red-throated model induces some fighting even in the horizontal position. A dummy not painted at all elicits some reaction only in the head-down position. This kind of additive effect of key-stimuli is called the *rule of heterogeneous summation,* described by Seitz (1940).

In the case of many animals, the key-stimulus comprises two components, a defined shape and a motion pattern. The males of wolf spiders and of fiddler crabs display characteristic waving movements of their specialized forelimbs when approaching females. The shape and the movement of the forelimb combined represent the key-stimulus that inhibits aggressive behavior by the females. Many key-stimuli similar to this operate in birds, too. They are referred to as *sign stimuli* in current scientific terminology.

Beside key-stimuli, the *search image* represents another important mechanism for connecting the animal with its environment. While recognition of key-stimuli is determined by genetic memory, the mechanism of the search image is based on neural memory. Many people have probably experienced not noticing an object they were searching excitedly for although it was right under their nose, but not exactly in the form imagined. Uexkuell (1934) described how he was searching for a water jug on the table, a clay one, but did not notice it standing right in front of him because it was made of glass. In analyzing his own experience he named the engram recalled from memory during the searching process a search image. The search image controls the action of the brain while looking for a given object. For instance, if we are looking for a name in a book it is not necessary to read letter by letter; it is enough just to scan the pages, "searching" for the given word

picture. A trained person has usually only to glance at a page to be able to decide with considerable certainty whether a given name is on that page or not.

Based on Uexkuell's many other observations it is most probable that the animal brain also makes use of search images. He observed, for example, that, if he fed a hungry toad an earthworm, during the next minutes the animal was inclined to snap at any long, worm-like object. But if the toad ate a spider first, it would be more inclined to snap at ants or insect-like objects. If a finch or a jay catches a caterpillar imitating a little branch, for a period of time it will be inclined to peck at twigs similar to the caterpillar.

Cowie, Krebs, and Sherry (1981) investigated how the hunting of insects by tits depends on the availability of different insect species. They discovered that if tits are provided with various but rarely occurring insects, then they hunt randomly. If the number of individuals of one of the insect species increases above a well-defined encounter rate, the tits begin to eat more of this species than would be theoretically expected. Tits become "accustomed" to hunting the species spread abundantly and to neglecting others. If in the meantime the number of the preferred species decreases, the tits continue to gather them for a while even though it is no longer economical. As time passes, they encounter this species only rarely, and begin to hunt another species. This behavior can also be explained by the development of a search image. While the tits are prepared to hunt for a variety of insects, a search image cannot be formed, but if members of a given species are encountered more frequently, a search image will develop based on memory. It helps the animal to concentrate on perceptual patterns similar to the object searched for, and this considerably increases efficiency.

In field experiments with crows, Croze (1970) demonstrated the development of the search image. Over a relatively large area on a seashore, he placed empty shells painted in different colors. He hid pieces of meat under differently colored shells at different rates. It was observed that when the crows arrived they first turned up each of the colorful red, blue, and yellow shells, one after the other. If one of the colors signaled food more frequently than the others, they began to search over the whole area but turned up only shells of the color under which they had found most food before. This behavior can also be explained by the development of a search image, and shows simultaneously how efficient behavior can be. The crows did not waste their time and energy by investigating seemingly hopeless varieties of shell.

Although the search image can serve in the short term, I. S.

Beritashvili, a Georgian neurophysiologist, discovered *image memory*, which has a different function. Beritashvili (1971) studied a variety of vertebrates ranging from fish to chimpanzees. The experimental protocol was usually the following: a food source was shown to the animal under investigation for a short time, although the animal was not permitted to get to the food immediately but only after some time had passed. It was then noted whether it tried to go directly to where it had seen the food before, or whether it searched at random. From the behavior of the animal it was possible to determine how long it remembered the position of the food. With fish, the investigation was performed in an aquarium divided into several compartments. The hungry fish was placed into a start-box, and a piece of food in one of the other boxes. The fish was then cautiously directed, using a net, to the box where it could eat the food. After feeding, the fish was placed back into the start-box. In the beginning the fish were frightened by this process, but they gradually became accustomed to it, and when the door of the start-box was opened, they swam out voluntarily. According to Beritashvili, the fish were able to remember the box where they had been fed for approximately ten seconds. If the time between feeding and the return to the start-box was less than ten seconds, the fish found their way back to the box where they had been fed before. If the time was longer, they swam at random or went mostly to the central compartment.

Beritashvili conducted similar experiments with frogs. They were able to remember for several minutes which box had previously contained food. This was also the approximate time limit for turtles. In an experiment with pigeons it was found that they could remember the location of food shown once, for two to three minutes. However, if they were permitted to go there and even eat some grains, the time increased considerably and the pigeons remembered the location of the food for several days.

Beritashvili also performed experiments with mammals, mostly dogs. One such experiment was conducted in a large room where the dog was placed in a cage. From behind one of several wooden screens in the room the experimenter showed a bowl containing food and drew the attention of the animal to it. Sometimes the experimenter not only showed the food but also gave sound signals, by tapping the bottom of the bowl, for example. In other experiments the animal was led to the screen and allowed to sniff at the food, and occasionally to eat some pieces. After this the animal was left alone for a given time in the cage. When the dog was allowed to come out again, Beritashvili observed

how it tried to find the food, which had been hidden behind the screen again. The experiments demonstrated that the dog would immediately run to the proper place, even after about two hours, and even when the food had been shown only from a distance. If more than two hours passed between showing and releasing, the dog would remember the food as something that "had to be somewhere in the room" but it would have forgotten the exact place and would run around searching at random. The image memory increased strongly, however, if the dog had been allowed to go to the place and to eat some pieces. In this situation the dog would hurry immediately to the proper screen, even after eighteen days. Of course, in these long-term experiments, the waiting time was not spent in the room.

Beritashvili found the memory of baboons to be even better: they remembered the exact position of food behind the screens even after six weeks, provided they had eaten there before.

These observations are of great value to us because they show what an important role a picture stored in memory can play in the regulation of animal behavior. Following its formation, the picture may be effective for hours, days, or even weeks (the duration is important because it clearly distinguishes between image memory and the search image; the latter is a short-term memory trace formed during searching). We must emphasize the importance of these findings, since other experiments on conditioned reflexes or operant conditioning have mainly concentrated on direct responses elicited by stimuli. The animals have been treated as a reflex machine from which an external stimulus can always elicit some response. The most important consequence of the experiments of Beritashvili is that it is the internal representation of the stimulus that influences the animal, and that this effect may last for a long time independently of the external environment.

Beside the search image and the image memory, we know of other mechanisms of the nervous system, also connected with memory, that are used for orientation within an animal's close surroundings. Even insects make use of these, despite the fact that their behavior is mainly directed by rigid rules fixed in genetic memory. Many insects return to the same location repeatedly for a special purpose, in which case it is the neural memory that directs their orientation. When a bee leaves the hive, it can be seen to fly some exploratory circles around the hive. It has been shown experimentally that, during this flight, it memorizes larger, conspicuous objects, like trees and houses, surrounding the hive. Is some form of "representation" of the environment formed in the brain of the bee or other insects that is able to orient them?

An earlier study by Tinbergen (1932) dealt with this kind of learning in the case of the digger wasp (*Philanthus triangulum*). The female digger wasp digs a burrow in the soft sand and supplies her growing larvae daily with immobilized bees, which are her special prey. Tinbergen and Kruy (1938) demonstrated that before flying off the wasp makes an "orienting flight" for some seconds in the vicinity of her burrow, during which she stores the characteristic points of the area in her memory. When she comes back after some hours with prey, her memory helps her to find the burrow. In the course of experiments for his 1932 paper, Tinbergen marked the burrow while the wasp was inside, ringing the exit with twenty pine cones. After the wasp had flown off, he placed all of the cones in the same arrangement but further away, at a distance of about 30 cm from the hole. The wasp now sought her burrow at the center of the cone ring but failed to find it until the original situation was restored. Beusekom (1946) has shown that the digger wasp uses several orienting cues simultaneously. In one of the experiments, he marked the burrow using a wooden cube and a shrub twig. When he moved the cube and turned it by 45 degrees before the wasp returned, the insect sought the entrance of her burrow according to the actual position of the twig. We can conclude from this and similar experiments that the wasp fixes a visual pattern in her memory and also fixes the position of the burrow in relation to this pattern. The more an object stands out from the surroundings, the more important is its contribution to the pattern. Consequently, certain elements or features of the pattern are selected by the animal's senses based on genetic memory, while their representation is later transferred to neural memory. The nervous system makes a comparison between the memory pattern and the actual perceptual pattern. (In principle, the innate releasing mechanism works similarly, but in the case of stimulus patterns formed in memory under the influence of the environment, they are compared by the brain to the pattern of key-stimuli in the genetic memory.)

Orientation, supported by external stimulus patterns, is used actively by most animals who seek to return to the nest or home. Of course, they need not only the stimulus pattern of their destination but also stimuli that help them find each step of the way back. Therefore external stimulus patterns must overlap each other. When an animal is placed in a new surroundings it can often be observed to return repeatedly to the point where it was first placed, using it as a starting base for the exploration of the new environment. Gradually it forms the memory patterns necessary for its proper orientation.

Higher animals not only have to orient themselves in their natural

environment if they are to survive, they must also be ready to escape the attacks of their enemies, to obtain food and shelter, to take care of their offspring—and all of these in a permanently changing world. Everything changes in the local environment: enemies, possibilities of obtaining food and even the most elementary physical conditions change with the change of the seasons. Consequently, higher animals must solve complex tasks that utilize their various capabilities simultaneously.

The cognitive maps of these animals are extremely complex and must be of a rather dynamic, continuously changing nature. A very large part of an animal's activity is devoted to constructing cognitive maps. Emil Menzel (1978) performed experiments with juvenile, 3-year-old chimpanzees in order to study the formation of dynamic cognitive maps. The "environment" consisted of a 0.4 hectare bushy, grassy enclosure with several trees in the middle. In a preliminary experiment, the animals were transported in cages to the margins of the area and released daily for one or two hours. Their behavior was registered from an observation tower and analyzed in detail. On entering the new place the animals became very excited. They first examined the whole area and then occupied a central position, which allowed them to observe the area in all directions. Using these places as "headquarters," the apes began systematically to explore the whole area in detail. This activity lasted several weeks, and the main experiment was begun when the animals had finished it.

The experimenters added twenty different toys and household utensils (durable enough to resist the intense interest of the chimpanzees) to the numerous other objects found on the ground. The animals became acquainted with the new objects during the 30-minute daily sessions run every second day (the total duration of these sessions was 5 hours). The 10-day period of familiarization was followed by a 10-day testing period, with daily sessions of 30 minutes. On each of these days, an additional new object was placed among the others. Thus, on the eleventh day of the experiment, twenty-one objects could be found in the area, while on day twenty, there were thirty. During the first five days the newest objects were placed in a separate location from the former; during the next five days they were placed among the older objects. Thus, the effect of both the new object and the new location could be observed. Finally, some older objects were removed and the position of other objects was changed.

The chimps noticed each new object immediately, and went to it and examined it carefully within 15 seconds of their entry into the

experimental area. Finding an old object in a new place also provoked a little interest, but the object was investigated only briefly. Other experiments also demonstrated that chimpanzees remember very precisely the location of objects for weeks. As was pointed out by Menzel, their capabilities are not inferior to the corresponding ones in humans. Field observations have demonstrated that chimpanzees know their environment in great detail. The dynamic cognitive map formed in their brain could instead be considered a cognitive model, as it contains not only a map of the physical environment but also the changes and the possible alternatives.

Based on similar observations, a new concept regarding the role of the brain has emerged. According to this concept, the main function of the brain is the formation of a dynamic model of the environment. The chimp's brain, with its huge memorizing capacity, is able to represent surrounding objects and places exactly, and to register changes minute by minute. Thus, the chimp's environmental model is "up to date" at all times.

The Neurological Basis of Cognitive Maps

Of course, we know of the existence of cognitive maps not only from ethological and psychological experiments but also from neurological investigations. With the help of micro-electrodes implanted into the brain, it is possible to map which neurons respond to particular stimuli affecting the animal, and how these are arranged within the perceptual areas of the brain. Through the investigation of mammalian hearing, it has been shown that in the auditory cortex, large and quite specific neurons can be found that fire only if the animal hears a specific sound from an extremely narrow frequency range (e.g. Uttal 1973). At the same time, other, more broadly tuned neurons cover the whole frequency range. The sound-detector neurons are arranged alongside each other on the surface of the brain according to the frequency ranges. Similar arrangements are quite common in the nervous systems of higher animals. For example, in the visual cortex, we find a topographical map of the retina's receptors with each neuron responding to stimuli coming from a given segment of the visual field. Since the cortex of the brain processes the two-dimensional picture on the retina in various ways (according to the direction of movement, the angles between edges compared to each other, and so forth), it seems to be most convenient for processing if the receptor neurons of the brain accurately represent the spatial localization of the receptor cells of the

retina. In this case we have an example of the physical realization of a cognitive map.

In the examples above, the central nervous system "transcribes" the two-dimensional stimulus patterns arriving at the sensory surface onto the neuron networks of the brain. One explanation for this might be that it is the simplest way to organize the processing of two-dimensional patterns during development. In recent years, however, it has been shown that a spatial representation of the environment is present in the central nervous system in an analogous form, even if the sense organs do not produce a two-dimensional pattern. Thus a "real" model of the environment is formed. The hearing of owls is very refined, since this is their most important sense for locating prey. There is a region in the owl's midbrain in which a precise spatial representation of the direction of sounds, similar to the neural representation of visual images in mammals, can be found, even though the owl's ears are not stimulated by a sound pattern arranged spatially, but rather by a sequence of sounds (Knudsen 1981). Each neuron in this cognitive map responds to sounds coming from a particular location, so that the different neurons are "listening" to different spatial areas. Whereas in vision the position of a stimulus is determined by the horizontal and vertical coordinates of the retina, in hearing the direction of a sound is determined by comparing the times of arrival and the intensities at the two ears. This makes it possible to create a three-dimensional map of the sources of the sounds. In the case of the owl, about half of the brain region processing sound maps is devoted to an area of 15 degrees just in front of the owl, which represents the most sensitive area for spatial hearing. Also, the area of the owl's brain that processes sounds coming from below is larger than the area that processes those coming from above. From the predatory viewpoint of the owl the information coming from below is more important.

A similarly elegant example of the physical existence of cognitive maps is provided by electrophysiological investigations of the auditory cortex of bats (Suga, Kuzirai, and O'Neil 1981). A model of the physical environment is constructed by analyzing the echoes from the ultra-sounds that bats emit. Thus, those parts of the bat's brain that analyze sounds are considerably enlarged in comparison with other animals. The auditory cortex can be divided into several parts with different physiological functions. These provide important information about insect prey crossing the bat's path. Separate regions are concerned with the distance, size, relative velocity, and the wing-beat frequency of the prey (the latter helps to identify it). From the delay between the

emission and the echo of the orientation pulse, the bat is able to compute distance with astonishing precision. In one area of the auditory cortex, we can find neurons which are "tuned" (sensitized) to the delay of emitted and echoed sounds. These neurons respond neither to emitted nor to echoed sound alone, but fire only to pairs of sounds. The remarkable feature of this mechanism is that individual neurons respond to different delays, from a fraction of a millisecond to about 18ms, and that based on this, the animal is able to locate prey at a distance of just under 10cm to 3m.

In investigations of spatial orientation in mice, it was found that various senses participate in the perception of space, including the visual, the auditory and the tactile (for example, the whiskers transmit tactile cues to the appropriate receptors). Accordingly, neuron layers can be found in the brain that map spatial information for each modality, and these neuron layers are situated in relation to each other in such a way as to provide accurate models of the mouse's environment (Drager and Hubel 1975).

Another problem in neurophysiology that has been intensively investigated is the question of how stimuli are transformed into action, and how the animal's brain generates the commands for the motor organs. We give two examples here to illustrate the organization of these mechanisms.

The German ethologist J. P. Ewert (1980) and his team have investigated the prey- and predator-recognizing mechanisms of the European toad (*Bufo bufo*). These toads prey upon smaller animals and are themselves preyed upon by predators that hunt specifically for them, thus presenting them with a considerable perceptual problem. The toad should choose the largest prey-stimulus possible, as within certain size limits catching large prey is the most economical activity, but at the same time it must also be able to recognize the smallest predator that could represent a danger. The toad carefully observes the size of all moving objects passing before it. If the toad is presented in an experiment with some dark squares varying in size, it will react within certain size limits by turning towards them, which is the first action in taking prey. If, however, the squares are above a certain size the toad will stand up tall, displaying one part of its repertoire of escape behaviors.

How can the toad estimate the size of an approaching object? The simplest way would be to calculate the size of the picture projected on to the retina on the basis of the visual angle. The visual angle of an object of a constant size changes with distance, appearing larger close up

and smaller further away. At the start of their terrestrial life, toads are unable to establish the distance of objects correctly; instead, they have a preference for objects of a given visual angle. The toads require some weeks of learning in order to be able to estimate the distance of objects correctly.

In addition to the size of a moving object, its shape also provides the toad with important information. If a moving black stripe is shown to the animal against a white background, it reacts in two different ways, depending on the direction of movement of the black stripe. If the stripe moves horizontally, like a worm, the toad immediately turns toward it and tries to catch it. However, if the stripe moves in the direction of the shorter axis, then the toad displays a defensive reaction, puffing itself up. In the first case, the moving stripe was named a *worm*, and in the second case an *anti-worm*.

The neuroanatomical basis of this behavior has been successfully analyzed. The information originating from the image projected onto the retina of the toad is transmitted through the axons of the optic tract to the opposite visual tectum and thalamus. If the neurons of the retina-projection layer of the optic tectum are stimulated electrically, then a freely moving toad will perform an orientation movement in exactly the same direction as it would if the picture of the worm were projected to the proper site of the retinal surface. In contrast, if the retinal projection to the thalamus is stimulated, then the animal produces an avoidance reaction similar to that elicited when a picture of the anti-worm appears.

Two kinds of visual neuron have been found in the tectum. Both types have receptive fields of about 27 degrees and respond to moving objects projected onto the retina. The activity of one type (the t1 cells) does not alter if the stimulus object is enlarged at right angles to the direction of movement (anti-worm), but the firing frequency increases considerably if the object is elongated (worm). The t2 cells increase their activity on the appearance of a worm stimulus, but they decrease it when the anti-worm is presented. In the thalamus, cells have been found (tp1) that have extremely large receptive fields in the retina (46 degrees), and can only be activated by larger objects or by the anti-worm. The different neurons also influence each others' activity. It has been recorded that the firing frequency of the t1 cells increases on presentation of the worm-stimulus, and that this activity stimulates the firing of the t2 cells. On presenting the anti-worm, however, the enhanced activity of the tp1 cells inhibits the firing of the t2 cells. Thus, the t1 and tp1 neurons act as stimulus filters, indicating whether the

stimulus is worm-like or anti-worm-like. The interaction between the two kinds of filter neuron strictly separates the neural information eliciting the orientating and defense responses.

Experiments such as these have proved beyond doubt the hypothesis, originating from the behavioral sciences, that one of the most important biological functions of the animal brain is the formation of an internal representation of the external environment in the form of an active dynamic model. The behavior is directed by the neural system, which receives instructions directly from this internal model. Furthermore, the investigation of environmental models in different species has revealed that such models are always species-specific, and that the genetic memory determines from the beginning which aspects of the environment will be built into the neural model constructed by the brain. The environmental model then obtains its final shape from the interaction of the genetic and neural memories.

Genetic Restrictions in the Application of Cognitive Maps

In animals, memory plays an important role in the creation of such cognitive maps of the environment. Cognitive maps, however, are only one of the factors that influence behavior. It is well known that cognitive maps are influenced by behavioral instructions that are determined by the genetic memory.

Observing animals in their natural environment, the American ethologist Alan Kamil has revealed that the cognitive map is of great importance in the life of the nectar-eating honey-bird (Kamil and Balda 1985). The energy requirements of this bird are supplied entirely by sugar derived from floral nectar. Since searching for flowers requires energy, the efficiency of searching is very important; these birds are territorial and defend their flowers. Kamil observed that the honey-bird visits flowers regularly and never returns to the same flower twice in a day. After careful observation, Kamil concluded that a cognitive map that localizes the flowers is formed in the memory of the honey-bird, which makes use of this map during gathering.

Kamil's conclusion is supported by laboratory experiments (Cole et al. 1982), which reveal another very important thing: a cognitive map can be used only for definite purposes and only in a definite way. In the laboratory, honey-birds were presented with a learning task similar to that solved under natural conditions. Colored plastic flowers containing sugar syrup were arranged in a way similar to real flowers in the natural environment. Birds learned easily the features and location

of the flowers. Two different tasks were then given to them. In the first experiment, birds were rewarded (with food) only if they chose flowers not visited previously. This task was very similar to the natural one and so the birds were able to learn it easily. After an average of 120 trials they rarely tried to visit the same flower twice. In contrast, the honey-birds in the second experiment were rewarded only when they visited the same flower a second time. The birds had difficulty adapting to this task, and even when they succeeded in learning it, they made many mistakes.

Considering the natural environment, this behavior is quite logical. Nectar production is a slow process. The replenishment of the nectar takes about a day and it is therefore quite pointless to waste energy in visiting flowers that have already been visited on the same day. It is especially interesting that the honey-bird is virtually unable to learn a task that is impractical in its natural environment.

In terms of game theory, the gathering behavior of the honey-bird is referred to as a *win–shift* strategy. The reverse is called a *win–stay* strategy, and these strategies control the behavior of many species. Aside from the shift and stay strategies, several additional rules have been demonstrated to complement the use of cognitive maps.

The most detailed laboratory experiments have been performed using rats. These experiments played a very important part in the discovery of the cognitive map and in the identification of its character-istics. In their experiments, D. S. Olton and co-workers used a radial maze with eight arms made of thin wood. A piece of food was hidden in a hole at the far end of each arm. A hungry rat was placed in the center of the maze and allowed to explore the new environment until it had discovered the covered food at the end of one of the arms. Thereafter, the rat visited the other arms for food. Searching could be performed in several ways: the animal could memorize, for instance, where it had already been and subsequently check only the arms not visited before. Another solution would be to follow a simple rule, such as "go clockwise and check the places one after another." It very quickly became clear, however, that the rat memorizes features of the environment outside the maze, and bases its orientation on these spatial landmarks. When the maze is rotated, the animal continues searching according to the original position.

Using a more complex maze with seventeen arms (built from linen tubes), it has been shown that, although the cognitive map plays the most important role in finding the food, the rat also uses additional behavioral instructions (Olton and Samuelson 1976). The role of

memory was demonstrated by an experiment in which rats were forced to wait before entering an arm; in this situation the next choice was random relative to the previous visit. However, efficiency did not decrease and only one or two mistakes were recorded during the course of visiting all seventeen arms. The special behavioral instructions were revealed when the delays were omitted. Under these conditions, rats often moved in a single direction, visiting the arms in a clockwise sequence, for instance. However, this rule seems not to be rigid; rather, it says, "go clockwise (or anticlockwise) into one of the next three or four arms." As we mentioned above, these additional instructions are not seen if a delay of several minutes interrupts searching. In this case, the animal's choice depends exclusively on its memory. It is not simple for a rat to solve the task without the help of the behavioral instructions. However, the animals are able to perform the task successfully using memory traces alone.

In lower animals behavioral instructions play the leading role, since memory is less developed. In experiments with the Siamese fighting fish (*Betta splendens*), a maze-like aquarium was built, with a reward of a tubifex worm placed at the end of each arm. The fish was able to learn to gather the worms, but only when entry to the arms was not delayed. In this case the performance of the animal was, on average, about seven correct choices out of eight opportunities. The fish applied a very effective behavioral instruction. After leaving an arm it always swam into the neighboring compartment. When the search was stopped for only half a minute, the fish was able to remember where the search had been interrupted, and its performance did not decline. However, after a delay of five minutes, the fish forgot everything, and it continued the search randomly, making numerous mistakes. Thus, it can be concluded that the Siamese fighting fish was not able to form a long-lasting cognitive map of the eight-armed aquarium, and that searching was guided only by the behavioral instruction ("go to the neighboring arm") and by the memory trace of the arm last visited (Roitblat, Tham, and Golub 1982).

It has been noted that rats, too, apply the win–shift rule. In one experiment, an eight-armed maze was used. Following the first four choices, the search was stopped for a while. Two experimental groups were formed. The first group was rewarded in the previously unvisited arms, while the animals of the second group could find food only in the arms visited before. The learning performance of the two groups showed a striking difference. The members of the first group acquired the task quickly; approximately thirty trials were sufficient to

produce 3.5 right choices on average. In contrast, the second group was unable to learn the task. Their performance only slightly exceeded the success of random choices (as expected without learning), even after fifty trials. It can be concluded that rats use the win–shift strategy (required for solving the first problem) and are unable to learn the win–stay strategy.

The experiment was repeated under more natural conditions. A large chamber was furnished with smaller chambers of various sizes, with tubes (excellent hiding-places), and also with three small towers in which food was hidden. The towers were continuously observed. In the first experiment, all three towers contained food and the rats were seen to visit all the towers and eat some food from each, even though there was plenty of the same food in each of them. The rats did not stop searching for food after consuming food in the first tower. Their behavior was even more unusual when only one of the towers contained food. Rats that chose an empty tower first continued to search as normal, and that tower was not visited again on the same day. The behavior of rats visiting the food-containing tower first was quite similar; the animals consumed some food, after which they left the food-containing tower and visited the other ones. They did not eat for the rest of the day, and failed to return to the tower already visited.

Barnett and Cowan (1976) studied the behavior of rats reared in the central compartment of a cross-shaped maze. The rats were allowed to investigate the rest of the maze for one hour daily. In this experiment, it was also observed that the animals never returned on the same day to the arms already explored. Thus, field exploration in rats is organized according to the win–shift strategy.

The rigidity of the animal mind is striking. The rat can form correct cognitive maps of its environment and has excellent learning abilities, as demonstrated in the seventeen-armed maze. The animal, however, is able to use these precise cognitive maps only in accordance with the genetically coded behavioral strategies. The win–shift strategy is obviously "logical" for rats. When they are searching for food they have to examine their cognitive map for places not visited before. The reverse strategy is illogical for rats; the idea of returning to where they were before simply does not enter their mind. It is likely that the food-searching strategy of the rat is a result of evolution. Rats show no food preferences, and the win–shift strategy ensures the consumption of a large variety of food—although at first sight it exposes them to the danger of eating toxic food. As we will show later, rats learn easily to avoid toxic baits. This type of learning is effective only if the animal

consumes small quantities of any kind of new food or of the food found at a new place. The win–shift strategy fulfills these requirements.

The meaning of such behavioral strategies can be understood only in the natural environment of the animal. In honey-birds, only the win–shift strategy ensures the required amount of energy; while the win–stay food-searching strategy is appropriate for ovenbirds, since maggots are always located in patches. These strategies reflect certain characteristics of the natural environment. They are elements of an environmental model formed in the brain and represent definite and specific relations between the components of the environment. Using "ready-made" model-elements, the animal is able to create a model that describes its environment exactly. It is obvious that if the animal is removed from its environment or the environment is changed in some way, the behavior of the animal may become completely inappropriate and meaningless.

Animal Cultures

Recent investigations have suggested that the transmission of experience may be an important factor for survival in animals that live in groups. The main features of the transmission of experience are as follows:

(1) a given behavior spreads within the group by learning;
(2) the transfer of experience also occurs between generations; and
(3) remote or separated populations show different forms of the given behavior.

Since these are similar to the most important features of human culture, the term *animal culture* has recently been accepted for various forms of transmitted experience within animal groups: the imitation of movement patterns, transmission of foraging techniques, transmission of song dialects from one generation to the next, recognition of special kinds of food by learning, and other similar behavioral forms (Mundinger 1980). In the following pages we describe several examples of animal culture in which imitation (copying) plays the leading role in the spread of experience.

A resident of the seashore, the oystercatcher (*Haematopus ostralegus*) forages mostly on mussels and refines its foraging technique by intensive learning. At first, parents feed their young in the nest, then in the close vicinity of the nest, and finally on the seashore. The birds use two different techniques to open the shells—both of them are the result of

repeated attempts and intensive learning. Birds using the "hammer-stroke" technique place the mussel on firm ground, knock a hole with their bill in the thinnest part of the shell, and then pull out the edible parts through the hole. The other technique is called "stabbing." In this case, birds attack the shellfish under the water, when the water-perfusing siphon of their prey is just visible. The birds stab their bills suddenly into the opening and cut the hinge of the shells with a skillful movement.

A given bird uses only one of the two available techniques. For a long time it was believed that oystercatchers form two different sub-species, with the two techniques resulting from genetic differences. It was the English ethologist Norton-Griffiths (1969) who demonstrated, by clever experiments, that youngsters learn the technique from their parents. When chicks were exchanged between parents using different techniques, the young always acquired the technique used by their foster parents.

Just as oystercatchers learn the difficult shell-opening technique, so several species of passerine birds learn their songs from their parents. In the course of "mobbing," birds also learn which species to regard as predators by imitating conspecifics. It can be predicted exactly what, when, and how a given animal will learn from conspecifics.

In this section, we shall deal with learning forms that are occasional rather than predictable. These demonstrate that higher animals, at least, are able to acquire special behavioral patterns purely by observing the behavior of conspecific animals. Learning of this type occurs mainly when it results in a well-defined benefit.

An illustrative example is seen in the behavior of a group of African elephants, as documented by Curio, Ernst, and Vieth (1978). In 1919, orange groves were established on an area that was often rifled by a resident population of more than a hundred elephants. The farmers hired an elephant hunter to kill off the animals. The hunter killed the animals one by one, so that their death and suffering were observed by their companions. One year later only twenty to twenty-five elephants were still living. The farmers made a concerted attempt to get rid of the remaining population, but the task of the hunter became more and more difficult because the elephants learned to be extremely cautious. They noticed the smallest movement from a great distance, and they switched to nocturnal activity. After numerous attempts, the hunter and the farmers had to acknowledge that they were not able to exterminate the elephants completely. They founded the Addo park, a closed bushy area of 10,000 hectares in the hills, which represented a suitable shelter

for the surviving elephants. More than sixty years have passed since that time, and presumably none of the animals surviving the original massacre is now living. Despite this fact, this elephant population is the most dangerous one in the whole of Africa. They have continued to live nocturnally, and they still respond with extreme aggression to humans even though nobody has assaulted them since the foundation of the park.

In the laboratory it is easy to carry out experiments demonstrating the ability of animals to learn from one another. There are popular legends about the bait-recognition ability of rats, which were discussed in detail above. This knowledge is thought to be transmitted from one generation of rats to the next. B. G. Galef, the Canadian ethologist, decided to check the validity of this legend by laboratory experiments. Using Norwegian rats, he asked whether poison-avoidance would appear in the offspring of a mother conditioned previously by poisoned food. A large room was divided into several compartments, each equipped with television cameras to observe the rats. In the course of the experiments, the legend was shown to be true. Young rats avoided the food that was avoided by the parents, particularly the mother. Imitation was demonstrated to be based on three factors. Young rats initially prefer the feeding grounds of their parents, and in this way they consume almost exclusively the food consumed by their parents. Later, when they forage alone, they still show a preference for these familiar foods. The second factor is the mother's milk. By clever experiments, Galef succeeded in demonstrating that preferences related to various food flavors are literally "sucked in with the milk," since young prefer the foods consumed by their mother during the suckling period. The flavoring compounds penetrate into the milk, and later guide the taste preferences of the young. The third factor had already been observed by previous investigators of poison-avoidance. Rats often urinate on unpalatable foods (or on foods that, through conditioning, they have learned to be unpalatable), and these foods are avoided even by in-experienced animals. Together, these experiments clearly demonstrate that rats are able to transmit food-preferences to future generations by social learning. However, considering the phenomenon as a whole, food-avoidance is clearly based on the contribution of several inherited behaviors. The role of learning is only to ensure the remembrance of places and flavors. The animals do not learn food-avoidance itself by observing the behavior of other animals, and in this type of social learning genetic memory plays the leading role (Galef 1976).

Two Italian researchers, Gandolfi and Parisi, noticed that among rat

populations living along the Po river, there are some animals that obtain their food in a quite special way (see Olton and Samuelson 1976). They dive into the river for clams, which they then open and eat on the bank. At the same time, Gandolfi and Parisi also observed sympatric populations in which this habit was completely unknown. According to the Italian researchers, this represents an unusually clear case of observational learning. It is highly probable that the rats learn this new way of foraging from each other. The knowledge survives within a relatively restricted colony, and its spread into other colonies is very slow. It would be almost impossible to demonstrate the validity of this theory by field observations, which persuaded Galef to perform appropriate laboratory experiments.

The experimental apparatus consisted of a home cage connected to a small swimming pool by a tunnel. Food and water were provided ad libitum in the home cage and the rats were also allowed to visit the swimming pool freely through the tunnel. The behavior of the animals was continuously recorded on videotape. The first question Galef asked was whether adult animals are able to learn underwater foraging from each other. Instead of clams, he used chocolate, a favorite food of rats. A particular animal was trained to dive into the 15cm-deep water for chocolate pieces previously placed there. The chocolate pieces were not covered by water at first; then they were covered by a thin layer of water, the depth of which was increased by 1–2cm each day. After the rat had learned to gather the chocolate pieces quickly and skillfully, untrained animals (adult siblings of the same age) were placed in the cage. The experiment lasted several weeks. Galef wanted to find out whether the inexperienced animals would imitate this technique of chocolate-gathering. None of the twenty naive animals used in the experiment was able to imitate the trained one, despite the fact that they often followed the trained individual into the swimming pool, observed his behavior, and even tried to steal the just-collected chocolate.

In a further experiment, Galef trained several female rats to gather the chocolate hidden under the water. When the females were able to perform the task, their 3-week-old offspring were placed in the cage for several weeks. Four out of eighteen young animals succeeded in imitating the behavior of their mother, and acquired the technique of chocolate-gathering. This experiment demonstrated clearly that rats are in fact able to learn new foraging techniques, although only during their youth. Later it was revealed that some young rats are able to acquire the new technique by themselves, especially those previously used to swimming. Animals able to swim showed much greater willingness to

search spontaneously under water. These experiments confirmed the Italian researchers' hypothesis regarding the appearance and spread of clam-foraging rat populations in nature.

Similar experiments have been performed by psychologists using the popular Skinner box (e.g. Schwartz 1984). The box used in these experiments was divided into two equal parts by a transparent wall. A small lever was placed symmetrically on each side of the partition, and a group of animals was trained to obtain water by pressing the lever. After a short period of water deprivation, the trained rats were placed individually in one side the box, and naive animals in the other. The trained rats immediately began to press the lever to obtain water, and drank the small portions of water greedily. Observing this, sooner or later the naive animals began to show similar behavior and learned how to obtain water much faster than control animals, which were allowed to operate the lever but had no neighbor or only an inexperienced partner on the other side of the wall. This experiment clearly supports the idea that the rat brain is somehow able to transform visual information about the behavior of another animal into its own behavioral instructions.

Since this time, similar experiments have been performed in birds. By watching trained animals, dwarf quail (*Excalfactoria chinensis*) are quickly able to learn to peck an illuminated spot to obtain food. The Hungarian ethologist L. Sasvári (1979) performed similar experiments with tits. He revealed that tits easily learn from trained animals to obtain food hidden in a cloth-covered hole by drawing the cloth aside. An extremely interesting observation made by Sasvári was that tits show a willingness to learn mainly from conspecifics. If one great tit (*Parus major*) observes the new foraging technique in another great tit, it is highly probable that it will acquire the technique. If the tutor animal is a blue tit (*Parus caeruleus*), then the probability of imitation is reduced. Young animals tend to imitate more easily the example of another species.

Japanese ethologists have established a group of Japanese macaques (*Macaca fuscata*) on a small sea island and observed them over a long period. One of their findings has become world famous: they reported that a juvenile female, named Imo, "discovered" a new foraging technique. The researchers fed the animals regularly on seeds strewn over the bare ground. The macaques liked this kind of food very much, and therefore picked the seeds from out of the dust one by one. Imo discovered that if she took sand and seeds to the beach and threw them into the water, the sand and the dust would sink down, and the clean

seeds remain on the surface, to be gathered easily. However, the most interesting phenomenon occurred later. Imo was very young when she discovered the technique, and therefore, as the observations confirmed, none of the group members living at that time imitated her. Had the monkeys lost their famous imitative ability? Several years later the new, young members of the group (lower ranking than Imo in the social hierarchy) began to imitate her, and in the next ten to fifteen years the habit became widespread in the group (Kawai 1965).

Thus even the fate of such a "discovery" is under genetic control. The acquisition of useful skills may be started by particular individuals and in definite ways, even in monkeys. In fact, only in the last few years has the interest of ethologists turned toward the mechanism of imitative learning. In the 1950s, English ethologists had already reported that in England tits "discovered" how to open milk bottles covered by aluminum foil (Hinde and Fischer 1952). By this means, they could steal the cream floating at the top of the bottles, which were brought to the houses each morning and placed on the doorsteps. The habit presumably spread by observational learning. When it was first noticed, the behavior was characteristic of only a small area; later it spread out concentrically among the tits at a speed of approximately 30km per year. All this was reported thirty years ago, and only recently have proper laboratory investigations of the phenomenon been performed, by two Canadian ethologists, Palametta and Lefebvre (Schwartz 1984). They investigated the existence of similar observational-learning mechanisms in pigeons.

The task was very similar to that performed by the tits. Seeds were hidden in a small box, and the box covered with a sheet of thin paper. At first, inexperienced pigeons did not know what to do with the box placed in their cage, and probably could not even suppose that it contained food. However, the pigeons could be trained to peck a hole in the paper to reach the seeds. As a first step, the experimenters cut a small hole in the paper covering the box, and put a seed into it. The pigeons discovered the seed and began to enlarge the hole to obtain additional seeds. Later they were able to make a hole by themselves. The experiment described below was performed using similarly trained pigeons.

Twenty naive pigeons were divided into four groups and were placed individually into the left side of a large cage divided in two by a transparent plastic wall. In a control group, naive animals had no visual contact with the trained ones, and none of them opened a seed-filled covered box placed in the cage. In the three remaining groups, a

trained "tutor" pigeon was placed in the opposite side of the cage. However, only one trained group was provided with the same seed-filled, covered box. As they had learned, the tutors in this group opened the box and consumed the seeds, and all the naive pigeons able to observe their behavior quickly learned to open their own box. In the third group, the tutor animals were provided with an already opened box, and thus began to eat immediately, without first pecking a hole. Their naive counterparts also learned to open the box, although they required more time for this learning than the previous group. Finally, the tutor pigeons of the fourth group were provided with covered but empty boxes. Of course they could not know this in advance, and consequently opened the box. As a result, their naive counterparts could observe only the opening phase, without information concerning the purpose of the action, and the naive pigeons of this group did not acquire the task.

The experiment leaves no doubt that pigeons are able to learn a complex food-obtaining technique by observation only. However, this occurs only when all phases, including food-consumption, are presented. Let us consider what a complex task must be performed here by the pigeon's brain. It demonstrates that a pigeon is able to include into its environmental model neutral stimuli like the box, the hole-preparing movements, and the image of the feeding conspecific, in such a way as to place itself in the position of another animal performing the observed actions. These facts lead inevitably to the conclusion that pigeons must possess the ability to think.

In the preceding pages we have seen that the ability to transmit learned behavior from generation to generation, and so to influence the behavior of whole groups or societies, is not unique to human experience. Human beings, however, have elevated this ability to a unique level with unprecedented consequences for human cultures, as we will see in Chapter 2, on the cognitive maps of societies.

Cognitive Maps in Children

We can now move back to humans and briefly examine the development of cognitive maps during childhood.

Perhaps the earliest maps that infants acquire are behavioral. In plain English, this means that very early in their lives infants acquire the ability to imitate simple motor activities that they have seen their parents, for example, perform. The details of the development of these

early maps have been studied by the psychologists Mandler (1988) and Bandura (1989). The latter emphasized the importance of the child's attention. What catches the attention is what is retained in the memory and later reenacted through imitation. This form of learning—imitation learning, or learning to behave like a parent or other model—is coming to be recognized as a central feature of infant and childhood learning, and may well play an underestimated role in adult behavior.

Perhaps no one has investigated the development of the overall spectrum of cognitive abilities in children as thoroughly as the Swiss psychologist Jean Piaget. Piaget (Piaget and Inhelder 1971) and the American psychologist Jerome Bruner (Bruner, Olver, and Greenfield 1966) have described the growth of mental representations in children in terms so similar that we will describe them both together as a single account. According to this account, the first year of life is marked by the early appearance of *sensory–motor* depictions of actions, or in other words behavioral reenactments exactly as described in the paragraph above.

According to Piaget and Bruner, the second year of life is marked by the appearance of static, *iconic,* images or maps that the child has little ability to manipulate. Such images center rigidly on the child's own perspective, whether it be of the physical or of the social environment. A child can be asked, for example, to describe a table-top landscape that includes several farm animals, a small lake, and a papier-mâché mountain, all as seen from the eyes of a doll placed nearby on the table. He will do a passable job of this, if he is near the doll and his own perspective is also that of the doll. When asked to walk to the other side of the table, however, and again to describe the landscape as seen by the doll, which has not been moved, his description changes dramatically to his own physical perspective, and utterly disregards the view from the side of the table where the doll remains, and where he was in fact just standing. The child is said to be *perceptually bound.* Switching momentarily to the level of social maps, is it any wonder that such a child may also appear to be self-centered, inflexible, and without true empathy, though he may, in fact, be kind and even compassionate?

By about seven years of age, the child develops the beginnings of a system of flexible symbol manipulations based on a growing language facility. As this system interacts with the internal imagery of the child, a compliant mapping facility develops, able to be manipulated and projected as anticipations of future situations. In this agility we see the beginnings of the full adult potential to create cognitive maps.

Along these lines, Harvard psychologist Stephen Kosslyn (1980),

the foremost researcher on visual imagery, observes a notable increase in the ability of adults, over children, to access specific information swiftly and efficiently from internal representations. Thus, an adult, for example, can quickly zoom in on a particular region of a memorized road map, or page of written notes, to gain the desired details.

Cultural Maps

Starting from earliest infancy and continuing throughout life, human cognitive maps accumulate an increasingly rich array of representations that, taken as a whole, portray a person's entire cultural experience. The cultural landscape encoded in such maps includes not only society's conventional patterns of behavior, but its moral values, aesthetic preferences, and spiritual aspirations. In adults, this wondrously complex panorama is divided into overlapping sectors that chart individual life domains such as professional activities, family roles, and religious commitments.

In the 1950s, social theorist Kenneth Boulding (1956) suggested the thoroughly postmodern notion that people project images of cultural reality that then become reality itself, a point we have already touched on earlier in this book. Such an idea is suggestive of a cybernetic circuit, or positive-feedback loop, in which maps of reality are projected out from the person, who then meets up with them in the physical and social environment, and in so doing is forced to affirm or reject their authenticity. This process of authentication, however, depends on the situational context, as well as on the existing maps and the flexibility and creativity of the individual. A piece of driftwood is not a work of art until someone brings it into the house and puts it on the coffee table. Only then does it begin to disclose its aesthetic subtleties. The treatment of women as an underclass is not a moral problem until someone "recognizes" it as such, and then it begins to present itself in increasing clarity.

Like the two apparent sides of a Möbius strip, realities and the maps that project them are one and the same thing. This is a rolling process in which map and reality are transformed into each other. We discover in this image the *process* aspect of both reality and cognitive maps. Both are subject to constant change as they are updated, either by new experiences with the world outside the individual, or by shifts in perspective brought about by ongoing changes within the person.

With these ideas in mind, we might well expect to find that within

a single culture, different individuals would have significantly different cognitive maps, depending on their own unique experiences and personalities. We know this to be true from our own personal experience. Moreover, in the large societies of today's world, there are many subcultures with their own attitudes, value systems, and so on. Studies have shown, for example, that within the subcultures of a single city, people from different social and economic groups draw surprisingly different physical maps of the city (Lynch 1960).

In an informal demonstration of the individual variability of cognitive maps, an associate of one of our colleagues asked undergraduate college students to draw maps of the university campus. Those who commuted to the university tended to include sizable parking lots on their maps, while those who lived on campus often omitted the parking lots entirely. Interestingly, the maps seemed to differ according to the student's field of study. Literature and philosophy students drew a large library building near the center of the campus, while business and accounting students displayed a disturbing tendency to include no library at all! Physics and math students sketched in a sizable computer center, while students of literature were likely to leave it out. The building where each student spent most of his or her time was likely to be represented near the center of the campus, while other buildings often got pushed out to the edges. But let us return to the matter of cognitive maps and culture.

Human cultures are represented in many physical objects. These range from works of art, to books, clothing, cities, and instruments of technology. A living culture, however, must also survive in the minds of the people who comprise it. In other words, the knowledge and cultural heritage that is encoded in physical objects such as art, books, and technology, does not comprise a living culture without the active participation of the subjective knowledge that is available only to the mind.

It is useful to consider a human culture as a flowing evolutionary system that involves both physical cultural objects and the ever-changing cognitive maps of individuals (Laszlo 1987a; Artigiani 1988). This whole fluid structure can be seen as an organic configuration that changes over time, thriving or dying out like other evolutionary processes. As we will emphasize below, a growing and vigorous culture undergoes constant transformation, adjusting to changes such as technological developments, influences from other cultures, and events in the natural environment. One thinks, for example, of the classical Greek culture at the time of Pericles, or of the European Renaissance. Cultures

that fail to make such adjustments become static and rigid, and are likely to die out if confronted by major challenges.

If we look at a culture as an evolving system, one formed on one side by the physical objects of the culture, and on the other by the cognitive maps of its members, we begin to see how it recreates itself from day to day, year to year, and generation to generation. Cultural objects such as books and works of art play an obvious and important role in transmitting culture, but on their own they are static and inert. The life of a culture is communicated directly by its members, their stories, their myths, their dances, their crafts and skills, passed directly from individual to individual. The entire cycle is animated and carried forward in the projected realities, or maps, of the people who comprise the culture. This process of continuous recreation places human cultures in a broad category of complex and flexible systems, the hallmark of which is their ability and passion for self-creation.

Human cultures, like the eddies of the mountain stream, are cyclic patterns that never quite repeat themselves. The overall form of the culture is always in a state of dynamic change or evolution. Such change may be relatively rapid, as is the case in the art world of New York City, or it may be slow, as was the case with ancient Egypt, which changed amazingly little over the entire millennia. Viewed from a particular moment in history, however, each culture represents a unique dynamic pattern, a particular configuration that usually remains relatively stable from year to year, decade to decade, and sometimes from century to century.

Each culture has its own unique qualities, which it transmits forward as it creates itself into the future. Some cultures, like the Europe of the Middle Ages, are strongly religious, while others are dominantly secular. Some, like classical Greece, place a high value on artistic expression, while many others do not. Some, like historical China, place significant value on tradition, while many modern cultures lack this emphasis. Some value democracy, while others prefer monarchy.

Given such obvious variation in style between different cultures, and realizing that these represent particular attractors, leads naturally to the question of whether certain general types of cultures can be distinguished within the remarkable diversity of past and present societies. So far, at least two notable efforts have been made to model a wide range of cultures in terms of dynamic systems. One of these efforts is by pioneering systems mathematician Ralph Abraham (1989, 1992), and the other is by the social theorist Riane Eisler (1987). Abraham's work is predicated, in turn, on certain thoughts of the prominent anthropologist Ruth Benedict (Maslow and Honigmann

1970), which date back to as long ago as the early 1940s. This story is worth telling.

It seems that Ruth Benedict was haunted by the realization that certain cultures were simply "nicer" to live in than others. Life in these nicer cultures seemed to be pleasant if not downright joyful. People worked together for the good of all, and few if any individuals were permanently rejected or condemned by others. These societies typically believed in benevolent cosmologies, ones in which, for instance, gods and goddesses looked favorably upon human beings.

The cultures that were not nice to live in were those in which individuals strove for power and status at the expense of others, and in which people could be humiliated or entirely rejected by the community. Typically, such cultures lived under oppressive cosmologies in which, for instance, angry, cruel, or indifferent gods required endless appeasement.

Searching for a theme that could clarify the essential difference between these two types of cultures, Benedict came up with the concept of *synergy*. She explained it in her 1941 Bryn Mawr lectures, in which she stated:

I shall need a term for this gamut, a gamut that runs from one pole, where any act or skill that advantages the individual at the same time advantages the group, to the other pole, where every act that advantages the individual is at the expense of others. I shall call this gamut *synergy* . . . I shall speak of cultures with low synergy, where the social structure provides for acts that are mutually opposed and counteractive, and of cultures with high synergy, where it provides for acts that are mutually reinforcing. (Maslow and Honigmann 1970: 324)

In the early 1940s, however, such thoughts were tantamount to heresy. Anthropology, much by dent of Benedict's own efforts, had recently discredited the whole business of ethnocentrism. To suggest that some cultures were in any way superior to others would have been to open a Pandora's box of criticism and misinterpretation. Perhaps for these reasons, or perhaps because of her ensuing involvement in the war effort, Dr Benedict chose not to publish the sizable manuscript on which she had based her lectures. Instead, she gave it for safe-keeping to a friend, Abraham Maslow. He was later to become the leading force in humanistic psychology, but in those days he was still a graduate student. A few years later he suffered a heart attack, and grew concerned that he was not a safe custodian for it. He returned it to Benedict, but when she died in 1948, it was nowhere to be found and, indeed, has not been found since. Fortunately, one of Maslow's

own graduate students, John J. Honigmann, had the opportunity to read it while it was in Maslow's possession. Recognizing its importance, he copied sizable portions of it on a manual typewriter. These were to be its only record. Later, he himself became a prominent anthropologist, and in 1970, with Maslow, published these portions of Benedict's manuscript in *American Anthropologist*, from which the above quote is taken.

Maslow had been fascinated by the humanistic implications of the synergy concept, and wrote of it in *Eupsychian Management*, published in 1965. At that time it received considerable discussion in management circles, but it has since fallen into obscurity. Ralph Abraham's (1989, 1992) recent mathematical treatment of synergy brings new vitality to it by exploring its meaning as a cultural attractor. Abraham approaches synergy from the point of view of dynamic systems theory. His work is mathematically sophisticated and will not be treated in detail here, but it is hoped that, when actualized as computer simulations, it will provide a powerful method of social analysis.

It is a general characteristic of highly complex systems, whether they be businesses, individual organisms, or ecologies, that they exhibit certain sensitive pivot points at which a small pressure applied in judicious fashion can dramatically influence the future evolution of the system. It is Abraham's hope that sufficiently large and complex simulations of human societies, and ultimately the world culture, will disclose the sensitive points at which the action of even a few people, applied judiciously, can influence this culture toward a better world.

Riane Eisler's (1987, 1995) work, like that of Ruth Benedict, is also based on a broad review of human societies. While Benedict considered a wide geographic range of societies that still existed during the first half of the twentieth century, Eisler developed her ideas from a penetrating analysis of history. This history goes all the way back to the ancient Magdalenian culture that produced the cave paintings of southern Europe.

The basic idea in Eisler's thought is that the major human cultures have tended to fall into two distinguishable configurations, which are centrally defined by differing gender orientations. She terms these configurations the *dominator* and the *gylanic* ethics. The dominator ethic is already familiar to us. It is characterized by the rule of a small, elite class of individuals, almost always male, who control the major assets of the culture. These individuals tend to dominate the other members of the society in hierarchically ordered regimes, with women forming an underclass that has little control over its own fate. In such societies, weapons represent the leading technologies, and war is a principal

means of the acquisition of wealth. Dominator societies value the obedience of their members, who find safety only in conformity. Leaders are
threatened by the appearance of creativity, individualism, and deep
inquiries after truth. They rule by dint of fear. Women are often the
object of the unsolicited aggression of males, and the men are largely
unaccountable for acts of brutality against women.

Gylanic cultures are fundamentally egalitarian. The term *gylany* is
taken from the Greek word *gyne*, or woman, here connected to *an*, from
andros, the Greek word for man (Eisler 1987). The defining characteristic of gylanic cultures is a balanced relationship between men and
women. Relationships in general are characterized by partnership and
lateral linkage rather than by dominance and hierarchy. Value is placed
on individual creativity, education, and the pursuit of truth. Technology
is directed toward the mutual benefit of the members of the society,
and war plays no role whatsoever unless it is inflicted from without.

Eisler's basic notion is that these two types of societies represent
major attractors into which cultural systems can be drawn. The description of dominator culture above seems all too familiar in Western
history and, unfortunately, is easily recognized in the world today. We
might even ask if there are any significant examples of gylanic societies
beyond exotic instances such as a few South Sea Island cultures. Can
we, in fact, find an instance of a major civilization that actually
flourished under the gylanic regime? It turns out that archeological
research seems to have unearthed just such a civilization, one that to
a striking extent fits the gylanic ideal.

In recent decades a significant re-evaluation of archeological findings
from the neolithic age in Eastern Europe and the Middle East has
brought to light an entire civilization that flourished prior to the rise
of ancient Egypt and Mesopotamia. The ascendance of this civilization,
which archeologist Marija Gimbutas (1982) calls *Old Europe*, lasted
for three thousand years, from roughly 6500 to 3500BCE. Agriculture
provided its principal source of material wealth. At its peak, Old
Europe produced religious art (pottery and frescoes), fine clothing, and
evidently had the time and energy for joyful celebration. The cosmology of this culture centered around images of the Earth Goddess. A vast
number of small statuettes from this period represent the goddess with
exaggerated breasts and hips, in some instances in the act of childbirth,
all suggestive of the nurturing, fertile, feminine aspect of the earth.

This civilization seems to have been remarkably egalitarian. Though
the feminine values of nurturance, mutual support, and creativity were
central, it was not a matriarchal society in the usual sense. In round

burial sites, for instance, women are found at the center, with men near the edge, suggesting that women were of higher status than men. Both sexes, however, were well dressed and in possession of ornaments and personal items that suggest that both were recipients of honor and respect. This contrasts dramatically with later burials in Greece and elsewhere, where the position of honor was held by a single warlord who was buried with his spears and shields.

Old Europe seems to have been peaceful beyond anything experienced since. Clean and comfortable cities and villages were positioned for beauty and convenience rather than for defense. There are virtually no weapons among the artifacts of this civilization, and the motifs of its art were of nature and the goddess rather than battles.

The point of all of this is that, if the evidence of three thousand and more years is to be believed, the gylanic way of life seems to be a major cultural attractor. Unfortunately, this attractor was gradually destabilized by the influx of increasing numbers of warlike nomadic tribes, who either conquered the Old Europeans or simply moved in on them, degrading their value system to that of their own. Many of these nomads originated on the steppes of Russia. Their migration has been traced by the southern and western spread of the barrow graves in which they buried their dead. Gimbutas (1982) called these invaders *kurgans*, after the Russian word *kurgan*, or barrow.

The demise of Old Europe was followed by a dark age that lasted until the rise of the "ancient world" of Egypt, Mesopotamia, and Greece during the last two to three millennia before Christ. The value system— indeed, the entire attractor for those new societies—however, was more kurgan than Old European. This was especially true of Mesopotamia and Greece. The warrior–king had replaced what had probably been a queen in the old culture. Warlike sky deities such as Zeus, Marduk, and Yahweh replaced the earth goddess. Hierarchies replaced equality, with male warriors and priests at the top and woman far down the line. Glory was to be achieved in battle, and aggression became institutionalized as noble and heroic. The entire dominator attractor had arisen in full ascendance.

This is not to say that there was nothing of deep value in the new civilizations or in their religions. They were the great cultural forebears of our own civilization. They gave us writing, art and architecture, and the great religious motifs that still remain with us today. The masculine visage of the transcendent carries a majesty, wisdom, and authority that is different from that of the feminine, though it can also be terrible in its destructive potency. The bottom line, however, is that the dominator

ethic, even at its best, amounts to good living for only a select few, and through its inherent tendency toward aggression, and its repression of individual freedom and creativity, inflicts a great cost on its members in terms of the loss of the life fully lived. And, in the world today, its penchant for aggression and war make it a grave danger for the entire human species, together with the whole web of life on Earth.

Moral Maps

Let us turn for the moment to a different topic, one of notable concern to the modern world. This is the matter of moral sensitivity. David Loye wrote:

If we look into the future, as we continually must, one thing above all is apparent. It is that of all the "cognitive maps" our species has evolved over more than a million years of living on this earth, we have at last reached a time where one map above all is of overriding importance. This is our cognitive map of what we call ethics, or moral development. (1990: 41)

By far the most prominent theory of moral development today is that of Harvard psychologist Lawrence Kohlberg (1984). The essential notion in Kohlberg's thought is that moral development follows a developmental progression through a sequence of stages not unlike Jean Piaget's stages of intellectual development. In support of his theory, Kohlberg and his students have conducted a considerable number of extensive interviews with individuals of many nationalities throughout the world. The approach used in these investigations is to present people with moral dilemmas and ask them to reason these through aloud. The maturity of their moral thinking is judged on the basis of the type of reasoning that they use, and not on the solutions themselves. For instance, the investigator might describe a situation in which a man cannot afford to buy medication for a seriously ailing spouse. Should he steal the medication or not, and why? The answer yes or no is not important to Kohlberg, but the reasoning behind it discloses the individual's level of moral attainment.

Kohlberg's theory sees moral development as passing through three major developmental levels. Although there has been more than one version of the theory, its most widely understood form posits three major levels of development, with two stages in each, thus giving a total sequence of six stages. This sequence can be observed in the development of moral maturity in the child (Lickona 1983). Few adults,

however, reach the highest levels, and indeed, Kohlberg's principal interest was with the moral judgments of adults, not children.

The three levels in Kohlberg's theory are referred to as *preconventional, conventional,* and *postconventional.* As the terms suggest, they indicate that the development of moral maturity passes from an early, preconventional level, through a conventional level, in which moral judgment is based on conventional social standards, and on to a level beyond the conventional standards of society. Preconventional morality is based simply on avoiding pain (stage one) or obtaining pleasure (stage two). The pop phrase "If it feels good, do it!" is an example of a preconventional moral attitude. It is not really a moral posture at all, but simply a self-serving rule for making decisions. Unfortunately, many adults do not pass beyond this level.

The first stage of conventional morality simply involves going along with the group. This orientation is frequently seen among adolescents. If a student at this stage is caught cheating on a test, he is likely to defend himself by pointing out that others cheat as well. In other words, he defends his behavior as complying with group standards. At the next stage, however, morality takes on absolute standards. These can be given by a parent, by religious dogma, or by the law. The important point is that the individual accepts these standards as absolute. Morality is a black-and-white affair, and there is no bargaining with it.

Kohlberg found that most adult Europeans and Americans, even college-educated ones, make moral judgments at the conventional level. A few, however, make judgments at the highest, postconventional level. Moral reasoning at the first of the two postconventional stages is based on the realization that it is, in fact, people who ultimately select moral standards. Laws, for instance, represent the considered judgment of society about right behavior. With this in mind, the person at this stage is likely to ask whether a particular act is in line with the law, and beyond this, whether it is in the spirit of the law as well. He or she might question a particular law, or church dogma, as contrary to the original intentions of those who formulated it. Thus, a person in this stage might engage in citizenly activities, including civil disobedience, directed at changing an unjust law. Not surprisingly, this stage is sometimes termed the *legalistic* orientation.

The highest stage of postconventional morality—the highest moral orientation in Kohlberg's system—involves what Kohlberg referred to as *individual principles of conscience.* This rare stage is most dramatically seen in persons such as Mahatma Gandhi and Martin Luther King, Jr. Though such individuals may sometimes seem to stand alone against

their peers, Kohlberg supposed that they represent abstract universal principles of compassion and concern for all of humanity.

Kohlberg believed that growth occurs when people with different moral orientations interact. When moral issues are discussed openly, the person with the lower standard is at a disadvantage beside one with the higher level of development, who, having once been at the lower level himself, is already familiar with his arguments. The result of such interactions is that the morally advanced individual is unlikely to be moved by the less mature person, while the latter experiences some degree of discomfort. In time, he is likely to find his own moral judgments ascending toward those of the more advanced person.

Interestingly, Kohlberg found that most of the time each individual operates from a single orientation, that is, from one particular stage. He or she has some feeling, however, for the stages immediately above and below. When in the company of others who are at one of these stages he is likely to fall in with them and behave as if he were at their stage, whether it is just above or just below his own. On the other hand, he does not really understand the morality of those who are two or more stages above. For instance, a person in either of the conventional stages of morality is unlikely to understand someone like Mahatma Gandhi as anything beyond an oddity. Such oddities can become quite annoying if, for example, they are petitioning for environmental conservation issues at the cost of preconventional rewards or conventional standards to which the forest, lake, or species has been subject.

Now, let us consider Kohlberg's overall system in terms of cognitive maps. Doing so presents us with a different kind of moral hierarchy. Preconventional morality, with its emphasis on rewards and punishments, seems to be governed by cognitive maps of the most concrete variety. These are of the sort studied by Tolman (1932) in rats, which represent the lay of the environment between me and the object of my pleasure or pain. There seems no reason to think that more abstract agendas are involved.

Conventional morality involves more abstract cultural maps. At the absolute morality stage, for instance, one must interpret the mandates of authority in terms of the particular situation in which one finds oneself. The results are neither flexible nor creative, but represent the use of the maps of cultural norms taken as absolute dictates of moral conduct. The first postconventional or legalistic orientation also draws on such maps, but seems to make use of them in a more flexible manner. Here, individuals seem to have acquired a certain ability to put distance between themselves and the map. They are able to make

some assessment of the general lay of the land, noting details that seem inconsistent with the whole—violations of the spirit of the law. In making such assessments, the postconventional person achieves the important recognition that cultural maps are human constructions. Thus, such a person can assume the prerogative to change them.

Individuals with the legalistic orientation are reflective, but are not necessarily self-reflective. They view the cultural map with an air of objectivity not possible for one who is entirely conventionally oriented. When such persons become self-reflective, however, they must consider their own relationship to the cultural map, a relationship that in time must come to include their own deepest personal feelings. If they continue to explore this relationship, they may begin to articulate a very personal value map that may or may not conform to cultural norms. If it does not, they must choose between their own standards and those of the collective. In this dialectic between self-reflective personal values and those of the culture at large, we find the genesis of Kohlberg's highest stage of moral development. In it, we have moved to a self-reflective consciousness that characterizes the very essence of the self. We might say that moral judgment at this stage arises directly from the recursive self, rather than from ordinary cultural maps.

One critic of Kohlberg's theory, psychologist Carol Gilligan (1982), argues that his entire approach to morality basically concerns *individuals* and how they resolve their differences, terming it a *morality of justice*, and contrasts it with an alternative system that she calls a *morality of care*. She suggests that the morality of justice is largely a male point of view, while concerns such as caring and compassion are more typically valued by women. She points out that much of Kohlberg's research was conducted with boys or men. In fact, his doctoral study was done solely with boys. Gilligan, on the other hand, interviewed a number of pregnant women about an eminent moral dilemma: their personal confrontation with the issue of abortion. She found only three distinct levels of moral growth, and these differed from those of Kohlberg.

The first of Gilligan's levels is characterized as *self-interest*. Here, the decision of whether or not to have an abortion is made on the basis of personal gain or loss. I will have an abortion, for instance, because a baby would be a burden to my life-style. The second level of moral development was that of *self-sacrifice*. For example, I will have the baby for my husband. The third and final level, *nonviolence*, represents a shift to a balanced regard for the well-being of everyone concerned, including oneself. For instance, one woman stated that going ahead with the pregnancy would not be a favor to either herself or the baby.

Viewing Gilligan's theory in terms of cognitive maps, we find that it has some features in common with Kohlberg's system. In particular, her lowest level of moral development, self-interest, is much like his preconventional level, and likewise would seem to utilize the most concrete variety of cognitive maps. Her self-sacrifice level seems at first sight to be different from Kohlberg's conventional morality. Given, however, that self-sacrifice has been a traditional role for women, it is not clear that this is not really another type of conventional behavior. The principal difference between the two systems would seem to lie at the very highest levels, namely Kohlberg's principles of conscience and Gilligan's level of nonviolence. Viewing them in terms of cognitive maps, however, suggests that even these have an essential feature in common. This is that both seem to arise from the self-reflective stance that brings one into relationship with both the cultural value maps and one's own inner feelings, leading to the discovery and articulation of authentic moral postures.

Gilligan's criticism that Kohlberg's model of moral development is largely a male-oriented one has not held up well empirically. Research has not generally supported the notion that men tend to score higher on Kohlberg's moral scale than do women (Thoma 1986). The failure to find significant gender differences, on the other hand, does not in itself invalidate her idea that there may be two styles of moral decision-making. Based on an extensive study of what he terms *moral sensitivity*, psychologist David Loye (forthcoming) has also discovered two styles of moral decision-making.

Loye chooses the expression *moral sensitivity* because it implies more than the idea of judgment; it also points to a level of moral awareness. Loye's investigation involves intensive scholarship in three fields. The first is the historical record of human culture. Here he focuses on the cultural attractors of the Old European gylanic and subsequent dominator social orders discussed above. Clearly these represent divergent moral principles, and it is not hard to see in them something along the lines of Gilligan's community-oriented or caring morality on the one hand, and Kohlberg's individual justice morality on the other. Though these may be metaphorically tied to notions of the masculine and the feminine, they apparently represent a broader set of motifs in human moral sensitivity.

The second field from which Loye draws strongly is research and clinical observation concerning the brain. The findings suggest that moral sensitivity is rooted in the very biology of the human nervous system. Most helpful here were the pioneering efforts of Alexander

Luria. From Luria's careful observations of psychological losses incurred when various regions of the brain are damaged, Loye is able to articulate a surprisingly distinct set of functions performed by the brain in appraising new situations and making plans to deal with them. One of these functions turns out to be moral sensitivity. That there is a biological foundation for moral sensitivity should not, perhaps, be surprising. Loye points out that precursors of human moral behavior can be found throughout the natural world, from symbiosis between single-celled organisms through cooperative interactions in many species of higher animals (Augros and Stanciu 1987, 1992).

The third area that Loye scrutinizes is the literature of previous scientific analyses of moral behavior. Here, he finds that, prior to Kohlberg, two distinct patterns of moral behavior had been discovered. These fit remarkably well with the two motifs already described. One emphasized individual right behavior, while the other stressed compassion, nurturance, and caring. These two motifs were described in one form or another by Marx and Engels (Engels 1972), in Piaget's (1965) studies of the moral development of children, in the writings of Wilhelm Reich (1972), in the intellectuals of the Frankfurt School (Jay 1973), and in the work of Erich Fromm (1947).

It would seem from all of the above that the two major cultural attractors, which we have identified with the gylanic and dominator social orders, correspond to two fundamentally disparate moral dispositions. These are the Gilligan and Kohlberg orientations. At their highest octave, they each bring the authentic inclinations of the individual into direct relationship and even confrontation with traditional cultural values. On the other hand, there is a tendency for the Kohlberg orientation to lead to a dogged insistence on particular moral attitudes in the face of all opposition. Such commitment is no doubt admirable in and of itself, but in a world of cultural cross-currents and social transformation it can be out of place and dangerous.

It is to be hoped that the new flexibility associated with a postmodern release from rigid perspectival maps will provide a field for the agile interplay of these modes, combining the strength and commitment of the one with the compassion and contextual appropriateness of the other.

Having examined the role of cognitive maps in the life of the individual, the following chapters will turn to an exploration of the evolutionary origins of such maps, and then to their role in human history. Finally, we will examine the potential that the understanding of such maps allows for a better world of the future.

The Cognitive Maps of Societies

In the first chapter of this book, we explored the importance of cognitive maps in the lives of individual human beings, the role they play in creating each person's unique reality, and the role they play in guiding social and moral behavior. All of this was seen from the perspective of the individual and his or her experience of the world, an experience intensely colored by the nature of his or her own cognitive maps. From this perspective we also examined the nature of human culture, finding in it a construction, a patchwork, of individual cognitive maps. More than this, however, it is a patchwork that emerges as a force in its own right, influencing the lives of individuals as surely as its own substance was woven originally from the maps of those individual human beings.

In the present chapter we return again to an examination of the fabric of social cognitive maps, but this time from a different perspective. Here, we emphasize the influence of society on the individual, rather than the other way round, thus bringing into context the enormously important influence of culture as history, evolving as a living dynamic system that carries in tow the lives of individual human beings.

The Swiss psychiatrist Carl Jung devoted much of his life to the study of powerful collective images, which he termed *archetypes*. He showed beyond reasonable doubt that these represent important determinants of the unconscious life of the modern human (Jung 1961). According to Jungian theory, such archetypes are projected outward on to other people, and on to society as a whole. Indeed, from Jung's perspective, a great deal of what is taken for granted, in both one's internal and external worlds, is formatted by projections of archetypal images. In later years, Jung became particularly concerned about the power of archetypes to pattern the realities of entire societies. For instance, he felt that the rise of the Third Reich represented the ascendance, at the

level of an entire nation, of what he called the *Odin archetype*, the image of ruthlessness and conquest. On a more positive note, in one of his last works, he speculated that widespread reports of flying saucers in the late 1940s and the 1950s were brought about by the collective influence of the *self*, the central archetype of the personality (Jung 1959).

Jung believed that archetypes gradually develop over long spans of human history. Recent scientific speculations that bear on the question of collective images suggest, however, that they may have the potential to develop considerably more rapidly (Sheldrake 1987; Laszlo 1987b, 1995). Laszlo (1993), for instance, has shown how the patterns of thought and behavior of even a single person might become the source of a formative influence, potentially available as a gentle patterning force on other persons, even in the future. This notion, which he calls the *psi-effect*, is rooted in contemporary quantum physics. It postulates that mathematical wave functions controlling the fate of individual subatomic particles are built up into increasingly higher-order or *nested* structures that have a direct influence on complex real-world events. In this case, such influence would be felt at the level of the neural processes in the brain. The nested quantum structures are "nonlocal," and stand beyond ordinary time as well. Such ideas are dramatically opposed to the mechanistic spirit of turn-of-the-century science prevalent when Jung was developing his original thoughts on archetypes. The realities of modern quantum physics, however, make them considerably more credible today (Combs and Holland 1990).

Evidently, cognitive maps exist on many levels. Social cognitive maps are supported by many minds acting in concert, any one of which contains only a part of an entire cultural map. At the same time, we have discovered the possibility of patterning fields that could mediate collective influences between minds themselves. A tentative conclusion regarding such fields is that they could effectively constitute subtle cognitive maps that might influence whole populations of people. It is, of course, difficult to observe such maps as pure instances beyond the rich surrounding influence of ongoing communications between individuals. Indeed, it is precisely the nesting of such collective maps within the buzz of ordinary discussion that seems to amplify their effectiveness. When the world's stock markets take a dip, or a regional or global recession sets in, a variety of levels of communication immediately become active. These range from many sorts of electronic transmissions to conversations carried on over lunch. The atmosphere of the event, however, seems larger, more foreboding, than the sum of the bits of information transmitted in all of these ongoing channels.

We must evidently enlarge our concept of culture to include not only the overlapping projections of individual cognitive maps, but the possibility of the projections of collective ones. One implication of all this is that collective maps carry the culture forward into the future with a greater momentum than the cumulative effects of individual maps could muster. The spirit of an age, for example, is more than an abstracted description of the general themes and individual experiences that characterize it. It is a collective map that embodies the unique themes of that particular moment in history. In terms of physics, such collective maps may well represent an objective process—one that asserts itself, via the brain, on the mental life of individuals.

Of Brains and Societies

The notion of social cognitive maps implies an analogy between social systems and brains, whether human or otherwise. It is problematic enough to suppose that what happened in the brain of a rat running through mazes in Tolman's laboratory is equivalent to what happens in a human brain flying an airplane or writing a book, but at least the two organisms have physiological material in common. There are no neurons in societies, no eyes or ears, no speech centers or limbic systems. How then can we claim that societies establish representations that orient them in space and guide their behavior in time?

Of course, the analogy has to be approximate. For the sake of convenience, the term *cognitive map* is being used to refer to both personal and public representations, and this may lead to some confusion. The analogy, however, is not as preposterous as it may initially seem, and terminological symmetry can have certain advantages. The name we apply to a phenomenon influences how we think about it, and the search for underlying unities implied by a universal term may lead to valuable insights.

To begin with, let us just think about a few facts. It is true, for instance, that children understand their parents, even in the midst of so-called "youth rebellions." The mere fact that generations can share a common language indicates that behavioral skills can be passed on pretty much uncorrupted from one period of time to another. Parents and children may not agree on much at given moments. Nevertheless, they tend to agree about which programmed response is appropriate to a shared experience, and do it using the same words (Connerton 1989; Fentress and Wickham 1992).

More dramatic examples abound, some of them seemingly trivial, but all instructive. What these examples tend to demonstrate is that collective, social realities actually do exist; that a new level of reality does emerge with human social systems. Organized human entities like teams, fire fighters, or military units are as real as biological individuals. In all of these organisms, a system-level reality has emerged. They each acquire, store, and process environmental information on the organizational level. In them, what happens to one happens to all, and the society acting as a whole can solve problems individuals cannot solve for themselves. Individual interests are subordinated to collective goals, and individual accomplishments transcend private skill. No player on a team, for instance, can advance to a world championship—no matter what his or her skill—if the team is defeated.

The firemen who raced into the burning nuclear reactor at Chernobyl had no biological advantage and little individual interest in what they were doing. In fact, most of them fully realized that by entering the plant they were exposing themselves to levels of radiation that would inevitably prove fatal. It is doubtful that many of them would have entered the blazing structure if left to themselves, just as men in combat will flee once their unit identity has been shattered after attrition rates approach a third. But in disasters, team sports, and wars, men are not alone. Nor are they acting on biological impulses. They will do what their society wants for as long as they believe that their society continues to exist.

In sport, disasters, and war, people are members of social systems. Those systems redefine their biological components, giving them attributes they do not have individually. In games, players may run faster or move more quickly; in disasters, firemen may sacrifice themselves with great nobility; in war, solders may kill with "inhuman" viciousness. On their own, athletes may be only moderately well coordinated, and they are never as much fun to watch in practice as in games. Firemen may be as reluctant to pay taxes individually as junk bond salesmen. And in their barracks soldiers may be only marginally harder to get along with than civilians. But during games, in crises, or in battle, all these people will display characteristics that are functions of their social identities, not their biological, or psychological, selves.

As members of societies, people will do to varying degrees what the social system wants, not what they want to do themselves. The things people do constitute what a social system is, and if successive generations of people display a characteristic set of distinguishing behaviors it is fair to say that the social system is a self-organized, or autopoietic,

system. Society "knows" how to do certain things, and it will "teach" those things to young people as they replace their elders in approved social roles, in the same way that replicating cells in a biological organism learn to be parts of livers or kidneys or brains.

It is hard for us to recognize the emergent level of a social process, for we are observing social systems from the perspective of just one of their parts. The mere fact that we do not recognize the existence of a social brain, therefore, is no more significant than the (presumed) fact that an individual neuron does not know it is part of a biological brain—let alone that it, the separate neuron, is having a great idea! We can see evidence that something is going on, however, from history as well as from an average person's point of view.

Perhaps the best place to begin is with technology. Technology is one of the ways that every society perceives its environment, but its form varies wildly from place to place and time to time. Moreover, we tend to associate it with individual inventiveness and skill. So technology should be an example of how social systems change, rapidly and significantly because of innovations in their basic organs of perception.

But V. Gordon Childe (1951), the Australian archaeologist who rattled so many academic cages, noticed that there are, of course, many ways to form a crude stone implement, and that people in different places and at different times have tried many of them. In fact, people at different times in the same place used different techniques to produce stone tools, weapons, and artifacts. But at any one time, he discovered to his surprise, all the manufactured implements in a particular location are made in exactly the same way. At any given level of any particular dig only one technique for manufacturing is ever discovered. The homogeneity of chosen methods suggests that a social group has a shared, approved procedure for manufacture, and that every youth raised in its bosom will be taught that technique and discouraged from exploring others.

Making implements is a behavior that requires knowledge of an environment and the skills needed to survive in it. People have to know whether to use flint or sandstone in making an ax, whether to flake or grind it, and how to use the ax in gaining food. No individual in a single lifetime is likely to be able to discover that axes made from stone collected at some particular spot can be used to hunt a certain kind of game in another spot later in the year. This kind of knowledge is accumulated over long periods of time, probably with a high degree of trial and error, through the observations of many people. Somehow they have to share that knowledge.

But when knowledge is shared something wonderful and not immediately obvious happens—people are thinking in each other's brains. The effects can be quite spectacular. An Aboriginal Australian, for example, can travel from one end of the continent to the other without ever being lost, despite the fact that he may never previously have wandered more than a few miles from his birth place (Chatwin 1988). He can do that because he has received, with the social equivalent of his mother's milk, knowledge gained by generations of explorers. During a "walkabout," the native Australian is guided by the experiences of people who may have died centuries earlier and whose lives were spatially remote. But the record of what they saw and learned can be passed on to him, and the contemporary walker has virtually the same experiences as the ancestors during the Dreamtime lost in history.

When people can think in one another's brains, it is obvious that the constraints of physics, chemistry, and biology are being transcended; that, in fact, a new level of reality has emerged. How that process happened exactly is unknown and unknowable. But we can speculate with reasonable intelligence about it, at least in general terms. But just because we are forced by the absence of historical documentation to think on a general level, we need not lose an appreciation for the distinctly individual flavor of Sumerian or Egyptian or Mayan civilization.

As we have shown in Chapter 1, human societies have their origins in biological capacities that people share with other animals. But it is clear that human societies represent differences in kind from the groups and societies of other creatures. They are more tightly organized than herds of cattle and more flexible than insect colonies. So the questions for us have to begin with why and how human societies emerged in their peculiar forms. The lessons derived from studying self-organization in the rest of nature suggest that human action triggered a series of positive-feedback loops that, eventually, transformed the nature of human action.

Working together in loosely coupled, small groups, people, we may suppose, released some energy flow that drove an aggregate of human individuals through some critical barrier, at which point a bunch of "yous" and "mes" became an "us." That critical boundary would involve increasing population supported by greater energy resources produced by domesticating animals, agriculture, new technology, and improved communication media. According to Denise Schmandt-Besserat (1986), the critical stage was reached about 8000BCE in Asia Minor, when settled agricultural communities reached populations of

about 350 people. It is after this point that the first artificial "tokens" were created.

Artificial tokens are important because they indicate the need to communicate information over macroscopic distances, significant periods of time, and in large amounts. People were no longer living in such small numbers and in such close proximity that each of them knew what the others were doing by direct contact. Moreover, in a sedentary agricultural society supported by specialized technical skills, people had become more dependent upon one another; they had reached a point where whatever happened to one happened to all.

In these circumstances, a social whole emerged, a system literally greater than the sum of its human parts. From now on, things would have to be done for the good of the system, upon the survival of which depended the survival of its members. Farmers would have to irrigate fields, plant seeds, and harvest crops even when they personally would have preferred lounging around lazily. Soldiers would have to fight and die at great distances from home for "rational" causes in which they had little or no emotional stake. New classes of political, military, economic, and spiritual leaders emerged, who took profits and benefits for collective accomplishments vastly disproportionate to their personal contributions. Humanity had stepped out of nature, entering into an artificial environment where an affluent minority coerced the impoverished majority to work for the collective good.

This dramatic symmetry-break with prehistoric developments was recorded in a great variety of myths, whose attractiveness continues to lure Rousseauistic thinkers to this day. But it seems clear that, like it or not, the Edenic garden was lost irretrievably. We can continue to wax poetic about how relationships in this earlier time were superior to those of the present, how people lived closer to nature, how much more respect for the land the ancients displayed. But the more we wallow in this sort of romanticism, the more inconceivable the leap to civilization appears (Schmookler 1984). Why would these noble savages ever have left the garden? Why were they foolish enough to create societies that were hierarchical, unequal, coercive, and militaristic?

The disconcerting answer, of course, may be that people did not organize civilized societies—the societies organized themselves. Like every other step up the evolutionary ladder, civilized societies did not ask the existing life-forms for permission to punctuate the established equilibrium and create a new level of reality. Rather, nature simply took the available resources—biological humans speaking languages and using specialized tools—and mixed them together. In François Jacob's

(1982) terms, also embraced by Claude Lévi-Strauss, nature is a *tinkerer* that works by *bricolage*. Evolution is not planned in advance, and whatever emerges depends upon what is available at the moment. What is available was usually developed for its own purposes, independently of everything else and with no long-term intentionality. The available is an example of what Stuart Kauffman (1993) calls *random grammars*, any sequence of information created in whatever isolated circumstances that later proves able to interact with other strings of information to interpret one another in completely unexpected forms.

But mixing the available strings of information—for example, how to make individual humans domesticate animals, plant seeds, make tools, and educate children—can produce a structure with attributes that are underdetermined by the histories of their component parts. There is nothing about the early development of human organs, for instance, that implies what their ultimate use would be. Our eyes did not incrementally, gradually, and continuously develop from rudimentary vision sensors into the miraculously refined instruments they are today. They began as parts of our primitive brains that suddenly changed their functions when other parts of the brain developed.

The same process is true of human societies, only the social process takes on an unexpected moral dimension. We make judgments about the past—for example, adoring prehistory and condemning modern civilization. That is a perfectly reasonable thing to do, but it is a consequence of civilization itself. The idealized gardens of prehistory, where people had not yet eaten of the Tree of Knowledge, are, by definition, amoral states. People are supposed to have lived in blissful self-assurance and unity with nature because they made no moral claims; they did not even know what a moral judgment was. Moral judgments are only possible after a phase change has occurred, after people have become so mutually dependent that their societies create a behavioral space in which individual actions are evaluated in terms of their public consequences. Only after the social whole upon whose survival individuals depend emerges can there be a moral judgment.

But now people are forced to make existential choices, for they must select between actions that are immediately profitable to themselves biologically and actions that are socially beneficial to the collective in the long run. The tug of self-service and self-sacrifice produced a strain that had to be overcome. No doubt, as the people being whipped in very early Sumerian clay tablets indicate, many individuals failed to make the socially approved choice. But their actions were no longer

strictly private and biological. Nor were human actions merely evaluated at the collective level; emergent social wholes possessed negative-feedback loops quite able to enforce public judgments upon private selves. The human beings through whom societal negative-feedback loops operated had to be convinced to swing their whips. Slave-drivers were almost as cruelly exploited as the driven slaves. It was the moral authority of social systems that inspired some people to coerce others.

Morality, Maps, and Social Reality

The point of the discussion above is to introduce a major idea, namely that morality is the language in which social cognitive maps are expressed. This does not come as a surprise, since the importance of moral cognitive maps was discussed in Chapter 1. Here, however, we consider the role of morality not in terms of the moral behavior of individuals, but in terms of the fabric of society itself.

Just as we cannot describe everything that happens in chemistry in terms of physics, or everything that happens in biology in terms of chemistry, we cannot describe everything in society in terms of biology. Moral maps are needed to represent emergent reality on the social level, a reality that cannot be reduced to the language of physics, chemistry, or even biology. We have to describe the collective reality of social systems in the symbolic languages used by the people who make up the systems.

When the social level of reality emerges, a public, linguistic domain is created by shared information. Suspended in that public domain, people can know things of which they have no direct experience, the way an Aboriginal can know the distant reaches of Australia without having traveled to them. Other people's bodies are providing our "sixth senses." But henceforth people can only know things in terms of linguistically shaped perceptions; they will never again experience reality unadorned and unprocessed.

Two things are critical here. First is the simple fact that to communicate information it has to be encoded and decoded. If I want you to know about my red Ferrari, I will not give you direct experience of it by driving into you with it but will say the word *Ferrari*. That word is essentially arbitrary. It has nothing to do with automobiles. It will not carry you to Portofino, attract members of the opposite sex, consume a nonrenewable resource, or pollute the atmosphere. You cannot polish the word *Ferrari* or act out fantasies driving it. But my use of the word

may well excite your envy and resentment (if you had a red Ferrari, I would probably be envious and resentful). That is, despite its arbitrary nature, the word *Ferrari* entering your brain will be decoded as a representation of a sleek, powerful, expensive automobile. Through the use of an agreed code, you and I can share information. But what we share is not the Ferrari. We share the socially conditioned experience of what *Ferrari* means, and we can never experience an actual Ferrari independently of its socially determined meanings.

Secondly, with the emergence of societies, new kinds of information came to be communicated. It was no longer merely a matter of my telling you something about my experiences. In a society it is necessary to communicate information about our experience. Assuming that all our verbal pictures are designed to map the world, the emergence of societies marks a symmetry-break in which a new world has to be mapped. It is a world created when the natural environment is transformed by collective action. No aggregate of individual cognitive maps can represent the collective environment, for the social world is a whole greater than the sum of its parts. A way to encode information about the reality that transcended biology had to be found if even bricolage were successfully to find a way to glue people together into new wholes by communicating information about what happened to closely coupled social systems.

It is not irrational to suggest as an axiom that society constitutes a new level of reality, for it is perfectly reasonable to suppose that our ancestors acted cooperatively to affect their environment. Cooperation is not uncommon in prehuman species. All we need to suppose is that by cooperation our precivilized ancestors created positive-feedback loops with the environment. The result would be a release of energy that drove early human groups through a cascade of bifurcations until they self-organized into stable states that were, in part, decoupled from their original, natural environments. At that point, society could be readily distinguished from nature.

No doubt the first societies were relatively simple, which is one aspect that so endears them to Hippies. A simple system models its environment, as Bateson (1972) pointed out. But one definition of a complex system is that it also contains a model of itself (Nicolis 1986). The earliest societies of which any symbolic record remains have *cosmogenic* myths. That is, they have symbolic representations of their world and how it came to be. But it is interesting that only later do societies have *origin* myths, stories of how the people came to be. The cosmogenic myth is a representation of the world; the origin myth is a represent-

ation of a society in its world. Simple groups were models of their environments, but civilized societies were complex enough to have models of themselves. Since it takes time for the latter to be created after the former, we can postulate that social evolution involves increasing complexity in human history, as it does in the rest of nature.

In both the cosmogenic and origin myths, a people talk to themselves about their shared experiences. It is this discussion that reveals the social corollary of cognitive mapping. As we still consider how an environment is represented and how problems are to be solved in that environment, the term *cognitive map* remains appropriate. But we no longer talk about the environment experienced by individual biological creatures (Lynch 1960). Therefore, the cognitive map can no longer be recorded in the "wetware" of a brain; it can no longer be written in the "language" of biological cells or their electrochemical connections. We are now talking about the environment experienced as a result of cooperative human effort, and of the forces released by that effort into a social whole (Downs and Stea 1973; Gladwin 1970).

Collective Experience, Myths, and Maps

Respecting the fact that a social cognitive map must be encoded in symbolic human languages replete with moral terms, we can give the following definition: a *societal cognitive map* is the set of shared symbols describing a collective environment and prescribing the organized behaviors appropriate to preserving social stability in that environment. In its descriptions a societal cognitive map locates the principle physical aspects of the environment—mountains, valleys, rivers, etc. (Frankfort 1973). These descriptions are rarely in terms that moderns recognize as "scientifically" valid, but they are usually amazingly perceptive and often better informed than the modern white Westerners who ridiculed ancient cognitive maps.

Take the Sumerian cosmogenic myth as an example. It tells the story of how the world was delivered from the Earth Goddess after she was raped by the Wind God. Now obviously, the tale as we have it includes some later emendations. But while their sexist dominating attitudes can be decried, the validity of the basic representation cannot be disputed. The story reveals that the meanderings of the Tigris and Euphrates rivers outline a woman's body, that the wind blows off the Persian Gulf between the mouths of the two rivers, and that the heavy silt carried by the rivers builds up at a very rapid pace. Ur, for instance, was a

coastal town when the story was created, but is now over two hundred miles inland.

The use of divine symbols and the attribution to the divinities of animal lusts made Sumerian cosmogony appear irrational to "scientifically" minded Westerners. But the creators of the tale accurately described their territory, provided one knew how to decode the information communicated. Westerners who did not know how to read the tales laughed at them. However, Western geographers knew less about the course of the two rivers than the ancients until British intelligence flights over the area in World War II photographed it carefully. Only when an officer who happened to be an Oxbridge orientalist laid out the pictures on a plotting board could the wisdom of the ancients finally be appreciated.

Egyptian cosmogony is similar in kind but radically different in detail. That is because the environment Egyptians had to map socially was radically different from that of Sumer. In Egypt, the Nile provides a narrow ribbon of fertile green slashed from the barren desert. Naturally enough, Egyptians described the world as a sort of celery-dish. In addition to the rains that fall sideways—the Nile—the most dominant feature of the Egyptian environment is the Sun, who became the principal god once the empire was created. The Sun was the god of Heliopolis, now only a minor city near Cairo. But once the empire was united, the priests at Memphis blended Re, the Sun, with Amon, the Air God of Memphis, to produce Amon-Re, the father of the pharaoh. It follows that this god was dominant, for, after all, a social cognitive map is the record of collective experience. Once civilization and male domination became complete, Egyptians could even imagine the male Sun God producing the world by masturbating it into existence (Reilly 1980). But even in early versions, it is the power of the Sun that draws the Earth out of the primeval waters, perfectly describing the sight of hillocks covered with fresh silt appearing to rise as the annual flood recedes.

Compared to Sumer, Egypt offered a benign environment. The land between the Tigris and Euphrates was washed by highly irregular floods, had been exposed to foreign invasion, and was sustainable only by continuous labor. The Nile, on the other hand, flowed with a notable regularity and predictability, providing virtually the same floods at virtually the same time for millennia. Its currents permitted easy travel by boat downstream, while the winds sweeping gently down the valley from the Mediterranean cooled the land and made sail-powered travel up-river almost effortless. The surrounding desert protected Egypt from

attack. The result was a civilization so attractive that it was nearly heaven, which is why the Egyptians were so fascinated with the afterlife and so concerned to be prepared for it. The next world would be as perfect as this one, and all the clothes, chariots, tools, and artifacts used in Egypt would be appropriate there.

The harsh and unforgiving world of Sumer, by contrast, described its quality of life in negative terms. People were created by gods, for instance, because the gods were unwilling to toil eternally, hauling mud to clear irrigation channels or build dams. The work was thankless, since floods washed everything away in a flash or else drought left the fields to die, and only slaves could be forced to carry it out. Human beings were, therefore, the slaves of the gods, and the statues created in Sumer, bowed persons with prayerful hands and big frightened eyes, reveal the sense people had of their precarious, ever-threatened existence.

By describing people as well as places, social cognitive maps are representing collective experience. They are preserving a memory of the world experienced by the ancestral founders of a society. At the same time, by exploring what a human life means and what its worth is, social cognitive maps also prescribe the behaviors necessary for society to survive. They filter out vital information and stimulate learned responses to it. Value symbols prescribe behavior, and behavior creates social structure. Values excite emotional responses to particular persons, places, or actions. Values decide that a person is noble or craven, that a place is holy or cursed, that an action is moral or immoral. Young people are encouraged to emulate behavior that is noble and repudiate behavior that is craven, to travel to the holy places annually and avoid the cursed ones, and to replicate useful actions and eschew wasteful ones.

When successive generations tell themselves the same stories, which describe the same environment and excite the same behaviors, a complex society comes into being. Society is a model of an environment that did not exist until collective human effort created it. Precivilized peoples, no doubt, affected their environments, but the moral grandeur in which contemporary critics cloak the ancients depends upon their not having devastated the world in which they lived. Notwithstanding tales of slash-and-burn agriculture to the contrary, the point is that precivilized peoples left a limited mark upon the earth because they were not able to affect it more drastically. Wandering in small, loosely coupled bands, they lived off nature's bounty. To be sure, when their populations rose, even small bands could seriously tax a locality. But

when such local resources became hard to get, the early human bands fragmented and searched for new places to forage (Mann 1986). Plant and animal life left behind in the abandoned territory could recover rapidly.

In these original bands, people are likely to have served their separate biological needs, taking as much interest in the group as cattle or birds take in herds or flocks. Group and biological individual benefited from each other, but to such a limited degree that disintegration was not a major concern. But when people began to work closely together to domesticate animals and plant crops, they created an artificial environment. The primeval forests could be mapped by the brains of individuals humans; but the artificial worlds created by collective human effort were more multi-dimensional and dynamic than the environments presented by nature. The information about a human-made environment could not all be stored in an individual brain. Nor could an individual brain anticipate the dynamics of a new environment or control collective responses. When complex societies emerged from precivilized bands, they were wholes whose survival demanded the preservation of collective behavior.

To survive, social wholes had to create means of distributing responsibility for information-processing. Everyone in a given society had to learn to speak the same language, perceive the same realities, value the same responses, internalize the same behaviors. Then, in reality, everyone could act as if they knew what the others were doing: behaviors became correlated. Individual cognitive maps cannot produce these tightly coupled correlations, for there is no way to distribute the programs for information-processing. But our precivilized ancestors found a way to act together to change their environment, to stabilize the structures cooperative action created, and rapidly to communicate information about environmental changes by mapping the world created by collective action. Moreover, because social cognitive maps are written in symbolic languages, they are uniquely suited for distribution throughout a population of human brains (Craik 1943).

Maps, Songs, and Writing

A social cognitive map is a song sung by every member of a stabilized society. The Homeric poems that mapped Greece during its "Dark Ages" were literally sung, as were the legends Pacific Islanders used to navigate the open seas. By singing the same song, members of a society

are locating the same key environmental elements and triggering the behaviors necessary for the replication of the society in the future. That is, each generation learns from the song what game is available and how to hunt it, what crops to plant and where to plant them, what campsite to use and how to find it. Members of societies also learn how to relate to one another from their shared cognitive maps. When the same foods are produced and eaten by people acting out the same behaviors, the same society has been reconstituted. So, in effect, social cognitive maps are equivalent to DNA, which itself is a kind of encoded representation of an organism that represents an environment. Only now it is not the biological features of people that are being replicated. Rather, it is behavior patterns, based upon trained perceptions and excited by values shared on the collective level, that are being replicated.

A society's fitness is determined by its social cognitive map. Thus, by introducing the concept of social cognitive maps we can provide a logical explanation of human social evolution. A society survives when the description and prescriptions encoded in its cognitive map match its environment. Then the group is able to reproduce itself in competition with other groups. In other words, when people are brought up to see the world in a certain way, they survive if the world they encounter as adults is, at least within limits, as they expected. Similarly, people survive because the skills they were provided with as children prove useful in the world they exploit as adults. Finally, competing groups will be selected for or against depending upon how much of the environment they can adequately map and how relatively effective their orchestrated responses are. The group mapping more of the world and processing the information more efficiently will have an advantageous differential rate in reproducing itself and its products.

But if people are, for example, trained to hunt bears where there are no bears, or trained to worship gods too weak to defend them, their society will usually disintegrate. The map they have inherited does not match their territory and they are lost. This is an important consequence of the social cognitive map theory, for it indicates that societies are, as Childe (1951) pointed out, less adaptive than we sometimes think. It is probably true that cultural evolution is faster than biological evolution; but that is because words are cheaper than genes. We can explore the possible advantages of changing a cognitive map by manipulating word-symbols. If the members of our society approve of some metaphorical deviation, it will be endorsed and the society will evolve.

But it is less easy to change social cognitive maps in practice than it is in theory, especially after societies have become complex. Once cooperative human action has created a dynamic, multi-dimensional environment, the society embedded in it is unstable. Any fluctuation in its internal structure can reduce its capacity to process the vast amounts of environmental energy, matter, and information flowing through the society. Besides, if what we are trained to experience is what we do experience, then we may not even be conscious of altered possibilities—an ear trained to hear one kind of song may not even realize that the noise assaulting it is music! Unless a sense datum is capable of being processed by symbolic representation, it is ignored or repressed.

Of course, one reason societies do not change readily is that they have negative-feedback loops, institutionalized subsystems that model a remembered environment. Complex societies even have subsystems designed to preserve established organization by suppressing deviations. These subsystems, of which the Inquisition and the FBI are typical examples, are triggered by the values in a social cognitive map. Medieval people were encouraged to love God and obey His earthly representatives, and anti-papal heretics who deviated were sometimes burned. Americans were required to hate communists, and those who were even mildly sympathetic were followed, spied on, fired from their jobs, and frequently arrested. Burning or harassing fellow human beings must be hard work, but dedicated disciples of the Church and the American Way of Life risked their souls and mental health because they were so enamored of a particular social system that they were inflamed by any opposition to it. Inflaming those repressive passions is a way for societies to preserve their identities.

Social cognitive maps, in other words, not only teach people how to experience the world and what parts of the world to experience, but also form patterned responses to experiences. Societies sense or perceive their artificial environment through people and tools. But they shape both the people and the tools, so that they are effective filters for sorting through the "bloomin' buzzin' confusion" of external reality. There was nothing wrong with the eyes of precivilized nomads or with the noses of preindustrial Arabs. Biologically, their eyes and noses were the same as ours. Yet the nomads never exploited the agricultural resources of the river valleys and the Arabs paid no attention to the treasury of oil. Neither nomads nor Arabs were socially equipped to see the potential of these environments. Their social cognitive maps could not process the energy flows represented by irrigated agriculture or oil,

so for them, in a very real sense, neither the valleys nor the oil fields existed. They were not part of the collective myth, so they were not real. Nor could the agricultural or industrial resources of river valleys and oil fields be perceived, since cooperative human action had not created the environment in which their potentials were societal actualities.

When societies perceive key features of their external environments and orchestrate responses to them, they are to all intents and purposes "thinking," as anthropologist Mary Douglas (1986) says. Of course, societies do not think by illuminating neural networks, for they are not made of neural networks. They are made of individuals and subsystems or "institutions." Societies think by activating organized programs for dealing with perceived problems by energizing institutions. When, for instance, strangely costumed foreigners approach a society's boundaries and a specialized class of comparably costumed males march out to give battle, society is thinking. It has perceived a change in its environment and responded by activating a prepared program previously shown to be effective. And it should be admitted that, by going to war, society as a whole is solving problems its individual members cannot solve for themselves.

Societies remember which behaviors solved problems in the past by storing information. Information is stored in a variety of ways. The most obvious are written documents, but they came late. Preliterate bands recorded their experiences through rituals and sung myths (Goody 1977; Turner 1986). Modern anthropologists notice a peculiar quality to the mythical life of preliterate groups: they do not take their rituals and myths lightly; it is not enough for them to attend church for an hour on Sunday and ignore religion the rest of the week. Preliterate peoples, we are told, live in their rituals and myths. That is, by performing a ritual or singing a mythic tale, preliterate peoples are actually acting out the divine adventure they describe. By doing so, they recreate both the cosmos and the people in the present.

Ritual and myth, therefore, are not merely ways of remembering past experiences; they are techniques for structuring present behaviors in exact imitation of the remembered past, which is literally present in the ritual or myth. Ritual and myth transport information from the past to the present, and, by the religious reenactment, those behaviors are replicated in the present. Ritual and myth are able to replicate the people whose behaviors preserve the rituals and myths as surely as successful mating songs reproduce flocks of birds. Ritual and myths, the earliest forms of social cognitive maps, act as DNA, which is how societies endure over time.

Of course, advanced biological brains think by creating new ideas, which societies do as well. A new social idea is a new behavioral role, and when societies create ideas they "make up new people," in Ian Hacking's phrase (1985). The prophet, the poet, the philosopher, and the physicist are all identities that are not found in nature, or even in preliterate societies. They are specialized identities produced in response to enriched environments that cannot be read through the prism of a monolithic social role. New social roles imply that new aspects of the environment are being perceived, for patterned individual behaviors are one method that societies have of "sensing" their worlds. By making up new people, societies do more than endure. They evolve by demonstrating that they can learn—perceive, store, and process—new information.

Most of the time, however, societies "develop" rather than "evolve." They streamline themselves by learning how to perform established tasks better. Only on rare occasions do societies learn qualitatively new tricks, break the symmetry of their historical development, and experience a discontinuous leap to levels of increased complexity. Because most laboratory examples of this fundamental evolutionary process are much quicker, it is not well understood. But perhaps the slow time scale—relative to individual lifetimes—of societal transitions can be observed more completely. Then the difficulty of translating scientific models to society can be made worthwhile, for science might end up with a better understanding of some fundamental problems. Let us begin with a modest presupposition, namely that the earliest societies were relatively crude brains. That does not mean that the brains of the individuals making up the earliest societies were crude—they were the most refined biological learning machines ever evolved, at least as far as we know.

The biological brains in the earliest societies were human brains. But the networked interdependencies connecting them were few and loose. So the reality that was emerging in the symmetry break from biological to social evolution had not progressed very far. Even the first civilized societies, whether in Sumer, Egypt, China, or America, were all thinking systems that, like frog brains, relied more on genetic than on acquired memory. They had found particular roles and relationships that effectively modeled the artificial environments created by irrigation, for example. Having found the roles and relationships suited to processing this information, societies were determined to preserve the ability. It turned out that a hierarchical structure, informed by writing, gathered in cities, and with a ceremonial center, worked best.

It was able to distribute food, tools, and weapons, repress divergent behavior, and defend frontiers.

So far as anyone knew, the structured procedures embraced by a society were the only ones capable of anticipating environmental dynamics fast enough to preserve stability. In the social cognitive maps encoding information, all these societies included cautionary tales about how bold attempts to wrest power or knowledge from the gods invited disaster. They also recalled an earlier period of formless anarchy, which was negatively valued by being made frightening. The point of all this was to teach people to worship the existing form of society and not risk its collapse by experimentation. Durkheim was right: "Society is God." And by making knowledge divine, it was protected from sacrilegious experimentation.

The first civilized states, therefore, have a kind of crystalline appearance. They may have been wealthy, productive, and artistic beyond previous measure, but they were rigid and unyielding in their attempts to preserve an identity as near to that of their ancestors as possible. It is probably true that pre-civilized societies were equally rigid—in intent. But one of the unexpected consequences of writing was that civilized societies actually were better able to achieve a fixed identity of themselves than their precivilized predecessors.

Preliterate, "aural" societies were able to preserve vast amounts of information over long periods of time. They did it, as Homer did, and as fundamentalist preachers in the American South do to this day, by using a relatively small number of phrases, messages, and metaphors that are deeply entrenched in social tradition. Consequently, a bard or storyteller can recount incredibly long tales about ancient heroes and their adventures, frequently in great detail. The repetition of familiar phrases and phrasings permits the story to go on and on.

But every telling of a story connotes a slight difference in meaning, for meaning is established by the context in which a message is decoded. It is the social environment that ultimately decodes messages. In preliterate societies, the social environment is able to drift incrementally with every slight shift in routinized experiences. Auditors of a tale, therefore, do not detect any transformation in messages as they are ritualistically repeated. There is no fixed reference against which to compare today's retelling with yesterday's original. Consequently, as the society drifts, it slightly alters its defining tales without being aware of it.

But literate societies have perfectly preserved versions of original sources. The Code of Hammurabi is carved into a stone stela, to which

any literate Sumerian could easily refer. A lawyer or administrator who slightly modified the law to meet immediate contingencies, therefore, would quickly have the error of his ways pointed out—and there were written punishments for those convicted of falsifying the law. Once a legal system was preserved in written form, it could be modified only with great difficulty. Of course, it was not until societies became complex that they required writing to communicate information. But then writing had the tendency to freeze the society in a particular image. Any variation in the environment, however, would require adaptive responses. When these became difficult, societies tended to become less fitted to their environments, and hence less stable.

The Maps of the Religions

Complex civilized societies were able to survive because they created new types of cognitive map, maps able to represent dynamic social environments and to process vast flows of information. These new types of cognitive map include the "higher" religions, which, like all the cognitive maps of civilized societies, purport to be delivered to humankind from divine sources. It is this record of delivery from "on high" that is our best clue that an evolved level of reality emerged. People are recording their experience of an event which is not physical but which they nevertheless experience to the very core of their beings. This indicates a level of reality that is created by preserving collective knowledge of a shared environment in relationships that endure generation after generation. The laws delivered to Hammurabi or Moses by their respective gods on the mountain tops froze societies into rigid structural forms, any deviations from which were severely punished.

The higher religions give the impression that they came "out of the blue." But they are as much historical artifacts as the social structures with which they coevolve. In fact, it is relatively easy to read the history of the peoples who created the higher religions through their sacred documents (Fox 1992; Wilson 1992). Here we shall concentrate on the Western tradition, since that is the one which eventually departed from civilized conventions and created a new kind of cognitive map.

There are two basic roots of the Western religious tradition, Hellenism and Hebraism. These two traditions are radically opposed to one another, and it can be argued, as the German poet Heinrich Heine did, that the tension between these two opposing religious views is what gives the West its peculiar dynamism. The contrasts between Hellenic

and Hebraic religiosity exist on virtually every level, with the Jews usually being given the nod for having produced the more significant version. Greek gods were fairly typical pagan deities; numerous and anthropomorphic, they often appeared to Victorian commentators as personifications of every libidinal drive on perpetual holiday. They had sexual relations with each other and with humans, their sexuality was not confined to what later Western authorities considered normal, and their lust-driven betrayals of responsibility and decorum still seem offensive. Aphrodite, for instance, was married to Hephaistos but was sleeping with Mars. (Love, in other words, betrayed Technology for War.)

The Olympian gods left much to be desired from every ethical point of view. The male sky gods dominated. Like Homer's Achilles, they took what they wanted, when they wanted it, and by any available means. The only interests they served were their own. But the male sky gods were constantly being tricked, deceived, and otherwise manipulated by female earth goddesses. Their main figure, Hera, was an obstinate, spiteful, conniving personality, who was inclined to bathe only when planning to seduce Zeus, her husband, into some action he would live to regret.

But crude though it may have been, the Greek pantheon did effectively map experience and record history. What the Homeric gods describe is a social environment formed when nomadic raiders from the north spilled into Greece riding horses—cf., the "centaurs"—and conquered an older, sedentary agricultural society. The nomads, being travelers, worshipped sky gods, who are almost always male. The Chthonians, being farmers, worshipped female earth goddesses. The rapine and pillage of conquest is symbolized in the marriage of Zeus and Hera, the nomads' god and the farmers' goddess. Their stormy celestial relationship must have perfectly mirrored the domestic situation in many Greek homes.

There was really no ethical dimension to the pagan Greek religion. It was framed by conquering aristocrats, horsemen who carried bronze weapons. These were people who valued excellence, but who felt no compulsion to curb power in the interest of good. Hesiod's *Works and Days*, the only source comparable to Homer, reinforces this idea in the litany of complaints expressed from the farmers' point of view. The aristocrats' main value—*arete*—extolled virtuosity, not virtue. It proclaimed the ideal of glory won by the display of skill, not ethical conduct. And why not, since Olympus was where the gods of conquerors dwelled. The men whose world was mapped by Homer's songs

relied on their individual prowess to survive. They had no need for societal restraints to protect them. According to Homer and Hesiod, their only interest in the weak was to rob and exploit them.

By Homer's time, a mismatch between the Greek cognitive map and the environment was beginning to show. The *Iliad*, for instance, is a war poem, telling the story of a ten-year conflict to preserve Greek honor after a Trojan dandy violated the norms of aristocratic etiquette by absconding with the wife of his host. In specific descriptions, Homer details the martial prowess of his hero, the warrior Achilles. But it is clear from the spirit of the poem that Homer's real sympathies are with the Trojans, protectors of the city and its humane values. The tragedy of the *Iliad* is that the barbarians prevail, Achilles's *arete* proves victorious when linked with the amoral cunning of Odysseus.

The explanation for Homer's mixed mood, glorying in prowess but lamenting mindless destruction, is to be found in the shifting Greek environment. Homer lived about six hundred years after the nomadic conquest and well into the Greek "Dark Ages," at a time when Greece was slowly beginning to revive. Cities were again stable, and piracy was giving way to trade. The experience of Greek life was no longer adequately described by the oral tradition handed down from the days of Troy, and Homer's ordering of the verses probably reflects just the sort of incremental departure from convention that would usually go unnoticed in an aural society.

But Homer was so great a poet that he infatuated the whole of Greece with his versions of their national epoch, and pride was ever after taken in the ability to recite verbatim the poems as Homer had arranged them. Besides, it was not long after Homer's death that writing was reintroduced into Greece, making the official version hard to ignore. So, by the seventh century BCE, Greeks began to feel a certain unease as they tried to balance the needs of actual experience against the prescriptive values of tradition.

It was such creative thinkers as Thales of Miletus (?625–?547BCE) who exploited the gap between map and territory and articulated a philosophical alternative. As a merchant, Thales traveled widely, and knowledge was among the things he brought back to the *agora*, or marketplace. For example, he had seen the pyramids in Egypt and learned the skill of making a corner perfectly square. Transferring that technology proved problematic, for Thales needed an explanation for why stretching a rope with twelve equal spaces in it produced a perfect right-angled triangle. The Egyptians, of course, explained the phenomenon as a gift of their architecture god. But gods do not travel well from

culture to culture, even when information does. Nor could a people who were already "more moral than their [own] gods" (Murray 1951) attribute to them an accomplishment this grand, especially since Homer had not mentioned it. So Thales invented geometry by figuring out a logical argument to demonstrate why the spatial relationships between a three–four–five triangle necessitate that the angle opposite the hypotenuse is ninety degrees.

The breakthrough to a rational, secular view of the world has often been touted as the "Greek Miracle." The Greeks deserve much credit for their creativity, but the societal cognitive map concept suggests that there was nothing miraculous about it. In fact, by searching for rational proofs or explanations, the Greeks were as clearly mapping their new, stable urban and political environment as the Sumerians or Egyptians mapped irrigated valleys with their myths. But in Greece, which came to civilization late and was influenced by foreign sources, the inherited symbolic representation was inferior to others and, in any case, no longer reflective of actual experience. Greek merchants were not the same ruthless thieves their forefathers had been, and Greek soldiers were no longer aristocratic warriors.

Greece had changed in the centuries after Homer, and the change was nowhere more apparent than in military matters. Iron technology had replaced bronze for weapon-making, and iron made weapons cheap enough for middle-class farmers and tradesmen to purchase. These people greatly outnumbered the aristocrats, and if the townsmen could organize themselves into a disciplined infantry they would be able to sweep the noble cavalry from the rock-strewn floors of the narrow valleys separating the cities. The problem was figuring out a device for integrating an infantry in which peaceful individual shopkeepers would willingly risk life and limb for the public good. Traditionally, force was the means employed to coerce cooperation. But when everyone is armed, force becomes self-destructive, and if a policy decision was reached through violence it would not be sustained during battle. An infantry unit, called the *Phalanx* in Greece, that was forced to fight a foreign invader after a civil war would hardly be efficient. Having bullied its members into combat, the Phalanx could expect to dissolve once battle started.

So the Greeks, unwittingly, invented "democracy," the technique of talking themselves into battle by openly arguing among themselves until a consensus was reached. When words rather than swords are depended upon, opinion changes because of logical persuasion. The point here is obvious. When Thales began to explain the world independently

of the Greek gods as a logical structure where law controlled action, he was simply reading into nature a symbolic representation of his own political environment. And Thales knew that environment well, since he was the first statesman to perceive the Persian threat to Greece and to lobby for a defensive union between the Ionian cities. In the politicized Greek environment, men moved because of reason, and they moved with terrible efficiency, as the Persian hordes learned to their dismay. Why then should not the material elements of the physical world be similarly controlled by law and logic?

The possibility was so exciting that Greek thinkers explored its many nuances in a 150-year intellectual explosion of almost unequaled creativity. But when it was all over, Parmenides, Zeno, and Plato fairly well demonstrated the bankruptcy of the exercise. To be sure, we stand in awe of Greek "scientists" who "discovered" virtually everything from atomism to evolution. But the Greeks, who were after all still the highly competitive spiritual sons of Achilles eager for glory, were more struck by Zeno's demonstration that none of these thinkers could explain something as common as how an arrow reached its mark, or could even move. The thinkers had many arguments, and while all were persuasive none was compelling. During stable times, the leisured intellectuals could gleefully compete in public trying to shoot down each other's arguments and advance their own theories. But after the Peloponnesian Wars, in which Athens and Sparta devastated the whole peninsula, times were no longer stable. And the common person, after all, had never found much advantage in rigorously abstract, formalized demonstrations of ideas that no one could prove in practice. It is not surprising, after the middle of the fourth century BCE, either that an outsider like Alexander the Great could conquer the Greeks, or that most Greeks would begin looking for a social cognitive map that offered meaning, promise, and protection to the lives of ordinary people.

The basis of an alternative map was being forged in the hostile desert environment of the Middle East by the Hebrews, a people too few in number to conquer much of anything. They began in accordance with their sacred history as nomadic bands of shepherds organized into families and clans that each worshipped its animistic spirit. Wandering into the fertile crescent, they were marched over by a series of conquering armies and eventually taken to Egypt. After a period of several generations, they were led by Moses out of captivity and into the Promised Land. On the way they formed a covenant with the god of an extinct volcanic mountain, at the top of which they received their law.

Moses was a less effective navigator than his talk in Egypt promised, and by the time the Jews were Chosen by Yahweh they were lost and in danger of fragmenting. The Covenant with Yahweh was a critical device for ensuring loyalty, for all Jews were bound to obey the law, repudiate the syncretic tendencies inherent in their geographical position, and worship only this One God. Focusing the tribes on the One God enabled Moses and later leaders to hold society together.

But the god of Moses is hardly more edifying than those of the Greeks. He is distinctly human-like, depicted as walking through the Garden of Eden trying to find Adam and Eve. He is often spiteful, imposing arbitrary obligations such as the prohibition against eating fruit from the trees of Life and Knowledge on His followers and then punishing them for acts of disobedience the Greeks would have admired. His conduct could be capricious, as poor Job found to his dismay. And He was always suspicious, as the demand for Abraham to sacrifice Isaac indicates. But all of these traits merely indicate the kind of god a people living in the desert is likely to have invented to map their world. Their God, like the whirlwind or burning bush from which He spoke, was harsh, unpredictable, and ceaselessly demanding.

At the time of Moses, the Jews were not yet monotheistic; they were monolatrous. They worshipped only one god, but that does not indicate that they believed other gods were any the less real. However, the covenanted obligation not to worship other idols provided an opportunity for the Jews to understand the terrible things which repeatedly happened to them. They were, for instance, defeated in war and carried off into slavery in Babylon not because Yahweh was weaker than Baal, the Babylonian God, but because some Jews, tempted by syncretism, had begun offering libations and other sacrifices to the gods of a richer, more powerful people. Angered by this betrayal, Yahweh raised the Babylonian scourge as a punishment for the law-breaking Jews.

The capacity for Yahweh to change sides introduced a certain spirituality into his identity. It was never possible for a wandering people to worship at a particular spot or cart about a heavy totem, but as Yahweh tracked the experiences of his people he acquired an ever more intangible quality. Building on this development, the prophets in Exile—who still had the problem of holding together a society without territorial boundaries—took an even bolder step. If Yahweh's power raised the Babylonians against Israel as just punishment for violating the Covenant, then there was no need for Baal at all. He was superfluous. In fact, argued Isaiah, there is really only one God, and that God is pure spirit and universal.

A purely spiritual, universal, single god is usually taken as representing the "higher" religions. But the Jews had even more to offer, for in their law they also introduced the concept of ethics. Unlike the Homeric Greeks, the Jews did not do things because they could, which would have been limiting indeed, given their environmental circumstances; they did things because they were good. It was virtue, not virtuosity, that Yahweh demanded. The poor and weak, the homeless and downtrodden, the orphaned and widowed, all these were groups that Jews were morally bound not only to respect, but to help. Again, it is obvious (as Nietzsche suggested) that these ideas should map the experiences of a small, frequently conquered and politically weak people. Ethics sheathed the sword of the powerful in Israel, just as democratically rooted nationalism reduced the propensity for discord among the middle-class members of the Phalanx in Greece. In either case, a value symbol was developed for reducing internal social violence.

But the ancient Jews were not interested in reducing violence between themselves and other peoples. On the contrary, their brief period of political independence and cultural dominance under King David and his heirs wet the Hebrew appetite to own their own territory and control their own destiny. The prophets assured them that, sticking strictly to the letter of the law, God would reward them with a Messiah or Savior who would carve out an empire for them.

Unfortunately, the rising Roman star was destined to eclipse Jewish political ambitions by a series of increasingly bloody, ruthless repressions. But just as the Greeks were able to adapt the Homeric value of *arete* from its original militaristic expression and moderate it into an intellectual skill in debate, members of the Jewish community began to explore other meanings of the term "Messiah." If it could not prove functional in political and military terms against superior Roman strength, perhaps it could acquire a spiritual and ethical meaning. Groups like the Essenes, who authored the Dead Sea Scrolls, began to search for a style of life that would lead to identity and community on a higher plane than politics.

It seems probable that Christ emerged out of this environment, and his teachings were a mapping of a transformed Romanized world using the language of Hebrew tradition. Perhaps the most fundamental need his ideas addressed were the sense of purposelessness and alienation typical of the Hellenistic age. All over the Mediterranean world, Rome was restoring peace. But it was a peace established only after two centuries of civil war had demonstrated the bankruptcy of republican institutions. What emerged in the Roman Empire—the same as in the

Alexandrian empire—was a bureaucratized society, governed from afar by managers with little knowledge of, and even less interest in, local affairs. There seemed no alternative to this solution, since only Roman power could establish law. Moreover, dictatorial or not, the Roman Empire ushered in two hundred years of prosperity from which most classes benefited.

But it must have been extremely difficult for men raised in the traditions of Achilles and Cincinnatus to yield dominion over their lives to emperors, generals, and bureaucrats. Seneca, whose high ethical ideals and republican sentiments could not control the power of Nero or abate its arbitrary exercise, fell on his sword. His suicide demonstrated the old Roman values in their noblest form—and their ineffectuality. To more average people, the situation was even worse. They lived in peace and plenty, fed bread and entertained by circuses. But they lived in an immense state over which they had no control and which was ruled for the benefit of a handful of military and civilian authorities.

People really cannot live by bread alone, at least not once their personalities have been transformed by the evolution of social complexity; they must have some sense of moral worth and purpose. But that comes from the match between their social cognitive map and their environment. When the match breaks down, people are confused, lost, and alienated, as they were in the Mediterranean when Alexander arose, and later with the ascendance of the Romans. People who had come to think of themselves in terms of their contribution to their cities, and who were responsible for their own actions, now had decisions made for them. They experienced the effects of external decisions over which they had no control.

The upper-class Greek response to this was suitably philosophical. The Cynics proclaimed the artificiality of all conventions and vowed to live like dogs as they searched for virtue. The Epicureans advised that the search be limited to a carefully controlled garden, populated with a few friends. And the Stoics proclaimed that, although there was a universal law, few of us ever got a glimpse into it or could predict its effects. All these schools, and the rhetoricians who proclaimed that truth was relative, were recording the experiences of people living in a world they could not map. The less articulate masses founded no schools, but in the resurrection of ancient chthonic fertility rites and the invention of new miracle religions they expressed a comparable sense that the Roman world held nothing of value for them—an escape to greener pastures was desirable.

There were, however, no greener pastures in this world—Rome had gobbled up all of them. But Rome had offered no spiritual benefits into the bargain. It had not even seriously undertaken to map its own reality cognitively. To be sure, a fair number of poets, including Virgil, had volunteered to cloak the imperial power in a robe of mythic authority. But while the *Aeneid* could extol the virtues of obedience, authority, and family, even its beauty could not conceal the intellectual vacuum behind the Roman purple. Augustus had made himself first citizen in name, but was emperor in fact. He knew Roman conservatism would never countenance an overt departure from tradition, so he hid his iron fist in the velvet glove of embalmed republican institutions. To complete the public-relations campaign behind which he grasped every lever of power absolutely, Augustus lived in humble housing, wore clothes of home-spun cloth, ate camp food, and held his family to puritanical standards.

Augustus's false advertising made Rome look as if it was still a republic, although, as Caligula's decision to make himself a god demonstrates, Augustus had made Rome an empire in the conventional civilized sense. But what his policies did was to force Rome to live a lie—clinging to the illusion of a rural republican virtue, the Romans felt themselves living the reality of imperial cosmopolitanism. They could not govern a universal empire on the basis of auguries and omens, but they would not repudiate the faith of their ancestors. So there was no map of the Roman territory, and despite the prosperity, people increasingly defined themselves as "corrupt." They began to look elsewhere for spiritual guidance. Christ's teachings were among the many possibilities they considered.

At first, it was mostly the poor, the enslaved, and the illiterate who rallied to the Christian message. Only the most alienated and helpless could have found it appealing. After all, Christ was a despised Jew, whose fellow countrymen were still rebelling against Rome. Unlike most Gods, he came from the humblest of backgrounds, and he met the most unsavory of ends. He was to bring a kingdom, but he died mocked on a Roman cross. Moreover, the basic ideas that the Christians announced were nonsensical. Theirs was a monotheistic religion, yet Christ was the divine son of a god who was also a holy spirit. Educated Romans found it difficult to equate three gods with monotheism.

However, as the sense of being uprooted in a world turned irrational deepened, it was this very absurdity, to use Tertullian's term, which made Christianity convincing. It now appeared to espouse a truth that surpassed mere human understanding. Since the fact that humans had

not given themselves much credit for understanding since the Hellenistic age revealed the mismatch between inherited social cognitive maps and the environment, the argument that Christianity made no logical sense seemed actually to intensify its appeal. If scientific reason could not explain an arrow's flight and political persuasion could not unite either Greece or Rome, how much credit did human reason deserve? Faith, a moral commitment that defied logic, now surpassed wisdom in prestige, and more and more educated, privileged upper-class people came to believe Jerusalem had surpassed Athens.

By the third century AD not even peace and prosperity were strong arguments for supporting the earthly city. Disease, economic depression, rising taxes, and political instability reduced the emotional appeal of Rome. When Diocletian tried to arrest the rot by force, he only accelerated the pace at which people exiled themselves. Now economic demands and military dangers added a physical factor to spiritual flight. St. Augustine was saying what everyone knew when he announced that Rome was not eternal. He became increasingly convincing when he argued that people had better look to the salvation of their eternal souls in the heavenly city. Committing themselves to a religious vision completely independent of time and space, people were decoupling themselves from Rome with ever greater totality.

Implementing the Jewish ethic in a less Spartan form, which St. Paul was able to make even more casual, Christ had urged a revolution upon humanity. Proclaiming the power of love and brotherhood, he gave people the promise of a world in which each could trust his neighbor. To accomplish that revolution, to bring God back in triumph upon the rainbow, each person had to look into his or her own heart. Purging it of greed, selfishness, violence, and lust, each person individually would save his or her own self. When all selves were pure, Jesus would return and the Kingdom of God would be at hand—not as a secular state but as an ever-lasting spiritual community.

The Medieval Cognitive Map

Invading barbarians must have delayed the transmutation of human nature, for even centuries after Christ's resurrection the Second Coming was yet to occur. But Christianity had not failed. It had planted a seed that would flower in the European Middle Ages and give rise to a new type of civilization. Of course, that had not been its intention. By contrast, the original, essentially communistic teachings of Christ

became institutionalized in a Church that saw itself as heir to Roman grandeur. It took almost 500 years to lay the foundations of the Christian state, but in the eighth century an alliance was forged that was to preserve Europe's independence from the Middle Eastern world by creating an empire like that of Sumer or Rome. Isolated on the periphery of civilization, the people of Europe began teaching themselves a new map and in doing so laid the foundations for a new type of society.

The popes joined forces with the Carolingians to domesticate Europe, while keeping it free from either Muslim or Orthodox interference. When Charlemagne was crowned Holy Roman Emperor, it looked as if the plan was well on its way to success. But two problems immediately presented themselves, and Europe found those problems impossible to solve using conventional techniques. The first was the problem of organizing a defense. The pope needed military force to remain independent of Constantinople, and the Franks needed an army to stop the Muslim advance. But neither had the money to pay for the soldiers, especially since Charles Martel had shown that mounted, armored warrior knights were the only military technology with a chance of success. Knights were dreadfully expensive, and land was the only source of wealth. Organizing a defense based on land meant that to save Europe it was necessary to fragment it.

It was easy to allocate each knight a parcel of land large enough to supply the horses, food, and labor necessary to equip him. But once a knight was ensconced behind a wall on his own land, he was essentially independent. He might owe moral obligation to his feudal lord, but the lord had no way to transport his land-based power and bring it to bear on the knight. Once in possession of the land needed to ensure that the knight could fight barbarians and Arabs, he could no longer be dependably controlled. He might obey a call to arms by baron, count, or king. But if the knight declined service, on his fief and behind his wall he was impregnable.

Knights could use promises of their support to play the major contenders for societal dominance off against each other, which was the second reason Europe failed to organize as a traditional civilizational state. In Rome, the pope wanted to be a god–king, and knights could always justify supporting his cause religiously. That is, whenever an emperor tried to extract the full measure of feudal obligations from his knights, they could find religion at the papal court and rebel against feudal authority. But in Germany, the emperor wanted to be a king–god, and other knights could rally to his side out of feudal obligation

or to circumvent religious interference in their secular affairs. Whenever a meddlesome cleric sought to inhibit knightly bloodlusts, knights could always yield to the pull of honor and obey their secular prince. The point is that, playing emperor and pope against each other, the knights shifted sides whenever it seemed that either was strong enough to dominate. The ensuing civil war kept Europe in turmoil even after the barbarians were suppressed, the Vikings were settled, and the Arabs were contained. The balance of power, however, permitted new centers of authority to gather strength.

Of course, the two contenders for control waged a propaganda war against each other, and neither popes nor emperors were above resorting to the most scurrilous charges and deceits. But in the educated clergy, the church had a distinct advantage, and, in the eleventh century, churchmen began to articulate a vision of European society that would eventually produce a cognitive map different from any previously seen. But churchmen were in the unenviable position of trying to bring some order out of chaos using purely verbal arguments. That meant they had to stick fairly close to the facts of experience, at least in the beginning.

It was during the eleventh century that churchmen began to describe medieval Europe as the "society of the three orders." The idea caught on quickly, for a clear class-distinction had developed during the turbulent period following Rome's collapse. The most important job had seemed to be religious, since it was into religion that people poured all their pent-up frustrations resulting from Roman governmental methods. When people no longer felt an allegiance to the earthly city, their only hope of identity was in the heavenly one. So Europe had worked desperately to preserve a group of men "who prayed." This was the first order.

Physical survival was similarly pressing, despite rumors that Christians eager for heavenly rewards offered their bared breasts to invaders. The knights who accepted the obligation to defend localities constituted the second "order" in the emerging medieval society, "those who fight." But fighters and prayers needed food, housing, equipment, and various buildings. They were too specialized actually to support all these activities directly, although the Cistercian monks made many contributions to rebuilding Europe. But a third "order" was available, "those who work," and it was to these enserfed farmers and craftsmen that Europe turned for material necessities.

The symbolic description of European society, once articulated, developed with increasing speed and precision. By the twelfth century,

a revival of learning began reintroducing clerics to classical thought, especially to the works of Aristotle. One of Aristotle's major themes, borrowed from Plato, was the idea that the universe was an interconnected hierarchical structure, a "Great Chain of Being." St. Thomas Aquinas, a Dominican monk of unequaled intelligence and learning, borrowed this conceptualization to refine the vision of a society of the three orders.

It was an apt choice, for everywhere classes of men were bound together in ladders of status and power. The pope was served by his archbishops, bishops, abbots, monks and priests. Kings depended on their counts, earls, barons, and knights. And both clerics and soldiers depended upon merchants, artisans, and serfs. Thus, Aquinas could argue that the universe began in God, pure spirit or intelligence, worked its way downward through the ranks of archangels and angels, passed through humankind, reached into the ranks of animals and plants, and ended in dead matter and the Devil. Each link on the Chain was distinct, but its unique identity depended upon the attributes of the links above and below it. Worms, for instance, were crawling matter, created by mixing the attributes of animals with dead matter. Human beings, who occupied the central link between heaven and earth, were physical creatures with bodies like animals and divine entities with souls like angels.

Of course, it followed from Aquinas's perspective that the pope should be dominant over the emperor, for spirit prevailed over matter. The Church officially embraced this idea in the doctrine of the "two swords." Moreover, in the organic quality of the Aquinian vision, most Europeans saw their world mapped realistically. A chain is only as strong as its weakest link, and the chain as a whole must take priority over any individual link. In the doctrine of the "just price," medieval economics practiced this idea. The price of any good was set by the Church acting for the community. It prevented gorging during poor harvests and bankruptcy during periods of abundance, because the just price fixed value in terms that could preserve the existing order.

Independent of market forces, prices were set in terms of costs plus the profit necessary to maintain the seller in his established position on the Great Chain. A serf could not be overcharged for bread following a drought, for example, since he might then starve to death and the community would be deprived of his services during the next agricultural cycle. But saving the soul of the seller was equally important, for inflating prices might make the seller rich and camels had less trouble passing through the eyes of needles than did rich men

entering the gates of heaven. Of course, by squelching ambition, the organic society of the three orders kept everyone in his proper hierarchical position and retained social stability despite the vagaries of harvests.

The initial conditions in which medieval society was forged were so unstable that freezing society in the rigid image of an interlocking chain made good sense. Amidst the turbulence of collapse and invasion, no risks could be taken. Every community needed to know that its knight would be in his castle, trained and eager to fight; every Christian needed to know that prayers would be said for his or her salvation; every priest needed to know where his next meal was coming from. There was no margin for error, especially after the Viking attacks began.

The Breakup of the Medieval Cognitive Map

By about AD1000, Europe had stabilized. Trade with the Middle East began to revive; silver was later discovered in central Europe. New crops, plows, and rotations generated agricultural surpluses and a population explosion. The knights who had crusaded in the Holy Land had acquired appetites for the finely manufactured luxuries Europe had not seen for nearly a millennium. Tradesmen sought to exploit those appetites by organizing fairs. Fairs gathered large populations that churches, miracles, and relics could exploit financially. And local princes began looking toward the new futures made possible by taxing trade in money.

But the merchant classes and towns that began to appear after AD1200 had no links on the Great Chain of Being, and social mobility was inexplicable in terms of a map that froze social relationships. The earliest cultural strains reflecting a mismatch between map and territory appeared, reasonably enough, in the few parts of Europe—such as southern France—where urbanization, prosperity, and commerce had flourished first. But the agents of the earthly shifts stirring beneath European feet were usually secular figures with limited learning. They were not equipped to praise the virtues of upward mobility based on material prosperity. Instead, they felt a growing sense of guilt, for their experience violated the norms and values of the Great Chain.

Naturally, the town-dwelling merchants of southern France expressed their own sense of misgiving by blaming the Church. They quickly passed from condemning clerical corruption to exploring a variety of

heresies encountered in the Middle East. Waldensians, Burgomites, Cathars, etc. all gathered members and intensified their followers' sense of alienation. But while these twelfth- and thirteenth-century heresies showed the seams were straining in the society of the three orders, established institutions were still powerful enough to repress them. The Church invented the Inquisition to destroy the Cathars, and the Inquisition was equipped with military might by inducing landless knights like Simon de Montford to unsheathe their swords in the interest of piety—and stability. The resulting bloodbath was so noxious that even some of the knights are thought to have protested. But the Church prevailed.

Challenges from inside were also effectively dealt with. Northern Italy revived soon after southern France, and its spiritual strains produced behaviors like that of Francis of Assisi. Rejecting the inherited wealth that might have jeopardized salvation, Francis embraced a religion of love and communal poverty that embarrassed Church authorities. Instead of destroying him, however, the Church domesticated the threat by letting the Franciscans organize a monastic order under papal control. It was a decision the popes later regretted, for by the fourteenth century Franciscan monks were among the most vociferous and ingenious critics of the official Church.

The papal ploy would probably have been more immediately effective had not the King of France grown angry at the Church's ability to tax commerce in France and siphon it into Roman coffers. King Philip IV needed that money, for it was only with money that he could overcome the fragmenting propensities of feudalism. Money was portable. It could be collected everywhere throughout the kingdom, transported to Paris, and there used to pay mercenary soldiers who would travel to any province and destroy the castles of recalcitrant knights. The destruction was more certain once gunpowder came into circulation, but cannons cost even more than soldiers. Every tithe that went to Rome, therefore, was a sapping of royal strength permitting the continuance of feudal decentralization.

Knights may have been the original markets for reviving European trade, but, by the fourteenth century, the explosive, violence-prone behaviors that had once secured survival from marauding bands of Vikings had become an obstacle to economic progress. Local knights demanded taxes, charged tariffs, abided by their own laws, and frequently broke out into feudal warfare—even in the marketplaces where the fairs were held. Knights, in other words, inhibited commerce and were bad for business. So kings had natural allies in the rising

middle classes, for if a centralized authority could be created, internal tariffs would disappear, only one tax would have to be paid, a single market would be created, just one set of laws would obtain throughout, and the internal violence that made business unpredictable would be repressed.

Businessmen would pay taxes to kings, provided kings supported their economic and social ambitions. Both were to the kings' advantage. Not only would establishing a stable market increase royal revenues; absorbing middle-class talents into royal bureaucracies would increase their effectiveness. Of course, any royal office meant that a bourgeois merchant had acquired social status, for the merchant or lawyer on a mission for the king was an "official" person. But moving up the social ladder weakened the organic structure of the Great Chain, which was being threatened by a variety of other forces as well.

Population growth from the mid-thirteenth century onward was necessitating the expansion of European agriculture into frontier areas. Serfs, of course, had little interest either in abandoning what few comforts they had acquired for rough frontier living or for trading the devils they knew for ones they had never met. So knights had to entice serfs into virgin territories. That was done by reducing the serfs' feudal obligations, meaning that even serfs were less trapped by their inherited identities than previously.

Thinking itself clever, the nobility accelerated the process by switching from rents in service and kind to fixed money payments. Money payments let the landlords buy the consumer goods for which they hungered from merchants at fairs. But increased demand sparked a cycle of inflation that, by 1300, left most knights in serious debt and many serfs virtually independent. When the Black Death struck in 1348, it devastated a medieval social structure that was already coming apart. By that point, the popes were already living in Babylonian exile in Avignon, having been reduced to employees of the French king. Towns and merchants had sprung up everywhere. Knights were no longer independent, and the emperor was as threatened by the emerging nationalism as the pope. Clearly, the Great Chain of Being no longer matched the European territory.

But no other image was available to make sense of experience. The plight of European intellectuals was made clear in the fifteenth century by both Nicholas of Cusa, a cardinal, and Pico della Mirandola, one of the first secular intellectuals. Nicholas of Cusa worked out the logical implications of the medieval cognitive map and found they contradicted themselves with a Gödelian viciousness. If God were the creator

and had infinite power, for instance, He ought to have made an infinite universe. But an infinite universe could not be mapped by the Great Chain. It would, to begin with, have the very sort of infinite regress whose logical impossibility St. Thomas had used to prove the existence of God. Similarly, Pico saw a world in which every day witnessed paupers becoming bankers, great families sinking into poverty, and everything in constant flux. He tried to extract a measure of hope from this pessimistic view by arguing that humankind was born at the center of the Great Chain but not locked into place. Rather, each of us was free to rise or fall according to individual abilities. We could rise to the very ranks of angels. But we could also, as so many Renaissance people so obviously did, sink into diabolical pits of sin and corruption.

This world of pure, rampant individuality was, like the Hellenistic age, an anarchy that could not be mapped. Consequently, neither could its future be predicted. Fortuna, the goddess of chance, was ultimately in charge, and no man's wit was powerful enough to control his destiny. People are, said Rabelais, more animal than human, and our greatest virtue is the ability to laugh—a virtue exercisable only behind the walls of an Epicurean garden. Agrippa was more cynical, arguing that "man is to man a wolf," and that whatever laws of nature there were got honored most regularly in the breach. Montaigne counseled that we withdraw, practice stoic virtues, and talk to our cats.

But while a world in cultural chaos distressed the sensitive, the more adventurous spirits set out to explore the possibilities of a wide-open social situation. Their guide was Machiavelli, who justified any means to achieve self-selected ends. Machiavelli's own examples, however, were, like Cesare Borgia, notable failures, and it is unlikely that Machiavelli himself aspired to an amoral world. Rather, as his many volumes on civil virtue in antiquity suggest, he was only willing to use ruthless means to build a new society in which people would again be moral. He rightly excused the "prince" from any inherited medieval moral restrictions during the creative phase of social reconstruction, since in the absence of a coherent society there was no foundation for morals, and in the absence of an accepted cognitive map no way to allocate virtue. But he dreamed of a united Italy in which citizens would demonstrate their commitment to public good over private advantage by, for instance, eager service in a volunteer army. He put his eggs in the wrong basket.

Machiavelli believed society could be reorganized from the top down. While it is possible to operate societies top-down, as traditional civilizations did, societies generate themselves bottom-up. Medieval

society, inspired by a carpenter and amplified by slaves, is the best historical example. But where were the people able to generate a coherent society to come from? The answer to that rhetorical question proves how unrealistic it is to try to control social evolution, or even to guide it. The people out of whom a new European society self-organized in the modern era were produced by the most backward-looking, self-consciously obstructionist personalities in sixteenth-century Europe: the fundamentalist leaders of the Protestant Reformation.

After Luther, Protestant clerics had shattered the Catholic Church's last vestiges of universal authority by denying the pope's power to control entrance through the Pearly Gates and the Church's role in directing behavior from the outside in. In Luther's theology, which expresses the bankruptcy of the medieval cognitive map by demonstrating that no rational path to understanding is possible, people would not be saved by "Good Works," the traditional Catholic theology. In the absence of a societal cognitive map, they did not know what was good, had no idea how to achieve it, and were too confused to choose good over evil. But, as Luther discovered in a blinding flash of inspiration, people could be saved through "Faith Alone." That was not supposed to be a license to immorality. Rather, Luther wanted "every man to be a monk his whole life through." Luther took the individual who had fallen through the tattered fabric of medieval culture and stood him on his own two feet again.

Calvin's contribution was even more extreme. Believing that people were too corrupt ever to control themselves or earn salvation, Calvin decided that this was predetermined by a divine fiat over which we had no control. Again, ruthlessly paring away the whole structure of medieval community that had safely nestled humanity, Calvin placed individual people alone and naked before the judgmental eye of an infinite and angry God. While this description of human experience reflects the alienation of social collapse, Calvin's other doctrines offered a way, in Erich Fromm's (1947) phrase, to "escape from freedom." In particular, Calvin taught that those few humans chosen by God for salvation would be the agents through which His will operated in the world. Since, by definition, God could not fail, those of us who prospered could expect to see worldly success as an outward sign of spiritual election. It does not take a Freudian psychologist to suppose that devout Calvinists would repress doubts about salvation by working hard to make money and living frugally to accumulate it.

But inwardly motivated people stimulated to work hard were a new component of societies. Civilized states had previously extracted more

work from the majority of their subjects than nomadic groups had, but civilized societies extracted work by what Herbert Spencer called "coercive cooperation." Calvinism did on a grand scale what only the Cistercian monks had previously accomplished on a small one— Calvinism motivated people throughout the ranks of secular society to work for themselves. But this dramatic change in human behavior was not entirely spiritual in origin. There were economic factors involved as well, the most important of which was the emergence of private property.

Like Protestantism, private property isolated people individually. A man on his own estate stood alone beyond the bounds of society. He could do whatever he chose, and no one had the right to invade his land and object. But while private property gave individual rights a material foundation, independence from the community also meant that the individual incurred private responsibilities. If he managed his land carefully and husbanded its resources well, a man could expect "to live off his own" quite comfortably. But should he be lazy, stupid, reckless, or rash, no one else was obliged to keep him. Private property meant that no one was anybody else's brother anymore.

Religious and economic individuality introduced the prospect of social anarchy, as sixteenth- and seventeenth-century conservatives repeatedly pointed out. Everyone was more-or-less free of inherited masters, but there was no way to communicate information from one person to another. People were so desperate that they had abandoned a society that could not solve problems for them and developed techniques for solving problems individually. In the great Renaissance figures, like Urbino or Leonardo, these highly individualized person-alities took great pride in their uniqueness. One of them, the goldsmith Benvenuto Cellini, even invented autobiography so that everyone else could appreciate just how fascinating his self-created identity was. But a world of mercenaries, confidence men, and cutthroats is not a society, nor is a world polarized by religious sectarianism. Some way had to be found to transcend religious differences and to map a world of competing individualists.

The religious movements that had done so much to destroy medieval society and lay the psychological foundations for a modern one made the reunification of society almost impossible. Intense commitments to the various forms of Christianity turned people against one another with a vindictiveness that exceeded Machiavelli's most bloody examples by several orders of magnitude. The first country to suffer was France. There, the Reformation made little initial progress, despite the fact that

many leading intellectuals and pious Christians shared Luther's basic ideas. But Luther had succeeded because his religious visions happened to coincide with the political aspirations of his local prince, Frederick the Wise. Aspiring to be independent of both the pope and the emperor, Frederick—like princes throughout the Germanic center of Europe—had rallied to the Protestants' cause. The eventual settlement, after decades of warfare and rebellion, was that every prince decided the religion of his region. In other words, Lutheranism helped create state churches throughout much of central and northern Europe.

But France had enjoyed the benefits of formal independence from papal power since the Pragmatic Sanction of Bourges was signed in 1438. No matter how compelling the theological arguments, therefore, French kings saw no advantage to rocking their political boat by engaging in religious polemic. Since Lutherans believed that the prince determined the religion of his domain, in France his followers had no alternative to obeying their Catholic king.

Calvin's more radical disciples had other ideas. They argued that social and political leaders, the magistrates, had a moral obligation to destroy a king whose false religion endangered the salvation of their subjects. They called it *tyrannicide.* How predestined salvation could be jeopardized by royal whimsy was never explained, but in the writings of several politically determined Calvinists it became the basis for the first justification of revolution in the West. The result was a decades-long civil war punctuated by some of the most ruthless savagery in European history.

Eventually, the first coolly modern heads prevailed in the writings of Jean Bodin and the *politiques.* Arguing that it made no difference whether France was Catholic or Protestant if all Frenchmen were dead, they concluded that national survival was more important than spiritual integrity. Their leader, the first Bourbon king, Henri IV, summed up the whole idea when he abandoned his Protestant faith to become king of a mostly Catholic France. "Paris," he said, "is worth a Mass." He issued the Edict of Nantes in 1598, guaranteeing to Huguenots, as French Protestants were called, the legal right to practice their own faith in their own churches free of interference from either Catholic vigilantes or the state. Religion was now a private matter of little interest to the state.

In England things were equally tumultuous. Henry VIII had embraced a kind of Lutheranism, although he was officially "Protector of the Faith" for having written a pamphlet denouncing Luther. But Henry believed that a divorce from his Spanish queen was essential to the

preservation of his dynasty, and a pope dominated by her uncle was unable to supply it. Henry won instant approval for repudiating Catholicism at home by breaking up the vast monastic lands and distributing them to bourgeois and lesser gentry who served him loyally and well. His daughter Elizabeth rode the tiger of religious dissension by studiously ignoring it, at least in public. "Open no windows into men's souls," she advised her minister Burghley. But when the Stuarts inherited the throne of England, the slide into anarchy was greased. James I managed to survive growing religious tensions by concealing his own beliefs. His son, Charles I, took the idea of the Divine Right of Monarchs so seriously that, simple-mindedly, he tried to ignore Parliament and smuggle Catholicism back into Britain. The civil war that followed led to his execution and the first successful revolution in European history. It was, more than the Renaissance, the point at which "Modern" society self-organized.

The Rise of the Cognitive Map of Modern Science

The process of cultural change in Europe can be tracked with special clarity by comparing the writings of Thomas Hobbes and John Locke, the two most prominent seventeenth-century English philosophers. Like other political philosophers, their whole arguments depended essentially on the definitions of human nature with which they began. But a definition of human nature is always a commentary on, or a "mapping" of, the people around the philosopher. Even though they appear to be writing in purely abstract theoretical terms, Hobbes and Locke were describing their world in their political analyses.

Writing during the bloodiest phases of the English Civil War, Hobbes described human nature as ruthlessly appetitive, cunning, and unrestrained. Every one of us, he thought, wants the same things, is equally capable of getting what he wants, and is uninhibited by any internal conscience or sense of limits. Since we all want the same apples, we fight with one another constantly in a "war of all against all." Life, therefore, is "nasty, cold, mean, brutish, and short." The only hope of survival lies in the erection of a Leviathan state, whose absolute power stands like the hangman beside every human being. The fear that certain death immediately follows any transgression alone inhibits human avarice and makes society possible.

Writing after the Civil War had been over for a generation, Locke postulated a human nature that was inherently rational and capable of

learning from experience. Thus, if people are bad it is not because they have to be bad, but because society has taught them to be. In the absence of society, of course, people would still want apples. In fact, Locke offered the first moral defense of private property by claiming that we have a natural right to anything with which we mix our own labor. Thus if I pick some apples they are rightly mine, not anybody else's.

But what happens when someone else comes along who wants my apples? Locke admitted a Hobbesean response was possible. The apple-less person might attack, trying to steal what is mine by natural right. But that was a risky business, Locke said, and hardly worth the trouble when barter is so easy and so much safer. To be sure, one trader might not offer what the other feels is fair, but that does not mean that war necessarily results. On the contrary, since war is threatening to both parties, it is likely that rational men would turn to some neutral referee to arbitrate. In other words, Locke did not see human nature as loving, caring, and eager to share: in the state of nature there were likely to be disputes. But Locke did not believe "the howling of jackals" would frighten humanity into "the jaws of lions." People would not erect the Leviathan state and surrender all rights to it just to survive. That was unnecessary, for the people Locke was describing in his theory of human nature had learned—through Protestantism and the responsibilities of private property—to govern themselves.

If by Locke's time it was obvious that society had begun to self-organize in a new form that depended on inner-directedness and that respected individuality, the problem still remained of how that world was to be mapped collectively. But great steps forward had been taken, despite, if not because of, the confusion. In a simple sense, what was needed was a way to bridge the gap between polarized religious convictions. Equally, some way had to be found to view the world that private initiative had vastly expanded but that transcended inherited moral and spiritual issues. When people confronted one another over their heart-felt beliefs, there was little hope of joining them together if their hearts could be filled with different beliefs—especially since each person was responsible only for his or her self.

The passionate intensity with which even the most intelligent people interacted during the Renaissance and Reformation measured the desperation they felt in living in a world that inherited beliefs no longer mapped (Toulmin 1990). Medieval tradition, for instance, held that God governed the world, rewarding the just and punishing the ungodly. The indiscriminate slaughter associated with either the Black Death or the

religious wars rendered that faith transparently foolish. The Scholastic philosophers, quoting St. Augustine, had proved the world was flat, but Columbus and Magellan experienced its curvature in their own flesh, as Campanella pointed out. Obviously, before any reintegration could take place, the past had to be purged.

Francis Bacon and René Descartes led the campaign to liberate the present through the method of "radical doubt." According to them, nothing was to be taken on faith, no matter what its authority. Everything was to be examined skeptically and "put to the test." This would probably have amounted to little more than yet another philosophical argument, as it had in Greece, had not an Italian mathematician and engineer, Galileo Galilei, stumbled upon the telescope. The telescope, which had been invented as a toy and which Galileo sold as a maritime device, was turned by him on the heavens. There it proved remarkably suited for resolving disputes by the discovery of incontestable, "value-free" facts.

The most important test case was the dispute over the heliocentric universe. Copernicus had argued that the planets' motion around the sun means that Venus passes through phases. Near the earth it would appear large but only partially illuminated, while at its farthest distance from earth Venus would appear small but be fully illuminated. As these ideas were rejected by disciples of Aristotle and most religious authorities, a hot debate ensued. But while Copernicus's prediction puts his thesis in the category of scientific theory, the naked eye could not detect changes in either the apparent shape or size of distant Venus. So, as with religion, all people could do was to argue about what they believed.

Galileo's telescope brought Venus closer and made it larger. When telescopic observations showed that the planet passed through the predicted phases, Galileo took it as proof that the Copernican system was as real as Copernicus thought. But more importantly, the telescope brought in an apparently neutral observer. It was neither an Aristotelian nor a Copernican, neither a Catholic nor a Protestant. Having no mind, the telescope had no philosophy; having no heart, it had no emotionally excited beliefs. Here, then, was a method—instrumental observation—that could bridge the gap between human minds.

Galileo followed up this discovery of the scientific method with a series of brilliant experiments in which he demonstrated relative motion, the flaw in Aristotle's theory of motion, and the law of falling bodies. In all these cases, he began the positive work of building on the ground cleared by skeptical doubt. But to bridge the gap between

passionate beliefs, Galileo had to introduce a radical set of presuppositions. Basic to Galileo's philosophy was the idea that the world exists external to and independent of the people observing it. We can stand outside nature and, provided we depend upon unbiased instruments, can reconstruct it accurately in our minds.

The problem, Galileo thought, is that people had traditionally relied only upon their minds to construct an image of the world. But those images were always distorted because the human mind contains "secondary characteristics" like color and taste, values and morals. There is nothing wrong with that, of course; it is simply the way the mind is. But when we take our inner experience as a guide to external reality we get a faulty picture. In our minds, the secondary characteristics like color and taste, values and morals, represent the world. But sweetness, said Galileo, depends entirely on taste buds, odors on nostrils, and judgments on prejudices. These things do not exist in the real world: there only matter and motion exist. Matter and motion, which are describable quantitatively because they can be counted, weighed, and measured, represent the "primary characteristics" of the real world.

Of course, it is precisely over whether an object is blue or green, sweet or bitter, good or evil that people contend. If they concern themselves exclusively with these things, they can never reach agreement, and "the great organ of our philosophy," said Galileo, must remain forever "discordant." But if people learn to focus on what instrumental measures tell them about the world, then they get an undistorted picture about which they need not argue. To be sure, one scientist may report that a body of a certain mass and shape fell at a certain rate, while another may give entirely different results. But there are no grounds for argument here. It does not matter if we think the one rate is moral and the other immoral, the one body Protestant and the other Catholic. We need only to repeat the experiment and check the arithmetic. As Leibniz was soon to say, to resolve a scientific disagreement all we need to do is say "let us calculate."

A picture of the world from which all secondary, qualitative characteristics had been cut out was so abstract that it could be applied universally, as Newton soon showed. But, as with any other new idea, this one could only be amplified by public endorsement after its utility had been demonstrated. Interestingly enough, the message that emerged for the public was significantly different from what Newton had in mind privately.

Newton captured the public imagination, under pressure from

Halley, in the *Philosophiae Naturalis Principia Mathematica* of 1687. Chapter 2 of the *Principia* demonstrated with geometrical certainty and experimental clarity that planets did rotate around the sun in orbits described by Kepler's three laws. Newton himself did not believe, however, that geometrical descriptions explained in reference to matter and force were complete. A hermetic magus and religious mystic, he was sure that God played an active role in nature, which only mystical numerology could ferret out. But he had not had time to include all the relevant arguments in the *Principia.* That book was written under the threat of Hooke's claim to have already solved the riddle of the universe.

Following publication of the *Principia,* Newton suffered a nervous breakdown. For nearly two years he did no work and seems to have understood very little of what went on around him. With recovery, he began editing the *Principia,* intending to supplement it with lengthy discussions of his religious, numerological, and alchemic doctrines. But as the revised edition neared completion, Newton suddenly realized that he was famous throughout the Western world, for he was the genius who had explained the whole creation without reference to God, alchemy, or numerology. Newton was the personification of human genius at its pinnacle—"God said, 'Let Newton be' | And all was light," according to Alexander Pope. He now faced an agonizing choice: should he let his book stand as published and reap unequaled praise, or should he set the record straight and announce to the Republic of Letters that this is not what he meant after all? Newton chose the former course, while keeping a scout's eye out for opportunities to advance his true beliefs.

But the time for mysticism had passed. Newton's *Principia* was the nucleation that permitted the European cognitive map to evolve. It is easy to see why Newton's ideas successfully blossomed into a new-style cognitive map, but harder to understand how that cognitive map actually worked and what it accomplished. There were three reasons for Newton's success.

First and foremost, his ideas provided precisely the sort of "clear and certain" knowledge people had been looking for since the Black Death. Newton's principles were absolute. Deterministic and universal, they required that every particle in every corner of the universe behave exactly as the laws of motion indicated, yesterday, today, and tomorrow. Moreover, although some period of lingering uncertainty might be necessary while complete knowledge is being accumulated, the inevitability of a God's-eye view of the whole world had been established. To

be sure, not everything had been discovered: some things remained unknown even about the Newtonian system itself. Newton, for instance, did not know what gravity is. But he knew how to measure it now, and he could guarantee that following the Galilean method would ultimately resolve the definitional conundrum. Finally, when the method was followed systematically, and "crucial experiments" were carried out, the scientist had indisputable knowledge of the world. The modern cognitive map written in the language of science took the powers and characteristics the Middle Ages had attributed to God, and bestowed them on Nature.

Secondly, Newton's ideas were publicly endorsed because modern Europeans could recognize their own experiences in the model he articulated. He postulated a world made up of "corpuscles," atomized units of matter whose every action was quantifiable. Now individualized competitors operating in a market economy where reality was measured in money must have looked very much like Newton's descriptions of nature, even to themselves. Similarly, Newton's *Principia* was written at the time the "Bloodless Revolution" finally and definitively established a "Balanced Polity." Henceforth, in Britain, free men governed themselves according to law. Newton's *Principia* mapped nature in the constitutional terms with which a generation of civil strife had made a significant part of the British middle class all too familiar. They must have seen a solar system that governed itself because of the rational laws its bodies obeyed as promise and reward for their efforts.

The third reason for Newton's success was that his ideas appeared useful to the nation states that had emerged as successors to traditional societies. Charles II, the restored king of Britain, quickly realized that astronomical knowledge improved the navigational skills of both his merchant and his military fleets. Thanks to Newton, the heavens could be plotted and the future positions of the heavenly bodies predicted. British ships could henceforth sail to every corner of the Earth faster and more directly than their Dutch and French competitors. Of course, Galilean studies of motion, which Newton perfected, also made artillery fire more precise. Since wealth and power flowed from science, Charles II founded the Royal Society for the Advancement of Learning, and Continental monarchs quickly opened similar institutions of their own.

The consequences of Newton's new social cognitive map were both dramatic and rapid. A pessimistic culture seeking to escape from freedom now became an optimistic culture bent on expanding freedom, at least for its own people and institutions. Europeans felt confident that they possessed the key to unlocking the mysteries of nature, for seeing

behind the "bloomin', buzzin' confusion" of experience. As Fontenelle put it around 1700, the world appeared like the face of a clock. For millennia, ignorant and opinionated people had marveled at the movement of the clock's hands and made up stories to explain the apparent miracle. Thanks to Newton, Europeans acquired the capacity to look behind the face, to see the gears and pulleys at work, and to comprehend the mechanism underlying the surface appearances.

Inspired by Voltaire, scores of intellectuals, called *philosophes*, embarked upon the great adventure of bringing light to the world and of mapping its most hidden recesses. They railed against religious intolerance in the name of Nature's God, which was equally revealed to all peoples everywhere and never capriciously broke its own laws. They demanded, with Cesare Beccaria, the ending of judicial torture and the development of rational legal codes in which private rights were respected and "cruel and unusual punishments" were forbidden. With the wit and clarity of Diderot, they proclaimed the dawn of a "natural morality" in which humanity would finally be released from the artificial restraints of superstition and tradition. In Scotland, Adam Smith, the Newton of economics, discovered the social equivalent of laws of motion—the laws of supply and demand—and demonstrated how by arranging economies naturally the wealth of nations could increase.

The Enlightenment heirs to Newton thought that they knew how the world was constituted, what controlled its actions, and how to organize society in a scientific way. They were ushering in a new age in which, for literally the first time, human beings could be happy. All that was necessary was for human beings to approach society with the same attitude Newton had approached nature, discover its basic laws, and bring to earth the harmonies that stabilized the solar system. But that was not so easy: the Reformation and the spreading of private property created individuals who obeyed only their own inner directions. How was their behavior to be correlated so that a coherent society could self-organize?

Using modern science to organize societies proved more difficult than expected. On the one hand, it was possible to use scientific research to learn more about nature and apply that knowledge technologically. There are hints in the modifications of the steam engine by Watt that science was indeed being used to access more energy and process more matter as early as the eighteenth century. But real "progress" did not come until the advent of the German dye industry and the various electrochemical technologies of the later nineteenth century. It is reasonable to maintain that these developments contributed to improving the

material foundations of civilized life in the West. Certainly, applications of medical technology in the twentieth century have prolonged life. So in these areas, science seemed to be delivering on the Baconian promise to build an earthly utopia by harnessing the forces of nature to meet human needs. Arming itself with "Modern Western Science," European society began to out-compete its tradition-bound neighbors.

Though there were advances on the material side of the ledger, problems on the spiritual side rose quickly. The fundamental distinction between how people were thinking—qualitatively—and how nature was supposed to act—quantitatively—made the transfer of science to social and political sectors almost impossible. Qualitative thought involved subjective judgments about values and ideas. But scientific descriptions denied the objective reality of judgments, values, and ideas. Modern thinkers found themselves in the odd position of trying to reconstruct human society with a cognitive map from which, in Erwin Schrödinger's words, "the human personality had been quite cut out."

The major drawback from which modern science suffered as a societal cognitive map was that, despite its skill in describing the world, modern science was silent when called upon to prescribe action. Behavior is triggered or inhibited by value symbols, which "enframe" the actor (Goffman 1973). Ancient and medieval societies could enframe their relationships and institutions by appealing to God. But in a universe reduced to matter and motion, which was everywhere "conformable to itself," there was no external authority to enframe relationships or institutions. Erstwhile legislators, said Rousseau, had thus to "be as gods." They had to rise above the fray, envisage an idealized future, wrap it in the cloak of its own necessity, and do what was good for the world whether the world knew it or not (Camus 1956).

The first indications of how problematical it was going to be to reform society on the basis of a cognitive map "that cared no more for good over evil than for heat over cold" appeared during the French Revolution. Leaders like Robespierre and Saint-Just were convinced by the Age of Reason that human happiness was attainable in time and in history. But they ruled a country ravaged by poverty and torn by civil war. They found to their chagrin that force was needed to solve multiple crises simultaneously. But how could force be justified? The Committee of Public Safety could not appeal to any external authority—there was no God from whom they could receive The Law by climbing a mountain. They had to find in the cauldron of political action the justification for political action. If people had to be killed, it

could only be for the good of the People. The self-referentiality of the societal feedback loop became visible for the first time, and it launched generations of European intellectuals on a desperate ideological search for morally binding values. If society was, like everything else in nature, simply a mechanism, then clear and certain moral knowledge should be attainable. Moreover, if there were laws of motion that controlled the trajectories of people, then the future of society should be as transparent as the future of the solar system. The great "Laplacean Illusion" was as seductive in politics as it was in physics.

But the political ideologue had to be "scientific," he had to stand outside the political system, observe it objectively, and calculate its future. In the name of humanity, the ideologue had to dehumanize himself. Experience taught, from 1789 on, that the predicted future was not always fast in coming. Delay, however, meant that human lives were being wasted, broken by poverty, and crushed by superstition. In the absence of a Heavenly City, each wasted life was an insult to the whole of nature. These offenses to the smooth fulfillment of human destiny, enlightened thinkers concluded, were obviously the result of subjective values perverting the behavior of a handful of sick minds. Reformers, therefore, had to emulate Robespierre and Saint-Just. Ensuring first that their own hearts were pure, they had then to steel themselves to perform the revolutionary surgery history demanded by cutting away the people who stood in the way of progress.

Chernyshevsky in Russia was among the first to articulate the vision of the modern reformer as the self-appointed, self-disciplined hero who did the dirty work necessary to save the world. But his fictional hero, Rakhmetov, was merely a mapping of underworld figures like Babeuf, Buonarroti, Blanqui, Bakunin, Marx, and Engels. These were genuinely tragic figures, dedicated to a cause for which they sacrificed everything but which corrupted them as surely as a life of crime would have. They were the victims of the modern cognitive map, repressing their humanity because nature, they thought, is only a machine. Awed by the accomplishments of technology that transformed the world beneath their feet, they were convinced science was the royal road to Truth. Convinced that underlying laws permitted the future to be logically deduced, they were nevertheless inflamed by a passionate desire to accomplish the historical mission before more lives were lost to selfishness and ignorance.

The nineteenth and early twentieth centuries were riddled with revolutions, almost all of which failed. Some, like the Bolshevik, managed to gain power for their initiators, but their consequences

seem, if anything, even more ineffective. The problem is not merely the psychological agony of trying to justify the deeds of the people in the name of the People by constantly escalating the violence used to achieve the noble end of abolishing violence. The problem is also the choice of the strategy to bring about societal self-organization.

Another strategy was developed in the newly founded United States, where a constitution of a new type was written in 1787. Traditionally, constitutions were defined as the formal arrangement of the parts of a society, comparable to the parts of a biological body. Eighteenth-century theorists meant by "constitution" the fixed organization of a society inherited from its ancestors. How a society was "constituted," in other words, was determined by nature and by historical experience.

Most revolutionaries were "blue-print" thinkers (Popper 1962). They were convinced that scientific analysis could not only demonstrate that previous societies were unjustly constituted, but could also display the architecture for how future societies ought to be arranged. When the fifty-five Founding Fathers of the American republic gathered in Philadelphia, they intended to create a nation in that traditional sense, to determine what arrangement of classes, territories, and subsystems was right and proper. Most of them, like their European contemporaries, had a clear idea of what the internal relations defining society should be. The problem immediately became, however, that few of the delegates shared one another's visions. Big states wanted to dominate small ones, seaboard states to dominate frontier areas, slave states to dominate free ones—and vice versa.

The delegates could have argued interminably, as each of them sought coalitions to achieve their goals. But the foundling nation was perilously perched on the edge of collapse—bankrupt and torn by dissent, with the British lion lurking off-shore, eager to pounce—and extended argument would simply have meant political failure. The delegates therefore abandoned their attempt to shape the nation and decided instead to seek agreement about the rules by which the nation would, over time and through experience, shape itself. They decoupled the politico-legal structure from the culture (Berthoff and Murrin 1973). The U.S. Constitution broke symmetry with previous social systems because it did not establish the rules by which parties, factions, and sections shall be arranged once and for all. It did not, in the traditional sense, "constitute" a society by formalizing the relationships between parts of the body politic. Instead, the U.S. Constitution established the rules of procedure, the rules for making rules, by which the nation is to arrange itself over time and through experience.

The Constitution introduced the possibility that a society can represent itself in a new way. It does not describe what the society is but how the society works. By emphasizing rules for the making of rules, it does not commit the United States to any particular policy. As a result, the structure of American society can adjust to a variety of environmental situations. As collective action transforms the environment, increasing the flows of information, energy, and matter, the society can alter its internal relationships. Of course, to preserve stability amidst change, it is necessary for all participants to accept the rules for making rules, the rules of the game. But since these rules do not commit the society to any particular arrangement, it is in the best interest of all concerned to follow them.

There are collective benefits to be had from this kind of structural flexibility. One of the most obvious is the vast amounts of wealth that a society of freely acting, politically empowered individuals can generate. Each individual, privately rewarded for his or her own initiative, is encouraged to search out opportunities, even opportunities that may destabilize existing formal arrangements. The ability to locate and exploit wealth on a previously unequaled scale is, no doubt, the major key—and the indisputable proof—of modern Western society's evolutionary transformation of traditional civilization. Valuing knowledge of how things are done rather than what things are done, the West has been extremely adept at locating wealth and multiplying the population of its products.

Whether the West and other societies can continue to adapt to the changes their collective actions precipitate is an issue that we shall examine in the next chapter.

Current Changes in Cognitive Maps

No creature on earth is as concerned with creating images of the future as is the human. It is our passion and our obsession, and we are good at it. Our brains are uniquely designed for this work.

Of all the structures of the brain, it is the frontal lobe, the most recent evolutionary development of the neocortex, that is uniquely involved in creating images of the future, and with projecting ourselves as active agents into those images. In an exhaustive examination of observations made both in the clinic and in the laboratory, psychologist and systems analyst David Loye (1983) concluded that the frontal lobe acts in a managerial fashion, consulting the rational analytic faculty of the left hemisphere and the intuitive spatial capacities of the right hemisphere to formulate overall agendas for action, and to issue orders for their execution.

Tens of thousands of prefrontal lobotomies were performed on psychiatric patients between the invention of the procedure in the early 1940s and its demise in the 1960s. The operation could be carried out in the physician's office simply by inserting a surgical instrument through the thin bone above the eye socket and sweeping it back and forth laterally through the tissue of the forward-most aspect of the frontal lobe. The patient could return home immediately, exhibiting nothing more visible than a set of black eyes that returned to normal within a few days. Patients showed considerable reductions in anxiety and emotional agitation, and became much easier to manage. Psychiatrists said that no significant damage was done to the patients' abilities, and indeed in more than one investigation demonstrated that they themselves could not tell a lobotomized individual from a normal one! The families of the patients said they had lost their souls.

In his thoughtful review of this material, Loye reveals that a considerable number of abnormalities in fact surfaced in lobotomized

individuals. Besides losing interest in other people—a symptom that the psychiatrists took to be an improvement—they seemed to take no interest in the future. The Russian neurologist Alexander Luria observed that frontal lobe damage caused patients to lose the ability to plan for the future:

Although their movements are externally intact, the behavior . . . is grossly disturbed. They have difficulty creating plans, they are unable to choose actions corresponding to these plans, they readily submit to the influence of irrelevant stimuli, and they vary the course of an action once it has been started. (1966: 531)

It is perhaps not surprising that patients who can't think about the future have remarkably low anxiety levels. The capacity to worry seriously, or at least to ponder the future deeply, is one of the unique capacities of the fully functional human mind.

Not surprisingly, anxiety is a common feature of today's world. The fact is that, in the last decade of the twentieth century, we are living in an era of transition, as different from life in the recent past as the grasslands were from the caves, and settled villages from life in nomadic tribes. Living in an era of transition is also an unusual adventure. In the span of a single lifetime, patterns of existence have seldom if ever changed as profoundly and as rapidly as today. But, though the speed of change is exhilarating, the transformations it produces are not without danger. Science and technology have raised human living standards for some millions beyond all expectations, but social inequities, political stresses, and unreflective uses of technology are polarizing the great majority of humanity, and they are also exploiting and degrading nature. Global warming, the attenuation of the ozone shield, the menace of deforestation and desertification, the destruction of many species of flora and fauna, the extensive pollution of air, water and soil, and the poisoning of the food chain are threats that all people and societies have come to share in common.

There is no consensus as yet on how to tackle such mounting problems. The world around us is too new; we have not yet developed the personal and social cognitive maps to cope with it. The earlier maps are falling by the wayside at a vertiginous pace. We can no longer map our world as the struggle of capitalism and communism led by two superpowers; ours has become a more complex world, with more actors and different faces. The USSR has disappeared; the United States is preoccupied with economic problems at home. Japan's economic miracle is fading, and the "little dragons" of Asia are eager to take its place. Europe has become an economic but not political

power, with its post-1992 single market and an East–West economic area of over 380 million people—and a Balkan rent by violence. Issues of environmental degradation are moving from marginal intellectual and youth groups to the center stage of international politics and global business. At the same time, many parts of the "Third World"—the 130-plus countries that count among themselves some three-quarters of the human population—sink further and further into poverty.

Adherence to the classical cognitive maps of the recent past is increasingly counterproductive—instead of the expected results, it produces surprises and shocks. This is true first of all in the area of the economy. The current variety of economic rationality legitimizes short-term policies that maximize competitiveness and profit and disregard the consequences of its actions in the medium and the long term. Some Third World governments are reluctant to pursue policies that reduce the ability of their national industries to compete and to produce—they would rather tolerate high levels of environmental degradation through chemical fertilizers, toxic-waste-dumping, and CFC-emission than put a brake on economic wealth-creation by ecological sanctions and regulations. Other governments perceive the need to bolster the global competitiveness of their economy by developing a dominant military presence in their region, legitimizing the acquisition of vast stockpiles of armaments by the search for economic security. Still other countries, with some industrial capacity but also considerable foreign debt, look to weapons-production as a means of coping with their trade deficits and increasing hard-currency exports. And still others export metals, minerals, timber, and other natural resources in response to pressures to obtain foreign currency, notwithstanding the fact that they are irreversibly depleting the wealth of their national patrimony.

GNP and other indicators of the economic wealth-creation process create an illusion that the natural resource-base of the economy is practically inexhaustible. In some cases, economic indicators suggest that wealth is actually increasing, even as natural resources are diminishing. If a government were to cut down all its forests and sell them as timber, its accounting books would report that its national wealth had increased; the same if it permitted pollution to become rampant and fought it by creating incentives for anti-pollution industries.

Because the long-term costs of such activities remain outside the accounting system as "externalities," factories can pollute rivers as if the waters that flowed past them entailed no costs; power stations can burn coal without calculating the cost of pumping carbon dioxide into the atmosphere; loggers can destroy wildlife and disrupt ecological

cycles without factoring the costs into their balance sheets; and farmers can use chemical fertilizers, pesticides, and fuel-oil as though the self-regenerating capacity of the soil and the supply of fossil fuels were unlimited.

An obsolete cognitive map guides the operation of financial markets as well. There is, for example, the "Wall Street syndrome" of investing for short-term profit. Institutional investors, including managers of highly endowed mutual and pension funds, move around a great deal of capital in search of quick returns, deflecting funds from necessarily lower-yield socially and ecologically oriented projects.

There is yet another indication of the obsolescence of today's social cognitive maps, and that is the sectoral segmentation of the design and implementation of public policy. Governments act as if finance could be separated from trade, defense from development, and social justice from the degradation of the environment: they have departments or ministries attempting to cope with each such domain separately, often in direct competition with one another. Within the domain of the economy, they handle individual sectors as if finance dealt only with flows of money, trade only with flows of goods, and communication only with flows of messages. And they address environmental issues as if they were yet another specialty, assigning deforestation problems to forestry experts, soil-erosion issues to soil pathologists, atmospheric-pollution problems to chemists, and so on.

Dysfunctional social cognitive maps bias the actions of the international community as well. Financial flows are handled by the World Bank Group and the coordination apparatus established after World War II at Bretton Woods; security issues are assigned to the United Nations Security Council, and action in regard to the environment is entrusted to UNEP, the UN's environment program. Health issues have their own World Health Organization, and children their Unicef, just as weather has its World Meteorological Organization and the international mail system the International Postal Union. Even when an issue cuts across the fields of competence of several agencies—such as education, which, in addition to Unesco, is of concern to Unicef, UNDP, UNFPA, and half a dozen other UN bodies—the separation of mandates encourages bureaucratic narrow-mindedness and in-fighting, with the result that, instead of joining forces, territories are insistently claimed and jealously guarded, and the available funds are intensely fought for.

Despite labels such as "oneworld" and "spaceship Earth," an integrated and effective approach to the problems of our age still awaits

realization. Governments, businesses, the same as private individuals, act as if the world was a jungle where the survival of one is the demise of another—but a large jungle, serving as an inexhaustible source of resources and an infinite sink of wastes. As a consequence, we find ourselves in a crisis in the Chinese sense of the term: in a condition replete with danger as well as with opportunity. If we are to avert the dangers and seize the opportunities, we need better to understand the real nature of this world; we need a more reality-matching cognitive map in societies, as well as in individuals.

Changes in Individual Cognitive Maps

As the first two chapters have shown, both individual and social cognitive maps have changed throughout history. Though the dominant maps are still in place, waves of change have started in recent years, moving strongly from the periphery toward the center. They wash over people and societies all over the world, in the rich as well as in the poor countries.

In the industrialized world, dominant values and beliefs have been shaped by the experience of the recent past, and as the realities of that world are changing, the concepts that mapped its contours are becoming increasingly obsolete. Serious changes started in the 1960s, at the periphery, with the Hippie, the New Age, and the early Green movements, and they kept moving toward center stage in the 1970s and 1980s with mounting concern over public health and safety, and worries over the negative effects of intensifying global economic competition. By the 1990s, the great majority of the industrialized societies had been caught up in what is sometimes referred to as a "paradigm shift." Since it is affecting the thinking and behavior of citizens as well as of consumers, governments as well as businesses are paying growing attention to it.

A profound change in the cognitive map of everyday people is now in the offing. Some old and cherished ideas are being rejected and replaced, and some basic relationships between humans and nature, as well as between humans and other humans, are being questioned. The changes are manifold; here is a brief but perhaps representative sample (Laszlo 1991).

- *The human–nature relationship.* The hitherto dominant cognitive map depicted human beings as mastering and controlling nature for their

own ends. The emerging map calls attention to humanity as an organic part within the self-maintaining and self-evolving systems of nature in the planetary context of the biosphere.

- *The male–female relationship.* The mainstream map was male-dominated and hierarchical, conceiving of high concentrations of power and wealth as the best way to promote the interests and maintain the affluence of governments and enterprises. The emerging map places sharing and complementarity over top-down commands and blind obedience. It is orientated towards a male–female partnership, and is participatory rather than hierarchical.

- *Wholeness vs. fragmentation.* The cognitive map of the industrial age was atomistic and fragmented; it saw objects as separate from their environments, and people as separate from each other and replaceable in their surroundings. The emerging map perceives connections and communications between people, and between people and nature and emphasizes community and unity both in the natural and in the human world.

- *Competition vs. cooperation.* The cognitive map of classical industrial society looked at the economy as an arena for struggle and survival, and entrusted the coincidence of individual and public good to what Adam Smith called the "invisible hand." The alternative cognitive map emphasizes the value of cooperation over competition, and tempers the profit- and power-hunger of the modern work ethos with an appreciation of individuality and valuation of diversity.

- *Accumulating vs. sustaining.* In the map of the traditional industrial culture, the accumulation of material goods was considered the pinnacle of achievement and success; there was little concern with costs in terms of energies, raw materials, and related resources. The emerging map is becoming aware of the threats to the sustainability of the value-creating process, and is intent on flexibility and accommodation in the human–human as well as in the human–nature relationship.

These changes are part of a deeper shift in the worldview that underlies the cognitive map of contemporary people.

- The previous cognitive map of modern people was materialistic, seeing all things as distinct and measurable material entities. It conceptualized nature as a giant machine, composed of intricate but

replaceable machine-like parts. The emerging cognitive map looks at nature as an organism endowed with irreplaceable elements and an innate but non-deterministic purpose, making for choice, for flow, and for spontaneity.

- In its application to society and the economy, the previous cognitive map highlighted the application of technology, the accumulation of material goods, and promoted a power-hungry, compete-to-win work ethos. The emerging cognitive map emphasizes the importance of information, and hence of education, communication and human services over and above technological fixes, the accumulation of material goods, and the control of people and nature.

- In the previous view, sickness was seen as the malfunction of a machine that could be best corrected by factual diagnosis and impersonal treatment; the ills of the mind were thought to be separable from those of the body, and were to be separately treated. In the alternative cognitive map, body and mind are not separable, and safeguarding the integrity and development of the whole organism requires empathy as well as expertise, and attention to psychological, social, and environmental factors in addition to physical and physiological conditions.

- In the spiritual domain, the previous concept envisaged the world as the work of a god who is outside, and indeed above and beyond his creation, with only humans privileged enough to be created in his image, to encounter his countenance, and to merit his love. The alternative cognitive map seeks the divine within all things natural, human, living, and even non-living, and refuses to draw categorical distinctions between the diverse spheres of reality.

- The previous view was globalizing and hierarchical, conceiving of high concentrations of power and wealth as the best way to maintain and promote the interests and affluence of states and corporations. The emerging cognitive map is likewise globally oriented, but in a participatory rather than in a hierarchical vein. It places cooperation born of understanding over top-down commands and blind obedience.

- Last but not least, the previous cognitive map of people was Eurocentric, looking at Western industrialized societies as the paradigms of progress; the cognitive map that is now dawning is centered on humanity.

A number of traditional conceptions and preconceptions are not only questioned, but are actually replaced by new insights. It is widely admitted, for example,

- that in this world those who survive are not necessarily those who are the strongest, but those who are the most symbiotic with their fellow humans and the systems of nature;

- that the trickle-down theory is a myth, and the only way to help the poor and the underprivileged is to create better conditions for their life and better opportunities for their advancement through higher levels of participation in economic, social and political processes;

- that specialists who know more and more about less and less need to be balanced by generalists who have sufficient overview to see the forest and not only a multiplicity of trees, and therefore make better guides in today's complex and interdependent world;

- that true efficiency is not simply maximum productivity but the creation of socially useful and necessary goods and services;

- and that ideas, values, and beliefs are not idle playthings but have a vital catalytic role in the world, not only in producing technological innovations but, even more importantly, by paving the way for the social and cultural advances that are the basic precondition of progress in the current transition toward a new world in the twenty-first century.

Changes in Social Cognitive Maps

In the political sphere, the mutation of the dominant cognitive map came late, but then it came forcefully. Until about 1988, ecopolitics was not popular in government circles. The governments of the industrialized countries underplayed environmental issues, fearing negative impacts on economic growth and global competitiveness. The former Marxist regimes of Eastern Europe had rejected ecological measures outright: there could be no environmental degradation under socialism. In turn, the governments of the developing countries claimed that environmental problems are due to pollution produced by the industrialized nations, and those nations should shoulder the responsibility for overcoming them.

Then, in 1988, the public media in the industrialized world seized

on the environment as a topic of major public interest. Within a single year, the National Geographic Society published *Earth '88, Time* magazine devoted its 1989 New Year's edition to "Earth, Planet of the Year," *The Economist* published a special survey on "Costing the Earth," *Scientific American* dedicated an issue to "Managing Planet Earth," and *The New Yorker* published a 35-page article on "The End of Nature."

Public opinion began to come around, and politicians were quick to note the changed mood of their electorate. Almost half of Margaret Thatcher's September 1988 speech to the Royal Society was devoted to the issue of environmental imbalances and the need to accept the concept of sustainable economic development. In his December 1988 speech to the UN, Mikhail Gorbachev spoke of the ecological catastrophe that would follow on traditional types of industrialization. Queen Beatrix of the Netherlands dedicated her entire Christmas speech to the nation to environmental threats confronting life on earth. And George Bush appointed professional environmentalist and former president of the World Wildlife Fund William Reilly to his cabinet, as Administrator of the Environmental Protection Agency (EPA).

Related changes have been occurring in the cognitive map of business, surfacing as the "new corporate culture." They concern issues such as:

- *Hierarchical vs. distributed decision-making.* The philosophy of the classical corporation was to create a disciplined hierarchy in which top managers decided all the essential parameters of the organization's activity. The new corporate culture moves toward decentralizing decision-making through network-like structures in which people closest to a given problem have the task and the responsibility of making the day-to-day decisions.

- *Control vs. self-regulation.* Old-style management applied rigorous external controls in all phases of work, making use of supervisors, specialists, and automated control procedures. The new style relies on self-regulation by semi-autonomous task-groups and broadly networked subdivisions.

- *Human vs. machine.* Classical management viewed the human being as an extension of the machine, and whenever possible substituted "reliable" machines for "unreliable" people. The emerging corporate culture views the human being as an uneliminable and vital complement to machines, and as irreplaceable by automation in all phases of business activity.

- *Routine tasks vs. responsible jobs.* The old-style corporation broke down tasks into simple and narrow-range skills, mechanizing the work process in the way Charlie Chaplin caricatured in *Modern Times.* The new corporation makes use of semi-autonomous task-groups and optimizes their contribution by assigning broad responsibilities to them, corresponding to their multiple skills and many-sided performance.

- *Complementary sex roles.* Mainstream corporate culture typically viewed women as unskilled or semi-skilled labor, and assigned simple or routine tasks to them—on the assembly-line, in cleaning up, and in routine secretarial jobs. The new corporate culture brings women into all levels of decision-making; it recognizes the complementarity of male and female personalities, skills, and concerns.

The fact is that, in the last few years, an entire new industry has been arising. It deals with biodegradable and organic products, environmentally harmless substances, the recycling of reusable materials, and the clean-up of existing pollution. By 1991, the US "Earth Age Industry" generated over US$100 billion in turnover and employed some 200,000 people.

Not surprisingly, the top management of globally operating transnational corporations now includes directors for environmental affairs. By 1990, one hundred percent of Dutch international companies, and the majority of German and Japanese companies, had a board member entrusted with environmental responsibilities. In some industry sectors, chief executives now devote as much as a third of their time to ecological issues, and many companies undertake costly alterations in product-design and manufacturing to meet self-imposed ecological standards.

The Evolutionary Map of the Sciences

In our science-infused and technology-dominated world, the contribution of science to the creation of a new and more adequate cognitive map remains essential. Science is a major—perhaps *the* major—force shaping contemporary industrial civilization. The revolutions of our time are driven by the social and technological implications of scientific breakthroughs rather than by the will of politicians or dictators. Scientific discoveries are extending the human life span, making it possible to reduce working hours and increase leisure-time, and to travel anywhere on the six continents in a matter of hours in considerable comfort

and safety. Scientific discoveries are also bringing to our fingertips ideas, images, and information on practically everything, from local events to global problems, in every conceivable field of public and personal interest.

At the same time, the products of industrial technologies are altering vital balances in the biosphere, changing the chemical composition of soil, water, and air, and wreaking havoc with the global climate; and the elemental power liberated by nuclear science, stockpiled in national arsenals, is endangering all life on the surface of this planet. Breakthroughs in microelectronics make for the quasi-instantaneous processing of a staggering amount of information, and the distribution of the information quasi-instantaneously to almost anyone, anywhere on the globe, while breakthroughs in biotechnologies make possible the manipulation of the genetic heritage of our species, with untold consequences for good as well as for bad.

Despite the shifts in values and worldviews already noted, the view of the world conveyed by scientific discoveries remains unclear to most people. Misconceptions about the nature of the cognitive map elaborated by science lead to mistaken applications and misguided practices. To this day, the absolutist and mechanistic worldview of Newtonian physics dominates interventions in society and in nature; most leaders believe that the world can be engineered to suit human wishes, much like the structure of a building or a bridge. The concepts of classical Darwinism inspired Hitler's social Darwinism and still underlie attempts to govern according to the principle that only might is right. Power and wealth can still be looked upon as signs of fitness; poverty and marginalization as signs of being a misfit. Even Einstein's theories have been misinterpreted to mean that everything is relative, including freedom, health, justice, and morality.

It is noteworthy, then, that for the past decade or so, an increasing number of scientists have been at pains to clarify a very different and in some respects diametrically opposite cognitive map suggested by the latest discoveries in the sciences. The new physics and the new cosmology, and the new sciences of nature and complexity, elaborate and specify the vision of a self-evolving, dynamic, and essentially unified reality in which life and mind, and human beings and human societies, are not strangers or accidents but integral co-evolving elements.

Today mathematical physicists, and not only poets and philosophers, are attempting to produce an integrated evolutionary map of the world. Many scientists have been fascinated by the notion that there is a

vantage point from which the 200-odd elementary particles and the four universal forces of nature can be seen as evolving from a single "supergrand unified" force—the force that is the origin of all that is. Ten or twenty three-dimensional universes, Big Bangs, black holes, supersymmetries, and superstrings are strange notions that scientists do not hesitate to espouse to prove the unity of the universe in theories that have come to be popularly known as TOEs—"theories of everything."

As physicists have been turning their eyes to the cosmos, the public has been turning its eyes to the new physics. Stephen Hawking's *Brief History of Time* sold over a million copies; James Gleick's *Chaos: Making of a New Science* made the bestseller lists. One large Manhattan bookstore devoted an entire window to new books on physics and cosmology; another displayed Paul Davies' *The Cosmic Blueprint* next to the latest collection of "Garfield" cartoons; and Bantam science editor Leslie Meredith declared that we are entering science's golden age.

In the new sciences, a new and different picture of the world has indeed been emerging: a highly unified picture. In this picture, the particles and forces of the physical universe originate from a single "supergrand unified force" and, although separating into distinct dynamic events, they continue to interact. Space–time is a dynamic continuum in which all particles and forces are integral elements. Every particle, every element affects every other. There are no external forces or separate things, only sets of interacting actualities with differentiated characteristics.

The new physicists have given up trying to explain the world in terms of laws of motion governing the behavior of individual particles. A coherent and consistent set of abstract and unvisualizable entities has replaced the classical notion of passive material atoms moving under the influence of external forces. This is important, because it is unlikely that phenomena of the level of complexity typical of life could be described by equations that center uniquely on the motion of the universe's smallest building blocks, no matter how thoroughly these entities and their laws are unified. A focus on a basic level of reality is unnecessary baggage left over from a classical theory that attempted to explain all things in reference to a combination of the properties of ultimate entities—entities that it has long believed to be atoms. The new scientists no longer maintain that nature can be explained in terms of groups of fundamental entities, even if the entities are not atoms but quarks, exchange particles, or strings.

The cognitive map emerging in the new physics is that of a universe

that is whole and self-organizing. This map is likely to remain valid, notwithstanding the high attrition rate of the hypotheses that expound it. It is difficult to see how science would ever regress to a universe of separate material things and dynamic forces, to a mosaic of unrelated events in mechanical equilibrium.

To have a good map of the world does not require having a map of *every thing* in the world; it only calls for having a sound grasp of the fundamental nature of the *processes* by which every thing that is in the world *came to be*. This is the essence of the emerging evolutionary map.

Let us retrace our steps, now, to the beginnings of the cosmic process some fifteen billion years ago. That was the epoch of universe creation by the primal explosion that became popularly known as the *Big Bang*. Although cosmologists disagree on the details of the process, it is clear that the universe we now observe had a beginning in time, and that since that beginning it has continued to evolve toward the order and complexity that now meets our eye.

Imagine, if you will, a cosmos of pure structure without things and movement. It is a "hypervacuum" made up of pure, potential energy. Except for tiny fluctuations, it is quiescent and unimaginably concentrated. Then one of the fluctuations suddenly nucleates and the pinpoint universe explodes. Within the smallest fraction of a second, the structure becomes fiery, and inflates to billions of times its former size. It begins to fly apart, and as it expands it cools. The continuous field of potential energy breaks up at myriad critical points, and nodules of real, actualized energy spring forth. The nodules have opposite charges, and as they meet they annihilate each other. Some survive, and establish themselves in space and time. Now there is something there: the material universe has been born. The nodules of persistent actualized energies bind together and form larger patterns that endure in time and repeat in space. "Things" emerge from the background of potential energies like knots on a fishing net, and they interact across the expanding substructure, contorting it by their presence. They are, in Einstein's theory, "electromagnetic disturbances" in the matrix of four-dimensional space–time.

Let us suppose that there are a vast number of such knots tied across the reaches of space–time, and that these knots are at uneven distances from one another. They do not form isolated units but parts of a continuum, and they communicate with one another through the continuum. Their primary mode of communication is attraction and repulsion, depending on the distance that separates them from one another. Attraction is the dominant mode of communication at all but

extremely close intervals, and thus the knots in relative proximity move closer together. Many of them come to be concentrated in such close quarters that ordinary attraction breaks down and more complex strains and stresses are created between them. Some of the elementary units achieve cohesion in balancing the energy flows that constitute them in a joint pattern. They constitute "superknots" of a much more complex kind.

A population of such complex entities transforms the character of space–time in the region of their concentration. There arises a material object—a star. These macro-objects continue to be connected through the continuum on which they are superimposed, but now they act as integrated masses: they form complexes constituted by the balance of their joint attractions and repulsions. The relatively stable superunits thus emerging further associate among themselves. Eventually, the entire universe is dotted with balanced knots-within-knots in space–time, affecting each other and reaching further orders of delicate balance. The universe itself takes on the character of a vast system of balanced energies, acting in some discernible form of cohesion. Thus the whole universe expands, or expands and then re-contracts, or maintains itself in a dynamic steady-state—we are not sure which, at this stage of theoretical cosmology.

In some cosmic regions—such as on planetary surfaces—further processes of structuration occur. Neighboring nodules interact and accommodate one another's internal flow-patterns. The new integration of already-integrated energies results in more complex flows along relatively stable pathways. The pathways themselves are the result of previous integrations; they themselves consist of energy-flows of established pattern. But now they serve to channel fresh flows of energy, and act as "structure" in relation to "function." Hence, new waves of formative energy course over stabilized structures, produced by foregoing waves. And the process continues; the beat goes on. Established structures jointly constitute new pathways and these, as they become established as structures in time, serve as templates for the production of new systems of flows. The patterns become complex; the cosmic cathedral of systems grows.

The known entities of science are interfaces located on various levels of the rising cathedral.

Electrons and nucleons are condensations of energies in the space–time field, based on the integration of quarks. They in turn are capable of integration into balanced structures: stable atoms. Here, the inte-

gration of diverse forces within the nucleus produces a positive energy, which is matched by the summed negative energy of the electrons in the surrounding shells. Uncompleted shells make the atom chemically active; that is, capable of forming bonds with neighboring atoms. We thus get systems produced by the integration of the energies of several atoms: chemical molecules. The tremendous potentials of electronic bonding, as well as of weaker forces of association, permit the formation of complex polymer molecules and of crystals, under energetically favorable conditions. In some regions, under especially favorable conditions, the level of organization reaches that of enormously heavy organic substances, such as protein molecules and nucleic acids. Now the basic building blocks are given for the constitution of self-replicating units of still higher organizational level: cells. These systems maintain a constant flow of substances through their structures, imposing on it a steady-state with specific parameters. The inputs and outputs may achieve coordination with analogous units in the surrounding medium, and we are on our way toward multicellular phenomena.

The resulting structures (organisms) are likewise steady-state patterns imposed on a continuous flow, this time of free energies, substances (rigidly integrated energies), and information (coded patterns of energies). The input–output channels of organisms can further solidify into pathways of definite structure, and the nature of these pathways, plus the variety of locally interacting organic systems, defines the ecological system. In some instances, where highly interacting organisms congregate, the pathways cohere into a system made up of but one variety of organism: this is a social system. And where the interacting organisms are conscious, symbol-using creatures, the system that emerges in the wake of their intercourse is sociocultural. Ultimately the strands of communication and interaction straddle the space–time region in which they occur and form a system of their own. This is Gaia, the system of the global bio- and sociosphere.

Here, then, is an evolutionary vision of the largest "forest" of all, the cosmos in its totality. Visions of this scope were once the province of poets and mystics, and perhaps of theologians and metaphysicians, but certainly not of scientists. Not so today. As we have just seen, a basically unified cognitive map is emerging today in the laboratories and workshops of the new physics, the new biology, the new ecology, and the avant-garde branches of the social and historical sciences. The new evolutionary map is practical and applicable: focusing on the forest does not prevent anyone from seeing the trees.

Practical Utility of the Emerging Evolutionary Map

The new cognitive map of the sciences offers a powerful way to look at the world; a way that can promote effective and responsible behavior.

As early as 1975, Erich Jantsch noted that the reward for the elaboration of an evolutionary vision will be not only an improved academic understanding of how we are interconnected with evolutionary dynamics at all levels of reality, but also an immensely practical philosophy to guide us in a time of creative instability and major restructuration of the human world. Jonas Salk (1972) affirmed in turn that having become conscious of evolution, we must now make evolution itself conscious. And in *The New Evolutionary Paradigm*, David Loye outlined the foreseeable basic benefits of the development of a natural-science-based evolutionary cognitive map in regard to society.

1. *The benefits of improved forecasting.* While the study of evolution through chaos in the natural sciences has uncovered specific limits for predictability during transitional states, it is now also discovering new possibilities for improving forecasting within these limits by identifying patterns that foreshadow either impending chaos or potential order out of chaos. The new advances suggest how more effective early-warning systems may be developed for identifying impending food, financial, political, and environmental crises. The need for such systems became crystal clear when, basically unprepared, the leaders of the international community faced the great waves of system transformation that began mid-century with decolonization in the Third World, continued in the 1990s with the dissolution of the Second, and led to the series of crises in the 1990s, including the wars in the Persian Gulf, in Somalia, and in Bosnia.

2. *The benefits of improved interventional guides.* As important for effective and responsible behavior as the forecasting of impending crises and transformations is the identification of fruitful routes that could lead out of the crises. Indeed, one of the greatest problems faced by people in decision-making positions today is knowing where, when, and how to intervene to prevent social, economic, political, or ecological crises— or, if prevention is no longer possible, how to alleviate and ultimately overcome the crises. The new cognitive map holds out an important promise in this regard: mathematically formulated dynamic systems theories enable the creation of computer graphics that allow scientists to reduce vast quantities of otherwise confusing data into a comprehensible form. This can simplify the understanding and communication of problems and the visualization of swift and effective intervention

strategies to overcome them. According to Ralph Abraham (1992), evolutionary modeling—especially in the form known as *modular dynamics*—can provide contemporary civilization with the means to transcend coming crises.

3. *The benefits of participatory rather than authoritarian problem-solutions.* The traditional recipe during times of trouble has been to turn to specialized experts for advice and to implement the advice through top-down authoritarian strategies. As the failed Soviet coup of August 1991 has shown, attempted solutions that disregard the participation and motivation of the wider masses whose life and well-being are affected exacerbate the problems they were meant to solve and create a new range of difficulties. The promise of the new cognitive map in this regard is that it permits broad segments of the population to share the concept underlying the proposed solutions. Hence, the new map could bring about a wide level of public comprehension of both problems and proposed solutions.

4. *The benefits of providing clearer long-term goals and humanistic images.* Futurists and social scientists have remarked that, in contrast to the fervent visions of a better future that animated the revolutions and re-forms of the eighteenth and nineteenth centuries, in the present century a confused and fearful humanity seems to be running out of positive vision. Romantic utopias have been dismissed as unscientific, the Marxist vision has failed, and visions inspired by religious tenets seem too otherworldly to motivate practical strategies. The utility of the emerging evolutionary cognitive map includes the promise of rectifying this situation. When adequately articulated and widely understood, it could revitalize currently atrophying images of the future and recharge public motivation in reaching for long-term objectives that are humanistic in intent and realistic in attainment.

Bibliography

Abraham, R. (1989). Social synergy and international synergy: A mathematical model. *IS Journal, 17*, 27–31.

——(1992). Mathematical cooperation. In A. L. Combs (Ed.), *Cooperation: Reaching for a new order* (pp. 68–75). New York: Gordon & Breach.

Anderson, T. W. (1990). *Reality isn't what it used to be.* San Francisco, CA: Harper & Row.

Artigiani, R. (1988). Scientific revolution and the evolution of consciousness. *World Futures: The Journal of General Evolution, 25*(3–4), 237–281.

——(1990). Post-modernism and social evolution: An enquiry. *World Futures: The Journal of General Evolution, 30*(3), 149–163.

Augros, R., & Stanciu, G. (1987). *The new biology: Discovering the wisdom in nature.* Boston: Shambhala.

—— ——(1992). Competition and enculturation in science. In A. L. Combs (Ed.), *Cooperation: Reaching for a new order.* New York: Gordon & Breach.

Bandura, A. (1989). Social cognitive theory. In R. Vasta (Ed.), *Annals of child development: Vol. 6. Six theories of child development: Revised formulations and current issues.* Greenwich, CT: JAI Press.

Barnett, S. A., & Cowan, P. E. (1976). Activity, exploration, curiosity and fear. *Interdisciplinary Scientific Review, 1*, 43–62.

Bateson, B. (1972). *Steps to an ecology of mind.* New York: Ballantine.

Beritashvili, I. S. (1971). *Vertebrate memory, characteristics and origin.* New York: Plenum Press.

Berthoff, R., & Murrin, J. M. (1973). Feudalism, communalism and the yeoman freeholder. In S. G. Kurtz & J. H. Hutson (Eds.), *Essays on the American Revolution.* Chapel Hill, NC: University of North Carolina Press.

Beusekom, G. van. (1946). *Over the Orientate van de Bijenwolf (Philanthus triangulatum Fabre).* Leiden.

Boulding, K. (1956). *The image.* Ann Arbor, MI: University of Michigan Press.

Bruner, J. S., Olver, R. O., & Greenfield, P. M. (1966). *Studies in cognitive growth.* New York: Wiley.

Campbell, J. (1988). *Historical atlas of world mythology: Vol. 1. The way of the animal powers: Part 1. Mythologies of the primitive hunters and gathers.* New York: Harper & Row.

Camus, A. (1956). *The rebel: An essay on man in revolt* (A. Bower, Trans.). New York: A. A. Knopf.

Chance, M. R. A. (Ed.). (1988). *Social fabrics of the mind.* Hillsdale, NJ: Lawrence Erlbaum.

Chatwin, B. (1988). *The songlines.* New York: Viking Penguin.

Childe, V. G. (1951). *Man makes himself.* New York: Mentor.

Cole, S., Hainsworth, R., Kamil, A. C., Mercier, T., & Wolf, L. L. (1982). Spatial learning as an adaptation in hummingbirds. *Science, 217*, 655–657.

Combs, A. C., & Holland, M. (1990). *Synchronicity: Science, myth and the trickster.* New York: Paragon House.

Connerton, P. (1989). *How societies remember.* Cambridge: Cambridge University Press.

Cowie, R. J., Krebs, J. R., & Sherry, D. (1981). Food storing by marsh tits. *Animal Behavior, 29*, 1252–1255.

Craik, K. (1943). *The nature of explanation.* Cambridge: Cambridge University Press.

Croze, H. (1970). Searching image in carrion crows. *Zeitsrift for Tierpsychology, 5*, 1–86.

Csányi, V. (1986). How is the brain modelling the environment? A case study by the paradise fish. In G. Montalenti and G. Tecce (Eds.), *Variability and behavioral evolution: Proceedings, Accademia Nazionale dei Lincei, 259*, 142–157.

——(1987). The replicative evolutionary model of animal and human minds. *World Futures: The Journal of General Evolution, 24*(3), 174–214.

——(1988a). *Evolutionary systems and society: A general theory of life, mind, and culture.* Durham, NC: Duke University Press.

——(1988b). Contribution of the genetical and neural memory to animal intelligence. In H. Jerison and I. Jerison (Eds.), *Intelligence and Evolutionary Biology* (pp. 299–318). Berlin: Springer-Verlag.

——(1989). Origin of complexity and organizational levels during evolution. In D. B. Wake & G. Roth (Eds.), *Complex organizational functions* (pp. 349–360). London: John Wiley & Sons.

——(1990). The shift from group cohesion to idea cohesion is a major step in cultural evolution. *World Futures: The Journal of General Evolution, 29*, 1–8.

——(1992). The brain's models and communication. In T. A. Sebeok & J. Umiker-Sebeok (Eds.), *The Semiotic Web.* Berlin: Moyton de Gruyter.

Curio, E., Ernst, U., & Vieth, W. (1978). Cultural transmission of enemy recognition. *Science, 202*, 899–901.

Davies, P. C. W. (1988). *The cosmic blueprint: New discoveries in nature's creative ability to order the universe.* New York: Simon and Schuster.

Dawkins, M. (1971). Perceptual changes in chicks: Another look at the search image concept. *Animal Behavior, 19*, 566–574.

Douglas, M. (1986). *How institutions think.* Cambridge: Cambridge University Press.

Douglas-Hamilton, I. O. (1976). *Among the elephants.* New York: Viking Press.

Downs, R. W., & Stea, D. (Eds.). (1973). *Image and environment.* London: Edward
  Arnold.

Drager, U. C., & Hubel, D. H. (1975). Responses to visual stimulation and
  relationship between visual, auditory and somatosensory inputs in mouse
  superior colliculus. *Journal of Neurophysiology, 38,* 690–713.

Eccles, J. C. (1989). *Evolution of the brain: Creation of the mind.* New York:
  Routledge.

Eibl-Eibesfeldt, I. (1970). *Ethology: The biology of behavior.* New York: Holt,
  Rinehart and Winston.

——(1989). *Human ethology.* New York: Aldine de Gruyter.

Eisler, R. (1987). *The chalice and the blade: Our history, our future.* San Francisco,
  CA: Harper & Row.

——(1995). *Sacred pleasures: Sex, myth, and the politics of the body.* San Francisco,
  CA: HarperSanFrancisco.

——& Loye, D. (1990). *The partnership way: New tools for living and learning,
  healing our families, our communities, and our world.* San Francisco, CA: Harper
  Collins.

Engels, F. (1972). *The origin of the family, private property and the state* (Ed. E.
  Leacock). London: Lawrence & Wishart. (Original work published 1884)

Ewert, J. P. (1980). *Neuroethology.* Berlin: Springer-Verlag.

Fentress, J., & Wickham, C. (1992). *Social memory.* Cambridge, MA: Blackwell.

Fox, R. L. (1992). *The unauthorized version.* New York: Knopf.

Frankfort, H. (1973). *Before philosophy.* Baltimore, MD: Penguin.

Fromm, E. (1947). *Man for himself: An inquiry into the psychology of ethics.* New
  York: Holt, Rinehart and Winston.

Galef, B. G., Jr. (1976). The social transmission of acquired behavior: A
  discussion of tradition and social learning in vertebrates. *Advances in the Study
  of Behavior, 6,* 77–100.

Gazzaniga, M. S. (1985). *The social brain: Discovering the networks of the mind.* New
  York: Basic Books.

Gibson, J. J. (1966). *The senses considered as a perceptual system.* Boston, MA:
  Houghton-Mifflin.

Gilligan, C. (1982). *In a different voice: Psychological theory and women's development.*
  Cambridge, MA: Harvard University Press.

Gimbutas, M. (1982). *The goddesses and gods of old Europe.* Los Angeles, CA:
  University of California Press.

Gladwin, T. (1970). *East is a big bird.* Cambridge, MA: Harvard University
  Press.

Gleick, J. (1987). *Chaos: Making a new science.* New York: Viking.

Globus, G. (1987a). Three holonomic approaches to the brain. In B. Hiley &
  D. Peat (Eds.), *Quantum implications.* London: Routledge & Kegan Paul.

——(1987b). *Dream life, wake life: The human condition through dreams.* Albany,
  NY: State University of New York Press.

Goffman, I. (1973). *The presentation of self in everyday life.* Woodstock: Overlook
  Press.

Goody, J. (1977). *The domestication of the savage mind.* Cambridge: Cambridge University Press.

Hacking, I. (1985). *Restructuring individualism.* Stanford, CA: Stanford University Press.

Hawking, S. W. (1988). *A brief history of time.* New York: Bantam.

Hediger, H. (1976). Proper names in the animal kingdom. *Experientia, 32,* 1357–1488.

Hinde, R. A. and Fischer, J. (1952). Further observations on the opening of milk bottles by birds. *British Birds, 44,* 306–311.

Hofstadter, D. R. (1979). *Gödel, Esher, Bach: An eternal golden braid.* New York: Basic Books.

Jacob, F. (1982). *The possible and the actual.* New York: Pantheon.

James, W. (1983). *The principles of psychology.* Cambridge, MA: Harvard University Press. (Original work published 1890)

Jantsch, E. (1975). *Design for evolution: Self-organization and planning in the life of human systems.* New York: George Braziller.

Jay, M. (1973). *The dialectical imagination.* Boston: Little-Brown.

Jaynes, J. (1976). *The origin of consciousness in the breakdown of the bicameral mind.* Boston, MA: Houghton Mifflin.

Jerison, H. J. (1973). *The evolution of the brain and intelligence.* New York: Academic Press.

Jouventin, P. (1982). *Visual and vocal signals in penguins, their evolution and adaptive characters.* Berlin: Verlag P. Parley.

Jung, C. G. (1959). *Flying saucers: A modern myth of things seen in the skies.* New York.

——(1961). *Dreams, memories, reflections.* New York: Random House.

Kahler, E. (1956). *Man the measure: A new approach to history.* New York: George Braziller.

Kamil, A. C. and Balda, R. P. (1985). Cache recovery and spatial memory in Clark's Nutcrackers (*Nucifraga columbiana*). *Journal of Experimental Psychology and Animal Behavior, Proceedings, 11,* 95–111.

Kauffman, S. A. (1993). *The origins of order: Self-organization and selection in evolution.* New York & Oxford: Oxford University Press.

Kawai, M. (1965). Newly acquired precultural behavior of the natural troops of Japanese monkeys on Koshima Island. *Primates, 6,* 1–30.

Kendrick, K. M. and Baldwin, B. A. (1987). Cells in temporal cortex of conscious sheep can respond preferentially to the sight of faces. *Science, 2436,* 448–450.

Kierkegaard, S. (1954). *Fear and trembling, and The sickness unto death.* (Walter Lowrie, Trans.). Garden City, NY: Doubleday Anchor. (Original work published 1849)

Knudsen, E. I. (1981). The hearing of the barn owl. *Scientific American, 245*(6), 82–91.

Kohlberg, L. (1984). *The psychology of moral development.* New York: Harper & Row.

Korzybski, A. (1958). *Science and sanity: An introduction to non-Aristotelian systems and general semantics.* 4th edn. Shore, CT: Institute of General Semantics.

Kosslyn, S. M. (1980). *Image and mind.* Cambridge, MA: Harvard University Press.

Lack, D. 1939. The display of the blackcock. *British Birds, 32,* 290–303.

Laszlo, E. (1987a). *Evolution: The grand synthesis.* Boston: Shambhala.

——(1987b). The psi-field hypothesis. *IS Journal, 4,* 13–28.

——(1991). *The age of bifurcation: Understanding the changing world.* New York: Gordon & Breach.

——(1993). *The creative universe: Toward a unified science of matter, life and mind.* Edinburgh: Floris.

——(1994). *The choice: Evolution or extinction.* Los Angeles, CA: Tarcher/ Putnam.

——(1995). *The connected universe.* London: World Scientific.

Leider, D. (1990). *The absent body.* Chicago, IL: University of Chicago Press.

Lickona, T. (1983). *Raising good children.* New York: Bantam.

Lovelock, J. E. (1979). *Gaia: A new look at life on Earth.* Oxford: Oxford University Press.

Loye, D. (1983). *The sphinx and the rainbow.* Boulder, CO: Shambhala.

——(1990). Moral sensitivity and the evolution of higher mind. *World Futures: The Journal of General Evolution, 30,* 41–52.

——(forthcoming). *The glacier and the flame: Of science and moral sensitivity.*

Lumann, N. (1986). *Love as passion.* Cambridge, MA: Harvard University Press.

Luria, A. (1966). *The human brain and psychological processes.* New York: Harper & Row.

Lynch, K. (1960). *The image of the city.* Cambridge, MA: Harvard University Press.

McFarland, D. J. (1985). *Animal behaviour.* London: Pitman.

MacKay, D. M. (1951). Mindlike behavior of artifacts. *British Journal of Philosophy of Science, 2,* 105–121.

Mandler, J. M. (1988). How to build a baby: On the development of an accessible representation system. *Cognitive development, 3,* 113–136.

Mann, M. (1986). *The sources of social power.* Cambridge: Cambridge University Press.

Maslow, A. H. (1965). *Eupsychian management.* Homewood, IL: Irwin.

——& Honigmann, J. J. (1970). Synergy: Some notes of Ruth Benedict. *American Anthropologist, 72,* 320–333.

Maturana, H. R., Lettvin, J. Y., McCulloch, W. S., & Pitts, W. H. (1960). Anatomy and physiology of vision in the frog (*Rana pipiens*). *J. Gen. Physiol., 43* (Suppl. 6), 129–175.

——& Varela, F. J. (1987). *The tree of knowledge: The biological roots of human understanding.* Boston, MA: Shambhala.

————& Uribe, R. (1974). Autopoiesis: The organization of living systems, its characterization and model. *Biosystems, 5,* 187–196.

Menzel, E. W. (1978). Cognitive mapping in chimpanzee. In S. H. Hulse, H.

Fower, & W. K. Honig (Eds.), *Cognitive Processes in Animal Behavior* (pp. 375–422). Hillsdale, NJ: Lawrence Erlbaum.

Mundinger, P. C. (1980). Animal cultures and a general theory of cultural evolution. *Ethology and Sociobiology, 1*, 183–223.

Murray, G. (1951). *The five stages of Greek religion.* Garden City, NY: Doubleday Anchor.

Neisser, U. (1976). *Cognition and reality.* San Francisco, CA: W. H. Freeman.

——(Ed.). (1982). *Memory observed: Remembering in natural contexts.* San Francisco, CA: W. H. Freeman.

Nicolis, J. N. (1986). *The dynamics of hierarchical systems.* New York: Springer-Verlag.

Norton-Griffiths, M. (1969). The organization, control and development of parental feeding in the oystercatcher (*Haematopus ostralegus*). *Behaviour, 24,* 55–114.

Olton, D. S., and Samuelson, R. J. (1976). Remembrance of places past: Spatial memory in rats. *Journal of Experimental Psychology and Animal Behavior, Proceedings, 2,* 97–116.

Payne, T. L. 1974. Pheromone perception. In M. C. Birch (Ed.), *Pheromones.* Amsterdam: North Holland.

Perret, D. I., Smith, P. A. J., Potter, D. D., Mistlin, A. J., Head, A. S., Milner, A. D., & Jeeves, M. (1985). Visual cells in the temporal cortex sensitive to face view and gaze direction. *Proceedings of the Royal Society of London, B223,* 293–317.

Piaget, J. (1965). *The moral judgment of the child.* New York: Free Press.

——& Inhelder, B. (1971). *Mental imagery in the child.* New York: Basic Books.

Popper, K. R. (1962). *The open society and its enemies.* New York: Harper Torchbooks.

Pribram, K. H. (1991). *Brain and perception: Holonomy and structure in figural processing.* Hillsdale, NJ: Lawrence Erlbaum.

Reich, W. (1972). *Sex-pol: Essays, 1929–1934.* New York: Vintage.

Reilly, K. (1980). *The West and the world.* New York: Harper & Row.

Roeder, K. D., & Treat, A. E. (1961). The detection and evasion of bats by moths. *American Scientist, 49,* 135–148.

Rogers, C. R. (1961). *On becoming a person.* Boston, MA: Houghton-Mifflin.

Roitblat, H. L., Tham, W., & Golub, L. (1982). Performance of *Betta splendens* in a radial arm maze. *Animal Learning and Behavior, 10,* 108–114.

Sackett, G. P. (1966). Monkeys reared in isolation with pictures as visual input: Evidence for an innate releasing mechanism. *Science, 1954,* 1468–1473.

Sasvári, L. 1979. Observational learning in great marsh and blue tits. *Animal Behavior, 27,* 767–771.

Schleidt, W. M., Schleidt, M., & Magg, M. (1960). Störungen der Mutter-Kind-Beziehung bei Truthünern durch Gehörverlust. *Behaviour, 16,* 254–260.

Schmandt-Besserat, D. (1986). The origins of writing. *Written Communication, 3*(1), 31–45.

Schmookler, A. B. (1984). *The parable of the tribes: The problem of power in social evolution.* Berkeley, CA: University of California Press.

Schneirla, T. C. (1953). Modifiability in insect behavior. In K. D. Roeder (Ed.), *Insect Physiology* (pp. 723–747). New York: John Wiley & Sons.

Schwartz, G. (1984). *Psychology of learning and memory.* London: W. W. Norton.

Seitz, A. (1940). Paarbildung bei einigen Cichliden I. *Zeitsrift for Tierpsychology, 4,* 40–84.

Sheldrake, R. (1987). Part I: Mind, memory and archetypes: Morphic resonance and the collective unconscious. *Psychological Perspectives, 18*(1), 9–25.

Suga, N., Kuzirai, K., & O'Neill, W. E. (1981). How biosonar information is represented in the bat cerebral cortex. In J. Syka and L. Aitkin (Eds.), *Neuronal mechanisms of hearing* (pp. 197–219). New York: Plenum Press.

Taylor, C. (1989). *Sources of the self.* Cambridge, MA: Harvard University Press.

Thoma, S. J. (1986). Estimating gender differences in the comprehension and preference of moral issues. *Developmental Review, 6,* 165–180.

Tinbergen, N. (1932). Über die Orientiering des Bienenwolfes (*Philanthus triangulum*). *Zs. vergl. Physiol., 21,* 699–716.

——(1951). *The study of instinct.* London: Oxford University Press.

——(1960). *The herring gull's world.* New York: Harper & Row.

——& Kruyt, W. (1938). Über die Orientierung des Bienenwolfes (*Philantus triangulum Fabr.*) III: Die Bevorzugung bestimmter Wegmarken. *Zs. vergl. Physiol., 25,* 292–334.

Tolman, E. C. (1932). *The purposive behaviour in animals and men.* New York: Appleton.

——(1948). Cognitive maps in rats and men. *Psychological Review, 55,* 189–209.

Toulmin, S. (1990). *Cosmopolis: The hidden agenda of modernity.* New York: Free Press.

Turner, V. (1986). *The anthropology of performance.* New York: PAJ.

Uexkuell, J. von 1934. *Streifzüge durch die Umwelten von Tieren und Menschen.* Berlin: Springer-Verlag.

Uttal, W. R. (1972). *The psychobiology of sensory coding.* New York: Harper & Row.

Vattimo, G. (1988). *The end of modernity.* Baltimore, MD: Johns Hopkins University Press.

Wilson, A. N. (1992). *Jesus: A life.* New York: W. W. Norton.

Index

DATE DUE

ISBN 0-275-95676-8

90000>

EAN

9 780275 956769

HARDCOVER BAR CODE